A

# BIOGRAPHICAL HISTORY

OF

# THE FINE ARTS

BEING MEMOIRS OF

THE LIVES AND WORKS OF EMINENT

## PAINTERS, ENGRAVERS, SCULPTORS

AND

## ARCHITECTS,

FROM THE EARLIEST AGES TO THE PRESENT TIME.

*Alphabetically arranged, and condensed from the best Authorities. Including the works of*

VASARI, LANZI, KUGLER, DR. WAAGEN, BRYAN, PILKINGTON, WALPOLE, SIR C. EASTLAKE, AND MRS. JAMESON.

With Chronological Tables of Artists and their Schools, Plates of Monograms, etc.

BY

S. SPOONER, M.D.

FOURTH EDITION.

VOL. II.—M TO Z.

NEW YORK:
LEYPOLDT & HOLT.
1867.

A

# BIOGRAPHICAL AND CRITICAL DICTIONARY

OF

# PAINTERS, ENGRAVERS, SCULPTORS, AND ARCHITECTS.

## M.

MAAN, or MAN, Cornelius de, an eminent Dutch painter, born at Delft in 1621. After receiving some instruction in the art in his native city, he went to Paris while young, where he met with sufficient encouragement to enable him to visit Italy. He traveled through Lyons to Lombardy, and spent two years in Florence. Then proceeding to Rome, during a residence of three years in that metropolis of art, he applied himself to study with great assiduity, and became an able designer. He next went to Venice, where he carefully studied the works of Titian, particularly his portraits, and strove to imbibe his delicacy and glowing colors. After an absence of nine years, he returned to his own country, and settled in his native city, where he distinguished himself as an historical and portrait painter. He excelled in portraits. One of his admired paintings is a large picture in the Hall of the Surgeons at Delft, in which he introduced the portraits of the most eminent medical men of his time. His compositions partake more of the Italian than of the Dutch school, and his coloring is founded on that of the Venetian. Brulliot, who erroneously calls his name Charles, says he engraved several portraits in a style approaching that of Jean Morin, but doubtless the prints he refers to were engraved by another artist of the name of Maan. He died in 1706.

MAAS. See Maes.

MAAT. See Blankhof.

MB MABUSE, John de, a Flemish painter, born at Maubeuge, a small town in Hainault. There is an astonishing contradiction among authors as to the name, time of nativity, death, merits, and works of this artist. He is called by some Jan (James) and others John de Mabuse, Maubeuge, and Malbeugius. From a singular whim of the artist, his name is found differently written on his works, as *Joannes Melbogius, Joaes Malbogius, Johannes* or *Joannes Malbodius*, and *Joaes Malbogi.* We cannot discuss these matters here, but proceed to give what is authentic. His family name was Gossaert or Gossard. It is not known under whom he first studied. He went to Italy when very young, where he made extraordinary improvement, and was the first among the Flemish masters who treated historical and allegorical subjects according to strict rules of art, and introduced the nude into his compositions. To appreciate the extraordinary merits of this artist, it is necessary to see some of his genuine works, instead of the wretched remains of Gothicity which are attributed to him, and which have caused the contradictions as to his merits. His design surpasses his cotemporaries of the Flemish school; his coloring is fresh and clear, and his pictures are not surpassed by the productions of Mieris or Douw. There can be no greater proof of his merit than the fact that the fame of his Descent from the Cross, in the great church at Middleburg, induced both Albert Durer and Lucas van Leyden to make a journey to that city expressly to see the picture, and that they both expressed their admiration of the work in the strongest terms. He bestowed extraordinary labor in finishing his works. His Wise Men's Offering, painted for the church of the Abbey of Grammont, according to the register of that Abbey, occupied him seven years, and he received 2000 golden pistoles for it. This picture, after having passed through the hands of various princes and nobles, is now in the possession of the Earl of Carlisle. His history is very confused. It is probable that he led a short and merry life. The earliest authenticated picture bearing his signature is dated 1516, and the latest discovered, 1527. By the general concurrence of most writers of authority, he was born between 1496 and 1500. If so, he must have painted his Neptune and Amphitrite, now in the Royal Museum at Berlin, dated 1516, at a very early age. Descamps says he died in 1562; but it is believed that he died in 1532, from the latest date found on his pictures, 1527, and from a print of his portrait published by Philip Galle, on which is inscribed *Fuit Hanno patria Malbodensis, obiit Antwerpiæ anno* 1532. Yet, if he bestowed as much labor on all his pictures as he did on his Wise Men's Offering, he could never have executed a tenth part of the pictures considered genuine. There are fifty-nine pictures by, and attributed to him.

MAC ARDELL. See Ardell.

MACCHI, Florio, an Italian painter, who studied under Lodovico Caracci, and was an able dis ciple of his school. He executed many works for the churches at Bologna. His greatest work is a grand fresco, representing the Annunciation, in the church of Il Spirito Santo, which has often been taken for a work of his master. Malvasia states that he was a native of Bologna, and flourished about 1620. Orlandi speaks of him also as an engraver, but he does not specify any of the productions of his burin.

MACCHIETTI, Girolamo, called del Crocifissaio, from his father having been a carver of crucifixes, was born at Florence in 1535. After studying under Michele Ridolfi de Ghirlandaio, he became the pupil of Giorgio Vasari, whom he assisted for some years in the execution of his works in the Ducal Palace at Florence. He then went to Rome, remained there two years, and returned to Florence, where he acquired considerable reputation, and executed some excellent works for the churches, the chief of which is the Adoration of the Magi, in the church of S. Lorenzo; and the Martyrdom of St. Lorenzo, in the church of S. Maria Novella. His best works are said to be at Naples, Pisa, and Benevento. He also painted some battle-pieces in the Hall of the Albani, at S. Giovanni in Urbino.

MACÉ, or MASSÉ, Charles, a French designer and engraver, born at Paris about 1631. He was much employed by M. Jabach to make designs for his celebrated collection of drawings, and to etch them. The set consists of two hundred and eighty prints, engraved by him in conjunction with his brothers, Corneille and Rousseau M., and Jean Pesne. There is a set of twelve etchings of landscapes and figures illustrative of biblical subjects, after Benedetto Castiglione, executed in a bold, free style, which M. Huber attributes to this artist. They are marked *C. Macê sculp.*, in the margin. Dumesnil gives a list of one hundred and twenty-three prints by him.

MACEDRATA, Giuseppino da, an Italian painter born at Macerata about 1600. He is said to have studied under Agostino Caracci. His works have a strong resemblance to the school of the Caracci in grandeur of style and chastity of composition. Two of his works remain in his native place; the Virgin and Infant, surrounded with a Glory of Angels, with Sts. Nicola and Girolamo, in the church of the Carmelites, and St. Peter receiving the Keys at that of the Capuchins. Both these pictures are in the Caracci style; the latter is so much like Guido's picture of the same subject in the church of the Fillippini at Fano, that it may be considered a copy. It is signed *Jos. Ma. faciebat.* 1630.

MACHELLI, Rolando, a Genoese artist, born in 1664, and died there in 1728. He was a reputable painter of portraits and history.

MACHEREN, Philip van, a Dutch marine painter, who flourished at Middlebourg in the latter part of the 17th century. In 1672 he entered one of the vessels of war, for the express purpose of seeing and depicting the horrors of a naval combat. His works are rarely seen with his name. Nothing further is known of him, except that Balkema says that he died at Amsterdam, and Immerzeel at Rotterdam.

MACHUCA, a Spanish architect, who flourished in the latter part of the 16th century, and erected, according to Milizia, the royal palace of Granada, entirely of wrought stone, by order of Charles V. The principal façade is rustic, with three large gates, and eight Doric columns on pedestals, sculptured with historical bas-reliefs. The second story is Ionic, with eight columns, and above them pilasters. The internal vestibule is circular, with a portico and gallery, on columns of the same order; the architraves are one single piece of marble. Unfortunately there are arches springing from the columns; but the rest of the work is well arranged; the vestibule, especially, is ingeniously managed, and of good proportions.

MACOURT, C., a German artist who, according to Lord Orford, resided several years in London, was a member of the Chartered Society of Artists, in whose rooms he exhibited his works from 1761 to 1767. He painted portraits in oil and in miniature. One of his best works is a three-quarter portrait of Morier, the animal painter, which has great merit. He died in 1768.

MACRET, Charles François Adrien, a French engraver, born at Abbeville in 1752, and died at Paris in 1783. He studied under N. G. Dupuis, at Paris, and engraved several plates in a neat and pleasing style.

MACRINO, d'Alba, a native of Alladio, and a citizen of Alba, whence he signed his name *Macrinus de Alba.* Lanzi says his real name was Gio. Giacomo Fava, but he is known at Turin and other places by the name of Macrino. He was an excellent painter, and there are many of his works, both large and small historical pictures, at Turin and other places, especially at Asti and Alba, which are held in high esteem. It is not known with whom he studied, or when he was born or died, but some of his works are dated about 1508.

MADDERSTEG, Michael, a Dutch painter, born at Amsterdam in 1659. He studied under Backhuysen, and, according to Houbraken, was his ablest scholar. His sea-pieces and storms approach so near the works of his master that they have been mistaken for them. He was invited to the Court of Berlin, where he passed the greater part of his life. His works are mostly confined to the collections at Berlin, and other parts of Germany. He died in 1709.

MADERNO, da Como, a painter of Como, who flourished about 1700. Lanzi says he painted interiors of kitchens, with all kinds of household utensils, in the taste of the Bassani, with whom less experienced judges are apt to confound him. His works of this kind display great ingenuity and beauty. He also painted flower-pieces, tastefully composed, and beautifully executed.

MADERNO, Carlo, an eminent Italian architect, born at Bissone, in the Comasco, in 1556. He was a nephew of Domenico Fontana, and visited Rome to study under that master. According to Milizia, his first profession was that of stuccoing, but from practising with Fontana, and studying his works, he became an architect; though he always retained an attachment to his original pur-

Several fine examples exist in American galleries, including those of Mr. Lenox and Mr. Donaldson of New York; others have been sent to England to take advantage of the rise in value that his paintings have experienced. His autobiography, and a selection from his correspondence, was edited by Tom Taylor, 2 vols., 1861.

LEWIS, Frederick Christian, an English engraver, born in London in 1779, died at Enfield, December 18, 1856. He studied at the Royal Academy, and was afterwards articled to an engraver. On starting in business on his own account he was for years employed by Mr. William Young Ottley in engraving facsimiles of the drawings of Raffaelle, Michael Angelo, &c., for his illustrated work, the Italian School of Design. This employment, in which he was eminently successful, determined the future career of Mr. Lewis, and he was for many years occupied almost entirely in engraving the exquisite chalk drawings of Sir Thomas Lawrence, celebrated for their beauty and refinement, qualities that no engraver had ever succeeded in rendering with equal fidelity. He was also a landscape painter of no ordinary excellence, and exhibited his pictures regularly at the Royal Academy for many years. He engraved a series of views of Devonshire river scenery from his own drawings. His eldest son is John F. Lewis, President of the Society of Painters in Water Colors.

McIAN, Robert Ronald, a Scotch painter, born in Scotland, 1802, died at Hampstead, Dec. 13, 1856. He was a true Scottish Highlander, one of the ancient race of the Mac Ians or Macdonalds of Glencoe. His earlier years were passed on the stage, and he attained to great eminence as a delineator of characters associated with his native country, as Rob Roy, &c. He afterwards quitted this profession and adopted that of art, in which he arrived at considerable excellence, applying himself to it with the indomitable energy that was the leading feature in his character. His pencil never seemed so much at home as in delineating the wild scenes of his native land, or the still more violent and stormy conflicts that diversify her annals. Among his finest pictures are the Battle of Culloden, An Encounter in Upper Canada, in which a party of the Clan Fraser made a gallant stand against a greatly superior force of French, and American Indians; The Coronach, &c. Mr. McIan's fame was greatly extended by his beautiful drawings for various illustrated works devoted to the scenery, costume, and character of the Scottish Highlands, including the "The Clans of Scotland," 2 vols. folio; "Gaelic Gatherings," folio, &c. Indeed, his extensive acquaintance with the land and the people, derived from intense sympathy and affection, gave him almost a monopoly of these subjects, during his professional career.

MARTIN, John, an English historical painter, born near Hexham, Northumberland, July 19, 1789, died at Douglas, Isle of Man, February 9, 1854. His early ambition being to become a painter, Martin was articled by his father to a coach painter at Newcastle, but did not long remain there. He was next placed with Mr. C. Muss, a painter on glass and china, of some merit. "Here," says Martin, "in some autobiographical notes, "by close application till 2 and 3 o'clock in the morning, in the depth of winter, I obtained that knowledge of perspective and architecture which has since been so valuable to me;" and there is little doubt that from his practice in glass painting he derived many of the startling effects of light and shade that gave such novelty to his style. Martin married at the age of nineteen, and being stimulated by growing expenses to further effort, he painted, in 1812, his first picture, Sadak in search of the Waters of Oblivion. It is remarkable as proving how early he had created in his own mind the peculiar walk of art on which his reputation was founded. It met with a purchaser for fifty guineas. He followed up this success by exhibiting his works for several years. In 1819, The Fall of Babylon was painted, and in 1820 Belshazzar's Feast, by many called his masterpiece. The novelty and striking character of these works took the town by surprise. They were multiplied all over Europe by engravings, and bid fair at one time to create a new school of art. Though the taste for them palled somewhat in the lifetime of the painter, they will always retain admirers among the class who can more easily appreciate the material sublime than the intellectual manifestations of the passions. Martin's popularity as a painter led to his employment for the production of numberless designs for standard authors and books published at the time. He engraved his own drawings in mezzotint, rendering their peculiarities with masterly effect. A series of illustrations to Milton's Paradise Lost met with great popularity; for them he received £2,100. A folio series of Bible illustrations also engraved by himself, met with great success. Martin was an indefatigable worker, and at the time of his death was engaged on three grand Gallery pictures: The Last Judgment; The Great Day of Wrath; The Plains of Heaven. These have since been exhibited in the United States. He was also much interested in architectural and engineering plans for the improvement of London, the supply of pure water, &c., and to him must be awarded the credit of many reforms since carried out, as the embankment of the river Thames, the erection of central railroad depots, &c. As an artist Martin is distinguished for originality and imagination, and has never been excelled in representations of the vastness and might of nature. He was deficient in drawing of the human figure, and his coloring was crude and conventional, but he has unquestionably made his mark on the art history of the century, and though he had many imitators, maintains a decided superiority to them all.

MULREADY, William, R. A., an English painter, born at Ennis, in Ireland, in 1786, died in London, July, 1863. His father was a small tradesman, and little is known of the circumstances of Mulready's youth. It was rumored that he left Ireland when a boy, for reasons connected with the disturbed state of the country, when in his fifteenth year. By some means he had acquired sufficient proficiency in drawing to gain admittance to the school of the Royal Academy, and he soon became noticed among his cotemporary scholars for patient industry and perseverance. His first attempts at painting were in the grand or historical style, Failing in this he seduously set to work to study the leading masters of the Flemish school, and from them derived the impressions which gave a character to his future works. At this period he painted many landscapes, remarkable for mellowness and truth of color and sober breadth of effect. Cottage interiors and rustic figures gradually led him into the style of art that he was henceforth to excel in. One of his first efforts of this character was The Rattle, exhibited at the Royal Academy in 1811. This was followed by The Music Lesson, The Roadside Inn, &c. His picture of Idle Boys, caused his election as Associate in 1815, and next year, after the exhibition of The Fight Interrupted, he became Academician. From this time his popularity never waned, and he continued till his death a constant favorite with the public. The Wolf and the Lamb, exhibited in 1820, and purchased by George IV., marks the maturity of his power. It is well known from the splendid engraving by Robinson. His pictures were not numerous, his careful style of execution forbidding the rapid multiplication of his works, but they were always regarded as the gems of the exhibitions where they appeared. In 1840, Mr. Mulready prepared a series of twenty designs illustrative of the Vicar of Wakefield. They were engraved by Thomson, for an embellished edition of that work. They excited general admiration, as few drawings had ever been executed that so truly entered into and exemplified the very spirit of the author. Many commissions were given to the painter for pictures from these designs. One of them, Choosing the Wedding Gown, painted for Mr. Sheepshanks, and now in the National Gallery by the bequest of that gentleman's collection, is among the most perfect works of the English school, in color, expression, and composition. To the evening before his death Mulready continued his attendance at the Academy schools, constantly drawing from the life model, and producing finished sketches in red and black chalk, which are now the wonder of artists, for their elaboration and mastery of form, texture, and chiaro-scuro. His pictures, indeed, exhibit the highest art applied to subjects that sometimes strike the beholder as scarcely worthy of the mental power and artistic resources lavished on them by the painter; but they all rise into importance from the careful earnest study bestowed upon them, the felicity of expression, and the grace of sentiment they display, truly reflecting the personal character of the artist. Two collections of Mulready's works have been brought together, and exhibited in London, the first in 1848, which led to the more general recognition of his genius, the latter since his death. The National Gallery possesses sixteen of his finest pictures, through the liberality of Mr. Sheepshanks and Mr. Vernon.

NIXON, Samuel, an English sculptor, born in London, 1803, died there, July 8, 1854. Mr. Nixon was regularly educated to his art, and for many years was one of the most popular bust and monumental sculptors of the day. Many public commissions were entrusted to him; the most prominent of these is the statue of King William IV., erected on the completion of the approaches to the new London Bridge. This is sculptured in granite, and successfully overcomes the difficulties offered by so impracticable a material. Statues of four Children, representing the Seasons, in Goldsmith's Hall, London, are very charming and graceful conceptions, carved with much delicacy. Several of Mr. Nixon's monumental sculptures were executed for Canada. He was devoted to his art, and careless of pecuniary profit in comparison with professional renown.

PEALE, Rembrandt, an American painter, born in Bucks county, Pennsylvania, February 22, 1778, died at Philadelphia, October 3, 1860. He was the son of Charles Wilson Peale, an American painter of reputation, who had studied under Copley and West, and practised his art during the Revolutionary War. At an early age he showed great talent for drawing, and in 1796 established himself as a portrait painter at Charleston, South Carolina. The period of his life between 1801 and 1809, was spent in Europe, chiefly in London and Paris. In the former capital he enjoyed the benefit of Benjamin West's instruction. On his return to Philadelphia he painted The Roman Daughter, and The Court of Death, the latter founded on a poem by Bishop Porteus. These had much celebrity in their day, and were exhibited in the chief cities of the United States. He finally, however, adopted portrait painting as his exclusive branch of art, and, during his long life, numbered among his sitters the most eminent men in the country. A portrait of Washington, made from life studies, was his best-known head, and is perhaps the most authentic representation of The Father of his Country, in the prime of life. Mr. Peale published an account of his European travels, and a book, entitled "Graphics," to show the identity of the best measures for teaching both writing and drawing.

PRADIER, Jean Jacques, a French sculptor, born in Geneva, 1790, died at Paris, June, 1852, was the son of parents who discouraged his early taste for the arts, and apprenticed him to a watchmaker. Here the taste he displayed in the ornamental branches of the art led to his becoming a pupil of the School of Design, from whence he proceeded to Paris, and entered the studio of the sculptor Lemot, who became so much interested in him that he procured him a pension through M. Denon, from the Emperor Napoleon, to be continued during the period of his study. He assisted Lemot in the sculptures of the Louvre, gained the first prize of the Academy for a bas-relief in 1813, and went to study at Rome, where he remained until 1819. His popularity was established on his return to Paris, and he was henceforward engaged in the great public works that decorate that capital, as the Arc de L'Etoile, the Palais of the Corps Legislatif, the Fontaine Molière, the Place de la Concorde, &c. One of his finest works, Niobe, exhibited in 1822, is now in the Luxembourg, as is also his Psyche, a statue distinguished for the *pose* and grace of its movement. His Prometheus is in the gardens of the Tuileries, his group of The Graces at Versailles. The last statue he exhibited was Sappho, in 1852, shortly before his death. Pradier is accused of treating the female form with too much voluptuousness; but his powers of concep tion and execution were equally great. He was an indefatigable laborer, and did much to popularize art. He ranks among the best sculptors of the present century.

PROUT, Samuel, an English water-color painter, born at Plymouth, September 17, 1783, died in London, February 10, 1852. From early childhood he evinced a fondness for drawing, and his aspirations in art were confirmed by the companionship of his youthful friend and townsman, Benjamin Haydon. His first employment was the task of making a series of views of Cornish scenery for Mr. John Britton's "Beauties of England." These were executed with so much freedom and boldness that they led to the young artist's removal to London in 1805. Here at first he taught drawing, and made sketches for the printsellers; and, perceiving the capabilities of the infant art of Lithography, published several series of drawing books and landscape views, executed in that medium, then a novelty in art. His pictures were regularly exhibited at the rooms of the Society of Painters in Water Colors, and steadily progressed in attraction. In 1818 he first visited the Continent, and saw before him a mine of artistic treasure in the quaint scenery, architecture, costumes, &c., of Normandy, Brittany, the Rhenish provinces, Switzerland, and other parts of Europe lying off the highway of modern travel, that he never ceased working until his death. His reputation as an architectural draftsman was increased by the unmeasured encomiums of Mr. Ruskin, who gives him the highest praise in that department. He excelled in representing the crumbling and mouldering remains of Gothic magnificence, and by a style of his own invention combined breadth of effect with the suggestion of a multitude of details incapable of being literally rendered. His coloring is pure and harmonious, and his chiaro-scuro broad and simple. His paintings are numerous and highly valued. He published several lithographic folio volumes of scenery, figures, &c., for artists, &c., all of which stand high in public estimation. He was a confirmed invalid, and his works were executed amidst constant suffering from ill health.

PUGIN, Augustus Welby Northmore, an English architect, born in London, 1811, died at Ramsgate, September 14, 1852. His father was an eminent architectural draftsman, under whose instructions young Pugin traveled in England and Normandy, collecting materials for the "Specimens of Gothic Architecture," a work which had important influence in the revival of mediæval art. He was afterwards employed in making drawings for silversmiths of designs for plate and jewelry, and as assistant to Messrs. Grieve, the scene painters of Covent Garden Theatre. A passion for Gothic architecture finally led to his establishment as an architect, and having joined the Roman Cat'.olic church, he assisted materially by his great artistic powers in the revival of Catholicism in England. In every part of the country, churches, chapels, convents, and schools after his designs were being erected, and his wonderful facility of execution, innate feeling for and perfect knowledge of Gothic art, gave an original character to his works that rendered them perfectly unique among the tame imitations of the period. He also designed and superintended the execution of much of the ornamental work of the new Houses of Parliament at Westminster, and published more than twenty distinct works on architecture, antiquities, polemical discussions of Catholic and Protestant doctrines, &c. Though he died in his fortieth year, he had been three times married, and latterly his intellect had given way under pressure of an amount of work, professional, artistic, controversial, and literary, that seems beyond the capacity of the longest life to accomplish. He was buried at Ramsgate, where he had founded a religious house, church, schools, &c., dedicated to St. Augustine. No one has ever approached Mr. Pugin in his intense sympathy for the works of the great mediæval architects and knowledge of the remains that still speak of their power and skill. Rapidity of execution made him somewhat of a mannerist in his designs; but they are all distinguished by wonderful familiarity with the resources of his art.

RAUCH, Christian, a German sculptor, born at Arolsen, Waldeck, January 2, 1777; died at Berlin, December 3, 1857. He early showed an aptitude for art, and received instruction in it from Professor Ruhl, of Cassel. In his twentieth year he went to Berlin, and obtained an office in the court of the Queen of Prussia, still steadily devoting all his leisure hours to sculpture. In 1804 he traveled through France and Italy, and when at Rome, by the advice of William Humboldt, then Prussian minister there, commenced the study of the antique, aided by the counsel of the two chief living sculptors, Canova and Thorwaldsen. He now began to produce original works, and was recalled to Berlin in 1811, by the King of Prussia, to execute a monumental statue of the Queen Louise. This was completed with so much success, that Rauch's reputation was assured, and until his death he continued at the head of the German school of sculpture. Nearly all the great men of the time, distinguished in war, statesmanship, and literature, were among his sitters. As early as 1824 he had executed with his own hand seventy marble busts, twenty of them being of colossal size. His full length statues of Goethe, Schiller, Schleiermacher, and others of his cotemporaries, have great historic value for their truth and absolute fidelity to nature. His chief work, however, is the grand monument of Frederick the Great, of Prussia, erected on the finest site of Berlin. The general model was completed in 1839, but the entire group was not finished till 1851. It was inaugurated with great pomp in May of that year. Rauch ranks among the first of portrait and monumental sculptors. The number and high quality of his works are amazing, considered as the production of one man, but his long life was entirely dedicated to the practice of the art he loved.

RETZSCH, Moritz, a German artist, born at Dresden, December 9, 1799; died there, June 11, 1857. He manifested as a child unusual talent for drawing and modeling, and having determined to devote himself to art, entered in 1798 the schools of the Berlin Academy. Here he made steady progress, and was elected member of that institution in 1826, and in 1828, professor of painting. His artist life was uneventful, and was nearly all spent in the neighborhood of his native city. He commenced his professional career by historical painting, and also painted portraits, held in great estimation for their fidelity and delicate execution. Early in life, however, he adopted the line of art on which his reputation was founded, and will always rest: outline illustrations of the works of the great poets. His first effort in this style, the illustrations to Goethe's Faust, met with extraordinary success all over Europe, and determined his future career

They were followed by his outlines to Schiller's Fridolin, and the Song of the Bell, Burger's Ballads, and various minor works, among which Pegasus in Harness, and the Game of Chess, will always be remembered. His series from Shakspeare's dramatic writings was the last that he was engaged on. Eight parts, comprising illustrations to six plays, appeared, the last in 1846. The outlines to "Hamlet" formed the most admired of the series. Retzsch's easel pictures are scarce. His outlines have been repeatedly copied in France and England, but the original German editions, the work of his own hand, are in every respect preferable.

ROBERTS, David, R. A., an English landscape painter, was born at Stockbridge, Edinburgh, 24th October, 1796; died in London, December 25, 1864. He was early distinguished by a taste for drawing, and at the age of fourteen was apprenticed to a house painter and decorator in Edinburgh, but still continued to improve himself in the practice of art. A view of Abbotsford, painted towards the end of his apprenticeship, introduced him to the notice of Sir Walter Scott. Through his influence, Roberts procured an engagement to paint scenes for the Edinburgh and Glasgow theatres. From Scotland he removed to London, in 1822, when in his twenty-sixth year; and being furnished with letters to Elliston, the manager of Drury Lane Theatre, he was at once engaged at that establishment, in a similar capacity. Here his talent had full scope to operate, and he soon carried the art of scene painting to a degree of perfection never before witnessed. The extraordinary power of painting and covering large spaces of canvas in a short time, thus acquired, always continued to be a characteristic of the artist, and many anecdotes are recorded illustrating his wonderful rapidity and facility of execution. Being desirous of cultivating the higher branches of his art, Roberts first appeared as an exhibitor at the British Institution in 1824. In 1825 he visited the Continent, and painted a view of Notre Dame, Rouen, which was his first picture seen at the exhibition of the Royal Academy, where it appeared in 1826. For the next few years he increased in fame, applying himself sedulously to painting, and making frequent foreign tours, from whence the subjects of his pictures were derived. In 1838 he was elected an Associate of the Royal Academy. In August of the same year he started for a tour in Egypt, Nubia, and the Holy Land. Twelve months were occupied in these countries; during this time he made many hundred sketches. The most remarkable of them were reproduced on stone by Mr. L. Haghe, in the magnificent work in four volumes, atlas folio, known as "Roberts' Sketches in the Holy Land, Egypt," &c. They contain two hundred and fifty plates; for the copyright of them the artist received £3,000. The publication was one of the most successful speculations of the kind ever undertaken, and has since been reproduced in a smaller form. After his return he became, until the time of his death, a regular exhibitor at the Royal Academy. His pictures were in great demand, and were always sold before completion. One of the most popular, The Destruction of Jerusalem by the Romans, was exhibited through England, and copied in chromo lithograph, yielding a very large sum of money. During the lifetime of Roberts his pictures increased enormously in price, and are now among the choicest ornaments of galleries of modern artists. He was a constant worker, and painted on the day of his death, which was occasioned by an attack of apoplexy. Roberts as an artist was remarkable for his skill in delineating the picturesque aspects both of nature and art. He was equally at home in representing the burning deserts of Syria, the monumental grandeur of ancient Egypt, or the gloomy splendors of the gorgeous cathedrals of continental Europe. Effect was what he chiefly aimed at, and this he attained by breadth of light and shade and freedom of execution in the absence of minute detail. He is understood to have left memoirs of his life, which will probably be published.

ROSS, Sir William Charles, R. A., an English miniature painter, born in London, 1794; died there, January 20, 1860. He inherited from his parents an inclination towards art, and at ten years of age entered the schools of the Royal Academy. His first tendency was to historical painting, and from 1810 to 1817, he gained nearly twenty academical prizes, medals, &c., for paintings and drawings of that description, many of which were exhibited with great success. Notwithstanding, he determined to relinquish the prospects of a historical painter, remote and unlucrative as experience had proved them to be in England, for the more profitable pursuit of portrait painting in miniature. In this branch of art he met with the most distinguished patronage, and during his whole career held the same position, with respect to miniatures, that Sir Thomas Lawrence did to portraits in oil. Up to the year 1849, the list of portraits so executed by him, reached the number of 2050, including the royal families of England and France, and most of the leading aristocracy, particularly the female portion, as the portraits of Ross were remarkable for exquisite grace and delicacy and purity of color. He was elected Associate of the Royal Academy in 1838, and Academician in 1848, the same year in which he was knighted by Queen Victoria. In 1843, at the cartoon competition in Westminster Hall for the decoration of the New Houses of Parliament, Sir William Ross's drawing of the Angel Raphael discoursing with Adam was one of the ten selected for a premium by the judges, showing that he still retained his ability for historic composition. He was remarkable for the most winning and gentle manners, and a high Christian character in every respect.

SCHADOW, Frederick Wilhelm von, a German painter, born at Berlin, September 6, 1789, died there, 1862. He was the second son of I. G. Schadow, the famous sculptor, and being left to follow the bent of his own strong inclination for art, he went to Rome while young, and joined the school then forming under Cornelius and Overbeck, which has exercised such a powerful influence over the art of painting in Europe. Schadow adopted to their fullest exent the views of Frederick Schlegel, and was one of the German students who abjured Lutheranism, with their master Overbeck, and joined the Romish church. On his return to Berlin, he was appointed professor in the Academy of the Fine Arts of that city, and soon gathered about him numerous attached scholars. He also found time for the execution of original works that were much admired. When Cornelius in 1826 removed from Dusseldorf to Munich, Schadow succeeded him as Director of the Dusseldorf Academy, whither most of his Berlin students followed him, and he quickly found himself at the head of a flourishing school. Here for twenty years was the scene of his labors, and here he succeeded in building up a school of art founded on the practice of the early German and Italian masters, yet modified by the attempt to "reproduce from the bosom of antiquity, fresh, living, and blooming, a new art meet for the new time." From this school have proceeded many of the ablest and most brilliant of the living German painters, as Lessing, Hubner, Hildebrant, Achenbach, &c., and high as Schadow's name stands as a painter it may be questioned whether his fame is not still higher as a teacher. His pictures are mostly at Dusseldorf and Berlin; one of his best works, the Wise and Foolish Virgins, is in the Museum of Frankfort.

SCHEFFER, Ary, a French painter, born at Dordrecht, Holland, in 1795; died at Paris, June 15, 1858. The father of Scheffer was a Flemish artist of some repute. His son Ary was sent to Paris at an early age to study painting under Baron Guerin. His first picture, Abel singing a Hymn of Praise, was exhibited in 1812, and raised high expectations of his future career, from the talent it displayed. He continued the laborious and energetic study of art, exhibiting annually pictures that met with much notice, and showed a steady progress until 1822, when his painting of Francesca da Rimini gained him universal applause, and was even said to mark an epoch in French art, when the painters of that country abandoned the classical teachings and traditions of David and his school, and sought their inspiration more directly from nature itself. This was followed by his Suliot Women, and Gaston de Foix, which were equally successful. History, sacred and profane, poetry, *genre* subjects, and portraiture were alike practised by Scheffer, and in each class he has left works among the most popular produced in this century, that will immortalize his name, and through their general diffusion by the art of engraving are perhaps the most widely circulated examples of modern art. Christus Consolator, Christ and the two Marys, Christ blessing little Children, are the best known of his sacred subjects, and for spiritual expression, purity of drawing, and imaginative conception do honor to the school of painting from whence they proceed. Mignon and Margaret, from Goethe; Beatrice, from Dante, the King of Thule, from Schiller, &c., show with what admirable facility Scheffer could embody the finest and most subtle imaginings of the poets. A head of Charles Dickens, exhibited at the Royal Academy in 1856, is a striking instance of his skill in portraiture. His aim was always a high one; many technical merits of texture, execution, &c., he purposely neglected, preferring to fascinate by depth of poetic feeling, and appeal to the tenderest emotions by touching and pathetic sentiment. As a man no less than as a painter, the memory of Scheffer is equally estimable; his high moral character, the dignity yet simplicity of his life, and the genuine nobility of his nature, impressed all who came in contact with him. He was brought into intimate relations with, and remained devoted to, the royal family of France of the Orleans dynasty, and counted among his pupils the amiable and accomplished Princess Marie, whose well-known statue—Joan of Arc—shows how much she had profited by his instruction. Scheffer married an English lady, who died some time previously to his last illness, inflicting a shock on his sensitive nature which it never overcame. He was generally regarded on the continent of Europe as a leader in devotional art, and received from the different governments the honors which reward marked success. In France he was a member of the Legion of Honor. His personal character was distinguished by the same delicacy, ideality, and tenderness that his works are remarkable for. The great popularity of his works has led to unprincipled piratical copies, imitations, &c., by which the author has suffered. Scheffer's life was written by Mrs. Grote, 8vo, London, 1860, who enjoyed the advantage of confidential friendship and intercourse with the painter whose career she illustrates.

STARK, James, an English landscape painter, born at Norwich, 1799; died in London, March 24, 1859. When young he was placed as a pupil with the elder Crome, a prominent artist, whose landscapes have lately acquired much celebrity. He made rapid progress, and in 1817 came up to London and studied at the Royal Academy. His first picture, Boys Bathing, was exhibited about this time, and his success in delineating English landscape, particularly the scenery of the eastern counties, led to a rapid demand for his paintings, and secured him the patronage of the best judges of art. In the midst of his success, he was compelled, by a severely painful affliction, to leave London and return to the care of his family at Norwich, where for three years he remained incapable of practising his profession. On his recovery he remained there, and continued exercising among his native haunts the branch of art that he excelled in. He afterwards returned to London, and for a time took up his residence at Windsor, where the scenery of the Thames offered congenial subjects for his pencil. Mr. Stark's landscapes are distinguished by truthful detail and sober, natural coloring, delineated with a careful, firm pencil, and are the ornaments of some of the finest galleries in England. "Scenery of the Rivers of Norfolk," engraved from his picture, was published in folio, 1834.

STONE, Frank, an English painter, born at Manchester, August 23, 1800, died in London, November 18, 1859. His father was a cotton spinner and manufacturer, by whom he was educated with a view to commercial pursuits. He was employed in his father's business till his twenty-fourth year, when he adopted art as a profession. Mr. Stone came to London in 1831, and became a member of the Society of Painters in Water Colors, and for the next fifteen years it was at their exhibition that his pictures were seen and attracted much attention from their graceful and spirited rendering of scenes from the poets, or original subjects imagined with a finesse and delicacy that was new to English art at the time. He practised at intervals oil painting, and in 1840 sent his first easel picture to the Royal Academy Exhibition, The Legend of Montrose. Its success was so great that he gradually abandoned water-color painting, and became one of the most admired and popular contributors to Exhibitions of the Royal Academy, of which he was elected an Associate in 1851. His paintings of a sentimental cast, as The Heart's Misgivings, The Bashful Lover and the Maiden Coy, The Impending Mate, &c., have been widely reproduced by engraving, and are among the most popular pictures of the present century. He did not confine himself entirely to this style, but painted several scripture subjects, and a few years before his death, during a visit to France, made careful studies of the peasantry, which afforded him matter for some of his last and best pictures. Mr. Stone's coloring is rich and pleasing; his feeling for grace and beauty of form and feature, refinement of style, and delicacy of touch will always secure to his pictures a high place among the most charming works of the English school.

THOMAS, John, an English sculptor, born in 1813, at Chalford, in Gloucestershire; died at Kensington, April 9, 1862. He was brought up as a stone mason, but showing an extraordinary degree of talent, energy, and industry in all that related to the artistic branches of his profession, he attracted the notice of Sir Charles Barry, about the time when the rebuilding of the new House of Parliament commenced, and was by him entrusted with the superintendence and execution of the sculptured decorations of that edifice. His great success in this department led to extensive general employment both as a sculptor and architect. Prince Albert especially patronized him, and he executed commissions for many of the nobility, besides designing and erecting many public buildings, particularly in Scotland, including the National Bank of Glasgow, the Life Assurance Building at Edinburgh, and many others. As a sculptor, his group of Boadicea and her daughters, Musidora, Lady Godiva, Una and the Lion, &c., were distinguished. His wonderful facility of invention, rapidity of execution, and great knowledge of ornamental and architectural sculpture, were exercised in various ways all over the kingdom, to the advancement of the arts. One of his best-known ornamental works was the great Majolica Fountain designed by him for the International Exhibition of 1862. His death was caused by over labor and anxiety connected with the production of his grand national monument to Shakspeare, also in the International Exhibition.

UWINS, Thomas, R. A., an English painter, born in London, February 25, 1782; died at Staines, August 25, 1857. He commenced his acquaintance with art when apprenticed to an engraver, and during that time studied at the Royal Academy and attended the anatomical lectures of Sir Charles Bell. When his time was out and it became necessary that he should support himself, he practised designing in water colors, and in this style produced many drawings from standard authors that met with great favor as book plates from publishers, by whom he was much employed in conjunction with Stothard, Smirke, and Westall, then the great book illustrators of the day. In 1811 Mr. Uwins was elected a member of the Water Color Society, and afterwards became its Secretary. In 1814 he visited the Continent for the first time, bringing back many sketches from the south of France, afterwards employed in his works. Shortly afterwards he became involved in pecuniary difficulties through the defalcations of a friend, and so injured his eyes and health by intense application to work for the purpose of meeting the liabilities incautiously incurred, that for some years he was debarred from the practice of his art, and even when he resumed his pencil found his eyesight so much impaired that he was unable to execute, as before, delicate drawings in water colors. This led him to practise in oil. In 1826 he visited Italy, and remained absent five years. The fruits of his study are seen in a series of pictures sent home to the Royal Academy Exhibition, representing the manners and customs of the Neapolitan peasantry, delineated with a truth and graceful sense of beauty, feeling, and expression that took the public by surprise, and conferred on Mr. Uwins the high position as an artist that he henceforth maintained. He was elected a Royal Academician in 1836, and was one of the artists selected to execute frescos on the Queen's Palace. In 1842 he was appointed by her Majesty Surveyor of the royal pictures, and in 1847 keeper of the National Gallery, which office he held until 1855, when his last illness commenced. Mr. Uwins' pictures are characterized by graceful composition, pure color, and delicate execution. Whatever he did was done carefully and conscientiously, and his works will always be valued as examples of simple and unaffected art. His "Memoirs and Correspondence" were published by his widow, in two vols., 1858.

VERNET, Jean Emile Horace, a French painter, born at Paris, June 30, 1789; died there, January 17, 1863. He was descended from a race of painters—Joseph Vernet, the celebrated marine painter, being his grandfather—and inherited the family taste for art. As a boy he was remarkable for the freedom and facility of his sketches, though in competing for the traveling prize of the Academy of the Fine Arts, with the view of prosecuting his studies in Rome, he was unsuccessful. The exigencies of the times, however, rudely interrupted his artistic pursuits, and in 1807 he joined the army, whether of his own free will, or as a conscript, is not rightly determined. He made the campaigns of that and the following year, when he retired from the service, married, and resumed the profession of a painter. Previous to his military experience the style of his pictures was tinged with the prevailing classicality of the school of David. He soon proved its inadequacy to embody the scenes and events that he had been an eye witness of, and struck out for himself a path to the hearts of his countrymen, by the adoption of the bold and daring realistic style in which he commemorated the feats of their glory. His first exhibited picture, Capture of a Redoubt, appeared in the salon of 1809, and from that time to the fall of the first empire he worked with a zeal and energy that nothing could depress, on a multitude of large paintings illustrative of striking incidents or episodes of the wars of Napoleon or the Republic. During the hundred days he was enrolled in the Legion of Honor, for the active part he had taken in the defense of Paris. After the restoration his pictures were denied admission to the annual exhibitions of the Louvre, on the ground of their inflammatory tendency and unmistakable effect in reviving the souvenirs of the Empire. His talents, however, made way against the interdiction, and he was appointed an officer of the Legion of Honor by Charles X. In 1826 he was elected a member of the Institute, and in 1828 the Directorship of the French Academy at Rome was conferred on him. This office he held till 1839, discharging its duties with singular care and conscientiousness, greatly to the advantage of his pupils, besides executing many large and important works. At the revolution of 1830 he was appointed diplomatic representative of France to the Papal See. The resolution of Louis Philippe to create out of the abandoned Chateau of Versailles, a museum or temple dedicated "to all the glories of France," supplied Vernet with a field for the exercise of his peculiar talent, which he embraced with avidity. He is in fact the presiding artistic genius of the place, and remembrances of his numerous and colossal paintings are among the most vivid that spectators carry away from that peculiarly national institution. The Hall of Constantine, devoted to the successful campaign against that city, and the triumphs of the French arms in Algeria, contains the Battle of Isly, the Capture of the Smala, &c., probably among the largest oil paintings ever executed. During their progress Vernet made frequent visits to Africa and the East, and produced some pictures of biblical subjects, more remarkable for their fidelity to Oriental scenery and costume than for the higher qualities of expression. Vernet continued in high favor with the new dynasty, and was a personal friend of Louis Napoleon. The last works he was engaged upon were illustrations of the campaigns of Italy and the Crimea. He painted with extraordinary rapidity at once on the canvas, without making any preliminary sketches, and never changed his original conception, or had occasion to retouch a stroke. So well stored was his mind with the form of the object he was painting that he dispensed with models, drapery, or any other aid. His coloring is inferior to his drawing. His pupils were numerous, and his intercourse with them of the most attached character. He was a man without pretense or affectation, and at his death stood confessedly at the head of his profession in France.

VISCONTI, Louis Joachim, a French architect, born at Rome, February, 1791, died at Paris, November, 1853. When an infant he was taken by his father Ennius Quirinus Visconti, the celebrated antiquarian, who followed the plunder of the Italian Galleries, to Paris. Here he studied with great success under MM. Percier and Fontaine, the famous architects at the Academy of the Fine Arts, where he gained numerous prizes. In 1826 he entered the public service as Deputy Inspector of Works, and through all subsequent changes of dynasty, seems to have secured the confidence of the reigning powers, and to have been constantly engaged on the most important public works. Under the Bourbons he was appointed in 1825, architect to the Royal Library in the Rue Richelieu, and most of the subsequent improvements in the capital were designed by him, or executed under his supervision. By Louis Philippe he was entrusted with the design for the tomb of the Emperor Napoleon in the under chapel of the church of the Hotel des Invalides, and by Louis Napoleon with the task of uniting the Palaces of the Louvre and the Tuileries, a gigantic undertaking, that had foiled the powers of all preceding monarchs. M. Visconti only lived to commence the work now recently concluded. His designs show him to have possessed great fertility of conception and richness of imagination, but they are deficient when judged by the severity of a pure taste.

WARD, James, R. A., an English painter, born in London 1770; died there November 17th, 1859. He was articled in early life to a mezzotinto engraver, and practised that art for many years with marked success, combining with it the practice of oil painting, to which his inclination strongly led him. From his intimacy with Morland, the landscape and animal painter, who became his brother-in-law, Mr. Ward's attention was gradually drawn to the painting of cattle, and this class of subjects became his specialty during his long life. His landscapes also were much esteemed. For many years he was the patriarch of his profession in England, connecting two generations by his own experience and continuing the traditions of the earliest school of British art, almost to the present day. Independently of his connexion with Morland he was the brother-in-law of Jackson, the portrait painter, and a granddaughter is married to E. M. Ward, R. A., the historical painter. One of his finest works, a Bull, painted in emulation of Paul Potter's masterpiece, The young Bull, in the King of Holland's Gallery, at the Hague, has been purchased since his death by a committee of his friends, and presented to the National Gallery. Mr. Ward retained the use of his powers to an advanced age, and exhibited pictures at the Royal Academy in 1855, when he was in his 86th year. He was remarkable for simplicity and sincerity of character, and stood high in the estimation of all.

WESTMACOTT, Sir Richard, R. A., an English sculptor, born in London 1775; died there September 1, 1856. He studied under his father who was in business as a statuary, and showing early signs of talent was sent to Rome in 1793. There he entered the studio of Canova, and made such progress that he obtained the first gold medal of the Academy of St. Luke, for a bas-relief of Joseph and his Brethren. The year following his arrival in Rome, after four years' foreign study, he returned to London, and marrying at an early age, established himself in the practice of his art. He soon rose in public favor; was elected an associate of the Royal Academy in 1805, and Academician in 1812. He succeeded Flaxman as Professor of Sculpture in 1827, and was knighted in 1837. Westmacott executed a very large proportion of the monumental sculptures voted by Parliament in commemoration of the heroes of the long war with France, in St. Paul's and Westminster Abbey, and many of the statues in the public places of the capital, the two Universities, &c. His poetical and ideal sculptures were also numerous, including Psyche and Cupid for the Duke of Bedford, the Distressed Mother, &c. His works are always chaste, dignified, and impressive, distinguished by a purity of taste that rejected all superfluous ornament, and leaned rather to a naturalistic than to an idealistic treatment. He was highly accomplished in all that related to his art; and his lectures set forth in simple and forcible language the great truths that he endeavored to exemplify in his practice.

WILLMORE, James Tibbetts, an English engraver, born near Birmingham, September, 1800; died in London, March 12, 1863. He was the son of a farmer, by whom he was apprenticed to an engraver at Birmingham. At the expiration of the term he went to London, and entered the studio of Mr. Charles Heath. Here he first was engaged on plates from the works of Turner and Brockedon, and succeeded so well as to gain the friendship and patronage of these two artists. His first large plate was from Sir Charles Eastlake's picture, Byron's Dream. On its appearance Turner sought out the engraver and proposed the engraving of one of his paintings as a joint speculation. In this way was executed the fine plate Mercury and Argus, one of the most beautiful landscapes of modern times. The next plate was from Turner's Ancient Italy, fine early proof impressions of which are very rare and valuable. Willmore's name continued associated with that of Turner, as in the opinion of the great landscape painter, he was the only engraver who could transfer his pictures to copper or steel with proper effect. The Old Temeraire, Venice, the Golden Bough, and others, were thus rendered with great success. He was elected Associate of the Royal Academy in 1843. He also engraved Landseer's Return from Deer Stalking, and some paintings by Stanfield, Callcott, &c. His work was rapidly executed, and is distinguished for infinite variety of tone and color, reproducing the pictorial effects of his originals, as far as was possible with the graver. Latterly his eye-sight failed from intense application to his profession.

WYATT, Matthew Cotes, an English sculptor, born in London, 1778, died there January 3, 1862. He was a member of a family distinguished for their ability in art, especially architecture, of which profession his father, James Wyatt, was one of the most distinguished ornaments, well known as the designer of the Drury Lane Theatre, Apsley House, and other public and private buildings in London. He was educated at Eton, and displaying a taste for sculpture soon acquired the patronage of the Royal Family. He was employed by George IV. in numerous works, including the beautiful cenotaph in St. George's Chapel, Windsor, to the memory of the Princess Charlotte. This is one of the most generally admired productions of modern sculpture. In it the departing spirit of the Princess is represented ascending from the body, which lies prostrate, surrounded by weeping mourners beneath. The equestrian statue of the Duke of Wellington, of colossal proportions, erected on the arch at Hyde Park corner; the monument to Lord Nelson in the Quadrangle of the Exchange, Liverpool; the statue of King George III., in Pall Mall, London, are among his best known works; the latter has been much ridiculed from its strict adherence to the minutiæ of modern costume. He was also extensively employed in monumental sculpture at St. Paul's Cathedral and Westminster Abbey. Mr. Wyatt was highly and universally esteemed for his amiable and social qualities. To his son, James, a sculptor of distinction, he confided for completion the works left unfinished at his decease.

suit, his buildings being invariably loaded with stuccoes. Like the Fontanas and others, he fell into the extravagancies of Buonarotti, without his excellencies, and erected many works which gained him great reputation in his time, but which cannot stand the test of enlightened criticism. He completed the church of S. Giacomo degl' Incurabili, and made the façade of two orders of pilasters, the first Doric, with plain metopes, very improperly placed; the second Corinthian, with separated pedestals, but at very small distances. The whole work abounds in defects. His façade of Santa Susanna is grand and rich in travertine and sculpture, but is a group of absurdities.

Maderno was appointed to complete the building of St. Peter's, in which nothing remained to be done but to finish that part toward the entrance, giving it the same form as that at the upper end, and thus complete the Greek cross, which had been the intention of Bramante, Peruzzi, and Buonarotti. Instead of doing this, however, he changed the Greek into the Latin cross, and destroyed the harmony of the whole edifice. According to Milizia, this work is exceedingly disproportioned. He says, "the effect produced on the spectator who enters St. Peter's for the first time will be that of an ordinary church, appearing much less than it really is. It is easy to see whence this grand defect arises, when we consider the disproportion between the two lateral aisles added by Maderno, and the grand centre nave planned by Buonarotti, the former being no wider than one of the many altars which are in them. This result, by incorrect judges, has been attributed to the beauty of the proportions; and even Montesquieu, in his Treatise on Taste, subscribes to this singular opinion. But the real effect of just proportions is to make an edifice appear larger than it really is, as is the case in the Sforza chapel in S. Maria Maggiore; that of the Medici in S. Lorenzo at Florence; the Library in the same church; the temple of the Madonna degli Angeli, near Assisi, reduced by Michael Angelo to its present proportions. When one enters these or similar edifices, the heart expands, becomes ennobled, and more capable of receiving the grand impressions which the building is calculated to inspire. Were one to enter St. Peter's with the eyes closed, and not open them until he reached one of the lateral arms, in which is the altar of St. Simon and St. Jude, or that of Sts. Processo and Martiniano, he would be astonished at the surrounding grandeur, magnificence, and vastness, which are not evident upon entering the principal gate." In addition to the above, Milizia severely criticises the façade, and many other additions by Maderno, and concludes by calling him "a perfect master of distorted architecture."

Notwithstanding the imperfections of Maderno, his work at St. Peter's gained him such great reputation, that scarcely an edifice was erected without his designs and advice. His reputation extended beyond Rome, and many of his designs were sent to the first cities in Italy, Spain, and France. He completed the palace at Monte Cavallo; removed a column from the ancient Temple of Peace, and erected it in the square of S. Maria Maggiore. He was commanded by the Pope to examine the different ports of the State, and to take the plan of the fortress of Ferrara. Among his other works are the church and monastery of Santa Lucia in Selce; that of Santa Chiara; the choir and cupola of Santa Andrea della Valle, characterized by simplicity; and the Palazzo Mattei, which does great honor to the architect, being majestic and well disposed, and the doors and windows well set out. His last work was the magnificent Barberini palace of Urban VIII., which he did not live to finish. He died in 1629.

MADERNO, Stefano, an Italian sculptor, born in Lombardy in 1576. During the first years of his professional career, he made many models after the antique, which were afterwards executed in bronze. In the Pauline chapel of S. Maria Maggiore, he executed a marble bas-relief, representing a Battle; also the model of a bas-relief in bronze, representing the History of the Foundation of S. Maria Maggiore. After executing a large number of good works, he was presented by Count Gasparo Rivaldi with a commission in the civil government of Ripetta, which completely occupied his time, so that he relinquished the art. Maderno died at Rome in 1636.

MADIONA, Antonio, a Sicilian painter, was born at Syracuse in 1650, and died in 1719. He studied under Agostino Scilla, at Rome, and afterwards accompanied Cav. Preti to Malta. According to Lanzi, he was an able artist. He painted some pictures at Malta, and more after his return to his native country, executed in a strong, vigorous style, resembling those of both his masters.

MADONNE, Dalle, an epithet applied by Italians to some artists who excelled or had some peculiarity in painting Madonnas. Thus Carlo Dolci and Carlo Maratti were called *Carlo dalle Madonne*, and Lippo Dalmasio, *Lippo dalle Madonne*, &c.

MADONNINA, Francesco, a painter who flourished at Modena about 1550. According to Vidriani, he was one of the most celebrated artists of that city, but Lanzi says there are not enough of his works remaining in Modena to form a judgment of his style.

MAENNL. See Mannl.

MAES, or MAAS, Arnold, a Dutch painter, born at Gouda in 1620. He studied under David Teniers the younger, and for a time imitated his style and subjects with considerable success and spirit, and it is supposed he would have arrived at eminence, had he devoted his powers in this line; but aspiring to a higher department of art, he went to Italy for the purpose of studying the works of the great Italian historical painters.—After a residence of several years at Rome, he returned to Holland, and died soon after his arrival; Balkema says in 1664, while on his way home. He left a large number of designs, which are still preserved and esteemed in the collections of connoisseurs. Descamps states that he etched several plates, and that he studied engraving under Renier Persyn, but he does not specify any of his prints. Zani also mentions him as an engraver.

MAES, or MAAS, Dirk or Theodore, a Dutch painter, born at Haerlem in 1656. After studying some time under Hendrick Mommers, disliking his style and subjects (markets and still-life), he placed himself under Nicholas Berghem, whose works were then held in the highest estimation, and with which he was highly delighted, and it is supposed that he would have become eminent had he confined himself to this master, and adopted his subjects; but happening to see some of the works of John van Huchtenburg, he quitted Berghem for that master, whose style and subjects he adopted, and painted ever afterwards, battles, skirmishes, huntings, horse-fairs, &c. His pictures are ingeniously composed, and touched with an intelligent and spirited pencil. He particularly excelled in his horses, which he designed and drew in various attitudes, with surpassing spirit and correctness. He went to England in the reign of King William, where he met with some encouragement, and, among other works, painted the Battle of the Boyne for the Earl of Portland, of which there is a print engraved in two sheets. He also etched some spirited prints, from his own designs, among which is a Cavalier on Horseback, fine and scarce. He died at Haerlem in 1715.

PM MAES, or MAAS, Peter, a Dutch engraver, and probably a painter, who flourished about 1578. Little is known of him. He etched a few prints in a slight but spirited style. There are some by him, copied from Henry Goltzius, marked with his name, *Peter Maes.* Bryan mentions a print by him, representing the Virgin and Child, signed *P. Maas, fecit, in aqua forti.* Brulliot gives two prints marked with his monogram, dated 1577 and 1578, one of which is a portrait of Mary Queen of Scots.

MAES, or MAAS, Nicholas, a Dutch painter, born at Dort in 1632. After learning the rudiments of the art in his native city, he went to Amsterdam, and entered the school of Rembrandt. Under that master he became an excellent colorist, and, on leaving him, distinguished himself as a painter of historical subjects of small size, in which he imitated with great success the richness of tone and harmony of effect to be found in the works of Rembrandt. Finding portrait painting a more profitable pursuit, and possessing great facility of execution and a spirited pencil, he devoted himself afterwards almost exclusively to this branch of the art, in which he found such abundant employment that it was accounted a great favor to get a portrait painted by him. His cabinet pictures are very scarce. Smith, with all his research, specifies only forty-five in his Catalogue raisonné and supplement. They are chiefly found in public galleries, and the private collections of opulent persons, and they are so much esteemed that they bring very high prices when they appear in the public sales. There are some of his finest subjects in the public galleries and the collections of the nobility of England, particularly the Idle Servant, and a Girl seated by a Cradle with a Child asleep, in the National Gallery. His works so nearly approach Rembrandt, that it requires a connoisseur to distinguish them from those of that master. He signed his name *N. Maes,* not Maas. He died in 1693.

MAES, or MAAS, Godfrey, an eminent Flemish painter, born at Antwerp in 1660. He was the son of an obscure painter, who instructed him in the elements of the art. Possessing genius and a deep love of art, and being surrounded with the grand productions of Rubens and other eminent artists, he studied them so attentively that he became one of the most eminent artists of his time. He painted sacred and historical subjects in the grand Flemish style, which are to be found in the churches and public edifices of the different cities of the Netherlands, especially of Antwerp, where his works appear to the greatest advantage. In the Cathedral of that city is a fine picture by him, representing the Death of St. Lucia; in the church of St. George is his celebrated altar-piece of the death of that Saint; and in the church of the Hospital is his Assumption of the Virgin, composed and executed in the great style of Rubens. In 1682, when he was admitted a member of the Academy at Antwerp, he painted for his reception picture a subject emblematical of the Liberal Arts, which is one of the most admirable works in the Hall. His compositions are ingenious and abundant, his design more correct than is usual with the Flemish painters, and like the generality of his countrymen, he was an excellent colorist. He draped his figures elegantly, with broad folds, and was a strict observer of the propriety of costume. His back-grounds were enriched with noble architecture, or the vestiges of ancient magnificent buildings in appropriate landscapes. He was constantly employed in executing works for the churches, the palaces of the nobility, and for several foreign princes. He was appointed to the honorable office of Director of the Academy of Antwerp. He died in 1722.

There are many other artists of the name of *Maes*, whose biography has not been written, but the foregoing are the principal.

MAFFEI, Francesco, was a native of Vicenza, and studied under Santo Peranda, some of whose pictures left unfinished at his death, he completed. He afterwards adopted the manner of Paul Veronese with considerable success. His style is on a lofty scale, insomuch that Boschini calls him a great mannerist and a painter of giants. According to Lanzi and other authors, he displays so much originality of design, with so much grace, that he cannot be ranked among the mannerists. His coloring too, exhibits the true glow of the Venetian school. Lanzi says his picture of St. Anna at San Michele di Vicenza, besides many works produced at the same place for the public edifices, and elsewhere, extremely poetical, full of fine portraits, and colored in the best Venetian style, show that he was able to compete with his ablest cotemporaries. His great fault was that he did not finish his works, or at least some of them, with sufficient care, often leaving some of his heads and figures incomplete. He was scanty in his coloring, employing dark grounds, and painted rather for immediate effect, than for permanence. His grand picture of Paradise, in the church of S. Francesco at Padua, owing to this method, has lost almost every trace of color, so that the praise of Boschini, that with four strokes of his pencil he could make the beholder raise his eyes in admiration, should rather be a warning to our expeditious artists who wish to preserve their reputation to posterity. He died at Padua in 1660.

MAFFEI, Jacopo, a Venetian painter, who, according to Lanzi, was an admirable painter of marines and incidents at sea, some of which were engraved by Boschini. He flourished in 1663.

MAGAGNOLO, Francesco, a painter of Modena, who flourished there about 1500. According to Tiraboschi, he was an excellent artist, and one of the first who drew his countenances in such a manner as to appear looking at the spectator at whatever point of view he might observe them.

MAGANZA, Gio. Battista, the elder, was born at Vicenza in 1509. He was brought up in the school of Titian, whose style he imitated with great success, especially in portraits, which are his best works, though he left some historical pictures at Vicenza which evince a chaste and refined taste. He was the head of a family of artists who did honor to their country. He was also quite famous as a poet, and wrote verses in the rustic idiom of Parma, under the name of "Magagno," while such cotemporaries as Tasso, Trissino, Sperone, and other celebrated wits, not ignorant of the dialect, applauded the excellence of his rude sylvan strains. He died in 1589.

MAGANZA, Alessandro, the son of the preceding, was born at Vicenza in 1556. After receiving instructions from his father, he studied with Gio. Antonio Fasolo, who inspired him with his own taste. He was also a fine imitator of Zelotti and Paul Veronese, as he has shown by his Adoration of the Magi, in the church of S. Domenico, and the Martyrdom of S. Giustina, in S. Pietro, at Vicenza. Lanzi says he executed many works which are to be found in the private and public edifices at Vicenza, and in the provinces and adjacent cities. He had great facility of execution, was judicious in his composition, and pleasing in his countenances, which are often repeated in different works. He enriched his pictures with noble architecture. Lanzi says that his flesh tints incline towards white, the folds of his draperies are somewhat hard and monotonous; and that he not unfrequently presents us with the same features, and the same attitudes and motions. This last could not be from want of genius, which some of his works show to have been of a high order, but from the necessities of a numerous family for whom he had to provide. He was exceedingly unfortunate as a father! His son Gio. Battista died in 1617, leaving a young family to the care of their grandfather. His second son, Girolamo, who had also to provide for his own children, and Marc' Antonio, his third son, then a youth, afterwards assisted their father in his works, and began to acquire distinction themselves, when the great plague that ravaged Italy in 1630, swept the whole family away, first his two sons, then all his grandchildren, one after another, until, "left the last of his race," to lament over the destruction of his kindred, he soon followed them to the tomb, in the same year, aged 74.

MAGANZA, Gio. Battista, the younger, was the son of Alessandro M., born at Vicenza in 1577, and died in 1617. He studied under his father, whom he afterwards assisted in many of his principal works, and whom he nearly equalled, as is proved by his fine picture of St. Benedetto in the church of S. Giustina at Padua.

MAGATTI, Pietro, a native of Varese, who flourished at Milan about 1770. He was a good artist, and executed some works for the churches. Lanzi says his works are somewhat tinctured with the greenish hues, introduced by Solimena in Naples, and which spread over Italy.

MAGGI, Giovanni, an Italian painter and engraver, who flourished at Rome in the last part of the 16th, and first part of the 17th centuries. He painted landscapes and architectural views but is more known as an engraver. In 1618, in conjunction with Domenico Parasachi, he published a series of plates representing the principal fountains of Rome. He also undertook to engrave a plan of Rome, with its principal edifices, on a very extended scale, but it was abandoned for want of patronage. The following prints are also by him: A Landscape with Ruins and a Waterfall, with figures; *J. Maius, in. et. fec.* 1595. Figura della Vita humana; *Joh. Maius, fec.* 1600. The portrait of a Cardinal; as large as life.

MAGGI, Pietro, a Milanese painter, who studied under Filippo Abbiati, whose manner he imitated. He was a reputable artist, and flourished about 1700.

MAGGIERI, Cesare, a painter of Urbino, who, according to Lazzari, was a good and an industrious artist, and executed many works for the churches of his native city and other places. Lanzi says his style inclines to that of Barocci and the Roman school. In a picture of St. Agostino, at Castel di Castello, he signs his name *Maccerius.* He died in 1629.

MAGGIERI, Basilio, a painter of Urbino, probably a brother of the preceding, who flourished about the same time, and excelled in portraits.

MAGGIOTTO, Domenico, a Venetian painter, who studied under Gio. Battista Piazzetta, whose style he adopted, though much subdued. He painted history with considerable reputation, and some of his works have been engraved at Venice and in Germany. He died in 1794, at an advanced age.

MAGISTRIS, Simone de, a native of Caldarola, who flourished in the Roman States about 1585. He acquired considerable eminence, both as a painter and a sculptor, and left many works in the provinces. His best works are at Ascoli; and his Madonna del Rosario in the church of S. Domenico, and another of the same subject at S. Rocco, are highly commended by Orsini. None of his sculptures are mentioned.

MAGLIAR, Andrea, an Italian engraver, born at Naples in 1692. He engraved some plates *after Franceso Solimena.* He had a son named Gioseffo, whom he instructed in the art, and who gave promise of uncommon ability, but died very young. He engraved a plate representing Christ appearing to St. Guglielmo, *after Solimena*

MAGLIONE. See Benincasa.

MAGNANI, Cristoforo, a native of Pizzighettone; studied under Bernardino Campi. He was an artist of great promise, but died young about 1580. Antonio Campi laments the shortness of his career, and Lamo mentions him and Trotti as the two greatest geniuses of the school of Cremona. He painted some considerable frescos in conjunction with Cav. Molosso and Mainardi. Lanzi says nothing of his works remain that has not been questioned. His chief talent lay in portraits, and it is said his memory was so retentive that he could draw the portrait of any person he had ever seen.

MAGNASCO, Alessandro, called *Lissandrino,* was born at Genoa in 1681. He was the son of Stefano M., a pupil of Valerio Castello, who died while he was in his infancy. He studied under Filippo Abbiati at Milan, and though he painted different subjects, on a smaller scale than those of his master, yet he acquired much of the boldness and spirit of his touch. He was very fond of painting military evolutions, public processions, schools of girls and boys, chapters of friars, artists' shops, Jewish synagogues, &c., which he painted with great humor and delight. His figures are seldom more than a span in length, executed with a bold, simple stroke of the pencil. Lanzi calls him the *Cerquozzi* of the Genoese school. There are many of his works in the private and public collections at Milan, and especially at Florence, where he resided many years, and was a great favorite with the Grand Duke Gio. Guastone, and all his court. Several are in the Pitti Gallery. He was an eccentric character, and when he inserted the figures in the works of his brother artists, which he was often solicited to do, he frequently added the most opposite subjects, which produced a most comical effect. This he did in the architectural ruins of Clemente Spera, and in the landscapes of Tavella and others. He died in 1747.

MAHUE, WILHELM, an eminent Dutch portrait painter, born at Brussels in 1517, and died there in 1569. Little is known of the events of his life. He is said to have enjoyed great reputation in his day. His works are rare, and mostly confined to his own country.

MAIA, GIOVANNI STEFANO, a native of Genoa, was born in 1672, and died in 1747. According to Ratti, he went to Naples and studied under Solimena. He was a reputable painter, and excelled in portraits.

MAIANO, GIULIANO DA, a Florentine architect, a native of the village of Maiano, near Fiesole. His father was a stone cutter, and wished him to pursue a literary career; but the son first devoted himself to sculpture, and afterwards to architecture. Invited to Naples by King Alfonso, he erected the magnificent palace of Poggio Reale, in the form of a square, with an arched portico in the centre, at the wings of which are Ionic pilasters, on high pedestals. The second floor has Corinthian pilasters, between which are windows, with a pediment. He erected a noble gate to the Castel Nuovo of Naples in the Corinthian style, like a triumphal arch, enriched with large figures and bas-reliefs. He also made designs for various works, particularly for many fountains in private palaces, contrived in a very ingenious manner. Being invited to Rome by Paul II., he made a court yard in the Vatican palace, which appears, according to Milizia, to be that now called S. Damaso, surrounded on three sides by three galleries of three orders. His principal work, however, was the palace and church of St. Mark, where he employed a great quantity of travertine stone taken from the ruins of the Coliseum. The pope sent him to Loretto, to adorn the body of that church, and he then returned to Naples, to complete the edifices he had commenced in that city. Vasari says that he died at Naples in 1447, in the reign of King Alfonso; but this statement is evidently incorrect, from the fact of Giuliano being employed by Paul II., who was pope from 1464 to 1471. Rumohr has clearly ascertained that Maiano was living at Florence in 1471.

MAIANO, BENEDETTO DA, the nephew of Giuliano da M., was born in 1444. He studied sculpture and architecture with success, and also gained great reputation for his performances in inlaid work, of which several specimens may be seen in the sacristy of S. Maria del Fiore at Florence, remarkable for their richness, good taste, and finished ornaments. King Alfonso of Naples invited him to that city, where his uncle was at that time employed, and he executed several works; but on receiving an invitation from Matthias Corvinus, King of Hungary, he visited that country, and remained some time in the King's service. Returning to Florence, he was commissioned to erect the grand entrance to the Hall of Audience, and executed the sculptures, besides the admirable portraits of Dante and Petrarch in inlaid work. By order of Lorenzo the Magnificent, he executed a marble bust of Giotto, placed in the church of S. Maria del Fiore. He was invited to Naples, and commissioned with many works, among which were a marble bas-relief of the Annunciation, in the monastery of Monte Oliveto. He afterwards returned to Florence, and executed the grand marble pulpit in the church of Santa Croce, representing the History of St. Francesco, which has been engraved in the *Notizie delle Chiese Florentine*, by P. Richa, vol. I., plate 56. Maiano died in 1498, and was buried with honors in the church of S. Lorenzo at Florence.

MAILLET, JOSEPH, a French engraver, who flourished at Paris about 1775. There are some plates of landscapes engraved by him in a neat, pleasing style.

MAINARDI, LATTANZIO, a Bolognese painter, who studied in the school of the Caracci, and went to Rome where he was employed in the Vatican in the Pontificate of Sextus V. He possessed genius, and the works he conducted there, gave promise of great renown, but he died at the early age of 27 years. Baglione calls him Lattanzio Bolognese.

MAINARDI, ANDREA, called IL CHIAVEGHINO, was a native of Cremona, where he exercised his art from 1590 to 1613. He was brought up in the school of Bernardino Campi, was one of his ablest scholars, and instructed several pupils. In conjunction with his nephew, Marc' Antonio Mainardi, he executed several considerable works at Cremona. One of his best pictures is the Marriage of St. Anna in the church of the Eremitani, which is pronounced an admirable performance in design, coloring, and execution. Unfortunately for his reputation, he did not always bestow equal care and attention upon his works, some of which show negligence in design, and haste in execution.

MAINARDI, MARC' ANTONIO, was a native of Cremona, and studied under Campi. He was an excellent artist; assisted his uncle Andrea M. in many of his works, and also painted several pictures from his own designs, one of which, at Castel Buttano, in the Cremonese, is dated 1629.

MAINARDI, BASTIANO, a reputable mosaic painter, and a native of Florence, who studied under Domenico del Ghirlandaio.

MAINERO, GIO. BATTISTA, a Genoese painter born in 1610. He studied under Luciano Borzone, under whose instruction he made rapid progress, and at an early age distinguished himself by some cabinet pictures of historical subjects, which were much admired. He excelled in portraits, and meeting with ample patronage from the nobility and gentry, he afterwards made this branch his exclusive occupation. He died of the plague in 1657.

MAIR MAIR, an old German engraver, who flourished about 1499. From resemblance of style, it is supposed that he was a disciple of Martin Schoen, though greatly inferior to that master. Their design is equally Gothic. He is said to have been the inventor of that species of engraving called chiaro-scuro. There are some fifteen or sixteen prints attributed to him, generally marked with his name, and dated 1499, among which are the following:

Samson carrying the Gates of Gaza. The Wise Men's Offering. The Martyrdom of St. Sebastian. A Man talking to a Woman, seen through the door of a house, with a Dog snarling at a Monkey. The Virgin and Infant, with St. Anne. The Virgin and Infant, with St. Joseph holding a Candle; in chiaro-scuro.

AM MAIR, ALEXANDER, a German engraver on wood and copper, who flourished at Augsburg about 1600. He was chiefly employed in engraving plates and frontispieces for the booksellers, some of which are executed in so masterly a manner, that it is regretted his talents had not been employed on more important subjects. He usually marked his plates with a monogram of his initials, as above.

MAIR, a German painter of insects, serpents, lizards, and other reptiles, in the manner of Otho Masseus or Marcellis, to whom his works are generally attributed, though they are painted on a lighter ground. He particularly excelled in painting butterflies. Little is known of him, except that he lived at Nimeguen in the 18th century.

MAISON-NEUVE, a modern French engraver, briefly mentioned by Basan. He engraved several portraits, among which is one of Jacques Theodore Klein. He also engraved the French Parnassus, from a bronze.

MAITRE, ROUX. See ROSSO.

MAJOLI, or MAJOLA, CLEMENTE, a painter of Ferrara, was born about 1640, and studied at Rome under P. da Cortona. He acquired considerable reputation, and there are some of his works in the Rotunda at Rome, and many in the churches at Ferrara and other cities, which are commended, especially a picture of S. Maria Maddalena de' Pazzi in the church of S. Paolo, and S. Niccolo da Tolentino, supported by an Angel, in the church of S. Giuseppe at Ferrara.

MAJOR, ISAAC, a German painter and engraver, born at Frankfort about 1576. He went to Prague, and studied painting for some time under Roland Savery, the painter to Rodolphus II. He afterwards studied engraving under Giles Sadeler, in whose style he engraved several plates, which have considerable merit, though they are greatly inferior to the works of his master. In the execution of his plates he united the point and the graver. The following are among his best prints:

A set of six Landscapes, Views in Bohemia; *after P. Stephani.* A set of nine romantic Views, numbered; *Isaac Major, fec.* A very large Landscape, with the figure of St. Jerome; *after Roland Savery. Isaac Major, sul., Viennæ.* 1622. The Emperor in a Triumphal Car, with Swans and Eagles; inscribed *Ite Triumphalis felices,* &c.

MAJOR, THOMAS, an English engraver, born about 1715. According to Strutt, he went to Paris while young, where he learned the art, and engraved several plates after Berghem, Wouwerman, and others. On his return to England he settled in London, where he distinguished himself by a variety of plates of portraits, landscapes, and other subjects, executed in a neat, firm style. In 1768 he published a set of twenty-four prints, entitled *The Ruins of Paestum, otherwise Posidonia, in Magna Græcia,* after the designs of J. B. Borra. On some of his earlier prints after Berghem and others, he put his name in an anagram, as *Jorma,* or *Jor. sculp.* The following are his best plates:

PORTRAITS.

John Carteret, Earl of Granville, 1757. Cardinal Pole.

VARIOUS SUBJECTS.

The Departure of Jacob; *after F. Lauri.* The Good Shepherd; *after Murillo.* Two Landscapes; *after Gaspar Poussin.* A Landscape, with a Man driving Sheep; *after Rubens.* Two Flemish Festivals; *after Teniers.* The Manege; *after Wouwerman.* The Travelers; *after N. Berghem.* Two Landscapes; Morning and Evening; *do.* The Four Seasons; *after Ferg.* A View near Haerlem; *after Vander Neer.* A Sea-port; *after Claude* A View of Ponte Mole, near Rome; *do.*

MALAGAVAZZO, CORIOLANO, born at Cremona about 1555, was a pupil of Bernardino Campi, whom he assisted in his great work in the church of S. Gismondo, at Cremona. He is more known as the coadjutor of that eminent artist than from any original productions of his own. His principal work is a picture of the Virgin and Infant, with Sts. Francis and Ignatius, in the church of S. Silvestro at Cremona, which is a fine picture, and supposed by Lanzi, Zaist, and others, to have been executed from the designs of Campi. It is dated 1585.

MALBONE, EDWARD G., an American portrait painter, was a native of Newport, Rhode Island. He early manifested an inclination for art, and during boyhood, he delighted in sketching objects from nature. Possessing few advantages for improvement, he was accustomed to frequent the theatre, to witness the illusions of scenery, and finally attracted the attention of the scene-painter, who gave him opportunities of exercising his talent. He occupied his leisure hours in drawing heads, and finally devoted his entire energies to painting miniature portraits. He practised the art with considerable success in Boston, New York, and Philadelphia; and in the winter of 1800, he went to Charleston, where he received considerable patronage. In May, 1801, he visited England, and passed several months at London, studying the best works of art in that city. Mr. West, the president of the Academy, gave Malbone free access to his study, and showed him every attention. He even encouraged the young artist to remain in England; but Malbone returned to Charleston in the winter of 1801, and practised the art with success in different American cities, until 1806, when he was obliged to relinquish it, on account of ill health. He died at Charleston in 1807.

MALDUCCI, MAURO, a priest of Forli, who, according to Guarienti, studied with Carlo Cignani, and was a reputable artist.

MALEUVRE, PIERRE, a French engraver, born at Paris in 1740. He first studied under Beauvarlet, and afterwards went to London, and placed himself under Sir Robert Strange. On his return to Paris, he engraved some plates of portraits and other subjects, in a neat, pleasing style, among which are the following:

PORTRAITS.

Gustavus Adolphus, King of Sweden. Count d'Aranda. M. d'Alembert. M. de Lalande.

VARIOUS SUBJECTS.

The Dozer; *after Craesbeck.* The Satyr and the Peasant; *after Dietricy.* The Spoiled Child; *after Greuze.* A Sea-storm; *after Backhuysen.* Boors regaling; *after Brower.* The Bath of Diana; *after Marillier.*

MALINCONICO, ANDREA, a Neapolitan painter, born about 1600. According to Dominici, he studied under Cav. Massimo Stanzioni, and was one of his ablest scholars. His frescos are almost entirely perished, but there are many of his works in oil in the churches and public edifices of Naples, particularly in the church de' Miracoli, where he painted almost all the pictures himself. The best of these are the Four Evangelists, and the Doctors of the Church. Dominici says they are most beautiful pictures; the design is original, the attitudes noble, and the whole painted with the spirit of a great artist. Lanzi says there are other works by this artist, but several are feeble and spiritless, and not worthy of his reputation.

MALLERY, CHARLES DE, a Flemish designer and engraver, born at Antwerp about 1576. It is not known with whom he studied, but from his style being founded on that of the Wierixes, it is supposed he was instructed by them. He wrought entirely with the graver, in a highly finished style, though his drawing is sometimes incorrect. He was an extremely laborious artist, and executed a multitude of prints, with the greatest delicacy. The Abbé de Marolles possessed three hundred and forty-two prints by him. Vandyck painted his portrait among the celebrated artists of his time, which was engraved by Lucas Vorsterman. The following are some of his best prints:

The infant Jesus, with two Angels, in a landscape; *C. de Mallery, fec.* The Adoration of the Magi. The Holy Family, with Mary Magdalene. St. Francis. Several Heads of Christ, the Virgin, Saints, the Apostles, and other devotional subjects; *from his own designs*, and *after Anthony Salaert*, and other masters. Part of the plates of the great Huntings; *after Stradan;* engraved in conjunction with the Collaerts, the Galles, and others. The History of the Silkworm; in six plates; *after Stradan.* A set of plates of Horses, for a book entitled *La Cavalerie Francoise.* 1603. Four plates of the Miller, his Son, and the Ass; *after Ambrose Franck;* scarce.

MALLERY, PHILIP DE, a Flemish engraver, the scholar, and probably the son, of Charles de M., born at Antwerp in 1600. His plates are executed with a precision, delicacy, and taste resembling that of his instructor. He engraved the plates for a work entitled *Typus Mundi*, published at Antwerp in 1627, and afterwards in 1652. Among other prints there are by him the following: The portrait of John Lelio, Archbishop of Prague; the Crucifixion, with a Table at the foot of the Cross, where a number of Men and Women are engaged in merriment; twenty-three prints, entitled *Ara Cœli;* but the first one is by Anthony Wierix.

MALO VINCENT, a Flemish painter, born at Cambray about 1625. He first studied under Rubens, and after the death of that great master, with David Teniers the Elder. Under those masters he acquired such excellence of design and beauty of coloring, that his works were eagerly sought after. He afterwards went to Italy, where he passed the remainder of his life, and where his reputation rose so high that he could scarcely execute all the orders he received, and almost every cabinet in Genoa, Florence, and Rome, possessed some of his works. He painted some sacred subjects for the churches at Genoa, but his forte lay in landscapes and battles, and humorous pieces He died at Rome about 1670.

MALOMBRA, PIETRO, a Venetian painter, who studied under Giuseppe Porta, called Salviati. Born in easy circumstances, he acquired an excellent education, and imbued with a deep love of art, he strove to reach excellence, adopting the axiom, that "honor is better than gain." Meeting with reverses, he entered upon the art as his profession, and acquired considerable distinction. He made the works of Palma his model, but he was no servile imitator. His composition and design are more studied and correct than is usual with the Venetian painters. He was much employed in decorating the churches, and the public and private edifices of Venice. Among his most admired works are his four pictures in the church of S. Francesco de Paolo, representing the miracles of that saint, which Lanzi says display such an originality of design, precision of contours, elegance and grace, as to lead us to doubt whether they can belong to that epoch and to the Venetian school. He is still more admired for his easel pictures of historical subjects; and he painted portraits with equal success. He also painted architectural views of noted places in Venice, as the grand Piazza, and the great Hall of the Council, enriched with assemblages of figures, representing sacred and civil ceremonies, public audiences, processions, and grand spectacles, with such grandeur, truth, and spirit, that they extorted the plaudits of all ranks. He was born at Venice in 1550, and died in 1618.

MALOSSO. See TROTTI.

MALPIEDI, DOMENICO, a native of San Ginesio, and a painter of the Roman school who, according to Colucci, studied under Federigo Baroccio. There are several of his works in the churches of his native place, especially two pictures of the Martyrdom of Saints Ginesio and Eleuterio, in the Collegiate church, are highly commended. He was esteemed an excellent artist, and received high prices for his works. He was living in 1596.

MALPIEDI, FRANCESCO, another painter of S. Ginesio, who flourished about the same time as the preceding at S. Ginesio. Lanzi mentions a Deposition from the Cross by him in the church of S. Francesco di Osimo, inscribed *Franciscus Malpedius di S. Ginesio*, which he says is feeble in composition, and little resembles the school of Baroccio, except in coloring.

MALTESE, FRANCESCO, an artist so called from the place of his nativity. There are no particulars of his life recorded. He flourished about 1670. His subjects were fruit, caskets, jewels, shells, books, and musical instruments, placed upon tables covered with rich cloths and tapestry, which he executed with great truth and spirit. He was a perfect master of chiaro-scuro, and by a judi cious distribution of his masses of light and shadow, he gave every object a surprising relief. His touch is bold and free, and his tone of coloring natural. The manner of his penciling was peculiar, being rough or smooth, according to the objects represented. Some of his compositions appear crowded, and he did not always make the most agreeable choice and disposition of his objects. Sandrart mentions two of his pictures in the gallery at Munich. There are some in England, others have been brought to the United States.

MALTON, Thomas, an English designer and engraver, born in 1748. He wrote a "Treatise on Perspective, in Theory and Practice," and a "Picturesque Tour through London." He also engraved some aquatint plates of many of the principal edifices of London. He died about 1804.

MAN, Cornelius. See Maan.

MANAIGO, Silvestro, a Venetian painter, born about 1680, and a scholar of Gregorio Lazzarini. He possessed a fertile invention, which was matured by an attentive study of nature and the antique, and his compositions evince both genius and taste; but his love of gain too often seduced him to negligence of design and rapidity of operation, so that he fell into the tameness and repetition of a mannerist. Lanzi says his works have a fine character, but he was too rapid, and too much of a mannerist. Zanetti praises his Joseph sold by his Brethren, formerly in the possession of Giuseppe Pedrini at Venice, in which the characters are so true to nature, as to make it a work "worthy of the greatest painter." Other fine works by this artist are Christ driving the Money Changers from the Temple, in the church of S. Felice, and a grand picture of St. Matthew in the church of S. Eustachio at Venice.

MANASAR, Daniel, a German engraver, who flourished at Augsburg about 1626. He engraved chiefly architectural views, plans of buildings, &c., executed with the graver in a neat, but formal style. In conjunction with Wolfgang Kilian, he engraved the plates for a work entitled ***Basilicæ S. S. Udalrici et afræ Augustæ Vindelicorum Historiæ***, published at Augsburg in 1626. He usually marked his plates with his initials, D. M. F.

MANCHETTI, Michele, a native of Genoa, born about 1550; who, according to Dominici, studied under Marco di Pino at Naples, and acquired considerable reputation as an historical painter. He executed some works for the churches of Naples, the best of which was a picture representing the Virgin and Infant, with St. John, Mary Magdalene, and Lucia, painted in 1586.

MANCINI, Annibale, an historical painter, extolled by Marini, who flourished at Turin about 1610.

MANCINI, Francesco, an eminent painter, was a native of S. Angelo, in Vado, and studied under Carlo Cignani at Bologna. Lanzi says, when he went to Rome he did not adhere exclusively to his master's manner, but rather attached himself to the facility and freedom of Franceschini. He designed well, colored in a charming manner, and was numbered among the first artists of his age in Rome. He executed many works for the churches at Rome and in various places in the dominions of the church. He painted the miracle of St Peter, at the Beautiful Gate of the Temple, a picture which is now in the palace of Monte Cavallo, and is copied in mosaic in St. Peter's. This picture is a spirited and grand composition, and is considered his master-piece. He painted many pictures for foreign collections, and he was especially commended for his large compositions. He was elected a member of the Academy of St. Luke in 1725, and died in 1758.

MANDER, Karel Van. See Vanmander.

MANDROCLES, an ancient architect, who flourished about B. C. 500; and constructed the great bridge of boats across the Thracian Bosphorus, by order of Darius, King of Persia. It was joined together in such a firm and ingenious manner, that the army passed over it in safety. Herodotus mentions a picture in the Temple of Juno at Samos, representing the Bosphorus with the Bridge, King Darius enthroned, and the Persian army. Upon it was inscribed, *Mandrocles, after having constructed a bridge of boats over the Bosphorus, by order of the King Darius of Persia, dedicated this monument to Juno, which does honor to Samos, his country, and the artificer.*

MANDYN, John, a Dutch painter, born at Haerlem about 1450. He painted drolls, incantations, and grotesque subjects, conflagrations and rocky landscapes, with great ingenuity and wit, in a style resembling that of Jerome Bosche, of whom he is said to have been the imitator; yet Bosche was born in 1470, twenty years after him. There are great discrepancies among authors about this artist. He is called *Jan* and *Johann Mandyn*, *Mandin*, *Madyn*, and *Madin*. Balkema says he was born in 1450, and died in 1568, making him 118 years old. Immerzeel places his birth in 1568, and says he instructed Bartholomew Spranger, who was born in 1546, and it is generally stated by authors in their biography of Spranger, that he first studied under John Madyn, which makes an error somewhere of an hundred years. Zani says, Mandyn died in 1500. So it is evident, from these and other contradictions, that there were two Mandyns, or a Mandyn and a Madyn, who lived a hundred years apart.

MANENTI, Vincenzio, an Italian painter, born at Canimorto, in the province of Sabina in 1600, and died in 1674. He was the son of Ascanio M., who instructed him in the rudiments of the art. He afterwards studied at Rome, first under Giuseppe Cesari, and next Domenichino. Lanzi says there are several of his works at Tivoli, which, though they do not exhibit an artist of great genius, show one assiduous and expert in coloring, and he specifies his St. Stephen in the Duomo (cathedral), and his St. Saverio in the church of Il Gesu. In coloring he imitated Domenichino, and it should be recollected that when a severe critic and a connoisseur like Lanzi, (a profound scholar, brought up amidst the gems of ancient and modern art, and one who pays more attention to *academy*, or the strict rules of art, than to coloring,) commends such an artist, in some countries he would be called a *Domenichino*, whose pictures, the Italians say, will bleed if pricked.

MANETTI, or MANNETTI, Rutilio, an eminent Sienese painter, born in 1571, and died in 1637, according to Lanzi, from authentic documents. He studied under Francesco Vanni, and at first imitated his graceful style and pleasing coloring, but he afterwards adopted much of the manner of Michael Angelo da Caravaggio, whose fame was then captivating Italy. He acquired great reputation, and executed many works for the churches and monasteries at Pisa, Florence, and Siena. There is considerable discrepancy among authors as to his merits, but it is allowed that he was a man of genius, had a fine invention, was correct in design, and disposed his figures with elegance and grace. He enriched his pictures with noble architecture, and hence, at times he approaches nearer to Guercino than to Caravaggio. Lanzi says his pictures are easily recognized by a tenebrosity that injures a just balance of light and shade,—a fault that is doubtless partly owing to changes wrought by time, from an injudicious mixture of colors, for the historian of the cathedral of Siena, in describing his Elijah under the Juniper Tree, in that edifice, commends the force of the coloring, and says it is juicy and natural. Lanzi further says that in private collections, where pictures are better preserved than in churches, we find very beautiful Madonnas by this artist; and he mentions "a most exquisite Lucretia in the possession of the Bandinelli family." There are many of his works at the Certosa, and the Carthusian monastery at Florence; his chef d'œuvre is the Repose of the Holy Family, in the church of S. Pietro, at Castelvecchio.

MANETTI, Domenico, a Sienese painter, probably a relative of the preceding, who acquired considerable reputation for his easel pictures of historical subjects, many of which are found in the private collections of Siena. Lanzi says his Baptism of Constantine, in the Casa Magnoni at Siena, has been highly commended.

MANFREDI, Bartolomeo, an Italian painter, born at Mantua in 1574. He first studied under Cristoforo Roncalli, but afterwards became a disciple of Michel Angelo da Caravaggio, whose style he imitated with such precision, that his works were often attributed to that master, though his pictures show a superior choice of forms, and a more dignified taste of design. He did not work much for the churches, but painted easel pictures representing corps-de-garde, soldiers or peasants gaming with cards and dice, fortune tellers, banditti; which he represented with appropriate ferocity of character, and an extraordinary effect of light and shadow. His pencil was free and firm, and his knowledge and skill in chiaro-scuro, enabled him to give his pictures a very striking effect of broad masses of light and shadow. He is said to have shortened his days by a dissolute and irregular life. Zani, whose dates are often incorrect, says he was born in 1580, and died in 1617.

MANGIN, Charles, a French architect, born at Mitry, near Meaux, in 1721. His uncle caused him to be instructed in mathematics and design, and placed him under several good architects. After passing the period of his tutelage, he visited Paris, and was commissioned to erect several important works, among which were the primitive *Halle au Blé;* the *Seminaire du Saint-Esprit;* the church of Gros-Caillou; and the restoration of the grand entrance to S. Sulpice. He was much esteemed by Soufflot and Chalgrin, and projected a plan for the embellishment of Paris, which gained him an honorable notice, and a gold medal. He died at Nantes in 1807.

MANGLARD, Adrien, a French painter and engraver, born at Paris in 1688, or, according to Dumesnil, at Lyons in 1696. He went to Rome early in life, where he acquired a great reputation for his sea-pieces and landscapes, and met with considerable employment. He executed some of his choicest works for the Villa Albani, and the Palazzi Colonna and Rospigliosi at Rome. Joseph Vernet was his scholar, and far surpassed him. He executed quite a number of spirited and pleasing etchings after his own designs. Dumesnil describes forty-four pieces by him. He died at Rome in 1761.

MANINI, Gaetano, a Milanese painter, born in 1730. He painted history in a gaudy and frivolous style, went to England about 1774, assumed the title of Cavaliere, occasionally exhibited with the Chartered Society of Artists, and died about 1790.

MANLIO, Ferdinando, an Italian architect of the 16th century. He was probably a pupil of Giovanni da Nola. According to Milizia, by order of the Viceroy of Toledo, he opened the road to the Porta Nolana; built a royal summer house at Pozzuoli; and drained a number of marshes. He also executed the regulations of the Viceroy, duke d'Alcala, in opening the noble road of Monte Oliveto, and erecting palaces where there were originally only the gardens of monks. He enlarged the grotto of Pozzuoli, and built the bridge of Capua.

MANNINI, or MANINI, Giacomo Antonio, a Bolognese painter, born in 1646. He studied under Domenico Santi, and according to Zanotti, became a very eminent painter of perspective and architecture. He was exceedingly accurate, but slow in his work. Lanzi says that he was employed to decorate a chapel at Colorno for the Duke of Parma, in which the Cavaliere Draghi was employed as figurist, whose genius was as eager and rapid as Mannini's was slow. Much like two steeds of opposite temper, yoked to the same vehicle, their sole occupation seemed to be biting and kicking each other, till it became necessary to separate them, and the slow one was sent back to Bologna, where, owing to this blemish, he never met with the encouragement he deserved. He etched some plates of architectural designs and perspective views, full of taste and spirit. Bartsch gives a detailed account of sixteen perspective views by him.—(P. Gr. tom. xix. p. 322.)

MANNL, or MAENNL, Jacob, a German mezzotinto engraver, born at Vienna about 1695. In 1720, Christopher Lauch, the Inspector of the Imperial Gallery, which had been augmented by the purchase of the collection of the Archduke Leopold, undertook to have all the pictures engraved, and employed Mannl for that purpose. But the death of both Lauch and Mannl happening about the same time, prevented the completion of the project, and only thirty-one were engraved. Heineken, in his idea of a complete collection of prints, gives a particular description of them. They are as follows:

The Portrait of the Emperor Charles VI. The dead Christ, supported by an Angel; *after Palma.* The Virgin with the infant Christ, who is caressing St. John; *after Vandyck.* Mary Magdalene penitent, accompanied by an Angel; *after Correggio.* St. Francis praying; *after Bassano.* St. Clara kneeling; *do.* The Repentance of St. Peter; *after Spagnoletto.* The Martyrdom of St

Bartholomew; *after L. Giordano.* Christ praying in the Garden; *after M. A. Caravaggio.* Venus, with Cupid holding a mirror; *after Titian.* Judith leaving the Tent of Holofernes; *after P. Veronese.* Christ disputing with the Doctors; *after Spagnoletto.* Samson delivered to the Philistines; *after Vandyck.* The Ecce Homo; half-length; *after Titian.* The Virgin, or Mater Dolorosa; *do.* A Philosopher meditating on a Skull; *after L. Giordano.* A Geometrician; *do.* St. Margaret treading on the Dragon; *after Raffaelle.* Tobit restoring Sight to his Father; *after M. A. Caravaggio.* Christ taken in the Garden; *after B. Manfredi.* Susanna at the Bath; *after Tintoretto.* Susanna and the Elders; *after Ann. Caracci.* Jupiter and Mercury, with Baucis and Philemon; *after Carlo Lotti.* Diana and her Nymphs; *after Willeborts Boschaert and John Fyt.* The Virgin and Infant; *after Titian.* A Warrior giving his Hand to a Man; *after Giorgione.* A dying Magdalene; *after the younger Palma.* Christ bearing his Cross; *after Bassano.* Judith with the Head of Holofernes; *after A. Varotari.* Judith; *after Carlo Veneziano.* A Child holding a Dog; *after P. Veronese.*

MANNOZZI, Giovanni, called Giovanni da San Giovanni, from the place of his nativity, near Florence, was born in 1590. He studied under Matteo Roselli. He did not follow the chaste, correct, and finished style of his master, but possessing a lively imagination, ready invention, and great facility of execution, he struck out into a style of his own, which, though sometimes marked with absurd extravagancies, gained him an immense reputation, and he was considered one of the ablest fresco painters in Italy. He was employed by the Cardinal Bentivoglio at Rome, to paint a picture of Night, as a contrast to the Aurora of Guido. This excited envy among his enemies, and after he had made considerable progress with his work, one morning, he had the misfortune to find it entirely effaced; but the miscreants being detected, he commenced and completed a new one, which gained him immense applause. Lanzi says that, although he did not begin to study till he was eighteen years old, and died in his forty-eighth year, yet he executed an incredible number of works at Rome, in the Pontifical States, and at Florence. He died in 1636.

MANNOZZI, Giovanni Garzia, was the son of the preceding, born about 1620. He was instructed in the art by his father, in whose style he painted with considerable reputation. There are some of his works in fresco in the churches at Pistoja. Time of his death not recorded.

MANRIQUE, Miguel, a native of Flanders, probably of Spanish descent, who flourished about 1650. He is said to have studied under Rubens, and having obtained a commission in the Spanish service, he went to Spain, and finally settled at Malaga, where he practised the art, and executed some works for the churches. He was a good colorist, and his works have the characteristics of the school of Rubens.

MANS, F. H. (Franz Herman?) a Dutch painter, by whom there are many pictures, small in size, of views of towns, villages, coast scenes, winter-pieces, &c., spiritedly executed, and signed with his name, and some of them dated about 1677. His winter pieces are in the manner of Klaas Molenaer, and painted with great truth and beauty.

MANSARD, François, an eminent French architect, was born at Paris in 1598, and received instructions in architecture from his paternal uncle, Germain Gaultier. At the age of twenty-two he began to distinguish himself by his restoration of the Hotel Toulouse; and a short time afterwards he was commissioned to erect the portal of the church des Feuillants, in the Rue St. Honoré, since destroyed; the chateau de Berni, near Paris; and those of Balleroi, in Normandy, Blerancourt and Choisy. His only fault was instability, which frequently led him, while aiming at perfection, to alter his designs during their execution, and to demolish what was done, in order to begin afresh. This characteristic lost him the finishing of the fine abbey of Val-de-Grace at Paris, founded by Anne of Austria, which he had commenced in 1645, but when raised to the first story, the queen was informed that large sums were being uselessly expended on the edifice; and when Mansard was interrogated, he answered her Highness with some rudeness. The direction of the church was immediately taken from him and given to others, who altered the design, and decorated the edifice with heavy sculpture. Notwithstanding this defect, Mansard was endowed with an exquisite taste, a strong mind, a habit of meditation, a fertile imagination, and great industry. His ideas for the general design of an edifice were noble and grand; and his choice in the outlines of all the members of architecture which he used was delicate and appropriate. He was employed by the President de Longueil to build his great Chateau de Maisons, near St. Germain en Laie; and when a part was erected, he pulled it down without the knowledge of the proprietor; but he afterwards completed it in a very noble style, and it is reckoned one of the finest architectural monuments of the age. Colbert applied to him for a plan of the principal front of the Louvre, and Mansard produced several sketches of great beauty; but when told that he must fix upon one to be invariably followed, if approved, he declined subjecting himself to such a condition. Milizia says that this was the reason why Bernini was invited to Paris. Mansard completed the chateau de Blois, which had been left unfinished by Gaston de France, Duke d'Orleans. In the palace of Fesora he afterwards built a chapel, which is considered a perfect model; and he invented the curb roof, called *à la Mansarde.* He adorned Paris and its environs, as well as several of the provinces, with fine edifices, of which the last was the portal of the church des Minimes in the Place Royale. He seems to have approved this work more than any other of his productions, but it is very likely he would have changed his opinion, had he not died soon after, in 1666.

MANSARD, Jules Hardouin, an eminent French architect, nephew of François M., born at Paris in 1645. He studied under his uncle, and became the favorite architect of Louis XIV., whose taste he suited through the variety and magnificence of his ideas. Though superior to his uncle in fortune, he did not equal him in merit. Milizia says he was too exuberant in his ideas, incorrect in his application of the orders; but ingenious in composition and the forms of his cupolas. His greatest work, the famous Palace of Versailles, has been severely, though perhaps justly criticised. Milizia says, "the taste of the exterior decoration is trifling, and full of defects; the palace imposes on the sight at a distance, from the large number of buildings, and its richness, the roof being all gilt, but our admiration diminishes on a nearer approach, and entirely disappears on arriving at that miserable court called *La Cour du Marbre.*" Christopher Wren described it as composed of "heaps of littleness." It has also been denominated "a favorite without merit"; but the Orangery has Tuscan columns, and is managed in the most magnificent style. The chapel is also an admirable work, being adorned with isolated columns, with bold architraves. Among other important works of this architect, are the chateau de Clagny; the chateaux of Marly and Trianon; the Mansion of St. Cyr; the Gallery of the Palais Royal; the Place Vendôme; the Places of Louis le Grand and des Victoires; and the dome and finishing of the Hotel des Invalides, commenced by Liberal Bruant. Jules Hardouin Mansard amassed an immense fortune under Louis XIV., who appointed him royal architect, cavalier of St. Michael, and general superintendent of the royal buildings, arts, and manufactures. He died suddenly at Marly, in 1708, and was buried in the parish church of St. Paul at Paris, where his tomb was sculptured by Coysevox.

MANSFELD, John Ernest, a German engraver, born at Prague in 1738. He went to Vienna when sixteen years of age, and learned design in the Imperial Academy. He engraved some portraits after eminent personages, and a few other subjects, mostly executed with the graver among which are the following:

PORTRAITS.

The Empress Maria Theresa; *J. E. Mansfeld, sc.* The Emperor Joseph II.; *do.* Pope Pius V.; *Hagenauer, pinx.* 1782. Wenceslaus, Prince Kaunitz; *after Vinazer.* Francis Anthony, Count Kollowrat; *do.* Maurice, Count Lacy; *after Kollonitz.* 1776. Frederick, Baron Trenck; *J. E. Mansfeld, fec.* Joseph Haydn; *do.* Anthony Stoerk; *do.* 1773. Sir Robert Murray Keith; *after Graff.*

SUBJECTS.

A Waterfall on the Danube; *after Wenzely.* The Coronation of the Emperor Leopold; *after Schutz.*

MANSUETI, Giovanni, a painter of the Venetian school, who flourished at Trevigi about 1500, and painted for the churches and private collections. He was a good artist, though Lanzi says he did not observe the proprieties of costume, and that there is not sufficient delicacy in his contours.

MF MANTEGNA, Cav. Andrea. There is a great deal of fiction interwoven in the history of this great artist, which our limits will not allow us to discuss. He was born at a small village near Padua, according to his picture in the church of S. Sofia at Padua, in 1431. Lanzi says he was born in 1430, and died in 1505 in his text and 1506 in his index; Pungilione 13th August 1506, and Zani 15th of September in the same year. He was the son of a poor herdsman, and Squarcione, observing him, then a lad, making some rude sketches on flat stones while tending his flock, took the lad to his own house, and instructed him in painting. He showed such extraordinary talents and made such progress, that he adopted him as his son. At an age when others usually commence the study of the art, he painted his celebrated altar-piece in the church of S. Sofia at Padua, which is inscribed *Andreas Mantinea Patavinus annos VII. et X. natus sua manu pinxit*, 1448. He soon after painted the Four Evangelists in the same church. The celebrity of these performances, it is said, induced Jacopo Bellini, the rival of Squarcione, to bestow upon the young artist his daughter in marriage. This alliance with the bitter enemy of Squarcione is said to have changed his love for Mantegna into gall, and that he became as inveterate in his detraction of the merits of his pupil as he had been lavish of his praise; and that his severe and sarcastic criticism on his works proved of the greatest advantage to him, by stimulating him to reform his manner. But this must be taken with considerable allowance. Lanzi says that "Squarcione was so pleased with the early genius of Mantegna, that he adopted him as his own son, but afterwards regretted his generosity, when he found he repaid him with ingratitude by marrying the daughter of his rival, so that he blamed him, yet continued to instruct him better than ever." The truth doubtless is that Andrea, having been bred in an academy which adopted the study of marbles (for Squarcione had a rich museum of designs, statues, and busts, which he had spared no expense to procure in his travels throughout Italy and Greece; and his academy was at that early period the most famous in Italy, at one time frequented by one hundred and thirty students), and for which he indulged a profound admiration, neglected the study of nature, and being bent upon that chasteness of contours, the beauty of the ideas and of the figures, he not only adopted that straightness of the garment, those parallel folds, and that study of parts which so easily degenerate into stiffness and formality, but that he also neglected that portion of the art which animates the otherwise lifeless images—expression. This was the case with his Martyrdom of St. James, in the church of the Eremitani, which drew down upon the artist the sarcastic criticisms of Squarcione, and led him to change his manner in the picture of St. Mark writing his Gospel executed soon afterwards, in the church of S. Giustina, where he represented in the head of the Evangelist an admirable expression of the most fervid devotion. His relationship with the Bellini also doubtless contributed to this result. A knowledge of his defects also led him to the study of nature and of the works of the celebrated masters; for, during his short residence at Venice, Lanzi says "he did not fail to avail himself of the best portion of that school, and we thus perceive that some of his pictures, landscapes, and gardens have a Venetian character, besides showing a knowledge of colors not inferior to the best Venetian masters of his age."

Mantegna settled with his family at Mantua, where, under the patronage of the Marchese Lodovico Gonzaga, he acquired an immense reputation. He was invited to Rome by Pope Innocent VIII., and employed to paint several considerable works, among which a chapel in the Vatican still exists, though much injured by time. Some of his best works, executed both in oil and fresco in the maturity of his powers, are still to be found at Mantua. Of these, the most celebrated is a picture of Victory, painted on canvass in 1495, for the chapel of Gonzaga in the church of the Filippini, in commemoration of a victory gained by that prince over Charles VIII. of France, at the Battle of Formoni. Another famous picture by him is one of the Virgin, surrounded by the Archangel Michael and various saints, protecting

Francesco Gonzaga. Speaking of this picture, Lanzi says "Mantua boasts no other specimen equally sought after and admired by strangers; and though painted in 1495, it is still free, in a conspicuous degree, from the effects of three centuries, which it has already survived. It is truly wonderful to behold carnations so delicate, coats of armor so glittering, draperies so finely varied, with ornamental fruits still so fresh and dewy to the eye. Each separate head might serve as a school, from its fine character and vivacity, and not a few from an imitation of the antique; while the design, as well in the naked as the clothed parts, expresses a softness which sufficiently repels the too general opinion that the *stiff style* and that of Mantegna are much the same thing. There is also a union of coloring, a delicacy of penciling, and a peculiar grace, that appears almost the last stage of the art towards that perfection which it acquired from Leonardo da Vinci." This gem was taken to Paris by the French, and restored in 1815. His master-piece, according to Vasari, was his Triumph of Julius Cæsar, represented in a series of nine pictures, painted for the great hall of the Palazzo S. Sebastiano. This work was taken to Germany when Mantua was sacked, and from thence found its way to England, and now adorns the royal collection at Hampton Court. For this picture he received the honor of knighthood from his patron. The style of Mantegna greatly influenced that of his age, and imitations of it are to be seen beyond his school, which was extremely flourishing at Mantua.

As an engraver, Andrea Mantegna claims our veneration as one of the earliest practisers of the art, and as having contributed more than all his cotemporaries in perfecting it, by his superior knowledge of design. Cotemporary with Antonio Pollajuoli, he resembles him in style of handling, but he greatly surpasses him in the drawing of his figures, particularly in the naked parts. His plates are generally executed by single strokes from one corner of the plate to the other, in a manner resembling drawing made with a pen, without hatching or cross-lines. His prints engraved after his own designs are distinguished by a simplicity and correctness of outline unusual before his time. He sometimes marked his plates with one of the above monograms, which are similar to those afterwards employed by Marc' Antonio Raimondi, and have led to some dispute as to which artist some plates should be attributed. Lanzi says that the science of foreshortening, originally attributed to Melozio, was greatly improved, and nearly brought to perfection, by Mantegna and his two sons. His Dead Christ, with the two Marys weeping, now in the Pinacoteca at Milan, is a model of excellence in this respect. "The foreshortening is so perfect, and the perspective so correct, that from whatever point it is viewed the body is still seen extended in its full proportion in length." There is a great deal of dispute as to the extent of his engravings. Vasari says, "Mantegna, having decorated the chapel of Innocent VIII. at Rome about 1490, from that date is entitled to the name of engraver, computing it from about his sixtieth year. He flourished more than sixteen years after this, during which period it is believed he executed that amazing number of engravings, amounting to more than fifty, of which about thirty appear to be genuine, on so grand a scale, so rich in figures, so finely studied and Mantegnesque in every part," &c. Our limits will not allow us to pursue this inquiry farther than to say it is now the opinion of the best critics that Mantegna commenced his career as an engraver at a much earlier period (though this cannot be positively decided, as there are no dates on his prints), and that he did not engrave above thirty plates. Bartsch describes twenty-three prints by him, and there are two more in the British Museum, one of which is of large dimensions, representing St. George and the Dragon, and cost £60 sterling. The following are his principal prints, as far as known:

The Virgin seated, with the infant Jesus in her Arms. The Scourging of Christ. The Entombing of Christ, inscribed, *Humani generis Redemptori*. Christ descending into Hell. Christ holding the Standard of the Cross between two Saints. Judith with the Head of Holofernes. A Battle of Sea Monsters, with the figures of two armed Warriors. A Battle of Sea Gods, with the figure of Neptune. Hercules between Virtue and Vice. This print is sometimes attributed to Marc' Antonio. Hercules strangling Anteus, inscribed, *Divo Herculi invicto*. Four Female Figures dancing. Bacchus, supported by Fauns and Satyrs. The Triumph of Julius Cæsar; in nine plates; after his pictures now in the King's collection. It is difficult to meet with a complete set of these plates. They have been copied in chiaro-scuro by Andrea Andreani.

MANTEGNA, Francesco. The most perfect imitators of Andrea Mantegna were his two sons, Francesco, and another whose name is not mentioned, nor is the time of his birth or death recorded. Their father left many frescos unfinished, which they completed, particularly the Camera degli Sposi, in the castle at Mantua. Andrea painted the walls, and his sons the dome, or as Lanzi terms it, the beautiful vaulted recess. "In the same work appear several exquisitely drawn infantile figures, under different points of view, and admirably foreshortened." They also added two laterals to an altar-piece by their father, in a chapel in the church of S. Andrea at Mantua; and in the same place they erected a superb monument to his memory in 1517, which has led some to suppose that his death happened in that year.—These sons were exceedingly eminent artists, and acknowledged the best disciples of Mantegna's school, and it is singular that so little should now be known of them and their works. Lanzi says that Francesco certainly gave instructions to Correggio. The glory of the father has completely eclipsed that of the sons.

MANTEGNA, Carlo del, a Lombard, who was a favorite pupil of Andrea Mantegna, and one of the most successful followers of his school. Lanzi says he is supposed to have assisted the sons of Mantegna in the completion of his unfinished works at Mantua, and afterwards went to Genoa, where he "not only painted but taught, with a success that would appear almost incredible, were it not that the works of his imitators (at Genoa) were still in existence." None of his works are now clearly identified, most of them having perished, and others confounded, from resemblance of style, with those of his master, and of course attributed to him. No imitator of an eminent painter may ever hope for a lasting reputation; for names and dates are easily effaced, and others as easily supplied, when this will enhance the value of a work.

MANTOUANO, or MANTOVANO. See ANDREANI, see VENUSTI, see GHISI.

MANTOUANO, TEODORO. See GHIGI.

MANTOVANO, RINALDO. This painter was a native of Mantua; studied under Giulio Romano, and was one of his most distinguished scholars. He died very young; his premature death is regretted, as his compositions display a sublimity of conception and beauty of execution far beyond his age. His best work is a picture of the Virgin and Child, with St. Agostino and St. Girolamo, in the church of S. Agnes, in that city, so beautifully designed and executed that it gave rise to a suspicion of its having been painted from a design of his instructor.

MANTOVANO, CAMILLO, a painter of Mantua, whom Vasari commends for his landscapes. He was educated in the school of Giulio Romano, and was an excellent artist. Lanzi says he wrought chiefly at Venice and Urbino. There are still some of his frescos in his native place. In a chamber of the Ducal palace at Pesaro he painted a grove, executed with so much truth and taste that it seemed nature in reality. He flourished about 1540.

MANUEL, NICOLAS, a Swiss painter, born at Berne in 1484. It is said that he visited Venice, and studied under Titian, but as he only painted in fresco, his productions are lost. A Dance of Death, at Berne, is mentioned as by him, the figures of which represented persons living at the time; it has been copied by Kauw and Stettler. There were also two pictures of the Passion of Christ and the Seduction of Solomon by his Wives. Manuel was among the most zealous defenders of the Reformation. He died in 1530. (*See Deutsch.*)

MANZINI, RAIMONDO, a Bolognese painter, was born in 1668, and died in 1744. He excelled in painting cabinet pictures of fruit, flowers, birds, and animals. Lanzi says he was most successful in his cartoons or drawings, which were executed with such a truth to nature that, when exposed to a certain light, they deceived even painters themselves. For this excellence, Zanotti extols him as a modern Zeuxis.

MANZONI, RIDOLFO, a native of Castelfranco, was born in 1675, and died in 1743. He painted small historical pictures with great reputation and profit, which are prized in the best collections at Turin and in his native place. He also painted flowers and birds, tastefully composed and beautifully executed.

MANZONI, DA FAENZA, a young painter of great abilities and rising reputation, who is said to have been assassinated by Ferraù da Faenza, merely out of professional jealousy. There are several of his altar-pieces in the churches at Faenza, which are highly esteemed. Lanzi says he would have shone a distinguished ornament of the art, had his life not been untimely cut short by envy. His death happened about 1625.

MANZUOLI, MASO, called MASO DI SAN FRIANO, from the place of his nativity, near Florence, where he was born in 1536. He first studied under Pier Francesco di Jacopo, and afterwards with Carlo Portelli. Vasari does not hesitate to rank this artist with Battista Naldini and Alessandro Allori. His most capital picture was the Visitation of the Virgin to St. Elizabeth, painted for the church of S. Pietro Maggiore at Florence. This picture was painted when the artist was only thirty years old, and is regarded the ablest production of the Florentine school at the period in which he lived. It was transported to Rome, and now adorns a gallery in the Vatican. There are other works by him in the churches and public edifices at Florence, especially in the church of S. Trinità and in the Ducal gallery, though his works are not numerous, as he died in the prime of life, in 1575.

MARACCI, GIOVANNI. See MARRACCI.

MARAIS, HENRI, a French engraver, born at Paris in 1764. He first attained distinction by engraving several plates for the magnificent folio edition of Racine and P. Didot the Elder. He also materially assisted Wicar in his *Galerie de Florence*, and engraved the frontispiece of that work, *after Moitte;* also the Dance of the Muses, *after Giulio Romano;* the Triumph of Amphitrite, *after Luca Giordano;* the portrait of Mieris, painted by himself; the Three Fates, *after Michael Angelo;* Andromeda, *after Furino.* Marais died in 1800, at the age of 36.

MARASCA, JACOPINO, a painter of Cremona, commended by Zaist as an excellent artist of his age, who enjoyed the friendship and patronage of Francesco Sforza. He flourished about 1430.

MARATTI, CAV. CARLO. This eminent painter was born at Camurano, in the Marquisate of Ancona, in 1625. At a tender age he showed a natural taste for the fine arts, and when he was twelve years old, his father sent him to Rome, and placed him in the school of Andrea Sacchi, where he studied several years, and became his most favored disciple. By the advice of his master he made the works of Raffaelle his chief study. He rose to great distinction, and during his life-time was considered one of the first artists in Europe. Mengs assigns to him the enviable distinction of having "sustained the art at Rome, where it did not degenerate as at other places." At the commencement of his career, he confined himself to painting Holy Families, pictures of the Virgin, and Madonnas, on which account the cotemporary artists, particularly Salvator Rosa, thought him incapable of higher productions, and satirically called him *Carluccio dalle Madonne.* To counteract the evil efforts of his enemies, Sacchi obtained for him a commission to paint a picture for the Baptistery of St. John of Lateran, where he represented Constantine destroying the Idols, a performance which stifled calumny and established his reputation as one of the ablest artists of his time. It also procured him the patronage of Alexander VII., under whose protection, and that of his successors, he became the most popular and the most employed artist at Rome. He was commissioned to restore the great frescos of Raffaelle in the Vatican and the Farnesian palace, which had begun to suffer from the effects of time—a task, says his biographer Bellori, "requiring infinite care and judgment, and which he performed to the satisfaction of his patron." Lanzi says that "Maratti was no machinist, therefore neither he nor his scholars ever distinguished themselves in frescos or in large compositions. At the same time, he had no fear of engaging in works of that kind, and willingly undertook the decoration of the Duomo of Urbino, which he peopled with his figures."—This work, with the cupola itself, was destroyed by an earthquake in 1782, but the sketches of it are preserved in the Albani palace at Urbino.—Though Carlo Maratti painted some pictures of extraordinary magnitude, as his St. Carlo in the church of that Saint at the Corso, and the Baptism of Christ in the Certosa, yet his pictures for the most part are on a smaller scale. He had a predilection for cabinet pictures and altar-pieces, of Holy Families, Madonnas, and other sacred subjects, of which he executed a multitude, which are to be found not only in the churches and every private collection at Rome, but in the State, as well as at Florence, Genoa, and other places. He was a chaste and elegant designer, but his forms discover too little acquaintance with the antique. His compositions are rich and magnificent, but they bear the character of coldness and languor, and appear rather the productions of labor than the inspirations of genius. He prided himself on the copious castings of his draperies, but in this he displays a species of mannerism, and the multiplicity of his folds exhibits little of the beauty of the figures. His coloring is generally silvery and pleasing, but towards the latter end of his life it became somewhat cold and chalky. Yet it is admitted that some of his productions are exquisitely beautiful; the forms of his female saints lovely; his Madonnas dignified, and his angels *angelic*.—It were useless to specify his numerous works. Lanzi says his pictures approaching nearest to Sacchi are most prized at Rome, among which are the Baptism of Christ, in the Certosa, which is copied in mosaic in the Basilica of St. Peter's; the Death of St. Francis Xavier, in Il Gesu, engraved by J. Frey; the Visitation, in La Pace; and the Conception, in S. Isidore. Among his most charming compositions are St. Stanislaus Kostka at the altar where his ashes repose, and David's first view of Bathsheba, which last is a work inexpressibly beautiful. His master-piece is the Martyrdom of St. Biagio at Genoa, which Lanzi pronounces worthy of the ablest imitator of the school of Sacchi. He died in 1713.

Carlo Maratti executed a few free, spirited etchings, after his own designs and other Italian masters, though they are more highly finished than is usual with painters. The following are the principal:

A set of ten plates of the Life of the Virgin; *from his own compositions.* Several Holy Families, and subjects of the Virgin; *do.* Heliodorus driven from the Temple; in two sheets; *after Raffaelle.* Christ with the Woman of Samaria; *after Ann. Caracci.* The Flagellation of St. Andrew; *after Domenichino.* Joseph discovering himself to his Brethren; *after Mola.* St. Charles Borromeo interceding for the persons afflicted with the Plague; *after Cavaliere Perugino.*

MARC. See MARCH.

MARC' ANTONIO. See RAIMONDI.

MARCA, DELLA, GIO. BATTISTA LOMBARDELLI, was born at Montenuovo, in 1532; hence he is sometimes called Il Montano di Montenuovo. According to Baglioni, he first studied under Marco Marchetti da Faenza, but afterwards went to Rome, and became the pupil of Raffaellino da Reggio, whose style he adopted, and whom he assisted in the execution of his frescos in the Vatican, for Pope Gregory XIII. Lanzi says he possessed great natural talents, which were rendered unavailing for want of application. He executed, at Rome, a series of pictures from the life of St. Francis, in the church of S. Pietro Montorio, and one of the Resurrection in S. Maria de' Monti. His best works are in his native city. There are also some of his frescos at Perugia. He died, according to Orlandi, about 1587. Zani says he was a native of Perugia, and that he was living in 1592.

MARCA, LATTANZIO. There is considerable dispute about the real name of this artist, which we cannot discuss, and which is of no importance, since he is known in the history of art by the name of Lattanzio Marca. He flourished at Perugia about 1550. Vasari says he studied in the school of Perugino, and others, of Giovanni Bellini; and he is thought to be the same as Lattanzio da Rimino, who painted a picture at Venice in rivalship with Conegliano. Mariotti has proved, by authentic documents, that he was the son of Vincenzio Pagani of Monte Rubbiano, a celebrated painter, and probably the instructor of Lattanzio.

On the death of Pietro Perugino, he succeeded to his fame and fortunes at Perugia, and received all the most important orders. He painted the great works in the churches of the Castle, in which he was assisted by Raffaelle dalle Colle, Gherardi, Doni, and Paparello. Of these works the most important, perhaps, was the S. Maria del Popolo, a large composition, with a multitude of figures in the act of prayer. Lanzi says that the figures are well disposed, with a fine expression in the countenances; the landscape beautiful; the coloring clear and strong; and the taste, on the whole, different from that of Perugino. He was a man much respected by his fellow-citizens, and when somewhat advanced in years, he was appointed to the then honorable office of Sheriff of his native city, in 1553, when he renounced the art. It is not stated of which of the cities claiming his birth he was appointed sheriff—Perugia, Rimini, or Monte Rubbiano, but doubtless of the former, where he flourished. *See Vincenzio Pagani.*

MARCEL, N., a German painter of fruit, flowers, and still-life, was born at Frankfort in 1628, and died in 1683. He was a disciple of George Flegel or Vlughels, whose manner he adopted, though he far surpassed him. His subjects are usually vases filled with different kinds of fruit or flowers, beautiful shells, books, and other table ornaments, which he always designed from nature. His pictures are highly finished and delicately colored, and are held in considerable estimation in his own country.

MARCELLIS, OTHO, a Dutch painter, born at Amsterdam in 1613. It is not known under whom he studied, but he acquired great celebrity by his excellence in a singular branch of the art. He painted curious plants, insects, serpents and other reptiles to the life, and finished them with extraordinary care. He painted everything from nature, and is said to have kept a museum of serpents, vipers, rare insects, exotics, and other curiosities, which he copied with unexampled precision, and a wonderful beauty of penciling, so that his works were sought after not only in his own country, but wherever he went; and they are still found in the choicest collections. He resided some time at Paris, and was greatly patronized by the Queen Mother, who magnificently rewarded him.

He afterwards went to Italy, and passed several years at Florence, Rome, and Naples, in all which cities his works were equally admired, and he was patronized by princes and nobles. Füessli says his real name was *Snuffelaer*. He signed many of his pictures *O. Masseus*. He died at Amsterdam in 1673.

MARCENAY, Antoine de Ghuy, a French engraver, who flourished about 1760. He was one of the most successful imitators of the style of Rembrandt. He executed quite a number of portraits and other subjects, in which the dry point is used with remarkable dexterity. The following are his principal prints:

PORTRAITS.

Henry IV. of France; *after Janet*. The Duke of Sully; *after Porbus*. The Chevalier Bayard. The Maid of Orleans. Viscount Turenne; *after Champagne*. Prince Eugene; *after Kupetzki*. Marshal Villers; *after Rigaud*. General Paoli. Stanislaus Augustus, King of Poland; *after Bacierelli*. Marshal Saxe; *after Liotard*. The Portrait of Tintoretto; *after a picture by himself*. A half-length of Rembrandt, with a Palette.

VARIOUS SUBJECTS.

Sun-set; *after Vernet*. A View of the Sea-cast, with Fishermen; *do*. A Land-storm; *after Vanuden*. A Skirmish of Cavalry; *after Parrocel*. The Testament of Eudamidas; *after N. Poussin*. Tobit recovering his Sight; *after Rembrandt*. The Lady with the Pearl; an oval, with the date 1768; *after Rembrandt*. The (lady) Gardener; *after G. Douw*, with the date 1766; and others, to the number of sixty-six.

MARCH, Estéban, a Spanish painter who, according to Palomino, was a scholar of Pedro Orrente. He painted history with reputation, but he was more celebrated for his battle-pieces, which are vigorously designed, and executed with a free pencil, and an effective style of coloring. His works are chiefly at Valencia and Madrid. In the former city is an altar-piece of the Last Supper, in the church of San Juan de Mercado, highly commended; and in the Bueno Retiro a large picture of the Marriage at Cana, and one of his most capital battle-pieces. He died at Valencia in 1660, at an advanced age.

MARCH, Miguel, the son and scholar of the preceding, was born at Valencia in 1633, and died there in 1670. He imitated the style and subjects of his father, though he was greatly inferior to him. He executed some works for the churches at Valencia, among which his Death of St. Francis, in the church of the Franciscans, is considered the best.

PM. or PM. or PM MARCHAND, or MARCHANT, Pierre, a French engraver who, according to Florent le Comte, flourished about 1577, and engraved both on wood and copper. Professor Christ also attributes to him some prints bearing the above monogram, dated 1577.

MARCHANT, J., an obscure English engraver, by whom there is a portrait of Mrs. Cibber, *after Hudson*, dated 1749.

MARCHANT, Pierre, a French engraver, by whom there is a book of goldsmiths' ornaments, executed with the graver in a neat, free style, signed *Petrus Marchant, fecit*. 1623.

MARCHELLI, Rolando, a Genoese painter, was born in 1664, and died in 1751. He studied under Carlo Maratti, and, according to Ratti, he possessed fine abilities, and executed a few excellent works; but, having a very favorable opportunity to engage in merchandise, he abandoned painting.

MARCHESI, Girolamo da Cotignola, an Italian painter, born, according to Baruffaldi, in 1480, at Cotignola in the Bolognese state. He studied under Francis Francia, and, according to Vasari, was one of the most eminent portrait painters of the day. He also painted history, and there are a number of historical compositions by him at Bologna and elsewhere, which prove him worthy a high rank among the artists of his time. Lanzi mentions among his best works a picture in the possession of the Serviti at Pesaro, where the Virgin is seen on a throne, before which, in a kneeling posture, is the Marchesa Ginevra Sforza, with her son Constantinus II. The design of this work is somewhat dry, but the coloring is extremely agreeable, the draperies well disposed. He visited Rome and Naples in the pontificate of Paul III., but did not gain any reputation in those cities, being somewhat behind the times. Vasari says he died between the years 1534 and 1549.

MARCHESI, Giuseppe, called Il Sansone, was born at Bologna in 1699. He first studied under Marc' Antonio Franceschini, and afterwards with Aureliano Milani. Lanzi says his style partakes of both his masters. To the vigorous coloring and bold foreshortening of his first instructor, whom he nearly approaches, he added the correct design of Milani, and distinguished himself by many excellent works in the churches at Bologna and Rimini, among which some of the most admired are the Birth of the Virgin, in the Madonna de Galleria; the Resurrection, in the church of S. Croce at Bologna, painted in the grand style of Franceschini. Another fine picture is in the church of S. Pietro, representing St. Ambrose refusing the Emperor Theodosius the entrance of the Temple. The Martyrdom of St. Prisca, in the Cathedral at Rimini, is highly commended. It "is an altar-piece," says Lanzi, "of many and fine figures, and good tints, for which the St. Agnes of Domenichino supplied him with some ideas. He painted much for the Galleries, and among other pieces, one representing the Four Seasons is reputed among the best works of the modern Bolognese school." He died in 1771.

MARCHESINI, Alessandro, a Veronese painter, born in 1664, and died in 1738. He first studied under Biagio Falcieri, at Verona; and at the age of sixteen went to Bologna, and became the pupil of Carlo Cignani, whose style he adopted. On his return to Verona he executed a few works for the churches of S. Biagio and La Madonna della Scala. He afterwards went to Venice, where he employed himself in painting easel pictures of historical and mythological subjects for private collections, with considerable success; but Lanzi says he afterwards "addicted himself to those compositions as a trade, and despatched them with more facility than care."

MARCHETTI, Marco, sometimes called Marco da Faenza, from the place of his nativity. It is not known where he was born, or with whom he studied, but he flourished at Rome, in the pontificate of Gregory XIII., and greatly distinguished himself. Vasari says "he was particularly experienced in regard to frescos; bold, decided, and terrible; and especially in the practice and manner of drawing grotesques, not having any rival there equal to him. He succeeded Sabbatini in the works of Gregory XIII. He decorated the loggia of the Vatican with small sculptured histories, decorated with beautiful grotesque and arabesque ornaments. Such is his Murder of the Innocents, "which," says Lanzi, "are full of spirit and elegance, and are his best works. His figures form a school for design. In the church of the Trinità de' Monti, he painted a series of pictures of the Life of St. Francis di Paola. His masterpiece is the Feast of Christ in the house of the Pharisee, in the Communal Collection. He afterwards entered the service of Cosmo I. of Florence, for whom he decorated the Palazzo Vecchio. He died in 1588.

MARCHI, Giuseppe Filippo Liberati, a native of Rome, who studied with Reynolds in that city, and afterwards accompanied him to England. Failing to meet with any encouragement, he continued with that master until his death in 1792, and rendered him much assistance in painting draperies, and forwarding his numerous pictures. Marchi had little energy, and could never have risen above mediocrity. He engraved a few plates in mezzotinto from portraits of Sir Joshua. He died in 1808.

MARCHIONE, an Italian sculptor and architect, was a native of Arezzo in Tuscany, and flourished in the 13th century. He was chosen by Pope Innocent III., to erect the church of S. Spirito in Sassia at Rome, afterwards rebuilt by Paul III.; the church of S. Sylvestro; the Tower of the Conti; and in S. Maria Maggiore the chapel of the Presepio, afterwards restored by Sextus V. At Arezzo he erected the parish church and bell-tower. The façade of this edifice had three orders of columns, and was redundant in fanciful ornament, devoid of taste.

MARCHIONE, Carlo, a talented Italian sculptor and architect, born at Rome in 1704. He attained a high reputation, and was employed to execute a number of works at Rome and Siena. His principal work in sculpture is the mausoleum of Benedict XIII., in the church della Minerva. As an architect he erected, among other works, the Albano palace at Rome, and the new sacristy of St. Peter's. He had a remarkable talent for designing with the pen, and his sketches of scenes from low life are in request among amateurs. He died at Rome, in 1780, greatly esteemed for his private character, as well as for his talents.

MARCHIONI, La, a paintress of Rovigo, who flourished in that city about 1700. Lanzi says she possessed singular skill in flower painting, and is considered the Bernasconi of the Venetian school. Her works are found in the choicest collections of her native city.

MARCHIS, Alessio de, a Neapolitan painter, who flourished about 1710. He imitated the style of Salvator Rosa, and painted landscapes, seaports, and conflagrations. His principal works are at Perugia and Urbino. Lanzi says that, in order to imitate nature with greater exactness in his conflagrations, he set fire to a barn at night for the purpose of study. Being detected, he was sent to the galleys for some years, till he was released by Pope Clement XI. on account of his great abilities, who employed him in his palace at Urbino, which he adorned with some of his choicest works. One of his most celebrated pictures is the Destruction of Troy, in the Palazzo Semproni. He died in 1742.

MARCILLA, or MARSIGLIA, Guglielmo da. This painter was born at Marseilles in 1475. Nothing is known of his real name. According to Vasari, he was engaged in a fatal duel when young, and fled to the Dominicans for protection, and became a monk. He afterwards went to Italy, became a secular priest, and finally a citizen of Arezzo, where he endeared himself to the people by his exemplary conduct and his talents as an artist, and was made prior of the convent. He excelled in painting on glass, and executed many works of this kind for the Cathedral and other churches of Arezzo, so beautifully designed and colored that Lanzi says that they might "excite the envy of much larger cities." To very good drawing and uncommon expression he joined tints that partake of the emerald, the ruby, and of the oriental sapphire, and when illuminated by the sun, exhibit all the brilliancy of the rainbow. They are so finely wrought with subjects from the New Testament and other scriptural histories, that they seem to have reached the perfection of the art." Vasari, speaking of his Vocation of St. Matthew, in the great window of the Cathedral, as he saw it, says, "it exhibits perspectives of temples and flights of steps, figures so finely composed, landscapes so well executed, that one can hardly imagine they are glass, but rather something sent down from heaven for the delight of mankind." The fame of these works induced Pope Julius II. to invite him to Rome, for whom he executed some considerable works on glass, as well as some works in fresco. While at Rome he entirely changed his style in fresco painting by studying the works of Michael Angelo, and on his return to Arezzo he painted the Four Evangelists in the dome of the Cathedral, and decorated the ceilings and arches of the same edifice with scriptural subjects in fresco, in the grand style of Angelo. Lanzi says, "his frescos at Rome seem the designs of the 14th century, while those at Arezzo appear the work of a modern. In design, he followed Angelo as near as he could, but his coloring is not so fine." There is great variation in authors as to the time of his birth and death, but Lanzi and Vasari both say that he died at Arezzo in 1537, aged 62; doubtless taken from authentic documents in his convent. (See the article *Guillaume* for the French account of this artist.)

MARCOLA, Marco, a painter of Verona, was born in 1728, and died in 1790. Lanzi says he was a universal painter, of great fertility of invention and rapid in his execution. His style is not given, nor is it known with whom he studied.

MARCOLINI, Francesco, an Italian wood engraver, born at Forli about 1500. There is a book entitled *Il Giardino de Pensieri*, illustrated with well executed wood cuts by him, after designs by *Giuseppe Porta*, published at Forli in 1540.

MARCONI, Marco, a painter of Como, who flourished about 1500. He was a good painter, and executed some works for the churches, much in the style of Giorgione. It is not known under whom he studied, but it is supposed he was educated at Venice.

MARCONI, Rocco, a painter of Trevigi, who flourished about 1505. Ridolfi classes him as a pupil of Palma, but Zanetti says he was one of the best disciples of Giovanni Bellini, which accords with Lanzi. The last named author says "he excelled in accuracy of design, taste of coloring and diligence of hand, though he is not sufficiently easy in his contours, and for the most part, exhibits a severity approaching to a plebeian coarseness of countenances." He executed many works for the churches and public edifices of his native city, the best of which is the Adulteress before Christ, in the Chapter of San Giorgio Maggiore, which is entirely in the style of Giorgione. There are several copies of this picture at San Pantaleo and other places, attributed to him. His easel pictures are quite numerous. Kügler in his *Italy*, mentions two fine pictures by him at Venice, viz., an altar-piece, of Christ between two Angels, in the church S. S. Giovanni e Paolo, and the Descent from the Cross, in the Academy. There is also a picture of The Supper at Emmaus, having his signature, and dated 1507, in the Museum at Berlin. There is a great difference in his works, and from the above it appears that he was not always mean in his expression, and Lanzi himself says that his Adulteress before Christ is entirely in the style of Giorgione.

MARCUARD, Robert Samuel, an English designer and engraver, born in 1751, and died in 1792. He studied with Bartolozzi, and was considered one of his best scholars. He died in the prime of life. He executed a few plates after the noted English painters of his time.

MARCUCCI, Agostino, a native of Siena, born about 1570, who studied under the Caracci at Bologna, until a schism arose in that school, when he arrayed himself with the foremost adherents of Faccini, who had the boldness to set up a new Academy in opposition to the Caracci. He continued to reside at Bologna, and to teach till the time of his death. He executed some works for the churches, among which the Death of the Virgin in la Concezione, is highly commended. Malvasia reckons him among "the first men" of that age.

MARENI, Gio. Antonio, a Piedmontese painter, who studied under Baciccio, and flourished at Turin about 1680, where there are some of his works, which are highly commended in the *Guida di Torino*.

MARESCALCO, Giovanni. See Buonconsigli.

MARESCALCO, Pietro, a painter, whose birth place is uncertain, but who flourished at Feltre about the middle of the 16th century. He was surnamed Lo Spada (the sword), and Lanzi says that in the MS. history of Feltre, he is claimed as a native of that city. There is one of his altar-pieces in the nunnery of the Angeli at Feltre, signed *Petrus Marescalcus P.*; a work of such merit as to entitle him to an honorable rank in art.

MARESCOTTI, Bartolomeo, a Bolognese painter, brought up in the school of Guido Reni, whose style he endeavored to imitate. Lanzi says he was a corrupter of the Guido manner, rather than an imitator, and that he is scarcely worthy of notice; still, he executed some works for the churches and public edifices at Bologna, among which are the Martyrdom of St. Barbara in S. Martino Maggiore; the Crowning of the Virgin, in S. Stefano; and the altar-piece of St. Sigismondo condemned to Death, in the church of that saint. He died in 1630.

MARGARITONE, d'Arezzo, an old Italian painter, sculptor and architect, born at Arezzo in 1198, and died in 1275, according to Vasari, though there is considerable discrepancy among authors on this point. Lanzi says he died *after* 1289, aged 77, and Zani places his birth in 1240, and death in 1317. It is agreed on all sides that he was born before Cimabue, who was born at Florence in 1240. He was a disciple and imitator of the Greeks. Vasari says he painted on canvass, and made the first discovery of a method to render his pictures more durable, and less liable to crack; for this purpose he extended his canvass on panel secured with strong glue, and covered the whole with a ground of gypsum before he began to paint. He formed diadems and other ornaments of plaster, giving them relief by gilding and burnishing. Some of his Crucifixions on a gold ground are at Arezzo, and there is one in the church of the Holy Cross at Florence, near one by Cimabue. Lanzi says both are in the old manner, and not so different, but that Margaritone may be pronounced as well entitled to the name of a painter, as Cimabue.

Margaritone practised sculpture and architecture, and executed. among other works, a marble statue for the mausoleum of Gregory X., who had died at Arezzo, on his way from Avignon to Rome. He decorated the chapel of that pope with his portrait and other paintings. He is said to have invented the art of gilding with leaf-gold upon Armenian bole. As an architect, he erected the governor's palace and the church of St. Ciriaco, at Ancona; and was commissioned in his own city to execute a design of Lapo, for the cathedral; but, according to Milizia, the building was nearly stopped, in consequence of the great expenditure of money in the wars between the Florentines and Argentines. During the latter part of his life, he had the mortification of finding his own credit diminishing in proportion as that of other professors increased. He died in 1289.

MARGHUCCI, Giacomo, an Italian engraver, of an uncertain age, who executed some plates of antique statues and busts.

MARI, Alessandro, a painter, born at Turin in 1650. He first studied under Domenico Piola, at Genoa, and afterwards went to Venice and became the pupil of Cav. Liberi. He then visited Bologna, and spent some time in the school of Lorenzo Pasinelli, and, on leaving this master, painted a few pictures for the churches, the most admired of which is the Martyrdom of St. Sebastian, in the church of S. Barbaziano. He ultimately became a celebrated copyist, and a successful designer of *capricci* and symbolical representations, by which he gained great reputation at Milan, where he chiefly resided. He went to Spain, and died at Madrid in 1707.

MARI, Antonio, a painter of Turin, some of whose works are mentioned in the *Guida di Torino*. Count Durando Villa, believes Alessandro and Antonio Mari to be the same.

MARIA, Cav. Ercole, a Bolognese painter, sometimes called Ercolino di Guido, from his having been a favorite disciple of that master.

He imitated and copied the works of his instructor with such precision, that Malvasia says he deceived the master himself, by substituting his copy for the original. Lanzi says his master willingly employed him in multiplying his own designs, two of which copies, extremely beautiful, are still to be seen at Bologna, though they do not display the same freedom as others which he executed for individuals at a more advanced age. In those there appears a decision and flow of his pencil which imposed upon the best judges,—a talent that procured him admiration at Rome, and the patronage of Urban VIII., who conferred on him the honor of knighthood. He died at Rome about 1640, in the flower of his life.

MARIA, Francesco di, a Neapolitan painter, born in 1623, and died in 1690. He was a disciple of Domenichino, while that artist resided at Naples, and imitated his manner so closely that Dominici says his works command great prices, and are bought by the inexperienced as the works of Domenichino. Lanzi says that he resembled his master in every quality except grace, which nature denied him. Hence Giordano said that "his figures were like a man whom consumption had reduced; the muscles and bones, might be correct and beautiful, but still insipid." Maria retorted by declaring the school of Giordano "heretical, and that he could not endure works that owe all their merit to ostentatious coloring and vigorous design." His works are not numerous, but they are held in the highest estimation for their excellence, particularly his History of St. Lorenzo at the Conventuali at Naples. He excelled in portraits, and Lanzi says that one of the latter being exhibited at Rome, together with one by Rubens, and one by Vandyck, the preference was given by the judges, Niccolo Poussin, Pietro da Cortona, and Andrea Sacchi, to that of Maria.

MARIANI, Camillo, an Italian painter and sculptor, born at Vicenza in 1565. He devoted himself orginally to painting, but subsequently turned his attention to sculpture. The grand theatre of Vicenza, which had been partially erected from the designs of Palladio, was completed about this time; and Mariani was commissioned to execute all the works of sculpture for its decoration. He afterwards traveled through Italy, and left in different cities proofs of his abilities in both arts. He finally settled at Rome, where his first productions were two figures in stucco for the church of St. John of Lateran; and he subsequently executed the colossal marble statues of the apostles St. Peter and St. Paul, which were admired by the connoisseurs. Among his other works, were eight colossal statues in stucco, in S. Bernardo de' Termini, characterized by great elevation of design. It seems that he continued the practice of painting during his whole life, and, according to Baglioni, excelled in easel pictures. He died at Rome in 1611.

MARIANI, Domenico, a Milanese painter, who, according to Orlandi, flourished at Milan about the middle of the 17th century, where he practised with considerable reputation, and established a school for the instruction of young artists.

MARIANI, Gioseffo, was the son and scholar of Domenico M. Lanzi says, he went to Bologna, where he greatly improved his manner, and distinguished himself throughout Italy and Germany

MARIANI, Gio. Maria. This painter was a native of Ascoli, and studied under Domenico Fiasella at the same time as Valerio Castelli, and in conjunction with the latter, distinguished himself by several works in oil and fresco for the churches in that city. Lanzi says he painted in the Oratory of S. Jacopo, the Baptism of that saint, in competition with the chief of his cotemporaries, and eclipsed them all, with the exception, perhaps, of Castiglione. He went to Rome, and was admitted into the Academy of St. Luke in 1650. He acquired great celebrity, and his easel pictures were much sought after for the best collections at Rome, Genoa, and Florence. His Rape of the Sabines in the Florentine Gallery is highly esteemed. He repeated this picture on a more extended scale in the Palace Brignole. His works are rare, as he died young.

MARIE, Rene Elizabeth. See Lepicie.

MARIENHOF, A., a Dutch painter, born at Gorcum in 1650. It is not known under whom he first studied, but Descamps says he passed the early part of his life in studying and copying the works of Rubens. He settled at Brussels, where he was much employed in copying the works of that master. He also painted small historical pictures, designed, touched, and colored in the manner of Rubens. The time of his death is uncertain, though Balkema places it in 1712.

MARIESCHI, Michele, a Venetian artist, who excelled in painting architectural views and perspective. He passed the greater part of his life in Germany, where he acquired great reputation. On his return to Venice, he painted the most remarkable views of that city, some of which he etched in a spirited and pleasing style. He died in 1743.

MARIESCHI, Jacopo or Giacomo, was the son of the preceding, born at Venice in 1711. After being instructed in design and perspective by his father, he became the scholar of Gasparo Diziani to improve himself in drawing the human figure. He painted architectural subjects and views in Venice, in which he imitated the style of Canaletto so closely that his works are frequently taken by the inexperienced for those of that master. Lanzi commends his pictures, and says that he was a good figurist. Some of his works are in the Algarotti collection at Venice, with those of Canaletto and Francesco Guardi, another imitator, who painted with more freedom of touch than either Canaletto or Marieschi. He died in 1794.

MARIETTE, Jean, an eminent French engraver and printseller, born at Paris in 1654. He studied drawing and design with J. B. Corneille, his brother-in-law, with the intention of becoming a painter, but on application to Charles le Brun, by his advice, he devoted himself to engraving. He executed a great number of engravings, mostly vignettes and other book plates, some of them after his own designs; but he engraved some large plates after the best masters, which possess considerable merit, though his drawing is not very correct. He wrought with both the point and the graver. He died in 1742. The following are his best prints:

The Descent from the Cross; *after le Brun*. The Angels ministering to Christ in the Desert; *do*. St. Peter delivered from Prison; *after Domenichino*. Moses saved from the Nile; *after N. Poussin*. Joseph making himself known to his Brethren; *after M. Corneille*. Christ curing the Paralytic; *do.* St. Louis receiving the Communion, *after J. B. Corneille.* St. Louis received into Heaven; *do.*

MARIETTE, Pierre Jean, was the son of the preceding, and died at Paris in 1774. He was instructed in the art by his father, who left him an ample fortune, and an extensive collection of prints and drawings, which, by continual additions, he rendered the most numerous and select of any private collection in Europe. For his amusement, he etched a few places of landscapes *after Guercino*, and some heads and studies *after Caracci* and *Pierino del Vaga.* He also published a work in two vols. folio, illustrated with 250 engravings of antique gems, entitled *Traité des Pierres Gravées.*

MARIGNY, Michel, a French historical painter, born at Paris in 1797, and died there in 1829. He first studied under M. Lafont, afterwards under the Baron Gros. He acquired considerable reputation, and executed several large works for the churches and public edifices at Paris and Rouen; among which, his Moses as the Legislator, in the council-chamber at the Louvre, is highly commended. Also his Wounded Soldier, his last production, which was exhibited at the Luxembourg in 1830.

MARILLIER, Clement Pierre, a French designer and engraver, born at Dijon in 1740. He studied painting under an artist of his native place, after which he visited Paris, and entered the school of Hallé; but being in narrow circumstances, he was compelled to devote himself to designing and engraving book illustrations. Possessing an excellent acquaintance of his art, with great delicacy of taste, he soon attained eminence, and was much employed. He made designs for the Bible of Defer Maison Neuve; two hundred designs for the Fables of Dorat; also many for the works of Prévost, de Roucher, and other authors. He designed and engraved in a spirited style, the landscapes for *Les Voyages en France, á Naples et en Grèce*, and for various other works. He died in 1808.

MARIN, Joseph Charles, a French sculptor, born in 1773. In 1812, he drew the grand prize in sculpture, and visited Rome, from whence, about four years after, he sent a Sleeping Cupid, copied from the antique. On returning to France, Marin gained encouragement. Among his principal works was the colossal statue of Tourville, which decorated the Pont Louis XVI., now the Pont de la Concorde, and was subsequently transported to the court of the Chateau de Versailles. In 1819, he was commissioned to execute a statue of M. de Tourny, for the city of Bordeaux. During many years he discharged the duties of Professor of the School of Fine Arts at Lyons. He died at Paris in 1834.

MARINALI, Horatio, an Italian sculptor, born in 1643, at Bassano, in the Venetian State. After acquiring considerable knowledge from his father, a reputable sculptor of Bassano, Marinali visited Venice, but finding the art in a comparatively low state in that city, he went to Rome, and studied under the best masters. In 1676, he returned to Venice, and executed for the church of the Augustini two statues of saints, and a bas-relief of Christ bearing the Cross. In 1681, he was commissioned to execute a statue of St. Bassano, to be elevated on a column in the public square of his native city, which he completed by the assistance of his two brothers, mentioned in the succeeding article. Marinali then settled at Bassano, and was much employed. He executed many works for the churches and palaces of Venice, Vicenza, Padua, Verona and other cities. The sculptures in the beautiful gardens of Cornaro, called "the Paradise," at Castelfranco, are by this artist. His works evince elevated genius and great facility of execution. They are mostly of life size, characterized by considerable expression, lively attitudes, and an agreeable cast of the draperies. While engaged in executing a number of statues and bas-reliefs for the church of Monte Berico, he was attacked by sickness, and died in 1720.

MARINALI, Francesco and Angelo, Italian sculptors, were brothers of the preceding, born at Bassano; the former in 1647; the latter in 1654. As they wrought almost entirely in concert with their brother Horatio, they attained but little distinction. There are however, several works of merit, to which their names are attached. For minute information of these artists, consult Verci's *Notizie sopra i pittori, gli scultori e gl' intagliatori, delle citta di Bassano*, 8vo. Venice, 1775.

MARINARI, Onorio, an Italian painter, born at Florence in 1627, and died there in 1715. He was the cousin and disciple of Carlo Dolci, and for a long time imitated the finished and labored manner of that master so closely, that his pictures readily passed for the genuine works of Dolci, and it is supposed that many works in the public and private galleries of Europe, now attributed to Dolci, were really executed by him. He afterwards formed a style of his own, more dignified, more ideal, and less constrained, executed with a firm pencil, and his coloring was life itself. He did not confine himself to saints and madonnas, but showed a high degree of merit in historical compositions, with an admirable chiaro-scuro. His principal works are in the churches of S. Maria Maggiore and S. Simone, at Florence. He also excelled in portraits. Two of his most charming pictures were the Judgment of Paris, and Diana and her Nymphs, now said to be in England. After the death of Carlo Dolci, he completed some of his unfinished pictures, not to their disadvantage. His known works are not numerous, though he was industrious, and lived to the great age of eighty-eight years.

MARINAS, Henrique de las, a Spanish marine painter, born at Cadiz in 1620. His real name is not known, nor that of his master; but he obtained great celebrity for his marines, storms at sea, sea views, sea-ports, &c., executed with great truth and beauty; whence his name. His embarkations in the bay of his native city are highly commended for their spirit and truth, for the transparency of the water, and the aërial perspective. He acquired an ample fortune, and traveled through Italy. He died at Rome in 1680.

MARINELLI, Girolamo, a native of Assisi, who painted in 1630. There are some of his works in the church of S. Francesco at Perugia, as mentioned in the description of that church.

MARINETTI, Antonio, called Il Chiozzotto, from the place of his nativity. He studied at Venice, under Gio. Bat. Piazzetta, in whose style he painted, but with much more softness of manner. He was a good artist, and flourished in the first part of the 18th century.

MARINI, Antonio, a painter of Padua who flourished about 1700. He chiefly painted landscapes, which he executed in a grand and classical style. His works are to be found in the public and private collections of his native city, where they are highly esteemed.

MARINI, Benedetto, a painter who flourished at Urbino about 1625. According to Lanzi, he was one of the most distinguished scholars of Claudio Ridolfi, and on leaving that master, he went to Piacenza, where he distinguished himself by several altar-pieces and other subjects, for the churches, in which he united the style of Baroccio with the Lombard and Venetian. His most celebrated work is the Miracle of the Loaves in the Desert, painted in oil, in the refectory of the Conventuali, in 1625. This is an immense composition, well grouped and well contrasted, and displays uncommon powers. Lanzi does not hesitate to prefer him before his master, in grandeur of ideas and vigor of execution, though perhaps inferior to him in the fundamental principles of the art; he says, also, that the history of his life and his works scattered abroad, in the neighborhood of Pavia and elsewhere, are worthy of research and commemoration. In the Oretti correspondence, written in 1777, in a letter from Andrea Zanoni to Prince Ercolani, Marini is classed as a scholar of Ferraù da Faenza, and Lanzi says there are many works by him in the style of that master.

MARINI, Gio. Antonio, a Venetian artist who wrought in mosaic, after the designs of Salviati, Tintoretto, the younger Palma, and other eminent artists. He was a scholar of Bartolomeo Bozza, according to Zanetti, and flourished about 1600.

MARINI, N., a painter of San Severino, who flourished about 1700. He was a scholar of Cipriano Divini, whom he surpassed. He executed some works for the churches in his native place, and obtained considerable celebrity.

MARINUS, Ignatius, a Flemish engraver, who flourished at Antwerp about 1630. Little is known of him, except some plates after the Flemish and Italian masters, engraved in a neat but singular style; they are executed entirely with the graver, with very delicate strokes crossing each other, with long dots in the intervening spaces. They are highly finished, but the drawing is not very correct, and the draperies are rather stiff. Fine impressions of his prints are nevertheless held in considerable estimation. The following are the principal:

The Flight into Egypt; a night-piece; *after Rubens.* St. Ignatius curing the Diseased; *do.* St. Francis Xavier resuscitating a Dead Person; *do.* The Adoration of the Shepherds; *after Jordaens.* Christ before the High-priest Caiaphas; *do.* The Martyrdom of St. Apollonia; *do.* Village Children forming a Concert; *after C. Sachtleven.* 1633.

MARIO DA FIORI. See Nuzzi.

MARIOTTI, Gio. Battista, a Venetian painter, who probably studied under Antonio Balestra, when that artist resided and taught in Venice. At all events, Lanzi says he was an excellent imitator of his style. There are some of his works at Venice and Padua. He also etched some plates after his own designs and others, in a spirited and painter-like manner. He died about 1765.

MARK, Quintin, or Quirinus, a German engraver, born at Littau in 1753, and died in 1811. He went to Vienna while young, and studied engraving under Schmutzer. He rose to distinction, and was elected a member of the Imperial Academy. He engraved quite a number of plates, in a neat and pleasing style, of which the following are among the best:

The Virgin and Infant, with St. John; *after L. Giordano.* Susanna and the Elders; *after Rubens.* Alexander and Diogenes; *do.* Herodias with the Head of St. John; *after T. van Thulden.* Cleopatra showing Augustus the Bust of Julius Cæsar; *after P. Battoni.* Venus and Cupid asleep; *after Franceschini.* The Amorous Miser; *after Braun.* 1786.

MARLET, Jean Henri, a French painter, born at Autun in 1771. He first studied in the Academy at Dijon, and afterwards with the Baron Regnault. His works are numerous, embracing a great variety of subjects, as history, poetry, fancy, and portraits. He published some works in Lithography, among which are *Les Tableaux de Paris.* He was living in 1831.

MARLIANO, Andrea, a native of Pavia, who, according to Lamo, studied painting under Bernardino Campi. He was a reputable artist, and executed some works for the church in his native city. He flourished in the latter part of the 16th century.

MARLOW, M., an obscure English engraver, who lived about 1674, and executed some indifferent plates for the booksellers.

MARLOW, William, an English landscape painter and engraver, born in 1740. He studied with Samuel Scott, the marine painter. He painted English scenery, usually views on the banks of the Thames, and in the neighborhoods of Richmond and Twickenham, in a pleasing manner, and sometimes approaching the style of Wilson in his English subjects. He painted and etched some Italian views, which he marked *Wm. Marlow, F. S. A.* He died in 1800.

MARMION, Edmund, an English designer and engraver of little note, by whom there are some slight etchings of domestic subjects of ladies and gentlemen, from his own designs. He also engraved a few portraits for the booksellers.

MARMITTA, Francesco, a painter of Parma, of whom there are notices from 1494 to 1506. He was esteemed an excellent artist in his time, and was the supposed master of Parmiggiano.

MARMOCCHINI, Giovanna Cortesi, a Florentine paintress, born in 1670. Her family name was Cortesi. She studied first under Livio Mehus, and afterwards Pietro Dandini. She showed so much talent that the Grand Duchess took her under her protection, and had her instructed in miniature painting by Ippolito Galantini, in which she became eminent, and found abundant patronage at the court. Her likenesses were striking and lifelike, her coloring pleasing and natural, and her pencilling very neat and delicate. She usually worked in oil, but she painted equally well with crayons, and gave to those pieces all the warmth and tenderness of life. She died in 1736.

MARMOLEJA, Pedro de Villegas, a Spanish painter; born, according to Bermudez, at Seville, in 1520. It is not known under whom he studied in his own country ; but he went to Italy for improvement, where he made the works of Raffaelle his especial study, and formed on them a grand style of design, which has led some authors to assert that he was a pupil of that great master, whereas Raffaelle died the same year in which Marmoleja was born. On his return to Seville he acquired great distinction, and executed many works for the churches and public edifices, especially in the Cathedral and the Hospital of San Lazaro, which are said to be distinguished for grandeur of design, beauty and symmetry of the figures, and dignity of character. Bermudez ranks him among the greatest artists of his country. He died at Seville in 1599.

MARNE, Louis Antoine de, a French engraver, born at Paris in 1673. Little is known of his personal history, but he attained sufficient distinction to be appointed engraver to the king. He is chiefly known by his work entitled *Histoire sacrée de la Providence.* Paris, 1728, 3 vols., 4to. in five hundred plates of subjects from the Old and New Testaments, after Raffaelle and other masters. In the Cabinet of the Duke de Vallière was a collection of one hundred designs by de Marne, entitled *Les Belles Statues de Rome*, copied very correctly from the antique. The *Biographie Universelle* notices de Marne as an architect, but does not mention any of his works. He died in 1755.

MARNE, Jean Louis. See Demarne.

MAROLI, Domenico, a Sicilian painter, born at Messina in 1612. He studied at Messina, under Antonio Ricci, called Il Barbalunga, and on leaving the school of that master went to Venice, where he resided several years and studied diligently the works of the best masters, and acquired considerable reputation for his pastoral and rural subjects. He was intimate with Boschini, who extols him as a new Bassano, and as a specimen of his talent, inserted in his "Carta del Nevega" an engraving after one of his designs. It represents a beautiful landscape, a shepherd with his flocks, several cows, and a dog, forcibly and beautifully drawn, and is one of the best designs in the work. On his return to Messina, he did not confine himself to these subjects, but devoted at least a part of his time to painting sacred subjects, in which he showed himself an accomplished artist in that branch. He painted some excellent works for the churches in that city, which are highly commended for beauty of design, freshness of color, delicacy of tints, and for the dignity of his heads, which are full of expression and character. Such are his pictures of the Martyrdom of St. Placido, in the church of S. Paolo ; and the Nativity, in the Chiesa della Grotta. This eminent painter was killed during the revolution in Sicily, in 1674.

MARON, Theresa Mengs da, a sister of the celebrated Antonio Raffaelle Mengs, was born at Auszig, in Bohemia, in 1726, and died at Rome in 1806. She showed great talents, even in her youth, and excelled in enamel, crayon, and miniature painting. She exercised her talents in full vigor till her death, at the great age of 80 years. She was the wife of the Cavaliere Maron, an eminent Italian artist. *See Mengs.*

MARONE, Jacopo, an Italian painter, and a native of Alessandria, who flourished at Genoa about 1480. Little is known of him. Lanzi says there is an altar-piece by him in the church of S. Jacopo at Savona, painted in distemper in several compartments, in the midst of which is a Nativity in a landscape, conducted with exquisite care in every part. In the church of S. Brigida at Genoa are two beautiful altar-pieces by the same artist, dated 1481 and 1484.

MAROT, Jean, a French architect and engraver, born at Paris in 1620. He applied himself more particularly to the theory than to the practice of his art, but was employed to design several important works, among which were the façade of the church des Feuillantines, of the Faubourg St. Jacques ; the Hotel de Mortemart ; and the façade of the Hotel de Pussort. He was appointed architect to the king, and with many other artists presented a plan for the façade of the Louvre. In concert with his son, Daniel M., he published in 1691 a collection of two hundred plates of the plans of different edifices, ancient and modern. The same plates were afterwards reprinted by Mariette, under the title of *L' Architecture Francaise.* Marot also engraved several plates for the great cabinet of the King of France. He died about 1697. The following are his principal prints :

A set of thirteen plates of Churches and public edifices at Paris ; designed and engraved after their measurement by *J. Marot.* A second set of twelve plates of the same. Twenty-one plates of Views of the Chateau de Richelieu. The Plans and Elevations of the Louvre ; three plates. The Plans and Views of the Chateau de Vincennes ; three plates. The Plan and Elevation of the Chateau de Madrid ; two plates.

MAROT, Daniel, a French architect and engraver, the son of the preceding, was born at Paris about 1660. He studied under his father, and assisted him in his works ; but after the revocation of the Edict of Nantes, he quitted France for Holland, where he gained considerable distinction, and was appointed architect to William, Prince of Orange, whom he accompanied to England. After the death of William III., Marot returned to Holland, and in 1712 published his *Recueil d'Architecture.* A number of his plates, with some by his father, were published at Paris under the title of *Recueil des planches des Sieurs Marot, pere et fils.* The following are his principal prints :

The great Fair at the Hague, with the Burghers under arms, saluting the Prince and Princess of Orange ; in two sheets. The great Fair at Amsterdam, with the Citizens under Arms. The Festival of the Birthday of the Prince of Orange. 1686. The Interior of the Audience-chamber at the Hague. A perspective View of Voorst.

MAROT, François, a reputable French painter, born at Paris in 1667. He studied under Charles de la Fosse, and painted history in the style of that master. Among other excellent works by him, is a picture of Christ appearing to Mary, in the church of Notre Dame. He was chosen a Royal Academician in 1702, and died in 1719.

MARQUEZ, Esteban, a Spanish historical painter, born at Estremadura, and, according to Bermudez, studied under his uncle, Joya Fernando Marquez, at Seville, who followed the school of Murillo. His instructor dying young, and being thrown upon his own resources, he engaged himself in an establishment where *pictures were manufactured to export to America*, but not having had sufficient practice and experience in that sort of work, he became the butt of his companions, so that he became disgusted, quitted Seville, and returned to his native place. He afterwards returned to Seville, where by close application in studying and copying the works of Murillo, he acquired a correctness of design and a knowledge of coloring that enabled him to imitate that master with considerable success. He executed some good works for the churches and public edifices in that city. He died in 1720.

MARQUEZ, Joya Fernando, a Spanish portrait and historical painter, who followed the style of Murillo, and flourished at Seville from 1649 till his death in 1672. He was an excellent portrait painter, and his picture of Cardinal Spinola was engraved by van Goyen.

MARRACCI, Giovanni, a painter born at Lucca in 1637. After acquiring the rudiments of design under Pietro Paolini, he went to Rome at the age of fourteen, and entered the school of Pietro da Cortona, and before the age of twenty-five he had acquired considerable distinction as a historical painter. He returned to Lucca, where he soon acquired distinction, and executed some works for the churches and convents. Lanzi says that "although little known beyond Lucca, he is reckoned one of the most eminent scholars and most successful imitators of Cortona, and merits this honor, either when he painted in fresco, as in the dome of S. Ignatius at San Giovanni, or when he wrought in oil, as in several pictures in the possession of the brotherhood of S. Lorenzo, in the church of S. Michele, and in other places." He died in 1704.

MARRACCI, Ippolito, was a younger brother of the preceding, and studied under Giuseppe Maria Metelli, at Bologna. Lanzi says he was a successful rival of his master, either when he painted by himself, as he did in the Rotunda at Lucca, or in conjunction with his brother. Time of his birth and death not recorded.

MARREBECK, J., an engraver, probably a native of Holland, who flourished about 1700, and engraved a few portraits in mezzotinto.

MARSHALL, William, an English engraver, who flourished in the first half of the 17th century, and is said to have practised the art upwards of forty years. He was wholly employed by the booksellers. He engraved a great number of plates, executed with the graver in a coarse, stiff, tasteless style, supposed to be after his own designs. His best prints are his portraits, and though indifferently executed, they are interesting on account of the personages they represent. The following are the principal:

Sir Thomas More, Chancellor. Desiderius Erasmus. William Cecil, Lord Burleigh. Robert Dudley, Earl of Leicester. Nicholas Ridley, Bishop of Rochester. Lady Jane Grey. James I. William Camden, Historian, &c. William Shakspeare. Benjamin Jonson. Charles I.; three prints. Francis, Lord Bacon. George Villiers, Duke of Buckingham. Robert Devereux, Earl of Essex; scarce. William Alexander, Earl of Stirling; do. William Laud, Archbishop of Canterbury. Nathaniel Bernard, Rector of Ramenham; scarce. Dr. Donne, when 18 years of age. 1635. The Reverend Dr. John Taylor. The Reverend John Sym. The Reverend Josia Shute. James, the first Duke of Hamilton. John Milton. James Shirley, Poet. Sir Robert Stapleton, Poet. 1646. Sir John Suckling, Poet. The Frontispiece to the Arcadian Princess. 1635. The Frontispiece to the Evangelical Harmony. The Frontispiece to Virgil's Works, by Ogilby. 1649

MARSIGLIA, Guglielmo. See Marcilla.

MARSY, Balthasar and Gaspar, were brothers, and distinguished French sculptors, born at Cambray; the former in 1624, and the latter in 1628. They were instructed by their father, who was probably an artist of little note. In 1648, they visited Paris, and after remaining for some time in the employ of a wood carver, their talents were noticed by Sarrazin and Buyster, who engaged their assistance. Commissioned to execute the decorations of the Hotel de la Vrilliere (now the Bank of France,) they acquitted themselves with great honor. For the Abbey of Montmartre they executed a statue of St. Denis, in alabaster, of life-size. At Versailles, however, they produced their finest works, among which was a group of two Tritons watching the Steeds of Phœbus. Among their other productions was the mausoleum of the king of Pologne Casimir, in the church of S. Germain des Pres, at Paris. Balthasar died in 1674, leaving his brother Gaspar, who afterwards executed a number of works for the Park of Versailles, and the bas-relief of the Porte St. Martin, representing Mars bearing the French Crown and pursuing an Eagle. Gaspar Marsy died in 1681.

MARTEAU, Giles de, the Elder, a Flemish engraver, born at Liege in 1722. He went to Paris while young, where he acquired considerable reputation as one of the most successful revivers of stipple engraving, which he brought to great perfection. He was elected a member of the Academy of Paris in 1764. He engraved quite a number of plates, mostly after eminent French masters, among which are the following:

The Portrait of C. Vanloo, painter. The Education of Cupid; *after Boucher*. Venus and Cupid; *do.* The Head of Heliodorus; *from a design by Pierre; after Raffaelle.* The Bust of the Virgin; *after Pierre.* The Entombing of Christ; *after Stellaert.* Justice protecting the Arts; *after Cochin.* Lycurgus wounded by a Plebeian; *do.*; his reception plate. An allegorical subject on the Death of the Dauphin; *do.* A set of six Landscapes; *after J. Houel.*

MARTEAU, Giles de, the younger, was the nephew and pupil of the preceding, born at Liege about 1750. He engraved some plates in the style of his uncle, which possess considerable merit. Among others we have the following by him: Innocent Pleasure, *after Huet;* the favorite Lamb, *do.;* two Hunting-pieces, *do.;* Cupid crying, *do.*

MARTELLI, Lorenzo. Lanzi says that the applause which Salvator Rosa received during his seven years' residence in Florence, induced many young men to copy and imitate him, and among the most successful were Lorenzo Martelli and Taddeo Baldini.

MARTENASIE, Peter, a Flemish engraver, born at Antwerp about 1730. He went to Paris and studied under Jacques Philippe le Bas. He executed some prints, chiefly after the Flemish masters, among which are the Rape of the Sabines, *after Rubens;* the Watering-Place, *after Berghem;* and the Father of a Family, *after Greuze.*

MARTIN, David, an English portrait painter and mezzotinto engraver of little note, who flourished from about 1765 to about 1780. He engraved a few portraits, among which is one of L.

F. Roubillac, sculptor, *after A. Carpentiers;* 1765. Lady F. Manners, daughter of the Marquis of Granby. 1772. David Hume. J. J. Rousseau, *after Ramsay.* Dr. Franklin, from a half-length portrait by himself.

MARTIN, JEAN BAPTISTE, a French painter, born at Paris in 1659. His father was a contractor of buildings, and placed him under Lahire, where he remained several years, and was then engaged as a draughtsman by Marshal Vauban. After the latter became sensible of the talents of Martin, he warmly recommended him to Louis XIV., who placed him under Vandermeulen, the eminent painter of battles. At the death of the latter, he was appointed Director of the Gobelins, with a pension. He painted the battles in all the campaigns of the Grand Dauphin, and a part of those in which the King commanded in person. His numerous battle pieces in the chateau of Versailles gained him the title of *Martin des Batailles.* By order of Leopold, Duke of Lorraine, he executed twenty pictures of the principal events in the reign of Charles V., which were placed in the chateau of Luneville. He died at Paris in 1735.

MARTINELLI, GIOVANNI, a Florentine historical painter, who flourished about the middle of the 17th century. Lanzi says historians do not allow him the praise to which his merits entitle him. There is a grand picture by this artist in the Florentine Gallery, representing Belshazzar's Feast, and in the church of S. Lucia de' Bardi, another fine picture of the Guardian Angel. His masterpiece is the Miracle of St. Anthony at the Conventuali di Pescia.

MARTINELLI, LUCA and GIULIO, two brothers, who studied under Jacopo Bassano, whose style they adopted, and were esteemed excellent artists. They were natives of Bassano, and flourished in the latter part of the 16th century.

MARTINELLI, DOMENICO, an Italian architect, born at Lucca in 1650. He visited Rome, where he gained great distinction; was appointed Keeper of the Academy of St. Luke, and public lecturer on perspective and architecture. He was invited to Vienna, where he designed a palace for the Prince of Lechstentein; and he erected a number of bridges, fortifications, and palaces in various parts of Germany. According to Milizia, his works are characterized by symmetry, and evince an excellent judgment in the combination of ancient solidity with modern elegance. His drawings in water-colors are much esteemed. He died in 1718.

MARTINET, a French lady who married the son of Nicholas Dupuis, and flourished about 1760. Her father-in-law instructed her in the art of engraving, and among others by her hand is a large print of Venus and Adonis, *after Bianchi.* She had a brother, who was also an engraver, and executed some plates of vignettes, views, and animals for the booksellers.

MARTINETTI, GIOVANNI BATTISTA, an Italian architect, born at Bironico in 1764. At the age of eleven years he visited Bologna, where he found a generous protector in the Marquis Zambeccari. After the completion of his course he settled in that city, and soon received several important commissions, the execution of which gained him great reputation. Among them are the Collegio Montalto; the Villa Ravona, erected for the Marquis Zambeccari; and the magnificent Villa Aldini, on the hill called Adel Monte, near Bologna. Martinetti was appointed architect to the city; and subsequently pontifical inspector of engineering. He was a member of many learned societies of Italy. He died in 1829.

MARTINEZ, AMBROSIO, a Spanish painter, born at Granada about 1630. He was educated in the school of Alonso Cano, and acquired considerable reputation as an historical painter. He executed some works for the churches and convents of his native city. His best works are in the church of the monastery of San Geronimo, and at the Carmelites. He died at Granada in 1674, in the prime of life.

MARTINEZ, SEBASTIAN, a Spanish historical painter, born at Jaen in 1602. According to Palomino, he passed the early part of his life at Cordova, where he painted several works for the churches, particularly three altar-pieces in the convent of Corpus Christi, representing the Conception of the Virgin, the Nativity, and St. Francisco di Assisi, which gained him much reputation. On the death of Velasquez he went to Madrid, and was appointed court painter by Philip IV. His best works are his cabinet pictures of historical and other subjects, which are to be found in the collections at Jaen, Cordova, Seville, and Madrid, where they are highly prized. He was also an excellent landscape painter. He died at Madrid in 1667.

MARTINEZ. See MAZO.

MARTINEZ, DOMINGO, a Spanish historical painter, born about the end of the 17th century. He studied under an unknown painter, named Juan Antonio, whom he soon surpassed, and attained considerable reputation. His works possess considerable merit, but are faulty in invention and composition; and he supplied his lack of ingenuity by having recourse to his large collection of prints. Notwithstanding these defects, his pictures were quite popular at Seville, and may be seen in many of the churches. When King Philip visited that city, he commissioned Martinez to execute a number of works, and he was promised the office of king's painter if he would go to Madrid, but he declined, preferring to reside at Seville. Martinez deserves honorable mention for establishing a School of Painters in his own house, and for devoting a portion of his fortune and talents to the education of young artists. He died in 1750.

MARTINEZ, GREGORIO, a Spanish painter, a native of Valladolid, flourished towards the close of the 16th century. He painted landscapes with success, but attained more reputation for his small historical subjects. There is mentioned a charming picture by him, on copper, representing the Virgin and Infant, with St. Joseph and St. Francis of Assisi, remarkable for its delicacy of tints.

MARTINEZ, JOSÉ, a Spanish historical painter, born at Saragossa in 1612. He visited Italy, and after studying at Rome for several years, he returned to Spain, and attained such distinction as to be appointed painter to the King in 1642. He painted a number of considerable works for the churches and convents of Saragossa, among which, Palomino mentions a series of pictures of the Life our Saviour. His works are distinguished for beauty of coloring more than for the higher qualities of art. He engraved a portrait of Mathias Piedra, from a picture painted by himself in 1681. He died in 1682.

MARTINEZ, TOMMASO, a Spanish painter, born at Seville about the close of the 17th century. He studied under Juan Simone Guttierez, a disciple of Murillo, and followed the admirable style of the latter. For the convent de la Merced at Seville, he painted a most beautiful picture of a Mourning Mother, entirely in the style of Murillo, which by reason of its rare merit, was afterwards transferred to the Alcazar.

MARTINEZ, DON JOSÉ LUXAN, or LUZAN, a Spanish painter of history and portraits, born at Saragossa in 1710. Patronized by the noble family Pignatelli, he was sent to Naples, and studied for five years, gaining improvement from the great works of the Italian masters. On returning to Spain, he executed several works for his patrons, among which were the portraits of the family. In 1741, he visited Madrid, having previously been appointed painter to the King. On returning to Saragossa, he was appointed Inspector of Paintings by the Inquisition. His pictures are characterized by facility of execution and harmony of coloring, as well as a good degree of excellence in invention, composition, and design. Many of them are in the churches of Saragossa, Huesca, Calahorra, and Calatyud. Martinez established a successful school of design, from whence issued Bayeu, and many other artists who have gained distinction in the 18th century.

MARTINEZ, D., BERNARDO, DEL BARRANCO, a Spanish painter, born in 1738, in the village of Cuesta. After acquiring a knowledge of the art at Madrid, he visited Italy in 1765, and spent some time in Turin, Parma, Naples, and Rome, studying particularly the antique and the works of Correggio. After an absence of four years he returned to Spain, and in 1774 was chosen a member of the Academy of San Ferdinando. Antonio Mengs being at that time first painter to the King, and having the direction of all matters relating to the Fine Arts, confided to Martinez the execution of several important works. Among them were a portrait of King Charles III.; and the Decollation of St. John, for the Academy of Painting, of which Martinez was one of the most zealous professors. He designed some of the figures for an edition of Don Quixote, published by the Academy, in 1788. He died in 1791.

MARTINI, GIOVANNI, a painter of Udine, of whom there are notices from 1501 to 1515. According to Vasari, he studied at the same time with Pellegrino di San Daniello, under Giovanni Bellini. There are some of his works in the churches at Udine, the best of which is his St. Mark, in the cathedral, painted in competition with Pellegrino, which, in the opinion of Vasari, is little inferior to that master.

MARTINI, INNOCENZIO, a reputable painter, who according to Affo, flourished at Parma about the middle of the 16th century. He painted some frescos in the churches of S. Giovanni and the Steccata.

MARTINI, PIETRO ANTONIO, an Italian engraver, born at Parma in 1739. He went to Paris while young, and there etched some plates after Teniers and other Flemish artists, which were finished with the graver by le Bas. He afterwards went to London, where he resided some time, and practised engraving. The following are the best:

Heliodorus driven from the Temple; *after Solimene.* Christ driving the Money-changers from the Temple; *do.* Architectural Ruins; *after Robert.* The Pleasures of Summer; *after Vernet.* A View of Spoletto; *do.* A View of Porto Ercole; *do.* A View of Avignon; *do.* The Augurs; *after Sal. Rosa;* etched by *Martini*, finished by *le Bas.*

MARTINI, SIMONE. See MEMMI.

MARTINO, BARTOLOMEO DI, an old painter of Siena, by whom there are some paintings in the churches of Siena, particularly one in the cathedral, representing the Translation of the body of St. Crescentius, dated 1405; and another fine picture in S. Antonio Abate.

MARTINO, MARCO SAN, an Italian painter and engraver who flourished about 1680. There is some dispute whether he was a native of Venice or Naples. He is also variously called by writers *Sanmartino, Sanmarchi;* and Guarienti divides him into two artists, *Sanmartino*, a Venetian painter, and *Marco Sanmarchi*, a landscape and figure painter much extolled by Malvasia, who flourished at the same time as San Martino. Bartsch settles the question by giving a description of thirty-three of his prints, many of them bearing his name *Marco San Martino.* Lanzi says he resided at Rimini, where his pictures are frequently met with. He was more eminent for his landscapes, but he also painted subjects of a higher order, as his Baptism of Constantine, in the cathedral at Rimini, and St. John preaching in the Desert, in the College of S. Vincenzio, at Venice.

MARTINOTTI, EVANGELISTA, a Piedmontese painter, was born at Castel Monferrato in 1634, and died in 1694. According to Lanzi he studied under Salvator Rosa, and painted landscapes with small figures and animals in a style of great excellence, in a manner partaking that of his master. His works are found in the collections of Turin, where they are highly esteemed. Lanzi mentions him as an historical painter, and commends his Baptism of Christ in the Cathedral of Casale.

MARTINOTTI, FRANCESCO, was a brother of the preceding, and also a disciple of Salvator Rosa, whose style he adopted. He painted landscapes and history. He died in 1674.

MARTIRELLI. See MARTORIELLO.

MARTIS, or MARTINI, OTTAVIANO, a painter of Gubbio, who matriculated at Perugia in 1400, and was living in 1444. Lanzi says there is a fresco in the church of S. Maria Nuova, in his native city, dated 1403, which represents the Virgin surrounded by a choir of Angels, certainly too much resembling each other, but in their forms and attitudes, as graceful and pleasing as any cotemporary productions.

MARTORANA, GIOVACCHINO, a Sicilian painter, who flourished at Palermo about the middle of the 18th century. There are four large pictures by him, from the life of St. Benedict, in the chapel de' Crociferi, and S. Rosalia.

MARTORIELLO, (sometimes mispelled MARTORELLI, or MARTIRELLI,) GAETANO, a Neapolitan painter, born about 1670, and died in 1723. According to Dominici, he studied under Giacomo del Po. He first attempted historical painting, but not succeeding in this, he devoted his attention to landscape painting, as better suited to his powers, and became the pupil of Niccola Massaro, a scholar of Salvator Rosa. He imitated Rosa in the romantic wildness of his scenery, as well as in the figures he introduced to embellish his pictures. Lanzi says he "was a landscape painter of a free style, but often sketchy, and his coloring not true to nature," which criticism might be applied to Rosa himself.

MARTOS, Ivan Petrovitch, an eminent Russian sculptor, born in 1755, at Itchnia, in Little Russia. He was munificently patronized by the Empress Feodorowna, who sent him to Rome to study at the expense of government. His works are numerous, and among the most important are, the bronze colossal group of the patriots Minim and Pozharsky, at Moscow; the monument to the Emperor Alexander, at Taganrog; the statue of the Duke of Richelieu, at Odessa; Potemkin's monument, at Cherson; and that erected in honor of Lomonosov, at Archangel. They are characterized by nobleness of conception, truth of expression, and freedom of execution, devoid of negligence. In the draping of his figures he is esteemed superior to Canova, and he had a particular talent in bas-reliefs. One of the most admired of these is that which adorns the monument of the Grand Duchess Helena Paulovna, representing Hymen extinguishing a torch. In the church of Grusino, are several statues of saints, executed by Martos. He was Counsellor of State, and Director of the Academy of Fine Arts, at Petersburg. He died in 1835, aged eighty years.

MARTSS, or MARSSEN, Jan, called de Jonge, a painter and engraver, who flourished about 1632. Little is known of him, except a few rare prints by him, engraved in a peculiar manner, which consists of short strokes, a little bent, and rarely crossed with counter strokes; the marks of the graver are but little apparent. Bartsch describes six prints of battles by him, and others are mentioned by Brulliot and Nagler. Bartsch observes that he is learned in the ordonnance of his groups and skilful in his drawing; but his horses are not correctly designed, and their limbs are heavy, resembling those that are condemned in the prints of Peter de Laer. He marked his prints *J. M. D. Jonge fecit*, or *J. M. D. J. fe.*

MARUCELLI, or MARUSCELLI, Giovanni Stefano, an Italian painter, born, according to Baldinucci, in the province of Umbria, in 1586, and died in 1646. Others say he was a Florentine; and, according to his epitaph, he died in 1656, aged seventy-two. He studied under Andrea Boscoli, at Florence, and soon distinguished himself, so that he was invited to Pisa to paint a grand altar-piece in the cathedral, which he executed in a manner that added to his reputation. Another admirable picture by him was one representing Abraham entertaining the Angels. It is said that he was more eminent as an architect and engineer, and that he invented many useful machines.

MARUCELLI, Valerio, a reputable painter, who, according to Baldinucci, studied under Santo di Titi, and flourished about 1600.

MARULLO, Giuseppe, a Neapolitan painter was born at Casale d'Orta about 1620, and died at Naples in 1685. According to Dominici, he studied under Cav. Massimo Stanzioni, and was one of his ablest scholars. His best works approach so near to his master in manner, that Lanzi says, artists themselves have sometimes ascribed them to Massimo. There are some of his best works in the churches at Naples, particularly in S. Severino. He afterwards changed his style of coloring for one of his own, so that he gradually lost public favor, and there is a great difference in his works. Lanzi says his example may serve as a warning to every one, not to estimate his own powers too highly, and not to affect genius when he does not possess it.

MARZI, or MAZZI, Ventura, a native of Urbino, who, according to Lazzari, studied under Federigo Baroccio, and flourished there in the first half of the 17th century. He painted in the style of his master, but there is a great difference in his works.

MARZIALE, Marco, a Venetian painter, who, according to Lanzi, flourished from 1488 to 1506. He was a scholar, or at least an imitator of Giovanni Bellini. In the Conservatorio delle Penitenti, at Venice, is a picture of the Purification by him, signed *Marcus Martialis Venetus*, 1488, and another of Christ with the Disciples at Emmaus, in the Contarini collection, dated 1506.

MASACCIO, or MASO DI SAN GIOVANNI. This great artist is reckoned one of the Fathers of Painting. His real name is not certainly known, though Zani says it was Tommaso Guidi. In his youth he was called Maso di San Giovanni, from the place of his nativity in the Florentine territory; and afterwards the name of Masaccio was given to him from his total disregard of all the comforts and conveniences of life, while eagerly striving to improve himself, or deeply engrossed in the studies of his profession. There is also a great deal of discrepancy as to the time of his birth and death, but Lanzi says he was born in 1401, and died in 1443, which would seem to be near the truth. Vasari says he was born in 1402, but does not mention the precise time of his death; Baldinucci places his birth in 1417, and his death in 1443.—Landrino, the commentator on Dante, who was his cotemporary, says he died at the age of 26, and according to the inscription on his monument, he died in 1443, aged 26; others say he died *very young*. It is probable that his monument was erected long after his death; and it seems improbable that an artist could have gone through the difficulties he had to encounter, executed so much, and acquired such distinction at the early age of 26 years. He first studied under Masolino da Panicale at Florence, and on the death of that master he finished some works left incomplete by him in the chapel of S. Pietro al Carmine. He formed his principles by studying the works of Ghiberti and Donatella. He learned perspective from Filippo Brunelleschi, and went to Rome to improve himself in design by the study of the antique. He had a genius calculated to make an era in art, and he is regarded as the founder of a new style, characterized by the incipient grandeur of the Florentine school. Mengs assigns to him the highest place among those who explored the untrod paths of art; and Vasari says "what were executed before his time might be called paintings, but his pictures seem to live, they are so true and natural"; and in another place he adds, "no master of that age so nearly approached the moderns." He considered painting the art of representing nature truthfully, by the aid of design and coloring, and therefore made nature his constant study. He was the first who removed the difficulties that impeded the progress of art, by judicious observations, and by setting an example of their importance in his own works. He showed the beauty which arises from a proper and agreeable choice of attitudes and motions, and the grandeur which arises from a greater boldness and freedom of execution, and a better chiaro-scuro than had before been practised. He was also the first who studied to give his figures more dignity by draping them with broad, loose folds, instead of the multitude of small ones so commonly practised by preceding artists, and by adapting the color of his draperies to the tint of his carnations, so as to make them harmonize with each other. He was also skilled in perspective, as is seen in his picture of the Annunciation in the church of S. Niccolo at Florence, in which the eye is pleasingly deceived by the receding of different objects, in such a manner as to excite general admiration.

Masaccio's earlier performances retain much of the dryness and stiffness that prevailed before his time. Such are his St. Anna in the church of S. Ambrogio at Florence, and his series of pictures of the Passion of our Saviour in the chapel of S. Caterina in the church of S. Clemente at Rome. But his celebrated frescos of scriptural subjects, in the church of S. Pietro del Carmine at Florence, are distinguished by a beauty and grandeur of style before unknown. Speaking of those works, Lanzi expresses his admiration by quoting Pliny, "*Jam perfecta sunt omnia.*" Mengs also says, "the compositions are studied and judicious, the design daring but correct, the foreshortenings of his figures diversified and complete beyond those practised by Paolo Uccello. The air of the heads is in the style of Raffaelle (should be, the air of Raffaelle's heads is in the style of Masaccio, for he copied him); the expression is so managed that the mind seems no less forcibly depicted than the body. The anatomy of the figure is marked with truth and judgment. The figure so highly extolled in the Baptism of St. Peter, which appears shivering with the cold, marks, as it were, a new era in art. The garments divested of minuteness present a few easy folds. The coloring is true, properly varied, delicate, and surprisingly harmonious, and the relief is in the grandest style."—His most celebrated work was Christ curing the Demoniacs. Vasari gives a long catalogue of painters and sculptors who formed their tastes and improved their arts by studying the works of this great master; among them he enumerates Michael Angelo, Leonardo da Vinci, Pietro Perugino, Andrea del Sacchi, Il Rosso, Pierino del Vaga, and Raffaelle. The last named artist was not ashamed to adopt largely from Masaccio's designs, and from them he took the figure of St. Paul preaching at Athens; the figure of the same Saint chastising the sorcerer Elymas; as well as that of Sergius Paulus, and of another figure among the listeners, whose head is sunk on his breast, and his eyes shut, as though deeply wrapt in thought; and for the Sacrifice of Lystra, he took the whole ceremony.

Such was Masaccio—well, indeed, entitled to the appellation of a Father of Painting. His early life, at least, was one of privation, and he was remarkable for enthusiasm for his art, and untiring industry. He cared nothing for food, raiment, or luxuries, beyond the simplest wants of nature. His name, instead of being a reproach, is his glory. His works procured him universal admiration; but the same merit which promoted his fame, excited envy, and he died deeply lamented by every lover of art, not without strong suspicion that some malignant demon had cut him off by poison.

MASCAGNI, Donato, called Fra Arsenio, a Florentine painter, born in 1579, and one of the ablest scholars of Jacopo Ligozzi. Soon after leaving that master, he became a monk of the Order of the Servi, taking the name of Fra Arsenio, by which he is commonly known. He painted some pictures for the churches of Florence, particularly for that of his Order. His manner is rather distinguished for minuteness and precision than for grandeur of design or softness of coloring. Lanzi commends his pictures of the Miracles in the Nunziata, but more especially one in the library of the monastery of his Order at Vallombrosa, which he says "is a picture full of subject, and the chief glory of this master." It represents, as some suppose, the donation of the state of Ferrara to the Holy See by the Countess Matilda. He executed some easel pictures before he became a monk, which are found in the private collections at Florence. He died in 1636.

MASCALL, Edward, an English portrait painter who flourished about 1650. He painted a portrait of Oliver Cromwell, which was in the possession of the Duke of Chandos.

MASCHERINO, Ottaviano, a Bolognese painter and architect, who visited Rome about 1572, in the time of Gregory XIII. He executed several pictures in the Vatican, among which was the Marriage at Cana; but soon devoted himself entirely to architecture, and attained such eminence as to be appointed pontifical architect. To the palace at Monte Cavallo he added the portico at the extremity of the court, with the loggia, the small façade of double pilasters, and the elliptical winding staircase. Among his other works were the palace now called the Monte della Pieta; the church of S. Salvatore in Lauro; and the façades of La Scala and Santo Spirito. The latter work is particularly characterized by simplicity. Mascherino died at the age of 82, in the pontificate of Paul V. He was often honored by the Academy of St. Luke, to which he bequeathed all his designs and his wealth.

MASÉ, F. de la, a French engraver of whom little is known. Mr. Strutt mentions a print by him, representing St. Jerome in a Cavern, *after L. de la Hire*, which he says proves him to have been an artist of ability.

MASINI, Giuseppe, a Florentine painter, who flourished about 1658. He studied under Giacomo Chiavistelli, and assisted him in his works in the Ducal Gallery. He was chiefly employed in painting for the cabinets.

MASO, di S. Friano See Manzuoli.

MASOLINO, DA PANICALE. See PANICALE.

MASON, JAMES, an eminent English engraver, born in 1710, and died in 1780. He engraved a large number of plates after Claude Lorraine, Gaspar Poussin, Swanevelt, Hobbema, Wilson, Lambert, Scott, and Zuccarelli, which are held in considerable esteem. Two of his best plates are the Landing of Æneas in Italy, *after Claude;* and Venus at the Bath, *after Andrea Sacchi.* He was much employed by Boydell.

MASQUELIER, LOUIS JOSEPH, a French engraver, born at Cisoing in 1741, and died in 1811. He went to Paris, and studied under J. P. le Bas, and executed many plates in the neat, spirited style of his instructor. He engraved several plates of French victories, after Vernet and Monnet; some of the plates for the Voyage of La Peyrouse; many plates illustrative of the Metamorphoses of Ovid and the Fables and the Kisses of Dorat; and, in conjunction with M. Née, the work entitled *Tableaux de la Suisse*, consisting of two hundred and sixteen folio prints. He was also the director of the work entitled *La Galerie de Florence*, and engraved some of the plates. His works possess much merit, and the following are among the best:

The Arrival of Voltaire in the Elysian Fields; *after le Barbier.* An old Man kneeling near a Skull, called Diogenes; *after G. Douw.* A View in Flanders; *after Teniers;* etched by *Masquelier*, and finished by *Le Bas.* A Landscape, with Cattle; *after P. Potter.* A pair of Landscapes; *after Ruysdael;* by *Masquelier* and *Le Bas.* A View in Italy; *after Vernet.* A Shipwreck; *do.* Two Views of Ostend; *after le May.* A Landscape, with a Waterfall; *after Dietricy.*

MASQUELIER, NICOLAS FRANÇOIS JOSEPH, called the Younger, was a relative and scholar of the preceding. He was born at Lisle in 1760, and died in 1809. He wrought in the style of his instructor, and his prints possess considerable merit. He engraved a number of plates for the Musée Robillard, among which are a Corps-du Garde, *after Leduc;* Cæsar at the Tomb of Alexander, *after S. Bourdon;* Extreme Unction, *after Jouvenet;* and Christ at the Column, *after Vouet.* He also engraved some of the cameos and bas-reliefs for the *Galerie de Florence.*

MASSA, D. GIOVANNI, a priest who flourished at Carpi about 1700. Lanzi says he excelled all other artists in works in *scagliola*, and produced some wonderful specimens of the art in his native city, and the adjunct places of Guastalla, Novellara, and elsewhere. He represented distant views, gardens, architectural designs, monuments, and altars, so as to reach the perfection of the art. The most dignified objects in Rome were the subjects he most delighted to introduce into his views, such as the facade of the temple of the Vatican, its colonnade, and its piazza. The Duke of Guastalla took singular pleasure in similar works, and at his desire Massa prepared those two little tables, so much praised by Tiraboschi. Lanzi says "no objects appeared to him more remarkable than such works, abounding in almost every church throughout those parts, and it were to be desired that this plan of representing architectural views should become more frequent." See *Del Conte.*

MASSARD, JEAN, an eminent French engraver, born at Belesme in 1740. He studied under J. G. Wille, and attained a high reputation. His plates are executed in the neat, finished style of his instructor, and are greatly admired, particularly his plates of the Family of Charles I., and the Beautiful Mother, *after Vandyck;* the Death of Socrates, *after David;* also a number of plates after Raffaelle, Domenichino, Cignani, and Rembrandt. Several prints in the *Galerie de Florence* and the *Musée of Filhol* are also by him. Massard was chosen a member of the Academy of Painting in the time of Louis XVI., and on the restoration of the Bourbons in 1814 he was appointed engraver to the king. He died in 1822. Nagler mentions a number of his plates, among which are the following:

PORTRAITS.

The Family of Charles I.; *after Vandyck.* Louis XVI. of France, when Dauphin. Marie-Antoinette, his consort. Nicholas de Livri, Bishop of Callinique; *after L. Toqué.*

VARIOUS SUBJECTS.

The Virgin and Infant; *after Vandyck.* Abraham and Hagar; *do.* Eve presenting the forbidden Fruit to Adam; *after Cignani.* The broken Pitcher; *after Greuze.* The Benevolent Lady; *do.*

MASSARD, JEAN BAPTISTE RAPHAEL URBAIN, the son and scholar of the preceding, was born at Paris in 1775. He studied design in the school of David. He was an excellent artist, and engraved many plates for the beautiful editions of Virgil and Racine, published by Didot, and some of the plates for the *Musée Robillard* and *Musée Francais.* Among his most esteemed works are St. Cecilia, *after Raffaelle;* Apollo and the Muses, *after Giulio Romano;* Hippocrates refusing the presents of Artaxerxes. He engraved many excellent works, which entitle him to a high rank as an engraver.

MASSARI, LUCIO, a Bolognese painter, born in 1569. He first studied under Bartolomeo Passerotti, and afterwards in the great school of the Caracci, at the same time as did Guido and Albano; and with the last named artist he formed a strict and lasting friendship. After leaving the Caracci, he went to Rome to complete his education by the study of the antique, after which he returned to Bologna, where he settled, soon gained an established reputation, and executed some excellent works for the churches and public edifices. His style nearest resembled that of Annibale Caracci, and he copied some of his works to admiration. Lanzi says there also shines in his countenances the spirit of his first master, Passerotti, and frequently the gracefulness of his dear friend Albano, whose society he enjoyed, both in his studio and at his villa, and in works undertaken in conjunction with him. His S. Gaetano at the Teatini is crowned with a glory of exquisitely graceful cherubs, that seem from the hand of Albano. In point of beauty, the *Noli me Tangere* at the Celestini, and the Nuptials of St. Catherine in S. Benedetto, are among his most esteemed pieces, to say nothing of his New Testament Histories at the Cortile of S. Michele in Bosco, where he left many very elegant specimens. Malvasia says his Marriage of St. Catherine in the church of S. Benedetto, Christ appearing to Mary Magdalene in the Celestini, and two altar-pieces in S. Michele in Bosco, are so much in the manner of Annibale Caracci that they might readily be taken for the works of that master. In treating tragic subjects, he was less successful. Lanzi says, "although he had a real knowledge of art, he conducted them without that extreme study of foreshortenings and naked parts of which others make such lavish display. Yet he showed noble clearness and decision, fine coloring, a grand spirit, enlivening them with light and graceful figures. Such is the Slaughter of the Innocents at the Bonfigliuoli palace, and Christ bearing the Cross at the Certosini—a most imposing production, from the number, variety, and expression of the figures, whose pictoric fire surpasses all we could mention from the hand of Albano." Massari also painted cabinet pictures of historical subjects in a style of excellence. He died in 1633.

MASSARO, Niccolo, a Neapolitan painter, and scholar of Salvator Rosa. According to Dominici, he painted landscapes in the style of that master, adopting his forms, and the sublime picturesque, more than his coloring, which was tame and insipid. He could not design the human figure well, so he employed Antonio de Simone, a painter of battle-pieces, to insert his figures. Lanzi says he was a good landscape painter. He died in 1704.

MASSAROTTI, Angelo, a painter of Cremona, born in 1655. He first studied under Agostino Bonisoli, in his native city, and afterwards went to Rome, where he became the scholar of Carlo Cesi. Though he resided many years at Rome, his works partake more of the Cremonese than the Roman school. He had little imagination, and therefore introduced portraits, rather than ideal forms, into his pictures, and by this servile habit, fell somewhat into the faults of a mannerist. His draperies too, are sometimes heavy. Lanzi says "he boasts a more rich and oily coloring than was then prevalent at Rome, which gives his pictures an appearance of freshness and roundness, while it adds to their preservation." He executed some works for the churches, the chief of which is a vast picture in the church of S. Agostino, representing that saint distributing his regulations to his different orders. He died in 1723.

MASSCEUS, or MASSEUS, Otho. See Marcellis.

MASSÉ, Charles. See Macé.

MASSÉ, Jean Baptiste, a French engraver and miniature painter, born at Paris, according to the Abbé Fontenai, on the 29th Dec., in 1687, and died 26th Sept., 1767; others says 1681, and 1752. Doubtless the first dates are correct. He distinguished himself as an engraver, which procured his admission to the Academy at Paris. He also painted portraits in miniature, with so much success that he made it his principal business. He was a correct designer, and undertook the direction of that great work entitled *La grande galerie de Versailles et les deux salons qui l' accompagnent, dessinée par J. B. Massé et gravée par les meilleurs maitres du tems*, Paris, 1752. This work consists of fifty-two immense plates, after the great works of le Brun, in the Royal Gallery at Versailles. Among others, he engraved the following plates:

Mary de Medicis, Queen of Henry IV.; a frontispiece to the Luxembourg gallery; *after Rubens*. The portrait of Anthony Coypel, Painter; *after a picture by himself*; engraved by *Massé* for his reception at the Academy. Mercury sent by Venus to dispose Dido in favor of Æneas; *after J. Cotelle*. Minerva showing the Portrait of Louis XIV.; *after Rigaud and Coypel*.

MASSE, Samuel, a French painter, born at Tours in 1671; he went to Paris, where he acquired distinction as a miniature painter, and died in 1753.

MASSEI, Girolamo, a painter of Lucca, who, according to Baglioni, flourished at Rome in the pontificate of Paul V., where he executed many works for the churches and public edifices, among which the most noted are an altar-piece of the Martyrdom of St. Sebastian, in the church of S. Luigi de Francesi, and several pictures representing the life and miracles of St. Francis in the Trinitá de Monti. He was a correct designer, and an excellent colorist. Lanzi says he was one of the artists who reflected a ray of honor on the age when the art had much declined from its former glory at Rome. No better proof can be required, than the fact that the Padre Ignazio Danti, an eminent designer and connoisseur, who had been selected by the pope as a fit person to conduct the works then going on at the Vatican, that the best talent should be secured without favoritism, chose him as one of the artists to execute the works; and he was employed several years in decorating the chambers and loggie of the Vatican. He returned to his native place in his old age, to die in tranquillity among his friends, and his death happened in the pontificate of Paul V., at the age of eighty.

MASSI, D. Antonio, a Bolognese painter and priest, who, according to Colucci, flourished at Bologna about 1580, and executed some works for the churches. None of his works are specified, but he was a reputable artist.

MASSI, G., an Italian engraver, of whom little is known. Mr. Stuart mentions a portrait of Cardinal Alaman Salviati, *after P. Nelli*, by him, dated 1730.

MASSINI, C., an engraver, and probably painter, by whom there are some slight etchings executed in a free, painter-like style, without date.

MASSON, François, a French sculptor, born at Vieille Lyre, in Normandy, in 1745. He learned the elements of design from a priest, and manifested such fine talents, that his elder brother placed him under Cousin, a sculptor of Pont Audemer, who had studied under Nicolas Coustou. Masson made rapid progress, and executed two excellent medallion portraits of Marshal Broglie, and his brother, the Bishop of Noyon, which gained him the patronage of this family, who sent him to Paris to study under Guillaume Coustou. At the termination of four years, Masson was commissioned by the Bishop of Noyon to execute a fountain for the Palace de l'Evechê. In two years it was completed, and pleased the prelate so highly, that he sent Masson to Italy, and maintained him at Rome for five years. By studying the noble remains of antiquity, he greatly improved his style, and on returning to France, was commissioned by Marshal Broglie to decorate the government palace at Mentz, where he executed among other works, an immense bas-relief, forty-two feet in length, with figures of colossal size. When the revolution broke out, public works being suspended, Masson devoted his energies to executing portraits in plaster and in marble, characterized by truth of resemblance, admirable expression, and careful execution. He executed the bust of Dufresne, from memory, after death, and produced an excellent likeness. Among his other works, was a group of Hector tied to the Car of Achilles, exhibited in 1792; a monument to Jean Jacques Rousseau, formerly in the garden of the Tuileries, but subsequently removed to the Luxembourg; the statue of General Caffarelli, executed in 1805; and a very beautiful statue representing Flora, or Youth, which was greatly admired, and after his death, was purchased by the government. Masson died in 1807.

MASSON, Antoine, an eminent French engraver, born near Orleans in 1636; died at Paris in 1700. He was bred to the business of an armorer, and first exercised the burin by engraving ornaments on steel. He visited Paris while young, and settled in that city, where he assiduously devoted his energies to drawing, and gained considerable distinction in designing and painting portraits. As an engraver, however, he gained much greater eminence, and some of his portraits have scarcely been surpassed. His plates are executed almost entirely with the graver, which he handled with surprising firmness and facility, and at the same time with the greatest delicacy. Among his historical plates, that of Christ with the Disciples at Emmaus, *after Titian*, usually called *The Table Cloth*, may be considered a master-piece in that style. His portrait of Brisacier, termed the Grayheaded Man, is a most admirable work. The following is a list of his principal prints:

PORTRAITS.

Anne of Austria, Queen of France; *after P. Mignard.* Maria Theresa of Austria, Queen of France; *after N. Mignard.* Maria Anne Victoria of Bavaria, Dauphiness. Louis Augustus, Duke du Maine, *ad vivum, sc.* John James de Mesmes, Count d'Avaux. 1683. Francis de Beauvilliers, Duke de St. Aignau. Francis Rouxel de Medavi, Archbishop of Rouen. 1677. Maria de Lorraine, Duchess de Guise; *after N. Mignard.* The Count D'Harcourt, called the *Cadet de la perle*; *after N. Mignard;* extremely fine. Nicholas de Lamoignon, Count de Courson. 1676. Jerome Bignon, Librarian to the King. 1686. Denis Marin, Secretary to the King. 1672. Louis Verjus, Count de Crecy. 1679. Frederick William, Elector of Brandenbourg. 1683; scarce. Guido Patin, Med. Doct.; engraved in a singular style; rare. Charles Patin, his son, M. D. Francis Maria, Doge of Genoa. 1685. Harr douin de Beaumont, Archbishop of Paris; *after N. Mignard.* Emanuel Theodore, Duke d'Albert; *do.* Gaspar Charrier, Secretary to the King; *after Blanchet.* Alexander du Puy, Marquis of St. André; *after de Seve.* Louis, Duke de Vendome; *after P. Mignard.* G. de Brisacier, Secretary to the Queen, called the Grey-headed Man; very fine. Olivier le Fevre d'Ormesson, President of the Parliament. 1668; very fine. Peter Dupuis, Painter to the King; *after N. Mignard.* Anthony Masson, engraver to the King; *se ipse fecit.*

The following heads, as large as life, though finely engraved, are less happy in the execution than the preceding portraits:

Louis XIV. with a Hat; *ad vivum fecit.* 1687. Louis XIV.; a large oval; *after C. le Brun.* Louis the Dauphin, his son, with a Hat. Philip, Duke of Orleans. John Baptist Colbert, Prime Minister. 1677. Francis de Harley, Archbishop of Paris. 1684. Claude du Housset. 1681. Henry de la Tour d'Auvergne, Viscount de Turenne.—Nicholas Potier de Novion, President of the Parliament. 1679. William de Lamoignon, President of the Parliament. 1675. Charles Colbert, Marquis de Croissi; *after H. Gascar.*

SUBJECTS.

St. Jerome in Meditation; *Masson, sc.* The Holy Family; *after N. Mignard.* Christ with the Pilgrims at Emmaus; *after Titian.* This print is celebrated by the name of the *Table-cloth;* very fine. The Assumption of the Virgin; *after Rubens;* fine and scarce. The Brazen Serpent; *do.;* in two sheets; fine.

MASSON, Magdalene, a French lady, the daughter of Antoinė Masson, was born at Paris about 1660. She studied under her father, and engraved several fine portraits, of life size, in the style of that master. Among them are the following:

Elizabeth Charlotte, Duchess of Orleans; *Mad. Masson, sc.* Elizabeth of Orleans, Duchess of Alençon; *after P. Mignard.* Maria Theresa of Austria, Queen of France; *after Habert.* Elizabeth Maria Josephine, Infanta of Spain. Victor Amedeus II., Duke of Savoy. Louis Henry de Gondrin de Montespan; *after a picture by A. Masson.*

MASSONE, Giovanni, a native of Alessandria, who painted in the church erected by pope Sextus IV., at Savona, about 1490, for the sepulture of his family. Little is known of him. Lanzi says that, although not mentioned in history, he must have been a distinguished artist to have received such a commission. The picture referred to is a small altar-piece, representing the Virgin, with pope Sextus, and Cardinal Giuliano his nephew, afterwards pope Julius II., kneeling at her feet. It is exquisitely executed, and the artist received 192 gold ducats for his labor.

MASTELLETTA, Il. See Donducci.

MASTROLEO, Giuseppe, a Neapolitan painter, who, according to Dominici, was born about 1744, and studied under Paolo de' Matteis, and was his ablest scholar. He painted some works for the churches, and his master-piece is a picture of St. Erasmus, in the church of S. Maria Nuova, which is highly commended. Time of his death not recorded.

MASTURZO, Marzio, a Neapolitan painter, who, according to Dominici, first studied under Falcone; and afterwards, Salvator Rosa at Rome, and was one of his ablest scholars. He painted battle-pieces and landscapes in the style of Rosa. Lanzi says he is sometimes rather crude in his figures, rocks, and trunks of trees. His flesh tints are not painted like those of Rosa, as in those he followed Giuseppe Ribera.

MASUCCI, Agostino, a painter, born at Rome in 1691. He studied under Carlo Maratti, and was the last pupil instructed by him. He painted Holy Families, pictures of the Virgin, Madonnas, &c., in the serene and dignified style of his master, rather than one of affability and loveliness, though he sometimes adopted the latter, through intercession. Lanzi says he was a good fresco painter, and decorated an apartment in a summer house erected in the garden of the Quirinal by pope Benedict XIV. He painted many altar-pieces for the churches, and his angels and children are designed with great elegance and taste. His most celebrated works at Rome are a picture of St. Anna, in the church of Il Nome S. S. di Maria, and the Holy Family, in S. Maria Maggiore. There is also an admirable picture of St. Francis in the church of the Osservanti, at Macerata, and one of the Conception in S. Benedetto, at Urbino, which he pronounced "a noble composition, full of fine portraits, (in which he was long considered the most celebrated painter in Rome) and finished with exquisite care. He died in 1758.

MASUCCI, Lorenzo, was the son and scholar of the preceding. He painted in the style of his father, but did not possess his merits, nor acquire much distinction.

MASUCCIO, an old Neapolitan architect and sculptor, born in 1230. According to Milizia, he completed the Castel Nuova, and S. Maria della Nuova, commenced by Giovanni da Pisa. He erected the archiepiscopal palace in the Gothic style; but evinced an improved taste in the church of S. Domenico Maggiore; and a still better style in S. Giovanni Maggiore. Among the palaces erected by Masuccio, is that now in the possession of the Princess of Colombrano.

MASUCCIO, Stefano, called Il Secondo, an Italian sculptor and architect, the scholar of the preceding, born at Naples in 1291. He visited Rome, and studied the monuments of antiquity, attaining a purity of style greatly surpassing his instructor. King Robert, of Naples, recalled him to that city, to erect the church of Santa Chiara; but being prevented from immediately complying, the edifice was commenced in the Gothic style, which is greatly to be regretted. One of his pupils, Giacomo de' Sanctis, commenced the church of S. Maria delle Grazie, in the same manner, but Masuccio corrected its defects, as far as possible. He erected the church and monastery della Croce de' Palazzo; the magnificent Carthusian monastery of San Martino; and the Castle of San Elmo. Masuccio completed the church of S. Lorenzo, which had been commenced by his instructor; erected the church of S. Giovanni at Carbonaro, and sculptured a number of tombs for that edifice. The bell-tower of Santa Chiara, is his work, and was intended as a specimen of the five orders of architecture, with five stories; the first, Tuscan; the second, Doric; the third, Ionic; the fourth, Corinthian; the fifth Composite. Unfortunately, this grand tower was only erected to the third story. Masuccio died in 1388.

*M excud.* or MA. MATHAM, James, or Jacob, an eminent Dutch engraver, born at Haerlem in 1571. He studied under Henry Goltzius, married his daughter, and by his advice, went to Italy for improvement, where he resided some time, and executed some plates after the best masters. On his return to Holland, he executed a great variety and number of plates under the eye of Goltzius. He worked entirely with the graver, which he handled with great freedom and facility, though his design is somewhat incorrect. He sometimes marked his plates with the above monogram, of his initials, I. M. A., and at others, with his name. He died in 1631. The following is a list of his best plates, some of which are scarce and valuable:

PORTRAITS.

Philip William, Prince of Orange; *after M. Mirevelt.* Henry of Nassau, Prince of Orange. 1610. Bust of Philip Winghius, inscribed *Henricus Goltzius Amicitiæ ergo delineabat Romæ.* Michel Angelus, Buonarotus. Abraham Bloemaert; *after Paul Moreelze.*

SUBJECTS AFTER VARIOUS MASTERS.

The Holy Family with St. Anne; *after Raffaelle.*—Mount Parnassus, with Apollo and the Muses; *do.* The Holy Family, with St. Catherine; *after Titian.* 1592. The Alliance of Venus with Bacchus and Ceres; *do.* The Visitation of the Virgin; *after Salviati.* Christ washing the Feet of his Disciples; *after Taddeo Zuccaro.* Christ praying on the Mount; *do.* The Nativity; *do.* The Assumption of the Virgin; *do.* The Adoration of the Kings; *after Fed. Zuccaro.* Christ curing the Sick; *do.* Christ raising the Widow's Son; *do.* The Visitation of the Virgin; *after Paolo Veronese.*

SUBJECTS AFTER GOLTZIUS.

The Fall of our first Parents. The Visitation of the Virgin to St. Elizabeth. The Crucifixion, with the Virgin and St. John. Christ appearing to Magdalene. 1602. Christ with the Disciples at Emmaus. The Loves of the Gods, Jupiter and Europa, Apollo and Leucothoë, Mars and Venus, and Hercules and Dejanira; four plates. Perseus and Andromeda. 1597. The Four Seasons; in four circular plates. 1589. Faith, Hope and Charity. 1590. The seven Cardinal Virtues; in seven plates. The seven Mortal Sins; in seven plates. The Type of Human Life; in three plates; scarce. 1592.

SUBJECTS AFTER GERMAN AND DUTCH MASTERS.

Abraham sending away Hagar; *after Ab. Bloemaert.* The Annunciation; *do.* The Adoration of the Shepherds; *do.* Jupiter and Danaë; *do.* Cupid and Psyche; *do.* Samson and Dalilah; *after Rubens.* The dead Christ, with the Marys; *after Jer. Franck.* The Crucifixion; *after Albert Durer;* scarce. Venus asleep, surprised by Satyrs; *after Rottenhamer.* A set of five prints of Fruit-pieces, and the Interiors of Kitchens; *after Peter van Aertsen,* called *Long Peter;* scarce.

MATHAM, Theodore, was the son and scholar of the preceding, born at Haerlem, according to Nagler, in 1589, others say about 1600. After engraving a few plates at home, he went to Italy, and entered the school of Cornelius Bloemaert; and afterwards, in conjunction with Michael Natalis, Renier de Persyn, and others, he engraved the marbles in the Palazzo Giustiniani. On his return to his native city, he engraved a considerable number of plates, executed with the graver, occasionally assisted with the point, in a clear, free style. He usually marked his plates T. M. *fecit,* or *sculpsit.* The following are the principal:

PORTRAITS.

Michael le Blon, Agent to the Crown of Sweden; *after Vandyck.* Joost van de Vondel, Dutch Poet; *after Sandrart.* Vopiscus Fortunatus Plempius, Med. Doct.; *after Backer.* D. Gerardus Vossius, Canonicus Cantuariensis; *after Sandrart.* Philip William, Count Palatine of the Rhine; *after J. Spilberg.* Wolfgang William, Count Palatine; *do.* Stephen Vacht, Dean of Sarten; *do.*—Claudius a Salmasi; *after Dubordieu.* Henricus Regius, Med. Doct.; *after H. Bloemaert.* D. Leonardus Marius Goezanus, Professor Coloniensis; *after N. Moyaert.* Gaspar Barlæus, Med. Doct.; *after Sandrart.*

SUBJECTS.

The Virgin and Infant, with St. John; *after Bassano.* The Holy Family; *after J. Sandrart.* Diana and Acteon; *Th. Matham, fec.* The Descent from the Cross, with the Marys, St. John, and Joseph of Arimathea; *after Gerardus Leydanus;* fine.

MATHAM, Adrian, is supposed to have been the second son of James M., born at Haerlem about 1600. He studied with his father, and engraved part of the plates for the *Academie de l'Espée,* published at Antwerp in 1628. He also engraved some portraits, and a few plates of grotesque subjects. He worked entirely with the graver, in a style resembling that of J. de Gheyn the Elder, though much inferior to that artist. There is a good deal of discrepancy among Italian authors about these artists. Zani says that James M. had three sons; *Jan,* the eldest, a portrait painter; *Adrian,* the second, and *Theodore,* the third, both engravers. Lanzi says that *Theodore* Matham, a native of Haerlem, was a portrait painter, and that he was employed at the court of Turin towards the close of the 16th century. The following are Adrian's best prints:

PORTRAITS.

James Graham, Marquis of Montrose. Peter Bor

Christiaensz, Historian; *after F. Hals.* D. Sibrandus Sixtius Oistervirius; *after N. Moyaert.*

SUBJECTS.

The Golden Age; *after H. Goltzius.* 1620. An old Man caressing a Woman, to whom he presents his Purse; *do.* Two Beggars, the Man playing on a Viol, the Woman singing; *after A. vander Venne.* A Combat of six grotesque Figures; *do.*

MATHEUS, a French designer and engraver, who flourished at Paris about 1620. He was chiefly employed by the booksellers, and engraved some frontispieces and other book ornaments, in a neat, finished style, which possess considerable merit. They are mostly after his own designs. Among others, are the following by him:

The Adoration of the Magi; *from his own designs.* The Frontispiece to a *General History of France:* published at Paris in 1619. A Frontispiece to the *Works of Thomas Aquinas.* 1622. Another Frontispiece to *Amours d'Endimion et de la Lune.* 1624.

MATHEY, C., an English engraver of no note, by whom there is a portrait of Arcangelo Corelli, the Musician, *after Howard.*

MATHIEU, or MATTHIEU, PIERRE, a French painter, born at Dijon in 1657. He went to Paris, where he acquired considerable reputation as an historical painter, but his works are now little known or valued. He died at Paris in 1719.

MATHYSSENS, ABRAHAM, a Flemish painter, born at Antwerp in 1570. According to Descamps, he painted landscapes and history with reputation, and executed some works for the churches. In the cathedral at Antwerp, is a picture of the Death of the Virgin by him, and an altar-piece, representing the Virgin and Infant, with St. Francis, in the church of the Recollets. He died at Antwerp in 1619.

MATHIAS, GABRIEL, an English painter, born about 1725. He went to Rome to complete his studies, and on his return to London practised the profession for some time, and for several years contributed to the Exhibition in the Strand. One of his pictures exhibited in 1761, representing a Sailor splicing a Rope, was engraved by Mac Ardell. Through the influence of his brother, Vincent M., a gentleman of distinction at court, he got an office in the royal household, when he abandoned painting. He was afterwards appointed deputy paymaster in the Board of Works, and died at Acton in 1804.

MATON, B., a Dutch painter of whom little is known, except that he was a copyist and imitator of Gerard Douw and William Mieris. He was very successful in copying the candle-light pieces of Douw, giving them great force and brilliancy, but less finish than the originals. His pictures are of small size, and painted on panel. They are found in the best collections in Holland, sometimes with his name, but generally where his pictures have changed hands, his name has been erased, and that of the painter imitated often substituted.

MATSYS, METSYS, or MESSIS, QUINTIN, an eminent Flemish painter, born at Antwerp in 1450, and died there in 1529. Authors vary as to the minutiæ of this artist's life, the truth of which is mixed up with a good deal of fiction and romance. Suffice it to say, here, that he was bred up to the trade of a blacksmith, or farrier, which business he followed till he was in his twentieth year. It is not known with certainty what caused him to abandon his devotion to Vulcan, and become a humble worshipper at the shrine of the Muses. Some say that the sight of some prints, others that his copying some prints for his amusement while confined by sickness, lit up the latent fire; and others that the ardent passion he bore for a blue-eyed lass whose cruel father, an artist, refused her hand to any one but a painter, inspired him. This last supposition is probably nearest the truth, as it is known that he married the daughter of an artist. This account of his conversion to art seems to be confirmed by the verses of Lampsonius, affixed to Matsys' portrait engraved by Jerome Cock; and by the inscription on his monument in the Cathedral at Antwerp, *Connubialis amor de Mulcibre fecit Apellem.* It is not known under whom he studied, or whether he had any instructor, but it is highly probable, from the above account, that his intimacy with an artist's family first directed his attention to art, and that he received instruction from the artist whose daughter he married. At all events he possessed uncommon talents and genius, and became one of the most eminent artists of his time, in the dry, minute style prevalent at that period in his country; and it is believed that, had he enjoyed the advantages of travel in Italy, to study the antique and the works of the great masters, he would have become one of the most distinguished painters of the Flemish school. His manner was peculiar, and unlike that of any other master; and his pictures are strongly colored and highly finished, though somewhat hard and dry. One of his most considerable works is an altar-piece with two folding doors, in the chapel of the Circumcision in the Cathedral at Antwerp. The centre picture represents the Dead Christ on the knees of the Virgin, with Mary Magdalene and other saints. On one of the doors is the Daughter of Herodias with the Head of the Baptist, and on the other St. John in the cauldron of boiling oil. Sir Joshua Reynolds thus describes this curious performance: "In the Pieta the Christ appears starved to death, in which manner it was the custom of the painters of that age always to represent a dead Christ; but there are heads in this picture not exceeded by Raffaelle, and indeed not unlike his manner of painting portraits, hard and minutely finished. The head of Herod, and that of a fat man near the Christ, are excellent. The painter's own portrait is here introduced. In the Banquet, the daughter is rather beautiful, but too skinny and lean." One of his most remarkable pictures, the Two Misers, is in the royal collection at Windsor, but there are others of the same subject, in other collections. Matsys was also a medalist; his most celebrated work of the kind is a medallion bust of Erasmus. There are some curious iron vessels at Antwerp, Arschot, and in England, attributed to him; probably they were executed by some other person from his designs. His works, about seventy in number, are widely scattered in the different collections in Europe, highly prized and much sought after for their unique character.

MATSYS, JOHN, was the son and scholar of the preceding, born at Antwerp about 1480. He painted in the manner of his father, though he is said to be greatly inferior to him. Some of his best works are in the collections at Antwerp and Amsterdam. Van Mander mentions one of two Old Men counting Money, which favorably compares with his father's works. Some of his pictures are certainly wrongly attributed to his father, so that it is evident that historians and connoisseurs differ as to his real merits.

MATSYS, or METENSIS, Cornelius, a Flemish engraver, who flourished at Antwerp about the middle of the 16th century. He executed a large number of plates, generally after his own designs, executed in a style somewhat resembling that of Francis de Babylone. Nagler gives a list of eighty-three prints by him. It is supposed he visited Italy, from the manner of his design and some of the subjects he engraved. It was a long time supposed that prints with this monogram were by two different engravers, the first by Matsys and the second by Metensis, but connoisseurs now consider them to be by one and the same artist. His prints are sometimes marked with one of his monograms, and at others with his name in full or its contractions, as *Cornelius Matsys* or *Metensis fecit*, or *Corn.* or *Cornel. Met. fec.* Among others, the following are attributed to him:

The Portrait of Ernest, Count de Mansfield, and his wife Dorothea. The Cardinal Virtues. Portrait of Henry, King of England, with the date 1544. The Death of Cleopatra. 1550. An old Man, with two old Women, one of whom holds a Basket of Eggs. 1549. Judith with the Head of Holofernes. 1539. A Battle; *after G. Penz.* The Holy Family, with St. Elizabeth; *after Raffaelle, Corn. Met.* The Miraculous Draught of Fishes; *do.; Cornel. Met. fec.* The Entombing of Christ; *after an etching by Parmiggiano.* A set of Prints from the Old Testament; on some of these he has put one of the above monograms, and also signed his name at length, *Cornelius Matsys, fecit.* They are dated 1549 and 1550.

MATTEIS, Paolo de, a Neapolitan painter, born in 1662, and died in 1728. According to Dominici, he studied under Luca Giordano, and was his most celebrated scholar. But Pascoli reckons him among the best scholars of Morandi, an artist who might vie with the first of his age. He probably studied first under Morandi, but his works partake more of the manner of Giordano. He acquired distinction; was invited to Paris, where he resided three years, and obtained considerable celebrity at the French court. He was next engaged by Pope Benedict XIII. to come to Rome, where he painted at the Minerva and the Ara Cœli. He was also employed in various other cities, particularly at Genoa, where there are two fine pictures by him in the church of S. Girolamo, one of which represents that Saint appearing to St. Saverio in a dream, and the other the Immaculate Conception, with a Choir of Angels, which Lanzi characterizes as an admirable production, "with figures as graceful as ever were painted." His principal residence was at Naples, where he distinguished himself by numerous works in the churches and public edifices. Lanzi says "he there decorated with his frescos the churches, galleries, halls, and ceilings in great numbers, after reaching the celebrity without attaining the merit of his master (Giordano). It was his boast to have painted in sixty-six days the immense cupola of the Gesu Nuovo, (a few years since taken down in consequence of its dangerous state); a boast which, when Solimena heard, he sarcastically replied that the work declared the fact itself without his mentioning it. Nevertheless, there were so many beauties in it, in the style of Lanfranco, that its rapid execution excited universal admiration.—When he worked with care, as in the Pii Operai, and in the Matalona Gallery, and in many pictures for individuals, he left nothing to desire in his compositions, in the grace of his contours, and in the beauty of his countenances, though there is little variety in the latter, or in any of the other estimable qualities of a painter. His coloring was at first *Giordanesque;* afterwards he painted with more force of chiaro-scuro, but with a softness and delicacy of tint, particularly in his Madonnas and Children, in which he sometimes displays the sweetness of Albano, and a trace of the Roman school, in which he had also studied."

MATTEUS, Cornelius, a Dutch painter and engraver, who flourished about 1637. Little is known of him. He painted landscapes and animals, and there are a few spirited etchings of landscapes by him, executed in a style resembling that of Herman Swanevelt.

MATTHIEU. See Mathieu.

MATTHIEU, Baldassare, a native of Antwerp, who painted at Turin in 1656, and by whom, according to Lanzi, there is a highly prized Supper of our Lord, in the refectory of the Eremites at Turin.

MATTIOLI, Lodovico, a Bolognese engraver, born in 1662. He first learned design in the school of Carlo Cignani, with the intention of becoming a painter; but having made some essays at etching, he showed so much talent that, by the advice of his master and others, he directed his attention to engraving. He executed a large number of spirited etchings, after the best Bolognese masters, as well as some from his own designs. Bartsch and others mention upwards of one hundred and sixty prints by him. Among others are the following:

The Annunciation; *after Lod. Caracci;* scarce. The Circumcision; *do.* The Nativity; *after Agos. Caracci.* Christ and the Woman of Samaria; *after An. Caracci.* The Death of St. Joseph; *after Franceschini.* The Presentation in the Temple; *after G. M. Crespi.* The Martyrdom of St. Peter; *do.*

MATTIOLI, Girolamo, a Bolognese painter of the school of the Caracci, who flourished about 1577. He executed some works for private houses of Bologna, particularly for the noble family of Zani. He is highly commended by Malvasia as an artist, enthusiastic in his profession, and of good abilities, but he died young.

MATURINO, an eminent Florentine painter, born in 1490. He was one of the favorite scholars of Raffaelle, and assisted him in decorating the Loggie of the Vatican. He was the intimate friend and partner of Polidoro da Caravaggio, with whom he applied himself diligently in studying the antique bassi-relievi, and other relics of Grecian sculpture, and became one of the most correct and graceful designers of his time. Lanzi says that he, in conjunction with Polidoro, "filled Rome with the richest friezes, façades, and ornaments over doors," most of which have perished from exposure. One of the most celebrated of their united works is the fable of Niobe and her Children, in the Maschera d'Oro at Rome, which Lanzi says "has suffered less than any other of their works from the ravages of time and the hand of the barbarian." Fortunately some of their most beautiful designs have been preserved by the prints of Cherubino Alberti and Santi Bartoli, who engraved them before they perished. Maturino and Polidoro lived together, as inseparable in their affections as their labors; they had the same taste of design, composition, and choice of subjects; and the ideas as well as the handling had so close a resemblance that it seemed impossible to determine the pencil of one from the other in their united performances. No painters could design the ancient manners, customs, arms, vases, statues, &c., better than these artists; and though they borrowed their hints from the most celebrated Grecian sculptors, yet they adopted them with so much taste that the antique style appeared wonderfully original in their compositions. The sacking of Rome in 1527 separated the two friends, and Maturino died soon after of the plague, as it is said, aged 37 years; which makes his death to happen in the same year.

MAUBERT, JAMES, supposed to be a French painter, who, according to Lord Orford, went over to England in the reign of George I. He distinguished himself not only by taking the portraits of the living English poets, as Dryden, but by copying those of all the dead ones he could find. He died in 1746.

MAUCOURT, CHARLES, a French mezzotint engraver, born at Paris about 1743. He went to London and executed some prints, among which is one of the Expulsion of the Jesuits from Spain, *after his own design*, and signed with his name. He died at London in 1768.

MAUPERCHE, HENRI, a French painter and engraver, born at Paris in 1606. He acquired considerable reputation as a painter, decorated several apartments in the palace at Fontainbleau with frescos, and was admitted into the Academy at Paris in 1655. He also painted landscapes, and etched a considerable number of plates after his own designs, and Swanevelt. Dumesnil enumerates fifty-one prints by him, many of which he says have become scarce, on account of the extreme lightness of his point, which he did not strengthen by the aid of the graver. The following are the principal. He died in 1686.

A set of six plates of the History of Tobit. A set of six plates of the History of the Virgin, from the Annunciation till the Flight into Egypt. Twelve Landscapes; *after Hermann Swanevelt.* Two plates of the Prodigal Son. Four Landscapes, with Figures and Ruins.

MAURER, JOSHUA, a Swiss painter in distemper, and more especially on glass, who flourished at Zurich in the middle of the 16th century. Little is known of him, though he is said to have been an artist of considerable genius.

[monogram] or [monogram] MAURER, CHRISTOPHER, was the son of the preceding, born at Zurich, in 1558. He was instructed in design by his father, and he afterwards went to Strasburg, and studied under Tobias Stimmer, a fresco painter and wood engraver of distinction. He painted in distemper and on glass with reputation, but he distinguished himself more as an engraver on wood and copper. In conjunction with Stimmer, he published a set of animals of the chase. He executed a set of wooden cuts for the Bible, which are admired for their neatness. He also etched a set of forty plates of emblems, which were published after his death, entitled *Emblemata miscel. nova.* &c. Zurich, 1622. He sometimes marked his prints with the above monogram. He died at Zurich in 1614.

MAURER, J., a Swiss engraver, who went to England about 1745. He engraved some views of buildings in London, which are neatly executed with the graver.

MAYER, MLLE. CONSTANCE, a French paintress, who acquired considerable distinction by her portraits and fancy subjects, some of which appeared in the annual exhibitions at the Louvre, from 1800 to 1821. She is said to have had the advantage of instruction from Suvée, Greuze, and Prud'hon. Among her most popular works were, Venus and Cupid asleep, caressed by the Zephyrs; the Torch of Venus; Innocence between Love and Riches; the Happy Mother; a young Naiad repeling a troop of Lovers; a Dream of Happiness, &c.

MAYNO, GIULIO, a Piedmontese painter, who, according to Lanzi, was a native of Asti, and flourished at Turin from 1608 to 1627. He was a reputable artist.

MAYNO, JUAN BAPTISTA, a Spanish painter, born at Toledo in 1594. He studied under Domenico dalle Greche Teoscopoli, under whose able instruction he became an eminent artist. He joined the Monks of the order of Predicatores, or as others say, of St. Dominici, at a very youthful period, but this did not preclude the exercise of his genius, and he was reputed one of the ablest artists of his time and country. In the convent of San Pedro, at Toledo, there are four of his most esteemed works, viz., the Nativity, the Resurrection, the Descent of the Holy Ghost, and the Mystery of the Trinity, and in the church of the same Order a fine picture, representing the Repentance of St. Peter. He had the honor of being drawing master to Philip IV., and also instructed him in painting, of which that monarch was a true lover and quite a proficient in the art. Philip also employed Mayno to paint a battle-piece in his palace, the Bueno Retiro, a grand composition, in which he introduced the Duke d' Olivarez animating his troops to victory by showing them a portrait of their king. He died at Toledo in 1654. Stanley says he was born in 1569, and died in 1649, at the age of 80, but he does not cite his authority.

MAZO. See VERMEYEN.

MAZO, DON JUAN BAPTISTA, or DEL MAZO MARTINEZ, a Spanish painter, born at Madrid in 1620. He studied in the school of Velasquez, whose daughter he married. According to Palomino, he was a general artist, and excelled equally in history, landscape, and portraits. He possessed an extraordinary talent for copying the works of the most eminent masters. Philip IV. employed him to copy the best works of the Venetian masters, particularly of Titian, Veronese, and Tintoretto, in the royal collection, which he performed with such surprising correctness in every particular that it was impossible to distinguish them from the originals. His landscapes are usually of a large size, and are considered by his countrymen as works of the highest merit. He died Feb. 10, 1687, according to the inscription on his monument, and not as Palomino says, in 1670.

MAZOT, an obscure engraver of little note, by

whom there are some indifferent portraits, and among them one of Christian IV., King of Denmark.

MAZZA, Damiano, a painter of Padua, who studied under Titian, whose style he imitated with great precision. Lanzi says he painted a few pictures for the churches in Venice, executed in the manner of Titian, with striking power and relief, if not with much delicacy of hand. He died soon after his return to Padua, in the flower of life, and the only work he left there was a picture of Ganymede borne away by the Eagle, in the Casa Sonica, a work of such exquisite beauty that it was attributed to Titian, and removed from the place.

MAZZANTI, Cav. Lodovico, an Italian painter, born at Orvieto in 1674. He studied under Gio. Battista Gaulli, called Baccicio, and followed the style of that master. His reputation gained him an invitation to Naples, where he is said to have painted a number of pictures in concert with Solimena. According to Ratti, he attained sufficient distinction to be honored with the order of knighthood. He visited Rome, and painted many pictures, both in oil and in fresco, particularly in the church of S. Ignazio. Lanzi says that his talents were not commanding, and that his abilities were inferior to his ambition. He died at Viterbo in 1766.

MAZZAFORTE, M. Pietro da, an old painter who flourished at Foligno about 1460. Lanzi says that in the church of S. Francesco di Cagli, there exists a most beautiful composition, painted by Pietro da Mazzaforte and Niccolo Deliberatore in 1461, for which they received one hundred and fifteen gold ducats.

MAZZAROPPI, Marco, a Neapolitan painter commended by Dominici, who was a native of S. Germano, and flourished at Naples from 1590 to the time of his death, in 1620. He painted landscapes and figures in an animated and natural style, with a pleasing tone of coloring, almost in the Flemish manner.

MAZZELLI, Giovanni Marco, a celebrated worker in *scagliola,* who flourished at Carpi about 1709. See *Guido Fassi.*

MAZZI. See Marzi.

MAZZIERI, Antonio di Donnino, a Florentine painter who flourished about 1520, and was the scholar of Francia Bigio. According to Vasari, he distinguished himself as a painter of landscapes and battle-pieces. He was a man of fruitful invention, a bold designer, and particularly excellent in his horses. His works also possess great vigor and strength of coloring.

MAZZOCCHI, Paolo. See Uccello.

MAZZOLINI, Lodovico, called Mazzolini di Ferrara, a painter born at Ferrara about 1481, and a student of Lorenzo Costa. There is a great confusion of names among Italian authors as applied to this artist. Lanzi says he must not be confounded with Mazzolino (nosegay), an epithet applied by Lomazzo in his *Idea del Tempio della Pittura,* to Francesco Mazzuoli, as if in sport. Vasari calls him Malini; another Marzolini; and a third divides him into two painters, Malini and Mazzolini. There is also much discrepancy as to his real merits. Lanzi thus describes his manner, after a careful examination of his best works: "It displays an incredible degree of finish, sometimes appearing in his smallest pictures like miniature; while not only the landscape, but the architecture and the bassi-relievi are most carefully executed. There is a spirit and clearness in his heads to which few of his cotemporaries could attain, though they are wholly taken from life, and not remarkably select; in particular, those of his old men, which in the wrinkles and the nose sometimes border on caricature. The color is of a deep tone, not so soft as that of Ercole da Ferrara, with some gilding, even in the drapery, but sparingly applied." His works are scarce, and highly prized. In the church of S. Francesco at Bologna is one of his altar-pieces, representing Christ disputing with the Doctors; in the Florentine Gallery a small picture of the Virgin and Child, with other saints; some small Histories in the Aldobrandini Gallery at Rome, and others in the Campidoglio. There are two of his pictures in the English National Gallery. He died about 1531.

MAZZONI, Cav. Guido, called also Paganini, and Il Modanino, a celebrated painter, sculptor, and architect, highly commended by Vasari, was a native of Modena. Little is said of his works, but he was twenty years in the employment of Charles VIII. of Spain, and returned to his own country with riches and honor, to spend his remaining days.

MAZZONI, Cesare, a Bolognese painter, born in 1678. He studied successively under Lorenzo Pasinelli, and Gio. Giuseppe dal Sole. According to Crespi, he was a commendable artist, and was much employed in painting for the churches, not only at Bologna, but at Faenza, Turin, and Rome. Among his principal works at Bologna, is an altar-piece, in the church of S. Colombano, representing that saint kneeling before the Virgin and Infant; in S. Tommaso di Strada Maggiore, the Crucifixion; and in S. Giovanni, St. Peter delivered from Prison. He died in 1763.

MAZZONI, Giulio, a painter of Piacenza, who studied at Rome under Daniello di Volterra. Vasari speaks of him in terms of high commendation. His chief work is the Four Evangelists, in the cathedral at Piacenza. Lanzi says he failed to acquire a knowledge of foreshortening, as seen from below, in the school of Daniello, though respectable in every other part. He was living in 1568.

MAZZONI, Sebastiano, a Florentine painter and architect, who flourished at Venice about 1685. As a painter, Lanzi says he belonged to the class of naturalists, though he possessed a certain delicacy, and roundness of style, and ease of handling. He was more eminent as an architect, and among other fine buildings, he erected the Palace for the Cavaliere Liberi, which, in magnificence, appears to exceed the fortunes of a painter.

MAZZUCHELLI, sometimes miscalled MAZZONI, and MORZONI. See Morazzone.

MAZZUOLI, Annibale, a fresco painter, born at Siena, who, according to Della Valle, acquired considerable reputation in his native city, and afterwards in Rome, so that his name was inserted in the Eulogies of Pio. Lanzi says he was rapid in his execution, and possessed but little merit. Most of his works are at Siena. He died in 1743, at an advanced age.

MAZZUOLI, MAZZUOLA, or MAZZOLA

Pier Ilario, an old painter of little note, who flourished at Parma about 1533. There are a few of his pictures in the churches at Parma. Lanzi says his real name was Mazzola, and he was the father of Parmiggiano. He had two brothers, Michele, and Filippo, also painters of little note, some of whose works are still to be found at Parma.

MAZZUOLI, Francesco, called Il Parmiggiano, from the place of his nativity, was the son of Pier Ilario M., born at Parma in 1503, according to the Padre Affò, who wrote his life. His real name was Mazzola. His father dying while he was very young, his uncles, Filippo and Michele, brought him up, and gave him what instruction they possessed in the art; but to his own genius and his assiduity, he owed his success, without the advantage of superior instruction. At the early age of fourteen, he painted his Baptism of Christ, in the church of the Annunziata, which was the astonishment of artists. Surrounded by the admirable works of Correggio, he made them his model, and at the age of nineteen, he had executed several works for the churches, both in oil and fresco, which raised his reputation to a high rank, and excited the highest expectations of his future career. His earlier works are entirely in the manner of Correggio; but he had too much confidence in his own powers, to servilely imitate the works of any master; therefore he was ambitious to travel to study the works of the best masters, and having painted three small pictures as a sort of introduction abroad, one of which was an exquisite portrait of himself, he set out for Rome, at twenty years of age. He diligently studied the works of the best masters, particularly of Raffaelle and Giulio Romano, and formed a style that was pronounced original, and which Lanzi says "is at once great, noble and dignified; not abounding in figures, but rendering a few capable of filling a large canvass; the prevailing character, however, in which he so greatly shone, was grace of manner, a grace which won for him at Rome the most flattering of eulogies, that "*the spirit of Raffaelle had passed into Parmiggiano.*" His talents recommended him to the patronage of Clement VII., for whom he painted a picture of the Circumcision, for the palace of the Vatican, which was considered a wonderful performance. It was not only admirable for the composition, coloring, and execution, but remarkable for the introduction of three different lights without destroying the harmony of the whole. The light diffused on the principal figures was from the irradiation of the Infant Jesus; others were illuminated by a torch carried by one who attended the sacrifice; and others again in the open air, were enlightened by the early dawn, which showed a lovely landscape with villas. When Rome was sacked in 1527, by the Emperor Charles V., the story of Protogenes of Rhodes, in similar circumstances, is repeated as having happened to this artist; at all events, he soon fled for safety to Bologna, where he executed some altar-pieces for the churches, among which was his celebrated picture of the Virgin and Infant, with St. John, St. Margaret, and St. Jerome, in S. Margherita, that was the study and admiration of the Caracci, and was preferred by Guido to the St. Cecilia of Raffaelle. The French connoisseurs also selected this picture as one of the gems of Bologna, to grace the gallery of the Louvre. In the church of S. Petronio, is another grand picture of St. Rocco, a noble and dignified performance. At Bologna also, he executed many of his choicest easel pictures. On his return to his native city, he was engaged to decorate the vaulted ceilings of la Madonna della Steccata, where he represented Adam and Eve, some of the Virtues, and his famed chiaro-scuro of Moses breaking the Tables of the Law, in which work the sublimity of the ideas, and the great style of the design, render it one of the grandest productions of the Lombard school. Unfortunately for his reputation, this great artist was addicted to that fatal delusion of the times, alchymy; he wasted his substance and his health, in the absurd pursuit of the philosopher's stone. This infatuation occasioned him to neglect, and finally to abandon the important works he was engaged to perform in the Steccata; and as he had been paid in advance, he was prosecuted and imprisoned by the confraternity. He was released on condition of his proceeding with the work, but offended or disgusted with the treatment he had received, he fled to Casale Maggiore, where he died of a fever, brought on by disappointment and chagrin, in 1540, at the age of thirty-seven years. There is a great contrariety of opinion as to the merits of Parmiggiano, much of which had its origin in enmity, and by taking a single picture, instead of several works as a standard of just criticism. It is, however, conceded by connoisseurs, that he had a truly fine and admirable genius, that his invention was ready, his design learned, though at times somewhat mannered, and that he had a peculiar talent in giving beauty, elegance, sweetness, and grace, to his figures. His coloring was excellent; some have called it enchanting; Lanzi says "it was moderate, discreet, and as well tempered as if the artist feared that too much brilliancy would offend the eye and diminish grace." He was a perfect master of chiaro-scuro. His carnations receive a remarkable lustre from the yellow and green draperies which he frequently used; his cherubs and angels are so exquisitely designed and executed, as to appear truly celestial. His attitudes are always chosen so as to show the most beautiful parts, and they are so judicious as to give life and motion to his figures. His outline is true and firm, and the light, easy flow of his draperies, gives an inexpressible beauty to his pictures. Lanzi says "he was accustomed to form the whole piece in idea before he once handled the pencil; though he was rapid in his execution. Strokes of his pencil may sometimes be traced so very daring and decided, that Albano pronounces them divine, and declares that to his experience in design, he was indebted for that unequalled skill which he always united to great diligence and high finish." Lanzi says too, that, if we admit Albano as a good judge, Parmiggiano was not very studious of expression, unless, indeed, we consider the grace which animates his characters and other delicate figures as meriting the name of expression; yet in another place he says that several of his works are conducted with so much feeling and enthusiasm as to have been ascribed to Correggio himself; such were his pictures of Cupid fabricating his bow, with two cherubs at his feet, one weeping, and the other laughing; and Ganymede and Leda, which were positively assigned by Boschini to Correggio, and still countenanced by many persons. Mengs and Algarotti accused him of being sometimes guilty of affectation, and of carrying his grace so far as to make his heads border upon effeminacy. Agostino Caracci too, said that "a painter should have a little of Parmiggiano's grace", not all, because he conceived he had too much. According to the opinion of others, his excessive study of what was graceful, led him sometimes to select proportions somewhat too long, in stature, in the fingers, and the neck. This is the case with his celebrated picture in the Pitti Palace, called *la Madonna collo lungo*, or *long neck;* but he might have pleaded the example of the ancients, who, in their draped statues, observed similar proportions, to avoid falling into vulgarity. The length of the figures was also a subject of praise among the ancients, as noticed in the commentators of Catullus. A long neck in virgins is also inculcated by some modern writers; Malvasia lays it down as a precept of art; and Cav. Lazzarini drew his Madonnas according to this rule. Parmiggiano, notwithstanding the shortness of his life, executed many works, which are to be found in the royal and noble collections of Europe. Some of his more favorite subjects he repeated several times, as his Cupid fabricating his Bow; his Holy Families and Madonnas, frequently somewhat varied. He also excelled in portraits.

Parmiggiano also distinguished himself as an engraver. It was claimed by his countrymen that he was the inventor of etching, but this art was practised in Germany by Durer and others long before his time; yet he has the merit to be considered the first artist who employed the point in Italy. This is rendered very probable from the appearance of his earliest prints, which show that he did not thoroughly understand the mechanical part of the process, such as laying the ground, and the use of acids; for those plates not being well corroded, are retouched with the graver without much delicacy of execution, while his later ones are clear and perfect, and every way superior. It was also said that he engraved on wood, but it is now well known that the wooden cuts formerly attributed to him, were executed after his designs, by Ugo da Carpi, Andrea Andreani, Antonio da Trento, and others. Some of the etchings marked F. P., attributed to him, are supposed to have been executed by cotemporary artists.—(See Meldolla.) Bartsch gives a description of only fifteen prints, which he considers genuine, and of twenty-six more, marked F. P., which, with others, given to this artist, he considers to have been executed by others, after his designs :

*List of prints by Parmiggiano, as given by Bartsch.*

1. Judith holding the Head of Holofernes and the Sword, &c.
2. The Annunciation, with the Holy Spirit descending, &c.
3. The Nativity. The Virgin seated and covering the Infant.
4. The Holy Virgin holding the Infant in her Arms.
5. The Entombment of Jesus Christ.
6. The Resurrection of Christ.
7. St. Peter and St. John curing the Lame Man at the Temple Gate.
8. St. James the Great.
9. St. Philip.
10. St. Thais, or some other holy recluse.
11. Love Asleep.
12. A Shepherd standing, supporting himself with a Stick.
13. A young Man and two old Men.
14. The two Lovers.
15. The Astrologer.

Of these, No. 9, St. Philip, is not by Parmiggiano; Bartsch himself describes it among the prints of Guido; neither is the print of the Astrologer, No. 15, by this master. There are two other prints by Parmiggiano which were unknown to Bartsch; a Judith, and the Study of an Arm.

MAZZUOLI, Girolamo, was the son of Michele M., and the cousin and scholar of Parmiggiano, whose graceful style he followed. He did not accompany Francesco to Rome, but continued to reside at Parma, where he made the works of Correggio his model, and executed many excellent works for the churches and convents, both in oil and fresco. Lanzi says "he was more attached to the school of Correggio than Francesco was, and in his style composed his picture of the Marriage of St. Catherine, in the church of the Carmine; a piece full of the characteristics of that great master. He was also excellent in perspective, and in his picture of the Supper of our Lord, painted for the Refectory of S. Giovanni, he represented a colonnade so beautifully and so well adapted to produce illusion, as to compete with the best specimens from the hand of Pozzo. He could, moreover, boast ease and harmony, with a fine chiaroscuro, while in his larger compositions in fresco, he was inventive, varied, and animated." Girolamo also executed some works for the churches at Mantua and Pavia, though he wrought mostly in his native city, where he executed more works for the churches than any other native artist. He also painted many easel pictures; and it is believed that some of the works attributed to Parmiggiano, were executed by him, especially those displaying warmer and stronger tints, than those usually employed by that master, for Girolamo was remarkable for his strong impasto, and few equalled him in his knowledge of coloring. This is rendered still farther probable by the early death of Parmiggiano, the numerous works attributed to him, and the great age attained by Girolamo, (he was living in 1580) his industrious life, and the few oil paintings now given to him. He also finished some of the works left incomplete by Francesco, especially his frescos in the Steccata. Among his other great fresco works, are a part of the Ten Colossal figures of children, in the arches of the cupola of the cathedral at Parma, six of which are by Correggio, and four by Girolamo; and the Multiplication of the Loaves in the church of S. Benedetto, at Mantua. Amidst all his beauties, Lanzi says this artist had not a few defects; he was sometimes careless in designing his naked figures, carried his grace to a degree bordering on affectation, and his more spirited attitudes are violent. These defects he attributes to his rage for accomplishing too much, and his often painting in competition with other artists. He is supposed to have died about 1590.

MAZZUOLI, Alessandro, was the son and scholar of the preceding artist. He was a weak imitator of the family style, and executed some works for the churches. In 1571 he was employed in some fresco works in the Cathedral at Parma, which was a great honor, in an edifice abounding in the works of Correggio and other great artists.

MAZZUOLI, Giuseppe, called Il Bastaruolo, or *Vender of Grain*—his father's occupation, not his own. He was born at Ferrara about 1525, and studied in the school of Dosso Dossi, where Gio.

Francesco Surchi was his fellow pupil. He had two manners; in the first he designed his figures too large, and was defective in his perspective, which injured his rising reputation, and his rivals considered him an artist of mediocrity; but by study and industry he formed a second manner, more elevated in design, with a softness of coloring, especially in his flesh tints and extremities, that approached Titian, with a breadth and intelligence of chiaro-scuro worthy of the school of Correggio. He rose to great distinction, and his works were held in such estimation that there is scarcely a public edifice in his native city which does not possess some of his works; and at this day he ranks as one of the most eminent painters of the Ferrarese school. Among his most celebrated works at Ferrara are, the Virgin and Infant crowned by Angels, in the Cathedral; the Ascension, in the church of S. Maurelio; the Annunciation, a Holy Family, and a Crucifixion, in Il Gesù; and in the Conservatorio of St. Barbara, an altar-piece representing that Saint and St. Ursula, and a number of female figures, designed and executed with such unequaled elegance and chastity that Lanzi says the figures seem to live and breathe. He also painted easel pictures for the collections. This great artist was drowned while bathing for his health, in 1589.

MECHAU, Jacob Wilhelm, a German painter and engraver, born at Leipsic in 1745. He studied under Bernard Rode, at Berlin, and afterwards improved himself by frequenting the Academy in his native city. He painted landscapes and history with considerable reputation in his own country, but he is better known as an engraver. He executed quite a large number of plates, many of them after his own designs, and engraved some plates of Views in Italy in aqua-tinta. He died in 1808. The following are among his prints:

St. Michael vanquishing the Demon; *Mechau, fec. aqua forti.* The Resurrection of Lazarus. *Mechau, fec.* 1761. The Adoration of the Shepherds; *after C. Schut.* A Dance of Nymphs and Fauns; *after Giulio Carpioni.* A set of six Italian Landscapes; in the style of *Swanevelt.* 1792. A set of six Views in and near Rome. 1792, 1793.

MECHEL, Christian von, an eminent Swiss engraver, born at Basle in 1737. He went to Paris, and studied under J. G. Wille, and afterwards returned to his native city, where he engraved a great variety of plates, and carried on a considerable commerce in prints. He engraved and published the Dusseldorf Gallery, with a catalogue raisonné; the Medals of Hedlinger; the Works of Hans Holbein, with explanatory and critical remarks; and many pictures of cotemporary painters. His prints are numerous, and remarkably well executed. He died in 1818.

MECHELN, or MECKENEN, Israel von, father and son, two old German artists, about whom and whose works there has been a great deal of disquisition, nor is the matter yet settled. Our limits will not allow us to enter into a dissertation on the subject, farther than to give facts, and refer the curious in such matters to Bartsch's P. G. tom. vi., and Zani's Enciclopedia delle belle Arti, parte i. vol. xiii., in which works all the points are fully discussed. According to M. Heineken, there are about two hundred and fifty prints, all bearing the same characteristics, and usually marked I. M., or I. V. M., or *Israhel* V. M., or sometimes *Israhel von Meckenen, Goldschmit,* or *Israhel tzu Bockholt,* the letters being in the Gothic character. All these prints were, until recently, attributed to one and the same artist; but on account of a great difference observable in the style of the different prints, as well as the dates found on them, Heineken and other critics conclude that there were two Meckenens who practised engraving, father and son. Israhel von Meckenen the Elder is stated by M. Huber to have been born at Mecheln, a village near Bockholt, a small town in the bishopric of Munster, in Westphalia, about 1424. He was regarded as one of the earliest engravers of whom we have any account, and immediately succeeded or was rather a cotemporary of Martin Schoen. That he was not a disciple of Schoen, is evident from the total difference in their styles. It has not been found practicable to distinguish precisely the prints of the elder Meckenen from those of the son, but it is reasonable to conclude that the ruder part of them in point of design and execution, and those having the earliest date, should be ascribed to the father. If any further proof were wanting of the existence of the two Meckenens, the two first prints in the list below—the portraits of the father and son—fully establish the point. It is also ascertained that the younger Meckenen died in 1523. There are quite a number of curious antique pictures at Cologne, Berlin, Munich, and other places, painted in oil, which have been long attributed to Israel von Meckenen, from similarity in design to his engraved subjects; but that able connoisseur, Dr. Franz Kügler, is clearly of opinion that these works must be given to some *unknown artist.* We copy from Kügler's Hand-Book of the History of Painting, part the second; London edition. 1846: "First in the school of Cologne, about the latter half of the 15th century, we meet with an excellent artist, who, with many traces of the elder Cologne school, unites a conscious familiarity with the models afforded by that of van Eyck. *The name of this artist is unknown;* formerly, though, without sufficient ground, that of a cotemporary goldsmith and engraver, *Israhel von Mecheln* or *Meckenen* was given to him. His chief work, a representation of the Passion, on eight panels, is in the possession of Herr Lyversburg, at Cologne, and it is now usual to designate him as the *Master of the Passion.* His pictures have still, indeed, a gold ground, and resemble the older school in this circumstance, as well as in the style of coloring, which is lively, powerful, and clear; but they are painted in oil, and moreover, the manner of treatment, the attitudes, and the arrangement, are generally borrowed from the school of van Eyck. He appears to have been an able, intelligent, and highly gifted artist, earnest in seeking an insight into life, zealous and careful, but for the most part, it must be confessed, devoid of original inspiration. The general character of his drawing is precise and hard; his efforts to mark character in the lower classes of persons, such as the persecutors of Christ, degenerates into exaggeration. Besides this excellent work of the Passion, there are several paintings evidently by the same hand. The most important of those in Cologne are, a Descent from the Cross, of the year 1488, in the City Museum, less powerful than the Passion, and probably of the latest time of the artist; the wings, added later, are probably by a scholar or imitator;

—two very good pictures in the possession of Herr Zanoli;—the paintings in the windows and on the walls of the Hardenrath chapel in Sta. Maria, in Capitolio, of the year 1466; the first of which, however, are injured, and the last considerably retouched. The Crucifixion, on the walls of the same place, belongs to a later period. There are, besides, excellent altar-pieces by him in the churches of Linz and Sinzig; and a considerable number at Munich, in the former Boisserée collection, particularly an altar-piece with very dignified figures of the apostles (John the Baptist in the place of Judas). Several are in the chapel of St. Maurice at Nuremberg; and a beautiful picture, with female Saints, is in the Berlin Museum. The influence of this artist on his cotemporaries was very important, as is proved by the various works of his scholars or imitators, extant at Cologne, and in the neighborhood, or in the Boisserée collection and Berlin Museum. Of those in the Berlin Museum, two panels with male and female Saints are particularly remarkable, being distinguished as much by the dignity of the figures and their noble drapery, as by the powerful painting and expression of their heads." Now, with all due deference to the eminent critic quoted above, is it not far more reasonable to give these works, as heretofore by many excellent critics, to Israhel von Mecheln, but to the younger, rather than to a supposed unknown "Master of the Passion"? because it is certain that there were two artists of this name, the elder a goldsmith and an engraver, two professions often combined in those days; the younger an engraver, certainly instructed in engraving by his father, and who might, and probably did, learn painting of the van Eycks, and the period of whose life agrees with the dates found on these pictures. The following is a list of their most remarkable prints:

The Portrait of Israel von Mecheln the elder, with a beard, and a kind of turban; signed *Israhel von Meckenen, Goldschmit.* The Portraits of Israel von Mecheln the younger and his Wife; inscribed *Figuracio facierum Israhelis et Ide Uxoris*, I. V. M. A set of Prints of the Life of Christ; these, as well as two following prints, are supposed to be some of the earliest works of the elder Mecheln. The Descent of the Holy Ghost. St. Luke painting the Virgin. Judith with the Head of Holofernes; in the back-ground is a battle, with cannon, and other warlike instruments. The Death of the Virgin; M. Schoen and others have engraved this subject. The Virgin standing upon a Crescent, crowned by Angels. The Annunciation; the Angel holds a Scroll, on which is inscribed *A VE. GRA.* The Virgin seated, in a landscape, embracing the Infant, and St. Joseph reposing; on the right of the print is a Grasshopper, on which account it is called the Virgin with the Grasshopper. The same subject has been engraved by Albert Durer, and copied from him by Marc' Antonio. The Virgin and Infant surrounded by four Angels. 1480. The Virgin seated, holding the Infant, with a garden-wall in the back-ground, inscribed in Gothic letters, *Ave potissima Maria.* The same is engraved by M. Schoen. The Feast of Herod; Herodias with the Head of St. John.—Herod's Cruelty. Christ bearing his Cross. The Scourging of Christ. The Crucifixion; *Israhel*, M.; with a light ground. The Crucifixion; *Israhel*, V. M; with a dark ground. St. George and the Dragon; I. V. M. St. Jerome seated in a Room, pointing to a Skull which lies on the table. This is considered one of their best prints. It has been copied by Lucas van Leyden. St. Anthony tormented by Devils. The same subject is engraved by Martin Schoen. The Death of Lucretia. A Man and a Woman walking, with Death behind a tree, shaking an hourglass. This print has been copied by Albert Durer and others. Several single Figures of male and female Saints. A Woman singing, and a Man playing on the Lute. A Man playing on the Organ. Three naked Women, with a Globe hanging above them. Albert Durer and others have copied this print. A Man holding a Skull, inscribed *Respice finem.* A Cup, richly ornamented. The same has been engraved by M. Schoen. A variety of goldsmith's ornaments, and a great number of other subjects.

MECHELN, a painter, doubtless a German, whose name is affixed to a portrait of Pope Urban VIII., dated 1623.

MECHERINO. See Beccafumi.

MECHOPHANES, a Greek painter, who, according to Pliny, was a disciple of Pausias. His manner was rather dry and hard, but this defect was in a measure compensated by his rigid correctness of design, which was appreciated by his cotemporary artists.

MEDA, Giuseppe, a reputable painter, who, according to Morigi, flourished at Milan about 1590, where he was employed in the churches. He was also an architect. He represented upon an organ in the Metropolitan church, the figure of David playing before the Ark, a work highly commended.

MEDA, Carlo, a Milanese painter, perhaps a brother of the preceding, who painted for the churches at Milan in 1595. He does not seem to have gained much distinction.

MEDICI, Pietro, a member of the illustrious house of the Medici, was born at Florence in 1586, and died in 1648. Having a passion for the fine arts, he studied under Lodovico Cardi, and became a reputable painter of history. He painted several altar-pieces for the churches, which are commended for correctness of design, a strong and pleasing tone of coloring, and a very truthful expression.

MEDINA, Juan Baptista, called in England Sir John Baptist M., was the son of Medina de l'Asturias, an officer in the Spanish service, born at Brussels in 1660. He studied under Francis du Chatel, and afterwards greatly improved himself by studying the works of Rubens. He painted history and landscapes with reputation, but he devoted himself mostly to portraits; and, after acquiring considerable reputation in his native city, he went to London, where he met with considerable employment. He went to Scotland under the patronage of the Earl of Leven, who procured him many commissions; and he painted the portraits of most of the Scotch nobility, and acquired great reputation in his day. He was knighted by the Duke of Queensberry, then Lord High Commissioner of Scotland. At Wentworth Castle is a large picture by him, of the Duke of Argyle and his two sons, painted in the Italian style, and according to Lord Orford superior to the works of most of his cotemporaries. His portraits, however, are generally in the style of Kneller, never equaling his best, nor sinking so low as his worst. He painted with great freedom of touch, and produced striking likenesses. His portrait, painted by himself, was sent by the Duke of Gordon to the Grand Duke of Tuscany, and was placed in the Florentine Gallery. He died at Edinburgh in 1711.

MEEL. See Miel.

MEELE, Matthew, a Dutch portrait painter born at the Hague in 1664. He went to England, and practised for some time under Sir Peter Lely

He afterwards returned to the Hague, where he acquired considerable distinction, was appointed one of the Directors of the Academy, and died there in 1724.

MEER, GERARD VANDER, a Dutch painter of low life and landscapes in the old Gothic style, born in 1450, and died in 1512. His works do not possess sufficient merit to deserve attention.

MEER, or MEEREN, JOHN VANDER, THE ELDER, a Dutch painter, said to have been born at Schoonhoven, but with more probability at Haerlem, in 1627. It is not known under whom he first studied, but when young he went to Italy. On his return to Holland he gained great reputation, and his works were much sought after for the best collections. His subjects were landscapes and figures, sea-pieces, and views on the sea-shore, which he painted with great truth and spirit, as he was accustomed to sketch every scene from nature. His sea-pieces are particularly admired, in which the vessels are designed with great correctness and neatness, the skies bright with light, fleecy clouds, and the water clear and transparent. His tints are warm and tender, and there is a sunny brilliancy in his coloring that reminds one of the sea-ports of Claude Lorraine. His landscapes are very pleasing, the scenes well chosen, the forms of his trees easy and natural, his distances well observed, and the whole scenery has a striking effect by a happy opposition of lights and shadows. He also painted battle-pieces with considerable success; his figures and horses in particular were designed with great fire and animation, and executed with a spirited pencil. He has been reproached for too great a predominance of blue in his backgrounds, a peculiarity not uncommon to those who have studied in Italy, where nature frequently assumes a brightness of atmosphere unknown in more northern climates. He died at Haerlem in 1691.

MEER, JOHN VANDER, DE JONGE (the Younger), was the son of the preceding, born at Haerlem in 1655. After studying with his father, he placed himself under Nicholas Berghem, and became one of his most celebrated scholars. He made the works of Berghem his model, took great pains to imitate his delicate style, and tried to improve himself by a diligent study of nature. He painted landscapes in the manner of Berghem, with cottages and peasants at their rural occupations and diversions. His works are well designed, correctly drawn, and delicately finished. His skies, trees, and figures are in good taste, and there is a freshness in the verdure of his plants and the foliage of his trees, that render his pictures very agreeable. He seldom introduced horses or cows, but he was so successful in painting sheep and goats, that in those he equaled, and some say, surpassed his master; his sheep, in particular, are so exquisitely and naturally depicted that it has been said one could imagine he heard the bleat. His works are highly finished, and though they are much inferior to those of Berghem, they command very high prices, and are admitted into the choicest collections. He died in 1688, in the flower of his life, greatly lamented, as he was considered one of the most promising artists of his country. His genuine works are seldom seen out of Holland, but they have been much imitated and passed on the undiscerning for originals. He executed a few charming etchings after his own designs, which are now extremely scarce. Among them is a set of four landscapes, and a Ewe suckling a Lamb, signed *I. v. der Meer, de Jonge fecit.* 1683.

MEER, JOHN VANDER, a Dutch painter, born at Schoonhoven in 1650. He was taught design and coloring at Utrecht, but went early to Rome, accompanied by Lieven Verschuur, where he first studied under his countryman, N. Drost, and afterwards with Carlo Lotti, and is said to have become an excellent historical painter. He designed his subjects on a grand scale, with figures as large as life, executed in a bold style, with a firm, broad pencil, and excellent coloring. On his return to his own country, he settled at Utrecht, where, falling into the possession of an ample fortune, he practised his profession more with a view of acquiring a lasting reputation, than augmenting his riches. He was also a good portrait painter. He died at Utrecht in 1711.

MEER, JOHN VANDER, a son of the preceding, was born at Utrecht in 1665, and died at Haerlem in 1722. He is called *de Jonge* (the Younger); is said to have first studied under his father, and afterwards with Berghem; and the whole history of the other John vander Meer the younger (if this was another) is applied to him. In short, the lives of these artists are mixed up in such admirable confusion, even by writers of their own country, that it is impossible to say with certainty whether there were two or four John vander Meers. Nevertheless, it seems evident from the difference of dates, and total difference of style and history, that there were two families of this name—the one landscape painters, residing at Haerlem; the other historical painters, of Utrecht.

MEER, N. VANDER, a Dutch engraver, who resided at Paris about 1760, and engraved some of the plates for le Brun's Gallery, consisting of interiors of churches, flowers, &c., which are neatly executed.

MEER, VANDER, of Delft. See VERMEER.

MEERT, PETER, a Flemish portrait painter and engraver, born at Brussels, according to Descamps, in 1618. In portraits, he imitated the style of Vandyck, and acquired considerable reputation. In the Museum at Brussels are some of his portraits of the magistrates of that city. It is said there are prints by him dated as early as 1621, which would make Descamps in error as to the time of his birth.

MEGLIO, DI, a Florentine painter, supposed to be the same as Coppi, which see.

MEHEUX, JAMES, a Dutch engraver, who flourished about 1680. He engraved some plates in mezzotinto, among which is a copy of the Rat Catcher, by Cornelius Visscher.

MEHUS, or MEUS, LIVIO, an eminent Flemish painter, born at Oudenarde, in 1630. The war which took place in Flanders soon afterwards compelled his family to flee the country, and they settled at Milan, where young Livio, discovering a genius for painting, received some instruction from a Flemish artist then resident in that city. At an early age he went to Florence, where he had the good fortune to obtain the protection of Prince Mattias, who placed him under the instruction of Pietro da Cortona, at that time employed by the

Grand Duke Ferdinand II. in decorating the Pitti palace. He accompanied his master to Rome, where he diligently studied the antique and the works of the best masters, and became a correct and skillful designer. He afterwards went to Venice and Lombardy, and improved his coloring by contemplating the works of the best masters of the Venetian school. By these means he formed a style of his own. He possessed a fertile and inventive genius; retained little of the manner of Cortona; and imitated the Venetians less in coloring than in the light but firm touches of his pencil. His coloring was chaste and harmonious, his attitudes lively, and his shadows most beautiful. On his return to Florence, he immediately acquired distinction and abundant patronage, for though he executed few works for the churches, he painted a great many cabinet pictures, was pensioned by the prince and employed by the nobility, in whose palaces his works are often to be met with. His most celebrated works are the Repose of Bacchus and Ariadne, painted for the Marquis Gerini in emulation with Ciro Ferri; the Sacrifice of Abraham, painted for the Grand Duke in the Pitti palace; the History of Hagar and Ishmael; the Engagement of Achilles with the Trojans; the Triumph of Ignorance, &c. His most capital work is in the dome of the church of La Pace, in which he appears to have outdone himself; and Lanzi says, "in this he surpassed Cortona, and approached the Lombard school." His portrait, painted by himself, was placed in the Florentine Gallery by the order of the Grand Duke. He died in 1691.

MEI, Bernardino, a Sienese painter, whose works bear date from 1636 to 1653. It is not known under whom he studied, but Lanzi says he was cotemporary with Cav. Raffaello Vanni, and assisted that master in his works at S. Maria della Pace at Rome. His works are mostly at Siena. The Padre della Valle highly commends his genius, and compares his works sometimes to the Caracci, at others to Paul Veronese, and to Guercino; very much as the eclectic philosophers adopt or change the maxims of the different schools. One of his best works was a fresco in the Casa Bandinelli, with an Aurora in a ceiling, surrounded with several elegant figures and designs.

MEIGEL, Christopher, a German engraver, who resided at Nuremberg, where he published a folio volume of prints, designed and engraved by himself, representing the follies of different people, and of all professions. They are indifferently executed.

MEIGHAN, R., an English engraver of little note, who carried on the business of bookseller and publisher in St. Dunstan's churchyard, about 1628.

MEIL, John Henry, a German engraver, who flourished in the latter half of the 18th century. He settled at Leipsic, and wrought for the booksellers. Among other plates, he engraved one hundred and twelve subjects from the Fables of Gellert.

MEIL, John William, a German engraver, the younger brother of the preceding, born at Altenbourg in 1732; died in 1805. He went to Berlin, where he was much employed in engraving vignettes and other book ornaments, from his own designs, for the publishers. He engraved a great number and variety of plates in a neat, spirited style, somewhat resembling that of Della Bella. He was Vice-Director of the Academy of Fine Arts at Berlin. Among others, the following are by him:

A set of eight small plates of Heads and Caricatures; scarce. Four of Quack-doctors and Ballad-singers; in the manner of Dietricy. A set of ten vignettes for the Poem of Joseph and his Brethren; by *Bitaubé*. Twelve Allegorical Vignettes. Hercules playing on the Lyre. A set of four Landscapes, with figures. Fifty-two subjects, entitled, *Spectaculum Naturæ et Artium*; published at Berlin in 1765.

MEIRE, Gerard vander, an old Flemish painter, a native of Ghent, who flourished about 1450. Little is known of him with any certainty. He is said to have been one of the earliest painters in oil, after the van Eycks, in whose style he painted, and of whom he probably learned the art. Van Mander highly commends a picture by him, representing the Death of Lucretia, which he says was well designed, beautifully colored, and admirably finished.

MEIRE, Jan vander, was a brother of the preceding, and is said to have studied with the van Eycks. He is also said to have painted a picture of the Institution of the Order of the Golden Fleece, for Charles the Bold, Duke of Burgundy, whom he followed in all his campaigns, and that he died at Nevers in 1471. If this be true, Hans Hemling and Jan vander Meire were fellow soldiers.

MEIRERPECK, M. Wolfgang, a German designer and engraver on wood, who flourished about 1550. He went to Italy, where, in conjunction with Giorgio Liberali, he designed and executed the wooden cuts illustrating the *Commentaries of Matthiolus on Dioscorides*, in Latin, published at Venice in 1548, and in Germany in the Bohemian language, in 1560.

MEIS, B., an engraver, by whom there are some etchings, somewhat in the style of Benedetto Castiglione, marked *B. Meis fecit.*

MEISSONIER, Justus Aurelius. This artist was born at Turin in 1695. He was a goldsmith, painter, sculptor, and architect. He visited France, and obtained the patronage of Louis XV., who appointed him his designer and goldsmith, in which employment he exhibited the most beautiful specimens of ingenuity and skill. Had he confined his energies to that branch, it would have been far better for the other departments of art in which his versatile talents were employed. As a painter, he executed among others, the portraits of Vicomte Turenne, and Baron J. V. de Besenval, a colonel in the Swiss Guards. The first has been engraved by Larmessin, and the second by Claude Drevet. His design for the façade of St. Sulpice, at Paris, is characterized by Milizia as ridiculous in the extreme. He died in 1750.

MELAN. See Mellan.

MELANI, Giuseppe and Francesco, two brothers, eminent fresco-painters, and natives of Pisa. Giuseppe was a pupil of Camillo Gabrielli, but painted history in the style of Pietro da Cortona. Francesco excelled in perspective and architecture, and was one of the ablest artists of his time in that branch. They usually painted in conjunction, and executed many beautiful works for the churches and public edifices of Pisa, Siena, and other places, in the splendid style of Cortona. They were both learned in design, and each excelled in his particular branch. One of their most capital works is the ceiling of the church of S. Matteo, at Pisa, executed entirely in the style of Cortona, a work greatly admired for the richness of the composition, the gracefulness of the figures, the harmony of the coloring, the magical effect of chiaro-scuro, and the inimitable perspective. Giuseppe was made a knight of the Golden Spur; he was also a good figurist in oil. His best work of this kind is a large picture in the cathedral at Pisa, representing the Death of St. Ranieri, a work that Lanzi says does honor to its author, who was worthy of painting in that sanctuary, so full of the gems of art. Giuseppe died in 1747, and Francesco in 1742.

MELANTHUS, an eminent Greek painter of the school of Pamphilus at Sicyon, was a fellow disciple of Apelles, and like that master, paid a talent of gold for ten years instruction in the art. According to Quintilian, Pliny, and Plutarch, Melanthus attained the highest rank among the painters of his time, deserving a place with Apelles, Protogenes, Nicomachus, Antiphilus, and Euphranor. Like his instructor, he excelled in the chaste propriety of his compositions, and even Apelles conceded to him the palm in the judicious grouping of his figures. Quintilian particularly mentions his skill in the designs of his pictures; and Pliny observes that he was one of those painters, who, with only four colors, produced pieces worthy of immortality. His works commanded very high prices in the cities of Greece and Asia Minor; and their estimation is also evinced by the act of Aratus, a good judge of art, who collected from every quarter, the pictures of Pamphilus and Melanthus, and presented them to Ptolemy III., King of Egypt. He left a Treatise on Painting, a fragment of which has been preserved by Diogenes Laertius; and of which Pliny availed himself in writing the 30th book of his Natural History.

MELAR, Adrian, a Flemish engraver, who flourished at Antwerp about 1650. He executed some plates of portraits and other subjects, in which he attempted to imitate Paul Pontius.

MELCHIORI, Giovanni Paolo, a Roman painter, born in 1664. He was brought up in the school of Carlo Maratti, to which he proved an ornament. According to Orlandi, he had a lively and fertile invention, and possessed much of the grandeur and sweetness of his master's style, to which he added a remarkable correctness of design, with an expression full of propriety and spirit. He painted easel pictures in the style of his master, and executed some works for the churches and public edifices of Rome, the most esteemed of which is a picture of the prophet Ezekiel, in the Basilica of St. John of Lateran. He died in 1721.

MELCHIORI, di Castelfranco, was the father of Matteo Melchiori, who wrote the Lives of the Venetian Painters. He painted history with reputation at Castelfranco, and especially at Venice, where he wrought in competition with Cavalier Liberi, in the Casa Morosini, which alone shews that he must have been an artist of distinction. He died in 1686.

MELDER, Gerard, a Dutch painter, born at Amsterdam in 1693. He showed an early inclination for art, and when a boy, preferred drawing and copying from prints and books, to play. He was a self-taught artist, and after painting many pictures in oil, he devoted himself to miniature painting, as best suited to his taste, and as most likely to afford him more employment and fewer competitors. He became possessed of some miniatures of Rosalba, and by copying them he acquired great proficiency in that branch of the art, and could imitate her style to perfection. He also imitated the works of Rottenhamer and vander Werf with equal success. He painted historical and allegorical subjects, designed in such good taste, and so beautifully executed that they were much sought after, and commanded high prices. He received many commissions from the King of Poland. He also painted small landscapes, composed in an agreeable style, and enriched with figures exquisitely designed and executed. He painted the portraits of many distinguished personages of his time. He also painted in enamel, and was much employed in copying the works of Mieris, vander Werf, and others, in water colors, which he finished with surprising delicacy; but he abandoned this branch of the art, as he found it prejudicial to his sight. He however acquired most distinction for his miniatures, and is accounted one of the ablest artists of his time in that branch. He died at Utrecht, according to Sandrart and others, in 1740, but Balkema says in 1746, and Immerzeel in 1754.

MELDOLLA, Andrea, an Italian designer and engraver, who flourished, according to dates on his prints, from 1540 to 1550. Nothing is known of his history. About one hundred and twenty prints are now ascribed to him by connoisseurs, many of which were formerly attributed to *Andrea Schiavone*, called *Medula;* or to Francesco Mazzuoli, better known as Parmiggiano, because many of them are from pictures or drawings by that celebrated master. Zani has the honor of making the discovery that Meldolla (or Meldola, for it is written both ways) was a different artist from Schiavone, or Parmiggiano; and the subject has been ably investigated by other eminent critics, and Zani's opinions confirmed. Zani says he was acquainted with one hundred prints by Meldolla, Bartsch enumerates and describes eighty-seven, Nagler mentions one more, and the Messrs. Smith, Brothers, the eminent dealers in ancient prints, London, possess one hundred and ten, and have a descriptive account of nine others in foreign cabinets. It is generally believed that the plates on which Meldolla etched were made of *pewter*, which will account for the scratches and corrosions that appear in the later impressions, and for the frequent alterations made in the treatment of the subject, and in the accessories. Good impressions of these prints are now exceedingly rare and valuable. They are sometimes marked with his name, but more frequently with one of the following monograms, often very slightly scratched in, and of unequal size, sometimes being very small. There are variations in many of the prints, owing to alterations in the plates, and repairs, when they had sustained injury. The following is a list of his prints as given by Bartsch and the Messrs. Smith, omitting the descriptions. which would occupy several pages

A M or M. or M. or AP.
MF. or M

PRINTS DESCRIBED BY BARTSCH.

1. Jacob's Ladder. 2. Moses saved from the Nile. 3. God appearing to Moses. 4. Moses showing the Quails to the Israelites. 5. The Annunciation. 6. The Nativity. 7. The three Kings. 8. Another of the three Kings. 9. The Flight into Egypt. 10. The Presentation in the Temple. 11. Another Presentation; very rare. 12. The Circumcision. 13. Another Circumcision. 14. Jesus with the Woman on the steps. 15. Christ healing the Sick; very rare; only two known—one in the Collection of the Archduke Charles at Vienna, the other in the Ortalli Collection at Parma. 16. Christ healing the Leper. 17. The Entombment. 18. Another Entombment. 19. Another Entombment. 20. The Miraculous Draught of Fishes; *after Raffaelle.* 21. St. Peter and St. John curing the Lame Man. 22. St. Paul preaching at Athens. 23. The Descent of the Holy Ghost. 24. The Saviour giving his Benediction. 25. St. Peter. 26. St. Andrew. 27. St. James the Great. 28. St. John. 29. St. Philip. 30. St. Bartholomew. 31. St. Matthew. 32. St. Thomas. 33. St. James the Less. 34. St. Simon. 35. St. Judas Thaddeus. 36. St. Matthias. 37. St. Paul. 38. The Saviour. 39. St. Peter. 39.* St. Peter; the same in design, reversed. 40. St. Andrew. 41. St. James the Great. 42. St. John. 43. St. Philip. 44. St. Bartholomew. 44.* St. Bartholomew; the same, but reversed. 45. St. Matthew. 46. St. Thomas. 46.* St. Thomas; the same, but reversed. 47. St. James the Less. 48. St. Simon. 48.* St. Simon; the same, with slight variations. 49. St. Judas Thaddeus. 49.* St. Judas Thaddeus; the same reversed. 50. An Anonymous Saint. 50.* Do.; but different composition. 50.** Do.; same as preceding, with slight variations. 51. The Saviour; a repetition of No. 38, with variations. 52. St. Andrew; a repetition of No. 40, reversed, with variations. 53. St. James the Great. 54. The Holy Family. 55. The Christian Religion triumphant over Heresy. 56. The Marriage of St. Catherine. 57. The Virgin. 58. The Virgin surrounded by several Saints. 59. Do., Saints, similar to the preceding, but reversed. 60. Do.; similar to the last, with variations. 61. The Holy Family. 62. The infant Jesus in a Cradle, surrounded by Saints. 63. The infant Jesus and St. John embracing, in the presence of several Saints. 64. The Virgin and Infant, with St. John paying homage, and several Saints. 65. Saints adoring the Infant Jesus in his Cradle, same as 62, with slight variations in size. 66. The Present of Flowers. 67. Heliodorus driven from the Temple; *after Raffaelle.* 68. Bellona. 69. Diana. 70. The Coronation of Pegasus. 71. Mercury. 72. Hercules, Dejanira, and Nessus. 73. Mars and Cupid. 74. Ganymede and Hebe. 75. Venus after Bathing. 76. Bellona. 77. Do., another. 78. Mars. 79. Minerva and the Muses conversing on Parnassus. 80. The Judgment of Paris. 81. The Rape of Helen; signed *Andrea Meldolla inventor.* 82. Virtue victorious over Vice. 83. A Prophet, with a long Scroll in his hands, and a Glory in the distance. 84. A Woman carrying a Vase. 85. Ganymede and Hebe; same composition as No. 74. 86. A Woman accompanied by a Child. 87. A Woman writing.

*Prints described by the Messrs. Smith and others, not mentioned by Bartsch.*

88. Eleazer at the Well. 89. The Adoration of the Shepherds. 90. The Adoration of the Kings; a grand composition of 16 figures. 91. The Holy Family. 92. Marriage of St. Catherine. 93. The Holy Family. 94. Christ and his Disciples. 95. Christ healing the Lepers. 96. Boy bending a Bow. 97. Mars. 98. Return of the Prodigal Son. This subject has been copied by Reveidinus. 99. Mercury. 100. Apollo and Daphne. 101. Do., another. 102. Judith. 103. Judith; a copy from an etching by Parmiggiano. 104. St. James. 105. St. Paul. 106. Nymph Bathing. 107. Cupid. 108. Bellona, throwing a Javelin. 109. Do., the same reversed. 110. The Virgin and Child, with St. John. 111. Apollo and the Python. 112. Diana. 113. Bellona. 114. A female Figure walking, and holding up a portion of her dress with both hands; doubted genuine. 115. Five Figures. 116. Faith. 117. Neptune appeasing the Storm; a copy of the centre compartment of the celebrated print by Marc' Antonio. This print is in the Louvre. 118. St. Christopher; at Paris. 119. A Woman pouring Water from a Vase. This print is in the British Museum.

MELEUN, COUNT DE, a French nobleman, who, according to Basan, for his amusement, etched some plates from Berghem, Callot, and other masters. He flourished about 1760.

MELINI, CARLO DOMENICO, an Italian engraver, born at Turin about 1745. He went to Paris, and studied under Beauvarlet. He executed some plates in a neat, finished style, among which are the following:

PORTRAITS.

The King of Sardinia. The Children of the Prince of Turenne.

SUBJECTS.

La belle Source; *after Nattier.* The Education of Cupid; *after Lagrenée.* Morning, a landscape; *after Loutherbourg.*

MELISSI, AGOSTINO, a Florentine painter, born at Florence in 1658, and died there in 1738. According to Baldinucci, he acquired distinction for the beauty of his designs for tapestry, and was much employed by the Grand Duke to paint cartoons in the manner of Andrea del Sarto, for this purpose. He also painted in oil, and the author above mentioned highly commends his picture of Peter denying Christ, in the Palazzo Gaburri.

MELLAN, CLAUDE, an eminent French designer and engraver, born at Abbeville, according to the *Biographie Universelle*, in 1598. Bryan says that he was sent to Paris, where he acquired the elements of design in the school of Simon Vouet, and subsequently visited Rome for improvement, at the age of *sixteen.* But Vouet did not return from his first foreign tour until 1627, consequently Bryan is in error; and the authority above cited, says that Mellan studied the art at Paris, under Thomas de Leu and Leon Gaultier; after which he visited Rome, in 1624, at the age of *twenty-six*, where he gained great improvement under the direction of F. Villamena, assisted by the advice of Simon Vouet. He executed several plates which were highly esteemed, and was commissioned to engrave part of the plates of the antique statues in the Giustiniani collection, the whole of which consists of three hundred and twenty-two prints, published in two vols. folio, Romæ, 1640. The principal part of the plates he engraved at Rome, are executed in the usual manner, with the strokes crossed a second and third time, as the strength of the shadows require. He subsequently adopted a novel mode of operating, with single parallel lines, without any cross strokes over them, the shadows being expressed by the same lines being made stronger, and consequently nearer together. In this new mode of engraving, Mellan acquired considerable celebrity, and many of his plates are characterized by a clear, soft, and agreeable effect. His success in this style appears to have been the result of his singular dexterity in handling the graver, rather than of the peculiarity of the process. The perfect master, which he attained over his instrument, is admirably evinced in his plate of the Face of Christ, called the Sudarium of St. Veronica, executed entirely with a single line, commencing at the extremity of the nose, and continued, without quitting, over the whole face and background. His print of Rebecca, *after Tintoretto*, is evidently from the work of a great colorist; and the artist appears to have seized the very tones of the painter, but without introducing any cross strokes, except in the accessories. Mellan died at Paris in 1688, aged ninety. He executed quite a large number of prints, among which are many admirable portraits, several of them from his own designs, as well as the greater part of his historical subjects. His prints are generally signed with his name in full, although he sometimes used the initials C. M.; or the abbreviation C. Mel., or Cl. Mell. He executed a part of the plates after the antique marbles in the royal palaces of France, which were completed by S. Baudet. The following are his principal plates:

PORTRAITS.

Urban VIII.; *after Bernini*. 1631. Cardinal Bentivoglio. The Marquis Justiniani. Anne of Austria, Queen of France. Henry, Duke of Montmorency. The Cardinal Duke de Richelieu. The Cardinal de Mazarin. Francis de Villemontée, Bishop of St. Malo. 1661. Peter Seguier, Chancellor of France. Nicholas Cœffeteau, Bishop of Marseilles; *after Du Moustier*. The Cardinal du Perron; *after Herbin*. Victor le Bouthillier, Archbishop of Tours. 1658. Nicholas Claude Fabri de Peiresc; one of his finest portraits. Charles de Crequis Lesdigueres, Marshal of France. 1633. Peter Gassendi, Professor of Mathematics. Louisa Maria de Gonzaga, Queen of Poland. 1645. Claude Mellan, painter and engraver. 1635.

SUBJECTS FROM HIS OWN DESIGNS.

Lot and his Daughters. Rome, 1629. Samson and Dalilah. Moses and the Burning Bush. 1663. The Miracle of the Manna. The Annunciation; inscribed *Ecce Virgo concipiet*. 1666. The Virgin with the infant Jesus on her knee. 1659. The Holy Family. Rome, 1635. Christ praying in the Garden; a night-piece; fine. Christ seized by the Soldiers, inscribed *Pater ignosce illis, &c.* St. John, with Magdalene embracing the Cross. Rome. The Crucifixion, with the Virgin, Magdelene and St. John. The Entombing of Christ, with an inscription, *Terra mota est.* The Resurrection; inscribed *Per se resurgens*. 1683. The Face of Christ, called the Sudarium of St. Veronica; executed entirely by a single spiral line, begun at the extremity of the nose, and continued, without quitting, over the whole face and back-ground. St. Peter Nolasque, supported by two Angels; one of the finest and the rarest prints of the artist. Four large plates of the Life of St. Bruno. St. Bruno praying in the Desert. St. Francis praying. 1638; very fine. Several other Saints in acts of Devotion. Mary Magdalene expiring, supported by Angels.

SUBJECTS AFTER VARIOUS MASTERS.

Herodias with the Head of St. John; *after S. Vouet.* The Roman Charity; *do.* The Death of Lucretia; *do.* St. Catherine kneeling, to whom an Angel is presenting the palm of martyrdom; *do.* Rebecca meeting the Servant of Abraham; *after Tintoretto;* esteemed the finest of his prints.

MELLING, Anthony Ignatius, a German painter and architect, born at Carlsruhe in 1763. He was the nephew of Joseph Melling, a painter of the Academy of Strasburg. After acquiring a knowledge of painting under that master, and having studied architecture under his brother, he went to Italy for improvement, at the age of nineteen. After visiting the different cities of that country, he travelled to Egypt, Smyrna, and then to Constantinople, where he settled. In 1795, he was appointed architect to the Sultana Hadidgé, the sister of Selim III., which office he held for five years. His leisure hours were mostly employed in making drawings of the principal views in Constantinople. In 1800, he went to Paris, and commenced the publication of his work entitled *Voyage pittoresque de Constantinople, et des rives du Bosphore*, which had excellent success and gained him the honor of being appointed landscape painter to the Empress Josephine. Several pictures exhibited at the Louvre gained him a gold medal. The Minister of Foreign Affairs, appointed him his designer and painter; and after the Restoration, he was appointed landscape painter to the King's Cabinet. After the publication of his pictorial work entitled *Voyage pittoresque dans les Pyrenées Francaises*, he was honored with a membership in the Legion of Honor. He painted a few subjects of history, among which were the Entry of Louis XVIII. into Paris; and the Distribution of the Standards of the National Guard. He died in 1831.

MELONE, Altobello, a painter of Cremona, whose works date from 1497 to 1520. He painted both in oil and fresco. In 1497, he was employed in completing the frieze of the cathedral. According to Vasari, he painted a series of pictures of the Passion, in fresco, in one of the churches, truly beautiful, and deserving of commendation; but Lanzi says he was not consistent in point of style, introducing figures of large and small proportions in the same piece, and coloring them in a manner that now gives them the appearance of tapestry; but time has doubtless wrought a great change in this respect. Lanzi himself, says he excelled in oil painting. Speaking of Christ descending into Limbo, in the sacristy del Sacramento, he says, "the figures are numerous, of somewhat long proportions, but colored with great softness and strength. His knowledge of the naked is beyond that of his age, combined with a grace of features and of attitudes, that conveys the idea of a great master." He also painted easel pictures. Morelli, in his Notizia, mentions a Lucretia by him, painted in the Flemish style, and he says he was a pupil of Armanino, perhaps a Fleming.

MELONI, Francesco Antonio, an Italian painter and engraver, born at Bologna in 1676. He first studied painting under Marc' Antonio Franceschini; but not succeeding to his wishes, he etched some plates after his master, in which he showed so much taste, that by his advice, he afterwards devoted himself entirely to engraving. He was a correct and pure designer, and his plates are executed with neatness and spirit, and carefully finished with the graver. His works are not numerous, though Bartsch, Nagler, and others, mention about thirty prints by him. He died young in 1713.

MELONI, Marco, a native of Carpi, who flourished in that city about 1537. He is supposed to have been a pupil of Andrea Costa. He painted in the manner of the Caracci, and was exceedingly accurate and studied in his design. There are some of his works in the churches at Carpi, especially in S. Bernardino, which are highly commended by Tiraboschi.

MELOZZO, da Forli, a native of Forli, and one of the Fathers of the Italian school of painting. There is much discrepancy about the minutiæ of his life. Zani states that he was born in 1436; Oretti that he died in 1492, aged fifty-six; Vasari that he was best known at Forli about 1472, and Luca Paccioli, in a work on geometry, &c., published in 1494, mentions him as one of the most excellent painters, *men famous and supreme*, then living. He is said by some to have studied under Ansovino da Forli, and others, Piero della Francesca. Lanzi doubts whether he could have been a scholar of Ansovino, and thinks it at least possible that he was acquainted with Françesca, and Agostino Bramantino, when these artists were employed at Rome by Nicholas V., about 1455. At all events, his name is revered among his countrymen, as the first who applied the art of foreshortening, the most difficult and the most severe, to the painting of vaulted ceilings. Considerable progress had been made in perspective, from the time of Paolo Uccello, with the aid of Piero della Francesca, a painter, and celebrated geometrician, and of a few Lombards. But the ornamenting of ceilings with that pleasing art and illusion which was afterwards brought to such perfection, was reserved for Melozzo. About the year 1472, he painted his famous work of the Ascension in the great chapel at the Santi Apostoli at Rome, for the Cardinal Riario, nephew to pope Sextus IV. Vasari says of this work, "the figure of Christ is so admirably foreshortened, as to appear to pierce the vault; and in the same manner, the angels are seen sweeping through the fields of air in two opposite directions." In 1711, when the chapel was rebuilt, this painting was cut out of the ceiling with the greatest care, and placed in the Quirinal Palace, where it still remains with this inscription, *Opus Melotii Foroliviensis qui summos fornices pingendi artem vel primus invenit vel illustravit.* Several heads of the Apostles which surrounded it were also cut out and deposited in the Vatican. The style of Melozzo resembles, in point of taste, that of Andrea Mantegna and the Paduan school, nearer than any other. His heads were finely formed, his coloring good, his attitudes well chosen, and his foreshortening admirable; the lights are well disposed and graduated, and the shadows judicious, so that his figures seem to stand out and act in space. He painted his works also with delicacy of hand, diligence and grace, in every part. There are few of his works now in existence. There is an apothecary's shop painted in arabesque, and a figure compounding drugs over the door, at Forli, venerated as the work of Melozzo. Vasari states that Francesco di Mirozzo of Forli, was employed in the villa of the Dukes of Urbino, called the Imperial, about the time Melozzo flourished; and Lanzi is clearly of opinion that "we are here to substitute the name of Melozzo, to correct one of those errors which we have so frequently before remarked in Vasari." Lanzi also calls him in his index, F. Francesco M., perhaps from the above circumstance. Lanzi, speaking of his great work of the Ascension, before mentioned, with the feelings of a true connoisseur, exclaims, "what a pity that so rare a genius, pronounced by his cotemporaries 'an incomparable painter, and the splendor of all Italy,' should not have had a correct historian, to have described his travels and pursuits, which must have been both arduous and interesting, before they raised him to the eminence he attained, in being commissioned by Cardinal Riario, to execute so great a work."

MELZI, Francesco, il Conte, a Milanese painter of noble birth, the friend and scholar of Leonardo da Vinci. He practised the art of painting as a delighful employment, for he was rich, and he approached nearer to the manner of da Vinci than any other of his scholars or imitators; and so near indeed, that most of his works are now attributed to his master. Nagler says that the picture of Vertumnus and Pomona, in the Berlin Museum, formerly attributed to da Vinci, bears the signature of Francesco Melzi, and another now in England, called "The Flora of Leonardo da Vinci," is supposed to be by Melzi, as Lomazzo mentions his having painted an exquisite picture of that subject, in the style of da Vinci. He was a man of the most amiable disposition, and loved da Vinci as his father, and accompanied him in his last visit to France. His master rewarded his affection by giving him all his designs, instruments, books and manuscripts, which he nobly used by furnishing both Vasari and Lomazzo with notices of his life, and depositing the numerous volumes of his manuscripts in the Ambrosian Library for the benefit of posterity, which conclusively show the profound acquirements of that great artist, not only in painting, but in statics, hydrostatics, optics, and anatomy. Melzi was living, according to Vasari, in 1568, at an advanced age.

MEMMI, Simone, an eminent Sienese painter, and one of the earliest who distinguished themselves after the revival of the art, was born in 1285. He is sometimes called *Simone di Martini*, and Lanzi says his father's name was *Martino*, and that of his father-in-law, *Memmo*, a corruption of *Guglielmo*, and that he sometimes assumed the one name, and sometimes the other. He signed several of his works *Simon de Senis*, the last in 1344. He died in 1345, and this inscription is on his tomb, *Simoni Memmio, pictorum omnium, omnis ætatis celeberrimo. Vixit ann.* 60, *mensibus duobus, diebus tribus.* These facts are given because of disputes as to his name and time of birth. Vasari says he was a pupil of Giotto, but this is also disputed, and the writers of Siena claim that he was a disciple of their own venerable artist, Maestro Mino. Lanzi thinks the claims of the Sienese good, and that he derived much advantage from the study of the large frescos of that master, though he thinks that, when he assisted Giotto in some of his works at Rome, he studied him closely, as many eminent painters have done with the most eminent masters. At all events, he imitated Giotto so admirably in his works in the church of St. Peter, that the pope invited him to his court at Avignon, where it seems he painted several portraits of the pope, and many portraits of Cardinals and other distinguished personages, among whom were Petrarch and his far-famed Laura, and Petrarch introduced his name in two of his sonnets, and eulogized him in his letters. He also decorated a manuscript copy of Virgil for his friend Petrarch, which is now in the Ambrosian Library, a gem of attraction. His great picture in St. Peter's has perished, but there are several of his works in the churches at Florence and Pisa, as well as at Siena. In the Campo Santo of Pisa, are several frescos of the history of St. Ranieri, and the far-famed Assumption of the Virgin amid a choir of angels, so beautifully executed that Lanzi says, they "seem actually floating in the air, and celebrating the triumph." Some of his larger works may be seen in the chapter-house of the Spanish friars at Florence, among which are several histories of Christ, of St. Peter the Martyr and St. Domenico, with others representing the Order of the Preaching Friars, engaged in the service of the church. There are more of this class of pictures, in which he excelled, in the churches of Siena. Vasari says "his works do not appear those of a master of that age, but of a most excellent modern artist." Lanzi says, "his coloring is more vivid than that of Giotto, and in floridness, seems a prelude to that of Baroccio."

MEMMI, Lippo. This artist was a native of Siena, the brother-in-law and scholar of the preceding. Although he was not equal in genius to Simone, he succeeded admirably in imitating his manner, and probably assisted him in many works; and, aided by his designs, he produced pictures that might have passed for the works of the former, had he not inscribed them with his own name. When he wrought from his own designs, there is a manifest mediocrity in his invention and design, but he is still a good colorist. He sometimes painted in conjunction with Simone, as appears from a picture formerly in the church of S. Ansano de Castel Vecchio at Siena, now in the Florentine Gallery, inscribed, *Simon Martini et Lippus Memmi de Senis, me pinxerunt*, A. D. 1333. He finished several works begun by Simone, at Ancona, Assisi, and other places. He also painted some from his own designs, at Siena and Pisa. He was living in 1361.

MENA, Felipe Gil de, a Spanish painter, born at Valladolid in 1600. He is said to have studied under vander Hamen, a Flemish painter settled at Madrid, where he made rapid progress, and soon surpassed all his fellow scholars. His instructor confided to him the execution of a number of important works, and his reputation increased to such a degree that he could hardly execute his commissions. He excelled particularly in portraits, characterized by natural and animated expression. Invited to his native city, he was commissioned to execute a large number of works, among which are several in the community of the Orphelins, and the convent of St. Francisco, at Valladolid. Mena deserves great credit for establishing a free school of design in his own house, and provided for its use a large number of designs and models, subsequently sold for a thousand ducats. He died in 1674.

MENA, Don Pedro de, a Spanish sculptor, born at Adra, in Alpujurra, about 1620. He studied the art under his father, and subsequently visited Granada, to complete his artistical education under Alonso Cano. His first work of any importance was a group representing the Conception, executed for the church of Algendin, near Granada, which gained him considerable reputation, and he received many commissions from the cities of Granada, Malaga, Madrid, Cordova, and Toledo. Among them are St. Antonio holding in his arms the infant Jesus, at Granada; and a Magdalene penitent, at Madrid, admired for its truthfulness of expression. For the Prince Doria of Genoa, he executed a statue of Christ agonizing, regarded as his master-piece. He died at Malaga in 1693, leaving a number of distinguished scholars, among whom was Miguel de Zayas.

MENABUOI. See Giusto Padovano.

MENAGEOT, François Guillaume, an eminent historical painter, born at London, of French parents, in 1744. At the age of six years his father took him to France, and afterwards placed him in the school of Augustin. He subsequently studied under Deshays, Boucher, and Vien. In 1766, he carried off the grand prize of painting, and visited Rome with the royal pension, where he remained five years, studying the antique, and the works of the great masters. On returning to Paris, he gained the favorable notice of the Academy by his grand picture of the Parting of Polyxenus and Hecuba; and in 1780 was chosen an Academician, for his painting of Study detaining Time. He was afterwards appointed Assistant Professor and in 1787 Professor of the Academy. Appointed by the King to the Directorship of the French Academy at Rome, he discharged the duties of that important office during the stormy times which led to the dissolution of the institution, in 1793, when he went to Vicenza, and resided there eight years. Although receiving several invitations to visit foreign courts, he declined them all, and about 1800 returned to Paris. He was honored with a membership in the Institute, and the Legion of Honor, and was appointed Professor of the Academy of Painting. Menageot employed his talents in painting easel pictures, but is chiefly known by his grand historical works. They evince an ardent love of nature, and are full of sweetness and grace. His compositions are characterized by excellent judgment; his design is elevated and pure; draperies skillfully cast; and coloring very harmonious. Among his principal works are Astyanax torn from the Arms of his Mother; Cleopatra at the Tomb of Antony; Diana searching for the young Adonis, and fearing to decide between the two children placed before her by Venus, lest she should choose Cupid; the Death of Leonardo da Vinci; and King Dagobert I. giving orders for the erection of the church of St. Denis. The latter picture is placed in the sacristy of that church. Menageot died in 1816.

MENAGEOT, Robert, a French engraver, born at Paris in 1748. He at first studied painting under Boucher, and practised that art for some time; but afterwards devoted himself entirely to engraving. He visited England, and executed several plates for Boydell. Among others, there are the following by him: Friendship, a circular print, *after Correggio;* Innocence, the companion, *Menageot fecit;* the Virgin and Infant, with St. Elisabeth, *after Guido;* an African Woman, *after Loutherbourg*.

MENANT, P., a French engraver, who flourished at Paris about 1715. In conjunction with Fonbonne, Scotin, Regnard, and others, he engraved part of the plates for the Views of the Palaces and Gardens at Versailles. They are neatly executed, but in a formal style, without much effect.

MENAROLA, Cristoforo, a painter of Vicenza, who flourished about 1727. According to Melchiori he first studied under Volpato, and afterwards Carpioni, whose manner he chiefly followed. He was esteemed an excellent artist, and his works were in much request.

MENENDEZ, Michael Hyacinth, a Spanish painter, born at Oviedo in 1679. He studied painting at Madrid, and is said to have attained equal skill in invention, design, and coloring. In 1712 he was appointed by Philip IV. painter to the King. There are many of his paintings at Madrid, among which are two subjects from the life of

Elijah, in the Carmelite monastery; a Magdalen at the Reccoletos; and the Apostles, in the church of St. Giles. He made designs of all the paintings in the church of S. Felipe le Royal, which were painted after his death, by his scholar, Andrea de Colleja. There is a print by John Barnabas Palomino, representing St. Isidore on horseback, clothed in the pontifical robes, and exterminating the Moors.

MENENDEZ, Francisco Antonio, was a Spanish painter, the son of Michael Hyacinth M., born at Oviedo in 1682. He acquired the elements of the art at Madrid, and afterwards visited Genoa, Milan, Venice, Rome and Naples. Possessed of no fortune, and without a protector, he became involved in difficulties, and was obliged to enter the Spanish infantry. During his leisure hours, however, he devoted his attention to art, and acquired much important knowledge. After a few years, in consequence of a change in the affairs of Naples, he was released from the army, and immediately went to Rome for improvement. In 1717 he returned to Spain, and commenced painting portraits in miniature, with considerable success. In 1726, he addressed a memorial to the Spanish king, praying him to establish an Academy of Design, Painting, Sculpture, and Architecture; but it was not until 1744 that he attained any success. In that year a School of Design was organized, and Menendez appointed Director.—This small beginning at length resulted in the foundation of the Academy of St. Ferdinando, which was not firmly established until after the death of Menendez. He deserves high credit, and the grateful remembrance of every lover of art, for his endeavors in this work. The masterpiece of Menendez is a Marine View, representing a tempest through which he passed while returning from Italy, characterized by great vigor and striking resemblance to nature. This beautiful picture was in the church of Our Lady d'Atocha, but is now in the church of the Rosary at Madrid. Menendez had three sons, whom he instructed in the art. The time of his death is not recorded.

MENESES. See Osorio.

MENGAZZINO, Il. See Domenico Santi.

MENGOZZI, Girolamo Colonna, or Colonna Mengozzi, a painter of the Ferrarese school, and a native of Tivoli, was born in 1688, and died about 1766. He was a very eminent ornamental and architectural painter. He resided at Venice many years, and was much employed in painting for the churches and public edifices. In the church of the Tolentini, and in the Tiepolo at the Scalzi, he painted the architectural and ornamental parts, while Zompini painted the figures. He conducted the architecture in the Ducal palace, and in other edifices. Guarienti extols him as the first architectural and ornamental painter of the age, which praise he evidently merited.

MENGS, Cav. Antonio Raffaelle, one of the most distinguished painters of the 18th century, was born at Auszig, in Bohemia, in 1728. His father, Ishmael Mengs, a Dane by birth, and an indifferent miniature painter, settled about this time at Dresden. He early instructed his son in the rudiments of art, and perceiving in him superior talents, he compelled him to exercise himself constantly in drawing, made him forego all recreation, and set him tasks which he was required to perform in a given time, and severely punished him if he failed. As he advanced, he instructed him in oil, miniature, and enamel painting. In 1741, when he was thirteen years of age, he took him to Rome, where he was employed in copying some of the works of Raffaelle in miniature for Augustus III., Elector of Saxony and King of Poland, which were sent to Dresden, where they were greatly admired. While engaged in executing these works, his father exercised the greatest tyranny over him. He was left in the Vatican, to pass the day at his work, with no other food than bread and water, and at evening his studies were examined with great severity. In 1744, his father returned with him to Dresden, when he was appointed court painter by Augustus, with a salary. His royal patron permitted him, soon after, to make a second visit to Rome, to pursue his studies. His first great work was an original composition, representing the Holy Family, on a large scale, which was exhibited at Rome, and gained him great reputation. Here he committed an act of indiscretion, by marrying the pretty servant girl who had served him for a model. He was desirous of fixing his residence at Rome, but his father compelled him to return to Saxony in 1749, after an absence of four years. He remained three years at Dresden, when the tyranny of his father rendered his situation so distressing that his health became impaired, and he asked and received permission of his royal patron to return to Rome, and execute a commission he had received from him for an altar-piece for the Royal chapel. Soon afterwards he was deprived of his pension, from the low state of the king's finances, occasioned by the seven years' war, and being thrown upon his own resources, he wrought at low prices for the support of his family. He copied Raffaelle's School of Athens for the Duke of Northumberland, and executed some easel pictures; but his reputation continued to increase, and he soon found abundant patronage. In 1754, he received the direction of the new Academy at Rome, and in 1757 was employed by the Celestines to paint the ceilings of the church of S. Eusebius, which were his first works in fresco. He soon afterwards executed his admired fresco of Mount Parnassus, in the Villa Albani, which has been finely engraved by Raphael Morghen. He also painted some easel pictures for Englishmen and other foreigners at Rome. About this time, also, he made an excursion to Naples, to execute a commission for the Elector of Saxony, where his merits were made known to the king of Naples, who soon afterwards succeeded to the throne of Spain as Charles III., and in 1761 invited Mengs to his court at Madrid, and granted him a liberal pension. His first undertaking was the ceiling of the King's ante-chamber, which he decorated with the Graces; and afterwards the Queen's apartment, where he painted one of his most celebrated works, the Aurora, a grand and beautiful composition. He also executed other works, among which were a Descent from the Cross, and the Council of the Gods. The air of Spain proving inimical to his health, he obtained permission to return to Rome for its reëstablishment, where, immediately on his arrival, he was engaged by Clement XIV. to paint in the Vatican a picture of Janus dictating to History, and a Holy Family which have been engraved by Cunego. After an absence of three years, he returned to Madrid, where he was received with every demonstration of respect by his royal patron, who loaded him with favors. He now commenced his celebrated work in the dome of the grand saloon of the royal palace at Madrid, where he represented the Apotheosis of the Emperor Trajan, a composition of extraordinary ingenuity and beauty. Throughout his whole life, Mengs devoted himself with the most untiring industry to the study and practice of his art, without taking necessary relaxation of exercise or society. Being naturally of a feeble constitution, his strength again failed him, and perceiving that the climate of Spain disagreed with him, he obtained permission from the king to return to Italy, with an increased pension. On his way, he stopped at Manaco to recruit, and while there painted his picture of the Nativity, in the Royal Collection of the King of Spain, in the style of the famous Notte by Correggio, in which the light emanates from the infant Saviour—one of his finest productions. It was so highly valued by his royal patron, that he ordered it to be covered with glass for its protection. It measures nine feet ten inches by seven. His feeble frame began to invigorate, and, as he approached Rome, his spirits brightened at the thought of passing the rest of his days in tranquillity with his family, in that world of art and taste. But his visions of happy years were not realized, for the death of his wife, whom he tenderly loved, happened soon after his arrival, and threw him into a most melancholy state of despondency, and he sunk into his grave in 1779, in the fifty-first year of his age, leaving a family of seven children. He left little property, besides his splendid collection of works on art, drawings of great masters, engravings, vases, and other articles of virtû, though he had received 180,000 scudi during the last eighteen years of his life. A splendid monument was erected to his memory by his friend Count d'Azara, by the side of Raffaelle's; and another by the Empress of Russia, in St. Peter's.

The talents of men of genius are seldom properly appreciated during their life-time, and when they are, they are sure to gain rancorous and bitter enemies, as well as warm friends. Hence there is great dispute as to the merits of Mengs. The indiscreet zeal of his friends has not hesitated to rank his powers on a level with those of Raffaelle, and the Abbe Winkelmann places him in a still more elevated rank. They call him the great luminary of modern times, and attribute to him the purity of the antique, the composition and expression of Raffaelle, the grace and chiaro-scuro of Correggio, and the coloring of Titian. On the other hand, his enemies call him a plagiarist in his writings; an artist who had seen much and invented little; that he dispenses neither life nor death to his figures; excites no terror, rouses no passions, and risks no flights; that by studying to avoid particular faults he fell into general ones, and his execution bears the stamp of tameness and servility; that the contracted scale and ideas of a miniature painter are observable in most of his compositions, in which the delicate finishing shows the hand of an artist, but manifests no emanations of soul in the master. If it be beauty, it does not warm; if sorrow, it excites no pity. Pompeo Battoni called his pictures "looking glasses," i.e. that he was an enamel painter. But we are not to judge Mengs by his oil paintings, or his earlier works. There can be no doubt that posterity will award him a distinguished position; and Lanzi thinks that he even made an era in art. To form a just estimate of his ability, it is necessary to contemplate his best works, which are undoubtedly his frescos in Spain. His composition is simple, noble, and studied; his drawing is correct and ideal; his expression founded on the dignified model of Raffaelle; and his coloring in every respect excellent. He finished his pictures with the greatest care. If his works do not surprise us by the fiery soarings of a lofty imagination, or by the display of a novel and inventive genius, they satisfy the most scrupulous by the chaste arrangement of his ideas, and his careful and learned attention to propriety of costume. His acquaintance with the antique is profound, and his characters are distinguished by a quiet correctness, and a placid expression of tranquil beauty.

As a theorist, and a writer on art, Mengs is entitled to a distinguished reputation. His writings were published at Rome, by his friend, the Cav. d'Azara, in 1783, and are highly instructive to the artist, especially his remarks on the antique and his criticisms on Raffaelle, Correggio, Titian, and other great masters. The libels in regard to his being a plagiarist, have been completely demolished by Winckelmann, Lanzi, and others. They have different titles, but all the same aim—the discrimination of real perfection in art. "The artist," says Lanzi, "as characterized by Mengs, may be compared to the orator of Cicero; both are endued by the authors with an ideal perfection which the world has never seen, and probably never will see. It is the duty of an instructor to recommend excellence, that, in striving to attain it, we may at least acquire a commendable portion of it; therefore I should defend his writings when, in the opinions of others, he seems to assume a dictatorial tone in the judgment he passes upon Guido, Domenichino, and the Caracci, the very triumvirate he proposes as models in art. Mengs was assuredly not so infatuated as to hope to surpass these great men; but because he knew that no one does anything so well that it cannot be done still better, he shows where they attained the summit of art, and where they failed. The artist, therefore, as described by Mengs, to whose qualifications he aspired, and was anxious that all should do the same, ought to unite in himself the design and beauty of the Greeks, the expression and composition of Raffaelle, the chiaro-scuro and grace of Correggio, and to complete all, the coloring of Titian. This union of qualities Mengs has analyzed with equal elegance and perspicuity, teaching the artist how to form himself on that ideal beauty which is itself never realized." Lanzi thus concludes his notice of Mengs, which is full of instruction to the artist: "As far as regards myself, I cannot but extol that inextinguishable ardor of improving himself by which he was so particularly distinguished, and which prompted him, even when he enjoyed the reputation of a first-rate master, to proceed in every work as if he was only commencing his career. Truth was his aim, and he diligently studied the works of the best luminaries of the art, analyzing their colors, and examining them in detail, till he entered fully into the design and spirit of those great models. While employed in the Ducal Gallery at Florence he did not touch the pencil until he had attentively studied the best pieces there, and especially the Venus of Titian in the tribune. In his hours of leisure, he employed himself in carefully studying the frescos of the best masters of that school which is so distinguished in this art. He was accustomed to do the same by every work of celebrity which fell in his way, whether ancient or modern; all contributed to his improvement, and to carry him nearer to perfection. He was, in short, a man of most aspiring mind, and may be compared to the ancient who declared he wished 'to die learning.' If maxims like these were enforced, what rapid strides in the art might we expect! But the greater part of artists form for themselves a manner which may attract popularity, and then relax their efforts, satisfied with the applause of the crowd; and if they feel the necessity of improving, it is not with the design of acquiring a just reputation, but of adding to the price of their works."

MENGUCCI, Domenico, a painter of Pesaro, who studied under Gio. Andrea Donducci, at Bologna, and painted landscapes much in the style of his master. He flourished at Bologna about 1660, where his works were held in considerable estimation, and according to Malvasia, are found in the best collections.

MENGUCCI, Gio. Francesco, a native of Pesaro, who studied at Rome under Cav. Lanfranco. According to Malvasia, he was an able artist, assisted his master in the execution of some of his grand cupolas, and afterwards painted much in oil for the collections. His works were highly esteemed.

MENHEERE, Cornelius Laurens, a Dutch marine painter, who flourished in the first part of the 18th century. He went to England, and resided a long time at Flushing, where he painted many pictures, representing views of the city and sea-coast.

MENICHINO, del Brizzio. See Ambrogi.

MENINI, Lorenzo, a Bolognese painter, the scholar and assistant of Francesco Gessi. According to Dominici and others, Guido Reni had received a commission to paint the chapel of S. Gennaro at Naples. Belisario, leagued with Spagnoletto and others, threatened his life if he did not instantly quit Naples, which Guido immediately complied with. The commission was then offered to Gessi, the scholar of Guido, who, regardless of the threats of the intriguers, set himself about his work, when they inveigled his two assistants, Lorenzo Menini and Gio. Battista Ruggieri, on board a galley, which instantly set sail. They were never heard of afterwards,and are supposed to have been murdered. Gessi was then compelled to take his departure. It was this infernal band that drove all foreign artists of talents from Naples, and compelled Domenichino to fly to Rome, in spite of the protection of the government; and on his second return they are said to have caused his death by the constant excitement of their intrigues, or by poison.

MENISECLES. See Mnesicles.

MENJAUD, a French painter, the son of a Parisian notary, born about 1772. He gained the grand prize of the Academy, and visited Rome with the royal pension. In 1822 he exhibited at the Louvre a picture of the Death of the Duke de Berri, and another of the portraits of Raffaelle, Tintoretto, and Aretino. In 1827 he also exhibited two pictures, Francis I. holding a wild boar, and Girodet bidding farewell to his Atelier. His masterpieces are said to be the Crowning of Tasso, and the Communion. He died in 1831.

MENODORUS, or MONODORUS, an Athenian sculptor, who lived in the time of Nero, about A. D. 60. He was principally distinguished for his statues of warriors, hunters, wrestlers, and priests. His masterpiece, however, was the marble figure of Cupid, executed for the Thespians, in imitation of the famous Cupid of pentelic marble, sculptured for that city by Praxiteles. The latter was first carried to Rome by Tiberius, and subsequently restored by Claudius; but being retaken to Rome by Nero, it was shortly after destroyed in a conflagration. This Cupid has been frequently copied.

MENTON, Francis, a Dutch painter, born at Alkmaer in 1550. According to van Mander, he studied under Francis Floris, and painted history and portraits with reputation. The encouragement he met with as a portrait painter, induced him to devote himself almost exclusively to that branch. The few historical pictures by him are well designed, colored, and finished. He died in 1605. He established a successful school, and instructed many young artists. He is also said to have engraved a number of plates in a tasteful and delicate style.

MENTOR, an eminent Greek sculptor of the age of Pericles, who wrought principally in gold and silver, which he chased with unrivalled skill. Cicero and Pliny allude to his works; and the vases and goblets carved or chased by him are mentioned with high commendation by Propertius, Juvenal, and Martial. Some of the finest productions of his chisel adorned the temple of Diana at Ephesus. Crassus is said to have paid for two goblets of his workmanship the enormous sum of 100,000 sesterces.

MENZANI, Filippo, a Bolognese painter, who flourished in 1660. According to Malvasia, he studied under Albano, and was his attached disciple and faithful copyist, whose works might readily pass among strangers for those of his master.

MERA, Pietro, a Flemish artist who, according to Ridolfi, flourished at Venice about 1600, and received many commissions for the churches, particularly for Sts. Giovanni and Paolo, and La Madonna dell' Orto. He was an able artist, and appears to have been educated in Venice, as his style is purely Venetian.

MERANO, Giovanni Battista, a painter born at Genoa, in 1632. He studied under Valerio Castelli, by whose recommendation he went to Parma, to study the works of Correggio and other great masters in that city, where he was employed by the Duke, and painted much for the nobility. On his return to Genoa, he painted some works for the churches, among which his Murder of the Innocents, in the church of Il Gesu, is one of his best performances. Lanzi commends it as a copious and careful composition, extremely well arranged and colored. He died, according to Zani, in 1698.

MERANO, Francesco, called il Paggio, a painter of Genoa, was born, according to Soprani, in 1619, and died in 1657. He studied under Domenico Fiasella, and was a reputable follower of his style.

MERCATI, Giovanni Battista, a Florentine painter and engraver, born at Citta San Sepolcro, in the latter part of the 16th century. Some of his earlier prints are dated 1616, and his latest 1637. He was an imitator, if not a scholar, of Pietro da Cortona, and painted history in the style of that master, though he sometimes resembles the Caracci. He gained great reputation in his native city, where he painted several works for the churches, among which, his two frescos of the history of the Virgin, in the church of S. Chiara, and an altar-piece in S. Lorenzo, are highly commended by Lanzi. They resemble the Caracci in composition and design, in the variety and expression of the heads, and especially in the draperies, which are well cast in ample folds, and skilfully varied. There are some of his works at Venice, Rome, and Leghorn. In the cathedral in the latter city, is a picture by him of the Five Saints, executed with great care.

He also etched quite a number of plates in a free and spirited style, finished with the graver in a bold manner, which gives them a vigorous and brilliant effect. The following are by him:

A set of fifty-two plates of Ruins and Views in Italy; engraved in the manner of Sylvestre; *Gio. Bat. Mercati, fec.* Four Antique Figures, from the arch of Constantine; engraved in the style of Gallestruzzi; circular; *Gio. Bat. Mercati.* The Marriage of St. Catherine; *after Correggio.* St. Bibiana refusing to sacrifice to false Gods; *after P. da Cortona.*

MERCIER, Philip, a painter of French extraction, was born at Berlin in 1689, and was brought up in the Academy of that city. After visiting France and Italy for improvement, he went to Hanover, where he painted the portrait of Prince Frederick, and some of the nobility. He afterwards went to England, and when his Royal Highness came over, Mercier was appointed his painter, was taken into his household, and painted the portraits of several of the royal family. After nine years, he fell into disgrace and was dismissed from his service. He afterwards lived in Covent Garden, and painted portraits and domestic subjects, in the style of Watteau. He was a good portrait painter, and blended the manners of Rigaud and Kneller. He died in 1760.

MERCIER, Jacques le, an eminent French architect, born at Pontoise about 1590. After acquiring the elements of the art in his native country, he visited Italy, and remained there several years, studying with great assiduity the noble remains of antiquity, and the creations of modern genius. On returning to France, in 1629, he was commissioned by Cardinal Richelieu to erect the college de la Sorbonne, and six months after, the church of that name, which is considered one of the finest architectural works of the age. He was appointed architect to the king, and erected many important works, among which is the Palais Royal; the church de l'Oratoire, in the Rue St. Honoré; the church of the Annunciation, at Paris, &c. He commenced the church of St. Roch at Paris, but died before its completion in 1660. Dumesnil mentions three very rare prints engraved by this architect. They are a design of the statue of Henry IV., erected at S. Giovanni de Laterano, in 1608; the design of a model (not executed) by Michael Angelo, of the church of S. Giovanni dei Fiorentini, 1607; and the Catafalco at Rome, for the obsequies of Henry IV., July 1, 1610.

MERCIER, Antoine le, a French engraver of little note, who flourished about 1633, and engraved among other prints, several slight but spirited etchings of architectural ornaments, &c., after the designs of *P. Collo.*

MERIAN, Matthew, the elder, an eminent Swiss designer and engraver, was born at Basle in 1593. Discovering an early inclination for art, he was sent to Zurich, and placed under the instruction of Dietrich Meyer, an engraver and glass painter, with whom he remained four years. On leaving that master he went to Frankfort, where he formed an intimacy with Theodore de Bry, whose daughter he married, and by whose instruction and advice he greatly improved himself. He executed a great number of plates of views in Germany, France, and Switzerland. His best works are a set of topographical plates of views in the environs of Heidelberg, Stuttgard, Schwalbach, and other places, which he afterwards published at Frankfort. They are all from his own designs, etched in a slight, free style and finished with the graver. They give a perfect idea of the places they represent, though without much taste in the execution. He was the instructor of the celebrated Hollar. He died at Frankfort in 1651. His plates are usually marked with one of his monograms. For a full list of his works the reader is referred to Nagler's Kunstler-Lexicon. The following are his best prints:

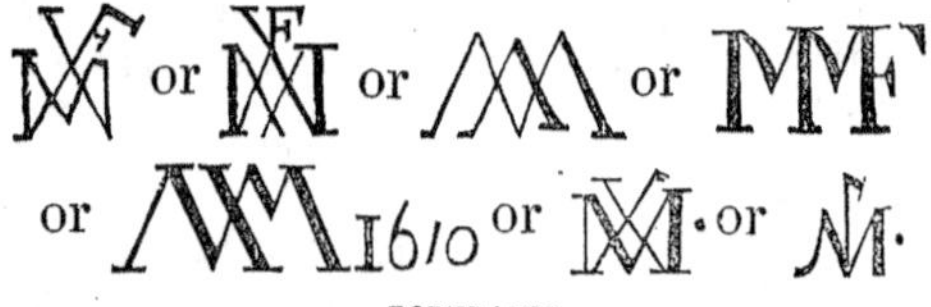

PORTRAITS.

David Pareus; *Prof. Academiæ Heidelberg.* Daniel Sennertus; oval. Arnold Weickerdus, Med. Doc. 1626.

SUBJECTS.

A set of plates from Sacred History. The Last Supper, inscribed, *Accepit Jesus panem;* a large plate; very scarce. A large plate of the Picture of Human Life; inscribed, *Tabula Cebetis, continens totius vitæ humanæ descriptionem;* scarce. A set of seven Views in France. Six Views in Germany. Sixteen Views in Germany and Switzerland. Twelve Views of Gardens, &c. Twenty-four Picturesque Landscapes, with figures.

MERIAN, Matthew, the younger, was the son of the preceding, born at Basle in 1621. He is said to have studied painting successively under Sandrart, Rubens, and Vandyck. Fuessli, his countryman, commends him as a good painter of history, and excellent in portraits, to which latter branch he devoted most of his attention, and was employed by many of the most distinguished personages in Germany. He was famous for his equestrian portraits, among the best of which is one of Count Serini, in an Hungarian uniform, with his right arm bared, and a sabre in his right hand, ready for the bloody strife; a picture admirably designed, and executed full of fire, with a coloring said to unite the depth of Rembrandt, with the tone of Rubens. His best historical pictures are the Martyrdom of St. Lawrence, in the cathedral of Bamberg, and Artemisia mixing the ashes of Mausolus in her Cup. In dignity of conception, he has seldom been surpassed; his design was correct; and his coloring partook of the vigor of the Flemish school. He also etched a few plates. Time of his death not recorded.

MERIAN, Maria Sybilla. This celebrated paintress was the daughter of Matthew M., the Elder, born at Frankfort in 1647. Her father dying when she was four years old, her mother married Jacob Murel, a reputable painter of fruit and flowers, who, discovering in the child a taste for painting, took great pains to instruct her. She made surprising progress, and became skilful in painting fruit, flowers, insects, and still life in miniature. She afterwards studied with Abraham Mignon, and acquired great neatness of handling and delicacy of coloring. Her genius led her particularly to the study of natural history, and she designed every thing from nature. She usually painted in water-colors on vellum, and she soon made an extensive collection of drawings of butterflies, caterpillars, and other insects, in the various changes they undergo, with remarkable beauty and fidelity. She also drew frogs, toads, serpents, and other reptiles. In 1665, she married John Andrew Graff, an ingenious artist of Nuremberg, who had studied with Murel, and settled in that city. Not satisfied with the description of insects, and the metamorphoses, which she found in the works of the naturalists of the time, she formed the design of giving to the world her own observations and researches, illustrated with plates from her own designs, and partly etched by herself. In 1679, she published the first volume of her interesting work at Nuremberg, in German, under the title of *The History of the Insects of Europe, drawn from nature, and explained, by Maria Sybilla Merian, with their Generation and Changes, with the Plants on which they feed.* The second volume appeared in 1683. Her zeal in pursuit of her favorite study induced her to make a voyage to Surinam, in 1698, for the express purpose of designing from nature the insects and plants peculiar to that climate. Soon after her return to Holland, she published at Amsterdam, in 1705, the fruits of her researches in a work in Latin, entitled *Dissertatio de Generatione et Metamorphosibus Insectorum Surinamensium*, illustrated with sixty plates. This work was augmented in a later edition by her daughter, Dorothea Graff, with twelve additional plates. Her drawings are executed with a truthfulness, delicacy, and beauty of coloring, that have seldom been surpassed. There are two large volumes of her drawings in the British Museum, one of the Insects of Europe, and the other of those of Surinam, which were purchased by Sir Hans Sloane, at the enormous price of five guineas for each drawing. Her pictures commanded high prices in her life time, and were much sought after. She died at Amsterdam in 1717.

MERIAN, Gaspar, a German engraver, probably a relative of the preceding family, who flourished about 1660, and published in that year a set of plates, representing the Ceremonies of the Election of the Emperor Leopold.

MERIMÉE, J. F. L., a French historical painter, who flourished during the present century. His principal merit consisted in the gradations of light and shadow, which he represented with the greatest delicacy imaginable. This excellence is well evinced in his picture of Travelers discovering the bones of Milo of Crotona, and endeavoring to ascertain, from the position of the arms, the manner of his death. His picture of Innocence, is well known at Paris, and has been finely engraved by Bervic. Merimée gained considerable distinction by his treatise on oil painting, which evinces an excellent knowledge of chemistry, and great research. It is entitled *De la peinture à l'huile, ou des procedés matériels employés dans ce genre de peinture, depuis Hubert et Jean van Eyck jusqu' à nos jours.* Paris, 1830, 8vo.—Merimée was appointed perpetual secretary of the Academy des Beaux Arts. He died at Paris in 1836.

MERLI, Gio. Antonio, an old painter of the Milanese school, who flourished at Novara in 1488. He was an excellent portrait painter, for his age, and painted many distinguished personages.

MERLIANO, Giovanni, an Italian sculptor and architect, born at Nola in 1478. He studied at Naples, under Agnello Fiore, and subsequently visited Rome for improvement. On his return to Naples, he wrought with great assiduity, and produced so many excellent works in sculpture, that his reputation exceeded that of any cotemporary Neapolitan sculptor. This is the judgment of Milizia, who says that the principal chambers of that city are decorated with the works of Merliano, among which are the Tomb of Andrea Bonifazio, in S. Severino; and the mausoleum of the Viceroy, Don Pedro di Toledo, in the choir of S. Giacomo. He also adorned La Punta del Molo with a fountain, in which were represented the four principal rivers of the world.

As an architect, Merliano erected, among other works, the church of S. Giacomo degli Spagnuoli; and the church of S. Giorgio degli Genovesi. He reduced the Castel Capuano to a hall of justice; and designed the palace of the Prince S. Severo; which Milizia characterizes as "magnificent and well arranged." He also erected a triumphal arch in honor of the return of Charles V. from Tunis. At the invitation of the Viceroy, Don Pedro Antonio, he visited Spain, in company with other Italian architects, to embellish the gardens of that nobleman. Merliano was universally esteemed for his modesty and mildness of character. He passed a very tranquil life until his eighty-first year, and died in 1559.

MERLIN, James and Theodore van, two engravers, probably brothers, who, according to Florent le Comte, flourished about 1600, and engraved conjointly, some plates after Martin de Vos and other masters.

MERSION, Madeleine le, a French lady, who engraved some plates of landscapes and cattle, somewhat in the style of Dankerts, when he engraved after Berghem.

MERZ, James, a Swiss painter, born at Besch, in the canton of Zurich, in 1783. He early manifested a strong inclination for art, and studied the elements of design under Lips, an engraver of Zurich. After progressing under that master with great rapidity for some time, he visited Vienna for improvement, and was greatly assisted by the counsels of Fugger and Rod. Fuessli. He executed a number of portraits and historical subjects, characterized by correctness of design and delicacy of expression. His engravings of Canova, Lavater, and others, are fine specimens of the art. Merz would doubtless have attained great eminence, had he not died in 1807, at the early age of twenty-four. His premature decease was deeply regretted by the friends of art. The engraving of the monument erected at Vienna, in 1806, in memory of the Emperor Joseph II., was his last work.

MESA, Alonso de, a Spanish painter, who, according to Palomino, was born at Madrid in 1628, and studied under Alonso Cano. He painted history with reputation, and executed several works for the churches, convents, and public edifices in Madrid, of which, the most admired are a series of pictures of the life of St. Francis, in the monastery of the Franciscans. He died at Madrid in 1668.

MESA, Juan de, a Spanish painter, who flourished at Madrid about 1605. He painted for the college of the Jesuits de Alcala de Henares, a series of pictures illustrating the life of St. Ignatius Loyola, which were engraved in Flanders.

MESNIL, E., a French engraver, mentioned by Basan, who flourished about 1760, and engraved some plates after Mieris, Karel de Moor, and other Dutch masters.

MESSINA, Antonello da, an Italian painter, born at Messina, about whose history no two authors agree. He was the first to practise oil painting in Italy, and for this reason, some of the old Italian authors claim for him the invention of the art. According to Vasari, he was born at Messina in 1426, which most probably is not far from correctness; though others place it in 1414, and others again as late as 1447. The fame of Masaccio drew him to Rome, where he studied some time. He afterwards went to Naples, where he saw some oil paintings by John van Eyck, or John of Bruges, which had been brought to Naples from Flanders by some Neapolitan merchants, and presented or sold to Alphonso I., King of Naples. The novelty of the invention, and the beauty of the coloring, inspired Antonello with so strong a desire to become possessed of the secret, that he went to Bruges, and so far initiated himself into the graces of van Eyck, then advanced in life, that he instructed him in the art, with which he returned to Italy, and was the first who painted in oil in that country. From him the secret was communicated to Domenico Veneziano. Such is the account given by Vasari, and Lanzi, who had carefully investigated the subject, saw no reason to doubt its correctness in the main, though others give very different accounts. Lanzi and others have clearly demolished the claims of the Italians to the discovery of oil painting, and give it to the van Eycks. Those old paintings at Milan, Naples, Pisa, and other places, painted in oil, as was claimed, before the time of the van Eycks, have been carefully examined; and some of them being analyzed, were found to have been painted in distemper. Those at Pisa, were analyzed by the able chemist Bianchi, and though apparently colored in oil, the most lucid parts gave out only wax, clearly proving that they had been painted in the Greek encaustic manner. Lanzi says this method fell into disuse after 1360, and was succeeded by a vehicle that carried no gloss. Others were examined at Venice and Vienna, and no traces of oil were found; but the vehicle seemed to have been certain gums and yolks of eggs, which might easily deceive the eye of the less skillful. Lanzi says that after Antonello returned to Venice from Flanders, he concealed the discovery from every one, except Domenico Veneziano, who is known to have availed himself of it for many years, both at Venice and elsewhere. During this period, Antonello visited other places and more especially Milan, whence he returned to Venice for the second time, and, as it is said, "received a public pension," and then he divulged the method of painting in oil to the Venetian professors, which, according to the inscriptions on his pictures, appears to have taken place about 1474. Other signatures are met with as late as 1490. So that he must have run a longer career than Vasari and Ridolfi assign to him. Two altar-pieces by his hand, are recorded, which were painted for the two churches of the Dominante; besides several Madonnas, and other sacred subjects, for individuals, and about four productions in fresco.—There is no doubt that he produced many others, both for natives and foreigners, relieving himself from the multiplicity of his commissions by the aid of Pino da Messina. His works are still preserved in many Venetian collections, and they display a very correct taste, united to a most delicate command of the pencil. Among others, is a portrait in the possession of the family Martinengo, inscribed *Antonellus Messaneus me fecit*, 1474. In the Council Hall of the Ten, is also a Pietà half-length, subscribed *Antonius Messinensis.*

MESSINA, Pino da, was a scholar, and probably a relative of Antonello da M., whom he accompanied to Venice, and was an able assistant in the execution of his numerous commissions. He also painted some works of his own in the style of his master.

MESSINA, Salvo da. This painter, according to Hakert, was a nephew of Antonello da M., and flourished about 1511. He was a successful follower of Raffaelle, and, according to the above author, his Death of the Virgin in the sacristy of the cathedral at Messina, is *in the pure Raffaellesque style.* Lanzi says he was liberally educated, and bred to the law, which he abandoned, went to Venice, studied with Antonello, became the friend of Giorgione, and improved himself by the study of the works of the best masters. After many years' residence at Venice, he went to Milan to study the works of Leonardo da Vinci, where he corrected his former dryness of style; but the story of his having visited, or studied with da Vinci, Raffaelle, and Correggio, cannot be true, as the first left Milan in 1499, the second was then a youth in Urbino, and the third in his infancy; but farther on he says that Salvo arrived at Messina in 1514, so that he might have seen Raffaelle, who was invited to Rome by Julius II., in 1508. At all events, he was an excellent artist, and executed some works for the churches of Messina in the style of Raffaelle, and was the first to introduce the style of that master into Sicily. The history of art is so full of contradictions, that we must often be satisfied with an approximation to truth.

MESSINA, Padre Feliciano da, a Capuchin

monk, was born in 1610. He first studied painting under Abraham Casembroodt, while that artist resided at Messina. He afterwards studied under Guido, in the convent of Bologna, and imbued himself with his style. He painted some works in S. Francesco, the church of his order, at Messina, which are highly commended by Hakert, who assigns the palm to him "among the painters of his order, which boasted not a few."

MESSINESE. See GIULIO AVELLINO and GABRIELLO.

METAGENES. See CTESIPHON.

METELLI. See MITELLI.

METENSIS. See CORNELIUS MATSYS.

METGER, J. J., an obscure engraver, who flourished about 1672. There is a portrait of Cardinal Giovanni Nitardo by him, in *Priorata's History of the Emperor Leopold*, indifferently executed.

METEZEAU, CLEMENT, a French architect, was a native of Dreux, and flourished in the 16th century. He settled at Paris, and was employed by Louis XIII. He acquired high fame by carrying into execution, conjointly with Jean Tiriot, a Parisian mason, the bold plan which Richelieu had formed for reducing Rochelle, by means of an immense dyke, in imitation of what Cæsar had done at Durazzo, and Alexander the Great at Tyre. This amazing work was completed in less than six months, and proved the principal means of compelling the surrender of the city. In honor of Metezeau's successful exertions in this grand undertaking, an engraved portrait of him was circulated in France, underneath which were the following lines:

"Dicitur Archimedes Terram potuisse movere,
Æquora qui potuit sistere, non minor est."

METHODIUS. This painter was a native of Thessalonica, in Macedonia, and flourished in the latter part of the 9th century. In the year A. D. 853, while residing at Constantinople, he was invited to Nicopolis by Bogoris, the King of the Bulgarians, to decorate a banqueting hall in his palace. That prince left the choice of the subject to the artist, limiting him to those of a tragic and terrible character. The sister of Bogoris, during a long captivity at Constantinople, had become a convert to the Greek church, and greatly desired that her brother should renounce paganism; therefore it was probably at her instance in this case, that Methodius painted the Last Judgment. The terror excited by the representation of this awful subject, had the effect of inducing Bogoris, and subsequently the whole Bulgarian nation, to unite with the Greek church. From this time, Methodius appears to have laid aside the pencil. In concert with St. Cyrillus, he preached the doctrines of his religion to the Moravians and other Sclavonian nations. He became archbishop of the Moravians and Pannonians, and died at an advanced age. The Greeks and Russians celebrate his holy-day on the 11th of May.

METRANA, ANNA, an Italian paintress, who, according to Orlandi, flourished at Turin about 1718, and acquired great reputation from her portraits. Her mother also was a paintress.

METRODORUS, an Athenian painter and philosopher, who flourished about B. C. 168. None of his works are mentioned, but Pliny says that, when Paulus Æmilius, the Roman Consul, vanquished Perseus, King of Macedonia, he demanded of the Athenians two men, one to educate his children, the other to paint his triumph. In acceding to this demand, they sent him Metrodorus, with the message that he greatly excelled in both philosophy and painting, which judgment was subsequently approved and confirmed by the Consul. Doubtless his merits were very great.

METTIDORO, MARIOTTO and RAFFAELLO, two Florentine painters, were brothers, and flourished about 1568. They were eminent ornamental painters, particularly in grotesque, and were the associates of Andrea Feltrini, which see.

METZ, CONRAD MARTIN, an eminent Swiss engraver, born at Bonn, in 1755. He went to London, and studied under Bartolozzi, and distinguished himself by the execution of a multitude of engravings in the chalk manner, and in aquatint, in imitation of the drawings of the old Italian masters. His principal plates are a set of fac similes of the drawings of Parmiggiano, in the Royal collection; another of those of Polidoro da Caravaggio, in the possession of Sir Abraham Hume, and numerous detached pieces, from authentic drawings in various cabinets. In 1801 he went to Rome, where he continued to exercise his ready talent at imitation, and otherwise engraving from works of the highest order, till his death in 1827. Nagler enumerates upwards of two hundred prints by him; nor is his list complete. His works are valuable, as they are correctly drawn, and convey a good idea of the originals.

METZU, or METSU, GABRIEL, an eminent Dutch painter, born at Leyden in 1615. It is not known under whom he studied, though he made the works of Gerard Terburg his model, whom he equals in the silky softness of his pencil, and surpasses in elegance and correctness of design. At an early period he settled at Amsterdam, where he soon rose to distinction, and his works were eagerly sought after. His pictures represent domestic scenes; conversations; ladies at the toilet, or playing on musical instruments; sick persons attended by the doctor; chemists in their laboratories; painters' shops and drawing schools, hung with pictures and drawings; still life and market-scenes, as women selling fish, game, fowls, fruit, vegetables, &c. These subjects have been frequently treated by Dutch and Flemish painters, but by few more successfully than by Metzu. He carefully studied the works of Douw and Mieris, and avoided their defects; he is less minute in detail, and less labored in his finishing than those masters, and at the same time he excels them in lightness and spirit of touch, and in the chasteness and harmony of his coloring. Though his works are of small dimensions, he has been compared to Vandyck in the correct drawing of his heads and hands, the delicacy of his carnations, and the breadth and facility of his pencil. His works are rarely seen out of Holland, where they are held in the highest esteem, and command very high prices; but, for these reasons, they have been much imitated, to satisfy the foreign demand. Smith, in his Catalogue raisonné and supplement, gives a descriptive catalogue of one hundred and sixty pictures by Metzu. On the few pictures that bear his name, it is written *Metsu*, not Metzu. He was sadly affected with the stone—brought on, as is said, by his great assiduity and sedentary habits—which made necessary an operation that terminated fatally, in 1658, in the prime of his life. Balkema says this happened in 1669, and there is a picture in the Dresden gallery, bearing his signature, and dated 1667, which if genuine would corroborate this statement.

MEUCCI, VINCENZIO, a Florentine painter, was born in 1694, and died in 1766. He studied under Gio. Gioseffo dal Sole, and according to Lanzi, was one of the ablest fresco painters of his time. He was much employed in the churches at Florence and other places in Tuscany, and also at Bologna. In oil painting he did not succeed as well, for he wrought in too hasty a manner—an error into which all fresco painters, accustomed to rapid execution, are apt to fall.

MEULEN, ANTHONY FRANCIS VANDER, an eminent Flemish painter, born at Brussels in 1634.—His parents, being affluent, to gratify his passion for art, placed him under Peter Snayers the battle-painter, under whose instruction he made great progress, and surpassed his master before he left his school. Some of his works having been sent to Paris, they attracted the attention of Charles le Brun, at that time the arbiter of art in the French Capitol, who recommended him to M. Colbert, minister of State, as a proper person to immortalize the victories of his master, Louis XIV., and he was accordingly invited to Paris by the King, who gave him a pension of 2000 livres, besides a remuneration for his work. He attended the King in most of his campaigns, designing on the spot the sieges, battles, encampments, and marchings of the royal armies; also taking views of the towns and places rendered memorable by success. From these sketches he painted the principal battles and sieges of that monarch in Flanders, to decorate the royal chateau of Marly. Vander Meulen carefully studied and copied every object after nature; hence his pictures have a pleasing effect, although it is to be regretted that he was confined to the representations of modern military tactics and evolutions, and monotonous uniforms, than which nothing can be less picturesque. His works are admired for an exact and local representation of events, a bold design and animated pencil, and a clear and silvery tone of coloring. His landscapes are distinguished by the freshness of the verdure and foliage, the clearness and brilliancy of his skies, and the pleasing degradation of his distances. His figures are designed and grouped with great judgment, his touch is free and full of spirit, and the effect is heightened by a judicious distribution of his lights and shadows. If his pictures are less effective than those of Borgognone and Parrocel, it may perhaps be attributed to the restrictions under which he wrought, and they certainly have more nature and sweetness. Few painters could excel him in the various attitudes, motions, and actions of his horses. Vander Meulen also painted some pictures of huntings and cavalcades with equal success. His principal works are at Versailles and Marly, though there are many of his easel pictures dispersed through France, Flanders, and England. He is usually classed among the French painters, as he passed most of his days in that country. The battles and sieges of Louis XIV. by vander Meulen have been engraved in a set of large plates, some of them by Hughtenberg, and also in a set of smaller size. He was chosen a member of the French Academy in 1673. He died at Paris in 1690.

MEULEN, PETER VANDER, was the brother and scholar of the preceding, in whose style he painted battles and hunting-pieces. In 1670 he went to England, where he was employed by King William, the rival of Louis XIV., in celebrating his exploits. He was originally bred a sculptor, but abandoned the chisel for the pencil. He did not acquire much distinction. Time of his birth or death not known.

MEUNIER, LOUIS, a French architectural designer and engraver, who flourished about 1665. His works consist chiefly of views of royal residences and public places in Spain. Dumesnil gives a list of eighty-eight prints by him.

MEURS, J. V., a Dutch engraver, who was employed chiefly in engraving frontispieces and other plates for the booksellers, which are executed in a neat, finished style. He engraved a portrait of Tycho Brahe, the astronomer.

MEURS, C. H. VAN, a Dutch engraver, who flourished at Amsterdam, about 1760. According to Basan, he engraved some plates after Mieris, Vanderwerf, and other masters.

MEUSNIER, PHILIPPE, an eminent French painter of perspective and architectural views. He studied under Jacques Rousseau, and on leaving that master went to Rome, where he resided several years, designing the most magnificent edifices in that metropolis. On his return to France, he was patronized by Louis XIV. and his successor. He was elected a member of the Royal Academy, and his works were held in high estimation. He was a skillful and correct designer. He died at Paris in 1734.

[monogram] or [monogram] or [monogram] MEYER, ANDREW, a Swiss painter and engraver, of whom little is known. According to Professor Christ, he was a native of Zurich, where he practised both painting and engraving. There are some prints of views of towns by him, which are marked with the above curious monogram.

MEYER, DIETRICH, a Swiss painter and engraver, born at Zurich in 1571. He engraved a set of portraits of the illustrious persons of his country, which are marked with one of the following monograms. He died in 1658.

DM or DM 1599, or DMF. or DM

RMF. MEYER, RODOLPH, was the son and scholar of the preceding, born at Zurich in 1605. He painted history and portraits with considerable reputation, but he was more distinguished as an engraver. He executed quite a number of prints after his own designs, some of which are portraits and emblematical subjects. He made the designs for Death's Dance, engraved by his brother Conrad.

MEYER, CONRAD, was the younger brother of Rodolph M., born at Zurich in 1618. After receiving instruction from his father, he went to Frankfort, and studied with Matthew Merian

He was a man of wonderful industry, and executed a multitude of plates, in a free and spirited manner. Caspar Fuessli endeavored to make a complete collection of his prints, and got together upwards of nine hundred, and yet it was far from embracing all his works. He also painted a few historical subjects, and many portraits, well designed and colored, and executed with a spirited pencil. He died at Zurich in 1689. His prints embrace a great variety of subjects, as portraits, views, landscapes, emblematical pieces, sports, &c. The following are among his principal works:

A set of thirty portraits of the Burgomasters of Zurich. Twenty portraits of the Clergy of Zurich. Forty portraits of Laicks and Artists, some of which are from the designs of his father and brother. One hundred and three portraits of the Reformers, Ecclesiastics, and literary characters. A set of sixty-one plates of the Dance of Death; principally from the designs of *Rodolph Meyer*. A set of fifteen prints; entitled *the Mirror of a Christian*. Twenty-six prints of the Sports of Children. Ten plates of the Ages of Man. One hundred and twenty-two subjects from the Old Testament.

MEYER, John. This artist was probably of the same family as the preceding. He resided chiefly at Nuremberg, where he practised painting and more especially engraving. He painted history and portraits, and executed many prints after his own designs, the principal of which are a set of battles, finished in a peculiar and beautiful manner, and a set of the Fountains of Rome, published at Nuremberg in 1600.

MEYER, Felix, a Swiss painter, born at Winterthur in 1653. He was the son of a clergyman, who intended him for the church; but his passion for the fine arts occasioned him to neglect his studies, till at length he was permitted to follow the bent of his genius, and was sent to Nuremberg, where he became the pupil of John Francis Ermels, a landscape painter. He made surprising progress, and was soon able to draw from nature with facility and correctness. In company with Roos and Rugendas, he was indefatigable in designing the most picturesque scenery of Switzerland, so favorable to the studies of a landscape painter. He afterwards went to Italy for improvement, and carefully studied and sketched the beautiful scenery and ruins that environ Rome. The climate proving inimical to his health, he returned to Switzerland, and pursued his studies among his own native mountains, till he acquired an extraordinary facility of hand. He designed everything from nature, and being indefatigable in the pursuit of excellence in his art, he made a multitude of sketches of the prospects, mountains, craggy rocks and precipices, with rivers and waterfalls, in Switzerland, sufficient to satisfy any painter of romantic compositions. From these and other drawings he had made in Italy and Germany, he executed many noble landscapes, which procured him high reputation. He possessed an uncommon facility of invention, and Descamps relates the following instance of his extraordinary powers. In his travels through Germany, he visited the celebrated Abbey of St. Florian, at a time when the abbot was desirous of having two of the apartments decorated with landscapes in fresco. An artist of the country had been applied to for the purpose, and having been occupied several months in preparing designs, the abbot became impatient of his dilatory way; and on Meyer's being introduced to him as an eminent artist, he took the liberty to consult him on the best manner in which the work could be accomplished. Our artist being shown the apartments, surveyed them for a few moments, and then taking a long stick, to which he attached a piece of charcoal, immediately began to design, and in a few moments sketched the outline of a noble landscape on the wall, explaining as he proceeded to the Superior, who beheld in mute astonishment the elegance and taste of the design sketched before his eyes without any time allowed for reflection. At the Abbott's urgent request, Meyer undertook to decorate the rooms, which he did in a shorter time than the other painter had been employed in making his drawings. This adventure spread his reputation throughout Germany, and he was employed by several princes, as well as many nobles, in decorating their palaces.

In the earlier part of his life, Meyer designed everything from nature, and finished his pictures with great care and attention; and, as he could not design figures well, he often employed his friends, Melchior Roos and George Philip Rugendas, to insert them in his works, and these are esteemed his best performances. After he began to paint his large works in fresco, and found abundant employment, he no longer designed from nature, and finished his works with negligence and haste, so that his later easel pictures do not compare with his earlier works. He etched a few landscapes after his own designs, among which are a set of twelve views in Switzerland, nearly square, signed *Felix Meyer, fec.;* four Italian landscapes, with ruins and figures; *same mark*, 1701; four Views in Switzerland, with figures; and four mountainous Landscapes, with buildings. He died in 1713.

MEYER, or MEYERLE, Francis Anthony, a German painter, born at Prague, in 1710. It is not known under whom he studied, but he went to Italy, where he passed the rest of his life, and where his works are to be found. He painted historical subjects and domestic scenes, of small size, in the exquisite style of the Flemings. Lanzi says the royal collection at Turin was enriched by the addition of nearly four hundred pictures by the best Flemish masters. About this time, Francisco Antonio Meyerle, commonly called Monsieur Meyer, from Prague, was court painter at Turin. He did not acquire so much fame from his larger works, as from his small pictures, in the Flemish style, which indeed were excellent. He was also a fine painter of portraits. The Bishop of Vercelli possesses one of an old man, scrutinizing some object with an eye-glass, executed with great truth and humor. In the same city, where he spent his latter days, his works are frequently met with, and the smaller they are in size, the more are they prized. He died at Vercelli in 1782.

MEYER, Heinrich, a Swiss painter and designer, born at Zurich in 1759. He produced few pictures in oil, but he obtained a high reputation for his works in water-colors, and other drawings from antique remains and from the works of the great Italian masters, which he executed in an exquisite manner. His principal work is an allegory of human life, represented by children, as a painted frieze, in the palace at Weimar. He also distinguished himself as a writer on art. He died in 1832.

MEYER, Hendrick, a Dutch painter, born at Amsterdam in 1737. He painted landscapes, chiefly in water-colors and India ink, and these works are held in high estimation. His design is correct, his compositions easily understood, and his landscapes are well furnished with objects; but his oil paintings are somewhat deficient in vigor, from his having practised so much in water-colors. He resided a long time at Haerlem, where he was appointed one of the Directors of the Academy. Late in life he went to England, and died in London in 1793.

MEYER, Henry, an English engraver, born in London in 1782. He studied under Bartolozzi, and engraved both with the point and in mezzotint. His best prints are his portraits, which he managed very skillfully, and to which he chiefly devoted himself. He died in 1846. The following are among his best prints:

Admiral Nelson and Lord Cathcart; *after Hoppner.* The Princess Charlotte and Prince Leopold; *after Chalon.* Miss O'Neal in the character of Belvidera; *after Devis.* Mr. Matthews in various characters; *after Harlowe.* Sir John Nicholl; *after Owen.* Mary anointing the feet of Jesus; *after Hilton.* Sir Roger de Coverly; *after Leslie.* The Proposal and the Congratulation; *after Harlowe.* The Stolen Kiss; *after Kidd.* The Dancing Bear; *after Witherington;* and other popular subjects of the day.

MEYER, Joachim, a German wood engraver, who flourished at Strasburg about 1570. There is a set of sixty-two wooden cuts by him, representing a variety of combats with the sword.

MEYER, Jean Louis, de Knonan, was born at Zurich in 1705, and died there in 1785. His life was chiefly devoted to science, but he designed and engraved the prints to illustrate his Book of Fables, published at Zurich in 1758.

MEYERING, Albert, a Dutch painter, born at Amsterdam in 1645. He was instructed in the rudiments of the art by his father, Frederick Meyering, an indifferent artist. When about twenty years of age, he went to Paris, where he resided some time with no great encouragement; but he contrived, by perseverance and rigid economy, to raise money enough to enable him to proceed to Italy. At Rome, he met with his friend and countryman, John Glauber, with whom he studied with great assiduity the most remarkable views in the vicinity of that city. His abilities procured him the esteem and friendship of some of the first artists at Rome, and he met with sufficient employment to induce him to continue his residence in that capital for several years. After an absence of ten years, he returned to his own country an accomplished artist, with his friend Glauber; and they were immediately employed by William, Prince of Orange, in painting the ceilings and otherwise decorating the palace of Loo and the chateau of Soesdyk. He now found abundant employment in decorating the halls and saloons of the wealthy and the nobility. In Italy he had acquired a free pencil and a ready hand, which peculiarly fitted him for that kind of compositions. His views are agreeably varied, frequently embellished with the ruins of ancient architecture, and decorated with figures representing historical or mythological subjects, in the style of Gerard Lairesse. There is a grandeur in the taste of his trees and buildings, a richness in his ornaments, a clearness in his skies, and a transparency in his water that gives singular satisfaction to the beholder. He painted many easel pictures, which were handled in an excellent manner. He also etched a few plates of landscapes, after his own designs, in a free and painter-like manner. Bartsch describes twenty-six prints by him. He died at Amsterdam in 1714.

MEYERS, Jeremiah, a German painter, born at Tubingen about 1728. He went to England when he was about fourteen years of age, and became a pupil of Zinck, who at that time had acquired great fame for his miniature and enamel paintings. Meyers acquired great reputation for his miniatures, and was considered one of the ablest artists of his time in his particular branch. He was honored by being appointed miniature painter to the Queen, and was one of the forty original members of the Royal Academy, at its foundation in 1768. He died at London in 1789.

MEYNIER, Charles, a French historical painter, born at Paris in 1768. He first studied engraving under Choffard; but was afterwards placed by an elder brother, Meynier St. Phal, under Vincent. In 1789 he gained the grand prize of the Academy, and visited Rome with the king's pension. After studying the antique, and the best works of art in that city, he returned to Paris. His pictures are often too highly labored, and evince considerable mannerism, particularly in the similarity of his heads; but they are characterized by excellent judgment of composition, and correctness of design. Meynier was appointed member of the Institute, of the Academy of Fine Arts, and of the Legion of Honor; also Professor in the Ecoles Royales. He established a school of painting exclusively for ladies, which produced many scholars, among whom was Madame Hersent. Among the principal works of Meynier are three pictures of subjects from French history, in the Museum Historique at Versailles; Phorbas presenting Œdipus to the Queen of Corinth, in the Louvre; Telemachus in the Isle of Calypso; and Wisdom preserving for Youth the lineaments of Love. Meynier died in 1832.

MEYSSENS, John, a Flemish painter and engraver, born at Brussels in 1612. He first studied painting under Anthony van Opstal, and afterwards with Nicholas vander Horst. He painted both history and portraits, but was particularly successful in the latter, and having painted that of Prince Henry of Nassau, his reputation was established, and he executed the portraits of the Countess of Stirum, Count de Bentheim, and other noble personages of the court. His greatest excellence consisted in producing a striking resemblance, while at the same time, he finished his pictures with great care, giving them a lively and good expression. One of his best pictures, is a portrait of Admiral van Tromp, in the Museum at Amsterdam. He afterwards settled in that city where he not only painted portraits, but carried on an extensive commerce in prints, and engraved many plates after his own designs, as well as other masters, among which are several portraits of eminent artists. As an engraver, he is not entitled to much praise. His plates are executed in a style every way inferior to what might have been expected from his abilities as a painter. It is proper to observe here, to put readers on their guard, that Balkema gives this artist a double life, applying the same facts to two persons, under the names of Jan Meyssens and Jan Meytens; and Immerzeel mentions him as Jan Mytens. Pilkington, and all his editors, have copied these errors. He died at Brussels in 1666. The following are his principal prints:

PORTRAITS.

Charles I. Henrietta Maria, his Queen. Henry de Keyser, Architect and Sculptor; *J. Meyssens, fec.* Guido Reni; *se ipse pinx. J. Meyssens, fec.* Francesco Padouanino, Painter; *se ipse pinx.* Daniel Segers, flower painter; *after Lievens.* Cornelius de Bie; *after Eras. Quellinus.* William de Nieulant, painter. Mary Ruthven, wife of A. Vandyck; *after Vandyck.* John Meyssens, Painter and Engraver; *se ipse pinx.*

SUBJECTS.

The Virgin and Child; *after Titian.* Meleager presenting the Boar's Head to Atalanta; *after Rubens.*

MEYSSENS, Cornelius, was the son of the preceding, born at Antwerp about 1636, though Nagler says in 1646, which is doubtless an error, as his print of Charles II. is dated 1660, and others bear earlier dates. He was instructed in engraving by his father. He engraved many plates of portraits, some of them after designs of John Meyssens. They are executed with the graver in a stiff, tasteless style He also engraved several frontispieces and other book ornaments; the following are his best works:

A set of Portraits of the Emperors of the House of Austria; entitled *Effigies Imperatorum domûs Austriacæ, delineatæ per Joannem Meyssens, et æri insculptæ per filium suum Cornelium Meyssens.* The Portraits of the sovereign Princes and Dukes of Brabant; entitled *Les Effigies des Souverains Princes et Ducs de Brabant.*—A part of these are engraved by P. de Jode, Waumans, and others.

DETACHED PORTRAITS.

Charles II.; for the History of Leopold. Octavius, Duke of Aremberg; *C. Meyssens, sc.* Cardinal Antonio Barberini. Cardinal Rinaldo, Principe Estense. John de Witt, Pensionary of Holland. David, Count of Weisenwolff, &c.

MEYSSONIER. See Meissonier.

MEYTENS, Martin de, a Swedish painter, born at Stockholm in 1695. He studied in Italy, and afterwards settled at Vienna, where he painted portraits with sufficient reputation to be appointed painter to the Imperial Court. He died in 1770.

MEZIOS, M., an engraver, of whom little is known. Mr. Strutt says he executed some portraits in a neat, clear style, which possess great merit; among others, is one of Petrus Lothicus, Medicus et Poeta, prefixed to his works published in 1626.

MEZZADRI, Antonio, a Bolognese painter, who flourished about 1688. Lanzi says that he so excelled in fruit and flowers, that the works of the famous Il Gobbo de' Caracci were scarcely superior to many of his productions.

MIAZZI, Giovanni, an Italian architect, born, according to Milizia, at Bassano, in 1699. He was originally bred to his father's trade of a carpenter; but by studying the works of Vignola, Scamozzi, Palladio, and others, he attained considerable ability in architecture, and erected a small theatre in his native town, a casino for the Signori Caffi, of Bassano, and the church of La Trinità, in the Borgo of Angarano. It was not until the age of forty, that he applied for regular instruction in the art, and availed himself of the abilities of Francesco Maria Preti, who was two years his junior. Placing himself entirely under the direction of that eminent architect, he adopted his plans and style, especially the proportions of the harmonic medium in the height of buildings, which he subsequently used in works of his own invention. He was commissioned to rebuild the church of S. Giovanni Battista at Bassano, and executed the work in a highly satisfactory manner, notwithstanding the numerous obstacles arising from the peculiarity of the site, and the conditions annexed to the commission. The Spineda Palace, at Venegazza, in the Trevegiano, excited much admiration for its elegant design, but has since been greatly injured by the demolition of the chapel and corresponding wing, and the arcades uniting them to the principal edifice. Miazzi also erected the beautiful theatre at Treviso. The design of this admirable work was by Bibiena, but was greatly improved by Miazzi, to whom are attributed the internal arrangements, the vestibule, and the façade. Even Milizia says that the work of Miazzi "corresponds exactly with that elegance and correctness which predominates throughout the whole interior building." Among his other works, are the Collegiate church at Schio; that at Valdagno; another at San Vito; and a fourth at Simonzo; besides that at the convent of Monte Gargano, in Puglia. Miazzi continued active and vigorous during his old age, and died about 1780.

MICARINO. See Beccafumi.

MICHAELIS, J. W., an indifferent German engraver of portraits, who flourished at Frankfort about 1700. He engraved several heads for a work entitled *Notitia, Universitatis Francofertanæ*, published in 1707.

MICHALLON, Claude, a French sculptor, born at Lyons in 1751. He early manifested a strong inclination for art, and visited Paris for improvement, where he was successively instructed by Bridan and Coustou. Devoting his entire energies with incredible assiduity to the prosecution of his art, he was successful in gaining the grand prize of the academy, and visited Rome with the royal pension. He formed an intimate connexion with Drouais, the historical painter, and at his death, was commissioned to execute the mausoleum erected in honor of that artist, in S. Maria in Via Lata. On returning to Paris, he practised the art with reputation for a number of years, and carried off several prizes in sculpture. He was killed by a fall in 1799, while laboring on a bas-relief in the Theatre Français.

MICHALLON, Achille Etna, a French landscape painter, the son of Claude M., born at Paris in 1796. Losing his father during infancy, he was reared in the family of his mother, daughter-in-law to Francine, sculptor at the Louvre, who attended to his education with the greatest care. Michallon studied under David, Valenciennes, and Bertin. He evinced such remarkable talents, that the Russian Prince Youssoupoff gave him a pension to assist him in his studies. In 1811, he drew the second gold medal of the Academy, and in 1817, the grand prize, which entitled him to the royal pension. He immediately went to Rome, where he spent five years, studying the works of the great masters. In 1819 he sent to Paris his picture of Roland at Roncesvalles, in the style of

Salvator Rosa. His next production was the Combat of the Lapithæ and Centaurs, in the style of Poussin, evincing excellent progress, both in the disposition of his groups, and skill in the figures. After traveling through Italy and Sicily, Michallon returned to Paris in 1822, and exhibited a number of landscapes, among which were the Ruins of a Roman Circus, a Swiss Cascade, and a View near Naples. He died very suddenly, in the month of September, of the same year.

MICHAU, Theodore, a Dutch painter, born at Brussels in 1676. He studied under Francis Bout, and painted landscapes and merry-makings, village festivals, &c., in which he attempted to imitate David Teniers the younger, with but very little success. He also painted landscapes and cattle. His earlier pictures are his best; his later ones are sketchy and insipid. It is said he became blind some years before his death, which happened in 1755.

MICHAULT, George, a French engraver, born at Abbeville in 1752. He studied under Francis Aliamet, and engraved some plates in the style of his master, among which are a part of the views of the Garden of Monceau, near Paris; Acis and Galatea, *after la Fosse;* and the Dead Christ, in the Orleans Collection, *after Schiavone.*

MICHEL, Jean Baptiste, a French engraver, born at Paris in 1738. He studied under Chenu, whom he greatly surpassed. He went to England about 1780, and engraved several plates for Alderman Boydell. He died at London in 1804. The following are his best prints:

PORTRAITS.

Sir Thomas Gresham; *after Sir A. More.* Rubens' Wife; *after Rubens.* Francis Hals; *after a picture by himself.* La Joconda; *after L. da Vinci.* M. F. A. de Voltaire.

VARIOUS SUBJECTS.

Two prints of the Bath of Venus; *after Boucher.* The Death of Dido; *after M. A. Challes.* The Death of Hercules; *do.* Abraham, Sarah, and Hagar; *after P. da Cortona.* The Prodigal Son; *after Salvator Rosa.* Hercules and Omphale; *after Romanelli.* Venus and Cupid; *after Carlo Maratti.* The Death of St. Joseph; *after Velasquez.* The Three Graces; *after Rubens.* Faith, Hope, and Charity; *do.* The Nativity; *after Carlo Cignani.* The Adoration of the Shepherds; *after Guido.* Clytie; a circular print; *after Ann. Caracci.* Cupid stung by a Bee; *after West.* Alfred dividing his last Loaf with a Pilgrim; *do.* The Continence of Alfred; *do.*

MICHELA, an Italian painter, mentioned by Lanzi. He flourished about 1740, and painted perspective pieces, ornamented with figures, in the royal castle at Turin, in competition with Lucatelli, Marco Ricci, and Gio. Paolo Pannini, all celebrated artists of the time.

MICHELE, Parrasio, a Venetian painter, who studied under Paul Veronese, and was an exact imitator of his style of design and coloring. He painted several works for the churches, which, according to Zanetti, were worthy of his master, especially a Pietà, in a chapel of the church of San Giuseppe, into which he introduced a portrait of himself. He flourished about 1590.

MICHELINI, Gio. Battista, a native of Foligno, was a scholar of Guido Reni, in whose style he painted. He wrought in the churches of the Romagna, and Lanzi says there are several of his works at Gubbio, particularly a Pietà, or Dead Christ, worthy of the school of Guido. He flourished about 1650.

MICHELINO, an old Milanese artist, ranked by Lomazzo among the best painters of his time; flourished at Milan about 1435. He retained the ancient style of making his buildings small and his figures large, a practice blamed by Lomazzo, even in the oldest painters; but his figures were spirited, and he painted animals wonderfully well.

MICHELOZZI, Michelozzo, an eminent Florentine sculptor and architect, born about 1402. He studied under Donatello, and obtained a patron in Cosmo de' Medicis, for whom he erected the edifice since denominated the Palazzo Riccardi, at Florence, a noble monument of the older Florentine style, simple and severe, but characterized by an air of grandeur and even magnificence. The façade consists of a lofty rusticated basement, with comparatively small apertures, above which are two ranges of large arched windows, seventeen on a floor, each divided into two lesser arches resting on a central column. The whole is crowned with a very rich cornicione. The interior court has upper and lower porticos, with arches resting upon columns, and with an enriched frieze between the first and second arcades. Michelozzi was so sincerely attached to his patron Cosmo de' Medicis that, in 1433, he followed him into banishment, to Venice, where he resided some time; made designs for many public and private edifices, and erected the celebrated Library in the convent of S. Giorgio. On their return to Florence, Michelozzi greatly improved the court of the Palazzo Vecchio (originally built by Arnolfo,) in a rich, though somewhat fanciful style, inclining to Gothic. He was employed by Cosmo to enlarge and embellish a palace at Milan, bestowed upon him by Lodovico Sforza. Among his other works at Florence, is the Palazzo Tornabuoni, now Corsi; in the vicinity of that city, the villas Cafaggiuolo and Carregi; also a palace at Fiesole, for Giovanni de' Medicis, son of Cosmo I. His last work was the monumental chapel of the Annunciation, erected by Piero de' Medicis, in honor of Cosmo, in the Chiesa dei Servi, at Florence. Michelozzi died at the age of sixty-eight, probably about 1470.

MICOCARD, an old French wood engraver. Papillon mentions a wooden cut by him representing Diogenes, *after Parmiggiano.* It is probably a copy of a wooden cut of the same subject by Ugo da Carpi.

MICON, an eminent Greek painter, and a sculptor of some distinction, was the son of Phanochus of Athens. He flourished about B. C. 450, and was the cotemporary of Phidias and Polygnotus. His history is less known than that of many other ancient Greek painters, but he was the most celebrated of them all, for painting horses. The Athenians selected Micon to perpetuate their great victories in the colonnades of the Ceramicus, which was enlarged or rebuilt by Cimon, after his victory over the Persians; and he was also appointed to paint the walls of the temple of Theseus at Athens; which sufficiently evince his high reputation.

Micon painted the Battle of the Amazons and the Athenians under Theseus, in the gallery of the Ceramicus. In the temple of Theseus he painted another battle of the Amazons and Athenians; and opposite to it the battle of the Centaurs and the Lapithæ. A third wall also was painted by Micon in this temple, but Pausanias says it was nearly defaced by age, so that the subject could not be ascertained. In concert with Polygnotus, Micon decorated the temple of the Dioscuri; he painted there the return of the Argonauts to Thessaly with Medea, Æsteropea and Antinöe, the daughters of Pelias. Pausanias remarks that the best part of these paintings was Acastus and his horses. It is observable that all of Micon's subjects are such as admit of introducing horses; and he showed so much skill in painting these animals, that one Simon, an Athenian writer, from whose knowledge of horses, according to Pliny, there was no appeal, could only say of Micon, that he represented his horses with lashes on their under eyelids. The criticism is correct, but Micon could not receive higher praise.

As a sculptor, Micon executed, according to Pausanias, the statue of Callias, the Athenian pancratiast, at Olympia. None other of his works are mentioned, and it is probable that they have all been destroyed.

MICON, a Syracuse sculptor, the son of Niceratus; flourished about B. C. 215. At the request of the children of Hiero II., he executed two statues of that monarch, one representing him on horseback, and the other on foot. They were both sent to Olympia.

MICONE, Niccolo, called Lo Zoppo, *the Cripple*, was born at Genoa in 1650, and died in 1730. He excelled in landscapes, which, according to Ratti, he executed in the style of Carlo Antonio Tavella, with warm skies, beautiful distances, and pleasing effects of light and shadow; the trees, flowers, and animals, were gracefully touched, and true to nature. His works are much esteemed at Genoa.

MIDDIMAN, Samuel, an eminent English engraver, born in 1746. He studied first under Woollett, and afterwards with Bartolozzi, and he excelled in all the various modes of engraving. His forte was landscape, of which he left many beautiful examples; his two large plates for Boydell's Illustrations of Shakspeare, The Storm Scene in Winter's Tale, and the melancholy Jacques, in As You Like It, both engraved in line, vie with the best productions of Woollett; he also engraved several other plates, both for the larger and smaller Illustrations of Shakspeare; and others, after Berghem, Gainsborough, Barret, Zuccarelli, and Hearne. His Select Views in Great Britain, are admirably engraved, and were very popular, both in England and on the continent. He died at London, in 1818.

MIEL, Cav. John, (not Jan,) called also Bicker, and by the Italians, Giovanni della Vite, was born at a small village near Antwerp, in 1599. He studied under Gerard Seghers, and was one of his ablest scholars. Lanzi says he also studied under Vandyck. On leaving his master, he went to Rome, and entered the school of Andrea Sacchi, where he gave such proofs of his genius, that Sacchi employed him to assist in his works at the Palazzo Barberini, where he represented a Procession of the Cavalry of the Pope. Miel, whose disposition and education naturally led him to the grotesque, introduced something ludicrous, which was deemed inconsistent with the dignity of the subject. This occasioned a dispute, and his dismissal. Stung with the reproaches of Sacchi, and stimulated by the advice of his friend Bernini, Miel visited Lombardy, for the purpose of improving himself by the study of the works of Correggio and the Caracci, and he also passed some time at Parma and Bologna. On his return to Rome, he was employed by pope Alexander VII. to paint a picture of Moses Striking the Rock, for the gallery of Monte Cavallo. He also painted a picture of the Baptism of St. Cyrillio, for the church of S. Martino de' Monti; and the Annunciation, and some frescos of the Life of St. Lamberti, in S. Maria dell' Anima. In these, and other considerable works at Rome and Turin, he showed himself capable of treating historical painting with dignity and success, though his genius and inclination turned to those familiar and lighter subjects, for which the Flemings were prëeminent, and which, a short time before, were so successfully treated in Italy by Peter de Laer and Cerquozzi. On his first arrival at Rome, he adopted the subjects and manner of Bamboccio with great success, and his best works are his easel pictures of huntings, carnivals, fairs, markets, gipsies, beggars, conversations, and pastoral scenes, which are admired for their spirit and truth of design, the brilliancy of their coloring, the clearness of their tints, the delicacy of their penciling, and the great intelligence of their chiaro-scuro, in which respects, he is not inferior to Bamboccio, though he has less dignity in his heads, is less select in the choice of his forms, and less graceful in his attitudes. He was invited to Turin by Charles Emanuel, Duke of Savoy, who appointed him court painter, and retained him in his service during the rest of his life. It was at this time, that he painted his celebrated hunting pieces and fables, in the saloon of the chateau of the Venerie, which were engraved by Tasniere. The Duke was so much pleased with the execution of these works, that he made him a knight of the Order of St. Mauritius, and presented him with a cross set with diamonds of great value, as a mark of his esteem. His pictures of huntings are particularly admired, in which he designed the figures, and every species of animals of the chase with uncommon beauty, spirit, and nature. His best works are said to be in the Grand Saloon of the Ducal Palace at Turin, and in the Imperial Gallery at Vienna. He was elected a member of the Academy of St. Luke in 1648. He died at Turin in 1664.

John Miel etched a few plates from his own designs, in a masterly style, and with a charming effect. His point is free and playful, and his figures and animals are designed with great spirit. The following are by him: The Holy Family. The Assumption of the Virgin. A set of Four Pastoral Subjects; in one of them is a figure seated on a bank, picking a thorn from his foot. These are charmingly etched. Three Battle Pieces; for the History of the Wars in Flanders, by Flaminius Strada.

MIERHOP, Francis van Cuyck de, a Flemish painter, born at Bruges in 1640. He was of a noble family, and at first studied painting only for amusement. The vicissitudes of fortune at length reduced his family to indigence, when he experienced the benefit arising from his cultivation of the art. Unable to bear the shock, or from a feeling of false pride, he left Bruges, and settled at Ghent where he acquired great reputation and abundant patronage. He particularly excelled in pictures of still-life, such as game, fish, fruit, and animals, in which he imitated the manner of Francis Snyders; and some of his best works approach those of that admired painter. In the monastery of the Alexines, at Ghent, is one of his pictures portraying dogs, dead game, and fish, which has frequently been mistaken by judges for a work by Snyders. He died at Ghent in 1701.

FM MIERIS, Francis, the Elder, one of the most eminent of the Dutch painters, born at Leyden in 1635, and not at Delft, as asserted by Descamps. He was the son of a goldsmith and lapidary, who, discovering in his son an early inclination for painting, placed him with Abraham Toornvliet, an eminent painter on glass, and one of the best designers in the Low Countries, with whom he learned the elements of design. He next entered the school of Gerard Douw, with whom he made extraordinary progress, and was called by his master *the prince of all his disciples.* Being eager for improvement, he left Douw and went to study with Adrian vander Tempel; but not finding his expectations realized, he again returned to that master, whose taste and genius more nearly corresponded to his own, and he continued with him until he wanted no farther instruction, except in studying after nature. In fact, before he left Douw, his fame was bruited abroad as the prodigy of the age. His first work was executed at the commission of the Archduke of Austria, and excited universal admiration. It represented the interior of a mercer's shop, with a beautiful young woman showing various silks to a gentleman, who was evidently admiring the bonnie lass more than the goods. The Archduke was so much pleased with the performance, that he immediately invited him to Vienna, and offered him a munificent establishment, which his engagements or inclinations did not permit him to accept. When the Grand Duke of Tuscany visited Leyden, he was struck with admiration at the exquisite finishing of his works, and engaged him to paint a picture, which is regarded as one of his most admirable productions. It represents a young lady dressed in white satin, playing on a lute, with another female and a young man seated on a couch, to whom a domestic presents a silver salver with refreshments. He also painted for that prince his own portrait, which was placed in the Florentine Gallery. The works of Mieris are similar to those of Douw, though on a more extended scale. He sometimes painted portraits, but oftener conversations, mercer's shops, persons playing on musical instruments, chemists in their laboratories, patients attended by the doctor, &c. He had an unusual sweetness of coloring, a neat and wonderfully delicate touch, and the same transparency that characterizes the paintings of Douw, and they say he excelled him in several particulars; his design is more extensive, his drawing more correct, his pencil more free and spirited, and his coloring, by being less disturbed, is more pure and delicate, and that Douw only excelled him in the extraordinary finishing of his pictures. This, doubtless, is too high praise, and his warmest admirers ought to be satisfied to place him next in rank to that great artist. His manner of painting silks, velvets, stuffs, and carpets, was so remarkable that the different kinds and fabric of any of them could easily be distinguished. His works are exceedingly scarce, and command enormous prices whenever they are offered for sale. Most of them are now in the royal galleries of Europe. Smith, in his catalogue raisonné, vols. i. and ix., gives descriptions of one hundred and fifty pictures by him. He died in 1681.

MIERIS, John, was the eldest son of the preceding, born at Leyden in 1660. He was instructed in the art by his father, but despairing of ever being able to equal him in the minuteness and delicacy of his finishing, without which he knew he could never hope to acquire any reputation in that line, he devoted himself to a different pursuit, and painted history and portraits, as large as life. After his father's death he went to Germany, and thence to Italy. He stopped first at Florence, where the fame of his father procured him a most honorable reception from the Grand Duke, who offered to retain him in his service. But Mieris declined the offer, and proceeded to Rome, where his abilities were already well known. He was unfortunately affected with the stone, and applying himself with great assiduity to his studies, his malady increased, and he died in the flower of life, in 1690.

MIERIS, William, called the Younger, was the second son of Francis M., born at Leyden in 1662. He studied under his father, whose style he adopted with great success, so much so that some of his best works have been attributed to the elder Mieris, though he was much inferior to that master in every respect. At the age of nineteen, he was already an able artist, when the death of his father occurred. At first he continued to pursue the same course which had led his father to such excellence and renown; but afterwards he was induced by the fame of Gerard Lairesse, whose works at that time excited universal admiration, to aim at a more elevated style, and to attempt to paint historical and mythological subjects, and also landscapes. This attempt, however, was not very favorable to his reputation, for his incapacity for designing the naked, and his ignorance of the proprieties of costume, rendered him totally inadequate to the dignity of history. His extreme labor in finishing, was also prejudicial to the effect of the whole; and his carnations, from their smoothness and polish, have the appearance of ivory. He did not succeed much better in landscapes. His best pictures are his domestic subjects, which are deservedly held in high estimation, and are admitted into the choicest collections. Smith gives a descriptive list of one hundred and sixty pictures by this master. He also modeled in clay and wax, in so sharp and accurate a manner as to show that he would have distinguished himself as a sculptor, had he devoted himself to that art. He died in 1747.

MIERIS, Francis, called the Younger, was the son of William Mieris, born at Leyden in 1689. He was instructed in the art by his father, painted similar subjects, and endeavored to imitate his style, but with comparatively little success. His design is heavy and tasteless, his touch dry and hard, and his coloring false and unnatural. He was industrious, however, and bestowed a great deal of time in copying the works of his father; and though these are said to be so much inferior that the least experienced collector cannot mistake them for the works of William M., yet there can be little doubt, from reading the accounts of different authors, that at least some of the works of this artist are attributed to his father, and greatly tend to injure his reputation; for there is a great contradiction about the real merits of William Mieris, some ranking him nearly equal to Francis Mieris the Elder in his best works, while others put as wide a distinction between them as they do between William Mieris and his son Francis. Time of his death not known.

MIERS, a Dutch painter who, taking a part in the revolutionary troubles, fled to London in 1788, where he acquired considerable reputation by his landscapes, with figures and cottages, which are well designed and executed; his figures and trees are finished with care and neatness. He also excelled in water-colored drawings. He died in 1793.

MIGER, SIMON CHARLES, a French engraver, born at Paris in 1736; died in 1820. He studied under Charles Nicholas Cochin the younger, and engraved a number of plates of historical subjects, in a neat, clear style. He acquired considerable distinction, and was a member of the Academy of Painting. He executed most of the portraits which illustrate the *Histoire de la maison de Bourbon;* all the designs for the *Menagerie du Museum;* and several plates for the *Voyages* of Cassas. The following are among his principal plates:

PORTRAITS.

David Hume, Historian; *after Cochin.* John Stanley, Musician; *do.* Count Maurice de Bruhl; *do.* Christopher Gluck, Musician; *after Duplessis.* Laurent Cars, Engraver; *after Perenneau.* John James Rousseau; *after Le Moyne.* Francis Mieris, Painter; *after a picture by himself.*

VARIOUS SUBJECTS.

Hercules strangling Anteus; *after Voiriot;* engraved for his reception into the Academy in 1777. The Flaying of Marsyas; *after C. Vanloo;* his other reception plate. Hercules and Omphale; *after Dumont.* The Rape of Europa; *after Hallé.* A View of the Coast near Civita Vecchia; *after Vernet.*

MIGLIARA, GIOVANNI, an eminent Milanese painter of the present century, born in 1785. He excelled particularly in painting interiors of ancient edifices, and his pictures of the Cathedral at Milan, and the Portico of the church of S. Ambrogio in the same city, have been highly praised. At Paris, in 1817, there were exhibited by the purchasers three of his paintings, representing the Interior of the grand court of the Milanese Hospital; a View of the Canal of Milan; and a colonnade of the Baths of Maximus Aurelius. Migliara subsequently executed many excellent works, which were exhibited at Turin, Milan, and Paris. He was appointed painter to the King of Sardinia, and Cavalier of the Order of Civil Merit, instituted in 1831, by the King, Charles Albert. He died at Milan, in 1837.

MIGLIONICO, ANDREA, a Neapolitan painter, and a scholar and imitator of Luca Giordano. According to Dominici, he acquired considerable reputation, and executed many works for the churches at Naples, the Descent of the Holy Ghost in the church of S. S. Nunziata, which is highly commended. He had a fertile invention, a correct design, harmonious coloring, and great facility of handling, though he was somewhat deficient in grace. He died about 1710.

MIGNARD, NICOLAS, an eminent French painter, born at Troyes in Champagne, in 1608. After receiving some instruction in his native city, he went to Fontainbleau, where he had the advantage of studying the works of Primaticcio and Il Rosso, the antique statues, and other works collected by Francis I. He afterwards went to Italy to complete his education, and studied diligently two years at Rome. On his return to France, he stopped at Avignon, where he married, settled, and acquired considerable distinction in his profession. From his long residence in that city, he was called Mignard of Avignon, to distinguish him from his brother, Pierre Mignard, who was called the Roman. By the advice of Cardinal Mazarin, he was invited to Paris, and employed to execute several important works in the palace of the Tuileries, among which are Apollo crowning the Muses of Poetry, Painting and Music; Apollo and Daphne; and Mercury presenting a Lyre to Apollo. He acquired considerable distinction, was elected a member of the Royal Academy, and afterwards appointed Rector, which office he held till the time of his death. He had a good invention, his composition is ingenious, his design dignified and correct, his coloring agreeable, his carnations lively, his attitudes and expressions graceful, and there is an abundance of union and harmony in his works. He also painted many portraits of distinguished personages, though his genius inclined him more strongly to historical compositions, and more especially to classic and poetic subjects, particularly those which call for an expression of the gentler emotions. Some of his works have been admirably engraved by Antoine Masson and others. He also etched a few plates in a bold and spirited style, among which are a set of eight prints after pictures of *Annibale and Agostino Caracci*, in the Farnesian Gallery. He died at Paris in 1668.

MIGNARD, PIERRE, called the Roman. This eminent painter was the younger brother of Nicolas M., born at Troyes in 1610. His father intended him for the profession of medicine, and after giving him the preliminary education, sent him to Bourges, and placed him with an eminent practitioner of that city; but young Mignard paid more attention to drawing than to physic, and without the help of an instructor painted the portraits of the professor and his family, which excited surprise. The commendation he received for these performances induced him to abandon his medical studies, and to place himself under the tuition of Jean Boucher, a reputable painter in that city, with whom he continued two years. He then proceeded to Paris, and entered the school of Simon Vouet, where he studied some time. About this time the Marquis de Crequy, the French ambassador to Rome, returned to Paris, and brought with him some valuable paintings by the Italian masters. Mignard being allowed to study them, soon perceived that Italy was the great centre of the art; and he accordingly proceeded to Rome, where he resided twenty-two years, and hence acquired the name of *Mignard the Roman.* He lived in habits of the closest intimacy and friendship with Charles Alphonse du Fresnoy, who had been his fellow-student with Vouet, during the residence of the latter in that metropolis, and derived much advantage from the counsels of that excellent theorist. He studied diligently the works of the best masters, particularly of Raffaelle and Annibale Caracci. His pictures of the Virgin and other holy subjects, designed and executed in the graceful and dignified style of Raffaelle, were greatly admired at Rome. He acquired a distinguished reputation in that city, and found abundant employment. He also distinguished himself as a portrait painter, and was patronized by Pope Urban VIII., Alexander VII., and many of the nobility. He executed some works for the churches, the principal of which is a picture of the Trinity, in S. Carlo; and a Holy Family, in S. Maria in Campitelli. He was invited back to Paris by Louis XIV., and on his way, passing through Tuscany, Modena, and Parma, he was honored by the princes of those cities, whose portraits he painted. Louis sat to him ten times for his portrait, and had such a respect for his talents that he ennobled him, and after the death of le Brun appointed him his principal painter and director of the manufactories. Mignard was chosen a member of the Academy, and was successively appointed professor, rector, director, and chancellor of that institution. His principal historical works in France are his great cupola in the church of Val-de-Grace, and twelve frescos in the Gallery at St. Cloud, which are highly commended. He also painted the portraits of many of the nobility. The works of Pierre Mignard are not distinguished for commanding genius, or great originality of invention, but they claim our approbation for richness of composition, a learned and correct design, a classic elegance of forms, an amiability of expression, and a harmonious coloring, though not rich, nor very vigorous. Several of his works have been engraved by some of the most distinguished French engravers, as Gerard Audran, Poilly, Roullet, Nanteuil, &c. There is a spirited etching by him, representing St. Scholastique kneeling before the Virgin. He died at Paris in 1695.

MIGNARD, Pierre, a French architect, the son of Nicolas M., and the nephew of Pierre Mignard the painter, was born at Avignon in 1640. He traveled through France and Italy, studying and copying the finest monuments of architecture, after which he settled at Paris, where his father was residing. He was commissioned to erect the Abbey de Montmajour, near Arles, which gained him great reputation; and he was intrusted with many important works. Among them were the façade of the church of St. Nicolas, and the Porte St. Martin. The Abbey de Montmajour was subsequently destroyed by fire, and was rebuilt precisely according to the designs of Mignard. He was one of the six architects who founded, in 1671, the French Academy of Architecture, of which he was appointed professor, and continued to discharge the functions of that office until his death, in 1725.

MIGNON, or MINJOHN, Abraham, an eminent German fruit and flower painter, born at Frankfort in 1639. His father was a merchant, but failing in his business, and being reduced to necessitous circumstances, his friend Jacob Murel, an eminent flower painter, took the child, and discovering in him a genius for painting, instructed him in his art, in which he made such progress that at the age of seventeen he surpassed his master. Murel carried on a considerable commerce in works of art; and about this time, his business leading him to Holland, he took his pupil with him, and recommended him to the especial care of John David de Heem, whose works were held in the highest estimation. Under the instruction of this able master he made such progress, and deported himself with so much urbanity, that he won his friendship and favor, so that he rendered him every assistance in his power. The pictures of Mignon were soon universally admired, and so much sought after, that with all his industry he could hardly execute all the commissions he received. He founded his manner on that of de Heem, but he improved himself by studying nature with the most curious and exact observation. He has seldom been surpassed in the selection of his objects, in the picturesque manner of his composition, and in the beauty and freshness of his flowers and fruit, which have all the bloom of nature. His butterflies and other insects seem to live and feed, and the dew drops on the leaves have all the transparency of real water. He died in 1679.

MIGNON, Jean, an obscure French engraver who executed a few plates. Among them is one of Abraham purchasing the Cave of Machpelah, signed *Io. Mignon. fec.*

DMF or DM. or DM. MIGNOT, Daniel, a French engraver, who flourished about 1593. He engraved a few plates, among them a set of ornaments for goldsmiths, marked with one of the above monograms.

MIKCKER, John, a Dutch landscape painter, who flourished at Amsterdam about 1650. He painted well wooded landscapes, ornamented with cottages, or gentlemen's parks with country residences, in rather a dark tone of color. He was the first instructor of J. B. Weeninx, whose earliest pictures are painted in his style, for which reason the works of Mikcker are sometimes passed upon the ignorant for those of Weeninx.

MILANESE, Il. See Cittadini. See Guglielmo della Porta.

MILANESE, Felice, an Italian painter, by whom there is a spirited etching of the Virgin and Infant seated on a throne, with a Bishop, and several children, signed *Felice Milanese, fec.*

MILANI, Giulio Cesare, a Bolognese painter, born in 1621. He studied under Flaminio Torre, and was the most successful and the most eminent follower of his style. He executed many works for the churches at Bologna, and in the adjacent cities. His most esteemed productions in his native city are the Marriage of the Virgin, in the church of S. Giuseppe; St. Antonio di Padova, in S. Maria del Costello; and a Holy Family at the Servi, which are pronounced such excellent performances as not to be "disgraced by the proximity of such powerful competitors." Lanzi says "he was the most eminent of Torre's disciples, and he was rather admired in the churches at Bologna, and extolled in many adjacent states." He died in 1678.

MILANI, Aureliano, was the nephew of Giulio Cesare M., born at Bologna in 1675. He first studied with Cesare Gennari, and afterwards with Lorenzo Pasinelli. He did not attach himself to the style of either of these masters, but enamoured with the works of the Caracci, he devoted himself a long time in copying their compositions entire, as well as in part, repeating his designs of the heads, the feet, the hands, and the outlines, till he caught the spirit, without borrowing the forms. Crespi remarks that no one showed more of the manner of the Caracci in the naked figure, and in the symmetry and whole character of his paintings; and, next to Carlo Cignani, no one did more to maintain the dignity and credit of the Bolognese school. Lanzi says he was not so excellent in his coloring. His principal works at Bologna are the Resurrection, in the church of La Puritá; the Stoning of St. Stephen, in S. Mascarella; and St. Jerome, in S. Maria della Vita. He went to Rome, where he resided a long time, and found abundant patronage from the churches and individuals. The best at Rome, perhaps, is the Beheading of St. John the Baptist, in the church of the Bergamaschi. He died in 1749.

MILANI, Gioseffo Maria. This painter was born at Pisa in 1678. He studied under Camillo Gabrielli, and following the example of his instructor, he attached himself to the style of Pietro da Cortona. On leaving his master, he applied himself to the study of perspective, and made designs after the most magnificent buildings, ancient and modern, in Pisa and elsewhere, which he afterwards introduced into his compositions with great effect. He excelled in perspective and architecture, which he embellished with figures elegantly designed, and grouped with great ingenuity, and his coloring was rich and harmonious. He acquired great reputation, and executed many works in fresco for the churches at Pisa and in other cities. One of his best works is a grand ceiling in the church of S. Matthew, in his native city. He borrowed so much from Cortona that he has been accused of plagiarism.

MILANO, Agostino. See Agostino di Bramantino.

MILANO, Andrea, a painter of Milan, who flourished in 1495. He was an able painter, and his altar-piece at Murano extorted the admiration of Zanetti. There is no certainty about this artist. Vasari's annotators call him Andrea Salai, and Battoni says his name was the same as Andrea del Gobbo, mentioned by Vasari in his life of Correggio. Lanzi thinks otherwise, and that he was a Venetian painter, or at least had studied in Venice, from his style and coloring.

MILANO, Andrea da. See Solari.

MILANO, Francesco da, a painter whose name is found on an exquisite altar-piece in the parish church of Soligo, quite in the style of Titian, dated 1540.

MILANO, Giovanni da, was a favorite pupil of Taddeo Gaddi, and one of his ablest scholars. He painted much at Florence and in Lombardy. To him, and to Jacopo di Casentino, Taddeo on his death-bed commended his two sons for their protection. He flourished about 1370.

MILBERT, Jacques Gerard, a French landscape painter, born at Paris in 1766. He early manifested a strong inclination for art, which he cultivated with assiduity; and in 1795, he was appointed professor of the Ecole des Mines. In that capacity he was sent by government to the Pyrenees, to design the various localities supposed to be rich in mineral wealth. In 1798 he was appointed a member of the scientific commission to Egypt, but was unavoidably prevented from visiting that country. In 1800 he was appointed chief designer of the Australian expedition commanded by Baudin, composed of the two corvettes *Geographe* and *Naturaliste.* Ill health compelled him to stop at the Isle of France, where he remained two years, and collected the materials for his pictorial work, published in 1812, entitled *Voyage pittoresque à l'Ile de France, au cap de Bonne Esperance et à l'ile de Teneriffe.* Paris, 1812; 2 vols. 8vo. In 1815, Milbert visited the United States, in the suite of the French Consul General, commissioned by the French Minister, M. Hyde de Neuville, to make researches in natural history. After employing nine years in this mission, he returned to Paris; and his discoveries gained him great reputation, being highly praised by Baron Cuvier. Milbert subsequently published his pictorial work, entitled *L'Itineraire pittoresque du fleuve Hudson et des parties laterales de l'Amerique du Nord, d'apres les dessins originaux pris sur lieux.* Paris, 1827—1829; 2 vols 4to., with an atlas. Milbert died at Paris in 1840

MILÉ, Francis, sometimes called Francisque, and often wrongly written *Millé* or *Millet,* was born at Antwerp in 1644. His father was a Frenchman, and had accompanied the Prince of Condé, to whom he was attached, into the Netherlands, at the time of the revolt. He showed an early inclination for art, and his father placed him with Laurent Franck, under whom he made great progress, and whose daughter he married at eighteen years of age. Having contracted a friendship with Abraham Genoels, they studied together after nature, and increased each other's ardor by a friendly emulation, which, with an unreserved communication of observations, ideas, and sentiments, greatly tended to the advantage of both. Milè was remarkable for such a tenacious memory that he could copy any scene he had observed in nature, or any particular picture which had struck his fancy, and what was still more extraordinary, he could readily recollect every remarkable aspect of nature, as the form of any particular cloud, or tints in the skies, and those evanescent beauties that pleased his eye and imagination. Soon after his marriage he went to Paris, where he made the works of Nicholas Poussin his study and his models. According to D'Argenville, he traveled through England and Holland, leaving in those countries abundant proofs of his ability. On his return to Paris he acquired much distinction, was received into the Academy, and his works were held in high estimation. The favorite subjects of Milé were heroic landscapes, in the style of Poussin; and though he was unequal to that master, he approached him nearer than any of his countrymen, or perhaps any other painter; like that master, his scenery is always appropriate to and in harmony with his subject. He was a strict observer of the propriety of costume, his pencil was broad and facile, and his coloring appropriate and agreeable, though in some of his pictures there is too great a monotony, and a want of intelligence in the distribution of his masses of light and shadow. He died in 1680, in the prime of his life, as some say, by poison administered by some one of his profession, envious of his merit and reputation. There are a few etchings by this able artist, after his own designs, which are much admired for their picturesque subjects, and their light and spirited execution. Among others are the following:

A Landscape, with Egyptian Ruins, with the subject of Moses saved from the waters of the Nile; *Francisque, inv.* Another grand Landscape, with the History of Cephalus and Procris. A Mountainous Landscape, with figures, and a town in the middle. Six other Landscapes, of various sizes. The Two Friends. The Voyagers. An Ancient City.

MILIZIA, Francesco, an eminent Italian writer on architecture, of a noble and opulent family, born in 1725, according to his own authority, at Oria, a small town in the province of Otranto, in the kingdom of Naples. At the age of nine years, he was placed under the charge of his maternal uncle, who was practising the medical profession at Padua. After remaining with the latter until the age of sixteen, he ran away from Padua to Rome, and joined his father, who sent him to Naples, to study logic and metaphysics under the celebrated Genovesi, and physics and geometry under Padre Orlandi. Desiring to see more of the world, he quitted Naples with the intention of going to France; but the low state of his finances prevented his going farther than Leghorn. After this, he was obliged to content himself with living a half studious, half indolent life at Oria; but at the age of twenty-five, he married a young lady of good family at Gallipoli, and having obtained a handsome allowance from her father, he went to Rome, and ultimately settled with his wife in that city, in 1761. He then began to apply his energies to the study of architecture, and published his Lives of the Architects, entitled *Vite dei piu celebri Architetti, antichi e moderni*, Rome, 1768, 8vo. The second edition appeared under the title of *Memorie degli Architetti antichi e moderni*, Parma, 1781, 8vo. It may rather be termed a history of the art, than a biography of architects. In 1772, Milizia published his *Trattato Completo formale e materiale del Teatro*, Rome, 1772. This work excited so much scandal on account of certain observations in it, as to cause its suppression by withdrawing the copies; but it was subsequently reprinted at Venice. His next work was the *Principi d' architettura civile*, Finale, 1781; Bassano, 1785; Ibid. 1825, 3 vols. 8vo.—This was considered the best production of Milizia, and greatly extended his reputation, being almost the first attempt to base the art upon rational principles, and to expose the pedantry with which it had been taught. It is moreover written in an attractive style, and the criticisms are characterized by highly caustic qualities. On the latter account, although admired by young artists, it was censured by many more advanced professors, who charged the author with speaking too freely of many eminent names, with attacking high authorities, and propounding his own views without regard to the example of others. His work entitled *L'Arte di Vedere nelle Belle arti del disegno*, Venice, 1781, is perhaps more fearless and unsparing than the preceding. It is written with great eloquence, and attacks Michael Angelo and others, in a very spirited style. For a specimen of his criticisms, the reader is referred to the article Buonarotti. He was appointed Royal Superintendent of the Buildings in the States belonging to the King of the two Sicilies, but he resigned the office in 1786, preferring to be free from the responsibility.

Milizia published a work entitled *Roma delle Belle Arti di Disegno*, Bassano, 1787, 8vo.; and his *Dizionnario delle Belle Arti*, Bassano, 1797, 2 vols., 8vo., which latter is chiefly a translation from the French work *Encyclopédie Méthodique*. After this, disgusted with the attacks upon his *Roma*, he desisted from publishing the first and second parts which he had prepared of this work, abandoned the Fine Arts, and devoted himself to the study of Natural History. He died at Rome in 1798.

The works of Milizia are pervaded with great severity of criticism, and a general tone of causticity, which render it highly improbable that he possessed an impartial judgment. He seems to delight in finding as much fault as possible with every work of architecture, and gives the good qualities but a slight prominence. Notwithstanding this hyper-critical disposition, he undoubtedly possessed an intimate knowledge of architecture; his works have overthrown many incorrect ideas based upon false principles, and sanctioned by nothing but the prestige attached to great names. They have greatly promoted the dissemination of the principles of pure architecture. His criticisms, if taken with proper allowance for his peculiarity of temper, may be safely relied upon. His *Lettere Inedite*, addressed to the Count San Giovanni, first published at Paris in 1827, serves to portray his disposition, and abundantly proves that he abhorred pedantry, dogmatism, quackery, and false enthusiasm. Milizia's writings were published in one entire collection at Bologna, in 1826, 9 volumes 8vo.

Pommereul has translated his first work into French, under the title of *Essai sur l'histoire de l'architecture, précédé d'observations sur le bon gout et les beaux arts*, La Haye, 1819, 3 vols. 8vo. Mrs. Cresy has also translated this work into English, under the title of Milizia's Lives of Celebrated Architects, Ancient and Modern, London, 1826, 2 vols., 8vo.

MILLER, Andrew, an Irish engraver, who flourished at Dublin about 1740. He executed some portraits in mezzotinto, which possess considerable merit; among others are the following:

Dean Swift; *after F. Bindou.* 1743. Robert Boyle, Philosopher. Charles Lucas, M. D. of Dublin. Robert Josleyn, Lord of Newport, Chancellor of Ireland. 1747.—Josiah Hort, Archbishop of Taum. Eaten Stannard, Recorder of Dublin. Joseph Baudin, Painter. Joseph Miller, Actor, in the character of Teague. John Harper, in the character of Jobson. Snowdon, in the character of Caled, in the siege of Damascus. Turbutt, in the Character of Sosia, in Amphitrion.

MILLER, J., an English engraver, who flourished in London about 1760. He engraved many plates, chiefly portraits, which possess considerable merit. The following are the most interesting:

King George III.; *ad vivum.* Queen Charlotte; *do.* Jeffrey, Lord Amherst. George Bridges Rodney, Lord Rodney. Charles Townsend, Chancellor of the Exchequer. Thomas Gray, Poet. Charles Churchill, Poet. Sir John Vanbrugh. John Wilks, M. P. and Chamberlain of London.

MILLER, John Sebastian. See Muller.

MILN, Robert, a Scotch engraver, who flourished at Edinburgh about 1710, and engraved some plates of Scottish antiquities for a work entitled *Miscellanea quædam Eruditæ Antiquitatis, quæ ad Borealem Britanniæ majoris partem pertinent, &c.*

MILOCCO, Antonio, an eminent painter of Turin, the friend and companion of the Cav. Claudio Beaumont, in whose style he painted, but with far less merit. He flourished in the first part of the 18th century. Lanzi says he was more dry in his design than Beaumont, less cultivated in his taste, and inferior to him in all the qualities of a painter; but from his peculiar facility, he was much employed by individuals, and sometimes by the court.

MILOT, an obscure French engraver, who flourished at Antwerp about 1620. He engraved some frontispieces, portraits, and other book plates, in a rather neat, but stiff and tasteless style.

MINDERHOUT, Hendrick, a Flemish painter, born at Antwerp in 1637. It is not known under whom he studied, but he painted marines and seaports, particularly views of Antwerp and Bruges, and other ports in the Netherlands. His works evidently show that he designed every thing from nature; his shipping in particular, are drawn with great accuracy and precision. His works are usually of a large size, and possess the merit of a bold design, a spirited pencil, a pleasing tone of coloring, and an intelligent management of the chiaro-scuro, which give them a fine effect.—He was elected a member of the Academy of Antwerp, and painted for his reception piece a splendid view of the port of Antwerp, with a variety of shipping, and many figures, which adorns their hall. He afterwards settled at Bruges, where he practised his profession the rest of his days.—There are some of his best works in the public edifices of that city. He was elected a member of the Society of Painters of Bruges in 1660. He was an unequal painter, and in the latter part of his life, seems to have painted with negligence and haste. His best works are highly esteemed, and are found in the principal collections in Flanders. He died at Bruges in 1696.

MINGA, Andrea del, a Florentine painter, who studied under Ridolfo del Ghirlandaio, and who is recorded by Orlandi and Bottari, as a fellow student with Michael Angelo. His works are generally indifferent. Lanzi says his Prayer in the Garden, in the church of the Holy Cross, rivals the works of any of his cotemporaries; hence it is alleged that he was assisted in its execution by his friends. He was living in 1568.

MINGOT, Teodosio, a Spanish historical painter, and a native of Catalonia, born in 1551. Palomino erroneously states that he studied under Michael Angelo at Rome, for Angelo died when he was only thirteen years of age; but he was a pupil of Gaspar Becerra, at Madrid, an eminent painter, who had studied with Buonarotti. It is believed, however, that he visited Italy, where it is said he acquired a correct and elevated style of design. He was also a vigorous colorist. He was employed by Philip II. in the palace of the Prado, where he executed some excellent works, all of which perished in the conflagration that destroyed the edifice. He died in 1590.

MINI, Antonio, a Florentine painter, and a favorite pupil of Michael Angelo Buonarotti. He did not acquire much distinction for original works, which was difficult in that glorious age of painting, but there is an anecdote, connected with his history, worth recording. Angelo, when he had finished his famous picture of Leda for Alphonso, Duke of Ferrara, offended at the manner of one of the courtiers who came for it, refused to sell it to that prince, and gave it to Mini, who took it with him. to Paris. Vasari describes it as "a grand picture, painted in distemper, that seemed to breathe on the canvass." Mariette also asserts that he saw the picture, and that in coloring "it approached the tone of Titian." Mariette is probably describing a copy in oil, as D'Argenville informs us that the original was destroyed by fire in the reign of Louis XIII.

MINNEBROER, Frans, a Flemish historical painter who flourished at Malines about 1540. Little is known of him. There is a Flight into Egypt in the church of Notre Dame in that city, and the Visitation to St. Elizabeth in the church of the same name in Hanswick, by him, which are considered remarkable productions.

MINIATI, Bartolomeo, a Florentine painter, was a scholar and able assistant of Il Rosso. He accompanied that artist to Paris, and assisted him in the great works he executed for Francis I.

MINIERA, Biagio, a reputable painter, commended by Orsini, was born at Ascoli in 1697, and died in 1755. Some of his works are to be found in the churches in his native place.

MINNITI, Mario, a Sicilian painter, born at Syracuse in 1577, and died in 1640. According to Hackert he was a good artist, and executed several works for the churches in his native city.

MINORELLO, Francesco, an Italian painter, born at Estè in 1624. He studied under Luca Ferrari at Padua. According to Lanzi, on the death of his master, he contributed to support the reputation of the Bolognese school in that city, where are some of his works. He died young in 1657.

MINOZZI, Bernardo, a Bolognese painter, born in 1699, and died in 1769. He studied landscape painting under Nunzio Ferraiuoli, and struck out into a style of his own, which gained him considerable reputation. He painted in fresco, distemper, and water colors. He was distinguished most for his landscapes in water colors, painted on fine paste-board, which were much admired and sought after, both at home and abroad.

MINZOCCHI, Francesco, called Il Vecchio di San Bernardo. This painter was born at Forli in 1513. He first studied the works of Marco Palmigiani in his native place, and his earlier productions, as the Crucifixion, at the Osservanti, are designed in the stiff formal style of that master. He afterwards changed his manner by studying with Girolamo Genga, and, as some writers add, with Pordenone, assuming, in his subsequent productions, a more correct, graceful, and animated style, with an expression that looks like nature herself. He acquired great reputation, and executed many works for the churches in his native city and elsewhere. Lanzi says his works are so much esteemed at Forli, that whenever a chapel was taken down, his pictures were carefully cut out of the walls and replaced elsewhere. Among his best works are two pictures in a chapel of the cathedral of Loretto, representing the Sacrifice of Melchisedec and the Miracle of the Manna, in which the prophet and principal characters have all the dignity of character, nobleness of drapery, and splendor of coloring belonging to the school of Pordenone; but Lanzi says he represented the crowd in the most popular features and attitudes, almost sufficient to excite the envy of Teniers, and the most popular painters of the Flemish school; his various and numerous animals are painted to the life, and his baskets and different utensils appear like reality, though the attempt to excite mirth in treating a serious subject always detracts from its dignity. Scannelli extols one of his frescos in the church of S. Maria della Grata at Forli, representing the Deity on a ceiling, surrounded by angels; the figures are full of spirit, majestic, varied, and painted with a power and skill of foreshortening which entitles him to greater celebrity. There are other excellent works by him in the cathedral and the church of S. Domenico at Forli. He also painted many easel pictures for the collections. He died in 1574.

MINZOCCHI, Pietro Paolo, and Sebastiano, were the sons and scholars of the preceding, but far inferior to him. They painted easel pictures of historical subjects, and executed some works for the churches at Forli. Lanzi says they "painted in the same natural style as their father, but they were not above mediocrity in invention, not select in their forms, and their works had little relief."

MIO, Giovanni di, an eminent artist of whom little is known with certainty, save that, from the archives of Venice, he painted in the Library of St. Mark about 1556, in competition with such eminent artists as Schiavone, Porta, Zelotti, Franco, and with Paul Veronese himself. He is supposed to have been a native of Vicenza, and perhaps a pupil of Gio. Battista Maganza. Lanzi thinks he may be the same as one Fratina, recorded by Ridolfi, as one of the assistants in ornamenting the Library. But this degrades him in the face of the authentic document before cited.

MIOZZI, Niccolo, and Marc' Antonio, two reputable painters of whom little is known, who, according to the *Guida di Rovigo*, were natives of Vicenza, and flourished about 1670. They painted in the style of Giulio Carpioni, of whom they were probably scholars.

MIRADORO, Luigi, commonly called Il Genovesino, a painter of Genoa, who, according to Lanzi, after having learned the first principles of the art in his native city, went young to Cremona, towards the beginning of the 17th century, and began to study the works of Panfilo Nuvolone. He afterwards formed a manner partaking much of the Caracci, though less select and studied, but bold, large, correct in coloring, harmonious, producing a fine effect. He settled at Cremona, where he opened a school for the instruction of young artists, and executed some excellent works for the churches and public edifices of that city and elsewhere. Among his most esteemed works are a picture of St. Gio. Damasceno, in the church of S. Clemente, at Cremona; and a Pietà, or Dead Christ in the Lap of the Virgin, in the Merchants' College at Piacenza. In all subjects he was successful, and remarkably so in those of a terrific cast. He also painted some excellent works for the collections. Lanzi says that, though this artist is unknown in his native city, and is not mentioned by Orlandi, he nevertheless is held in high repute in Lombardy, and particularly in Cremona. The time of his birth or death is not known, but one of his works in S. Imerio, bears date, 1651.

MIRANDOLA, Domenico, an eminent Bolognese painter and sculptor, who, according to Malvasia, was educated in the school of the Caracci, and acquired much distinction. Lanzi says, that when Pietro Facini opened his academy at Bologna, Mirandola quitted that of Lodovico, and entered the former, became a celebrated sculptor, enriched himself with the spoils of both, and kept an open studio, regulated according to the method of his first masters, which, for this reason, was called by some, the school of the Caracci. Mirandola had possessed himself of the casts, &c., of the Academy of the Caracci, which was closed on the death of Lodovico. But Lanzi must be in error, for Facini died in 1602, Lodovico in 1619, and Mirandola in 1612, according to his monument in the church of S. Tommaso at Bologna. According to Lanzi, he was one of those kind of men who gain more reputation, by management and address, than by true merit.

MIRANDOLESE, Il. See Pietro Paltronieri, and Giuseppe Perraccini.

MIRE, Noel le. See Lemire.

MIRETI, or MIRETTI, Girolamo, a reputable old painter of Padua. There are authentic notices of him and his works from 1423 to 1441. Lanzi says this artist is the famous Nicolo Moretto commended by Vasari, which see.

MIRETTO, Giovanni, an old artist of Padua, supposed by Lanzi to have been a brother of the preceding. There is one of the largest pictures in the world in the great Hall at Padua, consisting of a mixture of sacred and historical subjects, the signs of the Zodiac from Igino, and of the various operations carried on during the respective months of the year, besides some curious ideas evidently suggested by some learned man. This work was formerly attributed to Giotto; but Morelli, in his *Notizia*, upon the authority of Campagnuola, says it was executed conjointly by an artist of Ferrara and Gio. Miretto of Padua. Lanzi says this discovery justifies his previous opinions of his being unable to prevail upon himself to ascribe such a work to Giotto, although executed in his style.

MIREVELT, or MIREVELDT, Michael Jansen, an eminent Dutch painter, born at Delft in 1568. He was the son of a goldsmith, who, perceiving in him an early inclination for art, placed him with Jerome Wierix, an eminent engraver. When he was twelve years of age, he executed a plate of Christ and the Woman of Samaria, and soon after another of Judith with the Head of Holofernes. These juvenile performances attracted the attention of Anthony de Montfort, called Blocklandt, who advised him to apply himself to painting, and took him into his school. On leaving that master, he at first devoted himself to historical painting, and executed some altar-pieces for the churches at Delft; but having painted the portraits of some of the princes of the House of Nassau, which were universally admired, he ever after gained such abundant and profitable employment in that branch that he devoted himself entirely to it. He executed an incredible number of portraits

Houbraken and others say five thousand; but Sandrart, Descamps, and others, swell it to ten thousand—which number, though he is supposed to have lived to a great age, was assiduous and wrought with great facility, is beyond credibility. He studied and imitated nature exactly, and gave a striking likeness; designed his portraits in good taste; and finished them with great care. His pencil is free, his touch neat, and his coloring good. He obtained so great celebrity that he was invited to England by Charles I.; though the great plague, then raging in London, prevented his accepting an offer so much to his interest and honor. He never left Delft, except at particular times, when he went to the Hague, to paint the portraits of the princes of Nassau, who held him in the highest esteem. He received a very high price for his portraits, for the time in which he lived, obtaining one hundred and fifty guilders for the smallest size; and for full size, half and whole lengths, his charges were proportionably large. The portraits of Mirevelt are finely drawn and full of expression. Several of them were admirably engraved by his brother-in-law, James William Delft. He died in 1641.

MIREVELT, Peter, was the son and scholar of the preceding, born at Delft in 1596, and died young, in 1632. He painted portraits exactly in the style of his father, and in his best pictures was accounted no way inferior to him. One of his most esteemed works is in the Hall of the Surgeons of Delft, representing the portraits of the principal members of that institution at that time.

MIROU, Anthony, a Flemish painter, who flourished about 1640. Little is known of the events of his life. He painted landscapes and scriptural subjects, correct in design, and executed with a spirited pencil.

MIRUOLI, Girolamo, an Italian painter, who, according to Vasari, was a native of Romagna, and flourished about 1570. He studied under Pellegrino Tibaldi, and executed several works in fresco for the churches at Parma. He acquired so much distinction that he was appointed court painter by the Duke, and died in his service. He also painted at Modena and Bologna, in which latter city are some of his frescos, in the church of the Servi.

MISCIROLI, Tommaso, called Il Pittor Villano (rustic painter), was born at Faenza in 1636, according to Orlandi; died in 1699. He gained considerable reputation in his time, and executed some works for the churches. Lanzi says he owed his reputation rather to his genius or management than to any precepts of the art. In other words, he was what Fuseli terms *a bold adopter*. He took his attitudes and coloring from Guido, his draperies from the Venetians; and Lanzi says that his best works are equal to many of the Venetian school. This remark applies only to a few of his best works, executed with much care. His chief works are in the church of St. Cecilia at Faenza, particularly an altar-piece of the Martyrdom of that Saint, in which he introduced an executioner stirring up the flames—a figure almost copied from Lionello's grand picture of the Martyrdom of St. Domenico, in the church of that Saint at Bologna.

MISEROTTI, Domenico, an Italian engraver, who flourished about 1750, and engraved several plates for the collection of prints from the paintings in the Gallery of the Grand Duke of Tuscany.

MITCHELL, J., a Scotch engraver, who flourished at Glasgow about 1765. He engraved a few plates of historical subjects, most of them executed entirely with the graver.

MITELLI, Agostino, an eminent fresco painter, born at Bologna in 1609. According to Passeri, he acquired a knowledge of the human figure in the school of the Caracci, and was well grounded in perspective and architecture under Falcetta. He was not only one of the first perspective and architectural painters of his time, but an able figurist. Lanzi says, "his first labors proved very attractive to the public; not that they equaled the force, solidity, and reality of Dentone, but on account of their peculiar beauty and grace, such as to almost obtain for him the name of the Guido of ornamental architecture. Employing his own taste, he softened down the harder features of the art, made his elevations more delicate, the tints more mild, and added a style of foliage, scrolls, and arabesques, decorated with gold, which seemed to breathe of grace and elegance. The style of his ornaments was adapted to the nature of the edifice, and suited to the solemnity of the temple, the elegance of the saloon, or the splendor of the theatre. Each ornament filled its appropriate place at just intervals, and was executed with such delightful symmetry and harmony as to surprise and entrance the beholders, by the perfection of the illusion, and to remind them as it were of the enchanted palaces of the romancers." Mitelli's first assistants were two of his fellow pupils, Andrea Sighizzi and Gio. Paderna, with occasionally the figurist Ambrogi. But Michael Angelo Colonna alone seemed born to associate with him, as he did on the death of his favorite Curti (Dentone), and an intimacy and friendship sprung up between them, strengthened by interest and mutual esteem, which lasted till the death of Mitelli, and they wrought conjointly for twenty-four years, producing many magnificent works at Bologna, Rome, Parma, Modena, Genoa, in which Mitelli executed the ornamental, perspective, and architectural parts, and Colonna the figures. Among their most celebrated performances are the chapel of Rosario and the Palazzo Caprara, at Bologna; the Palazzo Spada, at Rome; and in the latter, Lanzi says, "they enlarged the ample hall, as it were, and dignified it by means of feigned colonnades, artful recesses, and magnificent steps, on which numerous figures, arranged in varied and novel drapery, were seen ascending and descending." In 1658, they were invited to Madrid by Philip IV., whose palace they decorated with several works, among which were a grand saloon in the royal palace at Madrid, in which Colonna painted his celebrated Fable of Pandora. Mitelli died at Madrid in 1660. He etched some plates of architectural ornaments, and a set of forty-eight friezes dated 1645, admirably designed, and executed in a spirited style. See *Michael Angelo Colonna*.

MITELLI, Giuseppe Maria, was the son of the preceding, born at Bologna in 1634. After having received instruction from his father, he entered the school of Flaminio Torre. He painted history with considerable success, and occasionally introduced the figures into the perspective pieces of his father. He executed several works for the churches at Bologna, the principal of which are St. Reniero healing the Sick, in S. Maria della Vita; a Pietá, in the Nunziata; and Christ taken in the Garden, at the Cappuccini. But he was more distinguished as an engraver, and he etched a great number and variety of plates from his own designs, and after some of the most celebrated masters. They are executed in a slight, feeble style, and the drawing is often incorrect. He possessed, however, a fruitful and inventive genius, which renders his works valuable. Bartsch describes one hundred and sixty-two prints by him, and Nagler has increased the list. He died in 1718. The following are his best prints:

GMF. or GMM or GMA. MTI F.

A set of twelve plates after the most esteemed pictures in the churches at Bologna. The history of Æneas, in twenty plates; *after the pictures by the Caracci*, in the Palazzo Favi, at Bologna. The Cries of Bologna, in forty-one prints; *after An. Caracci.* The Adoration of the Shepherds; called the *Notte; after Correggio.* The Martyrdom of St. Erasmus; *after Poussin.* David and Goliah; *after Titian.* The finding of the Cross; *after Tintoretto.* The Rich Man and Lazarus; *after P. Veronese.* The twenty-four Hours of Human Felicity.—There are two additional prints, making a set of twenty-six, probably from his own designs. They were published at Bologna in 1675, and are now become scarce.

MNESICLES, an eminent Greek architect, who flourished in the time of Pericles, the golden age of Grecian art. He was chiefly distinguished by that magnificent portico, the Propylea, which formed the façade and entrance to the Acropolis or citadel of Athens. It was commenced B. C. 437, and completed in five years, at a cost of about $2,500,000. Each front had a Doric hexastyle portico, raised upon three steps; the columns were nearly five feet in diameter, and twenty-nine feet high, including the capital. From the west front was entered a vestibule fifty-nine feet two inches wide, which was divided into three aisles by Ionic columns, three on each side; these supported a marble ceiling, divided into lacunaria; these lacunaria are formed of blocks twenty-two feet long, and extended from the walls to the columns; some of them are now remaining. The wall at the end of the vestibule had five openings, in which were hung the gates of the Acropolis; the central one is much the widest. The eastern portico, to which there was an ascent by five steps, was entered through these gates: from hence there was a descent of three steps, to the level of the ground before the interior front. The whole was of white marble, with Doric columns; and the façade was ornamented with equestrian statues, on isolated pedestals. Among the ruins may be observed some of the members of the cornice, which were gilt, and other parts painted with a reddish ochre. Although the Turks have greatly injured this masterpiece of art, sufficient remains to immortalize the name of its architect.

MOCETTO, Girolamo, or Hieronymus Mocetus, an old painter and engraver, a native of Verona, who studied under Giovanni Bellini at Venice, and hence some call him a Venetian. Lanzi says he was one of the earliest and least polished of the disciples of Bellini, and that the Veronese boast the possession of his portrait, among those of the painters of the town in Scuola del Nudo, and an altar-piece in the church of S. Nazario e Celso, bearing his name, and dated 1493. He died about 1500. He is chiefly worthy of notice as an engraver. His works in this line are extremely scarce and valuable, as early specimens of the art. They are executed with the graver, in a neat but stiff style, and marked with one of the accompanying monograms. We have about a dozen prints by him, among which is the Resurrection, with four Soldiers; the Sacrifice, with many figures, from an antique bas-relief; the Virgin and Child, with St. John the Baptist and another Saint, now in the British Museum; the Virgin and Child seated on a Throne, with lattice work and trees; Men sacrificing a Pig; Judith, in a landscape with trees; a wooden cut of the Entry of Christ into Jerusalem. Mr. Ottley attributes two prints to him—the Calumny of Apelles, and a Nymph sleeping on a Bank, bearing a curious inscription. He also engraved some battle pieces and other subjects. Bartsch describes eight pieces by him under the name of Jerome Mozzetto. Zani denies that Mocetto engraved on wood.

HROM, or HE:ROM or HERO M or HE·RoM or HERoM.

MODANINO, Il. See Cav. Guido Mazzoni.

MODENA, Barnaba da, an old painter of Modena, some of whose works are still found in excellent preservation. Lanzi says he was one of the first artists of his time. Two of his works are in the church and convent of the Conventuals, at Pisa. One represents the Coronation of the Virgin, and the other, the Virgin surrounded by St. Francis and other Saints of the Order. Morona praises the beautiful character of the heads, the draperies, and the coloring, and prefers him to Giotto. Della Valle mentions another fine altar-piece of the Virgin, in the possession of the Conventuals at Alba in Piedmont, which he says is painted in a grander style than any of his cotemporaries. This picture bears his name, and date 1357.

MODENA, Pellegrino da. The real name of this eminent painter was Pellegrino Munari. He is also sometimes called Aretusi, but generally Pellegrino da Modena, from the place of his nativity. According to Tiraboschi, he was born about 1485, which is evidently an error, as there is an altar-piece by him at Modena, dated 1497. Lanzi says he studied with his father, Giovanni Munari, who was also an able artist. In 1509, he painted an altar-piece for the church of S. Giovanni at Modena, which gained him great reputation. The celebrity of Raffaelle, then in the zenith of his fame, drew him to Rome, where he became the pupil of that sublime master, who, quickly perceiving his talents, employed him to assist him in the great works in the Vatican. He was first employed in the open galleries, but he afterwards executed from the designs of Raffaelle the histories of Jacob and Solomon in the Vatican, which Lanzi says were painted entirely in the style of his master, in an incomparable manner. After the death of Raffaelle he remained some time at Rome, and executed some admirable works for the churches from his own designs, particularly some fresco histories of St. James, in S. Giacomo degli Spagnuoli. On his return to Modena, with a distinguished reputation as one of Raffaelle's ablest scholars, he found abundant employment in the churches and public edifices, till his brilliant career was cut short by a melancholy event. His son happening to quarrel with one of his companions, slew his antagonist in the fight that ensued. Pellegrino, apprized of the fatal accident, ran into the street to save his son from the vengeance of the relatives of the deceased, who, directing their fury against him, slew him on the spot. This tragic event happened in 1523, and was deeply deplored by his fellow-citizens. Another of his sons Tiraboschi conjectures to have been Cesare de Pellegrino Aretusi, the same artist who is called by many writers *Modenese;* but Zani says he was the son of another Pellegrino, a painter of Bologna, and a nephew of the present, which is contrary to the opinion of Lanzi, and the name *Modenese* would seem to contradict it. (See *Aretusi.*) Pellegrino was the only pupil of Raffaelle who came near him in sublimity of style, and purity and elegance of design. Titi says that several of his pieces in the church of S. Giacomo degli Spagnuoli at Rome "boasted figures designed and executed so truly in the manner of Raffaelle, that the modern retouches they have received is a circumstance greatly to be deplored"; and Lanzi says that his celebrated picture of the "Nativity of our Lord, in the church of S. Paolo at Modena, seems to breathe, in every part, the graces of him of Urbino."

MODENA, Niccoletto da, an old Italian painter and engraver, who flourished at Modena from 1500 to 1515. He painted perspective and architecture, but is better known as one of the earliest engravers in Lombardy. His plates are well designed, but are rudely executed with the graver, which clearly proves that he received no instruction in the art, but was obliged to work out his own system. Bartsch gives a list of sixty prints by him, of which thirty-six have his monogram, but in this matter he was very capricious, using various characters, rebuses and initial letters, as well as his name in full; and sometimes he omitted the distinguishing mark altogether. His prints are very rare, and much sought after by the curious collector. The following are the principal:

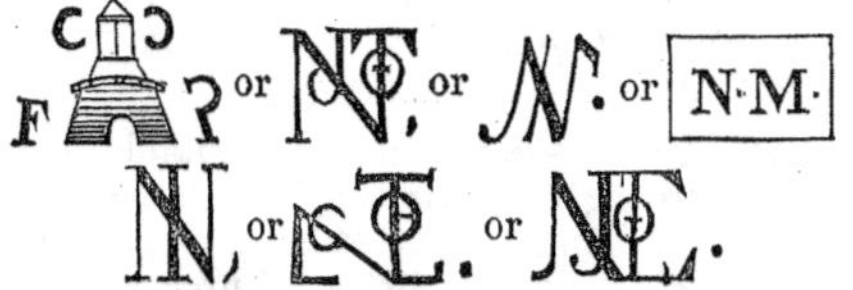


The Adoration of the Shepherds, marked with his name. St. Sebastian, with *Niccoletto* on a tablet. Another St. Sebastian, inscribed *Ora pro nobis, Sancte Sebastiane.* St. Jerome reading, with monogram. St. George, with name. A Triton embracing a Syren, marked N. M. on a tablet. A whole-length figure of Christ, with monogram. St. Sebastian, his arms tied over his head to a column, and body pierced with six arrows; marked with name. Another St. Sebastian, similar to the preceding, except that it is much larger, and body pierced with three arrows; marked with monogram. St. George in complete armor, with monogram; *in the British Museum.* St. Catherine with name. Mars in armor, name on a tablet hung to a tree. Three Children, with name on a scroll. A Female wearing a Helmet, pouring incense on an altar; no mark. Perseus and Pegasus, marked N. M. The Nativity. St. Cecilia. Christ crowned with Thorns. St. Jerome in penitence. A group of four Women, *copy from Albert Durer.* Hercules and the Cretan Bull. Two whole length figures on one plate. Two winged figures, supporting a Standard; in the *British Museum.* St. Roch. A Marine Monster holding a Sea-horse; a Boy with a Torch and Olive Branch, sitting on his tail; marked N. M. on a tablet. A Man crowned with Laurel, looking at some Geometrical figures; in the *British Museum.* David with the Head of Goliah, marked with monogram. St. Anthony, marked with monogram. A Saint, running with a large bag on his back; with monogram. Victory; a winged female figure, standing on the ruins of a large edifice; marked Victoria, N. R. Fame; a winged figure, sitting on some armor, writing Fama Volat on a shield; marked N. M. Neptune, holding a Trident, and sitting on a chair, on which is written Neptuni Simolacron; marked with the letters ONRM. Mercury standing, marked NJ. RO Another Mercury, marked N. R. on a vase. Four Children; *Opus Niccoletti de Mutina* on a tablet. The Vestal Lucia carrying Water in a Sieve, to prove her Virginity; marked with monogram. A Vase surrounded with a wreath of Roses, for a goldsmith's ornament; marked N. R. Another do., smaller size; same mark.

MODENA, or MUTINA, Tommaso, an old painter who flourished at Modena in 1352. There has been a great deal of disquisition about this artist, among the Italian and German writers, arising from the fact that his altar-piece, in three compartments, representing the Virgin and Child, with Saints Wenceslaus and Palmatius, patron saints of Bohemia, was claimed to be an oil painting, and to have been executed in 1297. This picture was formerly at Carlestein, but is now in the Belvidere Gallery, at Vienna. The two following lines are inscribed upon it, in ancient characters:

> Quis opus hoc finxit? Thomas de Mutina pinxit,
> Quale vides lector *Barisini* filius auctor.

It was, therefore, eagerly caught up by the German and Italian authors, to vindicate the claims of their respective countries to the honor of the invention of oil painting, in opposition to the Flemings. The indefatigable German historians traced his origin to Muttersdorff, and made him master of Theodoric of Prague, followed in succession by Wemser, Schoen, Wolgemut, and Albert Durer. Von Michel reads *Rarisini* in the last line quoted, but Federici, Tiraboschi, and Lanzi show that Barisini is the true reading, and Zani clearly shows that the date was 1357, which Michel read erroneous, 1297. At Trevigi, in the chapter house of the Padri Predicatori is a very extensive work by him, representing the saints and learned men of the order, bearing this inscription: "*Anno Domini* MCCCLII. *Prior Travisinus ordinis prædicatorum depingi fecit istud Capitulum, et Thomas Pictor de Mutina pinxit istud.*" This again led to warm disputes as to his real name, and whether the artist was a native of Modena or Trevigi. Federici, in his learned work on the Antiquities of Trevigi, thus admirably proves the paternity of Tommaso, and that he was a native of Trevigi, from the archives of the city. He says "he discovered that the father of Tommaso, named Borasino or Bizzarrino, an abbreviation of Buzzaccarino, became nominated to the citizenship, and to the public notaryship of Trevigi in 1315, in all which his family was called di Modena, as that of Girolamo Ferrarese was called di Carpi." In conclu sion, it will be sufficient to satisfy most persons, to add that the picture at Vienna has been proved by analysis to have been painted *in tempera*, and not in oil; and that Lanzi pronounces the works at Trevigi, judging from the engravings done by the Dominican, Father Federici, "tolerably good in design for those times." (See the articles *van Eyck*, and *Antonello da Messina*.) Those who are fond of such profound and intricate disquisitions, are referred to Bartsch, Nagler, Zani, Lanzi, and a host of others, where they can pursue the subject *ad libitum*.

MODIGLIANI, Francesco, a painter of Forli, who flourished about 1600. Lanzi says he was a scholar of Pontormo, and, though he was not remarkably powerful, nor always consistent, yet he was very graceful and beautiful, and deserves a place in pictoric lexicons. He executed some good works at Urbino, where he is known under the name of *Francesco da Forli*, the chief of which is a Descent from the Cross, in oil, in the church of S. Croce, and a ceiling in fresco, of some angels, in S. Lucia, which are much commended. His best works are in the churches at Forli and Rimino, among which are Adam driven from Eden, the Deluge, the Tower of Babel, with similar Old Testament histories, previously painted by Raffaelle at Rome, and by Agresti at Forli.

MODONINO, Gio. Battista, a painter, of Modena, who, according to Tiraboschi, acquired a distinguished reputation at Rome for his frescos of perspective and architecture, and is supposed to have executed some works in the Palazzo Spada. He died of the plague at Naples, in 1656.

MOELART, Jacob, a Dutch painter, born at Dort in 1649. He studied under Nicholas Maas, applied himself with great assiduity, and became a reputable painter of history, but he most distinguished himself as a portrait painter, and was much employed in that branch by many of the most distinguished persons of that country. Houbraken commends two of his historical works, Pharaoh and his Host drowned in the Red Sea, and Moses striking the Rock. He died in 1727.

MOERIKHOFER, John Melchior, a Swiss medalist, born at Frauenfeld in 1706. He attained sufficient excellence to be honored with the friendship of Hedlinger. During the latter part of his life, he was employed in the mint at Berne, where he engraved the dies. Among his best medals, are those of Haller, Voltaire, Frederic II., and George II. He died at Berne in 1761.

MOERIKHOFER, John Gaspard, a Swiss medalist, the nephew and scholar of John Melchior M., born at Frauenfeld in 1733. In 1759, he visited Paris for improvement, and at the death of his uncle he was appointed to succeed him in the mint at Berne. Among his best medals, are those of Catherine II., Stanislaus II., and the Count de Caylus.

MOFFEI, C. F., an obscure engraver, by whom there is an indifferent etching of the Death of St. Francis, signed *C. F. Moffei fecit.*

MOGALLI, Como, or Cosimo, an Italian designer and engraver, born at Florence in 1667. He was instructed in the elements of design by Gio. Battista Foggini, a Florentine sculptor; but he afterwards applied himself to engraving. He engraved a part of the plates for the book of Florentine Antiquities, published at Florence in 1724, by Thomas Dempster. He was employed in conjunction with Antonio Lorenzini, and others, to engrave the plates for the *Museo Florentino*. He also engraved some plates after Santo di Titi, F. Perucci, and others. He died about 1730. The following are from pictures in the Florentine gallery, and are among his best works:

The Holy Family reposing; *after Albano*; circular. Apollo and Marsyas; *after Guercino*. Magdalene carried up to Heaven by an Angel; *after Guido Cagnacci*. The Holy Family; *after Correggio*. Eve presenting the Apple to Adam; *after Gab. Cagliari*. Adam and Eve driven from Paradise; *do*. Christ and the Disciples at Emmaus; *after Palma*. The Marriage of St. Catherine; *after Fra. Bartolomeo*. David and Bathsheba; *after Salviati*. The Annunciation; *after Andrea del Sarto*. The Adoration of the Shepherds; *after Titian*. A Bacchanalian Dance; *do*. Philip II., King of Spain; *do*.

MOGALLI, Niccolo, was the son of the preceding, born at Florence in 1723. Losing his father at a tender age, he was placed with Francesco Conti, to learn the elements of design, and he was afterwards instructed in engraving by G. D. Picchianti. About 1750, he went to Rome, where he was employed by the Abbé Winckelmann to engrave from the designs of Casanova, the plates for his work entitled, *Monumenti antichi, inediti, spiegati et illustrati da Giovanni Winkelmann, Roma*, 1767. He also engraved some plates for the Florentine gallery, and for the Cabinet of Portici.

MOHEDANO, Antonio, an eminent Spanish historical painter in fresco, born at Antequera, in Andalusia, in 1561. He studied under the celebrated Pablo de Céspedes, at Cordova, but preferring *fresco* to oil, he became one of the most eminent artists of his country at that time. He followed the practice of his master, and designed every thing after nature; he first meditated, next studied his composition, and then proceeded to trace his figures after nature, or from models arranged by himself, and with the assistance of the *lay figure*. Hence, he was happy in his compositions, learned in the art of contrasting groups, and gave fine character and grandeur to the forms of his figures. He ornamented his works with *grotesques* in the manner of Giovanni da Udine, in the Vatican. He distinguished himself by many works for the churches and convents at Seville, particularly by four large pictures in the convent S. Francisco de Seville, and some other works painted in the same place, in conjunction with Alonso Vasquez. He also painted some excellent works in the cathedral at Lucena. He died in that city in 1625. He was a poet, as well as a painter, and specimens of his poetic talents may be found in a work published by Pedro Espinosa, in 1605, entitled *Flores de poetas ilustres de Espana*.

MOI, Peter van. See Mol.

MOIETTA, Vincenzio, a reputable painter, who, according to Morigia, was a native of Caravaggio, and flourished at Milan about 1500. He painted some pictures for the churches, but more for the collections.

MOINE, François le, an eminent French painter, born at Paris in 1688. He showed an early inclination for art, and studied with Louis Galloche, under whom he made great progress, and drew the first prize in the Academy, which entitled him to go to Italy with the king's pension, but the difficulties of the times prevented his enjoying this advantage; and his parents, being in indigent circumstances, had not the means of supporting him abroad. But he studied with great assiduity the best works in his own country, and soon acquired the distinguished reputation of being the most promising young artist of his country. He was admitted a member of the Academy at Paris in 1718, on which occasion he painted his picture of Hercules and Cacus. This picture, though not one of his best performances, is remarkable for correctness of design, and materially added to his reputation. In 1724, he accompanied his friend and patron M. Berger, to Italy, and during a short residence at Rome, he seems to have been more captivated with the splendor of Pietro da Cortona and the celerity of Lanfranco, than the sublime talents of Michael Angelo, or the elegance and grace of Raffaelle. On his return to Paris, he was chosen to paint the cupola of the chapel of the Virgin in St. Sulpice, where he distinguished himself by his elegance of grouping, and the beauty and freshness of his coloring. This work, which occupied him three years, established his reputation, and he was appointed by Louis XV. to paint the ceiling of the grand saloon at Versailles, where he represented the Apotheosis of Hercules, one immense fresco, deemed the largest in Europe, being sixty-four by fifty-four feet. It consists of nine compartments, and occupied him four years. At the death of Louis de Boullongne, in 1734, he was appointed painter to the King, with a large salary. Notwithstanding this distinction, and the liberal patronage he met with, he fell into a state of melancholy and despondency, and was afflicted with a monomania, so that the officers of justice were in search of him to convey him to prison. His friends endeavored in vain to console him and dissipate his fears. One day, being called upon by his old patron, M. Berger, for the purpose of inviting him to his country seat, he imagined the day of his doom had come, and seizing his sword, he stabbed himself in several places, and fell dead as his friend entered the apartment, in 1737.

MOINE, or MOYNE, Francis le, a French engraver, who flourished at Paris about 1660. In conjunction with Berain and Chaveau, he was employed in designing and engraving the ornaments of painting and sculpture in the gallery of Apollo in the Louvre. His plates are executed with the graver in a neat, but rather stiff and formal style.

MOINE, Jean le, a French painter, born at Paris in 1635, and died in 1713. He painted history and portraits, but did not acquire much distinction.

MOINE, Le, a French painter, born at Rouen in 1740; died in 1803. He studied under Descamps, and executed a number of good works in his native city, among which is the Apotheosis of Corneille, in the vault of the Theatre des Arts.

MOINE, Pierre Antoine le, was born at Paris in 1605, and died in 1665. He excelled in flower and fruit pieces, especially the latter, which were admired for their tasteful design, fresh and beautiful coloring, and natural expression.

MOINE. See Moyne.

MOITTE, Pierre Etienne, a French engraver, born at Paris in 1722. He studied under P. F. Beaumont, and engraved quite a number of plates of portraits and various subjects, executed with the graver, in a clear neat style. His principal works are the plates he engraved for the Dresden Gallery and the Cabinet of Count Bruhl. He was chosen an academician in 1770, upon the presentation of his portrait of Restout. He had two daughters, Angelique Rose, and Elizabeth Melanie, who practised the art with success. He died about 1780. The following are among his best portraits:

PORTRAITS.

J. Restout, Painter to the King; *after de Latour* Charles John Francis Hénault, Historian; *after St. Aubin.*

SUBJECTS AFTER VARIOUS MASTERS.

The Holy Family; *after Andrea del Sarto;* Dresden collection. Another Holy Family; *after F. Vanni;* do. The Marriage of St. Catherine; *after Correggio.* Christ praying on the Mount of Olives; *do.* A Halt of Travelers; *after Wouwerman.* The Watering-place; *do.* The Dutch Cook; *after Gerard Douw.* The Fish Woman; *do.* Æneas saving his Family from the Burning of Troy; *after M. Corneille.* The Triumph of Venus; *after Boucher.* The Pleasures of Summer; *do.* Several Prints after *Greuze, Cochin,* and other masters.

MOITTE, François Auguste, a French engraver, the son and scholar of Pierre Etienne M., was born at Paris in 1748. His plates are distinguished for neatness of the graver, and delicacy of the execution. He engraved a number of plates after Greuze and other masters, among which are a set of twenty-four plates entitled *Divers habillements, suivant la coutume d'Italie, dessinés d'aprés nature, par J. B. Greuze, ornès de fonds, par J. B. Lallemande, et gravês par A. Moitte, d'aprés les dessins tirés du cabinet de l'Abbé Gougenot;* also a pair, Poetry and Painting, *after Greuze;* and a Flemish Repast, *after Jordaens,* his best plate.

MOITTE, Jean Baptiste Philibert, the brother of the preceding, was an able professor of architecture in the school at Dijon. He gained considerable distinction for his plan of a cathedral and also for one of a triumphal arch, which drew a prize in 1792. He died in 1808.

MOITTE, Jean Guillaume, an eminent French sculptor, the brother of the preceding, born at Paris in 1747. He early manifested a strong inclination for design, which was increased by the meetings of artists, held frequently at his father's house. At the request of Pigalle, he was placed under that master, and devoted all his leisure hours to studying the living model. After the death of his instructor, he entered the atelier of Jean Baptist Lemoyne. He drew several prizes at the Academical exhibitions, and finally, in 1768, carried off the grand prize of sculpture, for his statue of David with the head of Goliah, which entitled him to the royal pension, and he immediately departed for Italy. On arriving at Rome he abandoned his former ideas of the art, and proceeded at once to the study of the antique. By a five years' course of assiduous study in the metropolis of art, he acquired a correct and exquisite taste of design; and his works are characterized by elegance of the forms, beauty of proportions, appropriate choice of draperies, and great variety of expression. In 1773 he returned to France, and was received by amateurs and artists with great enthusiasm. For some time after his return, Moitte was engaged in designing figures for M. Auguste, goldsmith to the King, which were greatly admired. Associated to the Academy in 1783, for a statue of a Priest, he was soon employed in many important works among which were a Vestal scattering the Holy Water, for M. Joubert; a statue of Arian. for Mr. Brackford; the bas-reliefs of many of the Parisian Barriéres; and his admirable statue of Cassini. In 1794 a prize was offered for the finest model for a bronze statue of Rousseau, to be cast in bronze. Moitte was the successful competitor, and he gained the prize, but the project was never completely executed. After the Battle of Marengo, he was commissioned to execute the mausoleum of Gen. Desaix, which is lacking in vigor, but has been greatly admired for its elegance, grace, and finished execution. His statues of Moses and Numa, and the Historical Muse, in the court of the Louvre, are in a more elevated style. Moitte was a member of the Legion of Honor. He died in 1810.

MOL, Jan Baptist van, a Dutch painter, of whom little is known. He was a cotemporary and imitator of Rembrandt, and for this reason his works are highly prized.

MOL, Peter van, a Flemish painter, born at Antwerp in 1590. He studied in the school of Rubens, and painted many excellent works for the churches in Flanders and Brabant, in the style of his master. In the cathedral at Antwerp is his Adoration of the Magi, beautifully executed in the manner of Rubens. Another fine picture by him, representing Christ after the Crucifixion, with the Marys, Joseph of Arimathea, and St. John, adorns the gallery of the Louvre. He painted many easel pictures of large size, in the manner of Rubens, which, though they are but coarse imitations, have frequently been sold as originals by that great master, and it may be safely affirmed that of the many paintings sold in the United States as the works of Rubens, not one of them is genuine; because his time was wholly occupied by church and state, and princes, and it is known where all his works are to be found.

MOLA, Pietro Francesco, an eminent painter, born, according to Passeri, at Lugano, in the diocese of Como, in 1612, and died in 1668; though, according to Pascoli, Mariette, and Desaix, at Coldré in the Milanese territory, in 1621, and died in 1666. Others place his birth in 1609, and death in 1665. He was the son of an architect, who first placed him under the instruction of Giuseppe Cesari d'Arpino, at Rome, with whom he continued several years. He afterwards went to Bologna, studied with Albano, and became his most distinguished disciple. He did not however, adopt the principles of either of his masters, but sought a bolder style of design and a more vigorous coloring. The works of Guercino were particularly the objects of his admiration, and he was ambitious of acquiring the energy and powerful effect of his chiaro-scuro, and the magic of his relief. Aiming at a fresher and more harmonious style of coloring than found in the works of Guercino, he went to Venice, where he assiduously studied the works of Titian, Tintoretto, Bassano, and Veronese. From all these, he formed a charming style peculiar to himself, at once bold, vigorous, elegant and graceful, which spread his fame throughout Italy. He returned to Rome in the pontificate of Innocent X., by whom he was immediately employed in several considerable works, particularly in a chapel of the church del Gesu, where he painted in fresco, St. Peter delivered from prison by the Angel, and the Conversion of St. Paul, which gained him great reputation. He was not less patronized by Pope Alexander VII., for whom he painted his most celebrated work of Joseph making himself known to his Brethren, in the pontifical palace of Monte Cavallo, for which he received the highest commendation and a noble reward. He painted many other works in the churches at Rome. He also painted at Milan, where, in the church of S. Maria della Vita, are two of his most admired performances, representing St. John in the Wilderness, and St. Paul the Hermit; these works are designed with a dignity and correctness worthy of the Caracci, and in the latter he introduced a noble landscape, resembling that in the famed St. Peter Martyr, by Titian. Besides the many fresco works he executed for the churches, he painted many pictures in oil, both of historical subjects and landscapes, which are to be found in the private collections in Italy. Lanzi says that, "after having diligently studied coloring at Venice, he attached himself to the school of the Caracci, but more particularly to Albano; he never equaled his master in fresco, though he had a bolder tone of coloring, greater invention, and more vigor of subject." Although Mola reached a distinguished rank as an historical painter, he is still more esteemed for his admirable landscapes, to which his genius and inclination seem to have particularly directed him. His scenery is generally solemn and sublime, but where his sites are more pleasing and extensive, they are always marked with a grandeur which is hardly surpassed in the best productions of the Caracci or Domenichino. His touch is firm and free, his coloring usually vigorous and glowing; his figures are introduced so as to represent subjects of history or fable, and with such taste, intelligence, and grace, that it is doubted whether they were executed by himself or Albano. He died suddenly at Rome in the prime of life, as he was preparing to set out for Paris, where he had been invited by the King of France, and appointed his painter, with a liberal pension. He executed a few spirited and masterly etchings, as follows:

The Virgin suckling the infant Jesus; *after his own design*. The Holy Family, with Angels; this plate was first etched by Mola, and was afterwards finished with the graver by a clumsy, unskillful hand. Joseph discovering himself to his Brethren; this print has been sometimes attributed to *Carlo Maratti*. The Holy Family, with Angels presenting Flowers to the infant Jesus; *after Albano*.

MOLA, Giovanni Battista, or Jean Baptiste. This artist is said by some authors to be a brother of Pietro Francesco M.; but, according to Malvasia, Orlandi, and others, he was a Frenchman, and born about 1620. This opinion is followed by Lanzi, and adopted by D'Argenville and other French writers. At all events, he studied under Simon Vouet at Paris, afterwards went to Bologna, and became the scholar of Albano, with whom he continued many years, and accompanied him to Rome. Boschini says he resided for some time "with Pietro Francesco Mola, at Venice, where they copied a vast work by Paul Veronese for Cardinal Bichi." Lanzi says "he displayed surprising skill in drawing rural scenes and trees; and being preferred by many in this branch to Albano, he often added landscapes to his master's figures, and occasionally adapted figures to his own landscapes, very beautiful, in Albano's style, but without his softness." While at Rome, he studied carefully the works of the best masters, particularly those of Annibale Caracci, in the Farnesian Gallery. Among his best performances at Rome are four large landscapes in the Palazzo Salviati, painted so entirely in the charming style of Albano that they are universally taken for the works of that master. There is an exquisite Repose in Egypt by him, in the collection of the Marchesi Rinuccini, at Florence. Though he is said to have been far inferior to the other more famous Mola in style, dignity, taste, and coloring, yet his works are rare, being doubtless attributed to his namesake and to Albano. He executed a few spirited etchings, among which is one of Cupid in a Car, drawn by two little Loves; *after Albano.* Malvasia says he died at Rome in 1678, but Oretti finds his death inscribed in the Register of the Chiesa della Lame, where he was buried in 1661, aged 45; and Zani says that he was born in 1616, and died in 1661, which accords with Oretti.

MOLENAER, Cornelius, a Flemish landscape painter, surnamed the *Cross-Eyed*, was born at Antwerp in 1540. His talents were unquestioned; his facility was so great that he could paint a large landscape in a single day; and he was highly esteemed by his cotemporaries: but his intemperate habits reduced him to so low a condition that he was obliged to paint the backgrounds in the pictures of other artists, at the miserable pittance of thirty sous per day! He at length sunk so low in vice as to work for six or seven sous per day, and subsequently died, at Antwerp, in obscurity and disgrace.

MOLIGNY, C. D, a French engraver, who flourished at Paris about 1760, and engraved several portraits of distinguished persons, principally *after Cochin.*

MOLINAER, John or Jan. There were several Dutch artists of the name of Molinaer or Molenaar, whose history and subjects are so mixed up by the Dutch writers themselves, that is difficult to distinguish them. They were probably relations, if not brothers, and flourished at Amsterdam about the same period. John Molinaer is said to have painted drolls and merry-makings, ingeniously composed, and colored with a richness and harmony approaching the admirable productions of Adrian van Ostade, though greatly inferior to him in the beauty of penciling, and the expression of the heads. The name of J. Molinaer, and sometimes it is spelled *Molenaar*, is frequently found on paintings, not only of the subjects above attributed to him, but on winter pieces, with figures skating, and practising other winter amusements, which are spirited and faithful representations of winter scenes in Holland.

MOLINAER, Nicholas Miense or Mins, a Dutch painter, born at Amsterdam in 1627, and died there in 1686. He painted interiors of farmhouses, and rustic sports and employments, admirably depicted, in a manner approaching Adrian van Ostade.

MOLINAER, Nicholas, a Dutch painter, born at Amsterdam in 1629. He also painted landscapes in the manner of Ostade.

MOLINAER, Jan Miense, a Dutch painter, whose subjects are the same as those of John Molinaer, and who is probably the same artist.

MOLINARETTO, Il. See Dalle Piane.

MOLINARI, Gio. Battista, a Venetian painter, was born, according to Melchiori, in 1636. He studied under Pietro Vecchia, and was a good artist.

MOLINARI, Antonio, was a son of the preceding, but lost his father at a tender age. He studied under Antonio Zanchi, but, according to Lanzi, almost wholly renounced the maxims he had learned, and struck out into a style of his own. He acquired considerable reputation, and executed some excellent works for the churches at Venice and other places, though he wrought with an unequal hand. Lanzi says his best works, "as the History of Hosea, in the Corpus Domini at Venice, he displays a style no less solid than pleasing, which equally satisfies the judgment and the eye. There is a study of both design and expression; ample beauty of forms; richness of drapery; with a taste, and a harmony of coloring not surpassed by any artist of the time." He was employed at Venice in 1727.

MOLINARI, Giovanni. This eminent painter was born at Savigliano in 1721, and died in 1793. He studied under Cavaliere Beaumont, and executed some works for the churches at Turin and other places, which gained him great reputation. On his death, he was honored with an elegant eulogium by the Baron Vernazza, which will confer lasting honor on his memory. He also painted history and portraits with great reputation. Lanzi says that, owing to his naturally timid, reserved, and modest character, he did not paint history as much as he ought. His historical works are mostly in the collections at Turin. Among his best portraits was one of the king, which was highly applauded, and has been frequently copied.

MOLITOR, Martin von, an eminent German painter and engraver, born at Vienna in 1759, and died there in 1812. He studied under Christian Brand, and painted landscapes, both in oil and water-colors, which were greatly admired, and much sought after by connoisseurs and others. He also executed a considerable number of etchings, after his own designs, marked M.M. Bartsch gives a list of fifty-two pieces by him, which Nagler has copied into his Lexicon. Bartsch engraved some plates after his designs, which are marked M. M. inv., *A. Btch, f.*; also Gabet, marked M.M.d.G.S., signifying *Martin von Molitor delineavit*, (François) *Gabet sculpsit.*

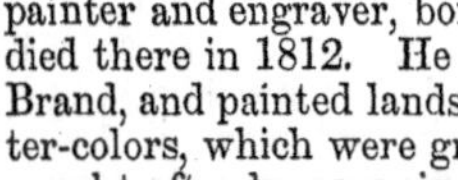

MOLYN, Peter, the Elder, a Flemish painter and engraver, born at Haerlem about 1600. He painted landscapes in a very pleasing style. His pictures are well designed, his coloring pleasing and natural, his penciling light and free, but delicate, his perspective and distances portrayed with fidelity and airy gracefulness, his fore-grounds are enriched with ruins or edifices in a picturesque manner. He executed a few spirited etchings after his own designs, erroneously attributed to his son Peter Molyn, called Tempesta. They are generally marked with his name, the P. and M. formed into a monogram, as above. Among others are the following: A set of four Landscapes;

inscribed *P. de Molyn, fecit et exc.* 1626. Another set of four Landscapes; *P. Molyn, fecit.* 1626. Several Candle-light pieces and dark subjects.

MOLYN, Peter, the Younger, called by the Italians first Il Tempesta, next Cavaliere Tempesta, and last Pietro Mulier, was the son of the preceding, born at Haerlem in 1637. He studied under his father, but having seen some of the hunting pieces of Francis Snyders, he applied himself with great assiduity to imitate the manner of that master, and with such success that his pictures were scarcely less esteemed than those of Snyders. He traveled through Flanders and Holland, to observe the works of the best Flemish and Dutch masters, and soon changed his subjects for sea pieces. At the age of twenty-five he went to Rome, where he soon obtained great reputation for his surprising pictures of sea-storms, which acquired him the name of Il Tempesta. His compositions of this class are executed with such wonderful truth and force, that they inspire the beholder with real terror. The devoted ships are seen overtaken by the tempest and darkness, fired by lightning, or driving helpless before the demons of the storm, now rising on the mountain waves, and again submerged in the abyss of the ocean, or splitting on the rocks, while all on board are stricken with horror and dismay. At Rome, he changed his religion from Calvinism to Popery, which, together with his great talents, recommended him to the nobility, and secured him the friendship of Count Bracciano, who became his patron. At length his commissions became so numerous that he called in the assistance of a young Roman artist, who in consequence was called *Tempestino*, whose sister, a beautiful woman, became the wife of Molyn. At Rome, he not only painted storm-pieces, but huntings and animals, for which purpose he kept a great variety of them about his house. He also painted landscapes with equal celebrity, in some of which he showed himself a not unworthy follower of Claude Lorraine in invention, enriching them with a great variety of scenery, hills, lakes, and beautiful edifices, although far behind that inimitable master in tone of color and finishing. At length he grew rich, and received the title of Cavaliere, and a golden chain from the pope. Having spent many years at Rome, he received the most flattering invitations to visit Genoa, whither he proceeded, met with an honorable reception, and found abundant employment. Here a fatal passion blasted all his prospects, and from an enviable height of public esteem and admiration, he sunk into the abyss of guilt, infamy, and remorse.—Having become deeply enamored of a Genoese lady, he left no art untried to seduce her, but failing in this he proposed to marry her, though it was well known that he had a wife at Rome.—When this objection was urged by the lady and her friends, he was exceedingly mortified, and resolved secretly to put his wife out of the way. For this purpose, he wrote her an affectionate letter, desiring her to come to him at Genoa, and murdered her by means of the very messenger he had sent to accompany her, an hired assassin. His crime did not long escape the vigilant eye of justice; he was arrested on suspicion, and so many circumstances appearing to confirm his guilt, he was condemned to death; but by the powerful intercession of the nobility, and in consideration of his extraordinary abilities, his sentence was commuted to imprisonment for life, and he probably never would have been released, but for a critical accident. When Louis XIV. bombarded Genoa, and the city was in danger of being burned, the prisons were thrown open, and Tempesta seized the opportunity to escape to Piacenza, after a confinement of sixteen years. From this affair he was nicknamed *Pietro Mulier* or *De Mulieribus*, (wife or mistress). He passed the remainder of his days at Parma, Bergamo, Piacenza, and Milan, where his works are numerous, especially in the latter city, and held in the highest estimation. During his long confinement, he wrought diligently, and executed many of his best works; indeed, his pictures of storms painted at that time, which were his favorite subjects, seem to have acquired additional gloom from the horrors of his dungeon. Tempesta was the first at Rome to decorate his landscapes with battles and skirmishes, which he did with great spirit and effect. He died in 1701. Balkema, differing from all authors of credit, says he was born in 1643, and died in 1699.

MOMBASILIO, Cavaliere, an eminent portrait painter of Turin, who flourished there in 1675. Little is known of him, except that his splendid portraits are frequently met with at Turin and elsewhere.

MOMBELLI, Luca, a painter of Brescia, who according to Orlandi, studied under Alessandro Bonvicino, in whose style he painted with considerable reputation. Lanzi says that after a time he changed his style, and by adopting too great delicacy of manner, his productions became somewhat tame and feeble. He was living in 1553.

MOMMERS, Hendrick, a Dutch painter, born at Haerlem in 1623. After studying in his own country, he went to Rome for improvement, where he was called by the Bentivogli Society *Meleager*, from his hunting pieces of the wild boar. He painted a variety of subjects, as Italian markets, with peasants; hunting pieces; landscapes, with figures and animals, seldom without an Ass. He also painted sea-ports, which might easily be taken for the works of Weeninx. His coloring is warm and harmonious, his touch vigorous and clear, and his pictures have a pleasing effect. After his return to Holland, he acquired considerable reputation, and instructed several scholars, among whom were Brackenbourg, Thierry Maes, and Bernard van Schendel. He signed his pictures sometimes with his initials, H. M., and sometimes with his name. Balkema mentions an artist of this name, who, he says, was a scholar of Karel du Jardin, went to Italy, and painted the same subjects; but says he was born at Haerlem in 1650, and died in 1708. He was doubtless the same painter.

MOMPER, or MOMPERT, Joos or Jodocus, a Flemish painter, born at Antwerp in 1580. It is not known with whom he studied, but as his manner differs from that of any other painter of his country, he must have founded his style from a close observation of nature. He painted mountainous landscapes in a bold, free style, and appears to have taken his views from the romantic scenery of Switzerland, rather than from the confined prospects of his own country. Contrary to the usual style of the Flemish artists, his works have nothing of the minute and precise finishing so much admired in the works of Breughel and Savery. His pencil is broad and facile, his coloring clear and of an agreeable effect, though in the forms of his trees and mountains there is occasionally an appearance of stiffness and formality. His landscapes often show an immense tract of country, and the imagination is agreeably amused with the vast extent of the prospect, which is admirably conducted. He was an unequal painter; but his best works are much admired, and admitted into the choice collections. His pictures were frequently decorated with figures by the elder Teniers, Francks, and John Breughel. Vandyck painted his portrait among the eminent artists of his country. Momper etched a few plates of landscapes from his own designs, as well as his own portrait, *after Vandyck*. They are executed in a free, spirited style, and are very scarce.

MONA, or MONNA, Domenico, a painter of Ferrara, born in 1550, and a disciple of Giuseppe Mazzuoli, called Il Bastaruolo. Baruffaldi read on his tomb, Domenico Mona, though he is variously called by writers Mona, Monna, Moni, and Monio. After studying the various professions of law, medicine, and theology, he attached himself to painting, in which he became eminent, and executed an extraordinary number of works for the churches and public edifices of Ferrara. His earliest productions were indifferent, but he applied himself with diligence to correct these faults, by studying the works of the best masters. Lanzi says he possessed fervor and richness of imagination, was learned in design, and wrought with a rapid hand. There is a surprising inequality in his works, and in viewing his best productions, works of a high order, as the Birth of the Virgin and the Nativity of our Saviour, in S. Maria in Vado; the Deposition from the Cross, in the Cathedral; and the Entombment, at the Servi, it appears unaccountable that, with the possession of such powers, he could be so negligent of his fame as to expose to public view the mediocre productions which form the majority of his works. Lanzi attributes this to an occasional derangement of his mind, to which he at length became a victim; in a fit of insanity, he slew a courtier of the Cardinal Aldobrandini, and ended his days in banishment from his native place. This, however, was by some attributed to enmity. He sought refuge at Modena, and then at Parma, where he is said to have afterwards painted some of his best works. Orlandi highly extols two of his pictures, representing the Conversion and Martyrdom of St. Paul, in the church of S. Paolo at Ferrara. He died in 1602.

MONACO, Pietro, an ingenious Italian engraver, born at Belluno in 1720. He visited Rome and other Italian cities, after which he settled at Venice, and soon gained encouragement. He was appointed Inspector of the Mosaics of St. Marco, and held that office until his death, about 1804. His plates possess considerable merit. Among them are a collection of fifty-five prints, published in 1743, engraved after the finest pictures in the Venetian collections, and entitled *Raccolta di stampe copiate da gli originali*, folio. In 1763 he published a similar work, containing one hundred and twelve plates. His plates are quite unequal in merit. Among them are the following:

PORTRAITS.

Giovanni Battista Tiepolo; *after a picture by himself* Jacopo Tatti, called Sansovino, Sculptor; *after Titian.*

VARIOUS SUBJECTS.

Tobit restoring his Father's Sight; *after Dom. Feti.* The Adulteress before Christ; *after P. Veronese.* The Nativity; *after Seb. Ricci.* The Murder of the Innocents; *after Giulio Carpioni.* The Last Supper; *after Pittoni.* Lot and his Daughters; *after P. Liberi.* Christ conducted to Mount Calvary; *after Gio. Bat. Tiepolo.* Christ with the Disciples at Emmaus; *after Bellini.* The Presentation in the Temple; *after Anto. Balestra.*

MONALDI, a scholar of Andrea Lucatelli, who flourished at Rome about 1700. He painted landscapes, in the style of his master. Lanzi says, "in some collections we find the works of Monaldi approaching those of Lucatelli, though somewhat inferior to them in design, coloring, and that natural grace which may be termed the *attic salt* of this mute poetry."

MONAMY, Peter, an English marine painter a native of Jersey, born about 1670. He was sent to London when young, and apprenticed to a house painter on London Bridge. He acquired considerable reputation in his time for his sea-pieces, which were compared to those of W. Vandervelde; but Stanley says, "the pictures of Monamy should not be named with those of W. Vandervelde; they are very inferior productions, and are seldom admitted into choice collections."

MONANNI, Monanno, a Florentine painter, who, according to Baldinucci, studied under Cristoforo Allori, and acquired considerable reputation as an historical painter. He went to Rome, where he seems to have resided a long time, and was admitted a member of the Academy of St. Luke, in 1652. In the church of S. Giovanni Decollato at Rome, is a picture by him, representing the Baptism of Christ.

MONCALVO Il. See Guglielmo Caccia.

MONCE, Ferdinand de la. This architect was born at Munich in 1678, of French parents. His father was Paul de la Monce, first painter and architect to the Elector of Bavaria. After acquiring the elements of design from his father, he went to Paris for improvement, and subsequently visited the principal cities of Italy. During his sojourn at Rome, the Duke d'Orleans commissioned him to purchase the celebrated cabinet of Queen Christina, then in the possession of the Duke de Bracciano. On returning to France, he stopped at Grenoble, and executed several works which gained him considerable reputation. In 1731 he concluded to marry, and settle at Lyons. Among his principal works are the Church des Chartreux, considered one of the finest edifices of that city; the gate of the church of St. Juste, highly esteemed by connoisseurs for its simple and elevated style; and the grand Hotel Dieu, which is reckoned his finest work. In his old age, when prevented by bodily infirmities from practising the art, he occupied his time in designing for the engravers.—Among these productions were the illustrations for Pope's Essay on Man, published by Lausanne. La Monce died at Lyons in 1753.

MONCHINO, Il. See Antonio dal Sole.

MONCORNET, Balthazar, a French engraver

born at Rouen, according to Nagler, in 1630, and died in 1670. Basan styles him one of the most indifferent engravers of his country; but France has produced many engravers inferior to him. He chiefly resided at Paris, where he engraved an incredible number of portraits and other subjects, and carried on quite an extensive commerce in prints. Nagler gives a long list of his portraits, which possess no interest aside from the persons they represent. His best prints are the Battle between Constantine and Maxentius, *after Rubens;* the Triumph of Constantine, *do.;* a set of goldsmith's ornaments; and a small etching of Rabbits, in imitation of the style of Hollar.

MONDINI, Fulgenzio, a Bolognese painter, and a pupil of Guercino. He acquired considerable reputation in his native city, and executed several frescos for the churches, the principal of which are two pictures in the Annunziata, representing the Angel appearing to Joseph in his Dream, and the Repose in Egypt; and in S. Antonio di Padoua, two subjects from the life of that saint, which are highly commended. He went to Florence where his merits recommended him to the patronage of the court, and was employed by the Marchesi Capponi to decorate their villas of Colonnata. He died in the flower of his life in 1664. Malvasia honors his memory in a long eulogy, in which he declares that he knew none more gifted with qualities that promised so much in that age, and he conjectures that, had his life been prolonged, he would have become the first fresco painter of his age.

MONEGRO, Juan Baptista, a Spanish sculptor and architect of Toledo, who flourished in the latter part of the 16th century. He studied under Alonso Berruguette, and afterwards visited Rome for improvement. On his return to Spain, he gained considerable encouragement and reputation. By order of Philip II., he made six statues for the porticos of the Escurial; and to him are attributed the architecture and sculpture of the Evangelists, which are in the gardens of the cloister of that edifice. Among his other works, is the chapel of the Sacrament at Toledo, erected in 1600.

MONERI, Giovanni, a Piedmontese painter, born at Visone, a small town near Acqui, in 1637. He studied in the school of Romanelli at Rome. He did not acquire any great distinction, but executed many good works for the churches in the provincial towns. In 1657, he returned to his native place, and was employed in the cathedral at Acqui, where he painted two frescos representing the Assumption of the Virgin and Paradise, in the style of his master, which were much commended. He executed other works for the churches in the neighboring cities, in which he continued to improve, exhibiting a greater copiousness of composition, a more correct design, a finer expression, and a stronger relief. One of his most esteemed works is a picture of the Presentation, in the church of the Capuchins at Acqui, executed at a more advanced period of his life. He was also employed in the churches at Genoa, Milan, and in their dependencies; also in several places in Piedmont. He died in 1714.

MONGEROUX, M. de, a French amateur engraver, who, for his amusement, etched a few plates, among which is a landscape with figures and animals, *after Casanova.*

MONI, J., an engraver who, according to Papillon, was a native of Lyons, and flourished about 1570. He was an eminent engraver on wood, and executed a set of plates from his own designs, for the *Bible History,* published at Lyons by Guillaume Rouille in 1570. He also copied the engravings on wood from the Bible, executed by Solomon Bernard, called *Little Bernard,* which copies were published at Lyons in 1570. He sometimes marked his plates with the initials of his name, J. M., and at others with the above monogram.

MONI, Louis de, a Dutch painter, born at Breda in 1698. He studied successively under van Kessel, Emanuel Biset, and Philip Vandyck. He painted small pictures, in which he endeavored to imitate the manner of Gerard Douw. His compositions are simple and animated, and deserving of high commendation. He understood the principles of light and shadow, and the harmony of color; and his handling is free, light, and firm. His pictures are occasionally found in the best collections in Holland. He died at Leyden in 1771.

MONICA. See Cavagni.

MONNICKS, or MONNIX, a Dutch painter, born at Bois-le-Duc in 1606. It is not known by whom he was instructed, but he went early to Rome for improvement, where he resided till advanced in life, and acquired great distinction. He designed everything from nature, and painted the most remarkable views in that capitol, as the Coliseum, the Columns of Trajan and Vespasian, the Campo Vaccino, the public fountains, and other noble edifices, ancient and modern. He embellished his pictures with numerous figures, representing people engaged in different occupations or amusements, sports, carnivals, or processions. He was a perfect master of perspective, and had an excellent knowledge of chiaro-scuro. His figures are well designed and grouped, though the airs and countenances partake somewhat of the Flemish school. His penciling is free, but delicate, and his coloring transparent. At Rome and throughout all Italy, his works were universally esteemed. His talents recommended him to the patronage of pope Urban VIII., in whose service he continued for thirteen years. His best works are entirely confined to Italy, as he did not return to Holland until upwards of seventy years of age; and though he painted a few perspective pieces afterwards, his powers had much declined. He died at Bois-le-Duc in 1686.

MONNOT, Pierre Etienne, a distinguished French sculptor, born at Besançon about 1660. He went to Italy early in life, and by studying the antique, assisted by the instruction of the best masters, he attained a high excellence in the art. In 1690 he was commissioned to execute the marble tomb erected to pope Innocent XI., in one of the side chapels of St. Peter's, which gained him so much reputation that he had plentiful encouragement. Among his principal works are two colossal statues of St. Peter and St. Paul, in St. John of Lateran. Monnot was employed by the Emperor Leopold, and by the Elector of Hesse, the latter of whom commissioned him to execute a number of copies after the finest antique statues, which are still to be seen in the palace and gardens at Cassel. He was ennobled by the pope; honored with the title of Cavaliere; and was one of the directors of the Academy of St. Luke. He died at Rome about 1730.

MONNOYER, John Baptiste, called Baptiste, an eminent Flemish fruit and flower painter, born at Lisle in 1635. It is not known under whom he studied, but he went to Antwerp, and at first devoted himself to historical painting, but afterwards, following the bent of his genius, he painted fruit and flowers, in which branch he acquired great fame. He went young to Paris, where the beauty of his works soon brought him into notice. In 1663, he was received into the Academy with distinction. He was employed in the royal palaces at Versailles, Trianon, Marly, and Meudon. At the invitation of Lord Montague, the English ambassador, he accompanied that nobleman to London, where he first displayed his talents in painting some of his choicest works, for the embellishment of Montague House, now the British Museum. During a residence of nearly twenty years, he found abundant employment, and executed a multitude of pictures which are now in the collections of the nobility and persons of distinction. He was much employed at Hampton Court, Windsor, and Kensington. His pictures are not so exquisitely finished as those of van Huysum, Rachel Ruysch, and Mignon, but his composition and coloring are in a bolder style. His flowers have a remarkable freedom and looseness, as well in the disposition as in the penciling, with a tone and brilliancy of coloring, that rivals nature herself. The disposition of his objects is surprisingly elegant and beautiful. A celebrated work of this artist is a looking-glass in Kensington palace, which is decorated with a garland of flowers, for Queen Mary II., who sat by him during the greater part of the time he was engaged in painting it. He also produced a few etchings after his own designs, representing vases of flowers, executed in a tasteful and spirited style; and about eighty prints were afterwards engraved by others after his designs, and published in a folio volume. He died in 1699.

MONNOYER, Anthony, called Young Baptiste, was the son and scholar of the preceding, whose subjects and style he imitated with considerable success, though his works are far inferior to those of his father in every respect.

MONODORUS. See Menodorus.

MONOSILIO, Salvatore, a Sicilian painter, born at Messina about 1700. He went to Rome and studied under Cav. Sebastiano Conca, whose style he adopted with great success. Lanzi says he very nearly approached him, both at Rome and in other places. His most esteemed productions at Rome are the ceiling in a chapel of S. Paolino della Regola, the Conversion of St. Paul, in the church of the Priests of the Mission, and other works at S. S. Quaranta, and in the Polacchi. At Piceno, where Conca was held in great estimation, Monosilio was also in high repute, and was employed both in public and private edifices. An altar-piece of St. Barnabas in the church of that saint, is highly commended. The time of his death is not known, though it is supposed he returned to Messina late in life.

MONSIAU, Nicolas Andre, a French historical painter, born at Paris in 1754. He was a scholar of Peyron, who is said to have been very fond of his pupil. Little is recorded of the circumstances of his life. In 1787 he was admitted to the Royal Academy, and exhibited his pictures of Alexander and Bucephalus, the Death of Cato Uticensis, and the Death of Phocion. His design was often incorrect, and his coloring defective; but his compositions were arranged with judgment; and although his abilities would never have ranked him among eminent historical painters, yet in conversation pieces he evinced considerable talent. Monsiau made many designs for book illustrations, particularly for the works of Delille. His pictures of St. Vincent de Paul, and Moliere reading the Tartuffe to Ninon l'Enclos, have been highly praised. Among his principal historical works, are Philoctetes in the Isle of Lemnos, exhibited in 1810; Alexander and Diogenes, exhibited in 1819, now in the chateau of Versailles; Ajax and Ulysses disputing for the Arms of Achilles, exhibited in 1827. Monsiau died in 1837.

MONSIGNORI, Francesco, a painter of Verona, born in 1455, and brought up in the school of Andrea Mantegna, by whose precepts he acquired a good taste for historical painting, as well as portraits. His talents procured him the patronage of the Marquis of Mantua, an excellent and learned critic, who employed him for several years. Lanzi says of this artist, that, "if he does not exhibit the beautiful forms and the purity of design so remarkable in the works of his master, he approaches nearer to the modern taste; his contours are full, his drapery less formal, and his coloring softer and more studied." He was a master of perspective, and in the Refectory of the Franciscans, is a picture of Christ, surrounded by the Apostles, in which the architecture produces a grand effect.

MONSIGNORI, Fra Girolamo, was a brother of the preceding, born at Verona about 1460.—When young, he became a monk of the order of the Dominicans. He executed several works for the church of his monastery. In the great Library of S. Benedetto, is a fine copy of the Last Supper of Leonardo da Vinci, by this artist, which, according to Lanzi, is considered the best ever executed of that miracle of art. He died in 1520.

MONT, Deodato del. See Delmont.

MONTAGNA, Bartolomeo, an old Italian painter, was a native of Vicenza, and studied under Andrea Mantegna. According to Lanzi there are many of his works in his native city, and some in Venice, which rank him at least among the chief of his cotemporaries. His subjects are sacred and scripture pieces. He is exact in his design, and skilful in his naked parts, and his coloring is fresh and warm. His cherubs are particularly pleasing and graceful, and in his altar-piece at the church of S. Michele at Vicenza, he has introduced architecture, which recedes from, and deceives the eye with a powerful illusion, sufficient of itself to have rendered him conspicuous. There are notices of him up to 1507.

BM. MONTAGNA, Benedetto, was a younger brother of Bartolomeo, with whom he is often confounded. He is said to have flourished at Vicenza about 1500, but Zani gives the inscriptions and dates on two of his pictures, 1524 and 1533. According to Ridolfi, he painted some works for the churches of Vicenza, so much in the style of Giovanni Bellini, that they might easily be mistaken for the works of that master. He is however, better known as an engraver, and though his prints are feeble and imperfect, both in design and execution, they are deserving of notice, as among the earliest specimens of the art in Italy. It is probable that the fame of the works of Albert Durer, at that time considered a wonder at Venice, encouraged him to attempt the art, then in its infancy in Italy. Marc' Antonio had made considerable progress, and successfully imitated some of Durer's prints at Venice, though he did not arrive at his zenith till some years after, at Rome. The prints of Montagna have a slight resemblance to the earliest and rudest engravings of Marc' Antonio. They are from his own designs, and usually marked with his name in full, but sometimes with his initials, B. M., on a tablet, and sometimes B. M., without the tablet. They are now very scarce, and their antiquity and scarceness renders them valuable to the collector of rare prints. The following are the principal:

The Virgin seated, holding the infant Jesus, St. John standing by her side, and St. Joseph below. In the background is a town, with a river and a bridge over it. A young Man sitting on a Rock. Venus punishing Cupid. The Rape of Europa. The Judgment of Midas. A naked Figure standing by a Tree. Two figures, an old man playing on the bag-pipes, and a young man on the violin. Three Women in a landscape, one of them taking a Child from a Tree, representing the Birth of Adonis. A landscape with a Cottage, and an old Man seated on a Bank. The Nativity, with St. Joseph at the Well; copied from Durer, and marked B. M. on a tablet. St. Anthony standing praying; marked B. M. Two Hunters observing a wounded Stag. Venus standing naked, holding a mirror in her hand. A River God seated on a Rock on the right, Cupid on the left. The Saviour standing in a landscape after his resurrection, a banner in his right hand and scroll in his left, with Jerusalem in the distance. A Woman, with two Children, and a Man, seated in a landscape. A Nymph with two Children and two Satyrs. The Holy Family seated near a Fountain. A River Goddess, with a winged Boy holding a Sphere; *in the British Museum.* The Sorceress; copy from Durer, marked B. M. An old Man in a turban, with a book in his hand, sitting on a Bank. Christ in the Manger, with the Ox and Ass near him, with the Virgin, St. Joseph, St. Catherine, and an Angel. The Repose in Egypt. St. Catherine. Christ showing himself to his Disciples, after his Resurrection; marked B. M.—The Saviour. The Virgin nursing the Infant; copy from Durer, marked B. M. The Satyr and his Family; three figures.

MONTAGNA, MARCO TULLIO, a Roman painter, who flourished in the pontificate of Clement VIII. He studied under Federigo Zuccaro, and assisted him in his works both at Rome and Turin. He painted both in oil and fresco, and executed a few works for the churches at Rome and elsewhere. Lanzi says "he painted at Rome in the church of S. Niccolo in Carcere, in the vaults of the Vatican, and in many other places, in a tolerable style, but nothing more."

MONTAGNA, IL, an eminent painter of sea-pieces, of whom little is known with certainty, except from his works. Lanzi says he was a native of Holland, and "left many works in Italy, especially at Rome and Florence, where he is sometimes mistaken for Tempesta, in the galleries and in the picture sales; but Montagna is more serene in his skies, and darker in his waves and the appearance of the sea." Malvasia says he was a Frenchman, calling him, Mons. Rinaldo della Montagne, and states that he was held in high esteem by Guido, for the excellence of his sea views. Felibien says he was a Venetian, and calls him Montagna di Venezia. There is a magnificent picture of the Deluge in the church of S. Maria Maggiore at Bergamo, in which the figures were inserted by Cav. Liberi, supposed to be by this artist, painted in 1668. Lanzi doubts its authenticity, as this Montagna is known to have died at Padua, and a MS. by a cotemporary author says he died there in 1644. Others confound him with Matthew Plattenberg, who styled himself in Italy *Plate Montagne*, but the style of Plattenberg was entirely different, besides, he did not reside in Italy many years, and died at Paris in 1660.

MONTAGNA, MATTHEW. See PLATTENBERG.

MONTAGNANA, JACOPO, an old Italian painter, a native of Padua, where he flourished in the zenith of his fame, from 1495 to 1508. Vasari and Ridolfi erroneously call this artist Jacopo Montagna. He is supposed to have studied with Giovanni Bellini at Venice. He was accounted by his townsmen the Apelles of his age. There are several of his works in the Episcopal palace at Padua particularly worthy of notice. They represent Christ risen from the dead, together with the portraits of all the Paduan Bishops, the busts of the Apostles, and several histories of their acts. Lanzi says they are executed with much elegance in chiaro-scuro. There is also a very extensive altar-piece at the Santo, with glowing colors, in the Venetian style, though in design and expression, it partakes more of the precise and formal principles of the Paduan school. There is also a celebrated picture by him in the Council Hall at Belluno. It is an immense production, representing Roman Histories. Lanzi says it so much resembles Andrea Mantegna, in composition, design, drapery, and expression, that at first view, one would be apt to attribute it to the pencil of that master. The following laudatory epigram is inscribed upon it:

Non hic Parrhasio, non hic tribuendus Apelli,
Hos licet auctores dignus habere labor.
Euganeus, vixdum impleto ter mense, Jacobus
Ex Montagnana nobile pinxit opus.

MONTAGU, a French engraver, who flourished about 1760. Little is known of him. He went to Rome, where he appears to have resided some time, and engraved several plates of the principal edifices and views in that metropolis.

MONTALTO. See DANEDI.

MONTANI, GIOSEFFO, a painter of Pesaro, born in 1641. According to Malvasia, he studied at Venice, where he flourished about 1678. He was an excellent landscape painter.

MONTANINI, PIETRO, called PETRUCCIO PERUGINO, a painter, born at Perugia in 1619. He first studied under Pietro Barsotti, and afterwards with Ciro Ferri. Lanzi says that, ambitious of the higher walks of art, he attempted the decoration of a church, but failing in this, he followed the natural bent of his genius, and restricted himself to landscape. He then studied under Salvator Rosa, whose style he imitated with great success, though his figures are more spiritedly than correctly drawn. He was nevertheless a pleasing painter, and his pictures were much sought after by foreigners. There is an abundance of his works in the collections at Perugia; there are some in the church of the Eremitani, which may be said to discover a Flemish style. He died in 1689.

MONTANO, IL. See DELLA MARCA.

MONTANO, GIO. BATTISTA, an Italian sculptor and architect, born at Milan about 1545. He was thrown upon his own resources early in life, but by great exertion he gained a knowledge of design and modeling. Visiting Rome in the pontificate of Gregory XIII., he soon became distinguished for his talents in sculpture. He gained great improvement by studying the antique. He practised the art with reputation at Rome for many years, and died in 1621. His scholar, J. B. Soria, published his designs after his death, under the title of *Architettura con diversi ornamenti cavati dall' antico*, Rome, 1684 and 1691.

MONTE, GIOVANNI DA, was a native of Cremona, and a scholar of Titian. He painted some works for the churches in his native city. Torri mentions him as one of the most distinguished artists who ornamented Milan. Lanzi says he was an excellent artist, and deserves to be better known. He flourished about 1580.

MONTELATICI, FRANCESCO, an Italian painter, supposed by some to have been a Pisan, and others, a Florentine, studied under Giovanni Bilivert at Florence, in whose style he at first painted; but Lanzi says he afterwards abandoned it, or rather blended it with that of Passignano. He was a fanciful and spirited designer, and a good colorist. He acquired considerable reputation, painted some for the churches, but more for private, and sometimes for royal collections. There is a very fine painting by this artist in the church of S. Simone at Florence, representing the history of St. Niccolo Vescovo, and another of the Fall of Lucifer, in the Teatini. He was invited to Inspruck, and appointed court painter, which office he held till his death, in 1661. He was surnamed Il Cecco Bravo, from his quarrelsome disposition.

MONTEMEZZANO, FRANCESCO, a painter of Verona, born about 1555. He studied under Paul Veronese, whose style he followed in the copiousness of his compositions, the airs of his heads, the beauty of his figures, and the splendor of his draperies; but his coloring in comparison with that of his master was languid and feeble. He nevertheless acquired great reputation, and was employed in several of the churches, and in the Ducal Palace. His picture of the Annunciation in the church of the Osservanti alla Vigna, at Venice, is highly commended. Another fine work by him, is Christ appearing to Mary Magdalene, in the church of San Giorgio, at Verona. He died in the prime of life in 1600.

MONTEN, DIETRICH, an eminent German painter, born at Dusseldorf in 1799. He showed from early youth a passion for depicting battles, and Homer, Tasso, and Ariosto, were his favorite authors. In order to acquire some practical military knowledge, he entered as a volunteer in the Prussian army for twelve months. At the expiration of his term of military service, he entered the Academy at Dusseldorf, and after studying two years in that institution, he went to Munich and placed himself under the instructions of Peter Hess. His talents attracted the attention of Cornelius, then at the head of the painters at Munich, who entrusted him with the execution of three of the frescos in the arcade of the Hofgarten, where he represented the Storming of the Turkish Entrenchments by the Bavarians, in 1717; the Battle of Arcis sur Aube, and the granting of the Bavarian Constitution by Maximilian Joseph in 1818. He painted many other large battle pieces representing the victories of his country, as well as many easel pictures of the same subjects, in which he is said to have displayed extraordinary spirit in the design and execution, with correct drawing and good coloring. His horses in particular were very spirited in their motions and attitudes. His faults were an occasional extravagance of action, and the want of necessary patience for elaborate modeling and uniform finish, some parts of his pictures being too sketchy and undefined.

MONTENAT, J., a French engraver on wood, who executed some cuts from the designs of Simon Vouet and others. Dumesnil mentions a print by him of the Virgin and Infant, inscribed *J. Montenat fecit.*

MONTEPULCIANO. See MOROSINI.

MONTEREAU, PIERRE DE, a French architect, who flourished under the reign of St. Louis, about the middle of the 13th century. He erected the Holy chapel at Vincennes, the Refectory, the Dormitory, the Chapter-house, and the chapel Notre Dame des Pres. These were all in the Gothic style, but distinguished for beauty of proportions and delicacy of ornament. His master-piece, however, was the Sainte Chapelle at Paris, commenced in 1245, and finished in three years. De Montereau was a man of learning, and was highly esteemed in his day. He died in 1266, and was buried in the chapel built by him in S. Germain des Pres; his portrait was carved on the tomb, with a rule and compass in his hand.

MONTERO, DE ROXAS, JUAN DE, a Spanish painter, born at Madrid in 1613. He studied under Pedro de las Cuevas, and then went to Italy to improve himself, and founded his style on that of Caravaggio, many of whose works he copied. On his return to Madrid, he acquired considerable reputation by the novelty of his style, and was much employed in the churches and convents.—Palomino highly commends several of his works, particularly the Assumption of the Virgin in the church of the Collegio de Atocha; the Angel appearing to St. Joseph, in San Juan de Alarcon; and the Destruction of Pharaoh's Host in the Red Sea, in the sacristy of the convent de la Merced. He died at Madrid in 1683.

MONTERO, DON LORENZO, a Spanish painter, born at Seville in 1656. He excelled in architecture, landscapes, fruit and flowers, which he painted in distemper, and was thus employed in decorating some of the churches at Seville and Madrid, especially in the Retiro at Seville. His works have mostly perished, but there are some traces of his skill in ornamental design in the church of St. Jerome, at Madrid. He was not equally successful in oil painting, and seldom practised it. His only work in oil worthy of notice is a portrait of Philip V., dated 1701. He died at Madrid in 1710.

MONTEVARCHI, IL, an Italian painter, so called from the place of his nativity. He was a scholar of Pietro Perugino, and executed some works for the churches of his own country, out of which Lanzi says he is unknown.

MONTFORT. See BLOCKLANDT.

MONTI, FRANCESCO, called IL BRESCIANO DELLE BATTAGLIE, a painter of Brescia, born in 1646. He first studied under Pietro Ricci, and afterwards with Borgognone, whose subjects and manner he adopted. He painted horses and battles, designed and executed with great spirit, but much inferior to Borgognone in point of coloring. He acquired considerable distinction, was called Il Bresciano Battaglie, or the Brescian Battle-painter, and was much employed for the collections at Rome, Genoa, and Parma. He settled at Parma, where he opened a school, and exerted a marked influence on the school of Parma. Lanzi says he was employed by the court, and painted for the churches as well as for individuals; and that his works are numerous, but in many collections they do not appear under his name, but are attributed to the school of Borgognone. He had a son whom he instructed in the art, and who painted similar subjects. He died, according to Orlandi, in 1712, but Zani says in 1703.

MONTI, FRANCESCO, called BOLOGNESE, a painter born at Bologna in 1685. He studied under Giovanni Gioseffo dal Sole. Lanzi says he was endowed by nature with an enthusiasm for ample and copious subjects. On leaving his master, he was patronized by the Count Ranuzzi, for whom he painted one of his finest pictures, representing the Rape of the Sabines. He was afterwards employed at the court of Turin, where he painted the Triumph of Mordecai—a copious composition, highly commended by Crespi. He also executed many oil paintings for the churches, as well as for different collections, at Turin, Bologna, and other places. Lanzi says, "his surprising merit is to be sought for in his frescos, particularly at Brescia, where he fixed his residence. He also executed many pieces for the adjacent cities, which are applauded for the fertility of his genius, and the masterly style of his coloring." He also decorated the palaces of many noble houses, on a very extended scale, particularly of the Martinengo, Avogadro, and the Barussi. There are many of his works in the churches and other edifices of Bologna, the most admired of which are Christ with the Disciples at Emmaus, at the Osservanti; the Virgin in Glory, St. Barbara and St. Filippo Neri, in the Madonna di Galeria; and the Martyrdom of St. Fidele, at the Cappuccini. He died in 1768.

MONTI, ELEONORA, was a daughter of Francesco Monti, of Bologna, born in 1727. She was instructed in the art by her father, and painted history, and especially portraits, with great ability. Lanzi says her portraits are held in high esteem, and that she received constant commissions from the nobility.

MONTI, GIOVANNI BATTISTA, a painter, born at Genoa about 1610. According to Soprani, he was the son of a poor mendicant, and, when a boy, exhibited an uncommon disposition for the art, by sketching rude designs of what he saw on the walls of buildings, which attracted the attention of a Genoese nobleman, who took him under his protection, and placed him under Luciano Borzone, with whom he made such rapid progress as to surpass his instructor. He became eminent in his profession, painted history with reputation, but was chiefly distinguished for his excellence in portraits; and he painted many of the principal personages of his country. He died in the great plague of 1657.

MONTI, GIO. GIACOMO, a Bolognese painter and architect. Lanzi, in his Index, places his birth in 1692, but says that he wrought in concert with Baldassare Bianchi, who died in 1679. He was undoubtedly born in the first half of the 17th century. He studied under Agostino Mitelli, and was an eminent painter of perspective and architecture. He traveled professionally with his partner, Baldassare Bianchi, the son-in-law of Mitelli, and they met with much employment, particularly at Mantua. The figures in their works were inserted by Gio. Battista Caccioli, a good disciple of Cignani.

As an architect, he attained deserved eminence, and erected a number of edifices which are highly esteemed. Among them are the church of S. Agostino at Modena; and the beautiful church of Corpus Domini at Bologna. He made the designs for the galleries of the choir of the Basilica of S. Petronio; and built a magnificent gallery in his own house, which is now the Palazzo Monti. His principal work, however, was the grand portico which led from the Saragossa gate at Bologna to the Monte della Guardia, a distance of two and a half miles. This great undertaking was commenced in 1674, and Monti was indefatigable in prosecuting the work, but died, according to Milizia, in 1692, before it was completed.

MONTI, INNOCENZIO. Crespi classes this artist among the Bolognese painters, but Orlandi among those of Imola, where he left some works, particularly one of the Circumcision at the Gesù of Mirandola, executed in 1690—a work highly commended. This artist went to Germany and Poland, where he is said to have met with great success, and executed many works.

MONTI, ANTONIO DE', a native of Rome, who flourished during the pontificate of Gregory XIII., and, according to Baglioni, was the first portrait painter of his age.

MONTI, DE', OR DALLE LODOLE. See GIUSEPPE FRANCO.

MONTICELLI, ANDREA, a Bolognese painter, born in 1640. He studied under Agostino Mitelli, and painted perspective and architecture in the style of his master; but his genius afterwards led him to practise in an entirely different branch, in which he excelled—that of easel pictures of fruit, flowers, vases, carpets, and other objects of still life, executed with freedom, spirit, and natural coloring. He also painted landscapes. He died in 1716.

MONTICELLI, MICHELE ANGELO, a Bolognese painter, born in 1678. He first studied under Marc' Antonio Franceschini, and afterwards with Domenico Maria Viani. He excelled in painting landscapes and battle-pieces, which his biographer Crespi highly extols. No painter of his time surpassed him in the composition of his subjects, the degradation of his distances, and the forms and foliage of his trees. He also enriched his pictures with noble edifices, and with figures correctly disposed, and touched with a spirited pencil. Unfortunately, he lost his sight in the prime of life, when his powers were in their perfection. He died in 1749. Zani says he was born in 1670, and died in 1748.

MONTMIRAL, Marquis de, a French nobleman, who, according to Basan, etched for his amusement a few plates of landscapes from his own designs, and others *after Albert*. They are dated about 1733.

MONTORFANO, Giovanni Donato, a Milanese painter, who, according to Zani, was born in 1440, and died in 1510. He executed some works for the churches at Milan, the chief of which is a Crucifixion, a grand composition, abounding in figures, in the Refectory of the Dominicans in the church of S. Maria delle Grazie, where Lanzi says "it is unfortunately thrown into the shade by the Grand Supper of Leonardo da Vinci. He cannot compete with a rival to whom many of the greatest masters are compelled to yield the palm. He excels in his coloring, which has preserved his work fresh and entire, while that of Vinci showed signs of decay in a few years. What is original in Montorfano, is a peculiar clearness in his features, as well as a dignity in his attitudes, which, if united to a little more elegance, would have left him but few equals in his line." He introduced into this picture a group of soldiers gaming, in whose countenances are depicted attention and a strong desire of gain. The architecture introduced of the walls, gates and edifices of Jerusalem, is both correct and magnificent, presenting those gradual retrocessions of perspective, upon which the Milanese school prided itself at that time. This work is dated 1495, and was painted before the Last Supper of da Vinci, which was executed about 1500. Lanzi says he retained the old custom, which continued at Milan till the time of Gaudenzio, though long before reformed in other places, of giving relief to his glories of Saints, and to arms and ornaments of men and horses, "by mixing with his pictures some plastic work in composition."

MONTORSOLI, Fra Giovanni Angelo, an eminent Italian sculptor and architect, born in 1507, at Montorsoli near Florence, a villa belonging to his father, Michele d'Angelo da Poggibonzi. He studied three years under Andrea Fiesole; and, after the death of his father, he found employment at Rome, Perugia, and Volterra, where he assisted in executing the monument to Raffaelle Maffei. He was next employed by Michael Angelo Buonarotti in the church of San Lorenzo, at Florence, and gained, according to Vasari, the admiration and lasting friendship of that great man. In 1530, Montorsoli became a friar of the Order dei Servi della Nunziata at Florence, and entered the convent of that fraternity; but he was shortly afterwards called to Rome by Clement VII., at the recommendation of Buonarotti, to restore several ancient monuments, much to the dissatisfaction of the brothers of the Nunziata. Montorsoli restored the Laocoon, to which he made the right arm; he made the left arm of the Apollo, besides several other restorations, and a statue of the Pope. After the death of Clement VII., Montorsoli again joined Michael Angelo at Rome, and assisted him in the monument of Julius II.; but while engaged in this work he was invited by Cardinal Turnone, and advised by Michael Angelo, to visit the court of Francis I. On arriving at Paris, he was commissioned to execute four colossal statues; but owing to difficulties with the treasury and servants of the court in the king's absence, Montorsoli left Paris, and returned to Italy, without executing the works. After completing several fine productions in Florence and its vicinity, he visited Rome by way of Naples, and there constructed the tomb of Jacopo Sanazzaro. He next finished, at Genoa, the statue of Andrea Doria, which was commenced by Baccio Bandinelli, and ornamented the church of S. Matteo in that city with many works. In 1547 he went to Messina, and executed the magnificent fountain in the square before the Cathedral. The successful completion of this great work induced the Messinese to commission Montorsoli to erect another fountain in front of the Custom House. He also designed at Messina the church of S. Lorenzo, a lighthouse, aqueducts, and many other important works in sculpture and architecture. In 1557, by a decree of Pope Paul IV., all persons who had taken religious orders, and were living at large in the world, were ordered to return to their convents and reassume their religious habits; and Montorsoli was accordingly obliged to leave many works unfinished, which he entrusted to his pupil Martino, and then returned to his convent at Florence. Shortly after, however, he was invited to Bologna, to construct the high altar of the church of the Nunziata, which he completed in the most splendid style in twenty-eight months. In 1561 he returned to Florence. Possessing an ample fortune, he erected a common sepulchre for artists in the chapter house of the Convent della Nunziata, with the requisite endowment for regular masses at appointed times; and gave the whole sepulchre, chapter, and chapel to the then almost decayed Society of St. Luke. At a solemn feast, celebrated by forty-eight Florentine artists in honor of the completion of the sepulchre, the Society was reëstablished by the consent and authority of Duke Cosmo I., upon a firmer and more permanent basis. The Society has since been considerably enriched, and endowed by successive Dukes of Tuscany, and still exists as the Academy of Florence. Montorsoli died, according to Vasari, in 1563.

MONTPETIT, Armand Vincent de, a French painter, born at Macon in 1713. He went to Paris, where he gained considerable distinction as a portrait painter. He also invented a method of painting in miniature, which he termed *Eludoric*. He had a great knowledge of and genius for mechanics, and produced several valuable inventions.

MONTREUL, Eudes de, an eminent French architect, who flourished, according to Felibien, in the latter half of the 13th century. His talents were highly esteemed by Saint Louis, king of France, whom he accompanied in the expedition to the Holy Land, and was employed to fortify the city of Jaffa. On returning to Paris, he was commissioned by the king to erect a number of churches, among which are those of St. Catherine du Val des Ecoliers; de l' Hotel de Dieu; des Blancs Manteaux; des Cordeliers; des Mathurins; and les Chartreux. He died in 1289.

MONVERDE, Luca, a painter born at Udine in 1501. He studied under Pellegrino di San Daniello and early exhibited such extraordinary talents that, according to Renaldis, "he was regarded as a sort of prodigy of genius"; but he died in 1522, aged 21 years. He painted an altarpiece for the church of S. Maria delle Grazie at Udine, representing the Virgin and Infant, with Sts. Gervasio and Protasio, which is highly commended. His premature death was lamented by every true lover of art.

MOOJAERT, MOOYAERT, or MOONYAERT. See MOYAERT.

MONZA, NOLFO DA, an old painter, who flourished at Milan about 1500, and studied under Bramante. Lanzi says, if he was not equal to the first painters of the time, he was, nevertheless, of a superior character. He is said to have painted at the church of S. Satiro and other places, from the designs of his master. In S. Satiro, near the beautiful temple of Bramante, are several old pictures, attributed to Nolfo.

MONZA, TROSO DA, an old painter much praised by Lomazzo, for his works in the Palazzo Landi, at Milan. "They consist of Roman histories," says Lomazzo, "quite surprising for the figures, as well as the architecture and perspective, which is stupendous." Resta, who saw them in 1707, says that "he was almost astounded by their surpassing excellence, beauty, and sweetness." He painted much at Milan and his native place, particularly at the church of S. Giovanni. In the same church are several histories of Queen Teodelina, executed in various compartments, in 1444, which are attributed to him. Lanzi does not think this artist worthy of so much praise as has been bestowed upon him, yet he admits that he had not seen his best works.

MONY, LOUIS DE. See MONI.

MOOR, CHEVALIER KAREL DE, an eminent Dutch painter, born at Leyden in 1656. He was intended by his father for one of the learned professions, but exhibiting an early and decided inclination for art, he was placed under the instruction of Gerard Douw, with whom he made considerable progress, but disliking his slow and tedious manner, and anxious to adopt a larger scale, he was sent to Amsterdam, and placed under Abraham vander Tempel. The death of that master happening soon afterwards, he returned to Leyden, and studied with Francis Mieris. On leaving this master, he went to Dort to practice with Godfrey Schalcken, though at that time he was superior to him as a designer, but wished to learn his method of handling. When he first began to practice his profession, he painted portraits and domestic subjects, and took the most effectual method to establish his reputation, by exhibiting in his works a greater regard to fame than fortune. His pictures were greatly admired, procured him abundant employment, and he was soon considered one of the ablest artists of his time. The states of Holland commissioned him to paint a picture for their Council Chamber, and left the selection of the subject to himself, with the proviso that it should relate to the administration of Justice. On this occasion, he proved himself capable of nobler exertions than had hitherto engaged his pencil, and represented the Judgment of Brutus, in the most sublime and impressive manner. Moor acquired immense reputation for his portraits, and being familiar with the manners of the best masters of his country, he sometimes imitated the dignity, force, and delicacy of Vandyck, and at others, the striking effect and spirit of Rembrandt. He was commissioned by the Emperor of Germany to paint equestrian portraits of Prince Eugene, and the Duke of Marlborough, which he executed so much to the satisfaction of that monarch, that he conferred on him the honor of knighthood. These works were regarded with universal admiration, and produced several poems laudatory of the artist. He also painted the portrait of Peter the Great, and of many other distinguished personages. The celebrity of Karel de Moor reached Italy, and the Grand Duke of Tuscany requested him to paint a portrait of himself to be placed in the Florentine gallery, on the receipt of which, he rewarded him with a gold chain and medal. One of his most capital performances is a large picture in the hall of the magistrates at the Hague, representing the Burgomasters and Echevins, in the year 1719. The pictures of Moor are ingeniously composed, his figures are correctly designed, and his coloring clear and transparent. His works are always very highly finished; yet his touch is firm and free, and they have nothing of the appearance of labor. Although he was mostly employed on large works, he often painted small easel pictures of history or conversations, elegantly designed and executed, which are exceedingly valued. He also etched a few portraits of eminent artists from his own designs, among which are those of Gerard Douw, Francis Mieris, and John van Goyen. He died in 1738.

MOORE, JACOB, or JAMES, a Scotch painter, born at Edinburgh about 1740, and brought up in the school of design established in that city under the direction of Alexander Runciman.—About 1770, he went to Italy and settled at Rome, where he continued to reside till his death in 1795. He acquired considerable reputation as a landscape painter, and appears to have founded his style by studying the works of Claude. He was much employed by the English nobility and gentry, who visited that capital.

MOORE, SAMUEL, an English amateur designer and engraver, who flourished about 1715. He executed a few plates from his own designs, among which are the Coronation Procession of King William III. and Queen Mary, coarsely etched, and retouched with the graver.

MOORTEL, or MORTEL, JOHN, a Dutch painter, born at Leyden in 1650. He excelled in fruit and flower-pieces, and other objects of still-life. He carefully studied and painted all his subjects after nature, which are elegantly designed, and executed with great delicacy and truth. There is a mellowness and relief in his pictures of fruit, and a freshness and brilliancy in flower-pieces, that rivals nature, and approaches to illusion. He copied de Heem and Mignon so skilfully as to deceive connoisseurs of his time. His works are chiefly confined to Holland, where they are highly esteemed.

MORA, GIOVANNI GOMEZ DE, an eminent Spanish architect, who flourished in the first part of the 17th century. About 1620 he erected the church and college of the Jesuits at Alcala, praised by Milizia for its correct and magnificent proportions. The façade is of granite, of two orders; one with pilasters, and the other with Doric columns. Among the other works of Mora, is the church and convent of the Franciscans at Madrid; and the royal convent of the Augustins in the same city. His greatest work, however, was the grand square at Madrid, in which the size and uniformity of the edifices are worthy of high praise. The royal house, called the Panaderia, has a portico of pilasters, with twenty-four columns of the Doric order.

MORA, Francisco de, an eminent Spanish architect, who flourished in the first part of the 17th century. At the death of Giovanni d'Herrera in 1597, he succeeded that architect in the erection of the Escurial, and built a chapel in the villa at the foot of the hill. Milizia says it is entirely of wrought stone, and is exceedingly attractive on account of its simple grandeur, being entirely destitute of ornament. Mora improved the cloister of the convent of S. Filippo el Reale; and erected at Madrid the Palace de los Consejos, the most superb edifice in that capital.

MORACE, Ernest, a German engraver, born at Stuttgard in 1766. He studied under J. G. Müller, and engraved quite a number of plates in the neat, finished style of his master. He went to Paris, where he resided a long time, and engraved several of the plates for the *Galerie de Florence*, the *Galerie d'Orleans*, and for the *Musée Francais*. He died in 1820.

MORALES, Luis, called El Divino, an eminent Spanish painter, born at Badajos in Estremadura in 1509. Palomino erroneously states that he studied with Pedro Campanna, for the latter did not arrive in Spain, according to Bermudez, till 1548, and there are pictures by Morales in the church of the Conception at Badajos, dated as early as 1546. His pictures generally represent the head of our Saviour crowned with thorns, or that of the Virgin in grief, and those of penitent Magdalens. He seldom painted beyond the bust, and it is supposed that he scarcely ever designed full length pictures. His heads are of the most admirable and touching character, and are finished with exquisite care, without weakening the force or diminishing the expression. His pictures of the Ecce Homo, exhibit the height of human suffering, endured with more than mortal resignation; while those of the Mater Dolorosa, are expressive of the deepest anguish, and Magdalenes of penitential sorrow. Hence he was called *El Divino Morales;* and hence too, his works are said to resemble in many respects those of Leonardo da Vinci. Yet it must be allowed that he was an artist of contracted genius, and barren of invention, never venturing beyond the delineation of a single figure, and seldom beyond a single head. His works are dispersed all over Spain, and seldom seen out of that country. His larger pictures are in the churches; his smaller ones are found in the best collections, and are usually painted on wood or copper. He died in 1586.

MORAN, Santiago, a Spanish historical and landscape painter who flourished at Madrid about 1640. According to Bermudez, he is deserving of more notice than he has received. He mentions three pictures by him, one of St. Jerome, in the possession of the Baron de Casa-Davalillo, in which the design, brilliancy of color, and anatomical science displayed, are admirable, and the landscape part, enchanting; another, the head of St. Jerome, was in the possession of Don Nicholas Lameyra, which le Brun mistook for the work of Albano; and a third, St. Jerome on his knees, quite naked, which has been engraved, but the engraver put the name of Guercino to the print. Moran designed the Muses which embellish the beautiful works of Quevedo, edition of 1670. He also painted many fine landscapes.

MORAND, Jean Antoine, a French architect, born at Briançon in 1727. His father intended him for the priesthood, but having a strong inclination for art, he left the paternal roof at the early age of thirteen, and went to Paris. He studied perspective and decoration under Servandoni, and subsequently entered the school of Soufflot, who treated him as a friend. He erected, after the designs of that master, the *Salle de Spectacle* of Lyons, of which the decorations gained him great reputation. In 1759, at the marriage of the archduchess of Parma, Morand was invited thither to erect a theatre with the necessary machines. His work was much admired by his patrons, as well as by the Italian artists. He subsequently settled at Lyons, and erected the great bridge over the Rhone, 640 feet long, with seventeen piers. During the siege of Lyons in 1793, Moran used all his art to protect this bridge from an *infernal machine*, and was successful. In the next year he was proscribed and led to the scaffold.

MORANDI, Giovanni Maria, an eminent painter, born at Florence in 1622. According to Pascoli he studied under Giovanni Bilivert, on leaving whom he went to Venice, where he resided sometime, studying and copying the works of the best Venetian masters. He afterwards went to Rome, where Lanzi says he established himself and formed a style of his own, Roman in design and Venetian in coloring, while some parts of it partook of the manner of Cortona. He acquired great reputation and executed several works for the churches, the chief of which are the Visitation of the Virgin to St. Elizabeth, in the church of La Madonna del Popolo, and the Death of the Virgin in La Pace. The latter may be considered his master-piece, and has been engraved by Pietro Aquila. He was also celebrated for his easel pictures of historical subjects. But he was more celebrated for his admirable portraits, which gained for him a great reputation, both at home and abroad, and he was much employed in that branch by the nobility of Rome and Florence. He was invited to Vienna by the Emperor Leopold I., whose portrait he painted, and those of the Imperial Family. He also painted the portraits of several of the lesser princes of Germany, and many of the nobility. He lived to the great age of 95, and died in 1717.

MORANDINI, Francesco, called Il Poppo, from the place of his nativity, a small town in the Florentine territory, where he was born in 1544. He was a scholar and imitator of Giorgio Vasari, though more minute in detail, and preferring more gay and cheerful compositions. He executed several works for the churches at Florence, the chief of which are the Conception in S. Michelino, and the Visitation of the Virgin, in S. Niccolo, which are highly commended by Vasari.

MORAZONE, Giacomo, a Lombard painter, who flourished at Venice about 1441, where there are some of his works. His name is variously given by Italian authors. Vasari calls him Girolamo Mazzoni, or Morzoni, and Orlandi and Guari enti call him Giacomo Marzone. Zanetti says his real name, as appears from his signature on his picture of the Assumption of the Virgin, in the Island of St. Elena, near Venice, is *Giacomo Morazone*, dated 1441. He was an artist of distinction in his time, as is evident from the fact that he painted at Venice in competition with Jacobello del Fiore.

MORAZZONE, IL, or CAV. PIER FRANCESCO MAZZUCHELLI, was born at Morazzone, in the Milanese territory, in 1571; hence he is usually called Il Morazzone. After painting for a period in his native place, he went to Rome, where he passed the early period of his life, and by studying the works of the great masters in that metropolis, he acquired a correct design, and executed some works for the churches, the chief of which are the Assumption of the Virgin, in S. Maria Maddalena al Corso, and the Adoration of the Magi, in S. Silvestro in Capite. He afterwards went to Venice, where he studied the works of the best Venetian masters, especially Titian and Paul Veronese, and greatly improved his style of coloring. On his return to Milan he executed several works for the churches, in which he entirely changed his manner, adopting the graceful style of the Roman school, with the glowing coloring and rich draperies of the Venetian, so that one who had seen his pictures at Rome, could not have recognized his hand. The Adoration of the Kings in S. Maria Abate, is pronounced an admirable production. Lanzi says the genius of Morazzone was not so well adapted to the *graceful* as to the *strong* and *magnificent*, as is exhibited in his Conquest of the Archangel Michael, over the rebel Angels, in the church of S. Giovanni at Como, which is designed in a grand and sublime style, and executed with a powerful effect. He was also much employed for the different collections, as well as for the churches of the neighboring places, and he received several commissions from the King of Sardinia, who conferred on him the honor of knighthood. In 1626, he was invited to Piacenza, to paint the great cupola of the cathedral, which he only lived to commence. It was finished by Guercino, and that magician of art made it one of his grandest productions.

MORE, CHEVALIER ANTHONY, an eminent Dutch painter, born at Utrecht in 1519. He studied under John Schoreel, on leaving whom he went to Italy, and spent some time at Rome in studying the works of the great masters, especially of Michael Angelo and Raffaelle, and thence proceeded to Venice, and improved his coloring by contemplating the works of the best Venetian masters. On his return to Holland he painted history, but more especially portraits, with great success, and soon acquired the reputation of one of the ablest artists of his time. In 1552, he accompanied Cardinal Granville to Spain, who recommended him to the patronage of the Emperor Charles V., whose portrait he painted, and that of Prince Philip, which gave so much satisfaction to the monarch, that he sent him to Portugal, to paint the portraits of King John III, Catherine of Austria his Queen, and sister to Charles, and that of their daughter, the Princess Donna Maria, then contracted to Philip; he also painted the portrait of Donna Catalina, Charles' younger sister; all of which gave entire satisfaction, and the artist was munificently rewarded, and the honor of knighthood conferred upon him. The Emperor next despatched More to England to take the portrait of the princess Mary, previous to her marriage with Philip of Spain. On this occasion he is said to have employed all the flattering aids of his art, and so captivated the courtiers of Spain, with the charms of Mary's person, that he was employed by Cardinal Granville and several of the grandees to make copies of it for them. He accompanied Philip to England, where he remained till the death of Queen Mary, who highly honored him, presented him a gold chain, and allowed him a pension of £100 a year. The Emperor Charles V., having abdicated in favor of his son Philip II., the latter returned to Spain, and made More his court painter, where his talents procured him great respect and abundant employment. The King was accustomed to honor him with frequent visits, and treated him with extraordinary familiarity, such as he was not wont to bestow on the highest dignitary of his realm, and one day, in a moment of condescension and admiration, the monarch jocosely slapped him on the shoulder, which compliment, the painter in an unguarded moment, playfully returned by smearing his hand with a little carmine from his brush. The King withdrew his hand and surveyed it for a moment, seriously; the courtiers were petrified with horror and amazement; the hand to which ladies knelt before they had the honor to kiss it, had never before been so dishonored since the foundation of the monarchy; at that moment, the fate of More was balanced on a hair; he saw his rashness, fell on his knees, kissed the King's feet, and humbly begged pardon for the offence. Philip smiled, and pardoned him, and all seemed to be well again; but the person of the King was too sacred in those days, and the act too daring to escape the notice of the Inquisition, from whose bigotry and vengeance the King himself could not have shielded him. Happily for More, one of Philip's ministers advised him of his danger, and without loss of time, he set out for Brussels, upon the feigned pretence of pressing engagements, nor could Philip ever induce him to return to his court. More was employed by most of the princes of Europe, who liberally rewarded him, and at every court his paintings were beheld with admiration and applause, but at none more than those of Spain and England. He acquired an ample fortune. When he was in Portugal, the nobility of that country, in token of their esteem, presented him, in the name of their order, a gold chain, valued at a thousand ducats. He closely imitated nature. He designed and painted in a bold masculine style, with a rich tone of coloring; he showed a good knowledge of the chiaro-scuro, and he finished his pictures with neatness and care; his style is said to resemble that of Hans Holbein, though not possessing his delicacy and clearness; and there is something dry and hard in his manner. His talents were not confined to portraits; he painted several historical subjects in Spain for the Royal Collection, which were highly applauded, but which were unfortunately destroyed in the conflagration of the palace of the Prado. While he resided in Spain, he copied some portraits of illustrious women, in a style said to approach Titian. His own portrait, painted by himself, charmingly colored, and full of life and nature, is in the Florentine gallery. His best work was a picture of the Circumcision, intended for the cathedral at Antwerp, but he did not live to finish it, and died there in 1575. There is a slight discrepancy among authors as to the time both of his birth and death.

MORE, John Gaspar, a Swiss engraver, who flourished at Zurich about 1694. He was principally employed in engraving portraits and other subjects for the booksellers, which are indifferently executed.

MORE, Jacob. See Moore.

MOREAU, Edme, a French engraver, who, according to Florent le Comte, flourished at Rheims about the end of the 17th century. He engraved some plates from his own designs, as well as from the works of other masters.

MOREAU, Louis, a French engraver, born at Paris about 1712. He was chiefly employed in engraving theses and ornamental subjects. He also engraved a few portraits and other subjects, among which are Lodovicus de Ponte Societatis Jesu; *L. Moreau fec.;* J. B. Bebel, *after Watteau*, and Christ raising the daughter of Jairus, *after La Fosse.*

MOREAU, Jean Michel, a reputable French engraver, born at Paris in 1741; died in 1814. He attained considerable eminence in the art, and was received into the Academy in 1781. There are a great variety of vignettes and other book ornaments by him, chiefly etched, and assisted with the graver, in a very neat style. He wrought with great industry, and is said to have executed about 2000 designs for illustrating the works of La Fontaine, Marmontel, Voltaire, Rousseau, and other French authors. Among others, we have by him the following:

The Bath of Bathsheba; *after Rembrandt.* The Consecration of Louis XVI. at Rheims. Four plates, forming a large print of the Fête given at Paris in 1782, for the Birth of the Dauphin. The Tomb of J. J. Rousseau; *J. M. Moreau, fec.* 1778. A set of twenty-five small plates for the first volume of the *Chansons de la Borde.*

MOREAU, P., a French architect of little note, who flourished from 1750 to 1760. He is chiefly known by his tasteful designs; and there are a few etchings by him of architectural subjects, from his own compositions.

1638 PM or PMoreelze. MOREELZE, Paul, a Dutch painter, born at Utrecht in 1571. He was a disciple of Michael Mirevelt, whose manner he adopted. He went to Italy, where he resided some time, and improved himself by a diligent study of the works of the great masters. On his return to his own country, according to van Mander, he distinguished himself as a painter, engraver, and architect. He painted history with reputation, but excelled in portraits, in which he was little inferior to Mirevelt, and obtained so much patronage, that he devoted his talents mostly to this branch. During his residence at Rome he carefully studied and drew the magnificent edifices in that city, and applied himself to the study of perspective, so that he painted architecture extremely well. As an architect, the only work mentioned by him, is the Gate of St. Catherine at Utrecht, which was built after his designs. As an engraver, he executed some wooden cuts in chiaro-scuro in a masterly style, after his own designs, which are very scarce and highly prized. The harmonious union of the three tints produces a very pleasing effect. They are sometimes marked with his monogram, and sometimes, with P. Moreelze, the P. and M. being formed into a monogram as above. He died about 1638.

MOREL, Antoine Alexandre, a French engraver, born at Paris in 1764. He studied successively under Pierre Charles Ingouf, and Jean Massard. He engraved quite a number of plates after David, Ingres, and other French masters, and some of the plates for the *Galerie de Florence*, and the *Musée Francais.* His plates are executed with the graver in a clear, neat, finished style, possessing considerable merit. He was living in 1827.

MOREL, François, a French engraver, who flourished about the middle of the 18th century and engraved some plates of landscapes after P. Hackert, and others.

MOREL, Jan Evert, a Dutch painter of fruit and flowers, born at Amsterdam in 1777. He had first studied under Thierry vander Aa at the Hague, and after his return to Amsterdam, with J. Linthorst. He made the works of John van Huysum his model, and became one of the best fruit and flower painters of his time, and is said to have very nearly approached that master in the lightness of his touch, and the brilliancy and delicacy of his coloring; which is high commendation. There is a superb vase of flowers by him in the Museum at Amsterdam. He died in 1808.

MOREL, Jean Marie, an eminent French architect, born at Lyons in 1728. In early youth he manifested a great love of art, and he vigorously prosecuted the study of mathematics and architecture. At the age of eighteen he was appointed architect to the Prince de Conti, who soon became convinced of his superior abilities, and gave him the entire management of his buildings. Morel showed his admirable taste, in arranging the gardens of the Isle Adam, which have been highly extolled. He subsequently transformed the Parc Guiscard into a beautiful landscape for the Duc d'Aumont, who obtained for Morel the appointment of architect des Menus Plaisirs, at the time of the marriage of Louis XVI. He preferred however, to remain with the Prince de Conti. After the death of that nobleman, Morel visited Holland, Germany, Switzerland, Italy, and Spain. He was constantly employed during a long life in designing and laying out gardens and parks in France, which gained him a wide reputation. His work entitled *Theorie des Jardins*, Paris, 1776, 8vo., has been highly praised for its originality and simplicity. He died in 1810.

MORELL, Nicholas, a Flemish painter, born at Antwerp in 1664. He studied with N. Verendael, an eminent painter of flowers and fruit, whose manner and subjects he imitated with great success. He also excelled in painting vases, bas-reliefs, and other objects of still-life. He obtained great celebrity, and was invited to the court at Brussels, where he found so much employment in painting for the nobility and the collections, and obtained such round prices for his works, that he was enabled to maintain a magnificent establishment, and to live on terms of intimacy with persons of the first rank, by whom he was great ly respected. The pictures of Morell are correctly designed, and elegantly disposed; his pencil is broad and facile, and shows great facility of execution; his touch is full of spirit; his coloring fresh and true to nature, and suitable to the subjects. In some respects he was superior to his master, especially in the foliage of his plants and flowers. Two capital flower-pieces by this master are painted on the folding doors of the cabinet in which are preserved the tapestries belonging to the church of the Abbey of St. Peter, at Ghent. They are composed in a grand style and beautifully executed. He died at Brussels in 1732.

MORELLI, Bartolomeo, called Il Pianoro, from his native place in the Bolognese Territory, was born about 1629. He studied under Francesco Albano, at Florence. He painted history with great reputation, and some of his works are compared by Crespi with those of Albano. He was particularly excellent in his frescos, and was much employed by the churches. Among his numerous works at Bologna, the most esteemed are his St. Teresa, in la Madonna delle Grazie; and the Resurrection, in the Buon Gesù. Lanzi says, "he succeeded so admirably in his frescos, more especially in the chapel of the Casa Pepoli, in S. Bartolomeo di Porta, decorated by him throughout in such exquisite taste, that, were History silent, it would be said to have been designed and executed by Albano's own hand." He died in 1683.

MORELLI, Francesco, a reputable Florentine painter, who flourished about 1600. He painted history; and also instructed pupils, among whom was the Cav. Giovanni Baglioni of Rome.

MORELLI, Cosimo, an eminent Italian architect, born at Imola in 1732. He was the son of Domenico Morelli, and the scholar of Domenico Trifogli. Fortunately for his success, he obtained powerful patronage at the very outset of his professional career; first, that of Gio. Carlo Bandi, Bishop of Imola, for whom he made designs for rebuilding the Cathedral of that city; and through him that of his nephew, Gio. Antonio Braschi, who was elevated to the pontifical office in 1775, with the title of Pius VI. The new pontiff, who had a personal regard for Morelli, appointed him city architect at Cesena; he also procured him a variety of commissions, among which was a design for a new sacristy at St. Peter's. The latter work, with several others, was not carried into execution; but the designs were universally admired.

Morelli executed a large number of works, which gained him great reputation. Among them are the cathedrals of Macerata and Imola; the metropolitan church at Fermo; the Conventuali, at Fossombrone, &c. It is somewhat singular that Morelli was almost as much employed in theatrical as in ecclesiastical architecture. Among his productions in the latter department of art, were the theatre of Imola (since destroyed by fire); those of Fermo, Jesi, and Osimo; also that of Ferrara, which he probably erected in concert with Foschini. Among his other edifices, are the Palazzo Braschi, at Rome; the Anguisola, at Piacenza; the Cappi, at Bologna; the Berio at Naples; the façades of the Ridotto at Cesena, and the Hospital at Imola; the façades of the Palazzo Pubblico, and the Palazzo Vescovile. He died in 1812.

MORELLON. See F. Morellon le Cave.

MORENO, Fra Lorenzo, a Genoese painter, who, according to Soprani, flourished in 1544. He was a Carmelite monk, and was a very skillful fresco painter. He painted the Annunciation in a cloister at the Carmine, which was so much admired, that it was cut out of the wall to preserve it, when the edifice was repaired.

MORESINI. See Fornari.

MORETTI, Cristoforo, a Cremonese painter, who flourished about 1460. According to Lomazzo, he painted a History of the Passion, representing our Redeemer before his Judges, opposite the Epiphany and the Purification of Bembo, in the Cathedral at Cremona. He was also employed with Bembo at the Court of Milan, and in the church of S. Aquilino. Lanzi considers him an able artist of the time, and one of the reformers of the art in Lombardy, particularly in perspective and design. In his History of the Passion, in which he excluded all kinds of gilding, he approaches the moderns. On one of his Madonnas in S. Aquilino, he signs his name *Christophorus de Moretis de Cremona.* The Cremonese writers call him the son of Galeazzo Rivello, and father and grandfather of several other Rivelli, all artists of Cremona, Moretti being only an assumed name.

MORETTO, Il. See Bonvicino.

MORETTO, Niccolo, a painter who, according to Vasari, was a native of Padua, where he flourished about 1495, and executed many good works. Lanzi says that Vasari is in error, and that this artist is no other than Girolamo Mireti; but the names and dates do not at all agree. Mireti flourished from 1423 to 1441.

MORETTO, Gioseffo, a painter of Friuli, who flourished about 1588. He studied under Pomponeo Amalteo, whom he assisted in his works, and whose daughter Quintilia he married. This lady had the reputation of a fine genius, and practised both painting and engraving, or rather etching. Lanzi says there remains only a single altarpiece of his at Friuli, inscribed *Inchoavit Pomponius Amalteus, perfecit Joseph Moretius, anno* 1588. He was a good artist.

MORETTO, Faustino, was a native of Valcamonica, in the Brescian territory. According to Orlandi he was a reputable artist, and painted for the churches, both at Venice and Brescia, but mostly in the former city. He flourished about the middle of the 17th century.

MORGENSTERN, Johann Ludwig Ernst, a German painter, born at Rudelstadt in 1738. He excelled in painting views of the interiors of churches and other edifices, in which the perspective is excellent. His subjects are similar to those of Peter Neefs, but have no appearance of imitation. They are painted with a full, rich pencil, a spirited touch, and a good knowledge of light and shade. His pictures are also ornamented with figures, elegantly designed and skillfully introduced. He died at Frankfort in 1819.

MORGHEN, Giovanni, an Italian engraver, the son of a lace merchant of Montpellier of German origin, who settled at Florence. Giovanni Morghen was born in that city, flourished about the middle of the last century, and was the uncle of the celebrated Raphael Morghen. He was employed by the Marquis Gerini to engrave part of the plates after the works of the Florentine artists, in the Ducal Gallery. In 1767, he published six plates of the Antiquities of Paestum, after the designs of Antonio Joli.

MORGHEN, FILIPPO, an Italian engraver, the brother of the preceding, and the father of Raphael Morghen, flourished about 1757. He married the daughter of Francesco Liani, painter to King Charles III. of Naples, where he permanently settled. He executed part of the plates for the Antiquities of Herculaneum, published at Naples in 1757; also a number of other prints, among which are a set of the Twelve Apostles, after the statues of *Baccio Bandinelli* at Florence; and thirty-one Views and Ruins in the environs of Naples.

MORGHEN, RAPHAEL SANZIO, a preëminent Italian engraver, born at Florence, June 19, 1758, by his own account, according to the authority of Niccolo Palmerini, his favorite pupil, who published a complete catalogue of his works. His grandfather was a lace merchant of Montpellier, of German origin, who married a Genoese wife, and settled at Florence, where he had two sons, Filippo and Giovanni. They both devoted themselves to art; Filippo, the preceding artist, being an engraver. He early settled at Naples, and married the daughter of Francesco Liani, court painter to Charles III., by whom he had several daughters, and one son named Raphael, the subject of the present notice. Filippo must have made a visit to Florence some time after his marriage, and before the birth of Raphael, as the latter was born in that city.

Raphael Morghen was early instructed by his father in the elements of the art, and he made such rapid progress as to be able to engrave a tolerable plate when he had reached the age of twelve years. He first gained distinction by seven engravings from the masks of the carnival of 1778, the Pilgrimage of the Grand Signior to Mecca. This work possessed such extraordinary merit that his father determined to give him the best advantages, and accordingly sent him to Volpato at Rome. The latter first set him at copying Sadeler's print of Christ and Mary Magdalene in the Garden; and he shortly afterwards engraved Gavin Hamilton's allegorical figure of Painting, for the brothers Hackert. In 1781, he engraved Raffaelle's allegorical figures of Poetry and Theology, from the Vatican, and in the same year he married Volpato's only daughter, Domenica. Morghen then wrought in concert with his father-in-law, and assisted him in his plate of Raffaelle's Parnassus, or the Historical Illustration of Poetry, in the Stauze of the Vatican. In 1787 he engraved the Aurora of Guido, painted in fresco in the Rospigliosi palace, which was greatly admired, though inferior to many of his works. The impressions taken without the words *In Ædibus Rospigliosis*, and those taken before the plate was retouched by the Volpato school, are much the most valuable. In 1790 Morghen visited Naples, and engraved a portrait of his father. The Neapolitan court, in 1792, wished him to remain permanently at Naples, and offered him a salary of 600 ducats; but Morghen chose to accept an invitation from the Grand Duke of Tuscany, and accordingly settled at Florence in 1793, with a salary of 400 scudi and free apartments in the city, under the sole condition that he should keep a public school; with the privilege of engraving what he might choose, his prints remaining his own property.

The fame of Morghen soon rose to a great height, and he received many commissions from the royal family of Florence. In 1795, he commenced the celebrated Madonna del Sacco, after Andrea del Sarto; and the Transfiguration of Raffaelle. The latter was not completed until 1812, when it appeared, with a dedication to Napoleon. This print was originally sold at twenty scudi, or about twenty dollars; but the price was much increased, and some impressions commanded one hundred, and even one hundred and fifty dollars. He was occupied three years on his print of the Last Supper, after Leonardo da Vinci, which is his master-piece. Later impressions are retouched; the first, and by far the most valuable, have no comma after the words *vobis-dico vobis*, &c. The last impressions are also without the comma, which was removed. All the prints of Morghen have been described by his pupil Palmerini, to whom it was his custom to give an impression in every stage of the plate, from the first outline to the finished proof. Morghen was associated with the French Institute after the year 1803, and he visited Paris in 1812, at the invitation of Napoleon, who honored him with many presents. By Louis XVIII. he was honored with the decoration of the Legion of Honor, and the cordon of St. Michael.

Although Raphael Morghen cannot, perhaps, be ranked with Marc' Antonio, Edelinck, Nanteuil, and Gerard Audran, he yet holds a very high rank among engravers. He deserves great credit for his correctness of design, vigorous and characteristic expression, not less than for the delicacy and harmony of his execution. His facility of execution was wonderful; no engraver ever had a more perfect control of his instrument. He is also said to have been the first to use the point in executing the flesh parts. His plates all appear to be after one master, consequently they can give no idea of the styles of those artists after whom he engraved. His execution is generally flat, lacking tone and aerial perspective.

Morghen married three times, and left several children. He died at Florence in 1833. His pupil, Palmerini, published at Florence in 1824 a life and portrait of him, with a catalogue of his works, entitled *Catalogo delle Opere d' Intaglio di Raffaello Morghen, raccolte ed illustrate da N. Palmerini.* According to this catalogue, Morghen has engraved seventy-three portraits; forty-seven religious subjects; forty-four historical and mythological pieces; twenty-four views; and thirteen vignettes and crests—in all 201 pieces. M. Feuillet de Conches, in the Biographie Universelle, says his entire work amounts to two hundred and fifty-four pieces, eighteen of which are after Raffaelle. Among his portraits are those of Dante, Boccaccio, Petrarch, Ariosto, Tasso, Raffaelle, the Fornarini, Leonardo da Vinci, and a magnificent plate after Vandyck, of the Duke de Moncada. Among his other plates are, Lot and his Daughters, *after Guercino;* the Repose in Egypt, and Angelica and Medora, *after Teodoro Matteini;* the Virgin sleeping, with the infant Jesus, *after*

*Titian ;* Magdalene penitent, *after Murillo ;* Charity, *after Correggio.* Besides these are the following:

PORTRAITS.

Francesco Moncado, Duke of Ossono, on horseback; *after Vandyck.* The Family of Earl Spencer; *after Angelica Kauffman.* The Family of Holstien Beck; *do.*

SUBJECTS AFTER VARIOUS MASTERS.

The Miracle of the Mass of Bolsena; *after Raffaelle.* The Transfiguration; *do.* The celebrated Madonna della Seggiola; *do.* La Madonna del Sacco; *after A. del Sarto.* The Virgin and Infant with a Book; *after Fra Bartolomeo.* St. John crying in the Wilderness; *after Guido.* The Aurora; after the celebrated painting by *Guido* in the Rospigliosi palace. The Seasons dancing before Time; *after N. Poussin.* The Holy Family reposing; *do.* Diana and her Nymphs; *after Domenichino.* Apollo and the Muses on Mount Parnassus; *after Mengs.*

MORIER, David, a Swiss painter, born at Berne in 1705. He distinguished himself as a painter of battle-pieces, managed horses, &c. He went to England soon after the battle of Dettingen, where he procured, through the interest of Sir Edward Faulkener, an introduction to the Duke of Cumberland, who took him into his service, and settled upon him a pension of £200 a year. He also painted portraits with reputation. He died in London in 1770.

MORIN, Jean, an eminent French painter and engraver, born at Paris about 1612. He studied painting under Philippe de Champagne, practised the art for some time, and executed many portraits, as well as some historical subjects. He afterwards abandoned it, and devoted himself entirely to engraving, in which he became very eminent. His plates are executed in a singular style, being a mixture of strokes and dots; but they are so harmonized as to produce a very pleasing effect. They are executed chiefly with the point, in a masterly manner; and though they are not finished with all the neatness and delicacy which the graver is capable of producing, yet they are etched with uncommon taste, and great freedom of hand, possessing extraordinary merit. His portraits are the most esteemed. He died in 1666. The following are his best prints:

PORTRAITS AFTER PHILIP DE CHAMPAGNE.

Louis XIII. King of France; octagon. Anne of Austria, Regent; octagon. Armand, Cardinal de Richelieu. John Baptist Amador, Abbé de Richelieu. Julius, Cardinal de Mazarin. Cornelius Jansenius, Bishop of Ypres. John Paul de Gondy, Cardinal de Retz. Francis de Sales, Bishop of Geneva. S. Charles Borromeus, Cardinal and Archbishop of Milan. John Peter le Camus, Bishop of Bellay. John du Verger, Abbé de St. Siran. Michael de Morillac, Keeper of the Seals. Michael le Tellier, Secretary of State. James Tubœuf, President of the Chamber of Accounts. René de Longueuil, President à Mortier. Henry de Lorraine, Count d'Harcourt. Nicholas de Neufville, Marquis de Villeroy. Charles de Valois, Duke d'Angoulême. Robert Arnauld, Seigneur d'Andilly. Vincent Voiture, of the French Academy. James le Mercier, Architect to the King. Anthony Vitré, celebrated Printer of Paris.

PORTRAITS AFTER VARIOUS MASTERS.

James Augustus de Thou, President of the Parliament; *after Ferdinand.* Francis Augustin de Thou, President; *do.* Guido, Cardinal de Bentivoglio; *after Vandyck.* The Countess de Bossu; *do.* Margaret Lemon; *do.*—Charles de Mallery, Engraver and Printseller; *do.* Jerome Franck, Painter; *se ipse pinx.*

SUBJECTS AFTER VARIOUS MASTERS.

The Adoration of the Shepherds; *after Ph. Champagne.* The Virgin and infant Jesus; *do.* The Crucifixion, in three sheets; *do.* The taking down from the Cross; *do.* The Assumption of the Virgin; *do.* Two half-lengths of St. Peter and St. Paul; *do.* The Virgin with the infant Jesus on her Knee, holding a bouquet of flowers, inscribed *Dilectus meus mihi ; after Raffaelle* The Virgin adoring the infant Christ; *after Titian.* This is a fine specimen of the artist's ability. The Virgin, with the dead Christ; *after Caracci.* A Landscape, with Ruins; *after Cl. Lorraine.* A Landscape, with a Man driving two Cows; *after Fouquieres.* Another Landscape, with figures; *do.* A set of four Landscapes, with Ruins and Figures; *after Cornelius Poelemburg.* A Landscape, with Ruins and a Fountain; *after J. B. Corneille.*

MORINA, Giulio, a Bolognese painter, who flourished in the latter part of the 16th and first part of the 17th centuries. According to Malvasia, he studied under Lorenzo Sabbatini, but formed his style of design by an attentive study of the works of the Caracci, and the airs of his heads show that he was emulous of imitating the expression of Correggio. He acquired considerable reputation, and executed many works for the churches at Bologna, the most esteemed of which are the Presentation, at the Servi; the Visitation of the Virgin to St. Elizabeth, in S. Uomobono; and the Crucifixion, in SS. Sebastiano e Rocco. He was also considerably employed at Parma, and was some time in the service of the Duke.

MORINELLO, Andrea, a native of Val di Bisagno, in the Genoese territory, according to Soprani, flourished about 1516. Lanzi says he was very graceful in his countenances, soft and clear in his outlines, and one of the first in those parts to open the way for the modern manner. There is a fine altar-piece by him at S. Martino di Albaro, dated 1516. He also excelled in portraits.

MORINI, Giovanni, a native of Imola, who studied under Giuseppe Maria Crespi, at Bologna, and whose manner he imitated. He was living in 1769.

MORIS, R., a scholar and imitator of Godfrey Schalcken. Little is known of him. He died young.

MORLAND, Henry Robert, an English painter, born at London in 1724, and died in 1797. He was the son of an obscure painter, who instructed him in the art. He painted portraits, both in oil and crayons, and scraped a few mezzotinto plates. He also painted domestic subjects, and was very successful in representing scenes by candle-light. He found considerable employment in cleaning and repairing ancient pictures. Embarking in the business of picture dealing, he became a bankrupt.

MORLAND, George, was the son of the preceding, born in London in 1764. He possessed, naturally, extraordinary talents for painting, which, if they had been improved by judicious instruction, assiduous study, and a noble ambition, would have led him to the very pinnacle of fame and fortune; but unfortunately his early mental and moral culture was neglected, and his professional instruction was defective; his early companions were dissipated and worthless, and he sunk a victim to intemperance almost as low as the swine he delighted to depict. After he had acquired distinction, and his works commanded high prices, he was surrounded by harpies, who took advantage of his necessities and misfortunes. Many of his best pictures were painted in sponging houses, to clear him from arrest; or in ale-houses, to discharge his reckoning. He died in one of the former, and his wife survived him only two days. He had no other instruction than what he received from his father, who early discovered in his son a genius for painting, and employed it for his own advantage; he had him indented to him, and kept him constantly employed in making pictures and drawings for sale. By these means, young Morland acquired a wonderful facility of execution, but wholly neglected academic studying. Owing to the narrow and illiberal manner in which his talents were employed, he fell into low habits, and formed bad connexions. On the expiration of his indenture, he left his father's house, and the remainder of his life is the history of genius degraded by intemperance and immorality, which alternately excites our admiration at his great talents, and our regrets at the profligacy of his conduct. Morland's subjects are usually from low life, such as pig-sties, farm-yards, landscapes with cattle and sheep, fishermen or smugglers on the sea-coast. He seldom or never produced a picture perfect in all its parts, but those parts adapted to his knowledge and taste were exquisitely beautiful. He knew well his faults, and usually selected those subjects best suited to his talents. His knowledge of anatomy was extremely limited; he was totally unfitted for designing the human figure elegantly or correctly, and incapable of large compositions. He also possessed little mental refinement, and perhaps lost the little inherent feeling he possessed by associating with low company, and indulging in slothful inebriety. In portraying the broad and vulgar walks of life he was inimitable, but his landscapes were not always critically exact, nor his coloring uniformly good, for he had not devoted sufficient time to acquire a true knowledge of nature, or to develop the powers he possessed. Never having traveled, even in his own country, nor seen any romantic scenery, his landscapes generally consist of fields, hedges, ponds, and clay-banks, introduced as backgrounds to his figures. His most admirable pictures are his interiors, those comprising inland scenery, sheep, pigs, and asses. The more confined the subject the greater his success; and his faults increase as the scene expands. He was peculiarly happy in depicting a flock of sheep under a dwarf oak. He selected those animals that require the least correctness of drawing, as sheep, hogs, asses, and old clumsy horses, being unacquainted with the anatomy of that noble animal. An old white horse was a favorite subject with him, from its affording a mass of light, with a most favorable opportunity for a display and contrast of coloring. But the hog was his favorite animal, and that which he introduced most frequently and with the greatest success; his touch was well adapted to the representation of its bristly hide, and he seldom failed to depict to the life the appearance and character of that lazy and gluttonous animal. According to his biographer, Mr. George Dawe, who wrote an impartial and excellent life of Morland, he arrived to the full maturity of his powers about 1790, in the short space of six years after he left his father, and from that time they began and continued to decline, till the day of his death. His earlier works are hard, formal, labored, and carefully finished; as he acquired confidence in his powers, he adopted a broader style and greater freedom of execution, and he wrought with extraordinary facility. During the last few years of his life he was seldom sober, and only painted to supply his animal wants and to escape from arrest; and it was a common practice of the sharpers about him to get him in debt, shut him up in a room, and thus compel him to paint for a guinea a picture which they could readily sell for thirty. Though Morland wrought with extraordinary facility, it is falsely said that he painted four thousand pictures. Even in his life-time his works were so much admired and sought after that they were imitated by some of his cronies, with his consent and connivance. Stanley says that his brother Henry "kept a regular manufactory of them." His best works now command very high prices. He died in 1804. What a melancholy history, and how full of admonition!

MORMANDO, Gio. Francesco, an Italian architect, born at Florence in 1455. He studied architecture under Leon Battista Alberti, and subsequently went to Rome for improvement. After studying the remains of antiquity in that city, he settled at Naples, and became the friend and competitor of Novella da S. Lucano and Gabriello d' Agnolo. He erected the church of S. Severino, and gained so high a reputation for this admirable work, that King Ferdinand invited him to Spain, and appointed him first royal architect. On returning to Naples, he continued the church of S. Severino, and made some additions to the monastery. The Duke de' Viestri commissioned him to erect a massive palace, subsequently called Filomarini, which has been greatly injured by various insurrections. Among the other works of Mormando is the small church della Stella, near S. Severino; and the Palazzo Cantalupo, erected from his design. He died, according to Milizia, in 1552.

MORO, Anthony. See More.

MORO, Il. See Torbido.

MORO, Gio. Battista d'Angelo, a painter, born at Verona about 1512. He was a scholar of Francesco Torbido, called Il Moro, but afterwards went to Venice to improve his coloring by studying the works of Titian. He painted both in oil and fresco, acquired considerable distinction, and executed several works for the churches at Verona, sometimes in competition with Paul Veronese. His design was graceful, and his coloring rich and vigorous. His picture of St. Paul before Ananias in the church of S. Eufemia, is so highly prized that it was sawed out of the wall with great care and expense, and removed to a place of safety, when that edifice was repaired. Another fine picture by him, is an Angel presenting the Palms of Martyrdom to the Innocents, in S. Stefano. He also painted at Venice, where his most capital work is an altar-piece in S. Maria Maggiore, representing the Virgin between St. John and St. Mark, surrounded with several figures in ducal robes, which are the portraits of the Marcello family, for whom it was painted. He also executed some slight, but spirited etchings, from his own designs, in which the extremities in particular, are drawn in a very masterly manner. In conjunction with Battista Vicentino, he engraved a set of fifty landscapes, mostly after Titian, executed in a bold, free style. We have also the following prints by him:

The Nativity, or Adoration of the Shepherds; *after Parmiggiano*. The Virgin, with the infant Christ and St. John; *B. A. del Moro, fec.* The Holy Family, with

St. Elizabeth and St. John; *after Raffaelle.* Another Holy Family; *do.* The Martyrdom of St. Catherine; *after Bernardino Campi.* The Baptism of Christ by St. John; *do.*

MORO, MARCO D'ANGELO, was the son of the preceding, who instructed him in the art. He assisted his father in some of his works at Venice, and Lanzi says he possessed excellent abilities, as is shown by his picture of Paradise, in the church of S. Bartolomeo at Venice. He died young about 1560.

MORO, GIULIO D'ANGELO, was a younger brother of Marco M. He studied under his father, whose style he followed, and whose reputation he justly sustained. Zanetti calls him the *dotto pittore*, the *learned painter*, and says that he distinguished himself alike in all the arts. His chief works at Venice are the Four Coronati, in the church of S. Apollinare, which discover an elegance and precision of design, sufficient to rank him among distinguished artists.

MORO, LORENZO DEL', a Florentine artist, who studied under Jacomo Chiavistelli, and, according to Orlandi, was a spirited painter of fruit, flowers and animals. He was living in 1718.

MORONI, DOMENICO, an old painter of Verona, born in 1430. According to Vasari, he was instructed in the art by one of the pupils of Stefano Veronese. There is an altar-piece by him in the church of S. Bernardino at Verona, which is highly esteemed and preserved with great care. He died about 1500.

MORONI, FRANCESCO, was the son and scholar of the preceding, born at Verona in 1474. Vasari says he excelled his father, and commends him for the graceful style of his design, and the harmony and suavity of his coloring, "in which he was inferior to none." Lanzi says he was bound by the strictest ties of friendship with Girolamo da' Libri from his youth, and that they were frequently employed together in the same labors. The latter part of his life was spent at Rome, where he executed several altar-pieces for the churches and convents, which hold a respectable rank even in that emporium of art. There are several pleasing pictures of Madonnas and Saints, inscribed with his name in the Museum at Berlin. He died at Rome in 1529.

MORONI, GIOVANNI BATTISTA. This painter was born at Albino, in the Bergamese Territory, in 1528. He was a pupil of Alessandro Bonvicino, called Il Moretto, and, according to Tassi, was one of his ablest disciples, and the most successful follower of his style. He executed many works for the churches at Bergamo, and other places in the vicinity. He was an excellent colorist, but was inferior to his instructor in invention and design, and in the graceful airs of the heads, which distinguish the productions of Il Moretto. Among his most esteemed works at Bergamo are, the Crowning of the Virgin, in the church of La Trinità, the Assumption, in S. Benedetto, and a Pietà, or a Dead Christ in the lap of the Virgin, surrounded by several saints, at the Cappuccini. He was one of the best portrait painters of his time, excelled only by Titian. He died in 1578.

MORONI, PIETRO, called MORONE BRESCIANO, was the son of the preceding, by whom he was first instructed. According to Averoldi, he afterwards became the disciple of Paolo Veronese.—Lanzi says, "he studied a good deal the works of Titian, and was one of the most accurate and elegant designers the Venetian school could boast at that period, nor does he yield to any of his cotemporaries in the strong body and clearness of his coloring." He executed some works for the churches of Venice and other places, particularly at Brescia; hence he is sometimes called Morone Bresciano. His picture of Christ bearing his Cross, in the church of S. Barnaba at Venice, is commended as one of the most masterly productions of the time. He was considered one of the ablest artists of the Venetian school. His name is improperly written by some authors, *Marone.* He died at Riva di Soldo about 1625.

MOROSINI, FRANCESCO, called IL MONTEPULCIANO, from the place of his nativity. According to Baldinucci, he studied under Orazio Fidani, whose style he adopted. He executed some works for the churches at Florence, but was chiefly employed by individuals. His best work is a picture of the Conversion of St. Paul, in the church of S. Stefano, at Florence. He flourished in the last half of the 17th century.

MORTIMER, JOHN HAMILTON, an English historical painter of considerable eminence, born at Eastbourne, in Sussex, in 1739. His father was a collector of customs, and his uncle is said to have been a painter of talents, whose studio he frequented. He was sent to London, and placed under the tuition of Hudson, but their tastes being different, he did not derive much advantage from his instructions. He was indebted for his greatest improvement to his constant attendance in the Duke of Richmond's gallery, which that nobleman liberally opened for the study and advancement of the young artists of the time. He soon after gained the pension of one hundred guineas, given by the Society for the Encouragement of Arts, &c., for the best historical picture, which was adjudged to his St. Paul converting the Britons. This picture established his reputation as an able artist, and he successively increased his celebrity by the production of several admirable works, among which are, King John granting the Magna Charta to the Barons, the Battle of Agincourt, Vortigern and Rowena, &c. He was a member of the Society of Artists for many years, and exhibited at their room in the Strand. In 1779, without solicitation or expectation, he was elected a royal academician. He executed a few etchings from his own designs, and after others, in a bold, free style, among which are a Set of twelve circular plates of characters from Shakspeare; Nature and Genius introducing Garrick into the Temple of Shakspeare; the Virgin teaching St. John, *after Guercino;* a set of fifteen plates of Studies, *after S. Rosa, Lairesse,* and other masters.

MORTO, DA FELTRO. See FELTRO.

MORVILLO, SILVESTRO, called IL BRUNO, a Neapolitan painter, whose works date, according to Dominici, from 1571 to 1597. He was a good artist, and was considerably employed by the churches.

MOSCA. There seem to have been several artists of this name, but they are so vaguely mentioned that it is difficult to distinguish them. Malvasia mentions a Giovanni Maria Mosca, of Padua, or Milan, who flourished in the first part of the 16th century, and executed some works in sculpture at Orvieto. Also a Mosca of Mantua, a painter, who lived about the same time. Lanzi, in his history of the Roman school says, "Mention is made of one Mosca, whether a native or a foreigner, I know not, as a disciple of this school; his Christ on the way to Mount Calvary, now in the Academy of Mantua, is certainly a Raffaellesque picture; but we may rather consider Mosca an imitator, and a copyist, than a pupil of Raffaelle." Stanley mentions a picture of the Virgin and Child in a landscape, which is supposed to be by this master, from its being inscribed with *a fly*, his rebus.

MOSCATIELLO, Carlo, a Neapolitan artist, born in 1655, and died in 1739. He was an excellent perspective painter, and executed the architectural parts of some of the works of Luca Giordano, and other eminent artists of the time.

MOSER, George Michael. This artist was born in Switzerland in 1707, but went to England very young. He was by profession a gold chaser, in which he arrived at great eminence. He did not confine his talents to this art, but painted in enamel with considerable success. He was also a skillful draughtsman, and had a good knowledge of the anatomy of the human figure, which perfectly qualified him for the office of Keeper of the Royal Academy, which he held from the foundation of that institution in 1768, till his death in 1783. The occupation of the Keeper principally consists in superintending and instructing the students who practise drawing and modeling from the antique statues.

MOSER, Mary, was a daughter of the preceding, who painted fruit and flowers in an exquisite manner, was much patronized by the nobility, and was elected a member of the Royal Academy;—an honor never conferred upon any other lady, except Angelica Kauffmann. It is said that Queen Caroline entertained so high a regard for her virtues and talents, that she paid her the highest respect, and frequently visited her studio. Miss Moser decorated an entire room at Frogmore with flowers, for Queen Charlotte, and received £900 for the work. She subsequently married a Mr. Lloyd, after which she practised only as an amateur. She died at an advanced age in 1803.

MOSES, called Little Moses. See Uytenbroeck.

MOSIN. See Mouzyn.

MOSLEY, Charles, an English engraver, who flourished in London about 1760. He was chiefly employed by the booksellers. His portraits are his best prints, of which King Charles I. on horseback, *after Vandyck*, and Marshal Belleisle on horseback, are worthy of notice.

MOSNIER, Jean, a French painter, born at Blois in 1600. He was the son of a painter on glass, who instructed him in his own profession. He afterwards went to Italy, and studied under Cristofano Allori at Florence. On his return to his native country, he settled at Paris, where he acquired considerable reputation as an historical painter. He executed some works for the churches and public edifices, the best of which are in the church of St. Martin at Paris. He died in 1656.

MOSTAERT, John, a Dutch painter, born at Haerlem in 1499. He was of an honorable family and studied under Jacob van Haerlem. His personal accomplishments, and the politeness of his address, together with his professional merits, procured him the esteem and patronage of persons of the highest rank, and he acquired great reputation as an historical and portrait painter. The Princess Margaret, sister to Philip I. of Spain, retained him in her service eighteen years. He painted the portraits of many of the nobility, and other distinguished personages of his country. Van Mander commends several of his historical works, which remained in his time in the churches and public edifices of Flanders, particularly a Nativity in the church of the Jacobins, at Haerlem; an Ecce Homo, in another church; and the Banquet of the Gods, a grand composition, full of dignity, and beautifully executed. He died in 1555. Balkema and Immerzeel both state that he was born in 1474, but they differ from all other authors.

MOSTAERT, Francis and Giles, twin brothers and Flemish painters, born at Hulst, near Antwerp, in 1520. Francis studied with Henry de Bles, and Giles with John Mandyn; the former excelled in landscape, the latter in figures, so they mutually assisted each other. They settled at Antwerp, where they gained considerable reputation. Francis died in 1557, and Giles, as variously stated, in 1579, 1598, or 1601. Giles was a good historical painter, and in the Museum at Antwerp is a picture by him of the Crucifixion, with the Virgin, St. John, and eight other large figures.

MOT, François Frederic le, a French sculptor, born at Lyons in 1773. He early manifested a strong inclination for art, and was sent to Paris, where he entered the Academy of Painting and Sculpture. While occupied one day in designing the Hercules of Puget, in the gardens of Sceaux Penthievre, he attracted the attention of Dejoux, who received him into his school. Here le Mot made rapid advances, and at the age of seventeen gained the grand prize of sculpture, for his bas-relief of the Judgment of Solomon. He then visited Italy with the royal pension. Recalled to Paris in 1795, he was employed on the statue of the French Hercules, but it was never completed. He gained a high reputation, and was successively appointed member of the Institute; Professor of the School des Beaux Arts; Member of the Legion of Honor; Baron; and Chevalier of St. Michael. Among his principal works are the bas-relief which decorates the grand façade of the colonnade of the Louvre; the marble bas-relief for the tribune of the Chamber of Deputies; and the colossal equestrian statue of Louis XIV., at Lyons. He died in 1827.

MOTTA, Raffaello, called Raffaellino da Reggio, was born at Reggio in 1550. He studied under Lelio Orsi, and, according to Tiraboschi, he was one of the most promising artists of his age. He painted a few frescos in his native city, but his principal works are at Florence, where his two fables of Hercules in the Ducal Hall, and two Gospel histories in the Ducal Gallery, are highly commended. He also painted at Capraruola in competition with Zuccari and Vecchi, with such success that his lively figures make those of his competitors seem inanimate. He also painted in oil for the collections. Lanzi says he possessed an astonishing genius, deserving of Rome for its theatre of action. Nothing was wanting in this artist except a greater knowledge of design. His works are full of delicacy, relief, and spirit. He died in 1578, aged 28 years, deeply lamented like another Raffaelle, prematurely passing away.

MOUCHERON, Frederick, called the Old, an eminent Flemish painter, born at Embden in 1633. He showed an early inclination for art, and was placed with John Asselyn, an eminent landscape painter, under whose able instructions, united with indefatigable application, he made extraordinary progress. When he was about twenty years of age he went to Paris, and met with such flattering encouragement that he abandoned the visit he had projected to Rome by the recommendation of his instructor. After a residence of several years at Paris, he returned to Antwerp, and afterwards settled at Amsterdam, where he acquired great distinction, and met with abundant employment. He designed everything after nature; consequently, though there is a great difference in the choice of his subjects, there is always an air of truth in his works. His landscapes are generally well chosen, and exhibit pleasing scenery; his touch is light and free; and his coloring generally agreeable; the forms of his trees well chosen, and his foliage light and apparently in motion. His foregrounds are clear and well finished, though his distances have frequently the appearance of mistiness or vapor, but they are in keeping with his subject. He frequently introduced waterfalls rushing through the different plans of his pictures, and enriched them with picturesque buildings and other architecture. He sometimes painted architectural views on a grand scale, with a magnificent effect. He did not succeed in his figures so well, and therefore employed other eminent artists to insert them for him, as Theodore Helmbrecker at Paris, and Adrian Vandervelde and John Lingelbach at Amsterdam. The works of Moucheron, though inferior to those of Berghem, Both, and other distinguished artists of the Dutch and Flemish schools, are yet esteemed worthy of a place in the choicest collections. He died at Amsterdam in 1686.

MOUCHERON, Isaac, called the Young, was the son and scholar of the preceding, born at Amsterdam in 1670. Although he lost his father at the age of sixteen, he had already made such progress, and was so thoroughly grounded in the principles of the art, that he needed no further instruction, but only an attentive study of nature. After having acquired the reputation of an able artist in his native city, desirous of further improvement, he went to Italy, where he resided four years, contemplated the works of the best masters, and filled his portfolio with the choicest designs of the picturesque scenery and ancient ruins in the vicinity of Rome and Tivoli. He thus acquired an extraordinary readiness for designing, and facility of execution, and was enabled to exhibit truth in all his compositions. On his return to Amsterdam he acquired great reputation, and was chiefly employed in decorating the grand saloons and halls of the nobility and wealthy persons with landscapes on a grand scale, in which the figures were usually inserted by Nicholas Verkolie, de Witt, and others. In the scenery, as well as the style of his landscapes, he seems to have emulated the grand manner of Gaspar Poussin. His pictures are enriched with figures and animals, and noble architecture. He was a perfect master of perspective and architecture. His coloring is extremely fresh, clear, and natural, with an abundance of harmony and union, and his touch is full of ease and spirit. He executed many easel pictures, which are exceedingly prized in Holland, and in every part of Europe. He also etched quite a number of plates, in a neat and very spirited style, after his own designs and those of G. Poussin, as follows. He died at Amsterdam in 1744.

A set of four Views of Gardens, with buildings and figures; inscribed *J. Moucheron inv. pinx. et fec.* Another set of four Views of Gardens and Buildings; inscribed *J. Moucheron, inv. et fec.* Four Landscapes, with Figures; *after Gaspar Poussin;* inscribed *EinigeLandschapen gescheldert door G. Poussin, &c.* A set of nineteen Views of Heemstede in the Province of Utrecht; *J. Moucheron, inv. et fec.*

MOUCHET, François Nicolas, a French painter, born at Grai, in Franche Comte, in 1750. He visited Paris, and entered the school of Greuze. In 1776 he gained the grand prize of the Academy, and then devoted his talents to miniature painting. When the Revolution broke out, he took an active part, and was successively elected member of the municipality, and justice of the peace. In 1792 he was sent to Belgium, to select the finest works of art for the Louvre. During the reign of terror he opposed its bloody excesses, and was imprisoned fourteen months, during which time he painted miniatures for the support of his family. Liberated in 1794, he retired to his native place, and established a school of design. His portraits are distinguished for a broad, free, and vigorous pencil. There were two compositions by Mouchet exhibited at the Louvre: the Origin of Painting, and the Triumph of Justice. He died in 1814.

MOUCHY, Martin de, a French engraver, born at Paris in 1746. He studied with Augustine de St. Aubine, in whose style he executed quite a number of prints, chiefly for the booksellers, among which are the following:

A pair of Views in the environs of Triel; *after Hackert.* A View of Marienberg, near Stockholm; *do.* Another View in Sweden; *do.* A set of sixteen plates from the History of Telemachus; after the designs of *Cochin* and *Monnet.*

MOUZYN, or MOSIN, Michael, a Dutch engraver, born at Amsterdam about 1630. He endeavored to unite the point with the graver, in the execution of his plates, but with no great success. His drawing is incorrect, and his style appears heavy and labored. The following are among his best prints:

PORTRAITS.

Jacob van Wassenaer, Admiral of Holland. Michael Ruyter, Dutch Admiral; *after H. van Alde.* Cornelius de Witt, Pensionary of Holland; *do.* John van Galen, Admiral of Holland; *after J. Livius.*

SUBJECTS.

Venus sleeping; *after J. A. Backer.* The Four Elements under the empire of Venus; *after C. Holsteyn.* A Satyr presenting a Bunch of Grapes to a Woman and Child; *do.*

MOYA, Pedro de, a Spanish painter, born at Granada in 1610. After acquiring some knowledge of the art in his own country, an ardent desire to view the works of the best Flemish painters induced him to go to Antwerp, where he was captivated with the style of Vandyck, and set out for England to place himself under that master

He did not enjoy this advantage long, for Vandyck died a few months after his arrival in London. On his return to Spain he acquired considerable reputation, and executed several good works for the churches of Granada, of which the most admired is an altar-piece of the Conception, in the church of Nuestra Sennora de Gracia. He died there in 1666.

MOYAERT, or MOOJAERT, Claas or Nicholas, a Dutch painter and engraver, born at Amsterdam about 1600. It is not known under whom he studied, but he is said to have formed his style by studying and imitating the works of Adam Ælzheimer. At all events, he could imitate Ælzheimer, Rembrandt, and Lievens so closely that some of his pictures have been sold for the genuine works of those masters. He was an eminent artist in his time, and taught many pupils, among whom were some of the most distinguished masters of the Dutch school, as Berghem, vander Does, Salomon de Koninck, John Baptist Weeninx. The pictures of Moyaert bear a strong resemblance to those of Weeninx. He also etched some spirited plates after his own designs, among which are a set of six different Animals, a Landscape with Cattle, and Lot and his Daughters, in the style of Ælzheimer.

C. L. M. MOYART, Christian Louis, a Dutch painter and engraver, born at Amsterdam about 1600. He is said to have engraved a set of eight emblematical plates of the History of Mary de Medicis, marked with the above monogram. But Brulliot and Zani both assert that he and Claas are one and the same artist, and that the part of the monogram composed of C. L. signifies Claas, and not Christian Louis, as supposed. It is also ascertained, beyond a doubt, that the plates of the History of Mary de Medicis, published by Blaeu at Amsterdam in 1639, were engraved by Peter Nolpe, from the designs of Claas Moyart.

MOYNE, Jean Louis, a French sculptor, born at Paris in 1665. He studied under Coysevox, and executed a number of esteemed works. He was chosen a member of the Academy, and was also honored with the office of rector of that institution. Among his best productions are his heads of distinguished personages, as the Duke d' Orleans, Mansard, and Largilliere; also two statues of Angels, in the church des Invalides; and a bas-relief in the church at Versailles, representing Christ bearing his Cross. He died at Paris in 1755.

MOYNE, Jean Baptiste le, an eminent French sculptor, the son and scholar of Jean Louis le Moyne, born at Paris in 1704. He was also a scholar of his uncle, Jean Baptiste le Moyne, a reputable sculptor; and of Robert le Lorrain. At the age of twenty, he gained the grand prize at the Academy, for a bas-relief, representing the Sacrifice of Polyxena. Although entitled to the royal pension, he did not visit Rome, his father being very unwilling to part with him. In 1729, he executed a group of St. John baptizing Christ, for the church of S. Jean in Greve, which gained him so much reputation that the city of Bordeaux commissioned him to execute the bronze equestrian statue of Louis XV. For this work, the king settled upon le Moyne a pension of 1500 francs. His works have nothing of the purity and simplicity of the antique, which he regarded as feebleness of design; they are in a theatrical taste, and deserve no credit, except for mechanical execution. Besides those mentioned, there are many others, among which are the mausoleums of Cardinal de Fleury, Mignard, and Crebillon; the statues of St. Gregory and St. Teresa, at the Invalides; besides many heads of distinguished individuals; that of Coysevox is in the Musée des Monuments Français. Le Moyne died at Paris in 1778.

MOYREAU, Jean, a French engraver, born at Paris in 1712. His plates are very unequal in merit, but some of them possess considerable excellence. In 1736 he was chosen an academician, and engraved two fine plates on that occasion, a Halt of Hunters and the Rendezvous of the Chase, *after van Falens.* Moyreau also executed eighty-nine plates after Philip Wouwerman, which give an inferior idea of his correctness of design, and the spirit and elegance of his pencil. The following is a list of his best prints:

Rebecca receiving the Presents from the Servant of Abraham; *after Paolo Veronese;* for the Crozat collection. The Resurrection of Lazarus; *after Bon Boullongne.* The Parting of Hector and Andromache; *do.*—Bacchus and Ariadne; *do.* A Halt of Hunters; *after van Falens.* The Rendezvous of the Chase; *do.* (The two last plates were engraved for his reception into the Academy in 1736, and are among his best prints.) A Seaport; *after Claude.* La Partie Quarrée; *after Watteau.* A Waterfall; *do.* Of his best prints *after Wouwerman,* may be mentioned those entitled Le Colombier du Maréchal; La grande Chasse a l'oiseau; La Fontaine du Dauphin; La Fontaine de Neptune.

MUCCIOLI, Bartolomeo, an old artist of Ferrara, who flourished about the middle of the 15th century. His works have mostly perished.

MUCCIOLI, Benedetto, was the son of the preceding, and flourished at Urbino in 1492, where it seems the family had settled. According to Lazzari, there is a fine altar-piece by him in the chapel of the Muccioli, their descendants, in the church of S. Domenico at Urbino, signed *Benedictus quondam Bartholomæi de Fer. Pictor.* 1492.

MUDO, El, an eminent Spanish painter, born at Logrono in 1526. His real name was Juan Fernandez Navarette, or Juan Fernandez Ximenes de Navarette. He was called El Mudo after he had acquired distinction as a painter, from his having been deaf and dumb from his infancy. He showed a talent for art early in life, and first studied under Fray Vicente de Santo Domingo, a monk of the Order of the Geronomytes, under whom he made such rapid progress, and exhibited so much genius, that his parents, by the advice of his instructor, sent him to Italy to study with Titian, with whom he remained several years, and thoroughly imbibed his principles and manner of coloring, so that he was called by his countrymen the *Spanish Titian.* He remained in Italy twenty years, visiting all the principal cities, Rome, Florence, Naples, &c., studying the works of the best masters, and frequenting the studios of the most eminent painters, who entertained for him the highest respect for his eminent abilities, perhaps heightened by his infirmity. He had already acquired a distinguished reputation in Italy, when, in 1568, he was summoned to Madrid by Philip II., to paint in the Escurial, and on his arrival he was appointed painter to the king, with a pension of two hundred ducats, in addition to the price of his works. He was naturally of a delicate constitution, and he had hardly commenced his labors, when a severe malady compelled him to retire to his native place, Logrono, with the permission of his royal patron, where he remained three years, during which time he painted four magnificent pictures, and brought them with him to Madrid in 1571. These were the Assumption of the Virgin, the Martyrdom of St. James the Great, a St. Philip and a St. Jerome, which were placed in the Escurial, and the artist rewarded with five hundred ducats, besides his pension. The head of the Virgin in the Assumption is supposed to be a portrait of his mother, the Donna Catalina Ximenes, who in her youth was very beautiful. In 1575 he added four more pictures, the Nativity, Christ at the Pillar, the Holy Family, and St. John writing the Apocalypse, for which he received eight hundred ducats. In the Nativity, El Mudo successfully overcame a formidable difficulty in painting—the introducing of three lights into the picture, as in the famous Notte of Correggio; one from the irradiation proceeding from the infant Jesus, another from a glory of Angels above, and a third from a flaming torch. It is related that Pellegrino Tibaldi, on seeing it, exclaimed, *Oh! i belli pastori!* This exclamation gave name to the picture, and it continues to be known to this day as *the beautiful Shepherds*. In 1576, he painted his famous piece of Abraham entertaining the three Angels, for which he received five hundred ducats. He now undertook a stupendous work, and was engaged to paint thirty-two pictures for the Escurial; twenty-seven of which were to be seven feet and a half in height, and seven feet and a quarter in breadth; and the other five thirteen feet high and nine feet broad. He did not live to complete this vast undertaking; he painted eight, representing the Apostles, the Evangelists, and St. Paul and St. Barnabas; the others were finished by Alonso Sanchez Coello, and Luis de Caravajal. He died in 1579. El Mudo's pictures are extremely scarce, and little known, as all his works in Spain, except a small picture of the Baptism of Christ in the Museum at Madrid, are buried in the royal solitude of the Escurial, where they are almost inaccessible. There were two other Spanish painters, of little note, called El Mudo, one Pedro el Mudo, and the other Diego Lopez, who must not be confounded with the illustrious Navarette.

MUET, Pierre le, a French architect, born at Dijon, in 1591. He practised the military as well as the civil branch of the art, and was employed by Cardinal Richelieu in fortifying a number of situations in Picardy. He was commissioned to complete the church of Val de Grace at Paris, and erected a façade of two orders, Corinthian and Composite, with windows richly decorated with columns and a balustrade. Among his other works were the designs for the hotels Luynes, Laigle, and Beauvilliers; the chateau of Pont en Champagne, and Chavigny en Touraine. He commenced the church des Augustins, in the Place des Victoires, but died before its completion, in 1669. Muet composed a treatise on architecture, and translated Palladio's work on the Five Orders; also the work of Vignola, adding to both a number of his own inventions and reflections. He published a work in folio, containing many plans, entitled *Le Maniere de Batir pour toutes sortes des Personnes*.

MUGELIO, Andrea del Castagno di, a Venetian painter, born in 1655, and died in 1726. He was deemed a good painter of history.

MUGNOZ, or MURENOS, a Spanish painter, so called by the Italian writers. See *Munoz*.

MULDER, J., a Dutch engraver, who flourished at Amsterdam about 1720. He engraved a set of Bible plates from the designs of Picart, published at Amsterdam in 1720, entitled *Figures de la Bible*. They are executed with the graver in a stiff, tasteless style, and the drawing is incorrect. There is a set of small plates by him, entitled *Vues de Gunterstein*, inscribed *J. Mulder ad vivum del. et fecit*. He also engraved some plates of churches and public edifices, which are his best prints.

MULIER, Pietro, or De MULIERIBUS. See Peter Molyn the Younger.

MULINARI, Giovanni Antonio, called Il Caraccino, a painter born at Savigliano, in Piedmont, in 1577. His name is often erroneously written Mollineri. There is considerable discrepancy about the history of this artist and his merits. His works are highly esteemed in his native place. He is said to have studied under the Caracci, and hence his surname of Caraccino. This is denied by Della Valle and others, who say that he only studied the prints of the Caracci, and never visited either Rome or Bologna. Lanzi says he acquired great celebrity in his native place, and was considerably employed at Turin; he is correct, energetic, and if not dignified, yet animated and varied in his male heads, though his females are all deficient in grace. His coloring is also good, though not resembling the Caracci; his tints being clearer, differently disposed, and sometimes feeble. His Deposition from the Cross, in the church of S. Dalmasio, is considered one of his best performances at Turin. But his best works are at Savigliano, his native place, where he passed the greater part of his life, and where his works are to be found in almost every church. In fact, his talents and his merits are only known in his native place. He died about 1640.

MULINARI, Stefano, an eminent Italian engraver, born at Florence about 1740. He studied with Andrea Scacciati, whom he assisted in a series of engravings after the most beautiful drawings in the Florentine Gallery. He is chiefly known by his numerous engravings after the best Italian masters. Nagler gives a list of 200 of his prints in his Kunstler Lexicon, among which are four after Leonardo da Vinci, five after Michael Angelo, twenty-two after Raffaelle, eight after Giulio Romano, six after Polidoro da Caravaggio, twenty-six after Parmiggiano, five after Daniello di Volterra, eight after Baroccio, seven after Giulio Cesare Procaccini, three after Guido, three after Andrea Sacchi, and thirteen after Guercino. His works are executed in a masterly style, and possess great interest and merit. His name is frequently but erroneously written, Molinari. He died about 1800.

MULLER, Hermann, an engraver who is said by Huber to have been a native of Amsterdam, though he resided, during the greater part of his life, at Antwerp. He flourished about 1585. He is supposed, from his style, to have been a pupil of Henry Goltzius, and to have studied afterwards in Italy. His plates are executed entirely with the graver, in the labored and formal style which distinguished the Flemish school of that period. He engraved, in conjunction with Cornelius Cort, several plates for Jerome Cock; also in conjunction with the Galles, the Sadelers, and others, a set of Bible plates, after Martin de Vos, John Stradan, and other masters. His plates are marked with one of the accompanying monograms.—Among others, we have also the following prints by him:

MF, or ML, or MLFe or ML Fec

The Fates; *after Cornelius van Haerlem.* The Four Cardinal Virtues; *after Martin Hemskerk.* The Ten Commandments; *do.* A set of seven plates of the Creation; *after H. Goltzius.* The Death of Cleopatra; *after C. van Haerlem.* The Death of Lucretia; *after Cornelius Ketel.*

MULLER, John. This eminent engraver is supposed to have been of the same family as the preceding. He was born at Amsterdam about 1570, and studied under Henry Goltzius, whose vigorous style he followed with an enthusiasm bordering on extravagance. He handled the graver with the most extraordinary and daring facility, and his works are worthy of the careful study of those who wish to distinguish themselves in the free use of the burin, though it is to be regretted that his drawing is not more correct. His plates are numerous, and though inferior to those of Goltzius in taste, correctness of drawing, anatomy and finish, they are more freely executed, and are considered extraordinary productions. Many of his prints are from his own compositions, and are very creditable to him as a designer. The following are among his most admired prints:

PORTRAITS.

Bartholomeus Spranger, pictor celeberrimus; *J. ab Ach, pinx.* Maurice, Prince of Orange; *after Mirevelt.* John Neyen, of Antwerp, his hand resting on a Skull; *do.* Ambrose Spinola; *do.* Albert, Archduke of Austria; *after Rubens.* Isabella, Infanta of Spain; *do.* Christian IV. King of Denmark; *after P. Isachs.*

SUBJECTS FROM HIS OWN DESIGNS.

The Baptism of Christ. An Ecce Homo, with angels. Balthasar's Feast; fine and rare. The Adoration of the Magi; do.

SUBJECTS AFTER BARTHOLOMEW SPRANGER.

Hagar in the Desert, comforted by an Angel. Lot and his Daughters. The Nativity; *J. Müller, scul.* 1606. The Holy Family, with two Angels. Venus and the Graces. Venus, Bacchus, and Ceres. A Satyr taking a Thorn from the Foot of a Faun. Venus and Mercury. Perseus armed by Minerva and Mercury; one of his finest plates. Cupid and Psyche. The Apotheosis of the Arts. Fortune distributing her Gifts.

SUBJECTS AFTER VARIOUS MASTERS.

The Raising of Lazarus; *after Ab. Bloemaert;* fine. Cain slaying Abel; *after Cornelius van Haerlem.* The Rape of the Sabines; *after the sculpture of A. de Vries.* Mercury and Pandora; *do.* The Martyrdom of St. Sebastian; *after J. van Achen;* fine.

MULLER, Solomon, is supposed to have been a member of the same family, and, from his style, to have been brought up in the school of the Wierixes, whose neat, finished style, he imitated with considerable success, though his drawing is incorrect, and his heads often lack expression. Among other prints he engraved a set of small plates of sacred subjects, which, as they are without the name of the painter, are probably from his own designs. He flourished about 1610.

MULLER, G. A., a German engraver, born at Vienna about 1700. In conjunction with Andrew and Joseph Schmutzer, he engraved a part of the plates of the life of Decius, after the designs by Rubens in the possession of the Prince of Lichtenstein. Among others, are the following by him: Philip Louis, Count de Sintzendorf, Minister of State. Jacob van Schuppen, Director of the Academy at Vienna. The two Children of Rubens; from a picture by that master, in the Lichtenstein collection.

MULLER, Jacob, a German engraver of little note, who flourished at Augsburg about 1750, and engraved some frontispieces and other book plates, executed with the graver in a neat, but a dry and tasteless style.

MULLER, Chevalier John Gotthard von, an eminent German engraver, born at Bernhausen in the Duchy of Wurtemberg, in 1747. It is not mentioned under whom he first studied, but he showed so much talent that the King of Wurtemberg took him under his protection, and sent him to Paris to study under J. G. Wille, under whose able instruction he made rapid progress, and soon acquired distinction in his profession. He was admitted into the Academy at Paris in 1776. He soon afterwards returned to Stuttgard, and was appointed Director of the Academy of Design in that city. He was elected successively a member of the principal German Academies; was presented, in 1808, by King Frederick of Wurtemberg, with the order of Civil Merit; and in 1818, was made a knight of the Wurtemberg Crown. Müller engraved only thirty-three plates, a small number, but most of them are of large size, very elaborate, and engraved in a neat, finished, and masterly style. His print of the Madonna della Seggiola, after Raffaelle, engraved in 1804, for the Musée Français, is considered by many, superior to the print of the same subject by Raphael Morghen. He died at Stuttgard in 1830. The following are his most esteemed prints:

PORTRAITS.

Louis XVI. full-length; one of his finest plates. J. G. Wille, Engraver; *after Greuze.* Louis Galloche, Painter; engraved for his reception into the Academy. Louis Leramberg, Sculptor to the King; do. Augustus Gottlieb Spanganberg; *A. Graff, pinx.* F. Schiller; *do.*

SUBJECTS.

Ceres; *after Goltzius.* The Nymph Erigone; *after Jollain.* A Lady playing on the Guitar; *after P. A. Wille.* Lot and his Daughters; *after Gerard Honthorst.* A subject from the Life of Alexander; *after G. Flinck.*

MULLER, Christian Friedrich von. This extraordinary engraver was the son of the preceding artist, all whose genius he inherited, and whom he surpassed in his last great work, the Madonna di San Sisto, and equaled in some others. He was born at Stuttgard in 1783. He was carefully educated by his father in all those branches of the art which he knew, by experience, to be essential to constitute an excellent engraver, and in 1802, he sent him to Paris to complete his studies. In 1808, he engraved his admired plate of St. John about to write his Revelation, *after Domenichino.*

in which an eagle brings him a pen in its beak; and shortly afterwards, Adam and Eve, under the Tree of Life, *after Raffaelle.* His last and greatest work was the Madonna di San Sisto, after the picture by Raffaelle in the Dresden gallery. He had received a commission from Rittner, the celebrated printseller of Dresden, to engrave this work without any limitation as to time or expense. He concentrated all his powers upon it, in the execution of which, his soul and existence seemed to be wrapped up. He applied himself incessantly, day and night, and being naturally of a sickly constitution, the infallible result of such lengthened and constant application and excitement, made its appearance. He lived to finish the plate, but he never saw a finished proof from it. On its completion, it was sent to Paris to be printed, and he had just strength enough to permit his being carried to Sonnenstein, near Dresden, where he died in 1816, only a day or two before the proof of his plate arrived from Paris. It was suspended over the head of his bier, as he lay dead, thus reminding the spectators of the untimely fate of the great master of the original. C. F. Müller engraved only eighteen plates, most of them portraits, but the Madonna di San Sisto is a host in itself, and is considered one of the most masterly productions of the burin.

MÛLLER, or MILLER, JOHN SEBASTIAN, a German engraver, born at Nuremberg in 1715. After acquiring his art, he visited England with his brother Tobias, probably early in life. About 1760 he was employed by John Boydell, and executed several plates for his collection, which possess great merit. He engraved the plates for Smollett's History of England; Chandler's Arundelian Marbles; the Ruins of Paestum; &c. His principal work, however, was the *Illustratio systematis sexualis Linnæi*, London, 1777, 104 pl. Müller was living in 1783, and is said to have had twenty-nine children! The following are among his prints:

The Holy Family; *after Federigo Baroccio.* Another Holy Family; *after Murillo.* Nero depositing the Ashes of Brittanicus; *after le Sueur.* A Landscape, with Apollo and Marsyas; *after Claude.* A Moonlight; *after vander Neer.* Two Views in Rome; *after Gio. Paolo Pannini.*

MÜLLER, WILLIAM JOHN, an eminent English painter, born at Bristol in 1812. His father, a native of Germany, was Curator of the Bristol Museum, and from him he acquired a taste and knowledge of science, especially of botany and natural history. He received some instruction in painting from J. B. Pyne, but he owed most of his success to his own genius and an attentive study of nature. On leaving Pyne, he made the tour of Germany, Switzerland, and Italy, filling his portfolio with choice drawings after nature, and returned to his native city an accomplished landscape painter. Meeting with little encouragement, he went to Greece and Egypt, and made numerous sketches of the interesting scenes and objects he met with in those countries. In 1839, he returned and settled in London. In 1841, he published his "Picturesque sketches of the Age of Francis I.," which extended his fame beyond his own country. He next, at his own expense, joined the expedition to Lycia, projected by the government. On his return to London, he exhibited at the Royal Academy and at the British Institution during the last three years of his life, several excellent paintings from his sketches made in Lycia; but his pictures were placed in improper positions, of which he bitterly and justly complained, without however, obtaining any redress. He died in 1845, and then it was that his talents were appreciated, for at the public sale of his effects, some of the choice sketches he had made in Lycia brought extraordinary prices, varying from £20 to £60 each, and the whole amount of the sale was £4600; nor were these fictitious prices, for many of them were bought by dealers, who reaped a rich harvest, by their re-sales. His works are still greatly increasing in value; Stanley says, they are already being imitated and palmed off on the unwary at exorbitant prices, by unprincipled traffickers in the fine arts.

MUNARI, PELLEGRINO. See PELLEGRINO DA MODENA.

MUNARI, GIOVANNI, a painter who flourished at Modena in the latter part of the 15th century. Lanzi says he was commended by historians for his works. He was the father and instructor of the celebrated Pellegrino da Modena.

MUNERO, GIOVANNI BATTISTA, a painter, born at Genoa in 1613. He studied under Luciano Borzone, and chiefly excelled in portraits, in which branch he acquired distinction. He died in 1657.

MUNIER, JEAN, a French engraver on wood, who flourished at Toulouse about 1553. He was chiefly employed by the booksellers. Among others, he engraved a set of 100 emblems for a small octavo volume published at Lyons in 1553, entitled *La Morosophie de Guillaume de la Perriere Tolsain.* He also executed some cuts in conjunction with Jean Perrin.

MUNNIKHUYSEN, JOHN, a Flemish engraver, who flourished about 1680. He engraved some plates, mostly portraits, executed with the graver in a neat, clear style, which possess considerable merit. The following are among the best:

PORTRAITS.

Hendrick Dirksen Spiegel, Burgomaster; *after Limburg.* Francis Burmann, Professor of Theology; *after C. Maas.* Henry vander Graft. Cornelius Tromp, Admiral of Holland; *after D. vander Plaas.* Peter van Staveren, of Amsterdam; *after W. Mieris.* Peter Zurendonk, Rector of the Latin School at Amsterdam.

MUNOZ, SEBASTIAN, a Spanish painter, born at Navalcarnero in 1654. He first studied under Claudio Coello at Madrid. In 1680, he went to Rome, and studied in the school of Carlo Maratti six years. On his return to Spain, he settled at Saragossa, where he acquired great reputation, and in conjunction with his former master, Coello, executed some considerable works for the churches. In 1688, he was invited to Madrid by the King, who appointed him his painter, and employed him in decorating the Royal Palaces, in one of which, he painted a series of frescos, representing the fable of Cupid and Psyche. He imitated the manner of Carlo Maratti, but his coloring was gaudy, without dignity in composition, beauty in the forms, or expression in the heads. He was killed by a fall from a scaffold in 1690.

MUNOZ, EVARISTO, a Spanish painter, born at Valencia in 1671. He studied under Conchillos, and painted history with reputation. His works evince an abundant invention; but his design is often incorrect, and is lacking in elevation. He formed a school of design at Valencia, which was much frequented till his death, in 1737. Most of his pictures are in the churches of Valencia.

MUNTINCK, Gérard, a Dutch engraver, born at Groningen, where he flourished about 1640. He engraved some portraits, executed with the graver in a neat style, but without much effect.

MUNTZ, J. H., an English artist, of German descent, who was much employed by Lord Orford in making drawings for his villa at Strawberry Hill. He invented a method of painting in *encaustic*, concerning which he published a volume in octavo in 1762.

MUOLTSCHER, Hans, or John, an old painter of Ulm, in Suabia, of whom nothing is known except an altar-piece, dated 1436. This picture is now in England.

MURA, Francesco de, called Franceschiello, a Neapolitan painter, born in 1696. According to Dominici, he studied under Francesco Solimena, and was his ablest disciple, the most successful imitator of his style, and approached nearest to his fame; hence his acquired name. He was much employed in decorating the public and private edifices of Naples. Lanzi says perhaps none of his works procured him greater celebrity than his frescos in the Royal Palace at Turin, where he successfully competed with Cav. Claudio Beaumont, then in the height of his reputation. He decorated the ceilings of several apartments, particularly of those containing the Flemish pictures. The subjects which he treated with the greatest success were the Olympic Games and the Deeds of Achilles, in which his composition is rich and ingenious, his figures elegantly designed, and the airs of his heads expressive and graceful. His coloring unites tenderness with grace, and his draperies are judiciously cast. He died in 1759.

MURANO, da, a name given to several old Venetian artists from the place of their nativity, the Island of Murano, near Venice. The eldest of these was Quirico da M., whose name is found inscribed on ancient pictures, *Quiricius de Muriano*. The second was Bernardino M., of whose productions Zanetti saw nothing but a rude altar-piece. The third, and most eminent, was Andrea da Murano, who was an excellent artist of his time, and established a school, which, through the Vivarini, his disciples, was continued at Venice for nearly a century, with distinction. There is a fine altar-piece by him in the church of S. Pietro Martire, in his native place, in which a St. Sebastian forms so conspicuous a figure from the beauty of its *torso*, that Zanetti conjectures he must have copied it from an ancient statue. It is dated 1402.

MURANO, Natalino da, a Venetian painter, who studied under Titian. According to Ridolfi, he was a good composer of cabinet pieces, and particularly excelled in portraits, which he executed and colored in the style of his master. Lanzi says he executed many easel pictures, from which the Venetian dealers derived more profit than himself, and that he saw one of his Magdalenes, put up for sale at Udine, which, in spite of frequent retouching, preserved much of Titian's manner. It bore the name of Murano, and the date 1558.

MURANT, Emanuel, a Dutch painter, born at Amsterdam, according to Houbraken, in 1622, but probably later, as he was a scholar of Philip Wouwerman, who was born in 1620. Though he did not adopt the subjects of his master, he acquired from him that correctness of design, purity and brilliancy of coloring, and neatness of pencil, which rendered him deservedly eminent. His subjects were views in Holland, cities, towns, and villages, decayed castles, and ruined buildings, which he drew from nature, and finished with such astonishing accuracy and precision, that it has been said, that "every particular brick or stone might be counted in his buildings by the assistance of a convex glass," in which particular he was only excelled by John vander Heyden. He went to Paris, and resided some time in that city, where his works were greatly admired. On his return to Holland, he settled at Lewarde, where he died in 1700. His works are exceedingly valuable and scarce, owing to the extraordinary labor he bestowed upon them. They have the rare merit of exhibiting the most exquisite finish, without the appearance of stiffness and labor, and without the interruption of that harmony of color and union of effect, which are usually the attributes of a process so tedious and precise. His tones are artfully broken, and there appears a vagueness and neutrality in his tints, which are only to be found in the works of the most intelligent colorists.

MURATORI, Domenico Maria, a Bolognese painter, born in 1662. He studied under Lorenzo Pasinelli at Bologna, after which he went to Rome, where he resided the greater part of his life, and acquired a distinguished reputation for the grandeur of his compositions, correctness of design, good coloring, and excellent chiaro-scuro. He executed many works for the churches in that metropolis, as well as in other cities. His Christ Crowned with Thorns, in the church of the Stimate, was universally esteemed, and procured for him the commission to paint one of the Prophets in the Basilica of St. John of Lateran—a high honor. In the church of the Apostles, he painted the great altar-piece, said to be the largest in Rome, representing the Martyrdom of St. Philip and St. James, composed and designed in a grand style, with a fine effect of chiaro-scuro, though in coloring, it is not equal to some of his other works. In the cathedral of Pisa, he painted a large picture of St. Ranieri casting out a Demon, which Lanzi considers one of his best works. He also etched a few plates from his own designs, and others, executed in a spirited and masterly style. He died in 1749. Zani, whose work is full of errors, as to dates, and who seems to delight in contradictions, says he was born in 1655, and died in 1742; but the dates given, were furnished to Oretti by the son of Muratori, and Lanzi and others state the same.

MURATORI SCANNABECCHI, Teresa, a Bolognese paintress, born in 1662. She was the daughter of an eminent physician, and at an early age discovered an uncommon genius for drawing and music. She studied painting successively with Emilio Taruffi, Lorenzo Pasinelli, and Giovanni Gioseffo dal Sole. She acquired considerable distinction, and executed several reputable works for the churches of Bologna, the chief of which are, St. Benedetto restoring a dead child to life, in S. Stefano; the Annunciation, in S. Trinità; and the

Incredulity of St. Thomas, in La Madonna di Galleria. She died in 1708.

MUREL, or MOREELS, Jacob, a German painter of fruit and flowers, who, according to Füessli, was born at Frankfort in 1628, and died there in 1683. Little is known of his life, but incidents mentioned in the history of art show that he was not only a reputable artist, but a true lover of art, and an excellent man. He painted fruit and flower-pieces, married the widow of Matthew Merian the Elder, and was the instructor of at least two distinguished artists. See *Abraham Mignon*, and *Maria Sybilla Merian*.

MURENA, Carlo, an eminent Italian architect, born at Rome in 1713. He studied polite literature, philosophy, and the law, intending to follow the legal profession; but acquiring a strong inclination for architecture, he studied that art under Niccolo Salvi. In order that he might acquire a knowledge of hydraulics, the Cardinal Barberini, his patron, sent him to Luigi Vanvitelli, who was then building the Lazaretto at Ancona. Murena made such rapid progress as to be entrusted by his master with those buildings to which he could not personally attend; and he had the entire charge of the edifices of his Sicilian majesty, attached to the Caserta. He was subsequently employed to erect the building for the Olivetani monks of Monte Morcino at Perugia, and superintended the church of that order to its completion. He designed an isolated tabernacle for the cathedral of Terni, adorned with mixed stones and gilt metal, producing rather an elegant effect; and at Foligno, the church of the monks of the Holy Trinity.

Milizia says of Murena, that "he was a good man, possessing a highly cultivated mind, exceedingly industrious, and rapid in execution. His style of architecture was simple and rational. He fell into some of the prevailing errors, but never into absurdities." Besides the works previously mentioned, Murena erected an edifice for the Cistercians, near Santa Lucia della Chiavica, which is simple and solid in the exterior; the internal arrangements are distributed with great order, convenience and beauty. His sacristy of the church S. Agostino is in a very elegant style. He also built the rich Zampaj chapel in S. Antonio di Portoghesi at Rome; and acquired great honor by the façade which he designed for the French ambassador Rochecouart. Murena died in 1764.

MURILLO, Bartolomé Estéban, a preëminent Spanish painter, was born at Pilas, a small town about five leagues from Seville, on the 1st of January, 1613. There is a great deal of contradiction among authors, no two agreeing about the history of this great artist's life, which we cannot touch upon, farther than to say that the stories of his having gone to South America in the early part of his career, and that he studied in Italy, are wholly unfounded, for the later Spanish historians have proved that he never left Spain. He was descended from an ancient family, who once held ample possessions in the province of Andalusia, but were then in reduced circumstances. Young Murillo, discovering an early inclination and genius for art, was placed in the Academy of his maternal uncle, Don Juan del Castillo, a distinguished historical painter of Seville, who was the instructor of some of the greatest artists of the Spanish school, among whom were Alonso Cano and Pedro de Moya, the very mention of whose names will contradict some of the assertions with regard to Murillo. When Murillo left the school of Castillo which he did while young, when that master went to Cadiz, the first subjects he painted were rustics and beggar-boys, in which he discovered a faithful and accurate attention to nature, and a charming simplicity of character that was peculiar to him. His pictures of this description are vigorously colored, but with the dark and heavy shadows of his master, and lack that tenderness and suavity that distinguish his later productions. It was the custom of the young artists of that time to expose their works for sale at the annual fairs held at Seville, and many of his earlier productions, which were greatly admired, were produced in this manner, and exported to South America, and there can be little doubt that the pictures of the Virgin and Saints, said to be in some of the churches of Spanish America, were thus procured, and gave rise to the false tradition of his having proceeded thither in person. The fame of Don Diego Velasquez, then at its zenith, inspired Murillo with a desire to visit Madrid, in hopes to benefit by his instruction. On his arrival at the capital in 1642, he paid his court to Velasquez, who, perceiving his merits, not only received him into his academy, but procured him the best means of improvement beyond his own instruction, by obtaining for him access to the rich treasures of art in the royal collections. Some say that when he left Seville he was extremely poor, and having disposed of all his pictures and effects, set out for Italy, by way of Madrid, without the knowledge of his relatives, and that on his arrival there, Velasquez dissuaded him from his object; which is an improbable story. At all events, a new scene was opened to his view, which inspired him with such zeal for advancement that he redoubled his efforts to attain the highest excellence. His attention was particularly directed to the works of Titian, Rubens, and Vandyck, which he continually studied and copied, and thus greatly improved his manner of design and coloring. After passing three years under such favorable circumstances, with the advantage of the instructions and counsels of Velasquez, he returned to Seville in 1645, and resumed the practice of his art with redoubled alacrity, and with the most flattering success. His first great work was a fresco in the convent of San Francisco, or the Capuchins, consisting of sixteen compartments, in one of which is his celebrated picture of St. Thomas of Villanueva distributing Alms to the Poor. This subject suited the bent of his genius, and gave full scope for the display of his powers, which were peculiarly adapted to the representation of nature in her most simple and unsophisticated forms. The saint stands in a dignified posture, with a countenance beaming with benevolence and compassion, while he is surrounded by a group of paupers, eagerly pressing forward to receive his charity, whose varied character and wretchedness is portrayed with wonderful art, and truthfulness of expression. At the principal altar in the church of the same convent, is a large picture of the Jubilee of the Porciuncula, representing Christ holding his Cross, and the Virgin interceding for the supplicants, with a group of Angels of extraordinary beauty. These works produced emotions of the greatest astonishment among his countrymen, procured him numerous commissions, and proved him one of the greatest artists of that age, so prolific in renowned masters. About this time he was employed by the Marquis of Villamanrique, to paint a series of pictures from the life of David, in which the back-grounds were to be painted by Ignacio Iriate, an eminent landscape painter of Seville. Murillo rightly proposed that the landscape parts should be first painted, and that he should afterwards put in the figures, but Iriate contended that the historical part ought to be first finished, to which he would adapt the back-grounds. To put an end to the dispute, Murillo undertook to execute the whole, and changing the History of David to that of Jacob, he produced the famous series of five pictures, now in the possession of the Marquis de Santiago at Madrid, in which the beauty of the landscapes contends with that of the figures, and which remain a monument of his powers in these different departments of the art. In the same collection are two other pictures, which are considered among his finest works; one represents St. Francis Xavier in a dignified and sublime attitude, his eyes devoutly raised to heaven, and his countenance beaming with devotion and fervor, while a stream of light from above strikes him on the breast, as if receiving the divine inspiration previous to his entering on his mission to the Indians, a group of whom are seen in the distance; the other represents St. Joseph, leading by the hand the young Saviour, apparently eight or ten years old; over the heads is a Glory of beautiful Angels, and a fine landscape in the background. He painted for the Cathedral of Seville his admired picture of San Antonio and the Holy Infant, with a glory of Angels, and a background of noble architecture; the Miraculous Conception; and the portraits of Leandro and Isidore, archbishops of Seville, all of them executed in his finest manner. He painted in the church of the Hospital of Charity three admired works—Moses striking the Rock, the Miracle of the Multiplication of the Loaves and Fishes, both grand compositions of numerous assemblages of people, the principal figures full of dignity, and the people exhibiting a striking variety of character, grouped with surprising ability; and one of St. John supporting a poor old man, aided in his charitable office by an Angel, whom the Saint regards with a look of reverence and gratitude, beautifully expressed. It is impossible to specify here Murillo's numerous works. He resided most of his life at Seville, where he executed many works, not only for the churches, but for the private collections. He also painted several pictures for the churches at Cadiz, Granada, and Cordova. At Cadiz are two of his most admired works, an altar-piece of the Conception, in the church of San Felipe Neri, and a picture of St. Catherine at the Capuchins, which is not only remarkable for its beauty, but from its being the last picture he ever painted. In the Chapel of the Nuns of the Angel, at Granada, is one of his most celebrated pictures, representing the Good Shepherd. In 1670, Charles II. invited him to Madrid, with liberal offers; but his natural humility, love of retirement, and his attachment to Seville prevailed over every consideration of promotion or advantage, and he excused himself to the king. Murillo died at Seville, in 1685, his death being hastened by a fall from a scaffold while painting the St. Catherine at Cadiz. Few painters have a juster claim to originality of style than Murillo, and his works show an incontestible proof of the perfection to which the Spanish school attained, and the real character of its artists—for he was never out of his native country, and could have borrowed little from foreign artists; and this originality places him in the first rank among the painters of every school. All his works are distinguished by a close and lively imitation of nature. His pictures of the Virgin, Saints, Magdalenes, and even of the Saviour, are stamped with a characteristic expression of the eye, and have a national peculiarity of countenance and habiliments, which are very remarkable. There is little of the academy discernible in his design or his composition. It is a chaste and faithful representation of what he saw or conceived; truth and simplicity are never lost sight of; his coloring is clear, tender, and harmonious, and though it possesses the truth of Titian, and the sweetness of Vandyck, it has nothing of the appearance of imitation. There is little of the ideal in his forms or heads, and though he frequently adopts a beautiful expression, there is usually a portrait-like simplicity in his countenances. In short, his pictures are said to hold a middle rank between the unpolished naturalness of the Flemish, and the graceful and dignified taste of the Italian schools. The works of Murillo are numerous and widely scattered over the world. His greatest works, as before mentioned, are in the churches in Spain, some in the royal collection at Madrid, some in France and Flanders, many in England, and a few in the United States. They now command enormous prices. The National Gallery at London paid 4000 guineas for a picture of the Holy Family, and 2000 for one of St. John with the Lamb. Murillo was of a noble and charitable disposition, and though he received large and increasing prices for his works after his return from Madrid to Seville, he is said to have left but little property.

MURPHY, John, an English mezzotinto engraver, born about 1748, and died about 1810. He engraved some of the prints in the Houghton collection, and others after the Italian masters; also after Reynolds, West, Romney, Northcote, Stothard, and Ramberg. He was an excellent engraver in his branch of the art. The following are among his most esteemed prints:

The Brothers of Joseph showing his bloody Garment to Jacob; *after Guercino*. Joseph interpreting Pharaoh's Dream; *do*. Mark Antony's Oration over the Body of Cæsar; *after West*. Elisha restoring the Widow's Son; *after Northcote*. The Tiger; *do*.

MURRAY, Thomas, an eminent Scotch portrait painter, born in 1666. He went to London at an early age, where he studied with John Riley, at the time he was painter to William and Mary. He studied nature carefully, imitated his master in his coloring, to whom his pictures have a striking resemblance. He was patronized by the royal family and many of the nobility, and acquired a considerable fortune. His portrait, painted by himself, is in the Florentine Gallery. He died in 1724.

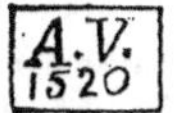
or MUSIS, Agostino de, called Agostino Veneziano, an eminent engraver, born

at Venice about 1490, and a disciple of Marc' Antonio Raimondi, of whose fine style he was one of the most successful followers. Several of his earlier plates were executed in conjunction with Marco da Ravenna, who had been his fellow-student under Marc' Antonio. After the death of Raffaelle in 1520, they separated, and each wrought alone. At the sacking of Rome in 1527, the artists in that capital sought refuge in other Italian cities, and Agostino went to Florence, where he is said to have applied to Andrea del Sarto for employment; but having previously engraved, in 1516, a plate from a picture by him, representing a Dead Christ supported by Angels, which did not meet the painter's approbation, he would not permit him to engrave any more of his pictures. Musis was one of the most eminent engravers of his time. His prints are equally neat and finished as those of Marc' Antonio, but they are inferior to him in the purity and correctness of his drawing, and the tasteful expression of his heads. Very many of his works are after Raffaelle. The earliest dates found on his plates are 1509, and the latest 1536, about which time he is supposed to have died. Fine impressions of his prints are extremely scarce and valuable. He sometimes marked them with a tablet, similar to that used by Marc' Antonio, but more frequently with a date and A. V., for *Agostino Veneziano*. The following are his principal plates:

PORTRAITS.

Pope Paul III., in profile; inscribed *Paulus III. Pon. Max.* 1534. The same Pontiff, with the papal crown; dated 1536. Charles V. holding a sword; *after Titian.* Another Portrait of Charles V.; dated 1536. Ferdinand, King of the Romans; inscribed *Proximus a summo Ferdinandus, &c.* 1536. Francis I. of France; dated 1536. The Emperor Soliman; dated 1535.

SUBJECTS OF SACRED HISTORY.

The Creation; engraved in conjunction with Marco da Ravenna; *after Raffaelle.* The Sacrifice of Isaac; *do.* The Benediction of Isaac; dated 1522; *do.*; very scarce. The same subject; dated 1524. The Israelites passing the Red Sea; *do.* The Israelites gathering the Manna; *do.* This plate is supposed to have been begun by Marc' Antonio. Samson bound by the Philistines; circular; *from his own design.* The Nativity; *after Giulio Romano.* 1531. The Four Evangelists; in four plates; *do.* 1518. The Murder of the Innocents; copied from the print by *Marc' Antonio.* A. V.; very scarce. The Nativity; copied from a wooden cut by *A. Durer;* very scarce. Christ bound to the Pillar; *do.;* very scarce. The Last Supper; *do.;* 1514. The dead Christ, with Angels; *after A. del Sarto.* 1516. The Archangel Michael; *after Raffaelle.* The Virgin and infant Christ, with St. John; *after Francia.* St. Jerome with the Lion; *after Raffaelle.*

HISTORICAL AND MYTHOLOGICAL SUBJECTS.

Diogenes seated by the side of a River; *after Baccio Bandinelli.* Tarquin and Lucretia; *after Raffaelle.* The Death of Lucretia; copied from the print by *Marc' Antonio; after Raffaelle.* Cleopatra; *after Baccio Bandinelli.* 1518. Vulcan giving Cupid's Arrows to Venus; *after Raffaelle.* 1530. Venus riding on a Dolphin, with Cupid holding a Torch; *do.* Jupiter and Leda. Apollo and Daphne; *after Raffaelle;* attributed by some to Marc' Antonio. The Fall of Phaeton; marked A. V. on a tablet. The Triumph of Silenus; *after Raffaelle;* do. The infant Hercules destroying the Serpents; *after Giulio Romano.* Hercules strangling Anteus; *after M. Angelo Buonarotti.* Hercules destroying the Nemean Lion; *after Raffaelle.*

VARIOUS SUBJECTS.

The Burying-place, an assemblage of emaciated figures with skeletons, and a figure of Death holding a book; *after Baccio Bandinelli;* inscribed *Augustinus Venetus de Musis faciebat.* 1518. A large print, called the Climbers; after the famous cartoon of Pisa, by *M. Angelo Buonarotti*, dated 1523. This print is very different from that of the same subject engraved by Marc' Antonio, which consists of many more figures. It is marked with the name of the painter on a tablet, and dated 1524. The Academy of Baccio Bandinelli, in which that artist is represented in the midst of his disciples. 1531. The Battle of the Sabre, so called from a sword which lies on the ground, fallen from the hand of a warrior, who is represented as dead, on the right-hand side of the print. An Emperor on horseback, with attendants, called by some the Triumph of Marcus Aurelius. This print is marked with the tablet used by Marc' Antonio, who is supposed to have partly engraved it. An old Philosopher, or Magician, seated on the ground, measuring with his compasses a circle, in which are seen the sun and moon; dated 1509; *after Dom. Campagnola.*

MUSIS, Lorenzo and Giulio de. These engravers are supposed to have been the sons of the preceding. They engraved some plates, in which they seem to have imitated Agostino de Musis, but with no great success. Their prints are marked with their names in full.

MUSS, Charles, a German painter in enamel, who ranked high in that branch. He also excelled in painting on glass. His picture of the Holy Family, after Parmiggiano, is the largest enamel ever executed. He died in 1824.

MUSSCHER, Michael van, an eminent Dutch painter, born at Rotterdam in 1645. He first studied under Martin Zaagmoolen, an obscure artist; and afterwards successively with Abraham vander Tempel, Gabriel Metzu, and Adrian van Ostade. He did not exactly follow the style of any of his instructors, but adopted one of his own, somewhat resembling Francis Mieris, without arriving at the harmony of his coloring, or the exquisite polish of his finishing. He painted conversations and small portraits, which are clearly and agreeably colored and highly finished, though his drawing is not very correct. He particularly excelled in portraits, which he executed with truth and fidelity; and he had the faculty of flattering his picture without spoiling the likeness, which doubtless was one reason for his great success. He settled at Amsterdam, where he found such abundant employment that he could hardly execute the numerous commissions he received. Descamps says he occasionally painted historical pieces, for which he received large prices. His works are highly esteemed in Holland, and are admitted into the choicest collections. His most remarkable work was a family picture of himself, wife, and children, which was sold for more than a thousand florins, and is now in the Museum at the Hague. He died at Amsterdam in 1705.

MUSSO, Niccolo, an Italian painter, born at Casalmonferrato. According to Orlandi, he went to Rome quite young, and studied in the school of Michael Angelo da Caravaggio. After spending two years at Rome, he returned to his native city, where he executed several altar-pieces for the churches, and wrought much for individuals.—Lanzi says, "his works possess an originality of style, though it leans to Caravaggio. His chiaroscuro, however, is more delicate and more transparent; he is very select in his figures, and in expression; and he is one of those admirable painters almost unknown, even to Italy itself." He also commends his picture in the church of St. Francis, representing that saint at the feet of Christ crucified, and a group of Angels, partaking in his lamentations and devotions. He flourished about 1618.

MUSTACCHI, IL. See REVELLO.

MUTEL, M., a French engraver little known, who executed a few portraits, among which is one of Thomas Fantel de Lagny.

MUTII, or MUCCI, GIOVANNI, a native of Cento, was the nephew and scholar of Guercino. According to Crespi, he was a faithful imitator of his master, and a distinguished engraver. None of his works are specified. He flourished about 1650.

MUTIUS, CAIUS, a Roman architect, who flourished about B. C. 100. He erected the Temple of Honor and Virtue at Rome, near the trophies of Marius. The ancient ruins near St. Eusebius are supposed by Milizia to be the remains of this temple. That author, quoting Vitruvius, says that the cell, the columns, and the entablature, were in strict accordance with the true laws of art; and had the richness of the materials been suited to the delicacy of the work, this temple would have been one of the most celebrated of all antiquity.

MUTO IL, DI FICAROLO. See ERCOLE SARTI.

MUTO IL, DI VERONA. See FRANCESCO COMI.

MUTTONI. See PIETRO VECCHIA.

MUYS, WILLIAM, a Dutch painter, born at Schiedam in 1712. He settled at Rotterdam, where he painted portraits, and cabinet pictures, somewhat in the style of Mieris and vander Werf. He died there in 1763.

MUYS, NICHOLAS, was the son of the preceding, born at Rotterdam in 1740. He was first instructed by his father, and afterwards studied with Aart Schouman at the Hague. He then returned to his native city, where he painted portraits and cabinet pictures, chiefly interiors, with considerable success. His pictures exhibit a fine genius in composition, are correct in design, well colored, and carefully finished. He died in 1808.

MUYS, R., an obscure Dutch engraver, who executed some portraits, among which is one of William, Prince of Orange.

MUZIANO, GIROLAMO, an eminent Italian painter, born at Aquafredda, in the territory of Brescia, in 1528. After learning the rudiments of the art under Girolamo Romanino in his native city, he went to Venice, where he diligently studied the works of Titian, and other great masters. He next visited Rome in company with Federigo Zuccaro, where he soon acquired distinction. His abilities recommended him to the notice of Pope Gregory XIII., who employed him to superintend the architectural works going on in the Vatican, and commissioned him to paint two pictures for St. Peter's church, representing St. Jerome and St. Basil, which gained him considerable reputation, and he was considered the great supporter of true taste. He derived his principles both in design and color from the Venetian school, and acquired such skill in landscape, that he was named in Rome *Il Giovane de' paesi.* The Cardinal Farnese employed him in competition with Zuccaro and Tempesta to decorate his villa at Tivoli, where he evinced the superiority of his talents over both his competitors. But he was ambitious to distinguish himself in a more elevated style; therefore he applied himself to study with such assiduity, that he shaved his head to prevent his going abroad. He soon afterwards produced his celebrated picture of the Raising of Lazarus for the church of S. Maria Maggiore, which was removed to the Pontifical Palace of the Quirinal, afterwards transferred to Paris by Napoleon, and again restored to its place in 1815. This capital production procured him the esteem and friendship of Michael Angelo Buonarotti, who assisted him with his instruction and advice. He soon afterwards painted his picture of the Circumcision for the church del Gesu, followed by many other admirable works in the churches and public edifices at Rome, the most remarkable of which are, the Ascension, in the Ara Cœli; St. Francis receiving the Stigmata, in the church della Concezione; the Descent of the Holy Ghost, in the Hall of the Consistory; the Nativity, in S. Maria de' Monti; Christ giving the Keys to St. Peter, in S. Maria degli Angeli, and a Troop of Anchorites attentively listening to a Saint, at the Carthusians. He also executed some excellent works for the churches in other cities, particularly in the cathedrals of Orvieto and Foligno. In the latter, he painted a fresco representing the Miracles of St. Feliciano, which Lanzi says were long covered up with smoke and dust, but a few years ago they were restored to all their original freshness and charm of color.

The works of Muziano exhibit a grandeur of design and an intimate acquaintance with anatomy, in which he appears to have emulated the learned design of Buonarotti. His composition is copious and ingenious, and the character of his heads is dignified and expressive. His coloring partakes of the truth and harmony of the Venetian school, and the back grounds of his pictures are often enriched with admirable landscapes, which remind one of the fine style of Titian. He particularly excelled in representing hermits and anchorites, men of severe aspect, with bodies attenuated by abstinence. He was also much employed in designing from the antique; and to him are we indebted for the engraving representing the basreliefs on Trajan's column. Giulio Romano had begun to copy them, and the laborious undertaking was continued, perfected, and prepared for the engraver, by Muziano. He died at Rome in 1592.

MUZIO, ANTONIO, a painter born at Verona in 1600. He studied under Enrico Fiammingo, at Bologna, the scholar of Guido, whose manner he adopted. He acquired considerable reputation, and was invited to Madrid, where he settled, and executed several works for the churches and palaces in that capital. He died there in 1648.

MY, JEROME VANDER, a Dutch painter, born at Leyden in 1688. He studied under William Mieris, whose manner he adopted; he paid great attention to the finishing, but his pictures are laborious, and deficient in vigor of effect. His subjects were history, portraits, and domestic scenes, interiors &c.

MYCON. See MICON.

MYIN, HENRY ARNOLD, a Flemish painter, born at Antwerp in 1760. He studied with Ommeganck, whose manner and subjects he adopted with considerable success. His pictures were highly esteemed, and are to be found in some of the best collections in his native city and country.

There are two fine landscapes with sheep, by him, in the Brentano collection at Amsterdam.

MYLNE, Robert, an eminent Scotch architect, born at Edinburgh in 1734. His father was also an architect, and a magistrate of that city. The son visited Italy for improvement, and resided several years at Rome, where he gained the first prize of architecture in the Academy of St. Luke, and was honored with a membership in that institution. He was also received into the Academies of Bologna and Florence. On returning to Great Britain, he settled at London; was commissioned to build Blackfriars' Bridge; and appointed surveyor of St. Paul's cathedral. Among other edifices which he erected or repaired, were Rochester Cathedral; Blaze Castle, near Bristol; Addington, the seat of the Archbishop of Canterbury; the Duke of Northumberland's pavilion at Sion, on the banks of the Thames; and Greenwich Hospital, where he was clerk of the works for fifteen years. He was consulted in regard to nearly all the harbors in England, and held a very high reputation during his long career. In 1762, he was appointed Engineer to the New River Head Company, which office he retained till his death, in 1811.

MYN, A. vander, a Dutch engraver, born at Amsterdam, who flourished about the middle of the 18th century. He engraved a few portraits and other subjects, indifferently executed.

MYN, George vander, a Dutch painter, born at Amsterdam in 1725. It is not known under whom he studied, but he imitated the manner and subjects of Watteau with considerable success. He was also a good portrait painter. He died young, at Amsterdam, in 1763.

MYN, Hermann vander, a Dutch painter, born at Amsterdam in 1684. He was the son of a clergyman, who intended him for the church, and educated him for that purpose; but his love of the fine arts induced him to study painting under Ernest Stuven, an eminent painter of fruit and flowers. Aspiring to a higher department of art, he quitted Stuven and flower painting, and devoted himself with assiduity to history. He made great progress, and acquired so much celebrity that he was invited to the court of the Elector Palatine, in 1716, where he continued some time. He afterwards returned to Holland, where he painted a picture of Jupiter and Danaë, which excited the admiration of the connoisseurs at the Hague. He also painted the history of Amnon and Tamar, in a noble style, as well as several other subjects from sacred and profane history, which were much admired for the beauty of the composition, elegance of expression, and excellence of the coloring; but, being excessively vain, he asked such enormous prices for his works that he could not find purchasers for them. He next visited Antwerp, and thence proceeded to Paris, where he was patronized by the Duke of Orleans, for whom he painted his picture of Peter denying Christ, which is considered his most capital work. In 1722 he went to London, at the recommendation of Lord Cadogan, where he was much employed in painting the portraits of the nobility, in which he carried to excess the laborious minuteness of his countrymen, imitating the details of lace, embroidery, fringes, &c., with the most patient precision. He painted the portraits of the Prince of Wales and the Princess of Orange; also a picture of the Duke and Duchess of Chandos, for which he received five hundred guineas. He lived in London for a long time in splendid magnificence; but, by indiscreet conduct and an unfortunate marriage, he sacrificed his fortune and reputation and died there, in misery and contempt, in 1741.

MYN, Agatha vander, was a sister of the preceding, and painted fruit, flowers, and dead game with considerable ability. According to Lord Orford, she accompanied her brother to London, where she practised her profession.

MYN, Robert vander, perhaps a son of Hermann vander Myn, born in 1724. He resided in London, where he painted many portraits, landscapes, and fruit and flower pieces.

MYNDE, J., an engraver who flourished in London about 1760. He was chiefly employed by the booksellers. He also engraved a few portraits, indifferently executed.

MYRIGINUS, or MYRICINUS, Peter, a Flemish engraver, who flourished at Antwerp about 1550. He engraved some subjects after Jerome Bosche, Breughel, and others, marked with the above monogram; also a portrait of Albert Durer, copied from another print. He is supposed to be the same as *Peter Martini*, an engraver and printseller of Antwerp, whose name appears on several prints published by Jerome Cock, marked *Pet. Merecinus, sc.*, one of which is dated 1567.

MYRON, an eminent Greek sculptor, born at Eleutheræ, in Bœotia, about B. C. 480. He studied under Ageladas, at the same time as Polycletus, and was therefore in the prime of life when Phidias died. At the commencement of the Peloponnesian war, Myron was settled at Athens, and in the height of his fame. Pliny says he first gained reputation by a brazen heifer. He also executed a Dog; a Quoit-thrower; Perseus killing Medusa; Delphic pentathletes; Pancratiasts; a Satyr admiring a flute; a Hercules, which was in the Temple of Pompeius in the Circus Maximus; also a statue of Apollo, taken from Ephesus to Rome by Marcus Antonius, but subsequently restored by Augustus.

Myron is said to have been the first sculptor who represented nature in a multiplicity of forms; he sculptured men and animals with equal success; and, according to Petronius, he imparted life itself to brass. Pliny says he was more varied than Polycletus, but not so exact in his proportions; curious in all corporeal detail, but paid little regard to expression. He appears to have adhered in the head and face to the earlier type; but Pliny appears to imply that he did this from taste, rather than from any want of the faculty of imparting expression.

The most celebrated of all Myron's works was his cow, lowing, and, according to some writers, suckling a calf. There are no less than thirty-six epigrams on this work in the Greek Anthology. No human figure has attracted so much notice, which probably arose from its novelty, for Athens abounded in statues of men and gods, with but very few animals, even the horses of Phidias being of a small size, and only bas-reliefs under a colonnade. It was of life-size, fixed upon a marble pedestal, in a public place in Athens, as it stood in the time of Cicero. Pausanias did not see it at Athens, however; and in the time of Procopius it was in the temple of Peace at Rome. Another celebrated work was the Dioscobolus or Quoit-thrower. The original was in bronze, and there are several similar marble statues existing, more or less perfect, supposed to be copies of Myron's work. One is in the Capitol at Rome; one in the Vatican; a third in the Villa Massimi at Rome; the one in the British Museum was found in the Villa Adriana near Tivoli, in 1791, and passed into the possession of Mr. Townley through the hands of Mr. Jenkins, a dealer in works of art. The Townley copy is said by some critics to be incorrectly restored, as it varies from the description of the original given by Lucian, which exactly corresponds with the Massimi copy. The variation, however, only concerns the position of the head; and Barry says that the deviation in the Townley copy is much more consistent with the necessary impetus of the throw, the head shooting upward and forward, instead of being turned toward the quoit-bearer. It should also be remembered that there is no proof whatever that any of these statues are really copies of Myron's work. Among the other productions of Myron, were four oxen in the temple of Apollo on the Palatine Mount; a statue of Hercules, brought by Verres to Italy; a statue of Apollo, with Myron's name in silver letters on the thigh, in the temple of Æsculapius at Agrigentum; Jupiter, with Minerva and Hercules, a very celebrated colossal work, in the Heræum at Samos. The latter was removed to Rome by Antonius, but the Minerva and Hercules were subsequently restored to their places by Augustus, who placed the Jupiter in the Capitol.

MYTENS, John. See John Meyssens.

MYTENS, Arnold, a Flemish painter, born at Brussels in 1541. It is not known under whom he studied, but he went to Italy for improvement, passing through Venice to Rome, where he resided several years, and became thoroughly imbued with the principles of that school. He afterwards went to Naples, where he painted an altar-piece representing the Assumption; also the Miraculous Conception, in the church of S. Lodovico, which gained him great reputation. At Abruzzo, he painted a grand composition, representing Christ crowned with Thorns, by the light of Flambeaux, in which the lights were judiciously and happily distributed, and the coloring excellent, with an admirable chiaro-scuro. On his return to Rome, he was employed in some considerable works in the church of St. Peter. He also painted much for the collections. He died at Rome in 1602.

MYTENS, A., a Dutch portrait painter, who flourished at the Hague from 1612 to 1660. Nothing is known of him except his works, which are well executed. Among other portraits at the Hague by him, are Frederick Henry, Prince of Orange; the poet Jacob Cats; his housekeeper, named Havius, and a picture of the Celebration of the Marriage of the Elector of Brandenbourg with the Daughter of the Prince of Orange.

MYTENS, Daniel, the Elder, a Dutch portrait painter, born at the Hague. It is probable that he studied in the school of Rubens, as he imitated that master in his portraits, and in his backgrounds. He went to England in the reign of King James, where he painted several of the Court. He was appointed court painter by Charles I., in 1625. At Hampton Court are several whole-length portraits by him of the princes of the House of Brunswick Lunenburg, and one of Charles Howard, Earl of Nottingham; at Kensington, a head of himself; and at St. James, a fine picture of Hudson, the king's dwarf, holding a dog with a string, in a landscape, warmly colored, and freely painted. Mytens continued in great reputation till the arrival of Vandyck, when the latter being appointed principal painter to the king, his pride was wounded, and he asked leave to retire to his own country. The king, learning the cause of his dissatisfaction, treated him with much kindness, and told him he could find sufficient employment for both him and Vandyck. He afterwards grew quite intimate with his rival, and Vandyck painted his portrait. It is supposed that he returned to the Hague about 1630, as none of his works in England bear a later date. Some of his portraits are so much in the style of Vandyck, that they have been taken for those of that master.

MYTENS, Daniel, the younger, was the son and scholar of the preceding, born at the Hague in 1636. Some authors confound his history with his father's. He went early to Rome, where he studied in company with his countrymen, William Doudyns, and vander Schuur. The works of Carlo Maratti, were particularly the objects of his admiration, and he formed an intimacy with that master, whose advice and instruction contributed much to his advancement; and he acquired considerable reputation at Rome, both as an historical and portrait painter. He returned to the Hague in 1664, where he continued to practise his profession with distinction, and was received into the Academy there; but having inherited a considerable property on the death of his father, he neglected his business, became dissipated, and towards the latter part of his life, degraded his talents, and impaired his health by habitual intemperance. He died in 1688.

MYTENS, Martin, a Swedish painter, born at Stockholm in 1695. He showed an early inclination for art, and before he left Stockholm, painted several works which excited the surprise of the best judges and principal nobility at that court; but feeling satisfied that he could not obtain a thorough knowledge of art in his own country, he determined to go to Italy, and on his way, to visit some of the principal cities of Europe. He first proceeded to Holland, and thence to London, where he carefully studied, and designed after Vandyck, and other masters. In 1717, he went to Paris, where he obtained the favor of the Duke of Orleans, and had the honor of painting the portrait of that prince, and of Louis XV. He also drew the Czar Peter, who made him liberal offers to induce him to settle at St. Petersburg, which he declined. In 1721, he arrived at Vienna, where he was well received, and painted the portraits of the Imperial Family. In 1723, he proceeded to Italy, stopping some time at Venice, to study the works of the best masters of the Venetian school. At Rome, he exerted all his powers to obtain a grand style of composition and a correct design. He next went to Florence, where the Grand Duke took him into his service for some time, showed him many marks of favor and esteem, and placed his portrait among the illustrious artists in his gallery. He afterwards returned to his own country, where he was received with high distinction. He painted the portraits of the Royal Family; and the King and Queen, both of whom presented him a gold chain and medal, as marks of their esteem. He finally settled at Vienna, where he was appointed court painter, which office he held, universally respected, till his death in 1755. He chiefly excelled in portraits, but he also painted several historical works of great merit. His picture of Esther and Ahasuerus, in the Imperial Collection at Vienna, is considered as an admirable performance.

# N.

NACHTGLAS, an engraver of uncertain age and country, who has executed a number of portraits, entirely with the graver, in a stiff, tasteless style, marked *Nachtglas, fecit.* It is probable, from the inscription, that they are from his own designs.

NADAT, a German engraver, who flourished about 1530. His style resembles that afterwards adopted by Theodore de Bry, from which it is supposed he instructed the latter in engraving. There are only three of his prints mentioned, executed entirely with the graver; marked with a mouse-trap, and the name NA DAT. Some authors have doubted whether Nadat was his real name, on account of the apparent division between the second and third letters. Zani calls him *Natalis Dati.* His prints are as follows:

The Virgin and Child, with St. Elisabeth; in an arch to the right is an Angel appearing to St. Joseph, and to the left an Angel appearing to St. Joachim. An Army on the march; dated 1530. An Army exercising. A Monstrous Infant, or two Infants joined back to back, inscribed *Duo Gemini*, &c.; H. 4 in., W. 6 1-8; not mentioned by Bartsch.

NAGEL, Peter, a Flemish engraver, who flourished at Antwerp about 1580. He is said to have been a disciple of Philip Galle, whose style he imitated at a very humble distance, his plates being incorrectly designed and coarsely executed. They are usually signed with his monogram, or, *P. N. fec.*, or *P. Na.* He engraved several sacred subjects, after Martin Hemskerk, and other Flemish masters, among which are the Seven Works of Mercy, *after M. Hemskerk.*

NAGLI, Francesco, called Il Centino, from the place of his nativity, Cento, where he was born about 1615. He studied under Guercino, and Lanzi says he was an excellent imitator of that master, in point of coloring and chiaro-scuro, though he was somewhat dry in his design, cold in his attitudes, and no way novel in his ideas. He executed many works for the churches at Rimini and other places.

NAGTEGEL, Arnold, an engraver of little note, who executed, among other prints, a mezzotinto portrait of Ishach Aboab Rabin, marked *Arnold Nagtegel, delin. et fecit.*

NAHL, John Augustine, a reputable German sculptor, born at Berlin in 1710. He acquired the elements of design from his father, and at the age of twenty, started on a tour through France and Italy. Returning to Berlin in 1741, he received several commissions to decorate the gardens of Potsdam and Charlottenburg. He finally settled at Hindelbanck, in Switzerland, where is one of his finest works, a monument to the memory of Madame de Langhans, wife of the minister of the town. This admirable production is well known, and is celebrated in the verses of Haller and Wieland. In 1755, Nahl removed to Cassel, and was appointed Professor of Sculpture. He executed many excellent works in that city, among which is the statue of the Landgrave William. He died in 1785.

NAIGEON, Jean, a reputable French historical and portrait painter, was born at Baune in 1757, and was living in 1831. He studied in the Academy at Dijon, and afterwards in the school of David. Among his principal historical subjects are, Æneas going to Battle; Numa consulting the Nymph Egeria; the Infant Pyrrhus presented at the Court of Closias; and the design for a grand vignette engraved by Roger, for the ordinances of the French Republic. He painted the portraits of several distinguished personages of his time; and also executed some theatrical decorations.—He was appointed Conservator of the Museum of the Luxembourg, and a member of the Legion of Honor.

NAIN, Le, a French painter, who flourished about 1650. He usually painted assemblages of peasantry, and other subjects of a domestic character. His composition is ingenious; his coloring is exceedingly sweet and simple; and there is an admirable appearance of nature and truth in the expression of his heads, which is peculiar to his works, and renders them highly interesting. (See the next article.)

NAIN, Louis and Antoine le, two brothers, were French painters, born at Laon, in the years 1583 and 1585. It is highly probable that the interesting subjects attributed to the artist mentioned in the preceding article, are the productions of Louis and Antoine le Nain. They always wrought in concert, and painted interiors of inns, domestic conversations, and the pleasures of the peasantry, which are characterized by a wonderfully natural and truthful expression, great simplicity, clear and agreeable coloring. Their best pictures are of cabinet size, and are found in the choicest collections of England, Germany, and France. Several of them have been engraved by le Bas, Daullé, Earlom, and Strange. The two brothers were chosen members of the French Academy. They maintained during life a remarkable attachment, and died only two days apart, in 1648.

NAIN, Matthieu le, was the brother of the preceding artists, born at Laon in 1593. Little is known of his life or works. He executed a portrait of Cardinal Mazarin, exhibited in the Academy, of which he was a member. He died in 1677.

NAIWINCK, NAIWYNCX, or NAUWINCX, Henry, or Hermann, a Dutch painter and engraver, born in 1620, at Utrecht, although Balkema says he was a native of Schoonhoven. He painted woody and mountainous landscapes, views of villages, and fortifications, in the style of Anthony Waterloo. The figures and animals in his pictures were inserted by John Asselyn. As an engraver he executed some admirable etchings, which are much esteemed, being engraved in a free and original style, with a very pleasing effect. Among them are two sets of landscapes, eight in each, one of upright plates, and the other lengthways. Both sets are numbered from 1 to 8. Plate I. in each is marked *H. Naiwinck inv. et. fe.*

NALDINI, Battista, an Italian painter, born at Florence in 1537. He first studied under Jacopo Carrucci, called Il Pontormo, and afterwards under Angiolo Bronzino. According to Baglioni, he visited Rome during the pontificate of Gregory XIII., and painted several altar-pieces for the churches, among which is a picture of the Baptism of Christ, in La Trinità de' Monti; and the Martyrdom of St. John the Baptist, in the church of that Saint. On returning to Florence, he was chosen by Vasari as a coadjutor in his works in the Palazzo Vecchio, and retained by him about fourteen years. Vasari makes honorable mention of Naldini, even when a young man, commending him as skillful, vigorous, expeditious, and indefatigable. He painted many pictures at Florence, especially the Deposition from the Cross, and the Purification, at S. Maria Novella, praised by Borghini for their judicious composition, correct design, elegant attitudes, beautiful coloring, and excellent perspective. His pictures are criticised by Lanzi as having the knee-joints too large, the eyes too widely opened, and generally marked with a certain fierceness; the coloring often characterized by changeable hues. In teaching his scholars, he followed the prevailing method of employing them to design after the chalk drawings of Michael Angelo, and giving them his own finished pictures to copy. He was living in 1590.

NANNI, Girolamo, called il Poco e Buono, a Roman painter, who flourished about 1643. His talents were by no means of a shining character, and he deserves little notice, except for his studious disposition, and slowness of execution. He was employed by Sixtus V. in several considerable works, and whenever requested by the director to hasten his operations, he always answered, "poco e buono" (little and good), which expression gained him his surname. There are a number of his pictures at Rome, among which are the Annunciation, in the church of the Madonna dell' Animâ; and two subjects from the Life of St. Bonaventura, in S. Bartolomeo dell' Isola.

NANI, Giacomo, a Neapolitan painter, who flourished about 1700. According to Dominici, he studied with Andrea Belvidere. He painted pictures of fruit, flowers, birds, and still-life, in the style of his master. In conjunction with Baldassare Caro, he was employed in decorating the palace of King Charles of Bourbon.

NANNI, Giovanni da Udine. See Udine.

NANNOCCIO, N., an Italian painter, commended by Vasari, who flourished about 1550. He was a scholar of Andrea del Sarto, whose style he imitated with success. He went to France, where he resided a long time.

NANTEUIL, Robert, a preëminent French engraver and painter in crayons, was born at Rheims in 1630. His father was a merchant, and gave him a classical education: but having a decided inclination for art, he studied engraving under his brother-in-law, Nicholas Regnesson, and became one of the most eminent engravers of his country. In his first productions, he appears to have imitated the style of Claude Mellan, in single strokes only, without being crossed; but he afterwards adopted a manner greatly superior, which, for clearness and beauty of effect, has never been surpassed. Nanteuil acquired considerable reputation as a painter of portraits in crayons, and his talent in that branch recommended him to the protection of Louis XIV., who commissioned him to execute his portrait, and appointed him designer and engraver to the cabinet, with a pension. His portraits will always be ranked among the finest productions of art. The larger ones, although of life-size, are remarkable for harmony of execution and admirable color. He married the daughter of Edelinck. It is evident that Nanteuil was exceedingly industrious; because, although he died in 1678, at the age of forty-eight, he executed about two hundred and eighty plates, in a highly finished style. Among them are the following:

PORTRAITS.

Anne of Austria, Queen of France; *after Mignard.* Several Portraits of Louis XIV.; *from his own designs, Mignard,* and others. Louis, Dauphin; son of Louis XIV. 1677. Louis Bourbon, Prince de Condé; *after his own designs.* 1662. Henry Julius de Bourbon, Duke d' Enghien; *after Mignard.* 1661. Christina, Queen of Sweden; *after S. Bourdon.* 1654. Louisa Maria, Queen of Poland; *after Juste.* 1653. Charles Emanuel, Duke of Savoy. 1668. Charles, Duke of Lorrain. 1660. John Frederick, Duke of Brunswick Lunebourg. 1674. Charles II., Duke of Mantua. 1652. William Egon, Prince of Furstenberg, Cardinal. 1671. N. Duke of Albret. 1649; scarce. Louis Dony d' Attichy, Bishop of Autun. 1663. Antonio Barberini, Cardinal, and Archbishop of Rheims. 1663. Pomponne de Bellievre, President of the Parliament; fine. Peter de Bonsy, Archbishop of Narbonne. 1678. J. B. Bossuet, Bishop of Meaux. 1674. Louis de Boucherat, Chancellor of France. 1676. Emanuel Theodore, Duke de Bouillon, Cardinal. 1670. Leon le Bouthellier, Minister of State; *after Champagne.* 1652. John Chapelin, the Poet. 1655. Charles d'Ailly, Duke de Chaulnes. 1676. Francis de Clermont, Bishop of Noyon. 1655. Peter du Cambut, Bishop of Orleans, afterwards Cardinal. 1666. James Nicholas Colbert, Archbishop of Rouen. 1670. John Baptist Colbert, Minister of State. 1676; *after Champagne.* Francis de Bonne, Duke de Crequy. 1662. Ferdinand de Foix de la Valette, Duke d'Espernon. 1650. Cæsar d'Etrée, Bishop of London, afterwards Cardinal. 1660. Francis de Harley de Chanvallon, Archbishop of Paris. 1675. Louis Hesselin, Counsellor of State; engraved in the style of *C. Mellan.* William de Lamoignon, President of the Parliament. 1659. Dominick de Ligny, Bishop of Meaux. 1654. René de Longueil, Minister of State and President of Parliament. Henry d'Orleans, Duke of Longueville; *after Champagne.* John Loret de Carenton. 1658; scarce. Francis Mallier, Bishop of Troyes; *after Velut.* Leonor de Matignon, Bishop of Lissieux. Julius Mazarin, Cardinal. 1655. Edward Molé, President of the Parliament. Charles de la Porte, Duke de Melleraye. 1662. John Francis Paul de Gondy, Cardinal de Retz. 1650. Armand John du Plessis, Cardinal de Richelieu; *after Champagne.* Henry de Savoye d'Aumale, Archbishop of Rheims. 1651. Peter Séguier, Chancellor of France; *after le Brun.* 1656. John Baptist Steenbergen, called the *Advocate of Holland;* one of his finest portraits. 1668. Charles Maurice le Tellier, Archbishop of Rheims. 1663. Michael le Tellier, Chancellor of France. 1662. Henry de la Tour d'Auvergne, Viscount Turenne. 1665; fine.

NAPOLI, Cesare di, a Sicilian painter, who flourished at Messina about 1583. According to Hackert, he studied in the Academy of Polidoro da Caravaggio, at Messina, and was one of his most distinguished disciples. He was a perfect imitator of his master's style, and executed some excellent works for the churches, but wrought more for individuals.

NAPOLITANO, IL. See FILIPPO D' ANGELI.

NAPPI, FRANCESCO, an Italian painter, born at Milan, according to Baglioni, in 1573. After attaining some proficiency in the art, he settled at Rome, during the pontificate of Urban VIII. He painted a number of pictures for the public edifices of that city, but they are little above mediocrity. Lanzi says, "he displays great variety; and when he painted in his Lombard manner, as in the Assumption at the cloister della Minerva, and the Annunciation and other works in the Monasterio dell' Umiltá, he showed himself a naturalist far more pleasing than the mannerists of his time." Nappi died in 1638.

NARDI, ANGELO, an Italian painter, who, according to Palomino, passed the greater part of his life in Spain, where he flourished about 1645. He studied under Paolo Veronese, and imitated the style of that master in all his works. It is probable that he attained a good degree of excellence, as Philip IV. appointed him painter to the court. There are a number of his pictures in the churches at Madrid, among which the most esteemed are the Annunciation, in the Society of S. Justo; the Nativity and Conception, in the church of the Franciscans; the Guardian Angel and St. Michael the Archangel, in the church of the Barefooted Carmelites. Nardi died at Madrid in 1660.

NARDINI, D. TOMMASO, an historical painter, born at Ascoli in 1658, and died in 1718. He studied under Lodovico Trasi, an excellent scholar of Carlo Maratti. He was much employed in decorating the churches of his native city, the best of which are in the church of S. Angelo Magno. The perspective was painted by Agostino Collaceroni, of Bologna. Nardini executed the figures, representing the Apocalypse, and other scriptural events. Lanzi says they display great spirit and harmony, richness of coloring, and facility of execution; which are the distinguishing characteristics of this master.

NASELLI, FRANCESCO, a distinguished Ferrarese historical painter, of noble birth, flourished about 1610. Lanzi says he practised drawing from the naked model with assiduity, and studied and copied the works of the Caracci and Guercino. By such practice he formed an excellent style of his own, on a large scale, soft, with vigorous coloring and rapid execution, inclining in those of his fleshes to a sunburnt hue. He made many excellent copies of the works of those masters, which are in the churches of his native place, and in private cabinets. Among these is his Communion of St. Jerome, from Agostino Caracci. He was exceedingly industrious and persevering, although in easy circumstances, and of noble rank. He painted at the Scala, in competition with one of the Caracci, Bonone, and Scarsellino; and, according to Lanzi, was deemed not unworthy of those eminent artists. Among his principal works are the Nativity, in the Cathedral; the Assumption, in S. Francesco; and several representations of the Last Supper, in private institutions. He died at Ferrara in 1630.

NASELLI, ALESSANDRO, was the son and scholar of the preceding artist, whose style he imitated, and executed according to Crespi, some works for the churches at Ferrara. He was an artist not above mediocrity.

NASH, JOHN, an English architect, born in 1752. He was at first a miniature painter, but subsequently devoted himself to architecture, and is chiefly known as the promoter and author of the important improvements in London, effected by the formation of Regent street and the Regent's Park. Among his other works, were the designs for Buckingham palace, the Pavilion at Brighton, the United Service Club House, the Haymarket Theatre, and the terraces in St. James' Park. He died in 1835.

NASINI, CAV. GIUSEPPE, an Italian painter, born at Siena, according to Della Valle, in 1664. He first studied under his father, Francesco N., an artist of little note; but afterwards entered the school of Ciro Ferri, and became one of his ablest disciples. He was deficient in correctness of design, and dignity of character, but possessed a fertile imagination, and a resolute and commanding execution, which peculiarly qualified him for grand fresco works. At the recommendation of Ciro Ferri, he was employed by the Grand Duke of Tuscany to paint in the Palazzo Pitti, from the designs of P. da Cortona, the Four Ages of Man. in emblematical subjects, which he finished to the satisfaction of his employer. There are many of his subjects at Siena, Foligno, and Florence, among which his masterpiece is supposed to be the St. Leonardo, in Madonna del Pianto, at Foligno. At Rome, he was commissioned to paint the ceiling of the Capella Bracciana, in the church de SS. Apostoli; in the large Prophets of the Lateran Cathedral, he competed with Luti, and the first artists then at Rome. Bartsch mentions a print by Nasini, representing the Virgin and the infants Jesus and John in a landscape, with Cherubs flying in the air; designed in the style of Ciro Ferri, and engraved with a delicate point in the manner of P. S. Bartoli. He died in 1736.

NASINI, CAV. APOLLONIO, born at Florence in 1697, was the son and scholar of the preceding, whom he assisted in the execution of his numerous works. Though he was inferior to his father in invention, he was an excellent artist, acquired distinction, and was much employed, not only by the churches, but by individuals. He died about 1754.

NASINI, D. ANTONIO, was a younger brother of Giuseppe, with whom he studied. According to Della Valle, he held an honorable rank among his cotemporaries. He was chiefly employed in painting portraits, in which branch he excelled. His likeness is in the Florentine Gallery. He entered the priesthood, but still continued to practise his art. He died in 1716.

NASMYTH, ALEXANDER, a Scottish landscape painter, born at Edinburg in 1758. He visited London, and became a pupil of Allan Ramsay; after which he went to Rome for improvement, and remained there several years, studying portrait, landscape, and historical painting. On returning to Edinburg, he painted the portraits of a number of persons, among which was that of Robert Burns; but subsequently devoted himself entirely to landscape. His favorite subjects were wild and mountainous views, usually designed from nature, and painted in a simple and picturesque style. He was much occupied in teaching the art. In 1813 he exhibited a View in Scotland, in the Royal Academy at London. He died in 1840.

NASMYTH, Patrick, a Scottish landscape painter, the son of the preceding, was born at Edinburg in 1787. He early manifested a decided inclination for art, and studied under his father, after which, at the age of twenty, he went to London, and attained considerable reputation. His landscapes are of a pleasing character. He often painted scenes from the wild, mountainous regions of Scotland, greatly wanting in that breadth of handling so necessary in grand landscapes, and remarkably injured by excessive detail. Had he confined his pencil to quiet, Arcadian scenes, his reputation would be greater than it is. Nasmyth had but little success. He died at Lambeth near London, in 1831.

NASOCCHIO, Giuseppe, a native of Bassano, who is said to have studied under Gentile da Fabriano at Venice, whose style he imitated. He was doubtless not a scholar, but an imitator of that master, as there is a picture by him dated 1529, whereas Fabriano probably died about 1423.—There were two other painters of this name, Bartolomeo and Francesco, who flourished about 1541. Little is known of these painters.

NASON, Peter, a Dutch painter, who flourished about 1670. He painted subjects of still-life, which are much esteemed, and are found in some of the principal German collections. It is said that he visited England, and painted the portrait of Charles II.; also that there are a number of portraits by him in that kingdom, colored in a delicate style, with considerable neatness of touch.

NATALI, Carlo, called Il Guardolino, an Italian painter and architect, born at Cremona about 1590. He studied successively under Andrea Mainardi and Guido Reni; and subsequently resided during a number of years at Rome and Genoa, observing all that was most valuable, and exerting his own talents in the art. Among his best paintings is his St. Francesca Romana, in the church of S. Gismondo at Cremona, which Lanzi ranks above mediocrity. Natali did not execute many works in painting, being principally devoted to architecture. His edifices are principally at Genoa and Cremona, but none of them are mentioned. He was living in 1683.

NATALI, Gio. Battista, an Italian painter and architect, the son of Carlo N., was born at Cremona about 1630. He was instructed in both arts by his father, and afterwards went to Rome for improvement, where he pursued his studies under P. da Cortona. On returning to Cremona, he was employed for the churches, and established a school of painting upon the principles of Cortona, though without many followers. There is a large picture by him in the Predicatori, displaying some skillful architecture, representing the Holy Patriarch burning heretical books, which Lanzi says is not unworthy a follower of Cortona. As an architect none of his works are mentioned. He died about 1700.

NATALI, Giuseppe, an eminent painter, born at Casal Maggiore, in the Cremonese territory, in 1652. According to Zaist, possessing a natural genius for the art, he went to Rome, notwithstanding the opposition of his father; and from thence to Bologna, where he assiduously studied the works of Dentone, Colonna, and Mitelli, the most famous perspective and architectural painters of the age. He flourished precisely at the period which the architectural painters consider the happiest for their art. Lanzi says "he formed a style at once praiseworthy for the grandeur and beauty of the architecture, and the elegance of the ornamental parts, judiciously introduced. He gratifies the eye by presenting those views which are the most charming, and gives it repose by distributing them at just distances. In his grotesques, he retains much of the antique, shunning all useless exhibitions of modern foliages, and varying the painting from time to time with small landscapes. The softness and harmony of his tints extorted great commendation." He found abundant employment, and decorated a great many churches and public edifices, as well as many halls and chambers for individuals throughout Lombardy. He also executed a great many small oil paintings, which were in the highest repute. He died in 1722.

NATALI, Francesco, was the brother and scholar of the preceding, whose style he adopted, and whom he nearly approached, and even surpassed in dignity. He executed many works on a large scale for the churches in Lombardy and Tuscany. He was also much employed at the courts of the Dukes of Massa, of Modena, and of Parma, in which latter city he died in 1723.

NATALI, Lorenzo and Pietro, were brothers of the preceding, whom they assisted in his works, but executed none of importance of their own.

NATALI, Gio. Battista, was the son and scholar of Giuseppe, whom he assisted in many of his works. He was afterwards appointed court-painter to the Elector of Cologne.

NATALI, Gio. Battista, was a cousin of the preceding, and the son and scholar of Francesco. He was an excellent artist in the same branch practised by his father and uncle. He was invited to the court of Charles, King of the Two Sicilies, in whose service he continued till his death, about 1750.

NATALINO DA MURANO. See Murano.

Mf or Mfe, NATALIS, Michael, a Flemish engraver, born at Liege about 1589. After acquiring the elements of design under Joachim Sandrart, he visited Antwerp, and studied engraving under Charles Mallery. From thence he went to Rome, and adopted the style of Cornelius Bloemaert, which he followed with some success. He engraved a number of plates after the great Italian masters; also part of the plates in the Giustiniani Gallery, in concert with Regnier Persyn, Theodore Matham, and others. On returning to Flanders, he was invited to Paris, where he resided some time. His plates are executed with the graver, in a free, open style, but deficient in taste. His drawing is usually incorrect, and the effect is generally cold and heavy; but his strokes are clear and regular, and he handled the burin with great facility. His portraits are his best productions. The following are his principal plates:

PORTRAITS.

Josephus Justinianus Benedicti Filius; *Mich. Natalis, fec.* Jacob Catz, Pensionary of Holland, and Poet. Eugone d'Alamond, Bishop of Ghent. Maximilian Emanuel, Elector of Bavaria; *after J. Sandrart.* Frederick, Count of Merode. Ernestine, Princess de Ligne; *after Vandyck.* The Marquis del Guasto, with his mistress represented as Venus; *after Titian.*

SUBJECTS AFTER VARIOUS MASTERS.

The Holy Family; *after Raffaelle.* The Virgin and infant Jesus, with St. Joseph seated behind, leaning his head upon his hand; *after A. del Sarto.* The Holy Family; *after N. Poussin*; the first impressions are before the nudity of the child was covered with linen. St. Paul taken up into Heaven; *do.* The Holy Family, with angels presenting Flowers; *after S. Bourdon.* The Marriage of St. Catherine; *do.* The Virgin holding the infant Christ, who is sleeping, with St. John by her side; *do.* The first impressions are before the bosom of the Virgin was covered with linen. St. Bruno at prayer; *after Bertholet Flemael.* The Assembly of the Carthusians; in four sheets; *do.* Mary washing the Feet of Christ; *after Rubens.* The Last Supper; *after Diepenbeck.* St. Francis with a Lamb; *do.*

NATOIRE, CHARLES, a French painter and engraver, born at Nismes in 1700. He studied under François le Moine, and was employed to finish several works left incomplete at the death of that master. Little is recorded of the circumstances of his life. His chief merit seems to have consisted in the correctness of his design; his coloring has been criticised as feeble and cold. The principal works of Natoire are those which adorn the apartments of the first story of the chateau of Versailles; those in the Hotel de Soubise; and in the chapel of *Les Enfans Trouvés*, at Paris. He was appointed Director of the French Academy at Rome, which honorable office he filled for twenty years, until 1775, when he retired on account of old age, and was succeeded by Vien. He died, according to Dumesnil, at Castel Gandolfo, in 1777. There are a few etchings by Natoire, executed from his own designs, in a free and spirited style. Among them are the following:

The Crucifixion, with Mary Magdalene at the foot of the Cross. The Adoration of the Magi. The Martyrdom of St. Fereol. Two, of the Sports of Children. Spring and Winter; etched by *Natoire*, and finished with the graver by *P. Aveline.*

NATTER, LAURENCE, a distinguished German medalist, and an engraver on precious stones, born at Biberach, in Suabia, in 1705. He studied design and engraving in the Academy of Fine Arts at Rome, and subsequently visited London, where he settled, and practised his art for a few years. He engraved several works for various persons, among which was a diamond for Lord Cavendish. In 1742 he went to the Hague, to execute a commission for the Prince of Orange. The next year he went to Copenhagen, and engraved a royal medal and several seals. He afterwards visited Stockholm and Petersburg, leaving proofs of his abilities in each of those cities, and then returned to London. He subsequently made another trip on the continent, similar to the first; and finally visited Paris, where he died, in 1763. Natter was chosen a member of the Antiquarian Society; and was appointed medalist to the King of the Low Countries. He published at London, in 1754, a treatise on the antique method of engraving on precious stones, as compared with the modern method, illustrated with plates. Mariette, in the first volume of his *Traité des pierres gravées*, has recorded the list of Natter's engravings on precious stones.

NATTIER, MARC, a French painter, born at Paris in 1642, and died there in 1705. He painted portraits, but attained little distinction.

NATTIER, JEAN MARC, a reputable French historical and portrait painter, the son and scholar of the preceding, was born at Paris in 1685. At the age of fifteen he gained the grand prize of the Academy, and received the royal pension, though it does not appear that he visited Rome. He made designs of the pictures by Rubens in the Luxembourg Gallery, which were subsequently engraved, and published, under the title of *La Galerie du Palais du Luxembourg, peinte par Rubens, dessinée par Nattier et gravée par les plus illustres graveurs*; Paris, 1710, in grand folio. He subsequently devoted his energies to portrait painting, and obtained great encouragement, being patronized by the royal family and many noble personages. His portrait of the Empress Catherine gained him the favor of the Czar Peter, who desired him to visit Russia, but Nattier declined the invitation. His works are praised for tasteful composition, brilliant coloring, and freedom of pencil. Among his principal portraits are those of the Princes of the House of Lorraine; Mlle. de Clermont; Marshal Saxe; the Duke de Richelieu; and that of Marie Leczinska, queen of Louis XV., engraved by Tardieu. In 1713, Nattier was chosen a member of the Royal Academy; he had a pension of 500 francs from the king; and in 1759 was elected a member of the Academy of Denmark. He died in 1766. He had a son, who bid fair to attain distinction in the art; but unhappily, while pursuing his studies at Rome, he was drowned in the Tiber at the age of twenty-two.

NAUCYDES, an eminent Greek sculptor, a native of Argos; who flourished, according to Pliny about B. C. 396. He was the son of Mothon, and the master of the younger Polycletus of Argos. According to Thiersch, he was one of the most important artists between Alcamenes and Praxiteles. Pausanias mentions six of his works; a statue of Hebe, in gold and ivory, placed near the celebrated chryselephantine statue of Juno by Polycletus at Mycenæ; a bronze statue of Hecate at Argos; and four bronze statues of victors at the Olympic games, one of Eucles at Rhodes, two of Chimon, one of which was at Olympia, the other in the temple of Peace at Rome, and the fourth of Bacis the wrestler. Pliny mentions by him a statue of Mercury, a Discobolus, and a man sacrificing a ram. Pausanias says that the two statues of Chimon were his best works. The well known Discobolus in repose, standing with a quoit in his hand, is sometimes said, incorrectly, to be the work of Naucydes.

NAUDET, THOMAS CHARLES, a French landscape painter, born at Paris in 1774. He studied under Hubert Robert, painter and designer for the royal gardens, and became one of his most distinguished scholars. He made a collection of nearly 3000 designs, embracing the most beautiful views and the finest monuments of ancient and modern times, in Italy, Spain, Germany and Switzerland. Naudet died in 1810, but a part of his work was published by his friend M. Bruun Neergard, under the title *Voyage pittoresque et historique du nord d'Italie; les dessins par Naudet, les gravures par Debucourt*, Paris 1812—1813; fol.

NAUDI, ANGELO, an Italian painter, a pupil and imitator of Paul Veronese. He went to Spain, where, according to Palomino, he passed the greater part of his life, and executed many works for the churches at Madrid, which are highly commended by the author above mentioned. He was also appointed court painter by King Philip, in whose service he continued a long time.

NAVARETTE. See EL MUDO.

NAVARO, JUAN, a Spanish engraver, mentioned by Strutt as residing at Seville about 1598. Among other plates he engraved several book frontispieces, executed with the graver, in a very indifferent style.

NAVARRO, JUAN SIMON, a Spanish painter, who flourished at Madrid about 1650. He attained considerable distinction as a flower painter; and also produced some indifferent historical works. There is a Holy Family by him, which is well colored, but inferior in other respects. In a convent of the Carmelites at Madrid, there are two of his pictures, representing a Nativity, and an Epiphany.

NAZZARI, BARTOLOMEO, an Italian painter, born, according to Tassi, in the territory of Clusane, in the Bergamese, in 1699. After studying at Venice, under Angelo Trevisani, he went to Rome, and finished his course under Benedetto Luti, and Francesco Trevisani. He settled at Venice, and became an excellent painter of history and portraits. He visited various capitals of different Italian and German states, and gained great reputation for his portraits of princes and of their courtiers; also for his heads of youths and old men, drawn from the life, very fancifully dressed and decorated. Among his best historical works, is a Holy Family, with St. Anne, at Pontremoli. He died in 1758.

NEALCES, an eminent Greek painter, cotemporary with Aratus of Sicyon; flourished about B. C. 213. He is said to have succeeded by accident in representing the foam on a horse's mouth, by a dash of his sponge. Few of his works are mentioned, but he was the most eminent painter of his time. Pliny mentions a Venus by him, and a battle between the Egyptians and the Persians on the Nile. To show the locality of this combat, Nealces painted an ass drinking at the river side, and a crocodile lying in wait. This ingenious application of accessories, has many other examples in the history of Grecian art.

Aratus, in his zeal against tyrants, resolved to destroy all their portraits which were preserved at Sicyon. This he accomplished with but one exception; at the earnest request of Nealces he spared the picture of Aristratus in his chariot, by Melanthus and Apelles, on condition that the figure of Aristratus should be defaced, which was accordingly done by Nealces, and a palm tree substituted in its place.

NEALE, JOHN PRESTON, an English painter, and a distinguished architectural engraver, was born in 1770. He painted landscapes of considerable merit, decorated with architecture; but subsequently devoted his energies to engraving. He executed many plates for the embellishment of various publications, and in 1818 he published the first part of the History and Antiquities of Westminster Abbey. In 1823 he published the second part, making in both sixty-one plates. Neale wrought with very great industry, and his plates possess considerable merit. Besides the works already mentioned, he published The Seats of Noblemen and Gentlemen of England, Wales, Scotland, and Ireland; and in 1829 a second series of five vols., making in the whole 737 plates. He died in 1848.

NEALE, THOMAS, an English engraver, who flourished about 1650. He resided at London, where he etched a good portrait of Bindo Altoviti, *after Titian*, in the style of Gaywood. It is said that he went to Paris, and engraved a number of plates in that city, among which are twenty-four pieces of Holbein's Dance of Death, the first of which is marked *Paris*, 1657; also several plates of Birds, after Barlow; *Paris*, 1659. Strutt supposes Neale had a share in engraving the plates for the octavo edition of Ogilby's Fables. His plates are usually marked with his name in full, or with the letters T. N.

NEAPOLI, FRANCISCO. See ARREGIO.

NEBBIA, CESARE, a reputable Italian painter, born at Orvieto about 1536. He studied under Girolamo Muziano, whose style he adopted, and assisted him in the important works he executed for Gregory XIII., in the Vatican, and the Capella Gregoriana. Assisted by Gio. Guerra da Modena, Nebbia superintended the works projected by Sixtus V., entrusting the completion of his designs to the younger painters. They were extensively employed during the five years' reign of that pontiff, in the chapel of S. Maria Maggiore, the Library of the Vatican, the Scala Santa, the Lateran and Quirinal palaces. Nebbia was very inferior to Muziano in dignity and grandeur, but possessed a very fertile invention, and great facility of execution. Lanzi says there are some beautiful pictures by him, finely colored, as the Epiphany, quite in Muziano's style, in the church of S. Francesco at Viterbo. Among his principal works at Rome, Baglioni mentions the Coronation of the Virgin, in S. Maria de' Monti; and the Resurrection, in S. Giacomo degli Spagnuoli. He died at Rome in 1614.

NEBBIA, GALEOTTO, an old Italian painter, a native of Castellaccio, near Alessandria, who flourished at Genoa about 1480. In the church of S. Brigida in that city, are two altar-pieces by him, which are esteemed for their antiquity and originality. The first represents the Archangels, and the second, St. Pantaleone and other Martyrs. Lanzi says they are remarkably well executed for the time, the figures represented on a gold ground, the draperies extremely rich, with stiff and regular foldings, not borrowed from any other school. The grado, or step, is ornamented with minute histories, somewhat crude, but displaying much diligence and care in finishing.

NECK, JOHN VAN, a reputable Dutch painter, born at Naarden in 1636. He was the son of a physician, who intended him for the medical profession; but manifesting a strong inclination for art, he was placed under the eminent Jacob de Backer. He settled at Amsterdam, and painted portraits and history in the admirable style of his instructor, which he followed with great success. He was very extensively employed in portraits. As an historical painter, Houbraken commends him in the highest terms, and mentions his capital picture of the Presentation in the Temple, in the Romish church at Amsterdam. His works are finely composed, and correctly drawn, particularly his subjects from the fable, where the female figures are designed with great elegance and taste, evincing a perfect acquaintance with the nude, unusual among his countrymen, and the draperies are distributed in easy and natural folds. He died in 1714.

NECKER, or NEGKER, JOBST, or JOSSE DE, a distinguished wood engraver of Nordlingen, flourished in the 16th century. He is supposed to be the same as Jobst Denecker who wrought at Augsburg about 1544, and engraved the prints for Holbein's Dance of Death, published in that year.—This is very probable, since the subject of this article executed part of the plates in the Triumph of Maximilian, by Hans Burgkmair, who flourished at Augsburg; and at the end of the Dance of Death is inscribed *Jobst Denecker Formschneyder.* Brulliot supposes that the engraver of Augsburg was the son of him of Nordlingen; but the dates agree so nearly, as to render this theory extremely improbable.

NEDEK, PETER, a Dutch painter, born at Amsterdam in 1616; died in 1678. He studied under P. Lastman, and painted landscapes, portraits, and history. His landscapes have considerable merit.

NÉE, DENIS, a French engraver, born at Paris about 1732. He studied under J. P. le Bas, and first gained distinction by restoring the plates of the *Recueil des peintres antiques*, published by Mariette and Caylus. Having formed a close intimacy with Masquelier, he executed in concert with that artist the vignettes for an edition of Ovid's Metamorphoses, and an Essay on Music. They were soon employed, however, upon more important works, among which were *Tableaux pittoresques de la Suisse*, 1 vol. fol., 430 plates; *Voyage en Grece*, by M. de Choiseul Gouffier; *Voyage de Naples et de Sicile*, by the Abbé de St. Non; and the elephantine *Voyage pittoresque de la France;* 12 vols. fol., 828 plates. The plates of Denis Née may also be found in Cassas' *Voyage d'Istrie et de Dalmatie;* and the *Voyage de Constantinople et des rives du Bosphore*, after the designs of Melling. He died in 1818. The following are a few of his best prints:

Several Views in Switzerland; *after Chatelet.* The Massacre of St. Bartholomew; *after Gravelot.* Three Views in Martinique; *after the Chevalier d'Epernay.* Benjamin Franklin; *after Charmontel.* A View of the City of Lyons; *after Lallemand.* The Environs of Frascati; *do.* A View of Tivoli; *do.*

NEEF, or NEEFS, PETER, THE ELDER, an eminent Flemish painter of interiors, born at Antwerp in 1570. He studied under Henry Steenwyck, and painted similar subjects to those of that master, representing interiors of churches and temples, which he finished with astonishing neatness and precision of pencil. All his architectural ornaments and various decorations of the churches, are designed with the utmost correctness, and touched with such delicacy as to render them objects of wonder rather than of imitation. Such was his knowledge of perspective, that he was accustomed to paint in the small space of a cabinet picture the largest and most magnificent Gothic edifices, in so masterly a manner, as to delude the spectator into the belief of the reality of the immense space the building represents. As the regularity of lines and great uniformity of tints would appear dull and insipid, Neefs was accustomed to introduce a variety of objects, to animate and diversify the scene; and by his admirable management of light and shade, he produced a lively and pleasing effect, where most artists would have been uninteresting and tame. Some of his interiors are represented by torch-light, with wonderful skill, and these are perhaps his most desirable productions. Neefs was not a good designer of the figure, and therefore employed John Breughel, the elder Teniers, and other eminent artists, to insert the figures in his pieces, which renders to them additional value. He died, according to Balkema, in 1651.

NEEF, or NEEFS, PETER, THE YOUNGER, was the son and scholar of the preceding artist, born at Antwerp, according to Balkema, in 1601. He painted interiors, similar to those of his father, but greatly inferior to that admirable master, both in correctness of perspective and neatness of finishing. According to Balkema, he died in 1658, but it is said there are pictures by him dated 1660, and even later.

NEEF, or NEEFS, JAMES, a Flemish engraver, born at Antwerp, according to Nagler, about 1610. There are various dates assigned for his birth, but Nagler is probably correct, as there are prints by him dated 1632 and 1633. His last print recorded is dated 1645. James Neefs was probably related to the preceding artists. He engraved a number of plates after Rubens, Vandyck, and other celebrated Flemish painters. His drawing is correct, but stiff and mannered, and his heads often have an extravagant expression; but his prints are much esteemed. They are executed entirely with the graver, which he handled with great facility. Among them are the following:

PORTRAITS.

Gaspar Nemius, Bishop of Antwerp; *after Gerard Segers.* John Tollenario, Jesuit; *after P. Fruytiers.* Francis Snyders, Painter; *after Vandyck.* Anthony de Tassis, Canon of Antwerp; *do.* The Marchioness of Barlemont, Countess d'Egmont; *do.* Josse de Hertoghe; *do.* Martin Ryckart, Painter; *do.*

SUBJECTS AFTER VARIOUS MASTERS.

The Fall of the Angels; *after Rubens.* The Meeting of Abraham and Melchisedec; *do.* The Crucifixion, with the Virgin and St. John; *do.* St. Augustine; *do.* The Martyrdom of St. Thomas; *do.* The Judgment of Paris, and the Triumph of Galatea, called the Ewer of Charles I.; *do.*; scarce. Christ and the six Penitents; *after Gerard Segers.* Job and his Wife; *do.* The Martyrdom of St. Lievin; *do.* Christ appearing to Magdalene; *do.* Christ brought before Pilate; *after J. Jordaens.* The Satyr, with the Peasant blowing hot and Cold; *do.* St. Roch interceding for the Persons attacked by the Plague; *after Erasmus Quellinus.*

or

NEER, ARNOLD VANDER, an eminent Dutch painter, born at Amsterdam in 1619. His instructor is not known. He sometimes painted sunsets, in which the glowing richness and harmony of his coloring approach the excellence of Rubens and Rembrandt. His pictures of winter scenes, with figures skating on the ice, are only surpassed by the works of Albert Cuyp; but his views by moonlight are undoubtedly his finest productions. They represent views of cottages or fishermen's huts, on the banks of a river with boats and figures, and the moon pouring a flood of effulgence over the landscape, while the sparkling radiance reflected from the water produces the most fascinating and picturesque effect. Vander

Neer died in 1683. There is a picture by him in the National Gallery, London, which brought $3,600. He used one of the above ciphers.

NEER, Eglon Hendrick vander, a Dutch painter, the son of the preceding, was born at Amsterdam in 1643. He first studied under his father, but his taste leading him to a different branch of the art, he was placed in the school of James Vanloo, an historical and portrait painter of Amsterdam. At the age of twenty he visited Paris, where he passed four years, and painted a number of small portraits and domestic subjects, which gained him considerable reputation. He afterwards returned to Holland, and painted some portraits and historical and fabulous subjects, colored with great delicacy, and carefully finished, although deficient in other respects. Among his portraits of life size, was that of the Princess of Neuburg, painted by order of the King of Spain, who was so highly pleased, that he desired vander Neer to visit Madrid, but he declined the invitation. He also painted conversation pieces and gallant subjects, in the style of Terburg, which are highly esteemed, and are considered his best works, being well colored, touched with great delicacy, and very highly finished, although less mellow and harmonious than those of Mieris or Metzu. Vander Neer was the instructor of Adrian Vanderwerf. He was employed for some time by the Elector Palatine at Dusseldorf, and died there, in 1703. His portrait, by himself, is honored with a place among those of the illustrious painters in the Florentine Gallery.

NEGKER. See Necker.

NEGRE, Matthias van. This painter was probably a native of Holland, and is mentioned by Descamps as living about 1625. He painted historical and architectural subjects. There is a Holy Family by him, in the cathedral of Tournay.

NEGRE, Nicolaus van, a portrait painter, who probably flourished in Holland about 1650. There are a number of plates after him, engraved by Suyderhoef, van Dalen, and Crispin de Passe.

NEGRI, or NERI, Pier Martire, a Cremonese painter, who flourished about 1600. According to Zaist he was a scholar of Cav. Gio. Battista Trotti, called Il Malosso. He painted history and portraits in the style of that master, but with more boldness, and vigor of light and shadow, as is evident from his admired picture representing Christ restoring Sight to the Blind, which Lanzi says is surpassed by his St. Giuseppe at Pavia. Negri passed some time at Rome, where he executed a number of works, and was received into the Academy of St. Luke.

NEGRI, Pietro, a Venetian painter, who flourished about 1680. He is supposed to have studied under Antonio Zanchi da Este, but Lanzi thinks he was rather an imitator of that master. He executed some works for the churches and public edifices of Venice, the most important of which is a picture in the College of S. Rocco, representing the Liberation of the city from the Plague in 1630, "in which," says Lanzi, "we perceive the peculiar ease and manner of Zanchi, somewhat improved and ennobled in the forms." This picture is placed opposite to the grand painting by Zanchi, representing the great Plague of 1630. He was also much employed in painting for the collections.

NEGRI, Gio. Francesco, an eminent Bolognese portrait painter, born in 1648. He studied under Odoardo Fialetti at Venice. On his return to Bologna, he acquired distinction for the excellence of his portraits. He is commended by Orlandi, Malvasia, and others. He was living in 1718.

NEGRONE, or NIGRONE, Pietro, called Il Giovane Zingaro (the young Gipsy) a painter of the Neapolitan school, born at Calabria about 1505. Dominici says he studied first under Gio. Antonio d'Amato; afterwards under Marco Calabrese; and he commends him as a diligent and accomplished artist. In S. Agnello at Naples, there is a picture of the Virgin and Infant in the Clouds, with Saints and a glory of Angels; also in S. Maria Donna Romata, are two pictures by him, representing the Adoration of the Magi, and the Scourging of Christ, painted in 1541. He died, according to Lanzi, about 1565, aged 60.

NEGROPONTE, Frà Francesco or Antonio, a monk of the order of the Cappuccini, who flourished at Venice in the early part of the 15th century. According to Kügler, his works resemble those of Jacobello del Fiore.

NELLI, Nello, an old painter of Pisa, by whom there is a Madonna painted on panel in the old church of Tripalle at Pisa, signed *Nerus Nellus de Pisa me pinxit*, 1299.

NELLI, Suora Plautella, an Italian paintress of noble family, born at Florence in 1523. She became a nun of the Dominican convent of St. Caterina at Florence, and without other assistance than a collection of designs by Fra. Bartolomeo di S. Marco, she attained considerable excellence in painting. Her pictures are generally in the style of that artist, although she also imitated other masters. Among them are a picture of the Crucifixion, with a number of small figures highly finished; a Descent from the Cross, said to be after a design by Andrea del Sarto, in the church of her order at Florence; and an Adoration of the Magi, of her own composition, possessing great merit. She died in 1588.

NELLI, Niccolo, a Venetian engraver, who flourished about 1568. There is an architectural frontispiece, with figures inscribed *Niccolo Nelli Veneziano f.*, engraved for a book of plans and views of the most illustrious cities and fortresses in the world, published in 1568. The figures are well drawn, and the plate is executed with considerable ability, somewhat in the style of Marco da Ravenna. It is observed by Strutt, that many of the prints without marks, of the above date, may be attributed to Nelli, particularly those in the style of Marco da Ravenna.

NELLI, Giovanni Battista, an Italian architect, and a writer on the art, born at Florence in 1661. He was of a noble family, and cultivated the Fine Arts, of which he was a zealous protector. He was appointed Director of the public roads and bridges in Tuscany. He died at Florence in 1725, leaving many manuscripts relating to literature and art, among which are his *Discorsi di Architettura*, Florence, 1753; 4to.

NELLI, Pietro, a painter of distinction, who flourished at Rome in the beginning of the 18th century. He was probably a scholar of Gio. Maria Morandi. He was a rival of Odoardo Vici nelli, whom Pascoli commends as the ablest scholar of Morandi, and Lanzi says that Nelli alone could dispute precedence with him at Rome.

NELLO, BERNARDO DI GIO. FALCONI, an old painter of Pisa, who flourished about 1390. He was a distinguished artist in his time, and Lanzi says he still merits consideration. He painted many pictures in the Cathedral at Pisa. He is supposed to be the same as Nello di Vanni, who, with other Pisan artists, painted in the Campo Santo in the 14th century.

NERANUS, A., a painter of little note, who flourished about 1650, and is said to have imitated the styles of van Vliet and Rembrandt. There was a picture by him in Cardinal Fesch's collection, representing Pilate washing his hands before the Jews.

NERI, PIER MARTIRE. See NEGRI.

NERI, GIOVANNI, a Bolognese painter, who was living in 1575. He excelled in painting all kinds of birds, fish, reptiles, quadrupeds, and other animals, which he did from life, with such precision and beauty that he was called *Giovanni degli Uccelli* (painter of birds). Masini says he filled seven folio volumes with these subjects, which he saw in the studio of Ulisse Aldovrandi.

NERITO, JACOPO, an old painter of Padua, who, according to Rossetti, subscribes himself a pupil of Gentile da Fabriano, on an altar-piece in the church of San Michele di Padova. He flourished about 1450.

NERO, DURANTE DEL, a painter born at Borgo San Sepolcro, who flourished at Rome about 1560, at which time he was employed in decorating the pontifical palace.

NERONI, BARTOLOMEO, called MAESTRO RICCIO, a distinguished Sienese painter, who flourished about 1573. He studied under Giovanni Antonio Razzi, whom he assisted in his works, and whose daughter he married. Lanzi says that Neroni, after the death of the four great pillars of the Sienese school, sustained its reputation, and probably educated one of its restorers. His pictures unite the style of Razzi with a certain resemblance to the manner of Vasari, in the distribution of his tints. He had excellent abilities in perspective, especially in representing scenery; Andreani has engraved a specimen. He was also greatly skilled in architecture, and had a pension from the magistrates of Lucca for his assistance in their public works. In Siena, at the Osservanti, is a Crucifixion by him, with a great number of figures; and in the church of the Derelitte, a Descent from the Cross, entirely in the style of Razzi.

NERVESA, GASPARE, a painter born in the Friuli, who, according to Ridolfi, was a scholar and imitator of Titian, and painted mostly at Spilimbergo. There are some of his works at Trevigi.

NES, or NEES, JOHN VAN, a Dutch painter, born at Delft, according to Immerzeel and Füessli, in the early part of the 17th century. He studied under Michael Mirevelt, and by his advice visited Italy for improvement, studying some time at Venice and Rome. On returning to Holland, he painted several historical pictures, which were much admired. He would probably have gained eminence in that branch of the art, had he not, for the sake of emolument, devoted himself to painting portraits, in the admirable style of Mirevelt. His works are distinguished for dignity of character, chaste and vigorous coloring, and accurate resemblance. Probably they are generally ascribed to Mirevelt, as the portraits of the latter are estimated at from 5,000 to 10,000! According to Immerzeel, Nes died in 1650; but Füessli says he flourished in 1670; and Balkema, that he died in 1692. It is probable that he lived longer than until 1650, as Mirevelt died in 1641.

NETSCHER, GASPAR. According to D'Argenville, this eminent painter was born at Prague, in Germany, in 1636; but Houbraken says he was born at Heidelberg in 1639. His father, a sculptor, and an engineer in the Polish service, died when he was only two years old, leaving a widow with three children, of whom Gaspar was the youngest. In consequence of the calamities of war, she was obliged to leave Germany and retire to Holland; but while on the way, two of her children perished with hunger, and she arrived at Arnheim, in Guelderland, in a state of abject wretchedness. Happily, she was met by the hand of charity; her wants were relieved by the compassionate people of that place, and her child was taken under the protection of an opulent physician, named Tullekens, who reared him as his own son. Netscher received an education fitted for his entrance into the medical profession; but manifesting a strong inclination for art, he was placed under Koeter, an obscure painter of still-life. Preferring some other department of art, he soon afterwards entered the school of Gerard Terburg, and made such rapid progress that, in a few years, his pictures were almost as highly esteemed as those of his instructor. On leaving the school of Terburg, he set out for Italy, sailing from Amsterdam to Bordeaux. Meeting some encouragement in portrait painting, and falling in love with the niece of the person with whom he lodged, Netscher remained rather longer in that city than he intended. He finally relinquished his project of visiting Italy, married the young lady and returned to Holland, where he settled permanently at the Hague. He sometimes painted historical and fabulous subjects, but was more successful in small portraits. His reputation in this branch was so great that he was patronized by nearly all the best families, and the foreign ambassadors residing at the Hague. His best works, however, represent domestic subjects and conversations, characterized by a delicacy of pencilling and a lustre of coloring similar to the exquisite productions of Terburg and Metzu. They are more tastefully composed and correctly designed than the pictures of Terburg. His touch is spirited, yet mellow, as is evident from his representations of silk, ermine, and white satin, so faithfully painted as almost to produce illusion. Netscher is said to have visited London, at the invitation of Sir William Temple, in the reign of Charles II.; but his stay in England was short. Among other portraits, he painted one of Lord Berkeley of Stratton, and his lady, dated 1676. In the royal collection at Paris, there are two pictures by Netscher; one a Lute-player, the other a Musician giving a Lady lessons on the Bass-Viol. He died at the Hague in 1684.

NETSCHER, THEODORE, a distinguished Dutch portrait painter, the son of the preceding, was born at Bordeaux in 1661, during the residence of his father in that city. He studied under that master, and attained such excellence that he was patronized by Count Davaux, ambassador from France to Holland, who induced him to visit Paris, and recommended his abilities to the people of that metropolis. Netscher was greatly encouraged, and acquired both fame and fortune. After an absence of twenty years, he returned to Holland, and settled at the Hague, where he was employed by the principal personages of the court. He sometimes introduced fruit and flowers into his larger pictures, and his peaches and grapes were colored with great transparency and beauty. According to Descamps, when the states of Holland sent six thousand troops to England, at the time of the rebellion in 1715, Netscher accompanied them as paymaster, and resided there six years, meeting great encouragement as a portrait painter. He returned to Holland in 1722, where he died in 1732.

NETSCHER, Constantine, a distinguished Dutch portrait painter, born at the Hague in 1670. He was the younger son of Gaspar Netscher, and acquired the elements of art from his father, who died when Constantine was fourteen years of age. It does not appear that he took lessons of any other master, but by assiduously studying the designs and pictures left by his father, he became an able and successful follower of his style, was extensively employed in portraits, and was patronized by the principal personages of his time. His talents were admirably adapted for success in portrait painting, combining accuracy of resemblance with the most flattering and favorable representations of his model, particularly in his female portraits, which are gracefully designed and beautifully colored. He also painted domestic subjects and conversations, but in these he was greatly inferior to Gaspar N. In 1699, he was chosen a member of the Society of Painters at the Hague; and was subsequently honored with the office of Director. One of his best performances is a family picture of the Baron Suesso, consisting of seven or eight figures, into which was introduced a dog, painted by vander Does. Among his other patrons, were the families of Wassenaer and Duivenvoorden, whose portraits he painted, together with those of the Earl and Countess of Portland. Descamps says that the Earl endeavored to induce Netscher to visit England, but he declined, on account of the infirm state of his health. He died in 1722.

NEUFFORGE, Jean François de. This artist was the descendant of a noble family, born at Camblain, near Liege, in 1714. He early manifested a decided taste for architecture, and visited Paris to acquire a knowledge of the art, after which he commenced, in 1755, his great work entitled, *Recueil elementaire d'architecture, contenant plusieurs etudes des ordres d'architecture*, 8 vols. folio, illustrated with plates. It was completed in 1776, and gained for its author considerable praise. In 1770, Neufforge was chosen a member of the French Academy of Architecture. He died in 1811.

NEURAUTTER, A., a German engraver, who flourished at Prague, and executed, among other plates, a set of figures entitled *Statuæ Pontis Pragensis*, entirely with the graver, in a stiff, labored style; published at Prague in 1715.

NEVE, Francis de, a Flemish painter, born at Antwerp, according to Balkema, in 1625. He studied for some time the works of Rubens and Vandyck, and afterwards visited Rome for improvement, where he resided several years. On returning to Flanders, he painted a number of good historical works, which gained him considerable reputation; but he afterwards painted heroic landscapes, with subjects from history or the fable, in which he evinces great fertility of invention, and refinement of taste. Bartsch mentions fourteen etchings by this artist, executed in a slight, but very masterly style, embellished with figures correctly drawn and ingeniously grouped. Several of them are marked *Fran. de Neue.* He died in 1681.

NEVEU, or NAIVEU, Matthew, a Dutch painter, born at Leyden in 1647. He first studied under Abraham Toren Vliet, but afterwards under Gerard Douw. He gained considerable distinction for his pictures of domestic subjects and conversations, in the style of his instructor, which, though inferior to the works of Douw, are correctly drawn and well colored. They are principally confined to Holland, where they are highly esteemed. Among others there is one at Amsterdam, representing the Seven Works of Mercy, highly commended by Houbraken for its ingenious composition, and fine expression and character in the heads. Neveu died in 1721.

NEWTON, E., an engraver, who executed among other plates, a portrait of William Tansur the musician, published with his *Melodia Sacra* inscribed *E. Newton j. ad vivum f.*

NEWTON, James, an English engraver, who resided at London about 1778, and executed, among others, the following plates:

PORTRAITS.

Sidney Parkinson, Draftsman on board of the Endeavor, Capt. Cook. William Newton, Clerk of the Works at Greenwich Hospital. Edward Sargeant, Secretary to the Protestant Association in 1780.

LANDSCAPES.

Two Views in Italy; *after Marco Ricci.* A Landscape, with Cattle passing a River; *after Claude.* The Herdsman, a pastoral Landscape; *after Zuccarelli.*

NEWTON, Francis Milner, an English painter, born at London about 1720. He studied under M. Tuscher, and devoted himself to painting portraits, in which he gained considerable encouragement. In 1768, at the foundation of the Royal Academy, Newton was appointed Secretary, and discharged the duties of that office for a period of twenty years, until 1788, when he resigned. He died in 1794.

NEWTON, Gilbert Stuart, a distinguished historical painter, was born in 1794, at Halifax, in Nova Scotia, where his father was collector of the customs. He studied at Boston, under his maternal uncle, Gilbert Stuart. About 1820, he visited England, and then proceeded to Italy, where he spent some time, afterwards returning to England, where he studied in the Royal Academy. He adopted the manner of Watteau in some degree, and produced several excellent pictures of a small size, in a style resembling the works of that master, but displaying great expression and character. He soon after painted two pictures of the Forsaken, and the Lover's Quarrel, which attracted considerable attention, and the latter was engraved in the Literary Souvenir of 1826. The Duke of Bedford commissioned him to paint the Visit of the Prince of Spain to Catalina, for which Newton received $2,500. His talents were greatly admired, and in 1833 he was chosen a member of the Royal Academy. He painted slowly, and finished his pictures with great care. Besides the works already mentioned, Newton painted a small picture of Abelard in his study, full of expression and sentiment; Macheath, purchased by the Marquis of Lansdowne for $2,500; Shylock and Jessica; Portia and Bassanio; King Lear attended by Cordelia and the Physician; and the Vicar of Wakefield restoring his Daughter to her Mother. In 1832, Newton visited America and married; after which he returned to England. In the next year he exhibited symptoms of insanity, and died in 1835. His talents were undoubted, and had his life been spared, he would have attained a high degree of eminence in the art.

NEWTON, William, an English architect, who flourished at London in the latter part of the 18th century. He published a translation of Vitruvius, London, 2 vols. 8vo., 1771—1791; also a second edition in 1793, folio, illustrated. In 1790, Newton published the second volume of James Stuart's Athenian Antiquities, with notes and explanations.

NEYN, Peter de, a Dutch painter and architect, born at Leyden in 1597. He studied painting under Esaias Vandervelde, and gave promise of attaining eminence in landscape, in the style of his instructor; but subsequently applied his talents to architecture. He attained considerable distinction in that art, and was appointed architect to the city of Leyden. He died in 1639.

GY NEYTS, Giles, a painter and engraver of little note, who flourished about 1681, as appears from the date on one of the pictures by him, preserved in the gallery at Dresden. Bartsch mentions ten plates by Neyts, and Nagler eleven more, etched and finished with the graver in a good style. A number of small pen drawings of landscapes, washed with India ink, with the trees in the style of Swanevelt, are ascribed to this artist, being marked *A. E. Neyts*, perhaps for *Ægidius* instead of *Giles*. Brulliot supposes that pictures of landscapes, with the accompanying monogram, are by this artist.

NICASIUS, Bernard, a Flemish painter, born at Antwerp in 1618. He studied under F. Snyders, and imitated the style of that master in fruit, still-life, huntings, and landscapes. He traveled through France and Italy for improvement, and finally died at Paris in 1678. Like other imitators, his reputation was transient, and nearly all his works are now ascribed to Snyders.

NICCOLA, da Pisa, an eminent Italian sculptor and architect, the precise dates of whose birth and death have not been ascertained. It is probable, however, that he was born near the commencement of the 13th century, as he was greatly advanced in years in 1273. He is distinguished among the earliest restorers of sculpture, which he elevated to a much higher state of perfection than he found it. He quitted the hard, dry, and mechanical style of his predecessors, and introduced a style which, though falling far short of the antique, was based upon similar principles, and evinced a vigorous mind and much feeling, if not always the most refined taste. In 1225 he was employed to execute the *arca* or tomb of St. Domenico at Bologna, which he embellished with a series of bas-reliefs and figures, truly admirable for the time. Several of these subjects are given by Cicognara, in his *Storia della Scultura*, and many of the heads and countenances are finely expressed. Among his other works in sculpture, are the pulpit in the Baptistery at Pisa, executed in 1260; and the pulpit in the Cathedral at Siena. These are highly praised by Cicognara, and are sufficient of themselves to prove the great excellence of Niccola in this department of art.

As an architect, Niccola seems to have acquired no less distinction. In 1231 he erected the celebrated church of S. Antonio at Padua. He was subsequently commissioned to build the church Dei Frari at Venice; and his reputation extended so widely that he was successively employed at Florence, Pistoia, Volterra, Naples, and Pisa.—Among his most important works at Florence, is the church and monastery of Santa Trinita, highly extolled by Michael Angelo as an edifice of surpassing excellence for its simple grandeur, and the nobleness of its proportions. In 1240 he commenced the cathedral of Pistoia; and likewise improved and embellished that of Volterra. Among his other works in architecture were the convent of S. Domenico at Arezzo; the church of S. Lorenzo at Naples; the campanile of S. Niccola at Pisa; and the magnificent abbey on the plain of Tagliacozzo, erected by Charles I. of Anjou, in 1268, in commemoration of his decisive victory over Corradino, and thence called Santa Maria della Vittoria.

NICCOLO, del Abati. See Abati.

NICCOLO, Maestro, an old painter of Friuli, some of whose works are still preserved at Gemona, among which are the façade of the Cathedral, and an altar-piece, signed *Magister Nicolaus pintor me fecit.* MCCCXXXII. To this artist is ascribed, by some writers, that vast and meritorious production, representing the solemn scene of the Consecration, which decorates the Cathedral of Venzone, and which is still in a fine state of preservation. This, however, is a matter of mere conjecture, founded on the resemblance of manner, vicinity of the place, and time of execution.

NICHOLS, Sutton, an obscure English engraver, who resided at London about 1710. He executed a number of plates of shells and other trifling subjects for the booksellers, which possess little merit.

NICIAS, an eminent Greek painter, a native of Athens, flourished in the latter half of the 4th century B. C. He lived in the time of Alexander, and though probably younger than Apelles, he was a cotemporary of that master. He excelled in elegance of design, beauty of coloring, and in effect of light and shade. He was famous above all the artists of his time, for the beauty and grace of his female forms, which were executed with such admirable relief that Pliny says "they appeared ready to leave the ground they were painted upon, and walk out of the frames."

The most celebrated work of Nicias was the Region of the Shades, described in Homer's Odyssey, where Ulysses invokes the departed spirits.

Plutarch says that Ptolemy I. of Egypt offered the artist sixty talents (about $75,000) for this picture, but was refused by Nicias, who presented it to his native city, Athens. Pausanias says that on the way from Pharæ to Tritæa, there was a sepulchre of white marble, decorated with the paintings of Nicias. He also painted in encaustic; and, according to that author, he was the most excellent animal painter of his time. Among the other works of this artist was a picture in the Cura Julia, of Nemea sitting on a Lion; Alexander; Io; Andromeda; a sitting Calypso; another Calypso, in the Hall of Pompey; Bacchus; Diana; and an elegant Hyacinthus, in the Hall of Concord. The latter work was brought from Alexandria to Rome by Augustus, and was subsequently consecrated by Tiberius in the temple of Augustus. Nicias appears to have been a very studious and absent man; Ælian says he used to forget to take his meals. At his death, he was honored with a public burial, and was interred in the road from Athens to the Academy, the cemetery of all great Athenians, where his tomb was erected.

NICOLAI, G. D. C., a German engraver, who lived at Vienna about 1760, and, in concert with A. J. Prenner, executed part of the plates from the pictures in the Imperial Gallery, published in four sets in folio.

NICOLAY, Isaac, a Dutch painter, born at Leyden in 1539. He designed correctly, and gave great animation to his figures. He died in 1597, leaving two sons, whom he had instructed in the art; Nicholas Isaac Nicolay, born at Leyden in 1566, painted history in the style of his father, and died at Amsterdam in 1640; and James Isaac Nicolay, born at Leyden in 1569, painted in the style of his father, gained improvement by visiting Italy, and died at Utrecht in 1639.

NICOLAY, Jan Hendrick, a Dutch painter, born at Leeuwarde in 1766. His forte was in painting dead birds, which he represented in a very skillful manner. His works were frequently exhibited at Amsterdam, and they are highly esteemed in Holland. He died in 1826.

NICOLE, Nicolas, a French architect, born at Besançon in 1701. Being of a poor family, he was first apprenticed to a blacksmith, but on visiting Paris, he determined to relinquish his occupation; and accordingly he entered the free school of Blondel. After studying some time under that master, he returned to Besançon, and was commissioned to erect the church du Refuge, of which the beautiful façade has been often engraved. He afterwards executed the plan for the collegiate church of S. Anne of Soleure, and was invited by the authorities of that city, to superintend the execution of the works. The church of the Magdalen, at Besançon, is also the work of Nicole, but has never been completed. These two latter works have been justly criticised as to the details. He had a very lively imagination, and drew his designs with great facility; but his edifices have none of that ever attractive simplicity, which preëminently distinguishes the antique.—Nicole was honored with the confidence of several successive intendants of the province of Franche Comte, and was consulted concerning all architectural projects. He died at Besançon in 1784.

WR. NICOLE, D. This name is affixed to a set of views slightly etched, in the style of a painter, and also marked with the accompanying monogram, which probably represents the initials of the designer.

NICOLET, Bernard Anthony, a Swiss engraver, born at St. Imer, in the bishopric of Basle, in 1740. He visited Paris while young, and engraved several plates after the marines of Vernet, in concert with Longueil; also a number of plates for the Abbé de St. Non's *Voyage Pittoresque du Royaume de Naples*. There is some confusion among writers about this artist, as his name is sometimes written Benedict Alphonsius A., and the dates of his birth are differently stated: but the above is the account of Nagler, who places his death in 1807. The following are among his best works:

PORTRAITS.

Noel Hallé, Painter to the King. 1775; *after Cochin.*
Thomas le Sueur, Professor of Mathematics at Rome; *do.*
Francis de Paul Jacquier, Professor of Mathematics; *do.*
Nicholas de Monthonon; *do.*

VARIOUS SUBJECTS.

St. Apollonia; after the picture by *Guido;* in the Orleans collection. Milo Crotoniate; *after Giorgione;* do. Susanna and the Elders; *after Deshayes.* A View of Naples; *after Vernet.* A Shipwreck; *do.* A View of the Interior of the Church of St. Januarius at Naples; *after Dupres.*

NICOLETTO. See Niccolo Cassana.

NICOMACHUS, an eminent Greek painter, a native of Thebes, flourished in the latter part of the fourth century B. C. Plutarch compares his paintings with the lines of Homer; Cicero says that, in the works of Nicomachus, Echion, Protogenes, and Apelles, all things are perfect. He was the most celebrated of all the Greeks for facility of execution. In illustration of this quality, Pliny relates that he executed, in a few days, the decorations of the monument to the poet Telestes, with remarkable beauty, and to the entire satisfaction of Aristratus, tyrant of Sicyon, who shortly before was exceedingly angry with the artist, because he thought the works would not be finished within the specified time. Nicomachus was the first artist who represented Ulysses with the cap of Liberty. Stobæus relates of Nicomachus that, hearing some one say he saw no beauty in the Helen of Zeuxis, he observed, "Take my eyes, and you will see a goddess."

Among the principal works of Nicomachus, Pliny mentions a picture of Scylla, in the Temple of Peace; Bacchantes, with Satyrs creeping up to them; Cybele sitting on a Lion; Apollo and Diana; a Victory in a Chariot, consecrated in the Capitol by Plancus; a Rape of Proserpine, in the Temple of Minerva on the Capitol; and an unfinished picture of the Tyndaridæ, which was in greater repute than his finished works.

NICOPHANES, a Greek painter, who flourished about B. C. 300. He studied under Nicomachus, and although little is recorded of his works, Pliny ranks him among the most eminent artists of his time. He possessed a lively genius, great facility of invention, and rapidity of execution. From his practice of frequently choosing courtesans for his models, he was called "the Painter of Courtesans."

NIEULANT, Adrian, a Flemish painter, a native of Antwerp, flourished in the latter part of the 16th century. He painted landscapes of considerable merit, and decorated them with small figures. Among other works, he executed a winter-piece, with masked figures skating on the moat of the citadel of Antwerp, which is now in the Museum at Brussels. He died about 1601.

NIEULANT, John, a Flemish painter, born at Antwerp in 1569. He studied under Peter Fransz and Francis Badens, and painted landscapes and historical subjects of small size, very highly finished. He died at Amsterdam in 1628.

NIEULANT, William van, a Flemish painter of landscapes with architecture, born at Antwerp in 1584; died in 1635. He acquired the elements of design from Roland Savery, and afterwards went to Rome, where he studied for three years under Paul Bril, and followed the style of that master. On returning to the Low Countries, he settled at Amsterdam, and adopted a more bold and expeditious manner of operating. He was much employed in painting views of the ruins of ancient architecture in the vicinity of Rome, from the designs he had collected in Italy. His coloring is bold and effective; his buildings are drawn with neatness and precision; and his figures are designed with tolerable correctness. There are a number of plates of architectural landscapes etched by Nieulant in a free and spirited style, occasionally assisted with the graver. Among them are the following:

A Landscape, with ruins, and figures representing the Merciful Samaritan; *P. Bril, inv. G. Nieulant, fecit.* A Mountainous Landscape, with Tobit and the Angel; *do.* Two Views of the Sea Coast; *do.* Three Views of Ruins in and near Rome; *Guil. Nieulant.* A large print, representing three Bridges on the Tiber, and part of the City of Rome; in three sheets, inscribed *Guilielmus van Nieulant, fecit et excud. Antverpiæ*, 1600.

NIGETTI, Matteo, a Florentine architect, who flourished in the first part of the 17th century. He studied under Buontalenti, and materially assisted that master in the erection of the Strozzi palace at Florence. According to Milizia, he erected a number of works in that city, among which were the cloister of the monks degli Angeli, completed by Silvani; and he made the design and model for the church of Ogni Santi, belonging to the brothers Osservanza. Nigetti also erected a beautiful edifice after the design of Vasari, near S. Lorenzo, intended as a sepulchre for the Grand Dukes. This architect was also an engraver on precious stones. Among his works in this branch of the art, was the wonderful shrine in the chapel of S. Lorenzo at Florence. He died in 1649.

NIKKELEN, J. van, a Dutch painter of interiors, who flourished about 1660. He was a good artist in perspective, and painted interiors of churches in the style of van Vliet, which possess considerable merit. They are signed *J. van Nikkelen.*

NIKKELEN, John van, a Dutch painter, the son of the preceding, was born at Haerlem in 1649. He studied the elements of design under his father, but did not pursue the same branch of the art. He applied himself to landscape painting, and acquired considerable distinction, being invited to the court of the Elector Palatine, for whom he painted several pictures, and was afterwards made painter to the Prince of Cassel. His works are said to resemble those of Karel Dujardin. He died in 1716. His daughter, *Jacoba Maria*, was a pupil of vander Myn, and excelled in fruit and flowers. She painted several pictures at Dusseldorf, which are erroneously ascribed to her father. She married William Troost, a portrait painter.

NILSON, John Elias, a German miniature painter and engraver, born at Augsburg in 1721. He engraved in a stiff, formal style, several portraits of eminent personages, among which are the following:

PORTRAITS.

Clement XIII. Pontif. Max.; *Nilson, inv. et fec.* Petrus III., Russorum Imperator. Catherina Alexiewna, Russorum Imperatrix. Stanislaus Augustus, Rex. Pol.

NIMECIUS, Balthasar Meneius, an obscure German wood engraver, is said to have been a native of Saxony. There are a number of wooden cuts, sometimes marked with the initials B. M. N., and sometimes with the accompanying monogram, which Prof. Christ attributes to Nimecius.

NIMEGUEN, Elias van, a Dutch painter, born at Nimeguen in 1667. He studied the elements of design under his elder brother, an inferior painter of portraits and flowers; but as his instructor died when Elias was only fourteen, he decided to dispense with farther assistance, and devote himself chiefly to the study of nature. By great assiduity he became a good designer of the figure, acquired a competent knowledge of architecture and perspective, and attained excellence in landscape and flowers. In concert with his younger brother Tobias, he executed an extensive series of decorations in the palace of Baron van Wachtendonk, which gained for the artists such high reputation, that they were employed by the Princess of Orange for several years, in painting emblematical and historical subjects on the walls and ceilings of her palaces, embellished with bas-reliefs and other accessories. The two brothers subsequently separated, Tobias going to the court of the Elector Palatine, and Elias to Rotterdam, where he was fully employed. His style was happily adapted to his subjects, being characterized by fertility of invention, great promptness and facility of execution, clear and agreeable coloring. Some writers place his death in 1745, aged 78; others in 1755, aged 87.

NIMEGUEN, Tobias van, the younger, the brother of the preceding, born at Nimeguen in 1670. Like his brother Elias, he studied under his elder brother, and wrought in concert with Elias, as detailed in the preceding article, until invited to the court of the Elector Palatine. He was retained in the service of that Prince during the rest of his life.

NIMEGUEN, Dionysius van, a Dutch painter, the son of Elias N., was born at Rotterdam in 1705; died in 1798. He studied under his father, and painted similar subjects to those of that master. He also excelled in portraiture, and is said to have painted at the age of 81, without spectacles, a perfect likeness of a young lady.

NIMEGUEN, Gerard van, a Dutch portrait and landscape painter, the son and scholar of Dionysius N., was born at Rotterdam in 1735. He manifested considerable ability in portraits, and was much employed, even by Prince William V., whom he painted at a very early age. He formed his style in landscape from the works of Everdingen, Ruysdael, and Pynacker. His pictures of mountains, landscapes, and forest scenery with rivulets, decorated with figures and animals, are highly esteemed, and are placed in the best collections. Nimeguen made many drawings and copies after Hackert, Hobbema, Wynants, and Ruysdael. Brulliot mentions twelve etchings of landscapes by him. He died at Rotterdam in 1808.

NINFE, Cesare dalle, a Venetian painter, mentioned by Zanetti among the imitators of Tintoretto. He flourished about 1595. He possessed the fertility of invention, and facility of execution, which characterized his great model; and though inferior to him in design, he was an excellent colorist. His works, probably, are mostly attributed to Tintoretto.

NINO, Don Juan. See Guevara.

NIQUET, the Elder, a French engraver, who flourished in the present century, and was living in 1831. He was employed by Filhol on the *Galerie du Musée Napoleon.* Among his principal plates, are the Triumph of Flora, *after N. Poussin;* Diana hunting; the Laocoön; Cupid and Psyche; the Death of St. Bruno; and Raffaelle's Transfiguration.

NIXON, an English engraver, who flourished about 1750, and executed, among other plates, a number of portraits, in a very neat style, the faces entirely finished with dots. Among them are the following:

PORTRAITS.

Frederick, Prince of Wales. William Augustus, Duke of Cumberland; two plates. Archbishop Tillotson. John, Earl of Granville.

NOBILI, Durante de', a painter born at Caldarola, who formed his style on that of Michael Angelo. Lanzi commends a Madonna by him, in the church of S. Pietro di Castello, at Ascoli, inscribed with his name, and dated 1571.

NOBLESSE, a French designer and engraver, mentioned by Basan as residing at Paris, where he died at an advanced age, in 1730. He excelled in pen-drawings, and appears to have formed his taste from studying the works of Callot. There are a few etchings by him, in the neat and spirited style of that master.

NOBLET, an engraver mentioned by Strutt, who says he executed a number of vignettes, and other book ornaments.

NOBLIN, H., an obscure engraver, who flourished about 1680. Among other plates, he executed the portrait of Cardinal Howard.

NOCHER, J. E., a French engraver, who flourished at Paris about 1760. He studied under Stephen Fessard, and engraved several book ornaments and portraits, among which is that of Jean Jacques Rousseau.

NOCRET, Jean, a French painter and engraver, born at Nancy in 1618. He studied under Leclerc, and afterwards visited Italy for improvement. On returning to France, he was much employed at the Tuileries and St. Cloud, and painted the portraits of several members of the royal family, which have been engraved. He is also said to have painted historical subjects. Felibien praises his abilities, and Dumesnil mentions a print by him, characterized by simple and graceful attitudes, draperies finely cast, and excellent gradation of the distances. Nocret was appointed rector of the French Academy. He died at Paris, according to Nagler, in 1672, though another authority says in 1676. His son and scholar, Charles Nocret, was born at Nancy in 1647; painted portraits with reputation; and died in 1719.

NOEL, a French marine painter, who flourished in the present century. He studied under Silvestre and Joseph Vernet, and painted several marine pieces, of views on the coasts of Spain and Portugal, with falls of snow, gales of wind, fogs, tempests, and conflagrations. He also executed views of Lisbon and Gibraltar, and exhibited many pictures up to the year 1822. He was living in 1831.

NOFERI, Michele, a Florentine painter, who flourished about 1660. According to Baldinucci, he studied under Vincenzio Dandini, and was a reputable artist.

NOGARI, Giuseppe, a reputable Venetian painter, born in 1699. He studied under Antonio Balestra, and attained such excellence in portraits and half-length figures, that, according to Lanzi, he was much patronized by the court of Turin for many years. His portraits are characterized by truth to nature, vigor of expression, and richness of coloring. He also painted history with considerable reputation, among which Lanzi commends his S. Pietro, in the cathedral at Bassano, combining the styles of Balestra and Piazzetta.

NOGARI, Paris, a Roman painter, born in 1512. He imitated the style of Raffaellino da Reggio, and painted a number of frescos in the Vatican Gallery, during the pontificate of Gregory XIII. He also executed several oil paintings. Among his principal works is a picture of Christ bearing his Cross, in the church della Madonna de' Monti; the Deposition from the Cross, in the Trinità de' Monti; and the Circumcision, in S. Spirito in Sassia. He died at Rome, in 1577, aged 65.

NOIR, Nicolas le, a French architect, born at Paris in 1726. He studied under Blondel, and having gained the grand prize of the Academy, visited Rome, where he devoted himself with great assiduity to the study of the admirable remains of antiquity. On returning to Paris, he soon gained reputation, and was commissioned by Voltaire to erect an edifice at Ferney. His principal work is the theatre of the Porte St. Martin. He was much employed, and died in 1810.

NOLIN, Jean Baptiste, a French engraver, born at Paris in 1657. He studied under Poilly, and afterwards visited Rome for improvement, where he engraved several plates after the great masters, among which was the Miracle of the Loaves, *after Raffaelle.* He also executed several plates in the work entitled *Vues, Plans, Coupes et Elevations du Chateau de Versailles.*

NOLLEKENS, Joseph Francis. This painter was born at Antwerp in 1706, and was the father of Joseph Nollekens, the sculptor. He visited England while young, and studied painting under Peter Tillemans. He painted landscapes, and musical and fashionable conversations; was much employed in copying the works of Watteau and the architectural views of Gio. Paolo Pannini. He was patronized by the Earl of Tilney, and executed several ornamental works for Lord Cobham. He died at London in 1748.

NOLLEKENS, Joseph. This eminent sculptor was the son of the preceding, born in London in 1737. He acquired the elements of the art under Scheemakers, and subsequently visited Italy for improvement, where he studied under Ciavetti, and remained nine years. He executed the busts of many distinguished Englishmen, among whom were Garrick and Sterne; and he also turned his attention to a lucrative, though rather undignified branch of the art—that of manufacturing antiques, by vamping up fragments; finding either heads and limbs for bodies, or bodies for heads and limbs. One of the statues thus compounded was the Minerva, afterwards purchased for a thousand guineas, and now in the Newby collection at Yorkshire. His skill in repairs of this kind was subsequently displayed in the Townley marbles. While at Rome, he also purchased for a mere trifle, from the workmen by whom they were discovered, a number of fine terra cottas, which he afterwards disposed of to Mr. Townley, and which are now let into the walls of the British Museum. He also obtained the patronage of Lord Yarborough, and the Earl of Besborough, for the former of whom he executed a group of Mercury and Venus chiding Cupid. During his residence at Rome, he gained a gold medal from the Academy of St. Luke.

Nollekens returned to England in 1770, and soon after married Mary, the youngest daughter of Justice Welch, with a handsome fortune. He soon took the lead in his profession, and attained a high reputation. Without the advantages of education it is rather surprising that he accomplished what he did in the superior branches of the art, than that his poetical subjects display so little of the higher powers of the imagination. His chief excellence was in executing busts, and he gained an extensive patronage in this branch of the art. Among his pieces in poetic sculpture were no fewer than five Venuses, one of them since known as the Rockingham Venus; and one representing the goddess anointing her hair. The latter was considered by the artist his master-piece. Among his groups were a Pætus and Arria, and a Cupid and Psyche. His best monumental sculpture was executed for the tomb of Mrs. Howard of Corby Castle. It is pathetic in composition, and elegant and tasteful in execution. In 1772, Nollekens was chosen a royal academician. He was a great favorite with George III. Eccentric in many points of his character, he was also distinguished for great penuriousness during his whole life, until the age of eighty, and the death of his wife, in 1817, when he began to relax a little of that economy which had always prevailed in his establishment. His whole history abundantly proves that he had a most contemptible idea of the art, regarding it merely as a means of acquiring wealth. During the few remaining years of his life, he was beset by a swarm of greedy legacy-hunters, all professing sympathy and attachment. He died in 1823, leaving a fortune of about $1,000,000, excepting a few small legacies, to his friends Francis Palmer, and Francis Douce, the antiquary.

NOLLET, Dominick, a distinguished Flemish painter, born at Bruges in 1640. He studied under Jacob van Oost the elder, and painted history with reputation; but was more distinguished for landscapes in a grand style, and for sieges and battle pieces, with figures and horses correctly drawn, and touched with great freedom and spirit. On a close inspection, his pictures appear crude; but when viewed at a proper distance, they have a fine effect. His style greatly resembles that of vander Meulen, and his talents nearly equaled those of that master. Nollet was patronized by Maximilian, Duke of Bavaria, the governor of the Low Countries, who appointed him his principal painter. He was chosen a member of the Society of Painters at Bruges, in 1687. There are a number of his works in the Flemish collections; and in the church of the Carmelites, at Bruges, is his picture of St. Louis embarking for the Holy Land. He died in 1736.

NOLLI, Gio. Battista, an Italian engraver, who flourished about 1755, and executed, among other plates, several plans and views of buildings.

NOLLI, Carlo, an Italian engraver, the son of Gio. Battista N., flourished at Naples about 1760, and was employed upon the plates engraved by command of the king, representing the Antiquities of Herculaneum. He is said to have etched several plates in imitation of the drawings of Parmiggiano.

NOLPE, Peter, a Dutch painter and engraver, born at the Hague in 1601. Little is known concerning his pictures, but he engraved a number of plates, etched with the point and finished with the graver, in a style of considerable ability; although his drawing is often incorrect, and his chiaro-scuro is ill managed. His best works are his landscapes, engraved in a free, bold, and masterly style. Nagler is of the opinion that he flourished until 1670. The following are his principal plates:

N. f. or N fe or N fe

The Portrait of John Adler Salvius, Swedish Minister Plenipotentiary. A set of eight Cavaliers; etched, scarce. A set of eighteen etchings of Beggars; in the style of *P. Quast.* St. Peter delivered from Prison; *after J. V. Vucht* Judah and Tamar, in a large landscape; *from his own design.* The same figures were afterwards introduced into another landscape, of a smaller size. The Broken Dyke; *from his own design.* The fine impressions of this print are very scarce; it is one of his most esteemed plates.—Daniel in the Den of Lions; *after Blancert.* The Departure of King William from Holland to England in 1660 An Emblematical Print on the Marriage of the Prince of Orange with the Princess Mary of England. A set of six Landscapes; *after Adrian van Nieulant;* fine. A set of six Landscapes; *after R. Rogman;* fine. Eight Months of the Year; *Peter Nolpe, fec. et exc.;* fine.—The Prophet Elias speaking to the Widow of Sarepta. St. Paul, the Hermit, fed by an Eagle in the Desert; *after Peter Potter.* The Cavalcade made in 1638 by the citizens of Amsterdam, on the entry of Mary of Medicis into that city; *after C. Molyn;* a large print in six sheets.

NON, Richard Abbé de St., a distinguished French author and amateur engraver, born at Paris in 1730; died in 1792. He edited and published a large pictorial work, entitled *Voyage Pittoresque des Royaumes de Naples et de Sicile.* Paris, 5 vols. folio; embellished with engravings by the most eminent French artists of the day. He also etched a variety of subjects, from his own designs and those of other masters; and engraved several plates in a style resembling washed drawings. Among them are the following:

ETCHINGS FROM HIS OWN DESIGNS.

A set of six Landscapes, with rural occupations and amusements; oval. A set of seven Landscapes and Cottages. Six Views in Italy, with figures; in the style of *Sal. Rosa.*

ETCHINGS AFTER VARIOUS MASTERS.

Six Views in and near Rome; *after Robert.* Six Views near Rome and Tivoli; *after Fragonard.* Two Landscapes, with figures; *after Boucher.* Two, a Village Festival, and a Cattle Market; *after Bernard.* A Landscape, with a figure drawing; *after Berghem.* A variety of Views and other subjects, in aquatinta; *after Boucher, Le Prince, Robert, Fragonard,* and other artists.

NONNOTTE, DONAT, a French painter, born at Besançon in 1707. He early manifested an inclination for art, and acquired the elements of design under a relative, an artist of little note, whom he soon surpassed. In 1728 he visited Paris, and entered the school of Lemoine. With increased advantages he made rapid progress, and was soon honored with the particular notice and encouragement of his instructor, who employed him to paint the backgrounds and accessories in several of his works. Nonnotte painted an historical subject, representing the Protestants attacking Besançon, which deserves considerable praise for its design and coloring. The Duke d'Antin had promised to use his influence to obtain a pension to enable him to visit Rome, but that nobleman died; and Lemoine also died soon after; so that Nonnotte was obliged to devote his energies to portrait painting. In 1741, he exhibited a portrait of such excellence as to gain him admission to the Academy. In 1754 he was appointed painter to the city of Lyons, where he established a free school of design, and sustained it for some time from his own resources, for which he deserves the grateful remembrance of every lover of art. He was subsequently assisted by the liberality of Mathon de la Cour. Nonnotte died in 1785. He left several treatises on art, which are preserved by the Academy of Painting at Lyons.

NOP, GERRIT, a Dutch painter, born at Haerlem in 1570; died in 1622. He studied the elements of design in his own country, and afterwards visited Germany and Italy for improvement.

NOOMS, REMY or RENIER, called ZEEMAN, a Dutch painter and engraver of marine subjects, born at Amsterdam in 1612. Being the child of poor parents, he was obliged to gain a livelihood as a common sailor; but having a great inclination for art, he quitted maritime pursuits, and acquired a knowledge of design. From his original occupation, he acquired the surname of Zeeman (sailor), by which he is often known. He excelled in painting sea views and shipping, which he designed with great correctness and precision; his figures are well drawn, and touched in a very free and spirited style. He attained so high a reputation as to be invited to Prussia; and during his residence in that kingdom he executed many works for the public edifices of Berlin, and for the royal palaces. Nooms etched a number of prints in a bold and free style, among which are the following:

A set of eight plates of Shipping; designed and engraved by Remy Nooms. 1632. A set of four Views in Amsterdam. 1636. A set of four Sea Ports in Holland; published at Amsterdam in 1656; The Four Elements, *Reinier Zeeman, fec.* Two Views in Paris, one of the Faubourg St. Marceau, the other of the Gate of St. Bernard. A set of twelve Views of Shipping; published at London by Ar. Tooker.

NOORDT, J. VAN, a painter and engraver, who lived about the middle of the 17th century. He painted portraits, nymphs bathing, and emblematical subjects; of which some have been engraved. Strutt mentions him as an engraver of great merit, and notices a spirited etching by him, of a landscape with ruins, executed in a broad, masterly manner, with figures well designed. This plate is supposed the same as a landscape *after P. Lastman,* 1645, mentioned by Bartsch, who also notices another, after P. de Laer. Both are very scarce. There is a portrait of Cornelius Noordt, engraved by himself, who was probably a relative of J. van Noordt.

NORDEN, JOHN, an English engraver of topographical subjects, probably born in Wiltshire, about 1546. His principal work was his *Speculum Britanniæ,* or An Historical and Chorographical Description of Middlesex and Hertfordshire, with a frontispiece and maps. He resided at Hendon, in Middlesex; was patronized by Lord Burleigh, and his son Robert, Earl of Salisbury; was Surveyor of the King's Lands in 1614.

NORISINI. See PARASOLE.

NORTHCOTE, JAMES, an eminent English historical painter, born at Devonport in 1746. He was the son of a watch-maker, who would not allow him to indulge in his desire to study painting, but brought him up to his own business. On attaining his majority, he followed the inclination of his genius, and after producing some pictures that were commended by his townsmen, he went to London and entered the school of Sir Joshua Reynolds, in which he continued five years; and by his assiduity, talents, and urbane deportment, he gained the esteem and friendship of his master. In 1777, he went to Italy, where he gained so much distinction that he was elected a member of the imperial Academy of Florence, of the Ancient Etruscan Academy of Cortona, and of the Academy del Forti at Rome. He also painted a portrait of himself, at the request of the Grand Duke of Florence, to be placed among those of distinguished artists in the Florentine Gallery. In 1780, he returned to England, visiting the various academies and collections of note in Holland and Flanders. He settled in London, and soon gained distinction in his profession. Though he mostly confined himself to portraiture from necessity (as there was little encouragement at that time for any higher branch of the art in England), he executed a considerable number of historical works which materially added to his reputation. When Boydell projected the Shakspeare Gallery, Northcote entered into the project with enthusiasm. "It was this memorable occasion," says Gould, himself a painter, "that enabled Northcote to develope his powers. The public excitement at the opening of the Shakspeare Gallery exceeded the expectations of even the most sanguine. All the fashionable world, and crowds of every class, flocked to Pall-Mall to behold the interesting sight, and subscriptions poured in from all quarters in support of the glorious enterprise. Among the most splendid efforts of British art which were thus collected together, none were more justly attractive than the compositions of Northcote." The most celebrated of these were Prince Arthur and Hubert; the Murder of the Princes in the Tower; the Burial of the Princes; and the Entry of Bolingbroke and Richard II. into London. These pictures procured his being elected an Associate of the Royal Academy in 1787. Among his other principal works are the Death of Wat Tyler; the Death of the Earl of Argyle; the Landing of the Prince of Orange; Romulus and Remus; Prospero and Miranda; Jacob blessing the sons of Joseph; the Angels appearing to the Shepherds; Christ the Good Shepherd; the Disobedient Prophet slain by the Lion; Joseph and his Brethren. He also painted some fancy pieces, among which are a Bacchante; the Cradle Hymn; the Mother's Prayer; the Girl Reading; Girl going to the Show of Animals; Girl going to the Market; a Lady crossing the Alps; the Vulture and the Snake; the Leopards; Tiger Hunting; Buck Hunting; the Two Monkeys; &c. He excelled in painting animals, particularly the horse. He also painted a series of pictures intended to convey a great moral lesson, as follows: 1. The Modest Girl and the Wanton, fellow servants in a gentleman's house; 2. the Wanton reveling with her Companions; 3. Good advice given to both by an old Servant; 4. The Wanton in her bed-chamber; 5. The Modest Girl in her bed-chamber; 6. The Wanton turned out of doors for misconduct; 7. The Modest Girl rejecting the illicit advances of her Master; 8. The Wanton dying in poverty and disease, visited by the Modest Girl; 9. The Modest Girl receiving the addresses of her Master; 10. The Modest Girl, married to her Master, is led to her couch, while the Wanton, having died in misery, is laid in her grave.

As an author, Northcote also distinguished himself. Besides several essays on various subjects connected with the Fine Arts, he wrote a Life of Sir Joshua Reynolds, published in 1813, in quarto; with a Supplement in 1815, and an enlarged octavo edition in 1819. In 1828, he published an octavo vol. of "One Hundred Fables," original and selected, and illustrated with numerous beautiful wood cuts, from his own designs. In 1830, appeared his "Life of Titian," and after his decease, a second volume of Fables, published under the title of "The Artists' Book of Fables," and illustrated with numerous wood cuts, from his own designs, executed under the direction of Harvey, by the most eminent engravers in that department. Northcote's life was one of indefatigable industry and perseverance. He was rather haughty in his deportment towards his brother artists, perhaps not without reason, and he was rather feared than beloved by them;—no one trod on his toes without receiving a kick in return. Few artists have encountered more severe, if not bitter and rancorous criticism. They say that he was a good portrait painter, to which branch he should have confined himself, and when he attempted historical painting, he aspired beyond his capacity. They say also that he wanted invention, that his compositions are formal and his heads lack expression. Yet his fables at least show that he had invention enough, and it is notorious, that his Hubert and Arthur, and the Murder of the Princes, drew tears from many beholders, that he often displeased his sitters, by giving them too exact a likeness. While with Reynolds he painted the portrait of one of the servant girls, whose evil genius was a large macaw, belonging to her master, and upon the picture being brought into the room where the bird was, it flew at it in a rage. It is also admitted that he was a good colorist and a "tolerably correct designer," and he died leaving an ample fortune. It would seem therefore fair to infer, that his critics have overlooked the fact, that with the exception of Boydell, there was little encouragement for the historical painters of his day; that he painted history more for the love of it, in his leisure hours, than for profit; that they measure him by a false standard, and demand from him too much, without duly considering his earlier and later disadvantages. Smith, in his Life of Nollekens, says of Northcote (vol. II, p. 424,) "There is one most honorable circumstance, which this celebrated artist has to boast of, namely, that his pictures, whenever they have been resold at auctions, have always been knocked down for more than *four* times their original price, and what is more, they have generally been purchased by men of rank and taste." He died in 1831.

NOSADELLA, Il. See Gio. Francesco Bezzi.

NOTHNAGEL, Johann Andreas, a German painter and engraver, born at Buch, near Saxe Cobourg, in 1729. He resided at Frankfort, where he painted a number of good landscapes, with the sports of the peasantry, in the style of Teniers. As an engraver, however, he gained more distinction; Nagler notices sixty-six prints by him, among which are several heads and busts, in the style of Rembrandt, which he imitated with great success. He died in 1800.

NOTRE, Peter Francis van, a Flemish painter and engraver of the present century, born at Waelhem, near Malines, in 1779. He studied sculpture for some time under van Geel, but in 1811 devoted his energies to painting, and attained considerable eminence in landscape and marines, but was particularly distinguished for his winter scenes and views of the interiors of cities. His pictures are characterized by a faithful imitation of nature, and great delicacy of penciling. Three of his works are in the Museum of Brussels, and many more are preserved in the richest collections of his country, where they are highly esteemed. As an engraver, Notre published a collection of landscapes, among which, several after Hobbema are in request. His talents were much esteemed; he was honored with many medals from different societies; was chosen a member of the Academy at Amsterdam; and Professor of Painting in the Academy at Ghent. He died in 1842.

NOTRE, Hermann Augustus van, was the son and scholar of the preceding, born at Ghent in 1806; died in 1839. He painted landscapes, winter scenes, marine views, and other subjects.

NOTRE, Andrea le. This architect was born at Paris in 1613. He visited Italy for improvement, and devoted his talents to the planning of gardens, in which he attained great eminence. He was appointed superintendent of the gardens of the Tuileries. Among his finest performances, are the terraces of St. Germain en Laie; the woods of the Trianon; the natural porticos of Marly; the espaliers of Chantilly; the walks of Meudon; the gardens of Versailles, unrivalled in their richness and extent. Le Notre evinced his genius in the management of a morass near Versailles, the waters of which he united into a beautiful canal, enclosing the royal gardens. He was appointed Pro-curator-General of the royal buildings, and chevalier of the order of St. Michael. He died in 1700.

NOTTI, Gherardo dalle. See Honthorst.

NOVA, Pecino and Pietro de, two old painters of Bergamo, who were conjointly employed many years, subsequent to 1363, in decorating the church of S. Maria Maggiore in that city.—Lanzi says they very nearly approached Giotto. Pecino died in 1403. There are notices of Pietro up to 1402.

NOVARA, Pietro da. "There are some pictures at Domodossola," says Lanzi, "that make us acquainted with an able artist of Nova. They are preserved in Castello Sylva, and in other places, and have the following inscription, *Ego Petrus filius Petri Pictoris de Novaria hoc opus pinxi* 1370." Doubtless he is the same as Pietro de Nova.

NOVELLANI, Simone. This engraver was probably an Italian. In concert with Francis Hogenberg, he etched, in a coarse style, twenty-one plates, representing the funeral ceremonies at the death of Frederick II., King of Denmark, published in 1592. He also etched several plates for Braun's *Civitates Orbis Terrarum*, published at Cologne in 1572.

NOVELLARA, Lelio da. See Lelio Orsi.

NOVELLI, Gio. Battista, a painter, born at Castelfranco in 1578. He studied under the younger Palma, in whose manner he executed many excellent works for the churches and public edifices at Castelfranco, and the adjacent places. Lanzi says he was a man of wealth, and painted more for amusement than for gain. He also instructed several pupils. He died in 1652.

NOVELLI, Cav. Pietro, called Il Monrealese, from the place of his nativity, an eminent painter and architect, who flourished at Palermo about 1660. He left many works both in oil and fresco in his native city, the most remarkable of which is his great picture of the Marriage at Cana, in the Refectory of the PP. Benedettini, which is particularly commended. He resided a long time at Palermo, where he painted many works for the churches, the most noted of which is the vault of the church of the Conventuals, wholly executed by himself in several compartments. Guarienti eulogizes him for his style, and says he was diligent in studying nature, correct in design, graceful in his forms, and rich in his coloring, with a slight imitation of Spagnoletto. Lanzi says, "the people of Palermo confer daily honor on him, since, whenever they meet a foreigner of taste, they show him nothing else in this city than the works of this great man."

NUCCI, Allegretto, an old painter of Fabriano, by whom, in the church of S. Antonio in that city, are some histories of that Saint, divided into pictures in the early style, resembling the school of Giotto, inscribed *Allegrettus Nutii de Fabriano hoc opus fecit.* 1366.

NUCCI, Avanzino, a painter born at Città di Castello, in 1552. After studying in his native place, he went to Rome, and became the pupil of Niccolo Circignano, and was his ablest scholar. He assisted him in almost all the works he executed in the Vatican. He also painted many works by himself in the churches and palaces at Rome. He afterwards went to Naples, where he painted for the churches. He wrought with great facility and despatch, in a style resembling his master, though he was inferior to him in grandeur. Lanzi commends his Murder of the Innocents, in the church of S. Silvestro at Fabriano. He died in 1629.

NUNEZ, Juan, an old Spanish painter, who flourished at Seville about 1505. He was a scholar of Sanchez de Castro, and probably attained great eminence in his day; but most of his works have been destroyed. There is a picture by him in the Cathedral of Seville, in an excellent state of preservation, representing the Body of Christ in the Arms of the Virgin, with St. Michael, St. Vincent, and other figures. This work is in the stiff, Gothic style prevalent at that time; but it deserves praise for its rich and beautiful draperies.

NUNEZ, Don Pedro Villavicencio, a Spanish painter, born at Seville, of a noble family, in 1635. He studied design as an accomplishment, but made such excellent progress, that he was induced to enter the school of Murillo, although without the intention of practising painting. He was greatly beloved by that master, and studied for some time in his school, after which he visited Malta in discharging his duties as a Knight of St. John, and studied under Mattio Preti, called Il Calabrese. He followed for a short time the vigorous style of that master, but afterwards returned to the tender and harmonious coloring of Murillo. According to Bermudez, he was distinguished in portraits, and painted children in a very beautiful manner, little inferior to Murillo. He presented several of his pictures to the Academy of Seville, where he died in 1700. There is a Holy Family by him at Alton Tower, the seat of Lord Shrewsbury, which partakes of the dark style of Preti.

NUNEZ, Pedro, a reputable Spanish painter of history and portraits, born at Seville in 1614. He studied under Juan de Soto, and afterwards visited Rome for improvement, where he is said to have studied under Guercino. His design was correct, and his coloring good, with a firm and vigorous execution. According to Palomino, he was one of the artists employed to paint the portraits of the Kings of Spain, in the Saloon of the Theatre at Madrid. There are several pictures by him in the church of the convent de la Merced. He died at Madrid in 1654.

NUNEZ, Mateo. See Sepulveda.

NUTTING, Joseph, an English engraver of little note, who resided at London about 1700, and engraved a number of portraits for the booksellers, among which are the following:

PORTRAITS.

Charles I., with the persons who suffered in his cause. Mary Capel, Duchess of Beaufort; *after Walker*. Matthew Mead, father of Dr. Mead. Sir John Cheke. Lucius Cary, Vicount Falkland. Robert Pierpont, Earl of Kingston. George St. Loo, Commissioner for the Navy; scarce. Henry Sacheverel, D. D. John Locke. Aaron Hill. G. Parker, the Almanack-maker. *after Melchior Fusslinus.* William Elder, Engraver; *after Faithorne.*

NUVOLONE, Panfilo, a Cremonese painter who flourished, according to Zaist, about 1608.—He studied under Cav. Gio. Battista Trotti, called Il Malosso, and was among the ablest disciples of that master. Lanzi says he afterwards followed a more solid and attractive style. Among his principal works is one in the monastery of Sts. Domenico and Lazzaro, at Milan, representing Dives and Lazarus; and the Assumption of the Virgin, in the church of La Passione.

NUVOLONE, CARLO FRANCESCO, a distinguished Italian painter, the eldest son of the preceding, was born at Milan in 1608. He studied under his father, but finished his education in the school of Giulio Cesare Procaccini, although he did not adopt the style of either, but became a follower of Guido. According to Lanzi, the forms of his figures are elegant, and the airs of his heads graceful, with a remarkable sweetness and harmony of tints, so that he deserved the name which he still enjoys, of the Guido of Lombardy. His Madonnas are in high request for private collections. Nuvolone also painted many portraits for the nobility, which possess great excellence; and he was selected to paint the Queen of Spain, when she visited Milan in 1649. Lanzi mentions his fine picture of the Miracle of St. Peter, in S. Vittore at Milan; and says he painted many other works in excellent taste, at Milan, Parma, Cremona, Piacenza, and Como. He died, according to Orlandi, in 1651; though Bryan says in 1661.

NUVOLONE, GIUSEPPE, called IL PANFILO, was the younger son of Panfilo N., born at Milan in 1619. Like his brother, Carlo Francesco, he studied first under his father, and afterwards under Giulio Cesare Procaccini. Lanzi says that in his works may everywhere be traced a composition and coloring derived from the school of Procaccini. His compositions are copious, and the oppositions of his lights and shadows are conducted with great intelligence and vigor; but his taste is often inferior to that of his brother, and his shadows are occasionally harsh and sombre. He wrought with great facility, and was indefatigable in the practice of his profession during a long life, painting until his eighty-fourth year. His latter works bear traces of infirmity. There are many of his paintings in the cities of Lombardy; also in Brescia and other Venetian cities, among which Lanzi mentions his fine picture of St. Domenico resuscitating a Dead Man, in the church of that Saint at Cremona, animated by the most natural expression, and adorned with beautiful architecture. He died in 1703.

NUVOLSTELLA, or NIVOLSTELLA, JOHANN GEORG, a German wood engraver, born at Mentz, in 1594; died in 1624. Among other prints, he executed several of the Holy Fathers, after the designs of Tempesta; a set of cuts for Virgil's Æneid; and other poetical subjects.

NUYEN, WYNAND JAN JOSEPH, a Dutch painter, born in 1813. He studied under A. Schelfhout, and in his sixteenth year exhibited a landscape at Ghent, which attracted much attention. He subsequently gained the first prize of the Society at Amsterdam; and in 1838, exhibited a Winter Scene at Ghent, distinguished for its beautiful coloring, and faithful imitation of nature. This picture gained him admission to the Academy of Fine Arts at the Hague, and he would probably have attained great excellence in the art, had he not died in 1839, at the early age of 26. There is an admirable landscape by him, in the Pavilion at Haerlem.

NUZZI, MARIO DEI LA PENNA, called MARIO DA' FIORI, an eminent Italian flower-painter, was born at Penna, in the diocese of Fermo, in 1603. He studied under Tommaso Salini, and settled at Rome, where his pictures were highly esteemed, and were purchased at high prices. He was also much employed in painting garlands, to decorate figures of the Virgin and Saints, in the pictures of other artists. Unhappily for his posthumous fame, he made use of treacherous colors, which, after a number of years, lost their original freshness, and assumed a black and squalid appearance. He died in 1673.

NYTS, J., a French engraver, who flourished in the latter part of the 16th century. Among other plates, he executed several neat and spirited landscapes, and a View of the city of Lisle, in French Flanders.

## O.

O, LEON HENRY VANDER, a German engraver, who flourished about 1660. He engraved part of the portraits for Priorata's History of the Emperor Leopold, among which are James, Duke of York, J. C. de Konigsmarch, Gualter Leslie, and Pietro Strozzi.

OBERTO, FRANCESCO DI, the earliest painter of the Genoese school, whose works are still extant. Lanzi mentions an altar-piece by him in the church of S. Domenico at Genoa, representing the Virgin between two Angels, signed *Franciscus de Oberto.* 1368.

OBREGON, PEDRO DE, a Spanish painter, born at Madrid, according to Bermudez, in 1597. He studied under Vincenzio Carducci, and gained a high reputation in historical painting, especially in works of an easel size. Palomino commends a large picture by him, representing the Trinity, in the refectory of the convent de la Merced; and another of the Immaculate Conception in the church of Santa Cruz. There are some of his easel pictures in the collections at Madrid, where they are highly esteemed. Bermudez says he was also an excellent engraver. He had two sons, *Diego* and *Marcos*, whom he instructed in the art. He died in 1659. There was another Pedro de Obregon, who was a miniaturist, and illuminated books of devotion. He flourished about 1564.

OCCHIALI. See FERRANTINI. See VANVITELLI.

OCHOA, FRANCISCO, a Spanish painter, born at Seville in 1644. He studied under Murillo, whose manner he so successfully imitated, that his works have frequently been mistaken for those of his instructor, even by connoisseurs. The time of his death is not known.

OCHTERVELDT, JOHN, a Dutch painter, of whom little is known, except by his works. He is supposed to have studied under Gerard Terburg, whose manner and subjects he imitated so closely, that his pictures have frequently been taken for the works of that master. They usually represent domestic subjects, ladies at their toilet, musical parties, &c. They are well colored and highly finished. He excelled in his draperies, particularly in white satin, in which he equalled Terburg. He sometimes painted fish stalls, and other familiar outdoor objects in the towns of Holland, in which he imitated Peter de Hooge. His pictures seldom exceed the small cabinet size. He flourished about 1670.

OCTAVIAN, Francesco, a painter, born at Rome in 1690. He went to Paris, where he acquired considerable distinction as an historical painter. He died there in 1736.

ODAM, Girolamo, a Roman artist born in 1681. He studied under Carlo Maratti, and is eulogized by Orlandi, in a long and pompous article, as a painter, sculptor, architect, engraver, philosopher, mathematician, and poet, accomplished in every art and science. Lanzi says he should suppose he was superficial, as nothing remains of him except some engravings, and a slender reputation, not at all corresponding to such unqualified commendation. He was living in 1718.

ODAZZI, or ODASI, Giovanni, a painter, born at Rome in 1663. He first studied under Ciro Ferri, and on the death of that master became the pupil of Gio. Battista Gaulli, called Baciccio. The liveliness of his genius, and his remarkable industry, gained him great distinction, and a multitude of commissions, not only for the churches and public edifices, but for individuals. He was one of the twelve artists selected to paint the prophets in fresco in St. John of Lateran. The prophet produced by Odazzi was Hosea, which was highly commended for correctness of design and dignity of expression. His most remarkable works are the Fall of Lucifer and his Angels, in the church of Santi Apostoli, and St. Bruno, in S. Maria degli Angeli. By aiming at the celerity and rapid execution of Baciccio, without possessing his powers, he proved but a feeble imitator of his style, and his design is frequently careless and incorrect, though he had a commanding facility and great freedom of pencil. He died in 1731.

ODDI, Giuseppe, a painter of Pesaro, who flourished about 1675. He studied under Carlo Maratti at Rome, and on his return to his native place, executed some reputable works for the churches, but wrought more for individuals.

ODDI, Mauro, a painter and engraver, born at Parma in 1639. After learning the elements of the art in his native city, he went to Rome and studied with Pietro da Cortona. On returning to his native city, his talents recommended him to the patronage of the Duchess of Parma, who employed him in decorating the Ducal Palace and the Villa di Colorno. He executed several other pieces in the churches of Parma, Piacenza, and Modena. He was also an eminent architect, and etched a few plates from his own designs, marked with the above monogram. He died in 1702.

ODEKERKEN, W., a Dutch painter, who flourished at Nimeguen about 1650. He painted subjects of still life with considerable success. He is also mentioned as having copied a picture by Metzu, representing a Cook in a Kitchen, surrounded by various culinary utensils, so exactly, that it could with difficulty be distinguished from the original.

ODERICO, Canonico, a priest and miniaturist, who flourished at Siena in 1213. There is a manuscript book entitled *Ordo officiorum Senensis Ecclesiæ*, preserved in the library of the Academy at Florence, written on parchment, and dated 1213, in which the initial letters are illuminated with little histories, ornaments of animals, &c., by this old painter. There are also other similar books, illustrated on the borders of the parchment by him, preserved at Siena. They are esteemed valuable, not only on account of their antiquity, but as showing the state of the arts at that early period.

ODERICO, Giovanni Paolo, a Genoese painter of noble family, born in 1613. Soprani says he studied under Domenico Fiasella, and gained great reputation as an historical painter, though he chiefly excelled in portraits. He was a correct and tasteful designer, select in his forms, and rich and harmonious in his coloring. His principal historical work is a picture of the Guardian Angel in the church of the Padri Scolopi at Genoa. Lanzi says his easel pictures are rare, and only to be found in the choicest collections. His portraits, which display great talents, are of more frequent occurrence, as he received numerous commissions. He died in 1657.

ODERIGI. See Da Gubbio.

ODEVAERE, Chev. Joseph Dionysius, an eminent Flemish historical painter, born at Bruges in 1778. After receiving a good scholastic education in the college of the Augustins, and obtaining several prizes in the Academy of Design in his native city he went to Paris, and studied successively under Suvée and David. In 1804 he drew the grand prize of the French Academy, for his picture of the Death of Phocion, which entitled him to go to Rome, as a pensioner of the government. This distinction, so honorable to him, was duly appreciated by the artists and inhabitants of Bruges, and he was received in triumph on his return; escorted to the city by the students on horseback, in fanciful costume, preceded by a band of music; complimented by the Mayor, and the president of the Academy; presented with a gold medal and chain, and a silver tea service; feasted at the Hotel de Ville, and was honored in the evening with a grand ball and illumination of fire-works, amidst continual acclamations of *Vive Odevaere!* Shortly after this magnificent reception, he returned to Paris; and the following year went to Italy, where he remained about eight years, and executed several pictures of large dimensions, which gained him great reputation. On his return to Paris, he was presented with a gold medal by the Emperor Napoleon. In 1814, he painted for William I., King of the Netherlands, a picture representing the Union of Utrecht; and after the Battle of Waterloo, another, representing the action at the time the hereditary prince (now king of Holland) received his wounds. He also executed for the same monarch several other works relating to the history of the country, for which he received special marks of royal favor, and was made a Chevalier of the order of the Belgic Lion. His pictures are numerous, and are to be found at Paris, Brussels, Bruges, and Ghent. They are generally of large dimensions; one, painted for the King of the Netherlands, measures twenty-four by sixteen feet. Odevaere cultivated letters as well as the arts, was a member of the Royal Institute, and while in Italy, prepared a history of the arts in that country, from the time of Cimabue to that of Raffaelle. He died at Brussels in 1830.

ODIEUVRE, Michel, a French engraver and printseller, who flourished at Paris about 1735. He engraved and published in 1738, a set of portraits of illustrious personages, entitled, *Portraits des Personages illustres de l' un et de l' autre Sexe, recueillis et gravés par les soins de Michel Odieuvre, marchand d'estampes à Paris.* They are usually found in the large quarto editions of the *Memoires de Sully* and *Memoires de Commines.*

OEHLMULLER, Daniel Joseph, an eminent German architect, born at Bamberg in 1791. He studied under Carl Fischer, and then visited Italy and Sicily, where he passed four years in studying and copying the principal edifices, until he was summoned home in 1819, to superintend the erection of the Glyptotheca at Munich, after the designs of Klenze. In 1831 he was commissioned to make designs in the Gothic style for a church in the suburbs of Munich, which gained him great reputation. He erected in the same style the national monument at Wittelsbach, and the Otto chapel at Kiefersfelden. Among his other works, is the church of S. Theresa at Halbergmoos, in the Italian style, commenced in 1833. At the death of Domenico Quaglio, in 1837, Oehlmuller was employed to complete the works at the Castle of Hohenschwangau. He died in 1839. In 1823 and 1825, he published a work containing designs for funeral monuments.

OERI, Peter, a Swiss painter, born at Zurich in 1637. After studying in his native city, he went to Italy, where he resided six years. According to Füessli, he was a correct and graceful designer, possessed a ready invention, and wrought with a spirited pencil. For lack of patronage, he abandoned painting, for the occupation of a gold-chaser.

OESER, Friedrich, an eminent German historical painter and engraver, born at Presburg in 1717. He early showed an inclination and talent for art, and first studied with one Kamauf, an indifferent artist, who made him copy prints; on which account he ran away from him and went to Vienna, where he frequented the Academy, and continued to support himself by the sale of his sketches. At the age of eighteen, he gained the first prize of that institution. His talents attracted the notice of Raphael Donner, an eminent sculptor, who befriended him, taught him to model, and made him acquainted with the antique. In 1739, he went to Dresden, where his abilities procured him the esteem and friendship of several artists of distinction, as well as eminent literary men who resided in that city. He formed an intimate acquaintance with the celebrated Winckelmann, who mentions him in these flattering terms in his work on the imitation of the Grecian painters and sculptors, "These reflections are the result of my conversations with my friend Oeser, the successor of the Theban Aristides, who sketches the soul and paints the mind." In 1764, he was appointed Director of the Academy of Leipsic, where he settled, and passed the rest of his days. He painted both in oil and fresco. His works are mostly to be found in Dresden and Leipsic, especially in the latter city, where are many of his best productions in the churches and public edifices, as well as in private collections. He also etched a large number of plates from his own compositions, and after other masters, executed in a free and spirited style. Nagler calls his name Adam Friedrich, and gives a list of forty-five of his principal engravings. He died at Leipsic in 1799.

OESER, John Louis, was the son of the preceding, born at Dresden in 1751. He was instructed in the art by his father. He was a good landscape painter, but devoted most of his time to engraving. His principal plates are after Rubens, Rembrandt, and Salvator Rosa. He died in 1792.

M Sculp or M. OESTEREICH, Matthew, a German designer and engraver, who flourished at Dresden about 1750. His principal works are a set of twenty-four caricatures from the designs of Cavaliere Ghezzi, published at Dresden in 1750; afterwards republished at Potsdam in 1766, with the addition of eighteen more, from the designs of Gio. Battista Internari and others; a set of forty plates from the drawings in the collection of Count de Bruhl, published at Dresden in 1752. He also engraved part of the plates from the pictures in the Dresden Gallery. He usually marked his plates with one of the above monograms.

OGBORNE, John, an English designer and engraver, born at London about 1725. He studied with Bartolozzi, whose manner he followed. He engraved quite a number of plates, most of them of large size, after some of the most celebrated English painters of his time, particularly Romney, Stothard, Westall, Smirke, Hamilton, Kauffman, &c. He was much employed by Alderman Boydell, and engraved several plates for the Shakspeare Gallery. He died about 1795.

OGGIONE, Marco da. See Uggione.

OHMACHT, Landelin, an eminent German sculptor, born at Dunningen, near Rottweil, in Wurtemberg, in 1760. He studied under J. P. Melchior, and during his earlier years executed a good bust of Lavater, and several sculptures for the Kreuzkirche at Rottweil. In 1790, he visited Rome for improvement, and remained two years in that city, studying and copying the antique, and the works of the great masters. On returning to Germany, he soon gained reputation, and was employed on several important monumental works, the first of which was the monument to the Burgomaster Rhode, in the Cathedral at Lubec. In 1801 he settled at Strasburg, and soon after executed the monument to Gen. Desaix, erected on the Rheininsel near that city. His abilities were highly esteemed by the celebrated sculptor David, who is reported to have said that Ohmacht was the Correggio of Sculpture, and that his works could not be sufficiently admired. He executed four monuments in the church of St. Thomas, of which that to Prof. Oberlin is greatly admired. Among his other works are, the monument to the historian Koch; the monument to Dr. Blessig; another to Gen. Kleber, in the Cathedral; and a colossal statue in honor of Adolph von Nassau, in the Cathedral of Speyer. Ohmacht was an intimate friend of Klopstock, and executed several busts of that celebrated poet. Among his classical sculptures, are the statues of Hebe, Flora, Venus, Psyche, and the Judgment of Paris. The latter work is at Nymphenburg. Ohmacht practised the art at Strasburg for many years, and died there, in 1834.

OLDONI, Boniforte and Ercole, two old

painters of the Milanese school, who, according to Della Valle, flourished at Vercelli about 1466, and executed some works for the churches.

OLEN, or OLIS, JOHN VAN, a Dutch painter, who flourished at Amsterdam about 1680. He painted conversations, game, fruit, and flower-pieces, and interiors of kitchens, ornamented with various culinary utensils, all of which are painted with a broad, free pencil, well colored, and carefully finished. He is also said to have painted landscapes, with sportsmen and dogs. Little is known of him except his works, and as his name is variously spelled by different writers, he may be the same as John van Alen, which see.

OLGIATI, GIROLAMO, an Italian engraver, who flourished about 1572. It is not known under whom he studied, though his style is evidently founded on that of Cornelius Cort. His drawing is incorrect, and his heads lack expression. One of his best plates is an arched one, representing the Trinity, with a number of Saints and Angels; *after Federigo Zuccaro*, inscribed *Hieronymus Olgiatus f.* 1572.

OLINDO, MARTINO DE, a Spanish architect of no great eminence, who flourished in the 16th century. According to Milizia, he erected the parochial church of Liria, of which the lower story has four Doric columns, on pedestals, with niches, statues, and bas-reliefs; the second order has the same number of Corinthian columns; the third order has two fluted, twisted columns, with a statue of St. Michael in the centre. Olindo also completed the monastery of S. Miguel at Valencia, commenced by Cobarrubias.

OLIVA, PIETRO, a painter of Messina, who flourished about 1491. He executed some works for the churches, which are highly commended by Hackert for correctness of design, and lively and natural expression.

OLIVER, ISAAC, an eminent English miniature painter, born about 1556. Lord Orford states that he first studied under Nicholas Hilliard, and afterwards received some instruction from Federigo Zuccaro. Vertue conjectures, from the variety of his drawings after Italian masters, that he visited Italy, which is doubtful. His principal employment was miniature painting, in which branch he acquired great distinction, and was patronized by the most distinguished personages of his time. Many fine miniatures by this master are to be found in the collections of the English nobility and gentry, among which are portraits of himself, Queen Elizabeth, Mary Queen of Scots, Prince Henry, James I., and Ben Jonson. In the particular branch which he mostly practised, it is said, by his countrymen, that he has hardly been surpassed by any artist of any country. He sometimes painted historical subjects, and executed many exquisite drawings after Raffaelle, Parmiggiano, and other Italian masters. He sometimes worked in oil, but did not succeed so well. He died in London in 1617.

OLIVER, PETER, was the eldest son of the preceding, born in London in 1601. He was instructed in the art of miniature painting by his father, whose excellence he nearly equalled. He not only painted portraits, but historical subjects, in water-colors. He was much employed by Charles I., in copying the finest pictures in the Royal collection, as it appears by the catalogue of that monarch and of James II. that there were thirteen historical miniatures by him in the royal collection, several of which are still preserved in Kensington palace. Vertue says he etched some small plates of historical subjects, but they are not specified by him, or any other writer. He died in 1660.

OLIVER, JOHN, an eminent painter on glass, is supposed to have been the nephew of Peter Oliver, born at London in 1616. He practised his art to a great age, as appears from an inscription on a window painted by him, in Christ's church, Oxford, representing the Angel liberating St. Peter from Prison, inscribed *J. Oliver, ætat. suæ* 84, *anno* 1700, *pinxit deditque.* He also engraved several plates, some of which are etched and others executed in mezzotinto. Among them are the following:

PORTRAITS.

King James II., in mezzotinto. Judge Jeffries, styled Earl of Flint. Thomas White, Bishop of Peterborough. John Woremberg, the Dutch Dwarf.

SUBJECTS.

A Boy sleeping, with a Skull by him; *after Art. Gentileschi.* A View of Tangiers; *J. Oliver, fec.* 1676. A View of the Hot Wells at Bath; *J. Oliver, fec. aqua forti.* 1676.

OLIVIER, M., a French painter of little note, born at Paris. He painted history and portraits. He went to London, and in 1772 exhibited in the Royal Academy six pictures, two of which were historical, representing the Murder of the Innocents and the Death of Cleopatra. Not meeting with much encouragement, he went to Spain about 1783.

OLIVIERI, DOMENICO, an Italian painter, born at Turin in 1679. According to Della Valle, he excelled in painting drolls, fairs, markets, merry-makings, in imitation of the style of Peter de Laer, in which he displayed a humorous talent for caricature which has seldom been surpassed. Lanzi says, "In his time the royal collection was enriched, at the death of Prince Eugene, by the addition of nearly four hundred Flemish pictures; and none profited more than Olivieri from the study of these works." He was a man born to amuse, from his singular personal appearance, his lively conversation, and the humorous productions of his pencil. He was extremely happy in his subjects, strong in his colors, and free in his touch. In the gallery of the court are two large pictures by him, one of which represents a fair with quack-doctors, drawers of teeth, villagers sporting or quarreling, and the variety of incident usually furnished by a busy assemblage of the vulgar, composed with an admirable variety of expression in the heads. Although he chiefly painted in what the Italians style *Bambocciate*, yet he was perfectly competent to tread in the higher walks of history, as is proved by his Miracle of the Sacrament, in the sacristy of Corpus Domini, in his native city. He died in 1755.

OLOTZAGA, GIOVANNI DE, an eminent Spanish architect, was a native of Biscay, and flourished during the latter part of the 15th century. His instructor is not mentioned, but he attained great excellence in the art. He erected the Cathedral of Huesca in Arragon, on the site of the celebrated mosque of Mislegda. This work gained him great reputation, and is greatly admired for its fine proportions. Milizia says "the principal façade is grand, with fourteen statues larger than life, on each side the entrance, placed on pedestals within niches; above these are forty-eight smaller statues, a foot in height." Under the reign of Ferdinand and Isabella, the Grecian style of architecture became prevalent in Spain, and was adopted by Olotzaga. Among his principal works in that manner, were the great college of Santa Cruz, at Valladolid, commenced in 1480, and completed in 1492; also the Foundling Hospital at Toledo; and the great college of St. Idelfonso, founded by Cardinal Ximenes.

OMMEGANCK, Cav. Balthasar Paul, one of the most eminent landscape and animal painters of modern times, was born at Antwerp in 1755. He studied with H. Antonissen. He was not one of those artists who astonish us by their precocity; his powers were long in being developed to full maturity, but he studied nature with wonderful assiduity, and carefully observed and noted every changing scene, and so impressed them upon his works that they truly represent not only the season, as the humidity of spring, the glowing heat of summer, and the picturesque alternations of autumn, but the very time of the day is perceptible, from the first roseate blush of the morning to the splendors of the evening sun. In his scenes of spring, all is dewy freshness; in those of summer, it is breathless sultriness—the ground is parched, the verdure withered and tinged, the atmosphere glowing with heat, and the very streams seem oppressed by its power. He enriched his pictures with figures and animals, especially with sheep and goats, which he painted to admiration, not only in the forms, but he represented their character and habits, to the life. Ommeganck acquired immense reputation, and though his pictures commanded such prices in his lifetime that only the rich could afford to buy them, they have more than trebled their value since his death, and are only to be found in the choicest collections in Holland, France, and England. He received many honors, was made a knight of the Order of the Belgic Lion, elected a member of several learned societies, and appointed in 1815, by Belgium, one of the commissioners to reclaim from France the works of art which Napoleon had acquired by force of arms, during the previous wars. He died at Antwerp in 1826. It is proper to caution amateurs that his works have been largely imitated and copied by several clever Dutch artists, many of which have been sent to England and to the United States, and sold as the genuine works of this master.

ONATAS, a Greek painter and sculptor, a native of Ægina; the son of Micon; cotemporary with Polygnotus; and flourished about B. C. 450. As a painter he executed, in concert with Polygnotus, the pictures on the walls of the vestibule of Minerva's temple at Platæa. He also painted the first Argive expedition against Thebes; and probably the picture of Eurygaņea lamenting the death of her sons Eteoches and Polynices, which, according to Sylburgius, is by a MS. error attributed to one Onasias, otherwise not mentioned.

As a sculptor, Onatas attained great excellence, according to Pausanias; although Pliny does not mention him. Pausanias observes that Onatas was not surpassed in his own time by any sculptor of Attica, since the days of Dædalus. That author speaks of a group of Homeric heroes near the great temple at Olympia; Thiersch attributes them all to Onatas, but his name was inscribed only on one of them—the statue of Idomeneus. The Thasians also dedicated a bronze statue of Hercules by Onatas at Olympia, which was ten cubits high. Among the other works of Onatas, was a statue of Apollo at Pergamus; and the bronze statue of Hiero, at Olympia.

ONATE, Miguel, a Spanish portrait painter, born at Seville in 1535. His parents, being in good circumstances, placed him while young under the Chev. Anthony More, then in high favor at the court of Madrid. He accompanied his instructor to Portugal, whither that painter was sent by the King of Spain to paint the royal family. He became one of the most celebrated portrait painters of his time, and found abundant employment at the Spanish court. His manner was exactly like that of More. He died at Madrid in 1606, leaving a considerable fortune to his heirs, which he had acquired by his profession.

ONOFRIO, Crescenzio di, a painter born at Rome in 1650. He studied under Gaspar Poussin, and painted landscapes in the charming style of that master. Lanzi says "he is alone considered the true imitator of that master." He resided chiefly at Florence, where he was much employed by the court, and by individuals. It is said he painted much for the Ducal villas. There are few of his works remaining, either at Rome or Florence, as he painted many frescos, which have all perished. Lanzi says that the Sig. Cancelliere Scrilli, at Florence, possesses several exquisite landscapes and a portrait of his ancestor by him inscribed with his name, and dated 1712. He etched some plates of heroic landscapes, from his own designs, executed in a beautiful and peculiar style, somewhat resembling those of Il Bolognese. The time of his death is not exactly known, and there are many contradictions as to the time of his birth and death, which are evidently erroneous. Thus Bartsch says he was born in 1613, and died in 1688; and Nagler copies him; while Lanzi and Zani both say he was living in 1712, and there are prints by him dated as late as 1696.

OOLEN, John van. See van Alen.

OORT, Lambrecht van, a Flemish painter and architect, born at Amersfort, about 1520. He acquired considerable reputation as an historical painter, but was more distinguished as an architect. He resided chiefly at Antwerp, where he was received into the Academy in 1547. In the Museum at Antwerp, is a picture of the Resurrection of Christ by him, and in that of Brussels are two, representing the Adoration of the Shepherds and the Descent from the Cross.

OORT, Adam van, was the son of the preceding, born at Antwerp in 1557. He was instructed by his father, possessed excellent abilities, and, had his habits been good and his ambition noble, he might have been one of the most distinguished artists of his country; but he was the slave of intemperance, by which he degraded his talents, and brutalized his disposition. His academy at one time was the most frequented at Antwerp, and he had the honor of instructing several of the most distinguished artists of the Flemish school, among whom were Rubens, Jordaens, Franck, and van Balen, but his outrageous conduct disgusted and drove all his pupils from his school except Jordaens, whose tender regard for his daughter, whom he afterwards married, induced him to remain. Notwithstanding the violence of his temper, and the depravity of his habits, van Oort executed numerous works for the churches in Flanders and Brabant, many of which have great merit, and are still highly esteemed. His compositions were agreeable, his coloring excellent, and he had great freedom of handling. His earlier works are studied, and the drawing tolerably correct, but his love of the art diminished as his excesses increased; he fell into mannerism, and wrought with negligence and haste, so that his later pictures have little to recommend them. Rubens used to say that van Oort would have surpassed all his cotemporaries had he seen Rome, formed his taste by studying the best models, and been regular in his habits. He possessed a giant constitution, and, notwithstanding his dissipated life, he lived to the great age of eighty-four years. He died in 1641.

OORTMAN, Jan Joachim, a Dutch engraver, born at Amsterdam in 1777. He studied successively with W. Kock, C. H. Hodges, and L. A. Claessens. He resided most of his life at Paris, where he acquired distinction for many excellent works after Rembrandt, Gerard Douw, van Ostade, and other eminent Dutch masters. He also engraved some plates after Titian, Giulio Romano, Caravaggio, and Valentino, as well as others of the more modern French painters.

OOST, Jacob van, the Elder, an eminent Flemish painter, born at Bruges about 1600. It is not known under whom he first studied, but in 1621 he painted an altar-piece for one of the churches in his native city, which excited the surprise and admiration of cotemporary artists. Being ambitious of further improvement, he went to Rome, where he attentively studied the works of the great masters, and made those of Annibale Caracci the particular objects of his imitation. During his residence in that metropolis, he produced several works of his own composition, so much in the style of that great artist that they astonished the best connoisseurs at Rome, and gained him great reputation. After a residence of five years in Italy, the love of country induced him to return to Bruges, though he had flattering prospects before him to remain. His talents had excited the most sanguine expectations of his fellow citizens before he went abroad; they were impatient to witness the improvement he had made in his travels, and they immediately loaded him with commissions. Van Oost is justly ranked among the ablest artists of the Flemish school. His first studies were the works of Rubens and Vandyck, and from them he acquired that freshness and purity of coloring for which his works are distinguished. Following the example of the greatest masters, his compositions are simple and studied, and he avoided crowding them with figures not essential to his subject. In his design, and in the expression of his heads, he seems always to have had in view the great style of Annibale Caracci. The back-grounds of his pictures are generally enriched with noble architecture, of which he was a perfect master. He had a ready invention, and wrought with extraordinary facility of pencil, though his works are well finished. During a long life he continued to exercise his talents with undiminished reputation, and always abounded with commissions. He executed an incredible number of works for the churches and public edifices, as well as for the private collections of his country, particularly of Bruges. He also excelled in portraits, and painted many distinguished personages. His most famous works are the Nativity, in the church of S. Saviour; the Resurrection, in the Cathedral—a grand composition; and the Descent from the Cross, in the church of the Jesuits at Bruges, which last is considered his master-piece. Most of his pictures are of large size. He died at Bruges in 1671.

OOST, Jacob van, called the Younger, was the son and scholar of the preceding, born at Bruges in 1637. At twenty years of age, his father sent him to Italy to complete his education, where he resided several years, and then returned to Flanders an able and accomplished designer. After painting some pictures for the churches at Bruges, he settled permanently at Lisle, where he acquired a distinguished reputation, and where are the greater part of his works. His historical pictures, like those of his father, are admirably composed, partaking more of the Roman than the Flemish school. Among his best works are the Martyrdom of St. Barbara, in the church of St. Stephen; and the Transfiguration, in the church of St. Saviour at Lisle. He was less eminent than his father as an historical painter, but excelled him in portraits, which some have not hesitated to rank with those of Vandyck. He died in 1713.

OOSTEN, John van, a Dutch painter of whom little is known. He painted small landscapes, with figures and animals, in the manner of Velvet Breughel. They are pleasing and spirited little pieces, and when they appear in sales, without his signature, they are invariably ascribed to Breughel.

OOSTERHOUDT, Thierry van, a Dutch painter, born at Tiel in Guelderland, in 1756. He went to Dusseldorf, where he studied under R. van Eynder. He frequented the Electoral Academy, and carefully studied the works of Raffaelle, Carlo Dolci, Rubens, Vandyck, and other masters in that famous collection. He afterwards returned to his native city, where he acquired considerable reputation as an historical and portrait painter, and executed numerous works, particularly domestic scenes, which are to be found at Tiel and Utrecht. He wrought much in water-colors, and his works in this line are highly esteemed. He died in 1830.

OOSTERWYCK, Maria van, a celebrated paintress of fruit and flowers, born at Nootdorp, a small town near Delft, in 1630. She was the daughter of a clergyman, who, perceiving in her an early disposition for the art, placed her under the tuition of David de Heem, the most celebrated flower painter of his time, under whose able instruction she made rapid progress, and in time produced works that nearly approached the beauty and delicacy of her master. Her pictures of fruit, flowers, and still-life found their way into the choicest collections, and she not only found abundant employment, but received commissions from many of the sovereigns and princes of Europe. She painted a picture for the Emperor Leopold, with which he was so much pleased that he sent her his miniature, with that of the Empress, set in diamonds, as a mark of his approbation. William III. and Louis XIV. were among the most munificent patrons of this celebrated lady. She is ranked among the most successful imitators of nature in the particular branch to which she devoted her talents. She grouped her flowers with great taste, and finished her pictures with extraordinary neatness and delicacy. Her coloring is clear and transparent, and her touch is admirably adapted to the various objects she represented. She imitated the freshness and bloom of flowers, and the luscious richness of fruit, with a truth and harmony that rivalled nature. Her works are extremely scarce and valuable, and are held in the highest estimation. She died in 1693.

OPIE, John, an eminent English historical and portrait painter, born at St. Agnes, a small town in Cornwall, in 1761. The life of this artist is no less instructive than interesting. He was the son of a master carpenter, who designed to bring him up to his own business, to which his aspiring genius could not submit. Prince Hoare, who wrote an excellent sketch of his life, says "he was very early remarkable for the strength of his understanding; at ten years of age he was able to solve many difficult problems in Euclid; at twelve, he kept an evening school, and taught arithmetic and writing to some pupils twice his age." At this time he "could write many various hands with admirable ease and accuracy." He had an unconquerable passion for painting, and sought every opportunity to indulge in it, which his father thought would prove his ruin, and endeavored to restrain. It happened, on one occasion, that his father was employed to repair a gentleman's house, at Truro, and the youth accompanied him. In the parlor hung a picture representing a farm-yard scene, which so captivated young Opie that he stole in to contemplate it, which his father perceiving, severely corrected him; but this had little effect, and he was soon at the door again. By the intercession and kindness of the lady of the house, he was permitted to view the picture without further molestation. On his return home in the evening, he began to copy it from memory. The next day he returned to the house, and in the evening again resumed his task; in this manner, in the course of a few days, he transmitted to his own canvass a very tolerable copy. In the same way he copied a picture of several hunting figures, which he saw exposed for sale in a window. The love of painting had now so thoroughly established its dominion over his mind, that nothing could divert him from engaging in it as a profession, and at the earnest solicitation of his uncle, a man of sound mind, and an excellent arithmetician, with whom he was a great favorite, and who used to call him the little Sir Isaac, in consideration of his talent for mathematics, his father was induced to allow him to follow the bent of his genius. He therefore prosecuted his new studies with ardor,and soon obtained considerable skill in portrait painting. He soon decorated his father's house with all the family portraits, as well as some of his youthful companions. His talents attracted the attention of Dr. Wolcott, so celebrated under the title of Peter Pindar, then residing at Truro, who kindly aided him with his advice, allowed him to copy some pictures in his possession, and recommended him to the patronage of the public. Thus assisted, his fame found its way through the surrounding country, and he commenced his career as a portrait painter, visiting many of the neighboring towns, with letters of introduction to all the principal families. "One of these expeditions," says Prince Hoare, "was to Padstow, whither he set forward, dressed as usual in a boy's plain short jacket, and carrying with him all the necessary apparatus for portrait painting. Here, among others, he painted the whole household of the ancient family of Prideaux, even to the dogs and cats. He remained so long absent from home, that some uneasiness began to arise on his account; but it was dissipated by his returning dressed in a handsome coat, with very long skirts, laced ruffles, and silk stockings. On seeing his mother, he ran to her and kissed her, and then taking out of his pocket twenty guineas which he had earned by his pencil, he desired her to keep them, adding that in future he should maintain himself." Young Opie's fame soon spread abroad, and about 1777 he was introduced to Lord Bateman, by whom he was much employed in painting pictures of old men, women, beggars, &c., which he designed with uncommon vigor, colored well, and gave great truthfulness of expression. In 1780, at the age of nineteen, he went to London under the auspices of Dr. Wolcott, where his merits, and the extraordinary circumstances of his career, excited universal admiration. His partisans were zealous in their praise of the "Cornish Wonder," as he was called, and commissions poured in upon him from many persons of distinction. The powers of Opie, however, were not calculated to flatter the frivolities of fashion. He lacked the polish of the courtier, and his portraits were rather distinguished by identity and truth than by dignity of character; his female portraits lacked elegance and grace, as well as that softening down of harsh features so essential to success. Some artists, too, were jealous of his fame. It was not long before the curiosity excited by his arrival in the metropolis began to subside; but as his talents were not confined to portraiture, he continued to meet with considerable employment in painting portraits and rural subjects, in which last he was particularly succesful. Opie now aspired to the highest branch of the art, historical painting, and bent all his energies to this object. The great artistical undertakings, viz.: Boydell's Shakspeare Gallery, Macklin's Poets' and Biblical Galleries, Boyer's Illustrations of English History, and the other enterprises of the day, opened a new field for the exercise of his abilities. In all these he was much employed, and the pictures he executed on these occasions are among the most admired productions of the British school. Among the most esteemed of these were the Murder of James I. of Scotland, the Death of Rizzio, Jephtha's Vow, the Presentation in the Temple, Arthur supplicating Hubert, Juliet discovered in her Bed-chamber, the Countess of Auvergne and Lord Talbot, &c.

The works of Opie are distinguished by great simplicity in the composition, masterly boldness of effect, and uncommon strength of character, though sometimes defective in dignity, and faithful expression of individual nature. His best works possess, in an eminent degree, what artists term *breadth*. Few painters have shown so perfect an eye to the purity of color, and in some of his works he appears to have emulated the rich and harmonious tones of Rembrandt and Titian; and even Fuseli says that nature had endowed him with an exquisite eye for color, and pronounces his coloring in the Murder of James I. unrivalled among the productions of his cotemporaries, and approaching the excellence of Titian. His conduct of the chiaro-scuro was intelligent and masterly. His faults resulted from the lack of academic tuition. He was a self-made man; and, self-instructed, he had to find out everything appertaining to his art, which is next to invention. Narrowed in his acquaintance of design, he was constrained to copy with precision the model before him. There is little of the ideal, also, in his works, and Fuseli observes of him that he rather bent his subject to the figure, than his figure to the subject. Although his works are deficient in grace of attitude and elevation of character, they invariably exhibit an appearance of reality and truth, which almost compensates for the absence of the more refined characteristics of elegance and grace. He has also been censured for laying on his color too thick, as though it were spread on with a palette-knife, rather than a brush; but this, as with Reynolds and others, was only an occasional experiment—a practice that is always to be condemned in oil paintings, unless they are viewed at a great height, as such parts are liable to crack, and produce unsightly seams. In fact, all unscientific experiments in vehicles, varnishes, and colors, especially vegetable colors, to produce a striking and brilliant effect, cannot be too highly condemned, as they are subject to chemical reaction, producing changes that destroy the harmony, and injure the reputation of the master.

Opie was a man of a strong mind, ambitious to distinguish himself; kind and generous, but bold and resolute, scorning all sycophancy or flattery; indefatigable in the pursuit of knowledge and excellence in his profession. Prince Hoare says, "wherever eminence appeared, he felt and eagerly showed himself its rival. He was forward to claim the honors which he was still more diligent to deserve. He regarded every honorable acquisition as a victory, and openly expressed the delight he experienced in success. On the Professorship of Painting becoming vacant by the dismissal of Barry, he offered himself as a candidate, and being told that he had a competition with an artist whose learning and talents preëminently entitled him to the office, he replied that he abstained from farther interference, but that the person who had been proposed was the only one in whose favor he would willingly resign his pretensions; consistently with this declaration, on Mr. Fuseli's appointment to the office of Keeper, he renewed his claim, and was elected." He delivered two courses of lectures before the Royal Academicians, and one before the Royal British Institution, which showed a profound knowledge of his subject. He also contributed several articles, intended to promote the advancement of the fine arts in Great Britain, to the various periodicals of the day. He died in the prime of life in 1807, deeply lamented for his talents, and his many excellent qualities. His remains were interred in St. Paul's Cathedral, near those of Sir Joshua Reynolds. His widow, Mrs. Amelia Opie, well known as an authoress, wrote an impartial and excellent life of her husband.

OPPENORD, Gilles Marie, a French architect, born at Paris in 1672. He studied under Jules Hardouin Mansard, and afterwards visited Rome with the royal pension, where he remained eight years. On returning to France, he first gained reputation by the grand altar in the church of S. Germain des Pres; and by the altar in S. Sulpice, which is highly praised by Milizia. The Duke of Orleans, Regent, was so much pleased with the abilities of Oppenord, that he appointed him director-general of the royal buildings and gardens. Among his principal works were the decorations of the Gallery of the Palais Royal, the interior of the house of the grand prior of France, the choir and altar of the church of S. Victoire, and the southern façade of S. Sulpice. In the decorative branch of the art he possessed great abilities, but had little merit otherwise; and to him has been attributed, perhaps with some degree of truth, the decadence of the art in the time of Louis XV. Oppenord was the instructor of Jacques François Blondel. He left a number of designs of considerable merit, some of which were published by M. Huquieres. He died in 1742.

OPSTAL, Gaspar James van, a Flemish painter, born at Antwerp in 1660. It is not known under whom he studied, but he painted history, landscapes, and portraits, with considerable reputation. He executed several works for the churches in Flanders and Brabant, in which his design is correct, his composition good, his coloring agreeable, and his touch brilliant and free. He copied the famous Descent from the Cross by Rubens, in the Cathedral at Antwerp, for the Marshal Villeroy, in which he imitated in a perfect manner the admirable coloring and the freedom of touch which distinguish the original painting. In the Cathedral of St. Omer is a grand picture by him, representing several Fathers of that church. He excelled in portraits, many of which are to be found at Antwerp, where they are highly esteemed. In the Hall of the Royal Academy is a noble portrait of one of the Directors of that institution. He also frequently inserted the figures in the works of the cotemporary artists. He died in 1714.

ORAM, William, an English architect and painter, who flourished about 1740. He was bred an architect, but finding little encouragement in that profession, he devoted his attention to landscape painting, and produced some works possessing considerable merit. Through the influence of Sir Edward Walpole, his principal patron, he was made Superintendent of the Board of Works.

ORAZZI, Niccolo, an Italian engraver, who flourished about 1760. Among other works, he engraved a part of the plates for the *Antiquities of Herculaneum*, published by the authority of the King of the two Sicilies.

ORBETTO, L'. See Alessandro Turchi.

ORCAGNA, Andrea. This eminent Italian painter, sculptor, and architect, was a native of Florence. According to some authors he was born about 1315 or 1320; although Vasari places his birth in 1329. His real name was Andrea di Cione; but according to Rumohr, he acquired the surname of L'Archagnuolo, which was afterwards contracted. Lo Archagnuolo, Lo 'rchagnio, L'Orchagno. Vasari calls him Orgagna. He was probably first instructed by his father Cione, a celebrated goldsmith; after which he entered the school of Andrea Pisano. He studied painting under his elder brother Bernardo Orcagna, and executed several works in the hard, dry style of the time, inferior to Giotto both in design and coloring. In concert with his brother he painted the frescos in the Strozzi chapel in the church of S. Maria Novella at Florence, representing Paradise and the Infernal Regions. Lanzi says "the two brothers imitated Dante; and that style was more happily repeated by Andrea in the church of Santa Croce, where he inserted portraits of his enemies among the damned, and of his friends among the blessed. Andrea discovers fertility of imagination, diligence, and spirit, equal to any of his cotemporaries. In composition he was less judicious, in attitudes less exact, than the followers of Giotto; and he yields to them in drawing and coloring." In the Campo Santo at Pisa, is a painting by Andrea Orcagna, representing the Last Judgment. Bernardo also painted a representation of the Infernal Regions in the same edifice; and both these paintings were engraved by Lasinio on a single plate, in his *Pitture del Campo Santo di Pisa.* Andrea was accustomed to sign his pictures *Fecc Andrea di Cione, Scultore.*

As a sculptor and architect, Orcagna attained, according to Vasari, much greater eminence than as a painter. According to the prevailing custom, he practised both arts in connection with the same works. He designed the celebrated tabernacle of the Virgin in Or San Michele, which is a high Gothic pyramidal altar of white marble, free on all sides, and richly ornamented with figures and other sculptures. It is inscribed on the base *Andreas Cionis pictor Florentinus Oratorii archimagister extitit hujus*, MCCCLIX. It is engraved in Richa's *Notizie delle Chiese di Firenze*, after a drawing by Andrea himself. In sculpture he was a worthy follower of the Pisani; and in architecture he attained great eminence. He erected the church of Or San Michele at Florence, and the elegant Loggia de' Lanzi in the Piazza Granduca, which is in a perfect condition. It was built entirely of stone, with great care; and, according to Milizia, had elegant semicircular arches, instead of the pointed ones, which had before been universal. Between the arches of the front façade were seven figures in half-relief, in allusion to the cardinal virtues. Michael Angelo was so highly pleased with this loggia, that, when asked by Cosmo I. for a design for the Senate-House, he answered that he should only continue the loggia of Orcagna round the square, as he never could produce anything superior. This great work, with the sculptures which adorn it, was engraved by Lasinio in Masserini's *Piazza della Granduca di Firenze, con i suoi Monumenti*, Florence, 1830. The portrait of Orcagna, published in Vasari's work, was taken from one of the figures of the Apostles in the above mentioned Tabernacle of the Virgin, which was understood to be his own. Orcagna died at Florence, according to Vasari, in 1389; though Manni says in 1375.

ORDONES, Gasparo, a reputable Spanish architect, who flourished about 1600, and erected, among other works, the church of S. Martino at Madrid.

ORIENT, Joseph, an eminent German landscape painter, born towards the close of the 17th century, at Buebach, near Eisenstadt, in Lower Hungary. He studied under Faistenberger, and became one of the most eminent landscape painters of his time. He passed much time in the study of nature, and gained great improvement from the works of art in the gallery of the Prince of Lichtenstein. He was accustomed to represent nature in her various appearances, as among the wild mountains of the Tyrol, or on the flowery banks of the Rhine; but his favorite subjects were storms of wind, and tempests. He sometimes imitated the styles of Breughel, Savery, Sachtleven, and Griffier. He wrought with great facility; his works are characterized by great fertility of invention, and a faithful imitation of nature. The figures in his landscapes were usually painted by Ferg, Janneck, Querfurt, or Canton. Orient settled at Vienna, and executed most of his works in that city. He was the instructor of a number of excellent artists, among whom were Ferg, Lauterer, and Thurner. His portrait has been painted in large and small by Ganneck. He died at Vienna in 1747.

ORIOLI, Bartolomeo, a painter who flourished at Trevigi about 1616. He executed numerous works for the churches in his native city, which are commended by Federici. He was also a good portrait painter, and frequently introduced portraits into his pictures, instead of ideal forms. There is a picture of this class in the church of S. Croce, representing a numerous procession of the people of Trevigi. Lanzi says he painted more pictures for public exhibitions at Trevigi, than any other artist, and that he belonged to that "numerous tribe of painters, who in Italy, were ambitious of uniting in themselves, the power of poetry and painting; but who, not having received sufficient polish, either in precept or in art, gave vent to their inspirations in their native place, by covering the columns with sonnets, and the churches with pictures, but without exciting the envy of the adjacent districts."

ORIZZONTE. See Francis van Bloemen.

ORLANDI, Odoardo, a Bolognese painter, born in 1660, and died in 1736. He was a scholar of Pasinelli. He executed a few works for the churches, but did not acquire much distinction.

ORLANDI, Stefano, a Bolognese painter, born in 1681, and died in 1760. He studied under Pompeo Aldrovandini. According to Crespi, he excelled in architectural and perspective painting, and in conjunction with Gioseffo Orsoni, painted many able frescos in the churches of Bologna and other Italian cities, besides decorating several theatres in the same places. In these Orlandi painted the architectural parts, and Orsoni the figures.

ORLANDINI, Giulio, a painter of Parma, who flourished in the latter part of the 17th century. He executed some works for the churches which are commended by Orlandi, but Lanzi says he was better qualified to show the succession of the Parmese school, than that of eminent painters.

ORLANDO, Bernardo, a Piedmontese painter, who flourished at Turin in the first part of the 17th century. At this time, the rich collections of pictures and drawings in the royal galleries at that court were made subservient to the instruction of young artists, which was intrusted to a painter of the court. Orlando was invested with this charge, and appointed painter to the Duke in 1617. He also painted some pictures for the churches.

ORLEY, Bernard van, called Bernard of Brussels, an eminent Dutch painter, born at Brussels, according to the best authorities, about 1490, and died in 1560; though there is considerable contradiction on these points. Michiels says he was born in 1471, and died in 1541; and Zani, differing from all others, places his birth in 1500, and his death in 1550. All however, are agreed that he went to Rome at an early age, and studied under Raffaelle, under whose instruction he made extraordinary progress, and soon acquired distinction. He designed in the manner of Raffaelle, and it is said that he not only assisted him in his works, but that "he was employed in finishing many of the grand compositions of that inimitable master"! Michiels says that he was sent by Raffaelle to superintend the execution of the tapestries manufactured at Arras from the cartoons designed by him in 1513 and 1514, for pope Leo X., which work was completed in 1519. At all events, he returned to Brussels with a distinguished reputation. He was employed by the Emperor Charles V., and appointed his court painter. He painted history, landscape, and animals. He was much employed in painting cartoons for tapestries for the court. In these he represented hunting pictures of Charles and his nobles in the forest of Soignes, which were composed and designed in a grand style. He also painted several altar-pieces for the churches, and some sacred and historical pictures for the collections. He painted sixteen cartoons for the Prince of Nassau, intended to decorate the palaces of Breda: each consisted of only two figures,—a knight and a lady on horseback,—being representations of the Nassau family. The design was exceedingly correct and grand, worthy of the school of Raffaelle; they were afterwards copied by Jordaens in oil. To give brilliancy and transparency to his colors, he frequently painted on a gold ground. A celebrated picture of this kind is his Last Judgment, formerly in the cathedral at Antwerp. As many pictures are falsely attributed to him, the following list of his works considered genuine by connoisseurs, will prove interesting:

The Sabeans carrying off Job's Cattle; the King of Holland. Job's Children feasting; do. Job in his Affliction; do. The Death of the Just; do. A Lady of Rank; do. The Restoration of Job; do. The Virgin and infant Jesus; do. Portrait of a Woman; do. The Holy Trinity; do. Neptune and Amphitrite; the Duke of Devonshire, at Chiswick. Venus and Adonis; at Berlin. Bust of Lucretia; at Prague. Antiochus erecting an idol in the Temple of Jerusalem, the right wing of a picture; at Vienna. The Marriage of the Virgin; in the Louvre. The Annunciation, and several circumstances in the life of Christ; in the Museum at Berlin. Connoisseurs are not agreed on its authenticity. The Nativity; formerly in the church of S. Gery, at Brussels. The Adoration of the Magi; formerly in the refectory of the abbey of Premontres, at Dileghem. The Presentation of Mary in the Temple; at Chatsworth. This picture, till recently, was attributed to Jan van Eyck. St. Anne blessing the Virgin, an imitation of Raffaelle; at Berlin. Mary with the infant Jesus, Sts. John, Joseph, and Elisabeth; Lord Scarsdale, at Keddleston.—Mary with the infant Jesus, under a *baldachin*, St. Joseph gathering dates from a Palm Tree; Liverpool Institution. A *riposo* during the flight into Egypt, in a rich landscape with pilgrims; at Vienna. Christ curing a Sick Person, eighteen figures; a drawing in black lead. (Mentioned by Thore, *Alliance des Arts.*) Christ on the Cross, between the two Thieves; in the church of St. Catherine at Brussels. The dead body of Christ on the knees of the Virgin, attended by the Magdalene, St. John, and five other figures; formerly in the church of S. Gudule, at Brussels. Mentioned by Descamps in *Voyage pittoresque.* Dead Christ mourned by his friends; Museum at Brussels. Descent of the Holy Spirit, left wing of a picture; at Vienna. The Last Judgment, a central panel; in the hospital of St. Elizabeth, at Antwerp. In Karel van Mander's time it belonged to the Almoners; and when Descamps wrote, it was in their chapel in the cathedral. The Works of Mercy; wings of the preceding. The Last Judgment, central panel; in the church of St. Jacques, at Antwerp. The Trinity, St. Peter, St. Paul, St. Teresa, and the Magdalene; exterior wings of the preceding. The Last Judgment; at Berlin. Connoisseurs not agreed. Death of the Virgin; in the hospital of St. John, at Brussels. St. Jerome; at Berlin. St. Luke painting the Virgin and Child; the central panel of a sumptuous architectural monument, the wings of which are painted by Michael Coxcie; in the church of St. Viet, at Prague. St. Norbert refusing the heresy of Tanchelin; in the Pinacothek. Lithographed by Bergman. Two wings of a Triptique; mentioned by Descamps as being formerly in the church of St. Martin, at Alost. Anne of Cleves, the bust only; Lord Spencer, at Althorp. The left wing of a Triptique, in the church of St. James at Antwerp, representing the donor and his three sons, under the protection of St. George. The right wing of the same, in the same church, representing the wife and her eleven daughters under the protection of St. Catherine. Portrait of a Female; Duke of Devonshire, at Chiswick. A young Girl reading near a Golden Vase; at Prague. *In his style.* A Woman holding a Serpent to her Breast, and supposed to represent Cleopatra; Duke of Devonshire, at Chiswick. Six Men and a Dog under Trees; a drawing in the collection of the Archduke Charles, at Vienna. Sportsmen on horseback and foot, with a Dog, under Trees; do. Paintings in the Piccolomini Palace; at Vienna. Cartoons for tapestry, designed for Charles V., Marguerite of Austria, and for the house of Nassau.

ORLEY, Richard van, a Dutch painter, born at Brussels in 1652. He was the son of Peter van Orley, an indifferent landscape painter, who first instructed him in the art. He possessed great talents, and first applied himself to miniature painting with considerable success, but being ambitious to distinguish himself in a higher branch of the art, he applied himself to the study of design and nature with great assiduity, and became a celebrated painter of historical subjects of a small size, which he designed and executed so much in the Italian style, that one might imagine he had studied in that country, though it is not known that he was ever in Italy. He painted a prodigious number of works, portraits, historical subjects, and landscapes, which are correctly designed, agreeably colored, and well executed. He enriched his backgrounds with elegant architecture and fine perspectives, and his figures are elegantly and appropriately grouped. Some of his works are said to bear a strong resemblance to those of Albano; others to Cortona, and his landscapes to Poussin. He also distinguished himself as an engraver, and etched a number of plates from his own designs, and after other masters, executed in a free and painter-like manner, among which are the following. He died in 1732.

The Fall of the Rebel Angels; *after Rubens.* Bacchus inebriated, supported by Satyrs; *do.* The Marriage of the Virgin and St. Joseph; *after L. Giordano.* Vertumnus and Pomona; *from his own design.* Twelve Pastoral subjects, *from Guarini's Pastor Fido; do.* Part of a set of twenty-eight plates of subjects from the New Testament; *after the designs of John van Orley,* who etched the remainder himself.

ORLEY, John van, was a younger brother of the preceding, born at Brussels in 1656. He first studied with his father, but afterwards devoted himself to historical painting, with considerable success, and was much employed in painting for the churches in the Netherlands. In the church of St. Nicholas at Brussels, is a picture by him, representing St. Peter delivered from Prison, and in the parochial church of Asch, a picture of the Resurrection, which are highly commended. His master-piece is a large picture of the Adoration of the Magi in the Refectory of the abbey of Dillighem. He etched a part of the plates from his own designs, for the New Testament, mentioned in the list of the preceding artist. He died in 1740.

ORNERIO, Gerardo, a native of Frisio, who, according to Orlandi, was one of the most famous painters of his time on glass. He especially commends his windows in the church of S. Pietro at Bologna, executed about 1575.

ORRENTE, Pedro, a Spanish painter, born at Montealegre, in Murcia, in 1560. It is not known under whom he studied in his own country, but he went to Italy and became the pupil of Giacomo da Ponte (Bassano), whose manner of coloring he adopted, though his style of composition and design was very different. Some authors say that he was not a pupil of Bassano, and that he never went to Italy, supposing that he was a pupil of El Greco, and afterwards imitated the manner of Bassano, from seeing his works in Spain; but Lanzi conclusively shows that he visited Italy, where he painted some works which Conca pronounced superior to those of Bassano. On his return to Spain he was favored with the protection of the Duke of Olivarez, who employed him to paint several pictures for the palace of Bueno Retiro. He painted many works for the churches and convents at Valencia, Cordova, and Toledo. His works are numerous, and are to be found in most of the principal cities of Spain, where they are held in high estimation. In the cathedral at Toledo, is an admired picture by him representing Santa Leocadia, coming out of the Sepulchre, and in the chapel of Los Reyes Nuevos, in the same church, was a picture of the Nativity, since removed to the Royal collection at Madrid; it is a grand composition, admirably executed. In the same church are some superb landscapes, and a picture of Orpheus charming the brute creation, one of his most celebrated works. He died at Toledo in 1644, and was interred in the same church as El Greco.

ORSI, Benedetto, a native of Pescia, who flourished about 1660. Lanzi says he was an eminent pupil of Baldassare Franceschini, called Il Volterrano. There is a fine picture of St. John attributed to him in the church of S. Stefano at Pescia. He also painted the Seven Works of Mercy for La Compagnia de Nobili, which were shown to strangers as among the curiosities of the city till the suppression of the Order, when they were dispersed. There still exists a large circular picture in the church of S. Maria del Letto at Pistoia, which was enumerated by good judges among the finest works of Volterrano, till an authentic document proved the real painter to be Benedetto Orsi.

ORSI, Bernardino, a painter of Reggio, who flourished there in the latter part of the 15th century. According to Tiraboschi, he was an eminent artist in his time. Most of his works have perished. Lanzi says that Reggio still boasts a Madonna of Loretto, painted by him in the cathedral, in 1501.

ORSI, Lelio, called Lelio da Novellara, a painter, born at Reggio in 1511. Banished from his native city for some unknown reason, he established himself at Novellara, where he acquired great distinction, whence his acquired name. Notwithstanding he was one of the ablest artists of his time, and his works have been the admiration of succeeding times, very little is known of his life with any certainty, and his history is mostly founded on supposition. The Cav. Tiraboschi wrote his life, compiled from a variety of sources. The Italian writers sáy that he was "in pittura grande, in architettura ottimo, e in disegno massimo"; *in painting grand, in architecture excellent, and in design pre-eminent.* Tiraboschi conjectures on the authority of a MS., that he imbibed his taste of design at Rome; others suppose he was a pupil of Michael Angelo, or that he studied the designs and models of that master; and others again, that he was a pupil of Giulio Romano. There is great similarity in his style to that of Correggio, though of a far more robust character; his works having the same grace in his chiaro-scuro—in the spreading of his colors, and in the beauty and delicacy of his youthful heads; hence some suppose, with great probability, that he was a pupil of that master. At all events, it is certain that he was on friendly terms with Correggio, that civilities passed between them, and that he attentively studied his works, some of which he copied, as is evident from his fine copy of the celebrated Notte, now in the possession of the noble house of Gazzola at Verona. Tiraboschi says he painted several works for the churches at Rome. It would therefore seem probable, as Tiraboschi asserts, that he first studied at Rome, and afterwards improved his style, by contemplating the works of Correggio; for Lanzi says, "his design is evidently not of the Lombard school, and hence the difficulty of supposing him one of the scholars of Correggio, in which case his earlier works at least, would have partaken of a less robust character." He painted many noble frescos in the churches at Reggio and Novellara, most of which have perished. Lanzi says, "we are indebted to Francesco III., of glorious memory, for such of his works as are now to be seen at Modena, who had them transferred from the fortress of Novellara, to the ducal palace, for their preservation. Few of his altar-pieces now remain in public, at either Novellara or Reggio, the most having perished or been removed, one of which last, representing Sts. Rocco and Sebastiano along with S. Giobbe, I happened to meet in the studio of Signor Armanno at Bologna." There are a few others of doubtful authenticity, claimed to be genuine by him, at Parma, Ancona, and Mantua. He died in 1587.

ORSI, Prospero, a Roman painter, born in 1560, who, according to Baglioni, was employed by pope Sixtus V. in the palace of St. John of Lateran, where he painted two ceilings, one representing the children of Israel passing through the Red Sea, and the other, Isaac blessing Jacob. He was the particular friend of the Cav. Giuseppe Cesari d'Arpino, whose manner he imitated. He afterwards abandoned historical subjects for grotesques, for which he had extraordinary talents, and for this reason was called *Prosperino dalle Grottesche.* He died in 1635, in the pontificate of Urban VIII.

ORSONI, Gioseffo, a Bolognese painter, born in 1691, and died in 1755. According to Crespi, he was a disciple of Pompeo Aldrovandini, and a fellow pupil of Stefano Orlandi, with whom he formed an intimate friendship, and afterwards wrought in conjunction with him. See Orlandi.

ORSOLINI, Carlo, an Italian engraver, born at Venice about 1724. He carried on a considerable commerce in prints, and engraved some of the plates for the Museo Fiorentino.

ORTEGA, St. Juan de, a Spanish architect, who flourished during the eleventh century. According to Milizia, he was the son of Vela Velasquez, and a native of Fontana d'Ortunno, near Burgos. He is said to have made a pilgrimage to Jerusalem, and to have erected at Montesdosa a church, a monastery, and a hospital, still existing. De Ortega also built a great many bridges in Spain, among which was one on the Ebro, near Longronno, and one near St. Domingo.

ORTOLANO, L'. See Gio. Battista Benvenuto.

ORVIETANO, Andrea and Bartolomeo, two painters, probably brothers, mentioned by Della Valle, who flourished at Orvieto about 1405, and were there employed in painting for the churches.

ORVIETANO, Ugolino, an old painter of Orvieto, who, in 1321, according to Della Valle, was employed in conjunction with Gio. Bonini di Assisi, Lello Perugino, and Fra. Giacomo da Camerino, in decorating the cathedral of that city. He was an artist of distinction in his time.

OS, John van, a Dutch painter, born at Middelharnis in 1744, and died in 1808. He settled at the Hague, where he acquired great distinction for his fruit and flower pieces, in which he imitated the manner of John van Huysum with great success, though he had not the tenderness and delicacy of touch, of that great master. His works are highly esteemed, and are to be found in the best collections in his own country. He also painted marines, but not with equal success. His son, George Jacob John van Os, still living, is preëminent for his flower pieces. There are two magnificent flower pieces by him in the Museum at the Hague, which are said never to have been surpassed in artistic execution, brilliancy of coloring, and powerful effect.

OS, Peter Gerard van, was a son of the preceding, born at the Hague in 1776. He studied with his father, but he afterwards formed a style of his own, by studying and imitating the works of Paul Potter and Karel du Jardin. He acquired distinction, and his works are found in the choicest collections in Holland. He also executed quite a number of spirited etchings from his own designs, and others after Potter, Berghem, and Ruysdael, which are held in high estimation. His prints are sometimes marked ***P. G. van Os fec. et exc.***, and sometimes with his initials ***P. G. V. O. f.*** He died at the Hague in 1839.

OSORIO, Francisco Meneses, a Spanish painter, a native of Seville, flourished in the latter part of the 17th century. He studied under Murillo, and became one of the most successful imitators of that great artist. In concert with Juan Garzon, one of his fellow disciples, he painted several pictures in the churches and convents of Seville. In 1668, Osorio was chosen Majordomo of the Academy of that city, and presented his picture of the Conception, which was greatly admired. At the death of Murillo, in 1685, he was employed to finish the works at Cadiz, left incomplete by that master. He copied the works of Murillo to perfection, particularly his pictures of children. Among his principal works are, Elijah fed in the Desert, in the church of San Martino at Madrid; and the picture of St. Catherine, in the Capuchin monastery at Cadiz—his finest production. Osorio died at Seville about 1700.

OSSENBECK, John or Josse, a Dutch painter and engraver, born at Rotterdam in 1627. After studying in his own country, he went to Rome, where he passed the greater part of his life, and acquired distinction for his pictures of landscapes and animals, fairs and huntings, in the style of Peter de Laer, called Bamboccio, whose works were then greatly admired at Rome. Though his works are greatly inferior to those of de Laer, they are ingeniously composed; and he designed his figures, horses, and other animals, with abundance of nature and truth. The back grounds of his pictures are generally embellished with fragments of antiquity, such as ruins of ancient edifices, vestiges of superb monuments, caves, or waterfalls, so exactly designed from scenes in and about Rome, that Sandrart says, "he seems in his works to have transplanted Rome to his own country." His works have the elegance and correctness of design of the Roman school, combined with the coloring and high finish of the Flemish school, executed with a delicate, but spirited pencil. He also distinguished himself as an engraver, and executed some free and spirited etchings after his own designs and others. He also engraved a part of the plates for the collection called the Gallery of Teniers, among which are the following. He died at Regensburg in 1678.

The Children of Niobe; *after Palma*. The Children of Israel gathering the Manna in the Desert; *after Tintoretto*. Orpheus playing to the Animals; *after Bassano*. The Four Seasons; *do*. A set of twelve plates of different Animals; *from his own designs*. A set of four different subjects; *do*. Two Views in and near Rome; *do*. A Boar-hunt; *after Peter de Laer*. Six large prints; *after Salvator Rosa*, *Peter de Laer*, and *S. de Vlieger*; scarce. A grand Festival given at Vienna, with a great number of figures on horseback and on foot; *A. Lartucci, inv. J. Ossenbeck, sc.*; fine and scarce.

OSTADE, Adrian van, a preëminent Dutch painter, born at Lubeck in 1610. He went very young to Haerlem, and studied under Francis Hals, whose works were then in high repute. He was a fellow student of Adrian Brower, with whom he contracted an ardent friendship. He had great talents and a lively genius, and adopted a style peculiar to himself, in which he equalled the best masters of his own country, and acquired a brilliant reputation for his admirable representations of subjects, which, in less skillful hands, would only have excited our disgust. His subjects are always taken from low life, and usually represent interiors of kitchens or ale-houses, with Dutch peasants smoking, dancing and regaling themselves, drunken frolics or quarrels; but he has treated these grotesque subjects with such infinite humor and spirit, and has given such a lively and natural expression to the various characters of his heads, that we forget the low vulgarity of his subjects, in admiring the truth and finesse with which he animates the uncouth actors in the scene. His coloring is rich, clear, and glowing, and he was a perfect master of the principles of chiaro-scuro.

His pencil is uncommonly light and delicate, and though his pictures have the most polished finishing, his touch is free and spirited, and wonderfully neat. There is an uncommon transparency in all his works, and there is such a harmony in the tone of coloring, as captivates the beholder. His figures were so much admired that the eminent cotemporary artists often solicited him to insert the figures in their works, which adds greatly to their value.

Ostade, after leaving his master, resided many years at Haerlem, where his works were so much admired and sought after, that he could scarcely supply the demand, at his own prices. The approach of the French troops, in 1662, excited the greatest alarm at Haerlem, and Ostade sold all his pictures and effects, and set out for his native city. On his arrival at Amsterdam with the intention of embarking for Lubeck, he was prevailed upon to abandon his fears and settle in that city, where he continued to practise his profession with great distinction till his death, in 1685. Notwithstanding he received high prices for his works, they have continued to increase ever since, and now are only to be found in the choicest collections, and whenever one is offered for sale, no price is accounted too exorbitant. In Smith's Catalogue raisonnè of the works of the Dutch and Flemish masters, vol. I., and the Supplement, may be found a full description of about three hundred and eighty paintings by Adrian van Ostade, together with the prices they have brought at various sales at different periods, the names of the purchasers in many instances, the present possessors, or the collections and galleries in which they are to be found. In addition to the large number of oil paintings, he made a considerable number of drawings, in semi-opaque color, which in richness and harmonious effect, are little inferior to his oil pictures, and are so highly esteemed by connoisseurs, that they command very high prices. The commercial value of his works has increased to an astonishing degree within the last fifty years, as may be seen by one or two examples taken from the Catalogue above referred to. In the year 1800, the picture described as No. 57, was sold in the famous Geeldermester Collection, for £229; in Penrice's sale in 1844, it brought £1375 10s. No. 104, was sold in 1802 for £340; in 1844 it brought in Mr. Harman's sale £1386.

Adrian van Ostade also executed upwards of fifty plates of charming etchings from his own designs, which are justly admired, and held by connoisseurs in high estimation. Some of them are etched in a bold and spirited manner, and printed without the assistance of the graver; others are very neatly etched and finished with the graver in the manner of Rembrandt. He sometimes signed his prints with his name, and sometimes marked them with one of the following monograms of his initials A. V. O. The most accurate account of his prints will be found in Bartsch's Peintre Graveur, tom. i. page 351. The following are his most esteemed prints:

AVO, or AVo. or AVØ. or AVØ

The Painter seated at his Easel. The first impressions of this plate are with the high cap considerably above the eyes; in the second impression, a lower bonnet nearly touches the eyes. An Assemblage of Peasants, occupied in killing a Pig; a night-piece, producing a fine effect of the chiaro-scuro. A Family of Peasants at table, saying grace. 1647. A Mountebank surrounded by several figures. Several Peasants at the door of a Cottage, with a fair in the back-ground. Several Peasants fighting with Knives. The Cottage Dinner. 1653. The Cobbler's Shop. 1671. A Man standing on a Bridge angling. The Interior of a Dutch Ale-house, with figures drinking and dancing. The Inside of a Cottage, with a Woman suckling a Child. The Spectacle-seller. A Man, Woman, and Child at the Door of a Cottage. 1652. Several Peasants at a Window; one of them is singing a ballad, and another holds the candle. A Man blowing a Horn, leaning over a hatch. A village Festival, with a great number of figures diverting themselves at the door of an ale-house. His largest plate.

OSTADE, Isaac van, was the brother of the preceding, born at Lubeck about 1617; some say in 1613, but it was probably even later than 1617, as he was the scholar of his brother, and is said to have died young, before he reached the full maturity of his powers. He probably died about 1654, as there are none of his works bearing a later date, though Houbraken says he died at Amsterdam in 1671, which is rendered improbable by the above facts, and the comparative scarcity of his works.

He at first imitated the manner and subjects of his brother, and, though they are every way inferior to the works of that great master, some of his own compositions, as well as the copies he made of his brother's works, have frequently been imposed upon the inexperienced as the genuine productions of the elder Ostade. But he afterwards adopted a style of his own, which led him to excellence and renown, in painting out-door scenes, such as travelers halting at an inn, winter-scenes of Dutch villages, frozen rivers and canals, with figures skating and otherwise amusing themselves on the ice. To these subjects he confined himself, but varied his scene and treatment so much that his pictures have no appearance of self-imitation or repetition. They are faithful representations of nature, and somewhat resemble the bold and admirable productions of Albert Cuyp. They are held in the highest estimation, and are found only in the choicest collections. Smith, in his catalogue, gives a descriptive account of 112 of his works. One of these, in the collection of M. Robit, was sold in 1801 for £361. The same picture, in the Duchess de Berri's collection, sold in 1837 for £1306. Many others have equally progressed in value.

OSTERWYCK. See Oosterwyck.

OTHO, Venius. See Venius.

OTTAVIANI, Giovanni, an Italian engraver, born at Rome in 1735; died in 1808. He visited Venice, where he studied under Wagner, and engraved several prints. On returning to Rome, he soon gained reputation, and became highly esteemed. His principal work was his collection of engravings after the pictures by Raffaelle in the Loggie of the Vatican, of which the first part appeared in twelve numbers, folio, at Rome, 1769—1770; the second in thirteen numbers, in 1776. Among his other prints are the following:

St. Jerome with a Crucifix; *after Guercino.* St. Cecilia; *do.* Angelica and Medora; *do.* Mars and Venus *do.* Three Women bathing surprised by a young Man *do.* Diana and Acteon; *do.* Twenty-three plates, from the paintings by *Raffaelle*, in the Vatican. Four plates from the pictures by *Raffaelle*, in La Farnesia, represent ing Jupiter and Ganymede, Juno on her Car, Neptune on the Ocean, and Pluto and Proserpine.

OTTAVIANI, Carlo, an Italian engraver, the brother of the preceding. He engraved ten of the thirty-three plates published under the following title: *Le pitture della capella pontificia Quirinale, opera di Guido Reni, disegnate da Pietro Angeletti ed incise da Giov. e Carlo fratelli Ottaviani.*

OTTENS, Francis, a Dutch engraver of little note, who flourished about 1760. He engraved some book plates and a few portraits.

OTTINI, Felice, a Roman painter, who, according to Pascoli, was a pupil of Giacinto Brandi. He possessed excellent talents, a fine taste, and was employed, almost in his youth, to decorate the chapel of P. P. di Gesù e Maria, at Rome. He died young, in 1695.

OTTINI, Pasquale, sometimes called Pasqualotto, was born at Verona in 1570. He studied with Felice Riccio, called Brusasorci, whose manner he imitated so happily that he was employed to finish some works by his master, left incomplete at his death. Lanzi says "he was a good artist in regard to forms, and of no common expression, particularly in the works he conducted after having seen Raffaelle's. Of this we have a striking example in his Murder of the Innocents at S. Stefano, and his picture of St. Niccolo with other saints, at S. Giorgio, in the best style of Venetian coloring. In other instances, his coloring is somewhat languid—a defect most probably arising from time and unfavorable situation." He was in high repute in his native city, and the learned Alessandro Carli, in his History of Verona, says that he approached nearer to Paul Veronese than any other artist of that city. He died of the great plague, in 1630. He is said to have executed some beautiful etchings. Bartsch has given a description of only one known print by him, which he commends in the highest terms. It represents the Burial of Christ, and is signed, *Pasq°. Ottii, Ver^s. inv.*

OTTMER, Carl Theodore, an eminent German architect, born at Brunswick in 1800. After acquiring the elements of design and perspective in his native place, he went to Berlin in 1822, where he executed designs for the new Königstadt Theatre, which were so highly valued that the work was entrusted to him. He next erected the Musical Academy at Berlin, which was completed in 1827. He then visited Italy, where he remained, studying and copying the antique, for two years, when he was summoned to Dresden, to prepare designs for the new Opera House in that city; but, for some cause, the structure was not erected. In 1830 he published the first part of his work on architecture, entitled *Architektonischen Mittheilungen.* In 1833, he commenced the erection of the new palace at Brunswick, which was three years in completing, and is regarded as one of the most magnificent and imposing edifices of the kind in Europe. Ottmer also erected at Brunswick several other excellent works, but the Palace is regarded as his master-piece. He died at Berlin in 1843.

OTTO, H. F., a German engraver, said to have been a native of Berlin. He resided at Frankfort, and was chiefly employed by the booksellers. He engraved a part of the heads for the *Notitia Universitates Francofertanæ,* published in 1707 They are indifferently executed.

OUDENARDE. See Audenarde.

OUDENDYK, Evert, a Dutch painter, who flourished at Haerlem about 1650. He painted landscapes, stag-hunts, and similar subjects, with considerable reputation.

OUDENDYK, Adrian, was the son and scholar of the preceding, born at Haerlem about 1648. He painted landscapes and views of towns, in some of which the figures were inserted by Dirk Maas. His chief skill lay in copying, or perhaps pillaging, the works of Adrian Vandervelde and Thomas Wyck, for which reason he was surnamed *Rapianus.* He was living in 1696.

OUDINET, Marc Antoine, a French medalist, born at Rheims in 1643. He at first studied law in his native city, but subsequently relinquished his profession to go to Paris with his relative Rainssant, as keeper of the medals in the King's cabinet. The skill with which he arranged this valuable collection obtained for him a pension, and the honor of a seat in the Academy of Belles-Lettres. He wrote three dissertations upon medals, of great merit. He died in 1712.

OUDRY, Jean Baptiste, a French painter and engraver, born at Paris in 1686. He studied under Nicholas Largilliere. He was an able designer and a respectable colorist, and for some time practised historical painting with considerable ability, as is shown by his picture of the Nativity, in the church of S. Leu, and the Adoration of the Magi, in the chapter of S. Martin des Champs. He afterwards adopted a different branch of the art, in which he acquired distinction. These were hunting pieces, cavalcades, and other similar subjects, in which the figures, horses, and other animals are designed with great correctness and spirit, and touched with a facile and vigorous pencil. There are many of his works of this class in the royal palaces, and the collections in France, where they are highly esteemed. He also painted portraits, landscapes, architecture, fruit, and flower-pieces. He also executed some etchings, from his own designs, in a bold, free, and masterly style. Bartsch gives a descriptive list of 66 prints by him. There are some others, of doubtful authenticity, attributed to him. He died at Beauvais, in 1755.

OUGRUMOFF, G., a Russian painter, born in 1764. He studied in the Academy of Fine Arts at Petersburg, and, in 1785, gained a prize in painting. He is said to have attained a high rank among the artists of his country. Among the principal works of Ougrumoff, are his Conquest of Kasan by the Czar Iwan IV.; and the Coronation of Michael Romanoff. In 1797 he was chosen a member of the Academy, and attained the rank of Director in 1820. He died in 1833.

OUVRIER, Jean, a French engraver, born at Paris in 1725. He was chiefly employed by the booksellers, and engraved a variety of landscapes, vignettes, and other subjects, neatly executed with the graver, though somewhat too dark in the shadows. He died in 1754. The following are among his best prints:

The Villagers of the Appenines; *after Pierre.* A View of the Alps; *after Vernet.* A View of the Appenines; *do.* The Magic Lantern; *after Schenau.* The Flemish

School; *after Eisen the elder*. The Dutch School; *do.* The Genius of Design, an emblematical subject; *after Cochin.*

OUWATER, or OUTWATER, ALBERT VAN, an old Dutch painter, born at Haerlem, according to van Mander, in 1444, and died in 1515; though this is disputed by others. Zani says he was born in 1370; Balkema places his birth in 1366, and death in 1424. There is great uncertainty as to the time in which he flourished; nor is this of much importance, as little remains by him that is authentic. Van Mander and Sandrart extol an altar-piece by him in the principal church at Haerlem, representing St. Peter and St. Paul, in which the figures are carefully and correctly designed, and richly colored, though stiff and labored in the finishing; and they describe another of his works, representing the Resurrection of Lazarus, with several figures, designed in a style superior to what was usually practised at that early period. Very old pictures of the Dutch school, which do not accord with the van Eycks and Hugo vander Goes, are often attributed to Ouwater.

OUWATER, ISAAC, a Dutch painter, born at Amsterdam in 1747. He painted views of the chief cities in Holland, especially of Amsterdam, Haerlem, and Utrecht, ornamented with numerous figures, somewhat in the style of vander Heyden. In his larger pictures, in addition to pedestrians he introduced carriages and horsemen. His representations are accurate, his perspective of streets fine, and the shadows and reflections of buildings and vessels in the water produce a fine effect. His penciling is minute and neat, his coloring rich and harmonious; and, though his works are far inferior to those of vander Heyden, they possess much merit, and are held in considerable estimation.

OUWATER, JACOB, a Dutch painter of fruit and flowers, of whom little is known except his works, which denote a painter of very high order in this branch of the art. His pictures are admirably composed, correctly designed, finely colored, and highly finished. It is conjectured that he flourished about 1750.

OVENS, JURIAN, a Dutch painter, born at Amsterdam in 1600, according to Nagler, who cites his portrait, dated 1666, *anno ætatis* 66. He studied in the school of Rembrandt, and acquired from him an excellent knowledge of coloring, and of the principles of chiaro-scuro. He excelled in painting night-pieces and subjects by torch-light. His portraits are particularly esteemed for their uncommon truth, and expression of character, as well as for the beauty and harmony of their coloring. He also painted history with considerable reputation. In the Stadt-House at Amsterdam are several of his pictures, representing subjects from ancient history, painted in the vigorous style of his master. One of these represents Julius Civilis in the consecrated grove, exhorting and animating the Batavians to shake off the Roman yoke and fight for their liberties. As the consultation of the Batavians was held at night, it afforded the painter an opportunity of exhibiting his genius in his favorite style of painting, in representing the transaction by the light of flambeaux and fires. This performance alone is accounted sufficient to establish his reputation as a great master. In 1665, he was invited to the court of the Duke of Holstein, in whose service he continued until his death, in 1678.

OVERBECK, BONAVENTURA VAN, a Dutch painter, born at Amsterdam in 1660. His parents were in affluent circumstances, and gave him a liberal education. While at college, he distinguished himself by the rapid advancement he made in his studies. On leaving the University, having a strong predilection for painting, he placed himself under Gerard de Lairesse. He afterwards went to Rome, where he applied himself with great assiduity in studying and drawing after the works of the best masters, and the remains of antiquity. He formed a rich collection of drawings and casts during his residence of several years at Rome, with which he returned to his native city, where he was warmly received by his friend and instructor Lairesse, and was visited and caressed by all the artists of Amsterdam. He executed some historical works, which were greatly admired. He possessed superior talents, with a thorough knowledge of art, and might have become one of the most distinguished artists of his time, had he not given way to an unfortunate disposition to dissipation and excess. His attention was also diverted, and his time greatly occupied in the preparation of a work he designed to publish, with plates engraved by himself, from the designs he had made and collected at Rome. He died of a fever brought on by a debauch, in 1706. Before his death, he engaged his nephew to undertake the publication of the work, which he desired to be dedicated to Queen Anne of England. It was published in 1709, in French, under the title *Les restes de l'ancienne Rome.*

OVERBECK, FRIEDRICH, one of the great leaders of the present German school, was born at Lubeck in 1789. In 1809 he went to Rome, where he remained till 1831, when he made a journey to Munich, to exhibit some of his beautiful designs at the Academy of the Fine Arts in that city, the grandeur of which caused a great sensation among the artists and connoisseurs. He was among the first to give impulse to the present aspiring state of painting in Germany, by reverting to the almost forgotten principles which guided the old masters. He has produced many works which prove him an artist truly inspired with a love of the grand and the beautiful. He was not in a hurry to distinguish himself, but spent many years in acquiring a profound knowledge of art. After ascertaining his strength, he commenced his picture of Christ's Entry into Jerusalem, now in the principal church of the city of Lubeck, which at once established his reputation. He next painted the Adoration of the Magi for the Queen of Bavaria, and Christ visiting Mary and Martha, for his friend Vogel the painter, of Zurich. He afterwards returned to Rome, where he still resides. He gained immense reputation at Rome for his fresco works, and was selected by Canova to ornament a part of the walls of the Vatican. He represented there the Coliseum, and placed the Virgin in the centre, appearing to a pilgrim, thus ingeniously contrasting the different states and feelings of the people of ancient and modern Rome. Among his most admired productions in fresco are the Joseph sold by his Brethren, and the Seven Years of Famine, which decorate La Salle Bartoldi, at Rome; a series of subjects from Tasso's Jerusalem Delivered, in the Villa Massimi; the Vision of St. Francis di Assisi, in the church of S. Maria degli Angeli, which last is considered one of the greatest works of the present epoch. His later productions of Christ in the Garden, Judith, and some frescos at Frankfort, have tended to increase his reputation. His drawings are numerous, of rare merit, and have widely spread his excellence and fame. His works have been criticised as deficient in knowledge of coloring, and his carnations are said to want life and energy; but Overbeck, like Niccolo Poussin, is of opinion that talent and tendency that way are more injurious than favorable to the perfection of art. Though critics will allow this in the classical productions of the latter, they will hardly grant it in the different class of subjects adopted by the former. Overbeck married the daughter of Schlegel, the great German critic. The school of which he may be considered the founder, is ably supported by several living German artists, among whom are Cornelius, Schadow, Bendeman, Weit, Schnorr, and Hess, all of whom are emulous of sharing the glory of their chief, and handing down their own names to posterity.

OVERBECK, Leendert, a Dutch painter and engraver, born at Haerlem in 1752, and a pupil of H. Meyer. At first he devoted himself mostly to painting designs for tapestry. He afterwards abandoned painting for engraving. He etched a number of landscapes, a list of which may be found in Nagler's Lexicon. He died at Haerlem, in 1815.

OWEN, William, an eminent English painter of portraits and fancy subjects, born at Ludlow, in Shropshire, in 1769. About 1786, he went to London, and studied under Catton, and afterwards had the benefit of the advice and instruction of Sir Joshua Reynolds. Though he was not a *fashionable painter*, he acquired distinction, and painted the portraits of many eminent persons, among whom were William Pitt, Lord Grenville, the Marquis of Stafford, Sir William Scott, Cyril Jackson, Vicary Gibbs, Chief Justice Abbot, the Earl of Bridgewater, Viscount Exmouth, John Soane, &c. These he executed in a bold, vigorous style, with good coloring; and he gave a striking likeness. He was less successful in his female portraits. He also painted many fancy pictures, which are ranked among the finest of that class of works by the English artists of that time. Among these are the Beggar's Daughter, the Sleeping Girl, the School Mistress, the Girl at the Spring, the Road-Side, the Cottage Door, Children in the Wood, Cupid, the Fortune-Teller, &c., some of which have been engraved. In 1806 he was elected a Royal Academician; in 1810 he was appointed portrait painter to the Prince of Wales, and afterwards "principal portrait painter to the Prince Regent," who offered to knight him, which honor he declined, as it promised to be more expensive than advantageous. His professional income, when at the height of his career, was about £3,000 per annum. During the last five years of his life his health gradually declined. He died on the 11th of February, 1825, by poison, taken by mistake for an aperient draught, through the carelessness of an apothecary's boy, who wrongly labelled the bottle. He was a man of estimable character, and his death was deeply lamented.

OZANNE, Nicholas, a French engraver, born at Paris about 1724. He engraved a number of plates of landscapes, marines, and sea-ports, from his own designs, executed with the graver in a neat, finished style. His vessels, in particular, are designed with great precision. Among the others by him, are a set of four landscapes, two views of the port of Brest, and a set of four marines, signed *Ozanne, fec.*

OZANNE, Jane Frances and Mary Jane, were sisters of the preceding artist, and learned engraving of Aliamet. They engraved, in a neat style, some plates of marines, sea-ports, pastoral subjects, and landscapes, after Vernet, Hackert, Wouwerman, and others. They are marked *J. F. Ozanne*, or *M. J. Ozanne*.

# P.

PACCELLI, Matteo, called della Basilicata, a Neapolitan painter, born about 1660. According to Dominici, he was the favorite disciple of Luca Giordano, and one of his most successful imitators. He executed some works for the churches, more distinguished for brilliant coloring and facility of execution, than for correctness of design. When Giordano was invited to Spain in 1692, by Charles II., he selected Matteo Paccelli and Aniello Rossi, his two favorite pupils, to accompany him as his assistants. They continued with him during his ten years sojourn at that court, and rendered him such valuable assistance in the execution of his numerous works, that, on their return to Naples with their master, the King settled upon them handsome pensions, which enabled them to pass the rest of their days in independence. Paccelli died in 1731.

PACCHIAROTTI, Jacopo, a painter of Siena, who flourished in the first part of the 16th century. It is not known under whom he first studied, but he formed his style by an attentive study of the works of Pietro Perugino, whom he at first closely imitated. Lanzi says, "Siena possesses several cabinet pictures and altar-pieces by him, in the style of Perugino," and that he so closely imitated that master that many of his works have passed under his name, or that of his school. He afterwards greatly improved himself by studying the works of Raffaelle. His best works are his frescos in the churches of S. Caterina and S. Bernardino, in which Lanzi says he emulated the ablest artists of Siena; the chief of these is a picture in the church of S. Caterina, representing that Saint visiting the Body of St. Agnes di Montepulciano—a grand composition, in which the airs of the heads are said to approach those of Raffaelle. There is much contradiction about the real merits of this artist. Speth, a German critic, says the works last referred to, can be justly compared to those of Raffaelle alone, and that great injustice is done to him by classing him in the school of Perugino; but no Italian author gives him any such rank, and Vasari only mentions him incidentally in his life of Razzi, under the name of Girolamo del Pacchia, "a rival of Razzi himself." In 1535, he headed an insurrection against the government, and only escaped an ignominious death by seeking refuge in the monastery of the Osservanti, where he was concealed till an opportunity was found for him to flee into France, where he is supposed to have died. It is probable that he never saw the best works of Raffaelle, as Lanzi thinks it doubtful if he had ever been out of Siena before 1535.

PACE, DEL. See PACI.

PACECCO, or PACICCO. See FRANCESCO DI ROSA.

PACHECO, FRANCISCO, a Spanish painter, born, according to Cean Bermudez, at Seville, in 1571. He studied under Luis Fernandez, a painter of serges and flags, to which occupation, and that of painting and gilding statues or images, he first devoted himself. In 1611 he visited Toledo and Madrid. He attentively studied the works of the great masters in the Escurial, and greatly improved himself. On his return to Seville, he opened an academy for the instruction of young artists, and had the honor of instructing Alonso Cano and Don Diego Velasquez, the last of whom married his daughter. His works are not worthy of much notice. Palomino says he was a correct and rigid designer,his compositions are studied and appropriate, and the airs of his heads noble and dignified; but his execution was feeble, his coloring indifferent, and his manner crude and dry—the last part of which criticism effectually destroys the first. He painted some pictures for the church of the Barefooted Carmelites, in competition with Alonso Vasquez, in which he was greatly surpassed by his rival. In 1623 he again visited Madrid, in company with his scholar and son-in-law, Velasquez, where he resided two years, and "dressed, gilded, and painted a statue of the Virgin by Juan Gomez de Mora,for the Duchess of Olivarez"; a work that was greatly admired, the decoration of which cost 500 ducats! He wrote an elementary treatise on painting, which is considered in Spain indispensable for the instruction of students, and the best in the language. He died at Seville in 1654.

PACHECO, CRISTOFORO, a Spanish portrait painter, of the school of Madrid, flourished in 1568. He was patronized by the Duke of Alba, and executed a number of works for his palace, which were destroyed in the conflagration of that edifice. His portraits are characterized by a good style of design and beautiful coloring; and the draperies are painted with a faithful adherence to the style of dress prevailing in his time.

PACI, RANIERI, called DEL PACE, a native of Pisa, who studied under Antonio Domenico Gabbiani, whose manner he adopted. According to Morrona, he executed some works for the churches of his native city in a reputable manner; but Lanzi says that by carelessness and inattention, he degenerated into a complete mannerist. He flourished in 1719.

PACOT, a French engraver, who flourished about 1690. He engraved some plates of battles and sea-fights, etched in a spirited style, and neatly finished with the graver.

PADERNA, GIOVANNI, a Bolognese painter, born, according to Malvasia, about 1600, and died in 1640. Lanzi says he died at the age of 40, but does not give the date; and Zani says he was living in 1647. He studied under Dentone (Girolamo Curti), under whose instruction he became an eminent painter of perspective and architecture, and after the death of that master he was much employed in decorating the churches,and the public and private edifices of that city. Lanzi says he was an accomplished imitator of Agostino Mitelli, one of the most eminent painters of perspective and architecture of his time. Yet this master was accounted inferior to Dentone, and he was born in 1609,nine years later than Paderna,as above stated Others say that his success excited the jealousy of Mitelli. Lanzi also says that he associated himself with Baldassare Bianchi, who on the death of Paderna married the daughter of Mitelli. Of his numerous works at Bologna, the decorations of the Capella Zagoni, in the church la Madonna della Liberta, are considered among the best.

PADERNA, PAOLO ANTONIO, a Bolognese painter, born in 1649. He first studied under Guercino, but on the death of that master he entered the school of Carlo Cignani. Although he was a reputable painter of history, he chiefly excelled in landscapes, in which Lanzi says "he was an admirable imitator of the manner of Guercino." He was much employed in painting for the collections. His pictures are designed and executed in a bold and vigorous style, his scenery is grand, his coloring clear and harmonious, and his chiaro-scuro excellent. He died in 1708.

PADOVA, GIROLAMO DA, called also GIROLAMO DAL SANTO, a painter born at Padua, where he died about 1550, aged 70. He was celebrated in his day for his small pictures of historical subjects, which he decorated with bassi-relievi, sarcophagi, and other antique ornaments, with inscriptions copied for the most part from the Paduan marbles. On the death of Bernardo Parentino in 1531, he was commissioned to continue the admirable works executed by that master in a cloister of the monastery of Santa Giustina. In these Lanzi says he showed himself greatly inferior to Parentino in his design and expression, but he commends his elegant accessories, designed from the antique.

PADOVA, MAESTRO ANGELO, a painter of Padua, who painted about 1489, in the Refectory of the monastery of Santa Giustina, a picture of the Crucifixion, which Lanzi says is designed in a grand style, and executed with great spirit. He was a close imitator of the style of Andrea Mantegna.

PADOVANINO. See ALESSANDRO VAROTARI.

PADOVANINO, FRANCESCO, a painter born at Padua in 1552. It is not known with whom he studied, but he painted history with considerable reputation. He possessed inventive genius, and was a correct and graceful designer. He painted some works for the churches, one of the best of which is a picture in the church of la Madonna del Carmine at Venice, representing a Saint interceding for two criminals condemned to death. He excelled in portraits, which were admired for their truth, dignity, and excellent coloring. He was much employed in this branch of the art, and painted the portraits of many distinguished persons. He died in 1617.

PADOVANINO, OTTAVIO, was the son of the preceding, born at Padua in 1582. After studying with his father, he went to Rome for improvement. He acquired some celebrity for his historical works, but more for his admirable portraits. He died in 1634.

PADOVANO, or PATAVINUS. See AVIBUS.

PADOVANO, GIUSTO, an old painter who lived at Padua, and died there in 1397, at an advanced age. He was a native of Florence, and his name was Giusto Menabuoi; but he was called Padovanc from having been naturally a citizen of Padua, where he chiefly resided. Vasari says he was a disciple of Giotto, and attributes to him the very extensive works which adorn the church of S. Giovanni Battista in that city. In the picture over the altar are represented various histories of St. John the Baptist; on the walls are represented various scriptural events and Mysteries of the Apocalypse; and in the cupola, is a choir of Angels, where we behold, as in a grand consistory, the Blessed, seated upon the ground, arrayed in various garments. Lanzi says the composition of these works is very simple, but they are executed with an incredible degree of diligence and felicity.

PADOVANO, Giovanni and Antonio, two old painters, probably brothers, to whom Morelli attributes the works in the church of S. Giovanni Battista, mentioned in the preceding article. In his *Notizia*, he says that formerly there was the following inscription on one of the gates, *Opus Johannis et Antonii de Padua*, for which reason he conjectures that they were the painters of the whole temple.

PADOVANO, Lauro. In the *Venezia Descritta* by Sansovino, this painter is said to have been a native of Padua, and a scholar of Francesco Squarcione. He was one of the most successful imitators of the manner of Andrea Mantegna. There are some of his works in the church of La Caritá, at Venice, representing subjects from the life of St. John, which rank among the best productions of his time. He also painted at Padua. He flourished about 1460. Lanzi calls him Lauro da Padova, and applies the same history to him. Others call him Lauro or Lauri da Padova. Zani says he painted from 1470 to 1500, but he is often inaccurate in his dates, and evidently often *guesses* at them. Many of the old Italian artists are called after the places of their nativity or chief residence, and this is always the case when the real name is not known; thus Lauro da Padova, or Padovano, or Padovanino, means Lauro of Padua, or Lauro the Paduan, or Lauro, the admired Paduan. In the latter case, the word is a diminutive, having a signification of eminence, and endearment. Thus, Francesco Mazzuoli, is generally called by the Italians, Parmiggiano, from Parma, his native place, but his fellow citizens endearingly call him Parmiggianino.

HP PADTBRUGGE, H. L., a Swedish engraver, who flourished at Stockholm about 1700. He engraved a part of the plates for a work entitled *Suecia Antiqua et Hodierna*, containing 350 plates. The first edition was published at Stockholm in 3 vols. fol. in 1693, and the second in 1714.

PAELINCK, an eminent Belgian painter, born at Oostacker, near Ghent, in 1781. He first studied under Verhaegen, then professor of painting in the Academy at Ghent. He next went to Paris, and entered the school of David. On his return to Ghent, he contended for the prize offered by the Academy, which he obtained for his Judgment of Paris, and he was appointed Professor of Design in that institution. He shortly afterwards resigned his professorship, and went to Rome, where he remained eight years, diligently studying the antique and the works of the great masters. While at Rome, he distinguished himself, and painted a large picture representing the embellishments of Rome by Augustus, by the commission of the Pope, for his palace at Monte Cavallo. On his return to his own country, he executed many works for the churches and public edifices, as well as for individuals, which justly rank him among the most eminent of the modern Belgian painters. Among his most esteemed works were, The Finding of the Cross, in the church of S. Michael at Ghent; The Adoration of the Shepherds, in the convent of La Trappe, near Antwerp; The Flight into Egypt, at Malines; The Departure of Tobit, at Opbraekel; The Return of Tobit, for Maria Oudenhove; The Assumption of the Virgin, at Muysen; The Disciples at Emmaus, at Everghem; The Calvary, at Oostacker, &c. These works are designed in a grand and elevated style, and display a profound knowledge of art. He is accused of over-fondness of academic display, and this blemish is more apparent in his profane subjects, although those of a sacred character, are not entirely free from it. Among his other most beautiful productions are, The Dance of the Muses; The Judgment of Midas; The Abdication of the Emperor Charles V., and the Toilet of Psyche, in the Museum at the Hague. He died at Brussels in 1839.

PAESI, da', a name given to several painters of landscapes and rural subjects. See Francesco Bassi, Antonio dal Sole, Girolamo Muziano, and Girolamo Vernigo.

PAGANELLI, Niccolo, a painter born at Faenza in 1538, and died in 1620. It is not known under whom he studied, but according to Oretti, he was an excellent artist of the Roman school. Lanzi says that some attribute to him a fine picture of S. Martino, in the cathedral, supposed to be the work of Luca Longhi, and that his genuine works are recognised by the initials N. X. P.

PAGANI, Francesco, a painter born at Florence in 1531. According to Baldinucci, after learning the rudiments of the art in his native city, he went to Rome, where he studied the works of Polidoro da Caravaggio and Maturino, but Lanzi says he imitated the works of Polidoro and Michael Angelo, and that he painted several such admirable imitations of those masters for individuals of Florence, while he was at Rome, that they could scarcely be distinguished from the genuine works. On his return to Florence, he executed several works which gained him great reputation. He died in 1561, in the flower of his life, greatly lamented, as one of the most promising artists of his time.

PAGANI, Gregorio, was the son of Francesco P., born at Florence in 1558. He first studied under Santo di Titi, and afterwards with Lodovico Cardi, called Cigoli, whose style he adopted. Lanzi says he was praised by strangers as a second Cigoli, and that he was much employed by them; hence there are few of his pictures at Florence. His most celebrated work, the Finding of the Cross, in the Carmine, which has been engraved, was destroyed with that edifice by fire. He painted a few frescos, all of which have perished, except one in the cloister of S. Maria Novella, commended by Lanzi, though injured by time. He died in 1605.

PAGANI, Gasparo, a painter of Modena, who flourished there in 1543. It is not known under whom he studied, but he adopted the manner of Raffaelle, for which reason Lanzi supposes he was instructed by Munari or the Taraschi, who succeeded in the school of that master. Few of his historical works now remain. He was also an excellent portrait painter.

PAGANI, Paolo, a painter born at Valsolda, in the Milanese territory, in 1661. He went to Venice, where he formed a style of his own, founded on the works of the best Venetian masters, which gained him considerable reputation in that city, where he executed several fine works for the churches and opened an academy for the instruction of young artists. After a residence of some years at Venice, he returned to Milan, and was employed in the churches and public edifices, and painted much for private collections. There are several of his best works in the Dresden gallery. He died in 1716.

PAGANI, Vincenzio, a native of Monte Rubbiano, in the Picenum, of whom there are notices from 1529 to 1553. Colucci, in his "Memorie de Monte Rubbiano," says he was a scholar of Raffaelle. He executed many works for the churches in the Roman territory, particularly in his native place, at Fallerone, and at Sarnano. One of his most beautiful works is the Assumption of the Virgin, in the collegiate church at Monte Rubbiano, designed and executed entirely in the manner of Raffaelle. The Padre Civalli highly extols two of his works in the church of his order at Sarnano. In 1553 he was employed to paint the altar-piece of the Capella degli Oddi, in the church of the Conventuals at Perugia. which is highly commended. Little is known of this artist except his works, which are of a high character; probably arising from his secluded life. Lanzi, and others, doubt whether he was really a scholar of Raffaelle, but rather think he formed his style by contemplating his works.

PAGANI, Lattanzio. See Marca.

PAGANINI. See Cav. Guido Mazzoni.

PAGANINI, Guglielmo Capodoro, a painter born at Mantua, according to Orlandi, in 1670, and a scholar of Antonio Calza. His genius leading him to paint battle-pieces, skirmishes of cavalry, encampments, &c., he went to Florence, where he carefully studied the works of Borgognone, whose manner he imitated with much success. His pictures are ingeniously composed, and executed with great freedom and spirit. The time of his death is not known.

PAGGI, Giovanni Battista, an eminent painter, born at Genoa in 1554. He was a patrician by birth, and having a passion for painting, he indulged in it from his earliest years, in spite of the opposition of his father. He was highly accomplished in letters, and his various attainments in history, poetry, philosophy, all served to assist him in the composition of his pictures. He studied painting under Luca Cambiasi, and improved himself by copying the antique statues and bas-reliefs. He had already acquired considerable reputation as an historical painter, when he was obliged to flee from Genoa, in consequence of a duel, in which he slew his antagonist. He sought refuge at Florence, where he was protected and employed by the court for twenty years. Florence at that time abounded with men of genius, whom the liberality of the Grand Duke Francis I. had drawn to his court Among them were Lodovico Cardi, and several other artists of distinction, who contributed to reform the Florentine school from the languid state into which it had fallen, by the introduction of the more rich and vigorous style of the Lombard school. Paggi's first productions were rather distinguished by elegance and grace, than energy, in which he seems to have imitated the suavity of Baroccio. Such is his Holy Family, in the church degli Angeli. Lanzi says, "the great merit of Paggi at this time was not vigor, but a certain nobleness of air, which always continued to be his characteristic, and a delicacy and grace which have led some to compare him with Baroccio and Correggio; as is seen in his History of St. Catherine, in the cloister of S. Maria Novella, a grand composition, ornamented with beautiful buildings, and so pleasingly executed, that I have heard it preferred to all others in that court." As he advanced, he adopted a more vigorous style, which gained him immense reputation. Lanzi pronounces his Transfiguration in the church of S. Marco, "a stupendous work, which seems almost beyond his powers." He afterwards painted for the Certosa at Pavia, three pictures from the Passion of our Saviour, in the same grand style, which are considered among his best works. About 1600, his great reputation induced the republic of Genoa to recall him; at the same time, he was invited to the courts of Pavia and Madrid, but his love of country prevented him from accepting these honorable appointments, and he returned to his native city, where he passed the rest of his days, and executed many of his best works. Perhaps his master-piece is the Murder of the Innocents, in the Palazzo Doria, painted in 1606, in competition with Rubens. He contributed greatly to the revival of the art at Genoa, wrote some excellent treatises on the art, and instructed several pupils who distinguished themselves. He died in 1627.

PAGGIO, Il. See Francesco Merano.

PAGLIA, Francesco, a painter born at Brescia in 1636. He was a scholar of Guercino, whose manner he imitated. Lanzi says he was excellent in laying on his colors, admirable in his chiaroscuro, but he displayed little spirit, and his proportions were frequently too long and slender. His best work is an altar-piece in the church of La Carità. He excelled in portraits, which are distinguished for dignity and truth of character, great purity of color, and uncommon relief. Orlandi says he was living in 1700; others, that he died about 1700; and Zani, that he died in 1713.

PAGLIA, Antonio and Angiolo, were sons and scholars of the preceding, and were reputable artists. Antonio was born in 1680, and died in 1747. Angiolo was born in 1681, and died in 1763.

PAGNI, Benedetto, was a native of Pescia, and studied in the school of Giulio Romano at Rome. He accompanied that master to Mantua, where he assisted him in his works. He acquired considerable distinction as an historical painter, and executed some works for the churches. Lanzi says his picture of the Martyrdom of S. Lorenzo in the church of S. Andrea, at Mantua, is worthy of the school of his master. Many pictures are claimed to have been executed by him in his native city, but Lanzi thinks that the Marriage at Cana, in the collegiate church, and the façade of the house of the Pagni family, are the only gen uine ones. Zani says he painted from 1525 to 1570.

PAIGEOLINE, an Italian engraver of whom nothing is known. There is a slight, but spirited etching, bearing his name, after the picture by Paul Veronese, representing the Mother of Moses brought to Pharaoh's Daughter, as a nurse for her son. Zani spells his name *Paigeloine*.

PAIOT, a French engraver of little note, who flourished about 1627. He was chiefly employed in engraving frontispieces, vignettes, and other book plates for the booksellers. They are indifferently executed.

PAJOU, Augustin, a distinguished French sculptor, was born at Paris in 1730. He early manifested a strong inclination for art, and was placed in the school of Lemoine, where he made such rapid advances that, at the age of eighteen, he gained the grand prize of the French Academy, and went to Rome with the royal pension. After pursuing his studies in that city for twelve years, he returned to Paris, and was admitted to the Academy, on the presentation of his group of Pluto holding Cerberus chained. This production gained for Pajou a great reputation, and he was soon extensively employed. His style was natural and masterly, and he far surpassed the sculptors of the preceding generation. In 1767 he was appointed Professor of Sculpture in the French Academy; and during the rule of Napoleon he was a member of the Institute. In 1768 he exhibited a sketch of the tomb of Stanislaus, King of Poland, father-in-law of Louis XV.; a leaden statue of life size, representing Love as the Ruler of the Elements; and four colossal figures in stone, for the garden of the Palais Royal, representing Prudence, Liberality, Mars, and Apollo. Among his principal works are the statues of Bossuet, and Descartes; Psyche abandoned, in the Luxembourg; the sculptures for the façade of the Palais Royal, ordered by Louis XVI.; the sculptures of the Opera House at Versailles; the ornaments of the Bourbon Palace, and of the cathedral of Orleans; and the Naiads of the south and west sides of the Fountain of the Innocents. Pajou died at Paris in 1809.

PALADINI, Filippo, a painter commended by Hackert, who flourished about 1600, and executed several works for the churches in Syracuse, Palermo, Catania, and other places. Lanzi thinks this artist the same as Filippo Palladino, which see.

PALADINI, Filippo, a painter born at Pisa about 1570. He was a reputable painter of history, but chiefly excelled in portraits.

PALADINI, Arcangela, was the daughter of the preceding, born at Pisa in 1599. She was instructed by her father, and acquired much distinction in her time, for the excellence of her portraits, and her beautiful embroidery. She excelled also in music. Maria Magdalena, Archduchess of Austria, took her under her protection, and she resided at the court of Florence many years, universally esteemed. She was also much employed by the nobility. Her portrait, painted by herself, is in the Florentine gallery.

PALADINI, Cav. Giuseppe, a Sicilian painter, who flourished at Palermo about the middle of the 17th century. Little is known of him, as the lives of the Sicilian artists have never been properly written. Hackert makes honorable mention of two of his works in the church of S. Joseph at Castel Termini, representing the Madonna and an Altar-piece of the titular Saint.

PALADINI, Litterio, a Sicilian painter, born, according to Hackert, in 1591. He studied at Rome under Sebastiano Conca, and afterwards improved himself by a diligent study of the antique models. On his return to Messina, he was employed on several considerable fresco works for the churches, the chief of which is the ceiling of the church of Monte Vergine. This work is on a grand scale, and is highly commended for correctness of design. He died of the great plague which ravaged Messina in 1743.

PALAMEDES. See Staevaerts.

PALENIER, Joachim, a Flemish painter, born at Dinant in 1490. He excelled in landscapes with small figures. He settled at Antwerp, where he acquired distinction, and was elected a member of the Academy in that city, in 1515. He died there in 1548.

PALING, Isaac, a Dutch painter, who, according to Houbraken, flourished about 1670. He was a scholar of Abraham vander Tempel, and painted portraits and conversation pieces in the style of that master. He went to London in the reign of Charles II., where he practised portrait painting some years, and returned to his own country in 1682.

PALLADINO, Adriano, a painter, born at Cortona in 1610. According to Orlandi, he was the scholar of Pietro Berretini, whose style he imitated with success. He executed several works for the churches and public edifices of his native city, which are commended. He died at Cortona in 1680.

PALLADINO, Filippo, a painter born at Florence about 1544. It is not known by whom he was instructed, but Lanzi says he seems to have studied the Lombard more than the native artists, and to have been acquainted with Baroccio. After acquiring considerable reputation by his picture of the Decollation of St. John in the church of that saint, at Florence, and an altar-piece at S. Jacopo a'Corbolini at Milan, he was obliged to fly from that city on account of some disturbance. He sought refuge at Rome, where he was received by the Prince Colonna; but being pursued, he went to Sicily, and resided at Mazzarino, on an estate belonging to the Colonna family. There, as well as at Syracuse, Palermo, Catania, and other places, he executed works for the churches, which Lanzi says are elegantly designed and finely colored, though they are not free from mannerism. He died at Mazzarino in 1614.

PALLADIO, Andrea, a celebrated Italian architect, born at Vicenza, in the Venetian territory, in 1518. Little is certainly known of his family, or his first studies; but, according to Milizia, he acquired a knowledge of literature, and afterwards devoted himself with great diligence to the study of Vitruvius and Alberti. He found an encouraging patron in his countryman Gio. Giorgio Trissino, who took Palladio three times to Rome, where the young architect made the greatest possible use of his advantages, measuring and taking drawings of all the ancient edifices of Rome and the vicinity. He appears to have returned from the last of these journeys in 1547, in his twenty-ninth year, when he settled at Vicenza, and was employed on the Palazzo Pubblico at Udine, commenced by Gio. Fontana, an architect of Vicenza. His first important work, however, was the grand Portico surrounding the ancient Basilica on three sides. It is all of fine stone; the first floor is Doric; the second Ionic, both ornamented with arches and columns, with entablatures of exquisite symmetry. The principal excellence of this work consists in making the new agree with the old, as the columns of the new exterior necessarily come in contact with the Gothic pilasters of the interior, requisite for its support. Notwithstanding this difficulty Palladio produced such an elegant and well proportioned edifice, that his reputation immediately rose to a great height, and he was invited to Rome by Paul III., who wished to consult him in regard to the works in progress at St. Peter's. On returning to Vicenza, he seems to have been overwhelmed with commissions for mansions and villas, of which class of subjects his works chiefly consist. Among the numerous private mansions designed or erected by him at Vicenza, are the Palazzi Tiene, Valmarana, Chieracati, Porti, Capitanale, Barbarino, &c.; also the celebrated Villa Capra or Rotonda near the city, and a great many villas along the Brenta.

The increasing fame of Palladio caused him to be invited to Venice, as Sansovino was then growing infirm. His first work there was the monastery of the Lateran Canons della Carita, of which the entrance was through a beautiful Corinthian portico. He afterwards erected two churches at Venice,—S. Giorgio Maggiore, and Il Redentore. The first is built on the plan of a Latin cross, with three naves, elevated from the ground on seven steps. The façade is adorned with a Composite order on a pedestal, which runs entirely around, terminated by a proportionate pediment, under which are two half pediments, indicating the lateral naves. This edifice is characterized by unity and simplicity in the ornaments, producing a majestic effect. The church of the Capuchins, called Il Redentore (the Redeemer), is entirely Corinthian, with a single nave, ninety two feet long, and forty-six wide. Palladio was invited to the court of Duke Emanuel Philibert of Savoy, who received him with distinguished honors. His designs were in great request throughout Italy. Besides the works by him already mentioned, there are the following: the façade of the church della Vigna, at Venice; the magnificent Palazzo Barbaro, at Maser in the Trevigiano; and a noble Palace at Montagnana for Francesco Pisani. His last work was the Olympic Theatre at Vicenza, which he did not live to complete. He died in 1580, aged 62.

The merits of Palladio have been extravagantly extolled by Göethe, Quatremére de Quincy, Forsyth, Hope, Beckford, and others; but these authorities do not attempt to show wherein his excellencies consist. It cannot be denied that his works abound in imperfections, chiefly relating to details. Among them may be mentioned such errors as windows cutting into architraves, windows within friezes, doors lower than windows, ornamented and unornamented windows in the same composition, extremely wide intercolumniations, heavy pediments, and a certain dryness, mannerism, and monotony of detail. It is very probable, however, that most of these defects arose in the execution, as Palladio designed many works which were executed by others; also, Milizia instances a number of edifices attributed to Palladio, which were probably not of his execution. He says, "It is in the beauty of architecture that he merits particular attention. Having always before him the noble style of the ancients, he acquired simplicity and majesty. He never used recesses or reliefs on the pedestals; he seldom sculptured the architraves; and carried his upper ornaments straight, and without projections. His doors, windows, and niches, were simple, and their pediments never broken. He preserved the exact character of each order, never loaded the members of the cornice, nor without reason introduced any new ones. He was extremely accurate in the setting out or measurement of his entablatures. He varied the proportions of the orders according to the nature of his buildings, and also the internal proportions of his rooms, halls, and temples, using the arithmetical, geometrical, and harmonic proportions. Amid the various proportions found among the ruins of antiquity, he well knew how to select the most perfect. His outlines are bold and easy; none of his buildings want character; and in them the serious, the grand, and the elegant, are all used with equal success. He made use of the five orders as they might be required, but appears most attached to the Ionic, and in it most closely followed Vitruvius. He always placed two faces on the capitals. In the Corinthian capital he attached the leaves to the drum, which makes it appear rather heavy. Instead of pediments to the first story, he sometimes placed three courses of quadrangular stone, diminishing towards the top, and producing a very fine effect. All his cupolas are hemispherical. Palladio was the Raffaelle of architecture, and most justly deserves to be studied over every other authority. Had a proper opportunity been afforded him for displaying his genius upon sumptuous and magnificent structures, his simple and majestic style would have triumphed over every other."

Palladio's Treatise on Architecture, in four books, folio, was first published at Venice in 1570, and has often been reprinted. A magnificent edition in 3 vols. fol. was published at London in 1715, in Italian, French and English. Another splendid edition has since been published at Venice in 4 vols. fol., with the edition of his inedited buildings. Lord Burlington published at London in 1730, *I Disegni delle Terme Antiche di Andrea Palladio.* Palladio also composed a small work entitled *Le Antichitâ di Roma,* published after his death.

PALLAJUOLO. See Pollajuolo.

PALLAVICINI, Leo, an Italian engraver, who flourished at Milan, according to several writers of authority, about 1604; Zani says about 1616; Professor Christ says about 1664, and that his prints are marked L. P. f. These prints are supposed to be of an earlier date, and to have been engraved by Luca Penni. There is no certainty, however, about this, as there are many prints bearing these initials, L. P. or L. P. f., sometimes on a tablet, all of which were evidently not executed by the same engraver. See *Luca Penni.*

PALLIERE, Louis Vincent Leon, a French painter, born at Bordeaux in 1787. He went to Paris, and studied under Vincent, under whom he made great progress, and showed uncommon tal ents. In 1812 he gained the first prize of the Academy, for his picture of Ulysses slaying the suitors of Penelope, which entitled him to go to Rome, on a pension from the government. At Rome he painted Argus slain by Mercury, Prometheus chained to the Rock, Juno borrowing the Girdle of Venus, and the Flagellation of Christ, which were commended. After a residence of several years at Rome, he returned to Paris, and in 1819 exhibited in the Louvre, St. Peter curing the Lame Man, Tobit restoring sight to his Father, a Shepherd in repose, a Nymph coming from the Bath, Preaching at night in Rome, and other subjects, and obtained the gold medal of the first class. He died in 1820, in the flower of his life, deeply regretted as an artist of great promise.

PALLONI, or POLLONI, Michael Angelo, a native of Campi nel Fiorentino, and a scholar of Volterrano. Orlandi calls his name *Palloni*, and Baldinucci *Polloni*. After acquiring considerable reputation at Florence, he was invited to the court of the King of Poland, in 1674, where he is said to have found abundant employment.

PALMA, Jacopo, called il Vecchio (the elder), to distinguish him from his great nephew, called il Giovine (the younger), was a native of Serinalta, in the Valle Brembana in the Bergamese Territory. There is a perfect chaos of contradiction, not only among English, French, and German writers, but also the Italian, as to the time this artist flourished, and the real merits of his works, owing to his having been confounded with the younger Palma, and his works extensively imitated. Lanzi, in his last edition, puts the question in the true light. He says, "Jacopo Palma, called il Vecchio, was invariably considered the companion and rival of Lorenzo Lotto, who was born about 1490, and died in 1560, until M. La Combe in his *Dictionnaire Portatif* confused the historical dates relating to him. By Ridolfi, we are told that Palma was employed in completing a picture left unfinished by Titian at his death, in 1576. Upon this and other similar authorities, Combe takes occasion to postpone the birth of Palma until 1540, adding to which the forty-eight years assigned him by Vasari, he places the time of his decease in 1588. Others place his death in 1596 and 1623. In such arrangements, the critics seem neither to have paid attention to the style of Jacopo, still retaining some traces of the antique, nor to the authority of Ridolfi, who makes him the master of Bonifazio Veneziano, who died in 1553; nor to the testimony of Vasari, who, in his work published in 1568, declares that he died at Venice several years before that period, aged 48. He does even consider, what he might more easily have ascertained, that there was another Jacopo Palma, great nephew of the elder, who, according to the authority of Boschini, was a pupil of Titian as long as he lived, and that on the occasion referred to, Ridolfi called him *Palma*, without the addition of the *younger*, without thinking that any could confound him with the elder Palma." Lanzi still further settles the matter by the date 1514, which he read on one of his pictures at Milan, representing the Saviour with several Saints, which he pronounces a *juvenile production*.

His manner, at first, according to Ridolfi, partook of the formality and dryness of Giovanni Bellini. He afterwards attached himself to the method of Giorgione, and aimed at attaining his clearness of expression, and rich and harmonious coloring, visible in his celebrated picture of St. Barbara, in the church of S. Maria Formosa, at Venice. In some of his other pieces he more nearly approaches Titian in the tenderness and *impasto* of his carnations, and a peculiar grace which he acquired from studying the earlier productions of that great master. Of this kind is his Last Supper, in the church of S. Maria Mater Domini at Venice, and a Holy Family in S. Stefano at Vicenza, esteemed one of his happiest productions. Lanzi says "the distinguishing character of his pieces is diligence and a harmony of tints so great as to leave no traces of his pencil; and it has been observed by one of his historians, that he long occupied himself in the production of each piece, and frequently retouched it. In the mixture of his colors, as well as in other respects, he often resembles Lotto, and if he is less animated and sublime, he is, perhaps, generally more beautiful in the forms of his heads, especially of those of women and boys. It is the opinion of some, that in several of his countenances he expressed the likeness of his daughter Violante, very nearly related to Titian, a portrait of whom, by the hand of her father, was to be seen in the Gallery of Sera, a Florentine gentleman. A variety of pictures intended for private rooms, met with in different places in Italy, are attributed to Palma; besides portraits, one of which was commended by Vasari as truly astonishing for its beauty; and Madonnas, chiefly drawn along with other Saints, on oblong canvass, a practice in common use by many artists of that age." The genuine pictures of Palma are exceedingly scarce and highly prized. They are found in all the principal collections on the continent, particularly at Paris, Dresden, Munich, Berlin, and St. Petersburg. But, above all, England is richest in works considered genuine by him, and they are not only to be found in the royal collections, but in many of those belonging to the nobility. It is evident that many of these are spurious, for he never could have executed half so many, even had his process been less tedious.—Lanzi explains this. "The least informed among people of taste, being ignorant of his cotemporary artists, the moment they behold a picture between the dryness of Giovanni Bellini and the softness of Titian, pronounce it to be a Palma; and this is more particularly the case when they find the countenances well rounded and colored, landscape exhibited with care, and roseate hues in the drapery occurring more frequently than those of a more sanguine dye. In this way Palma is in the mouths of all, while other artists, also very numerous, are only mentioned when their names are attached to their productions." Vasari describes, in high terms of commendation, a picture of his in the church of S. Marco at Venice, representing the ship in which the body of St. Mark was brought from Alexandria to Venice, exposed to a frightful tempest. "The picture is designed with great judgment; the vessel is seen struggling against the impetuous tempest; the waves burst with violence against the sides of the ship; the horrid gloom is only enlivened by flashes of lightning, and every part of the scene is filled up with images of terror, so strongly and naturally represented that it seems impossible for the power of art to rise to a higher pitch of truth and perfection."

Lanzi says his most beautiful work is a picture preserved at the Servi. It represents the Virgin, with a group of beatified spirits and a choir of angels, and other angels at her feet, engaged in playing in concert upon their harps. "It is an exceedingly graceful production, delightfully ornamented with landscape and figures in the distance, very tasteful in the tints, which are blended in an admirable manner, equal to the most studied productions of the cotemporary artists of Bergamo (Lorenzo Lotto and Giovanni Cariani), thus forming a triumvirate calculated to reflect honor upon any country." Another admirable picture is his Adoration of the Magi, formerly in the Isola di S. Elena, now in the I. R. Pinacoteca of Milan.

P or R. PALMA, Jacopo, called il Giovine, to distinguish him from the preceding artist, his great uncle, was born at Venice, according to Ridolfi, in 1544. There is a good deal of contradiction and discrepancy about this artist, as well as the elder Palma, and we shall therefore take Lanzi for our guide. He was the son of Antonio Palma, an artist of confined genius, who instructed him in the rudiments of the art. He early exercised himself in copying the works of Titian and other Venetian painters. Ridolfi says he studied with Titian, and others say that he was the scholar of Tintoretto; the last assertion is highly improbable. At the age of fifteen he was taken under the protection of the Duke of Urbino, and accompanied him to his capital. He afterwards sent him to Rome, where he resided eight years, and laid a good foundation by designing from the antique, copying the works of Michael Angelo and Raffaelle, and particularly by studying the chiaro-scuros of Polidoro da Caravaggio. The last was his great model, and next to him came Tintoretto, he being naturally induced, like them, to animate his figures with a certain freedom of action, and a spirit peculiarly his own. His abilities were noticed by the Pope, and he was employed to decorate an apartment in the Vatican. On his return to Venice, he distinguished himself by several works conducted with extraordinary care and diligence, which gained him much reputation. Lanzi says, "there are not wanting professors who have bestowed upon him a very high degree of praise, for displaying the excellent maxims of the Roman school, united to what was best of the Venetian." Though he made the greatest exertions to bring himself into notice, he was little employed; the post was already occupied by two men of consummate ability—Tintoretto and Paul Veronese—and they monopolized all the most lucrative business. Palma, however, obtained the third rank, chiefly through the means of Vittoria, a distinguished sculptor and architect, who was considered the principal judge and arbiter of works of art. The indignation which an able artist feels at having his works submitted to the capricious tribunal of a professor, who did not even practise painting, had caused some animosity betwen Vittoria and the two distinguished painters before mentioned, so that he began to encourage Palma, assist him with his advice, and to trumpet abroad his fame. Palma now came rapidly into notice, and on the death of his antagonists, he was overwhelmed with commissions. Lanzi observes of Palma that he was an artist who might equally be entitled the last of the good age and the first of the bad. When he found his reputation established, and himself almost without a competitor, he began to relax his diligence for such rapidity of execution that Lanzi says many of his works may be pronounced rough drafts, a title bestowed upon them in ridicule by the Cav. d'Arpino. "In order to prevail upon him to produce a piece worthy of his name, it became requisite not only to allow him the full time he pleased, but the full price he chose to ask. Upon such terms he executed the fine picture of S. Benedetto, for the church of SS. Cosmo and Damiano, for the noble family of Moro. Such are his Santa Apollonia at Cremona; his St. Ubaldo and his Annunciation at Pesaro; his Finding of the Cross at Urbino; and other valuable specimens scattered elsewhere. In these his tints are fresh, sweet, and clear—less splendid than those of Veronese, but more pleasing than in Tintoretto; and though they are scantily applied, they are more durable than those of certain other painters more heavily laid on." In short, the merits of his best works may thus be briefly summed up. His compositions are more copious than judicious, and his design more bold than correct; his coloring distinguished by suavity and freshness, and though less brilliant than that of Veronese, it approaches nearer to the truth and tenderness of Titian.—Among his best works at Venice, are the Deposition from the Cross, in the church of S. Niccolo dei Frari; the Martyrdom of St. James, in S. Giacomo del Orio; Christ taken in the Garden, in La Trinitá; the Visitation of the Virgin to St. Elizabeth, in S. Elizabetta; and the Plague of the Serpents, at S. Bartolomeo. The last, though a revolting subject, which strikes horror to the beholder, is one of his most masterly productions, and equal to Tintoretto. He died in 1628. We have quite a number of etchings by this eminent artist, executed in a spirited and masterly style. Bartsch gives a list of twenty-seven. They are sometimes marked with his name in full, and sometimes with a monogram composed of a P. crossed with a palm branch. The following are the principal:

Samson and Dalilah. Judith putting the Head of Holofernes into a sack, held by an attendant. The Nativity. The Holy Family, with St. Jerome and St. Francis. St. John in the Wilderness. The Decollation of St. John. The Tribute Money. The Adulteress before Christ. Christ answering the Pharisees who disputed his authority. The Incredulity of St. Thomas. An emblematical subject of Pallas presenting Victory. St. Jerome in conference with the Pope Damasius; scarce. An Ecclesiastic and a naked Figure, with two boys.

PALMA, Lodovico, a portrait painter and engraver, who, according to Zani, was living at Volterra in 1650. There are some etchings by this master, among which are eight prints and a frontispiece, in a work published at Avignon, entitled "La voye de Lait, ou le chemin des Heros au palais de gloire à l'entre triomphante de Louis XIII. en la Cité d'Avignon, 1622." They are inscribed *Palma Ludovicus Lusitanus f.*

PALMAROLI, P., (Pietro?) an Italian painter, who has rendered his name famous, and conferred a great benefit on art, by transferring to canvas, and thus preserving, some of the frescos of the great Italian masters which were in a perishing condition. In 1811, he thus transferred from the wall the famous Descent from the Cross by Daniele da Volterra, erroneously said to be the first effort of the kind, which gained him immense reputation, and he was employed in transferring and restoring quite a number of great works at Rome, as well as in other places. He freed the frescos of the Sibyls, by Raffaelle, in the church of S. Maria della Pace, from the destructive restorations in oil made by order of Alexander VII., and brought them back to something like their pristine beauty, though before, the objects were so obscured as to be scarcely distinguishable. He was also employed in Germany, and among others transferred and restored the famous Madonna di San Sisto by Raffaelle in the Dresden Gallery. As to his claims of the invention and the process, see *Antonio Contri.* He died at Rome in 1828.

PALMEGIANI, Marco, called Marco da Forli, a painter of much merit, scarcely known till the researches of Lanzi brought him before the world. He was a native of Forli, and the favorite disciple of Francesco Melozzo. He had two manners; the first dry and formal, extremely simple in composition, with gilt ornaments, as was the custom of the *quattrocentisti*, or artists of the 14th century. In his second, his composition is more copious and of greater proportions, his outline bolder, and he dispensed with the gilded ornaments. He was accustomed to add to his principal subject, some others unconnected with it, as in his picture of the Crucifixion in the church of S. Agostino di Forli, in which he inserted two or three groups on different grounds, one of which represents St. Paul visited by St. Anthony, and another representing St. Augustine convinced by the Angel on the subject of the incomprehensibility of the Supreme Triad. Lanzi says that "in these diminutive figures, which he inserted either in the altar-piece or on the steps, he displayed an art extremely refined and pleasing." He often enriched his back-grounds with animated landscapes and beautiful architecture. His works are numerous in Romagna, and are to be found in the Venetian states. In the Palazzo Vicentini, at Vicenza, is one of his most beautiful pictures, representing a Dead Christ, between Nicodemus and Joseph. He excelled in painting Madonnas and similar subjects. Lanzi says he generally signed his name *Marcus Pictor Foroliviensis*, or *Marcus Palmasanus P. Foroliviensis Pinsebat.* He seldom adds the date, but there are two pictures in the collection of Prince Ercolani dated 1513 and 1537. Vasari calls this artist Parmegiano. Others call him Palmezzano. Zani says he signed his pictures *Marcus Palmasanus*, *Palmisanus*, or *Palmezanus*, *Foroliviensis, &c.* Kügler says there are several pictures by *Marco Palmezzano* in the Museum at Berlin.

PALMEGIANI, Filippo, an eminent portrait painter, a native of Forli, who flourished about 1550. It is supposed that he was the son of the preceding.

PALMERINI, da Urbino, a painter of Urbino, of whom little is known. Lanzi says he was a cotemporary of Raffaelle, and probably his fellow scholar under Pietro Perugino. There is an altar-piece by him in the church of S. Antonio at Urbino, which Lanzi pronounces truly beautiful, approaching to a more modern style.

PALMERUCCI, Guido, a painter of Gubbio, who flourished about 1345. According to the Abbe Ranghiasci, he was an eminent artist in his time. He was employed in the churches, and in the palace of his native city. Lanzi says, "there remains one of his frescos in the hall of the palace, much injured by time; but some figures of saints are still preserved which do not yield to the best style of Giotto."

PALMIERI, Giuseppe, a Genoese painter, born in 1674. He studied at Florence, but it is not known under whom. Orlandi extols him as one of the first painters of his age. He excelled in painting pictures of animals, in which he found much employment, and received several commissions from the King of Portugal. Lanzi thinks Orlandi too extravagant in his praise, unless he refers to his merit in the subjects above mentioned. He adds, "still, in the human figure he is a painter of spirit, and of a magical and beautiful style of color, very harmonious and pleasing when the shades do not predominate; he is however, frequently incorrect in his drawing; yet he was capable of better things; for in his picture of the Resurrection, in the church of S. Domenico at Genoa, and in other works more carefully painted, judges of the art find little to reprove." He died in 1740.

PALOMBO, Bartolomeo, a painter born at Rome about 1610, and a pupil of Pietro da Cortona. He is highly commended by Orlandi; and Lanzi says he was one of the best scholars of that master. There are only two pictures by him at Rome, an altar-piece in the church of S. Giuseppe, and another of S. Maria Madalena de' Pazzi, now placed in the church of S. Martino a' Monti. These works are well designed, strong in coloring, excellent in chiaro-scuro; and the figures are extremely graceful. He probably painted much for the collections. He was living in 1666.

PALOMINO, Don Antonio. See Velasco.

PALTHE, Gerard John, a Dutch painter, born at Degenkamp, in Overyssel, in 1681, and a scholar of Juriaan Pool. He painted portraits, familiar subjects, and interiors by candle or torch-light, in the manner of G. Schalken. He died about 1750.

PALTHE, John, a Dutch painter, born at Deventer in 1719. He is supposed to have been a son of the preceding, and painted similar subjects. He settled at Leyden, where he gained considerable reputation, and died there in 1769. There were two other artists of little note, of the name of Palthe.

PALTRONIERI, Giovanni Francesco, a native of Carpi, and a celebrated worker in *scagliola.* He introduced the art into Romagna, where it still continues to flourish. He was living in 1737. See *del Conte.*

PALTRONIERI, Pietro, called Il Mirandolese dalle Prospettive, a painter born at Bologna in 1673. According to Oretti, he founded his style on that of Marc' Antonio Chiarini, and doubtless was his pupil. He was the Viviano of his age; his architectural pieces are numerous, and are to be found not only at Bologna, where he resided, but at Rome, and in many other cities. They consist of ancient temples, ruins, arches, fountains, aqueducts, tinged with a certain reddish color, which serves to distinguish his works from those of many others. To these he adds skies, fields, and waters, which appear real. He frequently employed other artists to insert his figures, among whom was Ercole Graziani. He acquired great reputation, and his works are highly esteemed. He is universally called by the Italians Il Mirandolese dalle Prospettive *The wonderful painter of perspectives.* He died at Bologna in 1741. This eminent artist must not be confounded with Giuseppe Perraccini, also called Il Mirandolese, which see.

PAMPHILUS, a celebrated Grecian painter, a native of Amphipolis, flourished from B. C. 388, to about B. C. 348. He studied under Eupompus of Sicyon, and succeeded in establishing the school founded by that master, which he elevated to the height of the most famous school of painting in Greece. Pamphilus seems to have been principally occupied with the theory of his art, and with teaching, as the notices of his works are very scanty. His pictures were usually of large dimensions. Aristophanes mentions one—the Heraclidæ; Pliny mentions three—the Battle of Phlius and victory of the Athenians, Ulysses on the Raft, and a "Cognatio," probably a family portrait. According to Quintilian, he and his pupil Melanthus were the most renowned among the Greeks for composition. Pliny says he was the first painter who was skilled in all the sciences, particularly arithmetic and geometry, without which he denied that the art could be perfect. By this it must doubtless be understood that Pamphilus reduced the art to rules; and that he particularly excelled in the sciences of optics and perspective. Flaxman well remarks, "How geometry and arithmetic were applied to the study of the human figure, Vitruvius informs us from the writings of Greek artists, perhaps from those of Pamphilus himself—'a man,' says that author, may be so placed with his arms and legs extended, that, his navel being made the centre, a circle may be drawn around, touching the extremities of his fingers and toes. In like manner, a man standing upright, with his arms extended, is enclosed in a square, the extreme extent of his arms being equal to his height.'" Flaxman also observes, "it is impossible to see the numerous figures springing, jumping, dancing, and falling, in the Herculaneum paintings on the painted vases, without being assured that the ancient painters and sculptors must have employed geometrical figures to determine the degrees of curvature in the body, the angular and rectilinear extent of the limbs, and to fix the centre of gravity."

Pamphilus raised the art to so high a position, that, chiefly through his influence, noble youth were taught the art of drawing before all others; it was considered the first among the liberal arts, and was practised exclusively by the free born. His school was characterized by a stricter attention to dramatic truth of composition, and a finer and more systematic style of design. The progressive courses of study occupied the period of ten years, comprehending instructions in drawing, geometry, and the different branches of painting. Daily practice was required; hence the maxim acquired there by Apelles, *Nulla dies sine linea.* According to Pliny, the fee of admission was an Attic talent, (about $1000); and he says that Apelles and Melanthus both paid this fee. Pamphilus left writings upon painting and famous painters; but they have unfortunately been lost.

PAMPURINI, Alessandro, a painter of Cremona, who, according to Zaist, was employed in the cathedral of that city in 1511. He was at least a reputable painter, and executed some frescos for the churches, which have perished.

PANÆNUS, an eminent Greek painter, a native of Athens, flourished about B. C. 450. According to Pausanias and Pliny, he was the brother of Phidias, although Strabo says he was the nephew of that sculptor. Panænus has been termed the Cimabue of the Greeks; but although among the first artists who attained great eminence in painting, he was many years the junior of Polygnotus, Micon, and Dionysius of Colophon. He assisted Phidias in decorating the Temple of the Olympian Jupiter, where he painted Atlas supporting the World, with Hercules near him, about to relieve him of his burden; Theseus and Pirithous; Figures representing Greece and Salamis, the latter bearing in her hands the rostrum of a ship; the Combat of Hercules with the Nemean Lion; Ajax and Cassandra; Hippodamia, with her mother Œnomaus; Prometheus chained, and Hercules preparing to destroy the Vulture which preyed upon him; Penthesilea dying, supported by Achilles, with Hesperian nymphs bearing fruit.

The most famous work of Panænus, however, was his grand painting in the Pœcile at Athens, representing the Battle of Marathon. It was in four great divisions; the first representing the position of the two armies before the battle; the second and third the principal incidents during the conflict; and the fourth the Overthrow of the Persians. The portraits of the Athenian generals Miltiades, Callimachus, and Cynægyrus, were introduced, as were also those of Datis and Artaphernes among the Persians. It has been asserted that these were painted from the life; but this is impossible, as the Battle of Marathon was fought about sixty years before the time of Panænus; Callimachus and Cynægyrus were both killed in the conflict, and Datis and Artaphernes had returned to Persia. If these *Iconics* or portrait figures are to be taken as portraits in the fullest sense of the term, then they must have been drawn from portraits painted during the life time of the generals.

PANCOTTO, Pietro, a Bolognese painter, brought up in the school of the Caracci, who flourished about 1590. According to Malvasia, he was an eccentric genius. His principal work is a grand fresco representing the Last Judgment, in the church of la Madonna di S. Colombano at Bologna, in which he attempted to revenge himself on the parish priest by introducing his portrait, in caricature, which excited the indignation of the clergy, and probably lost him any further employment from them. Lanzi places him in the third rank, among the Bolognese painters, Domenichino and Guido holding the first.

PANDEREN, Egbert van, a Dutch engraver, born at Haerlem, according to Nagler, in 1575, though others say in 1606. Nagler gives a list of thirty-three prints by him. They are executed with the graver in a formal style, with little effect, and the drawing is incorrect. Some of them are interesting from the subjects. The following are the best:

The Virgin interceding with Christ for the salvation of mankind; *after Rubens.* The Four Evangelists; *after Peter de Jode.* St. Louis, with a border, representing his Miracles; *do.* Three circular plates of Minerva, Juno, and Venus; *after Spranger.* The Portrait of Maurice, Prince of Orange, on horseback, with a battle in the background; *after Tempesta.* Four plates of the Sick Man and the Doctor; *after Goltzius;* scarce. Part of the Plates for the Academie de l'Espée; by *G. Thibault.*

PANDERIT, a painter mentioned by Balkema, as one of the best scholars of Rembrandt. He says he was a native of Saxony, born in 1601, and died in 1662. He afterwards notices John Paudits, also a scholar of Rembrandt, who, he says, was born in Saxony in 1618, and died in 1659, and was an excellent portrait painter. Both are doubtless the same as *Christopher Paudits*, which see.

PANDOLFI, GIOVANNI GIACOMO, a painter of Pesaro, who flourished about 1630. He was a scholar of Federigo Zuccaro. Lanzi says, "his works are celebrated in his native city, and do not yield the palm to those of Zuccaro, as seen in his pictures of S. Giorgio and S. Carlo in the cathedral." He also decorated the whole chapel in the Nome di Dio, with various subjects in fresco from the Old and New Testament.

PANDOLFO. See RESCHI.

PANETTI, DOMENICO, a painter of Ferrara, born in 1460. It is not known under whom he studied, but, according to Baruffaldi, he painted in the dry, formal style of the time, till his pupil, Benvenuto da Garofolo, returned from Rome after acquiring the new style under Raffaelle. The instructor now became the pupil of his former disciple, and although somewhat advanced in years, entirely changed his manner, and became one of the ablest artists of his time. He executed many works for the churches of Ferrara, which Lanzi says are worthy of competition with the best masters of the fourteenth century. Among his best works is the Descent from the Cross, in the church of S. Niccolo; the Visitation of the Virgin to St. Elizabeth, in S. Francesco; and a picture of St. Andrea, at the Agostiniani. There is one of his pictures in the Dresden gallery, and Kügler mentions by him a beautiful picture of the Entombment in the Museum at Berlin. He usually inscribed his name in full upon his pictures, which Lanzi says bear evidence of change in pictoric character without an example. He died in 1530.

PANFILO. See NUVOLONE.

PANICALE, MASOLINO DA, an eminent sculptor and painter, born at Panicale, in the Florentine Territory, in 1378. He first studied modeling and sculpture, under Lorenzo Ghiberti, who at that time was unrivalled in composition, in design, and in giving animation to his figures. Being already a distinguished artist, he studied coloring under Gherardo Starnina. Thus uniting in himself the excellence of two schools, and diligently cultivating the art of chiaro-scuro, he produced a new style, not wholly exempt from dryness, but grand, determined, and harmonious beyond any former example; but which was carried to higher perfection by his scholar, Masaccio. The chapel of S. Pietro al Carmine is a monument of his genius. He there painted the Four Evangelists, the Vocation of St. Peter to the Apostleship, the Denial of Christ, Curing the Lame Man at the Gate of the Temple, and the Preaching to the Multitude. He died in 1415, before the completion of the chapel, and the rest of the acts of St. Peter, as the Tribute Money, Baptism conferred on the Multitude, and the Healing of the Sick, were afterwards painted by Masaccio. Some of his works have been engraved.

PANICCIAGI. See PANNICCIATI.

PANICO, ANTONIO MARIA, a Bolognese painter, who, according to Bellori, was a disciple of Annibale Caracci, whom he accompanied to Rome at an early age, and whose manner he emulated. He was much employed by Mario Farnese in decorating his country seats at Castro and Latera. His most celebrated work is a picture of the Mass, in the cathedral of Farnese, in which Lanzi says he was assisted by Annibale, who even conducted some of the figures. This, however, seems doubtful, as Caracci died in 1609, and Panico in 1652. It is not probable that he would have been entrusted with so important a commission almost in his youth, which must have been the case were it true.

PANICO, CONTE UGO DA. See UGO DA CARPI.

PANNEELS, WILLIAM, a Flemish painter and engraver, born at Antwerp about 1600. Little is known of him as a painter, but it appears that he was a disciple of Rubens, from the inscriptions on some of his prints. He etched quite a number of plates after Rubens, and from his own designs. They are executed in a spirited and masterly style, but his drawing is frequently incorrect, particularly in the naked. The following, after Rubens, are his most esteemed prints:

SUBJECTS AFTER RUBENS.

The Portrait of Rubens, in an octagon border. Esther before Ahasuerus. The Nativity. The Adoration of the Magi. Mary washing the Feet of Christ. The Assumption of the Virgin. The Holy Family, with the infant Christ and St. John playing with a Lamb. St. John baptizing Christ. Samson killing the Lion, with a companion, David killing the Lion and the Bear. St. Sebastian. Jupiter and Juno. Jupiter and Antiope. Bacchus drunk, supported by a Faun and a Satyr. Bacchus supported by Satyrs and Bacchante. Meleager presenting the Head of the Boar to Atalanta.

PANNEELS, JOHN, a Flemish engraver, probably a brother of the preceding. Nagler describes only one print by him, *after Annibale Caracci.*

PANNICCIATI, JACOPO, a painter of Ferrara, who, according to Baruffaldi, was of noble birth and studied under Dosso Dossi, whose style he imitated very closely. He died in the flower of his life, in 1540.

PANNINI, CAV. GIOVANNI PAOLO, an eminent painter of perspective and architecture, born at Piacenza in 1691. He went early to Rome, where he studied under Pietro Lucatelli. He had an early passion for painting, and applied himself with great assiduity in designing the remaining monuments of antiquity, wherever he found them, especially at Rome. He formed his style, not on that of Lucatelli, but of Giovanni Ghisolfi. He was a perfect master of the art of perspective, in which he surpassed all his cotemporaries. He designed every vestige of ancient magnificence—the ruins of superb edifices, cenotaphs, columns, arches, obelisks, and some of the most ancient buildings which ornament modern Rome. His composition is rich, and his perspective critically correct. His works are universally admired for the grandeur of his architecture, the clearness of his coloring, the neatness and freedom of his touch, the beauty of his figures, and the elegant taste with which he disposed them, although he sometimes designed his figures of too large a size for his architecture which injures the effect that would otherwise be produced by the immensity of the buildings. This was contrary to the practice of Ghisolfi, whose works always afford a pleasing deception to the eye, by the exact proportions observed between the figures, buildings, and distances. This fault, however, is only occasional in Pannini's works. He generally painted his pictures of a large easel size, but sometimes he wrought on a grander scale. Lanzi highly commends a picture of this class in the church of the Signori della Missione, representing Christ driving the Money-changers from the Temple, in which the architecture is truly magnificent, and the figures designed with great spirit and variety of character, and of much larger size than he usually painted. His works are numerous, and are not only to be found in the principal collections of Italy, but in other countries of Europe. At Rivoli, in the pleasure house of the king of Sardinia, and in the pontifical palace of Monte Cavallo, are some of his choicest works. Many of his pictures have been engraved by Lempereur, le Bas, J. S. Müller, Vivares, Benasech, Bartolozzi, and other eminent engravers. He died in 1758.

PANSERON, Pierre, a French architect, a native of Brie, flourished in the latter part of the 18th century. He studied at Paris, under J. F. Blondel; was appointed professor in the military school; and was chosen by the Prince de Conti as inspector of his buildings. He is chiefly known by his treatises on the art, which gained him considerable reputation. Among them are *Elements d'Architecture*, Paris, 1772, 4to.; *Nouveaux Elements d'Architecture*, Paris, 1775—80, 3 vols., 8vo., with plates.

PANTOJA, de la Cruz, Juan, a Spanish painter, born at Madrid in 1551. He studied under Alfonso Sanchez Coello, and acquired so much distinction as a portrait and historical painter, that Philip II. named him one of his painters. He painted many portraits of the Royal Family, some of which are to be found in the Escurial, the Retiro, and in the tower of the Parada. He also painted the decorations for the funeral ceremony of Charles V., the original designs of which were in the possession of Palomino. On the death of Philip II., he continued in favor with his successor, Philip III., whose portrait he painted, and that of his Queen, which are dated 1606, and still preserved in the palace of the Dukes d'Uceda at Montalvan. He also painted an equestrian portrait of the king, as a model for the famous sculptor Giovanni di Bologna, then residing at Florence, who executed an equestrian group in bronze, placed in the garden of La Casa del Campo. It is difficult to form any correct opinion of the style of this eminent artist, from the accounts of the Spanish writers. Palomino says he was greatly distinguished in the school of Coello. Bermudez describes his picture of the Adoration of the Shepherds, in which he introduced the portraits of Philip II. and his family, as blending the qualities of Lucas Cranach and Bronzino, two very opposite masters. Again, he is said to strongly resemble Anthony More in his portraits. Many of his works were destroyed in the conflagration of the Prado. He died at Madrid, in 1610.

PANVINUS, Onulph, an engraver who lived at Antwerp, and published a set of 27 portraits from his own designs, entitled *Elogia et Imagines Pont. Max. ad viv. delin.* 1568. Zani mentions *Onofrio Panvinus*, a designer and engraver of Verona, who flourished about the same period.

PANZACCHI, Maria Elena, a paintress, of noble family, born at Bologna in 1668. According to Orlandi, she was instructed by Emilio Taruffi, and acquired great reputation, particularly for her landscapes, and was much employed in painting for the collections. Lanzi says her landscapes are now scarcely known at Bologna, and Crespi mentions only two. She died in 1737.

PAOLETTI, Niccolo Gasparo, an Italian architect, who flourished, according to Milizia, in the latter part of the 18th century. He was principally distinguished for the restoration of the imperial villa of Poggio, near Florence, in 1773. In the course of completing this work, it was necessary to dismantle an arched roof, twenty-two feet long and twelve feet wide; but the Grand Duke Peter Leopold, of Austria, would not consent to its destruction, because it was decorated with paintings by Matteo Rosselli. Paoletti conceived an ingenious plan, by means of which he removed the roof entire, greatly to the satisfaction of the Grand Duke, who presented him with one hundred sequins in token of his approval.

PAOLETTI, Paolo, a painter born at Padua, who excelled in painting fruit, flowers, dead game, fish, and other objects of still-life. He passed much of his life at Udine, and was employed many years in the house of the Conti Caiselli, which family possesses many specimens of his works. His pictures are quite numerous throughout the Friuli, and are held in considerable estimation. He died at Udine in 1735.

PAOLI, Francesco da, an Italian engraver, who flourished at Rome about 1640. There is a large plate engraved by him, representing a View of the City of Rome.

PAOLILLO, a Neapolitan painter, who flourished about 1530. According to Dominici, he was the ablest scholar of Andrea Sabbatini, whose style he imitated so closely that all his works were attributed to that master, until Dominici discovered his name on one of his pictures, and restored them to the right master. He says "he would have been a great ornament of this school, had he not died young."

PAOLINI, Pietro, a painter born at Lucca in 1603. He went early to Rome, where he entered the school of Angelo Caroselli, by education a follower of the school of Caravaggio, but exceedingly expert in copying and imitating other masters. Under him, Paolini acquired a manner that shows correct drawing, and a style of coloring more resembling that of the Venetian than the Roman school, uniting the richness and harmony of Titian and Pordenone. Lanzi says his Martyrdom of St. Andrea in the church of S. Michele at Lucca and the grand picture sixteen cubits long in the Library of S. Frediano, would be alone sufficient to immortalize a painter. The latter work represents the pontiff St. Gregory entertaining some pilgrims "It is a magnificent picture, ornamented in the style of Veronese, with a grand architectural perspective, full of figures, and possessing a variety harmony, and beauty that have induced many poets to extol it." He also excelled in cabine pictures of conversations and rural festivals, which are numerous at Lucca. Baldinucci especially commends two pictures of the Massacre of Valdestain, in the possession of the Orsetti family, and remarks that he had a peculiar talent for tragic themes. He was accused of being too energetic, and censured for making the action of his females too strong. To prove the contrary, and to show that he pursued his method from choice, and that he was not inferior to his rival Biancucci in his own style, he painted his large work in the church of the Trinity, in the *graceful style.*

PAOLINI, Pio Fabio, a painter born at Udine. He went to Rome, where he studied under Pietro da Cortona, and acquired considerable reputation, for some historical works, especially for his fine fresco of San Carlo, which adorns the Corso. In 1678, he was elected a member of the Academy of St. Luke. He afterwards returned to his native city, where he executed several altar-pieces and other works for the churches, which Lanzi says entitle him to a high rank among the followers of Cortona. He also painted much for the collections.

PAOLINI. See Paulini.

PAOLO, Maestro, and his sons Jacopo and Giovanni. Lanzi says that Maestro Paolo is the earliest painter in the national manner (i.e. different from the Greek artists of the time), of whom there exists a work with the indisputable name of its author. It is to be seen in the church of S. Marco at Venice, consisting of a tablet, or, as it is otherwise called, *ancona*, divided into several compartments, representing the figure of a dead Christ, with some of the Apostles, and historic incidents from the Holy Evangelist. There is inscribed underneath, *Magister Paulus cum Jacobo et Johanne filiis fecit hoc opus.*" There is no date upon it, but Zanetti found his name recorded in an ancient parchment, bearing the date 1346. Sig. Morelli also discovered a painting in the Sacristy of the Conventuali at Vicenza, inscribed *Paulus de Venetiis pinxit hoc opus.* 1333.

PAON, Du, a French painter, the son of a peasant, was born in the vicinity of Paris about 1740. He early enlisted in the army, and passed through several campaigns; but, having at length obtained his discharge, he went to Paris, intending to devote himself to art. He showed his designs to Carlo Vanloo, then first painter to the King, and to Boucher, both of whom encouraged his resolution. He entered the school of Casanova, and, according to the *Biographie Universelle*, subsequently became the rival of that master. Inferior to Casanova in coloring and spirit, he surpassed him in correctness of design, and faithful imitation of nature. He executed a number of works for the Bourbon palace, and the Salle du Conseil of the Royal Military School. He died in 1785.

PAPA, Simone, called il Vecchio (the elder), a Neapolitan painter, born about 1430. He studied under Antonio Solario, called il Zingaro, whose works were then held in high estimation. He excelled in painting altar-pieces with few figures, grouped in a pleasing style, and finished with exquisite care, in which he sometimes equalled Zingaro himself. His chief works are the Triumph of St. Michael over the Apostate Spirits, in the church of S. Maria Nuova—his greatest effort; the Annunciation, in S. Niccolo alla Dogana; the Virgin and infant Saviour, with several Saints, in S. Lorenzo. He died in 1488.

PAPA, Simone, called il Giovine, (the younger), a Neapolitan painter, born in 1506. He was the son of a goldsmith, who desired to bring him up to his own business, but showing an early passion for painting, he was placed under the instruction of Gio. Antonio d'Amato. He acquired distinction, and executed several works for the churches, the principal of which are the Annunciation, and the Assumption of the Virgin, in S. Maria la Nuova. He died in 1569.

PAPARELLO, or PAPACELLO, Tommaso, a painter of Cortona, who was living in 1553. He was a scholar of Giulio Romano, whom he assisted in his works. Little further is known of him.

PAPE, Adrian de, a Dutch painter, who, according to Balkema, was a scholar of Gerard Douw. He mentions several of his works, one of which is an Interior, in the Museum at the Hague, which he says is worthy of the school of Douw, but he gives no particulars of his life.

PAPILLON, Jean, the Elder, a French wood engraver, born at Rouen in Normandy, in 1639. He studied under du Bellay. His prints evince good natural talents, and are well executed, with clear and firm strokes; but in consequence of his incorrect design, he never attained distinction.—His works are marked J. P. He died at Paris in 1710.

PAPILLON, Jean, the Younger, a French wood engraver, the son of the preceding, was born at St. Quentin, in 1661. After receiving some instruction from his father, he visited Paris, and studied engraving under Noel Cochin, who gave him every advantage for improvement. He was the first who ever engraved on wood without using the pen. His prints are correctly designed, and executed in a harmonious style. Among them are a great variety of vignettes and other book ornaments; also portraits of the popes Paul III., Julius III., Pius IV., and that of James II. of England. Papillon is said to have invented, about 1688, the art of printing papers in imitation of tapestry, commonly called *Paper Hangings.* He died at Paris in 1723. He had a younger brother, named Jean Nicolas P., born in 1663; died in 1714. He attained but little distinction in the art.

PAPILLON, Jean Baptiste Michel, a French wood engraver, the son and scholar of the preceding, born at Paris in 1698. He gained considerable distinction in the art, particularly for his cuts executed in concert with N. le Sueur, from the designs of J. J. Bachelier, for the fine edition of *Les Fables de la Fontaine*, 4 vols. fol. Several of his cuts represent ornamented foliage, flowers, and shells, executed with great delicacy and skill. Papillon published a work relating to wood engraving, in two volumes, entitled *Traité Historique et pratique de la Gravure en bois.* The first volume treats of the history of the art, in which his re searches were extensive; and though there are many errors, yet it should be remembered that the author had little light or assistance in his labors. Doubtless his work proved of great assistance to Heineken, and other later writers, who condemn it. The second volume treats of the practical department of the art, and contains much interesting and important matter, besides many beautiful wood engravings, some of which are executed with single strokes, without cross-hatchings, producing a clear and pleasing effect. Among them are two specimens of figures in chiaro-scuro, executed with four blocks each, one of which, between the pages 154 and 155 of the second volume, he gives proofs of, from the separate blocks, followed by the figure complete. Bryan says, "there is, perhaps, no method by which the sketches and tinted drawings of the great masters can be more successfully represented." Up to the year 1722, Papillon marked his prints with the same initials as those of his father, but afterwards with his name in full. He died in 1776.

PAPINI, or DE PAPINI, Giuseppe Benedetti, an Italian engraver, born, according to Zani, in 1707, and died in 1782. He engraved several plates of ceilings and other decorations, for the Tuscan Gallery, published by Ignazio Orsini; and others for the Museum Capitolinum; and for the Museo Etrusco, published by Gori.

PAPPANELLI, Cav. Niccolò, a painter of Faenza, born in 1537. It is not known under whom he studied, but he went to Rome, where, such was his enthusiasm for improvement, that he attended all the most distinguished masters in that metropolis. On his return to Faenza, he executed some works for the churches of an exquisite character. Such is his picture of S. Martino in the Cathedral, which Lanzi says is "so well executed in point of design, force of coloring, and expression, as to be truly admirable." He was a very unequal painter, and some of his works are of a mediocre character. He died in 1620.

PARADISI, Niccolo, an old Venetian painter, by whom there is a picture of the Crucifixion, with the Symbols of the Four Evangelists, in the monastery of the Agostiniani, in the territory of Veruchio. It is inscribed *Nicholaus Paradixi miles de Venetiis pinxit*, 1404.

PARADISO, Orazio dal. See Castelfranco.

PARADOSSO, Il. See Giulio Trogli.

PARASACCHI, Domenico, an Italian designer and engraver, who flourished at Rome about 1630. He engraved a set of plates of the Fountains of Rome published in 1618. This collection, with additions, was republished at Rome in 1636, under the title, *Raccolta delle principale Fontane delle Città di Roma, disegnate e intagliate da Domenico Parasacchi.*

PARASOLE, Leonardo, called Norsini, from Norcia, the place of his nativity, was an engraver on wood, who flourished at Rome about 1570. He distinguished himself by a set of cuts of the plants for the Herbal of Castor Durante, physician to Pope Sixtus V., engraved by order of that pontiff. He also engraved some cuts after the designs of Antonio Tempesta and others.

PARASOLE, Isabella. This ingenious lady was the wife of the preceding. She executed a part of the cuts for an Herbal published under the direction of Prince Cesi of Aquasparta. She also wrote and published a book on the method of working lace and embroidering, illustrated with cuts engraved by herself, from her own designs.

PARASOLE, Bernardino, was the son of Leonardo P. He studied painting under Giuseppe Cesari. He had great natural talents, and had begun to distinguish himself as an historical painter when he died in the flower of his life. He executed a few wooden cuts, mostly after his own designs.

PARASOLE, Hieronima. This lady was of the same family as the preceding. She executed some engravings on wood, among which is one of the Battle of the Centaurs, *after Tempesta*.

PARCELLES, John, called the Old, a Dutch painter, born at Leyden in 1597. He studied under Henry Cornelius de Vroom, and acquired distinction for his marines, in which he excelled. His best pictures are those representing storms and tempests with lightning, violent agitation of the water, with all the horrors of shipwreck, and vessels in the utmost peril and distress, which he touched with extraordinary fidelity and effect. His pictures of calms also have considerable merit; they generally represent views on the coast of Holland, with fishing smacks and fishermen drawing their nets, and groups of figures on the strand. The pictures of Parcelles are delicately and carefully finished, and his figures are correctly drawn, and touched with great neatness and spirit. He signed his pictures with his initials, J. P. He also executed some spirited etchings from his own designs, among which are a set of twelve sea-pieces, with the figure of a Dutch boor on each, and a set of twelve plates of the different shipping used in Holland, with a Latin inscription. Balkema says he died at Leyerdorp in 1641, but others think his death happened at a later date, as he is known to have instructed his son Julius.

PARCELLES, Julius, called the Young, was the son and scholar of the preceding, born at Leyerdorp in 1628. He painted the same subjects as his father, whose manner he imitated so closely that most of his works are attributed to him, and the inexperienced are more liable to be deceived from the fact that both used the same mark. Although his pictures are inferior to those of John Parcelles in delicacy of touch and in clearness and transparency of coloring, yet they are correctly designed, and have great vigor and truthfulness.

PAREJA, Juan de. This painter was the slave of Don Diego Velasquez. The accounts of him are quite contradictory. According to Palomino and others, he was born a Mestizo, in Mexico, a name given by the Spaniards to people born of a Spanish father and an Indian mother. But Cean Bermudez says with more probability, that he was born at Seville in 1606, at which time there were many slaves in Spain. He accompanied Velasquez to Madrid, when he was called to that court in 1623. From being employed in his master's studio to attend on him, grind his colors, clean his palette, brushes, &c., he imbibed a passion for painting, and sought every opportunity to practice during his master's absence. He spent whole nights in drawing and in endeavoring to imitate him, for he durst not let him know of his aspiring dreams. At length he had made such proficiency, that he resolved to lay his case before the King Philip IV., who was not only an excellent judge, but a true lover, of art. It was the King's custom to resort frequently to the apartments of Velasquez, and to order those pictures which were placed with the painted side to the wall, to be turned to his view. Pareja placed one of his own productions in that position, which the King's curiosity caused to be turned, when the slave fell on his knees and besought the monarch to obtain his pardon from his master, for having presumed to practice painting without his approbation. Philip, agreeably surprised at his address, and well pleased with the work, bid Pareja to rest contented. He interceded in his behalf, and Velasquez not only forgave him, but emancipated him from servitude; yet such was his attachment and gratitude to his master, that he would never leave him till his death, and afterwards continued to serve his daughter with the same fidelity. He is said to have painted portraits so much in the style of Velasquez, that they could not easily be distinguished from his works. He also painted some historical works, as the Calling of St. Matthew, at Aranjuez; the Baptism of Christ, at Toledo, and some saints at Madrid. Bermudez says he was not emancipated till 1651. He died at Madrid in 1670.

PARENTANI, Antonio, a painter of Turin, who flourished about 1550. It is not known under whom he studied, but he received or completed, his education at Rome, and was a follower of the Roman school. There is a grand picture of Paradise with numerous Angels, by him, in the Chapter-house of the Consolata at Turin.

PARENTINO, Bernardo, called also Fra Lorenzo, a painter born at Parenzo, in Istria, in 1437. He was a pupil of Andrea Mantegna. Lanzi says that he approached so near to Mantegna, that his works might easily be mistaken for those of that master. In the Cloister of Santa Giustina, at Padua, are ten Acts from the life of St. Benedetto, with several little histories in chiaro-scuro, which are highly commended by Lanzi. He became a monk of the order of the Augustines at Vicenza, where he died in 1531.

PARIA. See Perrier.

PARICOLA, Masolino da, a Florentine painter, born in 1403, and died in 1440. It is not known under whom he studied, but he was accounted a good painter of history in his time, especially in fresco.

PARIGI, Giulio, a Florentine architect and engraver, flourished during the first part of the 17th century, and died in 1635. He was the son of Alphonso Parigi, an architect of ordinary merit; who, after the death of Vasari, completed the building of the Uffizi Nuovi at Florence, and died in 1590. Giulio Parigi was a disciple of Buontalenti, and became a civil and military architect of considerable eminence. He was selected by the wife of the Grand Duke Ferdinand II., to instruct the four princes in design and architecture. On the occasions of the marriage of Cosmo II., and the reception of Queen Maria, in 1612, Parigi was entrusted with the direction of the festivals. He established a successful school at Florence, where were taught mechanics, architecture and perspective. Among his scholars were Ottavio Piccolomini, Duke d'Amalfi, and the three brothers, Remigio, Antonio, and Gio. Francesco Cantagallina. He gained great reputation for the Imperial Villa at Poggio, the convent of the Padri Agostini, at Florence, that of La Pace, belonging to the Padri di S. Bernardo, and the Marucelli palace, at Florence.

As an engraver, Bartsch and Nagler mention three prints by Parigi; the Garden of Love, the Temple of Peace, and a Landscape, *after Cantagallina*, his pupil. In the ***Biographie Universelle***, are mentioned five plates by him, of the Interludes of the Comedy of Flora, with a great many figures, similar to the plates of Callot, who acquired a knowledge of engraving under this master. Giulio Parigi died in 1635. He had seven sons, of whom only one followed architecture.

PARIGI, Alphonso, a reputable Florentine architect, was the son and scholar of Giulio P. He entered the army as an engineer, where he remained several years; but subsequently devoted himself entirely to architecture. He completed a number of edifices left unfinished by that master, and particularly distinguished himself by his ingenuity in restoring the principal façade of the Palazzo Pitti, which had inclined eight and half inches from the perpendicular. He made several holes through the inclined wall, through which he passed chains, and fastened them externally with bolts; then by means of screws turned by levers, inside the apartments, he drew the wall back to a perpendicular position. Among his other works, is the Scarlati palace at Florence, with three well divided stories. He died in 1656.

PARIS, Domenico and Orazio di. See Alfani.

PARIS, Pierre Adrien, a French architect, born at Besançon in 1747. He acquired the elements of design from his father (also an architect), and afterwards visited Paris for improvement. He studied under Trouard, architect to the King, and followed for several years the course prescribed by the Academy. In 1767 he visited Rome with the Royal pension, and studied and designed the most remarkable remains of antiquity. On returning to France, he soon gained reputation, and in 1778 was appointed designer to the King's Cabinet. He was charged with the management of the fêtes at Versailles, Marli and Trianon, and soon after succeeded Soufflot in the Academy of Architecture. About this time Paris made a second trip to Italy, whence he brought many designs. While absent he was appointed to superintend the decorations of the Opera House, and about 1783 erected the beautiful gate of the Orleans Cathedral. In 1788 Louis XVI. appointed him Chevalier of the order of St. Michael. During the stormy scenes which followed this period, Paris remained in retirement. In 1806 he visited Italy for his health and on arriving at Rome, was appointed director of the French school in that city; an honor never since accorded to any architect. He was commissioned by the French government to treat for the acquisition of the antiques in the Villa Borghese; which he satisfactorily accomplished. In 1811, Paris superintended the excavations of the Coliseum; and made many drawings of that celebrated edifice. In 1817 he returned to France and retired to Besançon, where he died in 1819. He left a manuscript work entitled, *Examen des edifices antiques et modernes de la ville de Rome* Paris translated several works into French, and gained considerable reputation for his *Recueil des dessins et etudes d'architecture de Paris*, 9 vols fol.; also for his *L'Amphitheatre Flavien, vulgairement nommé le Coliseum, restauré d' apres les details encore visibles de la construction*, etc. 45 plates fol.

PARISET. D. P., a French engraver, born at Lyons in 1740. He is supposed to have been a pupil of Marteau. He went to London in 1766, where he executed quite a number of plates in the chalk style. He executed some of the plates for the collection of prints after the drawings of the great masters, published by Rogers. He also engraved several portraits of English artists and others from the designs of Falconet, among which are the following:

Sir Joshua Reynolds; *P. Falconet, del.* 1768. Benjamin West, with his family; *after West.* Francis Cotes. William Ryland. Paul Sandby. Ozias Humphrey. J. Meyer. Oliver Cromwell; *after Cooper.* The Death of Admiral Coligny. The Death of the Duke of Guise.

[monogram] or [monogram], or [monogram] PARISINI, AGOSTINO, an Italian engraver, who flourished at Bologna in the first part of the 17th century. In conjunction with J. B. Coriolano and Olivieri Gatti, he engraved a book of emblems from the designs of Paolo Macchi, published at Bologna in 1628. He also engraved a variety of other book plates, which are executed with the graver in an indifferent style. His prints are sometimes signed with his name Latinized (*Augustinus Parisinus,*) but generally with one of the above monograms.

PARIZEAU, PHILIPPE LOUIS, a French engraver, born at Paris in 1740. He engraved a number of plates after Salvator Rosa, and other masters, executed with the graver in a neat and spirited style, among which are the following. He died in 1801.

An Assembly of Roman Soldiers; *after Sal. Rosa.* Marius seated on the Ruins of Carthage; *do.* The Martyrdom of St. Andrew; *after Deshays.* The Martyrdom of St. Bartholomew; *do.* Psyche refusing the Honors of Divinity; *after Boucher.*

PARKER, JAMES, an English engraver, born in London about 1750. He studied with Bartolozzi, in whose style he engraved quite a number of plates after the eminent English artists of his time. He died in 1805.

PARKER, JOHN, an English painter of whom little is known. He went to Rome, where he resided several years, and was employed to paint an altar-piece for the church of S. Gregorio in Monte Celio, the subject of which was the history of St. Silvia. He returned to England about 1762. In 1763 he exhibited at the Rooms of the Society for the Encouragement of the Arts, &c., two pictures; one of the Death of Rizzio, and the other, his own portrait. He died soon afterwards, at Paddington.

PARKER, JOHN, another English painter of the same name, who first studied in the Duke of Richmond's Gallery, and afterwards received some instructions from the Smiths of Chichester. He went to Rome in 1774, but returned to London the following year, where he practised landscape painting with some success.

PARMA, LODOVICO DA, a painter of Parma, who, according to Malvasia, was a scholar of Francesco Francia, but the Padre Affò says he studied under Lorenzo Costa, the pupil of Francia. Lanzi says his pictures of Madonnas, executed in the style of Francia, are common at Parma.

PARMA, CRISTOFORO DA. See CASELLI.

PARMENSIS, BATTISTA. See PENSIERI.

PARMENSIS, JACOBUS, an Italian engraver, whose real name is not known. There are a few prints *after Parmiggiano,* and other masters, executed with the graver in a slight style, somewhat resembling those of Gio. Giacomo Caraglio, to whom they are attributed by some writers, but Caraglio signed his prints *Jacobus Veronensis.* See *Caraglio.*

PARMENTIER, JACQUES, a French painter, born at Paris in 1658. He was a relative of Sebastian Bourdon, by whom he was instructed in the art. After the death of Bourdon he went to England, in 1676, where he was employed by Charles de la Fosse to assist him in his works at the Montague House. He was sent to Holland by William III., to assist in decorating his palace at Loo, but quarreling with Marot, the superintendent of the works, he returned to London. Not meeting with much employment, he went to Yorkshire, where he painted some historical subjects, as well as portraits. He died in London in 1730.

PARMENTIER, L., an engraver of little note. He engraved a title for the works of Philip Wouwerman, with the portrait of that painter at the bottom, from a design by J. de la Jove.

PARMIGGIANO. See FRANCESCO MAZZUOLI.

PARMIGGIANO, FABRIZIO, called also FABRIZIO DA PARMA, a landscape painter, born at Parma in 1555. Baglioni commends him among the landscape painters of his time. Lanzi says he was much employed in painting for the collections, in which he was assisted by his wife Ippolita, and that he visited various places before his arrival at Rome, where he was employed in adorning a few of the churches with his wood scenes, and views with hermits, &c., in which there is more of the ideal than the natural. In the church of St. Cecilia at Trastevere, are eight large pictures by him, painted in fresco. His subjects are designed in a grand style, and executed with a spirited pencil. He died at Rome in 1600.

PARMIGGIANINO. See FRANCESCO MAZZUOLI, GIROLAMO SCAGLIA, and MICHELE ROCCA.

PAROCEL. See PARROCEL.

PARODI, FILIPPO, an Italian sculptor, born at Genoa about 1640. He attained the reputation of one of the most able artists of his age. There is a beautiful statue of the Virgin by him, in the church of S. Carlo at Genoa; also a statue of St. John the Baptist, executed in concert with the celebrated Puget. He executed for the Italian church of Loretto at Lisbon, a number of statues which surpass all others in that edifice. There are also several of his works at Venice and Padua. He died at Genoa about 1708.

PARODI, DOMENICO, a sculptor, architect, and painter, was the son of Filippo P., born at Genoa in 1668. His father, discerning in him an uncommon genius for the fine arts, gave him an excellent classical education, and instructed him in his own profession; but having a partiality for painting, he went to Venice and entered the school of Bombelli, improving his coloring by studying and copying the works of the best Venetian masters. Lanzi says there are several excellent copies of the Venetian pictures by him in the Casa Durazzo. He next went to Rome, where he resided many years, diligently studying design, but he did not forsake the Venetian style of coloring. He attached himself more to Carlo Maratti's manner of design than of any other master. "He painted," says Lanzi, "in a good Marattesque style, the noble picture of S. Francesco di Sales, at the Filippini, and other works; but of him, as well as of the Caracci, we find works partaking in an extraordinary manner of the style of Tintoretto and Veronese." His most celebrated performance is in the Palazzo Negroni at Genoa, where he decorated the walls in a style peculiarly his own, in which he displays a correct design, great vigor and harmony of color, a remarkably poetic invention, and a beautiful disposition and grouping of the figures. The whole is devoted to the glory of that noble family, whose escutcheon is crowned by the several symbols of Prudence, Continence, and other virtues; there are also fables of Hercules slaying the Lion, and Achilles instructed by Chiron, which indicate the honors acquired by this family in letters and in arms. Portraits are added to these decorations, and every part is so well connected, so well varied, and so enriched by vestures, draperies, and other ornaments, that Lanzi says "some professors have not hesitated to declare it the first performance in Genoa, and Mengs' attention was there arrested for several hours, by a painter he had never heard of before." He also decorated other noble houses at Genoa with his frescos. He embellished the Gallery of the Sig. Marcello Durazzo with stories, fables, and chiaro-scuri, much in the style of the one just described. The chiaro-scuri in particular are so admirably executed as to produce illusion, and appear like real bassi-relievi. He painted many altar pieces for the churches and chapels in other cities of Italy as well as Genoa. He also painted the portraits of the Duke and other distinguished personages, which added to his fame. Parodi was likewise a good sculptor. He executed the statues of the king of Poland and other members of the royal family, and several of the nobility, which were greatly admired. He also etched a few plates from his own designs. He died in 1740.

PARODI, Battista, was the brother of the preceding, born at Genoa in 1674. He studied at Venice, and his style partakes much of the Venetian school, both in design and coloring. He possessed a fertile invention, was expeditious, free, and brilliant in his coloring, but he was not sufficiently select in his forms. He executed some works for the churches at Milan and Bergamo, but wrought more for individuals. He died in 1730.

PARODI, Pellegrino, an eminent Italian portrait painter, was the son of Domenico P. To the merit of correct resemblance he added beautiful coloring, and easy and elegant attitudes. There are many of his works in England, Germany, and Spain. In 1741, he executed the portrait of Spinola, the Doge of Genoa, which has been engraved by Gregori. He resided some time at Lisbon, and was living, according to Lanzi, in 1769.

PARODI, Ottavio, a painter born at Pavia in 1659. He first studied under Andrea Lanzano, and afterwards went to Rome, where he resided many years. On his return to Pavia he executed some works for the churches, which are highly commended by Orlandi. Lanzi also says he was one of the ablest scholars of his master. He was living in 1718.

PAROLINI, Giacomo, a painter born at Ferrara. According to Baruffaldi, who wrote his life, his father dying when he was five years old, his maternal uncle took him under his protection, and, perceiving in him a genius for painting, placed him with the Cav. Peruzzini at Turin, with whom he remained till he was eighteen, when he entered the school of Carlo Cignani. On his return to Ferrara, he finished some pictures left incomplete at the death of Maurelio Scannavini, who had been his fellow-student under Cignani. He did this out of regard to his friend, for the relief of his orphan family. He executed many works for the churches, and a multitude for the collections.—Though inferior to Cignani in the grandeur of his conceptions, and the masterly conduct of his chiaroscuro, yet he sustained the credit of his school by the elegance of his design and the suavity of his coloring, particularly in his flesh tints, in which he excelled, for which reason he was fond of introducing into his compositions the naked figure. He was unusually successful in the design of his female figures, children, and cherubs. Lanzi says his pictures of Bacchanals, festive dances, and Capricci, partake much of the playful and elegant style of Albano, and are found in almost every collection at Ferrara. His principal works for the churches are three altar-pieces in the Cathedral, and a grand fresco, representing St. Sebastian mounting into Glory, amid a group of Angels, in the church of that Saint at Verona. Lanzi pronounces this work a grand production, well executed, which greatly raised his reputation. He died in 1733, and "with him (says Lanzi), was buried for a season the reputation of the Ferrarese school in Italy." Zani, differing from all others, calls him *Giacomo Filippo*, and says he was born in 1667 and died in 1737.

PAROLINI, Pio, a painter of Udine, who, according to the Ab. Titi, resided chiefly at Rome, and was admitted a member of the Academy of St. Luke in 1678. He painted the ceiling of one of the chapels of S. Carlo al Corso, representing an allegorical subject, which was ingeniously composed and well colored.

PARONE, Francesco, a Milanese painter, born about 1600. According to Baglioni, he was the son of an obscure artist, who taught him the rudiments of the art. At an early age he went to Rome, where he had the good fortune of being taken under the protection of the Marquis Giustiniani, for whom he painted several pictures. He studied the works of the best masters with great assiduity, and had already begun to distinguish himself, when he died, in 1634, in the flower of his life. His principal work is an altar-piece in the church of the monastery of S. Romualdo at Rome, representing the Martyrdom of that Saint—a grand composition, of many figures, executed in the style of Caravaggio.

PAROY, Jacques de, a French painter on glass, born at St. Pourçain-sur-Allier, towards the close of the 16th century. After acquiring the elements of design and painting, he visited Rome for improvement, and studied under Domenichino. It is probable that he gained his knowledge of glass-painting in his native country, as that art had already been practised in the south of France in great perfection, by Frére Guillaume, or Guglielmo de Marcilla. Paroy executed several fine works in Venice, and then returned to France. At Paris he painted the windows in the choir of the church of S. Merry; and designed the Judgment of Susanna for a chapel of the same church, executed on glass by Jean Nogare. There are four beautiful paintings by Paroy in the parish church of S. Croix, at Gannat, representing St. Ambrose, St. Jerome, St. Augustine, and St. Gregory.

PARR, Remi, or Remigius, an English designer and engraver, born at Rochester in 1723. He engraved a few plates for the booksellers, which are indifferently executed.

PARRASIO, Angelo, an eminent painter of Siena, who was employed at the court of the Marchese d'Este in 1449. He also painted the Nine Muses in the Palazzo Belfiore, near Ferrara.

PARRHASIUS, a celebrated Greek painter, the son and scholar of Evenor, was a native of Ephesus, but afterwards became a citizen of Athens; flourished about B. C. 390. He raised the art to a much higher degree of perfection than it had before attained. Comparing his three great predecessors with each other, he rejected that which was exceptionable in them, and adopted that which was admirable. The classic invention of Polygnotus, the magic tones of Apollodorus, and the exquisite design of Zeuxis, were all united in the works of Parrhasius. Plutarch instances Parrhasius' picture of Ulysses feigning insanity, as an improper subject for the pencil, yet reconciled to our taste through the spirit of the conception, and the truth of the execution. Pliny says he gave his figures more relief and roundness, with an air of life and motion unknown before him. According to Quintilian, he so circumscribed and defined all the powers and objects of art, that he was termed *the Legislator;* he reduced to theory the practice of former artists, and all cotemporary and subsequent painters adopted his standard of heroic and divine proportions. Parrhasius gave to the divine and heroic character in painting, what Polycletus had given to the human in sculpture, by his Doryphorus, namely, a canon of proportion. The branch of the art in which he chiefly excelled was elegance of outline; his figures of children were greatly admired for their simplicity, and his young men and women for their beauty and grace. When Euphranor remarked that the Theseus of Parrhasius had fed upon roses, and his own upon beef, he seems to have alluded particularly to the style of design, rather than to the coloring; for, as Winckelmann remarks, the word used by Plutarch, γλαφυρῶς or *elegantly*, relates expressly to form. It will be observed that, according to the taste of Euphranor, the figure of Parrhasius was too elegant and delicate for heroic beauty. Pliny praises him for the beauty of his figures; the "sweetness and lovely grace about the mouth and lips"; the softness and fullness of the hair; and the blended tints that melted away in the outline. He quotes two ancient writers on painting, Antigonus and Xenocrates, now lost, who praised Parrhasius, especially for the delicacy with which he painted the extremities of the fingers. They cited many portraits on panel, and drawings on parchment, which served as examples to other painters, and as proofs of his wonderful skill in this part of the art.

One of the most celebrated works of Parrhasius was his Demos, or allegorical figure of the Athenian People. Pliny says that it represented, and expressed equally, all the good and bad qualities of the Athenians at the same time; one migh trace the changeable, the irritable, the kind, the unjust, the forgiving, the vain-glorious, the proud the humble, the fierce, the timid. Supposing it to have been a single figure, this description of Pliny is scarcely creditable. His Theseus, after the general spoliation of Athens, was removed to Rome. Among the other works of Parrhasius Pliny enumerates a Naval Commander in his Armor; a picture of Meleager, Hercules, and Perseus; Ulysses feigning insanity; Castor and Pollux; Bacchus and Virtue; a Cretan Nurse, with an Infant in her Arms; a Priest officiating, with an attendant Youth bearing incense; two Boys, in which were admirably depicted the innocent simplicity of the age, and its happy security from all care; a Philiscus; a Telephus; an Achilles; an Agamemnon; an Æneas; and two famous pictures of Hoplites, or heavily armed warriors, one in action, the other in repose. Parrhasius was also distinguished for his small libidinous subjects. The Archigallus mentioned by Pliny was most probably of this description, both from the particular favor of Tiberius with which it was honored, and from the peculiar nature of the rites of Cybele, whose chief priest was called Archigallus. To this class may be added the picture of Meleager and Atalanta, mentioned by Suetonius. This picture was bequeathed to Tiberius on the condition that, if he were offended with the subject, he should receive in its stead 1,000,000 sesterces (about $40,000). The emperor not only preferred the picture, but had it fixed up in his own chamber, where the Archigallus was also preserved, which was valued at 60,000 sesterces. These productions entitle Parrhasius to the epithet of *Pornograph*, and prove that this style of painting was in vogue long before the decay of Grecian art.

The story told by Seneca, of Parrhasius having crucified an old Olynthian captive, when about to paint a picture of Prometheus chained, cannot relate to this artist, and is probably a fiction, as it is found nowhere but in the Controversies. Olynthus was taken by Philip, in the year B. C. 347; which is nearly half a century later than the latest accounts of Parrhasius. This great artist was well aware of his powers, but he became extravagantly carried away with pride and vanity. He assumed the title of *The Elegant;* styled himself the Prince of Painters; wrote an epigram upon himself, in which he proclaimed his birthplace, celebrated his father Evenor, and pretended that he himself had carried the art to perfection. He also declared himself descended from Apollo, and even went so far as to dedicate his own portrait as Mercury in a temple, and thus received the adoration of the multitude. From these considerations, it would appear that Pliny justly terms him the most insolent and most arrogant of artists. That author also mentions a contest between Parrhasius and Timanthes of Cythnos, in which the former was beaten; the subject of the picture was the contest between Ulysses and Ajax. The proud painter, indignant at the decision of the judges, is said to have remarked that the unfortunate son of Telamon was for a second time, in the same cause, defeated by an unworthy rival. Another anecdote is well known, respecting his contest with Zeuxis. The latter painted grapes, in the hands of a boy, so true to nature that the birds endeavored to peck them—no great compliment to his abilities in figure painting. Parrhasius painted a curtain so admirably that it deceived Zeuxis himself.

PARROCEL, Barthelemi, a French painter, was born at Montbrison, in the first part of the 17th century. He was at first intended for the church, but on account of a strong inclination for art, was permitted to study painting. After acquiring a knowledge of design in his own country, he set out for Italy; but, during his journey, he became acquainted with a Spanish grandee, who was greatly pleased with his talents, and invited him to visit Spain. The proposal was accepted, and Parrocel spent several years in that country; after which he again started for Italy, but was captured by Algerian corsairs. Happily, his confinement was of short duration; and upon being released he went to Rome. He passed several years in that city, and then settled at Brignoles, in France, where he died in 1660. The French writers do not state what subjects he usually painted, or what reputation he attained. He left three sons, who studied painting; the eldest died very young; the second, Louis Parrocel, practised the art with some distinction in Provence and at Paris. He afterwards settled in Languedoc. The third son, Joseph P., is the subject of the following article.

PARROCEL, Joseph, an eminent French painter, born at Brignoles in Provence, in 1648. He was the son of the preceding painter, who instructed him in the rudiments of the art, but died when he was twelve years of age. Without any further assistance, he went to Paris, where he greatly improved himself by studying the works of the best French masters. His talents and lively disposition recommended him to the notice of some of the most distinguished artists in that city, who aided him with their advice, and recommended him to go to Italy. On his arrival at Rome, he found the works of Borgognone in the highest estimation, and he had the good fortune to be admitted into the school of that distinguished master. He applied himself with great assiduity to acquire his principles. After a residence of several years at Rome, he went to Venice, where he improved his coloring, which at that time partook of the dark, cold style of Borgognone, by studying the works of the great Venetian masters. He had already acquired distinction at Venice, and such was the encouragement he received, and such the homage paid to his talents, that he resolved to establish himself in that city; but, in 1675, an extraordinary circumstance made it prudent for him to return to his own country. As he was returning to his apartments one night, he was assailed by assassins, on the Rialto, posted there, as is believed, by persons jealous of his merit and success, and he escaped death only by his personal valor. He therefore returned to Paris, where he immediately met with public favor and encouragement. He was elected a member of the French Academy in 1676, on which occasion he painted for his reception piece the Siege of Maestricht, which greatly increased his reputation. He was soon afterwards commissioned by the Marquis de Louvois, minister of state, to decorate one of the four refectories of the Invalides with the conquests of Louis XIV., in which he succeeded so admirably that he was employed in some of the works in the royal galleries at Versailles. Louis XIV. appointed him his state painter with a liberal pension, and he continued in his service till his death. The fame of Parrocel rests mostly on his battle-pieces, which are designed in the grand style of Borgognone, and although they cannot stand in competition with that great master, they possess so much merit as to rank him with any other artist of his time. His battle-pieces are ingeniously and copiously composed, designed with great correctness and skill, and executed with a spirited pencil, admirably adapted to the subjects he represented; his figures and horses have attitudes perfectly natural and full of fire, and the variety of passions are properly expressed. His talents were not limited to these subjects; he painted history and portraits with such excellence as plainly shows that he would have excelled equally in these branches, had he devoted his talents to them. He executed several works for the churches and public edifices, which display an excellent genius for historical composition. They are elegantly designed, his tints are unusually clear, his touch is free and clean, and there is a happy disposition of the lights which produces a pleasing effect. Such are his St. John in the Wilderness, in the church of Notre Dame at Paris; and several historical works in the Hotel de Toulouse. Parrocel also executed a large number of spirited etchings from his own designs. Dumesnil gives a list of ninety prints by him, among which are a set of forty-eight prints of the Life of Christ; the four Times of the Day; and four battle-pieces. They are marked *J. Parrocel inv. et fec.* He died in 1704.

PARROCEL, Charles, the son of Joseph P., was born at Paris in 1689. He studied the elements of design under his father, but as the latter died when Charles was only sixteen years of age, he entered the school of Charles de la Fosse. On leaving that master, he visited Italy, and painted a picture of the Finding of Moses, which he sent to Paris, and thereby gained the royal pension. During his residence in Italy he continued to cultivate the historical branch of the art, but on returning to France, he determined to become a painter of battles. In order to acquire a better knowledge of his favorite subjects, he entered a regiment of cavalry, and served for several years; but without relinquishing the practice of his profession. In 1721, by order of the King, he painted two pictures twenty-two feet in length, representing the Entrance of the Turkish Ambassador to the Gardens of the Tuileries, and the Exit of the same distinguished personage, after an audience, at the Pont Tournant. These fine works gained for Parrocel, a suite of apartments in the Gobelins, and a pension of 600 livres. In 1744 and 1745, he was appointed to accompany Louis XV. in his campaigns in Flanders, to paint the successful battles of the French forces. His pictures are inferior to those of his father in brilliancy, though superior in truth, of coloring. He was chosen a member of the Royal Academy. There are a number of spirited etchings by him, after his own designs, representing horse and foot soldiers. He died in 1752.

PARROCEL, Ignace, a French painter, the son of Louis P., and the nephew of Joseph P., was born at Avignon, according to Zani, in 1664; according to Nagler, in 1688. He studied under his uncle, and painted huntings and battle pieces in the admirable style of that master. He travelled through Italy and Austria, and was commissioned by the Emperor and Prince Eugene to paint a number of battle pieces. The Duke d'Aremberg invited him to the Low Countries, whither he went, and died at Mons, in 1722. Seven of his pictures were taken from the Imperial Gallery at Vienna, and placed in the Louvre; but they were restored in 1815.

PARROCEL, Pierre, a French painter and engraver, the younger brother of the preceding, was born at Avignon in 1664. He was first instructed by his uncle Joseph P., after which he visited Rome, and entered the school of Carlo Maratti. After returning to France, he travelled through Languedoc and Provence, and the Comtat of Avignon, leaving in the various cities through which he passed, numerous proofs of his abilities, among which were the Resurrection and the Ascension of Christ, in the chapel of the White Penitents at Avignon. His reputation soon extended to Paris, and gained him an invitation to that city, where he executed a number of fine works. His pictures are distinguished for graceful design, beautiful coloring, vigorous execution, and harmonious effect. Among his principal works are sixteen pictures of subjects from the History of Tobit, in the Gallery of the Hotel de Noailles, at St. Germain en Laie; and the Coronation of the Virgin in the church of S. Maria at Marseilles, which is considered his master-piece. As an engraver, he etched a number of plates, with rare dexterity and infinite spirit, in a style analogous to that of A. Rivalz. He was not equally successful with the graver. Dumesnil describes eighteen prints of his execution.

PARROCEL, Etienne, a French painter, the son of Pierre P. was born at Paris about 1720. He painted subjects of history, but attained little reputation. He exhibited several works, among which were Cephalus and Procris, and Christ on the Mount of Olives. There are several etchings by him, in a free bold style, among which are a Bacchanalian Subject,, from his own design; the Triumph of Mordecai, after de Troy; Bacchus and Ariadne, *after Subleyras*.

PARROCEL, Joseph Ignace, was a native of Avignon and a son of Pierre P. He was a member of the Royal Academy, and the last painter of the Parrocel family. According to Nagler, he died in 1781. He left several daughters, of whom the eldest, Madame de Valranseaux, was distinguished for painting flowers and animals.

PARRY, William, an English painter, born at London, in 1742. He first learned the rudiments of design in Shipley's drawing school; he next studied in the Duke of Richmond's Gallery, and afterwards with Sir Joshua Reynolds. He obtained several prizes from the Society for the Encouragement of Arts, &c. On leaving Reynolds, he was favored with the patronage of Sir Watkin Williams Wynne, by whose liberality he was enabled to visit Italy in 1770, where he resided four years, and painted for his patron, among other things, a copy of the Transfiguration by Raffaelle. He returned to London in 1775, and was chosen an associate of the Royal Academy in 1776. Not meeting with much encouragement he returned to Rome in 1778, where he resided till 1791, when the state of his health compelled him to return to his native country, where he died soon after his arrival. At Rome he was principally employed in executing commissions for his countrymen, who happened to stop at that city.

PARS, William, an English designer and painter, born at London about 1742. He learned the rudiments of art in Shipley's drawing school, and afterwards frequented the Academy in St. Martin's Lane, from which institution, in 1764, he drew the third premium of twenty guineas, for historical painting. Soon afterwards the Dilettanti Society sent him to Greece to make further researches into the remains of antiquity, on which expedition he was absent three years. On his return he was employed by Lord Palmerston to accompany him in a tour through Switzerland and Italy, to make drawings of the most remarkable views and antiquities. In 1770, he was elected an associate of the Royal Academy. In 1775 the Dilettanti Society sent him to Rome, on a pension, to study painting, where he resided till his death, in 1782. Some of his views made in Greece were engraved by Byrne, and some of those in Switzerland and Italy were executed in aquatinta by Paul Sandby.

PARSONS, Francis, an English portrait painter, who flourished in London about 1763. He was an indifferent artist, and afterwards turned his attention to restoring and dealing in old pictures.

PARSONS, William, an English painter, but more distinguished comedian, born at London in 1736. At the age of fourteen he was apprenticed to an architect, and so much distinguished himself by his architectural drawings and designs, that he obtained several premiums from the Society of Arts, &c. On attaining his majority, he took to the stage, and became one of the most popular comedians of his time. He is said, however, never to have relinquished his pencil, but painted a variety of landscapes, architectural subjects, and fruit pieces, which he gave to his friends. He died in 1795.

PASCH, John, a Swedish painter, born at Stockholm in 1706. He acquired the elements of design in his native country, and subsequently visited Holland, France, and Italy, for improvement. During his travels, he made a valuable collection of drawings and pictures. On returning to Sweden, he settled at Stockholm, and practised the art in that city for many years. He painted flower-pieces, landscapes, and marine views. Among his most important works, is the cupola of the Royal Chapel at Stockholm. His knowledge and taste were of great service to the Academy of Fine Arts, founded at Stockholm in 1734. He died in 1769.

PASCH, Lawrence, a Swedish painter, flourished at Stockholm in the first part of the 18th century. He was distinguished in portrait; and was appointed to the office of Director of the Academy of Fine Arts, which he filled for many years. His daughter, Ulrika Frederika Pasch, was born in 1735. She evinced remarkable talents, and in 1773 was admitted to the Academy. She died in 1796.

PASINELLI, Lorenzo, a Bolognese painter, born in 1629. He first studied under Simone Cantarini, and next with Flaminio Torre. He afterwards went to Venice, where he became enamoured of the ornamental and brilliant style of Paul Veronese, and he made the works of that master his model, though he did not servilely imitate him.

Lanzi says, "he borrowed from Veronese his effective and magnificent composition, but the airs of his heads and the distribution of his colors he obtained from another source; and though he never acquired the correctness of design which distinguishes the works of Torre, yet in this respect he surpassed Paolo." On his return to Bologna, he found abundant employment in painting for the churches and the collections. He was naturally inclined to create surprise by the display of copious, rich, and spirited compositions; such are his two pictures at the Certosa, representing Christ's Entrance into Jerusalem, and his Return into Limbo; and such, too, is his History of Coriolanus, in the Casa Ranuzzi—a piece found repeated in many collections. No one can behold these paintings without granting to Pasinelli a true painter's fire, great novelty of ideas, and an elevated character. With these gifts, he was sometimes too extravagant in his imitation of the attitudes, pompous spectacles, strange and novel draperies of Veronese, which he is thought to have carried to the extreme, as in his Preaching of John the Baptist in the Wilderness, which gave occasion to his rival Taruffi sarcastically to remark that, instead of the desert of Judea, he discovered in it the piazza of St. Mark at Venice. He, nevertheless, knew how to moderate his fire according to his theme, as in his Holy Family, in the church of the Barefooted Carmelites, which partakes of the elegance and grace of Albano. He painted more for private collections than for the public edifices, though there are several other works by him in the churches at Bologna, the most esteemed of which are the Resurrection, in S. Francesco; and the Martyrdom of St. Ursula and her companions, in the Palazzo Zambeccari. Lanzi says, "his private pictures are uniform in spirit, rich and varied in the composition, and they boast such a delicacy of handling and peculiar brilliancy of coloring, that they might be taken for the works of the Venetians or the Lombards; in particular some of his Venuses, which are supposed to be the portraits of one of his three wives. He died in 1700. Basan erroneously says that Pasinelli etched some plates, and mentions two—St. John preaching in the Wilderness, and the Martyrdom of St. Ursula and other Saints; but these plates were engraved by Lorenzini, a scholar of Pasinelli. See *Bartsch's P. G., tom. XIX., pp.* 415—417, *Nos.* 6 *and* 8.

PASITELES, a Grecian statuary, mentioned by Pliny as flourishing in the time of Pompey the Great. He executed a statue of Jupiter for the first temple erected in Rome by Metellus Macedonicus, and wrote an account of the finest monuments of art extant at the time.

PASQUALI, FILIPPO, a painter of Forli, who studied under Carlo Cignani at Bologna. He afterwards associated himself with Marc' Antonio Franceschini, in conjunction with whom he painted many works at Bologna, Rimini, and other places, in which he executed the ornamental parts. Some of his earlier works are to be seen in the portico of the Serviti at Bologna. Lanzi highly commends his altar-piece in the church of S. Vittore at Ravenna, which he executed alone, at a more advanced age. He is supposed to have died about 1690.

PASQUALINI, FELICE, a Bolognese painter, who flourished about 1575. According to Malvasia, he was the scholar of Lorenzo Sabbatini, whose style he adopted. He executed some works for the churches, which Lanzi thinks might be justly attributed to Sabbatini, such was the part he took in their execution.

PASQUALINI, or PASCALINI, GIOVANNI BATTISTA, an Italian painter and engraver, born at Cento, near Bologna, in the latter part of the 16th century. His earliest print is dated 1619, and the latest 1630. He studied painting under Ciro Ferri, but he does not seem to have acquired much eminence in that art. He executed many etchings, mostly after Guercino, in which he endeavored to imitate with the point the masterly pen-drawings of that master, but he did not possess a sufficient command of his instrument to accomplish it with much success. He frequently signed his plates *J. B. Centensis.* Nagler gives a list of forty prints by him, of which the following are the principal:

SUBJECTS AFTER GUERCINO.

Christ dictating the Gospel to St. John. The Resurrection of Lazarus. Christ giving the Keys to St. Peter. Christ taken in the Garden. Angels showing Mary Magdalene the Instruments of the Passion. Christ with the Disciples at Emmaus. The Incredulity of Thomas. The Virgin and Infant, with an Angel presenting Fruit. The Virgin and Infant, to whom St. John presents an Apple. St. Charles Borromeus. St. Felix resuscitating a Dead Child. Tancred and Erminia. Tithonus and Aurora.

VARIOUS SUBJECTS.

St. Felix kneeling before the Virgin and Infant; *after L. Caracci.* St. Diego working a Miracle; *after Ann. Caracci.* The Death of St. Cecilia; *after Domenichino.* The Aurora; *after Guido.*

PASQUALINO. See PASQUALE ROSSI.

PASQUALOTTO, CONSTANTINO, a painter of Vicenza, who flourished about 1700. He studied at Venice, and on returning to his native city he executed some works for the churches, but more for individuals, in which Lanzi says he was more distinguished for the richness of his draperies and the brilliancy of his coloring, than for the correctness of his design.

PASQUIER, JEAN JACQUES, a French engraver, born at Paris, and a pupil of Lawrence Cars. He engraved a variety of book plates and others, after the French masters, among which are two Pastoral Subjects, and Arion upon the Dolphin, *after Boucher;* the Graces, *after C. Vanloo;* and a set of twelve Academical Figures, *after Natoire.* He died in 1784.

PASS, or PASSE, CRISPIN DE, called THE ELDER, an eminent Dutch engraver, born at Utrecht in 1650, according to the best authorities, though there is great discrepancy as to the place and time of his nativity. He is said to have studied under Theodore Cuernhert. He was a man of letters, and not only a lover of his art, but fond of promoting it, as is evident from his Drawing Book, published at Amsterdam in 1643, when he was an octogenarian, in Italian, French, and Dutch, entitled *Della Luce del dipingere e disegnare.* In this work, he mentions his intimacy with the most eminent artists of his time, as Rubens, A. Bloemaert, Freminet, P. Moreelze, and P. vander Berg. This also farther appears from his having incurred the expense of publishing *Holland's Heroloogia,* in which it is ex pressly stated *Impensis Crispini Passe.* His tai-ants recommended him to the notice of Prince Maurice, who sent him to Paris, where he taught drawing in the Academy of M. Pluvinel, riding master to Louis XIII., at which time he designed and engraved his celebrated set of prints entitled, *Instruction du Roi en l'exercise de monter à cheval, par Messire Antoine de Pluvinel.* These plates represent the different exercises of the horse, the manner of tilting at the barriers, &c.; and into them he introduced the portrait of Louis XIII., the Duke de Bellgarde, and many of the great personages of the court. He went to London, where he resided a long time, and executed many plates. It is supposed that he returned to his own country about 1635, as there are none of his plates engraved in England, bearing a later date. The plates of Crispin De Passe are executed entirely with the graver, in a neat, clear, and original style, and though there is occasionally an appearance of stiffness and formality, his prints possess great merit, and are highly esteemed. Many of them are designed from the life, and the greater part of his historical and other subjects are engraved from his own designs. His portraits are his best prints. Nagler and Bartsch give copious lists of his works, which are very numerous, and show a life of extraordinary industry. The following are his most esteemed prints. They are generally marked with a monogram composed of an S., V., and a P., united as above.

ENGLISH PORTRAITS.

Queen Elizabeth, sumptuously attired, with the Crown, Sceptre, and Globe; *after Isaac Oliver.* A Head of the same Queen; oval. James I. with the Sceptre in his hand. James I. with a Hat and Ruff; oval. Anne of Denmark, his consort; do. Henry, Prince of Wales; do. Charles, his brother, afterwards Charles I.; do. Frederick, Count Palatine, consort of Princess Elizabeth. Elizabeth, daughter of James I., his wife. Sir Philip Sidney. The Earl of Essex on horseback. Thomas Percy, the conspirator; scarce.

FOREIGN PORTRAITS.

Henry IV.. King of France. Mary of Medicis, his Queen. Philip. King of Spain. Henry Frederick, Prince of Nassau. Albert, Archduke of Austria, and Maurice, Prince of Nassau, on horseback. Louisa Juliana, Countess of Nassau; circular. Andrea Doria, Genoese Admiral. Adolphus, Baron of Schwartzenberg. Alexander Farnese. A set of fourteen Portraits of women, with a frontispiece, entitled *Speculum illustrium feminarum.*

SUBJECTS FROM HIS OWN DESIGNS.

Adam and Eve. Susanna and the Elders. Three small circular plates of Busts, representing Faith, Hope and Charity; fine. Cleopatra. The Inside of a Tavern, with Men and Women quarrelling; *C. van Pass inv.* 1588, one of his earliest prints. The Seven Liberal Arts. The Nine Muses.

SUBJECTS AFTER VARIOUS MASTERS.

The History of Tobit, in six plates; *after M. de Vos.* The Twelve Months, in twelve circular plates; *do.* The Four Evangelists, in four plates; *after Goltzius Geldorp;* very fine. The Angels appearing to the Shepherds; *after A. Bloemaert.* The Crucifixion; *after Jod. de Winghe.* The Judgment of Paris; *after C. vander Broeck.* The Siege of Troy; *do.* A set of four Landscapes, with figures; *after J. Breughel.*

PASS, or PASSE, Crispin de, called the Younger, was the eldest son of the preceding, born at Utrecht about 1585. Little is known with certainty of him, and there is much discrepancy as to the time of his birth. He studied design and engraving with his father. Zani says he was living in 1659, and quotes one of his prints bearing that date. There are only a few prints by him, among which are the following:

PORTRAITS.

Frederick, Elector Palatine; inscribed *Crispin Passeus, jun., fig. et sculps.;* oval. Johannes Angelius Werdenhagen; *C. de Passe filius, fec.* 1600.

SUBJECTS.

Three, of a set of four plates of the History of the Rich Man and Lazarus; the fourth was engraved by his father.

PASS, or PASSE, William de, was the second son of Crispin de Pass, born at Utrecht, about 1590. He was instructed by his father, whom he very nearly equalled. It is supposed that he accompanied his father to England, where he resided the greater part of his life, and engraved a great number and variety of plates, which are highly esteemed. His best prints are his portraits. The times of his birth and death are altogether uncertain. His birth is variously placed in 1572, 1580, and 1590. Zani says he operated in 1640. There is a portrait of Oliver Cromwell, attributed to him, dated 1660. He sometimes marked his plates with his name, and at others with a monogram of his initials. The following are his best prints:

PORTRAITS.

James I. and his family, inscribed *Triumphus Jacobi Regis Augustæ que ipsius prôlis;* scarce. James I., with Henry Prince of Wales. After the death of that prince the face was erased, and that of Charles his brother substituted in its place. Robert Dudley, Earl of Leicester; oval, with the cipher. George Villiers, Duke of Buckingham, on horseback, with shipping in the background; scarce. Robert Devereux, Earl of Essex, on horseback; scarce. Frances, Duchess of Richmond and Lenox; very highly finished; inscribed *Anno.* 1625, *insculptum Guliel. Passeo Londinum.* Sir John Haywood; *W. Pass, f.* Sir Henry Rich: very fine. Darcy Wentworth. 1624. The King and Queen of Bohemia, with four of their children; inscribed *Will. Pass. fecit ad vivum figurator.* 1621. The Palatine Family, in which the youngest child is playing with a rabbit; without the name of the engraver.

PASS, or PASSE, Simon de, was the youngest son of Crispin de Passe the Elder, who instructed him in the art. He resided in England about ten years, and engraved quite a number of portraits and other subjects, which are highly esteemed. He was also employed by Hilliard to engrave counters of the English Royal Family. The earliest prints he engraved in England are dated 1613, and the latest 1623. On leaving England, he entered the service of the King of Denmark. Nagler mentions two Danish portraits, dated 1644. He marked his prints variously. with his name and the above monogram. His portraits are his best prints. The following are his principal works:

PORTRAITS.

Queen Elizabeth; whole length. James I. crowned, sitting in a chair. The same, with a hat. Queen Anne on horseback, with a View of Windsor; scarce. The same; dated 1617. Prince Henry with a lance. Philip III. King of Spain. Maria of Austria, his daughter, the intended bride of Charles I.; scarce. The same, as sister of Philip IV.; very fine. General Edward Cecyll, son to the Earl of Exeter; very scarce. George Villiers, Duke of Buckingham, 1617, when Earl. The same, when Marquis, 1620. Robert Carr, Earl of Somerset. Frances Howard, Countess of Somerset. Francis Manners, Earl of Rutland. Thomas, Earl of Arundel; *after Mirevelt.* Sir Walter Raleigh. Sir Thos. Smith, Ambassador to Russia. William, Earl of Pembroke; *after Van Somer.* Richard, Earl of Dorset Archbishop Abbot, with a View of Lambeth. R. Sidney

Viscount Lisle; scarce. Charles, Earl of Nottingham. Mary Sidney, Countess of Pembroke; scarce. Henry Wriothesly, Earl of Southampton. Edward Somerset, Earl of Worcester. Count Gondomar, Ambassador from Spain; very fine. Frederick Henry, Prince of Orange, inscribed *Liberum Belgium;* very fine. Four whole-length portraits of the Dukes of Burgundy—John the Intrepid, Philip the Bold, Philip the Good, and Charles the Rash; etchings; scarce.

PASS, or PASSE, Magdalena de, was the daughter of the elder Crispin de Passe, born about 1583. She learned engraving of her father, and engraved some small plates of portraits and other subjects, in a neat finished style, which possesses considerable merit. The following are by her, marked with one of the accompanying monograms:

PORTRAITS.

Her own Head; scarce. Catherine, Duchess of Buckingham, with a feather in her hand.

VARIOUS SUBJECTS.

The Wise and the Foolish Virgins; *after Elsheimer;* fine and scarce. The Four Seasons; *after the designs of her father.* Cephalus and Procris. Salmacis and Hermaphroditus. Latona changing the Lycian Peasants into Frogs. Alpheus and Arethusa. A pair of Landscapes: *after Roland Savery.* A pair, one a Storm with a Shipwreck, and the other a Landscape with a Windmill; *after A. Willeres;* fine.

PASS, or PASSE, Simon de. It is said that C. de Passe the younger had a son of this name, and that he went to Copenhagen, where he engraved some plates, among which were a portrait of Frederick III. King of Denmark; an Ecce Homo, dated 1639; and a Woman with three Children, dated 1643; but it seems more than probable that he is no other than Simon de P., the son of the elder Crispin de P.

PASSANTE, Bartolomeo, a Neapolitan painter, who, according to Dominici, was a scholar of Spagnoletto, whose style and subjects he imitated with great success, but with a more finished design and expression. Lanzi justly remarks that "those masters who are mannerists form scholars who confine their powers to the sole imitation of their master, and thus produce pictures that deceive the most experienced." He painted mostly for the collections, and flourished about the middle of the 17th century.

PASSAROTTI. See Passerotti.

PASSARI. See Passeri.

PASSERI, Andrea, a painter of Como, who flourished about 1505. In the cathedral of his native city is a picture of the Virgin surrounded by the Apostles, in which the composition and expression of the heads are good, but Lanzi says there is a dryness in the hands, with the use of gilding unworthy of the age in which he painted.

PASSERI, Giovanni Battista, a painter born at Rome about 1610. He is supposed to have been a pupil of Domenichino; at all events, in the early part of his life, he lived on terms of intimacy with that master at Frescati, and adhered much to his style in his historical works. Lanzi says there are few of his works in public, as he wrought mostly for the collections. In the church of S. Giovanni della Malva at Rome, is a picture by him of the Crucifixion. In the Palazzo Mattei are some of his pictures, representing butcher's meat, birds, and game, touched with a masterly pencil; to these are added some half-length figures and some sparrows (*passeri*), in allusion to his name. There is also by his hand, in the Academy of St. Luke, the portrait of Domenichino. He was a man of letters, possessed a profound knowledge of art, and wrote the lives of the *Painters, Sculptors, and Architects who were employed at Rome, now deceased, from* 1641 *to* 1673, published at Rome in 1772. Lanzi pronounces him one of the most learned and authentic writers on Italian art. He was President of the Academy of St. Luke in 1641, when Domenichino died, and pronounced his funeral oration. Malvasia erroneously states that it was Passerino. Towards the close of his life he entered the priesthood, and in 1675 obtained a benefice in the College of S. Maria in Via Lata. He died in 1679.

PASSERI, Giuseppe, was a nephew of the preceding, born at Rome in 1654. According to Pascoli, he was a scholar of Carlo Maratti, and one of the most successful followers of his style. He painted many works for the churches at Rome, and at different places in the Roman territory. In the church of the Vatican, he painted a pendant to the Baptism of Maratti, representing St. Peter baptizing the Centurion. This work, after being copied in mosaic, was sent to the church of the Conventuals at Urbino. It was executed under the direction of Maratti himself, and is admirably colored; but in his other works at Rome, such as the Conception, in the church of S. Tommaso in Parione, the coloring is comparatively feeble. At Pesaro is one of his most esteemed works, representing St. Jerome meditating on the Last Judgment. He painted much for the collections, and was also an excellent portrait painter. Passeri lived in general esteem, and his house was much frequented by persons of the first rank for taste and literature. He died at Rome in 1714.

PASSERI, PASSARO, or PASSARI, Bernardino, an Italian painter and engraver, who flourished at Rome about 1580. There is a great deal of contradiction and confusion about this artist, from his having flourished nearly at the same time with Bartolomeo Passerotti, and using the same mark. It is said that he studied painting under Taddeo Zuccaro, whose style he adopted; but there is no certainty of this, though it seems probable. He is more distinguished as an engraver, and he executed a large number of plates, mostly of devout subjects, from his own designs, which prove him to have possessed a fertile and ready invention. They are sometimes marked with his name, and sometimes with a monogram of his initials, the B. being reversed. Bartsch says he was not a painter, but a designer and engraver, and he gives a list of seventy-eight etchings by him; but many of the prints heretofore attributed to him he gives to Passerotti, *which see.*

PASSEROTTI, Bartolomeo, a Bolognese painter, born about 1540, and died according to the register of the church of S. Martino Maggiore, where he was interred, in 1592. He studied under Taddeo Zuccaro at Rome, and is mentioned by Vasari as one of the assistants of that master. He is also commended by Borghini and Lomazzo. He resided in the early part of his life at Rome, where he executed some works for the churches, the most esteemed of which is the Martyrdom of St. Paul, in S. Paolo alle Tre Fontane. On his return to Bologna, he painted many altar-pieces for the churches, the most celebrated of which are the Adoration of the Magi, in S. Pietro; the Annunciation, in S. Martino Maggiore; the Virgin, on a Throne, surrounded by St. John the Baptist and other Saints, in S. Giacomo Maggiore, which last work was avowedly painted in competition with the Caracci, and elicited their praise. The exquisite degree of diligence and refinement which he displayed in this work he rarely used; but he generally painted in a bold, free style, with remarkable facility of execution. He also excelled in portraits, and in this branch Guido ranked him next to Titian, preferring him before the Caracci themselves. Lanzi says the name of the Caracci, in several galleries, is attached to the portraits of Passerotti. The most commendable of all his portraits are those he executed for the noble family Legnani, which are full-lengths, extremely varied in costume, action, and attitudes, and, though correct likenesses, they appear like true ideal pictures. He opened a school at Bologna, which was attended by many distinguished masters. Lanzi says "he was the first at Bologna to make a grander display, and began to vary Scripture histories by drawing from the naked torsi. He possessed remarkable skill in designing with his pen; a gift which drew to his school Agostino Caracci, and *which assisted the latter as a guide in the art of engraving;* he likewise wrote a book, from which he taught the symmetry and anatomy of the human body essential to the artist. The pictures of Passerotti are distinguished by a sparrow, in allusion to his name —a custom derived from the ancients, and practised by many modern artists. It is a well known fact relating to the two ancient sculptors, Batrarchus and Saurus, that they indicated their proper names, the former by a frog and the latter by a lizard. Zani describes Passerotti as a designer and engraver. He says, also, that he is called *Il Maestro al Passero* (the Master of the Sparrow), from his having used a sparrow between the letters B. and P., as his rebus; but this is not mentioned by any other writer. Bartsch commends him highly for his ability as a designer, and for the freedom and boldness of his manner of engraving. He enumerates and describes fifteen prints by him; also two mentioned by Gori and Rost, and one doubtful, but he does not consider the catalogue complete. He says that his prints have at all times been sought for by artists and connoisseurs, and that they have become extremely scarce, the richest collections possessing one or two at most.

*A list of Passerotti's etchings, as given by Bartsch, Peintre Graveur, tom. xviii.*

1. The Chastity of Joseph; *after Parmiggiano.* 2. The Visitation; *after F. Salviati.* 3. The Virgin, with the infant and St. John, marked P. F. 4. A similar subject, with the letters B. P. 5. The virgin sitting on the ground, with the infant Jesus on her knees; signed B. PASAROT. 6. Jesus Christ holding a Banner; B. PASAROT. This and the five following are supposed to be part of a suite of thirteen, representing Christ and his Apostles. 7. St. Peter; the letters B. P. on the left at bottom. 8. St. Andrew; B. PASAROT at bottom. 9. St. John the Evangelist; do. 10. St. Bartholomew; do. 11. St. Paul; the letters B. P. on the right at bottom. 12. Religion, represented by a Woman seated, and surrounded by the sun; the letter B. on the right at bottom. 13. Painting represented by a young Female with Wings; the letters B. P. on the right at bottom. 14. A young Woman in Bed; B. PASSAROTO written backwards, the letter B. reversed and joined to the P. 15. The Sacrifice, in which there are eight figures.—The letters B. P. on the left at bottom. A Charity, mentioned by *Gori.* The Marriage of Isaac and Rebecca; *after Perugino;* mentioned by *Rost.* A Holy Family, doubtful. St. Peter delivered from Prison by an Angel. St. Peter is seated and the Angel, without wings, has placed the left hand on Peter's shoulder, and directs the way with the right. At the bottom, in the corner, are the letters B. P.

PASSEROTTI, TIBURZIO, was the eldest son of the preceding, born at Bologna, in 1575. He was instructed by his father, whose manner he adopted, though he wrought with a less bold, free, and rapid pencil. He executed some works for the churches, which were admired for their beautiful composition, and which Lanzi says possess real merit. The principal are the Assumption, in S. Maria Mascarella; the Virgin, with St. Francis and St. Jerome, in S. Cecilia; the Annunciation, in S. Cristina; and the Martyrdom of St. Catharine in S. Giacomo Maggiore, which last is his most celebrated performance. He was also an excellent portrait painter. He died in the prime of life, in 1612.

PASSEROTTI, AURELIO, was the second son of Bartolomeo. He acquired distinction for his small pictures of historical subjects. He died at Rome about 1605. The third son, Passarotte P., died in his youth.

PASSEROTTI, VENTURA, was the fourth son of Bartolomeo, born at Bologna, in 1586. He was instructed by his brother Tiburzio, whom he assisted in his works, but did not acquire any distinction as a historical painter. He, however, painted portraits equal to any of his cotemporaries. His greatest delight was in drawing with a pen or crayons, such subjects as occurred to his imagination, in which he aspired to express the proportions of the naked figure, and the muscular action, in the grand and terrible manner of Michael Angelo. He died in 1630.

PASSIGNANO. See CAV. DOMENICO CRESTI.

PASTERINI, JACOPO, an excellent mosaic painter, who wrought for the churches at Venice, in the latter part of the 16th century. There are notices of him up to 1618.

PASTI, MATTEO, an old artist of Verona, who, according to Maffei, was a painter, sculptor in marble and bronze, gem and wood engraver, who flourished about the middle of the 15th century. He is supposed to have executed the wood cuts for a folio volume published at Verona in 1472, entitled, *Roberti Valturii opus de re Militare.* They possess considerable accuracy and spirit, and show a considerable improvement in the art. This was the second book illustrated with engravings published in Italy, the first being the Meditations of Cardinal Turrecremata, published at Rome in 1467, by Hans Ulric, or as he is called by the Italians, Ulderico Han.

PASTILL, J. DE, a French engraver, who flourished about the middle of the 18th century. He seems to have employed himself mostly in copying the prints of other masters, which he did in an indifferent manner. Among other plates of this description, is one of the murder of the Innocents.

*after the engraving of Louis Audran*, from the picture of le Brun.

PASTORINI, B., an Italian engraver, who resided at London about 1770. He engraved some plates in imitation of the style of Bartolozzi, among which are the following:

L'Allegro; *Angel, Kauffman, pinx. B. Pastorini fec.* Il Penseroso; the Companion. A View of London; *from his own design.* Guntherus and Griselda; *J. F. Rigaud, pinx. B. Pastorini, fec.* Griselda returning to her Father; the companion.

PASTORINO, DA SIENA, an eminent painter on glass, who flourished at Rome about 1547. His greatest works were the windows in the State Saloon of the Vatican, and of the cathedral of Siena.

PATAROL, LAWRENCE, an engraver who flourished at Venice, in 1702. He engraved some book plates, among which was a frontispiece for a book on coins, published there in that year.

PATAS, JEAN BAPTISTE, a French designer and engraver, born at Paris in 1748. He engraved several of the plates for the Galerie de Florence, Galerie d'Orleans, Musée Français, Cabinet Poullain, and other works of importance. His prints are executed with the graver, in a neat, pleasing style. He died in 1817.

PATAVINUS. See AVIBUS.

PATCH, THOMAS, an English engraver, who flourished about 1770. He passed much of his time in Italy, and it is supposed that he died there. He engraved a set of twenty-six plates, *after pictures by Masaccio.* He also engraved some plates *after Giotto, Frá Bartolomeo*, and other old Italian masters.

PATEL, PIERRE, an eminent French landscape painter, was born in 1654. His instructor is unknown, but he probably visited Rome, as his pictures generally represent views in the vicinity of that city. His style is formed on that of Claude Lorraine, and in many of his works he imitated that master with success. His verdure is fresh and agreeable; his distances retire with a pleasing gradation; his scenery is grand and striking; his skies clear and brilliant. His landscapes are usually embellished with ruins of ancient architecture, and decorated with figures correctly drawn, touched in a very spirited style. Although the works of Patel are inferior to those of his great model in purity of aërial tints, and grandeur of composition, yet they entitle him to a high rank among the artists of his country. According to Dumesnil, he usually signed his pictures with a monogram composed of the letters A. P. T., followed by his name and the date. He etched two plates; a Landscape, with architectural ruins, and Travelers in a Forest, marked A. P. PATEL, *in et fecit.* He died 1703. In the Louvre collection there was one of his works, representing a landscape with a river and waterfall, the ruins of a superb Corinthian Temple in the foreground, and adorned with figures and animals. There were also three of his pictures in the gallery of the great Trianon.

PATEL, BERNARD, called by the French *Patel le jeune*, was the son and scholar of the preceding, whose manner he imitated. Although his works possess considerable merit, they are very inferior to those of his father. Some of his pictures have been engraved by Daulle, Vivares, Benasech, and others.

PATENIER, JOACHIM, a Flemish painter, born at Dinant, in the principality of Liege, in 1480. It is not known under whom he studied, but he settled at Antwerp, where he acquired distinction for his landscapes, and was admitted into the Academy in that city in 1515. His pictures are usually of small size, so exquisitely finished as to appear labored. He introduced into them a great number of small figures, which are correctly designed and neatly touched. His distances are charmingly preserved, and the foliage of his trees, the trunks and the branches appear like nature. He also painted battles and huntings which were highly esteemed. When Albert Durer was at Antwerp, he was so charmed with the works of this artist, that he painted his portrait. His works were greatly admired and much sought after, yet they are very scarce, as he bestowed much labor upon them, and was a man of low dissipated habits, spending most of his time in the ale houses. There is also much discrepancy as to his merits, which has doubtless arisen from spurious imitations of his works, as his genuine pictures in the Imperial Gallery at Vienna and other places, fully justify the above account. Van Mander mentions one of his pictures, representing a battle, in the possession of Melchior Wijntges at Middelburg, so delicately wrought that no miniature could surpass it. He is said to have died in 1548, though there is no certainty as to the exact time of either his birth or death, there being much discrepancy among authors on these points.

PATER, or PATERRE, JEAN BAPTISTE, a French painter, born at Valenciennes in 1695. He went to Paris early in life, and became the pupil of Anthony Watteau, whose subjects and manner he imitated with considerable success, though his works are greatly inferior to those of that master. He was an excellent colorist, but a negligent and incorrect designer, and his heads lack expression. He died in 1736.

PATERNO, IGNAZIO VINCENZIO CASTELLO, Prince of Biscari. This distinguished Sicilian nobleman flourished in the latter part of the 18th century, and deserves honorable notice in a work relating to architecture, for designing and erecting at his own expense, the great bridge of thirty-one arches, 1450 feet in length, over the Simeto, not far from Catania. Besides serving for the transit of freight and passengers, this bridge supports an aqueduct. The government of Sicily confided to Paterno the superintendence of the bridges, streets, and other public works.

PATICCHI, ANTONIO, an Italian painter, born at Rome in 1762. He acquired the elements of design from his father, and made such rapid progress, that, at the age of twenty he was commissioned to execute the paintings in the Refectory of the carnes at Veletri. On one of the walls he painted the Last Supper; on another, the Virgin, surrounded by Saints; and in the vault, Elijah ascending to Heaven in a Chariot of Fire. This great work gained for Paticchi so high a reputation, that Count Toruzzi of Veletri immediately commissioned him to paint the gallery of his palace, where he represented the Car of Night, and several fabulous subjects. He wrought with wonderful rapidity; and, perceiving that his facility of execution had led him to neglect excellence of coloring, he devoted his energies patiently to this branch of the art. Undoubtedly he would have attained great eminence, but he died in 1788, at the age of twenty-six. Paticchi possessed a great talent for imitating the designs of the great masters, and he executed very many in the style of Polidoro da Caravaggio, which, according to the *Biographie Universelle*, are attributed to that master by the best judges, and have a place in many fine collections.

PATIGNY, Jean or Giovanni, a French engraver, who flourished from 1650 to about 1670. He went to Italy, and appears to have imitated Agostino Caracci, but with little success. He executed some prints after Annibale Caracci and other Italian masters.

PATIN, Jacques, a French painter and engraver, who flourished about 1581. According to Dumesnil, he was employed by Louise de Lorraine, queen of Henry III. of France, to paint the decorations necessary for a masque, or ballet, given by her on the marriage of her sister Marguerite de Vaudemont with the Duc de Joyeuse, in 1581. Patin executed twenty-seven spirited etchings, to illustrate a book describing the same ballet, published in 1582.

PATON, Richard, an eminent English painter of marines and sea-fights, born in 1720, and died in 1795. He painted the principal naval battles of his time, which were very popular, and many of them were engraved by Woollett, Fittler, Lerpiniere, and Canot. He also executed a few spirited etchings of similar subjects, among which are the following:

The Victory gained by the English over the French, 21 September, 1757. The engagement of the Monmouth with the Foudroyant, in which the French ship was taken, 28 February, 1758. The Engagement between the Buckingham and Florissant, supported by two Frigates, 3 Nov. 1758.

PATOUR, Jean Augustin, a French engraver, born at Paris about 1730. He studied under Hallé and Flipart, and engraved some plates in a neat, pleasing style, among which are the following:

The Little Lyar; *after Albert Durer.* Le doux Sommeil; *after Halle.* Le doux Repos; *do.* Hercules and Omphale; *do.* Two Views of La Rochelle; *after Lallemand.*

PATTE, Pierre, a French architect and engraver, born at Paris in 1723. After acquiring the elements of design in his own country, he visited Italy for improvement. During the principal part of his life he was devoted rather to the theory than to the practice of the art; and during the stormy scenes of the revolution he lived in retirement. The Duke des Deux Ponts, appointed Patte his architect, and he designed for him the Chateau de Jaresbourg. The Hotel Charost at Paris, is also by him. His writings are quite voluminous. Among the principal are *Memoires sur les objets les plus importants de l'architecture*, 4 to.; *Traite de la construction des Batiments*, 3 vols. 8vo. intended as a supplement to Blondel's *Cours d'architecture;* and *Etudes d' architecture*, 1755, fol., illustrated with twenty plates. As an engraver, he executed the plates in the latter work; also several plates for Blondel's *Architecture Francaise;* Perspective Views, *after Piranesi*, and the Temple of Venus, *after Claude.* He died at Nantes in 1814.

PAUDITZ, or PAUDITS, Christopher, a German painter, born in Lower Saxony about 1620. After receiving some instructions from an obscure German painter, he went to Amsterdam and entered the school of Rembrandt. He applied himself with great assiduity, and became one of the ablest disciples of that master. On leaving the school of Rembrandt, he was employed by the Bishop of Ratisbon, for whom he painted some historical works as well as portraits, which gained him considerable reputation. He was next taken into the employment of the Duke of Bavaria, in whose service he continued several years, and for whom he painted some of his finest works. His subjects are well composed, his coloring is vigorous, and his heads, especially of old men, are marked with dignity and expression. He was particularly excellent in portraits, in which he was much employed. Sandrart relates that his death was occasioned by the unfortunate issue of a contest with one Roster, a painter of Nuremburg, who challenged him to paint a picture of the Wolf and the Lamb, in competition with him. Pauditz showed in his work great superiority in design, force, truth and expression, which gained him the approbation of the best judges. But the majority gave the preference to the picture of Roster, because it was so highly finished that they could count the hairs of the wolf, and appreciate the delicacy of the wool. This decision so mortified Pauditz and depressed his spirits that he died soon afterwards. His works are to be found at Munich, Vienna, and other principal German cities. He marked his pictures C. P.; the latest date known is 1665, about which time he is supposed to have died.

PAUL, or de PAULIS, a Flemish engraver, who flourished about 1640. Nagler says he was born in Holland in 1598. He engraved some prints after the Flemish masters, among which are Peter Denying Christ, *after Gerard Segers;* Titian and his Mistress, *after the etching by Vandyck;* the Tooth Drawer, *after Theodore Roelants.*

PAUL, I. S., an English mezzotinto engraver, who flourished at London about 1760. He scraped some portraits, among which are Mrs. Barry the actress, *after Kettle;* Lady Georgiana Spenser and her daughter, *after Reynolds.*

PAUL, Robert, a Scotch engraver, who flourished at Glasgow about 1762. He engraved some views of that city, which are neatly executed, and bear the above date.

PAULINI. See Paolini.

PAULINI, or PAOLINI, Giacomo, a Neapolitan engraver, who flourished about 1600. He engraved some plates from his own designs, and others, which he marked with his name.

PAULUTZ, Zachariah, a Dutch painter, born at Amsterdam in 1600, and died there in 1657. He was a good portrait painter.

PAULUZZI, Stefano, a painter who flourishished at Venice, and executed some works for the churches, which are highly commended by Boschini. Lanzi says his works have deteriorated so much, perhaps from the badness of his grounds, that it is impossible to form a correct opinion of his merits. He was living in 1660.

PAULY, Nicholas, a Flemish painter, born at Antwerp in 1660. He distinguished himself as a miniature painter, and settled at Brussels. where he died in 1748.

**PAULYN**, Horatius, a Dutch painter, born at Amsterdam, according to Descamps, about 1643, though probably at an earlier period. Balkema says he died there in 1686. It is not known under whom he studied, but he excelled in painting conversations and gallant subjects, in which he occasionally gave way to a culpable breach of decorum and decency. Some of his pictures are gross enough to cause the avowed libertine to blush. His pictures are exquisitely colored, his touch exceedingly neat and delicate, with a sweetness of tone that is capable of deluding any lover of the art to admire, what modesty must compel him to detest. In some of his works he imitated the manner of Rembrandt. Though his indecent subjects lessened him in public estimation, they brought large prices from the class for whom he pandered.

**PAULYN**, Isaac, a Dutch painter, born at Amsterdam about 1630. He studied under Abraham vander Tempel, and became an eminent portrait painter, in which capacity he visited England, where he resided several years. In 1682, he returned to Holland, and settled at the Hague, where he practised his profession with great encouragement.

**PAUSIAS**, an eminent Greek painter, the son of Brietes, was a a native of Sicyon, and flourished about B. C. 450. After acquiring the elements of the art from his father, he studied encaustic painting in the school of Pamphilus, where he was the fellow disciple of Apelles and Melanthus. He was the first painter who acquired a great name for encaustic with the *cestrum*. He particularly excelled in managing the shadows. His favorite subjects were small pictures, usually of children; but he also painted large compositions. Some of his rival artists pretended that he made choice of these subjects as best suited to the slow and labored style of his execution. To contradict the calumny, and to prove that he was capable of greater exertions, he finished in a single day a large picture of the infant Hercules. Pausias was the first who introduced the custom of painting the walls and ceiling of private apartments with historical and dramatic subjects, although the practice of decorating the ceilings of temples with stars and arabesque figures, was of very ancient date.

Pausias undertook the restoration of the paintings of Polygnotus at Thespiæ, which had been greatly injured by the hand of Time. In this work he was judged inferior to the original artist, perhaps unfairly, since he contended with foreign weapons, being accustomed to using the cestrum, instead of the pencil, as he doubtless did in this instance. His most famous work was a picture of the Sacrifice of an Ox, which in the time of Pliny, was in the Hall of Pompey. The figure of the animal was foreshortened; but, to show the ox to full advantage, the artist judiciously threw its shadow upon a part of the surrounding crowd; and he added to the effect by painting a dark ox upon a light ground. In this manner he doubtless produced a very powerful contrast of shadows; and some of the modern masters have followed in the same track.

During the younger days of Pausias, he loved a native of his own city, called Glycera, who gained a livelihood by making garlands of flowers and wreaths of roses. Her skill in this art induced Pausias, probably in a loving rivalry, to compete with her; and he eventually became an admirable flower painter. A portrait of Glycera with a garland of flowers, called the Stephanopolis, was reckoned his master-piece; a copy of it was purchased at Athens, by Lucius Lucullus, at the price of two talents, about $2000. Pausanias mentions two of his paintings at Epidaurus, the one a Cupid with a lyre in his hand, the other the figure of Methe, or Drunkenness, drinking out of a glass, through which his face is seen. The Sicyonians were obliged to part with the pictures which they possessed of so distinguished an artist, to free themselves from a heavy debt. They were purchased by M. Scaurus, when ædile, and were taken to Rome to adorn the new theatre which he erected. From the observation of Horace (Sat. II. 7, 95), we may collect that the works of Pausias were well known at Rome.

**PAUSON**, a Greek painter, who flourished about B. C. 420. He seems to have been an artist of little merit, being unfavorably compared by Aristotle with Polygnotus and Dionysius. "Polygnotus," said Aristotle, "drew men more perfect than they were, Dionysius such as they really were, and Pauson worse than they were." It may be inferred, then, that Pauson degraded nature by a selection of her most vulgar and ignoble forms. His abilities seem to have been properly rated, for he was reduced to beggary, so that his poverty passed into a proverb.

**PAUTRE**, Jean le, a distinguished French engraver, born at Paris in 1617; died in 1682.—While young, he was placed under an architect, with whom he learned to draw plans and ornamental designs, in which he manifested excellent powers of invention, and astonishing facility of execution. He subsequently devoted his talents to engraving, both with the point and graver, and met with great success. His plates principally consist of architectural decorations, friezes, ceilings, vases, and other ornaments; also several historical and devout subjects. In 1677 he was chosen a member of the Royal Academy. His plates are so very numerous that Mariette estimates them at fourteen or fifteen hundred; yet, with the exception of a few prints from the designs of Paolo Farinati, they are all after his own designs—a striking proof of his industry and facility. They are usually marked with his initials I. P. or I. le P. Among them are the following:

PORTRAITS.

John le Pautre, with a border of flowers, supported by Genii. 1674. Louis XIV. in Roman attire. 1684. John Robert.

VARIOUS SUBJECTS.

A set of ten plates of the History of Moses. Twenty-two of Mythological Subjects. Twelve of Landscapes, Views of Gardens and Grottos. Six plates of Italian Fountains. Six of Friezes, Mythological Subjects. Twelve of Antique Vases. Six plates of Sea-ports and Vessels. The Sacre of Louis XIV., in the Cathedral at Rheims; in three sheets. The Baptism of the Dauphin. Two perspective Views of the Canal of Fontainbleau.

**PAUTRE**, Antoine le, a French architect, born at Paris in 1614. He was appointed architect to Louis XIV., and designed a number of edifices, among which are the Pont Neuf; the church of the Port Royal, in the Fauxbourg St. Jacques; the Hotel de Beauvais; and the wings of the palace of St. Cloud. In 1671, at the formation of the Academy of Architecture, he was chosen a member. His taste lay in the decorative branch of the art, which he carried to excess. In 1652 he published a work on architecture, which is still held in high estimation. He died in 1691, of chagrin, because Lenotre preferred Mansard to himself as architect of the Chateau de Clagny, designed to be erected for Madame de Montespan.

PAUTRE, Pierre le, a French sculptor, the son of Antoine P., born at Paris in 1660. He gained the grand prize of the Academy, and then visited Rome, where he remained fifteen years. His best work is the marble group of Æneas and Anchises, executed in 1716, which was in the gardens of the Tuileries. There are also a number of other works by him, as a marble group of the Death of Lucretia. Most of his sculptures are in bad taste. He died in 1744.

PAVIA, Giacomo, a painter born at Bologna, Feb. 18th, 1655, according to authentic documents. There is much discrepancy as to the time of his birth, and about his instruction. He is said to have studied under Antonio Crespi, who was twenty-six years his junior. Lanzi says he was the pupil of Cav. Giuseppe Maria Crespi, ten years his junior; and the Canon Luigi Crespi, the son of Giuseppe, states, in the 3d volume of the Felsina Pittrice, that he was instructed by Gio. Gioseffo dal Sole, four years his junior. He acquired considerable reputation at Bologna, and executed several works for the churches, which were admired for the fine taste displayed in their composition. The most esteemed of these is a picture of St. Anne teaching the virgin to read, in S. Silvestro; and the Nativity, in S. Giuseppe. He went to Spain, where he distinguished himself, and executed many works for the churches. He died in 1740.

PAVIA, Donato Bardo da, a native of Pavia, who flourished in Savona about 1500. He was a reputable artist. There are some of his works in that city, on which he inscribed himself, *Donatius Comes Bardus Papiensis.*

PAVIA, Lorenzo da, a native of Pavia, who, flourished at Savona about 1513. There are some of his works in that city, inscribed *Laurentius Papiensis.*

PAVIA, Giovanni di, a native of Pavia, who according to Malvasia, was a pupil of Lorenzo Costa, and executed some works for the churches in his native city and elsewhere. He flourished about 1530.

PAVON, Ignatius, an excellent engraver, who studied under Raphael Morghen. His works are well known, though little is known of him, as his life has not been written, and he may yet be living. His master died in 1833. He has copied some of the best prints of Morghen, and engraved quite a number of plates after the Italian masters. They are executed in the manner of his master, and though greatly inferior to them, they possess much merit. The following are among his best works:

Mater Amabilis; *after Sasso Ferrato.* The Virgin and infant Christ, with St John, in a landscape; *after Raffaelle*; but copied from the engraving by *R. Morghen.* La Madonna del Trono; *after Raffaelle.* La Madonna del Foligno; *do.* La Vierge au Papillon; *do.* La Vierge a l'Oiseau; *do.;* copied after *R. Morghen.* The Transfiguration; *do.; do.* The Communion of St. Jerome; *after Domenichino.* St. John writing; do.—The Magdalene; *after Schidone.* Leda; *after Correggio*, and several others *after Caracci, N. Poussin, &c.*

PAVONA, Francesco, a painter born at Udine, according to Renaldis, in 1692. He first studied under Gio. Gioseffo dal Sole. He afterwards studied at Milan, and thence proceeded to Genoa. He next went to Spain, Portugal, and Germany, at all which courts he was well received and executed many works. He resided some time at Dresden, where he married and had a family. He subsequently returned to Bologna, where he resided some time, and executed some works for the churches. Lanzi says he was an excellent painter in oil, and better in crayons. He painted many large altar-pieces, well designed and colored. He also excelled in portraits. He died at Venice in 1777.

PAYNE, John, an English engraver, born about 1606. He studied under Simon de Passe the Elder, when that artist was in England, and was the first English engraver who distinguished himself. Had his application been equal to his genius, he would have ranked among the first of his profession. But he was indolent and dissipated; and, though recommended to Charles I., he neglected his fortunes and his fame, and died in poverty, in 1647 or 1648. He engraved portraits, frontispieces, and other book plates, as well as a variety of other subjects, such as landscapes, fruit, flowers, birds, animals, &c. His plates are executed entirely with the graver, in a free, open style, that produces a pleasing effect. His greatest work was an engraving of the Royal Sovereign, a ship of the line, built in 1637; it was engraved on two plates, and when joined together was three feet long, by two feet two inches high. His portraits are his best prints, of which the following are the most esteemed:

Henry VII., prefixed to his Life by Lord Bacon. Henry VIII. Robert Devereux, Earl of Essex, with a Hat and Feather. Sir Benjamin Rudyard; *after Mytens.* Dr. Alabaster; *after Cornelius Jansen*; scarce. Hugh Broughton. Alderman Leate; *after C. Jansen*; scarce. Roger Bolton. 1632. Arthur Lake, Bishop of Chichester. Sir Edward Coke. 1629. Algernon Percy, Earl of Northumberland. George Withers, the Poet, with a hat on (for his Emblems, published in 1635). William Shakspeare. Ferdinand of Austria; *after Vandyck.* Count Ernest de Mansfield. Elizabeth, Countess of Huntingdon.

PAZZI, Pietro Antonio, an Italian engraver, born at Florence in 1706. It is not known under whom he studied, but he executed many plates of portraits and other subjects, after the Italian masters, which are held in estimation. His works are to be found in the Museo Fiorentino, Museo Capitolino, and the Museo Etrusco. Among them are the following:

PORTRAITS.

Francesco Albano, Bolognese Painter; *se ipse pinx.* Federigo Baroccio, Painter; *se ipse pinx.* Giacomo Bassano, Painter. Giovanni Bizelli, Painter; *from a picture by himself.* Andrea Boscoli, Painter, *do.*

SUBJECTS AFTER VARIOUS MASTERS.

The Holy Family; *after L. Cambiasi.* The Assumption of the Virgin; *after Raffaelle.* The Virgin and infant Christ; *after Vandyck.* St. Zanobi resuscitating a dead person; *after Betti.* St. Philip refusing the Popedom; *do.* A Sibyl; *after Crespi.*

PEACHAM, Henry, an English amateur artist, who is said to have "distinguished himself by his skill in music, painting and engraving." He was born at South Mimms, in Hertfordshire, and studied at Trinity College, Cambridge, where he took the degree of Master of Arts. He was the author of a book entitled *The Gentleman's Exercise; or an Exquisite Practice, as well for drawing all manner of Beasts in the true Portraiture, as also the making of Colors for Limning, Painting, Tricking, and Blazoning Coats of Arms;* 1630, 4to. The only work mentioned by him, was a plate of Sir Thomas Cromwell, *after Holbein.* He died about 1650.

PEACKE, Edward, an English engraver, who flourished about 1640. In conjunction with Robert Peacke, probably his brother, he executed a set of plates of friezes, and other architectural ornaments, published in that year.

PEACKE, William, an English artist, mentioned by Strutt as the engraver of two portraits, one of the Earl of Holland, and the other of the Earl of Warwick.

PEAK, James, an English engraver, born in 1732, and died in 1782. He engraved some plates of landscapes, and a few prints from his own designs, among which are the following:

A View of Waltham Abbey, in Essex. Two Landscapes; *after Pillement.* Two Views of Warwick Hall, in Cumberland, and Ferry Bridge, in Yorkshire; *after Bellers.* A Landscape, with Mercury and Battus; *after Claude.* Morning, a Landscape; *do.* A Landscape, with Ruins; *after G. Smith.* A Landscape, with a Waterfall; the companion; *do.* Four Views; *after R. Wilson.* Banditti in a rocky landscape; *after Borgognone.* The Beggars; the companion; *do.*

PEARSON, Margaret, an English lady, whose maiden name was Paterson. She married an artist by the name of Pearson, a painter on glass. She devoted herself to the business, and acquired distinction. Among other fine specimens of her skill were two sets of the Cartoons of Raffaelle, one of which was purchased by the Marquis of Lansdowne, and the other by Sir Gregory Page Turner. She died in 1823, and her husband in 1805.

PECCHIO, Domenico, a painter of Verona, born about 1700. He studied at Venice, in the school of Antonio Balestra. He afterwards devoted himself to landscapes, which he executed in a style of excellence. He died about 1760.

PECHWELL, Carl von, a German engraver, who flourished at Vienna in the latter part of the 18th century. He engraved the portrait of the Emperor Joseph II., *after P. Batoni;* and the portraits of several German princes and distinguished personages. The following subjects are particularly noticed as among his best works:

La vieille Amoureuse; *after J. Toornvliet.* The Judgment of Paris; *after A. vander Werff,* with a dedication to the Graces of Europe. Venus uncovered by a Satyr. The Magdalene in a Grotto; *after P. Batoni's* picture at Dresden. The angry Mother and her Daughter; *after P. della Vecchia.*

PECORI, Domenico Aretino, a painter of Arezzo, who studied under Don Bartolomeo della Gatta, and afterwards improved himself by studying the works of other masters. In the parochial church of his native city is a picture by him of the Virgin receiving under her mantle the people of Arezzo, who are recommended to her protection by their patron saint. Lanzi says it is a judicious composition, enriched with good architecture, the airs of the heads resembling those of Francia. He used less gilding than was usual at the time. He flourished about 1450.

PEDRALI, Giacomo, a painter of Brescia, born about 1590. It is not known under whom he studied, but he associated himself with Domenico Bruni, in conjunction with whom he executed some perspective pieces for the churches in his native city, and also at Venice, which are highly commended by Orlandi. He died about 1660.

PEDRETTI, Giuseppe, a Bolognese painter, born in 1694. He studied under Marc' Antonio Franceschini, whose manner he adopted. Soon after leaving his master, he passed through Germany to Poland, where he resided many years, in the employment of the court. He afterwards returned to his native city, and painted a great many pictures and altar-pieces for the churches, the most esteemed of which are the Martyrdom of St. Peter, in S. Petronio; Christ bearing the Cross, in S. Giuseppe; and St. Margaret, in the Annunziata. He died in 1778.

PEDRINI, Giovanni, a Milanese painter, stated by the Padre Resta to have studied under Leonardo da Vinci. Little is known of him or his works.

PEDRONI, Pietro, a painter born at Pontremoli, in the Florentine territory. He first studied at Florence, and afterwards at Parma and Rome. He executed a few excellent works for the churches at Florence, and in his native place; but in consequence of ill health, he opened an academy under the protection of the Senator Martelli, which produced many able artists. "If not a rare painter," says Lanzi, "he was at least an able master; profound in theory, and eloquent in conveying knowledge to his pupils, of whom history will treat in the ensuing age. Their success, their affection and esteem for Pedroni, is the best eulogium on him which I can transmit to posterity." He died in 1803.

PEE, Engelhart van, a Dutch painter, who flourished in the first part of the 17th century. He was an excellent portrait painter, and was patronized by the court at Munich, where he died about 1605.

There were several other artists of this name. but of little account. *Emanuel van Pee* painted subjects from low-life, and copied the works of other masters with considerable success. *John van Pee* was the son of the preceding, born at Brussels in 1640. He painted the same subjects as his father, and is said to have copied the works of the Italian masters for the picture-dealers.

Theodore van Pee was the son of Justus van P. He is said to have painted ceilings, portraits, and various subjects, with no great success. He went to England, where he dealt largely in Dutch and Flemish pictures, and realized a snug little fortune, with which he returned to the Hague, where he died, in 1747.

PEHAM, George, a German engraver, and probably a painter, who flourished at Munich from 1592 to 1604, by the dates on his prints. There are a few etchings by him, executed in a bold, free, painter-like style, from his own designs, which are variously signed, with his initials G. P., or *Georges Peham,* or *Georges Peham Monachi.* Among them is one of Neptune rising from the Sea, and one of Hercules and Anteus.

PEINS. See PENZ.

PEIROLERI, PIETRO, an Italian engraver, born at Turin about 1738. Little is known of him except his prints. Nagler gives a list of twenty prints by him, of which the following are the principal. He was living in 1777.

Portrait of the Fornarina; *after Raffaelle*. Portrait of Raffaelle; *do*. Philip de Champagne; copied from *Edelinck*. The Holy Family; *after Scarsellino*. The Finding of Moses; *after Lazzarini*. The Roman Charity; *do*. Abraham's Offering; *after Bellucci*. Jupiter and Calisto; *after Amiconi*. Zephyrus and Flora; *do.*; and others, *after Rembrandt*, *Mieris*, *Nogari*, *Beaumont*, *and C. Ruthart*.

MP *fec.* PELAIS, MICHAEL, an engraver of whom little is known. There are some prints signed *Palais, fec.*, and others after the younger Palma and Federigo Zuccaro, marked with a monogram of his initials, M. P. *fec.*, which are attributed to him. His manner approaches that of Cornelius Cort, and he is supposed to have flourished at Rome about 1625, as some of his prints are dated at that city. He also engraved the portraits of Cardinal d'Ossat, and J. de Gastebois.

PELÉE, PETER, a Swiss engraver, born at Courtedoux, in the canton of Berne, and studied under von Schenker. Nagler mentions the following prints by him: The Evangelist St. John, *after Domenichino;* the President Duranti, *after Delaroche*; several Portraits and Vignettes for the works of Voltaire and Rousseau, *after Desenne* and *Deveria*. He was living in 1838.

PELEGRET, THOMAS, an eminent Spanish historical painter, born at Toledo at an uncertain time. After learning the elements of the art in his native place, according to Palomino, he went to Italy, and studied successively with Baldassare da Siena, and Polidoro da Caravaggio; from the last he derived his admirable chiaro-scuro, and he imitated his manner. He returned to Spain in the time of Charles V., established himself at Saragossa, and acquired considerable reputation for his frescos, but more for his black crayon drawings (*en grisaille*.) He had a fertile invention, was well versed in perspective, and, above all, was an excellent designer; which, together with the novelty of his works, made them highly prized by artists and amateurs. His drawings were purchased with avidity by painters, sculptors, decorators, and goldsmiths. He is said to have been an excellent fresco painter, but the only examples remaining are some pictures in the monastery of Santa Engracia, at Saragossa, executed in the manner of Caravaggio. His other works have perished. He instructed many pupils, and among them was Pedro de las Cuevas, who assisted him in painting the sacristy of the Cathedral of Huesca, and some other works. He died at the age of 84 years, but neither the time of his birth or death are known; but from the facts above mentioned, he must have been born about 1516, and died about 1600, as Caravaggio died in 1543, and Cuevas was born in 1548. "With him," says the historian, "died the art of painting chiaro-scuro in Spain."

PELHAM, PETER, an English engraver, born about 1684, and died about 1738. He executed quite a number of portraits in mezzotinto, among which are the following:

King George I.; *after Kneller*. King George II.; *do*. Anne, consort of the Prince of Orange; *do*. Oliver Cromwell; *after Walker*. Thomas Holles, Duke of Newcastle. Robert, Viscount Molesworth; *after Gibson*. John, Lord Carteret; *after Kneller*. James Gibbs, Architect; *after Hysing*. Peter Paul Rubens; *after Rubens*. Edward Cooper; *after vander Vaart*. Dr. Edmund, Bishop of London; *after Murray*.

PELHAM, J. C., was the son of the preceding, born in 1721. He painted history and portraits, with so little reputation, that his works are scarcely known.

PELKIN, CORNELIUS, a Dutch engraver, who flourished at Middleburg about 1663. He engraved some plates for the booksellers in a very indifferent style.

PELLEGRINI, ANTONIO, a painter born at Venice in 1674. He studied under Sebastiano Ricci. He was one of those fortunate men who acquire a greater reputation than their merits deserve. On leaving Ricci, it is said that he received some instructions from Paolo Pagani; at all events, that artist recommended him to Angelo Cornaro, for whom he executed some frescos, which gained him considerable applause, and laid the foundation of his fame. At the invitation of the Duke of Manchester, he went to England, where he decorated the palace of that nobleman, and others of the English nobility, for which he was roundly paid. In 1719 he went to Paris, where he was employed in embellishing the celebrated Hall of the Mississippi, and was chosen a member of the Royal Academy. He was next employed at the courts of the Electors Palatine and Brunswick. He afterwards returned to Venice, where he followed his profession with great success till his death in 1741. His wife was Angelica Carriera, sister to the celebrated Rosalba. Lanzi says, "the surprising success he met with in some of the most civilized kingdoms in Europe, is to be attributed to the decline of the art, and to the lively and mannered style he assumed, which procured him a welcome reception every where. He may be pronounced an artist of some ingenuity, facility, and sprightly conception, but he was not well grounded in the art, and he expressed his ideas with so little decision, that the objects appear to float in a kind of half existence, between visible and invisible. He was so superficial a colorist, that even in his own time, it was said his works would not continue half a century." His best works are the ceiling of the church of the Capuchins, and that of San Moisè, at Venice. In the first he represented the Israelites gathering Manna, and in the second, the Brazen Serpent. He executed many works in oil, in the same feeble and languid manner of coloring.

PELLEGRINI, FRANCESCO, a Ferrarese painter mentioned by Barotti, who flourished about 1740. He studied under Gio. Battista Cozza, and executed a number of works for the churches of Ferrara, among which is a picture of the Last Supper, in S. Paolo; and another of St. Bernardo, in the Cathedral.

PELLEGRINI, FELICE, a painter, born at Perugia in 1567. He studied under Federigo Baroccio, under whose able instruction he became a correct and skilful designer. He was invited to Rome by Clement VIII. to assist in the works going on in the Vatican. On his return to his native city he executed some good works for the churches. He died in 1630.

PELLEGRINI, VINCENZIO, was the brother of

Felice P., born at Perugia in 1575. He also studied in the school of Baroccio, and painted several pictures for the churches of Perugia, which Lanzi says appear dry and dead, and do not partake much of the style of his master. He was called *Il Pittor Bello*, for the beauty of his person, not that of his paintings. He died in 1612.

PELLEGRINI, Girolamo, a painter of Rome, who flourished there, according to Zanetti, in 1674. None of his works are mentioned at Rome, but he was employed at Venice, where he executed several frescos on a large scale for the churches, which Lanzi says indicates a painter sufficiently elevated, though not very select, varied, or spirited in his forms.

PELLEGRINI, Andrea, a Milanese painter, who flourished in the last part of the 16th century. He is commended by Lomazzo, and executed some works for the churches, particularly the choir of S. Girolamo.

PELLEGRINI, Pellegrino, an eminent Milanese painter and architect, the cousin of the preceding, born about 1570. After acquiring considerable reputation, he was invited to the court of Madrid, where he was employed both as painter and architect. He executed some works in the Escurial which are highly commended by Palomino. He died in 1634.

PELLEGRINI, Lodovica, a Milanese lady, who, according to Morigia, was very celebrated for her works in embroidery. She wrought not only fruit and flowers, but scripture histories. Lanzi says "she was the Minerva of her time. She devoted herself wholly to her needle, and embroidered the great pallium (vestment), and other sacred furniture, preserved in the sacristy of the cathedral, and still exhibited to strangers with other curious specimens of ancient learning and the arts. In the new Guide of Milan, she is called Antonia P." She was living in 1626.

PELLEGRINO, da Bologna. See Pellegrino Tibaldi.

PELLEGRINO, da Modena. See Pellegrino Munari.

PELLEGRINO, di San Daniello. See Udine.

PELLET, David, a French engraver, whose name is affixed to a plate representing Louis XIII. when young, on horseback, with the portrait of Henry IV., and Mary de Medicis, in small ovals at the top. It is executed with the graver in a neat, but formal style.

PELLETIER, Jean, a French engraver, born at Paris about 1736. He engraved quite a number of plates after the Dutch, Flemish, and French masters. They are executed with the graver in a neat, clear, and pleasing style. Among them are the following. His wife also engraved some plates, two of which are *after A. Ostade*, and one *after Wouwerman*.

The Watering-place; *after Berghem.* Ruins and Figures; *do.* The Fish Market; *after Pierre.* The Green Market; *do.* Diana reposing; *after Boucher.* The Rape of Europa; *do.* Two Pastoral subjects; *do.* The Union of Design and Painting; *after Natoire.* Young Bacchus; *after C. Vanloo.* The Travellers; *after Wouwerman.* Ladies going to the Chase; *do.* The Tipplers; *after Ostade.*

PELLI, Marco, an Italian engraver, born at Venice about 1696. There are no particulars concerning him. He engraved some plates of saints, a few portraits, and some other subjects, among which are a Charge of Cavalry, *after Borgognone*, and a Landscape, *after D. B. Zilotti*, marked *M. Pelli, exc.*

PELLIER, Nicolas François, a French engraver, born at Besançon in 1782.—There are some plates of landscapes by him, engraved with the point in a spirited and pleasing manner, from his own designs, marked with the above monogram. He died in 1804.

PELLINI, Andrea, a painter born at Cremona, of whom little is known, except some works at Milan. He is supposed to have been a scholar of Bernardino Campi. Lanzi says that "Pellini, though unknown in his native city of Cremona, is celebrated at Milan for his Descent from the Cross, in the church of S. Eustorgio." This is a grand composition, correctly designed and well colored, dated 1595.

PELLINI, Marc' Antonio, a painter of Pavia, born, according to Orlandi, in 1664. He first studied under Tommaso Gatti, at Pavia, and afterwards visited Bologna and Venice for improvement. He executed a few works for the churches in his native city, but did not rise above mediocrity. He died in 1760, at the great age of 96 years.

PEMBROKE, Thomas, an English historical painter, of little note, born in 1702, and died in 1730. He was a protegé of the Earl of Bath, for whom Walpole says he painted several pictures.

PEN, or PENN, Hispel, a supposed German engraver, to whom the Padre Orlandi erroneously attributes some prints, marked with the monogram of Hans Sebald Beham. Strutt, and others, have been led into the same error. It is satisfactorily ascertained that the prints in question were executed by Beham; and they are included in the lists of his works.

PEN, Jacob, a Dutch painter, mentioned by Balkema, who went to England, and was employed by Charles II. He says that he composed with intelligence, and to correct drawing added beautiful coloring. He died in 1674.

PENALOSA, Juan de, a Spanish historical painter, born at Baeza in 1581. He was one of the ablest scholars of Pablo de Cespedes at Cordova, and assiduously imitated his style. He painted some works for the churches and convents, but more for the collections. His picture of St. Barbe, in the cathedral at Cordova, is said to be a magnificent performance, executed entirely in the style of his master. He died in 1636.

PENCHARD, J., a Dutch engraver, who flourished at Leyden about 1678. He was chiefly employed by the booksellers. He engraved the anatomical plates for the works of Reg. de Graaf, with the portrait of the author, published at Leyden in 1678.

PENCHAUD, Michel Robert, an eminent French architect, born at Poitiers in 1782. He studied under his father, who was distinguished in the art, and assisted him in the chateau de Verrière, belonging to the Duc de Mortemart; and the chateau de Dissais, erected for M. de Sainte Aulaire, Bishop of Poitiers. Penchaud afterwards visited Paris, and studied under Percier and Fontaine with such assiduity, that in 1799 he was appointed designer to the Council of Civil Buildings. In 1803 he was made director of the public works at Marseilles; and was afterwards appointed head of the Department of the Mouths of the Rhone. He was employed for many years in embellishing the city of Marseilles with promenades, fountains, and public monuments, which gained him great reputation. During his engrossing cares, he found time to write a number of excellent memorials relating to art, which he furnished to the Academy of Inscriptions. The Institute awarded him a gold medal for a memorial on the Antiquités du Midi. Among his principal edifices, were the grand hospital on the Island of Ratonneau; a triumphal arch at the entrance of Marseilles, with a number of buildings in that city; the Palais de Justice at Aix; and a beautiful church at St. Remy. Penchaud died at Paris in 1832.

PENNACCHI, Pietro Maria, a painter of Trevigi, who, according to Zanetti, flourished at Venice about 1520. He painted some works for the churches at Venice and Murano, which Lanzi says are more excellent in coloring than design.

PENNEMAKERS, the Recollet, a Flemish artist of whom little is known. Balkema says he was a scholar of Rubens. In the Museum of Antwerp, there is a picture of the Ascension, attributed to him.

PENNENSUS, F., an engraver, probably an Italian, by whom there are some spirited etchings of devout subjects after the Italian masters, and from his own designs, marked with his name, among which are the Holy Family, with St. Catherine, and an Angel in the air, *after Parmiggiano;* and the Marriage of St. Catherine, from his own design. There is a fine expression in his heads, but he was negligent and incorrect in designing the extremities.

PENNEY, N., a French engraver, by whom there are some plates of devout subjects, from his own designs, executed with the graver in a very neat style, but without much effect, among which is one of the Virgin appearing to St. Bartholomew. They are marked *N. Penney, fecit.*

PENNI, Giovanni Francesco, called Il Fattore. This eminent painter was born at Florence in 1488. He went to Rome when a boy, and entered the studio of Raffaelle, in the capacity of a servant, as some say, but more probably, as *an apprentice*, which Il Fattore signifies. At all events, his talents, assiduity, integrity, and urbane deportment gained for him the confidence and affection of his master, who made him his most intimate disciple, took especial pains to instruct him, and confided to him the management of his household affairs. Had he derived his appellation from this last circumstance, it would have been Il Maggiordomo, *the Steward.* He became one of his principal scholars, and assisted him more than any other in his cartoons and his tapestries. The first work on which he was employed by Raffaelle was in decorating the Loggie of the Vatican, from his designs, where Giovanni da Udine, Pierino del Vaga, and other excellent artists were associated with him. There he executed the histories of Abraham and Isaac in such an admirable manner, as gave entire satisfaction to his master. Raffaelle conceived such an affection for him that he made him joint heir with Giulio Romano, to his estate. After the death of Raffaelle, he was employed conjointly with Giulio Romano, in finishing the frescos of the Histories of Constantine, in the saloon afterwards called after the name of that Emperor. Among other works left incomplete by his master, which he assisted in finishing, is the Assumption of Monte Luci in Perugia, the lower part of which, with the apostles, was painted by Giulio, and the upper part, which abounds with the graces of Raffaelle, by Penni. He had also the principal share in the history of Cupid and Psyche, in the Farnesina. Of his own compositions, those executed in fresco at Rome, have mostly perished, and he painted so few pictures in oil that they are seldom to be met with. Soon after the death of Raffaelle, some coldness between him and his co-heir, Giulio, caused them to separate. After this, he decorated the Chigi Palace in a manner so nearly resembling Raffaelle, that they might easily have been mistaken for the works of that master. He went to Naples at the invitation of the Marquis del Vasto, taking with him his admirable copy in oil of the Transfiguration of Raffaelle, which he sold to that nobleman, and he executed for him some considerable works. He died there in the prime of life in 1528. He possessed an admirable taste for design, which he imbibed from his instructor, and his execution was facile and graceful. He particularly excelled in landscape and architecture, with the advantages of which, in embellishing historical painting, he was well acquainted. Kügler says that Penni could work well, only when under the instruction of Raffaelle; and that when left alone he was weak and ineffective. This is contrary to the concurrent testimony of the best Italian authors, and it is unfair to judge from the few remains of his works. Lanzi says that, notwithstanding the shortness of his career at Naples, he greatly contributed to the improvement of art in that city. Kügler and Passavant conjecture that the celebrated Madonna del Passeggio, in the Bridgewater Collection, attributed to Raffaelle, was executed by Penni.

PENNI, Luca, was the brother of the preceding, born at Florence about 1500. Orlandi says he studied in the school of Raffaelle, which Lanzi thinks highly probable. According to Vasari, he united himself to Pierino del Vaga, and worked with him in the churches at Lucca, Genoa, and other cities; that he afterwards accompanied Il Rosso into France, and ultimately passed into England, where he was employed for some time by Henry VIII. On his return to Italy, he is said to have quitted painting for engraving. There are quite a number of prints, attributed to him.—There are mostly after the works of Il Rosso and Primaticcio, and usually marked with one of the accompanying monograms. Among them are the following:

Two Satyrs presenting Wine to Bacchus; *after Il Rosso.* Leda drawing out the Arrow from Cupid's Quiver; *do.* Susanna and the Elders; *do.* Abraham sacrificing Isaac; *after Primaticcio.* The Marriage of St. Catherine; *do.* Penelope at work, surrounded by her women; *do.*

PENNING, Nicholas Louis, a Dutch painter, born at the Hague in 1764. He was a scholar of

Thierry vander Aa, and painted landscapes, marines, and interiors of stables, with horses, with some success. He also executed finished drawings, which are held in considerable estimation. He died at the Hague in 1818.

PENNONE, Rocco, a distinguished Lombard architect, who flourished at Genoa in the 16th century. Milizia does not mention his instructor, but he warmly commends his abilities, as evinced in the enlargement of the government palace at Genoa, particularly in the arrangement of a grand portico, flanked by two courts, which, although differing in size, satisfy the eye by their perfect symmetry. These courts are surrounded by two orders of galleries; the first supported by Doric, the second by Ionic columns. Among the other works of Pennone, was a part of the church of S. Sacramento, which he completed after the designs of Galeazzo Alessi.

PENNY, Edward, an English painter, born at Knutsford, in Cheshire, in 1714. He went early in life to London, and studied under Hudson, on leaving whom he went to Rome, and became the pupil of Marco Benefiali. On his return to England, he joined the Society of Artists, of which he was for some time Vice President. At the foundation of the Royal Academy, he was one of the original members, and was appointed the first Professor of Painting. This situation he continued to fill with great respectability, and he delivered an annual course of lectures, till 1783, when ill health compelled him to resign the office. About this time he went to reside at Chiswick, where, having previously married a lady of fortune, he lived in quiet retirement till his death in 1791. He was principally employed in painting small portraits in oil, which were admired. He also painted a few historical works and fancy pictures, some of which have been engraved; the principal of these is the Death of General Wolfe.

PENOZZI, B., an engraver on wood, mentioned by Papillon, who does not specify any of his works.

PENSABEN, Frà Marco, and Frà Marco Maraveia, his assistant, two old painters of the order of the Dominicans at Venice, who exercised their talent at Trevigi in 1520 and 1521. Lanzi says Pensaben was an artist of singular merit, wholly unknown in the history of art till the P. M. Federici discovered some documents relating to him in the convent of the Dominicans at Treviso, whither he had been invited from Venice. "In this style, partaking of the ancient and modern taste is a large picture of St. Nicholas, in a church of the Dominicans at Treviso; in which the cupola, the columns, and the perspective, with a throne, on which is seated the Virgin, with the Infant Jesus, surrounded by saints standing, the steps ornamented by a harping seraph, all discover the composition of Bellini. It was painted by P. Marco Pensaben, assisted by P. Marco Maraveia, both Dominican priests, engaged for this purpose from Venice." Nothing further is known of their works. Pensaben was born about 1485, and died in 1530.

PENSIERI, Battista, an Italian engraver, who flourished in the latter part of the 16th century. He was a native of Parma, and is usually called Baptista Parmensis, from his signature. Zani calls his name Battista Pensieri da Parma. He says he was a designer, engraver, and a seller of books and prints; he gives four inscriptions from his prints, as follows: *Romæ Battista da Parma*, 1583,—*Battista Pensieri Parmensis fecit Romæ* 1590,—*Baptistæ pensier parmensis formis*,—*Baptista panzera formis*, 1601. He chiefly resided at Rome, where he engraved several plates after various masters, and others from his own designs, executed in a style resembling that of Cornelius Cort. Among others are the following: The Portrait of Philip II., King of Spain. 1589. The Virgin and Infant appearing to St. John, *after Baroccio, Baptista Parmensis, fec.* 1588. The Baptism of Christ. *Bapt. Parmensis, del.* The Chastity of Joseph. 1593. The Crucifixion, in two sheets, *Bapt. Parmensis, formis.* 1584.

GP or GP PENTZ, or PEINS, George Gregory, an eminent German painter and engraver, born at Nuremberg in 1500. His name is variously written George, or Gregory, Pentz, Peins, Penez, and Pens. On the plate of the portraits of himself and wife he signs himself *Gregori Peins*, and on that of the Taking of Carthage, *Georgius Pentz*. He studied painting and engraving under Albert Durer. On leaving that master he went to Italy, where he acquired a correct and tasteful design, which distinguishes him from the cotemporary artists of his country. Little is known of his works as a painter. Huber says there are some of his pictures in the Imperial Gallery at Vienna, where they are greatly admired. His prints are numerous and highly esteemed.—His plates are executed with the utmost neatness and delicacy, and though they are wrought with great care and precision, they have nothing of the stiffness and formality which distinguish the productions of the artists of his time. His drawing is correct, and the character of his heads is finely expressed. The greater part of his plates are of small size; hence he is reckoned among the *little masters*, as such artists are termed by connoisseurs, although perfectly competent to execute plates on a large scale, as is seen in his print of the Taking of Carthage, after Giulio Romano. While in Italy, in conjunction with Marc' Antonio, he engraved several plates after the works of Raffaelle. His style of engraving resembles the best manner of Raimondi, though his plates are more delicately wrought and finished. He usually marked them with a monogram of his initials, G. and P., joined together as above.

PORTRAITS.

The Artist and his Wife, on the same plate, inscribed *Imago Gregori Peins. Imago Duxore Gregori Peins.* John Frederick, Elector of Saxony, inscribed *Spes meus in Deo est.* 1543; scarce.

BIBLE SUBJECTS FROM HIS OWN DESIGNS.

Two small prints—Job tempted, and Esther before Ahasuerus. Two, Judith in the Tent of Holofernes, and Judith with his Head. Two, the Judgment of Solomon, and Solomon's Idolatry. Two, Lot and his Daughters, and Susanna and the Elders. Four, of the History of Joseph. 1544. Seven, of the History of Tobit. 1543. (Considered among his best.) Two of the Merciful Samaritan, and the Conversion of St. Paul. 1545. The Four Evangelists. The seven works of Mercy; circular. Twenty-five plates of the Life and Miracles of Christ; very fine.

VARIOUS SUBJECTS.

Two, Tarquin and Lucretia, and the Death of Lucretia. Cephalus and Procris. Medea and Jason. The Death of Dido. Thomyris causing the head of Cyrus to be put in a vessel of blood. The Death of Virginia. Mutius Scevola putting his hand into the Brasier. Marcus Curtius precipitating himself into the gulf. The Death of Regulus. Sophonisba drinking the Poison.—Artemisia drinking the Ashes of her Husband. (Both highly esteemed by amateurs.) The Triumph of Bacchus. A set of six plates of the Triumphs of Human Life. The Five Senses. The Seven Liberal Arts. The Seven Mortal Sins. The taking of Carthage; *after Giulio Romano*, inscribed *Georgius Pentz Pictor Nuremberg faciebat, anno* 1549; an admirable specimen of his great ability.

PENZEL, John George, a German painter and engraver, born at Hersbruck, near Nuremberg, in 1754, and died at Leipsic in 1809. He first studied under Schellenberg at Winterthur, and afterwards at Dresden. Nothing further is said of him as a painter, and he soon devoted himself entirely to engraving. He executed many plates for the publishers at Dresden. He also engraved many of Chodowiecki's designs.

PEONIUS. See Daphnis.

PEPIN, or PEPYN, Martin, a Flemish painter, born at Antwerp in 1574, as appears from the inscription on his portrait hereafter mentioned. It is not known under whom he studied, but after learning the principles of the art, he went to Italy, where he is said to have so much distinguished himself by his grandeur of composition, correctness of design, and vigorous tone of coloring, that Rubens himself regarded him with jealousy, and dreaded his return to Antwerp, fearing his reputation would suffer from his rivalship. The absurdity of this story is evident. Pepin resided most of his life at Rome, yet his name is unknown in Italy. In the church of the hospital at Antwerp, are two of his works, which are highly extolled; they are altar-pieces, with folding doors, as was customary with some of the old Flemish masters; the centre picture of one represents the Baptism of St. Augustine, and the laterals on the doors, that saint giving alms to the poor, and curing the sick; the other is a similar work, representing St. Elizabeth giving alms to a group of miserable objects, who are struggling to approach her. His portrait, by Vandyck, in the private collection of the King of Holland, is described by C. J. Nieuwenhuys, in his Catalogue; it is inscribed *Me Pictorem Pictor pinxit D. Ant. Vandyck Eques illustris. A. D.* 1632. Æt me lviii. Nieuwenhuys, who saw several of his pictures, says that his talents were but second rate, that his first manner partook of the school of Otho Venius, but that the works he executed in Italy are in a more elevated style. He died at Rome in 1641.

SP or S.P.F PERAC, Etienne du, a French painter, engraver, and architect, born at Paris about 1540. He went to Italy when he was young, and resided some years at Rome, where he made many designs from the vestiges of ancient architecture, and views of Tivoli and Frascati, which he engraved and published at Rome in 1569, 1573, and 1575. On his return to France he was appointed architect to Henry IV., and painted some architectural pieces for the palace at Fontainbleau. He also executed some etchings after Michael Angelo, Raffaelle, and other Italian masters, as well as from his own designs. Nagler gives a list of twenty-nine prints by him; the latest is dated 1583. Zani says he died in 1601.

PERANDA, Santo, a Venetian painter, born in 1566. According to Ridolfi, he first studied under the younger Palma, and afterwards with Leonardo Corona, of Murano. In his first performances, he followed the prompt and hasty manner of Palma; but he afterwards went to Rome, where, by diligently studying the antique and the works of the great masters, he formed a style of his own, more finished and correct. On his return to Venice he improved his coloring, by contemplating the works of Titian, Tintoretto, and Veronese, so that he became as accomplished in coloring, as he was before in design. He executed many works for the churches and public edifices, and was employed in decorating the ducal palaces at Venice, Mirandola, and Modena, with various subjects from history. "His usual manner," says Lanzi, "very much resembles Palma, while in the large histories, which he produced at Venice and Mirandola, he appears in a more practical character of his own. Yet he was of a more slow and reflective turn, and more studious of art, qualities that, in the decline of age, led him to adopt a very delicate and labored manner. He was not ambitious of equalling his cotemporaries in the number of his works, but his aim was to surpass them in correctness, nor did he any where succeed better in his object than in his Christ taken down from the Cross, in the church of San Procolo, at Venice." He had several disciples, among whom was Matteo Ponzone. He died at Venice in 1638.

PERCELLES. See Parcelles.

PERCIER, Charles, an eminent French architect, was the son of a colonel of dragoons, born at Paris in 1764. His name and works are so intimately associated with those of his friend and colleague, Pierre Louis François Fontaine, that the reputation of the one is inseparable from that of the other. Percier was first instructed in the elements of the art by an obscure designer named Poirson. In 1783 he entered the school of the architect Peyre, and afterwards studied under the elder Gisors, an architect of considerable reputation. In 1786, he gained the grand prize of the French Academy, and went with the royal pension to Rome, where his friendship with Fontaine first commenced. He also became acquainted with Flaxman, Canova, and other artists who subsequently rose to eminence. During their residence at Rome, Percier and Fontaine made the drawings which form the subject of their first publication; *Palais, Maisons, et autres Edifices modernes, dessinés à Rome*, Paris, 1798, folio; illustrated with 100 plates, beautifully delineated and engraved in outline. Previous to the publication of this work, however, and for some time after their return to Paris, they were obliged to contend with difficulties; the agitated state of public affairs being exceedingly unfavorable for their success.—With laudable energy and perseverance they commenced making designs for various articles of ornamental furniture and manufacture; and their careful study and superior taste soon brought their talents into notice. Various decorations, executed by them at Malmaison for the First Consul and Madame Bonaparte, secured for them the powerful patronage of Napoleon; and soon after his gaining the Imperial Crown, they were employed to restore, complete, and embellish, the two palaces of the Tuileries and the Louvre. The latter work was exceedingly extensive and complicated, occupying their attention for a number of years, until some time after the restoration of the Bourbons. They enjoyed imperial and royal patronage, with a very high reputation, for many years, but executed only a few original works; and their fame as practical architects is consequently merged, to a great extent, in that of the original authors of the works which they restored. They erected, however, a few edifices, as the arch in the Place du Carrousel, before the east façade of the Tuileries; the Chapelle Expiatoire in memory of Louis XVI.; and the regular and handsome line of houses termed the Rue Rivoli.

Percier and Fontaine gained great reputation from their publications, among which was the *Recueil de Decorations Interieures, contenant tout ce qui a rapport à l'Ameublement*, Paris, 1812, fol. This was a collection of designs for rooms and various articles of furniture in the prevailing style, which Percier outlived. About the same time, they published a series of views of Roman villas with their gardens, entitled *Choix des plus belles Maisons de Plaisance de Rome et ses environs;* also two magnificent works, one representing the ceremonies of the coronation of Napoleon, and the other those which took place upon his marriage with Maria Louisa. There is another work attributed to Percier, which seems not to be generally circulated, entitled, *Parallèle entre plusiers Residences des Soverains de France, d'Allemagne, de Suede, de Russie, et d'Italie*, Paris, 1833, illustrated with thirty-eight plates. Charles Percier died in 1838.

PEREDA, Antonio, an eminent Spanish painter, born at Valladolid in 1599. He first studied under Pedro de las Cuevas, and showed so much ability that he was taken under the protection of Don Francisco de Texada, who sent him to Madrid, where he had an opportunity of studying the works of the great masters in the Royal collections. At the age of eighteen he produced a picture of the Immaculate Conception, in which the Virgin appeared on a Throne of Clouds, supported by angels, executed so admirably that no one could believe it the work of so young an artist. The reputation he acquired by this performance induced the Duke de Olivarez, who had the direction of the works going on in the palace of the Retiro, to employ him and place him among the artists of the highest rank. He performed his part to the satisfaction of his patron, and was munificently rewarded. He acquired great reputation, and is said to have executed many works for the churches at Madrid, Toledo, Alcala, Cuenca, and Valladolid. He also painted much for individuals, and no collection was considered complete without a specimen of Pereda. It is also said that he was a universal artist, painting history, familiar life, vases, tapestry, musical instruments, and other objects of still-life. His pictures were well designed, his drawing correct, and his coloring rich and glowing, in the Venetian style, with an admirable *impasto*. Few of his works are known to remain at the present day. There are two in the Royal Gallery at Madrid, one of which represents St. Jerome meditating on the Last Judgment; one of Christ asleep on the Cross, with flowers and skulls, in the collection of Marshal Soult; one of St. Anthony and Christ in the Esterhazy Gallery in Vienna, and three or four in the gallery at Munich. He died at Madrid in 1669.

P PEREGRINI, da Cesena, or Pellegrino da Cesio, an Italian goldsmith, engraver, and worker in *niello*, who flourished in the latter part of the fifteenth and first part of the sixteenth centuries. He is one of those artists about whom and whose works there is a great deal of conjecture, and very little that is certain. Bartsch gives a descriptive account of ten prints by him (Peintre Graveur, tom. xiii.), five of which are marked with the monogram as above, three defective in the part where the monogram should be, and two have the additional letters O. P. D. C. These letters are interpreted by Duchesne *Opera Peregrini da Cesina*, and Zani says he read on some prints by him, *Opus Peregrini de Ces.* Duchesne discovered his name on some admirable works by him in *niello*, which he describes (*Essai sur les Nielles*). Ottley describes ten prints, which he supposes to be by the artist who used the above marks, but he does not mention Peregrini. Nagler, from these and various other authorities, gives a list of sixty-four pieces, which he attributes to him, as follows:

*List of Peregrini's Prints, from Nagler.*

[Where it is stated that the print is marked with the letter P., it is to be understood in the form indicated above; a P. crossed in the middle, as an abbreviation.]

1. Abraham loading an Ass for his journey to Mount Moriah. 2. Abraham, Isaac, and two servants, on their way to the Mount. 3. Abraham and Isaac on the Mount, the servants sitting below. 4. Abraham with a knife and torch, Isaac bearing a bundle of wood. 5. Abraham about to immolate Isaac, is prevented by an Angel; the head of a Ram is seen at the right hand corner. 6. David conquering Goliah; a very fine plate. According to Duchesne, it is probably by Peregrini. 7. Judith with the head of Holofernes in her left hand. This print has not Peregrini's mark, but the words *lvde te* on a scrap of paper. 8. The Holy Virgin with the Infant on a throne, attended by Sts. Paul and Francis d'Assisi. Peregrini's mark in the centre. 9. The Baptism of Christ. In the foreground to the right and left are St. Stephen and St. Francis. 10. The Resurrection of our Lord, signed DE—OPVS—PEREGRINI—CES. An impression of the unfinished plate, in which some parts of the figure of Christ are white, was sold in Sir Mark Sykes's sale, in 1824, for about £20 sterling. 11. The Annunciation, in two small medallions. 12. John the Baptist with the Cross, on which is a medallion with the Lamb, and the words ECE AGNUS. Duchesne is of opinion that this is the work of Peregrini. 13. St. Sebastian standing by a Tree, his hands tied above his head. 14. St. Jerome kneeling before a Crucifix, the lion behind him. Peregrini's mark in the margin. 15. St. Roch. On the right hand the first person of the Trinity blessing him. Attributed to Peregrini by Duchesne. 16. St. Margaret seated on a large winged Dragon, holding in one hand a cornucopia, and in the other a cake. In the dark back-ground are four trees, and the mark P. Bartsch calls the subject *Providence.* 17. The Triumph of Neptune; marked O. P. D. C. (*Opera Peregrini da Cesena*). 18. Minerva, with Lance and Shield; on the latter the head of Medusa. Duchesne considers this a work of Peregrini, though it has not his mark. 19. The Triumph of Mars. On a globe, surmounted by a figure of Cupid, is the letter P. Nagler notices that on an early impression of this subject it is difficult to distinguish the figure on the shield of Mars; on a later, it is seen plainly. The back-ground is very dark. A second impression sold in Sir Mark Sykes's sale for £31. 20. A Sacrifice in honor of Mars. Bartsch describes this among the prints of the old Italian masters, P. G. tom. xiii. p. 139, No. 69; but Duchesne considers it to be the work of Peregrini. An impression sold in Sir Mark Sykes's sale for 17 guineas. 20*b*. A Muse playing on a Flute. Around her are other instruments. Attributed to Perigrini by Duchesne. 21. A Muse playing on the Lyre, with other musical instruments lying around her. Attributed to Peregrini by Duchesne. 22. A winged Cupid standing on a Vase, which is ornamented with four figures of

Children; attributed to Perigrini. 23. Two Cupids by a Monument. Duchesne thinks it is by Marc' Antonio. 24. Psyche at the foot of a Tree, Cupid behind her; in the back-ground, on the sea, is a monster about to devour her. At the bottom is a mark which resembles that of Peregrini. 25. Leda and the Swan. According to Duchesne, by Peregrini. In the centre is a mark resembling Peregrini's. 26. A Nymph bound to a Tree by a Satyr and a Faun. 27. A Triton caressing a Nymph. The workmanship of this niello is fine, and resembles that of Peregrini. 28. A Woman with three Men and a Satyr. Duchesne considers it to be by Peregrini. 29. Hercules strangling Anteus. Attributed to Peregrini. 30. Hercules and Dejanira. HERCVLE—DEJANIRA—with Peregrini's mark. 29*b*. Hercules combating the Hydra. With Peregrini's mark. 30*b*. Hercules killing the Hydra. Duchesne says certainly by Peregrini. 31. Orpheus with a Guitar, surrounded by Animals. On the margin the letters O. P. D. C. 32. Arion on the Dolphin; in the back-ground the ship from which he was cast. Duchesne is certain that it is by Peregrini. 33. Arion on the Dolphin, with a violin in his left hand, arriving at Piræus. 34. Diomede naked, armed with helmet and shield, holding the Palladium in his left hand. O. P. D. C. in the margin. 35. Mutius Scævola before Porsenna, holding his hand over the fire. The letter P. by the throne. 36. An Apotheosis. On the right hand a naked Man with a Helmet before an Altar, on which is an Eagle, and a Woman on the left preparing a libation. In the centre of the margin the letter P. 37. A Standard bearer, with Peregrini's mark, P., by the trunk of a tree. Ottley thinks this piece was copied from the drawing of a German master. 38. Two Knights fighting. Duchesne thinks it is by Peregrini. 39. Two naked Men fighting with Boughs of Trees. Attributed to Peregrini. 40. Three Women dancing. In the margin below, the mark P. 41. Three Children dancing. At the bottom the mark P. 42. An Allegory of War; three naked Men with helmets on their heads, &c. The mark P. in the margin. 43. An Allegory of Union. A king on a throne; a young man and two soldiers before him. On the throne is written VN. FO. DI. F. Duchesne interprets these *Un Fondamento di Fraternità*. 44. An Allegory of Fame. Considered by Duchesne the work of Peregrini. 45. An Allegory of Seamanship. In the margin O. P. D. C. 46. An allegory of Plenty; same mark. 47. A Woman with a Sword and an Apple. Bartsch, tom. xiii. p. 206, No. 2. 48. A naked Man sitting under a Tree, a Snake in each Hand. The mark in the Margin. 49. Half-length figure of a Man with a fur Cap; ornaments on both sides. 50. Half-length figure of a young Man with a Cap. No mark. 51. Arabesque, with Acanthus and Grapes; do. 52. Arabesque, with winged Sphynx under two Satyrs. The mark P. 53. Arabesque, with flying Chimæra carrying a Veil. Do., on the shield. 54. Arabesque, with two Boys riding on Chimæric Birds; do. 55. Arabesque, with Helmet and Cuirass in the centre, above a winged Sphynx. Do., and the initials S. C. 56. Arabesque, with the Symbols of Seamanship; in the lower part two marine deities on dolphins; between them a Ship. 57. Arabesque, with two Goats. In the margin a mark which may be taken for a P. 58. Arabesque, with a female Satyr suckling two Children. 59. Arabesque, with the mark of a river Deity. Duchesne thinks this niello is by Peregrini, although without the mark. 60. Arabesque, with two Dolphins; in the centre above a winged head. 61. Arabesque, with two Trophies, chimæric birds, a faun sitting on a basket and playing a flute. On a tablet the letters SCOF. 62. A Coat of Arms with three Nails. On the right hand the letter C., on the left Z. or S. Therefore only probably by Peregrini. 63. Two Knife-handles with Arabesques. On one a head of Medusa in a medallion, and at the end two Satyrs, with the initials, P. C. 64. A Knife-handle, with two Guitars and two Rings. The letters S. C. in tablets, identify this piece as the work of Peregrini, in the opinion of Duchesne.

PERELLE, Gabriel, an eminent French designer and engraver, born at Paris, according to Nagler, in 1610. It is not known under whom he studied, but he executed a prodigious number of plates, from his own designs, as well as other masters, which prove much fertility of invention and extraordinary facility of execution, rather than an attentive study of nature, though his views are well composed, and enriched with architecture, ruins, and other objects which give a pleasing variety to the scenery. His plates are executed with neatness and taste, though there is a defect in the management of his masses, and his lights are scattered and spotty, which injure the effect of the prints. He wrought both with the point and the graver. He is considered the *Hollar* of France, both in his style of engraving, and in the estimation of his works. His large views of public buildings and gardens in France, Spain, and Italy, were published with those of Silvestre in 1680, and there is a smaller set of the same by these artists. In addition to the prints from his own designs, he executed many after Paul Brill, Gaspar Poussin, Asselyn, Poelemberg, Silvestre, and other masters. He died, according to Nagler, in 1675, and to Zani, in 1680. The following are among his principal prints after the works of other masters:

A set of four Views, the Church of St. Michael at Dijon, the Palace in that city, the Bridge of Grenoble, and the Porte Royale at Marseilles; *after Silvestre*. Four Views in Paris, the Arsenal du Mail, the Pontneuf, the Louvre, the Mail and the surrounding country; *do*. A set of four Views, the Baths of Bourbon d'Archambaud, the Castle of Bourbon Lancy, with the Baths of Julius Cæsar, and the great Chartreuse near Grenoble; *do*. Six Views of the Garden de Ruel; *after Israel Silvestre*. Two Mountainous Landscapes, with biblical subjects; *after P. Brill*.—Six Views of the Vestiges of Rome and its Environs; *after J. Asselyn*. A view of Ruins, with the Adoration of the Magi; *after Poelemberg*.

PERELLE, Adam and Nicolas, were the sons and scholars of the preceeding, whom they assisted in his numerous works; and, after his death, engraved a great number of plates of landscapes, architectural views, &c. Their works are inferior to those of their father. According to Nagler, *Adam* was born in 1638, and died in 1695; but Zani applies these dates to *Nicolas*.

PERERIETTE, an engraver whose name is attached to a coarse etching of the Holy Family, *after Paul Veronese*.

PEREYRA, Diego, a Portuguese painter, born about 1570. His instructor is not mentioned, and little is known concerning his life; but according to the *Biographie Universelle*, he was one of the most distinguished painters of his country. His usual subjects were landscapes; but he had a rare talent for painting conflagrations and infernal scenes. He often painted the Burning of Troy, and the Overthrow of Sodom, but always in a different manner. He excelled in painting pictures of fruit and flowers; also rural scenes, illuminated by the radiance of torches or the lightning's flash. His landscapes are painted in a spirited style, ornamented with small figures in excellent taste. They are said to be much in the style of Teniers, with the silvery tones of that master. Notwithstanding the merits of Pereyra, he met with little encouragement, and was finally received into the mansion of a nobleman, where he died in 1640. Soon after his death, his works rose into general esteem. There are many at Lisbon; the cabinet of the Duke d'Almeida contains about sixty.

PEREYRA, Manuel, a Portuguese sculptor was born in 1614. He settled at Madrid, where he attained great distinction, and is regarded a one of the most able artists that Portugal has produced. He was commissioned to execute a great number of works. His masterpiece is a statue of our Saviour, in the Church of the Rosario at Madrid. It is said that, in his old age, having become blind, he made the model of a statue of St. John the Divine, and directed its execution. This statue is one of his finest works. He died in 1667.

PEREZ, Bartolomé, a distinguished Spanish painter, born at Madrid in 1634. He studied in the school of Don Juan de Arellano, and attained great excellence in flower-painting. His pictures of this kind are composed in a tasteful and delicate style, with a brilliancy and harmony of coloring deserving of high praise. He also succeeded in the figure, following the style of Don Juan de Carreno. There were many of his flower-pieces at the Retiro, which were subsequently removed to the Rosario; and one of his best productions is mentioned, which combines his talents in both branches of the art, representing St. Rosa de Lima kneeling before the Virgin and infant Jesus, with two Angels, one of whom is crowning the Saviour, while the other is presenting him a vase of flowers. Perez was also distinguished for the excellence of his theatrical decorations, and he was employed by the King to paint the scenery in the Royal Theatre. The Duke de Monteleone commissioned him to paint a grand ceiling in fresco in his palace at Madrid; but, while occupied upon the work, he unfortunately fell from the scaffold and was killed, in 1693.

PEREZ, Francisco de Pineda, a Spanish painter, who flourished at Seville about 1660. He studied under Murillo, and followed his style with considerable success. Among other works, he painted several pictures for the churches and convents at Seville, which show that he was an able disciple of that great master. Perez was a member of the Society of Professors who established the Academy of Fine Arts at Seville.

PEREZ, Andres, a Spanish painter, the son and scholar of the preceding, born at Seville, in 1660. He painted historical subjects; also flower-pieces, in which he was more successful. Among his principal works were three sacred subjects in the sanctuary of S. Lucia at Seville, signed *Andres Perez*, 1707; and in the sacristy of the Capuchins of the same city, a picture by him of the Last Judgment, dated 1713. He died in 1727.

PEREZ, Pietro, an old Spanish architect, who flourished in the thirteenth century, and died in 1290. He is chiefly known as the architect of the Cathedral of Toledo, which measures 404 feet in length, and 202 feet in breadth. It has five naves, surrounded by chapels of white stone; the principal nave is 116 feet high.

PERICLES. This celebrated Athenian deserves mention in a work relating to art, for the liberal patronage he extended to painters, sculptors, and architects. Having obtained almost regal power in Athens about B. C. 450, he endeavored to inspire the people with a taste for the Fine Arts. By means of the wonderful talents of Phidias, and other famous artists, he embellished the city of Athens with those magnificent works which have been the admiration of all succeeding ages. (For a description of several of these, see the articles Phidias and Ictinus.) Pericles also designed the Odeum, a building constructed so as to give the greatest possible effect to sound, where the musicians used to assemble to rehearse their rival performances. It was of an elliptical figure, surrounded by a colonnade, except upon the southern side. After a period of several hundred years, it had suffered much from the ravages of time, but was restored by the munificent Herodes Atticus to its ancient beauty and magnificence.

PERIGNON, Nicolas, a French painter and engraver, born at Paris, according to Zani, in 1727; died in 1782. He painted flowers and landscapes in distemper; and also etched several plates, after his own designs, among which are a set of pleasing Landscapes, in the style of a painter; also four large Landscapes, inscribed *Perignon, fecit.* 1771.

PERIN, Lié Louis, a French miniature painter, born at Rheims in 1753. He entered the free school of design in that city, taught by Clermont; and, though opposed by many obstacles, he triumphed over them all. At the age of twenty-five he visited Paris, and commenced practising his profession. He was employed by Rosslyn, a Swedish artist, to copy a number of his works in miniature; and he gained such improvement by studying the works of Greuze, and other masters, that his practice greatly increased. He exhibited a number of fine miniatures; and painted, among others, the portraits of the Duchesses d'Orleans and de la Rochefoucauld. During the stormy scenes of the Revolution, Perin was constantly employed by the friends of condemned persons to visit the prisons and paint their portraits. In 1799 he quitted Paris, and retired to his native city, where he practised the art with success for many years, occasionally visiting Paris. He also painted a number of miniatures at Lyons. He died at Rheims in 1817.

PERINI, Giuseppe Sforza, an Italian engraver, born at Rome about 1748. He engraved some of the statues in the *Clementine Gallery*, and also some of the plates for the *Scuola Italica* of Gavin Hamilton. He was living in 1795. Among others, the following are by him:

The Frontispiece to the *Scuola Italica*, with two figures by *M. Angelo*. Jupiter and Antiope; *after Jacopo Palma*. Charity; *after Bartolomeo Schidone*. Christ bearing his Cross; *after Lanfranco*.

PERINI, Lodovico, an Italian engraver of little note, by whom there are a few prints, very indifferently executed with the graver, and possessing little interest of subject.

PERINO, del Vaga. See Vaga.

PERINO, da Perugia. See Pietro Cesarei.

or or PERISIN, PERSINUS, or PERRISIM, Jacques, an old French engraver; born, according to Nagler, in 1530. In concert with Jean Tortorel, he designed and engraved, partly on wood, and partly on copper, a set of twenty-four large prints, to illustrate a History of the Wars of the Huguenots, 1559 to 1570. This book is exceedingly rare. The copper-plates are etched in a coarse, incorrect style; the wooden cuts are executed with more attention. When Perisin and Tortorel engraved in concert, they marked their prints with the second monogram at the head of this article; when Perisin engraved alone, he used the first monogram. Malpé attributes to the latter a series of Tritons and Marine Monsters, small pieces lengthways, marked with his monogram reversed.

PERJECOUTER S. a real or supposed artist, said to have been a native of Italy, residing there about 1535, to whom were formerly attributed some prints bearing the above monogram, executed with the graver, in the style of Marco da Ravenna. Strutt and Bryan have fallen into the same error. The prints referred to were executed by some unknown Italian engraver, who flourished about that time. (See Bartsch P. G., vol. xv., p. 496. See also *Serwouter.*)

PERLA, Francesco, a painter of Mantua, supposed by Volta to have studied under Giulio Romano. There are two fine frescos in the dome of the chapel of S. Lorenzo, in that city, attributed to him. Little besides is known of this artist. He flourished about the middle of the sixteenth century.

PERMOSER, Balthasar, a German sculptor, was born at Cammer, in Bavaria, in 1650. He acquired the elements of the art at Saltzburg, and then went to Italy for improvement, where he remained fourteen years. His works are principally at Dresden and Vienna. He had so high an idea of his art that he was never satisfied with any of his works, and often destroyed them in disgust. They are consequently extremely rare. He was much employed by Prince Eugene, for whom he executed a statue of Charity, and a group of Painting and Sculpture. He also made the fine statue at Vienna of Prince Eugene, represented in the act of preventing Fame from publishing his exploits, by taking away her Trumpet. Permoser died in 1732.

PERNA, Peter, an engraver who flourished towards the close of the 16th century. There are no particulars of him. There are some wood cuts, marked P. P. which Strutt and others attribute to him.

PERNET, an obscure engraver, who lived about 1620. He engraved a few plates of portraits, very indifferently executed with the graver.

PEROLA, Juan and Francisco, two brothers, Spanish painters, sculptors, and architects, were natives of Almagro, and flourished about 1600. They visited Italy; studied under Michael Angelo; and finished their artistic education in Spain, under Gaspar Becerra. After leaving that master, they gained considerable distinction, and were commissioned by the Marquis de Santa Cruz to erect his palace at Viso, near the Sierra Morena, and to decorate it with paintings and sculptures of their own execution. They painted history, landscapes, portraits, battle-pieces, and marines, in a style of excellence, evincing a thorough acquaintance with the principles of art. Of their works in sculpture, the *Biographie Universelle* mentions the busts decorating the above mentioned palace, and the mausoleum of the Marquis of Santa Cruz, in the church of the Franciscans at Vico. They also painted the grand altar-piece in the same church: and, in concert with Mohedano, they painted several frescos in the sanctuary of Cordova and the convent of Seville. There was an architect, named Esteban Perola, a native of Almagro, and cotemporary with the preceding. He designed, and probably erected, the convent of S. Francisco at Seville, commenced in 1623.

PERONI, Giuseppe, a painter born at Parma, about 1700 (Zani says 1710). According to the Abate Affò, he first studied under Felice Torelli, at Bologna; next with Donato Creti; and afterwards went to Rome, where he became the pupil of Agostino Masucci. According to Lanzi, he designed much in the style of Carlo Maratti, but his coloring partakes much of the verds, and other false coloring of Conca and Giaquinto, who were then very popular at Rome. Such are his picture of St. Philip, in the church of S. Satiro, at Milan, and the Conception, in the possession of the Padri dell' Oratorio, at Turin. Lanzi also says that his best works are his frescos in the church of S. Antonio Abate, at Parma, which rank him among the good painters of his age. There he also painted an altar-piece of the Crucifixion, in competition with Pompeo Battoni. He executed several other works for the churches of his native city; adorned its Academy; and wrought much for the collections. He died at Parma in 1776, at an advanced age. Lanzi calls him the Abate Giuseppe Peroni, a title probably conferring some favor upon him.

PERONI, Giuseppe, an Italian sculptor, born at Rome in 1627. He early manifested a strong inclination for art, and entered the school of Algardi, who soon perceived in him more than ordinary talents. Peroni met with every encouragement; but his unrestrained passions involved him in many private intrigues, so that his professional improvement was sadly neglected. Finally, he became so irregular as to disgust Algardi, and soon after left his academy. He went to Sweden, and was patronized by Qeeen Christina, for whom he executed a bust in marble; but returned before long to Rome, married, visited Naples, and executed there a statue of Neptune, life-size, intended by the viceroy for a fountain at Madrid. He subsequently settled at Rome, where the Prince Camillo Pamfili patronized him extensively. The path to honor was open before him, but he chose to adhere to vicious habits, and died in 1663, aged 36.

PEROXINO, Giovanni, a Piedmontese painter, who flourished about 1517. According to Della Valle, he was a good artist; and Lanzi says "he is well known for the pictures he left in the church of the Conventuals at Alba."

PERACCINI, Guiseppe, called Il Mirandolese, a painter born at Mirandola, in 1672. According to Crespi, he studied under Marc' Antonio Franceschini, whose style he adopted. He executed some works for the churches at Bologna. He must not be confounded with Pietro Paltronieri, called *Mirandolese dalle prospettive.* (See *Paltronieri.*) He died in 1754.

PERRACHE, Michel, a French sculptor, born at Lyons in 1685. At the age of sixteen he visited Italy for improvement, and also went to Flanders, where he executed a number of sculptures for a church at Malines, and was honored with the freedom of the city. In 1717 he returned to France, and settled at Lyons, where he practised the art for many years, and executed a variety of sculptures for the churches and gardens. He died in 1750, leaving a son, who was also a sculptor.

PERRAULT, Claude, an eminent French architect, born at Paris in 1613. He was the son of an advocate, and was bred to the medical profession, but extended his studies to other branches of science, particularly mathematics and architecture. His attention became more especially directed to this art, upon being engaged by Colbert to undertake a translation of Vitruvius, the first edition of which appeared in 1673, in a folio volume, with plates after his own drawings. Before the completion of this work, Perrault gave indisputable proof of his practical ability and superior taste in architecture, in his designs for the east façade and colonnades of the Louvre. On a very beautiful basement, containing a range of apartments, the windows of which are without much decoration, and with circular heads, rests the famous colonnade, 525 feet long, of coupled Corinthian columns, and fluted, three feet seven inches in diameter, supporting bold architraves, twelve feet long. This colonnade has three breaks—one at each of the extremities, and one in the centre. Over this is a pediment, embracing eight of the coupled columns; and the two inclined planes forming the pediment are remarkable, each being fifty-four feet long, eight feet wide, and fourteen inches high. The whole edifice is surmounted by a balustrade. This superb façade fronts the church of S. Germain. Its excellence was a matter of surprise to Bernini, and Milizia says it may be ranked among the finest pieces of architecture in Europe.—Among the other works of Perrault, are the Observatory, and the grand triumphal arch at the entrance of the Faubourg St. Antoine. The foundations of the latter work were laid, but it was unfortunately only executed in stucco. It was 146 feet long in front, and 150 feet high; dimensions far superior to the arches of Constantine or Septimius Severus. The order was Corinthian; the columns ten and a half diameters instead of ten—an addition which appeared necessary, to give a greater degree of elegance, and to harmonize with the light sculpture which adorned the work. The ornaments were admirably selected, and none but such a master as Perrault could have used so many without overloading the architecture; every part displayed excellent taste. Milizia says that, had it been executed in marble, it would have conferred immortal honor on the French nation. Perrault was a member of the Royal Academy of Sciences. He published an abridged edition of his Vitruvius in 1674; an enlarged edition appeared in 1684; his work on the Five Orders, folio, was published in 1683; *Essais de Physique*, 2 vols. 4to., 1680, and a work on natural history; to which may be added a posthumous work, published in 1700, giving an account of several machines of his own invention. Perrault died at Paris in 1688.

PERRET, Peter, an engraver born about 1550. It is uncertain whether he was a native of France or the Low Countries. His Christian name is variously written Pierre, Pedro, and Pieter, and at Rome he signs himself *Pieter Perret*, which seems to confirm Basan's assertion that he was a Fleming. He went to Rome, where he studied under Cornelius Cort. On his return to his own country, he was appointed engraver to the Duke of Bavaria and the Elector of Cologne. He engraved the plates of the monastery of San Lorenzo in the Escurial, from the designs of Juan de Herrera, which gave so much satisfaction to Philip II. that he invited him to Madrid in 1595, and appointed him his engraver, which office he retained under Philip III. and Philip IV., till his death, which happened at Madrid in 1637. His chief works are a set of portraits of the Kings of Spain, signed *Pedro Perret sculptor Regis, fecit.*

PERRIER, François, a French painter and engraver, born at Macon, in Burgundy, about 1590. His father was a goldsmith, and instructed him in the elements of design, but was unwilling that he should become a painter. Opposed in his wishes, young Perrier left his native place; and, being without the means of a livelihood, he became the conductor of a blind mendicant, who was traveling to Italy, and in this manner succeeded in reaching Rome. On arriving there, he was employed by a picture dealer to copy several paintings, and some of his work was shown to Lanfranco, who encouraged him to persevere, and admitted him to his school. After several years' residence at Rome, Perrier returned to France, and passed some time at Lyons, where he painted the Decollation of St. John, a Holy Family, and other works for the cloister of the Carthusians. Not content with a provincial field for the exercise of his abilities, Perrier went to Paris, and, associating himself with Vouet, was employed by him to paint, from his design, the chapel of the chateau de Chilly. Meeting with little encouragement, he revisited Italy in 1635, and applied himself to engraving the principal antique statues and bas-reliefs; also a number of plates after the Italian masters. After the death of Simon Vouet, he returned to Paris in 1645, and was commissioned to paint the Hotel de la Vrilliere (now the Bank of France), where he represented Apollo in his Chariot; the Four Elements; Jupiter and Semele; the Rape of Proserpine; Neptune and Thetis; and Jupiter demanding of Eolus the destruction of the Trojan Fleet. He also painted landscapes, in the taste of the Caracci, but defective in perspective. His pictures evince great warmth of imagination, but the design is often incorrect; the airs of his heads lack elegance and dignity, and his coloring is too dark. Perrier was a member of the Academy, and died at Paris, according to D'Argenville, in 1650. There are a number of etchings by him, incorrectly and negligently designed, and executed in a slight, hasty style, usually marked *Paria*, or with his monogram. Among them are the following:

A set of one hundred prints from the antique statues, published at Rome. A set of fifty, taken from the ancient bas-reliefs. Ten plates of the Angels in the Farnesina; *after Raffaelle*. Two plates of the Assembly of the Gods, and the Marriage of Cupid and Psyche; from the paintings by *Raffaelle* in the Farnesina. The Communion of St. Jerome; *after Agos. Caracci*. The flight into Egypt; *do.* The Nativity; *after S. Vouet*. The Portrait of Simon Vouet; *F. Perrier, fecit.* 1632.

SUBJECTS FROM HIS OWN DESIGNS.

The Holy Family, with St. John playing with a Lamb. The Crucifixion; inscribed *Franciscus Perrier, Burgundus, pinx. et scul.* St. Roch curing the People afflicted with the Plague. The Body of St. Sebastian, supported by two Saints. Venus and the Graces. Time clipping the Wings of Love, engraved in chiaro-scuro; fine.

PERRIER, Guillaume, a painter and engraver, the nephew and scholar of François P., flourished about the middle of the 17th century, and died in 1655. His works are executed in the style of his uncle. Among the principal are several pictures in the sacristy des Minimes at Lyons, where he had taken refuge, having killed his antagonist in a duel. There are a few etchings by him in the style of François Perrier, among which are an emblematical subject; the Portrait of Lazarus Meyssonier; the Death of the Magdalen; and the Holy Family.

PERRIN, Jean, an obscure French engraver, who, in conjunction with Jean Munier, executed a set of one hundred wooden cuts, for a work entitled *La Morosophie de Guillaume de la Perriere Tolsain, contenant cent Emblemes*, published at Lyons in 1553.

PERRISSIM. See Perisin.

PERRONEAU, Jean Baptiste, a French painter in crayons, and an engraver, born in 1731. He studied under Lawrence Cars. Little is known of him as a painter. Stanley says he was in England for a short time, and exhibited some portraits drawn in crayons. He engraved some plates after Boucher, Vanloo, Bouchardon, and Natoire.

PERRONET, a distinguished French architect and engineer, was born in 1708. He studied under Beausire, and made such rapid progress that, in 1745, he was appointed inspector of the school of engineers, and afterwards became director. He attained great eminence in constructing roads and bridges, and executed several admirable and important works of this kind in France, besides the canal of Burgundy. He wrote a description of his bridges, in 2 vols. 12mo.; and some memoirs on the method of constructing grand arches of stone, from two hundred to five hundred feet. Perronet was honored with the Order of St. Michael, and with a membership in the Academy of Sciences at Paris, the Academy at Stockholm, and the Royal Society of London. He died in 1794.

PERRY, Francis, an English painter and engraver of little note. He engraved some plates for the magazines, and a few of coins and medals.

PERSON, Nicholas, a German engraver, who flourished about 1696. He engraved a set of twenty portraits of the Archbishops of Germany, published in that year. They are indifferently executed.

PERSYN, or PERZYN, Regnier de, an engraver who flourished at Rome about 1650, and, in conjunction with Cornelius Bloemaert, Theodore Matham, and M. Natalis, engraved the statues in the Palazzo Giustiniani. He also engraved some other plates, among which are the portraits of Ariosto, *after Titian;* Balthazar, Count Castiglione, *after Raffaelle*. His plates are executed with the graver, in a neat, clear, and pleasing style. There is considerable discrepancy about him, arising from a variety of signatures found on prints attributed to him, as *Regnier de Persyn fec.*, *R. a Persyn sculp.*, and *Regnerus a Persyn sculp. Lusit.* (Lusitanius), which last signature is found on a plate of Leander taken to the shore by Marine Deities, and would seem to indicate that he was a Spaniard. Nagler says that Regnier de Persyn or Perzyn, surnamed *Narcissus*, was a native of Amsterdam, born in 1600. Zani says he was born in 1639, and was living in 1690. Zani also mentions another Renato or Reniero Perzyn, whom he calls a Roman, and says he operated in 1642. He quotes two inscriptions from prints, *R. a Persyn sculp.*, *R. a Persyn fec.* 1642. There can be but little doubt that they all refer to one and the same person, as some artists frequently use various signatures.

PERUCCI, Orazio, a painter of Reggio, born in 1548. According to Tiraboschi he was a good artist, executed some works for the churches in his native city, and painted much for the collections. Lanzi says there remain various pictures by him in the private houses, and an altar-piece in the church of S. Giovanni at Reggio; and, judging from his style, he thinks he was a pupil of Lelio Orsi. He died in 1624.

PERUGIA, Giovanni Niccolo da, a painter of Perugia, born, according to Pascoli, about 1478. He was probably a scholar of Pietro Perugino. Lanzi says "he was a good colorist, and therefore was willingly received by Pietro to assist him in his works, however inferior to that artist in design and perspective. His works are recognized in the Capella del Cambio, near the celebrated Sala of Perugino, where he painted the Life of St. John the Baptist. In the church of S. Tommaso is his picture of that Saint about to touch the wounds of our Saviour, and with the exception of a sameness in the heads, it possesses much of the character of Perugino." He died in 1544.

PERUGIA, Mariano da, a painter who, according to Mariotti, was a reputable artist, and executed some works for the churches at Perugia and Ancona. There are notices of him from 1547 to 1576. He commends an altar-piece by him in the church of S. Domenico at Perugia, and another picture by him in the church of S. Agostino at Ancona. He is also called Mariano di Ser Eusterio.

PERUGIA, Sinibaldo da, a painter of Perugia, highly commended by Mariotti, who flourished in the first part of the sixteenth century. There are notices of him from 1505 to 1528. Lanzi says "he must be esteemed an excellent painter, from his works in his native place, and still more from those in the Cathedral at Gubbio, where he painted a fine picture in 1505, and a gonfalon still more beautiful, which would rank him among the first artists of the ancient school."

PERUGINI, Petruccio. See Montanini.

PERUGINI. There are several other painters, natives of Perugia, called by this name. The Cav. Ratti, in his life of Alessandro Magnasco, makes mention of one Perugini, who flourished at Milan at the same time as Magnasco, who inserted the figures in his landscapes. He flourished in the first half of the seventeenth century. Lanzi mentions another of the same name, who died at Milan in 1560.

PERUGINO, Sante Pietro. See Bartoli.

PERUGINO, Luigi. See Scaramuccia.

PERUGINO, Paolo. See Gismondi.

PERUGINO, Il Cavaliere. See Gio. Domenico Cerrini.

PERUGINO, Domenico, a painter of Perugia, who, according to Baglioni, flourished in the latter part of the 16th and first part of the 17th centuries. Lanzi says he painted small wood scenes or landscapes, and that he is scarcely known at Perugia; though it is believed that one of his pictures remains in the church of S. Angelo Magno at Ascoli. His name also occurs at Siena, and he is mentioned by authors as the master of Antiveduto Grammatica. He probably painted history, as well as landscapes, and wrought in various cities for individuals.

PERUGINO, Lello, an old painter of Perugia, who, in conjunction with Ugolino Orvietano and other artists, decorated the Cathedral of Orvieto in 1321. See *Orvietano*.

PERUGINO, Pietro. The family name of this eminent artist was Vannucci, but he is universally known in the history of art as Pietro Perugino, and when authors speak of *Perugino*, they always refer to him. There is a good deal of contradiction about the place of his nativity, and his master. The signatures on several of his earlier works show that he was a native of Città della Pieve, a small place near Perugia, where he was born in 1446. His parents soon afterwards removed to Perugia, and, being extremely poor, placed him under the tuition of an obscure painter in that city. It is generally believed by authors that he afterwards studied under Andrea Verocchio, at Florence. Mariotti raised a doubt whether he went to Florence and became the scholar of Verocchio, as writers report, but thinks he received his principal instruction from Benedetto Bonfiglio, at Perugia; and afterwards improved himself by studying the works of Masaccio. Pascoli, Bottari, and Taja are of opinion that Verocchio was never his master; and the Padre Resta, after reviewing the whole subject, comes to the same conclusion. Notwithstanding all the facts and ingenious arguments advanced by them, Lanzi thinks it highly probable that Perugino, on his arrival at Florence, attached himself to that celebrated artist, was instructed by him in design, and particularly in the plastic art; also in that fine style of painting with which Verocchio imbued both Vinci and Credi. Traditions generally have some foundation in truth. At all events, he first distinguished himself at Florence by his picture of the Deposition from the Cross, with the Virgin, St. John, and other Saints, painted for the church of S. Chiara, which was considered one of the finest productions of the art at that early period, and gained him such immense reputation that he was invited to Rome by Sixtus IV., to decorate the Sistine Chapel, where he executed several works, the most esteemed of which was that of Christ giving the Keys to St. Peter. Lanzi gives the following admirable critique on his manner, works and scholars, which places Perugino in the true light, and explains away many adverse opinions.

"The manner of Pietro is somewhat hard and dry, like that of other painters of his time; and he exhibits a poverty in the drapery of his figures, his mantles and garments being curtailed and confined. But he atones for these faults by the grace of his heads, particularly of his boys and women, which have an air of elegance, and a charm of color, unknown to his contemporaries. It is delightful to behold, in his pictures and in his frescos which remain at Perugia and at Rome, the bright azure grounds which afford such relief to his figures; the green, purple, and violet tints so chastely harmonized; the beautiful and well-drawn landscapes and edifices—a thing, as Vasari says, until that time never seen in Florence. In his altar-pieces he is sufficiently varied; there is, in the church of S. Simone at Perugia, a Holy Family, one of the finest specimens of a well-composed and well-designed altar-piece. In other respects, Pietro did not make great advances in invention; his Crucifixions and his Descents from the Cross are numerous, and of a uniform character. He has represented, with little variation, the Ascension of our Lord, and of the Virgin, in Bologna, Florence, in Perugia, and in Città di San Sepolcro. Reproached with this circumstance in his life-time, he defended himself by saying that no one had a right to complain, as the designs were all his own. There is also another defence for him, which is that compositions, really beautiful, are still beheld with delight when repeated in different places. Whoever saw, in the Sistine chapel, his St. Peter invested with the Keys, will not be displeased at finding at Perugia, the same landscape in a picture of the Virgin; on the contrary, this picture is one of the finest objects that noble city affords, and may be considered as containing an epitome of the various styles of Pietro. In the opinion of some writers, his frescos exhibit a more fertile invention, and greater delicacy and harmony of color. Of these, his master-piece is in his native city (Perugia), in the Sala del Cambio. It is an evangelical subject, with Saints from the Old and New Testaments, in which he inserted his own portrait, to which his grateful fellow-citizens attached an elegant eulogy. He is most eminent, and adopts a sort of Raffaellesque style, in some of his later pictures. I have observed it in a Holy Family in the Carmine, at Perugia. The same may be said of certain small pictures, almost of a miniature class, as in the Grado of St. Peter at Perugia; than which nothing can be more finished and beautiful; and in many other pieces on which he spared no pains, but which are few in comparison to the *multitude by his scholars which are attributed to him.*"

"In treating of the school of Pietro Perugino, it is necessary to advert to what Taja and the authors of the 'Lettere Perugine' notice respecting his scholars—'that they were most scrupulous in adhering to the manner of their master; and, as they are numerous, they have filled the world with pictures, which both by painters and connoisseurs are commonly considered as his.' When his works at Perugia are inspected, he generally rises in the estimation of travellers, of whom many have only seen paintings incorrectly ascribed to him. At Florence, there are some of his pictures in the Grand Duke's collection, and in the church of S. Chiara his beautiful Descent from the Cross, with other works; but in private collections, many Holy Families are ascribed to him which were executed by some of his numerous scholars. The Papal States also possess many works by his scholars, who were of higher reputation, and not so wholly attached to his manner."

Pietro Perugino died at Perugia in 1524. His name is illustrious in art, not only for his works, but for his having been the instructor of Raffaelle.

PERUNDT, George. See Pfründt.

PERUZZI, Baldassare, da Siena, a preëminent Italian painter and architect, born at Accajano, in the territory of Siena, according to Della

Valle, in 1481. According to Lanzi, he was the child of poor parents; was nurtured amidst difficulties; but succeeded in obtaining a knowledge of painting from some unknown master in his native city, and then went to Rome for improvement, in the pontificate of Alexander VI. He formed an intimacy with Raffaelle, whose style he admired and imitated, particularly in his fresco works. Peruzzi gained great eminence at Rome; was patronized by many of the nobility, particularly by Agostino Chigi, and also by Pope Alexander. In his Judgment of Paris, in the Castello di Belcaro; and in his picture of the Sibyl foretelling to Augustus the Birth of Christ, Peruzzi manifested such a divine enthusiasm, according to Lanzi, as Raffaelle himself never surpassed in treating the latter subject, nor Guido, nor Guercino, of whom so many admirable Sibyls are exhibited. Lanzi says that, in great compositions, he also evinced remarkable talents; as in his celebrated fresco of the Presentation in the Temple, in la Madonna della Pace at Rome, in which he showed himself a perfect master of the delineation of the passions, and unequalled in the excellence of his architecture. This magnificent work was a favorite study of Annibale Caracci. His oil paintings are extremely rare; Lanzi mentions one at Torre Babbiana, eighteen miles from Siena, containing three half-length figures, of the Virgin, St. John the Baptist, and St. Jerome.

Peruzzi was preëminently distinguished in perspective and architecture, which he painted with such fidelity and precision, and so judicious a management of chiaro-scuro, as to produce perfect illusion. Lanzi says that if other artists surpassed him in the vastness of their works, they never did in regard to excellence. He was eminently skilled in ornamenting façades—painting sacrifices, bacchanalian scenes, and battles, so as to represent bas-reliefs, and real architecture; which was afterwards so successfully practised by Polidoro da Caravaggio and Maturino. One of his most admired perspectives at Rome, is in the same apartment of the Farnese palace where Raffaelle painted his Galatea, and represents the History of Perseus, embellished with ornaments in imitation of stucco, executed in such admirable style that Titian himself was deceived by them, and could only be convinced of his error by changing the point of view. Peruzzi produced a similar ocular deception in a hall of the same palace, by painting a colonnade, the intercolumniations of which make the hall seem much larger than it really is. Of this work Pietro Aretino said that "the palace contained no picture more perfect in its kind." Lanzi remarks, "had the scenes he painted for the plays, represented in the Apostolical palace for the amusement of Leo. X., survived to our days, the perspective paintings of Peruzzi would have obtained greater fame than the Calandra of Cardinal da Bibiena. It would have been said of him, as of the ancient, that he discovered a new art, and brought it to perfection."

Peruzzi also attained great excellence in grotesques—a style of painting which, being the offspring of a whimsical fancy, affords abundant play for the imagination. Lanzi says: "Graceful in all his works, he was most elegant in grotesque; and, amid the freedom inspired by a subject entirely of a capricious character, he preserved an art to comprehend its principles. He employed every species of idea—satyrs, masks, children, animals, monsters, edifices, trees, flowers, vases, candelabra, lamps, armor, and thunderbolts; but he bridled his caprice by his judgment, in the actions represented, in the general arrangement, and in every other circumstance. He distorted and connected these images with a surprising symmetry, and adapted them as devices emblematic of the stories which they surround."

Baldassare Peruzzi is said to have engraved on wood; and a print is attributed to him representing Apollo, Minerva, and the Muses, with Hercules, driving before him a female figure loaded with treasure, supposed to represent Avarice. It is executed on three blocks, in a fine, bold style; marked *Bal. Sen.*, and at some distance the word *Perugo.* According to Papillon, he wrote a treatise upon the Antiquities of Rome, and a Commentary on Vitruvius, which he intended to embellish with engravings upon wood, but died before it was ready for publication.

As an architect, Peruzzi attained great excellence. He is said to have studied under Bramante, and, through the liberal patronage of the celebrated Agostino Chigi, he was enabled to acquire a thorough knowledge of the art. Milizia says he was a learned and talented architect. Serlio commends him for a sound taste, facility, and elegance, both in the general design and the ornaments of his edifices. Lanzi says he ranks among the first architects; that he is even preferred to Bramante; and evinces a lively imagination in all his works. He was employed in the building of St. Peter's, by Pope Leo X., who, thinking the idea of Bramante too vast, employed Peruzzi to make a fresh model. According to the account of Serlio, it was to have been of a Greek cross, with a cupola one hundred and thirty-eight feet in diameter; and was conceived with such judgment, that every part served as a model to the succeeding architects.—He designed many elegant façades at Rome, and gave proof of his superior ability in the Palazzo Massimo, which is one of the most original and tasteful edifices in that city. Instead of being perplexed at the awkwardness of the site, Peruzzi availed himself of it to curve the front of the building, and thereby produced so happy an effect that this particular form seems rather the result of choice. The loggia and small inner court are extremely beautiful, and the whole of this admirable work deserves the attention it has received in a folio work by Suys and Haudebourt, Paris, 1818, containing engravings of all its parts and details. The tomb of Adrian VI., in the church dell' Anima, was also erected by Peruzzi. For Agostino Chigi, at Longara, he erected the famous palace now called La Farnesina, which is highly praised by Milizia. Among his other works were the gat of S. Michele in Bosco, and the Cathedral of Carpi. He left a number of original manuscripts relating to architecture, and bequeathed them to hi scholar Serlio, who declares, in his fourth book that whatever merit his work possesses is due, no to himself, but, to Baldassare da Siena. He die in 1536, poisoned by a rival who endeavored to obtain his appointment of architect to St. Peter's Artists of every denomination assisted at his obsequies, and he was buried in the Pantheon, by th side of Raffaelle.

Lanzi judiciously remarks that "Baldassare Peruzzi is one of the numerous individuals whos merit must not be measured by their good fortune." His life was an uninterrupted series of misfortunes and injustice. Although his surpassing talents gained him the patronage of Agostino Chigi to enable him to pursue his studies, yet he was reckoned inferior to his rivals, because he was as modest and timid as they were arrogant. As architect of St. Peter's, he received two hundred and fifty crowns per annum; and for his labors in the Cathedral of Siena, he had the yearly pittance of thirty crowns! He derived but little benefit from private commissions, for even wealthy nobles took advantage of his modesty, either rewarding him scantily or paying him nothing at all. Despoiled of all his property in the sacking of Rome, he was cut off in the prime of life, just as his merits began to be appreciated. When lying at the point of death, the Pope sent him one hundred crowns, with offers of further assistance. His death demonstrated to the world the greatness of his talents; and his epitaph, comparing him to the ancients, is pronounced by posterity a just tribute to his wonderful genius.

PERUZZINI, Domenico, an Italian engraver, born at Pesaro or Ancona, flourished, according to the dates on the prints attributed to him, from 1640 to 1661. He is supposed to be the elder brother of Gio. Peruzzini, and like him, to have studied under Simone Cantarini. Lanzi says that in a MS. at Pesaro, it is mentioned that Domenico was a native of that city, and a scholar of Pandolfi. There is much confusion and contradiction about both artists, and still more uncertainty about Domenico; the list of prints given below were formerly attributed to Domenico Piola; but Bartsch repudiates the idea, and adduces several cogent reasons for transferring them to Domenico Peruzzini.—They are etched in a masterly style, resembling those of Cantarini. It would seem that both brothers were natives of Pesaro, but preferred to be called after Ancona, the place of their adoption. The following are the prints attributed to him by Bartsch. For full particulars see Bartsch, P. G., tom. xxi.

1. The Holy Virgin, half-length, with the infant Jesus. D. P. 1661.
2. The Virgin seated, with the Infant on her knees. D. P. 1661.
3. Christ tempted by the Devil, in the form of an old man. D. P. 1642.
4. Christ bearing his Cross, with other figures, half-lengths. D. P. P. F. engraved on the Cross. (Circular.)
5. The Holy Family and Saints. *Domus Pernus Anconæ* 1661. The figures in this print are half-lengths. Heineken, in his Dictionnaire des Artistes, attributed this print to *Gio. Dom. Cerrini,* known under the name of *Il Cavaliere Perugino.*
6. St. Anthony of Padua praying, and the infant Jesus appearing to him in a cloud, supported by three cherubim. *Dom. P.F.* This print has been erroneously attributed to *D. Cresti.*
7. The Assassination. A man in his shirt on a bed, assailed by three soldiers, one of whom thrusts a lance into his body. D. P. 1640.
8. to 11. Landscapes. The first is signed *D. P. f. Anconæ;* the others *D. P.* only.
12. St. Jerome doing Penance in the Desert. The letters D. P. F. are on a plant to the right. Bartsch, however, considers it doubtful whether it belongs to Domenico Peruzzini, as there is a sensible difference in the style from that of the others.

PERUZZINI, Cav. Giovanni, a painter of Pesaro or Ancona, born in 1629. The Canon Lazzarini asserts that both Domenico and Giovanni P. were natives of Pesaro, and that they transferred their services to Ancona, their adopted country. He studied under Simone Cantarini, acquired distinction, and painted several pictures for the churches at Ancona, Bologna, and other places. He was invited to the court of Turin, where he executed several works both in oil and fresco, so much to the satisfaction of his protector, that he made him a knight of the order of St. Maurice. He possessed a lively imagination, a ready invention, and a great facility of execution. He formed a style of his own, founded on those of Cantarini, the Caracci, and Guido. He was vain of his facility, as appears on one of the lunettes of the portico de' Servi at Bologna, on which he inscribed *Opus* 24 *Hor. Eq. Jo. P.*, (the work of twenty-four hours, by Gio. Peruzzini, knight,) which caused many sarcastic remarks from his brother artists. His best works are finished with more care. The principal at Ancona are the Decollation of St. John, at the Spedale, and St. Teresa, at the Carmelitani; at Bologna, the Descent of the Holy Ghost, in the church of S. S. Vitale ed Agricola, and an altar-piece of St. Cecilia, in the church dedicated to that Saint. Lanzi says, in his picture of St. Teresa are traces of Baroccio's manner; that of the Beheading of St. John is extremely beautiful, and there he appears a scholar of the Bolognese. He afterwards took to a wandering life, and painted in various churches and theatres, if not with much study, yet with tolerable correctness, a knowledge of perspective, and with a certain facility, grace and spirit, which delight the eye. His paintings are dispersed through various places in the Picenum, even as far as Ascoli, where are a number of his works. There are also some of his works at Rome and Milan. He died at Milan in 1694.

PERUZZINI, Paolo, was the son and scholar of the preceding. Lanzi says that, in the MS. at Pesaro, from which he had obtained much of the information respecting the father, the son is commended as a *good and decided painter*. He resided a long time at Rome, where there are some of his works. No further particulars are given of him.

PESARI, Giovanni Battista, a painter of Modena, who painted there about 1650. Tiraboschi says that he was either a pupil of Guido, or made that master his example. Lanzi says he resembles Guido very closely in his picture of the Madonna in the church of S. Paolo, at Modena, and in other works. He afterwards went to Venice, where he died, in the flower of his life.

PESARO, Simone da. See Cantarini.

PESARO, Niccolo Trometto, or Niccolo da, a painter of Pesaro, who studied under Federigo Zuccaro, whose style he at first closely followed. He executed some works for the churches at Rome, the principal of which are the Nativity in the Basilica; a Pieta in S. Francesco; the Nativity and the Circumcision, in S. Maria da Aracæli. Lanzi says his best piece is the Last Supper, in the church of the Sacrament at Pesaro. "It is a picture so well conceived and harmonized, and so rich in pictorial effect, that Lazzarini has descanted upon it in his lectures, as one of the finest works in that city." It is said that Baroccio beheld this artist with esteem, and Baglioni commends him for his earlier works. He afterwards fell into a mannered, insipid style, which injured his reputation and fortune. He died at Rome in the pontificate of Paul V., aged 70 years.

PESCI, Gaspero, a Bolognese painter who was living in 1776. He painted easel pictures of landscapes with figures, and views of architectural ruins. Little is known of him, further than that Count Algarotti was his friend and patron, with whom he corresponded, and for whom he executed two pictures of ancient architecture, which are described in the *Catalogo Algarotti.*

PESCIA, Mariano da, a painter of Pescia, whose real name was Mariano Gratiadei. He was a scholar of Ridolfo Ghirlandaio, (not, as is said, of Domenico G., who died about 1493), whom he assisted in many of his works. He also painted some pictures from his own compositions, of which the principal are an altar-piece in the Capella della Signoria, in the Palazzo Vecchio at Florence, and a picture of the Virgin and Infant Jesus, with St. Elizabeth and St. John, in the Florentine gallery. It is agreed by all that he died young, but the time of his birth and death is variously stated. Zani says he died in 1520; others that he was born in 1520 and 1525, and died at Florence in 1550. See *Ridolfo Corradi.*

PESELLO, Francesco, a Florentine painter, born in 1380, and died in 1457. He studied with Filippo Lippi, and was a good imitator of his style. There is a fine picture by him of the Epiphany, in the Ducal Gallery.

PESELLO, Pesellino, was the son of the preceding, born at Florence in 1426. Lanzi says he imitated Lippi more closely than his father. "He painted the Grado for the apartments of the Novices of S. Croce, where he represented the histories of S. Cosmo, S. Damiano, S. Antonio, and S. Francesco, denominated by Vasari most wonderful productions. Perhaps this is not too much to say when we recollect the period." He died in the flower of life in 1457. There is a great deal of contradiction about these artists, whose history is evidently confounded with another artist of the same name, noticed in the next article.

PESELLO, a Florentine painter, born in 1404, and died in 1481. It is said that he studied under Andrea del Castagno, who was born in 1409. He excelled in painting animals, which he designed from nature, and kept a great variety about him to serve as models. His history is mixed up with the two preceding artists in the most admirable confusion, and their names, dates, and works, are all applied to him by different authors.

PESENTI, Galeazzo, called Il Sabbionetta, a painter and sculptor of Cremona, who flourished, according to Zaist, in the first half of the 16th century. He was a cotemporary and friend of Galeazzo Campi, and they probably studied painting under the same master. He seems to have acquired more distinction as a sculptor, than as a painter. There are some of his works in his native city, but they are not particularly specified.

PESENTI, Martire, called Il Sabbionetta, a painter and architect of Cremona, who flourished in the last half of the 16th century. There are notices of him up to 1582. None of his works are specified, but he must have been an artist of reputation in his native city, as Lanzi says that his fellow citizens always consulted him when a valuable picture began to exhibit marks of decay, or an edifice required repairing, by which means many fine works were preserved.

PESNE, Jean, a French engraver, born at Rouen in 1623. It is not known under whom he studied, but he went to Paris, where he acquired distinction by the excellence of his works. His execution is not dexterous nor picturesque, but his outline is correct, and he rendered with remarkable fidelity the precise character of the different painters whose works he engraved, which makes his prints interesting and valuable to the collector. Dumesnil mentions 166 prints by him, the best of which are those he engraved after Niccolo Poussin. The following are his most esteemed prints. He died about 1700.

PORTRAITS.

Two of Niccolo Poussin; *after pictures by himself.* Louis le Comte, Sculptor to the King. Francis Langlois; *after Vandyck.*

SUBJECTS AFTER POUSSIN.

Esther before Ahasuerus. The Adoration of the Shepherds. The dead Christ, with the Virgin and St. John. The Entombing. The Death of Ananias. The Holy Family, with a dedication to le Brun. The Vision of St. Paul. The Triumph of Galatea. The Testament of Eudamidas; one of his best prints. The Seven Sacraments, in seven plates, of two sheets each. The Labors of Hercules, in nineteen plates; from paintings in the Louvre.

SUBJECTS AFTER ITALIAN MASTERS.

The Holy Family; *after Raffaelle.* A set of fifteen Landscapes; *after Guercino,* and other masters; fine.

PESNE, Thomas, was a younger brother of the preceding, and painted history and portraits, in which latter capacity he acquired at Paris considerable reputation.

PESNE, Antoine, a French historical and portrait painter, born at Paris in 1683. He was a son of one of the preceding, but authors differ. Dumesnil says he was a son of Jean P., and others with more probability, of Thomas. After learning the principles of the art under his father, he studied under Charles de la Fosse, and then went to Italy for improvement. On his return to Paris he acquired distinction, both in history and portrait. He was invited to Berlin by Frederick the Great, who appointed him his chief painter, and conferred on him a liberal pension. He painted the portrait of the King and other members of the Royal family, and of many distinguished personages at the court, where he died in 1757. The same history is erroneously applied to another Antoine Pesne, born at Paris in 1710, and died in 1770, who is said to have been a son of Charles Pesne, an engraver.

PEETERS, or PETERS, Bonaventura, an eminent Flemish painter, born at Antwerp in 1614. It is not known by whom he was instructed, but he distinguished himself as one of the most eminent marine painters of his time. His best pictures are his storms and tempests, which he has represented with wonderful truth and effect. The lowering sky, the glare of the lightning, the awful and terrific agitation of the water, the alarm and movements of the mariners, the vessels foundering or dashing to pieces on the craggy shore, are described with a fidelity and feeling that fill the imagination with horror, and show that he must have frequently witnessed these disastrous scenes to have enabled him to delineate them with such affect ing precision. He also painted calms and prospects of towns and castles on the sea shore, with nearly equal success. These represent scenes on the coast of Holland, with fishing boats at anchor, and fishermen drawing their nets; or views on the Scheldt, with vessels sailing under a gentle breeze, in which he exhibits a freshness of atmosphere and a transparency in the water, that is admirable. His vessels and figures are correctly drawn, his pencil is light, his touch is neat and full of spirit, his coloring exceedingly transparent, his water, whether calm or agitated, has great truth and delicacy, and his management of the chairo-scuro is admirable. His pictures are held in the highest esteem in Flanders, and are to be found only in the choicest collections. His works have been greatly imitated, and passed upon the unlearned in such matters, greatly tending to injure his reputation in foreign countries. This is particularly the case in England, and in the United States; many such, with his signature, well calculated to deceive, have been sold in this country for his genuine works. He died, according to Descamps, in 1652; most other authors, following him, give the same date; but Balkema says he died in 1671, and a picture in the Museum at the Hague, considered genuine, dated 1667, would seem to confirm the latter. He also executed a few spirited etchings from his own designs, which are exceedingly scarce.

PEETERS, or PETERS, John, was the brother and scholar of the preceding, born at Antwerp in 1625. He painted the same subjects as his brother, and imitated his manner so closely that his works have frequently been sold for those of that admirable master. Though his pictures are well composed, his figures correctly designed, his coloring clear and transparent, his penciling neat and delicate, he is very unequal to him in grandeur of effect, and in judicious management of the chiaro-scuro. He sometimes painted sea-fights, in which he showed great ingenuity in the composition, and his figures are correctly drawn and spiritedly touched. He died in 1677.

PEETERS, or PETERS, Francis Lucas, a Flemish painter, born at Mechlin in 1606. He was the son of an obscure painter, from whom he learned the elements of the art. He afterwards studied with Gerard Segers, but did not follow the style of that eminent master. He subsequently abandoned historical painting, and devoted himself to landscapes, which he executed in a pleasing style, and decorated with small figures correctly drawn and touched with great neatness and spirit. He acquired distinction, and was taken into the service of the Archduke Leopold, in whose employment he passed the greater part of his life. He died at Brussels in 1654.

PEETERS, or PETERS, Gerard, a Dutch painter, born at Amsterdam in 1580. He first studied with James Lenards, an eminent painter on glass, who, perceiving in his pupil an uncommon genius for the art, advised him to place himself under a more able master in a different branch of the art. He accordingly became the disciple of Cornelius Cornelisz, with whom he remained five years. He made such progress and showed so much genius, that that eminent master advised him to go to Italy. After a residence of some years at Rome, he returned to Holland, where he distinguished himself, but in a very different branch from what his master had anticipated. Karel van Mander extols him as a correct designer of the figure, and commends some of his historical works; but he is chiefly celebrated for his pictures of conversations and gallant assemblies, which are composed in an elegant and agreeable style, and finished with great neatness and delicacy. He also painted portraits with considerable success. He died in 1626.

PETER, the Long. See Peter Aertsen.

PETER, Wenceslaus, a German painter and sculptor, born at Carlsbad, in Bohemia, in 1742. Early in life he was apprenticed to an armorer; but having engraved upon steel some beautiful designs, he attracted the notice of the Prince of Kaunitz, who furnished him the means of visiting Rome. Arriving in that metropolis of art, Peter devoted himself to the study of the antique, and executed, not long after, a bas-relief of twenty figures in terra cotta, which was purchased by Lord Bristol, and sent to England. Notwithstanding this success, Peter resolved to gratify his strong inclination for painting; and he devoted his attention principally to representing animals, although by no means neglecting the study of the nude, which is evinced by his pictures of Daniel, Hercules, and Juno. In the branch of animal painting, he attained such excellence as to surpass most artists. His master-piece was a representation of the Terrestrial Paradise, with various animals distributed in pairs, comprising all the varieties which he had ever had the opportunity to design. He was offered large sums for this work, but would never dispose of it. Among the patrons of Peter, was Prince Antonio Borghese. He was honored with a professorship of Painting in the Academy of St. Luke; and died at Rome, in 1829.

PETERS, Matthias, and Nicholas, two Dutch engravers who flourished at Amsterdam about 1660. They were brothers, and executed conjointly the plates for the *Atlas Major*, published by Blaeu, in that city, in 1660.

PETERS, William, an English clergyman, who flourished in the last part of the 18th century, and distinguished himself as a painter. He was a man of wit, and possessed a lively imagination and great conversational powers, which made him a great favorite. Having a passion for painting, he practised it at first as an amusement, and by associating much with the eminent artists of the time, he greatly improved his manner, and distinguished himself by the production of many beautiful works, which were greatly admired. He painted for the Shakspeare Gallery, two scenes from the Merry Wives of Windsor, two do. from Henry VIII., and one from Much Ado about Nothing; also several for Macklin's Gallery, as the Resurrection of a Pious Family; the Guardian Angel and the Spirit of a Child; the Cherubs, &c., all of which were very popular. He executed many fancy subjects from his own imagination, which are pleasingly sentimental. He was much patronized by the nobility, and he sometimes painted subjects not strictly in accordance with just notions of propriety, and very different from those of the Cherubs and the Resurrection of the Pious Family. His pictures are well composed and his coloring rich and harmonious, with an admirable *impasto*, in which he imitated Reynolds. Many of his works were engraved by Bartolozzi, Thew, Simon, Smith, Marcuard, and others. He is generally called the Rev

W. Peters. The Duke of Rutland was his principal patron, and presented him with a valuable living; the Bishop of Lincoln gave him a prebendal stall in his cathedral. He died in 1814.

PETERZANO, or PRETERAZZANO, SIMONE, a Venetian painter, who, according to Lomazzo, was a pupil of Titian, and flourished at Milan in 1591, where he executed some works for the churches, both in oil and fresco. Lanzi says, "On his Pietá, in S. Fedele, he inscribed himself *Titiani Discipulus;* and his close imitation seems to confirm the truth. He produced several works in fresco, particularly several histories of St. Paul, in S. Barnaba. He there seems to have aimed at uniting the expression, the foreshortening, and the perspective of the Milanese, to the rich coloring of the Venetian artists; noble works, if they were thoroughly correct, and if the author had been as excellent in fresco as in oil painting." There is a fine picture by this master, of the Assumption of the Virgin, in the Chiesa di Brera.

PETHER, ABRAHAM, an English painter, born at Chichester in 1756. He was the son of William Pether, an engraver; and studied painting with George Smith. He painted landscapes and moonlight scenes, with considerable success, though without sufficient attention to nature. He did not confine himself to painting, but was a sort of universal genius, and withal a skillful musician. He died in 1812.

PETHER, SEBASTIAN, was the son of the preceding, born at Chichester in 1790. He was instructed by his father, and painted similar subjects, in a style not beyond mediocrity. He died in 1844.

PETHER, WILLIAM, an English engraver, born at Carlisle in 1731. He was a scholar of Thomas Frye, and was an excellent engraver in mezzotinto. He executed some fine plates after Rembrandt, Teniers, Rubens, and other masters, as well as a few from his own designs. The following are the principal:

PORTRAITS.

The three brothers, Smith, Painters of Chichester; *W. Pether, pinx, et fec.* 1765. Benjamin West; *after Lawranson.* Samuel Chandler, D. D.; *after Chamberlin.* Francis du Quesnoy, Sculptor; *after C. Le Brun.* Carlo Tessarini, Musician; *after Palthe.* Rembrandt's Wife, as the Jew Bride; *after Rembrandt.* Rubens' Second Wife; *after Rubens.*

SUBJECTS AFTER VARIOUS MASTERS.

The Rabbi; *after Rembrandt.* An Officer in Armor; *do.* An old Man with a beard; *do.* The Lord of the Vineyard; *do.* A Village Festival; *after Teniers.* A Warrior; half-length; *after Giorgione.* The Descent from the Cross; after the picture in King's College, Cambridge; by *Daniello da Volterra.* The Philosopher; *after Jos. Wright.* The Statuary; *do.* The Academy; *do.* The Continence of the Chevalier Bayard; *after Penny.* The Hermit; do. The Alchymist; *do.*

PETIT, GILES EDME, a French engraver, born at Paris in 1696. He studied under J. Chereau, and executed many plates in the neat, finished style of his instructor. Nagler gives a list of fifty-two prints by him, among which are the following. He died in 1760.

PORTRAITS.

Francis I., King of France; *after Titian;* for the Crozat Collection. Louis Philip, Regent of France; *after Liotard.* Louis XV., King of France; *after C. Vanloo.* Charles Edward Stuart, the Pretender; *after Dupra.*—Philibert Papillon, Canon of Dijon. René, Charles de Maupeon, President of the Parliament. Peter Bayle, Author of the Historical and Critical Dictionary. Maria Theresa, Queen of Hungary. Armand Julius, Prince of Rohan; *after Rigaud.* Henry Charles de Pomponne, Abbé of St. Medard. John Frederick Philipeaux, Count of Maurepas. Joachim Francis Potier, Duke of Gesvres.

SUBJECTS.

The Disciples at Emmaus; *after J. Andre.* The Visitation; *do.*; The Virgin of the Rosary; *do.* St. Catherine; *do.*

PETIT, LOUIS, a French designer and engraver, born at Paris in 1760, was a scholar of N. Ponce. He was much employed in designing and engraving vignettes and other subjects for the booksellers. He also engraved several plates after various masters, which possess considerable merit. The following are the principal. He died in 1812.

The Portrait of Peter Bayle, Author of the Dictionary. La belle Jardiniere, jointly with *Mansard*; *after Raffaelle.* The infant Jesus asleep, finished by *Bovinet; do.* Aurora; *do.* A Holy Family; *do.* St. Romualdus; *after A. Sacchi;* finished by *Dambrune.* The Dancing Nymphs; *after Vanderwerf.* And several for Ligni's History of the Life of Christ; among which are the Transfiguration, *after Raffaelle;* and the Last Supper, *after Leonardo da Vinci.*

PETIT-RADEL, LOUIS FRANÇOIS, a French architect, born at Paris in 1740. He studied under de Wailly, and carried off a number of medals at the exhibitions of the Academy. He visited Italy for improvement, and on returning to Paris, established a successful school, devoting his energies principally to the theoretical department of the art. He was a correct designer, and an adept in perspective; executed many excellent architectural designs; held an office in the Academy of Architecture; and was appointed Inspector General of Civil Edifices. In 1799, he published his *Projet pour la restauration du Pantheon Français.* He died in 1818. There are a number of plates representing ruins and other architectural subjects, engraved after his designs.

PETITOT, JOHN, THE ELDER, an eminent Swiss painter in enamel, was born at Geneva in 1607. He was the son of a sculptor and architect, who placed him with a gold worker and enameller, to learn that business. Having frequent occasion to make use of enamel, he succeeded in obtaining such beautiful tones of color, that he was advised to apply himself to portrait painting in enamel, in which he succeeded admirably, and afterwards carried it to a perfection before unknown. In company with his friend and associate, Peter Bordier, who afterwards became his brother-in-law, he went to Italy in search of improvement, where, during a residence of several years, he carefully studied the treasures of art, and consulted the best chemists, to discover some desirable colors that would stand the fire without change. Petitot and Bordier wrought together, the former painting the heads and hands, and the latter the hair, drapery, and backgrounds. They next went to England, where they had the good fortune to become acquainted with Sir Theodore Mayerne, physician to Charles I., an excellent chemist, who had bent his attention to the subject of enamels, and had discovered the principal colors to be used in painting, and the manner of vitrifying them, so that they surpassed the boasted enamelling of Venice and Limoges. Mayerne not only communicated his secrets to Petitot, but introduced him to the King, who took him into his service, and gave him apartments at Whitehall.

He painted the portrait of that monarch and of the royal family, several times. He copied several pictures after Vandyck, who assisted him with his advice; and these are considered his finest works. The beautiful portrait of the Countess of Southampton, now in the collection of the Duke of Devonshire, is considered one of the finest specimens of the art that exists. It is a whole length, nine inches and three quarters high, by five inches and three quarters wide, and was painted from the original in oil by Vandyck. The execution is bold, and the coloring is the most rich and beautiful that can be imagined. It is dated 1642. King Charles, who took great pleasure in his success, often honored him with his presence while at work. The tragical death of his royal patron was a dreadful stroke to Petitot, who would not quit the exiled family, but followed them into France, where he was one of their most faithful adherents.—Prince Charles, afterwards Charles II., took great notice of him, and recommended him to Louis XIV., who took him into his service, appointed him his painter in enamel, and gave him apartments in the Louvre. He painted that monarch several times, Maria Anne of Austria, his mother, and Maria Theresa, his queen. Petitot being a zealous Protestant, and dreading the consequences of the revocation of the edict of Nantes in 1685, which tolerated the Hugenots, he solicited the King's permission to retire to Geneva. Louis, unwilling to part with such a favorite artist, fearing his escape, ordered him to be arrested and imprisoned in the fortress of l'Evêque, and sent the Bishop of Meaux to convert him to the Catholic faith; but neither the eloquence of the Bishop nor the terrors of the dungeon could prevail on him to abjure his faith. His confinement threw him into a fever, on learning which, Louis ordered his release, and Petitot lost no time in escaping with his wife to Geneva, where he settled. There he continued to practise his profession, though wealthy, and at an advanced age. The King and Queen of Poland, desirous of having their portraits copied by him, sent the originals to Paris, believing him to be there; but the messenger, finding he had gone to Geneva, proceeded thither, and Petitot executed them in the most beautiful manner, though he was then above eighty years of age. The concourse of his friends and the curious was now so great, that he was obliged to retire to Vevay, a small town in the canton of Berne, that he might pass the rest of his life in quiet. He wrought to the last day of his life, and died suddenly, while he was engaged on a portrait of his wife, in 1691, aged 84 years.

Petitot may almost be considered the inventor of painting in enamel; at least he was the first artist who brought it to complete perfection. He was much assisted by his friend Bordier, but it is evident that he owed his success entirely to his own ingenuity, for, after they separated, little more is heard of Bordier. He made use of gold and silver plates, and seldom enamelled on copper. His custom was to sketch out his work from the portrait, and then finish after life. When he painted the kings of England and France, he selected their best portraits, and afterwards they gave him a sitting or two to finish his work. He labored with the greatest assiduity, *con amore*, and never laid down his pencil for any recreation, except with reluctance, saying that he always found more beauties in his art to charm him. When his works first came into vogue, his price was twenty louis-d'ors a head, which he afterwards raised to forty, and then to fifty. His works are exceedingly scarce and valuable. In the Apollo Gallery of the Museum at Paris, are about sixty of his finest works, consisting of portraits of Louis XIV., and several members of his family; ladies of his court, celebrated for their beauty, attachments, or literary acquirements; and some of the statesmen and military commanders of France. The following are the most interesting:

Several of Louis XIV. at different periods. Three of Anne of Austria. Two of Madame de Maintenon. Three of Maria Theresa of Austria. La Duchesse de la Valliere. Ninon de l'Enclos. Madame de Sévigné. Madame Deshouliéres. The Duchess of Portsmouth. Madame de Ludre in the character of a Magdalene. Christina of Sweden. The Duchess de Mazarin. The Cardinal de Richelieu. Madame de Montespan. Mademoiselle Montpensier. Maréchal de Villars. Jean Chardin, the Traveller.

PETITOT, John, the Younger, was the son and scholar of the preceding. Nothing is known of the time of his birth or death. He settled at London, where he practised his profession with considerable success till his death, when his family removed to Dublin. His works are said to possess great merit, though very inferior to those of his father.

PETRAZZI, Astolfo, a painter of Siena, born about 1590. He studied successively under Francesco Vanni, the younger Salimbeni, and Pietro Sorri. He acquired distinction, and executed many works for the churches and public edifices of his native city, as well as for the private collections. He also opened an Academy there, which was much frequented by the artists of Siena, and honored by the attendance of Borgognone, who stopped some months with Petrazzi before he proceeded to Rome. Lanzi says he seems to have adhered more to the manner of Vanni than that of any other master. He frequently aims at pleasing, and not unfrequently chose his models from the schools of upper Italy. His Marriage feast at Cana brings Veronese strongly to our recollection. His Communion of St. Jerome, at the Agostiniani, is painted much after the manner of the Caracci. He excelled in painting children, and his pictures are generally adorned with choirs of angels. His cabinet pictures are ingeniously composed, and have a lively and pleasing effect. His pictures of the Four Seasons, at Volte, a seat of the noble family of Chigi, are admired for the playfulness and elegance of the groups of Cupids introduced. He died in 1665.

PETREOLO, Andrea, a painter of Venzone, who, according to Renaldis, was employed in the cathedral of his native city, about 1586, where he "decorated the panels of the organ with very beautiful histories of S. Geronimo and S. Eustachio, together with the parable of the wise and foolish Virgins, surrounded with fine architecture."

PETRI, Pietro de', a painter born in Premia, a district of Novara, in 1671. He studied under Carlo Maratti, at Rome, and painted some works for the churches in that metropolis. Lanzi says he formed a style of his own, by engrafting on that of Maratti, a portion of the manner of Cortona. He did not, however, obtain the reputation which his merits deserved, on account of his infirm health and extreme modesty. His best works are a picture of the Crucifixion, in the church of S. S. Vincento e Anastasio, and some frescos in the tri bune of S. Clemente. He was called at Rome de' Pietri. Orlandi calls him a Roman, others a Spaniard; but Lanzi says he was a native of Premia. He died at Rome in 1716, in the prime of life. There are a few etchings heretofore attributed to him, but Bartsch gives them to another artist of the same name.

PETRI, or PITRI, Pietro Antonio de, an Italian engraver, to whom Bartsch attributes some etchings, heretofore given to the preceding artist. Zani also makes the distinction, and says he was born at Rome. All this, however, rests upon supposition, and is not worth disquisition here. Those interested are referred to Bartsch, P. G. tom. xxi. p. 289.

PETRINI, Cav. Giuseppe, a painter of the Milanese school, born at Carono about 1700. Lanzi says he studied under Prete of Genoa, but he adopted the manner of Francesco Solimena, then much in vogue, not only in Naples, but in other parts of Italy. He acquired distinction, and executed many works for the churches at Milan, and elsewhere. He seems to have been more anxious to captivate the eye than the judgment, by the brilliancy and contrast of the coloring, in which the greenish tints predominate. He died in 1780.

PEUTEMAN, Peter, a Dutch painter, born at Rotterdam in 1650. He excelled in painting objects of still-life, such as vases, books, musical instruments, &c., which he executed with surprising precision, with beautiful coloring, and a judicious management of the chiaro-scuro. He also painted allegorical subjects, emblematical of the shortness and misery of human life. His death happened in an extraordinary manner, in 1692. Receiving a commission to paint a picture emblematical of mortality, representing human bones and skulls, with rich gems and musical instruments to express the vanity of the world, he went to an anatomical lecture room to make some sketches, when an earthquake happening to occur, he was frightened into a fever, of which he died. Balkema says his Christian name was *Nicholas*, and that he also painted history.

PEYRE, Maria Joseph, a French architect, born at Paris in 1730. At the age of twenty-one he gained the grand prize of the Royal Academy, and visited Rome for improvement, where he made many designs of the ancient architectural monuments, published in 1765, under the title *Œuvres d'Architecture*. He also published a dissertation on ancient art, compared with that of the moderns, which was highly esteemed. Peyre was appointed architect to the king, and in concert with Wailly, erected the Nouveau Theatre Français, afterwards known as the Odeon, and one of the finest edifices in Paris. In 1767, he was received into the Academy of Architecture. He died in 1785.

PEYRE, Antoine François, the Younger, a French architect, the brother and scholar of M. J. Peyre. He made rapid progress in the art, and finally gained the grand prize, which entitled him to a residence at Rome, with the royal pension. Arriving in that capital in 1763, he commenced a diligent study of the antique, and afterwards executed a remarkable design, representing the interior of St. Peter's as it would appear if the front façade were removed. It is now preserved in the Musée Royal. After spending some time in Rome, Peyre returned to Paris, where he was appointed superintendent of the royal buildings at Fontainbleau, and subsequently of those at St. Germain, where he constructed two small churches, remarkable for excellent distribution, and correct proportions. In 1777 he was chosen a member of the Royal Academy of Architecture. In 1779, he was invited by the Elector of Treves to complete the palace of Coblentz; which he accomplished, greatly to the increase of his reputation. On returning to Paris, he received various important commissions from government, but was prevented from fulfilling them by the breaking out of the Revolution, when he retired to Fontainbleau, where he still retained his post of superintendent of the buildings. Manifesting much solicitude to preserve various works of art from the popular fury, particularly portraits and statues of the French kings, he was suspected of royalist tendencies, and was imprisoned for a short time. Under the rule of Napoleon, he was also distinguished in the art, being chosen a member of the Institute, and of several Councils of Architecture. During his latter days, he instructed several eminent architects of the present time. He died in 1823. Peyre composed several works relating to art, among which were his *Œuvres d'Architecture*, folio, 81 plates. Paris, 1819—1820.

PEYRON, Jean François Pierre, a distinguished French painter, and also an engraver, born at Aix, in Provence, in 1744. After acquiring a knowledge of the elements of design in his native place, he visited Paris in 1767, and entered the school of Lagrenée. He gained great improvement from the works of Poussin, and in 1773 drew the grand prize in the Royal Academy, for his picture of the death of Seneca, which entitled him to a four years' residence in Rome, with the king's pension. The reform in the French school had already been commenced by Vien; and Peyron on arriving at Rome determined to follow those correct principles derived from the Greeks, and the great masters of modern times. He painted at Rome a picture of Cimon taking from prison the dead body of his Father, and sent it to Paris, where it was greatly admired, and was placed in the Musée Royal. After a seven years' residence at Rome he returned to France, in 1781. He soon gained a high reputation, and was received into the Academy in 1783. In 1785, he was appointed Director of the Gobelins, and painted many pictures for that establishment. In 1787, he exhibited his pictures of Curius refusing the Gifts of the Samnites, and the Death of Socrates. A picture of the latter subject, by David, was also exhibited in the same year; and this period is said to have been the commencement of the new era in the French school, so eminently illustrated by the talents of David. The compositions of Peyron are said to be well arranged; his chiaro-scuro is managed with address; his draperies are broad and simple; his touch is firm, yet free and spirited; his coloring vigorous and harmonious, although his latter works have a purplish hue. Besides the pictures already mentioned, Peyron executed many others, among which are Paulus Æmilius; Antigone; the Daughters of Atheus, and Pythagoras with his Disciples. As an engraver, he executed nine plates, of which four are from his own designs—the death of Seneca; Cimon taking the dead body of his Father from Prison; Socrates and Alcibiades; and the Death of Socrates. Four after Poussin—a Sheep-Fold; Faustulus presenting Romulus and Remus to his wife Laurentia; the Rape of the Sabines; and the Despair of Hecuba. One after Raffaelle—a Holy Family. Peyron died in 1815.

PFEFFEL, John Andrew, a German engraver, born at Vienna in 1674. His works are chiefly confined to architecture, and ornaments for jewellers. In conjunction with C. Engelbrecht, he engraved a set of plates of ornaments for the jewellers. He also engraved a part of the plates for J. H. Fischer's *History of Architecture*, published at Vienna in 1721. His plates are neatly executed with the graver. He died in 1750. He had a son called by the same name, whom he instructed in the art, and who was similarly employed in engraving for the publishers. He was born at Vienna in 1715, and died in 1768.

PFEIFFER, Carl Hermann, a German engraver, born at Frankfort in 1769. He studied in the Imperial Academy at Vienna, under Professor Ch. Brand. He wrought with the point, and executed a great many portraits of the nobility, and other distinguished persons. He also engraved a number of plates after Raffaelle, Correggio, Rubens, and other masters.

PFENNINGER, Henry, a Swiss painter and engraver, born at Zurich in 1749. He studied painting under John Balthasar Bullinger, with whom he continued five years. He afterwards went to Dresden, where he improved himself by studying the works of the best masters, in the Electoral Gallery, particularly of Rembrandt and Vandyck. On his return to Switzerland, he painted portraits with reputation, and etched a great number of plates of portraits and views in Switzerland, which are executed with spirit and taste. He designed and engraved a part of the plates for Lavater's Physiognomy, and also some of the portraits for Füessli's Supplement to the Lives of the Swiss Painters. He was a very industrious artist, and, besides his numerous engravings, painted many portraits. He died in 1815. The following are his other principal prints: A set of seventy-five portraits of Illustrious Personages of Switzerland, accompanied with an abridged history of their lives by Leonard Meister. 1781. Thirty-four portraits of the most celebrated German Poets, with their characters, by L. Meister. 1785. A set of six Views in Switzerland.

PFENNINGER, Matthew, a Swiss designer and engraver, born at Zurich in 1739; died about 1810. He was of the same family as Henry P. He studied at Augsburg, under Emanuel Eichel, and afterwards visited Paris for improvement. He engraved a number of plates for Charles de Mechel, and several of the compositions of Loutherbourg; after which he returned to his own country. Among his principal plates are the portraits of Geis, Kleinjogg, and Shottenseps; a view of the tomb of Virgil, near Naples; and the statue of Marcus Aurelius at Rome.

PFRUNDT, George, a German sculptor, architect, and engraver, born in Franconia in 1603. Little is known of him as a sculptor or architect, but he executed quite a number of plates of architectural and geographical subjects, from his own designs. He died in 1663.

PHEAX, or PHEACES, a distinguished ancient architect, who flourished about B. C. 500, and constructed a number of edifices in Sicily, particularly at Agrigentum. He built the subterranean conduits; and also embellished the city by several fine edifices. It is probable that he was the architect of the celebrated Temple of Jupiter, near Agrigentum, described by Diodorus Siculus, of which the remains are still visible. It is said to have been 340 feet long, 60 feet wide, and 120 feet high: constructed in admirable style, with square pillars within, and circular without, thirty-two feet in circumference, and the flutings so deep as to admit of a man standing within them.

PHIDIAS, the most celebrated sculptor of antiquity, was the son of Charmidas, born at Athens, probably between the years B. C. 490 and 480. It is said that in early life he studied painting; but it does not appear that he ever practised that art to any extent, although he painted at Athens a picture of Pericles, represented as the Olympian Jupiter. According to the concurrent testimony of most ancient writers, he studied sculpture under Ageladas, one of the most eminent sculptors of the age. The times in which Phidias lived were peculiarly favorable to the development of his genius; and his talents must have been shown at a very early age, as it appears he was extensively employed upon great public works, even during the administration of Cimon. Subsequently, when Pericles attained the height of his power, Phidias seems to have been consulted in regard to the conduct of all works in sculpture as well as architecture. Plutarch says, "it was Phidias who had the direction of these works, although great architects and skillful sculptors were employed in erecting them." Among the most remarkable objects upon which his talents were exercised, the Parthenon, or Temple of Minerva, claims preëminence. It was built by Callicrates and Ictinus, under the superintendence of Phidias. For a description of this magnificent edifice, see *Ictinus*. Within the temple, Phidias executed his celebrated statue, in gold and ivory, of Minerva, represented standing erect, holding in one hand a spear, and in the other a statue of Victory. The helmet was highly decorated, and surmounted by a sphinx; the naked parts were of ivory; the eyes of precious stones; and the drapery throughout was of gold. It is said there were forty talents weight of this metal used in the statue. The people, being desirous of having all the glory of the work, prohibited Phidias from inscribing his name upon it; but he contrived to introduce his own portrait as an old bald-headed man throwing a stone, in the representation of the combat between the Athenians and Amazons, which decorated the shield. A likeness of Pericles was also introduced in the same composition. The exterior of the Parthenon was enriched with admirable sculptures, many of which were from the hand of Phidias, and all of them executed under his direction. A portion of these, termed the Elgin marbles, from their having been taken to England by the Earl of Elgin, are now in the British Museum. They have been highly commended by the most excellent judges; and the eminent sculptor Canova, after visiting London, declared that "he should have been well repaid for his journey to England, had he seen nothing but the Elgin marbles."

The time of Phidias is justly esteemed the grand

and golden age of Sculpture. The artists of the previous centuries are represented as having a dry, hard, and stiff manner. Phidias made a more careful selection of the finest models in nature, and brought to perfection the grand and sublime in sculpture. Quintilian calls him the "Sculptor of the Gods," from the character of grandeur and sublimity which he threw into his works. His skill in optics he probably acquired from his study of painting, and it is admirably attested by a curious circumstance. It was intended to place a statue of Minerva on a column of very great height; and both Phidias and his contemporary Alcamenes were employed to produce images for the purpose, which were to be chosen by the citizens. When the statues were completed, the universal preference was given to the work of Alcamenes, which appeared elegantly finished, while that of Phidias appeared rude and sketchy, with coarse and ill-proportioned features. At the request of Phidias, the statues were successively exhibited on the elevation for which they were intended; all the minute beauties of his rival's work completely disappeared, together with the seeming defects of his own; and the latter, though previously despised, seemed perfect in its proportions, and was surveyed with wonder and delight. Although he exercised his talents in all the materials generally used in art, yet his works in gold and ivory, called *chryselephantine* sculpture, appear to have been the most highly esteemed. The enemies of Pericles, with the view of implicating that statesman, accused Phidias of having misapplied part of the gold entrusted to him for the statue of Minerva, and desired that he should be brought to trial.—The sculptor, however, by the prudent advice of Pericles, had executed the work in such a manner that the gold might easily be removed, and it was ordered by Pericles to be carefully weighed before the people. As might have been expected, this test was not required, and the malicious accusation was overthrown. They then declared the sculptor guilty of sacrilege in placing his own portrait upon the shield of Minerva; and some writers state that he was thrown into prison; others, that he was banished. Some assert that there was no sentence passed; but that Phidias, fearing the consequences of the charge, fled from Athens to Elis, where he was employed to execute a costly statue of the Olympian Jupiter, for the temple in Altis. This statue was the most renowned of all the works of Phidias. It was of colossal dimensions, being sixty feet in height; and seated on a throne; the head was crowned with olive; the right hand held a small statue of Victory, in gold and ivory; the left hand grasped a golden sceptre of exquisite workmanship, surmounted by an eagle: the sandals and mantle were also of the same material, the latter sculptured with every description of flowers and animals; the pedestal was also of gold, ornamented with a number of deities in bas relief. In the front of the throne was a representation of the Sphynx carrying off the Theban youths; beneath these, the Fate of Niobe and her Children; and, on the pedestal joining the feet, the Contest of Hercules with the Amazons, embracing twenty-nine figures, among which was one intended to represent Theseus. On the hinder feet of the throne were four Victories, as treading in the dance. On the back of the throne, above the head of the god, were figures of the Hours and Graces; on the seat, Theseus warring with the Amazons, and Lions of gold. Its base, which was of gold, represented various groups of Divinities, among which were Jupiter and Juno, with the Graces leading on Mercury and Vesta; Cupid receiving Venus from the Sea; Apollo with Diana; Minerva with Hercules; and, below these, Neptune, and the Moon in her Chariot. On the base of the statue, was the inscription *Phidias, the son of Charmidas, made me.* Quintilian observes that this unparalleled work even added new feeling to the religion of Greece. It was without a rival in ancient times, all writers speaking of it as a production that none would even dare to imitate. There is an interesting tradition connected with this celebrated work. Phidias, after the completion of his design, is said to have prayed Jupiter to favor him with some intimation of his approbation, whereupon a flash of lightning darted into the temple, and struck the pavement before him. This was hailed as a proof of divine favor, and a brazen urn or vase was placed upon the spot, which Pausanias mentions as existing in his time. It is pretended that Phidias was again accused of robbery, by the people of Elis, and that he died in prison; but there are strong reasons, not only for thinking that these accusations against Phidias were false, but that the accounts of his disgrace and death are incorrect. From an expression in Aristophanes it is evident that an unjust feeling had been excited against Phidias; though it is not clear whether he fled or was exiled; and it seems highly probable that he died at Elis. The honor which was paid to his memory, would go far to disprove the assertion that he suffered the death of a criminal. The care of his master-piece was entrusted to his family, under the title of *Phaidruntai.* His studio, near the temple, was also preserved with great reverence, and an altar was erected therein, consecrated to the gods. Pausanias says that the Phaidruntai still existed in his time—six hundred years after the execution of the statue. Among the other works of Phidias were eight or nine statues of Minerva, of which one was the Minerva Areia of the Platæans, of wood, gilt; the extremities were of Pentelic marble. Besides these, he executed a number of admirable statues in marble, but chiefly in bronze, of Venus, Apollo, Mercury, an Amazon, etc., mentioned by Pausanias, Pliny, and Lucian.

PHILESIUS, Rigman, an old German wood engraver, and carver in wood, who, according to Papillon, flourished at Strasburg about 1508. He executed a set of twenty-five cuts of the Life and Passion of our Saviour, published at Strasburg by John Knoblauch, in 1508. These cuts are said to be very scarce. He is also called Rigman and Phillery, which see.

PHILIPPE, Peter, a Dutch engraver, who flourished at the Hague about 1660. He engraved a few plates of portraits and festivals, among which are the following:

PORTRAITS.

Louis Henry, Prince of Nassau; *P. Philippe, fec.* Henry Charles de la Tremouille, Prince of Tarente; *after Vanderbank.*

SUBJECTS.

The Assembly of the States-General of Holland; *after Tornvliet.* A grand Festival; *do.* A set of Merrymakings; *after vander Venne.* 1660.

PHILISCUS, a famous sculptor of Rhodes, who,

according to Pliny, executed statues of the Nine Muses in marble. These statues were carried to Rome by Fulvius Nobilior. Some of these, or copies of them, are now in the Vatican.

PHILLERY, an old engraver on wood, said to have been a German, but probably a Fleming, by whom there is a middle-sized print, representing two Soldiers standing before a Woman, who is seated, holding a Dog in her lap. It bears the following inscription in old Flemish characters, **Gheprint t'Antwerpen by my Phillery de figursnider**,(printed at Antwerp, by me Phillery, the figure-cutter). Heineken supposes this print to be very ancient, but Nagler quotes the same, and ascribes it to Anton Phillery, who flourished at Antwerp in 1530. There is considerable dispute about this *Phillery* and *Philesius*, whose works are not worth any disquisition, either on account of merit or antiquity, and there can be but little doubt that they are one and the same artist, *Rigman* being the surname, and *Phillery* the Christian name, which, latinized, is *Philesius.* Artists, too, are frequently whimsical, and often ignorant, in their signatures; and some use several signatures. *See Key to Monograms and Ciphers*, p. xix.

PHILLIPS, Charles, an English mezzotinto engraver, who flourished about 1765. He engraved some prints after Reynolds and Loutherbourg, and a few from the old masters, among which are the following:

A Boy holding a Pigeon; *after Mola.* A Woman plucking a Fowl; *after Rembrandt.* The Philosopher; *do.* The Holy Family; *after Parmiggiano.* Venus and Cupid; *after Salviati.* Isaac blessing Jacob; *after Spagnoletto.*

PHILLIPS, Thomas, an eminent English portrait painter, born at Dudley, in Warwickshire, in 1770. He first learned the business of a glass stainer at Birmingham. In 1790 he went to London, with a letter of introduction to Benjamin West, who employed him in painting the glass for the windows of St. George's chapel, Windsor. He soon turned his attention to oil painting; but whether he received any instruction from West is not mentioned. For several years he exhibited some of his pictures at the Royal Academy, among which were the Death of Talbot, Earl of Shrewsbury, at the Battle of Cassillon; Ruth and Naomi; Elijah restoring the Widow's Son; Cupid disarmed by Euphrosyne, &c. He afterwards devoted himself chiefly to portrait painting, in which branch he acquired distinction, notwithstanding he had such powerful competition as Beechey, Hoppner, Owen, Jackson, and Lawrence. He was not a *fashionable painter*, but he executed the portraits of many persons, distinguished for their intellectual, literary, or other attainments, a circumstance which, in future time, will add great interest to his works. It will be sufficient to mention the names of Lord Byron, Sir Walter Scott, Thomas Moore, Thomas Campbell, Southey, Coleridge, Crabbe, Sir Humphrey Davy, Lord Thurlow, Lord Brougham, Count Platoff, Earl Grey, Sir Joseph Banks, Sir E. Parry, Sir J. Brunell, Sir David Wilkie, Sir F. Burdett, Lord Lyndhurst, Sir Nicholas Tindal, and many more such men. His portraits are distinguished for dignity, truthfulness and excellent coloring. Nicaise de Keyser, a distinguished foreign artist, called him the English Vandyck, for the excellence of his works,—a very great compliment, whether deserved or not. In 1808, he was elected a member of the Royal Academy, and in 1824, succeeded Fuseli in the professorship of painting, which office he held till 1832. On his appointment to the professorship, he made a tour on the continent, visiting France, Italy, and Germany He published his "Lectures on the History and Principles of Painting," in one 8vo. vol. in 1833 He died in 1845.

PHILON, or PHILO, an eminent Grecian architect, who flourished about B. C. 330. According to Vitruvius, he erected various temples, and enlarged the vestibule of the temple of Ceres and Proserpine, built by Ictinus. He also designed and partially erected the white marble theatre at Athens, which was finished by Ariobarzanes, and rebuilt by Adrian. According to Plutarch, Philon was employed by Demetrius Phalereus to enlarge the port and arsenal of the Piræus, which he completed in excellent style. In giving to the Assembly an account of his operations, he expressed himself with such precision, purity, and eloquence, that the Athenian people—excellent judges of those matters—pronouced him equally a fluent orator and an admirable architect.

PHILOXENES, an eminent Greek painter, a native of Eretria, flourished about B. C. 316. He studied under Nicomachus of Thebes, whom he imitated, and probably surpassed in facility of execution. He was the most rapid painter of antiquity, and is said by Pliny to have discovered some more expeditious methods of operation in painting. Philoxenes gained great distinction by a picture painted for Cassander, King of Macedon, representing the Defeat of Darius by Alexander. According to Pliny, this work was not surpassed by any of the productions of ancient art. That author also describes another picture by Philoxenes, representing a lascivious subject, in which were three satyrs feasting. In 1831, there was discovered at Pompeii a large mosaic, apparently representing the Battle of Issus, which is supposed to be a repetition of the work of Philoxenes. It is still preserved in the house "Del Fauno," where it was first found.

PIACENZA, Gio. Battista, an Italian architect, born in 1735, at Pollone, near Vercelli. He studied under Count Alfieri di Sostegno, and was afterwards sent to Rome, at government expense. In 1777 he was appointed Architect to the King; in 1788, a magistrate of Turin; and in 1796, First Civil Architect to the Crown. He was employed in various works in the State, and in 1816, was chosen a member of the Academy at Turin. He died in 1818. His adopted son, Giuseppe Giovello, also an architect, completed a work commenced by Gio. Battista P. in 1768, published at Turin in six volumes, containing biographical sketches of artists from the time of Cimabue. It is mainly a reproduction of Baldinucci's work, but embraces many important additions and excellent annotations, which are justly appreciated by Cicognara.

PIAGGIA, Teramo or Erasmo, also called Teramo di Zoagli, a painter born at Zoagli, in the Genoese state, and who painted at Genoa in 1547. He was a scholar of Lodovico Brea, and painted in conjunction with Antonio Semini, several pictures for the churches at Genoa, the most esteemed of which is an altar-piece of the Martyrdom of St. Andrea, in the church of that saint. Lanzi highly commends this work, and says "none can witness this very beautiful altar-piece without seeing traces of Brea's style, already enlarged and changed into one more modern." He also painted several works by himself at Genoa and at Chiavari.

PIANE, Giovanni Maria delle, called Il Molinaretto, a Genoese painter, born at Genoa in 1660. According to Ratti, he studied under Gio. Battista Gaulli, whose style he adopted, and distinguished himself by some excellent works, which he executed for the churches at Genoa, but more by the excellence of his portraits. Lanzi highly extols his Decollation of St. John the Baptist, at Sestri di Ponente. He also says that he was particularly excellent in portraits, and that Genoa is full of his works in this branch. He was also invited to Parma and Piacenza, where he furnished the court with portraits, and executed some works for the churches. He was afterwards invited to Naples by King Charles of Bourbon, who appointed him his painter, with a liberal pension, and he continued in his service till his death in 1745.

PIANORO. See Bartolomeo Morelli.

PIASTRINI, Giovanni Domenico, a painter born at Pistoja about 1700. He studied under Cav. Benedetto Luti at Florence. and afterwards went to Rome, where he distinguished himself by some works in the church of S. Maria in Via Lata, in which Lanzi says he rivaled the best followers of Carlo Maratti. He also painted some works for the churches in his native city, particularly in la Madonna della Umiltà, where he filled two large spaces with pictures illustrating the history of that church.

PIATTI, Francesco, an Italian painter, born, according to Füessli, at Teglio, in the Valteline, in 1650. He executed many works for the churches in the neighborhood, and painted much for the collections. He particularly commends a picture of Cleopatra, in the possession of a noble family at Delebio.

PIATTOLI, Gaetano, a Florentine painter, born in 1703. He studied under Francesco Riviera at Leghorn. Lanzi says he is particularly extolled for the excellence of his portraits. He found abundant employment at Florence, in that branch of the art, and was not only patronized by the inhabitants, but was employed to take the portraits of the foreign nobility who visited that city. His portrait is in the ducal gallery. He also painted Conversazioni and Turkish ballets, which were very much prized in the collections for their excellence. He died in 1770.

PIAZZA, Callisto, a painter born at Lodi, who flourished from 1524 to 1556, as appears from the dates on his pictures. According to Orlandi, he was one of the most successful imitators of Titian. Lanzi says that his picture of the Assumption of the Virgin, in the Collegiate church of Codogno, is worthy of any of the disciples of Titian. It is a grand composition, containing figures of the apostles and two portraits of the Marchesi Trivulzi. In the church of the Incoronata, at Lodi, he painted three chapels in fresco, each ornamented with four beautiful histories. One contains the Mysteries of the Passion, another the Acts of St. John the Baptist, and the third, the Life of the Virgin. "It is currently believed," says Lanzi, "that Titian, in passing through Lodi, painted several of the heads—a story probably originating from the exceeding beauty that may be observed in them." He sometimes imitated the style of Giorgione, as may be seen in his altarpiece in the church of S. Francesco at Brescia, representing the Virgin among several saints, which is esteemed one of the most beautiful productions in that city. He executed many works for the churches in other cities, particularly at Crema and Alessandria; in the cathedral of the latter city are several of his best works. Lanzi rebukes Ridolfi, who commends him for nothing except his coloring, whereas, "he boasts a very noble design, is tolerably select in his forms, and rich and harmonious in his coloring. His Nuptials at Cana, in the Refectory of the Padri Cisterciensi, at Milan, is truly a surprising production, no less for its boldness of hand, than for the number of its figures, which seem to live and breathe, though the whole of them are not equally well studied, and a few are really careless and incorrect." Lomazzo also, speaking of his Choir of the Muses, in which he introduced the portraits of the president Sacco and his wife, for whom it was painted, says, "I may, without fear of temerity, observe that it is impossible to produce anything more perfectly graceful and pleasing, and more beautiful in point of coloring, among works in fresco."

PIAZZA, Paolo, commonly called Padre Cosimo, was born at Castelfranco, in the Venetian territory, in 1557. He studied under the younger Palma, and Baglioni commends him as one of his best pupils. He did not follow the style of his master, but adopted one of his own, which, though not distinguished by great vigor or energy, was graceful and pleasing, and gained him so much reputation, that he was successively employed by Pope Paul V., the Emperor Rodolph II., and the Doge Priuli. He executed many works both in oil and fresco for the churches and public edifices at Rome, Vienna, Venice, and other places. He was employed several years by the Emperor Rodolph. Among his best works are the Descent from the Cross, in the Campidoglio, and the history of Antony and Cleopatra, in the Palazzo Borghese at Rome. After he had acquired distinction, he joined the Capuchin friars, and took the name of Padre Cosimo, by which appellation he is usually known. He died at Venice in 1621.

PIAZZA, Cav. Andrea, born at Castelfranco about 1600, was the nephew and scholar of the preceding, whom he accompanied to Rome, and whose style he adopted, though somewhat modified by an attentive study of the works of the great masters. He acquired distinction, and was patronized by the Duke of Lorraine, in whose service he continued many years, and received from him the honor of knighthood. He afterwards returned to Venice, where he executed some works for the churches, the best of which is the Marriage at Cana, in the church of S. Maria, a grand composition of many figures, which Lanzi says is one of the best works in the place. He died there in 1670.

PIAZZETTA, Giovanni Battista, a Venetian painter, born in 1682. According to Zanetti, he was instructed in the rudiments of the art by his father, a reputable sculptor in wood, and afterwards became the scholar of Antonio Molinari. His first style was distinguished for a clear and brilliant tone of coloring, but on visiting Bologna, he employed himself with Spagnoletto, and by diligently studying the works of Guercino, he imitated his strong contrasts of lights and shadows, and boldness of relief, with considerable success. Lanzi says it is supposed that he had long observed the effects of light applied to statues of wood and images in wax, and by this means he was enabled to draw with considerable judgment and exact precision, the several parts that are comprehended in the shadowing; owing to which art, his designs were eagerly sought after, and his works repeatedly engraved by Pitteri, by Pelli, and by Monaco, besides other prints that were executed in Germany and elsewhere. His method of coloring, however, diminished in a great measure the chief merit of his pictures. His shades have increased and changed, his lights sunk, and his tints become yellow, so that there remains an inharmonious and unformed mass. There are a few of his pictures still in good preservation, as the Decollation of St. John the Baptist, in the church of that saint at Padua, placed in competition with those of the first artists of the state, and at that period esteemed the best of all. "Yet if we examine him closely, he will not fail to displease us by that monotonous and mannered coloring, of lakes and yellows, and by that rapidity of hand, by some called spirit, though to the judicious it often appears neglect, as if the artist was desirous of abandoning his labor before it was completed." He executed many chalk drawings which were held in great estimation. He also etched a few plates from his own designs. He died at Venice in 1754.

PICART, JEAN, a French engraver, who flourished at Paris about 1640. He is supposed to have studied under Crispin de Passe, whose style he imitated, though not with much success. He was principally employed in engraving vignettes, frontispieces, and other book ornaments. He also engraved a few portraits.

PICART, ETIENNE, called the ROMAN, an eminent French engraver, born at Paris in 1631. It is not known under whom he studied; but, after learning the art at Paris, he went to Rome, where he resided a long time, on which account some say he was called *Picart the Roman;* others, that he assumed this appellation to distinguish his works from those of an inferior engraver of the same name, probably the preceding artist. While at Rome, he executed some plates after the Italian masters. On his return to Paris he was employed, with other celebrated artists, to engrave the pictures in the King's Collection. His plates are generally executed with the graver, in the style of the elder Poilly, though he sometimes used both the point and the graver, and in a few of his prints the point predominates. His plates are neatly executed, with a fine expression in the heads, though his drawing is not very correct, and there is frequently a want of harmony in the effect of his engravings. His prints are very numerous; the following are esteemed the best.—He died at Amsterdam in 1721.

PORTRAITS.

John Francis Paul Gandy, Cardinal de Retz. 1652. Bust of Cardinal Fachenettus; *after Morand.* Melchisedeck de Thevenot, famous traveler; *after Chaveau.* Francis Tallemant, Abbé de Vlachretien; *after Nanteuil.* Andrew Hameau, Doctor of the Sorbonne. Nicholas Pavillon, Bishop of Aleth. Nicholas Choart de Busanval, Bishop of Beauvais. Claude de Brion, President of the Parliament. Peter Loisel, Doctor of the Sorbonne. Frances Athenais de Rochechouart, Marchioness de Montespan

SUBJECTS AFTER VARIOUS MASTERS.

The Ecce Homo, with three Angels; *after Albano.* The Birth of the Virgin; *after Guido.* The Marriage of St Catherine; *after Correggio.* Virtue triumphant over Vice; *do.* The Sensualist; *do.* St. Cecilia; *after Domenichino.* A Concert of Music; *do.* The infant Jesus sleeping, with the Virgin holding up her finger to St. John; called the Silence; *after An. Caracci.* The Holy Family; *after Palma.* The Separation of St. Peter and St Paul; *after Lanfranco.* The Plague among the Philistines; *after N. Poussin.* Christ curing the Blind; *do.* The Adoration of the Shepherds; *do.* The Martyrdom of St. Gervais and St. Protais; *after le Sueur.* St. Paul directing the burning of the Books of the Ephesians; *do* The Martyrdom of St. Andrew; *after le Brun.* The Stoning of St. Stephen; *do.* The Adoration of the Magi; *after Courtois.* The Virgin and Infant; *after Noel Coypel.* St. Anthony of Padua adoring the infant Jesus; *after Vandyck.*

PICART, BERNARD, was the son of the preceding, born at Paris in 1663. He was instructed in design and engraving by his father, and at the age of sixteen, gained the prize at the Academy of Paris. He distinguished himself not less as a designer than an engraver, and he executed a multitude of plates, which evince the fertility of his genius, and the excellence of his taste. He used both the point and the graver; his drawing is correct, and his prints have a very pleasing appearance. His works chiefly consist of book illustrations. In 1710 he left Paris, and settled at Amsterdam, where he found abundant employment. He engraved a set of seventy-eight plates, in imitation of the different styles of the old engravers, which were published after his death, in 1738, under the title of *Les Impostures Innocentes.* He died at Amsterdam in 1733. His prints are said to amount to about 1300. The following are the most esteemed:

PORTRAITS.

Charles I.; *after Vandyck.* 1724. Charles II.; *after Kneller.* 1724. James II.; *after Largilliere.* 1724. William III.; *after vander Werf.* George I.; *after Kneller.* Edward Hyde, Earl of Clarendon; *after Zoust.* 1724. William, Lord Russel; *after Kneller.* 1724. Frederick, Duke of Schomberg; *do.* 1724. Gilbert Burnet, Bishop of Salisbury; *after Hoadly.* 1724. Eugene Francis, Prince of Savoy; *after van Schuppen.* 1722. Don Louis, Prince of Asturias. John de Wit, Pensionary of Holland. 1727. Francis Peter, Cardinal de Foix. 1713. Philip, Duke of Orleans, supported by Minerva and Apollo; *after A. Coypel.* 1706. Stephen Picart, the Roman, Engraver to the King. Roger de Piles; *ipse pinx. B. Picart, fec. aqua forti.* 1704.

SUBJECTS FROM HIS OWN DESIGNS.

The Murder of the Innocents. The first impressions are before the crown was placed upon the head of Herod; fine. A set of twelve Prints, called the Epithalamiums; fine. Truth, the Research of Philosophy; a Thesis in honor of Descartes. The Triumph of Painting. The Death of the Infants of Niobe. The Feast of the Gods and the Cæsars. A set of Prints of the Annals of the Republic of Holland. The Frontispieces to Cérémonies Religieuses, 11 vols. 1723—1743. Do. to the Bible of vander Marck. Do. to the Roman Antiquities. Do. to Ovid. 1732. Do. to Temple des Muses. 1733. Do. to the Historical Dictionary.

SUBJECTS AFTER VARIOUS MASTERS.

Time discovering Truth; *after the picture by Poussin,* in the Louvre. An Allegory on Human Life; *do.* Two Arcadian Shepherds; *do.* Two Prints of the Muses, Calliope and Terpsichore; *after le Sueur.* Abraham sending away Hagar; *after le Brun.* The Discovery of the

Pregnancy of Calisto; *after An. Caracci.* Neptune calming the Sea; *after An. Coypel.*

PICAULT, PIERRE, a French engraver, born at Blois in 1680. He is supposed to have studied under Gerard Audran, as he imitated the style of that master, and copied, on a smaller scale, the celebrated Battles of Alexander, engraved by Audran after le Brun. He also engraved a few portraits, and the Visitation of the Virgin to St. Elizabeth, *after Carlo Maratti.* He died in the flower of his life, in 1711. He usually signed his plates, *P. Picault Blesensis, sculp.*

PICCHI, GIORGIO, a painter born at Castel Durante, who flourished in the latter half of the 16th century. He is supposed to have studied under Baroccio, whose style he adopted; but Lanzi thinks he was only an imitator of that master. He executed many works, both in oil and fresco, for the churches in his native city, at Cremona, and at Rimini. Some of these are painted on a vast scale, embracing whole oratories and churches, more distinguished for facility of execution than for correctness of design. Lanzi found it stated in a MS. at Castel Durante, that he was one of the artists employed at Rome in the pontificate of Sixtus V., in decorating the Library of the Vatican, the Scala Santa, and the Palazzo di S. Giovanni.

PICCHIANI, FRANCESCO, called PICCHETTI, an Italian architect, a native of Ferrara, flourished in the latter part of the 17th century. He was the son of Bartolomeo P.—also an architect, and probably his instructor—who had erected the church del Monte della Miseracordia at Naples. Francesco settled in that city, and gained a high reputation for his talents, as well as for his courteous and pleasing address. The Viceroy Don Pedro Arragona, had employed an architect named Bonaventura Presti to construct a basin for the royal galleys and other vessels; but while the excavations were in progress, the water flowed in so rapidly that Presti was unable to stop it. Accordingly Picchiani was employed, in concert with one Carfero; they removed the water by means of wheels, similar to those used in the process of irrigation, providing a number of fountains for the convenience of the royal vessels. Picchiani also executed the beautiful and majestic avenue leading from the basin to the piazza of the palace, and adorned it with elegant fountains. Among his other works, were the church and monastery of S. Giovanni della Monache, without the Porta Alba; S. Agostino; La Divino Amore; the church and monastery de' Miracoli; and the Monte de' Poveri, in the Strada di Toledo. He died in 1690.

PICCHIANTI, GIOVANNI DOMENICO, an Italian designer and engraver, born at Florence about 1670. He was taught the rudiments of drawing by Gio. Battista Foggini, a sculptor of little note. He afterwards learned engraving, and executed some plates both with the point and the graver. In conjunction with Lorenzini, Mogalli, and other artists, he was employed in engraving a set of plates from pictures in the Florentine Gallery. Among others are the following by him:

PORTRAITS.

Sebastiano del Piombo; *after Titian.* Cardinal Bentevoglio; *after Vandyck.* Pope Leo X., with the Cardinals Rossi and Giulio di Medici; *after Raffaelle.*

SUBJECTS AFTER VARIOUS MASTERS.

The Madonna della Seggiola; *after Raffaelle.* The Virgin and infant Jesus, with St. John; *after An. Caracci.* The Tribute Money; *after Titian.* The Virgin and Infant; *do.* Abraham sending away Hagar; *after P. da Cortona.*

PICCINI, GIACOMO, an Italian engraver, born at Venice in 1617. It is not known by whom he was instructed. He engraved a set of thirty portraits of the principal painters of the Venetian school, for the account of their Lives by Ridolfi, published in 1648. He also engraved a few plates after the Italian masters, among which are Diogenes with his Lantern, and the Holy Family, *after P. Liberi;* Judith with the Head of Holofernes at her feet, and the Holy Family, *after Titian.* His plates are executed in a stiff, disagreeable style. He was living in 1669.

PICCINI, GUGLIELMO, a Venetian engraver, the brother of the preceding. He engraved a few portraits and other subjects, in an indifferent style. He had a daughter named Isabella Piccini, whom he instructed in the art. She engraved a set of portraits of the Illustrious Personages of Italy, for the *Conchilia Celeste* of G. B. Fabri. She afterwards became a nun.

PICCININO, NICOLAO, a Milanese painter, who flourished about 1500. According to Morigia he was a good artist, and was considerably employed in decorating the palaces of the nobility in the Milanese territory, as well as painting for the collections.

PICCIONI, MATTEO, a painter and engraver, born at Ancona, according to Nagler, in 1615. Little is known of him as a painter, save that he flourished at Rome, and was elected a member of the Academy of St. Luke in 1655. Lanzi says he was a fellow-student with Gio. Antonio Galli. Bartsch gives a list of twenty-three prints by him, among which are the following:

St. Luke painting the Virgin; *after Raffaelle.* The Adoration of the Shepherds; *after P. Veronese.* The Holy Family; *do.* The Virgin and infant Jesus, with St. John; *after A. Camassei.* The Exposing of Moses in the Waters of the Nile; *do.*

PICCOLA, NICCOLA, or NICCOLA LAPICCOLA, a Sicilian painter, born at Crotone, in Calabria Ultra, in 1730. He studied under Francesco Mancini, at Rome; acquired considerable reputation; executed several works for the churches in that city; and decorated the cupola of a chapel in the Vatican, so much esteemed that it was afterwards copied in mosaic. He also painted much for the churches in the State, particularly at Veletri. None of his works are particularly specified. He died in 1790.

PICENARDI, CARLO, called THE ELDER, a painter who, according to Zaist, flourished at Cremona about 1600. He was of a patrician family, and one of the favorite pupils of Lodovico Caracci. He executed some works for the churches in his native city, and painted some burlesque histories which gained him considerable applause. He died young.

PICENARDI, CARLO, called THE YOUNGER, was the son of the preceding. It is not known by whom he was instructed; but, after studying at Rome, he went to Venice, and formed a style of his own, Roman in design, and Venetian in coloring. On his return to Cremona, he executed some works for the churches and public edifices, but painted more for the collections. Lanzi says he was very successful in burlesque histories, in imitation of the elder Picenardi. Zaist says he died aged 70, but he does not give the date. As one of his pictures is dated 1660, it must have happened about 1680.

PICKAERT, Peter, a Dutch engraver, who flourished about 1688. His name is affixed to a set of coarse etchings, representing the Flight of James II. from England. As the word *fecit* is added to his name, they are probably from his own designs.

PICOLET, Cornelius, a Dutch painter, who flourished at Rotterdam about 1680. He painted portraits and conversations with reputation, and was the first instructor of Adrian vander Werf.

PICOT, Victor Maria, a French engraver, born at Abbeville in 1744. He went to London about 1770, where he engraved several plates for Boydell. Nagler gives a list of thirty-six prints by him, among which are the following. He died about 1805.

The Four Evangelists; *after Rubens.* Diana and her Nymphs; *do.* The Nurse and Child; *after Schidone.* A young Man holding a Flute; *after B. Luti.* Apollo holding a Branch of Laurel; *after S. Cantarini.* A Landscape and Figures; *after Zuccarelli.* Two Sea-pieces; *after D. Serres.* Two Landscapes, Morning and Evening; *after Barralett.* Several other Subjects; *do.*

PICOU, Robert, a French engraver, who flourished about 1630. His name is sometimes erroneously written *Piquot.* According to the Abbé Marolles, he was a native of Tours. He went to Italy, and resided some time at Rome. He had the title of *Peintre du Roi*, though no paintings by him are mentioned. His prints are so scarce that Marolles could only collect three different specimens. Dumesnil describes seven as follows, which are etched with a firm point, with little dots intermixed, and finished with the graver. They are all evidently from his own designs except the last, which is the best.

1. Love asleep; *R. Picou, fe.* 2. Two Cupids caressing; *R. Picou, fe. Romæ.* 3. Two Infants; *do.* 4. Three Infants; *R. Picou, fe.* 5. The little Wrestlers; *R. Picou, fecit.* 6. Two couples of Infants; *R. P., &c.* 7. Jesus Christ delivered to his Enemies. On the margin to the left inscribed *Jacobus de poto Bassan pinxit, R. Picou, sculpsit*; and on the right, *Ciartres formis Cum Priuilegio.* In a second impression *Ciartres formis* is erased, and *Mariette Excudit* substituted.

PICQUET, Jean, a French engraver of little note, by whom there is a print representing Juno, Pallas, and Venus, half-length figures. It is inscribed *Joan Picquet, ft.*

TP PICQUOT, Thomas, a French engraver, who flourished about 1637. He executed some plates of ornaments for goldsmiths, designs for embroidery, damasking, and the like; also, a portrait of Marin le Bourgeois, painter and valet de chambre to Henry IV. and Louis XIII. His prints are marked with the above monogram.

PICQUOT, Henry, a French painter and engraver of little note, who flourished about 1640. He is supposed to be a brother of the preceding. He studied painting under Simon Vouet. None of his works as a painter are mentioned, but Dumesnil describes three prints by him, etched in a style resembling that of Michel Derigny.

PIEL, Louis Alexandre, a French architect born at Lisieux, in 1808. At the age of twenty four he entered the school of Debret at Paris; and in 1835, visited Germany to study the Gothic edifices. Having made the tour of that country, he published the result of his observations in *L'Européen*, a Parisian periodical, under the title of *Voyage en Allemagne.* This gained him considerable reputation, and he was commissioned, in 1837, to restore the church of S. Nicolas at Nantes in the Gothic style. Among his other works, was a church in the environs of Pontarlier, and the choir of the Cathedral at Sens. Piel assumed the Dominican habit in 1841, and died in the same year.

PIELLA, Francesco Antonio, a painter of Bologna, born in 1661, and died in 1719. It is said that he excelled in painting landscapes and seaports. There are no further particulars of him or his works.

PIEMONT, Nicholas, a Dutch painter, born at Amsterdam in 1659. He first studied under Martin Saagmolen, an obscure painter; and afterwards with Nicholas Molenaer. He next went to Italy, and resided several years at Rome, where he diligently studied after nature, and filled his portfolio with many choice designs of the picturesque scenery, views, and ruins, in the vicinity of that city, Tivoli, and other places. On his return to Amsterdam, he obtained a high reputation and abundant patronage for his views in Italy, which he executed in a manner strongly resembling that of John Both; and, though his works are much inferior to those of that celebrated master, they are deservedly admired, and admitted into choice collections. He died in 1709.

PIEMONTESE, Cesare, a Piedmontese painter, who flourished at Rome, in the pontificate of Gregory XIII. According to Taia, he was an excellent painter of landscapes, in which he attached himself to the manner of Paul Bril.

PIENE, A. de, a French engraver of little note, who flourished about 1672. He engraved a few plates of portraits and other subjects, for the booksellers.

PIERCE, Edward, an English painter, who flourished at London in the reigns of Charles I. and Charles II. He is said to have been eminent in history and landscape, and to have excelled in architecture and perspective. Few of his works now remain, the greater part of them having been destroyed in the great fire in London in 1666—probably not a very great loss. Lord Orford attributes to him eight plates of friezes, published in 1640.

PIERI, Stefano, a Florentine painter, born, according to Zani, in 1513, and a pupil of Battista Naldini. He seems to have passed much of his life at Rome, where he was patronized by the Cardinal Alessandro Medici, by whom he was employed in the church of S. Prassede, where he painted the Annunciation, and some pictures of the Apostles. He executed other works for some of the churches at Rome and Florence, in which latter city he assisted Vasari in the cupola of S. Maria del Fiore. Lanzi says one of his best works is the Sacrifice of Isaac, in the Palazzo Pitti. Another fine picture is the Assumption of the Virgin, in the church of S. Maria in Via, at Rome

His works are well designed, but Baglioni censures them as being very dry and hard. He died at Rome, in the pontificate of Clement VIII., at the great age of eighty-seven years; Zani says in 1600.

PIERI, ANTONIO DE', called LO ZOTTO or ZOPPO DA VICENZA, a painter of the Venetian school, and a native of Vicenza, who flourished in the first half of the 18th century; one of his pictures is dated 1738. It is not known under whom he studied, but he executed some works for the churches and public edifices at Vicenza and Rovigo, which, according to Lanzi, are more distinguished for brilliancy of coloring and facility of hand, than for correctness of design.

PIERINO, DEL VAGA. See VAGA.

PIERINO, SIG. GUIDO DEL. See GALLINARI.

PIERMARINI, GIUSEPPE, an eminent Italian architect, born at Foligno in 1734. His father was a merchant, and intended his son for the same business, which he followed for a number of years; but, as he manifested a strong inclination for mechanics and scientific pursuits, at the recommendation of the celebrated mathematician, Boscovich, his father was induced to send him to Rome, to pursue his studies under proper instruction. Accordingly, about the age of twenty, Piermarini went to Rome, and devoted himself to the study of mathematics and architecture, which last he studied under Poggi, and subsequently under Vanvitelli, who conceived for him a particular regard. He gave the young architect every means of advancement, particularly in the practical department of the art, which was, of course, the most difficult for him to acquire, while yet a student.—On Vanvitelli's going to Naples to erect the palace of Caserta, he took Piermarini with him as his principal assistant in that extensive work. Subsequently, when Vanvitelli was invited to Milan by the Austrian government, for the purpose of altering and embellishing the palace now called the Imperiale, Piermarini accompanied him, which proved the foundation of his fortunes. Meeting with obstacles, and having other engagements that demanded his attention, Vanvitelli contented himself with making some general designs, and explaining his ideas, recommending his pupil as fully competent to supply his place. The work was accordingly transferred to Piermarini, in 1769; and he thus found himself established at Milan, with the title of Architect to the Archduke, and Inspector-General of Buildings. His abilities fully sustained the high recommendation of Vanvitelli, and for thirty years he was constantly employed at Milan. He introduced a more correct taste than had hitherto been observed in the edifices of that city, and erected a large number of fine buildings, besides altering and improving so many others as greatly to enhance the architectural character of the city. His theatre Della Scala is sufficient to prove his great merit. Among his other works are the Palazzi Greppi, Moriggia, Lasnedi. Sannazari, Litta. Cusani; a façade of the archbishop's palace; the extensive and magnificent façade of the Palazzo Belgioioso; the Monte di Pietà; the Monte Napoleone; the Luoghi Pii; the Teatro della Canobbiana; and the Porta Orientale. He also conducted many general improvements, as several new streets, the Piazza del Tagliamento, and almost the whole of the new quarter called the Contrada di S. Redegonda; and the public gardens and their buildings. At Monza, he erected the elegant Imperial Villa; the Villa d' Adda at Casano; and the Villa Cusani at Desio. In the latter part of his life, Piermarini withdrew from active labors, and retired to his native place Foligno, where he lived in quietness until his death, in 1808. The Academy of the Brera at Milan erected a monument to his memory.

PIERRE, JEAN BAPTISTE MARIA, a French painter, born at Paris in 1715. It is not known by whom he was instructed; but he went to Rome when young, and resided there some years. On his return to Paris, he distinguished himself as a painter of history, and executed several works for the churches and public edifices, which gained him great reputation. He was appointed painter to the King, and was elected a member of the Academy at Paris. One of his greatest works was the ceiling of the chapel of the Virgin, in the church of S. Sulpice, which has been engraved by Nicholas Dupuis. He also etched a few spirited plates from his own designs and others. He died in 1789.

PIERSON, CHRISTOPHER, a Dutch historical and portrait painter, born at the Hague in 1631. He studied under Bartholomew Meyburg, with whom he traveled into Germany. Happening to visit the Swedish camp, he was engaged by General Wrangel to paint his portrait, and those of the principal officers of the army. These performances were so much admired for their striking resemblance, clearness of coloring, relief, and neatness of pencil, that the general endeavored to persuade him to go to the court of Sweden. He, however, returned to his own country, and settled at Gouda, where he found abundant employment, and acquired both reputation and riches. Observing that the pictures of Leemans, which represented dead game, and sporting apparatus, as guns, pouches, powder-horns, nets, bird-calls, &c., were greatly admired, and brought high prices, he applied himself entirely to that branch, with such success that he not only surpassed Leemans, but has scarcely been equalled by any other master. These subjects he usually painted on a white ground, and gave them such a just degree of light and shadow as produced perfect illusion, and made every object seem to stand out in relief from the canvass. He died at Gouda, in 1714.

PIET, a Dutch engraver, who flourished about 1608. He engraved the plates for a work entitled, *Le Maniement d'Armes de Nassau, &c.*, by Adam V. Brien, published in 1608. They are indifferently executed.

PIETERS, JOHN, a Flemish painter, born at Antwerp in 1667. After studying the art under Peter Eyckens, he went to England in 1685, and was employed by Sir Godfrey Kneller to paint the back-grounds and draperies of his portraits, in whose service he continued many years. He is said to have painted history with reputation, and to have excelled in copying Rubens; but the above facts render these statements very doubtful. He died in London in 1727.

PIETERS. Under this head are mentioned, for some unknown reason, the three sons of Peter Aertsen, commonly called *Peter the Long*, viz., Peter, Arnold, and Dirk, or Theodore. They were instructed by their father, and were good portrait painters. Peter was born at Haerlem in 1541, and died at Amsterdam in 1603. Arnold is said to have excelled in this branch; he died at Amsterdam in 1614. Theodore went to France, and died at Fontainbleau in 1602. See Peter Aertsen.

PIETERS. See PEETERS.

PIETRI, PIETRO DE'. See PETRI.

PIGALLE, JEAN BAPTISTE, a celebrated French sculptor, the son of a carpenter, was born at Paris in 1714. He first studied under Robert le Lorrain, and subsequently in the school of Lemoyne. He visited Rome, and studied for three years in that city; after which he returned to Paris. His statue of Mercury first brought him into public notice, being a most admirable work, in the antique style, full of ideal beauty. A statue of the Virgin, which he executed for the Invalides, gained him the patronage of the Minister Argenson, who commissioned him to execute a statue of Louis XV. Pigalle was also much employed by Madame de Pompadour, for whom he executed a statue of herself, one of Silence, and a fine group of Friendship and Love. King Louis ordered of him a large statue of the Mercury, with a Venus to accompany it, and presented the group to King Frederick the Great of Prussia. The latter statue gained the artist admission to the Academy; and the group is now at Sans Souci. Pigalle was considered one of the best sculptors of the last century. His manner in his earlier works is full of ideal beauty; but he subsequently forsook the antique style, and adhered to truth of resemblance. His principal work at Paris, is the tomb of Comte d'Harcourt, in the church of Notre Dame. Among his smaller productions, a figure of a Child holding a Cage from which a bird has escaped, was greatly admired for its animation, innocence, and simplicity. He completed and erected the bronze equestrian statue of Louis XV., commenced by Bouchardon. His master-piece, however, is the grand allegorical monument in memory of Mareschal Saxe, in the church of S. Thomas at Strasburg, commenced by order of Louis XV., in 1765, and finished in 1776. It is a group of five figures against a pyramid, which proclaims the glory of the warrior, who is represented in his own costume, and crowned with laurel, entering a tomb; on one side is Hercules mourning; on the other, Death as a skeleton; an impersonation of France is endeavoring to restrain the Marshal and avert Death; a weeping Genius is also in attendance, with an inverted torch, and many military trophies are introduced as accessories. The figure of the Marshal is very elaborately modelled, and the whole work has been several times engraved. In 1744, Pigalle was chosen an academician; was assistant-professor in 1745; professor in 1752; received the Cordon of St. Michael in 1769; was assistant-rector of the Academy in 1770; rector in 1777; and chancellor in 1785, in which year he died.

PIGNÉ, NICOLAS, a French engraver, born at Chalons in 1690. He was a pupil of Bernard Picart, and is said to have visited England, where he published ninety heads from the Cartoons, in 1722. Among his other plates are, a portrait of Richard Fiddes, D. D., prefixed to his *Divinity*, dated 1718; the Woman of Canaan kneeling at the feet of Christ, *after Ann. Caracci;* and the Virgin, with the Infant asleep in a cradle, St. John and four Angels, engraved for the Crozat Collection, *after F. Trevisani.*

PIGNONE, SIMONE, a painter born at Florence, according to Oretti, in 1614. He first studied with Fabrizio Boschi; next with Passignano, and afterwards with Francesco Furini, whose manner he adopted, though he improved his coloring by visiting Venice and studying the works of the great Venetian masters, particularly those of Titian and Tintoretto. On his return to Florence, he acquired distinction, and executed several works for the churches, which were greatly admired for the delicacy and beauty of the coloring, especially in the naked parts. The most esteemed of these are, St. Michael discomfiting the rebel Angels, in the Nunziata, St. Louis, King of France, distributing his wealth to the Poor, in S. Felicita, and an altar-piece at Monte Oliveto. His most admired works are sacred subjects of small size, to be found in the collections of the nobility. There are also some of his pictures in the Florentine Gallery. He was fond of painting mythological subjects, as their peculiar character gave him a fine chance of displaying his skill in the flesh tints, which are very tender and seductive. He sometimes treated them with unwarrantable licentiousness, and is said to have deeply lamented at his death, that he had prostituted his pencil to unworthy objects. Lanzi says he was the best of all Furini's numerous scholars. Carlo Maratti esteemed Gabbiani and Pignone only, among all the Florentine painters of the time. He died in 1698.

PIKLER, JOHN ANTHONY, a reputable engraver on precious stones, was born at Brixen, in the Tyrol, in 1700. He acquired a knowledge of his art at Naples, and attained a high reputation in that city, being patronized by the King and Queen, as well as distinguished personages of the court. In 1743 he settled at Rome, and executed a number of works, among which were a head of Homer in cornelian, and other copies from the antique, closely resembling ancient gems. He died in 1779.

PIKLER, CAV. GIOVANNI, an engraver on precious stones, was the son of the preceding, born at Naples in 1734. He studied design under Domenico Corvi, and copied the antiques at Rome with great assiduity. At the age of fourteen he executed a gem, representing Hercules vanquishing the Nemean Lion, which was much admired by the connoisseurs, and gained him great reputation and encouragement. In 1769, while the Emperor Joseph II. was at Rome, Pikler took an opportunity to design his portrait, and afterwards executed it in cameo. The monarch was so highly pleased with the work, that he appointed Pikler a cavalier, and invited him to Vienna. For some unknown reason, the artist declined this honor. He was greatly patronized, and could scarcely fulfil his commissions. Among them are many copies of ancient gems, statues, and bas-reliefs. He repeated twelve times his work representing Leander swimming towards a tower where Hero is holding a lamp; and also his Achilles dragging the body of Hector round the walls of Troy. Many of his gems probably pass for genuine antiques; and he is said to have sold for 100 sequins to the Cavaliere d'Azara, a head of Sappho, as an ancient work, which was in reality his own execution. Pikler commenced two works relating to art, but was prevented by death from completing them. He died in 1791.

PILAJA, Paolo, an Italian engraver, who flourished at Rome from 1727 to 1747. He executed a set of plates for a book entitled *Storia di Volsena*, by the Abate Adami, with a portrait of the author, published at Rome in 1737. He also engraved a few other subjects, among which are the following:

The Portrait of Pope Benedict XIII.; *after Brughi.* The Martyrdom of St. Fedele; *after S. Conca.* A Miracle wrought by S. Thoribio; *do.* St. Liberale, with two Children; *do.* The Statue of the Prophet Elias; *after the sculpture by Ag. Cornachini*, in St. Peter's at Rome.

PILES, Roger de, a French painter and writer on art, born at Clameci in 1635. He had a thorough knowledge of art, though he seems to have practised painting more for recreation than as a profession. He was tutor to the son of President Amelot, and afterwards accompanied him as secretary in several embassies. He had a good taste in coloring, was a master in chiaro-scuro, and possessed a remarkable talent for imitation. Rubens was his pictorial idol. He painted some portraits, among which were those of Boileau and Madame Dacier. He is better known as the author of several works on the lives of the most eminent painters, reflections on their works, &c. He died in 1709.

PILGRIM, John Ulric, an old engraver on wood, who is supposed to be the inventor of engraving in *chiaro-scuro.* Little is known of him, except a few prints which are marked with two pilgrims' staves crossed between the initials, Jo. V., as above; but whether these staves were used by him in allusion to his name is not satisfactorily ascertained. The French call him *Le Maître aux bourdons Croisés.* He must not be confounded with Ulderico Hans, or Hans Ulric of the Italians, who published the first illustrated book in Italy at Rome, in 1467. (See page xiii.) Bartsch (P. G. tom. vii.) describes the following ten prints by him.

1. Christ on the Cross, with the Magdalene kneeling at the foot, and the Virgin and St. John standing, one on each side.
2. The Virgin seated in a Garden, with the Infant on her knees.
3. The Virgin, half-length, with the Infant in her Arms.
4. St. Jerome in the Desert, with a book in one hand, and a stone in the other.
5. St. Sebastian tied to a Tree.
6. A Death's head seen in front, in a niche, with the inscription, *Mundanae foelicitatis gloria.*
7. Thisbe and the dead body of Pyramus, with an inscription, *Quid Venus in venis possit*, &c.
8. Orpheus charming the Brutes; inscription, *Orpheus vates.*
9. Alcon, a famous Archer of Crete, delivering his Son from a monstrous Serpent.
10. A Warrior on horseback, armed cap-à-pie, accompanied by a Halberdier on foot.

PILKINGTON, Sir Wm., an English amateur painter, born in 1776. He practised the art with great assiduity, constantly devoting a certain portion of his time to its prosecution. He chiefly excelled in landscapes, forming his style in a great measure on that of Richard Wilson, and his works exhibit breadth and truthfulness of effect, combined with depth and transparency of coloring. He died in 1850.

PILLEMENT, Jean, a French painter, who went to London about 1760, where he resided many years, and acquired considerable reputation for his drawings of landscapes and other subjects in water or body colors, many of which were engraved by the eminent engravers of the time, as Woollett, Mason, Elliot, Canot, Ravenet, and others. He also painted landscapes in oil, but these were very inferior to his water-color drawings. It is said that he died at Lyons about 1808, at the age of 80 years.

PILLEMENT, Victor, a reputable French engraver, the son of Jean P., was born at Vienna in 1767. He was principally distinguished for his plates of landscapes, and in 1801 he gained the first prize of the French Academy. There are many of his engravings in Robillard's *Galerie du Musée;* Melling's *Rives du Bosphore;* Denon's *Voyage en Egypte;* also a larger work entitled *Œdipe a Colone*, after Valenciennes; and many plates after Bourgeois. Pillement died at Paris in 1814.

PILON, Germain, a celebrated French sculptor of the 16th century, to whom, with Jean Goujon, the French writers ascribe the honor of the restoration of sculpture in France, was born at Loué, a small village near Mans. The date of his birth is not known; it was probably about 1520. There are very few facts ascertained concerning this artist. His father was a sculptor of little note, and instructed Pilon in the elements of the art. He executed a number of works in the vicinity of his native place, which evince his natural abilities; among them are the statues which adorn the convent of Soulesmes, near Sable, in Maine, known as the Saints of Soulesmes; also a statue of St. Bernard, in the church of Epau, near Mans. About the year 1550, he visited Paris, where Goujon was then in reputation. He became the emulator of that artist, and executed many works for the churches of Paris, also various monuments in the province of Normandy. Soon after attaining some reputation, he was commissioned to execute the mausoleum of Guillaume Langei du Bellay, in the cathedral at Mans. The sculptures which adorn this work, are much in the style of the antique. Pilon was the favorite sculptor of Henry II., and there are still many works at Paris, executed by him in that reign. Catherine de Medicis wishing to erect a monument to that monarch, Philibert de Lorme made the designs, and the execution was entrusted to Pilon, who seemed to surpass himself. The statues of Henry the II. and his queen were draped in robes of state; four bas-reliefs representing Faith, Hope, Charity, and Good Works, sufficiently attest his talent. Charity is represented entirely nude, having given all her clothing to the poor; with two infants suckling at her breasts. All the sculptures in this work are deserving of praise, but the reclining statues of Francis II., and Catherine de Medicis, are considered the best. The latter is represented as divested of drapery; both works are said to combine the vigor of Michael Angelo with the grace of Primaticcio: doubtless too high praise. The master-piece of Pilon, is his group of the Three Graces, on a triangular pedestal, supporting on their heads an Urn, which contains the hearts of Henry and Catherine. This admirable work was sculptured from a single block of marble, and is hardly surpassed for the ease and lightness of its draperies, in which Pilon especially excelled; it was former ly in the convent church of the Celestines, but is now at the Louvre, in the *Musée des Sculptures de la Renaissance*. There are also other works extant by Pilon, in clay, stone, alabaster, bronze, and marble. The date of his death is uncertain. For a long time it was supposed he died about 1606, on account of an epitaph to his memory, by President Maynard, published in that year; but the indefatigable le Noir, after all his researches, has discovered no work by Pilon, after the year 1590.

PILOTTO, GIROLAMO, a Venetian painter, who flourished about 1600. According to Zanotti, he studied under the younger Palma, whose style he closely imitated. He acquired considerable reputation, and executed some works for the churches at Venice and elsewhere. His most celebrated performance, is a large picture in the saloon of the Ducal Palace at Venice, representing the Marriage of the Adriatic, which is highly extolled by Orlandi, though others prefer his San Biagio, at the great altar of the Fraglia, at Rovigo, a picture displaying great sweetness of manner. He lived to an advanced age, and died, according to Zani, in 1649.

PILSEN, FRANCIS, a Flemish painter and engraver, said to have been born at Ghent about 1676, though probably at a later period, as there is a print by him dated 1770. He studied painting and engraving under Robert van Audenarde. Little is known of him as a painter, but there are a few prints by him, among which are the following: the Virgin and infant Jesus, the Conversion of St. Bavon, and the Judgment of Midas; *after Rubens*. St. Francis; *do.;* signed *F. Pilsen, sculp. G.* 1770. The Martyrdom of St. Blaize; *after G. de Crayer.*

PINACCI, GIOSEFFO, a painter of Siena, born in 1642. He first studied under Livio Mehus at Florence, and afterwards with Borgognone. According to Orlandi, he did not follow the manner of either of his masters. He devoted himself mostly to portraits, in which branch he acquired distinction, and made a considerable fortune. He was employed at the court of Carpio, Viceroy of Naples, and afterwards by the Grand Duke of Florence, where there are several of his works. He had an excellent knowledge of the pencilling of the old masters, which enabled him to imitate them very successfully. He was living in 1718.

PINAGIER, THOMAS, a French painter, born at Paris in 1616, and died there in 1653. Little is known of him; he is said to have been a good painter of landscapes.

PINAIGRIER, ROBERT, a French painter on glass, supposed to have been a native of Tours, born about 1490. He executed many works for various churches of France, among which were those in S. Hilaire at Chartres; and at Paris, in the churches of S. Victor, S. Jacques de la Boucherie, the Hospice des Enfants Rouges, S. Gervais, and S. Mederic. Most of his works have been destroyed; but in the Chapelle de la Vierge, at Paris, is preserved a History of the Virgin by him, characterized by beautiful heads, splendid coloring, and vigorous execution. Some of his works in the church of S. Mederic are also preserved. Pinaigrier left three sons—Nicolas, Jean, and Louis; of whom the first was most distinguished. At Chartres, in the church of S. Aignan, there are by him two glass paintings, representing Christ bearing the Cross, and the Last Judgment. There was a grandson of Robert P., named Nicolas, who adorned several Parisian churches with his works in the same art, from 1618 to 1635.

PINAS, JOHN, a Dutch painter, born at Haerlem in 1597, according to Descamps; though Nagler says in 1570. After learning the rudiments of the art at home, he went in company with Peter Lastman to Italy, where he studied some years. On returning to his native country, he became eminent as a painter of history, portraits, and landscapes. The most esteemed of his historical works is a picture in the great church at Haerlem, representing Joseph sold by his Brethren. His style of coloring was vigorous, but rather inclining too much to the deep brown or blackish tints, in which manner he had many admirers, and some imagine that even Rembrandt imitated him in that respect. He died in 1660.

PINAS, JACOB, was a younger brother of the preceding, born at Haerlem in 1599. He had not the advantage of studying in Italy, but after the return of John Pinas, he received considerable advantage from his instruction, and painted landscapes with reputation. He died at Amsterdam in 1659.

PINCHARD, P., an engraver, probably a Frenchman, who resided at Genoa about 1687, where he engraved some book plates.

PINE, JOHN, an English designer and engraver, to whom we are indebted for several splendid and interesting works, the principal of which are the Ceremonies used at the Revival of the Order of the Bath by George I.; the prints from the tapestry in the House of Lords, representing the destruction of the Spanish Armada; a superb edition of Horace, the text engraved, and illustrated with ancient bas-reliefs and gems; the Pastorals and Georgics of Virgil, ornamented in a similar manner, with a printed type. The last were published by his son, after his death, which happened in 1756. He was a man of letters; and designed and engraved many of the plates for the above works. He also engraved a few portraits among which is one of himself, and another of Garrick.

PINE, ROBERT EDGE, was the son of the preceding, born in 1742. It is not known by whom he was instructed, though Pilkington says by his father, who died, according to his statement, when Pine was fourteen years old. Nagler says he was born in 1730, and died in 1795. In 1760 and 1762, he drew the prizes from the Society for the Encouragement of the Arts, &c., for the best historical designs. He painted portraits with some reputation, and in 1782 exhibited a series of pictures of scenes from Shakspeare, some of which were engraved by McArdell, V. Green, C. Watson, and others. He afterwards went to America, where he died in 1790.

PINEDA. See PEREZ.

PINELLI, ANTONIA BERTUCCI, a Bolognese paintress, a favorite scholar of Lodovico Caracci, who admired her, says Lanzi, for her singular modesty and attachment to art. She executed several works for the churches, among which were the Guardian Angel, in S. Tommaso; and two altar-pieces of St. James and St. Philip, in the churches dedicated to those Saints. But her most celebrated performance is a picture of St. John the Evangelist, in the Nunziata, in which she introduced her own portrait with a bonnet, and that of her husband. It was painted from the design of her instructor. She also painted cabinet pictures of sacred subjects, which were admired. Her maiden name was Pinelli, and she married Gio. Battista Bertucci. She died, according to Malvasia and Zani, in 1644, though others say in 1640.

PINELLI, Bartolomeo, a modern Italian painter, designer, and engraver, who resided chiefly at Rome, and distinguished himself for his numerous designs and etchings of Roman history, Italian manners and costumes, and views of the environs of Rome, with groups of Banditti, which in all amount to upwards of two hundred prints, besides numerous other subjects. The works by which he is best known to foreigners, are *Istoria degli Imperitori inventata ed incisa in cento rami* (100 plates); *Raccolta di Costumi pittoreschi; Nuova Raccolta di cinquanta Costumi pittoreschi* (50 plates); *Istoria Greca* (100 etchings); *Istoria Romana* (152 etchings). He also designed and etched many other plates of illustrations to Virgil, Dante, and Tasso. He engraved the frescos painted by Pinturicchio in the dome of S. Maria Maggiore; the Life and Miracles of St. Francis di Paula, *after Marco da Faenza and others;* the Friezes by *Giulio Romano*, in the Farnesina; also, Picturesque Views of Tivoli, &c. His plates are etched in a bold and free style, and there is great spirit and vivacity in his figures. His drawings in chalk and water-colors are much esteemed for beauty of design and spirited execution. His life was one of extraordinary industry. He died at Rome in 1835.

PINI, Eugenio, a painter of Udine, born about 1600. It is not known under whom he studied, but he executed many works for the churches in his native city, and in the Venetian state, which Lanzi says show an artist "extremely diligent and skilled in every office of a painter, if we except, perhaps, his want of a more perfect harmony of tints." The Abate Boni pronounces his Repose in Egypt in the Cathedral of Palma, and his San Antonio in that of Gemona, noble productions, and among his best works. He was living in 1655.

PINI, Paolo, a painter born at Lucca, who, according to Orlandi, flourished shortly after the Caracci, and excelled in painting perspective and architectural pieces, with small figures, for the collections. Lanzi says he has seen only one of his pieces, representing a history of Rahab, in the church of S. Maria di Campagna at Piacenza; in which the architecture is very fine, the figures light, and touched with a spirited pencil.

PINO, Marco da, also called Marco da Siena, an eminent painter and architect, born at Siena about 1520. He seems to have studied under a number of masters. According to Baglioni, he received his first instruction from Domenico Beccafumi, and afterwards studied under Daniello da Volterra. Baldinucci places him among the disciples of Baldassare Peruzzi. It is, however, agreed that he completed his studies at Rome, where Lomazzo states he received instruction from Michael Angelo Buonarotti. Lanzi says he studied with Pierino del Vaga, and assisted him in his cartoons, and that he was a favorite with Michael Angelo, but not his scholar, as some have asserted; though doubtless he benefitted from his friendly instructions. At all events, he made the works of Angelo his model. Lanzi says: "Of his merits as a painter, I believe I do not err when I say that among the followers of Michael Angelo, there is none whose design is less extravagant, and whose color is more vigorous." He painted some pictures for the churches at Rome, which gained him considerable reputation, the most esteemed of which is a Dead Christ, in S. Maria di Aracæli. But the principal theatre of his fame was Naples, where he settled in 1560, and distinguished himself by many works which he executed for the principal churches and public edifices in that city, and in other parts of the kingdom. The most celebrated of these is the Descent from the Cross, in S. Giovanni dei Fiorentini, which he repeated on several occasions, with many variations. In the same church is an admired picture of the Annunciation. Other celebrated works are the Circumcision, in the Gesù Vecchio, into which he is said to have introduced the portraits of himself and wife; and the Adoration of the Magi, in S. Severino. He enriched many of his pictures with noble architecture. He was greatly respected at Naples, and many favors were conferred upon him. He instructed many pupils, the most celebrated of whom was Gio. Angelo Criscuolo.

Marco da Pino practised architecture at Naples. He remodernized the church of La Trinità di Palazzo, and erected the church and college del Gesù Vecchio, which is now used as the university of Naples. It is a well arranged and magnificent edifice, and gained for him the reputation of an able and talented architect. He was also distinguished for his literary labors for the promotion of art, and published a large work upon architecture, as well as a collection of the lives of Neapolitan artists. He died at Naples in 1587.

PINO, Paolo, a Venetian painter, whose history is generally confounded with that of Paolo Pini, *which see.* Lanzi says this similarity of names has frequently led authors into errors. He painted a picture of the Virgin with four Saints, for the church of S. Francesco at Padua, in a style between that of the moderns and the Bellini, to which he affixed his name, *Paulus Pinus, Ven.* 1565. In the castle of Noale, in the territory of Trivigi, he adorned the public hall, both interior and exterior; and that part of it where the judges are accustomed to hear causes and decide differences, with historical subjects adapted to the place. "Whoever is acquainted with the 'Dialogue on Painting,' published by this professor as early as 1548, where in the dedication he professes himself a Venetian, and whoever has seen his works, will be in no danger of confounding him with Paolo Pini of Lucca, who studied under the Caracci."

PINO, da Messina. See Messina.

PINSON, Nicolas. This painter was born at Valence, in the department of Drome, about 1640. He studied at Rome, where he remained some time, and imitated the style of P. da Cortona. Little is known of his history or works. There was a picture by him of Tobit and the Angel, in the collection of Boyer d'Aguilles, engraved by Coelmans. Pinson also etched two prints, now extremely rare representing a Dead Christ, marked *N. P. In. f.*

and the Assumption of the Virgin; marked *N. Pinson. Inuent. et Sculp.*

PINSSIO, Sebastian, a French engraver, born at Paris in 1721. Little is known of him, except that he engraved a few portraits and other subjects.

PINTELLI, Baccio, surnamed Urbinas, a reputable Italian architect, flourished at Rome from 1471 to 1484, during the pontificate of Sixtus IV. He was appointed principal architect to that pontiff, and in 1473 erected the Sistine chapel, which possesses little architectural interest, being principally distinguished for the grand works of art with which it is decorated. The style of Pintelli resembles that of Brunelleschi, and his designs have some characteristics of the previously pointed style of architecture. His works are well constructed, as appears from the cupola of S. Agostino and Ponte Sisto, still in perfect preservation. From 1472 to 1477, he erected the church and convent of S. Maria del Popolo; a beautiful chapel in that edifice for Domenico della Rovere, nephew of Sixtus IV.; a palace for the same at the Borgo Vecchio; and the Old Library of the Vatican. He also built the Hospital of S. Spirito in Sassia; the Ponte Sisto over the Tiber; the churches S. Pietro in Vinculis; S. Agostino; S. Maria della Pace; S. Apostoli (since rebuilt); and probably designed S. Jacopo and S. Pietro in Montorio. In 1480, Pintelli strengthened the celebrated church and convent of S. Francesco di Assisi, by erecting enormous buttresses against the northern walls.

According to the discoveries of Dr. Gaye, Pintelli left Rome after the death of Sixtus IV., in 1484, and went to Urbino, for the purpose of finishing the Ducal palace of Urbino, upon which Lucianus Lauranna had been employed from 1468 to 1483, for Federigo II., Duke of Urbino. It is supposed that he became a citizen of that place, as he assumed the surname of Urbinas. In 1491, he erected the church of S. Maria della Grazie at Urbino, for the Duke Giovanni della Rovere. The time of his death is not recorded.

PINTURICCHIO, Bernardino, a painter born at Perugia in 1454. He studied under Pietro Perugino, and assisted him in many of his principal works, both at Rome and Perugia. He was one of the most distinguished artists of his time, as is evident from the fact that he was selected by the Cardinal Francesco Piccolomini, who soon afterwards became Pope Pius III., to decorate the Sacristy of the Cathedral of Siena, and the chapel of his family, "with works of such magnitude," says Lanzi, in his life of Raffaelle, "as perhaps had never been before entrusted to a single master." Yet never was a painter so unfortunate in his reputation, and every author, from Vasari to Lanzi, sacrifices his just fame to Raffaelle, "the god of their idolatry." Vasari calls him "a pretty good painter." Lanzi is disposed to do him justice, and gives him more credit than any other author; therefore we will give his own account. Speaking of the second epoch of the Sienese school, he says that the Cardinal Francesco Piccolomini, a native of Siena, was the most distinguished patron and promoter of the Sienese school at that period. "For the purpose of decorating the sacristy of the cathedral, and the chapel of his family with various pictures from the Life of Pius II., he invited Pinturicchio to Siena. This artist carried along with him other scholars of Perugino, and even Raffaelle himself, who is reported to have designed either wholly, or in a great measure, those historical pictures." Let it be recollected that this was about 1500; Pinturicchio was forty-six years old. "Having painted with so much applause at Rome," says our author in another place, "before Raffaelle was born," who was a youth of seventeen, unknown at that time in the history of art. In his life of Pinturicchio he says, "Bernardino Pinturicchio, the pupil and assistant of Perugino in Perugia and in Rome, was a painter little valued by Vasari, who has not allowed him his full share of merit. He has not the style of design of his master, and retains more than is consistent with his age, the ornaments of gold in his draperies; but he is magnificent in his edifices, spirited in his countenances, and extremely natural in everything he introduces into his composition. As he was on familiar footing with Raffaelle, with whom he painted at Siena, he has imitated his grace in several figures, as in his picture of S. Lorenzo, in the church of the Francescani di Spello, in which there is a small St. John the Baptist, thought by some to be by Raffaelle himself. He was very successful in arabesques and in perspective, in which he was the first to represent cities in the ornaments of his fresco painting, as in an apartment in the Vatican, where, in his landscapes, he introduced views of the principal cities of Italy. In many of his paintings, he retained the ancient custom of making a part of his decorations of stucco, as the arches, a custom observed in the Milanese school till the time of Gaudenzio. Rome possesses some of his works, particularly in the Vatican and in Aracœli. There are three good pictures by him in the chapel of the Holy Sacrament, in the cathedral of Spello, consisting of three subjects from the Life of Christ—The Annunciation, the Nativity, and Christ disputing with the Doctors, the best of the three. In one of these he introduced his own portrait. But his best works are in the magnificent sacristy of the cathedral of Siena. They consist of ten historical subjects, containing the most memorable passages in the life of Pius II., and on the outside is the eleventh, representing the Coronation of Pius III., by whom this work was ordered." And yet, in his life of Raffaelle, Lanzi gives the glory of these works to that inimitable master, as though he had not accomplished enough of himself to immortalize his name.* "Raffaelle now became the admiration of his master and his fellow scholars; and about this time Pinturicchio, after having painted with so much applause at Rome before Raffaelle was born, aspired to become, as it were, his scholar, in the great works at Siena.† He did not possess a genius sufficient-

* Raffaelle, at the age of seventeen, had just executed a picture representing the Holy Family, in which the Virgin is lifting a Veil from the infant Jesus, who is sleeping in his cradle; which, says Lanzi, must have been the first attempt of the design which he finished at a more mature age.

† Mark the inconsistency in these assertions. "*The Cardinal Piccolomini was the most distinguished patron and promoter of the fine arts at Siena,*" but only as an instrument of blazoning to the world his own illustrious house. He did not employ the artists of his own city, but sought a foreigner whom he had known at Rome, *distinguished before Raffaelle was born*, and whom he judged most competent to conduct those great works. Raffaelle did not acquire any distinction till eight or nine years afterwards, when he was invited to Rome by Julius

ly elevated for the sublime composition which the place required; nor had Perugino sufficient fertility or power of conception equal to so novel an undertaking. It was intended to represent the life and actions of Silvius Piccolomini, afterwards Pope Pius II.; the embassies to various princes entrusted to him by the Council of Constance, and by Felix, the anti-pope, to Frederick III, who conferred on him the laurel crown; and also, the various embassies which he undertook for Frederick himself to Pope Eugenius IV., and afterwards to Callistus IV., who created him a cardinal. His subsequent exaltation to the papacy, and the most remarkable events of his reign were also to be represented; the canonization of St. Catherine; his attendance on the Council of Mantua, where he was received in a princely manner by the Duke; and finally, his death, and the removal of his body from Ancona to Rome. Never, perhaps, was an undertaking of such magnitude entrusted to a single master.* The art itself had not yet attempted any great flight. The principal figures generally stood isolated, as Pietro exhibited them at Perugia, without aiming at composition. In consequence of this, the proportions were seldom true, nor did the artists depart much from sacred subjects, the frequent repetition of which had already opened the way to plagiarism. Historical subjects of this nature were new to Raffaelle, and to him, unaccustomed to reside in a metropolis, it must have been most difficult in painting so many as eleven pictures to imitate the splendor of the different courts, and the manners of all Europe, varying the composition agreeably to the occasion; nevertheless, being conducted by his friend to Siena, he made the sketches and cartoons of *all* these subjects, says Vasari, in his life of Pinturicchio; and that he made the whole is the common report at Siena.† In the Life of Raffaelle, Vasari states that he made *some of the designs and cartoons for these works*, and that the reason for his not continuing them was his haste to proceed to Florence, to see the cartoons of da Vinci and Buonarotti. But I am more inclined to the first statement than the subsequent one. In April, 1503, Raffaelle was employed in the Library, as is proved by the will of Cardinal Francesco Piccolomini. While the Library was yet unfinished, Piccolomini was elected Pope, and his coronation following on the 8th of October, Pinturicchio commemorated the event‡ on the outside of the Library, in the part opposite to the duomo. Bottari remarks that in this façade we may detect not only the design, but in many of the heads the coloring of Raffaelle. It appears probable, therefore, that he remained to complete the works, the last subject of which, might perhaps be finished in the following year, in 1504, when he departed for Florence.* We may here observe, that this work, which has maintained its color so well, that it appears almost of recent execution, confers great honor on an artist of twenty years of age, as we do not find a composition of such magnitude in the passage from ancient to modern art, conceived by any single painter.† So that, if Raffaelle stood not entirely alone in this work, the best part of it must be assigned to him, since Pinturicchio himself was improving at this time, and the works which he afterwards executed at Spello and Siena, incline more to the modern, than any he had before done; which will justify the conclusion that Raffaelle had already, at that early age, far outstripped his master; his contours being more full, his composition more rich and free, accompanied by a more ornamental and grander style, and an ability unlimited, capable of embracing every subject presented to him."

It is evident that the kindness of Pinturicchio to Raffaelle, and the discernment which he evinced in selecting him as one of his assistants, has acted most injuriously to his reputation. If Raffaelle did not altogether paint the picture, he is said to have made the designs, and if authors are compelled to allow Pinturicchio a large share in the execution, they select the most graceful figures and attribute them to Raffaelle. As if this absurdity and gross injustice were not sufficient, they must blacken his fair fame, by making him a miser, and confirming his avarice by a ridiculous story of the cause of his death. He was employed, say they, to paint an altar-piece for the Franciscans at Siena, and the monks had taken everything out from an apartment for his better accommodation, except an old chest, which appeared so fragile that they judged it proper not to displace it. But Pinturicchio insisting on its removal, it was broken in pieces in the attempt, when, *mirabile dictu*, there fell out 500 ducats, which had been secreted in the chest many years. The poor artist was so mortified at missing the opportunity of finding the treasure, and appropriating it to himself, that he fell sick, and died soon afterwards of grief.

PINUS, Cornelius, a Roman painter, who

II., not for any reputation he had then acquired, but at the instigation of Bramante, the famous architect of St. Peter's, who was Raffaelle's uncle. There is good reason to believe, too, that Raffaelle's education at this time was very defective, and entirely unqualified him for any great historical composition. He had not been even in Florence, nor thought of any other style than that of Perugino. Lanzi himself, speaking of his literary attainments, and of a letter he wrote in 1508, requesting the Duke of Urbino to use his influence with the Gonfaloniere Soderini, to give him a commission in the Palazzo Pubblico at Florence, says, "if we were to judge from his letter just cited, now in the Museo Borgia, we might consider him grossly illiterate."

* Many grand historical works had been painted before the time of Raffaelle.

† Vasari had no just authority for making this assertion, further than supposition; common report, too, at Siena, is a very natural one—the pride of possessing works by so great a master.

‡ This work was executed at the express command of Cardinal Piccolomini, then elevated to the papacy under the title of Pius III.

* This is contrary to the express declaration of Vasari, who says Raffaelle hastened to Florence before the works were completed, to see "the cartoons of Michael Angelo and Leonardo da Vinci, which had been prepared in competition by those two great artists, in consequence of the prize offered by the city of Florence." These cartoons were then being publicly exhibited in that city, and attracted the greatest interest. If the advocates of Raffaelle admit that Pinturicchio painted the last and the most beautiful of the series, they must give the glory of the whole to him.

† Michael Angelo was a great inventor; Raffaelle a great composer, and what Fuseli terms a bold adopter. He seized upon the ideas and forms of others, and introduced them into his designs with such matchless skill as made them all his own; whereas the same course, pursued by any other master, would sink his name into plagiarism. Instance his celebrated cartoons, in which he copied the ancient Sacrifice of Masaccio into the cartoon of Paul and Barnabas at Lystra; also his grotesques, adopted from the antique.

flourished in the time of Vespasian, and was employed by him in concert with Accius Priscus, to execute some works in the Temple of Virtue and Honor.

PINZ, or PINTZ, JOHN GEORGE, a German engraver, born at Augsburg in 1697, and died there in 1767. He was chiefly employed by the booksellers, for whom he executed a variety of prints, in the style of those which ornament the numerous publications of Vander Aa. Among others, he engraved an emblematical plate, *after P. Decker*, in honor of the King of France, entitled *Gallus und Germanus*.

PIO, GIOVANNINO DEL. See BONATTI.

PIOLA, GIOVANNI GREGORIO, a Genoese painter, born in 1583. According to Soprani, he excelled in miniatures, or small cabinet pictures. He went to France, and died at Marseilles in 1625.

PIOLA, PIETRO FRANCESCO, a painter of Genoa, born in 1565. He was of the same family as the preceding, and had the reputation of being one of the best imitators of Cambiaso. He died young in 1600.

PIOLA, PELLEGRO, or PELLEGRINO, a painter born at Genoa in 1617. It is not known by whom he was instructed, but he studied diligently the works of the best masters, and selected from them what was most beautiful. Lanzi says, "he then tried a wider flight, and pursued it with great diligence, and a taste which charms us; and whatever style he adopted, he seems to have grown grey in it. A Madonna by him, in the great collection of the Marchese Brignole, was considered by Franceschini an original of Andrea del Sarto; his S. Eligio was by Mengs ascribed to Lodovico Caracci." He possessed wonderful talents, a keen perception of the beautiful, and aspired to the highest ranks of the art; he would have reached a transcendant rank, had he lived to mature his faculties. He was assassinated by an unknown hand, supposed a jealous rival. in 1640, aged twenty-three years.

PIOLA, DOMENICO, was the younger brother of Pellegro P., born at Genoa in 1628. He is said to have received his first instruction from his brother, which must have been at a very tender age; and he afterwards studied under Gio. Domenico Capellini. He associated himself with Valerio Castelli, and in conjunction with that master, executed some works for the churches and public edifices of Genoa. He next imitated Castiglione, and finally adopted a style of his own, in which he imitated that of Pietro da Cortona, in the lustre of his coloring, the splendor of his composition, and his uncommon facility of hand. Lanzi says, "he had a singular talent for the representation of children, and he refined it by the imitation of Fiammingo. He enlivened every composition by their introduction, and in some places he interwove them in elegant friezes. From this soft and easy manner, examples of which are to be found in every part of the Genoese territories, he occasionally departed, as in the picture of the Miracle of St. Peter, at the Beautiful Gate of the Temple, painted at Carignano, in which the architecture, the flesh tints, and the gestures are highly studied, and there is a force of effect, which seems to emulate a picture by Guercino, placed opposite to it in the same church. He also departs from his ordinary style in the Repose of the Holy Family, at the Gesù." He painted a multitude of pictures for the churches and palaces of Genoa, and in the state. He executed a few etchings from his own designs. Bartsch describes five, two Nativities; the Virgin on a throne, with the Infant Jesus on her knees, and St. John kneeling; the Judgment of Paris; and an Old Man with a beard. Nagler mentions another, St. Anthony of Padua, dated 1640, when he was only twelve years old; these are marked with his name. Other prints marked, D. P. or D. P. F., formerly attributed to him, Bartsch assigns to Domenico Peruzzini. He died in 1703.

PIOLA, ANTONIO, was the son of Domenico P., born at Genoa in 1654, and died in 1715. According to Ratti, he studied with his father, whose style he followed with commendation for some time, but afterwards changed his profession.

PIOLA, PAOLO GIROLAMO, was the second son of Domenico P., born at Genoa in 1666, and died in 1724. He studied with his father, and, according to Ratti, fully sustained his reputation; he executed many works for the churches and palaces at Genoa, and other places in the vicinity. Lanzi also ranks him among the best artists of the Genoese school. He died in 1724.

PIOLA, GIO. BATTISTA, was the third son of Domenico P. He assisted his father and his brother in their works, but did not acquire any distinction. Lanzi says he could copy or follow the designs of others well enough, but he had not sufficient invention to do much beyond.

PIOLA, DOMENICO, was the son of Gio. Battista P., born at Genoa in 1718. He possessed excellent abilities. Lanzi says, "while he was beginning to emulate the glory of his family, he was cut off by death in the flower of his life, and with him was extinguished a family which for the course of nearly two centuries had conferred great honor on the art." He died in 1744.

PIOMBO, FRÀ SEBASTIANO DEL. This eminent painter was born at Venice in 1485. His real name was Sebastiano Luciano; Vasari calls him Sebastiano Veneziano, by which name he was designated till Clement VIII. bestowed upon him the office of Keeper of the Seal of his Chancery, to fill which it was necessary for him to take the religious habit, and he assumed the title of Frà Sebastiano del Piombo (of the Leaden Seal), by which appellation he is universally known in the history of art. He first studied with Giovanni Bellini, then far advanced in years; and afterwards with Giorgione, and became the most distinguished disciple of his school, the most successful imitator of the harmony of his coloring, the breadth of his chiaro-scuro, and the fulness of his forms. He first distinguished himself as a portrait painter, to which his powers were peculiarly adapted. His portraits were admired for the striking resemblance, the sweetness of the coloring, and the roundness and boldness of relief, which made his figures appear to stand out from the canvass. Thus, in taking the portrait of Pietro Aretino, he distinguished five different tints of black in his dress, imitating with exactness those of velvet, satin, and other kinds of stuff. His portrait of Giulia Gonzaga, the mistress of Cardinal Hippolito de Medici, was called a *divine performance*.

But his powers of invention were contracted, and unfitted him to undertake by himself large historical compositions. His first great work was an altar-piece for the church of S. Gio. Crisostomo at Venice, executed so entirely in the manner of Giorgione that it was often mistaken for the work of that master, and it is supposed that Giorgione furnished the design. Lanzi, speaking of this performance, says: "It may be presumed, indeed, that he was assisted in the design, for it is well known that Sebastiano possessed no surpassing richness of invention; was slow in the composition of most of his figures; irresolute; eager to undertake, difficult to commence, and more difficult in the completion. Hence we rarely meet with any of his histories or his altar-pieces, at all comparable to the Nativity of the Virgin, in the church of S. Agostino in Perugia; or the Flagellation of Christ at the Osservanti of Viterbo, which is esteemed the best picture in the city. Pictures for private rooms, and portraits, he painted in great number, and with comparative ease; and we nowhere meet with more beautiful heads, more rosy flesh tints, and more novel accessories than in these."

He had already acquired the reputation at Venice of one of the finest colorists of his time, when Agostino Chigi invited him to Rome, and employed him in conjunction with Baldassare Peruzzi, in decorating his palace, where Raffaelle himself had painted his famous Galatea, and furnished the designs for the History of Cupid and Psyche. The rival labors of all these artists are still preserved in the same edifice, now the palace of the Farnesina. In this competition, Sebastiano discovered his inferiority in design, but endeavored to remedy his defects by the study of the antique, and the instruction of Michael Angelo. Vasari relates that "this great artist had felt some uneasiness at the growing fame of Raffaelle, and he gladly availed himself of the powers of Sebastiano as a colorist, in the hope that, assisted by his designs, he might be enabled to enter the lists successfully with his illustrious antagonist, if not to drive him from the field. With this view he furnished him with the designs for the Pietà in the church of the Conventuali at Viterbo, and the Transfiguration and Flagellation in S. Pietro in Montorio at Rome, which, as he was very tedious in his process, occupied him six years." The grandeur of the design, and the extraordinary beauty of the coloring, excited universal surprise and applause. Lanzi, though he notices Vasari's statements, is unwilling to believe that Buonarotti could have been so wicked. It was at this juncture that Cardinal Giulio de Medici commissioned Raffaelle to paint his immortal picture of the Transfiguration; and being desirous of presenting an altar-piece to the Cathedral of Narbonne, of which he was archbishop, he engaged Sebastiano to paint a picture of the same dimensions, selecting for the subject the Raising of Lazarus. On this occasion he was again assisted by Buonarotti, by whom it was composed and designed. Raffaelle died before the entire completion of the Transfiguration, and after his death both pictures were publicly exhibited in competition; and, notwithstanding the wonderful composition of Raffaelle's chef-d'œuvre, which was pronounced inimitable for design, expression, and grace, yet Sebastiano's performance excited universal admiration. After the death of Raffaelle, he was accounted the most distinguished painter in Rome. He was particularly esteemed by Clement VII., whose portrait he drew with amazing resemblance. The Pope rewarded his talents and services with a lucrative benefice, and appointed him to the office of Keeper of the Seals of his Chancery. He was the inventor of the art of painting upon walls with oil colors, which he performed by first covering the wall with a composition of lime, pitch, and mastich. The Resurrection of Lazarus, before mentioned, was purchased by the Regent of France from the Cathedral of Narbonne, for 24,000 francs, and removed into the Orleans Gallery. When that collection was sold in London in 1798, it was purchased by M. Angerstein, for 3,500 guineas. He subsequently refused £15,000 for it. It is said that the French government was desirous of obtaining this picture, to hang beside the Transfiguration of Raffaelle, then in the Louvre. It now adorns the English National Gallery; also his own portrait, holding the seals of his office in his hand. Those of the Cardinal Ippolito de Medici and Giulia Gonzaga are in the same institution, though the authenticity of the two last is doubted by some writers. He died at Rome in 1547.

PIORT, V., an obscure Dutch engraver, mentioned by Strutt, who engraved a plate representing an old Woman and Boy with a pot of lighted Coals, *after Rubens.*

PIPER, Francis, an English amateur artist, born in Kent in 1698. He was a man of fortune, and amused himself in sketching ugly faces and caricatures. He was a wayward and comical genius, and traveled on foot through France, Italy, Germany, and Holland. He drew landscapes, which he etched on tobacco boxes for his friends. He died in 1740.

PIPPI. See Giulio Romano.

PIRANESI, Cav. Giovanni Battista, a preëminent architectural designer and engraver, was born at Venice, according to Zani, in 1713; although Milizia and Gandellini place his birth in 1707. At the age of eighteen he was sent by his father to study architecture at Rome; and devoted himself with great enthusiasm to acquire a knowledge of his profession. He studied engraving under Giuseppe Vasi, a Sicilian. On receiving a summons to return to Venice, he refused, replying that Rome with her monuments was the birth-place of his talent, the adopted land of his affections. Upon this, his father withdrew his allowance; but Piranesi was not dismayed, and prosecuted his favorite art with the greatest ardor. In 1741, he published his first work on triumphal arches, bridges, and other antique architectural remains. This admirable work immediately established his reputation, the engravings being executed in such a masterly style, so decidedly superior to any former representations of similar subjects, as to form an era in chalcography, and architectural delineation; which latter had till then, particularly in Italy, been uniformly exceedingly coarse and tasteless.

Piranesi was of a fiery and impetuous genius. He wrought with marvellous facility, usually making his drawing at once upon the plate itself, and completing it almost entirely by etching in aquafortis, with very little assistance from the graver. His plates, therefore, are distinguished for an astonishing freedom and spirit, and great vigor of execution; although the warmth of his imagination at times impelled him to produce an occasional exaggeration of effect. It is difficult to determine whether the fecundity and spirit of his invention and composition, or the ardor and brilliancy of his execution, should be most admired. His skill in associating different objects, and arranging them for pictorial effect, and the vigor which he gave to the most important by his skillful arrangement of light and shade, gained him the designation of the Rembrandt of Architecture. Possessing such a facility of execution, unexampled in the art of engraving, Piranesi has left an astonishing number of plates. They amount to over two thousand, most of them of very large dimensions, and full of detail. Some of them are published on double elephant paper, the plates opening ten feet in length. Their contents afford an inexhaustible collection of the remains of antiquity, both in architecture and sculpture. His *Magnificenza*, containing many specimens and fragments of ancient architecture till then little known, with the astonishing merit of its execution, would alone have established his fame. He had three sons and three daughters, as well as several pupils, who were all reared to assist him in his labors; but the unmistakeable touch of his master genius runs through all his works, and has not been caught by any of his scholars, which is conclusive evidence that they only performed the strictly mechanical parts of the work.

Piranesi was elected an honorary member of the Society of Antiquaries at London; and also a member of the Academy of the Arcadi, under the name of *Salcindio Tiseio*, according to the custom of that association to give new names to their members. He was also knighted by Clement XIII. In addition to his numerous and extensive labors, he found time, at the particular request of that pontiff, to repair and decorate the church of Santa Maria del Popolo, and the Priory at Malta, where a statue was erected to his memory, executed by Angolini. He died at Rome, November 9th, 1778. His portrait, engraved in 1750, by Polanzani, in the style of a mutilated statue, is prefixed to some of his works. Francesco Piranesi, the son of Cav. Gio. Battista P., settled at Paris after the death of the latter, and transported thither his father's plates. He published a complete edition in that city, in thirty volumes, without the letter-press. The following is a list of the works of this great artist:

Antichità Romane, 4 vols. 1756. Raccolta di Tempi Antichi, viz. di Vesta; della Sibilla; dell' Onore e della Virtu, 1776. Panteon di Marco Agrippa, detto la Rotonda. Monumenti degli Scipioni, 1785. Romanorum Magnificentia et Architectura, 1761. Opere Varie di Architettura Grotescha. Trofei di Ottaviano Augusto. Carcere. Vedute di Archi Trionfali. Rovine del Castello del Acqua Giulia, 1761. Lapides Capitolini, sive Fasti Consulares, &c. Antichita di Cora, 1762. Campus Martius, 1762. Antichita d'Albano e di Castel Gandolfo, 1764-5. Vasi, Candelabri, Cippi, Sarcofagi, Tripodi, Lucerne ed Ornamenti Antichi, 2 vols. 1778. Colonna di Trajano, 1770. Colonna Antonina. Colonna dell' Apoteosi di Antonino Pio. Rovine di Pesto. Vedute di Roma, 2 vols. Teatro d'Ercolano, 1783. Diverse Maniere d'Adornare i Camini, 1769. Statue Antichi, 1781-84. Variæ Tabulæ celeberrimorum Pictorum: Raccolta di Disegni del Guercino. Schola Italica Picturæ, cura et impensis Gavini Hamilton, 1773. Stampe Diverse. Peintures de la Villa Lante; Sala Borgia; Jules II.; Farnesina; Villa Altoviti. Antiquités de la Grande Grèce, gravées par Fr. Piranesi d'aprés les Dessins du feu J. B. Piranesi. (Paris, 1804.) 1807.

PIRANESI, Cav. Francesco, an Italian engraver, the son of Cav. Gio. Battista P., was born at Rome in 1748. He studied design and architecture under his father, whom he assisted in his numerous works, and imitated his style with success. After the death of his father, Francesco transported all his plates to Paris, where he published a complete edition, in thirty volumes. He also engraved several plates of architectural views, and also of antique statues, somewhat in the style of Gio. Marco Pitteri. He died at Paris in 1810. Among others are the following by him:

Jupiter seated; from the statue in the Clementine Gallery; *after a drawing by Piroli.* The Venus of Medicis; *do.* Cupid and Psyche; from the Antique Sculpture in the Gallery of the Capitol. Papirius and his Mother; from the group in the Villa Ludovisi.

PIRANESI, Laura, the daughter of Cav. Giovanni Battista P., was born at Rome in 1750. She studied under her father, and etched a number of plates in his style. After his death, she assisted her brother Francesco in conducting the business, and is supposed to have retired with him to Paris. She engraved several architectural views in Rome, with great taste and delicacy, among which are, the Capitol; the Ponte Salario; the Temple of Peace; and the Arch of Septimius Severus.

PIRINGER, Benedict, a German designer and engraver, born at Vienna in 1780. He engraved numerous plates of landscapes, romantic scenery, views of cities, &c., after various masters and from his own designs. Some of them were published collectively. Nagler gives a list of one hundred and eighty prints by him. He worked in aquatint, and with the graver. He died at Paris in 1826, where he had resided many years.

PIRINI, Louis de, an obscure French engraver, by whom there is a coarsely executed print of the Card-Players, *after Cornelius van Tienen.*

PIRNRAUM, Alexis, an engraver on wood, who, according to Papillon, flourished at Basle about 1545, and whom he supposes was a pupil of Hans Holbein. He does not specify any of his works. Nagler is of opinion that he is the same as Adam Petri, a bookseller of Basle. Zani calls him Pirnbaum, and describes him as an excellent engraver on wood.

PIROLI, Tommaso, an Italian designer and engraver, born at Rome in 1750. He studied under Cav. Gio. Battista Piranesi, and executed numerous prints, etched in outline and in the chalk manner. The following are his most interesting works: the Prophets and Sibyls of Michael Angelo in the Capella Sistina; a copy of Metz's prints of the Last Judgment, in the same chapel; the Story of Cupid and Psyche, from the frescos of Raffaelle in the Farnesina; the frescos of Masaccio in the Brancacci chapel, at Florence; and the outlines for the original editions of Flaxman's designs, illustrative of Homer, Hesiod, Æschylus and Dante, published at Rome. He also executed several sets of engravings from the remains of ancient art, part of which were published at Rome and Paris by Francesco and Pietro Piranesi, sons of the celebrated Gio. Battista P. He died in 1824.

PIROLI, Prospero, an Italian historical painter

and engraver, born in 1761, at Berzonno, in the territory of Novara. He studied at Rome, under an elder brother, a print-seller in that city, and devoted himself to studying the antique, as well as the works of Raffaelle and Michael Angelo. In 1794 he settled at Milan, and was occupied for some time in restoring pictures, until recommended to the Russian prince Rozumowski, who invited him to Moscow. Piroli visited that city, and was employed three years by the Prince. The Emperor invited him to St. Petersburg, and appointed him picture-restorer to the Imperial Gallery, which office he filled eleven years, and acquired a handsome fortune. In 1817 he returned to Italy, and settled at Milan, where he died in 1831. The *Biographie Universelle* states that Piroli painted about twenty-four pictures, and engraved them in an old fashioned method, similar to that of Andrea Mantegna. He presented this collection of prints to the Emperor Nicholas, who acknowledged the compliment by presenting him a splendid ring.

PISA, Niccola da. See Niccola.

PISA, Giovanni da. See Giovanni.

PISANELLI. See Vincenzio Spisano.

PISANELLI, Lorenzo, a Bolognese painter, who studied under Cesare Baglioni, whose manner he adopted, and acquired considerable reputation as an ornamental and perspective painter. He also painted landscapes in the style of his master. He flourished about 1600.

PISANELLO, Vittore, an old painter and medalist, a native of St. Vito in the Veronese territory. There is a great deal of contradiction about this artist, as to the time he flourished, and his merits. Vasari says he was a pupil of Castagno, and dates his death about 1480; whereas dal Pozzo asserts that he possessed one of his pictures dated 1406, before Castagno was born. There are several little altar-pieces, containing the History of St. Bernardino, finished in the style of the old miniaturists (painters of histories with small figures), in the sacristy of S. Francesco at Verona, dated 1473, which are attributed to him, but Lanzi says he does not scruple to pronounce them by another hand. Zani quoted several of his works, dated from 1406 to 1447. His admirers have not hesitated to place him on a rank with Masaccio. Most of his great works, so highly commended by Vasari, have perished. He was an eminent artist in his time, and greatly contributed to the advancement of art. He struck many medals of different princes, possessing rare merit, which are to be found in the Museums and rare collections.

PISANO, Andrea. See Andrea.

PISANO, Giunta, an old painter of Pisa, of whom there are notices from 1210 to 1236. He was the first native painter of Pisa, who distinguished himself. Signor Tempesta wrote a fine eulogium on him about 1800. His works have mostly perished, but there are a few remains at Pisa and Assisi, particularly at the latter city, where he was invited to paint by Frat' Elia di Cortona, Superior of the Minori, about 1230. In the church of the Angioli is a Crucifixion inscribed with his name, Ivnta Pisanus, Ivntini me *fecit.* Lanzi says "this piece shows a knowledge of the naked figure, an expression of pain in the heads, and a disposition of the drapery, greatly superior to the efforts of the Greeks, his cotemporaries. The handling of his colors is strong although the flesh inclines to that of bronze; the local tints are judiciously varied; even the chiaro-scuro shows some art, and the whole is not inferior, except in proportions, to Crucifixions usually ascribed to Cimabue." He painted at Assisi another Crucifixion, which has perished; also a portrait of Frat' Elia, still preserved, signed *Juncta Pisanus me pinxit, An. D.* 1236. He also executed some frescos in the great church of the Franciscans, in which, according to Vasari, he was assisted by certain Greeks. These have mostly perished, except some busts and historical pieces, remaining in the gallery and the contiguous chapels among which is the Crucifixion of St. Peter. These remaining works are so much injured by time, and have been so often retouched, as is supposed, that no just opinion can be formed of their original merit. Morrona asserts that a *Giunta di Giuntino* is mentioned in the records of Pisa, who flourished at the same time; but Lanzi gives good reasons to show that he was the same as *Giunta Pisano.*

PISBOLICA, Jacopo, a Venetian painter, who flourished in the latter part of the 16th century. Vasari, in his life of Sansovino, records his name with praise. There is a fine picture by him of the Ascension, in the church of S. Maria Maggiore at Venice.

PISTOJA, Gerino da, a painter born at Pistoja, who studied under Pietro Perugino, whom he assisted in his works. He afterwards assisted Pinturicchio at Rome and Siena. He executed some works by himself for the churches at Pistoja, San Sepolcro, and even at Rome. Vasari gives him credit for his diligence; but he was meagre in his composition, and cold in his coloring. He flourished in the first part of the 16th century. There are notices of him down to 1529.

PISTOJA, Giovanni da, a painter who studied under Pietro Cavallini at Rome, and was his best scholar. Vasari only briefly mentions him. He flourished about 1350.

PISTOJA, Leonardo da, a painter born at Pistoja, who studied under Gio. Francesco Penni, a distinguished disciple of Raffaelle. His real name was Grazia, as appears from his signature on a picture of the Annunciation, in the chapel of the Canons of Lucca, *Leonardus Gratia Pistoriensis.* In the *Notizie di Napoli* he is called Guelfo dal Celano, and by others, Malatesta. Lanzi is of opinion that there were two painters of this name: of one of them there are notices in 1516; the other is the one to whom this article is devoted. He is called by the Italians Il Pistoia. He accompanied his master to Naples when he was invited to to that court, and assisted him till his death. He was afterwards much employed at Naples and Rome, in painting history and portraits. Lanzi says he was a "respectable painter;" and, in another place, he says the Annunciation before mentioned, his only work in Lucca, "is a picture worthy of a descendant of Raffaelle." Zani says he flourished from 1516 to 1540.

PISTOJA, Leonardo da. In the Cathedral of Volterra is a fine altar-piece, representing the Virgin seated on a throne, with the titular saint and other saints standing around the throne. It is inscribed *Opus Leonardi Pistoriens, an.* 1516. The Cavaliere Tolomei first raised the question whether there were not two artists of this name, who flourished nearly at the same time. Lanzi is decidedly of this opinion, and thinks they were of different families. He says, "the painter of the piece at Volterra was not Grazia who went to Naples, since his master Penni, if we are to believe Vasari, was in that year (1516) still the scholar and assistant of Raffaelle; nor does it seem probable that he educated a pupil of so much merit. This Leonardo, who painted at Volterra, must therefore have been some other, of more proficiency."

PISTOJA, or PISTOJESE, Fra Paolo da, was the favorite scholar and assistant of Fra Bartolomeo. Lanzi says he was his colleague, and that he was honored in his own country with a medal, which he saw at Pistoja, with those of many eminent men in that city. Paolo also inherited the rich collection of designs prepared by Fra Bartolomeo, and, according to Vasari, executed many pictures from them at Pistoja, in accordance with the injunction of his master. These designs were afterwards carried to Florence, and deposited in the Dominican convent of St. Catherine, where they were preserved in the time of Vasari. There is an altar-piece by him in the church of S. Paolo at Pistoja, and others in that of S. Domenico. He flourished in the first part of the 16th century. See Baccio della Porta, called Fra Bartolomeo.

PITAU, Nicholas, the Elder, an eminent Flemish engraver, born at Antwerp in 1633. It is not known by whom he was instructed, but it is supposed that he studied under Francis de Poilly at Paris, whose style he followed, though his plates are executed with more vigor and spirit. He engraved a considerable number of portraits and historical subjects, after various masters, which are deservedly esteemed for the correctness of his drawing, the firmness, dexterity, and vigor of his burin, and the beauty and expression in his heads. His print of the Holy Family, after Raffaelle, is considered a masterpiece of the art. The time of his death is uncertain. Nagler says he died in 1696; Watelet and Zani in 1676, which is probably nearer the truth, as the latest date found on his engravings is 1677. It would be an extraordinary circumstance that an artist possessing such commanding talent should cease to labor in the prime of his life, and twenty years before his death. The following is a list of his most esteemed prints:

PORTRAITS.

Louis Henry, Duke de Bourbon, supported by Wisdom and Religion. Oliver Cromwell; *after vander Werf N. Pitau the younger.* Pope Alexander VII.; *after Mignard.* Louis XIV., King of France; *after le Fevre.* 1670. Louis, Dauphin, his son; *do.* James Fabier du Bulay, Master of Requests; *after Champagne.* H. L. H. de Montmort, of the French Academy; *do.* Theodore Bignon, Master of Requests; *do.* Peter Seguier, Chancellor of France. 1668. Alexander Paul Pitau, Advocate in Parliament. Gaspar de Fieubet, Chancellor. 1662. Nicholas Colbert; *after le Fevre.*

SUBJECTS AFTER VARIOUS MASTERS.

The Holy Family, with St. Elizabeth and St. John; *after Raffaelle;* very fine. The Entombing of Christ; *after L. Caracci.* The Virgin holding the infant Jesus in her arms and reading; *after Guercino.* The Dead Christ, with Angels weeping over him; *do.* The Virgin interceding for St. Bruno and his order; *after Champagne.* Christ and the Woman of Samaria; *do.* Mary Magdalene penitent; *do.* St. Sulpitius in Council; *do.* The Holy Family, with the infant Jesus embracing St. John; *do.* The Holy Family, with an Angel presenting a Basket of Flowers; *after Villequin.*

PITAU, Nicholas, the Younger, was the son and scholar of the preceding. Neither the time of his birth or death is known. He engraved a few plates of portraits, in a manner greatly inferior to that of his father. He probably did not practise the art long. A list of his prints may be found in Nagler's Lexicon.

PITOCCHI, Matteo da'. This painter, according to Melchiori, was a native of Florence, where he is unknown, from his having resided abroad. He excelled in painting small pictures of beggars, bandits, markets, and burlesque subjects. He also painted on a larger scale for the churches, in several cities, particularly at Rovigo and Padua. Lanzi says "he displayed most talent in representations of mendicants, and burlesque and fanciful subjects, which are to be found in the galleries of many noble houses in Venice, in Verona, in Vicenza, and elsewhere. He painted likewise for the churches, particularly at Padua, where he most probably died." Melchiori says he died at Padua, about 1700, at an advanced age; others say he flourished about 1650.

PITTERI, Giovanni Marco, an Italian designer and engraver, born at Venice in 1703. He studied under Gio. Antonio Faldoni, but did not follow the style of his instructor. His plates are executed in a very singular manner, by single strokes, but very different from the method of Claude Mellan. His strokes run from the top to the bottom, and his shadows are produced by strengthening them as the occasion requires. The effect produced by this whimsical operation is rather pleasing, and not inharmonious. He engraved several plates for the Dresden and Florentine Galleries, and others after various masters. He died about 1786. Nagler gives a list of fifty-two prints by him. The following are the most esteemed:

PORTRAITS.

The Bust of Giovanni Marco Pitteri; *after Piazzetta.* Giovanni Battista Piazzetta, Painter, of Venice; *do.* Carlo Goldoni, comic Poet; *do.* Giuseppe Nogari, Painter; *do.* Giovanni Mocenigo, noble Venetian; *do.* Count Schulenbourg, Field Marshal of Venice; *after Rusca.* Cardinal Quirini. Marquis Scipione Maffei. Clara Isabella Fornari.

SUBJECTS AFTER VARIOUS MASTERS.

The Holy Family; *after Pietro Longhi.* The Seven Sacraments; *do.* The Crucifixion; *after Piazzetta.* The Twelve Apostles; *do.* Religion overthrowing Heresy; *do.* St. Peter delivered from Prison; *after Spagnoletto.* The Martyrdom of St. Bartholomew; *do.* St. Catherine of Siena; *after Tiepolo.* Mary Magdalene, penitent; *do.* A set of six Plates of Huntings, in the environs of Venice; *after Pietro Longhi.* Twelfth-Night; *after Teniers.* Two Rustic Subjects; *do.*

PITTONI, Battista, an Italian painter and engraver, born, as is supposed, at Vicenza, about 1508, though there is considerable discrepancy among authors. Nagler says he was born in 1520. He was living in 1585, and his prints bear date from 1561 to 1585. His engravings consist of landscapes, with ancient ruins, fabulous subjects and arabesques, and were published at Venice under the title of *Imagini favolosi, &c. intagliati in Rami da M. (Messer) Battista Pittoni, in Vene tia presso Fran. Ziletti*, 1585. There is no account of his paintings.

PITTONI, FRANCESCO, a painter of Vicenza, who flourished in the first part of the 18th century. He painted small historical pictures and portraits, but did not acquire much distinction.

PITTONI, GIOVANNI BATTISTA, a painter born at Vicenza about 1690. He received his first instruction from his uncle, Francesco P., but afterwards went to Venice, where he diligently studied the works of the great Venetian masters, and formed a style of his own, which Lanzi says displays some novelty in the warmth of his coloring, with a certain pictorial amenity and attraction prevailing throughout the whole, which is very pleasing; and, though his forms cannot be termed select, he is generally correct, ingenious, polished, and intelligent. His figures are generally smaller than life, and he was less successful when he drew on a larger scale. He particularly shone in easel pictures of historical subjects, which are abundant in the various galleries at Venice and in the State. He also painted many altar-pieces, which Lanzi says appear to increase in beauty as they diminish in size. "This we perceive at the Santo at Padua, where he painted, in competition with the best of his cotemporaries, the Martyrdom of S. Bartolomeo, which he colored on a small canvass." Two of his finest works are the Martyrdom of St. Thomas, in the church of S. Eustachio at Venice; and the Multiplication of the Loaves, in S. Cosmo della Guidecca. He also executed a few spirited etchings from his own designs, which are sometimes marked with his initials *G. B. P.*, and sometimes *Johannes Baptista Pittonus Vicentinum fecit.* He died at Venice in 1767.

PITTOR, BELLO, IL. See VINCENZIO PELLEGRINI.

PITTOR, SANTO, IL. See GIO. BERNARDINO RODERIGO.

PITTOR, VILLANO, IL. See TOMMASO MISCIROLI.

PITTORI, LORENZO, a painter born at Macerata, whom Colucci classes among the scholars or imitators of Pietro Perugino. There is a picture of Christ by him, in the church of the Virgin at Macerata, in which the architecture is admirable, but the figures are in the manner termed by the Italians *antico-moderno*. It is dated 1533.

PITTORI, BARTOLOMEO and POMPEO, were sons of the preceding, and flourished at Fano, where they painted in conjunction a picture of the Resurrection of Lazarus, in the church of S. Michele, dated 1534. Lanzi says it is wonderful to observe in this work how little they regarded the reform which the art had recently undergone. This, however, was an early performance, and Pompeo afterwards improved his manner, acquired considerable reputation, and executed some works which are commended by Civalli. He also instructed some pupils, the chief of whom was Taddeo Zuccaro.

PITTORI, PAOLO, DEL MASACCIO, a painter born at Ascoli, of whom there are notices from 1556 to 1590. He is commended by Colucci, who says he painted many works for the churches and public edifices of his native city and its vicinity.

PIZZARO, ANTONIO, a Spanish painter, who flourished at Toledo in the commencement of the 17th century. According to Bermudez, he was a scholar of El Greco, and became a correct designer and a good colorist. He painted several pictures for the convent of the Trinitarios, representing the history of the Order, and other works for the churches of San Justo and San Pastor at Toledo; also a picture of the Nativity of the Virgin, in the church of Santa Maria at Cassarubios. He designed three subjects, which were engraved by Alardo Pompo, for the life of St. Idelfonso, by Salazar de Mendoza, published in 1618.

PIZZOLI, GIOVACCHINO, a Bolognese painter, born in 1651, and died in 1733. According to Zanotti, he was the pupil of Michael Angelo Colonna, and assisted him in many of his works. He was an excellent painter of perspective, and also excelled in landscapes.

PIZZOLO, NICCOLO, a painter and a native of Padua, who died about 1500. According to Vasari, he was a fellow pupil with Andrea Mantegna, under Squarcione, and an imitator of his style. There is an altar-piece of the Assumption of the Virgin by him, in the chapel of the Eremitani at Padua, signed *Opus Niccoletti;* also other figures on the wall, and a fresco in one of the façades. Lanzi says these works approach near the composition and manner of Mantegna.

PLAAS, DAVID VANDER, an eminent Dutch portrait painter, born at Amsterdam in 1647. After learning the principles of the art in his native city, he went to Italy, where he resided several years, and made the portraits of Titian his especial models. He aimed to produce the effect of that great master, though by a very different method of pencilling; as he laid on his colors with a strong body, and so judiciously placed his lights and shadows as to produce a lively and natural effect, without breaking the masses or scumbling together his colors. This method not only gave more power to his figures, but also preserved his colors in lasting beauty. Hence, though his pictures will not bear a close inspection, they have the appearance of life when viewed at a proper distance. On his return to Holland, he acquired great reputation, and painted many of the most distinguished personages of his time. His portrait of Admiral van Tromp, is considered a masterpiece in this branch of the art, and represents, to the life, the spirit, and resolute boldness of the old veteran. His portraits are said to partake of the vigor of Rembrandt, and the truth of Titian; the drawing of his heads and hands is remarkably correct. He died at Amsterdam in 1704.

PLACE, FRANCIS, an English amateur painter and engraver, born at Dimsdale, in the county of Durham, about 1645. His father was a wealthy gentleman, and educated him for the bar; but he abandoned that profession, and amused himself in painting a few pictures of landscapes, flowers, birds and fish, and in designing, etching, and mezzotinting some plates. He possessed talents, and had stern necessity compelled him to greater application, he might have distinguished himself. It is said that he was offered a pension of £500 in the reign of Charles II., to draw for the Royal Navy, which he refused, as he could not endure confinement. He died in 1728.

PLACES, LOUIS DES. See DESPLACES.

PLANO, Francisco, a Spanish painter and architect, was born at Daroca, and flourished at Saragossa in the latter part of the 17th century. He acquired great reputation, both as a painter and an architect. He painted history and portraits, and particularly excelled in ornamental and perspective painting; in the latter branch, Palomino says he was equal to Colonna and Mitelli, an assertion which doubtless ought to be received with many grains of allowance. There is a grand picture by him in the parochial church at Santiago, representing the battle of Clavijo. None of his edifices are mentioned.

PLASS, or PLAS, Peter vander, a Dutch painter, who, according to Descamps, was born about 1570. He resided many years at Brussels, and painted history with great reputation. There are several of his works in the public edifices of that city. Balkema says he died there in 1626.

PLASSARD, Vincent, an obscure French engraver, by whom there is a print of the Holy Family reposing in a landscape, signed *V. Plassard in. et fe.* 1650.

PLATEAU, Antoine, a French painter, born at Tournay in 1759, and died in 1815. He was an excellent decorative painter, and excelled in painting fruit and flower pieces.

PLATTENBERG, or PLATTEN, Matthew van, a Flemish painter, born at Antwerp in 1600. After studying in his native city, he went to Italy for improvement. He resided some time at Florence, where, in conjunction with John Asselyn, called Crabbetjie, he painted some sea pieces and landscapes, which were greatly admired. About 1630 he visited Paris, where his works were held in no less repute, and where he settled for life. There is a good deal of confusion about this artist, as he changed his name from *Plattenberg* to *Platte Montagne*, and marked his prints *M. Montagne*. He etched some spirited plates of marines and landscapes from his own designs. Dumesnil describes twenty-nine prints by him; the greater number are marked *Montagne fecit, Morin ex. cum privil Re.* Some are marked *M. Montagne fecit*, or, *in. et f.* Some writers say his Christian name was *Michel*, but print No. 27, described by Dumesnil, is marked *Matthieu*, which settles the question. He married the sister of Jean Morin. He is confounded by the Italian authors with another artist, named Montagna, who excelled in marines. Malvasia calls him *Mons. Rinaldo della Montagne;* and Lanzi, copying Felibien, *'Niccolo de Plate Montagne.* See *Il Montagna.*

PLATTENBERG, Nicholas van, was the son of the preceding artist, born at Paris in 1631. He is said to have studied painting under Philip de Champagne, and engraving under his uncle, Jean Morin, though it is highly probable that he received his first instructions from his father. He acquired distinction, both as a painter and an engraver, and was elected a member of the Academy at Paris in 1681. His principal works as a painter are in the churches of Notre Dame, St. Sacrament, and St. Nicholas des Champs, at Paris. He was also a good portrait painter. As an engraver, he surpassed his instructor, and his prints are highly commended for correctness of drawing, and boldness and freedom of execution. Dumesnil gives a descriptive list of twenty-eight prints by him. He died at Paris in 1706.

PLATZER, or PLAZER, John George. According to Füessli, this painter was a native of Switzerland, born at Epan, in the Tyrol, in 1702. He first studied with his step father, named Kesler, and afterwards with an uncle on the father's side, a painter residing at Passau. In 1721 he went to Vienna, where he formed an intimate friendship with an artist named Janneck, and as they painted similar subjects, a spirit of rivalry sprang up between them, which proved beneficial to both, without in the least weakening their friendship. Platzer painted cabinet pictures of histories, and public festivals, with a multitude of excellent figures. His best pictures are exquisitely finished, his penciling very beautiful, his coloring gorgeous; and his pictures are very attractive to the uneducated eye. Hence he obtained abundant patronage, and his pictures are said to be found in many grand collections in Germany, and also in England. But his works are criticised as totally deficient in chiaro-scuro, and fantastically colored, without any just harmony of tints. His compositions abound with figures in theatrical action, and in the representation of his story, he frequently violates chronology, and the proprieties of costume. There are many of his works at Vienna, Breslau, and Glogau. He afterwards returned to his native place, where he was living in 1755.

Zani notices a *Giovanni Giorgio Platzer*, doubtless the same artist, a native of Trent, born in 1702, and died in 1760. He painted conversations; there are two of his pictures in the Imperial Gallery at Vienna, in which the figures are habited in Spanish costume.

PLATZER, John Victor. Nagler says this artist was a painter and sculptor, born in Vintschgau, probably at Mals, in 1704. He first studied with Kessler at Inspruck, and afterwards with Christopher Platzer, court painter at Passau. He afterwards established himself at Vienna, where he painted cabinet pictures of histories, conversations, and assemblies, mostly with many figures, which were received with great applause, both at home and abroad. He bestowed immense labor on his pictures, and his intense application weakened his sight and diminished the firmness of his hand, so that he was obliged to use a machine to steady it while painting. The pictures he painted under these circumstances are greatly inferior to his earlier productions. None of his works as a sculptor are mentioned. He returned to his native place in 1755, where he died in 1767. By comparing the names of this and the preceding painter, the dates, subjects, style, &c., it will appear evident that they were brothers, if not one and the same artist.

PLATZER, Joseph, a German painter, born at Prague in 1752. He was the son of Ignatius P., the celebrated sculptor. After the completion of his studies at the University, he devoted six years to the study of drawing, particularly in architecture, under the instruction of F. Wolf. In oil painting he was his own master. His attainments were noticed by Prince Kaunitz, who honored him with his patronage. Thus favored, he went to Vienna, and devoted six years more to assiduous study, when he thought himself qualified to undertake greater works than those on which he had been employed. In hopes to attract public attention, he executed a grand triumphal arch thirty-six feet high, and erected it on a holiday at St. John's hospital. It was universally admired, and produced the desired result. In 1781, he was employed to decorate the new theatre at Prague, and was soon afterwards selected by the Emperor Joseph II. to embellish the Royal Theatre at Vienna. On the accession of Leopold II., he was appointed one of the court painters, and notwithstanding much opposition proved himself worthy of the situation. In 1790, he was appointed principal cabinet painter, which office he held till his death in 1810. He did not confine himself to decorative painting, but painted cabinet pictures of historical subjects with great ability. He also excelled in moonlight scenes.

MP. or MP:F. PLEGINCK, Martin, a German engraver on wood and copper, who flourished about 1590. He executed quite a number of prints of small size, which do not possess sufficient interest for insertion here; for a description of his works the reader is referred to Bartsch, P. G., tom. ix. He engraved a set of copper plates representing various figures engaged in different kinds of combat, in a style resembling that of Virgilius Solis; also a set of small wood cuts representing ecclesiastical orders and dignities, cavalry and foot soldiers, *after J. de Gheyn.* Also some cuts of animals and ornaments for goldsmiths. His prints are usually marked with one of the above monograms. Zani says he operated in 1606, but the latest date found on his prints is 1594.

PLEYDENWURFF, William, an old German wood engraver, who flourished at Nuremberg in the latter part of the 15th century. In conjunction with Michael Wolgemut, he executed the cuts for the *Nuremberg Chronicle*, a heavy folio, compiled by Herman Schedel, and published in Latin at Nuremberg in 1493. It is illustrated with about 2000 cuts, representing views of ancient cities, figures of various kinds, and other subjects, which, though drawn in the stiff, formal, and incorrect manner of the time, are nevertheless spiritedly and boldly cut, with much expression in many of the heads.

PLIN, E., a French engraver, who flourished about 1780, and executed some plates of conversations and domestic subjects, etched and finished with the graver, in a neat, clear style.

PLINIUS, Secundus, Caius, usually called the Younger Pliny, was the nephew and adopted son of Pliny the Naturalist, and flourished about A. D. 100. He deserves mention in a work relating to architecture, for a number of excellent edifices which he caused to be erected, although not an architect by profession. While consul in Bithynia, he built the baths in the city of Nicomedia; rebuilt many public and private edifices in various parts of Asia Minor; erected a magnificent theatre at Nicæa; and cut a canal of communication from lake Nicæa to the sea. He was appointed by the Emperor Trajan to the general superintendence of the Roman aqueducts, and erected a number of beautiful edifices in Italy.

PLONICH, Vedastus du, a Dutch engraver, who flourished about 1660, and executed a few plates of views in Holland, in a neat, though formal style.

PLOOS, Cornelius van Amstel. See Amstel.

PLOTT, John, an English miniature painter, born at Winchester in 1732. He was bred to the law, but disliking that profession, he went to London in 1756, and became the pupil of Richard Wilson, the admirable landscape painter; but his genius leading him to portraiture rather than landscape, he left that master and placed himself under the tuition of Nathaniel Hone. He afterwards turned his attention to miniature, both in enamel and water colors, in which branch he was very successful, and met with considerable employment. He had a taste for painting history, and his drawings in that line possess great merit. He sometimes painted portraits in oil. Towards the close of his life he retired in easy circumstances to Winchester, where he was chosen a member of the corporation of that city. He died there in 1803.

PLUMIER, an artist, probably a Frenchman, by whom there are some spirited etchings, from his own designs, signed *Plumier fecit*, which show him to have possessed talent, though his drawing in the naked parts of his figures, is not very correct.

PO, Pietro del, a Sicilian painter, born at Palermo in 1610. After learning the rudiments of the art at Palermo, he went to Naples, and studied under Domenichino, during the residence of that celebrated painter in that city. On his return to Palermo, he executed some works for the churches, and afterwards proceeded to Rome, where he also wrought some for the churches, but distinguished himself more for the pictures which he painted for the collections, and especially for his spirited engravings. He had a thorough knowledge of art. His chief work at Rome is a picture of S. Leone, in the church of the Madonna di Constantinopoli, which Lanzi says does not do him so much honor as some of his easel pictures, especially his small cabinet pictures, executed in the manner of miniatures with exquisite taste; some of them are to be found in the collections at Rome and Piacenza, and some were sent to Spain. He afterwards settled at Naples with his son, Giacomo, where he died in 1692. He executed some spirited etchings, finished with the graver, from his own designs, and after other masters, which are highly esteemed. Bartsch gives a list of thirty-two prints by him, which he believes to be a complete catalogue, though there are three or four others attributed to him, which do not bear his name. The following are the best:

St. John in the Wilderness; *after An. Caracci.* The Woman of Canaan before Christ; *do.* The Dead Christ on the Lap of the Virgin; *do.* The Virgin seated on a Throne with the Infant, and a Choir of Angels; *after Domenichino.* The four Cardinal Virtues, with their attributes; *do.* St. Jerome kneeling; with an Angel; *do.* The Annunciation; *after N. Poussin.* The Flight into Egypt; *do.*

PO, Giacomo del, was the son of the preceding, born at Rome in 1654. He received his first instructions from his father, but afterwards studied under Niccolo Poussin. There are only two of his pictures in the churches at Rome, one in S. Marta, and the other in S. Angiolo. He went to

Naples, where he settled, and found abundant employment in ornamenting the halls and galleries of the nobility with frescos of allegorical and fabulous subjects. His intimacy with letters aided the natural poetic taste with which his pictures are conceived, and his varied and enchanting colors, fascinated the eye of every beholder. He was singular and original in his lights and in their various gradations and reflections. His inventive genius, extraordinary facility of hand, and abundant employment, led him into negligence and incorrectness in design, especially in his figures and draperies; so that he fell into a kind of mannerism, as is usually the case with confident and rapid operators. He also executed a few works for the churches; but his genius chiefly shines in the gallery of the Marchese Genzano, and in the Palace of the Duke of Matalona; and still more in seven apartments of the palace of the prince of Avellino. He died in 1726.

PO, Teresa del. This paintress was a daughter of Pietro del Po, who instructed her in the art. She painted cabinet pictures in the style of her father, and was skilled in miniatures. She also etched some plates in a manner so closely resembling that of her father that they can scarcely be distinguished, except by the signature. Bartsch describes sixteen prints by her, and enumerates six more, mentioned by Füessli. The time of her birth is not known. She acquired so much distinction, that she was elected a member of the Academy of St. Luke at Rome. She died at Naples in 1716.

POCCETTI. See Bernardino Barbatelli.

POCO E BUONO, Il. See Girolamo Nanni.

PODESTA, Andrea, a Genoese painter and engraver, born about 1620. He went early in life to Rome, where he studied under Giovanni Andrea Ferrari. He is scarcely known as a painter, but he executed some spirited and masterly etchings from his own designs and after other masters, for the Giustiniani Gallery, which prove him to have been an artist of ability. He is called by most writers, *Giovanni Andrea P.;* and Zani says his true name was *Giacomo Andrea*, but he marked his prints AND. P., or *And. P. in. et fec.*

or POEHAM, Martin, an old German engraver, to whom Professor Christ attributes some plates marked with one of the above monograms. They chiefly consist of indifferently executed copies of other prints by Aldegrever, Hans Sebald Beham, and others.

POEL, Egbert vander, a Dutch painter, of whom little is known, except by his works. His favorite subjects were conflagrations, representations of fire-works, with numerous figures, interiors by candle-light, &c., which he treated with great ability. His pictures are well designed, his pencil is free and firm, his coloring vigorous, and his chiaroscuro excellent. He is said to have been nearly related to Brower, and was perhaps his pupil, whose manner, as well as that of Teniers, he sometimes imitated with considerable success. In the Museum at Amsterdam is a fine picture by him, representing the explosion of a powder magazine at Delft in 1654, which he repeated several times. In the same collection is an interior of a cottage with females engaged in domestic employment. There are many of his cabinet pictures in the various collections in Holland, where they are highly esteemed. His name is generally found on his pictures, though he sometimes marked them only with his initials, E. V. P. His works date from about 1660 to 1690, at which time Balkema says he died.

POELEMBURG, Cornelius, an eminent Dutch painter, born at Utrecht in 1586. He first studied under Abraham Bloemaert, and afterwards went to Italy for improvement. He at first adopted the style of Adam Ælsheimer, but afterwards quitted it, on beholding the works of Raffaelle, as we are sagely told by Houbraken, "to study and imitate the grace of that incomparable master, particularly in the naked"! He formed for himself a style entirely new, partaking of both the Flemish and Italian schools; Flemish in landscape, and Italian in accessories. He adopted a pleasing style of painting small cabinet pictures of landscapes, into which he introduced some small figures, usually naked, illustrative of fable, poetry, or mythology, enriched with ancient ruins and edifices. His skies are clear, light, and transparent, and he generally made choice of agreeable scenery. He frequently ornamented his backgrounds with vestiges of magnificent Roman edifices, carefully copied from nature; his figures were more remarkable for the neatness of his pencil and the clearness of his carnations, than for correctness of design. His composition is pleasing, and there is a polish and seductive brilliancy in his finishing, that captivates the generality of observers. He soon gained an immense reputation at Rome; his works were held in the highest estimation, and it is said that some of the cardinals and other great personages frequented his studio. This flattering encouragement could not subdue his desire to return to his own country, and he set out, via Florence, where he was received by the Grand Duke with distinguished honors, who commissioned him to paint several pictures, and endeavored in vain to retain him in his service, by the most marked liberality and munificence. Soon after his arrival at Florence, Rubens himself honored him with a visit, purchased several of his pictures and bespoke others, by which generous conduct, he greatly benefitted the artist, instructing others how to estimate and encourage his talents. On his return to his native city, he was received with joy, and his countrymen, impatient for his presence, and anxious to possess his works, loaded him with more commissions than he could execute at the time. In 1637, Poelemburg visited England at the invitation of Charles I., where it is supposed he resided several years. He painted several pictures for the King, and others for the nobility. In King Charles' catalogues are mentioned the portraits of his Majesty, and of the children of the King of Bohemia; and in that of James the II., are sixteen pictures by him. The success he met with could not induce him to remain in England, and he returned to Utrecht; where he died, in 1660. The works of Poelemburg have been largely imitated, and one of the most successful imitators of his manner was John vander Lys, whose works are often attributed to Poelemburg. He also sometimes inserted the figures in the works of eminent cotemporary artists, as Steenwyck, Kierings, and John Both; and they probably returned him a like compliment, by painting his landscapes. Descamps and Watelet assert that Poelemburg etched some spirited prints from his own designs, but these were probably executed by *J. G. Bronkhorst*, after his designs.

POERSON, CHARLES, a French historical and portrait painter, born at Metz. He went to Paris, where he settled, and practised his profession with considerable reputation till his death, in 1667.

POERSON, CHARLES FRANÇOIS, was the son of the preceding, born at Paris in 1653. He learned the rudiments of the art from his father, and after his death became the pupil of Noel Coypel. He painted history and portraits, but was more successful in the latter branch; though he had an excellent general knowledge of art. His promising talents recommended him to the patronage of M. Mansard, through whose influence he was appointed portrait painter to Louis XIV., whose portrait he painted so much to the satisfaction of that monarch, that he honored him with the order of St. Lazarus. He was also employed to decorate the hospital des Invalides with some historical works, but these gave so little satisfaction, that Mansard caused them to be obliterated, and replaced by the frescos of Bon Boullongne, which obtained much applause. This sad failure threw Poerson into deep despondency, but his friend Mansard contrived to raise his spirits by inducing the King to appoint him professor of the French Academy at Rome, which office he filled with great honor. On the death of Carlo Maratti, he was made President of the Academy of St. Luke. He died at Rome in 1725.

POGGINO, ZANOBI DI, a Florentine painter, who studied under Gio. Antonio Sogliani. According to Baldinucci, he executed many works for the churches and edifices of Florence, in the style of his master. Lanzi says his works are now hardly known in that city.

POILLY, FRANÇOIS, THE ELDER, a very eminent French engraver, born at Abbeville in 1622. He was the son of a goldsmith and engraver, who instructed him in the rudiments of art. He afterwards went to Paris and studied with Pierre Daret three years. He then visited Rome, where he resided three years, greatly improved his design, and executed several plates after the Italian masters, in which he adopted the fine style of Cornelius Bloemaert, as his model. On his return to Paris, he distinguished himself as one of the most celebrated engravers of his country, and was appointed engraver to the King in 1664. His plates are executed entirely with the graver, which he handled with uncommon firmness and dexterity. The correctness of his drawing corresponds with the beauty of his burin, and his heads have a fine expression. Though he had the assistance of some able pupils, it is surprising that he could have produced so many plates, many of them of large size, in a manner that requires both time and patience, and so uniform, that it is difficult to establish a ground of preference, except by the subject. There are about 400 prints which bear his name; the following are the most esteemed. He died in 1693.

PORTRAITS.

Pope Alexander VII., with accessories. Louis XIV. when young; *after Nocret.* Cardinal Mazarine; *after Mignard.* Henry D'Arnaud, Bishop of Angers. Jerome Bignon, Counsellor of State; *after Champagne.* Abraham Fabert, Marshal of France; *after Ferdinand.* William de Lamoignon, with Allegorical Figures; *after Mignard.* Bust of William de Lamoignon; *after le Brun.*

SUBJECTS FROM HIS OWN DESIGNS.

The Virgin and Child. The Holy Family, with St. John embracing the infant Christ. St. Ignatius of Loyola. The Death of St. Francis Xavier. The Crucifixion. The Triumph of Augustus.

SUBJECTS AFTER VARIOUS MASTERS.

The Vision of Ezekiel; *after Raffaelle.* The Holy Family, in which the infant Christ is standing upon the cradle; *do.* The Virgin lifting up a Veil, to show to St. John the infant Christ sleeping; *do.* The Flight into Egypt; *after Guido.* The Nativity, or Adoration of the Shepherds, in an octagonal border; *do.* The first impressions of this plate are before the two angels which appear above were inserted. Christ praying in the Garden; *do.* The dead Christ on the lap of the Virgin, at the foot of the Cross; *after L. Caracci.* The Repose in Egypt, in which the Virgin is represented sleeping, with two Angels kneeling; *after An. Caracci.* The Holy Family; *after N. Poussin.* The Marriage of St. Catherine; *after P. Mignard.* The Holy Family; *do.* The Baptism of Christ; *do.* St. Charles Borromeus administering the Communion to the Persons infected with the Plague; *do.* The Visitation; *after C. le Brun.* St. John in the Isle of Patmos; *do.* The Crucifixion; *do.* The Parable of the Wedding Garment; *after Champagne.* The Crucifixion; a large print, in three sheets; *do.* The Trinity; *do.* Joseph's Bloody Garment presented to Jacob; *after Antoine Coypel.* Nymphs Bathing; *after Giulio Romano.*

POILLY, NICOLAS. This engraver was the brother of the preceding, born at Abbeville in 1626. It is said that he studied under his brother, but it is evident that he first studied under some other master, and that on the return of François from Rome, he improved himself by his instruction. He executed quite a number of prints in the style of his brother, and, though much inferior to them, they are executed in a clear, neat manner, and possess considerable merit. He died at Paris in 1696. The following are his principal plates:

PORTRAITS.

Louis XIV., in a frame of laurels, with Children bearing emblems; *after N. Mignard.* Bust of Louis XIV., as large as life. 1683. Maria Theresa, Queen of France; do. 1680. Louis, Dauphin, the son of Louis XIV.; do. Louis Bourbon, called the Great Condé; do. Francis de Coetlogon, Bishop of Rennes. René Potier, Duke de Gesvre; *after le Fevre.* Nicholas Edward Olier, Counsellor of State.

SUBJECTS AFTER VARIOUS MASTERS.

St. Augustine holding a Crucifix. The Holy Family, with two Angels holding a Basket of Flowers; *after S. Bourdon.* The Marriage of St. Catherine; *do.* The Presentation in the Temple; *after C. le Brun.* The Holy Family, with the infant Jesus sleeping on the Knee of the Virgin; *do.* The Repose in Egypt; *after Chapron.* The Crucifixion; *after N. Poussin.*

POILLY, JEAN BAPTISTE, was the son and pupil of Nicolas P., born at Paris in 1669. After studying with his father, he went to Rome, where he resided several years. On his return to Paris, he executed a considerable number of plates, which gained him distinction. He was elected a member of the Royal Academy at Paris in 1714. His style of engraving was very different from that of his father or uncle. He forwarded his plates with the point, and finished them with the graver. His prints are distinguished for correct drawing, fine expression of the heads, and a pleasing and picturesque effect. The following are his most esteemed works. He died in 1728.

PORTRAITS.

Clement XIII. Pontifex Max. Louis XIV.; *after Mignard.* Charles James Edward Stuart, son of the Pretender; *after Dupra.* Francis de Troy, Painter; *from a picture by himself;* his reception plate at the Academy. Cornelius van Cleve, Sculptor; *after Vivien:* do.

SUBJECTS AFTER VARIOUS MASTERS.

The Nativity; *after Gaudenzio Ferrari;* for the Crozat collection. The Virgin adoring the infant Jesus, who is sleeping; *after Benvenuto Garofalo;* do. The Martyrdom of St. Cecilia; *after Domenichino.* The Adoration of the Shepherds; *after C. Maratti.* The Rod of Aaron devouring the Rods of the Magicians; *after N. Poussin.* The Israelites worshipping the Golden Calf; *do.* The Holy Family; *do.* The Judgment of Solomon; *after A. Coypel.* Susanna and the Elders; *do.* Jupiter and Danaë; *after Giulio Romano;* for the Crozat collection. Eleven Plates from the paintings by *P. Mignard,* in the saloon of St. Cloud. The Four Seasons; *do.;* from the paintings in the Gallery of St. Cloud.

POILLY, FRANÇOIS, THE YOUNGER, was the younger son of Nicolas P., born at Paris in 1671. He received instruction from his father, and accompanied his brother to Paris, where he engraved a plate of St. Cecilia distributing her wealth to the poor, *after Domenichino,* a companion print to the martyrdom of that saint by the same master, engraved by Jean Baptiste Poilly. Nothing further is mentioned of him. He died in 1723.

POILLY, NICOLAS JEAN BAPTISTE, according to Basan, was the son of Jean Baptiste P., and was instructed by his father in the art, which he soon abandoned for some other employment. According to Nagler, he was born in 1712, and executed a few portraits, one of which is dated 1758, contradicting Basan's statement.

POINDRE, JACOB DE, a Flemish painter, born at Malines in 1527. He studied under Schwagers Marc Willems. He painted history and portraits, in which latter branch he excelled. He went to Copenhagen, where it is said he was employed to paint the portraits of some of the Kings, probably as historical recollections; but it seems more probable that he painted the portraits of the King and other members of the Royal family. He died there in 1570.

POINSART, J., a French engraver, who flourished about 1630. He was principally employed by the booksellers, for whom he executed a variety of views of cities, castles, &c., executed with the graver, in a neat, but incorrect and tasteless style. Among other prints by him, is one of the Entry of Charles VII. into Rheims.

POINTE, F. DE LA, a French engraver, who flourished at Paris about 1678. He engraved a plan of Paris in nine parts; and, in conjunction with Israel Silvestre, engraved some of the views of the Palace of Versailles.

POL, CHRISTIAN VAN, a Dutch painter, born at Berkenrode, near Haerlem, in 1752. He obtained great reputation for his arabesques, which he rendered very agreeable by the introduction of birds, flowers, and fruit. In 1782 he went to Paris, and was employed in decorating the palaces of Bellevue, Chantilly, and St. Cloud. He also painted flower-pieces, in oil, in a style of excellence. He sometimes painted groups of flowers on snuff-boxes, so delicately executed that they might be mistaken for the works of the greatest masters in that line. He died in 1813.

POLANCOS, two Spanish painters, brothers, who flourished at Seville about 1646. Little is known of them except by their works. They studied under Francisco Zurbaran, whose style they so closely imitated that their works are often attributed to that master. This is particularly the case in the church of San Esteban at Seville, where Zurbaran painted the pictures of St. Peter, St. Stephen, and St. Hermenegildo, and the brothers Polancos an altar-piece of the patron Saint, a picture of the Nativity, and another of St. Fernando. They also painted several large pictures for the churches and convents of Seville, among which are the Angels appearing to Abraham, Jacob wrestling with the Angel, Joseph's Dream, and Tobit and the Angel, in the convent of St. Paul; and St. Teresa conducted by Angels, in the church of the Guardian Angel, belonging to the Barefooted Carmelites and Franciscan Friars.

POLANZANI, FELICE, an Italian engraver, who flourished from 1745 to 1766. He engraved some prints after Vandyck and other masters, a list of which may be found in Nagler's Lexicon.

POLANZANI, FRANCESCO, an Italian engraver, born at Andale, near Venice, about 1700. He resided chiefly at Rome, where he engraved a set of twenty-two plates of the Life of the Virgin, from designs which are attributed by some to Niccolo Poussin, and by others to Jacques Stella, whose style they more nearly resemble. He also engraved several plates after Cignani, Marco Benefiali, and other masters. There was another engraver of this name, who was a native of Verona, and flourished about 1750.

POLAZZO, FRANCESCO, a Venetian painter, born in 1683, and died in 1753. Lanzi says he was a good painter in the manner of Gio. Battista Piazzetta, softened down with that of Antonio Ricci, called Il Barbalunga. He could also imitate the touch of various masters, and for this reason was much employed in restoring ancient pictures.

POLESTANI, ANDREA, an Italian artist, probably a painter, by whom there is a slight and spirited etching of a Bacchanalian subject, from his own design, signed *Andrea Polestanus, fecit.* 1640.

POLETNICH, J. F., an engraver who flourished at Paris, from about 1760 to 1780. He engraved several plates after the works of Vandyck, Boucher, Lagrenée, and other masters.

POLI, two brothers, natives of Pisa, who flourished about the middle of the 17th century. Lanzi briefly notices them among the landscape painters of the fourth epoch of the Florentine school, and says, "they executed many pleasing landscapes, which are to be found in the collections at Florence and Pisa."

POLIDORE. See JOHN GLAUBER.

POLIDORINO, IL. See FRANCISCO RUVIALE.

POLIDORO, DA CARAVAGGIO. See CARAVAGGIO.

POLIDORO, VENEZIANO, a Venetian painter, born in 1515, and died in 1565. His real name is not certainly known, though in the Necrologio of S. Pantaleone, he is expressly called Polidoro Pittore. According to Zanetti, he was a disciple of Titian, and an imitator of his style. He painted Holy Families, Madonnas, and other sacred subjects, for the collections, and wrought some for the churches and convents. Lanzi says he was for the most part a feeble imitator of Titian, who supplied the shops with an abundance of his Madonnas and other sacred subjects; one who made a trade of his profession. "To judge from an altarpiece at the Servi, and some other pictures by him at Venice, we may pronounce him a tolerably good composer, though he never distinguished himself much in the rank of his cotemporaries; yet, when the school declined, his labors acquired more esteem, and were exhibited in the studios of some artists, much in the same manner as sculptors collect specimens of ancient marbles, however inferior, as advantageous in the pursuit of their art";—by which he means that his pictures were used by artists as models in coloring.

POLLA, Bartolomeo da, a painter of the Venetian school, who flourished about 1500. Little is known of him. He decorated the panels in the Choir of the Certosa, at Pavia, with figures of the Apostles and other Saints, which Lanzi says are designed in the style of Leonardo da Vinci.

POLLAJUOLO, Antonio, an eminent Italian sculptor, painter, and engraver, born at Florence in 1426. He was brought up to the business of a goldsmith and designer, under Bartolucci. He afterwards studied modeling and casting, under Lorenzo Ghiberti, whom he assisted in executing the celebrated gates in the church of S. Giovanni at Florence, which were the admiration of Michael Angelo. He executed in bronze the tombs of Sixtus IV., and Innocent VIII. His younger brother having distinguished himself as a painter, he became his disciple, and executed several pictures for the churches and public edifices, which rank him as one of the ablest artists of his time. The most celebrated of these is the Martyrdom of St. Sebastian, in the chapel of the Marchese Pucci, in the church of the Servi at Florence. Lanzi says, "this is the finest picture of the 15th century I have seen; the coloring is not in the best style, but the composition rises above the age in which he lived, and the drawing of the naked figure shows what attention he had bestowed on anatomy. He was the first Italian painter who dissected bodies in order to learn the true situations of the tendons and muscles." He was also one of the earliest Italian artists who practised engraving. Cotemporary with Maso Finiguerra, he is supposed to have learned the art from him. He engraved a few plates, executed in a style similar to that of Finiguerra, which are now extremely scarce. He died in 1498. The following prints are known to be by him, and bear his signature:

Hercules strangling Anteus.

A large plate, representing ten Naked Figures fighting with swords and other weapons. It is inscribed *Opus Antonii Pollajoli Florentini*, without a date. The background is a forest, very rudely represented. The design shows that he had paid some attention to the figure, and the heads are not without expression.

The Holy Family, in which the Virgin is seated, with the infant Jesus on her knee; St. Joseph appears on the right hand, leaning on his staff; on the left is St. Elisabeth, with St. John presenting a flower to the Child.

The following are also generally attributed to him:

Hercules combating the Giants. There is no signature to this print, but Bartsch and Ottley both describe it, and think there is every reason to believe it to be by him.

The Battle of the Centaurs with the Lapithæ, described by Ottley. Bartsch gives this print to Gasparo Reverdino, but there seems to be little doubt among connoisseurs that it is by Pollajuolo. This print, formerly in the Palazzo Riccardi, is now in the British Museum.

The niello of the Martyrdom of St. Lawrence, described by Duchesne.

POLLAJUOLO, Pietro del, was the younger brother of the preceding, born at Florence in 1433, according to Vasari, though others say in 1428. He studied under Andrea Castagno, and distinguished himself chiefly for his admirable portraits. He painted many of the great personages of his time, as large as life, which gained him immense applause. Among his best historical works, were the Labors of Hercules, in the Medicean palace. He died at Rome in 1498, the same year as his brother, aged 65 years.

POLLAJUOLO, Simone del, called Il Cronaca, a distinguished Italian architect, was born at Florence in 1454. The surname Il Cronaca (the Chronicle), was given him on account of his ability in relating stories. He visited Rome at an early age, where he resided with his relative, Antonio del Pollajuolo, and studied the remains of antiquity with great assiduity. On returning to Florence, he gained great reputation, and, according to Milizia, was employed to finish the Palazzo Strozzi, commenced by Benedetto da Maiano. He erected the beautiful façade in the Tuscan order, and at the top placed a Corinthian entablature, from his own design, which Milizia characterizes as the most magnificent that was ever seen. He adorned the court of this palace with a Composite order below, and a Corinthian above, with exceedingly beautiful columns, windows, and doors, all from his own designs. On the hill of S. Miniato, near Florence, Pollajuolo designed the church of S. Francesco, of such exquisite proportions that Michael Angelo was accustomed to call it his *bella Villanella*, or beautiful country seat. His sacristy of S. Spirito, at Florence, is of an octangular figure, elegant and well proportioned. Among his other works were the convent Dei Servi, and the great Council Hall of Florence. He was a follower of Savonarola. He died in 1509, and was entombed in S. Ambrogio.

POLLIO, Vitruvius, a Roman architect, and a celebrated writer on the art, who flourished in the age of Augustus. According to Milizia, he was a native of Fornia, now called Mola di Gaeta. Other authorities say that he was a native of Verona. During the civil war, Augustus employed him in constructing military engines; and, after peace was restored, appointed him Inspector of Buildings. It is said that he designed the Theatre of Marcellus, although its arrangement was inconsistent with his precepts. The Temple of Justice at Fano, was unquestionably erected by him; the centre nave was one hundred and twenty feet long, and sixty feet wide, supported by eighteen Corinthian columns fifty feet high; the lateral naves were twenty feet wide. The reputation of Vitruvius chiefly rests on his celebrated treatise upon architecture, in a historical form, containing the names of many eminent architects with their works. At the request of Augustus, he commenced his celebrated work on Architecture, availing himself of the Grecian rules, as well as his own matured experience. It is divided into ten books; seven of which treat of architecture in its proper sense; the last three of hydraulic architecture, gnomonics, and mechanics. The style of Vitruvius is unostentatious and concise. It is also sometimes obscure, which is easily explained by reflecting that, being the first Roman writer upon this subject, and compelled to use many new terms and forms of expression, he was, in a limited sense, the inventor of a new language, which was necessarily imperfect, and subsequently underwent many alterations. It is the only ancient production of the kind that has been preserved to modern times, and, though defective in some respects, is well worthy of its numerous translations and commentaries, which for several centuries have been the study of architects. Vitruvius was learned in both the civil and military branches of the art, and reduced the latter to very simple principles. It is evident that he had an elevated idea of the art, believing that it should be practised for honor rather than profit. Milizia says that he allowed certain liberties with the orders—such as making the shaft of the Ionic equal to the Corinthian—which cannot be justified by the principles of correct taste.

POLO, Bernardo, a Spanish painter of fruit and flower pieces, who flourished at Saragossa in the latter part of the 17th century. Zani says he operated in 1680, and died about 1700. He painted his subjects from nature, in a style of excellence. His works are found in the collections at Saragossa and Madrid, where they are highly esteemed.

POLO, Diego, the Elder, a Spanish painter, born, according to Palomino, at Burgos, in 1560. He studied under Patricio Caxes, at Madrid, and acquired considerable reputation as an historical and portrait painter. There are some of his works in the Escurial and the Royal Palace at Madrid, which prove him to have been a correct designer, and an excellent colorist. His best works are the portraits of the Kings of the Goths; St. Jerome chastised by the Angel, for taking too much pleasure in reading Cicero; and a Penitent Magdalen. He died at Madrid in 1600.

POLO, Diego, the Younger, was the nephew of the preceding, born at Burgos in 1620. He studied under Antonio Lanchares, but profited more by a diligent study of the works of Titian in the Royal collection, by which means he became an admirable colorist. He executed several works for the churches and convents at Madrid, the most esteemed of which are the Baptism of Christ, in the Church of the Carmelites, and the Annunciation, in S. Maria. He also excelled in portraits. He was an artist of great talents, but died young in 1655.

POLONY, Ziaraka, an obscure engraver, who flourished at Paris about 1615. He executed a few etchings of various subjects.

POLVERINO, Romualdo, a Neapolitan painter, born in 1701. He studied under Francesco Solimena, and began to acquire distinction for his historical pictures, when he died, in the flower of his age, in 1731.

POLYCLES, a Greek sculptor mentioned by Pliny and Pausanias, who flourished in the 102d Olympiad, or about B. C. 370. He was cotemporary with Cephisodotus, Leochares, Praxiteles, and Lysippus. Little is recorded of him; although the notices by the above mentioned authors are so indefinite, that it is not always certain whether they refer to this artist, or to the one in the subsequent article.

POLYCLES, a distinguished Greek sculptor flourished about B. C. 170. He was the son of Timarchides, an Athenian statuary; but studied, according to Pausanias, under Stadieus. He appears to have often wrought in concert with his brother Dionysius, and Pliny says that their productions were carried to Rome, among which was a statue of Juno, in the temple of that goddess within the portico of Octavia, and near it a statue of Jupiter, also the work of Polycles and Dionysius. From the passage in Pliny, *Polycles hermaphroditem nobilem fecit*, this sculptor is supposed to have been the author of the original statue of the Hermaphrodite, from which the well known existing representations are copied, especially that usually termed the Borghese Hermaphrodite, from its having belonged to that collection, although now in the Louvre. Pausanias mentions a statue by Polycles, of Amyntas, a conqueror in the games, which was preserved at Olympia. Among his other works, were several statues of the Muses. He left several sons, who followed the profession of sculpture.

POLYCLETUS, a preëminent Grecian sculptor and an able architect, a native of Sicyon, flourished about B. C. 440. He studied under Ageladas of Argos, and was cotemporary with Myron, Alcamenes, and Phidias. The judgment of antiquity has given to Polycletus the reputation of one of the most remarkable sculptors of the golden age of Grecian art. It is evident that he was a worthy competitor and rival of Phidias; for, on one occasion, when five of the most eminent artists of the time, Phidias being among them, executed five statues in competition, that of Polycletus was preferred. He did not possess the grandeur of imagination of Phidias, but excelled rather in the beautiful. Phidias has been termed the Æschylus, and Polycletus the Sophocles of Sculpture. He finished his statues with the greatest care. Polycletus is said to have carried alto-relievo to perfection; and also the *toreutic* art commenced by Phidias, probably that of uniting metals with any other material. A correct estimate of his merit may be formed from the high eulogiums of the best ancient writers, and from the fact that among his scholars were Pericletus, Canachus the second, Asopodorus, Alexis, Aristides, Phryno, Dino, Athenodorus, and Demeas. Pliny says he succeeded best in statues of a soft and gentle character. Myron and Polycletus were always considered rivals; and one used the bronze of Delos in his works, while the other used that of Ægina.

Among the chief works of this eminent artist, was the colossal statue of Juno, in the temple of that goddess at Argos, which was considered in many respects equal to the finest productions of Phidias. It was chryselephantine, or composed of gold and ivory; all the naked parts being of ivory, while the gold was used for drapery and accessories. It was not as large as the Olympian Jupiter or the Minerva of Phidias. The goddess was represented seated on a throne; in one hand she held a sceptre, and in the other a pomegranate. The accompanying subjects and ornaments were of the richest description and of the most elaborate workmanship. The other works of Polycletus were almost as famous as his Juno. Among them were two statues of young men one, called Diadumenos, fastening a band around his head; the other called Doryphorus, of a more manly character, carrying a lance. Pliny says the former work was valued at the enormous sum of 100 talents. A group of two naked boys, called Astragalizontes, playing at a game of dice, was in the possession of the Emperor Titus at Rome, and was greatly admired. His statues of Canephoræ (female figures carrying baskets on their heads), were so greatly admired, that Cicero says the strangers at Messene crowded to see them, and that "the house in which they were preserved, was less its master's than the ornament or attraction of the whole city." Among the most important of the works of Polycletus, however, was the statue of a Life-Guard of the King of Persia, termed *The Canon*, or Rule of Art, of such perfect proportions that other artists referred to it as a standard for executing their own works. Among the other works of Polycletus, were the statues of an Amazon, Mercury, and several Athletes; also a group of Hercules lifting Antæus, and the image of a Voluptuary, languidly reclining on a couch, which was held in the highest estimation.

As an architect, Polycletus acquired considerable distinction. One of the monuments of his skill was a marble building erected at Epidaurus, called the Tholus. Pausanias mentions a theatre erected within the precincts of the Temple of Æsculapius, also at Epidaurus, and says it was superior for symmetry and beauty, to any theatre extant.

POLYCLETUS, a Greek sculptor, probably a native of Argos; was the brother and scholar of Naucydes, and flourished about B. C. 380. It is supposed that he was the author of several bronze tripods dedicated at Amyclæ, and two celebrated statues described by Pausanias; namely, the Jupiter Philius, erected at Megalopolis, and the Jupiter Milichius, a marble statue at Argos.

POLYGNOTUS, a preëminent Grecian painter. He was a native of Thasos, an island of the Ægean sea, the son of the painter Aglaophon. Plutarch's account of his friendship for Cimon, and his love for Cimon's sister Elpinice, would indicate that his career commenced about B. C. 460. As Thasos was conquered by the Athenians under Cimon in B. C. 463, it is probable that Polygnotus left his native island at that time, and went with Cimon to Athens. At first he acquired a knowledge of sculpture, but subsequently studied painting under his father, and devoted his energies permanently to that art. He seems to have contributed more largely to the advancement of the art than any preceding painter. Before his time, the human countenance was represented without animation, and a kind of leaden dullness pervaded the features. Polygnotus kindled expression in the face, and threw intellect and feeling into the whole frame. He also first painted the mouth open, so as to display the teeth; and in this way, caused the lips to contribute their full share to the general expression. He first clothed his figures in light, airy, transparent draperies, which he elegantly threw about the light forms of his women. From the expressions of ancient writers, his coloring seems to have been superior to his design; but he was the author both of delicacy and expression in the paintings of Greece. Aristotle calls him *Ethicos*, one who conveyed an idea of character and moral qualities by his works; in the "Poetics," he contrasts this distinctive quality of Polygnotus with the want of such excellence in Zeuxis; and he also says that Polygnotus made his figures superior, Pauson inferior, and Dionysius equal, to Nature.

Pausanias gives an elaborate description of the pictures by Polygnotus in the Lesche at Delphi. They represented the Capture of Troy, the Return of the Greeks, and the Visit of Ulysses to the Shades. The variety of age and sex, and the passionate expressions portrayed, indicate a discrimination of character and a power of expression, fully equal to the eulogisms of the ancient writers. Although these memorable events comprehended so many interesting circumstances, and such terrible situations, that it appeared beyond the power of human genius to depict and unite them, yet the master mind of the artist, filled with the sublime conceptions of Homer, overcame all obstacles, and produced such effects as filled the mind with astonishment. His celebrated picture of Cassandra was sufficient to rank his name as the first painter of Greece. He represented her at the moment when brutally outraged by Ajax, in the temple of Minerva. The face of the unfortunate captive was partially veiled, but the glowing blush of outraged modesty was visible in her countenance. This admirable work is cited by Lucian in his description of the portrait of a perfect woman. "Polygnotus shall open and spread her eyebrows, and give her that warm, glowing, decent blush, which so inimitably beautifies his Cassandra. He likewise shall give her an easy, tasteful, and flowing dress, with all its tender and delicate wavings, partly clinging to her body, and partly fluttering in the wind." In the portico called the Pœcile, at Athens, Polygnotus painted the Battle of Marathon. In the foreground of the picture, the Greeks and Persians were represented as combating with equal valor; but in extending the view to the middle of the composition, the Barbarians were seen flying to the Phœnician ships, which were visible in the distance. The Athenians were so delighted with his work, that they offered to reward him with whatever sum he might please to ask. Upon his declining this generous offer, the Amphictyonic council ordered that he should be maintained at the public expense wherever he went. Among the other works of Polygnotus, were a picture of Ulysses after the slaughter of the Suitors, in the temple of Minerva Area, at Platæa; and the paintings on the Walls of Thespiæ, subsequently restored by Pausias.

POMARANCE, DALLE. See CAV. CRISTOFORO RONCALLI.

POMARANCE, DALLE, or IL POMERANCIO. See NICCOLO and ANTONIO CIRCIGNANO.

POMAREDE, SYLVIUS, an Italian engraver, to whom Professor Christ attributes some prints marked S. P. F., the F for *fecit*, and says he flourished in 1720. Strutt says he lived in 1620, instead of 1720. Zani calls him (or another artist) Silvio Pomarede, and says he flourished from 1740 to 1768. Nagler calls him Silvestre Pomarede, and gives the same details as Zani, with a list of his prints, the chief of which are, the Triumphs of Time, Fame, Death, and the Christian Religion, *after Titian*.

POMPADOUR, THE MARCHIONESS OF. This

celebrated lady amused herself with engraving. She etched some small plates after Boucher, Eisen, and others. She also engraved a set of sixty-three plates, from gems by Gay.

POMPEI, CONTE ALESSANDRO, an Italian amateur painter, and an eminent architect, born at Verona in 1705. He was of noble descent, and was sent while very young to the college of noblemen at Parma, where he manifested a strong inclination for design. Having completed his education, he devoted his attention to cultivating the sciences, and also studied painting, under Antonio Balestra, but practised it only as a recreation. In 1731, being desirous of rebuilding his palace in the Villa Illasi, and not finding in Verona an architect equal to the undertaking, he turned his thoughts to architecture. According to Milizia, he studied the best authorities, and acquired the requisite knowledge, not from masters, but from his own reasoning; and soon attained great excellence, both in theory and practice. In 1735 he published his work entitled *I Cinque Ordini dell' Architettura, Civile di Michele Sanmicheli*, containing descriptions of the five orders as employed by Sanmicheli, with a parallel between them and the orders practised by Vitruvius, Leon Battista Alberti, Serlio, Palladio, Scamozzi, and Vignola. This production is highly praised by Milizia for its correct taste. Among the principal edifices of Pompei, are his palace at Illasi, universally admired; the Palazzo Pindimonti, in the village of Vo; the Palazzo Giuliari, at Sessino; and the Merchants' Exchange, at Verona. In the latter city his abilities were frequently in request; and he was also chosen President of the Academy of Painting.

PONCE, NICHOLAS, an eminent French engraver, born at Paris in 1746. He first studied painting under M. Pierre, but abandoned it for engraving, which he learned of Fessard and Delaunay. He distinguished himself in this branch, and was employed on several of the grand publications which do honor to the French nation, such as *Le Musée Laurent; Le Cabinet de Choiseul; La Galerie du Palais Royal; Les Campagnes d'Italie; the folio edition of Racine by Didot; the edition of Ariosto by Dussieux*, of which all the prints after Cochin's designs are engraved by Ponce; *Les Illustres Francais, avec les Notices historiques*, 56 plates; *Les Bains de Titus et du Livie*, 75 plates; and *La Guerre d'Amerique*, engraved conjointly with Godefroy. He edited an edition of the Bible, with 300 plates *after Marillier;* and the beautiful edition of the Charter, dedicated to Louis XVIII. In addition to these numerous works, he executed some detached pieces after various masters, among which are Christ curing the blind Man, *after le Sueur;* the Battle of Marengo, *after C. Vernet;* the Virgin and Child, *after Vouet;* the Marriage of the Virgin, *after Vanloo*, &c. He also distinguished himself as an author; wrote and translated several works on the Fine Arts; was elected a member of various academies and literary societies, a corresponding member of the Royal Institute of France, and a member of the Legion of Honor. His life was one of extraordinary industry and great usefulness. He died in 1831.

PONCE, ROQUE, a Spanish painter, who flourished at Madrid about 1690. He studied under Juan de la Costa, and painted landscapes in a style of excellence.

PONCHEL, CHARLES EUGENE DU, a French engraver, born at Abbeville, in 1748. He studied with Jacques Nicholas Tardieu, at Paris, and engraved several plates of portraits and historical subjects, among which are the Madonna della Seggiola, *after Raffaelle;* and a Holy Family, *after Andrea del Sarto.* He went to England about 1779, where he resided some time, and engraved a few plates.

PONCHINO, GIOVANNI BATTISTA, called IL BOZZATO, a painter born at Castelfranco in 1500. There is considerable discrepancy about him, but the following is Lanzi's account: "He was a friend of Paolo Veronese, and an excellent pupil of Titian, whom, in some things, he imitated. He has been erroneously denominated by historians. He is called by Vasari, Zanetti, and Guarienti, *Bazzacco* and *Brazzacco da Castelfranco*, and Guarienti makes him the scholar of Badile. My information respecting him, as well as other artists of Castelfranco, has been obtained from a MS. communicated to me by the learned Dottore Trevisani. He took the name of Gio. Battista Ponchino, and the surname of Bozzato, a city of his native country, where several of his paintings in fresco still exist, together with his celebrated piece of the Limbo, in the church of S. Liberale—the finest work, if we except those of Giorgione, which that city has to boast, and it is greatly admired by strangers. He painted also at Venice and Vicenza, during the lifetime of his wife, a daughter of Dario Varotari; but at her death, he assumed the ecclesiastical habit, and afterwards paid little attention to the art." He died in 1570.

POND, ARTHUR, an English painter and engraver, of whom little is known. He was evidently a learned man, as Pilkington says he was a member of the Royal and Antiquarian Societies. He is said to have contributed greatly to the encouragement of art in England, but in what manner we are not told. He painted portraits, both in oil and crayons, and, in conjunction with George Knapton, published a collection of heads of illustrious persons, engraved by Houbraken and Vertue; the memoirs were written by Dr. Birch. He engraved and published, in conjunction with Knapton, a set of ninety-five plates from the drawings of the great Italian masters, in a tasteful and spirited style, in imitation of the originals. He also engraved a set of twenty-five caricatures, *after Cav. Ghezzi*, and etched a few portraits in a style resembling that of Rembrandt. He died in 1758

PONSE, JORIS, a Dutch painter, born at Dort in 1723. He studied under A. Schouman, in whose style he painted cabinet pictures of birds, fruit, and flowers, more remarkable for elaborate finishing, than for elegance of composition. He died at Dort in 1783.

PONT, NICHOLAS DU, a Flemish painter, born at Brussels in 1660, and died there in 1712. He painted landscapes and architectural pieces, in which the figures are attributed to Bout, the coadjutor of Boudewyns. There is a perspective of a grand palace by him, with figures by Bout, in the Museum at Ghent.

PONTE, FRANCESCO DA, called also THE ELDER BASSANO, was the head of a family and school of artists called the Bassans, highly distinguished during and beyond the 16th century. He was born at Vicenza, about 1475, and is supposed to have studied at Venice, under Giovanni Bellini, whose style he at first imitated. He afterwards settled at Bassano, on the Brenta, from which town he and his descendants obtained their surname. He was well versed in polite literature and philosophy. He gradually abandoned the dry and gothic style in which he had been instructed, and adopted one of greater freedom, softness, and harmony of coloring, approaching the moderns. The styles of his altar-pieces, when compared with each other, manifest his progress, from the earliest to the latest specimens of his pencil. He is diligent, but dry, in his S. Bartolomeo at Bassano; more soft in another in the church of S. Giovanni; but best in his Descent of the Holy Ghost, in a church at the village of Oliero, near Bassano, a grand composition, with rich and harmonious coloring, and a fine expression in the heads. He died at Bassano in 1530, according to Verci, who wrote the Anecdotes of the lives and works of the artists of Bassano.

PONTE, Giacomo da, commonly called Il Bassano, was the son of the preceding, born at Bassano in 1510. He received his first instruction from his father, and some of his youthful efforts are in the church of S. Bernardino in his native place, which bear the impress of his early education. He went to Venice for improvement, and was recommended to Bonifazio Veneziano—a master equally jealous of the secrets of his art as Titian and Tintoretto—from whom he obtained no advantage in seeing him color his pictures, except by secretly watching him through the keyhole at the door of his studio. He derived much advantage, however, in designing from the cartoons of Parmiggiano, and in copying the pictures of Bonifazio and Titian. It has been supposed by some that he studied a short time under Titian; and Lanzi says, "if conformity of manner—not always a sure guide—were sufficient evidence, we might admit the truth of the supposition, his second style being altogether that of Titian; and some of his youthful productions, as the Nativity and Flight into Egypt, seemed to promise a second Titian, so richly were they imbued with his sweetness of taste." At this period, too, he drew some of his figures larger than life, and aspired to a greatness of style of which he showed himself not incapable.

No correct idea of the style and real merits of Bassano can be formed from the generality of his biographers, as for the most part they copy Vasari, who could find more faults to condemn than beauties to commend in the works of this artist, and who certainly has not judged him with the candor his merits deserve. He was the head of a great school, which had more imitators than almost any other in the history of art. We have nowhere read so able, just, and learned a criticism upon his works as that of Lanzi; for which reason, and in consideration of his school, we give his own words, somewhat abridged, but strictly preserving the sense.

"Upon the death of his father, he was compelled to return to Bassano, a city at this day rich and populous, and in those times considerably esteemed, its situation being delightful, abounding with flocks and herds, and well adapted for fairs and the sale of merchandise From these elements arose, by degrees, his formation of a third style, full of simplicity and grace, which gave the first indications in Italy of a taste altogether foreign—that of the Flemish school. In the use of his pencil, Jacopo may be said to have pursued two different methods. The first of these is much softened by a fine union of tints, and at last determined with fine strokes; the second, resulting in a great measure from the other, was formed by simple strokes of the pencil, with clear and pleasing tints, and a certain command, or rather audacity of art, that, nearly viewed, appears a confused mixture, but from a proper distance, an enchanting effect, of coloring. In both methods, he displays the originality of his own style, chiefly consisting of a soft and luscious composition, partaking at once of the triangular and circular forms, and arriving at a certain contrast of postures; so that if one of the figures is in full face, the other turns its shoulders, and if there are several figures in the composition, they are so arranged that the heads shall meet in the same line; in want of these, some of the objects are elevated in the same direction. In regard to his lights, he appears partial to such as are confined to one part, and he displays a masterly power in rendering it subservient to the whole; for with these rare lights, with the frequent use of middle tints, and the absence of deep obscure, he succeeded admirably in harmonizing the most opposite colors. In the gradation of his lights, he often contrives that the shadow of the interior figure shall serve as a ground for the one more forward, and that the figures should partake of few lights, but extremely bold and vivid at the angles; as, for instance, on the top of the shoulder, on the knee, and on the elbow, for which purpose he makes use of a flow or sweep of the folds, natural to all appearance, but in fact highly artificial, to favor his peculiar system. In proportion to the varieties of his draperies, he varies the folds with a delicacy of judgment that falls to the lot of few artists. His colors everywhere shine like gems; in particular his greens, which display an emerald tinge peculiar to himself.

"At the outset, Jacopo aspired to a grander style, which is apparent from some of his pictures remaining in the façade of the Casa Michieli at Venice. Among these, a Sampson slaying the Philistines meets with much praise; and indeed they all partake of the boldness of Michael Angelo. But, whether the result of disposition or judgment, he afterwards confined himself to smaller proportions, and to subjects of less power; even the figures in his altar-pieces are less than life size, and little animated. We do not meet with any of that noble architecture in his paintings, that adds so much to the dignity of those of the Venetian school. He appears rather anxious to find subjects into which he can introduce landscapes, cottages, candle-lights, animals, copper vessels, and all such objects as passed under his eye, which he copied with surprising accuracy. His ideas were limited, and he often repeated them—a fault to be attributed to his situation, it being an indisputable fact that the conceptions of both artists and writers become enlarged and increased by a residence in large capitals, and diminished in small places. All this may be gathered from his pictures produced for private ornament, the most familiar occupation of his life, inasmuch as he executed very few large altar-pieces. He conducted these works at his leisure in his studio, and, with the assistance of his scholars, having prepared a great number of various dimensions, he sent them to Venice, sometimes to the most frequented fairs; and produced so many as to render it a disgrace to a collection not to possess pictures by his hand rather than an honor to have them. In these may be viewed, almost invariably, the same subjects, consisting of acts from the Old and New Testaments; the Feasts of Martha, of the Pharisee, of the Rich Man, with a splendid display of brazen vessels; the Ark of Noah, the Return of Jacob, the Annunciation of the Angel to the Shepherds, with a great variety of animals. To these we may add, the Queen of Sheba, the Adoration of the Magi, with regal pomp of dress, and the richest array; then the Deposition of our Lord from the Cross, by torchlight. His pictures upon profane subjects exhibit the sale of beasts, and brazen vessels; sometimes rural occupations and husbandry corresponding to the seasons of the year; sometimes without human figures, merely a kitchen with furniture, a fowl-yard, or similar subjects. Nor is it the histories or compositions themselves that recur in every collection to the eye, but even countenances taken from individuals of his own family; for instance, arraying his own daughter as a queen of Sheba, a Magdalen, or a Villager presenting fowls to the infant Jesus. I have likewise seen an entire piece, entitled the *Family of Bassano*, sometimes in small size, and sometimes in large. Of the former, I remarked a specimen in possession of Sig. Ambrogio Durazzo at Genoa, where the daughters of the painter are seen, intent upon their feminine occupations, while a little boy is playing, and a domestic lighting a candle. One of the second kind, representing an Academy of Music, may be seen in the Medicean Museum.

"By this method, Bassano seemed to confess the poverty of his invention, though he derived from it a very remarkable advantage. By dint of continually repeating the same things, he brought them to the very utmost point of perfection of which they were susceptible, as we may gather from his picture of the Nativity in the church of S. Giuseppe at Bassano, which is not only the masterpiece of Jacopo, but in force of colors and the chiaro-scuro, surpasses everything that modern painting has to boast. The same is seen in his Burial of Christ, at the Seminario of Padua, which seems to breathe a spirit of pity and holy terror. Finally, in his Sacrifice of Noah in Santa Maria Maggiore at Venice, he represented all the birds and animals he had ever drawn elsewhere, producing a work so greatly admired by Titian that he wished to purchase a copy for the ornament of his own studio.

"Hence it happens that the works of Bassano, conducted at a certain age and with singular care, are estimated very highly and purchased at large sums, though not exempt from errors of perspective, awkwardness of postures, and faults in composition, particularly in point of symmetry. Indeed, it was the general belief that he possessed little skill in designing the extremities, thus avoiding as much as possible the introduction of hands and feet into his pictures. These accusations, and others before alluded to, might be greatly extenuated by producing such examples of his works as fully prove that he could, when he pleased, draw much better than he was accustomed to do. He knew how to vary his compositions, as evinced in his Nativity at the Ambrosiana at Milan, and he might as easily have varied his other pieces. He was also capable of conceiving with equal novelty and propriety, as we gather from his S. Rocco at Vicenza; and he might, if he would, thus have shone on other occasions. Moreover, that he knew how to draw the extremities, appears from his picture of St. Pietro in the church of the Umiltà at Venice; and he could give dignity to his countenances, as in his Queen of Sheba at Brescia. But whether he found such a task irksome, or from whatever other cause, he rarely displayed his full powers. He was generally content with reaching his peculiar method of coloring, of illuminating, and of shading, with a sovereign skill. So universally was he admired that he received numerous commissions from various courts, and an invitation to that of Vienna. What is more honorable, notwithstanding his defects, he extorted the highest praise, if not from Vasari, yet from many of the most renowned artists of his time, from Titian, from Annibale Caracci, who was so deceived by a book he painted upon a table that he stretched out his hand to take it up; and from Tintoretto, who commended his coloring, and in some measure wished to imitate him. Above all, he was honored by Paul Veronese, who intrusted him with his son Carletto for a pupil, to receive his general instructions, 'and more particularly in regard to that just disposition of lights reflected from one object to another, and in those happy counterpositions, owing to which the depicted objects seem clothed with a profusion of light.' Such is the flattering notice given by Count Algarotti to the style of Jacopo da Ponte."

It will be perceived, from the above account, that this artist had three manners; his first, or early one, partaking of that of his father; his second, resembling Titian; his third, original and peculiar to himself. It is to this artist that authors refer when they speak of *Bassano*, and to his last manner when they speak of the imitators of the style of *Bassano*, or of the *Bassans*. Jacopo Bassano designed and wrought with wonderful facility, and executed a multitude of works, which are to be found in the collections of every civilized country. His pictures have also been copied and imitated *ad infinitum*. His best works were held in great estimation, even in his own day, and he was invited to the court of the Emperor Rodolphus II., with the offer of a liberal pension; but he declined, preferring his own delightful retreat on the banks of the Brenta, to any prospect of emolument or honor. He also distinguished himself in portraits, and painted those of the Doge Sebastiano Venerio, Ariosto, and Tasso. Bassano educated four of his sons to his profession, and liberally instructed many pupils. He died in 1592.

PONTE, Francesco da, called the Younger, was the eldest son of Giacomo da P., born at Bassano in 1548, and was brought up in the school of his father. Lanzi says that of the "four sons of Jacopo, Francesco and Leandro were the best endowed to follow in his footsteps, and he was accustomed to pride himself upon the inventive talents of the former, and the singular ability of the latter in portraits. Of his two other sons, Gio. Battista and Girolamo, he used to observe that they were the most accurate copyists of his works." Francesco afterwards established himself at Venice, where he greatly distinguished himself by the admirable works he executed for the churches and public edifices. He was employed to paint a series of pictures, for the ducal palace called the Palazzo Grande, illustrating the history of the Republic. Lanzi says, "his father assisted him with his advice in these works, himself attending on the spot, and instructing him, when he found occasion, how to add force to his tints, to improve his perspective, and to bring the whole work to the most perfect degree of art. His pencil may be very clearly traced in that of his son, as well as his style, which, in the opinion of some critics, is somewhat too much loaded, especially in his shades." It is no slight proof of his distinguished talents, that these ingenious productions sustain their claim to admiration, although in the immediate vicinity of some of the most esteemed works of Tintoretto and Paul Veronese. He painted several altar-pieces and other works for the churches at Venice and in the State, which sustained his reputation, though less vigorous than those of his father. There is also a fine picture of Paradise, in the church of Il Gesù at Rome, and another of St. Apollonio in S. Afra at Brescia. He would have achieved still greater things, had he not been afflicted with fits of melancholy so severe as to deprive him of reason. Finally, while under this influence, he threw himself from a window, and was immediately killed, in 1591, in the prime of life.

PONTE, Giovanni Battista da, was the second son of Giacomo da P., born at Bassano in 1553, and died in 1613. He was instructed by his father, and imitated his subjects and manner, with a precision that deceived the most experienced. He copied the works of Jacopo, and Lanzi says there is no original work attributed to him, except an altar-piece with his name, in the church of S. Gallio at Bassano, painted in the style of his brother Leandro. Doubtless he painted many works from his own compositions, but they are now all attributed to Jacopo—the inevitable fate of every successful imitator.

PONTE, Cav. Leandro da, was the third son of Giacomo da P., born at Bassano in 1558. He also studied and followed the same maxims of art; but, by his skill and practice in portrait painting, he acquired more originality of expression. Lanzi says that "in the management of his pencil, he approaches nearer to the first than the second style of Jacopo. He is, moreover, more variable in it, and inclines somewhat to the mannerism of the age." One of his best performances is a picture of St. Caterina crowned by our Lord, in the church of S. Francesco at Bassano, with figures much larger than customary with the Bassanese school. Other fine pictures are the Resurrection of Lazarus at La Carità, afterwards placed in the Louvre; and the Nativity of the Virgin in S. Sofia, in his native city. He also produced several works for the churches at Venice, and in the State, distinguished by large proportions. He finished some of his brother's works in the Ducal palace, left incomplete at his death. Lanzi says, "if familiar with his father's productions, we may frequently detect domestic plagiarisms in Leandro, who often repeats the Family of da Ponte, copied in innumerable pieces, by Jacopo, by his sons, and by their imitators. Even in his pictures for private ornament, conducted according to his own style and fancy, he was fond of adopting paternal subjects and examples, being very skillful in drawing animals of every kind from nature." He, however, acquired most reputation for his admirable portraits, and executed an immense number, of princes and distinguished persons. He was invited to Vienna by Rodolph II., and painted the Imperial family, so much to the satisfaction of that monarch that he offered to make him his court painter; but Leandro declined, being more ambitious of enjoying fame at Venice than Vienna. He painted a noble portrait of the Doge Grimani, who conferred on him the honor of knighthood. Leandro was fond of display, supported his dignity with an imposing demeanor, and lodged, dressed, and maintained his table in princely splendor. He appeared in public, decorated with a gold collar and the insignia of St. Mark, accompanied by a train of disciples, one of whom bore his gold cane, and another the repertory in which he noted down all that was to be done during the day. Being suspicious of poison, he had his *tasters*, who took something of everything he ate or drank. Like his brother, he was at times afflicted with fits of melancholy. He died in 1623.

PONTE, Girolamo da, was the youngest son of Giacomo da P., born at Bassano in 1560. Like his brother, Gio. Battista, he copied and imitated his father's works so perfectly as to make them pass at the time for originals by his father, to whom they are now mostly attributed. He, however, painted some works for the churches at Bassano, and other places in the vicinity, in which he excelled his father in the graceful airs of his heads. These compositions are very simple, and the coloring sweet and harmonious. Such is his picture of St. Barbara, in the church of S. Giovanni at Bassano. He also painted an altar-piece at Venice, after the composition of Leandro. He died in 1622. There were others of this name, the descendants of the preceding artists, but they are unknown in the history of art. The works of the Bassani, and those of their imitators, which possess sufficient resemblance of style and manner of execution, are all attributed to Jacopo.

PONTE, Giovanni da, an old painter, born at Florence in 1306. He was a scholar of Buffalmacco, and acquired distinction in his time. Most of his works have perished. There are some remains of his pictures in the church of S. Francesco at Arezzo. He died in 1365.

PONTE, Giovanni da, an eminent Italian architect, born at Venice in 1512. He attained great distinction in his native city, in an age illustrated by several preëminent professors of the art. According to Milizia, when the great Council Hall was burned, and the Ducal palace much injured, Giovanni da Ponte rebuilt the whole, notwithstanding the contrary opinion of Palladio, who desired a new palace, thinking any repairs would be useless; but the restoration was so admirably conducted, that the edifice still remains beautiful and strong. The greatest triumph of da Ponte was the bridge over the Rialto, for which his design was preferred to those of Scamozzi and Palladio. Milizia says the mechanical arrangement was highly ingenious, although the work was thought to be weak, and operations were consequently suspended for some time; but, upon examination it was pronounced perfectly sound, and was safely completed in the third year from its commencement, without having settled in the least. It is built of Istrian stone. Da Ponte also built the well known prison united to the Ducal palace by the famous "Bridge of Sighs"; highly praised for its solidity and magnificence. Among his other works at Venice were the warehouse of the Arsenal; the gate of the church degl' Incurabili; and the church of Santa Croce. He died in 1597.

PONTIUS, Paul, a very eminent Flemish engraver, born at Antwerp about 1596. He studied engraving under Lucas Vostermans, but he greatly improved his design, and the effect in his prints, through the advice and friendship of Rubens, and engraved many admirable plates from his works, in the execution of which he seems to have possessed the mind of that great master. Few engravers have equalled him in correct and faithful imitation of their models, and in preserving in his figures the character and expression of the originals. In his fine portraits after Vandyck, he seems to have adapted his style to the character of the persons represented. His plates are executed with the graver, in a clear, bold style; and, though he did not possess the facility of Bolswert, or the delicacy of Vostermans, his plates will be ranked among the ablest productions of the Flemish engravers. The following is an ample list of his principal works; a full catalogue may be found in Nagler's Lexicon.

PORTRAITS AFTER VANDYCK.

Paul du Pont, or Pontius, Engraver. Peter Paul Rubens. James de Breuck, Architect. John Wildens, Painter, of Antwerp. John van Ravesteyn, Painter, of the Hague. Palamedes Palamdessen, Dutch Painter. Theodore Vanloo, Painter, of Louvain. Theodore Rombouts, Painter, of Antwerp. Cornelius vander Gheest, celebrated Connoisseur. Gerard Honthorst, Painter, of the Hague. Henry van Balen, Painter, of Antwerp. Adrian Stalbent, Painter, of Antwerp. Daniel Mytens, Painter, of Holland. Gerard Seghers, Painter, of Antwerp. Simon de Vos, Painter, of Antwerp. Gaspar de Crayer, Painter, of Ghent. Henry Steenwyck, Painter, of Antwerp. Gaspar Gevartius, Jurisconsult, of Antwerp. Nicholas Rockox, Magistrate, of Antwerp. John vanden Wouwer, Counsellor of State. Cæsar Alexander Scaglia, Abbot of Stophard. Gustavus Adolphus, King of Sweden. Mary of Medicis, Queen of France. Francis Thomas, of Savoy, Prince of Carignan. John, Count of Nassau. Don Alvarez, Marquis of Santa Cruz. Don Carlos de Colonna, Spanish General. Don Diego Philip de Gusman, Marquis de Leganez. Mary, Princess of Aremberg. Henry, Count de Berghe, in armor. Sir Balthasar Gerbier, Ambassador from Spain. Frederick Henry, Prince of Orange.

PORTRAITS AFTER RUBENS.

Philip IV., King of Spain. 1632. Elizabeth of Bourbon, his Queen. Isabella Clara Eugenia, Infanta of Spain. Ferdinand, Infant of Spain, on horseback. Gaspar Gusman, Duke of Olivarez; very fine. Christoval, Marquis of Castel Rodrigo; fine and scarce. Manuel de Moura Cortereal, Marquis of Castel Rodrigo; do. The Mother of Manuel, Marquis of Castel Rodrigo; do.

SUBJECTS AFTER RUBENS.

Susanna and the Elders. 1624. The Adoration of the Shepherds. The Murder of the Innocents; in two sheets. 1643; very fine. The Presentation in the Temple. Christ bearing his Cross; fine. The Crucifixion, with Angels, one of which is overcoming Sin and Death. The dead Christ, supported by the Virgin, with Mary Magdalene, St. Francis, and other figures; very fine. The Descent of the Holy Ghost. The Assumption of the Virgin. The Virgin suckling the Infant. St. Roch interceding with Christ for the Persons afflicted with the Plague; very fine. Thomyris causing the Head of Cyrus to be put into a Vessel of Blood; fine

SUBJECTS AFTER VARIOUS MASTERS.

The Flight into Egypt; *after Jordaens.* Twelfth-Night; *do.*; fine. The Adoration of the Magi; *after Gerard Seghers.* The Virgin with the infant Christ and St. Anne; *do.* St. Francis Xavier kneeling before the Virgin and Child; *do.* St. Sebastian, with an Angel drawing an Arrow from his breast; *do.* A dead Christ, supported by the Virgin; *after Vandyck.* St. Rosalia receiving a Crown from the infant Jesus; *do.* The Holy Family; *after J. van Hoeck.* The Entombing of Christ; *after Titian.*

PONTONS, Pablo (Paul), a Spanish painter, born at Valencia in 1606. He studied under Pedro Orrente, a scholar of Bassano, and followed the style of his instructor, both in design and coloring. He executed several works for the churches and convents of Valencia, of which the most considerable are a series of subjects from the life of San Pedro de Nola, in the church and cloister of the convent de la Merced. He painted some altarpieces for the monastery de la Cartuja del Puche; and in the church of S. Maria de Morella, there are by him a Nativity and an Adoration of the Magi. He was also a good painter of portraits. He died in 1670.

PONTORMO, Jacopo. See Carrucci.

PONZ, Don Antonio, a Spanish painter, and a distinguished promoter of art, born at Bexix, in the province of Valencia, in 1725. He was intended for a literary career, but manifesting a strong inclination for art, was placed in the school of Antonio Richart at Valencia. In 1746 he visited Madrid for improvement, and afterwards went to Rome. On returning to Spain he was commissioned to paint for the Royal Library, the portraits of the most eminent Spanish authors. He was chosen by the King to select from the pictures in the convents of Andalusia, those most desirable for the Academy of San Ferdinando. In 1776 he was chosen secretary of that institution, and discharged the duties of his office during a period of fourteen years. It was to Ponz that Raphael Mengs addressed his descriptions of the pictures in the palace at Madrid, inserted in the sixth volume of his works. Ponz procured the publication of Guevara's work, entitled *Comentarios de la Pintura.* He wrote a large work of Travels in Spain, illustrated with numerous plates from his own designs; of which eighteen volumes were published. He instructed a large number of scholars, with great care; and was elected a member of nearly all the Academies of Fine Arts in Europe. The time of his death is not recorded; but his obsequies were celebrated with great pomp, by the Academy of San Ferdinando.

PONZ, Moyses Jacob, a Spanish painter, born at Valls, near Tarragona, towards the close of the 17th century. He studied under Juncosa, and acquired considerable reputation for his works, designed in a good taste, and agreeably colored. In 1722 he was commissioned to paint a great part of the pictures in the Carthusian monastery. In 1732 he painted several frescos, and a fine picture of Christ reposing in the arms of the Virgin, in the Hermitage of Our Lady, near Reus.

PONZIO, Paolo, an Italian sculptor, a native of Florence, who flourished about 1550. He visited France, and was employed under Primaticcio, upon the works executed in the reign of Francis I. He was first employed in the sculptures at Meudon; and afterwards at Fontainbleau, where he executed most of the sculptures which decorate that magnificent edifice. His mausoleum of Louis XII. and Anne of Bretagne, is praised by M. Alexandre Lenoir, for its elevated design and studied execution; although a correct taste will scarcely approve of representing the bodies of a monarch and his consort as they appeared after death. This mausoleum is now in the church of St. Denis. Among the other works of Ponzio, were a bronze statue of Alberto Pio, prince of Carpi, who died at Paris in 1530; and a statue of Charlemagne, which was greatly esteemed by Bernini.

PONZIO, Flaminio, a distinguished Lombard architect, who flourished about 1600. He visited Rome, where he was extensively patronized, and gained eminence in the art. He was commissioned by the Borghese family to erect the celebrated Pauline chapel in S. Maria Maggiore, similar to the Sistine chapel, but more profusely ornamented with intaglios and sculpture. Milizia highly praises his façade of the Palazzo Sciarra Colonna, as a shining example of the simple, correct, and majestic style of architecture. In this beautiful work, the windows are justly disposed; the ornaments are simple; there are no superfluous cornices, no breaks or projections, but a single entablature crowns the whole. Among the other works of Ponzio, are the sacristy in S. Maria Maggiore; and the grand double staircase in the Quirinal palace. He died, aged forty-five, during the pontificate of Paul V., who filled the papal chair from 1605 to 1621.

PONZONE, Cav. Matteo, a painter of the Venetian school, and a native of Dalmatia. He studied under Santo Peranda, and assisted him in his great works at Mirandola. He at first adopted the manner of his instructor, but afterwards formed an original style, which Lanzi says surpassed Peranda in sweetness of coloring, though inferior to him in elegance of design. He was fond of copying from life without attempting much to add to its dignity. He acquired considerable distinction, and executed many works for the churches and public edifices of Venice, and also for the collections. It is generally, but erroneously, said that he was born at Venice. He was called Il Cav. Dalmatino; perhaps on account of his native country. He flourished about the middle of the 17th century, and perhaps later. He is said to have died about 1700, if so, he lived to a great age, as his instructor died in 1638.

PONZONI, Giovanni de', a Milanese painter, who flourished about 1450. He was a reputable painter in his time, and executed, among other works, a picture of S. Cristoforo, in the church called Samaritana.

POOL, Juriaen, a Dutch painter, born at Amsterdam in 1666. He was distinguished as a portrait painter, and passed the early part of his life at the court of the Elector Palatine, by whom his works were much esteemed. On the death of his patron, he returned to Holland, where he is said to have abandoned painting and engaged in mercantile pursuits. He married Rachel Ruysch, the celebrated paintress of flowers and fruit. He died in 1745.

POOL, Matthew, a Dutch engraver, born at Amsterdam in 1670. He went to Paris, where he learned the art of engraving, and on his return to Amsterdam executed a variety of plates after the Italian, Flemish, and French masters, in a style resembling that of Bernard Picart. He was living in 1727. Among others are the following by him:

The Portrait of Barent Graat, Painter. The Infancy of Jupiter; *after B. Graat.* Cupid taken in a Net by Time; *after Guercino.* A Bacchanalian subject; *after N. Poussin.* A set of twelve subjects; *from designs by Rembrandt.* A set of one hundred and three plates, entitled *The Cabinet of the Art of Sculpture*, by *Francis van Bossuit;* from drawings by *B. Graat.* Three burlesque representations of the Ceremonies adopted by the Flemish painters at Rome; *do.*

POOL, Rachel. See Ruysch.

POOST, Francis. See Post.

POPELS, John, a Flemish engraver, born at Tournay about 1630. He engraved some of the plates from pictures in the gallery of the Archduke at Brussels, for the collection of prints called the *Cabinet of Teniers*, among which are the following:

Hagar and Ishmael; *after Titian.* St. George and St. Stephen; *after Gio. Bellini.* St. John Baptist and St. Roch; *after Palma Vecchio.* The Virgin and infant Christ, with St. John and St. Catherine; *after Palma Giovine.* A dead Christ, supported by Joseph of Arimathea; *after Schiavone.*

POPOLI, Cav. Giacinto de', a painter of the Neapolitan school, according to Dominici, and a native of Orta. He studied at Naples under Cav. Massimo Stanzioni, and was one of his most celebrated scholars. He formed a style for himself, founded on that of his master, which was more admired for fertility of invention and elegance of composition, than for the grace of the figures. He acquired great reputation, and executed many works for the churches and public edifices at Naples. He died in 1682.

POPPI, da. See Francesco Morandini.

POR, Daniello de, called also Daniello da Parma, a painter of whom little is known. According to Vasari, he was an assistant of Correggio, and acquired from him and Parmiggiano, a certain softness of manner. The only work he mentions by him is a fresco in the church of S. Vito, where he invited Taddeo Zuccaro to join him as an assistant. He died at Rome, according to Bottari, in 1566.

PORBUS. See Pourbus.

PORCELLO, Giovanni, a Sicilian painter, born at Messina, according to Hackert, in 1682. He studied under Cav. Francesco Solimena at Naples, and adopted his manner. On returning to his native city, he found the art at an extremely low ebb, and attempted to revive it by opening an academy in his own house, to diffuse the taste and principles of his master, which he fully possessed. He executed some works for the churches, and died in 1734.

PORCIA, Il. See Apollodoro.

PORDENONE. See Licinio.

PORETTANO, Pier Maria, a Bolognese painter, who, according to Malvasia, was a scholar of the Caracci, and executed some works in their style for the churches at Bologna and the adjacent cities. Lanzi also briefly commends him as an excellent disciple of that school. He died in the first part of the 17th century.

PORFIRIO, Bernardino di, an eminent worker in mosaic, born at Leccio, in the Florentine state. He executed a picture for Francis I., from the design of Vasari, "composed of Oriental alabaster, and large slabs of jasper, heliotrope, cornelian, lapis-lazuli, agate, and other precious stones and gems, valued at 20,000 crowns." He was living in 1568.

PORIDEO, Gregorio, a Venetian painter, whom Lanzi supposes to have studied under Titian. There is a beautiful Madonna, executed in the manner of Titian, in the noble collection in the Casa Pisani, signed *Gregorius Porideus*, "most probably the production of one of Titian's imitators, whose name is now fallen into oblivion."

PORINUS. See Antistates.

PORPORA, Paolo, a Neapolitan painter, who, according to Dominici, was a scholar of Aniello Falcone, and at first painted battle-pieces, in the style of his master; but the impulse of his genius led him to paint pictures of fish, shells, and other marine productions, in which he succeeded to admiration. He was also skilled in painting flowers and fruit. He was elected a member of the Academy of St. Luke in 1656, and died in 1680.

PORPORATI, Carlo Antonio, an eminent Italian engraver, born at Turin in 1741. He was intended for the profession of an architect, but manifesting a strong inclination for engraving, by copying with the pen all the prints he could find, he was encouraged by Count Bogino, minister of the Sardinian King, who commissioned him to design the Capture of Asti. He succeeded so well that the King assigned him a pension, and sent him to Paris for improvement. He studied under J. G. Wille, Chevillet, and Beauvarlet; and acquired considerable celebrity for his portrait of Charles Emanuel III., and other plates. He adopted an original style, and was the first of the Italian engravers who availed himself of the elegance and purity of line attained by the use of the graver alone. The flesh parts of his plates are exceedingly delicate; the heads are expressive and graceful; and the general effect harmonious. His many excellencies gained him a high reputation; but the draperies, animals, and landscapes in his plates are treated in a monotonous style, destitute of variety. In 1773, Porporati was chosen a member of the French Academy, and presented his plate of Susanna and the Elders, as his reception piece. Returning to Turin, he was appointed engraver to the King, and gained a high reputation. He was invited to Naples to establish a school of engraving; and during his residence in that city, he employed four years in engraving Raffaelle's picture of the Madonna with the Rabbit. In 1797 he returned to Turin to complete his plate of the Bath of Leda, *after Correggio*. This was his last production, on account of enfeebled eyesight; and from this time until his death, in 1816, he instructed a number of pupils in the art. The following are his principal plates:

Abraham sending away Hagar; *after Philip Vandyck*. Tancred and Clorinda; *after C. Vanloo*. Erminia asking shelter of a Shepherd; *do.* Cupid in Meditation; *after Angelica Kauffman*. The Death of Abel; *after A. vander Werf*. The Madonna with the Rabbit; *after Raffaelle*. Venus caressing Cupid; *after Pompeo Battoni*. Jupiter and Leda; *after Correggio*; very fine. Leda and the Swan, and Leda bathing; *do.* La Zingarella; do. The young Girl with a Dog; *after Greuze*. The Lady preparing for Bed, and Paris and Helen.

PORRO, Girolamo, an Italian engraver on wood and copper, born at Padua about 1520. He wrought in various Italian cities, and engraved many plates in a tasteful and delicate style, for various works, among which were those in the edition of Orlando Furioso, published at Venice in 1548; one hundred prints in Camillo Camilli's *Impressi degli uomini illustri*; and his last work, a set of wooden cuts for *I Funerali degli antichi di diversi popoli e nazioni*, by Tommaso Porcacchi, published in 1574.

PORRO, Maso, an eminent painter on glass, and a native of Cortona, who flourished about 1560. He was employed in decorating the windows of the churches in Tuscany and elsewhere.

PORTA, Baccio della, called also Il Frate, and Frà Bartolomeo di San Marco. This celebrated painter was born in the territory of Savignano, near Florence, in 1469. While very young he became the disciple of Cosimo Rosselli, and acquired the name of Baccio della Porta, from his residence near the gate of St. Peter. After passing some years under the instruction of that master, he applied himself with great assiduity to studying the works of Leonardo da Vinci, whose admirable chiaro-scuro and grandeur of relief were the particular objects of his admiration. In company with his friend Mariotto Albertinelli, he modeled and copied from the ancient bassi-relievi, by which means he acquired a breadth of light and shadow that forms one of the most striking characteristics of his style. His first works were of small size, gracefully composed and designed, and highly finished; such are his two cabinet pictures in the Florentine gallery, representing the Nativity and the Circumcision. But he afterwards adopted a grander style, and in his fresco of the Last Judgment, in the chapel of S. Maria Nuova, he evinced powers of a superior order. About this time, he became acquainted, and formed an intimate friendship, with the famous monk Jerome Savonarola, whose preaching had such an effect upon his mind that he is said to have destroyed all the studies he had previously made from the naked figure. He was employed in the convent of S. Marco, when the officers broke into the monastery by order of Pope Alexander VI., to seize the person of Savonarola, who was condemned to the stake. The execution of his friend preyed upon the mind of della Porta, and he entered the convent of S. Marco in 1500, at the age of 31, assuming the name of *Frà Bartolomeo*, and was called *Il Frate*. Like Botticelli and Credi, he abandoned the pencil for nearly four years; but after resuming it he seems to have made constant improvement during the remainder of his life; so that his earlier productions, though very beautiful, are inferior to the last. His improvement was accelerated by the friendship he contracted with Raffaelle, who visited Florence for improvement about 1504. Il Frate instructed him in coloring and the folding of draperies, and in return Raffaelle taught him the rules of perspective. Some years afterwards he went to Rome, to view the works of the two great rivals of the age, Michael Angelo, and Raffaelle, and greatly elevated his style. "In that place," says Baldinucci, "he appeared with diminished lustre, in presence of those two great luminaries of the art, and speedily returned to Florence—a circumstance which also happened to Andrea del Sarto, Il Rosso, and other truly eminent masters, whose modesty was equal to the confidence of innumerable artists of mediocrity, who frequently enjoyed at Rome much ill placed patronage. Il Frate left there only two figures of St. Peter and St. Paul, in the Quirinal palace; the St. Peter he left unfinished, and it received its last touches from the hand of Raffaelle." The following admirable critique is extracted from Lanzi. "His manner at all times was more conformable to that of his friend (Raffaelle), than to that of his fellow citizen (M. Angelo), uniting dignity with grace in his heads, and in the general design. His picture in the Pitti Palace, painted before he went to Rome, is a proof of this. His most finished productions are in Tuscany, which boasts various altar-pieces, all of them very valuable. Their composition is in the usual style of the age, which may be observed in the productions of every school, not excepting Raffaelle, and which continued in the Florentine until the time of Pontormo; viz: a Madonna, seated with the Infant Jesus, and accompanied by saints. But in these hackneyed subjects, Il Frate distinguished himself by grand architecture, magnificent flights of steps, and the skillful grouping of his saints and cherubs; some of which are seated in concert, and some poised on their wings, to minister to their King and Queen, while others support the drapery, and others again have charge of the pavilion, a rich and happily conceived ornament, which he readily connected with such thrones, even in his cabinet pictures. He departed from this mode of composition in a picture he left in the church of S. Romano of Lucca, called la Madonna della Misericordia, who sits in a very graceful attitude, amid a crowd of devotees, shielding them with her mantle from the wrath of heaven. His rivals occasioned the production of two more altar-pieces, differing from his usual style; according to the example of other eminent men, he answered them by his classic performances, a retort the most galling to the invidious. They had stigmatized him as unequal to large proportions; and he filled a large piece with a single figure of St. Mark, which is admired as a prodigy of art in the Ducal Gallery, and is described by a learned foreigner (the Abbé Winckelmann), as a Grecian statue transformed into a picture. He was accused of being ignorant of the anatomy of the human figure; and to refute this calumny, he introduced a naked St. Sebastian into another picture, in the church of that saint, which was so perfect in drawing and coloring that it received the unbounded applause of artists, but being too much admired by the female devotees, it was removed by the fathers into a private room, and afterwards sold and sent into France. In short, Il Frate knew how to excel in every department of painting. His design is most chaste; his youthful pieces are more full and fleshy than was usual with Raffaelle, and according to Algarotti, they are little elevated above the standard of ordinary men. His tints at an early period abounded with shadows produced by lamp-black or ivory-black, which impairs the value of some of his pictures; but he gradually acquired a better manner, so as to be able to instruct Raffaelle. In firmness and clearness, he yields not to the best of the school of Lombardy. He was the inventor of a new method of casting draperies, having taught the use of the wooden figure, with moveable joints, which serves admirably for the study of the folds of drapery. His works are to be seen in several private collections at Florence, but they are rare beyond the precincts of that city; they are eagerly sought after by foreigners, but very rarely sold. The Fathers of St. Mark have a considerable number of his paintings in their private chapel, and among them a St. Vincenzio, said by Bottari, to resemble a work by Titian or Giorgione. His best and rarest performances are in the possession of the Prince, in whose collection is his last work, considered a model of art, a large picture in chiaro-scuro, representing the patron Saints of the City, surrounding the Virgin.

"The method of Il Frate was first to draw the figure naked, then to drape it, and form a chiaro-scuro, sometimes in oils, that marked the distribution of the light and shadow, which constituted his great study, and the soul of his pictures; the large chiaro-scuro before mentioned demonstrates such preparatives, and it has as high a value in painting as the antique plaster models have in sculpture, in which Winckelmann discovers the stamp of genius and compass of design, better than in sculptured marbles."

Several of the most celebrated works of Frà Bartolomeo were transferred by Napoleon from Florence to the Louvre, but they were afterwards restored. He gave the most of his designs to del Piombo, who deposited them with a Nun, as related by Vasari, in the convent of St. Catherine, at Florence. They came into the possession of Sir Benj. West, and afterwards into that of Sir Thomas Lawrence, at whose death, they were purchased by the Messrs. Smith, print dealers at London, and scattered over the world. See Introduction, p. vi., and del Piombo. Frà Bartolomeo died at Florence in 1517.

PORTA, Giuseppe, called also Salviati. This painter was born at Castel Nuovo, in the Grafagnana, in 1535. He was sent to Rome while young, and placed under Francesco Salviati, an eminent Florentine painter, from whom he acquired such an excellent taste of design, that he was called after the name of his master. He had already made considerable progress, when Salviati being invited to Venice, took with him his favorite pupil. Here he formed a style of his own, founded on that of his master, combining the energetic design of the Florentine school with the fine coloring of the Venetian, in which he acquired great reputation, and was ranked among the ablest artists of his time. His works were so much admired at Venice, that he was induced to settle in that city, where he met with the most flattering encouragement. He was approved by Titian, and was selected with Paul Veronese and other eminent artists to decorate the Palace and Library of St. Mark, where he painted the Prophets, the Sibyls, and the Cardinal Virtues. In the Piazza, he represented Alexander III. bestowing his benediction on Frederick Barbarossa, where he indulged his taste for splendid architectural ornament in the Venetian manner; and in the chapel he painted a Dead Christ with the Marys. He was invited to Rome by Pius IV., where he painted in the Sala Reale, the Emperor Frederick I. doing homage to Alexander III. Having finished these and other considerable works for the pontiff, who honored him with a munificent reward, he returned to Venice, and continued to reside there till his death. He executed several altar-pieces and other works for the churches and public edifices, of which the most esteemed are, the Assumption, in the church of the Padri Servi, and the Annunciation, in the chapel of the Incurabili. At Murano, in the church degli Angeli, is one of his finest works—a Descent from the Cross, with the Virgin, Mary Magdalene, and St. John, a favorite subject with him, which he repeated several times. His style was distinguished for fine and fertile invention, excellent taste of design, and tender and harmonious coloring. Lanzi says his best pictures display great powers of invention, are wholly original, full of expression, with an air of majesty unusual in the productions of the Venetian school. There is, however, in some of his works a sameness of style, and a deficiency of strength in coloring and shadowing; he was also occasionally strained and extravagant in the delineation of the muscles, emulating the daring contour of Michael Angelo. Towards the close of his life he was more languid and monotonous. There were a few spirited engravings on wood attributed to him, which are variously signed *Giuseppe Salviati*, *Joseph Porta Grafagninus*, or *Joseph Grafagninus*.—These however, are believed to have been executed by an anonymous hand from his designs. He died at Venice in 1585. There is considerable variation among authors as to the exact time of his birth and death, but the dates given, are from the best authorities.

PORTA, Andrea, a Milanese painter, born in 1656. According to Orlandi, he studied with Cesare Fiori, and afterwards gained improvement by contemplating the works of Legnanino. He formed for himself a style of coloring so vigorous and agreeable, as to excite general admiration. He executed some works for the churches, but more for individuals, in which, according to Lanzi, "he aimed at catching the manner of Legnanino." He died in 1744.

PORTA, Ferdinando, was the son of the preceding, born at Milan, according to Oretti, in 1689, and died in 1767. He first studied under his father, and distinguished himself for a number of works for the churches, in imitation of the manner of Correggio. He also painted history with applause, for the collections. Lanzi says he "was too inconstant, and often unequal to himself."

PORTA, Frà Guglielmo della, called Milanese, an Italian painter, and a distinguished sculptor, was the nephew of Giacomo della Porta; and flourished about the middle of the 16th century. He was born at Porlizza, in the diocese of Como, and studied the elements of design under his uncle; but afterwards went to Genoa, and entered the school of Pierino del Vaga. According to Lanzi, he assisted in painting four apartments in the Palazzo Doria, from the cartoons of that master. The latter became warmly attached to him, and offered him his daughter in marriage; but della Porta declined, having decided to enter the priesthood. His instructor in sculpture is not mentioned. He afterwards visited Rome, where he became intimately attached to Sebastiano del Piombo, and acquired the esteem of Michael Angelo. He attained a high reputation for his admirable works. When the famous Farnese Hercules was discovered, della Porta was commissioned to restore the legs, and performed the difficult task in so masterly a manner, that, when the original limbs were discovered, Michael Angelo preferred to let the statue remain as it was. At the death of Sebastiano del Piombo in 1547, he was appointed to the office left vacant by the latter, of Keeper of the Seal to the pontifical Court. He was commissioned to sculpture the monument to Pope Paul III., and displayed great talent in its execution.

PORTA, Cav. Gio. Battista della, an Italian sculptor, a relative and scholar of the preceding, born at Porlizza in 1542. He resided chiefly at Rome, and attained a high reputation among the sculptors of his day. He was patronized by the noble Farnese family, through whose influence he was honored with the Order of the Golden Spur. Among his principal works are several sculptures in the church of Notre Dame di Loretto; a group of Christ giving the Keys to St. Peter, in S. Pudore; and a colossal statue of St. Domenico, in S. Maria Maggiore. The *Dizionario Istorico* of Bassano, erroneously places his death in 1547;—he died at Rome in 1597.

PORTA, Tommaso della, an Italian sculptor, was the brother of the preceding, and a scholar of Guglielmo della P. He was principally distinguished for the admirable bronze statues of St. Peter and St. Paul, placed on the Antonine and Trajan columns. Among his other works, was a group sculptured from a single block of marble, representing the Descent from the Cross, placed in the church of S. Ambrogio al Corso.

PORTA, Giacomo della, an eminent Italian architect, born at Milan about the commencement of the 16th century. During his early youth he studied design under the sculptor Gobbio, and was occupied in making bas-reliefs in stucco. He afterwards studied architecture under Vignola, and soon gained considerable reputation. He was commissioned to continue the buildings of the Capitol, and to erect the Gregorian chapel, according to the designs of Michael Angelo; also the Church of the Greeks, of good form, in the Strada del Babbuino; the façades of the Madonna de' Monti, and S. Maria in Via. Della Porta was invited to Genoa, to erect the chapel of S. Giovanni Battista, in the cathedral of that city. In concert with Domenico Fontana, he was commissioned by Sixtus V. to erect the grand cupola of St. Peter's, after the model of Michael Angelo. Six hundred men were employed for twenty-two months upon this stupendous work. Milizia says "it combines originality, beauty, and grandeur;—the world has never seen its equal." Among the other works of Giacomo della Porta, are the church del Gesu, at Rome, after the designs of Vignola; the Palazzo Serlupi; the elegant Palazzo Gottofredi; the Palazzo Niccolini, noble in its simplicity; the majestic Pallazzo Marescotti; and the design for the Villa Aldobrandini, at Frascati. The latter is justly considered one of the most celebrated palaces in the vicinity of Rome. Della Porta designed a number of fountains in Rome, at Piazza Navona, at the foot of the Capitol, at the Rotonda, &c. He died at the age of sixty-five, near the close of the 16th century.

PORTA, Orazio, a painter of the Florentine school, and a native of Monte Sansovino, was living in 1568. He was a reputable artist, and executed several works for the churches of his native city, and other places in the vicinity.

PORTELLI, Carlo, a painter of the Florentine school, a native of Loro, in the Valdarno, and a scholar of Ridolfo Ghirlandaio. He flourished about the middle of the 16th century. He was much employed at Florence, and Vasari commends him as an able artist. Lanzi says that he sometimes painted with little harmony, but that his picture of S. Romulus, at the Santa, proves him an artist of ability.

PORTENGEN, Peter, a Dutch painter, who flourished at Utrecht about 1638, and studied under Paul Moreelze. He painted landscapes in imitation of John Both; but, though his pictures possess considerable merit, they are every way greatly inferior to the works of that master, especially in the handling of his trees.

PORTER, Sir Robert Ker, was the son of a British officer, born at Durham in 1780. His father dying while he was a child, his mother removed to Edinburg, where he exhibited such an extraordinary passion for sketching battle-pieces, that his parent was induced to take him to Mr. West at London, then President of the Royal Academy, who procured his admission as a student of that institution. He made rapid progress, and in 1793, painted an altar-piece for the Shoreditch church; in 1794 a picture of Christ stilling the Tempest, which he presented to the Roman Catholic chapel at Portsea; in 1798, St. John preaching, for St. John's college at Cambridge; and in 1800, he astonished the public by the exhibition of his Storming of Seringapatam, a very large picture, twelve feet by ten, *executed in six weeks*, "representing with Homeric fire and animation," says Stanley, "the details of an exploit of British valor never surpassed." He also painted several other renowned actions, among which are the Battle of Agincourt, the Battle of Alexandria, and the death of Sir Ralph Abercrombie. In 1804, he went to St. Petersburg, and was appointed painter to the Emperor, in whose service he continued several years. In 1808, he accompanied Sir John Moore to the Peninsula, and attended him throughout the campaign, till that hero's death at Corunna, but whether as a commissary, or as a designer of the principal battles, is not mentioned. Soon afterwards, Porter made a second visit to Russia, where he married the princess Mary, daughter of Prince Shorbatoff. On his return to England in 1813, he published an Account of the Russian Campaign, and was knighted by the Prince Regent. He afterwards published an account of his travels in Georgia, Armenia, Persia, ancient Babylon, and other places, illustrated with numerous engravings of portraits, costumes, and antiquities. He was afterwards appointed consul for Venezuela, and during his residence at Caraccas, he painted a portrait of Bolivar, and three other pictures, representing the Last Supper, Christ blessing little children, and an Ecce Homo. In 1841, he paid a last visit to St. Petersburg, and died there of apoplexy, in 1842. The above account, from which little idea can be formed of the merits of Porter as an artist, is extracted from Stanley. It is fair to infer that he received some benefit from family influence, for had he preëminently distinguished himself as a painter, he would not have roamed over the world, and certainly not have accepted the situation of consul at Caraccas.

PORTIO, Aniello, an Italian engraver, who flourished about 1700, and according to Zani executed a few portraits and other book plates.

PORTO, Gio. Battista de, an Italian engraver, who, according to Zani, flourished about 1503, and executed a few etchings marked *J. B. with a bird.*

PORZEL, Elias, a German carver and engraver on wood, who, according to Nagler, was born at Isny in Suabia, about 1622, and died at Nuremberg in 1722. He engraved some Bible plates, marked with one of the above monograms.

POSI, Cav. Paolo, a distinguished Italian sculptor and architect, born at Siena in 1708. He visited Rome at an early age, where he settled permanently, and attained a high rank among the professors of the day. He was extensively employed for many years, and was appointed pontifical architect. Milizia says he had naturally great talents, but was not a good architect; he gives him no credit for professional excellence, and criticises his edifices with such severity, as might lead some to suppose there had been personal jealousy between the parties. The peculiarities of Milizia, (see the sketchof his life), compel the candid connoisseur to receive his criticisms with caution; and it is clear that the merits of Posi were of no common order, since his reputation stood very high for many years; he was appointed architect of St. Peter's, and honored with the Order of the Golden Spur. His works in sculpture were chiefly mausoleums, of which he designed a great number. Among them was that of the Cardinal Caraccioli, at Aversa; the Cardinal Imperiali, in S. Agostino, at Rome; the Cardinal Caraffa, in S. Andrea de la Frate; and the Princess Chigi, in La Madonna del Popolo. Among his principal edifices, were the modernizing of the Colonna Palace; the church of S. Caterina at Siena; the church and house of the Jesuits at Sinigaglia; and the two Case del' Projetti, at Narni and Viterbo. He died in 1776.

POSSENTI, Benedetto, a Bolognese painter, who, according to Malvasia, was brought up in the school of the Caracci, and excelled in painting landscapes, sea-ports, embarkations, fairs, festivals, &c., for the collections, which were held in considerable estimation. He also painted battle-pieces. His pictures are well designed, and the figures spiritedly executed.

POST, or POOST, Franz, a Dutch landscape painter, born at Haerlem in 1620; died in 1680. He was the son of John Post, a painter on glass, who taught him the elements of design. Before the age of twenty, he manifested such good abilities, that Prince Maurice of Nassau employed him to accompany him as draughtsman on a voyage to the West Indies and South America. During a residence of two years, he made numerous drawings of the most interesting views in that country, from which, on returning to Holland, he painted several large pictures for the palace of Ryksdorp, near Wassenaer. According to Houbraken, his pencil is light, yet firm; his coloring clear and agreeable; and his trees and plants touched in a neat and spirited style. Humboldt says that several of his paintings, representing

Views on the banks of the Amazon, are to be seen in the picture galleries at Schleissheim, Hanover, Prague, and Berlin. His pictures sometimes occur in commerce. There are several spirited etchings by Post, among which are the following: A set of Views in Brazil; from designs by himself. A View of the Gulf of All Saints; *Fr. Poost, fec.* 1645. A View of Cape St. Augustine; *do.* A View of the Isle of Thamaraca; *do.*

POT, Hendrick Gerritz, a Dutch painter, born at Haerlem about 1600. It is not certainly known under whom he studied, but it is supposed he received some instructions from Francis Hals. He was a reputable painter of history, but more celebrated for his portraits. Houbraken celebrates a picture by him, representing Judith with the Head of Holofernes; and he commends a large picture of one of the princes of Orange in a Triumphal Car, in the Princenhof at Haerlem. In the Hall of the Society of Archers, at Haerlem, is a fine picture by him, representing the principal officers of that Society. He died in 1656.

POTENZANO, Francesco, an Italian painter and engraver, born at Palermo about 1550. His name is not mentioned in most works relating to art; but the *Biographie Universelle* notices him as an artist of decided merit. He visited Rome, Naples, and several cities of Spain, leaving everywhere proofs of his talent. His prints are after his own designs, in an elevated style, possessing considerable merit of execution. Among them are the Archangel Michael triumphing over Lucifer; the Adoration of the Magi, dedicated to King Philip II. of Spain; St. Christopher crossing a River, dedicated to Cardinal Za. From the inscription on the latter plate, it would appear that Potenzano was a member of the Florentine Academy. He also gained considerable reputation by his verses, particularly his *Destruttione di Gerusalemme;* Naples, 1600, 8vo. He died at Palermo in 1599.

POTHOVEN, Henry, a Dutch painter, born at Amsterdam in 1725. He studied under Philip Vandyck, and adopted his manner. In his small family pictures, he introduced very successfully, the accessories of satin, velvet, lace, carpets, &c. He also painted portraits, understood the nude, and designed his figures correctly. His pencil is neat and clean, and his coloring agreeable. Balkema says he applied himself much to engraving in mezzotinto, and Brulliot mentions a print by him of an old Man reading a Book, by candlelight. He died in 1795.

POTMA, James, a Dutch painter, born at Workum, in Friesland, about 1610. He was a scholar of Wybrant de Gheest, and painted history with reputation, but chiefly distinguished himself in portraits. He passed the greater part of his life at the different courts of Germany, where he was much employed. He died at Vienna in 1684.

POTRELLE, Jean Louis, a French engraver, born at Paris in 1788. He had the advantages of instruction under David, Tardieu, and Desnoyers, and manifested considerable talents. In 1806 he drew the second prize in engraving, from the Royal Academy. There are a number of portraits by him of distinguished individuals, also several subjects after the Italian masters, among which are the following:

Portrait of Giulio Romano; *after the picture in the Museum.* Portrait of Michael Angelo; *after the picture by himself.* Louis XVIII.; *after Gerard.* Cupids; *do.* Portraits of Raphael and N. Poussin. Portrait of David; *after the Picture by Navet.* Prince Schwartzenberg; *after Gerard.* Cupid and Psyche; after David. Portrait of Dr. Dubois. The Course of Love, in 6 plates; *after Gerard.*

POTTER, Peter, a Dutch painter, born at Enkhuysen about 1595. Little is known of him, except that he painted landscapes, decorated with figures, representing scriptural and other subjects. Some of them were engraved by Peter Nolpe, as the Four Seasons, the Four Elements, the Prophet Elias and the Woman of Sarepta, and St. Paul the Hermit nourished in the Desert by an Eagle. He is better known by the fame of his son, than by his own productions.

POTTER, Paul. This admirable painter of animals was the son of the preceding, born at Enkhuysen in 1625. He had no other instructor than his father, and early showed the most extraordinary talents, which he cultivated with such assiduity, that, at the age of fifteen, his works were held in high estimation, and he was regarded the most promising artist of the time. He carefully designed every object from nature, and it was his constant practice in his walks in the fields,—the only recreation he allowed himself,—to sketch every object that attracted his attention. He established himself at the Hague, where his works were in such demand, that he could scarcely execute all the commissions he received. The Prince of Orange was one of his greatest admirers, and purchased some of his finest pictures. His intense application was fatal to his naturally delicate constitution, and he died in 1654, in the 29th year of his age. He executed a great number of works for so short a life, considering their extraordinary merit; the subjects were landscapes, with different animals, but principally cows, oxen, sheep, and goats, which he painted in the highest perfection. His landscape is subordinate to his animals, and seldom extends beyond a pasture, with a stump of a tree, a farm house or a hovel. His pictures usually represent a brilliant effect of sunshine, with a lustrous glitter in his coloring that is peculiar to himself. His touch is free and firm, and his pencil usually full and flowing, although his pictures are highly finished. The best tests of the genuineness of his works are the wonderful correctness of his animals, which, in their attitudes and motions, seem to live and breathe; the natural verdure of his fields, and the careless manner of his leafing. His pictures are usually of small cabinet size, though he was not incapable of painting on a large scale, as is evinced in his picture of a herdsman and cattle, in the collection of the Prince of Orange, with figures as large as life, designed and painted with surprising energy and fidelity. This picture was transferred to the Louvre, but afterwards restored to its place. His cabinet pictures are, however, preferred to those of a larger size. His works now command enormous prices. One of the truest tests of the merits of a master is the progressive commercial value of his works after his decease, and it is interesting to observe this in those of Potter. In Smith's Catalogue raisonné of the works of the Dutch and Flemish Painters, vol. v., and the Supplement, may be found descriptive accounts of about 120 pictures by this master, with many curious particulars respecting them. A picture of Four Oxen in a meadow, now in the Hermitage at St. Petersburg, sold in 1750, for about £25; in 1812, it rose to £320, and in 1815, was purchased by the Emperor of Russia for about £2800. One of two Cows and a Bull in a Meadow, measuring 17 inches by 15, sold in 1771, for about £186; in 1823, it brought in London 1210 guineas. The Dairy Farm, 24 inches by 20, was sold in 1817, for £689; it rose progressively at different sales to £1228, in 1825. A pastoral scene, 23 inches by 21, was sold in 1765 for about £135; in 1783 it rose to £678, and in 1829, to 1205 guineas. The large picture referred to in the collection of the Prince of Orange, was sold at public auction at Haerlem in 1749 for only about £56! His drawings also are held in the highest esteem, and command proportionally enormous prices. At M. Goll's sale, a few years ago at Amsterdam, the Messrs. Woodburn of London, gave £200 for one in India ink, heightened with white chalk, measuring about 13 inches by 8; and the Chevalier Claussins gave £163 for another, drawn with a pen worked in India ink, about 10 inches by 7.

Paul Potter also produced some etchings, drawn with great correctness and spirit, and executed in a masterly style. Bartsch describes eighteen prints by him; and also a set of eight prints of cows, oxen, and other animals, generally considered spurious, which he attributes to John Visscher. A few have been added to the list by the Messrs. Smith and others. They are signed, *Paulus Potter, f.*, or *in. et fe.* A great number of the designs of Paul Potter were etched in a spirited manner by Mark de Bye, which see.

POTUIL, Henry, a Dutch painter, of whom little is known. He is said to have imitated Gerard Douw, with sufficient art to deceive good judges.

POULLEAU, a French engraver, who flourished at Paris about 1749, and engraved a few plates of ruins and other architectural subjects.

POURBUS, Peter, called the Old, a Dutch painter and architect, born at Gouda in 1510. It is not known under whom he studied. He settled at Bruges, and acquired distinction in history and portraits. He executed many altar-pieces and other works for the churches and public edifices at Bruges and other places in the Low Countries. There are some of his best works in the principal church in his native place, among which is one of St. Hubert. Another fine picture by him is a Crucifixion, in the church of Notre Dame, at Bruges. There are three of his works in the collection of the King of Holland. Michiels in his *Histoire de la Peinture Flamande et Hollandaise*, gives a catalogue of fifty pictures by this artist. He was also a geographer and geometrician, and executed for the magistrates of Bruges, an immense chart, an oil painting on canvass, still preserved in the Stadt-House, representing the minutest details of the whole territory under their jurisdiction. He was also an excellent portrait painter, and his portrait of the Duke of Alençon, is considered an admirable performance, not only for striking resemblance, but for its handling and coloring. He was originally a mason, and after acquiring distinction as a painter and an architect, he marked all his works with a trowel. None of his works in architecture are mentioned. He married the daughter of L. Blondeel and was President of the Corporation of Painters at Bruges. He died there in 1583.

P P 1551 or P P or P P

POURBUS, Francis, called the Elder, was the son of the preceding, born at Bruges in 1540. He received his first instruction from his father, but afterwards studied with Francis Floris; eventually surpassed both of his instructors, and was accounted one of the ablest artists of his time. He not only painted history, but also landscape and animals, and particularly excelled in portraits. He chiefly resided at Antwerp, where he was elected a member of the Academy in 1564. There are several of his works in the churches of that city, the most admired of which is a picture of the Circumcision in the Cathedral. One of his most esteemed works is the Adoration of the Magi, in the church of the convent at Oudenarde. Another fine picture is St. Aloisius preaching, in the Academy at Antwerp, into which he introduced several portraits. He painted animals extremely well, and was so exact in his landscapes, that every species of fruit and forest trees might be readily distinguished. One of his best works was a Martyrdom of St. George, painted for a confraternity of Dunkirk, and decorated with a landscape of great beauty. But his greatest excellence lay in portraits, which he executed with great truthfulness, life, and spirit, with admirable coloring. He died in 1580.

POURBUS, Francis, called the Younger, was the son of the elder Francis P., born at Antwerp in 1570. After studying with his father, he set out for Italy, via Paris, where he met with such encouragement in portrait painting, that he took up his residence in that city for life. He acquired great distinction, and painted the portraits of the royal family, and many of the most distinguished personages of the court. His talents were not confined to portraits, and he executed several works for the churches, which obtained for him a high reputation as a historical painter. Among these are the Annunciation, and a picture of St. Francis, in the church of the Jacobins; and the Last Supper, formerly in the church of St. Leu, now in the Louvre—a grand composition, admirably designed and colored. In the Hotel de Ville are two of his pictures, representing the Minority and Majority of Louis XIII., which he treated with great ingenuity, and the portraits which he introduced have the appearance of truth and nature. There are now six of his works in the Louvre, viz.: the Last Supper, previously referred to; St. Francis in ecstacy; a small portrait of Henry IV. in armor; another do. in black velvet; a portrait of Mary de' Medicis; and a portrait of Guillaume du Vair. There are also several of his works at Hampton Court, and in other collections in England. His portrait, painted by himself, is in the Florentine Gallery. He surpassed his father in elegance and grace, and in the noble simplicity of his drapery. His design was remarkably correct, and his coloring rich and harmonious. He died at Paris, in 1622.

POUSSIN, Nicholas. This distinguished paint

er was born at Andely, in Normandy, in 1594. He was descended from a noble family, originally of Soissons, whose fortunes had been ruined by the disastrous civil wars in the time of Charles IX. and Henry III. His father, Jean Poussin, after serving in the army of Henry IV., settled on a small paternal inheritance at Andely, where he cultivated a taste for literature and the sciences, and instructed his son in the same. Young Poussin had already distinguished himself for the solidity of his judgment, and his progress in letters, when a natural fondness for drawing, developed by an acquaintance he had formed with Quintin Varin, an artist of some eminence, induced him to solicit the permission of his father to adopt painting as a profession.

After learning the first principles of the art under Varin, he went to Paris in 1612, in search of improvement. The arts were at a very low ebb at that time in the French capital, and the only assistance which he appears to have received was from Ferdinand Elle, a Flemish portrait painter, but little qualified to forward him in the sublime ideas he had already conceived of the art. He remained with him only a few months, and then sought instruction from a painter named Lallemant, but perceiving that he could derive no benefit from him, he left him almost immediately, and devoted himself to the study of the best works to which he could gain access. Having obtained some prints after Raffaelle and Giulio Romano, he studied them with delight and admiration; he also improved his design by drawing after casts of antique statues. By these helps he acquired a fine taste and readiness of composition, which procured him employment from the Capuchins of Blois, and at the Chateau de Chiverny, where he painted several Bacchanalian subjects, which elicited considerable applause. His talents and the endowments of his mind procured for him the esteem of several men of letters and distinction, and among them Cav. Marino, the celebrated Italian poet, who happened then to be at Paris. Marino became his friend, and strongly urged him to accompany him to Rome, an invitation Poussin would gladly have accepted, had he not then been engaged in some commissions of importance, among which were six large pictures in distemper for the College of Jesuits, and the Death of the Virgin for the church of Notre Dame. Having completed these works, he set out in 1624 for Rome, where he was warmly received by his friend Marino, who introduced him to Cardinal Barberini. He however derived little advantage from this favourable notice at the time, as the Cardinal soon after left Rome on his legation to France and Spain, and the Cav. Marino died about the same time. Poussin now found himself a stranger, friendless and unknown in the Eternal City, in very embarrassed circumstances; but he consoled himself with the thought that his wants were few, that he was in the very place where he had long sighed to be, surrounded by the glorious works of ancient and modern art, and that he should have abundant leisure to study. Therefore, though he could scarcely supply his necessities by the disposal of his works, and was often compelled to sell them for the most paltry prices, his courage did not fail him, but rather stimulated him to the greatest assiduity to perfect himself in the art. He lodged in the same house with Francis du Quesnoy, called Il Fiammingo, the state of whose finances at that time were not more flourishing than his own, and he lived in habits of intimacy and strict friendship with that eminent sculptor, with whom he explored, studied, and modeled, the most celebrated antique statues and bas-reliefs, particularly the Meleager in the Vatican, from which he derived his rules of proportion. At first he copied several of the works of Titian, and improved his style of coloring, but he afterwards contemplated the works of Raffaelle, with an enthusiasm bordering on adoration. The admirable expression and purity of design which characterize the best works of Domenichino, rendered them particularly interesting to him, and he used to regard his Communion of St. Jerome as the second picture at Rome, the Transfiguration of Raffaelle being the first.

A brighter day now dawned upon Poussin. What had happened to him, which would have been regarded by most young artists as the greatest misfortune and sunk them in despondency and ruin, proved of the greatest advantage to him. The Cardinal Barberini having returned to Rome, gave him some commissions, which he executed in such an admirable manner as at once established his reputation among those of the greatest artists of the age. The first work he executed for his patron was his celebrated picture of the Death of Germanicus, which Lanzi pronounces one of his finest productions. He next painted the Taking of Jerusalem by Titus. These works gave the Cardinal so much satisfaction that he procured for him the commission to paint a large picture of the Martyrdom of St. Erasmus, for St. Peter's, now in the pontifical palace at Monte Cavallo. These works procured him the friendship and patronage of the Cav. del Pozzo, for whom he painted his first set of pictures, representing the Seven Sacraments, now in the collection of the Duke of Rutland. He afterwards painted another set of the same, with some variations, for M. de Chantelou, formerly in the Orleans collection, now in that of the Marquis of Stafford. In 1639, Poussin was invited back to France, by Louis XIII., who honored him with an autograph letter on the occasion; which invitation he accepted with great reluctance, at the earnest solicitation of his friends. On his arrival at Paris, he was received with marked distinction, appointed principal painter to the king, with a pension, and accommodated with apartments in the Tuileries. He was commissioned to paint an altar-piece for the chapel of St. Germain en Laie, where he produced his admirable work of the Last Supper, and was engaged to decorate the Gallery of the Louvre with the Labors of Hercules. He had already prepared the designs, and some of the cartoons for these works, when he was assailed by the machinations of Simon Vouet and his adherents; and even the landscape painter, Fouquieres, jealous of his fame, presumed to criticise his works and detract from their merit. Poussin, naturally of a peaceful turn of mind, fond of retirement and the society of a few select literary friends, was disgusted with the ostentation of the court and the cabals by which he was surrounded; he secretly sighed for the quiet felicity he had left at Rome, and resolved to return thither without delay. For this purpose, he solicited and obtained leave of the king to visit Italy to settle his affairs, and fetch his wife; but when he had once crossed the Alps, no inducement could prevail on him to revisit his native country, or even to leave Rome. During a period of twenty-three years after his return to Rome from Paris, he lived a quiet, unostentatious life, and executed a great number of pictures, which decorate the principal cabinets of Europe, and will ever be regarded as among their most valuable ornaments. He confined himself mostly to works of the large easel size, which were eagerly sought after, and usually disposed of as soon as they were executed. He never made any words about the price of his pictures, but asked a modest and moderate price, which he always marked upon the back of his canvass, and which was invariably paid. Many of his works were sent to Paris, where they were valued next to the productions of Raffaelle. He was plain and unassuming in his manners, very frugal in his living, yet so liberal and generous that at his death he left an estate of only 60,000 livres —about $12,000. Felibien relates an anecdote which pleasingly illustrates his simple and unostentatious mode of life. The Cardinal Mancini was accustomed to visit his studio frequently, and on one occasion, having staid later than usual, Poussin lighted him to the door, at which the prelate observed, "I pity you, Monsieur Poussin, that you have not one servant." "And I," replied the painter, "pity your Excellency much more, that you are obliged to keep so many."

The favorite subjects of Poussin were taken from fabulous or poetical history, and chiefly from Ovid. These he introduced into his landscapes, enriched with elegant architecture, designed after the magnificent edifices that abound in Rome and its environs; but he frequently painted subjects from the Bible and profane history. His figures are usually a palm and a half in length, as in his Seven Sacraments; and sometimes two or three palms, as in his picture of the Plague in the Colonna Gallery—but he did not succeed so well in large as in small figures. His invention was lively and happy, and he designed with great spirit and correctness. He was a perfect master of perspective and architecture, which he knew how to employ to the greatest advantage, enabling him to give a captivating air to his landscapes, the scenes and situations of which are always subordinate to, and in harmony with, his subject. His pictures are always highly pleasing from their choice of scenery, and possess peculiar interest and beauty from the novelty of the objects introduced and the variety of trees, buildings, and other ornaments, as arches, columns, antique vases, urns, &c., as well as for the spirit and delicacy of his pencil. When Poussin first arrived at Rome, he endeavored to imitate the coloring of Titian, but when he afterwards became an enthusiastic admirer of Raffaelle and the antique, his tone altered, and his carnations had no longer the warmth that distinguishes his earlier productions.

Perhaps the works of no painter have been the subject of so much and such divided criticism as those of Poussin. We cannot enter into any lengthened discussion on the subject, further than the main one—his coloring. Some critics contend that he was very unequal in coloring, that it was generally too cold and feeble; while others maintain a contrary opinion, and say that his coloring is that best adapted to his subject. In order to arrive at a just conclusion, it is necessary to look into the character of Poussin as well as his works. He was well versed in the classic authors of antiquity, and associated much with men of letters; his constant study of the antique statues and bas-reliefs inspired him with an attachment to them which partook of the fervor of devotion, and made him as intimately acquainted with the manners, rites, and ceremonies of the ancients, as he was with those of his own time. Lanzi says "he was very apprehensive lest his anxiety on that head (coloring) might divert his attention from the more philosophical part of his picture, to which he was singularly attentive; and to this point he directed his most serious and assiduous care. Raffaelle was his model in giving animation to his figures, in expressing the passions with truth, in selecting the precise moment of action, in intimating more than was expressed, and in furnishing materials for fresh reflection to whoever returns a second and a third time to contemplate his well conceived and profound compositions. He carried the habit of philosophy in painting further than Raffaelle, and often executed pictures whose claim to our regard is the poetical manner in which the moral is inculcated. Thus, in a picture at Versailles, called 'Memoria della Morte,' he represented a group of youths and a maiden, visiting the tomb of an Arcadian Shepherd, on which is inscribed the simple epitaph—'I also was an Arcadian.'" And again he says, "I think it may be safely asserted, without exaggeration, that the Caracci improved the art of landscape painting, and that Poussin brought it to perfection."

Poussin, in his directions to artists who came to study at Rome, says that "the remains of antiquity afforded him instruction that he could not expect from masters"; and, in one of his letters to M. de Chantelou, he observes that "he had applied to painting the theory which the Greeks had introduced into their music; the Dorian for the grave and the serious, the Phrygian for the vehement and the passionate, the Lydian for the soft and the tender, and the Ionian for the riotous festivity of his bacchanalians." He was accustomed to say "that a particular attention to coloring was an obstacle to the student in his progress to the great end and design of the art; and that he who attaches himself to this principal end will acquire by practice a reasonably good method of coloring." He well knew that splendor of coloring and brilliancy of tints would ill accord with the solidity and simplicity of effect so essential to heroic subjects, and that the sublime and majestic would be degraded by a union with the florid and the gay. The elevation of his mind is conspicuous in all his works. He was attentive to vary his style and the tone of his color, distinguishing them by a finer and more delicate touch, a tint more cheerful or austere, a site more cultivated or wild, according to the character of his subject and the impression he designed to make; so that we are not less impressed with the beauty and grandeur of his scenery, than with the varied, appropriate, and dignified characteristics which distinguish his works.

Notwithstanding this article has exceeded a proper length for a Dictionary, we cannot refrain from adding the following admirable critique from the 5th discourse of Sir Joshua Reynolds: "The favorite subjects of Poussin were ancient fables; and no painter was ever better qualified to paint such subjects, not only from his being eminently skilled in the knowledge of the ceremonies, customs, and habits of the ancients, but from his being so well acquainted with the different characters which those who invented them gave to their allegorical figures. Though Rubens has shown great fancy in his Satyrs, Silenuses, and Fauns, yet they are not that distinct, separate class of beings which is carefully exhibited by the ancients, and by Poussin. Certainly, when such subjects of antiquity are represented, nothing should remind us of modern times. The mind is thrown back into antiquity, and nothing ought to be introduced that may tend to awaken it from the illusion.

"Poussin seemed to think that the style and the language in which such stories are told is not the worse for preserving some relish of the old way of painting, which seemed to give a general uniformity to the whole, so that the mind was thrown back into antiquity, not only by the subject, but also by the execution.

"If Poussin, in imitation of the ancients, represents Apollo driving his Chariot out of the sea, by way of representing the sun rising, if he personifies lakes and rivers, it is noways offensive in him, but seems perfectly of a piece with the general air of the picture. On the contrary, if the figures which people his pictures had a modern air and countenance, if they appeared like our countrymen, if the draperies were like cloth or silk of our manufacture, if the landscape had the appearance of a modern one, how ridiculous would Apollo appear instead of the sun, and an old Man or a Nymph with an urn to represent a river or a lake?" He also says, in another place, that "it may be doubted whether any alteration of what is considered defective in his works, would not destroy the effect of the whole."

Poussin married the sister of Gaspar Dughet, but never had any children. He died at Rome of a palsy in 1665. In Smith's Catalogue raisonné may be found a descriptive account of upwards of three hundred and fifty of the works of this great artist, in many instances tracing the history from the time they were painted, the names of the present possessors, and the principal artists by whom they have been engraved, together with many interesting particulars of the life of the painter. There are eight of his pictures in the English National Gallery, fourteen in the Dulwich Gallery, and many in the possession of the nobility of England. The prices paid for those in the National Gallery vary from 150 to 1000 guineas.

POUSSIN, Gaspar, or Gaspar Dughet. This great landscape painter was born at Rome in 1613, according to Pascoli, Lanzi, and the best authorities; though others place his nativity in France in 1600. He was the son of a Frenchman settled at Rome, who had given his daughter in marriage to Niccolo Poussin. The latter adopted him as his son, instructed him in painting, taught him to select the beauties of nature and of art, so that he became an eminent, and in the opinion of many an unsurpassed, landscape painter. He was no servile imitator of his master, and considered merely as a landscape painter, certainly not his inferior. He selected the most enchanting scenery of the Tusculan, Tiburtine, and Roman territories, where, as Martial observes, nature has combined the many beauties she has scattered singly in other places. He also composed ideal landscapes; and following the example of Tasso in his description of the Garden of Armida, he concentrated in them all the beauties he had observed in nature. These enchanting scenes he decorated with appropriate edifices and figures; Italian scenes, with edifices in the beautiful proportions of antiquity, also arches, or broken columns, and other ruins; Egyptian scenes, with pyramids, obelisks, and the idols of the country: all displaying erudition and elegance. His figures sometimes represent shepherds with their flocks, but oftener subjects from ancient history and classic fable; poets crowned with laurel, hawking parties, and occasionally scriptural subjects, generally designed in a novel style, and finished almost as fine as minature. His distances recede from the eye with true beauty of perspective, his grounds are charmingly broken, and his figures, trees, and other objects are so judiciously arranged and proportioned to the distance, as to produce a most pleasing illusion. His trees are so faithfully depicted as to represent the exact species, showing a natural and proper degree of agitation, and every leaf in motion. He was very fond of the spreading palm and the graceful poplar. He not only succeeded in representing the rosy tints of the morning, the splendor of noon, the softness of evening twilight, and a sky tempestuous or serene, but the passing breeze whispering through the leaves, tempests rending the trees of the forest, lowering skies, clouds surcharged with rain and rent with forked lightnings that rive the towering pine and crumble the mouldering turret. His touch is firm and vigorous, yet delicate; the fertility of his invention is only equalled by the astonishing facility of his execution; and it is said that, like Salvator Rosa, he could paint a well-finished landscape, and insert all the figures, in a single day. He frequently suggests more than he expresses; for instance, we may occasionally observe an artful winding of the road, which in part discovers itself to the eye, but in other parts leaves it to be followed by the mental vision. He is only accused of not having sufficiently diversified his tints, of representing his verdure too green, and of occasionally using too dark colors in his foregrounds; but, notwithstanding such small imperfections, his pictures are always very beautiful.

Gaspar Poussin had three manners, which are distinguishable without any great nicety. The first was rather dry and hard, with the cold coloring of Niccolo; but after seeing the works of Claude Lorraine, he adopted a more mellow and agreeable tone. In his third, he is not as lively, nor are his last pictures as well studied and finished. His second, or middle style, is therefore the best by many degrees; and his pictures of this period are distinguished for such a simple and learned design, and a coloring so natural, truthful, fresh, and lovely, that no one can behold them without admiration. Being an indifferent designer of the human form, he frequently prevailed upon Niccolo to paint his figures, who always introduced them with the utmost propriety; and pictures of this class are more highly valued than any other of the landscapes of Poussin. No commendation can be bestowed upon his works superior to their merit, and the great prices they command in all enlightened countries, evince their high estimation wherever painting is cultivated or understood. His works are numerous; they are found in the great collections in Italy, and throughout Europe.—There are six of his pictures in the English National

Gallery, four in the Dulwich Gallery, three at Windsor Castle, and many more in the collections of the nobility, and gentlemen of wealth and taste, in England. His works have been constantly rising in value, and the prices paid for those in the English collections vary from 200 to 1000 guineas, according to the time when they were purchased, and the beauty of the picture. One of his best works would now bring at least 1000 guineas in London. Gaspar Poussin executed a few masterly etchings from his own designs, viz.: a set of four circular Landscapes, and a set of four Landscapes, length ways. These are all that are described by Bartsch, and probably the list is complete. He died at Rome in 1675.

POUSSIN, John Dughet, the younger brother of the preceding, was born at Rome about 1615. He was instructed in painting by Niccolo, but manifesting little talent, he followed the advice of his instructor, and devoted his attention to engraving, but never acquired much distinction. His best prints are those engraved after the works of Niccolo Poussin; the following are the most deserving of notice:

The Seven Sacraments; *from a picture painted by Nicholas Poussin,* for the Cavaliere del Pozzo, different from those formerly in the Orleans collection. Mount Parnassus; *do.* The birth of Bacchus; *do.* The Judgment of Solomon; *do.*

POUSSIN, Le Maire. There were two French painters, named Le Maire, who were the pupils of Niccolo Poussin, and assumed his name. Pierre le Maire, according to Dumesnil, was born at Dammartin, near Paris, about 1597, and died at Gaillon in 1659. He was an imitate friend of Niccolo, was called *Le Maire Poussin*, and being a corpulent man, was also known by the name of *Le gros le Maire.* Dumesnil describes (Le Peintre Graveur Français, tom. vi.) fifteen etchings by him, executed in the manner of Remi Vuibert. Nothing is said of his pictures.

François le Maire Poussin was born at Maison-Rouge, near Fontainbleau, in 1620. He went to Rome, and studied under Niccolo, who is said to have called him *Le petit le Maire*, to distinguish him from his corpulent friend. On his return to Paris, he followed the manner of his master, and acquired so much distinction that he was admitted into the Academy in 1656. Stanley says he is known in England by the name of *Poussin le Maire*, as a painter of landscapes with figures, evidently from the designs or drawings of Niccolo. They generally represent porticos or vestibules of temples, with few figures, well executed, somewhat brighter in coloring, but lacking the antique dignity of the originals. He died in 1688.

POWELL, C. M., an English marine painter, who flourished from about 1800 to 1820. Stanley says he was a sailor, and self-taught in the art of painting. "In the management of his vessels he shows his practical knowledge, and his compositions are well understood by seamen. His more carefully painted pictures are still esteemed, and obtain good prices."

POWLE, George, an English engraver of little note, who flourished about 1776. He engraved a few portraits and other subjects for the booksellers.

POZZI, Francesco, an Italian engraver, born at Rome in 1750. In conjunction with Coppa and Perini, he engraved some of the plates from the statues in the Clementine Gallery. Among other prints by him is a portrait of Pius VI., and the Aurora, *after Guercino.*

POZZI, Giovanni Battista, a Milanese painter, who flourished in the latter part of the 17th and first part of the 18th centuries. Not meeting with much encouragement at Milan, he went to Piedmont, where he painted a great number of frescos for the churches at Turin and other places. He wrought with great facility, and his works are more distinguished for brilliancy of coloring, than for elegance or correctness of design, yet some of them produce a fine effect, as in his picture of St Cristoforo at Vercelli.

POZZI, Giovanni Battista, a Milanese painter, who, according to Baglioni, evinced remarkable talents, and was employed by Sixtus V. in the palace of St. John of Lateran, and in the Library of the Vatican. In the Sistine chapel he painted the Visitation of the Virgin, and the Angel appearing to St. Joseph in his Dream; in Il Gesu, a Choir of Angels. He died in the pontificate of Sixtus V., aged 28, deeply lamented as the most promising young artist of his time. Lanzi says none approached so near to Raffaelling da Reggio as Pozzi, and as to ideal beauty, he may be considered the Guido of his day. Had he survived to the time of the Caracci, it is impossible to say what degree of perfection he might have attained."

POZZI, Stefano, a painter born at Rome, who first studied under Carlo Maratti, and afterwards with Agostino Masucci. Lanzi says he was more noble in his design than Masucci, and more natural and vigorous in his coloring. He acquired considerable distinction, and executed several works for the churches and public edifices at Rome. In the pontifical palace of Monte Cavallo is a fine picture by him, representing St. Gregorio, and in the church Il Nome S. S. di Maria an altar-piece of the Death of St. Joseph. He died in 1768. He had a brother named Giuseppe, who possessed excellent talents, but died young at Rome in 1765, before his powers were matured.

POZZI, Rocco, an Italian engraver, who flourished about 1750. He engraved some of the plates for the Museo Fiorentino, and others for the Antiquities of Herculaneum, published at Naples.

POZZO, Andrea, an eminent painter and architect, born at Trent in 1642. After learning the elements of painting under two indifferent artists in his native city, he went to Milan, where, by assiduously studying the works of the best masters, aided by the strength of his own genius, he made such progress as to be considered a young artist of great promise. But, falling into vicious company, he became extremely dissolute, until, disgusted by his course of life, and affected at the discourse of an eminent preacher, he resolved to retire from the world, and at the age of 23 joined the Society of the Jesuits, who, knowing his talents for painting, placed him under the instruction of Lodovico Scaramuccia, by whose precepts he acquired a grand and magnificent style of composition. He afterwards visited Rome and Venice, and greatly improved his design and coloring. At Rome, particularly, he diligently studied the works of Raffaelle, and other great masters; also the most superb edifices of that metropolis, so that he acquired a profound knowledge of architecture and perspective. He painted both in oil and fresco, and executed many works at Rome, Genoa, Turin, and other places, chiefly for the churches of his order, which gained him the reputation of one of the ablest artists of the time. His pictures are composed in a grand style, the figures elegantly designed, the coloring rich and harmonious, and the whole enriched with noble edifices, or grand perspectives. Few artists have excelled him in architecture and perspective, the principles of which he perfectly understood, and published an elaborate treatise on them. The Emperor Leopold I. invited him to Vienna, where he executed many admired works, and painted noble portraits of that monarch and the Archduke Joseph.

Pozzo not only excelled in history, but in portraits and landscape. He acquired such a wonderful facility of operating, especially in fresco, that Ciro Ferri used to say that, while the horses of other painters moved at a slow pace, those of Pozzo were always on the gallop. Yet he did not despatch his work too hastily, nor until he was satisfied with his performance. Among his best works in oil are St. Francesco Borgia, in the church of Il Gesù at Rome; the Wise Men's Offering, at Vienna; and four pictures from the Life of Christ, in the church of the Congregazione de' Mercanti, at Genoa. Lanzi says these last named pictures are executed in his best manner, and that "he imitated Rubens in those beautiful and playful lights which seem to irradiate the composition." He was more eminent and greatly distinguished in fresco. The ceiling of the church of S. Ignatius at Rome is regarded as one of the ablest productions of his time, not only for its ingenuity and copiousness of composition, and brilliancy of coloring, but for its animated freedom of execution. His portrait, painted by himself, is in the Florentine Gallery.

As an architect, Pozzo gained some distinction, and executed, among other works, the altar of S. Ignazio in the church del Gesù at Rome; and the altar of St. Luigi Gonzaga in S. Ignazio. The former is said to be the richest altar in Rome, or in all Europe. He died at Venice in 1709.

POZZO, Dario, a painter of Verona, who died in 1652, aged about 60, according to Lanzi, though others say in 1632. He painted a few excellent works for the churches at Verona and Urbino. He was learned in his profession, and instructed several pupils, among whom was Claudio Ridolfi, called also Claudio Veronese.

POZZO, Isabella dal, a paintress of whom little is known. There is a beautiful picture by her, representing the Virgin and Infant with several Saints, in the church of S. Francesco at Turin, bearing her name, and the date 1666. According to Lanzi, there were few better artists at Turin, at the time she flourished.

POZZO, Matteo dal, a painter of Padua, and a pupil of Squarcione, who flourished about 1480. Little is known of him, and his works have mostly perished.

POZZO, Conte Girolamo dal, an eminent Italian architect, born at Verona in 1718. According to Milizia, he combined noble descent with a good education, an excellent disposition, and superior talents. He studied philosophy and the fine arts under the brothers Don Pietro and Don Girolamo Ballerini, after which he applied himself to architecture; and by designing the antique with great care, assisted by the writings of Vitruvius, Palladio, and Scamozzi, he became an excellent architect. Milizia says that he endeavored to improve the extravagant fashion of the 18th century, and to establish a beautiful style after the antique. His style is a mixture of Sanmicheli and Palladio; his principal members are never broken; his ornaments are always well adapted; and his edifices are distinguished for grandeur and harmony of effect. Among his principal works is the elegant villa of the Counts Trissino, in the Vicentino, situated on a hill, and surrounded with beautiful gardens. The Count dal Pozzo wrote several works on Architecture, among which is a treatise entitled *Degli Ornamenti dell' Architettura Civile secondo gli Antichi;* also another, *Sopra i Teatri degli Antichi e sul Idea d' un Teatro adatto all' Uso Moderno.* He was celebrated for his literary attainments throughout all Europe, and was chosen associate of the academies at Parma and Bologna. He died in his prime, but Milizia does not mention the exact date.

POZZO, Juan del, a Spanish architect, who flourished about 1450. He was a Canon of the Cathedral at Cuenca, and the founder of the Dominican convent of St. Paul, near that city. He was principally distinguished for the celebrated bridge near the convent, over the river Huexar. It is admirably constructed, and with such solidity as to appear like a Roman work. It is 350 feet long, with five arches; the middle piers 150 feet high. Juan del Pozzo had a relative, named Pedro del P., who erected the convent of the Jesuits at Cuenca, now that of the Interpreters.

POZZOBONELLI, Giuliano, a Milanese painter, who flourished in the latter part of the 16th century. Lanzi says he was a good artist, and executed several works which approach the best of the Cerani. He was living in 1605.

POZZOSERRATO, Lodovico, called also Lodovico Pozzo, and da Trevigi. This artist was a native of Flanders, and was called Lodovico da Trevigi, from his long residence in that city. It is said that his family name was *Toeput.* He was cotemporary with Paul Brill, who then resided at Venice, and his landscapes were often put in competition with those of that master, and were sometimes preferred to them. Lanzi says, "he was equal to Brill in the representation of distant objects, and is more pleasing and select in the variations of his clouds and distinctions of light." Nothing can be finer than his representations of the rising and the setting sun, and the degradation of tint in his skies and distances. He painted landstorms and tempests with uncommon grandeur and effect. He was also celebrated for his altarpieces. He resided a long time at Trevigi, where he flourished, according to Federici, about the beginning of the 17th century, and left many of his finest works. He died at Trevigi, aged 60 years; the exact time is not known, although he was living in 1604, as appears from the date upon one of his pictures at Trevigi; and according to the *Guida di Rovigo* he painted in that city as early as 1587. As his name is unknown in his own country, it is probable that he passed most of his life in Italy.

POZZUOLI, Giovanni, a native of Carpi, an

eminent worker in *scagliola*, who studied under Annibale Griffoni. Lanzi says that, in conjunction with Giovanni Massa, he executed some wonderful specimens of this art in his native place, and in the adjacent cities of Guastalla, Novellara, and elsewhere. He died about 1734. See *del Conte* and *Gio. Massa*.

PRADIER, Charles Simon, a Swiss engraver, born at Geneva about 1790. He went to Paris, and studied under the celebrated Desnoyers. Among his principal plates are several landscapes, and a number of beautiful plates after the Italian, French, and Flemish masters, among which are La Vierge aux Ruines, *after Raffaelle;* Cupid and Psyche, Virgil reading the Æneid to Augustus, Zephyr caressing Flora, and several portraits, *after Gerard;* Raffaelle and Fornarina, and Antiochus, *after Ingres*. He was living in 1841.

PRADO, Blas de, a Spanish painter, born at Toledo, according to Palomino, in 1497. He studied under Alonso Berruguette, and executed some excellent works for the churches at Toledo, among which are several in the chapel of St. Blas, much injured by time and the dampness of the situation. There are also some fine pictures by him at Madrid, particularly a Descent from the Cross, in the church of San Pedro, which shows the hand of an able master. He also excelled in portraits, and was invited to the court of the Emperor of Morocco, to paint the portrait of the daughter of that monarch, who munificently rewarded him. He died at Madrid in 1557. Others say that he studied under Francisco Comontes, and that he was living in 1593, about which time he was sent to Morocco by Philip of Spain, for the purpose above mentioned; and that there is an altar-piece by him in the church of the Minimes at Toledo, dated 1591. Probably there were two artists of this name.

PRAET, Stephen de, a Dutch engraver, who executed a few portraits in a neat, but stiff and formal manner.

PRATA, Ranunzio, a Milanese painter, who flourished at Pavia about 1635. Lanzi says he executed some works for the churches in that city, which are highly commended.

PRATO, Francesco de, a painter who flourished at Brescia about the middle of the 16th century. There is an altar-piece, highly commended by Oretti, in the church of S. Francesco at Brescia, representing the Marriage of the Virgin, signed *Francisci de Prato Caravajensis opus* 1547. Lanzi thinks there were two artists of this name.

PRATO, Francesco del, a Florentine painter, who died in 1562. He was an eminent goldsmith, and an excellent artist in the inlaying of metals. He became inclined for painting when somewhat advanced in life, and studied under Francesco Salviati. He was soon able to execute cabinet pictures in the style of that master with great success. Vasari pronounces his Plague of the Serpents and Christ's Descent into Limbo "most beautiful productions." Lanzi thinks that some of the cabinet pictures ascribed to Salviati were very probably executed by this artist.

PRATT, Matthew, a native of Philadelphia, who went to London in 1764, and resided some time with Mr. West. In 1766 he exhibited a picture called the American School, consisting of the portraits of West, himself, and other American artists. He soon afterwards returned to his native city.

PRAXITELES, one of the most eminent Grecian sculptors, was cotemporary with Euphranor, and flourished, according to Pliny, in the 104th Olympiad, or B. C. 360. The place of his birth is not mentioned. He lived in the period immediately subsequent to the age of Phidias, but his genius took a different course from that character of elevation and sublimity which distinguishes the works of the Æschylus of Sculpture. Praxiteles was the founder of a new school. His style was eminently distinguished for softness, delicacy, and high finish; and he was fond of representing whatsoever in nature appears gentle, tender, and lovely. Consequently his favorite subjects were the soft and delicate forms of females and children, rather than the masculine forms of athletes, warriors and heroes. Perhaps in no work were his peculiar abilities so well displayed as in the Venus of Cnidus, which, with the exception of the Olympian Jupiter of Phidias, has received higher and more unqualified eulogiums from ancient writers, than any other work of Grecian art. These two great artists may therefore be considered, as standing at the head of their respective schools; Praxiteles, the delicate and beautiful—Phidias, the grand and sublime. Praxiteles acquired great skill in execution, and is said to have had some peculiarities in finishing his marble. He is said to have declared that he considered those to be his best works which had undergone the process of *circumlitio*, by Nicias. As the latter artist was a painter, it seems probable that this work cannot mean, simply rubbing or polishing the statues, but that some very thin transparent varnish was laid over the surface of the marble after it had passed through the sculptor's hands.

Praxiteles was eminent for his works both in bronze and marble, but he seems to have had the highest reputation for his skill in the latter. Among those in bronze, Pliny and Pausanias mention a statue of Bacchus, and one of a Satyr, so excellent, that it was called *Periboetos*, or, the Celebrated. He also made a statue of Venus; a statue of a Matron weeping; and one of a Courtesan laughing, believed to be a portrait of the celebrated Thespian courtesan Phryne. His Apollo Sauroctonos (or the Lizard Killer), was the finest of his works in bronze, and was greatly distinguished for purity of style, and graceful beauty of form. There is in the Vatican a well-authenticated marble copy of this celebrated work, which is justly considered one of the greatest treasures of that storehouse of art. Among the works in marble by Praxiteles, the famous Venus of Cnidus takes the preëminence. He executed two statues of that goddess, the one draped, and the other naked; the people of Cos chose the former; the Cnidians immediately purchased the latter. This work is mentioned by Lucian as the master-piece of Praxiteles; and it is also the subject of numerous epigrams in the Greek Anthology. Its fame was so great that travelers visited Cnidus on purpose to see it; and Nicomedes, King of Bithynia, offered to assume the payment of a heavy debt for the Cnidians, on condition of their giving up this celebrated work. To their honor be it said, they declined the offer. The original work was destroyed at Constantinople, in the fifth century, in the dreadful fire which consumed so many of the admirable monuments of art, collected in that city. Some idea of the action and general composition of this statue, may be gained from the figure of Venus on the ancient coins of Cnidus. Pliny mentions two figures of Cupids, as among his finest works; and he places one of them quite on an equality with the Venus of Cnidus. It was made of Parian marble. A Cupid in the Vatican is thought to be a copy of this work. Pausanias relates an anecdote in regard to this statue, which may properly be introduced here, as evincing that the opinion of Praxiteles in regard to it, coincided with that of the ancient writers, forming a stronger testimony to the merits of the work. "Phryne, whose influence over the sculptor seems to have been considerable, was anxious to possess a work of Praxiteles, and when desired to choose for herself, not knowing which of his exquisite works to select, devised the following expedient. She commanded a servant to hasten to him, and tell him that his workshop was in flames, and that, with a few exceptions, his works had already perished. Praxiteles, not doubting the truth of the announcement, rushed out in the greatest anxiety and alarm, exclaiming 'all is lost, if my *Satyr and Cupid* are not saved!' The object of Phryne was answered; she confessed her stratagem, and chose the Cupid." Among the other works of Praxiteles, were two statues of Phryne; one of marble, placed in the Temple of Venus at Thespiæ; the other of bronze, gilt, dedicated by her at Delphi, where it had the honor of a distinguished place. Praxiteles appears also to have executed some works of more extended character and composition, among which were some sculptures that decorated the pediments of the Temple of Hercules at Thebes, representing part of the labors of that demi-god. Praxiteles had two sons, Cephisodotus and Timarchus, both of whom were artists.

There was a painter of inferior note named Praxiteles, mentioned by Pliny; also a chaser and modeller, living at a later period.

PRECIADO, or PREZIADO, Don Francisco, a Spanish painter, born at Seville in 1713. After studying with Domingo Martinez, he went to Rome and entered the school of Sebastiano Conca, whose style he adopted. According to Lanzi, he resided at Rome the greater part of his life, and died there in 1789. He painted some good works, particularly a Holy Family, entirely in the style of Conca, for the Church of the Forty Saints. He was appointed painter of the Chamber to Ferdinand VI., and was for many years director of the Spanish Academy at Rome.

PREGLIASCO, Giacomo, an Italian architect, born in Piedmont in 1757. He gained great distinction in theatrical architecture, particularly by restoring the theatre of Canobiana, at Milan; also by erecting the theatre at Monza, the grand theatre at Naples, and several others. Pregliasco was eminent for his designs of gardens, in the English style, evincing an original and excellent taste. He died in 1825.

PREISLER, John Daniel, a German painter and engraver, who flourished at Nuremberg in the latter part of the 17th, and first part of the 18th centuries. He attained little distinction, but had several sons whom he instructed in his profession.

PREISLER, John Justin, the eldest son of the preceding, born at Nuremberg in 1698; died in 1771. He was instructed in design by his father, and afterwards went to Italy, where he resided eight years. On his return to Nuremberg he acquired considerable reputation as a painter, and his picture of the Entombment of Christ, in one of the churches, is commended. He is better known, however, as an engraver, and executed several plates after the French and Flemish masters, among which are the following:

The Four Elements; *after Bouchardon.* The Four Quarters of the World; *do.* A set of Fifty plates from the designs of *Bouchardon*; after the principal antique statues at Rome. Part of the plates from the ceilings painted by *Rubens*, in the church of the Jesuits at Antwerp, with the frontispiece, containing the portraits of Rubens and Vandyck.

PREISLER, George Martin, was the second son of John Daniel P., born at Nuremberg in 1700. He accompanied his brother to Italy, and resided there several years. On returning to Germany, according to Huber, he painted some portraits, but afterwards devoted himself to engraving, in which he acquired considerable eminence. He was employed to engrave some of the plates after the statues in the Dresden Gallery, and also by Stosch, for his work on Antique Gems. He engraved a set of twenty-one plates from the designs made by John Justin Preisler, after the antique and modern statues at Rome and Florence. He also executed many detached plates of portraits and other subjects, a list of which may be found in Nagler's Kunstler-Lexicon. He died in 1754.

PREISLER, John Martin, was the third son of John Daniel P., born at Nuremberg in 1715. He first studied with his brother George Martin P., and made considerable progress until 1739, when he visited Paris, and became a pupil of George Frederick Schmidt. In 1744 he was invited to the court of Denmark, appointed engraver to the King, elected a member of the Academy of Copenhagen, and resided in that city fifty years. He died there in 1794. He executed many plates of portraits and other subjects, a list of which is given by Nagler. The following are among the best.

PORTRAITS.

Frederick V., King of Denmark and Norway; *Tilo, pinx.* Christian VI., King of Denmark; *Wahl, pinx.* Jacobus Benzelius, Episcopus Upsal. 1751. Otto, Count de Thot; *after Krafft.* John Wiedewelt, Sculptor to the King; *P. Alst, pinx.* 1772. Klopstock; *Juel, pinx. Preisler, sc.* 1782. Equestrian Statute of Henry V.; *after a bronze by J. Saly.* The Cardinal de Bouillion; *after Rigaud.*

SUBJECTS AFTER VARIOUS MASTERS.

David and Abigail; *after Guido.* Semiramis putting the Crown of Ninus on her head; *do.* Christ bearing his Cross; *after P. Veronese.* These two prints were for the collection of the Dresden Gallery. Ganymede taken up by the Eagle of Jupiter; *after Pierre.* A Bacchanalian subject; *do.* Laban seeking for his Gods; *after Cazes.* The Triumph of David; *after Trevisani.* Jonas preaching to the Ninevites; *after Sal. Rosa.* The Madonna della Seggia; *after Raffaelle.*

PREISLER, Valentine Daniel, was the youngest son of John Daniel P., born at Nuremberg in 1717. He executed some indifferent portraits and other subjects in mezzotinto, of which Nagler gives a list of twenty-six pieces. He engraved some portraits of the Burgomasters of Zurich, after the designs of J. C. Füessli, which, from some caprice, he signed with the name of *S. Walch.* He also engraved some portraits and other subjects after pictures in the collection of the King of Denmark. He died about 1765.

PREISLER, John George, was the son of John Martin P., born at Copenhagen in 1757. After receiving instruction from his father, he went to Paris, and studied with John George Wille. He engraved some plates in the neat, finished style of that master, and when elected a member of the Academy at Paris in 1787, he engraved for his reception piece, Icarus, *after Vien.* He died in 1808.

PRENNER, Anthony Joseph von, a German engraver, born at Vienna about 1698. His instructor is not mentioned, but after the death of Mannl, he undertook to engrave all the pictures in the Imperial Collection, in conjunction with Andrew Altamont, Francis Stampart, John Adam Schmutzer, and others. These plates, 160 in number, were published at Vienna in four vols., each containing forty prints, under the title of *Theatrum artis Pictoriæ, &c.*, 1728, 1729, 1731, and 1733. He also engraved a few portraits; a complete list of his works may be found in Nagler. He died in 1761.

PRENNER, George Caspar von, was the son of the preceding, born at Vienna about 1722. After learning the rudiments of art under his father, he went young to Italy, and studied and practised painting at Rome for many years. There is an altar-piece by him in the church of S. Dorotéa. He executed a few spirited etchings, some of them neatly finished with the graver, after his own designs and those of other masters. He died about 1766.

PRENNER, John Joseph von, is said to have been the youngest son of Joseph Anthony P. After studying engraving with his father, he went to Italy, where he resided many years, and engraved a part of the plates of the Museo Fiorentino. He also engraved a set of forty-five plates after the paintings in the Castle of Caprarolla, by Taddeo Zuccaro, representing the most memorable actions of the Farnese family, entitled, *Illustri fatti Farnesiani*, published at Rome in 1744 and 1746. Nagler does not mention this engraver, but gives the works above mentioned to George Caspar P.

PRESTEL, John Gottlieb, a German painter and engraver, born at Grunebach, in Suabia, in 1739. After learning the rudiments of art in his own country, he went to Venice, where he studied painting under Giuseppe Nogari, and engraving under Joseph Wagner. On returning to Germany, he devoted himself almost entirely to engraving, and executed a great number of plates in various styles, most of them spiritedly etched, and finished in aquatinta. He resided chiefly at Nuremberg, and died at Frankfort in 1808. Nagler calls him *Johann Theophilus*, or *Gottlieb and Amadeus*, and gives a list of 140 prints by him, principally after the Flemish and Dutch masters.

PRESTEL, Maria Catherine, was the wife of the preceding artist, and assisted him in many of his best works. Some disagreement causing a separation, she went to London, and practised engraving there, until her death in 1794. Nagler gives a list of seventy-three prints by her, after the Italian, Dutch, and German masters, executed in the style of her husband, in a delicate and picturesque manner.

PRESTEL, Catherine, was the daughter and scholar of John G. P. She executed some plates in his style.

PRESTON, Thomas, an English engraver, who flourished about 1730. He executed a few book plates, possessing little merit.

PRETE, Genoese. See Galantino.

PRETI, Cav. Mattia, called Il Calabrese, an eminent Italian painter, born at Taverna, in Calabria, in 1613. After studying some time at Parma and Modena, he went to Rome and studied a short time under Gio. Lanfranco. The reputation of Guercino induced him to visit Cento, for the benefit of his instructions. Lanzi observes, that Calabrese was accustomed to boast that he had studied under Guercino, that he had visited almost every country, and seen and studied the best productions of every school, both in and beyond Italy. "Hence in his painting he may be compared to a man whose travels have been extensive, and who never hears a subject started, to which he does not add something new; and indeed the drapery, ornaments, and costumes, of Preti, are highly varied and original. He confined himself to design, and did not attempt coloring till he was twenty-six years old. In design he was more vigorous and robust, than delicate, and sometimes inclines to heaviness. In his coloring he was not attractive, but had a strong *impasto*, a decided chiaro-scuro, and an ashy tone, well adapted to his mournful and tragical subjects; for, following the bent of his genius, he devoted himself to the representations of martyrdoms, slaughters, pestilence, and the pangs of a guilty conscience. It was his custom, says Pascoli, to paint at the first conception, with fidelity to nature, and he did not take much pains afterwards in correction, or in the just expression of the passions."

Preti executed a multitude of works for the churches and public edifices, as well as the private collections of all the principal cities of Italy—at Rome, Florence, Naples, and especially at Bologna. His fame reached Malta, whither he was invited by the Grand Master, Cotoner, who commissioned him to decorate the cathedral with some frescos, representing subjects from the life of St. John the Baptist, which he executed in such admirable style, that Cotoner conferred on him the honor of knighthood. He afterwards passed some time at Naples, and executed some considerable works in fresco for the church of the Carthusians. According to Dominici, in conjunction with other eminent professors, Preti endeavored to resist the innovations of Luca Giordano, but the unprecedented popularity of that artist triumphed over all his cotemporaries. Disgusted at the perversion of taste, Preti returned to Malta, where he passed the remainder of his days. His figures are generally half-size, like those of Guercino and Caravaggio. His oil pictures in Italy are almost innumerable, as he had great readiness of invention, a remarkable facility of hand, and lived to an advanced age. Wherever he went, he was accustomed to leave some memorial of his talents; sometimes to the churches, but more frequently to the private collections. There are many of his works in the palaces and collections of the nobility at Bologna, as well as some in the churches. One of his mo finished altar-pieces is St. Bernardino preaching, in the cathedral at Siena. He painted three pictures in the church of S. Andrea della Valle, at Rome, representing subjects from the life of that saint; but unfortunately for his fame in that city, they were placed immediately under the Four Evangelists in the angles, so admirably painted by Domenichino. It is not considered derogatory to his character to allow that he was unequal to such competition. He died at Malta in 1699.

PRETI, Gregorio, was a younger brother and pupil of the preceding, whose manner he followed. He painted both in oil and fresco, but did not acquire much distinction. There is a fresco by him in the church of S. Carlo de' Catenari, at Rome.

PRETI, Francesco Maria, an eminent Italian architect, born at Castel Franco, in Trevigiano, in 1701. He was of noble descent, and received an excellent education in the college of Brescia. After completing his studies, he returned to Castel Franco, and decided to study architecture. He received much important information from the Count Giacomo Riccati, and applied himself with such assiduity, that in a short time he designed the church of S. Liberale, the cathedral of Castle Franco, which received general approbation. Encouraged by this success, Preti began to study the ancient and modern writers, and visited Padua to pursue a course of instruction. He proposed to collect all the rules of the best authors, adding his own reflections, to fix the harmonic medium of height, to supply what was wanting to a complete theory on that subject, and to write a treatise upon it. He also intended to explain by a series of designs, all that had been reduced to practice; also the method of preserving unity, solidity, harmony, elegance and majesty, in architectural works. He made a great number of designs for this treatise, which must have occupied him several years; but in consequence of his many commissions, and his delicate state of health, it was not published until after his death, in 1780, at Venice, under the title of *Elementi di Architettura*. His drawings were not printed with this edition; which is much to be regretted, as they contained solutions of several architectural difficulties, arranged with the greatest convenience and beauty.

Preti made many designs for palaces, rural dwellings, and additions to churches, which Milizia says are distinguished for simplicity, correctness, and majesty. Among the principal, are the façade of S. Giustina, at Padua; the parochial church of Valla, in the Ionic order; that of Salvatronda, in the Doric order, of the form of a Greek cross; those of Casselle and of Tombolo, in the Corinthian order; and a theatre at Castel Franco.

According to Milizia, Preti practised the art merely for the love of it, never receiving any recompense for his services. He was liberal and sincere in conversation, the friend of every professor of art, and distinguished for his integrity and honor. He died in 1774.

PREVITALE, Andrea, an eminent painter of Bergamo, whose works date, according to Tassi, from 1506 to 1528. He was one of the most distinguished disciples of Giovanni Bellini, whose dry manner he followed at first, but afterwards improved his design and coloring, and nearly approached the moderns, as is evident from his St. John preaching, in the church of S. Spirito, and his St. Benedetto, in the cathedral at Bergamo. One of his finest works is the Annunciation, at Ceneda, so beautifully colored and full of expression, that according to Ridolfi, it was the admiration of Titian, who always, in passing through the place, contemplated it with rapture, charmed by its expressive spirit of devotion. Lanzi says his Madonnas are held in the highest estimation; in the features he appears less a disciple of Bellini, than of Raffaelle, or da Vinci. Two of them, surrounded with figures of other saints, are in private collections at Milan. There are several of his works in the Carrara Gallery. Some of his pictures are signed Andreas Ber. Pin., i. e., *Andreas Bergomensis, Pinxit.* He died of the great plague in 1528.

PREVOST, Benoit Louis, a French engraver, born at Paris, according to Nagler, in 1740. He studied under Jean Ouvrier, and engraved a variety of vignettes and other book plates, in a clear, neat style, among which are a set of twelve pieces for the *Abregé chronologique du President Henault.* Nagler describes twenty-six prints by him. He died in 1804.

PREVOST, or PROVOST, Nicolas, a French engraver, who, according to Florent le Comte, studied under Claude Vignon, flourished about 1700, and etched six small plates. The Abbé de Marolles calls him Provost, in his catalogue of French artists. Dumesnil is of opinion that he is the artist of that name who painted the Decollation of St. John in the church of Nôtre Dame, at Paris. He also mentions an etching of a Holy Family, signed *N. Preuost, Jn.*

PREVOST, Pierre, a French painter, born at Montigni, near Chateaudun, in 1764. He visited Paris, studied under Valenciennes, and painted a number of easel pictures of landscapes, with ruins, in the style of his instructor, evincing considerable talent. In 1797, Robert Fulton, the celebrated American inventor of the steamboat, visited Paris, and projected the first panorama ever exhibited in that city. Prevost determined to enter upon this novel branch of the art, and soon devoted himself to it with great assiduity. According to French authority, he designed all his views on the spot, and carried the art to the highest perfection. He first produced his panorama of the city of Paris, and afterwards those of Rome, Naples, Amsterdam, Bologna, Tilsit, Wagram, Antwerp, and London. In 1817 he visited the East, and painted his fine panoramas of Athens and Jerusalem. While engaged upon a design of the city of Constantinople, he was prostrated by disease, and died, in 1823.

PREZ, F. des, a French engraver on wood, who flourished at Paris about 1573. His prints possess little interest.

PRICE, an obscure English engraver, who executed a few portraits in a very indifferent manner.

PRICKE, Robert, an engraver mentioned by Vertue, as one of the pupils of W. Hollar, while that artist was in England, whose style he endeavored to imitate. He engraved the plates for a book on architecture, by Pierre le Meurs.

PRIEST, Thomas, an English landscape painter, who lived at Chelsea about 1740, and chiefly painted views on the Thames. He also etched and published a set of eight views of Chelsea, Mortlake, and other places, executed in a rather coarse, but spirited style.

PRIMATICCIO, Francesco, an eminent painter, born at Bologna in 1490. He was of a noble family, and being a younger son was intended by his father for commercial pursuits; but manifesting a strong inclination for art, he was permitted to study with Innocenzio da Imola, and afterwards with Il Bagnacavallo, under whom he showed great talents, and made extraordinary progress. The fame of Giulio Romano drew him to Mantua, and he entered the school of that master, where he continued six years, and assisted him in his great works in the Palazzo del Te. He was the ablest of all Giulio's scholars, and when Francis I. applied to the Duke of Mantua for an artist to decorate the palace at Fontainbleau, he recommended Primaticcio. On arriving in France, he found Il Rosso engaged in the King's service, and invested with the office of Superintendent of the buildings. A violent animosity sprang up between these eminent artists, to terminate which the King sent Primaticcio to Italy, to make a collection of antique statues and other works of art. During his absence Il Rosso, called by the French Maitre Roux, died, and on returning he succeeded to his employment. He then commenced the great works in the Royal Palace at Fontainbleau, for which he had first been invited to France. In the ceiling of the great gallery he represented, in fifteen compartments, the Gods of Homer; and on the sides, in fifty-eight smaller compartments, the Adventures of Ulysses, taken from the Odyssey. These stupendous works were chiefly executed from his designs by Niccolo Abati, called also dell' Abati, as mentioned in the life of that painter, assisted by other artists, among whom was Ruggiero Ruggieri, the pupil of Primaticcio, whom he had brought with him from Mantua. These works gave so much satisfaction to the king that he munificently rewarded him, and bestowed on him the revenue of the Abbey of St. Martin, at Troyes in Champagne, worth 8,000 crowns a year, which he enjoyed through life. After the death of Francis, he continued in the service of his successors, Henry II., Francis II., and Charles IX.

Few of the works of Primaticcio now remain. He passed most of his life in France, and all his great pictures before mentioned, in the palace at Fontainbleau, were unnecessarily destroyed in 1738, when that edifice was repaired, through the ignorance and barbarism of the superintendent of the works, greatly to the regret of every lover of art. All that remains of his pictures at Fontainbleau are the frescos in the Saloon of the Guards, now called the apartment d'Estampes, representing the History of Alexander the Great.

There is much discrepancy about the real merits of this great artist. Some writers, who do not hesitate to give to Raffaelle the full merit of all the works executed from his designs by his numerous assistants, give a great share of the glory of the works at Fontainbleau to Primaticcio's assistant and coadjutor, Niccolo dell' Abati, although the latter had no hand in designing them. Their other objections are thus briefly summed up by Prof. Phillips, in one of his lectures: "Primaticcio and Niccolo dell' Abati wrought in the same brilliant and free style of design and composition; masterly, but false; able in art, but at variance with nature; manifesting far more science than feeling; freedom and ease of design being regarded by them as most worthy of attention." It is conceded, however, by the best authorities, that, though occasionally artificial, and somewhat incorrect from his expeditious manner, Primaticcio was distinguished for a fertile and inventive genius, judicious composition, a learned design, vigorous coloring, and a fine expression in his heads. It is also admitted that France was greatly indebted to him for the introduction of a better taste both in painting and sculpture. Vasari says, "the first stuccos and the first works in fresco of any consideration in France, took their rise from Primaticcio; he supplied the court with a rich collection of ancient statues, and moulds of many excellent sculpture, from which he afterwards took casts in bronze." Yet while he mentions that the King of France gave Il Rosso a pension of 1,000 crowns, he omits the fact that he was so impressed with the value of the services of Primaticcio that he rewarded him with a rich benefice of 8,000 crowns, for which omission Malvasia severely taxes him with malice, and Lanzi says he leaves the motives of Vasari to the judgment of his readers. The fact that Primaticcio was sent to Italy by the King to make a collection of antiques, shows the confidence that monarch reposed in his abilities. He ably acquitted himself, and brought back one hundred and twenty-five statues, busts, and mutilated figures; he also took moulds of the most celebrated antiques which he could not purchase, as the Laocoon, the Tiber, the Nile, Ariadne, Commodus, and others, which he subsequently cast in bronze. The works he conducted in France have been fully described by Felibien, who adds that "the geniuses of France are greatly indebted for many exquisite productions to Primaticcio and M. Niccolo (dell' Abati), who are entitled to the fame of first introducing Roman taste into France, with all the beau ideal of ancient painting and sculpture." His works are exceedingly rare in Italy. In the Ducal palace (Palazzo Te) at Mantua, are the exquisite stucco friezes so highly commended by Vasari, and a few pictures, the authenticity of which is questioned by Lanzi, who mentions only one genuine work by him in Italy. His pictures, indeed, are of the utmost rarity in Italy, even in Bologna itself. In the grand Zambeccari Gallery, there is a Concert by him, with three female figures, altogether enchanting; the forms, the motions, the coloring, the taste of the contours, and the easy and chaste foldings of the drapery, all combined with a certain originality pervading the whole composition, are well calculated to attract and rivet the eye at the first moment.

Primaticcio was also acquainted with architecture, and made a design for the palace at Meudon; but he never practised the art to any extent. He died at Paris in 1570. See *Niccolo Abati*.

PRIMI, Gio. Battista, a Roman painter, who, according to Soprani, was a scholar of Agostino Tassi. He painted landscapes in the style of that master with much success, and executed many works for the collections. He settled at Genoa, where he died in 1657.

PRIMO. See Gentile.

PRINA, Pietro Francesco, a painter of Novara, highly commended by Orlandi, as an excellent ornamental fresco painter. He excelled in perspective and architecture, and was engaged in several extensive works at Milan and other places. He was living in 1718.

PRINCE, Jean Baptiste le, a French painter and engraver, born at Metz in 1733. He went to Paris and studied painting, first with J. M. Vien, and afterwards with François Boucher. After acquiring considerable reputation at Paris for his conversation pieces, he accompanied the Abbé Chappe to Siberia, when that astronomer went to make observations on the transit of Venus. During an absence of several years he visited various parts of the Russian Empire, designing the various costumes, and taking sketches of the most remarkable views of scenery in the country through which he passed. On visiting St. Petersburg he painted a large picture of that city, of which he afterwards published an engraving. On returning to Paris with his extensive collection of drawings, he was very favorably received, painted many admirable pictures, and engraved about 160 plates from his own designs, a list of which may be found in Nagler's Lexicon. He was elected a member of the Royal Academy of Paris, and painted the ceremony of a Russian Baptism for his reception piece. He excelled in conversational pieces, interiors of guard-rooms, pastorals, rural festivals, &c., all which subjects he engraved. His prints are spiritedly etched, and usually finished in aquatinta. His works were so much admired that several of his countrymen occupied themselves in engraving from his designs. He died in 1781.

PRINS, J. H., a Dutch painter, born at the Hague, in 1758. His parents, being in good circumstances, intended him for the medical profession; but having a passion for painting, and being strongly opposed by his friends, he ran away from home, and traveled through Brabant and France, studying and making numerous sketches and drawings of the places through which he passed. He subsequently returned to the Hague, but afterwards visited Amsterdam, Utrecht, and Leyden, and practised his profession for a time in each of those cities. He acquired considerable reputation, and his pictures are compared by the Dutch writers to those of Berkheyden and Vanderheyden. There is not much resemblance, however, except in the subjects; and though his works have merit, they only suffer by a comparison with the productions of those admired painters. His pictures are generally of small size, and are faithful representations of the cities of Holland. They are executed in a lively and spirited manner, with a pleasing effect. His figures are correctly designed and introduced with judgment; the contrast of light and shade is striking, and the reflection of the objects in the water is admirable. His pictures are so very minutely finished, that it appears as if each separate piece might be counted, even the bricks in his edifices—showing less of the artist than the artisan. Nagler gives a list of 12 etchings by him, and says he was drowned in a canal in 1805.

PRINS, B. M., a Dutch artist who flourished at Amsterdam about 1824, and painted landscapes and marines with considerable reputation.

PRISCUS, Accius, a Roman painter, who flourished under Vespasian, and was employed by him in concert with Cornelius Pinus, to execute some works in the temple of Virtue and Honor. He is said to have approached the style of the ancients more closely than Pinus.

PRIWITZER, John, a painter born in Hungary, who went to England in the reign of James I., and was entertained at his court, where he painted the portraits of many of the nobility, among which is that of Sir William Russell, at Woburn Abbey, dated 1627.

PROBST, John Balthazar, a German engraver, born in 1673, and died in 1748. He worked with the graver, in a neat but formal style, and executed a part of the plates after the antique statues in the Dresden Gallery, and several plates of beasts and birds in the menagerie of Prince Eugene, published in 1734. He also engraved some detached pieces, after the Italian and German masters.

PROCACCINI, Ercole, the Elder, a painter born at Bologna in 1520. There is much discrepancy among Italian authors as to the details of this artist's life; but it is certain that, after acquiring distinction by executing many excellent works for the churches of his native city, he settled at Milan, and opened an academy, which became one of the most celebrated of his time. Besides his own sons, he educated some of the most distinguished artists of the Milanese school, among whom were Sammachini, Sabbatini, and Bertoja. Lomazzo extols him as a successful follower of the graceful design and admirable coloring of Coreggio. Lanzi, after pointing out the errors respecting him, says, "In my opinion, he appears somewhat minute in design and feeble in coloring, resembling the tones of the Florentines, a thing so common among his cotemporaries as to make it no reproach to him. For the rest, he is more accurate, diligent, and pleasing than most artists of his age, and perhaps his over-diligence acted as an obstacle to him at Bologna, where the rapid Fontana bore the chief sway; but this quality, besides exempting him from the mannerism then beginning to prevail, rendered him an excellent preceptor, one of whose principal duties is found to consist in checking the inspiration of young artists, so as to ground them properly in the principles of art, and accustom them to precision and delicacy of taste." The principal works of Ercole P. are in the churches at Bologna, the most esteemed of which are the Annunciation, in S. Benedetto; the Conversion of St. Paul, and Christ praying in the Garden, in S. Giacomo Maggiore; St. Michael discomfiting the Rebel Angels, in S. Bernardo; and the Deposition from the Cross, in S. Stefano. There are also some of his works at Milan, and at Parma. He was living in 1591.

PROCACCINI, Camillo, was the eldest son of the preceding, born at Bologna in 1546. As there is considerable discrepancy among authors as to the merits of this artist, we prefer to copy at length from Lanzi, who always ably investigates his subject, especially when there is any dispute. "He received his first instructions from his father, and often displays a resemblance in his heads, and in the distribution of his tints, though when he painted with care, he both warmed and broke them, as well as employed the middle col ors, in a superior manner. He studied other schools, and if we are to believe some of his biographers, he practised at Rome from the models of Raffaelle and Michael Angelo, besides being passionately devoted to the heads of Parmiggiano, an imitation of which is perceptible in all his works. He possessed a wonderful facility, both in conception and execution; added to nature, beauty and spirit, always attractive to the eye, though not always satisfactory to the judgment. Nor is this surprising, as he threw off the reign of paternal instruction, and executed works enough to have employed ten artists, in the various churches at Bologna, Ravenna, Reggio, Piacenza, Pavia, and Genoa. He was called by many the Vasari, and others the Zuccaro of Lombardy; although to say the truth, he surpassed both these artists in sweetness of style and coloring. He was particularly employed at Milan, a city boasting some of his finest productions, by which he obtained reputation there; as well as many of his worst, by which he satisfied those who valued his name. Of his earliest works there, the most free from mannerism are those adjoining the exterior of the organ at the Cathedral, along with various Mysteries of our Lady and two histories of David playing upon his harp. But he produced nothing at Milan equal to his Last Judgment, in the church of S. Procolo at Reggio, esteemed one of the finest specimens of fresco-painting in all Lombardy: and to his St. Roch administering to the sick and dying of the Plague—a picture which Malvasia says intimidated Annibale Caracci, when he was commissioned to paint a companion for it, to represent that Saint distributing alms to the poor. The pictures produced by Camillo in the Cathedral of Piacenza, where the Duke of Parma had placed him in competition with Lodovico Caracci, whose genius was then matured, are well and carefully executed. He there represented the Coronation of the Virgin, surrounded with a very full choir of Angels, in whose forms he displays the most finished beauty. It was the part of Lodovico to represent other Angels around and opposite to the Coronation, and the *Padri del Limbo*. Though Camillo occupied the most distinguished part of the tribune, he was esteemed by spectators then, as he is now, the least worthy of the two." Though Procaccini, in this contest, was unequal to his powerful antagonist in the dignity of his design, the novelty of ideas, and the expression of the heads, yet it is no mean proof of his abilities, that his pictures possess a powerful attraction, even in the neighborhood of so dangerous a competitor, and that they have elicited the applause of several travelers and historians. Other admired works by him at Milan are the Martyrdom of St. Agnes, in the sacristy of the Cathedral, and the ceiling of the Padri Zoccolanti, where he represented the Coronation of the Virgin, surrounded by a beautiful Choir of Angels. His other most esteemed works are the Adoration of the Shepherds in the church of S. Francesco, and the Annunciation, in S. Clemente, at Bologna; the Last Supper, in the façade of the Cathedral, a grand composition, with figures considerably larger than life; and the Circumcision, in S. Domenico at Genoa. It is generally admitted that Camillo P. possessed a fertile invention, and great facility of execution; that his coloring, especially in frescos, was clear and vigorous; that the airs of his heads were generally expressive and graceful; and that his draperies were cast with judgment and a noble taste; but his promptness and dispatch sometimes led him into incorrectness and extravagance, and he may be occasionally convicted of mannerism. He died at Milan in 1626. He executed a few spirited etchings from his own designs, among which are the following:

The Holy Family reposing, in which St. Joseph is represented lying on the ground, resting on the saddle of the ass. Another Holy Family, in which St. Joseph is presenting an orange to the Infant. 1493. The Virgin suckling the Infant. The Transfiguration. St. Francis receiving the Stigmata. 1593.

PROCACCINI, Giulio Cesare, was the second son of Ercole P., born at Bologna in 1548. After receiving some instruction from his father, he devoted himself to sculpture for some time with success, but he afterwards returned to painting, and is said to have studied in the school of the Caracci. Lanzi says it is evident that he directed his attention to the works of Correggio, and made them his models, and that, in the opinion of many, no one approached nearer to the grand style of that great artist. "In his small pictures, with few figures, in which imitation is more easy, he has often been mistaken for his original, though his elegance cannot boast the same clear and natural tones, nor his colors the same rich and vigorous handling. One of his Madonnas, in the church of S. Luigi de' Francesi at Rome, was in fact engraved not long since, by an eminent artist, for a work of Correggio; and there are other equally fine imitations in the Palazzo Sanvitali at Parma, in that of the Careghi at Genoa, and in other places." Cesare passed some time at Rome, where he diligently studied the works of Raffaelle, and it is said he occasionally imitated the rich, glowing coloring of Titian, though Correggio was evidently his great model. He settled at Milan, where he soon rose to distinction, and gained, by his merits, the friendship of the principal nobility. He executed an extraordinary number of well finished works for the churches and public edifices of Milan, Genoa, and other places, and more for private collections. He is esteemed the best of the Procaccini. Less prompt and capricious than his brother Camillo, his compositions are studied and judicious, his design dignified and correct, his masses broad and masterly, and his coloring rich and harmonious. In imitating the graces of Correggio, he sometimes attempted a tenderness of expression approaching to affectation; such are his pictures of the Virgin and infant Jesus surrounded with Saints, and a Choir of Angels gazing smilingly on him, in the church of S. Afra, at Brescia; and his Annunciation, in S. Antonio, at Milan, in which the Virgin and Angel are seen smiling at each other. In his attitudes, also, he was occasionally extravagant, as in his picture of the Martyrdom of St. Nazario, in the church of that Saint—a picture full of harmony and grace, though the figure of the executioner is depicted in a constrained attitude, with a ferocious expression. His most esteemed works in the churches at Milan are the Israelites passing through the Red Sea, in S. Vittore; the Transfiguration, in S. Celso; the Adoration of the Magi, and St. Francis receiving the Stigmata, at the Padri Zoccolanti. Some of his histories are of a very large size, as the Passage of the Red Sea, before mentioned. He died at Milan in 1626.

There is an etching attributed to this artist, representing the Virgin with the infant Jesus.

PROCACCINI, Carlo Antonio, was the third son of Ercole P., born at Bologna about 1555. He was instructed by his father, but afterwards devoted himself to landscape, flowers, and fruit, and acquired great distinction. He particularly excelled in landscape, and his works are highly commended by Malvasia and others, though Lanzi, who always considers such subjects as belonging to the lower branches of the art, hardly does him justice. He says, "he produced a variety of pieces for the Milanese Gallery, which happening to please the court, then one of the branches of Spain, he had frequent commissions from that country, insomuch that he rose, though the weakest in the family, into the highest repute." His works abound in Milan, and are found in many collections in other Italian cities. He also painted some pictures for the churches, one of the best of which is in S. Agata, dated 1605. He died about 1628.

PROCACCINI, Ercole, called the Younger, was the son of Carlo Antonio P., born at Milan in 1596. He first studied with his father, and afterwards with his uncle Giulio Cesare P., whose style he closely followed. Without possessing any remarkable powers, he enjoyed immense patronage, and executed many works for the churches of Milan and other places, but more for the collections. He also excelled in flower-pieces, and for an exquisite performance of this kind he was honored by the court with a gold chain. He opened an academy at Milan, instructed several pupils; and at the death of his uncle Giulio he was appointed Superintendent of the Academy. Lanzi considers that he contributed to the decline of the Milanese school, by neglecting design too much, and by promoting a servile imitation, or a rapid and mechanical execution. He says of the artists of the Milanese school, who immediately followed the Procaccini, "in general it may be remarked of the artists of this epoch, that though the pupils of different schools, they display a mutual resemblance, as much as if they had been instructed by the same master. They possess no character that strikes the eye, no beauty of proportions, no vivacity of countenances, no grace in the coloring. The whole composition appears languid; even their imitation of the head of the school does not please, as it is either deficient or overdone, or falls into insignificance"; and again:

"It is known that Ercole P., by public report, by his insinuating manners, and by the family reputation, arrived at a degree of consideration beyond his merit, and he lived to the great age of eighty. Hence he induced many to follow his maxims, and the more, as he kept an open academy in his own house for the study of the naked figure, and succeeded his uncles in their instructions; equal to them perhaps in rapidity, but not so well grounded in art. He painted much, and he maintains his place in the best collections in Milan, though he may not be in so much request as many others."

Lanzi admits however, that Ercole, in his more studied works, as the Assumption of the Virgin, in the church of S. Maria Maggiore at Bergamo, "exhibits dignity, spirit, and a happy imitation of the manner of Correggio." He died in 1676.

PROCACCINI, Andrea, a painter born at Rome in 1671. He studied under Carlo Maratti, and became one of his ablest scholars. He was one of the twelve artists selected by the command of Clement XI. to paint the Twelve Prophets in St. John of Lateran, on a trial of skill. On this occasion, Procaccini painted Daniel in such a masterly manner as gained him great reputation. He executed several other works for the churches at Rome; was invited to the court of Spain, and appointed painter to the King. During a residence of fourteen years at Madrid, he executed several works for the churches and royal palaces, which are highly commended. In his design and coloring he closely followed the manner of his instructor, though he painted in a grander style than was usual with Maratti. He painted both in oil and fresco, but his easel works are few. He executed a few spirited and graceful etchings from his own designs, and others after Raffaelle and Carlo Maratti. He died at St. Idelfonso in Spain, in 1734, and was buried with great pomp in the convent of San Francisco de Segovia.

PROFONDAVALLE, Valerio, a painter born in Louvain in 1533. According to Lomazzo, he settled at Milan about 1560, where he was much employed by the Court. He was distinguished for fertile invention and pleasing coloring, especially in fresco; but he was chiefly eminent for his paintings on glass, elegantly designed and brilliantly colored. Lanzi commends him as an able artist, who found abundant employment during his long residence at Milan, where he died in 1600.

PROKOPHIEV, Ivan Prokophievitch, an eminent Russian sculptor, born at Petersburg in 1758. At the age of twelve, he commenced studying under Gilet, one of the professors in the Academy of Fine Arts in his native city; and during the eight subsequent years he obtained medals and other prizes for a number of bas-reliefs. Having completed his academical course, he was sent at government expense, in 1779, to perfect himself under Julien at Paris. In 1780, he executed a bust in marble of Prince Gargarin, and a relief in terra-cotta, representing Moses. Having passed a few months at Stettin and Berlin, on his way home, he returned to Petersburg in 1784, and settled permanently in that city. He wrought with great industry, and executed a very large number of works, chiefly bas-reliefs, medallions, and other works on a small scale, mostly for private individuals, many of them being in terra-cotta. His productions evince considerable powers of invention and composition. Those executed in his earlier days have, with much beauty, somewhat of the French mannerism of that day, probably acquired from Julien; but he subsequently overcame this deficiency, and adopted a more noble and classical style. In the Petersburg Academy are his bust of Prince Gargarin, and his bas-reliefs of Moses and Morpheus. In the Imperial Library there are sixteen small caryatides and twenty-eight bas-reliefs by him. His last work was a bust of the Polish poet Trembecki. Soon after its completion, he was attacked by a complaint that rendered him incapable of using his right hand in modeling or designing. He died at Petersburg in 1828, aged 71.

PRONCK, Cornelius, a Dutch painter and engraver, born at Amsterdam in 1691. He was instructed in drawing under F. van Houten, and in painting by Arnold Boonen. He was excellent in portraits, and found considerable employment. He drew views of cities, and landscapes, in water-colors and India ink, which are highly esteemed by collectors. He also etched a few plates of views of cities and landscapes, from his own designs. He died in 1759.

PRONTI, Padre Cesare, a painter born at Rimini in 1626, according to most authors, though Pascoli says he was a native of Cattolica, of the family of Bacciochi. That author relates many interesting anecdotes of him, particularly one relating to his early passion for painting. When a boy, he accompanied his parents to a fair at Sinigaglia, where was a fine collection of pictures on exhibition. He gazed upon them for several hours, unmindful of his food or his parents, who were searching for him through the city, and when at length they found him, could hardly tear him from the spot. The impression made was indelible; he had resolved to become a painter, and his parents strongly opposing the fixed, determined resolution of his soul, he ran away to Bologna, and assumed the appellation of Pronti, the maiden name of his mother. He entered the school of Guercino, and adopted his style. At an early period of his life, he became a monk of the order of St. Augustine, and was afterwards employed in painting altar-pieces and sacred histories in fresco, for the churches of his order. He executed these in an excellent manner, generally enriching his back-grounds with admirable architecture. His principal works are at Rimini and Ravenna, and from his long residence in the latter city, he is frequently called *Padre Cesare da Ravenna.* Among his best works are a picture of St. Tommaso da Villanova, at Pesaro; and the Histories from the Life of St. Jerome, in the church of his order at Rimini, which Lanzi says are executed with abundant grace and spirit. He died at Ravenna in 1708.

PROTOGENES, was one of the most celebrated Greek painters. According to Pliny and Pausanias, he was a native of Caunus, a city of Caria, subject to the Rhodians. He was cotemporary with Apelles, flourished during the reign of Alexander the Great, about B. C. 330, and resided at Rhodes during the principal part of his life. Pliny says that Protogenes was originally in very poor circumstances, and that it was not known from whom he received instruction. He passed the earlier part of his life in obscurity, being principally employed in decorating ships. His fellow-citizens were totally insensible of his merit, until the generosity of Apelles roused the Rhodians from their indifference to the talent of their countryman. When that great painter visited Rhodes, he was struck with admiration at the works of Protogenes, and burned with indignation at the injustice of the Rhodians. He inquired what price he put upon his pictures, and when the Rhodian painter mentioned an inconsiderable sum, Apelles paid him fifty talents for a single picture, and publicly announced that he would make it pass and sell for his own. This liberality opened the eyes of the Rhodians, who immediately purchased back the picture at a still higher price, and thenceforward held Protogenes in the highest estimation. He finished his pictures with the greatest care, and consequently did not execute many works. Quintilian says that "cura" was the distinguishing characteristic of his paintings. The ancient writers always mention him in terms of the warmest approbation; and it is perhaps the highest proof of his merit, that Apelles declared Protogenes inferior to himself only in not knowing when "to take his hand from the tablet,"—i.e. in bestowing too much labor upon his paintings.

The most famous of all the paintings of Protogenes, was the picture of Ialysus and his Dog. Pliny says that he laid on four courses of color, lest it should be obliterated by age; and that he was occupied upon it seven years. The dog in this picture, represented as panting and foaming at the mouth, was greatly admired. It is related that Protogenes was for a long time unable to represent the foam in the manner he wished, till at length he threw his sponge in a fury at the spot, and produced the very effect he desired. The fame of this painting was so great, that, according to Pliny, Demetrius Poliorcetes, when besieging Rhodes, did not assault that part of the city where Protogenes lived, lest he should destroy the picture. His studio was situated without the walls, where, to the astonishment of the besiegers, he continued to paint with perfect tranquillity. This coming to the ears of Demetrius, he ordered the artist to be brought to his tent, and demanded how he could persist in the quiet exercise of his profession when surrounded by enemies? Protogenes replied that he did not consider himself in any danger, convinced that a great prince like Demetrius did not make war against the Arts, but against the Rhodians. During these hostilities he painted his famous picture of a Satyr playing on a Flageolet. At the recommendation of Apelles, the Athenians invited Protogenes to Athens, when he was about fifty years of age. He painted a picture of the Mother of Aristotle; one of Alexander; a picture of the god Pan; and the Thesmothæ, in the Senate House of the Five Hundred at Athens, mentioned by Pausanias. His famous picture of Ialysus and his Dog was still preserved in the time of Pliny in the Temple of Peace at Rome. According to Suidas, Protogenes wrote two books on the art.

PROU, Jacques, a French painter and engraver, born at Paris about 1639. He studied under Sebastian Bourdon, and followed his style in landscape painting. As an engraver, he executed a number of plates, among which are the following: A set of twelve Landscapes and Views, *after his own designs;* a set of six large Landscapes, *after Seb. Bourdon;* the Baptism of Christ, *do.;* the Flight into Egypt, *after Agos. Caracci.*

PROVENZALE, Marcello, a painter born at Cento in 1575. He studied under Paolo Rosetti, and acquired some distinction in history, but is chiefly celebrated for his beautiful portraits in mosaic. Baglioni describes some of his works, executed by command of Paul V., among which was the portrait of that pontiff, wrought with inimitable art and judgment. The face alone consists of more than two millions of pieces, many of them no larger than a grain of sand; it is esteemed one of the great curiosities of art at Rome. Another fine picture is Orpheus playing upon the Lyre, in the palace of the Cardinal Borghese. In conjunction with Rossetti, he executed several mosaics in the church of St. Peter, after the cartoons of the Cav. Roncalli. He died at Rome in 1639.

PROVENZALI, Stefano. According to Crespi, this artist was a native of Cento, and studied under Guercino. He devoted his talents mostly to battle-pieces, which are highly extolled by the author above cited, for their spirited design and vigorous coloring. He died in 1715.

PRUD'HON, Pierre Paul, an eminent French painter, was born at Clugny, according to Gabet, in 1760, although Nagler places his birth in 1768. He studied at Dijon, under Desvosges, and, having gained the prize at the exhibition, received a pension to enable him to visit Italy. At Rome he formed a friendship with the sculptor Canova, and remained in that city until 1789, when he returned to France. After painting miniatures and pastel portraits for some time, he produced his picture of Justice and Vengeance pursuing Crime, which was greatly admired, and placed Prud'hon in a high rank among modern artists. He was soon after chosen a member of the Institute and of the Legion of Honor, and teacher of design to the Empress Maria Louisa. His works are distinguished for richness of composition, elegance of design, beauty of coloring, and delicacy of penciling. The softness and harmony of his tints gained him the title of the French Correggio. He painted many subjects from poetry and history; also portraits and cabinet pictures, which are placed in the best French collections. Among the principal are, Psyche carried off by the Zephyrs; the portrait of the King of Rome; Venus and Adonis; Andromache; the Assumption of the Virgin; the Desolate Family; the Crucifixion; the Vault of the Musée, representing Diana; and a Zephyr hovering over the Water, sold in 1839 for 20,000f. Prud'hon died at Paris in 1823.

PRUNATO, Santo, a painter of Verona, born in 1656. According to Pozzo, he first studied under Voltolino, and afterwards with Falcieri, at Verona. He next went to Venice, and became the pupil of Gio. Carlo Loth. To acquire a more correct and dignified manner, he afterwards proceeded to Bologna, and studied the works of the Caracci. He acquired considerable reputation, and executed some works for the churches at Verona, and other places in the vicinity, among which is a picture of St. Francesco di Sales, in the Cathedral at Verona. Lanzi says that, in design, and in the expression of his heads, he displays too much of the naturalist, but his coloring is soft and harmonious. He was living in 1716.

PRUNATO, Michele Angelo, was the son of the preceding, born at Verona in 1690. He studied with his father, and imitated his manner with no great success. He executed some works for the churches, one of which is in the Cathedral, and compares unfavorably beside the one by his father, before mentioned.

PRUNEAU, Noel, a French engraver, born at Paris in 1751. He studied under Augustin de St. Aubin, in whose style he engraved some plates, chiefly portraits, from his own designs, and after other masters, among which are the following:

PORTRAITS.

Rosalia le Vasseur *after his own design.* Hermann Boerhave; *do.* Albert de Haller; *do.* Gerard, Baron van Swieten, Architect; *after A. de St. Aubin.* John Joseph Sue; *after A. Pujos.* Francis de la Peyronie, principal surgeon to Louis XV.

PUCCI, Giovanni Antonio, a painter who studied under Antonio Domenico Gabbiani. Lanzi says that honorable mention is made of him as a painter and a poet, in the eulogy of Gabbiani, in the *Lettere Pittoriche.* He was living at Rome in 1716, then young.

PUCCINI, Biagio, a painter of Rome, who flourished in that city in the first part, and perhaps to the middle of the 18th century. He painted some works for the churches, and Lanzi says he was esteemed an artist of good execution.

PUCHLER, John Michael, a German engraver of whom little is known. There are a few portraits by him, executed in a peculiar manner, the faces being stippled, and the hair and drapery formed of lines like writing. They are marked with the letters J. M. P. cursive, in a monogram.

PUCHLER, Michael, a German engraver, who executed a few portraits, among which are those of the Emperor Leopold and Eleonora Magdalena Theresa, his Empress.

PUGA, Antonio, a Spanish painter of familiar subjects, who flourished about the middle of the 17th century, studied under Don Diego Velasquez, and is said to have exactly imitated the early manner of that master. There were six pictures by him in the collection of Don Silvestre Collar de Castro, so much in the style of his master, that they might easily be taken for his works.

PUGET, Pierre Paul, a French painter, sculptor, and architect, termed the Michael Angelo of France, was born at Marseilles in 1622. His father, a painter and architect, gave him instructions in those arts, and at the age of fourteen he was placed under a ship-builder, named Roman, who employed him in carving ornaments for decorating vessels. Disgusted with the drudgery of his situation, Puget quitted Marseilles at the age of seventeen, and went to Italy. At Florence, according to Milizia, he met with attention and kindness from the Sculptor to the Grand Duke, and pursued his studies with great success. Attracted by the fame of Pietro da Cortona, he repaired to Rome, and entered the school of that master, where he made such rapid progress as to be selected to assist his instructor in painting the Pitti Palace at Florence. Instead of remaining in that city, however, he suddenly resolved to return to France, although aged only twenty-one years. On arriving at Marseilles he was very well received, and was shortly afterwards commissioned to design a vessel of extraordinary magnificence, named *La Reine*, in honor of Queen Anne of Austria, which was completed in 1646. That princess commissioned a monk of the Order des Feuillants to visit Rome and make designs of the most celebrated monuments of antiquity, and he selected Puget as his assistant. The latter accordingly proceeded a second time to Rome, and spent five or six years in that city; but it is not known what afterwards became of this valuable collection of drawings. On returning to Marseilles in 1653, Puget received commissions for several pictures, and he painted a number for the churches of Marseilles, Aix, Toulon, and other cities; besides some cabinet pictures. In the cathedral at Aix is a picture by him of the Annunciation, elegantly and gracefully designed, though cold and languid in the coloring; also the same subject in the Jacobin church at Toulon, differently composed, somewhat in the style of P. da Cortona. The excessive application of Puget to the art, proved so injurious to his health, that by the advice of his physicians he renounced painting, and thenceforward devoted his energies to sculpture and architecture.

The excellence of Puget in sculpture and architecture was very highly rated in his own day; although Cicognara says his sculptures betray inaccuracy as to proportions, want of refinement in taste, and evince more of the painter than the sculptor in their treatment, seldom producing a pleasing effect, but from a single point of view. His talents, however, were well esteemed by Bernini; his works are full of spirit and fire; they show the hand of a master, and gained him great applause from his countrymen and from cotemporary artists. His talents met with encouragement at Toulon and Marseilles; for which latter city he projected many embellishments, which established his reputation; and he gave further proof of his talents by various machines and inventions, which he introduced into the marine at Toulon. Milizia says that his two Termini, which support the Hotel de Ville at Toulon, although his first work in sculpture, received the applause of Bernini; and the Terra with Janus, and Hercules, which he sculptured at Paris, were still more admired. He was sent by Fouquet to Genoa, for the purpose of selecting marble for some of the works to be executed at Marseilles; but that minister being shortly afterwards disgraced, Puget preferred remaining at Genoa, where he produced several of his finest works, among which were the two statues of St. Sebastiano and St. Ambrogio; the grand bas-relief of the Assumption, in the chapel of the Albergo de' Poveri; the Madonna, in the private oratory of the Sauli. He also designed several fine architectural works, among which were the church of the Nunziata, erected at the expense of the Signor Lomellini; and the chapel of St. Lodovico, in that church. His talents were highly appreciated and rewarded by the Genoese. At length, after a residence of about eight years at Genoa, he was recalled to France by Colbert, who obtained for him the post of sculptor and director of the Works in ornamenting Vessels, with a pension of 1200 crowns, in consequence, it is said, of the earnest recommendation of Bernini. His two works in sculpture at Marseilles, the Milo of Crotona and the group of Perseus and Andromeda, gained him great reputation; the former is considered his master-piece, and a work that will bear comparison with the antique. Among his other works, were a bas-relief of Diogenes, a statue of Apollo, and a bas-relief of the Plague of Milan. He does not seem to have executed many works in architecture; besides those at Genoa already mentioned, he erected at Marseilles the church de la Charité, and that of the Capuchins. In 1688, Puget was presented to the King at Fontainbleau, and was graciously received. He was not, however, calculated for the meridian of a court; and, after residing a short time at Paris, he returned to Marseilles, where he erected an elegant house, in the style of a small palace, and occupied it till his death, in 1694, at the age of 72.

PUGH, Herbert, an Irish painter, who settled in London about 1758. He painted landscapes in a mannered and affected style, and also executed a few indifferent pictures in imitation of Hogarth. He died about 1775.

PUGLIA, Giuseppe, called Il Bastaro, a painter who, according to Baglioni, flourished in the pontificate of Urban VIII., and was employed in the Library of the Vatican. Lanzi reckons him among the second rate artists. He executed some works for the churches and public edifices at Rome, the chief of which are the Presentation, in the Cloister of the Padri della Minerva, and an altar-piece of the Assumption in the Basilica of S. Maria Maggiore. Baglioni says he died young; Zani says he wrought in 1600, and died in 1640; others say that he was born at Rome in 1620, and died in 1682.

PUGLIESCHI, Antonio, a Florentine painter, who flourished in the latter part of the 17th century. According to Baldinucci, he first studied with Ciro Ferri, and afterwards with Pietro Dandini. He was a reputable artist, and executed some works for the churches, but was mostly employed by individuals.

PULIGO, Domenico, a Florentine painter, born in 1475. He studied under Domenico Corradi, called Ghirlandaio, and was esteemed his ablest scholar. According to Vasari, he formed a strict intimacy with Andrea del Sarto, whose style he imitated in his Madonnas and Holy Families. He had an excellent taste of design and composition, but unfortunately for his fame, he was addicted to pleasure, and painted less for reputation than for immediate gain. He was also a good portrait painter. Lanzi says, "he was less skilled in design than in coloring. His tints are sweet, clear, and harmonious; but he aimed at covering the outline to relieve himself of the necessity of perfect accuracy; by this mask, he is sometimes recognized in Madonnas and cabinet pictures, which were perhaps designed by Andrea, and at first sight might pass for the works of that master." He died in 1527.

PULZONE, Scipione, called Gaetano, from the place of his nativity, was born at Gaeta in 1550. He studied under Jacopino del Conte, and acquired considerable reputation in history, but chiefly distinguished himself for his excellent portraits. He painted many of the most distinguished persons of his time, among whom were Gregory XIII., the Archduke Ferdinand, the Cardinal de Medici, and others. Lanzi says, "he formed his manner on those of Raffaelle and Andrea del Sarto, and though somewhat labored, he left behind him a great reputation, partly in portraits, of which he executed a great number for popes and princes, with so much success, that by some, he is called the Vandyck of the Roman school." His attitudes are elegant and graceful, and his heads full of life and expression. He finished his portraits very highly, representing in the pupil of the eye, the reflection of the windows and other objects, as minute and exact as in real life. He also painted some pictures in the finest style, as the Crucifixion, in the church of S. Maria in Vallicella, the Assumption, with the Apostles, in S. Silvestro in Monte Cavallo, and a Dead Christ, in the Lap of the Virgin, in del Gesu. In the Borghese Gallery, is a fine picture of the Holy Family, and in that of Florence, one of Christ praying in the Garden; and in other places are some of his cabinet pictures, which are deservedly esteemed. Lanzi says he died young, in his 38th year, in the pontificate of Sixtus V. Zani says he was born in 1562, and died in 1600.

PUNT, John, a Dutch painter and engraver, born in 1711; died about 1779. As a painter, he was principally employed in theatrical decorations and chiaro-scuro. He engraved some plates; Nagler gives a list of thirty-six of the principal, after the designs of Jacob de Witt, from the ceilings painted by Rubens in the church of the Jesuits at Antwerp, which are the more interesting, as the originals were destroyed by lightning.

PUNTORMO. See Jacopo Carrucci.

PUPILER, Anthony, a Flemish painter, who was employed in Spain by Philip II., about 1556. He is said to have been an artist of great ability, but no opinion can be formed of his merits, as all his works were destroyed in the conflagration of the Prado.

PUPINI, Biagio, a Bolognese painter, of whom there are notices from 1530 to 1540. He was a disciple of Francesco Francia, whose style he followed, though with a more modern air. He executed some works for the churches of Bologna, the most esteemed of which are the Coronation of the Virgin in S. Giuliano; the Virgin and Infant, with St. Orsola, in S. Giacomo Maggiore; St. John preaching in the Wilderness, in S. Maria della Baroncella, and the Nativity, at the Institute. He often wrought in conjunction with other artists, at Bologna and in other places. He is sometimes called Biagio dalle Lame, or Lamme.

PURCELL, Richard, an English engraver in mezzotinto, born in 1736, and died about 1800. He scraped some portraits after Vandyck, Reynolds, and others, among which are the following: John Manners, Marquis of Granby; Lady Fenhoulet, afterwards Countess of Essex; Elizabeth, Countess of Berkley; *after Reynolds*. The Children of Charles I.; *after Vandyck*. John Wilkes, Esq.; *after Pine*.

PUSCHNER, John George, a German engraver, who flourished at Nuremberg from about 1670 to 1720. He engraved a set of portraits for a folio volume entitled *Icones virorum omnium ordinum eruditione*, &c., published at Nuremburg.

PYE, John, an English engraver, born about 1745. He engraved quite a number of landscapes, etched and neatly finished with the graver, after Claude Lorraine, Swanevelt, and Cuyp, and some marines after Vernet. He was much employed by Alderman Boydell. His prints date from 1773 to 1775.

PYNAKER, Adam, an eminent Dutch landscape painter, born at the village of Pynaker, between Delft and Schiedam, in 1621. His first instructor is not mentioned; but he visited Italy while very young, and resided several years at Rome, studying the works of the best landscape painters, and designing the finest views in the vicinity of that capital. On returning to Holland, he soon gained distinction, and his works were held in great admiration. He was much employed in ornamenting the apartments of the nobility; he also painted easel pictures, which are very highly esteemed, and are placed in choice collections. His landscapes exhibit very pleasing scenery, frequently representing the sunny morning light breaking out from behind the woods or mountains, and diffusing a brilliant glow over the whole face of nature. His skies are clear, light, and floating; the foliage of his trees and plants is touched with unusual freedom and spirit; his pencil is firm and flowing, evincing remarkable facility of hand, with great breadth, richness, and brilliancy. His pictures are decorated with ancient architecture, figures and cattle, correctly drawn, and grouped in an elegant and tasteful style. Pynaker's easel pictures are not very numerous; Smith's catalogue contains a list of about seventy. Many of the finest are in England. He died in 1673.

PYNE, William Henry, an English designer and author, born at Holborn in 1769. As an artist, he confined himself to drawing, in which he manifested great facility, lively fancy, and delicate taste. In 1803, he published the first part of his interesting work entitled "The Microcosm; or a picturesque Delineation of the Arts, Agriculture, Manufactures, &c., of Great Britain," completed in 1806, illustrated with about 600 groups of small figures for the embellishment of landscapes. He afterwards published in three imperial quarto volumes, a "History of the Royal Residences," of Windsor, St. James, Carlton House, Kensington Palace, Hampton Court, Buckingham House, and Frogmore, illustrated with about 100 richly colored plates. He was much employed by the celebrated publishers, Ackermann & Co., in the Strand, in the supervision of their numerous publications. He died in 1843.

PYREICUS, a Grecian painter, who flourished about B. C. 200. His favorite subjects were scenes from low life; particularly interiors of the shops of tailors and shoemakers; also sheep folds, with groups of animals; asses going to market, laden with produce. His skill in representing scenes of the latter description, gained him the name of *Rhyparographus*. His pictures were of small size, exquisitely finished, and brought very high prices. Pliny thought that subjects from low life were beneath the dignity of painting, but the admiration universally conceded to them is sufficient evidence of their being proper subjects for the pencil. It is no small satisfaction to the lovers of art, that the ancients encouraged and appreciated every branch of painting.

PYRGOTELES, an eminent Grecian engraver on gems, who flourished in the time of Alexander the Great, about B. C. 330. He was cotemporary with the most distinguished painters and sculptors of Greece; as an engraver on gems, he was considered equal to Apelles in painting, and Scopas and Lysippus in sculpture. Alexander the Great conferred upon him the same honor as upon Lysippus and Apelles, who had the exclusive privilege of representing him in their respective arts. Among his principal productions, were the head of Alexander, the head of Phocion, and Hercules destroying the Hydra. There is no well authenticated work by this artist, which has reached modern times.

PYRRHUS. See Lacrates.

PYTHAGORUS, an ancient sculptor, a native of Rhegium. Some of his works exhibited a deeper sentiment and truer feeling than any that had yet appeared in works of statuary. His chief works were the statues of Euthymus and Asty lus, conquerors in the Olympic games. His statue of Philoctetes was remarkable for justness of proportions and delicacy of finish.

PYTHEUS, an eminent Grecian architect, who flourished about B. C. 324. He is principally distinguished for the celebrated mausoleum erected by Queen Artemisia in memory of King Mausolus of Halicarnassus, of which he had the entire direction, in conjunction with Satyrus; and both artists made the designs for the work.—(For a full description of this "wonder of the world," see the article Bryaxis.) Pytheus was also greatly distinguished for the famous pyramid, which surmounted the mausoleum, executed by himself. It was crowned with a car drawn by four horses abreast, representing the Chariot of the Sun. According to Vitruvius, Pytheus also erected at Priene, now Polazzo, a famous temple to Minerva Polias; which, though now in ruins, is an important evidence of Ionian elegance and grandeur. When entire, it overlooked the city, which was situated on the side of a mountain, on terraces cut out of the slope, descending in gradation to the edge of the plain. The communication from one terrace to another, was by steps cut in the solid rock, many of which are still remaining. The temple was surrounded by a wall, through which was a gateway. The plan of the edifice was a parallelogram, 122 feet six inches by 64 feet three inches, measured on the upper step, There were eleven columns in the flanks, and six in the fronts of the temple. The walls of the cell were four feet thick, ranging with the columns, and enclosing an area of sixty-five feet by thirty feet nine inches.

# Q.

QUAGLIA, Giulio, a painter, born at Como. According to Lanzi, he went to Friuli while young, towards the close of the 17th century, where he conducted works, principally in fresco, to an amount that almost defies enumeration. His histories of the Passion of our Saviour, in the Monte di Pietà, at Udine, are held in high estimation, although he conducted works on a much larger scale in the halls of many of the noble families, characterized by a fecundity of ideas, a decision of pencil, and a power of vast compositions, sufficient to distinguish him in his age, not only in the limits of Como, but also at Milan. Lanzi conjectures from his style, that he was a disciple of the Recchi.

QUAGLIATA, Giovanni, a painter of Messina, born in 1603. According to Hackert, he went to Rome, and studied under Pietro da Cortona. On returning to Messina, he acquired considerable distinction, and is said to have painted in competition with Rodriguez and Barbalunga. He died in 1673.

QUAGLIATA, Andrea, was the brother of the preceding, born at Messina in 1600, and died in 1660. It is not known under whom he studied, and he never visited Rome, but was considered a good artist at Messina.

QUAGLIO, Gio. Maria, an Italian architect and engineer, a native of Luino, probably the son, and certainly a relative, of Giulio Quaglia. He flourished in the first half of the 18th century. After acquiring a knowledge of the art in Italy, he visited Vienna, and was employed in the service of the Emperor. His son Lorenzo was born at Luino in 1730, accompanied his father to Vienna, and was instructed by him in architecture. Lorenzo erected a number of edifices in Germany, esteemed for their superior taste, among which are the Theatre of Manheim, and the Theatre of Frankfort. He died in 1804, leaving a son, named Giovanni Maria, born in 1772, who was a distinguished architectural and scene painter.

QUAGLIO, Domenico, a són of the elder Gio. Maria Q., the brother of Lorenzo Q., was a historical painter, and flourished in Germany about 1760. He had two sons—Giulio, an admirable scene painter, who flourished at Munich, and died in 1800—Giuseppe, born in 1747; died at Munich in 1828; was even more eminent than his brother, both in scene painting and general decoration. The latter had four sons; Domenico, Angelo, Lorenzo, and Simone. The two latter were born respectively in 1793 and 1795, but do not appear to have attained any distinction in art, if indeed they professed it at all. Angelo, born in 1788, was a scene painter of extraordinary genius. Some of his productions are described as producing an astonishing effect, particularly one representing the Illumination of St. Peter's at Rome, from studies made by him on the spot. He died in 1815. Domenico, the elder son, is the subject of the following article.

QUAGLIO, Domenico, an eminent architectural painter, the eldest son of Giuseppe Quaglio, was born at Munich in 1786. He early manifested a strong inclination for art, and was carefully instructed by his father. He made rapid advances, particularly in perspective and architectural painting, and also devoted considerable attention to drawing from the living model, to landscapes, and sketching from nature, as well as to etching and engraving. His versatility of talent had nearly prevented his attaining great excellence in any particular branch of art; but, following the advice of his brother Angelo, he devoted his energies to architectural painting. He was appointed to the office of scene painter of the theatre at Munich. Having imbibed a strong taste for the architecture of the Middle Ages from Angelo's drawings of the cathedral of Cologne (made for Sulpice Boisserée's magnificent pictorial work), he resolved to delineate chiefly the finest specimens of the edifices of that period. With this intent, he visited Freising and other places, and made many designs which he subsequently used in his compositions. His picture of the cathedral at Regensburg, gained him a high reputation, and was purchased by King Maximilian of Bavaria, who, as well as many other able judges, advised Quaglio to prosecute this department of the art. Accordingly, in 1819, he resigned his appointment as scene painter of the Munich theatre, and thenceforward devoted himself entirely to architectural painting. His reputation extended by degrees throughout Europe, and he received many commissions. His works, which are very numerous, are marked by striking picturesque effect. They are highly valued as representations of the finest specimens of German Gothic edifices, and have been partially instrumental in promoting that taste for the Arts and Architecture of the Middle Ages, which of late years has prevailed in Germany. In 1829, Quaglio accompanied Mr. Gally Knight, as architectural draughtsman, on his tour to Italy. While employed at Hohenswangau, in restoring and improving the Castle, he was attacked with apoplexy, and died April 9, 1837. There are a number of etchings and lithographic views by him; among the latter are a series of thirty subjects, entitled *Den Kwurdige Gebaude des Deutschen Mittelalters.*

QUAINI, Francesco, a Bolognese painter, born in 1611. He studied under Agostino Mitelli, and was one of his ablest scholars. He was much employed in decorating the churches, public edifices and palaces of Bologna with frescos of architectural and perspective views. Some of his most esteemed works are in the Sala Farnese, in the Palazzo Pubblico. He died at Bologna in 1680.

QUAINI, Luigi, was the son of the preceding, born at Bologna in 1643. After learning perspective with his father, he became the disciple of Guercino, and afterwards of his cousin Carlo Cignani, with Marc' Antonio Franceschini as a fellow pupil. Both these artists assisted Cignani in many of his works; and in distributing their labors he gave to Franceschini the fleshes, and to Quaini the more lively and spirited countenances and decorative parts, in which he succeeded so admirably that his painting could hardly be distinguished from that of his master. Franceschini and Quaini afterwards united their talents, the former painting the figures, and the latter the landscape, architecture, and other accessories, and thus in concert, they executed many admirable works for the churches and palaces of Bologna, Modena, Piacenza, Genoa, and Rome, in which latter city they made the cartoons for the cupola of St. Peter's afterwards executed in mosaic. Quaini also painted many historical pictures of his own invention, mostly for individuals. His pictures in public at Bologna, are the Visitation of the Virgin, in the church of S. Giuseppe; a Pietà, in la Carità, and an altar-piece of St. Nicholas visited by an Angel, in the church of that saint. He died in 1717.

QUARENGHI, Cav. Giacomo, an Italian architect, born at Bergamo in 1744. After receiving a liberal education, he studied painting under Mengs and Stefano Pozzi; but he subsequently gave his attention to architecture. According to the biographical memoirs published by his son Giulio, (entitled *Fabbriche e Disegni*, &c., Milano, 1821), he soon gained distinction in the art, and received many commissions at Rome. Unfortunately, none of these works are specified, nor is the chronology of his professional life recorded. Quarenghi was invited to Russia by the Empress Catherine II., who employed him to erect a variety of edifices, among which are the design for the triumphal arch erected in honor of the Emperor Alexander; the Theatre of the Hermitage; the Manège of the Imperial Guards, in the Isaac's Place at St. Petersburg; the Convent of Demoiselles Nobles; and the Palace of Prince Gargarin. Quarenghi attained a very high reputation in Russia; but his published designs afford little evidence of superior taste, or even of fertile invention. In comparison with many of his countrymen, he may be said to have been pure in his style of composition; but his merits are little more than negative;—if there is nothing glaringly offensive in his productions, there are no particular excellencies. They have insulated columns and ample prostyles, Ionic or Corinthian porticos, frequently attached to buildings in other respects naked and bare. His details evince a great deal of mannerism, being nearly the same on all occasions, as well as poor and meagre. He died in 1817.

[monogram] or [monogram] or [monogram] QUAST, Peter, a Dutch painter and engraver, born at the Hague in 1602; died in 1670. He painted humorous subjects, as beggars, drolls, assemblies of boors, merry-makings, &c., represented with great humor and spirit, not unmixed with vulgarity. He also executed some spirited etchings, after his own designs and those of other masters, in a manner resembling that of Callot, and usually marked them with one of the above monograms. Among others are the following:

The Five Senses; *P. Quast, fec.* 1638. The Four Seasons, in grotesque figures. A set of twenty-six plates of Beggars, Boors, &c. A set of twelve Grotesque Figures. A set of ten plates of Beggars, &c.; *S. Savery, exc.* A set of twelve fancy subjects, in imitation of *Callot.*

[monogram] QUATREPOMME, Isabella. This lady is mentioned by Papillon, as an engraver on wood, a native of Rouen, who flourished about 1521. He mentions one print by her, and Zani two more, marked with an apple and the figure 4, in allusion to her name.

QUEBOORN, or QUEBOREN, Crispin van der, a Dutch engraver, born at the Hague in 1604. He was chiefly employed in engraving small portraits for the booksellers, which possess considerable merit. He also engraved part of the plates for Thibault's *Academie de l' Epée*, published at Antwerp 1628. Among others, are the following portraits by him:

Queen Elizabeth. 1625. Charles I. 1626. William I., Prince of Orange; *after Visscher.* Mary, daughter of Charles I., consort of the Prince of Orange. Frederick V. Elector Palatine. Elizabeth, daughter of James I., his consort. Juliana, Princess of Hesse. Frederick Henry, Prince of Nassau. 1630.

QUELLINUS, Erasmus, a Flemish painter, born at Antwerp in 1609. According to Sandrart, he received a liberal education, and devoted himself for some time to the study of the Belles Lettres, in which he so far distinguished himself as to be appointed professor of Philosophy in the college of his native city. On becoming acquainted with Rubens, whose house was the resort of learned men, as well as distinguished artists, he was inspired with such a love of painting that he resigned his appointment, and entered the school of his friend. With a mind richly endowed by nature, and well stored with literature, he made rapid progress, and in a few years became one of the ablest artists of his country, at a period when Antwerp boasted the most celebrated painters of the Flemish school. He did not servilely imitate Rubens, like many of the scholars of that master, but formed a style of his own, abundantly evincing vivacity of genius, polished by study. His composition is good, his touch free and spirited, and his coloring rich and harmonious. His design, though considerably tinctured with the Flemish manner, is tolerably correct, and his ideas are generally just, learned, and elevated, though his drawing is sometimes inaccurate. He had an excellent knowledge of architecture and perspective, with which he embellished the backgrounds of his pictures. He was equally successful in history and landscapes, and painted many of the most distinguished personages of his time. He painted both in large and small size; his large works are executed with great vigor and freedom, but his cabinet pictures are more delicately pencilled and colored with greater transparency. His most celebrated works are Christ at the house of the Pharisee, with Mary Magdalen washing his feet, and the Guardian Angel, in the church of S. Andrew, at Antwerp; an altar-piece of the Holy Family reposing in Egypt, in the church of S. Saviour at Ghent; and the Nativity, in the church of S. Peter at Mechlin. The latter has often been mistaken for the work of Vandyck. Erasmus Quellinus died at Antwerp in 1678. He executed a few spirited etchings, chiefly after Rubens, among which are the following: Samson killing the Lion; the Virgin and Infant Jesus, *after Rubens.* A landscape, with a dance of children and young satyrs; *E. Quellinus fec.*; rare.

QUELLINUS, John Erasmus. This eminent painter was the son of the preceding, born at Antwerp in 1629. After receiving instruction from his father, he went to Italy, at the age of 21. Arriving first at Venice, he was captivated by the works of Paul Veronese, and made them his model. He afterwards visited Rome, Naples, and Florence, and found considerable employment in those places. He returned to Antwerp at the desire of his father, with a high reputation, and immediately received abundant encouragement in painting altar-pieces and other pictures for the churches at Antwerp. He also painted much for the private collections in other parts of the Low Countries. The ornamental style of Veronese is visible in all his works. His design is correct, his figures are elegant and graceful, with a lively expression, and disposed with propriety and judgment. His coloring is clear and brilliant, partaking of the Venetian and Flemish schools; his chiaro-scuro admirable; his draperies well cast in large and flowing folds, and his backgrounds enriched with noble architecture, obelisks and monuments. His most capital work is Christ healing the Sick, in the church of the Abbey of St. Michael at Antwerp. It is an immense composition, extending the whole height of the edifice, with a multitude of figures as large as life, yet so admirably arranged as to be free from the least appearance of confusion; the background is embellished with noble architecture. This picture is so much in the style of Veronese, that it might easily be taken for his work. In the Refectory of the same Abbey, he painted four pictures representing Christ feeding the Five Thousand; the Feast of the Pharisee; the Supper at Bethany; and the last Supper. In the cathedral at Antwerp is a fine picture of the Adoration of the Magi, and in the church of Notre Dame at Mechlin, the Last Supper, one of his finest works. The younger Quellinus is justly ranked among the ablest artists of his country, who succeeded the golden era of Flemish art under Rubens and Vandyck. He died at Antwerp in 1715.

QUELLINUS, Artus, a Flemish sculptor, the brother of Hubert, and the cousin of John Erasmus Q., was a native of Antwerp, and flourished about the middle of the 17th century. He visited Italy, and studied under Francis Duquesnoy; after which he returned to Flanders, and succeeded in attaining a high reputation. His principal sculptures are in the Stadt-House at Amsterdam, for which edifice he executed a large number of excellent works.

QUELLINUS, Hubert. This engraver was the brother of the preceding, born at Antwerp in 1608. It is not mentioned under whom he studied. He etched a set of plates in a singular style, resembling that of Peter Soutman, and neatly finished with the graver, from the marble statues of the sculptor Artus Quellinus, in the Stadt-House at Amsterdam. They are marked with the initials of both artists, A. Q. H. Q., and were published in a folio volume at Amsterdam in 1655. He also engraved some portraits, among which are Philip IV., seated on his throne, with the Prince Royal and several allegorical figures, and one of Artus Quellinus, from his own designs.

QUERFURT, Augustus, a German painter, born at Wolfenbuttel in 1696. After receiving instructions from his father, a reputable landscape painter, he went to Augsburg and studied under Rugendas. He painted encampments, skirmishes of cavalry, battle-pieces, and huntings, in which he appears rather an imitator than an original painter. Sometimes he adopted the manner of Borgognone and vander Meulen; at others he aimed at that of Wouwerman, but with less success. His pictures are well composed and colored, and executed with spirit. He died at Vienna in 1761.

QUESNEL, or QUENET, Francis. This painter is supposed to have been born at Edinburg about the year 1540. He passed his life in France, and was employed by Henry III., and Henry IV. Among others, he painted the portraits of those monarchs, and of Mary de Medicis. Several of his portraits have been engraved by Edelinck, T. de Leu, and van Schuppen. He died at Paris in 1619.

QUESNOY, Francis du. See Duquesnoy.

QUEVERDO, François Marie Isidore, a French engraver, born in Brittany in 1740, although some writers place his birth-place in Spain. He engraved a part of the plates for the *Voyage pittoresque d'Italie*, by the Abbé de St. Non. He also engraved some plates of portraits and other subjects, after his own designs and those of other masters. He was living in 1811.

QUEUX, Michel Joseph le, a French architect, born at Lille in 1756. His career was short, as he was assassinated in 1786, at the age of thirty; but he erected several fine edifices, in excellent taste, in his native city, and designed the Palais de Justice at Douay.

QUEWELLERIE, Guillaume de la, a French designer and engraver, who flourished about 1680. He engraved a set of small ornamental plates for jewelers, neatly executed. The frontispiece is inscribed with his name, *Guilhelmies de la Quewellerie, fecit, An. Dni.* 1680. The other plates are marked with the initials, G. D. L. Q.

QUILLART, Pierre Antoine, a French painter and engraver, born at Paris in 1711. He studied under Anthony Watteau, on leaving whom it is said he was invited to the court of Portugal, appointed painter to the Queen, and elected a mem ber of the Academy at Lisbon, where he died in the flower of his age. His principal work as a painter, was a beautiful ceiling in the Queen's bedchamber. He designed and engraved a set of plates representing the funeral pomp of Duke Don Nuno Olivares Pereira, published at Lisbon in 1730.

QUINKHARD, John Maurice, a Dutch painter, born at Rees, near Cleves, in 1687. He studied successively under Arnold Boonen, Lubinietski, and N. Verkolie. He painted familiar, allegorical, and mythological subjects, well designed and collored. He also excelled in portraits, and was much employed in that branch. He died in 1772.

QUINTILIEN, a French engraver mentioned by Florent le Comte. He executed some plates after Callot, but did not affix his name to them.

QUIRICO, Giovanni da Tortona, a Piedmontese painter, who flourished in the first part of the 16th century. There is an altar-piece by him, painted on a gold ground, in the Hospital of Vigevano, dated 1505.

QUIROS, Lorenzo, a Spanish painter, born at Santos, in Estremadura, in 1717. He studied under Bernard German Llorente, at Seville, with whom he made great progress, both in oil and fresco. He afterwards went to Madrid for improvement, where his talents recommended him to the notice of Carlo Corrado and Raffaelle Mengs, then in the service of the King of Spain, who offered him employment; but being of a turbulent disposition and a slave to his own fancies, he preferred imaginary liberty to fame and fortune. He afterwards retired to Seville, where he remained twenty years without making any one acquainted with his place of residence, and employed himself in copying and imitating the works of Murillo, which he sold, by means of an agent, for originals by that master. He is said to have been very successful, and doubtless many pictures in foreign collections, more recently smuggled out of Spain as the genuine works of Murillo, were by this master. He left some works at Madrid, in the Academy of San Fernando, at Cazalla, Granada, and other places in Spain. He died in 1789.

QUITER, Hermann Hendrick, a Dutch mezzotinto engraver, born about 1620, and died about 1700. He went to England, where he executed in an indifferent manner a few portraits after Sir Peter Lely and others, among which is that of Queen Catherine, consort of Charles II., *after Lely*.

QUITER, Hermann Hendrick, was the son of the preceding. He went to Rome, and studied in the school of Carlo Maratti. He afterwards returned to his own country, and was appointed painter to the Landgrave of Hesse. He died at Brunswick in 1731.

QUITER, Magnus, was a younger brother of the preceding. He visited Rome, and studied some time with Maratti, after which he went to England, where it is supposed he assisted Sir Godfrey Kneller. He afterwards returned to Holland, where he chiefly painted portraits, and occasionally historical subjects. He was appointed Keeper of the Gallery at Salzdalum, and died in 1744.

QUITER, E., a Dutch engraver in mezzotinto, who flourished in the latter part of the 17th century. He executed some portraits after John de Baan and others.

# R.

RABASSE, or RABAS, Jean, a French engraver and printseller, who flourished at Paris about 1650. Dumesnil attributes three prints to him: Judith, signed *Jean Rabas, avec Preuilege du Roy;* a Holy Family, marked with the initials J. R.; and a Repose in Egypt, with the same letters in a monogram. Brulliot attributes the mark on the last print to Jacob de Bray and Giuseppe Ribera.

RABBIA, Raffaelle, a portrait painter, born at Marino. Little is known of him except from the commendation of Cav. Marini, the poet, whose portrait he painted. He was living in 1610.

RABEL, Jean, a French painter and engraver, who flourished at Paris about 1588. As a painter, he is little known. Prof. Christ says he published several of his designs, engraved on wood, but does not specify the subjects, nor mention whether they were engraved by himself or some other artist. There is a copper-plate by him, representing the Martyrdom of St. Lawrence, copied from the print of the same subject by Marc' Antonio, *after Baccio Bandinelli.* It is less than the original, and is inscribed *Io. Rabel Bellonacus lute Parisii.* According to Basan, he was born in 1550, and died in 1608.

RABEL, Daniel, was the son of the preceding, who is supposed to have been his instructor. He painted landscapes in a pleasing style, some of which were engraved by cotemporary artists. He etched quite a number of plates from his own designs, in a style resembling that of Israel Silvestre, consisting of landscapes and views, with figures correctly drawn. Nagler places his death in 1628, but does not notice any of his prints. Zani says he operated in 1636.

RABEN, RAVEN, or RAEVEN, Servatius, a Dutch engraver, of whom little is known with certainty, except that he engraved the Twelve Cæsars, *after Stradanus*, one of which is marked with a monogram formed of the letters S. V. R., and the rest with his name in full, variously spelled, as above. There is also a plate of the Madonna della Seggiola, *after Raffaelle*, signed *Servatius Raeven.* Zani and others consider him the same as *Serwouter*, the accounts of whom are very contradictory, but the monogram of the latter is quite different, being composed of the letters P. and S. interlaced, followed by a W. See *Serwouter.*

RABIELLO, Parlo, a Spanish painter who flourished at Saragossa in the beginning of the 18th century. The accounts of him are contradictory. According to Bermudez, though not very correct in his drawings, he understood the great maxims of the painter, and excelled in battle-pieces, following the styles of Fray Juan Rizi and Juan de Valdes. There are several pictures in the Trinitarios Calzados de Terruel, attributed to him, and others in the chapels of San Marco and San Jago. In the Cathedral at Saragossa is one of his pictures, representing the Battle of Clavijo.

RABIRIUS, an eminent Roman architect, who flourished about A. D. 80, in the time of Domitian. He was much employed in the extensive architectural operations of that monarch, and erected a number of temples and triumphal arches, besides many works on the Capitol, and the famous palace of Domitian, on the Palatine Mount. Among the other works of this monarch, which Milizia attributes to Rabirius, was the public highway called Via Domitiana, forty miles long, from Pozzuolo to Sinvessa, crossing the river Vulturno by a bridge of white marble, richly ornamented. The Roman roads were generally surveyed in nearly a straight line, with but little allowance for obstructions—marshes were filled up, rivers were bridged, hills were levelled, mountains were tunnelled—several strata of stones were laid as the foundation, forming a mass of extraordinary depth and width, on which were placed large stones cut into regular forms, and fixed with great nicety upon the surface; the whole work constructed with such solidity that it seemed to bid defiance to the attacks of time. Gibbon remarks, "the firmness of the Roman roads has not entirely yielded to the attacks of fifteen centuries."

RABON, or REBON, Pierre, a French painter, born in 1616. He settled at Paris, and acquired considerable reputation in portraits. He died there in 1684.

RABON, or REBON, Nicolas, was the son of the preceding, born at Paris in 1644. He studied under his father, and painted history with considerable distinction. He died at Hermant in 1686.

RACCHETTI, Bernardo, a Milanese painter, born in 1639. He studied under his uncle, Giovanni Ghisolfi, whose manner he imitated so closely that his pictures are frequently taken for those of his instructor. They usually represent sea-ports embellished with shipping, and magnificent buildings, designed with accuracy, and touched with taste and spirit. His perspective is remarkably true, and none of his cotemporaries exceeded him in the artful management of the chiaro-scuro. He died at Milan in 1702.

RACINE, Jean Baptiste, a French engraver, born at Paris, according to Nagler, in 1747, and died in 1805, though Zani says he was living in 1807. He studied under François Aliamet, and engraved, in a neat style, some plates of landscapes after Breemberg, Pillement, and other masters; also a few subjects from pictures in the Orleans Gallery; and some vignettes and other book plates after the designs of Cochin.

RACLE, Leonard, a French architect and engineer, born at Dijon in 1736. He early manifested a strong inclination for art, and was instructed in the principles of architecture by Moutin de Saint Andre, engineer of the province of Bourgogne. He prosecuted his studies with great energy, and attained such excellence as to attract the attention of Voltaire, who employed him upon his works at Ferney. The recommendation of that celebrated author gained for Racle the patronage of the Duke de Choiseul, who commissioned him to design plans for the city and port of Versoix; but various circumstances prevented their execution. In 1786, Racle obtained a prize of the Academy of Toulouse; and he was soon after invited to Russia by the Empress Catharine, but declined the offer. Among his principal works were the canal of Pont de Vaux; and Voltaire's monument at Ferney. He was a member of the central administration for the Department de l'Ain, and prosecuted several projects for the improvement of that province. He died in 1791.

RACONIGI, Valentin Lomellino da, a Piedmontese painter, of whom little is known, except that he flourished at Turin about 1561, and was employed by the Duke as painter to the court.

RADEMACKER, Gerard, a Dutch painter, born at Amsterdam in 1672. He was the son of an architect, who instructed him in the rudiments of drawing and perspective, with the intention of rearing him to his own profession; but perceiving in his son an inclination for painting, he placed him with A. van Goor, a reputable artist in portraits. He had made considerable progress in his studies, when his instructor died; whereupon Gerard undertook to teach drawing and design, and was employed to instruct the niece of the Bishop of Sebasto. That prelate was so much pleased with his talents and amiable deportment, that he took him in his suite to Rome, where he spent three years in assiduously studying everything that could contribute to his advancement. On re turning to Holland, his merit procured him friends and abundant employment, and his works were eagerly purchased by persons of the first rank. His genius led him to represent views of the principal edifices, monuments, and ruins in Rome and its vicinity, which he designed with great accuracy and precision. He did not, however, confine him self to architectural views, but painted historical and allegorical subjects with considerable success. In the Stadt-House at Amsterdam is an allegorical picture by him, representing the Regency of that city. Another fine picture is a View of the Interior of St. Peter's church at Rome, accounted a master-piece for the accuracy of design, as well as the style of handling. He was fond of introducing bas-reliefs and embossed work into his pictures, which he designed with great truth and elegance. Rademacker is esteemed one of the good masters of the Dutch school; his works show a superior grandeur of ideas and a well cultivated genius. He designed and wrought with facility, and executed many works for the shortness of his life. He died at Amsterdam in 1711, aged 39.

RADEMACKER, Abraham. This artist was born at Amsterdam in 1675, and is generally supposed to have been a younger brother of the preceding. We are expressly told that he reached an eminent rank in the art of landscape painting, without the assistance of an instructor; wherefore some writers doubt whether he was of the same family as Gerard R. At first he spent whole days and nights in drawing and copying with India ink, and next in water-colors, till he arrived to a perfection in that branch that excited the surprise and elicited the approbation of the best artists of his time. He afterwards practised oil painting with equal success. He diligently studied nature, and the rules of perspective and architecture. He painted landscapes and views of towns in Holland, but oftener landscape compositions, enriched in a picturesque manner with edifices and vestiges of ancient ruins. His invention being remarkably fertile, he was never at a loss to furnish an endless variety of scenes and subjects; he filled his pieces with suitable figures and animals, well designed and grouped. His coloring is bright and clear, with a pleasing tone and degradation in his distance, though there is a little dryness observable in his larger works, probably caused by his habit of painting in small. He engraved from his own designs, in a masterly style, a set of three hundred plates of the most interesting views of ancient cities, monuments, &c., in Holland and the Netherlands, published at Amsterdam in six quarto volumes, in 1731. His oil paintings are numerous, and held in high estimation. He left an immense collection of drawings in water-colors and India ink, found in the collections of connoisseurs, by whom they are much prized for their neatness and delicacy of finishing, as well as their elegance of design. He finished a life of the most indefatigable industry in 1735.

RADI, Bernardino, an Italian designer and engraver, a native of Cortona, who flourished at Rome in the first part of the 17th century. He etched, in a slight and spirited style, a set of architectural ornaments, monuments, ruins, &c., published at Rome in 1618, under the title of *Varie invenzioni per depositi di Bernardino Radi Cortonese.*

RADIGUES, Antoine, a French engraver, born at Rheims in 1719. It is not known under whom he studied; but according to Basan, he went to England, and afterwards traveled through Holland and Germany to Russia, where he resided several years. At St. Petersburg he engraved the portraits of the Prince and Princess Gallitzin, and other persons of distinction. He also engraved a plate for the Dresden Gallery, representing Angelica and Medora, *after Alessandro Tiarini.*

RAEBURN, Sir Henry, an eminent Scotch portrait painter, born at Stockbridge, now a part of Edinburg, in 1756. At the age of six years he was left an orphan, and was placed in Heriot's Wark, the Christ's Church School of Scotland. At the age of fifteen he was apprenticed to an eminent goldsmith, but his propensity for drawing and sketching, manifested at school, seemed more to occupy his mind than the business of his master, who, on perceiving his inclination and examining some of his juvenile attempts at miniature, encouraged him to persevere, and took him to see Martin's pictures, the view of which astonished and delighted the young artist, and made a powerful impression upon his mind. He now devoted himself to miniature painting, and found sufficient employment to enable him to purchase the remainder of his apprenticeship. He also began to paint in oil, and obtained the loan of several pictures from Martin. The latter, however, soon grew jealous of his excellence, and is said to have unjustly accused him of selling one of his copies, when the latter indignantly refused any further assistance from so despicable an antagonist. Having begun to paint oil pictures, he gradually abandoned miniature, and became a professional portrait painter. At the age of twenty-two he married advantageously, and being ambitious to improve himself, he soon afterwards set out for London. Having introduced himself and his works to Sir Joshua Reynolds, the latter received him kindly, and advised him to study in Italy, at the same time proffering him all necessary funds and letters of introduction to distinguished artists and literati at Rome. Such disinterested and noble acts are worthy of immortality; yet how rarely they occur, and how much a calculating world has lost, and doubtless ever will lose, by rarely discriminating and encouraging the sons of genius, to whom it is indebted for the greatest conveniences, comforts, luxuries, and everything that ennobles the human mind! Young Raeburn gratefully accepted the last part of Sir Joshua's offer, and immediately set out with his wife, well furnished with every advantage. He spent two years in Italy, assiduously studying the great works of art. In 1787 he returned to Scotland, with his powers well matured, and settled at Edinburg, where he soon entirely eclipsed Martin, his former jealous friend, and completely drove him from the field into retirement. He became the only portrait painter of eminence in that city for a long time, and notwithstanding other able artists established themselves there, he continued to adorn both that and other branches of the art until his death. He was not in the habit of repairing to London, never having visited that metropolis but three times in his life, nor resided in it more than three months, consequently he saw little of the works of his cotemporaries; and, having stored his mind with ideas drawn from the purest school of modern art, he was indebted for his subsequent improvement solely to his own genius, reflections, and the study of nature. Hence the striking originality in his works. He made it his peculiar study to bring out *the mind* of his subjects. His penetration enabled him quickly to discover their favorite pursuits, and to engage them in topics of lively conversation, and while they spoke, he caught the features enlivened by the strongest expression of which they were susceptible. Thus, instead of an expression of mental vacuity, his portraits not only seem to live and breathe, but to *think*, looking as though they were about to speak on some favorite topic. This is the greatest merit of his works, though he was accomplished in every other necessary particular. His drawing was correct, his coloring rich and clear, and his lights well disposed; his pencilling bold and free; and his accessories, whether drapery, furniture, or landscape, were treated with elegance and spirit. He excelled in animals, particularly the horse, and his equestrian portraits are considered among his best performances; his portraits of Sir David Baird, the Duke of Hamilton, the Earl of Hopetown, and his own son on horseback, are among the most admired. He painted the portraits of all the most celebrated individuals of Scotland who flourished during the last forty years of his life, many of them full-lengths. The merit of Sir Henry was amply acknowledged, both by literary societies, and by those formed for the promotion of art. He was elected a member of the Royal society of Edinburg, of the Academy of Florence, of the Academy of New York, and various other institutions. In 1814, the Royal Academy of London, though unsolicited, elected him an Associate, and in 1815 an Academician. In 1822, when George IV. visited Scotland, he sat to Raeburn, conferred on him the honor of knighthood, and appointed him his painter for Scotland. His modesty was equal to his talents, and in his intercourse with young artists he was uniformly kind, communicative, and liberal. He was not only an artist, but a patron of art; and his gallery and study were always open to young artists. He died in 1822.

RAEFE, or RAEFUS, P., a French engraver on wood, mentioned by Papillon, who flourished at Paris about 1575. He engraved, in a spirited style, the greater part of two hundred cuts illustrating the Cosmographical work by André Thevet; the print of the Antiquities of Athens, page

796, is signed with his name, the others are marked with his initials, P. R. The rest of the cuts in the work were executed by O. Goujon, probably a brother of Jean Goujon, the celebrated sculptor. They are marked with the initials O. G.

RAFFAELLE, Raffaello, or Raphael Sanzio di Urbino. The name of this illustrious Italian painter is variously spelled; by the Italians, Raffaello; by the French, Raphael or Raffaello; by the Germans, Rafael; by the old English writers Raphael, and the moderns Raffaelle. The few works mentioned as bearing his signature, are inscribed in Latin, *Raphael Sanctius Urbinas pinxit; Raphael Urbinas Pingebat*, 1517; *Raphaelis Sanctij Urbinatis opus*, 1517. Two others with the last two signatures are dated 1518, and a medal struck in honor of Lucrezia Borgia, attributed to him, bears the name Raphael, in Roman capitals, in the exergue on the reverse. The Italians say that in his familiar correspondence, he always wrote his name Raffaello, and that this is the correct orthography.

By the general approbation of mankind, Raffaelle has been styled the prince of painters, and he is universally acknowledged to have possessed a greater combination of the higher excellencies of art, than has ever fallen to the lot of any other individual. He has had severe critics, but more able defenders. It has been remarked by Sir Joshua Reynolds and other authors, as well as by many travelers, as a remarkable fact, that the most capital frescos of Raffaelle in the Vatican do not at first strike the beholder with surprise, nor satisfy his expectations; but, as he begins to study them, he constantly discovers new beauties, and his admiration continues to increase with contemplation. This circumstance is accounted for by writers in various ways. De Piles attributes it to a want of strength of coloring proper for each object, and a deficiency in the chiaro-scuro. Montesquieu observes, that "the works of Raffaelle strike little at first sight, because nature is so well imitated that a spectator is no more surprised than he would be to see the object itself, which would excite no degree of surprise at all." Reynolds, after having expressed his first disappointment and subsequent admiration, says, "I am now clearly of opinion that a relish for the higher excellencies of the art is an acquired taste, which no man ever possesses without long cultivation, and great labor and attention." These quotations explain the contrariety of opinions often expressed by writers as to the merits of Raffaelle, especially by those superficial in art. Among other causes, doubtless, are the changes which time has wrought in depriving his frescos of their original beauty of coloring; and the fact that people who have read a great deal of any remarkable work of art or nature, frequently have their expectations so exalted that they are at first disappointed. Many persons, when they visit the cataract of Niagara, expect to see the water tumbling from the skies, with the noise of thunder and the shock of an earthquake, and find themselves disappointed; but when they begin to contemplate the wonder—its eternal, majestic, resistless current, that has cut its way for miles through the solid rocks, and formed for itself an impregnable barrier, as if afraid of deluging the world—they begin to realize, to be impressed with the sublimity of the scene.

There was nothing in the early life of Raffaelle, excepting fictitious accounts, more remarkable than in that of many others, nor anything that can afford much instruction. He did not acquire any marked distinction until his arrival at Rome in 1508. This very circumstance has led to endless disputes, and caused Michael Angelo and others to declare that he possessed no great originality of genius, but was rather a bold adopter; while others have zealously labored to prove that he was a prodigy from his birth, descended from an ancient noble house, and that he rather instructed his masters than received from them instruction. His life, therefore, will be briefly traced to the important epoch before mentioned.

He was the son of Giovanni Sanzio or di Santi, a painter of little celebrity, and was born on Good Friday, March 8, 1483. His father removed not long afterwards to Perugia, where, having instructed Raffaelle in the elements of design, and discovering his extraordinary talents, he sought for him a more able master, and placed him in the school of Pietro Perugino. Under this master he made great progress, soon surpassed all his fellow students, and even Perugino himself, if some historians may be credited, who cite in proof his first work of St. Niccolo da Tolentino crowned by the Virgin, at the Eremitani; a Crucifixion, with the Virgin, Mary Magdalene, and St. John, in S. Domenico, at Città di Castello; the Coronation of the Virgin, in the convent of the Franciscans at Perugia; and the Marriage of the Virgin. The last work was painted about his 18th year, entirely in the style of Perugino, but with a finer expression in the heads, particularly of the Virgin. About this time, Bernardino Pinturicchio was commissioned by Cardinal Francesco Piccolomini to execute his great works in the Cathedral of Siena, to illustrate the life and actions of Æneas Silvius Piccolomini, afterwards Pope Pius II.; the embassies entrusted to him by the Council of Constance to various princes; and by Felix the anti-pope to Frederick III., who conferred on him the laurel crown; and also the various embassies he undertook from Frederick himself to pope Eugenius IV., and afterwards to Callistus IV., who made him a Cardinal. No works of equal importance had hitherto been entrusted to any single master, and according to Vasari, Pinturicchio feeling himself incompetent to these vast undertakings, engaged the assistance of Raffaelle, who made the designs and cartoons for all the works. The glory of these performances, by general consent of authors, is thus given to Raffaelle, although they admit that he was a perfect novice in such matters, a stranger to the splendor of a metropolis, and wholly unacquainted with the manners and customs of the courts of Europe. This subject has been fully discussed under the head of *Pinturicchio*, which see. These great works were finished in 1504, about which time Raffaelle is supposed to have made his first visit to Florence, though this is uncertain, and very probably it was somewhat earlier. Vasari expressly says that he went to Florence before the completion of the Library; but Lanzi is of a different opinion. At all events, when Raffaelle learned that the cartoons of Michael Angelo and Leonardo da Vinci, which had been prepared in competition by those great artists in consequence of the prize offered by the city of Florence for the best designs for decorating the Palazzo Pubblico, were on exhibition in that city, he hastened thither to behold them. These cartoons, and many other invaluable treasures of art in Florence, made a deep impression on his youthful sensibilities, and he doubtless derived great advantage from the acquaintance of Ghirlandaio, Sangallo, and other distinguished young artists. Although Raffaelle's biographers do not expressly say that he assiduously studied at Florence the works of the earlier masters, Cimabue, Giotto, Masaccio, Verocchio, Ghiberti, as Michael Angelo and Leonardo da Vinci had done, yet this is abundantly evident from the pictures he executed there, among which is a Madonna and Child, now in the Tribune at Florence, as well as from the works he afterwards executed at Rome, where it is known he adopted largely from Masaccio. The death of his parents obliged him to hasten home, and while arranging his father's affairs he painted several pictures, among which were two Madonnas, St. George, and probably its pendant, the St. Michael, and Christ praying in the Garden, now in Paris; and in 1504 the Marriage of the Virgin, called *Lo Sposalizio*, in the church of S. Francesco at Città di Castello, now in the Pinacoteca at Milan. Lanzi and others speak of this picture in strains of rapture. He says the two espoused have a degree of beauty which Raffaelle scarcely surpassed in his mature age, in any other countenances. About this time, 1505, he executed several works at Perugia which sustained his reputation—a Madonna, for the church of the Servi, the Mater Dolorosa, over which he painted a second picture of God the Father, now in the Colonna palace at Rome, and a Crucifixion, preserved in the chapel of the Padri Camaldolensi. By these performances may be measured the progress he had made in his first visit to Florence. They partake of the style of Perugino, with little of the dignity, power, and grandeur of his later performances, but are distinguished for the sensibility and feeling belonging to the earlier school. That he had not made much progress in anatomy, is evident from his picture of the Crucifixion, in which the figure of Christ on the Cross does not discover any particular excellence in design, though affording him an excellent and appropriate opportunity to display his knowledge of that branch of the art. His desire for improvement drew him a second time to Florence, where he zealously pursued his studies of the old masters before mentioned, and derived great advantage from the acquaintance of Fra Bartolomeo, who returned to painting about this time. He communicated to Raffaelle a more correct knowledge of coloring; and in return, the latter taught him the rules of perspective. (See Baccio della Porta, called Fra B.) He seems to have spent in study the whole time of his residence in that city; at least it is known that he executed nothing there except a few portraits, and the cartoon for the Entombing of Christ; the picture itself he painted at Perugia, from whence it was afterwards transferred to the Borghese palace at Rome. It is a miracle of composition, design, and expression, surpassed in these respects by few of his subsequent performances. After completing this work, Raffaelle returned the third time to Florence, where his studies seem to have been his chief employment, as it is nearly certain that he executed at this time only two pictures—the Madonna called *La Bella Giardiniera*, now at Paris, and another Madonna with the Fathers of the Church, now at Brussels. His repeated residence at Florence exercised over him the greatest influence. He found that the Florentine artists, as Cimabue, Giotto, Fiesole and others, could not only compete with his teacher Perugino in all the departments of art, but that some of them, as Masaccio, Fra Filippo Lippi, Mariotto Albertinelli, Ghirlandaio, and Fra Bartolomeo, surpassed him in excellence of composition, correctness of design, and liveliness of coloring. In the works of Ghirlandaio, and above all of Masaccio, he found what he most desired, a grander style in the forms, drapery, and outline. Doubtless, too, he derived some advantage by contemplating the works of da Vinci and Michael Angelo, though the latter had not then executed his greatest performances, nor was his manner congenial to Raffaelle. Having previously acquired the excellencies of the greatest masters of the Romagna, he now possessed himself of those of the Florentine school, which he ever held in high estimation, evinced by his copying in the *Loggia*, without the least alteration, two figures by Masaccio, which may still be seen in the picture by the latter of Adam and Eve driven from Paradise, in the monastery of the Carmelites at Florence, as well as others in the Cartoons. (See *Masaccio.*) Raffaelle now considered himself competent to undertake greater works than he had hitherto attempted, and was ambitious of painting an apartment in the Palazzo Pubblico at Florence, which is evident from his letter to one of his uncles, desiring him to request the Duke of Urbino to write to the Gonfaloniere Soderini for this purpose. This letter, now in the Museo Borgia, is dated in April, 1508, and contains all the provincialisms then common to the inhabitants of Urbino. Lanzi says his biographers do not speak of his literary attainments, and that if we are to judge from this letter, we might consider him grossly illiterate; but he exculpates him on the ground that he was writing in the familiar dialect of his country, as is still done, even in the public acts of Venice, and that he might and did, when he chose, use a more correct language. His uncle Bramante, however, the famous architect of St. Peter's, procured him nobler employment at Rome, by recommending him to Julius II. to decorate the Vatican. We now behold him placed in that famous palace, with such advantages of time and circumstances as enabled him to rise to the position of the first painter of the world. It will assist the reader in forming an estimate of the powers of Raffaelle, to reflect on his attainments, and the new field open to his view. Possessing extraordinary genius and talents, he had already attained all that was excellent in his predecessors. His talents were immediately recognized at Rome, and if deficient in any necessary branch of knowledge, the whole literary and artistic world was at his command. He was inspired by the most unbounded ambition; the efforts of Michael Angelo to supplant him only stimulated him to greater exertions; and on his death-bed, he thanked God he was born in the days of Buonarotti. He was instructed in the principles of architecture for six years by Bramante, that on his death he might succeed him in superintending the erection of St. Peter's. He lived among the ancient sculptures, and derived from them not only the contours, drapery, and attitudes, but the spirit and principles of the art. Not content with what he saw in Rome, he employed able artists to copy the remains of antiquity at Pozzuolo, throughout all Italy, and even in Greece. It is also probable that he derived much assistance from living artists, whom he consulted in regard to his compositions. The universal esteem which he enjoyed, his attractive person, and his engaging manners, which all authors unite in discribing as incomparable, conciliated the favor of the most eminent men of letters, as Bembo, Castiglione, Giovio, Navagero, Ariosto, Fulvio, Calcagnini, &c., who set a high value on his friendship, and were doubtless ready to supply him with many valuable hints and ideas.

Raffaelle, on his arrival at Rome, says Vasari, was commissioned to paint a chamber in the Vatican, called *La Segnatura*, which, from the subjects of the pictures, was also called the Chamber of the Sciences. On the ceiling he represented Theology, Philosophy, Poetry, and Jurisprudence, and on each neighboring façade a grand historical piece illustrative of the same subject; on the basement, also, historical pieces belonging to the same sciences; and these smaller performances, and the caryatides and telamoni distributed around are monocromati or chiaro-scuri, an idea entirely original in Raffaelle, and afterwards continued, it is said, by Polidoro da Caravaggio. Raffaelle commenced with Theology, and imitated Petrarch, who in one of his visions assembled together men of the same condition, though living in different ages. He introduced the Evangelists, whose writings form the foundation of theology; St. Ambrose, St. Augustine, St. Gregory, and St. Jerome, the doctors of the church who continued the tradition; and the Fathers, St. Thomas Aquinas, St. Bonaventura, and other theologians; above all, the Trinity in the midst of the beatified, and beneath, on an altar, the Eucharist. This subject, which has since been denominated, with little reason, the Dispute on the Sacraments, retains traces of the ancient style, as gilded glories round the heads of the saints, with other similar ornaments, and the composition is more formal and restrained than in his later productions. The Pope was so satisfied with the performance that he ordered all the works of Bramantino, Pier della Francesca, and others to be effaced, in order that the whole Chamber might be decorated by Raffaelle. At the earnest solicitation of the latter, however, out of respect to his instructor, one picture by Perugino was preserved, as well as some ornamental parts by Sodoma. In the subsequent works of Raffaelle, and after the year 1509, no traces appear of his first style. He had abandoned every vestige of the antique gilding and manner, adopted a nobler style, and henceforth applied all his powers to bring it to perfection. On the opposite side of the chamber he represented Philosophy, now styled the School of Athens. In the upper part of the composition he introduced Plato and Aristotle expounding their systems to a number of surrounding disciples; in another group, Socrates is seen reasoning with Alcibiades; and below, Pythagoras in the midst of his scholars, one of whom holds a tablet, engraved with the harmonic consonances. In another part of the picture, Archimedes is seen instructing his pupils in geometry; Zoroaster is represented with a Globe in his hand; and on one side Diogenes is stretched on the ground with a book in his hand. In this magnificent work, representing the School of Philosophy, consisting of fifty-two figures, Raffaelle has given to the world a school of painting ever regarded as one of the most sublime productions of art, for its boldness of invention, its grandeur of composition, and perfection of design.

The third picture represents Jurisprudence, and is divided into two parts. On the left side of the window stands Justinian, presenting the book of civil law to Trebonianus, who receives it with an expression of submission and approval which no other artist can ever hope to equal. On the right side is seen Gregory IX., bearing the features of Julius II., delivering a book of the Decretals to an advocate of the Consistory. In the upper part of the picture are personified Prudence, Temperance, and Fortitude.

The fourth picture represents Poetry, where he introduced Apollo and the Muses on Mount Parnassus, surrounded by the most illustrious Greek, Latin, and Tuscan poets: Homer, seated between Virgil and Dante, is perhaps the most striking figure, appearing gifted with a divine spirit, uniting the characters of the prophet and the poet. The historical pieces in chiaro-scuro contributed, by their elegance, to charm the sight and preserve the unity of design; for instance, beneath the Theology, St. Augustine is represented on the borders of the sea, instructed by Angels not to examine the mystery of the Trinity, incomprehensible to the human mind; and under the Philosophy, Archimedes is seen surprised and slain by a soldier, while absorbed in his studies. The first chamber was finished in 1511, as appears from an inscription near the Parnassus.

It is proper to observe here, for the proper elucidation of this memoir, that Raffaelle had three manners; the first, that of his instructor Perugino; the second the same, modified by his residence and studies in Florence, which continued till the completion of the Theology, though constantly improving; and the third, his own grand, original manner, commencing with the School of Athens. It is also proper to notice the calumnies of the Florentine writers, who attempted to disparage Raffaelle in order to aggrandize their own countryman, Michael Angelo. The life of Buonarotti was written by two of his disciples, Vasari and Condivi, after the death of Raffaelle, and during the life of Angelo, which gave the latter decidedly the advantage; for, had Raffaelle been living when they attacked the originality of his style, he would have found no difficulty in confuting them. Vasari does not speak of the improvement in his manner until all the works above mentioned were completed. On the contrary, in his life of Raffaelle, he says, "although he had seen so many monuments of antiquity in that city, and studied so unremittingly, still his figures up to this time did not possess that breadth and majesty which he afterwards exhibited; for it happened that the breach between Michael Angelo and the Pope occurred about this time, and compelled him to flee to Florence; from which circumstance, Bramante, obtaining the keys of the Sistine chapel, exhibited it to his friend Raffaello, in order that he might make himself acquainted with the style of Buonarotti;" and he then proceeds to mention the Isaiah, the Sibyls, and the Heliodorus, painted after this period. In his life of Michael Angelo, he again mentions the quarrel which obliged the latter to depart from Rome, and proceeds to say that when, on his return, he had finished one-half of the work, the Pope suddenly commanded it to be exposed, "whereupon Raffaello di Urbino, who possessed great facility of imitation, changed his style, and immediately designed the Prophets and Sibyls della Pace." Thus originated the dispute, subsequently prosecuted with the greatest warmth, not only in Italy, but in other countries. Bellori attacked Vasari in a violent manner, and ably defended Raffaelle, in a work entitled *Se Raffaelle ingrandi e migliorò la maniera per aver vedute le opere di Michel Angiolo* (whether Raffaelle enlarged and improved his manner on seeing the works of Michael Angelo); Crespi also replied to him in three letters in the *Lettere Pittoriche*; and many other disputants have since arisen and started fresh arguments. It is impossible, in a brief biographical sketch, to pursue this subject, further than to observe that Raffaelle's defenders have shown that when Michael Angelo fled to Florence in 1506, Raffaelle was not even in Rome; that Angelo did not commence his works in the Sistine chapel before 1508, when he was invited to Rome by Julius II. for that purpose, and probably somewhat later, as it required some time to prepare his cartoons; that he did not finish the first half of it before 1511, when it was exhibited; and that in the meantime Raffaelle had completed his first chamber in the Vatican; that Raffaelle had studied the Torso of the Belvidere, as Angelo had done; that he formed his manner on the antique and on reason itself; and that the grand does not consist in enlargements of the muscles, or extravagance of attitudes, as practised by Buonarotti, but, as Mengs justly observes, "in adopting the noblest, and neglecting the inferior and meaner parts, and in exercising the higher powers of invention."* Lanzi says the objector to Vasari "would have proceeded to point out the grandeur of style in the School of Athens, in the majestic edifices, in the contour of the figures, in the folds of the drapery, in the expression of the countenances, and in the attitudes; and he would easily have traced the source of that sublimity in the relics of antiquity. If he appeared still greater in his Isaiah, he might have refuted Vasari from his own account, which assigns this work to a period anterior to 1511, and therefore cotemporary with the School of Athens; adding that he elevated his style by propriety of character and the study of Grecian art. The Greeks observed an essential difference between common men and heroes, and again between their heroes and their gods; and Raffaello, after having represented philosophers immersed in human doubts, might well elevate his style when he came to figure a prophet meditating the revelations of God." As to the rest, it is admitted that the works of Michael Angelo inspired him with a more daring spirit of design,* that in the exhibition of strong character, he did not hesitate even to imitate him, but Crespi observes that in this instance he rendered that very style more beautiful and more majestic; and Lanzi says, "whoever wishes to see what is wanting in the Sibyls of Michael Angelo, let him inspect those of Raffaelle; and let him view the Isaiah of Raffaelle who would know what is wanting in the Prophets of Michael Angelo."

Towards the close of 1512, Buonarotti finished the other half of his great work in the Sistine chapel, so that the Pope was able to perform Mass at the Feast of Christmas. Raffaelle was engaged in the same year in decorating the second apartment of the Vatican. The first subject was Heliodorus driven from the Temple by the prayers of Onias the high priest, one of the most celebrated pictures of the place, in which all the passions are wonderfully expressed. On the other side of the apartment are the Miracle of the Mass at Bolsena, the Deliverance of St. Peter from Prison, and Leo the Great stopping the progress of Attila. "In these works," says Mengs, "Raffaello gave to painting all the augmentation it could receive after Michael Angelo." Julius II. died in 1513, and was succeeded by Leo X., who, zealous for promoting the fine arts, and sensible of the extraordinary talents of Raffaelle, continued him in his employment. The two works last mentioned, as well as the remaining decorations of these chambers, were illustrative of the history of that pontiff, whose im-

* We have already mentioned the source whence Raffaelle derived his inspiration—the antique. The style of Angelo was not congenial to him. He had seen at least some of his cartoons and pictures at Florence, though not his greatest works, afterwards executed at Rome. Nor did Raffaelle study nature so attentively as some eminent masters have done, but he arrived at what nature should be; it was a maxim with him, which he taught his pupils, "We must not represent things as they are, but as they should be." Mengs says that "Raffaelle diligently studied the bassi-rilievi of the arches of Titus and Constantine which were on the arch of Trajan, and adopted from them his manner of marking the articulations of the joints, and a more simple and easier mode of expressing the contours of the fleshy parts." Raffaelle, like Shakspeare, did not hesitate to appropriate anything he found in ancient or modern art, that fitted his purpose; but, like the great poet, he threw around them the charm of his own incomparable genius. Michael Angelo scorned to borrow anything. It is a well known fact that the beautiful arabesques with which Raffaelle decorated the *loggie* of the Vatican were copied from antiques, which he discovered while making excavations by order of Leo X., though greatly improved by his own exquisite fancy. In compliance with the wishes of that pontiff, he made drawings of the ancient buildings of Rome, accompanied with descriptions, and employed the compass to ascertain the exact admeasurement. This valuable work was destroyed, and many of the edifices measured were destroyed in the sacking of Rome in 1527. The Abate Morelli (Notizia, p. 210), has made public a high eulogium on this work, written by Marc' Antonio Michiel, a cotemporary with Raffaelle, who asserts that "Raffaelle had drawn the ancient buildings of Rome in such a manner, and shown the proportions, form, and ornaments so correctly, that whoever had inspected them might be said to have seen ancient Rome."

* Lanzi says, "his rival Michael Angelo, too, and his party, contributed not a little to the success of Raffaello. As the contest between Zeuxis and Parrhasius was beneficial to both, so the rivalship of Buonarotti and Sanzio aided the fame of Michael Angelo, and produced the paintings in the Sistine chapel; and at the same time contributed to the celebrity of Raffaelle, by producing the pictures in the Vatican, and not a few others. Michael Angelo, disdaining any secondary honors, came to the combat, as it were, attended by his shield-bearer, for he made drawings in his grand style, and then gave them to Frà Sebastiano del Piombo, the scholar of Giorgione, to execute; and, by this means, he hoped that Raffaelle would never be able to rival his productions, either in design or color. Raffaelle stood alone, but aimed at producing works with a degree of perfection beyond the united efforts of Michael Angelo and F. Sebastiano, combining in himself a fertile imagination, ideal beauty founded on a correct imitation of the Greek style, grace, ease, amenity, and a universality of genius in every department of art. The noble determination of triumphing in such a powerful contest animated him night and day, and allowed him no respite. It also animated him to surpass both his rivals and himself in every new work."

prisonment at Ravenna, and subsequent liberation, are typified by St. Peter's deliverance from Prison by the Angel. It was in this picture that Raffaelle exhibited an astonishing proof of his knowledge of the effects of light; the figures of the soldiers who stand without the prison, are illuminated by the beams of the moon; a torch produces a second light; and a clear, celestial splendor, rivalling the sunlight, emanates from the body of the Angel. Here he also showed how art may convert impediments into advantages; for the place where he was painting being broken by a window, he imagined on each side of it a staircase which affords an easy ascent to the prison, and on the steps he placed the guard, overpowered with sleep, so that the painter does not seem to have accommodated himself to the place, but the place to have become subservient to the painter.

In the third apartment he painted four pieces, representing the Victory gained by St. Leo IV. over the Saracens in the port of Ostia; the Conflagration of the Borgo Vecchio; the Coronation of Charlemagne; and Leo III. vindicating himself before that monarch. These works, says Lanzi, justly entitle Raffaelle to the epic crown. It would require a volume to describe intelligently all the works of Raffaelle. The Incendio di Borgo, which is miraculously extinguished by St. Leo IV., is accounted a wonderful performance, alternately chilling the heart with terror, and warming it with compassion. The horrors of the conflagration are portrayed with all the truth and effect that art is capable of producing. The terror of the scene is increased by the darkness of the midnight hour; the flames, driven by a fierce wind, are spreading with fearful rapidity; the affright and sufferings of the inhabitants are carried to the highest pitch. Some rush forward with water, but are driven back by the scorching flames; others seek safety in flight, half naked, and with dishevelled hair; women turn an imploring look to the pontiff; mothers, less alarmed for themselves than their offspring, are solely intent in shielding them from danger. Amidst the confusion is seen an admirable group of a young man, like Æneas, carrying his aged father on his shoulders, sinking beneath the weight, but collecting his almost exhausted energies, to reach a place of safety. These three chambers, called the Stanze of Raffaelle, which name they still retain, occupied him nine years, and were finished in 1517. He introduced into them correct likenesses of many of the most distinguished personages of the age. Thus in St. Leo is represented Leo X., and in Charlemagne, Francis I. of France. In portraits, Raffaelle was transcendant, and his performances deceived persons the most intimately acquainted with the subjects; Cardinal Datary approached a picture of Leo X. with a bull and pen and ink for the pontiff's signature.

Having thus decorated the three principal apartments in the Vatican, Raffaelle turned his attention to the embellishment of the *loggie* (the galleries of the Vatican palace connecting the rooms) the architecture of which was begun by Bramante and finished by Raffaelle. These works were chiefly executed from his cartoons by his disciples, Giulio Romano, Gio. Francesco Penni, Pierino del Vaga, Pellegrino da Modena, Polidoro da Caravaggio, Giovanni da Udine, &c. The space of the present article will not even admit of mentioning all these productions. of which Vasari says 'it is impossible to execute or conceive a more exquisite work." The most important are the thirteen small ceilings, each containing four subjects from sacred history, the first of which, representing the Creation, was painted by Raffaelle himself, as a model to be followed by his scholars, and the whole were retouched and harmonized by Raffaelle, according to his usual custom. This series of subjects has been frequently engraved, and is generally denominated Raffaelle's Bible. He designed the famous cartoons for the tapestries of the papal chapel, representing the principal subjects of the Evangelists and the Acts of the Apostles. The tapestries were wrought in Flanders, and afterwards annually exhibited in the Vatican, on the festival of Corpus Domini, but have lately been dispersed. The cartoons, regarded as one of the most exalted monuments of art, were purchased in Flanders by Charles I., at the recommendation of Rubens, and are now in Hampton Court.

The immense works in the Vatican did not prevent Raffaelle from engaging in numerous other undertakings, to satisfy the desire of individuals to possess his works. He decorated the palace of Agostino Chigi, now the Farnesina, with admirable frescos, representing the Triumph of Galatea, and a series of pictures of the Loves of Cupid and Psyche, their Marriage, and the Assembly of the Gods; the first was painted by himself, and the others by his scholars from his cartoons. These pictures were treated with such admirable taste and learning, that they may be compared to the best works of antiquity.

Of his pictures in oil, the following are the most remarkable: St. Cecilia, formerly in the church of S. Giovanni in Monte at Bologna, now in the Louvre; La Madonna Pesce; the Holy Family, called La Perla; Christ bearing his Cross, called La Spasimo de Sicilia—an inimitable performance. The three last are in the Escurial. Christ in glory, surrounded by Saints, called I cinque Santi, in which he introduced his own portrait. The Portrait of Julius II., in the Palazzo Pitti at Florence, now at Munich. The Portrait of Leo X., at Paris. The Madonna della Seggiola, in the Florentine Gallery. The Madonna di San Sisto, at Dresden; and many other Holy Families and devotional subjects for churches and individuals, as well as portraits.

We come now to the last great work and master-piece of Raffaelle, the Transfiguration. It has already been stated in the Life of Frà Sebastiano del Piombo, that Michael Angelo, finding he could not successfully compete with Raffaelle, called in the assistance of that admirable colorist, and furnished him with designs for his most considerable works, hoping thereby to raise a rival to Raffaelle, who should drive him from the field, or at least, share with him the public favor; and that when the Cardinal de' Medici commissioned Raffaelle to paint the Transfiguration, he also commissioned del Piombo to paint an altar-piece of the Resurrection of Lazarus, of the same size, for the cathedral of Narbonne; that Buonarotti, to enable del Piombo to enter the lists with greater prospects of success, furnished him with the design; that this rivalship ended in a public exhibition of their works, and that the palm of victory was awarded to Raffaelle, over his united competitors. See *del Piombo*. This sublime composition represents the mystery of Christ's Transfiguration on Mount Tabor

At the foot of the Mount is assembled a multitude, among whom are the Disciples of our Lord, endeavoring in vain to relieve a youth from the dominion of an evil spirit. The various emotions of human doubt, anxiety, and pity, exhibited in the different figures, present one of the most pathetic incidents ever conceived; yet this part of the composition does not fix the attention so much as the principal figure on the summit of the mountain. There Christ appears elevated in the air, surrounded with a celestial radiance, between Moses and Elias, while the three favored Apostles are kneeling in devout astonishment on the ground. The head and attitude of the Saviour are distinguished by a divine majesty and sublimity, that is indescribable. This immortal production is generally considered the master-piece of Raffaelle. 'This is a picture,' says Mengs, 'that combines more excellencies than any of the former works of Raffaelle. The expression is more elevated, and more refined, the chiaro-scuro more correct, the perspective better understood, the pencilling finer, and there is greater variety in the drapery, more grace in the heads, and more grandeur in the style.' With this incomparable work ceased the labors and the life of Raffaelle; he did not live to entirely complete it, and the few remaining parts were finished by his scholar Giulio Romano. While engaged upon it, he was seized with a fever, of which he died on his birth-day, Good Friday, April 7th, 1520, aged 37 years. His body lay in state in the chamber where he had been accustomed to paint, and near the bier was placed the noble picture of the Transfiguration. The throngs who came to pay their respects to the illustrious artist were deeply affected; there was not an artist in Rome but was moved to tears by the sight, and his death was deplored throughout Italy as a national calamity. The gentleness of his nature, more than his extraordinary talents, had endeared him to every heart. Respectful to the memory of Perugino, and grateful for the instructions he had received from him, he exerted all his influence with the Pope, that the works of his master in one of the ceilings of the Vatican might be spared, when the other paintings were destroyed to make room for his own embellishments. Just and generous to his cotemporaries, though not ignorant of their intrigues, he thanked God, that he had been born in the days of Buonarotti. Gracious towards his pupils, he loved and instructed them as his own sons; courteous even to strangers, he cheerfully extended his advice to all who asked it, and in order to make designs for others, or to direct them in their studies, he had been known to neglect his own works, rather than refuse them his assistance. The funeral ceremony was performed with great pomp, and his remains were interred in the church of the Rotonda, otherwise called the Pantheon. The Cardinal Bembo, at the desire of the Pope, wrote the epitaph, which is now inscribed on his tomb. All cotemporary writers unite in describing Raffaelle as amiable, modest, kind, and obliging; equally respected and beloved by the high and the lowly. His beauty of person and noble countenance, inspired confidence and prepossessed the beholder in his favor at first sight. He never married, though by no means averse to female society. The Cardinal da Bibiena offered him his niece, which high alliance he is said to have declined because the honors of the purple were held out to him by the Pope, who favored him greatly, and made him groom of his chamber. Early in life he became attached to a young woman, the daughter of a baker at Rome called by way of distinction, La Bella Fornarina, to whom he was solely and constantly attached, and he left her in his will sufficient for an independent maintenance. The rest of his property he bequeathed to a relative in Urbino, and to his favorite scholars, Giulio Romano and Gio. Francesco Penni.

It said that Raffaelle executed some statues with his own hand, though only one is mentioned with certainty, the statue of a child, in the possession of Giulio Romano. In the Chigi chapel, in the church of S. Maria del Popolo, is a marble statue of the prophet Jonah, executed from a model by Raffaelle under his direction, by Lorenzetto. Raffaelle studied architecture under Bramante, and accompanied Leo X. to Florence. Among his principal works in that city, is the façade of S. Lorenzo, of two orders, and the Palazzo Ugoccioni, now Pandolfini, of two stories, the windows decorated with columns, supporting entablatures, with alternate triangular and circular pediments. At Rome he erected the stables of Agostino Chigi, in the Strada Lungara, near the Farnese palace. The first story has small double Doric pilasters, with an architrave of three faces, a plain frieze, and a cornice entire; the second floor has the same number of Corinthian pilasters. Near the church of S. Andrea della Valle, he built the Palazzo Caffarelli, now Stoppani, with a beautiful rustic basement, and over it an order of double Doric columns, between which are the windows, each with its balustrade of stone. After the death of Bramante, Raffaelle was appointed architect of St. Peter's and made a design for that edifice, in the form of a Latin cross, with three naves. Milizia criticises it as deficient in grandeur. Among his other architectural works were the designs for the Vatican gardens; his admirable drawings of the ancient Roman edifices have already been mentioned, with Vasari's high commendation. Marc' Antonio Raimondi engraved many of Raffaelle's designs, who assisted him with his counsel, and is said to have etched the outlines of several of his plates. He was also a poet, and there is an affecting sonnet written by him, only a day or two before his death, in which he compares himself to a sinking vessel abandoned by her crew.

When we consider the number of Raffaelle's paintings, the multitude of his designs, to which he devoted so much study, as is shown in his numerous sketches of Madonnas and Holy Families, &c., and especially his great works in the Vatican, in which, in many cases, he drew all the figures naked, in order the better to adapt the drapery and its folds to their respective attitudes; and further his supervision of the building of St. Peter's church, his admeasurements of the ancient edifices of Rome with exact drawings and descriptions, the preparation of designs for various churches and palaces, with several collateral tasks, it seems incredible even a long life were sufficient for their execution; and when we further reflect that he accomplished all this at an age, when most men only begin to distinguish themselves, we are struck with astonishment at the wonderful fecundity of his genius Raffaelle possessed in a high degree all those qualities necessary to constitute a preëminent painter and is universally acknowledged to deserve the place of supremacy. Volumes on volumes of descriptions and criticisms have been written on his works, but the author has nowhere read a more learned, judicious, and impartial critique than that of Lanzi, and for this reason, notwithstanding the great length of this article, he cannot forbear inserting it at length:

"Raffaello is by common consent placed at the head of his art; not because he excelled all others in every department of painting, but because no other artist has ever possessed the various parts of the art united in so high a degree. Lazzarini even asserts that he was guilty of errors, and that he is only the first, because he did not commit so many as others. He ought, however, to have allowed, that his defects would have been excellencies in any other artist, being nothing more in him than the neglect of that high degree of perfection which he was capable of attaining. The art, indeed, comprehends so many and such difficult parts, that no individual artist has been alike distinguished in all; even Apelles was said to yield to Amphion in disposition and harmony, to Asclepiodorus in proportion, and to Protogenes in application.

The style of design of Raffaello, as seen in those drawings, divested of colors, which form the chief ornaments of cabinets, presents us, if we may use the term, with the pure transcript of his imagination, and we stand in amaze at the contours, grace, precision, diligence, and genius which they exhibit. One of the most admired of his drawings I once saw in the gallery of the duke of Modena, a most finished and superior specimen, uniting in style all the invention of the best painters of Greece, and the execution of the first artists of Italy. It has been made a question whether Raffaello did not yield to Michael Angelo in drawing; and Mengs himself confesses, that he did, as far as regards the anatomy of the muscles, and in strong expression, in which he considers Raffaello to have imitated Michael Angelo. But we need not say with Vasari, that, in order to prove that he understood the naked figure as well as Michael Angelo, he appropriated to himself the designs of that great master. On the contrary, in the figures of the two youths in the Incendio di Borgo, criticised by Vasari, one of whom is in the act of leaping from a wall to escape the flames, and the other is fleeing with his father on his shoulders, he not only proved that he had a perfect knowledge of the action of the muscles and the anatomy requisite for a painter, but prescribed the occasion when this style might be used without impropriety, as in figures of a robust form engaged in violent action. He moreover commonly marked the principal parts in the naked figure, and indicated the others after the example of the better ancient masters, and where he wrought from his own ideas, his execution was most correct.

In chasteness of design, Raffaello was by some placed on a level with the Greeks, though this praise we must consider as extravagant. Agostino Caracci commends him as a model of symmetry; and in that respect, more than in any other, he approached the ancients; except, observes Mengs, in the hands, which being rarely found perfect in the ancient statues, he had not an equal opportunity of studying, and did not therefore design them so elegantly as the other parts. He selected the beautiful from nature, and as Mariette observes, whose collection was rich in his designs, he copied it with all its imperfections, which he afterwards gradually corrected as he proceeded with his work. Above all things, he aimed at perfecting the heads, and from a letter addressed to Castiglione on the Galatea of the Palazzo Chigi, or of the Farnesina, he discovers how intent he was to select the best models of nature, and to perfect them in his own mind.* His own Fornarina assisted him in this object. Her portrait, by Raffaello's own hand, was formerly in the Barberini palace, and it is repeated in many of his Madonnas, in the picture of St. Cecilia, at Bologna, and in many female heads. Critics have often expressed a wish that these heads had possessed a more dignified character, and in this respect he was, perhaps, excelled by Guido Reni, and however engaging his children may be, those of Titian are still more beautiful. His true empire was in the heads of his men, which are portraits selected with judgment, and depicted with a dignity proportioned to his subject. Vasari calls the air of these heads superhuman, and calls on us to admire the expression of age in the patriarchs, simplicity of life in the apostles, constancy of faith in the martyrs; and in Christ in the Transfiguration, he says, there is a portion of the divine essence itself transferred to his countenance, and made visible to mortal eyes.

This effect is the result of that quality that is called expression, and which, in the drawing of Raffaello, has attracted more admiration of late years than formerly. It is remarkable, that not only Zuccaro, who was indeed a superficial writer, but that Vasari, and Lomazzo himself, so much more profound than either of them, should not have conferred on him that praise which he afterwards received from Algarotti, Lazzarini, and Mengs. Leonardo was the first, as we shall see in the Milanese School, to lead the way to delicacy of expression; but that master, who painted so little, and with such labor, is not to be compared with Raffaello, who possessed the whole quality in its fullest extent. There is not a movement of the soul, there is not a character of passion known to the ancients, and capable of being expressed by art, that he has not caught, expressed, and varied, in a thousand different ways, and always within the bounds of propriety. We have no tradition of his having frequented the public streets, like Da Vinci, to seek for subjects for his pencil; and his numerous pictures prove that he could not have devoted so much time to this study, while his drawings clearly evince, that he had not equal occasion for such assistance. Nature, as I have before remarked, had endowed him with an imagination which transported his mind to the scenes of the event, either fabulous or remote, in which he was engaged, and awoke in him the very same emotions which the subjects of such a story must themselves have experienced; and this vivid conception assisted him until he had designed his subject with that distinctness which he had either observed in other countenances, or found in his own mind. This faculty, seldom found in poets, and still more rarely in painters, no one possessed in a more eminent degree than Raffaello. His figures are passions

* Lo dico con questa condizione che V. S. si trovasse meco a far la scelta del meglio: ma essendo carestia e di buoni giudici e di belle donne, mi servo di una certa idea che mi viene in mente.—Lett. Pittor. tom. i. p. 84.

personified; and love, fear, hope, and desire, anger, placability, humility, or pride, assume their places by turns, as the subject changes; and while the spectator regards the countenances, the air, and the gestures of his figures, he forgets that they are the work of art, and is surprised to find his own feelings excited, and himself an actor in the scene before him. There is another delicacy of expression, and this is the gradation of the passions, by which every one perceives whether they are in their commencement or in their height, or in their decline. He had observed their shades of difference in the intercourse of life, and on every occasion he knew how to transfer the result of his observations to his canvass. Even his silence is eloquent, and in every actor the smallest perceptible motion of the eyes, of the nostrils, of the mouth, and of the fingers, corresponds to the chief movements of every passion; the most animated and vivid actions discover the violence of the passion that excites them; and what is more, they vary in innumerable degrees, without ever departing from nature, and conform themselves to a diversity of character without ever risking propriety. His heroes possess the mein of valor; his vulgar, an air of debasement; and that, which neither the pen nor the tongue could describe, the genius and art of Raffaello would delineate with a few strokes of his pencil. Numbers have sought in vain to imitate him; his figures are governed by a sentiment of the mind, while those of others, if we except Poussin and a very few more, seem the imitation of tragic actors from the scenes. This is Raffaello's chief excellence; and he may justly be denominated the painter of mind. If in this faculty be included all that is difficult, philosophical, and sublime, who shall compete with him in the sovereignty of art?

Another quality which Raffaello possessed in an eminent degree was grace, a quality which may be said to confer an additional charm on beauty itself. Apelles, who was supremely endowed with it among the ancients, was so vain of the possession that he preferred it to every other attribute of art. Raffaello rivalled him among the moderns, and thence obtained the name of the new Apelles. Something might, perhaps, be advantageously added to the forms of his children, and other delicate figures which he represented, but nothing can add to their gracefulness, for if it were attempted to be carried further, it would degenerate into affectation, as we find in Parmiggiano. His Madonnas enchant us, as Mengs observes, not because they possess the perfect lineaments of the Medicean Venus, or of the celebrated daughter of Niobe; but because the painter in their portraits, and in their expressive smiles, has personified modesty, maternal love, purity of mind, and, in a word, grace itself. Nor did he impress this quality on the countenance alone, but distributed it throughout the figure in its attitude, gesture, and action, and in the folds of the drapery, with a dexterity which may be admired, but never rivalled. His freedom of execution was a component part of this grace, which, indeed, vanishes as soon as labor and study appear; for it is with the painter as with the orator, in whom a natural and spontaneous eloquence delights us, while we turn away with indifference from an artificial and studied harangue.

In regard to the province of color, Raffaello must yield the palm to Titian and Correggio, although he himself excelled Michael Angelo and many others. His frescos may rank with the first works of other schools in that line: not so his pictures in oil. In the latter he availed himself of the sketches of Giulio, which were composed with a degree of hardness and timidity; and though finished by Raffaello, they have frequently lost the lustre of his last touch. This defect was not immediately apparent, and if Raffaello's life had been prolonged, he would have been aware of the injuries his pictures received from the lapse of time, and would not have finished them in so light a manner. He is on this account, more admired in his first subject in the Vatican, painted under Julius II., than in those executed under Leo X.; for being there pressed by a multiplicity of business, and an idea of the importance of a grander style he became less rich and firm in his coloring. That, however, he excelled in these respects, is evinced by his portraits, when, not having an opportunity of displaying his invention, composition, and beautiful style of design, he appears ambitious to distinguish himself by his coloring. In this respect his two portraits of Julius II. are truly admirable, the Medicean and the Corsinian: that of Leo X. between the two cardinals; and above all, in the opinion of an eminent judge, Renfesthein, that of Bindo Altoviti, in the possession of his noble descendants, at Florence, by many regarded as a portrait of Raffaello himself. The heads in his Transfiguration are esteemed the most perfect he ever painted, and Mengs extols the coloring of them as eminently beautiful. If there be any exception, it is in the complexion of the principal female, of a greyish tint, as is often the case in his delicate figures; in which he is therefore considered to excel less than in the heads of his men. Mengs has made many exceptions to the chiaro-scuro of Raffaello, as compared with that of Correggio, on which connoisseurs will form their own decision. We are told that he disposed of it with the aid of models of wax; and the relief of his pictures, and the beautiful effect in his Heliodorus, and in the Transfiguration, are ascribed to this mode of practice. To his perspective, too, he was most attentive. De Piles found in some of his sketches the scale of proportion. It is affirmed by Algarotti, that he did not attempt to foreshorten his figures in ceilings. But to this opinion we may oppose the example we find in the third arch of the gallery of the Vatican, where there is a perspective of small columns, says Taia, imitated in that manner. It is true, that in his larger works he avoided it; and in order to preserve the appearance of nature, he represented his pictures as painted on a tapestry, attached by means of a running knot to the entablature of the room.

But all the great qualities which we have enumerated would not have procured for Raffaello such extraordinary celebrity, if he had not possessed a wonderful felicity in the invention and disposition of his subjects, indeed his highest merit. It may with truth be said that, in aid of this object, he availed himself of every example, ancient and modern; and that these two requisites have not since been so united in any other artist. He accomplishes in his pictures that which every orator ought to aim at in his speeches—he instructs, moves, and delights us. This is an easy task to a narrator, since he can regularly unfold to us the whole progress of an event. The painter, on the contrary, has but the space of a moment to make himself understood, and his talent consists in describing not only what is passing, and what is likely to ensue, but that which has already occurred. It is here that the genius of Raffaello triumphs. He embraces the whole subject. From a thousand circumstances he selects those alone which can interest us; he arranges the actors in the most expressive manner; he invents the most novel modes of conveying much meaning by a few touches; and numberless minute circumstances, all uniting in one purpose, render the story not only intelligible, but palpable. Various writers have adduced in example the St. Paul at Lystra, which is to be seen in one of the tapestries of the Vatican. The artist has there represented the sacrifice prepared for him and St. Barnabas his companion, as to two gods, for having restored a lame man to the use of his limbs. The altar, the attendants, the victims, the musicians, and the axe, sufficiently indicate the intentions of the Lystrians. St. Paul, who is in the act of tearing his robe, shews that he rejects and abhors the sacrilegious honors, and is endeavoring to dissuade the populace from persisting in them. But all this were vain, if it had not indicated the miracle which had just happened, and given rise to the event. Raffaello added to the group the lame man restored to the use of his limbs, now easily recognised again by all the spectators. He stands before the apostles rejoicing in his restoration; and raises his hands in transport towards his benefactors, while at his feet lie the crutches which had recently supported him, now cast away as useless. This had been sufficient for any other artist; but Raffaello, who wished to carry reality to the utmost point, has added a throng of people, who, in their eager curiosity, remove the garment of the man, to behold his limbs restored to their former state. Raffaello abounds with examples like these, and he may be compared to some of the classical writers, who afford the more matter for reflection the more they are studied. It is sufficient to have noticed in the inventive powers of Raffaello, those circumstances which have been less frequently remarked; the movement of the passions, which is entirely the work of expression, the delight which proceeds from poetical conceptions, or from graceful episodes, may be said to speak for themselves.

Other things might contribute to the beauty of his works, as unity, sublimity, costume, and erudition; for which it is sufficient to refer to those delightful poetical pieces, with which he adorned the gallery of Leo X., and which were engraved by Lanfranco and Badalocchio, and are called the Bible of Raffaello. In the Return of Jacob, who does not immediately discover, in the number and variety of domestic animals, the multitude of servants, and the women carrying with them their children, a patriarchal family migrating from a long possessed abode into a new territory? In the Creation of the World, where the Deity stretches out his arms, and with one hand calls forth the Sun, and with the other the Moon, do we not see a grandeur, which, with the simplest expression, awakes in us the sublimest ideas? And in the Adoration of the Golden Calf, how could he better have represented the idolatrous ceremony, and its departure from true religion, than by depicting the people as carried away by an insane joy, and mad with fanaticism? In point of erudition it is sufficient to notice the Triumph of David, which Taia describes and compares with the ancient bassi-rilievi, and is inclined to believe that there is not anything in marble that excels the art and skill of this picture. I am aware that on another occasion he has not been exempt from blame, as when he repeated the figure of St. Peter out of prison, which hurts the unity of the subject; and in assigning to Apollo and to the Muses instruments not proper to antiquity. Yet it is the glory of Raffaello to have introduced into his pictures numberless circumstances unknown to his predecessors, and to have left little to be added by his successors.

In composition also, he is at the head of his art. In every picture the principal figure is obvious to the spectator; we have no occasion to inquire for it; the groups, divided by situation, are united in the principal action; the contrast is not dictated by affectation, but by truth and propriety; a figure absorbed in thought, often serves as a relief to another that acts and speaks; the masses of light and shade are not arbitrarily poised, but are in the most select imitation of nature; all is art, but all is consummate skill and concealment of art. The School of Athens, as it is called, in the Vatican, is in this respect among the most wonderful compositions in the world. They who succeeded Raffaello, and followed other principles, have afforded more pleasure to the eye, but have not give such satisfaction to the mind. The compositions of Paul Veronese contain a greater number of figures, and more decoration; Lanfranco and the machinists introduce a powerful effect, and a vigorous contrast of light and shade: but who would exchange for such a manner the chaste and dignified style of Raffaello? Poussin alone, in the opinion of Mengs, obtained a superior mode of composition in the groundwork, or economy of his subject; that is to say, in the judicious selection of the scene of the event.

We have thus concisely stated the perfection to which Raffaello carried his art, in the short space allotted him. There is not a work in nature or art where he has not practically illustrated his own axiom, as handed down to us by Federigo Zuccaro, that things must be represented, not as they are, but as they ought to be; the country, the elements, animals, buildings, every age of man, every condition of life, every affection, all were embraced and rendered more beautiful by the divine genius of Raffaello. And if his life had been prolonged to a more advanced period, without approaching the term allowed to Titian or Michael Angelo, who shall say to what height of perfection he might not have carried his favorite art? Who can divine his success in architecture and sculpture, if he had applied himself to the study of them, having so wonderfully succeeded in his few attempts in those branches of art?

Of his pictures a considerable number are to be found in private collections, particularly on sacred subjects, such as the Madonna and Child, and other compositions of the Holy Family. They are in three styles which we have before described: the Grand Duke has some specimens of each. The most admired is that which is named the Madonna della Seggiola.* Of this class of pictures it is

* There are no less than eight portraits of Julius II. attributed to Raffaelle. 1. The original, by Raffaelle's own

often doubted whether they ought to be considered as originals or copies, as some of them have been three, five, or ten times repeated. The same may be said of other cabinet pictures by him, particularly the St. John in the Desert, which is in the Grand Ducal gallery at Florence, and is found repeated in many collections both in Italy and in other countries. This was likely to happen in a school where the most common mode was the following:—The subject was designed by Raffaello, the picture prepared by Giulio, and finished by the master so exquisitely, that one might almost count the hairs of the head. When pictures were thus finished, they were copied by the scholars of Raffaello, who were very numerous, and of the second and third order; and these were also sometimes retouched by Giulio and by Raffaello himself. But whoever is experienced in the freedom and delicacy of the chief of this school, need not fear confounding his productions with those of the scholars, or Giulio himself; who, besides having a more timid pencil, made use of a darker tint than his master was accustomed to do. I have met with an experienced person, who declared that he could recognize the character of Giulio in the dark parts of the flesh tints, and in the middle dark tints, not of a leaden color as Raffaello used, nor so well harmonized; in the greater quantity of light, and in the eyes designed more roundly, which Raffaello painted somewhat long, after the manner of Pietro Perugino."

RAFFAELLI, Francesco, an Italian engraver, who flourished about 1705. He engraved some plates of historical subjects, after the Italian masters.

RAFFAELLINO, del Colle. This artist was a native of Città San Sepolcro, born about 1490. He first studied under Raffaelle, and was employed by him in the Farnesina. He afterwards wrought for Giulio Romano in the Hall of Constantine. Hence he is considered rather a scholar of Giulio; and, after the death of Raffaelle, he assisted him in his works at Rome, and in the ducal palace called the *Te*, at Mantua. Taia ascribes the History of Moses in Horeb, in the Loggia, to "the bold pencil of Raffaellino del Colle." It is very singular that Vasari did not write a separate life of this artist; he only incidentally mentions his name, in several places, with scanty praise. Lanzi says his merit is little known to the public, as he painted mostly in his native place, and in the neighboring cities, where he executed many fine works, and instructed several pupils. At Città S. Sepolcro, in the church of S. Rocco, is a spirited picture of the Resurrection of our Saviour, "who, full of majesty, regards the soldiers with displeasure, which fills them with terror." The same subject is repeated in the Cathedral, and in the church of the Osservanti is an Assumption of the Virgin. At Città di Castello is another Assumption of the Virgin, beautifully designed and colored, and exquisitely finished, in the church of the Conventuali; an Entombment, at the Servi; an altar-piece full of grace and beauty in the church of S. Angelo, representing St. Michael and St. Sebastian, who humbly presents an arrow to the infant Jesus with the Virgin, as a type of his martyrdom; and a picture of the Virgin, with St. Sebastian, St. Roch, and a canonized bishop. Lanzi says the last piece, both in the figures and the landscape, much resembles the manner of Raffaelle. In the sacristy of the Cathedral at Urbino, he painted the Twelve Apostles, in small oblong pictures; they are noble figures, draped in a grand style, and finely colored. At Gubbio, in the chapel of the Olivet monks, is a Nativity and two pieces from the History of St. Benedict, painted in fresco, which he enriched with admirable architecture, and introduced into them several real portraits, and a figure of Virtue, which Lanzi says "seems a sister of the Sibyls of Raffaelle." He also painted in the castle of Perugia, and in the *Imperiale* at Pesaro, a villa of the Duke of Urbino, who held his works in high esteem, and preferred them to those of the two Dossi. He was remarkably modest, and diffident of his own abilities. The time of his death is not known, but one of his works at Città San Sepolcro is dated 1546, in his 56th year.

hand, is in the Palazzo Pitti at Florence, the best of all; 2. a scarcely inferior one in the Tribune of the Florentine Gallery; 3. one in the English National Gallery, from the Falconieri palace at Rome; 4. a very fine one, formerly in the Orleans Gallery; 5. an inferior one in the Corsini palace at Rome; 6. a very fine one in the Borghese Gallery at Rome; 7. one at Berlin, from the Giustiniani Gallery; 8. one in the possession of Count Torlonia at Rome. Most of these are doubtless copies by Raffaelle's scholars, some of them finished by himself. The original cartoon is preserved in the Corsini palace at Florence.

RAFFAELLINO, del. See del Garbo, Bottala, and Motta.

RAFFAELLINO, da Reggio. See Reggio.

RAGGI, Pietro Paolo, a painter born at Genoa, according to Ratti, in 1646. Tassi says he was a native of Vienna, born about 1650, and that his parents removed to Genoa when he was a child. It is not known under whom he studied, but Lanzi says he was certainly a follower of the Caracci, in his large picture of St. Bonaventura contemplating a crucifix, in the Nunziata del Guastato at Genoa. According to Ratti, who highly extols his works, he was of a restless disposition, irascible, and dissatisfied with every place he inhabited. This truant disposition induced him to lead a wandering life, carried him to Turin, thence to Savona, and back again to Genoa. He afterwards went to Lavagna, thence through Lombardy, and lastly to Bergamo. Some of his best works are in the churches at Bergamo, among which are the Annunciation in S. Lorenzo, and Mary Magdalene taken up into heaven by Angels, in S. Marta, highly commended for correctness of design and good coloring. He also excelled in landscapes, decorated with figures of pastoral and bacchanalian subjects, in which he sometimes imitated the style of Benedetto Castiglione, and at others Giulio Carpioni. He died at Bergamo in 1724.

RAGOT, François, a French engraver, born at Bagnolet in 1641. He engraved some plates after Charles le Brun, but chiefly distinguished himself by copying the best prints engraved by Bolswert, Pontius, and Vostermans, after the works of Rubens and Vandyck. He executed a considerable number of these copies, with such accuracy that they have often been mistaken by collectors for the originals. Nagler gives a list of thirty-four of his copies.

RAHART, Florent Delamere, a French

painter, born at Bayeux in 1630, and died at Versailles in 1718. He is commended for the excellence of his portraits.

RAIBOLINI, FRANCESCO. See FRANCIA.

RAIMBACH, ABRAHAM, an eminent English engraver, born at London in 1776. His father was a Swiss who had settled in London, and after giving his son a good primary education, he apprenticed him to J. Hall, an engraver. After the expiration of his apprenticeship, he entered the Royal Academy as a student, and occupied his time with his studies, engraving a few plates for the booksellers, and painting a few miniatures, but soon abandoned the latter occupation and devoted himself to engraving. His plates for Smirke and Forster's illustrated edition of the Arabian Nights established his reputation as an able artist. In 1812 and subsequent years he was employed by Sir David Wilkie to engrave many plates after his works, which proved very profitable both to the painter and the engraver. Among them are the Village Politicians, the Rent Day, the Cut Finger, the Errand Boy, Distraining for Rent, the Parish Beadle, and the Spanish Mother and Child. Raimbach is said never to have employed an assistant, but performed the whole work himself. His prints are executed in a bold style, and though deficient in freedom and delicacy of execution, especially in the extremities, they faithfully represent the spirit and expression of the original paintings, and were very popular. He died in 1843.

RAIMONDI, MARC' ANTONIO. This eminent engraver was born at Bologna in 1487 or 1488, and is generally known in art by the name of Marc' Antonio. He was instructed in design, and in the art of working in *niello*, by Francesco Francia, and next proceeded to engrave some of the productions of his master, the first of which was Pyramus and Thisbe, dated 1502. At first he imitated Andrea Mantegna, and next Albert Durer. According to Vasari, while on a visit to Venice in search of improvement, Raimondi met with a set of Durer's thirty-six wooden cuts representing the Life and Passion of our Saviour, and, being greatly pleased with them, he copied them on copper (affixing the cipher of Durer) with such precision that the prints were readily sold in Italy as originals. This deception reaching the ears of Durer, he went to Venice, and complained before the Senate of the plagiarism and injustice, but could obtain no further redress than an order forbidding Marc' Antonio to use his monogram on any future copies he might make of his works. Marc' Antonio copied both sets of Durer's prints, representing the Life of Christ and the Life of the Virgin; to the latter he affixed the mark of Durer, but not to the former, therefore Vasari made a slight mistake. He next proceeded to Rome, where his valuable talents immediately recommended him to the notice of Raffaelle, who employed him to engrave after his designs, and is said to have etched the outlines on some of the plates himself, to ensure greater correctness of drawing. It is well known that under the instruction of Raffaelle he acquired great improvement, and brought the art to a degree of perfection that has hardly been surpassed. This is shown in the prints he engraved after Raffaelle. The first was the Death of Lucretia, which, though neatly executed, was somewhat stiff and formal; the next, the Judgment of Paris, is executed in a more bold and spirited manner, and these were followed by others exhibiting marked improvement, until Raffaelle himself was satisfied with his performances, who is said to have sent some of his prints to Albert Durer, together with several of his own drawings, as a most acceptable present to that eminent artist, who had honored him by sending him his portrait. (See *Durer.*) Lanzi says that "Raffaelle not only assisted Marc' Antonio with his advice, but that he might devote his whole time to engraving, he permitted his own grinder of colors, Baviera, to manage the press." He was also assisted by his two pupils Agostino Veneziano and Marco da Ravenna, who succeeded him in the series of engravings from Raffaelle; which led Vasari to observe, in his life of Marc' Antonio, that "between himself, Agostino, and Marco, nearly all Raffaelle's designs and paintings had been engraved."

After the death of Raffaelle in 1520, he was employed by Giulio Romano, to engrave after his designs. It is said that he was prevailed upon to engrave a set of indecent subjects, with verses by Aretino. These prints so highly excited the indignation of Clement VII., that he ordered Marc' Antonio to be thrown into prison, and it was with great difficulty that Baccio Bandinelli and some of the cardinals procured his release. On recovering his liberty, Marc' Antonio, desirous of expressing his obligations to Bandinelli, engraved his celebrated print of the Martyrdom of St. Lawrence, after a picture by that painter, on which he exerted all his powers. The Pope, delighted at this masterpiece, quickly forgot the offence, and took him under his protection. He continued at Rome in full possession of public esteem, and favored with the patronage of the great, till the dreadful sacking of that city by the Spaniards in 1527, when he was despoiled of all his property, and obliged to flee to Bologna, where he continued to practise his art until 1539, when he engraved his last print, the Battle of the Lapithæ, *after Giulio Romano.* He is supposed to have died about this time. Malvasia says he was assassinated by a Roman nobleman, for having engraved a second plate of the Murder of the Innocents, *after Raffaelle*, contrary to his engagements—a highly improbable story.

Marc' Antonio is justly regarded as one of the most extraordinary engravers that have ever appeared. The purity of his outlines, the beautiful character and expression of the heads, and the correct drawing of his extremities, establish his merit as a perfect master in design. His prints are very numerous, and are held in the highest esteem; but there is a great difference in the impressions, owing to the plates having passed through a succession of hands, by which means they became greatly worn, and were frequently retouched. They first passed into the possession of Tommaso Barlacchi, and then successively to Antonio La freri, Nicholas van Aelst, and lastly Rossi or de Rubeis, at which time they were almost worn out. The best impressions are those without the name of any publisher. Lanzi says "he sometimes omitted every kind of mark, and every letter; sometimes he adopted the little tablet of Mantegna, either with or without letters. In some engravings of the Passion (rather the History of the Virgin) he counterfeited both the style and mark of Albert Durer; and not unfrequently he gave the initial letters of his own and Raffaelle's name and that of Michael Angelo, when he engraved after that master." For a complete account of the works of this artist, the reader is referred to Bartsch's Peintre Graveur, tom. xiv., the whole of which volume is devoted to an account of this artist, and of his two principal scholars, Agostino Veneziano and Marco da Ravenna, with a catalogue raisonné of their works; every known print being described, with all the variations. The Baron Heineken has also given a very complete catalogue of Marc' Antonio's prints, in his *Idea Generale d'une cellection d'estampes.* The following is an ample list of his most esteemed prints.—Some are without any marks, but on most of them are found one of the following monograms on the little tablet, and occasionally the tablet without any letters:

AF or MF 1506 R 9. or MF or MF,

·MF· or MAF 1506 .8 S, or MF

PORTRAITS.

Aretin, the poet; inscribed *Petrus Aretinus accerimus, &c.* A Man wrapped in a cloak, seated near a table, and on the left a pallette with colors. Malvasia calls this the portrait of *Raffaelle.* Charles V. when young; a medallion. Pope Clement VII.; do.

SUBJECTS OF THE OLD AND NEW TESTAMENTS.

Adam and Eve; *after Raffaelle.* This print has been copied by Mr. Strutt, and is placed as the title to the second volume of his Dictionary of Engravers. Adam and Eve driven from Paradise; after the painting by *M. Angelo,* in the Sistine chapel. Noah sacrificing after leaving the Ark; *after Raffaelle.* God appearing to Noah; *do.* God appearing to Isaac; *do.* Joseph and Potiphar's wife; *do.* David cutting off the Head of Goliah; *do.* David taking up the Head of Goliah; *do.;* very scarce. The Nativity, or Adoration of the Shepherds; *after Francia.* The Murder of the Innocents; *after Raffaelle.* He engraved this subject a second time, and has added in the second plate, towards the right of the print, a small pointed tree, resembling a yew tree, called in Italian *la felcetta,* in French *la fougere* or *le chicot.* The latter is considered the better print, and it is scarce. The Holy Family; the Virgin is seated, holding the infant Jesus on her lap, with St. John before him, and St. Joseph appearing behind; *do.* This print is usually called *The Virgin with the long thigh.* The Virgin seated, with St. Elizabeth and St. John, to whom the Infant is giving the Benediction. A large palm tree is seen in the back-ground, on which account the print is known by the appellation of *The Virgin of the Palm; do.* The Virgin seated near a cradle, presenting the infant Jesus to St. Anne. Behind it is an old woman with her arms extended, as if in admiration; *do.;* called *The Virgin of the Cradle.* The Virgin seated on a chair, embracing the infant Jesus; *do.* The Virgin holding the Infant, and reading; *do.* The Holy Family; after the painting by *M. Angelo,* in the Sistine chapel. The Virgin and infant Jesus, to whom Tobit, accompanied by an Angel, is presenting a fish. On the other side is St. Joseph reading in a book; *after Raffaelle.* The Virgin in the Clouds, holding the infant Jesus; *do.* Agostino Caracci, having got possession of this plate, retouched it, and added two beautiful heads of cherubim. A set of seventeen plates of the Life of the Virgin; copied from the wooden cuts by *Albert Durer,* with the monogram of that artist, and on the last plate the cipher of Marc' Antonio. Thirty-six plates of the Life and Passion of our Saviour; copied in imitation of the wooden cuts by *Albert Durer,* but without the mark of that master. Christ seated between two columns, upon the steps, with the Virgin and Mary Magdalene; *after Raffaelle;* called *The Virgin with the Steps.* Mary Magdalene at the feet of Christ, in the house of Simon the Pharisee; *do.* The Last Supper; *do.;* called *La piece des pieds.* The taking down from the Cross; *do.* The dead Christ laid on the Sepulchre, with the Virgin with her arms extended, and in the deepest affliction; *do.* The same composition, in which the Virgin appears younger, and has one of her arms naked, called *The Virgin with the naked arm.* The dead Christ, with his head on the knees of the Virgin, with the holy women and two of the disciples, with Nicodemus; *do.* Jesus Christ with a glory, between the Virgin and St. John, and below, St. Paul and St. Catherine; *do.* This print is called *The Five Saints.* The Death of Ananias; *do.* Elymas, the Sorcerer, struck blind; *do.* St. Paul preaching at Athens; *do.* (The three last are the subjects of three of the cartoons.) St. Cecilia, with Mary Magdalene, St. Paul, and two other saints; *do.* The best impressions of this plate have a strong shadow on the neck of St. Cecilia, resembling a necklace, on which account it is called *The St. Cecilia with the Necklace.* In the inferior impressions the shadow is more feeble. The Martyrdom of St. Felicita; *do.* St. Catherine holding the Palm of Martyrdom; *after Francia.* St. Catherine and St. Lucia; *do.* St. Martha holding the Palm of Martyrdom; *do.* The Martyrdom of St. Lawrence; called by the Italians *La graticola di S. Lorenzo; after Baccio Bandinelli.* A set of thirteen plates of Christ and the Apostles; *after Raffaelle.*

HISTORICAL AND OTHER SUBJECTS.

The four heroes, Curtius, Horatius, Scipio Africanus, and Titus Vespasian; supposed to have been among his first attempts on copper. The books of the Sibyls put into the tomb of Numa Pompilius; *after Raffaelle.* The Rape of Helen; *do.* Æneas saving his father Anchises from the burning of Troy, preceded by Ascanius; *do.* Venus appearing to Æneas in the form of a Huntress; *do.* The Death of Dido; *do.* The Death of Lucretia; *do.* The Battle of the Sabre; *do.* The same subject was engraved by Agostino Veneziano, called *de Musis.*

SUBJECTS OF THE FABLE.

Three of the Angels of the Farnesina; *after Raffaelle;* representing Jupiter caressing Cupid, Cupid and the Graces, and Mercury descending to earth from Olympus. The Judgment of Paris; *do.* Mars, Venus, and Cupid; *after Mantegna.* Vulcan, Venus, and Cupid; *after Raffaelle.* Apollo resting on the shepherd Hyacinth, accompanied by Cupid; inscribed 1506. *Ae.* 19. The Triumph of Galatea; *do.* The best impressions are without any name, the worst have the names of Van Aelst and Rossi. Mount Parnassus; *do.* Hercules strangling Anteus; after a design by some attributed to *Raffaelle,* by others to *M. Angelo.* The Battle of the Lapithæ; *after Giulio Romano.* 1539. Pyramus and Thisbe; *after F. Francia,* supposed to be his first engraving on copper. The two Sibyls; *after Raffaelle.* Neptune rising from the Sea, to calm the tempest in which Æneas and his companions were shipwrecked. It is surrounded by a border in which are nine compartments, containing subjects taken from the Æneid. The Pest, called *Il Morbetto; after Raffaelle.*

RAIMONDO, a Neapolitan painter, who flourished at Turin about 1477. Lanzi says there is a picture by him, in several compartments, in the church of S. Francesco di Chieri, esteemed for the lively expression of the countenances and the excellence of the coloring, but with much gilding in the draperies, according to the custom of the age.

RAIMONDO, Maestro, an old Italian architect, who was a native of Monforte, and flourished about the middle of the 12th century. He was principally distinguished for rebuilding the Cathedral of Lugo, a strongly built edifice of white marble, well worked, and supported on strong arches, with three naves, and four towers at the angles. Raimondo died before the work was finished, and was succeeded by his son. According to Milizia, the Cathedral was completed in 1177.

RAINALDI, Domenico, a painter who flourished at Rome about 1665. According to Titi, he was the nephew of the celebrated architect, Cav. Carlo Rainaldi, was patronized by the Pope, and executed some works for the churches. His name is also mentioned in the *Guida di Roma.*

RAINALDI, Tolomeo, an Italian architect, was the eldest son of Adriano R., a painter and architect, and is supposed by Milizia to have studied under Michael Angelo. He practised both the civil and military branches of the art, and was appointed architect to the royal house and fortifications of Milan. He had two sons, Domizio and Giovanni Leo, called *Tolomei*, who practised the same art, succeeded to the offices of their father, and erected a number of edifices and fortresses at Milan, in the States, and in the Valteline.

RAINALDI, Gio. Battista, a Roman architect, was a younger brother of the preceding. He erected a number of edifices at Rome, and was also employed in the fortifications at Ferrara, and the Ponte Felice, at Borghetto. He had a son named Domenico, a painter and architect.

RAINALDI, Girolamo, an Italian architect, the younger brother of the preceding artists, was born at Rome in 1570. He studied under Domenico Fontana, and gained the esteem of that master by his talents and application. When Fontana was commissioned by Sixtus V. to design a church at Montalto, being occupied with many engagements, he entrusted it to Rainaldi; and the young architect produced a design of such excellence that it was accepted by the Pope, who ordered him to erect the building. This was the commencement of Rainaldi's fortune, and he was much employed under successive pontificates. He finished the Capitol; built the gate of Fano, under Paul V., the house for the professor of the Jesuits at Rome, and the Jesuitical college of S. Lucia at Bologna. He was also employed by the Duke of Parma, and erected a palace in that city, as well as one in Piacenza and Modena. He constructed the bridge of Terni, over the Nera, of a single arch, and well proportioned. Among the most important works of Rainaldi, is the grand Palazzo Pamfili, in the Piazza Navona at Rome; and the beautiful church of the Padri Scalzi at Caprarola. He was employed to visit the Chiane marshes, on account of the difference concerning them between the Grand Duke and the Pope. died in 1655, and was buried in S. Martina.

RAINALDI, Carlo, an Italian architect, born at Rome in 1611. He was the son and scholar of Girolamo R., and gained great distinction in the pontificates of Innocent X. and Alexander VII. The former pope, after testing the abilities of Rainaldi by a number of designs and buildings, commissioned him to erect the church of S. Agnese on the Piazza Navona, which is highly praised by Milizia for the beauty of its design, in the form of a light, elegant, and well proportioned Greek cross. He designed and executed his works with rapidity; his ornaments were bold, though not always correct, especially in his façades of churches. The enemies of Bernini having suggested that his campanile over the façade of St. Peter's was in danger of falling, Rainaldi was named head of the Assembly appointed to investigate the affair, and used every effort, though unsuccessfully, to defeat the object of their attacks against that celebrated architect. He made four designs and models for the piazza before St. Peter's; one of a square figure, one circular, the third a long ellipsis, and the fourth hexagonal. On account of the death of Innocent X., they were never executed. Among his other works were the façade of Gesu Maria, on the Corso, and of S. Andrea della Valle, the most stately work in Rome, after St. Peter's; two beautiful temples for Cardinal Gastaldi; the Sepulchre of Clement IX., in S. Maria Maggiore; and the Palace of the French Academy. Rainaldi sent a number of designs to Charles Emanuel, Duke of Savoy, who honored him with several rich gifts, and the Cross of S. Maurizio and Lazzaro. He sent a design for the Louvre to King Louis XIV., who returned the compliment by sending the architect his own miniature, enriched with gems. He died in 1691.

RAINIERI, Francesco, called Lo Schivenoglia, a painter born at Mantua about 1680. He studied under Giovanni Canti, and adopted his style and subjects. Lanzi says he was equally distinguished for his landscapes and battle-pieces, and surpassed his master in design, though inferior to him in coloring. He died in 1758.

RAM, John de, a Dutch engraver, born about 1680. He studied under Romeyn de Hooghe, whom he surpassed in freedom and correctness of design. He was employed chiefly by the booksellers, and his prints are numerous in the Dutch publications of his day. He also engraved some portraits in mezzotinto, among which is one of Christian V. of Denmark.

RAMA, Camillo, a painter born at Brescia, who flourished about 1622. According to Orlandi, he studied under the younger Palma, and followed his style. He executed several works for the churches, convents, and public edifices of his native city, highly commended by the author above cited, though Lanzi does not deem them worthy of more than a passing notice.

RAMAZZANI, Ercole, a painter born at Roccacontrada, in the Roman territory. According to Lanzi, he studied under Pietro Perugino and afterwards under Raffaelle. He executed some works for the churches in his native place and in its vicinity, which, in the *Antichità Picene*, are commended for their beautiful style of coloring, charming invention, and a manner approaching to Baroccio. He was living in 1588.

RAMBALDI, Carlo, a painter born at Bologna in 1680. He studied under Domenico Viani, and adopted his style. He painted history with considerable reputation, and executed several works for the churches at Bologna, among which the principal are the Death of St. Joseph, in S. Gregorio, the Visitation of the Virgin, in S. Giuseppe, and St. Francis Xavier, in S. Lucia. He also painted many pictures for the collections. Lanzi says that his pictures, especially his half-length figures, are found in the select galleries at Bologna; and there are a few of his historical pictures in the royal collection at Turin. He died in 1717.

RAMBERG, John Henry, a German painter and engraver, born at Hanover in 1763. He went early in life to England, and studied with Sir Joshua Reynolds, under whom he showed great talents and made rapid progress. He acquired distinction, was patronized by the Royal Family, painted for the Prince of Wales at Carlton House, and was elected a royal academician. He afterwards made the tour of France, Italy, Germany, and Holland, and finally settled in his native city, where he practised his profession with distinction, and was chosen professor of painting in the Academy. He painted both history and portraits, and was employed by Boydell in painting for his Shakspeare gallery. He also engraved some prints from his own designs in aquatint, and in the chalk manner. He died at Hanover in 1840.

RAMELLI, Padre Felice, a painter born at Asti, in Piedmont, in 1666. He first studied under the Padre Abate Danese Rho, but finished his studies at Rome, where he took priestly orders, and was made one of the canons of the church of S. John of Lateran. He excelled in painting historical subjects and portraits in oil, as well as miniatures. He was invited by the King of Sardinia to Turin, where he executed for that monarch the portraits, in small, of the most celebrated artists, from the originals by themselves in the Florentine gallery. He finished his pieces with incredible neatness, and gave to each portrait in a small compass, the dignity and truth of nature. These works are preserved in the cabinet of the King of Sardinia, and among the heads, he took care to perpetuate his own, represented in the habit of his order. Most of his works are in the collections at Rome, where he chiefly resided, and died in 1740.

RAMENGHI, Bartolomeo, sometimes called Il or da Bagnacavallo, and by Vasari Il Bologna, was an eminent Italian painter, born, according to Baruffaldi, at Bagnacavallo, a small village near Bologna, in 1484. He first studied under Francesco Francia, and next imitated the manner of Girolamo da Cotignola, till he went to Rome, where he entered the school of Raffaelle and was employed, among other artists, in decorating the loggie of the Vatican. He afterwards returned to Bologna, where he executed many works for the churches, emulating the manner of Raffaelle, for which reason, Vasari and other authors give him less notice than his talents and merits deserve. Lanzi says, "in his composition he most affected Raffaelle, as may be gathered from his celebrated dispute of St. Augustine at the Scopetini, where the maxims of the school of Athens and of other copious and noble conceptions of Sanzio are apparent." (Why should not Bagnacavallo retort that Raffaelle copied into his cartoon of Paul and Barnabas at Lystra, the whole of the ancient Sacrifice of Masaccio?) "Indeed in those subjects treated by Sanzio, Bagnacavallo contented himself with being a mere copyist, declaring that it was madness to attempt to do better, and appearing to follow the opinion of Vida, and other poets of his age, who inserted in their pages fragments of Virgil, because they despaired of excelling them." Lanzi says however, that he was well grounded in the principles of art, and that he conducted some paintings on the strength of his own invention, which absolve him from the accusation of a copyist, as at S. Michele in Bosco, at S. Martino, and at S. Maria Maggiore. He also says that he was the first to introduce a better style at Bologna, and that, though he had not the depth of design of Giulio Romano and Pierino del Vaga, he nearly approached the latter, and was perhaps equal to him in the excellence of his coloring, while in the graceful airs of his heads, at least in the boyish and infantile, he surpassed him. It is also well known that his works were the admiration of Guido, Albano, and the Caracci, who at first made them their study and models. He died at Bologna in 1542. The times of his birth and death are variously stated, but the above dates are from authentic documents.

RAMENGHI, Giovanni Battista, was the son of the preceding artist. According to Malvasia, he was instructed by his father, and was employed as an assistant to Vasari in the palace of the Chancery at Rome; after which he accompanied Primaticcio to France, and assisted in his works at Fontainbleau. He afterwards returned to Bologna, where he executed some excellent works for the churches, and was chosen president of the academy in 1575. The notices of him are very scanty. He died in 1601. His son Scipione, was an excellent perspective and ornamental painter, and assisted his uncle Bartolomeo, the subject of the following article.

RAMENGHI, Bartolomeo, was the cousin of Gio. Battista R., and flourished in the latter part of the 16th century. His instructor is not mentioned. He excelled in perspective and ornamental painting, and found much employment at Bologna. Lanzi says he associated himself with Gio. Battista Cremonini, and in conjunction with that artist, decorated an astonishing number of public and private edifices at Bologna, in the neighboring cities, and at the different courts of Lombardy. Ramenghi painted the architectural parts, and Cremonini the histories, figures, statues, and animals. (See Cremonini.) He had a son named Gio. Battista, also an eminent painter in the same branch, who flourished at Bologna in the first part of the 17th century.

RAMIREZ, Geronimo, a Spanish painter, who flourished at Seville in the first part of the 17th century. He studied under Juan de las Roelas, and adopted his style. There is a fine picture by him, in the hospital de la Sangre, signed with his name, representing the Pope surrounded by Cardinals and other personages.

RAMIREZ, Felipe, a Spanish painter, who flourished at Seville about 1650, and was probably a relative of the preceding. His instructor is not mentioned, but according to Cean Bermudez, he was a correct and skillful designer of the human figure, as is evident from his picture of the Martyrdom of St. Stephen. He excelled in painting hunting-pieces, dead game, and objects of still-life, which are highly esteemed in Spain.

RAMIREZ, José, a Spanish painter, born at Valencia, according to Bermudez, in 1624. He studied under Geronimo de Espinosa, and followed his style. Palomino commends some of his best works in the convent of San Felipe Neri, particularly a picture of the Virgin. Bermudez says he was a learned ecclesiastic, and wrote the life of San Felipe Neri. He died, according to Bermudez, in 1692, and to Palomino, in 1686.

RAMIREZ, Juan, an eminent Spanish portrait painter, who flourished at Seville about 1550. He painted historical subjects, in the chapel of St. Christopher, and other places of note, but his works have all perished except his portraits.

RAMSAY, Allan, a Scotch portrait painter, the son of Allan Ramsay the poet, was born at Edinburg in 1709. After studying in London with Mr. Hyssidge, a painter of little note, he went to Italy, where he resided three years, chiefly at Rome, and studied successively under Solimena and Imperiali. Soon after his return to his own country, he settled at London, where he met with flattering encouragement. By the interest of Lord Bute, he was introduced to the Prince of Wales, afterwards George III., and painted his portrait. On the death of Shakelton in 1767, he was appointed principal portrait painter to the King. He painted several full-length portraits of George III., and Queen Charlotte, as well as others of the nobility, and persons of distinction, some of which were engraved. He visited Rome four different times, the last in company with his son, Major-General Ramsay. He died soon after his return, in 1784. Ramsay's portraits are distinguished for a calm, placid dignity, and a faithful representation of his subjects, devoid of the affectation that prevailed among his cotemporaries in London. Although he did not reach the highest rank in his profession, his works are esteemed, and he contributed to regenerate the art in his country. He was well versed in literature, and Boswell mentions him as a frequenter of the literary parties of Dr. Johnson, who said of him, "you will not find a man in whose conversation there is more instruction, more information, and more elegance, than in that of Ramsay."

RANBERT, Louis le, a French painter and sculptor, born at Paris in 1614. His father was keeper of sculptures to King Louis XIII., who consented to act as sponsor to the young artist. He studied painting in the school of Vouet, and afterwards under le Brun. He then entered the atelier of the sculptor Sarrazin, and soon gained distinction for the grace and beauty of his figures, and his facility of execution. As a painter, he executed several small portraits of Cardinal Mazarin, Marechal de la Meilleraie, and others. His principal work in sculpture was the tomb of Marquis Dampierre. For the park at Versailles, he executed several statues of Nymphs, &c., and for the cathedral at Blois, two bas-reliefs in white marble, representing Memory and Meditation. His works possess considerable merit of execution; but they want the simplicity of the antique. Le Ranbert died at Paris in 1670.

RANC, Jean, an eminent French portrait painter, born at Montpellier in 1674. He went to Paris and studied under Hyacinth Rigaud. After acquiring distinction, he was invited in 1724 to the court of Madrid, where he was appointed principal painter to the King, and painted the portraits of the King and other members of the royal family, besides those of the principal court personages. He also painted the portraits of the royal family of Portugal. He died at Madrid in 1735.

RANDA, Antonio, a Bolognese painter, who first studied under Guido, and afterwards with Lucio Massari. Malvasia observes that there is little good to be said of him, referring to his deed of homicide, originating in a quarrel, in which he slew his antagonist, and was obliged to flee from Bologna. In other respects, he ranks him among the best scholars, first of Guido, and next of Massari, to whose style he was most attached. On account of his reputation, the Duke of Modena granted him an asylum in his state, and made him his court painter in 1614. He executed many works for the Duke, which are highly commended by Orlandi, and was afterwards much employed in painting for the churches at Ferrara, besides many other places in the Polesine. He afterwards betook himself to a cloister, which, in the eyes of Orlandi covered a multitude of sins, and doubtless would have softened the asperity of Malvasia, had he been cognizant of the fact. Lanzi praises a St. Cecilia, that he saw in a private collection, as an exquisite production. There are some of his works in the churches at Bologna, and particularly at Ferrara, where are two of his best works,—St. Filippo Neri, in S. Stefano, and a grand altar-piece of the Virgin and Infant, with St. Francis, in S. Libera. He died in 1650.

RANDON, John, an engraver, probably a Frenchman, who flourished at Rome, from about 1710 to 1755. He engraved some plates of antique and modern statues for the collection published by Rossi; also several other subjects *after Passebon.*

RANSONETTE, Nicolas, a French engraver, born at Paris in 1753. His instructor is not mentioned, but he engraved some plates in a neat style. after his own designs and those of other masters, among which are the following. He died in 1810.

The new Palais-Royal at Paris. A View of the new Palace of Justice. The Rival Seducer; *from his own design.* The Lover Revenged; *do.* Cupid and Psyche; *after Raffaelle.* Italian Amusements; *after Watteau.* Diana of Poitiers; *after L. Penni.* Agnes Sorel; *do.* The Dream of Voltaire; *after St. Aubin.* Nostradamus showing Mary de Medicis the throne of the Bourbons. Several plates of fabulous subjects; *after Gabriel de St. Aubin.*

RAOUX, Jean, a French historical and portrait painter, born at Montpellier in 1677. He studied in the school of Bon Boullongne at Paris, where he made great progress, and obtained the grand prize of the Academy, which entitled him to visit Italy with the royal pension. He continued at Rome and Venice ten years, and practised his profession with credit in several Italian cities. On his return to Paris he acquired considerable distinction, and was admitted into the Academy in 1717, for his picture of Pygmalion and Galatea. Among his principal works are four pictures representing the different ages of Man, painted for the Prior of Vendome, Telemachus in the Island of Calypso, and a Sleeping Venus; the two latter have been engraved. He appears to have devoted his attention in France mostly to portraits and fancy pictures. It is said that he visited England, where he was sometime employed by Sir Andrew Fontaine. He died at Paris in 1734.

RAPHAEL. See Raffaelle.

RAPHON, or RAPHOHN, Johann, a German painter of whom little is known, and about whom considerable curiosity has recently been excited by the discovery of several pictures bearing his name. He is said to have been a scholar of Albert Durer, and to have died in 1528. There is an altar-piece by him in the Cathedral of Halberstadt, consisting of the Crucifixion, with laterals on the inside of folding-doors, representing the Annunciation, the Adoration of the Shepherds, the Adoration of the Magi, and the Presentation. The exteriors are decorated with figures of Saints. The composition is somewhat overcharged, and the heads are distinguished by energy and individuality of expression rather than by a manifestation of those inward feelings appropriate to the subjects. It is dated 1508. Another similar picture of a Crucifixion with laterals, is in the Library of the University at Gottingen. A third altar-piece is dated 1499, and M. Hausmann, of Hanover, possesses two wings of a fourth. It is probable that more will be discovered.

RATHBONE, John, an English landscape painter, born in Cheshire about 1750. By an assiduous study of nature, he acquired distinction as a painter of landscapes, and his pictures were frequently embellished with figures by Ibbeston, Anderson, and other cotemporary artists. He died in 1807.

RATTI, Gio. Agostino, a painter born at Savona in 1699. He went young to Rome, and studied in the school of Benedetto Luti, whose style he followed. He painted history, both in fresco and in oil, but was more eminent for his decorations of theatres with beautiful scenes, and cabinets with lively caricatures. He executed some works for the churches, among which are an admired picture of the Decollation of St. John the Baptist, in the church of S. Giovanni at Savona, and some frescos in the choir of the church of the Conventuali at Casale di Monferrato. Lanzi says, "subjects of humor were his forte. In these he had an exhaustless fancy, fertile, and ever creative. Nothing can be more amusing than his masks, representing quarrels, dances, and such scenes as form the subjects of comedy. Luti extolled him as one of the first artists in this branch, and even equalled him to the Cav. Ghezzi." Lanzi also says that he engraved some plates after his own designs. He died at Genoa in 1775.

RATTI, Cav. Carlo Giuseppe, a painter, and more eminent author, was the son of the preceding, born at Genoa about 1735. His principal literary works were, the Lives of the Painters, Sculptors, and Architects of Genoa; the Life of the Cav. Raffaello Mengs; and Historical Notices of Correggio; which last, in particular, brought down upon him the thunders of several writers, who accused him of plagiarism, and of having endeavored, by a change of style and the addition of trifling matter, to appropriate to himself what really belonged to Mengs. We cannot enter into the subject, further than to say that Ratti ably defended himself in an anonymous letter to a friend, which, however, did not satisfy the critics, and they carried the controversy to his works as a painter, so that it is impossible to form any correct estimate of his abilities. He first studied with his father, and afterwards with Mengs, rather as a friend, with whom he lived in his own house for four years, and who always entertained a warm friendship for him. Mengs proposed him as Director of the Academy at Milan, and some historical and national pictures being required in the royal palace at Genoa, Ratti was recommended to this honorable commission by both Mengs and Battoni, and he executed them to the entire satisfaction of the public, though his enemies could discover nothing in them but imitation and plagiarism. Ratti also wrote on art at the instigation of Mengs. He executed many works for the churches at Genoa, Rome, and other places, and painted much for individuals. He was knighted by Pius VI., made a member of the Academies of St. Luke, of Florence, and other places, extolled by poets and men of letters, and was offered the direction of the Academy at Genoa for life, which honorable office he declined. His friends admit that he did not hesitate to adopt from ancient or modern masters, when it suited his purpose. Lanzi says that he was an admirable copyist, and that Mengs himself paid him a considerable sum for a copy of the St. Jerome of Correggio, probably one of his earlier performances, which he had made at Parma. He died in 1795.

RAUCH, Christian, an eminent German sculptor, born at Waldeck in 1777. He acquired a knowledge of the art at Berlin, and afterwards visited Rome for improvement, in 1805. In 1811, the King of Prussia invited him to Berlin, to execute a mausoleum at Charlottenburg, in memory of the late queen. This splendid work was completed in three years, and is considered one of the finest productions of modern art. In 1815, Rauch was commissioned by the king to execute the statues of Scharnhorst and Bülow, which are now standing in Berlin, nearly opposite the King's palace. His works are principally distinguished for correctness of design. Besides those already mentioned, he has executed many others, among which are the bronze colossal statue of Blücher, at Berlin; and another of the same general at Breslau. In 1832, Rauch was Professor of Sculpture in the Academy of Fine Arts at Berlin. It is not ascertained if he is now living.

RAVENET, Simon François, the Elder, a French engraver, born at Paris in 1706, though Zani and Basan say in 1721. He studied under Philip le Bas, and after acquiring considerable reputation, he went to England, and settled in London about 1750, where he executed many plates after the Italian and French masters, which are highly esteemed. He gave both color and brilliancy to his engravings, and finished them with great neatness and precision. He died in 1774. The following are among his best prints:

PORTRAITS.

George I. George II.; *after Mercier.* Lord Camden; *after Reynolds.* Alexander Pope, Poet. James Thomson, Poet. David Hume, Historian. Mr. Garrick and Miss Bellamy, in Romeo and Juliet; *after B. Wilson.*

VARIOUS SUBJECTS.

The Emblem of Human Life; *after Titian;* Crozat collection. Venus and Adonis; *after P. Veronese;* do. The Adoration of the Shepherds; *after D. Feti;* do. Painting and Design; *after Guido.* The Virgin, with the infant Jesus sleeping; *do.* Charity; *after Carlo Cignani.* The Arcadian Shepherds; *after N. Poussin.* Sophonisba receiving the Nuptial Present; *after L. Giordano.* The Death of Seneca; *do.* Tobias' Nuptial Night; *after le Sueur.* Tobit anointing his Father's Eyes; *after Ag. Caracci.* The Lord of the Vineyard; *after Rembrandt.* The Prodigal Son; *after Sal. Rosa.* Phryne tempting Xenocrates; *do.* The Return of the Prodigal Son; *after Guercino.* Lucretia deploring her Fate; *after Cazali.* Gunhilda, Empress of Germany, acquitted of a charge of adultery; *do.*

RAVENET, Simon François, the Younger, was the son of the preceding, born in London in 1755. After learning engraving with his father, he went to Paris, and studied painting for a short time under François Boucher. On leaving that master, he went to Italy and settled at Parma, where he undertook the arduous enterprise of engraving and publishing plates from all the works of Correggio in that city, which occupied him several years His prints are executed with neatness and spirit He was living in 1813. The following are by him:

A set of twelve plates of the Cupola of the Cathedral. A set of plates of the Dome of S. Giovanni. The Madonna della Scodella. The Madonna della Scala. La Santissima Nunziata. The Madonna Incoronata. Christ bearing his Cross. The Descent from the Cross. The celebrated St. Jerome. The Martyrdom of St. Placido.—All of them *after Correggio.* Jupiter and Antiope; *after Rubens.* Theseus lifting the Stone; *after N. Poussin.*

MR. or SR RAVENNA, MARCO DA, an eminent Italian engraver, born at Ravenna about 1496. His family name was *Dente*, and Vasari calls him *Marco da Ravignano.* The fame of Marc' Antonio Raimondi drew many young men to Rome to study under him. Among them the most distinguished were Marco da Ravenna and Agostino de Musis, called Veneziano, both of whom assisted him in his works, and after his death engraved many admirable works by themselves. Ravenna imitated with precision the bolder style of engraving practised by his master, but was not equally successful when he attempted to follow him in his neatest and most finished works. He handled the graver with more freedom than his fellow-student Veneziano, though inferior to him in clearness and accuracy. He rarely signed his plates with his name, MRCUS RAVENAS, sometimes simply with an R., sometimes with a monogram composed of M. R., but more frequently with one composed of an R. and an S. interlaced as above. This last mark has led authors into a great deal of contradiction and confusion, which we cannot enter into, further than to say that some suppose there were two Ravennas, and that those plates marked R. or with the monogram M. R., were by Marco da Ravenna, and those with the monogram of R. and an S., were by an artist variously called *Silvestro*, *Simone*, or *Severo* da Ravenna. Others again interpret the monogram *Raffaelle Sanzio*, placed on the plate to denote that it was taken from a design by that master; but this opinion is confuted by the fact that he used the same mark on a print of the Murder of the Innocents, *after Baccio Bandinelli.* The prints in dispute are evidently by the same hand, and the best connoisseurs interpret the mark *Ravenna sculpsit.*—Those fond of such discussions are referred to Zani's Enciclopedia Metodica, parte prima, vol. xvi., and parte seconda, vol. v., where they will find the subject discussed *con amore*; and to Bartsch's Peintre Graveur, tom. xiv., who, with his usual critical acumen, has examined all the evidence of Zani, and placed the subject in as clear a light as practicable. The time of his death is not known. The following are his principal prints:

SACRED SUBJECTS.

A set of twelve plates of subjects from the Bible; after the paintings in the Vatican, from the designs of *Raffaelle.* The Murder of the Innocents; *after Baccio Bandinelli.* The Transfiguration; *after Raffaelle.* The Last Supper; *do.*; the same is engraved by *M. Antonio.* The Holy Family; *do.*; engraved also by *M. Antonio*, called *The Virgin with the long thigh.* The Virgin Mary holding the infant Jesus, seated on a pedestal with St. Joseph; *after Polidoro da Caravaggio.* A set of thirteen plates of Christ and the Apostles; *after Raffaelle*; the same were engraved by *M. Antonio*. St. Michael discomfiting the Evil Spirit; *do.*

SUBJECTS AFTER VARIOUS MASTERS.

The Remembrance of Death; an emblematical subject, in which a figure of Death is represented holding a book, surrounded by several emaciated figures; *after Baccio Bandinelli*; the same subject, with variations, was engraved by *Agostino Veneziano.* A Bacchanal subject, represented by children; *after Giulio Romano.* The Rape of Helen; *after Raffaelle.* Venus quitting Juno and Ceres; *do.* Two plates, the Interview between Scipio and Hannibal, and the Victory of Scipio; *after Giulio Romano.* The Triumph of Galatea; *after Raffaelle*; engraved also by *M. Antonio.* The Assembly of the Gods; *do.* Venus on the water, seated on a shell; *do.* Venus seated under a tree, taking a thorn from her foot, called *The Venus with the Rabbit.* Polyphemus pursuing Galatea; *do.* Galatea seated on a shell, flying from Polyphemus; *do.* Jupiter and Antiope; without the name of the painter. The Laocoon, after the antique statue; to this plate he has affixed his name nearly at length, MRCUS RAVENAS.

RAVESTEYN, HUBERT VAN, a Dutch painter of low subjects, born at Dort in 1647. He possessed uncommon abilities, and it is regretted that he had not devoted his pencil to more worthy objects. His pictures generally represent the interiors of slaughter houses, butcher's shops, and the inside of the miserable habitations of boors and villagers, with sheep penned up, slaughtering times, boys blowing up bladders, entrails of hogs, baskets of sausages, interiors of kitchens, with maids scouring utensils, &c. These disgusting subjects he treated with great address. His design is correct, his pencil neat and clear, his coloring transparent, his chiaro-scuro admirable, and every object is designed and touched with infinite nature and effect. His pictures, in point of color, light, and shadow, are compared to the admirable productions of Albert Cuyp. Immerzeel, differing from all others, says he was born in 1640. The time of his death is not known.

RAVESTEYN, JOHN VAN, an eminent Dutch portrait painter, born at the Hague about 1580. It is not known by whom he was instructed, but his works evince extraordinary merit, and he is said not to have been surpassed in his particular branch by any of his cotemporaries, with the exception of Rubens and Vandyck. He had an excellent knowledge of the palette, his lights and shadows are judiciously distributed, his coloring is clear and harmonious, and his touch broad and firm. Besides the portraits of many distinguished persons, which may be found in the private collections of Holland, he painted several large pictures, among which is a grand picture fifteen feet long, with twenty-six portraits of life-size, in the Banqueting Hall at the Hague, representing the magistrates of that city seated at a table. The figures are correctly drawn, admirably grouped, and the accessories are painted with great spirit and effect; the heads are full of dignity and expression, and the whole exhibits an appearance of truth and nature seldom surpassed; it is dated 1618. Another fine picture by him is in the Hall of the Society of Archers at the Hague, representing the officers and principal members of the Society. In the Town House is another, of the Burgomasters, in their robes of office, dated 1636. The time of his birth and death is variously stated. Houbraken says he was born in 1580, and died in 1649; Immerzeel, in 1572, and died in 1657. He was at the head of the forty-eight artists who, in 1655, presented a petition to be separated as a society from the company of house painters, at the Hague.

RAVESTEYN, ARNOLD VAN, was the son of John van R., born at the Hague in 1615. He was instructed in the art by his father, and though he did not equal him, he was accounted one of the greatest portrait painters of his time. He was chosen president of the Society of Artists at the Hague in 1661, and filled that office with honor till his death, in 1676.

RAVESTEYN, NICHOLAS VAN, a Flemish painter, born at Bommel in 1661. He was the son of Henry van Ravesteyn, a painter little known, who intended him for one of the learned professions, and gave him a classical education, but died before he had completed his course of study. Ravesteyn then turned his attention to painting, and having already learned the rudiments of design from his father, he went to the Hague, and first studied under Wm. Doudyns; but his genius leading him to portrait painting, he became the disciple of J. de Baan, who was then in high repute. He afterwards settled in his native place, where he found abundant employment. In 1694, he was sent for to the court of Kuilenberg to paint the princess of Waldeck, after her death. As no artist had been able to paint a satisfactory likeness of her while living, Ravesteyn had little hopes of accomplishing it after her death; yet he succeeded to the satisfaction of the court, and returned home liberally rewarded with his reputation greatly increased. Although his chief excellence lay in portraits, he painted history with reputation. For the most part, he painted his portraits *historically*, designed his figures in good taste, and obtained a striking likeness. He had a free and easy manner of handling, and his coloring was clear and harmonious. He enjoyed abundant patronage, and is said to have exercised his pencil to the last year of his long life, without showing any traces of the weakness or infirmities of old age. He died in 1750, aged 89 years.

RAVI, JEAN, a French architect and sculptor, who was employed at Paris, according to Felibien, upon the church of Notre Dame, for twenty-six years, and completed it in 1351. It is a magnificent Gothic edifice, the largest in France, being four hundred and thirteen feet long, one hundred and fifty-six wide, and one hundred and ninety-eight high. The nave is eighty-nine feet wide, of a beautiful elevation, well lighted, and regularly planned. The transept is of the same width, and equally beautiful with the nave, flanked by double aisles, leading to thirty-five chapels, magnificently decorated. The choir and sanctuary correspond in style to the rest. Above the double aisles are spacious and high galleries or porches, vaulted with stone. The façade is flanked by two square towers, two hundred and four feet high. The whole edifice is of stone, and is adorned with an infinite variety of beautiful specimens in painting and sculpture.

RAWLINS, J., an English engraver of little note, who flourished about 1760. He engraved a few portraits and frontispieces for the booksellers.

RAVIGLIONE, DI CASALE, a Piedmontese painter who, according to Orlandi, was a native of Casalmonferrato, and flourished in the first half of the 17th century. He executed some works for the churches in his native city and elsewhere. Lanzi considers him, after Niccolo Musso, the ablest artist Monferrato has produced, although his name, his age, and his school are unknown.

RAVIGNANO, MARCO. See MARCO DA RAVENNA.

RAYMOND, JEAN, a French engraver, born at Paris about 1695. Little is known of him. He engraved some of the plates for the Crozat collection, among which are the Holy Family, *after Raffaelle;* the Entombment, *after Taddeo Zuccaro;* and the Miracle of the Manna, *after Romanelli.* His prints are executed with the graver, in a bold, clear style, and his drawing is tolerably correct.

RAYMOND, JEAN ARNAUD, a French architect, born at Toulouse in 1742. He early manifested a strong inclination for art, and was sent to Paris at the expense of the liberal M. de Puymaurin. He studied successively under Blondel, Hilaire, and Leroi. In 1767 he gained the grand prize, and immediately went with the royal pension to Rome, where he was principally occupied in studying and copying the antique and the works of Palladio. He studied the writings of that master with great assiduity, carefully examined and designed his edifices at Venice, Padua, and Vicenza, and wrote many learned notices upon them. On returning to France in 1775, he intended to edit the works of Palladio, but was anticipated by Cameron, who published an edition from the designs of Lord Burlington. Raymond was employed for three years, soon after his return to France, at Montpellier, where he directed several public works. He also made many admirable designs, at the request of Joubert, for embellishing Nismes, and other cities of Languedoc, which were approved, but were never executed. In 1784, Raymond was chosen a Royal Academician, and afterwards a member of the French Institute, and the governmental Conseil des Batiments. He died in 1811.

RAZALI, SEBASTIANO, a Bolognese painter who, according to Malvasia, was a pupil of the Caracci, and followed their manner. Little is known of him or his works. Lanzi commends his picture of St. Benedict among the Thorns, in the church of S. Michele in Bosco at Bologna. He flourished in the first part of the 17th century.

RAZZI, CAV. GIOVANNI ANTONIO, called IL SODOMA. There is a good deal of dispute as to the place and time of birth, and the merits of this artist, which we cannot enter into further than to say that, according to the best authorities, he was born at Vercelli, in the Piedmontese, in 1479, not at Vergelle, a Sienese village, though he afterwards settled at Siena, and became naturalized. He studied under Giacomo dalle Fonte, but he formed his style on that of Leonardo da Vinci. Among his earliest performances were a series of pictures at Monte Oliveto, representing the history of St. Benedetto, painted about 1502. He afterwards went to Rome, where his talent recommended him to the notice of Julius II., who employed him in the Vatican, where he executed several works which were subsequently defaced to make way for the frescos of Raffaelle, though the latter spared the grotesques. He was also employed by Agostino Chigi to decorate his palace, now the Farnesina, with frescos from the life of Alexander the Great, of which the Nuptials of Roxana, and the Suppliant Family of Darius, are the most esteemed. Lanzi says of these works, "they do not exhibit the facility, grace, and the dignified heads that characterize the style of Vinci; but they show much of his chiaro-scuro, which was then much followed by the Lombards, and his perspective is conspicuous; they also abounded in gay images, little cupids with their arrows, and a pomp that is captivating."

The best works of Razzi are at Siena, the fruit of his studies at Rome, executed in the full maturity of his powers. The most celebrated of these are the Adoration of the Magi, in the church of S. Agostino, executed wholly in the style of da Vinci; the Flagellation of Christ, at the Franciscans, preferred by many connoisseurs to the figures of Michael Angelo; and the Swoon of St. Catherine of Siena, in the chapel of that saint, in the church of S. Domenico, in which he emulated the manner of Raffaelle; and St. Sebastian, now in the Ducal gallery, supposed to have been copied from an antique Torso.

Razzi, when advanced in life, by some misfortune which happened to him at Siena, was reduced to poverty; he then sought employment at Pisa, at Volterra, and at Lucca. The works he painted at these places, were frequently executed in a hurried manner, without preparatory study, and have greatly tended to injure his reputation. Vasari, the great enemy of his fame, generally styles him Mattaccio (*buffoon*), ascribing to chance or fortune whatever he performed well, as if his usual style had been that of a bad painter, and judging him from his last works, when misfortune, necessity, and advanced age oppressed him; yet he was so forgetful as incidentally to commend his works in high terms on several occasions. Thus in his life of Mecherino, he says that "Razzi possessed the grand principles of design," and in another passage he praises the brilliant coloring he brought with him out of Lombardy, and before noticing the works of his old age, often pronounced the others *beautiful*, and sometimes, *most beautiful*, and *wonderful* performances. It is sufficient to observe that public opinion at Siena, ranks him as one of the ablest artists of that city, and that his best works have received the unqualified approbation of both excellent writers and critics. Annibale Caracci, in passing through Siena, observed, "Razzi appears a very eminent master, of the greatest taste, and few such pictures are to be seen;" and Peruzzi affirmed of his St. Catherine, that "he had never seen a swoon so naturally represented." Lanzi says that, "the airs and various expressions of his heads are not borrowed from any artist, and on this account, he seems to have extorted the applause even of Vasari, and that he selected his models from among the Sienese, whose heads possess great innate gaiety, openness, and spirit." He died in 1554.

READ, Catherine, an English paintress, who gained considerable reputation for her portraits, both in oil and crayons. Among her best performances are mentioned the portrait of Queen Charlotte, and Mrs. Macaulay, the historian. Several of her paintings have been engraved in mezzotinto. She died at an advanced age about 1786.

READ, Richard, an English mezzotinto engraver of little note, who flourished about 1780, and executed a few portraits and other subjects.

REALFONSO, Tommaso, a Neapolitan painter, who, according to Dominici, was the most celebrated scholar of Andrea Belvidere. He excelled in painting still life, as dead game, fish, utensils, and similar subjects; also fruit, flowers, all kinds of confectionery and eatables, all which he painted with great truth and spirit. He flourished in the latter part of the 17th century.

RECCHI, Giovanni Paolo, and Gio. Battista, two brothers, painters of Como, who flourished about the middle of the 16th century, and perhaps later. They studied under Morazzone, whose manner they adopted. They acquired considerable reputation, and were employed conjointly in decorating with frescos the churches of their native city, at Varese, and other places in the vicinity. Gio. Battista was the most distinguished, became eminent beyond the state, and was much employed at the court of Turin; there are some of his works in the church of S. Carlo in the latter city, placed near those of his master, which do not suffer by the proximity. Lanzi says, "his style is solid and strong, his coloring forcible, and in his skill of foreshortening on ceilings, he yields to few artists of his time. Pasta, in his Guide to Bergamo, has deservedly praised him on this score when speaking of his Santa Grata, seen rising into heaven, a work, he observes, that is admirable and delightful." There was another Gio. Battista R., nephew of the preceding, who assisted him in some of the chambers of the Veneria at Turin. The elder Gio. Battista R., instructed several pupils in the art, some of whom acquired distinction.

RECCO, Cav. Giuseppe, a Neapolitan painter, born, according to Dominici, in 1634. He studied under Aniello Falcone, and became one of the most celebrated painters in Italy, of hunting, fowling, and fishing pieces, dead game, and similar subjects. His pictures are found in the best collections in Naples and other Italian cities, where they are admired for their excellence of composition, spirit of execution, and rich coloring of the Lombard school. Recco was invited to the court of Madrid, where he resided many years, whilst Luca Giordano was there. He died at Naples in 1695.

RECHBERGER, Franz, an eminent German landscape painter, designer, and etcher, born at Vienna in 1771. He studied under F. Brandt, with Martin von Molitor for a fellow student; the two young artists contracted an intimate friendship, and afterwards practised in conjunction. Rechberger is better known by his numerous designs and etchings, than by his paintings, though the latter are said to be executed in a pleasing and masterly manner. His etchings are so beautifully designed and spiritedly executed, that they rank with the choicest of modern times. They generally represent wild, romantic scenery, somewhat in the style of Jacob Ruysdael, or Albert van Everdingen. He also etched a number of plates of landscapes from drawings or paintings by Dietricy. Nagler mentions seventy-six plates by him, generally marked F. R., which has occasioned them sometimes to be attributed to Frederick Rehberg, a cotemporary artist, who used the same initials; but the works of the latter are historical, and belong rather to the Roman school. Rechberger was appointed keeper of the prints and drawings of the Archduke Charles at Vienna, and also had the care of the fine collection of prints formerly belonging to Count Fries. He was living in 1842.

RECLAM, Frederick, a German painter and engraver, was born at Magdeburg in 1734. After learning the rudiments of art in his native city, he went to Paris, and studied under J. B. Pierre. In 1755 he went to Italy, and resided several years at Rome, after which he returned to his own country, settled at Berlin, and painted landscapes and portraits with considerable success. He also executed a number of etchings from his own designs and those of other masters; of which Nagler enumerates twenty-nine. He died in 1774.

REDER, CHRISTIAN. There is some discrepancy among writers about the period of the birth and death of this painter, but the best authorities say he was born in Saxony in 1656, and died in 1729. According to Pascoli, he went to Rome in 1686, the year of the capture of Buda, and acquired considerable reputation for his representations of battles between the Christians and the Ottomans. Although his pictures were well composed and spiritedly touched, he executed so many of them, with little variation, that they soon depreciated in value. The best, in the opinion of Pascoli, was a grand picture in the gallery de' Minimi; and he left many in the palaces of the nobility. Lanzi says he was skilful in landscape and humorous subjects, in which he was assisted by Peter van Bloemen. He afterwards visited Venice, Hamburg, Amsterdam, and London, leaving specimens of his ability in each of those cities. Füessli calls his name *Reuter*. He is also called by the Italians *M. Leandro Sassone*.

REDI, TOMMASO, a Florentine painter, born in 1665. After studying under Domenico Gabbiani in his native city, he went to Rome and entered the Florentine Academy, established by the Grand Duke Cosimo III., then under the direction of Carlo Maratti and Ciro Ferri. He prosecuted his studies at Rome with ardor, and success, and afterwards visited the most celebrated schools for the purpose of studying and copying the works of the great masters. On returning to Florence, he was commissioned by the Grand Duke to paint several works for the Pitti palace, and soon obtained abundant employment for the churches, convents, and public edifices of Florence, as well as for the palaces of the nobility. He painted subjects from ancient mythology and sacred and profane history. He was also an excellent portrait painter. Redi designed with elegance and correctness, and his coloring partakes much of the sweetness of Carlo Maratti. He was well grounded in his profession, with a ready invention and great facility of hand. Peter the Great having seen some of his works, and being desirous of establishing an academy of the Fine Arts at Moscow, made very liberal offers to Redi to undertake the direction of it, but his engagements at Florence prevented his accepting the proposal. He died at Florence in 1726.

REDMOND, THOMAS, an English miniature painter, who died in 1785. He was the son of a clergyman, and a native of Brecknock, in Wales. He was almost entirely a self-made artist. He resided chiefly at Bath, and practised with considerable success.

REDOUT, PETER JOSEPH, an eminent Belgian flower painter, called by the French, the *Raffaelle des Fleurs*, was born in the province of Brabant, at St. Hubert, near Liege. After acquiring a knowledge of the elements of design, he visited various cities in the Low Countries for improvement. Meeting with the surpassing flower-pieces of John van Huysum, he greatly desired to devote himself to that branch of the art, and finally went to Paris, where he entered the studio of his elder brother Anthony, a painter of decorations. He shortly after commenced designing flowers, and entirely relinquished the other branches of the art. His merit soon became evident, and he was much encouraged by l'Heritier, who employed him to make a number of designs for the *Sertum Anglicum*, and by van Spaendonck, who commissioned him to paint the pictures of twenty rare plants, which he had engaged to furnish yearly for the collection of drawings on vellum, commenced in 1650, by Gaston, duke of Orleans, and continued to the present time by the *Musée d'Histoire Naturelle*. In 1792, Redout was appointed designer to the Royal Academy of Sciences, and afterwards a professor of the Institute, at its formation. In 1805 he was appointed flower painter to the Empress Josephine. In 1822 he succeeded to the office of van Spaendonck in the Royal Gardens. He was much employed in making designs for many pictorial works, such as the *Flora Atlantica*, of Desfontaines; and the *Jardin de Malmaison*, of Ventenat. He gained his principal reputation, however, by his *Liliacées*, and his *Roses*. The first were published with a descriptive text by Delaunay, from 1802 to 1816, in eighty numbers, embracing 480 plates of various specimens of the lily. The *Roses* were published from 1817 to 1824, in thirty numbers, embracing 180 plates. From 1827 to 1833, he published thirty-six numbers of selections of the most beautiful flowers and fruits; in 1835 and the following years twelve numbers of similar selections of flowers. In 1836, he published in fifteen numbers his *Choix de soixante Roses dediées a la reine des Belges*.

The many honors conferred upon Redout sufficiently evince his excellence. He was the instructor of many pupils, among whom were Maria Antoinette, Josephine, Hortense, Maria Louisa, the Duchess de Berri, the Queen of the French, Madame Adelaide, Madame Panckoucke, Mlle. Arson, Madame Chantereine, and others. Redout died in 1840. A number of his designs were published after his death, under the title of *Bouquet Royal*. The Belgian government erected a monumental fountain at St. Hubert, in 1846, in memory of this distinguished artist, surmounted by his bust.

REDOUT, HENRY JOSEPH, a Belgian painter, the younger brother of the preceding, was born in 1766. He practised flower painting with his brother for several years, but afterwards devoted his talents to animal painting. He accompanied the expedition to Egypt, and was subsequently appointed painter to the Museum of Natural History. His designs are distinguished for their fidelity, and have been the means of enriching the science of Zoology.

REGGIO, LUCA DA. See FERRARI.

REGILLO, DA PORDENONE. See LICINIO.

AL o REGNARD, VALERIAN, a French engraver, of whom little is known. He studied under Philip Thomassin at Rome, where he passed most of his life. He engraved some plates after various Italian masters, and some of the antique statues in the Giustiniani gallery. He was living in 1650.

REGNAULDIN, THOMAS, a French sculptor

born at Moulins in 1627. He studied under François Anguier, and gained considerable distinction in the reign of Louis XIV., who sent him to Rome, with a pension of one thousand crowns. His principal sculptures are those of Autumn, Faustina, and the three Nymphs in the Baths of Apollo, after the designs of Lebrun. In 1657 he was chosen a member of the academy, and presented his statue of St. John the Baptist, as his reception piece. In 1704 he made a marble statue of St. Catherine, for the church of that saint at Paris. According to French authority, his reputation seems to have surpassed his merit. He died in 1706.

REGNAULT, Jean Baptiste, an eminent French painter, born at Paris in 1754. When very young he manifested a strong inclination for art. He was taken by his parents to America, and afterwards entered the marine service without their knowledge, where he remained many years as a cabin boy; but during his wanderings, he constantly practised the art of design. At length, his mother, having lost her husband and her other children, returned to France, and used every endeavor to discover her long lost son. She was finally successful, and the young sailor artist was restored to his mother's arms. He soon devoted his attention to design, and attracted the notice of the painter Baudin, who took him to Rome. After studying in that city for some time with the greatest assiduity, he returned to Paris, and gained the grand prize in painting, for his splendid picture of Diogenes and Alexander. He then revisited Rome, with the royal pension, and passed his time in assiduous studies, until his second return to Paris. His picture of the Baptism of Christ, painted about this period, is highly praised for its fine coloring and masterly execution. In 1783, he was chosen an Academician, for his picture of the Education of Achilles. This work is treated in an elevated style, and has been engraved by Berwick. Regnault executed a large number of historical, poetical, and allegorical subjects, among which the most excellent, besides those already mentioned, are the Deluge, Jupiter carrying away Io, and the Descent from the Cross. The latter work is in the style of the Caracci, and is said to be not inferior to the same subject by Poussin. Regnault was a chevalier of the Order of St. Michael and of the Legion of Honor; he was also appointed Professor of Painting. He died at Paris in 1831. He left numerous studies, designs, and finished sketches illustrative of the works of Ovid and other poets.

REGNE, M., a French engraver, who flourished about 1760. Little is known of him. He engraved a few prints, among which are a set of plates of animals, neatly executed.

WR REICH, Wendel, a German engraver and bookseller, who flourished at Strasburg in 1540. He executed some wooden Cuts, bearing the above monogram. Prof. Christ says he lived at Lyons about 1515, where he engraved and published several cuts marked as above.

REINAGLE, Philip, an English painter, born about 1750. He studied under Allan Ramsay, and painted portraits for a while, but afterwards turned his attention to animals, and panoramic views, with some success. His pictures of huntings, with spaniels, shaggy ponies, and dead game, were the best of the day in England. He also copied the works of Paul Potter, Karel du Jardin, Berghem, and Adrian vander Velde, with considerable success. He assisted Barker in his panoramas of Rome, Naples, Florence, Gibraltar, Paris and Algesiras Bay. He is best known by the "Sportsman's Cabinet," engraved by John Scott, representing all the dogs used in field sports, drawn from life. He was elected a member of the Royal Academy in 1812, and died at London in 1834.

REINAGLE, Richard Ramsay, was the son and scholar of the preceding. His life has not yet been written, but he acquired distinction as a painter of animals, and English sporting scenes.

REINAGLE, George Philip, was the son of Richard Ramsay R., born about 1800. He studied with his father, and early manifested great tal ents for marine painting. After copying pictures by the best Dutch marine painters, he accompanied the expedition to Navarino, for the express purpose of giving a representation of the expected action, which he did with great applause. He died in 1833, in the flower of life.

REINER, Wenceslaus Laurent, a German painter, born at Prague in 1686. After learning the rudiments of design from his father, a sculptor of little note, he entered the school of Peter Brandel. Aided by his instructions, with a diligent study of nature and the works of the best masters, he became an accomplished and distinguished artist. He was a universal painter, and wrought both in oil and fresco. He painted history, landscapes, animals, and battle pieces with great credit, and executed several works for the churches and convents at Vienna, Breslau, and in other places. His best works are his landscapes with cattle, and battle-pieces, executed in a style resembling that of Peter van Bloemen. His pictures are well designed and colored, his figures and animals correctly drawn, and touched with great freedom and spirit. His works are chiefly confined to his own country, and are to be found in the best collections. There were several of his choicest works in the gallery of Augustus, King of Poland, and others in the collection of the late Count Bruhl. He died in 1743.

REINOSO, Don Antonio Garcia, a Spanish painter and architect, born at Cabra, in Andalusia, about 1623. He studied under Sebastiano Martinez, and executed a number of works in the churches—distinguished less for taste than facility of execution,—among which was a large painting in the vault of a chapel in the church of the Capuchins at Andujar, representing the Holy Trinity, with a number of the patriarchs, and below, St. Michael and St. George. At Linares, he painted a picture of Susanna at the Bath, in which the water was represented so truthfully as almost to produce illusion. As an architect, Reinoso erected various edifices, particularly at Andujar and Martos. He died at Cordova in 1677.

REINSPERGER, John Christopher, a German painter and engraver, born at Nuremberg in 1711, and died in 1780. He studied under Liotard, and painted portraits, some of which he engraved nearly as large as life, in a coarse, heavy, tasteless style. He practised some years at Vienna. Among his prints are the portraits of the

Emperor Joseph II., the Archduke Leopold, and the Empress Dowager, Elizabeth Christiana.

REITER, REYTER, or REUTER, BARTHOLOMEW, a German painter and engraver, who flourished at Munich in the first part of the 17th century. He was a scholar of Hans Ostendorfer the Younger. It is said, traditionally, that he was one of the best painters of Munich in his time, and instructed many pupils. None of his pictures are mentioned, and not a single name of his pupils is recorded. Nagler gives the following list of his prints, variously signed, *Reiter*, *Reitter*, *Reyter*, *Reytter*, *Reuter*, and with his initials B. R., or B. R. and F. for *fecit*.

1. Christ holding the Globe in his right hand. 2. Christ seated, crowned with Thorns; *Bartlme Reitter—Pictor inv. Monachy* 1615. 3. Christ carrying his Cross, group of half-length figures; *Georg Beham inv. Monachii. Bart. Reitter fec.* 1610. 4. Christ exposed to the People; inscribed *Ecce Homo, Bart. Reitter pictor figur. Monachy* 1612 *fec.* 5. The Holy Family, with St. Francis or St. Jerome, half-figures, a copy *after Palma*, with both monograms. 6. St. Jerome sitting in a Cavern, half-figure, the lion on the left; signed *Bart. Reytter pictor inv. et excud.* There is an impression signed *Bartholome Reuter*. 7. A Nymph sitting on the lap of a Satyr, Cupid at their feet; *Bart. Reiter, fec. Monachy* 1610. 7. Venus holding a Mirror, and seated with Cupid under a Tree, half-figures; *Georg Beham inv. B. Reyter fec.* 1610. 9. Neptune on a Sea-Horse, holding his Trident; *Georg Beham inv. Monachy*, with *Reiter's mark*, and the date 1610. 10. A Child seated on a Skull and blowing Bubbles; *B. R. F. Monachi Zimmerman Excud.* 11—18. Eight prints, a series of naked Children in different positions; marked B. R.

REITZ, E., a Swedish engraver, who flourished at Stockholm about 1700, and engraved some plates of coins and architecture, for a work entitled *Suecia Antiqua et Hodierna*.

REM, MATTHEW, a German engraver, who flourished about 1635. According to Prof. Christ, he engraved the plates for a work entitled *L'Architecture de Furtenbach*. He usually marked his plates with the initials of his name, M. R.

REMBRANDT, VAN RHYN, PAUL, was one of the most eminent painters and engravers of the Dutch school. He was the son of a miller, and was born in 1606, at a small village on the banks of the Rhine, between Leyderdorp and Leyden, whence he was called Rembrandt van Rhyn, though his family name was Gerretz. It is said that his father, being in easy circumstances, intended him for one of the learned professions, but was induced by Rembrandt's passion for the art to allow him to follow his inclination. He entered the school of Jacob van Zwaanenberg at Amsterdam, where he continued three years, and made such surprising progress as astonished his instructor. Having learned from Zwaanenberg all he was capable of imparting, he next studied about six months with Peter Lastmann, and afterwards for a short time with Jacob Pinas, from whom it is said he acquired that taste for strong contrasts of light and shadow, for which his works are so remarkable. He was, however, more indebted for his best improvement to the vivacity of his own genius, and an attentive study of nature, than to any information he derived from his instructors. On returning home, he fitted up an attic room with a skylight, in his father's mill, for his studio, where he probably pursued his labors for several years, as he did not remove to Amsterdam till 1630. Here he studied the grotesque figure of the Dutch boor, or the rotund contour of the bar-maid of an alehouse, with as much precision as the great artists of Italy have imitated the Apollo Belvidere, or the Medicean Venus. He was exceedingly ignorant, and it is said that he could scarcely read. He was of a wayward and eccentric disposition, and sought for recreation among the lowest orders of the people, in the amusements of the alehouse, contracting habits which continued through life; even when in prosperous circumstances, he manifested no disposition to associate with more refined and intellectual society. It will readily be perceived that his habits, disposition, and studies could not conduct him to the noble conceptions of Raffaelle, but rather to an exact imitation of the lowest order of nature, with which he delighted to be surrounded. The life of Rembrandt is much involved in fable, and in order to form a just estimate of his powers, it is necessary to take these things into consideration. It is said by some writers, that, had he studied the antique, he would have reached the very perfection of the art, but Nieuwenhuys, in his review of the Lives and Works of the most eminent painters of the Dutch and Flemish schools, in Smith's Catalogue raisonné, vol. xii. and supplement, says that he was by no means deficient on that point. "For it is known that he purchased, at a high price, casts from the antique marbles, paintings, drawings, and engravings by the most excellent Italian masters, to assist him in his studies, and which are mentioned in the inventory of his goods when seized for debt." He then goes on to give a list of the works so seized. Be this as it may, he certainly never derived any advantage from them. He had collected a great variety of old armor, sabres, flags, and fantastical vestments, ironically terming them his antiques, and frequently introducing them into his pictures.

Rembrandt had already brought both the arts of painting and engraving to very great perfection (in his own way), when a slight incident led him to fame and fortune. He was induced by a friend to take one of his choicest pictures to a picture-dealer at the Hague, who, being charmed with the performance, instantly gave him a hundred florins for it, and treated him with great respect. This occurrence served to convince the public of his merit, and contributed to make the artist sensible of his own abilities. In 1630 he went to Amsterdam, where he married a handsome peasant girl, (frequently copied in his works), and settled there for life. His paintings were soon in extraordinary demand, and his fame spread far and wide; pupils flocked to his studio, and he received for the instruction of each a hundred florins a year. He was so excessively avaricious that he soon abandoned his former careful and finished style, for a rapid execution; also frequently retouched the pictures of his best pupils, and sold them as his own. His deceits in dating several of his etchings at Venice, to make them more saleable, led some of his biographers to believe that he visited Italy, and resided at Venice in 1635 and 1636; but it has been satisfactorily proved that he never left Holland, though he constantly threatened to do so, in order to increase the sale of his works. As early as 1628, he applied himself zealously to etching, and soon acquired great perfection in the art. His etchings were esteemed as highly as his paintings, and he had recourse to several artifices to raise their price and increase their sales. For example, he sold impressions from the unfinished plates, then finished them, and after having used them, made some slight alterations, and thus sold the same works three or four times; producing what connoisseurs term *variations* in prints. By these practices, and his parsimonious manner of living, Rembrandt amassed a large fortune.

Though Rembrandt acquired a distinguished reputation for his historical works, he is more deserving of admiration as a painter of portraits. He was a perfect master of all that relates to coloring, distribution of light and shade, and management of the pencil; but he has no claims to the other great requisites of the true artist—correct taste, composition, grouping, dignified expression, design, perspective, and drapery. He drew, indeed, from the naked models, for which he used his scholars; but what sort of models they were, his works plainly show. In his composition and grouping, he followed common nature alone, and his momentary humor, which was often whimsical; in design he followed his model. He generally concealed the naked parts as much as possible, rarely allowing the hands or feet to be seen, because he was unable to draw them correctly, always making them too large or too small. In those works where he could not avoid naked figures, as in the Descent from the Cross, the Entombment, and several representations of Bathsheba in the Bath, his figures are entirely destitute of proportion, and it is only the magic tones and touch of his pencil that prevents these pictures from exciting disgust in every beholder of taste. Furthermore, he was the most outrageous violator of the proprieties of costume in the whole history of art, often introducing the Dutch dress of his time into subjects from ancient history. His drapery is fantastical, almost entirely destitute of taste, and sometimes ridiculous. His heads possess expression and character, but they have no dignity; his Christ is a man of the lowest class of the people, and his Marys are common women. On the other hand, the seductive simplicity of his arrangements, the glowing beauty of his coloring, the magic charm of his chiaro-scuro, almost conceal his gross imperfections; and it was these excellencies alone that gained him his great reputation, and even at the present day uphold the estimation of his works, which command such enormous prices. He was undoubtedly the greatest master of chiaroscuro that the world has ever produced, and one of the greatest colorists; in the harmony of his tones no other painter, with perhaps the exception of Titian, has equalled him. Although his portraits are without dignity or embellishment, they exhibit so much nature and animation, such truth and force of coloring, that it is allowed he has never been surpassed in this particular branch. Many of his heads are finished so minutely as to show, on a close inspection, every imperfection in the original, as moles, wrinkles, and even the hairs of the beard; yet, at a proper distance, the whole has such an astonishing relief and effect that every portrait seems ready to start from the canvass. Thus a picture of his house-maid, placed at a window of his dwelling, is said to have deceived the passers-by for several days, who wondered that she was always looking out of the window.

Rembrandt had two methods of handling. In the early part of his life, until some time after he settled at Amsterdam, he finished his pictures almost as highly as Gerard Douw, but with a more spirited pencil and a richer tone of color; such are his Esther before Ahasuerus, the Woman taken in Adultery, St. Peter in the Boat, St. John preachin the Wilderness, and others. He afterwards adopted a greater breadth of light and shadow, and a more commanding facility of execution; in his lights, he sometimes laid on his colors so unsparingly that they project far from the canvass, and thereby much increase the effect at a distance; it is said that he laid on his color with his stick, palette knife, or finger, according as they were capable of producing the desired effect. The invention of Rembrandt was very fertile, his imagination lively and active, and he designed and wrought with great facility. He always preferred a light from above, and had a small aperture made in the roof of his studio, by which alone his model was lighted. To this uniform method is ascribed the sameness in his coloring, which is always similar and somewhat monotonous. His paintings are numerous, and are dispersed in various public and private collections of Europe; and when they are offered for sale they command enormous prices. There are eight of his pictures in the English National Gallery; one of these, the Woman taken in Adultery, formerly in the Orleans collection, sold for £5000. In Smith's Catalogue raisonné is a description of six hundred and forty pictures by him, the public and private galleries and collections in which they were located at the time of the publication of the work, together with a copious list of his drawings and etchings, and much other interesting information. He left many studies, sketches, and drawings, executed in a charming style, which are now scarce and valuable.

Rembrandt holds a distinguished rank among the engravers of his country; he established a more important epoch in this art than any other master. He was indebted entirely to his own genius for the invention of a process which has thrown an indescribable charm over his plates. They are partly etched, frequently much assisted by the dry point, and occasionally, though rarely, finished with the graver; evincing the most extraordinary facility of hand, and displaying the most consummate knowledge of the effects of light and shadow. His free and playful point sports in picturesque disorder, producing the most surprising and enchanting effects, as if by accident; yet an examination will show that his motions are always regulated by a profound knowledge of the principles of light and shadow. His most admirable productions in both arts are his portraits, which are executed with unexampled expression and skill. For a full description of his numerous prints, the reader is referred to Bartsch's Peintre Graveur. The following is a list of his most esteemed and interesting prints. He died at Amsterdam in 1665, as is satisfactorily shown by Nieuwenhuys, though others say in 1674 and 1688

PORTRAITS OF REMBRANDT, BY HIMSELF.

Rembrandt with his mouth open. 1630. The Busts of Rembrandt and his Wife. 1636. A Bust of Rembrandt; highly finished. 1638. His Portrait, with a Crayon in his hand. His Portrait, in a Persian habit. 1654. There are no less than twenty-seven portraits of Rembrandt by himself.

SUBJECTS OF THE OLD TESTAMENT.

Adam and Eve in Paradise. 1638. Abraham sending away Hagar. 1637. Abraham and Isaac. 1645. Joseph relating his Dream. 1638. Jacob lamenting the Death of Joseph. Joseph and Potiphar's Wife. 1634. The Triumph of Mordecai. Tobit and the Angel. 1641.

SUBJECTS OF THE NEW TESTAMENT.

The Annunciation to the Shepherds. 1634. The Adoration of the Shepherds; there are three different impressions of this plate. The Circumcision; fine. The Presentation in the Temple. 1630. The Flight into Egypt. 1658. Another Flight into Egypt, in the manner of mezzotinto. The Flight into Egypt, in the style of Ælsheimer. The Holy Family. 1654. The little Tomb. The Tribute Money. Christ driving the Money-changers out of the Temple. Christ and the Samaritan Woman. The same subject, with the city of Samaria in the distance. 1634. The Resurrection of Lazarus. 1642. The great Resurrection of Lazarus; in the first impressions of this print, which are scarce, the figure running away affrighted is with his head uncovered; in the second he wears a cap. Christ healing the Sick; known by the name of *the Hundred Guilders print*. The Great Ecce Homo. 1636. The Descent from the Cross. 1633. Christ presented to the People. 1655. The Crucifixion. 1658. The Entombing of Christ. Christ with the Disciples at Emmaus. 1643. The Good Samaritan; in the first impressions of this plate the tail of the horse is white. St. Peter and St. John at the Gate of the Temple. The Baptism of the Eunuch. 1641. The Death of the Virgin. 1639.

DEVOUT SUBJECTS.

The Stoning of Stephen. 1635. St. Jerome sitting near the trunk of a Tree. 1654. The same, kneeling. 1634. The same, writing in a book. 1648. The same; an unfinished plate. St. Francis praying. 1657; very scarce.

VARIOUS SUBJECTS.

The Hour of Death. Youth surprised by Death. 1639. The Marriage of Jason and Creusa. 1648. The Star of the Kings. A Lion Hunt. Another Lion Hunt. The Blind Bagpiper. The Spanish Gipsy. The Rat-killer. 1632. The Goldsmith. The Pancake Woman. 1635. The Jewish Synagogue. 1648. The Corn-cutter. The Schoolmaster. 1641. The Mountebank. 1635. The Traveling Peasants. The Jew with the high cap. 1639. The Astrologer. The Philosopher. The Persian. 1632. The Skater.

BEGGARS.

Several small plates of Beggars, men and women; some of which are scarce. A group of Beggars at the door of a house. 1648.

ACADEMICAL SUBJECTS.

A Student drawing from the model, called the Statue of Pygmalion. The Bathers. 1631. The Woman before the Stove; there are four impressions of this plate. A Woman with her feet in the water.

LANDSCAPES.

The Bridge of the Burgomaster Six. 1643. A View of Amsterdam. The Sportsman. The three Trees. 1642. A Landscape, called the Milk Pails. The Coach Landscape. View of a Village near the high road, arched. 1650. Village with a square Tower, arched. 1650. A large Landscape, with a Cottage and Barn. 1641. The companion, a Village is seen in the distance. 1641. An arched Landscape, with Cattle. Do., with an Obelisk. Rembrandt's Father's Mill. 1641. The Goldweigher's Field. 1651. A Landscape, with a Cow drinking.

PORTRAITS OF MEN.

An old Man with a large beard. A Man with a Crucifix and a Chain. 1641. J. Antonides vander Linden, the Professor of Physic. Janus Silvius, Minister of Amsterdam. A young Man meditating. 1637. Manasseh Ben Israel. 1636. Doctor Faustus. Renier Hansloo, Minister of the Anabaptists. 1641. Clement de Jonge, Printseller. 1651. Abraham France. The old Haaring. The young Haaring. 1655. John Lutma, Goldsmith. 1656. John Asselyn, Painter. Ephraim Bonus, a Jewish Physician. Wtenbogardus; oval. 1635. John Cornelius Sylvius. The Banker, or Goldweigher. 1639. The little Coppenol, the Writing-master. The great Coppenol; there are impressions of this plate with the back-ground white, or unfinished, which are very scarce. The Advocate Tolling. The Burgomaster Six. 1647.

FANCY HEADS OF MEN.

Three Oriental Heads, inscribed *Rembrandt Venetiis* 1635. An old Man with a large beard. An old Man bald-headed. 1630. A young Man, half-length; in profile Bust of an old Man, with a square beard and a velvet cap 1637. The Turkish Slave. The Philosopher, with the hour-glass.

PORTRAITS OF MEN.

The great Jewish Bride. The little Jewish Bride. 1638 Two Portraits of old Women. A young Woman reading. 1634. An old Woman with a book. 1634. An old Woman in an Oriental dress. 1631. Rembrandt's Mother. 1631. Rembrandt's Wife. An old Woman sleeping. An old Woman with Spectacles.

REMSDYKE, a Dutch painter and engraver, of whom little is known. He visited England, and was much employed by Dr. William Hunter, in drawing and engraving subjects of natural history and anatomy. In conjunction with his son, he published a volume of plates in 1778, etched from various works in the British Museum.

REMSHARD, Charles, a German engraver, born at Augsburg, according to Zani, in 1678, and died in 1755. He executed a few plates, and copied some prints of other masters, generally marked with his initials, C. R.

RENANTO, J., an engraver of little note, mentioned by Strutt as the artist of a wooden cut of the Wise Men's Offering, indifferently executed.

RENARD, J., a French engraver, who flourished at Paris about 1710. He executed a part of the plates for the collection of views of the palace and gardens at Versailles.

RENARD, Simon de St. André, a French painter and engraver, born at Paris in 1614. He studied under Louis Bobrun, and painted portraits with considerable success. He is said also to have engraved quite a number of plates, the principal of which are a set of forty-six after the works of Charles le Brun in the gallery of Apollo in the Louvre. He died at Paris in 1677. Dumesnil doubts whether he engraved the plates after le Brun, as they were not published till 1695, eighteen years after his death; he supposes that they were executed by an engraver of the same name, probably his son.

RENARD, Jean Augustin, a French architect, born at Paris in 1744. He first studied painting under Hallé, but subsequently devoted himself to architecture, and acquired a knowledge of that art under the professor le Roi. In 1773 he gained the grand prize, and visited Rome with the royal pension. While busily occupied in designing the antique monuments of that city, he frequently encountered the Abbe de St. Non, who engaged him as a coadjutor in his famous *Voyage pittoresque d'Italie*, for which Renard made a number of excellent designs. On returning to Paris in 1784, he was appointed Inspector of the Royal Buildings, and the following year Inspector of the Quarries. In 1792 he was chosen a Royal Academician. Under the rule of Napoleon he held several appointments from government. Among his principal works were the grand stables erected by order of Louis XVI. at Sevres and St. Germain en Laie. His chief talent was in decoration, evinced in the Hotel d'Orsay the Hotel de Benevent at

Paris, and the chateau de Valençay. Renard died in 1807.

RENESSE, C. A., a Dutch designer and engraver, of whom nothing is known, except by a few etchings which bear so strong a resemblance to those of Rembrandt, that they might easily be mistaken for the works of that master, were it not for the signature. Bartsch has admitted one into his Catalogue (tom. ii. p. 104., No. 18.) Nagler describes six etchings by him; Brulliot says there are eleven known; and that only one bears his monogram, composed of the initials C. A. R., which he supposes to be the artist's portrait, as it represents a man seated at a table holding a burin in his hand; they are dated from 1649 to 1661; most of the prints are marked with his monogram, accompanied by *enesse*. The Dutch writers mention a J. Renesse, and an A. C. Renesse, who painted landscapes and sea-pieces. The following are the prints described by Nagler:

A half-length figure of a Man seated at table, with the monogram. A Clergyman seated at a table, with books, &c., signed *Renesse*. A half-length figure of a young Man. Full-face Portrait of a young Man, with long hair escaping from under his cap; signed *C. A. Renesse.* 1651. Christ bearing his Cross. A Village Fair, with Mountebanks and a crowd of People.

GR or GR RENI, Guido. This great painter was born at Bologna in 1575. He was the son of Samuel Reni, an eminent musician, who intended his son for the same profession, but manifesting an early and decided passion for art, he placed him in the school of Denis Calvart, where he made such rapid progress that his instructor, after slightly retouching his pictures, sold them for his own. Upon attaining his twentieth year, the great reputation of the Caracci induced him to enter their academy, and he was for some time the favorite disciple of Lodovico. He had already given proof of uncommon ability in several works for the Palazzo Bonfigliuoli, when some of the works of Michael Angelo Caravaggio were brought to Bologna. The novelty of the style, and the violent contrast of his light and shadow, astonished and pleased the generality of people, both at Rome and Bologna, and Guido was induced to adopt for a time, his singular principles. The applause bestowed upon the false style of Caravaggio, was extremely mortifying to the Caracci. Lodovico, familiar with the graces of Correggio, was disgusted with the praises bestowed on productions divested of dignity and grandeur, whose chief attractions were confined to a striking, but unnatural contrast of light and shade. In a conference held by the Caracci on this subject, at which Guido was present, Annibale proposed, as a means of bringing the new style into disrepute, to adopt one of an opposite character. "To the crudeness and violence of his tones," said he, "I would oppose tenderness and suavity. Instead of darkness and obscurity, I would represent my figures in the open day. Far from avoiding the difficulties of the art under the disguise of powerful shadows, I would court them by displaying every part in the clearest light. For the vulgar nature which Caravaggio is content to imitate, I would substitute the most select forms." The principles inculcated by Annibale, made a profound impression on the mind of Guido, and induced him to adapt a course which eventually conducted him to immortal distinction. He soon proceeded to put these principles into practice, but he had no sooner exhibited some specimens, than he encountered the violent animosity of his fellow students; they upbraided him with his insolence in aspiring to singularity, and adopting a new system, and even Lodovico, who had heretofore treated him with marked kindness, spoke of his new productions with harshness and severity, and at length dismissed him from his academy. From a pupil, he thus made Guido a rival, and in order to humble him, bestowed his favor on Guercino, an artist of quite another taste. By some critics Guido is esteemed the great genius of the Bolognese school, and the Caracci found sufficient reason for their jealousy, in his uncommon talents, his elevated and ambitious mind that aspired to something great and original from the outset of his career. When Guido painted his picture of St. Benedetto in the Desert, for the cloister of S. Michele in Bosco, where were several of the finest works of Lodovico, the public, astonished at the dignity and beauty of his picture, declared that the master had found a rival in his scholar. To the praise of that eminent artist, it is said that, notwithstanding his previous severe conduct, he expressed his approval of Guido's performance.

Guido had not yet visited Rome, though his works were well known and highly esteemed in that capital. He was invited thither by Giuseppino Cesari, with the intention of producing a rivalship between him and Caravaggio. Besides his desire of seeing and studying the works of Raffaelle and other great masters, he wished to visit Annibale Caracci, then engaged in decorating the Farnesian gallery, whose unkindness he had forgotten, and whose great talents he always highly respected. Albano, his friend and fellow pupil, accompanied him. His first production at Rome was the Martyrdom of St. Cecilia, for the church of that saint. Such was the infatuation that prevailed at Rome in favor of the works of Caravaggio, that when the Cardinal Borghese gave him the commission to paint his celebrated picture of the Crucifixion of St. Peter, he expressly stipulated that it should be painted in the manner of that master. Without departing from his engagement, Guido exhibited in the composition and design a correctness, dignity and grandeur, far superior to Caravaggio. He now rose rapidly in public estimation, and received such flattering encouragement as produced many enemies, the most furious of whom was Caravaggio, but the most dangerous was Annibale Caracci, who blamed Albano for bringing him to Rome, depreciated his talents, and put Domenichino in competition with him. Even Albano became his bitter enemy, when he found that Guido was esteemed his superior. But he triumphed over all his adversaries, and was chosen by Paul V. to decorate the private chapel of the palace of Monte Cavallo with histories of the Virgin, which materially added to his reputation. But being disgusted with the Cardinal Spinola, the Pope's treasurer, on account of the price he was to receive for his works, he returned to Bologna, where he executed his famous picture of the Murder of the Innocents for the church of S. Domenico, and the Repentance of St. Peter, for the Casa Sampieri, one of his most esteemed works. These distinguished performances increased his reputation. The Pope invited him back to Rome, received him in the most gracious manner, loaded him with favors, and commissioned him to decorate the chapel of S. Maria Maggiore. His most celebrated works in the palaces at Rome are, his fresco of the Aurora, in the Palazzo Rospigliosi, which has been admirably engraved by Raphael Morghen; his Fortune, in the Campidoglio; the Rape of Helen, in the Spada palace, and his Magdalen, in the Barberini collection. He was next invited to Naples to decorate the chapel of S. Gennaro. He had scarcely commenced operations when he was assailed by that desperate band, of which Bellisario and Spagnoletto were the head. Being warned that he must instantly quit Naples or prepare for death, he lost no time in returning to Bologna, where he resided during the remainder of his life, receiving so many commissions from all parts of Italy, that he was under the necessity of refusing many of them.

The following learned and admirable critique is extracted from Lanzi, somewhat condensed, but the sense strictly preserved. "The words of Annibale Caracci made a deep impression on the mind of Guido, nor was it long before he applied himself to the style thus indicated. Sweetness was his object; he sought it equally in design, in the touch of his pencil, and in his coloring; from that time he began to use white lead, a color avoided by Lodovico, and at the same time predicted the durability of his tints, such as they have proved. His fellow pupils were indignant at his presuming to depart from the method of the Caracci, and returning to the feeble, undecided manner of the past century. He did not pretend to be indifferent to their remarks or advice; he still preserved that strength of style so much aimed at by his school, while he softened it with more than its usual delicacy; and by degrees proceeding in the same direction, he attained in a few years, to that degree of delicacy he had proposed. For this reason, I have observed at Bologna, more than elsewhere, his first manner distinguished from his second, and it is made a question which of the two is preferable; nor do all agree with Malvasia, who pronounced the former the most pleasing, and the latter the most studied.

In these variations, however, he never lost sight of that exquisite ease which so much attracts us in his works. He was more particularly attentive to the correct form of beauty, especially in his youthful heads. Here, in the opinion of Mengs, he surpasses all others, and, according to Passeri's expression, 'he drew faces of Paradise.' Rome more richly abounds in them than Bologna itself. The Fortune in the Capitol, the Aurora in the Rospigliosi, the Helen in the Spada, the Herodias in the Corsini, the Magdalen in the Barberini, with other subjects in the possession of several princes, are regarded as the wonders of Guido's art. This power of beauty was, in the words of Albano, his most bitter and constant rival, 'the gift of nature,' though the whole was the result of his own intense study of natural beauty, of Raffaelle, and the ancient medals, cameos, and statues. He declared that the Medicean Venus, and the Niobe, were his most favorite models; and it is seldom we do not recognize in his paintings either Niobe herself, or one of her children, though diversified in a variety of manners, with such exquisite grace, as in no way to appear borrowed. In the same way did Guido derive advantage from Raffaelle, Correggio, Parmiggiano, and from his beloved Paul Veronese, from all whom he selected innumerable beauties, but with such happy freedom of hand, as to excite the envy of the Caracci. And in truth, this artist aimed less at copying beautiful countenances, than at forming for himself a certain general and abstract idea of beauty, as we know was done by the Greeks, and this he modulated and animated in his own style. When interrogated by one of his pupils, *in what part of heaven, in what mould*, he found these wondrous features, which he only drew, he pointed to the casts of the antiques, just alluded to, adding, 'you too may gather from such examples, beauties similar to those in my pictures, if your skill be equal to the task.' He took, moreover, for the model of one of his Magdalens, the vulgar head of a color grinder, but under his hand, every defect disappeared, each part became graceful, and the whole a miracle of art. Thus too, in his naked figures, he reduced them, whatever they were, to perfect form, more especially in the hands and feet, in which he is singular; and the same in his draperies, which he often drew from the prints of Albert Durer, enriching them, freed from their dryness, with those flowing folds, or that grandeur of disposition best adapted to the subject. To portraits themselves, while he preserved the forms and age of the originals, he gave a certain air of novelty and grace, such as we see in that of Sixtus V., in the Galli palace at Osimo, or that wonderful one of Cardinal Spada, in the possession of some of his descendants at Rome. There is no one action, position, or expression, at all injurious to his figures; the passion, grief, terror, sorrow, are all combined with the expression of beauty; he turns them every way as he lists; he changes them into every attitude, always equally pleasing, and every one equally entitled to the eulogy given him of displaying in every action and every step, the beauty which secretly animates it.

What most surprises us is the variety which he infuses into this beauty, resulting no less from the richness of his imagination, than from his studies. Still continuing to design in the academy up to the close of his career, he practised his invention how best to vary his idea of the beautiful, so as to free it from all monotony and satiety. He was fond of depicting his countenances with upraised looks, and used to say that he had an hundred different modes of thus representing them. He displayed equal varieties in his draperies, though invariably preferring to draw the folds ample, easy and natural, and with a clear meaning as to the origin, progress, and disposition, nor did he throw less diversity into the ornaments of his youthful heads, disposing the tresses, whether loose, bound, or left in artful confusion, always differently, and sometimes casting over them a veil, fillet, or turban, so as to produce some fresh display of grace; nor were his heads of old men inferior in this respect, displaying the inequality of the skin, the flow of the beard, with the hair turned up as we see on every side, and animating the features with a few bold, decided touches, and few lights, so as to give great effect at a distance, altogether with a surprising degree of nature, specimens of which are to be seen in the Pitti Palace, the Barberini and Albano galleries; and yet these are among the least rare of this artist's productions. He bestowed similar attention to varying his flesh colors."

These commendations will only apply to the best works of Guido. His exalted faculties were degraded by a fatal passion for gaming, which, though his gains were great, kept him in continual indigence. Towards the close of his life, to gratify his passion, and to supply his necessities, he sent into the world numerous works, executed with such negligence and haste, as to be totally unworthy of his reputation, and he even slightly retouched the pictures of his pupils and sold them as his own. This gave his enemies an opportunity to depreciate his merits, which they did not fail to employ, accusing him of being deficient in invention, incorrect in design and perspective, disproportionate in his figures, and mannered in his style, the latter accusation being strenuously insisted upon by the implacable Albano. Occasionally such were his necessities, that he sent his pictures to sale before their completion. Yet, says Lanzi, these pictures are not excluded from royal cabinets; that of Turin possesses one of Marsyas, a finely finished figure, before which is seen standing little more than the sketch of an Apollo. Therefore to form a fair estimate of his powers, we are to judge by his best works, such as the Crucifixion of St. Peter at Rome, the Miracle of the Manna at Ravenna, the Conception at Forli, the Murder of the Innocents, and St. Peter and St. Paul, at Bologna, the Purification at Modena, and the Assumption at Genoa, placed directly opposite the St. Ignatius of Rubens, by which contrast it does not suffer in the least, together with many other grand works at Rome, Bologna, and other places.

Some writers attribute to Guido two manners, and others three, at different periods; the first comprises those pictures which resemble the manner of the Caracci, and particularly that of Caravaggio, marked by deep shades, narrow and powerful lights and strong coloring; in short, an effort after great effect, distinguished his works at this period. The second manner is completely opposite to the first, and has already been fully described; the third commences soon after his return from Naples to Bologna, when he began to work more for profit than for fame. It is distinguished by a general carelessness in design and execution, with a greenish gray coloring, altogether mannered.

Guido is generally regarded as the most distinguished disciple of the school of the Caracci, with the exception of Domenichino, and some even give him the preference. The Italians say of him that "grace and beauty dwelt upon his pencil to animate his figures." The distinguishing characteristics of his style are elegance and grace, a singular facility of execution, a free but delicate pencil, an exquisite touch, and great suavity and harmony of coloring. He particularly excelled in tender, pathetic, and devout subjects, in which he could manifest the sweetness and delicacy of his thoughts. In one of his letters to a friend, he expressed a wish "that he had had the wings of an angel, to have ascended into paradise, and there to have beheld the forms of the beatified spirits, that he might have copied them into his pictures." He possessed an extraordinary faculty of being able to express grief, sadness or terror, without detriment to the beauty of his heads. His Madonnas and Magdalens are distinguished by a noble simplicity peculiar to himself. The heads of his figures are accounted not inferior to those of Raffaelle for correctness of design or engaging propriety of expression. De Piles says that "the great merit of Guido consisted in that moving and persuasive beauty which did not proceed so much from regularity of features, as from a lovely air he gave to the mouth, with a peculiar modesty, which he had the art to place in the eye." Guido instructed many pupils; he taught at Rome, and at Bologna, he opened a school, which, according to Crespi, was frequented by more than two hundred pupils. Even his rivals took advantage of it, as Domenichino, Albano, and Lanfranco, along with their best disciples, and Lanzi says it is an indisputable fact, that they derived from him that degree of delicacy in which they sometimes surpass the Caracci.

The works of Guido are numerous, and are to be found in all the principal collections in Italy, and throughout Europe; there are several in the English National gallery, but some of them are of doubtful authenticity, or if genuine, are among his poorest works. He was fond of amusing himself with the point, and we have a considerable number of his charming etchings, executed with great freedom and boldness, in the style of a perfect master. They exhibit the same beautiful expression in the heads and correctness in the extremities, which are so much admired in his pictures. Simone Cantarini, called Il Pesarese, imitated the etchings of Guido with such precision, as to mislead the inexperienced. Bartsch describes sixty-eight prints by him, marked with his monogram, or simply with his initials, G. R. He also modeled in clay, and is said to have executed several statues. Among those pupils who adhered most closely to his style, were Francesco Gessi, Giacomo Semenza, Guido Cagnacci, Simone Cantarini, Pietro Ricchi, Andrea Sirani, and Gio. Battista Bolognini. He died at Bologna in 1642.

RENOU, Antoine, a French painter, born at Paris in 1731. He studied successively under Pierre and Vien, and gained the second prize in painting. About 1760, he was invited to the court of Stanislaus, king of Poland, where he was appointed painter to the court, and also exercised his talents in the histrionic and poetic arts. At the death of his patron, he returned to Paris about 1766, where he gained considerable distinction for his picture of Christ disputing with the Doctors, exhibited in that year. In 1781, he was admitted into the Academy, upon the execution of his picture of Aurora, in the Apollo gallery of the Louvre. Among his other productions at Paris, were several well-arranged compositions, representing Agrippina with the ashes of Germanicus; the Annunciation, in the church of S. Germain en Laie; and a vault in the Hotel des Monnaies, or Mint. Renou wrote a tragedy entitled Tereus and Philomela, and translated Tasso's *Gerusalemme Liberata*, into French. He died in 1806.

RENOU, Louisa, a French lady, was born at Paris in 1754. She engraved several plates after the modern artists of her own country, among which is one of Alexander and his Physician, *after Colin de Vermont.*

RENTER, Bart. Mr. Strutt attributes to this artist a correct and spirited etching of Christ shown to the Jews by Pontius Pilate, inscribed *Bartt. Renter pictor figur. Monachii*, 1612. There is a print of the same date, and nearly the same inscription, described among the works of Bartholomew Reiter, and it is highly probable that they are both one artist.

RENZI, Cesare, a reputable Italian painter, was a native of S. Ginesio, in the Picenum, and flourished about the middle of the 17th century. Lanzi says he studied under Guido, and became a respectable pupil of that master. Among other works, he executed a picture of St. Tommaso, at the church of that saint in his native town.

RESANI, Arcangelo, a painter born at Rome in 1670. He studied under Gio. Battista Boncuore, and chiefly excelled in painting animals and huntings, decorated with large and small figures, in which, according to Lanzi, he had equal taste. His works were highly esteemed at Siena, Bologna, and Venice. His portrait is in the Medicean gallery at Florence, accompanied with a representation of still-life, in which he excelled. Resani died about 1740.

RESCHI, Pandolfo. This painter was born at Dantzic, in Germany, in 1643. He went to Italy while young, entered the school of Jacopo Borgognone, and attained great distinction by his battle-pieces in the style of that master. He also painted landscapes in the style of Salvator Rosa, and excelled in architectural subjects. Lanzi mentions a picture by him of surprising merit, with a view of the Pitti palace, decorated with figures in a spirited style; and there are several of his works in the Florentine collections.

RESTOUT, Jean, a French painter, born at Rouen in 1692. He studied at Paris under his uncle Jouvenet, whose style he followed with considerable success, and approached nearer to the merit of that master than any of the other artists of the time. He wrought with great facility, but with little true excellence; and his works are condemned even by French authority, as marking a most deplorable decadence of art in the French school. In 1720, he was chosen a member of the Academy, for his picture of Arethusa flying into the arms of Diana to escape from Alpheus. He passed through all the degrees of distinction in the Academy of Painting, until he was honored with the office of Chancellor. Among his principal works at Paris are, the Death of Ananias, and the Pool of Bethesda, in the church of S. Martin des Champs; and the ceiling of the Library of St. Genevieve. Restout died at Paris in 1768.

RETZSCH, Friedrich August Moritz, a German painter of the present century, was born at Dresden in 1779. Naturally of a roving and imaginative disposition, he spent his earlier years in the amusement of hunting and the contemplation of nature. About the age of twenty, however, he entered the Dresden academy, and acquired a knowledge of the art. He gained considerable distinction by his pictures illustrating the works of Goethe, Schiller, and Shakspeare, whose wild and luxuriant fancies were well adapted to his peculiar inclination. It is uncertain whether he is still living. His principal works have been engraved; among them are the following:

Sketches illustrative of Goethe's Faust. Illustrations of Schiller's Fight with the Dragon; Fridolin, or Walk to the Forge, Song of the Bell, Pegasus in the Yoke. Ditto to Bürger's Ballads. Outlines illustrative of Shakspeare's Macbeth, Hamlet, Romeo and Juliet, Lear, Tempest, Othello, Merry Wives. Various Fancies and Truths. Faust and Margaret. The Goblet, the Chess-players, &c.

REVELEY, William, an English architect who flourished in the latter part of the 18th century, and studied under Sir William Chambers. He accompanied Mr. Stuart to Greece, and completed the great work commenced by that eminent artist upon the Athenian Antiquities, which he published in folio. Among the principal structures of Reveley, are the church of All Saints at Southampton. He died in 1799.

REUVEN, Peter, a Dutch painter, born at Leyden in 1650. He studied at Antwerp, under Jacob Jordaens, but afterwards returned to Holland, and was much employed in decorating the halls of public and private edifices with historical and allegorical subjects. His pictures were distinguished for fertility of invention, freedom of pencilling, facility of execution, and a brilliancy of coloring equal to the best productions of the Flemish school. Among the principal, were the triumphal arches of the reception of William III., at the Hague; several pictures in the finest apartments of the palace at Loo; and an admirable composition in a ceiling of the mansion of M. de la Court Vandervoort. Reuven died in 1718.

REVELLO, Gio. Battista, called Il Mustacchi, a reputable Genoese painter, was born in 1672. He studied under Antonio Haffner, and formed a close friendship with Francesco Costa. According to Ratti, they wrought in concert for nearly twenty years, and executed the landscape, architecture, ornaments, and other accessories in the backgrounds of the works of various historical painters. Lanzi says they are both equally commended for their knowledge of perspective, their grace, brilliancy, and harmony of tints; but Revello surpassed his companion in the embellishment of flowers. Their master-piece is said to be at Pegli, in the Palazzo Grillo, the decorations of a saloon and several chambers. Besides their works in concert, they also conducted many separately, "being considered the Colonna and Mitelli of their country." Revello died in 1732.

REVERDINO, Cesare, an Italian engraver, concerning whom there is considerable doubt. Zani says he wrought from 1531 to 1554; Bartsch mentions a print by him dated 1531, and Bryan another dated 1602. Bartsch describes thirty-nine of his prints, and Nagler eleven more, executed in a very neat style, closely resembling that of Æneas Vico, with figures poorly drawn. Le Comte says he engraved several obscene subjects, which have probably been destroyed. The following are among his principal plates

Moses striking the Rock. The Wise Men's Offering. A small Frieze, representing a Bacchanalian subject; marked with his name. 1564. Venus coming to Vulcan for the Arms of Æneas; marked also with his name, and dated 1602.

REVETT, Nicholas, a distinguished English architect and designer, was born in the county of Suffolk, in 1721. In company with Stuart, he visited Rome in 1750, and studied design under Cav. Benefiali. The two artists subsequently continued their travels to Athens, Smyrna, Salonica, and the isles of the Archipelago. On returning to England, they commenced their valuable work upon the Athenian Antiquities, of which the last volume appeared in 1794. The whole contains 281 plates. In 1766, Revett started on a second expedition to Asia Minor, at the expense of the Dilettanti Society, in company with Dr. Chandler of Oxford, and Mr. Pars the designer and painter. After an absence of three years, the party returned to England with ample materials; and the publication of the Ionian Antiquities in two volumes, gave the public tangible evidence of their industry and skill. Besides his admirable drawings for the above mentioned works, Revett designed many edifices in England, among which is a church in the Grecian style at Ayot St. Lawrence, in the county of Hertz. He died at London, in 1804, aged 83.

REVOIL, Pierre Henri, a distinguished French painter of the present century, was born at Lyons in 1776. He early manifested a strong inclination for art, and was placed in the school of David, who was greatly pleased with his natural talents. The first work by Revoil that attracted public attention, was his grand allegorical composition, of the city of Lyons raised from its ruins by Gen. Bonaparte. He was afterwards commissioned to paint several sacred subjects in the church of S. Nizier at Lyons, and in 1809 was chosen professor of the School of Design in that city. In 1814, he exhibited two excellent pictures at the Louvre; in 1817 his simple and graceful picture of the Convalescence of Chev. Bayard, afterwards placed in the Luxembourg. His picture of Henry IV. playing with his children, drew a prize of 3000 francs, and was purchased by the Duke de Berri. In 1822, Revoil was chosen painter to the Dauphin and the Duchess de Berri; but the authorities of Lyons demanded the fulfilment of his duties as professor at the School of Design in that city, and he therefore returned thither. At the Revolution of 1830, he retired from Lyons for about three years, and executed his admired pictures of Charles V. at the Abbey of St. Juste, and Palamede de Forbin giving Provence to Louis XI. These were sent to Paris, and met with such admiration, that Revoil returned thither, and settled with an aged uncle, who had aided him in his youth. His success was proportioned to his expectations, and the court purchased some of his pictures for the palace at Versailles. Besides those already mentioned, he executed among others, a picture of Joan of Arc imprisoned at Rouen, purchased by the Count d'Artois; and Philip Augustus taking the Oriflamme at St. Denis, before his departure for the Holy Land. He died in 1842. His subjects were principally taken from the history of the Middle Ages, particularly of the days of chivalry. Revoil was a member of the Legion of Honor, and Correspondent of the Academy of Fine Arts.

REY, Antonio del, an excellent Spanish architect, who flourished about 1600, and studied under Giovanni de Herrera. He was employed to erect the college of Corpus Christi at Valencia, which is well proportioned, with a fine cupola. It has a court, ornamented with eighty-six columns, and a magnificent staircase.

REYN, John de, a distinguished Flemish painter, was born at Dunkirk in 1610. He visited Antwerp while young, and entered the school of Vandyck, where he made such rapid progress that the latter invited him to accompany him to England. He continued to assist Vandyck in his numerous works, until the death of that illustrious painter, in 1641, when he returned to Flanders, settled at Dunkirk, and received many commissions for portraits and historical works. His pictures are entirely in the style of Vandyck, exhibiting the same correctness of design, purity and delicacy of coloring, freedom and spirit of pencilling; distinguished for ingenious composition, masterly and effective lights and shadows. Doubtless many of the works and much of the reputation of Reyn are assigned to his great exemplar. Besides numerous admirable portraits in private collections, little inferior to those of Vandyck, there are by him in the church of S. Eloi at Dunkirk, the Death of the Four Royal Martyrs; in the church of the English convent, the Baptism of Totila; and the principal altar-piece in the parochial church of S. Martin, at Bergues St. Vinox, near Dunkirk, representing Herodias bringing the Head of St. John to Herod. Reyn died in 1678.

REYNA, Francisco de, a Spanish painter, was born at Seville about 1635. He studied in the school of Francisco de Herrera the elder, where he made rapid progress, and exhibited a high degree of talent in a picture of the Blessed Spirits, for the church of All Saints; but he died in the flower of his age, in 1659, greatly regretted by the friends of art.

REYNOLDS, Sir Joshua, an eminent English painter, was born at Plympton, in Devonshire, in 1723. He was the son of the Rev. Samuel Reynolds, the teacher of the grammar school in that town, and was intended for the medical profession; but, as he manifested a strong inclination for art, and executed several excellent likenesses, his father was induced to send him to London for superior instruction than he could obtain in the country. Accordingly, at the age of seventeen, Reynolds commenced studying under Hudson, and made such rapid improvement in the course of two years, that his instructor gradually became jealous of his excellence, and finally rendered his situation so unpleasant that he returned to Devonshire in 1743. During a residence of three years in his native county, he practised portrait painting with reputation, and then settled at Plymouth Dock, where he was greatly encouraged, particularly by Lord Mount Edgecumbe, who also recommended him to the favorable notice of Captain, afterwards Lord Keppel. The latter, appointed to the Mediterranean station, invited Reynolds to accompany him thither; and the young artist gladly embraced this opportunity, which promised a sojourn in Italy. On arriving at Rome, he devoted himself with great assiduity to the study of the best works of art, particularly those of Raffaelle and Michael Angelo; and he seems, from his own account, to have principally occupied his time in contemplating their peculiar excellencies, rather than in copying their productions. On leaving Rome, he visited various other Italian cities, passing two months at Florence, where he painted several portraits; and after a short stay in Venice, he returned to England in 1752, having been absent three years. He settled at London, where his talents before long attracted considerable attention, and his admired full-length portrait of his friend and patron, Admiral Keppel, elevated his reputation above that of any cotemporary English artist. He consequentry soon gained a large share of the public patronage and esteem, and was for many years considered the head of the English school of painting. Deficient in fertility of invention and correctness of drawing, he produced few large historical works; but in portraits he deserves very high commendation for his admirable coloring, which, though inferior to the excellence of the Venetian and Flemish masters, with whom he is sometimes compared, is highly distinguished for vigor, purity, truth, and harmony. His chiaro-scuro is justly praised; the expression of his portraits is dignified and characteristic; and their interesting air of history, in the landscape, accessories, and general execution, adds greatly to their value. His portraits of children are greatly esteemed for their attractive air of innocence. The attainments of Reynolds were the result of indefatigable industry; if his pencil was deficient in spirit, on account of successive efforts to improve the drawing, he yet added to the vigor and harmony of his coloring by every successive repetition.

At the formation of the Royal Academy in 1768, Reynolds being justly esteemed at the head of his profession, was appointed to the office of President, and shortly afterwards received from the king the honor of knighthood. On the annual occasions, during the twenty-one years of his presidency, of distributing prizes to the successful competitors, he was accustomed to deliver a lecture relating to art; and, according to his biographer, the entire collection of his discourses contains "such a body of just criticism on an extremely difficult subject, clothed in such perspicuous, elegant, and nervous language, that it is no exaggerated panegyric to assert that it will last as long as the English tongue, and contribute, not less than the productions of his pencil, to render his name immortal." Reynolds also contributed to the advancement and firm establishment of the Academy, by practical as well as theoretical labors; and he sent two hundred and forty-four pictures to the various exhibitions. In 1780, he completed his design for the great window in the New College Chapel at Oxford, containing in the seven divisions of the lower part, emblematical figures, with appropriate attributes, of Temperance, Fortitude, Justice, Prudence, Faith, Hope, and Charity; in the upper part he represented the Nativity, with the light emanating from the body of the Infant. In 1781, Reynolds visited Holland and the Netherlands, to examine the productions of the best Dutch and Flemish masters, by which he is said to have improved his coloring. In 1782, Mason's translation of Du Fresnoy's Art of Painting was published, with notes by Reynolds. In 1784, at the death of Ramsay, he was appointed principal painter to the king; and in that year he exhibited his picture of the Fortuneteller, and his celebrated portrait of Mrs. Siddons, as the Muse of Tragedy, now in the Grosvenor Gallery. About 1786, the Empress Catharine of Russia commissioned him to execute a subject of his own selection, and he chose the Infant Hercules, a picture highly praised for its excellent coloring and chiaro-scuro, for which the Empress sent him fifteen hundred guineas, and a gold box, with her picture set in diamonds. Several pictures for Boydell's magnificent Shakspeare Gallery were painted by Reynolds—the Death of Cardinal Beaufort, Macbeth with the Witches, in the Cauldron scene, and Puck, or Robin Goodfellow, from Midsummer Night's Dream. About 1789, he was obliged to relinquish practising the art, on account of weakened eyesight. In 1791, his health began to fail; his disease was ascertained to be an affection of the liver, and he died in the following year. His remains were deposited in the crypt of St. Paul's, near the tomb of Sir Christopher Wren. There are several pictures by Reynolds in the National Gallery, among which are the portrait of Gen. Elliot, and the Age of Innocence, formerly purchased by Mr. Vernon for 1520 guineas. In the collection of Sir Robert Peel there were, among others, the portraits of Dr. Johnson, Edmund Burke, and Admiral Keppel. Besides these, there are by him, in various collections, the portraits of Lady Charlotte Spencer, Charles J. Fox, the Earl and Countess of Bute, Dr. Beattie, Horace Walpole, Lady Montague, Sir Joseph Banks, Queen Charlotte, George III., and many other distinguished nobles and literati of the last century. He formed a splendid collection of works of art, which, after his death, brought at public sale about £17,000. The whole of his property amounted to about £80,000, the bulk of which he left to his niece, who married Lord Inchiquin, afterwards Marquis of Thomond. He never married, but his sister, Frances Reynolds, conducted his domestic affairs. She was an ingenious lady, painted miniatures in good style, and was esteemed by Dr. Johnson for her literary taste and acquirements. She died in 1807.

Sir Joshua Reynolds is called by his countrymen "the great founder of the British school of painting." If we are to believe some of his biographers, he was one of the greatest painters that ever lived. Burke says, in his eulogium, "in taste, in grace, in facility, in happy invention, and in the richness and harmony of coloring, he was equal to the greatest masters of the renowned ages. in portraits he went beyond them. * * * * In full affluence of foreign and domestic fame, admired by the expert in art and the learned in science; courted by the great, caressed by sovereign powers, and celebrated by distinguished poets, his native humility, modesty, and candor never forsook him, even on surprise or provocation; nor was the least degree of arrogance or assumption visible to the most scrutinizing eye, in any part of his conduct or discourse. His talents, of every kind, powerful from nature, and not meanly cultivated by letters, his social virtues in all the relations and habitudes of life, rendered him the centre of a very great and unparalleled variety of agreeable societies, which will be dissipated by his death. He had too much merit not to excite some jealousy, too much innocence to provoke any enmity." Dr. Johnson declared that he "should grieve to see Reynolds transfer to heroes and goddesses, to empty splendor and to airy fiction, that art which is now employed in diffusing friendship, in renewing tenderness, in quickening the affections of the absent, and continuing the presence of the dead." Such opinions, though emanating from men so distinguished in letters, can have little influence with connoisseurs. The following extract from the biography of Reynolds, in Rees' Cyclopedia, supposed to have been written by the late Prof. Thomas Phillips, R. A., is written with more knowledge and much candor, though few foreign critics will feel disposed to endorse the sentiments of the writer:

"It remains to speak of his style as an artist, which is precisely that denominated in his lectures the ornamental style, but which, beautiful and seducing as it undoubtedly is, cannot be recommended in so unreserved a degree as his industry both in study and practice: that which he characteristically terms his own uncertainty, both in design and execution, operates too frequently and too powerfully against its entire adoption. In the higher attainments of the art, coloring and chiaroscuro were undoubtedly elements which he favored, and in which he moved uncontrolled. Drawing, as he himself candidly confessed, was the part of the art in which he was most defective; and from a desire perhaps to hide this defect, with an over-solicitude to produce a superabundant richness of effect, he was sometimes tempted to fritter his lights, and break up his composition, particularly if it happened to be large, into too many parts; yet, in general, his taste in lines and forms was at the same time grand and graceful, and the taste and skill with which he drew and set together the features of the human face, has never been surpassed by any artist. We would be understood to speak of his finest productions; of the ordinary class among them, we must allow that the marking favors of manner, and the substance is not always characteristic of flesh. In execution, though he wanted the firmness and breadth which appertain to the highest style of art, yet the spirit and sweetness of his touch were admirable, and would have been more remarkable had he been more a master of drawing; but not being able readily to determine his forms, he was obliged to go over and over the same part, till some of the vivacity of his handling was frequently lost; his labor, however, was never wholly so, for he added to the force and harmony of his pictures by these repetitions; and frequently attained graces by them which would otherwise perhaps have remained unknown. The numberless instances in which he is known to have borrowed thoughts, both in actions of figures and effect of color, seem to impeach his power of invention. But surely it could not proceed from want of a sufficient portion of that high and necessary quality, that he who produced so many novel combinations, adopted that short-hand path to composition. We see it exemplified in a superior degree in most of his principal productions; and particularly in his whole-length and half-length portraits, the arrangements of which are no less beautiful and interesting than new, and entirely his own. These are composed in a taste far surpassing all that had ever been done by his predecessors, uniting the grandeur, simplicity, and fulness of Titian, and the grace and nature of Vandyck, with the artful and attractive effects of Rembrandt. One quality he had, which no other painter that ever breathed shares with him in an equal degree,—fascination. The effect of his best pictures acts like a charm, and arrests the tasteful beholder with irresistible power. On the works of others we look with approbation, and sometimes with feelings of admiration and delight, or even with a sensation of awe; but in those of Reynolds there is generally an indescribable unity and amenity which act upon us with the most fascinating power, and rivet the attention with superior gratification. No real connoisseur can deny the existence of this quality in his pictures, but wherein it specifically dwells, it is not easy to discover or define They are not labored to perfect imitation, indeed they stop very far short of that; yet they present a full image, with a degree of life and animation that has rarely been displayed upon canvass. It is a dangerous doctrine to advance, and may be abused; but, perhaps, this power may be in a great measure owing to his having painted less upon system than from feeling; and the latter governing the exercise of his pencil, not to the neglect of, but in a superior degree to the influence of, the former, necessarily imbued his works with a glow of nature, which, it will be allowed, attracts beyond the power of art. Whencesoever this fascination of which we speak proceeds, it must be acknowledged that no painter ever possessed it like Reynolds."

"This is just and masterly criticism," says Stanley, "as far as relates to the portraits by Sir Joshua Reynolds, and may be extended to his single figures in subjects of fancy, particularly of children; it applies also to the coloring and chiaroscuro of many of those compositions by him that are classed as historical. But it would be contrary to truth to claim for his attempts at poetical and historical compositions an equality even with the great masters of the Italian and Flemish schools. The greater part of his productions in these departments are failures. His picture of the Nativity is commonplace, partly borrowed; and the introduction of his own portrait and that of Jarvis in their European costume, a puerile absurdity. The allegorical figures of the Christian Virtues are prose versions of classical symbols; his Ugolino, without dignity, exhibits only the outward effects of punishment on culprits of the common herd; his Head of a Banished Lord belongs to the inmate of a lunatic asylum; his Holy Family* in *riposo* (in the National Gallery) is an egregious plagiarism, vulgarized by the adoption of forms deficient in beauty, grace, and intellect. His Macbeth with the Witches, and his Death of Cardinal Beaufort, are wholly deficient in that grandeur and sublimity that such subjects should have displayed. Even in that noblest of his productions, the portrait of Mrs. Siddons as the Muse of Tragedy, the genius of mischief interfered. The attitude and the expression are admirable; but the introduction of the two attendants

* Charles Lamb is exceedingly severe upon this picture. "Here, for a Madonna, Sir Joshua has substituted a sleepy, insensible, unmotherly girl—one so little worthy to have been the mother of the Savior, that she seems to have neither heart nor feeling to entitle her to become a mother at all." The coloring in this picture, though originally rich and glowing, is much injured in parts, and the harmony is entirely destroyed.

Mrs. Jameson says of the Infant Samuel in the National Gallery, "Call it a little boy saying his prayers, it is charming; but there is nothing here of the incipient prophet, nothing to bring before the imagination all that was grand, and supernatural, and tragic, in the incident it represents—the consecrated child waked from his innocent sleep in the dead of night by a divine voice, to be filled with a spirit beyond his own conceiving." Again, of the Graces sacrificing to Hymen, "The composition of this picture is rather fantastical than poetical. It is difficult to know what to say of the young ladies who personate the Graces, in silk gowns and high head-dresses, and are sacrificing to Hymen in a Wood. The picture, however, is beautiful, and full of that ladylike grace and sentiment which Sir Joshua gave to his female portraits."

with the dagger and bowl destroy the illusion; and, instead of the exalted personification of the highest order of poesy, we behold the figure of Medea meditating murder. It is vain to close the eyes of our understanding to these defects in our most admired painter; if *we* will not see them, *others* will; and it is better, therefore, to acknowledge it at once, than to be taunted by foreigners for blind or ignorant partiality. The fame of Reynolds, as a painter, is established on his numerous superlative portraits, and his enchanting representations of the innocence, simplicity, and natural habits of unsophisticated children: in these he stands alone. Let us not, by claiming too much, weaken that title to superiority which is justly his due, nor enter into a contest in which we might show zeal and pugnacity, but must fail of victory."

Sir Joshua Reynolds was confessedly deficient in the first principles of art—academic knowledge and skill—which totally unfitted him, had his talents been ever so great, for the highest order of historical painting. He frequently said with regret, that "he could not draw." This was a part of artistic education that he had not had the means of acquiring, or had neglected till too late. He could therefore only paint from his model. How different the case with the great artists, with whom he has been ranked and compared! Many of the great Italian masters were accustomed to study and to draw from the living model, not only in their youth, but all their days, like the skilful surgeon constantly practising dissection, "to keep his hand in." Before touching the brush to their canvass, they always prepared a cartoon of the same size as they intended the picture; they first drew each figure separate and naked, then grouped and draped them. (See Raffaelle.) This in art, is what plan and foundation are to the superstructure of an edifice. Again, his method of coloring is not to be commended. His palette, as given by Beechey in his Memoirs, is a curiosity of art. It might do well enough with his peculiar manner of handling, but would never answer in the hands of another. He was ignorant of chemistry, so much so that he sometimes employed mineral colors that reacted in a short time, also vegetable colors, and mixed with these various vehicles, as megilips, and different kinds of varnishes or glazes, so that he had the mortification of seeing some of his finest works change and lose all their harmony, or become checked with unsightly seams. He even *anatomized* several valuable pictures by Titian and other great colorists, to discover their peculiar methods of coloring—a practice which might be likened to the boy who cut open the bellows to find the wind. He lived to regret these experiments, and would never permit any of his students to practise them. These things are mentioned only to put others on their guard, for his system has been largely imitated, even in the United States. The true method for excellence and permanence in coloring, is to employ well prepared canvass, then to lay on a good heavy body color, and afterwards to employ only the best mineral colors which will not chemically react, giving the colors time to harden after laying on each successive coat, and above all to use no varnishes in the process, nor after the completion of the work, till it has sufficient age.

REYNOLDS, Samuel William, a distinguished English designer and engraver, was born in 1774. He studied under William Hodges, and attained considerable eminence for his plates in mezzotinto, as well as for his numerous sketches in oil, which are much esteemed. He engraved many portraits, historical, and fancy subjects, after pictures by modern artists, particularly those of Sir Joshua Reynolds, of whose works he engraved nearly three hundred. In 1826 he visited France, and executed several plates after Horace Vernet, Gericault, Delaroche, and others. He died in 1835. Among his principal plates are the portrait of Reginald Heber, bishop of Calcutta, *after Owen;* Lady Ellis Agar, *after Jackson;* the Chapeau de Paille, *after Rubens;* the Visit of the Poor Relations, *after Stephanoff;* the Lion and the Snake, the Vulture and the Lamb, and the Falconer, *after Northcote;* the Fisherman's Dog, and the Setters, *after Morland.*

REYNOSO, Don Antonio Garcia, a Spanish painter and architect, born at Cabra, in Andalusia, in 1623. He studied at Jaen, in the school of Sebastian Martinez, and gained considerable distinction by his pictures for the churches and private collections. Palomino mentions several of his works, particularly an altar-piece in the church of the Capuchins at Andujar, representing the Trinity with several saints. Reynoso also painted landscapes, and there are several of his pictures in the churches and private collections of Cordova. None of his architectural works are mentioned. He died at Cordova in 1677.

REYSSCHOOT, F. van, a Dutch engraver of whom little is known. He executed among other plates, several *after Teniers*, in a very neat and spirited manner.

RHELINGER, Welser, a German wood engraver, mentioned by Papillon as the artist of one hundred and twenty prints, illustrating a German book entitled *Patricium Stirpium Augustanarum Vindelicum, et earundem sodalitatis insignia.* The principal figures are all represented on horseback, in full armor, with their respective family arms inscribed on their shields.

RHODES, John, an English landscape painter, born in 1810. His father was a reputable painter of Yorkshire, and gave lessons to his son, who early manifested a strong inclination for the art His subjects were usually taken from scenes of rural life, and they possess much of the charm of nature. He chiefly resided at Leeds, but when about 30 years old, he went to London, where he met with some encouragement. His health, however, soon failed, and he was compelled to return to Leeds, where he died in 1843, at the age of 33.

RHŒCUS, an old Greek sculptor, a native of Samos, who flourished about B. C. 776, in the time of Dipenos and Scyllis. He obtained great celebrity in that early age, for his sculptures in brass. His son Telectes, and his grandson Theodorus, were also celebrated for their skill in the art. According to Pausanias, their works in wood, metal, and ivory, were extant in the age in which he lived. See *Theodorus.*

RHOLUS. See Theodorus.

RIBALTA, Francisco, a distinguished Spanish historical painter, was born at Castellon de la Plana, in the kingdom of Valencia, in 1551. After acquiring the elements of design from an artist of Valencia, he visited Italy for improvement, and is said to have studied under Annibale Caracci. He studied the works of Raffaelle, Sebastiano del Piombo and the Caracci, with great assiduity; and at the end of three years he returned to Spain so much improved, that his former instructor, who had previously refused him his daughter in marriage, now consented to the match. Ribalta soon acquired a high reputation, and executed many works for the churches and collections of Valencia, as well as for other parts of Spain. He made copies from the pictures of Sebastiano del Piombo, in the royal collection at Madrid, three of which are in the convent of the Carmelites in that city. Commissioned by the archbishop Don Juan de Ribera, Ribalta executed a picture of the Last Supper, for the grand altar of Corpus Christi, which was so greatly admired that Vincenzio Carducci visited Valencia on purpose to see it. His works are distinguished for admirable composition, excellent taste and elevation of design. There were two of his pictures in the Louvre, the Last Supper, and a picture of St. Peter; they were restored in 1815, and the former is now in the church of the Patriarch at Valencia, with many other of his works. In the chapel of the Magdalen college at Oxford, there is "a grand specimen" by Ribalta. He died at Valencia in 1628.

RIBALTA, Juan, was the son of the preceding artist, born at Valencia in 1597. He early manifested extraordinary abilities, and painted a picture of the Crucifixion, at the age of eighteen, which gave promise of great eminence. He also painted for Don Diego de Vich, about thirty portraits of eminent Valencians, and would probably have been a shining ornament to the Spanish school, had he not died young, in 1628. Many of his works are attributed to his father.

RIBAULT, J. F., a reputable French engraver, was born at Paris in 1767. He studied under Ingouf, and attained sufficient excellence to be employed on the Musée Napoleon, for which he engraved two plates, representing Paris and Œnone, *after Vanderwerf*, and a Young Lady playing on the Guitar, *after Metzu*. He also engraved several plates for the collections of Laurent and Robillard; portraits of Bernardin de St. Pierre, the poet Lebrun, and the Empress Maria Louisa; Marcus Sextus, *after Guerin*, and the Crowning of Thorns, *after Titian*. Ribault died in 1820.

RIBERA, José, called Il Spagnoletto, an eminent Spanish painter, born, according to authentic records cited by Bermudez, at Xativa, in the kingdom of Valencia, in 1588. He early manifested a strong inclination for art, and entered the school of Francisco Ribalta. After several years' study under that master, he visited Italy for improvement about the age of sixteen, supporting himself by the exercise of his talents. Arriving at Naples in 1606, while Caravaggio was residing in that capital, Ribera was greatly pleased with the vigorous style of that distinguished artist. Favored with his advice and instructions, he made rapid progress, and was soon denominated Il Spagnoletto, as a mark of distinction. On leaving Caravaggio, Lanzi says he "visited Rome, Modena and Parma, and saw the works of Raffaelle, and Annibale Caracci in the former place, and the works of Correggio in the two latter cities, adopting in consequence a more graceful style, in which he persevered for a short time, but with little success, as there were others in Naples, who pursued with superior skill the same path. He returned therefore to the style of Caravaggio, which, for its truth, and strong contrast of light and shade, was much more calculated to please the general eye. In a short time he was appointed painter to the court, and subsequently became the arbiter of its taste." His careful studies enabled him to surpass Caravaggio in invention, selection, and design. His subjects were generally austere, representing anchorets, prophets, apostles; and frequently of the most revolting character, such as sanguinary executions, horrid punishments, and lingering torments; which he represented with startling fidelity, and admirable correctness of design, particularly in delineating the muscles. His works are very numerous in Italy, and many of them were sent by the Viceroy to Spain, among which is his Ixion on the Wheel, in the Buon Retiro at Madrid. Giordano highly praises his Deposition from the Cross, in the Certosini at Naples. as alone sufficient to form a great painter, and worthy to compete with the highest luminaries of the art. Ribera seems to have sometimes departed from his severe manner, and Lanzi praises his Martyrdom of St. Januarius, in the Royal chapel, as beautiful beyond his usual style, and almost in the manner of Titian. He also painted portraits, which were highly esteemed. Among his other best productions, are St. Jerome and St. Bruno, at the Trinità; and Democritus and Heraclitus, in the collection of Sig. Girolamo Durazzo. Ribera's drawings with chalk or the pen, are much esteemed by the collectors. He executed about twenty etchings, in a bold, free style, producing a fine effect, correctly drawn, and the extremities marked in a very masterly manner. When not inscribed with his name, they are generally marked with one of the following monograms. Ribera died at Naples in 1656.

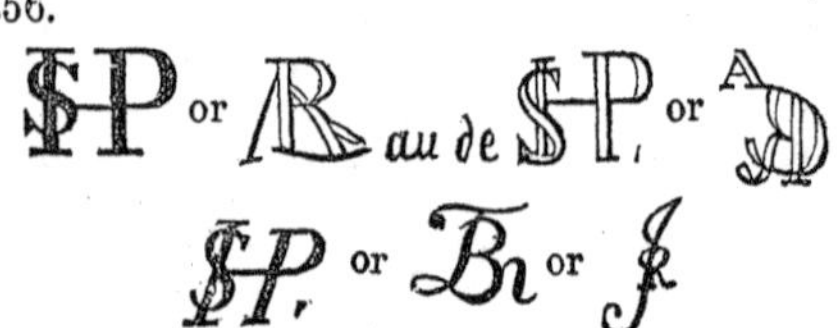


RICAMATORE. See Da Udine.

RICCA, or RICCO, Bernardino, an Italian painter, who flourished at Cremona about 1512. He executed, among other works, a Pietà, or Dead Christ, in the church of S. Pietro del Po at Cremona, which Lanzi says deserves commendation for the time.

RICCHI, Pietro, called Il Lucchese, a painter of Lucca, born, according to Baldinucci, in 1606. After studying under Passignano, he went to Bologna, and is said by Orlandi and Baldinucci to have entered the school of Guido, after which he resided many years at Venice. Lanzi says he frequently imitated the forms of the latter master, adhering to the manner of Passignano in design and coloring, combined with the principles of Tintoretto and other eminent Venetian masters. He was distinguished for fertility of invention and great facility of execution, but Lanzi seems inclined to charge him with introducing the oily and obscure mode of coloring, practised at Venice by the *Tenebrosi*, and says "it is at least certain that, besides having made use of bad priming, he was in the habit of covering his canvass with oil whenever he applied his pencil, which has occasioned the loss of so many of his works, that once produced an excellent effect, but which are now either defaced or perished. This is the case with those that remained at Venice, Vicenza, Brescia, Padua, and Udine; some of which, indeed, are not greatly to be regretted, being the production of mere mechanical skill, and that not always executed correctly. A few, however, are conducted with more care, as in his St. Raimondo, at the Dominicans of Bergamo, and his Epiphany in the patriarchal church at Venice, both highly deserving of commendation, no less for the union of their colors, than for the taste displayed in their whole composition." Ricchi practised the art in several cities of France, in the Milanese, and the Venetian states. There are many of his works at Udine, where he died, in 1675.

RICCHIEDO, Marco. This painter was a native of Brescia, but the time when he lived is not recorded. There is a fine picture by him, representing the Incredulity of St. Thomas, in the church of that saint at Brescia.

RICCHINO, Francesco, a Brescian painter, who flourished about 1568. Lanzi mentions him among the better disciples of Alessandro Bonvicino, called Il Moretto. His pictures evince an attempt to "extract improvement from the pictures, or at least from the engravings, of Titian." Among his best productions at Brescia, are several pictures in S. Pietro Oliveto.

RICCI, Antonio. See Barbalunga.

RICCI, Camillo, an eminent painter of Ferrara, born in 1580. He studied under Ippolito Scarsellino, and attained such excellence, according to Baruffaldi, that his master declared if Camillo had preceded him in the art, he would have chosen him as an instructor. Lanzi remarks, "the most skilful had difficulty to distinguish him from Scarsellino. His style is almost as tender and attractive as his master's, the union of his colors is even more equal, and has more repose; and he is principally distinguished by less freedom of hand, and by his less natural, and more minute folding." He manifested great fertility of invention in eighty-four pictures in the church of S. Niccolo, representing scenes in the life of that saint. There are many of his smaller pictures in the Palazzo Trotti, and Barotti mentions many admired works in the churches, among which are the pictures of St. Vincenzio and St. Margherita, in the cathedral; and the Annunciation, in S. Spirito. Ricci died at Ferrara in 1618.

RICCI, Gio. Battista, called da Novara, a painter born at Novara in 1545. He visited Rome at an early age, and studied under Raffaellino da Reggio, on leaving whom he was employed by Sixtus V. in the palace of St. John of Lateran, and in the Library of the Vatican. He was also appointed superintendent of decorations at the Quirinal palace, and according to Baglioni, was much employed in the pontificate of Clement VIII. Lanzi says that his works display great facility of pencil, beauty of forms, and attractive brilliancy and elegance; his style was that of Raffaelle reduced to mannerism, and he promoted the prevailing effeminate taste. His works are very numerous in Rome; among them are the Visitation, the Ascension, and the Assumption of the Virgin, in S. Maria Maggiore; and the Consecration of St. John of Lateran, placed in that Basilica. Orlandi mentions Ricci as an engraver, but does not specify any of his works. He died in 1620.

RICCI, Sebastiano, a painter born at Belluno, in the Venetian State, in 1659. After acquiring an excellent knowledge of art from Federigo Cervelli at Venice, he accompanied that master to Milan, and studied also under Alessandro Magnasco, named Lissandrino. He afterwards visited Bologna, and was patronised by the Duke of Parma, who employed him at Piacenza, and enabled him to visit Rome for improvement. On the death of his patron he quitted Rome, and visited Florence, Modena, Parma, and other cities, leaving proofs of his ability. Invited to the court of Vienna, he was employed to decorate the imperial palace of Schoenbrunn; and on returning to Venice, he went to England in the reign of Queen Anne, at the suggestion of his nephew, Marco Ricci, who was then residing in London. He was much employed by the nobility, and painted, among other works, the hall and several ceilings of Burlington House, and the altar-piece of the chapel of Chelsea College. After a residence of ten years in England, he returned to Italy, because, as it is said, Sir James Thornhill was preferred to paint the cupola of St. Paul's.

Lanzi says, "he did not early acquire a good knowledge of design, but he afterwards succeeded in this object, which he cultivated with extreme assiduity in the academies, even in mature age. The forms of his figures are composed with beauty, dignity, and grace, like those of Paul Veronese; the attitudes are more than usually natural, prompt, and varied; and the composition appears to have been managed with truth and good sense. Although rapid in the handling, he did not, like many artists, abuse this quality; his figures are accurately designed, and appear starting from the canvass, most frequently colored with a very beautiful azure, in which they shine conspicuous over all. His works in fresco have generally preserved their tints, but his other works appear to have suffered; his coloring was originally pleasing and spirited, and he perfected it in Flanders."

Ricci, like Luca Giordano, attained great skill in imitating the eminent Italian masters; one of his Madonnas at Dresden was for some time attributed to Correggio; and his imitations of Paul Veronese would deceive the best judges. His mind was greatly enriched by his travels, and he frequently adopted fine imitations of various masters into his works; but Lanzi absolves him from the charge of plagiarism. Among his principal works are the Apostles adoring the Sacrament, in the church of S. Giustina at Padua, containing many points of resemblance to Correggio's dome at Parma; and his St. Gregorio, in S. Alessandro at Bergamo, reminding the careful observer of Guercino's picture of the same subject at Bologna. Ricci died at Venice in 1734.

RICCI, Marco, was the nephew and scholar of the preceding, born at Belluno in 1680. He completed his studies at Rome, where he remained several years, designing the finest scenery and most remarkable ruins in the vicinity of that city. He was principally employed in painting landscapes, decorated with admirable architecture, which gained him great reputation. In 1710, he visited

England, and was much employed by the nobility; after which he traveled on the continent with his uncle Sebastiano R., and executed a number of works at Paris. He died at Venice in 1730, in which year were published in that city a set of twenty-one plates of landscapes with ruins, etched by him from his own designs.

RICCI, Natale and Ubaldo. These painters, natives of Fermo, are supposed by Lanzi to have studied under Lorenzino di Fermo before visiting Rome, where they entered the school of Carlo Maratti. They afterwards settled in their native place, and practised the art in the latter part of the 18th century. Ubaldo appears to have surpassed his companion; he is highly praised for his picture of St. Felice, at the Capuchins in Fermo, although Lanzi says he did not often transcend the bounds of mediocrity.

RICCIARDELLI, Gabriele, a reputable Neapolitan painter, who flourished at Naples, according to Dominici, in 1743. He studied under John Francis van Bloemen, called Orizzonte, and attained considerable distinction for his landscapes and marine views at the court of King Charles of Bourbon, where he was much employed.

RICCIARELLI, Daniele, called di Volterra, an eminent Italian painter, born at Volterra in 1509. After studying successively under Gio. Antonio Razzi, and Baldassare Peruzzi, he visited Rome, and became the assistant of Pierino del Vaga in the Vatican, and in the Massimi chapel, in the church of La Trinità de Monti. The style of Michael Angelo was congenial to his taste, and he studied with great assiduity the works of that master, who greatly esteemed his talents, appointed him his substitute in the works at the Vatican, and brought him forward into public notice.—Daniele soon rose to distinction, and was commissioned by Agostino Chigi to execute several frescos in the Farnese palace, in which he was much assisted by the designs and advice of Buonarotti. In the Orsini chapel in the church of La Trinità de Monti, he painted in seven years a series of frescos representing the History of the Cross, in which he was also assisted by Buonarotti. The principal painting was the wonderful Deposition from the Cross, which Lanzi classes with the Transfiguration of Raffaelle, and the St. Jerome of Domenichino. What higher praise could he give? "We seem to behold the mournful spectacle, and the Redeemer sinking with the natural relaxation of a dead body in descending; the pious men engaged in various offices, and thrown in different and contrasted attitudes, appear assiduously occupied with the sacred remains, which they seem to venerate; the mother of Jesus having fainted between the sorrowing women, the beloved disciple extends his arms and bends over her. There is a truth in the naked figures that seems perfect nature; a coloring in the faces and the whole piece that exactly suits the subject, and is more determined than delicate; a relief, a harmony, and, in a word, a skill that might do honor to the hand of Michael Angelo himself, had the picture been inscribed with his name." Unfortunately for the art, this sublime production was unintentionally destroyed by the French, while attempting to remove it from the wall; but some idea of it may be gathered from the fine print of Dorigny. Volterra also designed the Assumption of the Virgin and the Presentation in the Temple, painted by his scholars Michele Alberti and Gio. Paolo Rossetti, in another chapel of the same church. His last great work in painting was his famous picture of the Murder of the Innocents, from his own design, for the church of S. Peter at Volterra, which was subsequently purchased by the Archduke Leopold, and placed in the Tribune of the Royal Florentine Gallery—"an honor," says Lanzi, "that speaks more for it than my eulogy." At the death of Pierino del Vaga, in 1547, he was appointed by Paul III., at the recommendation of Buonarotti, to superintend the works in the Vatican. Naturally slow and irresolute, he did not complete anything in the course of two years, and was compelled to remove his scaffolding in 1549, at the death of the pope, to accommodate the college of cardinals. The unfinished work did not meet with public approval, and Volterra was removed from his employment by Julius III. He subsequently devoted his attention to sculpture. Under the pontificate of Paul IV., however, he was induced to add draperies to some of the nude figures in Michael Angelo's Last Judgment, which that pontiff considered as too freely treated for the sanctity of the Sistine chapel. He died in 1566.

RICCIO, Domenico, called Brusasorci, an eminent Italian painter, was born at Verona in 1494. According to Ridolfi, he studied under Gio. Francesco Carotto; but Lanzi ranks him among the pupils of Niccolo Giolfino. After completing his preparatory course, he visited Venice, and studied with great assiduity the works of Giorgione and Titian. According to Lanzi, he exhibited the style of the latter with great accuracy in a few of his pictures, particularly in the St. Rocco at the Padri Agostiniani at Verona, and several pictures of Nymphs and Venuses for private collections. Unlike many other followers of that great colorist, he did not confine himself to his style; and his works at Mantua partake of the depth of Giorgione, and the graceful design of Parmiggiano. In the Ducal Palace remains his Fable of Phaëton, which, though injured by the lapse of time, is greatly admired for its copious and ingenious composition, masterly foreshortening, and harmonious coloring. His greatest merit, however, was in fresco painting, and he executed many admirable works for the villas and palaces, displaying great poetical erudition, and a high order of pictorial talent. Among his historical works, the masterpiece is the Procession of Clement VIII. and Charles V. through Bologna, in the Casa Ridolfi. Lanzi remarks, "a nobler specimen cannot well be imagined; and although other specimens, both of this and similar subjects, are met with generally at Rome and Florence, none produce equal effect; combining in one piece a large concourse, fine distribution of figures, noble attitudes in the men and horses; variety of costume, pomp, splendor, and dignity; all bearing an expression of pleasure adapted to such a day." Riccio died in 1567.

RICCIO, Felice, called Brusasorci the Younger, was the son and scholar of the preceding, born at Verona, according to Ridolfi, in 1540. Losing his father when seventeen years of age, he completed his studies under Jacopo Ligozzi at Florence. On returning to Verona, he introduced a style extremely elegant and refined, as displayed in his Madonnas, with boys and beautiful cherubs, adorning various collections; and with features similar to those of Veronese, if not a little more spare. He also excelled in subjects requiring vigorous treatment; evinced by his picture of the Forge of Vulcan with the Cyclops, in the collection of Count Gazzola, which is designed in good Florentine taste, and powerfully colored. The churches of Verona possess many of Riccio's works, among which his St. Elena, in the church of that name, is greatly admired. His genius was inferior to that of his father, and he produced no fresco works; but some of his large pictures in oil are highly meritorious, particularly the Fall of Manna, in S. Giorgio at Verona. He also painted excellent portraits; and Lanzi mentions a number of his small pictures of sacred and other subjects, executed on stone or marble, which he colored with great skill, availing himself of the shades in the marble itself. Felice Riccio died in 1605. His sister Cecilia studied painting under her father, and attained considerable excellence in portraits.

RICCIO, Gio. Battista, called also Brusasorci, was the brother of the preceding. He studied under Paul Veronese, and painted a number of pictures for Verona, which were highly esteemed. He subsequently visited Vienna, and manifested sufficient abilities to be appointed painter to the Emperor. Nothing further is recorded of him, except that he remained in the Emperor's service during the rest of his life.

RICCIO, Mariano, a painter of Messina, born, according to Hackert, in 1510. He first studied under Alfonso Franco, but preferring the style of Polidoro da Caravaggio, he entered the school established by that master in Messina. He imitated his style so successfully that Hackert says his works pass for those of his instructor; but Lanzi remarks, "I think this can only apply to inexperienced purchasers, since if there be a painter, whose style it is almost impossible to imitate to deception, it is Polidoro da Caravaggio. In proof, the comparison may be made in Messina itself, where the Pietà of Polidoro, and the Madonna della Carità of Mariano, are placed near each other." Antonello, the son of Mariano, studied also under Caravaggio, and followed his style with considerable success. He flourished at Messina about 1576.

RICCIO, Il. See Bartolomeo Neroni.

RICCIOLINI, Niccolo and Michael Angelo. These two artists were born at Rome respectively in 1637 and 1654. They both executed a number of works for the churches of Rome. Lanzi says that the first had the reputation of a better designer than the second, and competed with Cav. Franceschini in the cartoons painted for several mosaics in the Vatican church. The second executed, among other works, several paintings in S. Lorenzo in Piscibus, and a ceiling in S. Maria in Campitelli. He died at Rome in 1715. Their portraits, painted by themselves, are in the Florentine Gallery.

RICHARDSON, Jonathan, an English portrait painter, was born about 1665. He was articled to a scrivener at an early age, but his master dying when six years of his apprenticeship had expired, he determined to gratify his natural inclinations, and commenced studying painting under John Riley After remaining four years with that artist, Richardson established himself as a portrait painter, married the niece of his instructor, and succeeded in gaining a good share of public patronage. During the lives of his cotemporaries, Kneller and Dahl, he was considerably employed; and, after their death, he was esteemed at the head of his profession in England. According to Walpole, his heads were distinguished for vigor and boldness of coloring, freedom and firmness of execution; but his pictures were destitute of imagination, his attitudes, draperies, and backgrounds were totally devoid of taste. He wrote three works relating to art, containing much excellent advice to artists, which he never reduced to practice. These were "The Theory of Painting"; "The Connoisseur"; and "An Account of some of the Statues, Bas-Reliefs, Drawings, and Pictures in Italy, &c., with remarks by Mr. Richardson, senior and junior. His son visited Italy, and wrote many notes, letters, and observations, from which, after his return, they prepared the last mentioned work for the press. Richardson retired from the practice of his profession long before his death, which occurred in 1745. There are a few etchings by him, among which are a portrait of himself, two portraits of Alex. Pope, one of Milton, and one of Dr. Mead.

RICHARDUS, Martin, a Flemish painter, born at Antwerp in 1591, and died there in 1636. He is said to have painted landscapes in a good style.

RICHART, F. J. de la Mare, a French engraver of little note, born at Bayeux about 1630, and died at Versailles in 1718. He executed, among other plates, one of St. Jerome, *after L. de la Hire;* two plates of the Ecce Homo and the Virgin, the former inscribed *F. de la Mare, fec.* 1650· and sixteen fancy heads, mentioned by Dumesnil in the style of Lievens, without marks.

RICHER, P., an engraver mentioned by Nagler, who flourished from 1630 to 1660, and executed, among other works, eleven plates of philosophical tables by Louis Lesclaches.

RICHIER, Ligier, a French sculptor, a native of Dagonville in Lorraine, who flourished during the 16th century. He visited Paris, and acquired a knowledge of sculpture; after which he returned to his native place, and practised the art with considerable reputation. His most distinguished work is a marble figure of the Holy Sepulchre, with thirteen statues surrounding it; which is now in the parish church of the town of St. Mihiel.

RICHIERI, Antonio, a Ferrarese painter of mediocre abilities, who flourished about the middle of the 17th century. According to Passeri, he studied under Giovanni Lanfranco, and afterwards accompanied that master to Naples and Rome, where he painted at the Teatini from his designs Passeri says he afterwards devoted himself to engraving, and executed several plates from the designs of his instructor. Strutt miscalls him A. Richer.

RICHMANS. See Ryckmans.

RICHOMME, Joseph Theodore, an eminent French engraver of the present century, was born at Paris in 1785. He acquired an excellent knowledge of design under Regnault the painter, and subsequently studied engraving under J. J. Coiny.

In 1806, he gained the grand prize at the Institute for the best engraving, and was subsequently chosen a member of that body, and of the Legion of Honor. Stanley classes his plates with those of the best modern Italian engravers. It is not ascertained whether he is still living. Among others, there are by him the following:

The Triumph of Galatea; *after Raffaelle.* The Five Saints; *do.* The Holy Family; *do.* Adam and Eve; *do.* Neptune and Amphitrite; *after Giulio Romano.* Venus at the Bath; *after the Antique.* Andromache; *after Guerin.* Thetis crowning Vasco de Gama; *after Gerard.*

RICHTER, Christian, was a Swedish painter, and visited England in 1702, where he painted portraits, both in oil and in miniature, adopting the forcible coloring of Michael Dahl. Towards the latter part of his career he applied himself to enamelling, but died before making much progress in that branch, in 1732.

RICKE, Bernard de. This painter was born at Courtray about 1520. His instructor is not mentioned; but he painted history in his native place with a high degree of reputation, and afterwards settled at Antwerp, where he was chosen a member of the Academy in 1561. In the church of S. Martin at Courtray, there are two pictures by Ricke, representing the Decollation of St. Matthew, and Christ bearing his Cross; the latter is highly esteemed.

RICKMAN, Thomas, a distinguished English architect, born at Maidenhead, in 1776. He was intended for the medical profession, which he pursued for some time, but subsequently entered into commercial pursuits, and afterwards engaged as clerk in an insurance office at Liverpool. Having abundance of leisure in the latter occupation, he devoted his attention to the study of architecture, and examined the ancient edifices with great diligence, pursuing his inquiries without the aid of an instructor. He made many excellent designs, and carefully noted the slighter peculiarities, which had escaped less discerning eyes. He also attempted original plans, and when Parliament granted £1,000,000 to erect new churches, Rickman sent in a design, which was accepted. He then determined to devote himself entirely to architecture, and removed to Birmingham. Possessing no practical knowledge of the art, he engaged Mr. Henry Hutchinson as assistant in all his matters of business, and after the death of the latter in 1830, he entered into partnership with Mr. Hussey. As a writer on the art, he was highly esteemed, and gained great celebrity by his "Attempt to discriminate the styles of Architecture in England." This production was originally written for "Smith's Panorama of Science and Art," but was subsequently much extended and improved as a separate publication, and has become a standard work, quite indispensable to the student. Its publication opened his way to an extensive practice, and procured him patronage in the most influential quarters. Rickman probably erected a larger number of churches than any other English architect. Among his other edifices are the new court and buildings of St. John's College, the restorations at Rose Castle, and the palace of the Bishop of Carlisle. He died in 1843.

RICO, Andreas, an ancient painter, a native of the island of Candia, who probably flourished about the middle of the 14th century. There is a Madonna in the Florentine Gallery, inscribed in Latin characters, *Andreas Rico de Candia pinxit.* Notwithstanding the rudeness of the composition, drapery, &c., this ancient work is still distinguished by such fresh, vivid, and brilliant coloring, that Lanzi says, "there is no modern work that would not lose by a comparison; the coloring is so extremely strong and firm, that, when tried with the iron, it does not liquefy, but rather scales off, and breaks in minute portions." He further remarks, "the Greeks were undoubtedly in possession of the best methods transmitted to them by a tradition, which, though in some measure corrupted, was confessedly derived from their ancestors." This opinion of a highly eminent and candid connoisseur may perhaps excite modern artists to investigate more closely the ancient methods of coloring, which were undoubtedly far more durable than those at present in use.

RIDINGER, or RIEDINGER, John Elias, a German painter and engraver of animals, was born at Ulm in 1695; died at Augsburg in 1769. He studied under Christian Resch, and subsequently settled at Augsburg. His animals are designed with admirable correctness, and his pictures possess considerable merit of execution. As an engraver, he was much employed by the booksellers, and executed many plates of animals, which have seldom been surpassed; the compositions are ingenious and animated, and each animal is drawn in its peculiar character and attitude, with surprising exactness. His two sons, Martin Elias and John James, were also engravers; the former was distinguished for his talents in delineating insects. Among the principal plates of John Elias R., are the following:

A set of twelve plates of the Creation. A set of Heads of Wolves and Foxes. Four plates of Boar huntings. A set of sixteen plates representing the mode of hunting different animals in Germany, with inscriptions in German and French. Eighteen plates of Horsemanship. Thirteen plates of various Wild Beasts. A Lion-hunting; *after Rubens;* for the Dresden Gallery.

RIDOLFI, Claudio, a painter born at Verona in 1560. According to Cav. Carlo Ridolfi, he was of noble birth, and first studied for amusement under Dario Pozzo, in his native place; but being afterwards compelled by necessity to practise the art, he became the scholar of Paolo Veronese, and the rival of the Bassans. Not finding much employment at Venice, he removed to Rome, and afterwards to Urbino, where he formed an intimacy with Federigo Baroccio, then in high reputation Aided by the advice and instruction of that master, he acquired an amenity of style, and a beauty in the airs of his heads, by which his subsequent works are distinguished. Ridolfi married at Urbino, and afterwards settled at Corinaldo, in the Marquisate of Ancona, where he painted many pictures for the churches of that place and its vicinity, which, according to Lanzi, "yield little in tone to the best colorists of his native school, and are often conducted with a design, a sobriety, and a delicacy, sufficient to excite their envy." His portraits, also, are distinguished for their dignity, character, and accurate resemblance. There are many of his works at Urbino, among which are his highly esteemed pictures of the Birth of St. John the Baptist, in S. Lucia; and the Presentation in the Temple, in S. Spirito Santo. At Rimini, Lanzi mentions by him a fine Deposition from the Cross; there are also some of his works at Venice, Verona, and Padua; in the celebrated church of S. Giustina, in the last city, is his admirable picture representing the honors rendered to the Benedictine order, distinguished for appropriate invention, rich ornaments, elegant and well finished execution. He died in 1644.

RIDOLFI, Cav. Carlo, a distinguished Italian painter and writer on the art, born at Vicenza, according to Orlandi, in 1602. He studied under Antonio Vassilacchi, called Aliense, and subsequently gained great improvement from the works of the best masters at Verona and Vicenza. He afterwards distinguished himself at Venice, and painted, among other works, the Visitation of the Virgin, in the church of the Ognissanti, "exhibiting," says Lanzi, "some novelty in the adaptation of the colors, a fine relief, and exactness in every part." There are also other specimens by him in the churches of Venice and the State, but most of his works were executed for private collections, consisting of portraits, half-length figures, and historical pieces. As a writer on art, Ridolfi deserves high commendation, and Lanzi ranks him among the best Italian biographers. His Lives of the Venetian Painters were published at Venice in 1648, entitled *Le Maraviglie dell' arte, ovvero le Vite degl' illustri pittori Veneti, e dello Stato.* Orlandi says he died about 1660; Boschini mentions him as among the *living* authors, in 1660; Zanetti records his epitaph, placing his death in 1658, at the age of 64.

RIDOLFO, Michele di, called Ghirlandaio, was a distinguished Florentine painter, and flourished about 1550. According to Vasari, he studied successively under Lorenzo Credi and Gio. Antonio Sogliani; after which he entered the school of Ridolfo di Domenico Ghirlandaio, assumed the name of that master, and was treated by him rather as a son than a companion. They painted many pictures in concert, which always pass under their names, among which is the St. Anne of Città di Castello, commended by Lanzi for its exquisite design, and peculiar fullness of coloring. Michele paid particular attention to coloring, and manifested his excellence in various fresco paintings over several gates of Florence; he was also employed by Vasari as the companion of his labors. His friend and coadjutor died in 1560, after which Michele is mentioned as operating in 1568.

RIDOLFO, Pietro di, a Florentine painter, who flourished about 1612, and is supposed to have studied under the last of the Ghirlandai. Lanzi says there is a large altar-piece at Florence by him, representing the Ascension. Strutt notices an engraver of this name, who flourished from 1710 to 1723, and executed, among other plates, a frontispiece to a collection of views in ancient and modern Rome, published at Venice in 1716, in a style resembling that of Cornelius Bloemaert, though very inferior.

RIEDEL, John Anthony, a German designer and engraver, born at Prague in 1732, and died, according to Nagler, in 1816. He was appointed Keeper of the Dresden Gallery, and engraved, in the style of Rembrandt, several plates from the pictures in that celebrated collection. Nagler enumerates fifty-two, among which are the following; the latest is dated 1772.

The Virgin and infant Christ; *after Baroccio.* The Seven Sacraments; *after Gio. Maria Crespi.* A portrait of Rembrandt; *after a picture by himself.* A Warrior, with a cap and feather; *do.* A Portrait of a Lady holding a Letter; *after Vandyck.*

RIETER, Henry, a Swiss landscape painter, born at Winterthur in 1751. He early manifested an inclination for art, and studied under a painter of his native place, but afterwards visited Dresden, and completed his professional education under Graf. He gained considerable improvement from the works in the Dresden Gallery, particularly the landscapes of Claude, Berghem, and Ruysdael. In 1775 he visited Holland; and two years after, he commenced practising at Berne. About this time, Aberli was prosecuting his work on the landscapes of Switzerland, and he engaged Rieter to accompany him in his excursions. The latter made many excellent designs of Swiss scenery, and in 1786, after the death of Aberli, he continued the publication of the work. He was appointed Professor of Design in the public school at Berne, and held that office for thirty-seven years. His landscapes possess considerable merit, particularly those of a wild and romantic character, such as his Cascade of Reichenbach, which has been engraved. He died in 1818, leaving several sons, one of whom continued the publication of the above mentioned work.

RIETSCHOOF, John Klaasz, a Dutch marine painter, was born at Hoorn in 1652. He studied under Ludolf Backhuysen, and attained great distinction for his admirable sea-pieces and storms, so much in the style of his instructor that they are sometimes mistaken for the works of Backhuysen. His calms possess considerable merit, with some resemblance to the works of Wm. Vandervelde; but his hurricanes and tempests are represented with the most impressive fidelity. Many of his pictures have been purchased for the private collections of England, and they are highly prized both there and in Holland. Rietschoof died in 1719. His son and scholar, Henry R., was born at Hoorn in 1678, and painted similar subjects, which, though unequal to the works of his father, possess sufficient merit to find a place in the Dutch collections. He also copied the works of Backhuysen with great exactness, and his works are probably mostly attributed to that master or to the elder Rietschoof.

RIGAUD, Hyacinthe, an eminent French portrait painter, surnamed the French Vandyck, was born at Perpignan in 1659. He acquired the elements of design from his father, Matthias Rigaud; but the latter dying while he was very young, he was placed under a portrait painter at Montpellier, where he continued till his eighteenth year, and then settled at Lyons. Notwithstanding the ample encouragement he received in that city, he was determined to attain greater excellence. In 1681 he visited Paris, to study historical painting in the Academy, and in the following year he obtained the grand prize, which entitled him to the royal pension. Instead of proceeding to Italy, however, he decided to accept the advice of Charles le Brun, and confine himself to portrait painting. Adopting the admirable style of Vandyck, he attained great excellence, and was very extensively patronized by Louis XIV., whose portrait he frequently painted; also by the French nobility, and many illustrious foreigners. His heads are full of character and expression, his touch is bold and free, and his coloring more chaste than usual among French artists. Unfortunately for the beauty of his portraits, they are mostly represented with enormous perukes and preposterous habiliments; but this was rather the fault of the times than the artist. In 1700, Rigaud was chosen a member of the Royal Academy, and presented, as the reception piece, his admirable portrait of Desjardins.—Among his few historical works are a picture of St. Andrew, in the hall of the Academy; and a Nativity, engraved by Drevet. Many of his portraits have also been engraved by the best French artists, among which are those of Bossuet, bishop of Meaux, by Drevet; and his own portrait, by Gerard Edelinck. Rigaud was honored with the Order of St. Michael; was appointed a professor, and afterwards director of the French Academy. He died in 1743.

RIGAUD, Jean, a French painter and engraver of landscapes and views, was born at Paris about 1700. He engraved many plates from his own designs, in a spirited and masterly style, with figures neatly and correctly drawn. Several of his etchings represent views in the vicinity of London, wherefore he is supposed to have visited England. Nagler says he died in 1754, and gives a long list of his plates, among which are the following. His son, Jean Baptiste R., engraved a view of the Bourbon palace, after a design by his father.

A pair of Views of Marseilles, at the time of the plague in 1720. A set of six Views of the Chateau and Gardens of Marly. The Garden of the Tuileries. A View of the Chateau of the Luxembourg. A View of Hampton Court. St. James' Park. Greenwich Park. Greenwich Hospital. A set of six Landscapes with figures. A set of six Views in France, with rural amusements.

RIGAUD, John Francis. This historical painter was probably of French origin. He visited England in the latter part of the last century, and practised the art there for a number of years. He painted a number of pictures for Boydell's Shakspeare Gallery; also several subjects of a sacred character, and subjects from the history of England. He was chosen a member of the Royal Academy, and presented his picture of Samson breaking his Bonds, in a style partaking more of the French than the English school. The reputation of Rigaud has been considerably diffused through many engravings of his pictures, and by his translation of Leonardo da Vinci's Treatise on Painting, illustrated with copper plates. His death is supposed to have happened in 1810.

RIGHETTI, Mario, a painter born at Bologna about 1590, who studied under Lucio Massari. There are several of his works in the Bolognese churches, among which are the Nativity in S. Lucia, and Christ appearing to Mary Magdalene in S. Giacomo Maggiore.

RILEY, John, an English portrait painter, born at London in 1646. He studied under Isaac Fuller and Gerard Zoust. Walpole considers him as one of the best English artists, but being very diffident of his own abilities, he was little noticed until after the death of Lely. He painted the portraits of Charles II., James II. and his Queen; also those of William and Mary, who appionted him their court painter. Several of his works, according to Bryan, would have done credit to either Lely or Kneller, particularly his portrait of Lord Keeper North at Wroxton. He died in 1691.

RILEY, Charles Reuben, an English painter was born at London about 1752. He studied under J. H. Mortimer, and drew the gold medal at the Academy in 1778, for his picture of the Sacrifice of Iphigenia. At the recommendation of his instructor, he was employed by the Duke of Richmond in the decorations at Goodwood; and subsequently embellished the mansion of Mr. Conelly, in Ireland. During the remainder of his life, he was principally occupied in making designs for the booksellers, evincing considerable fancy, taste, and ability. Riley died in 1798.

RIMINALDI, Orazio, an eminent painter, born at Pisa in 1598. After studying under Aurelio Lomi in his native place, he visited Rome, and entered the school of Orazio Lomi, called Gentileschi. During a residence of several years at Rome, he studied with great assiduity the antique and the productions of the great masters, and on returning to Pisa, became distinguished as one of the most promising artists of his time. He did not imitate either of the Lomi, but followed at first the style of Caravaggio, and afterwards adopted that of Domenichino, "to rival whom," says Lanzi, "he seems to have been intended by nature. From the time that the art of painting revived in Pisa, that city had not perhaps so eminent a painter, nor have many better been born on the banks of the Arno, a soil so propitious to the arts. Grand in contour and in drapery, after the manner of the Caracci, pleasing and agreeable in his carnations, full, free, and delicate in the management of his pencil, he would have been faultless, had not the wretched style of engraving raised prejudices against him." Among his principal works in the churches of Pisa, are two in the Cathedral, representing the Brazen Serpent, and Sampson destroying the Philistines, forming a perfect study to gain a knowledge of that epoch of painting. His Martyrdom of St. Cecilia is now in the Florentine Gallery. Lanzi says his last work, the Assumption, painted in oil, is one of the best conceived and most perfect works that Tuscany has ever beheld. Unfortunately for the art, Riminaldi was carried off by the plague, according to Morrona, in 1631, his Assumption was feebly completed by his brother Girolamo, and sold at 5000 crowns. Had this artist lived longer, it involves no great hazard to assert that he would have been a second Zampieri.

RIMINALDI, Girolamo, was the brother of the preceding, and flourished at Pisa about 1630. He gained considerable distinction in his time, and was invited to Naples, where he executed some works in the chapel of S. Gennaro. According to Morrona, he afterwards visited Paris at the request of Marie de Medicis, and was employed by the French court. There are a few of his works in the collections of Pisa and other places.

RIMINALDI, Domenico, an Italian sculptor in wood, was born at Pisa in 1595. He gained considerable distinction for his admired works in the Cathedral of Pisa, among which was a bas-relief of the grand altar, representing the Coronation of the Virgin, afterwards placed in a chapel of the Campo Santo. He died at Pisa in 1637.

RIMINI, Bartolomeo da. See Coda.

RIMINI, Lattanzio da. See Della Marca.

RINALDO, Santo, called il Tromba (the Trumpet), was a reputable Florentine painter, and flourished from about 1640 to 1660. He studied under Francesco Furini, and painted landscapes and battle pieces.

RINCON, Antonio del, a Spanish painter, born at Guadalaxara, in 1446. He is termed the founder of the Spanish school. He studied at Rome, and on returning to Spain was appointed painter to the court of Ferdinand and Isabella. Many of his works perished in the destructive conflagration of the Prado, in 1608; the principal that remain are two portraits of his royal patrons Ferdinand and Isabella, in the church of San Juan de los Reyes at Toledo; and an altar-piece in the church of Robledo de Chabela, a small town in the archbishopric of Toledo. Rincon was appointed groom of the king's chamber, and a knight of the order of Santiago. He died in 1500.

RING, Peter de, a Dutch painter of still-life, who flourished about 1650. His name is not mentioned by the writers of his country, but there is an admired picture by him in the Museum at Amsterdam, representing a table covered with blue velvet, upon which are various kinds of fruit, and shell-fish. His works are generally marked with a *ring*, probably in allusion to his name; several were taken to England a number of years ago, and are supposed to have been attributed to John David de Heem.

GR RINGGLI, Gothard, a reputable Swiss painter, born at Zurich, according to Füessli, in 1575. Little is known of the circumstances of his life, and his instructor is not mentioned. He was employed by the magistrates of Berne to paint several large pictures relating to the national history, such as the Foundation of the city of Berne, and the Arms of the Republic, sustained by allegorical figures of Religion and Liberty. Füessli praises them for ingenuity of composition, correctness of design, vigorous and beautiful execution. Among the other excellent works of Ringgli are his pictures of Christ at the Tomb, Susanna in the Bath, and Faith preserved from the Storms of Persecution. Nagler and Brulliot mention about twelve etchings by this artist, from his own designs, in a bold, free style, marked with a monogram composed of the letters G. R., or *G. Ringly u Zurich, fecit*, 1628. He died in 1635.

RIOJA, Domenico de la, a reputable Spanish sculptor, who flourished at Madrid about 1645, under the reign of Philip IV. Among other works he executed a statue of St. Peter, for a church of that city; and several bronze statues for the Octagon Saloon of the royal palace. He died about 1656.

RIPOSO, Felice. See Ficherelli.

RISTORO, F., was an old Florentine painter and architect, who flourished in the 13th century, and erected, in concert with F. Sisto, the grand bridges of the Carraja and the Holy Trinity, in 1264. Baldinucci says their pictures resemble those of Arnolfo, and proceeds to class them among the scholars of that master; but Lanzi thinks it more probable that Arnolfo, and even Cimabue, imitated them.

RISUENO, José, a reputable Spanish painter and sculptor, was born at Granada about 1640. He studied both arts under Alonso Cano, and attained considerable reputation. He painted a number of pictures in the churches of his native city, distinguished for their good taste of design, soft and harmonious coloring. His largest painting is in the cupola of the Carthusians, where he wrought in concert with his eulogist, Antonio Palomino. There are also many of his sculptures in the churches of Granada, in the style of Alonso Cano. Risueno died at Granada in 1721.

RITCHIE, John, a Scottish sculptor, was born at Musselburg in 1810. He was the brother of the distinguished sculptor Alexander Ritchie, who studied at Rome, under Thorwaldsen, and is now an Associate of the Royal Scottish Academy. He acquired a good knowledge of the art in his native country, and produced a number of works, which evince considerable skill and inventive genius. His statue of Sir Walter Scott, at Glasgow, is a work of uncommon merit; and his group from "The Deluge," exhibited at Edinburg in 1832, received much approbation. Upon the arrival of his brother Alexander from Rome, John Ritchie entered his studio as an assistant, and wrought with him for many years. At length Mr. Davidson of London, having seen Ritchie's model of "The Deluge," commissioned him to execute it in marble, whereupon he started for Italy, in order to prosecute his work with every advantage. Unfortunately, he died soon after his arrival, in the autumn of 1850.

RITRATTI, Santino da'. See Vandi.

RITUS, Michael, an obscure engraver, who lived about the middle of the 17th century, and executed, among other works, a plate of the Virgin and Infant, *after Annibale Caracci*. 1647.

RIVALZ, Jean Pierre, a French painter, born at Bastide d'Anjou in 1625. He had a strong inclination for art, and learned design from a monk, named Ambroise Fredeau, who had been a scholar of Simon Vouet. He afterwards visited Rome for improvement; and according to the *Biographie Universelle*, he attained such excellence, particularly in perspective and architecture, that Poussin employed him to assist him in some of his works. On returning to France, he settled at Toulouse, and was appointed painter to the city. He executed many works which compared favorably with contemporaneous productions of the French school; but they were nearly all destroyed in 1793. Rivalz instructed a number of scholars, among whom was la Fage. He died in 1706.

RIVALZ, Antoine, a distinguished French painter, the son of J. P. Rivalz, was born at Toulouse in 1667. After acquiring from his father the elements of design, he visited Paris for improvement, and afterwards went to Rome, where he studied the works of the great masters with assiduity, and succeeded in drawing the prize at the Academy of St. Luke, for his picture of the Fall of the Rebel Angels. On returning to Toulouse, he established himself in that city, and practised the art with reputation for many years. Inferior to his father in beauty of coloring, he surpassed him in fertility of invention and correctness of design; he also possessed an extraordinary talent for copying the productions of the great Italian masters. Rivalz was very active, both in words and deeds, in founding and establishing the Academy of Painting, in his native city, where most of his works are to be found. He died in 1735. There are by him a great number of drawings, executed in a very free style, resembling that of Raymond de la Fage; also a few spirited etchings, among which are the following: The Martyrdom of St. Symphorianus. An Allegorical subject of Vice driven away by Truth, as the enemy of the Arts and Sciences; in memory of *N. Poussin.* Four plates of Allegorical subjects for a treatise on Painting, by *Dupuy du Grez.*

RIVALZ, Jean Pierre, a French painter and engraver, was the son of Antoine P. After acquiring a knowledge of design in his own country, he visited Italy for improvement, and remained there eleven years. The Pope made him a knight of the Order of the Golden Spur. On returning to France he settled at Toulouse, and gained considerable reputation. Among his principal works in that city, are those at the Chartreuse, and at the hotel of the Grand Prior of Malta. He established a school of painting and engraving, and published a collection of prints in folio, engraved by his scholars, of a number of antiques, in his own possession. In 1770, he published a work entitled *Analyse des ouvrages de peinture, sculpture, etc., qui sont dans l'hotel de ville de Toulouse*, 8 vo. Rivalz died in 1785.

RIVALZ, Bartholomew, a French engraver, was the nephew and pupil of Antoine R., born at Toulouse in 1724. He executed a number of spirited etchings, among which are the following: The Fall of the Rebel Angels; *after Ant. Rivalz.* Judith and Holofernes, *do.;* Joseph and Potiphar's Wife, *do.;* The Death of Mary Magdalene, *after Benedetto Luti.*

RIVAROLA, Alfonso, called Il Chenda, a distinguished Italian painter, was born at Ferrara in 1607. He studied under Carlo Bononi, and became his most distinguished disciple. At the death of that master he was proposed by Guido Reni, to complete the Marriage of the Virgin, sketched by Bononi, for the church of S. Maria in Vado at Ferrara. Rivarola also painted a number of excellent works for the churches, which are highly esteemed; among them is his Baptism of St. Agostino, in the church dedicated to that saint, "exhibited," says Lanzi, "in a temple of noble architecture, in a style of foreshortening that displays a master"; also the Resurrection, at the Teatini; and the Brazen Serpent, in S. Niccolo. There are a few of his works in the private collections of Ferrara, but he seems to have aimed rather at popular admiration, and was frequently employed as architect and painter for arranging tournaments and other public festivals. Rivarola died at the premature age of thirty-three, in 1640.

RIVE, Peter Louis, a reputable Swiss portrait painter, born at Geneva in 1753. He studied under Chevalier Fassin, and afterwards visited Italy for improvement. He traveled through Switzerland and Savoy, making many designs of the most romantic scenery, which were of great use in his subsequent productions. His works were much esteemed, and are scattered over Germany, Russia, and England. Among the principal is a grand landscape, of a warm and vigorous coloring, presented by Rive to the Society for the Encouragement of the Fine Arts at Geneva; and a splendid View of Mont Blanc, in the Cabinet of Prince Galitzin, at St. Petersburg.

RIVELLO. See Moretto.

RIVERDITI, Marc' Antonio, a painter born at Alessandria della Paglia, who studied at Bologna, according to Lanzi, and flourished in that city, in the latter half of the 18th century.—He painted portraits with considerable success, and Lanzi commends his subjects of history for their clear, chaste style, and freedom from mannerism. He frequently imitated the style of Guido, particularly in his Conception, in the Padri Camaldolesi. He died, according to Lanzi and Zani, in 1774.

RIVIERA, Francesco, a French painter, who visited Italy, and flourished at Leghorn during the first half of the 18th century. According to Lanzi, he was much esteemed for his talents in painting conversations and Turkish ballets for the private collections. Having been extensively employed in painting portraits for the foreign nobility of Florence, his name must be well known in England and France, although not mentioned in the English dictionaries. There is a portrait of Riviera, executed by himself, in the Florentine gallery. He died at Leghorn about 1750.

RIVOLA, Giuseppe, a Milanese painter, born in 1740, was a scholar of Filippo Abbiati. He painted much for the private collections, and, according to Lanzi, was esteemed by his fellow citizens among the best pupils of his instructor.

RIZI, Francisco. This artist, the son of Antonio Rizi, a Bolognese painter, who had accompanied Federigo Zuccaro to Spain, was born at Madrid in 1608. He studied under Vincenzio Carducci, and early manifested great natural talents; but being allowed to indulge his abundant imagination, he neglected academic study, and soon fell into a dangerous facility of execution. His brilliant, though superficial talents, gained the approval of the public; Rizi was appointed painter to the cathedral of Toledo, and in 1656, court painter to Philip IV.; he was also continued in that office by Charles II., who added to it the honor of deputy Keeper of the royal Keys. There are many of his works in the palaces, churches, and cathedrals of Spain, which sufficiently evince that he contributed materially to the downfall of art in that country. His last design, probably his best, was a sketch for the esteemed altar-piece in the sacristy of the Escurial, completed after the death of Rizi, by his disciple Coello. He died in 1685.

RIZI, Fray Juan, the brother of the preceding, was born at Madrid in 1595. He surpassed his brother in correctness of design, and the conduct of the chiaro-scuro. In the latter part of his life, he went to Rome, and was appointed an archbishop by Clement X., in 1675, but died before entering upon his office. There are a number of his principal works in the Benedictine monastery of S. Martin at Madrid. During the peninsular wars, a painting representing St. Benedict celebrating mass, was removed to Paris, and placed in the Louvre; but it was restored in 1815.

RIZZO, Marco Luciano, an eminent Venetian artist in mosaic. This art was commenced in Italy by the Greeks as early as the eleventh century, and was subsequently continued by the Italians. Its gradual improvement may be traced by the invaluable specimens preserved in the church of S. Mark at Venice, first the antique, and afterwards the antique modern style. Finally, according to Lanzi, the art was completely reformed about 1517, by Marco Luciano Rizzo, and Vincenzio Bianchini, under whom, and the two Zuccati, it attained such perfection, that Vasari says "it would not be possible to effect more with colors." See *Bianchini.*

RÒ, GIOVANNI. See JOHN ROTTENHAMER.

ROBART, a Dutch painter who flourished during the last century, and is said to have been a scholar of John van Huysum. He painted fruit, flowers, dead game, and landscapes. His works are probably attributed to some more eminent painter.

ROBATTO, GIO. STEFANO, a painter born at Savona, in the Genoese state, in 1649. He studied at Rome under Carlo Maratti, and subsequently matured his genius by visiting other schools of Italy. After a visit in Germany, he returned to his native place, and executed a number of excellent works, which excited the unqualified praise of the Genoese professors, especially for their beautiful coloring. Unfortunately for the cause of art, he degraded his noble talents by a fatal passion for gaming, and produced many inferior works at a trifling price, so that, according to Lanzi, it may be said that Savona had not a better nor a worse painter than Robatto. One of his best frescos is in the cloister of the Capuchins, representing St. Francis receiving the Stigmata. He died in 1733.

ROBBIA, LUCA DELLA, a Florentine sculptor, who flourished about 1450. It is very probable that he was a scholar of Lorenzo Ghiberti, as he seems to have executed a part of the bas reliefs for the famous gates of the Florentine Baptistery. Together with his brother Agostino, and his nephew Andrea, he gained considerable reputation by his enamelled sculptures in terra cotta. At San Miniato, near Florence, there is a bas-relief by Luca, representing the Virgin and Infant; and in the Hospital of the Innocents at Florence, are several figures of children by Andrea, in demi-relief, commended by Vasari.

ROBERT, NICOLAS, a French painter, was born at Orleans in 1610. He gained considerable distinction for his miniature pictures of animals, insects, and plants, and was employed by Gaston, duke of Orleans, to paint the most curious beasts and birds in the royal menagerie. These miniatures are still preserved in the royal library at Paris; there are also by him several etchings of similar subjects, and a set of six plates of vases, after the designs of Charmeton. Robert died in 1684.

ROBERT, A., a French engraver, who flourished about the middle of the 18th century. He studied under J. C. le Blond, and is chiefly known by a number of good prints, colored according to the system of his instructor, by printing with four plates.

ROBERT, HUBERT, a reputable French painter, was born at Paris in 1733. After acquiring the elements of design in his native city, he visited Rome for improvement, and studied in the French Academy, then under the direction of Carlo Natoire. During a residence of several years at Rome, he made many accurate designs of architectural monuments in that city; he afterwards returned to Paris, and was principally employed in painting architectural and perspective views. Many of them represent scenes in the vicinity of Rome, which were highly esteemed, combining the styles of Gio. Paolo Pannini and Joseph Vernet. Robert was chosen a member of the Royal Academy, and was twice invited to St. Petersburg by the Empress Catherine II., in 1782 and 1791. There are by him several spirited etchings, among which is a set of ten architectural landscapes, entitled *Les Soirées de Rome.* He died in 1808.

ROBERT, NICOLAS, a French painter, who visited the court of Savoy at Chambery, and was employed, according to Lanzi, by the Duke (Philibert I.), from 1473 to 1477. His works have either perished, or remain unknown; and Lanzi thinks it probable that he was a miniature painter, or illuminator of manuscripts.

ROBERT, PAUL PONCE ANTOINE, a French painter, born at Sery en Porcien, in Champagne, in 1686. He studied under Pierre Jacques Cazes, and afterwards in Italy. On returning to Paris, he painted an altar-piece for the church of the Capuchins, representing the Martyrdom of St. Fidele, which is his principal work as a painter, and gained him a pension from Cardinal de Rohan. Robert etched several plates from the chiaro-scuros by Nicolas le Sueur, for the Crozat collection, which are described in the Manual of Huber and Rost. He died at Paris in 1733.

ROBERT, LOUIS LEOPOLD, a painter of the French school, was born in the Canton of Neufchatel, in Switzerland, in 1794. He early manifested a strong inclination for art, and was taken by the engraver Charles Girardet to Paris, where he entered the school of David, and made excellent progress in painting. He also studied engraving under Girardet, and in 1814 gained the second prize for a fine copper plate. He made strenuous exertions to gain the grand prize in painting; but the congress of Vienna having transferred to Prussia in 1815, his native province Neufchatel, he was declared a foreigner, and excluded from competition in the Academy. The banishment of his friend and instructor David, at the Restoration, induced Robert to leave France, and he accordingly returned to his native province, where he painted portraits for about a year and a half, and was then offered a pension to enable him to go to Rome, by M. de Mezerac. During his residence in Italy, he prosecuted his studies with the greatest energy and assiduity. The Roman government having captured a large number of bandits, with their wives and children, Robert frequently visited the prison, and made many faithful studies to illustrate their wild and romantic mode of life. In 1828, he returned and settled in his native place. Several of his pictures were sent to the Louvre, and were greatly admired; such as his Corinne singing on Cape Misenum, exhibited in 1822, under the title of *L'Improvisateur Napolitain,* and highly praised for its simplicity, grandeur, and varied expression in the figures. His Fête of the Madonna dell' Arco, and his Return of the Harvesters, are also much commended; the latter has been engraved. Robert was of melancholy temperament, and finally put an end to his life, in 1835.

ROBERTELLI, AURELIO, a painter who flourished at Savona, in the Genoese state, in the latter part of the 15th century. Lanzi mentions a picture of the Virgin by him, painted on a column of the old cathedral and subsequently transferred to the new one, where it excites the particular veneration of the people.

ROBERTS, James, an English engraver, was born in Devonshire in 1725, and executed several plates of landscapes and views from the pictures of Richard Wilson, George Barret, Smith of Chichester, and others.

ROBERTSON, George, an English painter, was born at London about 1742. After acquiring the elements of design in Mr. Shipley's drawing school, he visited Italy for improvement, and produced several landscapes of considerable merit. He subsequently made a voyage to Jamaica, and designed several views in that island, some of which were exhibited in the Academy in 1775. Meeting with little encouragement in landscape painting, he adopted the profession of a drawing-master, in which he was more successful. There are a few etchings by Robertson, from his own designs. He died in 1788.

ROBETTA, an old Italian engraver, concerning whom little is known. According to Huber, he was born at Florence about 1460; the researches of Vasari and Zani tend to show that he flourished also in the first part of the 16th century, cotemporary with Gio. Francesco Rustici, with whom and ten other Florentine artists he was accustomed to mingle in convivial entertainments, about 1512. Robetta followed the occupation of a goldsmith, and engraved a few plates in the rude manner practised in Italy before the time of Marc' Antonio. His prints are very scarce; Zani speaks of having seen thirty, signed *Robeta*, or *Robetta*, but more commonly Robta, or R. B. T. A. Bartsch gives a list of twenty-six, as follows:

*List of Prints by, and attributed to, Robetta.*

SUBJECTS FROM THE OLD TESTAMENT.

1. The Creation of Eve; *not signed.* 2. Adam and Eve driven from Paradise; *not signed.* 3. Adam and Eve, and their two Children; *signed* RBTA. There are two impressions of this plate. In the *first* the sky is white; the *second* is retouched, and there are several clouds in the sky, particularly to the right. 4. Adam and Eve, and their two Children; *no mark.* The *first* state before a round hole at the bottom of the plate. 5. Adam and Eve and their two Children; *no mark.*

SUBJECTS FROM THE NEW TESTAMENT.

6. The Adoration of the Kings; *signed* ROBETTA. 7. The Nativity; *not signed*, but undoubtedly his work. 8. Jesus Christ baptized in the river Jordan; *signed* RBTA. 9. Jesus Christ taking leave of his Mother; *do.* 10. The Resurrection of Christ; *do.* 11. The Virgin presenting her breast to the Infant; *signed* ROBTA. 12. The Virgin seated in a landscape, &c.; *signed* RBTA. 13. The Virgin with Angels, &c.; *not signed*, but considered one of the most beautiful pieces of the master. 14. St. Sebastian and St. Roch; *not signed.* 15. Faith and Charity, with their attributes; *signed* RBTA.

MYTHOLOGICAL SUBJECTS.

16. Ceres, with two goat-footed Infants; *signed* RBTA. 17. A young Man tied to a Tree, &c.; *do.* 18. Venus surrounded by Cupids; some traces of the name may be seen in a dark shadow. 19. Apollo and Marsyas; *signed* RBTA. 20. The young Hercules between Virtue and Vice; *not signed.* 21. Hercules killing the Hydra; *signed* RBTA. There are two impressions; in the *first*, the sky is left white; in the *second*, there are some clouds, and a falcon chasing a heron. 22. Hercules and Anteus; *not signed.* 23. The Lyrist; *signed* RBTA. 24 An old Woman and two amorous Couples, &c.; *not signed.* 25. A Man tied to a Tree by Cupid, &c.; on a tablet RORETA (*sic.*). 26 Mutius Scævola.; *signed* RBTA.

ROBINSON, R., an obscure English engraver, who left several plates in mezzotinto, among which are those of Sir James Worsley, knight; Thomas White, bishop of Peterborough; Charles II.; James II.; and Charles I., *after Vandyck.*

ROBINSON. This English painter was born at Bath, about 1715. He studied under John Vanderbank at London, and gained considerable distinction in portraits. He succeeded Jervas in his house in Cleveland Court, and obtained extensive employment. His draperies were painted in imitation of the style of Vandyck, but his coloring was feeble, and his abilities were of an inferior order. He died in 1745.

ROBSON, George Fennel, a distinguished English landscape painter in water-colors, was born at Durham in 1790. He early manifested a strong inclination for art, and was accustomed to observe, with intense interest, the operations of the artists who frequently visited his native town, to design the beautiful scenery in its vicinity. Encouraged by Mr. Wm. Daniell and Mr. Cotman, he produced several drawings of considerable merit, without the aid of regular instruction; and at the age of sixteen he visited London for improvement. For about a year, he maintained himself by the sale of his drawings, and then published a View of Durham, which brought him into public notice. He afterwards traveled through Scotland, Wales, and Ireland, designing many views of the most interesting scenery, distinguished for vigorous coloring and execution, and embellished with animals by the painter Hills. He was a member of the Water-Color Society, and sent a large number of drawings to the exhibitions of that association. His works were very popular during his life, and are still much esteemed. Robson died in 1833.

ROBUSTI. See Tintoretto.

ROCCA, Giacomo, a Roman painter, was probably born about 1520, and studied under Daniele Ricciarelli, called di Volterra. His pictures are mostly after the designs of other masters; and, according to Lanzi, they possess little merit of execution. Volterra, at his death, bequeathed to this artist a large number of designs by his instructor, Michael Angelo; and several pictures painted in concert with Rocca by Giuseppe Cesari, after some of these designs, established the reputation of the latter painter. Rocca died in the pontificate of Clement VIII., between 1592 and 1605.

ROCCA, Michele, called il Parmiggianino, a Roman painter, who flourished about the commencement of the 18th century. Lanzi says he gained considerable reputation, but does not mention any of his works. There is some danger, from the identity of their surnames, of confounding him with Mazzuoli and Scaglia.

ROCCADIRAME, Angiolillo, a Neapolitan painter, who flourished about the middle of the 15th century. According to Dominici, he was one of the best scholars of Antonio Solario, called Zingaro, and painted a picture in the church of S. Brigida, representing that Saint contemplating in a vision the Birth of Christ, which might pass with experienced connoisseurs for the work of his instructor.

ROCCHETTI, Marc' Antonio, a distinguished painter of Faenza, who flourished in the latter half of the 16th century. Lanzi supposes him to have been the same as Figurino da Faenza, enumerated by Vasari among the best disciples of Giulio Romano, but mentioned by no other writer. In the youth of Rocchetti, he executed for the church of S. Sebastiano at Faenza, many small pictures of subjects from the history of that saint, which were dispersed when the edifice was destroyed, and are now preserved with high esteem in private collections. He afterwards adopted a grander style, and imitated the manner of Baroccio with such simplicity of composition, and sweetness of coloring, that his works are quite conspicuous in the churches, particularly in S. Rocco, where he painted a picture of the titular saint, dated 1604. Lanzi also mentions another by him, in the Communal collection, which is highly praised, representing the Virgin with St. Francis, a bishop, and two portraits below. It is inscribed *M. Antonius Rochettus Faventinus pingebat.* 1594.

ROCHERS, Etienne des, a French engraver, who flourished at Paris in the first half of the 18th century. He was probably the pupil of P. Drevet, whose style he followed. His works do not possess much merit; but, according to the *Biographie Universelle*, he executed a set of 800 portraits of illustrious personages, was chosen a member of the Royal Academy, engraved a portrait of Charles VI., and was honored by that prince with a gold medal. He died in 1741.

ROCHFORD, P. de, a French engraver, who flourished about 1720. He practised the art for a number of years in his own country, and afterwards removed to Portugal, where he spent the remainder of his life. There are by him several plates after J. B. Santerre, and other painters; also part of the plates in the large folio collection of *Views of the Palace and Gardens of Versailles*, published by P. Menant.

ROCHIENNE, Pierre, a French engraver on wood, who flourished about the middle of the 16th century. According to Papillon, he executed, in concert with J. Ferlato, a set of indifferent wooden cuts for the New Testament in Latin, published in 1551. Several prints in the *Legende Dorée*, published in 1557, were also by him.

ROCQUE, J., a French engraver, who visited England, and executed, among other plates, two large plates of Wanstead House, in Essex.

RODE, Christian Bernard, a German painter and engraver, was born at Berlin in 1725. After acquiring the elements of design in his native city, he visited Paris, and studied under Charles Vanloo and Jean Restout. He subsequently passed some time in Italy, and then returned to Berlin. He painted history and portraits with flattering success; was employed for the churches of Berlin and other cities in Prussia; and executed a number of works for the royal palace of Sans Souci. As an engraver, he produced a large number of etchings, several of which are after his pictures in the public edifices. Rode died in 1797. Nagler gives a long list of his plates, among which are the following:

His Portrait; engraved by himself, *after Reclam.* Christ, with the Disciples at Emmaus. The Descent of the Holy Ghost. The Ascension; from his picture in the church at Rostock. St. Paul preaching. Christ in the Garden of Olives; from the picture in the church of S. Mary at Berlin. Joseph discovering himself to his Brethren

RODE, John Henry, a German engraver, the younger brother of the preceding, was born at Berlin in 1727. He first learned the business of a goldsmith, but afterwards devoted himself to engraving. After producing several admired plates at Berlin, he went to Paris, and studied under J. G. Wille, in whose finished style he executed several plates. On returning to Berlin, he published several prints from the designs of his brother, and soon acquired a distinguished reputation, but was cut off in the commencement of a flattering career, in 1759. The following are among his principal works:

The Portrait of John George Wille; *after Schmidt.* A Head of Epicurus; *after T. M. Preisler.* Jacob wrestling with the Angel; *after C. B. Rode.* An Ecce Homo; *do.* A Sacrifice of the Vestals; *do.*

RODERIGO, or RODRIGUEZ, Luigi, a Sicilian painter, probably of Spanish origin, who flourished, according to Hackert, in the first half of the 17th century. After acquiring a good knowledge of the art in Rome, he settled at Naples, and at first continued his studies under Bellisario Corenzio, whose style he subsequently relinquished for that of Giuseppe Cesari, called Cav. d'Arpino. There are many of his works in the public edifices of Naples, which have a degree of mannerism, but are distinguished for a certain grace and judgment superior to Arpino. Notwithstanding the amiable qualities of Roderigo, his former instructor—the treacherous and revengeful Bellisario—became jealous of his fame, and poisoned him in the flower of his life.

RODERIGO, Alonso, an eminent Sicilian painter, the brother of the preceding, was born at Messina in 1578. He attained a high reputation in his native place, and executed a large number of works for the churches and public edifices, which sufficiently evince, according to Hackert, his facility and excellence. Among his most admired works were the Probatica, in S. Cosmo de' Medici; and his capital picture of the two founders of Messina, in the senatorial palace, for which he received a thousand scudi. On the return of Antonio Ricci, called Barbalunga, to Messina, his fame and commissions began to decline; but being elevated above the influence of petty jealousies, he was nobly accustomed to term his rival the Caracci of Sicily. Roderigo died in 1648.

RODERIGO, Gio. Bernardino, called Il Pittor Santo, was the nephew and scholar of Luigi R., and flourished about 1650. He followed the style of Giuseppe Cesari with excellent success, and was commissioned by the Carthusian monks to complete a picture left imperfect at the death of that master.

RODERMONT, a Dutch engraver, who is also called *Rottermondt* and *Rotermans.* He flourished about 1640, and executed a number of plates, some of which are in the style of Rembrandt. Among others by him, are the portraits of Joannes Secundus, a Latin poet of the Hague, signed *Rodermont. fec.*; and Sir William Waller, with a Battle in the back-ground, *after C. Jansen.*

RODOLPH, Corrado. This artist was a native of Germany, the son of a sculptor, and flourished in the 17th century. After acquiring a knowledge of design from his father, he visited Paris, and afterwards Italy, where he studied in the school of Bernini. He then went to Spain, and gained great reputation at Valencia; he was also employed at Barcelona by the archduke, afterwards Charles III. One of his principal works was the façade of the Cathedral at Valencia, which is unmercifully criticised by Milizia.

RODRIGUEZ, Frate Adrian, a painter born at Antwerp in 1618. His name was originally Dierix, but upon visiting Madrid he entered the Jesuitical order, and changed it to Rodriguez. There are several pictures by him, probably in the churches of his order at Madrid, in the Flemish taste, among which are the Marriage at Cana, the Disciples at Emmaus, and the Feast of Simon. Rodriguez died in 1669.

RODRIGUEZ, Ventura, the most eminent Spanish architect of the 18th century, born at Cienpozuelos in 1717. He studied first under Estéban Marchand, who was then engaged in carrying on the works at Aranjuez. After the death of his instructor in 1733, he was engaged by Ivara to assist in making drawings for the design of the new palace at Madrid; and after the death of Ivara, he was employed by his successor Sacchetti, as principal superintendent of the works, in the erection of that edifice, in 1741. He soon rose to distinction, and in 1747 was chosen an honorary member of the Academy of St. Luke at Rome. In 1752, at the establishment of the Academy of San Ferdinando at Madrid, Rodriguez was chosen chief professor of architecture; and he discharged the duties of his office with admirable zeal and fidelity. Commissions poured in upon him from every quarter, and there was scarcely a work of importance throughout the country, in which he was not employed or consulted. His numerous engagements prevented his visiting Italy; but he collected all pictorial works relating to its ancient or modern edifices, and carefully studied the various monuments in the Peninsula, of Roman, Moorish, and Gothic architecture. He is highly praised by Ponz in the *Viage de Espana;* his talents were of surpassing excellence, and he doubtless merited the title accorded him by his cotemporaries, of "The Restorer of Architecture in Spain." Rodriguez was employed upon a variety of works, as hospitals, colleges, churches, and cathedrals, in the cities of Saragossa, Malaga, Granada, Toledo, Valladolid, and other places. Among the principal are, the Sanctuary at Cabadonga; the church of the hospital at Oviedo; that of S. Felipe Neri at Malaga; and the Palace of the Duke de Liria at Madrid. Rodriguez died at Madrid in 1785, and was buried in the church of S. Marcos, erected by himself.

ROELAS, Juan de las, an eminent Spanish painter, descended from a noble family of Flemish origin, was born at Seville in 1560. He first commenced the study of medicine, but after taking his degree he concluded to gratify a strong inclination for art, and accordingly went to Italy for improvement. He visited Venice, and is said by Palomino to have studied under Titian, but the latter died in 1576, when Roelas was only sixteen years of age. It is more probable that he studied under a scholar of that great master. On returning to Seville, he was much employed in ornamenting the churches, and produced many admirable works, which are compared with those of Palma and Tintoretto, being distinguished for ingenious and abundant composition, correctness of design, perfect delineation of the human figure, and the rich and harmonious coloring he had acquired in the Venetian school. Among his principal works is a picture of St. Jago riding over the Moors, a spirited and majestic composition, in the chapel of that Saint at Seville; the Conception, in the Academy; and the Death of St. Isidore, in the church of that saint, altogether in the style of Titian. This eminent artist entered the priesthood in the latter part of his life, and went as a canon to Olivares in 1624, where he died in the following year. He was termed *El Clerigo Roelas*, probably from his spiritual office; and *El Licenciado Juan*, probably from his doctor's degree. Palomino calls him Pablo, but Francesco Pacheco, his cotemporary, denominates him Juan.

ROEPEL, Conrad, an eminent Dutch painter of flowers and fruit, was born at the Hague in 1679. He studied portrait painting for some time under Constantine Netscher, but his delicate constitution obliged him to quit the city, and reside at a country mansion belonging to his father. Amusing himself in cultivating flowers, he made attempts at painting the beautiful objects of his care, and succeeded to admiration. He sent to the Hague one of his earliest productions, which was immediately purchased by a celebrated florist, who thereafter sent him the finest flowers of his garden. From these choice models, Roepel produced flower-pieces so agreeably disposed, and finished with such fidelity to nature, and clearness of coloring, that they were very highly esteemed, though not equal to the productions of Rachel Ruysch and John van Huysum. Invited to Dusseldorf in 1716 by the Elector Palatine, he was received with every mark of distinction, and painted several fruit and flower pieces for that prince, which were greatly admired, and gained him, besides a liberal reward, the decoration of a gold medal and chain. At the death of the Elector, he returned to the Hague with increased reputation, and was employed for some time in the service of Prince William of Hesse, and the families of Fagel and Lormier. In 1718, Roepel was chosen a member of the Society of Painters at the Hague. He was subsequently made Director, and discharged the duties of that office until his death, in 1748.

ROER, Jacob vander, a Dutch painter, was born at Dort in 1648. He studied under John de Baan, and afterwards went to England in the reign of Charles II. He practised the art for some time there, and then returned to Dort, where he died in 1699.

ROESEL, Augustus John, a German painter and engraver, was born near Arnstadt, in 1705. After acquiring a knowledge of art from a relative, he settled at Nuremberg and practised miniature painting and engraving for many years. He also passed two years at Copenhagen, and was patronized by the Danish court. He subsequently devoted his attention to natural history, and made designs of insects, frogs, and other reptiles, from which he engraved many plates, and published several pictorial works. He died in 1759.

ROESTRAETEN, Peter, a Dutch painter, was born at Haerlem in 1627. He studied under Francis Hals, and afterwards married his daughter. He painted portraits in the manner of his instructor, and also pictures of gold and silver vases, bas-reliefs, musical instruments, with other objects of use or ornament, correctly designed, well colored, and touched with delicacy and freedom. After gaining considerable distinction in Holland, the success of Sir Peter Lely induced him to visit England, during the reign of Charles II. Although Lely received him with great kindness, and presented him to the king, it does not appear that he was much employed at court. Probably doubtful of success in portraits, he applied his talents to the other branch of the art, in which he excelled, and was extensively employed by the nobility and gentry of the time. He died at London in 1698.

ROETTIERS, François, a French engraver of little note, of Flemish origin, was born at Paris in 1702. Several members of his family had held for many years the office of medalist at the French mint. There are a number of etchings by him, among which are two plates after *Nicolas de Largilliere*, representing the Crucifixion, and Christ bearing his Cross, executed with great spirit and effect. Roettiers died in 1770.

ROGER, of Bruges, an old Flemish painter, a native of Bruges, was probably born about 1390. He studied under John van Eyck about the time when he discovered oil painting, and executed historical works on a larger scale than those of van Eyck, well designed for that early period. According to van Mander, several of his works were preserved at Bruges in 1604. Among the names of several Flemish painters who practised the art in Italy in the 15th century, Vasari mentions that of Ruggieri da Bruggia, probably identical with Roger of Bruges. In the Palazzo Nani at Venice, there is a picture by him, representing St. Girolamo between two virgins, signed *Sumus Rugerii manus*. There is also at Venice a portrait of this artist, painted by himself, in 1462; and in the Vendramini collection is a picture by him, representing the Virgin and Infant, in a temple of Flemish architecture. The same artist is also highly commended by Bartolomeo Facio, in his work "De Viris Illustribus;" and, according to Lanzi, he appears to have acquired great reputation in Italy, from the cotemporaneous testimony of Ciriaco Anconitano, who saw in 1449 his picture of the Deposition from the Cross, in the possession of the Duke of Ferrara. There has been much useless disquisition in regard to this artist, to prove his identity with Roger vander Weyde of Brussels, which see.

W

ROGERS, William, an old English engraver, born at London about 1545. He engraved a number of frontispieces and portraits, in a neat, stiff style, among which are the following:

PORTRAITS.

Queen Elizabeth; a small upright plate. Henry IV. of France; a whole-length. The Earl of Essex, Earl Marshal of England. The Earl of Cumberland. Thomas Howard, Duke of Norfolk. Sir John Harrington; the title to his *Orlando Furioso*. Thomas Moffat; a frontispiece to his *Theatre of Insects*. John Gerarde, Surgeon; frontispiece to his *Herbal*.

ROGMAN, or ROGHMAN, Roland, a Dutch painter and engraver, born at Amsterdam in 1597. His instructor is not mentioned, but he became an eminent painter of landscapes. He traveled through several parts of Germany, designing the most agreeable scenery, architectural views, villages, figures and cattle, which he usually sketched on the spot. His pictures generally represent views in Holland and Germany, which are admired for their close resemblance to nature in the forms, though the coloring is dark and disagreeable. Rogman lived on terms of intimacy with Rembrandt, whose excellence in pencilling and chiaro-scuro he endeavored to follow—at a distance. He left a number of spirited pen drawings, and about thirty-three bold and masterly etchings of views of chateaux in ruins. There are six plates of "Views of the Wood at the Hague," in three sets of proofs; and it is supposed from the inscriptions, that the first was published by Rogman; the second, after retouching, by Peter Nolpe; and the third by N. Visscher and P. Schenck. Rogman probably died in 1689. His daughter, Gertrude R., engraved about twenty plates after him, among which is one entitled Le Chateau de Zuylen, in the style of Hermann Saftleven.

ROKES, Henry Martin, called Zorg, or, the Careful, a Dutch painter, was the son of Martin Rokes, the captain of the passage-boat from Rotterdam to Dort, who acquired the above appellation from his extraordinary attention to the comfort and interest of his passengers. The surname descended to his son, who was born at Rotterdam in 1621. After acquiring a knowledge of the art at Rotterdam from William Buytenweg, he visited Antwerp, and studied under the younger Teniers. He attained great reputation for his pictures of subjects similar to those of that master, representing interiors of Dutch apartments, with figures regaling and amusing themselves; also for his conversations, domestic subjects, fairs, and fish-markets. His pictures generally combine the styles of Teniers and Brower; the composition is ingenious, the design correct, the coloring warm and mellow, with good management of the chiaro-scuro. They are very highly esteemed, and the best are worthy of a place in choice collections. Rokes died in 1682.

ROLAND, Philippe Laurent, a distinguished French sculptor, born near Lille, in 1746. He early showed considerable talent, and visited Paris, where he was received into the studio of Pajou. Entrusted with a part of the works in the Palais Royal, he acquitted himself successfully, and afterwards visited Rome for improvement, where he remained five years. On returning to Paris, he manifested great progress, and gained considerable reputation by his statue of Cato Uticensis, executed in 1779. In 1781, he was chosen a member of the academy, for his fine statue of Samson; and he was soon after commissioned, by M. d'Angivilliers, to execute his statue of the great Condé. The works of Roland are distinguished for purity of design and facility of execution. Among the principal were, a bas-relief of the Nine Muses, for the queen's apartments at Fontainbleau; a bust of Pajou; and Homer playing on his Lyre, in the Louvre. The latter was exhibited in 1802, and is highly praised. Roland was appointed Professor of Sculpture in the Royal Academy, and a member of the Legion of Honor. He died in 1816.

ROLDAN, Pedro, an eminent Spanish sculptor, born at Seville in 1624. He visited Italy, and resided for a long time at Rome, where he gained several prizes in the Academy of St. Luke. On returning to Spain, he was much employed at Seville and Madrid. There are about thirty of his statues in the former city, and a number of groups, which are highly praised by Palomino. Among the principal are, the Burial of Christ, in the Charity church; and the Crucifixion, in that of St. Bernard. The latter work was considered equal to the same subject in the Basilica of S. Paolo, at Rome, destroyed in the conflagration of that edifice. Roldan died at Seville in 1700.

ROLDAN, Louisa, the daughter of the preceding, was born at Seville in 1654. She studied sculpture under her father, and assisted him in many of his works. She gained so much reputation that Philip IV. invited her to Madrid, commissioned her to execute a number of works, and assigned her a pension of six hundred ducats. There are a number of her works in the Escurial; also a fine group at Seville, representing the Body of Christ, with the Virgin and saints. She died at Madrid in 1704.

ROLI, or ROLLI, Antonio, a painter born at Bologna in 1643. He studied under Michael Angelo Colonna, and seems to have gained great reputation in his day, from the commendation of Cav. Titi, who extols his landscapes in the Certosa at Pisa, as "perfect miracles of the art." Roli died in 1696.

ROLI, Giuseppe, a painter born at Bologna in 1654. He studied under Domenico Maria Canuti, and subsequently went to Germany, where he remained several years. On returning to Bologna, he executed several fresco works for the churches. He died, according to Zani, in 1727. There are several plates by him, after the eminent Bolognese painters, among which are two, representing Charity, *after Lodovico Caracci;* and a Sybil, *after Lorenzo Pasinelli.*

ROLLO. Nothing is known of this artist, except by a picture of Christ crowned with Thorns, in the style of Guido, said to be so beautiful that it may be mistaken for the work of that master. It is inscribed *Rollo Gallois, F.;* from which it is supposed he was of French origin.

ROLLOS, Peter, a German engraver of little note, who resided at Frankfort and Berlin, and engraved a number of plates for books published in both those cities, among which is the frontispiece for a book of Emblems, by G. de Montenay, published at Frankfort in 1619.

ROMA, Spiridone, an Italian painter of little note, who flourished in the latter half of the 18th century. He visited England, and was chiefly occupied in the restoration of pictures, although he also painted a ceiling in the East India House. He died in 1786.

ROMAIN, —— de la Rue. The name of this painter has been Gallicized by French writers, although he was probably of Dutch origin. He is said to have imitated with great success the styles of John Asselyn, Swanevelt, and Both. His pictures pass for the works of those masters, and his name is almost lost in oblivion—a warning to all mere imitators.

ROMAN, Bartolomé, a Spanish painter, was born at Madrid, according to Bermudez, in 1596. He studied successively under Vincenzio Carducci, and Don Diego Velasquez. He painted historical subjects with great reputation, among which Palomino mentions several in the Sacristy of the Padres Cayetanos at Madrid, and compares them, in regard to coloring and effect, to the works of Rubens. His draperies are also very highly praised. In the church of the Franciscans at Alcala de Henares, there are several considerable works by Roman. He died at Madrid in 1659.

ROMANELLI, Gio. Francesco, a distinguished Italian painter, was born at Viterbo in 1617. Manifesting an early inclination for art, he was sent by his father to Rome, where he was patronized by the Cardinal Barberini, who placed him in the school of Pietro da Cortona. After several years of assiduous study under that master, he became one of his most distinguished scholars, and followed his style with such success, that, when Pietro started on a journey to Lombardy, he left him to supply his place in decorating the Barberini palace. On leaving his instructor, Romanelli altered his style, by the assistance of Bernini, adopting by degrees a more elegant and seductive manner in his figures, but manifesting less grandeur and science than that of Pietro. He painted a picture of the Deposition from the Cross, for the church of S. Ambrogio, which excited such universal applause, that Pietro was stimulated to paint opposite to it, his wonderful picture of the Martyrdom of St. Stephen, upon seeing which, Bernini exclaimed that he then perceived the difference between the master and the scholar. For the church of S. Peter, he painted the Presentation in the Temple, which has since been executed in mosaic; and the original is preserved in the Certosa. When Innocent X. succeeded to the papacy, Cardinal Barberini was obliged to quit Rome, and flee to Paris, where he recommended his former protegé to Cardinal Mazarin. On arriving at Paris, Romanelli was presented to Louis XIV., and was commissioned to execute several works, among which were a series of subjects from the Æneid, in the apartments of the Old Louvre, called the Queen's Bath. The King rewarded him in munificent style, and honored him with the order of St. Michael. According to Lanzi, Romanelli made two visits to France, and was preparing to start the third time, when he died at Viterbo, in 1662. He left numerous works in Rome and other cities, both in churches and private collections. The large copy of Guido's Triumph of Bacchus in Hampton Court, is said to be by Romanelli.

ROMANELLI, Urbano, the son and scholar of the preceding, was a native of Viterbo. After the death of his father, he completed his course under Ciro Ferri, and was subsequently employed for the churches of Veletri and Viterbo. According to Lanzi, his pictures from the life of St. Lorenzo, in the church of that saint at Viterbo, show that he might have attained great eminence, had he not been cut off prematurely, in 1682.

ROMANET, Antoine Louis, a French engraver, was born at Paris in 1748, and died in 1807 He studied under J. G. Wille, and was subsequently employed upon several great pictorial works such as the *Galerie du Palais Royal*, the *Galerie d'Orleans*, the *Cabinet Le Brun*, &c. He resided some time at Basle, and executed several plates under the direction of Christian von Mechel. There are also by him many detached pieces after various masters; the following are among his principal plates:

PORTRAITS.

Charles Theodore, Elector of Bavaria; *after P. Battoni.* Louis Francis de Bourbon, Prince of Conti; *after Le Tellier.* John Grimoux, Painter; *after a picture by himself.*

VARIOUS SUBJECTS.

The Death of Adonis; *after Kupetzky.* The Village Printseller; *after Seekatz.* The Ballad Singer; *do.*

ROMANI, da Reggio, a painter of Modena, who flourished in the latter part of the 17th century. According to Tiraboschi, he studied at Venice, attaching himself to the works of Paolo Veronese, and particularly to those of Tintoretto, whose rules he usually practised, with excellent success. Lanzi mentions a picture by him at Modena, in the style of Paolo, representing the Mysteries of the Rosario.

ROMANINO, or ROMANO, Girolamo, an eminent painter of the Venetian school, born at Brescia about 1504. After acquiring the elements of the art from Stefano Rizzi, he studied the works of Titian with great assiduity, and followed the styles of that master and Bassano, in many of his works. Cotemporary with Alessandro Bonvicino, called Il Moretto, he became his rival; Ridolfi ranks him at least equal, but Vasari inferior, to that master; and Lanzi endeavors to reconcile their judgments by observing that Romanino surpassed him in extent of genius and boldness of execution, but was inferior to him in delicacy of taste and careful execution, several of his works being painted with a hasty pencil. In general, however, he displays the qualities of a great master, in subjects from sacred and profane history, and also in burlesque compositions. His principal works are at Brescia and Verona; in the church of Sts. Faustino and Giovita at Brescia, is his Descent from the Cross, commended by Palma for its strong resemblance to the Venetian style; in S. Maria in Calcara, is his St. Apollonio administering the Sacrament, a surprising and delightful work, distinguished for great fecundity of invention, varied expression in the heads, and select choice of forms, combining many singular pictorial beauties within the limits of propriety and truth. In S. Giorgio at Verona, are his four histories from the life of that Saint, composed with surprising spirit and vigor. Vasari says he died before 1566; Ridolfi merely states that he died at an advanced age. Romanino sometimes signed his pictures *Hier. Roman, Hieronimi Rumani, and Hieronimus Rumanus.*

ROMANO, Giulio. The family name of this great painter was Pippi, but he is universally known in the history of art under the appellation of Giulio Romano. He was born at Rome in 1492, and manifesting an early genius for art, he was placed under the instruction of Raffaelle, soon after the arrival of that master at Rome, and became his most distinguished disciple. Raffaelle placed him at the head of his scholars, entrusted him with the execution of several of his greatest works, made him one of his heirs, and at his death confided to him and to Gio. Francesco Penni, the completion of his unfinished works. During the lifetime of Raffaelle he did not gain distinction by any original works, but afterwards he was enabled to develop his faculties, and soon displayed an elevated mind, poetic genius, unusual grandeur of conception, and remarkable correctness of design. He was particularly successful in battle-pieces and other warlike subjects, representing them with great spirit and correctness. In these subjects he imitated the grand design of Michael Angelo, commanding, with a master's hand, the whole mechanism of the human body, and rendering it subservient to his purposes. His chief fault is, that his demonstrations of motions are sometimes too violent. Vasari preferred his drawings to his paintings, as he thought the fire of his original conceptions partially evaporated in the finishing. Some critics have objected to the squareness of his physiognomies, and complained that his middle tints are too dark; but Niccolo Poussin was of a contrary opinion, and admired the asperity of the coloring in his Battle of Constantine, as suitable to the character of the subject. In sacred and other subjects he did not succeed as well. His figures lack the dignity and inimitable graces of his preceptor, his contours are harsh and severe, and his coloring cold, crude, and inharmonious. These defects are, however, in a great measure counterbalanced by the extraordinary fecundity of his imagination, and his learned acquaintance with ancient history and mythology.

After the death of Raffaelle, he was employed by Leo X. and Clement VII., in conjunction with Penni, to finish the Hall of Constantine in the Vatican, in which he painted the Apparition of the Cross, or the Harangue of Constantine, and the Battle wherein Maxentius is drowned and Constantine remains the Victor. The other two subjects, the Baptism of Constantine by St. Silvestro, and the Dotation of the city of Rome to that pontiff, were executed by Penni. They afterwards painted, or rather finished, the pictures of the Villa at Monte Mario, ordered by the Cardinal Giulio de' Medici, but suspended after the death of Raffaelle, till the second or third year after his elevation to the papacy, under the title of Clement VII., about 1525. He also painted a fine picture of Christ appearing to Mary Magdalene, for the church of La Trinità di Monte, and the Marriage of St. Catherine, for S. Andrea della Valle. It was about this time that he painted his celebrated picture of the Martyrdom of St. Stephen, for the church of S. Stefano at Genoa, which, for grandeur of composition, and pathetic expression, is regarded as a masterpiece of art.

Giulio had already distinguished himself as an architect, when he was invited to Mantua by the Duke to rebuild the Palazzo del Te. It was there that he won his greatest reputation, both as a painter and architect, and established a school in imitation of his master, which Rome herself might have envied. He erected many noble edifices, villas, palaces, temples, and decorated a considerable portion of them with his own hands, so that the Duke was heard to exclaim, in a transport of gratitude, that Giulio was in truth more the master of Mantua than himself. His time was now so much occupied in his architectural pursuits that he was obliged, like Raffaelle, after preparing the cartoons to leave the execution of his works to his scholars and assistants, afterwards carefully retouching them himself. The Palazzo del Te, which occupied him several years, is regarded as a lasting monument of his genius, both as an architect and a painter. His great abilities in painting are conspicuous in the two grand saloons, in one of which he represented the Fall of the Giants, and in the other the History of Cupid and Psyche. In the former it appears as if Romano, emulating Michael Angelo himself in grandeur of design, had soared to the utmost stretch of pictorial daring. He afterwards decorated the Ducal palace at Mantua with fresco histories of the Trojan war, in which he displayed the most capacious powers of invention and poetic fancy, aided by a profound knowledge of his subject. Sometimes, like Homer, he surprises by the heroic sublimity of his feats of arms; at others, like Anacreon, he captivates by the most seductive representations of festivity and love. Lanzi says these works have been so frequently retouched, that little remains of the original coloring.

As an architect, Giulio Romano gained great distinction. At Rome he designed the beautiful Villa Madama, on Monte Mario, about half a mile from the city; also the church of the Madonna dell' Orto, in the form of a Latin cross, with three naves, a well-proportioned and beautiful chapel at the back, and the two arms of the cross semicircular. He also erected the beautiful palace of Cicciaporci, on the Strada di Bianchi; and the Palazzo Cenci, over the piazza of S. Eustachio. By these works, he gained so much distinction that the Duke of Mantua invited him to that city, and employed him to erect the Palazzo del Te, which is regarded as the chief monument of his fame, being one of the most magnificent edifices in Italy. The room where he painted the Battle of the Giants, is of a circular form, and vaulted; the walls, windows, and angles are of rustic work, apparently split and broken, as if shivered and falling with the Giants, struck by the thunderbolts of Jove. Although this room is only thirty feet in diameter, it appears much larger, in consequence of its correct proportions. (See *Carlo Maderno.*) When the Emperor Charles V. arrived at Mantua, Giulio Romano erected several triumphal arches, of the most elegant designs. His design for the façade of S. Petronio, was preferred before those of a large number of competitors, although submitted to several celebrated architects. According to Milizia, this work "is of one order, a medium between the Gothic and the Greek, with a grand and picturesque effect, showing that Romano excelled in architecture more than in painting." The unqualified commendation which that author—usually so caustic in his criticisms—bestows upon the works of Romano, is a high evidence of their surpassing merit. His reputation at length rose so high, that the Duke forbid the citizens of Mantua to erect any edifice without consulting Romano. Among other works at Mantua, he restored the church of S. Benedetto; modernized and enlarged the Ducal palace; and erected another for the Duke at Marmiruolo, five miles from the city. He performed so many celebrated works there, in painting and architecture, that the Cardinal Gonzaga was accustomed to say that Mantua was created by Giulio Romano, and was his rightful property. Finally, he was honored by the pope with the appointment of architect to St. Peter's, and was earnestly entreated to repair to Rome, in order to commence operations upon that Basilica, which he doubtless would have done, had he not been prevented by death, in 1546.

ROMANO, Domenico, a painter of the Florentine school, of whom little is known. According to Vasari, he was a pupil of Salviati, whose manner he followed. He was living in 1568.

ROMANO, Virgilio, a painter who flourished at Siena about 1540. He studied under Baldassare Peruzzi, and executed some works for the churches and public edifices of Siena, which are commended by Vasari. There are also some grotesques at Siena, attributed to him.

ROMBORGH, a Dutch painter of whom little is known, who flourished in the commencement of the 18th century. He is said to have studied at Rome. He painted landscapes resembling those of Frederick Moucheron.

ROMBOUTS, Theodore, an eminent Flemish painter, born at Antwerp in 1597. He studied under Abraham Janssens, with whom he made great progress. On leaving his master in 1617, he went to Rome, soon attracted public notice by his assiduity and talents, and received several commissions, which he executed in a manner that augmented his reputation. From Rome, he went to Florence at the invitation of the Grand Duke, for whom he executed several excellent works, so much to the satisfaction of that prince, that he liberally rewarded him, and gave him several valuable presents as a mark of his esteem. After an absence of eight years he returned to Antwerp, whither his reputation had preceded him, and he was commissioned to paint several works for the churches, which excited universal admiration. Rubens was then residing at Antwerp, in the full enjoyment of his exalted reputation; and Rombouts, perceiving that his own performances were obscured by the perfections of that eminent master, had the vanity to think that he could successfully compete with him. This self-sufficiency, however, proved of great advantage to him, for the ambition of vanquishing so powerful an opponent stimulated him to extraordinary exertions, and his best productions were conceived and executed under the influence of this determination. He possessed a ready invention, a fine style of design, animated expression, warm and brilliant coloring, and uncommon facility of hand. His figures are usually as large as life. His most celebrated works are at Ghent—the Taking down from the Cross, in the Cathedral; St. Francis receiving the Stigmata, and the Angel appearing to Joseph in his Dream, in the church of the Recolets; and Themis with the attributes of Justice, in the Town House. The last named work is said to have elicited the commendation of Rubens himself. He occasionally painted cabinet pictures, gallant assemblies, concerts, merry-makings, mountebanks, &c., designed and executed with great ingenuity and spirit. He found a ready sale for these works, and they are still held in high estimation. He died at Antwerp in 1637, in the prime of life.

ROMEGIALLO, Giovanni Pietro, a painter born at Morbegno in the Valteline, in 1739. After learning the rudiments of art under G. F. Cotta, an obscure painter in his native city, he went to Rome, and studied with Agostino Masucci. He afterwards greatly improved himself by studying and copying the works of Guercino, Guido, and P. da Cortona. After returning to his native place, he painted many works, well designed and colored, with a fine expression in the heads, for the private collections, the churches, and public edifices of Como, and other neighboring cities. The time of his death is not recorded.

ROMEO, Don José, a Spanish painter, born at Cervera in Arragon, in 1701. He went to Rome at an early age, and studied with Agostino Masucci. On his return to Spain, he resided some time at Barcelona, where he executed several works for the church of the Mercenarios Calzados. He afterwards went to Madrid, where he was taken into the service of Philip V. He died at Madrid in 1772.

ROMEYN, William van, a Dutch painter, of whom little is known. He painted landscapes, with figures and cattle, much in the manner of Karel du Jardin, which occasionally occur in the collections of Holland. His pictures are generally of small size, well designed, delicately pencilled, and chastely colored.

ROMNEY, George, one of the most eminent painters of the English school, was born at Furness, near Dalton, in Lancashire, in 1734. His father was a builder; and George, in his twelfth year, was taken from the village school to superintend the workmen. He showed a passion for drawing from his earliest years, and at length prevailed upon his father to allow him to study painting, under one Steele, a portrait painter of little note, who barely taught him the use of the materials of the art. At the expiration of two years he left his instructor, married, and resided some time at York, where he met with considerable success; but aspiring to higher things, in 1762 he established himself in London. During the first year of his residence there, he painted portraits at the modest price of five guineas a head, and acquired considerable practice through the influence of Mr. Braithwaite, the comptroller of the foreign post-office. In 1763, he gained the second prize of fifty guineas from the Society for the Encouragement of Arts, &c., for his picture of the Death of General Wolfe. In 1764 he visited Paris, and on his return he settled at Gray's Inn. In 1765, he obtained the first prize from the Society for the Encouragement of Arts, &c., for his picture of the Death of King Edmund. In 1768 he removed to more eligible and convenient quarters, in Great Newport street, where his practice rapidly increased. Romney had hitherto confined himself to portrait painting, but being ambitious of gaining distinction in a higher department of art, and conscious of the necessity of cultivating his taste abroad, he set out for Italy in 1773, accompanied by Ozias Humphrey, the celebrated miniature painter. He resided there two years, chiefly at Rome, studying with enthusiastic assiduity the antique and the best works of the great Italian masters. In 1775 he returned to London, and took a house in Cavendish Square, where he resided during the remainder of his professional career. While abroad, the admiration and delight he experienced in contemplating the works of the old masters, made him resolve to devote his attention in future to historical painting; but soon after his return, the public taste, the persuasions of his friends, and the enticements of emolument, induced him to change his purpose. He soon became one of the most popular and most employed portrait painters in London, and even the rival of Sir Joshua Reynolds. When Boydell projected the Shakspeare Gallery, Romney entered into the scheme with enthusiasm, and executed four pictures for the work representing the Infant Shakspeare attended by Nature and the Passions, the Storm Scene in the Tempest, the Infant Shakspeare nursed by Tragedy and Comedy, and Cassandra in Troilus and Cressida. He also produced many fancy pictures which were among the most esteemed productions of the British school in his day. He painted upwards of thirty pictures of Magdalens, Bacchantes, Nymphs, and subjects from history or fable, for which the beautiful Emma Lyon, afterwards Lady Hamilton, served for his model, "for whose charms upon canvass, princes and peers contended." In 1797, Romney felt a paralytic stroke, which prevented him from continuing his professional labors. Finding his health declining, he revisited his native place in the following year, where he died in 1802.

It is a little singular that Romney was never elected a Royal Academician. This has been attributed to the spirit of rivalry between him and Reynolds, though the latter affected to ridicule the idea of Romney's pretensions. At all events, after the death of the president, the Academy feeling that they had done injustice to his talents, offered reparation, which Romney promptly declined. It has been said that he was *fortunate* in his biographers, but he ought rather to be regarded as *unfortunate;* for his friends extol him as one of the greatest modern painters, without any just discrimination of his real merits and defects; while on the other hand, his enemies make him "the best abused man in the world." Setting aside the sycophantic eulogies of Cumberland and Hayley, and the caustic critiques of Fuseli and Cunningham, it will be safe to give Romney the benefit of the opinion of an able and conscientious artist in another branch—Flaxman the sculptor: "When Romney first began to paint he had seen no gallery of pictures, nor the fine productions of ancient sculpture, but then women and children were his statues, and all objects under the cope of heaven formed his school of painting. The rainbow, the purple distance, or the silver lake, taught him coloring; the various actions and passions of the human figure, with the forms of clouds, woods, and mountains, or valleys, afforded him studies of composition. Indeed, his genius bore a strong resemblance to the scenes he was born in; like them, it partook of the grand and beautiful; and like them, also, the bright sunshine and enchanting prospects of his fancy were occasionally overspread with mist and gloom. On his arrival in Italy, he was witness to new scenes of art and sources of study, of which he could only have supposed previously that something of the kind might exist; for he there contemplated the purity and perfection of ancient sculpture, the sublimity of Michael Angelo's Sistine Chapel, and the simplicity of Cimabue and Giotto's schools. He perceived those qualities distinctly, and judiciously used them in viewing and imitating nature; and thus his quick perception and unwearied application enabled him, by a two years' residence abroad, to acquire as great a proficiency in art as is usually attained by foreign studies of a much longer duration. After his return, the novelty and sentiment of his original subjects were universally admired. Most of these were of the delicate class; and each had its peculiar character. Titiana, with her Indian votaress, was arch and sprightly; Milton dictating to his daughters, solemn and interesting. Several pictures of wood-nymphs and bacchants charmed by their rural beauty, innocence, and simplicity. The most pathetic—Ophelia, with the flowers she had gathered in her hand, sitting on the branch of a tree, which was breaking under her, while the melancholy distraction visible in her countenance, accounts for her insensibility to the danger. Few painters have left in their works so many examples of the tender and delicate affections; and several of his pictures breathe a kindred spirit with the Sigismonda of Correggio. His Cartoons, some of which have unfortunately perished, were examples of the sublime and terrible—at that time perfectly new in English art. As Romney was gifted with peculiar powers for historical and ideal painting, so his heart and soul were engaged in the pursuit of it, whenever he could extricate himself from the importunate business of portrait painting. It was his delight by day, and his study by night; and for this his food and rest were often neglected. His compositions, like those of the ancient pictures and basso-relievos, told their story by a single group of figures in the front; while the back-ground is made the simplest possible, rejecting all unnecessary episode and trivial ornament, either of secondary groups, or architectural subdivision. In his compositions the beholder was forcibly struck by the sentiment at the first glance; of which he traced the gradations and varieties through several characters, all conceived in an elevated spirit of dignity and beauty, with a lively expression of nature in all the parts. His heads were various—the male were decided and grand; the female lovely: his figures resembled the antique—the limbs were elegantly and finely formed; his drapery was well understood; either forming the figure into a mass with one or two deep folds only, or, by its adhesion and transparency, discovering the form of the figure, the lines of which were finely varied with the union or expansion of spiral or cascade folds, composing with or contrasting the outline and chiaro-scuro. Few artists, since the fifteenth century, have been able to do so much in so many different branches; for, besides his beautiful compositions and pictures, which have added to the knowledge and celebrity of the English school, he modeled like a sculptor, carved ornaments in wood with great delicacy, and could make an architectural design in a fine taste, as well as construct every part of the building."

ROMSTEDT, Christian, an obscure German engraver, who flourished at Leipsic from 1630 to about 1670. He engraved some portraits, indifferently executed, and marked with the above monogram. There was another artist of this name, probably a son of the above, who died in 1725. He engraved a few portraits, and several of the subjects in the Farnese palace, *after Annibale Caracci.*

RONCALLI, Cav. Cristoforo, called Il Cav. dalle Pomerance, was born at Pomerance, in the diocese of Volterra, in Tuscany, in 1552. He went to Rome and studied with Niccolo Circignani, called dalle Pomerance, by whose instructions and a diligent study of the antique, and the works of the best masters, he became an eminent painter of history, and one of the most popular and most employed artists of his time. As soon as his works were known at Rome, they immediately attracted public attention, and he was employed in decorating numerous churches and the palaces of the principal nobility. His performances gained him the highest applause, for their elegance of composition and correctness of design. He was employed by Paul V. in the execution of several important works, among which were the Death of Ananias and Sapphira, in the Certosa,—a picture so much admired, that it was afterwards copied in mosaic in St. Peter's, and other mosaics also were executed in the same edifice from his cartoons. In the Basilica of St. John of Lateran, he painted a grand composition of the Baptism of Constantine. He was also charged with the continuation of the gallery of Raffaelle, under the direction of the Padre Danti.—(See Danti). These works gave so much satisfaction to the Pope that he conferred on Roncalli the honor of knighthood. He executed several other important works for the churches of Rome, the principal of which are the Visitation of the Virgin in S. Giovanni Decollato, and St. Michael discomfiting the Rebel Angels in S. Andrea della Valle; but the most celebrated is the cupola of La Santa Casa di Loreto. He also painted in the treasury of the same edifice, several pictures representing the history of the Virgin. He obtained this vast commission, in competition with Caravaggio and Guido, through the powerful patronage of the Cardinal Crescenzi; which so much enraged Caravaggio, that he hired an assassin to murder him, but the intended victim escaped with a severe wound in his face. The distinction Roncalli gained by executing these works, soon brought his talents into great request, and he executed many works for the churches in the Picenum, besides others for the churches of Naples, Ancona, Genoa, and other Italian cities. He was also invited to several of the different courts of Europe, and visited Germany, Flanders, France, and England, leaving several specimens of his abilities in all those countries.

It is the opinion of Lanzi that Roncalli enjoyed a greater reputation than his merits deserved. He had many pupils, and Lanzi says "he learned to avail himself of the labors of others, and to content himself with mediocrity." This however, is contrary to the testimony of Baglioni, and several other excellent historians, and it is evident from Lanzi's memoir that he did not consider him an artist of mediocrity, but intended to censure him for not having attained to higher perfection, and for being more intent upon acquiring gain, that a lasting reputation. His style of design is a mixture of the Florentine and the Roman. In frescos, his coloring was fresh and brilliant, but in oil pictures his tints were more subdued, harmonized by a tone of general tranquillity. He had a lively invention, and designed and wrought with great facility, frequently enriching his back-grounds with landscapes treated with great beauty and effect. His faults were errors in perspective, occasional carelessness in design and frequent repetition, especially in his foreshortened heads, full and rubicund countenances and his backgrounds. He died at Rome in 1626.

RONCELLI. D. Giuseppe, a painter born at

Bergamo in 1677. According to Tassi, he acquired so high a reputation for his nocturnal scenes of landscapes and conflagrations, that Celesti added figures to his works, and Mazzoleni wrote his life. His works are also commended by Lanzi, and they are highly esteemed at Bergamo. He died in 1729.

RONCHO, Michele di, an old Milanese painter, who wrought in the cathedral of that city from 1375 to 1377. Lanzi says that remnants of his works still survive, and show that he approached nearer to the composition of Giotto, than the artists of Pavia.

RONDANI, Francesco Maria, a painter born at Parma about 1505. According to Affo, he was educated in the school of Correggio, and assisted him in two of his principal works, particularly in the dome of the church of S. Giovanni. In the church of S. Maria Madalena at Parma, is a noble picture by him of the Virgin and Christ, which has often been attributed to his instructor, and Lanzi says it might be really believed a work by Allegri, were it not for historic evidence. There is an altar-piece at the church of the Eremitani, representing saints Agostino and Girolamo, so much in the manner of Correggio, as to be esteemed one of the best works at Parma. There are also some frescos by him in a chapel of the cathedral, and in other churches and convents at Parma. Rondani was unable to reach the grandeur of the head of the school in historical works, and is also said to have been too careful and minute in the accessories, especially in his fresco works. His pictures are exceedingly rare in the collections. Lanzi had seen only two, a Madonna and Child, and a portrait; the latter designed in the style of Giorgione. He died at Parma about 1548.

RONDELET, Jean, a reputable French architect and writer on the art, was born at Lyons in 1734. He studied at Paris, under Soufflot, and was employed by the latter to assist in the execution of the church of S. Genevieve. Soufflot having died in 1780, before its completion, Rondelet was commissioned to finish the edifice, to which the National Assembly gave the name of the French Pantheon. In 1783 he visited Italy for improvement, and made many designs and architectural researches. He was subsequently employed by government in various important commissions; was a member of the Academy of architecture; and professor of Stereometry. He published a large number of valuable writings on the art, among which are his *Traité theoretique et pratique de l'Art de Batir;* and a number of articles in the *Encyclopedie Methodique*. His various labors at length rendered him totally blind. He died in 1829.

RONDINELLI, Niccolo, a painter born at Ravenna, about 1460. He studied under Giovanni Bellini, and assisted him in his works. His pictures were painted in the first manner of his instructor, but with greatly inferior abilities; the principal are in the churches and convents of his native city. He died, according to Vasari, at the age of 60.

RONDINOSI, Zaccaria, a painter of Pisa, of whom there are notices from 1665 to 1680. According to Morrona, he executed some works for the churches of his native city.

RONDOLINO. See Terenzi.

RONSERAY, Margaretta Louisa Amelia du, a French lady, born at Paris in 1730. She executed a few etchings after the French masters, among which are Venus rising from the sea *after Bouchardon;* The Fountain of Grenelle from the cartoon by Pierre, for the church of S Roch at Paris; a View of the Tower of Palmerana, *after Cochin;* a Sultan and a Sultana, *after B. Picart.*

RONTBOUT, J., a Dutch landscape painter, of whom little is known, though his pictures are quite common in Holland, and possess considerable merit. The landscape somewhat resembles the manner of Jacob Ruysdael, and the figures resemble those of Hobbema. He usually signed his pictures with his name, but sometimes with a monogram, resembling that of Ruysdael.

RONTBOUT, N., a painter of landscapes, highly commended by Pilkington. That author says he was of Flemish origin, and studied in Italy; but he is not mentioned by any of the Dutch or Flemish writers. Pilkington specifies only one picture by him, in the possession of Thos. Cobbe. Probably he is the same as the preceding artist.

RONZELLI, Fabio, a painter of Bergamo, who flourished, according to Tassi, about 1629, and executed some excellent works for the churches. Lanzi says, "if he was not sufficiently select and ideal, he was at least solid and robust." He commends his Martyrdom of St. Alessandro in the church of Santa Grata.

RONZELLI, Pietro, a painter of Bergamo, probably the father of the preceding, concerning whom there are notices from 1588 to 1616. He is chiefly commended by Tassi for the excellence of his portraits.

ROODTSEUS, Albert, a Dutch portrait painter of little note, was born in 1590, and died at Hoorn in 1648.

ROODTSEUS, John Albert, was the son of the preceding, born at Hoorn in 1615. After learning the rudiments of art, he studied with Peter Lastman, and became one of the most eminent portrait painters of his time. Some of his best pictures are said to equal the admirable productions of Bartholomew vander Helst. There are three large pictures by him in the Hall of the Society of Archers, in his native city, representing the portraits of the principal officers of that institution, executed with surprising truth and effect. He died in 1674.

ROODTSEUS, Jacob, was the younger brother of the preceding, born at Hoorn in 1619. He studied with John David de Heem, and painted flowers and still-life in his style. His works approach the merit of the admirable productions of his instructor. He died in 1669.

ROOKER, Edward, an English designer and engraver, born at London about 1712. He possessed excellent talents for engraving architectural views, evinced by his large plate of the Section of St. Paul's Cathedral, from a drawing by Wale. Among other plates by him are four views in Italy, *after Wilson;* six Views in London, and twelve do. in England, *after Paul Sandby.*

ROOKER, Michael Angelo, was the son of the preceding, born at London about 1743. He studied engraving under his father, and landscape painting under P. Sandby. He painted the scenery for the Haymarket Theatre for several years, and engraved a series of Views of the city of Oxford, for the Oxford Almanacs, which possess considerable merit. He died in 1801.

ROORE, Jacob de, a Flemish painter, born at Antwerp in 1686. His father was a goldsmith, and intended him for that occupation, but he died while Jacob was very young. His mother allowed him to follow the bent of his genius, and placed him under the instruction of Louis vander Bosch. He next studied two years with Nicholas van Schoor, and lastly with Gaspard Jacob van Opstal. He made such great progress under the last named master, that he copied for him a picture of St. Christopher by Rubens, to fulfil a commission from the court of France, with a precision and beauty that excited the surprise and satisfaction of his instructor, who scarcely had occasion to retouch it. At the age of twenty, he was admitted a member of the Academy of Antwerp. In the early part of his career, he painted history in the style of van Opstal, but possessing a happy talent for imitation, he adopted the subjects and manner of the younger Teniers, with such extraordinary success that he could scarcely execute all the commissions he received from the collections in Flanders, Brabant, and Holland. He was also much employed in embellishing the saloons of wealthy people, and the ceilings of the public edifices, distinguished for readiness of invention, and extraordinary facility of hand, although lacking that elegant taste of design which he might have acquired at Rome. Among his principal performances of this class were, the History of Achilles, Brennus besieging the Capitol, Antony presenting the crown to Julius Cæsar, and the History of Pandora, one of his most admired performances. His coloring is agreeable, and his easel pictures are executed with a free and spirited pencil, and delicately finished. He died at Antwerp in 1747.

ROOS, John Henry, an eminent Dutch painter of landscapes, figures and animals, and portraits, was born at Otterberg in 1631. He was the son of a poor weaver, who apprenticed him at the early age of nine years for the term of seven years, to a painter of little note, named Julian du Jardyn. He made little progress under this master, who employed him in drudgery, which was a part of the art quite uncongenial to his feelings. At the expiration of his indentures, he commenced studying under Adrian de Bie, an able designer of landscapes and animals, and soon manifested such extraordinary talent in painting landscapes, embellished with cattle, horses, sheep, goats, camels, and other animals, that he not only surpassed his instructor, but became one of the most celebrated animal painters of his time. He designed everything after nature with the utmost accuracy, and frequently placed his animals in attitudes the most singular and difficult to be represented. His landscape is pleasingly diversified with pleasant fields, woodlands, and shepherds' cots, or ruins more picturesque, rocks, mountains, and waterfalls, always adapted to the subject represented. His coloring is fresh and vigorous, his pencil firm and decided, and his conduct of the chiaro-scuro is excellent. For the most part he chose those sacred and historical subjects which admit of the greatest number and variety of animals, such as Jacob tending and Jacob driving his flocks and herds, Esau meeting his brother, Moses tending the flocks of Jethro, the Angel appearing to the Shepherds, &c. He was invited to the court of the Elector of Mentz, for whom he painted some of his choicest works. He also excelled in portraits, and painted those of that prince, and of the principal personages of his court, for which he was munificently rewarded. At the recommendation of his patron, he was employed in painting portraits at several of the courts of Germany, and had he been solely intent on the aggrandizement of his fortune, he would have confined himself to that lucrative pursuit, for his portraits deserved great admiration for their intrinsic excellence, and were rendered particularly attractive by the introduction of landscapes in the back-grounds, diversified with distant prospects of groves, hills, and groups of cattle, charmingly disposed, or incidents taken from sacred or profane history, giving force to the principal subject, and adding interest to the picture. But his predilection for his favorite subjects was not subdued by this seductive allurement, and having settled at Frankfort, he pursued his profession during the remainder of his life with the most flattering success. The Elector of Mentz honored him with a gold chain and medal, and several other princes testified their approbation by similar presents. In 1685, a dreadful fire broke out in the dead of night at Antwerp, and soon extended to the dwelling of Roos. While endeavoring to save a part of his valuables, he was suffocated, in the fifty-fourth year of his age. There are a considerable number of spirited and charming etchings by him, from his own designs. Bartsch gives a catalogue of thirty-nine; to which Weigel, in his Supplement to Bartsch, has added five more. The principal are a set of eight plates of Animals, dated 1665; a set of twelve plates of Domestic Animals; and several large plates of Landscapes, with ruins and animals, &c.

ROOS, Theodore, was the brother of the preceding, born at Wezel in 1638. He first studied under Adrian de Bie, and afterwards with his brother, whom he assisted in his works till 1659, when he was invited to the court of Manheim, and taken into the service of the Elector. His first performance was a large picture, representing the principal magistrates of Manheim, still preserved in the Council Chamber. He afterwards visited several other courts of Germany, particularly those of Baden and Hanau, and found much encouragement in painting the portraits of distinguished personages. The Elector Palatine employed him to paint the portraits of the Duke and Duchess of Orleans, for which he was liberally remunerated, and honored with a gold medal and chain. The Duke of Wurtemberg employed him on several historical works, and appointed him his principal painter. The pictures of this artist are chiefly confined to Germany, where they are highly esteemed, particularly his portraits, which are said to possess the merit of perfect resemblance. His manner was broad and free, and his coloring clear and vigorous, but he was deficient in design, and his drawing is frequently incorrect. He executed a few spirited etchings from his own designs. Bartsch describes a set of six upright landscapes, with figures and ruins, dated 1667; and Weigel adds a Holy Family, in the Dresden

Gallery, dated 1671. These prints are extremely scarce. He died in 1698.

ROOS, Philip, called Rosa da Tivoli, the son of John Henry R., was born at Frankfort in 1655. He early showed a passion for painting. Under the able instruction of his father he made great progress, and showed such extraordinary talents that the Landgrave of Hesse, in whose service the elder Roos was then engaged, took Philip under his protection, and sent him to Italy with a pension sufficient for his support. On his arrival at Rome, according to Lanzi, he commenced studying with Giacinto Brandi, whose daughter he afterwards married. He applied himself to his studies with such assiduity that he was regarded as the most laborious young artist of his time, and acquired a wonderful facility in design and execution, for which reason he was named *Mercurius* by the Bentvogel Society. A remarkable proof of this is recorded by C. le Blond, then a student at Rome. "It happened one day, that several young artists and myself were occupied in designing from the bassi-relievi of the Arch of Titus, when Roos passing by, was particularly struck with some picturesque object which had caught his attention, and he requested one of the students to accommodate him with a crayon and paper. What was our surprise when, in half an hour, he produced an admirable drawing, finished with accuracy and *finesse*." To facilitate his studies, he established himself at Tivoli (whence his name of Rosa da Tivoli), where he kept a kind of menagerie, and on account of the number and variety of the animals, his house was called Noah's Ark. He designed everything from nature, not only his animals, but the sites of his landscapes, ruins, buildings, rocks, rivers, &c.

His pictures usually represent pastoral subjects, with herdsmen and cattle, or shepherds with sheep and goats, which he frequently painted nearly as large as life. His groups are composed with great judgment and taste, and his landscape, back-grounds, kies, and distances, are treated in a masterly style. His cattle and animals, in particular, are designed with wonderful truth and spirit; his coloring is full of force, his lights and shadows are distributed with judgment, and his touch is remarkably firm, free and spirited. It is erroneously said by most of his biographers, that though he wrought with *wonderful rapidity*, yet his pictures show no appearance of negligence or inattention. There is indeed a *wonderful difference* in his works, as will readily be perceived by inspecting them, and by comparing the criticisms of the Dutch and Italian writers. The whole history of art does not show an example of such rapid execution, without its being accompanied with more or less defects, both in design and execution. In fact, the later productions of Rosa da Tivoli do not compare with his earlier works. He unfortunately fell into dissipated and extravagant habits, which frequently caused him great inconvenience; and, in order to supply his wants, he multiplied his pictures to such an extent as to depreciate their value. It is related that he would sit down, dispatch a large picture in a few hours, and send it directly to be sold, at any price; but his servant, possessing more discretion, usually paid him the highest price offered by the dealers, and kept the pictures himself, till he could dispose of them to more advantage. It is also related that Count Martinetz, the Imperial Ambassador, laid a wager with a Swedish General, that Roos would paint a picture of three-quarters size, while they were playing a game at cards; and in less than half an hour the picture was finished, though it consisted of a landscape, a figure, and several sheep and goats. Lanzi says, "we ought not to rest our decision of his merits on those hasty performances, which abound in Rome, but should examine his choicest pictures, conducted at his leisure, which are to be found in the galleries of princes." His best works are in the royal collections of Vienna, Dresden, and other cities of Germany, as well as in the best collections of Rome and Florence. There are also many of his works in England. Roos died at Rome in 1705. Huber says that he executed a few spirited etchings from his own designs, which are extremely scarce.

ROOS, John Melchior, was the younger brother of the preceding, born at Frankfort in 1659. After studying with his father, he went to Italy, and resided there several years. He afterwards returned to Germany, and settled at Nuremberg, where he painted history and portraits with considerable encouragement; but his taste leading him to landscapes and cattle, in the style of his brother, he soon devoted himself entirely to that branch. His principal patron was the Landgrave of Hesse Cassel, who employed him for many years, and gave the commissions for some of his choicest works. Roos painted subjects similar to those of Philip, but his coloring and handling were very different; he lacked his agreeable coloring and free, flowing pencil, and he laid on his colors with a body that seemed more like modeling than painting. Yet his pictures, at a distance, have a natural appearance, and produce a fine effect. There is an etching of a Bull by him, signed *J. M. Roos fec.* 1685; the only one known, and extremely scarce. He died in 1731.

ROOS, Joseph, a German painter, born at Vienna in 1728. He painted landscapes and cattle with considerable reputation, and was much employed by the Elector of Saxony. He was chosen a member of the Academy of Dresden, and afterwards was appointed Keeper of the Imperial Gallery at Vienna. His principal works are in the castle of Schoenbrunn. He executed a few neat and spirited etchings from his own designs, among which are a set of six plates of various animals, and another of ten plates of sheep and goats.

ROPER, an English painter of sporting pieces, race horses, dogs, and dead game, who died about 1762.

ROSA, Aniella, or Annella di, a Neapolitan paintress, born at Naples, according to Dominici, in 1613. She first studied under her uncle, Francesco di Rosa, and afterwards with the Cav. Massimo Stanzioni; at the same time, Agostino Beltrano was her fellow-student, whom she married. They wrought together, and prepared many pictures, which their master afterwards finished, and sold as his own. Some pictures, however, pass under her own name, and are highly extolled, as the Birth and Death of the Virgin at the Pietà; not however without a suspicion that Stanzioni had a share in their execution. She left numerous original drawings, which prove that she had a good knowledge of design, and several cotemporaneous artists and writers extol her as an excellent artist

She has been compared to Elizabeth Sirani for her talents, beauty, and tragical death; the fair Bolognese was inhumanly poisoned by some envious artist, and Aniella was murdered by a jealous husband in 1649.

ROSA, Cristoforo, a painter born at Brescia about 1520, and died of the plague at Venice in 1576. He excelled in painting perspective and architectural views, and lived upon terms of intimacy with Titian, who occasionally employed him to paint the architecture in some of his pictures. There are several of his works in the public edifices of Venice, particularly some perspective pieces, in the antechamber of the Library of St. Mark, so admirably executed that they deceive the eye by their relief, and surprise by their air of grandeur. He had a brother named Stefano, also an excellent painter in the same branch, who assisted him in his works. They established a school in their native city, which continued to flourish many years after their decease. They also executed many admirable works in oil and fresco, for the churches and public edifices of Brescia.

ROSA, Pietro, was the son of Cristoforo R. He studied under Titian, and was instructed by him with great care, on account of his friendship for Pietro's father. This extraordinary care was rewarded with excellent results, and few artists have approached so near the admirable principles of coloring practised by that great master. He executed several works for the churches of Brescia, which gained him great reputation. Unfortunately for the art, he fell a victim to the plague in the flower of his life, in 1576, the year of his father's death.

ROSA, Francesco, a Genoese painter, who flourished about 1670. According to Zanetti, he was a pupil of Pietro da Cortona. He painted several frescos and oil paintings for the churches, which Lanzi says show him to have been a follower of a different style; they resemble the works of Tommaso Luini and other dark mannerists of the age. He also painted in other cities. Lanzi says one of his best works is the Miracle of St. Anthony, in the church of the Frari at Venice, a grand composition of many figures, designed more in the style of the Caracci than of Cortona; displaying much knowledge of the naked figure, beautiful architecture, a fine effect of chiaro-scuro, with great vivacity in the heads.

ROSA, Francesco di, called also Pacicco or Pacecco, a Neapolitan painter, who, according to Dominici, was one of the ablest scholars of the Cav. Massimo Stanzioni. Lanzi says he is one of the few painters commemorated by Paolo de' Matteis, who never admits any inferior artists. "He declares the style of Rosa almost inimitable, not only from his correct design, but from the rare beauty of his extremities, and still more from the dignity and grace of his countenances. He had in his three nieces the most perfect models of beauty, and he possessed a sublimity of sentiment which elevated his mind to a high sense of excellence. His coloring, though conducted with exquisite sweetness, had a strong body, and his pictures preserve a fresh and clear tone." His style, like most of the scholars of Stanzioni, was founded on that of Guido, whose works he frequently copied, under the direction of his instructor, in the early part of his course. He lived to an advanced age, and executed a great many easel pictures, which are now preserved with high estimation in the collections of the Neapolitan nobility. He also painted some beautiful altar-pieces for the churches. He died at Naples in 1654.

ROSA, Giovanni, a Flemish painter, born at Antwerp in 1591. According to Soprani, he went early to Rome, and acquired great reputation for his exquisite paintings of landscapes and animals Lanzi says he studied at Rome, and was a happy imitator of nature in her most agreeable forms, especially animals. "Many artists of this period attached themselves to the painting of animals. Castiglione distinguished himself in this line; but he resided for the most part of his time in another country. Giovanni Rosa of Flanders is the most known at Rome, and in the State, for the great number of his paintings of animals, in which he possessed extraordinary talent. It is said of him that he painted hares so naturally as to deceive the dogs, thus reviving the wonderful story of Zeuxis, so much boasted of by Pliny. Two of his largest and finest pictures are in the Bolognetti collection. We must not confound this artist with Rosa da Tivoli, also an excellent animal painter, but not so celebrated in Italy." He afterwards established himself at Genoa, where he left many works, taught some pupils, and died in 1638. This artist is not mentioned by any of the Dutch or Flemish writers, doubtless because he passed his whole artistic life in Italy.

ROSA, Giuseppe. This artist is briefly mentioned by Lanzi in a note to his life of Rosa da Tivoli, of whom he was a descendant. He was appointed Director of the Imperial Gallery at Vienna, and published a catalogue of the Italian and Flemish pictures in 1784.

ROSA, Salvatore. This celebrated painter was born at Renella, a small village near Naples in 1615. His father, an archite and land surveyor, intended him for the church, and gave him a liberal education; but young Rosa left the Seminary of his own accord at the age of sixteen, and devoting himself to musical studies, became a skilful musician and a good composer. His eldest sister having married Francesco Fracanzani, a painter of considerable talent, Salvator imbibed an inclination for painting from frequenting his studio, and commenced studying under his brother-in-law. There is so much fiction mingled with the early history of this great artist, that it is impossible to arrive at the truth. It is certain, however, that he passed his early days in poverty, that he was compelled to support himself by his pencil, that he exposed his juvenile performances for sale in the public markets, and often sold them to the dealers for the smallest prices. To the honor of Cav. Lanfranco, it is related that while riding in his carriage one day along the streets of Naples, he observed one of Salvator's pictures exposed for sale in a shop window, and surprised at the uncommon genius which it displayed, he purchased the picture, and inquired the name of the young artist. The picture-dealer, who had probably found Salvator's necessities quite profitable to himself, refused to communicate the desired information, whereupon Lanfranco directed his scholars to watch for his pictures, and seek him out. When he had found him, he generously relieved his wants, and encouraged him in the pursuit of his studies. After receiving some instructions from Aniello Falcone, an eminent painter of battle-pieces, he was admitted, through the influence of Lanfranco, into the academy of Giuseppe Ribera, called Il Spagnoletto, and remained there until the age of twenty, when he accompanied that master to Rome. The Cardinal Brancacci, having become acquainted with his merits at Naples, took him under his protection, and conducted him to his bishopric of Viterbo, where Salvator painted several historical works, and an altar-piece for the Cathedral, representing the Incredulity of St. Thomas. On his return to Rome, the prince Gio. Carlo de' Medici employed him to execute several important works, and afterwards invited him to Florence. During a residence of nine years in that city, he greatly distinguished himself as a painter, and also as a satirical and dramatic poet; his Satires, composed in Florence, have passed through several editions. His wit, lively disposition, and unusual conversational powers, drew around him many choice spirits, and his house was the great centre of attraction for the connoisseurs and literati of Florence. He fitted up a private theatre, and was accustomed to perform the principal parts in his comedies, in which he displayed extraordinary talents. He painted many of his choicest pictures for the Grand Duke, who nobly rewarded him; also for the noble family of the Maffei, for their palace at Volterra. After his return to Rome, he demanded exorbitant prices for his works, and though his greatest talent lay in landscape painting, he affected to despise that branch, being ambitious of shining as an historical painter. He painted some altar-pieces and other subjects for the churches, the chief of which are four pictures in S. Maria di Monte Santo, representing Daniel in the Lion's Den, Tobit and the Angel, the Resurrection of Christ, and the Raising of Lazarus; the Martyrdom of St. Cosimo and St. Damiano, in the church of S. Giovanni.

The brightest era of landscape painting is said with truth to have been in the time of pope Urban VIII., when flourished Claude Lorraine, Gaspar Poussin, and Salvator Rosa. Of these, Salvator was the most distinguished, though certainly not the best; each was the head of a perfectly original school, which had many followers, and each observed nature on the side in which he felt impelled to imitate her. The first admired and represented nature in her sweetest appearance; the second, in her most gorgeous array; and the third in her most convulsed and terrific aspects. Salvator Rosa painted history, landscape, battle-pieces, and sea-ports; and of these he was most eminent in landscape. The scholar of Spagnoletto, he attached himself to the strong natural style and dark coloring of that master, which well accords with his subjects. In his landscapes, instead of selecting the cultured amenity which captivates in the views of Claude or Poussin, he made choice of the lonely haunts of wolves and robbers; instead of the delightful vistas of Tivoli and the Campagna, he adopted the savage scenery of the Alps, rocky precipices, caves, with wild thickets and desert plains; his trees are shattered, or torn up by the roots, and in the atmosphere itself he seldom introduced a cheerful hue, except occasionally a solitary sunbeam. These gloomy regions are peopled with congenial inhabitants, ferocious banditti, assassins, and outlaws. In his marines, he followed the same taste; they represent the desolate and shelvy shores of Calabria, whose dreary aspect is sometimes heightened by terrific tempests, with all the horrors of shipwreck. His battles and attacks of cavalry also partake of the same principle of wild beauty; the fury of the combatants, and the fiery animation of the horses are depicted with a truth and effect that strikes the mind with horror. Notwithstanding the singularity and fierceness of his style, he captivates by the unbounded wildness of his fancy, and the picturesque solemnity of his scenes. "He gives us," says Sir Joshua Reynolds, "a peculiar cast of nature, which, though void of grace, elegance, and simplicity, though it has nothing of that elevation and dignity which belongs to the grand style, yet has that sort of dignity which belongs to savage and uncultivated nature; but what is most to be admired in him is, the perfect correspondence which he observed between the subjects he chose, and his manner of treating them. Everything is of a piece; his rocks, trees, skies, even to his handling, have the same rude and wild character which animates his figures."

Although Salvator Rosa possessed a lively and inventive genius, his powers were better adapted to the scale of easel pictures than to more extensive compositions, with figures of large dimensions. "Owing to his frequent practice," says Lanzi, "he had more merit in his smaller than his larger figures. He was accustomed to insert them in his landscapes; and he composed his historical pictures in the same style as the Regulus, so highly praised, in the Colonna palace (this picture is now in the possession of the Earl of Darnley); also fancy subjects, as the Witchcrafts, specimens of which are to be seen in the Campidoglio, and in many private collections. In these he is never select, not always correct, but displays great spirit, freedom of execution, skill, and harmony of color. In other respects he has proved, on several occasions, that his genius was not confined to small compositions, evinced by some well conceived altar-pieces, executed with powerful effect, particularly when the subject demands an expression of terror, as in a Martyrdom of Saints in the church of S. Gio. de' Fiorentini at Rome, and in the Purgatory in S. Gio. delle Case Rotte at Milan. We have also some profane subjects by him, finely executed on a large scale; such is the Conspiracy of Catiline, in the possession of the noble family of Martelli in Florence, commended by Bottari as one of his best works." Salvator Rosa wrought with wonderful facility, and could paint a well finished landscape and insert all the figures in one day; it is impossible to inspect one of his bold, rapid sketches, without being struck with the fertility of his invention, and the skill of his hand that rivalled in execution the activity of his mind. He was also an excellent portrait painter. A portrait of himself is in the church degli Angeli, where his remains were interred, and he introduced his own portrait into several of his pictures, one of which is in the Chigi gallery, representing a wild scene with a poet in a sitting attitude (with the features of Salvator); before him stands a satyr, allusive to his satiric style of poetry. During his life-time, his works were much sought after by princes and nobles, and they are now to be found in the choic est collections of Italy and of Europe. There is a landscape in the English National Gallery which cost 1800 guineas; a picture in the collection of Sir Mark Sykes brought the enormous sum of 2100 guineas. Salvator Rosa also produced about ninety etchings from his own designs, executed in a spirited and masterly style. They are distinguished by intelligent management of the chiaroscuro, and uncommon vivacity and expression in the heads. They are usually marked with a monogram of his initials, as above. He also sometimes signed his paintings with the same mark. The following are his principal prints. He died at Rome in 1673.

A set of sixty-two Prints of banditti, soldiers, and other figures; single and in groups. The Fall of the Giants. The Death of Attilius Regulus. The finding of Œdipus. Democritus meditating. The Execution of Polycrates. Glaucus and Sylla. Jason charming the Dragon. Alexander with Apelles. Alexander and Diogenes. Diogenes throwing away his Bowl. Plato discoursing with his Disciples. Apollo and a Nymph. An allegorical subject; called *The Genius of Salvator*. A set of six Plates, in the form of friezes, representing Tritons, Sea Nymphs, &c.

ROSA, Sigismondo, a Roman painter, who flourished in the first part of the 18th century. He studied under Giuseppe Chiari, and adopted his style. He was a reputable artist, and executed a few works for the churches, but mostly painted easel pictures.

ROSA, Sisto. See Badalocchio.

ROSA, da Tivoli. See Philip Roos.

ROSALBA, Carriera, a celebrated Italian paintress, born at Chiozza, near Venice, in 1675. She was instructed in art by Giovanni Diamantini, and practised oil painting for some time, but afterwards abandoned it for miniature and crayons, in which last branch she became very eminent. In 1709, Frederick IV., King of Denmark, passing through Venice, sat to her for his portrait, which she executed so much to his satisfaction that he ordered several copies, and subsequently employed her to paint the portraits of twelve Venetian ladies, for which he rewarded her with princely liberality. She visited Paris in company with Pellegrini, her brother-in-law, where she painted the royal family, the princes of the blood, and the principal personages of the court. She was elected a member of the French Academy, and presented, as her reception-piece, a picture of one of the Muses. She was subsequently employed at several of the courts of Europe, and everywhere left many proofs of her extraordinary ability. On returning to Venice, she continued to practise her profession with undiminished success until the age of seventy, when, from incessant application, her eyesight completely failed. Few artists have equalled Rosalba in crayon painting. Her portraits, especially those of females, are gracefully designed, full of life and spirit, exceedingly natural, with an agreeable resemblance to the persons represented. Her coloring is soft, tender, and delicate, her tints are clear and admirably blended. She died at Venice in 1757.

ROSALIBA, Antonello, a Sicilian painter, who flourished at Messina in the first part of the 16th century. He executed some works for the churches, which, according to Hackert, are gracefully designed and well colored.

ROSASPINA, Francesco, an eminent Italian engraver, born at Bologna in 1760. His instructor is not mentioned, but he was equally skilful in operating with the burin, in the chalk manner, and in aquatinta. His drawing is very correct, and his plates are beautifully executed, with a fine effect of chiaro-scuro; they are also esteemed for the fidelity with which he copied the expression and characteristics of his originals. Among his most esteemed prints are, the Dance of Cupids, *after Albano;* the Dead Christ, *after Correggio;* St. Francis, *after Domenichino;* Cupid bending his Bow, *after Franceschini;* several portraits of illustrious Italians; and a series of twenty-five prints, *after Parmiggiano*, engraved in the crayon and tinted manner, in the finest taste. Rosaspina also engraved some of the Battles of Napoleon, *after the designs of Appiani*, in the style of bassi-relievi. He is also entitled to great credit for his able superintendence of the engraving and publishing of the work entitled *La Pinacoteca*, consisting of about seventy plates after the best paintings in the Academy of the Fine Arts at Bologna, of which institution he was professor. In these prints, the drawing and character of the originals are preserved with the greatest exactness. The time of his death is not recorded.

ROSATI, Rosato, an Italian sculptor and architect, who flourished in the first part of the 17th century. According to Milizia, he erected the church of the Jesuits in his native city, and the main portion of the church of S. Carlo de' Catenari at Rome, a Greek cross of one nave, with a cupola, to which was added a façade by Giovanni Battista Soria.

ROSE, Nicholas. See Liemaeker.

ROSE, Susan Penelope, an English paintress of miniatures, who, according to Lord Orford, was the daughter of Richard Gibson, called the Dwarf. She was born in 1652, and died in 1700. Her miniatures were of unusually large size, and are said to have possessed considerable merit.

ROSEL, John Augustus, a German painter of noble descent, born at Arnstadt in 1705. He at first practised as a miniature painter at Nuremberg, but afterwards devoted himself to the representation of insects, which he depicted with all the truth and accuracy of nature. He studied and wrote upon Entomology, and in 1746, published his celebrated work on that subject, entitled *Insekten-Belustigungen*, in 4 vols., 4to., illustrated with numerous plates from his own designs. He died at Nuremberg in 1759.

ROSELLI, Niccolo, a painter who flourished at Ferrara about 1568. Baruffaldi supposes that he was a scholar of the Dossi, but Lanzi says this is quite uncertain, as he could imitate many different masters. He executed many works for the churches at Ferrara. In his altar-piece of Christ with two Angels, at the Battuti Bianchi, he followed the Dossi, but in his twelve altar-pieces at the Certosa, he imitated Benvenuto Garofolo, Il Bagnacavallo, and several other artists.

ROSELLINI, Bernardo, a distinguished Italian architect, who flourished at Rome about 1450. He was highly esteemed by Pope Nicholas V., and was employed to execute many excellent edifices, among which were the church of S. Francesco at Fabriano; S. Benedetto, at Gualdo; and S. Francesco at Assisi. He also restored and embellished the Basilica of S. Giovani Laterano, of S. Paolo, and S. Lorenzo without the walls, at Rome, and the Baths at Viterbo. By a commission from the same pontiff, Rosellini repaired a great part of the walls of Rome, furnished them with towers, strengthened the Castle of St. Angelo, and restored the fortifications at Civita Vecchia, Narni, and Spoleto. Nicholas was a munificent patron of the Fine Arts, and conceived the idea of an immense architectural work in the suburbs of Rome, which was designed by Rosellini. It included a magnificent temple to St. Peter, with superb palaces for the pope and cardinals, beautiful villas, gardens and fountains. The death of the pope, in 1455, prevented the execution of this splendid project.

ROSER, M., a German painter, born at Heidelberg in 1737. After learning the rudiments of art, he studied under Loutherbourg. In 1764, he went to Paris, and chiefly devoted himself to copying the works of the Flemish painters, which he did with great success. His happy talent of imitating the touch and coloring of different masters, peculiarly fitted him for repairing ancient pictures in which he met with considerable employment. He restored Raffaelle's painting of the Virgin of Foligno, and several works by Correggio, Titian, and other great masters. He died at Paris in 1804.

ROSETTI, Domenico, a painter and engraver, born at Venice about 1690. It is not known under whom he studied. He painted perspective and architectural pieces with considerable success, but is chiefly known by his works as an engraver. He was invited by the Elector Palatine to Dusseldorf, where he engraved twelve large plates of the history of Alexander, after the works of Gerard Lairesse; these prints are now very scarce, as few impressions were taken. He executed some of the plates for a collection of prints after the most celebrated pictures at Venice, published by Domenico Louisa in that city, in 1720. He is said to have engraved a set of plates for a history of the Bible, printed at Venice in 1696; also a variety of plates after Palma Vecchio, Bassano, Tintoretto, P. Liberi, and others. Some of these bear a still earlier date, and Zani says he operated in 1675. He died about 1760. It is possible from the above dates, that there were two engravers of this name.

ROSI, Alessandro, a Florentine painter, born, according to Orlandi, in 1627. He studied under Cesare Dandini, and painted history with considerable reputation. He executed several works for the churches of Florence, and in the state, but painted more for the collections. In the cathedral at Prato, is a fine picture by him, of St. Francesco Di Paolo, and in the collection of the Grand Duke, are two Bacchanalian subjects, executed with great beauty and spirit. He died at Florence in 1697.

ROSI, Zanobi, a Florentine painter, who flourished in the first part of the 17th century. According to Baldinucci, he studied under Cristofano Allori, whose style he closely imitated, and at the death of that master he completed some of his unfinished works. Lanzi says he never obtained any reputation for originality of invention, but he was one of those artists to whom we owe the duplicates of Allori's most celebrated pictures, numerous in Florence, and over all Italy.

ROSI, Giovanni, a Florentine painter of landscapes, who flourished about the middle of the 17th century. Baldinucci says he closely imitated Gaspare Falgani, *which see.*

ROSIGNOLI, Jacopo, a painter born at Leghorn, of whom little is known. According to Lanzi, his works are frequently to be met with in Piedmont, resembling the style of Pierino del Vaga, especially in his grotesques. He attained sufficient reputation to be appointed painter of the court at Turin, where he died in 1604. He was buried in the church of S. Tommaso, and a monument, with a laudatory epitaph, was erected to his memory.

ROSITI, Giovanni Baptista, a painter of Forli, who flourished about 1500. Lanzi mentions only one picture by him, well designed and colored, in the church of S. Maria dell'Orto, at Veletri, representing the Virgin with the Infant Jesus in her arms. It is signed *Jo. Baptista de Rositis de Forlivio pinxit*, I. S. O. O. *de Mense Martii*, 1500.

ROSLER, Michael, an obscure German engraver, who flourished at Nuremburg, in the first part of the 17th century. He engraved several plates for a folio volume, published in that city in 1626, entitled *Icones Bibliopolarum et Typographorum.*

ROSS, James, an English engraver, who flourished about 1778. He engraved some views of the city of Hereford, neatly executed; also some plates after drawings by G. Powle.

ROSSELLI, Cosimo, a Florentine painter, born about 1416, who acquired great distinction without possessing commensurate merit. There is much discrepancy about his history, and his instructor is not mentioned. After acquiring considerable reputation in his native city, he was invited to Rome by Sixtus IV., to assist in ornamenting the Sistine Chapel, in conjunction with Domenico Ghirlandaio, Pietro Perugino, Sandro Botticelli, and other eminent artists. Lanzi says of his works at Rome, "Being unable to rival his competitors in design, he loaded his pictures with brilliant colors and gilded ornaments, which practice, though condemned at that time by an improving taste, yet pleased the pontiff, who commended and rewarded him beyond all other artists. Perhaps his best work there is Christ preaching on the Mount, in which the landscape is said to be the work of Pier di Cosimo, a painter more remarkable for his coloring than his design, as is evident from his picture in the church of the Innocents, and his Perseus, in the Florentine gallery. They are both however, celebrated in history, Rosselli, as the master of Baccio della Porta, and Cosimo, of Andrea del Sarto." Most of the works Rosselli executed in Florence have perished; there is, however, a fresco in the church of S. Ambrogio, representing the Miracle of the Sacrament, full of fine portraits, which discover variety, character and truth. Lanzi says he was living in 1496; Zani, that he died in 1506; others, that he was born in 1416, and died in 1484. Pier di Cosimo was born in 1441, and died in 1521, *which see.*

ROSSELLI, Matteo, a Florentine painter, born in 1578. He first studied with Gregorio Pagani and afterwards with Passignano, whom he accompanied to Rome, and gained improvement by studying the works of Raffaelle, Polidoro da Caravaggio, and other masters. On finishing his studies he returned to Florence, where he passed the remainder of his life, and acquired so much reputation, that he was invited to the court of the Duke of Modena. He remained, however, in the service of Cosimo II., Grand Duke of Tuscany, by whom he was much employed; he embellished his palace of the Villa di Coggio with several fine frescos, representing the history of the family of the Medici. He also executed many works for the churches and public edifices. The works of Rosselli are not distinguished by the vigorous design and animated expression which characterize the productions of some Florentine artists. His merit lies in correctness of design, and a close imitation of nature, with a peculiar harmony pervading the whole, which render his pictures agreeable and attractive, even when compared with works of the most brilliant coloring. He excelled in dignity of character; some of the heads of his apostles so strongly resemble the works of the Caracci, that even connoisseurs have sometimes been deceived. At other times he imitated the style of Lodovico Cardi, called Cigoli, as seen in his fine picture of the Nativity, in S. Gaetano, considered his most capital performance, and the martyrdom of St. Andrea at the Ognissanti, which has been engraved. His fresco paintings are greatly admired, and preserve their brilliancy, even to the present time. In the cloister of the Nunziata, are several semi-circular pieces by him, representing Alexander IV. confirming the Order of the Servi, which were considered grand productions by Passignano and Cortona. He opened a school at Florence, and instructed many pupils. Lanzi says he had few equals in the art of teaching; he possessed a remarkable talent for communicating instruction, and a judicious method of discovering the talents of each pupil and of directing his studies accordingly, so that his school, like that of the Caracci, produced almost as many different styles as he had scholars; he also preserved a fatherly regard for his pupils, who greatly loved and respected him. He died in 1650.

ROSSET, Joseph, a French sculptor, born at St. Claude, in Franche Comté, in 1706. He acquired a knowledge of the art without a master, by studying and modeling various works of sculpture. He was patronized by Voltaire, and executed several busts of that celebrated author. His subjects are principally of a religious character, some executed in ivory; among them are a number of beautiful statues of the Virgin; and one of St. Jerome, highly praised by Falconet, who supposed from its excellence, that the artist had studied in Italy. Rosset practised the art for many years in his native place, and died in 1786.

ROSSETTI, Cesare, a painter born at Rome, who, according to Baglioni, studied under Giuseppe Cesari, whom he assisted in many of his works, and whose manner he adopted. He also executed many works of his own for the churches, as well as for the collections. He flourished about 1830.

ROSSETTI, Giovanni Paolo, a painter born at Volterra, who flourished about 1568. He was a nephew of Daniele Ricciarelli, with whom he studied at Rome, and according to Vasari, painted history with considerable reputation. After the death of his uncle, he returned to Volterra, where he executed some altar-pieces for the churches, one of the most esteemed of which is the Descent from the Cross in S. Dalmasio. Zani says he operated in 1600.

ROSSETTI, Paolo, a painter of Cento, who, according to Baglioni, was an eminent painter in mosaic, and executed many beautiful works. He died in 1621, at an advanced age.

ROSSETTI. See Rovere.

ROSSI, Andrea, an Italian engraver, born at Rome in 1726, and died in 1790. He engraved several portraits of Popes and royal personages, and other subjects after various Italian masters, among which are the portraits of the Emperor Joseph II. of Austria, and the Archduke Leopold, *after Pompeo Battoni;* a Bust of the Virgin, *after Carlo Dolci;* and St. Margaret of Cortona, *after Pietro da Cortona.*

ROSSI, Antonio, a painter born at Bologna in 1700. He was the favorite disciple of the Cav. Marc' Antonio Franceschini, who recommended him in preference to his other pupils, to execute many of the commissions which he was obliged to decline on account of his constant occupation. He executed numerous works for the churches and public edifices at Bologna, one of the most esteemed of which is the martyrdom of St. Andrew, in S. Domenico. He was much employed in decorating with his figures, the architectural and perspective pieces of Orlandi and F. Brizzio. He died, according to Crespi and Lanzi, in 1753; others place his birth in 1697, and death in 1750.

ROSSI, Aniello, a Neapolitan painter, born about 1660, and died in 1719. According to Dominici, he was one of the favorite scholars of Luca Giordano, whose style he adopted. He accompanied his instructor to Spain, assisted him in the execution of his numerous works at Madrid, and returned with him to Naples, with a pension from the king that enabled him to pass the rest of his days in leisure and independence.

ROSSI, Antonio, called de Rubeis, a painter of the Venitian school, who, according to Lanzi, was a native of Cadore, flourished in the latter part of the 15th century, and from various authorities found in that city, is supposed to have been the instructor of Titian. He describes three pictures by him, inferior in design to Jacopo Bellini, though similar in style, and perhaps equal to the works of that master in elegance of coloring.

ROSSI, or ROSSIS, Angelo, a Florentine painter, born in 1742. It is not mentioned under whom he studied, but according to Lanzi, he acquired distinction as an architectural and ornamental painter, and was much employed at Florence, Bologna, and at Venice.

ROSSI, D. Angelo, a painter born in the Genoese territory, according to Ratti, in 1694, and died in 1755. Lanzi says he was the most distinguished scholar of Domenico Parodi, and a good follower of the style of Carlo Maratti. He executed but few works for the churches, but excelled in painting easel pictures of humorous subjects.

ROSSI, Carlo Antonio, a Milanese painter, born, according to Orlandi, about 1580, and died in 1648. He was educated in the school of the Procaccini, and executed some works for the churches, especially in the cathedral of Pavia "painted in the best Procaccini taste." He is described in the *Abbecedario*, as an eccentric man, but well versed in his art.

ROSSI, Enea, a Bolognese painter, who flourished about 1600, and, according to Malvasia, studied in the school of the Caracci. He was a skilful artist, and executed some fine works for the churches at Bologna and in the state.

ROSSI, Francesco. See Salviati.

ROSSI, Gabriele, a Bolognese painter of architecture and perspective, who flourished, according to Baruffaldi, about 1650. He attained eminence in that branch in his day, but his works have mostly perished. He was the instructor of Francesco Ferrari.

ROSSI, Giovanni Battista, called Il Gobbino (humpback), a painter of Verona, who, according to Pozzo, was an excellent disciple of Alessandro Turchi, surnamed Orbetto. He executed several works for the churches of Verona, but painted more for the collections. He flourished about 1630.

ROSSI, Giovanni Battista, a painter born at Rovigo about 1627, and died about 1680. He studied under Dario Varotari, called Padovanino, and adopted his style. He executed a few works for the churches at Padua and Venice, which are extolled by Boschini, but was mostly employed in painting for the collections.

ROSSI, Giovanni Battista, a Roman engraver, who flourished about 1640. He published in that year a set of perspective views of Rome.

ROSSI, Giovanni Stefano, a Genoese painter, born in 1719. He studied successively under Semini, Sorri, and Strozzi. He acquired considerable reputation, as a painter of history, and executed some works for the churches and convents. He died at Genoa in 1769.

ROSSI, Girolamo, a painter born at Brescia, who flourished about 1640. He is supposed from his style, to have studied under Camillo Rama, whose style he imitated, as appears from his altarpiece of the Virgin between various Saints, in the church of S. Alessandro, in his native city. Lanzi says he was either a pupil or an imitator of Rama, and displayed that master's manner better than any of his other pupils.

ROSSI, Girolamo, a Bolognese painter and engraver, who, according to Malvasia, was a pupil of Flaminio Torre, and flourished about 1660. Lanzi says he succeeded better in engraving than in painting. Perhaps he is the same as the following artist, though the accounts do not agree.

ROSSI, Girolamo, called de Rubeis the Elder, a painter and engraver, born at Rome about 1630. He studied at Bologna, under Simone Cantarini. Little is said of his works as a painter; he executed some spirited etchings after the Italian masters, which are marked *Hieronimus de Rubeis pictor, delineavit incidit. or fecit.* Bartsch asserts that his etchings amount only to six, but more are described by other writers.

ROSSI, Girolamo, called de Rubeis the Younger, was the son of the preceding, born at Rome about 1680. He studied with his father, and executed a number of plates after various Italian masters, also several for a set of portraits of the Cardinals of his time, which was afterwards continued by Pazzi, and others. His plates are engraved in a feeble style. Nagler gives a list of twenty-one prints by him. Zani says he operated as late as 1749.

ROSSI, Lorenzo, a Florentine painter, who, according to Orlandi, was a pupil of Pietro Dandini. He did not follow the style of that master but painted elegant small pictures, following the manner of Livio Mehus, which see. He died at Florence in 1702.

ROSSI, Muzio, a Neapolitan painter, born in 1626. According to Crespi, he studied with the Cav. Massimo Stanzioni, and afterwards entered the academy of Guido at Bologna. He possessed such extraordinary talents, that, at the age of eighteen, he was employed in competition with the first masters at the Certosa, where he painted an altar-piece of the Nativity, which was considered a prodigy of youthful ability, and is still held in high estimation. On his return to Naples, he was employed to paint the Tribune of St. Pietro in Majella, which he did not live to complete. He died in the flower of his life, deeply lamented, in 1651.

ROSSI, Niccolo Maria, a Neapolitan painter, born in 1645. According to Dominici, he studied under Luca Giordano, and became an excellent designer and colorist in the style of that master. He painted the ceiling of the Royal chapel, assisted by the designs of Giordano. He executed some works for the churches, which are commended in the *Guida di Napoli*, particularly several fine paintings in distemper, in Santi Sepolcri and Quarantore. There are several of his easel pictures in the collections, which are much esteemed for their correctness of design and spirited execution; he excelled in his representations of animals, in which branch he was considered next to the Cav. Giuseppe Recco. He died at Naples in 1700.

ROSSI, Pasquale, called Pasqualino da Vicenza, a painter born at Vicenza in 1641. According to Orlandi, he reached a respectable rank in historical painting, without the aid of a master, by studying the works of the best Roman and Venetian painters; but he early left his native city and passed many years at Rome, where he executed many excellent works for the churches, and is classed by Lanzi with the painters of the Roman school. Among his most esteemed pictures, are Christ praying in the Garden, in S. Carlo al Corso, and the Baptism of Christ, in S. Maria del Popolo at Rome; the Madonna and Child, at the Silvestrini in Fabriano, which Lanzi says is truly beautiful, and a picture of St. Gregory liberating souls from Purgatory, in the Cathedral at Matelica, one of his best works, executed in the style of Guercino. He also painted many cabinet pictures, representing gaming parties, conversations, concerts, and similar subjects, which are esteemed in the best collections. Lanzi says, "they are carefully finished, and little inferior to the Flemish pictures. I have met with numerous specimens of his cabinet pictures in various places, but in no place have I admired this artist so much as in the Royal gallery at Turin, where are several of his works, some of them of considerable size, chiefly scriptural subjects, executed in an animated and vigorous style, and with so much of the Roman school, that one would think them to be by some other master." Lanzi and several other writers say he was living in 1718; Zani, that he died in 1725; others place his death in 1700, but there are pictures by him bearing a later date.

ROSSI, JOHN CHARLES FELIX, an eminent English sculptor, was the son of an Italian of Siena, a resident of Nottingham, and was born in that town in 1762. He first studied sculpture under Luccatella, and afterwards visited London for improvement. He entered the Royal Academy as a student, and in 1781 gained the silver medal; in 1784 he drew the gold medal, which entitled him to a residence of three years at Rome, with a suitable pension. He went to Italy the succeeding year, where he studied with great assiduity, and in 1788 returned to England. He soon attained distinction, and received several commissions which decided his excellence. In 1800 he was chosen an Associate of the Royal Academy, and in 1802, a member. He executed many works of a classical description, as well as several celebrated monuments. Among the first, are a marble statue of Mercury, executed at Rome; a recumbent statue of Eve; Musidora; Zephyrus and Aurora; and Venus and Cupid. Sir Robert Peel owned his statue of the poet Thomson; and in the Exchange at Liverpool, is his statue of Brittania. These, however, are not the works by which Rossi is best known. His style is not remarkable for refinement of taste or delicacy of execution, but is distinguished for vigor and grandeur of effect. His peculiar talents are best displayed in his noble monuments in St. Paul's cathedral, upon which his reputation chiefly rests. They are the monuments of Lord Cornwallis, in the nave; Captain Faulkner, and Lord Heathfield, in the south transept; Lord Rodney, Capt. Riou and Capt. Mosse, in the north transept. The principal of these are those of Lords Cornwallis, Heathfield, and Rodney, and of Capt. Faulkner; all of which, excepting the second, are groups of three or more figures of the heroic size, in a grand style. The statue of Cornwallis stands on a pedestal forming the apex of a pyramid; below are three allegorical figures, Brittania, and impersonifications of the rivers Begareth and Ganges, denoting the British empire in the East. Lord Heathfield's is a single statue, represented in his regimentals; on the pedestal is an alto-relievo of Victory, descending from a castellated rock to crown a warrior on the sea-shore with laurel. In the monument to Capt. Faulkner, Neptune is represented seated upon a rock, in the act of catching the naked figure of a dying sailor, while Victory is about to crown him with laurel. Lord Rodney's monument is a pyramidal group, the statue of the Admiral forming the apex; below is Fame communicating with History.

Rossi was appointed sculptor to the Prince Regent, and was employed at Buckingham Palace. He was subsequently appointed sculptor to King William IV. He died in 1839.

ROSSI, ANGELO DE, an Italian sculptor, born at Genoa in 1671. He studied under Filippo Parodi, and afterwards visited Rome for improvement. He gained considerable reputation in that city, and was chosen a member of the Academy of St. Luke. Among his principal works, are a part of the sculptures of the Mausoleum of Alexander VII., in St. Peter's. His admirable bas-relief, which decorates this monument, was so highly esteemed by Louis XIV., that he ordered a model of it to be placed in the French Academy at Rome, as a study for the scholars. Among the other works of Rossi, are a number of sculptures in the chapel of S. Ignazio in the church del Gesu at Rome. He died in 1715

ROSSI, MATTEO DE, an eminent Italian architect, born at Rome in 1637. He was the son of Marc' Antonio Rossi, a reputable architect, from whom he received some instructions, and afterwards entered the school of Bernini, who esteemed him more highly than any of his other disciples. Selected to accompany that master to France he assisted him in all of his principal works and shared in his honors and rewards. He was also employed by Clement IX., at Lamporecchio and upon the church of the Scolopi, at Monterrano. His style was characterized by correctness of design, lively imagination, and excellent taste. At the death of Bernini, Rossi succeeded, according to Milizia, to the greater part of his employments, particularly to the appointment of architect of St. Peter's. He executed many works at Rome, such as the sepulchre of Clement X., in the Vatican temple; the façade of the church of Santa Galla; the custom house of Ripa Grande; and the Palazzo Monte Citorio. For the Prince Pamfili he built the cathedral of Valmontone. Rossi was greatly esteemed by Pope Innocent XII., and was presented by him with the cross of the order di Cristo. He died in 1695.

ROSSI, GIUSEPPE DE, a distinguished Italian architect and writer upon the art, was born at Rome in 1760. He was probably a descendant of Matteo de Rossi, as the *Biographie Universelle* says that his father and grand-father were both architects. While very young he was taken to Florence, where he acquired a knowledge of th art, and attained considerable distinction in the employment of Leopold I., the Grand Duke of Tuscany. In 1790 he visited Rome for improvement. The city of Siena, in 1798, having been seriously injured by an earthquake, Rossi was commissioned to superintend the principal restorations. At Florence, he restored the Palazzo Vecchio, the aqueducts, the Theatre, two towers of St. Maria Novella, a college, and a number of fountains. At Fiesole, he restored the ancient church of S. Fiesole. Rossi was appointed Professor of Architecture in the Florentine Academy, and was made a cavalier of the order of St. Giuseppe. His writings on the art are very numerous. He died in 1831.

ROSSI, GIO. ANTONIO DE, an Italian architect, the son of Lazzaro de' Rossi, was born at Rome in 1616. According to Milizia, he received the first rudiments of architecture from an obscure master; and, although defective in the elements of design, he attained considerable excellence by studying and copying the finest Roman edifices. His style of architecture was grand; he was ingenious in the distribution of his lights, in the solidity of his ornaments, and in adapting his building to its situation, to which, though it were really narrow, he succeeded in giving the appearance of much greater extension. He was much employed at Rome, and erected many works, such as the Palazzo d'Este, now called the Rinuccini, the façade of which is esteemed a masterpiece of art. He also erected the majestic Palazzo Altieri, on the Piazza Gesu, which is justly deemed one of the finest edifices in Rome. Among his other works, are the Palazzi Astalli and Muti, near the Capitol; the Hospital delle Donne, at St. Giovanni Laterano; the church of S. Pantaleo; and the elegant chapel of the Monte della Pietà. Rossi died at Rome in 1695.

ROSSMAESSLER, John Augustus, a German designer and engraver, born at Leipsic in 1752. He studied under Frederick Oeser, and engraved a great variety of vignettes and other book-plates, which are admired for the spirit and neatness of their execution. He also engraved a set of Views in the environs of Leipsic. He died in the flower of his life, much regretted, in 1783.

ROSSO, Il, called by the French Maitre Roux, was an eminent painter, born at Florence in 1496. It is not known from whom he received his first instructions, but by the efforts of his own genius, he arrived at distinction. He was intimate with Andrea del Sarto, and admired his manner. Lanzi says he was the most eminent disciple of his school, though he never studied with him as a pupil. He afterwards gained improvement by studying the works of Michael Angelo and Parmiggiano. Endowed with a ready invention, he scorned to be a servile imitator, even of Buonarotti, and at an early age he ventured to compete with the ablest of his cotemporaries in the cloister of La Nunziata, where he painted a picture of the Assumption of the Virgin, less distinguished for elegance and grace than for its great dimensions, and novel and intrepid style. After painting several other works for the churches of Florence, particularly the Marriage of the Virgin in S. Lorenzo, he went to Rome, where his talents were already known, and was commissioned to paint an altar-piece for the church of S. Maria della Pace, and the Decollation of St. John, for that of S. Salviati. These works increased his reputation; but the sacking of Rome by the Spaniards in 1527, compelled every eminent artist to quit that city, and Il Rosso sought refuge at Volterra, where he painted a picture of the Deposition from the Cross, one of his finest productions, for the Oratorio di St. Carlo. He next went to Venice, where he painted for Pietro Aretino, his celebrated picture of Mars and Venus, which was engraved by his disciple Domenico del Barbiere. Not meeting in Italy with the success he anticipated, he resolved to go to the court of Francis I. of France, who at that time was the great patron of art. He met a favorable reception from that monarch, who immediately engaged him in his service, and as he was skilled in architecture, he appointed him superintendent of the great works at the palace of Fontainbleau. He built the great gallery in that palace, and decorated it with twenty-four pictures, emblematic of the principal actions in the life of Francis I., some of which were subsequently destroyed to make way for the works of Primaticcio.

The style of Il Rosso, though singular, is characterized by grandeur, much originality, and dignity of character, animated expression in his heads, a tasteful arrangement of his draperies and ornaments, lively coloring, free and firm pencilling, with a broad and effective distribution of his light and shadow. The works of Il Rosso are very scarce, as he did not execute many in Italy, and those in France are confined to the palace of Fontainbleau. Thirteen of the latter still remain, and are fully described by the Abbé Guget, in his Memoir on the Royal Academy of France. Of these, the most remarkable is Ignorance banished by Francis I.; a picture that has been several times engraved. He was assisted in these works by several artists, among whom were Domenico del Barbiere, Bartolomeo Miniati, and Luca Penni. The death of Il Rosso happened from a singular circumstance, when he was in full possession of royal favor and public estimation. He had contracted a friendship with Francesco Pellegrini, a Florentine painter, who paid him frequent visits. His house happening to be robbed of a considerable sum, he suspected his friend, and rashly accused him of the robbery; Pellegrini was put to the rack to extort confession, but he endured the torture with heroic fortitude, constantly protesting his innocence, and was acquitted. Pellegrini then published an account of his case, and appealed for justice; whereupon Il Rosso, struck with shame and remorse, poisoned himself in 1541. See *Primaticcio.*

MR or M. ROTA, Martino, an eminent engraver, born at Sebenico, in Dalmatia. His instructor is not mentioned, and there is much contradiction about the time of his birth; the dates on his prints range from 1558 to 1586. He passed most of his artistic life at Rome and Venice. His design of the figure is remarkably correct, and his extremities are drawn with great precision. His plates are executed entirely with the graver; and though not very highly finished, they are wrought in a neat, clear style. Bartsch describes 114 prints by him, and considers it a complete list. His most celebrated print is the Last Judgment, after Michael Angelo which is held in the highest estimation, not only for its neatness of execution, but for its faithful representation of the drawing, expression, and other characteristics of the original; it is inscribed *Martinus Rota*, 1569. This admirable plate has been very closely copied by Leonard Gaultier, though the copy may be easily distinguished by the inferiority of its execution, and by the small oval portrait of Angelo at the top, the face of which is turned towards the left, but in the original towards the right. There is also another inferior copy by J. Wierix. Some of Rota's plates are from his own designs, but the majority are after the principal Italian painters. He sometimes marked his plates with his name in full, with and without the date, and sometimes with the monogram composed of the letter M, with a wheel, which is the Latin signification of Rota. The following are among his most esteemed plates:

PORTRAITS.

Maximilian II., Rom. Imper. 1575. The Emperor Rodolphus II. 1592; with the cipher. Ferdinand I. in the costume of his time. 1575. Henry IV., King of France. Albert de Lasco. Baron de Kaizsmarck.

SUBJECTS FROM HIS OWN DESIGNS.

The Resurrection; dated 1577. The same subject, differently treated. The Murder of the Innocents. The Last Judgment; dedicated to Rodolphus II. 1573. Another print of the Last Judgment. This plate was left imperfect at his death, and was finished by another hand. The Scourging of Christ. 1568. The Battle of the Lepanto; of the greatest rarity.

SUBJECTS AFTER VARIOUS MASTERS.

The Martyrdom of St. Peter; *after Titian.* Mary Magdalene penitent; *do.* Prometheus chained to the Rock; *do.* Christ appearing to St. Peter; *after Raffaelle.*

ROTAMER. See John Bottenhamer.

ROTARI, Conte Pietro, a painter of a noble family, born at Verona in 1707. He first studied design merely as an accomplishment, but he became so passionately attached to art, that he entered the school of Antonio Balestra, who, perceiving his talents, took unusual care in his instruction, and foretold his future excellence. Rotari remained with Balestra till the age of eighteen, and then went to Venice, where he spent two years in studying and copying the works of Titian and Paul Veronese. In 1727 he went to Rome, entered the school of Francesco Trevisani, and devoted four years to the study of the antique, and the works of the best masters. From Rome he travelled to Naples, to profit by the advice of Francesco Solimena, with whom he resided three years. By this course of study he acquired an elegant taste of design and composition, an uncommon correctness of drawing, and a very beautiful style of coloring, unsurpassed by any artist of his time. At first he confined himself to works for the churches, which gained him great applause, and princes soon became solicitous to possess his pictures. He visited some of the principal courts of Europe, and was every where received with the respect due to his talents. At Dresden he painted the portraits of the Electoral and Imperial family. At Vienna, his works gave so much satisfaction to the Emperor, that he ordered Rotari's portrait to be painted, and placed in the Florentine gallery. At St. Petersburg, he painted the Empress Catherine, and other members of the Imperial family; was appointed her principal painter, and received many marks of favor. He continued in the Imperial service the remainder of his life, and painted for the Empress several subjects from sacred and profane history. He died at St. Petersburg in 1762. His most admirable works in Italy are the Annunciation at Guastalla, and the Birth of the Virgin at Padua. He executed several etchings from his own designs, and after Antonio Balestra, among which are the following:

The Portrait of Filippo Baldinucci. 1726. St. Francis kneeling before a Crucifix; *from his own design*. The Education of the Virgin; *do.*

SUBJECTS AFTER ANTONIO SOLARIO.

Abraham and the Angels. David with the Head of Goliah. St. Jerome; half-length. Venus and Æneas.

ROTTENHAMER, John, a German painter, born at Munich in 1564. He received his first instruction from an obscure artist in his native city, named Donnaver, and afterwards went while young to Rome. He there distinguished himself by his small paintings on copper, delicately pencilled and agreeably colored; and at length he received a commission to paint a large picture, representing several Saints, with a glory of Angels. The ability he displayed on this occasion excited universal surprise, and inspired him with a strong desire to distinguish himself as a grand historical painter. To improve himself in coloring, he proceeded to Venice, where he made the works of Tintoretto his model, and imitated his style with great success. He painted in that city the Annunciation, in the church of S. Bartolomeo, and a picture of St. Christina in the Hospital of the Incurabili; and probably some works for individuals. The Duke of Mantua next employed him in several considerable works, the most admired of which was one representing a Dance of Nymphs. After a residence of many years in Italy, he returned to his own country with a high reputation, and established himself at Augsburg, where he received abundant employment from private individuals. His most remarkable work at Augsburg is an altarpiece in the church of the Holy Cross, representing an Assemblage of Saints, considered one of his most capital performances. He was patronized by the Emperor Rodolph II., for whom he painted an admirable picture, representing the Feast of the Gods, a grand composition of many figures, gracefully designed, with the rich coloring of the Venetian school.

Rottenhamer painted both in oil and fresco, preferring the latter for his great works. Though he had studied many years in Italy, he never entirely divested himself of the German taste; his design is formal and mannered, and frequently incorrect. He was fond of decorating his pictures with rich and splendid accessories, and of introducing the naked figure, which he piqued himself on designing with taste and coloring with delicacy. He had a lively invention, and usually made choice of agreeable subjects; his attitudes are graceful, and the airs of his heads expressive, though not sufficiently varied. His best works are his small cabinet pictures, often on copper, in which the back-grounds were frequently painted by John Breughel, and sometimes by Paul Brill; these are the most esteemed, and in his life-time commanded very high prices. Rottenhamer, notwithstanding his professional merits and abundant employment, died at Augsburg in 1606, so extremely poor from his reckless extravagance, that his funeral expenses were defrayed by some of his brother artists. His name is frequently written Rothenhamer, and the Italian writers call him Rô Rotamer, and Rothenamer.

ROUBILLIAC, Louis François, an eminent French sculptor, was born at Lyons about the commencement of the 18th century. He probably acquired a knowledge of the art in his native country; after which he visited England, and was first employed to execute several busts for Trinity College, Dublin, at the recommendation of Sir Edward Walpole, who afterwards procured him the commission for the monument of John, Duke of Argyle. In the latter work he was so successful that his claims to the honors of the profession were at once admitted, and he received a great many commissions, so as to surpass in his practice the most distinguished artists of his time Among his principal works are the monuments of Mr. Nightingale and his lady; the statue of Eloquence in the Argyle monument; the draped figure in Bishop Hough's monument; and the statue of Sir Isaac Newton. These productions evince great fertility of invention, truth of expression and finished execution; but they are deficient in the repose, unity, and simplicity, essential to lasting remembrance. In the statue of Newton, the drapery is divided into many folds, and the attitude of the figure is by no means that of a philosopher Among the other works of Roubilliac, is the monument of Sir Peter Warren, which, with the two others above mentioned, is in Westminster Abbey also that of the Duke and Duchess of Montague in Northamptonshire; the statue of Handel, the Composer, in Westminster Abbey; that of George II., in Golden Square, London; those of the Duk of Somerset, George I., and Sir Isaac Newton, at Cambridge. He also executed numerous busts. Roubilliac died in 1762.

ROULLET, Jean Louis, an eminent French engraver, born at Arles, in Provence, in 1645. He went to Paris, and first studied with Jean Lenfant, after which he entered the school of Francis Poilly the elder, and became the ablest of his scholars. On leaving that master, he went to Italy, where he resided ten years, and acquired a remarkable purity and correctness of drawing. His prints are neatly executed with the graver, faithfully representing the expression, and other characteristics of the originals. His print of the Marys with the Dead Christ, after the celebrated picture by Annibale Caracci, formerly in the Orleans Gallery, now in the possession of the Earl of Carlisle, is considered one of the most admirable productions of the art for correctness of drawing, firmness and beauty of the graver, and faithful preservation of the fine expression in the original. The following are his most esteemed prints. He died at Paris in 1698.

PORTRAITS.

Louis XIV.; a half-length. Francis de Poilly, Engraver to the King, *ad vivum.* 1680. John Baptist Lully, Musician to the King; *after Mignard.* Ascanius Philamarinus, Cardinal Archbishop of Naples.

SUBJECTS AFTER VARIOUS MASTERS.

The three Marys, with the dead Christ; *after Ann. Caracci.* The Virgin and infant Jesus; *do.* Two of the angles of the dome of the church of the Jesuits at Naples, representing St. Matthew and St. Luke; *after Lanfranco.* The two other angles. representing St. Mark and St. John, are engraved by *F. Louvemont.* The Visitation of the Virgin to St. Elizabeth; *after Mignard.* The Virgin, with the Infant Jesus in her arms, who is holding a Bunch of Grapes; *do.*, and inscribed to Madame de Maintenon.

ROUILLIERE, La, a French engraver on wood, who flourished according to Papillon, about 1700, and executed some cuts which possess considerable merit. He does not specify any of his works.

ROUSSEAU, Jacques, a French painter, born at Paris in 1630. After studying the elements of design, he went to Rome, and applied himself to the study of perspective and landscape, designing the most remarkable views in the vicinity of that metropolis. Here he formed an intimacy with Hermann Swanevelt, whose sister he married, and assisted by the advice and instruction of that able scholar of Claude Lorraine, he became an eminent and excellent painter of landscapes and perspective pieces. On his return to Paris, he was employed by Louis XIV. in decorating the chateaux of Marly and St. Germain en Laie, and was elected a member of the Royal Academy. At the revocation of the edict of Nantes, he had attained the height of his reputation; but, being a staunch Protestant, he was obliged to leave France, and sought refuge in Holland. So intolerant was the spirit of bigotry, that his name was expunged from the Academy roll, by order of the Court. He visited England, at the invitation of the Duke of Montague, who employed him in conjunction with Charles de la Fosse and Jean Baptiste Monnoyer, to decorate his mansion of Montague House, now the British Museum. He was employed in painting some landscape and perspective pieces for the palace of Hampton Court.

The landscapes of Rousseau generally represent select and classic scenery, embellished with magnificent architecture and ruins, in which he appears to have imitated the admirable productions of Niccolo Poussin, though his coloring is more warm and glowing. His figures are well designed, his perspective excellent, and his pictures have the appearance of classic elegance, nature, and truth combined. His works are rare, and when offered for sale they command high prices. He was a man of piety, integrity, and benevolence, and at his death he bequeathed the greater part of his property for the relief of his countrymen in England, who, like himself, had been exiled on account of their religion. He died at London in 1693. Dumesnil mentions eight masterly etchings by Rousseau, from his own designs, and eleven fine pictures in the cabinet of Jabach; the former are finished with the graver, in a bold style.

ROUSSEAU, Jean François, a French engraver, who flourished at Paris about 1760. He engraved a great number of vignettes and other book plates, after the French masters; also a few other subjects, among which are the Virgin and Infant, *after Vanderwerf;* and St. Jerome, *after Mola.*

ROUSSELLET, Giles, a French engraver, born at Paris in 1614. It is not known under whom he studied, but his style resembles that of Cornelius Bloemaert. His drawing is correct, and his prints possess considerable merit, though in some of them the lights are too much covered, which gives a heaviness to the general appearance. Nagler gives a list of seventy-four prints by him; the following are the most esteemed. He died in 1686.

PORTRAITS.

Charles de Valois, Duke d'Angouleme. Peter Seguier, Chancellor of France; *after le Brun.* Richard de Belleval, Chancellor of the University; *do.*

SUBJECTS AFTER VARIOUS MASTERS.

The Frontispiece to the Polyglot Bible; *after S. Bourdon.* The Holy Family; with St. Elizabeth and St. John presenting the infant Jesus with a Bird; *after Raffaelle.* The Holy Family; *do.;* called *La Belle Jardinière.* The Holy Family, with St. Elizabeth, St. John, and two Angels; *do.* G. Edelinck has engraved the same subject. St. Michael discomfiting the Evil Spirit; *do.* The Annunciation; *after Guido.* Four plates representing three of the Labors of Hercules and his Death; *do.* David playing on the Harp; *after Domenichino.* The Entombing of Christ; *after Titian.* Four plates of the Four Evangelists; *after Valentin.* The Servant of Abraham meeting Rebecca; *after N. Poussin.* Moses saved from the Nile by Pharaoh's Daughter; *do.* The Holy Family; *after S. Bourdon.* St. John the Evangelist; *do.* The Crucifixion; *after le Brun.* The dead Christ in the lap of the Virgin; *do.* The dead Christ supported by an Angel; *do.* The Holy Family; *do.* Mary Magdalene penitent; *do.* St. Bernard kneeling before the Virgin; *do.* St. Theresa in contemplation; *do.*

ROUSSELET, Marie Anne. This lady, probably a relative of the preceding, engraved a number of plates for Buffon's Natural History; also some sea-pieces and other subjects, after Backhuysen, William Vandervelde, Joseph Vernet, and Charles Vanloo. She married Peter Tardieu, the engraver. Her prints are dated from about 1760 to 1770.

ROUSSIERE, François de la, an obscure French engraver, who flourished about 1650. Little is known of him, except by a few indifferent portraits.

ROUX, Maitre. See Il Rosso.

ROVERE, Ricardo, a Flemish painter, who settled at Milan about 1565. He painted landscapes, but did not acquire much reputation, and is chiefly known as the father of several artists, sometimes called Rossetti, but more frequently termed Fiamminghini.

ROVERE, Giovanni Mauro, called il Fiamminghino, the son of the preceding, was born at Milan in 1570. According to Orlandi, he was educated in the school of the Procaccini, whose style he followed with distinction. Lanzi says he exchanged the manner of Camillo for that of Giulo Cesare P., and might be accounted a worthy disciple of the school of the Procaccini, had he not been induced by his impetuous temper to produce works of a careless execution. "He had all that fire which, when directed by judgment, is the soul of painting, but when abused, destroys the beauty of the art. It was very seldom that he was able to command it, though in a Supper of our Lord at S. Angelo, in which he used great care, he obtained corresponding success." He gained considerable reputation, however, and was much employed in decorating the churches and private houses with frescos. He also painted easel pictures of histories, perspectives, landscapes, and battle-pieces, which possess considerable merit. There are by him several spirited etchings, from his own designs, marked with the initials of his name, and F. for *fecit*, thus J. M. R. F.

ROVERE, Giovanni Battista and Marco, called also Fiamminghini, were the brothers of the preceding, whom they assisted in this numerous frescos. Lanzi says, "besides some works they left in fresco, they painted histories in oil, perspectives, battle-pieces, and landscapes, which are to be met with in almost every corner of Milan."

ROVERE, Giovanni Battista della, a Piedmontese painter, who flourished at Turin about 1626, and whose name occurs in the registers for several years after that date. Some of his works are also mentioned in the Turin Guide. There was another artist, cotemporary, of the same name, whose style was entirely different. Lanzi mentions only one picture by him, in the convent of St. Francis at Turin. The subject represented is the origin of death by the transgression of Adam and Eve, a picture of very original invention, in which, though sacred and profane ideas are confounded together, much ability is displayed. It is signed *Jo. Bapt. a Ruere, Taur. f.* 1627.

ROVERE, Girolamo, a Piedmontese painter, who flourished at Turin in the first part of the 17th century. According to Baglioni, he was a good artist in history, and received the appointment of court painter.

ROVIGO, da Urbino, a celebrated painter on porcelain, who flourished at Urbino about 1530.

ROVIRA Y BRÓCANDEL, Hippolito, a Spanish painter and engraver, born at Valencia in 1693. It is not known under whom he first studied, but according to Palomino, he attained excellence in engraving by frequenting the studio of Evaristo Munoz. At the age of thirty he went to Rome, and devoted himself with such enthusiasm to the study of the antique, that he passed whole days and nights in copying, without any other sustenance than bread and water. He acquired such facility of handling that he frequently said he had copied all the pictures at Rome which had given him pleasure. His great enthusiasm, and his fine copies in chiaro-scuro of all the works in the Farnese Palace, elicited the admiration of the professors, who highly commended them, and Sebastiano Conca publicly declared that Annibale Caracci could not have done better. After acquiring considerable reputation at Rome for several original works, he returned to Spain, and was invited to the court at Madrid; but soon after his arrival in that city, there began to appear the effects of his midnight studies, fastings, and other privations, on his physical and mental faculties, and all his bright prospects became speedily blasted. He gradually lost his reason, and died in the Hospital di Misericordia at Valencia, in 1765.

ROWLANDSON, Thomas, an English designer and etcher of caricatures, was born at London in 1756, and died there in 1827. He was educated in the Royal Academy, and afterwards studied at Paris. He had great talents, a lively imagination, and wonderful facility of execution; but he squandered a fortune, reduced himself to want, and wrought only when his necessities compelled him. His principal works are the illustrations, designed and executed by himself, for those popular volumes, "The Travels of Dr. Syntax," "The Dance of Death," "The Dance of Life," &c., published by Ackermann & Co.

ROY, Claude le, a French engraver, who flourished at Paris about 1709, and executed several portraits, among which are those of Fleury, Boileau, Bossuet, and Cardinal Dubois, *after H. Rigaud.*

ROY, Henry le, an obscure French engraver, by whom there is a set of six plates of butterflies, beetles, and other insects, inscribed *Henry le Roy, fecit, Æ.* 72. 1651.

ROY, John Baptist de, commonly called *De Roy of Brussels*, an eminent painter of landscapes and cattle, born at Brussels in 1759. Manifesting an early inclination for art, his father took him to Holland, that he might have the opportunity of studying the works of the best Dutch masters, which he is said to have done with assiduity, making the works of Paul Potter, Cuyp, and Berghem his models. He attentively studied nature, and formed a style of his own, more analagous to that of Ommeganck than to any other of the cattle-painters of the Dutch school. His subjects were generally horned cattle, standing in groups, grazing in meadows, or ruminating during meridian heat, accurately designed and skilfully grouped. His coloring is more warm and glowing than is usual with the Dutch school; he acquired a high reputation, and instructed several pupils He died in 1839, and left numerous sketches and studies, which are highly esteemed. His pictures are to be found in most of the best modern collections in Belgium.

ROYER, Jean le and Aubin Olivier, brothers-in-law, were French wood engravers, mentioned by Dumesnil, and flourished about the middle of the 16th century; they were also employed in the service of King Henry II., the former as a medalist, the latter as a printer. They executed in concert about sixty beautiful geometrical illustrations for Jean Cousin's "Book of Perspective." This work was printed and published in 1560, by Jean le

Royer, who executed many vignettes and other illustrations for the various works which he published.

ROZE, MADEMOISELLE, a Dutch paintress, born at Leyden in 1632. She gained great distinction by many exquisite imitations of oil paintings, executed with different colored threads of silk floss, or other material, so artfully disposed as to deceive the eye at a short distance. She united, softened, and blended the different colors with such consummate art as to rival nature, and to acquire the cognomen of "Sorceress." Her portraits were particularly admired; one of them in the Florentine Gallery, is considered a curiosity of art. She executed representations of landscape and animals with equal success, one of which sold for 500 florins. She died in 1682.

RUBBIANI, FELICE, a painter born at Modena in 1677. According to Tiraboschi, he studied under Domenico Bettini, and adopted his style. He accompanied Bettini in his travels, and, like him, painted fruit, flowers, birds, fish, &c., in which he excelled. Lanzi says he was a great favorite at the court of Montau, and in the cities of its vicinity. He was patronized by the Duke, and the Marchesi Riva of Mantua gave him commissions for thirty-six pictures, all of which he varied in an astonishing manner, and executed with a force and truth that rivalled nature.

RUBENS, PETER PAUL. This preeminent painter, accomplished scholar, and skilful diplomatist, was the son of John Rubens and Mary Pipelings, both descended from distinguished families in the city of Antwerp. His father was one of the principal magistrates of that city, at the time when the civil war obliged him to quit the Low Countries, about 1570, and seek refuge at Cologne. Rubens was born in that city in 1577, on the feast-day of St. Peter and St. Paul, for which reason he received, at the baptismal font, the names of those Apostles. When the city of Antwerp again came under the dominion of Spain, John Rubens returned to his native city, and renewed the administration of his office. Young Rubens, in his earliest years, discovered uncommon ability and vivacity of genius, literary taste, and a mild and docile disposition. His father gave him a very liberal education, and after the completion of his studies, placed him as a page with the Countess of Lalain, in order that his son might acquire graceful and accomplished manners, so important to success in a professional career. His father dying soon afterwards, Rubens obtained the permission of his mother to pursue the bent of the inclination he had discovered for painting, and she placed him under the instruction of Tobias Verhaecht, an eminent artist in landscape; but his genius inclining to historical painting, he soon left that master, and entered the school of Adam van Oort, whose works were then in high repute. The vulgarity and depravity of this master disgusted Rubens, and he soon left his school for that of Otho Venius, or van Veen, then one of the most eminent painters of the Flemish school, distinguished alike for pictorial talents, amiable and polished manners, and extensive literary attainments. These qualities, so congenial to the feelings of Rubens, rendered his engagement with Venius exceedingly pleasant; he conceived for his instructor profound respect and veneration, and ever maintained towards him the strongest attachment. It was from this master that he acquired that taste for allegory for which he was remarkable through life, though it certainly did not constitute his greatest merit. When he had reached his twenty-third year, Venius frankly assured him that his instructions could be of no further service to him, and that nothing more remained for his improvement but a journey to Italy, which he recommended as the surest means of ripening his extraordinary talents to the greatest perfection. Rubens had already contemplated such a project, and in following the advice of his master, he consulted also his own inclinations. There is a little discrepancy among authors about this part of Rubens' life, but Sandrart, who was intimately acquainted with him and traveled through Holland in his company. says that "the Archduke Albert, Governor of the Netherlands, who had conceived a high opinion of his talents, employed him to paint several fine pictures for his palace, and forwarded his designs by recommending him in the most honorable manner to the Duke of Mantua, that at his court he might have constant access to his admirable collection of paintings and antique statues, and thus have an opportunity of improving himself by studying as well as copying the former, and designing after the latter." At all events, he set out for Italy in 1600, and after spending a short time at Venice in examining the works of the Venetian masters, he proceeded to Mantua, and was received with the most marked distinction by the Duke, who took him into his service, and appointed him one of the gentlemen of his chamber, an honor which was the more acceptable to Rubens, as it gave him greater facilities for studying the great works of Giulio Romano, in the Palazzo del Te, which were the objects of his particular admiration. Giulio's masterly illustrations of the sublime poetry of Homer excited his emulation to the highest degree, and it is related that while he was engaged in painting the history of Turnus and Æneas, in order to warm his imagination with poetic rapture, he repeated with energy the lines of Virgil commencing

Ille otiam patriis agmen ciet, &c.

The Duke, overhearing his recitations, entered the apartment, and was surprised to find the young artist's mind richly stored with classic literature. After having spent two years in the service of the Duke of Mantua, he requested and received permission to revisit Venice, for the purpose of studying the works of Titian and Paul Veronese, from which he acquired that splendid manner of coloring so much admired in his works. On his return to Mantua, he painted three magnificent pictures for the church of the Jesuits, which evince the progress he made at Venice, and are considered among his finest works. The Duke commissioned Rubens to visit Rome, to execute copies of several celebrated works, which he performed in such admirable style, that the painter esteemed them little inferior to the originals. At the same time Rubens gladly availed himself of the opportunity of studying all the best works of art in that metropolis. He was also employed by the Archduke Albert to paint three pictures for the church of S Croce in Gerusalemme, representing the Finding of the Cross by St. Helena, Christ bearing his Cross, and the Crucifixion. The two last are considered among his most admirable productions.

In 1605, the Duke of Mantua, having occasion to send an envoy to the court of Spain, employed Rubens as a person eminently fitted for the delicate mission. He successfully accomplished the negotiations confided to him, painted the portrait of Philip III., and received from that monarch the most flattering marks of distinction. Soon after his return from this embassy, he again proceeded to Rome, and painted three admirable pictures for the tribune in the church of S. Maria in Vallicella, in which he appears to have adopted the style of Veronese. He next visited Genoa, where his distinguished reputation excited public curiosity, and he was employed to execute several works, which increased his celebrity; particularly two pictures in the church of the Jesuits, representing the Circumcision, and St. Ignatius working a Miracle, which were highly applauded. Rubens, having now been absent eight years, was suddenly recalled to Antwerp in 1608, by the severe illness of his mother, who died before his arrival. The loss of his dearly beloved parent was a severe affliction to him. He then concluded to return to Italy, but the Archduke Albert and the Infanta Isabella induced him to abandon his intention. He settled at Antwerp, where he married, built a magnificent house with a saloon in the form of a rotunda, which he embellished with antique statues, busts, vases, and pictures by the most celebrated painters. Amidst these select productions of art, he passed about twelve years in the tranquil exercise of his great abilities, producing an astonishing number of admirable pictures for the churches and public edifices of the Low Countries. He also instructed numerous pupils. In order to continue his mental improvement, to enjoy the sweets of friendly intercourse, and to economize his precious time, he regulated his affairs with a precision which nothing was permitted to derange. He received company at stated times, and it is said he never painted without having some one read to him from a work of history or poetry. He possessed an extraordinary memory, and understood the ancient and several modern languages, writing and speaking them with fluency. His familiar acquaintance with ancient and modern literature, had enriched his mind with inexhaustible resources. His great popularity naturally excited envy and created enemies; although generous and affable to all, and a liberal encourager of art, he found himself assailed by those who were most indebted to him for assistance. With the most audacious effrontery, they insinuated that he owed the best part of his reputation in the great variety of his works, for which he was celebrated, to the talents of two of his disciples, Snyders and Wildens, whom he employed occasionally in forwarding the animals and landscapes in his pictures. The principal of these vilifiers were Abraham Janssens, Cornelius Schut, and Theodore Rombouts; the first had the hardihood to challenge him to paint a picture in competition with him. Rubens treated these acts with a dignity and philanthropy that shows his exalted mind, and the goodness of his heart; he relieved the necessities of his accusers, and exposed his immortal production of the Descent from the Cross.

In 1650, Mary of Medicis commissioned Rubens to decorate the Gallery of the Luxembourg with a series of emblematical paintings, in twenty-four compartments, illustrative of the principal events of her life. The series was painted at Antwerp, except two pictures, which he finished at Paris in 1623, when he arranged the whole in the gallery. These great works, executed in less than three years, are alone sufficient to attest the abundant fertility of his genius, and the wonderful facility of his hand. It was at this time that he became acquainted with the Duke of Buckingham, as that nobleman was passing through France on his way to Madrid, who afterwards gave him £10,000 for his collection of antiques and paintings. On his return to Antwerp, his time was occupied in executing numerous commissions till 1628, when the Infanta Isabella dispatched him on a delicate political mission to the court of Spain, relative to the critical state of the government of the Low Countries, and for instructions preparatory to a negotiation for peace between Spain and England. On his arrival at the Spanish capital, he was received in the most gracious manner by Philip IV. acquitted himself in his diplomatic mission to the entire satisfaction of the Infanta and of the King, and completely captivated the monarch and his minister, the Duke de Olivares, by his magnificent productions. The Duke had just founded the convent of the Carmelites at Loeches, near Madrid, for which the king, as a mark of favor to his minister, commissioned Rubens to paint four pictures of large dimensions, which are not surpassed by any of his other works for admirable composition, grandeur of design, and richness of coloring. The first is an allegorical subject of the triumph of the New Law, which he personified in the most beautiful and graceful manner. The figure of Religion is seated on a superb triumphal car, drawn by four Angels, with others bearing the Cross, with characteristic symbols; four figures expressive of the various characters of Infidelity or Ignorance, over which religion is supposed to triumph, follow the car like slaves or captives, bound with chains. The group is crowded with beautiful cherubim hovering in the air, with chaplets in their hands, disposed with singular art, the whole producing the most charming effect. The companion picture represents the Interview between Abraham and Melchisedech. In the drapery of the priests and the armor of the soldiers, Rubens seems to have exhausted every resource that his rich fund of coloring could supply. The other two compositions, of equal size and not inferior in excellence, are distinguished for indescribable majesty and expression; they represent the four Doctors of the Church, and the four Evangelists, with their distinctive emblems. He also painted eight grand pictures for the royal palace at Madrid, which are regarded as matchless specimens of his coloring. They represent the Rape of the Sabines; the Battle between the Romans and the Sabines; Diana and her Nymphs bathing; Perseus and Andromeda; the Rape of Helen; the Contest between Juno, Minerva, and Venus; the Judgment of Paris; and the Triumph of Bacchus. He likewise painted an equestrian portrait of the king, and a picture of the Martyrdom of St. Andrew. For these great works he was munificently rewarded, received the honor of knighthood, and was presented with the golden key, as Gentleman of the Royal bed-chamber.

In 1627 he returned to Flanders, and was immediately dispatched to England on a secret mission by the Infanta, to ascertain the disposition of the government on the subject of peace. The king

Charles I., an ardent lover of the fine arts, received the illustrious painter with every mark of distinction, and immediately employed him in painting the ceiling of the Banqueting House at Whitehall, where he represented the Apotheosis of his father, James I., for which he received £3000. Here Rubens showed himself no less skilful as a diplomatist than as a painter. In one of the frequent visits with which the king honored him during the execution of the work, he alluded with infinite delicacy and address to the subject of a peace with Spain, and finding the monarch not averse to such a measure, he immediately produced his credentials. Charles at once appointed some members of his council to negotiate with him, and a pacification was soon effected. The king was so highly pleased with the productions of his pencil, and particularly with his conduct in this diplomatic emergency, that he gave him a munificent reward, and conferred upon him the honor of knighthood, Feb. 21, 1630. On this occasion, the king presented Rubens with his own sword, enriched with diamonds, his hatband of jewels, valued at 10,000 crowns, and a gold chain, which Rubens wore ever afterwards. He also painted the portrait of Charles I. in the character of St. George, and that of his queen, Henrietta Maria, as Cleodelinde, with a view of Richmond and the Thames in the distance. Having thus happily accomplished the object of his mission, he returned to Antwerp, and was received with all the honors and distinction due to his services and exalted merit. He still continued to exercise his pencil with undiminished industry and reputation till 1635, when he experienced some aggravated attacks of the gout, to which he had been subject, succeeded by an infirmity and trembling of the hand, which obliged him to decline executing all works of large dimensions. Though he had now reached his fifty-eighth year, and was loaded with deserved honors and wealth, he nevertheless continued to instruct his pupils, to correspond with his cherished friends, and to paint easel pictures when his torturing malady would permit, till his death, in 1640, aged 63 years. He was buried with extraordinary pomp and solemnity in the church of St. James, under the altar of his private chapel, which he had decorated with one of his finest pictures. A superb monument was erected to his memory.

There is an astonishing contrariety of opinion among writers, as to the real merits of this illustrious painter. While his countrymen generally account him the greatest of modern painters, the Italians refuse him the merit of an able designer. In order to arrive at a just conclusion, it is necessary to take many things into consideration, such as his genius, manner, habits; the genuineness of his works, and the changes that have taken place in them from the effects of time, together with frequent cleaning, restoring, and retouching of parts; his numerous scholars and their assistance in his works. Genius is always bold and daring, and while it commands attention and admiration, is sure to provoke criticism. The styles of the three greatest modern painters, Michael Angelo, Raffaelle, and Rubens, were entirely different, and it is very certain that, had they adopted any other, they never would have reached the excellence and renown which they achieved.

Rubens was undoubtedly one of the most original painters that ever lived, and his subjects were unlimited. He painted history, portraits, landscapes, animals, fruit and flowers, with such excellence, that it is difficult to decide in which he most excelled. He possessed inexhaustible fertility of invention, never copying himself or any other master, in so many and various productions, though accused of it in his famous Descent from the Cross, in which he is said to have exactly copied a print marked *Peter Passen invenit; Hieronymus Wierix sculpsit;* but this wants authentication. If he adopted the design of this picture, he certainly did it to show a skill in coloring that no one but a great painter would dare to attempt. His extensive knowledge of classical and polite literature, enabled him to excel in emblematical and allegorical compositions, of which he was very fond. His genius was adapted to the grandest compositions, and his powers appear to have expanded in proportion to the scale on which they were called to act. He did not, like Raffaelle, possess that mild inspiration of sentiment which manifests itself in dignified and noble, or graceful and beautiful forms, but he was animated with a poetic fire that displays itself in surprising and astonishing effects. The powers of his imagination were so abundant, that his most extensive compositions seem to have been produced without effort, and creation appears an operation of his will. This is evident from his admirable productions in the Luxembourg, and many other works too well known to need description. He is generally allowed to have carried the art of coloring to its highest excellence; he thoroughly understood the principles of chiaro-scuro, and managed it with such art as to give the utmost roundness, relief, and harmony to each particular figure, and the greatest effect to the whole composition; his groups are disposed with such skill as to conduct the eye of the spectator at once to the principal object. His draperies are simple, broad, and grand; his carnations have the appearance of nature, and the warmth of life. His greatest excellence appears in his grand compositions, for, as these were to be seen at a distance, he laid on a proper body of color with uncommon freedom, and fixed all his tints in their proper places, never impairing their lustre, by breaking them, but touching them only in such a manner as to give them lasting force, beauty and harmony. He is less chaste in his coloring than Titian, but is more brilliant, and excites our admiration by the splendor of his tints. Rubens, beyond comparison, was the most rapid of the great masters, and so many pictures bear his name, that it is impossible not to partially accord credit to what was asserted in his own day, that the greater portion of many of them were executed by his pupils. Rubens has been accused as defective in design, and it is generally allowed that he was frequently incorrect in his drawing, and that his figures, particularly those of females and children, are devoid of elegance, grace and beauty. There are apologies, however, to palliate, if not to excuse, these defects. He did not attempt the ideal, nor imitate the antique, but adopted the models of his own country from choice, not ignorant, for he could not have been deficient in knowledge of the antique and Roman schools. His beau-ideal of Venus and Cupid seems to have been a dumpy fat woman, with an equally fat child, as seen in his Judgment of Paris. It cannot be denied that he preferred brilliancy of effect to beauty of form, and frequently sacrificed correctness of design to the magic of coloring, probably from his impetuosity of conception and rapidity of execution. His drawing is generally grand and facile, his outline free and flowing, and he had a competent knowledge of anatomy. Some of his naked figures are as excellent for their design and drawing as for their inimitable coloring, as seen in his admirable picture of the Fallen Angels in the Dusseldorf gallery, of which Sir Joshua Reynolds says, "If we consider the fruitfulness of invention which is discovered in this work, or the skill which is shown in composing such an infinite number of figures, or the art of the distribution of light and shadow, the freedom of hand, the facility with which it is performed, and what is most extraordinary, the correctness and admirable taste of drawing of figures foreshortened in attitudes the most difficult to execute, we must pronounce this picture to be one of the greatest efforts of genius that the art has produced." The same author thus sums up his admirable criticism on the works of Rubens, in his Journal of a Journey to Flanders and Holland: "The works of Rubens have that peculiar property always attendant on genius, to attract attention, and enforce admiration in spite of all their faults. It is owing to this fascinating power that the performances of those painters with which he is surrounded, though they have perhaps fewer defects, yet appear spiritless, tame and insipid, such as the altar-pieces of Crayer, Schut, Seghers, Huysum, Tyssens, Van Balen, and the rest. They are done by men whose hands, and indeed all their faculties, appear to have been cramped and confined; and it is evident that every thing they did was the effect of great labor and pains. The productions of Rubens, on the contrary, seem to flow with a freedom and prodigality, as if they cost him nothing; and to the general animation of the composition there is always a correspondent spirit in the execution of the work. The striking brilliancy of his colors, and their lively opposition to each other, the flowing liberty and freedom of his outline, the animated pencil, with which every object is touched, all contribute to awaken and keep alive the attention of the spectator; awaken in him, in some measure, correspondent sensations, and make him feel a degree of that enthusiasm with which the painter was carried away. To this we may add the complete uniformity of all the parts of the work, so that the whole seems to be conducted, and grow out of one mind: every thing is of a piece, and fits its place. Even his taste of drawing and of form appears to correspond better with his coloring and composition, than if he had adopted any other manner, though that manner, simply considered, might be better: it is here as in personal attractions; there is frequently found a certain agreement and correspondence in the whole together, which is often more captivating than mere regular beauty.

"Rubens appears to have had that confidence in himself, which it is necessary for every artist to assume, when he has finished his studies, and may venture in some measure to throw aside the fetters of authority; to consider the rules as subject to his control, and not himself subject to the rules; to risk and to dare extraordinary attempts without a guide, abandoning himself to his own sensations, and depending upon them. To this confidence must be imputed that originality of manner by which he may be truly said to have extended the limits of the art. After Rubens had made up his manner, he never looked out of himself for assistance: there is consequently very little in his works, that appears to be taken from other masters. If he has borrowed any thing, he has had the address to change and adapt it so well to the rest of his work, that the theft is not discoverable." Reynolds also says he possessed in an eminent degree the true art of imitation. He saw the objects of nature with a painter's eye, and caught at once the predominant features by which every object is known and distinguished, and as soon as seen, executed them with astonishing facility. "This power," says he, "which Rubens possessed in the highest degree, enabled him to represent whatever he undertook, better than any other painter. His animals, particularly lions and horses, are so admirable, that it may be said they were never properly represented but by him. His portraits rank with the painters who have made that branch of the art the sole business of their lives; and of these he left a great variety of specimens. The same may be said of his landscapes; and though Claude Lorraine finished more minutely, as became a professor in any particular branch, yet there is such an airiness and facility in the landscapes of Rubens, that a painter would as soon wish to be the author of them as those of Claude or any other artist whatever.

"The pictures of Rubens have this effect on the spectator, that he feels himself in no wise disposed to pick out and dwell on his defects. The criticisms which are made on him are indeed often unreasonable. His style ought no more to be blamed for not having the sublimity of Michael Angelo, than Ovid should be censured because he is not like Virgil. However, it must be acknowledged that he wanted many excellencies which would have perfectly united with his style. Among these we may reckon beauty in his female forms; sometimes indeed they make approaches to it; they are healthy and comely women, but seldom if ever possess any degree of excellence. The same may be said of his young men and children; his old men have that sort of dignity which a bushy beard will confer, but he never possessed a poetical conception of character. In his representation of the highest characters in the christian or the fabulous world, instead of something above humanity, which might fill the idea which is conceived of such beings, the spectator finds little more than mere mortals, such as he meets with every day.

"The incorrectness of Rubens in regard to his outline, oftener proceeds from haste and carelessness, than from inability: there are in his great works, to which he seems to have paid more particular attention, naked figures as eminent for their drawing as for their coloring. He appears to have entertained a great abhorrence of the meagre, dry manner of his predecessors, the old German and Flemish painters, to avoid which, he kept his outline large and flowing; this carried to extreme, produced that heaviness which is so frequently found in his figures. Another defect of this great painter is his inattention to the foldings of his drapery, especially that of women; it is scarcely ever cast with any choice or skill." Algarotti says, "Rubens was more moderate in his movements than Tintoretto, more soft in his chiaro-scuro than Caravaggio; but not so rich in his composition, nor so light in his touches as Veronese. His carna tions are always less true than those of Titian, and less delicate than those of Vandyck; yet he contrived to give his colors the utmost transparency, and no less harmony, notwithstanding their extraordinary depth."

The number of works executed by Rubens is truly astonishing; Smith in his Catalogue raisonné, vols. II. and IX., describes about 1800 considered genuine by him, in the different public and private collections of Europe. There can be no doubt that a great number of these were executed by his numerous scholars and assistants, under his direction, from his designs, and then finished by himself. It is well known that he employed his pupils in forwarding many of his pictures, and that Wildens, van Uden, and Mompers, in particular, assisted him in his landscapes, and Snyders, in his animals. His principal scholars were Anthony Vandyck, Justus van Egmont, Theodore van Thulden, Abrahám Diepenbeck, Jacob Jordaens, Peter van Mol, Cornelius Schut, John van Hoeck, Simon de Vos, Peter Soutman, Deodato Delmont, Erasmus Quellinus, Francis Wouters, Francis Snyders, John Wildens, Lucas van Uden, and Jodocus Mompers. Several other distinguished Flemish painters of the period, who were not his pupils, imitated his style; the most eminent of whom were Gerard Seghers, Gaspar de Crayer, and Martin Pepin. Besides the genuine paintings of Rubens, there are a multitude of doubtful authenticity, attributed to him, most of which were executed by his pupils and imitators. Many such, fine pictures, are in the United States. There are upwards of 1200 engravings after works attributed to Rubens; some of which, however, are of doubtful authenticity. Those executed by the Bolswerts, Paul Pontius, and other cotemporary engravers who worked under Rubens' supervision, are undoubtedly genuine. There are a great number of his works in England in the public galleries and the collections of the nobility; there are nine in the National gallery, fourteen in the Dulwich gallery, and others at Windsor, Hampton Court, and Whitehall. The enormous value set upon his works at the present time, may be seen by referring to the catalogue of the National gallery; thus, the Brazen Serpent cost £1260; a Landscape, called Rubens' Chateau, £1500; Peace and War, £3000; the Rape of the Sabines, £3000; and the Judgment of Paris, 4000 guineas. Many of the works of Rubens, like those of other great masters, have suffered greatly from the effects of time, but more from improper cleaning and unskilful restoration, especially in retouching injured parts, by which the original harmony of coloring has been destroyed. Thus his pictures in the Banqueting-house at Whitehall, have been three times cleaned, repaired and painted over, so that little of the original splendor of coloring remains.

Rubens occasionally amused himself with the point, and executed a few etchings in a bold and masterly style, which show his profound knowledge of chiaro-scuro. It is well known that the masterly effects of light and shade, and characteristic expression, in the prints of Bolswert, were owing to the instructions and assistance he received from Rubens.—(See S. A. Bolswert.) The following etchings are by him:

St. Francis receiving the Stigmata. Mary Magdalen Penitent. St. Catherine; a design for a ceiling. An old Woman holding a lighted Candle, with a Boy lighting another by it. When Rubens had etched the plate, a few impressions only were taken off, which are now become extremely scarce. There is a copy of this print by *Cornelius Visscher*. The Portrait of an English Minister; signed *P. P. Rubens, fecit.*

RUBENSTEIN, or RIEBENSTEIN, a reputable German painter of still-life, dead game, and portraits. He went to England, and resided several years at London, where he died about 1763.

RUBIALES, Pedro de, a Spanish painter, born in the province of Estremadura. He went to Italy and studied under Francesco Salviati, whom he assisted in many of his works. He afterwards became the assistant of Giorgio Vasari. He resided chiefly at Rome and Florence, and executed some works by himself for the churches, the best of which is the Conversion of St. Paul in S. Spirito in Sassia at Rome. There are notices of him from 1545 to 1560. He is little known in his own country, and probably passed most of his life in Italy.

RUBINI, a Piedmontese painter who, according to Federici, flourished at Trevigi about 1650. He executed some works for the church of S. Vito in that city, which are commended by that author.

RUBIRA, Don Andres de, a Spanish painter, born at Escacena del Campo. He studied under Domingo Martinez at Seville, whom he assisted in several works for the cathedral of that city. When Francisco Vieira, painter to the King of Portugal, was passing through Seville on his way from Rome to Lisbon, he invited Rubira to accompany him home, where he profited greatly by the instructions of that excellent master. On his return to Seville, he was employed in executing several important works for the churches and convents. He also painted conversation pieces, drolls, and interiors, in a style of excellence. There is a picture of a blind man by him, singing and playing on the guitar, painted with such truth and power, that, at first view, it might be attributed to Velasquez. He died at Seville in 1760.

RUBIRA, José de, the son of the preceding, was born at Seville in 1747. He is said to have had no other instruction than what he received from his father, though he was only thirteen at his death. By diligently studying the works of Murillo, he became a good imitator of his manner, and an excellent copyist. Among others, he copied a magnificent picture of the Holy Family by Murillo, for Don Francisco de Bruno, so admirably executed, that many connoisseurs have taken it for the original. He died in 1787.

RUCHOLLE, Pierre, a French engraver, who flourished about 1690. He engraved a few indifferent portraits, among which are Charles Emanuel, Duke of Savoy, *after Vandyck*, and Louis XIV.. *after Rigaud.*

RUEDA, Gabriel de, a Spanish painter whose history is little known. He is said to have executed some excellent works for the churches at Granada and Toledo. He was appointed painter to the Holy church at Toledo in 1633, and died in 1641.

RUFO, José Martin, a Spanish historical and portrait painter, was born at Madrid and educated in the academy of S. Ferdinando, from which institution he drew several prizes by the superiority of his productions. He executed many works for the public edifices, particularly a series of histories of the life of S. Juan de la Cruz in the cloister of the Carmelitas Descalzos. His portrait of Ferdinand VI., formerly in the monastery del Paular, is in the Royal collection at Madrid. He flourished in the second half of the 18th century.

RUGENDAS, George Philip, a German painter and engraver, born at Augsburg in 1666. He studied under Isaac Fischer, a painter of history, with whom he continued five years; but his genius leading him rather to painting battles and skirmishes of cavalry, he formed his style by studying the works of Borgognone, and the prints of Antonio Tempesta. He had already acquired considerable reputation in his native city, when he went to Italy in 1692. He stopped some time at Venice, where he received some instruction and advice from Gio. Battista Molinari. From Venice he proceeded to Rome, where his talents soon became known, and he met with such flattering encouragement that he thought of establishing himself in that city, when he was suddenly recalled to Augsburg in 1695, by the death of his father. He then settled in his native city, where he passed the rest of his life, and executed a great many works, which are highly esteemed, and are found in the choicest collections of Europe.

Rugendas is reckoned among the good battle painters. He possessed an abundant imagination, he composed his subjects with taste, his design is correct, his perspective excellent, his coloring good, his pencilling free and spirited, and his execution exceedingly rapid. He had three manners. In the first he was less attentive to design than to the charm of coloring; in the second, his drawing is more correct, and his touch more free and animated, but his coloring is less attractive; in his last and best manner, he successfully combined harmonious coloring with accuracy of design and uncommon freedom of pencilling. During the bombardment of Augsburg by the French and Bavarians in 1703, when the citizens were overwhelmed with alarm, confusion and despair, Rugendas sallied forth with his pencils and sketch-book, to contemplate with a painter's eye, the attacks of the besiegers, exposed himself to the most imminent danger, and amidst the carnage and destruction, designed the military operations of the French and Bavarian armies in a very spirited and accurate manner, which he afterwards engraved and published. He could work with equal facility with both hands, on account of a disease of his right hand, which for some years compelled him to exercise his left. It is said that the most illustrious personages of Germany employed his pencil; if so, they illy rewarded him, for it is well known that he practised engraving to support his family; he devoted a considerable portion of his time to engraving; some say the whole of it, from 1719 to 1735, when he returned to painting. He executed a great number of etchings and mezzotinto plates after his own designs. He died at Augsburg in 1742. He was the ancestor of several painters and engravers of this name, some of whom are living at the present time. The following are among his most esteemed prints:

ETCHINGS.

A set of six Plates; entitled, *Capricci di Giorgio Filippo Rugendas.* 1698. Eight Plates; entitled *Diversi Pensieri fatto per Giorgio Filippo Rugendas, Pittore.* 1699. A set of eight plates, representing horsemen. Six Plates of Cavalry marching. The military operations of the French and Bavarian armies at the siege of Augsburg in six plates. 1704.

MEZZOTINTO.

Four plates of Skirmishes between the Prussian and Hungarian Hussars. Four plates of Huntings of the Lion, Tiger, &c.

RUGENDAS, Christian, was the son of the preceding, born at Augsburg in 1708, and died there in 1781. He engraved in mezzotinto about sixty plates after the designs of his father, representing marches, halts, battles, &c. He also executed about thirty etchings from his own designs, which are highly esteemed.

RUGGIERI, da Bruggia. See Roger of Bruges.

RUGGIERI, Antonio, a Florentine painter, who flourished in the first part of the 17th century. According to Baldinucci, he studied under Ottavio Vannini, was a good painter of cabinet pictures of historical subjects, and wrought much for the collections. There is a picture of St. Andrew by him in the church of S. Gaetano at Florence.

RUGGIERI, Antonio Maria, a Milanese painter, who flourished in the first part of the 18th century. He formed an intimate friendship with Francesco Bianchi, in conjunction with whom he executed many works in fresco for the churches and public edifices of Milan and other cities. Lanzi considers them mediocre artists, more intent on gain than applause. Ruggieri also painted in oil.

RUGGIERI, Giovanni Battista, called also Gio. Battista del Gessi, a Bolognese painter, who first studied under Domenichino, and afterwards became the disciple of Francesco Gessi, the pupil of Guido, whose style he adopted. He accompanied that master to Naples, and assisted him in some of his principal works in that city and at Bologna. He afterwards visited Rome, where he was patronized by the Marchese Giustiniani, and executed some works for the churches and the palaces of the nobility. His principal works at Bologna, are the Assumption of the Virgin, the Adoration of the Magi, and the Descent of the Holy Ghost, in the church of S. Barbaziano, which have sometimes been mistaken for the works of Guido. His most esteemed works at Rome are, a picture of the Nativity in S. Maria della Minerva, one of his finest works, and a fresco, representing Mary Magdalen and St. Catherine, with several other saints, in S. Caterina a Monte Magnanapoli. There is much discrepancy as to the time of his birth and death. According to Baglioni, he died aged thirty-two, in the pontificate of Urban VIII. Lanzi asserts the same, and says he was an artist of rare merit, particularly esteemed by Cortona, in whose arms he breathed his last. Zani says he was born in 1606, and died in 1640. Others say he was born in 1595, and died at Rome in 1659. Dominici says he was enticed on board a galley at Naples, kidnapped, and never heard of afterwards. See *Lorenzo Menini.*

RUGGIERI, Ercole, called also Ercolino del Gessi, or Ercolino da Bologna, was the brother of the preceding, and a scholar of Francesco Gessi, whose style he followed, according to Malvasia, with so much success, that, at first sight, his works are often mistaken for those of his master. Such are his pictures of the Death of St. Joseph, in the church of S. Cristina di Pietralata, and the Virgin and Infant, with several saints, at the Servi, at Bologna. The time of his birth or death is not known, but he is supposed to have died young.

RUGGIERI, Girolamo, a painter born at Vicenza in 1662. According to Pozzo, he studied with Cornelius Dusman, a Flemish painter, who had settled at Vicenza. Lanzi says Ruggieri established himself at Verona, where he painted history, landscapes and battle-pieces, in the Flemish style. He died there about 1717.

RF or GR or RF. RUGGIERI, Guido, called also Ruggiero Ruggieri, a Bolognese painter and engraver, who flourished about 1550. He studied under Francesco Raibolini, called Il Francia, and accompanied Primaticcio to France, where he assisted him in his great works at Fontainbleau. He is, however, better known as an engraver, and executed some plates after the designs of Primaticcio, in a style somewhat resembling that of Marco da Ravenna, from whom it is not improbable that he learned the art. His plates after Primaticcio are usually marked with a monogram composed of a G and an R, joined together, with F for fecit. There are other etchings attributed to him, bearing various marks, and partaking of the manner of Giulio Bonasone, Giorgio Ghisi, and Caraglio; but there is great uncertainty respecting them. Bartsch classes twenty-two under the monogram F. G. (No. 86, tom. ix.,) and mentions others with different marks, all of which Nagler attributes to Guido Ruggieri.

RUHL, John Christian, a German sculptor, born in Hesse Cassel in 1764. He studied sculpture under Nahl, and in 1787 drew the grand prize of the Academy at Cassel, which entitled him to travel at the expense of the state. He spent one year in Paris, studying in the atelier of Pajou, and then visited Rome, where he was rejoined by his instructor, Nahl. He copied many sculptures in that city, and executed a marble statue of Achilles dying, which is highly praised by Goethe. On returning to Cassel, in 1790, he was chosen an Academician, and was commissioned to execute a number of works. Among them were the monument to the Hessians who fell at the Siege of Frankfort, in 1792; and the Tomb of Baron de Hayn. At the establishment of the ephemeral kingdom of Westphalia, Ruhl was appointed sculptor to the court, and made many busts of King Jerome. After a career of half a century, he died, in 1842.

RUIDIMAN, or REUTTIMAN, or REUTLIMANN, John Conrad, a German goldsmith and engraver, who flourished at Augsburg in the first part of the 17th century, and designed and engraved some plates of ornaments for goldsmiths.

C ✻ RUINA, Gasparo, an Italian wood engraver, who flourished towards the end of the 16th century. There are a variety of historical, mythological, and allegorical prints attributed to him, executed in a peculiar manner; the shadows are produced by numerous fine hatchings, which make them in many places appear too black, and out of harmony. His prints are sometimes marked with the above monogram, and at others variously signed *Gasparo f.*, ; *Gaspar or Gasparo Ruina, f.*, or *fecit.* Zani and Brulliot say he was the engraver who marked his prints with *three darts crossed*, sometimes accompanied by the letter G.

RUISCH, or RUYSCH, Rachel, a celebrated Dutch paintress of fruit and flowers, born at Amsterdam in 1664. She was the daughter of Frederick Ruisch, the celebrated professor of anatomy. She early showed an extraordinary taste for depicting flowers, which induced her father to procure for her the instruction of William van Aelst, an eminent flower painter. She not only surpassed her instructor, but some have not hesitated to equal, and even prefer, her works to those of John Van Huysum. She grouped her flowers in the most tasteful and picturesque manner, and depicted them with a force and brilliancy that rivalled nature; Descamps says that, "in her pictures of flowers and fruit, she surpassed nature herself." The extraordinary talents of this lady recommended her to the patronage of the Elector of Palatine—a great admirer of her pictures-for whom she executed a considerable portion of her finest works, and received a munificent reward. She was admitted a member of the academy at the Hague in 1701. Though she is said to have exercised her talents to an advanced age, her works are exceedingly rare, so great was the labor she bestowed upon them. She spent seven years in painting two pictures, a fruit and a flower piece, which she presented to one of her daughters, as her marriage portion. She married Jurian Pool, an eminent portrait painter, by whom she had ten children; she is frequently called by his name, though she always signed her pictures with her maiden name. Smith, in his Catalogue raisonné, vols. vi. and ix., gives a description of only about thirty pieces by her—a proof of their great rarity. They now command very high prices when offered for sale. She died at Amsterdam in 1750, aged 86 years.

RUIZ DE LA IGLESIA, Francisco Ignacio, a Spanish painter, born at Madrid, about 1640. He first studied with Francisco Camillo, and afterwards perfected himself in coloring, in the school of Juan Carreño. He acquired distinction, was appointed painter to Philip V., in 1689, and painted his portrait several times. He was employed in conjunction with Antonio Palomino in decorating several of the churches and public edifices at Madrid, with paintings both in oil and fresco. He died in 1704.

RUIZ GIXON, Juan Carlos, a Spanish painter, who flourished at Seville about 1677. He is supposed to have studied under the younger Herrera, whose style he adopted. There is a grand picture by him of the Immaculate Conception, in the Cathedral at Seville, of which the grand taste, fine coloring, and bold execution, would make it pass for a work by Herrera, were it not signed with the name of Ruiz, as was his custom in all his productions.

RUIZ GONZALES, Don Pedro, a Spanish painter, born at Madrid in 1633. He did not commence the study of painting until the age of thirty, when he placed himself under the instruction of Juan Antonio Escalante. On the death of that master he became the disciple of Juan Carreno, under whose able instruction he made rapid progress, acquired considerable distinction, and was much employed by the nobility and the churches.

There are many fine works by him in the churches and Convents at Madrid. He particularly excelled in cabinet pictures, which he colored with all the richness of the Venetian masters. His works are found in the best collections in Spain, and are highly esteemed. Though he commenced painting so late in life. he acquired great facility of hand, executed many works, and acquired a fortune. He died at Madrid in 1709.

RUIZ, Ferdinando, a Spanish architect of the 16th century. He gained considerable distinction at Seville, and erected there a church and several other edifices, but was most distinguished for his restoration of the tower of Giralda. This famous structure is said to have been commenced in the 11th century by Geber, to whom is attributed the invention of Algebra, and the design of two similar towers at Rabata and Morocco. It was originally two hundred and fifty feet high, but was increased by Ruiz to the height of three hundred and fifty feet. In the centre is another tower, higher than the exterior one, and twenty-three feet thick; the interval between the towers is twenty-three feet, and serves for the ascent, by which two horsemen can mount abreast. The edifice is adorned with one hundred and forty columns, and the entablature is crowned by four large globes of gilt bronze, so resplendent that in the sunshine they were visible for twenty-four miles. In the earthquake of 1395 the globes fell, and the tower remained in its mutilated state until 1568, when Ruiz was employed to restore it. He performed his commission in the most admirable manner, and the Giralda still remains secure, notwithstanding the frequent earthquakes.

RUMALDE, an ancient French architect, who flourished about 840, in the time of Louis the Pious. According to Felibien, he erected the old Cathedral at Rheims, which is celebrated as the most magnificent of the age. Rumalde is said to have used for materials the ancient city walls, previously demolished by Charles Martel.

RUMOHR, Carl Friedrich Ludwig Felix, a distinguished German writer upon art, born at Reinhardsgrimma, his father's estate near Dresden, in 1785. He was educated at the high school of Holzmünden, in Brunswick, and was afterwards sent to the University of Gottingen; but already, at the age of fifteen, he neglected every other study for that of art, and finally quitted the University to place himself under J. D. Fiorillo, well known as the author of a general history of modern painting. After acquiring a good knowledge of the art, he visited many collections, particularly the Dresden Gallery, where he was particularly struck with the works of Raffaelle and Paul Veronese. In 1804, at the age of twenty, he first went to Italy, and visited various cities, enjoying at Rome the friendship of Wilhelm and Alexander Von Humboldt, Thorwaldsen, and other distinguished individuals. In 1805 he returned to Germany, in the company of Ludwig Tieck, and was honored with the confidence of the crown prince, afterwards King of Bavaria. His literary activity commenced about 1811. In 1815 he revisited Italy, and commenced his labors at Florence, for his celebrated work the *Italienische Forschungen*, or Italian Researches, a critical work on the history of art, compiled exclusively from the archives and other original MSS. at Florence. It is in three volumes; the first two were published at Berlin, in 1827, and relate to modern art in Italy, generally, from its origin to its decline in the 16th century; many errors of Vasari are corrected; much obscurity of the 12th, 13th, 14th, and 15th centuries is cleared up by authentic documents. The third volume was published in 1831, divided under two heads, which treat chiefly of Raffaelle and the architecture of the middle ages. It is a work of great interest, abounding in excellent critical and theoretical reflections, and has gained for its author a wide celebrity. Rumohr visited Italy again in 1828, and also in 1837. His taste and judgment in the Fine Arts were frequently consulted by German princes. He wrote a large number of works relating to painting and engraving, which are much esteemed. He died at Dresden in 1843.

RUNCIMAN, Alexander, a Scotch painter, born at Edinburgh in 1736. The accounts of his early life are conflicting. Some say that he was the son of an architect, who instructed him in the rudiments of design, and then apprenticed him to two landscape painters, named Norries. Fuseli says he served his apprenticeship to a coach maker; but at all events, he first painted landscapes. In 1766 he went to Italy with his younger brother John, who was also a painter, and died at Rome. Alexander resided there several years and pursued his studies under the patronage of Sir James Clerk. On his return, he exhibited some pictures in 1772. The following year he settled at Edinburgh, where he conducted the Academy of Arts recently established in that city. He executed a few historical works, among which are Ulysses surprising Nausicaa at play with her Maids, the Ascension, Lear and his Daughters, and Agrippina carrying the ashes of Germanicus. He also painted some subjects from Ossian for Sir James Clerk; and executed a few etchings. He died in 1780.

RUOPPOLI, Giovanni Battista, a Neapolitan painter of fruit, flowers, fish, shells, and other marine objects. According to Dominici, he studied under Paolo Porpora, whom he excelled in fruits, particularly grapes, and was little inferior to him in other subjects. He died about 1685.

RUOPPOLI, Giuseppe, a Neapolitan painter, born in 1600, and died in 1659. He studied with Giovanni Baptistello, and painted fruit and flower pieces in a style of excellence.

or

RUPERT, Prince Palatine of the Rhine, was for a long time considered the inventor of the art of engraving in mezzotinto; but Baron Heineken has shown with tolerable clearness that he learned the art of Lieut. Colonel de Siegen, an officer in the service of the Landgrave of Hesse, who first engraved in this manner, and executed a portrait of Amelia Elizabeth, Princess of Hesse, as early as 1643. Prince Rupert learned the secret of this gentleman, and introduced the art into England when he went over the second time with Charles II. Laborde also asserts the same thing in his *Histoire de la Gravure en manière Noire*, Paris, 1839. See Article Siegen.

Prince Rupert amused himself with etching and mezzotinting. Nagler describes sixteen prints by him which are very rare. They are usually marked with one of his monograms. There are several of his prints in the British Museum; one, an etching, is dated 1636, and another, a mezzotint called the Executioner, is dated 1658.

RUPPRECHT, Frederick Charles, a German painter, engraver, and architect, born at Oberzenn, near Anspach, in 1779, and died in 1831. After receiving some instruction at Nuremberg, he went to Dresden, and improved himself by studying the works of the great masters in the Dresden Gallery, particularly those of Claude, Titian, and Paul Potter. He also studied perspective and architecture. In 1802, he made a journey through the south of Germany to study landscape, which was his delight, after nature; but to support himself, he was compelled to have recourse to portrait painting. In his travels, he became acquainted with General Drouet, whose portrait he painted, and those of several of his officers, and accompanied that commander through Germany in the capacity of interpreter.

His best pictures are his landscapes, which are painted both in oil and water-colors. They are drawn with great minuteness, and finished like miniatures; yet they are not mannered, and have the appearance of originality and freedom. His works as a painter are little known out of his country. As an engraver, he executed about twenty-five spirited etchings, mostly from his own designs, which are highly esteemed, and about fifty wooden cuts, a few of them in chiaro-scuro, with two blocks. They are sometimes marked with his name in full, and sometimes with his initials, as F. C. R. *f.*, C. R. *f.*, or R. *f.* As an architect, he was employed to restore the old Cathedral of Bamberg to its primitive state, and he prepared the plans, drawings, and models for that purpose, but did not live to see the work completed. The Cathedral possesses about one hundred and thirty of his drawings, many of them interesting to the antiquary, as representing many curious objects of ancient date, destroyed or discovered during the progress of the restorations. An account of his life and works, with a portrait, was published at Bamberg in 1843, written by J. Heller.

RUSCHEWEYH, Ferdinand, an eminent modern German designer, engraver, and lithographer, born at Mecklenburg about 1785. He has distinguished himself by his masterly engravings after the works of the most distinguished painters of the modern German school, as Overbeck, Cornelius, Steinle, Schadow, Bendemann, Wagner, and others, whose fame has been widely diffused by his burin. He first studied at Berlin, and afterwards passed some time at Vienna. In 1808 he went to Rome, where he pursued his studies with enthusiasm and assiduity, associating with his talented countrymen, whose tastes were congenial to his own. He resided at Rome till about 1832, and distinguished himself by many admirable productions after Raffaelle, Michael Angelo, Giulio Romano, Fiesole, and the antique bassi-relievi, in which he imitated the manner of Marc' Antonio. He also engraved some beautiful plates of illustrations for Goethe's Faust, after designs by *Cornelius;* of Schiller's Eleusinian Festivals, *after Wagner;* some sacred and ecclesiastical subjects, *after Overbeck;* and some plates after the sculptures of Thorwaldsen. In 1832 he returned to his own country, since which time he has executed some admirable plates after the great modern German masters, among which are Christ in the Temple, and Ruth and Boaz, *after Overbeck;* and the Jews in Exile, *after Bendemann.* See *Frederick Overbeck.*

RUSCHI, or RUSCA, Francesco, a Roman painter, who flourished about the middle of the 17th century. According to Zanetti, he was a disciple of Michael Angelo da Caravaggio, whose manner he adopted, both in his forms and his style of coloring. He is little known at Rome, but he acquired considerable reputation at Venice, Vicenza, and Trevigi. Lanzi says his pictures are to be met with in quite good preservation, and are admitted into the collections.

RUSS, Charles, a German painter and engraver, born at Vienna in 1779. He acquired some knowledge of the art from two painters named Drechsler and Brand, and afterwards visited Munich in 1804, where he designed about one hundred pictures in the Gallery. On returning to Vienna, he devoted his energies to historical painting, and produced his picture of Tiresias foretelling to Alcmena the destiny of Hercules, which gained him several commissions from the Archduke John. In 1809, he drew the second prize in the Imperial Academy, for his picture of Hecuba on the Coast of Thrace. In 1810 he was appointed cabinet painter to the Archduke, and in 1818 Keeper of the Belvidere Gallery. He executed many drawings of subjects from Austrian history. His works are lacking in originality; but they evince great application, and profound acquaintance with the principles of art. Russ died in 1843.

RUSSELL, John, an English portrait painter, chiefly in crayons, born at Guildford in 1744. He studied with Francis Cotes, whose style he imitated. He published a work on crayon painting, which was considered valuable in his time, and went through two editions. He was also fond of Astronomy, and constructed a model showing the appearance of the moon, for which he obtained a patent, and published a description, with plates engraved by himself. In 1788, he was elected a member of the Royal Academy, and died in 1806.

RUSSI, Giovanni de, a miniature painter of Mantua, who flourished about 1455. He illustrated for the Duke of Modena the Bible of Este, in large folio, which Lanzi says is one of the rarest specimens of the art in the distinguished collection of that prince.

RUSSO, Giovanni Pietro, a painter of Capua, who died in 1667. According to Dominici, after studying in various schools, visiting Rome, Naples, Venice, and Florence, he settled in his native city, where he executed many excellent altar-pieces, and other subjects, for the churches and public edifices. He is also commended by Lanzi.

RUSTICI, called Il Rustico, a painter of Siena, who flourished about the middle of the 16th century. He studied under the Cav. Gio. Antonio Razzi. Lanzi says "he was an excellent painter of grotesque subjects, with which he filled Siena." He had a son named Cristoforo, who also excelled in the same line, and obtained great reputation. There was another painter, named Vincenzio R., who excelled in the same branch, and is supposed to have been a son of Il Rustico.

RUSTICI, Francesco, called Il Rustichino, was the son of Cristoforo R., born at Siena about 1595. He first studied with his father, and afterwards with Francesco Vanni. He afterwards went to Rome, where he studied the works of Annibale Caracci, Guido, and Michael Angelo da Caravaggio, and formed an original and graceful style of his own. He possessed great talents, and executed a few choice pictures, but died in the flower of his life in 1625. In the collection of the Grand Duke of Tuscany is a fine picture by him, of an expiring Magdalen, and in the Palazzo Borghese at Rome, an admired picture of St. Sebastian. He also painted some torch-light pieces in the manner of Gherardo dalle Notti.

RUSTICI, Gio. Francesco, a Florentine sculptor of the 16th century, who studied under Verocchio, at the same time with Leonardo da Vinci. Among his principal works are mentioned the statues of Leda, of Neptune, and of Europa; a figure of a woman, and a mounted horseman, both of colossal size. Rustici quitted Florence in 1528, on account of the civil commotions, and went to the court of Francis I., who employed him on the works at Fontainbleau. He remained in France during the rest of his life; the time of his death is not recorded.

RUTA, Clemente, a painter born at Parma in 1688. According to Oretti, he is supposed to have studied first with Ilario Spolverini, a painter of battles, &c. He afterwards studied in the school of Carlo Cignani, at Bologna. After his return to his native state, he entered the service of the Infant Charles of Bourbon, and accompanied that prince to Naples, where he executed many excellent works. He subsequently returned to Parma, where Lanzi says he continued to practise his profession with credit till he lost the use of his eyes, at an advanced age. He painted easel pictures of histories, battles, skirmishes of cavalry, banditti, &c., and his pictures hold a high rank in the collections of Parma. He died there in 1767.

RUVIALE, Francisco, called Il Polidorino, a Spanish painter who, according to Dominici, went to Naples, and studied under Polidoro da Caravaggio. This must have been about 1527, as Caravaggio fled to Naples at the sacking of Rome, which happened in that year. He made great progress, imitated his master very happily, and assisted him in his works in the Palazzo Orsini, with subjects illustrative of the history of that noble family. After Caravaggio left Naples, he continued to reside there, and executed some works for the churches and public edifices, the principal of which are a picture of a dead Christ, with the Virgin Mary and St. John, in the chapel of the Royal Tribunal; the Descent from the Cross, in that of the Vicaria Criminale; and others at Monte Oliveto. The greater part of his works have perished, as happened to those of Caravaggio at Rome, from the use of improper grounds or colors.

RUVIALE, Spagnuolo, a Spanish painter, who studied under Il Salviati, at Rome, and afterwards assisted Vasari in his works in the Chancery, on which occasion Vasari says he formed himself into a good painter. This was in 1544. Nothing more is known of him; Palomino does not mention him, therefore it is probable he did not return to Spain.

R. or R. 1661 RUYSDAEL, or RUISDAEL, Jacob, an eminent Dutch landscape painter, born at Haerlem, according to Houbraken and others, in 1636, though probably at an earlier date, as there are pictures by him dated in 1645. Balkema says he was born in 1640, a glaring error. There is also much uncertainty respecting his history. It is not known under whom he studied, but it is highly probable that he received instruction from his fellow townsman, Nicholas Berghem, who was born in 1624; and it is certain that he was intimate with that artist. Houbraken says that, though he had given extraordinary proof of his ability as a painter at the early age of fourteen, he did not follow the art as a profession till some years later, but devoted himself to the study and practice of surgery; that he afterwards lived in habits of intimacy with Nicholas Berghem, who advised him to devote his attention entirely to painting. Some say that he early showed the most extraordinary talents for painting, and that, at twelve years of age, he produced pictures that were the astonishment of artists; that Berghem and Ruysdael went to Italy, and improved their taste by studying at Rome, and designing from the beautiful scenery in its environs; but others maintain that neither one nor the other was ever in that country. The only thing that seems to favor this supposition is that there are some of Ruysdael's works in the collection of the Grand Duke of Tuscany, and the Palazzo Riccardi at Florence. Amid all this confusion, when we consider his subjects, style, place of nativity, time of birth, &c., there can be little doubt that he received instruction from Berghem, and afterwards, by an assiduous study of nature, formed a style of his own. However, there is little dispute about his works.

Ruysdael is justly considered one of the most eminent landscape painters of the Dutch school. His pictures generally represent the most interesting views in the vicinity of Haerlem, where he resided most of his life; or occasionally the rocky borders of the Rhine, with cascades and waterfalls, which he treated in a style so admirably picturesque, that in these last subjects he may be said to be unrivalled. He rarely painted a picture without a river, brook, or pool of water, and his general subjects are views of the banks of rivers, with windmills or water-mills; hilly grounds, with brooks and cascades, a country interspersed with cottages and huts; solemn scenes of woods and groves, with roads through them, &c. It is evident in his pictures that he designed everything from nature, and he is uncommonly happy in his selections. His grounds are agreeably broken, his trees are of the most pleasing forms and delicately handled, his skies are clear, with light floating clouds, and there is an agreeable freshness in his verdure. He perfectly understood the principles of chiaro-scuro and perspective; his distances have always a fine effect, and his masses of light and shadow are distributed with such judgment as equally to delight the eye and charm the imagination. His coloring is chaste and clear, and his pencilling free and spirited, yet delicate. His talents were not confined to landscapes; he painted sea-pieces with equal success, and his pictures of fresh breezes and gales of wind are admirable. His scenes of torrents and waterfalls are depicted with wonderful force, truth, and grandeur. The pictures of this admired painter are numerous, and are held in the highest esteem. Smith, in his Catalogue raisonné of the

Dutch and Flemish masters, vols. vi. and ix., gives a descriptive account of 448 pictures by him, but doubtless there are many more which have not come under his notice. His works have also been largely imitated. He did not design the human figure with elegance, and frequently employed Ostade, Vandervelde, and Wouwerman to insert the figures, and such pictures are the most valuable. He also executed a few spirited etchings from his own designs, which, though slightly etched, produce a very natural and masterly effect. He died at Haerlem in 1681.

RUYSDAEL, Solomon, was the elder brother of the preceding, born at Haerlem in 1616, and died in 1670, according to Houbraken, though there appears to be no certainty about it, as there are pictures by him dated 1673, and most Dutch writers say he was about twenty years older than his brother. He painted landscapes and river views, in which he imitated the manner of John van Goyen, and some suppose him to have been a pupil of that master. His pictures are poor affairs, and are not admitted into choice collections; but he imitated variegated marbles with exact precision.

RUYTER, N. de, a Flemish engraver of little note, who flourished about 1688. He engraved a few plates, in which he appears to have imitated the style of Paul Pontius, but with no great success.

RUYVEN, Peter van. See Reuven.

RY, Peter Dankers van, a Dutch painter, born at Amsterdam in 1605. He was a good portrait painter, and went to Stockholm, where he met with much employment, and was appointed court painter to the King Ladislaus IV. He died in 1659.

RYCK, Peter Cornelius de, a Dutch painter, born at Delft in 1566. He first studied with James Willems, next, with Hubert Jacobs, and afterwards went to Italy, where he studied the works of Giacomo Bassano. On his return to Delft, he painted historical and pastoral subjects in the manner of Bassano, which were esteemed in his day. He died at Delft in 1628.

RYCKAERT, Martin, a Flemish painter, born at Antwerp in 1591. Discovering an early taste for painting, he was placed under the tuition of Tobias Verhaecht, an eminent landscape painter. On leaving his master he went to Italy, where he resided several years, and filled his portfolio with choice designs of the most interesting scenery and objects he met with in his travels, particularly at Rome, and in its vicinity. On his return to Antwerp, he distinguished himself as one of the ablest landscape painters of his time. His pictures, especially in the scenery, resemble the Italian, more than the Flemish school, and he embellished them with architecture, ruins, rocks, mountains, waterfalls, &c., pleasingly diversified. His works are occasionally decorated with figures by John Breughel. He lived on terms of intimacy with Vandyck, who painted his portrait among the eminent artists of his country. He died at Antwerp in 1636.

RYCKAERT, David, was the son of the preceding, born at Antwerp in 1615, according to the best authorities. He was instructed in landscape painting by his father, but the great estimation in which the works of Teniers, Brouwer, and Ostade, were held, induced him to paint similar subjects, in which he was eminently successful. His pictures usually represent conversations, musical parties, assemblies of peasants regaling themselves, chemists' laboratories, &c., though he sometimes adopted subjects of a more elevated character. He gave a lively and expressive character to his heads, his coloring is clear and transparent, and his pencil is light and spirited. He was very fond of representing subjects by candle-light and flambeaux, in which he had a peculiar manner of managing the lights, so as to give them an extraordinary effect. He acquired great reputation, and his works were so much admired, that he could scarcely supply the demand. The Archduke Leopold, a great encourager of art, favored him with his particular protection. In 1651 he was appointed Director of the Academy of Antwerp. Towards the latter part of his life, he frequently painted grotesque and fantastical subjects, such as spectres, incantations, assemblies of witches and devils, and the Temptations of St. Anthony, somewhat in the manner of Peter Breughel. Notwithstanding the disagreeableness of these subjects, he treated them with so much spirit, beauty of penciling and coloring, liveliness of imagination, variety and humor of expression, that they had many admirers, and were eagerly purchased, even by princes. His first works were not so well colored as his later ones, the former being rather too gray, but the latter having a remarkable truth and warmth. The heads of his figures are painted with great art and precision, but he was negligent of his hands and extremities; doubtless to save labor. His pictures are found in the best collections of Flanders and Brabant, but they are rare out of those countries. He died at Antwerp in 1677.

RYCKMAN, Nicholas, a Flemish engraver, born at Antwerp about 1620. He engraved some plates after Rubens and other masters, in a style resembling that of Paul Pontius, and probably was a pupil of that master. They are executed with the graver in a neat but formal manner, and his drawing is generally incorrect. The following are among his best prints:

The Adoration of the Magi; *after Rubens*. The best impressions are before the address of either Gas. Huberti, or Corn. van Merlen. The Entombing of Christ; *do.* The Holy Family; *do.* Christ and the Twelve Apostles; *do.*; thirteen plates. The best impressions are before the address of E. Coninck. Achilles discovered by Ulysses at the court of Lycomedes; *do.*

RYDER, Thomas, an English engraver, born in 1746, and died in 1810. He studied under Bartolozzi, and executed quite a number of plates after the works of Wright, West, Fuseli, Northcote, Stothard, Smirke, Ramberg, Rigaud, Hamilton, and other eminent painters of his day. He was one of the artists employed by Boydell, to engrave the Shakspeare Gallery, for which he executed eight of the large plates. His plates are usually executed in the dotted manner, but sometimes with a combination of the line and stipple, and possess great merit.

RYLAND, William Wynne, an eminent English engraver, born at London in 1732. He first studied with Ravenet, who was at that time established in England. On leaving that master, he went to Paris, and studied design under François

Boucher, and engraving with J. P. le Bas. On his return to his native city he acquired distinction in his profession, and was appointed engraver to the King, with a pension of £200 per annum. He was the first who practised chalk engraving (lines composed of dots in imitation of drawings), in England. He executed a large number of prints of various subjects, after the old Italian and modern English masters, which are highly esteemed. He engraved a great many plates after the works of Angelica Kauffmann, which has been regretted, as there is little variety in them, and his time could have been better employed. He engraved fifty-seven plates for the work entitled "A Collection of Prints in imitation of Drawings," published by Charles Rogers, in 2 vols. folio. These, with few exceptions, are after the old Italian masters. He also executed some spirited etchings, sometimes finished with the graver, which Watelet says, one would suppose to be the work of a painter. He left many unfinished plates at his death. This eminent artist, having become involved in pecuniary difficulties, committed forgery, and though there were many mitigating circumstances, he was condemned and executed in 1783, as Dr. Dodd had been about six years before for a like offence. The following are his principal plates:

PORTRAITS.

George III., King of Great Britain, &c.; *after Ramsay*; whole length. Charlotte, Queen of Great Britain, &c.; *after Coates.* John Stuart, Earl of Bute; *after Ramsay.*

SUBJECTS AFTER VARIOUS MASTERS.

Antiochus and Stratonice; *after P. Da Cortona.* Jupiter and Leda; *after F. Boucher.* The Graces bathing; *do.* Charity; *after Vandyck.* Four plates representing the Muses, Urania, Thalia, Erato, and Clio; *after Cipriani.* King John signing the Magna Charta; *after Mortimer.*

SUBJECTS AFTER ANGELICA KAUFFMAN.

Patience; oval. Perseverance; do. Maria, from Sterne's Sentimental Journey. Telemachus recognized at the court of Sparta. Achilles lamenting the Death of Patroclus. Penelope awakened by Euryclea. Eleonora sucking the Venom from the Wound of Edward. Lady Elizabeth Grey imploring Edward IV. for her husband's lands. The Judgment of Paris. Venus on her Car. The Flight of Paris and Helen. Venus presenting Helen to Paris. Juno borrowing the Cestus of Venus. A Sacrifice to Pan. Cupid bound, with Nymphs breaking his Bow. Cupid asleep, with Nymphs awaking him. Cymon and Iphigenia. The interview between Edgar and Elfrida, after her marriage with Athelwold. This plate was left imperfect, and was finished by Mr. Sharp after his unfortunate death, for the benefit of his widow. Fourteen plates engraved for the edition of Walton's Angler, published by Sir John Hawkins in 1760.

RYN, or RHYN, REMBRANDT VAN. See REMBRANDT.

RYNE, JOHN VAN, a Dutch engraver, born in 1712. Little is known of him; he went to London about 1750, where he resided several years, and executed some plates of views in England and the East Indies. He died in 1760.

RYSBRACK, G., a Dutch painter of flowers, dead game, and still life, who flourished about 1650. Nothing is known of him, further than by his pictures, which are well executed and signed with his name and the date.

RYSBRAECK, or RYSBRECHTS, PETER, a Flemish painter born at Antwerp in 1657. He studied under François Milé, whom he accompanied to Paris. Following the example of his instructor, he studied the works of Niccolo Poussin, and made them his models, which is discernible in all his works. His pictures were so much admired at Paris, that he was solicited to settle in that city; but though he met with the most flattering encouragement, he preferred to return to his native city, where he exercised his talents with great reputation, and was made Director of the Academy there in 1713. The landscapes of Rysbraeck, are distinguished by a grandeur of style, which, though founded on that of Poussin, possesses sufficient originality to acquit him of the imputation of plagiarism. His coloring is clear and harmonious, his touch broad and free, his figures well designed, and he possessed great facility of hand. There is, however, a want of variety and classic elegance, which together with a certain monotony in his pictures, places them in a very inferior rank to those of Poussin. There are six etchings by this artist from his own designs; they are marked *P. Rysbraek pinx. fecit et excudit.* He died in 1716. This artist must not be confounded with another painter of the same name, who flourished at Brussels, and painted landscapes, in a style entirely different, possessing little merit.

RYSBRACK, MICHAEL, an eminent Flemish sculptor, the son of Peter Rysbraeck the painter, was born at Antwerp, according to Rogers, in 1693. He studied design under his father, and subsequently acquired a knowledge of sculpture under Michael vander Vorst, with whom he remained about six years. In 1720, he visited England, and first distinguished himself by his small models in clay. At that time, no sculptor had ever been extensively employed in England, but the admirable productions of Rysbrack soon roused the dormant taste for fine sculptures. The first production that brought him into general notice was his bust of the Earl of Nottingham. He was for some time engaged by Gibbs, who contracted with the original parties for monuments greatly to his own advantage, and undoubtedly for the artist. The latter, however, shook off all connection with Gibbs, and obtained an extensive practice. He studied exclusively nature and the antique; his figures are well disposed, and characterized by simplicity and grandeur. He wrought with the greatest energy and constancy, and executed a large number of works. For a period of nearly forty years, he was very extensively employed, and there was scarcely an important work of sculpture undertaken in England, that was not entrusted to his direction.

The first great public work of Rysbrack, was the bronze equestrian statue of William III., erected in Queen's Square at Bristol, in 1733. Scheemakers also competed for this statue, and produced so excellent a model that he was presented with £50; although it was rejected for the design of Rysbrack, who received, according to Walpole, £1800 for the work, though another authority says £3000. The monument to Sir Isaac Newton in Westminster Abbey, was executed by Rysbrack from a design of Kent. In 1735, he finished a colossal statue of George II., for the parade of Greenwich Hospital. His most celebrated work, however, is the monument to John, Duke of Marlborough and his Duchess, at Blenheim. They are represented with their two sons, who died young, supported by History and Fame; in the lower part is a bas-relief representing the surrender of Marshal Tallard. In Westminster Abbey there are also several other monuments by Rysbrack, among which are those of Admiral Vernon, and Richard Kane, governor of Minorca, in the north transept; James, Earl Stanhope, in the north aisle; Sir Godfrey Kneller, in the nave; John Gay, Ben Jonson, and John Milton, in the south transept, or Poet's Corner. Rysbrack also executed a large number of statues of nobles and distinguished personages, among which are those of the Duke of Somerset, at Cambridge; Sir Hans Sloane, in the Botanical Garden at Chelsea; Dr. Radcliffe at Oxford; Charles I., for George Selwyn. Among his principal busts, are those of Alex. Pope, the Duke and Duchess of Argyle, Cromwell, Milton, etc. During the latter years of his life, the practice of Rysbrack sensibly declined, in consequence of the rising fame of Scheemakers and Roubilliac. At the age of seventy, when he relinquished his profession, he was by no means wealthy, notwithstanding his extensive practice; and he disposed of his remaining works at a general sale, also his collection of prints, pictures, drawings, marbles, models, casts, &c., including a large number of his own drawings, which, according to Walpole, were designed in the true taste of the Italian masters. His chief amusement during the last three years of his life, was in making such drawings in bistre. Rysbrack died in 1770.

RYSEN, Wernard, or Werner van, a Dutch painter, born at Bommel about 1600. He studied under Cornelius Poelemberg, and afterwards went to Italy, where he resided some time. On his return to Holland, he painted landscapes with historical figures, in the style of his instructor, with considerable success. According to Descamps, he abandoned painting, and became a dealer in diamonds and jewels, in which capacity he went to Spain.

RYTHER, Augustine, an English engraver and printseller, who flourished at London in 1590. He engraved some plates of the Spanish invasion, a curious map of Yorkshire, with views of York and Hull in the corners, and a large plan or birds-eye view of London and Westminster, engraved on wood, about six feet long by four in height; do. of Cambridge, four feet by three; do. of Oxford on metal, dated 1578. The plates representing the Spanish fleets, and some plans of fortifications and batteries on the river Thames for the protection of London, heretofore attributed to Robert Adams the architect, are clearly shown by Stanley to have been executed by Ryther.

RYX, or RYCKX, Nicolas, a Flemish painter, born at Bruges in 1637. It is not known under whom he studied, but after having learned the art, he embarked for the Mediterranean, and traveled through several eastern countries, sketching the manners, customs, and habiliments of Oriental people, especially their caravans, camels and modes of traveling. He spent some time in Palestine, and made designs of the most memorable places, especially Jerusalem, and scenes in its vicinity. On his return to Bruges, he painted pictures of those subjects, much in the manner of Vander Kabel, which were much esteemed. He wrought with great facility, executed many works, and was received into the Academy at Bruges in 1667, where he died in 1695.

# S.

SAAL, T., a Dutch engraver, who flourished about 1672. He engraved a variety of vignettes and other book-plates, which are indifferently executed with the graver.

SABBATINI, Andrea, called also Andrea da Salerno, an eminent painter, born at Salerno, about 1480. According to Dominici, he was the son of an opulent merchant, who intended him for the same profession, but discovering in him a passion for painting, he took him to Naples and placed him under the instruction of Raimo Epifanio, a painter of little celebrity, with whom he continued some time. He was so much captivated with the Assumption of the Virgin by Pietro Perugino in the cathedral, which excited universal applause, that he solicited and received permission of his father to go to Perugia and study with that master. On his way, he met some artists, who recommended him to go to Rome, and place himself under Raffaelle, who had then begun to distinguish himself by his great works in the Vatican. He accordingly proceeded to Rome, entered the school of that illustrious painter, where he made such rapid progress, and showed so much ability, that he was entrusted by Raffaelle to execute from his designs some of the frescos in the Vatican, in S. Maria della Pace, and in La Torre di Borgia. Here too, he formed an intimate acquaintance with Polidoro da Caravaggio. While he was prosecuting his studies with eminent success, he was summoned to Salerno to attend the deathbed of his father, and he left Rome much sooner than he had intended; yet he had so thoroughly imbibed the principles of Raffaelle, that he became a successful emulator of his style. He afterwards established himself at Naples, where he distinguished himself by many works both in oil and fresco, painted for the churches and public edifices; also at Salerno, at Gaeta, and other cities in the kingdom. He likewise painted much for the collections. Lanzi says, "he was an accomplished copyist of his master's works, and a successful emulator of his style. Compared with his fellow scholars, although he did not rival Giulio Romano, he yet surpassed Raffaellino del Colle and others of that class. He had correctness in his design, selection in his heads and attitudes, a depth of shade, and the muscles rather strongly developed; a breadth in the folding of his drapery, and a coloring that still preserves its freshness after the lapse of so many years." Most of his frescos have unfortunately perished, but there are many oil paintings by him which fully sustain his reputation: of these, the following are among the most esteemed at Naples; the Assumption of the Virgin in the Cathedral; the Adoration of the Magi in S. Spirito; and the Madonna and Child, with St. Elizabeth and other saints, in S. Domenico Maggiore. His easel pictures of Madonnas, Magdalens, Holy Families, &c., of enchanting beauty, are frequently to be met with in the collections at Naples. He died about 1545, aged 65 years. There is a slight disagreement among writers as to the exact time of his birth and death, but the above dates are given by Dominici, Lanzi, and Zani.

Others place his birth about 1485, and death in 1550.

SABBATINI, Lorenzo, called also Lorenzo da Bologna, an eminent painter, born at Bologna, according to Malvasia, Lanzi, and others, about 1540; but Ticozzi says he was born in 1530, and Zani that he operated as early as 1553. It is not known under whom he studied. There is also some discrepancy as to his style and merits. The following sketch by Lanzi is to the point: "Lorenzo Sabbatini, called also Lorenzo da Bologna, was one of the most graceful and delicate painters of his age. I have heard him enumerated among the pupils of Raffaelle by keepers of galleries, deceived doubtless by his Holy Families, designed and composed in the best Roman taste, although invariably more feebly colored. I have also seen some of his Holy Virgins and Angels, painted for private ornament, which resemble Parmiggiano. Nor were his altar-pieces inferior, the most celebrated of which is that of St. Michael, engraved by Agostino Caracci, from an altar of S. Giacomo Maggiore, and which he held as an example of gracefulness and beauty to his whole school. He was moreover a fine fresco painter, correct in design, copious in invention, a universal master in the subjects of the piece; and what is still more remarkable, he was very rapid in point of execution. Endowed with such qualities, he was engaged by many noble houses in his native place. On proceeding to Rome in the pontificate of Gregory XIII., according to Baglione, he met with so much success, that even his fleshes and naked figures were highly commended, though this was by no means a branch of his pursuit at Bologna. In the Capella Paolina, he represented the histories of St. Paul; in the Sala Regia, the picture of Faith, triumphing over Infidelity; in the gallery and lodges of the Vatican, a variety of other pieces, always in competition with the best masters, and always with equal applause. Hence, in the immense list of artists, at that period congregated at Rome, he was selected by the Pope to preside over the works going on in the Vatican, in the enjoyment of which honorable post, he died at an early age in 1577." His most esteemed works in the churches at Bologna, are the Crucifixion in S. Maria delle Grazie; the Assumption of the Virgin in la Morte; St. Gioachino and St. Anna in S. Martino Maggiore; the Four Evangelists, the Four Doctors of the Church, and St. Michael vanquishing the Rebel Angels in S. Giacomo. Lanzi says he painted a Pietà for the sacristy of the church of S. Pietro, from a design by Michael Angelo, a work attributed by some to that master. It is abundantly evident that he possessed great imitative, as well as original powers, and made the works of Michael Angelo, Raffaelle, and Parmiggiano his models.

SABBATINI, Francesco, an eminent Sicilian architect, born at Palermo in 1722. After acquiring a liberal education, he studied architecture in his native city, and then visited Rome for improvement. He subsequently visited Naples, where he married the daughter of Luigi Vanvitelli, and was employed by him as superintendent of the magnificent Palazzo Caserta. He was also honored by the King with a Lieutenancy in the artillery, and commissioned to erect the Arsenal Armory, and the Cavalry Barracks near the Ponte della Maddalena. When the King succeeded to the Spanish throne as Charles III., at the death of his brother Ferdinand, Sabbatini settled at Madrid, in 1759, under the royal protection, and was very extensively encouraged. He was highly esteemed for his correct taste, and great professional judgment and skill. He made some additions and alterations at the Royal palaces at Madrid, Aranjuez, and at the Prado. Among his chief works in the capital, are the Custom-House, the magnificent gates of the Alcala and of S. Vincente, and the royal porcelain manufactory at the Buon Retiro. He also designed the mausoleum of Ferdinand VI., in the church de las Salesas; the chapel in honor of Palafox, in the cathedral of Osma; the grand altar in the cathedral at Segovia; besides making many designs for edifices erected in Spanish America, among which were a number of churches, and the Arsenal at Caraccas. Sabbatini rose to considerable military ranks in the Spanish army, being appointed lieutenant-general in 1790, and inspector-general in 1792. He died at Madrid in 1798.

SABBIONETA, Il. See Pesenti.

SABINESE, Il. See Generoli.

SABLON, Pierre, a French designer and engraver, born at Chartres, in the department d'Eure et Loire, in 1584. There are only three known prints by him, viz., Lamech and Cain, *after Lucas van Leyden;* the Good Samaritan, and a medallion portrait of Rabelais.

SACCHETTI, Gio. Battista, an Italian architect, was born at Turin in the early part of the 18th century, and a disciple of Ivara. The latter was employed by King Philip V. of Spain to rebuild the royal palace at Madrid which had been destroyed by fire in 1734, but was prevented by death from completing it, and therefore recommended Sacchetti as his successor. Accordingly, the King invited him to Madrid in 1736. The original design of Ivara was upon a most extraordinary scale, the plan being 1700 feet square; but as the King insisted that the new palace should be precisely as large as the old one, Sacchetti made a new design of 470 feet square, which pleased the monarch. The height of the entablature is 100 feet, although in some parts, owing to the inequalities of the ground, it is 150 feet. There are four projections at the four angles, and another in the centre of the northern façade, which contains the chapel. The ground story is a rustic basement, on which rises a species of order resembling the Ionic, containing three stories; this order consists of half columns, and pilasters on pedestals. In the whole edifice there are no less than nine different floors, which render it too much cut up or crowded, and give it an appearance of littleness, greatly impairing its grandeur. The whole is of granite, except the window ornaments, which are of white Colmenar stone. This great work occupied the attention of Sacchetti so entirely, as to leave him little leisure for any other works of importance, except completing the façade of the palace of St. Ildefonso from the design of Ivara. He was appointed director of the public architectural school at Madrid; and in 1752, at the establishment of the Academy of S. Ferdinando, he was appointed honorary director of that Institution, being unable, on account of his various avocations to discharge the duties of an acting director. In

1760, on account of ill health, he was obliged to relinquish the practice of his profession. He died in 1764.

SACCHI, Andrea, an eminent painter, born at Rome, according to Passeri in 1600, and died in 1661; Pascoli copied the inscription on his tomb in full, by which it appears he died 21st June, 1661, aged 62; Lanzi says "his epitaph in the Stato della Ch. Lateran, gives his age 63 years, 4 months. Others place his birth in 1594 and 1599, but all agreed that he died in 1661. He was the son of Benedetto Sacchi, a painter of little note, who instructed him in the rudiments of design. He afterwards studied under Francesco Albano, and was his most distinguished disciple. On leaving the school of Albano, he improved himself by studying the works of Raffaelle, Polidoro da Caravaggio, and the antique marbles. Lanzi says he was profoundly skilled in the theory of art, and after its chief, the best colorist of the Roman school. He was slow in his execution, as it was a maxim with him that "the merit of a painter does not consist in giving to the world a large number of works of mediocrity, but a few perfect ones"; hence his pictures are rare. "His compositions," says Lanzi, "do not abound with figures, but every figure appears appropriate to its place, and the attitudes seem not so much chosen by the artist as regulated by the subject itself. Though he did not shun the graceful, he seems to have been born for the grand style—grave miens, majestic attitudes, draperies with broad and simple folds, a sober coloring, and a general tone which gave all his objects a pleasing harmony and a grateful repose to the eye. He seems to have disdained minuteness, and after the example of the ancient sculptors, to have left some parts unfinished; so at least his admirers assert." Mengs, however, is of a different opinion, and ranks Sacchi nearly on a level with Pietro da Cortona; but this is contrary to the opinion of several excellent authors, and certainly, when judged by the strict rules of art, there can be no just comparison between them. The characteristics of Cortona are copiousness, magnificence, and brilliant coloring, to charm the eye, and he was often negligent of design; of Sacchi, simplicity, majesty, sober coloring, and correctness of design, which mainly constitute greatness in art. There was a strong competition between these eminent artists, both men of genius, equally ambitious of immortalizing themselves by their works. Sacchi formed for himself a manner which had no resemblance to that of any other master, and always adhered to it. He distinguished himself so much by his fresco paintings, that he was accounted to have no superior at that time. He was favored with the protection of the Cardinal Barberini, whose palace he decorated with several allegorical works in fresco, which were greatly admired. Several of the churches and public edifices of Rome are embellished with his oil paintings, some of which are ranked among the most admired productions of the Roman school. Such are his celebrated picture of the Death of St. Anna, in S. Carlo; the Angel appearing to St Joseph in a Dream, the principal altar-piece in S. Giuseppe; St. Andrew, in the Quirinal; St. Augustine, in St. Peter's; and his famous St. Romualdo, in the church of that Saint, which is considered his masterpiece, and is ranked as *one of the four great paintings of Rome.* This picture was removed from its place by the French, to decorate the Louvre, but was restored by the allies in 1815. It represents the venerable St. Romualdo seated in a solitary valley in the Apennines, surrounded by the monks of his order, expounding to them his reasons for retiring from the world. The subject was a very difficult one to treat (the dress of the order being white), as the great quantity of white drapery tended to produce a sameness of color. The means which he adopted on this occasion to obviate the difficulty have always been admired. He placed a large tree near the foreground, the shade of which serves to break the uniformity, and produce a pleasing variety in the colors, which otherwise would have been monotonous. Everything in the picture seems to breathe tranquillity and repose, the expression in the heads is admirable, and, taken altogether, this picture is the wonder and admiration of artists. There are also some beautiful altar-pieces by him at Perugia, Foligno, Camerino, and other places, which Lanzi says are the pride of those cities. He was a perfect master of perspective, and executed some fine compositions, with a multitude of figures and admirable architecture (perhaps to show that his usual manner was one of choice), which procured him as much applause as his other performances. One of these represented the military sports of the Roman youth on horseback, which was publicly exhibited by order of the pope. He had a great many scholars, and always enjoyed the reputation of a learned, able, and amiable instructor. He had a son named Giuseppe whom he instructed in the art, but he became a conventual monk. There is one of his pictures in the Sacristy of the Apostles at Rome.

SACCHI, Antonio, a painter of Como, who, according to Orlandi, studied at Rome, and possessed good abilities. On his return to Lombardy, he undertook to paint the cupola of a church in his native city, but fixing on too high a point of perspective, he made his figures appear so gigantic that the ridicule and mortification he experienced threw him into a fever, of which he died in 1694.

SACCHI, Carlo, a painter, born at Pavia in 1617. According to Orlandi, he studied with Il Rosso of Pavia, but Lanzi thinks rather with Carlo Antonio Rossi, a Milanese painter, who wrought in the Cathedral at Pavia about that time. He afterwards went to Rome, where he studied some time, and thence proceeded to Venice, where the works of Paul Veronese were the particular objects of his admiration and imitation, in which he was successful. There is a fine picture by him at the church of the Osservanti at Pavia, representing the Miracle of the Dead resuscitated by St. Jacopo, in which Lanzi says he succeeded admirably in imitating the manner of Veronese, showing himself an excellent colorist, splendid in ornament, and spirited in his attitudes, though somewhat extravagant. He painted mostly easel pictures for individuals, and Lanzi mentions an exquisite picture of Adam and Eve, he saw in the possession of the Cav. Brambilla at Pavia, which he says is entitled to a place in that fine collection. He executed a few etchings, among which are the Adoration of the Shepherds, *after Tintoretto;* and the Adoration of the Magi, *after Veronese.* He died at Pavia in 1706, at the great age of 89 years.

SACCHI, Gaspare, a painter born at Imola, who flourished in the first part of the 16th century. There is an altar-piece by him in the sacristy of Castel S. Pietro, in his native city, dated 1517, and another in S. Francesco in Tavola, at Bologna, dated 1521. According to Orlandi, he executed many works for the churches and convents at Ravenna, and other places in the Romagna.

SACCHI, M., a Piedmontese painter, and a native of Casale, commended by Della Valle as one of the ablest scholars of Guglielmo Caccia, called Il Moncalvo, whose style he followed. There are two of his works in the churches of his native city, which, according to Lanzi, show a more energetic pencil, and perhaps a more learned design than his master possessed. He flourished about 1625.

SACCHI, Pietro Francesco, called Il Pavese, and by Lomazzo Pierfrancesco Pavese, a painter born at Pavia, of whom there are notices at Milan about 1460, and at Genoa from 1512 to 1526. Lanzi says the style of Sacchi resembles that of Carlo del Mantegna. He was a good perspective painter, delightful in landscape, and a diligent and correct designer in history. There is an altar-piece by him of the Four Doctors of the Church in the Oratory of St. Ugo at Genoa. Lanzi thinks there is some error in the dates given, or that there were two artists of this name.

SACCHI, a family of Mosaic painters, who were employed in the monastery of the Carthusians at Pavia for many years previous to 1783. Lanzi says "they filled the great church of that convent with beautiful mosaic works."

SACCHIATI, Pietro, an engraver on wood, born at Ravenna about 1598. According to Basan, he executed some wood-cuts, part of them printed in chiaro-scuro, after various masters, but he does not specify them, nor is he mentioned by any other writer.

SACCO, Scipione, a painter, born at Cesena, who, according to Francesco Scannelli, was a pupil of Raffaelle, though this rests on tradition. There is a picture of St. Gregory, painted in a grand style by him, in the Cathedral of Cesena, inscribed *Cœsenas* 1545, and another of the Death of St. Peter the Martyr, in the church of S. Domenico. Lanzi says he was doubtless of the school of Raffaelle, but not remembered out of Romagna.

SACHTLEVEN, or ZACHTLEVEN. See Saftleven.

SADELER, John, an eminent Flemish engraver, born at Brussels in 1550. His father was an ornamental engraver on steel and iron, to be inlaid with gold and silver, and brought up his son to the same business. At an early period he applied himself to the study of design, and he drew the human figure correctly, but with the stiffness and formality of his time and country. At the age of twenty he began to engrave on copper, and executed some plates after the designs of Crispin vander Broeck, which met with so much success, that he devoted himself entirely to engraving. He traveled through Germany and Italy, and finally settled at Venice, where he divested himself in a great measure of the dry, hard manner discernible in his earliest works. His plates are executed entirely with the graver, in a neat, clear, and masterly style; his drawing is generally correct, and he gave a fine expression to his heads. His works are numerous and highly esteemed. His death is variously placed in 1600 and 1610, but the latest date found on his prints is one executed at Venice in 1600. His prints are sometimes marked with his name, and sometimes with the above monogram. The following are his most esteemed prints. For a full list the reader is referred to Nagler's Lexicon.

PORTRAITS.

Clement VIII., *Pont. Max.* Mary of Medicis. Charles, Hereditary Prince of Sweden. Otho, Henry, Connt of Schwarzenberg. Sigismund Feyerabend, famous Printer. 1587. George Hoefnagel, Painter of Antwerp; (*piece precieuse. Joubert.*) Martin Luther; in an arabesque border.

SETS OF PRINTS.

Eight plates of the Creation of the World; *after Crispin vanden Broeck.* Six of the History of Adam and Eve; *after Michael Coxis.* Sixteen subjects from the Book of Genesis; *after M. de Vos.* A numerous set of plates of the life of Christ; *do.* Seven plates of the Passion of our Savionr; *after Christopher Schwarz.* A very numerous set, called the Hermits; engraved in conjunction with his brothers; *do.* The Twelve Months of the Year; *after P. Stephens,* or *Stephani.* The Four Seasons; *after Hans Bol.* The Four Times of the Day; *after Theodore Bernard.*

SUBJECTS AFTER ITALIAN MASTERS.

The Rich Man and Lazarus; *after Bassano.* Christ entertained by Martha and Mary; *do.* These two prints, with a third, representing Christ with the two Disciples at Emmaus, engraved by Raphael Sadeler, *after the same painter,* are usually called *Sadeler's Kitchens.* The Angel appearing to the Shepherds; *do.* The Nativity; *after Polidoro da Caravaggio.* The Virgin, with the Infant sleeping, and an Angel; *after Ann. Caracci.* St. Jerome praying; *after Giles Mostaert.* Mary Magdalene in meditation; *do.* St. Roch, with two Pilgrims; *do.* Jesus calling to him the little Children; *after Jodocus de Winghe.* The Prodigal Son; *do.* The Annunciation; *after Peter de Witt,* called *Pietro Candido.* Christ at table with the Disciples at Emmaus; *do.* The three Marys at the Sepulchre; *do.* The Last Supper; *do.* The Martyrdom of St. Ursula and her Companions; *do.* The Nativity; *after J. van Achen.* The Holy Family, with Mary Magdalene; *do.* The Crucifixion; *do.* The Last Judgment; *do.* Mary Magdalene penitent; *after Federigo Sustris.* Christ appearing to Magdalene; *do.* Mankind surprised by the sudden advent of the Deluge; *after Theodore Bernard.* Mankind surprised by the coming of the Last Day; *do.* The Trinity; *after Antonio Maria Viani.* Several Landscapes; *after Paul Brill* and others.

SADELER, Raphael, was the younger brother of the preceding, born at Brussels in 1555, and brought up to the same business under his father. The success John S. met with as an engraver, induced Raphael to turn his thoughts to the same pursuit, and he became his disciple, traveled with him, and settled with him at Venice, where he died in 1616. His prints are nearly as numerous as those of his brother, equally esteemed, and like them, they are executed entirely with the graver, which he handled with boldness and precision. His drawing is generally correct, his extremities carefully marked, and the expression of his heads excellent. The following are his principal plates:

PORTRAITS.

Paul V., *Pont. Max.* St. Charles Borromeus, Cardinal Ernest, Archbishop of Cologne. Leopold of Austria. Bishop of Salzburg and Passau. Ferdinand, Archduke of Austria. Charles Emanuel, Duke of Savoy, on horseback John Dietmar, Abbot of Furstenberg. Hypolitus Guarinonius, M. D.

SUBJECTS AFTER VARIOUS MASTERS.

A set of four plates of the Life of the Virgin; *from his own design.* Twenty-eight plates of the Life and Passion of Christ; *do.* Mary Magdalene at the Sepulchre, with St. Peter and St. John; *after J. de Winghe.* Lot and his Daughters; *do.* The Holy Family, with St. Elisabeth and St. John; *after John van Achen.* The Entombing of Christ; *do.* The dead Christ in the Sepulchre, with Angels; *do.* Mary Magdalene penitent; *do.*—The Judgment of Paris; *do.* The Virgin and infant Christ; *after Peter de Witt,* called *P. Candido.* 1593. The Immaculate Conception; *do.* The Presentation in the Temple; *do.* 1591. The Resurrection of Lazarus; *after Rottenhamer.* The Marriage of St. Catherine; *after Henry Goltzius.* The dead Christ, attended by the Marys, St. John, and Angels; *after J. Stradan.* An emblematical subject on the uncertainty of life, represented by death seizing a Lady at a Feast; *do.* The Crucifixion; *after Palma.* The Virgin suckling the infant Christ; *after Ann. Caracci.* The Holy Family, with St. John presenting a Cross; *after Raffaelle,* without the name of the painter or his own; inscribed *Qui non accipit, &c.* The Annunciation; *after Federigo Zuccaro.* The Adoration of the Magi; *after Bassano.* 1598. Christ at table with the Disciples at Emmaus; *do.*; called one of *Sadeler's Kitchens.* The Four Seasons; *after J. Stradan.* A set of six Landscapes; *after P. Stevens or Stephani.* Two Landscapes, with figures; *after Matt. Brill.* Four Landscapes, with the History of the Prodigal Son; *after Paul Brill.* A numerous set of prints, entitled *Bavaria Sancta,* engraved conjointly with his son Raphael, and published by him at Antwerp in 1624 and 1628. Several emblematical and allegorical subjects; *after Martin de Vos.* The great Battle of Prague, in eight sheets; very scarce.

SADELER, Egidius or Giles. This eminent engraver was the nephew and disciple of the two preceding artists, though Zani thinks that he was their brother, born at Antwerp in 1570. He excelled his instructors in design, taste, and command of the graver. He passed some time in Italy, and engraved several plates after the Italian masters. He was afterwards invited to Prague by the Emperor Rodolphus II., who retained him in his service, and assigned him a pension, which he enjoyed till his death, in 1629. He handled the graver with commanding facility, sometimes finishing his plates very highly when the subject required it; at other times his burin is bold and free. His plates are very numerous, many of them from his own designs, and are highly esteemed, particularly his portraits, which are executed in an admirable style, full of expression. The following are his best prints:

PORTRAITS.

The Emperor Rodolphus II. on horseback, with a Battle in the back-ground; *after Ad. de Vries.* The Emperor Matthias. 1616. The Empress Anne, his consort. 1616. The Emperor Ferdinand II. on horseback; in two sheets. 1629. Burckhard de Berlihing, Privy Counsellor to Rodolphus II. Christopher Guarinonius Fontanus, Physician to the same. John George Goedelman, Jurisconsult. Joachim Huber, Aulic Counsellor. Jacob Chimarrhæus, Grand Almoner. Cardinal de Dietrichstein, Bishop of Olmutz. 1604. John Matthew Warenfels, Aulic Counsellor. 1614. Aaron, Baron de Trautmansdorf. Siegfried de Kolonitsch. Ferdinand de Kolonitsch. Torquato Tasso, *Poetarum Princeps.* 1617. Octavius Strada, Antiquary. Peter Breughel, Painter, of Brussels. 1606. Martin de Vos, Painter, of Antwerp. Sigismond Bathori, Prince of Transilvania.

SUBJECTS FROM HIS OWN DESIGNS.

A set of twelve plates representing Angels with the Instruments of the Passion. A set of fifty-two Views near Rome, entitled *Vestigi delle Antichità di Roma.* The Burning of Troy, an etching; *Æg. Sadeler, fecit, aqua forti.* Charity, represented by a female figure with three children. Narcissus admiring himself in a Fountain. Pan and Syrinx. St. Sebastian dying, with an Angel drawing out the Arrows from his side. St. Dominick receiving the Institution of his Order from St. Peter and St. Paul. The Scourging of Christ. The Crucifixion. The great Saloon at Prague; in two sheets.

SUBJECTS AFTER VARIOUS MASTERS.

The Virgin and Infant; *after Raffaelle.* The Angel appearing to the Shepherds; *after Bassano.* The Murder of the Innocents; *after Tintoretto.* The Last Supper; *do.* St. Peter called to the Apostleship; *after F. Baroccio.* The Entombing of Christ; *do.* The Scourging of Christ; *after Giuseppe Cesare d' Arpino.* The Martyrdom of St. Sebastian; *after the younger Palma.* The Rich man and Lazarus; *do.* Angelica and Medora; *after Carlo Cagliari.* Hercules and Omphale; *after B. Spranger.* The Marys at the Tomb of Christ; *do.* The Annunciation; *after Peter de Witt,* called *Candido.* The Virgin and infant Jesus; copied *from Albert Durer.* Christ bearing his Cross; *do.* Judith with the Head of Holofernes; *after John van Achen.* The Nativity; *do.* The Virgin and infant Christ, with St. John; *do.* Several sets of Landscapes; *after Breughel, Paul Brill, Roelant Savery, P. Stevens, &c.*

SADELER, Marcus, is supposed to have been a son of John Sadeler, and born at Munich, but there is great uncertainty respecting his paternity and whether he was an engraver at all. This much is certain, that he resided a long time at Venice, where he carried on the business of a print-seller, and it is probable that he inherited the plates of John, Raphael, and Giles S., as many of them were subsequently published by him; none of the first impressions bear his name. Heller ascribes to him a set of fifteen plates copied from Albert Durer's series of Christ's passion; but there is no certainty about this, as the prints are without any signature or date, and no other author mentions any prints by him. The prints referred to are easily distinguished from the originals by their being reversed.

SADELER, Raphael, the Younger, was the son and pupil of the elder Raphael S. Little is known of him, and neither the time of his birth or death are recorded. He accompanied his father to Munich, and assisted him in many of his works, particularly in the illustrations for Rader's "Bavaria Sancta et Pia." He also engraved some plates by himself, which are tastefully executed. His works are so blended with those of his father that it is difficult to distinguish them, but the following are particularized:

The Annunciation; *after C. Schwarz.* The Virgin and St. Anne caressing the infant Jesus; *do.* The Holy Family, with his name and date 1613. Venus endeavoring to dissuade Adonis from the Chase; *after Titian.* Forest Scenery; *after Breughel.*

SADELER, Tobias, is supposed to have been a son of Giles S. He flourished at Vienna about 1675. The following prints are by him. There were several other engravers and publishers of the name of Sadeler, of whom little is known; probably they were the descendants of those already mentioned.

Johann Christian Schulz, ambassader of Wurtemberg, dated 1675. Three pictures of the Virgin in the church of St. Francis at Bechin in Bohemia. The picture of the Virgin in the Dominican church at Budweis in Bohemia. The dancing Peasant and the young Bride; *after S. Beham's drawing*; signed *Tobias Sadeler sc.* 1670. This is described as a finely engraved and brilliant piece. The Vignettes to the first part of Priorata's History of Frederick III.

S or S SAENREDAM, JOHN, a Dutch designer and engraver, born, according to the best authorities, at Leyden in 1565, and died in 1607. According to Huber, he studied first under Henry Goltzius, and afterwards with James de Gheyn. He engraved a great number of plates, many of them from his own designs, executed entirely with the graver, in a clear, neat style, and, though his drawing is not very correct, he handled the burin in a very masterly manner. The plates from his own compositions prove him to have been an able and tasteful designer. Bartsch gives a catalogue of one hundred and twenty-three prints by him, of which the following are the most esteemed:

PORTRAITS.

Carl van Mander; *after Goltzius.* P. H. Hornanus, Poet and Physician; *after Van Mander.* John Cesaree, Philosopher. John de la Chambre, Writing Master.

SUBJECTS FROM HIS OWN DESIGNS.

Susanna and the Elders. Hercules between Minerva and Venus. Lycurgus giving Laws to the Lacedemonians. The Wise and Foolish Virgins, in five plates. 1606. An allegorical subject, relative to the government of the Low Countries by the Infanta Isabella. The portrait of that Princess is seen under a tree on the right of the print. 1602. The Prosperity of the United Provinces under the House of Orange; an emblematical subject. 1600. A representation of a large Whale which was thrown on the Coast of Holland. 1602.

SUBJECTS AFTER VARIOUS MASTERS.

Adam and Eve in Paradise; *after H. Goltzius.* Lot and his Daughters; *do.* Judith with the Head of Holofernes; *do.* Susanna and the Elders; *do.* Ceres, Venus, and Bacchus united: *do.* The Seven Planets, the Four Seasons, the Five Senses, the Four Ages, the Three Marriages at different times of life; *do.* The Bath of Diana; *do.* A set of six plates of the History of Adam and Eve; *after Ab. Bloemaert.* Four plates of the History of Elijah and Elisha; *do.* Elijah and the Widow of Sarepta; *do.* 1604. The Angel appearing to the Shepherds; *do.* 1599. The Prodigal Son; *do.* 1618. Vertumnus and Pomona; *do.* 1605. Mars and Venus; *after P. Isaacx.* Judith with the Head of Holofernes; *after Lucas van Leyden.* David carrying in Triumph the Head of Goliah; *do.* The Nativity; *after C. van Mander.* Paul and Barnabas; *do.* Adam and Eve in Paradise; *after Corn. van Haerlem.* St. John preaching in the Wilderness, *do.* Angelica and Medora; *do.* Vertumnus and Pomona; *do.* The Grot of Plato; inscribed *Lux venit in mundum*, &c.; *do.* The Death of Epaminondas; *after Polidoro da Caravaggio.* Camillus breaking the Treaty of Peace between the Romans and the Gauls; *do.* The History of Niobe and her Children; in eight sheets, forming a frieze; *do.* 1594. The Entombing of Christ; *after M. Angelo Caravaggio.* The Repast of our Saviour with Levi; *after P. Veronese.*

SAENREDAM, PETER, a Dutch painter, was the son of the preceding, born at Assendelft about 1597. He studied under Francis Peter de Grebber, but he did not follow the style of that master. He painted architectural pieces, particularly the interiors of churches, in a very neat and correct manner, which were highly esteemed in his own time, and are now extremely rare. He painted a View of the Town House of Haerlem, enlivened by a multitude of figures, representing the solemn entry of Prince Maurice; and in the Museum at Amsterdam, is another fine picture by him, representing the interior of the great church at Haerlem. There are few particulars recorded of him. He died in 1666. His name is sometimes erroneously written *Zaenredam* or *Zaanredam.* He signed his pictures *P. Saenredam.*

SAFTLEVEN, CORNELIUS, a Dutch painter, born at Rotterdam in 1606. His name is variously written Saftleven, Sachtleven, Zachtleven, and Zaftleven; the first is correct. It is not known under whom he studied, but he settled at Antwerp, where he acquired considerable reputation. He painted drolls and drunken frolics, in which he imitated the style of Adrian Brower; interiors of farm-houses and kitchens, village sports and festivals, in which he emulated David Teniers. Some of his best pictures represent corps de gardes, soldiers playing at cards or amusing themselves, embellished with armor, helmets, and other warlike implements in the foregrounds. These are well designed and drawn, and executed with great spirit. Though his coloring is less clear and harmonious, and his pencil less delicate and spirited than in the productions of the two eminent artists whose styles he followed, his pictures are esteemed, and thought worthy of a place in the best collections. He executed a few spirited etchings from his own designs, among which are a set of five grotesque subjects, representing the Five Senses; twelve small plates of Dogs, Cats, Fowls, &c.; and a Landscape, with Goats and a Goatherd, etched in a bold and masterly style. He died in 1673, though writers differ as to the exact time of his birth and death. He marked his prints with one of the following monograms:

C L 1650 or C L 1673 or C L

HL inventor SAFTLEVEN, HERMANN, was the younger brother of the preceding, born at Rotterdam in 1609. He studied under John van Goyen, but he did not follow the style of that master. He diligently studied nature, and applied himself to designing the most picturesque views on the borders of the Rhine and the Meuse; the windings of the rivers, the antique edifices, the woods, the waterfalls, broken grounds, and everything affording picturesque and agreeable materials for embellishing his landscapes, which he painted in a very neat and highly finished style. He decorated his pictures with numerous figures and boats, which are correctly drawn and touched with great neatness and spirit. His coloring is clear and transparent, his skies light and floating, and his distances recede with a pleasing and natural degradation. His works are highly esteemed, and are found in the choicest collections. His drawings also enrich the portfolios of connoisseurs. He executed a considerable number of spirited and masterly etchings from his own designs, of which Bartsch describes thirty-six, and several more are mentioned by other authors. He resided the greater part of his life at Utrecht, where he died in 1685.

SAGRESTANI, GIOVANNI CAMILLO, a Florentine painter and poet, born in 1660. Lanzi says he studied under Antonio Giusti, and that he was esteemed at Florence, even in the life time of Gabbiani and Gherardini. To profit by the instruction of the best masters, he visited different schools, and for some time attended that of Carlo Cignani, whose manner he adopted. There are some of his works in the churches and public edifices of his native city, having much of the ideal in the heads, and a more florid coloring than was usual with his cotemporaries of the Florentine school. Such is one of his Holy Families in the Madonna de' Ricci. He died in 1731.

SAHLER, Otho Christian, an obscure German goldsmith and engraver, who flourished in the 18th century. He executed some prints in imitation of drawings. There was a C. Sahler who engraved some portraits.

SAILLIAR, Louis, a French engraver, who flourished about the middle of the 18th century. He engraved a few plates, mostly portraits, after various masters. He went to England, where he was employed by the Messrs. Boydell.

SAILMAKER, Isaac, an English painter of marine subjects, born in 1633, and died in 1721. All that is known of him is that he was employed by Cromwell to paint a view of the fleet before Mardyke. It is also said that he painted a picture of the combined fleet under the command of Sir George Rooke, engaging the French, commanded by the Count de Toulouse, which was engraved in 1714.

SAINT ANDRÉ. See Renard.

SAINT AUBIN. See Aubin.

SAINT NON. See Non.

SAINT MAURICE, P. de, a French amateur engraver, who is said to have etched a few prints, among which is one of an old man playing on the flute, surrounded by five children. He was an officer in the French Guard.

SAINT OURS, a distinguished Swiss painter, born at Geneva, according to the *Biographie Universelle*, in 1762. After acquiring the elements of the art from his father, who was an excellent designer, he visited Paris at the age of sixteen, and entered the school of Vien. His progress was rapid; in the following year he drew a medal at the exhibition of the French Academy; and in one year afterwards he gained the grand prize for his picture of the Rape of the Sabines. Visiting Rome with the royal pension, he diligently studied the great works of art, and produced several esteemed pictures, among which was a contest of wrestlers at the Olympic Games. He settled at Geneva in 1792, and executed many estimable historical subjects, as well as portraits. He also painted the representation of an earthquake, distinguished for fine conception and great vigor of penciling. Saint Ours died at Geneva in 1809.

SAITER, or SEITER, Cav. Daniello, a German painter, born at Vienna in 1649. He went early to Italy, where he seems to have spent the rest of his life. He first stopped at Venice, where he resided twelve years, and studied under Carlo Loth. From Venice he proceeded to Rome, where he executed several works for the churches, which Pascoli says are incorrect in design, though finely colored. He was next invited to Turin, where he was employed by the court for several years, and distinguished himself so much that he received the honor of knighthood. He painted both in oil and fresco. Lanzi says his cupola in the great hospital is one of the finest frescoes in that capital. He executed many works for the churches at Turin and in various places in that state, and decorated the palaces and villas of the nobility. Lanzi says he formed a style of his own, by studying in all the schools of Italy, and that in his works at Turin we do not find that incorrectness of design attributed to him by Pascoli. "His works in oil are found in the palaces and in the villas, and he has no occasion to fear the proximity of Giovanni Miel himself. He yields to the latter indeed, in grace and beauty, but is superior to him and others in the force and magic of his coloring. His oil pictures are by far the most highly finished of his works, as seen in a Pietà in the royal collection, which we should say was designed in the Academy of the Caracci." His best works at Rome are St. John preaching in the Wilderness in the church of S. Maria in Vallicella, and a fine picture of the Death of Lucretia in the Spada Palace. He also painted at Venice, but his best works are at Turin. He died in 1705. Some writers call his name *Seuter*, place his birth in 1642, and say that he painted portraits and engraved; but it is evident that they refer to another artist.

SAITER, SEITER, or SEUTER, John Gotfried, a German designer and engraver, born at Augsburg in 1718. He was instructed in design by J. E. Ridinger, and in engraving by G. M. Preissler. He afterwards went to Italy, and was employed at Florence in engraving a part of the plates from the pictures in the collection of the Marchese Gerini; in the Florentine gallery, and that of Sans Souci. He also copied some mythological prints from Agostino Caracci, published at Venice, which he signed G. G. Saiter; this has led to some confusion (see table of christian names.) He simply rendered his name into Italian. He afterwards returned to his own country, and died in the hospital at Augsburg in 1800. Nagler gives a list of fifty-three prints by him. His name is variously writted by authors, as above.

SALA, Vitale, an Italian painter, was born at Cernusco, near Cano, in 1803. At the age of fourteen he visited Milan, and studied under the Professor Mazzola, who lost his right hand at the age of fifty, and afterwards painted with his left. In 1822 and 1823, Sala drew the grand golden medal at the exhibition of the Academy. Among his principal works are mentioned the Arrest of Bernardo Visconti; the Departure of Regulus; the Battle of Landriano; and several pictures for the churches. Sala died at Milan in 1835, aged 32 years.

[monogram] or [monogram] or [monogram] SALAERT, or SALLAERTS, Anthony, a Dutch painter and engraver, born at Brussels in 1571. It is not known under whom he studied, but he acquired considerable reputation as an historical painter, and executed several works for the churches in his native city, as well as many others for individuals. One of these, representing a procession of a Company of Archers, possessed sufficient merit to induce the French to carry it to Paris to embellish the Louvre. He also engraved on wood, and executed some cuts in a bold, free style, marked with one of the above monograms. There is some dispute about these prints, but they are considered genuine by the best connoisseurs. He died in 1632.

SALAI, or SALAINO. See Solari.

SALAMANCA, Antonio, a celebrated Italian print publisher, who flourished about the middle of the 16th century. There is some dispute whether he engraved or not. There is a plate of a Pietà after Michael Angelo, signed *Antonius Salamanca*

*Quod Potuit Imitatus Exculpsit.* Two more have been ascribed to him; a portrait of Baccio Bandinelli, and the Creation of Animals, after Raffaelle. All other prints with his name have *excudit*, or *excudebat*, or *A. S.*, i.e., *Antonius Scudebat.* He restored many plates by the old masters. The lovers of the fine arts are greatly indebted to Salamanca, Lafreri, and the three Rossi of Rome, for the preservation of many fine works by the old Italian engravers, and for the many engravings each had executed after works that might otherwise have been lost to posterity.

SALERNO, Andrea da. See Sabbatini.

SALIMBENI, Arcangiolo, a painter born at Siena, whose history is mixed up in the most admirable confusion. Baldinucci expressly says he was born in 1500, and studied under Federigo Zuccaro. Lanzi thinks he might rather have received instructions of Gio. del Tozzo, or Marco Bigio, two Sienese painters, as his principles are entirely different from those of Zuccaro. "He loved precision, more than fulness, in design, and we may even observe in him an attachment to the manner of Pietro Perugino, as has been observed by Della Valle, with regard to a Crucifixion with six saints in the parish church of Lusignano." It is known, however, that he studied at Rome, and during his residence in that city, he might have contracted a friendship with Zuccaro. He executed many works for the churches and convents of his native city, as well as for individuals. In these, Lanzi says he appears wholly modern, as in his picture of St. Peter the Martyr, in the convent of the Dominicans, which is dated 1579. "This date, says Lanzi, must be false, as the widow of Archangiolo married again, and bore Francesco Vanni in 1565, consequently the latter could not have been a scholar of Archangiolo, though such an idea is prevalent, and he could give lessons only for a short time to his son Ventura," (born in 1557! so carelessly do the best authors sometimes write), "or to Sorri and Casolani, if the period of their birth is true." Zani places his birth in 1536, and his death in 1583. Others place his death in 1563. The truth doubtless is, that Salimbeni married the widow of Vanni as is expressly stated by several writers in the life of Cav. Francesco Vanni, which reconciles the contradictory statement. See *Vanni.*

SALIMBENI, Cavaliere Ventura, called also Il Cav. Bevilacqua, was the son of the preceding, born at Siena in 1557. There is some discrepancy respecting the early history of this eminent artist, about which there is no certainty, and which is of no importance. All are agreed that he received his first instructions from his father, and afterwards improved hinself by visiting the different cities of Lombardy, and sketching the works of the best masters, especially those of Correggio and Parmiggiano at Parma and Modena. He afterwards went to Rome, where he executed many works for the churches, and was employed by Sixtus V. in the Library of the Vatican, and in the palace of St. John of Lateran. Baglioni enumerates several of his works at Rome, the principal of which are the Baptism of Christ, and Abraham entertaining the Angels in del Gesù; the Circumcision in S. Simeone de Lancellotti; and the Annunciation in S. Maria Maggiore. He also painted some ceilings in conjunction with his half-brother Francesco Vanni. He next visited Florence, where, in competition with Bernardino Barbatelli, called Il Poccetti, he painted several pictures of the history of the Virgin in the cloister of the Servi. He also executed many works for the churches and public edifices at Siena, Perugia, Foligno, Lucca, Pavia, Genoa, and other cities. His Marriage of the Virgin, in the cathedral of Foligno; and his St. Gregory in the church of S. Pietro at Perugia, are highly commended.

Cav. Ventura possessed a ready and fertile invention, an elegant and graceful taste in design, and a delicate, sweet, and harmonious coloring. Lanzi says, "in conjunction with Vanni, he executed some ceilings, and, perhaps, derived advantage from observing his practice. In many of his works he resembles him in his imitation of Baroccio, and hardly yields to him in grace of contour, in expression, and in delicacy and clearness of coloring." There is, however, a great difference in his works, as he fell into dissipated habits. He lived on terms of intimacy with Agostino Tassi, and that artist sometimes painted the landscapes and backgrounds of his pictures, especially those he executed at Genoa. He is sometimes called Il Bevilacqua, a surname conferred upon him by the Cardinal Bevilacqua, when he knighted him in Perugia. He also executed a few masterly etchings from his own designs; Bartsch gives a list of only seven, which he thinks is complete, as follows: the Marriage of the Virgin, the Salutation, the Baptism of Christ, the Destination of the Holy Virgin, the Virgin and Infant, St. Agnes and Sts. Anne and Joachim. He died at Siena in 1613.

SALINCORNO, Mirabello da, called also Cavalori, a Florentine painter, who flourished about the middle of the 16th century. He studied under Ridolfo Ghirlandajo, and painted chiefly cabinet pictures. Lanzi mentions one of the Annunciation, dated 1565. He also assisted in the decorations for the obsequies of Michael Angelo. Zani says he operated as late as 1578.

SALINI, Cav. Tommaso, a painter born at Rome about 1560. He was the son of a Florentine sculptor, who placed him under the instruction of Baccio Pintelli, a painter of little note. Without the advantage of superior instruction, by studying the works of the best masters, he became an excellent painter of history, and particularly excelled in flowers and fruits. He executed several works for the churches at Rome, which are commended by Baglioni, the principal of which are an altar-piece of the Martyrdom of St. Agnes in the church of that saint; St. Tommaso da Villanova giving alms to the Poor, and a picture of St. Nicholas, in that of S. Agostino. Lanzi says, "he was the first who composed vases of flowers, accompanied with beautiful groups of corresponding foliage and other elegant designs." He was principally employed in painting easel pictures for the collections, which were eagerly sought after, and purchased at high prices. He died at Rome in 1625. The above dates are given by Lanzi; Zani says he was born in 1581, and died in 1631. Others place his birth in 1575, and death in 1625.

SALIS, Carlo, a painter born at Verona in 1680. He first studied under Giuseppe dal Sole at Bologna, and afterwards with Antonio Balestra at Venice, whose style he adopted with success. He executed several works for the churches in the Venetian states. One of his most esteemed productions, is an altar-piece representing St. Vincenzio administering to the sick, in the church of that saint, at Bergamo, which Lanzi says "is finely mellowed, and uncommonly spirited, approaching very near to Balestra's style, especially in the handling of his colors." He died in 1763.

SALLIETH, Mathias de, a German designer and engraver, born at Prague in 1749. He first studied with J. E. Mansfeld at Vienna, and afterwards at Paris with J. Ph. le Bas. He resided several years at Paris, and engraved some of the plates for Choiseul-Gouffier's Voyage pittoresque en France; and for La Gallerie de le Brun. He afterwards went to Holland, and there engraved some marines and battle-pieces from his own designs and after the Dutch masters. The time of his death is not known.

SALM, A. van, a Dutch painter of marines and views in Holland, in black and white, in imitation of pen-drawings. His pictures are neatly executed, but have little more effect than a print. The elder Vander Velde designed many marines in a similar manner. They are esteemed by some as curiosities of art. Salm flourished about 1650.

SALMEGGIA, Enea, called Il Talpino, (the Mole, slow,) an eminent painter, born at Bergamo about 1556. After studying in the schools of the Campi at Cremona, and of the Procaccini at Milan, he proceeded to Rome, where, according to Orlandi, he devoted himself fourteen years to the models of Raffaelle, and emulated his manner during the rest of his life. Orlandi and other writers extol his picture of S. Vittore at the Olivetani at Milan, and some of his other works, as worthy of the school of Raffaelle, to whom they have even been ascribed. He executed many works for the churches at Bergamo and Milan; in the former city, the most remarkable are the St. Vittore before mentioned; the Adoration of the Magi, in S. Maria Maggiore; the Martyrdom of St. Agatha, at the Teatini; the Descent from the Cross, in S. Leonardo; the great altar-piece in Santa Grata, representing the Virgin and infant Jesus in the Clouds, crowned with glory, with a Choir of Angels, and several Saints below; another grand altar-piece of the same subject, in Santa Marta. In both the last named works he observed the same general composition; in that of Santa Marta, Lanzi says, "he introduced a splendid variety of foreshortenings, of attitudes, and of lineaments; he even inserted the city of Bergamo, with some fine architecture, in the style of Paolo Veronese. The figures are arranged with extreme care, among which appears a bishop, in his sacred paraphernalia, that reminds us of Titian himself." At Milan, in the church of La Passione, are two of his finest works, representing Christ's Sermon on the Mount, and the Flagellation. His pictures for private ornament are rare, extremely valuable, and only to be found in the collections of Bergamo and Milan; there are several in the Royal Gallery in the latter city. "Whoever attentively examines the best works of Salmeggia," says Lanzi, "will not feel inclined to refuse him one of the most distinguished places in the ranks of the followers of Raffaelle. The clearness of his contours, though sometimes bordering on the minute, the expression of his youthful countenances, the smoothness of his pencil, and the flow of his drapery, together with a certain graceful air in the expressions and the motions, sufficiently mark him for an admirer of that sovereign master, how much soever inferior to him in point of dignity, in imitation of the antique, and in felicity of composition. His method of coloring was also different; he affects a greater variety of colors in his draperies; the tints in a large portion of his works are at present faded, and the shades, as in the works of other painters of the same period, are much changed; yet it is probable that this great artist, as it has been observed of Poussin and of Raffaelle himself, did not always bestow the same degree of care upon his coloring, satisfied with displaying, from time to time, his surpassing excellence in this department." He died at Bergamo, according to Tassi, in 1626; Lanzi says he died old, in 1626; and Zani places his death in 1610.

SALMEGGIA, Francesco and Chiara, were the son and daughter of the preceding. Lanzi says of them, "although educated by their father, they succeeded rather in imitating his studies and his figures, than in thoroughly penetrating into the principles of his art. The fruits of a good education are sufficiently apparent in them, and when placed in competition with some of their cotemporaries they appear, if not very animated, at least very sedulous artists, and greatly exempt from the faults of the mannerists. Bergamo is in possession of many of their public works, in some of the best of which the father is supposed to have afforded them his assistance." They are also commended by the Conte Tassi, in his *Vite de Pittori Bergamaschi*. The times of their birth and death are not known. Several of their works are dated from 1624 to 1628.

SALMERON, Cristobal Garcia, a Spanish painter, born at Cuenca in 1603. He studied under Pedro Orrente, and acquired considerable reputation as a painter of history and animals. He executed some works for the churches, one of the most esteemed of which is a picture of the Nativity, in the church of San Francisco at Cuenca. He also painted a celebrated picture of a Bull Fight, by the order of Philip IV., given in honor of the birth-day of Charles II. of Spain. He died in 1666.

SALMERON, Francisco, was the younger brother of the preceding, born at Cuenca in 1608, and died in 1632. The account given of him by Cean Bermudez, is ridiculous. He studied under Pedro Orrente, and afterwards, "by *analyzing* the works of Titian, Veronese, Tintoretto, and the Bassans, he formed for himself a style of coloring so brilliant, that no other palette was ever equal to it; it was in effect dazzling."

AS SALMINCIO, Andrea, a Bolognese engraver, who studied under Gio. Luigi Valesio, and flourished about 1640. He engraved some plates, both on wood and copper, marked with the above monogram. They are indifferently executed.

SALOMON, Jean, called by the Italians, Giovanni Gallo, Johannes Gallus, l' Infante Gallo, and by other appellations indicative of his country. According to Zani, this artist was the son of Solomon Bernard, called *little Bernard*, whose real name he says was Bernard Salomon. He says that the elder Salomon operated from 1547 to 1580, and the younger from 1550 to 1590.

He denies that *Bernard* ever engraved on wood, but he calls *Jean* "the prince of the little masters on wood, or the *Callot* of engraving on wood." He pursues the subject *con amore*, but does not advance anything conclusive, as no prints are mentioned bearing his signature or mark. The Italian writers mention *Bernardo Gallo*, a Frenchman, as an engraver on wood, and it is evident that the prints attributed to him were executed by Solomon Bernard. See *Solomon Bernard* and *Bernardo Gallo*.

SALTARELLO, Luca, a painter born at Genoa in 1610. He studied under Domenico Fiasella, and gave early proofs of extraordinary talents. Soon after leaving his master, he went to Rome in search of improvement, where he fell a victim to his unremitting assiduity, in the flower of his life, about 1635. Lanzi says "he left a picture of St. Benedetto restoring a dead person to life, in the church of S. Stefano at Genoa, a picture of sober coloring, beautifully harmonized, and full of expression and knowledge, which sufficiently proves that he had capacity to have formed an epoch in his school, had he lived."

or SALTZBURGER, P., a German engraver on wood, who flourished about 1580. He executed some cuts, mostly after the designs of Jost Amman. They are usually marked with one of the above monograms, but sometimes with his initials, P. S., separate.

SALVESTRINI, Bartolomeo, a Florentine painter, who, according to Baldinucci, studied under Giovanni Bilivert, and was one of the most successful imitators of his style; but he was cut off in the prime of life by the great plague, in 1630, so disastrous to Italy and to art.

SALVETTI, Francesco, a Florentine painter, who flourished in the first part of the 18th century. According to Lanzi, he studied under Antonio Domenico Gabbiani, and was a successful imitator of his style. Little more is known of him.

SALVI, Tarquinio, a painter born at the castle of Sassoferrato, near Urbino, whose history is very obscure. There is a large picture in the church of the Eremitani at Sassoferrato, representing some monks at their devotions, dated 1573.

SALVI, Giovanni Battista, called Il Sassoferrato, from the place of his nativity. Though this eminent painter acquired distinction in his time, and his works are held in high estimation, especially in Italy, there is a surprising contradiction among writers, even of his own country, as to the time of his birth and death, history and merits; therefore, we shall give Lanzi's account, who, considering the life of this painter a desideratum, went to Sassoferrato after he had published the first edition of his History of Painting, where, assisted by the researches of Monsignore Massajuoli, Bishop of Nocera, he obtained much valuable and long desired information. He was the son of Tarquinio Salvi, was born at Sassoferrato, on the 11th of July, 1605, and died at Rome on the 8th of August, 1685. In his life of Carló Dolci, he says, "Dolci holds the same rank in the Florentine as Sassoferrato does in the Roman school. Both, though destitute of great powers of invention, obtained high reputation for Madonnas and similar small subjects, which have now become extremely valuable; for the wealthy, desirous of possessing pictures at once so estimable and religious, to hang up in their oratories, have brought these masters into great request. Carlo is not so celebrated for beauty (for he was a mere naturalist), as for the exquisite pains with which he finished everything, and the genuine expression of certain affecting emotions, such as the patient sufferings of Christ, or of the Virgin Mary, the penitential compunctions of a Saint, or the holy confidence of a martyr, devoting himself as a victim to the living God. The coloring and general tone of his pictures accord with the idea of the passion; nothing is turgid or bold; all is modesty, repose, and placid harmony."

Again, in his life of Sassoferrato, he says: "Sassoferrato excelled Dolci in the beauty of his Madonnas, but yields to him in the fineness of his pencil. Their styles were dissimilar, Salvi having formed himself on different models. He first studied under his father Tarquinio in his native place, then in Rome, and afterwards in Naples; it is not known precisely under what masters, except in his MS. Memoirs we read of one Domenico, at Naples. The period in which Salvi studied corresponds in a remarkable manner with the time in which Domenichino was employed at Naples, and his manner of painting shows that he adopted the style of that master, though not exclusively. I have seen in the possession of his heirs at Sassoferrato, many copies from the first masters, which he executed for his own pleasure. I observed several from Albano, Guido, Baroccio, and Raffaelle, reduced to a small size, and painted, as one may say, all in one breath. There are also some landscapes of his composition, and a vast number of portraits; several of St. John the Baptist, but more than all, of the Madonna. Though not possessing the ideal of the Greeks, he has yet a style of countenance peculiarly appropriate to the Virgin, in which an air of humility predominates, and the simplicity of the dress and the attire of the head corresponds with the expression of the features, without at the same time lessening the dignity of the character. He painted with a flowing pencil, and had a fine relief and chiaro-scuro; but in his local tints he is somewhat hard. He delighted most in designing heads with a part of the bust, which frequently occur in collections; his portraits are very often of the size of life, and of that size, or larger, is a Madonna by him, with the infant Christ, in the Casali palace at Rome. The picture of the Rosario, which he painted at S. Sabina, is one of the smallest pictures in Rome. It is nevertheless well composed, and conducted with unusual spirit, and is regarded as a gem. In other places, the largest picture by him is to be seen in an altarpiece in the Cathedral of Montefiascone." The above admirable account is entirely different from that given by any other author, and perfectly accords with his genuine works. There was another Sassoferrato, a disciple of Gio. Francesco Penni, born in 1504, and died in 1590. It is evident that many of the works attributed to Il Sassoferrato, "executed in a dry manner," were the productions of his father, or the other Sassoferrato. It also reconciles the contradictory accounts of those writers who state that he flourished at a much earlier period.

SALVI, Niccolo, an eminent Roman architec

was born in 1699. After acquiring a liberal education, he entered the school of Antonio Cannevari, where he studied the maxims of Vitruvius, and the best models, both ancient and modern. After making considerable progress, he was entrusted with the erection of a temporary edifice for a festal occasion, representing the Temple of Glory, one hundred and ninety feet high, with four façades of architecture in relief. Cannevari being invited to Portugal by King John V., all of his employments were entrusted to his pupil Salvi, who was appointed pontifical architect. He executed a large number of works at Rome, in a slender, elegant, and simple style, not exempt from defects; among which were the Baptistery of St. Paolo, without the walls, the grand altar of St. Eustachio; and the church of S. Maria in Grado, for the Dominicans of Viterbo. His greatest work, however, was the fountain of Trevi, erected during the pontificate of Clement XII. The Ocean is represented by a gigantic figure standing on a shell, drawn by two marine horses, guided by Tritons; these are in the midst of an immense mass of rocks, from which the water flows in various ways. In the centre is a beautiful niche, with Ionic columns, from which the principal figure appears to issue; on each side are two Corinthian columns, which contain two stories; and between the intercolumniations are the statues and bas-reliefs. Over the entablature are four statues, plumb with the four columns; above, there is an attic with the arms of the Corsini family, and a balustrade at the sides; receding a little on each side are four Corinthian columns, containing two orders of windows; and over the entablature is an attic, lower than that of the centre, with small windows, between which are festoons. According to Milizia, this fountain is rich, superb, and magnificent, justly considered the best work produced at Rome during the 18th century. It occupied Salvi thirteen years, partially in consequence of the intrigues of his enemies, who caused continual interruptions; in order to complete it, he declined designing the façade of the Cathedral at Milan, the superintendence of the royal edifice of the Caserta, and the Reclusorio; he also refused the invitation of the Turin court, to continue the works left unfinished by Ivara. Being constantly obliged to enter the aqueducts of the Acqua Virgine, his naturally delicate constitution was enfeebled by the exposure; he became paralytic, and died in 1751. Among his pupils was Signor Giansimone, afterwards architect of Rome.

SALVIATI, Francesco Rossi, called also Il Salviati, and sometimes Cecchino de' Salviati, an eminent Florentine painter, born in 1510. He was a fellow-student with Giorgio Vasari, first under Andrea del Sarto, and next under Baccio Bandinelli. The two young friends afterwards pursued their studies at Rome with the same intimacy, and adopted similar principles. The genius of Salviati, however, directed him to a more correct design, and to a grander and more animated style than that of his companion, and Vasari himself celebrates him as one of the ablest artists of his time. He soon acquired distinction, and was taken under the protection of the Cardinal Salviati, and permitted to bear the name of his patron. He painted the Annunciation, and Christ appearing to St. Peter, in the church of La Pace, and soon afterwards embellished the vault of the chapel of his patron with a series of frescos representing the History of St. John the Baptist, which added greatly to his reputation. He was employed by the Prince Farnese to execute the cartoons for the tapestry of his palace, in which he represented the History of Alexander. In conjunction with Vasari, he was employed by Pius IV. to decorate the apartments of the Cancellaria with several frescos; and it was the intention of the pope to have confided all the works in the Sala Regia to Salviati, but at the intercession of Michael Angelo, in order to expedite the work, he gave one-half to Salviati, and the other to Ricciarelli. From Rome Salviati, proceeded to Venice, where he executed several works for the public edifices, and others for individuals; the most remarkable of which is the History of Psyche, in the Palazzo Grimaldi, and which Vasari, with a partiality for his friend and countryman, styles *La piu bell' opera de pittura che sia in tutta Venezia.* He afterwards traveled through Lombardy, and made some stay at Mantua, where he was delighted with the works of Giulio Romano in the Palazzo del Te. He next visited Florence, and was employed by the Grand Duke to decorate a saloon in the Palazzo Vecchio, where he represented the Victory and Triumph of Furius Camillus. These works are designed and painted with great genius and spirit, and the accuracy with which he delineated the costumes, habiliments, and arms of the ancient Romans, is worthy of a learned antiquary. At the invitation of the Cardinal de Lorraine, he accompanied that prelate to France, where Francis I. had engaged some of the ablest artists of Italy in the decoration of the Palace at Fontainbleau. He was received with distinction by the French monarch, and treated with great kindness by Primaticcio, the superintendent of the works. He painted a fine picture of the Descent from the Cross, in the church of the Celestines, and was afterwards employed in the palace at Fontainbleau; but he soon quarrelled with his associates, and returned to Rome, where he fell into new contentions with Daniello da Volterra, Pietro Ligorio, and most of the artists of the time. He was a man naturally of a proud, haughty, overbearing, and turbulent disposition, which led him into continual strifes with his cotemporaries, and is said to have shortened his life. The continued agitation of his mind brought on a fever, of which he died at Rome, in 1563.

Salviati painted with equal success in fresco, in distemper, and in oil. His restless disposition did not permit him to remain long in one place after he first left Rome, and his works are widely scattered throughout Italy, in the public edifices, as well as in the palaces of the nobility. He also painted portraits with great success, and his picture of Aretino, the satirist, which was sent to Francis I., gained him immense applause. He possessed a rich and fertile invention, his compositions are original and abundant, and he embellished his works with magnificent architecture. He was one of the few who have been able to combine celerity of pencil with correctness of design, for which he was distinguished, though sometimes bordering on the gigantic. Although he is more esteemed as a designer than a colorist, his carnations are delicate and tender, his figures graceful, and the folding of his draperies broad and simple, without concealing the beauty of his forms. He particutarly excelled in the naked. With the possession of sucn powers, which might, perhaps, have placed him at the head of all his cotemporaries, his rancorous and envious disposition prompted him to vilify the works of others, and to extol his own, and by the injustice and impolicy of his conduct, he frequently had the mortification to find rivals preferred to him whose talents were unworthy of his competition.

SALVIATI, Giuseppe del. See Giuseppe Porta.

SALVIONI, Rosalba Maria, a Roman paintress, born in 1658, and died in 1708. She studied under Sebastiano Conca, but devoted herself entirely to portraits, which she executed in a style of excellence and truthfulness that gained her considerable distinction.

SALVOLINI. See Episcopio.

SALVUCCI, Mateo, a painter who, according to Pascoli, was born at Perugia about 1570, and died about 1628. After acquiring considerable reputation in his native city, he went to Rome, where he was kindly received by the Pope; yet from his inconstant disposition he did not remain long there. No authentic works are mentioned by his biographer.

SALWAY, N., an English mezzotinto engraver, who flourished about 1760, and executed some portraits, which possess considerable merit.

SALY, Jacques François, a French sculptor, born at Valenciennes in 1717. He was invited to the Court of Denmark, where he executed an equestrian statue of King Frederick V., of which there is a print by J. M. Preissler. He also executed several other statues in marble and bronze. He etched, in a spirited style, a set of thirty plates of vases, and four of monuments, from his own designs. He died in 1776.

SAM, Engel or Angelo, a Dutch painter, born at Rotterdam in 1699, and died in 1769. He was a good portrait painter, and is said to have excelled in familiar subjects, in which he imitated the manners of Vanderwerf and Metzu, two very opposite masters, with great success.

HS SAMBIN, Hugues, a French architect, a native of Dijon, who flourished in the latter half of the 16th century. According to the *Biographie Universelle*, he was a scholar of Michael Angelo. In concert with his son-in-law, Gaudrillet, he executed several good works at Dijon, among which were the beautiful portal of the church of S. Michael, and the domes surmounting its three arcades, erected after his designs. In 1572, Sambin published a folio work at Lyons, embellished with thirty-six plates, entitled *Œuvre de la diversité des termes dont on use en architecture.*

SAMACCHINI, Orazio, an eminent painter, born at Bologna in 1532. According to Malvasia, he was a disciple of Pellegrino Tibaldi, but improved himself by studying the works of Correggio, whose style he emulated with success. He was employed to paint in fresco the great chapel in the Cathedral at Parma, contiguous to the famous cupola by that distinguished master. He was invited to Rome by Pius IV., and employed in conjunction with Marco da Siena, and other artists of distinction, to decorate the Sala Regia. Having completed this engagement he returned to his native city, where he executed many admirable works for the churches and palaces, both in oil and fresco. The most remarkable are the Coronation of the Virgin in the church of Sts. Naborre e Felice, so much applauded by the Caracci; the famous Presentation in S. Giacomo Maggiore; the Crucifixion, in La Trinita; an altar-piece of the Last Supper, in the Certosa; and the Fall of Icarus, in the Palazzo Lambertini. The following admirable critique is condensed from Lanzi:

"He more nearly approached Correggio than any Bolognese artist of that age. On proceeding to Rome, he succeeded in catching a taste of the Roman school, for which he was praised by Vasari, and afterwards by Borghini and Lomazzo. In this new style, however, he contrived to please others more than himself, and on his return to Bologna he was accustomed to lament that he had ever removed from upper Italy, where he might have carried his early manner to greater perfection. Still he had no reason to be dissatisfied with what he had gathered and moulded by his own genius, so as to exhibit something novel and singular in every character. In his altar-piece of the Purification, in S. Jacopo, all is exquisite delicacy; the leading figures enchant us by a majestic yet tender expression of piety, while those of the infant figures, seen conversing near the altar, and that of a young girl holding a little basket with two doves, gazing on them in so peculiar a manner, delight us with their mingled simplicity and grace. Skilful judges, even, can take no exceptions, unless it be too great diligence, with which, during several years, he had studied and polished this single picture. This work, as one of the most celebrated of its school, was engraved by Agostino Caracci; and even Guido seems to have availed himself of it, in his Presentation in the Cathedral at Modena. Yet Samacchini was an equally powerful artist when his subject required it. His chapel in the Cathedral at Parma is highly commended, though his most vigorous effort is shown in the ceiling of the church of S. Abbondio, at Cremona. The grand and the terrible seem to strive for the mastery in the figures of the prophets, in all their actions and positions; the most difficult from confinement of space, yet the best arranged and imagined. There is, moreover, a truth in the shortening, and a skilful use of the *sotto in su* (foreshortening of the figures), which appears in this instance as though he had purposely selected the most difficult portion of the art in order to triumph over it. His forte is believed to have consisted in grand undertakings in fresco, on which he impressed, as it were, the seal of a vast spirit, at once resolute and earnest, without altering it by corrections and retouches, with which he labored his oil paintings." He died in 1577, in the prime of life. Vasari erroneously calls his name *Fumaccini*, and Lomazzo *Somachino*.

SAMENGO, Ambrogio, a Genoese painter, who, according to Soprani, studied under Gio. Andrea Ferrari, and was an excellent landscape painter. Lanzi commends his landscapes, which are rare, as he died at an early age.

SAMELING, Benjamin, a Flemish painter, born at Ghent in 1520, and died in 1571. He studied under Francis Floris, and painted history and portraits in the style of his instructor.

SAMMARTINO, SAN MARTINO, or SANMARCHI, Marco, an Italian painter, who flourished in the latter part of the 17th century. He painted landscapes, and history, but particularly excelled in landscapes, ornamented with beautiful little figures in exquisite taste. Lanzi says his works are frequently to be met with throughout Romagna, particularly at Rimini, where he resided some time. He also attempted more extensive works, as seen in his Baptism of Constantine, in the Cathedral of Rimini, and St. John preaching in the Desert, in the College of S. Vincenzio at Venice. He was less successful in these. There is some question as to his real name, and place of nativity. According to the *Guida di Rimino*, he was a Neapolitan, named Sammartino, and his picture in the Cathedral is dated 1680. Zanetti and Guarienti call him by the same name, and say that he was a Venetian; and the last declares that he passed most of his life at Venice. Guarienti, in his next article, gives the name of Marco Sanmarchi, a Venetian who flourished at the same time, and extols him as an excellent landscape and figure painter on a small scale. Malvasia gives the same account. Lanzi has no doubt but they are one and the same artist.

SAN-ANTONIO, Fray Bartolomé de, a Spanish painter, born at Cienpozuelos, in 1708. At the age of fifteen he became a monk of the order of the Trinitarios descalzos, at Madrid, and after studying philosophy and theology, he went to Rome to study painting, the elements of which he had already acquired at Madrid, having a taste and talent for painting. After a residence of six years in Italy, he returned to his convent in 1740, where he spent the rest of his life in embellishing it with many works of a sacred character, both in oil and fresco, which are said to possess great merit.—Those old monks were shrewd fellows; knowing the advantages which superb works of art conferred on their convents, and how much money they brought into their coffers by attracting visiters, they were always liberal patrons of artists, especially when they found a superstitious one, who would exchange his services for their prayers; or a talented novice, whom they could educate. San Antonio died in 1782.

SAN BERNARDO, Il Vecchio di. See Minzocchi.

SANCHEZ, Alonzo, a Spanish painter who, according to Bermudez, was employed in conjunction with three other artists, in painting the beautiful frescos in the University of Alcalá de Henares, founded by Cardinal Cisnéros. In 1508 he was employed in conjunction with Diego Lopez and Luis de Medina, in decorating the Cathedral of Toledo.

SANCHEZ, Clemente, a Spanish painter, who flourished at Valladolid about 1620. He executed some works for the churches and convents, which prove him to have been an able designer and a good colorist. He painted several pictures for the convent of the Dominicans, among which are the Visitation of the Virgin, the Marriage of the Virgin, the Virgin of the Rosary, a Magdalen, and a small oratory, representing the Virgin and Infant, with the infant St. John and other Saints.

SANCHEZ-COELLO. See Coello.

SANCHEZ-COTAN, Fray Juan, an eminent Spanish painter, born at Alcázar de San Juan in 1561. He studied at Toledo, under Blas de Prado, whose style he is said to have imitated. He excelled in painting subjects of still-life, called by the Spanish *bodegones*, consisting of fruit, flowers, fish, game, and vegetables of all sorts, profusely collected in the larder, like those of Snyders, De Vos, Van Utrecht, and other Dutch and Flemish masters. He also painted Madonnas with chaplets of flowers and other similar subjects.—The account of him is so bombastic and confused that no correct opinion can be formed of his merits. His principal works are in the Carthusian monasteries at Paular and Granada; at the Agustinos Calzados in the latter city, and at the Merced Calzada at Seville. He painted many subjects relating to the passion of Christ, the sorrows of the Virgin, sufferings and persecutions of saints, &c. According to Palomino, he painted a picture of the Crucifixion so naturally that (like Zeuxis' grapes) the birds came to light on the cross; and when he painted St. Ildefonso receiving the Miraculous Chasuble from the Virgin, she descended from heaven and honored the painter with a sitting (related on the authority of the monks of the convent). Vincenzio Carducho made a journey from Madrid to Granada, expressly to see him and his works, and he at once singled him out among the monks as the painter he sought for, from the serenity of his countenance being in accordance with the style of his pictures. "This amiable man and excellent artist died at Granada in 1627; he was reckoned one of the most venerable monks, and also one of the best painters of Spain."

SANCHEZ, Felipe, a Spanish architect, who flourished in the latter part of the 17th century. His principal work is mentioned by Milizia—the celebrated Pantheon or sepulchral chapel of the illustrious family dell' Infantado, in the church of S. Francisco at Guadalaxara. The chapel is elliptical, containing twenty-six urns, placed between eight pilasters, also a smaller chapel with four jasper columns; it is composed of the richest materials, and is said to have cost 2,000,000 crowns. Sanchez died in 1696.

SAN DANIELLO, Pellegrino di. See Udine.

SANDBY, Paul, an eminent English painter in water-colors, and engraver in aquatinta, was born at Nottingham in 1732. He went to London at the age of fourteen, and obtained admission into the drawing-room of the Tower, where he studied two years, and made such progress that the Duke of Cambridge, wishing to have a survey made of the north and west parts of the Highlands of Scotland, engaged him as draughtsman to accompany the expedition. During this tour, he made many drawings of the most beautiful and romantic scenery with which those regions abound. From these designs he made etchings, which were published on his return to London, by Messrs. Ryland and Bryce. In 1752 he went to Windsor, where he spent some time, and executed seventy drawings of the scenery, so accurately and tastefully designed that Sir Joseph Banks purchased them all at a liberal price. His reputation was now established, and he executed a great number of scenes in England and Wales, and views of the seats of the nobility and gentry, some of which he engraved himself in aquatinta, and others were engraved by Middiman, Milton, Byrne, and other artists. On the foundation of the Royal Academy, he was elected one of the first forty members. About the same time he was appointed chief drawing master of the Military Academy at Woolwich, which situation he held till his death. He contributed much to the English school of landscape painting, and especially in bringing into vogue water-colored designs, which branch is now highly esteemed in that country. His drawings are still admired, and are only to be found in the choice collections of his country. He also made improvements in the method of engraving in aquatinta. He died in 1809.

SANDRART, Joachim de, an eminent German painter and writer on art, was born at Frankfort in 1606. He was instructed in the elements of design by Matthew Merian and Theodore de Brye. At the age of fourteen he went to Prague, where for some time he devoted himself to engraving under Giles Sadeler, who, finding his genius better adapted to painting than engraving, recommended him to change the graver for the pencil. He accordingly proceeded to Utrecht, and became the disciple of Gerard Honthorst, under whose able instruction he made great progress, and being already well grounded in the first principles of the art, he was soon able to assist him in his works. Descamps asserts that when Honthorst was invited to England by Charles I., Sandrart accompanied him to that court, where he remained till 1627, and executed several works for the king; but this is discredited by Bryan, on the ground that none of his pictures are mentioned in King Charles' collection; what renders it still more improbable, is the fact that Sandrart takes no notice of it in his life of Honthorst, though he mentions that artist's journey to England, and gives an account of the works he executed there. It is certain that he went early in life to Italy, where he resided many years. He first stopped at Venice, where he copied the finest pictures of Titian and Paul Veronese. From Venice he proceeded to Rome, where he acquired a high reputation, as is evident from the fact that when the king of Spain sent an order to Rome for twelve pictures of equal size, to be executed by twelve of the most eminent masters in Italy, Sandrart was selected as one of them, on which occasion he produced his admired picture of the Death of Seneca. The distinguished twelve were Guido, Domenichino, Guercino, Cortona, Lanfranco, Valentino, Poussin, Sacchi, Gentileschi, D'Arpino, Massimi, and Sandrart. To be numbered with such artists was a high honor. Previous to this, however, he obtained the patronage of the Cardinal Barberini, through whose influence he had the honor of painting the portrait of Urban VIII. He was also employed by the Prince Giustiniani, and was entrusted with the superintendence of the engravings of the statues in his gallery. After a long residence at Rome, Sandrart went to Naples, thence to Sicily and Malta, returning by way of Lombardy to Frankfort, where he married. From that city he went to Augsburg, and lastly to Nuremberg, where he permanently settled and established an academy of painting. He executed several works for the Emperor Ferdinand, and for Maximilian, Duke of Bavaria. Here, towards the close of his life, he published several works on the fine arts, for which he had, during his life, been collecting materials, as follows: *Academia Tedesca della Architettura, Scultura, e Pittura*, 4 vols. in 2, folio, Nuremberg, 1675—79; *Iconologia Deorum*, 1680; *Admiranda Sculpturæ Veteris Vestigia*, 1680; *Romæ antiquæ et novæ Theatrum*, 1684; and *Academia Artis Pictoriæ*, 1683, collected from Vasari, Ridolfi, and Van Mander; this last is a Latin translation and abridgment of the *Academia Tedesca.* A uniform edition of all his works was published at Nuremberg, in 8 vols. folio, in German. 1769—75. He executed many works, well designed and colored, which are to be found in Italy, Germany, and the Low Countries. During his residence abroad, he made a multitude of sketches of views after nature, buildings, antiquities, statues, &c., which, together with his pictures and curiosities, brought at public sale after his death 22,721 florins. He died at Nuremberg in 1688, aged 72.

SANDRART, Jacob von, a German engraver, was the nephew of Joachim de S., born at Frankfort in 1630. He first studied with Cornelius Dankerts, and afterwards with William Hondius. He engraved a large number of plates of various subjects, executed with the graver in a neat, clear style. His portraits are his best prints, among which are those of the Emperors Rodolphus II., Ferdinand II., Ferdinand III., Frederick, Prince of Norway, Princess Sophia of Saxony; Ferdinand Maria, Duke of Bavaria; Joachim Sandrart, painter; and Joannes Paulus Auer, painter. A list of his works may be found in Nagler's Lexicon. He died at Nuremberg in 1708.

SANDRART, John Jacob von, was the son of the preceding, born at Ratisbon in 1655. He was instructed in engraving by his father, and derived much advantage in designing, from the lessons of his great uncle Joachim de S. He was an able designer as well as an expert engraver, and possessed a ready and fertile invention. He engraved a considerable number of plates, some of them from his own designs, executed with the graver in a neat, tasteful style. He engraved several of the plates for a work entitled *Suecia Antiqua et Hodierna.* He also executed a number of spirited etchings which embellish the publications of Joachim de S. He died at Nuremberg in 1698. The following are among his most esteemed plates, a full list of which may be found in Nagler:

PORTRAITS.

Elizabeth Henrietta, Princess of Brandenbourg; *after A. Le Clerc.* Silvius Jacob de Dunkelmann; do.

VARIOUS SUBJECTS.

The Holy Family; *after Joachim de Sandrart.* Two subjects of the Origin of Painting; *do.* Two subjects of the Customs and Amusements of the ancient Germans; *do.* Æneas saving his father Anchises from the burning of Troy: *from his own design.*

SANDRART, Lawrence. The name of this artist is affixed to a frontispiece to a set of prints from Ovid's Metamorphoses, by Engelbrecht, published in 1700. He was probably of the same family as the preceding. There was a painter in enamel of this name, who was living in 1710, supposed to be the same artist.

SANDRART, Susan Maria von, was the daughter of Jacob von S., born at Nuremberg in 1658.

She was instructed in the art by her father, and executed several plates to illustrate the works of Joachim de Sandrart. She also engraved a few other subjects, among which are the following: The Assembly of the Gods on the Marriage of Cupid and Psyche, *after Raffaelle;* the Nozze Aldobrandi, after a design *by Bartoli;* a Bacchanalian subject inscribed *Immoderatum dulce Amorum.* She died in 1718.

SANDRO, Jacopo de', a Florentine painter mentioned by Vasari, as an assistant of Buonarotti, in the Sistine chapel. Lanzi says he is the same as Sandro Botticelli, which see.

SANDRINO, Tommaso, a painter born at Brescia in 1575. He distinguished himself as a perspective architectural painter in fresco, and was a good painter of history. His great works are the ceilings of the cathedral, and the churches of S. Domenico and S. Faustino at Brescia. There are several of his works of a sacred character in the public edifices at Brescia, Milan, and Ferrara, skilfully composed, and well designed and colored. He died in 1630.

SANDYS, Edwin, an obscure English engraver, mentioned by Strutt, by whom there is a portrait of Sir William Petty.

SANFELICE, Ferdinando, a noble Neapolitan painter and architect, descended from the Normans, was born at Montagna in 1675. He studied under Solimena, and painted a number of good historical works; he also attained great excellence in representing fruit, landscapes, and perspective views. He patronized Solimena, who painted a saloon in his palace, which afterwards became a gallery for young artists, and was called *The Sanfelice*, after its original possessor. About the time when Philip V. succeeded to the Spanish throne, Sanfelice applied himself to architecture, and made many excellent designs for the festal decorations on the arrival of the monarch at Naples. He afterwards attained a high reputation, and was extensively employed. Among his principal works were the Palazzo Serra; the enlargement of the Palazzo Monteleone; two palaces in the Borgo delle Vergine, and near the Seggio di Montagna; and the façade of St. Lorenzo. He died in 1759.

SAN FRIANO, Maso di. See Manzuoli.

SANGALLO, or SAN GALLO, da, a family of eminent Italian architects, whose original name was Giamberti. Giuliano Giamberti, born at Florence in 1443, was the son of Francesco G., an architect of some repute in the service of Cosmo de' Medici. In concert with his brother Antonio, he first practised carving in wood, and attained some celebrity. Giuliano was next employed in the capacity of a military engineer, by Lorenzo de' Medici, who highly esteemed his abilities. He afterwords devoted himself to architecture, and was employed to erect the cloister of the court of S. Maria Madalena de' Pazzi at Florence, where he introduced an Ionic order, with capitals remarkable for an ornamental necking, at that time an innovation, but copied, according to Milizia, from an ancient capital found near Florence. While in the service of Lorenzo, he visited Naples to present the King a model for some architectural works near the Castel Nuovo; and the monarch was so highly pleased, that he offered him a rich present of horses, clothes, and other valuables, among them, a silver cup, containing a hundred ducats. The architect declined the gifts, saying that he was in the service of Lorenzo de' Medici, who did not value riches. The king, surprised at his honorable independence, insisted on his selecting whatever pleased him, and he therefore chose three antiques—a head of Adrian, a naked female figure, and a sleeping cupid—which, on his return to Florence, he presented to Lorenzo. He was afterwards commissioned by that nobleman to erect a large convent near the gate of San Gallo; whence he obtained the name of *da San Gallo*, at first jestingly bestowed by his patron, but subsequently adopted by himself and all his family. In 1490, Sangallo commenced the Palazzo Gondi for a wealthy merchant of that name, which is highly praised for the beauty of its façade and the elegance of its general proportions. He also erected the Palazzo Imperiale, and was invited to Milan, to build a palace for the Duke, but was prevented by the civil commotions. Sangallo was much patronized by Cardinal della Rovere, for whom he erected a palace at Savona, and several other edifices. During the pontificate of Alexander VI., he restored the soffite of St. Maria Maggiore; and adorned the national church dell' Anima with a square façade of three orders of pilasters. When his patron, the Cardinal della Rovere, became Pope Julius II., Sangallo expected to be appointed architect of St. Peter's; and when Bramante was chosen, he retired in disgust to Florence. He was afterwards recalled by the Pope, and returned to Rome; but not being successful in any important work, he returned to Florence. At the accession of Leo X., Sangallo returned to Rome, and was offered the appointment of architect of St. Peter's; but he declined it, on account of his age and infirmities. He died two years afterwards at Florence, in 1517, aged 74. His abilities were very great, and were very highly esteemed in an age so fruitful in eminent architects. Vasari mentions Francesco Sangallo, a son of Giuliano S., as a skilful sculptor. One of his principal works was the mausoleum erected at Monte Cassino, by order of Clement VII., in honor of Pietro de' Medici.

SANGALLO, Antonio, the brother of Giuliano S., probably born at Florence about 1450. In concert with the latter, he practised wood carving for some time, but was at length induced by him to study architecture. He completed the palace commenced by Giuliano at Savona, and afterwards visited Rome, during the Pontificate of Alexander VI., who commissioned him to convert the mausoleum of the Emperor Adrian into a fortress, called the Castle of St. Angelo. Sangallo displayed such excellent abilities in this work, that his reputation was immediately established, and Duke Valentino, the Pope's son, employed him to erect the fortress of Civita Castellana, and afterwards that of Montefiascone. Among his other works, was a beautiful temple to the Madonna at Montepulciano, and several churches at Monte Sansovino. Sangallo was intimately acquainted with the antique, and improved the Doric order. In the latter part of his life, he relinquished the practice of his profession, on account of bodily infirmities, and devoted himself to agriculture. He died at an advanced age, in 1534.

SANGALLO, Antonio, an eminent Italian architect, the son of Bartolomeo Picconi, was born at Mugello, in the Florentine state, about 1482. He was the nephew, on the maternal side, of the two preceding architects, and adopted their surname. He first learned the carpenter's trade, but dazzled by the fame of his uncles, he went to Rome, and entered their school, where he remained until they left Rome. He afterwards studied under Bramante, to whom, then advanced in years, he soon became of great assistance. According to Milizia, his first work was the church of the Madonna di Loretto, near Trajan's column. His talents attracted the attention of several distinguished personages, among whom was Cardinal Alexander Farnese, (afterwards Pope Paul III.,) who employed him to rebuild his palace in the Campo de' Fiori, the first beginning of that splendid pile, which alone would have established his fame. He afterwards greatly extended it when his patron became Pope, and carried it up to the majestic cornicione, which was subsequently added by Michael Angelo. This noble structure is one of the most magnificent edifices of Rome, and has received the applause of all succeeding ages. The Reform Club House, Pall-Mall, London, though differing in several details, is a good imitation of the Farnese Palace. Sangallo also erected a palace for the Marquis Baldassini, and the Palazzo Pasquino di Santo Buono. In the great island of Lake Bolsena he constructed two small temples, one octangular without, and circular within, the other square without and octangular within, with four niches, at the side faces, with a beautiful altar. In concert with Sanmicheli, he was sent by Clement VII. to fortify Parma and Piacenza. When the Emperor Charles V. passed through Rome, Sangallo directed all the festivals given in honor of that monarch. Before the palace of St. Mark at Venice, he erected a triumphal arch of four Corinthian columns, between which were two victories. In the pediment were two figures in relievo, representing emperors of the house of Austria. It was a most superb work, for invention, proportions, and embellishments in painting and sculpture. For the Duke de Castro he built the fortress of Nepi, raised the streets of that city, and designed a number of private mansions for the citizens. At Rome he executed a number of bastions, and the gate of St. Spirito, a solid and magnificent work, resembling a structure of antiquity. Among his other works at Rome, were the restoration of the Vatican, the erection of the elegant Pauline chapel, so greatly admired for its exact proportions, and a noble palace for himself in the Strada Giulia, now belonging to the Marquis Sacchetti. He was a masterly architect, not only for his taste and elegance, but particularly for the solidity of his works.

At the death of Baldassare Peruzzi, in 1536, Sangallo was appointed sole architect of St. Peter's. With the view of preventing those changes introduced by the preceding architects, the Pope ordered him to prepare a model so large and expensive, that there was no danger of its ever being destroyed or forgotten. After several years, it was completed, at the expense of 4184 crowns; it is fifty-five Roman palms in length (about twenty-eight and a half English feet), and is now preserved in the Vatican. Although Sangallo did not complete the edifice, he enlarged the piers of its foundations, and filled them with a very large amount of solid material, which greatly contributes to the firmness of this immense edifice. In the first volume of Wood's *Letters of an Architect*, there is an elevation of Sangallo's model, which appears very different from the building as subsequently completed. The cupola would have had two orders, one around the tambour, another carried up above the spring of the dome, which also would have been of much lower proportions than the present one; while two lofty and tapering campanili would have been very conspicuous, contrasting, yet harmonizing with the cupola. Although the design was broken into a multiplicity of parts, yet they were agreeably proportioned, tastefully combined, and consistent in character; which is more than can be properly affirmed of the present façade, by Carlo Maderno (q. v.), in which there is a want of agreement between the order itself and the other parts, and also a deficiency in variety of outline. In the latter part of his life, Sangallo was sent by the Pope to settle the disagreement between the inhabitants of Terni and Rieti, concerning their right to the lake of Marmora. He terminated the strife with extreme difficulty, by dividing the lake between them. While remaining at Terni, he was taken ill, and died in 1546. His remains were removed to Rome, and were deposited with great pomp in St. Peter's, near the Sistine Chapel.

According to Milizia, Sangallo had a brother, Antonio Battista Gobbo S., who attained considerable excellence in the art, and usually assisted him in his numerous commissions. He published an edition of Vitruvius, with many marginal notes and well drawn figures.

SANGALLO, Bastiano da, called Aristotile, from his skill in perspective, an Italian painter and architect, was a cousin of the more eminent Antonio S., and born at Florence in 1481. He first studied painting under Pietro Perugino; but after seeing Michael Angelo's cartoon of Pisa, he left the studio of his master, and, like many other artists, commenced studying and copying that celebrated production. Besides copying the principal parts separately, in detail, he made a copy of the entire composition, on a reduced scale, which after a few years became extremely valuable, the original having been destroyed by Baccio Bandinelli. According to Lanzi, he exercised himself for several years in figure painting; he copied several subjects from Michael Angelo and Raffaelle, and executed many Madonnas and other pictures of his own composition. At the instance of his friend Vasari, Sangallo afterwards painted a copy in oil, in chiaro-scuro, of Buonarotti's cartoon, and sent it to Francis I., who with his usual liberality, rewarded the artist in munificent style. The latter work is now in the Earl of Leicester's collection at Holkham and is engraved in Foster's "British Gallery." In the meanwhile, Bastiano began to apply himself to architecture, and joined his brother Giovanni Francesco at Rome, where the latter, then engaged upon the works at St. Peter's, employed him to oversee his business concerns. During his stay at Rome, Bastiano frequently visited Raffaelle, to whom he had been introduced by Giannozzo Pandolfini, bishop of Troia; and when the latter built himself a house at Florence, from the designs of Raffaelle, Giovanni Francesco was employed to conduct the work, which devolved upon Bastiano at his brother's death in 1530. This edifice, the Palazzo Pandolfini, is considered a master piece of art; but its excellence cannot properly be attributed to Bastiano, who was always employed upon works of a temporary character.

Upon settling at Florence, after his return from Rome, Sangallo applied himself to architectural and perspective painting. He was chiefly employed in designing and executing the decorations for numerous festivals, in which he displayed great skill. He afterwards visited Rome, and was employed by his cousin Antonio to superintend some of his works at Castro. For the Cardinal Farnese he executed a fine perspective, and then returned to Florence in 1547, where he died in 1551.

SAN GIMIGNANO, Vincenzio di, a Tuscan painter, who studied at Rome, and was a very successful imitator of Raffaelle. Vasari highly commends him for some façades he painted in fresco at Rome, which have now perished. According to the author above referred to, he returned to his own country on the sacking of Rome in 1527, so broken-hearted and dispirited that we have no account of his subsequent works.

SAN GIORGIO, Eusebio di, a painter who, according to Pascoli, was born at Perugia about 1478, and died about 1550. He was a pupil and imitator of Pietro Perugino, and executed some works for the churches at Perugia and other places, designed in the style of his master, but more feebly colored.

SAN GIOVANNI, Giovanni da. See Mannozzi.

SAN GIOVANNI, Ercole da. See Maria.

SAN GIOVANNI, Oliviero da, a painter who flourished at Ferrara about 1450. He painted both in oil and fresco, and, according to Baruffaldi, executed many works for the churches. His Madonnas and similar subjects were numerous, and much admired.

SANLUCANO, Novella da, a Neapolitan architect, who studied at Rome, and flourished in the latter part of the 15th century. He restored the church of S. Domenico at Naples, removing many of the Gothic parts. His principal work, however, was the palace of Roberto Sanseverino, prince of Salerno, who gave no other direction to the architect than to produce the most sumptuous edifice that had ever been seen. After ten years, in 1480, the palace was completed; it was built of travertine stone, worked so as to resemble the points of a diamond. The princess Isabella Feltri della Rovere afterwards presented this superb edifice to the Jesuitical order.

SANMARCHI. See Sammartino.

SANMICHELI, Michele, a celebrated Italian architect, equally famous in both the civil and military branches of the art, was born at Verona in 1484. He acquired some knowledge of architecture from his father Giovanni and his uncle Bartolomeo, but gained the most improvement by studying the amphitheatre and other remains of antiquity in his native city. At the age of sixteen he visited Rome, where he prosecuted his studies with great assiduity for many years, living on terms of intimacy with Bramante, Michael Angelo, the Sangalli, Sansovino, and others. His first works in that part of Italy, were the cathedral of Monte Fiascone, octangular, beautifully proportioned, with a graceful cupola (subsequently injured by fire, and *restored* in a very inferior style); the famous temple of St. Domenico at Orvieto; and a number of beautiful small palaces in both cities. Having acquired considerable reputation, Sanmicheli was sent, by Clement VII., in company with Antonio Sangallo, to visit the fortifications of the Ecclesiastical States. Having executed this commission, he revisited his native Venetian territory about 1525, and was employed by the republic to construct the new fortifications at Verona, where he introduced a number of improvements, which have been universally adopted throughout Europe, and have totally changed the system of military architecture. Before the time of Sanmicheli, the bastions were always either round or square. He introduced the triangular and pentangular bastions, with plain fosses, flanks, and square bases, which doubled the support. The particular feature of his improvement consists in defending every part of the wall by flanks, rendering the operations of besieging much more hazardous and difficult. Blondel, Vauban, and others, have modified the inventions of Sanmicheli, and have thereby gained a part of the glory which justly belonged to the original inventor. At Verona, he constructed five or six bastions in this manner, which have remained for more than 200 years. His military works are constructed with such solidity, that not a stone has moved. Not content with his first inventions, he went on making other improvements, instructed by his own works, until his fame increased to such a degree that the Duke of Milan repeatedly requested his services of the Venetian Senate, who at length granted him for three months only. While in the Milanese state, he visited Casale de Monferrato, to inspect that city and its strong castle, erected by his cousin Matteo Sanmicheli, an excellent sculptor and architect, who executed the noble marble sepulchre at the church of S. Francesco in that city. The Duke was so highly pleased with his designs and advice, that he loaded him with gifts and honors. Sanmicheli next visited all the fortifications of the Venetian state, restoring and improving them everywhere. At Zara, in Dalmatia, he left his designs to the execution of his nephew Gio. Girolamo S., who, after fortifying the city, erected the admirable fortress of St. Niccolo at the port of Sebenico. Michele also fortified Corfu, Cyprus, Candia, and other islands belonging to the Venetians. Perhaps his most famous military edifice, is the Castello di St. Andrea, built of Istrian stone, with a stately rusticated façade, on the shore of Venice. It appeared impossible that, on so marshy a situation, exposed to the ebb and flow of the tide, an immense fortress could be erected with any hope of security. Accordingly, when the structure was completed, it was reported, and generally believed, that the firing of heavy artillery would destroy the work; whereupon Sanmicheli requested that the fort should be supplied with two tier of the largest cannon, and that they all might be fired at the same moment; which was accordingly done, but without moving a single stone in the building. The Emperor Charles V., and Francis I. of France invited him and his nephew to enter their service, but they declined the alluring offers.

As a civil architect, according to Milizia, the genius of Sanmicheli was sublime. Solidity and convenience, unity, simplicity, and harmony, are conspicuous in all his works. Like Palladio, Michael Angelo, and other great architects, he was faulty in details, particularly in the use of the orders. Milizia says, "his Tuscan architrave and capital are composed of so many members, that they resemble the Doric. The flutes of his Doric columns are too small for the solidity of that order. To the Corinthian he invariably gave modillions and dentils. He also attached his columns in the walls, and placed them on pedestals, higher than those of Vignola, that is, more than a third of the height of the order. Finally, to the Doric he put immense pedestals, with a profusion of ornaments." His interior arrangements are often inconvenient, and sometimes very irregular. Notwithstanding these faults, his exterior architecture exhibits less of mannerism, and more of invention and fine taste, than that of Palladio, particularly in his lofty and majestic rusticated basements. Among his principal edifices at Verona, are the Palazzo Canossa; the Palazzo Bevilacqua, of which the façade is beautifully ornamented; the Palazzo Verzi, and the Palazzo Pompeii, designed in excellent taste. His Capella Guareschi, or Pellegrini, in St. Bernardino is greatly admired, and deserves a particular description. It is a small round Corinthian temple, with three altars, and four niches for statues. The altars, pedestals, pediments, cornices, and the arches themselves, are all circular. The light is admitted by four apertures, each decorated with two columns. Of the eight columns, four have flutes in the regular manner, and the others are entirely plain; all are plain to within about one-third of their length from the bottom, that they might be less liable to injury. The chapel is adorned with beautiful statues. Among his other works at Verona is the beautiful church of the Madonna di Campagna. At Venice, he erected the Palazzo Grimani, and the Palazzo Cornaro at S. Paolo.

During the latter part of his life, Sanmicheli enjoyed in tranquillity the honorable fruits of his labors, esteemed by all for his excellent character, and admired for his surpassing talents. He was suddenly surprised by intelligence of the death of his beloved nephew and pupil Gio. Girolamo Sanmicheli, at the age of forty-four, in the island of Cyprus. Overwhelmed by the shock of this affliction, his powers rapidly failed, and he died a few days after, in 1559, aged 75. His remains were deposited in the church of S. Francesco at Verona.

SANSONE, Il. See Marchesi.

SANSOVINO, Andrea. See Contuccio.

SANSOVINO, Jacopo. See Tatti.

SANTA-CROCE, Francesco Rizzo da. According to Tassi, this painter was a native of Santa Croce, in the Bergamese territory, and flourished from 1507 to 1529; Zani says from 1507 to 1545; Lanzi says the last date of which he can find any account is on a picture in the parochial church of Chirignano, dated 1541. In one of his pictures in the parish church of Endine, he signs himself *Franciscus Rizus Bergomensis habitator Venetiis*, 1529; and another in the parochial church of Serina, *Francesco da Rizo Santa Croce depense*, 1518. Without entering further into the disputes about this artist, suffice it to say that he studied at Venice, under Vittore Carpaccio, and, following the example of his instructor, he adopted a more modern style than was practised by his predecessors, the Bellini. He painted some altar-pieces, which are gracefully composed, delicately colored, and enriched with noble architecture. Zanetti divides him into two artists, but Lanzi says he is evidently in error.

SANTA-CROCE, Girolamo Rizzo da, was doubtless of the same family as the preceding; Federici says he was the father of Francesco; Ridolfi, that they were of the same family; and Tassi, that the dates on his pictures commence later and are traced up later than those of Francesco, viz., from 1520 to 1549; Zani gives the date of one 1549, and says he operated in 1552. Zanetti says he approached nearer to the styles of Giorgione and Titian than any other artist of his time. Others accuse him of retaining something of the ancient Venetian style, but Lanzi vindicates him from this charge, especially in his cabinet pictures of bacchanalian and other subjects. "They display a grace of composition, study of foreshortening and of the naked parts, and a harmony of coloring, forming a mixture of different schools, in which the Roman predominates, and least of all the Venetian. In his celebrated picture of the Martyrdom of St. Lorenzo, he availed himself of the engravings of Marc' Antonio, after Bandinelli and others, but without appearing a mere copyist, for he varied his figures, and especially his landscapes, in which he was very skillful." There are several of his works in the churches at Venice, and in the State, the chief of which are the Martyrdom of St. Lorenzo, in the church of S. Francesco della Vigna, and the Last Supper in S. Martino at Venice; the latter is inscribed *Hieronimo de Sancta Croce*, MDXXXXVIII.

SANTA-CROCE, Pietro Paolo, a painter who flourished at Padua about 1591. According to the *Guida di Padova*, he was of the same family as the preceding. There are some of his works in the churches of Padua, which Lanzi says show that he was attached to the school of Cavagna, or at least to the less mannered class of Venetian artists. He also painted pictures of Madonnas, Holy Families, &c., for the collections. There were several other artists of this name, of little note.

SANTAFEDE, Francesco, a Neapolitan painter who, according to Dominici, was the disciple of Andrea Sabbatini, whose style he followed with great success. He executed many works for the churches, which are well designed; his attitudes are elegant and select, his coloring fresh and vigorous, and his masses of light and shadow conducted with intelligence. Lanzi says that, in point of coloring, he has few equals in the Neapolitan school, and his works possess a singular uniformity of style. One of his best works is the Coronation of the Virgin, in the church of S. Maria la Nuova. He flourished in the last half of the 16th century.

SANTAFEDE, Fabrizio, was the son of the preceding, born at Naples in 1560. After receiving instruction from his father, he became the scholar of Francesco Curia, and next went to Rome, where he devoted two years to the study of the works of the best masters. On his return to Naples he acquired a high reputation, and was employed in executing many works for the churches and public edifices, which are highly commended by Dominici in his Lives of the Neapolitan Artists. The principal of these are the Nativity, and the Angel appearing to the Shepherds, in La Nunziata; the Adoration of the Magi, in S. Maria de Constantinopoli; and the Deposition from the Cross, in the possession of the Prince di Somma. Though he acquired a higher reputation than his father, the experienced discover in the works of the latter more vigor of expression, and a better effect of light and shadow. He died in 1636.

SANTAGOSTINO, Giacomo Antonio, a Milanese painter, born, according to Orlandi, about 1588, and died in 1648. He studied under Giulio Cesare Procaccini, whose style he adopted. He acquired considerable reputation, and executed several works for the churches at Milan, particularly in S. Lorenzo Maggiore, S. Maria del Lantazio, and in S. Vittore; but he wrought more for individuals. He had two sons, Agostino and Giacinto, both of whom he instructed in the art. Lanzi says they were good artists, and distinguished above most of their cotemporaries. They sometimes wrought together, as in the church of S. Fedele, where they painted two grand histories; at other times separately, and each executed several works for the churches. Agostino was the most distinguished; he wrote a work upon the paintings of Milan, entitled *L'Immortalità e Gloria del Pennello.* Lanzi says "his pictures exhibit him in the light of a good painter of his time; in particular a Holy Family in St. Alessandro, and a few others among the more highly finished, in which he displays expression, beauty, and harmony, although he is somewhat too minute."

SANTARELLI, Gaetano, a painter of noble birth, and a native of Pescia. Having a passion and a talent for painting, he studied with Ottaviano Dandini at Florence, under whom he made great progress. He next went to Rome for improvement, and executed some works which gave earnest of distinction, had he not died there in the flower of his life.

SANTARELLI, Giovanni Antonio, a distinguished Italian engraver on gems, was born at Manopello, in the territory of Abruzzo, in 1759. He was placed at an early age under a painter of Chieti; but having little inclination for that art, he determined to learn to engrave on gems, and accordingly set out for Rome. On arriving in that city, he made several attempts, which excited the admiration of Pikler, and Santarelli was admitted to the studio of that artist, who is said to have frequently attached his own signature to the works of his pupil. After remaining several years under Pikler, he established a studio at Rome, and soon attained distinction. Among his principal productions are the heads of Dante, Petrarch, Boccaccio, Michael Angelo, and Machiavelli, which are now in the Louvre; also a number of medals. In 1797 he visited Florence, and was appointed a Professor in the Academy of Fine Arts. He was honored with the knighthood of the Order of the Reunion by Napoleon, and with membership in the Legion of Honor by Louis XVIII.; was associated to the academies of Berlin, Vienna, and St. Luke at Rome. Santarelli resided many years at Florence, instructing his pupils in the art, until 1826, when he died.

SANTELLI, Felice, a painter of Rome, of whom little is known. He painted in competition with the Cav. Giovanni Baglioni, in the church of the P. P. Spagnuoli del Riscatto Scalzi at Rome. There are also some of his works in churches in the State, particularly in S. Rosa at Viterbo, which Lanzi says show a painter full of truth. He flourished in the first part of the 17th century.

SANTERRE, Jean Baptiste, a French painter, born at Magny, in Pontoise, in 1651. He was a pupil of Bon Boullongne, and, though deficient in readiness and fertility of invention, he studied after nature with great assiduity, and attained considerable excellence. He painted women and young girls with success, in portraits and domestic subjects, carefully and correctly designed, and colored with greater harmony than the works of his cotemporaries. He also painted several historical works, among which are St. Theresa, in the chapel at Versailles; a penitent Magdalene, in the King's collection; and Susanna and the Elders, his reception-piece at the Academy, formerly in the hall of that institution, and now in the Louvre. Santerre died at Paris in 1717.

SANTI, or SANTO, de Titi. See Titi.

SANTI, Antonio, a painter born at Rimini, who studied with Carlo Cignani at Bologna. Lanzi says there are some of his works at Rimini, where he is extolled as one of the best pupils of his master. He died young at Venice in 1700.

SANTI, Bartolomeo, a painter of Lucca, who flourished in the first part of the 18th century. He was an imitator of Pietro da Cortona, and excelled in ornamental and perspective painting. He was much employed in theatrical and other decorations.

SANTI, Domenico, called Il Mengazzino, an eminent perspective and architectural painter, born at Bologna, according to Orlandi, in 1621, and died in 1694. He studied under Agostino Metelli, whom he very nearly equalled. He executed many perspective and architectural pieces for the churches and palaces, in which the figures were sometimes inserted by Giuseppe Metelli, Gio. Antonio Burrini, but oftener by Domenico Maria Canuti. He also painted many pictures of a smaller size for the collections at Bologna, which are highly esteemed, and frequently mistaken for the works of his master. Bartsch attributes to him four prints, viz.: the portraits of Simone Cantarini, and of Lodovico, Agostino, and Annibale Caracci; the first only has his name in full, the second and third are marked *Canutus*, and the fourth with the word *Libertas.*

SANTIAGO - POLMÁRES, Don Francisco Xavier de, a Spanish painter and designer, born at Toledo in 1728, and died at Madrid in 1796. He painted, in oil, four views of Toledo, a number of landscapes, and several portraits of distinguished persons. He also designed many frontispieces, which embellish the books published in Spain in the last half of the 18th century.

SANTINI, called the Elder and the Younger, two painters, father and son, who flourished at Arezzo in the 17th century. Lanzi says there are some of their works in the churches at Arezzo, executed in a style much resembling that of the Florentine painters of the same epoch.

SANTIS, Orazio di, an Italian engraver, supposed to have been a native of Aquila, and flourished, according to the dates on his prints, from about 1568 to 1584. Bartsch describes 17 prints by him, mostly *after Pompeo dell' Aquila*, and supposes there are others which have not come to his knowledge, Nagler says that, in conjunction with Cherubino Alberti, he engraved a set of seventy-four plates after the antique statues in Rome, published in 1584. There is great inequality in the prints of this artist, both in the management of the burin, and the care with which they are executed; yet they have such a striking resemblance, in general effect, to those of Alberti, that they may easily be mistaken for his works, and it is very probable he was a pupil of that master.

SANTISSIMO-SACRAMENTO, FRAY JUAN DEL, a Spanish painter, born at Puente de Don Gonzalo in Cordova, in 1611. His real name was Juan de Guzman. After studying at Cordova, he went to Rome, where he does not seem to have profited much from the study of the antique, or the works of Raffaelle. He returned to Spain in 1634, and went to reside at Seville, where, taking part in a revolt, he was obliged to seek refuge in the convent of the Carmelites Calzados (shod Carmelites), and assume the habit of the order with the above name. His restless and turbulent disposition soon caused his superior to send him to the convent of the Carmelites Descalzos (barefooted Carmelites), at Aguilar, where a severe discipline converted him into a *humble and pious monk*. He was employed in decorating that convent and others of his order. In 1666 he went to Cordova, and spent eleven years in executing works for the convent of his order, and for the palace of the bishop, and other places in his diocese. He returned to Aguilar in 1677, where he died in 1680. His works gave great satisfaction to his brethren, but they possess little merit beyond brilliant coloring, in which he is said to have emulated Rubens and Vandyck. He had a poor invention, and made up his compositions by plagiarisms from prints, and his drawing is very defective.

SANTO-DOMINGO, FRAY VINCENTE DE, a Spanish painter who died about 1550. Little is known of him. He was a monk of the order of the Geronomytes, decorated the walls of his cloister with chiaro-scuros, and executed some paintings for the convent of S. Catalina de Talavera de la Reyna at Logrono. He was the first instructor of the illustrious Navarette, called El Mudo. The four superb paintings in the church de la Estrella, formerly attributed to Santo Domingo, are now ascertained to have been painted by El Mudo while he resided at Logrono, for the benefit of his health, by the permission of Philip II., in 1569.

SANTOS, JUAN, a Spanish painter, who flourished at Cadiz about 1662. No idea can be formed of his style or merits from the account given by his biographer, Bermudez, which is, in substance, that he was a fresco painter, and much employed in painting standards for vessels sent to Spanish America and elsewhere. "He also painted pretty little pictures to please certain ladies of Andalusia, who in point of taste are not inferior to those of any country, and consequently such pictures taxed both the ingenuity and delicacy of the painter to give satisfaction to his amiable employers." He probably decorated their fans.

SANTO, GIROLAMO DA. See PADOVA.

SANTVOORT, ANTHONY. There were two obscure Dutch painters of this name; the first flourished about 1550, and the second about 1661. Strutt mentions a print representing an Almanac-seller, with a town and church in the back-ground, neatly etched in a style resembling that of Hollar, signed *A. Santvoort.*

SANTVOORT, DIRK VAN, a Dutch painter, supposed to have been a son of the latter Anthony S.; but this is very doubtful, as there are prints after his works by Theodore Matham and Jonas Suyderhoef, which show that he must have flourished long before the death of his supposed father. He painted history and portraits, somewhat in the manner of Rembrandt. The accounts of him are very meagre. There were two other obscure painters named Santvoort, who flourished at a later period.

SANUTO, or SANUTUS, GIULIO, an Italian engraver, who flourished at Venice from about 1530 to 1540, and probably later. Zani says he was living in 1580. He engraved quite a number of prints, which are executed in a coarse, heavy style, with single strokes without any hatching, resembling a wooden cut. The following are all that are mentioned by Bartsch, Nagler, and others:

A print of the Birth of a monstrous Child, inscribed *Jul. Sanutus Venet, fec.* Venus and Adonis; *after Titian.* Apollo and Marsyas; *after Correggio*; in three sheets. The Marriage of the the Virgin; *after Raffaelle;* with the engraver's mark. The Massacre of the Innocents, signed BACCIUS BRANDIN INVEN., and Marc' Antonio's cipher. The monstrous Child, signed *Jul. Sannutus Venet Fac.* The birth of this monstrous child took place at Venice in 1540; the mother was a German. Two winged Genii in the air, supporting a Globe, on which Cupid stands discharging an Arrow to the left of the print; no name of engraver. Dance of Bacchanals in a Wood; signed JULIUS SANNUTUS, F. Apollo and Marsyas, *after Correggio*, with the Parnassus, *after Raffaelle*, in three sheets. The story of Apollo and Marsyas, from which the engraving was taken, ornamented the case of a harpsichord. The Martyrdom of St. Lawrence. St. John the Baptist. The Tree of Life. Venus restraining Adonis. A Vase with two handles, ornamented with festoons and figures. The Punishment of Tantalus. The dead body of Christ supported by the Virgin and Angels; *after Michael Angelo;* it is in the collection of H. R. Willet, Esq.

SANZ, AUGUSTIN, an eminent Spanish architect, born at Saragossa in 1724. He studied the theory of his profession in the School of Design established in his native city at the expense of the sculptor Ramirez, and acquired a knowledge of the practical part under Raymundo Cortes, surveyor-general of the public buildings. He gained his greatest advantage, however, from the advice and instruction of Ventura Rodriguez, when the latter was engaged at Saragossa in erecting the chapel del Pilar. His reputation gradually increased, and he was employed by government and by private individuals. In 1775 he was chosen a member of the Academy of S. Ferdinando, and in 1792, at the formation of the Academy of St. Luis, he was appointed Director of that institution. He discharged the duties of his important office with fidelity, doing much towards eradicating the prejudices and corrupt taste of the preceding period, and towards introducing a better style. He was appointed by government to inspect all designs for public buildings proposed to be erected in Arragon. Among his principal works are the churches at Urrea and Binaces; and the church of Santa Cruz at Saragossa, in the form of a Greek cross, of the Corinthian order. Sanz died in 1801, leaving a son named Matias S., who was also an architect. He erected, among other works, the façade of the church at Epila, left incomplete by his father.

SANZIO, RAFFAELLE. See RAFFAELLE.

SARABIA, Diego Sanchez, a Spanish architectural designer and painter of familiar subjects, who resided at Granada, and in 1762 was elected a member of the Academy of San Ferdinando in that city. By the desire of that body, he made plans of that magnificent monument of Moorish art, the Alhambra, and of the elegant Greco-Roman Circus of Charles V., at Granada. He also copied all the ornaments, bassi-relievi, and ancient oil paintings that adorn those edifices. These works were presented to Charles III., who was so pleased with their execution, that he commanded the originals to be preserved in the Academy, and copies to be made for himself. Sarabia executed some cabinet pictures of various subjects, in all of which his predilection for architecture is exhibited. He died at Granada in 1779.

SARABIA, José de, a Spanish painter, born at Seville in 1618, according to Palomino, but Bermudez says in 1608. He first studied with Augustin del Castillo, and on the death of that master, with Francisco Zurbaran. He acquired a high reputation in his day, and executed many works for the churches and convents of Seville and Cordova. Though he was not deficient in merit, he was a shameless plagiarist. He frequently took his subjects from the prints of the Sadelers and others, and imposed them on the ignorant as his own inventions. He thus copied the Nativity and another picture from prints *after Rubens*, for the monastery of S. Francisco at Seville, and the Elevation of the Cross, by the same master, for the convent de Arrizaffa. His best original work is the Flight into Egypt, in the convent de la Victoria at Seville. It is so beautifully designed, colored, and handled, as to cause regret that he had not avoided such glaring acts of piracy, and confined himself entirely to his own compositions. He died at Cordova in 1669.

SARACINO, or SARACENI, Carlo, called also from his birth-place, Carlo Veneziano, a painter born at Venice, according to Orlandi, in 1585. He first studied at Venice, and then went to Rome, and placed himself under the instruction of Camillo Mariani, but he afterwards adopted the manner of Caravaggio. He acquired considerable reputation, and was employed to execute many works, both in oil and fresco, for the churches of Rome, and the palaces of the nobility. Lanzi says he displayed a Venetian taste in his figures, dressing them richly in the Levant fashion, and was fond of introducing into his compositions corpulent persons, eunuchs, and shaven heads. In conjunction with the Cav. Lanfranco, he painted several frescos for the pontifical palace of Monte Cavallo, which are considered his best performances. His other principal works at Rome are the Death of the Virgin, in the church of S. Maria in Trastavere; and the Virgin and Infant, with St. Anne, an altar-piece in a chapel of the church of S. Simone. He was next invited back to Venice, to paint a grand picture in the Council Chamber, but he did not live to finish it. He died in 1625. Baglioni says he died in 1585, aged about 40—evidently an error or a misprint into which others have fallen, as Lanfranco was born in 1581. Zani says he was born in 1585, and died in 1625, which dates are doubtless correct. He is said to have executed a few spirited etchings from his own designs, but there is no certainty with regard to the prints attributed to him.

SARAZIN, Jacques, a French sculptor, born at Noyon in 1590. He studied under the elder Guillain at Paris; and afterwards visited Italy for improvement. Finding a protector in the Cardinal Aldobrandini, nephew of Clement VIII., he was commissioned to execute for the villa of that prelate, at Frascati, two colossal statues of Atlas and Polypheme. He studied the works of Michael Angelo, and was assisted by the counsel of Domenichino, when executing some sculptures at the portal of S. Andrea della Valle, while the latter was engaged in painting the vault of that church. After a residence of eighteen years at Rome, Sarazin returned to France, and while stopping at Lyons, executed the statues of St. John and St. Bruno, for the Carthusian monastery. On arriving at Paris, in 1628, he soon gained reputation, and was employed by the Cardinal de Richelieu, the Marechal d' Effiat, and others. At the instance of Desnoyers, he executed eight grouped Caryatides for the Louvre, which were distinguished for lightness and elegance of the figures, and gained for the artist a pension from the king, with apartments in the Louvre. Queen Anne of Austria commissioned him to execute a group in gold and silver, of an Angel presenting the Infant to the Virgin; and in 1643 he modelled the statues of two Angels in silver, supporting the heart of Louis XIII., in the church of S. Louis de la Rue St. Antoine, distinguished for elegant proportions and beautiful draperies. Sarazin acted an important part in the establishment of the Royal Academy of Painting, and was appointed Rector, at the establishment of that office in 1655. Besides the works already mentioned, he executed the following, highly praised by French writers. The mausoleum of Cardinal de Berulle, adorned with bas-reliefs representing the Sacrifice of Noah; two groups of Children playing with goats, formerly at Marly; the mausoleum of Henry de Bourbon, Prince of Condé, decorated with figures of Religion, Justice, Piety, and Strength, and several bas-reliefs of the Triumphs of Fame, Time, Death, and Eternity. Sarazin made some attempts at painting, and produced several pictures of very inferior merit. He died at Paris in 1660.

SARDI, Giuseppe, an Italian architect, was a native of Morco, near Como, and flourished in the latter part of the 17th century. He was appointed architect to the Venetian republic, and executed a number of works in that city, among which were the façades of the church of the Carmelites, of S. Maria de Zobenigo, and of the Beggar's Hospital. Sardi died in 1699.

SARRABAT, D., a French painter, was born at Paris in 1667. He flourished chiefly at Lyons, where he left many historical paintings in oil and fresco. He died at Lyons in 1747.

SARRABAT, Isaac, a French mezzotint engraver, born at Andely, according to Laborde, in 1670, though others say in 1680. One of his best prints, the portrait of M. Choiseul Praslin, is dated 1695. He was one of the earliest artists of his country who practised that method of engraving. Dumesnil gives descriptions of twenty-eight prints by him, mostly portraits. Bryan says his prints are indifferently executed, but Laborde ranks him among the most eminent engravers in mezzotinto.

SARRAGON, John, a Dutch engraver, who flourished about 1645. Only two prints are known by him, the portraits of Adrian Hoffer, and G. U. Bergizomius. They are neatly executed in the style of James William Delft.

SARTI, Antonio, a painter who, according to Baldassini, flourished about 1600, and executed some good works for the churches in Romagna. Lanzi also commends him particularly for his picture of the Circumcision in the collegiate church of Massaccio.

SARTI, Ercole, called Il Muto di Ficarolo, an eminent painter born at Ficarolo, in the duchy of Ferrara, in 1593. He was deaf and dumb from his nativity, and, notwithstanding this misfortune, he early exhibited a passion for the fine arts, and the only amusement that seemed to interest him was the attempt to imitate prints and other objects that fell in his way. At the age of fifteen, without any aid or assistance, and without the knowledge of any person, he painted a picture representing the Adoration of the Magi, and on the occasion of a festival and grand procession, he placed it in front of his father's house. The excellence of the production, under the circumstances, excited universal admiration and astonishment, and the young aspirant was immediately placed in the school of Carlo Bononi, an eminent historical painter at Ferrara, under whose instruction he made rapid progress. He afterwards studied with Ippolito Scarsellino, whose works he particularly admired. He acquired a high reputation for the merit of his works under the singularity of his circumstances, and his praise was celebrated by the poets of his country. He executed several works for the churches of Ferrara and Ficarolo, particularly for the church of the Benedictines in the latter city. His best works are said to combine the correct design of Bononi with the rich coloring of Scarsellino. He also excelled in portraits, and was much employed by the nobility and wealthy citizens of Ferrara. The time of his death is not exactly known; some place it in 1637; Zani says he was living in 1650.

SARTO, Andrea Vannuchi del, a celebrated painter, born at Florence in 1488. His real name was Andrea Vannuchi, but he was called *del Sarto* from the occupation of his father, who was a tailor. Showing an early taste for drawing and designing, he was placed with a goldsmith, to learn ornamental plate engraving. In this situation he was found by Gio. Barile, a wood engraver and a painter of little note, who persuaded his fathe to entrust his son to his instruction. He studied with this master three years, and then became the disciple of Pietro di Cosimo. He, however, derived more advantage from studying the works of Masaccio, Il Ghirlandaio, Leonardo da Vinci, and Michael Angelo, particularly the two latter, than from his instructors. While with Cosimo, it was his custom to devote every holy-day to designing after the cartoons of da Vinci and Buonarotti. On leaving Cosimo, which the morose temper of that painter compelled him to do sooner than he would have done, he formed an intimacy with Francesco Bigio, who had been a disciple of Mariotto Albertinelli, and in conjunction with him, he executed several works for the churches and convents of Florence, both in oil and fresco, and each successive work showed decided improvement, and added to his reputation. Lanzi says, "this artist demonstrates the ascendancy of native genius over precept. When a boy, he was put under the tuition of Gio. Barile, a good carver on wood, employed on the ceilings and doors of the Vatican, after the designs of Raffaelle, but a painter of no celebrity. While still a youth, he was consigned to Pier di Cosimo, a practical colorist, but by no means skillful in drawing or composition; hence the taste of Andrea in those arts was formed on the cartoons of Vinci and Buonarotti, and as many circumstances indicate, on the frescos of Masaccio and Ghirlandaio, in which the subjects were more suited to his mild disposition; it is also certain that he went to Rome, and improved himself by contemplating the works of Raffaelle. His progress from one perfection in art to another was thus not sudden, as has happened to some artists, but was gradually acquired during many years at Florence." This is illustrated in his frescos in the Compagnia dello Scalzo, and in the convent of the Servi, where his pictures executed at different periods are to be seen. At the Scalzo, he painted a series of twelve pictures from the life of St. John the Baptist, in chiaro-scuro, the cartoons of which are still preserved in the Palazzo Rinuccini. The first of the series, the Baptism of Christ, discovers some palpable imitations, and even some whole figures, copied from Albert Durer; the Visitation of the Virgin, painted some years after, shows a conspicuous improvement; and the Nativity of St. John, the last of the series, is painted in his best and broadest manner. The same thing is to be observed in his works in the convent of the Servi, where he painted a series of ten pictures from the Life of St. Filippo Benizi, which Lanzi says are very beautiful productions, though among the earlier efforts of his genius. In the same edifice are his pictures of the Epiphany and the Birth of the Virgin, which are among his most finished works. Also the *Madonna del Sacco*, so called from the sack of grain on which St. Joseph leans, than which few pictures are more celebrated; it has frequently been engraved, but justice was never done to its merits till Raphael Morghen executed his famous print from it, as a companion to the Transfiguration of Raffaelle. "Both prints," says Lanzi, "are in the best collections, and to those who have not been at Rome or Florence, Andrea appears rather a rival than an inferior to the prince of painters. On examining this picture closely, it affords an endless scope for observation; it is finished as if intended for a cabinet; every hair is distinguished every middle tint lowered with consummate art each outline marked with admirable variety and grace; and amidst all this diligence, a facility is conspicuous that makes the whole appear natural and unconstrained." There is a good deal of contradiction among writers as to the history of this artist's life. Some assert that immediately after he dissolved his connexion with Bigio, he was commissioned to execute the works at the Scalzo, before mentioned, and next the ten pictures from the life of St. Filippo Benizi for the Servi. But it is evident from the above account, taken from Lanzi that they were executed at different times, and some of them when he was at the very height of his career. It has been erroneously asserted by some that he never went to Rome. Vasari expressly asserts that he did visit that city, though he does not mention the time, and that "on seeing the works of the scholars of Raffaelle, his natural timidity induced him to despair of ever being ab to equal them, so that he suddenly returned to Florence." Lanzi says, "he went to Rome, I know not in what year, but that he was there appears not, as in the case of Correggio, to admit of dispute." Others say that, notwithstanding his constant employment at Florence, he could not resist the temptation to see the works of Raffaelle at Rome, whither he went, and examined everything with attention and a critical eye, not only the frescos of Raffaelle, but those of Buonarotti, and the antique sculptures. It is probable that he did not remain long in that metropolis, as it is not known that he executed any work there. It is said that soon after his return from Rome he executed his Descent of the Holy Ghost and the Birth of the Virgin, for the church of the Servi, and his Last Supper, for the monastery of St. Salvi, one of his greatest works. Lanzi reports of this picture, that, "at the siege of Florence in 1529, the soldiers, after having destroyed the suburbs of the city where the convent was situated, and demolished the church and a part of the monastery, on approaching the refectory they were astonished at beholding this Last Supper, and had not the resolution to destroy it; thus imitating Demetrius, who at the siege of Rhodes respected nothing but a picture of Protogenes."

He executed many works both in oil and fresco for the churches, convents, and palaces of Florence, and he received commissions from other cities. In the Ducal palace at Poggio a Caiano there is a fresco representing Cæsar seated in a grand hall, ornamented with statues, to whom a great variety of exotic birds and wild animals are presented as the tribute of his victories. Lanzi says, "this picture alone is sufficient to mark Andrea as a painter eminent in perspective, in a knowledge of the antique, and in every excellence in the art." There are also other frescos in the same edifice. The order for decorating this edifice came from Leo X.; and Andrea having for his competitors Francesco Bigio and Pontormo, exerted all his energies, and with such success, that they retired from the field. Francis I. of France gave him a commission for a picture, and he executed and transmitted to that monarch the admirable Pietà, or Dead Christ, with the Virgin, St. John, and Mary Magdalene, which now adorns the Louvre. This picture was universally admired at the court of France, and the King invited him to Paris. Andrea, at that time, reduced to a state of penury by the troubles of his country, and the small remuneration he was enabled to obtain for his works, or, perhaps, by the extravagance of a termagant wife, gladly accepted the alluring invitation of a prince characterized for his munificence and liberal encouragement of the arts. On his arrival at Paris, he was received with the most flattering distinction. He painted a portrait of the Dauphin, and an exquisite picture of Charity, now in the French Museum, for which he was munificently rewarded. He also executed some works for the nobility, and the Queen mother gave him a commission for a picture of St. Jerome. In the midst of all this prosperity, he received letters from his wife, which determined him to return to Florence. It is said that under pretext of his domestic affairs requiring his presence in Italy, he solicited and obtained the King's permission to depart with a promise of a speedy return with his family to Paris, and that the monarch, anxious to profit by his judgment and taste, confided to him a large sum to purchase for him rare works of art; that he forgot his engagements, violated every tie of honor, and squandered the King's money, till at length reduced to indigence and distress, and stung with the recollection of his folly, perfidy and ingratitude, he fell into a state of despondency, which was increased by his jealousy of his wife; that he was ultimately abandoned by her and all his false friends with whom he had wasted his substance, and that his miseries were finally terminated by the great plague which devastated Florence in 1530. The misfortunes of Andrea, could they be truly related, would doubtless vindicate his character in a great measure, and excite compassion for his lot. He was naturally of a mild and timid disposition. He married a woman of exquisite beauty, of whom he was passionately fond, and who ruled him with an iron rod. She was a very shrew; her extravagance kept him in continual poverty, and her conduct excited his jealousy. Vasari, who had been his pupil, and could not but know the truth, expressly says, in the first edition of his work, that, "Andrea was despised by his friends, and abandoned by his employers from the time of his marriage with this woman, (Lucrezia del Fede); the slave of her will, he left his father and mother to starve; through her arrogance and violence, none of his scholars could continue with him long." In his second edition, though he omitted this censure, he repeated, that she was a perpetual source of misfortune to her husband. He repeated that Andrea was invited to the French court by Francis I., "where, caressed and rewarded, he might have excited the envy of every artist, but influenced by the womanish complaints of Lucrezia, he returned to Florence, and remained in his own country, in violation of his faith solemnly pledged to that monarch. He afterwards repented, and was anxious to regain his former situation, but his efforts were ineffectual, and he dragged out a miserable existence amidst jealousy and domestic wretchedness, until abandoned by his wife, and every other individual, he was infected with the plague, and died in 1530, in the forty-second year of his age, and had a very mean funeral." Lanzi says, in concluding the life of this artist, "so much genius merited success; and a book written on the misfortunes of painters, as has already been done on those of authors, would awaken compassion for the fate of Andrea. The poverty of Correggio is exaggerated, or perhaps, untrue; the misery of Domenichino had a termination; the Caracci were illy rewarded, but they lived in easy circumstances; Andrea, from his marriage with Lucrezia del Fede, until his death was almost always pressed with griefs."

There is also considerable discrepancy as to the real merit of this painter. It has been asserted by some, that had he possessed the advantages of better early instruction, a longer residence at Rome, and more fortunate domestic relations, he would have equalled the greatest masters of the art; others declare that he was barren of invention, and that he wanted that elevation of conception, which constitutes the epic in painting as well as in poetry. Vasari says "he was the most faultless painter of the Florentine school. He perfectly understood the principles of chiaro-scuro, representing the indistinctness of objects in shadow, and painting with a sweetness truly natural. He taught how to give a perfect union to frescos, and in a great measure, obviated the necessity of retouching them when dry, a circumstance which gives all his works the appearance of having been finished in one day." Lanzi says "he undoubtedly wanted that grandeur of conception which constitutes the highest rank in painting. Deficient in this talent, Andrea is said to have been modest, elegant, and embued with sensibility; and it appears that he impressed this character on nature, wherever he employed his pencil. The portico of the Nunziata, transferred by him into a gallery of inestimable value, is the fittest place to judge of his chaste outlines that procured him the surname of *Andrea the faultless*. Conceptions of graceful countenances, whose smiles remind us of the simplicity and grace of Correggio; appropriate architecture; draperies adapted to every condition, and cast with ease; popular expressions of curiosity, of astonishment, of confidence, of compassion, and of joy, never transgressing the bounds of decorum, understood at first sight, and greatly affecting the mind without agitating it, are charms that are more readily felt than expressed."

The fresco works of Andrea del Sarto abound in the churches, public edifices and palaces of Florence, and his easel pictures are numerous, and scattered throughout the principal galleries of Europe. He possessed an extraordinary talent for imitating and copying the works of other masters. Of this Vasari relates a remarkable instance, of which he himself was an eye witness, while studying with Andrea, and which affords a striking lesson to those connoisseurs who pretend to infallibility. Raffaelle had painted for the Cardinal Giulio de' Medici, afterwards Clement VII., the portrait of Leo X., seated between that prelate and Cardinal Rossi. Frederick II., Duke of Mantua, in passing through Florence to Rome, having seen this picture, and being captivated with it, requested Clement VII. to give it to him, whereupon the Pope gave directions to Ottavio de' Medici to send it to Mantua. Unwilling to deprive Florence of so interesting a work, Ottavio employed Andrea to make a copy of it, which he sent to the Duke of Mantua, while Giulio Romano was in his service, who had painted the background and draperies in the original picture. No person suspected the deception; even Giulio himself was deceived, and could only be convinced of the fact, by Vasari's assuring him that he had seen it painted, and by his pointing out to him the private mark of Andrea del Sarto. There is an etching of a Holy Family, in which the Virgin is represented kneeling before the Infant Christ, with St. Joseph and St. John, inscribed *Andrea del Sarto in Roma;* though neatly executed, it is considered spurious.

SARTORIUS, Francis, a painter of horses, dogs, and sporting pieces, who flourished in England in the latter part of the 18th century. Many of his pieces were engraved in mezzotinto and aquatinto.

SARTORIUS, Jacob Christopher, a German engraver, who flourished at Nuremberg, according to the dates on his prints, from about 1670 to 1737; so that there were probably two engravers of this name, father and son. The prints referred to consist of portraits and other book illustrations indifferently executed.

SARZANA, Il. See Fiasella.

SARZETTI, Angiolo, a painter of Rimini, who flourished in the latter part of the 17th century According to the *Guida di Rimini*, he was a pupil of Carlo Cignani. There are some of his works both in oil and fresco, in the churches of that city. He was living in 1700

SAS, Christian, a German engraver, who flourished, according to the dates on his prints, from about 1628 to 1660. He engraved a variety of plates after Pomarance and other masters; also a set of forty-five plates of the life of St. Filippo Neri, after Stella.

SASSI, Cav. Giovanni Battista, a Milanese painter, who, according to Orlandi, studied with great assiduity under Solimene at Naples, and acquired a high reputation. He painted both in oil and fresco, and executed many works for the churches of Milan, Pavia, Varese, and other places. Lanzi says he gained more reputation for his small pictures intended for private ornament, than for the works he produced for the churches. He was living in 1718.

SASSOFERRATO, Il. See Salvi.

SATYRUS, an ancient Greek architect, who flourished about B. C. 324. In conjunction with Pytheus, he had the direction of the famous tomb erected by Queen Artemisia, in memory of King Mausolus of Halicarnassus. These two artists made the designs for the work, and left a particular description of it; for which, see Bryaxis.

SAUBERLICH, Lawrence, a German engraver, who, according to Professor Christ, engraved and published some wooden cuts at Wittemberg in 1599, bearing the above monogram. Very little is known of him; he is supposed to have died in 1613.

SAURUS. See Batrarchus.

SAUERWEID, Alexander, a German painter and engraver, born at Courland in 1782. It is not known under whom he studied, but he is said to have received some instructions in the academy at Dresden. He painted battle-pieces and skirmishes of Cossack cavalry in a very spirited manner. He settled at St. Petersburg, where he passed most of his life; he was patronized by the Emperor Alexander, and died there in 1844. He is little known out of Russia, except by the numerous prints from his designs, executed in aquatint and colors, which are numerous and interesting, as faithful representations of European military costume, and lively records of warlike operations during the wars of Napoleon.

SAUVAGE, J. P., a French painter, born at Tournay in 1744. He studied in the academy at Antwerp, and adopted the style of painting in bas-relief, which art he is said to have carried to such a state of perfection, as to produce perfect illusion. He resided a long time at Paris, where his works were held in high estimation. He imitated marbles and ancient Terra-cottas with great success. He returned to Tournay in 1808, and died there in 1818.

SAUVÉ, Jean, a French engraver, who according to Basan, flourished in the latter part of the 17th century, and executed some plates after Guido, Pietro da Cortona, and other masters; also a few portraits.

SAVAGE, J., an English engraver and printseller, who flourished in London about 1680. He engraved a number of portraits of noted malefactors, and some of exemplary character, who fell in a better cause, for which reason they are interesting. The following are deserving of notice:

PORTRAITS.

Bishop Latimer. John a Lasco. Algernon Sidney. Archibald Campbell, Earl of Argyle. Henry Cornish, Sheriff of London. Sir Edmundbury Godfrey. John Gadbury, Astrologer. James Fitzroy, Duke of Monmouth. Sir Thomas Armstrong. Sir Henry Chauncey, Antiquary. Sir Henry Pollexfen, Chief Justice of the Common Pleas. Arthur, Earl of Torrington. Charles Leigh, M. D.

SAVART, Peter, a French engraver, born at Paris in 1750. He engraved quite a number of plates, executed with the graver in a neat, finished style, among which are some portraits of illustrious personages of France. The following are his most esteemed prints:

PORTRAITS.

Louis XIV.; *after Rigaud.* 1771. Louis de Bourbon, Prince of Condé; *after le Juste.* 1776. John Baptist Colbert; *after P. de Champagne.* 1773. De la Motte Fenelon; *after Vivien.* 1771. J. B. la Bruyere; *after St. Jean.* 1778. Peter Bayle; *do.* 1774. Jean Racine; *after Santerre.* 1772. Nicholas Boileau Despreaux; *after Rigaud.* 1769. Rabelais; *after Sarrabat.* 1767. Cardinal Richelieu; *after P. de Champagne.* Nicholas de Catinat, Mareschal de France. Comte de Buffon; *after Drouais.* 1776. Bossuet; *after Rigaud.* 1773. D'Alembert; *after Lusurier.* 1780. Montesquieu. 1779.

SAVERY, James, a Flemish painter, born at Courtray about 1545. He studied under Hans Bol at Amsterdam, and painted landscapes and cattle in the style of his master. He finished his pictures with great labor and neatness, though in a hard dry style. He died of the plague at Amsterdam in 1602.

SAVERY, Roland, was the son of the preceding artist, born at Courtray in 1576. He was instructed by his father, and it has been supposed from his style, that he afterwards became the disciple of Paul Bril, but this cannot be reconciled with chronology, as that artist left Flanders for Italy when Savery was an infant, where he passed the rest of his life. The resemblance of his style to that of Bril is not more apparent than to that of Breughel or other eminent Flemish landscape painters of the time. He visited France in the reign of King Henry IV., and was employed by that monarch in decorating the royal palaces with his landscapes. He afterwards returned to the Low Countries, where he met with great encouragement. He was invited to Prague by the Emperor Rodolphus II., in whose service he passed the greater part of his life. By the direction of that monarch, he traveled through the grand and picturesque regions of the Tyrolese, and during a residence of two years in that country, filled his portfolio with numerous sketches of the most beautiful wild and romantic scenery. From these designs he executed for his patron many compositions, decorated with animals and figures, in a highly finished and effective style, with a pleasing and natural tone of coloring. His small easel pictures are the best, and in neatness of touch, are accounted little inferior to those of Bril or Breughel. On the death of the Emperor, he settled at Utrecht, where he died in 1639.

SAVERY, John, a Flemish painter and engraver, born at Courtray in 1597. According to Huber, he was a nephew of Roland S., and probably was his disciple, as he painted landscapes in his style, which, though inferior to them, possess considerable merit. He executed some spirited etchings from his own designs, among which are a set of six mountainous Landscapes, marked *J. Savery, fec. Nic. de Clerc. exc.*; a Landscape, with a Stag-hunt, and a Landscape, with Samson killing the Lion. He died at Utrecht in 1655.

SAVERY, or SAVRY, Solomon, a Dutch engraver, who flourished at Amsterdam about 1650. He engraved quite a number of plates of portraits and other subjects, mostly after the Dutch and Flemish masters, among which are a set of seventeen plates from Ovid's Metamorphoses. He also engraved several portraits of Englishmen, among which are Charles I., Oliver Cromwell, Lord Fairfax, and John Speed, the historian, from which circumstance it is supposed he went to England. A list of his prints may be found in Nagler's Lexicon.

SAVOLDO, Girolamo, an artist of Brescia, of a noble family, who painted in 1540. It is not known under whom he studied, but Lanzi classes him among the pupils and imitators of Titian, and says, "upon transferring his residence to Venice, he is known to have become one of Titian's most formidable rivals; not. indeed. in works on a large scale, but in smaller pieces, conducted with an exquisite degree of care, which may, in a measure, be said to have been his chief characteristic; with such as these, he beguiled his time, presenting them gratuitously to the churches." Paolo Pino ranks him among the best painters of his age. Zanetti describes his little Presepio, or Christ in the Manger, in the church of S. Giobbe, at Venice, "as a truly beautiful picture, exquisitely colored, and the whole composition conducted with singular care." Ridolfi says that in Venice, this painter is known under the name of Girolamo Bresciano, and that he cannot possibly be confounded with Romanino, or Muziano, as neither of those artists were ever employed in that city. Lanzi says his happiest production is an altar-piece painted for the church of the Predicatori at Pesaro, now in the I. R. Pinacoteca, at Milan. "Our Lord is seen placed on high, seated upon a cloud, which appears truly illuminated by the sun, and in the foreground are seen four saints drawn with a force of coloring that appears to bring them as near to the eye as the soft color of the perspective in the upper part of the picture, throws its objects into the distance. It is wholly *Titianesque*, and is only wanting in a more choice selection of the figures in the foreground." There is also a beautiful picture of the Transfiguration by him in the Florentine gallery. His works are very rare, as he only wrought for amusement. Zani says he operated in 1548, when he was very old; others say he was living in 1590.

SAVOLINI, Cristoforo, a painter born at Cesena, who was living in 1678. According to Malvasia he studied with Cristoforo Serra, a faithful scholar and imitator of Guercino. He executed some works for the churches of his native place, and at Rimini. Lanzi classes him among the followers of the style of Guercino.

SAVONA, Il Prete di. See Bartolomeo Guidobono.

SAVONANZI, Emilio, a painter of noble descent, born at Bologna in 1580. He studied successively under Denis Calvart, Cremonini, Lodovico Caracci, and Guido at Bologna; next with Guercino at Cento, and lastly with Algardi the sculptor at Rome. Lanzi says, "by such means he became a good theorist, and an able lecturer, applauded in every particular of art, nor was he wanting in good practice, uniting many styles in one, in which, however, that of Guido most prevails. Still he was not exactly correct in all his pieces, even betraying feebleness of touch, and not scrupling to denominate himself an artist of many hands." He executed a variety of works for the churches at Ancona, at Camerino, and the adjacent cities. He afterwards went to Spain, where he met with great encouragement. He died at Bologna in 1660, aged 80, not in 1638, as erroneously stated by some writers.

SAVORELLI, Sebastiano, a painter of Forli, who, according to Guarienti, studied under Carlo Cignani, whose style he adopted, and executed some works for the churches of Forli, and the adjacent cities. He was a priest, and flourished in the latter part of the 17th century.

SAVOYE, or SAVOYEN, Charles van, a Flemish painter, who, according to Balkema, was born at Antwerp in 1619, and died in 1669. Zani says he was living in 1680. He was very fond of painting the nude figure, and he painted a great many small cabinet pictures of subjects taken from Ovid. His works are beautifully colored and highly finished, though his drawing is not very correct.

SAVOYE, Daniel, a French painter, born at Grenoble in 1644, and died at Erlangen in 1716. He studied under Sebastien Bourdon, and painted portraits with reputation. He etched some small plates of soldiers, and costumes of the time of Louis XIII., marked D. S., *sc.* There is also a Repose in Egypt by him, in which the Virgin is seated near a fountain, attended with three angels; on the left an ass is tied to a tree.

SAY, William, an eminent English engraver in mezzotinto, born at the small village of Lakenham, near Norwich, in 1768. He studied with James Ward, and executed a great number of plates, many of them of large dimensions. He engraved several plates after the old masters, but most of his prints are from the English school; many of them half and full length portraits, after Reynolds, and others; several for Turner's River Scenery, two of Brigands, *after Eastlake;* the Raising of Lazarus, *after Hilton*, &c. The whole number of his plates is about 330. He died in 1834.

SBARBI, Antonio, a painter born at Cremona, according to Zani, in 1661; others say he flourished from 1701 to 1750. He first studied under Bernasconi at Milan, and afterwards with Lorenzo Pasinelli at Bologna. He painted history and animals, but was most eminent in the latter, which he drew from life with great spirit and accuracy. He acquired sufficient reputation to induce the Duke Ranucci Farnese, to invite him to Piacenza, and take him into his service, for whom he executed some of his best works.

SCACCIANI, Camillo, a painter of Pesaro, who flourished there towards the latter part of the 18th century. He executed some works for the churches, but he wrought mostly for the collections. Lanzi says he was a good artist, and painted in the style of the Caracci, allied to the modern. There is a fine picture by him of St. Andrea Avellino, in the cathedral of Pesaro.

SCACCIATI, Andrea, a painter born at Florence in 1642. He first studied under Marco Balassi, but afterwards with Lorenzo Lippi, who, perceiving that his genius was best adapted to the representation of fruit and flowers, persuaded him to devote himself entirely to that branch, which advice he followed, and became very eminent. He was much patronized by the Grand Duke of Tuscany and the principal nobility, and his pictures were sought after in foreign parts. He was living in 1704.

SCACCIATI, Andrea, an Italian designer and engraver, born at Florence, according to Zani, in 1725, and died there in 1771. In 1766 he published a set of forty-one plates in aquatinta, after the works of the great masters in the collection of the Grand Duke of Tuscany. He also engraved some other plates after the Italian masters.

SCAGLIA, Girolamo, called Il Parmiggianino, a painter born at Lucca, who studied first with Pietro Paulini at Lucca, and afterwards with Giovanni Marracci. He executed some works for the churches of his native city and of Pisa, which Lanzi says exhibit extreme industry, but little taste; in his architecture, he imitated Pietro da Cortona, and in his coloring, he followed Paulini, particularly in his shadows, in which he approached Ricchi. He flourished in the latter part of the 17th century.

SCAICHI, Gotefred, a Florentine engraver, who flourished in 1623. There is a set of views of the palaces and gardens of the Grand Duke, by him, etched in a slight style.

SCAIARIO, Antonio, a painter of Bassano, who studied under Gio. Battista da Ponte, whose style he imitated, and whose daughter he married. He also inherited his property. For these reasons he sometimes signed his pictures Antonio da Ponte, and Antonio Bassano. His works are held in considerable esteem. He died, according to Verci, in 1640.

SCALABRINI, Marc' Antonio, a painter born at Verona, who flourished in 1565. He executed some works for the churches of his native city and elsewhere, in which he imitated the Venetian school in design and coloring. Pozzi says he distinguished himself, and particularly commends two altar-pieces of scriptural subjects by him, in the church of S. Zeno.

SCALABRINO, Lo, a painter said to have been born at Siena, but probably was a native of Pistoja. He studied under the Cav. Gio. Antonio Razzi, called Il Sodoma, and is said by Della Valle to have excelled in grotesque subjects. In the church of S. Francesco, at Siena, without the Tuscan gate, are seven beautifully painted altar-pieces, inscribed *Scalabrinus Pistoriensis*. Lanzi says that Scalabrino was a man of genius, a poet, and a good painter. It is uncertain whether he was a native of Siena or Pistoja; if the altar-pieces referred to are not by the scholar of Razzi, then a skillful painter of Pistoja has been overlooked. He thinks, however, that there was but one artist of that name, and if he was a native of Siena, he preferred to be considered a Pistoiese.

SCALBERGE, Peter, a Flemish painter and

engraver, of whom little is known, except by his prints. He resided at Paris about 1638, where he executed quite a number of plates from his own designs and after other masters. Dumesnil describes forty-seven prints by him. Zani says he operated as late as 1650.

SCALBERGE, or SCALLE BERGE, Frederic, a Flemish engraver, and probably painter, who flourished, according to the dates on his prints, from about 1623 to 1636. Four of his etchings are marked at Rome, 1623; others are dated at Paris, 1636. His prints consist mostly of landscapes, etched in a spirited manner; some of them in the style of Paul Bril, and others more nearly resemble that of Nicolas Moyaert. He variously signed his prints *Scalberge*, and *Scalle Berge*. He was probably a relative of the preceding artist, but his prints are executed in a more scientific manner.

SCALFURATIO, Giovanni, an Italian architect, who is merely mentioned by Milizia as the restorer of the church of S. Rocca at Venice, originally erected by Bartolomeo Buono, in 1495.—Scalfuratio died in 1764.

SCALIGERO, Bartolomeo, a painter born at Venice, according to Zani, in 1630, though Zanetti and others say he was a Paduan, and Lanzi, that he is claimed by the people of Padua as one of their fellow citizens. At all events, he studied under Alessandro Varotari, called Padovanino, and ranks among the most celebrated pupils and imitators of that master. He resided mostly at Venice, where he executed many works for the churches, the most beautiful of which, according to Lanzi, are at the Corpus Domini. There are four of his works at Padua. The time of his death is not known, and it is very probable that he was born much earlier than 1630. See *Varotari*.

SCALIGERO, Lucia, a Venetian paintress, born at Venice in 1637. She was distinguished for her knowledge of the learned languages, skill in music and taste in painting. She is said to have studied painting under Alessandro Varotari; if so, it was at a tender age, as Varotari died in 1650. Boschini is of opinion that she learned the art of Chiara Dario, a celebrated paintress, much employed by the Grand Duke of Tuscany. Lucia acquired considerable reputation for her portraits, was much employed by the nobility of Venice, and her beauty, merits and accomplishments, were extolled by the poets of her time. She also painted several pictures for the churches. She died in 1700.

SCALVATI, Antonio, a painter born at Bologna in 1559. He studied under Tommaso Lauretti, accompanied that master to Rome, when he was invited there by Gregory XIII., and assisted him in his works in the Sala di Constantino. Scalvati was afterwards employed among other artists, by Sixtus V., in decorating the Library of the Vatican, and in the execution of several other important works. He however chiefly excelled in portraits, in which branch he was very distinguished, and during the pontificates of Clement VIII., Leo XI., and Paul V., he painted the portraits of many of the most distinguished personages at Rome, among whom was Clement VIII. He died in 1622.

S
RAF. F.

SCAMINOSSI, Raffaelle, a painter born at Borgo San Sepolcro, about 1570, though authors disagree on this point. He studied under Raffaellino del Colle, and painted history with considerable reputation, though he is more celebrated as an engraver. Orlandi commends a picture by him in the cathedral at Bologna, and Lanzi says his compositions display great simplicity; he drew his ideas chiefly from nature, and he attended sufficiently to coloring. Bartsch describes in *Le Peintre Graveur* tom. xvii., 137 prints by him. They are executed in a bold, effective style; his drawing is tolerably correct, and there is a fine expression in the heads; some of them are from his own designs, and others after other masters. He sometimes marked his prints with a monogram composed of R. A. S. F., as above; at others, with his name in full, variously written, *Raphael Schaminossi*, *Schiaminossi*, or *Sciamonossi*, frequently Latinized, as *Raphael Schaminossius, Pictor, et Sculp.* He is also called by writers, by all the above names, to which *Scaminossi* is added. The time of his death is not known; he was living in 1620, as appears from the dates on some of his prints.

SCAMOZZI, Vincenzio, an eminent Italian architect, the cotemporary and countryman of Palladio, was born at Vicenza in 1552. He was the son and scholar of Giovanni Domenico S., an architect of small reputation, who practised at Vicenza. After displaying proofs of his taste and ability in several designs for Count Verlati and others, Scamozzi visited Venice, where he is said, though very improbably, to have studied under Palladio. He gained great improvement, however, by attentively studying the works of Palladio and Sansovino, then being erected at Venice; and Milizia says "he particularly admired Palladio," although in his writings Scamozzi rather detracts from the merit of that master. When seventeen years old, he was employed to remedy certain defects in the church of S. Salvatore at Venice, and at the age of twenty-two he composed a treatise on perspective, in ten books, enlarging particularly upon the subject of scene-painting. Not contented with his attainments in the art, he visited Rome in 1579, studied mathematics under the Padre Clavio, inspected the monuments of antiquity with the greatest assiduity, and made exact and elaborate drawings of the most famous edifices, especially the Coliseum, and the Baths of Antoninus and Diocletian. After spending about eighteen months at Rome, he revisited Venice, and studied the remains of antiquity in that city and its environs.

On returning to Venice, Scamozzi at first devoted his attention to the theoretical department of his art, and composed the explanations to a series of plates by Pittori, with an Essay in three chapters, relating to Roman antiquities. This work was received with great and deserved applause by the best judges of the time. The recent death of Sansovino and Palladio (1570 and 1580), were not unfavorable to his rising distinction, and he began to be considered as their successor in the public esteem. Accordingly, after completing his admirable monument to the Doge Niccolo da Ponte, in the church of S. Maria della Carita, Scamozzi was commissioned to complete the public library of S. Marco, commenced by Sansovino, and was afterwards employed in a similar commission on Palladio's Teatro Olimpico at Vicenza, adding a fixed *scena*, with its three avenues of buildings, shown in perspective, but executed in relief. In 1585, at the reception of the Empress Maria of Austria at Vicenza, Scamozzi was appointed to direct the festivals. For Vespaziano Gonzaga, Duke of Sabionetta, he erected a theatre similar to that at Vicenza, which was honored by the perfect approbation of the learned, but has since been destroyed. In 1593, he erected the famous fortress of Palma, near Friuli.

A deputation being sent from the Venetian republic to congratulate Sigismund on his accession to the throne of Poland, Scamozzi availed himself of the offer of the Senator Duodo to visit that country, as well as various parts of Germany and France. During this journey, he studied every specimen of Gothic architecture with the greatest assiduity, and conceived the idea of his treatise on all the different styles of European architecture. While spending a short time at Saltzburg, he was presented to the archbishop, who subsequently employed him to design the Cathedral of that city. This celebrated edifice was completed from his design in 1628, and is described by Temanza as one of the noblest temples of modern times, greatly superior in architectural excellence to the world-renowned St. Peter's. Scamozzi was deeply learned in his profession; his edifices were simple, correct, and majestic. On returning to Venice from his northern tour, he was very extensively employed, and erected, among other edifices, the Palazzo Cornaro, in the Doric, Ionic, and Corinthian orders at Venice; the church of S. Niccolo di Tolentino; and that of SS. Simone e Giuda. At Florence, he was employed upon the Strozzi palace; and at Genoa he superintended the Ravaschieri palace, of three stories, rustic, Ionic, and Corinthian. One of his most celebrated works, however, is the stately range of buildings on the south side of St. Mark's Place, called the Procuratie Nuove, commenced by him in 1586. The design itself, however, may be said to belong to Sansovino, all the lower part as far as the entablature of the second order being a continuation of the façade of the adjoining public library; while the excessively deep frieze and cornice of Sansovino's second order are moderated, and a beautiful Corinthian story is added to the whole, forming a most tasteful and elegant structure, sufficient alone to perpetuate the fame of the architect. Scamozzi was almost overwhelmed by commissions and applications for designs, from princes and distinguished individuals, so that he had little time to devote to the favorite project of his life, his *Architettura Universale*. This great undertaking was to have been completed in ten books, but only six appeared. The sixth treats on the different orders of architecture, and, according to Milizia, is a masterpiece, showing his deep knowledge of his profession. Scamozzi died in 1616, and his remains were deposited in the church of SS. Giovanni e Paolo, at Venice.

SCAMOZZI, Ottavio. See Bertotti.

SCANNABECCHI. See Dalmasio and Muratori.

SCANNAVINI, or SCANNAVESI, Maurelio, a painter born at Ferrara in 1655. He first studied under Francesco Ferrari, but afterwards visited Bologna, where he entered the school of the Cav. Carlo Cignani, and became one of his most distinguished disciples. Lanzi says, "he emulated his master with the most scrupulous exactness. He was naturally slow, and never could prevail on himself to send a picture from his studio till he beheld it complete in every respect; though impelled by domestic penury to greater haste, he never varied from this method; nor did he envy the more fortunate Avanzi, who abounded with commissions while he was destitute. The noble house of Bevilacqua assisted him much, and it redounds to its honor that, in remunerating him for some figures in an apartment where Aldrovandini had conducted the architecture, a very large sum was added to the price agreed upon." He painted both in oil and fresco, but he conducted only a few fresco pieces, as that method requires artists of a more expeditious hand. The greatest work of this master is in the refectory of the Dominicans at Ferrara, consisting of a series of fourteen pictures from the life of St. Dominic. His other principal works in the churches are, the Annunciation, in S. Stefano; St. Brigida swooning before a Crucifix, supported by an Angel, in S. Maria della Grazie; and St. Tommaso di Villanova distributing Alms to the Poor, at the Agostiniani Scalzi, which last is considered his most capital performance. He wrought much for the collections, and Lanzi says the noble families of Bevilacqua, Calcagnini, Rondinelli, and Trotti, possess several of his pictures, painted for private ornament, among which are portraits that display Maurelio's singular talents in that branch; and histories of half-length figures, in the manner of Cignani. "They possess gracefulness, union of coloring, and a strength of tints, which leaves him nothing to envy in the artists by whom he is surrounded, except their fortune." He died in 1698.

SCARAMUCCIA, Gio. Antonio, a painter born at Perugia in 1580. According to Pozzo, he studied under the Cav. Roncalli, whose manner he adopted. Lanzi says his works are frequently to be met with at Perugia. "The spirit and freedom of his pencil are more to be commended than his tints, which are too dark, and which in the churches easily distinguish him amidst a crowd of other artists. It is probable that he used too great a quantity of *terra d' ombra*, like others of his day." He died at Perugia in 1650.

SCARAMUCCIA, Luigi, called Il Perugino, was the son of the preceding, born at Perugia in 1616. After receiving instruction from his father, he went to Bologna, and entered the school of Guido, and, according to Malvasia, he afterwards studied with Guercino. He however founded his style on that of Guido. Lanzi says, "he displays grace and elegance in every part of his work, and if he does not soar, he never falls to the ground." He rose to eminence in his profession, and executed many works for the churches and public edifices at Perugia, Bologna, and Milan; he also painted much for the collections. Among his principal works are the Presentation, in the church of the Filippini, at Perugia; St. Barbara, in the church of S. Marco, at Milan; and the Coronation of the Emperor Charles V. by Clement VII.; composed and designed in a grand style, in the Ducal palace at Bologna. Lanzi says his works abound at Perugia both in public and private, and there are more at Milan than at Bologna. He executed a few etchings, in a free and spirited style, resembling that of Guido; only four, with their variations, are known, viz.: Christ crowned with Thorns, *after Titian;* St. Benedict praying, *after L. Caracci;* the Virgin, and Venus and Adonis, *after Ann. Caracci.* He died at Milan in 1680, though some say at Pavia.

SCARPACCIA, Vittore, an old Venetian painter, born in 1410, and died at Verona in 1469. He was eminent in his time, both in history and portraits, and is said to have understood the principles of perspective.

SCARSELLA, Sigismondo, called Il Mondino, a painter born at Ferrara in 1530. He went to Venice, studied in the school of Paul Veronese three years, and afterwards continued there thirteen years, engaged in studying the best works of the Venetian school, with the rules of perspective and architecture. He returned to Ferrara, where he acquired distinction, and was called by his fellow-citizens *Il Mondino.* He executed many works for the churches and public edifices, as well as for the collections of his native city, in which he imitated the manner of Veronese. Lanzi says, "he wrought in a good *Paolesque* style, but at a considerable distance as a disciple." Most of his works in public have perished, or been greatly injured by retouching. The only one retaining anything like its original beauty is the Visitation to St. Elizabeth, in the church of S. Croce. His easel pictures are in better preservation, and are highly esteemed; but Lanzi says they are mostly attributed to his son, Ippolito. He died in 1614.

SCARSELLA, Ippolito, called Lo Scarsellino, an eminent painter, was the son of the preceding, born at Ferrara, according to Baruffaldi, in 1551. After receiving instruction from his father, he went to Venice, where he became the pupil of Giacomo Bassano, and afterwards diligently studied the works of the great Venetian masters, particularly those of Paul Veronese. After a residence of six years at Venice, he returned to Ferrara, where he acquired an immense reputation. Lanzi says he "executed more pictures for the churches and individuals in his native city, than by many other artists together. His fellow-citizens call him the *Paolo* of their school, but his character is different; he seems the reformer of the paternal taste; his conceptions are more beautiful, and his tints more attractive. On comparison with Veronese, it is evident that his style is derived from that source, though it is different, being composed of the Venetian and the Lombard, of native and foreign schools, the offspring of an intellect well founded in the theory of the art, of a gay and animated fancy, of a hand, if not always equal, yet always prompt, spirited, and rapid. Hence we see a great number of his pictures in different cities of Lombardy and Romagna, to say nothing of those at Ferrara. There, his pictures of the Assumption and the Nuptials at Cana, at the Benedettini; the Pietà and the Decollation of St. John, in the church of the same convent; and the Noli me Tangere, at S. Niccolo, are among the most celebrated; also his Pentecost, his Annunciation, and his Epiphany, conducted in competition with the Presentation of Annibale Caracci, at the Oratorio della Scala. A number of repetitions or copies of these and others, on a smaller scale, are to be seen in private houses. His works, too, are frequently met with at Rome; some are at the Campidoglio, and at the palaces of the Albani, Borghesi, Corsini, and in greater number at the Lancellotti. I have sometimes examined them in company with professors who never ceased to extol them. They recognized various imitations of Veronese, in the inventions and the copiousness of Parmiggiano in the lightness and grace of the figures; of Titian in the fleshes, particularly in a Bacchanal at the Casa Albani; of Dossi and Carpi in the strength of color, in those fiery yellows, in those deep rose colors, and also in that bright tinge given to the clouds and the air. What sufficiently distinguishes him, too, are a few extremely graceful countenances, which he drew from two of his daughters; a light shade which envelopes the whole of his objects without obscuring them, and that slightness of design which borders almost upon the dry, in opposition perhaps to Bastiano Filippi, who is sometimes reproached with exhibiting coarse and heavy features." He also painted portraits with great success. Bartsch describes a single print by him, representing a female Saint with Angels, signed with his name, but without date. He died in 1621. The above dates are given by Baruffaldi and Lanzi, and are doubtless correct, though there is some disagreement on these points; Zani says he was born in 1551, and died in 1621; Ticozzi, that he died, in 1621, aged 70; others place his birth about 1560 and 1570.

SCHADOW, John Godfrey, a German sculptor, was born at Berlin in 1764. After acquiring a good knowledge of the art he married, and was enabled, through the liberality of his father-in-law, to visit Italy in 1785. After studying at Rome with assiduity for two years, Schadow was recalled to Berlin, and appointed sculptor to the court. His busts, statues, and monuments are quite numerous, and evince considerable talents. Among them are the colossal statue of Gen. Ziethon; that of Frederick the Great, at Stettin; the monument to Gen. Blucher, at Rostock; and the superb monument to the young Count de la Marche, the natural son of Frederick the Great; also the model of the four-horsed chariot over the Brandenburg gate at Berlin. Schadow left two sons; Frederick William, born in 1789, has attained considerable eminence in painting, and in 1826 was appointed Director of the Dusseldorf Academy. The elder son, John Rodolph, is the subject of the following article.

SCHADOW, John Rodolph. This sculptor was born at Rome in 1786. He was the son of Godfrey Schadow, an able German artist, who returned to Berlin in 1788, and was appointed sculptor to the king. The young Schadow acquired from his father the elements of the art, and executed, at the age of eighteen, a copy of the Apollo Belvidere. In 1810 he visited Rome with the royal pension, and studied with such great assiduity under Canova and Thorwaldsen that he soon gained distinction, and produced his graceful statue of Paris debating on his Decision, which was executed in bronze at Vienna, for Count Schoenborn Wiesentheid, a patron of the young artist. His next production was a marble statue of a Girl fastening her Sandals, greatly admired by connoisseurs for its simplicity, grace, and exquisite proportions; also two other figures, a young Girl spinning, and a winged Cupid hesitating which of the two he shall honor with a crown. Schadow received many commissions for single copies of these exquisite statues; some of them were in the collections of Prince Esterhazy and the King of Prussia, and several are in England. He commenced a work in the latter part of his life, said to have combined the grandeur of Thorwaldsen with the grace of Canova, representing Achilles protecting the body of Penthesilea. The Prince Hardenberg of Prussia offered him 64,000f. for the complete work upon viewing the model; but, unfortunately for the art, Schadow died soon after, in 1822, universally regretted. Among his other works are a statue of St. John the Baptist; the Virgin bearing the infant Jesus; Diana; Bacchus; a Discobolus, or Quoit-Thrower; a bas-relief at the tomb of the Austrian general, Koller, representing that commander reclining on a couch, with Faith, Hope, and Charity above; also a similar bas-relief at the tomb of the Marquis of Lansdowne, with a representation of Night above, and a figure of Sleep and Death in her bosom. His group of Achilles and Penthesilea was completed in Carrara marble, by Wolf, the cousin of Schadow, and a scholar of his father.

HLS or HLS. SCHAERER, H. L., a Dutch engraver, who, according to Professor Christ, engraved a small landscape marked with a monogram composed of his initials, H. L. S., as above. He also copied some prints by Saftleven and J. Saenredam, which are signed *H. L. Schaerer, sculp.* There are other similar prints, signed *A. L. Schaerer.* He flourished about 1627.

HS. SCHAEUFLEIN, Hans or John, the Elder and Younger. There is much contradiction and uncertainty about these old German artists. Bartsch, after having examined the subject with his usual critical acumen, says, "that there were two artists of this name, an elder and a younger, seems to rest merely on conjecture." The curious inquirer, after having consulted that author, Nagler, Brulliot, Heineken, Jackson's History of Wood Engraving, and many others who have discussed the subject, will doubtless come to the same conclusion. Bartsch, in "Le Peintre Graveur," tom. vii., gives a descriptive account of one hundred and thirty-two prints, by or after the designs of Hans Schaeuflein, and Nagler has increased the number to one hundred and seventy-seven. They are mostly wooden cuts, dated from about 1515 to 1540. They are usually marked with one of the accompanying monograms, composed of an H. and an S., to which a baker's peel or, shovel, often two crossed, are frequently added as a rebus to the name, *Schaeuflein* in German, signifying *little shovel.* These prints are designed in the dry, stiff, formal manner of the time, yet they are executed in a bold, spirited style. There is, however, a considerable difference in the merit of the prints; hence, Bartsch infers that many of them were executed by other engravers after his designs. It is certain that he was a coadjutor of Hans Burgkmair, in the work known as the "Adventures of Tewrdanck," published in 1517, the greater part of the designs for which he is supposed to have made for the engravers, and some of the cuts bear his mark, H. with S. on the cross-bar and a *single peel.* The same may be said of the "Triumphs of Maximilian." His principal works are, "The Life and Passion of Christ," in thirty-seven cuts, published at Frankfort in 1537; and "The Miracles, Parables, &c., of Christ," in thirty-six cuts. The generality of writers, especially the older German, mention only one Schaeuflein, but Huber and some others say there were two, the Elder and the Younger. The elder, they say, flourished about 1480, and they suppose, from the style of the prints they attribute to him, marked simply H. with an S. on the cross-bar, that he was a disciple of Martin Schoen. The younger was born at Nuremberg about 1487, and distinguished himself as a painter as well as an engraver on wood; and they suppose that he was a disciple of Albert Durer, whom he imitated both in his paintings and engravings. All this, however, rests merely on conjecture. If there were any good grounds for believing that there were two Schaeufleins, from history or style, Bartsch would not have failed to have made the distinction, and to have separated and classified their prints. The prints attributed to the younger S. are of little account, and of very doubtful authenticity. The name, too, is variously written *Schaeuflein, Schaufflein, Schauffelin.* The younger S. is said to have died at Nordlingen in 1539.

HS, ro HS. ro SH,

SCHAFFNABURG, or SCHAFFNABURGENSIS, Matthew or Mattheus, an old German engraver on wood, who executed the cuts for a bible published at Wittemberg, in 1545. He engraved some other pieces, which are marked with his name, or his initials M. S. on a tablet. There is little certainty about the prints attributed to this artist, as well as the works of several other German artists who flourished about 1550, and used the initials M. S. The accounts are exceedingly contradictory, and the information sought for is for the most part "as two grains of wheat hid in two bushels of chaff."

SCHAFFNER, Martin, a German painter, who flourished at Ulm from 1502 to 1539, as appears from the records of that city. He painted history and portraits, and ranks among the best German masters of that period. There are several of his works at Ulm, Nuremberg, Augsburg, Vienna, and other places. Some of his best works were in the Gallery at Schleissheim, among which are the Annunciation, the Presentation, the Descent of the Holy Ghost, and the Death of the Virgin. His pictures are well designed, with a fine expression in the heads, but his coloring is feeble and defective. He sometimes signed his pictures with a monogram composed of his initials, an M. with an S. in the centre, and sometimes with the letters MSMZV., which Brulliot interprets *Martin Schaffner Mahler zu Ulm.* This last mark is on a picture of the Annunciation, now in the collection of the king of Bavaria. Some of his works were formerly attributed to Martin Schoen or Schöngauer, from the similarity of mark.

SCHAGEN, Giles van, a Dutch painter, born at Alkmaer in 1616. He first studied with Solomon van Ravesteyn, and afterwards with Peter Verbeck. He traveled through Germany for improvement, and first went to Dantzic, where he resided some time, and painted interiors of kitchens, ale-houses, and conversations, in imitation of Ostade, with considerable success. At Elbing, he contracted an intimacy with Strobel, through whose influence he was introduced to Stanislaus, king of Poland, whose portrait he painted. Schagen next went to Paris, where he met with much encouragement, and his pictures were greatly admired. He was also employed in copying the works of the best Italian and Flemish painters, for which he possessed a remarkable talent. He copied a picture of the Virgin and Child after Rubens, with a force and brilliancy of coloring, and a freedom of penciling little inferior to the original. He afterwards returned to his native city, where he practised with equal success till his death. One of his most remarkable pictures was a representation of the engagement between the Dutch and Spanish fleets under admirals van Tromp and Oquendo, which he sketched during the fight, at the request of the Dutch admiral, it is said, but more probably it was his own desire, as he was an eccentric man, fond of novelty and excitement. The picture was executed with great spirit and freedom. He died in 1668.

SCHALCH, John Jacob, a German landscape painter, born at Schaffhausen in 1723. Little is known of him. He is said to have painted landscapes, cattle, and figures, in the manner of Breughel. He visited Holland and England, and died in 1770. His works are unknown in England.

SCHALCKE, a Dutch painter of whom nothing is known except a few pictures of river scenery and landscapes, with cattle and figures, said to be "painted with the spirit and freedom of Teniers, and an effect of light similar to Rembrandt." There is a fine marine by him in the Gallery at Prague. Nagler suggests whether he is not the same as Godfrey Schalcken. He flourished in the second half of the 17th century.

SCHALCKEN, Godfrey, a Dutch historical and portrait painter, born at Dort in 1643. His father was rector of the college in that city, and intended to give his son a liberal education, but finding that he possessed a passion for painting, he allowed him to follow the bent of his genius, and placed him under the instruction of Solomon van Hoogstraten. He afterwards went to Leyden, and entered the school of Gerard Douw, with whom he continued some years, and acquired that delicacy of finishing, and that knowledge of the principles of the chiaro-scuro which distinguishes his works. At first he confined himself to small cabinet pictures, chiefly represented by candle-light, subjects which his instructor treated with distinguished success. On leaving the school of Douw, he attempted to aggrandize his style by studying the works of Rembrandt, but unequal to attain the vigorous touch and magical effect of that extraordinary artist, he pursued his first principles, and his pictures were sought after with avidity.

On settling in his native city, he soon gained a high reputation, and was much employed in painting portraits. He was remarkable for painting in a variety of ways, in all of which he excelled, but most in night subjects. He knew how to distribute the light of a flambeau or taper with extraordinary skill, so as to diffuse a brightness over his objects by a proper opposition of shadow, which only nature could equal; in this line he was without a competitor. Houbraken mentions one of his pictures of this sort which was exceedingly admired; the subject was St. Peter denying Christ, in which the maid is represented as holding up a light to the face of the apostle. It was a composition of many figures, more correctly designed, and with a better expression than was usual with him, and the whole picture, from the powerful distribution of light and shadow, produced a wonderful effect. To give the most natural effect to his night-pieces, it was his custom to arrange his models, or the objects he desired to paint, in a dark room attached to his studio, with the light properly adjusted; then, observing the effect through a small aperture, he painted what he saw in the darkened chamber. Schalcken met with the most flattering success at Dort, especially in small portraits; he had painted the principal families in that city, when the extraordinary success of his countryman, Sir Godfrey Kneller, in England, induced him to visit that country in the reign of King William. He had the honor of painting that monarch, but did not meet with much success, and soon left the country in disgust and settled at the Hague, where he found a prodigious demand for his small pictures, and sold them at a high price. A ridiculous and preposterous anecdote is related of the cause of his failure in England, on the authority of Campo Weyermans, which is not entitled to the least credit. "When Schalcken had the honor to paint King William III., it was the monarch's wish to be painted by candlelight, from the reputation the painter had acquired in pictures of that sort. Schalcken presented him with a taper to hold in a particular position, which, during the progress of the work, accidentally melted, and dropped on the fingers of the king, who, unwilling to disconcert the artist, bore it with great composedness for some time. This ignorant and disrespectful conduct of Schalcken disgusted the courtiers, and entirely lost him their favor." The true causes doubtless were that Kneller and others monopolized the business of portraiture—the only branch which occupied public attention at that time in England, and to satisfy the taste of the country, he was obliged to paint his figures as large as life, to which he had not been accustomed, and in which he was not very successful.

The chief merits of the pictures of Schalcken consist in the neatness and spirit of his touch, the delicacy of his finishing, and a perfect intelligence of the chiaro-scuro, as it relates to objects under the influence of a fixed and local light. In his sun-light pictures, his pencilling has been compared to that of Mieris and Vanderwerf; his coloring was warm and gilded, and his tones sweet and harmonious. His works, however, are generally defective in design, expression, and drawing.—There is a great discrepancy among writers as to the real merits of Schalcken; and his works, or at least some of them, do not sustain his reputation. But this may be said of many of the old masters, for time often produces great changes in pictures, and this is the case with some of those of Schalcken. His works have also been largely imitated, and many considered genuine are doubtless spurious. It is said by some that he was an expert mechanical painter, who labored and finished his pictures with great care; but this objection might be urged against his instructor, Douw, and other eminent artists of his country. His daylight pictures are the rarest, and consequently bring the highest prices. His works are to be found in the choicest collections, and are highly esteemed. Some of them have been engraved by Wille and other eminent artists. Smith, in his Catalogue raisonné, vol. iv., and Supplement, gives descriptions of one hundred and thirty-seven pictures by him. Brulliot ascribes to him a single etching, of a laughing peasant, hiding the greater part of his face with his right hand. It is a three-quarters bust, oval, inscribed *Quam meminisse juvat.* Balkema says he had a nephew named Jacob Schalcken, whom he instructed in the art, and who imitated his manner successfully. He also had a sister, named Maria, who practised painting, and was doubtless instructed by her brother. He died at the Hague in 1706. His name is often incorrectly written *Scalken.*

SCHAPFF, Jorg, one of the oldest German wood engravers. The Baron Heineken says he executed a part of the cuts for a book on Chiromancy, by Dr. Hartlieb, published in 1448. In his *Idea of a complete collection of Prints,* that author has given a copy of one of these cuts, and nothing can be more rudely executed. The book consists of twenty-four pages, printed on both sides, the discourse being cut on blocks of wood. The name of the engraver is inscribed on the bottom of one of the leaves, **Jorg Schapff in Augsbourg,** 1448. On the last page is *Jorg Schapff zu Augsbourg.*

SCHATEN, Hubert, an engraver, who resided at Copenhagen, and engraved some portraits of distinguished Danish personages, which bear date from 1675 to 1694.

SCHAUR, Philip, an engraver mentioned by Strutt, by whom there is an etching of an old Man with a bushy beard, in spectacles, mending a pen, with books and an hour-glass before him.

SCHEDONE. See Schidone.

SCHEEMAKERS, a Flemish sculptor, who attained great celebrity in England. He was born at Antwerp in 1691. After studying under his father, and a sculptor named Delvaux, he went to Denmark, and wrought for some time as a journeyman. About 1728 he visited Rome for improvement, and before long went to England, where he obtained considerable employment.—About 1733 he revisited Rome, where he remained two years, and returned to England in 1735. At this time, Rysbrack and Roubilliac were flourishing; but Scheemakers gradually rose in public esteem, and received many important commissions. His numerous works are distinguished for elaborateness of design, beauty of execution, and vigor of effect. Among the principal are, in Westminster Abbey, the greatly admired monument of Shakspeare; also those of Dryden, the Duke of Albemarle, the Duke of Buckingham, Admiral Watson, &c. He executed several busts and other sculptures for the gardens of Stowe; also the statue of Sir John Barnard, in the old Royal Exchange; the statues in the India House of Admiral Pocock and Lord Clive; the bronze statue of Guy, in Guy's Hospital; and that of Edward VI. in St. Thomas' Hospital. In 1756 and 1757 there were two sales of his effects, in Covent Garden, among which was a beautiful small copy of the Laocoon in marble, purchased by the Earl of Lincoln. There have been many excellent casts made of this work. Smith, following the authority of Nollekens, a pupil of Scheemakers, says that he returned to Antwerp in 1770, and soon after died in that city.

SCHEINDEL, or SCHEYNDEL, George van, a Dutch designer and engraver, who flourished at Rotterdam, according to the dates on his prints, from about 1635 to 1660. He engraved quite a number of plates from his own designs, and after other masters, executed in a neat and agreeable style, resembling that of Callot. His landscapes with figures, correctly drawn and executed with spirit, are deservedly admired. He was a cotemporary of William van Buytenweg, and engraved some plates after his designs. Among other prints are the following by him:

A pair of Landscapes, with Peasants amusing themselves. The Tooth-drawer. A Village Festival, with Boors fighting. The Companion, with a Quack-doctor. A Winter piece, with Skaters on the ice. A Landscape, with a Waterfall. A Landscape, with a Bridge. A set of four views of a Castle and the environs, one of them with a Windmill. A set of twelve Landscapes, with a Dutch inscription. A set of twelve plates of European, Turkish and Grecian figures. Twelve plates of Habits of the Countrymen of the several Cantons of Holland.

SCHEITZ, Matthew, a German painter, born at Hamburg about 1646. According to Huber, he was a scholar of Philip Wouwerman, whose style and subjects he followed for some time, but afterwards abandoned them for those of David Teniers. He etched some plates from his own designs, executed in a bold, free style, among which are the following:

The Four Seasons, represented by the Sports of Children; in four plates; *M. Scheitz fec.* 1671. Two Landscapes, with figures dancing and amusing themselves. An old Man playing on the Violin, and a Woman singing before the door of a Cottage. The Spectacle Merchant.

SCHEITZ, Andrew, a German engraver, was the son of the preceding. He executed some plates after the works of his father and others, which bear date from 1657 to 1678.

SCHELLENBERG, John Rudolph, a Swiss designer and engraver, was born at Winterthur in 1740. He was the son and scholar of an obscure painter of portraits and landscapes, named John Ulric S., born in 1709, and died in 1770. Entomology being his favorite study, he made about 2000 colored designs of insects, and sold them to the king of Bavaria; after which he made a similar collection of 4500 designs of insects, making 60 vols. in 8vo. Among his principal plates are some in Lavater's work on Physiognomy, after the designs of Chodowiecki; several of the portraits and ornamental prints for the Lives of the Swiss painters, by J. C. Füessli; and twenty-four plates of insects, for a work entitled *Les Caracteres des Insectes, suivant le systeme de Linnée.* Schellenberg died, according to Nagler, in 1806.

SCHELLENBERGER, or SCHOLLEMBERGER, John Jacob, a German engraver, who flourished from about 1660 to 1674. He engraved some portraits of distinguished personages, and executed a part of those for Priorato's History of the Emperor Leopold.

SCHELLINKS, William, a Dutch painter, born at Amsterdam, according to Descamps, in 1632 From the style of his pictures, he is supposed to have studied with John Lingelbach. He afterwards traveled through France, Switzerland, Italy, and England. He painted landscapes and seaports, decorated with figures well designed, and touched with great neatness and spirit. His animals are correctly drawn, and his groups are tastefully composed. The brilliant and sunny effect in some of his pictures reminds us of the charming productions of Karel du Jardin. He also had an excellent knowledge of perspective, as is evinced in some of his extensive views, in which the nicest gradations are observed. He resided chiefly at Amsterdam. His works are little known out of his own country, though there, they are to be found in the choicest collections, and are highly esteemed. He wrote his name, as appears from several of his drawings, *Schellinks* and *Schellings;* others write it *Schellincks.* He died in 1678.

SCHELLINKS, Daniel, was the brother of the preceding, born at Amsterdam in 1638, and died in 1701. He is said to have been instructed in the art by William S., in whose style he painted landscapes and sea-ports with some reputation. The Dutch writers mention him very briefly.

SCHELTEMA, Taco, a Dutch painter, born at Harlingen in 1760. It is not known under whom he studied, but he improved himself by diligently studying after nature, and copying the works of the best masters, particularly those of Vandyck, whom he made his model. After visiting Dusseldorf and Dresden, in which places he painted the portraits of several persons of distinction, he returned to his own country, where he practised portrait painting with great success in the manner of Vandyck. He resided alternately at Amsterdam and Rotterdam. He painted numerous family pictures of life size, some of which he enriched with landscapes and various accessories. At Amsterdam, he painted the portraits of all the founders and directors of the Batavian Society, which are, or were in one of the chambers of the Bourse.

SCHENAU, John Eleazer, a German painter and engraver, who resided at Paris in 1765, where he etched a set of twelve plates with a frontispiece, which he published under the title of *Achetez mes petites eaux fortes à la douzaine*, 1765.

SCHENCK, Peter, a Dutch engraver, and an eminent printseller, born at Elberfeld in 1645. He went to Amsterdam, where he learned the art, and formed an intimacy with Gerard Valck, who taught him mezzotinto. In 1683 they became partners, and having purchased the stock of J. Jansens, then dead, they added their own, commenced business, and published a multitude of prints, engraved by themselves, as well as others; hence it is difficult to distinguish their actual performances. Their catalogue contains a list of several hundred prints, after Ochterveldt, Netscher, Toornvliet, Kneller, Lely, Terburg, Schalcken, Lairesse, and others; also a set of 100 views in and near Rome, entitled *Roma Æterna*, many of which were engraved by Schenck himself. The King of Poland, Augustus II., Elector of Saxony, honored him, by naming him engraver to his court. Nagler gives a list of his prints. He is more celebrated as a publisher, than for his skill as an engraver, though he was a very industrious man, and executed a multitude of plates himself, most of them in mezzotinto. He died at Amsterdam in 1715.

SCHENDEL, Bernard, a Dutch painter, born at Haerlem in 1634. He studied with Hendrick Mommers, and painted conversations, merry-makings, markets, &c., in the style of his instructor. His pictures are correctly designed and well colored. He died about 1693.

SCHEVENHUYSEN, Anthony, a Dutch engraver who flourished about 1695. He engraved a set of 100 small plates, representing the different trades of Holland.

SCHIANTESCHI, Domenico, a painter born at Borgo San Sepolcro, who flourished there in the first part of the 18th century. He studied under Ferdinando Galli, called Bibiena, at Bologna, whose style he imitated. On his return to his native city he found some employment in painting perspective and architectural pieces for the public edifices, but he wrought mostly for individuals. Lanzi says "his perspectives are to be found in the houses of many of the nobility of Borgo San Sepolcro, where they are much esteemed."

SCHIAVONE, Andrea, called Medula, a painter born at Sebenico, in Dalmatia, in 1522. He evinced a passion for painting, which exhibited itself in childhood, as he was walking through the streets of Venice with his father; nothing afforded him so much pleasure as the contemplation of pictures. There is some discrepancy about the history of his early life. Lanzi says that, "his father, as soon as he became aware of his passion, instantly applied to the artists, and devoted him to the profession, but fortune proving unfavorable to him, he was compelled by penury to obtain a subsistence rather as a daily hireling than as an artist." Others assert that his father being extremely poor, placed him as a servant, or assistant to a house painter. This much is certain, that being destitute of the means of procuring a technical education, he employed the best means within his reach to accomplish his object. He derived his knowledge of design from copying the etchings of Parmiggiano, and his taste of coloring from Titian and Tintoretto. For some years he continued to support himself by executing the ornamental parts for wall and house painters, decorating household furniture, and perhaps painting for the picture dealers. Some of these performances attracted the attention of Titian, who, perceiving his talents, and learning his wretched situation, took him into his academy, and subsequently employed him in conjunction with other artists, to assist him in his great works in the Library of S. Marco. There he had an opportunity of displaying his talents, and he executed three entire ceilings from the designs of Titian, which are still to be seen in that repository of art. In competition with Tintoretto, he painted his Visitation of the Virgin, in the church of the Padri della Santa Croce, and though he was unable to compete with his powerful antagonist from his imperfect knowledge of design, yet he retired from the contest with applause. His talents were highly respected by Tintoretto, who considered him one of the best colorists of the Venetian school, and he is said to have kept one of his pictures in his studio as a model in coloring, and he was accustomed to say that, "it would be well for colorists to follow Schiavone's example in coloring, though he would do ill not to design better than his model." Robusti, moreover, imitated him with such success in an altar-piece of the Circumcision, in the church of the Carmini, that Vasari mistook it for a work by Schiavone. Yet the same historian held him in such slight esteem, as to say that it was only by mistake that he occasionally painted a good picture; a sentence, says Bottari in his Life of Franco, severely criticised by Agostino Caracci, who considered him one of the greatest geniuses of the Venetian school. Notwithstanding the possession of such extraordinary talents, Schiavone passed his days in poverty, and his necessities compelled him to accept any commission offered to him, and even to work for speculators for the most paltry remuneration. Lanzi says, "his fame after his death increased, and his paintings, for the most part, of a mythological character, were removed from *the chests and benches* to adorn the cabinets of connoisseurs. Guarienti cites three of these in the collection of Dresden; and Rosa four in the Cesarean gallery at Vienna; I have seen several very graceful specimens in the Casa Pisani at San Stefano, and in almost every gallery in Venice. In Rimini, also, I saw two of his pictures painted as companions at the Padri Teatini; they represent the Nativity and the Assumption, and the figures, on the Poussin scale, are among the most beautiful he ever drew."

There is a great difference in the works of Schiavone. So slender was the emolument he received, that he was frequently obliged to adopt a slight and expeditious mode of operating; and he was confessedly deficient in drawing, hence his surname *Medula*, or *Meldolla* (faulty), and hence too, the diversity of opinion as to his merits. The deficiency of his early education, his poverty, and lack of appreciation, plead an ample apology for all his faults. His best works, with the single exception of correctness of design, possess almost every other excellence of the art. His compositions are copious and agreeable, his attitudes graceful and elegant, resembling those of Parmiggiano, whose works he studied; his draperies are cast with judgment and taste; the heads of his females are beautiful, and those of his old men dignified and expressive, and his coloring had much of the glow of Titian, with the sweetness of Andrea del Sarto. He wrought with facility, and had a neat and flowing pencil. He possessed an excellent knowledge of the chiaro-scuro, and gave his carnations such freshness, warmth, and relief, that his figures seemed to live and breathe. His works are now only to be found in the best collections in his own country and throughout Europe. There are several in the public galleries in England, and others in the collections of the nobility.

Schiavone executed some spirited etchings from his own designs, and after Titian. The names and the works of *Andrea Schiavone* and *Andrea Meldolla* have, until recently, been confounded together as one artist. Zani first discovered that Meldolla was a different artist from Schiavone, and many of the prints formerly attributed to the latter, are now given to the former.—(See *Meldolla.*) The similarity of names was the cause of this error. The only prints attributed to him by Bartsch (P. G. tom. xvi.,) are the twelve Cæsars, *after Titian*, signed simply Titiano V., and twenty-one other subjects, apparently from his own designs, some of which are signed *Andrea Schiaon. f.* He died in 1582.

SCHIAVONE, Gregorio, a painter born a Padua about 1430. He was a fellow pupil with Andrea Mantegna under Squarcione. Lanzi says he is a very pleasing artist, whose pictures are frequently to be met with in the collections, ornamented with architectural views, with fruit and flowers, and above all, with joyous little cherubs. His style is between those of Mantegna and the Bellini. He read the following inscription on a charming picture by him at Fossombrone, *Opus Sclavonii Dalmatici Squarzoni S.*, the S. meaning Scholaris. Zani says he flourished from 1460 to 1490. Ridolfi erroneously calls him *Girolamo.*

SCHIAVONE, Luca, a Milanese artist, who, according to Lomazzo, flourished about 1450. He carried the art of pictorial embroidery, then in great repute, to the highest degree of perfection. He executed in embroidery, not only portraits, but landscapes with animals, and histories. He was the instructor of Girolamo Delfinone, which see.

SCHIAVONETTI, Luigi, an Italian designer and engraver, born at Bassano in 1765. He was the son of a stationer, and showing a taste for art, his father placed him under the tuition of Giulio Golini, a painter of some eminence at Bassano, by whom he was instructed in design; but preferring engraving, he devoted himself to that art, and with the assistance of an obscure engraver named Lorio, he acquired so much skill as to be enabled to execute a line plate of the Holy Family, *after Carlo Maratti*, so successfully as to procure him the patronage of Count Remaudini. The works of Bartolozzi, in the chalk manner, were then in great repute at Bassano, and Schiavonetti imitated his style. He went to England, and placed himself under Bartolozzi, and afterwards practiced in his style with great success. His prints are executed with spirit and freedom, his drawing is remarkably correct, and he faithfully gave the character and expression of his originals. He engraved quite a number of plates, some of them of large size, after the old masters, as well as others after the painters of the English school. He was much employed by Boydell, and he executed several plates for the Shakspeare Gallery. He died in 1810. The following are among his most admired prints:

Four plates, representing the most interesting events which preceded the murder of Louis XVI.; *after the designs of Benazech.* The celebrated cartoon by *M. Angelo Buonarotti*, representing the Surprise of the Soldiers on the Banks of the Arno. The Portrait of Vandyck in the character of Paris. The Mater Dolorosa; *after Vandyck.* The Landing of the British troops in Egypt; *after Loutherbourg.* A set of etchings, illustrative of Blair's Grave; *after the designs of Blake.* The etching of the Canterbury Pilgrimage; *after Stothard.* Dead Christ; *after Vandyck.* The Portrait of Berchem; *after Rembrandt.* The Death of General Wolfe, engraved from a gem by *Marchant*, in the original unpublished Museum Worsleyanum. There is a copy of this print in the smaller edition. The Portrait of W. Blake; *after T. Philips.* Several in "The Italian School of Design," published by *Ottley.* Also, among the original designs of celebrated Italian masters, published by *Chamberlaine;* and several of the "Specimens of Ancient Sculpture," published by the Society of Dilettanti.

SCHIAVONETTI, Niccolo, was a younger brother of the preceding, by whom he was instructed in engraving, and whom he assisted in many of his works. He also executed a few plates of his own in the style of his brother.

SCHIAVCNI, Natale, an Italian painter and distinguished engraver, born at Chiozza in 1774. He studied engraving under Raphael Morghen, and engraved a number of plates which gained him great reputation. His Assumption of the Virgin after Titian, is considered a master-piece of the art. His life has not yet been written, nor is it known whether he is now living.

SCHICK, Gottlieb, a German painter, born at Stuttgard in 1779. He went to Paris and entered the school of David, and afterwards proceeded to Rome, where he diligently studied the works of Raffaelle and the antique. On his return to his native city, he acquired considerable reputation for his historical pictures, heroic landscapes, and portraits. His principal historical pictures are the Sacrifice of Noah, David playing before Saul, and Apollo with the Shepherds, which last is in the palace at Stuttgard. He excelled in portraiture, and executed the likenesses of several distinguished persons, among them, the Baron von Humboldt. His landscapes are embellished with subjects from the ancient poets. His works are highly commended by his countrymen for correctness of design and beauty of coloring. He possessed a fine imagination, and his pictures are generally distinguished for noble simplicity and purity of sentiment. His religious pictures, however, exhibit more of the poet than of the devout worshipper. He died at Stuttgard in 1818.

SCHIDONE, Bartolomeo, an eminent painter, born at Modena in 1560, according to Malvasia and others, though there seems to be no certainty about it. His early history is very contradictory. Malvasia says he studied in the school of the Caracci, but Lanzi is of a contrary opinion, as his works show few traces of the style of the Caracci; he says, "if such be the fact, we must conclude either that his first productions are not known, or that he merely saluted that school, as it were from the threshold." If he was born in 1560, it is not probable that he would have received his first instruction from the Caracci, as Lodovico was born in 1555, Agostino in 1558, and Annibale in 1560. Therefore it seems more probable, observes Lanzi, that he employed himself in following the successors of Raffaelle in his native place, but more particularly Correggio, by whom there are many original pieces at Modena. Again, it is said that he had gained considerable reputation by some juvenile performances in the public edifices at Modena, when the Duke Ranuccio, a great patron of art, took him under his protection, and gave him his villa at Felegara, as a place of residence, that he might pursue his studies more commodiously, and with greater tranquillity. But the first pictures known to have been conducted by him in public, are the celebrated frescos of the history of Coriolanus, and the Seven Sisters, emblematic of Harmony, painted in competition with Ercole Abati, in the Palazzo Pubblico at Modena, about 1604, in which he emulated the grand style of Raffaelle and Correggio. These works, and others in the same edifice, still exist, and sufficiently evince, that he was not then a *juvenile artist*, but that he had reached the full maturity of his powers. It is also agreed that he died in the latter part of 1615. Lanzi, Tiraboschi and others, say that he died *young* about the end of 1615; Zani, that he operated in 1604, and died in 1615. If he was born in 1560, it cannot be said that he died young, at the age of fifty-five. As for the rest, and most important part, there is no dispute. His genius was noble and elevated, and he emulated the style of Correggio so closely, that some of his works have been mistaken for the productions of that great master; he approached very near him in the graceful and expressive airs of his heads, and in the elegant attitudes of his figures; his management of the chiaro-scuro exhibits the breadth and intelligence, and his coloring the purity and *impasto*, of that admirable painter; his touch is light and delicate, and he finished his pictures in an exquisite manner. Though his outlines are not always critically correct, he conceals the deficiency by the loveliness of his attitudes, and the enchanting harmony of his tones. He was accounted one of the ablest masters of his time. He was taken into the service of the Duke of Modena, for whom he executed many of his most admired works of subjects taken from the scriptures and ancient history; he also excelled in portraits, and painted those of the Duke, and all the members of his family. He painted both in oil and fresco; his coloring in the latter is very vivid and lively even at the present day; in oil, it is more subdued, but more harmonious, though not always free from the ill effects produced by the bad grounds usual in the age of the Caracci. His pictures on a large scale, such as his Pietà, now in the academy at Parma, and the Conception in S. Francesco at Piacenza, are extremely rare; also his historical pieces, as the Nativity of Christ and the Birth of the Virgin, placed for lateral ornaments to an altar-piece by Filippo Bellini. There are some of his Holy Families, Madonnas, and little sacred pieces in the galleries at Modena and elsewhere, which are held in the highest estimation, and are exceedingly valuable. Tiraboschi mentions the sum of 4000 crowns as having been paid for one of them. The court of Naples is extremely rich in his works, having purchased all those he executed for the Duke of Modena, his principal patron. In the cathedral at Modena is an admirable picture by him, representing St. Geminiano restoring a dead Child to life, which has often been mistaken for a work by Correggio. Two of his pictures, a Holy Family, and a sleeping Cupid, formerly in the Orleans collection, are now in the Dulwich gallery. His works are very rare, and only to be found in the collections of princes, though many spurious ones are attributed to him. Like Guido, he had a fatal passion for gaming, and it is said that his death was occasioned by the distress of mind brought on by losing a large sum of money, and more than he could pay, in a single night. Bartsch attributes an etching of a Holy Family to this artist, which he conjectures to be a youthful production; it is signed *Barto. Schidono*. His name is variously written *Schidone, Schedone, Schedoni* and *Schidoni*; the first is correct.

SCHINKEL, Karl Friedrich, a Prussian painter and an eminent architect of the present century, was born in 1781, at Neu-Ruppin, in Brandenburgh. He studied at Berlin, under David Gilly, an architect of reputation, but gained the most improvement from the advice and instruction of Friedrich Gilly, the son of David G., who returned from his travels about a year after Schinkel commenced his studies, and communicated to the young archi tect liberal and enlightened views of the art. Gilly employed him to erect several buildings, from his designs, and at his death in 1800, Schinkel was employed, notwithstanding his youth, to complete several of his unfinished edifices. Instead of following the common course, he steadfastly continued his theoretical and artistic studies, supporting himself by making designs of various ornamental articles for modellers and artisans. In 1803 he visited Vienna, Prague, and Dresden; and then went to Italy; extended his travels to Naples and Sicily; and returned to Berlin in 1805. In consequence of the civil commotions, all architectural works were suspended, and Schinkel therefore applied himself to painting landscapes. The studies of scenery he had made in Italy, were of great use in his compositions, and he produced a number of excellent pictures, usually adorned with architecture, besides a large panorama of Palermo, and a number of scenes for the theatre, afterwards engraved and published, with those for the *Zauberflote Die Brant von Messina*, &c. His various artistical labors during this period, were of great service in developing his imagination, and refining his taste, so that he came to look upon architecture more in the light of a fine art, than did most of the German professors. At the general restoration of peace, Schinkel was employed by the King of Prussia to design a great national cathedral, in commemoration of that event; but, although his design excited general admiration, the work, for various reasons, was not erected. However, from the year 1815, he was incessantly employed. Among his earliest edifices at Berlin, were the Hauptwache Theatre, and Museum, all of them treated in the pure Grecian style. The façade of the Museum is particularly distinguished for severe simplicity of outline, with a fulness of refined ornament, unknown to any modern examples of what is termed the Grecian style. The external elevation consists merely of a single row of eighteen columns in antis (Erechtheum Ionic), raised on a lofty stylobate, with a flight of steps in the centre, enclosed by pedestal walls (in continuation of the stylobate), and forming the ascent to the colonnade. Great power and variety of effect is given to the whole design by the inner elevation, or background behind the outer row of columns, which present in the centre portion a second colonnade (four columns in antis), with a screen-wall rising about half its height, and beyond that the upper half of the open staircase; whereby the whole composition acquires singular movement and play of both perspective, and light and shade. In addition to this, Schinkel intended to have decorated the screen-wall with splendid frescos, and actually designed some masterly cartoons; but they were not completed. There is reason to suppose that his idea will be finished, Cornelius having been mentioned as the artist; and not till then, will the contemplated effect of this novel design be completely realized. The two other above mentioned edifices also, have not received their complement of sculpture, which is evident from Schinkel's *Entwurfe*, a publication containing a full and extensive series of designs for all his principal buildings, with ample explanations. He has been termed the Luther of Architecture; he effected much by his personal exertions, and perhaps more through his influence and example, since, by venturing to think for himself, he has led others to do the same. He has been criticised as being too limited in his reforms; but this probably resulted rather from the prejudices of the age, than from his own inclination. Among Schinkel's principal works, are the Werder Kirche (Gothic), Bauschule and Observatory, at Berlin; the Theatre at Hamburg; and the church of S. Nicholas, at Potsdam. The latter would have been a most imposing structure, had the original design been executed, instead of omitting the cupola. There are a number of magnificent designs in his *Entwurfe*, which, for various reasons, were never executed. Among these, were several for a monument to Frederick the Great, remarkable for freedom of imagination, and architectural luxuriance. Another publication, entitled *Werke der Hoperen Baukunst*, contains a series of designs for a palace at Athens, to be erected on the Acropolis, which was greatly superior to a similar design by Klenze. His latest poetical conception was a design for a summer palace at Orianda, in the Crimea, on a lofty eminence commanding a prospect of the Black Sea, and surrounded by terraces and hanging gardens. In 1839, Schinkel was promoted to the highest rank in his profession, that of Ober-Landes-Baurector. He died in 1841.

SCHIVENOGLIA, Lo. See Rainieri.

SCHIZZONE, a young artist commended by Vasari, as one of the most promising followers of the school of Raffaelle. At the sacking of Rome in 1527, he was obliged to flee from the city; nothing more is recorded of him.

SCHLEY, Jacob vander, a Dutch engraver, born at Amsterdam in 1715, and died there in 1779. He studied under Bernard Picart, in whose style he executed some portraits, and a variety of plates for the book-publishers. He also finished some plates by Picart, left incomplete at his death. Among others, are the following by him:

PORTRAITS.

John Baptist Boyer, Marquis d' Argens; *after van Pée.* Anthony Bernard Prevot, Almoner to the Prince of Conti; *do.* Bernard Picart, Engraver; *after M. des Angles.* 1734. Henry de la Tour d'Auvergne, Viscount de Turenne; *do.* The prints *after Coypel*, for the edition of Don Quixote, published at Amsterdam in 1746.

SCHLICHT, Abel, a German painter, architect, and engraver, born at Manheim in 1754. He studied perspective under L. Quaglio, and was appointed professor in the Academy at Dusseldorf. Nothing is recorded of his works as a painter or an architect. As an engraver he executed some plates in aquatinta, among which are the following. He died in 1826.

A Storm and Shipwreck; *after Vernet.* A Calm; *do.* A Landscape, with cattle; *after A. Vandevelde.* A Landscape, with figures and animals; *after Berghem.* A Landscape; *after Pynaker.* Several architectural Views; *after Bibiena, Pannini,* and others.

SCHLOTTERBECK, William Frederick, an eminent Swiss designer and engraver, born at Hartingen in 1777. He studied with C. von Mechel at Basle. He had a great predilection for the aquatinto style of engraving, which was then a novelty, and his great success may be said to have made that branch of the art very popular in Germany. He engraved many large plates in that manner, after the works of Claude, John Both, P. Hackert, and others, as well as many of views from his own designs. In 1798 he went to Dessau, where he joined the Chalcographic Institution, and engraved the four landscapes by Claude, then at Cassel, but now in the Hermitage at St. Petersburg. In 1801 he went to Vienna, and was employed several years in engraving for Mollo's Repository of Arts. From 1808, till the time of his death in 1818, he occupied his time in making drawings of the picturesque scenery in the Tyrol, at Salzburg, in various other parts of Germany, and in Hungary, from which he engraved many plates for Mollo. His prints are beautifully executed, producing a fine effect, and are highly esteemed. Dr. Giulio Ferrario, in his account of classical prints, describes two large prints by him in aquatinto, after J. Both, published at Vienna in 1804, which he considers very rare and fine, as he had not seen any others elsewhere. He writes his name erroneously, *Scheletterbek*.

SCHLOTTERBECK, Christian Jacob, a German painter and engraver, born at Brehlingen in Wurtemberg in 1755. Little is known of him as a painter, but he executed a number of plates of portraits, some after antique sculptures, and a number of frontispieces, vignettes, and other book plates. Among his principal prints are, the portraits of Lavater, F. Kobell, J. J. Moser, Titian's Mistress, Herodias with the Head of St. John the Baptist, the Laocoon, Castor and Pollux, Minerva, Mercury, and Diana.

SCHLUTER, Andrew, a German sculptor and architect, born at Hamburg in 1662. He acquired the elements of the art from a sculptor of Dantzic, named Sapovius, and is supposed to have completed his studies in Italy. In 1691, he was employed at Warsaw, by the king of Poland; and the Elector of Brandenburg invited him to Berlin in 1694, with a considerable pension. In the following year he was appointed a Director of the Academy of Fine Arts, and erected for Sophia Charlotte, the wife of his patron, the grand and beautiful chateau of Liezenburg, near that of Charlottenburg. In 1697 he executed his bronze statue of the Elector, and was appointed architect to the king. Charged with rebuilding the royal chateau, he proceeded in his work for some time; but, in consequence of the intrigues of his rivals, he lost his appointment of royal architect, although retaining that of sculptor. His works in the latter branch of art are distinguished for correctness of design, purity of outline, and truth of expression. Among the principal are the bronze statue of Frederick I.; that of Hohenzollern; and above all, his equestrian statue of the Grand Elector, distinguished for its noble expression, easy and lively attitude. Schluter visited St. Petersburg in 1713, and was commissioned by Peter the Great to erect several palaces; but he died there in the following year.

SCHMIDT, George Frederick, an eminent Prussian engraver, born at Berlin in 1712. He first studied under G. P. Busch, an obscure artist in that city. He afterwards went to Paris, where he became the pupil of Nicholas Larmessin. Under the able instruction of that eminent artist he acquired a skill in handling the graver, with a neatness and firmness seldom surpassed. In 1742 he was received into the Academy at Paris, and engraved for his reception-piece his fine portrait of P. Mignard. In 1744 he returned to Berlin, and was soon after appointed engraver to the king. In 1757 he went to St. Petersburg, at the invitation of the Empress Elizabeth, and executed several portraits and other plates, with great success. In 1762 he returned to Berlin, where he discovered a new talent in etching and engraving several plates in the manner of Rembrandt, which were greatly admired; he also engraved in the manner of Della Bella and Benedetto Castiglione, with equal success. He died at Berlin in 1775. His prints amount to about two hundred, of which the following are the most esteemed:

PORTRAITS.

The Empress Elizabeth of Russia; *after L. Tocqué* Michael, Count de Woronzow; *do.* Nicholas Esterhazi, Count of the Roman Empire; *do.* Frederick Henry Louis, Prince of Prussia; *after A. Vanloo.* John Paul Bignon, Abbe de St. Quentin; *after Rigaud.* Constantine Scarlati, Prince of Moldavia. Charles Gabriel de Caylus, Bishop of Auxerre; *after Fontaine.* Louis de la Tour d'Auvergne, Count d'Evreux; *after Rigaud.* Charles de St. Albin, Archbishop of Cambray; *do.* Peter Mignard, Painter to the King; *do.* Anthony Pesne, Painter to the King of Prussia; *after a picture by himself.* Maurice Quentin de la Tour, Painter to the King; *do.*

SUBJECTS AFTER VARIOUS MASTERS.

The Virgin and infant Christ, with St. John; *after Vandyck.* The Presentation in the Temple; *after Pietro Testa.* Alexander and his Physician; *after Ann. Caracci.* Timocleus justified by Alexander; *do.* A Bust of the Virgin; *after Sassoferrato.* Dutch Boors regaling; *after A. Ostade*, in the style of *Visscher*.

PRINTS ETCHED IN THE STYLE OF REMBRANDT.

His own Portrait, drawing. The Portrait of Rembrandt, *after a picture by himself.* Christ resuscitating the daughter of Jairus; *after Rembrandt.* Christ presented to the People; *do.* The Presentation in the Temple; *after Dietricy.* A variety of Busts and Portraits; *after Rembrandt*, and in his manner. Lot and his Daughters; *do.*; very rare, before the letters. The Young Jewess and her Father; both *do.* The Mother of Rembrandt. The young Lord, and an old Man with a Beard; *do.*

SCHMIDT, Isaac, a Dutch painter, born at Amsterdam in 1740. He first studied under John van Huysum, and afterwards with J. M. Quinkhart, with whom he continued six years. He did not acquire much reputation as a painter, though he executed some good landscapes in concert with Juriaan Andriessen. He devoted much of his time to teaching, poetry, and music. He was one of the founders of the Drawing Academy at Amsterdam in 1759, and continued to be a director till his death, in 1818.

SCHMITZ. This engraver was a native of Germany, and flourished about 1780. He studied design at Dusseldorf, under Lambert Krahe, whose daughter he afterwards married. Having completed his engagement with that master, he visited Paris, and studied engraving under J. G. Wille; after which he returned to Dusseldorf, and practised the art with reputation and success. He was honored with a pension from the Elector of Bavaria. Among his principal prints are the following, after pictures in the Dusseldorf Gallery: A Group of Children, *after Rubens;* Jesus and St. John, *after Scarsellino;* Jesus appearing to Mary Magdalene, *after Baroccio.* He died about 1791.

SCHMUTZ, Johann Rudolf, a Swiss painter, born at Regensperg, in the canton of Zurich, in 1670. He studied under Mathias Füessli, and first applied himself to historical painting, but not meeting with much success, he bent his attention to portraiture. He went to England when Knelier was at his zenith, and, attaching himself to his style, he met with flattering success, and was rising rapidly into public favor when he died, in 1715.

SCHMUTZER, John Adam, a German engraver, the eldest son of an Austrian general, was born at Vienna about 1700. He did not attain much distinction in the art. He was commissioned to engrave several subjects after pictures in the Imperial Gallery; and his portraits of the three Empresses, Eleonora, Amelia, and Elizabeth, are not without merit. He died in 1739.

SCHMUTZER, Joseph and Andrew, German engravers, and younger brothers of the preceding, were born at Vienna about 1702. They frequently wrought together on the same plate; and their prints are sometimes signed *Joseph-Andreas*, and sometimes *Andreas-Joseph*. Andreas imitated the manner of van Dalen and Bolswert, and handled the graver in a clear, bold style. Among other prints by these artists are the following:

PORTRAITS.

The Emperor Charles VI.; *after Meytens*. The Empress Elizabeth Christina; *after Averbach*. Gustavus Adolphus, Baron de Gotter.

SUBJECTS AFTER VARIOUS MASTERS.

Two Views of a Temple; *after G. Galli Bibiena*. Three subjects from the History of Decius; after the pictures by *Rubens* in the gallery of the Prince of Lichtenstein.

SCHMUTZER, Jacob Mathias, a German engraver, the son of Andrew S., was born at Vienna in 1733. Losing his father when only eight years of age, he passed his youth in trials and struggles; acquired a knowledge of architecture through the patronage of Matthew Donner, an engraver of medals, and practised it in Hungary; and finally, through the kind offices of the Prince of Kaunitz, by order of the Empress Maria Theresa, he was sent to Paris, and placed in the school of J. G. Wille. After studying four years at Paris, Schmutzer returned to Vienna, and was appointed Director of the Academy established by Maria Theresa. He deserves to be ranked among the most famous engravers of his time; and several excellent scholars were produced under his instruction. His plates are executed very skillfully with the graver, in a neat, clear style, resembling that of his instructor. Nagler gives a list of forty-seven prints by him, among which are the following:

PORTRAITS.

Francis I., Emperor of Germany. Maria Theresa, his Empress. Joseph Winceslaus, Prince of Lichtenstein. Wenceslaus, Prince of Kaunitz; very rare. Martin de Meytens, Painter to the Emperor. C. W. E. Dietricy, Painter.

VARIOUS SUBJECTS.

Mutius Scævola before Porsenna; *after Rubens*. St. Gregory refusing the Emperor Theodosius the entrance into the church; *do*. Venus rising from the Sea; *do*.

SCHNEBBELIE, Jacob. This artist was the son of a Swiss officer, who went to England, and settled in the parish of St. Martin-in-the-Fields, where Jacob was born in 1760. Having a taste for the fine arts, he learned drawing and landscape painting, without any other assistance than nature and books; for some time he taught drawing, and obtained considerable employment. While sketching in Hertfordshire, he attracted the notice of the Earl of Leicester, who became his patron, and gave him commissions for several landscapes from nature. In 1781, he began a set of views of St. Augustin's monastery; in 1788, he designed, engraved and published four views of the town and abbey of St. Albans. Soon after this he set on foot a work entitled "The Antiquary's Museum," and he became an associate of Mr. Moore in the "Monastic Remains," &c. He was next engaged by the Society of Antiquaries, in designing for their "Vetusta Monumenta"; by Mr. Gough for his "Sepulchral Monuments in Great Britain," and by Mr. Nichols for his "History of Leicestershire." He projected a work under the title of the "Antique Dresses since William the Conqueror," but he did not live to complete it, and died in 1792.

SCHNELLHOLTZ, Gabriel, a German designer and engraver, the accounts of whom are exceedingly contradictory. Some say he was born at Merseberg, others at Wittemberg, in 1536; others again that he flourished at Wittemberg about 1590. According to Nagler, he carried on the business of a printer and bookseller, as well as engraving, and published several books at Wittemberg in 1562 and 1563, one of which is entitled *Illustrium Ducum Saxoniæ vivæ effigies ab anno nativitatis Christi* 824 *usque ad annum* 1563. This work was reprinted in German in 1570. He marked his prints with an S. and an arrow placed perpendicularly, which is the *rebus* of his name. Zani says he was a wood engraver, and operated in 1590; Strutt that he engraved a considerable number of excellent prints, marked with the above monogram. His name is variously written, *Schnellholtz*, *Schnellboltz*, and *Schnellbotz;* the first is the correct spelling.

SCHNITZER, John, an old German wood engraver, born at Arnsheim, who flourished at Ulm about 1486. He executed the cuts of the *Geographical Chart for the edition of Ptolemy*, published at Ulm in that year. The map of the world is ornamented with ten heads, representing the winds, rudely cut. It is inscribed, *Insculptum est per Johannem Schnitzer de Arnsheim.*

SCHNORR VON CAROLSFELD, Johann Veit, commonly called Hans Veit, a German artist, born at Schneeberg in 1764. His father was a member of the common council in that city, and gave his son a liberal education; he afterwards studied jurisprudence till he was twenty-five years of age, when his strong predilection for the fine arts induced him to abandon that profession, and he entered the school of Frederick Oeser, at Leipsic, an eminent painter and engraver. He distinguished himself by his multifarious works. He painted history and portraits, made designs and drew in chalk, India ink, sepia, and in water-colors. He modeled in clay and plaster, and in short exercised his abilities in every branch of art. He is known however, beyond the limits of his own country, only by his works as an engraver. He executed many spirited and beautiful plates in aquatinto, and in the chalk manner. His subjects consist of portraits of distinguished persons, poetical illustrations and vignettes, from his own designs, antique statuary, bas-reliefs, &c., of which an ample list may be found in Nagler's Lexicon, with many interesting particulars. He died at Leipsic in 1842.

SCHOEN, or SCHONGAUER, Martin an

old German painter and engraver, about whose history and works there is a great deal of contradiction and uncertainty. His countrymen claim that he was one of the earliest engravers. His birth is variously placed about 1420, 1445, and 1453, and his death in 1486 and 1499; the place of his nativity, Culmbach, Colmar, and Augsburg. Huber calls him the father of engraving in Germany, and says he was born at Culmbach about 1420, and died at Colmar, where he chiefly resided, in 1486. Bartsch and Zani place his birth at Colmar, in or about 1445; Ottley in 1453, and they all concur that he died in 1499. Bartsch engraved the portrait of Martin Schongauer, and prefixed it to the sixth volume of "Le Peintre Graveur," taken from a painting formerly at Nuremberg, afterwards in the collection of Count Fries, and now at Schleissheim or Munich, on which is inscribed, *Hipsch Martin Schongauer Maler*, 1483, with an escutcheon of arms, bearing a crescent gules on a field argent. On the back of the picture is written, in old German characters, "Master Martin Schongauer, painter, called Hipsch (handsome) Martin on account of his art, born at Colmar, but of a citizen family of Augsbourg. Noble by origin, &c. Died at Colmar, in the year 1499, the 2nd of February. May God show him mercy. And I, Hans Largkmair, was his disciple in the year 1488." Albert Durer is said to have had such a strong desire to be personally acquainted with Schongauer, that he went to Colmar in 1492 on purpose to see him, but was disappointed, Martin being absent from the city. Yet he was kindly received by his brothers, Gaspar, Paul, and Louis. The Baron Heineken describes a drawing in his possession, on the back of which is written in German, "This piece was designed by Hübsch Martin in 1470, being then a youth. I, Albert Durer, have learned that, and have written this to his honor, in the year 1517." Bartsch says that "all the prints of Martin Schongauer exhibit an almost equal perfection in the management of the burin, which induces the belief that he had not commenced engraving on copper, or rather that he had not taken impressions, till after he had acquired a thorough command of the instrument, by great practise in ornamenting plate; for it is said that he united the art of the goldsmith with that of the painter." Ottley remarks, on this supposition of Bartsch, "If the truth of this observation be acknowledged, it will follow, as highly probable at least, that none of the engravings of Schongauer now known appertain to a period more remote than about the year 1475; at all events, there seems every reason to believe that by far the greater portion of them were executed in the last twenty years of the century in which he lived." So much for supposition. This much appears certain, that he was one of the earliest, if not the very first German artist who engraved on copper-plates. Wood engraving had been practised many years before there is anything authentic concerning him. (See Introduction, page xii.) He carried the mechanical part of the art to an astonishing degree of perfection. Although his drawing is incorrect, and his compositions partake of the stiffness and formality which characterize the works of the old German artists, his productions prove that he possessed a fertile imagination, and exhibit both genius and judgment. In his print of the Death of the Virgin, there is a fine expression in the heads, and the accessories are finished with a beauty and delicacy of execution which has scarcely been surpassed. It is stated that Michael Angelo, in his youth, was so captivated with the wildness and variety of his print of St. Anthony tormented by Demons, that he copied it in colors. His prints are numerous, and are principally from his own designs. He usually marked them with one of the following monograms of his initials, an M. and an S. in the old German letter, with a kind of cross between them. With regard to his paintings there is much uncertainty. There are works attributed to him in the Galleries at Nuremberg, Munich, Schleissheim, and Vienna, but connoisseurs are divided as to the authenticity of several. There are two, doubtless genuine, in the church of the Hospital at Colmar, representing the Nativity, and the Adoration of the Magi, both of which subjects he engraved. There is another, called the Virgin in the Rosebush, placed behind the altar in the Cathedral of the same city. It is celebrated for its large size, composition, and excellent state of preservation. It is painted on a gold ground, as almost all the works attributed to him are; the Virgin is represented seated among Roses, with the infant Jesus in her lap, while two Angels are in the act of crowning her. The figures are of life size, the whole picture is carefully executed, and the colors are so blended that the touch of the pencil is imperceptible. The Crucifixion, at Vienna, is also one of his approved pictures; it is full of expression, and is thought to partake of the school of Cologne. The following are his most esteemed prints:

M + S, or M + S, or M S
M + S, or M + S.

SACRED SUBJECTS.

The Life of the Virgin; twelve plates. Twelve plates of the Passion of our Saviour. The Annunciation. The Nativity. The Adoration of the Magi. The Flight into Egypt. The Wise and the Foolish Virgins; ten plates. The Last Judgment. Christ bearing his Cross. The Crucifixion. The Death of the Virgin; this was also engraved by Israel van Mecheln, Wenceslaus, and others. A small set of the Apostles. St. Anthony carried into the Air by Demons. St. Sebastian tied to a Tree.

VARIOUS SUBJECTS.

Two Alchymists fighting. A set of twelve subjects of Ornaments for goldsmiths. A Ciborium. An incense Cup, or Censer. Engraved also by J. van Mecheln. A Bishop's Crosier. The Battle of the Saracens against the Christians, in which St. James appears on the side of the latter. This was probably his last plate, as it was not entirely finished.

b x 8 SCHOEN, Bartholomew. According to Professor Christ, this artist was a brother of Martin Schoen, but Bartsch and others express a doubt of this, and even whether there was ever an artist of this name, as it is expressly said that the celebrated Martin S. had four brothers, Gaspar, Paul, Louis, and George, but there is no mention of Bartholomew; therefore they think that the prints bearing the above monogram were executed by an artist whose name has been lost. It would seem more probable, that he was the brother or a relative of Martin, inasmuch as there is a great simi ιarity in their styles and marks, and he moreover copied some of his prints, particularly the twelve prints of the Passion of Christ. There are about thirty prints attributed to him by Bartsch and others, all of which bear the above monogram, composed of a B. and an S. in the old German characters, with a cross between them. They have a strong resemblance to those of Martin S., though they are not executed with so much neatness and expression. Prof. Christ mentions one with the date 1479.

SCHOEN, or SCHÖN, Erhard, a German engraver on wood, who flourished at Nuremberg from 1516 to 1550, as appears from the dates of several books published there during that period, embellished with frontispieces or other engravings from his designs. Bartsch attributes thirty-three prints to him. In 1538 he published a book on the proportions of the human figure, for students, which, though illustrated with coarse wood cuts, had a great sale, and went through three editions in five years. Jackson, in his treatise on wood engraving, asserts that Erhard Schoen, like many others of the 16th century called wood engravers, only made the designs for the prints bearing his mark, and that he never engraved; this assertion, however, is founded on mere supposition, though there can be little doubt that several of the old German wood engravers employed assistants, as is done at the present day. Schoen marked his prints with a monogram composed of an E. and an S., with a knife underneath, as above.

J. H. S. P.

SCHOENFELD, or SCHOONFELD, John Henry, a German painter, born at Biberach, in Swabia, of a noble family, according to the best authorities, in 1609. After studying with John Sichelbein, an indifferent artist, in his native city, he traveled through Germany, and then went to Italy for improvement. At Rome he painted two altar-pieces, which gained him considerable reputation, and he was employed in executing some of the embellishments in the Palazzo Orsini. On his return to his own country, he distinguished himself as an historical painter, and executed many works at Vienna, Munich, Salzbourg, and other cities. He was also much employed in portraiture, and painted landscapes, decorated with figures and architecture, which were greatly admired. Among his most esteemed historical works, are Christ conducted to Calvary, and the Descent from the Cross, in the church of the Holy Cross at Augsbourg, where he resided in the latter part of his life. In the Senate-house of the same city, is another fine picture by him, representing the Race of Hippomenes and Atalanta. His works show a ready and fertile invention, and an extraordinary facility of hand; but his drawing is often incorrect, and his figures are generally too long; his coloring is vigorous, though occasionally crude and glaring. He executed quite a number of etchings from his own designs. Nagler gives a list of twenty-three prints by him, and there are others of landscapes with figures and rich architecture. They are etched in a slight style, and the figures, as in many of his pictures, are out of proportion to the other objects. Zani and Füessli place his death at Augsbourg in 1680; Nagler in 1675, and others, his birth in 1619, and his death in 1689 He marked his prints with initials as above.

SCHOENMACKER, or SCHOENMAKERS John Peter, a Dutch painter, born at Dort in 1755, and died there in 1842. His life has not yet been written. He painted views of the cities of Holland in the manner of Vander Heyden, with great success, and his pictures are to be found in the best collections of his country, where they are highly esteemed. He was on intimate terms with several eminent artists of his country, and sometimes employed them to insert his figures and animals. In one of the exhibitions at Dort, there were four of his most admired pictures, in which the figures and vessels were painted by J. C. Schotel; these additions enhance their value.

SCHOEVAERDTS, M., a painter born about 1667. The accounts of this artist are very contradictory—some make him a native of Flanders or Holland; others of Germany. He painted village festivals, merry-makings, &c., in which he appears to have imitated Teniers, though there is little resemblance in their works except similarity of subjects. His pictures are generally crowded with figures in full activity, and he frequently introduced horses and wagons and horned cattle. His pictures are well designed, his touch is neat and spirited, his coloring pleasing, and his works, though very inferior to those of Teniers, are held in considerable estimation. There are two village scenes by him in the gallery of the Louvre, under the name of *N. Schowaert*. Balkema confounds him with *Christopher Schwarts*, a totally different artist. He signed his pictures and his etchings *M. Schoevaerdts;* hence it is conjectured that his christian name was *Martin* or *Michael*. Some write his name *Schovaerts*. Two of his pictures have been engraved under the titles of *Fête de campagne Hollandaise*, and *Retour de la Fête Hollandaise*. He executed a few etchings in a slight, but spirited style, from his own designs and after other masters.

SCHOLLENBERG, H. J., a German engraver, who flourished about 1630, and engraved some portraits, executed in a neat, but hard and formal style. Nagler says his name was *Hans Jacob Schollenberger*, and that he flourished at Nuremberg from 1670 to 1690; but this artist was probably his son, as there are prints by Schollenberg dated 1630, and Zani says he operated from 1622, to 1674.

SCHOONEBECK, Adrian, a Dutch engraver, born at Amsterdam in 1650. He studied under R. de Hooghe, whose manner he followed at first, but afterwards practised mostly in mezzotinto. He engraved a variety of frontispieces and other book plates; also the costumes of all the religious orders of Europe, published in two volumes. He went to Russia, and died at Moscow in 1714.

SCHOONJANS, Anthony, a Flemish painter, born at Antwerp, according to Descamps, in 1650. While young, he was placed under the tuition of Erasmus Quellinus, with whom he continued till he was nineteen years of age, when he went to Italy for the completion of his artistic education. During a residence of two years at Rome, he diligently applied himself to the study of the best works of art, and executed several pictures for the churches, which gained him so much reputation, that the Emperor Leopold I., invited him to Vienna in 1678, appointed him his cabinet painter, and honored him with a present of a gold chain and medal. He painted the portraits of the Emperor, of the Imperial family, and of the principal personages of the court, which were greatly admired. He also executed several grand altar-pieces and other works for the churches and convents. Having a desire to visit England, he obtained leave of the Emperor to absent himself for a time from his service, and he went to that country in the reign of William III., where he met with considerable employment in painting the portraits, and decorating the mansions of some of the nobility. In returning to Vienna, he passed some time at Dusseldorf, where he painted several pictures for the Elector Palatine, who munificently rewarded him, and presented him with a gold chain and medal. On his return to Vienna, he continued in the service of the Emperor till his death, in 1726. His pictures are correctly designed and carefully executed. He had a thorough knowledge of the principles of chiaro-scuro, which enabled him to give his pictures a remarkable roundness and relief.

SCHOOR, Nicholas van, a Flemish painter, born at Antwerp in 1666. It is not known under whom he studied. He painted nymphs, genii, and children sporting, taken from fabulous history, which he represented in a pleasing and lively style; he was employed in introducing these subjects, as accessories, into the flower pieces of Nicholas Morell, and the landscapes of Rysbraeck. His chief business was in making designs for tapestry for the manufacturers at Antwerp and Brussels. In the Museum at Ghent, there is an equestrian portrait of Charles II. of Spain, by him, painted when that prince was about the age of eighteen. He is said to have died rich, at Antwerp, in 1726.

SCHOORE, J. V., a Flemish engraver, who flourished about 1650. He executed a few plates, among which is one of St. Vincent, *after Anthony Salaert.*

SCHOOTEN, George van, a Dutch historical and portrait painter, born at Leyden in 1587. He was a scholar of Conrad vander Maas. He was a painter of considerable eminence in his time, though his works are little known at present except a few portraits. Suyderhoef engraved one of his portraits, and J. G. van Vliet, his picture of Christ and the Woman of Samaria, one of his best prints, which is inscribed J. (Jorg) van Schooten, 1635. He is supposed to have been one of the instructors of Rembrandt. He died in 1658.

SCHOOTER, Francis van, a professor of mathematics and philosophy at Leyden, who flourished about the middle of the 17th century. He designed and engraved the portrait of Des Cartes, which is inscribed *Franciscus a Schooten Pr. Mat. ad vivum delineavit et fecit, anno.* 1644. It is prefixed to an edition of the "Geometria," published at Leyden in that year.

SCHOREL, or SCHOOREEL, John, a Dutch painter, born at Schooreel, a small village near Alkmaer, in 1495. There is a great deal of romance mixed up with his life, but there is not, according to Waagen, a single well authenticated picture in existence by him; therefore we shall be brief. After studying, as is said, successively with Cornelisz at Amsterdam, John de Mabuse at Utrecht, and Albert Durer at Nuremberg, he went to Venice, where, meeting with a number of pilgrims, and an ecclesiastic of Gouda, with whom he was acquainted, bound to Jerusalem, he was persuaded to accompany them. He designed some of the most interesting scenery in the Holy Land. In 1520, he embarked for the Isle of Rhodes, thence he sailed to Venice, and traveled to Rome, where he resided three years, designing after the antique, and the great Italian masters. He also painted the portrait of Pope Adrien VI. On his return to Holland, he settled at Utrecht, where he acquired great reputation for his scriptural subjects, embellished with the scenery he had sketched on the spot. Such were his celebrated pictures of Christ entering into Jerusalem, and the Baptism of Christ, in which he is said to have imitated the grand style of Raffaelle. Many of his works were destroyed during the civil wars in the Low Countries. He was the first who attempted to reform the taste of his country by the introduction of a more elevated style. He died at Utrecht in 1562.

ISF 1609 SCHORER, John Frederick, a German designer and engraver, born at Augsburg, at what time is not known, but he flourished at Nuremberg about 1619. Nagler describes nine prints by him, representing the Four Elements, the Four Seasons, and an ornament for goldsmiths, dated from 1615 to 1619. Brulliot notices several drawings by him, marked with the above monogram, bearing dates from 1609 to 1639. He is supposed to have resided chiefly at Nuremberg and Cobourg, and from his initials to have been called *Hans Friedrich Schorer.*

SCHORN, Charles, an eminent German painter, born at Dusseldorf in 1803. He studied under Cornelius at Munich, and afterwards with Gros and Ingres, at Paris. Returning again to Munich, he assisted Cornelius in some of his important works, and was afterwards occupied in the *atelier* of Wach, in the same city. He gained distinction, and practised the art at Munich for many years, with great success. His imagination was discursive, and his invention ready and fertile. His works generally are not what may be termed historical, but rather from subjects like his two pictures of Monks carousing at a Tavern, and a Group of Puritans. He painted a large picture of Paul III. contemplating the portrait of Luther, for the Consul Waggener at Berlin; a fine composition, and full of dignified character. His picture of Salvator Rosa among the Brigands is a most admirable work. He was appointed Professor of the Academy at Munich, and was chosen by the king to form the collection of pictures for the Munich Gallery. He died in 1850.

SCHORQUEUS, John van, a Dutch engraver who went to Madrid, where he appears to have flourished from about 1600 to 1630, and executed many frontispieces and other plates for the book publishers. The Spanish writers call him *Juan Scorquens*, but he inscribed some of his plates *J. van Schorqueus fecit in Madrid.*

SCHOTEL, John Christian, an eminent Dutch marine painter, born at Dort in 1787. He first studied with A. Meulemans, and afterwards with Martin Schouman, with whom he continued three years, and chiefly devoted his time to drawing in water colors and India ink, under the direction of that master. On quitting Schouman, he devoted himself to the study of nature with great assiduity, for which purpose he was accustomed to embark in an open boat, in all kinds of weather, and carefully sketch and note every appearance of the sea. His first exhibition of two pictures in oil at Amsterdam, was eminently successful; they were received by the artists as well as the public with applause, and were immediately purchased at high prices. This was a stimulus to still greater exertion, and made him emulous of rivaling his renowned countryman, Backhuysen. From 1814 to 1817, he executed two pictures representing the precipitous retreat of the French from before Dort, and the Bombardment of Algiers by the allied fleets in 1816. He soon rose to great distinction, and his works were eagerly sought after, not only by his own countrymen, but by foreigners. In 1827, he painted two magnificent pictures for the Prince of Orange, as a present to the Emperor of Russia. He received honors from his own sovereign, and other crowned heads, and was elected a member of several academies and societies of art.

Schotel designed everything from nature; hence it is that his pictures have an air of truth which excites universal admiration. In his calms and river views, he is said to have equalled the younger Vandevelde in the smoothness and transparency of the water, and in the reflections of his objects; and in his storm-pieces, almost to have rivalled Backhuysen in the sublime and terrific conflict of the elements. His pictures are distinguished for excellence of perspective, correct drawing, neatness and freedom of touch, and admirable chiaroscuro. He died at Dort in 1838. His son, Peter John Schotel, still lives at Dort, and practises marine painting in the style of his father; and, though his subjects are usually of smaller dimensions, representing breezes, calms, and river views, they very nearly approach the elder Schotel in excellence.

SCHOUMAN, Artus, a Dutch painter and engraver, born at Dort in 1710. He studied under Adrian vander Burg, and painted history, portraits, and landscapes. His small cabinet pictures of histories and poetical subjects, chiefly taken from Ovid, and landscapes with figures and animals, are well designed and colored. He settled at the Hague, where he acquired considerable reputation. He also engraved some plates in mezzotinto, after the works of Gerard Douw, Paul Potter, Frank Hals, Schalcken, and others. He died in 1792.

SCHOUMAN, Martin, a Dutch painter, who flourished at Dort in the last part of the 18th, and the first part of the present century. His life has not yet been written. He painted landscapes, marines, and river views, with considerable reputation.

SCHRODER, Hans, a Dutch engraver, who flourished about 1600. Little is known of him, except that he engraved some ornamental plates of foliage, &c., for goldsmiths.

SCHROEDER, Frederick, a German engraver, born at Hesse Cassel in 1768, or, as some say, in 1772. He studied under Sebastian Ignatius Klauber at Nuremberg. He went to Paris, where he was employed to engrave for several publications of the day, as Le Musée Laurent et Robillard, and Le Voyage à Constantinople, &c. He confined himself chiefly to landscape, and engraved several plates after Swanevelt, Vernet, La Hire, Karel du Jardin, and Wm. van Bemmel. His plates are executed in a neat, pleasing style. He was living at Paris in 1831.

SCHROETER, Frederick Charles Constantine, a German painter, was the son of a veterinary surgeon in a Saxon regiment, born in 1794. He was early apprenticed to a carpenter, but having considerable inclination for design, he quitted that employment, and commenced studying painting in the Academy at Leipsic. Through the patronage of Keyl, the Receiver General of the provincial excise, Schroeter was sent for improvement to Dresden, where he gained two prizes at the exhibitions, and was admitted to the studio of Pochmann. After completing his studies, he settled at Leipsic, and painted many esteemed cabinet pictures of familiar subjects. He subsequently settled at Berlin, and exhibited, in 1828, two pictures, the Sermon and the Music Teacher, which were greatly admired for their fidelity to nature. In 1832 he painted a picture representing the Sale of the Effects of a deceased Painter, which is considered his masterpiece, the composition being abundant, the groups happily disposed, the expression animated, and the gradations of coloring extremely delicate. Schroeter practised the art at Berlin with success, for many years. He died in 1835.

SCHUBART, Peter, a German engraver, who went to Venice, where he flourished about 1696. Professor Christ attributes to him several plates, marked P. S. d E., which he interprets *Peter Schubart de Ebrenberg*.

SCHUBLER, A. G. J., a German engraver, who flourished at Nuremberg about 1626. He engraved some portraits for the booksellers; also a part of the plates for the work entitled *Icones Bibliopolarum et Typographorum*, published at Altdorff and at Nuremberg in that year. His prints are indifferently executed.

SCHULZE, Johann Gottfried, a German engraver, born at Dresden in 1749. After learning the rudiments of design of Charles Hutin, and engraving of Giuseppe Camerati, he went to Paris, and studied with J. G. Wille. On his return to his native city, he engraved some portraits and other subjects, particularly several plates for the Dresden Gallery, which are executed in a neat, firm style, and possess considerable merit. He died in 1818. Nagler calls his name *Christian Gotfried*, and gives a list of 36 prints by him.

SCHUMANN, Johann Gottfried, a German engraver, born at Dresden in 1761. He studied design in the Academy in that city, and engraved a number of landscapes after Ruysdael, Klengel, Both, and others, executed in a neat, spirited style. He went to London, where he resided some time, and engraved some plates in conjunction with Byrne. He died at Dresden in 1810. Nagler gives a list of 26 prints by him.

SCHUPPEN, Peter van, the Elder, a Flemish designer and engraver, born at Antwerp in 1628, according to the best authorities, though some variously place it in 1623, 1625, and 1630. After learning the rudiments of design in his native city he went to Paris, where he studied with Nanteuil, and resided the most of his life. He engraved a large number of plates of portraits and other subjects, some of them from his own designs, executed with the graver in the style of his instructor. His design is correct, and he handled the graver with great dexterity and firmness. A list of 119 prints by him may be found in Nagler's Lexicon. His death is variously placed in 1702, 1710, and 1715.

SCHUPPEN, Peter van, the Younger, was the son of the preceding, born at Paris, according to Füessli and Zani in 1669, though others say in 1673. He studied painting under Nicholas de Largilliere, and acquired considerable reputation at Paris as an historical painter. He was invited to the court of Vienna, where he was appointed painter to the Emperor, whose portrait he painted, and those of the Imperial family, and the principal nobility. He was also appointed Director of the Academy in that city. He died there in 1751. Some writers call his name *Jacques van S.*

HSV SCHUPPEN, H. van, an engraver of whom nothing is known, except some prints of landscapes, *after Giovanni Maggi*, who flourished at Rome in the early part of the 17th century. Some of them are signed ***H. v. Schuppen***, and others marked with a monogram composed of his initials, H. V. S., as above.

SCHURMANS, Anna Maria. This extraordinary lady, descended of a noble family, was born at Utrecht in 1607. If the half of what is recorded of her be true, she must be regarded as one of the most wonderful prodigies the world has produced. From her earliest infancy she discovered an extraordinary quickness of parts, and her father took every care to have her instructed, not only in every female accomplishment, but in the languages, literature, science, and arts. She not only understood the modern and dead languages, but spoke them with fluency, and corresponded in them with the most learned persons of her time. She spoke the German, Italian, French, and English; also the Latin, Greek, and Hebrew languages. She made great progress in the Oriental languages, having an affinity to the Hebrew, as the Syriac, Arabic, Chaldean, and Ethiopic. She was also a poetess. She was well versed in ancient and modern literature, in geography, astronomy, the arts and sciences. She was deeply read in divinity and theology. She excelled in music, both vocal and instrumental. She embroidered beautifully; cut out of paper with her scissors, all kinds of images and objects. She painted history, portraits, flowers, birds, insects, and excelled in all; modelled in clay and wax, and executed several marble busts, said to be still preserved in the cabinets of the curious. She etched and engraved several plates of portraits and other subjects. Her hand-writing was very beautiful, of which there is abundant proof in the many existing letters, written in several languages, addressed to the most learned personages of her time. Her literary works, in Latin, Greek, Hebrew, and French, have been published in one volume. Unfortunately none of her works in art are specified, except a bust and an engraved portrait of herself, inscribed *Anna Maria Schurmans an. ætat.* CIƆ.IƆ.CXL. A. M. S. *fec.*, with these lines:

> Cernitis hic pictâ nostras in imagine vultus:
> Si negat Ars formam, gratia vestra dabit.

Her bust, modelled in wax by herself, is said to be preserved in Holland, to which she appended the following verses:

> Non mihi propositum est humanam eludere sortem,
> Aut vultus solido sculpere in ære meos;
> Hæc nostra effigies, quam cerâ expressimus, ecce
> Materiæ fragili, mox peritura, damus.

This learned lady died, unmarried, at Altona, in 1678.

CNS SCHURTZ, Cornelius Nicholas, a German engraver, who flourished at Nuremberg from about 1670 to 1689, according to the dates on his prints. He engraved some plates of portraits, among which are several of eminent physicians; also some frontispieces, emblematical subjects, and other book plates, indifferently executed. His prints are sometimes marked with his name in full, and sometimes with his initials, C. N. S., or the same letters formed into a monogram, as above.

SCHUT, Cornelius, an eminent Flemish painter, born at Antwerp. There is a great deal of confusion and contradiction among writers as to the history of this artist, arising partly from the fact, unknown to some of them, that there were two artists of this name. His birth is variously placed in 1590 and 1600, and his death in 1649, 1660, and 1675; but, according to the best authorities, he was born in 1600, and died in 1660. It is also generally stated that he was a scholar, and one of the ablest and most distinguished followers of Rubens. Possessing a lively and inventive genius, disciplined by a liberal education, it was not long before he distinguished himself among his fellow students. On leaving the school of Rubens, he was employed to execute several works for the churches, which gained him great reputation, and he was accounted worthy of the school in which he was educated. It is said by some that this success rendered him so self-sufficient and presumptuous that he had the temerity to offer himself as a rival to his illustrious instructor, whose works he criticised, accusing the author of a want of genius and invention, and asserted that the best part of his pictures were executed by his disciples. Others say that disappointment at the lack of appreciation and employment inspired him with an implacable enmity towards his master, who, instead of expressing any resentment, commended his performances and procured him employment. It is hardly credible, that a pupil could be so rash and so ungrateful to an instructor who always treated his scholars with paternal regard. It would therefore seem more probable that he received at least his first instruction from some other master, and that Rubens, perceiving his talent, employed him as an assistant, as he did other painters of talents who were not strictly his pupils, in executing some of his numerous commissions. The manner in which his conduct towards Rubens is mentioned in the life of that master, would certainly lead to this conclusion; at all events the magnanimous conduct of Rubens conciliated him, which is another argument in favor of this supposition.

Schut had a poetic and fertile invention, and he generally chose to paint subjects from ancient fable, though he painted sacred and profane history with equal reputation. He had a free, firm pencil, and his coloring plainly indicates the school of Rubens, yet his works are depreciated by a prevailing greyish tint, an incorrectness in design and out-

.ine, and a want of an attentive study of nature. He also had a facility of hand (dangerous to the reputation of most artists who practice it) which qualified him for the functions of a machinist. This is particularly evident in his frescos in the cupola of the Cathedral at Antwerp, and in other large works of that description in the public edifices of that city. Of his altar-pieces and other pictures in the churches, the most deserving of notice, are the Nativity, and the Assumption of the Virgin, in the church of the Jesuits; a Dead Christ with the Virgin and St. John, in the church of James, often mistaken for a work by Vandyck; and the Martyrdom of St. George in the Cathedral at Antwerp. There are also some of his works in the churches at Ghent. He painted many historical and fabulous pieces for the collections, ingeniously composed, though occasionally the groups are too much scattered or confused. Schut etched a large number of plates from his own designs, executed in a spirited style, resembling that of Benedetto Castiglione, a list of which is given in Nagler's Lexicon.

SCHUT, Cornelius, the Younger. According to Bermudez, this artist was the son of Peter Schut, the brother of Cornelius, and born at Antwerp, at what time is not known. He studied with his uncle, and accompanied his father to Madrid, who was an engineer in the service of the king of Spain. He passed the rest of his life in that country, and settled at Seville, where he acquired a high reputation, and executed many works for the churches, which are highly commended by the author above cited. He also executed many drawings in imitation of Murillo, which frequently pass for the works of that master. He was one of the founders of the Academy at Seville, and contributed liberally to its support. He filled the office of consul to that institution from 1663 to 1666, and President from 1670 to 1674. He died there in 1675. It is said that the elder Schut visited his brother at Madrid, and painted a large picture in the Imperial College, representing St. Francis Xavier baptizing the Indians, but as it is said that the artist died in Spain in 1675, it was evidently executed by the nephew. There are also some battle-pieces attributed to Cornelius Schut, but as neither of the preceding artists are mentioned as ever having painted any such subjects, and as the name is spelled *Schuyt*, they were doubtless executed by another artist.

SCHUTER, an engraver, probably a German. He engraved the portrait of Rembrandt for the first volume of prints from the paintings in the collection of the Marquis Gerini, at Florence, dated 1760.

SCHUTZ, Christian George, a German landscape painter and engraver, born at Floresheim, in the Electorate of Mentz, about 1730. He painted small cabinet pictures of landscapes and views on the Rhine, which are neatly touched and very highly finished, though the style is somewhat dry and hard. He also etched some plates from his own designs and after other masters.

SCHUUR, Theodore vander, a Dutch painter, born at the Hague in 1628. After learning the rudiments of the art in his native city, he went to Paris, and studied with Sebastian Bourdon three years, after which he proceeded to Italy. He arrived at Rome in 1651, and applied himself incessantly in copying and designing after the works of the best masters, particularly those of Raffaelle and Giulio Romano, in which he succeeded so happily that his performances attracted the notice and commendation of the best judges. He had acquired considerable reputation by some historical works he had exhibited, when he was favored with the patronage of Christina, Queen of Sweden, who, on the abdication of her throne in favor of Prince Charles Gustavus, had taken up her residence at Rome. He executed for her several historical works, which were highly commended, and for which he was liberally rewarded. In 1665, after a residence of fourteen years at Rome, he returned to his native city, where he was received by his fellow-citizens with the most flattering distinction. He painted the ceiling of the hall of the Burgomasters in the Town House, representing emblematically Justice, Temperance, and Fortitude. This work was highly applauded, and gained him extraordinary honor. He executed many works for the churches and public edifices, and for individuals. One of his most esteemed works is a large picture in the Town House, representing the Officers of the Armed Citizens, painted in 1675. His works are designed rather in the Roman than in the Dutch style, his coloring is sweet and harmonious, and he had an excellent knowledge of perspective and architecture. He enriched his backgrounds with ruins of ancient Grecian and Roman edifices, introduced with the skill of a painter and the knowledge of an antiquary. He died at the Hague in 1705.

SCHUYT, Cornelius. See Cornelius Schut the Younger.

SCHWABE, Lambert. See Suavius.

SCHWANTHALER, Lewis, an eminent German sculptor, born in 1802. He was the son of Franz S., a sculptor of little note, who placed him in the Royal Academy at Munich. The young artist attracted the attention of King Maximilian, who engaged him to decorate a silver table-service with bassi-relievi, which represented the Entrance of the Younger Deities to Olympus. About this time the sculptor Cornelius arrived in Munich, and on seeing this table-service, he engaged Schwanthaler to execute different bassi-relievi for the Glyptotheca. The career of the young artist was now opened; he immediately went to Rome, where he was cordially received by Thorwaldsen. In a year after, he returned with the elegant and beautiful bassi-relievi of "the Birth of Venus," and of "Cupid and Psyche," which are now in the Glyptotheca; and afterwards he executed the other relievi for the same edifice, the "Battles between the Trojans and the Greeks," and between "Achilles and Pantheus, and the other river-Gods." The first of his statues was that of Shakspeare, in the theatre at Munich, and the first great basso-relievo, that of the Triumph of Bacchus, for the palace of the Duke Maximilian. In 1832 he visited Rome a second time, and in 1835, was appointed Professor of the Academy at Munich. His imagination was inexhaustible, and his facility of execution almost incredible. He produced an immense number of works, among which, are twelve statues of the most celebrated ancestors of King Louis, to adorn the throne of the festal hall in his new palace at Munich; the Battle of Arminius, for the northern tympanum of the same palace one of the finest works of modern art; and his celebrated shield of Hercules, in bronze, containing 136 figures, a master-piece of the finest taste, and full of beauty and fancy. He executed the monumental statues of Mozart, for Saltzburg; of Jean Paul, for Bayreuth; of Göethe, for Frankfort; of the Grand Duke of Baden, for Carlsruhe; a beautiful fountain, for the city of Vienna; the Nymph of the Danube, for the Prince Schwartzenburg; the statues of Venus, Diana, Vesta, Ceres, Apollo, etc., for the Duke of Nassau. In his latter days, he was occupied with the decoration of the celebrated Bavarian Ruhmeshalle, the two tympana of which, as well as the metopes, are ornamented with his bassi-relievi. He died in 1848.

SCHWARTS, CHRISTOPHER, a German painter, born at Ingolstadt in 1550. He learned the elements of the art in his native city, and then went to Venice and studied in the school of Titian. After a residence of several years in Italy, he returned to Germany, where he distinguished himself, and was invited to Munich by Albert V., Duke of Bavaria, who appointed him his court painter, in whose service he continued during the rest of his life. He executed many works for his patron; and many, both in oil and fresco, for the churches and public edifices at Munich; some of which have been engraved by John Sadeler. His countrymen honored him with the title of the *Raffaelle of Germany*, with what propriety it is difficult to discover; as his works have little of the dignity or grandeur of the Roman or Florentine schools. His principal merits consist in the abundance of his composition and the splendor of his coloring; the airs of his heads are neither beautiful nor expressive, his drawing is incorrect, and there is a national stiffness and formality in his design, of which he could never divest himself. His manner is a mixed one, partaking of the Venetian, Roman, and German schools. Two of his best works are the Virgin and Child in the grand hall of the Jesuits at Munich, and the Entombment, in the Dusseldorf gallery. He died at Munich in 1594.

SCHWARTS, a German engraver, who flourished at Nuremberg about 1626. He engraved some portraits and book plates, and a part of the plates for a work entitled *Icones Bibliopolarum et Typographorum*, published at Nuremberg in that year. His plates are indifferently executed.

SCHWARTZ, JOHANN, an old Dutch painter and engraver on wood, was born at Groningen in 1480. Zani denominates him *Giovanni di Groningen*, called *Giovanni Vredeman*. He visited Italy for improvement, and resided several years at Venice. On returning to Holland, he painted landscapes and history, and contrived to introduce somewhat of the Italian taste into his native country. He is said to have followed the style of Schorel in landscape; but as the latter was born in 1495, he more probably imitated Schwartz. He was residing at Gouda in 1522 and 1523. There are two of his landscapes in the Louvre, one of which is decorated with a large number of figures and animals. The *Biographie Universelle*, mentions two of his prints; Christ standing in a bark, preaching to the multitude on the shore; and a Troop of Turkish Cavaliers. Schwartz died in 1541.

SCHWARTZENBERG, MELCHIOR, an old German wood engraver, who flourished from 1530 to 1550. He executed some cuts of frontispieces and other subjects for Feyeraband, the bookseller.

SCHWEGMAN, HENDRIK, a Dutch painter and engraver, born at Haerlem in 1761, and died there in 1816. He studied under P. van Loo, and painted flower pieces with considerable success. He etched some plates of landscapes after E. van Drielst and others, in the style of Anthony Waterloo. He also engraved and colored the plates for the work entitled *Icones Plantarum rariorum*, &c.

SCHWEICKHARDT, HENRY WILLIAM, a German painter, born at Brandenburg in 1746. He painted landscapes and cattle, and particularly winter pieces, which were held in considerable estimation. He went to England in 1786, where he passed the rest of his life. He etched and published a set of plates of animals, which he dedicated to Mr. West, in 1788. He died at London in 1797.

SCHWEICKART, JOHN ADAM, a German engraver, born at Nuremberg in 1722. After acquiring a knowledge of the art under George Martin Priesler, he visited Italy for improvement, and resided eighteen years at Florence, where he engraved among other plates, several of the antique gems in the cabinet of Stosch, and was admitted a member of the Academy of Fine Arts. He gained considerable distinction by his discovery of the method of imitating washed designs, by means of the graver.

SCHWEIZER, JOHN, a German engraver, who flourished at Heidelberg about 1660. He engraved some plates of portraits, and some of animals, after J. H. Roos. He also engraved the frontispiece and plates for a work entitled *Parnassus Heidelbergensis, omnium illustrissimæ hujus academiæ professorum icones exhibens*, some of which are from his own designs. His prints are indifferently executed.

SCHYNDAL, or SCHENDAL, BERNARD, a Dutch painter, born at Haerlem, according to the best authorities, in 1659, and died in 1716, though some place his birth in 1634, and his death in 1693. He studied under Hendrick Mommers. He painted scenes from low life, such as assemblies of peasants regaling themselves, fairs, merry-makings, interiors of kitchens, ale-houses, &c., in the style of John Molinaer. He treated these subjects with much humor; his pictures are ingeniously composed, his coloring is rich and harmonious, and his penciling neat and clean; though his works are greatly inferior to the similar productions of Brouwer and Ostade, they are held in considerable estimation.

SCHYNVOET, JACOB, a Dutch engraver, of whom little is known. He went to London about 1700, where he engraved some birds-eye views of gentlemen's seats, from his own designs.

SCHIVENOGLIA, LO. See FRANCESCO RAINIERI.

SCIACCA, TOMMASO, a Sicilian painter, born at Mazzara in 1734. He studied under Antonio Cavalucci at Rome, and assisted him in some of his works. He also painted some large frescos in the cathedral, and in the church of the Olivetani at Rovigo. On his return to Sicily, according to Hackert, he executed "some vast works in fresco which are to be seen in the churches at Palermo." He died in 1795.

SCIAMERONI, Lo. See FRANCESCO FURINI.

SCIARPELLONI. See LORENZO DI CREDI.

SCILLA, or SILLA, AGOSTINO, a Sicilian painter, born at Messina, according to Hackert, in 1629. He showed an early genius for painting, and studied under Antonio Ricci, called Il Barbalunga, at Messina, under whose able instructions he made rapid progress. His talents raised such high expectations in Barbalunga, that he procured a pension for him from the Senate, to enable him to visit Rome and study with Andrea Sacchi. After a residence of four years in that metropolis, where he diligently studied the antique and the works of Raffaelle under the direction of Sacchi, he returned to Messina, an accomplished artist, and executed many works for the churches and public edifices in that city and elsewhere, both in oil and fresco. He also opened a school for the instruction of young artists, which was much frequented, till the stormy times of the revolution obliged him to fly from Messina in 1674. He then went back to Rome, where he does not seem to have met with much encouragement, at least in historical painting, though according to Orlandi, he was elected a member of the Academy of St. Luke in 1679. Lanzi says he excelled in figures and in heads, particularly in the heads of old men; he designed in the grand Roman style, and his coloring was rich and harmonious. He excelled in the inferior branches of the art, as landscapes, animals, fruit and flowers, and after his return to Rome, confined himself pretty much to those subjects, though he executed a few historical works. He went to Turin, where he was employed by the court to paint some frescos of the Cardinal Virtues. His principal works are his frescos in the churches of S. Domenico and the Nunziata di Teatini at Messina. One of his best works in oil, is St. Ilarione dying, in the church of S. Ursula, one of the most esteemed pictures in that city. He died at Rome in 1700.

SCILLA, GIACINTO, was a younger brother of the preceding, born at Messina. He studied first with Barbalunga, and afterwards with Agostino, whom he assisted in his numerous works at Messina, and accompanied him to Rome in 1674, where he painted easel pictures of landscapes and animals, in a style of excellence. He died there in 1711.

SCILLA, SAVERIO, was the son of Agostino. He was instructed by his father, in whose style he painted easel pictures of landscapes, animals, fruit, and flowers, but he did not reach the excellence of his father or his uncle. The time of his birth and death are not recorded.

SCIORINA, LORENZO DELLO, a Florentine painter, who flourished about 1568. He studied under Bronzino, and afterwards assisted Vasari in some of his works at Florence. Lanzi says that honorable mention is made of him among the academicians of Florence.

SCIPIONE, JACOPO, a painter born at Averara, in the Bergamese territory, who flourished at Bergamo from 1507 to 1529. According to Tassi, he executed some works for the churches in that city, "in a style between the ancient and the modern taste." His design was very simple, but his coloring very beautiful.

SCLAVO, LUCA, a painter born at Cremona, who flourished about 1460. Zaist briefly mentions him as one of the "excellent artists," of the Cremonese school of that period.

SCOLARI, GIUSEPPE, a painter generally supposed to have been born at Vicenza, though the Cav. Pozzo says he was a native of Verona. At all events, he studied with Gio. Battista Maganza at Vicenza, and executed many works for the churches in that city, Verona and Venice. Lanzi says "he excelled in works in fresco, and in chiaro-scuro, enlivened by certain yellowish tints, at that period in great vogue. He was a good designer, as appears from his works both at Vicenza and Verona; and he likewise produced several large pictures in oil at Venice, much commended by Zanetti." According to Papillon, he executed some wood cuts, which, though rudely executed, evince the hand of a master; among them are the Entombment, a Pietà, St. Jerome holding a crucifix, and the Rape of Proserpine.

SCOPAS, a celebrated Greek sculptor and architect, was a native of Paros, an island of the Ægean Sea. Pliny, (Hist. Nat. xxxiv. 8.), places him as cotemporary with Ageladas, Polycletus, Myron, and other eminent artists who flourished about B. C. 430; but from various circumstances, he appears to have flourished during the succeeding century. The Temple of Minerva Alea, rebuilt by Scopas, was destroyed, according to Pausanias, about B. C., 388; and a part of his work upon the tomb of Mausolus, was performed after the death of Queen Artemisia, which happened B. C. 350.

The works of Scopas were held in the highest esteem by the ancients, and his talents seem to have been little inferior, if not fully equal, to those of Polycletus or Myron. He was employed with three others, by Artemisia, Queen of Caria, in erecting a magnificent monument to the memory of her husband Mausolus, in the city of Halicarnassus, ranked among the seven wonders of the world. Each of the builders chose and undertook to complete one of the four sides—Bryaxis the North, Timotheus the South, Leochares the West, and Scopas the East. Before the work was finished, Artemisia died; but the architects determined, for the sake of their own fame, to complete it. Its dimensions on the north and south sides were sixty-three feet; the east and west sides were a little shorter, and the extreme height was one hundred and forty feet. It was surrounded with thirty-six splendid marble columns. A fifth sculptor was added to the others, named Pythis, who carried up the sides in a pyramidical form, and placed at the top a chariot and four horses in marble. Scopas was appointed to execute one of the columns for the Ephesian Temple of Diana, and his work is said to have been the most beautiful of the whole. His statues were very numerous; among the most remarkable, were those representing Love, Passion, and Desire, in the Temple of Venus at Megara, mentioned by Pausanias; also a statue mentioned by Strabo, called the Rat-killer, represented in the act of crushing a rat with his foot, in the temple of the god surnamed Smintheus, at Chrysa in the Troad. Many of his compositions were among the noblest ornaments of Rome in the days of Pliny, particularly a large group of figures, representing Neptune, Thetis, Achilles, Nereids riding on tritons and dolphins, with a train of marine monsters. It was preserved in the chapel of Cneius Domitius, in the circus Flaminius at Rome, and, according to Pliny, was a splendid work, (præclarum opus), sufficient for the fame of his whole life. His colossal image of Mars, and his beautiful statue of Venus, were also greatly admired at Rome, and the latter was preferred to a similar statue by Praxiteles, which is supposed to have furnished the idea of the Venus de Medicis. Pliny says there was a doubt in his time, whether some statues representing the dying children of Niobe (*Niobæ liberos morientes*), in the Temple of Apollo Sosianus at Rome, were by Scopas or Praxiteles. The well known group of this subject in the Florentine gallery, is generally believed to be the identical work mentioned by Pliny. Whether it be an original production of one of these great artists, or as some critics have supposed, only a copy, it will ever be considered worthy of their genius, as one of the sweetest manifestations of that deep and intense feeling of beauty which the Grecian artists delighted to preserve in the midst of suffering. The admirable criticism of Schlegel (Lectures on the Drama, III), developes the internal harmony of the work. "In the group of Niobe, there is the most perfect expression of terror and pity. The upturned looks of the mother, and the mouth half open in supplication, seem to accuse the invisible wrath of Heaven. The daughter, clinging in the agonies of death to the bosom of her mother, in her infantile innocence, can have no other fear than for herself; the innate impulse of self-preservation was never represented in a manner more tender and affecting. Can there, on the other hand, be exhibited to the senses, a more beautiful image of self-devoting, heroic magnanimity than Niobe, as she bends her body forward, that, if possible, she may alone receive the destructive bolt? Pride and repugnance are melted down in the most ardent maternal love. The more than earthly dignity of the features are the less disfigured by pain, as from the quick repetition of the shocks, she appears, as in the fable, to have become insensible and motionless. Before this figure, twice transformed into stone, and yet so inimitably animated—before this line of demarcation of all human suffering, the most callous beholder is dissolved in tears." Among the other works of Scopas, were a statue of Apollo, on the Palatine Mount; Vesta seated, with two female attendants sitting on the ground beside her, in the gardens of Servilius; also a group of the same description, and a Virgin bearing on her head a basket of relics, in the collection of Asinius Pollio.

Scopas seems to have possessed as great merits in architecture as in sculpture. According to Pausanias, the temple erected by him at Tegea, in honor of Minerva Alea, far exceeded in its dimensions and the excellence of its decorations, all the other temples of Peloponnesus. The outside was built in the Ionic order; the inside was decorated with Doric columns. In the pediment in front was represented the hunting of the Macedonian boar, with Atalanta, Meleager, Theseus, and numerous other figures. The other pediment exhibited the contest between Telephus and Achilles.

SCOPPA, Orazio, an Italian designer and engraver who flourished at Naples about 1642. He engraved a set of fifteen plates of designs for chalices, crosses, and other ecclesiastical ornaments, etched in a spirited style.

SCOR, Giovanni Paolo, a German painter, briefly mentioned by Lanzi and Taja among the foreign artists who resided at Rome about the middle of the 17th century, but in such a manner as to show that he was an artist of distinction. He excelled in landscapes and animals. He painted a picture representing Noah's Ark, in the Quirinal palace, which "excited the most enthusiastic encomiums." He was elected a member of the Academy of St. Luke in 1653. Taja calls him Gian. Paolo Tedesco Scor, and commends him as one of the ablest artists of his time, in the branch of the art he followed. He had a brother named Egidius, who was employed for a considerable time in the Gallery of Alexander VII. These artists are not mentioned by the German or Dutch writers, therefore the name is wrongly spelled by the Italian writers, as frequently happens, or else they passed their whole artistic life in Italy.

SCORODOMOFF, Gawril (Gabriel), a Russian designer and engraver, born at St. Petersburg about 1748. He went to England when young, and studied under Bartolozzi, whose manner he followed. While in that country, he engraved several plates after Reynolds, West, and others, and some from his own designs. On his return to St. Petersburg, he engraved the portraits of the Empress Catherine, the Grand Duke, and other princes of the country, *after F. Rocotoff*. He died there in 1792. He is said to be the first Russian who acquired any reputation as an engraver.

SCORZA, Sinibaldo, a painter born at Voltaggio, a small town near Geneva, in 1589. He studied under Gio. Battista Paggi, and excelled in painting landscapes, which he decorated with figures and animals, tastefully composed, and touched with great neatness and spirit. Lanzi says, it would be difficult to find in Italy a pencil which engrafted so successfully the neatness of the Flemish execution with the taste of the Italians in design." He painted easel pictures of historical and fabulous subjects, in a style of excellence that procures their admission into the choicest collections at Genoa. He also excelled in drawing with pen and ink. He is said to have copied some of the prints of Albert Durer, with such accuracy that some of the best judges in Italy were deceived by them, and supposed they were original engravings by that master—a very questionable assertion.

SCORZINI, Pietro, a painter of Lucca, who flourished about 1750, and acquired a great reputation for his elegant decorations of many theatres.

SCOTIN, Gerard, the Elder, a French engraver, born at Gonesse, near Paris, in 1642. He studied under Francis Poilly the elder, whose style he imitated with considerable success, though his works are very inferior to the admirable productions of that master. He died in 1718. The following are among his best prints: The Marriage of St. Catherine, *after Alex. Veronese;* the Communion of the Magdalene, *after Domenichino,* the Circumcision, *after P. Mignard;* the Baptism of Christ, *do.;* the Presentation in the Temple, *after C. le Brun;* the Country Life, *after Dom. Feti.*

SCOTIN, Gerard, the Younger, was the nephew of the preceding, born at Paris in 1690. He studied with his uncle, and executed quite a number of plates, chiefly for the booksellers. He went to London, where he resided several years. In 1740, in conjunction with Ravenet and Baron, he engraved the six plates of the Marriage à la Mode, *after Hogarth.* Among other prints, are the following by him: The Birth of Adonis, *after Boucher;* Notre Dame des Victoires, *do.;* Belisarius, after the supposed picture by *Vandyck* at Chiswick. Vortigern and Rowena, *after Blackeney;* Alfred receiving the account of the defeat of the Danes, *do.*

SCOTIN, Jean Baptiste, a French engraver, who flourished at Paris in the first half of the 18th century. He engraved some prints after H. Rigaud, Boucher, Watteau, Lancret, and other French painters. Some of them are dated as early as 1710. He also engraved the anatomical plates for *Boudon's Anatomy*, published at Paris in 1734. He is supposed to have been the son of the elder Scotin.

SCOTT, John, an English engraver, born at Newcastle in 1774. He went to London, and studied under Pollard, an engraver of little note. He engraved some plates for the publications by Tresham and Ottley, Britton's Cathedral Antiquities, Westall's Illustrations for the Book of Common Prayer, and other works. His best prints are those he engraved for the "Sportsman's Cabinet," and a "Series of Horses and Dogs," in which he excels, as an engraver of animals, all the English artists that had preceded him. He died in 1828.

SCOTT, Samuel, an English marine painter, called the "English Vandervelde," whom he is said by Lord Orford and Pilkington to have equalled in marines, and to have excelled in sea-ports and buildings. He was born at London in 1710, and died there in 1772. Stanley says, "Scott was an excellent painter in his style, and his pictures are deserving of more attention than has been bestowed on them; but no comparison can be instituted between his works and those of W. Vandervelde."

SCOTTO, Felice, a painter of the Milanese school, who flourished at Como in the latter part of the 15th century. Lanzi says "he painted a good deal for private individuals at Como, and left a number of pictures in fresco in the church of S. Croce, relating to the life of St. Bernardino. His genius is varied and expressive, he displays judgment in composition, and is one of the best artists of the 15th century in those parts. He was probably a pupil of some other school, his design being more elegant, and his coloring more clear and open, than those of the Milanese."

SCOTTO, Stefano, a Milanese painter, who flourished in the last part of the 15th, and first part of the 16th centuries. According to Lomazzo, he painted history, both in oil and fresco, and particularly excelled in arabesques. He was one of the instructors of Gaudenzio Ferrari. Lanzi thinks he was of the same family as the preceding.

SCOTTO, or SCOTTI, Francesco, an Italian designer and engraver, born at Venice about 1760. He studied with Vincenzio Vangelisti. He engraved some fine prints after Raffaelle, Leonardo da Vinci, and other masters. He is principally known by his admirable *fac similes* of original drawings by the celebrated Italian masters, particularly those of Raffaelle. These, with others by Rosaspina, form the splendid work published by the Abate Celotti, under the title, "Desegni Originali di Raffaello per la prima volta publicata, esistenti nella Imp. Academ. di Belle Arti di Venetia," 1829, folio. The painter Bossi bought the drawings and plates after the death of Scotto, and intended to have published them, but dying, they fell into the hands of Celotti, who published them as above mentioned. The time of the death of Scotto is not recorded.

SCOTTO, or SCOTTI, Girolamo, an Italian engraver, born at Milan in 1780. He studied under Giuseppe Longhi, and was one of the ablest disciples of that distinguished master. He executed quite a number of plates in the style of his instructor, after the great Italian masters, among which are the following:

The Virgin in the Clouds, with the Child in her arms; *after Raffaelle.* Madonna di Foligno (the Virgin and Child only); *do.* Mater pulchræ dilectionis, after a picture by *Raffaelle* discovered at Genoa in 1823. Madonna with the Child in her lap, the young St. John, and another little Boy, from a picture by *Raffaelle*, in the possession of the Duke of Terranuova. Mary Magdalene anointing the feet of Christ; *after P. Veronese.* The healing of the Children by virtue of the Garments of St. Philip; *after A. del Sarto.* This print is dedicated to Charles Albert, King of Sardinia, 1834.

SCRETA, Charles, an eminent German painter of a noble family, born at Prague in 1604. He showed an early passion for painting, and after learning the rudiments of the art in his native city, he went young to Italy, and studied several years at Venice, Bologna, and Florence. In 1634, he went to Rome in company with his friend William Bauer, where he diligently studied the antique and the works of the great masters. He also frequented the schools of eminent cotemporary artists, and studied their different manners. By his talents and application he acquired a high reputation in Italy, and was appointed one of the professors in the Academy at Bologna. On his return to his native country, he was received with distinction, and the Emperor Ferdinand III. and the nobility honored him with many commissions. In 1644, he was elected a member of the Academy at Prague, and in 1652 the president of the institution. The emperor confirmed the title of his family to nobility, and he spent the remainder of his life in that city, honored and admired.

He painted history, allegory, and portraits; his works are numerous, and many of them have been engraved. Several of his historical works are said to rank among the best productions of his time, though they are not so remarkable for originality of conception, as a judicious selection from the antique and the best modern masters. Like the eclectic philosophers of old, he was of opinion that excellence did not consist in propounding new theories or practices, but in a judicious selection and appropriation of old ones. He also had a remarkable talent of imitating the styles of the great masters of the Italian, Spanish, and Flemish schools, particularly in single half-length and three-quarters figures, some of which are said to be a perfect deception. They are not copies, but imitations. He imitated the Caracci, Guido, Domenichino, Lanfranco, Murillo, and Rubens, so as to deceive connoisseurs. He also imitated Raffaelle, Titian, and Paul Veronese, but with less success. His works are numerous, and are to be found in the churches, palaces, and private collections at Prague, Vienna, Dresden, Salzburg, and Schleissheim. Many of his subjects are taken from sacred history, and legends of saints. In portraiture, he delighted to represent his sitters in imaginary characters. Thus it is said that he painted his own portrait twice under saintly guise—once as St. Giles, in the church of St. Martin; and again as St. Luke painting the Virgin, in the church of St. Mary at Prague. One of his portraits in the Gallery at Prague is particularly admired; it represents a lapidary and glass cutter in his workshop. He engraved a large philosophical thesis, on two plates, entitled *Philosophia Universa in Universitati Pragensi.* It is an allegory formed of busts and statues of the members of the house of Lobkowitz, signed *Car. Screta fec.* 1666. He died at Prague in 1674.

SCRIVEN, EDWARD, an English engraver in the chalk and dotted manner, born in 1775. He studied under Bartolozzi, whose elegant style he adopted. He engraved a great many plates of portraits and other subjects, after the eminent painters of his time, and was much employed by Boydell and other publishers of prints. Among his principal works are "Specimens of Ancient Sculpture," published by the Dilettanti Society, in Dibdin's Aedes Althorpianæ, in Tresham's Gallery of Pictures, and other expensive publications of the day; the Studies of Heads, from West's picture of Christ rejected; a series of portraits, chiefly after Sir Peter Lely, of the Ladies commemorated by Hamilton in his Memoirs de Grammont. Most of the expensive publications of the day were embellished with his prints. In all his works he faithfully preserved the character and expressions of the originals. He died in 1841.

SCUTELLARI, ANDREA, a reputable painter, born at Viadana, in the Cremonese territory, who, according to Zaist and others, flourished at Cremona about 1588, and executed some works for the churches. There was another painter of the same name, probably his brother, who resided at Cremona about the same period. Lanzi says "few of their works remain, and those of no great merit."

SCYLLIS. See DIPENOS.

SEBASTIANI, LAZZARO, a Venetian painter, who flourished in the early part of the 16th century. He studied under Vittore Carpaccio, and followed his style. He painted a number of pictures for the churches and public edifices of Venice, among which was the Entrance of Filippo Mazeri into Venice, bringing a piece of the true Cross, placed in the hall of the knights of St. John of Jerusalem. In the church of S. Salvatore is a picture by him in five compartments, in one of which is represented St. Agostino surrounded by a great number of religious perpersons. According to Lanzi, although flourishing so near the golden period of Italian art, Sebastiani did not succeed in freeing himself from the influence of the old and uniform taste; for which reason his works are frequently confounded with those of Veglia, Mansueti, and other followers of Carpaccio. His pictures, however, possess much merit, being distinguished for several noble traces of the style of Gentile and Carpaccio, especially in the architecture; and although his coloring is considered cold and languid in the Venetian school, it would be termed, in several of the others, sufficiently soft and animated for that period.

SEBASTIANO, FRA. See PIOMBO.

SEBILLE, GYSBERT, a Dutch painter, who flourished at Weesp about the middle of the 17th century. There are several of his works in the Town House of that city, among which is a picture of the Judgment of Solomon, and another representing an Assembly of the Magistrates in 1652, of which he was a member. Nothing more is recorded of him.

SECANO, GERONIMO, a Spanish painter and sculptor, was born at Saragossa in 1638. After acquiring the elements of design from an obscure artist, he visited Madrid for improvement, and studied with great assiduity the best works of art in that city. On returning to Saragossa, he soon manifested uncommon abilities, by executing several pictures for the church of S. Pablo. He was also employed in S. Miguel, and painted several works for the government edifices, in oil and in fresco, distinguished for correct design and excellent coloring. At the age of fifty, he acquired a knowledge of sculpture, and practised it with ability. He established a school, in which were educated some able professors of both arts. Secano died at Saragossa in 1710.

SECCANTE, SEBASTIANO, a painter of the Venetian school, who flourished at Udine about 1576. According to Renaldis, he studied with Pomponeo Amalteo, a painter of a noble family, which yet boasts its descendants at Uderzo. He married the daughter of his instructor, and settled in his native city, where he executed several altar-pieces and other works for the churches, and two grand historical pieces in the castle, embellished with several fine portraits. One of his most esteemed altar-pieces is in the church of S. Giorgio, "representing the Redeemer suffering under the Cross, between several figures of cherubs, holding other instruments of the Passion; a piece that displays all the excellent maxims derived from his education." He also painted many excellent works for individuals. Lanzi says: "This artist may be pronounced the last of the great school (the Venetian) whose productions do credit to a good collection." He had a brother named Giacomo, who practised the art at Udine in 1571, but he did not acquire much reputation. Giacomo had a son, called also Sebastiano, whom he instructed in the art, and of whom there are notices from 1571 to 1629. They had a relative, whom they instructed in the art, called Seccante de' Seccanti, who flourished at Udine about 1621. None of these last named painters acquired any distinction.

SECCHI, GIO. BATTISTA, called also IL CARAVAGGIO, a painter of the Milanese school, who flourished at Milan about 1619. He executed some few works for the churches in that city, in which Lanzi says he approaches the best of the Cerani. Little is known of him. In the *Pitture d' Italia* he is called Caravaggino, and he signed himself *Jo. Bapt. Sicc. de Caravag.*, which shows that he was a native of Caravaggio.

SECCHIARI, GIULIO, a painter born at Modena

He first studied in the school of the Caracci at Bologna, and afterwards proceeded to Rome, where he diligently studied the works of the great masters, and acquired so much reputation that the Duke of Mantua invited him to his court. He executed for that Prince some of his best works, which were destroyed, or taken away in the sacking of Mantua in 1630. There are some of his works in the churches of his native city, which are commended by Tiraboschi, particularly an altar-piece representing the Death of the Virgin, in the Cathedral. Lanzi also commends him as an able disciple of the school of the Caracci, though his works are rare, and little known. He died in 1631.

SECU, or SEEUW, Martin de, a German painter, born at Romerswalen in 1520. He studied under Francis Floris, and painted history with reputation. He settled at Middlebourg, where he met with considerable encouragement, and where his principal works are to be found. He had a free, delicate, and rapid pencil, and his compositions are not deficient in grace, though his drawing is frequently incorrect. He died in 1574.

SEDELMEYER, Jeremiah James, a German painter and engraver, born at Augsburg in 1704. He first studied engraving under Pfeffel, and attained considerable excellence in managing the point and the graver, combining the styles of Dorigny and Audran. Receiving some ill treatment from his instructor, Sedelmeyer fled to Vienna, and entered the school of his brother-in-law, Keukel, who instructed him in miniature painting. He formed an intimate friendship with Gaspar Füessli, in concert with whom he engraved a number of plates, and painted portraits in oil and miniature. He executed several plates of landscapes, after pictures in the Imperial Gallery, by Daniel Gran; also many plates of portraits and historical subjects.

SEGALA, Giovanni, a painter born at Venice in 1663. According to Zanetti, he studied with Antonio Zanchi, and acquired considerable reputation as a historical painter. He was a man of genius, and though, like his master, addicted to the use of strong shades, he possessed sufficient intelligence to derive some advantage from a wrong direction of his powers. Lanzi says, "he made use of dark grounds, which he contrasted with very spirited lights, and with a skill that enlivens, while it enchants us. His style seemed adapted to grand works, and he had genius enough to conduct them well." Lanzi particularly commends his picture of the Conception in the college of La Carità, in which he competes with, if he does not surpass, some of the first painters of the age. He died in 1720.

SEGERS, or SEGHERS, Gerard, an eminent Flemish painter, born at Antwerp in 1589. After having studied successively with Henry van Balen and Abraham Janssens, he went to Rome, where, being captivated by the vigorous style of M. Angelo da Caravaggio, he became the disciple of Bartolomeo Manfredi, who had studied under that master, and whose manner he followed. To the striking opposition of light and shadow, and the broad relief of Caravaggio, he added the rich coloring of the Flemish school, and his pictures, though exhibiting a violence of contrast not authorized by a legitimate observance of nature, eclipsed in point of effect every work placed near them. Sandrart, who was intimately acquainted with him, observes that he avoided using the "bright blues, yellows, greens, and glaring colors, being always careful to observe a general harmony in his coloring; and yet his pictures have so great a degree of force that they make most other paintings look weak and faint." He acquired so much reputation at Rome that the Cardinal Zapara, the Spanish ambassador, invited him to accompany him to Madrid, and presented him to the king, who took him into his service, and gave him a liberal pension. He executed several historical works, musical conversations, and other subjects which were greatly admired, and so much to the satisfaction of the monarch, that he liberally rewarded him, and made him several magnificent presents. After a residence of some years at the court of Madrid, the desire of revisiting his native country, where the reputation he had acquired both in Italy and Spain, rendered his fellow citizens impatient to possess his works, induced him to ask permission of the king to return to Flanders, who would gladly have retained him in his service. On his arrival at Antwerp, he executed several works for the churches, in imitation of the style of Caravaggio, which were not so favorably received by the public as he expected. The clear and brilliant coloring of Rubens and Vandyck were so deeply rooted in public estimation, that he was compelled to adopt a system more tender and agreeable than he had heretofore practised. The facility with which he effected this change in his manner, proves the flexibility of his powers, and some of his later works are ranked among the most estimable productions of the Flemish school, vieing in brilliancy and harmony of coloring with Rubens and Vandyck. Sandrart says that when he visited Segers, and first saw some of his later performances, he could scarcely believe them to be by his hand, till Segers declared that he was under the necessity of changing the style he most approved, to comply with the taste of the world, and to sacrifice his fame and fortune, as the public preferred the coloring of Rubens and Vandyck to the best artists of the Venetian and Roman schools. However this may be, the public certainly showed their good taste in preferring the rich and harmonious coloring of their own great masters to the artificial one of Caravaggio, and Segers also in knowing it; but he had no just cause to complain of lack of patronage, for he is said to have met with constant employment, and received such liberal prices that he was enabled to live splendidly, and to expend 60,000 florins in the purchase of the works of the great masters. He also painted conversation and musical parties, soldiers playing at cards, &c., which were exceedingly admired, and eagerly sought after. He composed his subjects well, was more correct in his design than the generality of his countrymen, and excellent in expression; his coloring was warm and full of force, and the oppositions of his lights and shadows evinced a perfect knowledge of the chiaro-scuro, which enabled him to give his figures a surprising roundness and relief. Among his most celebrated works at Antwerp are the famous Elevation of the Cross, in the church of the Jesuits; the Adoration of the Magi, in the Cathedral, admirably engraved by Vostermans; Peter denying Christ, engraved by Bolswert; and the Marriage of the Virgin, in the church of the Barefooted Carmelites, which is esteemed his masterpiece. It is asserted by Descamps and others that Segers visited England, but Bryan says there is no evidence of his ever having been in that country. Vandyck painted his portrait among the eminent artists of his country. He died at Antwerp in 1651.

SEGERS, or SEGHERS, Daniel, was the brother of the preceding, born at Antwerp in 1590. Having a passion for depicting flowers when a youth, he was placed under the instruction of John Breughel, at that time famous for his flower-pieces, but afterwards more distinguished for his landscapes. At the age of sixteen he was persuaded to join the society of the Jesuits. When the time of his probation had expired, his superior, knowing his talents and alive to his interest, permitted him to visit Rome, where his brother had already distinguished himself. Wherever he traveled, he was curious to observe the flowers, fruits, plants, and insects peculiar to each place, all which he accurately designed and transferred to his portfolio, so that on his return to Flanders, he had an abundant supply of beautiful objects for his future compositions. During his residence at Rome, also, he diligently studied everything that could contribute to his own particular branch of the art, and the improvement he made proves that a sojourn in that metropolis of art is beneficial to every painter, whatever may be the department to which he devotes himself. Segers painted flower-pieces, elegantly and tastefully composed, and executed with a brilliancy, variety, and beauty that rivalled nature. His usual manner of disposing his subjects was in garlands or festoons, round elegant vases of marble, on which were often represented historical subjects by the most distinguished masters; even Rubens himself did not disdain to lend him his assistance. His pencil was light, his touch free and delicate, and his flowers have all the freshness and bloom of nature, sparkling with dew-drops. He particularly excelled in depicting lilies and roses. His tints are transparent and natural, and the insects and butterflies which he introduced among the flowers appeared as perfect as life. It was his custom to cultivate the most beautiful flowers for models, and he also made a large collection of insects for the same purpose. His pictures were eagerly sought after by princes and others, and proved a source of honor and profit to his confraternity. The Prince of Orange deputed Boschaert, his principal painter, to visit Segers and endeavor to procure a picture by him, on which occasion he painted two of his choicest works, which were presented in the name of the society to the Prince, who munificently repaid the gift. His most capital performance was in the church of the Jesuits at Antwerp. It represented a garland of the most beautiful flowers, in the centre of which was a picture of the Virgin and Child, painted by Rubens. He died in 1660. The works of Segers are very rare and valuable; the demand for them caused them to be largely imitated, and many are attributed to him which are totally unworthy of his pencil.

SEGERS, SEGHERS, or ZEGERS, a Dutch painter, born, according to Balkema, in 1625, and died in 1679, though others place his birth in 1629, and his death in 1675. It is not known under whom he studied, but he painted landscapes and cattle, in which, according to some writers, he imitated Paul Potter; but others say that, like Potter, he only copied nature, and while he equalled that master in cattle, he greatly excelled him in landscape; the last part of this assertion might be readily granted, as Potter paid little attention to landscape, which he used only as an accessory; but the first part should be received with many scruples of allowance. However, he had a fine invention, a ready genius, and a clear judgment. His composition is rich, and full of pleasing variety of mountains, valleys, and villages; his aerial perspective is so excellent that his distances appear exceedingly remote, and the scene of his landscape uncommonly extensive; his play of light and shadow, according to the divisions, is scientifically true, and, like Jacob Ruysdael and Philip de Koningh, he made a flat country appear interesting by his artistic management. Every object is touched with delicacy and spirit, and the sweetness and harmony of his coloring was scarcely inferior to any artist of his time. Notwithstanding the possession of these excellencies, he lived in comparative obscurity, and it is said was oppressed with poverty all his days, his works not being appreciated during his lifetime, though after his decease they were more sought after and rose greatly in value. He is also said to have invented a method of stamping landscapes on cloth with colors, so that every object appeared of its natural color and in its proper place; but this wants authentication. In the British Museum there are nineteen etchings, with six variations, making twenty-five in all, by this artist. There are three more in the Bibliothêque at Paris, and doubtless more will be discovered; Stanley supposes that some of the prints now attributed to Rembrandt, on a critical examination, may be transferred to him. These prints are executed in a free and masterly, but peculiar style, and some of them appear to have been experiments. They are all from his own designs, and represent scenery similar to that in his landscapes.

SEGOVIA, Juan de, a Spanish painter, who flourished at Madrid about 1650. Little is known of him. He painted marine pieces in a spirited style, which are held in high estimation in that capital.

SEGURA, Antonio de, a Spanish painter and architect, of whom little is known. In 1580, Philip II. commissioned him to copy the celebrated picture by Titian, known as the Apotheosis of Charles V., or the Glory of Titian, as an altar-piece for the monastery of San Yuste. He died in 1605, and Philip III. settled a pension on his widow.

SEIBOLD, Christian, a German painter, born at Mayence in 1697. He is said to have acquired his knowledge of art without the aid of an instructor. In 1759, he was appointed cabinet painter to the Empress Maria Theresa. His works are principally half-length portraits, with historical accessories; they deserve credit for their choice of attitudes and correctness of design. The portrait of Seibold, painted by himself, is in the Louvre. He died at Vienna in 1768.

SEILLER, John George, a German engraver who flourished at Schaffhausen about the end of the 16th and commencement of the 17th centuries His plates are said to be executed in mezzotinto if this is so, the claims of Prince Rupert and Lieutenant Colonel de Siegen to the invention of engraving in mezzotinto fall to the ground, unless there be some mistake as to the time he lived; for the earliest print mentioned by Siegen was the portrait of Amelia Elizabeth, Princess of Hesse, engraved in 1643. The invention, however, is not attributed to Seiller. Laborde specifies several of his prints, among which the following have his approbation: Portrait of the Emperor Joseph I. *C'est un bon travail.* Portrait of the Empress Eleonora. *Bonne execution.* Portrait of Kilian, the engraver. *Belle planche.* Portrait of J. H. Heidegger. *Assez belle planche.* A Monk attempting to kiss a Girl. *Très bon travail.* His prints are inscribed *J. G. Seiller, fecit*, or *J. Georg Seiller fecit et ex.*, or *Joh. Georg Seiller scaffusianus fecit.*

SEIS, Paul Pontius Anthony Robert de, an artist, probably a painter, by whom there is a masterly etching, representing Lot and his Daughters, executed in the style of Rembrandt. It is inscribed *P. P. A. Robert de Seis, fecit.*

SEITER. See Saiter.

SELIGMAN, Johann Michael, a distinguished German engraver on wood, was born at Nuremberg in 1720. He early manifested an inclination for design, and studied in the Academy of Painting, under the able tuition of two of the brothers Preisler. Rapidly attaining excellence in the art, he was invited to Rome in 1744, and afterwards to St. Petersburg. He subsequently settled in his native city, and was extensively employed, particularly upon works of natural history. Among his most esteemed productions were thirty-four engravings, representing the Nutritive Vessels in the Leaves of Trees, with explanations by C. J. Trew, published at Nuremberg in 1748; the *Hortus Nitidissimus* of the same author, embellished with one hundred and ninety plates; and a Collection of rare Birds, in nine volumes, folio, published at Nuremberg in 1749, and subsequent years. Seligman died in 1762.

SELLITTO, Carlo, a Neapolitan painter, who flourished in the first part of the 17th century. According to Dominici, he went to Rome and studied with Annibale Caracci, whose principles he adopted. Little more is known of him, though Guarienti records his name in the Abbecedario, and Lanzi says he finds him commended in some MS. notices of eminent artists of the Neapolitan school.

SELMA, Fernando, an eminent Spanish engraver, born at Valencia in 1750. He is said to have studied under Emanuel Salvador Carmona, and engraved a number of plates in a style of excellence, resembling that of Carmona, though in his latest manner he is said to have imitated Edelinck. He engraved several fine plates after the great masters in the Escurial, among which the most celebrated are La Madonna del Pesce, the Virgin and Child, and Christ bearing the Cross, called Lo Spasimo di Sicilia, *after Raffaelle;* and the portrait of the Emperor Charles V., *after Titian.* He also engraved several portraits of distinguished personages, as Cortes, Solis, Magellan, and others. He engraved the plates for the "Maritime Atlas of Spain," which occupied him several years. He was also a man of considerable literary acquirements. He died at Madrid in 1810.

SEMENTI, or SEMENZA, Giovanni Giacomo, a painter born at Bologna, according to Baglioni, in 1580. He was a fellow-student with Francesco Gessi, first under Denis Calvart, and afterwards with Guido Reni. According to Malvasia, he was one of the most successful followers of the style of Guido, and painted several works for the churches at Bologna, which have sometimes been mistaken for the productions of that master. Such are his pictures of the Martyrdom of St. Cecilia, in S. Elena; the Marriage of St. Catherine, in S. Francesco; and the Crucifixion, in S. Gregorio. He went to Rome in the pontificate of Urban VIII., and was favored with the protection of Cardinal Prince Maurice of Savoy, for whom he executed several admired works. He also painted some pictures for the churches. There are several fine frescos by him in S. Carlo a Catinari, and an oil painting, representing the Virgin and Infant, with Sts. Gregory and Francis, in the Capella Cavalieri. The authors above cited, and Lanzi, say he died at Rome in the prime of life; others place his death in 1638.

SEMINI, or SEMINO, Antonio, a painter born at Genoa in 1485. He was a pupil of Lodovico Brea, but afterwards studied the works of Pietro Perugino, according to Soprani, and was a successful imitator of his style. He executed several works for the churches at Genoa. His picture of the Nativity, in the church of S. Domenico at Savona, has been compared to the best productions of that master, and even to the early performances of Raffaelle. He died at Genoa in 1549.

SEMINI, Andrea, was the son of the preceding, born at Genoa in 1510. He first studied with his father, and afterwards with Pierino del Vaga, who had sought refuge at Genoa after the sacking of Rome in 1527. He showed such talents that Vaga advised him to visit Rome, whither he proceeded, and during a residence of eight years in that city made the works of Raffaelle the especial objects of his study. On his return to Genoa, he acquired considerable reputation, and executed several works for the churches and public edifices, the most esteemed of which are the Nativity, in S. Francesco; and the Adoration of the Magi, in La Nunziata. In these, as well as his other productions, he was a faithful follower of Raffaelle, though not always sufficiently correct in his design. According to Baldinucci, he painted portraits with great success. He died in 1578.

SEMINI, Ottavio, was the younger son of Antonio S., born at Genoa in 1515. He also studied under Pierino del Vaga, and accompanied his brother to Rome; and, like him, he studied the works of Raffaelle. He also copied the antique bas-reliefs of Trajan's column with great accuracy. He returned to Genoa with Andrea, and assisted him in several of his works. He also decorated the façade of the Palazzo Doria with statues and architecture, designed in the finest taste, and painted some frescos in the interior, particularly the Rape of the Sabines, so much in the style of Raffaelle that, according to Soprani, it was mistaken by Giulio Cesare Procaccini for a work of that master. He was invited to the court of Milan, where he passed the rest of his days and executed some of his principal works. He decorated the chapel of St. Girolamo in S. Angelo with several choice works, the most admired of which was a nob composition of the obsequies of that Saint. He was more correct in his design, and possessed a more lively imagination than his brother. He died at Milan in 1604.

SEMINI, Michele, a Roman painter, who was a pupil and imitator of the Cav. Carlo Maratti, whom he assisted in some of his works. He is commended in the life of that eminent artist, but Lanzi says little is known of him or his works.

SEMITECOLO, Niccolo, an old Venetian painter, by whom there is a picture of the Virgin, with some histories of St. Sebastian, in the Chapter Library at Padua, signed *Niccolo Semitecolo da Veniexia impense* 1367. This picture is in excellent préservation, and a fine specimen of the time and school. Lanzi says, "the naked parts are tolerably well drawn, and the proportions of the figures, though somewhat extravagant, are bold and free; and what is more important, the picture discovers no resemblance to the style of Giotto, being inferior in design, though equal to him in coloring."

SEMOLEI, Il. See Franco.

SEMPELIUS, D. G., a German engraver, who flourished about 1580. He copied some of the prints of Albert Durer with great success; one of the best is the Descent of Christ into Hell, from the set of plates of the Life of Christ, by that master. It bears the date of the original, 1512, as well as the year in which it was engraved. 1580.

SEMPLICE, Fra. See da Verona.

SENAVE, Jacob Albert, a distinguished Belgian painter, was born at Loo in 1758. The Canon of the Abbey of Loo perceiving in him a strong inclination for art, prevailed upon his father to send him to the Academy of Painting at Dunkirk. After studying there for three years, he gained the first prize, and then visited Paris for improvement. On returning to Belgium, he received several commissions from the Bishop of Ypres; after which he revisited Paris; frequented the Royal Academy; received the counsels of Suvée; and finally settled in that city. His pictures are distinguished for originality of composition, purity of design, and faithful imitation of nature. They generally represent feasts of the peasantry and other scenes from low life; they are highly esteemed, and have been extensively purchased for the collections of Belgium, France, Germany, Russia, Switzerland, England, and the United States. In 1821, Senave visited Belgium, and painted a picture representing a Reunion of Artists in the Studio of Rembrandt, for the Academy at Ypres, which chose him an honorary director. In the church at Loo is another work by him, representing the Seven Works of Mercy. In 1822, the Royal Society of Literature and the Fine Arts honored him with a membership in that institution. He had one son, who gave fair promise of great excellence in the art, but died at the age of twenty-two. Senave died at Paris in 1823.

SENEFELDER, Alois, the inventor of lithography, was the son of a performer at the Royal theatre of Munich, where he was born in 1771. His father placed him in the University of Ingoldstadt, as a student of jurisprudence, but after his death, he attempted a theatrical career in 1791; not succeeding in this he became an author, though his poverty prevented his publishing his works. He tried many plans with copper plates and compositions as substitutes for letter press, in order to be his own printer. He found, in the course of his experiments, that a composition of soap, wax, and lampblack, formed a good material for writing on plates; that when dry it became firm and solid, and that it resisted the action of aquafortis.—Wanting facility in writing backwards on the plates, he polished some pieces of Kelheim stone, as cheap materials on which he could practice. One day, being desired by his mother to take an account of some linen about to be sent to be washed, and having no paper at hand, he wrote the account on a polished stone, with his composition ink, intending to copy it at his leisure. When he was about to efface the writing, it occurred to him that by eating away the stone with acid, he could obtain impressions; having done this to the depth of an hundredth part of an inch, he charged the lines with ink, and found he could take successive impressions. This new mode of printing, instantly struck him as being very important, and he persevered through all difficulties in applying his discovery to practical purposes. In the course of a multitude of experiments, he found that it was not necessary to have the letters raised above the surface of the stone, but that the chemical principles by which grease and water were kept from uniting, were alone sufficient for his purpose. This point obtained, lithography may be said to have been fully discovered. All that was required was the improvement of the materials, and the mode of working with them, and the construction of a proper press for taking impressions. The perseverance with which he followed up his experiments in order to overcome the difficulties which successively arose in his progress was very remarkable, and the more so, considering the want of method in his proceedings. Often did he waste days and months in surmounting a difficulty which a little knowledge, or apparently a very little reasoning, would have enabled him to conquer immediately. Invention and application, however, are two different matters; the simplest things have sometimes been the most difficult to discover; it took the world nearly six thousand years to find out the use of moveable metalic printing types. Senefelder's first essay to print for publication, was some pieces of music, in 1796. Afterwards he attempted drawings and writings. The difficulty he experienced in writing backwards, led him to the process of *transfer;* and the use of dry soap, which he found to leave permanent traces that would give impressions, naturally led him to the mode of chalk drawings. Having made considerable progress in his invention, Senefelder, in 1799, obtained a patent privilege for Bavaria, when he made known his process. He afterwards entered into a partnership with M. André of Offenbach, who proposed to establish presses and take out patents in Vienna, Paris, and London. For this purpose, Senefelder went to London with the brother of André, and introduced his invention under the name of *Polyantography.* Several of the principal English artists made trials of it; but unfortunately, the difference between the materials of Germany and those of England, used for the purposes of drawing and printing and the art of printing from stones being imperfectly understood, caused constant failures, and they successively abandoned its practice. In

August, 1800, Senefelder, who had dissolved his connection with André, went to Vienna, where, after much difficulty, he obtained a patent, and extensive preparations were made for applying his process to printing cottons; but bad management and some unfortunate circumstances prevented his success, and he returned to Munich in 1806, leaving the establishment in other hands. In October 1809, he was appointed Inspector of the Royal lithographic establishment at Munich, and after that time till his death in 1834, he devoted himself to experiments, to instructing numerous pupils, and to writing a history of his invention. In 1819, he published his *Elements of Lithography* in German. In 1826, he invented a new process for taking impressions on colored sheets, so as to imitate oil painting, which art he called *Mosaic Painting*. Notwithstanding the difficulties he had to encounter, not the least of which were the opposition, and libels on his invention by persons who supposed their interests would be affected by his success, he completely triumphed, and lived to see his art brought to great perfection, and to be regarded as one of the most useful inventions of modern times, from its facility, cheapness, and general application. See *Lithography*, page xvii. of this work.

SENEX, John Christian, an English engraver, who flourished about 1720, and was employed by the booksellers. He engraved the plates for the London almanacs, from 1717 to 1727.

SENNAMAR, an eminent Arabian architect, mentioned by Milizia, who flourished in the fifth century. His chief works were two wonderful palaces called Sedir and Khaovarnack, concerning which many fabulous stories have been handed down in the Arabian chronicles.

SEPP, John Christian, a Dutch naturalist and painter, born at Amsterdam in 1739, and died there in 1811. He painted insects in water colors, with the greatest accuracy. He published some works on Entomology, in which he was assisted by his son. The principal is "The History of the Insects of Holland," published in five vols. quarto, illustrated with upwards of two hundred and fifty fine colored plates.

SEPPEZZINO, Francesco, a painter born at Genoa in 1530, and died there in 1579. He studied successively under Luca Cambiasi, and Gio. Batista Castelli. None of his works are specified, but he is said to have painted history with reputation.

SEPTIMUS, Hercules. See Setti.

SEPULVEDA, Mateo Nunez, a Spanish painter, who flourished about the middle of the 17th century. In 1640, Philip IV. appointed him painter and gilder of the Royal Navy of Spain, "in consideration of his talents as an artist," says Bermudez, "and for his *contribution* of 500 ducats towards the expenses of the war in which his majesty was engaged.' His patent, among other privileges, gave him the sole right of painting all the banners and standards required in the navy.

SEQUEIRA, Domingos Antonio de, a Portuguese painter, born at Lisbon, according to Count Raczinski, about 1760, but Nagler says in 1768. After studying in his native city, he was taken under the protection of the Marquis Marialva, who sent him to Rome to complete his artistic education, where he became the disciple of Antonio Cavallucci. After a residence of several years in Italy, he returned to Lisbon, where he executed several works for the churches and public edifices, and was considerably employed by the nobility. Most of his works are of a sacred character; but he painted some pieces from profane history, and others relating to the family of his patron Marialva. In 1823, he went to Paris to exhibit his picture of the Last Moments of the Poet Camoens, which elicited the applause of Gerard Vernet, and other French artists. He afterwards went to Rome, where he is said to have continued to paint with all the vigor of his youth. He had a great facility of design, and his drawings in crayons and India Ink were much sought after by amateurs. He is said to have succeeded better in oil when he painted figures of a small, rather than those of a full size. It is impossible to form any correct opinion of his style or merits from the accounts given.

SEQUENOT, L., a French engraver, who flourished about 1671. He engraved some frontispieces and other book plates, indifferently executed.

SERAFIN, Pedro, called El Griego, a Spanish painter, who flourished at Barcelona, and in conjunction with one Pedro Pablo, painted the doors of the organ of the cathedral at Tarragona, for which they received three hundred pounds, Catalonian money. On the inside of the doors they painted the Nativity and the Resurrection; on the outside, the Annunciation, and on one side of the organ, the figures of Faith, Hope, and Charity, and on the other, Sts. Thecla and Catherine. Nóthing more is recorded of them.

SERAFINI, Serafino de' an old painter of Modena, by whom there is a picture in the cathedral of that city, representing the Coronation of the Virgin, painted in the style of Giotto, inscribed *Serafinus de Serafinis Pinxit*, 1385, *die Jovis* 23 *Martii.*

SERANO, or rather CERANO, Il. See Gio. Battista Crespi.

SERENARI, Abate Gaspero, a Sicilian painter, born at Palermo, where he flourished about the middle of the 18th century. He went young to Rome, and studied with the Cav. Sebastiano Conca. Lanzi says he was considered a young man of talents at Rome, and after he left Conca, he painted some frescos in the church of S. Teresa, in competition with the Abate Peroni of Parma. On his return to Palermo, he became a celebrated master; and besides many oil paintings, he executed some vast frescos for the churches, particularly the cupola of the monastery of La Caritá. He also instructed several pupils.

SERGELI, Johann Tobias, an eminent Swedish sculptor, was born at Stockholm in 1740. He was the son of an embroiderer and manufacturer of gold lace. Apprenticed to a stone mason while quite young, he wrought as such in the palace at Stockholm, and attracted the notice of the sculptor Larcheveque, who received him into his studio. He soon manifested unquestionable talents, and after assisting his instructor in modelling the two statues of Gustavus Vasa and Gustavus Adolphus, he obtained a traveling pension in 1767, and visited Rome for improvement. He spent about twelve years in the Metropolis of art, and produced many admirable works. After this he visited Paris, and was admitted to the Royal Academy, upon presenting the statue of a wounded Greek soldier, termed "Othryades," of half life size, subsequently placed in the Luxembourg. From Paris he proceeded to London, but was directly afterwards summoned to Stockholm by Gustavus III., who appointed him court sculptor. In 1784, he accompanied that monarch on a visit to Rome, and was frequently consulted in reference to the purchase of a number of antiques for the Royal Museum at Stockholm. The talents of Sergell were very highly esteemed, and he received the most flattering offers from Catharine II. of Russia, but being indifferent to riches, and ardently attached to his sovereign and his native land, he declined her invitations. His works are distinguished for energy and vigor, with elegance and grace of design, and perfect freedom from the mannerism and disgusting affectation which distinguish the works of his immediate predecessors and cotemporaries. His busts and portrait medallions are highly esteemed for their faithful likenesses and artistic excellence. Among his principal statues are the group of Cupid and Venus; Diomed carrying off the Palladium; Othryades; a Faun; Gustavus III.; Oxenstierna dictating to the Historical Muse the deeds of Gustavus Adolphus; and Mars and Venus. Most of these are in the Royal Museum. One of his finest productions, a composition in alto-relievo for the Adolph-Frederick church at Stockholm, has never been executed in marble.

The untimely end of his friend and patron, Gustavus Adolphus, affected Sergell with so deep a melancholy, that for a long time he was unable to practise his profession. At length, a few years before his death, he nearly regained his wonted mental composure, but so late in life as to render it impossible to retrieve the time that had been lost to the art. He died at Stockholm in 1814, aged 74. Byström, an eminent Swedish sculptor of the present day, was a pupil of Sergell.

SERI, Robert de. See Seis.

SERICCUS, Philip, a Flemish engraver, according to Huber, who was a cotemporary and disciple of Cornelius Cort, and resided at Rome, about 1568, in which year he engraved in a formal style a set of twenty-eight half-length portraits of the Popes, from the year 204 to 1568. This artist is differently denominated Sericeus, Sericus, Syticus, Sytius, Soius, and Soye; various plates marked with these signatures, are evidently by one hand. Other marks have also been attributed to him, as the letters P. S. interlaced, and P. S. in a circle, with the dates 1535 and 1538; but they appear quite doubtful, and the *Biographie Universelle* places his birth in the latter year. The following are among his principal prints.

The Angel appearing to Joseph in his Dream; *C. Cort, inv. Ph. Soye, fec.* St. Francis receiving the Stigmata; *F. Zuccaro, pinx. Soye, fec.* The Virgin with the infant Christ sleeping; *after M. Angelo Buonarotti. Philippus Sericcus.* 1566. The Crucifixion; *do.* Adam and Eve in Paradise; *after P. del Vaga, P. Sericus fecit.* Judith with the Head of Holofernes; *after Giulio Clovio. Phil. de Soye, f.* Adoration of the Shepherds; *after F. Zuccaro. Ph. Sericus fecit.* The Angel appearing to Joseph; *do.* A Pietà; *after Michael Angelo.* St. Jerome in a Landscape; *after H. Muziano.*

SERIN, N., a Dutch historical painter, who flourished at Ghent in the last half of the 17th century. He studied with Erasmus Quellinus, and executed several works for the churches at Ghent. There is also a fine picture attributed to him in the church of S. Martin at Tournay, representing that saint dividing his cloak with a Beggar. Balkema has confounded this artist with his son John S., who he says was a pupil of Quellinus, and he attributes to him all the works executed by his father, which is evidently an error, as John was born in 1678, the year in which Quellinus died.

SERIN, John, was the son of the preceding, born in 1678, and doubtless was instructed by his father. He is said to have excelled in portraits, and in 1748, at the age of seventy, he painted the portrait of Marquis de Fenelon, ambassador at the Hague, and that of the Marchioness. He is also said to have painted several works for the churches, but he is so generally confounded with his father, that it is impossible to distinguish with certainty, their respective performances.

SCRIVANO, Pirro Luigi, was a knight of Malta, mentioned by Milizia, who gained considerable distinction by his works in civil and military architecture. His principal work in the latter branch, was the new castle of Aquila, in the Neapolitan state, which he executed at the commission of Charles V., in 1534.

SERLIO, Sebastiano, an Italian architect, chiefly celebrated for his writings on the art, was born at Bologna in 1475. According to Vasari, he was a disciple of Baldassare Peruzzi. The study of Vitruvius inspired him with an eager desire to obtain more knowledge of ancient edifices, and he accordingly proceeded to the Venetian states, where he employed himself in examining and measuring the amphitheatre and bridges at Verona. He subsequently erected a theatre at Vicenza, and designed the church of S. Francesco della Vigna at Venice. During his residence in the latter city, he formed the acquaintance of Sanmicheli, Sansovino, and other architects of note, and was also favored with the notice of the Doge Andrea Grilli. Had Serlio remained at Venice, he would undoubtedly have gained plentiful encouragement. He passed over to Pola, and examined its architectural remains. On returning he studied the antiquities of Ancona, Spoleto, and Rome. While in the latter city, he composed his work entitled "Regole Generali di Architettura di Sebastiano Serlio, sopra le cinque maniere de gli edifici, cioe Thoscano, Dorico, Ionico, Corinthio, e Composito, con gli Essempi dell' Antichita che per la maggior parte concordano con la dottrina di Vitruvio." This work evinces great learning and research, and has generally been regarded of great authority. Milizia says "he was devoted to Vitruvius, and showed himself equally well acquainted with theory and practice." Serlio sent a copy of his book to Francis I. of France, who acknowledged the compliment by a present of three hundred gold crowns, and invited the author to visit Paris. He accordingly went thither in 1541 with his family, and was appointed architect at Fontainbleau. He was also commissioned to undertake the court of the Louvre, but generously declined in favor of Lescot, whose design he recommended as superior to his own. At the death of his patron, and the commencement of the civil war, Serlio retired to Lyons, and remained there for some time, in straitened circumstances; but he afterwards returned to Fontainbleau, where he died in 1552.

SERMEI, Cav. Cesare, a painter born at Orvieto in 1516. It is not known under whom he studied, but, according to Orlandi, he married and settled at Assisi. He executed many excellent works both in oil and fresco, for the churches and public edifices at Assisi and Perugia, and at Spello. Lanzi says "he painted in fresco, if not in a grand style, still with a felicity of design, with spirited and graceful attitudes, and a vigorous pencil. He wrought with great facility, and his oil paintings possess great merit. At Spello I saw a picture by him of the Beatified Andrea Caccioli, and it seemed to me that few other painters of the Roman school had at that time equalled him. His heirs at Assisi possess some pictures by him of the fairs, processions, and ceremonies which occur in that city on the occasion of the Perdono, and the numbers, variety, and grace, of the small figures, the architecture and the humor displayed are very captivating." He died at Assisi in 1600, aged 84.

SERMOLEI, or SERMELEI, Il. See Battista Franco.

SERMONETA, da. See Siciolante.

SERODINE, Giovanni, a painter born at Ascona in Lombardy. According to Baglioni, he was a pupil of Michael Angelo da Caravaggio, whose style he followed with considerable success; he enumerates many of his works, executed chiefly for individuals. Lanzi says his pictures are more remarkable for their facility of execution than their excellence, and that he died young in the pontificate of Urban VIII.

SERRA, Cristoforo, a painter born at Cesena, who, according to Malvasia, was a pupil of Guercino, whose style he adopted, and executed some excellent works for the churches in his native city, but wrought mostly for individuals. Lanzi also commends him, and says he was an imitator of Guercino. He was living in 1678.

SERRA, Miguel; in French, *Michel Serre.* This painter was born at Catalonia, in Spain, about 1653. At the age of eight years he left his home on account of ill treatment, and went to Marseilles. Destitute of resources, he applied to an obscure painter of that city, who relieved his wants, and gave him instructions in the art. Two years after, the precocious young artist started for Rome, and remained in that city several years, studying the works of the best masters. At the age of seventeen he returned to Marseilles, and soon after painted his picture of the Martyrdom of St. Peter, which gained him great reputation. Commissions flowed upon him in abundance, and he painted many pictures for the churches and private collections. Serra's works are distinguished for great fertility of invention, spirited execution, and such astonishing facility of operation, that he is reported to have painted an altar-piece entire, in a few hours! As might be expected, his works show many marks of neglect. He sent a picture to Paris, which gained him admission to the Academy, and the appointment of painter to the King. In 1721, during the plague at Marseilles, he nobly devoted the whole of a large fortune to relieving the sick; and after the plague ceased, he resumed his pencil, adopting for subjects the mournful scenes he had recently witnessed. His easel pictures are very numerous in private collections; among his other works were several in the Carmelites at Aix, the convent of St. Claire, and the church of the Magdalen at Marseilles. Serra died in 1728.

SERRES, Dominic, a marine painter, born a Auch, in Gascony. He went to England about 1765, where he acquired considerable reputation for his marines and landscapes. When the Royal Academy was founded in 1768, he was chosen one of the first 40 members, and some years afterwards was appointed marine painter to the King. In 1792 he was appointed Librarian to the Royal Academy. One of his best works is a representation of Lord Howe's victory over the combined fleets of France and Spain, off Gibraltar, in 1782. He was a large contributor to the annual exhibitions of the Royal Academy, and during the first ten years he exhibited about 40 pictures, all of them representations of English naval engagements. Many of his works were engraved by Canot, Mason, Fittler, Vivares, and others, and were very popular in their day. He was compared to Vernet, but Stanley says that his pictures as works of art, possess very little value, but are still looked at with respect for the gallant deeds they commemorate. He died in 1793.

SERVANDONI, Cavaliere Giovanni Girolamo, an eminent scene painter and architect, was born at Florence in 1695. He studied painting in the school of Gio. Paolo Pannini, where he became expert in landscape and architectural scenery, and painted a number of pictures in the style of his instructor, which are preserved in various collections. He afterwards acquired a knowledge of architecture under De Rossi. After painting a number of admirable scenes at Lisbon, for which he was honored with the order di Cristo, he visited Paris in 1724, and was extensively employed. He greatly improved the former mode of scene painting, and also produced an entirely new system of it, aiding and heightening the effect by machinery and every possible artifice. His scene exhibitions were received by the public with the greatest enthusiasm, and they were highly praised by men of genius and taste, well capable of appreciating the artist's poetical invention and profound classical study. Even in the most magnificent architectural fancies, Servandoni, unlike many others, never outraged probability by exhibiting mere gorgeous chimeras. Among his most celebrated scenes were the representation of the fable of Pandora (at the Tuileries in 1738), and the Descent of Æneas into the Infernal Regions. His talents were greatly in request at all public festivities, especially those held at Stuttgard, and the festivals held at Paris, in 1739, in honor of the marriage of Philip V. of Spain with the princess Elizabeth. There are a number of paintings by him, representing architecture, ruins, &c., preserved in French and English collections, among which is a picture of ancient ruins in the Louvre, painted in the style of Gio. Paolo Pannini. As an architect, Servandoni was also distinguished, and his fame would have been much greater than it now is, had he been allowed to realize various magnificent projects, such as an extensive amphitheatre, of which the arcades and galleries alone were to contain 25,000 persons. His most important work is the façade of S. Sulpice, commenced about 1732, and greatly superior to the taste of the times. Unlike the frittered and unmeaning decorations of that age, the façade of S. Sulpice is distinguished for a considerable degree of simplicity and harmony. The arrangement of the loggia formed by the Doric order below, where the columns are coupled one behind the other, has a good effect, but the second order appears more solid and heavier, in consequence of the intercolumniations being filled in with arcades and piers. Among his other works praised by Milizia, are the gate of the Maison de l'Enfant Jesu; the magnificent staircase of the Hotel du Cardinal Auvergne; the round isolated chapel of M. de Live; and the Rotunda, in the form of an ancient temple, with twelve Corinthian columns, for the Mareschal de Richelieu. He made a number of designs for important edifices at Brussels; also several for the court of Portugal; and some in England for the Prince of Wales, the father of George III. Servandoni died at Paris in 1766.

SERVI, Constantino de', an Italian painter, gem-engraver, architect, and engineer, was born at Florence in 1554. According to the supposition of Baldinucci, he studied under Santo di Titi; and Lanzi says he excelled especially in portraits. He visited nearly every European court, and practised the art with plentiful encouragement. In his earlier productions he followed the style of Titi, but upon seeing the works of Pourbus, during his sojourn in Germany, he adopted the style of that master. At the request of the Prince of Wales, he visited England, and was appointed to superintend the erection of a number of bridges and machines, with a salary of 800 crowns. In 1609 he was invited by the Grand Sophy of Persia, to visit that country, and he remained there about a year; but it is not known on what he was employed. On returning to Florence, he was appointed, according to Milizia, superintendent of all the commercial companies, the works at the Chapel of St. Lorenzo, and the Florentine gallery, and also of the great mosaic manufactory, established by the Grand Duke Francesco I. Lanzi says he contributed to the improvement of this curious art. At the invitation of the States General, Servi visited Holland, and was commissioned to erect a palace at the Hague for Prince Maurice of Nassau, who favored him with many marks of esteem. This versatile artist finally returned to Tuscany, and was appointed by the Grand Duke to the vicarship of Lusignano. He died in 1622.

PS W SERWOUTER, Peter Van, a Flemish engraver, who flourished at Antwerp, according to the dates on his prints, from 1608 to 1628. There are also a number of prints attributed to him by several writers, marked with a monogram, composed of a P. and an S., with a W., as above, which, from its being similar to the mark used by a supposed artist, called *Perjecouter*, *Persecouter*, or *Persecuteur*, has led to his being confounded with that artist, who, from the dates on his prints, flourished seventy or eighty years before the time of Serwouter. The prints marked with the above monogram, among which are a set of twelve Huntings *after Vinckenbooms* were evidently executed by a Dutch or Flemish engraver. Nagler gives a list of Serwouter's prints, most of which are marked with his name in full and only one with a monogram composed of his initials, P. V. S. He does not mention the P. S. monogram, nor the W., as being marks found on any of his prints. He is also called *Sevouter*, *Servatius*, and *Raeven*, from the same confusion of marks. The prints in question are of little consequence.

SESSONE, Francesco, an Italian engraver, who flourished at Naples in the latter part of the 18th century. He engraved part of the plates for the Antiquities of Herculaneum, published at Naples.

SESTO, Cesare da, called also Cesare Milanese. There is a singular paucity of information respecting this eminent artist. He is generally regarded as the most distinguished disciple of Leonardo da Vinci. The time of his birth and death are not exactly known; some say that he was born at Milan about 1480, and died in 1524. Others that he flourished about 1500, and Zani, that he operated in 1524. It is known that he went to Rome, where he improved himself by the study of the antique, and an intimacy with Raffaelle, and that he was there employed by the Pope and some of the principal nobility. The following admirable account from Lanzi embraces all that is known of him or his works. In his account of Vinci and his followers he says: "One who approached nearest to Vinci's style at a certain period, was Cesare da Sesto; though not recorded by Vasari or Lomazzo in the list of his disciples, still, he is admitted by more modern writers. In the Ambrosian collection at Milan, is the head of an old man, so extremely clear and studied, in the Vinci manner, by this artist, as to surprise the beholder. In some of his other works he followed Raffaello, whom he knew in Rome; and it is reported that this prince of painters, one day said to him, 'It seems to me strange that, being bound in such strict ties of friendship as we two are, we do not in the least respect each other with our pencils,' as if they had been rivals on a sort of equality. He was intimate, too, with Baldassare Peruzzi, and was employed with him in the Castle of Ostia. In this work, which was one of the earliest efforts of Peruzzi, Vasari seems inclined to yield the palm of excellence to da Sesto. He was esteemed Vinci's best pupil; and he is more than once held up by Lomazzo as a model in design, in attitude, and more particularly in the art of using his lights. He cites an Herodias by him, of which I have seen a copy in the possession of the Consiglier Pagave, in which the countenance bore an extreme resemblance to the Fornarina of Raffaello. The original, formerly in the gallery of the Archiepiscopal palace, was in the first occupation of the French adjudged to Madame la Pagerie, wife of the then General Bonaparte, and passed into France. The Cav. D. Girolamo Melzi, has likewise one of his Holy Families, in the manner of Raffaello, which he obtained a few years since for the enormous sum of 600 sequins, as well as that celebrated altar-piece painted for the church of S. Rocco. It is divided into compartments; in the middle of it is seen the titular saint, and the Holy Virgin with the Infant, imitated from a figure by Raffaello, which is at Foligno; he likewise borrowed the figures of St. John the Baptist and St. John the Evangelist, seated on a cloud, from the Dispute of the Sacraments. These decorate the upper part of the picture, the lower being occupied by two half naked figures of Sts. Cristoforo and Sebastiano, both appropriately executed, and the latter exhibiting a new and beautiful foreshortening. They are on a larger scale than the figures of Poussin, and with such a resemblance to those of Correggio, that in the opinion of the Abbe Bianconi, they might easily have been attributed to that master, were it not for the superscription of the artist, such is the softness, union, and brightness of the fleshes, such their beauty of coloring, and the harmony pervading the whole painting. It used to be closed with two doors, on which, with a certain correspondence of subjects, were painted the two princes of the Apostles, with St. Martin and St. George on horseback; all of which display the same maxims, though not the same diligence in the art. Hence we may infer that this artist did not, like Vinci, aspire at producing master-pieces as an invariable rule, but was content, like Luini, with occasional efforts of the kind. I ought not to separate the name of this noble figurist from that of Bernazzano, the landscape painter, as they were united no less in interest than in friendship. It is uncertain whether he was instructed by Vinci; he doubtless availed himself of his models, and in painting rural landscapes, fruit, flowers, and birds, he succeeded so admirably as to produce the same wonderful effects as are told of Zeuxis and Apelles in Greece. This indeed Italian artists have frequently renewed, though with a less degree of applause. Having represented a strawberry bed in a courtyard, the pea-fowls were so deceived by the resemblance, that they pecked at the wall till the painting was destroyed. He painted the landscape part of the picture of the Baptism of Christ, and on the ground he drew some birds in the act of feeding. On its being placed in the open air, the birds were seen to fly towards the picture, as if to join their companions. This beautiful painting is still one of the chief ornaments in the gallery of the distinguished family of the Trotti at Milan. As Bernazzano had the sense to perceive his own deficiency in figures, he cultivated an intimacy with Cesare, who added to his landscapes fables and histories, sometimes with a degree of license that is reprobated by Lomazzo. These paintings are held in the highest esteem, where the figure-painter made a point of displaying his powers."

At the church of Sarono, situated between Pavia and Milan, are to be seen the figures of four saints, painted in fresco, on four narrow pilasters; the two equestrian saints on the doors of the altar-piece above mentioned, are saints Sebastian and Rocco, to whom especial invocations are made against the plague. They are signed *Cesare Magnus f.* 1533. These pieces are generally assigned to Cesare da Sesto, and many infer from the incription, that he belonged to the family of the Magni, but this is doubted by others, as his works do not sustain his high reputation, though excellent in their way. Lanzi finds much conformity of ideas in the frescos and the altar-pieces, which, together with other probable circumstances, induces him to believe Cesare da Sesto and Cesare Magni, to be the same artist.

SESTRI. Antonio da. See Travi.

SETLEZKY, Balthazar Sigismund, a German engraver of Polish origin, born at Augsburg in 1695, and died there in 1770. He engraved some plates of portraits and other subjects, after Watteau, J. M. Roos, H. Roos, and others, executed in a stiff and formal style.

SETTI, Ercole, an Italian painter and engraver, of whom there are notices from about 1560 to 1593. Lanzi says that he was an excellent engraver, and a painter of considerable merit. "There are a few of his altar-pieces at Modena, and I have seen some little pieces painted for the galleries, dignified, rather than beautiful, in point of design. He is cautious and studied in the naked parts, nearly equal to the style of the Florentines, spirited in his attitudes, and strong in his coloring. We find his name subscribed *Ercole de' Setti*, and also in Latin, *Hercules Septimus*." He is said to have etched several historical subjects, and some architectural ornaments, which he usually marked with the initials H. S. and the date.

SETTIGNANO, Desiro de, an Italian sculptor, born at Florence in 1457. His instructor is not mentioned, but after acquiring a knowledge of the art, he gained great improvement by studying the works of Donatello. The figure of an infant, in relief, executed by him for the chapel of S. Sacramento, in the church of S. Lorenzo, gained him great reputation, and he was commissioned to execute a number of works among which was the statue of the Beautiful Villana, surrounded with graceful figures of angels, in the church of S. Maria Novella at Florence. His works are distinguished for graceful simplicity, animated expression, and beautiful finishing. Among his other productions, are the mausoleum of Carlo Marsupini d'Arezzo in the church of S. Croce; the Arms of Florence, sculptured on the façade of the Palazzo Gianfigliazzi; and the bust of Marcotta Strozzi. During the short career of Settignano, he continued to make good progress, and would probably have attained great eminence, had he not died at the age of twenty-eight years, in 1485.

SEUPEL, J. A., a German engraver, born at Strasburg in 1660, and died there in 1714. He engraved a number of portraits, some of them from his own designs from life, executed with the graver in a neat but formal style. He is said also to have engraved seven plates with the burin, so as to produce an effect similar to mezzotint.

SEUTER. See Saiter.

SEVE, Gilbert de, a French painter, born at Moulins in 1615, and died at Paris in 1698. It is not known under whom he studied, but he painted history, allegory, and portraits, with considerable ability. There are several of his works in the galleries at Versailles and Fontainbleau. Some of his portraits of distinguished personages were engraved by Edelinck, van Schuppen, Masson, and other eminent engravers.

SEVE, Pierre de, was the brother of the preceding, born at Moulins in 1623, and died at Paris in 1695. He was instructed in the art by Gilbert, and painted similar subjects. Edelinck engraved a Holy Family by him, and other subjects were engraved by Simmoneau, Landry, Gantrel, and Dolival.

SEVERUS. See Celer.

SEVILLA, Romero y Escalante, Juan de, a distinguished Spanish painter, was born at Seville, according to the *Biographie Universelle*, in 1627. He acquired the elements of design from Andres Alonso Arguello of Granada, and subsequently entered the school of Pedro de Moya. Through the excellent advice and instruction of the latter, Sevilla acquired a taste for the works of Vandyck, and gained great improvement by studying them, as well as by copying the drawings of Rubens. He received numerous commissions for the churches and private collections, and executed many admired works, distinguished for lively and rapid conception, coloring in the style of Rubens, free and vigorous penciling, and great facility of execution. Among his principal productions was a large picture of the Last Supper, in the refectory of the Jesuits, several others in the Carmelite and Augustine churches, and the convent of St. Geronimo at Granada. Notwithstanding the excellent system of coloring adopted by Sevilla from the Flemish school, he instructed no pupils. He died at Grenada in 1695.

SEVIN, Pierre, a French painter and engraver, who flourished at Lyons about 1689. Little is known of him. Some of his works were engraved by Cossin, Gantrel, and le Moine; the last engraved his portrait of Madame la Valliere, which shows that he was an artist of some distinction. He also engraved some plates from his own designs for the booksellers.

SEYDELMANN, Jacob Crescentius, a German artist, celebrated throughout Europe for his admirable drawings in Sepia (India ink, from sepia, the cuttle-fish), was born at Dresden in 1750. After studying with Bernardo Bellotti and Casanova in his native city, he went under the patronage of the Elector to Rome, where he formed a friendship with Antonio Raffaelle Mengs, who directed his attention to the most renowned works of ancient and modern masters, which he copied in sepia in a style entirely his own, possessing so much novelty and beauty of execution that they readily sold at high prices. Many were purchased by English visitors, and some by Baron von Riesch, and other noblemen of his country. He also drew the portraits of several persons of distinction in the same manner. On his return to his native country he was received with distinction, and appointed Professor of Drawing in the Academy of Dresden. The Academy at Berlin sent him a diploma, and he was elected a member of several foreign academies. In 1788, he commenced copying the principal pictures in the Dresden Gallery for the Duke of Gotha, among which were the celebrated Notte, by Correggio, and the Madonna di San Sisto by Raffaelle; also the Venus by Titian, for the Winkler Cabinet. Soon afterwards, he again went to Rome, where he copied some of the works of the great masters, particularly of Raffaelle, of the same size as the originals. From Rome he proceeded to Naples for the same purpose. In 1792, he returned to Dresden, and was employed by the Countess Radczivil to copy some of the finest pictures in the Dresden Gallery to embellish the chapel of her country seat. In 1794 he made a third trip to Rome, and executed two large drawings after Raffaelle. After an absence of eight months he returned to superintend the continuation of the work called the *Dresden Gallery*, for which he made many of the drawings for the engravers. In 1804 he went to Rome for the fourth time, to execute a commission for Count Marcolini. On his return, he was commissioned by the Emperor Alexander to make copies of the Notte and St. George of Correggio, the Madonna di San Sisto by Raffaelle, and several others, of the same size as the originals, for which he was munificently rewarded. For the copy after Raffaelle he received 1000 ducats. He was afterwards invited to St. Petersburg to retouch the pictures which had received some injury in their transit; at the same time he received a commission from the Emperor to make two other drawings after the Magdalene of Correggio and the Venus of Titian, in the Dresden Gallery. Besides the copies enumerated after the great Italian masters, he made many others after the Dutch and Flemish masters, particularly after Chevalier Vander Werf, in which he imitated the polished manner of that painter to perfection. His high reputation continued till his death in 1829. There is an etching by him of a Figure bathing in a Cavern, *after J. F. Bloemen.* E. G. Krüger engraved an allegorical piece representing the Genius of Truth, and twelve plates of antique heads, after his designs; also several of his portraits were engraved by other artists.

SEYDELMANN, Apollonia, of the family of de Forgue, was the wife of the preceding, born at Venice in 1767. She was instructed by her husband, and not only assisted him in his works, but acquired distinction for her own copies in sepia after the most distinguished Italian masters. She also excelled in miniature painting. In 1789 she accompanied her husband to Italy, and assisted him in forwarding his larger pieces—a practice which she continued with so much ability that no difference is discernible. She made an admirable copy of Raffaelle's Fornarina, in the Borghese palace at Rome, executed entirely by herself in 1823, and many smaller pieces, which she marked with her name. She was elected a member of the Academy at Dresden.

SEYMOUR, James, an English painter of animals, born at London in 1702, and died in 1752. He excelled in painting horses, in which he was thought superior to Wootton.

SEYNES, Alphonse de, a French architect and designer, who flourished at Nismes during the present century. He was chiefly distinguished for his researches among the antiquities of that city, and published a work relating to them, entitled *Monuments Romains de Nimes, dessinés d'apres nature et lithographies*, Paris, 1818. De Seynes died at Nismes in 1844.

SEZENIUS, Valentine, a German engraver, who flourished about 1620. He engraved some plates of ornaments and grotesque subjects, which he usually marked with his initials V. S., and the date.

SGUAZZELLA, Lo, Andrea, a native of Città di Castello, who flourished about 1550. He studied with Andrea del Sarto, in company with a painter named Nannoccio, whose manner they followed. Vasari makes honorable mention of them, and says they went to France, where they resided a long time. Lanzi attributes to them some of the fine copies of the works of del Sarto, which often pass for originals at Florence. After mentioning the names of Domenico Puligo, Domenico Conti, Jacopo di Sandro, and Sguazzella, as followers of del Sarto, he says, "the fine copies that so often pass for originals by Andrea del Sarto in Florence and other places, are chiefly the work of the above-named artists; it does not seem hardly credible that Andrea copied so closely his own inventions, and reduced them from the great to smaller dimensions. I have seen one of his Holy Families, in which St. Elizabeth appears, in ten or twelve collections, and in other pictures in private houses. I found the St. Lorenzo surrounded by other saints, at the Pitti palace, in the Albani Gallery; the Visitation, in the Giustiniani palace; the Birth of our Lady in the convent of the Servi, in the possession of Sig. Pirri at Rome. All these are beautiful pictures, painted on small panels, all of the old school, and all believed to be the work of Andrea. It seems not improbable that the best of these were painted in his own studio, and retouched by him, a practice adopted by Titian, and even by Raffaelle."

SHARP, William, one of the most celebrated English line engravers, was born at London in 1749. His father was a gun-maker, and apprenticed him to a bright engraver (ornamental plate engraver), named Barak Longmate, who was also skilled in heraldry. His first essays, when an apprentice, were the embellishment of pewter pots; his flatterers qualify this assertion by substituting silver tankards, but Sharp always insisted on the veracity of this humble employment. After the expiration of the term of his apprenticeship, he commenced business for himself as a writing engraver, but he soon aspired to higher things. One of his first attempts in a superior branch of the art, was to make a drawing of the old lion Hector, who had been an inmate of the tower of London for thirty years, which he engraved on a small quarto plate, and exposed the prints in his shop-window for sale. He studied with great assiduity, and made such rapid progress that he was employed to engrave several plates from Stothard's designs for the "Novelist's Magazine," published by Harrison, a work on which Heath, Collyer, Angus, and other eminent artists were employed. By this means, his merits as an engraver were widely diffused; he soon distinguished himself among his cotemporaries, and was employed on works of art of the highest order, in the execution of which he proved himself a worthy successor of Woollett. As proofs of his extraordinary abilities, it is only necessary to adduce his prints of the Doctors of the Church, *after Guido*, in which he blended all the freedom of Giacomo Frey with the careful practice of Raphael Morghen; the portrait of John Hunter, *after Reynolds*, in which is shown his just discrimination and skill in the quality and texture of the draperies and objects; and Lear in the Storm, *after West*, which last is considered his master-piece, and has been held up as a model for line engravers; proof impressions of this plate have been sold for fifteen and twenty guineas each. His style is always masterly, not servilely borrowed from any of his predecessors or cotemporaries, but formed by a judicious selection of the merits of all who excelled, improved by an attentive study of nature. He gave to his plates all the expression, fire, and energy of his originals. The half-tints and shadows of his best works are peculiarly rich, and his lines combine with the utmost freedom, a regularity and accuracy seldom attained. He was particularly distinguished for his power of imitating the various textures of the draperies. He conferred great honor on the fine arts in his country, yet he was not admitted a member of the Royal Academy. He was proposed by Sir Joshua Reynolds as an *Associate*, but it is related that he rejected the offer with disdain, warmly espousing the cause of those distinguished engravers of his country who considered themselves and their art slighted in not being allowed to become Royal Academicians; yet the Imperial Academy of Vienna, and the Royal Academy of Munich, deemed him worthy of being ranked among their honorary members, and he was elected by both. There are many amusing anecdotes told of this artist. Being suspected of revolutionary principles, he was examined before the privy council. At one of these meetings, being annoyed by questions which he considered irrelevant, he deliberately pulled out of his pocket a prospectus for publishing the portrait of Kosciusko, after West, which he was engraving, and with great gravity handed it to Pitt and Dundas, requesting them to have the goodness to put their names to it as subscribers, and then to give it to the other members of the council to add theirs. The singularity of the proposal, under the circumstances, set them all to laughing, and relieved him from an unpleasant, and at that time, dangerous, predicament. With all his genius, Sharp had an erratic mind. He was a firm believer in the reveries of Emanuel Swedenborg, the divine mission of the madman Richard Brothers, and the immaculate conception of Johanna Southcote. Sharp engraved the portrait of Brothers, and Smith, in his life of Nollekens, relates a ludicrous mistake which occurred in the inscription. Sharp had written below, as now appears on the prints, "Fully believing this to be the man appointed by God, I engrave his likeness. W. Sharp." The writing engraver, Smith says, put the comma after the word "appointed," and omitted it in the subsequent part of the sentence. The mistake was not discovered till several impressions had been taken, when it was rectified; but the unrectified impressions are in the greatest request. There is a complete collection of the prints of this eminent engraver, in every state of progress, in the British Museum. He died at Chiswick in 1824, and was buried in the same churchyard as Hogarth and de Loutherbourg. The following is a list of his principal plates:

The Doctors of the Church; *after Guido*. Ecce Homo; *do.* Portrait of John Hunter, two plates, one large and one small; *after Sir Joshua Reynolds*. The Holy Family, two plates, one large and one small; *do.* The Witch of Endor; *after B. West*. Alfred dividing his Loaf with a Beggar; *do.* Lear in the Storm; *do.* The Children in the Wood; *after Benwell*. St. Cecilia; *after Domenichino*. The Siege of, and Sortie from, Gibraltar; *after Trumbull*. Some plates in Cook's Voyages; *after Webber*. Portrait of Thomas Paine; *after Romney*. The Portrait of Mr. Boulton. Sir Francis Burdett; *after Northcote*. Sir William Curtis; *after Lawrence*. Charles I., three faces; *after Vandyck*. The Earl of Arran; *do.* Boadicea haranguing the Britons; *after Stothard*. The three Marys and dead Christ; *after Ann. Caracci*, from the picture at Castle Howard, but left unfinished.

SHAW, James, an English painter, born at Wolverhampton. He went to London, and studied with Edward Penny. He painted portraits with considerable reputation till his death, in 1784. There was another artist of this name, who exhibited at the Royal Academy at its first establishment, as a painter of horses. He died in 1772.

SHAW, Joshua, an English landscape painter

of little note, born at Bellingborough in Lincolnshire, in 1776. He was a self-taught artist, and went to London for improvement, but not meeting with any encouragement, he painted for the dealers, and is said to have copied for them some pictures by Berghem, Both, and Cuyp. He afterwards emigrated to America.

SHEE, Sir Martin Archer, an eminent English portrait painter, born at Dublin in 1770. He was placed early in life in the Academy of West, in that city, where he soon distinguished himself. He drew several chief medals for drawings of the figure, landscapes, and flowers; and was honored by the Dublin Society with a silver palette. At the early age of sixteen, he lost his father, and being obliged to provide for his own support, he established himself as a portrait painter at Dublin, where he gained reputation and encouragement. Two years after, he removed to London, where he made the acquaintance of Reynolds and Burke, and was admitted as a student of the Royal Academy. In 1798, he was elected an associate, and in 1800 an academician. He soon attained high distinction, and gained great encouragement. In 1830, at the death of Lawrence, he was elected president of the Royal Academy, on which occasion he received the customary honor of knighthood. Devoting his energies from the first to the practice of portrait painting, under the auspices of Reynolds, he never, during the long period of his career, deviated from the path which he had marked out; hence he acquired a position beyond any of his cotemporaries, except Lawrence; nor was he far behind his predecessor in the presidential chair in attracting the nobility and other distinguished characters to his studio, the ladies only excepted, for whom Lawrence's graceful pencil possessed a charm with which no other painter could vie with the least chance of success. A list of the great names who sat to Sir Martin would fill several columns of this work. He never attempted any works of an ideal or fanciful nature, unless a few portraits of celebrated actors and actresses, in their favorite characters, may come under this denomination. His first picture was exhibited in 1789; his last in 1845; and for half a century he enjoyed a large share of public patronage. He died in 1850.

SHEPHERD, Robert, an English engraver, who flourished about 1660. He engraved some portraits, and copied on a smaller scale the Battles of Alexander by Gerard Audran, *after le Brun.* His prints are indifferently executed.

SHERLOCK, an English engraver of little note, who flourished about 1760. He engraved some portraits and landscapes.

SHENTON, Henry Chawner, an English sculptor, born in 1825. He early manifested an inclination for art, and was placed under the tuition of Mr. Behnes, with whom he made rapid progress. In 1843, at the age of eighteen, he was admitted as a student of the Royal Academy; and he exhibited in the same year a group of "Christ and Mary"; and the next year, in Westminster Hall, a group entitled the Burial of the Princes in the Tower of London, which possesses considerable merit. In 1845 he exhibited two works, "Archbishop Cranmer," and "The Penitent." He afterwards commenced a fine group of the Crucifixion, but its completion was interrupted by the death of the artist, in 1846.

SHERWIN, John Keyes, an eminent English engraver, born in Essex or Sussex, where his father carried on the business of a cutter of wood pins or bolts, for shipping, which business young Sherwin followed till he was about seventeen years of age, when by accident variously stated, he showed a talent for drawing that excited interest in his favor, and he was sent to London to study with Bartolozzi. Under this eminent master he made rapid progress in drawing and engraving, and in 1772 gained the gold medal at the Royal Academy, for a drawing of Coriolanus taking leave of his family. From that time to 1780, he exhibited at the annual exhibitions of the same institution a number of chalk drawings, some of them copies, others originals, which attracted considerable attention, particularly one called the "Joys of Life," executed in red and black chalk, with a mixture of color, in the manner of Bartolozzi.—This composition consisted of a beautiful female, and a figure of Bacchus surrounded by Cupids strewing flowers. In his larger works, his style of engraving has a greater resemblance to that of Woollett, than of Bartolozzi. One of his best works, and supposed to be his last, was a print from his own design, called the Finding of Moses, in which he introduced the beautiful Duchess of Devonshire as the Daughter of Pharaoh, and several ladies of rank as her attendants. Stanley says this print would have made his fortune had he been prudent, but unfortunately he contracted bad habits, plunged himself into debt, and in order to escape the importunities of his creditors and arrest, he was obliged to secrete himself, and finally died in a small ale-house, called "The Hog in the Pound," in 1790. The following is a list of his best prints:

PORTRAITS.

William Pitt, Earl of Chatham. George Nugent Grenville Temple, Marquis of Buckingham; *after Gainsborough.* Dr. Louth, Bishop of London; *after Pine.* Captain James Cook; *after Dance.* Sir Joshua Reynolds; *after a picture by himself.* William Woolett, Engraver to the King. Mrs. Siddons, in the character of the Grecian Daughter.

VARIOUS SUBJECTS.

The Holy Family; *after N. Poussin.* Christ bearing his Cross; *after the picture in the chapel of the Magdalene College, Oxford.* Christ appearing to Magdalene; *at All Souls' College, Oxford.* The Holy Family; *after N. Beretoni.* The Fortune Teller; *after Reynolds.* The Death of Lord Robert Manners; *after Stothard.*

SHERWIN, William, an English engraver, who flourished from about 1669 to 1711. It is not known by whom he was instructed. He is said to have been a royal engraver by patent, the only English artist known to have received that honor, a distinction to which his merits did not entitle him. He engraved some portraits in a stiff, formal style; also some frontispieces and other book plates, among which are most of the plates for a work entitled *God's Revenge against Murder*, published in 1669. He also scraped a few mezzotintos. The following are his best prints:

Charles I. on horseback, with a view of Richmond. Oliver Cromwell. Charles II.; three plates, one a whole-length; prefixed to Ashmole's Order of the Garter. Catherine, his Queen. Christopher, Duke of Albemarle. William III. when Prince of Orange. Henry, Duke of Norfolk. George I. when Elector of Hanover. Richard Atkyns, Typograph. Reg.; scarce. Slingsby Bethell, Sheriff of London; scarce. Henry Scudder, B. D. Presbyt. William Ramesay, M. D. William Bridge, A. M. Presbyt. William Sermon, M. D.; inscribed, *W. Shirwin, ad vivum, del. et sculp.* 1671. John Gadbury, Astrologer. Judge Powell. 1711.

SHIPLEY, William, an English artist, born at London in 1714. He was a drawing master, and kept a school for teaching drawing many years in London. He chiefly deserves notice for his public spirit. He was the founder of the "Society for the Encouragement of Arts, Manufactures, and Commerce," an institution that has proved highly beneficial to his country. In 1758, he received a gold medal as a token of acknowledgment for his exertions. He afterwards settled at Maidstone, where he died in 1804, at the great age of ninety. He was a brother of Dr. Jonathan Shipley, bishop of St. Asaph.

SIBELIUS, G., a Dutch engraver, who went to London about 1775, where he was chiefly employed by Sir Joseph Banks in engraving plates for his great botanical work. He also executed a few portraits.

SIBMACHER, John, a German engraver, who flourished at Nuremberg from about 1596 to 1611. He engraved, among other plates, a part of the antique statues for Boissard's collection. They are executed in an indifferent style.

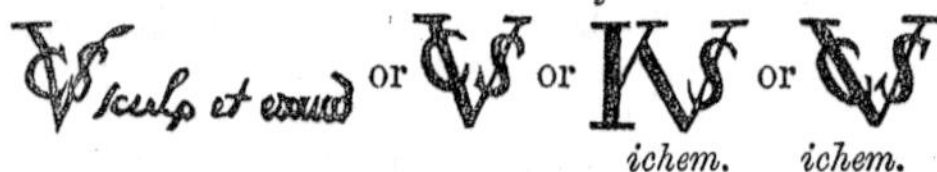


SICHEM, Christopher and Charles van, two Dutch engravers, who flourished at Amsterdam in the first part of the 17th century. They engraved both on wood and copper, and, though their works are exceedingly numerous, there is such a perfect chaos of confusion among writers that it is impossible to distinguish their respective works. According to Baron Heineken, there were three Sichems, Christopher, Cornelius, and Charles. To Cornelius, he attributes about six hundred prints from the Old and New Testaments, marked with a monogram of C. V. S. and K. V. S., though he admits that it is impossible to separate the prints of Cornelius and Charles, from the similarity of monograms and style; but other writers suppose there were only two, Christopher and Charles. The prints in question are usually marked with one of the preceding monograms, composed of the initials C. V. S. and K. V. S., sometimes with *ichem* below, which has led several writers to confuse the Sichems with a supposed engraver of the name of *Vichem;* the V. in the monogram being the largest, they have erroneously concluded that it was the principal letter. The truth doubtless is, that there were but two Sichems, Christopher and Charles, as there are some prints signed C., Ch., or Christ. van Sichem, and none with the name of Corn. or Cornelius; K., also, is frequently used by the Dutch writers for Karolus or Karl, but never for Christopher or Cornelius; and doubtless those prints marked with the monogram composed of C. V. S. were executed by Christopher, and those with K. V. S. by Karl or Charles. According to Malpe, Christopher was born about 1580, and his prints are dated from 1601 to 1637, and there are prints marked K. V. S. from about 1600 to 1629. Many of them are from their own designs, and the others after various masters. Their wooden cuts are the best, and are executed with great vigor and spirit.

SICIOLANTE, Girolamo, a painter born at Sermoneta in 1504; hence he is generally called Girolamo da Sermoneta, though sometimes Girolamo Siciolante da or di Sermoneta, and Girolamo di Sermoneta. He was one of the ablest disciples of Pierino del Vaga, whom he assisted in his works at the Castle of St. Angelo. As there is some discrepancy as to his style and merits, we prefer to give Lanzi's account. After stating that he was a pupil of del Vaga, whom he assisted in his works, and that he was one of the successors of Raffaelle employed to complete the works in the Sala Regia, he says, "Girolamo Siciolante da Sermoneta, who adopted Raffaello's style, may be enumerated among the scholars of that great man, from his felicitous imitation of their common master. In the Sala Regia, in the Vatican, he painted Pepin, King of France, bestowing Ravenna on the church, after having made Astolfo, King of the Lombards, his prisoner. But he approaches Raffaello in some of his oil paintings, as in the Martyrdom of St, Lucia, in the church of S. Maria Maggiore; in the Transfiguration in the Ara Cœli, and in the Nativity in the church della Pace, which last he repeated in the most graceful style in the church of Osimo. His master-piece is at Ancona, on the great altar in the church of S. Bartolomeo, a vast composition, original and rich in invention, and commensurate with the grandeur of the subject, and the multitude of saints introduced into it. The throne of the Virgin is seen above, amidst a brilliant choir of angels, and on either side, a virgin saint in the attitude of adoration. To this height, there is a beautiful ascent on each side; and the picture is thus divided into a higher and a lower part; in the latter of which is a titular saint, a half-naked figure vigorously colored, together with Saint Paul and two other saints; the whole designed and executed in a truly *Raffaellesque* style. This altar-piece possesses so much harmony, and such a force of color, that it is esteemed by some, the best picture in the city. If anything is wanting in it, it is perhaps a more correct observance of the perspective." Siciolante also excelled in portraits. His easel pictures painted for the private collections are extremely rare. There is much discrepancy as to the time of his death, but the best authorities place it in or about 1580. Baglioni says that he died in the pontificate of Gregory XIII., who ascended the papal chair in 1572, and it is stated by every author, that he was employed by that pontiff. Lanzi says he was living in 1572, as appears from an inscription on a monument he erected to his son. It is therefore evident that those who place his death in 1550, are greatly in error. It seems probable also that there is an error as to the time of his birth, as it is agreed that he was a pupil of Vaga, who was born in 1500, only four years previously.

SIEGEN, Lieut.-Colonel von, was born in Holland of a noble family, according to Laborde, in 1609. He went to Germany in 1620, where he received his education. He returned to Holland in 1626, and remained there till 1637, when he entered the service of the Landgrave of Hesse, and attained the rank of lieutenant-colonel. His name was Louis von Siegen, or de Siegen, and it is now generally admitted that he was the inventor of the art of engraving in mezzotinto. It was for a long time attributed to Prince Rupert, till the Baron Heineken proved that he learned the art of Siegen, while in the service of the Landgrave of Hesse, which he afterwards introduced into England. Siegen produced his first print, a bust portrait of Amelia Elizabeth, Landgrave of Hesse, in 1643. Many interesting particulars of this amateur artist may be found in Laborde's "L'Histoire de la gravure en manière noire." He gives a descriptive account of seven prints by him, as follows: 1. Bust portrait of Amelia Elizabeth; 2. Eleonora Gonzago, wife of the Emperor Ferdinand III., called by others the Queen of Bohemia; 3. Portrait of the Prince of Orange, *after Honthorst;* 4. Portrait of the Princess of Orange, *do;* 5. The Emperor Ferdinand III. in an oval; 6. St. Bruno, a full length figure kneeling; 7. The Holy Family, *after Ann. Caracci.* They are marked *L. à S.*, or *L. à Siegen inv. et fec.* Laborde, in his account of John George Seiller, who flourished about 1600, says he engraved in mezzotinto, and commends several of his prints; if this is true, Siegen's claim to the invention falls to the ground, as well as that of Prince Rupert. There is a fine collection of the works of Siegen, Prince Rupert, and other early engravers in mezzotinto, in the British Museum. Siegen died in the service of the Duke of Wolfenbuttel, about 1680. See *Rupert* and *Seiller*.

SIENA, Agnolo, or Angelo and Agostino da. See Angelo.

SIENA, Ansano, or Sano, da, a painter of Siena, of whom there are notices from 1422 to 1462. According to Della Valle, when Pope Pius II. erected the cathedral in Pienza (the new name of his native place, Corsignano), in 1462, he invited the best artists of Siena there to decorate it, among whom were Ansano and his son Matteo. Lanzi says their style was laborious and minute, the universal character of that age.

SIENA, Baldassare da. See Peruzzi.

SIENA, Duccio da, called also Duccio, or Guiduccio di Boninsegna, or Buoninsegna. See Duccio.

SIENA, Francesco, called by Vasari Francesco Sienese, a painter of Siena, who flourished about 1530. He studied under Baldassare Peruzzi, and is commended by Vasari for his frescos in the grotesque style of Peruzzi, most of which have perished, though there are some grotesque subjects in Siena attributed to him.

SIENA, Berna, or Bernardo da, an old Italian painter, who flourished at Siena about 1370. According to Vasari, "he was the first who painted animals correctly;" and he also attained uncommon excellence in the human figure, particularly in expression. Lanzi mentions a fresco painting by him, in the parish church at Arezzo, as deserving more praise for the execution of the extremities, in which he surpassed his cotemporaries, than for the drapery or coloring. He attained such reputation that he was invited to Florence, and commissioned to execute several paintings in the chapel of S. Niccolo, in the church of S. Spirito, which was afterwards destroyed by fire. The Canons of Siena possessed a collection of small pictures by this artist, which were better colored than his frescos. He also painted at Venice and Cortona, and finally died at San Gimignano, in 1380, after making considerable progress in a copious work, illustrative of sacred subjects, still remaining in the parish church. It was continued by his scholar Giovanni d'Asciano, with a superior coloring, but less pure design.

SIENA, Francesco Antonio da, a painter who flourished at Siena in the first part of the 17th century. Little is known of him except by a picture of the Last Supper in the convent of the Angioli, near Assisi, inscribed *Franciscus Antonius Senensis*, 1614. Lanzi says the style resembles that of Baroccio enough to lead him to suspect that he was a pupil of Vanni or Salimbeni. The picture is well colored, with a fine and appropriate expression in the different countenances.

SIENA, Francesco di Giorgio da, a painter of Siena, who flourished in the first half of the 16th century. According to Della Valle, he was one of the ablest scholars of Baldassare Peruzzi, whose style he followed. He painted grotesque subjects, in which, like his instructor, he introduced every species of ideas, as edifices, trees, fruit, flowers, vases, candelabra, lamps, armor, thunderbolts, satyrs, masks, animals, and monsters, in which he bridled his exuberant fancy with judgment. Lanzi says that, though he did not equal Peruzzi, he acquired great reputation in this style of painting. He was also a skillful architect.

SIENA, Giorgio da, a painter of Siena, who flourished about 1550; probably somewhat earlier. He studied under Domenico Beccafumi. Lanzi says he imitated Giovanni da Udine, both in his own country and at Rome. He was doubtless the father of the preceding artist.

SIENA, Giovanni, or Gianella da, a painter and architect of Siena, probably a brother of Giorgio, with whom he studied under Beccafumi, according to Della Valle. Little is known of him. Lanzi says he turned his attention from painting to architecture. He flourished about the middle of the 16th century.

SIENA, Giovanni, di Paolo, a painter employed among others by Pope Pius II. to embellish the cathedral of Pienza, where he showed himself deserving a good reputation among the artists of his time. His notices range from 1422 to 1462. About four years after his performances in the cathedral of Pienza, he painted a Descent from the Cross, in the Osservanza at Siena, commended by Lanzi for his excellence in the naked figure, surpassing the productions of most artists of the time.

SIENA, Guido Guidone, an old Sienese painter, whom the writers of Siena and the learned and celebrated Cav. Marini of Florence claim to have made great improvements in painting, over the raw and feeble manner of the Greeks, before the time of Cimabue and Giotto. Lanzi says, "Guido left the art not very far behind (Cimabue and Giotto) in his picture of the Virgin, now hung up in the Malevolti chapel, in the church of S. Domenico. On it is inscribed the name and the date:

Me Guido de Senis diebus depinxit amenis.
Quem Christus lenis nullis velit agere poenis.
An. 1221.

And this example (of name and date) was often

followed by the masters of the Sienese school, to the great benefit of the history of painting. The countenance of the Virgin is lovely, and participates not in the stern aspect that is characteristic of the Greeks. We may also discover some trace of a new style of drapery. The Madonnas of Cimabue which are at Florence, the one in the church of the Trinity, and the other in S. Maria Novella, are not however inferior. In them we may discover the improvement of the art (over the Greeks)—a more vivid coloring, flesh tints more true, a more natural attitude of the head of the Infant, while the accompaniments of the throne and of the Glory of Angels proclaim a superior style." Lanzi then goes on to confute Marini, by showing that while Guido only painted single figures, only one specimen of which is known, the paintings of Cimabue are numerous and full of subject.

SIENA, Marco Da. See Pino.

SIENA, Matteo di Giovanni da, an eminent Sienese painter, of whom there are notices, according to Della Valle, from 1462 to 1491. Lanzi says he far surpassed all his predecessors (of the Sienese school) in the extent of his genius. "This is the Matteo designated by some the Masaccio of this school, although there is a great distance between him and the Florentine Masaccio. The new style of Matteo begins to be recognized in one of his two pictures in the Cathedral. He afterwards improved in his works in S. Domenico, in Madonna della Neve, and in some other churches at Siena. It was he who excited the Neapolitan school to attempt a less antiquated style. Having learned the art of oil painting, he imparted softness to his figures; and from his intimacy with Francesco di Giorgio, a celebrated architect (also a sculptor and painter; see Giorgio), he imbibed a good taste in buildings, and diversified them very ingeniously with alto and basso-relievos. He foreshortened level objects well, and he cast his draperies with more nature and less frippery than was common in that age; if he imparted little beauty to the features, he attained variety of expression, and was attentive in marking the muscles and veins in his figures. He did not always aim at novelty and display; on the contrary, after painting the Murder of the Innocents, his best composition, which is engraved in the third volume of the *Lettere Sanesi*, he often repeated it at Siena and at Naples, but always with variations and improvements. His most studied picture on this subject is that at the Servi in Siena, painted in 1491, which must have been near the close of his life. He was accustomed to introduce some episode, unconnected with the principal story, in small figures, a style in which he excelled. The noble house of the Sozzini, and other families of Siena, possess several of his small pictures. As an artist, he is inferior to Bellini, to Francia, or Vannucci, but he surpasses many others."

SIENA, Matteo da, called by the Sienese writers Matteino, to distinguish him from the preceding, was born at Siena in 1533, and died at Rome in 1588. He painted landscapes and perspective in fresco, and was much employed in conjunction with other artists in decorating the public and private edifices. He went to Rome in the pontificate of Gregory XIII., where he was employed to paint many landscapes in the Vatican, in which the figures were inserted by other artists. In conjunc tion with Niccolo Circignani, called Pomerancio, he painted a series of thirty-two pictures of the History of the Martyrs, at S. Stefano Rotondo, which have been engraved by Cavalieri. (See Gio. Battista Cavalleriis). It is said that he painted at the Casino at Siena about 1551, and in the Palazzo Lucarini with Rustichino. Many of his works still exist. Lanzi says they are beautiful, though executed in the old, dry style.

SIENA, Maestro, Mino da, called Minuccio, to distinguish him from Fra Mino da Turrita. There is a picture in the Council Room of the public palace, or City Hall, at Siena, painted in 1289, which Lanzi attributes to him. Lanzi, after showing that he was a different artist from Fra Mino, says of the picture above referred to, "He there represented the Virgin and Child surrounded by angels, and under a canopy supported by apostles and the patron saint of the city. The size of the figures, the invention, and the distribution of the work, are surprising for that age; of the other qualities one cannot speak with certainty, as it was repaired in 1321 by Simone da Siena." There are other works attributed to him of an earlier date.

SIENA, Michael Angelo da. See Anselmi.

SIENA, Segna, Boninsegna, or Buoninsegna, an old Sienese painter, of whom there are notices in 1305, according to Lanzi. There is no authentic work by him remaining at Siena, though he was eminent in his time. He was the instructor of Duccio di Buoninsegna, who painted as early as 1282, and died about 1340. See *Duccio*.

SIENA, Ugolino da, an old painter of Siena, who died old in 1339. Vasari insinuates that he was a disciple of Cimabue, and says, "he painted pictures and chapels all over Italy." Baldinucci engrafts him on his *tree* as a pupil of that master; others assert that he was a pupil of Guido da Siena. Lanzi is of a contrary opinion, as he adhered too closely to the style of the Greeks. There were several other old artists called da Siena, of little note, the accounts of whom are very contradictory. Some of them were pupils of those already noticed, and flourished from about 1350 to 1400.

SIENA, Simone da. See Simone Memmi.

SIERRA, Francisco Perez, a painter born at Naples in 1627. His father was a Spanish officer, who, following the career of arms in the kingdom of Naples, married the daughter of the Governor of Calabria, for which reason, and that Francisco passed most of his life in Spain, he is ranked among the Spanish painters. Having a taste for painting, his father permitted him to study with Aniello Falcone; at the same time he received the appointment of page to Don Diego de la Torre, Secretary to the Council of Santa Clara, which was a great hindrance to his progress in art, as he could only devote to painting such time as he could snatch from his duties. He afterwards accompanied his patron to Madrid, where he entered the school of Juan de Toledo, a painter of battles, and by great assiduity became such a proficient as to attract the notice of Francisco Rizi and Juan Carreno, who obtained employment for him in the house of the Marquis de Heliche. His patron, la Torre, employed him to copy several pictures by

Spagnoletto, which he had brought with him from Naples; also to paint a series of pictures of saints to decorate a chapel in the church of the Angels, which he had founded at Madrid. He also painted for the same church a picture in honor of Santa Rosa of Lima. He painted landscapes, battles, and pictures of Saints. Later in life he received the appointment of General Manager of the Prisons of Spain, when he abandoned painting as a profession, though he painted flower-pieces for amusement, some of which found their way into the palace of the Buon Retiro, and the houses of the nobility. He died at Madrid in 1709.

SIGALON, Xavier, a reputable French historical painter, born in 1790, at Uzés, in the old province of Languedoc. After acquiring the elements of the art at Nismes, he executed several pictures for the church of Aigues Mortes, and then visited Paris, to enter the school of Guerin. In 1822 he exhibited at the Louvre his admired picture of the Courtesan, which was purchased by the Government for the Gallery at the Luxembourg. Sigalon resided about twenty years at Paris, and painted many meritorious productions; but not being properly encouraged, he retired to Nismes, and commenced painting portraits, and teaching design. At the request of M. Thiers, however, the Minister of the Interior, he visited Rome, and commenced copying the Last Judgment by Michael Angelo. In 1837, at the completion of the work, it was placed in the old church of the Augustines at Paris, now the Hall of the School of Fine Arts. Sigalon gained considerable reputation by this work, and was commissioned to copy the Prophets of Michael Angelo in the Sistine chapel; but soon after his return to Rome, he was attacked by the cholera, and died on the 10th of August, 1837. Besides his works already mentioned, he executed a picture entitled *La Locuste*, now in the Museum at Nismes; and the Vision of St. Jerome, in the Luxembourg.

SIGHIZZI, Andrea, a Bolognese fresco painter of some eminence, who, according to Malvasia, was living in 1678. He was employed by Agostino Mitelli to insert the figures in some of his perspective pieces. He was also employed at Turin, Mantua, and Parma, where he was appointed court painter, with a salary. Nothing more is recorded of him.

SIGISMONDI, Pietro, a painter born at Lucca, commended by the Cav. Titi as a scholar or imitator of Pietro da Cortona. He commends the great altar-piece by him in the church of S. Niccolo in Arcione, at Rome.

SIGNORELLI, Luca, an eminent painter, born at Cortona in 1439, and died in 1521, according to the best authorities, though there is a slight discrepancy; Vasari says he was born about 1440, and died in 1521; Lanzi, the same; Zani, that he was living in 1525. He studied under Pietro della Francesca, and was one of the ablest artists of his time. He contributed much to the advancement of the art, as his works served as types to some of the illustrious painters, his cotemporaries or immediate followers. Lanzi says that he was the first of the Tuscan artists who designed the human figure with a true knowledge of anatomy. His greatest work is his celebrated fresco in the chapel of the Virgin in the Cathedral of Orvieto, representing the final Dissolution and Judgment of the World—an immense composition, exhibiting a surprising variety and originality of ideas, and designed in a bold and daring style, in which he evinces a profound knowledge of anatomy and of foreshortening. This performance, though not entirely divested of the dry, stiff manner that preceded him, was greatly admired by Michael Angelo, and Lanzi says that great artist did not disdain to imitate his naked figures in his Last Judgment in the Sistine chapel. In this work, too, Signorelli introduced the portraits of many of his friends and benefactors. In the greater part of his works he is not so remarkable for beauty of form or harmony of coloring, as for fertility of invention and correctness of design, though Lanzi cites an exception to this, in his picture of the Communion of the Apostles, in the Church of the Jesuits at Cortona, in which there is beauty and grace, and harmony of tints approaching to modern excellence. He wrought equally well both in oil and fresco, and painted many works for the churches of his native place, Urbino, Volterra, Florence, and other cities. He was invited to Rome to assist in decorating the Sistine chapel, where he painted the Journey of Moses with Zippora, and the Promulgation of the Old Law—paintings full of incident, and greatly superior in composition to the confused style of his age. Vasari and Taja have assigned him the first place in the great assemblage of artists employed at Rome before the time of Buonarotti and Raffaelle, and Lanzi says he seems to him to have at least equalled the best of them, and to have improved his usual style. Zani quotes two of his inscriptions, *Lucas Aegidii Signorelli Cortonensis*, 1502, and *Lucas Coritius*. There is considerable discrepancy as to his real merits, but whoever will refer to the print of the Last Supper, after him, in the *Etruria Pittrice*, and those of the Descent from the Cross, and a part of the Last Judgment in Rosini's *Storia della Pittura* (plates 65 and 82), will perceive an original mode of composition and design, and an energy of expression unknown before his time.

SIGNORELLI, Francesco, a painter of Lucca, of whom there are notices from 1520 to about 1560, was the nephew of the preceding. He is commended by Bottari as an able artist, and Lanzi says that, "though unnoticed by Vasari, he shows himself a painter worthy of praise, by a circular picture of the patron saints of the city, which was executed for the Council hall in 1520, after which period he exercised his art at least forty years."

SIGNORINI, Guido, a Bolognese painter who, according to Orlandi, was the cousin and scholar of Guido Reni, and inherited his effects. Little is known of him. He died about 1650.

SIGNORINI, Guido, another Bolognese painter, mentioned by Crespi as a scholar and imitator of Carlo Cignani. He chiefly painted for individuals. Lanzi says he must not be confounded with another Guido Signorini, heir to Guido Reni.

SIGRILLI, B., an Italian engraver who flourished about 1760. He engraved a part of the plates for the collection of prints after the paintings in the Gallery of the Marchese Gerini.

SILANION, a distinguished Greek sculptor, who probably flourished about B. C. 346, in the time of Alexander and Lysippus. He executed a statue of the sculptor Apollodorus, holding a hammer in his hand, and about to strike an object before him; Pliny says it expressed the passion with such truth, that it seemed to personate Anger itself. It appears that Silanion was an adept in representing vivid passions. Cicero mentions his statue of Sappho, in the Prytaneum at Syracuse, as highly finished, delicate, and beautiful, and deemed worthy of Verres' rapacity. He executed a bronze bust of Plato, of which that in the Florentine Gallery is probably a copy. Among his other works were the statues of Corinna, Theseus, and Achilles; and also a bronze statue of Alexander the Great, said to have been ordered by a Persian satrap named Mithridates, and consecrated by him to the Muses, in the shade of Academus.

SILO, Adam, a Dutch painter, designer, engraver, and *ship-builder*, born at Amsterdam in 1670. He was probably the man who instructed Peter the Great in ship-building; at all events, it is said that the Czar sent to him five young Russians to learn the art of naval architecture, for whose instruction he paid him one hundred ducats each. He painted several marine pieces for the Czar, in which the drawing of the vessels was correct, but the sky and water not in *accordance with nature;* probably these were designs for ships. He also painted a Storm at Sea, for the Dutch admiral Grave, which is said to have been a learned composition, and gained him great reputation. There are nine etchings by him, of fishing boats and other vessels, signed *A. Silo, inv. et fecit.* He is said to have died in 1760, aged 90.

SILOE, Diego, a distinguished Spanish architect, a native of Toledo, who flourished in the latter part of the 15th century. According to Milizia, he studied under Alonso Cobarrubias, and assisted that master in restoring good taste in architecture. He erected the Royal Hospital at Granada, and several other edifices, among which are the Cathedral, adorned with Corinthian columns and a magnificent cupola; also the great chapel of S. Geronimo, with the royal monastery, founded in 1496, and considered one of the finest in Spain. It is decorated with a Corinthian order, and the cloister is graceful and well arranged. This edifice was purchased of Charles V. by the Duchess of Terra Nuovas, Donna Maria Maurique, wife of the famous Gonsalvo de Cordova, otherwise known as "the Great Captain."

SILVANI, Gherardo, an eminent Florentine architect, born in 1579. His instructor is not mentioned, but he gained great distinction in his native city, and was highly esteemed by the Grand Duke Ferdinand; he wrought with indefatigable industry, and, according to Milizia, with unquestionable ability. In Via San Gallo, he erected a noble palace for Signor Castelli, now belonging to the Marucelli family, and one of the most beautiful edifices in Tuscany. In Via Guelfonda, he built the magnificent Riccardi palace, a truly royal residence. Silvani also made a noble design for enlarging the Palazzo Pitti, with a large square in front; but, on account of the intrigues of his rivals, it was never executed. The Grand Duke commissioned him to strengthen the Cathedral, for the façade of which he made a design of two orders, which was preferred to those of Buontalenti and other eminent architects, although the edifice still remains without a façade. During a long life of ninety-six years, Silvani erected a large number of edifices besides those already mentioned, among which were the Albizzi palace at Florence; the church of the Compagnia delle Stimmate; the Capponi palace; the Salviati palace at Pinti; the Bardi palace at Verbellezza; the Sapienza palace at Pistoja, &c. He died in 1675. His son, Pier Francesco S., studied the art under his father, and was much employed in the Cathedral at Florence; he also erected a number of edifices, among which the church of the Padri dell' Oratorio is deemed by Milizia as deserving much commendation.

SILVESTRE, Israel, an eminent French designer and engraver, born at Nancy in Lorraine, in 1621; died at Paris in 1691. He visited Paris, and studied under his uncle Israel Henriet. He engraved a great variety of landscapes and views, after his own designs, in a neat, tasteful manner, with charming effect, founded on the styles of Callot and Della Bella. His plates are decorated with small figures, correctly drawn, and touched with uncommon spirit; his style appears to have been followed by Sebastian le Clerc. The excellence of his performances gained him the patronage of Louis XIV., and he was employed to engrave views of the royal palaces, the public festivals, and the cities conquered by the king; was appointed drawing master to the Dauphin, with a pension, and apartments in the Louvre, and elected a member of the Royal Academy. Silvestre visited Italy twice, and made many designs there, which he afterwards engraved. His plates number about one thousand, among which are a collection entitled *Paysages Diverses*, containing seventy-four views of palaces, churches, gardens, fountains, &c., in Italy and France; *Vues diverses de Rome et d' Italie*, containing one hundred and five views of Italian scenery; and the following:

A set of twenty-one Views of Italy and France, representing edifices, ruins, and landscapes, with inscriptions in French. A set of thirteen Views in Rome and the environs; inscribed *Faites par Israel Silvestre, et mises en lumiere par Israel Henriet.* Twelve Views of gardens and fountains; entitled *Alcune vedute de Giardini e Fontane di Roma e di Tivoli, &c.*, with descriptions in Italian. Four Views of the Kingdom of Naples, in the form of friezes. A set of six Views of Sea-ports in the Kingdom of Naples; circular. Twenty-four circular plates of Views of Italian and other Sea-ports, with descriptions in French. Twelve of the most remarkable Views in Paris and the environs, some of which are engraved by *la Bella.* A View of Paris from the Bridge of the Tuilleries. A large View of Rome; four sheets. Two Views of Campo Vaccino, and the Coliseum at Rome; the latter is scarce. The grand Carousal, or Royal Entertainment at Paris in 1662; in one hundred and eight prints. *F. Chaveau* engraved some of these plates. The Pleasures of the Enchanted Island; nine plates, with a vignette. A great variety of other views and Landscapes.

SILVESTRE, Louis, a distinguished French painter, was the son of the preceding. There are great discrepancies in the accounts of the sons of Israel Silvestre. Bryan says that Louis was his eldest son, born at Paris about 1651; Zani says he was his third son, born in 1675; others place his birth in 1644. After acquiring the elements of design from his father, he studied painting under le Brun and Bon Boullongne, and subsequently visited Italy for improvement. On returning to Paris, he was chosen a member, and afterwards a professor of the Royal Academy. After gaining considerable reputation by various works in portrait and landscape, for the refectory of S. Martin des

Champs, the churches of S. Roch and Notre Dame, &c., he was invited to the court of Dresden by Augustus III., king of Poland and elector of Saxony, who honored him with letters of nobility, and made him principal painter to the court. Appointed director of the Dresden Academy, he remained twenty-four years in that city, and then returned to Paris, where Louis XV. assigned him apartments in the Louvre, with a pension of 1000 crowns. Silvestre died in 1760; though some place his death in 1728.

SILVESTRE, Alexandre. This engraver was born at Paris, according to Nagler, in 1650. Zani says he was the eldest, and Bryan the younger son of Israel Silvestre. Among other plates, he etched several from the designs of his brother, Louis S., which possess considerable merit, though greatly inferior to the productions of his father.

SILVESTRE, Nicolas Charles, grandson of Israel S., was born at Paris, according to Basan, in 1700. He obtained sufficient distinction to be appointed drawing master to the king and royal family of France; and engraved, among other plates, a hunting-piece, *after Audray;* and Ubaldo and the Danish knight searching for Rinaldo in the Palace of Armida, *after Lemoine.* He died in 1767.

SILVESTRE, Susanna. This lady was the daughter of Israel S., and became the wife of Lemoine the painter. She engraved a number of plates, among which are several copies of other plates of heads and portraits, *after Vandyck.* One of them is signed *Susanna Silvestre Lemoine, sculp.*

SILVESTRO, an old Florentine painter, and a monk of Camaldoli, who died about 1350. According to Vasari, he was a pupil of Taddeo Gaddi. He was one of the miniaturists. He devoted his time mostly to ornamenting missals, which Lanzi says still exist, and are among the best that Italy possesses.

SILVIO, Giovanni, a Venetian painter, who flourished in the first part of the 16th century. Lanzi conjectures from his style that he was a pupil of Titian. He says, "Gio. Silvio, a Venetian, though omitted in the history of his native place, still vindicates his title to notice by numerous works dispersed throughout the state of Trevigi; there is a very elegant altar-piece by him in the collegiate church of Piovi di Sacco, a municipality of the Padovano, executed in 1532. It represents St. Martin in his episcopal chair, between the two Apostles Peter and Paul; three angels form the accessories, two in the act of raising his pastoral staff, and the third playing upon a harp, at the foot of the throne, extremely graceful, like the rest, the whole displaying a design of taste and nature, such as are found in Titian."

*A* SILVIUS, or SYLVIUS, Anthony, a real or supposed designer and wood engraver, who according to Papillon, flourished at Antwerp from about 1553 to 1580. He was much employed by Christopher Plantin, an eminent printer and bookseller of that city, to execute cuts to illustrate his publications; also by other publishers. The prints are marked with the above monogram. Nagler says that the prints in question were executed by an unknown artist, and that Papillon mistook for the engraver the name of *Antoniano Silvio*, professor of Belles Lettres at Rome, afterwards a Cardinal himself, who dedicated an edition of Faerno's Fables to Cardina Borromeo, published at Antwerp in 1567, illustrated with cuts marked with a monogram composed of an A. and an S.

SILVIUS, or SYLVIUS, Balthasar, an engraver who flourished about 1555. He engraved some plates from his own designs, and others after Francis Floris, Karel van Mander, Jerome Bosch, and others. They are coarsely executed with the graver, and are marked with his initials, B. S.

SIMMONS, or SIMMONDS, John, an English painter, born at Nailsea, in Somersetshire, about 1715. He served his apprenticeship to a house and ship painter at Bristol. He afterwards devoted his attention mostly to portraiture, and acquired considerable reputation at Bristol. His portrait of Ferguson the astronomer, and several others, have been engraved. He was one of the earliest exhibitors at the Royal Academy, and in the catalogue his name is sometimes printed *Simmonds of Bristol.* There is an altar-piece of the Annunciation by him, in All-saints church, Bristol, and another of the Resurrection, in St. John's church, Devizes. He died at Bristol in 1780.

SIMON, Jean, a French engraver, born in Normandy about 1675. He learned the art of line engraving in his own country, and afterwards went to London, where he engraved several portraits of distinguished personages, in line. The success of John Smith in mezzotinto, then coming into vogue, induced him to adopt that method of engraving. The following are his principal prints:

Queen Elizabeth; *after Hilliard.* Charles I.; *after Vandyck.* William III.; *after Kneller.* Mary, his consort; *after vander Vaart.* Queen Anne; *after Kneller.* George, Prince of Denmark. George I.; *after Kneller.* George II., when Prince of Wales; *do.* John, Lord Cutts; *do.* William, Earl of Cadogan; *do.* John Tillotson, Archbishop of Canterbury; *do.* John, Lord Sommers; *do.* Sir Richard Temple; *do.* William, Earl of Cadogan; *after la Guerre.* Horace, Lord Walpole; *after Vanloo.* Henry Rouvigny, Earl of Galway; *after de Graves.* William Shakspeare. John Milton. Joseph Addison. Richard Steele.

The following are his principal works in mezzotinto:

Half-length of the Princess Mary, daughter of George II. Peter delivered from Prison; *after Berchet.* The Cartoons at Hampton Court. Christ and his Apostles; *after Baroccio.* Christ restoring sight to the Blind; *after la Guerre;* excellent. The Samaritan Woman; *do.* Portrait of the Hon. Mrs. Walpole; *after M. Dahl:* excellent. Maria Stuart; the expression infantine. Dorastus and Fannia; *after Berchet.* A Pastoral Scene, of which the foliage and landscape are remarkable.

SIMON, Pierre, a French engraver, who flourished at Paris about 1680. He is supposed to have studied under Robert Nanteuil, whose style he adopted. His works, though inferior to those of Nanteuil, possess considerable merit. Among other prints, are the following by him:

PORTRAITS.

Louis XIV.; *after C. le Brun;* the size of life. Louis de Bourbon, Prince of Condé; *from his own design.* Anna Maria Louisa of Orleans, Duchess of Montpensier; *do.* Elizabeth Charlotte, Duchess of Orleans; *do.* Charles d'Ailly, Duke de Chaulnes, Peer of France; *after Laborde.* Jacobus Cardinalis Rospigliosus; *after C. Maratti.* Federigo Baroccio, Painter,

SUBJECTS.

The Martyrdom of St. Cosmus and St. Damien; *after S. Rosa.* Moses at the burning Bush; *after N. Poussin.*

SIMON, John Peter, an eminent English designer and engraver, born at London in 1750. It is not mentioned under whom he studied, but he acquired a high reputation for his engraving in the chalk and dotted manner, after the eminent English painters of his time. He engraved the following from the Shakspeare Gallery, which are among his best works. He died in 1810.

A scene from the Tempest; *after Fuseli.* The Merry Wives of Windsor, two plates, one *after Smirke*, and the other *after Rev. W. Peters.* Scene from Measure for Measure; *after T. Kirk.* Scene from Much Ado about Nothing; *after W. Peters.* Midsummer Night's Dream; *after Fuseli.* Scene from the Merchant of Venice; *after Smirke.* Scene from As You Like It; *after W. Hamilton.* Scene from the Taming of the Shrew; *after F. Wheatley.* Another from the Introduction to the Play; *after Smirke.* Scene from Henry IV.; *after R. Westall.* Scene from Romeo and Juliet; *after Miller.* The Woodman; *after Gainsborough.* The Philosopher Square, discovered by Tom Jones, and the Companion; *after Downman.* The Sleeping Nymph; *after Opie.* Frances Isabella Ker Gordon; *after Sir J. Reynolds.* The Three Holy Children; *after W. Peters.* Bust of Clytie; *after J. B. Cipriarni.* Fair Emmeline, and a subject from the Vicar of Wakefield; *after Stothard.*

SIMON, Thomas, an eminent English engraver of medals and seals, who lived in the time of Charles I., Cromwell's protectorate, and Charles II., by all whom he was employed. He was also employed for some time in the service of Christina, Queen of Sweden. His great Seal of the Commonwealth is mentioned as an exquisite specimen of the art. He died soon after the Revolution. He had a brother named Abraham Simon, who was a medalist, and assisted him in his works. Abraham was also a celebrated modeler in wax.

SIMONE, Maestro, an old Italian painter, of the time of Giotto, about whose history there is much discrepancy. He is variously called *Maestro Simone*, *Simone da Bologna*, and *Simone da Crocifissi*, and is said by some to have been a disciple of Filippo Tesauro; by others of Giotto. Lanzi, after stating that Giotto was invited to Naples in 1325 by Robert King of Naples, to decorate the church of S. Chiara, with subjects from the New Testament, and the mysteries of the Apocalypse, says, "Giotto selected for his assistant in these labors, a Maestro Simone, who, in consequence of his enjoying the esteem of that master, acquired a great name at Naples. Some consider him a native of Cremona, others a Neapolitan, which seems nearer the truth. His style partakes both of Tesauro and Giotto, whence some consider him a disciple of the first, others of the second master; and he may probably have received instructions from both. However that may be, on the departure of Giotto, he was employed on many works which King Robert and the Queen Sancia were prosecuting in various churches, particularly in S. Lorenzo. He there painted that monarch in the act of being crowned by Bishop Lodovico, his brother, to whom, upon his death and subsequent canonization, a chapel was dedicated in the episcopal church; Simone was commissioned to decorate it, but death prevented his accomplishing it." Dominici extols a picture by him of a Deposition from the Cross, painted for the great altar of the Incoronata, and thinks it will bear comparison with the works of Giotto. In other respects he confesses that his conception and invention were not equally good, the airs of his heads less graceful, and less suavity in the tone of his coloring.

SIMONE, Francesco di, was the son and scholar of the preceding, of whom there are notices from 1340 to 1360. He executed some works in the church of S. Chiara, all of which have been effaced, together with those of Giotto, except a Madonna, in chiaro-scuro, which is highly extolled by Dominici.

SIMONELLI, Giuseppe, a Neapolitan painter, born about 1649, and died in 1713. According to Dominici, he was originally a servant of Luca Giordano, but showing a talent for painting, his master instructed him in the art. He became an accurate copyist of his works, and an excellent imitator of his coloring. When he attempted original works, he was generally deficient in design, though the author above cited highly extols his picture of S. Niccolo di Tolentino, "which approaches the best and most correct manner of Giordano both in design and handling."

SIMONET, Jean Baptiste, a French engraver, born at Paris in 1742, and died there in 1810. It is not mentioned with whom he studied, but he engraved a considerable number of plates after the works of Greuze, Moreau, Baudoin, Aubry, and other artists of his country. His plates are executed in a neat and pleasing style.

SIMONETTI, Domenico, a painter of the Roman school, born at Ancona, where he flourished in the latter part of the 18th century. Lanzi says he was a reputable artist, and executed many works for the churches of his native city, and particularly distinguished himself in the church of the Suffragio. He decorated the gallery of the Marchesi Trionfi, and was much employed by individuals. He is also called *Magatta*, for what reason is not stated, for his real name was *Simonetti.*

SIMONI. See Simonini.

SIMONINI, Francesco, an eminent battle painter, born at Parma in 1689. According to Lanzi and others, he studied with Ilario Spolverini, and painted battles, skirmishes of cavalry, attacks of banditti, &c., in the style of his master. His pictures are designed and executed with great fire and spirit. He chiefly resided at Venice, where he painted in the Sala Capello, a series of battles and warlike achievements, which are highly commended and greatly admired. There are many of his works in the collections at Venice, which Lanzi says abound with figures, and are ornamented with fine architecture. There are also some of his works at Rovigo. Orlandi says he studied with Francesco Monti, called delle Battaglie, and was educated at Florence, upon the model of Borgognone. Lanzi says he was living in 1753; others that he died at Venice about 1760. His name is sometimes written *Simoni.*

SIMONNEAU, Charles, an eminent French engraver, born at Orleans in 1639; died at Paris in 1728. He learned design from Noel Coypel; and studied engraving under Guillaume Chateau. His first plates were executed entirely with the graver, in a style resembling that of Poilly; but he afterwards introduced the point, particularly in the demi-tints and distances, reserving the burin for the more prominent and vigorous parts. Chosen a member of the Royal Academy, he presented, as the reception piece, the portrait of Jules Hardouin Mansard; and was afterwards appointed engraver to the King, with a pension. He engraved numerous historical subjects, portraits, and vignettes, in a neat, agreeable, and spirited style. Among them are the following:

PORTRAITS.

Henrietta Maria, consort of Charles I. Charlotte Elizabeth, Duchess Dowager of Orleans; *after Rigaud.* Charles Francis de Brienne, Bishop of Constance; *after Dumée.* Julius Hardouin Mansard, Architect to the King; *after de Troy.* George Villiers, Duke of Buckingham.

SUBJECTS AFTER VARIOUS MASTERS.

The Holy Family, with St. Elisabeth and St. John; *after Raffaelle.* The Virgin and infant Jesus, with St. John; *do.* The Adoration of the Shepherds; *after Ann. Caracci.* Christ and the Woman of Samaria; *do.* Hagar and Ishmael; *after Andrea Sacchi.* The Virgin and infant Christ, with Angels; *after Frà Bartolomeo.* The Stoning of Stephen; *after Caracci.* Christ with Martha and Mary; *after Domenichino.* Christ's Entry into Jerusalem; *after C. le Brun.* Christ bearing his Cross; *do.* The Nativity; *after Noel Coypel.* Christ among the Doctors; *after Ant. Coypel.* The Triumph of Galatea; *do.* Venus curing the Wound of Æneas; *after C. de la Fosse.* The Journey of Mary of Medicis to Pont-de-Cé; *after Rubens;* for the Luxembourg Gallery. The Conquest of Franche-Comté; *after le Brun.* This is esteemed his best print.

SIMONNEAU, Louis, a distinguished French engraver, the younger brother of the preceding, was born at Orleans, according to Zani, in 1660, and died in 1727. His style seems to have been formed in imitation of the Audrans. He nearly attained the excellence of his brother; his drawing is correct, particularly in the extremities, and by combining the point with the graver, he gave a pleasing variety to his plates. He was chosen a member of the Royal Academy. The following are among his principal plates:

PORTRAITS.

Giacinto Serroni, Archbishop of Albi. Anthony Arnauld, famous Theologian; *after Ph. de Champagne.* Anthony le Maitre, Advocate in Parliament; *do.* Martin de Charmois, Counsellor of State; *after Seb. Bourdon.*

SUBJECTS AFTER VARIOUS MASTERS.

Susanna and the Elders; *after Ant. Coypel.* Lot and his Daughters; *do.* Christ with Martha and Mary; *do.* Christ bearing his Cross; *after Ant. Dieu.* The Elevation of the Cross; *do.* The Crucifixion; *do.* The Assumption of the Virgin; after the ceiling by *le Brun* in the chapel of St. Sulpice. Four plates of the Four Times of the Day; *do.* The Four Seasons, in fonr plates; *do.* The ceiling of the Pavilion of Aurora, in the garden de Sceaux; in four plates; *do.*

SIMONNEAU, Philippe, was the son of Charles S. He studied design and engraving under his father, and executed several plates, but subsequently relinquished the art, either from the lack of application or ability. Three prints of moderate merit are mentioned by him, which are:

Two friezes, on one sheet, representing the Rape of the Sabines, and the Peace between the Romans and the Sabines; after the pictures by *Giulio Romano* in the Orleans collection. The three Goddesses preparing for the Judgment of Paris; after the picture by *Pierino del Vaga* in the same collection. Venus and Adonis; *after Albano.*

SIMPSON, William, an indifferent English engraver, who flourished about 1635. He was chiefly employed by the booksellers, and among other things, engraved the plates for *Quarles' Emblems.*

SIMPSON, Joseph, the elder, an English engraver of little note, who flourished, according to Lord Orford, about 1710. His chief employment was to engrave coats of arms and other embellishments.

SIMPSON, Joseph, the younger, was the son of the preceeding. He died young in 1736. He engraved a plate of a Holy Family, with St. John, St. Sebastian, and several angels, *after Filippo Lauri*, dated 1728.

SIMPSON, William, a Scotch painter, born at Dundee in 1800; studied in the Academy at Edinburgh. About 1829, he commenced painting portraits, and was so successful that in three or four years he was enabled to visit Italy. On his return in 1838, he exhibited in the Royal Academy at London, "A Camaldolese monk showing the Relics of his convent," which was engraved by the Art Union; also "Cimabue and Giotto," which was purchased by Sir Robert Peel for one hundred and fifty guineas. From this time till 1844, he exhibited a number of works, of which his "Columbus asking charity for himself and Child" is esteemed the best. Few of the rest possess merit. Had he devoted himself to portrait painting, he would have attained considerable eminence. This artist died in 1847.

SINGHER, John, a painter born at Hesse Cassel about 1510. He settled at Antwerp, where he painted landscapes with figures, in a free, bold style, with considerable reputation. He was elected a member of the Academy there in 1543. He was much employed in making designs for the manufacture of tapestry. He died in 1558.

SINGLETON, Henry, an English designer and painter, born at London in 1766. He first studied with his uncle, a miniature painter. He afterwards became a student of the Royal Academy, and gained the gold medal in 1788, for the best historical painting; the subject was taken from Dryden's Ode on Alexander's Feast. Among his most esteemed works are Christ entering Jerusalem; Christ healing the Blind; Coriolanus and his Mother; and Hannibal swearing eternal enmity to the Romans; all which were engraved in mezzotinto. His paintings of the Storming of Seringapatam, the death of Tippoo Saib, and the Surrender of Tippoo's sons as hostages, were engraved by Schiavonetti and Cardon, and were very popular. He painted many poetical and fancy subjects, and made many designs to embellish the various publications of the day. His conceptions are commonplace, his style mannered, and his execution exceedingly rapid. "Propose a subject to Singleton," said West, "and it will be on canvass in five or six hours." Stanley says there is an extensive series of small paintings by him of scenes from Shakspeare's Plays, which, if they were engraved, would enhance his reputation. He died in 1839.

SINJEUR, Govert, a Dutch painter who resided at Rotterdam, and is said to have been a successful imitator of the style of Philip Wouwerman. No particulars are recorded of him.

SINTZENICH, Heinrich, an eminent German engraver, born at Manheim in 1752. After learning the elements of the art in his native city, he was sent to England at the expense of the Elector, to complete his studies under Bartolozzi, with whom he continued four years. On his return to his native city, he was appointed engraver to the court, and executed many works in the chalk and dotted manner, and in mezzotinto. Among these are the portraits of several noble and distinguished personages of his country; also subjects after Frà Bartolomeo, A. Caracci, P. Veronese, Domenichino, Carlo Dolci, Solimena, Rubens, le Brun, and other eminent painters of later times. He acquired a high reputation, and was elected a member of the academies of Munich and Berlin. Nagler gives a descriptive catalogue of fifty-four of his principal works. He died at Munich in 1812.

SIRANI, Giovanni Andrea, a painter born at Bologna in 1610. According to Crespi, Oretti, and others, he was one of the favorite disciples of Guido Reni, and one of the most successful emulators of his style. Lanzi says, "another good copyist and master of Guido's style appeared in Gio. Andrea Sirani. On his master's death, he completed the great picture of St. Bruno, left unfinished at the Certosini, with several others throughout the city in the same state. Whether owing to Guido's retouches, or his want of freedom, Sirani's earliest works bear much resemblance to that master's second manner, more particularly in his Crucifixion, in the church of S. Marino, which seems like a repetition of Guido's St. Lorenzo in S. Lucina, or that in the Modenese Gallery. In process of time, Sirani is supposed to have aimed at the stronger style of Guido in his early career; he conducted in such a taste his pictures of the Supper of the Pharisee, at the Certosa; the Nuptials of the Virgin, in S. Giorgio at Bologna; and the Twelve Crucifixions, in the Cathedral of Piacenza, an extremely beautiful picture, ascribed by some to Elizabeth Sirani, his daughter and pupil." Lanzi means that Sirani, in these last works, followed the style of Guido founded on that of Michael Angelo da Caravaggio. (See Guido.) At Rome is a very beautiful picture of the Last Supper by him, alone sufficient to establish his reputation as a great master. He usually painted in a large size, and in a grand style, like his master. There are a number of spirited etchings marked G. A. S. and I. A. S. heretofore attributed to him, but Bartsch considers only two genuine—Apollo and Marsyas, signed *Sirani fecit*, and the Death of Lucretia. He died in 1670.

SIRANI, Elizabetta. This extraordinary lady was the daughter of the preceding, born at Bologna in 1638. She was instructed in the art by her father, and showed such talent, and made such rapid progress, that she was accounted a prodigy at fifteen years of age. She attached herself to an imitation of the best style of Guido, which unites great relief with the most captivating amenity. It is almost incredible that in a short life of not more than twenty-six or twenty-seven years, she could have executed the long list of works enumerated by Malvasia, copied from a register kept by herself, amounting to upwards of one hundred and fifty pictures and portraits; and our astonishment is increased when we are told that many of them are pictures and altar-pieces of large size, and finished with a care that excludes all appearance of negligence or haste. Her first public work appears to have been painted in 1655, when she was seventeen years of age. Her compositions are elegant and tasteful, her design correct and firm, and there is a freshness and suavity in her coloring, especially in her demi-tints, that strongly resembles the best works of Guido. The airs of her heads are noble, beautiful, and graceful. She was particularly successful in the expressive character which she gave to her Madonnas and Magdalens, which were her favorite subjects. Her penciling was more delicate, but less free and spirited than that of her father. Her most admired works in the churches at Bologna, are the Baptism of Christ at the Certosa; St. Antonio of Padua kneeling before the infant Christ, in S. Leonardo; the Virgin with St. Anne, contemplating the infant Christ sleeping, in S. Maria di Galiera. Lanzi says that in her smaller works, painted by commissions, she still improved herself, as may be seen by the numerous pictures of Madonnas, Magdalens, Saints, and the infant Christ, found in the Zampieri, Zambeccari, and Caprara palaces, at Bologna, and in the Corsini and Bolognetti collections at Rome. She also painted some small histories on copper, exquisitely finished and extremely valuable, which are to be found in the palaces at Bologna and Rome. She received many commissions from several of the sovereigns and most distinguished personages of Europe. Lanzi mentions an exquisite specimen of her art which he saw, in the possession of Counsellor Pagave at Milan—a portrait of herself, in the act of being crowned by a cherub. She died by poison, August 29th, 1665, administered by one of her own maids, instigated, as is supposed, by some jealous young artist. Her melancholy death was bewailed with demonstrations of public sorrow. Her remains were interred in the same vault in the church of S. Domenico where reposed the ashes of Guido. She executed some spirited etchings, mostly from her own designs, which she usually signed with her name, but sometimes marked with her initials, E. S. F. Bartsch describes only ten prints by her; some are signed and others are not, but none have E. S. F. Some of them are dated as early as 1655, when she was only seventeen years of age. Lanzi says she instructed, besides her two sisters, many other ladies, the most talented of whom were Veronica Franchi, Vincenzia Fabri, Lucrezia Scarfaglia, and Ginevra Cantofoli.

SIRANI, Anna and Barbara, were the younger sisters of the preceding. They were doubtless instructed both by their father and sister, though Crespi and Lanzi say they were instructed in the art by Elizabeth, whose fame was so great, according to Lanzi, that "she is nearly the sole individual of the family whose name occurs in collections out of Bologna"; by which he doubtless means that the works of her father and her sister are generally attributed to her. This would account for the extraordinary number of works attributed to her throughout Italy, but more especially at Bologna, Rome, and Milan. Lanzi says they imitated the style of Elizabeth, and that there are some pictures by Barbara in the churches and collections of Bologna.

SIRCEUS, Philip, an artist mentioned by Florent le Comte and others, as the engraver of some prints after Michael Angelo. He is the same as Serriccus or Soye, which see.

SIRIES, Violante Beatrice. This ingenious lady was born at Florence in 1710. She was first instructed in crayon painting and in water-colors by the celebrated paintress Giovanna Fratellini. At the age of sixteen, she accompanied her father to Paris, who was an eminent goldsmith, and had been invited to that court and appointed goldsmith to the King. In that city she learned from a Flemish artist, the practice of oil painting, in which she made rapid progress, and during her residence of five years there, she painted the portraits of several persons of rank. These performances were so much admired, that flattering offers were made to induce her to remain at Paris, under the royal patronage. She, however, preferred to return with her father, who was recalled by the Grand Duke to Florence, where she acquired a high reputation, and was much patronized by the court and the nobility. Though she chiefly confined herself to portraits, she occasionally painted history, and fruit and flower-pieces. Her works are correctly designed, her pencil light, delicate, and free, her carnations warm and life-like, her draperies well chosen, varied, and remarkable for noble simplicity, her perspective excellent, and she enriched her pictures with magnificent architecture. One of her most capital performances is a picture of the Imperial family, consisting of fourteen portraits. The Grand Duke ordered her portrait to be placed in the Florentine Gallery, among those of illustrious artists, on which occasion she took the opportunity of introducing the likeness of her father into the picture, a proof of her filial piety and distinguished merit. Most of her works are in oil. She died in 1770.

SIRLET, Flavius, an eminent gem engraver, who died at Rome in 1737. Some of his works are accounted little inferior to the finest specimens of antiquity. One of his best performances is the famous group of Laocoon and his children, cut upon an amethyst.

SISTO, F. See Ristoro.

SIXDENIERS, M., a distinguished French line engraver, born at Paris in 1795; died in 1846. He studied under Villerey, and soon acquired distinction. In 1816 he gained the second prize for line engraving; in 1824, a gold medal at the Salon. Besides many line engravings, he also executed, in concert with Maile and Reynolds, many of the best mezzotints of the time. He was much patronized, and gained great reputation. Among his line engravings the following are most worthy of note:

Honors rendered to Raffaelle after his death; *after Bergeret.* 1822. Properzia di Rossi; *after Ducis.* 1824. Vignettes for various works; 1827. Endymion; *after Girodet.* Sleep; *after Mlle. Pagés.* The Bath, and the Surprise; *after Rioult.* 1831. Pacha de Janina, Don Juan, the Visit, the Invasion. 1833. Edward in Scotland; *after Delaroche.* Combat de Navarino; *after Langlois.* 1834. The Departure, and the Return; *after Mlle. Pagés.* Young Girls and Faune; *after Rioult.* Group of Louis XVI.; *after Bosio.* 1835. Charles I. and his Children; *after Colin.* 1836. The Broken Contract; *after Destouches.* 1837. Portrait of Arago. 1839. The Rural Virtuoso; *after Bouterwek.* Boatmen attacked by Bears; *after Biard.* 1840. Charlotte Corday; *after Scheffer.* Hospitality; *after Latit.* Mlle. Rachael; *after Charpentier.* 1841. Napoleon and the King of Rome; *after Steuben.* 1842. Funeral of Gen. Marceau; *after Bouchot.* 1843. Arab in Prayer and Posting in the Desert; *after Horace Vernet.* 1844. Head of Christ; *after Colin.* 1845. The Village Bride; *after Greuze.* Portrait of Brother Philip; *after H. Vernet.* 1846.

SKELTON, William, an English engraver, born at London in 1763. He studied with James Basire, and afterwards with William Sharp. He acquired considerable reputation as a line engraver, and was much employed by Boydell, Macklin, and others. He executed several plates for the Dilettanti Society, and some of his best engravings are from the antiques published in their valuable works. Towards the close of his professional labors, he engraved and published his series of Royal Portraits, embracing every member of the Royal family, from the time of George III. to the accession of Queen Victoria. He was a most worthy and exemplary man, and by his professional skill and industry, acquired a moderate independence, which he expended in deeds of charity. For nearly sixty years he was a guardian of the Asylum of Female Orphans, and such was his devotion to the interests of the institution, that he was called the father of that noble charity. He died in 1848, in the 86th year of his age.

SKILLMAN, William, an English engraver, who flourished about 1655. Among other plates, he engraved the façade of Albemarle House, and a view of the Banqueting House.

SKIPPE, John, a modern English artist, of whose history, singularly enough, little is known. There are about thirty wooden cuts by him, printed in chiaro-scuro, with three and four blocks, after Raffaelle, Corregio, Parmiggiano, Giorgione, Titian, Tintoretto, Pierino del Vaga, Salvator Rosa, Andrea del Sarto, Baccio Bandinelli, and Rubens. His prints are dated from about 1771 to 1809. Jackson, in his "Treatise on Wood Engraving," says, "from the year 1754, the date of John Baptist Jackson's tract '*On the Invention of Engraving and Printing in Chiaro-Scuro*,' to 1819, when the first part of Mr. Savage's *Hints on Decorative Painting* was published, the only chiaro-scuro wood engravings which appear to have been published in England, were executed by an amateur of the name of John Skippe."

SLABBAERT, or SLABBARD, Karl, a Dutch painter, of whom little is known, except by a few pictures which are elaborately finished and well colored, though labored and incorrectly drawn. He painted interiors and familiar subjects. With respect to the time of his birth and death, the Dutch writers are silent. Zani mentions him or another artist of the same name, as a designer and engraver who *operated* in 1645.

SLATER, T., an obscure English engraver, who flourished about 1630. He engraved some portraits for the booksellers.

SLINGELANDT, Peter van, a Dutch painter, born at Leyden in 1640. He studied under Gerard Douw, whose manner he imitated, and in the opinion of some judges, he surpassed that master in the delicate and labored polish which he gave to his pictures, though they are deficient in the characteristic expression, the magical effects of the chiaro-scuro, and the correctness of design, which distinguish the works of Douw. His chief merits seem to consist in Dutch patience and perseverance. Houbraken relates that he was occupied three years without intermission in painting a small picture of the portraits of the Meerman family; that he was employed a month in finishing the lace of a ruff; and that when he painted a dog, cat, or mouse, which he was fond of introducing into his pictures, he was not satisfied till he had represented each particular hair. Yet his stiff and tasteless compositions were much sought after, still command high prices, and are only to be found in the collections of the great. One of his works, now in the Louvre, was bought of a brewer for £480, and has been valued at 20,000f. Smith, in his Catalogue raisonné, vol. I. and Supplement, gives a descriptive account of 70 pictures by him. There are several of his works in the Royal galleries and the collections of the nobility in England. He died in 1691.

SLODTZ, Sebastian. This sculptor was born at Antwerp in 1655, and gained considerable distinction among the artists employed in embellishing the palace of Louis XIV. His productions are more distinguished for beauty of execution, than for elevation of design. Among the principal are the statue of St. Ambrose, and the group of St. Louis sending missionaries to the Indies, at the Invalides; and a marble statue of Hannibal measuring with a bushel the rings of the Roman knights slain in the battle of Cannæ. Slodtz died at Paris in 1736.

SLODTZ. There were several sons of the preceding artist, who gained in France considerable distinction in sculpture. Sebastian Slodtz, the eldest, practised the art with success, in concert with his younger brother Paul Ambrose, who was born in 1702, and died in 1758. Among the works executed by them were, the grand altar of the church of St. Bartholomew; the altar of the chapel of the Virgin, in S. Sulpice; also several decorations for the fêtes celebrated at Versailles in 1751, on occasion of the birth of the Duke de Bourgogne. Paul Ambrose was appointed professor of sculpture in the Academy, and designer to the King's Cabinet. His abilities, however, were surpassed by his younger brother René Michel, generally known among his cotemporaries as Michael Angelo Slodtz. He was born at Paris in 1705; at the age of twenty-one he gained a prize from the Academy of Sculpture, and visited Rome with the royal pension. He remained seventeen years in that city, and was commissioned to execute a statue of St. Bruno, for St. Peter's; the tomb of the Marchese Capponi, in S. Giovanni dei Fiorentini; and the mausoleum in the cathedral of Vienna in Dauphiny, in honor of M. de Montmorin, archbishop of that city. In 1747, Slodtz returned to Paris, where he soon gained reputation, and was commissioned to execute a number of works. Many of his productions evince the decadence of the arts under Louis XV., particularly his monument to Languet in S. Sulpice, which, though possessing little true merit, gained for Slodtz so great reputation, that King Frederic II. of Prussia commissioned him to execute two statues, and invited him to his court. In 1755, he received a pension from the King of France, and in 1758 succeeded his brother Paul Ambrose as designer to the King's Cabinet. He died in 1764.

SLUYS, Jacob vander, a Dutch painter, born at Leyden in 1660. He first studied with Ary de Voys, and afterwards with Peter van Slingelandt, whose polished style he imitated, though with less laborious finishing. He copied the works of Slingelandt, and painted conversations, domestic subjects, and modish assemblies, composed and treated in an agreeable style, though his drawing is incorrect. His works are principally confined to Leyden, where he constantly resided and died in 1736.

SLUYTER, P., a Dutch engraver, who flourished about 1700. He was principally employed in engraving frontispieces and other book plates, for the publications of Peter vander Aa.

SMEATON, John, an eminent English architect and engineer, born at Ansthrope, in Yorkshire, in 1724. His father, who was an attorney, gave him a classical education, intending him for his own profession, but young Smeaton having a passion for mechanics, he placed him with a mathematical instrument maker to learn that business. He afterwards studied architecture and engineering, acquired distinction, and was much employed by government in executing some difficult works, one of the most important of which was to rebuild the Eddystone light-house. He erected this famous edifice in a novel, and so substantial a manner, that it may justly be pronounced a work unparalleled in its kind; it has withstood the contest of the elements, contrary to predictions, ever since, and bids fair to continue a monument to his genius for ages to come. He published a curious account of this structure and its history in one vol. folio. In 1753, he was elected a fellow of the Royal Society, and in 1759 he obtained its gold medal for his valuable paper on "The Natural Powers of Wind and Water, to turn Mills and other Machines, depending on a Circular Motion." He constructed the improvements in Ramsgate harbor, of which he published an account. He died in 1792.

SMEES, John, a Dutch landscape painter and engraver, of whom little is known. He died about 1729. There are some spirited etchings by him, of landscapes, with figures and animals, enriched with edifices and ruins, in the manner of John Both. Bartsch describes five, signed *J. Smees, in. et fecit.*

SMIBERT, See Smybert.

SMILIS, the earliest sculptor of Egina, of whom we have any account. His works are distinguished for a gravity and severe grandeur, which marked the school of Egina. Pliny mentions a statue of Juno by him, considered the most ancient of that goddess.

SMIRKE, Robert, an eminent English historical painter, born at Wigton in 1752. It is not mentioned under whom he first studied, but it is said that he first painted coats of arms on coach panels. In 1771, at the age of 19, he became a student at the Royal Academy, but he did not exhibit there till many years after, in 1786, as he was extremely diffident, and a severe critic on his own performances. His merits, however, were soon acknowledged, and he was elected a member of that institution in 1792. His favorite subjects are from Scripture, English history and poets, Don Quixote, and the Arabian Nights. He was employed by Alderman Boydell to paint several pictures for the Shakspeare Gallery, of life size, which he treated in an admirable and very humorous manner. He was more successful in his cabinet pictures, which are numerous, than in those of a large size. His works are correctly designed, his figures arranged with judgment and skill, and he gave to his countenances an admirable and appropriate expression. He particularly excelled in the representation of comic subjects, in which he displayed a rich humor in his characters that never degenerates into buf foonery; he is always the gentleman when representing the ridiculous, the affected, or the grotesque. He makes the observer to think and smile, but never to laugh outright. It is said that he was in the habit of sketching every marked face he met with, which he transferred to his portfolio; thus he had an ample collection of *real heads*, from which he could select one appropriate to every character; hence the striking originality in all his works, in which the figures appear to be *real portraits*, though sometimes a little caricatured to fit the *dramatis personæ*. His coloring is pleasing, and his chiaro-scuro excellent. He made many designs for the various publications of the day, which abound with humor, pathos, and sentiment. Many of his works were engraved by eminent artists, and were very popular, not only in England, but on the Continent. He continued to practice his art till advanced in life. It is said that his last works were the designs for the admirable bas-reliefs which embellish the front of the Oxford and Cambridge Club House, in Pall-Mall, erected by Sir Robert Smirke, jr., the eminent architect. Though he was not fully appreciated till late in life, his works greatly increased in value, and are now held in high estimation. He died in 1845.

SMIT, Andrew, a Dutch marine painter, who flourished about 1650. There is a capital picture by him in the Berlin Gallery, resembling the manner of Backhuysen. It represents an approaching Storm; the sea is rising with a heavy swell, and several vessels are seen making preparations to encounter the tempest. Stanley says there are some of his works in England, but they are attributed to other artists.

SMIT, Arnold, a Dutch painter, who flourished about the middle of the 17th century. He painted landscapes and marines; the latter resemble the darkest manner of Backhuysen. There are pictures signed *A. Smit*, *And. Smit*, and *Arn. Smit*, and from the similarity of style, subjects, and the time they flourished, it may reasonably be conjectured that *Andrew* and *Arnold* are one and the same artist, especially as there are no authentic particulars recorded of either.

SMITH, Anker, an excellent English line engraver, was born in London in 1759. After receiving a good education, he was articled to an attorney. As he was an excellent penman, and had a taste for the fine arts, he amused his leisure hours in copying line engravings with his pen, which he did with such accuracy that on some of them being shown to James Heath, he mistook them for prints. This induced his friends to place him with an engraver named Taylor, who instructed him in the mechanical part of the art, and his natural talent soon enabled him to surpass his instructor. He afterwards became an assistant to Heath, in whose name he is said to have executed several works, among which the Apotheosis of Handel is named. Bell was then engaged in publishing an edition of the British Poets, and he employed Smith to engrave the illustrative plates; other publishers also employed him, and his name soon became familiar to the public. His plates are much esteemed for correctness of drawing and beauty of execution.

He executed many plates to embellish the various publications of the day, among which may be mentioned Smirke's Edition of Don Quixote, Wood's small edition of Shakspeare's Plays, Coombe's Ancient Marbles and Terracottas in the British Museum, &c. He was also much employed by Boydell; he engraved several of the plates for the smaller edition of the Shakspeare Gallery. His print of the Death of Wat Tyler, *after Northcote*, obtained for him the honor of being elected an associate of the Royal Academy. He engraved several fine plates after Leonardo da Vinci, Titian, and the Caracci. He died in 1819.

SMITH, Benjamin, an eminent English engraver in the chalk manner, born in London about 1750. He studied with Bartolozzi, whose style he followed. He engraved a considerable number of plates, chiefly after the eminent English painters of the day; most of them are of large size, beautifully executed, with the character and expression of his originals carefully preserved. He was employed by Boydell to engrave several of the plates for the Shakspeare Gallery, which are elaborately executed, and rank among his best works. He died in 1810. The following are among his principal works:

Christ healing the Sick; *after B. West*. St. Peter's first Sermon; *do.* An Allegory of Providence; *after J. F. Rigaud*. An Allegory of Innocence; *do.* Sigismunda; *after Hogarth*. Bacchus; *after Sir J. Reynolds*. Shakspeare nursed by Tragedy and Comedy, and the infant Shakspeare attended by Nature and the Passions; *after Romney*. An equestrian Portrait of George III.; *after Beechey*. The Portrait of Napoleon; *after Appiani*. William Hogarth and his Dog; *after Hogarth*. The Marquis Cornwallis; *after Copley*. The Annual Ceremony of administering the Oath of Allegiance to the Lord Mayor elect, &c. Scene from Richard II.; *after Matthew Brown*.

SMITH, Charles John, an English engraver, born at Chelsea in 1803. He was the son of an eminent surgeon, who placed him with Charles Pye to learn engraving. He became a skillful artist, and was much employed in engraving plates for the various expensive publications of the day, among which are Stothard's Sepulchral Effigies, Cartwright's Rape of Bramber, Murray's Illustrations of Johnson, Dibdin's English Tour, and other similar works, some of them for private circulation only. In 1828, he engraved and directed the publication of a volume in imperial quarto, comprising a series of fac simile autographs of royal, noble, and distinguished personages, from the reign of Richard II. to that of Charles II., to which biographical notices were furnished by John Gough Nichols, F. S. A. At the time of his death, he was engaged on the work entitled "Historical and Literary Curiosities," of which six numbers were published; the remaining two to complete the work were left unfinished. He was a member of the Society of Antiquaries. He died in 1839.

SMITH, Francis, an English landscape painter of little note, whose name occurs as an exhibitor at the Royal Academy, in the catalogues of that institution, from about 1770 to 1779, when he is supposed to have died.

SMITH, Gabriel, an English engraver, born in 1724, and died in 1783. After learning the rudiments of the art, he went to Paris, where he acquired the method of engraving in imitation of chalk drawings. On his return to London, he practised this method with considerable success. He was much employed by Boydell, for whom he executed his principal works.

SMITH, Jacob, an obscure English engraver, who flourished about 1730, and executed a few portraits, among which are those of Sir Isaac Newton and Sir Hans Sloane, on one plate. The engraving is executed in a singular manner, with one spiral line, begun in the centre, and continued to the border of the plate.

SMITH, John, an eminent English mezzotinto engraver, who died about 1720. Little is known of him except by his works. He is said to have first studied painting under an obscure artist, named Tillot or Tillet. As soon as he became his own master, he learned the art of engraving in mezzotinto of Isaac Becket and J. vander Vaart. He surpassed every engraver in his line who had preceded him, and was employed by Sir Godfrey Kneller to engrave many of his portraits. His works are very numerous; Nagler gives a catalogue of five hundred prints by him. The following are his most esteemed works:

PORTRAITS AFTER KNELLER.

Charles II. with a Star. James, Duke of York, leaning on an Anchor. The Duke of Schomberg on Horseback. Meinhard, his Son, when Duke of Leinster. William III. Mary, his Queen. George, Prince of Denmark; an oval. Queen Anne, when Princess of Denmark. John Churchill, Duke of Marlborough. John, Duke of Buckingham. Charles Sackville, Earl of Dorset. Charles, Earl of Halifax. Arnold, Earl of Albemarle. William, Earl of Jersey. Catherine, Duchess of Rutland. Frances Bennet, Countess of Salisbury. Mary Somerset, Duchess of Ormond, with a black Boy. Henrietta, Duchess of Bolton. Sir Richard Steele. Joseph Addison. Alexander Pope. William Congreve; very fine. 1710. Johu Locke. Sir Godfrey Kneller. John Smith, holding a Portrait of Kneller; the engraver's own Portrait, painted by Kneller in 1696, engraved in 1716. Sir Christopher Wren. 1713. Lord Euston, whole length. 1689.

PORTRAITS AFTER VARIOUS MASTERS.

Queen Mary II. with a high head-dress; *after vander Vaart.* James Fitzroy, Duke of Monmouth; *after Wissing.* Thomas Herbert, Earl of Pembroke; *do.* Patrick Crawford, Viscount Garnock; *after Medina.* William Anstruther; *do.* Sir Henry Goodricke; *after J. Hill.* Mr. Sansom; *after Closterman.* Mrs. Cross, Actress; *after J. Hill.* Arcangelo Corelli, Musician; *after Howard.* William Penkethman, Comedian; *after Schutz.* Godfrey Schalcken; *after a picture by himself.* Charles XII.; *after D. Craft.* 1701-2. William, Duke of Gloucester, and Benj. Bathurst; *after T. Murray.* Anthony Leigh, in the character of the Spanish Friar. A beautiful print in folio. Isaac Becket; *J. Smith, fec.* Thomas Murray, Pictor, an oval. W. Wycherley; *after Sir Peter Lely;* remarkably fine. Gulielmus Cowper, Chyrurgus; *after J. Closterman;* excellent.

SUBJECTS AFTER VARIOUS MASTERS.

Ten Plates of the Loves of the Gods; *after Titian.* Venus standing in a Shell; *after Correggio.* Cupid and Psyche; *after A. Veronese.* Tarquin and Lucretia; *do.* Time conqnering Love; *after S. Vouet.* Venus and Adonis; *after N. Poussin.* The Virgin and infant Christ; *after F. Baroccio.* The Holy Family; *after C. Maratti.* A Woman asleep near a Light; *after G. Schalcken.* The Story of Acteon, small figures; *after P. Berchet.* M. Magdalene; *after G. Schalcken.* An admirable imitation of the manner of the original master. There are proofs of a second state, in which tears are introduced. The Angel and Tobit; *after Ælsheimer.*

SMITH, Nathaniel, an English sculptor, the friend and companion of Nollekens, flourished in the latter half of the last century. He entered the studio of Roubilliac in 1755, and in 1759 and 1760 gained several prizes from the Society of Arts. He afterwards wrought in the studio of Nollekens, and subsequently established himself as a printseller in St. Martin's Lane.

SMITH, John Thomas. This distinguished English artist, and writer on art, was the son of the preceding, born in 1766. The friendship existing between his father and Joseph Nollekens, occasioned young Smith to be frequently noticed by that sculptor, and at the age of thirteen he entered his studio. After remaining there three years, he entered the Royal Academy, and distinguished himself by several drawings in imitation of Ostade and Rembrandt. He afterwards studied engraving under Sherwin; and at the termination of his engagement with that artist, he was for several years employed as a drawing master. In 1791 he commenced his first work, the "Antiquities of London and its Environs," ninety-six plates, accompanied with brief descriptions. His next work relating to art was the "Antiquities of Westminster," representing the old Palace, St. Stephen's chapel, &c., containing engravings of two hundred and forty-six topographical objects, of which, at the time of its publication in 1807, only one hundred and twenty-four were remaining. This work also contains colored engravings of several curious old paintings discovered in 1800, on the wainscoting of the House of Commons, and soon after destroyed by the workmen in enlarging the building, but not before they had been copied by the prompt and energetic Smith. In 1809, he published a second volume of sixty-two additional plates. In 1815 he completed the publication of the "Ancient Topography of London," which is considered his best work, containing thirty-two plates, very boldly etched, in a style smewhat resembling that of Piranesi. In 1816, Smith received his appointment of Keeper of Prints in the British Museum, and discharged the duties of his office in an exemplary manner. His last literary production was "Nollekens and his Times," which appeared in 1828, and soon ran through three editions. The author was an executor of Nollekens, and was disappointed at not being a legatee; he therefore wrote under the influence of excited feelings, and appears to have made a discreditable use of the privileges of intimacy he so many years enjoyed in the home and studio of his old instructor. Although containing many details that should never have been made public, and characterized by a degree of high coloring that greatly impairs its credibility, it contains many curious anecdotes of artists and distinguished personages, with whom Smith had been more or less intimately connected in the course of his long and rather eventful life. He left in manuscript the materials for a history of his own life and times, which has never been published. He died in 1833. There is a portrait of Smith by Skelton, engraved after a drawing by Jackson.

SMITH, Samuel, a very talented landscape engraver, little known in the annals of art, as he wrought principally for other artists. The date of his birth or death is unknown; and nothing of his history has been ascertained, except that he never married. He executed the landscape in Sharpe's Holy Family, *after Reynolds*, and several engravings after Loutherbourg. Among his other works is a beautiful plate of Wilson's Niobe, in the National Gallery, of which the figures were inserted by Sharpe.

SMITH, Thomas, an eminent English landscape painter, who resided chiefly at Derby, and was usually styled Smith of Derby, to distinguish him from the Smiths of Chichester. He is said to have reached a distinguished rank in his profession, without any other instructor than nature and his own genius, and to have been the first English artist who explored and depicted the charming scenery of the country. He painted almost all the picturesque views of the Peak of Derbyshire; forty of these were engraved by Vivares, and published collectively by Boydell, in 1760; others were engraved by Mason and Elliot. He also painted sporting pieces. He died at the Hot Wells, Bristol, in 1769.

SMITH, John Raphael. This eminent artist was the son of the preceding, born about 1750. He was instructed by his father in painting, but he afterwards adopted engraving, in which he distinguished himself, particularly in mezzotinto. He executed about one hundred and fifty plates from his own designs, and after other masters. His portraits are the best, and are much admired. He also practised drawing in crayons. He died in 1812. The following are among his most esteemed prints:

PORTRAITS AFTER SIR JOSHUA REYNOLDS.

The Duke of Devonshire. William Markham, Archbishop of York. Richard Robinson, Archbishop of Armagh. Joseph Dean Bourke, Archbishop of Tuam. Lady Beaumont. Lady Caroline Montague, daughter of the Duke of Buccleugh. Mrs. Montague. The Marchioness of Thomond, when Miss Palmer. Lady Gertrude Fitzpatrick, daughter of the Earl of Ossory. Lady Catherine Pelham Clinton. Master Crewe, as Henry VIII. Master Herbert as young Bacchus. Lieut. Colonel Tarleton. Mrs. Musters. Lieut. General Sir William Boothby. The Duke of Orleans, called *Egalité*, father of Louis Philippe.

PORTRAITS AFTER VARIOUS MASTERS.

Hyde Parker, Vice-Admiral of the Blue; *after Northcote.* Miss Coghlan; *after Gainsborough.* Mrs. Siddons as the Grecian Daughter; *after Lawrence.* Edward Wortley Montagu, in an Oriental dress; *after Peters.*

SMITH, William, George, and John, three English painters, born at Chichester, where they resided, and hence called the Smiths of Chichester. William was born in 1707; George, in 1714; and John in 1717. William and John died in 1764, and George in 1766. It is not known that they had the advantage of any instructor in art, but they established a kind of domestic academy, and, by a diligent study of nature, acquired a high reputation in the age in which they lived. William devoted his attention chiefly to portraits, though he occasionally painted landscapes, flowers, and fruit. George excelled in landscape painting, and reached an eminent rank in that department; John also painted landscapes with nearly equal success. Their fame was widely spread by the admirable engravings by Woollett, Elliot, Peake, and others. John and George etched and finished with the graver fifty-three prints of landscapes painted by themselves, and of subjects from Rembrandt. There is also a collection of "Select Views in England and Wales," after their designs, by Vivares, and others.

SMITHSON, John, an English architect, who died in 1648. Little is known of him. He was early taken into the service of the Earl of Newcastle. He built part of Welbeck in 1604, the riding house there in 1623, and the stables in 1625. He made great additions to Bolsover Castle for William Cavendish, Earl and afterwards Duke of Newcastle, who, it is said, sent him to Italy to collect designs. He left a great many drawings and designs, some of which were purchased by Lord Byron from his descendant who lived at Bolsover.

SMITS, Ludolf, or Ludewyk, called Hartcamp, a Dutch painter, born at Dort in 1635, and died there in 1675. He acquired considerable reputation for his fruit and flower pieces, but his works, from his bad system of coloring, have mostly perished.

SMITS, Nicholas, a Dutch painter, born at Breda about 1672, and died there in 1731. Little is known of him. There are a few of his pictures at Breda, which are said to evince considerable talent.

SMITZ, Gaspar, called by the English *Magdalen Smith*, a Dutch or Flemish painter, who we t to London soon after the Restoration, where he acquired considerable reputation and employment. He painted several portraits in oil, and fruit and flower-pieces, which were admired. He also painted some beautiful pictures of Magdalens, and for these penitents his model was a beautiful English woman, whom he called his wife. He also taught drawing and painting. An Irish lady of rank, whom he had instructed, persuaded him to go to Dublin, where, at her recommendation, he found abundant employment at high prices. He received £40 for a picture of a single bunch of grapes. In his Magdalens, he always introduced a thistle in the foreground. Pilkington says that, though his reputation as an excellent painter was fully established, and he had as many commissions as he could possibly execute at high prices, yet his extravagance kept him always necessitous, and he died at Dublin in miserable circumstances in 1707. Graham, in his Lives of the Painters, says he died in 1689. He engraved a few plates in mezzotinto, from his own designs, among which are a Portrait, a Magdalen in a Grotto, and Hagar in the Wilderness.

SMYBERT, John, a Scotch painter, born at Edinburgh about 1680. He served his apprenticeship to a common house painter; but aspiring to higher things, he went to London, where he studied diligently, and contrived to support himself by copying for the dealers, and ornamenting coaches. His enthusiasm carried him to Italy, where he spent three years in copying the works of Titian, Vandyck, and Rubens. He then returned to London, and commenced portrait painting. When his industry and ability had surmounted many difficulties, he was induced to engage in Bishop Berkeley's famous scheme of founding a universal college in Bermuda for the instruction of the heathen. He accompanied the Bishop to America; but the scheme failing, he settled in Boston about 1725, where he married, and continued to practise portrait painting till his death in 1751. There is a large picture by him of Bishop Berkeley's family at Yale College. Dunlap says he painted the portraits of the most eminent magistrates of New England and New York, who lived from 1725 to 1751. He is said to have lived on terms of friendship with Allan Ramsay, the author of the "Gentle Shepherd," with whom he corresponded after his settlement in America. His name is written *Simbert*, *Smibert*, and *Smybert;* the last was the way he wrote it.

SNAYERS, Peter, an eminent Flemish painter, born at Antwerp in 1593. He studied under Henry van Balen, and distinguished himself by many excellent works in history and portraits, battles, huntings, and landscapes. His pictures are well designed, his composition ingenious, his pencil free and delicate, and his coloring rich and harmonious, approaching that of Rubens. He particularly excelled in battles and huntings, in which his figures and horses are designed and painted with great spirit and animation. He was much patronized by the Archduke Albert, who appointed him his principal painter, with a large pension, and for whom he executed many of his choicest works. The Archduke sent some of them to the King of Spain, and Snayers afterwards received many commissions from that court. His works are found in the choicest collections of the Netherlands, and some in those of foreign countries, where they are highly esteemed. There are some of his pictures in the churches and public edifices of Antwerp and Brussels. He was esteemed by Rubens, and Vandyck painted his portrait among the eminent artists of his country. He died in 1670, though some say in 1662.

SNAYERS, Henry. See Snyers.

SNELLINCKS, John, a Flemish painter, born at Mechlin in 1544. It is not known under whom he studied. He painted history, but he chiefly excelled in depicting battles and skirmishes of cavalry, which are ranked among the ablest productions of his time. His compositions are judiciously grouped, his figures and horses correctly designed, his attitudes spirited and graceful, and his aerial perspective and chiaro-scuro excellent. His pictures are full of fire and energy, and produce a surprising effect; he expressed the hurry and confusion of an engagement with singular judgment and skill. He contrived to relieve and animate his figures in an artful manner, by contrasting them with the dark masses of clouds of smoke. According to van Mander, several princes and persons of the highest rank employed him incessantly; Vandyck esteemed him one of the ablest artists of the Low Countries, and painted his portrait, which was afterwards placed over his tomb in the church of St. James at Antwerp. He resided chiefly at Antwerp, and was appointed battle painter to the Archduke Albert and the Archduchess Isabella, governors of the Netherlands. He died in 1638, at the great age of ninety-four years. His name is variously written, *Snellincks*, *Snellinks*, *Snellinck*, and *Snellinx*. There is a single etching by this artist of his own portrait, *after Vandyck*.

SNYDERS, Francis, a very eminent Flemish painter, born at Antwerp in 1579. He studied under Henry van Balen, and confined himself for some time to painting subjects of fruit, flowers, and still life, in which he excelled, but his genius led him to paint animals and huntings, which he designed in a grand style, with surprising fire and spirit. It has been asserted by D'Argenville and others that he went to Italy, and improved himself by studying a long time with Benedetto Castiglione; a palpable error, for Snyders was an old man when that artist began to distinguish himself, who was born in 1616. It is very probable that he never left Flanders, and it is certain that he frequented the studio of Rubens, who was a great admirer of his talents, and often employed him to paint the animals, fruit, &c. in his pictures, though he himself represented those objects in so admirable a manner. The favorite subjects of Snyders were all kinds of animals, combats of wild beasts, and subjects of the chase, which he represented with wonderful truth and spirit. His pictures are designed in a grand style, his composition is rich, varied, and ingenious. He gave to every animal an expression adapted to its species and situation; nothing can be finer than his representations of the ferocious combats and attacks of wild beasts. His pencil is bold and free, peculiarly adapted to express the hairs, furs, and skins of the animals he introduced into his pictures; his coloring is clear, chaste, and vigorous; and his landscapes and accessories are designed and executed in fine taste. He also excelled in interiors of kitchens and larders, stored with all kinds of dead game, fish, fruit, vegetables, &c. When his designs required figures of a larger size than he was accustomed to paint, they were frequently inserted by Jordaens, and sometimes by Rubens, which gave an additional value to his works. He resided most of his life at Antwerp, and it is not known that he ever left that city, except for a short time, when he went to Brussels at the invitation of the Archduke Albert, who appointed him his principal painter, and for whom he executed some of his finest works. The Archduke sent some of these to Philip III. of Spain, who commissioned Snyders to paint several large pictures of subjects from the chase, and combats of wild beasts, which are now in the old palace Buon Retiro. Snyders acquired an immense reputation, and found abundant employment from princes and persons of the highest distinction; his works are now only to be found in public galleries and the choicest collections. Vandyck painted his portrait, which was in the Orleans collection. There is a set of sixteen spirited and masterly etchings of various animals, marked *Liure d'Animaux Peint et Gravé par Senedre*, which have heretofore been attributed to him, but Bartsch (Peintre Graveur, tom. iv.) has shown that they were executed by John Fyt. The first impressions from the plates are signed *Johannes Fyt, pinxit et fecit*, or *Fyt, pinx. et fec.* They were published by Fyt in 1642, dedicated to the Marquis de Solerio, and are extremely rare. The plates afterwards passed into the hands of some person who erased the name of Fyt, and substituted that of Snyders. There are also variations of these prints; particularly some in which the lettering is written backwards, and the prints reversed, attributed by some to imitators; but these are what the trade call *transfers;* they are produced by laying sheets of paper on the fresh impressions, and subjecting them to pressure, by which means the prints are duplicated, but the transfers are in *reverse.* The author has several transfers in his possession, after Rubens and other masters. Snyders died at Antwerp in 1657. His name is often erroneously written *Sneyders*.

SNYERS, or SNAYERS, Henry, a Flemish engraver, born at Antwerp in 1612. It is not known with whom he studied, but he imitated the manner of Scheltius Bolswert with considerable success, and probably was the pupil of that master. His drawing is pretty correct, and his prints exhibit much of the character of their originals. He engraved some portraits and other subjects, after

Rubens, Vandyck, Jordaens, Titian, and other masters. He is generally called *Snayers*, but he signed his prints, *Heinrich* or *H. Snyers*.

SOANE, Sir John, a distinguished English architect, born at Reading in 1753. His family was of very obscure origin. At an early age, he was taken into the service of Dance, and afterwards studied under Holland. The first work which brought him into public notice was a design for a triumphal bridge, which drew the gold medal of the Royal Academy. At the recommendation of Sir W. Chambers, in 1777, Soane was sent to Italy, with a pension. An octavo volume of his architectural designs was published the year after his departure. During a three years' residence in Italy, he studied the remains of antiquity and the finest modern edifices with great assiduity, and made several original designs, among others, for a British Senate House and a Royal Palace. He also made the acquaintance of Mr. Thomas Pitt, afterwards Lord Camelford, who assisted him by his influence. On returning to England, he was commissioned to execute several country residences in Norfolk, Suffolk, and other counties, the plans and elevations of which he published in a folio volume in 1788. At the death of Sir Robert Taylor, in the same year, Soane was appointed to the lucrative office of architect of the Bank of England. Other advantageous appointments followed; that of Clerk of the Works of St. James' palace, 1791; Architect of the Woods and Forests, 1795; Professor of Architecture in the Royal Academy, in 1806; and Surveyor of Chelsea Hospital, 1807. In addition to his public employment, he received many commissions for private buildings, and was constantly occupied for many years. He was industrious and indefatigable in the practice of his profession. His works are eminently distinguished for convenient arrangement, and have many striking beauties, though frequently marred by defects. He had great ingenuity and a surprising faculty of contrivance, often producing many happy combinations, particularly in regard to skylights; and he is entitled to no small praise, if not for inventing a new order of architecture, yet for being the first to apply and naturalize in England the Tivoli Corinthian. In the Bank, he used it with great success, and the northwest corner of that magnificent edifice surpasses all his other works. In 1828, Soane published his folio volume of "Public and Private Buildings," containing designs of many edifices erected by him in the preceding years. He made liberal donations to aid the progress of art, such as £1000 to the fund for building the Duke of York's monument, and similar sums to the Royal British Institution. He died at the age of 84, in 1837.

SOBLEO. See Desubleo.

SODERINI, Mauro, a painter born at Florence about 1690. He studied with Gio. Giuseppe dal Sole, and was one of his ablest pupils. He executed some works for the churches at Florence, but wrought mostly for individuals. Lanzi says he enjoyed the reputation of an able designer, and that he aimed at beauty and effect. There is a fine picture by him in the church of S. Stefano, representing St. Zanobi restoring a dead Child to life; and another of the Death of St. Joseph, in the Cathedral, attributed to him by some, but by others to his fellow-pupil, Gio. Domenico Ferretti. The time of his death is not known. He was living in 1730.

SODOMA, Il. See Razzi.

SODOMA, Giomo or Girolamo del', a Sienese painter, of whom little is known with certainty. According to Vasari, he studied with Gio. Antonio Razzi, called Il Sodoma. He is confounded by Orlandi and Bottari with Jacopo Pacchiarotti, the rival of Razzi, which has led to some discrepancy. Lanzi says he was without doubt a pupil of Razzi, and he supposes he died young.

SOENS, John, a Dutch landscape painter, born at Bois-le-Duc in 1553. He first studied with James Boon, and next with Giles Moestaert. He made great progress, and was considered one of the most promising young artists of his time. He went early to Rome, where he greatly improved himself, and his works are much admired. He was employed by the Pope and several of the nobility in embellishing their palaces. From Rome he went to Parma, where he was taken into the service of the Duke, for whom he executed many works. His landscapes are designed in a grand style, and his manner was prompt and full of vigor; he had an excellent knowledge of perspective, and his distances recede with a pleasing degradation; his figures are correctly drawn and touched with great spirit. He died at Parma in 1611. Zani says he was born in 1547.

SOEST, or ZOEST, Gerard, a German painter, born at Westphalia in 1637. He learned the art in his own country, and went to England about 1656, where he painted portraits with reputation, and found abundant employment. Pilkington says he was one of the rivals of Sir Peter Lely. His heads are animated and full of truth, his coloring warm, and he gave his figures great relief. At first he finished his pictures very highly, and painted his draperies, particularly satins, in the manner of Terburg. He, however, enlarged his manner, by studying the works of Vandyck, and painted with a bolder and freer pencil. He succeeded best in his male portraits; his manners are said to have been too coarse and ungraceful to recommend him to the softer sex. He died at London in 1681.

SOEUR, Hubert le, a French sculptor, according to Walpole, was probably born about 1580. He visited Italy, and studied under Giovanni da Bologna. Very little is known of the circumstances of his life, except that he visited England in the first part of the 17th century, and was employed in 1633 by the family of Howard Arundel, to execute the bronze equestrian statue of Charles I. at Charing Cross. At the commencement of the civil war it had not been erected, but was sold to a brazier named John Rivet, with orders to break it in pieces. The latter buried it in the earth, and kept it concealed until the Restoration. About 1678 it was placed in its present situation. The figure of the horse is heavy, and generally faulty in the model; but the statue of the monarch is exceedingly dignified and expressive, and reflects great credit upon the artist. Soeur executed many other works in brass and bronze in various places in England, most of which have been destroyed. Walpole mentions a bronze bust at Stourhead, representing Charles I., with a helmet and dragon.

SOGGI, Niccolo, a painter, born at Florence in 1474. He was a scholar of Pietro Perugino, whose manner he imitated, though his works are designed and executed in a more dry and labored style. He resided chiefly at Arezzo, where there are some of his pictures in the churches, and where he died in 1554.

SOGLIANI, Giovanni Antonio, a painter born at Florence in 1481, and died in 1533. He studied with Lorenzo di Credi for several years; but he afterwards imitated the manner of Bartolomeo di S. Marco, called della Porta, though not very successfully. His genius was better adapted to the simple and agreeable style of his instructor, than to the grand manner of Porta. Lanzi says he lived with Credi for twenty-four years, in imitation of whom he was content to paint less than his cotemporaries, that he might do it better. "Few of his scholars can compare with him for the natural appearance he gave the naked as well as the clothed figure, or for the conception, as Vasari terms it, of 'handsome, good-natured, sweet, and graceful features.' Like da Vinci, he possessed the rare talent of representing images of virtue by the faces of his saints, and of vice by those of his wicked characters. This is exemplified in his Cain and Abel, in the cathedral of Pisa, in which he introduced a landscape that would do credit to any painter. With equal felicity in the figures, and the back-ground, he painted the Crucifixion of St. Arcadius, in the church of S. Lorenzo at Florence. He entered into competition with Pierino del Vaga, Mecherino, and Andrea del Sarto at Pisa, where he was noted for his dilatoriness, but admired for that happy simplicity and elegance which he always preserved. Some have praised a few of his pictures, as inclining to the manner of Raffaello."

SOIARO, Il. See Bernardo Gatti.

SOITZ, G. C., a German engraver, who flourished at Vienna about 1530. He executed some plates for the booksellers.

SOIUS, Philip. See Seriocus.

SOLARI, Andrea, called also del Gobbo, and by Vasari, Andrea Milanese, a painter who flourished at Milan about 1530. Vasari, in his life of Correggio, commends him as a beautiful designer, and an excellent colorist; he mentions several of his works in private collections, and his Assumption of the Virgin in the church of the Carthusians at Pavia, where Torre says he wrought in conjunction with Salaino. Zani says he was born in 1458, and died in 1508, and thinks he is the same as *Andrea Salai* or *Salaino*, the scholar of Leonardo da Vinci, but he is evidently in error. Several writers have confounded the history of Solari with Salaino, who is also called Salai, and Solaino, from similarity of names. See *Salaino.*

SOLARIO, Antonio, called Lo Zingaro (the Gipsy), a painter born, according to Dominici, at Civita, in Abruzzo, in the kingdom of Naples, about 1382, and died about 1455. There is considerable discrepancy about this old painter. Lanzi says, "before Zingaro introduced a manner acquired in other schools, the art had made little progress in Naples and her territories. This is clearly proved by the works of Colantonio del Fiore (the scholar of Francesco di Simone), who lived until the year 1444." After giving the life of that painter and of Angiolo Franco, his scholar and an imitator of Giotto, he proceeds, "the art however, was more advanced by Antonio Solario originally a blacksmith, and commonly called Lo Zingaro. His history has something romantic in it, like that of Quintin Matsys, who, from his first profession, was called *il Fabbro* (the smith), and became a painter from his love to a young girl who promised to marry him when he had made himself a proficient in the art of painting. Solario, in the same manner, became enamored of the daughter of Colantonio del Fiore, and receiving from him a promise of her hand in ten years, if he became an eminent painter, forsook his furnace for the academy, and his file for the pencil. He went to Bologna, where he studied several years with Lippo Dalmasio, called Lippo delle Madonne, from his numerous and beautiful pictures of the Virgin. On leaving Bologna, he visited other parts of Italy, to study the works of the best artists in the various schools, as Vivarini in Venice, Bicci in Florence, Pisanello and Gentile da Fabriano in Rome. It has been thought that he assisted the two last, and Luca Giordano affirmed that among the pictures in the Lateran, he recognized some heads which were indisputably by Solario. He excelled in this particular, and excited the admiration of Marco da Siena himself, who declared that his countenances seemed alive. He became also a good perspective painter for those times, and respectable in historical compositions, which he enlivened with landscape in a better style than was practised by other painters before him; he distinguished, too, his figures by a drapery peculiar to the age in which he lived, and carefully drawn from nature. He was less happy in designing his hands and feet, often being heavy in his attitudes and crude in his coloring. On his return to Naples, he gave proofs of his skill, and is said to have married the daughter of Colantonio, and to have taught and painted there under the patronage of King Alfonso till about 1455, when he died." He painted numerous pictures, usually portraits of Madonnas, Magdalens, and Saints, for the churches of Naples, very beautiful in form and expression. His most celebrated work was the choir of S. Severino, painted in fresco, representing, in several compartments, the life of S. Benedetto, into which he introduced an incredible number and variety of figures and objects. In the church of S. Domenico Maggiore, he painted a Pietà, or Dead Christ in the lap of the Virgin, and in that of S. Pietro Martire, an altar-piece of St. Vincenzio with some subjects from the life of that saint, in which he is said to have surpassed himself. Thus he commenced in Naples a new epoch, which the Cav. Massimo Stanzioni termed *the school of Zingaro.* There are several of his works in the Museo Borbonico. Some writers assert that Solario was a Venetian, and Rosini gives an outline, (plate 37) of a picture of the Virgin and Infant Christ, with St. John, inscribed *Antonius da Solario Venetus, f.* The composition has the truth and simplicity of Raffaelle, and evidently belongs to a later age. Some writers have mixed up together the histories of *Andrea Salaino*, *Andrea Solari*, and Antonio Solario, but with regard to the last there can be no doubt as to his belonging to the Neapolitan school, the time he flourished, and the authenticity of his works.

SOLDANI, Massimiliano, an Italian sculptor and medalist, was born in Florence in 1658. During his infancy his parents removed to a country seat at Petriolo. As he grew up, he manifested great inclination for art, and was finally sent by an uncle to Florence, where a model in terra cotta, representing the Assumption of the Virgin, gained him the patronage of Baldassare Franceschini, who placed him under the instruction of Giuseppe Arrighi. After progressing rapidly for some time, he was sent by the Grand Duke Cosmo III., with a pension, to Rome, where he studied design under Ciro Ferri, and sculpture under Ercole Ferrata. Manifesting superior excellence in medal engraving, he was commissioned by Queen Christina of Sweden to execute one hundred medals, illustrating the events of her reign; but in consequence of his recall to Florence by the Grand Duke, he only completed five. Before his departure, however, he executed medals of the Cardinals Azzolino, Chigi, and Rospigliosi; also those of Ciro Ferri and Ercole Ferrata, his instructors. Innocent XI. was so greatly pleased with the beauty of these works, that he wished Soldani to engrave his head; but he was obliged to depart for Florence, being a pensioner of the Grand Duke. On arriving there, he received apartments in the buildings of the old mint, and proceeded to execute his magnificent bas-relief of the Decollation of St. John. He afterwards visited Paris, where he engraved a large medal of Louis XV., struck on occasion of the peace, representing on the reverse side, Hercules reposing after destroying the Hydra. In 1686, he returned to Florence, where he executed many medals, statues, and bas-reliefs, in silver and gold, with great delicacy and beauty. After the death of Cosmo III., Soldani found in his successor Ferdinand, the same favor. Among his principal works are, the magnificent bronze candelabras in gilded bronze, in the Nunziata, at Florence; the mausoleums of Marc Antonio Zondadari, and Don Manuel de Vilena, grand master of the Knights of Malta; also twelve busts, three bronze statues, and several bas-reliefs, executed by the commission of the Prince of Lechtenstein, for his rich Museum at Vienna. Soldani established a successful school, which produced a number of able artists, among whom was Gio. Battista Foggini. He died in 1740.

SOLDI, Andrea, a painter born at Florence about 1702. He went to Aleppo, where he painted the portraits of some English merchants, at whose recommendation he went to London, about 1735. He met with considerable employment there in portraiture, became a member of the Chartered Society of Artists, and exhibited with them till about 1766, when he is supposed to have died.

SOLE, Antonio dal, called Il Manchino, a painter born at Bologna in 1606. He studied with Francesco Albano, but afterwards devoted himself to landscapes, in which he became very eminent, and as he always wrought with his left hand, he was called *Il Manchino da' Paesi* (the left-handed landscape painter.) His pictures represent the most charming scenery, and delightful situations, his perspective is admirable, and his distances recede with a pleasing degradation; his coloring is clear and lively, and his touch delicate and free. He decorated his landscapes with groups of graceful and beautiful figures, designed and composed in the style of Albano. He died in 1684. Crespi and others place his birth in 1597, and his death in 1677; but Zani and Lanzi say that he was born in 1606, and died in 1684. Oretti copied the same dates from the Register of la Maddalena.

SOLE, Giovanni Giuseppe dal, was the son of the preceding, born at Bologna in 1654. He received his first instructions from his father, and next studied with Domenico Maria Canuti, whom he left to become the disciple of Lorenzo Pasinelli, by whose instruction and advice he gradually rose to great distinction. His life is full of instruction and encouragement to young artists. He did not early exhibit any extraordinary powers, and was diffident of his own performances. He labored incessantly to improve himself, and following the example of Pasinelli, he went to Venice to improve his coloring by studying the works of Paul Veronese. Even after he had executed several admirable works, and acquired distinction—when he was employed to paint the Martyrdom of St. Vittoria for the cathedral of Mirandola, in competition with his fellow pupil, Gio. Antonio Burrini, he was thrown into despair on beholding the picture of his rival so greatly superior to his own. Pasinelli, the common master, reassured him by predicting that he would become a better artist than Burrini, whose facility of genius would at length betray him into mannerism, which prediction was exactly fufilled, for though he practised with tolerable care for fifteen years, he at length formed his second style, that of a mere machinist. Lanzi, after giving the life of Burrini, and describing the means by which he lost his reputation, thus contrasts the picture of dal Sole with his: "Gio. Giuseppe dal Sole, on the contrary, burned each day to become more perfect, and gradually raised himself to one of the first posts among the artists of his age. He had constant commissions from noblemen, both native and foreign, and received invitations also from the courts of England and Poland. For some time he followed the style of Pasinelli, but in order to improve it from the same sources, he made frequent visits to Venice, though he never attained to that degree of beauty in his most elegant subjects that formed the boast of his master. In many particulars, however, he displays exquisite grace, as in the hair and plumes of his angels, and especially in his accessories, such as veils, bracelets, crowns, and armor. He seems also to have been more inclined to treat powerful themes than Pasinelli; more observant of costume, more methodical in his composition, and more learned in point of architecture and landscape. In these, indeed, he is almost unique, and the most beautiful specimens are to be seen in the Casa Zappi in Imola, representing Evening, Night, and Morning, all very pleasingly distributed with sober tints, such as the subject required. His other works in most instances, exhibit the most lively play of vivid fluctuations of light, more especially in his holy pieces, and celestial visions, as we see in St. Peter of Alcantara, in S. Angiolo at Milan. Moreover he was more exact and polished than Pasinelli, not that he was by any means deficient in celerity in conducting his works, but esteemed it unworthy of an upright character, to bestow upon them less perfection than he was capable of doing. Being employed at Verona by the noble family of Giusti, where he left several mythological pieces and Scripture histories, truly beautiful, he executed one of Bacchus and Ariadne, which artists pronounced excellent, in one week; yet he erased the whole and remodeled it according to his own taste, declaring that it was enough to have shown his rapidity of hand to satisfy others, but that it became his duty by additional accuracy to satisfy himself. Hence, his fresco in the church of S. Biagio at Bologna, cost him an infinite deal of labor in its execution; and in conducting his altar-pieces, which are few and valuable, as well as in his pictures for individuals, which are numerous, he called for high remuneration, persevering in his determination to paint only with care." Gio. Giuseppe dal Sole, like many artists, had two manners, the first founded on that of Pasinelli, and the other, which he practised later in life, on that of Guido, and which procured for him the surname of *the Modern Guido.* Very many of the pictures which he executed for the collections were painted in this style. Lanzi says a large portion of his pictures nearly approach the taste of Guido. He instructed many pupils. He executed many spirited etchings from his own designs, and after Pasinelli. He died at Bologna in 1719.

JF SOLEMACKER, J. F., a painter of whom nothing is known except by his pictures. He is said to have flourished in the time of Wynants, Ruysdael, and Berghem. He imitated the manner of Berghem sufficiently to make his pictures pass for the works of that master with the unlearned in such matters. He imitated his grouping, forms, and cattle, in some instances, with considerable success, but his handling is less delicate and free, his coloring less transparent, his shadows are dark, and the general appearance of his pictures heavy. His pictures, though they cannot be compared with the admirable productions of Berghem, possess considerable merit. His greatest skill lay in painting cows, sheep, and goats. There is a piquancy in his manner, a pleasing rural choice in his subjects, and a freedom in the distribution of his objects, which would make his pictures valuable, were it not for their opacity of coloring. He is also said to have sometimes imitated Wouwerman, and occasionally to have imitated the animals and figures in the landscapes of Wynants. His pictures are generally of small size, and always painted on panel. His name is sometimes written *Soolemaker*, and *Zoolemaker*.

SOLERI, Giorgio, a painter born at Alessandria, where he died in 1587. It is not known under whom he studied, but he married the daughter of Bernardino Lanini, for which reason some suppose he was his pupil, though he did not follow his style. He excelled in portraits, in which branch Malvasia ranks him equal to Bartolomeo Passerotti, Giuseppe Arcimboldi, and Gio. da Monte. Lanzi highly commends two of his historical works. One is an altar-piece in the church of the Conventuali at Alessandria, representing the Virgin, to whose protection Sts. Augustin and Francis are recommending the city; there is a fine landscape in the background in the style of Paul Bril. The other is in the church of the Dominicans at Casale, and represents St. Lorenzo kneeling before the Virgin with the holy Infant; near are three cherubs playing with a huge gridiron, the symbol of his martyrdom. Lanzi says in this picture we trace most distinctly a follower of Raffaelle in the chasteness of design, the beauty and force of the countenances, and the finished expression. He had a son named Raffaelle Angiolo, but he did not rise above mediocrity.

SOLFAROLO, Il, a German painter, who, according to Lanzi, flourished at Milan about the middle of the 17th century, where he acquired considerable reputation for his landscapes. His name was Gruenbrech, or Gruembroech, and he was called Solfarolo for his night-scenes, fires, and conflagrations. He is not mentioned by the Dutch or German writers.

SOLIMENA, Angelo, a Neapolitan painter, who flourished at Nocera de' Pagani, a place about eighteen miles from Naples, about the middle of the 17th century. He studied under the Cav. Massimo Stanzioni at Naples, and acquired some distinction in his time, but his fame was entirely eclipsed by his son Francesco.

SOLIMENA, Cav. Francesco, called L'Abate Ciccio. This eminent painter was the son of the preceding, and was born at Nocera de' Pagani, in 1657. His father being in easy circumstances, intended his son for the profession of law, and had him instructed in classical learning, in which he showed apt parts; he had a passion for poetry and design, and is said to have passed whole nights in the pursuit of his favorite studies. The Cardinal Orsini, afterwards Pope Benedict XIII., in passing through Nocera, honored Solimena with a visit, and expressed his approbation of the progress Francesco had made in his studies. Solimena complained of his son's unwise application of his time, which prevented him from making such progress as he might, and requested the Cardinal to remonstrate with the youth. The prelate desired to see the designs, and was so struck with the uncommon talents they evinced, that he advised the father not to thwart his son's inclination, but to allow him to follow a profession for which nature had evidently designed him. Angelo followed this advice, and began to instruct Francesco with great care, so that he was soon able to design from the naked figure. After studying two years with his father, he went to Naples in 1674, at the age of seventeen, and entered the school of Francesco di Maria, but soon left it, as he thought that master too exclusively devoted to design. He then entered the academy of Giacomo del Po, where he assiduously designed from the naked figure, and at the same time began to color. Thus, says Lanzi, he had the advantage of being the scholar of two of the best masters of the Neapolitan school, and he always studied and copied their works. He next proceeded to Rome, where the works of Pietro da Cortona were for some time the models of his imitation. Lanzi says, "at first he imitated Pietro da Cortona, but afterwards formed a manner of his own, still retaining that master as his model, and copying entire figures from him, which he adapted to his new style. This new and striking style of Solimena approaches nearer to that of Preti than any other. The design is not so correct, the coloring not so true, but the faces have more beauty; in these he sometimes imitated Guido, sometimes Maratti, and they are often selected from nature. Hence he is called by some il Calabrese *ringentilito* (ennobled). To the style of Preti he added that of Lanfranco, whom he named his master, and from whom he adopted that curving form of composition which, perhaps, he carried beyond propriety. From these two masters, he took his chiaro-scuro, which he painted strong in his middle age, but softened as he advanced in years, and then attached himself more to facility and elegance of style. He carefully designed every part of his picture, and corrected it from nature before he colored it; so that in preparing his works, he may be included among the most correct, at least in his better days, for he latterly declined into general facility and opened the way to mannerism. He possessed an elegant and fruitful talent of invention, for which he was celebrated by the poets of his day. He was also characterized by a sort of universality in every style he attempted, extending himself to every branch of the art; history, portrait, landscape, animals, fruit, architecture, utensils, &c.; and whatever he attempted, he seemed formed for that alone, he did everything so well. As he lived to the age of ninety, and was endowed with great celerity of pencil, his works, like those of Giordano, were spread over all Europe. Of that artist, he was at the same time the competitor and the friend, less powerful in genius, but more correct in principles. When Giordano died, Solimena became the first painter in Italy. Notwithstanding what his rivals said of his colors not being true to nature, he began to ask extraordinary prices for his pictures, and still abounded in commissions."

Solimena executed an incredible number of works, in oil and fresco, of large and small size, for the churches and public edifices of Naples, for the kings, princes, and nobility of Europe. The King of Naples held him in such esteem, that he not only commissioned him to paint several pictures, sat to him for his portrait, and conferred on him the honor of knighthood, but he desired him to paint a picture representing himself in familiar conversation with Solimena. He took delight in the instruction of youth, and had many scholars, to whom he pointed out, in the most familiar manner, the principles and practice of the art, and the observations he had made; he took especial pains to make his disciples acquainted with the perfections of the most celebrated masters, inculcated the advantage of seeking out the most beautiful features, forms, and proportions from nature, and uniting them with the correctness, elegance, and grace of the antique. Solimena, notwithstanding his great abilities and merits, is reckoned by Lanzi and other judicious critics, among those artists who caused the declension, and accelerated the downfall of Italian art. Pietro da Cortona, Carlo Maratti, Luca Giordano, Solimena, Sebastiano Conca, and Pompeo Battoni, regularly followed each other in depravity of style, and by the influence of their immense reputation, gradually reduced the art from the correctness, elegance, and dignity of Raffaelle, to a species of mannerism. With Solimena, this was not intentional; as he advanced in years, his facility led him imperceptibly to become less studied and correct, and at length, the gradual failure of his sight increased the difficulty, so that his later performances are not to be compared with his earlier works. Such was his reputation in his time, that anything from his hand was admired and esteemed. The history of art hardly furnishes an example of rapid execution which did not eventually prove injurious to the reputation of the artist; hence great facility of hand is termed by the best critics *dangerous*. Michael Angelo and Raffaelle, though they possessed the greatest facility of hand, never practised it, but curbed it within proper bounds.

Among the most celebrated works of Solimena are the Sacristy of the PP. Teatini in S. Paolo Maggiore; the arches of the chapel in the church of the Holy Apostles, particularly commended; the chapel of S. Filippo in the church of the Oratorio, conducted with extreme care; the Sanfelice, so called from his noble scholar Ferdinand; the great altar in the church of the monks of S. Gaudioso; four immense pictures in the choir of the church of Monte Cassino, and many others in the churches at Naples, and various places in the kingdom. His private pictures are to be found in all the best collections of Naples. At Rome, the princes Albani and Colonna, have some large compositions by him, and the Bonaccorsi family, a great number in the gallery of Macerata. One of his best works is a picture of the Last Supper, in the Refectory of the Conventuali at Assisi. He died at Naples in 1747. His name is generally, but erroneously written Solimene. Dominici read it *Solimena* on his tomb.

SOLIS, Juan de, a Spanish painter who flourished at Madrid in the first part of the 17th century. He studied with Alonso Herrera of Segovia. Little is known of him, or his works. Bermudez says he did not practise much as a professor.

SOLIS, Francisco de, was the son of the preceding, born at Madrid in 1629. According to Bermudez, his father intended him for the church, but his passion for painting induced him to instruct him in the art. At the age of eighteen he painted a picture for the Capuchins of Villarubia de los Ojos, which being exhibited on a public solemnity at the convent de la Paciencia at Madrid, attracted the notice of connoisseurs, and Philip IV. was so much pleased with the performance, that he directed the artist to sign it with his name and age. This incident brought him immediately into notice, and he soon gained abundant employment. When the Queen Louisa of Orleans, made her solemn entry into Madrid, he contributed to the splendor of the decorations by a series of paintings representing the labors of Hercules, from the designs of Claudio Coello; but the work which established his reputation was a picture representing the Immaculate Conception of the Virgin. Henceforward, says his biographer, his conceptions were all the vogue. He contributed much to the advancement of Painting in Spain. He opened an academy in his house, to which he admitted young artists, free of expense, to draw from the living model. He wrote an account of the Spanish painters, sculptors, and architects, and engraved several portraits for its embellishment, but he did not live to publish the work, and the manuscript was afterwards lost. He left books, prints, and drawings worth 6000 ducats. He died in 1684.

or or SOLIS, Virgil, a German engraver, born at Nuremberg in 1514, and was living in 1581. Little is known of him with any certainty, except by his prints, executed both on wood and copper, amounting to upwards of 800, which are usually marked with one of the above monograms. His prints are chiefly from his own designs, and of small size; hence he is classed with the *little masters.* His copper plates engraved in the early part of his life, resemble the works of Hans Sebald Beham, but when he afterwards engraved after the Italian masters, he adopted a style more open and spirited. His wooden cuts are similar to those of Jost Amman, both in respect to composition and execution. His works prove him to have possessed a fertile invention, and though the design is stiff and formal, some of them possess great merit. As with many of the old German artists, it is a disputed question, whether he engraved on wood himself at all, or employed others to execute the cuts from his designs. It is a profitless discussion, and adds or detracts little from the value of their productions. Doubtless Solis not only wrought himself, but employed others to assist him in the execution of his numerous works, as is done at the present day. There is a great difference in his prints, especially in his wooden cuts, and some of them bear the mark of the engraver or assistant, in addition to his own, which signifies that the print was designed and traced by himself, which made the work practically his own. The following are his principal prints:

A variety of small engravings on copper, representing hunting subjects; dated 1541. A set of Vases and Ornaments for Goldsmiths; do. The Marriage of Cupid and Psyche, the Assembly of the Gods, Mount Parnassus, and several other subjects; *after Raffaelle.* The Bath of the Anabaptists; copied from *Aldegrever.*

WOODEN CUTS.

Several sets of small historical subjects from the Bible. The Metamorphoses of Ovid, in one hundred and seventy cuts; published at Frankfort in 1563. A set of cuts for the Emblems of *Nicholas Reuser.* 1581. Another set of cuts for the Emblems of *Andreas Alciatus.* 1581.

SOLOMAYOR, Luis de. See Sotomayor.

SOLON, an ancient engraver on gems, who flourished at Rome in the time of Augustus, and was a cotemporary of Dioscorides. His name is affixed to an ancient portrait, which for a long time was supposed to represent the Athenian Lawgiver, but has since been attributed to this artist, and probably represents Mæcenas, whom he often portrayed. Among his other productions were, a portrait of Diomed sitting; a head of Medusa; Cupid standing; and a head of Hercules.

SOLVYNS, Francis Balthasar. This painter and engraver was born at Antwerp in 1760. After acquiring a knowledge of the art, he practised marine painting for some time, and executed, among other works, a View from the port of Ostend, engraved on a large plate by Daudet, and now in the palace at Vienna. His taste for travel induced him to embark in the squadron of Sir Home Popham, for the Red Sea and the Indian Ocean. He made many exact designs of the shores of the Red Sea; and on arriving at Calcutta, he commenced making designs to illustrate the manners and customs of the East Indians. A part of these he engraved and published at Calcutta in 1799, and according to his own account, they were favorably received. Solvyns afterwards returned to Europe, and published at Paris his entire work in four folio volumes, in 1809, and the three succeeding years, containing 288 colored plates, engraved by himself, with descriptions in English and French. It bears the marks of great care and expense; but it met with little encouragement, and involved the author in pecuniary embarrassment. The subscription price was $500. Solvyns died at Antwerp in 1824.

SOLY, Arthur, an obscure English engraver, who flourished about 1683. He was employed by Robert White, and engraved a few portraits for the book publishers.

SOMER, or SOMEREN, Mathias van, a Dutch engraver, who flourished about 1660. He engraved some portraits, and a set of landscapes, marked with the initials, M. V. S.

SOMER, John van, a Dutch engraver, supposed to have been a relative of the preceding, who flourished about 1675. He engraved some portraits and other subjects, after the Dutch masters, indifferently executed. He usually marked his prints with one of the accompanying monograms.

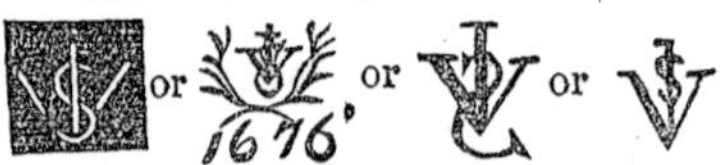


SOMER, Paul van, a Dutch engraver, probably of the same family with John van S. He went to Paris, where he resided some time. He finally settled in London, where he died in 1694. He executed quite a number of plates, from his own designs and after other masters, some of which are etched, and others engraved in line or mezzotinto.

SOMERS, or SOMEREN, Bernard and Paul, two Flemish painters, born at Antwerp—the first in 1579, and the last in 1581. Little is known of them. Bernard went to Italy, and on his return joined his brother at Antwerp, where it is said they painted history with reputation. Bernard died in 1632, and Paul in 1641.

SOMMERAU, Ludwig, a German painter and engraver, born at Wolfenbüttel in 1750. He studied engraving under Christian de Mechel, at Basle. He went to Rome, where he engraved several portraits, and some pieces after Raffaelle, Guido, Domenichino, and Guercino, the most important of which are twenty plates from the designs for tapestry in the Vatican, by Raffaelle. These were published at Rome in 1780. The same, with six additional plates, were published in London in 1837, by Cattermole, with explanations.

SOMPEL, or SOMPELEN, Peter van, a Flemish engraver, born at Antwerp, about 1600.—He studied with Peter Soutman, whose style he followed with success. His plates are neatly executed with the graver, and produce a pleasing effect. His portraits are the best. Among other are the following by him:

PORTRAITS.

Paracelsus, the famous Physician; *after Soutman.* Henry, Count of Nassau; *do.* Philip of Nassau, Prince o Orange; *do.* The Emperor Charles V.; *after Ruben* Cardinal Ferdinand, brother to Philip IV.; Governor o the Netherlands; *after Vandyck.* Isabella Clara Eugenia, Infanta of Spain; *do.* Gaston, Duke of Orleans, brother to Louis XII.; *do.* Margaret, his consort; *do.* Philip the Bold, Duke of Burgundy; *after J. van Eyck.* Frederick Henry of Nassau; *after G. Honthorst.*

SUBJECTS.

Christ with the Disciples at Emmaus; *after Ruben* The Crucifixion; *do.* Juno and Ixion; *do.*

SON, or ZOON, Joris van, a Flemish painter born at Antwerp in 1622. It is not known und whom he studied, but he excelled in painting fr and flower pieces. His pictures are well designed, his pencil light and flowing, and his coloring clear and natural. He died in 1676.

SON, or ZOON, John van, was the son of the preceding, born at Antwerp about 1650. He studied with his father, whom he greatly surpassed. He painted similar subjects, and designed everything from nature with a fidelity and precision that approaches to illusion. He went early in life to England, where he married the niece of Robert Streater, and succeeded to most of his business. He painted fruit, flowers, dead game, vases, curtains fringed with gold, Turkey carpets, and other objects of still life, which he composed in a picturesque manner, and executed with a free and spirited pencil. Lord Orford calls his name Francis van Son, but Descamps and others say his name was John. He died at London in 1700, though some say he was born in 1661, and died in 1723.

SON, Nicolas de, a French engraver of whom little is known, except by a few prints, in which he imitated Callot with considerable success, and doubtless he was a pupil of that master. He was a native of Rheims, and flourished about 1628. He is sometimes called *Anthony*, but he signed his prints *N. de Son, fecit.*

SONNIN, Ernest George, a German architect, born at Perleberg in 1709. While acquiring a liberal education at Altona, he formed an intimate friendship with an artist named Moller, who instructed him in design, and received from him in return instruction in mathematics. Several years afterwards, he was induced by a wealthy citizen of Hamburg, named Rahusen, to study architecture; and he made such rapid progress that he was soon commissioned to erect an edifice at Altona. The Senate of Hamburg, probably at the instance of his patron, appointed him second architect of the church of St. Michael, erected in place of the one consumed by lightning in 1750. In this work, notwithstanding Precy had the ostensible direction, the talents of Sonnin controlled the operations. He was subsequently employed on various edifices, and sustained a deserved reputation until his death, in 1794.

SONS, Giovanni. See Soens.

SOPHONISBA. See Angosciola.

SOPRANI, Raffaelle, a painter born at Genoa in 1612. He studied successively under Giulio Benso and Sinibaldo Scorza, after which he applied himself to landscape under Godefroi Vals. He painted landscapes, perspectives, and architectural subjects with applause, though he was rather an amateur than a professor of the art. He wrote the Lives of the Painters, Sculptors, and Architects of Genoa, published at Genoa after his death, in 1674, 4to. He died in 1672.

SORDO, DI SESTRI, Il. See Antonio Travi.

SORDO D' URBINO, Il. See Antonio Viviani.

SORDO, Giovanni Del, called also Mone Da Pisa, a painter who flourished at Pisa about 1650. It is not known under whom he studied, but he is commended by Morrona for some works in the churches at Pisa, particularly in the Cathedral. Lanzi says that his coloring seems superior to his invention.

SORE, Nicolas de, an excellent French engraver, who flourished at Rheims in the first part of the 17th century. Among his principal plates were the façade of the church of S. Nicaise, and the grand entrance to the Cathedral at Rheims, which were greatly admired. De Sore died in the prime of life, about 1625.

SORELLO, Miguel, a Spanish engraver, born at Barcelona about 1700. He went to Rome, and studied with Giacomo (James) Frey. He executed a part of the plates for the Antiquities of Herculaneum, published in 1757 and 1761. He also engraved several plates after the Italian masters, the principal of which are a set of eight plates from the tapestry in the Vatican, designed by Raffaelle, as follows:

The Nativity. The Purification of the Virgin. Christ giving the Keys to St. Peter. Christ descending into Hell. The Resurrection. Christ with the Disciples at Emmaus. Christ appearing to Magdalene. The Conversion of St. Paul.

SORGH, ZORG, or ZORGH. See Rokes.

SORIA, Gio. Battista, an Italian architect, born at Rome in 1581. His instructor is not mentioned, but he obtained considerable employment through the patronage of Cardinal Scipione Borghese. Milizia gives him little credit for excellence. Among his principal works are the façade of the church della Vittoria; that of S. Carlo de' Catenari; the porticos and façade of S. Gregorio; and the church of S. Caterina da Siena, on the Monte Magnanapoli. Soria died in 1651.

SORIANI, Carlo, a painter who flourished at Pavia about the middle of the 17th century. Little is known of him. He is commended by Bartoli for several works he executed for the churches at Pavia, particularly for his picture of the Rosario, accompanied by fifteen Mysteries, in the Cathedral. Lanzi says he deserves to be better known.

SORIANI, Niccolo, a painter who flourished at Cremona in the latter part of the 15th century. According to Baruffaldi, he was an artist of considerable note in his day at Cremona. He was the maternal uncle of Benvenuto Tisio, who, after having received his first instruction from Panetti at Ferrara, went to Cremona, and studied with Soriani till the death of the latter in 1499.

SORNIQUE, Dominique, a French engraver, born at Paris in 1707. He studied with Charles Simonneau, whose style he followed with considerable success. He engraved a variety of vignettes and other book plates, in a neat, clear, and pleasing style; also some larger plates of portraits and other subjects, among which are Cardinal Richelieu, and John Louis, Duke of Epernon, *after Nanteuil;* Admiral Louis Bourbon, *after Mignard;* Marshal Saxe, *after Rigaud;* Diana and her Nymphs, *after Correggio;* the Rape of the Sabines, *after Luca Giordano;* and Peasants regaling, *after Teniers.* A list of his works may be found in Nagler's Lexicon. He died in 1756.

SORRI, Pietro, a painter born at Siena in 1556. After receiving instruction from Arcangelo Salimbeni in his native city, he went to Florence, and became the disciple of the Cav. Passignano, whose system he adopted, which was characterized by a mixture of the Florentine and Venetian schools. He married the daughter of that master, and accompanied him to Venice, where he improved himself by studying the works of Paul Veronese, whose splendid and magnificent style is discernible in his best works. On his return to Florence, he received the highest marks of approbation and applause, for the elegance and taste of his composition and design, and the beauty and brilliancy of his coloring. Lanzi says, "he emulated the style of Passignano with such success that their works bear a perfect resemblance, and are held in equal estimation; though he wrought with less facility, his design was more graceful, and his coloring more durable." He executed many works for the churches of Florence, and all the cities of Tuscany, particularly at Pisa, where he painted for the Cathedral a vast picture on canvass, representing the ceremony of the consecration of that edifice, and another of Christ disputing with the Doctors—two of his best works, in which he imitated the grand style of Veronese, in his architecture and other accessories. He was employed in the convent of S. Sebastiano at Siena, in competition with the best Sienese artists. He was also employed in the convent of the Carthusians at Pavia, and appointed preceptor in the Academy of Genoa. He died in 1622.

SOSTRATUS of Cnidus, the son of Dexiphanes, was a celebrated ancient architect, and flourished in the time of Ptolemy Philadelphus. He constructed in his own country the noted hanging gardens, concerning which there have been formed so many conjectures. His greatest work, however, according to Strabo, was the celebrated light-house on the Isle of Pharos, considered among the seven wonders of the world. It was 450 feet high, divided into several stories, each decreasing in size; the ground story was hexagonal, the sides alternately concave and convex, each an eighth of a mile in length; the second and third stories were of the same form; the fourth was a square, flanked by four round towers; the fifth was circular. The whole edifice was of wrought stone; a magnificent staircase led to the top, where fires were lighted every night, visible from the distance of a hundred miles, to guide the coasting vessels. Sostratus is said to have engraved an inscription on stone, and covered it over with a species of cement, upon which he sculptured the name of Ptolemy, calculating that the cement would decay, and bring to light his original inscription. Strabo says it read, *Sostratus, the friend of kings, made me.* Lucian reports differently, and more probably, thus, *Sostratus of Cnidus, the son of Dexiphanes, to the Gods the Saviors, for the safety of Mariners.* It is also said that Ptolemy left the inscription to the inclination of the architect; and that by the *Gods the Saviors* were meant the reigning king and queen, with their successors, who were ambitious of the title of Soteros or Savior.

SOTO, Juan de, a Spanish painter, born at Madrid in 1592. He studied with Bartolomeo Carducci, whom he assisted in several of his works, and whose style he followed. He possessed great talents, and according to Bermudez, was "selected from among the great professors of his time to decorate in fresco the Queen's dressing room, in the palace of the Prado;" but this work was doubtless executed from the designs of Carducci, who was then in the service of the king. (See Carducci.) He painted several pictures in oil, which gained him great reputation, and he was rising rapidly in public estimation, as one of the most promising artists of his time, when he died in the flower of his life, in 1620.

SOTO, Don Lorenzo de, a Spanish painter, born at Madrid in 1634. He studied under Benito Manuel de Agüero, whose manner he followed. According to Palomino, he painted landscapes, decorated with figures of hermits and saints, with high reputation, till the government attempted to impose a tax on artists, when he abandoned painting, and retired to Yecla, in Murcia, where he obtained the post of collector of the royal rents. During this retirement, he made many sketches of the beautiful scenery of the country, and after an absence of about 50 years, he returned to Madrid and resumed his pencil, but his works were looked upon (as well they might be) with indifference, and the poor old man was under the necessity of selling them in the public places to gain a subsistence. He died in 1688, aged 54, so that the account is not only bombastic, but contradictory.

SOTOMAYOR, Luis de, a Spanish painter, born at Valencia in 1635. He first studied with Estéban March in his native city, and afterwards went to Madrid, where he entered the school of Juan Carreno. On his return to Valencia, he acquired considerable reputation, and executed several works for the churches and convents in that city, which are highly commended by Bermudez. He died in 1673.

SOUBEYRAN, Peter, a Swiss painter and architect, was born at Geneva in 1708. He visited Paris quite young, and resided there about twenty years, during which time he engraved most of the plates for Mariette's *Traité des pierres antiques gravées du Cabinet du Roi*, after the designs of Bouchardon. Among his other plates were a variety of vignettes and other book ornaments, after Cochin and others; also the portrait of Peter the Great, *after Caravac;* the Arms of the city of Paris, supported by Genii *after Bouchardon;* and the Fair Maid of the Village, *after Boucher*. On returning to Geneva, Soubeyran devoted himself to the study of architecture, and gained considerable distinction. He was employed for many years upon the most important edifices of Geneva; and he filled with distinction the office of director of the school of design, established in that city. He died in 1775.

SOUFFLOT, Jacques Germain, an eminent French architect, born at Irancy, near Auxerre, in 1713. After receiving a liberal education, he studied mathematics and drawing at Paris, and afterwards visited Rome for improvement. Through the influence of M. de St. Aignant, he was admitted as a pensionary in the French Academy, and soon attained distinction. Several new edifices having been projected in the city of Lyons, the commissioners requested the directors of the French Academy at Rome to send them an able architect, and they decided upon Soufflot. He erected several fine edifices in that city, among which are the Hotel Dieu, the Exchange (now the Protestant church), and the grand Hospital, an immense edifice, the façade being over 1000 feet in length. Having acquired considerable distinction by these works, Soufflot was invited to Paris, and was chosen a member of the Academy of Architecture. At the invitation of M. de Marigny (the brother of Madame de Pompadour) superintendent of the Crown Buildings, he visited Italy in 1750, and examined the antiquities of Paestum. In 1754 he was again employed at Lyons to erect the Grand Theatre.

The ancient church of S. Genevieve having fallen into decay, it was determined that it should be rebuilt. Among a number of designs for the new edifice, that of Soufflot obtained the preference; and in 1757 the works were commenced, but they proceeded so slowly that the ceremony of laying the first stone by Louis XV. did not take place until 1764. This magnificent work is distinguished for good proportions, elegance and beauty of outline, simplicity and grandeur. A single order, with Corinthian columns sixty feet high, forms a grand portico, crowned with a pediment filled with sculpture. The entablature is continued along the whole building, of which it constitutes almost the sole decoration, the interior being lighted by the dome, and several semi-circular windows above the internal colonnades, which are not visible externally. The lower part of the dome is encircled by a Corinthian peristyle of thirty-two columns, thirty-six feet high, on an unbroken podium or stylobate. The interior is in the form of a Greek cross, the breadth being uniform, 104 feet, the principal nave 295 feet, and the transept, 262 feet. Including the portico, the total length of the edifice is 352 feet. Instead of pier arches, the aisles are formed by insulated Corinthian columns, forty feet high, producing an air of great richness and lightness. Soufflot did not live to see his great work completed. It was afterwards generally known as the Pantheon. He was honored with the Order of St. Michael, and according to Milizia, his labors have greatly aided the progress of the art in France. Besides the edifices already mentioned, Soufflot erected others, among which were the treasury and sacristy of Notre Dame; the Ecole de Droit, in the Place du Pantheon; the Orangery at the Chateau de Menars; and several private hotels. He died in 1780. In the next year, his friend M. Dumont, Professor of Architecture, published a number of his drawings, under the title of *Elevations et coupes de quelques Edifices de France et d'Italie, dessinées par feu M. Soufflot, Architecte du Roi, et gravées par ses ordres.*

SOURCHES, Louis François du Bouchet, Marquis, grand marshal of France, was an amateur engraver, and is supposed to have learned the art of Stefano Della Bella, who resided at Paris from 1640 to about 1649. He copied some prints by that master, in which he imitated his style so successfully that proofs before the letter have sometimes been mistaken for the originals. In the print department of the Bibliothêque, at Paris, are nineteen pieces by him, all of them copied from Della Bella. They are entitled *Diuerses figures et Maneiges de Cheuaux Gravées par le Marquis de Sourches.* His prints are very rare. Dumesnil also attributes to him twelve pieces from his own designs, as follows:

1. Le Berger. 2. L'Homme de Qualité. 3. La Dame de Qualité. 4. Le Duel. 5. Le Porte-drapeau. 6. La Marchande de vieux Habits. 7. Le Depart pour la Chasse. 8. Le Promeneur. 9. Le Pêcheur. 10. Le Puits. 11. Les Ramoneurs. 12. Le Batelier.

SOUTMAN, Peter, a Dutch painter and engraver, born at Haerlem, according to Nagler, about 1580, and to others, 1590. He studied painting under Rubens, and painted history and portraits with considerable success, particularly at the courts of Berlin and Warsaw. He is, however, better known as an engraver. He executed a considerable number of prints from his own designs, and after Rubens and other masters, in which he aimed at producing a striking effect by keeping all the masses of light broad and clear; but by carrying this idea too far, some of his prints, though neatly executed, have a slight, unfinished appearance. He engraved several portraits of the Counts of Flanders, and other distinguished personages. A full list of his works may be found in Nagler's Lexicon. He operated as late as 1650. The following are his best prints:

SUBJECTS AFTER RUBENS.

The Fall of the Angels. The first impressions are before the address of the younger *Bouttat.* The Defeat of the Army of Sennacherib. Christ giving the Keys to St. Peter; from a design by *Rubens, after Raffaelle.* The Last Supper; from a drawing by *Rubens, after Leonardo da Vinci.* The Miraculous Draught of Fishes. The dead Christ at the Tomb, with the Holy Women; the first impressions are before the shadows were strengthened by Witdoeck. The Crucifixion. The Consecration of a Bishop. The Rape of Proserpine. The Triumph of Venus. Silenus supported by a Satyr and a Negress. A Boar-hunt. 1642. The Hunting of the Lion and Lioness. Do. of the Wolf. Do. of the Crocodile and Hippopotamus.

SOZZI, Olivio, a Sicilian painter, and a native of Catania, who flourished in the 17th century. According to Hackert, he studied at Naples, and executed many excellent works for the churches at Palermo, particularly in S. Giacomo, where all the altars have pictures by him, besides three large ones in the tribune, of subjects from the infancy of Christ. There was another Sozzi, named Francesco, who is highly commended for his picture of Five Saints, bishops of Agrigentum, in the Cathedral of that city.

SPADA, Lionello, a painter, born at Bologna in 1576. When a boy, he was employed in the school of the Caracci as a color-grinder. Possessing a lively imagination, it was not long before the display of genius by which he was surrounded inspired him with the ambition to become a painter. He accordingly occupied his leisure hours in imitating the objects before him, following the instructions given to the pupils, which, being observed by the Caracci, they commended him, and admitted him into the academy. His progress under their instruction was rapid, and he became one of the most eminent disciples of that distinguished school. Lanzi relates an interesting anecdote of his ready wit and quick parts. When Giovanni da Capugnano came from his native hills and settled at Bologna, misled by a pleasing self-delusion, and the flattery he had received, he imagined himself the greatest painter in the world. He requested the Caracci to send him a pupil from their school, that he might polish him in his studio. They accordingly sent Lionello Spada, an admirable wit, who went and copied some of his designs, affecting the utmost obsequiousness towards his new master. At length, thinking it time to put an end to the jest, he left behind him an exquisite picture of Lucretia, and over the door some fine satirical verses, in apparent praise, but real ridicule of Capugnano, who only accused Lionello of ingratitude for having acquired from him, in so short a time, such excellence in the art; but the Caracci at last acquainted him with the joke, which acted as a complete antidote to his folly. One of his first public works was a picture of Sts. Francesco and Domenico, kneeling before the Virgin, in the Chiesa de Poveri at Bologna, which excited general admiration. Malvasia relates that Guido, on seeing this performance, sarcastically observed that the powers of Lionello seemed to be confined to *decoration*, which so exasperated him that he determined to rival the graceful and delicate style of that master, by adopting a system more masculine and vigorous. Vindictively bent on this purpose, he had recourse to the novel and energetic style of Michael Angelo da Caravaggio, which at that time was exceedingly popular. He accordingly went to Rome, and studied some time under that master. This emulation, though it fell short of its object, carried Spada further than he otherwise would have reached. In adopting the daring contrasts of light and shadow which distinguish the works of Caravaggio, he avoided his incorrectness, and introduced something of the dignity and elevation which characterize the school of the Caracci, though his forms are neither beautiful nor select. On his return to Bologna he acquired great celebrity, and executed many works for the churches and public edifices of Bologna and Reggio, particularly in the latter city, where he resided a long time, and instructed many pupils. The latter part of his life was passed at Parma, in the service of the duke of Ranuccio, till the death of his patron, whom he did not long survive. Among his best works at Bologna are, the Miraculous Draught of Fishes, in the refectory of S. Procolo; and his celebrated altar-piece in the church of S. Domenico, representing that Saint burning heretical books, which last is considered his masterpiece. He sometimes marked his pictures with the letter L., crossed with a sword, which is the rebus of his name, *Spada* in Italian signifying *sword*. He died at Parma in 1622, in the prime of life.

SPADA, Veronica, an Italian paintress, who excelled in painting fruit, flowers, and birds. She flourished at Bologna about the middle of the 17th century.

SPADARINO, Gio. Antonio, a painter born at Rome in 1600, and died in 1648. Little is known of him. Orlandi says he was of the family of the Galli, and that he painted in the church of S. Pietro in Valeria with a talent that entitles him to more consideration than he has received from biographers.

SPADARO, Micco. See Gargiuoli.

SPAENDONCK, Gerard van, an eminent Dutch painter of fruit and flowers, was born at Tilburg in 1746. After studying under the elder Herreyns, a flower painter of Antwerp, he visited Paris at the age of twenty-four, and devoted himself to miniature painting. Through the kindness of Watelet he obtained, in 1774, the appointment of miniature painter to the king, and his excellence in flower-painting, which he constantly practised, soon gained him great reputation. His exquisite productions were distinguished for tasteful arrangement, correct design, and coloring natural, light, transparent, harmonious, and delicate.—They were in great request, and were purchased for the choicest collections. In 1781, Spaendonck was chosen a member of the Academy of Painting; and during the civil commotions of France, he discharged the office of Professor of Iconography at the Jardin des Plantes. At the formation of the Institute, he was appointed Professor, and discharged his duties with highly commendable ability, assiduity, and kindness. He published a work entitled *Fleurs dessinées d'apres Nature*. There are four of his pictures in the Louvre, which are greatly admired. Spaendonck died at Paris in 1822.

SPAGGIARI, Giovanni, a painter of Reggio, of whom little is known. According to Tiraboschi, he was a skilful painter of perspective and architecture, and was much employed in decorating theatres.. He died in the service of the king of Poland, in 1730.

SPAGGIARI, Pellegrino, was the son of the preceding, born at Reggio. After receiving instruction from his father, he studied with Francesco Galli, called Bibiena, and became one of the most skilful of the decorative painters of Lombardy. He went to France, where he died in 1746.

SPAGNOLETTO. See Ribera.

SPAGNUOLO, Giovanni, called Lo Spagno. This artist was a Spaniard. He studied with Pietro Perugino at Perugia, whose style he followed. In the opinion of Vasari, the coloring of Perugino survived in him more than in any of his fellow-scholars. He established himself at Spoleto, at which place and Assisi he left his best works. He excelled also in portraits. Lanzi says, "In a chapel of the Angioli below Assisi, there remains the picture described by Vasari, in which are the portraits of the brotherhood of St. Francis; and perhaps no other painter of this school painted portraits with more truth, if we except Raffaello himself, with whom no other painter is to be compared." He was living in 1524, and probably later. He is doubtless the same artist mentioned by Bermudez under the name of *Juan de Espana*, which see.

SPAGNUOLO, Il. See Giuseppe Crespi.

SPALTHOF, N., a Dutch painter, born at Haerlem, in 1636. After studying in his own country, he went to Italy, where he resided several years. He excelled in painting Italian fairs, markets, carnivals, and merry-makings. His pictures are ingeniously composed in the Italian taste, correctly designed, and neatly and spiritedly touched. He copied everything after nature, and had an excellent knowledge of chiaro-scuro, which enabled him to give his figures and objects a fine relief. He died in 1691.

SPECCHI, Alessandro, an Italian engraver, who flourished from about 1665 to 1706, and is supposed to have died in 1710. He engraved a large number of views of the palaces and public edifices in and about Rome, which are executed with the graver in a bold and spirited style. These were published at different periods, and a set was published by Dom. de Rossi, in 1699.

SPECKLIN, Vitus Rodolphus, a German engraver on wood, who flourished at Strasburg about 1540. He engraved a set of cuts for Fuchsius' Herbal, published in that year, with a whole-length portrait of the author, the engraver's own portrait, and those of Henry Fullmaurer and Albert Maher, the artists who designed the prints. The cuts are executed in a neat and spirited style. His name is variously written *Specklin*, *Speckle*, and *Spectle*.

SPECKTER, Erwin, an eminent German painter, was born at Hamburg in 1806. During the siege of that city, in the winter of 1813–14, his parents took refuge at Altona, in the house of the banker Dehn. A painter named Herterich was also residing in the house of Dehn, from whom the young Erwin acquired some ideas of art, and his taste was also developed by spending most of his time in contemplating a good collection of pictures in that city. In 1818, his father and Herterich established a lithographic press, and young Speckter made some attempts at designs and portraits. In 1822, Rumohr returned to Hamburg from his second visit to Italy, and was much surprised at the talents of Speckter, encouraged him to persevere, and gave him much valuable instruction. In 1825, he visited Munich, and entered the school of Cornelius, who greatly admired his talents, and commissioned him to decorate one of the vaults of the Pinacotheca, with subjects from the life of Fra Giovanni da Fiesole. Unfortunately, this building was not ready for the work until many years after. In 1827, Speckter returned to Hamburg, chiefly on account of his desire to be near Overbeck's celebrated picture of Christ's Entry into Jerusalem, in the Marian Kirche at Lubec, while painting his picture of Christ and the Samaritan Woman. The study of this work seems to have had a prejudicial effect, by inducing him to strive after abstract ideal representation. His inward dissatisfaction at his own attempts may be inferred from his immediate, though gradual, change of manner; for his next work, the Women at the Tomb, is in a more natural style, both in design and coloring. About this time, he also painted several beautiful miniatures of sacred subjects. In 1830, he appeared in an entirely new character, in his arabesque mythological representations of Syndicus Sieveking, near Hamburg. In the same year, he set out for Italy. His originally transcendental ideas of art had been gradually yielding to the dictates of experience, and the immortal productions of the Roman and Venetian schools finally drew him, by the essential attractions of art, from an abstract conventional system to the imitation of nature. At Rome he executed a number of studies, in the general spirit of Italian art; also two pictures of Albano Women, and a large painting of Samson and Delilah. After spending three years in Italy, he was commissioned to paint in fresco the villa of Dr. Abendroth, at Hamburg. Returning to his native country in the summer of 1834, he executed three of the principal cartoons, and commenced the frescos in the ensuing spring. The subjects were, Minerva receiving the winged Pegasus from the Muses, near the Hippocrene fountain; the Graces, in a grove of laurels, decorating the bow and quiver of Cupid, and offering him a cup of ambrosial drink; and the Fates reclining on cushions, lulled by the lyre of Cupid. The first of these admirable designs, distinguished for the exquisite beauty of its forms, was completed in fresco; the second was partially finished; the third was not commenced. Speckter had for some time been afflicted with the asthma, and his weak state finally obliged him to relinquish his operations, about the first of November, and he died on the 23d of that month, in 1835, deeply lamented by all the friends of art. The letters he wrote while in Italy, were published in two vols. 12mo., at Leipsic, in 1846, under the title of *Briefe eines Deutschen Kunstlers aus Italien*, or Letters of a German Artist from Italy. They are accompanied with an account by his friend Rumohr, of the character of Speckter's genius, and are full of interesting information and reflections upon art.

SPEERS, M., a German painter and engraver born at Regensburg (now Ratisbon), in 1700. Little is known of him with certainty. He is said to have visited Italy, and studied with Solimena; at all events he imitated the manner of that master in painting, and he engraved some of his allegories and martyrdoms. He painted several altar-pieces and historical pictures, and engraved several plates from his own designs, as well as other masters. His prints are marked *M. Speers inv. et fecit.* Hence, he is called *Martin* or *Michael S.* Some of his prints are dated 1742. The time of his death is not certainly known, though Zani says he died in 1762.

SPELT, Adrian vander, a Dutch painter, born at Leyden or Gouda (for writers differ) in 1630. He studied with W. Crabeth, and excelled in painting flower-pieces. He went to Germany, where he resided a long time, and was much patronized by the Elector of Brandenburg. He afterwards returned to Leyden, where he died in 1674. His works were held in great estimation in his time.

SPENCER, Jarvis, an English miniature painter, who died in 1763. He was a self-made artist, originally the servant of a gentleman, through whose influence and his own talents and application, he acquired considerable reputation and practice.

SPERA, Clemente, a painter who flourished at Milan in the first half of the 18th century. It is not known under whom he studied, but he excelled in painting landscapes, architectural ruins, and perspective views. These were sometimes decorated with figures by Alessandro Magnasco, which see.

SPERANZA, Giovanni, a painter of Vicenza, who flourished about 1500. He studied with Andrea Mantegna, and followed his style with success. Lanzi says there are a few of his pictures at Vicenza, which are highly esteemed, though not remarkable for strength of coloring.

SPERANZA, Giovanni Battista, a painter born at Rome in 1610. He studied under Francesco Albano, and afterwards greatly improved himself by studying the works of Raffaelle, and other great masters. He excelled in fresco, and in that manner painted a series of pictures of the Life of the Virgin, in the church of S. Caterina at Siena; and the ceiling of the church of the Orfanelli, where he represented the Passion of our Savior, in five compartments. He was an artist of great talents, but died in 1640, in the flower of his life.

SPERLING, Jerome, a German engraver, born at Augsburg about 1693. He studied with John Justin Preisler, at Nuremberg. He engraved part of a set of plates of the churches of Vienna, published by J. A. Peffel in 1724; and part of the plates from the marble statues in the gallery of the king of Poland, published at Dresden in 1733. He also engraved some plates of portraits, chiefly after the German painters, and a set of thirteen allegorical subjects, representing the Twelve Months of the Year, with a frontispiece. He signed his plates *H.* (*Hieronymus*) *Sperling.* He died in 1777.

SPERLING, John Christian, a German painter, born at Halle in Saxony, in 1691. He was the son of John Henry Sperling, a painter of portraits and fancy subjects, who was born at Hamburg, but settled at Halle. He first studied with his father, and afterwards with Adrian vander Werf at Rotterdam, whose manner he adopted. He excelled in portraits, and painted the likenesses of many persons of rank and distinction. He also painted cabinet pictures of poetical and historical subjects, with considerable reputation. There are some of his pictures in the galleries at Dresden and Salzdahlum. His works are little known out of his own country. He died at Ansbach in 1746.

SPEY, Martin, a Flemish painter, born at Antwerp, in 1777. He painted portraits, and excelled in painting fruit, flowers, dead game, and other objects of still life. He went to Paris in 1809, where he resided till 1815, and gained considerable reputation. On the entrance of the allied army, he disappeared, and has not been heard of since.

SPEZZINI, Francesco, a painter who, according to Soprani, flourished at Genoa about 1578; others say that he died young, of the plague, in or about 1590. He first studied in his native city, under Luca Cambiasi, and next with Gio. Battista Castelli. He afterwards went to Rome, and improved himself by studying the works of Raffaelle, Michael Angelo, and other great masters. On his return to Genoa, he executed several works for the churches and public edifices, which gained him considerable applause. His best work is an altarpiece in the church of S. Colombano.

SPICER, Henry, an English painter, born about 1744. He painted portraits in miniature and enamel, and acquired considerable reputation and patronage. He died in 1804.

SPICER, an English mezzotint engraver, who flourished at London about 1760. He engraved some portraits after Reynolds and other English painters.

SPIEGL, Joseph, a German engraver, born at Vienna in 1772. He studied in the academy in that city, and executed a few plates in mezzotinto, among which are a Female bathing, *after Rubens;* a Holy Family, *after Sassoferrato;* the Mater Dolorosa, *after Guido;* Venus and Cupid, *after N. Poussin;* and Bacchus and Ariadne, *after G. Hamilton.*

SPIERRE, François, an eminent French engraver, born at Nancy in 1643. He went to Paris, and studied with Francis de Poilly, whose style he at first followed with great success. He afterwards went to Italy, where he resided several years, and changed his style, adopting a novel method of handling the graver, which produced a pleasing effect, much admired. He did not long survive his return to Paris, where he died in 1681. The following are his most esteemed prints:

PORTRAITS.

Pope Innocent XI.; engraved with single strokes, in the style of Mellan; *Franciscus Spier, del. et sculp.* The Grand Duke of Tuscany; dated 1659. Lorenzo, Count de Marsciano; *after his own design.*

SUBJECTS AFTER VARIOUS MASTERS.

The Virgin suckling the infant Christ; *after Correggio.* This fine print is very scarce. The first impressions are before the drapery was inserted to cover the nudity of the child. St. Michael combating the Evil Spirit; *after P. da Cortona.* The Conception of the Virgin; *do.* The Virgin and infant Jesus, with St. Catherine; *do.* The Circumcision; *after Ciro Ferri.* St. John preaching in the Wilderness; *after Bernini.* The Miracle of the Loaves and Fishes; *do.* Christ on the Cross, suspended over a sea of blood, which flows from his wounds; *do.;* executed with single strokes. The first impressions are before the heads of the cherubs were added at the top.

SPIERINGS, N., a Dutch painter, born at Antwerp in 1633. It is not known under whom he studied; nor is his baptismal name known, though Balkema calls him *Nicholas.* He went young to Italy, where he painted landscapes so much in the style of Salvator Rosa, that his works have sometimes been mistaken for those of that master. His style is agreeable, though bold and eccentric; his scenery is well chosen; the forms of his rocks and trees grand and picturesque; his coloring good, and his touch firm and spirited. He was not so successful in designing the figure, and his pictures are usually decorated with historical subjects by other artists. In returning to his own country, he passed through France, and resided some time at Paris, where his pictures were greatly admired, and he was employed by Louis XIV. to execute several works to adorn the royal palaces. On his return to Antwerp, he found abundant employment, till his death in 1691. Houbraken calls his name *Henry,* but he signed his pictures *N. Spierings.*

SPIERS, Albert van, a Dutch painter, born at Amsterdam in 1666. He studied with William van Inghen, in his native city, and then went to Rome, where he resided some years, diligently studying the works of Raffaelle, and other great masters. He next proceeded to Venice to improve his coloring by studying in the Venetian school. In 1697, after a residence of ten years in Italy, he returned to Amsterdam, where he acquired great distinction, and was regarded one of the ablest artists of his time. He painted both in oil and fresco, and was much employed in decorating the ceilings and mansions of the nobility and gentry with poetical and historical subjects, which were greatly admired. His compositions are ingenious and abundant, his design correct, and his coloring rich and harmonious; his design partakes more of the Roman, and his coloring of the Venetian, than of the Dutch school. He had acquired a brilliant reputation, when he fell a victim to an assiduous application to his profession, in 1718.

SPILBERG, John, a German painter, born at Dusseldorf in 1619. He was the son of a glass painter, who was employed in the service of the Duke of Wolfgang. He early showed great talents, and his father instructed him in the rudiments of the art, with the intention to send him to Antwerp to study in the school of Rubens, for which purpose the Duke furnished him with a letter, commending him to the particular care of that great master. As he was on the eve of his departure, news came of the death of the head of the Flemish school, and he was sent to Amsterdam to study with Govaert Flinck. He prosecuted his studies under that able master with untiring assiduity for seven years, and on leaving his school, he soon distinguished himself as a painter of history and portraits. After acquiring a high reputation at Amsterdam, he was invited to Dusseldorf by the Elector Palatine, who appointed him his court painter, with a liberal pension. He painted the portraits of the Elector and his family, and of the distinguished personages of the court, and the Elector presented him with a gold medal and chain in token of his approbation. He executed several altar-pieces and other works for the churches, and a series of twelve pictures representing the Labors of Hercules, for the Castle of Dusseldorf, in which he discovered great fertility and originality of invention, and a commanding facility of execution. In these works the figures were of life size. At the same place he painted an allegorical picture representing the Alliance of Music and Poetry, designed and executed with judgment and taste. He was commissioned by the Elector to paint a series of pictures from the Life of Christ, but he did not live to complete them. His pictures are correctly designed, his coloring is rich and harmonious, and he wrought with a bold and free pencil. He died in 1690.

SPILBERG, Adriana. This lady was the daughter of the preceding, born at Amsterdam in 1646. She was instructed by her father, and excelled in painting portraits in crayons, though she sometimes painted in oil. These works were much esteemed for the correctness of her likenesses, the neatness and delicacy of her handling, and her lively and natural tone of coloring. She was most patronized at the court of Dusseldorf, where she was respected and beloved. She married Eglon H. vander Neer, an eminent artist of Amsterdam, then in the employment of the Elector Palatine.

SPILIMBERGO, Irene di, a paintress of the Venetian school, born at Spilimbergo. She flourished, according to Ridolfi, about 1550; Vasari says she died a short time before 1576. She was of a noble house, and is believed to have received instruction from Titian, who painted her portrait, and was familiar with her family. She practiced only for amusement, yet she is said to have applied herself to study with the enthusiasm of a professor. Her works are very rare. Lanzi mentions three pictures of sacred subjects by her, preserved by the noble family of Maniago, and a Bacchanal, at Monte Albodo, in the possession of the Claudi family; he says, "they display but little skill in design, though they are colored with a degree of masterly power not unworthy of the first artists of that happy period."

SPILMAN, Henry, a Dutch painter and engraver, born at Amsterdam, according to Nagler, in 1721, and to others, at the Hague, about 1738. Some of his prints, however, were published in 1745, and one after van Goyen, is said to be dated 1732. He painted portraits and landscapes with some reputation. He also engraved a few portraits and landscapes from his own designs and after other masters. Huber says he engraved three landscapes in the style of drawings in bistre, after Everdingen, van Borsum, and Berghem.

SPILSBURY, Inigo, an English designer and engraver, born about 1730. After acquiring a knowledge of the art, he established himself as a print-seller at London, and drew successively the first prize from the Society for the Encouragement of Arts, &c., in the years 1761 and 1762. He engraved several plates in mezzotinto, and in the dotted style; particularly a collection of gems in the latter manner. His plates are very numerous; among them are the following:

PORTRAITS AND HEADS.

A set of fourteen Heads and Busts; in the manner of *Rembrandt.* 1767 and 1768. George III. when Prince of Wales. 1759. Queen Charlotte. 1764. Christian VII. King of Denmark; *after Fesché.* 1769. Inigo Jones; *after Vandyck.* Lady Mary Leslie decorating a Lamb with Flowers; *after Reynolds.* A young Lady holding a Bouquet of Flowers; *do.* Frederick Howard, Earl of Carlisle; *do.*

SUBJECTS AFTER VARIOUS MASTERS.

A Boy eating Grapes; *after Rubens.* Two Monks reading; *do.* Abraham sending away Hagar; *after Rembrandt.* The Flight into Egypt; *after Murillo.* The Crucifixion; *do.*

SPINEDA, Ascanio, a painter born, according to Federici, at Trevigi, in 1588. He was of a noble family, and is included among the disciples of Jacopo Palma, called Il Giovine, whose style he followed so closely, that Lanzi says it is sometimes difficult to distinguish their respective performances. "His works abound at Trevigi; no artist of his district surpassed him in the number of his pieces in public, if we except indeed Bartolomeo Orioli. He was one of the most exact (of the artists of Trevigi), in point of design; he also colored with much sweetness and grace of tints." He is little known out of his own city, though Lanzi says his works are found in many churches at Trevigi and its vicinity, which display talents that entitle him to more consideration. He was living, according to Ridolfi, in 1648.

SPINELLO, Aretino, an old painter, born at Arezzo in 1308. He studied under Jacopo del Casentino, a disciple of Taddeo Gaddi. He was one of the most distinguished fresco painters of his time, and his fame spread throughout Italy. He excelled in portraits, and had the honor of painting those of Popes Innocent IV., and Gregory IX. In the Sacristy of S. Miniato at Florence, are still remaining several pictures by him of the life of S. Benedetto, which are among his best preserved works. He was employed in conjunction with the first artists of his time, in decorating the Campo Santo at Pisa, with historical paintings, and his pictures there, of the Martyrdom of St. Petito and St. Epiro, are ranked by Vasari as his best performances. Lanzi says he was inferior there to his competitors, both in design and coloring, and that his green and dark tints are too predominant. Others however, say that he was equal to Giotto in design, and surpassed him in the force and beauty of his coloring. Though his design was stiff and formal, as was usual at the time, he gave great force and expression to his figures. His picture of the Fall of the Rebel Angels still remains at Arezzo, in which he represented Lucifer so terrible, that it afterwards haunted him in his dreams, deranging both his body and mind, and hastening his death, which happened, according to Bottari, Lanzi, and others, in 1400, at the age of 92. As if this story were not improbable enough, some say that he executed this painting in conjunction with his son Parri in 1407, and that he represented the devil so hideous, that his satanic majesty appeared to him, and fiercely demanded satisfaction for the foul injustice done him, frightening the terror-struck artist into convulsions, of which he died!

SPINELLO, or SPINELLI, Parri (for Gasparri), was the son of the preceding, born at Arezzo in 1356. He first studied with his father, and afterwards with Lorenzo Ghiberti. Lanzi says he excelled in the art of coloring, but he was barbarous in the drawing of his figures, which he made extravagantly long and bending, in order, as used to say, to give them greater spirit. There are some of his works still preserved in the church of S. Domenico at Florence. Lanzi says he was the first to introduce the art of painting on glass for the windows of churches at Arezzo. There are notices of him as late as 1425.

SPINELLO, Forzore, another son of Aretino S., was a very eminent worker in niello, a species of engraved work on silver, filled up with a compound of silver and lead, called by the ancients *nigellum*, contracted by the Italians into *niello*. This substance being incorporated with the silver, and the whole being polished, produced the effect of shadow, which, contrasted with the clearness of the silver, gave the entire work the appearance of a chiaro-scuro in silver. Various things were ornamented in this way, as caskets, sword and dagger hilts, images, and particularly *paxes*, or images of Christ on the cross, which the people used to kiss after service, called the kiss of peace. Some of these works were executed with wonderful neatness and precision, representing flowers, portraits, and even historical subjects, and gained for the artist, called *Niellatore*, a high reputation. The art is very ancient, and was much practiced by the old Italian goldsmiths. See *Matteo Dei* and *Maso Finiguerra*.

SPINTHARUS, an eminent ancient architect of Corinth, who flourished about B. C. 550. The only work by his hand, was the temple of Apollo at Delphi. This magnificent edifice, originally erected by Trophonius and Agamedes, was destroyed by fire, and afterwards rebuilt by Spintharus.

SPIRINX, L., a Dutch engraver of little note, probably a relative of the preceding, who executed in an indifferent style, some frontispieces, portraits, and other book plates, which bear date from about 1641 to 1674.

SPIRITO, Monsieur, a French painter, briefly mentioned by Lanzi, as a portrait painter, who was employed by the court at Turin in the latter part of the 17th century. He is also commended for the excellence of his portraits in the *Pitture d'Italia*.

SPISANO, Vincenzo, called also Pisanelli and Lo Spisanelli, a painter born at Orta, in the Milanese territory, in 1595. According to Malvasia, he was brought up in the school of Denis Calvart, whose style he adopted, and followed without variations. Lanzi says, "he laid down for himself the maxim, never to alter with any other styles, that of Calvart. He however is inferior to that master in solidity and truth of design, and displays quite as much caprice and mannerism as any of the practitioners of his time; nor does he always preserve the colors of his school, but deadens them with a leaden hue, which is still not unpleasing. His altar-pieces executed for the churches at Bologna and in the neighboring cities, are less celebrated than his small pictures for private ornament, which abound at Bologna, and which he enlivened with very attractive landscapes." His best works at Bologna are the Death of St. Joseph in S. Maria Maggiore; the Visitation of the Virgin to St. Elizabeth, in S. Giacomo Maggiore; the Baptism of Christ in S. Francesco; and the Conversion of St. Paul in S. Domenico. He died in 1662.

SPOFFORTH, Robert, an English engraver and printseller, who flourished about 1707. He engraved a few portraits, among which are those of Queen Anne and George I.

SPOLETTI, Pietro Lorenzo, a painter born, according to the Cav. Ratti, at Finale, in the Genoese territory, in 1680. He was a scholar of the Cav. Claudio Beaumont, whose style he followed with considerable success. He died in 1726.

SPOLVERINI, Ilario, a painter born at Parma in 1657. Orlandi says that he was a scholar of Francesco Monti, and educated at Florence upon the model of Borgognone. He painted history, but chiefly acquired his reputation from his battle-pieces, in which Lanzi says he was not less eminent than Monti. He delighted in depicting battles, skirmishes of cavalry, attacks of bandits and assassins, which he designed with spirit and touched with a vehemence of pencil well adapted to the subjects. It is said that while the soldiers of Monti threatened, those of Spolverini seemed to kill. He was much employed by the Duke Francesco, for whom he executed many works, though he painted some large pictures both in oil and fresco for the cathedral, the Certosa, and other churches in Parma, and throughout the state. He died in 1734.

SPOOR, W. J. L., a painter born at Budel, in North Brabant. He studied under Henry Antonissen at Antwerp, whose style he followed for some time. He afterwards chiefly employed himself in copying and imitating the works of Paul Potter and other great landscape and animal painters of the Dutch school, which he did with considerable success. He also painted some original subjects in which he faithfully represented nature. There were some of his pictures, both copies and originals, in the collection of Prince William at the Hague. He flourished in the latter part of the last, and first part of the present century.

SPRANGHER, Bartholomew, an eminent Flemish painter, born at Antwerp in 1546. He was the son of Joachim Sprangher, an eminent merchant of that city, who intended to bring him up to commercial pursuits, but finding in Bartholomew a decided inclination for painting, he placed him under the instruction of John Madyn at Haerlem, with whom he continued about eighteen months, till the death of that master, when he became the pupil of Francis Mostaert. He is also said to have received instructions from van Dalen and other masters of his country. He afterwards went to Paris, and next to Parma, where he studied three years with Bernardino Gatti, called Il Sojaro, who had been a disciple of Correggio. From Parma he went to Rome, where he was favored with the patronage of the Cardinal Farnese, who employed him in decorating his villa of Caprarola, with several landscapes painted in fresco. The Cardinal also recommended him to Pius V., who appointed him his painter, and accommodated him with apartments in the Palazzo Belvidere—a high compliment. His first work for the Pope was a picture of the Last Judgment, executed on a copper plate six feet high, and containing above five hundred figures, which occupied him three years, and was so highly esteemed, that after the death of that pontiff, it was placed over his tomb. He was commissioned by the Pope to paint twelve pictures of the passion of Christ, which he did not accomplish before the death of his holiness. In 1575 he was invited to the court of Vienna by the Emperor Maximilian II., who appointed him his principal painter. That monarch dying the following year, he was continued in his office by his successor, Rodolphus II., who employed him to paint several considerable works, both at Vienna and Prague. Spranghe was greatly respected by the Emperor Rodolphus, not only for his abilities as a painter, but for his extensive literary acquirements, and great conversational powers. In 1588, that monarch ennobled him and his descendants, and honored him by placing round his neck with his own hands, a gold medal and chain.

With all his talents and advantages, Spranghe did not arrive at any great excellence in art, because he pursued a false system. His great success was owing more to several lucky circumstances, and his own pleasing address, than to his merits as a painter. He totally neglected the study of nature, and does not seem to have profited much by a residence of several years in Italy; it is very doubtful whether he ever made a single design from the antique or the great Italian masters, but contented himself with a superficial observance of those great models, and depended upon his memory for a retention of their beauties. His design has little of the dignity and elegance of the Roman school, his contours are constrained and unnatural, his outline hard, stiff, and ungraceful, his attitudes are affected, the extremities of his figures contorted, and his general style mannered. He had however, a lively and inventive imagination, and an alluring facility of execution, an extraordinary lightness of hand, and great sweetness of pencil, which always procured him many admirers. His later productions have fewer extravagances, and a more natural tone of color. Nagler attributes six etchings to him, from his own designs. They are executed in a slight, but agreeable style. He died at Prague in 1623.

SPRIETT, John vander, a Dutch mezzotinto engraver of little note. He studied under Verkolie at Amsterdam, and executed a few indifferent portraits. He went to London, where he died about 1700.

HSK SPRINGINKLEE, Hans. The only information respecting this artist, is derived from Doppelmayr, who states that he lived in the house of Albert Durer, from whom he learned the art of design and engraving, and that he died about 1540. He was formerly ranked among the wood engravers, and certain cuts marked with the above monogram, were attributed to him. Bartsch describes sixty-one of these cuts, to be found in a work entitled "Hortulus animæ cum horis beatæ Virginis," &c., published at Nuremberg in 1518, and afterwards in 1519 and 1520. Bartsch, Zani, and others, are of opinion that he only made the designs, and that the cuts were executed by another hand, as they are too indifferently executed for a pupil of Albert Durer. It has been conjectured that he was a painter, but no pictures by him are known, and all that can be affirmed is, that he was a cotemporary with Durer, and disgraced the subjects which bear his monogram.

SPRONG, Gerard, a Dutch painter, born at Haerlem, according to Balkema, in 1600, and died there in 1651; though others say he was living in 1661. He excelled in portraits; there is a half-length portrait of a lady by him in the gallery of the Louvre.

SPRUYT, Peter, a Flemish painter and engraver, born at Antwerp about 1740, and died, according to Nagler, about 1790. There is a singular paucity of information respecting him, for he must have been an artist of some distinction, as he was director of the Academy at Ghent, where he appears to have settled. Nagler describes thirteen etchings by him, after Rubens, Teniers, and van Goyen. Several of these are signed *E. P. Spruyt*, so that even his christian name is not certainly known.

SQUARCIONE, Francesco, an eminent painter, born at Padua in 1394. He was more celebrated as the founder of the most distinguished academy of his time, and for his excellent system of instruction, than for his works as a painter. After acquiring a high reputation and abundant employment at Florence and other cities, his desire to cultivate the art of painting in the most effectual manner, induced him to forego these advantages, and travel throughout Italy and Greece to design the most interesting vestiges of antiquity. On returning to his native place, he began to form a Museum, which proved the richest of any known at that period, not merely in designs, but in statues, torsos, bassi-relievi, and funeral urns. Here he opened a school which at one time was frequented by upwards of one hundred and thirty students from all parts of Italy, and such was his success in communicating instruction, and the paternal regard he had for his pupils, that he acquired the venerable name of *the Father of the young painters*. Thus devoting himself to the instruction of students, he continued to live in comparative affluence, and divided many of the commissions he received among his different pupils. Such was the respect entertained for him, that he was frequently visited by popes, sovereigns, princes, and cardinals. Of his productions as a painter, little remains. Lanzi notices a picture by him, formerly in the church of the Carmelites at Padua, afterwards in the possession of the Conte Cav. de' Lazara. It is executed in different compartments, the chief place being occupied by the figure of St. Girolamo, surrounded by several other saints. The work has been retouched in parts, yet sufficient of the original remains to establish the character of the painter. "Rich in coloring, in expression, and, above all, in perspective, it may be pronounced one of the best specimens of the art produced in those parts." This picture was executed for the noble family of the Lazara, of which the original contract is still preserved, dated 1449. It is signed *Francesco Squarcione*, 1452, thus correcting Vasari, who called his name *Jacopo*, an error repeated by many writers. Lanzi says, "in the church of the Misericordia at Padua, is preserved a book of anthems, illustrated with very beautiful miniatures, commonly ascribed to Andrea Mantegna, the ornament of the Lombard school; but so great is the variety of the different styles, that the most competent judges conclude it to be one of the works committed to Squarcione, and by him distributed among his disciples. Of these we are not yet prepared to treat, but the chief part of them are known to have flourished subsequent to the introduction of oil painting. Though little can be said of the productions of Squarcione as a painter, great respect is due to his labors as a master. Indeed he may be considered the tree, as it were, whose branches we trace through Andrea Mantegna in the great school of Lombardy; through Marco Zoppo in the Bolognese; while it extended some degree of influence over that of Venice itself, for Jacopo Bellini, having come to exercise his talents in Padua, it appears that he took Squarcione for his model." Rosini has given an outline of the above named picture of St. Girolamo, and another of a Madonna and Infant, in the same collection, in his "Storia della Pittura Italiana," which gives a good idea of his excellence in design. Zani strongly inclines to the belief that he also engraved. He died in 1474. See *Andrea Mantegna.*

STABEN, Henry, a Flemish painter, born at Antwerp in 1578. After learning the rudiments of the art in his native city, he went quite young to Italy, and entered the school of Tintoretto at Venice. He had not, however, the advantage of the instruction of that able master for any length of time, as he died before Staben was seventeen years old, nor is it known that he studied with any other painter. It is supposed also that he did not remain long in Italy, as he early established himself at Paris, where he acquired considerable reputation for his small pictures of interiors, decorated with figures, executed with great neatness and precision. His pictures are well composed, correctly designed, agreeably colored, and highly finished, more in the style of the Flemish, than the Italian school. One of his best performances was a picture representing the interior of the gallery of a Virtuoso, decorated with pictures and statues, in which he displayed an intelligent acquaintance with perspective. Above are several pictures of different subjects, arranged in regular order, every object being exquisitely finished, and placed in such exact perspective, that they produce a very agreeable deception. This work was formerly in the collection of Count de Morny, but is now in England. Stanley says it is a picture that would be an ornament to the richest collection of the Dutch and Flemish masters. He died in 1658.

STAEVAERTS, or STEVERS, Anthony Palamedes, a Dutch painter, born at Delft in 1604. He painted portraits; but was more frequently employed in painting conversation pieces, card and musical parties, &c. He executed many works, little distinguished for correctness of design, or judgment in composition. He died in 1680.

STAEVAERTS, or STEVERS, Palamedes, a painter of the Dutch school, the younger brother of the preceding, and the son of a Dutch engraver on precious stones, who was employed by James I. at London, where Palamedes was born, in 1607. He was taken to Delft while very young. After acquiring a knowledge of the elements of art, he gained considerable improvement by studying the works of Esaias Vandervelde, adopting his clear and transparent coloring, and excelled in painting similar subjects, representing battles and skirmishes, attacks of robbers, the plundering of villages, &c. His works are distinguished for ingenious composition and remarkable transparency of coloring, the figures and horses are spiritedly designed, and touched with a free and firm pencil. Staevaerts rose to a distinguished rank among the artists of his native country, and his works were highly esteemed; but he died in the prime of life in 1638.

STAINES, Robert, an English engraver, born at London in 1805. He studied under J. C. Edwards, and also with the Messrs. Finden. He wrought chiefly for the booksellers, and executed a number of good plates for the Annuals of the day, after Richter, Westall, etc. Two of his best plates, however, are "Sancho and the Duchess," and "Malvolio," which he executed in 1849 for the London Art Journal, from pictures in the Vernon Gallery. He died in 1849.

STALBENT, Adrian van, a Flemish painter and engraver, born at Antwerp in 1580. It is not known under whom he studied, but he painted landscapes decorated with small figures, in which he imitated Velvet Breughel. His scenes are well chosen, frequently solemn, his figures are well designed and touched with a free, delicate, and spirited pencil, his trees are well formed, and his coloring clear and natural, though his verdure is sometimes a little too green. According to Lord Orford, who calls his name *Stalband,* this artist visited England in the reign of Charles I., for whom he painted several pictures, among which was a View of Greenwich, and returned to Antwerp liberally rewarded. He also painted interiors, decorated with historical subjects in small. Some of his earlier performances resemble the manner of old Franck, for which reason some suppose that he was a pupil of that master. Vandyck painted his portrait among the eminent artists of his country, of which there is an engraving by Pontius. He also etched a few subjects. He signed his pictures A. V. STALBEMT, in Roman capitals, the letters A and V being joined together, and he signed his etchings *Adrianus van Stalbant.* Most writers call him *Stalbent.* He died at Antwerp in 1660.

STALBENT, John. This artist was a cotemporary, and perhaps a relative of the preceding. He is said to have painted landscapes in the manner of Peter Breughel the elder, which has caused some confusion in the accounts of both. Little is known of him or his works.

STAMPART, Francis, a Flemish portrait painter, born at Antwerp in 1675. He studied under the younger Tyssens, whose style he followed, though he improved by studying from nature and the works of Vandyck. He had acquired considerable reputation as a portrait painter in his native city, when he was invited to Vienna by the Emperor Leopold, who appointed him his principal painter, which office he held under his successor Charles VI. He there found abundant employment. As he was much employed in painting persons of distinction, who had neither the leisure nor patience, to undergo the tedium of the usual process of sitting, he was accustomed to sketch the features with white, black, and red crayons, which was soon executed, and then he worked on the portrait with color at his leisure and finished it at a single sitting. Another custom of his was to lay upon the canvass patches of flesh color, in proper places, which contributed to lessen his labor, and to assist him in getting the right tints. If we can form any correct opinion of his merits from this singular method of operating, we may safely conclude that his works have little of that air of life and nature which distinguish the portraits of his instructor. He died at Vienna in 1750.

STANZIONI, Cav. Massimo, an eminent painter, born at Naples in 1585. He first studied with Gio. Battista Caraccioli, a follower of Ann. Caracci, whose style is discernible in all his works; but he derived his best instruction in fresco painting from Belisario Corenzio, one of the ablest fresco painters of his time. When Lanfranco visited Naples, he profited by his instruction, and in one of his MS., he calls him his master. He also took lessons of Fabrizio Santafede in portrait painting, whose principles he adopted in that branch, and attained, says Lanzi, "an excellent Titianesque style." He next went to Rome, where he applied himself particularly to the study of the works of Annibale Caracci, and having formed an intimacy with Guido Reni, he became ambitious of imitating the design of the first, with the coloring of the second, in which he was so successful, according to Galanti, that he attained the appellation of *Guido Reni di Napoli.* On his return to Naples his talents enabled him to compete with the ablest of his cotemporaries, and to excite their jealousy. He painted in the Certosa a Dead Christ surrounded by the Marys, in competition with Giuseppe Ribera, which excited the envy and animosity of the latter to such an extent that, having persuaded the monks to allow him to clean it, as the picture had become somewhat obscure, he purposely applied a corrosive liquid which destroyed the beauty of the work. The Fathers applied to Stanzioni to restore it, which he positively refused to do, declaring that such an act of perfidy and malice ought to be perpetuated to public indignation. In the same edifice, which is a Museum of Art, in which the most distinguished masters successively vied to surpass each other, Massimo left several admirable works, particularly a stupendous altar-piece, representing St. Bruno presenting to his brethren the rules of his Order. He executed many works for the churches and public edifices of Naples, both in oil and fresco. The vaults of the Gesu Nuovo, and of S. Paolo, entitle him to a place among the most distinguished fresco painters. He painted many easel pictures for the collections, which are highly esteemed. The school of Massimo produced many celebrated scholars, his method and high reputation confirming the ancient proverb, *primus discendi ardor nobilitas est magistri* (the example of the master is the greatest incentive to improvement.)—Stanzioni was highly respected by the King, who, among other marks of his favor, conferred upon him the honor of knighthood. Lanzi says "he studied perfection during his celibacy, and finished his paintings very highly, but afterwards, marrying a woman of rank, in order to maintain her in an expensive style of living, he painted many hasty and inferior pictures; therefore it was not without reason that Cocchi took occasion to warn all artists against the perils of the wedded state." He died in 1656.

STAREN, or STERN, Dirk or Theodore van, a Dutch engraver, about whom there is much discrepancy. Like many of the old engravers, little is known of him except by his works. His prints are said to be numerous, and dated from about 1520 to 1550. But Bartsch has described only nineteen; a few others are mentioned by other writers, though doubtless some of them are the same as those given by Bartsch, under another name. Most of them are copper plates of small size, hence he is classed with the *little masters.* Only one wood cut, mentioned by Ottley, is known by him. Some of these are marked simply with his initials, and others with the same with a star between them, and the date sometimes on a tablet. There are other similar prints, bearing similar marks, except that a bird or starling is substituted for the star, which are generally attributed to him, but some give them to *Dirk Verster*, an artist unknown in the history of art. The following are the titles and dates given by Bartsch, P. G. tom. viii.:

1. Eve and the little Cain, 1522, *A. G.* (*Augusti*) 19. 2. The Deluge (L. 14 *p.* 6 *l.*; H. 10 *p.* 5 *l.*) 1544. 3. Christ calling Peter and Andrew, 1523, *Mey* 30. 4. St. Peter walking on the Water, 1525, *Des.* 30. 5. Christ tempted by the Demon, 1525, *D*V. April* II. 6. Christ and the Woman of Samaria, 1523. 7. The Virgin and St. Anne, 1522, *D. C.* (*Decembris*) 31. 8. St. Bernard, 1524, *Oct.* 3. 9. St. Luke painting the Portrait of the Virgin, 1526, *In Juli*, 28. 10. St. Elisabeth, 1524, *Nove.* 15. 11. Venus, 1524, *Oct.* 20. 12. The Faun, 1522, *Sept.* 14. 13. The Man with a chimerical Fish, 1522, *A. G.* (*Augusti*) 16. 14. The Goldsmith, *no date.* 15. The Man asleep, 1532, *Oct.* 10. 16. The Drunken Drummer, 1525, *Mert.* 8. 17. The Drummer and a Child, 1523, *Oct.* 14. 18. The Man holding a Shield, with armorial bearings, 1522. 19. The Woman holding an Escutcheon, of lozenge form, 1525.

FROM OTTLEY'S CATALOGUE NOT MENTIONED BY BARTSCH

20. St. Christopher, date not mentioned. 21. A wood cut of an Interior, with a Gallery, and numerous Figures The mark near the middle, 1526 on the left.

STARNINA, Gherardo, an old painter born at Florence in 1354. He was a disciple of Antonio Veneziano, and painted history in the dry, stiff style, which prevailed at that early period, though he improved over the immediate followers of Giotto. Vasari says that he was invited to the court of Spain, where he executed several grand pictures for the King, who liberally rewarded him, and loaded him with presents. Few of his works have escaped the ravages of time. There is a picture by him in the church of S. Croce at Florence, representing the dying St. Jerome exhorting his disciples, some of whom are listening to his discourse, others writing down his precepts. Another picture by him is a Descent from the Cross, of which Rosini has given an etching by Gatti, which proves him to have been an able designer. Lanzi says he painted in a gay style, and that his works are among the last efforts of the school of Giotto, which succeeding artists abandoned to adopt a better manner. The time of his death is not exactly known; it is generally placed in 1403, but it is certain that he was living in 1406, and Zani says he died in 1415.

STARRENBERG, John, a Dutch painter, who was born, according to Descamps, at Groningen, where he flourished from about 1650 to 1670. He painted in fresco, and executed some considerable historical works, chiefly on ceilings, which were well composed, and executed with facility.

STAVEREN, John Adrian van, a Dutch painter who flourished from about 1660 to 1680. He was a close imitator of Gerard Douw, and is supposed to have been his pupil. He chiefly excelled in painting subjects representing a saint or hermit contemplating a skull, reading a book, or at his devotions. The scene is generally a grotto, in a wild locality, and he usually introduced the trunk of an old tree, covered with ivy or moss. His execution is as elaborate as that of Douw, but his pencilling is not so soft and clear. There is one of his pictures in the Louvre, representing a Geographer in his Study. He is also said to have painted familiar scenes, conversations, and groups of family portraits; many such are attributed to him, but it is very doubtful whether they were executed by *the painter of hermits*, or another van Staveren, as none of the van Staverens appear to have signed their works with their christian names.

The Dutch writers mention three other van Staverens, Paul, Jacob, and E.; all of whom flourished about the same time with the preceding. Paul and E. are said to have studied with Douw, whose manner they followed. Jacob was a painter of fruit and flowers. Laborde mentions a mezzotinto print of a man counting money, a half-length, signed *P. Straverenus*, and asks *Que signifie ce nom?*

JS or JS or JS

STEEN, Jan, (James, not John, as frequently written), an eminent Dutch painter, born at Leyden in 1636. When we consider the great number and excellence of this master's works, which betray no want of diligence and care, it is impossible to credit the accounts given of his debauched and dissipated course of life. He was the son of a wealthy brewer at Leyden, who, perceiving his passion for painting, first placed him with Nicholas Knufer at Utrecht. Descamps, probably from similarity of subjects and character, asserts that he afterwards studied with Adrian Brower, and his account has been followed by Pilkington and others; but Brower died in 1640, when Jan Steen was only four years old. It seems very probable that he received instruction from John van Goyen, whose daughter he married, and who died in 1656, when Jan Steen was twenty years old. The rest of his life, if we are to believe his biographers, is soon told. His father, apprehending that he could not procure a comfortable subsistence by the exercise of his pencil, established him in his own business at Delft, where, instead of attending to his affairs, he gave himself up to dissipation, and soon squandered his means and ruined his establishment; his indulgent parent, after repeated attempts to reclaim him, was compelled to abandon him to his fate. He opened a tavern, which proved more calamitous than the former undertaking. He gave himself up entirely to reveling and intoxication, wrought only when his necessities compelled him, sold his pictures to satisfy his immediate wants, and often for the most paltry prices to escape arrest.

The pictures of Jan Steen usually represent merry-makings, and the frolics and festivities of the ale-house, which he treated with a characteristic expression of humorous drollery, that compensates for the vulgarity of his subjects. He sometimes painted interiors, domestic assemblies, conversations, mountebanks, &c., which he generally accompanied with some facetious trait of wit or humour, admirably rendered. Some of his works of this description are little inferior to the charming productions of Gabriel Metzu. His compositions are ingenious and interesting, his design is correct and spirited, his coloring chaste and clear, and his pencil free and decided. He also had a good knowledge of the chiaro-scuro, which enabled him to give his figures a fine relief. His works are invariably finished with care and diligence, and do not betray any haste or infirmity of hand or head. It is evident that, from some untoward circumstance, his works were not appreciated in his day, but after his death, they rose amazingly in value, and have continued to increase ever since,—a true test of a master's merit—till now they are scarcely to be found except in royal and noble collections and the public galleries of Europe. His pictures were, for a long time, scarcely known out of Holland, but now they are deservedly placed in the choicest collections. His works are very numerous, sufficient to have continually occupied the life time of not only a sober and industrious artist, but one possessing great facility of hand. Smith, in his Catalogue raisonné, vol. iv. and Supplement, gives a descriptive account of upwards of 300 genuine pictures by Steen, many of them compositions of numerous figures, and almost all of them executed with the greatest care. It cannot be believed that a man living in a state of continued dissipation and inebriety, could find time to produce so many admirable works, displaying, as they do, a deep study of human nature, and a great discrimination of character; or that the hand of an habitual drunkard could operate with such beauty and precision. Nor is it probable that a mind besotted by drink, and debased by low intercourse, could moralize so admirably as he has done on the evil consequences of intemperance and the indulgence of evil passions. Dr. Kügler, a judicious critic, thus sums up his character as an artist: "The works of Jan Steen imply a free and cheerful view of common life, and he treats it with a careless humour, such as seems to deal with all its daily occurrences, high and low, as a laughable masquerade and a mere scene of perverse absurdity. His treatment of the subjects differed essentially from that adopted by other artists. Frequently, indeed, they are the same jolly drinking parties, or the meetings of boors; but in other masters, the object is, for the most part, to depict a certain situation, either quiet or animated, whilst in Jan Steen is generally to be found action more or less developed, together with all the reciprocal relations and interests between the characters which spring from it. This is accompanied by great variety and force of individual expression, such as evinces the sharpest observation. He is almost the only artist in the Netherlands who has thus, with true genius, brought into full play all these elements of comedy. His technical execution suits his design; it is carefully finished, and notwithstanding the closest attention to minute details, it is as firm and correct as it is light and free." There is a single etching attributed to him, representing a woman seated, apparently in a drunken sleep, holding a small glass in her left hand, and a bottle in her right, with other figures in a chamber. It is signed *Pinxit J. Steen*, the J and S interlaced on the left, and on the right *H. Steen.* It is a poor affair, and is regarded spurious by the best judges. Jan Steen died in 1689.

STEEN, Francis vander, a Flemish painter and engraver, who flourished at Antwerp about 1604. Little is known of his works as a painter, but he distinguished himself by the plates he executed for the collection of prints known as the Teniers' Gallery. He was much employed by the Archduke Leopold, who assigned him a pension. He engraved quite a number of plates, besides those he executed for the Teniers' Gallery, among which are the following. A complete list of his works may be found in Nagler's Lexicon.

PORTRAITS.

Cornelius Cort, Engraver, of Antwerp. Theodore Coornhaert, Engraver, of Amsterdam. Andrew del Vaulx, Professor of the University of Louvain.

SUBJECTS AFTER VARIOUS MASTERS.

The Holy Family; *after Titian.* The Holy Family, called *La Madonna del Sacco; after A. del Sarto.* Michael Angelo's Dream; *after M. Angelo.* Soldiers playing at Cards; *after Manfredi.* The Martyrdom of the Eleven Thousand Virgins; from a drawing by *van Hoy*, after the picture by *Albert Durer*, in the imperial collection. Silenus drunk, supported by Satyrs and Bacchante; *after Vandyck.* (*Rubens?*) Cupid shaping his Bow; *after Correggio.* Jupiter and Io; *do.*; Ganymede; *do.*

1573 HVS STEENWYCK, Henry, the Elder, a Flemish painter, born at Steenwyck in 1550. He studied under John de Vries, an artist who excelled in perspective and architecture. Steenwyck painted similar subjects, but he far surpassed his instructor, and in neatness and accuracy, he has hardly been surpassed by succeeding artists. He settled at Antwerp, where he met with good encouragement. His pictures usually represent interiors of churches, and Gothic edifices, designed with surprising accuracy and precision. He frequently represented those superb edifices by torch-light, and by his perfect knowledge of the chiaro-scuro, he was enabled to produce a mysterious grandeur of effect, extremely picturesque. He did not succeed so well in his figures, and frequently employed other artists to insert them. His pictures are frequently decorated with figures by Franck. The time of his death is not exactly known; some say he died in 1603, and others that he was living in 1604. His name is also variously written *Steenwyck, Stenwyck*, and *Steinwyck.*

STEENWYCK, Henry, the Younger, the son of the preceding, was born at Antwerp in 1589. He was instructed by his father, and painted similar subjects, though he usually designed them on a larger scale. He acquired a high reputation, and lived in habits of intimacy with Vandyck, who painted his portrait among the distinguished artists of his country, which was engraved by Pontius. At the recommendation of Vandyck, Charles I. invited him to England, for whom he executed some of his choicest works, ten of which are described in the Catalogue of King James. He sometimes painted the backgrounds of Vandyck's pictures with ornamental architecture. He is said to have died in London, at what time is not known. There is a picture by him in the Museum at Berlin, dated 1642.

STEENWYCK, or STEINWYCK, Nicholas, a Dutch painter, born at Breda, according to Descamps, in 1640. He excelled in painting vases, musical instruments, books, and other objects of still life, which he composed in a pleasing manner and represented with great truth and precision. He also painted fish, dead game, &c., in an admirable style. He wrought with a bold, free pencil, yet his pictures are well finished.

STEFANESCHI, Giovanni Battista, a painter born at Ronta, in the Florentine state, in 1582. He was a monk, and is generally called *l'Eremita di Monte Senario.* Having a taste for painting, he studied with Andrea Comodi, and afterwards with Pietro da Cortona; he became an excellent miniature painter, and was very conspicuous among the portrait painters and copyists of his time. He was much employed by the Grand Duke Ferdinand II. in copying in small, some of the works of the great Italian masters, as Raffaelle, Correggio, Titian, and Andrea del Sarto. His coloring was lovely, his touch delicate, and his chiaro-scuro excellent. He died in 1651.

STEFANI, Tommaso de, an old painter, born at Naples about 1230. Dominici, in his Lives of the Neapolitan Painters, attempts to show that the art was practiced at Naples long before the time of Cimabue, even in the Dark Ages, and that this artist was equal, if not superior to Cimabue; but he signally fails to prove it, and his works will not bear him out in his assertions. Marco da Siena, who is the father of the history of painting in Naples, declares that, in respect to grandeur of composition, Cimabue was entitled to the preference. He however acquired great distinction in his time, and enjoyed the favor of King Charles of Anjou, and of Charles II., who employed him at Naples, as did also the principal personages of the city. He formed his style by studying the remains of Grecian art which had been preserved in the churches and public edifices. He had painted several pictures for the churches of S. Francesco and S. Maria della Grazie previous to 1260, at which time he was employed by the Archbishop of Naples to decorate the chapel of his palace with several pictures of the Passion of our Saviour. Several of his works still remain, which are particularly described by Dominici. He died in 1310.

STEFANI, Pietro de', the oldest sculptor of the Neapolitan school, and brother of the preceding, was born at Naples about 1228. He was frequently employed by Charles of Anjou and his son Charles II. He acquired some reputation as a painter, but was more celebrated as a sculptor. Among his principal works, are still preserved in the archiepiscopal palace, the tombs of Pope Innocent IV., and the Archbishop Filippo 'Minutolo. Stefani died about 1310.

STEFANI, Benedetto, an Italian engraver and printseller, who flourished at Verona about 1575. Little is known of him or his works. There is a print by him representing the battle of the Lapithæ, copied from Marc' Antonio. The style of engraving resembles that of Æneas Vico.

STEFANINI, Giovanni, an Italian engraver and perhaps painter, who flourished at Florence about 1760. There is an etching by him, representing the Purification of the Virgin, *after Bartholomew Sprangher.*

STEFANO, called Il Fiorentino, an old Florentine painter, born in 1301. He was the grandson and disciple of Giotto, whom, according to Vasari, he greatly excelled in every department of art. He was the first artist who attempted to show the naked under his draperies, which were loose, easy, and delicate. He established the rules of perspective, little known at that early period, on more regular principles. He was the first to attempt the difficult task of foreshortening. He also succeeded better than any of his cotemporaries in giving expression to his heads, and a less Gothic turn to the attitudes of his figures. He acquired a high reputation, and executed many works for the churches and public edifices at Florence, Rome, and other places, all of which have perished, according to Lanzi, except a picture of the Virgin and Infant in the Campo Santo at Pisa. He died in 1350.

STEFANO, Tommaso, was the son and scholar of the preceding, born at Florence in 1324. According to Vasari, he adhered so closely to the style of Giotto, that his fellow citizens called him *Il Giottino*, and used to say that the soul of Giotto had transmigrated and animated him. There are some frescos by him still remaining at Assisi, and a picture of the dead Christ with the Virgin and St. John, in the church of S. Remigio at Florence. He died at Florence in the flower of his life, in 1356.

STEFANO, Niccolo di, a painter born at Belluno, who flourished about 1530. He was an imitator, and perhaps a disciple of Titian. Lanzi says, "Niccolo di Stefano, a cotemporary with the Vecelli (the family of Titian), was a painter deserving commendation, no less for his having competed with the family of Titian, than for the reputation he acquired by such competition. His rivals among the Vecelli, were Francesco, the brother, and Orazio, the son of Titian, who approached him pretty nearly in point of style."

STEFANO, da Verona, or da Zevio, an old painter, who flourished at Verona about the commencement of the 15th century. There is a good deal of uncertainty and contradiction about him, though he was an eminent artist in his time. He studied with Angiolo Gaddi at Florence. Lanzi says that Vasari sometimes calls him Stefano da Verona, and at others, Stefano da Zevio, a territory adjacent to the former; he is also of opinion that the artist mentioned by Vasari under the name of *Sebeto*, must be the same as Stefano da Verona. He says, "Vasari makes honorable mention of him in several places, exalting him above the best disciples of Angiolo Gaddi, to whose style (judging from what I have myself observed of his works at San Fermo and elsewhere), he added a certain dignity and beauty of form, while such was his excellence in fresco, that Donatello extols him beyond any of the artists who were then known in those parts for similar compositions. Del Pozzo brings his labors down as late as 1463; an incredible assertion, as applied to a scholar of Gaddi (who was born in 1324, and died in 1387, though to this period might perhaps be referred Vincenzio di Stefano, apparently one of his sons, of whom nothing survives but his name, and the tradition of his having conferred the first lessons of the art upon Liberale da Verona."

STEFANONE, Maestro, a Neapolitan painter, who was born, according to Dominici, at Naples about 1325, and studied with Gennaro di Cola, in conjunction with whom he painted some grand frescos for the church of S. Restituta. He also says he painted in oil, and cites a beautiful picture still preserved in the church of S. Maria della Pietà, representing the Virgin Mary and Mary Magdalen weeping over the dead Christ. From this, and similar statements, authors have attempted to prove that oil painting was practiced in Italy before the time of the van Eycks. Lanzi, however, throwing aside all national pride, cites abundance of evidence to prove that all claims set up by the Italians to the invention of painting *pictures in oil*, are unfounded. Lanzi says also that Stefanone studied under *Maestro Simone*, and that Cola was his fellow pupil, which is the more probable, as they were nearly of the same age, and wrought much together. On the death of Simone they executed in conjunction, several large pictures in fresco, from the life of S. Lodovico, in the church of S. Giovanni da Carbonara, which had only been commenced by Simone when he died. They also painted in the same edifice some histories of the Virgin, which were preserved for a long time. The styles of Cola and Stefanone were very similar, and Lanzi says, "notwithstanding the similarity of their styles, we may perceive a difference in the genius of these two artists; Cola was more studied and correct, anxious to overcome all difficulties, and to elevate the art, on which account he appears occasionally somewhat mannered. Stefanone discovers more genius, more confidence, and a greater freedom of pencil, and he gave a spirit to his figures that might have assured him a distinguished place, if he had been born at a more advanced period of art." Stefanone died about 1390. See *Gennaro di Cola* and *John van Eyck*.

STEFANONI, Giacomo Antonio, a painter and engraver, who flourished at Bologna about 1630. Little is known of him as a painter, but he executed quite a number of spirited etchings, among which are the following:

The Virgin, with the Infant Christ, St. John, and two Angels; *after Lod. Caracci.* The Holy Family, with St. John; *after An. Caracci.* 1632. Another Holy Family, with St. John presenting Cherries; *do.* The Virgin and infant Christ, with St. John; *after Agos. Caracci.* The Murder of the Innocents; *after Guido.* The Martyrdom of St. Ursula; *after L. Passinelli.*

STEFANONI, Pietro, an Italian engraver and printseller, who flourished about 1620. There is a set of forty etchings by him, after the designs of the Caracci, intended as a drawing-book. He usually marked his plates P. S. F.

STEIDNER, D., a German engraver of little note, who died at Augsburg in 1760. He engraved some plates of devotional subjects.

STELLA, Fermo, a painter of the Milanese school and a native of Caravaggio. He studied under Gaudenzio Ferrari, whose style he followed with considerable success. Lanzi says there are some of his works in the chapels at Varallo. He flourished in the first part of the 16th century.

STELLA, Francis. This painter was born at Mechlin, in Flanders, in 1563. After acquiring a knowledge of the art in his own country, he visited Rome for improvement, and afterwards settled in France, in the city of Lyons. He executed a considerable number of works for the churches and private collections, among which are his frescos of the Virgin, St. Sebastian, St. Roch, and St. Anthony, in the church des Minimes; the Entombment, in the church of St. John; the grand altar-piece at the Celestines, representing a Descent from the

Cross; and the Seven Sacraments at the Cordeliers, considered his master-piece. Stella died in 1605.

STELLA, JACQUES, an eminent French painter, was the son of the preceding, born at Lyons in 1596. His father taught him the rudiments of design, and though he died when Jacques was only nine years old, he had made such proficiency that he was enabled to complete his education without the assistance of any other master. At the age of twenty he went to Italy, and first stopped at Florence, where he was employed by the Grand Duke to assist in the decorations for the solemnization of the marriage of his son Ferdinand II. The Grand Duke was so much pleased with his abilities that he took him into his service, assigned him apartments in his palace, and gave him a pension equal to that of Callot, who was at that time in his service. After a residence of seven years at Florence, he proceeded to Rome in 1623, where he formed an intimacy with Niccolo Poussin, by whose direction and advice, he particularly devoted his attention to a diligent study of the antique and the works of Raffaelle, by which means he acquired that remarkable correctness of design which distinguishes his subsequent works. He executed several works at Rome, which gained him so much reputation that he was invited to the court of Madrid. Having determined to accept this invitation, he resolved to first visit his native country, and after a residence of eleven years at Rome, he proceeded in 1634 to Paris, whither his reputation had preceded him. His talents recommended him to the patronage of Cardinal Richelieu, at whose solicitation he was induced to abandon his intended visit to Spain and settle at Paris, where, through the influence of the Cardinal, he was appointed painter to the King, with apartments in the Louvre and a pension of one thousand livres. The King also honored him by conferring upon him the Order of St. Michael. Stella executed many works for churches and public edifices, but succeeded best in easel pictures, particularly those of pastoral subjects, though he showed great skill in painting cherubs and boys, or dancing cupids. He had an extensive genius, which enabled him to paint all kinds of subjects with equal ease. His invention is noble; his design rigidly correct, and his attitudes natural; but his works appear cold and inanimate, and we look in vain for that sentiment and expression which characterize the admirable productions of his friend Poussin. He was however a perfect master of perspective, and often enriched his pictures with noble architecture. His principal works in the churches at Paris are the Baptism of Christ in St. Germain le Vieux; the Annunciation, in the chapel of the Nuns of the Assumption; and Christ with the Woman of Samaria at the Carmelites. He executed some spirited etchings, marked with a star, the rebus of his name, among which are the Descent from the Cross; the Ceremony of doing Homage to the Grand Duke of Tuscany on St. John's Day, dated 1621; a Madonna, a St. George, and some dancing children. There are also some wood cuts after his designs, marked with a star, but they were executed by Paul Maupain. He died at Paris in 1657, aged 61, according to Bardon; and not in 1647, as generally stated.

STELLA, FRANÇOIS, was the younger brother of the preceding born at Lyons in 1601. He was instructed by Jacques, accompanied him in his travels, and settled with him at Paris. He painted history, but never acquired any great distinction. He painted some works for the churches at Paris, among which is an altar-piece at the Augus tines, representing the Dead Christ with the Virgin and St. John. It is generally stated that he died at Paris in 1661, though Felibien says on the 26th of July, 1647, in his forty-fourth year, which changes the time of his birth.

STELLA, ANTOINE BOUSONNET, was the nephew of Jacques Stella, and born at Lyons in 1630. He was instructed by his uncle, and acquired sufficient reputation as an historical painter to procure his election as a member of the Royal Academy at Paris, where he died in 1682. He also etched some plates, among which is one of Moses defending the Daughters of Jethro, *after Poussin.*

STELLA, CLAUDINE BOUSONNET, was the sister of the preceding, born at Lyons in 1636. She studied design under her uncle Jacques S., and afterwards applied herself to engraving, in which she became greatly distinguished. Her plates are chiefly after the works of Jacques Stella and Niccolo Poussin. Her prints after the latter have hardly been surpassed by other artists, and she greatly excelled Jean Pesne. Her drawing is very correct, and the character of the heads is admirably expressed. She died at Paris in 1697. The following are her best prints:

A set of seventeen plates of pastoral subjects, including the title; *after James Stella.* Fifty plates of the Sports of Children, and rural subjects; *do.* The Marriage of St. Catherine; *do.* Moses found in the Bulrushes, in two plates; *after N. Poussin.* Moses striking the Rock; *do.*; very fine. St. Peter and St. John curing the Lame Man; *do.* The Crucifixion, called the Great Calvary; *do.*; very fine. The Holy Family, with St. Elizabeth and St. John; *do.* Another Holy Family, with children bringing flowers; *do.*

STELLA, ANTOINETTE BOUSONNET, was the sister of Claudine, born at Lyons about 1637. She was also instructed by her uncle, and though she did not equal her sister, she handled the graver with judgment and taste, her drawing is correct, and her prints possess considerable merit. She executed some plates after Jacques Stella, Giulio Romano, and other masters. She died at Paris in 1676.

STELLA, FRANÇOISE BOUSONNET, another sister of Claudine. She engraved a set of sixty-six plates of antique ornaments, and a set of fifty-six vases, after her uncle *Jacques Stella.* Finding she could not equal the reputation of her sister Claudine, she afterwards assisted that distinguished lady in many of her productions.

STELZER, JOHN JACOB, a German engraver, who flourished about 1730. He engraved a part of the plates for the collection of prints after the antique marbles in the Dresden Gallery, published in 1733. He also executed some other plates after various masters. Nagler says he operated as late as 1780.

STEMPSIUS. See SEMPELIUS.

STENDARDO, or STANDARD. See PETER VAN BLOEMEN.

STENREE, or STEENREE, G., was a nephew of Cornelius Poelemburg, with whom he studied, and whose style he followed. His name is called

George by some, and William by others. His birth is placed at Utrecht in 1600, and his death in 1648.

STENT, Peter, an English engraver and print-seller of little note, who flourished at London from 1640 to 1663. Only one print, a portrait of Andrew Willet, marked P. S., is certainly the work of his hand; other prints bearing his name, with *exc.*, only indicate him as the publisher.

STERN, Dietrich van. See Staren.

STERN, Ignazio, a painter born in Bavaria about 1698. Probably he learned the rudiments of design in his own country, but he went young to Bologna, where he entered the school of the Cav. Carlo Cignani. While in Lombardy, he painted some pictures for the churches, possessing great merit; particularly an Annunciation in the Nunziata at Piacenza, which Lanzi describes as a graceful and elegant composition, executed in a style peculiar to himself. He afterwards went to Rome, where he acquired a high reputation, and executed several works, both in oil and fresco, for the churches and public edifices, the most considerable of which are some frescos in the Sacristy of S. Paolino, and some oil paintings in S. Elizabetta. He however, excelled more in painting easel pictures from profane history, conversations, musical parties, and what the Italians call *Bambocciate*, as fairs, rural festivals, markets, masquerades, &c., which were greatly admired, and Lanzi says they are to be found even in royal collections. He died in 1746.

STETTLER, William, a Swiss painter, born at Berne, according to Füessli. He studied with Felix Meyer at Zurich, and afterwards went to Paris, where he learned miniature painting of Joseph Werner. He settled in that city, and was much employed in designing historical and other subjects for the publishers. He accompanied Charles Patin as draughtsman, in his travels through Holland and Italy, and made the greater part of the designs for the plates in his publications on medals and antiquities. He died in 1708.

STEUDTNER, Mark Christopher, a German engraver, born at Augsburg in 1698, according to Nagler; though this is doubtless an error, as there is a print bearing his signature, representing St. Catherine carried to Heaven by Angels, dated 1696. He engraved both on copper and wood, and scraped in mezzotinto. His works embrace a variety of subjects, the chief of which are a set of etchings, representing the Loves of the Gods, and other mythological subjects, from his own designs, which evince considerable talent. He died in 1736. He is sometimes called *Steudener*, but he signed his prints *M. C. Steudtner*.

STEVENS, Alexander, an able English architect and engineer, was born in the early part of the eighteenth century. He distinguished himself by a great number of excellent works, among which are Carlisle Bridge, over the Liffey, in Dublin; the locks and docks on the Grand Canal in Ireland; and the aqueduct over the Lune, at Lancaster. He died at an advanced age, in 1796.

STEVENS, or STEPHANUS, John, a German engraver, and probably painter, who flourished at Strasburg about 1585. He engraved a variety of plates from his own designs, which prove him to have possessed considerable genius. His prints are chiefly slight etchings, executed almost entirely with dots, and are frequently little more than outlines. He sometimes marked his prints with his name, but generally with his initials, J. and S., with the date.

STEVENS, John, an English landscape painter, supposed by Lord Orford to have been a scholar of Vandiest, whose style he imitated. He was principally employed in painting pieces for chimney ornaments. He died in 1722.

STEVENS, STEEVENS, or STEPHANS, a Flemish painter, born at Mechlin about 1540. Little is known of him. He painted both history and landscape, and was employed by the Emperor Rodolphus II. at Prague, where he died, at what time is not known. Several of his pictures, chiefly landscapes, were engraved by the Sadelers and H. Hondius.

STEVENS, or STEEVENS, Peter, another artist born at Mechlin, who flourished about 1650. He was a painter and engraver, but devoted himself chiefly to the latter art. He engraved several portraits, among which are John III., King of Poland; Lodovic, Marquis of Brandenburg; the King of Prussia; Philip, Duke of Orleans; Count Emeric Tekely, and other distinguished personages.

STEVERS. See Staevarts.

STIEGLITZ, Christian Ludwig, a distinguished German writer on architecture, was born at Leipsic in 1756. After receiving a liberal education, he studied the legal profession, but devoted his leisure hours to the study of architecture. In 1792, he published his "History of the Architecture of the Ancients," and in 1798, completed his "Encyclopedia of Civil Architecture." In 1804 he began to publish, under the title of *Zeichnungen aus der schonen Baukunst*, a series of engravings of select specimens of modern architecture, which was exceedingly well received. After producing two or three treatises on ancient coins and medals, he published, in 1820, his excellent work on "Ancient German Architecture," entitled *Alt Deutsche Baukunst*, which has had considerable influence towards inspiring and directing the present German taste for the monuments of mediæval art. His next work was his *Geschichte der Baukunst*, a valuable compendium of the history of architecture from the earliest periods, among all nations, published in 1827. Stieglitz died in 1836. His works evince profound research, and an intimate acquaintance with his subject.

STIGLMAYER, Johann Baptist, an eminent German sculptor, and the distinguished director of the Royal Brass Foundry at Munich, was the son of a blacksmith, born in 1791, at Furstenfeldbruck, a small town near Munich. Manifesting a strong inclination for art, he was apprenticed to a goldsmith at Munich, named Streissel; and he also attended the holiday school, where by his industry and good conduct he gained the first prize of 100 florins. This success attracted the notice of M. Leprieur, Director of the Bavarian Mint, who encouraged the young artist, and in 1810 procured him admission as a student at the Academy. From this time, Stiglmayer pursued the regular course of study in sculpture, and also practiced seal and medal engraving. In 1814, he executed an admirable medal, representing, on the obverse, von Langer, a Director of the Academy, and on the reverse, Moses striking the Rock, which gained him the appointment of engraver to the Mint. In 1819 he was sent to Italy at the king's expense, to complete his studies. At Rome, Ludwig, then crown prince and subsequently king of Bavaria, became cognizant of Stiglmayer's great abilities; and he seems to have first directed the sculptor's attention to those great undertakings which he had already projected. Accordingly, Stiglmayer visited Naples, to witness the operation of casting the colossal equestrian statue in bronze of Charles III., by Francesco Righetti and his son Luigi, from the model by Canova; but some petty jealousy prevented him from accomplishing his purpose. Undismayed by difficulties, after considerable trouble he obtained permission to erect a smelting oven in his own cellar; and, having procured the assistance of Beccari, an experienced founder, he undertook the casting of several works. The first wholly failed; but the second, a cast from Thorwaldsen's bust of Prince Ludwig of Bavaria, was so completely successful that the journeyman Pasquali, in his ecstacy kissed the lips of the bust before they were cool, and seriously burnt his own! After casting a few other works, and perfecting his acquaintance with the practical department of the art, he returned to Germany in 1822. During the succeeding two years, he was chiefly employed as engraver to the Mint, and in the execution of several works in sculpture, for the Glyptothek or Sculpture Gallery at Munich. Among his busts of this period, are those of Maximilian I., Queen Theresa, Count Dorring, and Bishop Streber. In 1824, he commenced making preparations for his great series of metal castings; and from this time he was exclusively employed in founding the numerous monumental works erected by the king of Bavaria, some of which are after his own models, and others after those of Schwanthaler, Thorwaldsen, and other eminent sculptors of the present century. Impelled by great energy and caution—qualities rarely united—he visited Berlin in 1824, to witness the casting of Rauch's statue of Blucher by Reisinger, who, influenced by liberal and generous sentiments, showed him everything in his power.

Stiglmayer's great activity commenced in 1826, at the accession of his patron, Ludwig I. His works are too numerous to admit the insertion of a complete list. Among the principal are, the monument of Maximilian I., in Bad Kreuth; and the Parting of Otto, king of Greece, from his mother Theresa, queen of Bavaria, at Aibling—both after his own designs; the twelve colossal fire-gilded statues of the ancestors of the king of Bavaria, in the palace at Munich; the colossal statues of Jean Paul in Bayreuth, Mozart in Salzburg, the Margrave Frederick of Brandenburg in Erlangen, and the Grand Duke Ludwig of Darmstadt—all after Schwanthaler; the statue of Schiller at Stuttgard; and the colossal statue of Maximilian I. of Bavaria at Munich—both after Thorwaldsen; the Obelisk, 100 Bavarian feet high, in commemoration of the 30,000 Bavarians who fell in the allied war; the bronze gates of the Glyptothek and the Walhalla; and the grand constitutional column at Gaibach. Stiglmayer was honored, in 1830, with the knighthood of the Bavarian order of St. Michael. He died in 1844, leaving a number of important works in progress, which have since been completed. Among them are the colossal statue of Goethe, for Frankfort, cast on the day of Stiglmayer's death; the enormous colossal impersonification of Bavaria, nearly sixty feet high, placed before the Bavarian Rumeshalle, or Temple of Fame, and the largest statue in the world, measuring with its pedestal about eighty feet; the monument of the Grand Duke of Baden—all after the designs of Schwanthaler.

T, or T. STIMMER, Tobias, a Swiss painter and designer, born at Schaffhausen in 1534, according to Bartsch and Nagler, and not in 1544, as stated by others. It is not known under whom he studied, but he had acquired considerable celebrity by decorating the principal mansions of his native city, Strasburg, and Frankfort, with historical subjects painted in fresco, when he was invited to the court of the Marquis of Baden, to paint a series of portraits of the ancestors of that prince, which, according to Huber, he executed in a grand style. All his frescos, however, have perished; but he designed a set of small wooden cuts for a Bible, published at Basle in 1586, entitled *Novæ Tobiæ Stimmeri sacrorum Bibliorum figuræ versibus Latinis et Germanicis expositæ*, and another set of cuts for the New Testament, printed at Strasburg in 1588. These cuts are numerous, and prove him to have possessed a ready and fertile invention. It is no mean proof of his ability that they were commended by Rubens, who declared that he had studied them with attention, and derived much instruction from them. The cuts in the Bible before mentioned, marked with the above monogram of his initials, have heretofore been attributed to him; yet Bartsch says that he made the designs, but never engraved on wood. This, however, rests upon conjecture, and as John C. Stimmer certainly executed a part of these cuts, and doubtless learned the art of his brother, it seems more than probable that Tobias engraved those bearing his monogram; otherwise, why should not his mark be found on all the prints, if it only indicates him as the designer? The title page clearly shows that he designed them all. The time of his death is not known, but he is supposed to have lived to an advanced age.

CSTM STIMMER, John Christopher, was the younger brother of the preceding, born at Schaffhausen, in 1552. He is supposed to have been instructed by Tobias. He is said to have distinguished himself as an engraver on wood, and to have executed many cuts in a clear, neat style, from his own designs, and after those of his brother, which he marked with a monogram composed of the initials C. S. T. M., as above. The accounts of him, however, are involved in much intricacy, confusion, and uncertainty. Those fond of vainly attempting to unravel such perplexities, are referred to Nagler's Lexicon, and Bartsch's P. G., tom. ix. Besides some of the cuts in the Bible mentioned in the preceding article, the following are attributed to him: A set of cuts for the New Testament, printed at Strasburg in 1588. A set of prints of learned persons and theologians of Germany, published by Bernard Jobio, at Strasburg, in 1587. A set of Emblems entitled *Icones Affabræ*, published by B. Jobio, at Strasburg, in 1591.

STOCCADE, Nicholas de Helt, a Dutch

painter, born at Nimeguen in 1614. He studied at Antwerp under Martin Ryckaert, whose daughter he married. He first practiced landscape painting in the style of his instructor, but his genius leading him to historical painting, he applied with great assiduity to that branch, and had acquired considerable reputation, when he went to Italy for improvement. He passed eight years at Rome, with unremitting application, where his talents soon recommended him to public attention, and he was employed to paint several pictures for the palaces and private collections, particularly for Christina, Queen of Sweden. From Rome he went to Venice, to improve his coloring by studying the works of the great Venetian masters. After a residence of several years at Venice, he set out for his own country; but visiting Paris on his way, he met with such distinguished encouragement that he was induced to establish himself for many years in that city, where he was appointed one of the painters to the king. It is said that he did not long survive his return to the Netherlands, where he died, according to Immerzeel, in 1669.

The historical pictures of Stoccade are generally of large dimensions, and his design bears the character of the Roman school. His compositions evince a ready and fertile invention, his figures are correctly designed, his manner of penciling broad and free, his coloring sweet and harmonious, and he sometimes showed a singularity of manner in expressing the actions and passions of his characters, different from other painters. Thus in the story of Andromeda, while many painters have represented her almost dying with fearful apprehension of her danger, Stoccade, on the contrary, depicted her in modest confusion, rather blushing from the consciousness of being exposed naked, than terrified at the horrors with which she was threatened. This picture, and those of Clelia passing the Tiber, and Joseph distributing Corn to his Brethren, were celebrated by the poets of his country. His principal works are at Rome, Venice, and Paris. He executed a few etchings, among which are Cephalus and Aurora, and Susanna and the Elders, *from his own designs*; and a portrait of A. van Opstat, *after Vandyck.*

STOCK, Ignatius vander, a Dutch painter and engraver, who flourished from about 1620 to 1660. Little is known of him as a painter, though he is said to have painted landscapes with ability. There are some spirited etchings by him, from his own designs, and after other masters, which evince considerable talent.

STOCK, Andrew, a Dutch engraver, born at the Hague, in 1590. He went to Antwerp, where he seems to have chiefly resided. He is supposed to have studied under James de Gheyn the Elder, whose style he imitated. He engraved several plates for the *Academie de L'Espée*, published at Antwerp by Thibeau, in 1625; he inscribed them *Andreas Stokius Hagæ Comitis, sculp.* Among others, are the following by him:

PORTRAITS.

Albert Durer, *Effigies Alberti Dureri. And. Stock. sc.* 1629. Hans Holbein; *Effigies Holbeini, Pictoris celeberrimi, se ipse pinx. And. Stock, fecit.* Lucas of Leyden; *from a picture by himself.* Peter Sneyers, Painter; *after A. Vandyck.*

SUBJECTS.

The Sacrifice of Abraham; *after Rubens.* Twelve plates of the Months in the Year; *after Wildens.* A set of eight Landscapes; *after Paul Brill.*

STOCK, H., an English engraver, who flourished about 1635. Only one print is mentioned by him—a portrait of Robert Cecil, Earl of Salisbury.

STOER, Lawrence, a German artist, who flourished at Augsburg, about 1567. According to Prof. Christ, he was a painter, and an engraver on wood. He executed several cuts, which are marked with the above monogram.

STOFFE, J. V. D., a Dutch painter of battle-pieces and skirmishes of cavalry, of whom nothing is known except by his pictures, signed with his name. They are of small size, painted on panel, and rarely exceed thirty-six inches by about twenty-four. His pictures are well designed, spirited in action, strongly colored, and highly finished.—They bear some resemblance to those of Stoop, or Esaias Vandervelde, to whom they are sometimes attributed. He flourished about 1650.

STOLKER, John, a Dutch painter, and an engraver in aquafortis and mezzotinto, born at Amsterdam in 1724. He studied painting under J. M. Quinkhard, with whom he remained till he was twenty-three years of age. He then went to the Hague, where he resided nine years, painting portraits and family groups. He next removed to Rotterdam, where he settled permanently, and acquired considerable reputation. He also painted cabinet pictures of familiar subjects, one of which, called *Rhynlande*, is highly commended for its admirable design, composition, expression, chiaroscuro, and elaborate finishing. He also engraved quite a number of prints after Rembrandt, Adrian van Ostade, Jan Steen, Frank Hals, Terburg, Schalcken, and other masters. He died in 1786.

STOM, or STOOM, Matthew, a painter, supposed to have been of Flemish origin, who died at Verona in 1702. He painted landscapes and battle-pieces with considerable reputation. There was another artist of this name who flourished about 1650. He painted sacred subjects, and there is an altar-piece by him in the church of St. Cecilia at Messina.

STOMME, a Dutch painter of still-life, supposed to have been a scholar of John David de Heem, whose style he imitated. There is a fine picture by him in the Museum at Brussels, representing a table covered, on which are a pitcher, a plate of broiled fish, and other objects. Nothing more is known of him.

STONE, Nicholas, an English sculptor and architect, born in 1586. He served his time with Isaac Jones, for whom he worked a considerable time. He afterwards went to Holland, where he was employed by one Peter de Heyser, whose daughter he married. On his return to England, he was much employed in executing monuments for persons of distinction. In 1616, he was employed at Edinburgh, in the King's chapel. In 1619, he was engaged in the Banqueting House at Whitehall, and in the beginning of the reign of Charles I. he received his patent as master mason. The following are a few of his principal works, given by Vertue: A tomb, for the Earl of Ormond, set up at Kilkenny, Ireland; a superb tomb for Lord Northampton, in Dover Castle; another for the Earl of Bedford, for which the artist received £1020; a monument to Spenser, the poet, in Westminster Abbey; four statues for the old Royal Exchange, London, of Edward IV., Richard III., Henry VII., and Queen Elizabeth, which were afterwards removed to Guildhall Gate. He executed many works at Windsor for Charles I., and built the front of St. Mary's church at Oxford. According to Stone's private memoranda, he received about £11,000 for his monuments. He died in 1647.

STONE, HENRY, was the son of the preceding, and usually called *Old Stone*, to distinguish him from his brother John. The time of his birth is not known. He probably studied with Michael Cross, an excellent copyist of the works of various masters, employed by Charles I. He made many excellent copies from the portraits of Vandyck, and many portraits now to be found in various collections, attributed to Vandyck, are supposed to have been painted by him. He also copied the Italian masters with great success. Stanley says that the picture of the Cornaro family, said to be by Titian, formerly at Northumberland House, and now at Hampton Court, is a copy by Stone. He died at London in 1653.

STONE, JOHN, was the brother of Henry. He chiefly followed the profession of his father as a statuary. He also copied some of the most esteemed works of the old masters with considerable success. He is said to have studied with Thomas Cross, an engraver; but it was more probably Michael Cross, mentioned in the foregoing article. He is said to have designed and engraved some plates, but only one is known. He died in 1653.

STONE, NICHOLAS, an English statuary, was the third son of Nicholas S. After receiving some instruction from his father, he visited Italy to complete his education, and modelled many excellent copies of celebrated foreign works, among which, according to Walpole, were the Laocoön, and Bernini's Apollo and Daphne, in terra-cotta, afterwards in the possession of the sculptor Bird.—He returned to England in 1642, and died in the same year as his father, in 1647.

STOOP, DIRK or THEODORE, and PETER. There is a great deal of contradiction and confusion among writers, especially the English, with regard to the Stoops. According to Bartsch and the best authorities, Theodore, Thierry, Dierick, Dirk, and Roderigo are one and the same artist. Roderigo in Portuguese is the same as Theodorus in Latin, from which the other names are derived, Dirk being the diminutive, or rather a corruption, of Theodore, used by the Dutch. Dirk Stoop was a designer and engraver, and probably a painter, born in Holland about 1610. There is a set of twelve plates of Horses, and a set of twelve masterly etchings of figures and animals, signed D. Stoop, which he engraved before he left Holland. He went to Lisbon, where he resided some time, and was patronized by Catherine of Braganza, whom he accompanied to England. While in Lisbon, he engraved a set of eight views in that city, from his own designs, which he dedicated to his patroness. They are signed *Ro. Stoop, f.*, and are dated 1661 and 1662. It is supposed by some that these were from pictures painted by himself, though this rests entirely on conjecture. On his arrival in London, he engraved and published a set of seven prints, representing the Queen's Journey from Lisbon to London. These are marked *Ro. Stoop, f.* Some time afterwards he engraved, conjointly with Hollar, the plates for the first part of Ogilby's translation of Æsop's Fables, after designs by Barlow, though several of those by Stoop are from his own designs. He engraved several other plates while in England, some of which he signed *Ro.*, and others *T. Stoop.* It is therefore evident that these prints are all by the same artist, and that he varied his signature according to the custom of the country in which he happened to be located when he published them. There are several other prints by him; and others are attributed to him, but they are of very doubtful authenticity. Some of his prints are extremely rare. Lord Orford, Pilkington, and Bryan, who call him Peter and Roderigo, say he died at London in or about 1685; others, that he returned to his own country about 1678.

STOOP, PETER, is supposed to have been the brother of Dirk, and born about 1612. He was a cotemporary of Peter de Laer, whose style and subjects he imitated with great success, and his best works are said to be little inferior to the productions of that admirable master. Bryan says, in his life of Dirk S., that "his pictures represent hunters and sportsmen on horseback, the halts of travelers, farriers' shops, &c., which are composed and designed with a spirit and taste which has scarcely been surpassed by Philip Wouwerman, for whose works the pictures of Stoop are not unfrequently taken." He then goes on to describe Peter S. as an engraver, and says that he painted battles, huntings, and sea-ports with considerable success. Pilkington gives nearly the same account. It is evident, however, that the imitator of Bamboccio was Peter, for such pictures are frequently met with, signed *P. Stoop.* The Dutch writers describe *Jan Pieter Stoop*, as a painter of similar subjects as those attributed by the English to Dirk Stoop. It seems very probable, too, that Dirk was also a painter as well as an engraver, and that he painted the battles, huntings, and halts of travelers. The Dutch writers also mention a J. Stoop, who they say imitated van Bloemen and Michael Carré, and he is commended for his good coloring, spirited penciling, and excellent chiaro-scuro. The reader who wishes to pursue this subject further, must be referred to Bartsch's Peintre Graveur, tom. iv., Weigel's Supplement to Bartsch, Nagler's Lexicon, and Robert Dumesnil Le Peintre Graveur Français, tom. v.

STOOPENDAAL, or STOOPENDAEL, B., a Dutch engraver, who flourished from about 1700 to 1720. He imitated the style of Cornelius Visscher, and copied some of his prints. He generally signed his plates *B. Stoopendael, fec.*, but sometimes with the contraction, B. Stoop., which has caused some confusion. There was another engraver who flourished about the same time, named D. Stoopendael, probably his brother. The following are by him:

Sixty Views in Holland, entitled *Les Delices du Diemer Meer*; engraved *from his own designs.* A set of twenty-four Views near the Hague. Four plates, representing the Departure of King William from Holland for England, his Arrival, his meeting the Parliament, and his Coronation; inscribed *B. Stoopendaal, fec.* The Robbers; *after Bamboccio*; *B. Stoopendaal, sc.* The Attack of a Military Convoy; *do.*; *do.* A Lime-kiln; *do.* The last three plates are very finely copied from the prints by Visscher.

STORALI, Giovanni, a Bolognese painter, who flourished about 1600. He studied with Cesare Baglioni, whose style he followed with considerable reputation. He painted landscape, fruit, flowers, and still-life.

STORCK, or STORK, Abraham, an eminent Dutch marine painter, born at Amsterdam in 1650. It is not known by whom he was instructed, but he studied nature with great assiduity, and carefully sketched every scene, vessel, and object which he intended to introduce into a picture; hence his works have a strong character of truth. His pictures usually represent views on the Y, or the Amstel, near Amsterdam, with a variety of shipping and boats, decorated with small figures, correctly drawn, and touched with great neatness and spirit. He also painted sea-ports, calms at sea with fishing smacks, and sometimes storms at sea, which he represented with great truth and fidelity. His pictures are ingeniously composed, his vessels and rigging are drawn with precision and accuracy, his coloring is clear and transparent, his skies light and floating, and his chiaro-scuro excellent. One of his most celebrated pictures was a representation of the reception of the Duke of Marlborough in the river Amstel, with a procession of vessels, yachts, and barges, superbly decorated, and crowded with figures in a variety of habits, adapted to their different dignities, ranks, and conditions, yet so ingeniously disposed and arranged that there is no appearance of confusion or want of room. His pictures are little inferior to those of Backhuysen and Vandervelde, and are now held in high estimation. Bartsch describes six etchings, which he attributes to him, signed *A. Storck.* His name is often written *Stork*, but he signed his pictures *A. Storck.* He died at Amsterdam in 1708.

STORCK, Jan, or Jacob, is supposed to have been the elder brother of the preceding. He painted similar subjects, but his works are far inferior to the admirable productions of Abraham Storck. His pictures are numerous, usually of small dimensions, and are signed *J. Storck*, or simply *Storck.* Jan or Jacob is merely conjectural.

STORER, John Christopher, a Swiss painter, born at Constance in 1611. He went to Milan, and studied in the school of Ercole Procaccini. Lanzi says that he produced some works of a solid taste, but subsequently he fell into mannerism, and not unfrequently adopted gross and common ideas. In other points he displayed much spirit, and was a good colorist. He was one of the artists employed on the decorations at Milan, on the occasion of the Entry of Philip IV. and Maria of Austria. There are many of his pictures in the churches and collections of Germany. Several of his pictures have been engraved by Bonacina, dal Sole, M. Küsel, B. Kilian, and Ph. Kilian. He also etched several plates of subjects from sacred and profane history, from his own designs, some of which are signed *Joan. Christ. Storer*, and others *Giov. Christ. Storer.* His name is sometimes erroneously written *Stoer* and *Stora.* He died at Constance in 1671, though Lanzi and others say at Milan.

STOSS, Francis, an old German engraver, who is supposed to have flourished as early as 1460, and to have practiced engraving before the time of Martin Schoen and Israel von Mecheln. He is said to have engraved a set of small plates representing the Life and Passion of Christ, which were copied by Schoen, who is believed to have been his pupil, as he imitated his style. He marked his plates with the initials F. and S., in old German characters, with a kind of cross between them, as above. Much of this, however, is merely conjectural. Bartsch (P. G., tom. vi.) describes only three prints bearing this mark, viz., the Resurrection of Lazarus, the Dead Christ, and the Holy Virgin. He says "the engraver who used this mark is very ancient, and absolutely unknown; for as to the names of *Francis Stoss*, *Stoltzhirs*, and *Stolzius*, which different writers have given him, they have as little foundation as the opinion that he was the master of Martin Schongauer." Nagler, however, is of a different opinion, and regards this artist of so much importance that he devotes eight closely printed pages concerning him and his supposed works, which, though interesting to the connoisseur, elicits nothing beyond conjecture.

STOTHARD, Thomas, an eminent English painter of historical, poetical, and fancy subjects, was born at London in 1755. His father was a coachmaker, and as Thomas was an only and a sickly child, he sent him to Acomb, a small village near York, when he was five years old, and placed him with an old Scotch lady, whose motherly care, with the healthy locality, soon restored him to strength. It was here that his natural genius for painting exhibited itself at a very tender age, and the artist used to relate, in his old age, an incident that induced him to adopt a profession which had afforded him pleasure full seventy years. "My Scotch friend had two sons in the Temple, London, who had sent her some of Houbraken's heads, with an engraving of Blind Belisarius and other prints from the graver of Strange; as they were framed, she had them hung up in a sort of drawing room, and rarely allowed any one to look at her treasures, as she called them. One day I ventured to follow her into her sanctuary. She was pleased with the earnestness with which I viewed the heads and groups, patted me on the head, and said I should see them often, since I seemed to like them so much. I became almost a daily visitor to her room, and I began to wonder how such things were done. I was told they were made with pencils. Though the old lady told me this, she little expected the result. In short, she missed me one day, and found me standing on a chair, trying to imitate with a pencil one of the heads before me. She smiled, patted me on the head, and bade me go on, adding, 'Thomas, ye are really a queer boy.' I did little else now but draw, and I soon began to make tolerable copies.

"I lived at Acomb till I was eight years old, when I left my old Scottish dame with tears in my eyes, and went to school at Stretton, the birth-place of my father. I continued drawing, and even attempted to make sketches from life. Some one told me that engravings were made from paintings in oil colors. I longed to see a painting, and shall never forget the delight with which for the first time I looked upon one. I resolved to paint in colors, and wrote to my father to send me some materials; I was, however, too impatient to wait their coming; but going to a cart and plow wright, I begged black, red, and white oil colors from him, and commenced to make a picture. I painted a man in black paint, and then tried with red and white to work it into the hues of life. It was a sad daub; but I still persevered, and soon learned to handle my brush with more skill, and to lay on my colors with better taste." Such are the simple and instructive circumstances which often lead men of genius to excellence and renown. His father dying about this time, his relatives apprenticed him to a weaver of brocades, but at his master's death, which happened when he was about seventeen years of age, he devoted his whole time to his favorite art, which he had never neglected. To improve himself, he became a student of the Royal Academy. He had already, by the force of his own genius and application, made great progress in art. He had, too, adopted the right path to excellence, which he ever pursued—a diligent study of nature. He delighted to roam over the fields, and sketch on the spot, in water colors, every curious and beautiful object that met his view, whether tree, plant, flower, or insect. In town, too, he was not less diligent in drawing every beautiful and pleasing form. Cunningham says, "His first recorded work is a Holy Family, painted in small, like almost all his pictures; it was exhibited in the Royal Academy in 1778; he was then twenty-three years old, and though an early beginner, his modesty equalled his talents, and he did not hurry, as many do, his first crude gropings after beauty before the public. In the following year, he exhibited a little picture of Banditti, and afterwards the retreat of the Greeks with the body of Patroclus; the Death of Sir Philip Sidney; King Richard returning from Palestine; King Richard's treatment of Isaac, King of Cyprus; and Britomart, from Spenser. The last of these intimates the commencement of that series of works, from our poetic and prose literature, which extend to several thousands, and exhibit the heroism, the pathos, the humor, and the spirit of the island genius, in a manner as easy, as graceful, and as brightly, as it shines in the purest prose, or the most vivid verse. In 1792, he was elected an associate of the Royal Academy, and two years afterwards he was admitted into the ranks as a Royal Academician. He moved at the same time from 39 East street to 28 Newman street—a neighborhood much frequented by brethren of the art.

"Of all our poets, Spenser was his favorite, and from his pages, and those of Chaucer and Shakspeare, he has embodied scenes and groups sufficient for his fame. To ensure the presence of nature in his compositions, it was his custom to walk frequently in the streets, and observe the men and women, girls and boys, the rich and the poor, the high and the humble, as they hurried or loitered along. He used to say that he transcribed their looks or their air from his memory into his studies, and that he never met with two faces or two forms exactly alike. He loved to extend his walks to the Tower, and often further, to study the heads of foreign mariners, who crowd the Thames from every point of the compass: and of these he loved the seamen from the Mediterranean most, for their ancient Grecian cast of countenance; and the Chinese and low Irish least, from their coarse looks and unpoetic airs. In all his pictures there is a natural action and a classic grace—the fruit of these studies, and his fine poetic talents. This is visible in his numerous scenes from the Grecian and Italian poets, over which the air of antique beauty is warmly, sometimes too glowingly, breathed; these consist chiefly of nymphs wandering in shady forests, reposing by falling streams, singing to the lute by silent fountains, walking with their favorite knights, or bathing singly or in clusters in lovely streams, with nothing save a song-bird or a wild fawn to see them.

"The Pilgrim's Progress and Robinson Crusoe were the sources from which he frequently drew his inspiration; Christiana and her Children was in the exhibition of 1797; Christian, the Pilgrim, followed, and both were admired for their simplicity and beauty; while Robinson Crusoe on his lonely isle, scared by the print of a man's foot in the sand, can never pass away from the memory. The illustrations of these romantic compositions tell the story of themselves; in a small compass, and at a glance of the eye, we find the bloom and essence of the great originals. There is scarcely an author of any mark whose pages he has left unembellished; nor is there a poet whose peculiar excellence he can be accused of not perceiving and feeling. In his scene from the Canterbury Pilgrimage, where he musters at sun-rise his motley yet select devotees, and directs their march to the shrine of Thomas à Becket, at Canterbury, we read in their looks the various characters described by Chaucer; and no man who has seen that fine picture, glowing with truth and life, can say he is unacquainted with the poet, though he only knows him by name. The same may be said of those fine pictures which he has hung, like summer garlands, on the Muse of Rogers; and of his illustrations to the Tales of Boccacio; in both of which he has shown a fancy teeming with images of innocence and loveliness. The sun never shone on more pure and lovely creatures; yet now and then, here and there, he has exhibited a touch of what the Puritans call the old Adam, and has just intimated, in some of his Nymphs, that they feel their steps unsteady, and the grass under their feet a little slippery.

"The chief excellence of Stothard lies in expressing virgin innocence and matronly grace—in depicting images of female loveliness, and rural or chivalrous life. He has humor of a quiet kind, and deep sensibility; he is without labored shapes or constrained postures; all, with him, is easy, graceful, and unaffected. He is the painter of thought, rather than form; and yet, where are fairer forms to be found than in his clusters of nymphs and bevies of ladies? His coloring is often bright and clear. He is very unequal, and what is called mannered; his smaller pictures are his best, and luckily they are very numerous."

Stothard's chief fame rests upon his almost innumerable designs and water-colored drawings, which he executed to embellish almost all the beautiful publications of his day. It is said that he made upwards of five thousand, more than three thousand of which were engraved by Charles Heath, and many other eminent engravers, by which means his fame was spread all over the world, even in his life-time. Among his larger works may be enumerated the pictures he painted for the Shakspeare Gallery, the Canterbury Pilgrims, the Flitch of Bacon, and the Wellington Shield. He also painted in fresco the staircase at Burleigh House, the seat of the Marquis of Exeter, the figures of which are seven feet high and occupied him near four years; and he executed the designs for the ceiling of the Advocates' Library, at Edinburgh. He made many excellent designs for workers in gold, silver, and other metals, to ornament rich services of plate, urns, vessels, &c., and drew the outlines of many celebrated works by the English sculptors, for the engravers. His designs are now highly esteemed, and eagerly sought after by collectors; and though they are so numerous, they are constantly rising in value—a sure proof of their merit. Some of his aquarel drawings are almost as valuable as his oil paintings. Of his numerous oil paintings, his cabinet pictures are the best, and less mannered than his larger productions. It is admitted that he succeeded better in illustrating domestic scenes and the poets of his own country, than the heroic subjects of antiquity; for he was a close observer of men and manners. In representing the sports, humors, and innocence of children, he is without a rival among modern artists. It is said that he gave the preference, before all his other works, to fifteen small pictures which he painted to illustrate the Pilgrim's Progress. He was very simple and unassuming in his deportment, and an unfortunate deafness prevented him from associating with his brother artists and men of genius as much as he otherwise would have done. He was a self-made man, and by the force of his genius, and untiring perseverance and industry, raised himself to a distinguished position, at a period when so many English artists flourished as to cause it to be designated "the golden era of English art." The history of such a man is full of instruction and encouragement to young artists. He died in 1834, aged 79 years.

STOTHARD, Charles Alfred, was the son of the preceding, born in London in 1787. His father gave him a liberal education, and instructed him in art; he afterwards studied in the Royal Academy, where he soon attracted attention for his chaste drawings, and the accuracy with which he drew from the ancient sculptures. In 1802, he accompanied his father to Burleigh, the seat of the Marquis of Exeter, and during the four years he was occupied there, young Stothard employed much of his time in making drawings from the monuments and antiquities in the various churches of that region. This awakened in him a predilection for a pursuit in which he distinguished himself. In 1811 he exhibited at the Royal Academy a spirited picture, representing the Murder of Richard II. at Pomfret Castle, in which the costume of the time was strictly observed, and the portrait of the monarch taken from his effigy in Westminster Abbey. In the same year he commenced and finished the first number of his great work, "The Monumental Effigies of Great Britain," under the auspices of the Society of Antiquaries, of which he became a member. This work required immense labor and research, as it was intended to bring together and preserve correct representations of the best historical illustrations extant, from the Norman Conquest to the time of Henry VIII., to be found in the cathedrals and churches. He therefore devoted his whole time to its prosecution, with great assiduity. He executed the designs with the utmost accuracy and precision, the heraldic emblazonry is of the highest order for correctness and beauty, and he etched all the plates himself, with a delicacy and fidelity before unknown in English art. The work is now considered indispensable to antiquaries, artists, and to every person who is desirous of being acquainted with the costumal history of those times, and the heraldic bearings of all those illustrious persons whose names are recorded for valorous achievements, or other deeds beneficial to their country. In 1816, he was sent by the Society to Bayeux, to make drawings from the famous tapestries preserved in that city. While thus engaged, he visited the Abbey of Fontevraud, where he discovered the effigies of the Plantagenets, the existence of which, after the revolutionary tempest, was considered doubtful. These were added to the work, and in the edition published by Bohn, are superbly illuminated in imitation of the originals. In 1818, he married Miss Kempe, a very ingenious lady, who accompanied him in his second visit to France, and wrote an interesting account of their tour through Normandy and Brittany, which was subsequently published, illustrated with twenty-one engravings from designs by her husband. In 1819, he made drawings for the Society, from the pictures discovered on the walls of the Painted Chamber. In prosecuting this work, he recovered the long lost art of embossing gold on the surface of the material, as practiced by the old Italian and German illuminators, and which contributes so much to the splendor of ancient missals and other manuscripts. His last undertaking, which cost him his life, was for illustrating Lysons' account of Devonshire in the Magna Britannia. He left London in May 1821, and after traversing some portion of that interesting county, came to Bere Ferrers on the 27th of the month. The next day he ascended a ladder, and began to make tracings of the stained glass window in the church, when his feet slipping, he fell, and his head striking against a monument in the chancel, he was instantly killed, aged 34 years.

STRAATEN, John Joseph Ignatius van, a Dutch painter, born at Utrecht in 1766. He studied under C. van Geelen, and painted fruit, flowers, dead game, and other objects of still life, in a style somewhat resembling that of J. Weenix. His pictures are well composed and highly finished; they are sometimes enriched with landscape backgrounds by his countryman Swagers. He died in 1808.

STRADA, or STRADANUS, John, an eminent Flemish painter, born at Bruges in 1536. He was first instructed in art by his father, an artist of little celebrity, and next studied under Peter Aertsen. He afterwards went to Rome, where he diligently studied the antique, and the works of the great Italian masters. He there became acquainted with Francesco Rossi, called Il Salviati whose style he in some measure adopted. In conjunction with that master and Daniello da Volterra, he was employed in decorating the pontifical palace of Belvidere, where he acquired considerable reputation. From Rome he proceeded to Naples, at the invitation of Don John of Austria, to represent his military achievements, in which he gave entire satisfaction to the monarch, and proved himself one of the ablest artists of his time. Vasari next engaged him to assist him at Florence, and in conjunction with that artist, he executed several considerable works for the Ducal palace, and the churches and public edifices. In that city are still to be seen some noble performances of

Strada. In the Nunziata is a grand picture by him, representing Christ on the Cross with the Virgin Mary, Mary Magdalen and St. John, with a number of other figures larger than life. Lanzi says this is considered his most capital performance. In S. Croce, is a fine picture of the Ascension, and in S. Maria Nuova, the Baptism of Christ. In the chapel of the Palazzo Pitti, are two small altar-pieces of the Nativity, and the Adoration of the Magi, which are much admired. He did not confine himself to sacred history, but painted battles, huntings, and processions, with great ability; and these are his most numerous works, executed in a noble and spirited style, with a ready hand and a free, firm pencil. He also made many designs for tapestry. He was an indefatigable artist, and his constant practice gave him an uncommon facility of hand, both in oil and fresco. He had a fertile invention, and his design was generally correct, though occasionally heavy and somewhat mannered, for notwithstanding his long residence in Italy, he could never entirely divest himself of his Flemish manner. His coloring was vigorous and effective, and sometimes very brilliant, especially in his cabinet pictures. His works are very numerous, and there are upwards of 400 engravings after pictures by him, many of them by Sadeler, Goltzius, Collaert, Wierix, Galle, and C. de Passe. In 1578, a work was published at Antwerp, entitled, *Stradani Venationes Ferarum, Avium, Piscium,*" &c., illustrated with 94 plates of all kinds of huntings and fights of animals, engraved by several of the above named artists. Lanzi says that he imitated the design of Salviati, and the coloring of Vasari, in whose employment he remained two years at Florence. He died in that city, according to Baldinucci, in 1605. He is called by the Italians *Giovanni Stradano.*

STRADA, Vespasiano, a painter who was born at Rome, according to Baglioni, of Spanish parents. It is not known whether he had any other instructor than his father, who was an artist of little note. He wrought chiefly in fresco, and had decorated several of the churches at Rome with his works, when his promising career was cut short by death in the prime of his life. His principal works are a series of pictures in the monastery of S. Onofrio, representing the history of that saint; the Visitation of the Virgin, and the Adoration of the Shepherds in S. Maria Maddalena al Corso. Bartsch describes twenty-one etchings by him, which he believes to be a complete list. Fifteen of these have his name in full, and one only is marked V. S. I. F. Others say that he usually marked his prints V. S. F., or V. S. I. F., and sometimes, VES. ST, I. FE., or VESP. STRA. I. F. There is great discrepancy as to the time of his birth and death. Baglioni and Lanzi say that he died in the pontificate of Paul V., aged 36; Malpe that he was born in 1591, and died in 1624; others that he died about 1615 and 1620. One of his prints is dated 1595; on which Bartsch remarks (P. G. tom. xvii), that supposing this print, which exhibits his greatest power, was done by him at the age of twenty, he must have been born about 1575.

STRAETEN, Henry vander, a Dutch painter, born about 1665. It is not known under whom he studied. Bryan says that, by an attentive study of nature, without the help of a master, he reached an eminent rank as a landscape painter. He went to England about 1690, where he painted landscapes in a style resembling those of Ruysdael and Hobbema, and might have found abundant and profitable employment had it not been for his dissipated habits. He is probably the same artist mentioned by Balkema, under the name of Nicholas vander Straeten, who, he says, was born at Utrecht in 1680, and went to London, where he died in 1722. The accounts of him are contradictory and exaggerated, and it is doubtful if there are any authentic pictures by him. Houbraken says he painted ten landscapes in a day, "each of them full of pleasing variety, with views of mountains, forests, water-falls, and other pleasing incidents"!

STRANGE, Sir Robert, an eminent Scotch engraver, born at Pomona, in the Orkneys, in 1721. He was a descendant of the family of the Stranges of Balcasky, in the county of Fife, who had settled in the Orkneys at the time of the Reformation. He was educated for the law, but having a passion for drawing, in which he evinced uncommon talents, his friends were induced to place him under the instruction of Mr. R. Cooper at Edinburg. His progress to fame, was, however, arrested for a time by the rebellion, for he joined the Pretender, Charles James Edward Stuart, and after the ruin of his affairs, he wandered for some time a fugitive in the Highlands, and had a narrow escape with his life, the incidents attending which, are in the highest degree romantic. After the battle of Culloden, being pursued by a party of the King's troops, he fled into a cottage, where, observing a young lady dressed in the full costume of the period, he besought her protection. As the soldiers were close at his heels, no time was to be lost, she raised her hoop and directed him to seek shelter under the ample folds of her petticoat, and there, "patulae sub tegumine recubans," he remained undiscovered, though the soldiers ransacked the house. After their departure, she concealed him till the troublous times were past. Filled with gratitude and admiration at her conduct, the youth begged her to wait for him till he should prove himself worthy of her hand. As soon as his fortunes were sufficiently prosperous, he married his protectress, and never was there a more devoted husband, or a more affectionate wife. When tranquillity was restored, he returned to Edinburg, and thence proceeded to London. Shortly afterwards he set out for Italy, but stopping at Rouen, he entered the academy there and drew the first prize for a design, though his competitors were numerous. He next went to Paris, where he became the pupil of le Bas, from whom he learned the use of what is called the *dry point*, which he afterwards improved, and used with such distinguished success. He now abandoned for the present, his projected visit to Rome, and returned to London, where he soon distinguished himself as an historical engraver. In 1761, he gratified the wish he had long entertained of visiting Italy for the purpose of making designs, and engraving some of the most celebrated pictures of the great Italian masters of the different schools. He was every where received with marked attention and respect, and elected a member of the academies of Rouen, Florence, Bologna, Parma, and Paris; he was also appointed Professor in the academy at Parma. The Royal Academy of London did not show him any favor, though it could not have added to his honor; yet the King thought him worthy of knighthood for the honor he had conferred upon the arts of his country, and accordingly knighted him in 1787. The works of Sir Robert Strange consist of about one hundred plates, more than one-half of which are after the most eminent Italian painters. They are distinguished by a bold and intelligent execution, exhibiting an admirable union of the point and the graver, producing a vigorous and harmonious effect. It is said that he retouched Dorigny's plates of the Transfiguration, and the cartoons of Raffaelle, in Hampton court; also that about 1790, he had 80 copies of selected proofs of his own works, bound, to which he prefixed a dedication to the King, and an introduction on the progress of the art of engraving, with remarks on the pictures he had engraved. There are *three states* of almost all the prints by Strange; 1st. the pure aquafortis, or single etching; 2d. the proof before the letter, or the plate finished with the graver; 3d. do. with the letter. The first are extremely rare, as they were only trial proofs; the second also are rare, as he never struck more proofs than were subscribed for. As an author, he published "An Inquiry into the Rise and Establishment of the Royal Academy of Arts," to which is prefixed a letter to the Earl of Bute, and "A descriptive Catalogue of a Collection of Pictures, and of thirty-two Drawings collected by him in Italy." He died at London in 1792. The following is a complete list of his works, except a few of his earlier productions:

PORTRAITS.

*After Vandyck.*—Charles I., whole-length, 1770; Charles, with a page and his equerry holding his horse, 1782; Charles I., half-length, 1775; Henrietta Maria, Queen of Charles I., with the Prince of Wales and the Duke of York; the Children of Charles I.; the Marquis of Montrose; the Earl of Stafford.

*After various Masters.*—A Bust of Raffaelle, *after a picture by himself*; inscribed *Ille hic est Raphael*, &c. 1787. A portrait of himself; *from a design by J. B. Greuze.* The Apotheosis of Octavius and Alfred, children of George III., who died in their infancy; *after West.* 1787. Charles James Edward Stuart, called the young Pretender. Mary Stuart, Queen of Scotland. Parmiggiani Amica, or the Mistress of Parmiggiano; *after Parmiggiano.* 1774. Thomas Cromwell, Earl of Essex; *after Holbein.* William Hamilton, Poet, 1760; for an edition of his Poems. Robert Leighton, Archbishop of Glasgow, for a selection from his works. 1758. Archibald Pitcairn Physician and Poet; a bust in medallion.

SUBJECTS AFTER VARIOUS MASTERS.

*After Raffaelle.*—St. Cecilia; after the picture formerly in the church of S. Giovanni, at Bologna. 1771. Justice; 1765. Meekness; 1765.

*After Guido.*—Mary Magdalene penitent. 1762. Do., another. 1773. The Death of Cleopatra. 1777. Fortune, a figure flying over a Globe. 1778. Venus attired by the Graces. 1759. The Chastity of Joseph. 1769. The Holy Virgin. 1756. The Angel of the Annunciation. 1756. The Annunciation. 1787. The Offspring of Love; from the picture in the collection of the Marquis of Westminster. 1766. The Magdalen. 1753. The Death of Cleopatra. 1753. Cupid sleeping. 1766. Liberality and Modesty. 1755.

*After Correggio.*—The Virgin and infant Christ, with Mary Magdalene, St. Jerome, and two Angels; from the famous picture in the Academy at Parma. 1768. Do., another. 1771. The Magdalen. 1780.

*After Titian.*—Venus reclining; after the famous picture in the Florentine Gallery. Danaë; from the picture in the collection of the King of Naples. 1768. Venus and Adonis; do. 1762. Venus binding Cupid. 1769.

*After Carlo Maratti.*—The Virgin with a Choir of Angels, *Te Deum Laudamus.* 1760. The Virgin with St Catherine, and Angels contemplating the infant Jesus sleeping. 1760.

*After Guercino.*—Christ appearing to the Virgin after the Resurrection. 1773. Abraham sending Hagar away. 1763. Do., another. 1767. Queen Esther before Ahasuerus. 1767. The Death of Dido. 1766.

*After Domenichino.*—The Martyrdom of St. Agnes. 1759. St. Agnes. 1759.

*After Pietro da Cortona.*—Romulus and Remus. 1757. Cæsar repudiating Pompeia. 1757. The Finding of Romulus and Remus. 1757.

*After Salvator Rosa.*—Belisarius. 1757. Laomedon, king of Troy, detected by Neptune and Apollo. 1775.

*After Carlo Dolci.*—Sappho consecrating her Lyre to Apollo.

*After Niccolo Poussin.*—The Choice of Hercules. 1759.

*After Philip Wouwermans.*—The Return from Market, the first plate he engraved at Paris. 1750.

*After Murillo.*—The infant Jesus platting a Crown of Thorns. 1787.

*After Vandyck.*—The Infant Jesus asleep. 1787.

*After Andrea Sacchi.*—Apollo rewarding Merit. 1755.

*After Schidone.*—Cupid. 1774. The first of Duties. 1781.

*After Vanloo.*—Cupid. 1750.

*After the Antique.*—Lips, an allegorical representation of the south-west wind; Zephyr, do. of the west wind; from the bassi-relievi which ornament the tower of Andronicus Cyrrhestes at Athens, for the first volume of Stuart's "Antiquities of Athens."

STRASTER, Fray Geronimo, a Franciscan monk, who lived in the convent of his order at Valladolid, where he practiced engraving. He engraved the plates for a work entitled "Historia del Monte Celia de nuestra Señora de la Salceda," written by D. Fr. Pedro Gonzalez de Mendoza, archbishop of Granada, published in 1613. The plates are executed with considerable ability.

STRATEN, George vander, a Flemish painter, of whom little is known. He went to Lisbon, where he flourished in 1556, and painted the portraits of some of the princes and principal nobility of Portugal. It is probable, from some documents, that he was painter to the court.

STRAUCH, Lorenz, a painter born at Nuremberg in 1554. He was a skillful portrait and architectural painter, and also painted on glass. Bartsch describes only one etching by him, dated 1599, but Nagler gives a list of twenty-two; some of which are signed with his name in full, and others marked with the above monogram, dated as late as 1614. There is some question whether the prints bearing this mark are really by him; some writers interpret it *Lorenz Schnitzner*, and *Lorenz Stoer*, but the first is a *supposed name*, and the second used a mark composed of the same initials, but of a different form. The question can only be settled by a critical examination and comparison. Bartsch and Zani place his death in 1630, and Nagler in 1636.

STREATER, Robert, an English painter, born at London in 1624. He studied with a French painter, named du Moulin. He painted history, portraits, landscapes, and still-life, with such reputation, that at the Restoration, Charles II. appointed him his serjeant painter. The King had a high respect for him, and when he was afflicted with the stone to such a degree as to render an operation necessary, the Monarch procured a surgeon from France to perform it, but it proved fatal, in 1680. His principal works were the theatre at Oxford; some ceilings at Whitehall, which were destroyed by fire; the Battle of the Giants at the Palace of Sir Robert Clayton; and two al tar-pieces of Moses and Aaron in the church of St. Michael, Cornhill. Some of his finest pieces are still preserved, and possess great merit. There are a few etchings by him, indifferently executed.

STREEK, JURIAN VAN, a Dutch painter, born at Amsterdam in 1632. He painted portraits with reputation, but chiefly excelled in objects of still-life. He painted dead game, musical instruments, books, vases, and other objects, correctly designed after nature, agreeably composed, finely colored, and finished with uncommon neatness. He had a good knowledge of the chiaro-scuro, and the effect of light and shadow in his works is very picturesque, giving his objects great force, relief, and truth. He frequently introduced a skull and sepulchral lamp into his compositions. He sometimes signed his pictures with his name, and at others with the above monogram. He died in 1678.

STREEK, HENRY VAN, was the son of the preceding, born at Amsterdam in 1659. He first studied with his father, and afterwards with Emanuel de Wit, whose manner he followed. His pictures generally represent the interiors of magnificent buildings, churches, temples, and palaces. He had perfect knowledge of the principles of perspective, which enabled him to design his works with great accuracy and precision. He did not succeed so well in figures, and frequently employed other able artists to insert them in his pictures. He died in 1713.

STRESI, PIETRO MARTIRE, a Milanese painter, who died in 1620. He studied under Gio. Paolo Lomazzo, and acquired some reputation as an historical painter, but chiefly excelled, according to Lanzi, in copying the works of Raffaelle.

STRINGA, FRANCESCO, a painter born at Modena in 1635, according to Tiraboschi, and to Oretti, in 1638. According to most writers, he studied with Lodovico Lana, an imitator of Guercino, but Lanzi says it is a question whether he was not rather a pupil of Guercino himself. "All that is certainly known is, that he formed himself upon this model (Guercino and Lana), and that of other excellent masters, whose works, during his direction of the great Este Gallery, he might consult at his pleasure. Endowed with a rich imagination, spirited and rapid in his execution, he produced many works in the cathedral and other churches, which were greatly commended. His distinguishing character is the depth of his shades, the somewhat disproportioned length of his figures, and an inclination to the capricious in his composition, and in his actions. When he was advanced in years, he began to deteriorate in style, a case common to most artists." He painted history, landscape, and architecture, and engraved in aquafortis. He executed some spirited etchings from his own designs, which he signed *F. Stringa, In. F.* He died in 1709.

STRINGA, FERDINANDO, an Italian engraver, who flourished at Naples about the middle of the 18th century. He engraved a part of the plates for the Antiquities of Herculaneum, published at Naples in 1750.

STROIFI, DON ERMANNO, a painter born at Padua in 1616. Lanzi says he studied with Il Prete Genovese, and afterwards with Titian, whose style he imitated with great success, although, owing to an excessive attention to chiaro-scuro, he deviated too much from the right path. According to Boschini, he traveled for the purpose of improving himself by observing the practice of other schools, and on his return to Venice, he still continued to rise in the estimation of the Venetians. He executed several works for the churches and convents at Venice, and at Padua. He was a monk, and the founder of the order of S. Filippo Neri at Venice. He died in 1693.

STROZZI, ZANOBI, a Florentine painter of a noble family, born in 1412. He studied under F. Giovanni da Fiesole, whose style he followed; his frescos have all perished, and Lanzi says he does not know that any of his works exist in the public collections. He was living in 1466.

STROZZI, or STROZZA, BERNARDO, called IL CAPPUCCINO, and sometimes IL PRETE GENOVESE, from his monastic and ecclesiastical character, was born at Genoa in 1581. He studied under Pietro Sorri, and at an early period of his life became a monk of the order of St. Francis. Lanzi gives the following admirable account of him. "The other great colorist of this school, and the scholar of Sorri, was Bernardo Strozzi, better known under the name of *Il Cappuccino*, or the Capuchin of Genoa, from his preferring that order. He is also called *Il Prete Genovese*, because he left the cloister when a priest to support an aged mother and a sister; but the one dying, and the other marrying, he refused to return to his order; and when forcibly recalled, and sentenced to three years' imprisonment, he contrived to effect his escape, and fled to Venice, where he passed the rest of his days as a secular priest. His larger compositions are only to be found at Genoa, in the houses of the nobility, and in S. Domenico, where he executed the great picture of Paradise, one of his best works. There are too at Novi, and at Voltri, several altar pieces by him; and above all, an admirable picture of the Madonna in the Palazzo Reale, at Genoa. There are also some of his works in the churches at Venice, where he was preferred to every other artist to replace a Tondo (an oval), executed in the best age of Venetian art, in the Library of S. Marco, and he there painted a figure of Sculpture. He however left few public works. Whoever wishes to see admirable productions, must observe his pictures in eminent collections, as the Incredulity of St. Thomas in the Palazzo Brignole. When placed in a room of excellent colorists he eclipses them all by the majesty, copiousness, vigor, nature, and harmony of his style. His design is not very correct, nor sufficiently select; in these respects we see a naturalist who follows neither Sorri nor any other master, but one who, after the example of that ancient master (Apelles), derives instruction from the multitude. There is a deep expression of force and energy in his heads of men, and of piety in those of his saints; but in the countenances of his women and his youths, he has less merit; and I have seen some of his Madonnas and angels vulgar and often repeated. He was accustomed to paint portraits, and in his compositions, derived all his knowledge from the study of nature, hence there is a want of ideality, and often a meanness in his heads. He often painted half-length figures in the style of Caravaggio. In the Royal Gallery at Florence, is a picture of Christ by him, called *della Moneta;* the figures are half size and exhibit great vivacity. He is esteemed the most spirited artist of the Genoese school; and in strong impasto, in richness and vigor of coloring, he has few rivals in any other; or rather, in this style of coloring, he is original and without an example." There are two admirable works by him in the Louvre, St. Anthony of Padua caressing the infant Jesus, and the Virgin and Infant in the clouds, surrounded with a choir of angels. Strozzi also excelled in portraits. He died at Venice in 1644, and his remains were deposited in the church of S. Fosca, with this inscription, "Bernardus Strozzius, Pictorum splendor, Liguriæ decus;" a high eulogium in the seat, and near the ashes, of the greatest colorists of the Venetian school.

STRUDEL, Peter von, an eminent Tyrolese painter, the time of whose nativity is variously placed in 1648, 1660, and 1680, which last date is evidently erroneous. The best authorities place it in 1660. He went to Venice, and studied with the Cav. Carlo Loti. On leaving the school of that master, he distinguished himself so much as an historical painter, that he was invited to Vienna by the Emperor Leopold, who appointed him his principal painter, and employed him to execute several grand compositions, which gave the monarch so much satisfaction, that he conferred upon him the title of a baron. The accounts of him are singularly brief. He is said to have executed many works for the churches, convents, and public edifices of Vienna, and other cities of Germany, which are correctly designed, warmly and vigorously colored, and evince great originality of taste and conception. He particularly excelled in the graceful airs he gave to his women and children. There are several of his works in the churches of St. Lawrence, and the Augustines at Vienna; and an altar-piece in the cloister Neuburg. There were also three pictures by him in the Dusseldorf gallery—an Ecce Homo, St. John and a Holy Family. He died at Vienna in 1717.

STRUTT, Joseph, an English engraver and a writer on art, was born at Springfield, in Essex, in 1749; died in 1802. At the age of fourteen he was apprenticed to Ryland the engraver, and afterwards studied design and painting in the Royal Academy. He engraved a variety of plates in the crayon and dotted manner, in a very neat and delicate style. In 1785 and 1786, he published his "Biographical Dictionary, containing an Account of all the Engravers from the earliest period to the present time, illustrated by engravings," 2 vols. quarto; a work very creditable to his industry and judgment. Strutt also published several works relating to the ancient and modern customs of England. Among other plates, he engraved twelve illustrations for the Pilgrim's Progress, *after T. Stothard;* the Birth of Venus, 1779; Pandora presenting the fatal Box to Epimetheus, 1779; Candaules presenting his Queen to his favorite Gyges, *after le Sueur;* and an allegorical picture of America, *after R. E. Pine.*

STRY, Abraham van, a Dutch painter, born at Dort in 1753. His father was an ornamental painter, and brought his son up to his own business, but when he attained his majority, he aspired to a higher branch, in which he attained considerable reputation. He painted interiors, with representations of various occupations of the middle class, particularly of shopkeepers and other dealers. He treated these subjects with much ability He is also said to have painted landscapes with figures and cattle, in the manner of Albert Cuyp, but probably he is confounded in this respect with Jacob van Stry. His pictures are well designed, and though his coloring is rather gay, his chiaro-scuro is excellent. There are two of his works in the Museum at Amsterdam, and others are to be found in the best collections of the Netherlands. He was also a good portrait painter. Balkema places his death in 1824, and Nagler in 1830; but Immerzeel says he died March 7th, 1826.

STRY, Jacob van, a Dutch painter, born at Dort in 1756. He was doubtless the brother of the preceding. After receiving instructions from his father, he went to Antwerp, and studied with Andrew Lens, and afterwards in the Academy in that city. He also diligently studied nature, made rapid progress, and was considered one of the most promising landscape painters of his time. He made the works of Albert Cuyp and Hobbema, particularly of the former, his model. Unfortunately for his reputation, instead of striking out into an original style, he imitated them so closely, that his name has been erased from many of his best works by unprincipled dealers, who have passed them upon the unlearned, for originals by those masters. The Dutch writers boast that his pictures have brought from four to seven hundred florins in Holland, and Stanley says they have been sold in England for as many *pounds sterling*. He was an artist of great ability, highly eulogized by several cotemporary writers, and was appointed corresponding member of the Royal Institute of the Netherlands. There are three capital landscapes with figures and cattle by him in the museum at Amsterdam. He died in 1815.

STUART, Gilbert Charles. This preëminent portrait painter was born at Narraganset, Rhode Island, in 1756. He received his first instruction from a Scotch painter at Newport, named Alexander, who was so much pleased with his talents and lively disposition, that he took him with him on his return to Scotland. His friend dying soon after, the youth found himself pennyless in a strange country, but undismayed, he resolved to return home, and found himself obliged to work his passage before the mast. He had already made considerable progress in art, and on his return commenced portrait painting, although without meeting with much encouragement. He was in Boston at the time of the battle of Lexington, but immediately left that city and went to New York, where he painted the portrait of his grand-mother from memory, though she had been dead about ten years, which is said to have been a capital likeness, and gained him some business. About this time he painted his own portrait, the only one he ever took of himself, to the excellence of which, his friend Dr. Waterhouse, bears ample testimony. He says, "it was painted in the freest manner, and with a Rubens' hat," and in another place, that "Stuart, in his best days, said he need not be ashamed of it." Not meeting with any adequate encouragement, and the country being in a deplorable state, in the midst of the Revolution, he set sail for London in 1778, at the age of twenty-two, to try his fortunes in that city. Stuart was a wayward and eccentric genius, proud as Lucifer withal; and on his arrival in that metropolis, he found himself full of poverty, enthusiasm and hope,—

often a painter's only capital. He expected to have found Waterhouse, who would have helped him with his advice, and purse if necessary, but he had gone to Edinburg. Instead of going directly to West, as he should have done, he wandered about the "dreary solitude" of London, as Johnson used to characterize the busy hum of that crowded city to the poverty-stricken sons of genius, till he had expended his last dollar. He had cultivated a taste for music, and was an accomplished musician. One day as he was passing a church in Foster-Lane, hearing the sound of an organ, he stepped in, and ascertaining that the vestry were testing the candidates for the post of organist, he asked if he might try. Being told he could, he did so, and succeeded in getting the place, with a salary of thirty guineas a-year! Dr. Waterhouse at length returned to London, and procured for him better lodgings, and "managed to keep him even with his landlord and washerwoman, which was better than he had done." All this time, for some unknown reason, he never once sought the acquaintance of West, but the moment that excellent man heard of the young painter and his circumstances, he immediately sent a messenger to him with money to relieve his necessities, and invited him to call at his studio. "Such was Stuart's first introduction," says Dunlap, "to the man from whose instruction he derived the most important advantages from that time forward; whose character he always justly appreciated, but whose example he could not, or would not follow." Stuart himself says, "On application to West to receive me as a pupil, I was welcomed with true benevolence, encouraged and taken into the family, and nothing could exceed the attentions of the great artist to me,—they were paternal." He was twenty-four years old when he entered the studio of West. Before he left the roof of his benefactor and teacher, he painted a full-length portrait of him, which elicited general admiration. It was exhibited at the Royal Academy, and the young painter paid frequent visits to the exhibition rooms. It happened that one day as he stood near the picture, surrounded by artists and students (for he had fine wit, and was an inimitable story-teller), West came in and joined the group. He praised the picture, and addressing himself to his pupil, said, "you have done well, Stuart, very well; now all you have to do is to go home and do better." Stuart always expressed the obligations he was under to that distinguished artist. When West saw that he was fitted for the field, prepared for and capable of contending with the best portrait painters, he advised him to commence his professional career, and pointed out to him the way to fame and fortune. But Stuart did not follow this wise counsel, preferring to indulge his own wayward fancy. He had a noble, generous, and disinterested heart, but he was eccentric, improvident, and extravagant, and consequently he was always necessitous. There are many amusing anecdotes told of him, some of which do not redound to his credit. He himself explains how he came to adopt a custom, which, where it can be adopted, commends itself to others. "Lord St. Vincent, the Duke of Northumberland, and Colonel Barre, came unexpectedly into my room one morning, shortly after my setting up an independent easel, and explained the object of their visit. They understood that I was under pecuniary embarrassment and offered me assistance, which I declined. They then said they would sit for their portraits,—of course I was ready to serve them. They then advised that I should make it a rule that half-price must be paid at the first sitting. They insisted on setting the example, and I followed the practice ever after this delicate mode of their showing their friendship."

Stuart married the daughter of Dr. Coates in 1786. Soon afterwards, he was invited to Dublin by the Duke of Rutland, who promised him his patronage and influence, but he died while the artist was on his way. Miss Stuart, his daughter, says, "he arrived in Dublin in 1788, and notwithstanding the death of his friendly inviter, he met with great success, painted most of the nobility, and lived in a good deal of splendor. The love of his own country, his admiration of General Washington, and the very great desire he had to paint his portrait, was his *only* inducement to turn his back upon his good fortune in Europe." Accordingly, in 1793, he embarked for New York, where he took up his abode for some months, and painted the portraits of Sir John Temple, John Jay, Gen. Clarkson, John R. Murray, Colonel Giles, and other persons of distinction. In 1794, he proceeded to Philadelphia, for the purpose of painting the portrait of Washington, who received him courteously. Stuart used to say that when he entered the room where Washington was, he felt embarrassed, and that it was the first time in his life he had ever felt awe in the presence of a fellow-man. Washington was then standing on the highest eminence of earthly glory, and the gaze of the world was steadily fixed upon the man whom Botta terms "the Father of Freedom." To leave to posterity a faithful portrait of the Father of his country, had become the most earnest wish of Stuart's life. This he accomplished, but not the first time; he was not satisfied with the expression, and destroyed the picture. The President sat again, and he produced that head which embodies not only the features but the soul of Washington, and from which he painted all his other portraits of that great man. This picture in now in the Boston Athenæum.

After the removal of Congress to Washington, Stuart followed and resided there till 1806, when he went to Boston, and passed there the rest of his days. He painted a great many portraits, which are scattered all over the country. The last work he ever painted was the head of the elder John Quincy Adams. He began it a full-length; but he was an old man, and only lived to complete the head, which is considered one of his best likenesses, and shows that the powers of his mind and the magic of his pencil continued brilliant to the last. The picture was finished by that eminent and highly gifted artist, Thomas Sully, who would not touch the head, as he said "he would have thought it little less than sacrilege." He died in 1828, in the seventy-fifth year of his age.

As a painter of heads, Stuart stands almost unrivalled in any age or country; beyond this he made no pretensions, and indeed bestowed very little care or labor. He used to express his contempt for fine finishing of the extremities, or rich and elegant accessories, which he used to say was "work for girls." Whether these were his real sentiments, or affectation, it is difficult to determine. He was, however, totally deficient in that academic education which is necessary to success in the highest branch of the art—historical painting. He had genius enough to have distinguished himself in any branch, but he could not, or would not, brook the necessary toil. All who have written about Stuart speak of his wonderful conversational powers. He read men's characters at a glance, and always engaged his sitters on some interesting topic, and while their features were thus lit up, he transferred them to the canvass. Hence his portraits are full of animation, truth and nature. This trait is well illustrated by the following anecdote. While he was in England, Lord Mulgrave employed him to paint his brother, General Phipps, who was going out to India. When the portrait was finished, and the General had sailed, the Earl called for the picture, and on examining it he seemed disturbed, and said, "This picture looks strange, sir; how is it? I think I see insanity in that face." "It may be so," replied Stuart, "but I painted your brother as I saw him." The first account Lord Mulgrave had of his brother, was that insanity, unknown and unapprehended by any of his friends, had driven him to commit suicide. Washington Allston, in his eulogium of Stuart, says, "The narratives and anecdotes with which his knowledge of men and the world had stored his memory, and which he often gave with great beauty and dramatic effect, were not unfrequently employed by Mr. Stuart in a way, and with an address peculiar to himself. From this store it was his custom to draw largely, while occupied with his sitters, apparently for their amusement; but his object was rather, by thus banishing all restraint, to call forth, if possible, some involuntary traits of natural character. But these glances of character, mixed as they are in all men with so much that belongs to their age and associates, would have been of little use to an ordinary observer; for the faculty of distinguishing between the accidental and the permanent, in other words between the conventional expression which belongs to manners and that more subtle indication of the individual mind, is indeed no common one; and by few, if indeed by any, has this faculty been possessed in so remarkable a degree. It was this which enabled him to animate his canvass, not with the appearance of mere general life, but with that peculiar, distinctive life which separates the humblest individual from his kind. He seemed to dive into the thoughts of man—for they were made to rise and speak on the surface. Were other evidences wanting, this talent alone were sufficient to establish his claims as a man of genius; since it is the privilege of genius alone to measure at once the highest and the lowest. In his happier efforts, no one ever surpassed him in embodying, if we may so speak, these transient apparitions of the soul. Of this, not the least admirable instance is his portrait of President Adams, whose bodily tenement at the time seemed rather to present the image of a dilapidated castle, than the habitation of the unbroken mind; but not such is the picture—called forth from its crumbling recess, the living tenant is there, still ennobling the ruin, and upholding it, as it were, by the strength of his inner life. In this venerable ruin, will the unbending patriot and the gifted artist speak of the first glorious century of the republic. In a word, Gilbert Stuart was, in its widest sense, a philosopher in his art; he thoroughly understood its principles, as his works bear witness—whether as to harmony of colors, or of lines, or of light and shadow—showing that exquisite sense of a whole which only a man of genius can embody Jealousy was unknown to him, but where praise was due he gave it freely, and gave it with a grace too which showed that, loving excellence for its own sake, he had a pleasure in praising it. To young artists he was uniformly kind and indulgent, and most liberal of his advice, which no one ever properly asked but he received, and in a manner no less courteous than impressive."

STUART, James, called *The Athenian*, was an English architect, born at London in 1713. His father, a Scottish mariner, died while James was very young, and the latter materially assisted his mother in the support of her family, by the profits of his ingenuity in designing and painting fans for an engraver named Goupy. By great application, he acquired a knowledge of anatomy and geometry, and also of the Greek and Latin languages. In 1742 he set out for Italy, by the way of Holland and France, defraying his expenses by exercising his talents on the route. At Rome, he formed an intimate acquaintance with Nicholas Revett, a painter and architect; and, after several years' study, they formed a plan for visiting Athens, and published proposals, soliciting assistance to carry it into execution. Having received from England the necessary aid, they quitted Rome in March 1750, proceeded to Venice, and thence to Pola in Istria, to examine the interesting remains of antiquity at that place. Returning to Venice, they sailed to Zante in the beginning of 1751, and thence to Corinth. In the month of March they reached Athens, and remained there about two years and a half, making drawings and exact measurements of the architectural remains. Stuart there became acquainted with Sir Jacob Bouverie, and Mr. Dawkins, the latter of whom proved a most liberal patron. From Athens, they visited Salonica, and several islands of the Ægean Sea, returning to England in the beginning of 1755. The result of their labors appeared in 1762, when the first volume was published of their work in folio, entitled, "The Antiquities of Athens, measured and delineated, by James Stuart, F. R. S., and S. A., and Nicholas Revett, Painters and Architects." In the drawings and measurements of this work, their labors were doubtless united; but the letter-press appears to have been Stuart's. It was received with great applause by the lovers of art and antiquity; and although anticipated by Leroy's *Ruines*, which surpassed it in picturesque beauty, yet its superior truth and depth of research gave it a more solid and permanent value. Stuart, on his return to England, was patronised by several persons of rank and influence, in the practical department of his profession. Lord Anson procured for him the appointment of surveyor to Greenwich Hospital. Among his principal works were, the seat of Lord Eardley, near Erith, Kent; Mrs. Montague's House, Portman Square; the chapel and infirmary at Greenwich Hospital; and the seat of Lord Anson, in Staffordshire. Stuart died in 1788. The second volume of the Athenian Antiquities was published by Mr. Newton, in 1790, the third by Mr. Revely, in 1794.

STUBBS, George, an eminent English painter of animals, was born at Liverpool in 1724. It is not known under whom he studied, but he went to Rome at the age of thirty for improvement, and on his return settled in London, where he soon distinguished himself as a painter of animals, particularly the horse, which he designed with the greatest anatomical accuracy, to ensure which he practiced dissection. In 1766, he published "The Anatomy of the Horse," all the plates of which he etched himself, from his own designs. Though he chiefly devoted his attention to this branch of the art, he was capable of higher exertions, as is proved by his picture of Phaëton with the Horses of the Sun. His pictures of the Lion and the Horse, the Lion and the Stag, &c., were highly applauded. He was the inventor of a method of painting large landscapes in a kind of enamel, on plates of iron, of little value. He etched and engraved in mezzotinto some fine plates of animals, from his own designs. Other pictures by him were engraved by Woollett, Earlom, Green, Hodges, and other eminent engravers. At the time of his death, he was employed upon a work entitled "A Comparative Anatomical Exposition of the Structure of the Human Body, with that of the Tiger and the Common Fowl." He was elected an associate of the Royal Academy, and died in 1806.

STUBBS, George Townley, was the son of the preceding, born in 1756, and died in 1815. He engraved some plates of animals, after his father's works, and other subjects after other English painters.

STUERBOUT. See Dirck van Haerlem.

STURMIO, Hernando, a Spanish painter, who flourished at Seville, according to Bermudez, about the middle of the 16th century. He painted the altar-piece of the Four Evangelists, for the chapel of the Evangelists, and another grand picture in the Cathedral, in several compartments, representing the Resurrection, St. Gregory saying mass, the patron saints of Seville, and other subjects. These works are well designed and colored.

STURMIUS, Leonard Christopher, an eminent German writer upon architecture, was born at Altorf in 1669. After receiving a liberal education, he studied divinity, but soon quitted it for the mathematics. In 1714 he published "Prodromus Architecturæ Goldmannianæ," and afterwards, in separate treatises, a new edition of Goldmann; the whole forming a "Complete Course of Civil Architecture," printed at Augsburg, in 16 vols. fol. His next work was "Sciagraphia Templi Hierosolymitani," in folio. In 1697, he started on a tour through France and the Netherlands, and published, in 1719, the result of his observations in a work in folio, illustrated with numerous plates from his own designs. At Mecklenburgh he erected the palace of Neustadt, on the Elde. He also made an unsuccessful attempt to form a sixth order of architecture. Sturmius was successively honored with the appointments of Professor of Mathematics at Wolfenbuttel, and in the University of Frankfort on the Oder; also of Counsellor of the Chamber of Finances, and Director of Buildings at the court of Frederick William, Duke of Mecklenburgh. He died in 1719

STURT, John, an English engraver, born at London in 1658, and died there in 1730. He was a pupil of Robert White, and his chief excellence consisted in engraving ornamental letters. His principal work is a Book of Common Prayer, published in 1717. The top of every page is ornamented with a small scriptural vignette, neatly executed.

STUVEN, Ernest, a German painter, born at Hamburg in 1657. He learned the rudiments of art in his native city, of an obscure painter named Hins, and at the age of eighteen went to Amsterdam, and studied with John Voorhout, a reputable painter of history. The fruit and flower pieces of Abraham Mignon were then held in the highest estimation, and Stuven having a taste for that branch of the art, he became the pupil of that master, and imitated his manner with considerable success. Though his works are not so exquisitely finished and delicately colored as those of Mignon, they are held in considerable estimation. He died in 1712.

SUARDI, Bartolomeo. See Bramantino.

SUÁREZ, or JUÁREZ, Lorenzo, a Spanish painter who was born at Murcia, and flourished there about 1600. In conjunction with Cristobal Acebedo, he executed several works for the convent of the Shod Carmelites in his native city, which are said to display considerable ability.

SUAVIUS. See Suterman.

SUBLEYRAS, Pierre, an eminent French painter, born at Usès in Languedoc, in 1699. After acquiring the elements of design from his father, Matthieu S., an artist of little note, he entered the school of Antoine Rivalz, at Toulouse, at the age of fifteen. In 1724, he went to Paris, and frequented the Royal Academy, where he obtained, two years after, the grand prize in painting, for his fine picture of the Brazen Serpent. He visited Rome for improvement, with the royal pension. According to Lanzi, when Subleyras entered the French Academy at Rome, it was distinguished for a certain mannerism, designated *spiritoso* by Mengs, which had brought it into disrepute, consisting in transgressing the limits of propriety and beauty, overcharging both the one and the other, and aiming at fascinating the eye rather than satisfying the judgment. Subleyras, though instructed in this false taste, had sufficient discrimination to reject it entirely; he reformed the prevailing manner, retaining the good, avoiding the feeble part, and added from his own genius what was lacking to make a truly original style. His pictures are distinguished for admirable fidelity of representation, an engaging variety in the airs of the heads and the attitudes of the figures, and great skill in the distribution of the chiaro-scuro, which gives them a fine general effect. His figures and drapery have a certain fullness and grandeur, which in him appears easy, because natural; but it was never emulated by his scholars. Upon leaving the Academy, he was already an accomplished artist; and he was commissioned, in preference to Masucci, to paint the portrait of Benedict XIV., which, according to Lanzi, established his reputation as the first painter at Rome. He was soon afterwards chosen to paint the History of St. Basil, for the purpose of being copied in mosaic, for the church of the Vatican. The original is at the Carthusians, and is a most admirable production, remarkable for the august representation of the Sacrifice solemnly celebrated by that Saint in the presence of the Emperor Valens, who is offering bread at the altar. Lanzi says, "the countenances are very animated; there is great truth in the drapery and accompaniments; and the silks, in their light and lucid folds, appear absolutely real." Subleyras settled permanently at Rome, and executed many altar-pieces for the churches in that city, and other places in Italy, among which his St. Benedict resuscitating an Infant, in the Olivetani at Perugia, is accounted his masterpiece. He also painted many portraits and easel pictures, which are highly prized, even in the choicest collections. He was chosen a member of the Academy of St. Luke about 1740, and presented a sketch of his picture of Mary Magdalene washing the feet of Christ; it was afterwards executed in oil for a monastery at Turin, and is now in the Louvre, with two other of his productions. Subleyras was subsequently received into the Academy of the Arcadi, with his wife (formerly Maria Felice Tibaldi, a paintress in miniature), under the names of Protogenes and Asteria. He died at Rome in 1749. There are two of his works in the Academy of the Brera at Milan; and one representing the Fall of Simon Magus, in England, at Alton Tower, the seat of the Earl of Shrewsbury. There are a few spirited and tasteful etchings by Subleyras, among which are the following, from his own designs: The Brazen Serpent. The Martyrdom of St. Peter. Mary Magdalene washing the Feet of Christ. A set of four plates from La Fontaine's Fables. The Holy Family, in an oval. St. Bruno restoring a Child to life. Martyrdom of St. Peter.

SUBTERMANS. See SUSTERMANS.

SUEUR, EUSTACHE LE, an eminent French painter, born at Paris in 1617. He was the son of an obscure sculptor, who, discovering in him a talent for painting, placed him under the tuition of Simon Vouet. He was, however, more indebted to a diligent study of the antique marbles, and the fine pictures of the Roman school which Francis I. had caused to be brought into France, and to which he had free access, than to the precepts of his instructor. Though he never visited Italy, and had not the advantage of studying the works of Raffaelle at Rome, he was an enthusiastic admirer of that great master, and in his laudable ambition of emulating him, he threw aside the frippery and affected style then prevalent in his country. The simplicity and grandeur of his compositions, and the purity of his design procured for him, among his countrymen, the honorable appellation of the *French Raffaelle.* The French biographers do not hesitate to compare his talents with those of Raffaelle, and M. Watelet, one of the least prejudiced of the French critics, elevates his talents to nearly a level with those of the illustrious head of the Roman school. Making every allowance for national partiality, it must be allowed that no painter of his country, N. Poussin only excepted (who ought to be regarded as a Roman rather than a Parisian), approached so nearly to the dignity and grandeur of the Roman school; yet there can be no justice nor advantage in comparing him to Raffaelle. He had an easy and fertile invention, his compositions are noble and elevated, his draperies are simple and grand, and in the manner of his folds he observed the order of the antique. Yet his close attention to his models, without a sufficient study of nature, contributed to give a hardness and dryness to his works. He never divested himself entirely of the manner of coloring which he had acquired under Vouet, and he knew but little either of chiaro-scuro, or of local colors. Though he had extraordinary merit, it was blended with great imperfections, so that in some parts of all his pictures he was unequal to himself. His taste of design and the airs of his heads are justly to be admired, but his nude figures are faulty in their disposition, as well as in the action of the muscles. His coloring is tender and delicate, yet it wants vigor and force, and the distribution of his lights and shadows is far from judicious. His attitudes, however, are noble, simple, and natural, his expression great, and well adapted to his subject, and he was ingenious in the choice of his objects. Upon the whole, he may be said to have had an uncommon mixture of the perfections and imperfections of the art; he excelled in the superior and most difficult parts, and erred in those which are least important, yet necessary to form a perfect whole.

Le Sueur never received that patronage and consideration to which his talents and great merits eminently entitled him. His dignified and unpretending style was less captivating than the gaudy and fantastic productions of some of his cotemporaries. In 1640 he was received into the Academy, and painted, for his reception piece, St. Paul casting out a Demon. He was soon afterwards engaged in his celebrated series of twenty-two pictures, representing the Life of St. Bruno, for the monastery of the Carthusians at Paris. These pictures were afterwards purchased by the king, and arranged in one of the apartments of the Luxembourg; they are now in the Louvre, with twenty other works by him of different subjects, among which are the famous pictures of St. Paul preaching at Ephesus, painted for the church of Notre Dame, and the Descent from the Cross, formerly in the church of S. Gervais. There is a single etching by le Sueur, representing the Holy Family, half-length figures, from his own design. He died in 1655.

SUEUR, PIERRE LE, called the Elder, a French engraver on wood, born at Rouen in 1636, and died there in 1716. According to Papillon, he studied with an artist named du Bellay, whom he greatly surpassed. He generally marked his prints with a monogram composed of his initials, P. L. S., as above.

SUEUR, PIERRE LE, called the Younger, was the son of the preceding, born at Rouen in 1663. He was instructed by his father, whom he surpassed. His drawing is tolerably correct, and his cuts are executed with great neatness and delicacy. He went to Paris, where he settled, and engraved some devout subjects, biblical prints, and other subjects, which he usually marked with his initials, P. L. S.

SUEUR, VINCENT LE, was a younger brother of the preceding, born at Rouen in 1668. After receiving instruction from his father, he went to Paris, and studied with Jean Papillon. He distinguished himself as an engraver on wood, and executed a variety of cuts, from his own designs and after other masters, some of which are printed in chiaro-scuro. He marked his prints V. L. S.

SUEUR, NICHOLAS LE, was the son of Pierre le S. the Younger, born at Paris in 1690. He studied with his father, excelled as an engraver on wood, and was the most eminent of the family

He executed some beautiful cuts, mostly in chiaroscuro, for the Crozat collection, which gained him great reputation. He also engraved in a very tasteful manner, the embellishments for an edition of La Fontaine's Fables, from the designs of Bachelier. The following are among his best prints, executed for the Crozat collection. He died at Paris in 1764.

Fishermen drawing their Nets; *after Giulio Romano.* The Mass; *after Polidoro da Caravaggio.* The Egyptians overwhelmed in the Red Sea; *after Gio. Fran. Penni,* called *Il Fattore.* Christ with the Apostles; *after Raffaelle del Colle.* The Man and the Lion; *after Bal. Peruzzi.* The Death of St. Francis Xavier; *after Lod. Gimignani.* The Descent of the Holy Ghost; *after G. B. Lenardi.* The Annunciation; *after G. M. Morandi.* The Virgin appearing to St. Philip Neri; *after L. Garzi.* The Virgin on a Throne, surrounded by Saints; *after P. Pietri.*

SUGGER. This architect was an abbot of St. Denis, and flourished about the middle of the 12th century. In 1140, he rebuilt the church of St. Denis, near Paris, with magnificent additions. Its length is 335 feet, and its width from the middle nave 39 feet. The vault is of an equal elevation in every part, and supported by slender columns; the entire edifice is lighted by three orders of windows.

SUISSE, Le, an engraver on wood mentioned by Papillon, who executed several cuts, particularly a large one representing a Turkish army arrayed in order of battle. He is probably the same as Christopher Stimmer, which see.

SUIZER, John, a Dutch engraver, who flourished about 1650, and executed some book plates. He is doubtless the same as John Schweizer, which see.

SULIVAN, Luke, an Irish miniature painter and engraver, of little note. He went to London, where he learned engraving of Thomas Major. As an engraver, he was principally employed by Hogarth, to engrave from his pictures, and he sometimes worked conjointly with that artist.

SUNMAN, or SOUMANS, William, a Dutch portrait painter, who went to London in the reign of Charles II., where, after the death of Lely, he acquired considerable practice. He was employed to paint several large pictures of the founders of the University of Oxford, which are preserved there in the picture gallery. He died about 1707.

SUPPA, Andrea, a Sicilian painter, born at Messina, according to Hackert, in 1628. He studied with Bartolomeo Tricomi, whom he excelled, particularly in portraits, which he executed with great truthfulness. Lanzi says "he studied landscape and architecture under Abraham Casembrodt; but he formed himself principally upon the antique, and by constantly studying Raffaelle and the Caracci, and other select masters, he acquired a most enchanting style of countenances, and indeed of every part of his composition. His works are as fine as miniature, and are perhaps too highly finished. His subjects, in unison with his genius, are of a pensive and melancholy cast, and are always treated in a pathetic manner. He excelled in frescos, and painted the vaults in the Suore in S. Paolo; he excelled equally in oils, as may be seen from the picture of S. Scolastica, there also. He died in 1671.

SURCHI, Giovanni Francesco, called Dielai, a painter born at Ferrara. He was a disciple of the Dossi, whom he assisted in some of the principal works in the palaces Belriguardo, Belvidere, Giovecca, and Cepario. Lanzi says, "Thus instructed by both brothers, he became, perhaps, the most eminent figurist among his fellow-pupils, and beyond question, the best ornamental painter. He left many specimens in the first branch, but few in the second. In rapidity vivacity, and grace in his figures, he approaches Dosso Dossi; also in his easy and natural mode of draping. In the warmth of his coloring, and in his strong lights, he even aimed at surpassing him; but, like most young artists who carry to excess the maxims of their schools, he became somewhat crude and inharmonious, at least in some of his works. Two of his Nativities at Ferrara are highly extolled, one at the Benedettini and the other at S. Giovannino, to which he added the portrait of Ippolito Riminaldi, a distinguished civilian of his age; both possess great merit." Barotti notices several other works by him in the churches at Ferrara, particularly the Marriage of St. Catherine in S. Anna, and the Adoration of the Shepherds in S. Giovannino. He died in 1590.

SURRUGUE, Louis, a French engraver, born at Paris in 1695. He was instructed in design and engraving by Bernard Picart, whose style he followed with success, and, like his instructor, united the point and the graver in a very agreeable manner. Though his drawing is not very correct, he acquired distinction, and was elected a member of the Academy of Paris. His prints are very numerous, and are after some of the greatest masters of the Italian, French, and Flemish schools. The following are among his best prints; for a full list the reader is referred to Nagler's Lexicon. He died in 1769.

PORTRAITS.

Louis de Boullongne, Painter to the King; *after Matthieu.* Joseph Christopher Veirier, Sculptor.

SUBJECTS AFTER VARIOUS MASTERS.

St. Margaret; *after Raffaelle;* for the Crozat collection. St. Jerome in the Desert; *after Bal. da Siena;* engraved by *N. Chateau,* and finished by *L. Surrugue;* do. Christ curing the ten Leprous Men; *after Girol. Genga;* do. Abraham sacrificing Isaac; *after A. del Sarto.* The Birth of the Virgin; *after P. da Cortona.* Abraham sending away Hagar; *after le Sueur.* Venus nursing Love; *after Rubens.* A Flemish Merry-making and the Fortune-Teller; two plates; *after Teniers.*

SURRUGUE, Pierre Louis, was the son of the preceding, born at Paris in 1717. He was instructed by his father, whose style he followed, though he was inferior to him. He executed quite a number of plates after Correggio, Guido, Coypel, Latour, Teniers, Pater, Chardin, and other masters. He died in 1771.

SUSTERMANS, or SUBTERMANS, Justus, an eminent Flemish painter, born at Antwerp in 1597. He first studied under William de Vos, and afterwards with Francis Pourbus. He next traveled through Germany to Italy, in search of improvement, and after stopping some time at Venice, he proceeded to Florence, where his talents recommended him to the patronage of the Grand Duke Cosmo II., who appointed him his painter. He continued in the service of that prince till his death, and was continued in his office by his successor, Cosmo III., to the end of his reign. Sustermans painted history and portraits, and in the latter branch he was considered little inferior to Vandyck. When that distinguished painter visited Florence, he expressed his admiration of the works of Sustermans, and painted his portrait, of which we have an etching by Vandyck himself. Rubens also esteemed him, and presented him with one of his own historical works, regarding him as an honor to his country. Lanzi says, "Sustermans painted all the living members of the Medicean family in a variety of attitudes; and when Ferdinand II. ascended the throne, he executed a stupendous picture, wholly composed of portraits. He represented in it the ceremony of swearing allegiance to the new sovereign; and portrayed with him his mother and grandmother, and the senators and nobility who were present. This picture is very large, has been engraved, and still remains in the Gallery. The artist had a neatness and elegance of pencil, extraordinary even in the school to which he belonged; and he possessed a peculiar talent of ennobling every countenance, without injuring the likeness. It was his custom to study the peculiar and characteristic air of the person, and to impart it to his work, so that when he would sometimes conceal the face of a portrait, by the bystanders it could certainly be told whom it represented, from the figure, and the disposition of the hands."

Sustermans was also employed by several other princes of Italy and Germany, as well as the nobility, who were ambitious of having their portraits painted by an artist scarcely less famous, or inferior to Vandyck. His historical works are composed in a grand style, and his design, refined by his studies in Italy, is elegant and correct. His coloring possesses all the clearness, brilliancy, and strength of his country, and he had an excellent knowledge of the chiaro-scuro, which enabled him to give his figures, and every object, a surprising relief.. His name is called by the Italians *Subtermans*; and he is sometimes confounded with *Suterman*, an entirely different artist, from similarity of names. His real name was *Sustermans*. He died in 1681.

SUSTRIS, or SUSTER, Lanzi says, is the surname of Federigo di Lamberto, called also F. del Padovano, a Fleming who flourished in 1568, at Florence, of which place he had become a citizen. Vasari also commends him, and says he was an ornament to the Academy there. This artist cannot be the same as Lambert Lombard, as some have supposed, from similarity of names, for that artist had returned many years before to Liege, where he is supposed to have died about 1565. See ***Lambert Lombard*** and *Suterman*.

SUTERMAN, Lambert, called also Suavius, a Flemish painter and engraver, born at Liege, where he flourished about the middle of the 16th century. He was a disciple of Lambert Lombard. Nothing is known of him with certainty as a painter, but there are quite a number of prints by him, after the works of his instructor, and from his own designs. He generally marked his plates with his initials, L. S., and the date.

The history of three Flemish artists, viz., Lambert Lombard, Lambert Suterman, and Justus Sustermans, has been mixed up, by some careless writers, in the most admirable confusion, under the names of *Lambert Suterman*, or *Sutermans*, or *Sustermans, Suavius, Suster*, or *Sustris.*—There is a picture in the Louvre attributed to *Lambert Suster*, who it is said was a pupil of Christopher Schwartz, and afterwards of Titian, and died at Munich in 1600. (See ***Lambert Lombard, Sustermans***, and *Sustris.*, Among others are the following prints by Suterman:

SUBJECTS AFTER LAMBERT LOMBARD.

The Resurrection of Lazarus; *Lambert Lombard, inv. L. S.* 1544. Christ with the Disciples at Emmaus. The Entombing of Christ. St. Peter and St. John healing the Lame Man at the Gate of the Temple. The taking down from the Cross.

SUBJECTS FROM HIS OWN DESIGNS.

The Twelve Apostles; dated 1545, 1547, and 1548. The Head of Christ; circular. 1559. The Head of the Virgin; do. Some portraits, among which is that of M. Angelo Buonarotti.

SUVÉE, Joseph Benoit, a distinguished painter of the French school, was born at Bruges in 1743. After acquiring the elements of design under Matthew de Visch, he visited Paris, and entered the school of Bachelier, where he made such rapid progress that, at the age of twenty-three, he was appointed to superintend the free school of design in that city. In 1771 he gained the grand prize, and went to Rome with the royal pension, by the way of Bruges, where he was honored with a public banquet by the city magistrates. After studying for seven years the antique and the works of the great masters, he returned to Paris, and in 1780 was chosen a member of the Academy. He exhibited several pictures at the Louvre, which were much admired. His compositions are more distinguished for graceful expression and harmonious effect, than for vigorous coloring and spirited touch. Among the principal are the Descent from the Cross, and the Adoration of the Magi, in a church at Ypres; the Origin of Painting, in the Academy at Bruges, and the Resurrection, in the church of S. Donat. Most of his pictures are to be found in France. In 1792, Suvée was appointed Director of the French Academy at Rome, but was prevented by the civil commotions from entering upon the duties of his office until 1801, when he proceeded to Rome. Finding the institution almost entirely abandoned, he labored several years with great assiduity to restore its reputation and prosperity, and had finally succeeded in establishing it with comparative stability, in the Villa de' Medicis, when he died suddenly, in 1807.

SUYDERHOEF, Jonas, an eminent Dutch designer and engraver, born at Leyden, the times of whose birth and death are not exactly known; several writers variously place his birth about 1600 and 1613; Zani says he operated from 1631 to 1668. He studied with Peter Soutman, whose style he followed, but excelled him in the delicacy and harmony of his execution. Although his plates are finished with uncommon neatness, they produce a vigorous and harmonious effect, and exhibit great knowledge of the principles of chiaroscuro. He advanced his plates with the point, and finished them with the graver, in a very picturesque and pleasing style. He executed a considerable number of plates of portraits and other subjects, after the Flemish masters, and some from his own designs, which are deservedly held in high estimation. The following are his best prints:

PORTRAITS.

The Emperor Maximilian; *after Lucas of Leyden.* The Empress Maria, his consort; *do.* Maximilian, Archduke of Austria; *after Rubens.* Philip III. King of Spain; *do.* Albert, Archduke of Austria, Governor of the Netherlands; *do.* Isabella Clara Eugenia, Infanta of Spain, his consort; *do.* Charles I., King of England; *after Vandyck.* Henrietta Maria, his Queen; *do.* Francis de Moncade, Count d'Ossonne; *do.* John the Bold, Duke of Burgundy; *after P. Soutman.* Charles the Warlike, Duke of Burgundy; *do.* Aldus Swalmius, the old Man with the Beard; *after Rembrandt.* René Descartes, Astronomer; *after F. Hals.* Anna Maria Schurmans; *after J. Lievens.*

SUBJECTS AFTER VARIOUS MASTERS.

The Fall of the Angels; *after Rubens.* The Virgin embracing the infant Jesus; *do.* A Bacchanalian subject; *do.* A Drunken Bacchus, supported by a Satyr and a Moor; *do.* The Hunting of the Lion and Tiger; *do.* The Peace of Munster, containing the Portraits of the Plenipotentiaries; *after G. Terburg;* one of his finest plates. Dutch Peasants quarreling; *do.* The Burgomasters of Amsterdam; *after Theod. de Keyser.* Three old Women regaling; *after Ostade.* Three Boors, one playing on the Violin; *do.* The Tric-trac Players; *do.* Dutch Boors fighting with Knives; *do.* Dutch Boors dancing, called the Ball; *do.*

SWAGERS, Francis, a Dutch painter, born at Utrecht in 1756. It is not known under whom he studied, but after acquiring considerable reputation in his native city as a painter of landscapes and marines, he went to Paris, where he resided till his death. His works are numerous, and consist mostly of views in Holland, in the vicinity of Utrecht, Haerlem, Rotterdam, and Dort, and mariners off the coast, with fishing smacks, &c. From his long residence in Paris, he imbibed much of the French taste, and his pictures executed there exhibit a mixture of the Dutch and French schools. They are, however, pleasing compositions, and are held in considerable estimation. He died in 1836.

SWAINE, Francis, an English marine painter, who lived in London from about 1770 to 1780. He painted small sea-pieces in the style of the elder Vandervelde, for the dealers. Stanley says, "he earned his bread, but got no reputation, though a clever painter. His very name is held in abhorrence when pronounced before one of his own pictures, as it deprives *old* Vandervelde of the honor, and endangers the dealer's profits. Many ***English Vanderveldes*** are certainly by Swaine." Stanley ought to have known, as he was one of the craft.

SWANENBURG, William van, a Dutch engraver, born at Leyden about 1581. Little is known of him except by his works. Huber says he was a disciple of John Saenredam, but his style has a greater resemblance to that of Henry Goltzius. He had a great command of the graver, and his plates are executed in a bold, free style, but his drawing is not very correct. The following are his most esteemed prints:

PORTRAITS.

Maurice, Prince of Orange Nassau. Ernest Casimir, Count of Nassau. John William, Duke of Cleves. Daniel Heinsius, Historian. 1608. Abraham Bloemaert, Painter.

SUBJECTS AFTER VARIOUS MASTERS.

Esau selling his Birth-right to Jacob; *after P. Morelsen.* The Resurrection; *do.* The Adoration of the Shepherds; *after Ab. Bloemaert.* The six Penitents; *do.* St. Jerome in the Desert; *do.* St. Peter penitent; *do.* Lot and his Daughters; *after Rubens.* Christ with the Disciples at Emmaus; *do.* The Judgment of Paris; *after M. Mireveldt.* Perseus and Andromeda; *after J. Saenredam.* A Village Festival; *after D. Vinckenbooms.* A set of fourteen Plates, entitled *The Throne of Justice; after Joachim Uytenwael.* 1605, 1606.

SWANEVELT, Hermann, a very eminent Dutch painter, born at Woerden in Holland, in 1620. He is said to have first studied with Gerard Douw, but this is very doubtful. He went young to Italy, where he passed the rest of his life, and from his studious and retired life was called the *Hermit of Italy.* On his arrival at Rome, he was indefatigable in the pursuit of his studies; he was seen to frequent the most sequestered places, and he designed the most interesting views and the most remarkable vestiges of antiquity in the vicinity of that metropolis. In 1640, he is said to have become the pupil of Claude Lorraine, whose productions he had contemplated with wonder and delight; this however, though highly probable, seems to rest merely on conjecture and assertion. At all events, he made the works of that great painter his model, and followed his precepts. He became one of the most celebrated landscape painters of his time, and his works were held in such estimation that he could scarcely supply the demand for them. Though the scenery of Swanevelt is less extensive and select, and his coloring less warm and glowing than that of his inimitable model, yet he nearly equalled him in the suavity and tenderness of his tints, in aërial perspective, in the delicate degradation of his distances; and he excelled him in his figures and animals. His pictures are usually enriched with the choicest relics of antiquity, as edifices, ruins, and monuments, and he decorated them with groups of figures and cattle, tastefully composed, and designed with elegance and correctness. Swanevelt approached Claude nearer than any other master; hence his pictures are held in the highest estimation, and are only to be found in the choicest collections, and mostly in Italy.

Hermann Swanevelt produced a large number of etchings from his own designs, executed in a free, spirited, and masterly style. Bartsch describes 116 (P. G., tom. ii.). He handled the point with uncommon neatness and dexterity, and his prints are held in the highest estimation. The following are the principal:

A set of eighteen small oval plates, representing Views in Italy, and rural subjects; entitled *Variæ campestri fantasiæ a Hermano Swanevelt, invent. et in lucem editæ.* A set of thirteen Italian Landscapes, including the title; dedicated to Gideon Tallement. A set of twelve Views in and near Rome; entitled *Diverses Vues dedans et dehors de Rome,* &c. 1653. A set of seven Plates of Animals, with landscape back-grounds and figures. A set of four Arcadian Landscapes, with Nymphs and Satyrs. A set of four Landscapes, with Biblical subjects. A set of four Mountainous Landscapes, with different representations of the Flight into Egypt. A set of four Views of the Appenines, with pastoral subjects. A set of six grand Landscapes, with the history of Venus and Adonis. A set of four Landscapes, with different Saints and Mary Magdalene.

SWEBACH, James, called also Fontaines, a Belgian painter, whose life has not yet been written. He flourished from about 1800 to 1824, and resided chiefly at Paris. He painted battles, marches, encampments, landscapes, and huntings, with ability. All his compositions of military subjects and huntings are remarkably spirited, and prove that he was well acquainted with the manœuvres of the field, either as a soldier or a sportsman. His pictures are numerous, and held in considerable estimation. Some of his works were engraved by Couché, Beauvinet, and Bertaux; and since his death many have been executed in mezzotinto, aquatinto, and lithography. Swebach etched a great number of his own compositions, which were published collectively at Paris, in five vols. quarto, under the title, "Encyclopedie Pittoresque; ou, Suite de compositions, caprices, et etudes utiles aux Artistes." He died at Paris about 1824. He left a talented son, Edward Swebach, whom he instructed in the art, and who painted and designed similar subjects.

SWEERTS, or SWERTS, MICHAEL, a Dutch painter and engraver, who flourished about 1655. Little is known of his history. He is said to have been a good portrait painter, but he is only known by his prints, of portraits and other subjects, chiefly from his own designs. Bartsch describes sixteen prints by him, some of which are signed *Michael Sweerts Eques pin. et fecit.*

SWELINCK, JOHN, a Dutch engraver, who flourished at Amsterdam from about 1620 to 1635. Among other plates, he engraved a set of emblematical subjects, *after A. vander Venne;* some subjects of the Life of the Virgin, the Resuscitation of Lazarus, and St. John the Evangelist. His plates are executed with the graver, in a style resembling that of the Wierixes, and he marked them with his initials, J. S.

SWIDDE, WILLIAM, a Dutch engraver, who flourished in the latter part of the 17th century. Little is known of him, except by his works. There are some large marines by him, dated about 1680; also a set of six landscapes, with figures and cattle, *after Dirk Dalens.* He went to Stockholm, where he resided about 1690. He engraved several plates for a work entitled *Suecia Antiqua et Hodierna*, containing views of the principal buildings in Sweden, and the plates for Puffendorf's Life of Charles Gustavus.

SWITZER, CHRISTOPHER, a German engraver on wood, who resided in England about 1614. He was employed by Speed to cut the coins and seals for his History of Great Britain, from the originals in the Cottonian collection. Speed calls him *the most exquisite and curious hand of that age.* He had a son, also named Christopher, who assisted him, and whose works are confounded with those of his father. Stanley says he is the same as Christopher Stimmer—a very doubtful assertion.

SWITZER, JOSEPH, a Swiss painter, born at Berne in 1570. He went to Rome, where he is said to have studied with John van Achen, whose style he followed with considerable success. He died at Rome in 1629.

SYBRECHT, JOHN, a Flemish painter, born at Antwerp in 1625. He was the son of an obscure painter, who instructed him in the art. He afterwards improved himself by studying nature, and the works of Berghem and Karel du Jardin, both which painters he is said to have imitated with great success. He painted both in oil and water-colors, and the latter are the most numerous. He painted landscapes with figures and cattle, and views on the Rhine. He went to England at the invitation of the Duke of Buckingham, who employed him at Cliefden. He died at London in 1703. His name is variously written, *Sybrecht*, *Sybrechts*, *Sibrecht*, and *Sibrechts.*

SYDER, DANIEL, called by the Italians, IL CAVALIERE DANIELLO, a German painter, born at Vienna in 1647. After receiving instruction in his native city, he went to Venice, and studied under Carlo Loti, whose style he emulated with so much success, that some of the works which he executed for the churches and private collections in that city have been mistaken for those of his instructor. He next proceeded to Rome, to improve himself by a study of the antique and the works of the great masters. Carlo Maratti was then at the height of his reputation, and Syder entered his school, where he distinguished himself so much that Maratti procured him the commission to paint two pictures—the Children of Israel gathering Manna, for the Chiesa Nuova, and the Last Supper, for the church of S. Filippo Neri. These works established his reputation, and his instructor recommended him to the patronage of the Duke of Savoy, who invited him to his court, appointed him his painter, conferred on him the honor of knighthood, and presented him with his own walking stick, richly set with diamonds. Syder also excelled in portraits. He died at Rome in 1721. The Italians apply the history of this painter to an artist variously called *Saiter*, *Seiter*, *Sauter*, *Seutter*, and *Schuter*. The accounts nearly agree, and they are doubtless one and the same painter. Zani, differing from others, says he was born at Vienna in 1642, and died in 1705. See *Seiter.*

SYLVESTRE. See SILVESTRE

SYMMACHUS, a learned Roman, who flourished in the early part of the 6th century, under the reign of Theodoric, the Ostrogoth. He was employed by that monarch, according to Cassiodorus, in superintending the erection and restoration of various edifices in Rome, which had been rapidly going into decay during the foreign and civil wars, particularly the famous Theatre of Pompey.

SYMPSON. See SIMPSON.

SYSANG, JOHN CHRISTOPHER, a Danish engraver, who flourished about 1746. He engraved several plates of portraits, in a neat, clear style, for a work entitled, "Portraits Historiques des Hommes Illustres de Danemark," published in that year.

SYTICUS. See SERICCUS.

# T.

TACCA, PIETRO GIACOMO, a sculptor of Carrara, who flourished in the first half of the 17th century. He studied under Giovanni da Bologna, and subsequently traveled into Spain and France, where he acquired great celebrity. He executed, among other works, a statue of Henry IV. at Paris, one of Jane of Austria, and a statue of Ferdinand III. of Tuscany, with four slaves chained at his feet, at Leghorn; his master-piece is said to be an equestrian statue of Philip IV. at Madrid. Tacca afterwards returned to Florence, and died there in 1640. His son Ferdinand, was esteemed an able sculptor.

TACCONI, INNOCENZIO, a Bolognese painter who, according to Baglioni, was a relative and disciple of Annibale Caracci, whom he accompanied to Rome, and assisted in many of his works. Lanzi says, "whether he was really the kinsman of Annibale or no, he certainly enjoyed his confidence, and he received from him designs and retouchings, tending to make him appear a greater artist than he really was. To judge from some of his histories of St. Andrew, painted for S. Maria del Popolo and S. Angiolo, he may be said to have rivalled the best of his fellow pupils. But abusing his master's goodness, and alienating himself from Agostino, from Albano and from Guido, by misrepresentations, he received the usual recompense of slanderers. Annibale withdrew from him his support, deprived of which, he became gradually more and more insignificant." His principal works are the histories of St. Andrew, above mentioned, and three large frescos, representing the Coronation of the Virgin, Christ appearing to St. Peter, and the Vision of St. Paul in the third Heaven, in the vault of the church of S. Maria del Popolo. He died at Rome in the prime of life, in the pontificate of Urban VIII.

TAFFI, or TAFI, ANDREA, an old Florentine painter, born in 1213, who was the first to introduce mosaic painting into his native city. According to Vasari, he went to Venice, where he learned the art of one Apollonius, a Greek, whom he induced to accompany him to Florence, where they executed in concert some scripture histories in mosaic, in the church of S. Giovanni, which the author above cited says "are without invention and without design." Lanzi says "he improved as he progressed, so that his last works were not so despicable as at the beginning." His most famous work was a Dead Christ, executed entirely by his own hand. He died in 1294.

TAGLIASACCHI, GIO. BATTISTA, a painter born at Borgo S. Donnino, near Piacenza. He studied with Giuseppe dal Sole. Lanzi says "he displayed a fine genius for elegant subjects, which induced him, after he left the school of dal Sole, to study the works of Correggio, Parmiggiano, and Guido. He was particularly ambitious of adding Raffaello to the list, but his parents would not permit him to visit Rome. He resided and chiefly employed himself at Piacenza, where there is a much admired Holy Family by him in the cathedral, which in its ideal cast of features, partakes of the Roman style, and is not inferior to the Lombards in point of coloring. He was an artist of far greater merit than fortune." He painted easel pictures for the collections, and excelled in portraits. He died, according to the *Guida di Piacenza*, in 1737.

TAILLASSON, JEAN JOSEPH, a French painter, was born at Blaye, near Bordeaux, in 1746. He early manifested a strong inclination for art, and though opposed by his parents, he finally obtained their consent to his entering the school of Vien at Paris, where he arrived in 1764, at the age of eighteen. After studying with assiduity for several years, he visited Italy about 1773. He returned to Paris four years afterwards, and gained considerable reputation for his picture of the Birth of Louis XIII. The works of Taillasson are distinguished for sensibility and expression, and possess considerable merit; but they often exhibit a labored appearance, which impairs their vigor. He was chosen a member of the Royal Academy, for his picture of Ulysses bearing to Philoctetes the arrows of Hercules. Among his other principal works were, Virgil reading the Æneid to Augustus; Timoleon visited at Syracuse by strangers the Death of Seneca; and Hero and Leander Taillasson wrote a work of considerable merit, entitled *Observations sur quelques grands peintres*, 1807, 8vo. He died in 1809.

TALAMI, ORAZIO, a painter born at Reggio, according to Tiraboschi, in 1625, and died in 1705. He first studied with Pietro Desani, in his native city, and afterwards traversed Italy for improvement. Lanzi says "he studied the models of the Caracci with unwearied care, and succeeded so well, that he might be mistaken for one of their scholars. While at Rome, which he visited twice, he devoted himself particularly to the study of perspective, and very scrupulously observed its rules in the noble and extensive edifices and ruins, with which he enriched his compositions. On his return to his native city, he executed many works for the churches and public edifices, as well as for individuals, which prove him an able artist. His works are more distinguished for solidity and correctness of design, than for amenity."

TALPINO, IL. See SALMEGGIA.

TALMAN, WILLIAM, a distinguished English architect of the 17th century, was a native of West Lavington, in Wiltshire. Although he was Comptroller of the Works during the reign of William III., little is known of him, except by a few private edifices, erected for the nobility, among which are Dynham House, in the county of Gloucester, commended for its elegant taste; Thoresby House, for the Duke of Kingston, in the county of Nottingham, erected in 1671, which has a basement of rusticated stone work, and a tetrastyle portico of the same material, in the Ionic order. In 1681, according to Walpole, Talman designed Chatsworth House, in the county of Derby, for the Duke of Devonshire. On the ground plan are the offices, a large hall, and a chapel, with a spacious court and two noble porticos in the centre; a magnificent staircase leads to the first range of state apartments, in which is a superb gallery, and a library; over these is a suite still more noble. The western façade is in the richest and best style of architecture, a rustic basement surmounted by an order of Ionic pilasters, with a tetrastyle portico in the centre, over which is a rich pediment. The whole edifice is crowned with balustrades, on the solid divisions of which are vases, producing a better effect than statues. There are a few of Talman's drawings in the library of the Antiquarian Society. His son, John Talman, was esteemed a good artist.

TAMBURINI, GIO. MARIA, a Bolognese painter who flourished about 1640. He first studied with Pietro Faccini, and afterwards entered the school of Guido, whose manner he adopted. He acquired considerable reputation, and executed several works for the churches of Bologna, the most esteemed of which are the pictures representing the history of St. Anthony of Padua in the church of La Morte, and the Annunciation in S. Maria della Vita. He also etched some plates from his own designs, and after other masters. Lanzi says he died old, at what time is not known.

TANCREDI, FILIPPO, a Sicilian painter, born at Messina, according to Hackert in 1655, and died at Palermo in 1725; but Zani says in 1722. He first studied at Naples, and afterwards proceeded to Rome, where he entered the school of Carlo Maratti. On leaving this master, he returned to Sicily, where he acquired a great reputation, and executed many works for the churches at Messina and Palermo, particularly in the latter city, where he settled. Hackert says he possessed a ready and fertile invention, a tolerably correct design, and a very sweet and agreeable style of coloring. He painted both in oil and fresco, and his best works are the ceilings of the churches of the Teatini, and of Il Gesù Nuovo at Palermo.

TANDINO, a painter of whom little is known, born at Bevagna, a place near Assisi. In the church of S. Giacomo at Spello, there is an altarpiece by him, representing that saint and St. Catherine before the Madonna, which is inscribed *Tandini Mevanatis*, 1580. This work is highly commended by Orsini, and Lanzi says, "it is a picture not to be passed over."

TANJÉ, PETER, a Dutch engraver, born at Amsterdam about 1700. It is not known under whom he studied, but he was a very industrious artist, and engraved a great number of plates of portraits and other subjects, as well as many vignettes and other book plates. His most considerable works are five large plates from the famous paintings on the windows of the church of St. John of Gouda, and several plates for the Dresden gallery. Zani says he was born in 1706, and died in 1760.

TANTERI, VALERIO, a Florentine painter, who flourished in the first part of the 17th century. He studied with Cristofano Allori, and was an excellent copyist of his works. Lanzi says, "To Valerio Tanteri, F. Bruno Certosino, and Lorenzo Cerrini, we owe numerous duplicates of Allori's most celebrated pictures, scattered through Florence, and over all Italy; more especially of that Judith, so beautifully and magnificently attired, a portrait of his mistress, while that of her mother appears as Abra, and the head of Holofernes is that of the painter himself, who permitted his beard to grow for the purpose." There is a Visitation of the Virgin by Tanteri, inscribed with his name, with the date 1606, in the church of S. Antonio of Pisa, executed in a weak style. He was also a good portrait painter.

TANZI, ANTONIO, a painter born at Alagna, near Novara, in 1574. It is not known with whom he studied, but Lanzi says he was an able and skillful designer, and distinguished himself by several public works at Milan, painted in competition with Carloni; and others for the churches at Varallo and Novara. He particularly commends his Battle of Sennacherib in the church of S. Gaudenzio, in the latter city, a work full of spirit and intelligence. He also painted much for the collections, and there are several of his histories and perspectives in the galleries at Naples, Venice, and Vienna. He died in 1644. He had a brother, named Giovanni Melchiore, who practiced the art, but there is nothing remaining by him worthy of notice.

TAPIA, DON ISIDORO DE, a Spanish painter, born at Valencia in 1720, and a scholar of Evaristo Munoz. In 1743 he went to Madrid, where he improved himself by studying the works of the best masters in that capital. He acquired considerable reputation, and executed several works for the churches and convents in his native city, which, according to Bermudez, are well designed and colored. The principal are a grand altarpiece in the church of San Bartolome, and the Oratory of the convent of the Carmelites, where he represented St. Teresa and the Four Doctors of the church. He died young at Madrid in 1755.

TARABOTI, CATERINA, a Venetian paintress, who studied, according to Lanzi, with Chiara Varatori, and painted history and portraits with considerable reputation. She was living in 1660. Others say that she was a native of Vicenza, and was instructed by Alessandro Varatori, the brother of Chiara. Pilkington says she was born at Venice in 1582, and died there in 1631; Zani, that she operated in 1659. She is also called *Tarabotti*, and *Tarabotta*. She was doubtless a pupil of Chiara V., who is highly extolled by Ridolfi, for the beauty of her portraits, and who is known to have instructed several Venetian ladies in the art.

TARASCHI, GIULIO, a painter of Modena, who, according to Tiraboschi, was a pupil of Pellegrino da Modena, whose style he followed with considerable success. Lanzi says he executed many works for the churches at Modena, entirely in the Roman taste, particularly some sacred subjects in S. Pietro. He had two younger brothers, whom he instructed in the art. He was living in 1546.

TARAVAL, THOMAS RAPHAEL, a Swedish painter, who resided at Paris some time; and on his return to Stockholm, he painted portraits with reputation. He died there in 1750. He had two sons, the first, John Hughes T., was born at Paris in 1728. He painted portraits and familiar subjects. He was also a designer, employed in the Gobelin manufactory, and died about 1785. Louis Gustavus T., was born at Stockholm in 1737. His father sent him to Paris, where he learned the art of engraving. Among other things, he engraved some architectural subjects from the designs of Dumont. He was living in 1790.

TARDIEU, ANTOINE FRANÇOIS, an eminent geographical engraver, born at Paris in 1757, and died there in 1822. His principal works are:

Les Cartes marine de l'Atlas de Commerce. Les Plans des Capitales de l'Europe. Cartes in the Atlas de Mentelle. Several plans in "le Voyage pittoresque en Grèce," by *Choiseul Gouffier*. Les Palatinats de Cracovie, Plack, Lublin, et Sandomir. The folio Atlas for the quarto edition of the "Voyage du jeune Anacharsis." Atlas du Voyage aux Terres Australes. Atlas for l'Histoire des Guerres des Français en Italie; *after Lapie*. A grand map of Russia in Europe, in six sheets.

TARDIEU, JEAN BAPTISTE PIERRE, probably a brother of the preceding, was born at Paris in 1746, and died in 1816. He executed many valuable geographical works, the principal of which are the following:

Cartes des Pays Bas, 53 plates, engraved for the Empress Maria Teresa. Cartes de Chasses du Roi, by direction of Louis XVI. Cartes du *Voyage de Sonini en Grèce et en Turquie*. Cartes de l'edition de *Volney*. Cartes Topographiques de la Saxe-Gotha, 25 plates.

TARDIEU, PIERRE, was the son of Antoine François, born at Paris in 1784, and died in 1837. He engraved several maps and plans after Humbolt, de Buch and Brousted; the Atlas for "l'Histoire Ancienne," of M. Segur; "La Carte des Routes de Poste de l'Empire," in 1811, by order of the Emperor Napoleon, and many other important works.

TARDIEU, NICHOLAS HENRI, an eminent French engraver, born at Paris in 1674. He first studied with P. le Pautre, and afterwards with Jean

Audran. He acquired distinction, and was elected a member of the Academy at Paris in 1720. He was engaged on some of the most important publications of his time, and engraved some of the plates for the Crozat Collection, the Gallery of Versailles, and other works. He is ranked among the most eminent engravers of his country. His design is correct, and by a judicious union of the point and the graver, he finished his plates in a very tasteful and effective style. He died at Paris in 1749. The following are among his most esteemed prints:

PORTRAITS.

Louis Anthony, Duke d'Antin; *after Rigaud;* engraved for his reception plate at the Academy in 1720. John Soanon, Bishop of Senez; *Nic. Tardieu ad vivum fecit.* 1716.

SUBJECTS AFTER DIFFERENT MASTERS.

Four subjects of Roman History, in the form of friezes, *after Giulio Romano.* Jupiter and Alcmena; after a cartoon *by the same.* The Annunciation; *after Carlo Maratti.* The Holy Family with Angels presenting Flowers and Fruit; *after Andrea Luigi d' Assisi.* Adam and Eve; *after Domenichino.* The Scourging of Christ; *after le Brun.* The Crucifixion; *do.* An Emblematical subject, representing the principal qualifications of a perfect Minister, Secresy, Fortitude, and Prudence; *after le Sueur.* This print is scarce. Christ and the Woman of Samaria; *after N. Bertin.* Christ appearing to Mary Magdalene; *do.* The Martyrdom of St. Peter; *after Seb. Bourdon.* The Crucifixion; *after Joseph Parrocel.* The Conception; *after Anthony Coypel.* Apollo and Daphne; *do.* The Wrath of Achilles; *do.* The parting of Hector and Andromache; *do.* Vulcan presenting to Venus Armor for Æneas; *do.* Venus soliciting Jupiter in favor of Æneas; *do.* Juno directing Æolus to raise a Tempest against the Fleet of Æneas; *do.*

TARDIEU, ELIZABETH CLARA, was the wife of the preceding. Her maiden name was Tournay. She engraved some plates in a neat and tasteful style, among which are the following:— The Concert, *after J. F. de Troy;* the Mustard Merchant, *after Charles Hutin;* two plates of the charitable Lady and the Catechist, *after P. Dumesnil;* the Old Coquet, *do.;* the Repose, *after Jeaurat.*

TARDIEU, JACQUES NICOLAS, was the son of Nicolas Henry T., born at Paris in 1718. He was instructed by his father, but in his mode of operating, he used the point less, and the graver more, than that master; hence his prints have a neater appearance, but they are much inferior in spirit and picturesque effect. His prints, however, possess considerable merit. He was admitted into the Academy. He engraved a part of the plates for the Gallery of Versailles, after the works of le Brun, and a considerable number of portraits and other subjects, among which are the following:

PORTRAITS.

Louis XIV.; *after Vanloo.* His Queen; *after Nattier.* Maria Henrietta of France; *do.* The Archbishop of Bordeaux; *after Restout.* Robert Lorraine, Sculptor to the King; his reception plate at the Academy. 1749. Bon Boullongne, Painter to the King; the companion.

VARIOUS SUBJECTS.

Christ appearing to the Virgin; *after Guido.* Mary Magdalene penitent; *after Paolo Pagani.* The Pool of Bethesda; *after Restout.* Diana and Acteon; *after F. Boucher.* The Miseries of War; *after Teniers.* A pair of Landscapes; *after Cochin the younger.*

TARDIEU, LOUISA, was the wife of the preceding. She was the daughter of the celebrated medalist du Vivier. She executed several plates of portraits and other subjects, in a neat style.

TARDIEU, JEAN CHARLES, an eminent French historical painter, was the son of Jacques Nicolas T., born at Paris in 1765. He painted a great many pictures by order of the government, for the galleries of the Luxembourg, Versailles, St. Cloud and Fontainbleau, and seems to have been fully employed during the reigns of Napoleon, Louis XVIII., and Charles X. There are several of his works in the Museum and the cathedral at Rouen. He also painted many poetical and classical subjects for individuals. He was living in 1831, and continued still to exercise his pencil.

TARDIEU, PIERRE FRANÇOIS, was the nephew of Nicolas Henry T., by whom he was instructed in engraving. He was born at Paris in 1720, and died in 1772. He engraved quite a number of plates, which, though inferior to those of his relative, possess considerable merit. He engraved a set of architectural Views *after Pannini;* a set of plates for La Fontaine's Fables, after the designs of Oudry, and some plates for Buffon's Natural History; also some large plates after various masters, among which are the Judgment of Paris, and Perseus and Andromeda, *after Rubens.* His wife, Marie Anne Tardieu, whose maiden name was Roussellet, was also an engraver, and executed some plates.

TARDIEU, PIERRE ALEXANDRE, an eminent French engraver, was a nephew of Jacques Nicolas T., born at Paris in 1756. He studied with J. G. Wille, whose style he followed. He executed some historical subjects, and a great many portraits of eminent persons. He was the successor of Bervic in the Institute of France, and was made Chevalier of the Legion of Honor in 1825. He instructed several pupils, among whom were Desnoyers, Bertonnier, and Aubert. Among his principal plates are the following:

Three of Henry IV. of France; *after Janet* and *Pourbus.* Two of Voltaire; *after Largilliere* and *Houdon.* The Earl of Arundel; *after Vandyck.* Mareschal Ney; *after Gerard.* Napoleon (for the Coronation); *after Isabey.* Maria Antoinette; *after Dumont.* Montesquieu, Paul Barras, and others. St. Michael overcoming Lucifer; *after Raffaelle.* The Communion of St. Jerome; *after Domenichino.* Judith and Holofernes; *after Allori.* Psyche abandoned; *after Gerard.*

TARICCO, SEBASTIANO, a painter born at Cherasco, in the Piedmontese, in 1645. The Padre Della Valle commits an extraordinary error with regard to this painter, into which others have fallen. After mentioning the time and place of his nativity, he says, "it clearly appears from his works that he studied with Guido and Domenichino in the great school of the Caracci," whereas not only the Caracci, but both Guido and Domenichino were dead before he was born. The probability is that he studied at Bologna, where he made the works of the Caracci his models. He acquired considerable reputation, and executed some works both in oil and fresco for the churches and palaces of Turin, Cherasco, and other places in the vicinity. Some say that he imitated Guido and Domenichino in his design and coloring. Lanzi, though he admits he has not seen his best productions, says that, judging from his works which he saw at Turin, he was rather a follower of Guido; he is select in the heads and sufficiently pleasing in general, but of too great facility, and without that refinement which distinguishes the classic painters; others of his works in his native city and elsewhere, are said to inspire a higher opinion of his talents." His name is sometimes erroneously spelled Tarrico. He died in 1710.

TARILLIO, Giovanni Battista, a Milanese painter, who, according to Lanzi, was an artist of great merit, as is evinced by his altar-piece painted for the church of S. Martino, dated 1575.

TARUFFI, Emilio, a painter born at Bologna, according to Crespi, in 1633, and assassinated in 1696; others place his birth in 1632, and his death in 1694. He was a fellow student with Carlo Cignani, under Francesco Albano. He assisted Cignani in decorating the Palazzo Pubblico at Bologna, and next at Rome, in his frescos in the church of S. Andrea della Valle, and others for private houses. After a residence of three years at Rome he returned to Bologna, where he was employed to execute several works for the churches, the most esteemed of which is the Virgin presenting the Rosary to St. Domenico, in S. Maria Nuova, and the Virgin with a glory of angels appearing to St. Celestino, in the church of that saint. Lanzi says, "no artist there better conformed to Cignani's style, than Taruffi, and he could at least second him in painting histories. But his genius lay more in minor compositions for the collections. He was an excellent copyist of any ancient master; a portrait painter of great spirit; and in landscape, one of the best pupils formed by Albano. In these three branches, he obtained his usual commissions, which he ever discharged with credit. He also conducted some altar-pieces, and that of S. Pier Celestino, yields to few of that period."

TASCA, Cristoforo, a painter born at Bergamo in 1667. After studying in his native city, he went to Venice, where he settled, and adopted the manner of Carlo Loti. He found considerable employment in painting for the churches and public edifices. His works most deserving of notice are the Birth of the Virgin in dell' Assunzione; the Death of St. Joseph, in SS. Filippo e Giacomo; the Nativity and the Baptism of Christ in S. Marta. He also painted much for the collections. He died in 1737.

TASNIERE, G., an engraver who, according to Basan, flourished at Turin about 1670. He engraved a part of a set of plates of huntings and portraits of the nobility, after the works of John Miel, in the palace of the Duke of Savoy, published at Turin in 1674, under the title of *La Venaria reale Palazzo di piacere*, &c. He also engraved some plates after other masters, some of which are signed *G. Tasniere Bourgundus scu. Mediolano*, or *G. Tasniere sculps. Taurini*, and dated as late as 1703. His plates are executed with the graver in a coarse, heavy style.

TASSART, Peter Joseph, a Flemish painter and engraver, born at Brussels in 1736. He is little known as a painter, though he painted some portraits. He etched some plates from his own designs, and after other masters, among which are the following, *after Rubens;* Jonas thrown into the Sea; the Parting of Venus and Adonis; the Woman taken in Adultery; the Martyrdom of St. Lawrence; and the Virgin and Child, with St. Elizabeth and St. John.

TASSI, Agostino, a painter born at Perugia, according to Lanzi and the best authorities, in 1566, and died at Rome in 1642; some place his birth in 1565, and his death in 1644. His real name was Buonamici. There is considerable contradiction as to his history, but none as to his works. He studied with Paul Brill at Rome, though Lanzi says he was ambitious of being thought a pupil of the Caracci. He however founded his style on that of Brill, and had already acquired a high reputation for the beauty of his landscapes,—which are elegantly designed, enriched with noble architecture, and exquisite figures, touched with a free and spirited pencil,—when he was condemned to the galleys at Leghorn for some unknown cause, though Passeri intimates that it was assassination. Lanzi says he was a man of infamous character, but the incidents recorded of him in the lives of his pupils, particularly that of Claude Lorraine, (whom he took into his house, when he was in poverty and obscurity, instructed him and treated him as his son,) show that he possessed a kind and generous heart. It seems more than probable that the crime which stigmatized his character, was a fatal duel, or the slaying of an antagonist in the heat of passion. At all events, his reputation had gained him friends sufficiently powerful to procure the remission of the laborious part of his sentence, and ultimately, his pardon. Lanzi says, "in this situation, he prosecuted his art with such ardor that he soon obtained the first rank as a painter of sea views, representing ships, storms, fishing parties, and the dresses of mariners of various countries with great spirit and propriety. He excelled in perspective, and in the papal palace of the Quirinal, and in the palace de' Lancellotti, he displayed an admirable style of decoration, which his followers very much over charged. He painted many pictures at Genoa in conjunction with Salimbeni and Gentileschi." Tassi, after his liberation, confined himself mostly to marine subjects and sea-ports, which last he enriched with noble edifices and abundance of shipping, and figures decked in the costume of all nations. He did not succeed so well in storms, as in scenes of tranquillity and repose. He painted both in oil and fresco equally well, and his works adorn the choicest collections of Italy. There are some spirited etchings by this artist from his own designs, of marines, storms and shipwrecks.

TASSINARI, Giovanni Battista, a painter born at Pavia, whom Orlandi supposes to have studied with Il Rosso of Pavia. He executed some works for the churches of that city, two of which are dated 1610, and 1613. He was a reputable artist.

TASSONE, Carlo, a painter of Cremona, born about 1640. He studied under Carlo Natali, and became an eminent portrait painter. Lanzi says "he flourished about 1690, and was much employed at Turin and other courts, where his portraits were much admired." Zaist says he died aged 70, but he does not mention the time or place.

TASSONI, Giuseppe, a painter born at Rome, according to Dominici, in 1653. It is not known by whom he was instructed, but he went to Naples, where he distinguished himself as a painter of animals. He died there in 1737.

TATTI, Jacopo, called Sansovino, an eminent

Italian sculptor and architect, was born at Florence in 1479. He was the son of Antonio Tatti, whose surname he exchanged for that by which he is more generally known, assumed out of compliment to his master, Andrea Contucci da Monte Sansovino. Contucci had just returned from Portugal, where he had acquired great reputation as a sculptor, when Jacopo, then twenty-one years of age, became his pupil, and afterwards greatly surpassed him; but his superior talents served only to increase his instructor's attachment. At this time Jacopo profited greatly by his intimacy with Andrea del Sarto; they almost pursued their studies in common, and both of them copied Michael Angelo's famous cartoon of Pisa. Becoming acquainted with Giuliano Sangallo, then architect to Julius II., he was taken by him to Rome, where his talents procured for him the notice of Bramante and other eminent artists, and also that of the Pope himself. He was probably indebted to Sangallo for instruction in architecture, which he did not commence practising until some years afterwards. On returning to Florence, he produced his Bacchus, a master-piece of modern sculpture, which is now only known by copies and drawings, it having been destroyed by a fire that broke out in 1762, in the Florentine Gallery, where it had been placed. While residing at Florence at this time, Jacopo displayed his talents in designing several triumphal arches, and erecting a temporary façade to the church of S. Maria del Fiore, in honor of the entry of Pope Leo X., in 1515. On a very large base he arranged couplets of columns in the Corinthian order, between which were niches with figures representing the apostles; the columns supported a cornice and pediment with various projections. Del Sarto painted several historical subjects in chiaro-scuro, and Jacopo executed the statues and bas-reliefs; the whole work, according to Milizia, was extremely well conceived, and the Pope complimented him by saying that the design ought to be executed in marble.

On returning to Rome, besides executing a number of statues, he erected a loggia on the Via Flaminia without the Porto del Popolo, for Marco Coscia; the church of S. Marcello; and a beautiful and convenient palace, near Banchi, for the Gaddi family, which afterwards passed into that of Niccolini. His greatest work in Rome was the design for the church of S. Giovanni dei Fiorentini, which he commenced erecting upon some ground near the Tiber. Not succeeding in laying firm foundations in the water, he transferred the works to Sangallo, who completed the foundations at immense expense, and erected the edifice after the original design. At the sacking of Rome in 1527, Sansovino quitted the city, and went to Venice; after which he visited France, whither he had been invited some years before by the King, but it does not appear that he executed any works in that country. Returning shortly after to Venice, he was appointed by the Doge, Andrea Gritti, to the post of principal architect to the Procurazie. One of his first works was the repairing of the cupolas of St. Mark's, which he performed with great credit, and afterwards erected many other public and private edifices, among which are the Scuola della Miseracordia, consisting of two magnificent halls, one above the other; the Palazzo Cornaro a S. Maurizio, one of his best works; the church of S. Giorgio de' Greci; the Loggia del Campanile; Palazzo Delfino; the Fabbriche Nuove, or New Buildings, in the quarter of the Rialto; the admired church of S. Francesco della Vigna; and the celebrated Zecca, or Mint, a magnificent work, built of Istrian stone, and one of his finest designs. The Library of St. Mark is perhaps the most highly esteemed of all his works; it has two orders, the first a highly ornamented Doric, the second an elegant Ionic with a grand frieze and noble partition. Over the cornice is a balustrade, with beautiful statues above, by the ablest scholars of the architect; on the ground floor is a portico, raised three steps from the level of the piazza: it has twenty-one arches, supported by pilasters, to which there are external columns, with other arches corresponding to the interior, sixteen of which, with their internal rooms, are used for shops. The centre arch conducts to the noble staircase, divided into two branches; at the top of this staircase is a hall, used as a museum for ancient statues; beyond this is the Library, occupying seven arches in length, by three in width. Scarcely was the vaulted ceiling of the Library completed, when it fell down; in consequence of which Sansovino was deprived of his office, imprisoned and fined 1000 crowns; but through the active exertions of his friends Pietro Aretino, and Mendoza, the Spanish ambassador, combined with his former exalted reputation, he was restored to his office, and his fine was remitted. The edifice, when completed, was the most highly ornamented building, according to Palladio, in the world; to its exquisite style of architecture is added every variety of elegant columns, bas-reliefs, stuccoes, and statues.

There are some inconsistencies in the works of Sansovino, as in those of all the great architects. In the Loggia del Campanile, the sculptures on the exterior represent heathen deities, while the Virgin Mary occupies the niche within; and in a magnificent bronze door in the sacristy of St. Mark's, the two principal compartments represent the Savior's death and resurrection, while the smaller panels are decorated with the heads of the Evangelists, and those of Sansovino's friends, including Pietro Aretino. Notwithstanding these errors, he possessed a fertile invention, and his architecture, though sometimes deficient in solidity, was full of elegance and grace. His ornaments are exceedingly correct, and he very frequently introduced the Doric and Composite orders; he sculptured the members of the cornices, and often introduced bas-reliefs and statues, thus adding much to the decoration and majesty of his buildings. In sculpture, Sansovino executed many works, most of which were for the decoration of his edifices; his design for the sepulchre of Sig. Podacataro, in the church of S. Sebastiano, is greatly admired for its simplicity and elegance; and that of the Doge Veniero, in S. Salvatore, is still more beautiful. He executed the two statues between the lateral niches of this sepulchre at the age of eighty, and five years before, he sculptured the two colossal statues of Mars and Neptune, which adorn the Giants' Staircase in the Ducal palace. Sansovino was held in such high esteem, that when an extraordinary tax was raised by the Senate, he and Titian alone were exempted; thus the architect was accounted equal in his department to the head of the Venetian school of painting. He enjoyed, according to Vasari, unimpaired health and strength to the great age of ninety-one, when he died, November 27, 1570. Scamozzi mentions a useful work by Sansovino, relating chiefly to the construction of floors, which is now unfortunately lost.

TATORAC, V., an old engraver on wood, who executed, according to Papillon, a set of one hundred and fifty cuts for an edition of Ovid's Metamorphoses, published in 1537, and a print of the Annunciation for a prayer book, dated 1530.

TAUNAY, Nicolas Antoine, a French painter, born at Paris, and died there in 1830. He studied with Casanova, but he painted more in the manner of the French school. He was a universal painter. He painted several large pictures of the battles and victories of Napoleon, among which are the Passage of the Alps, the Battle of Lodi, the Battle of Ebersberg, the Triumphal Entry of the Imperial Guard into Paris, and many others. He also painted history, landscapes, seaports, pastoral and poetical subjects, sentimental and humorous pieces, games and village festivals. His cabinet pictures are the most esteemed out of France.

TAURINI, R., a French artist, born at Rouen. According to Papillon, he was a disciple of Albert Durer, and a skillful engraver on wood, but none of his prints are mentioned. He was called *Monsieur Richard* and *Ricardus Gallus*. He is also said to have been a skillful *carver* in wood and stone, and an architectural designer.

TAURISCUS. See Apollonius.

TAVARONE, Lazzaro, a painter born at Genoa, according to Soprani, in 1556, and died in 1641, aged 85, though some place his death in 1631. He studied with Luca Cambiaso, and was his most distinguished disciple. He accompanied that master to Spain in 1583, at the invitation of Philip II., assisted him in his great works in the Escurial, and on the death of Cambiaso, he completed his unfinished pictures. He continued several years longer in the service of Philip, and afterwards returned to Genoa, rich in the designs of his instructor, which he inherited, and loaded with riches and honors. Lanzi says, "Luca seemed to live again in his scholar, so fully did he possess his style. He moreover distinguished himself by a method of coloring in fresco, which if I mistake not, raised him above all his predecessors in this school (the Genoese), and above all who succeeded him, except Carloni. This peculiarity consisted in a richness, brightness, and variety of color, which brings distant objects vividly to the sight, the whole composition appearing brilliantly illuminated, and the tints splendidly and harmoniously blended. One may, perhaps, occasionally wish them more soft, but in general they have all the richness of oil paintings." He executed many works for the churches, public edifices and palaces of Genoa, of sacred and profane histories, fables, and imaginary compositions, often so well preserved as to appear freshly painted. The principal of these are in the tribune of the cathedral, where he represented the patron saints of the city, and several subjects from the life of St. Lorenzo, which Lanzi says are the chef d'œuvres of his public works. Also the façade of La Dogana or the Custom House, where he represented St. George slaying the Dragon; "around it and above are numerous figures, portraits of eminent citizens, typifying the Virtues; of genii, with nautical weapons and the spoils of the enemy, some of which might pass for the work of Pordenone. It would have been fortunate, had his works been fewer and finished with equal care."

TAVELLA, Carlo Antonio, an eminent painter, born at Milan in 1668, and died at Genoa in 1738. Lanzi gives the following account of him. "The most justly celebrated landscape painter of this epoch (in the Genoese school), is Carlantonio Tavella, the scholar of Tempesta (Peter Molyn), at Milan, and of Gruenbrech, a German, who from the fires he introduced into his landscapes, was called Il Solfarolo. He at first emulated the last named artist; he then softened his style by studying the works of Castiglione, Poussin, and the best Flemish painters. Among the Genoese landscape painters, he ranks next after Il Sestri. His works are easily distinguished in the collections of Genoa, particularly in the Palazzo Franchi, which had more than three hundred pictures by his hand, and acquired for him the reputation of one of the first painters of the age. We are there presented with warm skies, beautiful distances in the landscape, and pleasing effects of light; the trees, flowers, and animals are gracefully touched, and with wonderful truth of nature. In his figures, he was assisted by the two Pioli, father and son, and often by Magnasco, with whom he was associated in the work. He sometimes inserted them in his pictures himself, copying them indeed from the originals, designed by his comrades, but identifying them by a style peculiarly his own. Tavella had a daughter, named Angiola, of feeble invention, but a good copyist of her father's designs. He also had many imitators, among whom Niccolo Micone, commonly called Lo Zoppo, most nearly resembles him."

TAVERNER, William, an English amateur painter, who was a proctor in the Doctors' Commons. Lord Orford mentions some pictures by him, in the possession of the Earl of Harcourt and Mr. Fauquier, which he says might have been mistaken for the works of Gaspar Poussin. He died in 1772.

TAVERNIER, François, a French painter, born at Paris in 1659, and died in 1725. There are no particulars recorded of his life, but he is said to have painted history with considerable ability.

TAVERNIER, Melchior, a French engraver and printseller, who flourished at Paris about 1630. He engraved some portraits; also a few plates of ornaments, from his own designs. On an equestrian portrait of Henry IV. of France, he signs himself engraver and printer to the king.

TAYLOR, Simon, an English painter of botanical subjects. He was much employed by Lord Bute and Dr. Fothergill. The collection of the latter, painted on vellum, was sold after the death of that eminent physician, to the Empress of Russia, for £2,000; but they cost the Doctor much more, as Taylor's charge was the round sum of three guineas for drawing a single plant. He died about 1794.

TAYLOR, T., an obscure English engraver, who flourished about 1735. He engraved some plates of portraits and other subjects, after various masters, which are indifferently executed.

TAYLOR, Sir Robert, an English sculptor and architect, was born in 1714. He was the son of a London stone-mason, who bestowed upon him only a common school education, and then placed him under Sir Henry Cheere, a sculptor. He was next sent to Rome, whence he was soon obliged to return, on the death of his father. He then commenced as a sculptor, and first attracted notice by Cornwall's monument; after which he executed a number of other works in sculpture, among which the principal are Guest's monument, near the north door of Westminster Abbey; the figure of Britannia, at the Bank of England; and the bas-relief in the pediment of the Mansion House, London. After this he abandoned sculpture for architecture. In 1756–58, he was employed in the alterations of the Old London Bridge, in connection with Dance, and he executed, among other works, the Stone Buildings at Gray's Inn, and Lord Grimston's seat at Gorhambury. He also obtained several lucrative appointments, and surveyorships to the Admiralty, Foundling Hospital, Greenwich Hospital, and the Bank of England. In 1783, he was appointed Sheriff of London, when he received the honor of knighthood. Taylor died in 1788, leaving a fortune of £180,000, which he left to his son, the late Michael Angelo Taylor, M. P., with the exception of a legacy to the University of Oxford, to accumulate for a term of years, and then to be applied to founding an institute for the study of the modern languages. This bequest having been incorporated with a similar one by Dr. Randolph for a picture and statue gallery, a building was begun in 1841, under the name of the "Taylor and Randolph Institute."

TAYLOR, William Sarsfield. This painter was born in Ireland in 1780, and in early life was attached to the Commissariat department of the British army. He afterwards devoted himself to art, and having been present at the siege of St. Sebastian, made that engagement a frequent subject of his pencil. His pictures, however, did not rise above mediocrity, and he is better known by his valuable writings, which consist of a Description of Trinity College, Dublin, in quarto, with plates after his own designs; a translation from the French of Merimée's Practice of painting; a History of the Fine Arts in England, in two vols.; and a History and Practice of Fresco Painting. Taylor was for many years Keeper of the Model Academy in St. Martin's Lane. He died Dec. 23d, 1850.

TECTÆUS, an ancient sculptor, who is invariably named in connection with his coadjutor, Angelion. They were of the Sicyonian school, and are supposed by Sillig to have flourished about B. C. 548. The ancient writers particularly mention a statue of Apollo by these artists, and Müller says they imitated a very ancient statue of the Delian Apollo, made, as Plutarch states, in the time of Hercules.

TEDESCO, Il. See Ælzheimer.

TEISSIER, John George, a Dutch artist, born at the Hague in 1750. He painted portraits and landscapes with reputation, but was more celebrated for his faculty of imitating and copying the works of the old masters, for which reason he was much employed in repairing old paintings, which had sustained injury. He was a Director in the Academy of Design at the Hague, and a sub-director of the Museum. He was an excellent teacher, and instructed several pupils, who have distinguished themselves; among them are Bésanger, Valois, Harry, and Carbenthus. He died in 1821.

TEISSIER, Jean, a French engraver of little note, who flourished at Paris about 1770. He studied under Philip le Bas, and engraved a few plates after Bénard and other masters.

TELFORD, Thomas, an eminent Scottish architect and civil engineer, was the son of a shepherd in the pastoral district of Eskdale, in Dumfriesshire, and was born in the Parish of Westerkirk, in 1757. He lost his father while yet an infant, and at the age of fourteen was apprenticed to a stone-mason in the neighboring town of Langholm. In 1780, he visited Edinburgh, and devoted much attention to drawing and architecture for two years, after which he removed to London, and was employed upon the quadrangle of Somerset House, then erecting by Sir William Chambers. About 1784 he was engaged to superintend the erection of a house for the resident commissioner in Portsmouth dock-yard, from the design of Mr. S. Wyat: and in 1787 he was invited by Sir William Pulteney to take the superintendence of some operations at Shrewsbury Castle. At Shrewsbury, he was also employed to erect a new gaol: and he was subsequently appointed to the office of county surveyor, which he retained until his death. In Shropshire, upwards of forty bridges were erected under his direction. In 1793, he was engaged to construct the Ellesmere Canal—a series of channels intended to unite the Severn, the Dee, and the Mersey, and extending altogether to a length of over one hundred miles. In 1801 he was deputed by government to make a survey of the coasts and interior of Scotland, and to report generally upon desirable public works for the improvement of the country. In consequence of his reports, commissions were formed to construct the celebrated Caledonian Canal, which was opened throughout in 1823. Several other important canals in England and Scotland, were constructed either wholly or partially under his superintendence, besides the Gotha canal in Sweden, at the completion of which Telford received the Swedish order of knighthood, and other honors. Under the commissioners of Highland Roads and Bridges, he constructed many works. His already elevated reputation was greatly increased by the ingenious alteration of Glasgow old Bridge, the erection of the new bridge at Glasgow, the light and elegant Dean Bridge at Edinburgh, the arch of 112 feet span over the Dee near Kirkcudbright, and the celebrated Menai Suspension Bridge. The latter work alone would be sufficient to establish his reputation. In 1803, Telford was elected a fellow of the Royal Society of Edinburgh; in 1820, president of the institution of Civil Engineers; and in 1827, a fellow of the Royal Society of England. He wrote several valuable articles in Brewster's Edinburgh Encyclopædia, under the titles Architecture, Bridge, Civil Architecture, and Inland Navigation. Telford never married, and had no fixed habitation until late in life. He died at his residence in Abingdon street, Westminster, in 1834, and was buried in Westminster Abbey.

TELLIER, Jean le, a reputable French painter, the nephew and residuary legatee of N. Poussin, born at Rouen in 1614. He painted history and portraits, and his works are much esteemed for their correct perspective, simplicity of style, and truthful imitation of nature, although they have little vigor of coloring. He executed many works for the churches and private collections of Rouen. Seventeen of his pictures were in the Museum of that city, among which were the Adieus of Paul and Silas; two Annunciations; two Assumptions; and St. Joseph carrying the infant Jesus in his arms, with the figures of life-size. In the church of S. Augustine are two pictures of great merit; a Holy Family, and the Miracles performed at the Tomb of St. Augustine. Le Tellier died in 1676.

TEMANZA, Tommaso, an Italian architect, and an eminent writer on the art, was born at Venice in 1705. Having studied mathematics in the school of Pádre Niccolo Comini and the eminent Marchese Poleni, he was appointed at the early age of twenty-two, one of the assistants in the commission of Engineers, and in 1742 became the chief of that body, at the resignation of Bernardino Zendrini. During the time of Temanza, there were few great architectural works erected in Venice, and he had little opportunity for displaying his abilities, except in the fine church of La Maddalena, in the Ionic order. His other principal works are the façade of St. Margherita, at Padua; the Rotonda, at Piazzolo, built at the expense of the Contarini family; and the bridge over the Brenta at Dolo. As a writer on the art, Temanza is more extensively known, especially by his *Vite de' piu Eccellenti Architetti e Scultori Veneziani*, 4to., Venice, 1778; considered one of the most copious and best-written works of the kind ever produced. He also published the *Antichità di Rimini*, folio, 1741; and left behind him another work, *Degli Archi e delle Volte, e delle Regole generali dell' Architettura Civile*, which was first edited in 1811. Temanza died at Venice in 1789.

TEMINI, Giovanni, an Italian engraver, and probably a painter, who flourished about 1622. There is a portrait by him of Carlo Gonzales, Duke of Mantua; it is slightly etched, and finished with the graver.

TEMPEL, Abraham vander, a Dutch painter, born at Leyden in 1618. He studied under George van Schooten, and painted small pictures of historical subjects and conversations, which are held in considerable estimation. He holds a respectable rank among the artists of his country who distinguished themselves by their high finishing, neatness of penciling, and delicacy of coloring. He particularly excelled in portraits, and in this branch few of his cotemporaries equalled him. He instructed several pupils, the most distinguished of whom was Francis Mieris the Elder. He died at Amsterdam in 1672.

TEMPERELLO, Il. See Caselli.

TEMPESTA, Il, called also Cav. Tempesta, and Pietro Mulier. See Peter Molyn the Younger.

A or Æ or EF or TA.

TEMPESTA, Antonio, a very eminent painter and engraver, born at Florence in 1555. He first studied with Santo di Titi, and afterwards with John Strada. Lanzi gives the following admirable account of him. "Antonio Tempesti, of Florence, a scholar both of Titi and Stradano, was among the first to acquire a celebrated name in Italy for landscapes and battles. He practised engraving, prepared cartoons for tapestry, and gave scope to his genius in the most fanciful inventions, in grotesque and ornamental work. He surpassed his master in spirit, and was inferior to none, not even the Venetians. In a letter on Painting, by the Marchese Giustiniani, he is adduced as an example of great spirit in design, a gift conferred by nature, and not to be acquired by art. He attempted few things on a large scale, and was not so successful in these as in small pictures. The Marchese Niccolini, the Order of the Nunziata, and several Florentine families, possess some of his battles, painted on alabaster, in which he appears the precursor of Borgognone, who studied his works attentively. He most frequently painted in fresco, as at Caprarola, in the Este Villa at Tivoli, and in some of the palaces at Rome, from the time of Gregory XIII., who employed him in the gallery of the Vatican, where most of the historical pictures are his work; in these the figures, a palm and a half high, display astonishing variety and spirit, accompanied by beautiful architecture and landscapes, with every species of decoration. He is not, however, very correct, and his tints are sometimes inclined too much to a brownish hue; but all such faults are pardonable in him, as being occasioned by the *pictoric fury* which inspired him, that fancy which hurried him from earth, and conducted him through novel and sublime regions, unattempted by the vulgar herd." Tempesta not only painted history, battles, and landscapes, but animals, huntings, cavalcades, processions, and grotesque ornaments, in all which he showed a wonderful fertility of invention; but his greatest excellence lay in his skirmishes and battles of cavalry, which are full of fire and spirit. One of his most celebrated works is the Murder of the Innocents, in the church of S. Stefano Rotondo at Rome. The extent of his genius, the variety of his powers, the fertility of his invention, and the vividness of his imagination, are evinced by the astonishing number of his etchings from his own designs, which his biographers say amounted to more than eighteen hundred. Bartsch (Peintre Graveur, tom. xvii.), gives a descriptive catalogue of fourteen hundred and sixty pieces by him, which he believes to be a complete list; Gori makes them amount to fifteen hundred and nineteen, according to the reports of different writers; but Brulliot inclines to the side of Bartsch. The earliest of his known etchings is dated 1589, and the latest 1627. With the exception of an occasional extravagance and incorrectness in design, they are very spirited and masterly performances, which both artists and connoisseurs may study with advantage. The principal are, a set of one hundred and fifty prints from Ovid's Metamorphoses; a very numerous set of subjects from the Bible, called Tempesta's Bible; a set of twenty-four plates from the life of St. Anthony; a set of thirteen plates of the Labors of Hercules, with a frontispiece; the four Ages of Man, in four plates; a great variety and number of huntings of different animals; many plates of battles, cavalcades, processions, and many from sacred and profane history. He sometimes signed his plates *Ant. Tempestes*, but usually marked them with one of the preceding monograms. His name is generally written *Tempesta*, bu sometimes by the Italians, *Tempesti*, *Tempestes*, and *Tempestino*. He died in 1630.

TEMPESTI, or TEMPESTINO, DOMENICO, a painter and engraver, born at Florence, according to Orlandi, in 1652. He studied with Volterrano, and afterwards traveled through Europe, and finally settled at Rome, where he painted landscapes, and engraved some views from sketches he had made during his travels. Lanzi says it would appear that he was the same as Domenico dei Marchis, called Tempestino.

TEMPESTINO, IL, a Roman painter who, according to Pascoli, flourished at Rome about 1680. All that is known of him is, that he assisted Peter Molyn in his numerous works at Rome, in which he followed his manner so closely that he was called after him *Tempestino*. Molyn married his sister, and afterwards assassinated her for the love of another woman. Lanzi says he not only assisted Tempesta, but often exercised his genius in landscape, in the style of Niccolo Poussin.

D or DT. TENIERS, DAVID, the Elder, a Flemish painter, born at Antwerp in 1582, and educated in the school of Rubens, who highly esteemed him for his assiduity and promising talents. For some time he applied himself to historical painting, and visited Italy for the purpose of studying the works of the most celebrated masters of the Italian school, but his genius leading him rather to landscape, he placed himself under the instruction of Adam Ælzheimer, at Rome, with whom he continued six years. Lanzi says he was one of the best imitators of Jacopo Bassano, *in small*, and that by his exquisite skill he acquired the surname of Bassano. Between the styles of his two masters, he formed an original one of his own, which, on his return to Antwerp, he practised with great success. He painted cabinet pictures of rural sports, merry-makings, fairs, festivals, fortune-tellers, mountebanks, conversations, chemists' laboratories, &c., which he treated with such humor and ingenuity that they were greatly admired, and purchased with avidity. His works would have been considered among the happiest efforts of the art in that particular branch, had they not been so much surpassed by the inimitable productions of his son. His design is correct and tasteful, his coloring clear and harmonious, his touch light and delicate, and his chiaro-scuro excellent. He executed some spirited etchings from his own designs, which are not easily distinguished from those of the younger Teniers, as they are similar in style, and both used the same monogram. He died in 1649.

TENIERS, DAVID, the Younger. This celebrated painter was the son of the preceding, born at Antwerp in 1610. There is a good deal of contradiction about his early history, as with many other eminent painters. It is a remarkable fact in the history of art, that there is a vast deal more contradiction in the lives of the most eminent artists, as Raffaelle, Rubens, and Claude Lorraine, than with artists of less note, such is the disposition of the human mind to romance. Young Teniers early showed a genius for painting, and he was carefully instructed by his father, whose style of design he always followed. It is said that he afterwards studied with Adrian Brower, and Rubens. That he was a pupil of Brower is in the highest degree improbable, because the latter was only two years his senior, and could not have been in Antwerp till Teniers had become an accomplished artist. Yet it is probable that he lived on friendly terms with him, frequented his studio, and profited by his example, for it is certain that he imitated that master's style in some of his pictures. It is also very certain that he frequented the school of Rubens, and probably received lessons from him in the principles of coloring; though he did not assist him in any of his works, he is known to have copied some of them. It is also said that his merit was so little regarded at first that he could not find sale for his works at Antwerp, and was obliged to make frequent visits to Brussels to dispose of them; and that he had the mortification to see the works of inferior artists, even of his pupil Tilburg, preferred to his own, till the Archduke Leopold, Governor of the Netherlands, chancing to see some of his productions, was so captivated with them that he took him into his service. Then it was that he became distinguished, and his works were appreciated and sought after. The absurdity of this story is sufficiently evident; his father was then a distinguished artist, whose works were sought after with avidity by the most distinguished persons, till he was eclipsed by his son. The probability is that his extraordinary talents had already excited universal admiration when the Archduke took him under his protection. At all events, the Governor conferred upon him extraordinary honor. He appointed him his principal painter, made him a gentleman of his bed-chamber, presented him with a gold medal and chain, and gave him the direction of his gallery, which contained the works of the most eminent masters of the Italian, Dutch, and Flemish schools. He copied, in small, the principal pictures of this collection, in which he imitated the style of each particular master so exactly that he was called the *Proteus* of painting. The powers of his pencil in this respect were incredible; he knew how to adapt it to the style of every eminent master, no matter how varied the touch and coloring, and he gave to these *pasticci* so strong a character of originality, that it was impossible to distinguish them, by sight alone, from the works of the very artists whose manner of thinking, composing, and pencilling he only imitated. These copies he caused to be engraved and published in a folio volume, dedicated to his patron. The first edition, containing about 200 engravings, was published at Brussels in 1660, and forms what is now called the *Teniers' Gallery*. He did not limit his mimic powers to merely copying, but he painted *pasticci*, or compositions of his own, so exactly in the styles of Rubens, Titian, Tintoretto, Bassano, and other eminent painters, that they have frequently been mistaken for original works by those masters. It was not, however, by his imitative faculties that he obtained his greatest celebrity. He was a constant and faithful observer of nature, which is discernible in all his works. His favorite subjects were landscapes with small figures, village festivals and merrymakings, Flemish fairs and kermesses, shooting at butts, playing at bowls, and other diversions, sports, and occupations of low life. That he might have an opportunity of studying from life the rustic character of the peasantry, their sports, rejoicings, quarrels, and combats, he established himself in a retired situation in the village of Perk, between Antwerp and Mechlin, where he could mingle with the people, and observe with a painter's eye their character under the impulse of the various passions; and it is surprising that he was able to give such an admirable variety to representations which, in their nature, appear confined and uniform. His landscapes, though perfect representations of nature, have an appearance of sameness and monotony, because he copied his scenery from the country where he resided, which was flat; but he amply compensates for this want of variety by the truth and simplicity of these homely views. His pencil is free and delicate, his trees are touched with a spirit and taste for which he is remarkable, his skies are light and floating, and there is a silvery charm in the coloring of his best works peculiar to himself. He is not less admirable in his interiors of cabarets, with peasants smoking, dancing, and regaling themselves, corps-de-garde, and chemists' laboratories, in which he surpassed Ostade in perspective, and equalled him in the chiaro-scuro. In all his works he shows a lively and fertile invention, and great facility of execution. It was not unusual for him to paint a landscape in a single day; and he used jocosely to observe, that to contain all the pictures he had painted, it would require a gallery two leagues long. Notwithstanding this facility, his pieces are always well finished in every part, his figures correctly drawn, and the passions remarkably expressed. His pictures are generally clear in all their parts, with a beautiful transparency; he had the art of relieving his lights, by the disposition of others, without the use of deep shadows, which produced a happy effect. This practice he is supposed to have learned of Rubens, who remarked that strong oppositions of light and shadow were not always necessary to produce effect in a picture, as is evinced by the coloring and tints of Titian.

David Teniers acquired an immense reputation, and his works were eagerly sought after by the princes and most distinguished personages of all Europe, even of Italy. The Archduke having sent some of his pictures to the king of Spain, that monarch was so much delighted with them that he employed his pencil for several years, and had a gallery built expressly as a repository for his paintings. He also received commissions from Don John of Austria, and Christina, Queen of Sweden. Lanzi says that the Duke of Savoy had a collection of nearly four hundred choice specimens of the Flemish masters, in which were many pictures by Teniers. His works, though exceedingly numerous, are justly held in the highest estimation, and whenever they are offered for sale, command enormous prices. Many of them have been sold at public sale in Europe, at sums varying from 300 to 1500 guineas, and some in royal and public collections are estimated at 2000 and upwards. Teniers was also of great service to the landscape painters of his time, in decorating their works with his admirable figures, and the value of some of the pictures of Artois, Vanuden, and others, is greatly enhanced by such embellishment. Some critics have accused Teniers of representing his figures too short and clumsy, with too much sameness in their costumes and countenances; but it ought to be considered that he designed every object from life, and formed his ideas from the scenes with which he was conversant, and that his forms are exactly those of his models. Though he generally painted small cabinet pictures, he was capable of executing works on a large scale. Descamps mentions an altar-piece by him of the Temptation of St. Anthony, in the church of Meerbeck, near Mechlin, in which the figures are of life size. Some of them are not only of a large size, but contain a multitude of figures; thus a Fair at Ghent has 340 figures, a village festival 150, another 93, and his great picture at Schleissheim, 13 feet 6 inches by 10 feet, contains 1138 figures, those in the foreground being 12 inches high. Smith, in his Catalogue raisonné of the works of the Dutch and Flemish masters, vol. iii. and supplement, gives a descriptive account of 900 pictures by him, which are doubtless authentic; but this must be far short of the real number of his genuine works, as there are 100 in the galleries of Schleissheim and Munich, and sixty-five in the royal collection at Madrid, not described by Smith, besides many others mentioned by various writers. There are also a multitude of spurious pictures attributed to him; Stanley says at least 500, which are considered genuine by the possessors. Some of his pupils imitated him very closely, and the rapacity of dealers has induced them to convert every picture having a sufficient resemblance in style, into an *original Teniers*, by erasing the name of the painter, and substituting the signature or monogram of that master. See *Abshoven.* The younger Teniers also etched some plates from his own designs, but it is difficult to distinguish them from those of his father, as they both used the same marks, and etched similar subjects. As far as the merits of the etchings are concerned, it is of no consequence; but G. du Vivier and Coryn Boel etched some imitations after pictures by Teniers, and marked them with his monogram. He died at Brussels in 1694, though some say in 1690.

TENIERS, Abraham, was the younger brother of the preceding, born at Antwerp about 1618. He was instructed in the art by both his father and brother, and painted Flemish festivals and conversations in the style of David Teniers the Younger, though not with equal excellence; yet they possessed sufficient merit to pass with the inexperienced for the productions of his brother. He died in 1691.

TEODOLI, Marchese Girolamo, a distinguished Roman architect, was born in 1677. Descended from a noble Roman family, he was well versed in belles lettres and the sciences; he was fond of the study of architecture, and by attention to the best books, became an architect both in theory and in practice. At Rome he erected the admirable church of Sts. Pietro and Marcellino; the façade is an order of Ionic pilasters; the internal plan is a beautiful Greek cross, covered in the centre with an elegant cupola, and decorated mostly with the Ionic order. Among the other works of Teodoli are the theatre of Argentina; the church of Vicovaro, and the Casa della Madonna de' Miracoli, on the Corso at Rome. His private character is highly eulogized by Milizia. He died in 1766.

TEOSCOPOLI. See Theotocopuli.

TERASSON, H., an English artist mentioned by Strutt as the engraver of some plates of Insects.

TERBRUGGEN. See Verbruggen.

BT or TB or GB TERBURG, Gerard, an eminent Dutch painter, born at Zwoll in 1608. He was the son of a painter, who instructed him in the art, of whom little more is known, except that he had studied at Rome. Some writers suppose that he perfected himself under another master at Haerlem, but others assert that he had no other instruction. At all events, after acquiring considerable reputation, he traveled through Germany, Italy, and France. He resided some time at Paris, where his works were greatly admired. On his return to Holland, he met with the most flattering encouragement, and was one of the most popular painters of his time. He attended the Congress assembled at Munster in 1648, for the negotiation of peace, on which occasion he painted his celebrated picture representing the portraits of the plenipotentiaries and principal personages assembled there, regarded as his masterpiece. At the invitation of Count Pigorando, the Spanish ambassador, he visited Madrid, where he was much employed by the court and the principal nobility. The King conferred on him the honor of knighthood, presented him with a gold chain and medal, and munificently rewarded him. He afterwards returned to his native country, and settled at Deventer, where he died in 1681.

The pictures of Terburg generally represent conversations, musical parties, ladies at the toilet, and similar domestic subjects. He particularly excelled in portraits. Though he had the most ample opportunities of studying the productions of the most eminent masters, he did not much improve his taste of design, which is neither correct nor elegant, nor did he change his manner of composition. He finished his pictures exquisitely, with a light and agreeable touch; his coloring is lively and transparent, and he shows a pleasing and skillful management of the chiaro-scuro. His greatest excellence lay in his draperies, and he was remarkable for introducing white satin in all his compositions, which he represented in an inimitable manner. The genuine works of Terburg are exceedingly scarce, and are only to be found in public, royal, and noble collections, where they are estimated enormously. Such was the labor he bestowed upon his pictures, that his known works, omitting portraits, do not exceed one hundred. Though he received high prices for his productions, their value has constantly increased; thus the *Music Lesson* was sold in 1767 for £112, and in 1826 it was bought by Sir Robert Peel at 920 guineas. Another, called *the Letter*, or *Female Curiosity*, was sold in 1762 for £144, and in 1837 it brought £640. The famous *Congress of Munster*, a picture only seventeen inches by twenty-two, in 1804 sold for £640, and in 1837 for £1890. For the fullest account of this master's works, the reader is referred to Smith's Catalogue raisonné, vol. iv. and Supplement.

TERENZI, Terenzio, called Il Rondolino, a painter born at Urbino, who flourished about 1600. He studied under Federigo Baroccio in his native city, and afterwards, according to Baglioni, visited Rome, where he obtained the patronage of Cardinal Montalto. He possessed an extraordinary faculty of imitating the works of the old masters, so as to deceive the best judges. Baglioni says he was a noted cheat, and that "after having sold to inexperienced persons many of his own pictures for those of ancient masters, he attempted to practise the same deception upon Cardinal Peretti, the nephew of Sixtus V., and his own patron, offering to his notice one of his own pieces as a Raffaelle; but the fraud was detected, and Terenzio in consequence banished from the court—a circumstance which he took to heart, and died while yet young." Others place his death in 1620.

Zani says there were two artists of this name: Terenzio d' Urbino, the scholar of Baroccio, whose history is recorded above; the other was a native of Pesaro, called Il Rondolino (the Swallow), an eminent artist, who flourished about 1550, which date is evidently an error, for Lanzi says "the *Guida di Pesaro* assigns Terenzio Terenzi called Il Rondolino to the school of Baroccio, whom it characterizes as an eminent painter, four of whose works are in public, and many more in the neighborhood of the city. It is also mentioned that he went to Rome, where he was employed by the Cardinal della Rovere, and that he painted a picture in the church of S. Silvestro. The picture in S. Silvestro *in capite*, which represents the Madonna attended by Saints, is ascribed by Titi to a Terenzio of Urbino, who, according to Baglioni, served the Cardinal Montalto." Lanzi then goes on to give his opinion that they are one and the same artist, and that at Rome he took his name from Urbino, the capital of Pesaro, though he was a native of the latter place.

TERLEY, N. van, a Dutch painter, born at Dort in 1636, and died there in 1687. Little is known of him. It is said that he was a scholar of Rembrandt, and that his pictures exhibit a fine taste in design and composition, and agreeable coloring.

TERMISANO, Dezio, a Neapolitan painter, who, according to Dominici, studied with Gio. Filippo Criscuolo. There is a picture of the Last Supper by him, in the church of S. Maria Chiazza at Naples, signed with his name, and dated 1597.

TERRY, G., an English engraver, who flourished from 1770 to 1788. He scraped some portraits in mezzotinto for the book publishers.

TERSAN, Comte de. See Campion.

TERWESTEN, Augustine, an eminent Dutch painter, born at the Hague in 1649. He had a natural genius for painting, and without any instruction he had made sufficient progress in design to be employed by goldsmiths as a chaser on gold and silver, which business he followed till he was twenty years of age. He then studied two years with Nicholas Wieling, till that artist was invited to the court of the Elector of Brandenburg, when he placed himself under the tuition of William Doudyns. He next traveled through Germany and Italy, studying with great assiduity the works of the best masters, particularly at Rome, Florence, and Venice. At Rome, he applied himself to designing after the antique, and the works of Raffaelle, and at Venice he made the works of Titian and Tintoretto the especial objects of his study. After a residence of six years in Italy, he returned to Holland, where he distinguished himself as one of the ablest artists of his time. His talents were chiefly employed in decorating the ceilings and apartments in fresco, of the mansions of the nobility at the Hague, Amsterdam, and Dort. His subjects were usually taken from Ovid, but he painted many from sacred and profane history. He possessed a lively genius, a ready invention, and a wonderful facility of hand; his design is correct, his draperies well cast, and his coloring chaste, natural, and brilliant. One of his most admired performances was a saloon he painted for the Burgomaster van Slingelandt at Dort, which Descamps commends in the highest terms. He was the principal reviver of the Academy at the Hague, which had fallen into decadence, and by his abilities and influence, he restored it to its former lustre. In 1690 he was invited to the court of the Elector of Brandenburg, afterwards king of Prussia, who appointed him his principal painter, and made him Director of the Academy at Berlin. He continued in the service of that monarch during the rest of his life, and decorated the royal palaces with many of his best works. He died at Berlin in 1711.

TERWESTEN, Elias, was the brother of the preceding, born at the Hague in 1651. He studied with Augustine, and for some time devoted himself to historical painting, but not succeeding to his expectations, he turned his attention to animals, fruit, flowers, and still-life, in which he was more successful. He painted birds admirably, for which reason he was called "The Bird of Paradise." He traveled to Italy, and settled at Rome, where he acquired considerable reputation, and was employed by the Elector of Brandenburg to procure the finest casts from the antique statues and sculptures for the Academy at Berlin; he purchased for that prince the valuable cabinet of gems, medals, and curiosities collected by the celebrated Bellosi. He died at Rome in 1724.

TERWESTEN, Matthew, was the younger brother of the two preceding artists, born at the Hague in 1670. He was first instructed by Augustine T., and afterwards studied with Daniel Mytens and William Doudyns. Possessed of a decided genius, and aided by the instruction of such able masters, he had made such progress, that at the age of twenty years, he was entrusted by his brother to finish some considerable works when the latter set out for the court of Berlin. He acquitted himself on this occasion with so much ability, that he received several important commissions, and met with the most flattering success. One of his earliest patrons was M. Schuilenberg, prime minister of the King of Holland, for whom he painted a ceiling, representing Diana and her Nymphs, which gained him great reputation. This encouragement, so far from rendering him self-sufficient and conceited, only inspired him with more ardor in cultivating his talents. He accordingly went to Italy, and arrived at Venice in 1694, where he frequented the school of Carlo Loti, and studied the works of Titian, Tintoretto, and Veronese with the greatest assiduity. He next went to Rome, where he found his brother Elias, and passed three years in designing after the antique, and the works of the great Roman masters. On his return to his native country in 1699, he was received with distinction, admitted into the Academy at the Hague, and found abundant employment. He was soon after appointed director of the Academy, which office he filled till his death, with great credit to himself and advantage to the students. Though he was chiefly occupied in decorating ceilings and grand apartments of the principal mansions of the city, with historical and fabulous subjects in fresco, he frequently painted altar-pieces and other sacred subjects for the churches, one of the best of which represents Christ's Agony in the Garden, in the Church of the Jansenists at the Hague. He also occasionally painted portraits, and there is one of the Princess Mary, afterwards Queen of England, and consort of William III., in the Museum at Amsterdam. He died in 1735.

TERZI, Cristoforo, a painter born at Bologna in 1692. He studied under Giuseppe Maria Crespi, and afterwards improved himself by a residence of several years at Rome. On his return to Bologna, he acquired considerable reputation as an historical painter, and executed several works for the churches, but wrought mostly for the collections. One of his most esteemed works is a picture of St. Petronio kneeling before the Virgin, in the church of S. Giacomo Maggiore. Lanzi says that from the outset, he boasted a decision of hand, and with a few bold strokes of the pencil, was able to sketch very spirited heads, though he did not often practise in this manner, but finished his pictures with sufficient care. "Many collections at Bologna possess some of his half-length figures, and heads of old men, which are mistaken by less experienced judges for those of Lana." He died there in the prime of life in 1743.

TERZI, Francesco, a painter born at Bergamo, about 1520. He studied under Gio. Battista Morani, and according to Tassi, he distinguished himself by two pictures he painted for the church of S. Francesco at Bergamo, representing the Nativity of Christ, and the Assumption of the Virgin. Lomazzo mentions two noble histories of our Lord with his Apostles, in the church of S. Sempliciano, in his native city. He was invited to Vienna by the Emperor Maximilian II., who appointed him his painter, and retained him in his service for many years. Lanzi says he also distinguished himself by his works in most of the capitals of Italy. He is said to have engraved a set of portraits of the princes of the House of Austria, but they were executed by Gaspar ab Avibus, who signed them *Gaspar Patavinus, incisor*, 1569. Terzi died at Rome in 1600, at an advanced age.

TESAURO, Filippo or Pippo, an old Neapolitan painter, born about 1260, and died in 1320. According to Dominici, he was a disciple of Tommaso de Stefani, whom he assisted in his works, and became one of the ablest artists of that period. The author above cited describes several of his works in the public edifices at Naples, but they have all perished except some frescos in the church of S. Restituta, representing the life of St. Niccolo, the Hermit.

TESAURO, Bernardo. This old artist of the Neapolitan school is supposed to have been a descendant of the preceding; born about 1440. He was a disciple of Silvestro Buono, and was an artist of great reputation in his time. Though his works have mostly perished, there are sufficient remaining in the churches of Naples to show that he was a man of extraordinary genius. Lanzi says, "he is supposed to have been descended from that Filippo who is commended as the second of the Neapolitan school, and the father or uncle of Raimo. He made nearer approaches to the modern style than any of the preceding artists, more judicious in his invention, more natural in his figures and drapery; select, expressive, harmonized, and displaying a knowledge in gradation and relief, beyond what could be expected in a painter who is not known to have been acquainted with any other schools, or seen any pictures beyond those of his own country. Luca Giordano, at a time when he was considered the Coryphæus of painting, was struck with astonishment at the painting of a *soffitto* by Tesauro at S. Giovanni de' Pappacodi, and did not hesitate to declare that there were parts in it which no one could have surpassed in his own age, so fruitful in fine works. It represents the Seven Sacraments, and the portraits of Alfonso II., and Ippolita Sforza, whose espousals he represented in it, affords some light in fixing the date of the picture about 1480." Another fine work by him is an altar-piece of the Assumption of the Virgin in S. Giovanni Maggiore.

TESAURO, Raimo Epifanio. This painter was the son and disciple of the preceding, according to Dominici, and flourished about 1490. He was much employed in decorating with frescos, the churches and public edifices of Naples, and some pictures by him still remain in S. Maria Nuova, Monte Vergine, S. Lorenzo, and the Nunziata, particularly the Visitation of the Virgin to St. Elizabeth in the Nunziata, and the great altar-piece in S. Lorenzo, representing the Virgin and Infant Christ, with St. Anthony, St. Jerome, and St. John the Baptist, dated 1494. He was living in 1501.

TESI, Mauro, a painter born in the state of Modena in 1730. He studied under an obscure painter at Bologna, but possessing strong natural genius, he greatly improved himself by studying the architectural works of Mitelli and Colonna, and others at Bologna, by which means, says Lanzi, "he restored the art of architectural painting, which had degenerated at Bologna, to a judicious and solid style, sparing in decoration as it had formerly been, and in some parts still more philosophical and learned." His principal patron was the learned Count Algarotti, who made him his companion in his tours, and encouraged him to study and make excellent observations on the works of the ancients. He executed some beautiful works for his patron, for the Marchese Zambeccari, and others, but he died at Bologna in the flower of life in 1766, and his friends erected a marble monument to his memory in the church of S. Petronio, with this inscription, "Mauro Tesi elegantiæ veteris in pingendo ornatu et architectura restitutori."

TESIO, a Piedmontese painter, who flourished at Turin in the latter part of the last century. He is supposed to have studied with the Cav. Beaumont. Lanzi says, "whether Tesio was instructed by Beaumont or others I cannot state; but I know that he repaired to Rome, and there became one of the best scholars of Mengs; and at Moncalieri, a delightful residence of the royal family, are to be seen some of the finest specimens of his talents." He died about 1800.

TESSIN, Nicodemus Valentinson, an eminent Swedish architect, was born at Stralsund in 1619. There is little recorded of his history, but he was appointed crown architect by Queen Christina, in 1645; visited Italy for improvement, and was honored with a patent of nobility in 1674 by Charles XI. Among his principal works are the mausoleum of Charles Gustavus, the Royal Villa of Stromsholm; and the palace of Drottningsholm, completed by the following artist. Tessin died about 1688.

TESSIN, Count Nicodemus, an eminent Swedish architect, the son of the preceding, was born at Nykoping in 1654. After completing his studies, first at Stockholm, afterwards at Upsala, he was sent to Italy, at the age of eighteen, in the suite of the Marquis del Monte. He studied four years at Rome, under Bernini, and, after making the tour of Italy, received from Charles XI. the appointment of future crown architect. On returning to Sweden, he was allowed by the King to prosecute his travels, conformably with his earnest wish for further improvement, and he spent three or four years in France and England. On finally settling in his native country, he received in addition to his former appointments, that of city architect to the magistracy of Stockholm. In 1697, the royal palace was destroyed by fire, and Tessin availed himself of this highly favorable opportunity to erect one of the noblest edifices of the kind in Europe. His talents were frequently employed upon splendid decorations for festivals, and works of a similar nature. The Queen-dowager Hedwig Eleonora employed him to complete the palace at Drottningsholm, and to lay out the gardens both there and at Ulriksdal. Besides the cathedral at Calmar, and Oxenstiern's monument, Tessin executed or designed a great number of other buildings, including a project for rebuilding the palace at Copenhagen, which was partly carried into effect, many years after his death, when it was curtailed, and injured in other respects. Elevations of the original design were published by his son under the title of *Regiæ Hafniensis Facies*, &c. In addition to his professional occupations, Tessin was engaged in several offices at Court, and took a considerable share in public and political affairs. In 1714 he received the title of Count, and in 1728, at the time of his death, he was Chancellor of the University of Lund. His son, Count Charles Gustavus Tessin, born at Stockholm in 1695, possessed considerable architectural talent, but did not practise the art, except in completing the palace at Stockholm, after his father's death. He was chiefly distinguished as a statesman and diplomatist, and exercised his extended influence for the encouragement of arts and manufactures, particularly in the foundation of the Swedish Academy of Painting and Sculpture, which he first established in 1735. He died in 1771.

TESTA, Pietro, a painter born at Lucca, and hence called at Rome, Il Lucchesino. There is a great deal of discrepancy about the history of this painter and his real merits as an artist. Passeri and the best authorities place his birth in 1617, others in 1611; but all are agreed that he died in 1650. Lanzi gives the following account of him. "It is highly probable that he learned the principies of the art from Pietro Paolini at Lucca before he came to Rome. He there had several masters, but chiefly Pietro da Cortona, from whose school he was expelled because he treated the maxims of his master with contempt. He then put himself under Domenichino, on whose principles, says Passeri, he gloried to rely, but his style, in despite of himself, approached nearly to that of Cortona. He has also some resemblance to his friend Poussin, in his figures (which at one time he made too slender), in his landscapes, and in his study of the antique, of which he was deeply enamored, having applied himself to designing the finest specimens in architecture and in sculpture that Rome afforded. The Death of St. Angelo, in the church of S. Martino a Monti, a picture of great force, is the only piece in public at Rome, though he is frequently recognized in the galleries; there is a Joseph sold to the Ishmaelites, by him, in the Capitol, and a Murder of the Innocents, in the Palazzo Spada; but there are not many of his pictures elsewhere, for he engraved more than he painted. He left some oil paintings at Lucca, in the church of S. Romano, and S. Paolino, in the Buonvisi Gallery, and in other places; also two works in fresco; viz., an allegorical picture of Liberty, in the Senate House, and the small, but very elegant cupola of the Oratory in the Lippi palace. He settled at Rome, where he lived unhappily, and either from despair or some affront, drowned himself in the Tiber. His fate may teach young artists of genius, not to overrate their own talents, nor to despise those of others. By these failings he alienated the minds of his cotemporaries, so that neither in reputation nor employment, was he so successful as many others, and his perpetual complaints occasioned doubts even of his sanity."

Others say that he had a passion for art from infancy; that he studied under Paolini; that in order to see the works of the great masters, he traveled on foot to Rome, disguised as a pilgrim; that he there first studied with Domenichino, and lastly with Cortona, till he was expelled for speaking disrespectfully of the talents of that master, when he devoted himself with the greatest assiduity to designing after the marbles and the remains of architecture; and it is said there was scarcely a vestige of antiquity in or about that capital, which he had not designed, and with which he was so familiar, that he could not draw from memory alone. He was also attentive in designing after the works of the most celebrated painters. Sandrart relates that he gave himself up entirely to these studies, suffering extreme poverty, destitute of all assistance and means, except what he could procure for his sketches and designs, which were not appreciated; that he found him in this condition, sketching among the ruins in the vicinity of Rome, when he took him home, fed, clothed, and lodged him, procured him employment in the gallery of the Prince Giustiniani, and recommended him to other persons of rank. Some writers do not hesitate to declare that Testa never produced anything worthy of commendation; that his pencil was hard, his coloring crude, his genius licentious, his compositions crowded and confused, and his figures extravagant in their proportions.

Much of this discrepancy doubtless arises from the prejudice of his cotemporaries, for it is conceded that he was of a melancholy and unsocial character, and probably this natural disposition was aggravated by disappointment and want of appreciation. Sandrart, himself a noted artist, and an excellent writer and critic on art, considered him an extraordinary genius; Passeri was a great admirer of his works, and thought that his tints and coloring, like those of Poussin, harmonized with his subjects. Whoever will examine his numerous prints, all of them from his own designs, must acknowledge that he possessed an extraordinary imagination, a perfect knowledge of the antique, and a wonderful facility of hand. His style of etching is bold, free, and masterly, resembling that of Antonio Tempesta, but of superior execution. Passeri says of his engravings, that he was a perfect master of invention, "such vigor of conception, such novelty, and such variety, were never the gift of any other artist. He is a poet in all his historic pieces; his composition is full of fancy; this however is not equally commended by all who look for the simple action without other accessories." Strutt says, "Pietro Testa drew with great taste, and marked the extremities of his figures in a very masterly manner. The characters of his heads are finely expressed, and the female faces are often very beautiful. When the extravagance of his fancy did not hurry him beyond the bounds of nature, his outlines are correct and elegant. The draperies of his figures are flowing and easy, and so contrived as to show the form of the figure very distinctly, yet these beauties are often obscured by ill chosen attitudes. He seems to have paid no attention to the management of the chiaroscuro; his lights are scattered, without forming any great masses, and so produce little effect."

In the collection of Mariette, there were ninety-two etchings by this master. He sometimes signed them with his name, and at others with the above monogram. The following are among his rarest and best prints. He was drowned in the Tiber in 1650, some say accidentally, while he was sketching, and others, that he threw himself into the river in a fit of despair; Sandrart says that while endeavoring to recover his hat, blown off by a sudden gust of wind, as he sat sketching on the bank, he slipt and fell in.

Abraham sacrificing Isaac; *P. Testa, fec.* The Holy Family, with Angels presenting refreshments; rare. The Virgin and Infant, who is embracing the Cross; rare. The Adoration of the Magi. The Crucifixion. Four plates of the History of the Prodigal Son; *P. Testa, fe. Romæ.* The Martyrdom of St. Erasmus. St. Jerome praying. St. Roch and two Bishops interceding for the Cessation of the Plague. Thetis directing the infant Achilles to be plunged into the river Styx; *P. Testa, fecit.* Achilles dragging the Body of Hector round the walls of Troy; *P. Testa, aq. for.* Socrates at Table with his Friends; *P. Testa.* 1648. The Death of Cato; *do.* The Sacrifice of Iphigenia. Four plates of the Seasons of the Year, with the Signs of the Zodiac. The Triumph of Bacchus. Faith, Hope, and Charity; one of his rarest prints. Magdalene in the Desert; very rare. A young Woman in a Swoon, surrounded by Cupids; exceeding rare.

TESTA, Giovanni Cesare, was the nephew of the preceding, born at Rome about 1630, and practised both painting and engraving. Little is known of him, however, as a painter. He executed quite a number of plates, chiefly after his uncle's designs, though some of them are from his own, and after the works of other masters. From resemblance of style, he is supposed to have studied with Pietro. His prints are usually signed with his name. Among others, are the following by him. Zani says he died young, in 1655.

The Portrait of Pietro Testa; *J. Cesar Testa, sc.* The Death of Dido; *after P. Testa.* The Centaur Chiron instructing Achilles to throw the Javelin; *do.* The Emperor Titus consulting Basilides respecting his expedition against Jerusalem; *do.* The Communion of St. Jerome after the celebrated picture by *Domenichino.*

TESTANA, Giovanni Battista, an Italian engraver, born at Genoa about 1645. He resided chiefly at Rome, where he engraved, in conjunction with William Vallet and Stephen Picart, the plates from medals and antique gems of the work of Canini. He also engraved some plates after Pietro da Cortona, Agostino Caracci, and other masters. He was living in 1700.

TESTANA, Gioseffo, an Italian engraver, probably a relative of the preceding, born at Genoa about 1650. He established himself at Rome, where he engraved a part of the plates for a work entitled *Effigies of the Cardinals now living*, dated 1680. He subsequently engraved some plates after the Italian masters.

TESTELIN, Louis, a French painter and engraver, was born at Paris in 1615. He studied under Simon Vouet, and was elected one of the original members of the French Academy at its establishment in 1648, although he was only 33 years of age. His presentation picture was a historical portrait of Louis XIV. In 1650 he was chosen a professor of the Academy. He painted, in 1652, a picture of the Resuscitation of Tabitha by St. Paul, which is considered one of the master-pieces of the French school; it is now in the church of Notre Dame, where is also another celebrated picture by him, of the Flagellation of Paul and Silas. His picture of St. Louis attending a sick Man, in the Hospital de la Charité is also greatly admired. Testelin was a very intimate friend of le Brun, who highly esteemed his knowledge of the principles of the art. He died in 1655, aged 40; consequently his works are scarce. He engraved a plate of the Holy Family, after his own design.

TESTELIN, Henri, a French painter and engraver, the brother of Louis T., was born at Paris in 1616. He studied under Simon Vouet, and attained sufficient reputation in portrait and historical painting, to be elected a member of the Academy. He was also appointed Secretary of that institution, and at the death of his brother, succeeded him as Professor of Painting. He wrote a work in folio, highly esteemed in his time, entitled "Sentimens des plus habiles peintres sur la pratique de la peinture et de la sculpture," &c., published in 1696, and embellished with plates engraved by himself. There are also about fifty plates, in sets, which D'Argenville attributes to this artist, although another authority says they were engraved by Louis Ferdinand, after Testelin's designs. The following are among his principal plates:

Studies of expression in Heads, in outline. Studies of antique Statues, with proportions. Studies of expression in Heads; *after le Brun*. The Israelites gathering Manna; *after N. Poussin*. The Holy Family; *after Raffaelle*. This is from the picture in the Louvre, in which there are angels scattering flowers; also engraved by *Edelinck*. St. Michael vanquishing the Evil Spirit; *after Raffaelle*.

TESTORINO, Brandolino, an old painter of Brescia, whose name is placed in competition with Gentile de Fabriano, and, according to Morelli, "perhaps preferred to him." He is supposed to have assisted Altichiero in decorating the great hall in Padua, called Sala de' Giganti. His works have mostly perished, and the exact time he flourished is not known, though it must have been in the last part of the 14th, and the first part of the 15th centuries.

TEUCHER, John Christopher, a German engraver of whom little is known. He resided at Paris about 1750. He engraved a print called the Virgin of the Rose, *after Parmiggiano*, for the collection called the Dresden Gallery.

TEXIER, G., a French engraver, born at Paris about 1760. He studied with Jacques Philippe le Bas, and engraved some plates of landscapes, conversations, and serenades; also views in Switzerland, vignettes, and other book-plates. His plates are executed with the graver, in a neat, clear style. He was living in 1824.

TEXIER, Victor, was the son of the preceding. He was one of the engravers employed on the Musée Français and Musée Royal. He also engraved some views of the Alhambra, chemists' laboratories, and other subjects. He wrought with the graver, in a very neat and pleasing style.

TEXIS, Jerome, an old engraver, by whom there is a print of Mount Calvary, with Christ upon the Cross, signed *Hieronimus Texis*, *Carmagnolie.* 1561.

THACKER, Robert, an English artist, who flourished in 1670. There is a large print by him, in four sheets, representing the Cathedral of Salisbury, signed with his name, with the title of *Designer to the King.*

THELOTT, Jacob Gottlieb, a German engraver, who flourished about 1730. He engraved some portraits, and a part of the plates for a work entitled "Representation des Animaux de la Menagerie de Prince Eugene, 1734." His plates are executed with the graver, in a neat, but formal style.

THEODORE, A., a Dutch artist, mentioned by Strutt as the engraver of a print representing a procession in Holland, dated 1636.

THEODORE, an artist who, according to Basan, was a scholar of Francis Milé, painted landscapes in the style of that master, and etched some plates from his designs, which are signed with his name. There is also a set of twenty-eight etchings after Milé attributed to him, but Barstch and Dumesnil say that they have a great resemblance to the prints of vander Cabel; Houbraken and Mariette attribute them to Gerard Hoet. It is probable that *Theodore* is the baptismal name of some unknown artist. The curious in such matters are referred to Bartsch, Peintre Graveur, tom. v., and to Robert Dumesnil, Peintre Graveur Français, tom. i., for full descriptions of the prints, and their opinions on the subject.

THEODORE CASPAR, Baron De Furstenbergh, one of the earliest mezzotinto engravers, of whom nothing is known with certainty, not even his family name. There are three or four prints by him, signed with his name, and a few others of very doubtful authenticity, attributed to him. He is variously called by writers Theodore Caspar, Theodore Caspar a Furstenbergh, and Theodore Caspar, Baron de Furstenbergh. His prints are not worth any disquisition, nor is it pretended that he was the inventor of the art, or that he improved it. He flourished in 1656, as appears from the date of one of his prints. See *Siegen.*

THEODORUS. There were several Grecian painters of this name, mentioned by Pliny and Diogenes Laertius. The principal was an Athenian painter of considerable eminence. Among his most important works were the following: Clytemnestra and Ægisthus slain by Orestes; a picture of Cassandra, preserved formerly in the temple of Concord; and several pictures of the events of the Trojan War, which were afterwards taken to Rome, and placed in the Philippian portico.

THEODORUS. There were two ancient Grecian artists of this name, who flourished between the years 800 and 700 B. C. One of them was the son of Rhœcus of Samos, a sculptor and architect, who executed a statue impersonating Night, in the temple of Diana at Ephesus, and erected, in concert with his son Theodorus, the famous Doric temple of Juno at Samos. According to the researches detailed in the "Antiquities of Ionia," it appears to have been a decastyle and dipteral temple like that of Apollo Didymeius, 344 feet by 166. Vitruvius mentions a description of this temple by Theodorus, who, according to Pliny, constructed, in concert with Zmilus and Rholus, the labyrinth at Lemnos, supported by fifty immense columns, and so ingeniously contrived as to surpass, in the opinion of Pliny, both the Candian and Egyptian labyrinths. These two artists deserve everlasting remembrance for having invented the art of modeling in clay.

The second Theodorus was the son of Telecles, and invented, according to Pausanias, the mode of casting statues in iron. He is said to have been the sculptor of one of two magnificent vases, which were presented to the temple at Delphi, by Crœsus, king of Lydia. Pliny mentions by him a work of great delicacy and minuteness—a brass statue of himself holding in one hand a file, probably in allusion to his profession, and in the other a quadriga, or four-horse chariot, so small that a fly might cover it with its wings.

THEOLON, Etienne, a French painter, born at Paris in 1739. He studied with Joseph Vien, and painted interiors and conversation pieces with great reputation. His pictures are highly finished and very rare, as he bestowed great labor upon them and died young. He was admitted into the Academy at Paris in 1774, and died in 1781.

THEON, an eminent Greek painter, was a native of Samos, and flourished about the time of Philip and Alexander of Macedonia. According to Quintilian, he was considered among the first masters of the age, on account of his powers of invention, and the gracefulness of his execution. Ælian mentions an admirable picture by Theon, representing a youthful warrior, animated by martial spirit, and eagerly hastening to the fight. Pliny speaks of two, representing Thamyris playing the cithera, and Orestes in the act of killing his mother.

THEOTOCOPULI, or TEOSCOPOLI, Domenico, called delle Greche, Il Greco, and El Griego. This eminent painter, engraver, sculptor, and architect, was a native of Greece, according to Palomino, and born in 1548. He quitted his native country, and visited Italy, where he studied painting under Titian, and also practised wood engraving. Little is known concerning his works in the latter art, but Lanzi briefly mentions his name in such a manner as sufficiently shows his eminence, thus: "the art of wood engraving continued gradually to advance, and was cultivated by many distinguished men; such as Albert Durer in Germany; in Italy by Mecherino di Siena, by *Domenico delle Greche*, by Domenico Campagnola," &c. That author also says that he was employed by Titian to engrave some of his designs, and that his print after that master, representing the Submersion of Pharoah, is a sufficient proof of his ability in wood engraving; also that Palomino was wrong in citing the date on this print as 1549, when Theotocopuli was only one year old. Zani, following Palomino's date, makes two artists; but Lanzi's correction explains the discrepancy.

None of the paintings of Theotocopuli have been certainly identified in Italy; but there are many in Spain, whither he went in company with Titian, at the invitation of Charles V. He remained in that country many years, during the rest of his life, and executed a large number of works in painting, sculpture, and architecture. His portraits and altar-pieces, in the style of Titian, Palomino says, appeared to be from the hand of that master himself. He afterwards attempted a different style, but failed entirely. In 1577, when he settled at Toledo, Theotocopuli painted for the cathedral, a remarkable picture of the Parting of Christ's Raiment, which has received very high commendation from Bermudez, and others, being entirely in the style of Titian, and scarcely inferior to that master. His picture of the Interment of Don Gonsalvo Ruiz, in the church of Santo Tomé, at Toledo, is commended as the finest picture in that city, and one of the noblest productions of Spanish art. He painted portraits in an admirable style, some of which are in the Royal Gallery at Madrid, and would do honor to Velasquez; his own portrait, and that of his beautiful daughter, are in the Spanish collection at the Louvre, where they are very highly valued.

As a sculptor and architect, El Greco gained considerable eminence, practising both these arts in the same works, according to the general custom of his time. He designed the Casa del Ayuntamiento, or mansion house, of Toledo; also the churches La Caridad, and of the Franciscan convent at Illescas; for which edifices he executed a great part of the paintings and sculptures. In 1590, he designed the church of the Augustines at Madrid, called De Dona Maria de Arragon. He designed, also, several admirable monuments; but his grandest work, according to Milizia, was the church and monastery of the Bernard monks at San Domenico di Silos, of which he executed the whole—painting, sculpture, and architecture. According to Palomino, he died at Toledo in 1625, and was buried with great pomp in the church of St. Bartholomew. His son, George Manuel Theotocopuli, was also distinguished in sculpture and architecture, and practised both these arts in the Cathedral of Toledo, in 1625 and the following years. Among his other works, is an octagon edifice attached to the Cathedral, termed the *ochavo;* it is decorated with precious stones, and is used as the treasure-house of the Virgin. He died at Toledo in 1631.

THEW, Robert, an eminent English engraver, was born in the small town of Patrington, in the East Riding of Yorkshire, in 1758. At an early age he was apprenticed to a cooper, and continued at that business for a number of years; Chalmers states that, during the war of American Independence, he served as a private in the Northumberland militia. According to the "Gentleman's Magazine," his attention was first directed to engraving about the age of twenty-six, when it is said he happened to see an engraver at work, and although destitute of any practical knowledge of drawing, he procured a copper-plate, and engraved an old woman's head, from a picture by Gerard Douw, with such extraordinary skill, that he was appointed historical engraver to the Prince of Wales, at the recommendation of Charles Fox, Lady Ducannon, and the Duchess of Devonshire. This story, however, is highly improbable, since considerable mechanical dexterity is indispensable to producing a good copper-plate engraving. A more credible account is, that about 1783 Thew settled at Hull, and commenced engraving shop-bills, cards, etc. Chalmers states that he engraved and published a plan of Hull, which is dated May 6, 1784; and that shortly afterwards he solicited subscriptions for two views of the Dock at that place. The latter are large aquatint plates, drawn and engraved by Thew, with the assistance of F. Jukes in the aquatinting department; and they were published in London, by Thew himself, in May, 1786. Copies of them are now preserved in the British Museum. In 1788, Thew was introduced to Alderman Boydell by the Marquis of Caermarthen, afterwards duke of Leeds, whose patronage he had obtained by the construction of a camera-obscura on a new principle; and Boydell immediately commissioned him to engrave Northcote's picture of the Interview between the young Princes, from Richard III., act iii., scene 1. This plate was published in 1791, at which time Thew held the appointment above alluded to, of engraver to the Prince of Wales. He subsequently engraved eighteen other plates for the Shakspeare Gallery, and part of a nineteenth; several of these are among the best in the collection, displaying an unusual amount of spirit and expression, as well as a high degree of mechanical skill. That of Cardinal Wolsey entering Leicester Abbey (Henry VIII., act iv., scene 2), from a picture by Westall, is particularly and deservedly celebrated as a fine specimen of stipple engraving; and in consequence of its superior beauty, proof impressions were charged double the price of any other in the entire work. Thew received but little instruction, and owed his success, according to Chalmers, to his native genius, aided by an industrious application, by which he rapidly attained great excellence in the art. The distinguishing characteristics of his practice consisted in most faithfully exhibiting the true spirit and style of each master; a most minute accuracy, a certain polish, and exquisite delicacy of manner; with the appropriate character given to all objects, while a mildness of tone and perfect harmony pervaded the whole piece. Thew died at Stevenage, in Hertfordshire, in 1802.

THIBOUST, Benoit, a French engraver, born at Chartres about 1655. It is not known under whom he studied, but he went young to Italy, where he seems to have passed the rest of his life. He engraved a set of thirty-five plates, representing the life of St. Turribius, *after Gio. Battista Gaetano*, entitled *Vita Beati Turribii, Archiepiscopi Limani in Indiis*, published at Rome in 1679. He also engraved a number of other plates, after the Italian masters, among which are the Crucifixion, *after Gaetano;* St. Teresa and St. Bibiena, *after Bernini;* St. Tommaso d'Aquinas, *after Calandrucci;* St. Rosa kneeling before the Virgin, the martyrdom of St. Peter, and St. Peter of Alcantara, *after A. Baldi.* His plates are executed with the graver, in a slight, open style, resembling that of Claude Mellan, though very inferior to those of that master. He was living in 1699.

THIELE, John Alexander, a German painter, born at Erfurt, in Saxony, in 1685, though some say in 1695. He is said to have first studied with an obscure landscape painter, named Manyoky, and afterwards with C. L. Agricola. He however chiefly owed his success to his own genius, and a diligent study of nature. His pictures represent the beautiful scenery on the banks of the Sala and the Elbe, which he depicted in a very natural and pleasing manner. He acquired considerable celebrity, and was appointed painter to the king of Saxony. He executed quite a number of spirited etchings from his own designs, consisting of views in Saxony, which are dated 1726 to 1743; those of the later dates are far superior to his earlier prints. He was the instructor of the celebrated Dietricy, and died at Dresden in 1752.

THIELEN, John Philip van, an eminent Flemish painter of flowers, born at Mechlin in 1618. He was descended of a noble family, and was Seigneur or Lord of Cowenberg, on which account he usually signed his pictures J. P. Cowenberg. After receiving a liberal education in every branch of polite literature, a passion for painting induced him to place himself under the instruction of Daniel Seghers, the celebrated painter of flowers, under whose able instruction he became one of the most famous painters of his time in that branch of the art. He usually composed his subjects in the manner of Seghers, in garlands of flowers around some historical designs, or in festoons that encircled vases enriched with bas-reliefs. He copied every object after nature, cultivated the most beautiful flowers, selected them when they appeared in their fullest bloom, and grouped them with elegance and taste. His pictures are well composed, and very highly finished, and though they are less spirited and brilliant than those of his instructor, his touch is as light, his pencil as neat, and his coloring as transparent. He was much employed by the king of Spain, and most of his works are in the royal collections at Madrid. In competition with Seghers, he was employed to paint a picture in the Abbey of St. Bernard, near Antwerp, on which occasion he exerted all his abilities, and his performance was judged little inferior to that of his master. Weyerman highly extols a garland of flowers by him, encircling a sleeping Nymph, with a Satyr watching her, by Poelemburg. There are two capital pictures by him at Mechlin, representing St. Bernard and St. Agatha, surrounded by garlands of flowers, with insects, as natural as life. He sometimes painted landscapes, huntings, and architectural pieces, but he was not so successful in these subjects. He died in 1667.

THIELEN, Maria Theresa, Anna Maria, and Frances Catherine van, were the daughters of the preceding, who carefully instructed them in the art, and they all excelled in the same branch. *Maria Theresa*, the eldest, was born in 1640. She painted portraits and flowers in such an excellent manner, that Weyerman says her pictures were worth their weight in gold. *Anna Maria* was born in 1641, and *Frances Catherine* in 1645; they were not inferior to their sister in elegance of composition, delicacy of penciling, or softness of coloring—commendation too gallant and uniform to be of much value.

THIELENS, John, a Flemish painter, who flourished at Antwerp, in the latter part of the 17th century. He painted the interior of chemists' laboratories, workshops of sculptors, studios of painters, &c., in which he imitated the manner of David Teniers.

THIEMON, otherwise Diethmar, a painter, sculptor, founder, and gilder of the Middle Ages, was born in Bavaria, of noble parentage, about 1045. He was as well versed in mechanics as in the Fine Arts, agreeably to the custom of his time. He executed many works in painting and sculpture for the churches, particularly for that of St. Blaise, near the city of Ems. In 1079, Thiemon was appointed abbé of the diocese of Saltzburg; in 1090, he was chosen archbishop of that city. About the year 1099, he started for the Holy Land, where he died in 1101. It is said that he was taken prisoner by the infidels, who, on learning his skill in sculpture, commanded him to restore the arms of a brazen idol. Upon his refusing to do it, on account of religious scruples, he was put to death; and the Catholic church has placed him among the martyrs.

THIERS, Baron de, a French amateur artist, who flourished about 1760. He etched a few plates of landscapes and other subjects, of small size, *after Boucher*.

M or M. THIM, Moses, a German artist, who flourished at Wittenberg about 1613. He is said to have practised both painting and engraving, and to have used the above monogram, but none of his works are specified. Zani says he was a printer, and denies that he ever engraved either on wood or copper.

THOMAN, or THOMANN, Christian Raymond, a German engraver, who was living in 1733. He engraved some of the plates for the collection of prints from the antique marbles in the Dresden Gallery.

THOMANN, Jacob Ernest, a German painter, born at Landau in 1588. After learning the rudiments of art in his native city, he went to Italy at the age of seventeen, and spent fifteen years at Rome, Naples, and Genoa. At Rome, he studied with Adam Ælzheimer, whose style he imitated with such success that it is sometimes difficult to distinguish their works. He acquired considerable reputation at Rome, and his works were much sought after. He afterwards visited Naples and Genoa, where his pictures were held in equal estimation. On the death of his friend and preceptor, he returned to Germany, and established himself at Landau, where he was appointed painter to the Emperor, and found abundant employment. Like the works of Ælzheimer, his subjects were usually landscapes of small size, decorated with small figures, from sacred and profane history; and he entered so completely into the spirit of that master in design, handling, and coloring, that his works have often been mistaken for those of his instructor. The German writers call him *Jacob Ernest Thoman von Hagelstein.* He died at Landau in 1653.

THOMANN, Philip Ernest, was the grandson of the preceding, born at Augsburg in 1657, and died in 1726. Little is known of him. He is said to have painted some works for the churches, and to have engraved some plates of portraits and other subjects in mezzotinto.

THOMAS, John, a Flemish painter, born at Ypres, in or about 1610. He studied in the school of Rubens, and afterwards went to Italy, in company with his fellow pupil Diepenbeck, where he studied the works of the great masters with assiduity, and greatly improved himself. On his return to his own country, he distinguished himself, and executed several works for the churches, one of the best of which is an altar-piece in the church of the Barefooted Carmelites at Antwerp, representing St. Francis kneeling before the Virgin and Infant. He was invited, in 1662, to the court of the Emperor Leopold, who appointed him his principal painter, with a liberal pension, and retained him in his service till his death. This artist executed some spirited etchings from his own designs, and engraved several plates of portraits and other subjects in mezzotinto, among which are the portraits of the Emperor Leopold and Titian. He died at Vienna in 1673.

THOMASIN, Philip, a French engraver, born at Troyes, in Champagne, about 1536. He went young to Rome, where he resided the greater part of his life. Huber says he there studied under Cornelius Cort, whose style he followed with considerable success. He wrought entirely with the graver, in a clear, firm style. His prints are numerous, and amount to more than two hundred; about fifty of them are after the antique statues at Rome. He was living in 1618. The following are his most esteemed prints:

The Portrait of Philip Emanuel of Lorraine, Duke de Mercœur. A set of fourteen plates, with the title, "Christ and the twelve Apostles;" *after Raffaelle.* St. Margaret; *do.* St. Cecilia; *do.* The School of Athens; *do.* The Dispute on the Sacrament; *do.* The Defeat of the Saracens in the Port of Ostia; *do.* The Conflagration of the Borgo Vecchio; *do.* The Holy Family; *after Federigo Zuccaro.* The Adoration of the Magi; *do.* The Miracle at the Marriage of Cana; *after Taddeo Zuccaro.* The Nativity; *after Ventura Salimbeni.* The Purification of the Virgin; *after F. Baroccio.* The Last Judgment; *after F. Vanni.* Apollo and the Muses; *after Bal. Peruzzi;* a frieze.

THOMASSIN, Simon. This artist is said to have been of the same family as the preceding, born at Troyes in 1638, though Zani places his birth in 1652, and his death in 1732. After learning the rudiments of design at Paris, he went to Rome, and studied in the French Academy in that city. He devoted himself to engraving, and acquired distinction. He was elected a member of the Academy at Paris, and appointed one of the engravers to the king. His plates are executed entirely with the graver, in a neat, clear style, but without much intelligence in the effect of light and shadow. His drawing is generally correct, though somewhat mannered, and his extremities are not marked with that freedom and lightness which distinguish the hand of a great master. His most considerable work is a folio volume of plates, from the statues and other marbles in the palace and gardens of Versailles. He also engraved a number of portraits and other subjects, among which are the following:

PORTRAITS.

Louis, Duke of Burgundy. 1698. Maria Adelaide of Savoy, Duchess of Burgundy. Paul Beauvillier, Duke of St. Aignou. 1695. Charles XII. of Sweden. Peter Corneille; *after le Brun.*

SUBJECTS AFTER VARIOUS MASTERS.

The Miraculous Draught of Fishes; *after Raffaelle.* The Transfiguration; *do.* St. Paul taken up in the third Heaven; *after N. Poussin.* Christ praying on the Mount; *after le Brun.*

THOMASSIN, Henri Simon, was the son of the preceding, born at Paris in 1688. After receiving instruction from his father, he became the pupil of Bernard Picart, and accompanied that master to Amsterdam, where he engraved several plates. On his return to Paris, he acquired considerable reputation, and was admitted into the Academy in 1728. His plates are executed with more freedom and spirit than those of his father, and he availed himself more of the assistance of the point. His prints are quite numerous, and some of them are considered very masterly productions. Among others are the following by him. He died at Paris in 1741.

PORTRAITS.

The Portrait of Louis XIV. presented to the Arts by Minerva; *after L. de Boullongne;* engraved for his reception into the Academy. 1728. Louis, Dauphin of France; *after Tocqué.* The Bust of Cardinal de Fleury, supported by Diogenes, who had at length found an honest man; *after Rigaud.* John Thierry, Sculptor to the King; *after N. Largillière.* Carlo Cignani, Painter; *after a picture by himself.*

SUBJECTS AFTER VARIOUS MASTERS.

Christ with the Disciples at Emmaus; *after P. Veronese;* for the Crozat collection. Adam and Eve driven from Paradise; *after D. Feti;* do. Melancholy; *do.;* do. The *Magnificat,* or Song of the Virgin; *after Jouvenet.* Coriolanus overcome by the solicitations of his Family; *after la Fosse.* The Plague at Marseilles; *after J. F. de Troy.*

THOMOND, Thomas, a French architect, born at Paris in 1759. He had scarcely acquired a knowledge of his profession, when the civil commotions obliged him and his family, with many other royalists, to quit France. He settled at St. Petersburg, and commenced practising the art of painting, to which he was much attached, particularly in architectural and perspective pieces. The taste he displayed in those subjects, led at length to his being employed by the government in that department of art which he originally intended to follow, and he was commissioned in 1804, to improve and partly remodel the great Theatre, first erected by the German architect Tischbein, in 1783. Although not altogether free from the peculiarities of the French school, the façade and octastyle Ionic portico which he added to that structure, is one of the noblest pieces of architecture of the kind and date in Europe; and had the architect executed nothing else, that alone would have entitled him to rank higher in his profession than many who owe their celebrity as much to the number as the merit of their works. Thomond also erected several private mansions and other buildings at St. Petersburg, the mausoleum of the Emperor Paul at Pavlovska, the theatre at Odessa, and the Pultava monument. His second important work was the grand Imperial Exchange, erected during the years 1804–1810, an insulated structure of the Roman Doric order, 256 by 300 feet, peripteral and decastyle at each end, though without pediments, and embellished with forty-four columns. Situated at the southern point of the Vassilievskii Island, immediately facing the Neva, it stands in the centre of a spacious square, upon a rich architectural terrace, which sweeps out so as to form a semi-circular esplanade in front, at each extremity of which is a flight of steps leading down to the river, and a massive rostral column, one hundred and twenty feet high. The architectural combination is exceedingly picturesque, and may be said to be unique. In 1808, Thomond published some of his buildings and designs, in a quarto volume; and he also wrote a treatise on painting. He died in 1813.

THOMPSON, Henry, an English historical and portrait painter, born at Portsea in 1773. Little is recorded of him. He was a member of the Royal Academy, and filled the office of keeper of that institution for several years. In 1828, owing to ill health, he retired to his native place, where he died in 1843.

THOMSON, William, an Irish portait painter, born at Dublin. He settled in London, where he practised with some reputation, and died there in 1800. His pictures are said to possess the merits of faithful likeness and a natural tone of coloring.

THOMSON, James, an excellent English engraver, was born at Mitford, in Northumberland, in 1789. He was the fourth son of the Rev. James Thomson, M. A., of Nunriding Hall, and as he evinced at an early age considerable talent for drawing, he was articled to Mr. Mackenzie, an engraver residing in Margaret street, Cavendish Square, London. After spending seven years under the latter, Thomson wrought for two years under Mr. Carden, after which he received commissions on his own account, and practised the art in London for many years. He lived universally respected, and died in 1850, regretted by a large circle of friends. Among the principal works of Thomson, are the Three Nieces of the Duke of Wellington, *after Sir Thomas Lawrence;* Lodge's Portrait Gallery; an equestrian portrait of Her Majesty, attended by Lord Melbourne, the Marquis of Conyngham, &c., *after Grant;* the Museum Townley Marbles; the Bishop of London, *after Richmond;* Prince Albert, *after Sir W. C. Ross;* Portraits of Louis Philippe and his Queen.

THORNHILL, Sir James, an eminent English painter, born at Weymouth, in Dorsetshire, in 1676. He was descended of an ancient family, but his father being in reduced circumstances, was compelled to sell his paternal estate, and young Thornhill was obliged to take care of himself. He accordingly set out for London, and having a genius for painting, his uncle Sydenham, the celebrated physician, rendered him assistance, and procured him instruction in art. The name of his master is not mentioned, but he was indebted more to his own talents and application, than to the precepts of his instructor. After acquiring some celebrity as an historical painter, he traveled through Holland and Flanders to France, and greatly improved himself. On his return to London his abilities soon attracted public attention, and his reputation rose to the greatest height.

He was commissioned by Queen Anne to decorate the cupola of St. Paul's cathedral, where he represented the principal events in the life of that apostle, in eight compartments, designed and executed in a grand style; these subjects were engraved in eight sheets by du Bosc, Beauvais, Baron, G. Vandergucht and Simonneau. These works gave so much satisfaction that the Queen appointed him her first painter of history. He was afterwards employed to execute several public works, particularly an apartment at Hampton Court, which he embellished with subjects emblematic of the history of Queen Anne, and her consort George, Prince of Denmark. He painted some altar-pieces for the churches, and was much employed in decorating the palaces of the nobility and gentry. Among his principal productions are the great saloon and the refectory in Greenwich Hospital. He was particularly patronized by George II., who conferred upon him the honor of knighthood. He sat in parliament several years, from his native town, and was elected a Fellow of the Royal Society. He copied the cartoons of Raffaelle in Hampton Court of the same size as the originals, which occupied him three years; he also made another set of one-fourth the size; he also made numerous studies of the heads, hands, and feet, which he intended to publish for the use of students, but the work never appeared. At the sale of his effects after his death, the small set brought 75 guineas, and the large one more than £200; the latter was purchased by the Duke of Bedford, and many years afterwards, was presented to the Royal Academy. Sir James had a genius for portrait and landscape, though he did not practise those branches much; he had a good knowledge of architecture, and erected several private edifices; he also etched some plates from his own designs, executed in a bold, free style. Though he received only moderate compensation for his services, he acquired a handsome fortune. His demands were contested for his paintings at Greenwich Hospital, and while la Fosse, the French painter, received £2500, for his work at Montague House, Thornhill could obtain only forty shillings the square yard, for the cupola of St. Paul's, and the same for the apartments at Greenwich! He had a son named James, whom he instructed in the art, and for whom he procured the appointment of sergeant painter to the King, but he did not acquire any distinction; also a daughter, who ran away and married the inimitable Hogarth. He died in 1734.

THORWALDSEN, Albert. This preëminent Danish sculptor was born at Copenhagen, November 19, 1770. He was the son of Gottschalk Thorwaldsen, a native of Iceland, and his wife, Karen Gronlund, the daughter of a priest of Jutland. He was descended from the most renowned warriors and princes—it being a well authenticated fact that his family goes back to the fabulous period of Danish history, as far as King Harold Hildetand (Harold of the Tooth of Gold), who was killed in 735, at the battle of Bravalla. The descendants of Harold removed to Norway, from whence a part of the race emigrated to Iceland. One among them, named Olaf Paa, was distinguished for the wise and magnificent use he made of his fortunes, in the encouragement of painting and architecture; the Savan Finn Magnussen alludes to him with great commendation in his Researches on Danish Archæology. A tradition had long been preserved, that "the gods had promised Harold a descendant whose fame should spread from the extremities of the North even to the sunny regions of the South." This tradition was at length fulfilled in the birth of the illustrious subject of this sketch. Almost the first things that drew his attention while an infant, were a sculptor's chisel, and a few pieces of work that bore resemblance to sculpture. He went to school but a short time during boyhood, and learned very little while there. He assisted his father at a very early age, and when only eleven years old commenced attending the free school of the Academy of Arts at Copenhagen. In two years he made such progress that he was enabled to improve his father's carvings, and he undertook to execute the head pieces of ships. At the age of 17, he obtained the silver medal of the Academy, for a bas-relief of Cupid reposing; and in 1791, when 20 years old, the small gold medal for a sketch of Heliodorus driven from the temple. At this time he was remarkably modest, and diffident of his own abilities. Two years after, he drew the grand prize, which entitled him to the royal pension; but as the latter privilege was then being enjoyed by another, he was obliged to wait three years, during which time he continued his professional pursuits, devoting also considerable time to general study, as he had much both to read and learn.

On the 20th May, 1796, Thorwaldsen set out for Italy in the Danish frigate Thetis, and after a voyage of almost interminable length, he reached Malta, where, losing all patience, he quitted the ship, and embarked in a vessel for Palermo, whence he sailed in the packet boat to Naples, arriving there in January, 1797. Without friends and ignorant of the Italian language, the young sculptor's heart failed him, and he longed to return to Denmark, which according to his own account he would have done, if he had found a Danish vessel about to leave Naples at that time. However, after a little while, he gained courage sufficient to engage a place in the coach of a vetturino for Rome, where he arrived March 8th. He brought letters of introduction to his distinguished countryman Zoëga who however did not give him much encouragement, nor did he estimate his abilities very highly The first years which Thorwaldsen passed in Rome were frequently saddened by painful experiences All Europe was agitated to such a degree tha none escaped the shock—not even the savant i his retreat, nor the artist in his studio. The roug spirits of war invaded the realms of art. Notwith standing this, the young sculptor prosecuted hi art devotedly and enthusiastically, but withou that encouragement which he had a right to ex pect. The term of his annuity was rapidly pas ing away, and he had not yet learned to depen on the strength of his own genius. In 1801, h prepared to return to Denmark; but before settin out he wished to complete a work designed as a gi to his country—Jason's Conquest of the Golde Fleece. He had already made the model, but b coming dissatisfied with it, he destroyed the wor and commenced another of larger dimensio When it was completed, and shown to Canova then arbiter in the art—he exclaimed, "Questa ap ra di quel giovane Danese è fatta di uno stilo nuo e grandioso!" The work was also highly prais even by Zoëga; but Thorwaldsen, feeling that me admiration, however gratifying, would not supply the place of ducats, determined to proceed immediately home; he made all necessary preparations, and the vetturino had already arrived at the door, when suddenly the sculptor Hageman of Berlin, his traveling companion, came to say that, in consequence of an informality in his passport, he could not yet begin his journey. This delay was followed by another, and not long afterwards the liberality of Thomas Hope relieved him from embarrassment. That English connoisseur having heard of Canova's praise of Thorwaldsen's work, visited his studio, and after regarding the model for a long time, asked the artist, "How much do you require to complete that statue in marble?" "Six hundred ducats," was the answer. "You shall have eight hundred," said the generous patron of art. Thorwaldsen remained in Rome.

From this time (1803), his star was in the ascendant; the statue of Jason was not indeed finished till many years after, but many celebrated works were done meanwhile; as the bas-reliefs of Summer and Autumn, and the Dance of the Muses on Helicon; Cupid and Psyche, and Venus with the Apple. His fame spread far and wide, and Christian, (then crown-prince), of Denmark, wrote him a pressing invitation to return to Copenhagen, communicating at the same time the discovery of a white marble quarry in Norway. Thorwaldsen was eager to return, but his numerous commissions rendered it impossible. During these busy years, he was accustomed to recreate at Leghorn during the summer seasons, at the beautiful villa of Baron Schubart, the Danish minister at Florence; he also executed some of his works there. In 1812, when arrangements were being made for Napoleon's entry into Rome, the architect Stern, who superintended the preparations, requested Thorwaldsen to prepare a plaster frieze for one of the large apartments in the Quirinal Palace. He undertook the commission, and in three months completed his plaster model, sixty feet in length, of his celebrated bas-relief of the Triumphal Entry of Alexander into Babylon. The Danes opened a subscription to enable him to reproduce this master-piece in marble, and their efforts were warmly seconded; it has been twice executed in marble, with slight variations, and is engraved in a series of plates by S. Amsler, of Munich, after drawings by Overbeck and others. During the course of his rapid and brilliant career, Thorwaldsen was occasionally disturbed by spells of deep melancholy, and it was in a single one of these sombre days that he modeled his celebrated bas-reliefs of Night and Morning, in 1815. At length, in July 1819, the entreaties of his countrymen determined Thorwaldsen to visit his native land. His progress through Italy and Germany was marked by many honors, and on arriving at Copenhagen, the 3d of October, he was received with acclamations by a vast multitude of his fellow citizens, and lodged in the palace of Charlottenburg. For a year he was entertained with public feasts and other demonstrations of gratitude from his countrymen; after which he started for Rome, visiting Berlin, Dresden, Warsaw, and Vienna, everywhere welcomed enthusiastically and overwhelmed with marks of distinction. At Warsaw he received several commissions, and executed a bust of the Emperor Alexander.

Thorwaldsen executed his principal works after his return to Rome—as Christ and the Twelve Apostles, and the large majestic statue of Copernicus, both placed in the church of Notre Dame at Copenhagen; also the monuments of Pius VII., Maximilian of Bavaria, the Poniatowski monument, and others. In 1823, he had a narrow escape of his life; a young lad, the son of his landlady, contrived to get hold of one of his pistols, which he had carelessly hung up loaded; ignorant of the danger, the boy discharged it at Thorwaldsen, but the ball, after grazing two of his fingers, passed through his dress without cauing further injury. In 1838, the statues of Christ and the Apostles, the group of St. John preaching, and other works for the church of Notre Dame at Copenhagen, besides others for the palace of Christianburg, were finally completed, and the Danish government sent the frigate Rota to convey them and their sculptor to Denmark. Though enriched by the proceeds of his works, surrounded with every luxury of life, and enjoying at will all the advantages to be derived from a people who truly appreciated his genius, Thorwaldsen yet resolved to return to Copenhagen. Having transferred the above mentioned works and the original plaster models of all his sculptures, which he had carefully preserved, he bade adieu to the metropolis of art, which had so long witnessed the triumphs of his genius. On arriving at the port of Copenhagen, as the frigate sailed up towards the city, the vessels in the harbor were decked with flags, the cannon thundered from the batteries, and when the illustrious sculptor had landed and entered his carriage, the people detached the horses, and drew their much loved artist, amid the enthusiastic cheering of the excited multitude, through the streets to the palace of Charlottenburg, where his studio was already prepared, decked with wreaths and garlands of flowers. After this princely ovation, festival succeeded festival, until Thorwaldsen at length withdrew from the city to the beautiful villa of Nyso, the seat of his friend Baron Stampe, who showed him the greatest attention and kindness. During his absence on an excursion to the island of Moe, a studio was built for him in the garden of the villa, directly facing the sea. Here he finished some of his last compositions, Christ bearing his Cross; the Entry into Jerusalem; Rebecca at the Well; his own statue; the busts of the poets Oehlenschlager and Holberg; and those of his friends the Stampe family. In 1841, finding the climate disagree with him, he returned to Italy in company with the Stampe family, and he executed at this time his group of the Graces for the King of Wurtemberg. He returned, however, to Denmark and Nyso the following year, and executed two bas-reliefs—Christmas Joys in Heaven, and the Genius of Poetry; the latter he presented to his friend Oehlenschlager, saying "It is your medallion." He intended to return to Rome in the summer of 1844, but was prevented by his death, which occurred very suddenly, on the 24th of March in that year, just after he had entered the theatre. The cause was subsequently ascertained to be disease of the heart. His remains lay in state in the Academy, and were interred with regal honors, beneath his own greatest productions in the cathedral church of Copenhagen. The news of his death was received with the deepest regret throughout Europe, and funeral honors were celebrated to his remembrance at Berlin and at Rome.

Thus ended the glorious career of Thorwaldsen.

fortune had favored him with her choicest honors. The great were proud to have him in their halls; and the people, knowing that he sprang from their ranks, were proud of his fame. His prosperity did not alter in the least his genuine native modesty and simplicity of character. He was generous to all who needed assistance; he had a tender and compassionate heart; and his genius was allied to a gentleness and sweetness of disposition which charmed all who had access to him. Age had conferred upon him beauty of a most impressive character; "his face," said the poet Holberg, "had the plastic characteristic of one of his admirable statues; when he moved in the midst of a crowd, it would separate as if it felt the pressure of a superior being."

There has much been written, and much more been said, respecting the artistic merits of Thorwaldsen. His warmest admirers consider him the greatest of modern sculptors, and many have not hesitated to place him above Canova, and even to compare him with the antique. On the other hand, some question his power or fertility of invention, consider his style monotonous, and even rank him inferior to Canova in heroic vigor or robust strength of character. Amid such contradictory opinions, it is perhaps difficult to arrive at a satisfactory conclusion; but it would be very difficult indeed to coincide with the latter opinion. Power of expression was Thorwaldsen's peculiar excellence. He distinguished his smallest medallion by peculiar force, and from the minutest treatment his mind could at once rise to colossal composition, without exhibiting the least trace of littleness of style. Not so with Canova; although he frequently excelled the Dane in beauty of the female forms, many of his works are enfeebled by affectation and excessive *finesse*—defects nowhere to be found in those of Thorwaldsen, whose chief characteristic was that energetic enunciation in his figures which claims at once all the senses of the spectator. His imagination was inexhaustible; and the exquisite feeling which he threw into his works, is nowhere better exemplified than in his basso-relievos, "Night" and "Morning." Contrary to poetical usage, he characterized Night as the Mother of Humanity: for her gemmy crest is substituted the fillet of poppies, her star-studded mantle is also cast aside, and she has gathered to her bosom her sleeping children. The figures are floating rather than flying through the air; and an aspect of repose is given to the whole composition by the quiet attitudes, even to the lower limbs of the principal one, crossed as at rest; the companion of their shadowy flight is the "bird that loves darkness." Morning is equally beautifully described as a buoyant winged figure, speeding gracefully through the air, and strewing roses over the earth, accompanied by a torch-bearer, who does not rest upon his associate, although poised on her shoulder; his own wings are bearing him forward through the freshening air, which expands and moves the draperies by its gentle influences. Both these master-pieces of art are in the Chatsworth Gallery of the Duke of Devonshire.

Thorwaldsen was the greatest master of his age in basso-relievo; his highest excellence in statues is surpassed by the learning he displayed in low-relief—the most difficult part of sculptural composition. It was therefore his favorite style, and a great proportion of his works are executed in this manner. Of this class, some of his minor works are most expressive; besides those above mentioned, are his admirable versions of Death, Justice, Power, and Wisdom; but the largest are—the Triumph of Alexander, and the Procession to Golgotha, which is the frieze of the cathedral church of Copenhagen; immediately below is the numerous group of St. John preaching in the Wilderness, in full relief, in the pediment: in the vestibule are the four great Prophets; Christ and the Twelve Apostles are above and around the altar. The Triumph of Alexander, of which there is a copy in marble in the palace of Christianburg, (the first marble copy was made for Count Somariva's villa on lake Como), is a long triumphal procession in two divisions, one meeting the other. In the centre, Alexander, in the chariot of Victory, and followed by his army, is met by the goddess of Peace, followed by Mazæus and Bagophanes with presents to the conqueror. The subject is taken from the work of Quintus Curtius; the frieze is mostly symbolical, and perspective is nowhere introduced. The whole arrangement is admirable, especially that portion represented as coming from Babylon, comprising the General Mazæus with his family; female figures strewing flowers; Bagophanes placing silver altars with burning incense; musicians and attendants leading horses, sheep, wild animals, and other presents for the conqueror; next to these are symbolical representations of the river Euphrates, and the peaceful occupations of the Babylonians. The horses are inferior to the other figures, but the human forms are admirable, as is also the management of the costumes. His vast Swiss Lion at Lucerne, was carved from a rock near Berne of between sixty and eighty feet in height. The Poniatowski monument, in the great square at Warsaw, is a beautiful allusion, wrought out in a vein of the most graceful poetry; it is an equestrian composition, surmounting a fountain, by the water of which the horse is terrified, as if at the current of the river Elster. In England, Thorwaldsen is chiefly known by the statues of Jason and Lord Byron. Many years ago some admirers of the poet raised a subscription for a monument to be erected to his memory in Westminster Abbey. Chantrey was requested to erect it, but declined on account of the smallness of the sum subscribed; Thorwaldsen was then applied to, and cheerfully undertook the work. About 1833, the finished statue arrived at the London Custom House, but to the astonishment of the subscribers, the Dean of Westminster, Dr. Ireland, declined giving permission to its being set up in the Abbey; and as his successor entertained the same views, the statue remained upwards of twelve years in the Custom House, and was finally removed in 1845 to the library of Trinity College, Cambridge. The poet is represented of life size, seated on a ruin, with his left foot resting on the fragment of a column; in his right hand he holds a style up to his mouth; in his left is a book inscribed "Childe Harold," he is dressed in a frock coat and cloak. Beside him on the left is a skull, above which is the Athenian Owl. The likeness is of course posthumous.

Thorwaldsen bequeathed all works of art in his possession, including plaster casts of his own works, to the city of Copenhagen, for the purpose of forming a distinct museum, to be called after his own name, on condition that the city furnished an appropriate building for their reception. The requisite sum was speedily raised, and the building nearly completed before his death. Besides the casts of his numerous works, which alone would constitute an imposing collection, the Thorwaldsen Museum contains many works of ancient and modern sculpture, numerous paintings by old and recent masters, casts, vases, engraved gems, cameos, terracottas, bronzes, medals, curiosities, engravings, prints of all descriptions, drawings, and books on the fine arts. With the exception of 12,000 dollars to each of his grandchildren, and the life-interest of 40,000 to their mother, Madame Poulsen (his natural daughter, born at Rome), to descend to her children, the whole of his personal estate, estimated at nearly 1,000,000 dollars, was to be converted into capital, and to be added to the 25,000 dollars already presented for the purpose by Thorwaldsen, to form a museum perpetual fund; for the preservation of the museum, and to add to the collection; for the purchase of the works of Danish artists, and for the encouragement of Danish art generally. On the day before his death, his monument was located, at his express desire, in the centre of this museum. His unfinished works were to have been completed by Prof. Bissen, of the Academy of Copenhagen, who was also appointed Superintendent of the Thorwaldsen Museum. The government is under five trustees, two of whom are always to be professors in the Academy, one a magistrate of the city, and one a lawyer. The president of the council is to be the senior trustee, and all questions are to be decided by a majority of voices.

or THOURNEYSER, John James, a Swiss engraver, born at Basle in 1636. He received his first instruction from Peter Aubry at Strasburg, and next went to Paris, where he resided many years. He engraved some portraits of distinguished personages and other subjects, some of which are executed in the style of Francis de Poilly, and others with single strokes, in the manner of Claude Mellan. He engraved a part of the plates for a set of prints from select pictures published by Catherine Patin in 1691; also a variety of vignettes and other book plates. There are several of his plates in the Academy of Sandrart, among which are Latona, the Laocoön, and Antinous. He usually marked his plates with one of the above monograms. His name is sometimes written *Thourneysen.* He died in 1718. He had a son, called also *John James*, whom he instructed in the art, and who assisted him in his works. He was living in 1736.

THUFEL, or TEUFEL, John, a German wood engraver, who, according to Professor Christ, was a native of Saxony, flourished about 1570, and executed some cuts marked with the initials I. T .F. He is also called the master of the *picklock* and the *trefoil*, and his prints date from about 1540 to 1568.

THULDEN, Theodore van, an eminent Flemish painter, born at Bois-le-Duc in 1607. He was educated in the school of Rubens, and was one of his most distinguished disciples. He assisted that master in some of his works, and is said to have had a considerable share in forwarding the famous pictures for the gallery of the Luxembourg. He went to Paris in 1633, where he was employed to paint a series of twenty-four pictures for the church of the Mathurins, representing the life of St. John of Matha, which he etched and published. On his return to Flanders, he painted many works for the churches and public edifices of Antwerp, Mechlin, Bruges, Ghent, and other cities, so much in the style of Rubens, that some of them have been mistaken for the works of that master. He also painted much for individuals. He did not confine himself to history, but sometimes painted village festivals and the pastimes of the peasantry, in which he excelled. He painted small figures with great spirit and vigor, and frequently inserted them in the works of his cotemporaries, as Peter Neefs, Wildens, Mompers, and even in the hunting pieces of Snyders. Among his most celebrated works are the Martyrdom of St. Sebastian in the church of the Bernardines at Mechlin; the Martyrdom of St. Adrian, in the church of St. Michael at Ghent, and the Assumption of the Virgin, formerly in the church of the Jesuits at Bruges, which is considered his master-piece. He executed a large number of etchings in a clear, firm, and painter-like style, the principal of which are a set of twenty-four plates of the life of St. John of Matha, from his pictures before mentioned, at Paris, 1633; a set of 58 plates of the history of Ulysses, after the pictures by Primaticcio at Fontainbleau, 1640; a set of eight plates of Triumphal Arches designed by Rubens, for the Entry of Cardinal Infant Ferdinand into Antwerp, and a set of eight plates of the Prodigal Son, from his own designs. His name is sometimes erroneously written *Tulden.* He died, according to the best authorities, in 1676, but Balkema says in 1686.

THURMER, Joseph, a reputable German architect, was born at Munich in 1789. In 1817, at the age of twenty-eight, he commenced applying himself professionally to architecture, and studied under Prof. Fischer, with Gartner, Ziebland, Oehlmuller, and many others for fellow students. The following year he visited Rome, and afterwards joined Hubsch, Heger, and Koch in a professional excursion to Greece, where he spent five months in studying and drawing the Athenian antiquities, some few of which he published on his return, with the title of *Ansichten von Athen und seine Denkmaler*, 1823-6. Unlike some others, he was not such a prejudiced admirer of the Grecian style as to have no relish for any other, and he considered the Italian style of the time of Leo X., as equally worthy of the architect's attention. Accordingly, he united with Gutensohn in bringing out the *Sammlung von Denkmaler*, &c., or a "Collection of Architectural Studies and Buildings at Rome, of the fifteenth and sixteenth centuries." The first number appeared in 1826; but not meeting with the encouragement it deserved, the work was discontinued. Its publication, however, was advantageous to Thurmer, since it recommended him to notice, and led to his receiving in 1827, at the same time, two different invitations, one from Frankfort, the other from Dresden, the latter of which he accepted, and was appointed professor-extraordinary, in the school of architecture. In 1832 he was promoted to the first professorship of architecture, in which post he effected much for the advancement of the art and the improvement of taste. He erected but few edifices in Dresden, the only public building there entirely by him being the Post-office; the *Hauptwache* or Guard House, was erected by him after Schinkel's designs. Thurmer died in 1833. In 1838 his friends and pupils erected a bronze bust and monument to his memory, in the Academy of Arts.

THURSTON, John, an English designer, born at Scarborough in 1774, and died at London in 1822. It is not known by whom he was instructed, but he was a tasteful and elegant designer, much employed by the booksellers in embellishing numerous editions of the British Poets and Novelists.

THYS, Gysbrecht, a Flemish painter, born at Antwerp about 1625. He studied with Adrian Hanneman, and according to Descamps, was one of the ablest portrait painters of his time, in which he imitated the style of Vandyck so successfully, that his works have sometimes been mistaken for the productions of that master. He also excelled in painting landscapes, decorated with small figures in the manner of Poelemburg. Balkema says he died in 1684.

THYS, Peter Joseph, a Flemish painter of flowers, born at Lier in 1749. He first studied in the Academy at Antwerp, where he gained several prizes, and afterwards with Koeck the flower painter, at whose house he became acquainted with Spaendonck, whom he accompanied to Paris. On his return he settled at Brussels, where he acquired considerable reputation. He was employed to paint some flower-pieces to decorate the orangery of the palace of Laeken, which possessed sufficient merit to induce the French to carry them to Paris in 1792. He was very skillful in imitating the touch and coloring of various masters, for which reason he was much employed in restoring old paintings. He died in 1823.

TIARINI, Alessandro, an eminent painter, born at Bologna in 1577. He first studied with Fontana, and next with Cesi, when he was obliged to fly from his native city on account of a fatal quarrel. He sought refuge at Florence, and became the pupil of Passignano, who conceived so high an opinion of his abilities, that he subsequently became his associate in several works in Florence, Pisa, and other cities in the state. After an absence of seven years, he was enabled to return to Bologna, through the influence of Lodovico Caracci, who highly esteemed him, leaving behind him a few paintings executed in his first easy style, resembling that of Passignano. The following admirable account is condensed from Lanzi: "In such a style (of Passignano) he conducted his first work at Bologna, of St. Barbara, in the church of S. Petronio, which failed to please the public. To give it greater attractions, he next proceeded to copy from, and to consult Lodovico Caracci—not to attain his manner, but to improve his own; for, though he sprung from another school, he profited as much by his example and advice as if Lodovico had really been his master. This was a short task to a man of genius, well grounded in the theory of his art, and perhaps more philosophical than any other artist in Bologna. He soon became a different painter, and in his novel taste of composing, of distributing his lights, and of expressing the passions, he shone like a disciple of the Caracci; still, he preserved a character distinct from the rest, grounded upon his naturally severe and melancholy disposition. With him, all is serious and moderate; the airs of his heads, his attitudes, and his draperies, varied with few but noble folds, such as excited the admiration of Guido himself. He avoided, moreover, very gay and animated colors, chiefly contenting himself with light violets or yellows, and tawny colors, tempered with a little red; but so admirably laid on and harmonized, as to produce the finest feeling of repose to enchant the eye. His subjects, too, were well adapted to his taste, generally pathetic or sorrowful, such as Magdalens penitent, St. Peters and Madonnas in grief, some of which drew tears from the beholders, and are held in high esteem. Subsequently he became expert in foreshortening, and in all the intricacies of the art, more particularly in point of invention. There is scarcely one of his works that does not exhibit a certain novelty and originality of idea. When he represented the Virgin in grief, in the church of S. Benedetto, he drew her seated together with St. John and the Magdalen; the one upright, the other kneeling, and intently contemplating the Redeemer's crown of thorns; other incidents of the Passion are alluded to; all are silent indeed, but every eye and attitude is eloquent in its silence. In his altar-piece of St. John and St. Jerome, in S. Maria Maggiore, he shunned the trite expression of drawing them in a glory; but he feigned an apparition, through which the holy doctor, intent on his studies, appears to receive lectures in theology from the beatified Evangelist. His most distinguished production, however, is a picture of St. Domenico raising a Man from the Dead, in the church of that Saint, painted in competition with Lionello Spada, a work abounding in figures varied in point of feature, attitude, and dress, and everything highly select. Lodovico expressed his astonishment at it, and declared that he knew no master then to compare with Tiarini. As he survived to his ninetieth year, his works are exceedingly numerous. He dwelt a long time at Reggio, whence he often proceeded to other cities of Lombardy, which possess many of his altar-pieces and cabinet pictures. The Modenese Gallery abounds with them, among which his St. Peter struck with remorse, as he stands outside of the prætorium, is more particularly extolled; the superb architecture, the depth of night lighted up by torches, Christ's judgment beheld in the distance, all conspire to raise the tragic interest of the scene. He was also employed by the Duke of Parma to decorate his garden with frescos from Tasso's Jerusalem Delivered, which were much extolled, but no longer exist. In short, Tiarini, next to the Caracci, was one of the most eminent artists of the Bolognese school, at least in point of composition, expression of the features and of the passions, perspective, power and durability of coloring, if not of the most exact elegance."

Other admirable works by this artist in the churches at Bologna are the Marriage of St. Catherine, and the Annunciation, in S. Agnes; the Nativity, in S. Salvatore; St. Catherine kneeling before a Crucifix, in S. Maria Maddalena; and a Dead Christ in the lap of the Virgin, in S. Antonio. Tiarini was also an excellent portrait painter, was several years in the service of the Duke of Mantua, who sat to him, and appointed him to paint all the members of his family, which gained him so much applause that all the nobility of Mantua flocked to him to be commemorated by his pencil. He died in 1668.

TIBALDI, Pellegrino, called Pellegrino da Bologna, an eminent Italian painter and architect, was born, according to Lanzi, at Valdelsa, in the Milanese, in 1527. He was taken to Bologna at a very early age, and was subsequently placed under the instruction of Bartolomeo Ramenghi, called Il Bagnacavallo. After copying some pictures of Giorgio Vasari in S. Michele in Bosco, and a few other select pieces, he went to Rome in 1547, and devoted his principal attention to the works of Michael Angelo. According to Baglioni, he executed a picture of the Archangel Michael, for the Castel St. Angelo, which gained him great reputation. He afterwards painted the ceiling of the chapel of St. Denis, in the church of S. Luigi de' Francesi, representing a battle, composed in a grand style; also, in concert with Marco da Siena, he painted the ceiling of the Capella Rovere, in the church of La Trinità de Monti, from the cartoons of Daniello da Volterra. The Cardinal Poggi was so highly pleased with these works, that he employed Tibaldi to ornament his villa near the Porta del Popolo, with some admirable works in fresco, and afterwards sent him to Bologna, to employ his architectural talents upon his own palace, now the Palazzo dell' Instituto, which is considered one of Tibaldi's principal works. Within this palace, he executed several subjects from the Odyssey, which are more highly commended by Vasari than the works he executed in the chapel of his patron in S. Giacomo Maggiore, although the latter were most esteemed by the Caracci, particularly his pictures of St. John in the Desert, and the Division of the Just and the Unjust, upon which those eminent artists and their pupils bestowed a great deal of study. They evince the greatest art of composition, and form a most admirable school of design and expression. He painted almost entirely in fresco; consequently his oil pieces are very rare. His style was principally formed upon the models of Michael Angelo—vast, correct in drawing, bold and happy in the foreshortenings, yet at the same time tempered with so much mellowness and softness, as to induce the Caracci to denominate him the "Reformed Michael Angelo." Lanzi says, "at the great merchant's hall at Ancona, Tibaldi exhibited, in his picture of Hercules, the true method of imitating the terrible in the style of Michael Angelo, which consisted in a fear of too nearly approaching him. At Loretto, and different other adjacent cities, he produced other histories, less celebrated perhaps, but all nearly as deserving of the burin as those at Bologna. Such is the entrance of Trajan into Ancona, in possession of the Marquis of Mancinforte; and various exploits of Scipio, which decorate the halls of Marchese Ciccolini. It is a work conceived in a more refined and graceful taste than we meet with in other compositions of Tibaldi; and of the same composition I have seen some of his pictures on a very small scale; but rare, like all his pieces in oil; wrought with the exquisite finish of a miniaturist; mostly rich in figures, full of fine spirit, vivid coloring, and decorated with all the pleasing perspectives that architecture could afford."

According to Lanzi and others, Tibaldi relinquished painting about 1566, and did not touch the easel for twenty years. It is not known who instructed him in architecture, but he gained great distinction in that art, first at Bologna, in erecting the Palazzo dell' Instituto, for the Cardinal Poggi. He afterwards designed the Palazzo della Sapienza, or Collegio Borromeo, at Pavia; erected the church of S. Lorenzo, and that of the Jesuits, at Milan; the famous Loggia, at Ancona; the church of the Madonna, near S. Celso, at Bologna; restored the Archiepiscopal palace at Milan; and was appointed chief architect of the Cathedral in 1570; also engineer of the Milanese State. He designed the façade of that celebrated edifice, combining the Gothic and Greek styles, which has obtained for him about an equal amount of praise and blame. Tibaldi visited Genoa, and erected a number of excellent works in that city, among which the house of the Jesuits, called the "Casa Professa," with its church, is esteemed his best performance. A Genoese critic thus praises this work. "A more than irregular situation, surrounded by narrow streets, was the area presented to Tibaldi, although the society required vast and commodious arrangements. Such, however, was the ability of the architect, that, in devoting the best part of the ground to a very elegant church, he did not omit the least convenience with regard to the other parts. Every difficulty disappeared before him, and in such a manner that it seemed as if he had chosen the situation himself. Commodious offices, a large and light refectory, noble corridors, with excellent and well arranged rooms, a beautiful internal chapel, a large hall for recreation, and a magnificent library; an ample and commodious surgery, with a a court and other conveniences, are unanswerable arguments that he not only possessed an uncommon genius, with an exquisite taste in decoration, but that he had a thorough knowledge of all that is required for the comfort and convenience of a great society. The building of the church is the most conclusive evidence of the sublimity of his talents, and his singular knowledge of decoration and proportion. It is divided into three naves. The large lateral chapels of the cupola are preceded by two others on each side, with smaller cupolas; as has also the other beyond the large chapel opposite the small door which leads to the side aisles. The proportions between the height, width, and length, are superior to any in Genoa. The principal decorations consist of the pilasters being encrusted with marbles, the base of which rests on the pavement at the presbytery, and the others on a simple plinth. What, however, is most astonishing, is the ingenious manner in which the principal entablature, with a majestic pediment, forming a portion of a circle, supported by six columns of black and yellow marble of Porto Venere, is continued over the great altar. These columns are each of a single block, and though lower than the pilasters, are beautifully proportioned, together with the architrave, frieze, and cornice, which is continued over the pilasters with admirable effect. The exterior façade is in equally good taste, and is carried up, perhaps judiciously, only to the first order, since the narrowness of the street would have prevented the second from being seen to advantage."

The fame of Tibaldi gained him, in 1586, an invitation from Philip II. of Spain to visit that country. He was employed both in architecture and painting; Milizia briefly states that he rebuilt the old royal palace, and several other works. Having expunged the unsuccessful productions of Federigo Zuccaro, in the lower cloister of the Escurial, by order of the king, he proceeded to paint several subjects in fresco, representing the Purification, the Flight into Egypt, the Murder of the Innocents, Christ tempted in the Wilderness, the Election of the Apostles, the Resurrection of Lazarus, the Expulsion of the Money-changers from the Temple, and the Resurrection of Christ. These works completely satisfied the king, being composed in a grand and copious style, the figures models of correctness, designed in a free and masterly style, with great attention to truth and nature. In the great church at Madrid are several pictures by Tibaldi, representing St. Michael with the Fall of the Angels, the Martyrdom of St. Lorenzo, and two very grand compositions of the Nativity and the Adoration of the Magi, executed to replace those of Zuccaro. His most esteemed work in Spain, however, is the ceiling of the library, somewhat resembling Raffaelle's School of Athens, where he has personified the Arts and Sciences, the Four Doctors of the Church, with the ancient philosophers Socrates, Plato, Aristotle, and Seneca, accompanied with their characteristic attributes and insignia, with beautiful groups of children and figures supporting the cornice and festoons, in a variety of attitudes and foreshortenings; the whole designed with such grandeur and expression as prove him a worthy follower of Michael Angelo. After remaining nine years in Spain Tibaldi returned to Italy, richly rewarded by Philip, who conferred upon him the title of Marquis of Valdelsa, his native place. The time of his death is variously stated; Zanotti makes it as early as 1591, but he did not return from Spain till 1595. It is therefore probable that Tiraboschi is correct, who says he died at Milan in 1598, aged 71.

TIBALDI, Domenico. This artist was the younger brother of Pellegrino T., born at Bologna in 1540; died in 1583. He acquired the elements of design in that city, and is said to have practised the art of painting, but on very slender authority, as not even a single portrait is exhibited from his hand. As an architect and engraver, however, he attained great excellence. At Bologna he erected the Magnani palace, of two orders, without entablatures between, producing an harmonious unity; although the edifice is rather diminutive, it is arranged with such skill as to appear much larger than it really is. His chapel in the Cathedral was so greatly admired by Clement VIII., that he accounted it superior to any similar edifice in Rome. Among his other works at Bologna, are the great door of the city palace; the small church of the Madonna del Borgo; and the admired Dogana, or custom house, praised by Milizia as surpassing any other similar work.

As an engraver, Tibaldi executed a number of spirited etchings; Bartsch mentions only nine, as follow, but thinks there must be many more, as these exhibit such a skillful management of the burin as is only acquired by long practice.

1. The Repose in Egypt; *from his own design.* 2. The Holy Trinity; *after Samacchini.* 1570. 3. The Virgin with a Rose; *after Parmiggiano.* 4. St. Francis of Assisi; copied from two prints by *C. Cort;* the landscape from one with the date 1567, and the figure from another with the date 1568, both after pictures by *Girolamo Muziano.* 5. The Penitent Magdalene; *after Titian.* 6. Peace; properly the Triumph of Peace; *after his own design.* 7. Portrait of Pope Gregory XIII.; *after Passarotti.* 1572. 8. View of the grand Fountain in the Piazza Scaffieri at Bologna. 1570. 9. The Palace. This view of a magnificent palace, ornamented with columns and statues, is from a design of *G. Alghisi.* It is in two plates, with the date 1566; but Bartsch is of opinion that there should be a third plate to complete the composition, as only the left wing and centre are shown, and there are borders to the tops and bottoms and the left side, but none to the right.

TIDEMAN, or TIEDEMAN, Philip, an eminent painter, born at Hamburg in 1657. His father being in opulent circumstances, intended him for one of the learned professions, and gave him a liberal education; but Philip having a passion for painting, he permitted him afterwards to follow the bent of his genius, and placed him with Nicholas Raes, a respectable painter of history, with whom he studied eight years. The fame of Gerard Lairesse next drew him to Amsterdam, where he became his disciple, and assisted him in the execution of some of his most important works. The talents he displayed recommended him to public notice, and on his leaving Lairesse, he soon acquired a high reputation at Amsterdam, and was much employed in decorating the public edifices and the principal mansions of the nobility with historical and mythological subjects. In the composition and handling of his subjects, he followed the style of Lairesse, and having had a classical education, he treated them with so much learning, judgment, and skill, that some of his compositions were regarded as models for the historical painters of his country. Among his most admired works was a saloon at Hoorn, painted for the family of Verschuur, in which he represented the leading incidents in the history of Æneas, with classical propriety, and great originality of invention. As he passed most of his life in Holland, he is ranked among the painters of the Dutch school. He died at Amsterdam in 1705.

TIEPOLO, Giovanni Battista, an eminent painter, born at Venice in 1697. Lanzi says: "he was the last of the Venetian artists who acquired for himself a great reputation, and became celebrated in Italy, in Germany, and in Spain." He studied under Gregorio Lazzarini, whose careful and academic style served to curb the natural impetuosity of his genius; he next studied the works of Gio. Battista Piazzetta, whose style he imitated for some time, as seen in his pictures of the Shipwreck of St. Satiro, in the church of S. Ambrogio at Milan. Lanzi says: "he subsequently became an assiduous imitator of Paul Veronese, whom, though inferior to him in the airs of his heads, he very nearly approached in his drapery and in his coloring. From the engravings also of Albert Durer, that store-house of composers, he derived no little advantage; he also diligently studied nature, in observing all the accidents of light and shade, and the contrasts of color best adapted to produce effect. In this branch he succeeded admirably, particularly in his frescos, for which he seems to have been endued by nature, with promptness, rapidity, and facility in great compositions. While others were accustomed to display the most vivid colors, he only availed himself in his frescos of what are termed low and dusky colors; and by harmonizing them with others of a common kind, but more clear and beautiful, he produced a species of effect, a sun-like radiance, unequalled perhaps by any other artist. Of this the grand vault of the Teresiani at Venice, presents a fine specimen

He there represented the Santa Casa (Heaven), accompanied by numerous groups of angels finely foreshortened and varied, surrounded by a field of light, that appears to rise into the firmament. An artist who could produce such works on so grand a scale would have been truly great, had he succeeded in observing equal correctness in every part; in the whole, he always produces an agreeable effect. He is more correct and careful in his oil pieces, which are scattered throughout the metropolitan city, as well as the state."

Tiepolo acquired an immense reputation, and executed many works for the churches and public edifices at Venice, Rome, Milan, Padua, and other cities. He was also invited to the courts of Vienna and Madrid. He decorated the New Palace in the latter city with several splendid frescos, which were so much admired by the public, as to excite the jealousy of Mengs, then the popular court painter at Madrid, in the height of his celebrity, who severely criticised his works as defective in design, fantastical in composition, and meretricious in coloring. He was also attacked by Cochin and others, but he was ably defended by his friends Rossetti and Algarotti. "Where there is smoke there must be fire," and we may doubtless take the account of the ever candid and judicious Lanzi as just and true. There are about sixty etchings by this master, executed with taste, neatness, and spirit, from his own designs, among which are a set of twenty-four fancy subjects, another of ten fancy subjects of smaller size, besides single plates after his principal works, of which the Adoration of the Magi is esteemed the best. An admirable account of his works at Madrid may be found in Cumberland's Catalogue of Paintings in the royal palaces at Madrid. He died at Madrid in 1770. Zanetti says he died in 1769, aged 77; others place his birth in 1693.

TIEPOLO, Giovanni Domenico, was the son of the preceding, born at Venice about 1725. He was instructed by his father, whose manner he followed. He painted some works of his own for the churches of Brescia and other places, but chiefly wrought in conjunction with his father, whom he accompanied to Spain, and assisted in his works in the Palace at Madrid. He is supposed to have died there in or about 1795. We have about 100 spirited etchings by this artist, mostly from his own designs, and after the works of his father, executed in a style resembling that of Benedetto Castiglione, among which are the following:

A set of twenty-seven plates of the Flight and Repose of the Holy Family in Egypt. The Passion of Christ; in fourteen plates. A set of twenty-six Heads; in the style of *Benedetto.* The Virgin appearing to St. Theresa; *after Gio. Bat. Tiepolo.* St. Ambrose preaching to the People; *do.* A set of eight pieces of Satyrs, Turks, and Arabs.

TIEPOLO, Lorenzo, was the youngest son of Gio. Battista T., by whom he was instructed in art, and whose style he followed both in painting and engraving. He etched quite a number of plates from his own designs, and after the works of his father. No further particulars are recorded of him.

TIERENDORFF, Jeremia van, a Flemish painter, of whom little is known. He flourished at Ypres about 1626, where are two pictures by him; one representing Christ delivering the Keys to St. Peter in the church of St. Peter, and another of the Nativity, in the church of St. James.

TILBURG, Egidius or Giles van, called the Elder, a Flemish painter, born at Antwerp in 1570, according to Balkema. He was a cotemporary of David Teniers, the Old, and painted similar subjects, as village wakes and festivals, conversations, and peasants regaling themselves, which were esteemed in his day. He settled at Brussels, where he died in 1622.

TILBURG, Giles van, the Younger, was the son of the preceding, born at Brussels in 1625. It is said that he received his first instruction from his father, at whose death he became the scholar of the younger Teniers, at the same time that Francis du Chatel studied with that master; and that he followed the style of Teniers with such success, that the latter had for some time the mortification to see the works of his pupil preferred to his own. The latter assertion is probably as correct as the first, for his father died when he was only seven years old, David Teniers was fifteen years his elder, and one of his pictures is now worth more than a dozen of Tilburg's. It is more probable that he studied with Brower, or rather, his pupil, Craesbecke, whose style he more closely followed. He painted similar subjects to Teniers, as assemblies of boors, fairs, feastings, cabarets, conversations, corps-de-garde, &c., but they bear no resemblance to his style. In his coloring he approached nearer the manner and tints of Brower, but in his pencil and touch he was infinitely less spirited and delicate. He had a good knowledge of the chiaro-scuro, and gave his figures and objects a fine relief, though some of his pictures are too dark. His works, however, are held in high estimation in his own country, and are admitted into the choicest collections. His name is sometimes written *Tilborch* and *Tilborgh.* He died in 1678.

TILIUS, John, a Dutch painter, born at Bois-le-Duc. He painted portraits and conversations in the highly polished manner of Terburg. There are no particulars recorded of him.

TILL, John Charles van, a German engraver, whose prints date as early as 1644, and who died in 1676. He was chiefly employed in engraving small portraits and other book-plates.

TILLARD, Jean Baptiste, a French engraver, born at Paris in 1740. He studied with Fessard, whom he greatly surpassed. His works are very numerous, chiefly book plates, executed in a very neat, pleasing style. The following are among his principal illustrative prints. He was living in 1786.

A portion of the views in Choiseul-Gouffier's Voyage de la Grèce. The Vignettes for an edition of Tasso; *after Cochin.* The figures for the quarto edition of Telemachus; *after Monnet.* The greater part of the prints for the Travels of the Abbé Chappe in Siberia. A suite of Savoyards, with the title "Mes Commissionnaires, mes Gens," &c. A Portrait of Pope Clement XIV.; *after D. Porta.* Hagar in the Desert; *after J. Vernet.* Russian Shepherds; *after le Prince.*

TILLEMANS, Peter, a Flemish painter, born at Antwerp in 1684. He is said to have excelled in copying the works of other masters, particularly the battles of Borgognone, and the landscapes of Teniers, in which last he preserved much of the freedom and spirit of the originals. He also painted landscapes with small figures, sea-ports, and views of his own composition or from nature, which were esteemed. He went to England in 1708, where he found considerable employment in painting views of country seats, huntings, and races, in which last he excelled, as he painted horses in great perfection. He was much patronized by the Duke of Devonshire and Lord Byron. He died at Norton, in Suffolk, in 1734.

TILLEMANS, Simon Peter, a German painter, born at Bremen in 1602. Little is known of his early history. He went to Italy, where he acquired so much reputation as a landscape and portrait painter, that he was invited to Vienna by the Emperor Ferdinand, whose portrait he painted, as well as other members of the Imperial family, and the most distinguished personages of the court. He died there in 1670.

TILLIARD, F., a French engraver, who flourished at Paris about 1760. He engraved some portraits, executed with the graver, in a neat, finished style.

TILSON, Henry, an English painter, who studied, according to Lord Orford, with Sir Peter Lely, till the death of that master, when he went to Rome in company with Dahl. After a residence there of seven years, he became an excellent painter of portraits in oil and crayons, but unhappily he went crazy, and shot himself. This happened about 1687, in the 36th year of his age.

TIMANTHES, an eminent Grecian painter, a native of Sicyon or Cythnos, was cotemporary with Zeuxis and Parrhasius, and flourished about B. C. 400. His works were distinguished particularly for their invention and expression, and it was one of the chief merits of his invention, that it suggested much to be supplied by the imagination of the spectator. Pliny says that, though in execution always excellent, his execution is invariably surpassed by his conception. As an instance of the ingenuity of his invention, that author mentions a picture of a Sleeping Cyclops, painted upon a small panel, but in which the painter had conveyed a perfect idea of the giant's huge size, by adding a few satyrs measuring his thumb with a thyrsus. Another work by Timanthes was the Stoning of Palamedes, the victim of Ulysses' revenge for having proclaimed his apparent insanity to be feigned; it was painted with such powerful expression, that Alexander shuddered when he beheld it at Ephesus. His most celebrated work, however, was that in which he bore away the palm from Colotes of Teos—the sacrifice of Iphigenia. The tender and beautiful virgin was represented standing before the altar, awaiting her doom, and surrounded by her afflicted relatives. Much has been written concerning the propriety of Agamemnon's face being covered with his mantle in this picture. Quintilian, Cicero, and some modern critics, have supposed that the artist, having represented Calchas sorrowful, Ulysses much more so, and having expressed intense sorrow in the countenance of Menelaus, was in consequence compelled to conceal the face of the father. This criticism, however, can hardly be received, since Timanthes, whose greatest forte was expression, would certainly not have omitted such an admirable opportunity of displaying his powers, had he not been aware of the manifest impropriety of representing the father in any other manner than precisely that described. It is well known that the ancients considered the expression of severe grief indecorous, and that when they found themselves unable to repress their emotions at severe affliction they concealed the face with the mantle. Moreover, notwithstanding many things might combine to render his presence indispensable at the sacrifice, it would be unnatural to suppose that Agamemnon could be an eye witness to his own daughter's immolation; although firmly convinced that his presence was necessary to sanction the dreadful deed, he could not look upon it. Timanthes' picture of a Hero, in the Temple of Peace at Rome, was so perfect in its proportions, and so majestic in its expression, that it appeared to reach the utmost height of the ideal. He competed with Parrhasius at Samos, and gained the victory; the subject of the painting was the Contest of Ajax and Ulysses for the Arms of Achilles.

TIMBRELL, H. This sculptor was born at Dublin in 1806. He studied under John Smith, and went to London in 1831, where he worked as an assistant in the studio of E. H. Baily for many years; at the same time studying his art in the Royal Academy, having become a student of that institution. In 1837 he obtained the gold medal for the best work in Sculpture, "Mezentius tying the Living to the Dead," and in 1843 was elected travelling student, which he gained by his group of "Hercules throwing Lichas into the Sea." In 1845 he executed a beautiful group of a mother and two children, life-size, representing "Instruction." He was also engaged upon several important commissions, when he died at Rome, in 1849.

TIMOMACHUS, an eminent Greek encaustic painter, and a native of Byzantium. In the common text of Pliny, he is said to have flourished in the time of Julius Cæsar (Julii Cesaris ætate); but Durand, in his *Histoire de la Peinture Ancienne*, &c., expresses an opinion that the word *ætate* is an addition of the copyist. According to Pliny, Cæsar purchased two pictures in encaustic by this artist, for eighty Attic talents (about $80,000), one representing Ajax, the son of Telamon, brooding over his misfortunes; the other, Medea about to destroy her children; both were dedicated in the temple of Venus Genetrix. The latter work was unfinished, which puts it beyond a doubt that it was not purchased of the painter himself; from a passage in Cicero (In Verr., i. iv. c. 60), it seems equally clear that both were purchased of the city of Cyzicus; and the enormous price of the pictures is only paralleled by the sums paid for the works of artists long before deceased. Pliny elsewhere mentions him, together with the more ancient and celebrated painters of Greece, with Nichomachus, Apelles, and Aristides; and it is quite probable that Timomachus lived cotemporaneously with Pausias, Nicias, and other encaustic painters, about B. C. 300. The two pictures above mentioned have been much celebrated by the poets; there are several epigrams upon them in the Greek Anthology, and in Ovid (Trist., ii. 525).

> Utque sedet vultu fassus Telamonius iram,
> Inque oculis facinus barbara mater habet.

"Ajax the son of Telamon is seated, showing his anger by his countenance; and the barbarous mother betrays by her eyes the intended crime." The unfinished picture of Medea was admired more than any of the finished works of Timomachus, as was the case with the Iris of Aristides, the Tyndaridæ of Nicomachus, and a Venus of Apelles. Pliny mentions also the following works by this artist: an Orestes; an Iphigenia in Tauris; Lecythion, a gymnasiast; a "cognatio nobilium"; two philosophers or others, with the pallium, about to speak, one standing, and the other sitting; and a very celebrated picture of a Gorgon.

TIMOTEO, da Urbino. See Vite.

TINELLI, Cav. Tiberio, an eminent painter, born at Venice in 1586. He first studied with Giovanni Contarini, and afterwards with Leandro Bassano, whose style he imitated. According to Ridolfi, he not only copied the works of Bassano, but imitated him so successfully in design, coloring, and handling, that some of his works are attributed to that master. He, however, abandoned historical painting for portraiture, in which branch he became the most eminent artist of his time. Lanzi says that he eclipsed his master Contarini, so famous in portraits, and that Pietro da Cortona, on beholding one of them, exclaimed that Tiberio had not merely infused into it the whole soul of the original, but added his own. He acquired an immense reputation, and found abundant employment at Venice, Rome, and Florence, among persons of the highest distinction, at his own prices. He treated his subjects in a novel manner, different from any other painter of his time. He generally represented his sitters under characters selected from sacred and profane history, and the classic poets, which, without injuring the likeness, gave interest to his pictures. Thus he represented Spinelli as Mark Antony, and his wife as Cleopatra, about to drink the dissolved pearls; young and beautiful females he portrayed as Aurora, Diana, Hebe, and other poetical deities and nymphs. He sometimes left his pictures unfinished, except the heads, or enveloped a part of the bust in clouds or wrapt it in drapery, at the desire of the parties, to diminish the price. He settled at Florence, where he lived, greatly respected, till some domestic calamity deprived him of his reason, when he opened a vein and expired, in 1638, aged 52. Among his historical works are mentioned, the Salutation of the Virgin, the Last Supper, and a Paradiso (Heaven), with a multitude of figures, executed so much in the style of Jacopo Bassano that they might be attributed to that master.

TINGHIUS, A. M., an artist who flourished about 1760, mentioned by Basan and Strutt as the engraver of a print of the Temptation of St. Anthony, from a drawing by Callot. Zani says he is the same as *Antonio Meitinghius*, a Florentine engraver, who flourished in 1627.

TINTI, Camillo, an Italian engraver, born at Rome about 1738. He engraved several plates after the Italian masters. He was employed by Gavin Hamilton, during his residence at Rome, to engrave several plates for his *Schola Italica Picturæ*.

TINTI, Giovanni Battista, a painter born at Parma, according to Affò, about 1550. He studied with Orazio Samacchini, at Bologna, but forming an acquaintance with the younger Caracci, he became attached to the school of Lodovico. He afterwards accompanied Annibale to Rome, where he resided some time. Lanzi says that he studied Tibaldi with great assiduity, and painted upon his model at S. Maria della Scala at Bologna, not without marks of plagiarism. "He subsequently established himself in his native city, where he selected for his chief model the works of Correggio, and next proceeded to study those of Parmiggiano. The city contains many of his productions, both in public and in private, among which the Assumption, abounding with figures, in the Cathedral, and the Catino (Dome) at the Old Capuchin Nuns, are accounted some of the last grand works belonging to the old school of Parma."

TINTI, Lorenzo, a painter born at Bologna, according to Zani, in 1626, and died in 1672; others place his birth in 1634, and his death about 1700. He studied with Gio. Andrea Sirani, in whose style he executed several altar-pieces and other works, for the churches at Bologna, the principal of which are the Scourging of Christ, in La Madonna del Piombo; and the Virgin and Infant, with several Saints, in S. Tecla. He etched several plates after the works of Elizabeth Sirani, Guido, Francesco Stringa, and others.

TINTORE, Cassiano, Francesco, and Simone del, three painters of Lucca, brothers, who were scholars of Pietro Paolini, and flourished in their native city in the latter part of the 17th century. Lanzi says, "Cassiano did not rise above mediocrity, and when one meets with an indifferent picture of the school of Paolini, it is usual to ascribe it to Cassiano. Francesco is recognized as an able artist in the Visitation of the Virgin, in the apartments of the Gonfaloniere, and pieces in the Motroni collection. Simone was expert in depicting birds, fruit, flowers, and other objects in the inferior walks of the art."

TINTORELLO, Jacopo, a painter of Vicenza, who flourished in the 15th century. Little is known of him. There are some of his works in the public edifices of Vicenza. Lanzi says he strongly resembles Vittore Pisanello in his style of coloring, though inferior to him in point of design, and that his picture of the Savior crowned with Thorns, at Santa Corona, reflects credit upon his school.

TINTORETTO, Il, or Giacomo Robusti. The name of this distinguished painter was Giacomo or Jacopo Robusti, but he was called Il Tintoretto because he was the son of a dyer. He was born at Venice, according to Ridolfi, in 1512. From his infancy, he discovered a passion for painting, which exhibited itself by his sketching upon the walls, with a piece of charcoal, everything that struck his fancy. His father, though very poor, far from curbing this propensity, encouraged him, had him instructed in the rudiments of design, and at length placed him as a disciple of Titian. How long he remained with that master is not known; Ridolfi says only ten days, which is evidently an error, as the best authorities agree that he studied with him long enough to thoroughly imbibe his principles of coloring, and to make such progress in design as to qualify him to pursue his studies without any further instruction. It is generally stated that he made such rapid progress, and showed such extraordinary genius, that Titian soon became jealous of his talents and banished him from his studio. Tintoretto had then arrived at manhood, and this unworthy treatment, instead of disconcerting him, only inspired him with the ambition and determination to rival his instructor. Lanzi gives the following admirable account of his course after this event. "He did not aspire, like many of his fellow-pupils, to the name of a follower of Titian; he burned with the ambition to become the head of a new school, which should carry the manner of that artist to perfection, adding to it all that was yet wanting; a vast idea, the offspring of a grand and fervid genius, as bold as it was great. Not even banishment from his master's school could damp his ardor. Constrained by circumstances to confine himself to an incommodious apartment, he ennobled it with specimens of his early studies. Over the door he wrote, 'Michael Angelo's design, and the coloring of Titian'; and as he was an indefatigable imitator of the latter, so he was equally studious, both day and night, in copying the models taken from the statues of the former at Florence. To these he added many more of ancient statues and bassirilievi. In a catalogue of ancient pieces of sculpture, cited by Morelli, is recorded a head of Vitellius, upon which he says Tintoretto was always employed in designing and learning. He was frequently in the habit of designing his models by lamp-light, the better to obtain strong shades, and thus acquire skill in the use of a bold chiaroscuro. With the same view, he wrought models in wax and plaster, and having draped them carefully, he adapted them to little houses made of paste-board and pieces of wood, supplying them through the windows with small lights, by which he might thus regulate his own lights and shades. He suspended the models themselves from the ceiling by means of cords, placing them in a variety of positions, and designing them from different points of view, the better to acquire a mastery of foreshortening as seen from below—a science then not so familiar to his school as to that of Lombardy. Nor did he neglect the study of anatomy by dissection, to obtain a thorough knowledge of the muscles and the structure of the human frame. He designed also the naked parts from life, as much as possible, in various shortenings and attitudes, in order to render his compositions as diversified as nature herself. By these studies he prepared himself to introduce the true method to be pursued by his followers, beginning with designing from the best models, and after having obtained the idea of a correct style, proceeding to copy the naked parts, and to correct their defects. To similar aids, he united a genius which extorted the admiration of Vasari, one of his severest critics, who pronounced it the most terrible of which the art could boast—an imagination fertile in ideas, and a pictorial fire which inspired him with vigor to conceive well the boldest character of the passions, and continued to support him till he had given full expression to them upon his canvass.

"Yet, what is the noblest genius, what are all the rarest qualities meeting in a single artist, without diligence, a virtue which of itself, says Cicero, seems to include all the rest? Tintoretto possessed it for a period, and produced works in which the most captious of critics could not find a shade of defect. Such is the Miracle of the Slave, adorning the college of St. Mark—a piece he executed in his 36th year, and which is held up as one of the wonders of Venetian art; the colors are Titian's, the chiaro-scuro extremely strong, the composition correct and sober, the forms select, and the draperies studied; while equally varied, appropriate, and animated beyond conception, are the attitudes of the men assisting at the spectacle, in particular of the saint who flies to succor, giving an idea of the swiftness of an aërial being. There, too, he painted other beautiful pieces, whose merit extorted from the lips of Pietro da Cortona these words: 'Did I reside in Venice, not a festival should pass without still resorting to this spot, to feast my eyes with such objects, and above all with the design!' His picture of the Crucifixion, in the College of S. Rocco, engraved by Agostino Caracci, is also esteemed a picture of extraordinary merit, displaying so much novelty upon a hackneyed subject. Nor are other examples wanting of his surpassing powers in the same place, filled with pictures as various as new; but for brevity, I shall only record the Supper of our Lord, now at the Salute, having been removed from the refectory of the Crociferi, for which it was painted. Those who beheld it in its place, write of it as a miracle of art, inasmuch as the construction of the place was so well repeated in the picture, and imitated with such knowledge of perspective, as to make the apartment appear double its real size. Nor are these three works, to which he affixed his name as his favorite productions, the only ones worthy of his genius; Zanetti enumerates many more, conducted with the most finished care, all exhibited to the Venetian public, without including those dispersed throughout the cities of Europe.

"But diligence is rarely found long united to a rage for achieving much; the true source in this instance, as in numerous others, of false, or at least, inferior composition. Hence Annibale Caracci observed that in many pieces Tintoretto was inferior to Tintoretto, while Paul Veronese, an ardent admirer of his talents, was in the habit of reproaching him with doing injustice to the professors of the art, by painting in every manner, a plan that went far, says Ridolfi, to destroy the reputation of his profession. Similar exceptions will be found to apply to such of his works as, conceived at a heat, executed by habit, and in great part left imperfect, betray certain errors, both in point of judgment and design. Sometimes there appears a crowd of superfluous or badly grouped figures, and most generally all in the most energetic action, without any spectators regarding them in quiet, as was practised by Titian, and all the best composers. Neither in these figures are we to look for that senatorial dignity which some discover in the works of Titian.

"Tintoretto aimed rather at liveliness than at grace, and from the studied observation of the people of his native state, perhaps the most spirited in Italy, he drew models for his heads as well as his attitudes, sometimes applying them to the most important subjects. In a few specimens of his Suppers, the apostles might easily be taken for gondoliers, just when their arm is raised, ready to strike the oar, and with an air of native fierceness, they raise the head to ridicule or dispute. He likewise varied Titian's method of coloring, making use of primary grounds no longer white and composed of chalk, but shaded, owing to which his Venetian pictures have felt the effects of time more than the rest. Neither was the choice nor the general tone of his coloring the same as Titian's; the blue or the ash-colored being that which predominates; one which assists the effect of the chiaro-scuro as much as it diminishes the amenity of the whole. In his fleshes there appears a certain vinous color, more particularly in his portraits. The proportions of his bodies are also different; he does not affect the fulness of Titian; he aims more at lively action than the latter, and sometimes attenuates his figures too much. The least correct portion of his pictures is the drapery, few of them being free from those long and straight folds, or flying abroad, or in some other way too common and obvious. It would be useless to insist on his want of judgment, or rather his pictorial extravagance."

Lanzi, after having animadverted upon Vasari's terrible criticisms and wholesale condemnation of his works, proceeds: "He ought to have tempered the severity of his criticisms, however, by admitting that, if the author of that great work (the Universal Judgment at S. Maria dell' Orto) had bestowed as much pains upon the several parts as upon the whole, it would have been a magnificent production. Even in those pictures in which he wished to display the talent, as it were, of an *improvisatore*, he still vindicated his title to the name of a great master, in the command and rapidity of his pencil, in the manifestation of original powers, where he seems to triumph in his play of light, in the most difficult foreshortenings, in fanciful inventions, in relief, in harmony, and in the best supported of his pieces, even in the beauty of his tints. But his sovereign merit consisted in the animation of his figures, it being a universal opinion, that has almost acquired the force of a proverb, that the power of action ought to be studied by artists in Tintoretto. Upon this point, Pietro da Cortona used to say that, if we observe the whole of those pictures which have been engraved, no artist will be found equal to him in the pictoric fire which he infused into his forms. He flourished for a long period, exerting his talents till he could with difficulty make a catalogue of his works, still giving the rein to his divine ardor in many pieces of great size, or abounding with a great variety of actors."

Few artists have encountered such a storm of criticism as Tintoretto, and yet his best works have always extorted the admiration of his severest critics. The impetuosity of his genius, and the extraordinary promptness of his hand, together with an ardent desire of embracing every opportunity of distinguishing himself, induced him to paint several large works for the convents and churches of Venice almost gratuitously, as on several occasions, the prices he received were little more than enough to defray the expense of the materials. It is therefore not to be wondered at that he gave Annibale Caracci occasion to observe that Tintoretto was sometimes equal to Titian, and at others inferior to himself. Of the merits of his works he was fully sensible, as he particularly distinguished three of them, which he and others regarded as his master-pieces, viz., the Crucifixion in S. Rocco; the Last Supper, now at S. Maria della Salute; and Il Servo, or the Venetian Slave, condemned to martyrdom by the Turks, invoking the protection of St. Mark. The last is regarded as his master-piece; it was carried to Paris by the French, but restored in 1815. Some of his works are of enormous size; the Crucifixion is forty feet in length; and two others, the Israelites worshipping the Golden Calf, and the Last Judgment, are each about sixty feet high, filled with figures drawn in a grand style, with powerful coloring and masterly execution. Tintoretto also excelled in landscape and portraiture. He painted both in oil and fresco; most of his great works are executed in fresco. A just idea of his merits can only be formed by contemplating his numerous pictures in the churches, convents, public edifices, and palaces at Venice. Most of his works elsewhere only exhibit his infirmities. Ridolfi asserts that he finished some of his oil paintings almost as highly as miniatures, and Lanzi says there are not wanting at Venice specimens to prove so improbable a story. He retained his powers to a great age. One of his last productions was his Paradiso in the hall of the Great Council Chamber of S. Marco, an immense composition, abounding in figures, which Lanzi says was greatly esteemed by the Caracci. He was probably the most expeditious painter that ever appeared: of this a memorable instance is related. The members of the confraternity of S. Rocco, at Venice, desired Paul Veronese, Tintoretto, Salviati, and Zuccaro to prepare each a design for a picture to represent the Apotheosis of their patron Saint, or as some say of the Crucifixion, for their selection. On the day appointed for their decision, instead of a design, Tintoretto sent in a finished picture, so admirably executed as to extort the commendation of his competitors, who termed him *Il furioso Tintoretto, un fulmine di Pennello* (the furious Tintoretto and the lightning of the pencil). Sandrart says that he frequently painted without any preparatory design, as if he only sported with his pencil, and he seems to have executed his ideas almost as quickly as he conceived them. He wrought so fast, and at so low a price, that few of the other painters at Venice could get employment. The churches and halls of the different communities are overloaded with his productions. That of St. Roch alone contains above sixty pictures of sacred subjects by him, exhibiting such an extraordinary combination of beauties and defects as sets all criticism at defiance. There is a single etching by this great painter, from his portrait of the Doge Pacale Ciconia. He died at Venice in 1594, aged 82 years.

TINTORETTO, Domenico Robusti, usually called Domenico Tintoretto, was the son and disciple of the preceding, born at Venice in 1562. Lanzi says that none conferred greater credit upon the school of Tintoretto than his son Domenico. "He trod in the steps of his father, but like Ascanius following Æneas, 'non passibus æquis.' Still he boasts much resemblance in his countenances, in his coloring, and in harmony, but there is a wide distinction in point of genius, though some of his most spirited pieces have been ascribed to his father, or at least suspected of having been chiefly indebted to his hand. Many works, however, upon a large scale, are attributed to the son; those which he filled with portraits are by far the most commended, his merit in that branch having been thought by Zanetti equal to that of his father. One of these is to be seen in the college of S. Marco, where, as in the rest of his compositions, the figures are disposed with more sobriety than those of Jacopo, as well as finished with more care, and with more enduring colors. As he grew older, his style degenerated somewhat into that of a mannerist, which at that time much prevailed. By these distinctions, his productions may be frequently known from those of his father and we may be able to refute the assertions of dealers, who, to obtain a higher price, indiscriminately attribute them to Jacopo. Yet Domenico produced many pieces, more especially portraits, for different collections, besides some mythological and scriptural histories, which he sometimes signed with his name, as in his picture of a penitent Magdalen, boasting such exquisite tints, adorning the Campidoglio." His principal works are in the Sala di Consiglio, and in the Scuola di S. Marco at Venice. He was very eminent in portraits, and painted many of the most distinguished personages of his time. His works must be numerous, as he continued to exercise his pencil till his death, in 1637, aged 75.

TINTORETTO, Marietta Robusti, was the daughter of Jacopo, born at Venice in 1560. She was instructed by her father, and displayed great talents in portraiture. She painted many of the principal personages of Venice, and acquired so much distinction that she was invited to the courts of both Vienna and Madrid, which honors she declined on account of her attachment to her father, who idolized her, and could not bear to be separated from her. She died in the flower of her life, in 1590.

TIO, Francesco, called Francesco Tio da Fabriano. See Fabriano.

TIODAS, a Spanish architect, very eminent and meritorious for his time, who flourished in the 9th century, in the reign of Alphonso the Chaste. About A. D. 840, by order of that monarch, he erected at Oviedo, the basilica of S. Salvador, with two other churches at the sides, one to the Madonna, the other to St. Miguel. The basilica was demolished in 1380, to make room for the present Cathedral, but the two others remain. That of Santa Maria is one hundred feet wide, divided into three naves, with six arches, all on pedestals; the great chapel and the two collateral ones are well proportioned, and adorned with famous marbles. The entrance to S. Miguel is from the Cathedral, by a flight of twenty-one steps, to a hall twenty feet high; from which twelve steps descend to a church ornamented with many delicate works, twenty-five feet long and sixteen wide, the vault of which, although resting on the walls, appears supported by six columns of different marbles, over which are the twelve Apostles, two to each column. Tiodas also built the royal palace at Oviedo, thus highly praised by King Alphonso in his Chronicles: "Cujus operis pulchritudo plus præsens potest mirari quàm eruditus scriba laudare." The church of S. Julius, erected by him without the walls, is said by Milizia to be a magnificent edifice, more resembling modern Greek than Gothic. Among the other works of this celebrated architect, were the churches of S. Maria and S. Miguel, at a short distance from Oviedo, erected by the desire of Don Ramiro, successor of Alphonso the Chaste. They are very highly praised by Milizia, particularly the latter, which he commends for its harmonious arrangement, and beautiful proportions. Tiodas was very highly honored, and richly rewarded by King Alphonso.

TISCHBEIN, John Henry, called the Elder, one of the most eminent painters of the last century, was the fifth son of a baker of Hayna, near Gotha, where he was born in 1722. He was first apprenticed to an uncle on his mother's side, who was a locksmith; but he displayed so much talent for drawing, that an elder brother, John Valentine, took him away from his uncle and placed him, in his fourteenth year, with a paper stainer and decorator of Cassel, named Zimmermann. He received, also, some instruction from van Freese, the court painter at Cassel, and soon gave proof of his ability. Tischbein met with an early and valuable patron in Count Stadion, through whose assistance he was enabled, in 1743, to visit Paris, where he remained five years with Charles Vanloo, and acquired his style of painting. From Paris he proceeded to Venice, and there studied eight months with Piazzetta; from Venice he went to Rome, where he remained two years; he again visited Piazzetta in Venice, and after a short time, in 1751, he returned to Cassel, where, in 1752, he was appointed cabinet painter to the Landgrave.

Tischbein excelled in historical and mythological subjects, which are his best pictures, painted from about 1762 to 1785. Many of his subjects are taken from the ancient poets, and some from Tasso; several of which are now in the Gallery at Cassel. He painted also a collection of female portraits, selected chiefly for their beauty, which is now in the palace of Wilhelmsthal, near Cassel. He also frequently copied his own pictures; but nearly all his works remain in his own country, on which account he is little known out of it. Of all the great galleries in Germany, the Pinacotheca at Munich is the only one that possesses a specimen of his works, and that is only a portrait. He painted very slowly, but was very industrious; generally commencing work at five o'clock in the morning, in the summer-time, and remaining at his easel until four o'clock in the afternoon. He painted in the French style; his coloring was a mixture of the French and Venetian, and in large compositions very gaudy; but his drawing and chiaro-scuro were excellent. In costume, like many of the Venetian painters, he was extremely incorrect; according to the critics, he generally contrived, in his ancient subjects, to make his actors look much more like Frenchmen and Germans than Greeks or Romans. In his religious pieces he was more successful: he was no follower of Lessing's theory of beauty, and considered beauty of little consequence.

Tischbein was chosen a member of the Academy at Bologna, and Director of the Academy of Cassel, which office he held at the time of his death, in 1789. In 1797, a biographical notice, with criticisms on his works, was published at Nuremberg, containing a list of one hundred and forty-four historical pictures by him, among which the following have been considered the best: the Resurrection, very large figures, painted in 1763, for the altar of St. Michael's church at Hamburg; the Transfiguration, in the Lutheran church at Cassel, 1765; Hermann's Trophies after his Victory over Varus, in the palace of Pyrmont, 1768; ten pictures of the life of Cleopatra, painted in the palace of Weissenstein, 1769–70; sixteen from the life of Telemachus, in the palace of Wilhelmsthal; an Ecce Homo, in the Roman Catholic chapel of Cassel, 1778; a Deposition from the Cross, and an Ascension, altar-pieces in the principal church of Stralsund, 1787; Christ on the Mount of Olives, an altar-piece presented by him to the church of his native place Hayna, 1788; the death of Alce tis, 1780; and the restoration of Alcestis to her husband by Hercules, 1777.

Tischbein was a man of very domestic habits; he had an old servant named Conrad Otto, without whom he used to say he would be perfectly helpless; he had a cook, also, who lived with him twenty-one years. Although twice married, he was a husband scarcely four years; he married his first wife in 1756, by whom he had two daughters; he lived with her three years, when she died; in 1759 he married her sister, with whom, however, he lived only a few months. His elder daughter Amalia, was a talented paintress; she was accustomed to sit to her father for many of the females in his historical works; the Academy of Cassel elected her a member of their body in 1780. After Tischbein's death, the Landgrave of Cassel purchased all the works that were in his house, and placed them together in the palace of Wilhelmshohe. There are a few etchings by this artist from his own designs, among which are the following: Venus and Cupid; Cupid stung by a Bee, complaining to Venus; Nymphs bathing; Hercules and Omphale; Menelaus and Paris; Thetis and Achilles; The Resurrection, after the picture he painted for the church of S. Michael at Hamburg.

TISCHBEIN, JOHN HENRY WILLIAM, called THE YOUNGER, the youngest son of John Conrad Tischbein, and nephew of the preceding, with whom he is sometimes confounded, was born at Hayna in 1751. He was instructed in historical painting by his uncle John Henry of Cassel; after which he studied landscape painting three years with his uncle John Jacob at Hamburg; in 1770 he went to Holland, where he remained two years, and in 1772 returned to Cassel, and painted portraits and landscapes; he visited also Hanover and Berlin, and painted many portraits in both places. In 1779 he left Cassel, by the desire of the Landgrave, for Italy, but he spent about two years in Zurich, where he painted many portraits, and made the design of his celebrated picture of Conradin of Suabia, playing, after his sentence to death, a game of draughts with Frederick of Austria. In 1781, Tischbein arrived at Rome, where his first studies were some copies in oil after Raffaelle and Guercino, and some drawings after Raffaelle, Domenichino, and Leonardo da Vinci. His first original picture was Hercules choosing between Vice and Virtue; after which he painted his picture of Conradin of Suabia, now in the palace of Pyrmont. In 1787 he went to Naples, and the next year painted the portrait of the crown prince for the queen, who presented Tischbein with a valuable snuff-box and 200 ducats, expressing her complete satisfaction with the picture. His reputation rapidly increased, and in 1790 he was appointed director of the Neapolitan Academy, with a salary of 600 ducats. In 1799, at the breaking out of the French Revolution, he lost his post, but was allowed by the French authorities to return to Germany with his effects, consisting principally of the plates of his illustrations of Homer, his designs for Sir W. Hamilton's second collection of Vases, and some other works of art; and after a troublesome journey of four months, he reached Cassel in safety.

After his return to Germany, Tischbein resided principally at Hamburg, and at Eutin, in Oldenburg, near Lubec. His drawing was correct, and his expression and coloring good; he chiefly excelled in drawing animals. Most of his pictures are in the possession of the Grand Duke of Oldenburg; the following are three of his most celebrated works: Ajax and Cassandra, painted in 1805; "Let the little children come unto me," painted in 1806, for the altar of the church of S. Angari at Bremen; and Hector taking leave of Andromache, painted in 1810. He also painted the portraits of Klopstock, Heyne, and Blucher.—While residing at Naples, he published in 1796, a remarkable work on animals, in two parts, folio, entitled *Têtes des differents Animaux, dessinés d'après Nature, pour donner une idée plus exacte de leurs caracteres.* The first part contains sixteen designs of animals, and the first plate of this part is the celebrated design called in Italy, Tischbein's Laocoön, of remarkable power and spirit, representing a large snake attacking and destroying a lioness and her young in their den; the second part contains eight plates only, consisting of characteristic heads of men and gods—Correggio, Salvator Rosa, Michael Angelo, Raffaelle, Scipio Africanus, Caracalla, Jupiter, and Apollo.

Tischbein's drawings for Sir W. Hamilton's collection of Vases, published at Naples in 1791, in 4 vols. folio, amount to 214; the work is entitled "A Collection of Engravings from Ancient Vases, mostly of pure Greek workmanship, discovered in Sepulchres in the kingdom of the Two Sicilies, but principally in the environs of Naples, during the years 1789 and 1790; now in the possession of Sir W. Hamilton, published by William Tischbein, Director of the Royal Academy of Painting at Naples." The text, which is in French and English, is by Italinsky. In Gottingen, in 1801–'4, he published in royal folio, his favorite work on Homer, with explanations by Heyne—*Homer, nach Antiken gezeichnet von Heinrich Tischbein, Direcktor, &c,, mit erlauterungen von Chr. Gottl. Heyne*, I. VI.; each number containing six plates, the portraits of the Homeric heroes being engraved by Morghen. Tischbein also published other works, and etched several plates, after Paul Potter, Roos, Rosa da Tivoli, Rembrandt, &c. He died in 1829. There are several other artists of this family, of various degrees of merit; but they are unknown out of their own circle.

TISCHLER, ANTHONY, a German engraver, who flourished from about 1750 to 1775. He engraved among others, a part of the plates for the collection of prints, from the pictures in the collection of Count Bruhl.

TISIO, or TISI, BENVENUTO, called IL GAROFOLO. This eminent painter ranked at the head of the Ferrarese school, was born in 1481. There is a good deal of discrepancy about him, which is thus explained by Lanzi: "Besides Benvenuto Tisio, surnamed Garofolo, from the place of his nativity, in the Ferrarese territory, there flourished at the same period, Gio. Battista Benvenuto, said by some to have been also a native of Garofolo, but called from his father's occupation, *Ortolano* (the Gardener); hence mistakes have been made as to his name, and our dilettanti have often been betrayed into errors, both from resemblance of name and style, so far as even to mistake the portrait of Ortolano for that of Tisio, and as such it is inserted in the edition of Vasari, published at Bologna. Several of the altar-pieces of the former have been transferred to the Roman galleries, where they are attributed to the latter, whose first manner, being more careful than soft and tasteful, may easily be mistaken for that of Ortolano.

"Tisio received his first education under Domenico Panetti, from whose school he went to Cremona and studied with Niccolo Soriani, his maternal uncle, and next under Boccaccio Boccaccino. On the death of Niccolo in 1499, he proceeded to Rome, where he resided fifteen months with Gian Baldini, a Florentine. Thence he traveled through various Italian cities, remained two years with Lorenzo Costa in Mantua, and then returning for a short time to Ferrara, finally proceeded back to Rome. These circumstances I relate, because there are a number of Benvenuto's works to be met with at Ferrara and elsewhere, which partake little or nothing of the Roman style, though not excluded as apocryphal, but attributed to his earlier age. After remaining a few years with Raffaello, (about two years according to most authors, and Lanzi himself says in another place, 'only a short time, but sufficient to enable him to become the chief of the Ferrarese school,') his domestic affairs recalled him to Ferrara. Having arranged these he prepared to return to Rome, but at the solicitations of Panetti, and still more, by the commissions of Duke Alphonso, he remained in his native place, and engaged with the Dossi in immense undertakings at Belriguardo and other places. It is observed by Baruffaldi, that the degree of Raffaellesque taste to be traced in the two Dossi, is to be attributed to Tisio. He conducted a great number of other paintings both in oil and fresco.

"The most happy period of Tisio dates from 1519, when he painted the Murder of the Innocents in S. Francesco at Ferrara; availing himself of earthen models, aud copying draperies, landscapes, and in short, everything from the life. In the same church, is his Resurrection of Lazarus, and his celebrated Taking of Christ, commenced in 1520, and finished in 1524. No finer works appeared from his hand; no better composed, more animated, or conducted with more care and softness of coloring; there only remain some slight traces of the fourteenth century in point of design, and some little affectation of grace,—if the opinion of Vasari be correct. The district formerly abounded with similar specimens of his works in fresco; and they are also met with in private, as that frieze in a chamber of the Seminary, which in point of grace and Raffaellesque taste is worthy of the burin. Many of his works in oil remain in the churches and private collections of Ferrara, at once so numerous and so beautiful as alone to suffice for the decoration of a city. His St. Peter Martyr, in the church of the Dominicans, supposed by some to have been painted in competition with Titian's great picture of the same subject, and in case of its loss, to have been able to supply its place, is a picture remarkable for its force; his Helen, too, of a more elegant character, at the same place, is greatly admired, this gracefulness forming one of Benvenuto's most peculiar gifts. And, indeed, not a few of his Madonnas, his Virgins, and his boys, which he painted in his softest manner, have occasionally been mistaken for the works of Raffaello. His picture of the Princes Corsini deceived good judges, as we are informed by Bottari, and the same might have happened with the portrait of the Duke of Modena, and others scattered throughout the Roman galleries, where are many of his pieces on a large scale, particularly in the Chigi palace. All these must be kept in view, in forming an estimate of the merits of Garofolo. His little pictures, consisting of scripture histories, are very abundant in different cabinets, the Prince Borghese alone being in possession of about forty; and although they bear his mark, a gilly-flower or violet, they were, I suspect, the productions of his leisure hours. Those in this style without this mark, are frequently the works of Panelli, who was employed along with him; others are copies or repetitions by his pupils, who must have been numerous during so long a period." Lanzi in again briefly noticing him under the head of the Roman school says, "He imitated Raffaello in design, in the character of his faces, and in expression, and also considerably in his coloring, although he added something of a warmer and stronger cast, derived from his own school.—Rome, Bologna, and other cities, abound with his pictures from the lives of the Apostles. They are of various merit, and not wholly painted by himself. In his large pictures he stands more alone, and many of these are to be found in the Chigi Gallery. The Visitation of the Virgin, in the Palazzo Doria, is one of the finest pieces in that rich collection. The artist was accustomed, in allusion to his name, to mark his pictures with a violet (clove pink), which the common people of Italy call garofolo. It does not appear from Vasari, Titi, and Taja, that Garofolo had any share in the works executed by Raffaello, and his scholars."

Tisio, though he devoted himself mostly to sacred history, was an universal painter. He was almost equal to Raffaelle in portraits, and he occasionally painted landscapes in the highest excellence, two specimens of which are in the Palazzo Zampieri at Bologna. His works are extremely valuable, and scarcely to be found out of Italy. There is a fine specimen of his easel pictures in the English National Gallery, called the Vision of St. Augustine. He is generally called by the Italian writers *Il Garofolo*, from his mark, though some say, *da Garofolo*, from the place of his nativity, near Ferrara. It is generally stated that he was born at Ferrara. He had the misfortune to lose the sight of one of his eyes, yet he contrived to paint with as much beauty and correctness as ever, till his sixty-ninth year, when he became totally blind. He survived nine years, and died in 1559.

TITI, Santo di, an eminent Italian painter and reputable architect, was born at Città San Sepolcro, in the Florentine state, in 1538. According to Lanzi, he studied under Agnolo Bronzino and Cellini. He visited Rome, where Baldinucci says he entered the school of Baccio Bandinelli, and studied for a long time in that city. While residing there he was employed upon some subjects in the chapel of the Palazzo Salviati, and painted a St. Jerome in S. Giovanni dei Fiorentini, besides executing several works in the Belvidere of the Vatican. By designing with great assiduity after the antique, and the works of the best masters, he returned to Florence with a style full of science and grace. Lanzi says "his beautiful is without much of the ideal; but his countenances exhibit a certain fulness, an appearance of freshness and health, that is surpassed by none of those who took nature for their model. Design was his characteristic excellence, and for this he was commended by his imitator, Salvator Rosa. In expression he had few superiors in other schools, and none in his own. His ornaments are judicious, and he introduced perspectives that imparted a dignity and a charm to his compositions. He is esteemed the best painter of this epoch, and belongs to it rather from the time in which he lived than his style; if we except his coloring, which was too feeble, and without relief." He seems to have devoted his chief attention to design and expression, and Borghini says that he was not deficient in coloring when he chose to exert his powers, as in the Feast of Emmaus, in the church of S. Croce at Florence, and in the Resurrection of Lazarus, in the cathedral at Volterra. There are also several of his works in the private collections at Florence, among which is his greatly admired Baptism of Christ by St. John, in the Palazzo Corsini, commended for its elegant and graceful composition, correct design, and vigorous coloring. Lanzi says that his picture of the Faithful receiving the Holy Spirit by the laying on of the Apostles' hands, may be viewed with pleasure, even after the three by Raffaelle, which adorn that city.

It is not mentioned who was the instructor of Titi in architecture, but as Lanzi says he studied under Benvenuto Cellini, it is probable that he obtained a knowledge of the art from that master, although the latter principally employed his talents in sculpture. Titi's architectural works were principally distinguished for correctness in the proportions. Among the principal were the Villa Spini at Peretola; his own house, and the Casa Dardanelli at Florence. He was frequently engaged upon the decorations of splendid festivals, particularly those celebrated at the nuptials of the Duke de Bracciano. Titi was honored by the Florentines with the freedom of the city. He died in 1603.

TITI, Tiberio, was the son of the preceding, born at Florence in 1578. He studied with his father, but chiefly devoted himself to portraiture, which he practised with success. He had a singular talent for painting small portraits in vermillion (some say red lead), and was continually employed by Cardinal Leopold de Medici, who admitted them into his collection, which now forms a single cabinet in the Florentine Gallery. He was, however, capable of exercising his talents in a higher branch; he finished a picture of the Last Supper, begun by his father and left incomplete at his death, in which he imitated the manner, touch, and tone of coloring so exactly, that it gained him general applause. He died in 1637.

TITIAN. The name of this illustrious painter was Tiziano Vecellio or Vecelli, and he is called by the Italians, Tiziano Vecellio da Cadore. He was descended of a noble family, and born at the castle of Cadore in the Friuli in 1477, and died in 1576, according to Ridolfi; though Vasari and Sandrart place his birth in 1480. Lanzi says he died in 1576, aged 99 years. He early showed a passion for the art, which was carefully cultivated by his parents. Lanzi says in a note, that it is pretty correctly ascertained that he received his first instruction from Antonio Rossi, a painter of Cadore; if so, it was at a very tender age, for when he was ten years old he was sent to Trevigi, and placed under Sebastiano Zuccati. He subsequently went to Venice, and studied successively under Gentile and Giovanni Bellini. Giorgione was his fellow-student under the last named master, with whom Titian made extraordinary progress, and attained such an exact imitation of his style that their works could be scarcely distinguished, which greatly excited the jealousy of Bellini. There is some little discrepancy among authors as to this period of Titian's history. It is universally stated that Giorgione was the first of the Venetian painters who broke through the dry and Gothic style that prevailed at that time in the Venetian school, and introduced a freedom of outline, a boldness of handling, a force of coloring, and a vigorous effect of chiaro-scuro before unknown; that Titian followed the manner of the Bellini till he saw the works of Giorgione, when he immediately changed his style; that when he was only eighteen years of age he painted the portrait of the head of the noble family Barbarigo in so admirable a style that it excited universal admiration; that, soon afterwards, he was employed in conjunction with Giorgione to paint the two fronts of the Fondaco de Tedeschi: and that his portion of the undertaking was preferred to his competitor, and established his reputation. Now Giorgione was certainly Titian's fellow-pupil under Gio. Bellini, whom Durer pronounced the best painter of his time; and he was of the same age if Ridolfi's statement is correct, both being born in 1477. It is also stated by Ridolfi and others, that Titian painted in the labored style characteristic of the school in which he was bred, until, seeing the works of Giorgione, he resolved to change his style, and accordingly formed an acquaintance with that master, and painted in conjunction with him till the friendship was dissolved by jealousy, never afterwards to be renewed; that Titian's first works in his own original style were a picture of the angel Raphael conducting the young Tobias, and another of the Presentation in the Temple; and that on the death of Giorgione in 1511, he succeeded him in several important commissions in which he was employed. One of his most extraordinary early performances was a picture of Christ and the Tribute Money, painted in competition with Albert Durer, finished in the minute style of that master. Lanzi says that all his earliest productions were executed in a more minute and labored style than that of Durer. He further says that a few of his early portraits can not be distinguished from those of Giorgione He also says that, "the first specimen he is known to have produced altogether in the Titian manner is preserved in the sacristy of St. Marziale, representing the Archangel Raphael with Tobias at his side, painted in the 30th year of his age." Here then we have a key to some important facts. Durer was in Italy twice—first in 1495, and next in 1506, in which year the Tribute Money must have been painted, and the Angel and Tobias in the following year 1507, or in 1510, according to the time of his birth. These facts are important, because they show that Titian did not manifest that precocity of genius claimed for him, except in imitation. He did not, like Giorgione, on leaving Bellini, strike out into a new, bold, and original style, but he followed in his course; and his own original manner was the result of a diligent study of nature, of patient labor, and mature judgment.

On the death of Giorgione, Titian rose rapidly into favor. He was soon afterwards invited to the court of Alphonso, Duke of Ferrara, for whom he painted his celebrated picture of Bacchus and Ariadne, and two other fabulous subjects, which still retained somewhat of the style of Giorgione. It was there that he became acquainted with Ariosto, whose portrait he painted, and in return the poet spread abroad his fame in the Orlando Furioso. In 1523, the Senate of Venice employed him to decorate the Hall of the Council Chamber, where he represented the famous battle of Cadore, between the Venetians and the Imperialists—a grand performance that greatly increased his reputation. This work was afterwards destroyed by fire, but the composition has been preserved by the burin of Fontana. His next performance was his celebrated picture of St. Pietro Martire, in the church of SS. Giovanni e Paolo, at Venice, which is generally regarded as his master-piece in historical painting. This picture was carried to Paris by the French, and subsequently restored by the Allies. Notwithstanding the importance of these and other commissions, and the great reputation he had acquired, it is said, though with little probability of truth, that he received such a small remuneration for his works, that he was in actual indigence in 1530, when the praises bestowed upon him in the writings of his friend Pietro Aretino, recommended him to the notice of the Emperor Charles V., who had come to Bologna to be crowned by Pope Clement VII. Titian was invited thither, and painted the portrait of that monarch, and his principal attendants, for which he was liberally rewarded. About this time he was invited to the court of the Duke of Mantua, whose portrait he painted, and decorated a saloon in the palace with a series of the twelve Cæsars, beneath which Giulio Romano afterwards painted a subject from the history of each. In 1543, Paul III. visited Ferrara where Titian was then engaged, sat for his portrait and invited him to Rome, but previous engagements with the Duke of Urbino obliged him to decline or defer the invitation. Having completed his undertakings for that prince, he went to Rome at the invitation of the Cardinal Farnese in 1548, where he was received with marks of great distinction. He was accommodated with apartments in the palace of the Belvidere, and painted the pope, Paul III., a second time, whom he represented seated between the Cardinal Farnese and Prince Ottavio. He also painted his famous picture of Danaë, which caused Michael Angelo to lament that Titian had not studied the antique as accurately as he had nature, in which case his works would have been inimitable, by uniting the perfection of coloring with correctness of design. It is said that the Pope was so captivated with his works that he endeavored to retain him at Rome, and offered him as an inducement the lucrative office of the Leaden Seal, then vacant by the death of Frà Sebastiano del Piombo, but he declined on account of conscientious scruples. Titian had no sooner returned from Rome to Venice, than he received so pressing an invitation from his first protector, Charles V., to visit the court of Spain, that he could no longer refuse, and he accordingly set out for Madrid, where he arrived at the beginning of 1550, and was received with extraordinary honors. He was appointed a gentleman of the Emperor's bed-chamber, who conferred upon him the order of St. Jago, and made him a Count Palatine of the Empire. He did not grace the great artist with splendid titles and decorations only, but showed him more solid marks of his favor, by bestowing upon him life rents in Naples and Milan of two hundred ducats each, annually, besides a munificent compensation for every picture he painted. He also frequented his studio, and treated him with extraordinary familiarity. On one occasion, the pencil falling out of Titian's hand, Charles picked it up and presented it to the astonished painter, saying, "It becomes Cæsar to serve Titian." After a residence of three years at Madrid, he returned to Venice, whence he was shortly afterwards invited to Inspruck, where he painted the portrait of Ferdinand, king of the Romans, his queen and children, in one picture. Though now advanced in years, his powers continued unabated, and this group was accounted one of his best productions. He afterwards returned to Venice, where he continued to exercise his pencil to the last year of his long life.

Such is the contrariety of opinion among the most eminent critics as to the real powers and merits of this illustrious painter, that the learned Lanzi himself, accustomed to contemplate his works all his days, modestly declines entering the contest, but gives the following admirable summary from the best authorities. He says: "From the works he painted in the zenith of his fame, his critics have gathered the general idea of his style, and the greatest contest they have among themselves relates to his design. In this contest of opinion between the true judges of art, I shall decline interfering with my own, observing only, in justice to so extraordinary a genius, that if happier combinations had led him to become familiar with more profound maxims of design, he would probably have ranked as the very first painter of the world. For he would have been allowed to be the first and most perfect in design, as he is by all allowed to have no equal in coloring.

"By Mengs he is denied the title to rank among good designers, considering him in this respect an artist of ordinary taste, by no means familiar with the antique, however well he might have succeeded in its study, had he devoted his attention to it, possessing so very exact an eye in copying objects from nature. Vasari appears to be of the same opinion, where he introduces Michael Angelo observing, after viewing the Danaë of Titian, 'that it was a great pity the Venetian artists were not earlier taught how to design.' The judgment formed of him by Tintoretto, though placed in competitio with him, was less severe, namely, 'that Titian ha produced some things which it was impossible t surpass, but that others might have been mor correctly designed.' And among these more ex cellent pieces he might have indisputably include his St. Pietro Martire, in SS. Giovanni e Paolo, piece, says Algarotti, 'which the best master have agreed in pronouncing free from every shad of defect'; besides that fine Bacchanal, and a fe others, ornamenting a cabinet of the Duke of Fer rara, and declared by Agostino Caracci prodigie of art, and the finest paintings in the worl Fresnoy was of opinion that in the figures of h men he was not altogether perfect, and that in h draperies he was somewhat insignificant; but th many of his women and boys are exquisite, both point of design and coloring. This commendation confirmed by Algarotti in respect to his female form and by Mengs in those of his boys. Indeed, it almost universally admitted that in such kind of fi ures no artist was ever comparable to him; and that Poussin and Fiammingo, who so greatly excelled in this particular, acquired it only from Titian's pictures. Sir Joshua Reynolds also affirms, that 'although his style may not be altogether as chaste as that of other schools of Italy, it nevertheless possesses a certain air of senatorial dignity; and that he shone in his portraits as an artist of the highest character'; and he concludes by observing that he may be studied with advantage even by the lovers of the sublime.

"Zanetti assigns him the first rank in design among all the most distinguished colorists; asserting that he was much devoted to the study of anatomy and copying from the best antique; but supposes that he was not ambitious of affecting an extensive knowledge of the muscles, nor aimed at displaying an ideal beauty in his contours. For the rest, he adds that the Titian manner was uniformly elegant, correct, and dignified in its female forms and in its boys; elevated, great, and learned for the most part, in those of its men; while in testimony of his naked figures, he adduces the history pieces in the sacristy of La Salute, whose beauty of design appears to triumph, even in the extremities, while it boasts the rare merit of a striking acquaintance with the science of foreshortening, both appearing blended together. Had the historian been desirous of extending his notice to such works as are to be found in foreign parts, he might have added much valuable matter upon the subject of his bacchanals, and his pictures of Venus, one of which in the Florentine Gallery, was justly thought to vie with that of the Medici herself, the most exquisite triumph of Grecian art. For his skill in draperies, Zanetti further cites the example of his St. Peter, painted on an altar of the Casa Pesaro, with a very artificially wrought mantle, adding, that he occasionally sacrificed the appearance of the drapery, purposely to give relief to some neighboring object.

"Many critics have pushed the inquiries from the artist, into the peculiar character of his chiaro-scuro, and the most copious among these is Signor Zanetti, who devoted years to its examination. I select some of his observations, premising however that he left a large portion of them to the more studious, desirous themselves of developing them, in the works of Titian. And in truth, his pictures are the best masters to direct us in the right method of coloring, but like the ancient classics, that are equally open and equally the subjects of commentary to all, they are only of advantage to those who are accustomed to reflect. I have already mentioned the lucid clearness predominating in Venetian paintings, more especially in those of Titian, whom the rest adopted for their model. I then pronounced it to be the result of very clear primary grounding, upon which a repetition of colors being laid, it produces the effect of a transparent veil, and renders the tints of a cast no less soft and luscious than lucid. Nor did he adopt any other plan in his strongest shades, veiling them with fresh color when dry; renewing, invigorating them, and warming the confines that pass into the middle tints. He availed himself very judiciously of the powers of shade, forming a method not altogether that of a mere naturalist, but partaking of the ideal. In his naked forms, he cautiously avoided masses of strong shade and bold shadows, although they are sometimes to be seen in nature. They certainly add to the relief, but they much diminish the delicacy of the fleshy parts. Titian for the most part affected a deep and glowing light; whence, in various gradations of middle tints, he formed the work of the lower parts; and having very resolutely drawn the other parts, with the extremities stronger perhaps than nature, he gave to objects that peculiar aspect which presents them, as it were, more lively and pleasing than the truth. Thus, in his portraits he centres the chief power in the eyes, the nose, and the mouth, leaving the remaining parts in a kind of pleasing uncertainty, extremely favorable to the spirit of the heads, and to the whole effect.

"But since the variations of depth and delicacy of shades are insufficient, without the aid of colors, in this branch he likewise found for himself an ideal method, consisting of the use, in their respective places, of simple tints, copied exactly from life, or of artificial ones, intended to produce the illusion required. He was in the habit of employing only few and simple colors, but they were such as afforded the greatest variety and contrast; he knew all their gradations, and the most favorable moments for their application and opposition to each other. There appears no effort, no degree of violence in them, and that striking diversity of colors which seems to strive, one above another, for the mastery, as it were, has all the appearance of nature in his pictures, though really an effect of the most bold and arduous art. A white dress, placed near a naked figure, gives it all the appearance of being mingled with the warmest crimson, while he employed nothing beyond simple terra rossa, with a little lake in the contours, and towards the extremities. Certain objects, in themselves dark and even black, produce a similar effect upon his canvass; and which, besides enlivening the adjacent color, give force to the figures, wrought, as before stated, with gradual middle tints. It is said to have been his favorite maxim, transmitted to us by Boschini, that whoever aspires to become a painter, must make himself acquainted with three colors, and have them ready upon his palette, namely—white, red, and black; and that an artist, while attempting the flesh parts, must not expect to succeed at once, but by repeated application of opposite tints, and impasting of his colors.

"Here I shall subjoin some observations by the Cav. Mengs, who entered so deeply into the Titian manner. He pronounces him the first who, subsequently to the revival of painting, knew how to avail himself of the ideal, as it were, of different colors in his draperies. Before his time, all colors had been applied indifferently, and artists used them in the same manner for the clear and for the obscure. Titian was aware, if indeed he did not acquire this knowledge of Giorgione, that red brings objects nearer to the eye, that yellow retains the rays of light, that azure is a shade, and adapted for deep obscure. Nor was he less intimate with the effects of juicy colors, and was thus enabled to bestow the same degree of grace, clearness of tone, and dignity of color, upon his shades and middle tints, as upon his lights, as well as to mark with great diversity of middle tints, the various complexions and various superficies of bodies. No other artist, likewise, was more accurately acquainted with the mutual power or equipoise of the above three colors, upon which the harmony of pictures so much depends; an equipoise, too, so difficult in practice, to which not even Rubens, however excellent a colorist, perfectly attained.

"Both Titian's inventions and compositions partake of his usual character; he produced nothing in which nature was not consulted. In the number of his figures he is inclined to be moderate; and in grouping them, he displays the finest unshackled art—an art he was fond of exemplifying by comparison with a bunch of grapes, where a number of single ones compose the figure of a whole, agreeably rounded, light through the openings, distinct in shades, in middle tints, and in lights, according as it receives more or less of the solar rays. No contrasts are to be met with in his compositions that betray a studied effect; no violent action that is not called for by the incidents of the story; the actors in general preserve their dignity, and a certain composure, as if each seemed to respect the assembly of which he formed a part. Whoever is attached to the taste of the Greek bassi-rilievi, in which all is nature and propriety, will invariably prefer the sober composition of Titian to the more fiery one of Paul Veronese and Tintoretto. Neither was Titian ignorant of those strong contrasts of limbs and action, then in such high vogue with his countrymen; but these he reserved for his bacchanals, his battle-pieces, and other subjects which called for them.

"It is admitted on all hands that as a portrait painter, he was quite incomparable; and to this species of excellence he was in a great part indebted for his fortune, smoothing, as it did, his reception into some of the most splendid courts of Europe. He was not less successful in depicting the passions of the mind. The Death of S. Pietro Martire, at Venice, and that of a devotee of St. Anthony, at Padua, display scenes than which I know not whether painting can afford us anything more terrific in the ferocity of those who strike, or more full of compassion in the whole attitude of the falling saint. And thus the grand picture of the Coronation of Thorns, in the Grazie at Milan, abounds with powers of expression that enchant us. He has also left us not a few examples of costume, and of erudition in the antique, every way worthy of imitation, as we may observe in the Coronation above mentioned, where, desirous of marking the precise period of the event, he inserted in the Prætorium a bust of Tiberius, an idea that could not have been better conceived either by Raffaello or Poussin. In his architecture, he sometimes availed himself of other works, particularly those of Rosa of Brescia; but his perspectives, like that of his Presentation, are extremely beautiful. He was equalled by none in landscape; and he was careful not to employ it as a mere embellishment, like some artists, who esteem themselves so highly in this particular, that they hardly scruple to present us with cypress trees growing out of the sea. But Titian always makes his landscapes subservient to history, as in that horrific wood, whose dreary aspect adds so much to the solemnity of St. Peter's death; or to give force to his figures, as we perceive in those pieces where the landscape is thrown into the distance. His natural manner of representing the various effects of light, may be best gathered from the Martyrdom of St. Lorenzo, belonging to the Jesuits at Venice, in which he displayed such an astonishing diversity in the splendor of fire, in that of torch-lights, and in that of a supernatural light falling upon the martyr. He likewise expressed, with the utmost felicity, the time of the day in which the event is supposed to have taken place, and he frequently selected night-fall, drawing forth all its most beautiful attributes for the canvass.

"From the whole of this it may be inferred that Titian is not to be included in that class of Venetian artists whose rapidity of hand overpowered their judgment, rendering them somewhat careless and inaccurate; though at the same time we must speak of his celerity with some degree of reservation. A freedom of pencil must doubtless be granted him, and he thus applied it without failing in point of design, to his paintings in fresco, as they are to be seen at Padua, and which in some measure compensate us for the loss of those in the Venetian capital, in which city there is nothing of the same kind preserved, except, perhaps, his St. Christopher in the Ducal palace, a majestic figure, both in character and expression. We are not, however, to look for the same degree of freedom in his oil paintings. Indeed, he was by no means ambitious of displaying it, but rather encountered much painful labor to arrive at a perfect knowledge of his subjects. With this view, after throwing off a rough draught of his intended works, with a certain freedom and resolution, he was in the habit of laying them aside for some time, and again returned to them with an eye prepared to detect the least defect. The noble Casa Barbarigo, among a fine collection of his most highly finished pictures, preserves also a few of these first sketches. It is well known that he underwent extreme labor in the completion of his works, and at the same time he was very solicitous to conceal the pains he bestowed upon them. Yet in some of his pieces, such spirited and resolute strokes of the pencil are to be met with, as seem to imprint upon every object the true character of nature, attain at once the points that have been long laboriously aimed at, and perfectly delight professors. To this practice he adhered in the zenith of his fame; nor was it till near the close of his life, that both his hand and his eyes failing him, his style became less elegant, being compelled to paint with repeated efforts of the brush, and with difficulty mingling his tints. Vasari, who saw him once more in 1566, even then was no longer able to recognize Titian in Titian, and it must have been more difficult in the few following years. Yet, as is customary with old age, he was not at all aware of his failings, and continued to receive commissions to the last year of his life. There remains at St. Salvatore one of these pictures, of the Annunciation, which attracts the spectator only from the name of the master. Yet when he was told by some one that it was not, or at least did not appear to have been, executed by his hand, he was so much irritated, that in a fit of senile indignation, he seized his pencil and inscribed upon it, "Tizianus fecit fecit." Still the most experienced judges are agreed that much may be learned, even from his latest works, in the same manner as the poets pronounce judgment upon the Odyssey, the product of old age, but still by Homer. Several of these last specimens, distributed throughout private collections, are nevertheless doubtful, as well as some copies made by his pupils, but retouched by his hand; and in particular some Ma donnas and Magdalens which I have seen in various places, displaying little or no variety. Upon this point we ought not to omit the account given by Ridolfi, of his having purposely left his studio open for the free access of his disciples, in order that they might secretly take copies of such pictures as he had placed there; that afterwards, when he found such copies became vendible, he retouched them with little trouble, and passed them for originals. The reporter of this incident added in a marginal note, 'behold what a degree of forecast!' and to this I might rejoin one of my own, 'note that the worth of Titian ought not to be estimated, as is too often the case, by this multiplication of originals.'

"Titian was by no means so excellent a master as an artist. Whether disliking the interruption and tediousness attaching to such a character, or apprehensive of meeting a rival, he was always averse to affording his instructions. He was extremely harsh with Paris Bordone, and even entered into decided hostility against him, an artist who burned with an ambition to resemble him. He banished Tintoretto from his studio, and artfully directed his own brother to mercantile pursuits, though he displayed uncommon talents for painting. 'Hence,' observes Vasari, 'there are few who can really be called his disciples, inasmuch as he taught little; but each learned more or less, according as he knew how to avail himself of the productions of Titian.' This great artist fell a victim to the plague in 1576, when within one year of completing a century."

In forming an estimate of Titian's design, it will be of service to compare the different systems practised by different schools at the time he flourished. The system of the Venetian school was to paint everything from nature without the preparation of a cartoon; this method, though well calculated to give the painter greater promptness of execution, and a more commanding facility of hand, was also the means of introducing a want of correctness in design and purity of forms. On the contrary, the Roman and Florentine painters never painted a picture without having first prepared a model or cartoon, and corrected every figure by the antique. Titian, following the system of his countrymen, painted immediately from nature, and satisfied with its exact imitation, he was little sensible to ideal beauty of form, or to that elevated and dignified expression so essential to the higher order of historical painting. Tintoretto, on being banished from his school, immediately threw this in his teeth, by affixing over his door this inscription, "The coloring of Titian, and the design of Michael Angelo." Sir Joshua Reynolds says, in his Discourses, "Raffaelle and Titian seem to have looked at nature for different purposes; they both had the power of extending their view to the whole; but one looked for the general effect produced by form, the other, as produced by color. We cannot refuse to Titian the merit of attending to the general form of his object as well as color, but his deficiency lay—a deficiency, at least, when compared with Raffaelle—in not possessing the power, like him, of correcting the form of his model by any general idea of beauty in his own mind." In short, it may now be considered an established fact, that Titian justly ranks as the greatest colorist of modern times, but in design he was far inferior to many other painters of the Roman, Florentine, and even of his own school. In fact, he has been accused of occasional anachronisms in his historical works. He neither presents us, like Raffaelle and Poussin, as a faithful historian, the precise locality of the scene, the strict costume of the time or country, nor the accessories best suited to the development of his subject. See *Raffaelle.*

Most writers observe that Titian had four different manners, at as many different periods of his life; first that of Bellini, somewhat stiff and hard, in which he imitated nature, according to Lanzi, with a greater precision than even Albert Durer, so that, "the hairs might be numbered, the skin of the hands, the very pores of the flesh, and the reflection of objects in the pupils seen:" second, an imitation of Giorgione, more bold and full of force; Lanzi says that some of his portraits executed at this time, cannot be distinguished from those of Giorgione: third, his own inimitable style, which he practised from about his thirtieth year; and which was the result of experience, knowledge, and judgment, beautifully natural, and finished with exquisite care: and fourth, the pictures which he painted in his old age. Sandrart says that, "at first he labored his pictures highly, and gave them a polished beauty and lustre, so as to produce their effect full as well when they were examined closely, as when viewed at a distance; but afterwards, he so managed his penciling that their greatest force and beauty appeared at a more remote view, and they pleased less when they were beheld more nearly; so that many of those artists who studied to imitate him, being misled by appearances which they did not sufficiently consider, imagined that Titian executed his work with readiness and masterly rapidity; and concluded that they should imitate his manner most effectually by a freedom of hand and a bold pencil; whereas Titian in reality took abundance of pains to work up his pictures to so high a degree of perfection, and the freedom that appears in the handling was entirely effected by a skillful combination of labor and judgment, and a few bold, artful strokes of the pencil to conceal his labor."

The works of Titian, though many of his greatest productions were destroyed by terrible conflagrations at Venice and Madrid, are numerous, scattered throughout Europe, in all the royal collections, and the most celebrated public galleries, particularly at Venice, Rome, Bologna, Milan, Florence, Vienna, Dresden, Paris, London, and Madrid. The most numerous are portraits, Madonnas, Magdalens, bacchanals, Venuses, and other mythological subjects, some of which are extremely voluptuous. Two of his grandest and most celebrated works are the Last Supper in the Escurial, and Christ crowned with Thorns at Milan. It is said that the works of Titian, to be appreciated, should be seen at Venice or Madrid, as many claimed to be genuine elsewhere are of very doubtful authenticity. He painted many of his best works for the Spanish court, first for the Emperor Charles V., and next for his successor, Philip II., who is known to have given him numerous commissions to decorate the Escurial and the royal palaces at Madrid. Palomino reports that when the palace of the Prado was burned, the king on learning the disaster, earnestly demanded if the Titian Venus had escaped, and on being told that it was one of the few that had been saved, he exclaimed, "then every other loss may be supported." There are numerous duplicates of some of his works, considered genuine, some of which he is supposed to have made himself, and others to have been carefully copied by his pupils and retouched by himself; he frequently made some slight alterations in the backgrounds, to give them more of the look of originals; thus the original of his Christ and the Pharisees, or the Tribute Money, is now in the Dresden Gallery, yet Lanzi says there are numerous copies in Italy, one of which he saw at St. Saverio di Rimini, inscribed with his name, which is believed to be a duplicate rather than a copy. There are more than six hundred engravings from his pictures, including both copper-plates and wooden cuts. He is said to have engraved both on wood and copper himself, but Bartsch considers all the prints attributed to him as spurious, though a few of them are signed with his name, only eight of which he describes. There are two of his works in the English National Gallery, namely, the Bacchus and Ariadne, and the Rape of Ganymede; the Gallery of the Louvre boasts about twenty of his compositions, including portraits. Although Titian spent much time abroad, he was exceedingly attached to Venice, where he lived in great splendor, and maintained the rank due to his genius and reputation. For the lives of Titian's son, brother, and relatives, see *Vecelli*.

TITO, Pompilio, an Italian engraver, who flourished at Rome, according to Prof. Christ, about 1685, and marked his plates with the initials P. T., and the date. He does not specify any of his prints.

TIVOLI, Rosa da. See Roos.

TIZIANELLO. See Tiziano Vecelli.

TIZIANO Il. See Girolamo Dante.

TIZIANO, Marco di. See Marco Vecelli.

TOBAR, Don Alonso Miguel de, an eminent Spanish painter, born at Higuera, near Aracena, in 1678. According to Bermudez, he went to Seville, and studied with Juan Antonio Faxardo, a painter of little note. He afterwards diligently studied and copied the works of Murillo, and became so exact an imitator of his style, in composition, heads, expression, coloring, handling, and every other peculiarity, that not only his copies, but his own compositions, have frequently been attributed to that master. One of his most celebrated copies is in the church of Santa Maria la Blanca at Seville, representing the Virgin, St. Joseph, and the Infant Jesus and St. John, which was considered a genuine production by Murillo till it was discovered that the original was in the Royal Palace at Madrid. In the church of S. Isidora at Seville, are two pictures representing the Good Shepherd and the Infant St. John, which Stanley says "are copies by him with variations, of the two originals by Murillo, so well known in England, formerly in the collection of Sir Simon Clarke, but now in those of the Baroness Rothschild, and the National Gallery." Probably the fathers of St. Isidora would dispute this assertion. It is said that he copied many of the easel pictures of Murillo, and that many of them, even in his time, were passed for originals. Of his original compositions, the most deserving of notice are the Virgin enthroned, holding the Infant in her lap, attended by Sts. Francisco and Antonio, called Our Lady of Consolation, in the cathedral of Seville, and the Divine Shepherdess, in the Queen of Spain's gallery, in which the Virgin is represented as a shepherdess feeding lambs with roses. He excelled in portraits, and painted many of the most distinguished personages of his time. In 1729 he succeeded Teodoro Ardemans as painter to Philip V., when he removed to Madrid, where he practised his profession with great distinction till his death in 1758.

TOBIN, J., an English artist, who flourished about 1770. He etched some plates of landscapes, and executed some tinted plates after Both, Ostade, and other masters.

TOCQUÉ, Jean Louis, a French painter, born at Paris in 1696. He first studied under Nicholas Bertin, and afterwards with Hyacinth Rigaud. He acquired distinction as a portrait painter, was made a member of the Academy at Paris, and invited by the Empress Elizabeth, to the court of St. Petersburg, where he met with the most flattering encouragement. The Empress appointed him her painter, and he painted her portrait and those of the most distinguished personages of her court. He died in 1772.

TOEPUT, Louis, a Flemish painter, born at Mechlin in 1550. According to Descamps, he went young to Italy, where he passed the rest of his life. He was a versatile artist, and particularly excelled in landscape; he also painted Italian fairs, markets, and similar subjects, which were well designed, spiritedly touched, and finely colored. He was called in Italy *Lodovico di Trevigi*, after the place where he chiefly resided. He was living in 1604.

TOGNONE, Antonio, called also Antonio da Vicenza, a painter of Vicenza, who studied with Zelotti. He is highly commended by Ridolfi for his uncommon talents, but he died in the flower of his life. There are several frescos by him in the churches at Vicenza.

TOL, Dominick van, was the nephew and disciple of Gerard Douw, and one of the most successful imitators of his style and subjects. He copied some of the works of his uncle so closely, that they might easily be mistaken for the originals, by the inexperienced. Stanley says that some of these copies, under his own name, have brought at public sale in England, prices varying from £150 to £350 sterling. He was not so successful in his original compositions, though some of his interiors, conversations, and domestic subjects, are highly wrought up and well colored. He was living in 1680. The Dutch writers mention *David* and *Peter* van Tol, but they are doubtless identical with Dominick, as he seems to be called by some simply van Tol, and by others, variously, Dominick, David, and Peter van Tol, the same history being applied to each.

TOLEDO, Juan de, a Spanish painter, born at Lorca, in Murcia, in 1611. According to Palomino, he was the son of Miguel de Toledo, an obscure artist, who instructed him in the rudiments of the art. Bermudez however says that he served in the army in his youth, distinguished himself for his gallantry, and was made a captain of dragoons. He went to Italy, and first studied under Aniello Falcone at Naples, afterwards proceeding to Rome, where he became the disciple and friend of Angelo Cerquozzi, called delle Battaglie.

On his return to Spain, he established himself at Granada, where he distinguished himself as a painter of battles and sea-fights, executed in the manner of Cerquozzi. His small easel pictures are numerous, spiritedly executed, and highly esteemed. He also painted history, and there are some of his works in the churches at Granada, Murcia, Madrid, and Alcalá de Henares, the most esteemed of which is the Assumption of the Virgin, in the Colegio de San Esteban at Murcia, and the Conception, in the church of las Monjas, at Madrid. He was not so successful in his sacred subjects as in his battle-pieces. He died in 1665.

TOLEDO. See GIOVANNI BATTISTA.

TOLMEZZO, DOMENICO DI, a painter of Udine, who flourished in the latter part of the 15th century. There is an altar-piece painted in several compartments, and a picture of the Madonna, in the cathedral of that city, signed with his name, and dated 1479. Lanzi says they are executed so much in the Venetian style, that one might believe him to have been a disciple of that school.

TOLOSANO. See JEAN BARON.

TOMBE, NICHOLAS LA, a Dutch painter, born at Amsterdam in 1616. It is not known under whom he studied, but he went young to Italy, and passed several years at Rome, diligently studying nature, and designing after the beautiful remains of antiquity which abound in that city and its environs. He painted landscapes and architectural pieces, but his usual subjects were conversations and assemblies of both sexes habited in the Italian costume. He was fond of introducing into his designs the ruins and remains of ancient edifices, caves, grottos, and antique sepulchres, whenever his subject would admit of them. His situations are agreeably chosen, his distances recede with a pleasing degradation, his coloring is lively, his pencil free and spirited, and he decorated his pictures with numerous small figures, correctly designed and spiritedly touched. He also painted small portraits with success. On returning to his own country, he settled at Amsterdam, where he acquired considerable reputation and employment. He died there in 1676.

TOMKINS, PELTRO WILLIAM, an English engraver, born at London, in 1760. He studied under Bartolozzi, whose manner he followed with distinction. He engraved several plates of portraits and other subjects, after the eminent English painters of his time, but his best plates are those he executed for the publications, entitled "The British Gallery of Pictures," being a selection of the choicest pictures of the old Dutch and Italian masters in the possession of the English nobility and gentry; and that of the "Stafford Gallery." Some of these were printed in colors, and for beauty and delicacy of tint, are almost equal to highly finished drawings. He also engraved the illustrations for a splendid edition of "Thomson's Seasons," and other similar publications. His prints are beautifully and tastefully executed in the chalk and dotted manner. He died in 1840.

TOMKINS, WILLIAM, an English landscape painter, born in London about 1730. He was much employed in painting views of gentlemen's seats in England. His principal patron was the Earl of Fife, for whom he painted several views of his estate in Scotland. He also copied some of the landscapes of Hobbema, and other Dutch painters. In 1763, he obtained the second prize of twenty-five guineas for a landscape from the Society for the Encouragement of Arts, &c., and on the institution of the Royal Academy, he was elected an Associate. He died in 1792. He had two sons who were reputable painters in the same line.

TOMMAZI, TOMMASO, a fresco painter, born at Pietra Santa, who flourished about the middle of the 18th century. He was a scholar of the Melani. Lanzi says he was a man of vast conceptions, worthy of his masters, whom he succeeded, after their death, in several important commissions. One of his finest works is the ceiling of the church of S. Giovanni in Pisa.

TOMOLIUS, LUCA, an Italian engraver, whose name is affixed to a small portrait of F. Lælius Contesino, executed with the graver in a coarse style.

TOMS, W. H., an English engraver of little note, who flourished about 1740. He engraved several views and architectural subjects, a few portraits, and some book plates, indifferently executed.

TOMS, PETER, an English painter, supposed to have been a son of the preceding. He studied under Hudson, was elected one of the first forty Royal Academicians, and held a situation in the Herald's Office. His chief excellence lay in his drapery, for which reason he was much employed in that department by Sir Joshua Reynolds. He went to Dublin, to practise portrait painting, but not meeting with any success, he put an end to his life, in a fit of despondency, in 1776.

TONDUZZI, GIULIO, a painter born at Faenza, who flourished in the first half of the 16th century. He was a pupil of Giulio Romano, whose style he followed with distinction. There is a fine picture by him, the Stoning of St. Stephen, in the church of S. Giovanni at Faenza, which has been attributed by some to his master; and another large altar-piece of the same subject, in the church of S. Stefano at Ravenna. He executed several works for the churches and public edifices of his native city, in competition with all the most distinguished artists of Faenza, who flourished at that time.

TONELLI, GIUSEPPE, a painter born at Florence, who flourished from about 1668 to 1718. He first studied with Jacopo Chiavistelli in his native city, and then went to Bologna, and became the disciple of Tommaso Aldrovandini. He acquired considerable distinction as a painter of perspective and architecture, and was employed in decorating several of the churches and public edifices at Florence and elsewhere.

TONI, MICHAEL ANGELO, a painter born at Bologna in 1640, and died there in 1708. He acquired considerable reputation for his copies and imitations of the great Italian masters, painted in small, for which he had a happy talent.

TONNO, a Sicilian painter, born in Calabria. According to Hackert, he was originally a servant to Polidoro da Caravaggio, who, perceiving in him a genius for painting, instructed him in the art. He painted a picture representing the Epiphany, in the church of S. Andrea, at Messina, in which he introduced the portrait of his master, and which evinces uncommon talent. His name is rendered infamous by the foulest ingratitude.

and the blackest crime—he murdered his benefactor to possess himself of his money, and was executed in 1543.

TOORNVLIET, James, a Dutch painter, born at Leyden in 1641. It is not known under whom he studied, but after acquiring considerable reputation as a portrait painter, he was induced to accompany his friend Nicholas Rosendael to Italy in 1670. On his arrival at Rome, he was inspired by a desire to distinguish himself as a painter of history. He made the works of Raffaelle his model in design, and studied them with enthusiasm. He next proceeded to Venice, where he was equally assiduous in contemplating the works of Titian, Tintoretto, and Veronese. After a residence of six years in Italy, he returned to his native city, where he commenced his new career with the most sanguine expectations; but he was sadly disappointed, for though he wrought in the Italian style, designed correctly, and colored sweetly, his works were not agreeable to his countrymen, so that he was obliged to return to portraiture. He frequently painted family groups in conversation, in which he was remarkable for judicious disposition of his figures, correctness of design, and agreeable style of coloring. His name is sometimes erroneously written *Torenfliet*. He died in 1719.

TOPINO-LEBRUN, François Jean Baptiste, a French historical painter, was born at Marseilles in 1769. His first master is not mentioned, but he visited Rome, and studied painting for some time. He there formed an intimacy with David, imbibing his political opinions; and on returning to Paris, he entered the school of that master. He made excellent progress until the Revolution broke out, and then, like his instructor, forsook the easel for the stormy career of politics and violence. His operations for several years after, are a matter of French political history; but in 1797 he resumed the pencil for a short time, and produced his admirable picture of the Death of Caius Gracchus, which gained a prize at the exhibition, and was purchased by government for the Museum of Marseilles. He subsequently figured among the Jacobins, and in 1800, when the conspiracy against Bonaparte's life was discovered, he was accused and condemned to death, but probably unjustly, since the Biographie Universelle states that all the charges against him were reduced to a single one, namely that the sculptor Ceracchi had previously said that Topino possessed a poniard intended to kill the First Consul; and Ceracchi, when brought before the judges, revoked his declaration. The career of the accused, however, marked him as dangerous to the ambition of Bonaparte, and he accordingly suffered death in the year 1801. His large picture of the Siege of Lacedæmon, he did not live to complete.

TORBIDO, Francesco, called Il Moro, a painter generally stated to have been born at Verona, about 1500, Zani says in 1504; but he was probably born earlier, as it is agreed that he studied a short time with Giorgione, who died in 1511. He afterwards became the pupil of Liberale da Verona. Lanzi says he was a distinguished follower of the tints of Giorgione, and a true imitator of the diligence and design of Liberale, and that he was deficient in nothing, except perhaps we could wish to see somewhat greater freedom of hand. He was a severe critic upon himself, and spared no labor to perfect his works in every part, hence they are very rare. He painted a few altar-pieces and other pictures for the churches, the most remarkable of which are several frescos representing the Life of the Virgin, and the best of these is the Assumption, which Lanzi pronounces truly admirable; but the designs are not his, Giulio Romano having prepared for him the cartoons. There is an admired picture by him in the church of S. Maria Maggiore at Venice, representing the Transfiguration. His easel pictures of sacred subjects are more frequently to be met with in the collections at Verona and Venice. He also excelled in portraits. He finished all his works with extraordinary neatness and precision, was one of the best colorists of his time, and had an excellent knowledge of the chiaro-scuro. He lived to a great age, and died about 1581, though the accounts are contradictory on this point; Fuseli says he died in 1522, aged 82 years, a palpable error, as Giulio Romano would have been only 32 at his death. Others say he died in or about 1581, aged 81.

TORELLI, Cesare, a Roman painter, who studied under Giovanni de' Vecchi, and was one of the numerous artists employed in the Vatican in the pontificate of Sixtus V., about 1585. Lanzi briefly notices him as a second class artist. He executed several works in fresco in the Vatican, in the Scala Santa, and in St. John of Lateran. There are two sibyls by him, larger than life, in the church of La Madonna del Orto, which are considered his finest works. He also wrought in mosaic. He died in 1615.

TORELLI, Felice, a painter born at Verona, according to Zanotti, in 1667, or to Zani in 1670. He first studied under Santo Prunato in his native city, and afterwards with Gio Gioseffo dal Sole at Bologna. Lanzi says he followed the style of Prunato in a great measure. He became a painter of strong character, fine chiaro-scuro, and no common merit in oil paintings for altars, which are to be found at Rome, Milan, Turin, and other cities of Italy. The most celebrated is one at the Dominicans of Faenza, representing St. Vincenzio casting out a demon from a female possessed. He died the 12th June, 1748.

TORELLI, Lucia, was the wife of the preceding, born at Bologna, according to Crespi, in 1677, and died in 1762. Her maiden name was Casalini. She painted some altar-pieces for the churches, but her chief excellence lay in portraits, in which branch she gained so much distinction, that her portrait was placed among those of celebrated artists in the Florentine gallery.

TORELLI, or TONELLI, Maestro. According to Ratti, he was a native of Milan and a pupil of Correggio, whom he assisted in some of his works. Lanzi says that in conjunction with Rondani he painted the frieze at San Giovanni in Parma, from the designs of Correggio, and adorned the first cloister in the same monastery with singular felicity.

TORELLI, Giacomo, an Italian architect, was born at Fano in 1608. He first gained considerable reputation in theatrical architecture, and invented a variety of scenic machines at Venice, and elsewhere, which were greatly admired. He visited Paris, where his talents gained him the favor of Louis XIV., and he was engaged as royal architect and machinist. He erected the famous theatre Le Petit Bourbon, and evinced so many novel and ingenious ideas in this and many other works, that he acquired fame and fortune. Having married Madame de Suez, a lady of noble birth, Torelli returned to Italy in 1662, and erected the theatre of Fortune at Fano, greatly admired for the size of its scenery, and the elegance of its architecture. Among his other works, was the Santa Casa at Fano, after the model of that at Loreto, presented by him to his native city. The King of France sent him repeated invitations to erect a theatre at Versailles, and other buildings; but he died in 1678, without performing the commission.

TORENBURG, Gerard, a Dutch painter, born at Amsterdam in 1737. He first studied under J. Ten Compe, and afterwards with C. Pronck. He painted landscapes and views of cities in the style of his instructor with considerable reputation. His drawings are also held in high estimation. There is a fine picture by him, in the Museum at the Hague, representing a View on the Amstel, near Amsterdam. He died at Nykerk, in 1785.

TORESANI, Andrea, a painter born at Brescia about 1727. Lanzi says he painted some pictures for the churches of his native city, of Venice, and Milan. "His chief merit, however, lay in an inferior branch, that of painting animals, sea views, and landscapes, in the Titian manner, often accompanied by figures in tolerably good taste." He died in 1760.

TORNIOLI, Niccolo, a painter of Siena, who flourished, according to Malvasia, about 1640. He resided some time at Bologna, where he painted two pictures for the church of S. Paolo, representing Jacob wrestling with the Angel, and the Death of Abel. He had a method of painting, or rather staining marble, with some chemical preparation, which struck into the stone, so that by sawing it in slabs, he duplicated his works, as is done in modern mosaic work.

TORRE, Bartolomeo, a painter of Arezzo, who flourished about 1600. According to Orlandi, he was much employed in decorating the houses and halls of the principal citizens of Arezzo and other places in its vicinity, with fresco histories, which he praises for the excellence of their coloring. He was assisted by his pupil Teofilo Aretini Torre.

TORRE, Flaminio, called Dagli Ancinelli, a painter born at Bologna in 1621, and died in 1661. He first studied under Jacopo Cavedone, next with Guido Reni, and afterwards with Simone Cantarini. His chief talent consisted in an easy and perfect imitation of every style. He copied the works of the most distinguished masters with such precision, that it was difficult to distinguish them from the originals, and he received a higher price for his copies, than many eminent artists could obtain for their productions. Though not learned in the theory of art, he painted some original compositions, designed in the manner of Cantarini, but colored more in the style of Guido. He was employed for some time at Modena as court painter, and executed some works for the churches at Bologna, the best of which is a Deposition from the Cross in S. Giorgio. He also painted some works for the collections, which Lanzi says are in better preservation than his church pictures, which he injured by an excessive use of rock oil. He executed some spirited etchings. Bartsch describes seven prints by him which he says are in great request among connoisseurs, being engraved with a fine point, in the taste of a designer who was consummate in his art, approaching the manner of Cantarini.—They are as follows:

1. Samson; *after Guido.* 2. The Virgin, accompanied by the infant Jesus and St. John; *his own design;* dated 1639. 3. The Virgin, with St. Jerome and St. Francis; *after Lodovico Caracci.* 4. The Virgin and patron Saints of Bologna; *after Guido.* 5. St. John the Evangelist; *from his own design;* signed F. T. F. 6. Three Children bearing a Plateau, on which are two vases and a glass; signed G. R. T. 7. Pan conquered by Love; *after Agos. Caracci.*

TORRE, Gio. Battista della, a painter born at Rovigo, and a disciple of Carlo Bononi. He painted history in the style of his master. Lanzi says he was a man of genius, and his works are held in high estimation in the collections at Ferrara, where he chiefly resided. He died young in 1631.

TORRE, Giovanni Paolo della, a painter born at Rome. According to Baglioni, he was at first an amateur, and a pupil of Girolamo Muziano, but he showed such talents, and attained such proficiency, that he was employed by Cesare Nebbia to assist in the great works in the Vatican, and other places. See *Nebbia.*

TORREGIANI, Bartolomeo, a Roman painter, who studied under Salvator Rosa. Lanzi says he excelled in landscape, but failed in his figures; therefore he usually employed some other artist to assist him in his pictures. He died young, according to Passeri, about 1673.

TORRIGIANO, Pietro, an eminent Italian sculptor, was born at Florence about 1472. He studied the antiquities in the gardens of Lorenzo the Magnificent, in company with Michael Angelo, but becoming jealous of the rising distinction of the latter, he one day assaulted him, and inflicted so severe a blow upon his nose, as to crush and disfigure that feature for life. Being obliged to quit Florence in consequence, Torrigiano went to Rome, where he was employed by Pope Alexander VI.; but he afterwards threw up his profession, and enlisted as a soldier, first under the Duke Valentino in Romagna, next under Vitelli and Piero de' Medici. According to the accounts of Vasari and Cellini, he was well suited to his new profession, being a large, handsome, and powerful man, gifted with great audacity, with more the air of a rough soldier than of an artist. But though he gained distinction by his prowess, and was promoted to the rank of an ensign, he entertained little expectation of rising higher, and accordingly returned to his original profession. He executed several bronze figures for some Florentine merchants, whom he accompanied to England. Having gained the favor of Henry VIII., he was employed in a variety of works, particularly the tomb of Henry VII., in Westminster Abbey, completed in 1519, for which he received the sum of £1,000. The tomb of Margaret, Countess of Richmond, in Henry VII.'s chapel, is also supposed to have been executed by him. While engaged upon Henry's tomb, he returned to Italy to procure assistants, and endeavored to prevail upon Benvenuto Cellini to accompany him; but the latter declares that he was so disgusted with Torrigiano, upon learning from him how brutally he had treated Michael Angelo, that he could not endure the sight of him.

After finally quitting England in 1519, Torrigiano visited Spain, where he executed several pieces of sculpture for convents, &c., and among others, a group of the Virgin and Infant, so beautiful that the Duke d'Arcos commissioned him to make a copy of it, at the same time promising a liberal recompense. When the work was finished, the Duke sent him two servants, bearing two bags of maravedis; but Torrigiano, on ascertaining that the vast heap of copper coin amounted to only thirty ducats, was so highly exasperated that he seized a mallet, and shivered his beautiful work into a thousand pieces. The Duke, filled with rage and shame, immediately accused him to the dreaded Inquisition, as a sacrilegious heretic, who had impiously destroyed a figure of the Holy Virgin. The unfortunate sculptor was accordingly condemned by that tribunal, but avoided the ignominious end which awaited him, by starving himself in the dungeon. Thus perished, in 1522, an artist of more than ordinary talent—a victim to the malice of an infamous noble, and the mercilessness of a most odious and sanguinary tribunal.

TORRENTIUS, John. There is considerable discrepancy about this artist; but the following is condensed from Houbraken, who obtained his information from authentic accounts at Haerlem, where Torrentius was born in 1589. It is not known under whom he studied, but he excelled in painting conversations, domestic subjects, and still-life, which were so admirably designed, exquisitely finished, and delicately colored, that they were eagerly sought after. While he continued to paint these subjects, he lived in affluence, and was highly respected. At length he became exceedingly licentious, was a leader in the infamous sect called *Adamites*, and prostituted his pencil to the most lascivious and indecent subjects. He was at length arrested, condemned to the torture, and finally sentenced to twenty years' imprisonment, and his obscene pictures to be burnt by the executioner. He was subsequently released, at the instigation of the English ambassador, when he went to London, but the profligacy of his conduct soon brought him into disrepute, and he returned to Holland, and died at Amsterdam in 1640, in obscurity and misery. Sandrart and others say that he was born at Amsterdam, and died under the torture in 1640.

TORRES, Clemente de, a Spanish painter, born at Seville in 1665. According to Palomino, he was a disciple of Don Juan de Valdes. He acquired considerable reputation, and executed many works, both in oil and fresco, for the churches and monasteries at Seville and other places, besides many easel pictures for the collections. He went to Madrid in 1724, where he formed an acquaintance with Palomino, whom he praised in a sonnet, and the latter returned the compliment by describing him as a distinguished painter and a laurelled scholar of the Muses. He afterwards went to Cadiz, where he died in 1730. It is said that he was a skillful draughtsman, and that his drawings so strongly resemble those of Murillo as to pass for the productions of that master.

TORRES, Matias de, a Spanish painter, born at Espinosa de los Monteros, in 1631. No correct opinion can be formed of his style or merits from the bombastic account of his biographer. He studied first with his uncle, an obscure painter at Madrid; next in the Academy; and afterwards received lessons in coloring from the younger Herrera. He executed several works for the churches and convents at Madrid, in which he attempted to emulate the daring style of Caravaggio, but missing his principles, he produced little more than blackness and obscurity. He, however, succeeded better in his easel pictures of landscapes and battle-pieces, executed in a free and graceful manner. "He challenged the arrogant Bocanegra to a trial of skill in any public place, the subjects to be selected by the spectators; but that boaster, after accepting the challenge, was fearful of the encounter, and slunk away from Madrid." He died in the public hospital in 1711. Stanley says there are some of his pictures in the Hermitage at St. Petersburg.

TORRI, or TORRE, Pietro Antonio, a Bolognese painter, who studied under Francesco Albano. According to Malvasia, he distinguished himself as an architectural and perspective painter, and executed some works, in conjunction with other artists, for the churches and public edifices at Bologna, Venice, and other places. In the Guide to Venice, he is called Torrigli. In the church of S. Giuseppe, in the latter city, in conjuuction with Ricchi, he executed some frescos, in which he painted the architectural parts, and the latter the figures.

TORRICELLI, or TORRICELLA, Il. See Buonfanti.

TORTEBAT, François, a French painter and engraver, born at Paris in 1610, though some say in 1600, and 1626. He studied under Simon Vouet, whose daughter he married. He was an excellent painter of portraits, to which branch he chiefly devoted his talents. He etched a few spirited plates, after the works of Vouet, and from his own designs. Dumesnil describes twenty-five, twelve of which are anatomical plates. He died in 1690.

TORTEBAT, Jean, was the son of the preceding, born at Paris in 1652, and died in 1718. He studied with his father, and was a good painter of portraits.

TORTELLI, Gioseffo, a painter born at Brescia, who, according to Orlandi, was a disciple of Francesco Paglia, whose style he followed. He painted easel pictures of historical subjects for the collections, in a very spirited manner, designed and colored in the Venetian style.

TORTIROLI, Gio. Battista, a painter of Cremona, who flourished in the first part of the 17th century. He studied with Andrea Mainardi in his native city; afterwards proceeded to Rome, and thence to Venice, where Lanzi says he formed a style which partakes most of that of the younger Palma, with an evident imitation of Raffaelle. He executed some works for the churches at Venice, the best of which is the Murder of the Innocents in S. Domenico. He possessed excellent abilities but died young. Zaist says he was born in 1621 and died aged 30; but Lanzi thinks he must have been born earlier, as he painted well in 1632.

TORTOREL, Jean. See Jacques Perisin.

TOSS, J. The name of this artist is affixed t

a spirited etching of the Adoration of the Shepherds, *after C. Hochfield.*

TOSSICANI, Giovanni, an old painter of Arezzo, who was a disciple of Giottino. He was an eminent artist in his time, and was employed in painting for the churches at Pisa, and over all Tuscany. His works have mostly perished; but his St. Philip and St. James still remain on the baptismal font in the church dedicated to those Saints at Arezzo. Lanzi says, "with him perished the best branch of the stock of Giotto."

TOURNIER, Robert, a distinguished French painter, was born at Caen in Normandy, in 1676. After acquiring the elements of the art under Lucas de la Haye, a Carmelite friar, he visited Paris, and entered the school of Bon Boullongne. He practised the art with success for many years, and painted history and portraits, but generally preferred to exercise his talents upon smaller subjects, following the styles of Gerard Douw and Godfrey Schalcken. He was patronized by several persons of distinction, whose portraits he painted, particularly the regent Duke of Orleans, who took delight in seeing him paint. Tournier was chosen a member of the Academy in 1721, and professor in 1735. He painted several pictures for the churches, and some of his portraits and other works have been engraved by Chereau, Drevet, Sarrabat, Daullé, and others. Late in life, Tournier returned to his native place, where he died in 1752. Some writers notice him under the name of *Tourniere*, and *Tournieres*. There was also an engraver of this name, a native of Toulouse, who studied in Italy under Moses Valentin. He followed the style of his instructor for some time, and etched several plates after Guido, and Polidoro da Caravaggio.

TOWNLEY, Charles, an English engraver in mezzotinto, who flourished in the last part of the 18th, and first part of the present century. He engraved some plates of portraits and other subjects, from his own designs, and after other masters, among which are Leonardo da Vinci, Annibale Caracci, Domenichino, Peter Paul Rubens, and Rembrandt.

TOZZO, Giovanni del, a painter of Siena, who flourished about 1530. He was a cotemporary of Marco Bigio, and Lanzi says that they had such an extraordinary similarity of style that it is not easy to distinguish their respective performances. They both painted histories with small figures.

TRABALLESI, Francesco, a Florentine painter, who, according to Baglioni, was a pupil of Ridolfo del Ghirlandaio, and flourished at Rome in the pontificate of Gregory XIII., who employed him in the Chiesa de' Greci (Greek church), which he had founded, where he painted two altar-pieces, representing the Annunciation, and Christ disputing with the Doctors. He died young. He had a brother, named Bartolomeo, who painted the fable of Danaë on the writing desk in the same edifice, and afterwards became the assistant of Vasari.

TRABALLESI, Giulio, an Italian designer and engraver, born at Florence about 1728. He made the greater part of the designs for the collection of portraits of the Illustrious Men of Florence, engraved by Allegrini and others. He executed some spirited etchings after the Caracci, Guido, Cavedone, F. Brizzio, and other eminent painters. He was living in 1808.

TRAINI, Francesco, a Florentine painter, who was the most distinguished disciple of Andrea Orcagna. He flourished in the latter part of the 14th century, perhaps as late as 1400, or even later. He could not have painted in 1341, as Orcagna was born, according to Vasari, in 1329, and died in 1389. He was far superior to his master as a painter, which is shown by his picture of St. Thomas Aquinas, in the church of S. Caterina at Pisa. It is a large composition, and the Saint stands in the middle of the picture, under the Redeemer, who sheds a glory on the Evangelists and him; and from them, the rays are scattered on a crowd of listeners, composed of popes, cardinals, bishops, doctors, and clergy. Arius and other innovators are at the feet of the Saint, as if vanquished by his divine doctrine; and near him appear Plato and Aristotle, with their volumes open—a circumstance not to be commended in such a subject. Lanzi says that though it exhibits little skill in grouping or knowledge of relief, abounding in attitudes too tame or too constrained, yet it pleases by a marked expression in the countenances, an air of the antique in the draperies, and a certain novelty in composition. Rosini has given a print of this picture in his "Storia della Pittura Italiana," plate 20. There are no other authentic works by Traini remaining. His name is sometimes written *Triano* and *Triani.*

TRAMAZZINO, Francesco, an Italian engraver, who flourished about 1561. Florent le Comte mentions a rare print by him, representing a solemn Entry into the city of Rome.

TRAMULLES, Francisco, a Spanish painter, born at Barcelona about the commencement of the 18th century. He was the son of a sculptor, who was employed in the Cathedral of Perpignan. He first studied under Don Antonio Viladomat, in his native city, and afterwards went to Paris, and from thence to Madrid, in each of which places he resided some time. In his style, he made the works of Luca Giordano his model, which he found at Madrid. On his return to Barcelona, he opened an academy, and had a great number of scholars. He executed some works for the churches and convents at Barcelona and Gerona, and others for the Cathedral of Perpignan, which gained him considerable reputation. He died at Barcelona in the 56th year of his age.

TRAMULLES, Manuel, was the younger brother of the preceding, born at Barcelona in 1715. He practised both painting and sculpture. He studied painting under Viladomat, whose manner he at first imitated so closely that their works may be confounded. He afterwards adopted a style of his own, which was less agreeable in point of coloring. Like his brother, he opened a school, to study from the living model, which was much frequented. He decorated the Opera House, and the Chapter of Barcelona commissioned him to paint six pictures for the sanctuary in which repose the ashes of St. Olegario; also a large picture, with many figures, representing Charles III. taking possession of the Canon's stall in the Cathedral, which pertains to the kings of Spain. He also distinguished himself by his perspectives, in the church of Santa Maria del Mar; and his monuments in Santa Semana de S. Pedro de las Puellas. His principal works are in the churches and convents at Barcelona, but there are a few in those of Tarragona and Gerona. He died in 1791.

TRASI, Lodovico, a painter born at Ascoli, in 1634. He was for several years a fellow pupil of Carlo Maratti, under Andrea Sacchi at Rome. He afterwards became the disciple of Maratti himself, and after frequenting his Academy for some time, he returned to Ascoli, where he executed a great number of works, both for the churches and for individuals, in various styles. In his easel pictures he emulated Maratti, and in his frescos and altar-pieces, he adopted the less labored and more spirited manner of Sacchi, in which Lanzi says we may discover traces of that of Cortona. Such are his fine pictures of St. Nicholas and the Enfranchisement of a Christian youth from servitude, in the church of S. Cristoforo. There are some remarkable pictures by him in the Cathedral, painted in distemper, particularly that of the Martyrdom of St. Emidio. He died in 1694.

TRAVERSE, Charles François de la, a French painter, born at Paris, was a scholar of Boucher. He gained the grand prize in the Academy, which entitled him to go to Rome with a pension from the crown, where he passed six years. He afterwards went to Naples to explore the excavations at Herculaneum. He next accompanied the Marquis D'Osson to Madrid, where he resided many years, and obtained considerable employment in painting small pictures of landscapes and flower-pieces. He afterwards returned to Paris, where he continued to practice his profession with reputation till his death, in 1778.

TRAVI, Antonio, a painter born at Sestri, in the State of Genoa, in 1613. When a boy, he was employed as a color-grinder in the studio of Bernardo Strozzi, who, perceiving in him a genius for painting, gave him lessons, and his taste inclining to landscape, he procured for him the instruction of his friend, Godfrey de Waal. Lanzi says he soon emulated both his instructors. From Waal, he learned the art of painting landscapes. with buildings in perspective and ruins, and from Strozzi to decorate them with spirited figures. He afterwards copied from nature, the beautiful country of the Riviera, with avenues of trees, rich fields, and fine orchards, which he embellished with beautiful and spirited figures, not so much painted as sketched by a few bold strokes of a master's pencil, to gratify the eye when viewed at a little distance. Although his pictures are not highly finished, they please us by their agreeable disposition, and degradation of distances; by their azure skies, the verdure of the trees, and their freedom of touch. Lanzi says his pictures abound in the State, and are found in all the best collections; but there are many bearing his name which were executed by his son Antonio, and are very inferior to his own productions. He is generally called Il Sestri, or Il Sordo di Sestri, on account of his deafness. He died in 1668.

TREBATTI, Paolo Ponzio, a Florentine sculptor, who flourished in the first half of the 16th century. He is said to have studied under Michael Angelo, and afterwards visited France, where he passed the greater part of his life. Vasari, in his life of Primaticcio, says that Trebatti was employed to execute many figures in stucco, in high relief, for the palace at Fontainbleau. There is much contradiction among various writers, as to the dates of his birth and death, and the authenticity of some of his works; but the researches of Sauval (*Antiq. de Paris*), have indicated him as the artist of several sculptures now deposited in the Musée d'Angoulême. Among them are the bronze tomb of Alberto Pio da Carpi, with a reclining figure of that prince, in high relief, executed in 1535, and evincing considerable ability. The monuments of Charles de Magny and André Blondel de Roquancourt, in the same museum, are likewise attributed to him, although their authorship is not certain. Trebatti seems to have wrought mostly in concert with other artists, particularly with Jean Goujon, in his works at the Old Louvre. His death is placed with much probability in 1562.

TREMOLLIERE, Pierre Charles, a French painter, born at Chollet in Poitou, in 1703. He went to Paris when young, and became the scholar of J. B. Vanloo, under whom he made remarkable progress. He gained the grand prize at the Academy, and went with the royal pension to Rome, where he studied six years. On his return from Italy, he stopped at Lyons, where he was employed to paint three pictures for the church of the Carmelites, representing the Nativity, the Presentation, and the Adoration of the Magi, which increased his reputation. In 1734 he returned to Paris, and in 1737 was elected a member of the Academy, on which occasion he painted for his reception picture, Ulysses shipwrecked on the Island of Calypso, which was admired. He painted several histories and fabulous subjects for the Hotel de Soubise, and was engaged in preparing a set of cartoons for tapestry for the king, representing the Four Ages of the World, but he died of consumption before their completion, in 1739. Tremolliere was considered one of the most promising artists of his country. He had an extensive genius; his compositions were noble and judicious, his design graceful and correct. He etched a set of studies after Watteau, and commenced the Seven Works of Mercy, from his own designs, but only lived to finish two of them.

TRENTO, Antonio da. This artist was born at Trent, in the Venetian States, about 1508. He first studied painting under Parmiggiano, but by the recommendation of that master, devoted himself to engraving on wood in chiaro-scuro. He is supposed to have learned the art from Ugo da Carpi, to whom the invention is attributed. He executed quite a number of cuts, mostly after the designs of Parmiggiano, though some of them are after the works of Andrea del Sarto, Beccafumi, Salviati, and others. He generally used three blocks to each print; the first for the outline, the second for the dark shadows, and the third for the demitints.

Bartsch is of opinion that Antonio da Trento and Antonio Fantuzzi are one and the same artist; Zani is of a contrary opinion. We cannot enter into the discussion further than to say that it is agreed that both flourished about the same time (from about 1530 to 1545), though it is contended that one was a native of Trent, and the other of Viterbo or Bologna. It is said that Fantuzzi, who worked under the direction of Parmiggiano, absconded from his master, taking with him many of his drawings, etchings, and wood cuts; and that he went to France, and connected himself with Primaticcio at Fontainbleau, who engaged him to engrave some of his works on copper. Among the thirty-seven prints described by Bartsch, and attributed by him to Fantuzzi, are several that go to corroborate his statement, could he prove them to have been executed by him. On the other hand, there are several strong circumstances against the supposition. Those who are fond of such disquisitions are referred to Zani, "Enciclopedia delle belle Arti," and to Bartsch, "Peintre Graveur," tomes xii. and xvi.

TRESHAM, Henry, an English painter and distinguished connoisseur, was a native of Ireland, and acquired the elements of design in West's academy in Dublin. He subsequently visited England, and painted small portraits for some time, after which he was favored with the patronage of Lord Cawdor, and was invited to accompany that nobleman in his travels to Italy. During a residence of fourteen years on the continent, he studied with great assiduity the antique, and the productions of the Roman school, and attained great correctness and elegance of design. He had a redundant invention, and great facility of composition, but paid less attention to coloring than to design. Tresham had already distinguished himself by several designs for the principal publications of his time, when Mr. Boydell projected his well known Shakspeare Gallery, and that liberal patron of art employed him to paint three scenes from the play of Antony and Cleopatra, which received the deserved approval of the public. Unfortunately for the art, his health became much impaired soon after this time, and prevented him from accomplishing much in the art. His long acquaintance with the works of the Italian masters, rendered him familiar with their merits and defects; consequently he was esteemed one of the ablest critics of his day, and his opinion was sought with earnestness by the connoisseur as well as the artist. His drawings with pen and ink, and in black chalk, evince uncommon ability; the latter, in particular, are executed with a spirit, boldness, and breadth not often found in such productions. During his latter years, Tresham superintended the publication of a collection of beautiful engravings, entitled "The British Gallery," from pictures by the old masters, of which he wrote the descriptions. The following tribute to his professional abilities and private character, is from the pen of an eminent cotemporary English connoisseur: "He was not less distinguished by the amiable qualities of his heart, than for the elegance of his taste as an artist, and he was equally beloved by a large circle of friends, as he was respected by his brother academicians." He died in 1814.

TREU, Catherine, a paintress of whom little is known. It is said that she was a daughter of Marquard Treu, an obscure painter, and born in 1747. She painted fruit and flower pieces in a beautiful style. There are some of her pictures in the Dusseldorf Gallery.

M or M or M. TREU, Martin, a German engraver, who flourished, according to Prof. Christ, about 1540. He was cotemporary with John Sebald Beham, and Henry Aldegrever, and from the small size of his prints, is ranked among the *little masters*. His plates are engraved from his own designs, and prove him to have been a man of genius. His prints, though inferior to the productions of the above named artists in clearness and precision of execution, are spirited, and possess much merit. They are sometimes marked with the initials M. T., and sometimes with one of the above monograms. Bartsch describes forty-two pieces by this artist; but Brulliot considers the list incomplete, and Malpe attributes to him thirteen large pieces of Christ and his Apostles, which are marked with the second or gothic monogram. Bartsch says also that there is no account of an artist of this name, and that it is a mere conjecture of Prof. Christ, and he supposes the prints to have been executed by an artist who flourished at the period mentioned, whose name is now lost. Some of the prints he describes are marked with the gothic monogram, so that it is not improbable that the prints in question were executed by two different artists.

TREVIGI, Antonio da, an old painter of Trevigi, of whom there are notices from 1402 to 1414. In the church of S. Niccolo in that city, is a picture of St. Christopher of gigantic stature, which Lanzi says is tolerably well executed.

TREVIGI, Dario da, a painter of Trevigi, who flourished about 1474. He was a pupil and imitator of Andrea Mantegna. There are some of his works in the church of S. Bernardino, at Bassano, placed opposite those of Mantegna, as if, says Lanzi, to exhibit their inferiority; elsewhere they would appear more respectable.

TREVIGI, Giorgio da, an old painter, who flourished about 1437. According to Rossetti, he was an artist of considerable note in his time. He was invited to Padua in 1437, to paint the celebrated tower of the Horologe.

TREVIGI, Girolamo da, a painter of Trevigi, whose pictures date from 1470 to 1492. According to Federici, he was a pupil and imitator of Squarcione, and his family name, Aviano. Lanzi says he found several of his works at Trevigi, signed *Hieronymus Tarvisio*, and judging from its style, "he was a very doubtful pupil of Squarcione." His pictures are very well designed, but poorly colored.

TREVIGI, Girolamo da, a painter of Trevigi, born, according to Ridolfi, in 1508, and died in 1544. His family name was Pennacchi. Zani says he was the son of Pier Maria Pennacchi, a painter of little note, and was born in 1496. He has been confounded by some writers with the preceding artist of the same cognomen. He went to Rome while young, where he studied the works of Raffaelle, and became a correct and graceful designer. He afterwards went to Venice, where little remains from his hand. He next went to Bologna, where about 1530 he was an assistant of Pupini. He afterwards painted a series of pictures in the church of S. Petronio, representing the life of St. Anthony of Padua, and the Presentation in S. Salvatore. Lanzi says that in these works he happily succeeded in uniting the excellencies of the Roman and Venetian schools, but did not live long enough to mature them, as he devoted himself to the occupation of a military engineer, to which service he fell a victim in England in 1544. According to Ridolfi, he went to England in the reign of Henry VIII., who employed him as a painter, architect, and military engineer. He attended the King in his expedition into Picardy, and was killed at the siege of Boulogne in 1544.

Stanley says there is a picture by him in the collection of Lord Northwick, representing the Virgin with the Infant on the throne, surrounded by saints and angels, formerly in the church of S. Salvatore, at Bologna; it is signed HIERONYMUS TREVISIUS, P.

TREVILIO, or TRIVIGLIO, BERNARDO DA. See ZENALE.

TREVILLIAN, WILLIAM. The name of this engraver is affixed to the portrait of Oliver Cromwell's Porter, dated 1650.

TREVISANI, ANGELO, a painter born at Trevigi, according to Lanzi, though some say at Venice. He was educated at Venice, where he passed the rest of his days, and is ranked among the Venetian painters. It is not known under whom he studied, but he painted history with reputation, as is evinced by his fine altar-piece in the church of La Carità, and other pictures in the churches at Venice; but he particularly distinguished himself as a painter of portraits, in which branch he acquired both fame and fortune. Lanzi says he formed a style of his own, not sublime but very select, founded upon nature, and in part conformble to the schools then in vogue. His pencil displays diligence and research, especially in his management of the chiaro-scuro. He was living in 1753.

TREVISANI, CAV. FRANCESCO, was born at Trevigi in 1656, according to Lanzi and the best authorities, though some say at Trieste, Castel Franco, Capo d'Istria, Venice, and Rome. He was the son of an architect, named Antonio Trevisani, who instructed him in the rudiments of art. He then became the disciple of Antonio Zanchi at Venice, whose principles he at first followed. Lanzi says he was called in Venice, Il Trevisani Romano, to distinguish him from Angelo T., the subject of the preceding article. After having acquired considerable reputation at Venice, a Venetian lady of noble family fell in love with him, and married him, but the lovers, fearing the displeasure of her parents, retired to Rome. Trevisani, possessing a happy talent of imitating the style of every master, soon abandoned his first principles, and adopted those of the most popular artists then resident in that city. At one time he appears a follower of Cignani, at another of Guido, or of other masters, and Lanzi says he was alike successful in all. He obtained the patronage of Cardinal Chigi, who employed him in several considerable works, and recommended him to the protection of Pope Clement XI. That pontiff commissioned him to paint one of the Prophets in St. John of Lateran, and afterwards employed him to decorate the cupola of the cathedral at Urbino, where he represented in fresco, subjects emblematic of the Four Quarters of the World, which Lanzi pronounces truly estimable for design, fancy, and coloring. After the death of Cardinal Chigi, he met with another powerful friend in Cardinal Ottobuoni, who employed him to adorn his gallery, for which he painted his celebrated picture of the Murder of the Innocents. The Duke of Modena employed him to copy several pictures by Correggio, Parmiggiano, and Paul Veronese, which he executed in such an exact and admirable manner, that he conferred upon him the honor of knighthood. He acquired an immense reputation, and abounded in commissions, more than he could execute; almost every person of distinction, passing through Rome, endeavored to procure a specimen by his hand. Lanzi says his pictures abound in the churches and the collections at Rome. The Albiccini family in Forli, possess many of his works in various styles, among them a small picture of the Crucifixion, an exquisite picture, which the artist considered his masterpiece, and subsequently offered a large sum to obtain it back again. His works generally exhibit much elegance of design, a fine pencil, and a vigorous tone of color. It is not a little remarkable, that, notwithstanding his numerous commissions, he always wrought with diligence and care. He possessed an extraordinary talent of imitating the works of other great masters, and frequently copied them on commission. He was also a universal painter, and could paint almost equally well, history, architecture, portraits, landscape, animals, fruit, and flowers. Among his best works at Rome are, the Death of St. Joseph, at the Collegio Romano; the Virgin contemplating the Instruments of the Passion in S. Maria in Vallicella; and his picture of Antony and Cleopatra, in the Spada palace, painted as a companion to Guido's Rape of Helen. There are many of his works in various cities in the state, as Foligno, Camerino, Perugia, and Forli. He died in 1746, at the great age of 90 years, and is said to have still retained his energies, working to the last year of his life.

TREZZO, GIACOMO DA, a famous painter in mosaic, of the Milanese school, who died in 1595. According to Abbé Conca, he was invited to the court of Philip II. of Spain to execute the Tabernacle for the church of the Escurial, which is esteemed the most beautiful and magnificent work of the kind in Christendom. For this, and other similar works, he was munificently rewarded, and acquired so much reputation, that the name of one of the principal streets, in which he lived, was changed to *Jacome Trezzo*.

TRIBOLO, NICCOLO DI, an able Italian sculptor, born at Florence in 1500. He was originally bred to the trade of a carpenter, but becoming acquainted with Sansovino, he commenced studying with him. On leaving that master, he was employed to execute two statues of Sibyls for the façade of S. Petronio at Bologna, which at once established his reputation. They have been engraved in Cicognara's *Storia della Scultura*. He also executed several bas-reliefs for the doors of that church, which possess great merit. In 1525 Tribolo was obliged to quit Bologna, on account of the plague, but he soon returned and continued practising the art until the death of his patron Bartolomeo Barbazzi, when he visited Pisa, and was employed by the sculptor Pietrosanta. While at Pisa, he was commissioned by Gio. Battista della Palla, who was collecting works of art for Francis I., to execute a statue of Nature, which, on being sent to Fontainbleau, was admired as a choice production of art. He seems afterwards to have practised in his native city, for when Florence was besieged by Pope Clement VII., in 1529, he treacherously furnished that pontiff with plans and models of the city and its outworks. His services on that occasion obtained him Clement's patronage, who among other things, employed him to assist Michael Angelo in the sculptures intended for the chapel of S. Lorenzo; and he had begun two figures, one representing Earth, and the other Heaven intended to decorate the tomb of Giulio de' Medici, when he was disabled from proceeding further by an attack of ague; and he had hardly recovered, when the Pope's death put a stop to the work. He was subsequently employed by the Grand Duke Cosmo I., in laying out gardens and designing the fountains and statues of the Villa di Castello, near Florence. Vasari, his friend and biographer, gives a minute account of this extensive scheme of embellishment, but partly on account of Tribolo's remissness it was prosecuted slowly, and never completed. On purchasing the Palazzo Pitti, the Grand Duke engaged Tribolo to improve the gardens and decorate them with various works in sculpture; but he had hardly commenced his labors, when he was seized with an illness that caused his death, September 7th, 1550.

TRICOMI, Bartolomeo, a Sicilian painter, who flourished at Messina about 1650. According to Hackert, he studied with Domenichino, though Lanzi says with Barbalunga. He devoted himself chiefly to portraiture, in which branch he greatly excelled.

TRIERE, P., a French engraver, who flourished about 1780. He engraved some plates of historical subjects and conversations, after various masters, which are executed with the graver in a neat and pleasing style.

TRINGHAM, an obscure English artist, mentioned by Strutt, as the engraver of a few portraits and other subjects for the booksellers. He flourished about 1750.

TRIPPEL, Alexander. This able sculptor was born at Schaffhausen, in Switzerland, in 1747. After acquiring the elements of design, he visited Copenhagen, and studied sculpture under Prof. Wiedevelt. He remained eight years in Denmark, and then went to Berlin, but meeting with little encouragement, he returned to Copenhagen, and gained several prizes at the Academy. He subsequently spent three years in Paris, and executed a fine model of his allegorical group of Switzerland, after which he settled at Rome in 1777, and practised the art in that city for many years, with good success. His works are distinguished for their noble simplicity and beautiful execution. He was most successful in bas-reliefs and busts, among which last he executed one of Goethe for the Prince of Waldeck, which is praised by the poet for the excellence of its style. Another of his works is the monument to Salomon Gessner, at Zurich. Trippel died at Rome in 1793.

TRISTAN, LUIS, a Spanish painter, born, according to Palomino, near Toledo, in 1594, and died at Toledo in 1649; Bermudez places his birth in 1586, and his death in 1640. He studied under Domenico Theotocopuli, called El Greco, whom he surpassed in design and the purity of his taste. El Greco, then somewhat advanced in years, far from being jealous of his talents, was the first to applaud his works, and to commend him to the public. He executed many works for the churches and convents of Toledo, the most esteemed of which are in the Cathedral, and in Santa Clara. There are some of his works at Madrid. He also excelled in portraits. It is no mean proof of his ability, that Velasquez professed himself his admirer, and quitting the precepts of Pacheco, his instructor, formed his style from the works of Tristan.

TRIVA, Antonio, a painter born at Reggio in 1626. He was a disciple and imitator of Guercino. and acquired considerable reputation for several works he executed for the churches at Reggio, Venice, and other cities in Italy, which were celebrated by his friend, the poet Boschini. He was invited to the court of the Elector of Bavaria, in whose service he died in 1699. He was remarkable for using both hands with equal facility. He executed a few spirited etchings from his own designs, and after other masters. Bartsch describes four, and Füessli mentions five more. He had a sister named Flaminia, who possessed considerable genius, and executed some good works, even for the churches.

TROGER, Paul, a German painter, born at Zell in the bishopric of Brixen, in 1695. After learning the rudiments of design in his own country, he went to Fiume, in the Venetian territory, and studied under Giuseppe Alberti. He established himself at Vienna, where he acquired considerable reputation as an historical painter, and was made Director of the Imperial Academy. He also executed some spirited etchings of historical subjects and landscapes from his own designs. He died at Vienna in 1777.

TROGLI, Giulio, a painter born at Bologna, according to Malvasia, in 1613, and died in 1685. He first studied under Francesco Gessi, but preferring perspective and architecture, he afterwards became the pupil of Agostino Metelli. He acquired considerable reputation, and published a work entitled "Paradossi della Prospettiva"; hence he was ever afterwards called Il Paradosso (the Paradox). He died in 1685.

TROMBA, Il. See Rinaldi.

TROMPETTA, Il. See Pesaro.

TRONCHON, A. R., a French engraver, who flourished from about 1740 to 1760. He engraved some plates after Coypel and other masters.

TROOST, Cornelius, a Dutch painter, born at Amsterdam in 1697. He studied under Arnold Boonen, and improved himself by a diligent study of nature. He painted history, comedies, conversations, and gallant subjects, in a very pleasing style, and was called the Dutch Watteau. His greatest excellence, however, lay in portraiture, and he was much employed in painting large pictures for the halls of the different societies and companies of Amsterdam, containing the portraits of the principal officers of the institutions. He there painted the Directors of the College of Physicians at Amsterdam, as large as life, and at full length, in one piece, which picture established his reputation. His most capital performance is a large picture in the Surgeons' Hall, representing the principal persons of that profession in Amsterdam, sitting round a table, on which is placed a subject prepared for dissection, while a professor appears as if explaining the parts previous to an operation. He was much applauded for his admirable portrait of Boerhaave, which is placed in the Anatomical Hall. His conversations, though occasionally broad, are true to nature, and faithfully portray the enjoyments of the high and the low, according to the manners and customs of the people of Holland in his day. His pictures are correctly designed and well colored. He painted in crayons as well as in oil, and his works are highly esteemed in his own country. The late Baron Verstolk de Soelen, Minister of State, possessed a large collection of his works, which were sold at public sale at Amsterdam in 1847, and brought large prices. Troost also engraved some prints in mezzotinto from his own designs. He died in 1750. He had a daughter named Sara, whom he instructed in the art. She painted portraits with reputation, both in oil and crayons, and made drawings of several of her father's works. She died in 1793.

TROOST, WILLIAM, a Dutch painter, born at Amsterdam in 1684. He first studied with John Glauber in his native city, and next went to Dusseldorf, where he became a disciple of J. van Nikkelen, painter to the court, whose daughter he married. At Dusseldorf, he is said to have painted the portraits of many persons of distinction. He afterwards returned to Amsterdam, where he settled, and devoted his talents chiefly to landscape, both in oil and India ink; the latter are considered the most valuable. His style in landscape resembles that of his first master, Glauber. His wife, Jacoba Maria van Nikkelen, excelled in painting fruit and flower pieces, which art she learned of vander Myn.

TROOSTWYCK, WALTER JOHN, a Dutch painter, born at Amsterdam in 1782. He studied both with Anthony and Juriaan Andriessen, and afterwards improved himself by copying the works of the best Dutch landscape and cattle painters, as Paul Potter, Adrien Vandervelde, and Karel du Jardin. He painted landscapes and cattle in the manner of those masters, which are much esteemed. He died in 1810.

TROPHONIUS. See AGAMEDES.

TROSCHEL, JAMES, a German painter and engraver of little note, born in 1583, and died in 1624. Prof. Christ attributes to him some indifferent prints marked with the initials I. T. F.

HT TROSCHEL, HANS, a German engraver, born at Nuremberg about 1592. He studied under Peter Isselburg, and gained considerable reputation by several plates, particularly a Set of Landscapes, the Court House at Nuremberg, and the portrait of Ferdinand II. In 1622, he went to Rome, and assisted Francesco Villamena in executing several important works. The *Biographie Universelle* praises him for his facility and delicacy of execution; Bryan says his style is greatly inferior to that of Villamena, both in design and execution, and that his plates, though neatly engraved, are stiff and labored. Troschel died at Rome in 1633, and was honorably interred in S. Maria del Popolo. His plates are generally marked with the above monogram, sometimes with the figure of a *thrush* added, in allusion to his name; among them are several emblematical subjects, portraits and frontispieces; also the following: The Conception of the Virgin, *after Bernardo Castelli*. A large Thesis, dedicated to Cardinal Prince Maurice of Savoy. The Emperor Julian, with a figure showing the heart of a Bull, upon which appears a cross surmounted by a crown, *after Antonio Circignano*. A portrait marked *Fortunius Licetus, Philosoph.* The portrait of Louis XIV., considered his best work.

TROSCHEL, PETER. This engraver was the son and scholar of the preceding, born at Nuremberg about 1620, and flourished until about 1661. His plates were chiefly engraved for the booksellers; among them are several frontispieces and other book ornaments, executed with the graver, in an indifferent style, usually marked with the initials P. T.

A TROST, ANDREW, a German painter of familiar subjects, was a native of Carniola. Little is known of him as a painter. He engraved some plates, which he marked with the above monogram. He was living in 1695.

TROST. See TROOST.

TROPPA, CAV. GIROLAMO, a painter who is supposed to have studied with Carlo Maratti. Lanzi says he was certainly his imitator, and a successful one too. He executed some works for the churches at Rome, both in oil and fresco, the best of which are in S. Giacomo delle Penitenti, where he painted in competition with Romanelli. There are also some of his works scattered in the churches throughout the state, particularly at S. Severino. He died in the prime of life.

TROTTI, CAV. GIO. BATTISTA, called IL MALOSSO, an eminent painter, born at Cremona in 1555. He was the most distinguished disciple of Bernardino Campi, whose niece he married, and inherited his valuable studio. He acquired a brilliant reputation, and executed many works for the churches and public edifices of Cremona, Parma, Piacenza, and other cities of Italy. He was employed by the court of Parma to paint in competition with Agostino Caracci, on which occasion, says Lanzi, Trotti being most applauded, Agostino with pleasantry observed, "that they had given him a hard bone to crack"; hence he was called Il Malosso, which name he adopted, and transmitted as an hereditary appellation to his nephew; he also sometimes made use of it in signing his name, thus, *Jo. Baptista Trottus dictus Malossus Cremon. faciebat*, 1594. "Thus, he converted into a sort of applause the satire, launched at him by Caracci, meant to convey that the people of Parma had preferred to him an artist of inferior worth; nor indeed was Malosso his equal in design or in solid judgment, though he could boast pictoric attractions which made him appear to advantage when opposed to other artists. He displayed little of Campi's taste except in a few of his first efforts; he afterwards studied Correggio, and most of all, emulated Sojaro, whose gay, open, and brilliant style, varied shortenings, and spirited attitudes, he exhibited in the chief part of his works. But he carried it too far, making an extravagant display of his white and other clear colors, without sufficiently tempering them with shade, insomuch that I have heard his paintings compared to those on porcelain, while he has been accused of want of relief, or, according to Baldinucci, of some degree of harshness. His heads, however, are very beautiful, smiling with loveliness, and of a graceful roundness, not unlike those of Sojaro, though he is apt to repeat them on the same canvass, nearly alike in features, colors, and attitudes. Here his rapidity of hand was alone at fault, for he was no ways deficient in fertility of ideas. When he pleased he could give variety to his lineaments, as is seen in his Beheading of St. John, in the church of S. Domenico at Cremona, as well as in his compositions, for he repeated his Conception of the Virgin in S. Francesco at Piacenza, on several occasions, abounding with fresh ideas in every instance, nor do we often meet with any of his paintings throughout the numerous cities in which he was employed, that have much resemblance in point of invention. He was equally varied in his imitations when he pleased."

Trotti wrought with extraordinary facility, and executed a multitude of works, both in oil and fresco; hence he frequently laid himself justly open to the accusation of incorrectness, want of harmony, and mannerism. His most esteemed works in fresco, for which he was honored with knighthood, are in the Palazzo del Giordani, at Parma. His labors in the cupola of S. Abbondio at Parma, are on a magnificent scale, though designed from Giulio Campi; but they display, says Lanzi, a masterly hand and a strength of coloring fully equal, if not superior, to the design. Among his other works, most deserving of notice, are the Crucifixion, executed in the best Venetian taste in the cathedral at Cremona; his St. Maria Egiziaca, in the church of S. Pietro, in the same city, much in the Roman style, and a Pietà, in S. Abbondio, in which he emulated the Caracci. He died in 1612.

TROTTI, Euclide, called also Il Malosso, was the nephew of the preceding, assisted him in his works, and was an able imitator of his style. The only works known, executed entirely by him, are two pictures of the history of St. James, in the church of S. Gismondo, at Cremona, and an altar-piece of the Ascension, in the church of S. Antonio at Milan, which Lanzi says displays much beauty, and a more serious and dignified manner, than is generally found in the works of the elder Malosso. Unfortunately he fell into extravagant and dissipated habits while young, committed a felony, was condemned to death, and died in prison, by poison, as is supposed, administered by his friends, to avoid the disgrace of a public execution. He is sometimes called *Il Cav. Euclide Trotti.*

TROUVAIN, Antoine, a French engraver, born at Montdidier in 1666. He is supposed to have been a pupil of Bernard Picart, whose style he imitated. His plates are executed entirely with the graver, which he handled with great neatness and dexterity, and his prints produce a very pleasing effect. He was living in 1707. Among others, are the following by him:

PORTRAITS.

Peter Daniel Huet, Bishop of Avanches. 1695. Francis le Bouthellier, Bishop of Troyes. John Pesne, Painter and Engraver. 1698. René Anthony Houasse, Painter; *after Tortebat*, John Jouvenet, Painter; *after a picture by himself.*

SUBJECTS.

The Annunciation; *after Carlo Maratti.* Christ restoring Sight to the Blind; *after Ant. Coypel.* The Marriage of Mary of Medicis with Henry IV., and the Minority of Louis XIII.; after the pictures by *Rubens* in the Luxembourg Gallery. Silenus drunk; *after Ant. Coypel.*

TROY, François de, an eminent French painter, born at Toulouse in 1645. He was the son of Nicolas de Troy, a painter of little note, by whom he was instructed in the rudiments of the art. He went to Paris while young, and studied under Nicholas Loir, where he made rapid progress, and soon distinguished himself. In 1674 he was admitted into the Academy, on which occasion he presented a picture of Mercury and Argus, which gained him so much reputation, that he received immediately several commissions for sacred and profane subjects. The brilliant success of Claude le Fevre as a portrait painter, induced him to devote himself more particularly to that branch, in which he became one of the most celebrated artists of the French school. He was sent by Louis XIV. to the court of Munich to paint the portrait of Maria Christiana of Bavaria, afterwards Dauphiness of France, which was subsequently placed in the gallery of Apollo, as an exquisite specimen of coloring and finishing. He also painted the portraits of many of the most distinguished personages of his time. His portrait, painted by himself, is in the Florentine gallery. His greatest historical work is in the church of Genevieve, representing the Magistrates of Paris invoking the protection of that saint, pronounced a grand performance. There is a very rare etching by him representing the *Catafalque* for the obsequies of Maria Teresa, Queen of Louis XIV. He died at Paris in 1730.

TROY, Chevalier Jean François de, was the son of the preceding, born at Paris in 1676. After receiving instruction from his father, he went to Italy, where he resided several years, diligently studying the works of the best masters. On his return to Paris, he soon gained a distinguished reputation, and was elected a member of the Academy. On the first exhibition of his works, they were generally admired, and the best judges of the art commended the taste, invention, coloring, neatness of finishing, and happy union of simplicity and grandeur, which appeared in his compositions. He was employed by Louis XIV. to paint a series of cartoons for tapestry, representing the history of Queen Esther, and to decorate the Hotel de Ville with several large emblematical subjects, which gave so much satisfaction to the monarch, that he conferred on him the order of St. Michael, and honored him with other marks of his peculiar esteem. He subsequently appointed him director of the French Academy at Rome, where he resided the greater part of his life, and discharged the duties of his office with much dignity and credit. He had a fruitful invention, and an extraordinary readiness of handling; his touch was firm and free, and his coloring extremely pleasing; and in all his works he showed a just and natural expression of the passions in his countenances, as well as in the attitudes and motions. He was not less distinguished as a painter of portraits than of historical subjects, and his own likeness, painted by himself, is in the Florentine Gallery. He died in 1752.

TROYA, Felix, a Spanish painter, born at San Felipe, near Valencia, in 1660. He studied with Gasparo de la Huerta, at Valencia, and painted history with considerable reputation. His works are numerous, and may be found in almost all the churches, convents, and public edifices at Valencia, San Felipe, and other places in that region of country, where he resided. He acquired a high reputation for the richness of his coloring, and the grand and imposing effect of his pictures, though his design is frequently incorrect. His best works are in the church of S. Agostino at Valencia, where he died in 1731.

TROYEN, John van, a Flemish engraver, who flourished about 1650. He engraved some of the plates from the pictures in the collection of the Archduke Leopold, called the Teniers' Gallery, among which are, the Daughter of Herodias with the Head of St. John, *after L. da Vinci;* the

Magdalene penitent, *after Correggio;* Christ healing the Sick, and the Adoration of the Magi, *after P. Veronese;* and the Entombment, *after Pordenone.*

TROYEN, ROMBOUT VAN, a Flemish painter, born at Antwerp about 1600. It is not known under whom he studied, but Harms, in his Chronological Tables, states that he went to Italy, and resided there some time; others say that he never left his own country. He distinguished himself as a painter of the ruins of ancient architecture, and other interesting objects in the neighborhood of Rome, which he embellished with figures representing subjects of sacred or profane history or fable. His style resembles that of Cuylenburg, and his pictures, like those of that master, have become much darkened in parts by age, from the use of improper colors. His cabinet pictures are the most esteemed. Balkema says he lived at Amsterdam, where he died in 1650.

TRUCHI, DOMINIC and L., two engravers, said to be French, but probably Italians, who flourished in London about 1730. They engraved some book plates.

TRUCHOT, a French painter of landscapes and architectural views, who lived in England some time, and died about 1823. Little is known of him except by his works, among which are a view of Canterbury Cathedral; a View of St. Michael's Mount; Abelard reading a Letter from Eloisa; Eloisa in Prayer before an Altar; the grand Staircase of the Palais Royal; Henry, Count de Bouchange, in a Cloister; also several interiors of churches and chapels, and views of ancient ruins in various parts of France. Some of his pictures are embellished with figures by Xavier le Prince.

TRUMBULL, JOHN. This eminent American painter was born at Lebanon, Conn., June 6th, 1756, and died in New York, November 10th, 1843, aged eighty-seven. His father was the first governor of Connecticut as an independent State, and the advantages of his birth gave to young Trumbull one of the best educations the country could afford. He graduated at Harvard College in the class of 1773, at the early age of seventeen; and having seen at Boston the works of Smybert and Copley, he determined to devote his time and talents to the profession of painting.

Boston and its environs had at this time become the seat of war; and the young artist, fired with a spirit which animated his countrymen, enrolled himself, at the age of nineteen, as an adjutant in the American Army, and marched to join the undisciplined forces which were assembling around the head quarters of General Gage. On the 17th of June, 1775, was fought the memorable battle of Bunker's Hill, at which time the young adjutant was stationed with his regiment at Roxbury. In July, General Washington arrived at Cambridge to take command of the troops which were besieging Boston; and being informed of the talent of Trumbull, he employed him to make a draft of the enemy's works, which he completed to the satisfaction of the commander-in-chief. In August, 1775, Trumbull was appointed aid to Washington; in the autumn of this year he was promoted to the office of brigade major, and in the succeeding year, 1776, he held the post of Deputy Adjutant General of the Northern Department under General Gates. Owing to some informality respecting the date of his commission, Trumbull became, at this time, dissatisfied with the service, and having witnessed many of the chief occurrences of the Revolution, he resolved to terminate his military career, and become the historiographer of these great events and of his early comrades.

With this view he resided some time at Boston, studying the works of Copley and others, until 1780, when he embarked for France, and having made a short stay in Paris, proceeded to London, where he was kindly received by West, with whom he pursued his studies uninterruptedly till about the middle of November, when the news of the death of Major André was received, and a violent irritation was occasioned in the public mind. It was Trumbull's misfortune to lodge in the same house with another American gentleman, who had been an officer, and against whom a warrant had been issued to apprehend him for high treason. Instructions had been given to the officer who was to execute the warrant, to arrest, meanwhile, the painter, and secure his papers in expectation of finding something of importance; and in accordance with this order, Trumbull was arrested on the night of the 19th November, and committed to prison. Immediately upon hearing of the arrest, West waited upon the king; represented the circumstances of his pupil's former and present situation; the long time which had intervened between his quitting the rebel army and his coming to England; and his present entire devotedness to the study of the fine arts. George the Third, after a moment's hesitation, replied, "this young gentleman is in the power of the laws, and I cannot at present interfere; but go to him, and assure him from me, that in the worst possible legal result he has my royal word that his life is safe." This assurance, of course, softened in a great degree the rigor of an eight months' imprisonment, during which period he made the fine copy from West's picture of Correggio's St. Jerome, now in the gallery at New Haven.

In June, 1781, a change had taken place in the affairs of the two countries; the English government had begun to relax their severity, and Trumbull was admitted to bail by a special order of the king, in council, on condition of quitting the kingdom within thirty days, not to return during the war. Making the best of his way to Ostend, and from thence to Amsterdam, he embarked for his native country, where he arrived, after much detention, about the middle of January, 1782. Fatigue, vexation, and disappointment brought on a fever, which confined him to his father's house the principal part of the ensuing winter.

In the spring of 1783, the news arrived of the preliminaries of peace having been arranged, and Trumbull immediately formed the resolution of again visiting England; he arrived there in the early part of 1784, and recommenced his studies with West, by whom he was again kindly received. In the year 1786, he produced his first considerable historical work, the Death of General Warren at the Battle of Bunker's Hill. This his first patriotic work of art, having been seen and appreciated by both Adams and Jefferson, the former of whom was residing at that time as American minister at London, and the latter at Paris, he communicated to them his project of painting a series of national pictures, in commemoration of the principal events of the Revolution, preserving, as far as possible, faithful portraits of those who had been conspicuous actors in the various scenes, as well as accurate details of the arms, dresses, and manners of the times, with all of which he had been familiar.

Finding that the Death of General Warren had given offence in London, and being desirous to conciliate, Trumbull determined to paint, before leaving England, a subject from British history; and selected the Sortie of Gibraltar, which was finished in the spring of 1789. In the autumn of this year, Trumbull returned to America, and devoted himself with great assiduity to the task of procuring portraits of all the distinguished characters in New York, then the seat of government, and in the summer of 1790, he was commissioned by the Corporation to paint a full-length of Washington, now in the Common Council room of the City Hall. It represents the General in full uniform, standing by a white horse, leaning his arm upon the saddle; in the background, a view of Broadway in ruins, as it then was, the old fort at the termination, and Staten Island in the distance. He passed the winter of 1790–1, in traveling through various parts of the country, to take portraits of illustrious individuals, and in the spring returned to New York, where he painted for the Corporation the whole length portrait of General Clinton, also in the Common Council room of the City Hall. In 1792, he was again at Philadelphia, and there painted the portrait of General Washington, now in the gallery at New Haven.

In May, 1794, he returned to England as Secretary to Mr. Jay, who had been appointed minister to Great Britain; and, in a residence of ten years, produced several pictures, the most celebrated of which are the Madonna au Corset rouge, from Raffaelle; the Infant Saviour and St. John; and a Holy Family, all of which are now in the New Haven gallery. He returned to the United States again in 1804, but in consequence of the embarrassments of trade, and the unsettled state of the country, the fine arts were but illy supported here; and in 1808, he returned again to London, and remained abroad until his final return to the United States in 1816.

During his last absence, a change had taken place in the state of the arts in this country. Stuart, Sully, and Jarvis were each enjoying a high and deserved reputation; and although Allston had not yet arrived, the fame of his success had preceded him. The Capitol at Washington was rebuilding, and Cougress, during the session of 1816–17, appropriated thirty-two thousand dollars for the purchase of four pictures, each eighteen feet by twelve, to be placed on the walls of the Rotunda. They selected for their subjects the Declaration of Independence, signed on the 4th of July, 1776; the Surrender of Burgoyne, on the 17th of October, 1777, to the American forces under General Gates, at Saratoga; the Surrender of Cornwallis at Yorktown in Virginia, Oct. 19, 1781; and the Resignation of General Washington, at Annapolis, Dec. 23, 1783. They authorized Trumbull to execute the work, which he performed in the space of seven years. These pictures are in the style of his master, West; and although some critics have found fault with the grouping of the figures, and the apparent stiffness of the principal officers, their merit in many particulars is of a high order, and they will ever be valuable for the faithful portraits they have handed down to us.

The last picture was scarcely finished in 1824, when Trumbull had the misfortune to lose his wife, the faithful and beloved companion of all the vicissitudes of twenty-four years. In his own words, "my best friend was removed from me, and I had no child. A sense of loneliness began to creep over my mind, yet my hand was steady, and my sight good; then why sink into premature imbecility?" He therefore resolved to begin a new series of his revolutionary subjects, on canvas six feet by nine, for the purpose of solacing his weary hours by occupation. The expenses necessarily incident to such an undertaking, soon diminished his pecuniary resources, and the thought occurred to him, that, although there was little probability of his being able to dispose of his pictures, either to individuals or to the State, it might be that some literary institution would be desirous of possessing them. An arrangement was finally concluded with Yale College at New Haven—a fireproof gallery was erected, in which the pictures were arranged under his direction, and an annuity of one thousand dollars for the remainder of his life was settled upon the artist, who made one noble condition in this final disposition of his works, that, after his death, the entire proceeds of the exhibition should be perpetually appropriated towards defraying the expense of educating indigent scholars in Yale College. "I thus," says he, "have the happy reflection that when I shall have gone to my rest, these works will remain a source of good to many a poor, perhaps meritorious and excellent young man."

Among other valuable productions, the Trumbull Gallery contains, besides the small copies of the pictures at the Capitol, fifty-three pictures by him, the principal of which are, the Battle of Bunker Hill; the Death of Gen. Montgomery, in the attack of Quebec; the Battle of Princeton, partly finished; the Capture of the Hessians at Trenton; the Death of Gen. Mercer, at the battle of Princeton; Portrait of General Washington, painted at Philadelphia in 1792, for the city of Charleston, S. C.; a copy of Correggio's celebrated St. Jerome of Parma; and a copy of the Transfiguration, the master-piece of Raffaelle. Five copies of his historical pictures, the Declaration of Independence, the Death of General Montgomery, the Death of General Warren, the Death of Gen. Mercer, and the Rout of the Hessians at Trenton, were purchased by the Wadsworth Athenæum at Hartford, and now adorn the walls of that institution. The Sortie of Gibraltar, and Priam receiving the Body of Hector, are the property of the Athenæum at Boston.

An association had been early formed in New York for promoting the Fine Arts, and Chancellor Livingston elected President. For a considerable period, the institution was sustained with some vigor, but it finally lost its vitality, and in 1816 it had nearly ceased to exist. During that year De Witt Clinton, who was then President of the Association, originated a plan, by which it was revived, under the name of the American Academy of Fine Arts. Delicacy required him to resign the presidency, and at his nomination, Trumbull was elected to occupy the chair, which he continued to do with great ability until the formation of the National Academy of Design, which went into operation in 1825, with Samuel F. B. Morse as President. During this period it may be said, no artist in this country gave instruction to so many scholars, and certainly no one displayed a warmer zeal in the cause of Art.

In the year 1837, Trumbull removed to New Haven, and resided there till 1841; when he returned to New York, in order to receive the advice of his favorite physician, Dr. Washington. He remained there until his death, in November, 1843. By his own request, his remains were interred in a sepulchre, built by himself, beneath his Monumental Gallery, at New Haven.

TSCHERNINGK, DAVID, a German engraver, who flourished about 1639. He engraved some frontispieces and other book plates, executed with the graver, in a poor style.

TSCHERNINGK, JOHN. There were two German engravers of this name; the elder was living in 1634, and the younger in 1685. They engraved some portraits and other book plates. There was a portrait painter named *Andrew T.*, who flourished about 1660. Little is known of them.

TUAIRE, FRANÇOIS, a French painter, born at Aix in Provence, in 1794. He studied under Prudhon with the greatest assiduity, and being obliged also to give lessons in the art, to gain a subsistence, his constitution was injured by incessant application. The Empress Josephine commissioned him to paint a picture of Venus and the Loves, which was greatly admired, and gained him considerable reputation. In 1821 he executed a picture for the palace at Fontainbleau, representing Psyche in prison, condemned to separate grains of corn, and succored by Cupid. It was much admired for its design, coloring, and expression, and gained the gold medal at the exhibition in 1822. Tuaire finally ruined his health by excessive labor, and died in 1823.

TUBI, GIO. BATTISTA, a reputable Italian sculptor, was born at Rome about 1630. He visited Paris, and was elected a member of the Academy of Painting and Sculpture. He was employed in copying works from the antique; and his excellent talents in this respect are evinced by the Laocoön in the Versailles Park. There are also a number of original compositions by him at Versailles, representing the Fountain of Flora, Cupid, Galatea; and also a marble vase, with bas-reliefs, illustrating the victories of Louis XIV., in Flanders. At Paris he executed a number of works, among which are a statue of Immortality, on the tomb of la Chambre, and that of Religion, on the tomb of Colbert; both in the church of S. Eustache. Tubi also executed the mausoleum of Turenne, after the designs of le Brun, with the exception of the statues impersonifying Wisdom and Valor, which are by Marsy. This mausoleum was formerly in the church of the Abbey of St. Denis, but was transferred in 1800 to the church of the Invalides. Tubi died at Paris in 1700.

TUCCARI, GIOVANNI, a Sicilian painter, born at Messina, according to Hackert, in 1667, and died there in 1743. He studied with his father, Antonio T., who was a feeble disciple of Barbalunga. Though he painted much in other branches, he chiefly distinguished himself as a painter of battles and skirmishes of cavalry, and by the extraordinary facility of his pencil, "he multiplied these subjects almost beyond number. Many of them were sent to Germany, where they were engraved." His name is frequently written Tucarri. He died in 1743.

TULDEN. See THULDEN.

TUNCOTTO, GIORGIO, an old Piedmontese painter, who was living, according to Count Durando, in 1473, when he painted in the church of S. Domenico at Alba. His works have mostly perished.

TURA, COSIMO, called COSMÈ DA FERRARA, an old painter, born at Ferrara in 1406, and died in 1469. He was a disciple of Galasso Galassi, and painted sacred subjects in the dry, gothic style which prevailed at that time. Several of his works are still preserved in the churches and public edifices of Ferrara. He was court painter in the time of the Duke Borso d' Este, and Tito Strozzi wrote a poetic eulogy upon him. His figures are treated in the style of Andrea Mantegna, the muscles clearly expressed, the architecture drawn with care, the bassirilievi highly ornamented, and the whole labored in the most minute and exact taste. This is remarkable in his miniatures, which embellish the choral books in the Cathedral and the Certosa, which are shown to foreigners as extreme rarities. He painted both in oil and fresco; his oil paintings are executed in the same labored manner, as seen in his Annunciation and Nativity, in the Cathedral, the Acts of St. Eustace in the monastery of S. Guglielmo, the Virgin with various Saints in the church of S. Giovanni, and Christ praying in the Garden at the Cappuccini. He decorated the palace of Borso, Duke of Ferrara, with a series of twelve frescos, emblematical of the months of the year, which are mentioned by Baruffaldi as very remarkable productions for that early period. The month of the year was scientifically indicated in each picture by astronomical symbols, and classical deities, adapted to each. In each month he introduced the Duke in his usual employment at such season; in the judgment hall, in the chase, at spectacles, &c., with a great variety of circumstances, full of poetry in the execution. There is a picture by him, representing the Madonna with Saints, under splendid but overloaded architecture, in the Berlin Museum. Rosini, in his *Storia della Pittura Italiana*, tom. iii., gives an outline of a Madonna and Child by him, which is a chaste and beautiful composition. His name is sometimes written *Turra*.

TURCHI, ALESSANDRO, called L'ORBETTO, an eminent painter, born at Verona, according to Pozzo, and died at Rome in 1648, aged 66; though Passeri places his birth in 1580, and his death in 1650. D'Argenville, and other French biographers, followed by Pilkington, place his birth erroneously in 1600, as his instructor died in 1605. Pozzo says that he was surnamed *Orbetto* because when he was a child he guided an old blind mendicant about the streets, but Passeri declares that he derived it from a defect in one of his own eyes, which Lanzi says is confirmed by his portrait, blind in the left eye. At all events, Felice Riccio, called Il Brusasorci, perceiving in him a fine genius for painting when a lad, took him into his studio and carefully instructed him in the art, so that in a few years, says Lanzi, he encountered a rival rather than a disciple. On leaving the school of Riccio, he went to Venice, where he studied some time with Carlo Cagliari, and acquired a chaste and natural style of coloring. He next proceeded to Rome, where he diligently studied the works of the great masters, and formed a style wholly his own, in which he attempted to combine the Roman taste of design with the coloring of the Venetian school. He established himself at Rome, where he painted some altar-pieces and other pictures for the churches, in competition with the best followers of the Caracci, with Sacchi and Pietro da Cortona, the most esteemed of which are in the church of La Concezione, executed in competition with Sacchi and Cortona, in which he displayed talents not unworthy of his rivals. Among his other principal works at Rome, are the Flight into Egypt, in S. Romualdo; the Holy Family, in S. Lorenzo; and St. Carlo Borromeo, in S. Salvatore. His best works in public, however, are at Verona, and of these the most worthy of notice are his pictures of the Forty Martyrs in S. Stefano, and a Pietà in La Misericordia, in which last he emulated the grand style of the Caracci in composition, expression, and coloring. He was chiefly employed in painting easel pictures for the collections. Lanzi says that the Marchese Girardini, who was his principal patron, possesses, in his gallery at Verona, enough to enrich several collections, in which it is amusing to trace his progress from the inferior to the most correct specimens. Some writers have not hesitated to rank Turchi with Annibale Caracci, but Lanzi says such assertions "ought not to be listened to anywhere." However, he admits that he succeeded in emulating the design of Caracci on several occasions, with great success; though generally in his naked figures, which in Annibale approach the ancient Greeks, he was far from equalling him. In conclusion he says, "Still he exhibits so many attractions that he never fails to please us in every subject. He seems to have aimed at forming a union of various schools, and added to it a certain originality in giving dignity to the portraits introduced into his histories with the most animated, yet the most delicate complexions. He excelled in the choice and distribution of his colors, among which he introduces a reddish tint, which much enlivens his pictures, and is one of the indications by which we may recognize him as the author. He is said to have exercised exquisite care in the application of his tints, and to have possessed some secret art, by means of which they continue to attract the envy of posterity; but the truth is, he selected, purified, and kneaded well his colors, besides consulting chemists upon the subject. (How few artists seriously consider the importance of this subject; and how many noble works, by great masters, have been lost to the world by the use of injudicious colors, particularly those which chemically react, and in a few years entirely change the original harmonious effect to a discordant mass!) His Passion of the Forty Martyrs, in the church of S. Stefano, in regard to depth of color and foreshortening, partakes much of the Lombard; in point of design and expression, of the Roman; and in its coloring, of the Venetian school. It is one of the most studied, finished, and animated pieces he produced; there is a choiceness in the heads that approaches Guido's; and a skill in composition that throws into the background of the picture a great portion of the multifarious history, as appearing in a field of vast extent, where his figures were admirably varied, according to the distances in which they are supposed to appear. Yet he does not belong to that class of artists who go about in search of personages to fill their histories with figures. On the contrary, he seems to take more pleasure in introducing a smaller number. Thus, in his Pietà at La Misericordia, he exhibits only a dead Christ, the Virgin, and Nicodemus, but the whole is so well designed, arranged, and animated, as well as colored, that it is esteemed by many his master-piece, and is certainly one of the best paintings in Verona."

TURCO, Cesare, a Neapolitan painter, born, according to Dominici, about 1510. He studied first with Antonio d'Amato, and afterwards with Andrea Sabbatini. He was a good painter in oil, but unsuccessful in fresco. There are some of his works in the churches at Naples, the most esteemed of which are the Baptism of Christ in S. Maria delle Grazie, and the Circumcision in del Gesu. He died in 1560.

TURESTIO, Francesco, a Venetian mosaic worker, who, according to Zanetti, was living in 1618. He executed some beautiful pieces from the designs of Tintoretto, the younger Palma, Leandro Bassano, and other eminent painters.

TURK, The. See Liotard.

TURNER, Joseph Mallard William, R. A. This eminent English painter of landscapes and marines, so highly distinguished during the present century, was born in Maiden Lane, Covent Garden, London, in 1775. His father, who carried on a respectable business as a hair-dresser, perceiving in him a strong inclination for art, permitted him to follow the bent of his desires. Young Turner was indebted for much sound advice, and the use of many valuable copies, to Dr. Munro, a distinguished connoisseur and amateur. In company with Girtin, he copied many water-colored drawings in his patron's collection; and they also produced at that time many admirable works in this branch of the art, so closely resembling each other in style, that their respective performances can hardly be distinguished, although Turner's exhibit more elaborateness of detail, yet no less breadth and richness of effect. It is said that the present elevated position of English painting in water colors is due in a great measure to the efforts of these two artists. In 1789, Turner entered as a student of the Royal Academy, and exhibited in the following year a View of the Archbishop's palace at Lambeth, executed in water colors. In 1793, he exhibited his first painting in oil; from 1790 to 1800, when he was elected Associate, he contributed to the exhibition of the Academy nearly sixty pictures. In 1802, he sent several works to the Academy, among which were the Tenth Plague of Egypt, and the Fall of the Clyde. In the same year he was chosen a Royal Academician, and for many years afterwards he painted a large number of pictures, by which he gained both fame and fortune.

Perhaps there is not a more difficult task for a writer on art, than to compose a criticism upon an eminent painter, a few months after his death; and from the novel course of Turner's genius, so many various opinions have been advanced by his detractors and admirers, that his true merits and demerits can hardly be ascertained. The points he most aimed at in his works were light and space; and their highly luminous qualities are their grand characteristics. He scarcely ever placed an important object in his foregrounds, but generally in the centre of his pictures, where also is the greatest mass of light; and opposed to the point of sight is the darkest and largest quantity of shade. These peculiarities are admirably illustrated in the "Golden Bough," an Italian landscape composition, engraved for the London Art Journal from the picture in the Vernon Gallery; while the effect of space and air in the same work, produced by the most delicate application of touch and tint, carries the eye over many miles of distance, where the exact character of the whole landscape can be discerned, till it is lost in the harmonious blending of earth and sky, into which fancy alone can penetrate.

Turner's breadth of effect and of shadow, and his brilliant representation of light, are often carried to extremes, which, though they may fascinate the eye of the uninstructed, can by no means satisfy the judgment of the connoisseur. His admirers ascribe the erratic course of his genius to his redundant imagination; they say that "great geniuses are always great experimentalists, and Turner's vast and comprehensive mind disdained to follow in the track marked out by others, however distinguished; hence he broke away from the trammels which the dogmas of schools would have interposed between him and his genius, and hewed out a way for himself through the world of nature, which none had ever passed before, and which few can hope to follow." Perhaps the true interests of art would have been better promoted, if his genius had been subjected to more severe discipline. Moreover, it is also said that "his mind was too poetically constituted to permit him to treat even the most commonplace subject in a common way; his faculty of conception was too expansive, his power of invention or creation too fertile, to permit him to become a mere imitator of nature; the pencil of the artist is like the pen of the poet, and we seem to be reading an epic when studying one of his pictures." Turner's abundant imagination is nowhere better exemplified than in his Venetian and other Italian views. These landscape compositions exhibit scenes of his own creation, decorated with every conceivable accessory, and invested with such a beauty and glory as they might have possessed in the Golden Age of the Poets. "In his Italian compositions," says Burnet, "the works of Virgil and Ovid were ransacked to people the scenes restored from the remains of ancient Roman architecture. If the sea-ports of England spring from his pencil, the heroes of Nelson, or of the songs of Dibdin, rise before the spectator, enlisting his feelings in the scene." His skies have been greatly admired; the variety of forms in the clouds, their respective elongation and diminution; the bursts of sunshine from the azure openings; the black masses, "charged with deluges of rain," pouring their burdens through the enshrouding prismatic curtains, all combine to produce an effect of the most enchanting variety and originality.

Turner's early compositions are of a simple character, containing fewer parts than his later works; which arose not only from his being engaged in representations of extensive scenery—such as the embellishment of engraved subjects demanded, where a multitude of objects was required to be given in a small space—but also from his changing his conduct of light and shade from a breadth of shadow to a breadth of light, which gradually expanded to almost a want of solidity in his last paintings; this was also the reason for adopting a more brilliant style of color, since objects could not be rendered sufficiently distinct without cutting up the breadth of light, except by the contact of warm and cold color. The works of Turner indicate three distinct styles. The first shows the closest attention to the most minute detail of nature, and a sober, unaffected application of color. He afterwards launched into a bolder and broader use of his pencil, still adhering closely to form, and using the colors of his palette with great vigor and richness. In his last manner, he appears to have paid his entire attention to color, neglecting form altogether. The second class of his works are probably those upon which his future reputation must rest.

During the unusually long career of this artist, he produced so many pictures that it is quite impossible to insert a catalogue. His marines are generally signed in the trough of the sea, each letter flowing into the motion of the element. It is probable that his coloring will change in the course of time, as many of his pictures were commenced in water color, which renders the oil portion liable to crack and peel off the canvass. His later productions have much less oil in the vehicle than the earlier ones. Many of his works have been engraved, generally under his own supervision; and no pictures lose less of their beauty in this process than Turner's. Several engraved publications have emanated from his pencil, among which is the *Liber Studiorum*, published in 1808, and now very rare, consisting of a large number of studies or sketches, made in a remarkably free and powerful manner, in imitation of Claude's *Liber Veritatis*. His "Rivers of England" were engraved after a very beautiful collection of drawings in his possession at the time of his death. Among the other most admired works of this kind, are the "Rivers of France," "England and Wales," "The Southern Coast," and his beautiful illustrations of the Poems of Scott, Byron, and Rogers.

The private life of Turner was quite eccentric, and many curious anecdotes are related of him, which cannot properly be recorded in this work. Notwithstanding his wealth, he lived on a very contracted scale; but the noble use to which he finally devoted his property—that of erecting an asylum for decayed and destitute artists—will cause his name to be remembered with blessings to the end of time. The annals of art contain the record of many a noble spirit, that has gone to ruin for the lack of such an institution, but who with its protection might have been the pride and delight of his country. All honor to the name of Turner, for his expansive benevolence! He bequeathed to the nation the whole of his finished pictures, on condition that a suitable gallery be erected for their reception within ten years. Turner died at London on the 19th of December, 1851, and was buried in the crypt of St. Paul's Cathedral, by the side of Sir Joshua Reynolds. Those who wish a more extended notice of the style and character of his works, are referred to the editorial remarks in the London Art Journal for February, 1852, together with a subjoined critique by the engraver Burnet; from which the materials of this sketch have been drawn.

TURPILIUS, a Roman Knight, who painte

several pictures, formerly preserved at Verona. Pliny gives no information concerning him, except that he painted with his left hand.

TURPIN, Pierre Jean François, an eminent French painter of natural history in water-colors, born in 1775. He made upwards of 6000 drawings in water-colors, beautifully executed on vellum, which were engraved to illustrate various works, among which may be mentioned the Travels of Humboldt and Bompland; the great works on Egypt; the Plants of New Caledonia; Les Icones de M. Decandolle; L'Iconographie Vegetale; L'Atlas du Dictionnaire des Sciences Naturelles; and Duhamel's beautifully illustrated treatise on Fruit Trees. He was living in 1831.

TURRITA, Fra Mino da, or Fra Jacopo Turrita, so called from the place of his nativity in the Sienese territory, an old painter in mosaic, about whose history, and the time he flourished, there is much discrepancy. Suffice it to say that Lanzi says it is now clearly ascertained that he was not a painter, but a worker in mosaic, and that he far surpassed the Greek artists of his time. The first work known to have been executed by him is in the tribune of the church of St. Giovanni at Florence, and is dated 1225. "On examining what remains of his mosaics in S. Maria Maggiore at Rome, one can hardly be persuaded that it is the production of so rude an age, did not history constrain us to believe it." This work is dated 1495, but Lanzi says this must refer to the time when it was repaired, for it was finished in 1289, and Turrita died soon afterward; he had commenced another work in St. John of Lateran, which was finished by Gaddo Gaddi in 1292. This explains much of the discrepancy as to the time he flourished, yet Lanzi says he was the most celebrated mosaic painter of his time in 1225, when he executed his work at Florence, which would prolong his life and faculties to more than one hundred years. There was another Sienese painter called Maestro Mino, or Minuccio, who flourished at Siena in 1289, as is shown by a manuscript in the Library of Siena of that date, in which is found the following memorandum. "Paid, on the 12th of August, nineteen lire to Master Mino, the painter, who painted the Virgin Mary and other SS. in the council-room of the public palace, the balance, &c." Thus, says Lanzi, we discover another eminent painter of the name of Mino, who flourished at Siena at the same time that Fra Mino was employed at Rome. "The picture alluded to remained in the Council Chamber even within my memory, with others, dated down to 1298. He there represented the Virgin and Child surrounded by angels, under a canopy supported by apostles and the patron saint of the city, a surprising production for the age." All these works are attributed by other writers to the one artist, Fra Mino, who, they say, was both a painter and a worker in mosaic. Granting that there were two, as seems evident, the discrepancy of dates is not obviated, unless we suppose that Maestro Mino also wrought in mosaic.

TUSCHER, Marcus, a German painter and engraver, born at Nuremberg in 1706. He studied with J. D. Preisler, and afterwards went to Italy, where he resided about ten years. He painted conversations and dramatic subjects, and engraved some plates of historical subjects, vignettes, portraits, and other book plates, from his own designs, and after other masters. He is said to have visited France, Holland, England, and Denmark, in all which countries he practised his profession. Füessli describes him as an universal artist, painter, engraver, sculptor, carver in wood, architect and gem engraver. Lord Orford says he was a painter, architect, and engraver. He sometimes signed his plates with his name, and at others with his initials, *M. T. fecit.* He is supposed to have died in Denmark about 1755.

TUTIANI, Bartolomeo, an engraver on wood, who is said to have executed some cuts marked with a gothic monogram of his initals. Bartsch describes only one cut with this mark, representing Christ scoffed at by the Jews, which occurs in a book printed at Nuremberg in 1515; but there is no evidence that it was engraved by Tutiani.

TUTILO, a celebrated monk of the convent of St. Gall in Switzerland, who flourished in the latter part of the 9th century. Tutilo, and Notker, of the same convent, were the most celebrated painters, sculptors, and goldworkers of their time in Germany. The former made for the Abbot Salomo of St. Gall, a golden crucifix, richly ornamented with bas-reliefs and precious stones. He also made a celebrated image of the Virgin Mary, in gold, for a church at Metz, by which he acquired great celebrity. In the church of St. Otmahr, also at St. Gall, the altar of St. Gall was decorated with some copper plates, on which the life of that saint was engraved or carved by Tutilo. He is said to have died in 896.

TYN, Lambert de, a Belgian painter, born at Antwerp in 1770. He studied with P. van Regemorter, and painted interiors with conversations by candle light, landscapes by moonlight, and familiar subjects, with considerable reputation. He died in 1816.

TYROFF, Martin, a German engraver and publisher, who flourished at Nuremberg about 1750. He engraved a considerable number of portraits and other book plates.

TYSON, Michael, a fellow of Bennet College, Cambridge, was born in Stamford in 1740. His principal researches were in history, biography, and antiquities, which he very ably illustrated, according to Chalmers, both as a draughtsman and engraver. He painted for amusement, and etched several plates, particularly the portrait of Archbishop Parker, taken from an illumination by T. Berg, preserved in the library of Bennet College. Strutt mentions two prints by Tyson, the portrait of Sir William Paulet, and that of Jane Shore, from an original picture at King's College, Cambridge; Chalmers also says he engraved the portraits of Michael Dalton, Jacob Butler, and several other of his private friends. Tyson died in 1780.

TYSSENS, Peter, a Flemish painter, born at Antwerp in 1625. It is not known under whom he studied, but he emulated Vandyck, and approaches so near the correct design, and chaste coloring which characterize the productions of that eminent master, that it is not easy to discriminate between their respective performances. He greatly distinguished himself both in portraits and history, and after the death of Rubens and Vandyck, was considered one of the ablest painters of his time. He was made director of the Academy at Antwerp in 1661. His compositions are copious and ingenious, his design more correct than is usual with the painters of his country, his coloring is strong, clear, and harmonious, and he usually enriched his backgrounds with magnificent architecture. He executed some altar-pieces and other works for the churches in Flanders, which sustain his reputation in the vicinity of the works of the greatest masters of the Flemish school. Among those most worthy of notice, are the Martyrdom of St. Benedict, in the church of the Capuchins at Brussels; the Crucifixion at the Barefooted Carmelites, and the Assumption of the Virgin, in the church of St. James at Antwerp; the last mentioned has frequently been mistaken for a work by Vandyck. He died, according to the best authorities, in 1692, though Balkema says in 1682.

TYSSENS, Augustine, was the son of the preceding, born at Antwerp about 1660, some say about 1655; Zani places his birth in 1660, and his death in 1710; Balkema says he was born in 1662, and died in 1722. He studied with his father, but his genius leading him to landscape, he made the works of Nicholas Berghem his model, and became one of the most successful followers of his style. His landscapes are embellished with ruins, figures, and cattle, correctly designed and neatly touched; they are highly esteemed, and admitted into the choicest collections. He was director of the Academy at Antwerp in 1691.

TYSSENS, Nicholas. This artist is variously said to have been the elder and the younger son of Peter Tyssens, but it is agreed that he was born at Antwerp in 1660. After receiving instruction from his father he went to Italy, and passed some time at Venice, Rome, and Naples. He devoted himself to still-life, but he does not seem to have met with any great encouragement, though his pictures are said to be well composed and executed; they represent fruit, flowers, armor, sabres, and other military weapons, which he rendered interesting by a correct and faithful delineation, picturesque and ingenious arrangement, and an intelligent conduct of the chiaro-scuro. He was an excellent judge of the authenticity of old paintings, and was frequently commissioned to purchase valuable paintings. The Elector Palatine sent him through the Low Countries to purchase rare works for his gallery at Dusseldorf, which commission he executed to the entire satisfaction of his employer. Balkema says he died at London in 1719.

# U.

UBERTI, Pietro, an eminent Venetian portrait painter, who flourished, according to Zanetti, about 1733. He was the son of Domenico U., an artist of little note. He is celebrated in the Guida di Venezia, for his portraits, particularly for eight, representing the *Avogadori* of his time, painted for the Avogaria (Court House); which was considered a very honorable commission, formerly bestowed upon Domenico Tintoretto, Tinelli, Bombelli, and other artists, all celebrated in the same branch.

UBERTINI, Francesco, called Il Bachiacca, or Bachicca, a Florentine artist, who flourished from about 1530 to 1557. He painted history with considerable reputation, and excelled in grotesque and ornamental subjects. One of his best historical works is the Martyrdom of St. Arcadio, in the church of S. Lorenzo at Florence. The latter part of his life was passed in the service of the Grand Duke, for whom he painted some historical works for his gallery, and executed some beautiful designs for tapestry. His historical pictures are generally of small size, with numerous figures, many of which, according to Lanzi, were sent to England. He also decorated various articles of rich furniture. Vasari says his best work was a cabinet, "ornamented divinely with flowers and birds in oil colors, for the Grand Duke."

UBERTINI, Antonio, was the brother of the preceding. He was a celebrated weaver of tapestry and embroidery. He executed some exquisite works from his brother's designs for the Grand Duke. He was also employed by the Prince Doria at Genoa.

UBERTINI, Baccio, another brother of Francesco U. He was a scholar of Pietro Perugino. Lanzi says, "he was a great colorist, and on that account was employed as an assistant to his master."

UCCELLO, Paolo Mazzocchi, an old painter, born at Florence in 1349, and a disciple of Antonio Veneziano. He was one of the first who cultivated perspective; before his time, buildings had not a true point of perspective, and figures appeared sometimes as if falling or slipping off the canvass. He made this branch so much his hobby, that he neglected other essential parts. To improve his knowledge, he studied with Giovanni Manetti, a celebrated mathematician. He distinguished himself as a painter of animals, and particularly excelled in depicting all kinds of birds, of which he formed a large collection of the most curious; hence he was called Uccello (bird.) He acquired great distinction in his time, and some of his works still remain in the churches and convents of Florence. In the church of S. Maria Novella, are several subjects from the Old Testament, which he selected for the purpose of introducing his favorite objects of beasts and birds; among them are Adam and Eve in Paradise, Noah entering the Ark, the Deluge, &c. He painted battles of lions, tigers, serpents, &c., with peasants flying in terror from the scene of combat. He also painted landscapes, with cattle, figures, and ruins, possessing so much truth and nature, that Lanzi says he may be justly called the Bassano of his age. He sometimes painted figures of a colossal size; in the cathedral is a gigantic equestrian portrait of Giovanni Aguto, painted in green earth, and at Padua he painted several figures of giants in the house of Vitali. He was much employed in ornamenting articles of furniture, and in the Florentine gallery are the Triumphs of Petrarch, painted on small cabinets, which are attributed to him. Some of his pictures are signed *Pauli Uccelli Opus*. Rosini, plate 30, gives an outline of his picture of the Deluge. He was living in 1436.

UCHTERVELT. See Ochtervelt.

UDEN, Lucas van. See Vanuden.

UDINE, Giovanni da, a painter born at Udine in 1494. His family name is variously called Manni, Nanni, and Ricamatore. Lanzi says that in the *Carte Antiche* of Udine, signed by him, there appears only the family name of *Ricamatore*, and that Nanni or Nani are contractions of Giovanni, used by the common people in some parts of Italy, which have again been corrupted by historians into Manni and Mani. He is, however, usually known in the history of art as Giovanni da Udine. According to Baldinucci, he was born in 1494, and died in 1564; but Renaldis, with better authority, places his birth in 1489, and his death in 1561. Discovering an early passion for painting, his father sent him to Venice, and placed him under the instruction of Giorgione. He had already acquired considerable reputation at Venice, when the fame of Raffaelle inspired him with a desire to visit Rome, to enjoy the benefit of his instructions. Through the influence of his protector, the patriarch Grimani, and Count Baldassare Castiglione, he was admitted into Raffaelle's studio, and was employed by him in painting the ornamental accessories in many of his works, consisting of animals, birds, fruits, and flowers, in which he particularly excelled. At the time he was thus engaged, the discovery was made of the precious remains of antiquity in the Baths of Titus, and Raffaelle selected him to make designs from the beautiful grotesque ornaments in stucco, found in the different apartments. He not only succeeded in this to the entire satisfaction of his instructor, but he discovered a process of compounding stucco, which had the same appearance, and probably the same durability as that used by the Romans. He was now employed by Raffaelle to execute the greater part of the arabesque and grotesque ornaments in stucco in the Loggie, and apartments of the Vatican, which he finished in so tasteful and masterly a style, that they have ever since been the objects of universal admiration. After the death of Raffaelle, he was employed by Clement VII., in conjunction with Pierino del Vaga, to decorate that part of the Vatican called La Torre di Borgia, where they represented the Seven Planets; the emblematical figures were designed by Vaga, and the grotesque ornaments and symbolical decorations by Udine. On the sacking of Rome in 1527, he fled to his native city, where he was employed some time. He was afterwards engaged by the family of the Medici at Florence, for whom he executed some considerable works. He also visited other cities of Italy, and everywhere left exquisite specimens of his hand. He returned to Rome in the pontificate of Pius IV., where he died, in 1561, and was buried, by his own request, in the church of La Rotonda, near the tomb of Raffaelle.

Giovanni da Udine chiefly excelled in painting in fresco every species of arabesque and grotesque ornament, fruit, flowers, foliage, shells, aviaries, birds, animals, and all kinds of objects of still life, which he imitated so exquisitely, as to deceive the eye; in animals and birds particularly, he is said to have reached the highest point of excellence. He was remarkable for counterfeiting with his pencil every species of furniture, and a story is told that a groom in the service of the Pope mistook one of his imitations of a carpet for a real one, and stooped down to take it up. He also painted occasionally these subjects in oil, and pictures claimed to be originals by him are to be found scattered in many collections in Italy, though Lanzi considers many of them of very doubtful authenticity; "not, indeed, that he produced no specimens in oil, although it is extremely difficult to discover any that are certain; nor that he was incapable of drawing larger figures than such as are seen in his satyrs, in his boys and nymphs, with which he diversified the little landscapes, and the tracery of his grotesques." Vasari mentions some of his Standards, one of which, executed at Udine for the fraternity of Castello, presents in large proportions the Holy Virgin with the infant Christ, and an angel making her an offering of the same castle. The original is still preserved in the chapel, though much defaced, with a copy made by Pini in 1653. There likewise remains in the archiepiscopal palace at Udine, among some grotesques, two scripture histories drawn in half-length figures, which, though not so perfect as the ornamental parts, are valuable for their rarity.

UDINE, Girolamo da, a painter of Udine, who flourished about 1540. Little is known of him; there is an altar-piece, representing the Coronation of the Virgin, in the church of S. Francesco at Udine, bearing his signature. Lanzi says it exhibits novel invention, though rather strained, with a vigorous and effective style of coloring.

UDINE, Martino da, called Pellegrino di San Daniello. There is some discrepancy about the name of this painter, and the place of his nativity; some say that he was born at Udine about 1480, and others at the castle of San Daniello, about ten miles distant from Udine. Lanzi says that his name was Martino da Udine, but his instructor, Bellini, in honor of his rare genius, bestowed upon him the name of Pellegrino, to which the name of the country where he afterwards long resided and executed many of his best works was attached, so that he came to be called Pellegrino di San Daniello. He studied with Giovanni Bellini during that artist's residence at Udine, and, according to Vasari, had for his fellow-pupil Giovanni Martini, also a native of Udine. They were both men of genius, emulous to excel each other, and afterwards executed many works in competition at Udine, which proved of advantage to the reputation of both. According to his biographer, Renaldis, he executed many works for the churches and public edifices at Udine and San Daniello, both in oil and fresco, which raised his reputation nearly to a level with that of his instructor, whose works were then held in the highest estimation. In the Cathedral at Udine is his picture of St. Joseph with the infants Christ and St. John, which was esteemed not inferior to the picture of St. Mark, in the same edifice by Bellini. His most celebrated performance is an altar-piece in S. Maria de Battuti, representing the Virgin with several female saints and St. John the Baptist, which displays a dawning of that breadth of style and mellowness of coloring afterwards carried to such perfection by Giorgione. In the church of S. Antonio at San Daniello, are several frescos of the life of Christ by him, which are highly commended. The Duke of Ferrara invited him to his court, held him in the highest esteem not only for his professional talents but for his various accomplishments, and loaded him with favors. He is allowed to have had a fine genius, a fertile invention, and in many respects to have been superior to Bellini. He died about 1545.

UGGIONE, or OGGIONE, or DA OGGIONE, Marco, a painter born at Oggione, near Milan, about 1480. He was a favorite disciple of Leonardo da Vinci, and may justly be regarded one of the ablest artists of the Milanese school. Lanzi says he was celebrated for his frescos, and his works in the church and refectory of S. Maria della Pace, still retain the outline entire and the colors bright. "Some of them are in the church, and a very magnificent picture of the Crucifixion is to be seen in the refectory, surprising for the variety, beauty, and spirit of the figures. Few Lombard artists attained the degree of expression that is here manifested, and few to such mastery of composition and novelty of costume. He aimed at elegance of proportions; but in those of his horses he is seen to be the disciple of Vinci. For the refectory of the Certosa at Pavia, he copied the Last Supper of Leonardo, and in such a manner as to supply in a measure, the loss of the original. Milan boasts two of his altar-pieces in oil—one at S. Paolo in Compito, and the other at S. Eufemia—both excellent performances, in the style of his master, though the manner which he observed in his frescos, is more soft and analogous to modern composition." Stanley says that Uggione's copy of the Last Supper, painted for the Refectory of the Carthusians at Pavia, is now in the Royal Academy of Arts at London; it was imported into that country by a foreigner, in conjunction with Mr. Jones, a dealer in old pictures, and it was placed in that institution, mainly through Stanley's influence. The original, in the refectory of the Padri Dominicani at Milan, was painted in distemper, and Lanzi, though he does not expressly state it, strongly conveys the idea that the copy by Oggione was painted in fresco, for while he commends this work, he speaks of his oil pictures as being far inferior to his frescos.

UHLICK, an obscure German engraver, who flourished from about 1719 to 1740. He engraved some portraits in a neat, but stiff and formal style.

ULDERICO, Hans. See John or Hans Ulric, John Ulric Pilgrim; Pasti, and Preface, p. xiii.

ULFT, Jacob vander, a Dutch painter, born at Gorcum, about 1627. It is not known with whom he studied, but his first occupation was painting on glass, and there are some of his windows in the churches of Gorcum and in Guelderland, which are little inferior to the works of the celebrated Dirk and Wouter Crabeth. He afterwards devoted himself to painting cabinet pictures of historical subjects, in which he acquired distinction. His pictures represent subjects from Roman history, processions and markets, in which he introduced the most remarkable views in Rome and its vicinity; hence it has been supposed by some that he visited Italy, but the Dutch biographers have proved that he was never out of his own country. He had a perfect acquaintance with perspective and architecture, and copied his scenery from the prints and drawings of others, which he selected with judgment and taste. His works are generally crowded with figures, tastefully grouped, and he observed a marked attention to the propriety of costume. His pictures are very highly finished, and so labored as to appear like paintings on glass; yet they are highly esteemed in his own country, out of which they are scarcely known. His works are very rare, as he bestowed great labor upon them, and much of his time was occupied in discharging the duties of his office as one of the Burgomasters of the city. He died at Gorcum, some say, in 1679, though there is no certainty as to the exact time of his birth or death.

ULIVELLI, Cosimo, a painter born at Florence in 1625, and died in 1704. He studied under Baldassare Franceschini, whose style he emulated so closely that Lanzi says his works have sometimes been mistaken for those of his master, though to the intelligent observer they will appear less elegant in the forms, less chaste and effective in the coloring, and somewhat mannered and labored in the execution. Some of his best works are in the cloister of the Carmine, and prove him to have been an artist of ability.

ULRIC, Hans or John, a real or supposed German artist, mentioned by Strutt as a skillful engraver on wood in chiaro-scuro. Baron Heineken conjectures that he flourished before the time of Ugo da Carpi. He is said to have marked his prints with the above monogram, composed of the initials I. and V. on a tablet, separated by two swords but there is no certainty about him, either as to name, country or the time he flourished, and a long dissertation, without further critical research, would amount to nothing. The monogram is very similar to that used by John Ulric Pilgrim, and it seems very probable that they are one and the same artist. See *Pilgrim*.

ULRICK, Henry, a German engraver, who flourished at Nuremberg from about 1590 to 1628. He engraved some portraits and other subjects, among which are twelve circular prints, one of them of the Crucifixion. They are executed with the graver, in a stiff, formal style.

UMBACH, Jonas, a German painter and engraver, born at Augsburg in 1624, and died in 1680, according to Zani; but Brulliot says in 1700. He painted history with reputation, and executed a great number of small but spirited etchings from his own designs. Some of these are marked with his name, and others with a monogram composed of his initials. He had a son, also named Jonas, but there are no particulars recorded of him, except that he painted portraits.

UNTERBERGER, Ignatius, a distinguished German painter, was born in 1744, at Karales in the Tyrol. The *Biographie Universelle* states that his family has produced many artists, but none of them are mentioned. After acquiring the elements of design from his father, he visited Rome at the age of twenty, and studied under the direction of his brother. He designed the remains of Greek and Roman antiquity, composed several good historical subjects, and was among the artists employed to copy the Loggie of Raffaelle in the Vatican, for the Empress of Russia. In 1776 he settled at Vienna, and exhibited several historical pictures and representations of cameos and arabesques, which were greatly admired. From this time, Unterberger became the favorite painter of the minister Kaunitz, and his works were in great demand. They are distinguished for an elevated style of composition; and the management of the groups and masses of light, the drapery and the coloring are highly praised. His figures are full of animated expression, and he enriched his subjects of history with landscapes, decorated with animals and vestiges of ancient architecture.—Among the principal works of Unterberger are the Descent of the Holy Spirit, in the principal church of Koenigsgratz; and an allegorical subject impersonifying Peace and Love, as a young girl caressing a lamb. His picture of Hebe presenting ambrosia to Jupiter under the form of an Eagle, was purchased by the Emperor Francis II. for ten thousand florins, and placed in his own chamber. Unterberger practised the art for many years, and died in 1797.

URBAIN, Ferdinand de St., an eminent French medalist, was born at Nancy in Lorraine, according to the *Biographie Universelle*, in 1654. His family had been ennobled by the Dukes of Lorraine. The accounts of his early life are very imperfect; he is said to have acquired a knowledge of design and painting without an instructor, and then to have left his native country for Germany. In 1671, he visited an uncle who was residing at Munich, and afterwards traveled through Germany and Italy for improvement. During this time, he must have attained considerable excellence as a medalist; for after arriving at Bologna he was received into the Academy, and appointed engraver to the municipal counsellor, who entrusted him with the direction of his cabinet of medals. After remaining in this position about ten years, Urbain was invited to Rome by Pope Innocent XI., who appointed him his medalist, and he discharged the duties of his office under that pope, and his successors Alexander VIII. and Innocent XII., executing many admirable medals and designs for the mint. He is also said to have been employed by the popes as an architect, but none of his edifices are mentioned. Finally, after twenty years spent at Rome, Duke Leopold I., wishing to recall him to Lorraine, succeeded in obtaining the pope's consent to his departure; and on Urbain's arrival, he received him with marks of great distinction, assigning him a liberal pension, with apartments in the mint at Nancy. During a period of thirty-five years spent in the service of Dukes Leopold I. and Francis III., he executed a large number of medals for the royal houses of Spain and of Orleans, for the Elector Palatine, for the Italian princes, for cardinals, prelates, and illustrious men. He commenced a set of medals of the popes, which he did not succeed in completing; but his set of the Dukes of Lorraine was entirely finished by his own hand. It is said that all the matrices from his burin are in the Imperial Cabinet of Medals at Vienna. During a very long career, Urbain executed a large number of beautiful works, and in 1735, he was honored by Clement XII. with the order di Cristo. He died at Nancy in 1738, aged eighty-five.

URBAIN, Michael Angelo, an eminent painter on glass, born at Cortona, who flourished about 1564. He was employed in painting the windows of the churches in Tuscany and other parts of Italy.

URBANIS, Giulio, a painter of San Daniello, who studied with Pomponeo Amalteo, and followed his manner. Lanzi mentions a fresco by him at San Daniello, representing the Virgin with the infant Christ, seated upon a throne, surrounded by St. Thomas the Apostle, St. Valentine, and other Saints, signed *Opus Julii Urbanis*, 1574; it partakes of the taste of Amalteo and Pordenone.

URBANO, Pietro, a painter of Pistoja, who flourished in the first half of the 16th century. He was a disciple of Michael Angelo, whose style he emulated. Lanzi says he was a man of genius, but very indolent. There are some of his works in the churches of his native city.

URBINELLI, a painter who flourished at Urbino in the first part of the 17th century. His works are found in the public edifices and private collections in that city. Lanzi says, "he was a vigorous painter, an excellent colorist, and partial to the Venetian school."

URBINI, or URBINO, Carlo, a painter of Crema, who flourished there in the last half of the 16th century. His will is dated 1585. He executed some works for the churches and public edifices of his native city, as well as others for the collections. He was employed at Milan and elsewhere. Lanzi says he was one of the least celebrated, but one of the most deserving artists of his age. Some of his principal works are in a public hall in his native city, which he decorated with a series of national battles and victories.

URBINO, Raffaelle Sanzio di. See Raffaelle.

URBINO, Il Prete, or Timoteo and Pietro di. See Vite.

URBINO, Terenzio di. See Terenzi.

URBINO, Crocchia di, a painter of Urbino, whom, according to Baldinucci, the citizens of Urbino claim to have been a scholar of Raffaelle, and assign to him a fine picture at the Capuchins in that city. He is a different artist from Della Vite.

URBINO, Giovanni and Francesco di, two painters of Urbino, whom Lanzi thinks were scholars of Federigo Baroccio, and though he is not positive, he says he feels a pleasure in restoring them to the glorious country from which they had been separated. "In the *Descrizione odeporica della Spagna*, we find Giovanni and Francesco di Urbino mentioned, who, about 1575, were both engaged by the court of Spain to decorate the Escurial. The latter came early in life to Spain, and being endowed with a noble genius, soon became an excellent artist, and is extolled by his cotemporary, P. Siguenza, and by all who have seen the Judgment of Solomon and his other pictures, in a choir in that magnificent place. He died young."

URBINO, Luca di, an Italian engraver, by whom there is a set of prints for a Drawing Book, from the designs of Michael Angelo, the Caracci, and other masters. On one of the plates in the book above mentioned he inscribed his name Lucas de Urbino, F.

URIA, Pedro de, a Spanish architect of the 16th century, by whom Milizia mentions only one work, the Bridge of Almaraz, over the Tagus, a few miles distant from Plasencia. It is a structure that may compare with the boldest efforts of this description. Two large Gothic arches form the bridge, 580 feet long, 25 feet wide, and 134 feet high. The piers are lofty towers, and that in the centre stands on a high rock. Another pier has a semicircular projection between the arches, forming a piazza at the top, on which is an inscription, importing that the work was erected in 1552, at the expense of the city of Plasencia, under Charles V., by Pedro de Uria.

UROOM, Enrico, called also by the Italians, Enrico di Spagna, and Enrico delle Marine. See Henry Cornelius de Vroom.

USTAMBER, Pedro de, an architect who flourished in Spain during the eleventh century. According to Milizia, by order of King Ferdinand of Castile, he toŏk down the old church of St. John the Baptist, of Leon; and erected another of stone, dedicated to St. Isidorus, whose remains were removed from Seville. Within this church is the sepulchre of the architect, a lofty tomb of polished stone, which imports that he also built the bridge called Ustamber.

UTRECHT, Adrian van, an eminent Flemish painter of subjects of still-life, was born at Antwerp in 1599. He painted fruit, flowers, shellfish, dead game, birds, &c., sometimes together, and sometimes separate, with such elegance of composition, and remarkable truth and freedom of touch, that he received many more orders than he could execute. He frequently assisted other artists by painting the fruit and flowers in their pictures, and according to Houbraken and Descamps, he excelled all the other Flemish painters of still-life, except Francis Snyders. His best pictures were purchased by the king of Spain. His works are now very scarce, and command high prices. Van Utrecht visited Spain, where he was much employed by Philip IV.; and it was there he painted the magnificent assemblage of fruit in the large picture by Rubens of Pythagoras and his Disciples, which is now placed in Buckingham Palace. He died wealthy, at Antwerp, in 1651.

UYTENBROECK, Moses, called Little Moses, from the small size of his prints. He was a native of the Low Countries, and according to the dates on his prints, flourished from about 1615 to 1646; some say he died in 1650, but this is uncertain. He painted small landscapes, embellished with subjects from history or fable, so much in the style of Cornelius Poelemburg that it is supposed that many of his works are now attributed to that master, and that he was his pupil. Of his etchings and engravings, Bartsch gives a description of fifty-eight (Le Peintre Graveur, tom. v.), to which Weigel, in his Supplements to Bartsch, has added nine more, with full particulars of the variations of those described by his predecessor. From some whimsical fancy, he variously signed his prints Uytenbroeck, Utenbroeck, Vytenbrouck, Vtenbrouck, Wtenbrouck, Wtenbroeck, Veit vander Broeck, Van Brouck, Brouck, and various other contractions, for which see monograms, plate xxiii.

UYTENWAEL, Joachim, a Dutch painter, born at Utrecht in 1566. He was the son of a painter on glass, who brought him up to his own business till he was eighteen years of age, when he became the scholar of Joseph de Beer, with whom he studied three years, and then went to Italy, where he resided some time. At Padua, he became acquainted with the Bishop of St. Malo, whom he accompanied to France, and remained in his employment two years, when he returned to his native city, where he passed the rest of his life. He painted history in the manner of Bartholomew Sprangher, and though his pictures are well colored and elaborately finished, his design, like that of his model, is generally incorrect, and his draperies often fantastical. His cabinet pictures of mythological subjects are the best. Van Mander commends two small pictures by him in the collection of the Elector Palatine, representing the Feast of the Gods, and Mars and Venus. They are elaborately finished and well colored. He died in 1624.

# V.

VAART, John Vander, a Dutch painter, born at Haerlem in 1647, and studied under Thomas Wyck. He went to England in 1674, where he painted landscapes, objects of still-life, and dead game, with considerable reputation, particularly the latter, in which he excelled. He also scraped a few indifferent portraits in mezzotinto. He died at London in 1721.

VACCA, Flaminio, a Roman Sculptor of the latter part of the 16th century. He is less known as a statuary, than as a restorer of statues, although many of his own works adorn the churches, squares, and fountains of Rome. He wrought in that capital in the pontificate of Sixtus V., and was also invited into Tuscany. In 1594, he completed his manuscript entitled *Memorie di varie Antichità di Roma*, which was published by Ottavio Falconieri at Rome in 1704. It is inserted in Montfaucon's *Iter Italicum*, in a Latin translation, and has gained considerable celebrity for its author.

VACCARINI, Bartolomeo, an old painter of Ferrara, who flourished, according to Baruffaldi, about 1450. There are some of his works at Ferrara signed with his name, executed in the dry and gothic style of his time.

VACCARO, Andrea, a painter born at Naples, according to Dominici, in 1598, and died there in 1670. He was a disciple of Cav. Massimo Stanzioni, on leaving whom, he adopted the style of Michael Angelo da Caravaggio, which he followed for some time, with such success, that some of his earlier works, especially his cabinet pictures, have been frequently mistaken by good judges for the productions of that master. Lanzi says "he was the rival of Massimo, but at the same time, his admirer and friend; possessing great imitative powers, he was afterwards induced by the advice of Stanzioni, to adopt the style of Guido, in which he succeeded in an admirable manner, though not equal to his friend. In this style he executed his most celebrated works at Certosa, at the Teatini, and at the Rosario, without enumerating his numerous productions in the collections." After the death of Massimo, he was considered the ablest artist of the Neapolitan school, and was without a rival until the return of Luca Giordano from Rome with a new style, from the school of Pietro da Cortona. Both artists were competitors for the large altar-piece in the new church of S. Maria del Pianti, representing the Virgin liberating the city from pestilence; the designs were submitted to Cortona as umpire, who decided against his own scholar, in favor of Vaccaro, observing that, as he was first in years, so he was first in design and expression. Giordano, however, soon carried all before him, and Vaccaro, now advanced in years, in attempting to compete with him in fresco, which he had not studied in his youth, lost his reputation.

VACCARO, Francesco, an Italian painter and engraver, said to have been born at Bologna in 1636, though probably at an earlier date, as Zani says he operated as early as 1650. He studied under Francesco Albano, but devoted himself chiefly to painting perspective and architectural pieces. He published a treatise on perspective, illustrated with plates engraved from his own designs. There is also a set of twelve perspective views of ruins, fountains, and other edifices in Italy by him, inscribed *Fr. Vaccaro fec.* He died in 1687.

VACCARO, Domenico Antonio. This artist was born at Naples in 1680, and is said by Milizia to have been a painter, sculptor, and architect; but he probably did not practise the first to any extent, as his name is not mentioned by Lanzi. After receiving a good education, he studied architecture, and attained considerable eminence. At Naples he built the church of the monastery of the Concezione, called di Monte Calvario, of nearly a circular form, interrupted by four arches, supporting four tribunes. He also constructed the Teatro Nuovo; modernized the church Monte Vergine near that of Gesu Vecchio; and built that of S. Michele Arcangelo, without the gate Spirito Santo. Vaccaro erected a number of other works at Naples, and in other parts of the kingdom, among which are the Tarsia palace, the little palace of Caravita, at Portici; and the church of S. Giovanni at Capua.

VACCELLINI, Gaetano. See Vascellini.

VADDER, Louis de, a Flemish painter, born at Brussels in 1560. It is not known under whom he studied, but he is ranked among the ablest landscape painters of his country. From the grandeur of his style and the picturesque beauty of his scenery, it is supposed that he visited Italy, where he appears to have made the works of Titian the particular objects of his study, as his best works have a striking resemblance to the admirable landscapes of that great master. His touch is uncommonly firm and free, and his coloring, though vigorous, is tender and chaste. He had a good knowledge of perspective, and proportioned every object to its distance; his grounds are pleasingly broken, the forms of his rocks and trees are noble and select, and his pictures are usually distinguished by a vapory degradation, which is only to be found in the works of the most faithful observers of nature. It was his custom to frequent the fields before sunrise, to observe the gradual diffusion of light and its effects in unfolding the hills and mountains by the gradual dispersion of the mists and vapors. His works are not much known out of his own country, where they are deservedly esteemed, and found in the choicest collections. He executed some spirited etchings from his own designs, in a style resembling that of Lucas van Uden. He died at Brussels in 1623.

VAFFLARD, Pierre Antoine Augustin, a French painter of the present century, whose career is now probably terminated, was born at Paris in 1777. He studied under J. B. Regnault, and subsequently practised the art with reputation for many years. Most of his works are poetical subjects, well chosen, and ably executed; besides which he painted portraits, and subjects from the history of his country. The government purchased many of his productions, and employed him in restoring many of the decorations of the galleries at the Tuileries and Versailles. Among the principal works of Vafflard are, the Barricades in July, 1830; Molière reading his *Tartuffe;* and subjects from the lives of Henry IV. and Napoleon.

VAGA, Pierino del. The name of this artist was Pietro Buonaccorsi, but he was called Pierino del Vaga, after one of his instructors, who conducted him to Rome, and was the means of introducing him into the school of Raffaelle, and thus leading him to distinction. He was born at a small village near Florence, in 1500, and having the misfortune to lose his parents during infancy, he was taken under the care of Andrea de Ceri, whose house was much frequented by the young artists of Florence. At an early age, he discovered a decided genius for art, and was placed under the instruction of Ridolfo Ghirlandaio, with whom he made great progress. In 1515, he accompanied del Vaga, a Florentine painter of some note, to Rome, where he had the advantage of studying the antique, and the works of Michael Angelo. His merits becoming known to Giulio Romano and Gio. Francesco Penni, two of the principal disciples and assistants of Raffaelle, they recommended him to the notice of that illustrious master, who received him into his academy, and employed him in the Loggie of the Vatican. Such was the versatility of his powers, that he was equally successful in assisting Giovanni da Udine in the stuccos and grotesque ornaments, and Polidoro da Caravaggio in his antique subjects in chiaroscuro, as well as in executing several scriptural histories from the designs of Raffaelle, the principal of which are, Abraham preparing to sacrifice Isaac, Jacob wrestling with the Angel, Joseph and his Brethren, the Battle of Joshua, the Passage of the Jordan, and the Capture of Jericho. On the death of Raffaelle, he was employed by Leo X. and Clement VII., in conjunction with Giulio Romano and Gio. Francesco Penni, to finish the great works in the Vatican. Lanzi says that he was a relation, as well as a fellow citizen of Penni. One of the earliest works which he exhibited at Rome from his own composition was the Creation of Eve, in the church of S. Marcello, designed in the grand style of Michael Angelo, which Lanzi characterizes as a "most finished performance."

Pierino del Vaga was in full possession of public esteem, when the dreadful sacking of Rome by the Spaniards in 1527, so disastrous to the arts and artists in Italy, compelled him to fly from that capital, and having lost all his property, he arrived at Genoa, in a state of distress in 1528, where he was liberally welcomed by the Prince Doria, who employed him for several years in the decorations of his magnificent palace, situated without the gate of S. Tommaso. It was here that he displayed the extent of his powers, and the fecundity of his invention; so that it has been a matter of dispute whether Giulio Romano, in the Palazzo del Te at Mantua, or Pierino, in the Palazzo Doria at Genoa, has done most honor to the great school in which they were educated. Lanzi says, "Pierino nowhere displayed his talents to such advantage as in the Doria Palace. He superintended the exterior decorations of the sculptures, as well as the interior ornaments of the stuccos, the gilding, the arabesques, the paintings in fresco and in oil. This place in consequence, breathes all the taste of the halls and loggie of the Vatican, the celebrated works of which attracted universal admiration, and in the execution of a part of which, Pierino had a considerable share. We find in the Doria Palace some small histories of celebrated Romans, of Cocles, for example, and of Scævola, which might pass for the compositions of Raffaello; a group of Boys at play, likewise, has all the air of that master; and on a ceiling, in the War of the Giants against the Gods, we seem to behold in conflict, the same persons whom Raffaello had represented as banqueting in the Casa Chigi. If the expression be not so noble, nor the grace so rare, it is because that grand specimen of art may be emulated by many, but equalled by none. It may be added that his style is less finished than Raffaello's, and that in his drawing of the naked figure, he, like Giulio Romano, partakes of the style of Michael Angelo." Pierino also decorated several apartments with subjects taken from Roman history, and the Metamorphoses of Ovid; he also designed for tapestry a series of cartoons of the history of Æneas. All these works are not, however, executed with equal care, and Lanzi says that his avidity for gain drew down upon him merited reprehension, for while Raffaello and Giulio Romano were indefatigable in their application, selecting only the best artists for their assistants, Pierino contented himself with preparing his cartoons, and entrusted their execution mostly or entirely to his pupils or assistants, some of whom were artists of inferior talents,—a practice which, though it added materially to his pecuniary advantage, was detrimental to his reputation. Vasari informs us that four of the chambers in the Doria palace were executed from the designs of Vaga by Luzio Romano, and some Lombards, his assistants. Nevertheless, Vasari considers him the best designer of the Florentine school, after Michael Angelo, and his partiality placed him at the head of all those who assisted Raffaelle. Lanzi says, "It is certain that no one could, like Pierino, compete with Giulio in that universality of talent so conspicuous in Raffaello; and the subjects from the New Testament, which he painted in the Papal Gallery, were praised by Taja above all others. In his style there is a great mixture of the Florentine, as may be seen at Rome in the Birth of Eve, in the church of S. Marcello, where there are some children painted to the life, a most finished performance." Del Vaga also executed some works for the churches and public edifices at Lucca, Pisa, Genoa, and elsewhere. In the convent at Tivoli is one of his best works, representing St. John in the Desert, with an admirable landscape. Towards the close of his life, he returned to Rome, where, Lanzi says, "he might have effected the restoration of art, if his magnanimity had corresponded with the sublimity of his mind, but he did not inherit the genius of his master." Lanzi then goes on to accuse him of making a traffic of art, contriving always to abound in commissions and money, and that he employed the best artists to paint from his designs in order to make them dependent upon him, and thus prevent them from interfering with his commissions and emoluments. He was much employed by Paul III., who granted him a life pension of 25 ducats monthly. About 1543, Vaga undertook the direction of the paintings in the Sala Regia; he ornamented the ceiling, and directed the preparatory operations, all in the style of a great master; after which he applied himself to design the subjects for his pencil, when he died in 1547.

VAGNUCCI, Francesco, a painter of Assisi, who flourished there in the first part of the 16th century. There are some of his works in the churches of that city, which Lanzi says are "executed in the spirit of the old masters," i. e., somewhat dry and hard.

VAIANI, Anna Maria, an Italian lady who flourished at Rome about 1650. She painted flower pieces, and engraved a part of the plates for the Justinian Gallery. Bartsch describes five prints by her, but with no great commendation.

VAIANO, or VAJANO, Orazio, sometimes called Il Fiorentino, a painter born at Florence, who flourished about 1600. He resided a long time at Milan, where he executed many works for the churches and for individuals, which Lanzi says display diligence and judgment, though they are somewhat feeble in point of coloring. According to Orlandi, some of his pictures have been confounded with those of the elder Palma, "for what reason," says Lanzi, "it is difficult to conjecture, as there is little resemblance of style. In the distribution of his lights he much resembles the Cav. Roncalli." Some of his best works are in the churches of S. Carlo, and S. Antonio Abate at Milan. There are also several of his works in the churches and public edifices at Genoa. Bartsch says his name was *Alessandro*, and that he flourished about 1628. He describes a print by him of a Dead Christ, and another of a Magdalen, engraved from his design, by *Sebastian Vajano;* but these were doubtless different artists, of whom little is known. The name is sometimes written *Vaiani.*

VAILLANT, Wallerant, a Flemish painter and engraver, born at Lisle in 1623. After studying in his native city, he went to Antwerp, where he became the disciple of Erasmus Quellinus. Finding his genius best adapted to portraiture, he applied himself to that branch, and met with great encouragement. He went to Frankfort at the time of the coronation of the Emperor Leopold, whose portrait he had the honor to paint, which gained him great reputation, and abundant employment. At the invitation of Marshal Grammont, the French ambassador, he accompanied him to the court of France, where he added to his reputation by his portraits of the Queen Mother, and the Duke of Orleans. He now met with such constant employment and liberal prices, that in a few years, he was enabled to return to Flanders with a competent fortune. He painted equally well both in oil and crayons. He is said to have visited England in the suite of Prince Rupert, who communicated to him the then newly discovered process of mezzotinto engraving. He engraved quite a number of plates in that manner, from his own designs and after other masters, which he usually marked with one of the accompanying monograms. His brother and pupil, John V., was born at Lisle in 1624, and followed painting for some time with great success; but having married a rich lady of Frankfort, he devoted himself to commerce. Among other prints by Wallerant V., are the following. He died at Amsterdam in 1677.

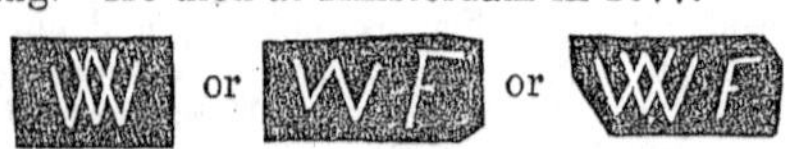


PORTRAITS.

Prince Rupert. His own Portrait. The Portrait of his Wife. Desiderius Erasmus. John Frobenius, the celebra ted printer of Basle. Sir Anthony Vandyck. Barent Graat, Painter.

SUBJECTS AFTER VARIOUS MASTERS.

St. Barbara; *after Raffaelle.* Judith; *after Guido.* The Holy Family; *after Titian.* The Temptation of St. Anthony; *after Cam. Procaccini.* The Bust of a Warrior; *after Tintoretto.* Venus lamenting the Death of Adonis; *after Eras. Quellinus.* The Prodigal Son; *after Mark Gerard.* Judith and Jael; *after Gerard Lairesse.*

BVF VAILLANT, BERNARD, was the brother of the preceding, born at Lisle in 1625, though some say in 1627. The success of his brother induced him to adopt the same profession, and he received his principal instruction in art from him. He chiefly excelled in painting portraits in crayons, and accompanied his brother to Frankfort and Paris, and found considerable employment in that branch. On his return to the Low Countries, he settled at Rotterdam, where he passed the rest of his life. He also engraved several plates of portraits from his own designs, and after W. Vaillant and other masters, which he sometimes signed with his name, and at others marked with the above monogram.

VAILLANT, JAMES, was also the brother and scholar of Wallerant V., born at Lisle in 1628. He went to Italy while young, and passed two years at Rome. On his return to Flanders, he was invited to the court of the Elector of Brandenburg at Berlin, where he practised both historical and portrait painting with considerable reputation. The Elector sent him to Vienna to paint the portrait of the Emperor, who presented him with a gold chain and medal. There is some discrepancy as to the time of his death; some say that he died young, without giving the date, others place his death in 1670; but Laborde and Zani, in 1691. This latter date may apply to the fourth brother, *John V.*, mentioned in the second preceding article.

VAILLANT, ANDREW, was the youngest brother of Wallerant V., born at Lisle in 1629. He was instructed by him both in painting and engraving, and engraved some portraits after pictures by his brothers, one of which is dated 1689.

VAL, DU, an artist mentioned by Papillon as an engraver on wood, who flourished about 1650. His prints are remarkable for neatness and delicacy of execution; they are chiefly after the designs of James Stella and Nicholas Cochin. There is a set of twenty cuts by him, engraved for a work entitled "The Miraculous History of Notre Dame de Liesse," which are highly esteemed.

VAL, MARK DU, an engraver on wood, who flourished from about 1560 to 1580. His cuts are very indifferently executed.

VAL, SEBASTIANO D'. Little is known of this artist. There are two spirited etchings by him, one of which is dated 5558, which Zani conjectures to stand for the age of the world; this would make the artist to have flourished, he says, in 1558. It represents Prometheus tormented by the Vulture, inscribed *Sebastiano D' Val, Ut.* 5558; the other, representing the Repose in Egypt, is inscribed on a tablet, *Sebastiano D.' VL.;* and on another tablet held by an angel, is written, *Piu alto non so dir che Mater Dei.* Zani interprets the signatures, *Sebastiano de Valentini Utinense.*

VAL, DU. See DUVAL.

VALDELVIRA, PEDRO DE, a Spanish architect, who flourished about the middle of the 16th century. According to Milizia, between the years 1540 and 1556, he erected in Ubeda the famous chapel del Salvador, by order of the Comendador, Don Francisco de los Cobos. He also erected a palace for that nobleman, which, like the chapel, is profusely ornamented. Among his other edifices, is the hospital and chapel of S. Giacomo in Baeza, erected in 1562, and considered one of the best buildings in Andalusia.

VALDES, DON JUAN DE LEAL, a Spanish painter, descended from an ancient family of Asturia, and born at Cordova in 1630. He studied in the school of Antonio del Castillo, and afterwards removed to Seville, where he became one of the most distinguished painters in that city, and lived on terms of intimacy with Murillo, who was a great admirer of his works. He was one of the founders of the Academy there, and succeeded Murillo as president of that institution. At the death of that master, he was esteemed at the head of his profession. His works are numerous in the churches at Seville, among which is the Triumph of the Cross, in La Caridad; there are also a number at Cordova, as the Martyrdom of St. Andrew, in the church of S. Francisco; and the history of the Prophet Elias, in the church of the Carmelites. Valdes is said to have distinguished himself as a sculptor and architect, but none of his works are specified. There are two prints attributed to him, one marked with his monogram, and the other with his name in full. He died in 1691.

VALDES, DON LUCAS DE, was the son of the preceding, born at Seville in 1661. He was instructed in the art by his father, and painted history and portraits with considerable reputation. There are some of his works in the churches and public edifices of his native city. He also engraved several plates from his own designs. He died in 1724. He had a son named *Juan*, who engraved some plates of devotional subjects, and a few portraits, mostly for the booksellers.

VALDES, DON SEBASTIAN LLANOS DE, a Spanish painter, who flourished at Seville about 1660. He studied under Francisco d' Herrera the Elder, and attained a high reputation among the artists of his time. His works are characterized by correctness of design and beauty of coloring, although they manifest some degree of mannerism. He aided greatly in establishing the Academy of Seville, and succeeded Murillo and Juan de Valdes in the presidency of that institution. Many of his pictures are to be found in the Spanish private collections. Among his large historical subjects, are a Magdalen, in the church of the Recollets at Madrid; and a picture of the Virgin surrounded by Saints and Angels, painted in 1669, for the church of St. Thomas at Seville.

VALDOR, JOHN, a Flemish engraver, born at Liege, who flourished from about 1620 to 1649. He went to Paris, where he chiefly resided, and engraved a considerable number of plates for the booksellers, representing Saints and devotional subjects, which are executed with remarkable neatness and precision. He also engraved a part of the plates for a book published at Paris in 1638, entitled *Les Triomphes de Louis le Juste*, which are his best performances.

VALENCIA, Fray Matias de, a Spanish painter, born at Valencia in 1696. His name was Lorenzo Chafrion. After acquiring some knowledge of the art in his native city, he went to Rome, where he became the disciple of Corrado Giaquinto, whose style he adopted. On his return to Valencia, he did not meet with much encouragement, and afterwards went to Granada, in hopes of being able to obtain some assistance from an uncle residing there, but being disappointed in his expectations and reduced to distress, he took refuge in a convent. There are some of his cabinet pictures in the collections at Valencia, and a picture of the Last Supper, in the refectory of his convent. He was drowned in 1749.

VALENCIENNES, Pierre Henri, an eminent French landscape painter, was born at Toulouse in 1750. His parents intended him for the study of music, but as he manifested a strong inclination for art, he was sent to Paris, and placed in the school of Doyen. Under that master, he acquired that historical style which forms the chief characteristic of his productions; but being more inclined to landscape painting, he visited Rome, and studied the works of N. Poussin and Claude Lorraine. On returning to Paris, he was chosen a member of the Academy, and formed a school which has produced the best French artists in landscape of the present day. He was an associate of the Academy at Toulouse, and a member of the Legion of Honor. The talents of Valenciennes, though unequal to those of his great models, were of a superior order; and he first, after Poussin, gave to his department in art that grandeur of style which elevates it to the rank of history. Among his best works are, Œdipus found on the island of Cythera; Œdipus before the Temple of Eumenides; Philoctetes in the Isle of Lemnos; the Vale of Tempe; a View of the ancient city Trezina; the Dance of Theseus; and his masterpiece in the Louvre, according to the *Biographie Universelle*, representing Cicero, while questor in Sicily, discovering the tomb of Archimedes. Valenciennes wrote an admirable work on perspective entitled *Traité de perspective et de l'art du paysage*, 1800, 4to. He died at Paris in 1819.

VALENTIN, Pierre, a French painter, born at Colommiers en Brie, near Paris, in 1600. It is generally stated that he acquired a knowledge of design under Simon Vouet, in his own country, but Vouet quitted France in 1602, and did not return until 1627. Valentin therefore probably studied under some other master, as he visited Rome while still young, where he passed the rest of his life. He was one of the most judicious followers of Michael Angelo da Caravaggio. He acquired a high reputation at Rome, and enjoyed the protection of the Cardinal Barberini, nephew of Urban VIII., through whose influence he obtained the commission to paint a picture of the Martyrdom of Sts. Processo and Martiniano, for the Basilica of St. Peter, which is esteemed his best performance. He also painted for his patron the Decollation of St. John, in the Barberini palace, and St. Peter denying Christ, in the Corsini palace, which Lanzi says is a "delightful picture." His other principal historical works are, Judith with the Head of Holofernes, the Judgment of Solomon, and Susanna and the Elders, in the Louvre. His easel pictures are his best works, and Lanzi says they are frequently to be met with in the collections at Rome; they usually represent concerts of music, corps-de-gardes, fortune-tellers, card-players, and similar subjects. He was an artist of great promise, but died in the flower of his life in 1632. The Italians call him *Pietro Valentino*.

VALENTINA, Jacopo di, a painter of the Venetian school, born at Serravalle. There are some altar-pieces and other pictures by him in the churches of his native place, Ceneda, and elsewhere, painted in the style of Squarcione of Padua. He flourished about 1500.

VALERIANI, Padre Giuseppe, a painter born at Aquila, who flourished at Rome, according to Baglioni, in the pontificate of Clement VIII. It is not known under whom he studied, but he imitated Sebastiano del Piombo, though Lanzi says he was too heavy in his design, and too dark in his colors. He afterwards entered the Society of the Jesuits, and much improved his first manner. His best works are in the Chiesa del Gesù, where he painted a fine picture of the Annunciation, and several subjects from the life of Christ.

VALERIANI, Domenico and Giuseppe, two painters, brothers, born at Rome, who studied under Marco Ricci, and flourished about 1730. According to Zanetti, Domenico excelled in landscape and perspective, and Giuseppe in figures; they wrought conjointly, each in his respective department, and were much employed in decorating the churches and public edifices, but more particularly the theatres, "in Venice, and indeed throughout Italy and other parts of Europe."

VALESIO, Francesco, an Italian painter and engraver, who flourished at Venice about 1612. Little is known of his works as a painter, but he engraved a variety of frontispieces and other book plates from his own designs, and some portraits and other subjects after Pietro Faccini and other masters. His most considerable work is a set of plates of Hermits, engraved for a work entitled *Illustrium Anachoretorum Elogia*, written by Jacobus Cavacius, a Benedictine monk, published at Venice in 1612. His plates are executed with the graver, in a neat but formal style. He sometimes marked his plates *Franciscus Valegius, f.*

VALESIO, Giacomo, an Italian engraver, born at Verona, who flourished in the latter part of the 16th century. His prints are dated from about 1574 to 1587. He engraved some plates after Paul Veronese and other masters, executed with the graver, in a style resembling that of Cornelius Cort. He also carried on the business of a printseller.

VALESIO, Niccolo, another engraver of Verona, probably a brother of Giacomo V. He flourished about the same time, engraved some book plates, and was also a publisher.

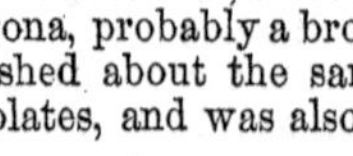

or VALESIO, Giovanni Luigi, an Italian painter and engraver, born at Bologna in 1561. He studied in the school of the Caracci and, according to Malvasia, and Lanzi, acquired a greater reputation than he deserved. He executed several works for the churches of his native city, the principal of which are, the Scourging of Christ, in S. Pietro; the Annunciation, at th

Mendicanti; and St. Roch curing the Sick of the Plague, in S. Rocco. Lanzi says these works have nothing of the grandeur of the school of the Caracci; they are dry in composition, and have little relief, yet they are executed in the exact method of the miniaturists. He afterwards went to Rome, where by his assiduity, ready wit, convivial and social qualities, he acquired much reputation and abundant employment. He was much patronized by the Lodovisi family, and his praise was sung by Marini and other poets of the day. "By means like these," says Lanzi, "he maintained his equipage in Rome, where Annibale Caracci, during many years, obtained no other stipend for his honorable toils than a bare roof for his head, daily pittance for himself and servant, with an annual payment of 120 crowns!" Bartsch, however, highly commends him as an engraver. He describes (P. G. tom. xviii.), one hundred and eleven prints by him, and mentions sixteen more on the authority of Malvasia. He approaches nearer to Agostino Caracci in his engravings, than any other artist of that school. He died at Rome in 1640.

VALET, or VALLET, Guillaume, a French engraver, born at Paris in 1636. He is supposed to have studied with François de Poilly. He afterwards went to Italy, and resided many years at Rome. He engraved a considerable number of plates after the Italian and French masters, which are executed chiefly with the graver, in the style of de Poilly, and though his prints are inferior to the works of that master, they possess considerable merit. He died in 1704. The following are among his principal prints:

PORTRAITS.

Charles Emanuel, Duke of Savoy. Louis, Duke of Mantua. Alessandro Algardi, Sculptor. Andrea Sacchi, Painter; *after C. Maratti.* The Bust of Peter Corneille, crowned by Melpomene and Thalia; *after Paillet.* Olympia Maldachini, Roma, 1657.

SUBJECTS AFTER VARIOUS MASTERS.

The Nativity; *after Raffaelle.* The Holy Family; *do.* Melchisedec bringing presents to Abraham; *do.* The Last Supper; *do.* The Holy Family; *after Guido.* Cornelius Bloemaert has engraved the same subject. The Holy Family; *after Albano.* A Repose in Egypt; *after C. Maratti.* The Virgin, with the infant Christ and St. John; *after An. Caracci.* The Annunciation; *after Courtois.* The Resurrection; *after N. Loir.* St. John the Baptist before Herod; *after le Brun.* The Adoration of the Magi; *after Poussin.* The Assumption of the Virgin; *after J. Miel.* The Holy Family; *after James Stella.* The Crucifixion; *do.*

VALK, or VALCK, Gerard, a Dutch engraver, born at Amsterdam about 1626. He studied with Abraham Blooteling, whose sister he married, and was afterwards taken into partnership with him. He went to England, where he was employed by David Loggan for some time. He also assisted Peter Schenck in his large Dutch Atlas, in 2 vols. folio, published in 1683. He wrought both with the graver and in mezzotinto, and some of his prints possess considerable merit. The following are among the best:

PORTRAITS WITH THE GRAVER.

Hortensia, Duchess of Mazarin; *after Lely;* one of his best plates. Robert, Lord Brooke. John, Duke of Lauderdale. Eleanor Gwyn; *after Lely.*

PORTRAITS AND SUBJECTS IN MEZZOTINTO.

William, Prince of Orange; *after Lely.* Mary, Princess of Orange; *do.* Louisa, Duchess of Portsmouth; *do.* Mary Davis, Actress; *do.* A Girl holding a Lamp; *after G. Douw.* David and Bathsheba; *after B. Graat.* A Trumpeter presenting a letter to a Lady; *after Terburg.* A Death's Head crowned with Laurel. Cupid asleep; *after Guido.* A Woman searching for Fleas.

VALK, Peter, a Dutch painter and engraver, born at Leuwarde in 1584. It is not known under whom he studied, but he at first imitated Abraham Bloemaert. He afterwards went to Italy, and passed several years at Rome. On his return to Holland, he acquired considerable reputation as a painter of history, portraits, and landscapes. He also engraved a few plates in the manner of Philip Galle, which are chiefly copied from the prints of that master.

VALKAERT, Waernaert vander, a Dutch painter and engraver, whose birth is variously placed at Amsterdam in 1572, 1575, and 1580. He studied under Henry Goltzius, and became a good painter of history and portraits, in the manner of his master. There are some pictures by him in the churches of Utrecht. He also etched some plates from his own designs, in a bold and spirited style. He died in 1625. His name is variously spelled, *Warner*, *Warnard*, and *Waernaert Valker*, *Valkert*, and *Valkaert.*

VALKENBURG, Lucas van, a Flemish painter, born at Mechlin in or about 1530. He painted landscapes and portraits in small, with considerable reputation. He was patronized by the Duke of Lintz, for whom he executed many works. His death is variously placed in 1582 and in 1625. His name is sometimes written *Valckenburg.*

M VV. VALKENBURG, Martin van, was the younger brother of the preceding, born at Mechlin about 1533, though some say in 1542. He accompanied his brother in his travels, and is said to have painted many pictures from the beautiful scenery in the vicinity of Liege and Aix-la-Chapelle. He frequently enriched his pictures with figures from ancient history or mythology. He sometimes marked his pictures with the above monogram. He died at Frankfort in 1574, though some say in 1636.

VALKENBURG, Dirk or Theodore, a Dutch painter, born at Amsterdam in 1675. He studied successively under Cuylenberg, Michael van Musscher, and John Weenix. He painted animals, huntings, and dead game, in the manner of Weenix, and his pictures, particularly of dead game, are accounted little inferior to the productions of that admired master. He was also an excellent portrait painter. In 1696, he set out to travel through Germany to Italy. He stopped some time at the court of Baden, where his pictures were greatly admired; he next proceeded to Vienna, with letters to the Prince of Lichtenstein, who received him in the most gracious manner. He soon acquired a distinguished reputation at that capital, and received so many commissions from the most distinguished persons, that he abandoned his projected visit to Italy, and in the course of a few years amassed a handsome fortune. The desire of revisiting his native country, induced him to abandon his brilliant and flattering career at Vienna, and he returned to Amsterdam, where his works were not less esteemed. He was employed by William III. to paint several pictures for his palace at Loo. He died of apoplexy in the prime of life, in 1721.

VALKENBURGH, Frederick, a German painter, born at Nuremberg in 1555. After studying in his native city, under an obscure artist, he went to Venice, where he studied the works of Titian and Paul Veronese, and formed a style of his own, agreeable and elegant, with rich and harmonious coloring, a light and clean pencil, and a delicate touch. His usual subjects were fairs, markets, sports, and dead game, though he sometimes painted history. He was also very successful in representing perspective views of public edifices and places in cities. He usually introduced a large number of small figures into his pictures, which he designed with tolerable correctness. His works are little known out of Germany, where they are held in considerable estimation. He died in 1623. His name is sometimes erroneously called *Vallenburgh.*

VALLE, Giovanni da, an old painter who flourished at Milan about 1460. According to Lomazzo, he made great improvements in perspective. "He was one of the great inventors in the art of correctly viewing objects." He had a brother, named Carlo, also a painter, who was sometimes called *Carlo Milanese.* Their works have mostly perished.

VALLE, Andrea della. This architect was a native of Padua, and flourished in the 16th century. From the high commendation of Milizia, it would appear that he deserved greater reputation than he attained. His principal work was the Carthusian monastery, two miles from Padua, which is admirably constructed, and of such a beautiful design that it has been attributed to Palladio. Della Valle published an edition of the unprinted works of Palladio, in which he inserted five plates.

VALLEE, or VALEE, Simone, a French engraver, who is said to have been born at Paris about 1700, although a print is mentioned with his signature, dated 1706. He studied under P. Drevet, and executed several plates, which are etched and finished with the graver, in a neat, tasteful style. Among them are the following:

PORTRAITS.

John de Troy, Painter to the King; *after Fras. de Troy.* John Francis Savery, Curate of St. Menehoult; *do.*

SUBJECTS AFTER VARIOUS MASTERS.

The Transfiguration; *after Raffaelle.* St. John in the Desert; *do.* The Flight into Egypt; *after Carlo Maratti.* The Resurrection of Lazarus; *after Girolamo Muziano.* The Finding of Moses; *after Francesco Romanelli.* Christ bearing his Cross; *after Andrea Sacchi.* The Death of the Virgin; *after M. Angelo da Caravaggio.* The Sacrifice of Abraham; *after Ant. Coypel.* Christ calling to him the little Children; *after P. J. Cazes.* The Descent of the Holy Ghost; *do.*

VALLET, Pierre, a French designer and engraver, who flourished at Paris in the first half of the 17th century. According to Dumesnil, he engraved one hundred and twenty-four plates for a work entitled "Les Aventures amoureuses de Theagene et Chariclée," published in 1613; a Plan of the City of Paris; and the Flowers in a work entitled "Le Jardin du Roy tres Chrestien Henri IV. Roy de France et Navarre. Dedie à la Royne." His prints are executed in a neat and beautiful style. He was living in 1642.

VALLORY, Chevalier de, a French amateur engraver, who flourished about 1760. He etched some plates of landscapes, *after Boucher.*

VALPUESTA, Pedro, a Spanish painter, born at Osma, in Old Castile, in 1614. According to Palomino, he was a disciple of Eugenio Caxes, and the most successful follower of his style. His principal works are in the churches and convents of Madrid; the most worthy of notice are a series of pictures representing the life of the Virgin, in the church of San Miguel; the Holy Family, in the Chapel of the Hospital del Buensuceso; and six pictures of the history of St. Clara, in the convent of the Franciscan Nuns. He died at Madrid in 1668.

VAN, VANDE, VANDEN, VANDER, and VON, are only articles prefixed to Flemish, Dutch, and German names, and when artists are not found in letter V. under one of these heads, they will be met with by referring to the proper initial letter, as Van Balen, see Balen; Vander Berg, see Berg; Vander Borcht, see Borcht; Von Müller, see Müller.

VANBRUGH, Sir John, an eminent English architect, of Dutch extraction, was born in 1666. His grandfather was a citizen of Ghent, and removed to England at the time when Alva persecuted the Protestants. His son Giles married Elizabeth, youngest daughter and co-heir of Sir Dudley Carleton, and had a family of eight sons, among whom was the subject of this sketch. Little is known of John until he commenced writing for the stage, and it appears rather doubtful if he was ever regularly educated in architecture. He was sent by his father to France at the age of nineteen, and is said to have studied the art in that country; he subsequently entered the French military service for a short time, and his professional progress for several years after remains in obscurity. It is evident, however, that he had attained considerable skill previously to 1695, for he was then appointed one of the commissioners for completing the palace at Greenwich, when it was about to be converted into an hospital. In 1702, Vanbrugh was employed by Charles, the third Earl of Carlisle, to erect a mansion for him in Yorkshire, on the site of the ancient Castle of Hinderskelf; and he erected the palace of Castle Howard, an extensive and noble pile, 660 feet in length; although, like all his other works of this class, more satisfactory in its general character than when examined in detail. His patron Carlisle, then earl marshal of England, signified his approbation by bestowing on him the honorable and not unprofitable appointment of Clarencieux king-at-arms, in 1703. His work of Castle Howard also recommended him as architect to many persons of rank or wealth, for whom he erected stately mansions in different parts of the kingdom. Among these were King's Weston, near Bristol, greatly admired for the effect produced by its chimneys; Duncombe Hall, Yorkshire; Eastbury in Dorsetshire, built for Bubb Doddington but subsequently demolished by Earl Temple; Seaton Delaval, Northumberland; Oulton Hall in Cheshire; and Grimsthorpe, Yorkshire, considered one of his most important works. Most of his edifices appear to have been country seats and mansions, except a theatre in the Haymarket which afterwards became the original Opera House.

About 1706, the nation voted, as a monument o

gratitude to the first Duke of Marlborough, a palace, to be named after the victory at Blenheim. Vanbrugh was appointed the architect, but although this high distinction and the excellence of his performance have greatly increased his posthumous fame, he was involved in great difficulties, in consequence of no specific appropriation having been provided by parliament, and being afterwards refused. During the queen's life, she furnished the necessary funds; but difficulties increased afterwards, and, to complete the architect's vexation, after the Duke's death, his wife Sarah discharged Vanbrugh from his post, and refused to pay him the amount due on his salary! The edifice was however completed according to the original model, and forms an honorable monument to the genius of the architect. Although Vanbrugh was greatly ridiculed by Swift and Pope, so that his merits were not appreciated in his day, posterity has at length afforded him full justice. Sir Joshua Reynolds was the first who ventured to bear testimony to the picturesque magnificence of Blenheim, besides which, the testimony of Sir Uvedale Price and others removed the prejudices against the architect. His works are distinguished for great variety of outline, although his style is occasionally somewhat heavy, as solidity and massiveness are its chief characteristics. The massive grandeur of the palace of Blenheim, is esteemed a fitting type of the talents of the hero, for whom it was erected.

Vanbrugh evinced great talent as a dramatic writer, and his masterly powers in comedy are so well evinced in several plays, that, were it not for their strong libertine tendencies, which have properly banished them from the stage, and almost from the closet, he would be regarded as a standard classic author in English dramatic literature. His private character seems to have been amiable, and his conduct tolerably correct. He died at his own house in Whitehall, in 1726.

VANDAEL, John Francois, an eminent Flemish painter of fruit and flowers, born at Antwerp in 1764. He went early to Paris, where he greatly distinguished himself. On one occasion he drew the grand prize of 4,000 francs, and on two others, the large gold medal. He was patronized by the empresses Josephine and Maria Louisa, the Duchess de Berri, and other distinguished personages. Many of his pictures were to be seen in the chateaux of St. Cloud and Trianon. He was made a Chevalier of the Legion of Honor, and a member of the academies at Antwerp, Amsterdam, and Paris, as well as of several learned societies. His pictures are elegantly composed, and executed with all the truth and brilliancy of nature. He did not strictly confine himself to fruit and flowers, but often painted other subjects, into which he could introduce these with propriety as accessories; thus, two of the pictures which he painted for the Empress Josephine, now at Munich, represent the Tomb of Julia, and an offering to Flora. He died at Paris in 1840. See, also, the article *Dael*.

VANDEN DYCK. See Dyck.

VANDERBURG. See Burg.

VANDERGUCHT. See Gucht.

VANDERLYN, John. This eminent American painter was born in 1776, in the town of Kingston, Ulster county, of the State of New York. After receiving an academical education in his native place, he visited the city of New York at the age of sixteen, in company with his brother; and while there, he was offered by Mr. Thomas Barrow, an extensive dealer in engravings, a place as clerk in his store. Young Vanderlyn accepted the offer, and remained two years in his employment, acquiring and improving a taste for the Fine Arts, and also taking drawing lessons in moments of leisure. During this period, he made the acquaintance of Stuart, who allowed him to copy some of his portraits; also of Colonel Burr, who advanced him the means of prosecuting his studies under the direction of Stuart, and subsequently of going to France.

In 1796, Vanderlyn went to Paris, where he continued his studies under the most eminent French artists, and made the acquaintance of several distinguished men, who predicted from his earlier efforts the highest success. After a residence of five years he returned to his native country, and soon obtained plentiful patronage. He painted two fine views of Niagara Falls, which were engraved, and gained him the warm friendship of Washington Irving, Allston, Monroe, and others. Notwithstanding this success, Vanderlyn revisited Europe in 1803, to purchase a large collection of pictures, and while sojourning at Paris, he executed his first historical composition, a work of great originality and vigor, representing the Murder of Miss McCrea by the Indians, during the early border wars of the State of New York. He then visited Rome, and applied himself to improvement with great assiduity, making copies after the Italian masters, which evinced considerable excellence, particularly a picture of Danaë, from Titian, Antiope from Correggio, and a female figure from Raffaelle's Transfiguration, which was retained for a long time in the collection of the late Philip Hone, Esq., but has recently passed into other hands. Among his original works, executed about this time, were his Ariadne, an original picture of singular beauty, which was greatly admired; and his large historical subject, "Marius on the Ruins of Carthage," which is considered his masterpiece. The strength, dignity, and truthfulness of the solitary general, as he sits baffled and disappointed, but not overcome, amid the fallen columns of the old African city, his wild eyes glaring around the desolation, but his face full of the great heart of the exiled Roman consul,—evinced a power of conception on the part of the painter, which gained the universal applause of his brother artists, while the depth and purity of the coloring excited their admiration. This grand work of art was removed to the Louvre, and in 1808 it drew the gold medal, and was honored by the praises of Napoleon, who highly complimented the author upon his genius.

Vanderlyn returned to this country in 1815, where his reputation was undoubtedly much higher than when he left it; and he soon received numerous commissions for portraits, among which were some of our most eminent men—Madison, Calhoun, Monroe, Clinton, &c. But he became interested in a plan for the introduction of panoramic exhibitions into the United States, and having obtained a privilege from the Corporation in New York city, he erected a building in the Park, to which he gave the name of the Rotunda. He exhibited there many fine views of the cities of Paris, Mexico, Versailles, Athens, &c.; but the project proved an unsuccessful speculation, and the Corporation resumed possession of the building. The effect upon Vanderlyn's finances was not less disastrous than upon his energies, and he never completely recovered himself in either respect. Had he devoted himself from the first to his proper department in the art, doubtless his reputation and success would have been much greater than they were.

In 1832 Vanderlyn was commissioned to paint a full-length portrait of Washington, for the Hall of Representatives; and as soon as it was completed, he was voted $1500 additional compensation. In 1839 he was chosen to fill one of the vacant panels in the rotunda of the Capitol, with a great national picture; he accordingly removed to Paris, and returned with his Landing of Columbus. The last work exhibited from his pencil was the portrait of President Taylor, at the National Academy of Design, in 1851. He died at his native place, Kingston, Ulster Co., Sept. 23, 1852.

VANDERMINE, VANDERMYNE, or VANDERMYN. See Myn.

VANDERVELDE, VANDENVELDE, or VANDEVELDE. See Velde.

VANDERVENNE. See Venne.

VANDERVERT, Henry, called by the Italians Enrico Vandervert, and in the *Catalogue of the Colonna Gallery*, Enrico Wandervert. All that is known of this painter is, that he was a native of Flanders, and went to Rome, where he became the disciple and imitator of Claude Lorraine. It is probable that he spent the rest of his life in Italy, as he is not mentioned by the writers of his country. Lanzi briefly notices him among the disciples and followers of Claude as an artist deserving commendation.

VANDERWERF. See Werf.

VANDI, Sante, sometimes called Santino da' Ritratti, a painter born at Bologna, in 1653. According to Crespi, few persons could compete with him in portraiture, and he was constantly employed by princes and persons of distinction. He was much employed by the Grand Duke of Tuscany, and Ferdinando Duke of Mantua invited him to his court and appointed him his painter, with a liberal salary, which situation he held till the death of that prince, when he returned to Bologna, and died there in 1716. He had the faculty of giving to his female sitters all the beauty, and to his male, all the dignity they possessed, without injuring the likeness. "With him," observes Crespi, "disappeared the manner of producing portraits at once so soft and powerful, combined with such natural expression."

VAN DIEST. See Diest.

AD F. VANDYCK, Sir Anthony. This eminent Flemish painter was born at Antwerp, March 22, 1599. His father was a glass-painter of Bois-le-Duc, in good circumstances, and early gave him instruction in drawing; he was also instructed by his mother, who painted landscapes, and was very skillful in embroidery. He studied afterwards under Henry van Balen, and made rapid progress in the art; but attracted by the fame of Rubens, he entered the school of that master, and showed so much ability as to be soon entrusted with the execution of some of his instructor's designs. Some writers, among whom D'Argenville was the first, assert that Rubens became jealous of Vandyck's growing excellence, and therefore advised him to devote himself to portrait painting; assigning the following anecdote as the immediate cause of this jealousy. During the short absences of Rubens from his house, for the purpose of recreation, his disciples frequently obtained access to his studio, by means of bribing an old servant who kept the keys; and on one of these occasions, while they were all eagerly pressing forward to view the great picture of the Descent from the Cross (although later investigations concerning dates, seem to indicate that it was some other picture), Diepenbeck accidentally fell against the canvass, effacing the face of the Virgin and the Magdalen's arm, which had just been finished, and were not yet dry. Fearful of expulsion from the school, the terrified pupils chose Vandyck to restore the work, and he completed it the same day with such success that Rubens did not at first perceive the change, and afterwards concluded not to alter it. Walpole entertains a different and more rational view respecting Rubens' supposed jealousy; he thinks that Vandyck felt the hopelessness of surpassing his master in historical painting, and therefore resolved to devote himself to portrait. One authority states that the above mentioned incident only increased Rubens' esteem for his pupil, in perfect accordance with the distinguished character for generosity and liberality, which that great master so often evinced, and which forms very strong presumptive evidence against so base an accusation. Besides, his advice to Vandyck to visit Italy—where his own powers had been, as his pupil's would be, greatly strengthened—may be considered as sufficient to refute it entirely. They appear to have parted on the best terms; Vandyck presented Rubens with an Ecce Homo, Christ in the Garden, and a portrait of Helen Forman, Rubens' second wife; he was presented in return by Rubens, with one of his finest horses.

At the age of twenty Vandyck set out for Italy, but delayed some time at Brussels, fascinated by the charms of a peasant girl of Saveltheim, named Anna van Ophem, who persuaded him to paint two pictures for the church of her native place—a St. Martin on horseback, painted from himself, and the horse given him by Rubens; and a Holy Family, for which the girl and her parents were models. On arriving in Italy, he spent some time at Venice, studying with great attention the works of Titian; after which he visited Genoa, and painted many excellent portraits for the nobility, as well as several pictures for the churches and private collections, which gained him great applause. From Genoa he went to Rome, where he was also much employed, and lived in great style. His portrait of Cardinal Bentivoglio, painted about this time, is one of his master-pieces, and in every respect an admirable picture; it is now in the Palazzo Pitti at Florence, hanging near Raffaelle's celebrated portrait of Leo X. Vandyck was known at Rome as the *Pittore Cavalieresco;* his countrymen there being men of low and intemperate habits, he avoided their society, and was thenceforward so greatly annoyed by their criticisms and revilings, that he was obliged to leave Rome about 1625, and return to Genoa, where he met with a flattering reception, and plentiful encouragement. Invited to Palermo, he visited that city, and painted the portraits of Prince Philibert of Savoy, the Viceroy of Sicily, and several distinguished persons, among whom was the celebrated paintress Sophonisba Anguisciola, then in her 92d year; but the plague breaking out, he returned to Genoa, and thence to his own country.

On returning to Antwerp, Vandyck was speedily employed by various religious societies, and his picture of St. Augustine for the church of the Augustines in that city, established his reputation among the first painters of his time. He painted other historical pictures, for the principal public edifices at Antwerp, Brussels, Mechlin, and Ghent; but acquired greater fame by his portraits, particularly his well-known series of the eminent artists of his time, which were engraved by Vorstermans, Pontius, Bolswert, and others. His brilliant reputation at length roused the jealousy of his cotemporaries, many whom were indefatigable in their intrigues to calumniate his works. In addition to these annoyances, the conduct of the canons of the Collegiate church of Courtray, for whom he painted an admirable picture of the Elevation of the Cross, proved too much for his endurance. After he had exerted all his powers to produce a masterpiece of art, the Canons, upon viewing the picture, pronounced it a contemptible performance, and the artist a miserable dauber; and Vandyck could hardly obtain payment for his work. When the picture had received high commendation from good judges, they became sensible of their error, and requested him to execute two more works; but the indignant artist refused the commission. Disgusted with such treatment, Vandyck readily accepted an invitation to visit the Hague, from Frederick, Prince of Orange, whose portrait he painted, and that of his family, the principal personages of his court, and the foreign ambassadors. Hearing of the great encouragement extended to the arts by Charles I., he determined to visit England in 1629. While there, he lodged with his friend and countryman, George Geldorp the painter, and expected to be presented to the King; but his hopes not being realized, he visited Paris; and meeting no better success there, he returned to his own country, with the intention of remaining there during the rest of his life. Charles, however, having seen a portrait by Vandyck, of the musician Nic. Laniere, director of the music of the King's chapel, requested Sir Kenelm Digby to invite him to return to England. Accordingly in 1631, he arrived a second time at London, and was received by the King in a flattering manner. He was lodged at Blackfriars, among the King's artists, where his majesty frequently went to sit for his portrait, as well as to enjoy the society of the painter. The honor of knighthood was conferred upon him in 1632, and the following year he was appointed painter to the King, with an annuity of £200.

Prosperity now flowed in upon the Fleming in abundance, and although he operated with the greatest industry and facility, painting single portraits in one day, he could hardly fulfil all his commissions. Naturally fond of display, he kept a splendid establishment, and his sumptuous table was frequented by persons of the highest distinction. He often detained his sitters to dinner, where he had an opportunity to observe more of their peculiar characteristics, and retouched their pictures in the afternoon. Notwithstanding his distinguished success, he does not appear to have been satisfied with eminence in portrait painting; and not long after his marriage with Maria Ruthven, grand-daughter of Lord Gowrie, he went to Antwerp with his lady, on a visit to his family and friends, and thence proceeded to Paris. The fame which Rubens had acquired by his celebrated performances at the Luxembourg, rendered Vandyck desirous to execute the decorations at the Louvre; but on arriving at the French capital, he found the commission disposed of to Nicholas Poussin. He soon returned to England, and being still desirous of executing some great work, proposed to the King through Sir Kenelm Digby, to decorate the walls of the Banqueting House (of which the ceiling was already adorned by Rubens), with the History and Procession of the Order of the Garter. The sum demanded was £8000, and while the King was treating with him for a less amount, the project was terminated by the death of Vandyck, December 9th, 1641, aged 42 years. He was buried with extraordinary honors, in St. Paul's cathedral. His high living had brought on the gout during his latter years, and luxury had considerably reduced his fortune, which he endeavored to repair by the study of alchymy. He left property amounting to about £20,000. In his private character, Vandyck was universally esteemed for the urbanity of his manners, and his generous patronage to all who excelled in any science or art, many of whose portraits he painted gratuitously.

According to Fuseli, Vandyck deserves the next place after Titian in portrait painting. Inferior to that master in richness and warmth of coloring, he surpassed him in almost every other respect. He is unrivalled for the delicate drawing and beauty of his hands; he was a perfect master of drawing and chiaro-scuro; he was admirable in draperies; with simplicity of expression and graceful attitudes, he combined both dignity and individuality; his heads are full of life and expression, without anything of the coldness and insipidity which are frequently found in the productions of the portrait painter. Although they are but little flattered, his portraits generally impress us with the feeling that he has not only selected the most suitable attitude for the figure, but that he has chosen the best view of the countenance. There are many fine portraits by him of distinguished personages, besides those of the King and royal family, in the mansions of the English nobility.

Although Vandyck acquired his great fame in portraits, he painted also many historical pieces, and he never at any time ceased operating in this department. Inferior to Rubens in boldness of conception and fertility of invention, he never could have equalled him in historical painting; but his compositions are arranged with judgment and propriety; he surpassed him in correctness of design, the delicate expression of his heads, and the truth, purity, and harmony of his coloring. His picture of St. Augustine, in the church of the Augustines at Antwerp, gained him great celebrity soon after his return from Italy; Reynolds observes that "it is of great fame, but that it in some measure disappointed his expectations; that it has no effect, from the want of a large mass of light, the two angels making two small masses of equal magnitude, while the figure of the saint is dressed in black." This is satisfactorily accounted for by the fact that Vandyck originally painted the drapery white, but was reluctantly obliged to alter it to black, on account of the prejudices of the monks, before he could obtain payment for the work; in P. de Jode's print of this picture, the idea of the artist is correctly followed, and the figure of the saint makes the principal light. His admirable picture of the body of Christ in the arms of the Virgin, with St. John and two Angels, is now in the Louvre, and is scarcely inferior to the Pietà of Annibale Caracci, in the exquisite expression of the head of the Virgin. Vandyck's best historical picture however, in the opinion of Reynolds, is the Crucifixion, in the church of the Recollets at Mechlin, of which he says, "This perhaps is the most capital of all his works, in respect to the variety and extensiveness of the design, and the judicious disposition of the whole. In the efforts which the Thieves make to detach themselves from the cross, he has successfully encountered the difficulty of the art; and the expression of grief and resignation in the Virgin is admirable. This picture, on the whole, may be considered one of the first pictures in the world, and gives the highest idea of Vandyck's powers: it shows that he had truly a genius for history painting, if he had not been taken off by portraits."

The works of Vandyck are very numerous, notwithstanding the shortness of his career; Smith describes upwards of 950 in the Catalogue raisonné, vol. III., and Supplement. Many of the best are at Windsor Castle, Hampton Court, Wilton House, Blenheim, &c. Walpole thinks his masterpiece is the dramatic portrait of the Earl of Strafford, and his secretary, Sir Thomas Mainwaring, at Wentworth House; there is also one of this subject at Blenheim, which is highly praised by Dr. Waagen. At Wilton House there are twenty-five pictures by him—"here," says Walpole, "Vandyck is upon his throne, and the great portrait of Philip, Earl of Pembroke, with his family, though damaged, would serve alone as a school of this master." Charles I. was painted several times by Vandyck, sometimes on horseback. The superb head of Gevartius, in the National Gallery, though attributed to Vandyck, is by some critics assigned to Rubens. His series of one hundred portraits of the most eminent artists and others his cotemporaries at Antwerp, were painted in small upon panels, in chiaro-scuro, before he left that city for the Hague. Walpole states that thirty-five of them were in his time in the collection of the Countess of Cardigan at Whitehall; the whole of the originals have been thrice published; the first edition by vander Enden, contains eighty plates; the second by Giles Hendricks, one hundred; the last edition is by Verdussen, who effaced the names and letters of the original engravers. The title is, "Icones Virorum doctorum, pictorum, chalcographorum, &c., numero centum, ab Antonio Vandyck pictore ad vivum expressæ, et ejus sumptu æri incisæ Antverpiæ." Vandyck etched some of the plates himself, besides a few other subjects, in a style of wonderful spirit and energy. Among them are the following:

Christ crowned with Thorns; *A. Vandyck, inv.* A Holy Family. A Bust of Seneca; and others.

PORTRAITS OF ARTISTS.

Adam van Oort, Painter; *Ant. Vandyck, fecit aqua forti.* Justus Suttermans, Painter of Antwerp. Peter Breughel, Painter. Lucas Vorstermans, Engraver. Jodocus de Momper, Painter. Paul de Pont, or Pontius, Engraver. John Breughel, Painter. Francis Frank, Painter. Jon de Wael, Painter. John Snellinx, Painter. Titian, with his Mistress, who is leaning on a casket, with a skull; *Titiano, pinx. A. Vandyck, fec.* Anthony Cornelissen, Amateur. Erasmus Rotterdamus. Anthony Vandyck. Philip le Roy, Eques. Francis Snyders, Painter. Anthony Triest, Bishop of Ghent. William de Vos, Painter. Paul de Vos, Painter. John Waverius, or Vanden Wouwer.

VANDYCK, Philip, a Dutch painter, born at Amsterdam in 1680. He was a scholar of Arnold Boonen, with whom he continued till he surpassed him, and then improved himself by studying the works of Mieris and Metzu. He painted small portraits in the style of his master, but his best pictures are his conversations, gallant assemblies, and ladies at their toilet, or playing on musical instruments. In 1710 he established himself at Middleburg, where he was much employed. He was afterwards invited to the Hague, where he soon acquired an immense reputation, and his works were so much sought after, that he could scarcely supply the demand. His fame spread throughout Holland, Flanders, and Germany, and he was considered one of the ablest artists of that day in his line. He was also an excellent connoisseur; the Prince of Hesse Cassel commissioned him to paint several pictures, and employed him to purchase some of the choicest works of art he could find in Holland and Flanders, for the rich collection he was then forming at Cassel, all which he executed with judgment and taste, to the entire satisfaction of his patron. His cabinet pictures, though inferior to the admirable productions of Mieris and Metzu, are highly finished and agreeably colored, and they are admitted into the choicest collections of his country. Two of his happiest productions, representing a young lady at her toilet, and another playing upon a guitar, were esteemed by the French connoisseurs worthy of a place in the gallery of the Louvre. These pictures were restored in 1815, and are now in the Museums at the Hague, and at Brussels. There are, however, two of his pictures in the Louvre, relating to the history of Abraham and Hagar. He also excelled in portraits, especially in those of a small size; he frequently painted family pictures, in which he introduced all the members of the family, even to the cats and dogs; he sometimes gave these subjects a historical turn; thus he painted a ceiling for M. Schuylenberg, representing the story of Iphigenia, into which he introduced the portraits of the whole family. He died at the Hague in 1752.

VANDYCK, Floris van, a Dutch painter, born at Haerlem in 1577. Schrevelius mentions him as an admirable painter of flowers, which he says would even deceive the birds. He was also distinguished for his subjects of history, but they are extremely rare, even in Holland. Two of them were in the Louvre, representing Hagar presented to Abraham, and Hagar sent into the Wilderness.

VANDYCK, Daniel, called by the Italians Daniele Vandyck. See Dyck.

VANETTI, Marco, a painter born at Loreto, who flourished about 1720. He was a disciple of the Cav. Carlo Cignani, and a reputable follower of his style. He wrote the life of Cignani, which was published at Bologna.

VAN EYCK, John, called by the Italians, Giovanni van Eyck, and Giovanni da Bruggia, or de Bruges, and by Facio, who wrote his eulogy, *Jo. Gallicus.* See Eyck.

VANGELISTI, Vincenzio, an Italian engraver, born, according to Zani, in 1738. He went to Paris when young, where he became a pupil of J. G. Wille. He acquired considerable reputation as an engraver, and executed some plates after Raffaelle, Caracci, Guido, and other masters, in a neat and finished style. He instructed several pupils, who distinguished themselves, among whom were Longhi and F. Anderloni. He was the first director of the school of engraving, instituted at Milan in 1790, by Leopold II., and Longhi succeeded him. According to Ferrario, he went crazy, and after having defaced all his plates, he killed himself, in 1798.

VANGHELS, Nicholas, a French historical painter, born in Paris in 1674. Little is known of him, though he must have been an artist of distinction, as he was appointed director of the French Academy at Rome, where he died in 1737. His works are said to be correctly designed, ingeniously composed, and agreeably colored.

VANLOO, James, a Dutch painter, born at Sluys in 1614. He was the son of John Vanloo, a painter of little note, who instructed him in the rudiments of art. He afterwards went to Amsterdam, where he greatly improved himself. He then went to Paris, where he settled, and acquired considerable reputation as a painter of portraits and fancy pictures; he was admitted into the academy there, on which occasion he painted as his reception piece an admirable portrait of Michael Corneille, the elder. Houbraken mentions several fine pictures by him, representing Diana in the Bath, the discovery of the Pregnancy of Calisto, and a young lady playing on the Lute. He was a correct designer and an agreeable colorist. He died in 1670. He had a son, *Louis Vanloo*, whom he instructed in the art, and who was a good painter of portraits and history. He settled at Aix, in Provence.

VANLOO, Jean Baptiste, was the son of Louis Vanloo, born at Aix in 1684. His father perceiving in him a genius for painting, carefully instructed him in the art. He went to Toulon, and executed several works for the churches, when the siege of that place in 1707, compelled him to return to Aix, where he continued five years, and found considerable employment in painting for the churches and convents, as well as for individuals, but he received so small a compensation that he could barely defray his expenses. The Prince of Carignan now took him under his protection, and enabled him to gratify his desire of visiting Rome, where he studied the antique and the works of the great masters with unremitting assiduity, and that he might not omit anything conducive to his advantage, he placed himself under the instruction of Benedetto Luti, one of the ablest artists of his time. He acquired considerable reputation at Rome, and executed several works for the churches and palaces, the most esteemed of which is the Scourging of Christ in S. Maria in Monticelli. He was invited to the court of Turin, where he distinguished himself by many works both in oil and fresco, for the royal palaces, the churches, and the palaces of the nobility. He also painted the portraits of the King and of the principal personages of his court. After realizing a handsome fortune, he went to Paris, where he lost it all in the famous Mississippi scheme. He was elected a member of the Academy, painting for his reception piece, Diana and Endymion; he was also chosen professor in that institution in 1735. He executed several works for the churches, the principal of which were, the Entry of Christ into Jerusalem, in St. Martin des Champs, and St. Peter delivered from Prison, in St. Germain des Prés. In 1737, he went to London, where he painted the portraits of the Prince and Princess of Wales, and several other persons of distinction. In 1742, the state of his health compelled him to return to Aix, where he died in 1746. He had a lively genius, a ready invention, and great facility of hand; his coloring was excellent, his touch light and spirited, and he gave his carnations a freshness and warmth, not much inferior to the tints of Rubens.

VANLOO, Charles André, called the Cavaliere Carlo Vanloo, was the younger brother of the preceding, born at Nice in 1705. He was first instructed by his brother, whom he accompanied to Rome, and studied some time under Benedetto Luti. He visited Paris in 1723, where he gained the first prize for historical composition, and was employed by his brother in repairing the paintings of Primaticcio in the palace of Fontainbleau. In 1727 he again went to Italy, and passed some time at Rome, diligently studying the works of the best masters. In that year, he drew the prize in design at the Academy of St. Luke, and afterwards painted his magnificent composition in a vault of the church of S. Isidore, representing the Apotheosis of that Saint. He also studied sculpture for some time, and gained a prize by his proficiency in that art. His pictures of St. Francis and St. Martha gained him a pension from the Duke d'Antin, and the Pope conferred on him the honor of knighthood. Thus elevated to distinction, he was invited to the court of Turin, where, according to Lanzi, he executed more works than his brother had done; the principal of these were a series of subjects from the Jerusalem of Tasso, in the royal palace. In 1734 he returned to Paris, and was admitted into the Academy the year following, on which occasion he painted his picture of Apollo and Marsyas as his reception piece. He soon acquired great distinction, and was one of the most popular artists of his time. After his admission to the Academy, he was successively appointed assistant professor, and afterwards director. In 1752, Louis XV. conferred upon him the honor of knighthood, and appointed him his principal painter, with a liberal pension, which situation he enjoyed till his death. He executed some works for the churches and public edifices at Paris, but wrought more for individuals; the principal are in the church of the Augustines. One of his most esteemed productions is the Marriage of the Virgin, in the gallery of the Louvre. By an attentive study of the antique and the works of the great masters during his long residence at Rome, he acquired a correctness of design and a simplicity of style, which had a useful influence in reforming the affected and gaudy manner then prevalent in the French school. His countrymen, in their enthusiasm and admiration of his talents, have not hesitated to attribute to him the design of Raffaelle, the grace of Correggio, and the color ing of Titian; but a juster homage would have been to compare him with the best of the more modern Italian painters. He often varied his style of painting, finishing some of his pictures with a bold, free pencil; others with softness and delicacy; he sometimes imitated the coloring and touch of Guido, of Carlo Maratti, or some other master. His imagination was lively and fertile, and he composed his subjects with care, judgment, and taste; his coloring is exceedingly natural, and his power in penciling enabled him to produce a pleasing effect, as well when his touch was strong and vigorous, as when it was tender and delicate. He died in 1765.

VANLOO, Louis Michel, was the son of Jean Baptiste Vanloo, was born at Toulon in 1707. After studying under his father, he visited Rome for improvement, and gained the prize in design at the Academy of St. Luke. On returning to France, he went to Paris, where he was admitted into the Academy, and painted for his reception piece, a picture of Apollo and Daphne. He acquired considerable reputation as an historical painter, though he was more distinguished by his excellence in portraiture. Philip V. invited him to the court of Madrid, and appointed him his principal painter. After the death of that monarch he returned to Paris, where he continued to practise his profession with great success till his death in 1771.

VANLOO, Charles Amédée Philippe, the brother of Louis Michel V., was born at Turin in 1718, and was honored in his infancy by receiving the baptismal rites while in the arms of the Prince of Piedmont and the Princess Carignan. The *Biographie Universelle* states that he accompanied his uncle Carlo, and his brother Louis Michel, to Rome, and there attained similar success. On returning to France, he was invited to Berlin, where he resided a long time, sustaining the honor of his family as a painter of history and portraits.

VAN MANDER, Charles, a Flemish painter, born at Meulebeke, near Courtray, in 1548. He was descended of a noble family, and received an education suitable to his rank. He early discovered a genius for painting, and after studying successively under Lucas de Heere at Ghent and Peter Vlerick at Courtray, he went to Italy, and spent three years in assiduously designing the vestiges of antiquity in the environs of Rome, and studying the works of the best masters. He there formed an intimate acquaintance with Bartholomew Sprangher, in conjuction with whom he executed several works for the public edifices, as well as for individuals. At Terni, he painted one of his best pictures, representing the Martyrdom of St. Bartholomew. He accompanied his friend Sprangher to Vienna, where he met with the most flattering encouragement. The Emperor would gladly have retained him in his service, but he declined the honor and returned to his native place. One of his first productions at Courtray, was a picture of Adam and Eve in Paradise, which gained him great reputation; the figures were elegantly designed, and finely colored, the landscape enchanting, and the animals executed with great spirit. He next painted a picture of the Deluge, which was highly applauded for the excellence of its composition, and the affecting manner in which he described the horrors of the scene, depicting in the most striking and pathetic manner the varied expressions of terror, grief, and despair.

Van Mander acquired a high reputation, had married, and was passing his days in tranquil prosperity, when the dreadful wars, which desolated the Low Countries, broke out and compelled him to seek refuge in Holland, which country had just shaken off the Spanish yoke, and he settled at Haerlem, where he formed an intimacy with Henry Goltzius, in conjunction with whom, he established an Academy in that city, into which he introduced the style of design which he had acquired in Italy. In 1604 he removed to Amsterdam, where he died in 1606. Among the principal works he executed for the churches in Holland were, St. John preaching in the Wilderness; the Adoration of the Magi, and Christ bearing his Cross. His works are well designed, agreeably colored, and full of spirit, though somewhat mannered, especially his later productions; he also excelled in landscape. He distinguished himself not only as a painter, but as a writer. He wrote an account of the painters of the Italian and Flemish schools from the year 1366 to 1604. He was also a poet, and composed several tragedies and comedies, some of which were acted with applause.

VANNI, Cav. Francesco, an eminent painter, born at Siena, according to Baldinucci and Lanzi, in 1565, though Malvasia, on the authority of Ugurgieri, places it in 1555, and others, in 1563. There is also considerable discrepancy about him in other respects, which we cannot enter into further than to say that, according to the best authorities, he received his first instruction from his father, a painter of little note, who dying when he was a child, his mother married for her second husband, Arcangiolo Salimbeni, (though there is some dispute on this point, and Niccolo Pio asserts that he was the uterine brother of the Cav. Ventura Salimbeni, who was born in 1557, see *Salimbeni*), who gave him further instruction, till he was twelve years old, when he went to Bologna, and became the pupil of Passarotti. At about sixteen he went to Rome, where he entered the school of Giovanni de' Vecchi, under whose direction he studied the antique, and made such rapid progress as to excite the jealousy of his fellow pupil Arpino. The works of Federigo Baroccio particularly attracted his attention; he made them his model, and imitated them with great success. On leaving Rome, he traveled through Lombardy, and improved his taste by studying the works of Correggio and Parmiggiano at Parma. On his return to Siena, he obtained much employment, and executed several works for the churches and convents, which gained him so much reputation, that he was invited to Rome by Clement VIII., who commissioned him to paint his admirable picture representing St. Peter rebuking Simon Magus. He painted this work on a slab of marble, for the church of St. Peter. It is designed and colored in the manner of Baroccio, and was prepared expressly to stand the humidity of the place. Lanzi says that, though somewhat injured by injudicious cleaning, it is still in good preservation, and an object of admiration. His works gave so much satisfaction to the Pope that he made him a knight of the Order of Christ. He painted several other works for the churches at Rome, the principal of which are St. Michael vanquishing the Rebel Angels, in S. Gregorio, a Pietà, in S. Maria in Vallicella, and the Assumption, in S. Lorenzo in Miranda. His best work however, are to be found at Siena, where he painted many pictures for the churches and public edifices, as well as for individuals, in which he approached nearer the elegant and graceful style of Baroccio. Lanzi says, "Vanni attached himself to the elegant and florid manner of Baroccio, in which he was eminently successful; this is to be seen not only in his works at Rome, but at Siena, and in other Italian cities, where he approaches the manner of that master, more closely than Viviani or any other of his pupils. His Marriage of St. Catherine, with a numerous group of angels, at the Refugio, is much praised in Siena; as is the Madonna surrounded by saints in Monna Agnese, and St. Raymond walking on the Sea, at the Dominicani, considered by some to be his best picture at Siena, where his works are very numerous. Among the finest pictures in the cathedral at Pisa, is the Dispute about the Seven Sacraments, painted in imitation of his brother Ventura Salimbeni, who had surpassed himself in his altar-piece of the angels. At the Umiltà of Pistoja, in the convent of the Camaldules of Fabriano, and at that of the Capuchins of S. Quirico, are some of his most exquisite performances; and they are so numerous in other places that I do not imagine a full catalogue has ever been made out. He is generally a follower of Baroccio, as before observed, and amateurs, deceived by his coloring and the heads of his boys, which appear to be cast in the mould of Baroccio, frequently confound the works of Vanni with those of that master; but one acquainted with Federigo, will observe in him more grandeur of design, and a greater freedom of penciling. The pictures of Vanni, executed negligently, or at low prices, of which there are several at Siena, can scarcely be recognized for his. By his example and lessons, for he taught many pupils, the honor of painting was long supported at Siena." He died at Siena in 1610. He executed a few correct and spirited etchings from his own designs, which are highly esteemed.

VANNI, Cav. Michael Angelo, was the eldest son of the Cav. Francesco V., by whom he was instructed in the art, and whose style he followed, though he chiefly acquired his reputation from the invention of a new process of painting on marble, or rather staining it, in imitation of mosaic. Lanzi says, "the secret of coloring marble was discovered by Michael Angelo Vanni, who has transmitted the memory of the invention to posterity. He erected a monument to his father, with columns, ornaments, festoons, and figures of children; accompanied by a genealogy of the family, all designed on a white slab, and every part carefully and appropriately colored, so as to resemble mosaic of different marbles. It is supposed that the colors were imparted to the marble by some mineral essences, because they penetrated a considerable way. He entitles himself the inventor of the art in the monumental inscription." There are some of his works in the churches and convents of Siena, but they are much inferior to the best productions of his father. He was living in 1656, at which time the monument above referred to was erected.

VANNI, Cav. Raffaelle, was the second son of Francesco V., born at Siena in 1596. He received his first instruction from his father, whom he had the misfortune to lose when he was fourteen years old. He afterwards went to Rome, where, according to Mancini, he entered the school of Antonio Caracci, under whose instruction he made such progress as even to surpass his father, —"an assertion," says Lanzi, "not sustained by the opinion of posterity." He is generally allowed to have been a bold and correct designer, and to have possessed an excellent knowledge of the chiaro-scuro. He imitated the style of Pietro da Cortona in the greater part of his works, which are numerous, and are to be found in the churches and public edifices at Rome, Siena, Florence, Pisa, and other cities. Lanzi says he not only strongly resembles Cortona in the fine taste of his shadows and in coloring, but several of his pictures have no small portion of the *ideas* of that master. Among his finest productions are the Birth of the Virgin, in La Pace, and the cupola of S. Maria del Popolo, at Rome; the Martyrdom of St. Catherine, in the church of that Saint at Pisa; and the Procession of our Saviour to Calvary, in S. Giorgio, at Siena. He was elected a member of the Academy of St. Luke, in 1655, and both he and his brother were honored with knighthood.

VANNI, Giovanni Battista, an Italian painter and engraver, born at Florence, according to the inscription on his monument, in 1599. The Pisans claim him as a native of their city. Lanzi says that, "after taking lessons from Empoli and other masters, he studied with Cristofano Allori, and was superior to any other scholar of his school; he imitated his master admirably in his coloring, and rivalled him in design; he also imbibed from him his lessons of intemperance. Had he conducted himself with more propriety, and adhered to fixed principles, the genius he possessed might have raised him to more celebrity. He visited the schools of Italy, and copied, or at least designed, the choicest productions of each. Many praise his copies of Titian, of Veronese, and of Correggio." He, however, soon degenerated into mannerism, so that Lanzi says he did not leave one truly classical work. His master-piece is his picture of St. Lorenzo, in the church of S. Simone, at Florence. He executed some masterly and spirited etchings, which are highly esteemed, although the drawing is not very correct. The principal are a set of fifteen plates from the paintings by Correggio, in the cupola of S. Giovanni at Parma; the Martyrdom of St. Placido, *after the same;* and the Marriage at Cana, *after Paul Veronese.* He died at Florence, in 1660.

VANNI, Andrea di, an old painter of Siena, of whom there are notices from 1369 to 1413. He was an eminent artist in his time, and executed many works for the churches and public edifices at Siena, Naples, and in other cities of Italy. There is a St. Sebastian in the convent of S. Martino, and a Madonna surrounded by Saints, in that of S. Francesco, at Siena, by him. Lanzi says, "He was likewise employed in public embassies, and like another Rubens, was a magistrate and ambassador of the republic to the pope."

VANNI. There were several artists of this name, who were natives of Pisa. From one Vanni, who flourished in 1300, sprung Turino di Vanni, who lived about 1343; also Nello di Vanni, who was employed, in conjunction with other artists, in decorating the Campo Santo. Bernardo di Vanni was the son of Nello, and a disciple of

Orcagna. He painted many pictures for the palace of the Primate at Siena, as well as others for the public edifices.

VANNI, Gio. Antonio and Gio. Francesco del, were the disciples, and probably relatives, of the Cav. Francesco Vanni. Some of their works are mentioned in the *Guida di Roma.*

VANNINI, Ottavio, a painter born at Florence, in 1585. After studying four years with Gio. Battista Mercati, in his native city, he went to Rome where he became the disciple of Anastagio Fontebuoni; he also diligently studied the works of Raffaelle and other great masters. On his return to Florence, he entered the school of Passignano, with whom he lived many years, and assisted him in his numerous works. Lanzi says he also painted many works for the collections, from his own designs, which, though well colored, are feeble in design, and labored in execution. He died in 1643.

VANNUCCHI. See Sarto.

VANNUCCI. See Perugino.

VAN OBSTAL, Gerard. This sculptor was born at Antwerp, in 1597, but seems to have gained his chief reputation at Paris. The Biographie Universelle states that he was chosen rector of the Academy of Painting and Sculpture. His bas-reliefs and works in ivory gained him considerable reputation, and his statue of Louis XIV., which was placed over the Porte St. Antoine, is esteemed his most remarkable work.

VANONE, Andrea, a Lombard architect of the 16th century. According to Milizia, he removed from his native country, Lancio, in the Comasco, to Genoa, where he built the ducal palace—a stately structure, fortified with chains of iron. He was employed by the government in fortifications and other works, and led a long and honorable life. Milizia does not mention the time of his birth or death.

VANSOMER, or VAN SOMEREN, Paul, a Flemish painter, born at Antwerp about 1576. According to van Mander, he resided in Amsterdam in 1604, with his brother Bernard, where they practised portrait painting with great success. The accounts of them are contradictory. Balkema says that both Paul and Bernard established themselves in Amsterdam, where they died—the former in 1641, and the latter in 1632. Paul Vansomer certainly visited England at the commencement of the 17th century, and died in London, January 5th, 1621, and was buried in St. Martin's-in-the-Fields. He acquired a high reputation in that country, and painted the portraits of many persons of distinction, which are dated from 1606 to 1620. Bryan says he was one of the ablest portrait painters who visited England before Vandyck. It appears that there were several artists named Vansomer. There was a Paul Vansomer, an engraver, who flourished at a much later date; he engraved a few prints in mezzotinto, an art not known in the time of the elder Paul.

VANTE, or ATTAVANTE, Fiorentino, an old painter of Florence, who was living in 1484, and was much employed in ornamenting books, with miniatures, for Matthias, king of Hungary, which were afterwards preserved in the Medicean and Estensean libraries at Florence. Lanzi mentions one he saw in the Library of St. Mark at Venice. "It is a work of Marziano Capella, where the subject is poetically treated by the painter. The Assembly of the Gods, the emblems of the Arts and Sciences, the grotesque ornaments, set off with little portraits, discover in Vante a genius that admirably seconded the ideas of the author; the design resembles the best works of Botticelli; the coloring is gay, lively, and brilliant, and the excellence of the work ought to confer on the artist greater celebrity than he enjoys."

VANUDEN, Lucas. This eminent artist wrote his name Lucas van Uden, but he is generally called by English writers, Vanuden. He was born at Antwerp in 1595, and learned the art of painting from his father, an artist of little note, but he derived his chief excellence from an indefatigable study of nature. He passed all his leisure hours in the fields, where he designed the most beautiful scenes and picturesque objects with remarkable precision; he was particularly attentive to note the appearances and changes of the atmosphere, perpetually occurring from the time the rising sun dissipates the vapors, till it sinks beneath the horizon. He watched the effects of light on different objects, and suffered no incident which might prove of advantage to his art to escape his notice, not even those almost instantaneous beauties seen in the forms and colors of clouds and vapors, which are lost almost the moment they are beheld. All these he sketched on the spot, and afterwards introduced them into his pictures with the happiest effect. His manner is soft, tender, and delicate; his coloring natural and pleasing; his skies clear, often with light, floating clouds, beautifully adapted to, and harmonizing with the scene, and every object beautifully reflected and mirrored in the water; the forms of his trees select, and his foliage apparently in motion. His pictures represent views in Flanders; and, though the flatness of the country does not admit the extensive vistas so much admired in the works of Claude Lorraine and Niccolo Poussin, yet his scenery is always pleasing, the degradation of his distances admirable, and his prospects as extensive as his design would admit. In short, he was considered one of the most delicate and natural landscape painters of the Low Countries. His extraordinary merit recommended him to the particular notice of Rubens, who not only approved but admired his style, and often employed him to insert the backgrounds in his pictures, which Vanuden adapted to the rest of the composition with such harmony and taste that the whole seemed to be the work of one artist. Rubens, in return, used also to enrich the landscapes of Vanuden with historical figures. Vanuden's small landscapes are esteemed his best works; some of them bear so strong a resemblance to those of Rubens that they are scarcely distinguishable from those of that master, except by their size, and a less daring execution; they have the effect of those of Rubens viewed through a diminishing glass. Some of the later works of Vanuden are decorated with the figures of the younger Teniers, and, though he designed small figures well, these embellishments by other eminent masters greatly enhance the value of his pictures. His works are justly held in the highest estimation, and are found in the choicest collections. There are some admirable pictures by him on a larger scale than he usually painted, in the chapels belonging to the Cathedral of Ghent.

Vanuden executed some admirable etchings of landscapes, from his own designs, and after the works of Rubens, Titian, and others, which he usually marked *L.* or *Lucas van Uden.* Bartsch describes fifty-nine etchings which he attributes to him; but he acknowledges that several of these have so strong a resemblance to those of Louis de Vadder, that the most experienced connoisseurs find it difficult to distinguish them. Dumesnil attributes some of them to *Jean Bonnecroy.* For further particulars, the reader must be referred to Bartsch, Peintre Graveur, tom. v., and Weigel's Supplement, and to Robert Dumesnil, Le Peintre Graveur Français, tom. iii. He died in 1660.

VANUDEN, James, was the brother and scholar of the preceding, whose manner he imitated. He was very inferior to Lucas, though his works have often passed with the unlearned for the productions of his brother.

VANVITELLI, Gaspare, called Dagli Occhiali. This artist was born at Utrecht in 1647, but he went to Italy while young, where he passed the rest of his life, and is ranked among the Italian painters. His family name was Witel, or Vanvitel, which he italianized to Vanvitelli. It is not known under whom he studied, but he painted architectural subjects, perspective pieces, and views of sea-ports, in the manner of Canaletto; and, though his works are inferior to the productions of that master in the spirit and animation of his touch, and in the lustre and brilliancy of his coloring, yet his drawing and perspective are correct, and his tints natural and agreeable. As Canaletto was the painter of modern Venice, so Vanvitelli may be called the painter of modern Rome; his pictures represent the magnificent edifices in that city, to which he added landscapes when the subject admitted of it. He also painted views of other cities, sea-ports, villas and farm-houses. He painted a few large pictures, but most of his works are of small size; and these are the best. Lanzi says, "He was correct in his proportions, lively and clear in his tints, and there is nothing left to desire, except a little more spirit and variety in his landscape or in the sky, as the atmosphere is always of a pale azure, or carelessly broken by a passing cloud." The greatest merit in his works consists in the accuracy of his design, and the excellence of his perspective, which Lanzi says made his works alike useful to painters and architects. He died at Rome in 1736.

VANVITELLI, Luigi. This eminent architect was of Dutch origin, and the son of the preceding artist, Gaspar van Witel, who, settling in Italy, was called *Vanvitelli.* Luigi was born at Naples, in 1700, and early manifested a strong inclination for art. At the age of twenty, he was employed by Cardinal Acquaviva to paint some frescos in the chapel of St. Cecilia; and he afterwards made some of the cartoons from celebrated pictures, preparatory to their being copied in mosaic on a larger scale, for St. Peter's at Rome. About this period also, he began to study architecture under Filippo Ivara, an eminent architect of that day. His first work in this art, was the restoration of the Palazzo Albani at Urbino, for the Cardinal di San Clemente; besides which he erected two churches in that city—S. Francesco and S. Domenico—that led to his obtaining the appointment of architect to St. Peter's at the age of twenty-six. He was also associated with Niccolo Salvi, in the undertaking for conducting the water Vermicino to Rome. About this time, there was a competition between all the most eminent architects of the day, for a façade to the church of St. John of Lateran; Salvi and Vanvitelli sent in designs, each of which were approved with an equal number of votes above all others, by the academicians of St. Luke; but, according to a memorial of Vanvitelli, the pope adopted the design of Galileo, not so much on account of superior merit, but rather for private reasons. However, neither Salvi or Vanvitelli was overlooked; the former was employed upon the Fountain of Trevi, and the latter was sent to Ancona, where he planned the Lazzaretto of a pentagonal form with a bastion, having first studied those at Leghorn, Genoa, and Venice. He also repaired and altered some churches and chapels in that city, and was occupied in a number of similar employments at Macerata, Perugia, Pesaro, and Siena. In 1745, according to Milizia, he went to Milan to design the façade for the Cathedral, which he intended to be of a style between the Gothic and the Greek; but the breaking out of the war prevented its execution. At Milan, he erected the archducal palace; at Rome, the convent of S. Agostino—his most important work in that city, and a most superb edifice—also an admirable chapel for the Portuguese ambassador, which was removed, and placed in the church of the Jesuits at Lisbon. In 1750, he arranged the ornaments of the tribune of St. Peter's, the illumination of the Cupola in a new style, the preparations for a consecration, the obsequies of the queen of England, and the removal of the Pietà of Michael Angelo.

By this time his reputation had increased to so great a degree, that when the king of Naples, afterwards Charles III. of Spain, determined to erect a palace at Caserta, that should be upon a scale hardly inferior to that of any other edifice of the kind in Europe, he at once made choice of Vanvitelli as the architect, and the corner-stone was laid with great pomp, in presence of all the court, Jan. 28th, 1752. This vast pile is an unbroken parallelogram of uniform design, all its fronts being nearly similar in their elevations; those facing the north and south are 730 feet, the others 570 feet in length; and the general height of the building is 102 feet, which is however increased to 162 feet at the angles, where there is a square pavilion enclosing a second order. The elevations consist of a very lofty basement, comprising a ground floor and mezzanine; and above that an Ionic order with two series of windows, and mezzanine windows in the frieze. Although it may be considered in some respects as the principal front, since it faces a spacious semi-elliptical piazza, enclosed by a uniform range of buildings for lodgings and stables, the south front is less decorated than that towards the gardens, for it has columns only in the centre and at the extremities; while in the other the order is continued throughout in pilasters, as well as in columns; yet the degree of unity thus kept up is attended with a very great drawback, for the narrower intercolumns between the centre and end breaks, cause the others to appear offensively wide, and those parts of the compositior where there ought to have been greater richness, to look poor and straggling: this is particularly the case with regard to the centre, which is only three intercolumns in width; therefore that and its pediment become insignificant in comparison with the entire mass, a defect which is still further increased by the end pavilions being so much loftier. Owing to the great height of the basement, the cornice of the order forms no adequate finish to the general elevation. The interior of the edifice is divided into four courts, 162 by 244 feet; the depth of building which surrounds these courts, in which are the rooms, passages, &c., is 80 feet; in this dimension is comprehended the thickness of the walls, which are in some instances 15 feet. The courts are formed by other ranges of building crossing from north to south and from east to west, at the intersection of which there is a large and lofty octagon vestibule, crowned by a dome. On one side of this vestibule is the grand staircase—a most magnificent structure—and the chapel on the other, decorated with isolated Corinthian columns on pedestals. The chambers throughout the whole edifice are vaulted, and admirably arranged. Milizia characterizes this stupendous edifice as "a rare assemblage of vastness, regularity, symmetry, richness, ease and elegance." Vanvitelli published in 1757, a large folio volume of the plans, &c., under the title of *Dichiarazione de' Disegni del Reale Palazzo di Caserta.*

Vanvitelli erected the great ranges of aqueducts for supplying the palace with water, forming one of the most stupendous works of the kind ever undertaken in modern times. He was also employed upon many other works at Naples, the principal of which are the cavalry-barracks, near the Ponte Maddalena, and the three churches of S. Marcellino, Della Rotonda, and La Nunziata. Among his works at other places, besides those already mentioned, are the public hall at Brescia, and the bridge at Benevento. For many years, Vanvitelli enjoyed a very prosperous career, and finally died March 1st, 1773.

VARCO, Alonzo de, a Spanish painter, born at Madrid in 1645. He studied under Don José Antolinez, and painted landscapes in the style of that master with considerable reputation. He died there in 1680.

VARELA, Francisco, a Spanish painter, said to have been born at Seville in 1606, though probably earlier, as Bermudez says he was employed by the convent of the Carthusians of Santa Maria, in 1618, and his Last Supper, in the Church of San Bernardo, one of his best works, is dated 1622. He was a disciple of Pablo de las Roelas, and acquired considerable reputation as an historical painter. He executed many works for the churches and convents, as well as for individuals at Seville, where he died in 1656.

VARGAS, Andres de, a Spanish painter, born at Cuenca in 1613. He went early to Madrid, and became the disciple, friend, and imitator of Francisco Camillo. He executed some works for the churches and convents of Madrid, Cuenca, and Hiniesta, but wrought more for individuals. He injured his reputation, by regulating the quality of his work by the price received. He died in 1674.

VARGAS, Luis de, an eminent Spanish painter, the accounts of whom are very contradictory. According to Palomino, he was born at Seville in 1528, and died in 1590; he says that, after learning the rudiments of the art in his native city, he went to Rome, where he studied some years, and directed his attention particularly to the works of Pierino del Vaga. On his return to Seville, finding himself unable to compete with Pedro Campana, whose works were then held in great esteem, he again went to Rome, and devoted seven years more to a diligent study of the works of Raffaelle and other great masters. He then returned to Seville, and soon gave proof of extraordinary abilities. Cean Bermudez gives an entirely different account. He places his birth in 1502, and his death in 1568. He went to Italy in 1527, where he resided many years, and by a diligent study of the works of the great masters, he became one of the most correct and skillful designers of his time. Pacheco says he resided in Italy 28 years, and returned to Seville about the middle of the 16th century. All, however, agree that on his return to Seville he greatly distinguished himself by several admirable works on a grand scale, painted in fresco, for the churches and convents, which have perished, or so little remains of them, that little opinion of their merits can now be formed. Bermudez says, "De Vargas executed many works both in oil and fresco, equal to the productions of the masters in Italy. Nothing can be more correct than his contours, grander than his forms, or better understood than his foreshortenings; for in these particulars he was superior to the most renowned of his countrymen who have followed him. If, in his smaller oil pictures, painted on panel, the aërial effect and gradations of light and tints had been equal to the splendor of his principal colors, the beautiful foldings of his draperies, the nobleness of the expression and of the attitudes, the graceful air of the figures, and the strict imitation of nature in the accessories, he would have been the best painter in Spain; but these defects were common in his time, and the greatest artists were not free from them." Among his chief performances were Adam and Eve in Paradise, Christ bearing his Cross, in the cathedral, and the Virgin holding a Rosary, in the church of the convent of San Pablo; productions said to be worthy of the hand of Raffaelle. He was accustomed to inflict scourgings and mortifications upon his body, and following the example of the Emperor Charles V., he used to lay himself in his coffin, to meditate on death.

VARIN, Jean, a sculptor and medalist, was born at Liege in 1604. During his earlier years, he served as a page in the employment of Comte de Rochefort, but having a strong inclination for design, he devoted his leisure moments to its study. He at length attained so much excellence in engraving, that he was invited to Paris and commissioned to engrave the seal of the French Academy, then recently established, in 1635. The merit of this performance gained him the friendship of Cardinal Richelieu, and he was soon after appointed keeper of the mint. He executed a set of medals commemorating various events in the reign of Louis XIII.; and after the death of that monarch, he was appointed, in addition to his former office, Intendant of Buildings to the Crown. Among his principal works in sculpture, are mentioned a Bust of Cardinal Richelieu; a marble statue of Louis XIII., placed in the palace at Versailles; and two colossal busts of that prince, one in marble, and the other in bronze. Varin was chosen one of the first members of the Academy of Painting and Sculpture, established in 1664. He died in 1672.

VARIN, Joseph, a French engraver, mentioned by the *Biographie Universelle*, who appears to have attained considerable celebrity. He was born at Chalons-sur-Marne, in 1740, and studied under his father, who was a graver on metals, descended from Jean Varin, and who taught a free school of design at Chalons. In 1755, Joseph assisted in executing a large map of the province of Burgundy, which gained him the honor of a medal. He visited Paris in 1760, in company with his brother, whose name is not mentioned, and found patrons in Crozat, Caylus, and others. They were engaged for many years upon various works, particularly the *Voyage pittoresque de Naples et de Sicile*, published by the Abbé de St. Non. The talents of Joseph Varin were also employed upon the *Voyage en Grèce*, by Choiseul Gouffier; the *Voyage pittoresque de Syrie, de Phenicie, et de Palestine*, by Cassas; and the *Tableau de l'Empire Othoman*, by Chev. Ohsson Mouradja. He also executed many views of cities and public buildings in France. This laborious artist unhappily lost the fruits of his labors during the civil commotions in France. He died in 1800.

VARLEY, John, an eminent English painter in water colors, was born at London about 1777. He was about to be apprenticed to a silver-smith, when the death of his father left him at liberty to choose his own profession, and he at first obtained employment with an obscure painter at Holborn. Afterwards, when about fifteen or sixteen, he received some instructions from a drawing master named Barrow, and they went in company on a sketching excursion, which was of material advantage to Varley, as a view that he then made of Peterborough Cathedral brought him into notice. He next became acquainted with Arnold, the landscape painter, with whom he made a tour through North Wales about 1799. On returning from that excursion, he was for some time employed by Dr. Monro in making sketches for him of the scenery in the neighborhood of his residence at Fetcham, in Surrey. Two other excursions through Wales, in 1801 and 1802, produced him numerous subjects, which occupied his pencil many years in London, and established his reputation as the first in that department of art he had chosen. He was certainly among the first, if not the very first, who began to advance the art of water-color drawing to that of water-color painting, and to give that mode of execution a solidity and force, a freedom and breadth, which it had not before attained, and of which it was not supposed capable. Up to that time, scarcely anything had been produced beyond washed or tinted drawings, very little superior to the colored prints of the same period—raw and feeble in effect. On the other hand, Varley gave to his paintings nearly all the vigor of oil pictures, and by a mode peculiar to himself, for he wrought with great rapidity, and does not appear to have produced his effects by repeated sponging and other processes now in use, or by admixture of body-color; his colors look as if they had been laid on at once, and hardly retouched. Varley was not an original member of the Water Color Society (established in 1804,) but he afterwards joined it, and sent many pictures to its exhibitions. Although he derived a good income from the sale of his works, and from his practice as a teacher, his numerous family, and want of either management or economy, kept him in continual embarrassment. He devoted much time to the study of judicial astrology, and is said to have made many extraordinary predictions. He was married twice, and died in 1842.

VAROTARI, Dario, a reputable painter and architect, was born at Verona, according to Ridolfi in 1539. He studied under Paul Veronese, and subsequently established himself at Padua, where he laid the foundation of a very flourishing school. According to Lanzi, his design is very chaste, and though his works occasionally resemble those of his instructor, his taste seems to have been formed on other models, particularly Titian, whom he frequently imitated in the airs of his heads. Although his coloring cannot boast the Venetian strength or beauty, it possesses great truth and harmony. He painted in the Polesine, at Venice, and at Padua, particularly in the church of S. Egidio in the latter city.

As an architect, Varotari erected a number of works, among which Milizia mentions a villa at Dola, for the Signori Mocenighi; a Casino on the Brenta for the famous Medico Acquapendente; and the graceful Montecchia de' Caodelista, not far from Praglia and Padua. While engaged in painting in this Casino, he accidentally fell from the first scaffold to the second, but without injury. His preservation appearing to him miraculous, he immediately went to Padua, and took the habit of the Santa Virgine. He died in 1596.

VAROTARI, Alessandro, called Il Padovanino. This eminent painter was the son of the preceding, born at Padua in 1590. His father dying when he was only six years old, he was instructed by some artist, not mentioned. He however, derived his principal improvement by studying the works of Titian, which were at Padua, and some of his juvenile copies excited the surprise and admiration of artists. He was sent young to Venice, where he pursued his studies with unremitting diligence, and soon began to distinguish himself. He was called Il Padovanino, by which name he is generally known in Italy. Lanzi gives the following admirable account of him: "He first studied Titian's works in fresco, such as he found in Padua, and his copies still continue to attract the admiration of the greatest professors. In Venice he persevered in his assiduous attention to the same incomparable master, penetrating so far by degrees, into his peculiar characteristics, as to be preferred by many to any of Titian's other disciples. But comparison is always disagreeable, and I am inclined to think those who personally receive from the lips of great artists a few brief and sound rules as to what ought to be avoided, or achieved, in order best to resemble them, are entitled to a high degree of respect; all the speculations of the finest geniuses upon their works are not half so valuable; for the second century is fast passing away, since the oral traditions of the best colorists wholly ceased, and we have been attempting to attain their method, in which we cannot succeed. Padovanino was always equal to the task of handling any subject that had been before treated by Titian; his softer ones with grace, his more powerful with strength, his heroic pieces with dignity, in which last, if I mistake not, he surpassed any other disciple of this great master. Women, cavaliers, arms, and the Loves (gli Amori), and let us add, boys, were the favorite subjects of his pencil, which he exhibited to the most advantage, and which he most frequently introduced into his compositions. And he knew how to treat landscape as well, in which he has succeeded admirably in some of his small pictures. He was familiar with the science of the *sotto in su* (foreshortening on a ceiling, so as to produce a correct point of view, as seen from below), of which he gave the most favorable specimens in the church of S. Andrea di Bergamo, in three admirable histories of that saint. It is a work embellished with beautiful architecture and replete with graces in every part. He has approached agreeably near his model in the sobriety of his composition, in the very difficult use of his middle tints, in his contrasts, in the color of his fleshes, and in smoothness and facility of hand. But Titian was still to remain unequalled in his art; and Varotari is not a little inferior to him in animation and in truthfulness of expression. Nor can I believe that his method of preparing his canvass, and of coloring it, was the same as that pursued by Titian's scholars, many of his pieces being much darkened, with the shades either deepened or altered. This is very perceptible even in his Dead Christ at Florence, a painting which the prince not very long since purchased for his gallery there. In other points, he appears to me to have observed the same method, in regard to his model, as Poussin did, who aimed at Raffaello's manner without reaching it, either from want of ability or a dread of falling into servility. His master-piece is said to be the Supper at Cana, formerly in Padua, now in the chapter of La Carità, at Venice, engraved by Patina, among the *Select Paintings*. It has few figures in proportion to the place, a rich display of costume and ornament, dogs that appear like those of Paul Veronese, full of life; grand attendance of women of the most exquisite forms, warmed with more ideal beauty than those of Titian, and drawn in the most graceful attitudes; still, not every one will approve of his introduction of them for the service of such a table, in preference to men, as is the general custom. The above picture, however, does not boast such fresh and lucid tints as his four histories of the life of S. Domenico in the Refectory of S. S. Giovanni e Paolo, containing, as it were, the flower of Padovanino's best style. This very elegant artist spent his time between Venice and his native province, where alone his pictures abound in public; in other cities, they are rarely to be met with, and are scarce even in private collections. In forming a correct opinion of his merits, it is necessary to be upon our guard against a variety of copies, many of his disciples having so happily imitated him, that Venetian professors themselves with difficulty distinguish their hand from that of their master." He died in 1650.

VAROTARI, Chiara, was the sister of Alessandro, and is said to have learned the rudiments of the art from her father. She is extolled by Ridolfi for the beauty of her portraits, and as fully deserving of the extraordinary honors conferred upon her by the Grand Duke of Tuscany, who invited her to his court, and placed her portrait, painted by herself, in the Florentine gallery. The poet Boschini also celebrated her beauty, talents, and accomplishments. She was living in 1660, according to Borghini and Lanzi, though some say she died at Verona in 1639.

VAROTARI, Dario, called Giovane, or the Younger, was the son and scholar of Alessandro V. According to Boschini, he was a physician, poet, painter, and engraver, but he seems to have practised the fine arts merely for his amusement. Lanzi says, "In the index to the *Carta del Navegar*, we find him ranked with the Dilettanti, from the circumstance of his producing little in art, and this more with the object of presenting his pictures as gifts than of gain. Nevertheless, we meet with an encomium upon them sufficient to satisfy his claims, even of a good professor; besides which some of his portraits, and pictures emblematic of the virtues, with an excellent body of coloring, are equally extolled for the spirit of the attitudes and exquisite taste, in the manner of Giorgione." Bartsch describes two prints by him—the portrait of his grandfather, Dario V., and of Vincentius Gusonus, Eq., both signed with his name.

VASARI, Lazzaro, an old painter of the Florentine school, who flourished about the middle of the 15th century. According to Lanzi, he was the intimate friend of Pietro della Francesca, and the imitator of his paintings; he was also the great-grandfather of Giorgio Vasari, the first biographer of Italian artists. There was another Giorgio V., uncle of the latter, who modeled admirable vases in plaster, reviving the forms of the antique, in their basso-relievos, and their brilliant coloring. There are specimens of his skill now in the Florentine Gallery.

VASARI, Giorgio. This eminent painter and writer on art, was born at Arezzo, according to Bottari, in 1512. He was descended from a family attached to the fine arts, and the great-grandson and nephew of the two artists mentioned in the preceding article. According to Lanzi's account, he was instructed in design by Michael Angelo and Andrea del Sarto; in painting by Rosso and Guglielmo da Marcilla, an eminent glass painter of that age. His chief improvement, however, was at Rome, whither he was brought by Cardinal Ippolito de' Medici, and introduced by that nobleman to his family, who afterwards loaded him with riches and honor. According to Lanzi, "after having designed all the works by Michael Angelo and Raffaelle at Rome, and much after other schools and the antique marbles, he formed a style in which we discover traces of his studies; but his predilection for Buonarotti is apparent. After acquiring skill in painting figures, he became one of the most excellent architects of the age; and united in himself the various branches which were known to Pierino del Vaga, Giulio Romano, and their scholars, who followed the example of Raffaelle. He could unaided direct the construction of a grand fabric, adorn it with figures, grotesques, landscapes, stuccos, gilding, and whatever else was required to ornament it in a princely style." By this means he became known in Italy; and was employed to exercise his talents in various cities. He painted a number of pictures in the Vatican; also in the Hall of the Chancery, where he executed a series of historical frescos from the life of Paul III., at the desire of Cardinal Farnese.

In 1544, according to Lanzi, Vasari was invited to Naples, to paint the refectory of the P. P. Olivetani, upon which he also exerted his talents in architecture, converting it from the Gothic into a better form; he altered the vault, and ornamented it with modern stuccos, which were the first seen in Naples. He remained in that city about a year, and painted a considerable number of subjects, with that rapidity and mediocrity which characterize the greater part of his works. In his own life, Vasari gives the idea of his being the restorer of taste in Naples; but, as Lanzi justly remarks, "it is not easy to conjecture why he should overlook many eminent painters, and even the illustrious Andrea da Salerno himself." The Neapolitan writers have always, and, as it seems, justly, complained of this neglect in his Lives of Italian Artists.

Besides his works at Rome and Naples, Vasari executed many others, among which are the Adoration of the Magi, in the Conventuali at Rimini; the Feast of Ahasuerus, in the church of the Benedictines at Arezzo; and three sacred subjects in the refectory of S. Michele in Bosco, at Bologna. Brought into public notice by these works, honored by the esteem and friendship of Buonarotti, and recommended by his multifarious abilities, he was invited to the court of Cosmo I. at Florence, whither he went with his family in 1553. He was employed by the Grand Duke in superintending the important works in the Palazzo Vecchio, among which the most considerable was the apartment of Clement VII., on the ceiling of which he represented that pontiff, in the act of crowning Charles V., and all around disposed the emblems of his virtues, his victories, and his most remarkable actions. The following criticism on his artistic merits is condensed from Lanzi. "Vasari aimed at too much, and for the most part preferred expedition to accuracy. Hence, though a good designer, his figures are not always correct; and his painting appears languid, from his meagre and superficial coloring. In his writings, he recommended the acquirement of compendious methods, and the 'expedition of practice'; in other words, to make use of former exercises and studies. This method is highly advantageous to the artist, because it increases his profits; but is prejudicial to the art, which thus departing from nature, degenerates into mannerism. Vasari often fell into this error, especially in his hasty productions, or where he borrowed the hand of others; as in the Hall of the Chancery at Rome, which he completed in one hundred days, to please the Cardinal, notwithstanding the admonitions of his friends, among whom Caro did not fail to remind him of the injury his reputation might sustain." Notwithstanding this, Vasari conducted several works with sufficient care to evince abilities of an uncommon order. Bottari does not scruple to compare some of his portraits to Giorgione; Borghini extols his Conception, in S. Apostolo at Florence; Lanzi praises his Decollation of St. John, in the church at Rome dedicated to that Apostle, and says that if all his works had perished but the above, and some of those in the Palazzo Vecchio at Florence, his reputation would have been much greater.

As an architect, Vasari attained greater excellence than as a painter. At Rome, he erected a great part of the palace for Julius III., without the Porta del Popolo, and near the Arco Scuro According to Milizia, the exterior parts of this edifice, taken separately, are not very correct; but as a whole, the proportions are elegant. He was engaged for many years at Florence on various works, particularly the Palazzo Vecchio, of which he improved the form, and made several alterations in the internal arrangements. His best edifice, and in Milizia's opinion the most elegant in Florence, is the Palazzo Uffizi, commenced in 1561 by order of the Grand Duke, and completed after Vasari's death by Alfonso Parigi. The façade has a portico, with openings alternately circular and level; the centre opening is supported by double insulated columns, and the others by large piers with niches. Over the entablature of this portico, which is Doric, with a plain frieze, and dentels above the cornice, is a lofty attic; the windows are small. This idea evinces an improved taste. According to Maffei, the archivolts on the arches are managed with so great skill, that although the interior façade rests upon them, even an experienced eye cannot perceive any settlement, nor is this arrangement in any degree prejudicial to the firmness of the building; and although another story has been added, containing an immense collection of busts, marble statues, &c., not a stone has moved from its original position. Vasari was of opinion that all archivolts, both ancient and modern, were fractured in the centre; he therefore took care to avoid this in his own work, by adopting the same plan as in the amphitheatre at Verona, where the key-stone is dove-tailed into the two lateral stones, which are so long and deep that they extend to the pilasters, and entirely through the walls. Vasari executed many other architectural works in various parts of Italy, among which were the designs for the palace and church of the cavaliers of Santo Stefano, at Pisa; and the beautiful cupola of the Madonna dell' Umilta, at Pistoja; he also restored the ancient church della Pieve, at Arezzo, besides many others. He was for many years employed to superintend the decorations in Florence, that were ordered by Cosmo I., and Prince D. Francesco. Lanzi says that the Florentine Academy of Design was reëstablished about 1561, principally through the exertions of Vasari. According to Bottari, he died in 1574, although his death is elsewhere placed in 1576.

As a writer on art, Vasari deserves considerable attention. He entered upon his work at the suggestion of Cardinal Farnese; and, according to Lanzi, his first intention was merely to collect anecdotes of artists, to be extended by Giovio; but when it was discovered that he could write better than the latter, the whole task devolved upon him, although he had the assistance of various literary characters, in order to render the work more worthy of the public. Lanzi says that "he reckoned Buonarotti the greatest painter that ever existed, exalting him above the ancient Greeks; and from his practice, held a bold and vigorous design as the summit of perfection, compared to which beauty and coloring were nothing. From such fundamental principles proceeded some of his obnoxious criticisms on Bassano, Titian, and even Raffaelle himself. But this was the effect of his education, and we may observe on a few passages of his work, that, while we condemn his principles, we admire his history. He was the father of the history of painting, and has transmitted to us its most precious materials. Educated in the most auspicious era of the art, he has in some measure perpetuated the influence of the golden age." There are many chronological errors in Vasari's work, and no writer on art has endured such a storm of criticism and hostility; but he has doubtless rendered greater service to art than any other. Had it not been for his indefatigable study, and his researches in various parts of Italy, the most valuable information concerning the old masters of the Venetian, Bolognese, and Lombard schools, would have been lost to us forever, unless indeed some other able writer had devoted his talents to produce so elegant and finished a history. It was published at Florence in 1550, in two volumes, entitled *Vite de' piu eccellenti Pittori, Scultori, e Architetti.* In 1566, Vasari undertook a new tour, to prepare for the second edition, which was published in 1568. The best subsequent editions are, that of Bottari, Rome, 1759, 3 vols., 4to.; those printed at Leghorn, 1767, 7 vols., 4to.; at Siena, 1791–98, 11 vols., 8vo.; at Milan in 1807, 16 vols., 8vo. Mr. Bohn has also recently published an English edition at London, in his Standard Library.

VASCELLINI, Gaetano, an Italian engraver, born at Castello S. Giovanni in the Bolognese state, in 1740. He was instructed in design by Ercole Graziani, and in engraving by Carlo Faucci at Florence. He engraved some portraits from those in the Florentine Gallery, and some historical and sacred subjects after Titian, Andrea del Sarto, Sebastiano Conca, Volterra, and other masters.

VASCO, Pereyra, a Portuguese painter, who flourished at Seville in the latter part of the 16th century, where he practised with considerable distinction. He painted the Decollation of St. Paul, for the convent of that order, in competition with Alonso Vasquez and Mohedano. He was employed in the Cathedral of Seville in 1598. He is said to have executed many works, both in oil and fresco, for the churches and convents in Spain and Portugal. He died about 1600.

VASCO, called by the Portuguese Gran-Vasco, or the Great Vasco. The accounts of this artist are very contradictory and uncertain. Whether he was the same as the preceding, or another artist is not known. It is said that his works are to be found in the churches and convents of Portugal, and that they are very numerous and held in the highest estimation. It would appear, also, that he had many imitators, whose works are frequently attributed to him. According to Berardo, who made diligent inquiries on the subject, but the result of whose researches has not yet been fully made known, he was the son of Francisco Fernandez, a painter of the city of Vizeu, where Vasco was born and baptized, on the 18th of September, 1552. For an account of his works, the reader is referred to "Les Arts en Portugal," by Count Raczynski.

VASCONI, Filippo, an Italian engraver, who flourished at Venice about 1720. He engraved some plates of views in Venice and its vicinity.

VASCONIO, Giuseppe, a Roman painter, who flourished about the middle of the 17th century. He is commended by Orlandi and the *Guida di Roma.* He executed some works for the churches, and was elected a member of the Academy of St. Luke in 1657.

VASELLI, Alessandro, a painter born at Rome, who flourished in the latter part of the 17th century. He was a scholar of Giacinto Brandi, whose style he followed, according to Orlandi, with considerable success. Some of his works are mentioned in the *Guida di Roma.*

VASI, Cav. Giuseppe, a Sicilian designer and engraver, was born in that island in 1710. His instructor in the art is not mentioned. He visited Rome, and passed most of his life in that city, where he was much patronized by Benedict XIV. He published several views of the port of Ancona, and afterwards engraved for Charles III., king of Naples, the decorations of the festival in honor of the birth of his eldest son, which pleased that monarch so highly, that he assigned Vasi apartments in the Farnese palace at Rome. Encouraged by this distinction, he applied himself to engraving the finest ancient and modern edifices, fountains, and other monuments in the metropolis of art, which he published in one grand collection of ten volumes in 1761, under the title *Delle magnificenze di Roma,* &c. The success of this work determined him to proceed further, and he published in six sheets a View of Rome in perspective, from Mount Janiculum, dedicated to Charles III.. which was greatly admired, and is now to be found in most European cabinets. Among the other works of Vasi, are his collection of plates in two volumes, entitled *Tesoro sacro, cioè: le Basiliche, le Chiese, i Cimiterj e i Sanctuarj di Roma,* &c., published in 1778. In 1777 he published a guide book, entitled *Itinerario istruttivo di Roma nella pittura, scultura, e architettura,* &c., containing a catalogue of all his plates up to that date. According to Bassano, Vasi died at Rome in 1785; although the Biographie Universelle places the date in 1782. Gio. Battista Piranesi, the celebrated architectural engraver, was his pupil.

VASQUEZ, Alonso, a Spanish painter, born at Ronda, according to Palomino, in 1589, and died in 1650. These dates, however, are doubtless incorrect, as Bermudez says he was one of the artists employed in the magnificent decorations for the obsequies of Philip II. in 1598, and he died before Pacheco published his work in 1649. He studied at Seville, under Antonio Arfian, a scholar of Luis de Vargas, and acquired considerable reputation as an historical painter. He also excelled in painting fruit, flowers, and subjects of still-life. He was particularly distinguished for his intimate acquaintance with anatomy; his works are correctly designed, and executed with freedom and facility. The principal are in the monastery of the Barefooted Carmelites at Seville. He died about 1645. Juan Batista Vasquez, probably a relative of the preceding, was born at Seville in the 16th century, and practised both painting and sculpture. His best performance in the former art is a picture of the Virgin and Infant, at the altar of the church of Our Lady of Granada.

VASSALLO, Antonio Maria, a Genoese painter, who flourished about 1670. He studied under Vincent Malo of Cambray, the scholar of Rubens. He painted landscapes and animals, but chiefly excelled in flowers and fruit, which he colored admirably, and touched with great freedom and spirit. He also designed the human figure correctly, and gave proofs of much talent for historical painting; but he died young.

VASSEUR, Jean Charles le, a French engraver, born at Abbeville in 1734. He studied first with Daullé, and afterwards with Beauvarlet. He engraved a considerable number of plates after the works of the French, Dutch, and German masters. Among others are the following by him. He died in 1816.

The Triumph of Venus; *after Boucher.* The Death of Adonis; *do.* The Continence of Scipio; *after Le Moine.* Diana and Endymion; *after J. B. Vanloo.* Apollo and Daphne; *after Luca Giordano.* The Triumph of Galatea; *after J. F. de Troy.* The Parting of Hector and Andromache; *after Restout.* Alexander and his Physician; *do.* Tarquin and Lucretia; *after A. Peters.* The Milkmaid; *after J. B. Greuze.* Thais, or the beautiful Penitent; *do.* The Step-Mother; *do.* The Widow and the Curate; *do.* The Will destroyed; *do.* Leonardo da Vinci expiring in the arms of Francis I.; *after Ménageot.* The Four Seasons; *after Gallet.* A Holy Family; *after R. Mengs.*

VASSILACCHI, Antonio, called L'Aliense, or Aliense da Milo, a painter born in the island of Milo, in the Archipelago, in 1556. According to Ridolfi, who wrote his life, he was sent to Venice when young, and placed under the instruction of Paul Veronese, under whom he made such progress and showed such a genius for historical painting, particularly for works of vast and imaginative character, as to excite the jealousy of that master, who dismissed him from his studio, at the same time advising him to confine himself to small pictures. Aliense, confident in his own powers, and suspecting that Veronese was practising towards him the same disgraceful illiberality which Titian had shown to Tintoretto, followed the example of the latter, and redoubled his efforts to attain excellence. He designed from the antique, day and night; he exercised himself in acquiring a knowledge of the human frame; he modeled in wax; copied Tintoretto with the utmost assiduity; and, as if wholly to forget what he had learned of Paolo, he sold all the designs he had made in his academy. He acquired great distinction, was patronized by the Doge and principal nobility of Venice, was invited to the court of Spain by Philip II., and Sigismond, king of Poland, earnestly solicited him to enter his service; but preferring to remain in Venice, he declined these honors and emoluments. He executed many works for the churches and public edifices of Venice; also in other cities of Italy, particularly Perugia, generally on a grand scale. At first, Aliense could not entirely divest himself of the style of Veronese, and his earlier productions in the church of La Vergine, display much of that master. He afterwards formed a style of his own, founded on that of Tintoretto, which in boldness and energy of design, freedom and spirit of pencil, and vigor of coloring, approaches the best productions of that master. Such are his pictures in the church of the Holy Apostles at Venice, representing Abraham sacrificing Isaac, Cain slaying Abel, and the Brazen Serpent. In the Sala dello Scrutinio are several of his best productions, particularly the Destruction of Troy, which prove him to have possessed a very fertile and inventive genius.

Lanzi says, "Aliense has been accused by historians of having abandoned the style of Veronese for one less adapted to his genius; and moreover, of having been misled by the innovations of the mannerists. Sometimes, however, he painted with extreme care, as in his Epiphany for the Council of Ten; though in general he abused the facility of his genius, without fear of risking his credit, inasmuch as his rivals, Palma and Corona, pursued the same plan. In order to oppose his great enemy, Vittoria, he attached himself to another architect who possessed great influence, named Girolamo Campagna, the disciple of Sansovino; he moreover enjoyed the favor of Tintoretto. In this manner he obtained many commissions, both for the public palace and for the churches of Venice, besides being engaged in many works for other cities." He died at Venice in 1629.

VAST, Vander. The name of this artist is affixed to some etchings of landscapes, executed in a spirited and tasteful style. Some writers conjecture, with little probability, that he is the same as Adrian de Weerdt, or Veert, which see.

VAU, Louis le, or Levau, a distinguished French architect, was born, according to D'Argenville, in 1612. Little is known of him, except by his works, but he acquired sufficient eminence to be appointed, in 1653, first Architect to Louis XIV., and Superintendent of Buildings to the Crown; and he discharged the duties of that office during the rest of his life. Milizia says, "his talents were of the highest class, and he practised his profession with that assiduity and activity which are requisite to undertake and execute great projects." He was occupied upon the enlargement of the Tuileries, and ornamented the great gallery with a Composite order. Among his other works were, various alterations in Cardinal Mazarin's Chateau de Vincennes; the Chateau de Vaux, erected for M. Fouquet; the Chateau of Livry, for M. Berdier; and the hotels Pons and Colbert. Le Vau died in 1670. The College des Quatre Nations was afterwards erected from his designs, by his pupil François d'Orbay.

VAUGHAN, Robert, an English engraver, who flourished about 1650. He was chiefly employed in engraving portraits of distinguished personages, for the booksellers, which are more praised for the characters they represent, than for the merit of the prints.

VAUGHAN, William, an English engraver, probably a brother of the preceding. He flourished about 1660, and, like Robert Vaughan, was probably employed in engraving portraits and other subjects for the booksellers. He also engraved a set of thirteen plates of animals. His prints are poorly executed.

VAUQUER, a French designer and engraver, by whom there is a set of plates of flowers and ornamental foliage for goldsmiths.

VAYMER, Giovanni Enrico, a painter born at Genoa in 1665, and died in 1738. He studied under Gio. Battista Gaulli. He painted history with reputation, but he chiefly excelled in portraits, in which branch he was very celebrated. Lanzi says he abounded in commissions, and that Genoa is full of his portraits. "He was called three times to Turin to paint the King and royal family, and was invited by very considerable offers to remain there, which, however, he always declined." So great was his reputation, that every foreigner of distinction, passing through Genoa, sat to him for his portrait.

VEAU, Francesco, a painter born at Pavia in 1727, and died in 1768. He was an excellent painter of perspective and architecture in the decorative style.

VEAU, Jean le, a French engraver, born at Rouen about 1736. He went to Paris when young, and studied under J. P. le Bas. He engraved quite a number of plates of landscapes and other subjects after the French, Dutch, and German masters, which are executed in the neat and spirited style of his instructor. Zani mentions Jean Jacques le Veau, a French designer and engraver of landscapes, born in 1729, and died in 1785, perhaps the same artist.

VECCHI, Giovanni de', a painter born at Borgo San Sepolcro in 1536. He went to Rome when he was young, and first studied under Raffaellino delle Colle, and afterwards with Taddeo Zuccaro, who was at that time employed by the Cardinal Alessandro Farnese in the embellishment of his palace at Caprarola, where, in conjunction with his instructor, Vecchi executed several considerable works. Lanzi says he was rather a competitor, than a scholar, of Zuccaro, that he was an eminent master, and that from the time he was employed by the Farnese family, he was considered a first rate artist. "He painted much for the churches at Rome, but chiefly excelled at Caprarola, when contending with Taddeo Zuccaro, and in the church of S. Lorenzo in Damaso, where he painted various histories of that martyr." Among his other principal works are the cupola of the Chiesa del Gesù, where he painted in fresco, the Four Doctors of the Church, and several histories of St. Jerome in the church of S. Maria d'Aracæli. He died at Rome in 1614.

VECCHIA, Pietro, a painter born at Venice in 1605. He was educated in the school of Alessandro Varotari, called Padovanino, but he did not follow the style of that master. He applied himself to an imitation of the works of Giorgione and Pordenone, with such success that his works have frequently been mistaken for the productions of those masters, even by connoisseurs. He also imitated Titian and other masters very accurately. Lanzi says he inherited from his master an admiration of the old masters, as well as the art of imitating them. His powers were better adapted to familiar and fancy subjects, than to the dignity of history, and his best pictures represent armed soldiers, banditti, corps-de-garde, which he painted with great vigor and effect in the manner of Giorgione, though often bordering on caricature. Lanzi mentions one of some soldiers, in the possession of the Senator Rezzonico at Rome, so exquisitely beautiful, that Giordano painted a companion of it, and Sandrart mistook another, in possession of the Count Palatine of the Rhine, for a genuine work by Giorgione, till he examined it, very critically. Lanzi says, "though his humor pleases us in some of his pieces, it disgusts in others, particularly in the Passion of our Saviour, in which the spectator ought never to be presented with cause for mirth; but Vecchia forgot this, and like Callot, introduced certain caricatures in his sacred pieces, of which specimens are to be seen in the church of the Ognissanti at Venice, and in various other places. In other points, with a style rather strong and loaded with shade, than pleasing, he showed himself an excellent artist, both in the naked parts and in his draperies, which he designed and colored at the same time, in the Academy. His fleshes are dark red, his handling easy, his color thick and heavy, the effect of his lights new and studied, and his whole taste so far from any appearance of mannerism and of such a composition, that to one unversed in pictorial history, he would appear to have flourished at least two centuries before his real time." His talent in imitating the works of the old masters, induced the Doge and Senate of Venice to employ him to copy in oil, some of the historical works in mosaic in the church of St. Mark, which he performed with great ability. He also painted two altar-pieces from his own designs, in the same edifice, representing the Crucifixion, and Christ driving the Money-changers out of the Temple, both accounted excellent performances. Melchiori bestows upon him particular commendation for his talent of restoring ancient paintings, as he could happily imitate the touch and color of any master; hence he conjectures that he acquired the appellation of Vecchia; his family name was *Muttoni*. He is variously called Pietro Vecchia, or Pietro da or della Vecchia. He died in 1678.

VECCHIETTA, Lorenzo di Pietro, called also da Siena, was a Sienese painter and sculptor, born, according to Vasari, in 1424. His pictures are characterized by that hardness of style, so common among the Sienese painters of that age; there are a few of them remaining at Siena, and one is mentioned by Lanzi, in the Medicean Gallery, dated 1457. He probably studied sculpture under Donatello, in which he attained much more distinction, and his superior talents gained him the commission to execute the bronze Tabernacle of the grand altar in the cathedral at Siena, with the marble ornaments. The beauty of this work excited the admiration of his cotemporaries, and gained him commissions for various works in sculpture in the edifices of Siena, among which were two statues of St. Peter and St. Paul, in the Loggia del Banco, tastefully designed, with great delicacy of execution; a statue of Christ, in the hospital of the Scala; and several works in bronze for the Baptistery of S. Giovanni. Vecchietta completed the latter edifice, and is said to have finished some of the works of Donatello. He died, according to Vasari, in 1482. The *Biographie Universelle* places the birth of this artist in 1482, and his death in 1540; but this is doubtless an error.

VECCHIO, Il, di San Bernardo. See Francesco Minzocchi.

VECELLI, or VECELLIO, Tiziano. Tee Titian.

VECELLI, or VECELLIO, Francesco, was the brother of Titian, born at Cadore, in the Friuli, in 1483. He was instructed by his brother, and is said to have shown such extraordinary talents as to excite the jealousy of his brother, who persuaded him to engage in other pursuits. Be this as it may, he entered the army, and followed the career of arms, for many years, till the restoration of peace in Italy, when he returned to Venice, and resuming his pencil, he executed several altar-pieces and portraits in the style of Titian, possessing so much merit as to excite the alarm of that master, who, dreading a powerful competitor in Francesco, artfully contrived to induce him to devote his attention to the decoration of cabinets with small historical pieces and other subjects, for which at that time, there was a great demand. In 1531 he wholly relinquished painting and devoted himself to mercantile pursuits. Though Titian was exceedingly jealous of the secrets of his art, and carefully withheld his instruction from those whom he might fear to educate as rivals; it is hardly credible that he could have treated his own brother with such duplicity and illiberality, and such a charge ought not to be tolerated without undeniable evidence. Titian was only six years older than Francesco, and if we are to believe his biographers, notwithstanding all his talents, he received such paltry remuneration for his works, till he was almost fifty years old, that he was not only poor, but in embarrassed circumstances;—grant this, and he could have little cause of jealousy. Francesco, moreover, was evidently an erratic and wayward genius, not apt to practise a profession long that merely afforded him his bread, he joined the army; when disbanded, he returned to painting for a time; then became a merchant, and finally, he threw away his time and money in the idle pursuit of alchemy, a chimera at that time thought attainable, in which many great minds were engaged. As to decorating cabinets, Titian and other great artists did not disdain such employment. His principal works are the Transfiguration, in the church of S. Salvatore at Venice, and the Nativity, in that of S. Giuseppe at Belluno, a picture frequently attributed to Titian. Some of his cabinet pieces are still preserved, and are generally attributed to Titian. The time of his death is not known.

VECELLI, Orazio, was the son of Titian, born at Venice in 1540. He studied with his father, and followed his style with great success. He particularly excelled in portraits, in which branch he was esteemed little inferior to his father. He accompanied his father in his travels to Rome, Madrid, and Germany. He painted in the palace of the Doge at Venice, in conjunction with Tintoretto and Paul Veronese, some excellent works, which were all destroyed in the conflagration of that edifice. Little is known of him, the glory of the father having entirely eclipsed the son; and none of his historical works are particularly recorded. The paucity of his works is accounted for by his untimely death; yet he lived to the age of Raffaelle, and enjoyed the advantages of early and most excellent instruction; therefore it is reasonable to suppose that his works are now mostly attributed to his father. He died in 1576, the same year as his father, which contradicts the story that, after the death of the latter, he devoted his life to pleasure, and squandered his patrimony in the ridiculous pursuit of the philosopher's stone. It were to be wished that historians would confine themselves to facts, dates, and probabilities, and not relate fables and suppositions for truths; the history of art would not then be so full of contradictions.

VECELLI, Marco, called Marco di Tiziano, was the nephew and scholar of Titian, born at Venice in 1545. He was the favorite disciple of his great instructor, and approached nearer to his style, both in composition and color, than any of his other relatives. He accompanied him in his journies to Rome and Germany, and assisted him in his works. There are some of his pictures in the Palazzo di S. Marco at Venice, one of the most esteemed of which is an allegorical subject on the Peace of Italy, in the ante-chamber to the Sala del Consiglio; another admired work by him represents the Doge Leonardo Donato, kneeling before the Virgin and Infant, in the Salla della Bussola. He also executed some considerable works for the churches at Venice, Trevigi, and in the Friuli, one of the most remarkable of which represents Christ fulminating the World, and the Virgin with several Saints interceding, in SS. Giovanni e Paolo at Venice. Another admired production is in the parish church of Cadore; it represents the Crucifixion, with two laterals of the Controversy and Martyrdom of St. Catherine. Lanzi says, "In simple composition and mechanism of the art, he was a good disciple of his master, but he had not the genius to inspire his figures and interest the eye of the beholder, like his great cotemporary." Marco also excelled in portraits. His known works are not numerous, and doubtless many of his productions are attributed to Titian, as he lived to the good age of 66 years, and died in 1611.

VECELLI, Tiziano, called Tizianello to distinguish him from his father, was the son of Marco. The time of his birth and death are not known. Lanzi says, "He flourished about the beginning of the 17th century, when mannerism began its innovation upon the Venetian school of painting. And those specimens by him, possessed by Venice at the Patriarchal church, at the Servi, and elsewhere, exhibit him in a very opposite taste to that of his predecessors; his forms are larger, but less imposing; his pencil full and free, but destitute of softness of hand;—so powerful is the influence of prevailing taste, over even family descent and education. In portraits, nevertheless, and in heads, very capriciously varied and ornamented, I find him to be in much esteem among artists." He died about 1650.

VECELLI, Fabrizio, was the son of Ettore Vecelli of Cadore, a relative and probably a brother of Titian. Lanzi says, "his name had hitherto been confined to his native place, Cadore, until brought to light by Renaldis, who traced his origin to another branch of the Vecelli, and gives an account of a fine picture he executed for the Council Hall of the parish, and for which he was paid sixteen gold ducats, no despicable price for the period when he flourished. He died in 1580."

VECELLI, Cesare, was the brother of Fabrizio, and flourished towards the close of the 16th century. The accounts of him are very contradictory, which Lanzi reconciles and explains. "He was the brother of Fabrizio, and like him, long unknown to pictorial history, although his productions are pointed out at Lintiai, at Vigo, at Candide, and at Padola. His name is more familiar to engravers, inasmuch as he gave to the world two works of etchings, during his residence at Venice. One of these, which is very scarce, contains *Ogni sorte di mostre di punti tagliati, punti in aria*, &c., the other *De gli Habiti Antichi e Moderni di diverse parte del mondo, Libri due fatti da Cesare Vecellio;* this last has been several times republished, and once in 1664, with a false title, where Cesare is mentioned as a brother of the great Titian." The false title above referred to is as follows: *Raccolta di figure delineate dal gran Tiziano, e da Cesare Vecellio suo fratello diligentemente intagliate.* There is a fine picture by him in the I. R. Pinacoteca of Milan, representing the

Father supporting the crucified Son, with the Holy Spirit hovering above, to complete the triad.

VECELLI, Tommaso. This artist was also a kinsman of Titian, brought to light by Renaldis, who highly commends his picture of the Annunciation, in the parish church of Lozzo; and another of the Last Supper, which he pronounces estimable. He died in 1620.

VECQ, James la, a Dutch painter, born at Dort in 1625. He studied with Rembrandt, whose style he followed for some time with considerable success, but he afterwards abandoned it for that of John de Baan. He painted history and portraits, particularly the latter, with reputation. He died at Dort in 1674.

VEEN, Martin van. See Hemskirk.

VEEN, Otho and Gilbert van. See Venius.

VEENHUYSEN, J., a Dutch engraver, who flourished at Amsterdam, about the middle of the 17th century. He engraved a set of views of the public edifices in that city, published with descriptions in Dutch and French, in 1656. They are executed in a neat but slight style. He was living in 1677.

VEGLIA, Marco and Piero, two painters of Venice, brothers, who flourished, according to Zanetti, in the first part of the 16th century. They were reputable painters, though their works partake much of the dry and gothic style of the Bellini.

VELA, Cristobal, a Spanish painter, born at Jaen in 1598. He studied successively under Pablo de Cespedes and Vincenzio Carducci. He settled at Cordova, where he was chiefly occupied in painting for the churches and convents. He was esteemed a correct designer, though he was languid and feeble in his coloring. His works have mostly perished, or been injured by unskillful restoration. In the cloister of the convent of San Augustin at Cordova is a series of the Prophets by him, designed in a grand style. He was drowned by falling into the well of his own house, at Cordova, in 1658.

VELASCO, Don Acisclo Antonio Palomino de Castro y, an eminent Spanish painter, was born at Bujalance in Valencia, in 1653. He is usually called Palomino by foreign writers. His parents afterwards removed to Cordova, where young Palomino was educated for the church, but having a passion for painting, which he had cultivated to some extent, he placed himself in 1672, under the instruction of Juan de Valdes, on the return of that painter from Seville to Cordova, under whom he made rapid progress. In 1675, he formed an intimacy with Juan de Alfaro, and in 1678 accompanied him to Madrid, where he assisted him in some of his works. He next formed a friendship with Juan Carreno, and with Coello; the latter employed him to assist him in painting the ceiling of the Queen's Gallery at the Alcazar; in which he displayed so much ability that Coello, having other works in hand in the Escurial, left him to complete the work, which he did so much to the satisfaction of the king that he named him one of his painters, but without a salary. On the marriage of Charles II. to Donna Maria Ana de Neoburg in 1690, he designed the arches and other decorations for the bridal entry into the city, which confirmed him in his office with its emoluments. The arrival of Luca Giordano at Madrid in 1692, according to Bermudez, caused some consternation among the Spanish painters, but Palomino maintained his position, and Luca not being so well versed in Christian theology as in heathen mythology, Palomino was able to instruct him in the subjects he was called upon to paint, which he did with such delicacy and perspicuity that the great Italian painter, embracing him, exclaimed, "the work is already finished"—a very improbable story. In 1697 he went to Valencia, where he executed some important works, the principal of which were some frescos in the presbytery of the church of San Juan del Mercado. In 1705, he was employed to decorate the convent of S. Esteban at Salamanca with some frescos, representing the Church Militant and Triumphant, accompanied with many allegories. On his return to Madrid, he was employed on many works for the churches and convents. In 1715, he published the first volume of his "Museo Pictorico," on which he had been engaged many years, and in 1724 the second volume appeared. He painted the Chartreuse of Granada, where he represented St. Bruno supporting the World, with a Glory of Angels and Saints; also five pictures for the grand altar at Cordova, and the hieroglyphics which adorned the funeral of Donna Maria Luisa de Saboya. He died at Madrid in 1726, and was buried with great pomp in the church of S. Francisco.

Palomino has not inaptly been termed the Vasari of Spain; like that artist, he abounded in commissions and degenerated into mannerism, and he was the first writer of any note on Spanish art. His employment was incessant, and he left the execution of many of his designs to his scholars, particularly to Dionisio Vidal. Palomino is better known out of his own country as a writer on art, than as a painter.

VELASCO, Luis de, a Spanish painter, who flourished at Toledo from 1564 to 1606, when he died. Little is known of him. He painted history and portraits, and there are some of his works in the Cathedral at Toledo, though most of his productions are attributed to other masters. His design is said to be noble, his drawing correct, and his coloring harmonious; his style exhibits a knowledge of the antique and of the best Italian masters.

VELASCO, Cristobal de, was the son of the preceding. He was instructed by his father, and followed his precepts. In 1598, he painted the portrait of the Archduke Albert. He also painted seven views of cities in Flanders for Philip III., to decorate his hunting residence in the woods of Valsain. He had a son, Matias de Velasco, whom he instructed in the art, and who accompanied the court of Philip III. to Valladolid, where he was employed to paint several histories of the Virgin, for the royal nunnery of the Carmelites.

VELASQUEZ, Don Diego Rodriguez de Silva y. This most eminent painter of the Spanish school, was born at Seville in 1594. He was descended from a noble family, originally of Portugal, which had been reduced by the troubles of their country, and had settled in Andalusia. Although his parents were in very narrow circumstances, they gave Diego a liberal education; and, as he manifested an extraordinary genius for art, he was placed under the tuition of Francesco Her rera the elder. The principles of that master, whose chief ambition was to obtain effects true to nature, are to be traced in all the works of his pupil. Herrera being of a very violent temper, he treated Velasquez so cruelly that he quitted him, and entered the school of Francisco Pacheco. The latter was learned in the theory of art, and an able designer; but he exercised no influence over the style of his pupil; and the reason why Velasquez remained five years in this school, was perhaps explained at the end of that time, when he married Pacheco's daughter. Meanwhile, he devoted himself faithfully to studying the theory of the art, and to the imitation of nature. Like Caravaggio, the leader of the naturalist school in Italy, he determined to represent things as they are, and not as they ought to be; he accordingly procured a peasant lad as a model, and painted his commonplace form, rags, and nakedness, under every aspect and attitude. He also made many designs from nature of peasants and ordinary people, in peculiar habits and occupations, and produced many faithful and striking representations of the manners and characters of the lower orders of the people, designed and painted with great fidelity and spirit. Like Murillo, Velasquez was taught to draw and color at the same time, beginning with subjects of still-life, and those the most ordinary, such as meat, vegetables, and kitchen utensils; hence the generic term *Bodegones*, by which they are still known. Thus he obtained an early mastery over his materials, a habit of close imitation, and a marvellous power of representing nature and texture. One of the most celebrated of these early productions is his picture, now in the new palace at Madrid, of the Old Water-Carrier at Seville, whose tattered garment exposes parts of his body through the rents, giving drink to a Boy out of his barrel; exhibiting considerable science in muscular anatomy, and a wonderful degree of nature and expression.

After painting subjects of this familiar description for a few years, his thoughts were turned towards the higher branches of the art by the contemplation of the paintings of Luis Tristan, whose style was a compound of Titian and El Greco; and he visited Madrid in 1622, for the purpose of seeing the treasures of art in the rich collections of that city. He was welcomed by Don Juan de Fonseca, and other Sevillians, and painted a portrait of the poet Gongora—a commission from Pacheco—after which he returned to Seville. Meanwhile, the influence of Fonseca was not idle, and Velasquez was recalled to Madrid the following year, by the Conde Duque de Olivarez, the prime minister of the tastes and pleasures of King Philip IV. Velasquez having painted the great man's portrait, immediately rose to that fortune which never deserted him during a long career of prosperity. As soon as the King saw the portrait of his favorite, he sat for his own, and the young painter, exerting all his powers, produced a picture of the King in armor, mounted on a magnificent steed, with a background of beautiful scenery. The picture was exhibited at Madrid in the open air; the connoisseurs joined in exalting Velasquez above all his predecessors; and the King—a true judge of art—ordained that none but the new Apelles should paint him. He was next employed to paint the infants Don Carlos and Don Fernando, and the equestrian portrait of Olivarez. He was appointed principal painter to the King, with a liberal salary, besides a munificent remuneration for his pictures.

Although thus greatly honored by his own and foreign princes (among the latter was Charles I., of England,)* Velasquez had not yet attempted any great historical composition; and as Vincenzio Carducci and Eugenio Caxes, his predecessors in royal favor, had distinguished themselves by painting the expulsion of the Moors by Philip III., he determined to depict that important event of Spanish history, and produced a magnificent composition, representing the King armed in the centre, commanding a party of soldiers, who are escorting a company of Moors of different ages and sexes, to an embarkation which awaits them in one extremity of the picture; on the other side is represented an impersonification of the kingdom of Spain, as a majestic matron in armor, with part of a stately edifice. It is signed *Didacus Velasquez Hispalensis Philip IV. Regis Hispan. pictor ipsiusque jussu fecit, anno* 1627. This celebrated performance established the fame of Velasquez, and he was appointed one of the King's chamberlains, with an additional stipend to support his new dignity. In the same year, 1627, Rubens visited Madrid, to discharge the duties of his embassy; and the two great masters formed an intimate friendship. Rubens associated with no other artist but Velasquez, and was accustomed to walk with him alone to the Escurial. His frequent dissertations upon Italian art, inspired the Spaniard with the greatest desire to visit that country, and he had no sooner expressed his wish to that effect, than the King directed Olivarez to supply him with a plentiful sum of money, and the warmest letters of recommendation.

Velasquez embarked at Barcelona in 1629, and on landing at Venice was lodged in the hotel of the Spanish ambassador. He contemplated with surprise and admiration the works of Titian and Tintoretto, and after a few months went to Rome, where he was very kindly received by Cardinal Barberini, nephew to Urban VIII., who procured him apartments in the Vatican. Here he had constant access to the works of Raffaelle and Buonarotti, which he studied with the greatest assiduity. From the Vatican he removed to the Villa de' Medici, but falling a victim to malaria, was soon carried down an invalid to the Piazza de Spagna below, and lodged in the palace of the Condé Monterey, the ambassador of Spain, who watched over his patient, and restored him to health. During his residence at Rome, he painted his two celebrated pictures of Jacob with the Garment of Joseph, and Apollo at the Forge of Vulcan; which he sent home to the King.

From Rome Velasquez passed to Naples, where he felt at home amid the works of Caravaggio, Stanzioni, and Ribera. With the last he lived in the closest intimacy, but preferred the flowing style and cheerful composition of Stanzioni, between whose manner and his own the resemblance cannot be mistaken, as is evident from comparing their works in the gallery at Madrid. He painted the portrait of Donna Maria of Austria, consort

* Velasquez painted a portrait of Charles I., which for many years was supposed to be lost; but it has been discovered within a few years, and in 1850 was in the possession of Mr. John Snare of Reading, England, who exhibited it in that year in the city of Edinburgh.

of Ferdinand III., and after an absence of a year and a half, returned to Spain. Philip IV. had meanwhile remained true to his promise of sitting for his portrait to no other painter, and he now appointed Velasquez one of the gentlemen of his wardrobe, with a studio in his palace, of which the King kept a private key, for the purpose of visiting him daily unceremoniously, as Charles V. had done to Titian.

Thus enjoying the sunshine of royal favor, Velasquez went on rapidly producing many admirable works. He painted the magnificent equestrian portrait of Philip IV., from which the great carver Montanez made a model in wood, in order to be sent to Florence, where it was cast in bronze by Pietro Tacca, and is now placed in the gardens of the Buon Retiro. This success led to new honors; Velasquez was appointed to an office about the King's person, and in that capacity followed Philip into Arragon and Catalonia in 1643 and 1644. In the former of these years the Conde Duque de Olivarez was disgraced, but Velasquez had the honesty and boldness to continue to show respect to his original patron, nor did Philip IV. resent this uncourtier-like gratitude. In November, 1648, he made a second journey to Italy on a particular embassy to the Pope; also to purchase modern pictures for the King, and to procure moulds from the best antique statues for the projected Academy. He embarked at Malaga, landed at Genoa, passed rapidly to Milan, Venice, Florence, and Parma, and thence hastened to embrace his friend Ribera at Naples. Returning to Rome, he was presented to Innocent X., and painted his portrait, which is now the gem of the Doria collection, and the only real specimen of his art in Rome. Lanzi says, "he renewed in this portrait the wonders which are recounted of those of Leo X. by Raffaelle, and Paul III. by Titian; for this picture so entirely deceived the eye as to be taken for the Pope himself." He was elected a member of the Academy of St. Luke, and received many flattering attentions and honors, among which were a gold medal, presented him by the Pope. He persuaded Michael Angelo Colonna and Agostino Mitelli to visit Spain, to assist in the decorations of the royal palaces.

The Inquisition had always persecuted nudity, and Spain was deficient in models from the antique. The lax and voluptuous Philip IV. protected the license of Greece and Italy, and Velasquez, feeling the value of exquisite form,—in which he was very deficient—and knowing that the opportunity might never again occur, collected a large number of casts from the antique, besides many admirable works by eminent modern masters. After three years' absence, he returned to Spain with his cargo, and was received by the King with his usual favor. He was now in his full power, and painted his finest pictures. In 1656 he received the much coveted cross of Santiago, which the King drew in with his own hand, upon a portrait of Velasquez, painted by the artist himself. The nobles resented this profanation of a decoration hitherto given only to high birth; nor were the difficulties removed without a papal dispensation, and a grant of Hidalguia. About this time, he was raised to the lucrative and honorable post of Aposentador Mayor, the duties of which were to superintend the lodgment of the King in his frequent migrations. Much of his precious time was thus taken from art. In 1660 he was sent to prepare the royal quarters during the journey from Madrid through the Castiles to the Bidassoa, when he erected on the island of Pheasants the temporary saloons for the conferences which terminated in the marriage of the Infanta Maria Teresa with Louis XIV. Velasquez appeared here for almost the last time, remarkable among the noble crowd for his tasteful costume and the arrangement of his diamonds. He returned to Madrid July 31, worn out with fatigue by preparations which any lord of the bed-chamber might have superintended. He died one week after, on the 7th of August, 1660, and was buried with the most distinguished funeral honors in the church of San Juan. Seven days after, his wife died, broken-hearted at the loss of her gentle and excellent husband, and was laid by his side in the same grave. In his private character he was most highly esteemed and beloved by all who knew him.

It is somewhat remarkable that the best English dictionaries of painting contain no criticism upon the characteristics of this great painter, at all commensurate with his extraordinary merits, and his position at the head of the Spanish school. The critical remarks in this article are derived from the various authorities of Mengs, Pacheco, Carducho, and Bermudez.

Velasquez drew nothing from the antique, and his visit to Italy produced no change in his style. He held up the mirror to his own age alone—all was his own, original, national, and idiosyncratic; he shrunk from any change by which loss might be risked; and notwithstanding the truth, character, and powerful painting of his works, they are singularly marked with the most ordinary forms, copied from nature as he observed her from day to day. His style was based on Herrera, Caravaggio, Ribera, and Stanzioni—a compound of all, not a servile imitation of any. His drawing was admirable, correct and unconstrained; his mastery over his materials unequalled; his coloring was clear and clean; he seldom used mixed tints; he painted with long brushes, and often as coarsely as floor-cloth; but the effects when seen from the intended distance were magical, everything coming out into its proper place, form, and tone. He painted with a rapid, flowing, and certain pencil, with the greatest ease, and absence of art or effort. There was no showing off of the artist;—loving Art for itself alone, he passed his whole soul into his subject, without one disturbing thought of self: having conceived his idea, he worked it rapidly out, taking advantage of everything as it turned up, correcting and improving it as he went on.

He pursued every branch of painting excepting the marine, and excelled almost equally in all. His portraits baffle description and praise;—they must be seen to be known. He depicted the *minds* of men; they live, breathe, and seem about to walk out of their frames. His power of painting circumambient air, his knowledge of lineal and aërial perspective, the gradation of his tones in light, shadow, and color, give an absolute concavity to the flat surface of his canvass,—we look into space, into a room, into the reflection of a mirror. The freshness, individuality, and identity of every person are quite startling; nor can we doubt the anecdote related of Philip IV., who, mistaking for the original the portrait of Admiral Pareja in a dark corner of Velasquez's room, exclaimed, as he had been ordered to sea, "What! still here?" He was inferior to Vandyck in representing female beauty, partially because he had not his advantages; the oriental jealousy of the Spaniards revolted at any female portraiture, and still more at any display of beauteous form: his talents, moreover, were most decidedly for depicting the *man*. He caught the high bred air of the Hidalgo, his grave demeanor and severe costume, with perfect truthfulness, never flattering any, not even royalty. In landscape he is said to surpass all other Spanish artists; his scenes are full of local color, freshness, and daylight, whether verdurous court-like avenues, or wild rocky solitudes. The animals in his pictures are perfectly admirable, and his beggars, urchins, and drunkards, are ranked with the performances of Murillo and Teniers.

Unlike most of the artists of Spain, Velasquez was patronized little by the church; his patrons were knights and kings. Consequently he comparatively neglected the religious and legendary; but his Crucifixion, painted in 1638, and now in the convent of S. Placido at Madrid, would be sufficient, if he had done nothing else, to have immortalized his fame. It is designed with his usual nature and simplicity, but with an expression in the features, an affecting air in the reclining of the head, and an harmonious tone of coloring, at once so tender, and of such effect, that it cannot be surpassed. In historical performances, Velasquez was most eminent. Mengs describes his famous picture of General Pescara receiving the keys of a Flemish citadel from the governor of the place. The group of generals, soldiers, citizens, and horses, &c., and the striking effect of the town and landscape, in the background, have established the fame of this great work, and Mengs calls it his master-piece, pronouncing it faultless in every respect, except that the lances are too long—a trivial remark, not to have been expected from such an authority, but tending rather to enhance than depreciate the merits of this celebrated performance.

The genuine and finest works of Velasquez remain at Madrid; in other cities of Spain they are quite as rare as in other parts of the world. This remarkable fact results from the unusual character of his career; he commenced in the royal service, and so continued to the end, rarely condescending to work for the church or for private patrons. All his great pictures were thus monopolized, and hung up in the royal palaces, not to be purchased, and nearly inaccessible to travellers. Unlike the works of the other Spanish masters, they were not scattered abroad in the French wars, and only two—the Jacob and the equestrian portrait of Philip IV.—were sent to Paris. The great gallery at Madrid contains a sufficient number of the pictures of Velasquez, to give the connoisseur a correct idea of his extraordinary power and universality of talent. Of his portraits and landscapes, quite a number have been transferred to the private collections in England, and the grand landscape with a representation of a Boar-hunt, according to the old Spanish fashion, is now in the National Gallery. It was formerly in the great palace at Madrid, but was presented by Ferdinand VII. to Sir H. Wellesley, afterwards Lord Cowley, and was purchased for the National Gallery for £2200.

VELASQUEZ, Alexandro Gonzalez, a Spanish painter and architect, was the son of a sculptor of little distinction, born at Madrid in 1719. He studied in the Academy of that city, and made such rapid progress, that at the age of nineteen he was commissioned to paint, in concert with his brother Luis, the decorations of the theatre of the Retiro. In 1744 he was entrusted to superintend all the works of painting and sculpture executed at St. Ildefonso, and was afterwards occupied during three years in making the plans and elevations of the palace at Aranjuez. In 1752, Velasquez was elected by the Academy sub-director in the department of architecture; and in 1762 he was chosen for the same office in that of painting. The *Biographie Universelle* states that there are a number of architectural works by Alexandro at Madrid, which do honor to his talents, and Milizia specifies only one, the modernizing of the church las Ballecas, where he ornamented the inferior part with Ionic pilasters, and placed Corinthian columns to the altars. He instructed many pupils, and died in 1772.

VELASQUEZ, Antonio Gonzalez, a distinguished Spanish painter of the last century, the brother of the preceding, was born at Madrid in 1729. He visited Italy with the King's pension, and studied in the school of Corrado Giaquinto, where he made rapid progress, and was commissioned to paint the frescos which adorn the church of la Trinità de Castelli. He returned to Spain in 1753, and painted the cupola of the chapel of Our Lady of the pillar, in the cathedral at Tarragona, which gained him considerable reputation. At Madrid he also executed a number of works, in concert with his two brothers, Luis and Alexandro, in the monastery de las Salesas, the convent of the Incarnation, and various other edifices, by which he gained so much reputation that Charles III. appointed him court painter in 1757. In 1765 he was chosen director of the Academy of Painting, and discharged the duties of that office until 1785. During this period he executed many fine works, particularly in fresco, which were greatly admired. Few painters of his country have possessed the qualities of grace and facility, in so high a degree as Antonio Velasquez, and his abundant imagination enabled him to produce a large number of sketchings and drawings of all kinds, among which his beautiful sketch of the Foundation of the Order of the Golden Cross, has been engraved by Salvador Carmona. He died in 1793, leaving three sons, who practised the Fine Arts with success.

VELASQUEZ, Luis Gonzalez, the brother of the two preceding artists, was born at Madrid in 1715. After acquiring the elements of design from his father, a sculptor of little note, he studied in the Academy at Madrid, and was afterwards commissioned to execute the decorations of the theatre of the Retiro, in concert with his brother Alexandro. About 1752, he painted the Cupola of the church of St. Mark in fresco, which occupied him several years, and was so greatly admired, that the King appointed Luis a sub-director of the Academy, and subsequently painter to the royal cabinet. He died in 1764.

VELDE, Adrian van de, an eminent Dutch painter, born at Amsterdam in 1639. The history of his brief life is very similar to that of Paul Potter. Discovering a passion for the fine arts, even in his infancy, which exhibited itself by his sketching upon walls, or whatever else came to hand, all kinds of animals and objects that struck his fancy, his father was induced to place him under the instruction of John Wynants, with whom he made extraordinary progress, and continued several years. Wynants was one of the ablest landscape painters of his time, accustomed to draw everything from nature, and he educated his pupil in the same excellent system. Young van de Velde's application was incessant, and he was accustomed to pass the greater part of his time in the fields, studying and sketching every object and appearance that could prove of advantage to his pursuit. The scenes and situations of his landscapes, his trees, skies, clouds, animals, &c., were all sketched from nature, a practice he continued as long as he lived, nor did he neglect to study the human figure, which he designed with great accuracy, and was soon able to embellish the landscapes of his instructor. Wynants did not design the figure well, and had heretofore employed Philip Wouwerman or John Lingelbach to insert them in his works. Some of the finest landscapes by Wynants are adorned with the figures and cattle of Adrian van de Velde, which greatly adds to their value. Such was his excellence in these auxilliary embellishments, that many of his cotemporaries applied to him for similar assistance; the pictures of van der Heyden, Hackaert, Hobbema, Ruysdael, Verboom, and Moucheron, are frequently decorated with his figures and animals.

The pictures of van de Velde are full of truth and nature; in the choice of his subjects, the agreeableness of his scenes, and the excellence of his coloring, he has hardly been surpassed by any of his countrymen. Though his landscape is confined to the pasture in which cattle are grazing, it captivates by its truth and simplicity. His trees are natural and well formed, the leafing sharply and accurately marked, his herbage and plants fresh and juicy; his skies clear and brilliant, and his pictures exhibit a sparkling glow of sunshine almost peculiar to himself; he was careful to depict the effects of light upon every particular object, and happily expressed its effects through the branches of the trees, on the surface of water, on his cattle, and every part of his scenery. His figures and animals are designed with remarkable correctness and precision, with great life and spirit in the actions and attitudes; he particularly excelled in the representation of cows, oxen, sheep, and goats. His touch is light and delicate, yet free and full of spirit. Though he had not the advantage of a regular education in the higher branch of historical painting, yet he executed several works for the Roman church at Amsterdam, which prove that he possessed an extensive and varied genius, and that he would have shone in that branch, had he devoted his attentions more to it. These represent several subjects taken from the Life and Passion of Christ, the chief of which is the Descent from the Cross, the figures being half life size. His pictures are deservedly held in the highest estimation, and are only to be found in the choicest collections. He wrought with great facility and unceasing application, as is evident from the large number of his genuine works, executed entirely by himself, besides the many pictures of Wynants, and others, which he decorated with figures and animals. Smith, in his Catalogue raisonné of the works of the Dutch and Flemish masters, vol. v., and Supplement, gives a descriptive account of about 180, which are considered authentic. The value of his works has increased amazingly within 70 or 80 years. Thus,

No. 2. A Mountainous Landscapé, in which Jacob, his family, and his servants, appear conducting their flocks and herds, sold in 1765 for £130; in 1811 it brought at M. le Brun's sale at Paris, £960.

No. 5. Watering Cattle, sold in 1754, for £135, in 1810, it brought £688; it is now in her Majesty's collection.

No. 8. Peasants with cattle fording a Stream, sold in 1771 for £280. In Sir Simon Clark's sale in 1840, it was bought by Sir Robert Peel for 760 guineas.

No. 15. A Landscape, with peasants, cattle, and sheep, sold in the famous Braamcamp collection in 1771, for £218; in 1822, it brought £746; it is now in the Museum at Amsterdam.

No. 26. La Chasse Royale was sold in the Lormier collection, in 1763, for £53, and at the Count Perregaux's sale in 1841, it was purchased by the Baron Rothschild for £1125!

Adrian van de Velde executed quite a number of charming etchings, from his own designs. Bartsch describes 21, to which Weigel, in his Supplement to Bartsch, has added four more. They are usually marked A. V. V. *f.*, or A. V. Velde, *f.*, though sometimes A.V.V., or A.V.V. *F.*, or Adrian Van de Velde *f.*, and one A. V. V. His name is variously written by English writers, *Vandevelde*, *Vandervelde*, and *Van de Velde*. He died at Amsterdam in 1672, in the flower of his life.

E v V

VELDE, Esais van de, a Dutch painter, born at Leyden in 1597, according to the best authorities, though some say about 1590. He studied under Peter Denyn, an artist of little note, and painted landscapes with figures and cattle, but his principal subjects, in which he excelled, were battles, skirmishes of cavalry, marchings of soldiers, attacks of banditti, &c. His pictures are usually of small size, ingeniously composed, agreeably colored, and touched with a light, neat, and spirited pencil. His expertness in small figures procured him almost constant employment from his cotemporaries, who were anxious to have their landscape or perspective views adorned by his pencil. He was remarkable for his fondness of draping his figures in the Spanish costume. His works during his lifetime were highly esteemed, and brought high prices, but they subsequently sunk considerably in value. He executed a number of neat and spirited etchings of landscapes and other subjects from his own designs, which are usually marked with his initials, or *Esijas Vander Velde, invent.* He died at Leyden, in 1648.

VELDE, James van de, was the younger brother of the preceding, born at Leyden in 1598, according to the best authorities, though some say about 1595. He painted landscapes and merrymakings, but was chiefly distinguished as an engraver. He engraved a great number of landscapes, views, and other subjects, chiefly from his own designs, which are executed in two entirely different styles, directly opposite to each other. His landscapes and views are chiefly etched, and his point is free and spirited; his lights are broad and clear, and though his shadows occasionally want strength, they generally produce a pleasing and masterly effect. His other prints are executed with the graver, sometimes assisted by the dry point, in a highly finished style, resembling that of Count Goudt; these chiefly consist of night pieces, or scenes by candle-light, and such subjects as require a great depth of shadow. He is generally called *John Van de Velde*, or *Vandervelde*, but usually signed his prints *Jan (James) van der Velde*. The time of his death is not known, but his prints are dated from about 1615 to 1645. The following are the principal:

A set of Thirty-six Landscapes, entitled *Playsante Landschappen, door Jan van der Velde*. Twelve plates representing the Twelve Months, 1616; another set of the Twelve Months, larger. The Four Seasons, in four plates; *after Valck*. 1617. Four plates of the History of Tobit; *after Uytenbroeck*. The Four Elements; *after Buytenwegh*. The Four Times of the Day. A set of six Landscapes with ruins, figures, and cattle; *after G. vander Horst*. A series of plates representing the Spanish Troops, marching in the Low Countries in the years 1638, 1641, and 1645, with other military scenes; *after Jacob Martss de Jonge*. Also a great variety of landscapes, views, portraits, and other subjects, from his own designs, and after other masters.

VELDE, William van de, the Elder, generally called the *Old*, an eminent Dutch marine painter, was born at Leyden in 1610. He is said to have been bred to the sea; this report, however, is very doubtful, and probably arose from circumstances connected with his profession. It is not known by whom he was instructed; but before he was twenty years of age, he had acquired considerable reputation as a painter of marine subjects, which he usually represented in black and white, in imitation of drawings in India ink. He drew everything after nature, and became one of the most spirited, correct, and admirable designers of marine subjects of his country. He made an incredible number of drawings on paper, heightened with India ink, all of them sketched from nature with uncommon elegance and fidelity. His talents recommended him to the notice of the States of Holland, and Descamps says, they furnished him with a small vessel to accompany their fleets, that he might design the different manœuvres and engagements; that he was present in various sea-fights, in which he fearlessly exposed himself to the most imminent danger, while making his sketches; he was present at the severe battle between the English and Dutch fleets, under the command of the Duke of York and Admiral Opdam, in which the ship of the latter, with five hundred men, was blown up, and in the still more memorable engagement in the following year, between the English under the Duke of Albemarle, and the Dutch Admiral de Ruyter, which lasted three days. It is said that during these engagements he sailed alternately between the fleets, so as to represent minutely every movement of the ships, and the most material circumstances of the actions with incredible exactness and truth. So intent was he upon his drawing, that he constantly exposed himself to the greatest danger, without the least apparent anxiety. He wrote over the ships their names and those of their commanders; and under his own frail craft *V. Velde's Gallijodt* or *Myn Gallijodt*. After having executed many capital pictures for the States of Holland, he was invited to England by Charles II., who had become acquainted with his talents during his residence in Holland. He arrived in London about 1675, well advanced in years, and the king settled upon him a pension of an hundred pounds per annum until his death, in 1693, as appears from this inscription on his tomb-stone in St. James's church. "Mr. William van de Velde, senior, late painter of sea fights to their Majesties, King Charles II. and King James, died in 1693." He was accompanied by his son, who was also taken into the service of the king, as appears from an order of the privy seal as follows: "Charles the Second, by the grace of God, &c., to our dear Cousin, Prince Rupert, and the rest of our commissioners for executing the place of Lord High Admiral of England, greeting. Whereas, we have thought fit to allow the salary of one hundred pounds per annum unto William van de Velde the Elder, for taking and making draughts of sea-fights; and the like salary of one hundred pounds per annum unto William Van de Velde the Younger, for putting the said draughts in color for our particular use; our will and pleasure is, and we do hereby authorize and require you to issue your orders for the present and the future establishment of said salaries to the aforesaid William van de Velde the Elder and William van de Velde the Younger, to be paid unto them, or either of them, during our pleasure, and for so doing, these our letters shall be your sufficient warrant and discharge. Given under our privy-seal, at our palace of Westminster, the 20th day of February, in the 26th year of our reign."

Many of the large pictures of sea-fights in England, and doubtless in Holland, bearing the signature, *W. van de Velde*, and generally attributed to the son, were executed by him from the designs of his father. Such are the series of twelve naval engagements and sea-ports in the palace at Hampton Court, though signed like the best works of the younger van de Velde; they are dated 1676 and 1682.

VELDE, William van de, the Younger, was the son of the preceding, born at Amsterdam in 1633. He received his first instruction from his father, but afterwards studied with Simon de Vlieger, an eminent painter of sea-pieces, whose works were then held in the highest estimation. He possessed extraordinary talents, and not only surpassed his father, and all his cotemporaries, but he arrived at a perfection in the particular branch to which he devoted himself universally allowed to be unequalled. "The palm," says Lord Orford, "is not less disputed with Raffaelle for history, than with van de Velde for sea-pieces." He had already acquired a distinguished reputation in his native country for his admirable cabinet pictures, when he accompanied his father to England, where his talents not only recommended him to the notice of the king, who settled upon him a pension of one hundred pounds, but to the principal nobility and personages of his court, for whom he executed many of his most beautiful works.

Like his father, the younger van de Velde designed everything from nature, and his compositions are distinguished by a more elegant and tasteful arrangement of his objects than is to be found in the productions of any other painter of marines. His vessels are designed with the greatest accuracy, and from the improvements which had been made in ship-building, they are of a more graceful and pleasing form than those of his predecessors; the cordage and rigging are finished with a delicacy, and at the same time with a freedom almost without example; his small figures are drawn with remarkable correctness, and touched with the greatest spirit. In his calms the sky is sunny and brilliant, and every object is reflected in the glassy smoothness of the water, with a luminous transparency peculiar to himself. In his fresh breezes and squalls, the swell and curl of the waves is delineated with a truth and fidelity which could only be derived from the most attentive and accurate study of nature; in his storms, tempests, and hurricanes, the tremendous conflict of the elements and the horrors of shipwreck are represented with a truthfulness that strikes the beholder with terror.

The works of the younger van de Velde are very numerous, and the greater part of them are in England, where Houbraken says they were so highly esteemed that they were eagerly sought after in Holland, and purchased at high prices to transport to London; so that they are rarely to be met with in his native country. Smith, in his Catalogue raisonné, vol. vi. and Supplement, describes about three hundred and thirty pictures by him, the value of which has increased amazingly, as may be seen by a few examples. The marines now in the Earl of Ellesmere's collection, one a View of the Entrance to the Texel, sold in 1766 for £80, now valued at £1,000: the other sold in 1765 for £84, now valued at £500. A Sea-View formerly in the collection of Sir Robert Peel sold in 1772 for only £31; brought in 1828, £300. The Departure of Charles II. from Holland in 1660, sold in 1781 for £82; it brought recently at public sale, £800. A View off the Coast of Holland sold in 1816 for £144; it brought, in Sir Simon Clarke's sale in 1840, £1,029. A View on the Sea-Shore, 16 inches by 12, sold in 1726 for £9, and in 1835 for £108. The picture known as *Le Coup de Canon*, sold in 1786 for £52, in 1790 for only £36, but in 1844 it brought 1,380 guineas.

The drawings, and especially the sketches and studies of the younger van de Velde are very numerous, and prove the indefatigable pains he took in designing his vessels, their appurtenances, and the ordonnance of his compositions. His sketches are executed in black lead only; his more finished drawings with the pencil or pen, and shaded with India ink. He executed these with wonderful facility; it is recorded that he was so rapid in his sketching, that he frequently filled a quire of paper in an evening. Stanley says that during the years 1778 and 1780, about 8,000 of his drawings were sold in London at public auction. Some of his choicest drawings in India ink, brought at the sale of M. Goll de Frankenstein at Amsterdam, in 1833, and at that of the late Baron Verstolk de Soelen, in the same city in 1847, prices varying from £27 up to £144 each. He inherited his father's drawings, and all these seem now to be attributed to him. He died in 1707.

VELDENER, John, a German book publisher, supposed to have been a designer and engraver on wood, who flourished about 1480. All that is known of him with any certainty is that he published at Louvain two works entitled "Fasciculus Temporum," 1474, and "Caroli Viruli formulæ Epistolare," 1476; also at Culembourg, "Speculum Humanæ Salvationis," 1483; and "Historia Santæ Crucis," in the same year; all of them in Latin, and embellished with wood cuts, executed in the rude style of the age. Whether he really designed and engraved the cuts which embellish these books, is a question that has exercised the industry and ingenuity of several able writers to maintain or refute, without eliciting anything positive. The cuts, not being the earliest specimens of the art, are not worth the disquisition, and those fond of such intricacies must be referred to the works of Heineken, Santander, Ottley, Zani, Jackson, and others, who have written learnedly and elaborately on the subject. His name is sometimes written *Veldner*, and the Italians call him *Giovanni di Westfalia.*

VELI, Benedetto, a Florentine painter who flourished about 1650. Little is known of him. Lanzi says he painted in the Cathedral of Pistoja, the Ascension of Christ, placed at the entrance of the Presbytery. It is the companion to one of the Pentecost by Gregorio Pagani, which sufficiently proves that it possesses uncommon merit. Zani calls his name *Velli*, and says he operated in 1588.

VELLANI, Francesco, a painter born at Modena in 1688, and died in 1768. According to Tiraboschi, he studied under Francesco Stringa, whose style he followed, though Lanzi says he was not a very accurate designer. He executed many works for the churches of Modena, and in the State.

VELLETRI, Andrea da, an old painter, born at Velletri. There is a picture by him in the Museo Borgia at Rome, representing the Virgin surrounded with saints, signed with his name, and dated 1334. Lanzi says that in execution it approaches the Sienese school. There was a Lello da Velletri, who painted an altar-piece in several compartments in a church at Perugia, about 1487. It is signed *Lellus de Velletro, pinsit.*

VELTRONI, Stefano, a painter born at Monte Sansovino, who was living in 1568. Lanzi says he was a man of slow parts, but very respectable in art. He assisted Vasari in some of his works at Rome, and afterwards accompanied him to Naples, Bologna, and Florence.

VENANZI, Antonio, a painter about whose Christian name and place of nativity there is much discrepancy; he is variously called *Giovanni*, *Giovanni Battista*, and *Francesco.* Suffice it to say that Oretti read on his picture of St. Onofrio, in the Carmine at Pesaro, *Ant. Venantius Pisauriensis*, 1688; and on his tomb, that he died on the 2d of October, 1705, aged 78. Lanzi says "Gio. Venanzi (or Francesco) had been already instructed by Guido, when he entered the school of Simone Cantarini, though he resembles neither of these masters so nearly as he does the Gennari. When we inspect his two beautiful histories of St Anthony, in the church of that Saint at Pesaro we might pronounce him their disciple." In the church of SS. Gervasio and Protasio at Bologna is a fine picture by him, representing the Descent of the Holy Ghost. It is said that he was employed at the court of Parma.

VENDRAMINI, Giovanni, an Italian engraver born at Roncade, near Bassano, in 1769. After studying in his native country, he went to England, where he became the pupil of Bartolozzi. In 1805 he went to St. Petersburg, where he remaine about two years, and was patronized by the Emperor. An accident is said to have hastened his return. Being employed by the Emperor to engrave a design upon a very valuable antique gem, representing Alexander and Olympia, the laurel that encircled the brow of Alexander was broken, and although it was privately repaired, he soon after returned to England, where he died in 1839. Among his principal plates are the Vision of St. Catherine, *after Paul Veronese;* St. Sebastian, *after Spagnoletto;* Leda, *after Lionardo da Vinci;* and the raising of Lazarus, *after Sebastiano del Piombo.*

VENENTI, Giulio Cesare, a Bolognese amateur artist, born about 1609, and died, according to Zani, in 1697. He studied painting under Filippo Brizio, and is said to have studied and practised art with the zeal of a professor. He executed a few spirited etchings after Ann. Caracci, Parmiggiano, Canuti, and others, which he marked with the above monogram.

VENEZIA, Jacometto da, a painter born at Venice, who flourished, according to Morelli, in 1472. He was very celebrated in his day for his small cabinet pictures of historical subjects, for private ornament, as well as for portraits and miniatures.

VENEZIA, Maestro Giovanni da, an old Venetian painter, who was living in 1227. He wrought in the old Greek style; little remains from his hand.

VENEZIA, Lorenzo da, a Venetian painter, who was living about 1358. He is commended by Zanetti for his altar-piece in the church of St. Anthony of Castello, signed *Laurentius de Venetiis*, 1358, for which he was paid 300 gold ducats. There are several other pictures bearing his signature—one in the possession of the noble family of Ercolani at Bologna, signed Manu Laurentii de Venetiis, 1368. Lanzi attributes to him a fresco, representing Daniel in the Lion's Den, in the church of Mezzaratta, near Bologna, inscribed *Laorentius, P.* The work bears no resemblance to the style of Giotto, and appears to have been completed about 1370.

VENEZIA, Niccolo da, also called Niccolo da Veneziano, an eminent Venetian artist in embroidering tapestry. He flourished in the time of Pierino del Vaga, and was in the service of the Prince Doria at Genoa, when that artist arrived there, and he introduced him to the court.

VENEZIA, Maestro Paolo da, an old Venetian painter of whom, according to Morelli, there are notices from 1333 to 1346. In the great church of St. Mark at Venice, is a very curious *Ancona* (tablet) divided into several compartments, representing the figure of a dead Christ, with some of the Apostles, and various historic incidents recorded by the Evangelist, which is thus noticed by Zanetti: "Among the specimens of simple painting in St. Mark's, the ball centre of the great altar is remarkable for several small tablets of gold and silver, on which are painted several figures, in the ancient Greek manner. San Pietro Urseolo had it constructed about the year 980 at Constantinople, and it was removed to this place in the time of the doge Ordelafo Faliero, in 1102, though it was afterwards renovated by the command of the doge Pietro Ziani, in 1209." Lanzi says this was certainly the work of Paolo and his two sons; underneath it bears this inscription, which escaped the notice of Zanetti: *Magister Paulus cum Jacobo et Johanne filiis fecit hoc Opus.* He mentions another work by him in the church of the Padri Conventuali at Vicenza signed *Paulus de Venetiis pinxit hoc opus*, 1333." "He is the earliest of the Venetian painters in the national manner (i.e. the old Greek style improved), of whom there exists a work with the indisputable name of the author."

VENEZIA, Fra Santo da, a Capuchin monk, who, according to Lanzi, flourished in 1640. Lanzi commends him as an artist worthy of notice, and says he was much employed in painting for the churches and convents within the Venetian territory.

VENEZIANO, Agostino. See Musis.

VENEZIANO, Carlo. See Saracini.

VENEZIANO, Sebastiano. See Piombo.

VENEZIANO, Antonio, a painter born at Venice, according to Vasari, in 1310, a scholar of Angiolo Gaddi; although Baldinucci, an excellent authority, asserts that he was a native of Florence, and acquired the surname of Veneziano from his long residence at Venice, where he executed many works, among which were several in the Ducal Palace. The latter were destroyed by fire in 1573. It is probable, however, that he was a scholar of some other master, as Angiolo Gaddi was not born until 1324. Baldinucci also states that he afterwards quitted Venice, on account of the intrigues of the painters in that city. His style was less dry and formal than the generality of his cotemporaries, and he is said to have attained a higher degree of perfection in fresco painting than the artists of that day. The principal works of Veneziano, are at Pisa and at Florence, among which are several subjects from the history of St. Ranieri, in the Campo Santo at Pisa; and his most celebrated performance at Florence, representing the Miracle of the Loaves and fishes. He died in 1384. The supposed portrait of him in the Florentine gallery, is considered by Lanzi as being in too modern a style for this age; and he thinks it represents another Antonio Veneziano, who flourished about 1500, and painted a picture of St. Francesco at Osimo, in the manner of the time. It was originally inscribed with his name, which has been erased, and that of Pietro Perugino inserted.

VENEZIANO, Domenico, an eminent Venetian painter, born in 1420. He was a favorite scholar of Antonio da Messina, who had learned the art of oil painting from John van Eyck, and communicated the secret to his pupil. He afterwards resided some time at Loreto and Perugia, and finally settled at Florence, where his works were greatly admired, both on account of their merit and the novelty of the process. He unfortunately formed a connection with Andrea del Castagno, an eminent Tuscan painter, who treacherously murdered him, in order that he might be the sole possessor of the secret. Castagno artfully concealed the atrocious deed until he was upon his deathbed, when he confessed the crime for which innocent persons had suffered. This catastrophe happened in 1476. His principal works are in the church of S. Lucia and the monastery degli Angeli at Florence. See *Antonio da Messina*, and *Andrea del Castagno.*

VENIER, Pietro, a painter born at Udine, who, according to Renaldis, died at an advanced age, in 1737. He studied at Venice, and executed many works both in oil and fresco. His best works are some frescos in the ceiling of the church of S. Jacopo at Udine, which are commended by Lanzi, who says he there appears to great advantage.

VENIER, Nicholas, an engraver, who executed a set of twelve plates, representing the months of the year, *after Bassano.*

VENIUS, or VAN VEEN, Otho, an eminent Dutch painter, born at Leyden in 1556. His parents being persons of distinction, gave him a classical education, and to gratify his passion for painting had him instructed in design by Isaac Nicholas, and painting by Jodocus van Winghen. Being compelled to leave his own country on account of the civil wars he retired to Liege to pursue his studies, where his talents recommended him to the notice of Cardinal Grosbeck, who advised him to go to Rome, and gave him letters of commendation to Cardinal Masuccio, who received him with the greatest kindness, and entertained him at his palace. He entered the school of Federigo Zuccaro, and at the same time studied the antique and the works of the great masters with assiduity. After a residence of several years in Italy, he set out to return to his own country, and passing through Germany, he stopped some time at Vienna, in the service of the Emperor, who endeavored to retain him by flattering offers, which he declined, and passing on to Munich and Cologne, he executed several works for the Duke of Bavaria and the Elector. On his arrival at Brussels, Alessandro Farnese, Prince of Parma, then Governor of the Netherlands, took him into his service, and appointed him principal painter to his court. He painted the portrait of his protector, and executed several historical works which established his reputation as one of the ablest artists of his time. On the death of the prince he went to Antwerp, where he established himself, and was employed to execute some works for the churches and public edifices. He also opened an academy, and had the honor of instructing Rubens. When the Archduke Albert, who succeeded the Prince of Parma in the government of the Low Countries, made his public entry into Antwerp, Venius designed the triumphal arches erected on the occasion, which displayed so much ingenuity and taste, that the prince invited him to Brussels, appointed him his principal painter, and master of the mint, which offices he filled with great reputation till his death.

Otho Venius had a lively and fertile invention, his compositions are learned and judicious, and his design, founded on that of the Roman school, was more elegant and correct than that of any of his cotemporaries of the Flemish school. The airs of his heads are graceful and expressive, his draperies are cast with ease and propriety, and he was one of the earliest artists of his country who had a thorough knowledge of the principles of the chiaro-scuro. Among his principal works are, the Last Supper, in the cathedral at Antwerp; the Marriage of St. Catherine, in the church of the Capuchins at Brussels; the Resurrection of Lazarus, in the church of St. Bavon at Ghent, and the Adoration of the Magi, in the cathedral at Bruges. He also distinguished himself in literature as well as in the arts, and published several works embellished with plates from his own designs, engraved by his brother Gysbert Venius; the principal are a history of the War of the Batavians against Claudius Civilis and Cerialis, from Tacitus; Horace's Emblems, with Observations; the life of Thomas Aquinas; and the Emblems of Love, divine and profane. He died at Brussels in 1634.

VENIUS, or VAN VEEN, Gertrude, was the daughter of Otho V., born at Brussels about 1600. She was instructed by her father, and painted cabinet pictures of historical subjects, and portraits, in which last branch she chiefly excelled. Her coloring was clear and lively, and her touch delicate. The portrait of her father, painted by herself, was engraved by Rucholle.

VENIUS, or VAN VEEN, Gysbert, was the younger brother of Otho V., born at Leyden in 1558. It is not known under whom he studied, but his style resembles that of Cornelius Cort. He engraved several plates after the Italian masters, for which reason some suppose that he accompanied his brother to Rome. His plates are executed entirely with the graver, his drawing is tolerably correct, and the character of his heads is well expressed. He engraved a great number of plates from the designs of Otho V., chiefly emblematical subjects, and some portraits which possess considerable merit. He died at Antwerp in 1628. The following are his best prints:

PORTRAITS.

Ernest, Duke of Bavaria; in a medallion, supported by Fame. Cardinal Alessandro Farnese; *after Otho Venius.* Giovanni da Bologna. 1589.

SUBJECTS AFTER VARIOUS MASTERS.

The Four Seasons; *after Raffaelle del Colle.* 1589. These have been incorrectly stated to be from the designs of Raffaelle d'Urbino. The Espousal of Isaac and Rebecca; *after Bal Peruzzi;* in five sheets, in the form of a frieze; fine and scarce. The Visitation of the Virgin to St. Elizabeth; *after F. Baroccio.* The Crucifixion; *do.* The Emblems of Horace; *after Otho Venius.* The Emblems of divine and profane Love; *do.* The Life of St. Thomas Aquinas; a set of several plates; *do.*

VENIUS, or VAN VEEN, Rochus, a Flemish painter, born at Antwerp in 1650, and died at Haerlem in 1706. He excelled in painting live and dead game, and birds, which he finished with great care.

VENNE, ABRAHAM vander, a Dutch portrait painter, born in 1586, and died in 1650. There is a portrait of William I. by him, in the Museum at Amsterdam.

 or  or 

VENNE, Adrian vander, a Dutch painter, born at Delft in 1589, and died at the Hague in 1662. He studied under Jerome van Diest. He possessed a lively imagination, and executed many beautiful designs to embellish the various Dutch publications of his time. He also painted history, battles and portraits. As he wrought with great facility, his works are very numerous, and are said to possess considerable merit. The subjects of some of the most interesting are the famous battles fought in Flanders, painted on canvass of immense size. His pictures are generally marked with one of the preceding monograms. There was a Hubert vander Venne, supposed to have been a relative of Adrian, who flourished at the Hague about the same time. He painted bas-reliefs, groups of children, vases, and other ornaments. Also a John vander Venne, who flourished at Brussels. He painted landscapes, which were sometimes decorated with figures by Bout.

VENTURINI, Angelo, a Venetian painter, who flourished in the first part of the 18th century. According to Zanetti, he was a pupil of Antonio Balestra, and painted both in oil and fresco. His principal works are in the church of Gesù e Maria at Venice, of which he decorated the ceiling, and various portions of the walls with frescos.

VENTURINI, Gasparo, a painter of Ferrara, who flourished about 1594. After having studied under Domenico Mona, as is conjectured by Baruffaldi, he went to Genoa, and became the disciple of Bernardo Castelli, whose style he followed. He executed some works for the churches, but wrought mostly for individuals. Lanzi says his coloring partakes of that ideal taste so pleasing in the works of Castelli.

VENTURINI, Giovanni Francesco, an Italian engraver, and probably a painter, born at Rome, in or about 1619. His style of engraving strongly resembles that of Gio. Battista Galestruzzi, and it is supposed that he was a disciple of that master. He etched a number of plates after the works of the Italian masters, among which is a set *after Polidoro da Caravaggio*, from the designs of Galestruzzi.

VENUSTI, Marcello, a painter born at Mantua in 1515. According to Baglioni, he first studied under Pierino del Vaga in his native city, and afterwards went to Rome, where his talent recommended him to the notice of Michael Angelo, who employed him to execute many works from his designs. Lanzi says, "he was a young man of great talents, but diffident, and probably standing in need of more instruction than Pierino afforded him; this he afterwards received from Michael Angelo, whose style he adopted, without affectation, and executed his designs in an excellent manner. He thus colored two Annunciations for altar-pieces, one of which was set up in the church of St. John of Lateran, and the other in Della Pace. He is also said to have painted some cabinet pictures after the designs of Buonarotti, as the Limbo * in the Colonna palace, Christ going to Mount Calvary, and some other pieces in the Palazzo Borghese, also the celebrated copy of the Last Judgment, which he painted for the Cardinal Farnese, that still exists at Naples. Although a good designer, and the author of many pieces, he obtained greater celebrity by clothing the inventions of Michael Angelo in exquisite beauty, especially in small pictures, of which Vasari says he executed a great many." These copies were executed on a much larger scale than the originals, and the beauty of his coloring and neatness of his finishing, won the admiration of Buonarotti, which, together with the fact that he employed Sebastiano del Piombo to assist him in competing with Raffaelle, shows that that great artist was not so insensible to the advantages of fine coloring, as some have pretended. Venusti executed many works for the churches at Rome, both in oil and fresco, from his own designs, which are greatly admired for the grandeur of their composition, correctness and elegance of design, excellence of coloring, and neatness of finishing. He is sometimes called by the Italians, *Mantuano.* Vasari and Orlandi erroneously call him *Raffaelle Venusti.* He died in 1576.

* Limbo, among theologians of the Roman church, is the place where the souls of just men, who died before the coming of our Saviour, and of unbaptized children, are supposed to reside, and the word means here, Christ preaching to the spirits in prison, or Hades.

VERAT, Darius, an engraver mentioned by Strutt as the engraver of a print signed *Alex. Verat, pinx. Darius filius sculp.* These names signify Alessandro and Dario Varotari, which see.

VERACINI, Agostino, a Florentine painter, who studied under Sebastiano Ricci, whose style he followed. He executed some works for the churches at Florence and elsewhere, which, according to Lanzi, gained him considerable reputation. He died in 1762.

VERALLI, Filippo, a painter of Bologna, who was living in 1678. According to Malvasia, he was a disciple of Francesco Albano, in whose style he painted landscapes, which were greatly admired. Lanzi also commends him as an excellent painter of rural views, which are much prized in the collections.

VERBEECK, or VERBEECQ, Philip, a Dutch painter and engraver, born at Haerlem, who flourished about 1620. Little is known of him, except that he engraved some plates, in a style said to so nearly resemble that of Rembrandt, that his prints have sometimes been mistaken, even by connoisseurs, for the productions of that master. If this be the case, *Rembrandt* was the imitator, as Verbeeck flourished before him, and it would seem probable that he was one of the several masters from whom Rembrandt derived instruction. There were several artists whose names are variously spelled as above, of whom little is known, but who seem to have flourished in the first half of the 17th century, and were probably of the same family.

VERBEECK, or VERBEECQ, Peter, a Dutch painter born at Haerlem, who flourished about 1640. He painted landscapes, hunting parties, halts of travelers, conversations, &c. He is said to have been one of the instructors of Philip Wouwerman, whose early pictures bear some resemblance to his style. There are a few etchings signed *P. C. Verbeecq*, which are dated from 1619 to 1639, perhaps the same artist. His style is also said to resemble that of Rembrandt. There are also some prints signed *G. Verbeecq.*

VERBIUS, or VERBUIS, Arnold, a Dutch painter, born at Dort, in or about 1646, and died in Friesland in 1704. He painted history, portraits, and lascivious subjects, from which last circumstance, he was called the *Libertine.*

VERBOOM, a Dutch painter, of whom little is known, except from his works. He flourished about the middle of the 17th century, and painted landscapes in a style partaking of those of Waterloo and Both, but not so warm as the latter. His pictures are very rare, and little known out of his own country. Bartsch describes two etchings by him, one of which is signed *V' Boom f.*, which are extremely rare. It is supposed that there are others, which do not bear his signature. There is a set of six landscapes engraved after him by Gronsvelt. Bartsch calls him *A. H. V. Boom;* others *Abraham Verboom.* He sometimes signed his pictures *A. Verboom.* His landscapes are occasionally enriched with the figures of Wouwerman, or Lingelbach. There is a fine landscape by him, with figures preparing for the chase by Lingelbach, in the Museum at Amsterdam.

VERBRUGGE, Andriesz Gysbert, a Dutch painter, born at Leyden, according to Immerzeel, in 1633; Füessli says he died at Delft in 1730, in his 77th year, which makes his birth twenty years later. He was a scholar of Gerard Douw, whose style he followed with considerable success. He passed some time in England, and afterwards settled at Delft, where, it is said, many of his portraits and cabinet pictures are to be found in the collections.

VERBRUGGEN, or TERBRUGGEN, Henry, a Dutch historical painter, born at Utrecht in 1588. After studying under Abraham Bloemaert, he went to Italy, where he resided ten years, chiefly at Rome and Naples. His talents recommended him to the patronage of several persons of distinction, and he executed several works for the churches, one of the best of which, was a Deposition from the Cross, in one of the principal churches of Naples. On his return to his native country, he settled at Middleburg, where he acquired a high reputation. When Rubens made his tour through Holland, he was particularly struck with the works of Verbruggen, and pronounced him one of the ablest artists of his country. His pictures are well composed, correctly designed, finely colored, and executed with a bold and spirited pencil. His name is generally written *Terbruggen*, and the best authorities agree that he died at Utrecht in 1629, but some say at Middleburg in 1640.

VERBRUGGEN, Gaspar Peter, a Flemish painter of fruit and flowers, born at Antwerp in 1668. He was the son and scholar of Peter Verbruggen, a painter of whom little is known except that he was director of the Academy at Antwerp in 1659. After having acquired considerable reputation in his native city, he established himself in 1706 at the Hague, where he was employed in conjunction with Matthew Terwesten in decorating the mansion of the Greffier Fagel, in which the figures were painted by Terwesten, and the festoons of flowers, fruit, and other ornaments, by Verbruggen. In 1708, he was elected a member of the Academy at the Hague. His works were greatly admired, and he found such abundant employment, that in the course of a few years, he amassed a competent fortune, with which he returned to Antwerp, where he is said to have devoted most of his time to company and amusements, painting chiefly at night, so that he became careless, and his later productions are inferior to his earlier ones. In his manner he exhibits the loose, free, and spirited touchings of John Baptist Monnoyer, rather than the polished finishing of van Huysum, and his coloring had more of brilliancy than of truth and nature. He particularly excelled in frescos, for which his style and great facility of hand were adapted. His manner of painting ceilings and saloons with festoons of flowers and fruit, was truly grand; and his coloring and grouping of objects, showed extraordinary skill and judgment. He died at Antwerp in 1720.

VERBRUGGEN, Peter and Henry Francis. There were two sculptors and wood carvers of this name, who executed various excellent works, according to Stanley, in the cathedral and churches at Antwerp, as pulpits and confessionals, and also many of the carved decorations in numerous noble mansions in Belgium. The time when they flourished is not stated, nor has the author been able to obtain any definite information concerning them. It is probable that their works were all of a decorative character, and executed in wood. During the civil commotions, some of them were sold, and sent to England.

VERCELLESI, Sebastiano, a painter born at Reggio, who was living in 1650. According to Tiraboschi, he was a disciple of Lionello Spada, and executed some works for the churches of his native city, but was mostly employed by individuals. He was a reputable follower of his master's style.

VERCELLI, Fra Pietro da, an old painter of the Milanese school, who, according to Della Valle, flourished at Vercelli about 1466. There is an altar-piece by him in the church of S. Marco, in that city.

VERCHIO. See Civerchio.

VERCRUYS. See Kruger.

VERDIER, François du, a French historical painter, designer, and engraver, born in 1651, and died in 1730. He studied under Charles le Brun, and copied many of the works of his master, by which he is better known than by his original compositions. His drawings in black and red chalk, heightened with white, in which he appears to have copied or imitated those of his master, are numerous in France. He also engraved some plates after le Brun, and others after his own designs. He is sometimes called *van Hawken*, for what reason is not mentioned.

VERDIZZOTTI, Giovanni Maria, a Venetian painter, poet, and disciple of Titian, was born at Venice in 1525, and died there in 1600. According to Ridolfi, he was an intimate friend of Titian, who instructed him and took every pains to make him a proficient in the art. He excelled in painting landscapes in the style of his master, usually of small size, which he enriched with figures representing some subject of history or fable. He showed Titian every mark of respect and affection, and acted as his secretary when he had occasion to correspond with persons of high rank. He translated the Æneid and Ovid's Metamorphoses into Italian, and on the death of Titian, wrote a Latin poem in honor of his memory. Lanzi says, "he was one of Titian's literary friends, who painted, under his direction, several landscapes which are much esteemed in different collections, where they are extremely rare."

VERDOEL, Adrian, a Dutch painter, born at a small village on the Meuse, in or about 1620, and died at Flushing in 1681. He is said to have first studied under Leonard Bramer; next one of the de Wittes, and lastly Rembrandt, whose manner he followed. His design was more correct, and his compositions more elevated, than those of Rembrandt, but in harmony of coloring, and in the effect of the chiaro-scuro, he was far inferior to him. His works are very rare, as he quitted painting for commercial pursuits.

VERDUSSEN, JOHN PETER, a painter who flourished from about 1743 to 1763, when he is supposed to have died. He painted hunting pieces, cavalcades, horse-fairs, and other subjects, in which animals form the principal objects, in a style of excellence. There are some of his works in the Munich collection.

VERELST, SIMON, a Flemish painter, born at Antwerp in 1664. It is not known under whom he studied, but he painted flowers and fruit exquisitely. He went to England early in life, in the reign of Charles II., where his works were extremely admired, and he gained abundant employment. He sometimes painted history, and oftener portraits; in which the beauty of the flowers always so entirely eclipsed the figures that they passed for *flower-pieces.* His conceit was unbounded. He called himself the king of painters, and used to exhibit an historical piece on which he had labored many years, and to boast that "it contained all the several manners and excellencies of Raffaelle, Titian, Rubens, and Vandyck." He died in 1710.

VERELST, HERMANN, is said to have been the elder brother of the preceding. He also excelled in painting fruit and flower-pieces. He went to Rome, and afterwards settled at Vienna, where he appears to have resided many years, till 1683, when that city being besieged by the Turks, the success of his brother induced him to go to England, where he remained till his death in 1700.

VERELST, CORNELIUS, was the son of Hermann, born at Vienna in 1667. He studied with his father, accompanied him to England, and painted similar subjects with success.

VERELST, MARIA, was the daughter of Hermann, and is said to have been born at Vienna in 1630, evidently an error of more than forty years. She studied with her father, but was chiefly indebted to the instruction of her uncle Simon, with whom she chiefly resided, for her proficiency in art. She excelled in painting portraits of a small size, which were admired for the delicacy of her touch, and the neatness of her finishing. She was an accomplished musician, performed on several instruments, and spoke and wrote the German, Italian, French, English, and Latin languages with fluency and elegance.

VERELST. See VERHELST.

VERENDAEL, N., a Flemish painter, born at Antwerp in 1659. It is not known under whom he studied, but he painted fruit and flower pieces in an exquisite manner, in which he appears to have emulated the delicate finishing of Abraham Mignon. His compositions exhibit both genius and judgment, and show that he studied everything after nature. His works are esteemed next to those of Mignon and van Huysum, and are to be found in the choicest collections of his country. His flower pieces are preferred to his pictures of fruit. He died in 1717.

VEREYCKE, HANS, a Flemish painter, born at Bruges in 1510. He painted landscapes in an agreeable and masterly style, and also portraits with considerable reputation. He was called by his cotemporaries *Little John.* He is supposed to have died in or about 1569.

VERGARA, NICOLAS DE, the ELDER, a Spanish painter and sculptor, born at Toledo about 1510 His works are chiefly to be found in the cathedral of Toledo, where he directed the works in painting and sculpture for thirty-two years, after 1542; and they are commended for an elevated taste of design, good taste in the accessories, and beauty of the forms. Vergara also executed a part of the paintings on glass in the same edifice, which were continued and completed by his sons, Nicolas and Juan, after his death in 1574.

VERGARA, JUAN DE, the son and scholar of the preceding, was born at Toledo about 1540. He distinguished himself as a painter, sculptor, and architect, and assisted his father and brother in executing the glass paintings in the cathedral, which occupied about forty years. He succeeded his father as director of the works in painting and sculpture in that edifice. Vergara contracted a close intimacy with El Mudo, who is said to have expired in his arms. He died at Toledo in 1606.

VERGARA, JOSÉ, a Spanish painter, was born at Valencia in 1726. At a very early age he manifested a strong inclination for art, and the *Biographie Universelle* states that he competed in the school of Evaristo Munoz for the prize offered for the best drawing after the living model, when only seven years old. He formed his style from the prints of Spagnoletto, and is also said to have studied the works of Coypel and Paolo de Matteis. His portraits are very numerous, and he painted many pictures for the churches of Valencia and the cities of that province, in oil, fresco, and distemper, generally characterized by correct design and excellent coloring. Among the most remarkable, are mentioned the Conception of the Virgin, in the Library of the convent S. Francisco at Valencia; and a picture of Telemachus and Mentor, placed in the Academy of that city, and afterwards transferred to the Academy of S. Ferdinando. Vergara was chosen director of the Academy of San Carlos at Valencia, and discharged the duties of that office until his death in 1799.

VERGAZON, HENRY, a Dutch painter of landscapes and ruins, who went to England in the reign of William III., where he was chiefly employed by Sir Godfrey Kneller, in painting the backgrounds to his pictures. He sometimes painted portraits of a small size.

VERHAECHT, TOBIAS, a Flemish painter, born at Antwerp in 1566. After studying in his native city and acquiring considerable reputation, he went to Italy for improvement. He resided some time at Florence, where his talents recommended him to the patronge of the Grand Duke of Tuscany, for whom he painted several large landscapes and views. He next went to Rome, where his works were much admired. On his return to Flanders, he acquired a brilliant reputation, and was considered one of the ablest landscape painters of his time. Rubens testified to his merit, and used to say that Verhaecht was his first and best instructor in that branch of the art. His scenery is grand and extensive, and he exhibited a more perfect acquaintance with aërial perspective than any of his cotemporaries. He frequently embellished his pictures with the ruins of ancient edifices, which he had designed during his residence in Italy. As he was not so successful in designing figures, he usually employed the eminent painters of his time, particularly Franck, to insert them in his pictures. He died in 1631.

VERHAGHEN, Peter Joseph. This historical painter was born at Aerschot, in South Brabant, in 1728, according to Immerzeel; although Balkema places his birth in 1720. The account of his life is contradictory, since it is stated that he studied under Kerckhove and Besschey, whereas the former died in 1724, and the latter was born in 1739. Verhaghen applied himself with great assiduity, and attained sufficient excellence to gain the patronage of Prince Charles of Lorraine. It would appear that he practised the art for a number of years at Louvain, a city not far from his native place, and painted many pictures remarkable for their coloring. At the expense of the government he visited France, Sardinia, and Italy; and while sojourning at Rome he painted two pictures which attracted much attention, representing Christ crowned with Thorns, and Christ with the Disciples at Emmaus. The latter was greatly admired for its rich composition and beautiful coloring, and gained for the artist an audience with the Pope, Clement XIV., who presented him with two gold medals. Verhaghen afterwards visited Vienna, and was patronized by the Empress Maria Theresa, to whom he presented his picture of Christ at Emmaus, placed in her Majesty's bed-chamber. She presented him with a gold snuff-box, and appointed him her principal painter; but these favors did not induce him to remain long at Vienna, and he accordingly returned to Louvain in 1773, where the citizens honored him with a general reception. Verhaghen painted with great rapidity, and executed many works for the churches and convents of his country, which, though finely colored, were often defective in drawing and finishing. He died in 1811.

VERHELST, or VERELST, Egidius or Giles, a German sculptor and engraver, was the son of a Bavarian sculptor, and born in that kingdom in 1742. He is said to have followed the profession of a sculptor for several years in various German cities; but none of his works are mentioned, and he probably gained greater distinction in the theoretical branch of the art, as he was appointed Professor of Design in the Academy at Manheim. It appears that he also practised engraving, but being desirous of further improvement, he visited Paris, and studied under J. G. Wille. On returning to Germany, he settled at Munich, and engraved various portraits and other subjects, in the neat and finished style of his instructor. Among them are the portraits of the Electors of Bavaria and of Treves; a set of five plates for a translation of Tasso's Jerusalem; and Two Heads, characteristic of Innocence and Simplicity, for the work of Lavater.

VERHELST, Peter or Paul, a Dutch painter, born about 1614. Little is known of him. He painted familiar subjects, in which he imitated the styles of Douw, Mieris, and Slingelandt, with considerable success. One of his pictures is signed *P. Verhelst*, 1659.

VERHEYDEN, Francis Peter, a Dutch painter, born at the Hague in 1659. He followed the profession of a sculptor till he was about forty years old, and was one of the artists employed in modeling the figures and ornaments for the triumphal arches erected on the public entry of William III. into that city in 1691. Soon after this, while associating with some artists who were employed with him at the King's palace at Breda, he tried his hand at painting, and with such success that he was induced to abandon sculpture and devote himself entirely to painting, against the advice of all his friends. Being captivated by the works of Francis Snyders, he made them his model, and by assiduous application was soon able to paint similar subjects, such as huntings of wild boars, stags, and other animals, in a style of such excellence as surprised everybody. His pictures are ingeniously composed, correctly designed, and executed with a freedom and spirit little inferior to the distinguished artist he adopted as his model. His coloring was good, and he acquired a freedom of touch and a boldness of penciling that is surprising when we consider the late period of life at which he commenced painting. He also excelled in painting fowls and dead game in the manner of Hondecooter, and he touched the plumage with a lightness and truth almost equal to that master. His pictures are scarcely known out of his own country, where they are found in the choicest collections. He died in 1711.

VERHEYDEN, Matthew, was the son of the preceding, born at Breda in 1700. His father dying when he was eleven years old, he studied successively under Michael Carré, Terwesten, and Netscher. He afterwards went to the Hague, and studied portraiture under the Chev. Karel de Moor. Little more is known of him, except that he is said to have practised portrait painting with a success that enabled him to live in comfort, and to acquire a competent fortune.

VERHOEK, Peter Cornelius, a Dutch painter, born at Boodegraven in 1642, according to the best authorities, though some say in 1633, which last date is evidently an error, as he studied under Abraham Hondius at Rotterdam, who was born in 1638. Orlandi calls his name *Verhuik*, saying that he was born at Rotterdam in 1648, and that he was living in 1718. After acquiring considerable reputation as an able designer of animals he went to Italy, and stopping at Bologna, he was so captivated with the works of Borgognone that he studied them incessantly, and distinguished himself as a painter of battles and skirmishes of cavalry in the style of that master He afterwards visited Rome, Naples, and othe cities, and his works were everywhere greatly admired. He painted both in large and small size his figures and horses are correctly designed, an touched with great spirit and animation; his coloring is lively and full of force. He also painte landscapes in a pleasing style, which he decorate with small figures in the manner of Callot. Lan says, "Cornelio Verhuik of Rotterdam was als a pupil of Cortese (Borgognone), and resided several years at Bologna. Besides his battle-piece in his master's manner, displaying strong and viv coloring, he painted in the Flemish style, market fairs, and landscapes, which he enlivened with sma figures, like those of Callot." It is evident th Cornelio Verhuik of the Italians is the same Peter Cornelius Verhoek of the Dutch, and not different artist, as some have supposed. He seems to have passed most of his life in Italy.

VERHOEK, GYSBERT (GILBERT), was the brother of the preceding, born at Boodegraven in 1644. He first studied under Adam Pynaker, but he did not follow his style. He is said to have studied afterwards with his brother, and to have painted similar subjects with success, though it is not known that he ever went to Italy. He painted battles, marches of cavalry, and encampments. He particularly excelled in drawing the horse in every action and attitude, and his pencil was very animated and peculiarly adapted to the subjects he painted. He was remarkably studious to improve himself, and took great pains to make numerous sketches of men and horses in different motions, actions, and attitudes, to introduce into his compositions. His works are little known out of his own country, where they are frequently met with in the collections. He died in 1690.

VERHULST, PETER, a Dutch painter, born at Dort. Little is known of him. He is said to have studied under William Doudyns, and to have painted fruit, flowers, and insects, in the style of Otho Marcellis.

VERKOLIE, JOHN, a Dutch painter and engraver, born at Amsterdam in 1650. He was the son of a locksmith, who brought him up to his own business till he was twelve years of age, when he met with an accident which confined him to his bed for three years. It was during this painful and tedious confinement that he discovered a genius for painting by amusing himself in copying prints, in which he showed great talent. After his recovery he was placed under the instruction of John Lievens, but he remained with him only about six months, and further improved himself by studying and copying the works of Gerard Pietersz van Zyl, whose works were then held in high estimation, and whose style he imitated so successfully as to be able to complete some of the unfinished works of that master. He painted historical subjects and conversations, which, though somewhat defective in design and deficient in elegance and grace, are well colored and executed with a neat, tender, and delicate pencil. He however chiefly excelled in painting portraits of small size, which were admired. Verkolie was one of the earliest engravers in mezzotinto in Holland, and executed some portraits and other subjects from his own designs, and after other masters. He died in 1693.

VERKOLIE, NICHOLAS, the son of the preceding, born at Delft in 1673. He studied under his father, and for some time painted small portraits and domestic subjects in his style, but afterwards applied himself to historical painting, and distinguished himself as one of the ablest artists of his time. Among his most esteemed works are three pictures formerly in the collection of M. de Neufville at Amsterdam, representing Moses rescued from the Nile, David and Bathsheba, and Peter denying Christ. His composition is simple and judicious, his design is more correct and graceful than is usual with the artists of his country; his coloring is tender and harmonious, and his pencil is firm, though delicate. His works are found in the choicest collections of his country, where they are deservedly admired. He sometimes painted night pieces, to which he gave a surprising effect. He also excelled in designing and drawing in India ink. He likewise distinguished himself as an engraver in mezzotinto, and carried that art to a much higher degree of perfection than his father. He engraved quite a number of portraits and other subjects from his own designs and after the Dutch masters. He died at Amsterdam in 1746.

VERMEER, JOHN. See MEER.

VERMEULEN, CORNELIUS, a Flemish engraver, born at Antwerp in 1644. It is not known under whom he studied, but he went young to Paris, where he passed some time. He afterwards returned and settled in his native city, where he executed with the graver in a neat clear style, a considerable number of portraits. He also engraved some historical subjects, but these are inferior to his portraits, as the drawing is incorrect. The following are his most esteemed prints:

PORTRAITS.

Anne Boleyn, Queen of Henry VIII.; engraved for Larrey's History. Catherine Howard; do. Catherine Parr; do. Lady Jane Grey; do. Robert, Earl of Leicester; do. Oliver Cromwell; do. William III.; do. Maria Louisa of Orleans; *after Rigaud.* Philip V. of Spain; *after Vivien.* Maximilian Emanuel, Elector of Bavaria; *do.* Louis de Luxembourg, Marshal of France; *after Rigaud.* Maria Louisa de Tassis; *after Vandyck.* Peter Mignard, Painter; *from a picture by himself.* Nicholas vander Borcht. Painter; *after Vandyck.*

SUBJECTS.

Bacchus and Erigone; *after Guido;* for the Crozat Collection. Mary of Medicis escaping from the city of Blois; after the picture by *Rubens*, in the Luxembourg Gallery.

VERMEULEN, CORNELIUS, a Dutch painter of little note, born at Dort in 1732, and died there in 1813. He was a good colorist, and chiefly occupied himself in copying the works of the Dutch masters. He was also a restorer and dealer in old paintings.

VERMEULEN, ANDREW, the son of the preceding, born at Dort in 1763, was instructed by his father, and painted landscapes with figures, horses, and cattle, in a lively and pleasing style. He also painted winter scenes with figures skating and amusing themselves on the ice. He died in 1814.

VERMEYEN, or MAYO, JOHN CORNELIUS, a Dutch painter, born at Beverwyck, near Haerlem, in 1500. He was the son of an obscure painter named Cornelius V., who probably instructed him in the art. The Emperor Charles V. appointed him his principal painter and honored him with many marks of his particular esteem. He attended that monarch in all his expeditions, was present at all his battles and sieges, and designed on the spot all the fortified places attacked, the different encampments of the army, and every memorable action of the whole war by sea and land. In 1535 he was present at the siege and capture of Tunis, and made designs of the principal events, from which he afterwards executed cartoons for the tapestry to adorn the Escurial. He was remarkable for having a long beard, which he is said to have cultivated with such care that it grew down to his feet, and the Emperor in his merry moods would tread upon it; hence he was called *Johannes Barbatus*, *Barbalonga*, *Barbato*, and other significant names.

He is said to have been skilled in mathematics, geometry, and architecture. Most of the works he executed while in the service of the Emperor, are supposed to have perished in the conflagration of the Prado. He passed the latter part of his life at Brussels, where he executed several works for the churches and public edifices, which are highly commended by Vanmander. There are two pictures by him in the church of St. Gery, representing the Nativity and the Resurrection. He was likewise a good portrait painter.

Vermeyen was also an engraver. Brulliot claims the credit of being the first to notice him as such, and he describes four prints by him, marked with the above monogram, which he says properly signifies *John Cornelisz.* They are of small size; three are dated 1545, and one, 1546. They represent the Virgin and Child, accompanied by an angel; a Man duped, a composition of several half-length figures; a young Woman with a Cat, half-length profile; a young Woman seated on a Couch, apparently sewing. He died in 1559.

VERMIGLIO, Giuseppe, a painter born at Turin, who was living in 1675. Little is known of him except by his works. Lanzi regards him as one of the ablest artists of the Piedmontese school. He highly commends his picture of Daniel in the Lion's Den, in the Library della Passione at Milan, and says that "for correctness of design, beautiful forms, expression highly studied, and colors warm, varied and lucid, it is one of the most valuable pictures painted at Milan since the time of Gaudenzio Ferrari. From the imitative style of the heads it is evident that he studied the Caracci, and was not a stranger to Guido, but in coloring he seems to have imitated the Flemish artists. It is improbably reported at Milan, perhaps from resemblance of style, that he instructed Daniello Crespi. I consider him as the finest painter in oil that the ancient state of Piedmont can boast, and as one of the best Italian artists of his day. Why he painted so near Turin, and yet had no success in that city, and why he was not distinguished by his own sovereign, though well received at the court of Mantua, I have not been able to discover." He executed several other fine works for the churches at Milan, Mantua, Alessandria, and Novara. He enriched the backgrounds of his pictures with beautiful landscapes, or magnificent architecture. Thus, his Daniel in the Lion's Den is enriched with architecture in the style of Veronese, and his Christ and the Woman of Samaria, in the Refectory of the P. P. Olivetani at Alessandria, is decorated with a beautiful landscape and a magnificent view of the city of Samaria in the distance. The latter is supposed to be one of his last works, and is dated 1675.

VERNET, Claude Joseph, a celebrated French marine and landscape painter, was born at Avignon in 1714. According to Fiorillo, at the age of five years he manifested great skill in drawing. After receiving instructions from his father Antoine Vernet, he visited Rome at the age of eighteen, and commenced studying under Adrian Manglard. The beautiful views of Genoa, Naples, and other parts of Italy, served to develope his talent, and are said to have determined him to fix upon marine landscape as his principal study. He subsequently studied with Bernardino Fergioni, and soon attained a high degree of excellence. For some time he lived in great poverty, glad to paint for the slightest remuneration; he executed a piece for a suit of clothes, which brought 5000 francs at the sale of the collection of M. de Julienne. He also painted several panels for coach-builders, which were subsequently taken out, and framed as works of great value. Vernet remained in Italy twenty years, including some time spent in Greece and the Greek islands; and made elaborate sketches of many of the most interesting and beautiful spots on classic ground. He painted a great variety of landscapes, sea-views, and other marine subjects, which gained him great reputation. They possess the beauty and freshness of nature, and are excellent in every respect, but mostly in the admirable management of light and shade, and aërial perspective. He was deficient only in a knowledge of the rigging and construction of ships; his figures are arranged with unusual taste, remarkably well drawn, and touched with great neatness and spirit. His moonlight effects are admirable, and likewise his representations of water, particularly when agitated and boisterous. The pictures painted by Vernet in Rome, for the palaces Rondanini, Borghese, and Colonna, are among his best works; those in the Palazzo Rondanini were executed much in the style of Salvator Rosa, whom he imitated with great success; but he afterwards forsook Salvator's manner for one as conspicuous for its delicacy of coloring as the other was for its force.

In 1743, Vernet was chosen a member of the Academy of St. Luke; and about the same time he married Miss Parker, the daughter of an English Roman Catholic, who was an officer in the Pope's marine. His reputation at length reached France, and he was invited to Paris in 1752, by Louis XV. Embarking at Leghorn in a small felucca, he sailed to Marseilles. A violent storm happened on the way, which terrified some of the passengers; but Vernet, struck with the grandeur of the scene, requested the sailors to bind him to the mast-head; and there he remained, absorbed in admiration, and endeavoring to transfer the scene to his sketch-book. His grandson, Horace V., painted an excellent picture of this scene, and exhibited it at the Louvre in 1816. About 1753, Vernet was chosen a member of the French Academy, and presented for his reception piece a Sea-port at Sunset, which is now in the Louvre. In the same year he was commissioned to execute pictures of the principal sea-ports of France, of which he painted fifteen views, occupying him ten or twelve years. These works are of large size, and are now in the Louvre; but he was only paid 7500 francs each, including his traveling expenses. In 1766 he was elected one of the Council of the Academy, and Louis XV. gave him apartments in the Louvre. From 1752, when he returned to France, until his death in 1789, Vernet painted upwards of 200 pictures, mostly from his designs made in Italy, which were held in the highest estimation. His extraordinary talents enabled him to surpass every landscape painter in Europe, Richard Wilson being the only one who disputed the palm with him. They had become acquainted in Rome, and exchanged pictures; Vernet kept Wilson's in his studio at Paris, and is said to have remarked to English connoisseurs who visited him, that they had no occasion to come to him for pictures when they had such a painter at home

There are a few neat and spirited etchings by him, among which are a Landscape, with a Bridge and part of a Village; a Shepherd and Shepherdess; a View of a market-place; and a Canal, with Fishermen.

VERNET, Antoine Charles Horace, a distinguished French painter, the son of Claude Joseph V., was born at Bourdeaux in 1758. He studied the art under his father, and at the age of seventeen gained the second prize in the Academy of painting. In 1782 he gained the grand prize, which entitled him to a residence in Italy, with the royal pension. After spending some time in Rome, he returned to Paris, and in 1787 was made a member of the Academy. Vernet excelled chiefly in battle and parade pieces of large dimensions, in which he commemorated the battles of Rivoli, Marengo, Austerlitz, Wagram, the Departure of the Marshals, and many other events of French history, which occurred during his artistical career. More pleasing to many are his smaller scenes, mostly referring to battles and camps; and there are also numerous small equestrian portraits by him, showing unusual skill in depicting the horse. His studies from nature, and his hunting pieces, especially the lithographical ones, are much sought after by connoisseurs, possessing a vivacity and boldness of conception, in which his only rival was his eminent son Horace, the following artist. The twenty-eight plates in folio, illustrating the campaign of Bonaparte in Italy, are esteemed among his most successful efforts. Vernet was made a Chevalier of the Legion of Honor, and the Order of St. Michael. He died in 1836. Many of his pictures have been lithographed.

VERNET, Horace. This eminent French battle painter of the present century, the son of Antoine Charles Horace V., was born at Paris, in the Louvre, in 1789. In early youth he manifested a strong inclination for art, and received his chief instruction from his father. He was obliged for some time to perform all kinds of illustrative work, in order to obtain a subsistence, and having failed in obtaining the grand prize, he turned his attention to that department of art for which he felt himself best adapted—the incidents of the camp and field. His pictures of the Taking of a Redoubt, the Dog of the Regiment, the Battle of Tolosa, the Barrier of Clichy, or Defence of Paris in 1814, (both of which last, exhibited in 1817, now hang in the Luxembourg gallery), besides many more, followed in quick succession, keeping up continually and incessantly, the public admiration. The critics violently opposed him, but the truth and spirit of his productions gained great admiration from the people. His pictures of the Battles of Jemmapes, Valmy, Hanau, and Montmirail, executed about 1820, were more satisfactory as works of art, than some others of his earlier works, particularly the Massacre of the Mamelukes, and they approach much nearer to historical painting. The details are executed rapidly, but with care and fidelity, the generals and personages in the front are speaking portraits, the whole scene is full of appropriate life and action, impressing the beholder with a most accurate and vivid conception of the event.

Vernet, from the first, paid little attention to the antique, and united his influence with that of the innovators against the school of David. It was perhaps for these reasons that his works were refused admission into the Louvre in 1822. Accordingly, he made an exhibition room of his atelier, and admitted the public to a numerous collection. In 1826, however, he was chosen a member of the Institute, and in 1830, director of the Academy at Rome. In the latter capacity he visited Italy for the first time, and resided five years among the works of the best masters. Inspired with ideas which he had not hitherto been able to gratify, he commenced studying those great productions, and sent a Judith and Holofernes to the Paris exhibition of 1831; but it obtained little success. His picture of the Arresting of the Princes at the Palais Royal, by order of Anne of Austria was much better received, and was placed in th Palais Royal by order of the King. Vernet alsc produced various other works while at Rome, but on returning to Paris in 1835, he found the public favor still turning to his usual and best subject, the French soldier life. Accordingly he recurred to his original study, and exhibited in the following year his battle pieces of Friedland, Wagram, Jena, and Fontenoy, in which were apparent all his usual excellencies. The Algerian war at this time afforded him an admirable opportunity of exhibiting his talents, and a whole gallery at Versailles was set apart to be decorated by his pencil, called the Constantine Gallery, after the most important feat yet performed by the French troops in Africa, the capture of the town of Constantine. For this he depicted many scenes from the Algerian war, besides various military events which occurred in Europe during the reign of Louis Philippe, such as the Occupation of Ancona, and the Entry of the Army into Belgium. The Taking of the Smalah, from the Algerian war, preserved in this gallery among many other of his works, is said to be the largest canvass in existence. There are also in the Gallery of French History at Versailles, several others by him, as the Battle of Bouvines, Charles X. reviewing the National Guard, and Marshal St. Cyr. These latter works are said to illustrate the peculiar excellencies of the artist, as well, if not better, than any others, being full of that vivacity, energy, and truthfulness, which he so eminently displays. Vernet's powers of memory were most remarkable, so that he rarely employed the model, and generally wrought out his subject at once in the definitive size, without making a smaller sketch beforehand, and painting with a rapidity that is truly wonderful. His knowledge of military tactics is unmistakeable, particularly in giving prominence to the chief aim of the victorious army, and for indicating the event of the battle by the movements of the lines. His domestic scenes, rural feasts, huntings, and caverns of robbers, are also much esteemed, and all his works are the more impressive on account of their perfect freedom from affectation. There are many of them in the public galleries and private collections throughout Europe, and the sketches for Dupont's magnificent edition of the *Henriade*, published in 1824, were also from his fertile pencil.

In 1850, Vernet started to Rome, for the purpose of making the necessary sketches for a finished picture of the siege of that city, which was intended to be much larger than any of his former works. He is living at this time, (1852,) aged 63.

VERNICI, Giovanni Battista, a Bolognese

painter, who was brought up, according to Malvasia, in the school of the Caracci. He painted history with considerable reputation, and was appointed principal painter to the Duke of Urbino, in whose service he died in 1617. His principal works are in the churches of Pesaro and Urbino. He was also a good portrait painter.

VERNIGO, GIROLAMO. a painter born at Verona, who died of the plague in that city in 1630. It is not known under whom he studied, but Lanzi ranks him among the eminent landscape painters of the Venetian school. He says "he was particularly celebrated in his native city for the beauty of his landscapes, for which reason he was called *Girolamo da' Paesi.*" See *Paesi.*

VERNIQUET, EDME, a French architect, was born at Chatillon on the Seine, in 1727. After completing his studies at Dijon, he commenced practicing his profession, and erected many churches, chateaux, bridges, and various other works throughout Burgundy, which surpass in taste and solidity all the other works in the province of that period. He also executed various works in Maine and Poitou, and finally settled at Paris in 1774. Appointed architect of the Royal Gardens, he carried out the projects conceived by Buffon, elevating them to their subsequent height of magnificence. Verniquet was engaged for many years upon a plan of the city of Paris, which was published in 1796, in a grand atlas of seventy-two sheets. It is a work of great beauty and merit, highly praised by Lalande, (*Bibliogr. Astronomique*, 694.) He died in 1804.

VEROCCHIO, ANDREA, a celebrated Italian painter, sculptor, and goldsmith of the fifteenth century, was born at Florence in 1432. Vasari says he had little genius, but was the most laborious man of his time; Baldinucci makes him a scholar of Donatello. He first distinguished himself as a goldsmith, both at Florence and Rome; he then devoted himself solely to sculpture in bronze and marble. His first work in marble was a monument in the Minerva at Rome, to the wife of Francesco Tornabuoni, which is now in the Florentine Gallery, and exhibits good expression in the figures, but very imperfect execution. His next work was a colossal bronze figure of David, now also in the Florentine Gallery. Verocchio executed several other works in metal, by which he acquired great reputation; the principal were the monuments in San Lorenzo, of Giovanni and Pietro, the sons of Cosmo de' Medici; and the Incredulity of St. Thomas, in the church of Or San Michele at Florence, finished in 1483; it is a colossal group of two figures, weighing 3981 pounds, and for which, according to Baldinucci, he was paid 476 gold florins, although Manni, in a note appended to that authority, says 800 heavy florins. According to Vasari, Verocchio left nothing to be wished for in this work; and having attained perfection in sculpture, he began to turn his attention to painting.

His practice in sculpture had made Verocchio an able designer; his academy was frequented by many disciples, among whom were Pietro Perugino and Lionardo da Vinci. He painted very few pictures, however, and finally relinquished painting upon finding himself surpassed by Lionardo da Vinci, whom he had ordered to paint the figure of an angel, in a picture of the Baptism of Christ by St. John. The work of the youth so greatly excelled that of Verocchio, that the latter thenceforward devoted himself to sculpture. Vasari mentions many designs and cartoons by him, some of which were copied and imitated by da Vinci.

Verocchio's fame having reached Venice, he was called to that city to cast an equestrian statue of Bartolomeo Colleoni, the celebrated general, but having completed the model of the horse, he was informed that Vellano of Padua was to execute the figure of the general; whereupon he was so greatly offended, that he immediately broke the head and feet of his horse, and quitted Venice without giving any notice to his employers. This independent spirit so exasperated the signory of Venice, that they wrote to Verocchio, and told him he had better not return to Venice, if he valued his head; and the artist replied that he should be mindful of their admonition, for they were as little capable of restoring him his head as they were of finding another head sufficiently beautiful for his horse! They now earnestly solicited his return, promising him twice the remuneration formerly agreed to; he therefore returned and cast his model, but caught cold in the casting, and died a few days afterwards, before the statue was quite completed, in 1488. This work was finished by Alessandro Leopardi, who cast the pedestal, and fixed it in its present position in the Piazza di Santi Giovanni e Paolo, in the year 1495. Verocchio's remains were taken by his favorite scholar Lorenzo di Credi to Florence, and were deposited in the vault of Michele di Cione, in the church of S. Ambrogio. The following inscription is over the vault: *S.* (for Sepulchrum) *Michaelis de Cionis et Suorum et Andrae Verocchi, filii Dominici Michaelis, qui obiit Venetiis* M. CCCC. LXXXVIII.

Verocchio had many distinguished scholars in sculpture, as well as in painting; among them were Lorenzo di Credi, Nanni Grosso, and Francesco di Simone. According to Bottari, he was one of the first who made plaster casts from the human body; but not the first, as Vasari states, for Pliny (Hist. Nat. XXXV. 12, 44.) says it was invented by Lysistratus, the brother of Lysippus, in the time of Alexander the Great. It is probable that Vasari referred only to the artists of modern times.

VERONA, BATTISTA DA. See ZELOTTI.

VERONA, STEFANO DA, called also STEFANO DA ZEVIO (Piacenza). See STEFANO.

VERONA, FRA GIOVANNI DA, a monk of Oliveto, born in 1469 and died in 1537. He was very celebrated in the art of decorating the choirs and sacristies of churches with inlaid work of wood. Lanzi says, "he surpassed all his predecessors, and practiced the art in various cities of Italy, and at Rome itself, in the service of Pope Julius II., but still more successfully in the sacristy of his own order, where his works are still to be seen in the best condition." At first woods of different colors were employed, and large edifices, temples, colonnades, and architectural views were represented; the art was afterwards improved by using artificially stained, as well as natural woods, and by adding figures. Many of the old churches in Italy and in other countries of Europe, are decorated in this manner, and many artists acquired distinction in the art. See Lendinara.

VERONA, JACOPO DA, an old painter, born at Verona, who was living in 1397. Lanzi says he is only known by his numerous paintings in fresco, in the church of St. Michele at Padua, executed in the style of Giotto, some of which still remain entire.

VERONA, Maffeo da, a painter born at Verona in 1576. He studied under Luigi Benfatto, but derived his chief improvement from studying and copying the works of Paul Veronese, whose style he adopted. According to Ridolfi he painted both in oil and fresco, and particularly excelled in the latter; he wrought with great facility and executed many works for the churches and public edifices of Venice. He also painted several works for the churches of his native city, and for the cathedral at Udine. Among his principal works at Venice are two altar-pieces, representing the Descent from the Cross, and the Resurrection, in the church of S. Marco; and Christ bearing his Cross and the Crucifixion, in the chapel of St. Isidore in the same church. He died in 1618.

VERONA, Padre Massimo da, a painter born at Verona in 1599 and died in 1679, aged 80. He was a Capuchin monk; hence he is sometimes called Il Padre Massimo Cappuccino. According to Melchiori, he was a disciple of Marc' Antonio Bassetti, whose careful style he followed, and executed many excellent works for the different churches of his order. He particularly commends four large pictures by him in the Cathedral at Montagnana.

VERONA, Fra Semplice da, a Capuchin monk, born at Verona about 1574, who, according to Melchiori, studied first under Brusasorci, and next with Fra Santo of Venice. He became a good artist, and executed some works for the churches and convents within the Venetian territory. He was also employed at Rome. Lanzi says there is a fine picture of St. Felice, by him, at Castel Franco, which was engraved in 1712. He died in 1654, at an advanced age.

VERONESE, Alessandro. See Turchi.

VERONESE, Claudio. See Ridolfi.

VERONESE, Paolo. See Cagliari.

VERRIO, Antonio, a painter born at Naples in 1634. It is not known under whom he studied. He went to France and settled at Toulouse, where he was probably employed in designing or directing the manufacture of tapestry, as he was invited to England by Charles II. to take charge of his manufactory of tapestry at Mortlake, but instead of engaging him in this business on his arrival, he employed him in decorating the ceilings of Windsor Castle. He was also employed by King James and William III., as well as by some of the nobility. Though he found much employment at liberal prices, he was a very indifferent artist, and his performances are not worth recording. He died at Hampton Court in 1707.

VERRYKE, Hans. See Vereycke.

VERSCHAFFELT, Chevalier Pieter, a Flemish sculptor, known among the Italians as Pietro Fiammingo, was born at Ghent in 1710. After acquiring the elements of the art from an obscure carver in wood, he visited Paris and entered the school of Bouchardon. In 1737 he went to Rome, where Benedict XIV. commissioned him to execute various works in sculpture, particularly a bust and a marble statue of himself, of life size. His works are found at Rome, Bologna, Naples, and Ancona, and are highly esteemed by the Italians. After leaving Italy, Verschaffelt went to London, and was invited by the Elector of Manheim to fill the office of sculptor to his court, and also to assume the directorship of the Academy of Fine Arts in that city. During the forty years of his subsequent career, he enriched Manheim and Schwetzingen with various works in sculpture, and also superintended the architectural operations carried on by the government. He died at Manheim in 1793.

VERSCHURING, Henry, an eminent Dutch painter, born at Gorcum in 1627. His father was a captain of infantry in the Dutch Service, and intended him for the profession of arms, but his naturally delicate constitution, with a genius for painting, induced him to place him under the instruction of Theodore Goverts, a portrait painter, with whom he continued till he was thirteen years old, when he went to Utrecht, and became the scholar of John Both. After studying six years under that eminent master, he went to Rome, where he frequented the Academy, to design from the living model, and diligently studied the antique, and the works of the best modern masters. He also designed the ruins and vestiges of superb architecture, not only in and about Rome, but in every part of Italy that he visited. His landscapes are copied from nature and generally show a judicious and agreeable choice of scenery. These he enriched with architecture, ruins, figures and animals, which always correspond to the locality of the scene, the time, manners and customs of the country. He also had a genius for painting huntings, battles, and animals, in which last he particularly excelled. His works were much admired at Rome, Florence and Venice, in all which places he passed some time. After a residence of ten years in Italy, he returned to his own country and settled at Dort, where he distinguished himself as a painter of landscapes, and more particularly of battle-pieces, attacks of banditti, plundering and sacking of villages, &c. The desolating wars which ravaged his country at this time, gave him frequent opportunities of designing his subjects on the spot. He followed the armies into the field, and was very curious in observing the actions, movements and attitudes of horses, and the engagements, retreats, and encampments of armies.

Verschuring possessed a fertile and inventive genius, and as he always designed every thing from nature, there is no appearance of mannerism in his works, but all looks like reality and truth. His landscapes are admirable, his scenery beautiful, his figures correctly designed and touched with spirit, his coloring remarkably transparent, his penciling neat, and he finished his pictures very highly. His battle-pieces are full of fire and truth, and his figures and horses are correctly designed and touched with lightness and spirit. He was a man of estimable character, much beloved by his fellow-citizens, who chose him one of their Burgomasters. He was drowned near Dort in 1690, by the upsetting of a boat. He also executed a few spirited etchings of battles, dogs, and other subjects from his own designs.

VERSCHURING, William, was the son of the preceding, born at Gorcum in 1657. He was first instructed by his father, but having a taste for a different branch of the art, he was allowed to follow his inclination, and he became the scholar of John Verkolie. He painted small portraits, conversations and domestic subjects, in the pleasing style of that master. After acquiring considerable reputation, he abandoned painting for commerce. He died in 1715.

VERSCHUUR, Lieven, a Dutch painter, of whom little is known. He was born at Rotterdam, probably about 1630, as he was the companion of John vander Meer in his travels to Italy. He excelled in painting sea-pieces, river views, and moonlight scenes; his style somewhat resembles that of Simon de Vlieger, equally free in execution, and perhaps more lively in color. There are two fine pictures by him in the museum at Amsterdam, one of which represents Charles II. of England entering the port of Rotterdam. He had a brother named Albert, who was a good portrait painter. They both died in the same year, 1691.

VERSTEEG, or VERSTEIGH, Michael, a Dutch painter, born at Dort, in 1756. It is not recorded by whom he was instructed, but he at first painted landscapes with figures and cattle in a very pleasing style, somewhat resembling that of Janson, though evidently aiming at the older and greater masters. His coloring though verdant is yet warm, and his pictures are elaborately finished, even to the foliage of his trees. He afterwards abandoned landscape, and painted interiors and conversations by candle-light, in which he distinguished himself. In his pictures of this class, without reaching the excellence of Schalcken in penciling, he often equals him in the effects of his light and shadow, and his works are found in the best collections of his country. He acquired distinction, and was elected a member of the Royal Institute of the Netherlands and of the Academy of Painting at Antwerp. His works are found in the best collections of his country. He lived to an advanced age, and died about 1840.

VERSTRAELIN, J., a Dutch engraver, who flourished about 1620. He engraved several plates, among which is one representing Maurice, Prince of Orange, lying dead, surrounded by his officers and guards.

VERTANGEN, Daniel, a Dutch painter, born at the Hague, in 1598. He studied under Cornelius Poelemburg, whose style he closely imitated. He painted landscapes with small figures, of Nymphs bathing, Bacchanals, and other subjects taken from Ovid. Though his pictures are far inferior to those of his instructor in force and beauty of coloring, yet they are so well composed, agreeably colored and highly finished, that they readily pass with the inexperienced for the genuine works of Poelemburg.

VERTUE, George, a distinguished English engraver and antiquary, was born at London in 1684. According to Walpole, he was placed at the age of thirteen with a French engraver of arms on plate, who had the chief business of London. Three or four years afterwards, his master left the country for France, and Vertue returned to his parents. After studying drawing for two years longer, he formed an engagement with Michael Vandergucht, the engraver, and remained with him seven years, acquiring a good knowledge of copper-plate engraving. He received instruction and advice from several painters, and commenced business on his own account in 1709. After operating for the booksellers about one year, he gained the patronage of Kneller, when his works began to draw attention, and Lord Somers employed him to engrave a plate of Archbishop Tillotson, which was much admired, and proved the ground-work of his reputation. In 1711, an Academy of Painting was instituted by Kneller and other artists of the day, and Vertue was among the first members. In 1717, at the revival of the Society of Antiquaries, he was appointed its engraver. For many years, the university of Oxford employed him to engrave their Almanacs; and in 1730, he published his twelve heads of poets, esteemed one of his capital works. In 1740, he published his proposals for the commencement of a valuable work, his historical prints, drawn with extreme care and fidelity, and executed in a most satisfactory manner.

Vertue deserves great credit for his industrious and protracted researches concerning the history of the arts and artists in England, which he continued for about forty years, and collected a large amount of information in many volumes of manuscript. These were purchased after his death by Horace Walpole, who compiled and digested from them his Anecdotes of Painting in England. Vertue died in 1756, and was buried in the cloisters of Westminster Abbey. His works are extremely numerous, and consist of portraits, copies from old pictures, and antiquities of every kind. Walpole has given a complete list of them, among which are the following:—

PORTRAITS.

King Richard II.; from the painting in the Westminster Abbey. Queen Elizabeth; *after Isaac Oliver.* Mary, Queen of Scots; *after Zuccaro.* Queen Anne; *after Kneller.* King George I.; 1715; very large. The same; smaller; 1718; a better print. George, Prince of Wales. The Princess of Wales, with an Angel bringing a Crown; *after Amiconi.* Frederick, Prince of Wales; *after Boit.* Princess Anne. William, Duke of Cumberland; *after Jervas.* Princess Mary. William Seymour, Duke of Somerset. Henry Somerset, Duke of Beaufort. William Cavendish, Duke of Newcastle. John, Duke of Marlborough. John, Duke of Buckingham. Philip, Duke of Wharton; *after Jervas.* Lionel, Duke of Dorset. Henry Howard, Earl of Surrey. Francis, Earl of Bedford. Edward, Earl of Dorset. Heneage, Earl of Winchilsea. Edward, Earl of Oxford, sitting; with many pieces of his collection round him. Sarah, Duchess of Somerset. Elizabeth, Countess of Shrewsbury. Dorothy, Countess of Sunderland. Sophia, Countess of Granville. Archbishop Warham. Archbishop Cranmer. Archbishop Parker. Archbishop Tillotson. John Robinson, Bishop of London. Edward Chandler, Bishop of Durham. Gilbert Burnet, Bishop of Salisbury. William Loyd, Bishop of Worcester, sitting in his library; one of his best prints. John Spencer, Dean of Ely. Humphrey Prideaux, Dean of Norwich. Sir Thomas More. Sir Nicholas Bacon. Sir Francis Bacon. Sir Joseph Jekyll, Master of the Rolls, sitting; fine. Sir John Vernay, Master of the Rolls; fine.

HISTORIC PRINTS, AND PRINTS WITH TWO OR MORE PORTRAITS.

Henry VII. and his Queen, with Henry VIII. and Jane Seymour. Three Children of Henry VII. Charles Brandon, Duke of Suffolk, and Mary, Queen of France. Frances, Duchess of Suffolk, with Adrian Stoke, her first husband. Thomas, Earl of Arundel, his Countess and Children; a private plate. Thomas, Earl of Suffolk, and his Secretary. The Earl of Stafford's three Children. William, Duke of Portland, his Duchess, and Lady Mary Wortley. The Procession of Queen Elizabeth to Hunsdon-house. The Tomb of Lord Darnley; James I. when a child, Earl and Countess of Lenox, &c., praying by it. The Battle of Carberry-hill. Edward VI. granting the palace of Bridewell for an hospital. The Court of Wards, with an explanation.

VERVEER, Ary Hubertsz, a Dutch painter,

born at Dort in 1646. He was much esteemed by his countrymen for his historical compositions, in which he usually designed the figures naked. In attempting to imitate the magical coloring of Rembrandt, his tints became gloomy and obscure. His best performances are painted in a rough, unfinished manner, and appear to be the productions of negligence and despatch.

VERWILT, Francis, a Dutch painter, born at Rotterdam in 1598. He first studied under Cornelius de Bois, a landscape painter of little note, and afterwards became the disciple of Cornelius Poelemburg, whose style and subjects he imitated successfully. His pictures are correctly designed and highly finished; his coloring is brilliant and clear, and though his works are much inferior to those of his master, they possess considerable merit, and readily pass with the unlearned for the genuine productions of Poelemburg. He died in 1655.

VERZELLI, Tiburzio, a painter born at Recanati, and died there about 1700. Lanzi commends him as an excellent painter of perspective and architectural pieces, little known beyond his native place. "The noble family of Calamini, of Recanati, possess, perhaps his best picture, the Elevation of S. Pietro in Vaticano, one of the largest and most beautiful works of this kind that ever I saw, which occupied him several years in finishing."

VEYTH. See Vyth.

VIA, Agostino A., an Italian engraver, by whom there is a print of Daniel in the Lions' Den, after *Pietro da Cortona*.

VIA, Alessandro della, an Italian engraver, who flourished at Venice about 1730. He engraved some portraits and other subjects, in an indifferent style, among which is one of the Virgin and infant Christ, with St. Sebastian and other saints, *after Paul Veronese.*

VIANEN, John van, a Dutch engraver, born at Amsterdam about 1660. He was chiefly employed in engraving frontispieces and portraits for the booksellers. His plates are executed with the graver in a neat style, though without much effect.

VIANI, Antonio Maria, called Il Vianino, an Italian painter, was a native of Cremona, according to Zaist, and flourished in the latter part of the 16th century. After acquiring a knowledge of the art from the Campi, eminent painters of Cremona, he was invited to Mantua by the Duke, Vincenzio Gonzaga, and commissioned to execute several pictures for the churches, among which were his St. Michael in S. Agnese, and the representation of Heaven, at the Orsoline; both in the style of his instructor. He was also employed in the ducal palace, and Lanzi mentions a group of most beautiful boys playing amidst luxuriant festoons of flowers, painted in chiaro-scuro on a golden ground, in the frieze surrounding the gallery of the court. This work also is in the style of the Campi, and is probably from the hand of Viani. It is said that he was employed by the Duke in the capacity of an architect, but none of his edifices are mentioned. After the Duke's death Viani was employed by his three successors. He was living in 1582.

VIANI, Giovanni Maria, an eminent painter, born at Bologna in 1637. He was a fellow student with Pasinelli in the school of Flaminio Torre. Lanzi says, "he was a learned painter, not inferior in design to any cotemporary of the Bolognese school, and added to his powers by assiduous drawing from the living model in the Academy and the study of anatomy as long as he lived. To such knowledge, he united elegance of forms, softness of coloring, engaging attitudes, lightness of drapery, studying much from nature, and giving it an air of grace, in the manner of Torre, or of Guido. That exquisite picture of St. John di Dio at the hospital of the Buonfratelli, is such a specimen of his art. In the Portico of the Servi, he represented, in a Lunette, St. Filippo Benizi borne up to Heaven by two angels; a figure which, both in countenance and action, breathes an expression of beatitude, conspicuous, even at the side of another history by Cignani. In other Lunettes of the same portico, he does not excite equal admiration, and gives us an idea of an artist able to compete with the best masters, though obliged to work with a larger share of study." Viani executed many works for the churches and public edifices of Bologna. He opened a school opposite to that of Cignani, and instructed several pupils. He also executed several spirited etchings from his own designs, and after the Caracci. He died in 1700.

VIANI, Domenico Maria, was the son of the preceding, born at Bologna in 1668. After receiving a thorough education in the art from his father, he went to Venice, where he diligently studied the works of the great Venetian masters. Guidalotti, who wrote his life, prefers him to his father. Lanzi says, "few will subscribe to this opinion, he not having attained to that exactness, much less that dignity of design exhibited by his father. He was also inferior to him in the nature, truth, and clearness of his coloring. Still, he possessed a grand character in his outline, a stronger execution, like Guercino's, and more splendid ornaments, like the Venetians. His St. Antony in the church of S. Spirito at Bergamo, in the act of convincing a skeptic by a miracle, is a surprising picture, extolled by Rotari and Tiepolo." He succeeded his father in the school which he had established at Bologna, and instructed several pupils. He executed many works for the churches at Bologna, and the adjacent cities, particularly Bergamo and Pistoia. The principal at Bologna are a series representing the Prophets and Evangelists in the church of the Nativity; and a legendary story of Christ healing a pilgrim, in the church of the Servi. Bartsch describes a single etching by him, of St. Joseph with the infant Saviour. He died at Pistoia in 1711. Some place his birth in 1670, and his death in 1716, but Lanzi and the best authorities, give the dates as above.

VICARO, Francesco, an engraver to whom a set of etchings of landscapes are attributed. He is the same as *Francesco Vaccaro*, which see.

VICENTE, Bartolome, a Spanish painter, born at Saragossa in 1640. He studied under Juan Carreno at Madrid. He was a reputable painter both in oil and fresco, and executed some works for the churches and convents of his native city. He is said to have chiefly employed himself in painting landscapes of a small size, and *teaching mathematics*, a proof that he did not acquire any great reputation, notwithstanding the high commendations of Bermudez. He died at Saragossa in 1700.

VICENTINI, Antonio, a Venetian painter, who excelled in painting perspective, architectural pieces, and views in Venice, in the style of Canaletto. He was born in 1688, and died in 1782, at the great age of 94 years. Lanzi says his views are frequently ornamented with the figures of Zuccarelli and Tiepolo.

VICENTINO, Andrea, a painter born at Venice in 1539, and died in 1614. He was a scholar of the elder Palma, whose style he followed. Lanzi says, that though not excelling in point of taste, he was very skillful in handling his colors, and showed great power of invention. He was a great plagiarist, and seldom painted a picture without borrowing in his perspective, architecture, or figures, or some ideas from others, though he had the judgment to select those of the best masters. He was one of the most popular artists of his time, and found abundant employment in painting for the churches and public edifices of Venice and other cities in the state, and even beyond the bounds of the Republic. He was also employed to paint several histories of the Republic, which still adorn the halls of the Palazzo Grande. Lanzi says, "he bestowed upon his plagiarisms a beauty of composition and a grand effect that does honor to his talents, applicable to every variety of subject. He could also use a very delicate, tasteful, and effective pencil whenever he chose. In his grounds he was less successful, many of his pictures being already defaced. In collections, always more favorable to the duration, than in public places, we find them in good preservation, and deserving of much commendation, as seen in his Solomon anointed King of Israel, in the Royal gallery at Florence."

VICENTINO, Marco, was the son and scholar of the preceding, born at Venice, where he practiced, according to Zanetti, with considerable reputation. He executed many works for the churches and for the collections. Lanzi says he acquired some celebrity by his *imitations*, but more by his father's name.

VICENTINO, Battista, an Italian engraver, born at Vicenza, who flourished at Venice about 1540. In conjunction with Gio. Battista del Moro, he engraved a set of fifty plates of landscapes, with ruins and architecture, which are executed in a bold, spirited style. He marked his prints *Battista P. V. F.* He is probably the same as *Gio. Battista Pittoni*, which see.

VICENTINO, Francesco, a Milanese painter, highly commended by Lomazzo for the excellence of his landscape, in which "he imitated nature so accurately as to show the dust blown about by the wind." Lanzi conjectures that he was a disciple of Bernazzano, and says that he was also a good figure painter, several specimens of which may be seen at the Grazie, and in other churches at Milan. He flourished about 1550.

VICENTINO, Francesco Maffei, a painter born at Vicenza about 1600. He studied under Santo Peranda at Venice, and afterwards improved himself by studying the works of Paul Veronese. He settled at Padua, where he executed many works for the churches and public edifices. He died there in 1660.

VICENTINO, Giovanni Niccolo, called Rossigliani, an Italian painter and engraver, born at Vicenza about 1510. Little is known of him as a painter, but he executed some wooden cuts after Raffaelle, Caravaggio, and other masters, in chiaroscuro, in which he made use of three blocks.—Bartsch says he variously signed his prints *Joseph Nicolaus Vicentini*, and *Nic. S. Vicentino, I.;* for the names of *Giovanni* and *Rossigliani*, he thinks there is no good foundation. He is also called *Gioseffo Scolari Vicentino*, which is evidently an error, as the signature simply means *Joseph, the scholar of Vicentino.* It would seem that there were two or more engravers of Vicenza, who signed their prints Vicentino. Niccolo Boldrini flourished about the same time, and was called Vicentino. See *Boldrini.*

VICI, Andrea del, architect to the Grand Duke of Tuscany, was born at Arcevia, in the Marca d'Ancona, in 1744. Having gone through the usual course of education at Perugia, he was sent to Rome to study painting and architecture, the first under Stefano Pozzi, the other under Carlo Murena, and it was the second of these arts that he decided on following as a profession. It would appear that he gave promise of more than ordinary talent, from the circumstance of Vanvitelli engaging him as his assistant, when he was about to commence the palace at Caserta; yet the latter part of this statement is evidently incorrect, because Vici could not have been more than eight or nine years old at that time. It is certain, however, that he was connected for some time with Vanvitelli, for he was commissioned by him to attend to matters of business connected with the Mola di Pontano; in consequence of which he became known at Rome as a skillful engineer. In 1780, the court of Tuscany appointed him hydraulic architect and engineer for the Val di Chiana, and in 1787, he was employed in a similar capacity by the papal government, in the work of draining the Pontine marshes, and preventing the inundations of the Teppia. In 1810 he erected the embankment to support the left bank of the Anio. His architectural works are considerable in number and importance; among them are the Palazzo Lapri at Bevagna; the church and monastery delle Salesiane at Offagna; the seminary at Osimo; the church of S. Francesco at Foligno; the Capella Gozzoli at Terni; the villa and casini at Monte Gallo; and the superb cathedral at Camarino. Vici died Sept. 10, 1817.

VICINELLI, Odoardo, a painter born at Rome in 1684. According to Pascoli, he studied under Gio. Maria Morandi, and was his ablest scholar. He does not hesitate to assert that he conferred more honor on his master, than any other of his scholars, and that Pietro Nelli alone could dispute precedence with him. He died in 1755.

VICINO, an old painter in mosaic, who was a native of Pisa, and flourished about 1321. Vasari says that he finished a mosaic commenced by Turrita, in which he was assisted by Taffi and Gaddi, and adds that he was also a painter.

ÆV

VICO, VIGHI, or VICUS, Enea, an eminent engraver and medalist, was born at Parma, according to Bartsch and Zani, about 1520. He studied under Giulio Romano, and afterwards visited Rome, where he entered the school of Marc' Antonio Raimondi. He made rapid progress, and was invited by the Grand Duke Cosmo I. to Florence, where he engraved several plates after Michael Angelo, also the portraits of Henry II. of France, Giovanni de' Medici and his son, Bembo, Ariosto, &c. From Florence, Vico went to Venice and Ferrara. On returning to Parma in 1554, he engraved and published the medals of gold, silver, and bronze, of the Twelve Cæsars, with explanations. In 1555, he published at Venice his *Discorsi soprà le Medaglie*, which was reprinted at Venice in 1558, at Paris in 1619, at Parma in 1691. Vico is esteemed as the first who wrote in Italy upon the science of Numismatics, or at least the first who attempted to reduce it to rules. His last work, *Imagine delle donne Auguste*, appeared at Venice in 1557; and a work in folio by him was published at Rome without a date, containing a number of plates after ancient gems. Vico was of a very ardent disposition, and although perfectly acquainted with design, his plates do not equal those of Raimondi, either in correctness of outline or beauty of finish. They are, however, held in considerable estimation. He is said to have executed some wooden cuts, among which is mentioned one of Charles V., Emperor of Germany, which evinces great ability, both in design and execution; but Bartsch and Zani are decidedly of opinion that he never engraved on wood. Bartsch describes about 500 prints by Vico, generally marked with his name in full, or with the initials Æ. V., sometimes upon a tablet, and sometimes without it. Among them are the following. He probably died about 1570.

PORTRAITS.

Charles V., surrounded by emblematical figures, inscribed, INVENTUM SCULPTUMQUE AB AENEA VICO PARMENSE, MDL. Bust of Giovanni de Medici, in a border. 1550. Bust of Cosimo de Medici, when young. Bust of Alfonso II., Duke of Ferrara.

VARIOUS SUBJECTS.

The Army of Charles V. passing the Elbe; *from his own designs*. The Battle of the Amazons; inscribed, *Bellum Amazonum*. 1543. A Female Figure, with her arms extended, over which appears an Owl flying in the air; *after Parmiggiano*. 1548. A free subject of Vulcan and Venus; *do*. 1643. The Battle of the Lapithæ and Centaurs; *after Il Rosso*. 1542. The Dispute of Apollo with Cupid; *after Baccio Bandinelli*. The Academy of Baccio Bandinelli; *do*. The Conversion of St. Paul; *after F. Salviati*. Judith with the Head of Holofernes; *after M. Angelo Buonarotti*. The Entombing of Christ; *after Raffaelle*. 1548. The Death of Lucretia. 1541. Jupiter and Leda; *after M. Angelo Buonarotti*. A Bacchanalian Subject; *do*. The Annunciation; *after Titian*. A set of twelve Vases; from the designs of *Polidoro da Caravaggio*. A set of fifty plates of the Habiliments of different Nations; *from his own designs*.

VICOLUNGO, DI VERCELLI, a painter born at Vercelli, who flourished there in the first part of the 17th century. He was an imitator of Bernardino Lanini. There are some of his works in his native city, which, according to Lanzi, have little to recommend them except the coloring.

VICTOR, or FICTOOR, JAN, a Dutch painter, supposed to have been born about 1600, and died about 1670. All that is known of him is that he painted subjects taken from the Old Testament, so much in the style of Rembrandt, that they have frequently been mistaken for the works of that master. Stanley says that there are pictures in the rich collections of England, considered the genuine productions of Rembrandt, which really owe their paternity to Jan Victor. His name is variously written, Victor, and Fictoor, and one of his pictures in the Louvre, is signed *Jan Fictoor*, 1650. Some say he was a pupil of Rubens, and others of Rembrandt. There were several other artists of this name who flourished about the middle, or last half of the 17th century, probably the sons of Jan Fictoor. *F. Fictoor*, is said to have painted familiar subjects; *Jacob*, animals, and *Lodovick*, still-life. There are a variety of subjects signed with their names, such as village sports, rural occupations, travelers refreshing at inns, fish-markets, fruit-stalls, dead poultry and game, landscapes and animals, with objects of still-life, &c.

VICTORIA, VICENTE, a Spanish painter, born at Valencia in 1658. He went young to Rome, where he entered the school of Carlo Maratti, and distinguished himself so much that he was taken into the service of the Grand Duke of Tuscany, who placed his portrait in the Florentine gallery. He is said to have painted some works for the churches and convents of his native city, which were doubtless executed in Italy, as he appears to have passed most of his life in that country. In his style, he emulated Maratti. He was also an engraver, and executed a great many etchings and engravings in a neat style. He died at Rome in 1712.

VIDAL, DIEGO, called the ELDER, a Spanish painter, born at Valmaseda in 1583. According to Bermudez, he studied at Rome, and was a reputable artist. He commends two of his pictures in the cathedral of Seville, of which he was a prebendary, representing a naked Christ, and the Virgin with the Infant in her arms. Pacheco also speaks of his drawings in terms of eulogy. He died at Seville in 1615.

VIDAL DE LIENDO, DIEGO, called the YOUNGER, was the nephew of the preceding, born at Valmaseda in 1602. Like him, he studied theology and painting at Rome, and was a canon of the cathedral of Seville. There are some of his works in the sacristy of the cathedral of Valencia, which evince considerable skill. He died at Seville in 1648.

VIDAL, DIONISIO, a Spanish painter, born at Valencia about 1670. He studied under Antonio Palomino, and assisted him in some of his works in different cities. On his return to Valencia, he was employed to paint the ceiling of the church of St. Nicolas, from the designs of Palomino. He also executed some works of his own composition in fresco, for various churches, some of which, according to Bermudez, have perished, and others are of little account. He died at Tortosa, while painting the chapel of the Virgin of the Girdle, at what time is not recorded.

VIDAL, GERALD, a French engraver, born at Toulouse in 1742. He settled at Paris, where he engraved a variety of plates after the modern French masters, among which are Jupiter and Io, Venus and Adonis, Jupiter and Antiope, Rinaldo and Armida, *after Ch. Monnet;* and Paris and Helen, *after David.*

VIDAL, JOSÉ, a Spanish painter of battle-pieces and familiar subjects, who flourished at Valencia about the middle of the 17th century. He was a disciple of Esteban March, whose free, vigorous and effective style he successfully followed. He had a son also named José, whom he instructed in the art, but he did not equal his father.

VIDAL, L., a Dutch painter, of whom nothing is known except by his works. He painted fruit, flowers, dead birds, and other objects of still life. His manner of composition resembles that of the Elder van Os, though he appears to have been an earlier painter. His drawing is very accurate, his penciling delicate, and his pictures are highly finished, though his tone of coloring is sometimes too low for effect. The dew-drops on his leaves are as transparent as those of van Huysum, and his bird's nests with eggs almost equal him.

VIEHL, Pierre, a French engraver, born at Paris in 1755. He studied under B. L. Prevost, and executed some plates after the French and Dutch masters, in the clear, neat, finished style of his master; among them are a pair of landscapes, *after Ruysdael*, the Judgment of Paris, *after Rottenhammer*, and the Bath of Diana, *after Mettai*.

VIEIL, Pierre le, an eminent French painter on glass, born at Paris in 1708. He was the son and scholar of Guillaume le V., a reputable artist in this branch. In 1734 he executed several excellent works for the church of S. Etienne du Mont, at Paris; and afterwards restored the glass paintings in the Cathedral of Notre Dame. Among his other productions are the paintings in the church of S. Victor. Le Vieil employed fifteen years in collecting materials for a work relative to the history and practice of glass painting, entitled, *Traité historique et pratique de la peinture sur verre.* He also wrote several other works of a similar nature, and a treatise on the art of Mosaic, entitled, *Essai sur la peinture en mosaique.* Paris, 1768. He died in 1772.

VIEIRA, Francisco, a Portuguese painter, born at Lisbon in 1699. When a boy he went to Rome, in the suite of the Marquis of Abrantes, where he entered the school of Trevisani, and improved himself by copying the works of Annibale Caracci in the Farnesian Gallery. After a residence of seven years at Rome, and gaining the first prize in the Academy of St. Luke, he returned to Lisbon, when only 16 years old, where, according to Count Raczynski, he astonished the people, by several youthful performances, the most remarkable of which was an elopement with a beautiful young lady of rank, whose heart he had won, but whose cruel parents had forbidden the bans. The lovers first fled to Spain, and thence to Italy, where they passed several years, during which time Vieira greatly improved himself by the constant exercise of his pencil. At length he was invited back to Portugal by the king, and during a residence of forty years at Lisbon, he executed a great many admirable works for the royal palace, the churches and convents of that city. In 1744 he entered the religious order of San Santiago; in 1755, on the death of his wife, he relinquished the pencil and retired to spend the rest of his days in pious meditation. It is said that many of his best works were destroyed in the great earthquake at Lisbon in 1755; no great loss, if any opinion of his merits can be formed from the bombastic account of his biographer. He died in 1783.

VIEIRA, Francisco, the Younger, was the son of the preceding, born at Lisbon. He probably was instructed by his father; he went to Italy, and thence proceeded to England, where he exhibited in the Royal Academy, in the years 1798 and 1799. During his residence in England, he lived with Bartolozzi, who is said to have instructed him in engraving. He married and returned to Lisbon, where he died in 1805.

VIEL, Charles François, a French architect, was born at Paris in 1745. After completing his studies at the College of Beauvais, he entered the school of Chalgrin, to acquire a knowledge of architecture. The first work that brought his name before the public, was a project for a monument, reviving in a superb colonnade the pomp of Greek and Roman architecture, to be erected to Natural History. During a long career, he erected many works, among which were the Bicêtre; the grand amphitheatre of the Hotel Dieu; and the Mont de Piété, with an imposing façade of beautiful proportions. Viel held the office of architect to the hospitals of Paris, for a period of forty years, and also wrote various estimable dissertations on the art. He died in 1819.

VIEN, Joseph Marie, one of the most eminent French painters of the 18th century, and the regenerator of art in France, was born at Montpellier, June 18, 1716. Being very sickly in youth, his parents endeavored to lead him to other pursuits, but his enthusiastic devotion to art overcame all obstacles, and he studied painting under several masters, among whom were A. Rivalz of Toulouse, and finally C. Natoire at Paris, whither he repaired in 1740. In 1743 he competed successfully for the grand prize of the Royal Academy, by his picture of the Plague of the Israelites in the time of David. In 1744 he departed for Rome, and passed several years in designing from the antique and the best masters of the Roman school. Besides numerous studies, he painted there many excellent pictures, including several altar-pieces of great merit, as the Slaughter of the Innocents, and the only two pictures by him now in the Louvre, a Sleeping Hermit, and St. Germain and St. Vincent receiving the Crown of Glory from the hands of an Angel.

Vien returned to Paris in 1750, and was chosen a member of the Academy in 1754, when he presented a picture of Dædalus attaching his wings. He painted a large number of works at Paris, many of them compositions of great excellence, and indicating a decided revival in the French school of painting, from the insipid and puerile state to which it had been reduced by Vanloo and Boucher. It was his object to restore the study of the antique, and of nature as represented in the works of the best Italian masters, and he succeeded to a considerable extent in both respects. His preference for the antique was carried to the extreme by his pupils Vincent and David. His pictures approach the style and artistic excellence of the scholars of the Caracci, although for some time they were much maligned by the scholars of Boucher and Vanloo, among whom was his former instructor Natoire. They pronounced Vien's picture of St. Denis preaching to the Gauls, (one of his best works,) inferior to Doyen's picture representing the tradition of St. Genevieve arresting the Conflagration of Paris; both of which are now placed in the church of St. Roch. A few years after, however, Vien was justified by his cotemporaries, and his reputation rose to a great height. His works are very numerous, considering that many of them are of large proportions. In 1775, after the completion of his picture of St. Denis, which was exhibited at the Louvre the previous year, he was decorated with the order of St. Michael, and was appointed director of the French Academy at Rome, where he resided from that time until 1781, and was meanwhile elected a member of the Academy of St. Luke. After returning to Paris, he was chosen one of the rectors and director of the Royal Academy, and was finally appointed principal painter to the king in 1789. At the Revolution, he of course lost this last post, but at the organization of the French Institute, he was chosen one of the original members. Napoleon also created him a member of the Senate, a count of the Empire, and a commander of the Legion of Honor. He died at Paris, March 27th, 1809, having nearly completed his ninety-third year; and was buried in the Pantheon.

Vien's subjects are chiefly taken from the Scriptures, from ancient and modern history, and from Greek mythology. Among the most celebrated are, Julius Cæsar contemplating the Statue of Alexander at Cadiz, and regretting that he was still unknown at an age when Alexander was already crowned with glory; the Consecration of the Equestrian Statue of Louis XV.; Marcus Aurelius causing Provisions to be distributed among the People; St. Louis vesting the Regency of the Kingdom in his Queen, Blanche of Navarre; St. Jerome; the Embarkation of St. Martha; Christ breaking Bread; the Resurrection of Lazarus; the Virgin attended by Angels; St. Gregory; Briseïs in the Tent of Achilles; the Parting of Hector and Andromache; Hector exhorting Paris to go out to Battle; Venus wounded by Diomed; Æneas pursuing Helen during the burning of Troy; Andromache showing the Arms of Hector to her Son; Mars forcing himself from the Arms of Venus; Cupid and Psyche; Sappho playing on her Lyre; Proserpine adoring the Statue of Ceres; Cupid flying from Slavery; and a Young Greek Girl comparing her Bosom with a Rose-bud. There are also many drawings by Vien, some in series, as the Sports of Nymphs and Cupids, in 20 pieces; and the Union of Cupid and Hymen, in 36 pieces. He executed a few etchings, among which are a set from a series of de Troy's designs of the Adventures of Lot and his Daughters; the same after his own designs; five Bacchanalian subjects; and 32 pieces representing a Fête or Masquerade given by Vien and other students of the French Academy at Rome, to the Cardinal de la Rochefoucauld, in 1748. It is entitled, "Caravane du Sultan à la Mecque, Mascarade Turque donnée à Rome par Messieurs les Pensionnaires de l'Academie de France et leurs Amis, au Carnaval de l'Année 1748." *Jos. Vien, inv. et. sc.*

VIEN, Madame, was the wife and pupil of the preceding artist. Her maiden name was Marie Reboul. She painted flowers, birds, and still-life, with distinguished reputation, and was chosen a member of the Royal Academy. She died in 1805, aged 77.

VIEN, Joseph Marie, the son of the preceding artists, was born at Paris in 1761. He was a distinguished portrait painter, but practiced only as an amateur. He exhibited several pictures at the Louvre until within a few years.

VIENOT, Nicolas, a French engraver, who flourished about 1630. He was probably a pupil of Paul Pontius, and he imitated his style with considerable success, and copied some of his portraits after Rubens, on a small scale. He also engraved some landscapes after John Both, Pellerin, and other masters. There was another engraver of this name, who flourished about 1680.

VIEUX, Renaud le, a French historical painter who flourished in the latter part of the 17th century. He visited Rome for improvement, and on returning to France, produced several pictures of considerable merit. His works are distinguished for correctness of design, and truth and brilliancy of coloring, particularly in the carnations. He painted several pictures for the church des Penitents at Avignon, of subjects from the history of St. John the Baptist; two of which were taken to Paris in 1793; two are in the Gallery at Nismes; and the rest are at Avignon.

VIGÉE, Marie Louise Elizabeth. See Lebrun.

VIGHI. See Vico.

VIGNALI, Jacopo, a painter born at Florence in 1592. He was a disciple of Matteo Rosselli. Lanzi says, "his style has some resemblance to that of Guercino, but less in the forms than in the dark shadows and the grounds. He is among those scholars of Rosselli, who are seldom mentioned, though he painted more than any of the rest for the Prince and the state; he is often weak, especially in attitudes; often, however, he appears praiseworthy, as in his two pictures at S. Simone, and in the S. Liborio. He is most conspicuous in his frescos, as seen in the chapel of the Buonarotti. He painted good historical pictures in the palaces of many of the nobility, and he even boasts noble pupils, none of whom did so much honor to his memory as Carlo Dolci." He died at Florence in 1664.

VIGNERIO, Jacopo, a Sicilian painter, who, according to Hackert, flourished at Messina about the middle of the 16th century. He studied under Polidoro da Caravaggio, whose style he followed. There is an excellent picture by him of Christ bearing his Cross in S. Maria della Scala, dated 1552.

VIGNOLA, Girolamo da, a painter of Modena, who flourished in the first half of the 16th century. Lanzi conjectures that he was a pupil of Pellegrino da Modena; at all events, he was a professed follower of the style of Raffaelle. Some of his frescos still remain in the church S. Piero, in his native city.

VIGNOLA, Giacomo. See Barozzi.

VIGNON, Claude, a French painter and engraver, was born at Tours in 1590, and died in 1670. He visited Italy for improvement, and studied there several years, following the style of Caravaggio with considerable success, although equally ignoble in the selection of his forms and lacking his excellence of coloring. Dumesnil mentions twenty-seven spirited and masterly etchings by him, among which are, St. John in the Desert; thirteen plates from the life of Christ; the Martyrdom of St. Andrew; Philip baptizing the Eunuch; and the Coronation of the Virgin.

VIGNON, Philippe, was the son of the preceding, born at Paris in 1634, and died in 1701. He was instructed in the art by his father, and painted history with reputation.

VIGNON, Claude François, was the second

son of Claude V., born at Paris in 1635, and died in 1703. He was also instructed by his father and confined himself to history with considerable success.

VIGRI, Caterina, a paintress born at Bologna in 1413, and died in 1463. Her father was a painter of little note and a native of Ferrara, and probably instructed her in the art. She was principally employed in illuminating missals and in painting miniatures. She was a nun, and from the sanctity of her life was called *Santa Caterina da Bologna.* She is also sometimes called *Beata Caterina Vigri.*

VILA, Senen, a Spanish painter, born, according to Palomino, at Valencia, and a disciple of Esteban March. He resided chiefly at Murcia, where he executed many works for the churches, convents, and public edifices, which are more remarkable for correctness of design and great expression in the heads, than for beauty of coloring. He died in 1708.

VILA, Lorenzo, was the son and scholar of the preceding: born at Murcia in 1682. He painted history in the style of his father, and gained considerable reputation by several works which he executed for the churches, when he became an ecclesiastic. He died in 1713.

VILADOMAT, Don Antonio, a Spanish painter, born at Barcelona in 1678, and died in 1755. It is not known by whom he was instructed, but at the age of twenty-one he had made such progress that he was employed to paint a series of pictures from the life of St. Bruno, for the monastery of the Carthusians, at Monte Allegri. He afterwards painted a similar set from the life of St. Francis for the monastery of the Franciscans, at Barcelona. He painted many other works for the churches and public edifices of Barcelona. He also painted landscapes, battle-pieces, and portraits with equal success. Mengs regarded Viladomat as the principal Spanish painter of his day, and his works are commended by several excellent critics.

VILADOMAT, Don José, was the son and scholar of the preceding. He was a reputable painter, though far inferior to his father. There are some of his works in the churches and convents at Barcelona.

VILLACIS, Don Nicolas de, a Spanish painter, born of a noble family of Murcia. After receiving some instruction in design, in his native city, he was sent to Madrid, and placed under the instruction of Don Diego Velasquez. He afterwards went to Italy for improvement, and on his return to Murcia, executed some considerable works for the churches and convents, which are highly commended by Palomino. The chief of these are a series of pictures of the life of San Blas in the convent of la Santissima Trinidad de Calzados, and the Martyrdom of St. Lorenzo in the church of the Dominicans. Being a nobleman and rich, he painted only for amusement; his works are therefore very rare. His correspondence with Velasquez is said to be still preserved. He died in 1690.

VILLAFRANCA, Malagon, Pedro de, a Spanish painter and engraver, whose prints date from about 1640 to 1676. He was born at Alcolea in La Mancha, and studied at Madrid under Vincenzio Carducci. Little is known of him as a painter, except that he was employed to execute some pictures for the church of San Felipe el Real, at Madrid. He chiefly devoted himself to engraving, and executed a great number of vignettes, title-pages, portraits, and other book-plates. He engraved the illustrative plates for the Books of Official Rules of the Orders of Santiago, Calatrava, and Alcantara, which are embellished with portraits of Philip IV. He was appointed engraver in ordinary to the King, with a pension of 100 ducats. His last print is a portrait of Calderon, dated 1676.

VILLAIN, Gerard Renard, a French engraver, who flourished about 1760, and executed a few portraits.

[monogram] or [monogram] VILLAMENA, Francesco, an eminent Italian designer and engraver, born at Assisi, about 1566. According to Baglioni, he went to Rome in the Pontificate of Sixtus V., where he applied himself to designing from the antique, and the works of the great masters, with great assiduity. He is supposed to have been a fellow-student with Agostino Caracci, under Cornelius Cort, whose style he emulated. His plates are executed entirely with the graver, in a bold, open and masterly style, and he handled the burin with uncommon facility. The effect of his prints is more clear than powerful, from the lights being too equally diffused over the whole subject. This defect, however, discernible in most of the productions of his time, is compensated in a great measure, by the correctness of the drawing and the admirable expression of the heads. His prints are numerous, and are sometimes marked with the above monogram, sometimes with his initials, F. V. F., and occasionally with his name in full. He died about 1626. The following are his principal works.

PORTRAITS.

Cæsar Baronius Soranus, Cardinal. 1602. Christophorus Clavius, Bambergensis e Societ. Jesu. 1606. Robertus Bellarminus Politianus. Christiern IV., King of Denmark. Galilee Galilei, of Pisa, famous Mathematician.

SUBJECTS FROM HIS OWN DESIGNS.

St. Theresa meditating in her Cell. Mary Magdalene penitent, crowned by an Angel. St. Francis praying before a Crucifix. A set of six grotesque Figures, one of which is a Monk begging, accompanied by two Children. A print called *The Boxers*, representing a Man fighting against a crowd of people. Another print, called *The Antiquary*, representing John Alto standing in one of the streets of Rome.

SUBJECTS AFTER VARIOUS MASTERS.

Moses showing the Brazen Serpent to the Israelites; *after Ferrau da Faenza.* The Virgin and infant Christ, with St. Francis; *do.* The Holy Family, with St. John, St. Elizabeth, and St. Anne; *after Raffaelle.* 1602. The same subject; engraved at Rome in 1611. St. Bruno, with his companions, doing penance in the Desert; *after Lanfranco.* The taking down from the Cross; *after Baroccio.* The Presentation in the Temple; *after Paolo Veronese.* This plate was begun by Agostino Caracci, and was finished by Villamena; it is scarce. St. Bernard with the Virgin in the clouds; *after Vanni.* A set of twenty Scriptural subjects, from the paintings by *Raffaelle* in the Vatican, called Raffaelle's Bible.

VILLAVICENCIO, Don Pedro Nunez. See Nunez.

VILLEGAS MARMOLEJO, Pedro de, a Spanish painter, born at Seville in 1520. It is not known under whom he studied, but it is supposed that he received his education in Italy. There is much discrepancy as to his merits among the Spanish writers. He executed a few works for the churches and public edifices of Seville, which, according to Bermudez, partake of the manner of Pedro Campana, and his best works are equal to the finest productions of that master. His Visitation of the Virgin Mary to St. Elizabeth, in the cathedral, has often been attributed to Campana. Others however, do not speak of him in terms of such high commendation. He died in 1597.

VILLEGUAIN, Etienne, a French painter, born at Ferrière in 1599, and died at Paris in 1668. Little is known of him. He is said to have painted history and portraits with considerable reputation. His name is also written *Villeguin* and *Villequin*.

VILLEREY, Antoine Claude François, a French engraver, born at Paris in 1768. He studied under Antoine Louis Romanet. He engraved part of the plates for the Musée Filhol; twenty-six plates for the Galerie de St. Bruno, *after le Sueur;* a great part of the vignettes for the edition of Voltaire published by Renouard, and some single plates after the French masters. His plates are executed with the graver in a neat, finished style. He was living in 1831.

VILLOLDO, Juan de, a Spanish painter, who, according to Bermudez, practiced his profession with great credit at Toledo, in the first part of the 16th century. In 1508, he was employed by the chapter of the cathedral, to paint several pictures for the Muzarabic chapel, which, with the assistance of Juan de Borgona and Amberes, he finished in 1510. Nothing more is heard of him till 1547, when he was employed by the bishop of Plasencia to adorn a chapel which he had rebuilt in the parish of St. Andrew at Madrid, with a series of forty-five pictures of sacred history, from the fall of Adam to the death of Christ. These works are commended by Bermudez for correctness of design, and for "purity in the antique style." He finished the chapel in 1548, "a proof of the fecundity of his imagination, and the extraordinary rapidity of his pencil." He is supposed to have died about 1551.

VIMERCATI, Carlo, a painter born at Milan in 1660. Some say his family name was Donelli; by others he is called Il Vimercati. He studied under Ercole Procaccini; but Lanzi says, "he owed his success to the most pertinacious study of the works of Daniello Crespi at the Certosa; he exhibited few of his pictures in public at Milan; he painted more at Codogno, and in his best manner, as well as others in a new one, in which he was greatly inferior." He died in 1715.

VINCENT, Hubert, a French engraver who went to Rome, where he flourished about 1690. He engraved some plates after Correggio, Paul Veronese, and other masters, which are indifferently executed.

VINCI, Gaudenzio. This painter, according to a MS. cited by Lanzi, was a native of Novara, in Piedmont. There is an altar-piece by him at Arona, executed entirely in the manner of Lionardo da Vinci, signed *Gaudenzio Vinci*, 1511, which Lanzi says is pronounced by all an astonishing performance. This is all that is known of him with any certainty, though some say he was a pupil of Pietro Perugino, and several works partaking of the style of that master, are attributed to him. It seems very probable that he is the same as *Gaudenzio Ferrari*, which see.

VINCI, Lionardo da. This illustrious artist, denominated by Lanzi, "the Father of Modern Painting," was also an eminent sculptor, architect, and engineer, the natural son of Pietro da Vinci, notary to the Florentine Republic. Vasari and his annotators, place his birth in 1445; but Durazzini, in his Panegyrics on Illustrious Tuscans, satisfactorily proves that he was born in Lower Valdarno, at the castle of Vinci, in 1452. At an early age he evinced remarkably quick abilities for everything he turned his attention to, but more particularly for arithmetic, music and drawing. His drawings appeared something wonderful to his father, who showed them to Andrea Verocchio, and that celebrated artist, greatly surprised at seeing productions of such merit from an uninstructed hand, willingly took Lionardo as a pupil. He was soon much more astonished when he perceived the rapid progress his pupil made; he felt his own inferiority, and when Lionardo painted an angel in a picture of the Baptism of Christ, in S. Salvi at Vallombrosa, so much superior to the other figures that it rendered the inferiority of Verocchio apparent to all, he immediately relinquished the pencil for ever. This picture is now in the Academy at Florence. The first original work by Lionardo, mentioned by Vasari, was the so-called Rotella del Fico, a round board of a fig-tree, upon which his father requested him to paint something for one of his tenants. Lionardo, wishing to astonish his father, determined to execute something extraordinary, that should produce the effect of the head of Medusa; and having prepared the rotella and covered it with plaster, he collected almost every kind of reptile, and composed from them a monster of most horrible appearance; it seemed alive, its eyes flashed fire, and it appeared to breathe destruction from its open mouth. The picture produced the desired effect upon his father, who thought it so wonderful that he carried it immediately to a picture-dealer in Florence, sold it for a hundred ducats, and purchased for a trifle an ordinary piece for his tenant. The talents of Lionardo soon attracted public attention at Florence. He was endowed by nature with a genius uncommonly elevated and penetrating, eager after discovery, and diligent in the pursuit, not only in what related to sculpture and architecture, but in mathematics, mechanics, hydrostatics, music, poetry, botany, astronomy, and also in the accomplishments of horsemanship, fencing, and dancing. Unlike most men of versatile talent, he was so perfect in all these, that when he performed any one, the beholders were ready to imagine that it must have been his sole study. To such vigor of intellect he joined an elegance of features and of manners, that graced the virtues of his mind, he was affable with strangers, with citizens, with private individuals, and with princes. This extraordinary combination of qualities in a single man, soon spread his fame over all Italy.

Lanzi divides Lionardo's life into four periods, the first of which includes the time he remained at Florence, until 1494. He says, "Lionardo retained traces of his early education through his whole life. Like Verocchio, he designed more readily than he painted; he assiduously cultivated mathematics; in his design and in his countenances he prized elegance and vivacity of expression, more than dignity and fulness of contour; he was very careful in drawing his horses, and in representing the skirmishes of soldiers; and was more solicitous to improve the art than to multiply his pictures. By his knowledge of sculpture, he gave that perfect relief and roundness, in which painting was then wanting; he imparted to it symmetry, grace, and spirit, and these and his other merits, gave him the title of the Father of Modern Painting, though some of his works participate in the meanness of the old school. He had two styles, the one abounding in shadow, which gives admirable brilliancy to the contrasting lights; the other more quiet, and managed by means of middle tints. In each style, the grace of his design, the expression of the affections, and the delicacy of his pencil, are unrivalled. Everything is lively, the foreground, the landscape, the adventitious ornaments of necklaces, flowers, and architecture; but this gaiety is more apparent in the heads. In this he apparently repeats the same idea, and gives them a smile which delights the mind of a spectator. To this first period of Lionardo's life may be referred the Medusa, and the few pictures mentioned by Vasari; others also, less powerful in the shadows, and less diversified in the folds of the drapery, present heads more delicate than select, apparently derived from the school of Verocchio. Such is the Magdalen in the Florentine Gallery, and that of the Aldobrandini palace at Rome; some Madonnas and Holy Families in the Giustiniani and Borghese Galleries; and some heads of the Redeemer and the Baptist in various places, although the multitude of his imitators must render all decision on their originality ambiguous. Of a different class, and without a doubt by his hand, is the picture of a Child playing on an ornamented bed, richly dressed and adorned with necklaces, which is in the apartment of the Gonfalonière at Bologna." Lionardo also executed several excellent works in sculpture, among which are the statue of St. Tommaso, in Or San Michele at Florence, the Horse, in the church of Sts. Giovanni and Paolo, at Venice, and the superior models for the three statues cast in bronze by Rustici, for S. Giovanni at Florence.

The second period of Lionardo's life commences with his residence at Milan. About 1490, he presented a memorial to the duke Lodovico Sforza, in which he set forth at considerable length his abilities in painting, sculpture, architecture, and engineering. Accordingly, in 1494, the Duke invited him to Milan, and appointed him director of the Academy of Painting and Architecture, which he had recently revived with additional splendor and encouragement. During his residence there, he painted but little, with the exception of his celebrated picture of the Last Supper, a description of which will be found in the latter part of this article. As director of the Academy, he banished all the dry, Gothic principles established by his predecessor, Michelino, and introduced the beautiful simplicity and purity of the Grecian and Roman style. Lanzi says that in this capacity, "he left a degree of refinement at Milan, so productive of illustrious pupils that this period may be reckoned as the most glorious era of his life." The Duke engaged Lionardo in the stupendous project of conducting the waters of the Adda, from Mortesana, through the Valteline, and the valley of the Chiavenna, to the walls of Milan, a distance of nearly two hundred miles. Sensible of the greatness of this undertaking, Lionardo applied himself more closely to those branches of philosophy and mathematics which are most adapted to mechanics, and he finally accomplished this immense work, greatly to the astonishment and admiration of all Italy. He executed the model for a colossal bronze equestrian statue of the Duke's father, Francesco Sforza, and would have completed it, but the Duke's affairs were becoming greatly embarassed, so that the necessary metal, (200,000 lbs.), was not furnished. In 1500, Lodovico Sforza was overthrown in battle by the French, made prisoner, and conducted to France, where he soon after died in the castle of Loches. The Academy was suppressed, the professors dispersed, and Lionardo, after losing all, was obliged to quit the city and take refuge in Florence.

The third period of Lionardo's life commences at the time of his return to Florence, about 1500. He was well received by Pietro Soderini the Gonfalonière, who had him enrolled among the artists employed by government, and settled upon him a pension. In 1502, Cesare Borgia, captain-general of the Pope's army, appointed him his chief architect and engineer, and Lionardo visited many parts of the Roman states in his official capacity. In 1503, however, after the death of Pope Alexander VI., he was again at Florence, and was employed by Soderini to paint one side of the Council-hall of the Palazzo Vecchio, while Michael Angelo, then in his twenty-ninth year, and already rising into eminence, was fixed upon as the artist to paint the other side. Lionardo selected the battle in which the Milanese general, Niccolo Piccinino, was defeated by the Florentines at Anghiari, near Borgo San Sepolcro. This composition, of which he only made the cartoon of a part, was called the Battle of the Standard; it represents a group of horsemen contending for a standard, with various accessories. Vasari praises the beauty and anatomical correctness of the horses, and the costumes of the soldiers. Lanzi says it was never executed, after his failing in an attempt to paint it in a new method upon the wall, but Lucini afterwards represented it in a painting which is in the Ambrosian Library at Milan, esteemed one of the finest works in that collection. The fame of this contest between the two great artists, caused great excitement, and induced Raffaelle, who had recently quitted the school of Perugino, to visit Florence. The grace and delicacy of Lionardo's style, compared with the dry and Gothic manner of Perugino, excited the admiration of the young painter, and inspired him with a more modern taste. In 1507, Lionardo again visited Milan, and painted in that year, in an apartment of the palace of the Melzi at Vaprio, a large Madonna and Child, which in part is still extant.

During this period of Lionardo's life, having attained his highest skill, and mostly unoccupied with other pursuits, he painted in his best manner. "Such," says Lanzi, "is the specimen that was preserved at Mantua, but which was stolen, and after many vicissitudes, was sold for a high price to the court of Russia; the subject is a Holy Family, and in the background is a woman of beautiful and majestic countenance, in an upright position. It bears the cipher of Lionardo, consisting of a D interlaced with an L and a V. His own portrait, in the Ducal gallery at Florence, surpasses every other in that room for energy of expression; also another head in a different cabinet, called a portrait of Raffaelle; the half-length figure of a young nun, so much commended by Bottari, and which he points out as one of the greatest treasures in the splendid mansion of Marchese Niccolini. In the same rank we may include the much admired specimens in the possession of some of the noble families of Rome; as the picture of Christ disputing in the Temple, and the supposed portrait of Queen Giovanna, ornamented with fine architecture, in the Doria Palace; the Vanity and Modesty in the Barberini Palace, the tints of which no pencil has been able to imitate; the Madonna of the Albani Palace, that appears to be requesting the lily which the infant Jesus holds in his hand, drawing back as if unwilling to part with it—a picture of exquisite grace, and preferred by Mengs to every other painting contained in that fine collection." Lionardo's cartoon of St. Anna, for the church of the Servi at Florence, is also esteemed among his most remarkable productions; and also his celebrated portrait of Mona Lisa, the wife of Francesco Giocondo, which occupied him four years. It was purchased by Francis I. for 4000 gold crowns, and is now in the Louvre at Paris. Lionardo visited Milan about 1512, and painted two portraits of the young duke Maximilian, the son of Lodovico, his former patron. In 1514 he quitted it again with several of his companions, and returned to Florence. The patronage extended to the arts by Pope Leo X., then recently elevated to the papal throne, inclined him to visit Rome, and accordingly he went thither in that year, in the train of the Duke Giuliano de Medici, by whom he was introduced to the Pope, who soon after signified his intention of employing Lionardo's pencil. Upon this, the painter began to distil his oils and prepare his varnishes, which the Pope seeing, he exclaimed with surprise, that "nothing could be expected of a painter who thought of finishing his works before he had begun them." This want of courtesy in the Pope offended Lionardo, and according to Vasari, was the reason why he immediately quitted Rome in disgust. It is probable, however, that the talents and fame of Buonarotti and Raffaelle had more to do with producing the dissatisfaction of this great painter, who was then declining into the vale of years.

Lionardo's final departure from Rome marks his relinquishment of the art of painting, and the commencement of the fourth period of his life. He set out for Pavia at the invitation of Francis I. of France, who received him with the greatest kindness, and took him into his service, with a salary of 700 crowns annually. Lionardo accompanied him to Bologna, where he went to meet Leo X., and afterwards, in the beginning of 1516, he accompanied him to Florence. The health of this great painter was so much enfeebled after leaving Italy, that he executed little or nothing more. The king could not prevail upon him even to color his cartoon of St. Anna, which he had brought with him; nor did he seem disposed to commence any new work which would require the exertion of his energies. During an indisposition of five years, he continued to receive marks of that monarch's esteem. His health gradually grew worse, and he finally expired at Fontainbleau on the 2d of May 1519, aged sixty-seven. Vasari relates that he died in the arms of Francis I., who happened to be visiting him at his chamber.

This great artist is esteemed the most eminent Italian of the 15th century. Says Hallam, "the discoveries which made Galileo and Kepler, Maestlin, Maurolicus, Castelli, and other names illustrious, the system of Copernicus, the very theories of recent geologists, are anticipated by Lionardo da Vinci, within the compass of a very few pages, not perhaps in the most precise language, or on the most conclusive reasoning, but so as to strike us with something like the awe of preternatural knowledge. In an age of so much dogmatism, he first laid down the grand principle of Bacon, that experiment and observation must be the guides to just theory in the investigation of nature." His scientific knowledge proved the means of conferring incalculable benefits upon the art of painting, one of the most important of which was the invention of the chiaro-scuro. His intimate acquaintance with mathematical studies enabled him to develope greatly the knowledge of optics, and no one was better acquainted with the nature of aërial perspective, which became a distinctive and hereditary characteristic of his school. Lanzi says, "being extremely well versed in poetry and history, it was through him that the Milanese school became one of the most accurate and observing in regard to antiquity and to costume. Mengs has noticed that no artist could surpass Vinci in the grand effect of his chiaro-scuro. He instructed his pupils to make as cautious a use of light as of a gem, not lavishing it too freely, but reserving it always for the best place. And hence we find in his, and in the best of his disciples' paintings, that fine relief, owing to which the pictures, and in particular the countenances, seem as if starting from the canvass."

"For a long period before the time of Lionardo da Vinci, the art had become gradually more refined, and considered its objects more minutely; in which Botticelli, Mantegna, and others had acquired great reputation. As minuteness, however, is opposed to sublimity, it ill accorded with that elevation in which the supreme merit of the art would seem to consist. In my opinion, Lionardo succeeded in uniting these two opposite qualities, before any other artist. In subjects which he undertook fully to complete, he was not satisfied with only perfecting the heads, counterfeiting the shining of the eyes, the pores of the skin, the roots of the hair, and even the beating of the arteries; he likewise portrayed each separate garment and every accessory with minuteness.—Thus, in his landscapes also, there was not a single herb, or leaf of a tree, which he had not taken like a portrait, from the select face of nature; and to his very leaves he gave a peculiar air, and fold, and position, best adapted to represent them rustling in the wind. While he bestowed his attention in this manner on the minutiæ, he at the same time, as is observed by Mengs, led the way to a more enlarged and dignified style; entered into the most abstruse inquiries as to the source and nature of expression, the most philosophical and elevated branch of the art; and smoothed the way, if I may be permitted to say so, for the appearance of Raffaelle. No one could be more curious in his researches, more intent upon observing, or more prompt in catching the motions of the passions, as exhibited either in the features or the actions. He frequented places of public assembly, and all places in which man gave free play to his active powers; and there, in a small book always ready at hand, he drew the attitudes which he selected; and these designs he preserved that he might apply them, with expressions more or less powerful, according to the occasion, and the degree of expression he wished to introduce. For it was his custom, in the same manner as he gradually strengthened his shadows until he reached the highest degree, so also in the composition of his figures, to proceed in heightening them until he attained the perfection of passion and of motion. The same kind of gradation he observed in regard to elegance, of which he was perhaps the earliest admirer; since previous artists appeared unable to distinguish grace from beauty, and still more so to adapt it to pleasing subjects in such a way as to rise from the less to the more attractive points, as was practiced by Lionardo. He even adhered to the same rule in his burlesques, always throwing an air of greater ridicule over one than another, insomuch that he was heard to say, that they ought to be carried to such a height, if possible, as even to make a dead man laugh. The characteristic, therefore, of this incomparable artist, consists of a refinement of taste, of which no equal example, either preceding or following him, is to be found; if indeed we may not admit that of Protogenes, who wrought seven years upon the picture of Jalysus and his Dog. It is prudent counsel that teaches us to aspire to the best, but to rest satisfied with attaining what is good. Vinci was never pleased with his labors if he did not execute them as perfectly as he had conceived them; and being unable to reach the high point proposed with a mortal hand, he sometimes only designed his work, or conducted it only to a certain degree of perfection. But as there was no limit to the discovery of fresh beauties in the work of Protogenes, so, in the opinion of Lomazzo, it happens with the perfections of Vinci's paintings, including even those which Vasari and others allude to as left imperfect. In regard to the reported imperfection of many of his works, it is certain that he left a number only half finished, but the report is most generally grounded upon his having left some portions of his pieces less perfectly finished than others; a deficiency, nevertheless, that cannot always be detected, even by the best judges. The portrait of Mona Lisa, upon which he wrought four years, and then, according to Vasari, left it imperfect, was examined by Mariette, in the collection of the King of France, and was decided to be carried to so high a degree of finish that it was impossible to surpass it. Lomazzo has remarked that, excepting three or four, he left all the rest of his heads imperfect. But imperfections and faults like his would have been accounted distinguishing qualities in almost any other artist."

"Even his grand Supper has been stated in history as an imperfect production, although at the same time all history is agreed in celebrating it as one of the most beautiful paintings that ever proceeded from the hand of man. It was painted for the Refectory of the Dominican fathers at Milan, and may be pronounced a compendium, not only of all that Lionardo taught in his books, but also of what he embraced in his studies. He here gave expression to the exact point of time best adapted to animate his history, which is the moment when the Redeemer addresses his disciples, saying, 'One of you will betray me.' Then each of his innocent followers is seen to start as if struck with a thunderbolt; those at a distance seem to interrogate their companions, as if they think they must have mistaken what he had said; others, according to their natural disposition, appear variously affected; one of them swoons away, one stands lost in astonishment, a third rises in indignation, while the very simplicity and candor depicted upon the countenance of a fourth, seem to place him beyond the reach of suspicion. But Judas instantly draws in his countenance, and while he appears as it were, attempting to give it an air of innocence, the eye rests upon him in a moment, as the undoubted traitor. Vinci himself used to observe, that for the space of a whole year he employed his time in meditating how he could best give expression to the features of so bad a heart; and that being accustomed to frequent a place where the worst characters were known to assemble, he there met with a physiognomy to his purpose; to which he also added the features of many others. In his figures of the two saints James, presenting fine forms, most appropriate to the characters, he availed himself of the same plan, and being unable with his utmost diligence to invest that of Christ with a superior air to the rest, he left the head in an unfinished state, as we learn from Vasari, though Armenini pronounced it exquisitely complete. The rest of the picture, the table-cloth with its folds, the whole of the utensils, the table, the architecture, the distribution of the lights, the perspective of the ceiling, (which, in the tapestry of S. Pietro at Rome, is changed almost into a hanging garden), all was conducted with the most exquisite care; all was worthy of the finest pencil in the world. Had Lionardo desired to follow the practice of his age in painting in fresco, the art at this time would have been in possession of this treasure. But being always fond of attempting new methods, he painted this master-piece upon a peculiar ground, formed of distilled oils, which was the reason that it gradually detached itself from the wall. About half a century subsequent to the execution of this wonderful work, when Armenini saw it, it was already *half decayed:* and Scanelli, who examined it in 1642, declared that it '*was with difficulty he could discern the history as it had been.*' Nothing now remains except the heads of three apostles, which may be said to be rather sketched than painted."

This great loss is in some measure compensated by several excellent copies, some of which are by Lionardo's most eminent disciples; the best are, that by Marco Uggione, at the Carthusians of Pavia; another in the Refectory of the Franciscans at Lugano, by Bernardino Luini; and one in La Pace at Milan, by Gio. Paolo Lomazzo. Fuseli, lecturing on the copy by Marco Uggione, says, "the face of the Saviour is an abyss of thought, and broods over the immense revolution in the economy of mankind, which throngs inwardly on his absorbed eye—as the Spirit creative in the beginning over the water's darksome wave—undisturbed and quiet. It could not be lost in the copy before us; how could its sublime expression escape those who saw the original? It has survived the hand of time in the study which Lionardo made in crayons, exhibited with most of the attendant heads in the British Gallery, and even in the feeble transcripts of Pietro Testa. I am not afraid of being under the necessity of retracting what I am going to advance, that neither during the splendid period immediately subsequent to Lionardo, nor in those which succeeded to our own time, has a face of the Redeemer been produced, which, I will not say equalled, but approached Lionardo's conception, and in quiet and simple features of humanity, embodied divine, or what is the same, incomprehensible and infinite powers." In 1825, Prof. Phillips examined the remains of this picture, and says, "Of the heads, there is not one untouched, and many are totally ruined. Fortunately, that of the Saviour is the most pure, being but faintly retouched; and it presents, even yet, a most perfect image of that Divine character.—Whence arose the story of its not having been finished it is now difficult to conceive, and the history itself varies among the writers who have mentioned it. But perhaps a man so scrupulous as Lionardo da Vinci, in the definement of character and expression, and so ardent in his pursuit of them, might have expressed himself unsatisfied, where all others could only see perfection."

Lionardo wrote several works on various subjects, the principal of which is a Treatise upon Painting, published in folio at Paris in 1651, entitled, *Trattato della Pittura di Lionardo da Vinci. Novamente dato in Luce; con la vita dell' istesso autore, scritta da Raffaelle du Fresne*, &c., Parigi, 1651, with figures designed by Nicholas Poussin. It was translated into English, and published by John Senex, London, 1721; there are also several other later editions of this work, which Count Algarotti held in such high esteem, that he thought it the only one necessary to be placed in the hands of a student of art. Besides this, Lionardo wrote five Treatises, on Hydraulics, Anatomy, Perspective, Light and Shadow, and the Anatomy of the Horse.

Lionardo left the whole of his designs, instruments, books, and manuscripts, to his friend and disciple, Francesco Melzi, who accompanied him on his last visit to France. His designs and writings were collected into thirteen volumes, which have been dispersed in various royal and noble collections. Several volumes of his MSS. are preserved in the Ambrosian Library, and Lanzi remarks that, as long as they exist, "the world must admit that he was one of the chief revivers, not only of painting, but of statics, hydrostatics, optics, and anatomy." The extracts upon which Hallam grounds the eulogium above cited, were published at Paris in 1797, by Venturi, in an essay entitled, *Essai sur les ouvrages Physico-Mathematiques de Leonard da Vinci, avec des Fragmens tirès de ses Manuscrits apportés de l'Italie.* The original MSS. were subsequently restored to the Ambrosian Library. One volume of his drawings has found its way into the English Royal collection, and contains a variety of heads, portraits, caricatures, single figures, horses, and animals; botany, optics, perspective, mechanics, and anatomical subjects.

It has been attempted to prove that Lionardo engraved a few prints on copper; in the British Museum are three prints attributed to him, the Bust of a young and beautiful Female, a study of the Heads of three Horses, and a Lady in a rich dress. The first two are much in the style of his drawings, and Ottley is quite confident that the former was designed and engraved by him. A print representing a species of ornament, is also mentioned, formerly in Sir Mark Sykes' collection, inscribed in Roman capitals, ACCADEMIA DI LEONARDO VINCI.

VINCK, J., a Dutch portrait and landscape painter, of whom nothing is known except by his works. His landscapes are in a mixed manner, partaking of the styles of Paul Brill and John Breughel. His portraits are only known by engravings that bear his name. He flourished in the first part of the 17th century.

DVB VINCKENBOOMS, DAVID, a Flemish painter, born at Mechlin in 1578. He was the son of Philip V., an obscure painter in distemper, who instructed him in the art. He painted landscapes of a small size, in the style of Roland Savery and John Breughel. These he decorated with subjects taken from the Bible, with fairs, merrymakings, rural festivals, conversations, &c., which are ingeniously composed, and designed with tolerable correctness, though his touch is dry and hard. One of his most considerable works is a picture in the hospital of the Old Men at Amsterdam, representing a crowd of people attending the drawing of a lottery by torch-light. He occasionally painted historical subjects, in which the landscape serves as the background. Such is his picture of Christ bearing his Cross, in the collection of the Elector Palatine, and another at Frankfort, representing Christ restoring blind Bartimeus to sight. Some of his pictures are decorated with the figures of Rottenhammer. He excelled in making drawings with the pen, washed with India ink, several of which are in the British Museum, representing the story of the Prodigal Son. Some of his landscapes were engraved by N. de Bruyn and others. He also engraved some plates of landscapes from his own designs, which he usually marked with the above monogram. His name is sometimes written Vinkoboon. He died at Amsterdam in 1629.

VINKELES, RENIER, a Dutch engraver, born at Amsterdam in 1741. He studied under J. Punt, and engraved some portraits and other subjects after the works of the Dutch masters.

VINNE, JOHN VANDER, a Dutch engraver who flourished at Haerlem about 1730. He engraved a set of twelve plates of views in the environs of Haerlem, executed in a very neat style, *after Peter Bout.* There was also an Isaac Vinne, who was an engraver and publisher, and flourished at Haerlem about the same time. He engraved some plates after T. Wyck.

VINNE, VINCENT LAWRENCE VANDER, a Dutch painter, born at Haerlem in 1629. He showed an early inclination for art, and had made considerable progress without any other assistance than his own genius, when he was placed under the instruction of Francis Hals, one of the ablest artists of his time. On leaving his master, he traveled through Germany, Switzerland, and France. In 1657, he returned to his native city, where he settled for life, and found abundant employment. He painted history, portraits, landscapes, and drolls, in the style of his instructor, and in each of these branches, he discovered a lively imagination, a fruitful invention, an admirable tone of coloring, a faithful imitation of nature, and an uncommon fa cility of hand. His best performances are his portraits, and some of these are accounted little inferior to those of Hals. Towards the latter part of his life, he neglected his fame, in his eagerness for gain, and accepted every commission offered him, which he dispatched with negligence and haste. He died in 1702.

VINNE, Lawrence vander, was the son of the preceding, born at Haerlem in 1658, and died in 1724; though Immerzeel says in 1729. He studied with his father, whose precepts he followed, but never rose above mediocrity. His chief merit consisted in painting flowers and plants, and he was much employed by the botanists of his time. He had two brothers, John and Isaac, who practiced the art, but they did not acquire any distinction. John studied under John van Hugtenburg, and painted landscapes and hunting-pieces. He went to England, where he resided some time. He died at Haerlem in 1721, and Isaac in 1740. There was also a John vander Vinne, an engraver, who flourished at Haerlem about 1730.

VINNE, Vincent vander, was the son of John vander Vinne (probably the engraver), born at Haerlem in 1736, and died there in 1811. He first painted fruit and flower pieces, and afterwards landscapes and cattle, with considerable success.

VINI, Sebastiano, a painter of Verona, who settled at Pistoja in the first part of the 16th century. Lanzi says, "his reputation and his pictures did honor to the country that adopted him. He left many works both in oil and fresco, but his most extraordinary production was in the suppressed church of St. Desiderio. The façade over the great altar was storied with the Crucifixion of the Ten Thousand Martyrs, a work abounding with figures and invention."

VINSAC, Claude Dominick, a French engraver, born at Toulouse in 1749. He engraved a few portraits, and a set of plates of ornaments for goldsmiths, neatly executed in the dotted manner.

VIOLA, Giovanni Battista, a painter born at Bologna, according to Lanzi and the best authorities, in 1576, though some say in 1572. He studied several years with Annibale Caracci, whose admirable manner of painting landscapes he successfully adopted. He accompanied his fellow pupil Albano to Rome, where, in conjunction with him, he was much employed in decorating the palaces of the nobility with landscape-frescos, in which Albano painted the figures. One of the works which first brought him into repute was a large landscape painted for the villa of Cardinal Montalto, in competition with Paul Brill, whose pictures were then highly esteemed. The grandeur both of style and subject of Viola's landscape, greatly excelled that of the Fleming, and gained him great reputation. Some of his finest works are in the Villa Pia, and the Villa Aldobrandini. Fresnoy, who was an able judge, considered the pictures of Viola "wonderfully fine and well colored." Lanzi says that he painted mostly in fresco, and that his portable works are rarely to be met with at Rome; "his landscapes however, were frequently introduced into the pictures of Albano, and may be recognized in that city by judges, as those of Viola, like Mola's in other pieces of Albano at Bologna." He died at Rome in 1622.

VIOLA, Gio. Battista, a painter of Bergamo, of little note, who flourished in the first part of the 17th century, and should be distinguished from the preceding.

VIOLA, Domenico, a Neapolitan painter, who, according to Dominici, died old, in or about 1696. He was a disciple and imitator of the Cav. Mattia Preti (Calabrese). He executed some works for the churches and collections, but did not pass the bounds of mediocrity.

VIRLOYS, Charles François Roland le, a French architect and writer on the art, was born at Paris in 1716. During the period of youth, he applied himself to the study of philosophy and jurisprudence; after which he studied architecture, and made rapid progress. He successfully competed for the erection of the theatre of Metz, and constructed that edifice in 1751. His reputation extended into foreign countries, and he was appointed architect to the King of Prussia, and subsequently to the Empress Maria Theresa; but no mention is made whether he accepted either of these honors. The principal production from the pen of Virloys, is his *Dictionnaire d'architecture, civile, militaire et navale, ancienne et moderne*, &c., Paris, 1770, 3 vols. grand quarto, with 101 plates. The *Biographie Universelle* commends it as superior to the work of Aviler, but adds, that it leaves much to be desired.

VISACCI, Antonio, called also, Il Visacci, a painter of Urbino, who, according to Lazzari, was a pupil of Federigo Baroccio, and flourished about 1600. His real name was Antonio Cimatori. In conjunction with the younger Viviani, Mazzi, and Urbani, he was employed to paint the arches, pictures, and other decorations, in honor of Giulia de' Medici, married to the Duke of Urbino. Lanzi says, "his forte lay in pen-drawing and in chiaro-scuro, as may be seen in his prophets, designed in a grand style, which were transferred from the cathedral to the Apostolic Palace. He did not leave many works in his native place, but among them is his fine picture of St. Monica at S. Agostino. His copies from Baroccio are to be found in various places, particularly at the cathedral of Cagli. He resided and practiced a long time at Pesaro, where he instructed several pupils."

VISCH, Matthias de, a Flemish painter, born at the village of Reningen in 1702. He studied under Joseph vander Kerkhove at Bruges; he also entered the Academy there and obtained the first prize in 1721. He went to Paris in 1723; and thence to Italy, where he resided nine years, and diligently studied the antique and the works of the great masters. On his return to Bruges, he executed several works for the churches, and opened a school of design. He distinguished himself more by his love of the art, the zeal he took in its advancement, and the instruction of youth, than by any superior talents he showed in its practice. He was a correct and able designer, and was appointed director of the Academy at Bruges. He collected materials for a history of painting in Belgium, which he gave to Descamps, who made use of them in his Lives of the Flemish Painters. He died in 1765.

VISCHER, Peter, a celebrated old German sculptor and founder, was probably born about 1460. He studied in Italy, and resided there sev eral years. On returning to his native country, he first distinguished himself by his monument to the Archduke Ernest of Magdeburg, erected in the cathedral of that place in 1497. Vischer ultimately settled at Nuremberg, and lived in the same house with his five sons, Peter, Hermann, Hans, Paul, and Jacob, with their wives and children. His master-piece is the tomb of St. Sebald, in the church of that saint at Nuremberg, which is esteemed worthy of any time or nation. It is beautifully designed and richly ornamented: among other figures are twelve small statues, eighteen inches high, of the apostles, remarkably well drawn, and conspicuous for their fine expression. In one part of it, Vischer introduced his own portrait in his working dress. Notwithstanding he was employed with his sons upon this monument from 1506 to 1519, he received only 2402 florins for the whole work. He executed some other excellent works at Nuremberg, and died, according to Doppelmayer, in 1530.

His son Hermann Vischer studied likewise in Italy, and was scarcely inferior to his father. According to Sandrart, no prince or gentleman that visited Nuremberg, left the place without having seen and conversed with Vischer. During these visits, he received many orders, and executed numerous works, which were sent to Bohemia, Poland, and other neighboring countries. He was killed by a sledge, while going home at night with a friend, in 1540.

VISENTINI. See VICENTINI.

VISINO, IL, a Florentine painter, who, according to Lanzi, was the best scholar of Mariotto Albertinelli. Little is known of his works, as he went to Hungary, where he was much employed. He died there in the prime of life about 1512.

VISO, FRAY CRISTOBAL DEL, a Spanish painter, who died at Madrid about 1700. He resided there at that time, and held the office of commissary-general of the Indies. He was a monk of the order of San Francisco, and painted all the Saints of his order for the chapter house of the convent of S. Francisco at Cordova, which are said to display considerable ability.

VISPRE, FRANÇOIS SAVERIO, a French painter and engraver of little note, born at Paris about 1730. He engraved a few portraits in mezzotinto. He went to London about 1765, where he resided some time.

VISSCHER, CORNELIUS, a celebrated designer and engraver, born at Haerlem about 1610. He studied under Peter Soutman, but he did not follow the style of that master; he adopted one of his own, formed by a combination of the point with the graver, in which he has hardly been equalled. His drawing is correct, and his execution is clear, delicate, and admirably harmonized. His works are very numerous, and those from his own designs are the most esteemed. Basan remarks that no master can be studied by young engravers with more advantage. His plates of the portrait of Gellius Bouma, the Pancake-woman, the Rat-catcher and the Bohemian Woman, may be cited as models of perfection in his style of engraving. He was less successful in his plates of historical subjects after the Italian and Spanish masters; those in particular which he engraved after Rubens, are inferior to the productions of Bolswert, Vostermans, and Pontius. There were two portrait painters of this name, who flourished at an earlier date. One of them was drowned about 1550, in his passage from Hamburg to Amsterdam. There are no particulars recorded of the other. Cornelius Visscher, the engraver, died in 1670. The following is an ample list of his best works. For a complete catalogue, the reader is referred to Bartsch and Nagler.

PORTRAITS.

A Portrait, supposed to be that of himself, with a high-crowned hat, and his hand on his breast; inscribed *Corn. Visscher, fecit. anno* 1649. Another Portrait of Cornelius Visscher, with a similar hat, and enveloped in his cloak; *Corn. Visscher, fecit. anno* 1651. Andreas Deonyszoon Winius, called the Man with the Pistol. The scarcest and most valuable of his portraits. [A proof of this portrait sold at M. Debois' sale in 1845 for 1660 francs.] Gellius de Bouma, Minister of the Gospel, at Zutphen; fine. William de Ryck, Oculist, of Amsterdam; fine. This portrait and the preceding one are commonly called the great Beards. [A proof of this sold in Debois' sale for 1020 francs.] Cornelius Vosbergius, pastor of Spaerwouw, with a book in his hand. 1653; fine and scarce. William vanden Zande, Theologian; *after Soutman;* fine; and very rare. David Peiterz de Vries, Grand-master of Artillery to the States of Holland; scarce. Jacob Westerbaen, Lord of Brandwyck, &c.; very rare. Coppenol, called the Writing-master. 1658. Constantine Huygens, Lord of Zuylichem; inscribed with his motto, *Constanter.* 1657; scarce. William, Prince of Orange; *after G. Honthorst.* 1649. Mary, daughter of Charles I., his consort; *do.* 1649. Charles II., King of England; *do.* 1650.

SUBJECTS FROM HIS OWN DESIGNS.

The Pancake-woman. The first impressions are before the address of Clement de Jonghe. The Rat-catcher. The best impressions of this plate are before the name of Clement de Jonghe, and without the title. The Bohemian Woman, with three children, one of which she is suckling. In the first impressions the name of Visscher is upon the margin, at the bottom of the print. It was afterwards effaced to make room for the inscription, and placed upon the upper part of the plate. A boy holding a Candle, and a Girl with a Mouse-trap. A Cat sleeping on a Napkin; fine, and extremely rare. A Cat sleeping, with a Rat behind her. The Coronation of Carolus Gustavus and the Queen of Sweden.

SUBJECTS AFTER VARIOUS MASTERS.

The Angel directing the Departure of Abraham; *after Bassano.* Abraham's Arrival at Sichem; *do.* Susanna and the Elders; *after Guido.* Magdalen penitent; supposed to be *after Parmiggiano;* very fine. The Entombment of Christ; *after Tintoretto.* The Resurrection; *after P. Veronese.* The Holy Family, with St. John presenting a Pear to the infant Christ; without the name of the painter. The Last Judgment; *after Rubens.* The best impressions of this plate are before the address of Soutman. The Virgin and Infant, crowned by Angels; *do.* Achilles discovered by Ulysses at the court of Lycomedes; *do.* The traveling Musicians; *after A. Ostade;* very fine. Two Men, and a Woman holding a Glass; *do.* The Skaters; *do.* The Surgeon; *after A. Brower.* A Man playing on the Violin, others singing; *do.* A Landscape, called the Attack of the Convoy; *after P. de Laer.* Another Landscape, called the Coach robbed; *do.* The Lime-kiln; *do.* A set of four Landscapes; *after Berghem.* Another set of four Landscapes; *do.*

VISSCHER, JOHN, was the younger brother of Cornelius V., born at Amsterdam in 1636. He was probably instructed by his brother, whose style he followed, though his plates are more forwarded with the point, and his style of etching is uncommonly picturesque and effective. Although he did not possess the extensive talents of Cornelius in design and in historical engraving, he equalled him in landscape, and some indeed prefer him before his brother in this branch; his landscapes after Berghem, Ostade, and Wouwerman are among the happiest productions of the art, and rank him among the most eminent engravers of his country. He also engraved some portraits, which show that he handled the graver with ability and facility. Of his numerous prints, the following are the most deserving of notice:

PORTRAITS.

John de Uytenbogaert; *Joh. de Visscher, sc.* Peter Proelius, Minister of the Gospel at Amsterdam. Abraham vander Hulst, Vice-Admiral of Holland. Peter Paul Rubens; *after Vandyck.* Michael de Ruyter, Admiral of Holland; *after Berchmans.* Portrait of a Negro, holding a Bow and Arrow in his hand; after a design by *Cornelius Visscher.*

SUBJECTS AND LANDSCAPES AFTER VARIOUS MASTERS.

Peasants playing at Trictrac; *after A. Ostade.* A Woman spinning and Man reeling; *do.* Peasants dancing; called Ostade's Ball; *do.* Peasants regaling at the door of an Ale-house; *do.* A Country Wedding, called Ostade's Bride; *do.* Several Peasants dancing in a Cottage, called Berghem's Ball; *after Berghem.* A set of four Landscapes, the Four Times of the Day; *do.* Several sets of Landscapes with figures and animals; *do.* A set of six plates of Figures and Animals; *after K. du Jardin.* A set of four plates of various Subjects; *after P. van Laer.* These prints have been sometimes incorrectly attributed to Cornelius Visscher. Several landscapes, &c.; *after Ph. Wouwerman.* A set of twelve Landscapes and Views; *after P. van Goyen.* A set of twelve Landscapes and Sea-ports; *after Herm. Swanevelt.*.

VISSCHER, Lambert. According to Huber, this artist was a brother of the preceding, and flourished about 1664. He went to Italy, and resided some years at Rome and Florence. In conjunction with Cornelius Bloemaert and Francis Spierre, he engraved several plates from the paintings of Pietro da Cortona, in the Florentine Gallery. He also engraved a few portraits, among which is one of Maria Theresa of Austria, Queen of France, *after Vanloo.*

VISSCHER, Nicholas John, was of the same family as the preceding, and flourished at Amsterdam about 1600. He engraved some portraits and other subjects after the Dutch masters. We have by him also a variety of etchings of small landscapes and views, with figures and animals, which are executed in a spirited manner. He usually marked his prints with the above monogram, composed of the initials C. I. V., the first letter signifying Class, an abbreviation of Nicholas.

VISSCHER, Theodore, a Dutch painter, born at Haerlem in 1650. He studied under Nicholas Berghem, whose style he imitated. He went to Italy, where he resided some years, and was called by his countrymen, from his dissipated habits, *Slempop.* His best pictures are painted in a superior manner, and much resemble the admirable works of Berghem; others appear to be the productions of inebriety and negligence. His death is variously placed in 1699 and 1707.

VISSELLET, M., an engraver who flourished about 1600. Dumesnil describes forty-three wooden cuts by him of subjects taken from the New Testament. They are executed in a coarse manner, resembling the wood cuts of J. Stella, from which they seem to have been copied. Some of them are marked MV. F., and one is signed *M. Vissellet, F.*

VITALBA, Giovanni, an Italian engraver, who studied under Joseph Wagner at Venice. He went to England in 1765, where he was employed by Boydell to engrave several plates, among which are Cupid with two Satyrs, *after Agostino Caracci;* a pair, Spring and Summer, *after Filippo Lauri;* Herodias with the Head of St. John, *after L. Pasinelli.* He was living in 1790.

VITALI, Alessandro, a painter born at Urbino in 1580, and died in 1630. He was the scholar and imitator of Federigo Baroccio. Lanzi says he copied the Annunciation of Loreto by Baroccio in such a manner that it might be easily mistaken for the original picture. "Baroccio was pleased with his talents, and willingly retouched some of his pictures, and probably favored him in this way in his St. Agnes in the cathedral, and St. Augustine, in the church of the Eremitani, at Urbino, in which he may be said to have surpassed himself."

VITALI, Candido, a painter born at Bologna in 1680. He was brought up in the school of Carlo Cignani, and by the advice of his instructor, who was always attentive to the particular genius of his disciples, he devoted himself to painting animals, birds, flowers, and fruit. His pictures of these subjects were greatly admired at Bologna and throughout all Italy, for his tasteful composition, beauty of coloring, and delicacy of penciling. He died in 1753.

VITALI, Giuseppe, a painter of Bologna, who flourished about 1700. He studied under Giovanni Gioseffo dal Sole, and painted history with some reputation. He executed some works for the churches of Bologna, the principal of which are, the Annunciation, in S. Antonio; St. Petronio, in S.S. Sebastiano e Rocco; and the Martyrdom of St. Cecilia, in the church dedicated to that saint. He was living in 1720.

VITE, Antonio, a painter of Pistoja, who flourished in 1463. He executed some works for the churches of his native city, and of Pisa, in the dry style of the time.

VITE, Timoteo, called also Timoteo della Vite di Urbino, a painter born at Urbino, according to Vasari, in 1470, and died in 1524. Lanzi says, "Timoteo della Vite of Urbino, after some years spent in studying under Francesco Francia at Bologna, (he remained there till he was twenty-six years old), returned to his native city, and thence repaired to the Academy, which his countryman and relative Raffaello had opened in the Vatican. He assisted Raffaello at the Pace, in the fresco of the sibyls, of which he retained the cartoons; and after some time, for some cause or other, he returned to Urbino, and there passed the rest of his days. He brought with him to Rome a method of painting which partook much of the manner of the early masters, as seen in some of his Madonnas at the Palace Bonaventura, and the Chapter of Urbino; and the Discovery of the Cross in the church of the Conventuali at Pesaro. He improved his style under Raffaello, and acquired from him much of his grace, attitudes and colors, although he always remained a limited inventor, with a certain timidity of touch, more correct than vigorous. His best works are the Conception at the Osservanti, at Urbino; and the Noli me Tangere, in the church of S. Angelo at Cagli." He died in 1524. His name is sometimes written *Viti* and *Vita.*

VITE, Pietro della, is supposed to have been the brother of the preceding, in whose style he painted, though in a very inferior manner. Lanzi conjectures that he is the same as Il Prete di Urbino, mentioned by Baldinucci, as a relative, and one of the heirs of Raffaelle.

VITE, Giovanni della. See Miel.

VITERBO, Fra Mariotto da, an old painter, born at Viterbo, of whom little is known. According to Della Valle, he was employed in the cathedral at Orvieto in 1444. Little now remains from his hand.

VITERBO, Tarquinio da, a painter of Viterbo, who, according to Baglioni, flourished at Rome in the pontificate of Pope Paul V. He excelled in landscapes, which were decorated with figures by his friend Giovanni Zanna, a Roman. They wrought in conjunction, and their works were held in considerable estimation.

VITO, Niccola di, an old Neapolitan painter, who studied under Antonio Solario, called Zingaro. Lanzi says he may be called the Buffalmacco of his school, from his singular humor and eccentric invention, though otherwise an artist deserving little commendation. He flourished about 1440.

VITTORIA, Alessandro, a distinguished Italian sculptor and architect, was born at Trento in 1525. He studied at Venice under Sansovino, and afterwards practiced for many years in the Venetian states. In statuary and modelling, Milizia says he attained such excellence as yielded only to that of Michael Angelo. In Venice he executed many works both in public and private, especially the statues and ornaments on the staircase of the Library of St. Mark, in the Ducal Palace, the Council Hall, and different churches. Vittoria also executed many busts, and various sculptures in other cities, among which is the monument of General Contarini, in the church del Santo at Padua. As an architect, he completed the church of S. Giuliano at Venice, the chapel of S. Fantino, and other works of Sansovino; also the chapel and altar of the Rosario, in S. Giovanni e Paolo; the monument of Priuli in S. Salvatore; the Oratory of S. Girolamo, with superb statues in bronze and in marbles; and the magnificent Palazzo Balbi, near the grand canal. He died in 1608.

VITRINGA, Wigerus, generally called William, a Dutch painter, of whom little is known, except that he painted marines in the manner of Backhuysen, who is supposed to have been his instructor. Some of his storm pieces are excellent. He also excelled in drawings in India ink, washed with bistre; some of these are signed with his name and dated about 1652. The accounts as to the time of his birth and death are very contradictory. Immerzeel and Balkema, say he was born at Leeuwarde in 1657, the latter that he died in 1721; others say he was living in 1744.

VITRUVIUS. See Pollio.

VITRULIO, a Venetian painter, of whom nothing is known except by his works, which are highly commended by Lanzi, who says that "several of his works bearing his signature, are the ornament of Monte Novissimo at Venice. He must be referred to the age of Titian, and seems to have lived in the time of Bonifazio, and to have been his competitor." Some of his pictures are mentioned in the *Guida di Venezia*.

VITUS, Domenico, an Italian engraver, of whom little is known. He is said to have been born about 1536, and to have become a religious of the monastery of Vallombrosa, in the Appenines, in the prime of life. He engraved some plates, in which he imitated Agostino de Musis, called Veneziano, from which circumstance he is supposed to have studied with that master. This however is an error, as Veneziano died about 1536. His prints possess considerable merit. Among others are the following:

St. Bartholomew; inscribed, *Dom. Vitus ordinis Valisumbrosæ Monachus excidit Romæ.* 1576. St. Joachim holding a Censer; *after A. del. Sarto.* Jupiter and Calisto; inscribed, *Dominicus V. F.* A River God; *after the antique.* A set of small plates, representing the Passion of our Saviour, with borders, ornamented with birds, beasts, &c. A set of plates from the Antique Statues; *Dom. Vitus, fec.*

VIVARES, Francis, a French engraver, born at Montpellier about 1712. After studying in his own country he went to London, where he became the pupil of J. B. Chatelain. Being a man of genius, he improved upon the style of his instructor, and became one of the most eminent landscape engravers of his time. He was particularly successful in his plates after Claude Lorraine, in which he preserved much of the air and picturesque beauty which distinguish the productions of that great painter. He died in London in 1782. His prints amount to about 150; among them are the following:

A set of four Views of Ruins; *after J. Smith.* Eight Views in Derbyshire; *after Thos. Smith of Derby.* A Landscape, called the Hop-gatherers; *after Geo. Smith.* A Landscape; *after Gainsborough.* A View in Holland, by moonlight; *after vander Neer.* A Land-storm; *after Gaspar Poussin.* A Tempest, with the history of Jonas; *do.* A Landscape, Morning; *after Claude Lorraine.* The Companion, Evening; *do.* The Enchanted Castle; *do.* A View in the Environs of Naples; *do.*

VIVARINI, da Murano. There was a family of artists of this name who flourished at Murano, about whom there is considerable discrepancy among writers. We shall, therefore, condense Lanzi's account. "The first among the Vivarini mentioned by historians is Luigi, by whom a painting is cited in the church of S. Giovanni e Paolo, at Murano, representing our Redeemer bearing his Cross, dated 1414.

"Next to this artist, according to Ridolfi and Zanetti, are Giovanni and Antonio Vivarini, who flourished about 1440. The authority they adduce for this is another piece in S. Pantaleone, inscribed, *Zuane e Antonio da Muran pense* 1444. But this Giovanni, if I mistake not, is the same who signs on another picture at Venice, *Joannes de Alemania, et Antonius de Muriano, pinxit*, or as it is written on another at Padua, *Antonio de Muran e Zohan Alamanus pinxit.* This Giovanni, therefore, was a German by birth, and the companion of Antonio, and traces of a foreign style are perceptible in his paintings. The reason for his omitting to insert his country in the picture in S. Pantaleone, arose, I suspect, from the fact, that his name and acquaintance with Antonio, were too well known to admit of doubt.

"After the year 1447 there is no more mention made of Giovanni, but only of Antonio, sometimes alone, and sometimes together with some other of the Vivarini. Thus, his name is subscribed alone in the church of S. Antonio Abate at Pesaro, upon an altar-piece of the Titular Saint, surrounded by the figures of three young martyrs, with some smaller paintings attached, the production of a very animated colorist and displaying forms inferior to none in the school of Murano. I have seen two other specimens, in which he is mentioned together with a second Vivarini. The least excellent of these is in the church of S. Francesco Grande at Padua, consisting of a Madonna with some saints in several compartments, inscribed *Anno* 1451, *Antonius et Bartholomeus fratres de Murano pinxerunt hoc opus.* Similar to this, the two brothers had produced another in the preceding year in the Certosa at Bologna, where it is still in a high state of preservation, beyond any other specimen I have seen belonging to the family. There is much in each figure in the whole piece, which is worthy of commendation; features dignified and devout, appropriate dresses, care in the disposition of the hair and beards, united to a warm and brilliant coloring.

"It would appear that Bartolomeo was held in less account than Antonio, until the discovery of oil painting; on its being introduced into Venice, he was one of the first to profit by it, and towards the period when the two Bellini appeared, was held in pretty high repute. The first specimen by him in oil, exists at the church of S. Giovanni e Paolo, and exhibits among other saints, P. San Agostino, with the date 1473. From that period he continued to distinguish himself, producing a great number of pieces, both in oil and in water colors, sometimes with more, and at others with less care, but always in the ancient taste for subdividing the altar-piece into several compartments, in each of which he represented separate heads or entire figures. These he often signed Vivarino, with the date, and occasionally added a finch or linnet in allusion to his name. In his last work, representing Christ risen from the dead, in the church of S. Giovanni, at Bragora, the date 1498, which Boschini read, is no longer apparent, but it is a piece which vies in every part with the best Venetian artists of that period.

"Cotemporary with Bartolomeo was Luigi (the younger,) Vivarini, one of whose productions was seen by Zanetti, in a collection of paintings dated 1490, and appeared to him strongly approaching, in point of taste, to the best style of the former. There is a half-length figure of the Saviour in the R. Pinacoteca, at Milan, a work finished with such care that it may challenge comparison with the productions of the cotemporary painters; it is inscribed *Alovisius Vivarinus de Muriano pinxit,* 1498. To Luigi, also, must undoubtedly be ascribed the altar-piece bearing his name in the church of S. Francesco, at Trevigi. There is also another at the Battuti, in Belluno, representing Sts. Piero, Girolamo and others, which cost that school 100 ducats, besides the expenses of the artist who attached his name to it. But superior to every other of his existing specimens, is that fine picture in the school of San Girolamo, at Venice, in which he represented a history of the Titular Saint, in emulation with Giovanni Bellini, whom he here equalled, and of Carpaccio, whom he surpassed.'

VIVIANI, Il. See Codagora.

VIVIANI, Antonio, called Il Sordo, a painter born at Urbino or Ancona, (for writers disagree,) who, according to Baglioni, was a scholar and imitator of Federigo Baroccio, and flourished at Rome in the pontificate of Paul V. There are also notices of him at Genoa, but there is considerable contradiction and uncertainty about him.

VIVIANI, Lodovico, a painter of Urbino, who, according to the Guida di Urbino, flourished in 1650. Lanzi says, there is a tradition at Urbino, that he was a brother or cousin of Antonio V.; and that he sometimes imitates Baroccio, as in his St. Girolamo, in the Cathedral, and sometimes approaches the Venetian style, as in his Epiphany at the monastery della Torre, at Urbino.

VIVIANI, Ottavio, a painter born at Brescia in 1599, and died in 1674, though there is some discrepancy on this point, and some uncertainty whether these dates should apply to him, or to Viviano Codagora, with whom he is very generally confounded. They both painted perspective and architectural pieces and landscapes, enriched with superb ruins and architecture, but Codagora studied in the Roman school, and was far superior to Viviani, who was educated in the Venetian. His instructor in architecture and perspective was Tommaso Sandrini, at Brescia, and in landscape, Agostino Tassi at Genoa. His pictures usually represent the remains of ancient edifices, selected and arranged for picturesque effect in a pleasing landscape, and generally show judgment and taste, though the composition is sometimes too much crowded, and perhaps overloaded with ornament. He was excellent in figures, and used them to great advantage in showing the relative size and height of his buildings and objects. There is a great variety in his coloring, too much for harmony, but producing a striking effect; and such pictures being intended for decoration, the richness does not offend. He had an excellent knowledge of perspective and chiaro-scuro, which he exhibited on all occasions, but time has darkened his shadows and given too solemn a gloom to his temples and arcades.

VIVIEN, Joseph, an eminent French painter, born at Lyons in 1657. He studied under Charles le Brun, and for some time painted portraits in oil with considerable success; but he afterwards adopted the method of painting in crayons, which he carried to a perfection unknown before his time. He not only obtained an excellent likeness, but his heads exhibited uncommon life, nature, and truthfulness of expression; his carnations were fresh and pure, his touch vigorous and spirited, the general tone of his pictures tender and harmonious, and he gave his figures an extraordinary relief. He particularly excelled in female portraits, to which he gave great grace and elegance in the airs of the heads and attitudes and an exquisite velvety softness in his tints. He frequently painted his portraits in the historical style, and the back-grounds decorated with agreeable vistas, or embellished with fabulous or mythological figures. He acquired great reputation, and was called by his countrymen, *the French Vandyck.* In 1701 he was chosen a member of the French Academy of Painting. He passed the latter part of his life in the service of the Elector of Bavaria, for whom he painted some of his choicest works. His portrait by himself is placed in the Florentine Gallery. His famous portrait of Fenelon is in the Louvre. He died in 1735.

VIVIER, JEAN DU, a French medalist, who flourished at Paris in the first half of the 18th century. In 1718 he was chosen a member of the Academy, and was appointed medalist to Louis XV. in 1735.

VIVIER, G. DU, a Dutch engraver, who flourished about 1666. Little is known of him except by a few prints bearing his signature, of which the following are described by Dumesnil in Le Peintre Graveur, tom iii.

1. Christ in the Sepulchre; *Anton. van Heuvel invent.; G. de Vivier, fecit.* Four verses in Dutch, beginning, "*Hier is het leven soet.*"
2. The Four Evangelists, in one piece, no mark.
3. The Temptation of St. Anthony; *Anton. van Heuvel invent.; G. de Vivier fecit.*
4. Thetis and Chiron; the Centaur holding the infant Achilles in his arms; no mark.
5. A Flemish Kitchen; *Ant. V. Heuvel pinxit; G. du Vivier fecit.*
6. The Flageolet Player; no mark.
7. The Tippler; in the manner of Rembrandt; no mark.
8. A Landscape outside of a fortified city; a winter scene. Many figures are skating, and otherwise amusing themselves on the ice; persons of condition, in coaches and on foot, dressed in the costume of the time of Louis XIII., or the minority of Louis XIV., are looking on; no mark.

VIVIO, JACOPO. This Italian artist flourished in the latter half of the 16th century, and distinguished himself by his models in colored wax. Fiorillo records a model by him in that style, of the Last Judgment, by Michael Angelo.

VLENGHELS, PHILIP, a Flemish painter, born at Antwerp, in 1620. Little is known of him. He is said to have painted history with reputation. He went to Paris, where he died in 1694.

VLERICK, PETER, a Flemish painter, born at Courtray in 1539. He was the son of a lawyer, who, perceiving in him a genius for painting, placed him under the instruction of William Snellaert, a painter in distemper. He afterwards became the disciple of Charles d'Ypres, a historical painter of some note who had studied in Italy, with whom he continued two years, but whose capricious disposition constrained him to quit his studio sooner than he intended. He had, however, made such progress that he was able to live on the proceeds of his talents. He traveled through France and met with such encouragement during a short residence at Paris, that he was enabled to proceed to Italy. At Venice he had the good fortune to secure the friendship and instruction of Tintoretto. After a residence of four years in that city, he went to Rome, where he designed after the antique and the works of the great masters, and sketched the beautiful scenery and views on the banks of the Tyber, and proceeding to Naples he designed the prospects about that city and Puteoli. During his residence in those cities, he executed some historical pictures both in oil and distemper, which gained him considerable reputation. In 1568 he returned to Flanders and settled at Tournay, where he resided the remainder of his life. He distinguished himself by many excellent works, the principal of which, according to Van Mander, were the Brazen Serpent, Judith with the head of Holofernes, the Four Evangelists, and the Crucifixion. In all his works the manner of Tintoretto is observable. He was skilled in perspective and architecture, with which he enriched his backgrounds. His design is correct, his coloring rich and harmonious, and his execution prompt and vigorous. He died in 1581.

VLIEGER, SIMON DE, a Dutch painter, born at Amsterdam about 1612. It is not known by whom he was instructed, but he acquired considerable reputation in his time as a painter of marine subjects and landscapes. He was the instructor of the younger Vande Velde, and though his fame was eclipsed by the brilliant talents of his disciple, his works possess great merit, and are found in the choicest collections. He executed some spirited and masterly etchings from his own designs, a description of twenty of which may be found in Bartsch (Peintre Graveur, tom. i.), representing views in Holland, rivers, canals, and animals; some of them approach the style of Waterloo. He died in or about 1670.

VLIET, WILLIAM VAN, a Dutch painter, born at Delft in 1584, and died there in 1642. Little is known of him, but he is said to have painted history and portraits with considerable reputation. His touch was firm and facile, and his coloring excellent.

VLIET, HENRY VAN, was the nephew of the preceding, born at Delft in or about 1608. He learned the principles of the art from his uncle, but afterwards studied with Mirevelt, the eminent portrait painter. For some time he practiced portraiture, in the style of that master, but he gradually abandoned it for another branch, in which he distinguished himself. He painted perspective views of the interiors of churches and temples, in the style of Emanuel de Wit, and his best pieces in this line are accounted little inferior to the admirable productions of that master. He frequently represented these subjects by torch-light, producing a picturesque and pleasing effect. He decorated his pictures with a great number of small figures, correctly drawn, and touched with neatness and spirit. He also painted moonlight scenes in a very agreeable manner. The times of his birth and death are not certainly known. Some say he died in 1646.

JGV or JV VLIET, JOHN GEORGE VAN, a Dutch painter and engraver, born at Delft, in 1610. He was one of the numerous disciples of Rembrandt. Of his works as a painter, little is known, but there are about ninety prints by him, mostly from his own designs, and after Rembrandt, with a few after J. Lievens. They are executed in the manner of his instructor, and produce a surprising effect; the lights are broad and clear, and the shadows dark. His drawing, however, is very incorrect, and his draperies clumsy and mannered, but notwithstanding these defects, his prints are held in considerable estimation. He sometimes signed them with his name, at others marked them with the above monogram of his initials, J. G. V. The following are his best prints; for a complete list, the reader is referred to Bartsch and Nagler:

PORTRAITS AND HEADS; AFTER REMBRANDT.

Bust of a Man, with his face in shadow. 1634. Bust of an old Man, with a turban and aigrette. The Head of a Warrior. An old Man with his hands joined, apparently in great affliction. 1634. Bust of an Oriental Character, with a fur cap. An old Woman reading. One of his best prints.

SUBJECTS AFTER REMBRANDT.

Lot and his Daughters; very fine. The Baptism of the Eunuch. St. Jerome praying in a cavern, with a book and crucifix. This is the finest print.

SUBJECTS AFTER J. LIEVENS.

Jacob obtaining his Father's Blessing instead of Esau. Susanna and the Elders. The Resurrection of Lazarus.

SUBJECTS FROM HIS OWN DESIGNS.

An Assembly of Peasants regaling. The Rat-catcher. A set of twenty-two plates of the Arts and Trades.

VOEIRIOT. See WOEIRIOT.

VOERST, ROBERT VANDER, a Dutch engraver, born at Arnheim, about 1596, though Zani places his birth in 1610, and his death in 1669. The first of Zani's statements is evidently erroneous, as he resided in England several years, where he executed quite a number of plates of portraits, mostly after Vandyck, the latest date found on which is 1635. He acquired so much reputation in that country that he was appointed engraver to the king. His plates are executed with the graver, in a clear, neat style, resembling that of Giles Sadeler, with whom he probably studied. The following are the principal plates he engraved in England:

Charles I. and his Queen; on one plate; *after Vandyck.* Prince Rupert. James Stewart, Duke of Lennox; *after Geldorp.* Robert, Earl of Lindsey; *after Mirevelt.*—Philip, Earl of Pembroke; *after Vandyck.* Ernest, Count Mansfeld; *do.* Simon Vouet, Painter; *do.* His own Portrait; *do.* Edward, Lord Littleton. James, Marquis of Hamilton. Henry Rich, Earl of Holland. William Fielding, Earl of Denbigh. Sir Kenelm Digby; *after Vandyck.* Inigo Jones; very fine; *do.* Christian, Duke of Brunswick; *do.* Sir George Carew; *do.* Elizabeth, Queen of Bohemia; *after Gerard Honthorst.*

VOET, ALEXANDER, a Flemish engraver, born at Antwerp in 1613. He executed quite a number of plates after the Flemish masters, in which he emulated the style of Paul Pontius; hence he is supposed to have been the disciple of that master. Though he handled the graver with ease and facility, his drawing is incorrect, and the general effect of his prints is far inferior to that of his model. The following are some of his best prints:

Judith with the Head of Holofernes; *after Rubens.* The Holy Family returning from Egypt; *do.* The Virgin and Infant, to whom Angels are presenting Fruit; *do.* The Martyrdom of St. Andrew; *do.* Seneca in the Bath; *do.* The Entombing of Christ; *after Vandyck.* Folly, holding a Cat; *after Jordaens.* The Card-players; *after De Vos.*

VOET, CHARLES BOSCHAERT, a Dutch painter, born at Zwolle in 1670. He was instructed in the rudiments of the arts by his elder brother, who was a Burgomaster of the city, and though not a professional artist, had learned drawing, and painting in water-colors, to assist in his studies of botany and natural history, and was a correct designer of flowers, plants, birds, and insects. Charles greatly improved himself by an attentive study of nature, and became one of the ablest artists of his time in painting flowers, fruit, plants, birds, and objects of still-life. His pictures are ingeniously composed, and exquisitely finished; his coloring is extremely natural, and his pencil delicate; some of his birds are esteemed scarcely inferior to those of Hondekoeter. He studied everything from nature, and cultivated in his garden the most beautiful flowers and exotics for models. Descamps asserts that he had made such proficiency, and acquired so high a reputation, at the age of nineteen, that the Earl of Portland, the favorite of William III., took him under his protection to England, where he was much employed by that nobleman, and patronized by the king. Bryan, however, doubts the truth of this story, as his name is not mentioned in Lord Orford's Anecdotes. It is certain, however, that he was much employed by William III. in decorating his palace at Loo. He died at the Hague in 1745.

VOGEL, BERNARD, a German engraver, born at Nuremberg in 1683, and is said to have died in 1737. He resided chiefly at Augsburg, and executed a number of plates, with the graver and in mezzotinto, among which is the portrait of John Kupetzky, dated 1737; and that of Christopher Weigel, *after Kupetzky*, dated 1735.

VOGHTER, HENRY, a German engraver on wood, who, according to Professor Christ, was born at Strasburg about 1507. Zani says he was born in 1497, and died in 1537. He is said to have imitated the style of Albert Durer with considerable success. He executed the cuts for a Drawing Book, entitled, "A book of the extraordinary and marvellous Art, very useful to all painters, sculptors, and goldsmiths," &c., printed at Strasburg in 1540. He marked his prints with the above monogram. Some say there was a Henry Voghter the Younger, who was born at Strasburg in 1513, and operated in 1545. There does not seem any good ground for such a supposition.

VOGLAR, CARLO, a Dutch painter, born, according to Pascoli, at Maestricht in 1653, and died at Rome in 1695. He excelled in painting flowers, fruit, and dead game, particularly the latter, and his works were greatly admired. He is sometimes called Carlo da' Fiori, from the beauty of his flowers. He is not mentioned by the Dutch writers, as he passed his artistic life in Italy.

VOISARD, ETIENNE CLAUDE, a French engraver, born at Paris in 1746. He engraved some plates after the French masters, which are executed with the graver, in a neat and pleasing style.

VOLANT, ANTOINE, a French artist, mentioned by Papillon as an engraver on wood, who operated in 1564. He does not specify any of his works. There was also a George Volant, a wood engraver, who was living in 1600.

VOLCKAERT, NICHOLAS, an old Dutch painter, born at Haerlem in 1450, and died there in 1519. He excelled in distemper, and designed in the dry, Gothic style of his time and country. It is said that he was much employed in making designs for painters on glass. Little or nothing remains from his hand. Some say he had a son named Klaas, who flourished from about 1480 to 1500; doubtless an error, Klaas, Klaus, and Class being merely contractions of Nicholas.

VOLIGNY, DE TONNERES, a French engraver, of whom little is known, except that he died in 1699. Florent le Comte mentions an engraver named Voligny, but whose principal talent, he says, was in drawing portraits with a pen, which he afterwards washed with India ink in a soft and delicate manner, that was greatly admired—probably the same artist.

VOLLERDT, or VOLLAERT, JOHN CHRISTIAN, or CHRISTOPHER, a German painter, born at

Leipsic in 1708, and died in 1769. He was a pupil of Alexander Thiele, and painted small landscapes, and views on the Rhine and in Switzerland, in a pleasing style.

VOLLEVENS, John, a Dutch painter, born at Gertruydenberg in 1649. He first studied under Nicholas Maas, and afterwards with John de Baan, one of the most eminent portrait painters of his time, with whom he continued eight years, and whom he nearly equaled. On the death of that master, he succeeded to most of his practice. The prince of Courland was his first patron, and procured him the advantage of painting all the officers of his regiment. The Prince of Nassau next employed him to paint a full-length portrait of himself, as large as life, which he executed in such an admirable manner as to effectually establish his reputation, and he soon became one of the most popular and most employed artists of his time. He gave to his portraits a striking resemblance, and life-like air and expression; his coloring was clear and chaste, and his touch bold and free. He died at the Hague in 1728. He had a son of the same name, whom he instructed in the art, and who was a good portrait painter, but there are no particulars recorded of him, except that he is supposed to have passed some time in England.

VOLPATI, Giovanni Battista, a painter born at Bassano, in 1633, and died there in 1706. According to Lanzi, he executed many works for his native state, in a style closely resembling that of Giulio Carpioni. He also left several MS. treatises on the pictoric art, which are preserved in the rich and select library of Count Giuseppe Remondini, and prove him an able theorist.

VOLPATO, Giovanni, a distinguished modern Italian designer and engraver, was born at Bassano, in 1738. Having learned from his mother the mode of tapestry embroidery, he at first practiced that art; but at the same time he occasionally occupied himself with engraving, without any regular instruction, and published some prints under the assumed name of Renard. The success of these attempts determined him to adopt engraving as a profession; he accordingly settled at Venice, and entered the school of Bartolozzi. According to Huber, he engraved many good prints, after Piazzetta, Maiotto, Amiconi, M. Ricci, Zuccarelli, and others. He afterwards visited Rome, and was employed as its principal engraver by a society of Dilettanti, who undertook to re-engrave all the works of Raffaelle in the Vatican. Volpato engraved, on a large scale, seven of the great works of Raffaelle in the stanze of the Vatican; an eighth, the Mass of Bolsena, was engraved by his son-in-law and pupil, Raphael Morghen. The prints were published colored, as well as plain; they are a very splendid and valuable set of engravings. Skilful in designing, and expert in the use of the graver and dry point, he gave to his prints great precision and powerful effect. He and Morghen were the best engravers in Italy, at the end of the 18th century. Volpato was employed by Gavin Hamilton, upon his *Scuola Pitture d' Italia*, and also published many prints after the celebrated Italian masters, among which are the Farnese Gallery, after Annibale Caracci; two Prophets and two Sibyls, after the paintings by Michael Angelo in the Sistine chapel. He also published many colored landscape etchings of Roman views, &c., in partnership with P. du Cros; and a set of fourteen views of the galleries of the Museo Clementino, with all its works of art. Volpato died at Rome in 1803. Huber, who wrote before his death, enumerates, as his principal works, 166 engravings. Among others, are the following:

PLATES ENGRAVED FOR THE COLLECTION OF G. HAMILTON.

The four Sibyls; from the paintings by *Raffaelle*, in the church of S. Maria della Pace. The Marriage of Alexander and Roxana; *after Raffaelle*. Modesty and Vanity; *after L. da Vinci*. Perseus and Andromeda; *after Polidoro da Caravaggio*. Christ praying on the Mount; *after Correggio*. Mary Magdalene at the feet of Christ, in the house of Simon the Pharisee; *after P. Veronese*. The Marriage of Cana; *after Tintoretto*. The Gamesters; *after M. Angelo Caravaggio*.

SUBJECTS AFTER GAVIN HAMILTON.

The Death of Lucretia. Innocence. Juno. Hebe. Melancholy. Gaiety.

ILLUMINATED PRINTS AFTER THE PAINTINGS BY RAFFAELLE.

The School of Athens. The Dispute on the Sacrament. Heliodorus driven from the Temple of Jerusalem. Attila stopped by the appearance of St. Peter and St. Paul. St. Peter delivered from Prison. Mount Parnassus. The Burning of the Borgo Vecchio. The Miracle of the Mass at Bolsena. This plate was engraved by his disciple *Raphael Morghen*.

VOLPI, Stefano, a painter of Siena, who flourished there in the first part of the 17th century. Lanzi supposes that he was a scholar of Cristofano Casolani, as he executed some frescos from the designs of that master, for the churches in his native city.

VOLTERRA, Francesco di. This architect, according to Milizia, was originally a carver in wood, but devoted himself to architecture, and erected, among other edifices, the church of S. Giacomo degli Incurabili, at Rome; the Lancillotti palace; and the nave of the church della Scala, which has a stately appearance, but a number of defects in the details, such as the projecting of entablatures, and the carving of pilasters. He died in 1588.

VOLTERRA, Daniele di. See Ricciarelli.

VOLTERRANO, Il. See Franceschini.

VOLTRI, Niccolo da, an old painter, born at Voltri in the Genoese territory, who flourished in 1401. He was a follower of Giotto, and an artist of distinction in his time; but Lanzi says there is no known surviving work by him.

VOLVINO, a Milanese artist of the 10th century, who produced the celebrated *Palliotto d' Oro*, or gold pallium or mantle. Lanzi says, "he produced the very celebrated altar-piece, wrought in gold, in the church of S. Ambrogio, at Milan; a work which may be pronounced, in point of style, equal to the finest specimens of the *dittici*, or small ivory altar-pieces, that the museums of sacred art can afford."

VONCK, or VONK, C., a Dutch painter, who flourished in the last half of the 17th century. Nothing is known of him, except by his works. He painted birds, animals, and objects of still-life, in the manner of Melchior Hondekoeter and Francis Snyders, which are said to possess extraordinary merit, and are found in the choicest collections. There was another painter of this name, of less merit, who resided at Middleburg about 1750. He painted the same subjects, in the manner of Artus

Schouman, of whom he was probably a pupil. He was living in 1778.

VOOGD, Hendrick, a Dutch painter, born at Amsterdam about 1766. He studied under Juriaan Andriessen, with whom he made such progress that M. D. Versteeg took him under his protection, and furnished him the means of visiting Italy. He designed the beautiful scenery in the environs of Rome with great assiduity. He sent one of his pictures to the "Societé des Sciences," at Haerlem, which procured him a pension of fifty ducats per annum, for three years. Thus encouraged, he prosecuted his studies with ardor, and acquired so much distinction for his beautiful landscapes of Italian scenery, which he enriched with ruins, and ancient temples and edifices, and peopled with appropriate figures from ancient history or mythology, that he was called the *Dutch Claude*. He frequently sent his pictures to the exhibitions in his native city, where they were admired greatly, but whether he ever revisited his own country is not mentioned. He died at Rome, in 1839.

VOORHOUT, John, a Dutch painter, born at Amsterdam in 1647. He first studied six years under Constantine Verhout, or Verbout (probably Voorhout, and his uncle), of Gouda, a painter of conversations and gallant assemblies. He next became the disciple of John van Noort, at Amsterdam, a reputable painter of history and portraits, with whom he continued five years more. He had already begun to distinguish himself, when the French army entered Holland, in 1672, and he sought refuge at Hamburg, where he met with the most flattering encouragement. On the restoration of peace, he returned to Amsterdam, where he found abundant employment till his death. He painted both history and portraits, and is ranked by Descamps among the ablest artists of his country. His historical subjects are usually selected from the Greek or Roman history, and he treated them with propriety and judgment. His works are highly esteemed, and are to be found in the choicest collections. He died at Amsterdam in 1710. The Dutch writers mention another John Voorhout, who painted similar subjects, and died in 1749—probably his son.

VOORT, Cornelius vander, a Dutch painter, born at Amsterdam in 1580, and died there in 1632, though some say he was a native of Antwerp. He excelled in portraits, which were admired for skillful arrangement, excellent likeness, and a fresh and natural tone of coloring.

VORONIKHIN, Andrei Nikophorovitch, a Russian architect, was born in 1760, among the peasantry of Count Alexander Stroganov. That nobleman, having heard of his talents in drawing, sent him to Moscow in 1777, in order to be properly educated as an artist; and he there received some instruction from Bazhenov and Kasakov, two eminent architects. He was then sent to travel with his patron's son, Count Paul Stroganov, and after visiting the southern provinces of Russia, Germany, and Switzerland, resided some time at Paris, laboring diligently to profit by this opportunity of pursuing his architectural studies. In 1790, he returned to St. Petersburg, and the protection of Stroganov soon brought him into notice and employment. In 1800, the Emperor Paul conceived the idea of building a magnificent Cathedral in the "Nevskii Prospect," to be dedicated to Our Lady of Kazan, and Voronikhin, who was then Professor in the Academy of Arts, was appointed architect. In the following year the first stone was laid by the Emperor Alexander; the edifice was completed and consecrated in 1815, and forms one of the finest architectural monuments in the city of the Czars. Voronikhin also erected many other edifices, public and private, among which were several villas at Gatchina and Pavlovsky. He died in 1814.

VORSTERMANS, John, a Dutch painter, born at Bommel in 1643. He was the son of a portrait painter, who instructed him in the rudiments of art, but having a genius for landscape, he studied under Hermann Zachtleven at Utrecht, and became one of the most admired landscape painters of his time. But great as his merit was, it fell short of his vanity. He went to Paris, where he assumed the title of Baron, and for a short time kept up the establishment of a person of rank. This extravagant course, however, could not last long, and his necessities soon compelled him to return to Holland. In 1672, on the approach of the French army, he removed to Nimeguen, where his talents recommended him to the patronage of the Marquis of Bethune, who employed him to collect some of the best works of art that could be obtained in Holland, and to paint several landscapes and views on the Rhine. Soon after the Restoration, he went to England, where he was employed by the king to paint a view of Windsor, and several other pieces, for which he demanded such an exorbitant price that he not only lost his patron, but the king's commissioners refused to allow him a moiety of what he demanded. Unable to support his extravagance, he was at length arrested for debt, and thrown into prison, where he remained till he was released by a contribution of some of his countrymen. On the accession of James II., Sir William Soames, being appointed ambassador to the Ottoman court, took Vorstermans in his train, with a view to employ him in painting the most remarkable scenes in the East, but that minister dying on the voyage, put an end to the project. Nothing more is known of Vorstermans, though he is supposed to have gone to Poland, whither he had been invited by his former patron, the Marquis of Bethune, before he left England.

Had Vorstermans been a prudent man, and his industry equal to his genius, he would have become one of the most famous painters of his country. He surpassed, by many degrees, all the landscape painters of his time, in neatness of touch and delicacy of finishing. His taste was Flemish; but he worked up his pictures in an exquisite manner, and enriched them with small figures, correctly designed, and touched with great neatness and spirit. His scenery is always well chosen, frequently taken from the borders of the Rhine, in which he constantly represents a large extent of country, diversified with hills, lawns, groves, and lovely windings of the river. His coloring is chaste and agreeable, and he was a perfect master of aerial perspective. The time of his death is not certainly known; some place it in 1699. His name is often written *Vosterman* and *Vostermans*.

V. or L. VORSTERMANS, Lucas, called the Elder, an eminent Flemish engraver, born at Antwerp about 1580. He first studied painting in the great school of Rubens, but by the advice of that master (who was quick to perceive the particular genius of his pupils, and careful to give it the right direction), he afterwards devoted himself entirely to engraving. No painter ever had the satisfaction of seeing so great a number of his best works engraved in so admirable a manner, as Rubens. He was surrounded by engravers of the greatest abilities, who worked immediately under his eye, and who had the advantage of his assistance and advice, which contributed in no small degree to the beauty and excellence of their prints. Of these, no one was more successful than Vorstermans. His drawing is correct, and his heads are full of expression. His plates are executed entirely with the graver, which he handled with great facility, though he was always more attentive to the general effect, than to neatness and regularity of execution; in his best prints he has transcribed, with surprising fidelity, the life and spirit of the original paintings. His plate of the Adoration of the Magi, after Rubens, is regarded as one of the finest productions of the art. He visited England in the reign of Charles I., where he resided eight years, from 1623 to 1631, and was employed by that monarch and the Earl of Arundel. The time of his death is not known. He usually signed his plates with his name in full, but he sometimes marked them with the above monogram of his initials, L. V. His prints are very numerous, of which the following is an ample list of the most esteemed. A full catalogue may be found in Bartsch:

PORTRAITS AFTER VANDYCK.

Charles I., King of England. Thomas Howard, Earl of Arundel. Isabella Clara Eugenia, Infanta of Spain. Gaston, Duke of Orleans. Ambrose Spinola, Governor of the Low Countries. Wolfgang William, Duke of Bavaria. Francis de Moncade, Count of Ossone. Nicholas Rockox, a Magistrate of Antwerp. Anthony Vandyck, Painter. Peter de Jode, the elder, Engraver. Charles de Mallerie, Engraver. James Callot, Engraver. Theodore Galle, Engraver. Wenceslaus Koeberger, Painter. Deodatus Delmont, Painter. Peter Steevens, Amateur, of Antwerp. John van Mildert, Statuary. Hubert vanden Enden, Painter. Lucas van Uden, Painter. Cornelius Sachtleven, Painter. Orazio Gentileschi, Painter. John Lievens, Painter and Engraver.

PORTRAITS AFTER VARIOUS MASTERS.

Thomas Howard, Duke of Norfolk; *after Holbein.* Sir Thomas More; *do.* Erasmus; *do.* The Emperor, Charles V.; *after Titian.* Charles, Duke of Bourbon; *do.* Charles de Longueval, Count of Busquoi; *after Rubens.*

SUBJECTS AFTER RUBENS.

The Fall of the Evil Angels. Lot and his Daughters leaving Sodom. Job tempted by his Wife, and tormented by Demons. Susanna and the Elders. The Nativity, or Adoration of the Shepherds. The Adoration of the Magi. One of his finest prints. The same subject, differently composed. The Holy Family, with St. Anne. Another Holy Family, in which the infant Christ is embracing the Virgin. The Return from Egypt. The Virgin and infant Christ, with St. John playing with a Lamb. The Tribute-Money. The Descent from the Cross. The first impressions of this fine print are before the address of *Corn. van Merlen.* The Angel appearing to the Holy Women at the Sepulchre. St. Francis receiving the Stigmata. The Martyrdom of St. Lawrence. Mary Magdalene renouncing the Vanities of the World. The Battle of the Amazons; a large print, on six sheets.

SUBJECTS AFTER VARIOUS MASTERS.

The Holy Family; *after Raffaelle.* The Entombing of Christ; *do.* St. George; *do.* Christ praying in the Garden; *after An. Caracci.* Lot and his Daughters; *after Orazio Gentileschi.* The Virgin and infant Christ, with two Pilgrims; *after M. Angelo da Caravaggio.*—Christ dead, supported on the lap of the Virgin, with Angels weeping; *after Vandyck.* St. Theresa; *do.* Christ bound to the Pillar; *after G. Segers.* The Death of St. Francis; *do.* St. Ignatius; *do.* The Fable of the Satyr, with the Peasant who blows hot and cold; *after J. Jordaens.* A Bear-hunt; *after F. Snyders.* A Concert, consisting of five persons, one of whom is a Girl playing on a Guitar; *after Adam de Coster,* being a companion to the Concert, engraved by *Bolswert; after Theodore Rombouts.*

VORSTERMANS, Lucas, the Younger, was the son of the preceding, born at Antwerp about 1605. Although he had the advantage of his father's instructions, his prints are far inferior in every respect, to the admirable productions of the elder Vorstermans. The following are considered his best prints:

PORTRAITS.

Lucas Vorsterman the elder; *after Vandyck.* Sir Hugh Cartwright; *after Diepenbeck.*

SUBJECTS AFTER VARIOUS MASTERS.

The Trinity; *after Rubens.* Part of the ceiling of Whitehall; *do.* The Virgin in the Clouds, surrounded by Angels; *after Vandyck.* The Satyr, and the Peasant blowing hot and cold; *after J. Jordaens.* This print greatly resembles that of the same subject engraved by his father. The Triumph of Riches; *after Holbein.* The greater part of the Plates for the book on Horsemanship, by the Duke of Newcastle. Several of the Plates in the collection called the Gallery of Teniers. Various other subjects from other masters, and some portraits from his own designs.

VOS, Peter de, a Flemish painter, who flourished at Antwerp in the first part of the 16th century. He painted history and portraits with reputation, and was elected a member of the Academy at Antwerp in 1519. He had two sons, whom he instructed in the art—Peter and Martin. Peter did not rise above mediocrity; Martin is the subject of the following article.

VOS, Martin de, was the son of the preceding, born at Antwerp according to the best authorities, in 1520, and died in 1604, aged eighty-four years; though some say he was born in 1531, and died in 1603. After receiving instruction from his father, he frequented the school of Francis Floris till he was twenty-three years old, when he went to Italy, and spent seven years at Rome, where he greatly improved his design by attentively studying the works of Raffaelle, and other great masters of the Roman school. He next went to Venice, to improve his coloring, where he had the good fortune to obtain the esteem and friendship of Tintoretto, who is said to have disclosed to him all the secrets relative to coloring, which he had either derived from Titian, or acquired by his own skill and experience, and to have explained to him the rules and principles on which he had founded his own practice. He also employed de Vos to paint the landscape in some of his works. Under the direction of his able instructor, de Vos soon became an excellent colorist, and he gained so much reputation, that he was employed by the illustrious family of the Medici, to paint several portraits. He also executed several historical works, which added to his reputation. After an absence of about eight years, he returned to his own country, whither the fame he had acquired in Italy had preceded him. He was received into the Academy at Antwerp in 1559, and executed several works for the churches, which established his reputation as one of the ablest artists of his time. He also excelled in portraits, in which branch he was much employed. He also received commissions for pictures to adorn the churches of other cities in the Netherlands. His principal works at Antwerp are the Marriage at Cana; the Incredulity of St. Thomas; the Miracle of the Loaves and Fishes; the Temptation of St. Anthony, in the Cathedral; and a fine picture of the Last Supper, in the church of St. James. He had a fruitful invention, composed with readiness, and wrought with facility; his manner resembled that of Tintoretto, but his composition had less variety, fire, and energy. His figures are often forced and exaggerated in their attitudes. Notwithstanding his long residence in Italy, he could never entirely divest himself of the peculiar characteristics of his native school. His works, both in portraiture and history, were numerous, and exerted considerable influence on the art in his time. In portraiture, he was the precursor of Rubens and Vandyck, who perhaps owe more to him than their admirers are willing to allow.

VOS, WILLIAM DE, was the nephew and scholar of Martin de Vos, whose style he followed, both in history and portraits, with distinction. His portrait was painted by Vandyck, among the eminent artists of his country, which he also etched, and it was finished with the graver by Bolswert. The times of his birth and death are not known.

VOS, PAUL DE, a Flemish painter, born at Aelst, about 1600. He is supposed to have been a disciple of Francis Snyders, as he painted battles, and huntings of the wild boar and other animals of the chase, in the style of that master; and his best works are esteemed little inferior to the admirable productions of that eminent artist. He traveled through Italy and Spain, and his works were everywhere admired, and he found abundant patronage. He was much employed by the King of Spain, and the Emperor of Germany; there are several of his finest works in the royal collection at Madrid, and in the palace of Bueno Retiro, which are deservedly held in the highest estimation. His animals, especially his dogs, are drawn with uncommon correctness and spirit, and his coloring is clear and harmonious. As he usually painted in a large size, his pictures were mostly the ornaments of magnificent halls, in the palaces of great personages. He died in 1654. He had a son named Paul de Vos, whom he instructed in the art, and who flourished at Aelst, in the latter part of the 17th century. He did not acquire much distinction.

VOS, CORNELIUS DE, was the son of Paul de Vos, born at Aelst in 1690, and died there in 1751. After being instructed in the art, he went to Italy, where he resided some time. On his return to Aelst, he painted history and portraits with reputation. There was another Cornelius de Vos, who was a scholar and imitator of Vandyck.

VOS, SIMON DE, a Flemish painter, born at Antwerp in 1603. He studied in the school of Rubens, under whom he became an eminent painter of history and portraits. He painted so much in the manner of his instructor, that some of his works in the churches at Antwerp have frequently been mistaken for the works of Rubens. Such are his picture of the Resurrection, in the Cathedral; the Descent from the Cross, in the church of St. Andrew; and St. Norbert receiving the Sacrament, in the abbey of St. Michael. Sir Joshua Reynolds highly commends this last picture, and speaks of him as a portrait painter, in the following terms: "De Vos was particularly excellent in portraits. There is, at Antwerp, his own portrait painted by himself, in black, leaning on the back of a chair, with a scroll in his hand, so highly finished in the broad style of Correggio, that nothing can exceed it." Simon de Vos was very diligent, and occupied himself continually in studying everything that might promote his knowledge, and he was one of the few who took pains to make the deepest researches into the true principles of the art. He painted equally well in large and in small size; his pencil is free, his touch light and firm, and his coloring lively and agreeable, producing a good effect. His figures are correctly designed, though sometimes a little too much constrained in the attitudes; and he often wanted dignity and elegance in his ideas, as well as grace in the airs of his heads. He sometimes painted pictures of the chase, in which he showed extraordinary power and truth. There is a fine specimen of his skill in this branch, in the collection of the Elector Palatine. The time of his death is not known; he was living in 1662.

VOS, LAMBERT DE. Little is known of this painter, except that he visited Turkey in 1574, and made many excellent water-color drawings of Turkish costume. A volume of these drawings was formerly preserved in the Gymnasium Library at Bremen, and it is probably there still.

VOS, DE. There were several other painters of this name, of little note, apparently of the same family, which continues down to the present day.

VOSMEER, James WOUTERS, a Dutch painter, born at Delft in 1584, and died there in 1641. It is not known under whom he studied, but he visited Italy, and on his return to Flanders painted landscapes, and especially fruit and flowers, with considerable reputation.

VOSTERMANS. See VORSTERMANS.

VOU, I. DE, a Dutch engraver, who flourished at Amsterdam about 1700, and engraved some plates of views and edifices in that city, which are etched and finished with the graver in a neat, clear style.

VOUET, SIMON. This eminent painter, generally considered the founder of the French school, was born at Paris in 1582. He was the son of Laurent Vouet, an obscure painter; and without the aid of better instruction than he could derive from his father, he made rapid advances in the art. The Biographie Universelle states that at the age of fourteen he was commissioned to visit England for the purpose of painting the portrait of a French noble, then residing in London. This performance gained Vouet considerable patronage. Baron de Sancy, French Ambassador to the Porte, took him, several years after, in his suite to Constantinople.—While there, he painted an excellent portrait of the Sultan, Achmet I., from memory, after seeing him at the ambassador's audience; which performance gained Vouet the munificent patronage of the Turkish nobles. From Constantinople he went to Venice, where he was attracted by the works of Paul Veronese; but he visited Rome in 1613, and adopted the style of Caravaggio. Some of his biographers assert that he chose Valentin as a model, but the latter was not born until 1600. The talents of Vouet gained him the patronage of Pope Urban VIII., and his nephew, the Cardinal, by whom he was employed to paint several pictures for St. Peter's and the Palazzo Barberini, which are among his best works, and are termed by Lanzi "charming productions." Louis XIII. hearing of his talents, allowed him a pension of 400 francs. He was also patronized by Prince Doria of Genoa, whither he went, and painted the portraits of the royal family. On returning to Rome he was chosen president of the Academy of St. Luke, in 1624.

In 1627, after a residence of fourteen years at Rome, Vouet returned to Paris, by invitation of the king, and was appointed his principal painter, with apartments in the Louvre. He was employed in decorating the palaces of the Louvre, the Luxembourg, and St. Germain's; also in many other commissions, so numerous that he was obliged to entrust nearly the entire execution of many of them to his scholars. He painted ceilings, galleries, altar-pieces, small religious subjects and other easel pictures, as well as portraits in oil and crayons. The multiplicity of his engagements induced Vouet to abandon the careful and vigorous style which he followed while in Italy, and during the first years after returning to France; after which he adopted a manner distinguished by surprising facility, and gay but inharmonious coloring. He was mannered likewise in his drawing, especially in the hands and the heads; his genius was unequal to grand compositions, he was also deficient in invention and expression. Had Vouet followed his Italian style, his reputation would have been much greater; but he nevertheless greatly improved the French school, and he is allowed by the French historians to have done as much for painting in France as Corneille did for the drama. The improved taste which he introduced, was still further exalted by his numerous disciples, among whom were le Brun, le Sueur, Mignard, du Fresnoy, Testelin, and others. Among his principal works in the churches of Paris, are the Assumption of the Virgin in S. Nicolas des Champs; and the Martyrdom of St. Agnes, in S. Eustache. He died in 1641. Dumesnil mentions an etching by Vouet, of the Holy Family, dated 1633. Aubin Vouet, the brother of Simon, painted in his style with tolerable success.

VOUILLEMONT, Sebastian, a French engraver, born at Bar-sur-Aube, about 1620. He studied under Daniel Rabel, at Paris, on leaving whom he went to Rome, where he resided several years. He engraved quite a number of plates after the Italian and French masters, as well as others from his own designs. His simple etchings are the best; when he attempted to finish them with the graver, he was less successful. He sometimes signed his plates with his name, and sometimes marked them with the above monogram. The following are among his best prints.

The Murder of the Innocents; *after Raffaelle.* 1641. Christ with his Disciples at Emmaus; *do.* Mount Parnassus; *do.* The Holy Family; *after N. Poussin.* The Virgin and Infant Christ; *after Parmiggiano.* The Marriage of St. Catherine; *after Albano.* A young Man presenting Money to a Fortuneteller.

VOYEZ, Nicholas Joseph, a French engraver, born at Abbeville in 1742. He went to Paris when very young, and became the pupil of Beauvarlet, his fellow-citizen. He engraved some portraits and other subjects, mostly after the French masters, in the neat style of his instructor. He had a brother named François, born at Abbeville in 1746, who was also an engraver.

VOYS, Ary de, a Dutch painter, born at Leyden in 1641. He first studied under Nicholas Knufer, at Utrecht, with whom he continued two years, when he returned to Leyden and became the disciple of Abraham vander Tempel; but he did not adopt the manner of either of his instructors. He formed an intimacy with Peter van Slingelandt, whose highly finished style he followed with the greatest success. Although he occasionally painted small cabinet pictures of history, his best and most numerous works are portraits, conversations, and domestic subjects, which are accounted little inferior to the productions of Metzu or Mieris. His pictures are exquisitely finished, his drawing is correct, his coloring is clear and transparent, and his conduct of the chiaro-scuro admirable. He acquired a high reputation, and his pictures were so much sought after that he could not supply the demand. It is said that he was naturally indolent, and that having married a lady of considerable fortune, he passed several years of his life in idleness and dissipation. His works are rare, and only to be found in the choicest collections. He died at Leyden in 1698.

VREE, or VREEM, Nicholas de, a Dutch painter, born at Utrecht in 1650, and died at Alkmaer in 1702. He was a good painter of landscapes, and excelled in flower-pieces, which were admired for the freedom and lightness of his pencil, and the fresh and natural tone of his coloring.

VRIES, John Fredeman de, a painter born at Leeuwarde, in East Friesland, in 1527. He was sent to Amsterdam when young, and placed under the instruction of Renier Gueritsen, with whom he continued five years. He afterwards studied perspective and architecture under another master, whose name is not mentioned. In 1549, he went to Antwerp, where, in conjunction with other artists, he was employed in painting the triumphal arches and other decorations for the celebration of the Entry of the Emperor Charles V. and his son Philip into that city, on which occasion he displayed so much ability, as to give him considerable employment in decorating the mansions of some of the principal nobility with perspective views, which he designed and painted with such truth and effect, as to produce complete illusion. He traveled through Germany and Italy, and everywhere met with abundant employment. He afterwards returned to Antwerp, where he settled, and continued to practice his profession till his death. His works are dispersed through Germany and the Low Countries, and some of them are in the English collections. They are frequently enriched with the figures of other celebrated painters of his time, which adds to their value. He was much employed in making designs of architectural and other subjects for the printsellers, particularly for Jerome Cock, who published a great variety of prints from his designs. He published a treatise on perspective, which was afterwards enlarged by Samuel Marolois. It is said that he was also an architect and engraver, and the same as *John Vredeman Frisius*, which see. This is very probable, as the date of their births is the same. There have been published twenty-six books of prints by Vries, illustrating various styles of architecture, with views of buildings, villas, &c.

VRIES, Paul de, was the son of the preceding, born at Antwerp in 1554, and died in 1598. He was instructed by his father, and followed his style with success. It is also said that he visited Prague, in Germany, and executed some extensive works in that city.

VRIES, Solomon de, was also the son and scholar of John F. de Vries, born at Antwerp in 1556, and died at the Hague in 1604. He painted landscapes and ruins much in the style of his father, except that his coloring is too dark.

VRIES, Adrian de, is supposed to have been a son or relative of John F. de V. Little is known of him, except that there is a set of large etchings of theatrical decorations by him, executed in a coarse, hasty style. He is said also to have been a painter of perspective and architecture.

VRIES, Peter de, was the son of Solomon de V., born at the Hague in 1587, and died in 1642. He painted the same subjects as his father, and followed his style completely.

VRIES, John Renier de, a landscape painter, who is supposed to have been a scholar of Jacob Ruysdael, whose style he followed. He painted a great number of small pictures on panel, generally woodland scenery, into which he generally introduced a cottage or a mill. His manner of handling resembles that of Ruysdael, but his coloring has the sombre hues of Decker. His pictures are usually signed with a monogram, bearing so strong a resemblance to that of Ruysdael, that many have been deceived by it. He flourished in the latter part of the 17th century. There were several other painters of this name of less note.

VROMANS, or VROOMANS, Nicholas, a Dutch painter, born in 1660. He painted serpents, toads, lizards, and other disgusting reptiles, with such truth that he was called "the painter of serpents."

VROOM, Henry Cornelius, a Dutch painter, born at Haerlem in 1566. He was the son of a sculptor, who dying when he was young, his mother afterwards married Cornelius Henricksen, a painter on china, who instructed him in the first principles of art. He visited Spain, Italy, and various other countries, and painted marines with considerable reputation. He executed the designs for tapestry illustrating the defeat of the Spanish Armada, for the Earl of Nottingham, Lord High Admiral of England. His works are now held in little estimation. His name is often written Vroon. He died in 1619.

VRYE, Thierry de, a Dutch painter, born at Gouda in 1530. He went to Paris, where he painted portraits and history with considerable reputation, and died there in 1582.

VUEZ, Arnold. This painter was born at Oppenois, near St. Omer, in 1642. He was the son of a turner in metals, who, when obliged by poverty to enlist as a soldier, placed him under a Jewish painter of St. Omer. Young Vuez here manifested so much ability that his instructor recommended him to visit Paris, and gave him a letter to an artist named Frère Luc, in whose school he remained three years, and then went to Italy On arriving at Venice, he sought out his uncle, a canon of St. Mark, who advanced him the means necessary to visit Rome. He studied the grand works of art in that city, and carried off the first prize at the Academy. A copy of Raffaelle's School of Athens, which he took to Venice, gained him new favors from his generous relative, and on returning to Rome, he recommenced his studies with new ardor. The Prince Pamfili took him under his protection, and procured him many commissions; but this success awakened envy among other artists, and various plots were formed for his destruction. At length, in a personal encounter, Vuez killed his intended assassin in self-defence. About this time, he received an invitation from le Brun to visit Paris, which he accepted, and was received by that painter with the greatest kindness. The King gave him a pension, and he executed many good works. He was patronized by the Duchess of Bouillon, and also by Louvois, who commissioned him to visit Lille to paint a picture of the Presentation in the Temple, for the church of the Hospital in that city. During his sojourn at Lille, Vuez received so many commissions, that he concluded to remain there permanently; and during the rest of his life, he executed numerous works for the churches of Lille, Cambray, and Douay. The pictures of Vuez evince great fertility of invention; and although the coloring is quite defective, they are correctly designed, and embellished with rich architecture. He drew his figures before draping them; his groups are admirably distributed, and he made nature his model. Among his principal works are mentioned the Resurrection; the Martyrdom of St. Andrew; the Judgment of Solomon; Daniel in the Den of Lions; the Discovery of the Promised Land, and the Descent from the Cross. Vuez was chosen an alderman of the city of Lille. He died in 1724, aged 82.

VUIBERT, Remi, a French painter and engraver, born at Paris in 1607. He is supposed to have studied under Vouet. He went to Italy, and passed many years at Rome, and probably died there. He executed quite a number of plates after Raffaelle, Domenichino, Poussin, Pietro da Cortona, Duquesnoy, and others from his own designs; which are dated from 1635 to 1663. His name is sometimes written Wibert, but he signed his prints *Remigius Vuibert Gallus*. Little is known of his works as a painter. Bartsch describes twenty-nine prints by him.

VYL, J. Den. There are some etchings of cows, oxen, bulls, sheep, and dogs, variously signed, *I.* or *J. den Vyl*, *Uil*, or *Uyl*, probably the work of one artist.

VYTH, or VEYTH, John Martin, a Swiss painter, born at Schaffhausen in 1650. After learning the rudiments of art in his native city, he went to Italy, and passed several years at Rome and Venice, and attached himself to the grand style of Michael Angelo, which is discernible in all his works. On his return to his native country, he acquired a high reputation as a painter of history, and executed many works for the collections of Berne, Basle and Schaffhausen, which are held in high esteem. Though his works prove him to have been one of the ablest artists of his country, his merits were not appreciated in his day, and he lived in poverty. He died in 1717.

# W.

WAAL. See WAEL.

WAARD, or WAERD, ANTHONY DE, a Dutch painter, born at the Hague in 1689. He first studied under Simon vander Does, and afterwards at Paris. He is said to have painted history, portraits, landscapes, and animals, with considerable reputation. His works are little known out of his own country, where they are esteemed. He died about 1752.

WAAS, or WAES, AART VAN, a Dutch painter, a native of Gouda, was a scholar of Wouter Crabeth. He went to Italy, where he resided some time. On his return to his native city, he painted conversations and familiar subjects with considerable reputation. He died at Gouda, according to Balkema, in 1646, and to Immerzeel, in 1650. There are nine etchings of grotesque subjects attributed to him in Hazzard's Catalogue of Prints.

WACH, KARL WILHELM, a Prussian painter, was born at Berlin in 1790, of highly respectable parentage. He commenced studying under Kretschmer, and executed a number of pictures which, compared with the average productions of that period, displayed superior talent. His studies were interrupted by the events of 1813, which occasioned him to serve as an officer in the Prussian militia. Even then, he did not entirely relinquish the pencil, and after the general peace he remained some time at Paris, studying the works of art then collected in that capital, and next visited Italy, where he allied himself with Overbeck, Schadow, and others who have since become famous in German art. On returning to Berlin in 1819, Wach immediately rose into high credit and favor with the public, more especially as a portrait painter, in which character he stood preëminent among his countrymen and cotemporaries. He also became highly distinguished in historical painting, and was one of those reformers who have contributed to establish the present German school. This eminent artist was chosen Professor of the Academy at Berlin, and discharged the duties of that office until his death, in November, 1845. His labors and researches in respect to the important subject of the chemical preparation of colors and varnishes, are said to have been attended by some valuable results.

WACHSMUTH, JEROME, a German engraver, who flourished at Vienna about 1730. He engraved several prints, among which are the Elements, and the Seasons, from his own designs, evincing an humble imitation of the style of Bernard Picart.

WAEGMAN, HENRY, a Swiss painter, born at Zurich, according to Füessli, in 1536. He is little known as a painter, but he executed many drawings, in a vigorous and spirited style, resembling that of Paolo Farinato, which possess great merit. He was also an engraver.

WAEL, or WAAL, JOHN DE, a Flemish painter, born at Antwerp in 1557. He was a disciple of the elder Frank, in whose style he painted history with considerable reputation, as is evident from two circumstances, namely, that he was elected a member of the Academy in his native city, and that Vandyck painted his portrait among the eminent artists of his country. His works are said to be very rare. He died, according to the best authorities, in 1602, in the prime of life; though Zani and Füessli say he died in 1633, aged 75 years. Bartsch says that John de Wael the Old, went to Paris in company with John de Mayer, where he acquired a fortune, and died in 1633. It is very probable that there were two artists of this name. (See *John Baptist de Wael.*) His name is variously written *Wael*, *Waal*, and *Weel*, but he wrote it *Wael*.

WAEL, or WAAL, LUCAS DE, was the son of the preceding, born at Antwerp in 1591. He received his first instruction from his father, but his genius leading him to landscape, he was placed under the tuition of John Breughel, with whom he made rapid progress, and adopted his style with great success. On leaving this master, he went to Italy, where he resided several years, and distinguished himself by some admirable works, both in oil and fresco, particularly at Genoa, where his works were highly esteemed, and he met with very flattering encouragement. Although he sometimes painted battle-pieces and attacks of cavalry, well composed, correctly designed, and touched with great spirit and animation, yet his most esteemed works are his mountainous landscapes, representing a great variety of precipices, craggy rocks, torrents, waterfalls, and other picturesque scenery, extremely pleasing; his coloring is chaste and natural, and his pencil neat and spirited. He died in 1676.

WAEL, or WAAL, CORNELIUS DE, was the younger brother of Lucas de Wael, born at Antwerp in 1594. He studied with his father, and accompanied Lucas to Italy, where he distinguished himself as a painter of battles, skirmishes of cavalry, marches, processions, and landscapes. He appeared most eminent in his battles and sea-fights, in which the fury of the combatants, the joy and exultation of the victors, the dejection and terror of the vanquished, and the sufferings of the wounded, are depicted with great force. His landscapes were also admired for the agreeable choice of his scenery, pleasing degradation of his distances, and for excellent keeping. His compositions are ingenious and abundant, his figures and horses are correctly designed, his coloring chaste and natural, his pencil free and masterly, and his touch peculiarly adapted to his subject. Though his taste was entirely Flemish in the forms, habits, character, countenances and airs of his heads, in his figures, as well as in his horses and cattle, he nevertheless acquired a high reputation in Italy, and was much patronized by princes and the nobility. The Duke d'Arschot (probably a Spaniard), appointed him his principal painter, for whom he executed many of his choicest works. He was also much patronized by Philip III., king of Spain, who held his works in the highest estimation; but whether he ever visited the Spanish court is not mentioned. The particulars of his life are too briefly recorded. It would seem that both Cornelius and Lucas passed most of their artistic lives in Italy. Cornelius is said by most writers to have died in 1662, but where, is not stated. Soprani and Lanzi say that he was living at Genoa in 1665. He executed some spirited etchings from his own designs.

WAEL, or WAAL, John Baptist de. This artist, according to Huber, was the nephew of Cornelius de Wael, but he does not say whether he was the son of Lucas, or of another brother. He executed some slight etchings from the designs of his uncle, among which are a set of eight prints, representing the History of the Prodigal Son. Bartsch, on the contrary, is of opinion that there were two artists of this name. He says, (Peintre Graveur, tom. v.,) "We have a series of *five* prints, representing the life of the Prodigal Son, which are engraved after the designs of Cornelius de Wael. *Three* of these plates are anonymous; the other *two* are by *John Baptist de Wael*, who has marked them with his name, and the date 1658. This artist, cotemporary with Cornelius de Wael, or perhaps his son, is absolutely unknown. In comparing the two *signed* prints, with the fourteen pieces of which we have given the description, and which also bear the name of John Baptist de Wael, it becomes evident that these latter cannot be the work of the *John* of 1658, so much difference is there in the composition, drawing, and point. There is, therefore, no doubt that the author of them is John Baptist de Wael, who, according to Descamps, was the father of Cornelius." Bartsch then goes on to give an account of John de Wael, whom he designates *the Old*, as above related, in the life of that artist. Be this as it may, there is no account of John de Wael ever having been in Italy, and the title page of the fourteen prints in question, clearly shows that they were engraved and published in Rome.

WAESBERGE, Isaac, a Dutch engraver, whose prints date from about 1650 to 1660. He engraved some portraits, among which is one of Admiral de Ruyter, *after H. Berckmans*, executed in a style resembling that of Cornelius Visscher.

HE W or HEW WAGNER, Hans Erhard, a German engraver, who was a native of Strasburg, according to Professor Christ, and flourished about 1690. He engraved a considerable number of plates of various subjects, which he marked with a monogram of his initials, as above.

WAGNER, James, a German engraver, probably of the same family as the preceding. According to Prof. Christ, he engraved some prints, which he usually marked *J. Wa. fec.*

WAGNER, John George, a German painter, born at Dresden in 1732. He was a disciple of the celebrated Dietrich, whose manner and subjects he imitated with such success, that his works frequently pass for the genuine productions of his master, especially in foreign countries. Stanley says his pictures have frequently been sold in England as the works of Dietrich. His drawings in water-colors are highly esteemed. He is sometimes called *the Younger*, to distinguish him from another artist of the same name, who painted portraits and history with some reputation, and flourished in the previous century. He died in 1767.

WAGNER, Joseph, a Swiss engraver, born at Thalendorf, on Lake Constance, in 1706. He first studied painting at Venice, under Jacopo Amiconi, who, perceiving that he had a better genius for engraving than for painting, advised him to devote himself to that art. He accordingly accompanied his preceptor to Paris, where he studied some time under Lawrence Cars. He also went with Amiconi to London in 1733, where he resided some time, and engraved several plates, among which were three of the princesses Anne, Amelia, and Caroline, daughters of George II. He afterwards returned to Venice, and established himself as an engraver, also carrying on a considerable commerce in prints. He instructed several pupils who distinguished themselves; among them were Bartolozzi, Flipart, and Berardi. His plates are numerous, and possess considerable merit. The following are the most esteemed. He died at Venice in 1780.

PORTRAITS AFTER AMICONI.

Peter the Great, Emperor of Russia, conducted by Minerva. Anne, Empress of Russia. Elizabeth Petrowna Empress of Russia. Carlo Broschi, called Farinelli, Musician.

SUBJECTS AFTER VARIOUS MASTERS.

The Education of the Virgin; *after Amiconi.* The infant Christ sleeping; *do.* The Holy Family; *after P. Veronese.* The Interview between Jacob and Rachel; *after L. Giordano.* Rebecca receiving the presents from Eliezer; *do.* The Death of Abel; *after Benedetto Luti.* Mary Magdalene in the House of the Pharisee; *do.* The Virgin and infant Christ; *after Solimena.* The Assumption of the Virgin; *after Piazzetta.* St. John in the Desert; *after C. Vanloo.* Twelve Landscapes and Pastoral subjects; *after Zuccherelli;* engraved by Wagner and his pupils.

WAILLY, Charles de, a distinguished French architect, was born at Paris in 1729. He early manifested a strong inclination for art, and studied successively under Blondel and Lejay; after which he completed his course under Servandoni, and gained the grand academical prize in architecture in 1752. This entitled him to three years' residence in Italy, at the expense of government, but he generously desired and obtained permission to divide this advantage with Moreau, one of his competitors, who drew the second prize. While residing in Italy, he attained sufficient reputation to be chosen a member of the Institute at Bologna. After his return to Paris, he was admitted to the Academy of Architecture in 1767, and in 1771 to the Academy of Painting, on which occasion he presented a perspective design of the staircase to the new theatre then projected, afterwards called the Odeon. Wailly was much employed in the distribution and ornamenting of the interiors of edifices, and he executed many elegant designs of this description, among which were the interiors of the Hotel d'Argenson at Paris, the chateau des Ormes, the Odeon Theatre, and the Palazzo Spinola at Genoa. The Landgrave of Hesse Cassel invited him to his court, and the magnificent plans which he made for the embellishment of the Capital and the State of that prince, are preserved in two folio volumes, in the Library at Cassel. He was an indefatigable designer, and gained such high reputation, that the Prince of Nassau invited him to his court, and the Empress Catherine offered him the presidency of the Academy of Architecture at St. Petersburg. After the conquest of the Low Countries, he was sent to select the finest works of art by the Dutch and Flemish masters, which were placed in the Louvre; and he was one of the original members of the Institute. Wailly died at Paris in 1798.

W  WALCH, Jacob, an old German engraver, who flourished about 1480 and is thought by some to have been the master of Michael Wolgemut—a supposition that is extremely questionable. Walch engraved on copper, whereas the greater part of the works of Wolgemut are wooden cuts, and his few copper plates are very unlike those by Walch, whose style bears a great resemblance to that of Israel von Mecheln. Besides, Wolgemut was probably the oldest, as he was born in 1434. The prints attributed to Walch are characterized by all the stiffness and formality of the primitive productions of the German school. They are usually marked with a W. and a kind of Gothic cross, as above. There are a few prints marked with a similar cross alone, which some attribute to him, but they are very rudely engraved, and resemble the more bold and determined style of Martin Schoen, of whom the artist was probably a cotemporary

WALCH, George, a German engraver, who flourished from about 1650 to 1678. There are some portraits by him, executed with the graver in a very indifferent style, and also several in mezzotinto. He appears to have resided chiefly at Nuremberg.

WALCH, Sebastian, a Swiss engraver in mezzotinto, who executed a series of portraits of the burgomasters of Zurich, from 1336 to 1740, from the designs of *J. C. Fuessli.* He was living in 1756.

WALDIE, Jane. See Watts.

WALE, Samuel, an English artist, born in London, who served an apprenticeship with an engraver on plate. He afterwards studied design in the Academy in St. Martin's Lane, and was chiefly employed in designing for the booksellers. He also practiced decorative painting, in which he imitated the manner of Francis Hayman. He was one of the first forty members of the Royal Academy, was appointed professor of perspective, and on the death of Wilson, was also made Librarian, both which situations he held till his death, in 1786. He etched a few vignettes from his own designs.

WALES, James, a Scotch artist, probably an amateur; born at Peterhead in 1748. He was educated in the University College, at Aberdeen. In 1791, he went to the East Indies, in what capacity is not mentioned, and died there in 1796. He designed twenty-four views of the Mountains of Ellora and the Hindoo Excavations, which were afterwards published in T. and W. Daniell's "Oriental Scenery." He is also said to have painted many portraits in India, some of them of Indian princes.

WALKER, Robert, an English portrait painter, who flourished in the time of the Protectorate, and died at London in 1660. He painted the portrait of Cromwell four times, and was much employed by the chiefs of the Republican party. He imitated Vandyck.

WALKER, Anthony, an English engraver, who flourished about 1760. He was chiefly employed in engraving vignettes, frontispieces, and other plates for the booksellers, some of which are from his own designs. He also engraved some plates for Alderman Boydell, among which are Curius Dentatus refusing the Presents of the Samnites, *after P. da Cortona;* the Village Lawyer and his Clients, *after Holbein;* and the Angel departing from the house of Tobit, *after Rembrandt.*

WALKER, William, was the brother of the preceding. He was much employed in engraving for the collection of Boydell, after the Italian, Dutch, and Flemish masters. Some of his prints possess considerable merit.

WALL, William Rutgaart vander, a Dutch painter, born at Utrecht in 1756, and died there in 1813. He painted landscapes with considerable reputation. His figures and animals are correctly designed, and touched with neatness and spirit.

WALLINT, Francesco, a Flemish painter, who appears to have passed his artistic life in Italy, and flourished at Rome in the first part of the 18th century, perhaps as late as 1750. Lanzi says, "Francesco Wallint, called Monsieur Studio, lived at Rome at the same time as Francis van Bloemen. He painted small landscapes and sea-views, ornamented with beautiful figures, in which he imitated Claude. He was, however, devoid of that sentiment which is the gift of nature, and that delicacy which charms in the Italian school." He had a son called Francesco Wallint the Younger, who attached himself to the same manner, with success, but he did not equal his father. See *Henry van Lint.*

WALMSLEY, John, an English landscape painter, born in 1763, and died at Bath in 1805 He was the son of Major Walmsley, who was stationed in Ireland with his regiment. Having a serious dispute with his friends, he went to London, where he was employed as scene painter, first at the King's Theatre, and afterwards at Covent Garden. He resided at Bath the last ten years of his life, where he painted landscapes of a small size, which Cunningham says are "truly excellent."

WALRAVEN, Isaac, a Dutch painter, born at Amsterdam in 1686, and died there in 1765. He first studied under Gerard Rademacker, and afterwards went to Dusseldorf, where he improved himself by copying the best works in the Gallery. He painted history and fancy pieces with considerable reputation. His pictures are well composed and colored, and he had a good knowledge of the chiaro-scuro, but his drawing is incorrect, and his pencil lacks precision and firmness. His pictures, however, are said to have brought good prices; two small pieces of Children sporting, brought, at the sale of his effects after his death, 800 florins each, and another, an historical subject, 1500. He also etched some small plates from his own designs, in which he appears to have imitated Stefano Della Bella.

WALSCAPELLE, Jacob, a Dutch painter of flowers, of whom little is known. He is supposed to have been a cotemporary, and perhaps a scholar of John David de Heem, whose style he imitated. His pictures are found in the best collections of his country, where they are held in high estimation. He particularly excelled in representing groups of flowers in glass bottles. His pictures are tastefully arranged, his coloring is fresh and transparent, his foliage and flowers sparkle with dewdrops, and the butterflies, moths, and other insects give them additional interest. His name is sometimes written *Waltskapelle.*

WALTER, Henry, an English painter of the present century. His subjects were chiefly land scapes and cattle. He exhibited occasionally at the Royal Academy, and the British Institution. He left quite a number of drawings, which are deserving of credit. He died in 1849.

WANDELAAR, John, a Dutch designer and engraver, born at Amsterdam in 1692. He studied under the elder Folkema, and became eminent in the art. He engraved some portraits, besides a variety of vignettes and other subjects, for the booksellers: but his best productions are a set of thirty-four plates for the great anatomical work of Albinus, entitled, *Tabulæ sceleti et musculorum corporis humani*, which he designed from the subjects, under the direction of the great anatomist himself. They are drawn with the greatest accuracy, and executed in a spirited and masterly manner. There is an English translation of this capital work, in which the plates were copied, of the same size as the originals, by Grigniôn, Ravenet, Scotin, and others. Wandelaar is also said to have painted portraits, some of which are said to have been engraved by Houbraken. He died at Leyden in 1759.

WANS, or WAMPS, a Flemish painter, who flourished in the first half of the 17th century. He was accounted a good landscape painter. He also copied some of the works of Vandyck.

WARD, William, an English engraver in mezzotinto, who flourished in the latter part of the 18th, and the first part of the present century. He was the brother-in-law of George Morland, and engraved many plates from his pictures, which had an extensive sale. He also executed many portraits after Reynolds, and other English painters, which display considerable talent. He was elected an Associate of the Royal Academy. He had a brother named James, who excelled in painting animals. There was also a *Captain* Ward, who held a commission in the service of the East India Company. He painted some landscapes and views in the East Indies, several of which were exhibited at the Royal Academy in 1772 and 1773.

WARD, William James, was the son of William Ward, born at London in 1801. He was instructed by his father, and engraved quite a number of portraits and other subjects, after Reynolds and other English painters. His prints were admired for their depth and richness of color, and artistic effect. He died in 1840.

WARNIR, John, a German engraver, who flourished about 1636, and is supposed to have died very young. He copied some prints after the old German masters, which, though neatly executed, have all the appearance of servile imitation. He copied the print of Albert Durer, representing St. Jerome seated before a crucifix, with a city in the background, which is inscribed *Jh. Warnir, Æ.* 16, 1636; also the Twelve Apostles, after the same master, in the following year, when he was seventeen, *Jh. W. Æ.* 17.

WARREN, Charles, an English engraver, who died in 1823. He engraved a great number of small plates, neatly executed, after Stothard, Westall, Smirke, and others, to illustrate the various editions of the British poets and novelists, published by Harrison, Bell, Cadell, and other enterprising booksellers of his day.

WASSEMBERG, John Abel, a Dutch painter, born at Groningen in 1689. He was the son of a lawyer, who intended him for the same profession, and gave him a classical education, but his passion for painting induced the father to place him under the instruction of John van Dieren, a painter of little note. After remaining with the latter till the age of twenty-three, he went to Rotterdam, and became the disciple of Adrian vander Werf, who aided him with friendly counsel, and took particular pains to instruct him in his method of coloring and penciling. On returning to his native city, Wassemberg soon gave proof of his abilities, and received many commissions to decorate the saloons and ceilings of the principal inhabitants. He was also much employed in portraiture, in which he excelled. His talents recommended him to the patronage of the Prince of Orange, who employed him to paint the portraits of himself and family, and the principal personages of his court. He was not less celebrated for his cabinet pictures from sacred and profane history, in which he imitated the polished style of vander Werf with such success, that his works of this class were accounted little inferior to the admirable productions of that master. It is not a little remarkable, that an artist who was accustomed to large works, both in oil and fresco, which must be viewed at a distance, to produce the desired effect on the eye, could adapt his touch, tints, and handling to such small pieces as required the nearest view, and even the use of the glass, to perceive their beauties. He died in 1750.

WASSEMBERG, Elizabeth Gertrude, was the daughter and pupil of the preceding. She painted cabinet pictures, similar to those of her father, finished in such an exquisite manner, that some of them are said to closely approach the productions of Gerard Douw. She died in 1782.

WASSER, Anna, an eminent Swiss paintress, born at Zurich in 1679. She early discovered a lively genius, so that before the age of twelve, she could speak and write the Latin and French languages correctly, and had made considerable progress in the Belles Lettres. She showed such a taste for painting, and had made such progress in design at thirteen years of age, that her father, who was a man of some distinction, and a member of the Common Council of the city, was induced to place her under the instruction of Joseph Werner of Berne, one of the most eminent artists of Switzerland, with whom she made surprising progress. At first she painted some pictures in oil, but manifesting peculiar talents for miniature, she applied herself entirely to that branch, and soon arrived at such perfection as almost rivalled Werner himself. Her fame spread throughout all Germany, and there was scarcely a court in Europe from which she did not receive commissions. The Duke of Wurtemburg and the Margrave of Baden-Durlach, were among her most distinguished patrons. Her talents were not confined to portraits, though she was mostly employed in this branch; she excelled in painting pastoral and rural subjects, composed with great ingenuity, and finished with uncommon delicacy. She died unmarried in 1713.

WATELET, Claude Henry, an eminent French amateur engraver and writer on art, born at Paris in 1718. His father was receiver-general of the finances, to which post he succeeded after his death. After receiving a liberal education, he traveled through Germany to Italy, and passed some time at Rome, where he made the acquaintance of M. Pierre, an eminent French painter, with whom he contemplated the most remarkable works of art in that metropolis. On returning to Paris, he devoted much of his time to an assiduous cultivation of the fine arts. He executed upwards of a hundred etchings after the Italian, French, and Flemish masters, some of which possess uncommon merit. In 1761 he published his poem on the *Art of Painting*, embellished with plates from the designs of M. Pierre, etched by himself, and finished with the graver by Lempereur. He was the principal author of a very laborious work published in 1792, four years after his death, with additions by M. Levesque, entitled *Dictionnaire des Arts de Peinture, Sculpture, et Gravure.* He died in 1788.

AXA or AW f or AW

WATERLOO, ANTHONY, an eminent Dutch painter and engraver, of whose early history nothing is known, and whose birth is variously placed at Amsterdam and Utrecht, about 1618. This much is certain, that he passed his artistic life in the latter city, and the scenery of his pictures is generally taken from its environs. His landscapes are characterized by the most interesting simplicity, sometimes representing the entrance into a forest; a broken road, with a few trunks of trees; a solitary cottage, or a watermill; all evidently the transcripts of simple nature, as he saw it, without any attempt at improvement. Yet he treated these subjects in such an admirable manner as to entitle him to rank among the best landscape painters of his country. His skies are light and floating, his coloring chaste and natural, the foliage of his plants and trees is touched with great spirit, as well as with a marked attention to their different species, so that they can be readily distinguished, and the reflection of his objects in the water is wonderfully transparent and natural. He did not design the human figure correctly; therefore he frequently employed Weenix and other eminent artists of his time to insert the figures and cattle in his pictures, which are sometimes found without these accessories. His pictures are exceedingly rare, as he devoted much of his time to engraving, and he is said also to have led a dissipated life. It is reported that he never signed his pictures with his name.

As an engraver, the works of Waterloo have long been the admiration of artists and connoisseurs. They are etched with great spirit and facility, in a very masterly style, and usually retouched with the graver, to harmonize the lights and invigorate the shadows. They consist of landscapes from his own designs, frequently embellished with figures from sacred and profane history, and mythology. He etched the whole design with equal strength, but slightly, and then finished in a bold manner those parts which he desired to be most effective. Therefore as the plates were worked off, the etching grew imperceptibly fainter, while that part executed with the graver, suffered little change; which accounts for the numerous poor impressions. Bartsch regards his prints of so much interest and importance, that he minutely describes *one hundred and thirty-six*, which he believes to be a complete catalogue. For further information on this subject, the reader must be referred to Bartsch, Peintre Graveur, tom. ii., and Weigel's Supplement to Bartsch. He usually marked his prints with one of the above monograms, but sometimes with the initials A. W. *f.;* and Stanley mentions one in the British Museum signed *A. Waterlo fec.* Some writers say that he died in the prime of life from dissipation, but Houbraken and Weyermans assert that he died in the hospital of St. Job at Utrecht, in 1679, which is doubtless correct.

HW WATMAN, HENRY, a Dutch or German engraver, of whom little is known. According to Professor Christ, he engraved some landscapes, which are marked with the above monogram.

WATSON, CAROLINE, an English lady, born at London in 1760, who distinguished herself as an engraver in the dotted manner, and in mezzotinto. She was instructed by her father, and executed quite a number of plates which possess great merit. Among others are the following by her:

PORTRAITS.

Prince William of Gloucester; *after Reynolds.* Lord Malmsbury; *do.* Mrs. Stanhope; *do.* Sir Joshua Reynolds; *do.* Earl of Bute; *after Gainsborough.* Ozias Humphry, Painter; *do.* Mrs. Drummond and Children; *after Shelley.* Mrs. Siddons, as the Grecian Daughter; *after Shirrif.* Miss Bover; *after Hoppner.* Benjamin West, Esq., P. R. A.; *after Stuart.* William Woollett; *do.* Sir Robert Boyd, Governor of Gibraltar; *after Smart.*

WATSON, THOMAS, an eminent English engraver in mezzotinto, born at London in 1750. He was probably of the same family as the preceding. Though he died at comparatively an early age, he is regarded as one of the ablest English artists in his particular branch. He died in 1781. The following are his most esteemed prints:

PORTRAITS.

Six, of the Windsor Beauties; *after Lely.* Lord Apsley and his Brother; *after N. Dance.* Frances, Countess of Jersey; *after Gardner.* Alderman Sawbridge, in the character of a Roman Senator; *after West.*

PORTRAITS AFTER SIR JOSHUA REYNOLDS.

Henry Frederick, Duke of Cumberland. Lady Bamfylde. Lady Melbourne. James Hay, Earl of Errol. Lady Broughton. Dr. Newton, Bishop of Bristol. Warren Hastings. Mrs. Sheridan, as St. Cecilia. Georgina Countess Spencer. Lady Townshend, and her two Sisters. Mrs. Crewe.

SUBJECTS AFTER VARIOUS MASTERS.

Jupiter and Mercury, with Philemon and Baucis; *after Rembrandt.* The Virgin, with the infant Jesus and St. John; *after Correggio.* The Death of Mark Antony, *after N. Dance.*

WATSON, JAMES. This artist was of the same family as the preceding. He greatly distinguished himself as an engraver in mezzotinto. His plates are very numerous, and are held in high estimation, particularly those after Reynolds. The following are the principal:

PORTRAITS AFTER SIR JOSHUA REYNOLDS.

Anne, Duchess of Cumberland. Elizabeth, Duchess of Buccleugh, with her daughter. The Duchess of Manchester, with her son, as Diana and Cupid. The Countess of Carlisle. Sir Jeffrey Amherst, Commander-in-Chief in America. Jemima, Countess Cornwallis. Robert Drummond, Archbishop of York. Barbara, Countess of Coventry. Sir John Cust, Speaker of the House of Commons. John, Marquis of Granby. John Hely Hutchinson, Secretary of State in Ireland. Doctor Samuel Johnson. Lord and Lady Pembroke, with their son. Vice-Admiral Sir George Bridges Rodney. Lady Scarsdale, with her Son. Isabella, Countess of Sefton. Frances, Marchioness of Tavistock. Miss Price. Henry Woodward, Comedian. Mrs. Abington, as Thalia.

PORTRAITS AFTER VARIOUS MASTERS.

Paul Pontius, Engraver; *after Vandyck.* Dr. Busby; *after Riley.* Charles, Duke of Richmond; *after Romney.* The Duchess of Leinster; *do.* John, Duke of Argyle; *after Gainsborough.* Miss Lascelles, with a Greyhound; *after Cotes*

SUBJECTS AFTER VARIOUS MASTERS.

A Madonna; *after Reynolds.* The Children in the Wood; *do.* Rubens and his Family; *after J. Jordaens.*

WATSON, Musgrove Southwaite, an English sculptor, born near Carlisle, in 1804. When quite young he went to London, and was advised by Flaxman to visit Italy. After remaining in that country about three years, studying and copying the sculptures of the best masters, he returned to London, where he was employed by Chantrey as a modeller. His merit now began to be known, and after a few years of persevering endeavors, he was commissioned to execute the magnificent group of Lords Eldon and Stowell, which gained him great reputation. He soon had plenty of employment, and executed a number of fine works, among which may be mentioned the colossal statue of the Earl of Lonsdale, the statue of Queen Elizabeth in the Royal Exchange, also two bas-reliefs of the Battle of St. Vincent, and Dante and Beatrice. The two latter works have been very much admired. He modelled and cast in plaster his beautiful Flaxman monument, but it was not completed till after his death. He exhibited at the Royal Academy a bas-relief monument to the memory of Allan Cunningham, entitled "Literature;" also another, "Death and Sleep bearing off the Body of Sarpedon;" and a bas-relief monument of Dr. Cameron. The three latter works have been highly praised by the critics. Watson died in 1847, at the age of 43.

WATTEAU, Anthony, an eminent French painter, born at Valenciennes, in 1684. He early discovered a passion for painting, but his parents being very poor, were unable to give him an education suitable to his genius. They however procured him the instruction of an obscure artist in his native city, with whom he continued until the latter could render him no further assistance. In 1702, he connected himself with a scene painter, and went to Paris, where they obtained employment for a short time, but Watteau soon found himself solitary and destitute in that great city, and he was compelled to work for the shops, for a scanty maintenance. While in this situation, he became accidentally acquainted with Claude Gillot, a painter and engraver of grotesque and fabulous subjects, who conceived such a friendship for Watteau that he took him into his house, communicated to him all the information he possessed, the observations he had made, and the precepts by which he had formed his own style. It was not long before Watteau surpassed his friendly instructor. Shortly after this, he was employed by Audran to make some designs from the pictures in the Luxembourg Gallery, where he was so strongly impressed by the splendid works of Rubens, that he was fired with the ambition to become an historical painter, and he studied them with great assiduity, by which means he acquired an admirable system of coloring, and a good knowledge of chiaro-scuro. He also entered the Academy, designed from the living model, and drew the first prize for a historical piece. Fortunately for his fame, he discovered that history was not his forte, and he struck out into a new and original style, in which he acquired a lasting reputation, and which gave rise to a host of imitators, without ever producing a rival. His subjects are usually comic conversations, musical parties, balls, masquerades, gallant and pastoral subjects, which he designed correctly, and with admirable finesse, ease, and natural grace. His coloring is fresh and splendid, and he is equally admired in the tenderness of his carnations, the brilliancy of his habiliments, and the verdure of his landscapes. His pencil is free and flowing, his touch neat and spirited, and his pictures are carefully finished in every part. The figures which he introduces into his compositions, in whatever character he designs them, have a peculiar *naiveté* and grace in the airs of the heads, in the attitudes and actions. The national taste of his country, however, prevails in all his productions. Watteau also painted the marchings, halts, and encampments of armies, with great success. Lord Orford makes the following admirable criticism upon his works. "Watteau painted imaginary nymphs and swains, and described a kind of impossible pastoral, a rural life, led by those opposites of rural simplicity, people of rank and fashion. His shepherdesses, nay, his very sheep are coquettes; yet he avoided the glare and *clinquant* of his countrymen; and, though he fell short of the dignified grace of the Italians, there is an easy air in his figures, and that more familiar species of the graceful which we call genteel. His nymphs are as much below the forbidding majesty of goddesses, as they are above the hoyden awkwardness of country girls. In his halts and marches of cavalry, the careless slouch of the soldiers still retain the air of a nation that aspires to be agreeable, as well as victorious."

Watteau found abundant employment, and was indefatigable in the exercise of his pencil. His works, though numerous, are rarely to be met with out of the collections of his own country, where they are held in great estimation. His reputation abroad has been injured by a multitude of imitations, many of which have been sold for his genuine works. He executed a few spirited etchings, from his own designs. He also left behind him a great number of drawings, in red and black chalk. Having injured his health by his intense professional application, he went to England, to consult the celebrated Dr. Meade, and resided there about one year. He died shortly after his return to France, in 1721.

WATTS, Jane. This highly gifted lady was the daughter of George Waldie, of Hendersyde Park, Scotland, where she was born in 1789. Almost in her infancy, she exhibited a passion for drawing. She painted landscapes in oil, which were greatly admired, and many of them were exhibited at the Royal Academy and the British Institution, with universal applause. She was also accomplished in literature, in which she displayed equal talent. She died in 1826.

WATTS, William, an English engraver, was born in 1752. His father was a master silk-weaver in the neighborhood of Moorfields, and placed him under the tuition of Paul Sandby and Thomas Rooker. While with the latter, Watts assisted in some of Woollett's plates; and after his instructor's death, he continued the publication of a periodical work commenced by Rooker, entitled, "The Copperplate Magazine," being the first English magazine ever embellished with copper plates. In 1779, he commenced a work entitled "Views of Gentlemen's Seats," published by subscription during the succeeding years, until completed in 1786. He then sold the plates to Boydell, and visited Naples in the same year, where he received much kindness from Sir Wm. Hamilton and his lady. After spending nine months in Italy, he returned to England, and published, about 1791, his twelve Views of the city of Bath, which are esteemed beautiful specimens of line engraving. For several years he relinquished the art, but having invested the greater portion of his property in French funds, he was compelled to return to it, in consequence of an act confiscating the property of British subjects. Between 1801 and 1805, he published his last work, containing sixty views in Turkey and Palestine, from drawings made by Luigi Mayer during the Embassy of Sir Robert Ainslie to the Sublime Porte. In 1814, he purchased a small property at Cobham, in Surrey, and at the peace of 1815 recovered about half of his investment in the French funds. He died at his residence, in 1851, aged about 100 years. Watts was formerly intimate with Bartolozzi, Middiman, Milton, and other eminent engravers of his day. His plates are esteemed for their beautiful selection, truth, simplicity, and fine artistic execution.

WAUMANS, Conrad. This Flemish engraver flourished at Antwerp, his native place, about 1642. He studied under Peter Bailliu, and executed a number of plates of portraits and historical subjects after the painters of his country, which are little inferior to those of his instructor.—Among them are the following:

PORTRAITS.

Frederick Henry, Prince of Orange; *after Vandyck.* Emilia de Solms, Princess of Orange; *do.* Don Antonio de Zuniga; *do.* John Both, Landscape painter; *after Willaerts.* Herman Zachtleven, Painter; *after a picture by himself.* David Bailli, Painter; *do.* Cornelius Jansen, Painter; *do.*

SUBJECTS AFTER VARIOUS MASTERS.

The Descent from the Cross; *after Rubens.* The Assumption of the Virgin; *do.* The Virgin and infant Jesus; *after Vandyck.* Mars and Venus; *do.*

WEBB, Westfield, an English painter, who died at London in 1772. He usually painted portraits, and sometimes flower-pieces; but he never rose above mediocrity.

WEBBER, John, an English painter, designer, and engraver, born in London in 1752. His father, a Swiss sculptor of Berne, sent him to Paris while young, where he received a part of his artistic education, and, on returning to London, he frequented the Royal Academy. Having acquired considerable reputation as a designer, he was appointed draughtsman to the last expedition made by Captain Cook round the world. On his return in 1780, he was employed by the Lords of the Admiralty to superintend the engraving of the prints made from his designs by Bartolozzi, and other eminent artists. When this work was completed, he published on his own account a set of views of the principal places he had visited, which he etched and aquatinted, and afterwards colored, producing a very pleasing effect. He afterwards devoted himself to landscape painting, usually representing scenes in the South Sea Islands, which, though gaudily colored, are well finished, and produce a pleasing effect. He was elected an Associate in 1785, and a Royal Academician in 1791. He died in 1793.

WEBBERS, J., a Dutch engraver, who flourished at Amsterdam about 1656, in which year he published a set of indifferently executed views of the churches and public edifices in that city, engraved by himself, with descriptions in Dutch and French.—There was a painter named Zachariah Webber, who flourished at Amsterdam, and died in 1697.

WEELING, Anselm, a Dutch painter, born at Bois-le-Duc in 1675. He was the son of an officer in the service of the States General, and was intended for the profession of arms; but discovering a passion for painting, he was placed under the instruction of one Delang, an obscure painter in his native city, with whom he continued till he had the satisfaction of being acknowledged his superior. He then went to Middleburg, to commence business for himself, where he became acquainted with Jacob Bart, an eminent picture dealer, who had a fine collection of the works of the most eminent masters of the Dutch school. The sight of these fine works made Weeling perceive his own inferiority, and in a fit of despondency, he resolved to go to the East Indies; but encouraged by Bart, who received him into his own house, he devoted two years, with great assiduity, in studying and copying the fine collection. His improvement equalled his industry; some of his pictures were highly commended, and sold for high prices. He was particularly attached to the productions of Godfrey Schalcken and Adrian vander Werf, whose styles he followed with great success. His most esteemed pictures are his candle-light scenes, in which he imitated Schalcken so closely that some of his works have been mistaken for the productions of that master. In his best works, his design is tolerably correct, his color is warm and glowing, and he evinced an excellent knowledge of the effects of light and shadow. In the latter part of his life, he became a slave to intemperance and debauchery, which destroyed his powers, and reduced him to poverty and wretchedness, so that his later performances are greatly inferior to his earlier ones. He died in 1749.

WEENIX, or WEENINX, John Baptist, called the Elder, an eminent Dutch painter born at Amsterdam in 1621. He was the son of John Weenix, an architect of considerable note, who intended him for the same profession; but the latter dying while he was young, his mother allowed him to follow the bent of his genius. He first studied with John Micker, a painter of little note, and next with Abraham Bloemaert, under whose able instruction he made surprising progress, and in a short time surpassed his instructor, by the facility and precision with which he designed the principal buildings, castles, and ruins about Amsterdam. He drew with equal spirit and accuracy all kinds of animals, as well as the human figure. On leaving the school of Bloemaert, he studied two years under Nicholas Moyaert, till he could imitate his style so closely that it was almost impossible to distinguish the works of the master from those of his pupil. At the age of eighteen, he went to Italy, and on his arrival at Rome, he was struck with the sublime edifices and ruins of ancient grandeur, and he applied himself to designing them with his wonted assiduity. His great talents recommended him to the patronage of the Cardinal Pamfili, who not only favored him with many commissions, and liberal remunerations, but also settled upon him a considerable pension, that he might pursue his studies without interruption. This prelate was very desirous to retain Weenix at Rome, and offered to engage him in the service of the Pope, but the solicitations of his family, and his love of country, induced him to forego the brilliant prospects before him, and he returned to Holland, after an absence of four years. He soon found abundant employment, and acquired the reputation of one of the ablest artists of his country.

Weenix possessed extraordinary and varied talents. He painted history, portraits, landscapes, sea-ports, animals, and dead game, in all which branches he showed uncommon ability; but his greatest excellence was in painting Italian seaports, of large size, enriched with noble edifices, and decorated with figures representing embarkations, and all the activity of commercial industry. In these subjects he has scarcely been surpassed, except by his pupil, Nicholas Berghem. His figures and objects are correctly designed, his coloring clear and harmonious, his pencil free and flowing, his touch bold and animated, and though he wrought with wonderful facility, he did not neglect to finish his pieces well. His portraits are vigorously executed, and he obtained excellent likenesses. Houbraken mentions several instances of his admirable facility of hand. He frequently painted a large landscape, and inserted the figures in a single day, and on one occasion, he commenced and completed three portraits on canvass, of three-quarters size, with heads as large as life, from sunrise to sunset, in a summer's day. He executed a few spirited etchings from his own designs; Bartsch describes two, to which Weigel has added five more, and doubtless there are others. The signatures on these are *Batta. Weenix; J. B. Weeninx*, the J. and B. interlaced; *Gio. Batta. Weenin;* and *J. Weenix;* the one with the last signature was doubtless executed by his son. He died in 1660, aged 39 years.

WEENIX, or WEENINX, John, called the Younger, was the son of the preceding, born at Amsterdam in 1644. He studied with his father until the age of sixteen, when his instructor died; yet he had made such progress that he was able to prosecute his studies, by the attentive study of nature, without any further assistance. Though of less universal talent than his father, he painted with great ability, landscapes, huntings, animals, dead game, flowers, and fruit. He particularly excelled in the representations of huntings and dead game, in which he may be said to have surpassed every artist of his country. His talents in this branch recommended him to the patronage of the Elector Palatine, who invited him to his court, appointed him his painter with a liberal pension, and employed him to decorate his palace at Bernsberg with many of his choicest works. Weenix painted in one gallery a series of pictures representing the hunting of the Stag, and in another the Chase of the Wild Boar, which gained him the greatest applause. There are also many of his best works in the Dusseldorf Gallery. He was equally successful in representing every species of animal, whether alive or dead. He painted all kinds of birds and fowls in an inimitable manner; the soft down of the duck, the glossy plumage of the pigeon, the splendor of the peacock, the magnificent spread of an inanimate swan, producing a flood of light, and serving as a contrast to all around it, are so attractive that it is impossible to contemplate one of his pictures of these objects without feeling admiration and delight at the painter's skill in rivaling nature. His living hounds and other dogs, as well as his dead game, are not less true, and his objects of still-life, such as sporting instruments, vessels, fruit, flowers, and other accessories with which he embellishes his principal subject, are all depicted with the same fidelity and beauty. It has been said that he did not equal his father in landscape, but it should be recollected that his landscape is always accessory to the principal subject with which it accords, and no more was required. In his large pictures, his compositions are ingenious, abundant, and picturesque, his touch is bold and animated, his coloring clear and brilliant, and he always exhibits a perfect intelligence of the chiaro-scuro. His works of a cabinet size are exquisitely finished, without impoverishing the spirit of his touch, or diminishing the breadth of his light and shadow. His works are numerous, and deservedly held in the highest estimation; and they are only to be found in the choicest collections. He continued to practice his profession to the last year of his life, without any apparent diminution of his powers. One of his finest pictures, in the collection of the king of Holland, is dated the year before his death. It is signed *J. Weenix, f.*, 1718. He died in 1719.

WEERDT, Adrian de, a Flemish painter, born at Brussels in 1510. He first studied under Christian Queburgh, at Antwerp, a landscape painter of little note; but he afterwards went to Italy, and made the works of Parmiggiano the particular objects of his study. On his return to Brussels, he painted history in the graceful style of that master with considerable success, till the troubles in the Low Countries compelled him to take refuge at Cologne, where he died, in or about 1566. There is considerable discrepancy among writers as to his name, and the time and place of his death. He is variously called *Adrian*, *Andrea*, and *Abraham de Weerdt*, and some say his family name was Hoste.

WEERT, J. de, an engraver, supposed to have been a native of Flanders, who flourished at Paris about 1605. He engraved some frontispieces, vignettes, and other book plates, in a neat, though tasteless style; also a set of plates from his own designs, representing the Life and Passion of Christ.

WEESOP. This painter, who was probably a native of the Low Countries, visited England, according to Walpole, in 1641, shortly before the death of Vandyck, whose style he imitated with such success, that several of his pictures have passed for the productions of that master. He quitted England in 1649.

WEIGEL, Hans or John, a German designer

and engraver on wood, who is said to have operated in 1535, and to have died at Nuremberg in or about 1590. He was also a printer. He engraved some ornamental book plates and a book of costumes, which are indifferently executed. He marked his cuts with his initials, H. W. His name is written on his book titles, *Hans Weygel.*

WEIGEL, CHRISTOPHER, a German engraver, born at Redwitz, in Bohemia, in 1654. After visiting various cities in Germany, he settled at Nuremberg, where he died in 1725. He engraved a set of Bible plates, from his own designs, entitled *Sacra Scriptura loquens in imaginibus*, &c., published at Nuremberg in 1690. They are executed with the graver, and each plate contains four prints; the plates amount to one hundred from the Old Testament, and one hundred and ten from the New. According to M. Heineken, he also engraved in mezzotinto. There is a portrait of Charles V. in mezzotinto, signed *C. Weigel, f. et ex.*, 1688. He is said to have carried on an extensive commerce in prints.

WEINBRENNER, FRIEDRICH, an eminent German architect, was born at Carlsruhe in 1766. He was the son of a carpenter and builder, who died before the destination of Friedrich was fixed; and his studies thereafter were rather irregular, but having obtained from his elder brother sufficient insight into the practical routine of the art, he started on a tour for improvement in the spring of 1788. Arriving at Zurich, he was employed there a considerable time, in superintending some timber constructions; but though his stay in that city was rendered very agreeable by the society of several artists and literary men,—among the latter Lavater,—he hastened as soon as engagements would permit to Vienna, and after examining the architectural monuments in that capital, he proceeded to Dresden and Berlin. This he had proposed to himself as the extent of his travels, but in Berlin he became acquainted with the brothers Genelli, architects of considerable repute and talent, who urged him to visit Italy. This advice was so strongly seconded by Weinbrenner's inclination, that he resolved to adopt it, and accordingly set out for Rome in June 1792, in company with Carstens, and another young artist named Cabot.

Soon after arriving at Rome, when he had viewed with delight the great monuments of art, Weinbrenner felt, if not disheartened, most anxiously conscious that the study he had imposed upon himself required system and perseverance, and also more historical and antiquarian knowledge than he then possessed. The time that was not occupied in examining and drawing buildings, was devoted to books and literary research; yet not entirely, as the state of his finances obliged him to give instruction in architecture. For some time, numerous strangers of distinction took lessons of him, but the commotions of 1793 drove many strangers and artists from the city. Nevertheless, Weinbrenner remained there until 1797, with the exception of a considerable interval spent by him at Naples. On returning to Carlsruhe, he was appointed Inspector of Buildings, and soon after had the opportunity of displaying his ability in the erection of the new synagogue, and one or two private mansions. Notwithstanding this favorable commencement, he relinquished his office two years after, and went to settle at Strasburg, where the relations of his wife (Margaretha Arnold, whom he had shortly before married) resided, and were many of them artists. The change proved imprudent: Strasburg became menaced by hostilities, and Weinbrenner found himself without other occupation or resource than teaching a few pupils. At this juncture, he was invited by the Hanoverian government, through the recommendation of Prince Augustus, to inspect and improve the prisons of that country; but his wife and her family dissuaded him from accepting the proposal, and on receiving the offer of his former appointment at Carlsruhe, he accepted it, and returned to that city.

From this time, Weinbrenner was continually employed on various improvements and embellishments in the capital of Baden, and other parts of its territory. His numerous works exhibit various degrees of merit, according to the respective opportunities afforded him; but taken collectively, they manifest a great improvement in style, with individuality of character, and fresh and masterly combinations, instead of the mere routine of design. He applied himself to his art with higher views of it than were entertained by the generality of his countrymen, and diffused a similar feeling for it through the next generation of the profession, having instructed a great number of the eminent living architects of Germany. Weinbrenner deserves to rank among the most eminent modern architects of his country, not only on account of the numerous edifices erected and professional works published by him, but for his extensive influence in founding a better school of the art. Among his principal edifices are many at Carlsruhe, among others the Catholic church, the Lutheran church, Theatre, Ettlinger gate, Standeshaus, Museum, Mint, and the Hochberg palace. At Baden he erected the Conversation-haus or Assembly Rooms, baths, and Antiquitaten-halle or Museum, &c., besides the Leopold summer palace, and various private houses and smaller buildings. There are also a very considerable number of churches, mansions, villas, &c., erected or designed by him in other places within the territory of Baden; and not a few in various other parts of Germany, Leipsic, Strasburg, Dusseldorf, and Gottingen. Notwithstanding his numerous engagements, Weinbrenner published treatises on different branches of architectural study, viz., two on the orders of architecture, *Zeichnungslehre*, 1810; *Optik*, 1811; *Perspectivlehre*, 1817-24; *Ueber Form und Schonheit*, 1819; *Ueber Architektonische Verzierungen*, 1820; besides a work on theatres, and a variety of papers on architectural and artistical topics in the *Morgenblatt*, and other literary journals. Weinbrenner continued his professional pursuits and studies almost to the last, and died March 1st, 1826.

HW WEINHER, HANS OR JOHN, a German painter and engraver who flourished in the first part of the 17th century. Little is known of him, but he is said to have been employed during boyhood in the service of the Duchess Maximilienne of Bavaria, in the capacity of valet de chambre. He learned engraving of Frederic Sustris, and executed some plates which are marked with the above monogram.

WEINHER, PETER, a German designer and engraver, was also the assayer of the mint of the Duke of Bavaria, and lived at Munich in 1580. Bartsch describes only twelve prints by him, but Brulliot mentions many more. They are usually marked with his name, to which he sometimes adds *Monachij* and the date.

WEIROTTER, FRANCIS EDMUND, an eminent designer and engraver, born at Inspruck in 1730. After learning the rudiments of design, he went to Paris, and became the pupil of J. G. Wille. He traveled to Italy, where he resided some time, and returned to Paris with a large collection of designs, of the most beautiful and picturesque scenery and views in that delightful country. In 1767, he was invited to the court of Vienna, where he was appointed professor of the Academy of Design. We have by him a great number of charming etchings from his own designs, executed in a free, spirited and masterly style, and consisting of landscapes, views of ruins, bridges, edifices, cottages, &c., which are admired for their correctness of design and harmonious distribution of light and shadow. He usually published them in sets of twelve. He died at Vienna in 1773. The following are among the most esteemed of his numerous prints:

A set of twelve Views in Normandy, with a Dedication. Twelve Views in Italy; dedicated to the Prince of Kaunitz. A set of twelve Views in Italy; dedicated to the Prince of Staremberg. Twelve Views in Italy; dedicated to the Duke Albert of Saxe-Teschen. A set of twelve Views in Italy; dedicated to the Archduchess of Austria.

WEISBROD, CHARLES, a German engraver, born at Hamburg in 1754. He went to Paris, and became the disciple of J. G. Wille. He engraved a great number of landscapes, in the neat, clear style of his instructor, after Ruysdael, Pynacker, Adrian vande Velde, Poullain, Choiseul, Praslin, and others.

WEISHUN, SAMUEL, a German engraver, who flourished at Dresden from 1630 to 1650. He engraved a considerable number of portraits, which are executed with the graver, in a neat, but stiff and formal style. According to Professor Christ, he engraved a set of portraits of the princes of Saxony, some of which are marked with his initials S. W. Zani says he was a goldsmith, as well as a designer and engraver.

WEISSE, GOTTHELF WILLIAM, a German engraver, born at Dresden about 1750. He studied under Giuseppe Canale, and executed quite a number of plates of portraits, historical subjects, and landscapes, which display considerable ability.—He was invited to the court of Hesse Cassel, where the Landgrave appointed him his principal engraver. He engraved the portraits of the Landgrave and Landgravine.

WELBRONNER, NICHOLAS, a German engraver, who flourished, according to Professor Christ, about 1536. He engraved some plates of ornamental foliage and small figures in the manner of Hans Sebald Beham, which he marked with a monogram of his initials. Bartsch describes eighteen etchings supposed to be by him, and Brulliot says he is acquainted with fourteen more by the same artist, one of which is signed *Nicolas Wilborn*, 1536, his real name. Brulliot remarks that Professor Christ has not only misnamed this artist, but erroneously explained the monogram, as signifying *Nicolas Manuel Deutsch*.

WELL, ARNOLD VAN, a Dutch painter, born at Dort in 1772, and died in 1818. He studied under Andrew Vermeulen, in whose manner he painted landscapes by moonlight, and winter scenes. with figures skating and amusing themselves on the frozen rivers and canals of Holland, with considerable success. His pictures are admitted into good collections.

WENCESLAUS, OF OLMUTZ, an old German engraver, of whom nothing is known except by some prints attributed to him. There is a great deal of contradiction and uncertainty about him, which we cannot discuss further than to say, that some writers maintain the opinion that Wenceslaus d'Olmutz, and Michael Wolgemut, are one and the same artist; but that eminent critic, Bartsch, is of a contrary opinion. He describes fifty-six prints which he attributes to him, and one more which he considers doubtful. Some of these are copies from the prints of Martin Schoen and Israel von Mecheln, and others from his own designs. His print of the Death of the Virgin from that of Schoen, is signed WENCESLAUS DE OLOMUCZ IBIDEM, 1481. Others are marked with a gothic W., and some have no mark at all. Those who wish to examine into the merits of the controversy, are referred to Bartsch, Peintre Graveur, tom. vi.; Zani's Enciclopedia Metodica delle belle Arti, parte prima, letters O. and W., vols. xiv. and xix.; and Ottley's Enquiry into the History of early Engraving. See *Wolgemut*.

WENG, J. G., an engraver, and probably a painter, who flourished about 1630. There is an etching by him of Minerva visiting the Muses, neatly executed, in the manner of de Hooghe.

WERDMULLER, RUDOLF, a Swiss painter, born at Zurich in 1639. He studied under Conrad Meyer, and had given promise of uncommon ability, both in history and portraits, when he was unfortunately drowned in 1668. The *Biographie Universelle* states that he also manifested considerable talents in sculpture, and modelled two busts of Apollo and Minerva, besides a figure of Milo of Crotona.

WERENFELS, RUDOLF, a Swiss painter, born at Basle in 1629. According to Füessli, he studied first at Amsterdam, and afterwards in Italy. He excelled in portraits, and was much employed at several of the courts of Germany. He died in 1673.

WERF, ADRIAN VANDER, an eminent Dutch painter, born at Kralinger-Ambacht, near Rotterdam, in 1659. He early showed a genius for painting, and first studied for two years under Cornelius Picolett, a painter of portraits and conversations; he afterwards became the scholar of Eglon vander Neer, with whom he continued four years He had made great progress under this master, when a picture by Francis Mieris being brought to vander Neer to copy, he entrusted it to his pupil, who executed the task so admirably, as to deceive the best judges. At the age of eighteen, he commenced his professional career at Rotterdam, and met with the most flattering encouragement. He formed an intimacy with M. Flink, who possessed an extensive collection of drawings by the best Italian masters, to which he had access at all times, and by a diligent study of these treasures and designing after the best casts of the antique he greatly improved himself, and formed a correct and elevated taste of design.

Vander Werf had already acquired a distinguished reputation, when the Elector Palatine, visiting Holland, and passing through Rotterdam, was captivated with his works, invited him to his court, and commissioned him to paint a picture of the Judgment of Solomon, and his own portrait, which last he intended to send to the Grand Duke of Tuscany, to be placed in the Florentine Gallery. Having finished his pictures, he went to Dusseldorf the following year, where he was received in the most flattering manner, and his pieces greatly admired. The Elector conferred on him the honor of knighthood, presented him with a gold medal and chain, and his portrait set with diamonds. That prince was desirous of retaining him in his service at Dusseldorf, but vander Werf excused himself, urging other engagements, and the necessity of his returning to his family and friends; but he engaged to devote six months in the year in painting for him, for which he received a liberal pension, besides liberal payment for his works. The same prince, on being presented with a picture of Diana and Callisto by the wife of vander Werf, gave her a magnificent toilet of silver, and presented her husband with six thousand florins. He continued to be employed by the Elector till the death of that prince in 1717, for whom he painted many of his most capital works.

Few painters have carried finishing to so high a pitch as vander Werf, yet his pictures produce a less pleasing effect than those of Gerard Douw and Francis Mieris. Sir Joshua Reynolds, in his Journey to Flanders and Holland, gives the following admirable critique upon the works of this eminent artist in the Dusseldorf Gallery. "The most distinguished pictures in this room are the vander Werfs, which are twenty-four in number, three of these are as large as life; a Magdalen, whole-length, and two portraits. The Magdalen was painted as a companion to the St. John of Raffaelle, but it was not thought, even by his friends and admirers, that he had succeeded: however, he has certainly spared no pains; it is as smooth and as highly finished as his small pictures; but his defects are here magnified and consequently more apparent. His pictures, whether great or small, certainly afford but little pleasure. Of their want of effect, it is worth a painter's while to inquire the cause. One of the principal causes appears to me, his having entertained an opinion that the light of a picture ought to be thrown solely on the figures, and little or none on the ground or sky. This gives great coldness to the effect, and is so contrary to nature and the practice of those painters with whose works he was surrounded, that we cannot help wondering how he fell into the mistake.

"His naked figures appear to be of a much harder substance than flesh, though his outline is far from cutting, or the light not united with the shade, which are the most common causes of hardness; but it appears to me that in the present instance, the hardness of the manner proceeds from the softness and union being too general; the light being everywhere equally lost in the ground or its shadow.

"In describing vander Werf's manner, were I to say that all the parts everywhere melt into each other, it might naturally be supposed that the effect would be a high degree of softness; but it is notoriously the contrary, and I think for the reason that has been given; his flesh has the appearance of ivory or plaster, or some other hard substance. What likewise contributes to this hardness is a want of transparency in his coloring, from his admitting little or no reflections of light. He had also the defect which is frequently found in Rembrandt, that of making his light only a single spot. However, to do him justice, his figures and his heads are generally well drawn, and his drapery is excellent; perhaps there are in his pictures as perfect examples of drapery as are to be found in any other painter's works whatever."

Vander Werf bestowed so much labor on his pictures, that they are exceedingly rare, and are consequently purchased at high prices, though they do not seem to excite the admiration they did in his lifetime. Smith, in his Catalogue raisonné, of the works of the Dutch and Flemish masters, vol. iv. and Supplement, gives a descriptive account of about 150 pictures by this master. He died in 1722.

WERF, Peter vander, was the younger brother of the preceding, born at Kralinger-Ambacht, near Rotterdam, in 1665. He was instructed by his brother, whose works he copied for some time, in the same tone of coloring and delicate manner of penciling. He afterwards painted small portraits and conversations, and occasionally history, from his own designs, in which he imitated his brother so closely, that his pictures have sometimes passed for Adrian's works, though they are inferior to them. One of his best works is in the Hall of the Dutch East India Company at Rotterdam, representing the portraits of the Directors at that time. He died in 1718.

WERNER, Joseph, an eminent Swiss painter, born at Berne in 1637. He was the son of a painter of little note, who instructed him in the rudiments of art, and afterwards sent him to Frankfort, where he became the disciple of Matthew Merian the Younger, under whom he made such progress, and showed such talents, that his instructor advised him to complete his education in Italy, and procured for him the protection of M. Muller, an amateur of fortune, who took him with him to Rome. During his residence in that city, Werner was indefatigable in designing from the antique, and the works of the great masters, and made an incredible number of designs. He painted both in oil and fresco, but having a predilection for high finishing, he afterwards devoted himself to miniature painting, which he carried to such a height of perfection, as has seldom been surpassed or equalled. His historical works are ingeniously composed and correctly designed, his coloring is clear and forcible, his heads have a fine expression, and the whole has great harmony, neatness, and elegance. His chief excellence lay in portraits, which he finished in an exquisite manner, and obtained a correct likeness. In returning from Italy, he passed through France, where his talents recommended him to the patronage of Louis XIV., who invited him to Versailles. He painted the portrait of the King, and those of the principal personages of his court; he was also much employed in painting historical and emblematical subjects, which were so much admired, that the most flattering proposals were offered to induce him to establish himself in France, but he had already accepted an invitation from the court of Inspruck, whither he proceeded. He painted the portrait of the Archduchess, for which he was liberally rewarded, and honored with a gold medal and chain. He resided some time at Augsburg, where he was incessantly employed by the princes and nobility of Germany. In 1696, Frederick, Elector of Brandenburg, and the first King of Prussia, invited him to Berlin, and appointed him director of the Academy there, with a liberal pension. He died at Berlin in 1710.

WESEL, TELMAN VAN, a German engraver of whom little is known. It appears from an inscription on one of his plates that he was a goldsmith, as well as an engraver. His prints are chiefly copied from the works of Albert Durer and other German masters; they are indifferently executed, and sometimes signed with his name, and at others T. W., or T. M. W.

WEST, BENJAMIN. This preëminent American painter was born at Springfield, in Pennsylvania, Oct. 10, 1738, and was the tenth child of John and Sarah West. His life is so full of interest and instruction, not only to the young artist, but to the public generally, that a more extended notice of it will be given, than the limits of this work will admit in most instances. Cunningham says, "John West, the father of Benjamin, was of that family settled at Long-Crendon, in Buckinghamshire, which produced Colonel James West, the friend and companion in arms of John Hampden. Upon one occasion, in the course of a conversation in Buckingham palace, respecting his picture of the Institution of the Garter, West happened to make some allusion to his English descent, when the Marquis of Buckingham, to the manifest pleasure of the king, declared that the Wests of Long-Crendon were undoubted descendants of the Lord Delaware, renowned in the wars of Edward the Third and the Black Prince, and that the artist's likeness had therefore a right to a place amongst those of the nobles and warriors, in his historical picture." The warlike propensities of this branch of the family, however, had long been extinguished; in 1669 they embraced the peaceful tenets of the Quakers, and emigrated to America. John West only remained behind till his education was completed, in the Quakers' Seminary at Uxbridge, when he followed his family to Philadelphia. He there married Sarah Pierson, whose grand-father was the confidential friend of William Penn, and aided him in founding the State of Pennsylvania. They settled at Springfield, where he carried on the mercantile business. One part of the marriage portion of his wife was a negro slave, an affectionate and faithful creature; but John West, in his intercourse as a merchant with the West Indies, witnessing the cruelties to which the unhappy Africans were frequently subjected, liberated his bondsman, and retained him as a hired servant. His example was followed by others, and the charitable feeling spread far and wide, till it came to be established as one of the tenets of the Quakers, that no person could remain a member of their Society, who held a human being in slavery. Benjamin's birth was brought on prematurely by a vehement sermon, preached in the fields, by Edward Peckover, on the corrupt state of the Old World, which he prophesied was about to be visited with the tempest of God's judgments, the wicked to be swallowed up, and the terrified remnant compelled to seek refuge in happy America. Mrs. West was so affected that she swooned away, was carried home severely ill, and the pains of labor came upon her; she was, however, safely delivered, and the preacher consoled the parents by predicting that "a child sent into the world under such remarkable circumstances, would assuredly prove a wonderful man," and admonished them to watch over their son with more than ordinary care. The first remarkable incident recorded of the infant prodigy occurred in his seventh year, when being placed to watch the sleeping infant of his eldest sister, he drew a sort of likeness of the child, with a pen, in red and black ink. His mother returned, and snatching the paper which he sought to conceal, exclaimed to her daughter, "I declare, he has made a likeness of little Sally!" She took him in her arms, and kissed him fondly. This feat appeared so wonderful in the eyes of his parents, that they recalled to mind the prediction of Peckover. When he was about eight years old, a party of Indians, who were always kindly treated by the followers of George Fox, paid their summer visit to Springfield, and being struck with the rude sketches which the boy had made of birds, fruit, and flowers, they taught him to prepare the red and yellow colors with which they stained their weapons and ornamented their skins; his mother added indigo, and thus he was possessed of three primary colors. The Indians also instructed him in archery. The wants of the child increased with his knowledge; he could draw, and had colors, but how to lay them on skillfully he could not conceive; a pen would not answer, and he tried feathers without any better success; a neighbor informed him that it was done with a camel's hair pencil, but as such a thing was not to be had, he bethought himself of the cat, and supplied himself from her back and tail. The cat was a favorite, and the altered condition of her fur was attributed to disease, till the boy's confession explained the cause, much to the amusement of his parents and friends. His cat's tail pencils enabled him to make more satisfactory efforts than he had before done. Soon after this, when he was only eight years old, a merchant of Philadelphia named Pennington, and a cousin of the Wests, was so much pleased with the sketches of little Benjamin, that he sent him a box of paints and pencils, with canvass prepared for the easel, and six engravings by Gribelin. The child was perfectly enraptured with his treasure; he carried the box about in his arms, and took it to his bedside, but could not sleep. He rose with the dawn, carried his canvass and colors to the garret, hung up the engravings, prepared a palette, and commenced work. So completely was he under this species of enchantment, that he absented himself from school, labored secretly and incessantly, and without interruption, for several days, when the anxious inquiries of his schoolmaster introduced his mother into his *studio*, with no pleasure in her looks. He had avoided copyism, and made a picture, composed from two of the engravings, telling a new story, and colored with a skill and effect which, to her eyes, appeared wonderful. Galt, who wrote West's life, and had the story from the artist's lips, says, "She kissed him with transports of affection, and assured him that she would not only intercede with his father to pardon him for having absented himself from school, but would go herself to the master, and beg that he might not be punished. Sixty-seven years afterwards, the writer of these memoirs had the gratification to see this piece, in the same room with the sublime painting of Christ Rejected (West's brother had sent it to him from Springfield), on which occasion the painter declared to him that there were inventive touches of art in his first and juvenile essay, which, with all his subsequent knowledge and experience, he had not been able to surpass." A similar story is told of Canova, who visited his native place towards the close of his brilliant career, and looking earnestly at his youthful performances, sorrowfully said, "I have been walking, but not climbing." In the ninth year of his age, he accompanied his relative Pennington to Philadelphia, and executed a view of the banks of the river, which so much pleased a painter named Williams, that he took him to his studio, and showed him all his pictures, at the sight of which he was so affected that he burst into tears. The artist, surprised, declared like Peckover that Benjamin would be a remarkable man; he gave him two books, Du Fresnoy, and Richardson on Painting, and invited him to call whenever he pleased, to see his pictures. From this time, Benjamin resolved to become a painter, and returned home with the love of painting too firmly implanted to be eradicated. His parents also, though the art was not approved by the Friends, now openly encouraged him, being strongly impressed with the opinion that he was *predestinated* to become a great artist. His notions of a painter at this time were also very grand, as the following characteristic anecdote will show. One of his school-fellows allured him, on a half holiday from school, to take a ride with him to a neighboring plantation. "Here is the horse, bridled and saddled," said the boy, "so come, get up behind me." "Behind you!" said Benjamin; "I will ride behind nobody." "Oh, very well," replied the other; "I will ride behind you, so mount." He mounted accordingly, and away they rode. "This is the last ride I shall have for some time," said his companion; "to-morrow I am to be apprenticed to a tailor." "A tailor," exclaimed West; "you will surely never be a tailor?" "Indeed but I shall," replied the other; "it is a good trade. What do you intend to be, Benjamin?" "A painter." "A painter! what sort of a trade is a painter? I never heard of it before." "A painter," said West, "is the companion of kings and emperors." "You are surely mad," said the embryo tailor; "there are neither kings nor emperors in America." "Aye, but there are plenty in other parts of the world. And do you really intend to be a tailor?" "Indeed I do; there is nothing surer." "Then you may ride alone," said the future companion of kings and emperors, leaping down; "I will not ride with one who is willing to be a tailor!"

West's first patron was Mr. Wayne, the father of General Anthony Wayne, who gave him a dollar a piece for two small pictures he had made on poplar boards, which a carpenter had given him. Another patron was Mr. Flower, a justice of Chester, who took young West to his house for a short time, where he was made acquainted with a young English lady, governess to Mr. Flower's daughters, who had a good knowledge of art, and told him stories of Greek and Roman history, fit for a painter's pencil. He had never before heard of the heroes, philosophers, poets, painters, and historians of Greece and Rome, and he listened while the lady spoke of them, with an enthusiasm which he loved to live over again in his old age. His first painting which attracted much notice was a portrait of Mrs. Ross, a very beautiful lady, the wife of a lawyer of Lancaster. The picture was regarded as a wonderful performance, and gained him so much reputation, says Galt, "that the citizens came in such crowds to sit to the boy for portraits, that he had some trouble in meeting the demands." At the same time, a gunsmith, named Henry, who had a classic turn, commissioned him to paint a picture of the Death of Socrates. West forthwith made a sketch, which his employer thought excellent, but he now began to see his difficulties, and feel his deficiencies. "I have hitherto painted faces," said he, "and people clothed. What am I to do with the slave who presents the poison? He ought, I think, to be painted naked." Henry went to his shop, and returned with one of his workmen, a handsome young negro man, half naked, saying, "There is your model." He accordingly introduced him into his picture, which excited great attention. West was now fifteen years old. Dr. Smith, Provost of the College at Philadelphia, happened to see him at Lancaster, and perceiving his wonderful talents, and that his education was being neglected, generously proposed to his father to take him with him to Philadelphia, where he proposed to direct his studies, and to instruct him in all the learning most important for a painter to know. The art of painting being regarded by the Quakers as not only useless, but pernicious, "in preserving voluptuous images, and adding to the sensual gratifications of man," Mr. West determined to submit the matter to the wisdom of the Society, before giving a positive answer. He accordingly sent for his son to attend the solemn assembly. The Friends met, and the spirit of speech first descended on John Williamson, who, according to Galt, thus spake: "To John West and Sarah Pearson, a man-child hath been born, on whom God hath conferred some remarkable gifts of mind; and you have all heard that, by something amounting to inspiration, the youth has been induced to study the art of painting. It is true that our tenets refuse to own the utility of that art to mankind, but it seemeth to me that we have considered the matter too nicely. God hath bestowed on this youth a genius for art—shall we question his wisdom? Can we believe that he gives such rare gifts but for a wise and good purpose? I see the Divine hand in this; we shall do well to sanction the art, and encourage this youth." The Quakers gave their unanimous consent, and summoned the youth before them. He came, and took his station in the middle of the room, his father on his right hand, his mother on his left, while around him gathered the whole assembly. One of the women first spake, but the words of Williamson, says Galt, are alone remembered. "Painting," said he, "has hitherto been employed to embellish life, to preserve voluptuous images, and add to the sensual gratifications of men. For this we classed it among vain and merely ornamental things, and excluded it from amongst us. But this is not the principle but the misemployment of painting. In wise and pure hands, it rises in the scale of moral excellence, and displays a loftiness of sentiment, and a devout dignity, worthy of the contemplation of Christians. I think genius is given by God for some high purpose. What the purpose is, let us not inquire—it will be manifest in His own good time and way. He hath in this remote wilderness endowed with rich gifts of a superior spirit this youth, who has now our consent to cultivate his talents for art; may it be demonstrated in his life and works, that the gifts of God have not been bestowed in vain, nor the motives of the beneficent inspiration, which induces us to suspend the strict operations of our tenets, prove barren of religious and moral effect!" At the conclusion of this address, says Galt, the women rose and kissed the young artist, and the men, one by one, laid their hands on his head. The scene made so strong an impression on the mind of West, that he looked upon himself as expressly dedicated to art, and considered this release from the strict tenets of his sect, as enjoining on his part a covenant to employ his powers on subjects pure and holy. The grave simplicity of the Quaker continued to the last in his looks, manners, and deportment; and the moral rectitude and internal purity of the man were diffused through all his productions.

West now proceeded to Philadelphia, where he studied till he was eighteen, except a short time, when he accompanied Major Sir Peter Halkert, as a volunteer to search for the remains, and bury the bones of the army which had been lost under General Braddock. He returned home from this expedition just in time to receive the welcome of the eyes and the mute blessing of his dying mother, whom he tenderly loved and honored; even when he was old and gray, he loved to recall her looks, and to dwell on her expressions of fondness and of hope, with a sadness which he wished neither to subdue nor conceal.

After this bereavement, he again proceeded to Philadelphia, where he commenced his profession. His extreme youth, the peculiar circumstances of his history, and his undoubted merit, brought him many sitters. His prices were very humble—$12.50 for a head, and $25 for a full-length; all the money he thus laboriously earned, he carefully treasured, to secure, at some future period, the means of travel and study; for his sagacious mind perceived that travel not only influenced public opinion, but was absolutely necessary for him if he wished to excel, especially in historical painting. There were no galleries in America; he knew that the masterpieces of art were in Italy, and he had already set his heart on visiting that delightful country. He made a copy of a picture of St. Ignatius, by Murillo, which had been captured in a Spanish vessel, and belonged to Governor Hamilton; he also painted a large picture for Mr. Cox, from the history of Susanna, the Elders, and Daniel, in which he introduced no less than forty figures. This work gained him great reputation, and West always considered it the masterpiece of his youth; it was afterwards unfortunately destroyed by fire. After having painted the portraits of all who desired it in Philadelphia, he proceeded to New York, where he opened a studio, and Dunlap says for eleven months he had all the portraits he could execute, at double the prices he had charged in Philadelphia. An opportunity now presented itself, which enabled him to gratify his long cherished desire of going to Italy. The harvest had partially failed in that country, and Mr. Allen, a merchant of Philadelphia, was loading a ship with wheat and flour for Leghorn. He had resolved to send his son as supercargo, to give him the benefit of travel, and West's invaluable friend, Provost Smith, made arrangements for the young painter to accompany the young merchant. It happened that a New York merchant, of the name of Kelly, was sitting for his portrait when this good news arrived, and West with joy spoke to him of the great advantage he expected to derive from a residence of two or three years in Italy. The portrait being finished, Mr. Kelly paid him ten guineas, and gave him a letter to his agent in Philadelphia, which, on being presented, proved to be an order from the generous merchant to pay him fifty guineas, as "a present to aid in his equipment for Italy."

West arrived at Rome on the 10th of July, 1760, in the 22d year of his age. Cunningham thus describes his reception: "When it was known that a young American had come to study Raffaelle and Michael Angelo, some curiosity was excited among the Roman virtuosi. The first fortunate exhibitor of this lion from the western wilderness was Lord Grantham, the English ambassador, to whom West had letters. He invited West to dinner, and afterwards took him to an evening party, where he found almost all those persons to whom he had brought letters of introduction. Among the rest was Cardinal Albani, who, though old and blind, had such delicacy of touch that he was considered supreme in all matters of judgment regarding medals and intaglios. 'I have the honor,' said Lord Grantham, 'to present a young American, who has a letter for your Eminence, and who has come to Italy for the purpose of studying the Fine Arts.' The Cardinal knew so little of the New World, that he conceived an American must needs be a savage. 'Is he black or white?' said the aged virtuoso, holding out both hands, that he might have the satisfaction of touching, at least, this new wonder. Lord Grantham smiled and said, 'He is fair—very fair.' 'What! as fair as I am?' exclaimed the prelate. Now the complexion of the churchman was a deep olive—that of West more than commonly fair; and as they stood together, the company smiled. 'As fair as the Cardinal,' became for a while proverbial. Others, who had the use of their eyes, seemed to consider the young American as at most a better kind of savage, and accordingly were curious to watch him. They wished to try what effect the Apollo, the Venus, and the works of Raffaelle would have upon him, and thirty of the most magnificent equipages in the capital, filled with some of the most erudite characters in Europe, says Galt, conducted the young Quaker to view the masterpieces of art. It was agreed that the Apollo should be first submitted to his view; the statue was enclosed in a case, and when the keeper threw open the doors, West unconsciously exclaimed, 'My God! a young Mohawk warrior!' The Italians were surprised and mortified with the comparison of their noblest statue to a wild savage; and West, perceiving the unfavorable impression, proceeded to remove it. He described the Mohawks, the natural elegance and admirable symmetry of their persons, the elasticity of their limbs, and their motions free and unconstrained. 'I have seen them often,' he continued, standing in the attitude of this Apollo, and pursuing with an intense eye the arrow which they had just discharged from the bow.' The Italians cleared their moody brows, and allowed that a better criticism had rarely been made. West was no longer a barbarian.

"West, however, soon attracted other attention than mere curiosity. He had shown his drawings to Mengs and Hamilton, but they were, as he confessed, destitute of original merit; nor could they be commended for neatness or accuracy. He therefore waited on Lord Grantham, and said, 'I cannot produce a finished sketch, like the other students, because I have never been instructed in drawing; but I can paint a little, and if you will do me the honor to sit for your portrait, that I may show it to Mengs, you will do me a great kindness.' His lordship consented, and the name of the artist being kept secret, the picture was placed in the Gallery of Crespigni, where artists and connoisseurs were invited to see it. 'It was known,' says Cunningham, 'that Lord Grantham was sitting to Mengs, and to him some ascribed the portrait, though they thought the coloring surpassed his other compositions.' Dance, an Englishman of sense and acuteness, looked at it closely; 'the coloring surpasses that of Mengs,' he observed, 'but the drawing is not so good.' The company eagerly engaged in the discussion; Crespigni seized the proper moment, and said, 'It is not painted by Mengs.' 'By whom, then?' they exclaimed, 'for there is no other painter in Rome capable of doing any thing so good.' 'By that young gentleman,' said the other, turning to West, who sat uneasy and agitated. The English held out their hands; the Italians ran and embraced him."

Mengs himself was surprised at the excellence of this performance, complimented the young artist highly, and advised him to "examine everything at Rome worthy of attention, making drawings of some half dozen of the best statues; then go to Florence and study the galleries; from there to Bologna, and study the works of the Caracci, and then proceed to Venice, and view the productions of Tintoretto, Titian, and Paul Veronese. When all this is accomplished, return to Rome, paint a historical picture, exhibit it publicly, and then the opinion which will be expressed of your talents, will determine the line of art which you ought to follow." West had previously entered the Academy, and he immediately proceeded to follow this common but sensible advice. The excitement to which he was subjected, and his anxiety to distinguish himself, brought on a fever, and for a time interrupted his studies; by the advice of his physicians, he returned to Leghorn, where, after a lingering sickness of eleven months, he was completely cured. But he found his funds almost exhausted, and he began to despair of being able to prosecute his studies according to the proposed plan. He called on his agents, to take up the last ten pounds he had in the world, when to his astonishment and joy, he was handed a letter of unlimited credit from his old friends in Philadelphia, Mr. Allen and Governor Hamilton; they had heard of his glorious reception at Rome, and his success with the portrait of Lord Grantham. At a dinner, one day, with Governor Hamilton, Mr. Allen said, "I regard this young man as an honor to his country, and as he is the first that America has sent out to cultivate the Fine Arts, he shall not be frustrated in his studies, for I shall send him whatever money he may require." "I think with you, sir," replied Hamilton, "but you must not have all the honor to yourself; allow me to unite with you in the responsibility of the credit." Those who befriend genius when it is struggling for distinction, are public benefactors, and their names should be held in grateful remembrance. The names of Hamilton, Allen, Smith, Kelly, Jackson, Rutherford, and Lord Grantham, must be dear to all the admirers of West; they aided him in the infancy of his fame and fortune, cheered him when he was drooping and desponding; and watched over his person and purse with the vigilance of true friendship. West always expressed his deepest obligations to these generous men, and it was at his particular request that Galt recorded their names, and their deeds.

West now proceeded with redoubled alacrity, to execute the plan recommended by Mengs. He visited Florence, Bologna, Parma, and Venice, and diligently examined everything worth studying. He everywhere received marked attention, and was elected a member of the Academies of Florence, Bologna, and Parma. In the latter city, he painted and presented to the Academy, a copy of the famous St. Jerome by Correggio, "of such excellence," says Galt, "that the reigning prince desired to see the artist. He went to court, and to the utter astonishment of the attendants, appeared with his hat on. The Prince was familiar with the tenets of the Quakers, and was a lover of William Penn; he received the young artist with complacency, and dismissed him with many expressions of regard." West returned to Rome, where he painted two pictures which were highly commended, one of Cimon and Iphigenia, and the other of Angelica and Medora. At Venice, he particularly studied the works of Titian, and Cunningham says "he imagined he had discovered his principles of coloring." We can only record one more of the interesting incidents which occurred to him while in Italy. He was conversing one evening with Gavin Hamilton, in the British Coffee House, when an old man with a long and flowing beard, and a harp in his hand, entered and offered his services as an improvisatore bard. "Here is an American," said the wily Scot, "come to study the fine arts in Rome; take him for your theme, and it is a magnificent one." The minstrel casting a glance at West, who never in his life could perceive what a joke was, commenced his song. "I behold in this youth an instrument chosen by heaven to create in his native country a taste for those arts which have elevated the nature of man—an assurance that his land will be the refuge of science and knowledge, when in the old age of Europe they shall have forsaken her shores. All things of heavenly origin move westward, and Truth, and Art, have their periods of light and darkness. Rejoice, O Rome, for thy spirit immortal and undecayed now spreads towards a new world, where, like the soul of man in Paradise, it will be perfected more and more." The predictions of Peckover, the fond expressions of his beloved mother, and his solemn dedication to art rushed upon West's memory, and he burst into tears; and even in his riper years, he was willing to consider the poor mendicant's song as another prophecy.

Having seen everything in Italy which he regarded as essential to his success, West set out for his native country, but resolved first to visit the land of his ancestors; he accordingly traveled through France in the company of Dr. Patoun, an eminent Scotch physician, whose acquaintance he had made in Italy, and who took a lively interest in his welfare. He arrived at London in August, 1763, where he was warmly received by several eminent artists and persons of distinction, to whom he had letters of introduction from Mengs and others; Dr. Patoun also spoke so highly of his works as to excite general curiosity among the admirers of the Fine Arts, to see his two pictures of Cimon and Iphigenia, and Angelica and Medora, which he had painted at Rome. Among others who visited him at this time was Mr. Reynolds, (afterwards Sir Joshua,) who, instead of looking upon him as a rival, at once acknowledged his merit, offered him his friendship, and urged him to exhibit his two pictures at the Society Rooms in Spring Gardens. They were accordingly exhibited there, and the praises which they elicited, far surpassed the most sanguine expectations of the artist. He also had the good fortune to meet with three of his best friends—Dr. Smith, Governor Hamilton, and Mr. Allen—who then happened to be in London, and who strongly recommended him to set up his easel. He now abandoned the idea of returning to America, at least for the present, although there was a powerful attraction to draw him thither. While he resided in Philadelphia, he had formed an acquaintance with Miss Elizabeth Shewell, the daughter of a merchant of that city. The intimacy had ripened into one of deep affection, but the intended marriage had hitherto been delayed by prudential motives. The sacred engagement was, however, never forgotten on either side; and no sooner had West formed the resolution of settling in England, and felt assured of success, than he wrote to his father, requesting him to accompany the young lady to London, that their union might take place. Miss Shewell accordingly sailed from Philadelphia with Mr. West, senior, and soon after their arrival, the nuptials were solemnized.

The paintings which West exhibited at Spring Gardens, and his love of serious and solemn subjects, attracted the notice of some of the dignitaries of the church, and other persons of distinction. He painted for Dr. Newton the Parting of Hector and Andromache; and for the Bishop of Worcester, the Return of the Prodigal Son. His reputation rose so much with these productions, that Lord Rockingham offered him a permanent engagement, with a salary of £700 a year, to embellish with historical paintings his palace in Yorkshire. West consulted with his friends, who advised him to *confide in the public*, and he followed for a time this salutary counsel. In 1765, the Society of Artists was incorporated by royal charter, and West became both a member and a director. The same year he exhibited two pictures, one of Jupiter and Europa, and the other of Venus and Cupid. The following year he had four pictures, viz.: the Continence of Scipio, Pylades and Orestes, Cimon and Iphigenia, and Diana and Endymion. The merit of West now became more extensively known, by the patronage and friendship of Dr. Drummond, Archbishop of York, a great admirer of painting, who invited him to his house, and commissioned him to paint a picture of Agrippina landing with the ashes of Germanicus. That liberal prelate was so much pleased with the performance, that he made an effort to procure the painter an annuity by subscription, so as to enable him to desist from portraiture, and confine himself to historical subjects. He proposed to raise £3,000; himself and friends subscribed £1,500, but the public coldly refused to coöperate, and the scheme was abandoned. The Archbishop, however, regarding the failure of his plan as a stigma on the country, sought and obtained an audience of the king, then a young man, and a lover of the fine arts; he informed him that "a devout American, and a Quaker, had painted, at his request, such a noble picture, that he was desirous to secure his talents for the throne of his country." The king was so much pleased with the story, that he desired he would send the young painter with his picture to him. West was well received by the king, who presented him to his Queen, and commissioned him to paint a picture of the Departure of Regulus from Rome. The king treated West, on this occasion, with extraordinary condescension; he took from the shelf a copy of Livy, and read to him that part of the history which describes the departure of Regulus. The talents, simplicity, candor, and dignity of the artist completely won his heart, and this was the commencement of a remarkable intimacy of nearly forty years' duration. The palace doors now seemed to open to him of their own accord, and the domestics attended with an obedient start to the wishes of him whom the king delighted to honor.

There are other minor matters, says Cunningham, which help a man on to fame and fortune. West was a skillful skater, and in America had formed an acquaintance on the ice with Colonel Howe. One day, the painter having tied on his skates at the Serpentine, was astonishing the timid practitioners of London by the rapidity of his motions, and the graceful figure which he cut. Some one shouted "West! West!" It was Colonel Howe. "I am glad to see you," said he, "and not less so that you came in good time to vindicate my praises of American skating." He called to him Lord Spencer Hamilton, and some of the Cavendishes, to whom he introduced West as one of the Philadelphia prodigies of skating, and requested him to show them what was called "the Salute." He performed this feat so much to their satisfaction that they spread the praises of the American skater all over London. West was exceedingly fond of this invigorating amusement, and used frequently to gratify large crowds by cutting the Philadelphia Salute. Cunningham says, "Many to the praise of his skating, added panegyrics on his professional skill, and not a few to vindicate their applause, followed him to his easel, and sat for their portraits."

While West was painting the Departure of Regulus, the Royal Academy was planned, and he was one of the principal founders. The Society of Artists had grown rich by the yearly exhibitions, and how to lay out this money, became the subject of vehement contention. The architects were for an edifice, the sculptors for statues, and the painters for a gallery of historical works. West, who was one of the directors, approved of none of these notions, and with Reynolds withdrew from the association. The newspapers denounced these indecent bickerings, and the king learning the cause from the lips of West, declared that he was ready to patronize any association formed on principles calculated to advance the interests of art. A plan was accordingly drawn up by some of the dissenters, and submitted to the King, who corrected it, and drew up some additional articles with his own hand. The Royal Academy was accordingly founded in 1768, and in the first exhibition appeared the Departure of Regulus.

A change was now to be effected in the character of British art. Hitherto, historical painting had appeared in a masking habit; the actions of Englishmen, says Cunningham, had all been performed, if costume were to be believed, by Greeks or Romans. West dismissed at once this pedantry, and restored nature and propriety in his noble work of "the Death of Wolfe." The multitude acknowledged its excellence at once, on its being exhibited at the Royal Academy; but the lovers of old art, or of the compositions called *classical*, complained of the barbarism of boots, buttons, and blunderbusses, and cried out for naked warriors, with bows, bucklers, and battering rams. Lord Grosvenor was so pleased with the picture, that, disregarding the frowns of amateurs, and the cold approbation of the Academy, he purchased it. Galt says that the king questioned West concerning this picture, and put him on his defense of this new heresy in art. "When it was understood," said the artist, "that I intended to paint the characters as they had actually appeared on the scene, the Archbishop of York called on Reynolds, and asked his opinion; they both came to my house to dissuade me from running so great a risk. Reynolds began a very ingenious and elegant dissertation on the state of the public taste in this country, and the danger which every innovator incurred of contempt and ridicule, and concluded by urging me earnestly to adopt the costume of antiquity, as more becoming the greatness of my subject than the modern garb of European warriors. I answered that the event to be commemorated happened in the year 1758, in a region of the world unknown to the Greeks and Romans, and at a period of time when no warriors who wore such costume existed. The subject I have to represent is a great battle fought and won, and the same truth which gives law to the historian, should rule the painter. If instead of the facts of the action, I introduce fiction, how shall I be understood by posterity? The classic dress is certainly picturesque, but by using it, I shall lose in sentiment what I gain in external grace. I want to mark the place, the time, and the people, and to do this, I must abide by truth. They went away, and returned again when I had finished the painting. Reynolds seated himself before the picture, examined it with deep and minute attention for half an hour; then rising, said to Drummond, 'West has conquered; he has treated his subject as it ought to be treated; I retract my objections. I foresee that this picture will not only become one of the most popular, but will occasion a revolution in art.'" "I wish," said the king, "that I had known all this before, for the objection has been the means of Lord Grosvenor's getting the picture; but you shall make a copy for me."

West had now obtained the personal confidence of the King, and the favor of the public—his commissions were numerous, but of course the works for the palace had the precedence. The King employed him to paint the Death of Epaminondas, as a companion to the Death of Wolfe, which he copied; the Death of the Chevalier Bayard; Cyrus liberating the Family of the King of Armenia; and Segestus and his Daughter brought before Germanicus; all of which gave great satisfaction to the monarch. The success of West, and the royal favors bestowed upon him, not only began to excite the envy of artists generally, but even of Reynolds himself, who, says Cunningham, thought a few rays of the royal sunshine, at least, should have fallen upon him. "The President was not fool enough to complain—but his friends did so for him, while West, too prudent to carry himself loftily, because of his good fortune, enjoyed his success in secret, and continued in the outward man submissive and thankful. To Reynolds had fallen the whole portrait department, of church and state, which lay without the gates of the Palace; while within, West reigned triumphant." The King now commissioned West to paint a series of eight pictures to decorate St. George's Hall in Windsor Castle; all the subjects except one, were taken from the victorious reign of Edward III., as follows: 1. Edward the Third, embracing the Black Prince after the Battle of Cressy. 2. The Instalment of the Order of the Garter. 3. The Black Prince receiving the King of France and his Son prisoners at Poictiers. 4. St. George vanquishing the Dragon. 5. Queen Philippa defeating David of Scotland in the Battle of Neville's Cross. 6. Queen Philippa interceding with Edward for the Burgesses of Calais. 7. King Edward forcing the passage of the Somme. 8. King Edward crowning Sir Eustace de Ribaumont at Calais. These works are of very large size.—They were the fruit of long study and much labor, and are among his best and most carefully preserved works. Cunningham says their lustre is fresh and unfaded, the coloring natural and harmonious, and they present a lively image of the times and the people.

After the completion of these works, West proposed to the King to paint a great series upon the Progress of Revealed Religion, to decorate the Royal chapel at Windsor; but the King, before consenting to the proposal, summoned some of the dignitaries of the church to consider the propriety of introducing paintings into a place of worship. "When I reflect that the Reformation condemned religious paintings in churches, and that the Parliament, in the unhappy days of Charles the First did the same, I am fearful of introducing anything which my people might think popish. Will you give me your opinion on the subject?" After some deliberation, bishop Hurd delivered, in the name of his brethren and himself, the unanimous opinion, that "the introduction of religious paintings into your Majesty's chapel, will in no respect whatever violate the laws or the usages of the Church of England. We have examined, too, thirty-five subjects, which the painter proposes for your choice, and we feel that there is not one of them that may not be treated in a way, that even a *Quaker* might contemplate with edification." The King conceiving this to be an impertinent and ironical allusion to West, replied, "the Quakers are a body of Christians, for whom I have a high respect. I love their peaceful tenets and their benevolence to one another and the world, and but for the obligations of birth, I would be a Quaker." The bishop bowed submissively and retired.

To the thirty-five subjects approved by the bishops, West subsequently added another, making thirty-six in all. He divided the series into four departments—the Antediluvian, the Patriarchal, the Mosaic, and the Prophetic. Half of the subjects were from the Old Testament, and half from the New. They were all sketched, and twenty-eight of them executed, for which the artist received £21.705. He painted, in the meantime, nine pictures of portraits of the Royal Family, for which he received 2000 guineas.

The war which broke out between Great Britain and her colonies, says Galt, was a sore trial to the feelings of West; his early friends and his present patrons, were involved in the bloody controversy. He was not, according to his own account, silent; he was too much in the palace, and alone with the King, to evade some allusion to the subject. After the death of Reynolds in 1792, West was unanimously elected President of the Royal Academy, on which occasion, the King sent his brother, the Duke of Gloucester to him, to enquire whether the honor of knighthood would be acceptable to him; he declined in so respectful and dignified a manner, that the Duke took him warmly by the hand and said, "you have justified the opinion the King had of you; he will be delighted with your answer."

In 1801, during the illness of George III., West met with a severe reverse. Mr. Wyatt, the royal architect, called upon him and told him, without any further explanation, that he was directed to inform him, that the pictures painting for the chapel at Windsor, must be suspended until further orders. "This extraordinary proceeding," says Galt, "rendered the studies of the best part of the artist's life useless, and deprived him of that honorable provision, the fruit of his talents and industry, on which he had counted for the repose of his declining years. For some time, it affected him deeply, and he was at a loss what steps to take. At last, however, upon reflecting on the marked friendship and favor which the King had always shown him, he addressed to his Majesty a letter, on the 26th of September." This letter was carried to the court by Wyatt, but he received no answer to it. When the King recovered, West sought and obtained a private audience, and he found that the King did not know of the order to suspend the paintings, and that he had not received any letter from him; he spoke very kindly to the troubled artist, and said "go on with your work, West; go on with the pictures, and I will take care of you." This was West's last interview with the King. "But he contrived," says Galt, "to execute the pictures, and in the usual quarterly payments, received his salary of £1000 per annum, till his Majesty's final superannuation; when, without any intimation whatever, on calling to receive it, he was told it had been stopped, and that the paintings for the chapel had been suspended! He submitted in silence—he neither remonstrated nor complained." The story of his dismissal from court was spread abroad with many exaggerations, and the malevolent enemies, whom his success had created—for there are always such reptiles—circulated papers stating that the fortunate painter had received from the King the enormous sum of £34,187; so that the public imagined that he must have amassed a fortune. This notion was dispelled by an accurate statement from the painter, by which it appeared that he had toiled incessantly during thirty-three years of the prime of his life in the service of the King, for this sum, giving an accurate list of the works executed, and the prices paid, by which it appeared that he had received but a poor compensation, and that his income was much less than would satisfy any successful portrait painter of the day.

After the peace of Amiens, West visited Paris, for the purpose of viewing the world's gems of art, which Bonaparte had collected together in the Louvre. He was received in that capital with the most marked respect, not only by distinguished artists, connoisseurs, and literary men, but by the officials of the government. Cunningham, who, while he takes his favorites by the beard, as if to kiss them, seldom fails to jerk them under the ribs, attributes all this courtesy and hospitality to the cunning of "the wily politicians who surrounded the future Emperor. In a series of entertainments, in which wine and flattery were poured out abundantly, the enemies of his country succeeded in persuading the simple Benjamin, that they were the most philanthropic of all nations, and their master the kindest and worthiest of men." The truth is, West was too liberal in his sentiments to please the court under the Prince Regent; hence his rude dismissal from court. That he was highly gratified with the tributes of respect which the French know so well how to bestow upon a man of genius, cannot be doubted. West had already conceived a project for establishing in England a national institution, for the encouragement of art, similar to that of the Louvre, and he took occasion one day, while strolling about the Louvre in company with Mr. Fox and Sir Francis Baring, to point out to them the advantages of such an institution, not only in promoting the Fine Arts, by furnishing models of study for artists, but he showed the propriety even in a mercantile point of view, of encouraging to a seven-fold extent, the higher department of art in England. Fox was so forcibly struck with his remarks, that he said, "I have been rocked in the cradle of politics, but never before was so much struck with the advantages, even in a political bearing, of the Fine Arts, to the prosperity, as well as the renown of a kingdom; and I do assure you, Mr. West, if ever I have it in my power to influence our government to promote the Arts, the conversation which we have had to-day shall not be forgotten." Sir Francis Baring also promised his hearty coöperation. Cunningham also sagely attributes this to his opinion that the "wily politicians," had wheedled the "simple Benjamin," into the belief that the "views of Napoleon were sublime and benevolent, and that he only conquered kingdoms out of love of liberty, and collected pictures in the towns which he stormed, to furnish models of study for the artists of all nations." He forgets that the Royal British Institution was mainly established through the influence and energy of West; that he battled for years against coldly calculating politicians for its accomplishment; and that at length his plan was adopted, with scarcely an alteration. These things are mentioned here, because Cunningham, perhaps unwittingly, has detracted from the great renown of West, more than any other writer. His criticisms too, not only on West, but on all the artists whose biography he has written, are frequently more poetical than just, more flippant than erudite.

Soon after West's return to England, he resigned the President's chair in the Academy, owing to stormy opposition among its members; he also fancied that the government looked coldly upon him for his admiration of Bonaparte. Wyatt, the royal architect, was put in his place, but the Academicians soon became wearied of the latter, and having displaced him in the following year, 1803, they restored West, almost unanimously. There was but one dissenting voice, supposed to be that of Fuseli, who voted for Mrs. Moser. When Fuseli was taxed by some of the members with having given this vote, says his biographer Knowles, he answered, "well, suppose I did; she is eligible to the office—and is not one old woman as good as another?" The impatient extravagance of Fuseli accorded little with the dignity and diligence of West.

West was sixty-four years old when he lost the patronage of the court, having in a great measure thrown away thirty-three years of the prime of his life, for a paltry pittance, when his talents are taken into estimation; for while Reynolds, in the inferior branch of portraiture, realized some £12,000 a year, the first historical painter of the 18th century, was toiling incessantly for £1000. His blameless and temperate life had preserved his strength unimpaired, and he had still the same composed and determined mind, by which he was distinguished in youth. He therefore commenced a series of great religious works, on a larger scale than any he had previously painted. The first was Christ healing the Sick, a picture painted for the Pennsylvania Hospital, an institution founded by the Quakers, who had solicited his assistance, and as he was far from being rich, he had promised them a picture. When this picture was exhibited in London, it was so highly commended, that the British Institution offered him 3000 guineas for it, which he accepted, on condition that he should be allowed to make a copy, with some alterations. He did so, and when the copy was exhibited in the United States, the profits ($20-000,) enabled the committee of the hospital to enlarge the building and receive more patients. It has since continued to add to their resources about $500 per annum. "The success of this picture," says Cunningham, "impressed West with the belief that his genius appeared to most advantage in pictures of large dimensions, and that royal commissions had interposed between him and fortune.* His mind, from long contemplation, was familiar with subjects of gigantic proportions, and he had soon sketched out several and finished some; but the sunny and comfortable houses of England could not contain this colossal progeny; the doors of our churches are generally opened to art with reluctance, our palaces had already admitted more of the President's works than perhaps were welcome; and the owners of our galleries were unwilling to make room for such enormous pieces of scripture subjects. There was no market for the manufacture." The next picture he painted was the Crucifixion, sixteen by twenty-eight feet; followed by the Descent of the Holy Ghost on Christ at the Jordan, Christ rejected by the Jews, the Ascension, and the Inspiration of St. Peter, all of very large dimensions. In 1817, he exhibited his sublime picture of Death on the Pale Horse, painted when he was seventy-nine years old! On the 6th of December of the same year, he lost his beloved wife; they had tenderly loved each other some sixty years, and had seen their children's children; the world had no consolation to offer, and he began to sink; though still to be found at his easel, his mind had lost its wonted alacrity, and it was evident that all this was to cease soon; that he was suffering a slow, general, and easy decay. The venerable old man sat in his study among his favorite pictures, a breathing image of piety and contentment, calmly awaiting the hour of his dissolution. Without any fixed complaint, his mental faculties unimpaired, his cheerfulness undisturbed, and with looks serene and benevolent, he expired on the 11th of March, 1820, in the eighty-second year of his age. He was buried with great pomp in St. Paul's cathedral, beside Reynolds, Opie, and Barry.

As West's life was long and laborious, his productions are very numerous. He painted and sketched upwards of 400 pictures in oil, mostly taken from sacred and profane history; he also left more than 200 original drawings in his portfolio. The following is Cunningham's critique. "His works were supposed by himself, and for a time by others, to be in the true spirit of the great masters, and he composed them with the serious ambition and hope of illustrating scripture, and rendering gospel truth more impressive. No subject seemed to him too lofty for his pencil; he considered himself worthy to follow the sublimest flights of the prophets, and dared to limn the effulgence of God's glory, and the terrors of the Day of Judgment. (Have not many great masters attempted the same?) The mere list of his works makes us shudder at human presumption—Moses receiving the Law on Sinai; the Descent of the Holy Ghost on the Saviour in the Jordan; the Opening of the Seventh Seal; St. Michael and his Angels casting out the Great Dragon; the Mighty Angel with one foot on the Sea and the other on the Earth; the Resurrection; and there are many others of the same class. With such magnificence and sublimity, who but a Michael Angelo could cope?

"In all his works, the human form was exhibited in conformity to academic precepts—his figures were arranged with skill; the coloring was varied, and often harmonious; the eye rested pleased on the performance, and the artist seemed, to the ordinary spectator, to have done his task like one of the highest of the sons of genius. But below

* Who can doubt it? Three of his most capital works are, Christ healing the Sick, Christ rejected by the Jews, and Death on the Pale Horse. The exhibition of either of these pictures would have brought him more money annually than his royal salary. There was very little encouragement for historical painters at that time in England, as the following extract from the Percy Anecdotes will show. Speaking of West and the excitement which his superb picture of Pylades and Orestes produced among the higher circles of London, the writer says, "But the most wonderful part of the story is, that notwithstanding all this vast bustle and commendation bestowed upon that justly admired picture, by which West's servant gained upwards of thirty pounds for showing it (it was exhibited gratuitously at West's house), no mortal ever asked the price of the work, or so much as offered to give him a commission to paint any other subject."

all this splendor, there was little of the true vitality;—there was a monotony too, of human character,—the groupings were unlike the happy and careless combinations of nature, and the figures frequently seemed distributed over the canvass by line and measure, like trees in a plantation. He wanted fire and imagination to be the true restorer of that grand style, which bewildered Barry, and was talked of by Reynolds. Some of his works—cold, formal, bloodless, and passionless,—may remind the spectator of the sublime vision of the valley of dry bones, when the flesh and the skin had come upon the skeletons, and before the breath of God had infused them with life and feeling.

"Though such is the general impression which the works of West make, it cannot be denied that many are distinguished by great excellence. In his Death on the Pale Horse, and more particularly in the sketch of that picture, he has more than approached the masters and princes of the calling. It is indeed, irresistibly fearful, to see the triumphant march of the terrific Phantom, and the dissolution of all that earth is proud of beneath his tread. War and Peace, Sorrow and Joy, Youth and Age, all who love and all who hate, seem planet-struck. The Death of Wolfe, too, is natural and noble, and the Indian Chief, like the Oneyda warrior of Campbell,

A stoic of the woods, a man without a tear,

was a happy thought. The Battle of La Hogue, I have heard praised as *the best historic* picture of the British school, by one not likely to be mistaken, and who would not say what he did not feel. Many of his single figures also are of a high order. There is a natural grace in the looks of some of his women that few painters have ever excelled."

West emulated the great head of the Roman school, or the combined excellencies of the antique and modern schools. In his Journal kept in Italy, he says, "Michael Angelo has not succeeded in giving a probable character to any of his works, the Moses, perhaps, excepted. The works of Raffaelle grow daily more interesting, natural, and noble." It is allowed that he drew correctly, that many of his works are finely composed, and that he has frequently shown great power of invention; but it is said that he was deficient in coloring, lacked expression in his heads, was monotonous in his features and countenances, and that his pictures want effect. In his grand historic pictures he doubtless considered, like Raffaelle and Poussin, that splendid coloring would detract from the dignity of his subject; since in some of his pictures, when the subject allowed it, and particularly in his female forms, his tints are clear, and very beautiful. This is illustrated in his Death on the Pale Horse, and Christ healing the Sick, in which less attention is paid to coloring than to expression. He always avoided having recourse to any meretricious tricks to catch the eye and raise admiration. It is a well known fact, that the great works of Raffaelle are not *striking*, but they *grow*, with contemplation. There has not yet appeared a *learned*, *just*, and *academic critique* upon the works of West, but there can be no doubt that such an one would pronounce him the greatest historical painter of the 18th century.

Benjamin West in person was above the middle size, of very fair complexion, and firmly and compactly built; his lofty brow beamed with goodness and benevolence. He was polished, but simple and unostentatious in his manners, and affable to all. Intercourse with courts and the world which changes so many, made no change in him. His kindness to young artists was great, and he aided them as freely with his advice and his purse, as though they were his own children; so generous was he, that his liberality seriously impaired his income. He had no secrets in his profession, whatever he knew in art, he readily imparted, and was happy to think that art was advancing; and no mean jealousy of other men's good fortune ever invaded his repose. He was so regular and simple in his habits, and careful to improve his time, that to describe one day of his life, is to describe years. He rose early, studied before breakfast, wrought upon one of his large pictures from ten to four, dressed and saw visitors, and having dined, recommenced his studies. For further information of this distinguished artist, the reader must be referred to Galt's "Life and Studies of Benjamin West," London, 1816 and 1820; Cunningham's "Lives of eminent British Painters," and to Dunlap's "History of the Rise and Progress of the Arts of Design in the United States," 2 vols., New-York, 1834.

WESTALL, Richard, an excellent English historical painter, and an eminent designer, was born in 1765, probably at London. At the age of fourteen, he was apprenticed to an engraver of heraldry on silver, named Thompson; but excelling his fellows in this humble department of the arts, he aspired to a higher order of distinction. By working an additional time in the mornings, he obtained the permission of his employer to draw at the Royal Academy in the evenings. He commenced his career as an artist in 1786, and first attracted public attention by a number of highly finished historical paintings in water colors, which manifested a brilliancy and vigor before unknown. In company with his friend Mr. Lawrence (afterwards Sir Thomas), he took a house in Soho Square, which they occupied for several years, until their success justified their forming separate establishments. Westall's book illustrations were very popular, and he was much employed by the publishers, particularly Alderman Boydell, for whom he executed the designs in the superb edition of Milton. He also designed the illustrations for Moore's Loves of the Angels, Crabbe's Poems, and many other works. His earlier works display considerable intelligence of chiaro-scuro, and elegance of coloring, but from the great facility with which his ready talent enabled him to produce book designs, he was led into a greater degree of mannerism than any of his cotemporaries, which detracted not a little from his reputation; but many of his works evince, notwithstanding, the possession of very uncommon taste and judgment.

As a painter of history, Westall deserves much higher commendation than seems to be generally accorded to him. He produced many excellent historical subjects, some of them to fulfil the commissions of Boydell, for his great work of the Illustrations of Shakspeare. Among these, his picture of Cardinal Wolsey entering Leicester Abbey, is perhaps deserving of the highest praise. This picture is finely composed, the light and shadow are admirably managed, the horses are full of fire and spirit, which, with the expression of childish wonder and compassion in the face of the little page at viewing the stricken Wolsey, are sufficient proofs of Westall's ability in this branch. This performance has been preserved to the world by the admirable plate of Thew, esteemed the masterpiece of Boydell's collection. His Lady Macbeth, and the Ghost of Cæsar appearing to Brutus in his tent, both portraits, are noble pictures, full of dignity and expression. In 1794, Westall was elected a member of the Royal Academy, at the same time as Lawrence and Stothard. In 1808, he published a volume of poems of considerable merit, entitled "A Day in Spring, and other Poems, embellished with four plates engraved by James Heath, A. E. R. A., and Charles Heath, from designs by R. Westall." By his professional exertions, Westall attained a handsome competence, but he became involved in an unsuccessful speculation in foreign pictures, and some improvident partnership engagements. During the latter part of his life, he was aided by the assistance which the Royal Academy assigns to its reduced members. His last occupation was in giving lessons in drawing and painting to the present Queen, while Princess Victoria. He died in 1837.

WESTALL, William, an English painter in water-colors, and an engraver in aquatinta, born in 1781. In 1801, through the influence of West, he was appointed draughtsman to the voyage of discovery to Australia, made by Capt. Flinders in H. M. S. Investigator. He also visited China, and made many drawings of landscapes, particularly a View of the Canton River, representing an incident he had witnessed, of which he afterwards painted a large picture, exhibited in 1814, at the Royal Academy. He also resided for about a year in the island of Madeira, whither he went during the delay of the expedition at the island of Mauritius; and he executed a number of landscapes, with views of the planters' villas, which realized a handsome return. In 1810, he was employed to prepare many designs for the engravers, for the publication of the discoveries of the expedition; and also in painting pictures, by order of the Admiralty, of several important incidents which occurred during the voyage. In 1812 he was elected an Associate of the Royal Academy. In 1816 he engraved, in aquatinta, a work descriptive of the noted caves in Yorkshire; and for many years subsequently, he produced a number of similar works, among which was one of the Isle of Wight; and he also executed several large paintings, among which was the Commencement of the Deluge, exhibited in 1848. He died in 1850.

WESTERHOUT, Arnold van, a Flemish engraver, born at Antwerp, in 1666. After having studied in his native city, he went to Italy, and established himself at Rome. He engraved quite a number of plates after the Italian masters, and from his own designs, executed with the graver, in a neat, clear style, resembling that of his countryman, Robert van Audenarde. He also engraved some portraits in mezzotinto. He died about 1725.

WESTMACOTT, Richard, a distinguished English sculptor, the eldest son of an artist in the same branch, was born at London about 1774. After completing his preliminary studies, he visited Italy for improvement, in 1792, and studied the antique, and the works of the great masters. The first work of importance which he was engaged upon after returning to England, was a statue of Addison, which was placed in Westminster Abbey about 1806. In 1809, he was elected an Associate of the Royal Academy, at which time he completed and erected in St. Paul's cathedral, the monument of Sir Ralph Abercrombie, and subsequently that of Lord Collingwood, in the same church. On his engagement to execute the bronze statue of the Duke of Bedford, in Russell Square, he personally attended to the whole management of the casting, and thereby acquired so much skill that, after erecting the statue of Lord Nelson at Birmingham, and of Mr. Fox in Bloomsbury Square, he was able to accomplish the immense bronze colossal statue of Achilles, erected in Hyde Park. In 1811 he was elected a Royal Academician, and subsequently a fellow of the Society of Antiquaries, and a member of the Dilettanti Society. In 1814, he completed his national monument to William Pitt, in Westminster Abbey, which is a work of great talent. Among the other works of Westmacott, are the beautiful statue of a Peasant Girl, exhibited at the Royal Academy in 1819, which is part of a monument erected to Lord Penrhyn; the Hindoo Girl, for a work to be erected at Calcutta, in memory of Alexander Colvin; and the statue of King George III. at Liverpool. The author has not been able to procure further information concerning Westmacott, since the year 1832, when his bronze colossal statue of Canning was erected in Palace Yard.

WET, Gerard de, a Dutch painter, born at Amsterdam in 1616, and died there in 1679. He was a disciple of Rembrandt, whose style he followed with some success; he also painted landscapes, and was accounted a good colorist. The Dutch writers mention a Jacob de Wet or Weth, who painted cabinet pictures of sacred subjects in the manner of Rembrandt; probably they are the same artist. There was also a John de Wet, who flourished at Haerlem, and was more noted as a dealer in old pictures than as a painter.

WET, P. F., a Dutch engraver, who flourished in the latter part of the 17th century. He etched a set of plates of ornamental foliage for goldsmiths and jewelers, executed in a slight style.

WEYDE, Roger vander, a Flemish painter, born at Brussels, according to Van Mander and Descamps, about 1480; and died there in 1529. His instructor is not mentioned, but he was one of the first painters of the country who improved the national taste, by divesting it of the dry, gothic manner, and introducing a more graceful style of design, and a better expression in the heads. Among his principal works were four pictures in the Town House at Brussels, representing subjects connected with the administration of justice. He painted a picture of the Descent from the Cross, for the church of St. Gertrude at Louvain, which was greatly admired. It was afterwards sent to the King of Spain, and a copy of it, by Michael Coxcis, substituted in its place.

There has been much disquisition among writers as to whether Roger vander Weyde and Roger of Bruges were the same or different artists. The dispute is of little consequence, as there is not a single well authenticated work by the former, and little remains by the latter, and that little of no importance. Roger of Bruges was certainly a scholar of the Van Eycks; his birth is variously placed in or about 1366, and 1390, the latter having the best authorities; and his death in 1418 and 1464. It is known that he was employed by the Town House of Brussels, and that he visited Italy. Now, in the Archives of the city of Brussels, the name of *Meester Rogieren vander Weyden* occurs in two or more instances; once in 1436, and again in 1449. In 1450, the year of Jubilee, he went to Italy, where he practiced some years, and was called *Ruggiero da Bruggia* or *da Bruxelles.* He died at Brussels, June 16th, 1464, and was buried in the church of St. Gudule; his name appears in the church register *Magister Rogerus vander Wyden, excellens pictor cum uxore,* &c. From these dates, it is contended that Roger of Bruges and Roger vander Weyde are but one artist. If this supposition be correct, then Van Mander and Descamps have made an error of about one hundred years in the dates. The discussion, at best, is "stale, flat, and unprofitable." See *Roger of Bruges.*

WEYDEMANS, Frederick William, a Dutch portrait painter of some distinction, born in 1668, and died in 1750. There was also a Charles Emilius Weydemans, born in 1685, and died in 1735. He painted portraits, and is said to have been a cousin or nephew of the former. Besides these, there was also a N. Weydemans, an engraver, of whom nothing is known, except by a few indifferent prints.

GW or GW or GW WEYER, Gabriel, a German painter and engraver, who flourished at Nuremberg from about 1610 to 1640, when he died. He is said to have painted some pictures, of which nothing is known; but he executed a great number of wooden cuts from his own designs, which are marked with one of the above monograms of his initials. It is disputed whether he engraved all the cuts, or merely furnished the designs and employed others to engrave them; a question of no importance, which applies to nearly all the old German designers and wood engravers.

WEYER, Hans, or John, a German painter and engraver, who was a native of Cobourg, according to Professor Christ, and flourished about 1610. He engraved some plates in an excellent style, admirably designed, and marked with the initials H. E. W. There is some question whether he really engraved all the plates attributed to him.

WEYER, Nicholas, an engraver to whom Professor Christ attributes some prints marked with his initials, and the date, thus, N. 1567 W. He gives no particulars of the artist, nor does he specify any of his subjects.

WEYERMAN, John, a Dutch painter of fruit and flower pieces, was born in 1636, and died in 1681. There are no particulars recorded of him, except that, after studying in his own country, he went to Italy.

WEYERMANS, Jacob Campo, a Dutch painter, born at Amsterdam, in 1679. He studied under Ferdinand van Kessell, and painted fruit, flowers, and still-life, but his productions are not above mediocrity. He published the Lives of the Dutch painters, in three volumes, poorly compiled and abridged, from Houbraken. He died in 1747.

WEYNERS, Johanssen, a German engraver, who flourished about 1611. According to Prof. Christ, he engraved some plates after the designs of Christopher Schwartz, which he marked with a bunch of grapes, in allusion to his name. He is the same as *Hans Weinher,* which see.

WHEATLEY, Francis, an English painter, born at London in 1747. He received his first instruction in Shipley's Drawing School; he evinced much talent, and while young, drew several premiums from the Society for the Encouragement of Arts, &c. Having afterwards improved himself by diligent study, and by associating with artists of distinction, he acquired considerable reputation as a historical painter. After practicing some time in London, he went to Dublin, where he painted a large picture, representing the Irish House of Commons, in which he introduced the portraits of the most distinguished political characters of the day. This work increased his reputation, and gained him considerable employment. On his return to London, he was employed by Alderman Boydell to paint several pictures for the Shakspeare Gallery. There being little encouragement for historical painting at that time in England, he chiefly devoted himself to rural and domestic subjects, for which he had a happy talent: and his productions of that description are highly esteemed. He was elected a member of the Royal Academy, and died in 1801.

WHITE, Robert, an English designer and engraver, born at London in 1645, and died in 1704. He was a pupil of David Loggan, for whom he designed and engraved several architectural views. He engraved an immense number of portraits of distinguished personages, from his own designs, and after Kneller, Vandyck, and other eminent painters. Most of his plates are executed with the graver, in a neat, clear style. They are chiefly valued for their subjects and their excellent likeness.—He also engraved a few heads in mezzotinto, but they are far inferior to his other prints. He excelled in drawing portraits with black lead upon vellum, in which he was much employed. White was busily employed for about forty years, and amassed about £5,000, according to Walpole; but from some cause he died indigent. At his death, a printseller purchased his plates, and realized a fortune from them. The following are his most esteemed prints:

James I.; *after C. Jansen.* George, Earl of Cumberland, habited for a tournament; fine. Charles I.; *after Vandyck.* Another of Charles I.; *after van Vorst.* Prince Rupert; *after Kneller.* Charles II.; *do.* 1679. Another of Charles II., whole length, in the robes of the Garter. James II. under a canopy, with Archbishop Sancroft and the Chancellor Jefferies. James II. when Duke of York, in the robes of the Garter. Maria Beatrix of Este, his consort; *after Kneller.* 1686. Henry, Duke of Gloucester. Lady Mary Joliffe; scarce. Heneage, Earl of Nottingham. Thomas, Duke of Leeds. Sir Edward Ward, Chief Baron. 1702. Sir George Treby, Chief Justice of the Common Pleas. 1694. Samuel Pepys, Secretary to the Admiralty; *after Kneller.* George, Earl of Melvil; *after Sir John Medina.* James, Earl of Perth; *after Kneller.* Another Portrait of the same; *after Riley;* fine Bishop Burnet; *after Mrs. Beale.* Sir Alexander Temple. Lady Susanna Temple. Lady Anne Clifford. Thomas Flatman; *after Hayls.* Sir John Fenwick; *after Wissing.* The Seven Bishops; seven small ovals in one plate. The Seven Bishops who suffered Martyrdom; five ovals in one plate. Duke of Norfolk, Mezzotinto; *after Kneller* John, Earl of Randor, *do.; do*

WHITE, George, was the son of the preceding, who instructed him in art. After the death of his father, he finished the plates left imperfect by him; he also engraved some portraits in the same style; but his best prints are in mezzotinto, in which he frequently etched the outline before the ground was laid upon the plate, which sometimes adds to the firmness of the effect. He also painted portraits, both in oil and miniature. His prints are dated from about 1700 to 1732, when he is supposed to have died. The following are his best prints:

PORTRAITS IN MEZZOTINTO.

Sir Richard Blackmore, M. D.; *after J. vander Bank.* Sylvester Petyt, Principal of Bernard's Inn; fine. Nicholas Sanderson, Professor of Mathematics, of Cambridge. John Baptist Monnoyer, Painter; *after Kneller.* John Dryden; *do.* Alexander Pope; *do.* Thomas Bradbury; *after Gibson.* George Hooper, Bishop of St. Asaph; *after Hill.* Colonel Blood, who stole the Crown. William Dobson, Painter; *from a picture by himself.* A Man playing on the Violin; *after Frank Hals.* 1732. Henry Purcell; *after Frank Hals?* 1732.

PORTRAITS IN THE STYLE OF HIS FATHER.

James Gardiner, Bishop of Lincoln; *after Dahl.* Charles II., King of Spain; begun by Robert White, and finished by George White, whose name is affixed. The Duke of Ormond. Lord Clarendon.

WHITE, Charles, an English engraver, born at London in 1751. He studied with Pranker, on leaving whom he quitted stroke engraving, and wrought chiefly in the chalk style. He was chiefly employed by the booksellers, and died young in 1785.

WHITE, Thomas, an English engraver, who died at London about 1776. He was much employed by Ryland, to assist him in his plates. He afterwards engraved the greater part of the architectural plates for the continuation of the "Vitruvius Britannicus," by Wolf and Gandon.

WIBERT. See Vuibert.

WICHMAN, J., a German engraver, and probably a painter, who flourished about 1683. There is a large print by him, etched in a slight, coarse style, representing the *Besieging and Taking of Stadtwien by the Emperor of Germany.* At the bottom of the print are represented the portraits of the Emperor of Germany, and the Grand Sultan; at the top, those of the generals of the German and Turkish armies.

WICKENBERG, M. This Swedish painter was born in 1812. After acquiring a knowledge of art in his own country, he visited Paris in 1837, where he obtained considerable success. His pictures consist chiefly of winter scenes, delineated with great truthfulness to nature; one of his best performances is in the Luxembourg Gallery. He exhibited annually at the Louvre, until 1846, when he died of consumption, on the 19th of December.

WIDEMAN, Elias, a German designer and engraver, who flourished at Augsburg about 1648. He engraved a great number of portraits, title-pages, vignettes, and other plates for the booksellers, executed with the graver, in a stiff, formal style. His chief work is a set of plates of illustrious personages, published at Augsburg in 1648, entitled, *Comitium Gloriæ centum qua Sanguine qua Virtute illustrium Heroum Iconibus instructum, &c. E. Wideman, del. et sculp.*

WIDITZ, a German engraver on wood, who flourished at Strasburg, according to Professor Christ, about 1570. There are no reliable particulars recorded of him.

WIEBEKING, Chevalier Carl Friedrich. This eminent German engineer, and writer on hydraulic and civil architecture, was born at Wollin in Pomerania, in 1762. He attained very great eminence as a practical engineer, and was employed many years by the Prussian, Austrian, and Bavarian governments, until 1818, when he retired from the service of the latter, with a pension. He is chiefly mentioned here on account of his large work on a general course of Civil Architecture and its History, entitled *Theoretisch-practische Burgerliche Baukunde*, 4 vols. 4to., with a very large folio atlas of plates, 1821–6. This is esteemed a very valuable contribution to architectural study, particularly on account of the fund of fresh information it supplies relative to the architecture of Germany, Holland, Poland, Russia, and some other parts of Europe. The Chevalier von Wiebeking, as he was usually called, (being knight of several German and foreign orders,) was also a member of nearly all the academies and learned societies in Europe. He died at Munich in 1842. There is by him a work entitled, *Analyse Historique et Raisonné des Monumens de l' Antiquité, des Edifices les plus remarkables du Moyen Age*, &c., published in 1840, and dedicated to Queen Victoria, of England.

WIEDEMANN, Ludwig, a German sculptor and founder, was born at Nordlingen in 1690. His principal work mentioned in the Biographie Universelle, is the equestrian statue of Augustus II. of Poland, placed in 1735 near the river Elbe at Dresden. The king is represented in Roman costume, and the likeness is good; but the horse is better executed than any other part of the composition. In 1738, Wiedemann was invited to London by the Duke of Cumberland, to take charge of a foundry. He made an improvement in the manufacture of muskets, and afterwards went to Vienna, in 1750, where he was made a colonel of artillery. His last work in sculpture was the statue of the king of Denmark, executed at Copenhagen. He died in 1754.

WIELANT, or WILLANT, an engraver who is said to have executed several portraits. The name is probably a corruption of *Vaillant*, which see.

WIELING, Nicholas, a historical and portrait painter, supposed to have been a native of Holland. Little is known of his history, except that he was invited to the court of Frederick William, Elector of Brandenburg, who appointed him his court painter in 1671. He died at Berlin in 1689. His style is said to resemble that of Vandyck. He had a son of the same name, whom he instructed in the art, but there are no particulars recorded of him.

WIENBROUCK, M. V. The name of this artist is affixed to a few slight etchings, executed in a painter-like style, among which is one representing an Old Man seated, to whom a Youth is relating a Message.

WIERENGEN, Cornelius Nicholas van, a Dutch painter, born at Haerlem about 1600. He excelled in painting sea-pieces and storms, which he represented with great truth and effect. He was also a good painter of landscapes, fourteen of which were engraved by Nicholas John Visscher. He etched many plates of sea-pieces and landscapes from his own designs, in a neat and spirited style. He died at Haerlem, according to Balkema, in 1658.

WIERINGA, Gerard, a Dutch painter, born at Groningen, probably about 1770. After learning the rudiments of the art from his father John W., an ornamental painter of little note, he went to Dusseldorf, to study the pictures in the Gallery there. In 1790 he returned to his native place, where he painted landscapes, sunsets, and winter-pieces, with considerable success. For one of his pictures, he obtained the gold medal from the Academy at Leyden. He died in 1817.

WIERIX, John, an eminent Dutch designer and engraver, born at Amsterdam in 1550. His name is variously written Wierix, Wierx, and Wierinx, but he wrote it *Wierix*. It is not known by whom he was instructed, but he appears to have formed his style by an attentive study of the works of Albert Drurer, as he copied several of the prints of that master with great precision. His plates are executed with the graver, in a neat and highly finished, though somewhat stiff and formal style, and his drawing is generally correct. His prints are very numerous, and are held in considerable estimation by the curious collector; some of them are from his own designs, but those after other masters are the best. He rarely signed his plates with his name, but usually marked them with the initials, I. W. F., and sometimes I. H. W. F. with the date. He was living in 1601. The following are among his most esteemed works:

PORTRAITS.

Rodolphus II., Emperor of Germany. Philip William, Prince of Orange. Eleanora de Bourbon, Princess of Orange. James I., King of England, and his Queen; scarce. Philip II., King of Spain. Catharine de Medicis, Queen of Henry II., of France. Henry III., King of France. The Countess de Verneuil.

SUBJECTS FROM HIS OWN DESIGNS.

The Resurrection; inscribed *Insanus Miles*. Mary Magdalene seated at the entrance of a Grot; *J. Wier, inv. et fec.* An allegorical subject, representing the Redemption of Mankind. The Four Elements; *Wierix*. 1601.

SUBJECTS AFTER VARIOUS MASTERS.

The little Satyr; copied from the print of *Albert Durer*, when he was only twelve years of age. Adam receiving the forbidden fruit from Eve; copied from the celebrated print of the same subject by *Albert Durer;* upon a Tablet is inscribed *Albert Durer, inventor, Johanes Wierix, fec. aet.* 16. St. Hubert kneeling before the Stag, with a Crucifix on its forehead; a copy, reversed, from the print by *Albert Durer*, marked with the cipher of that artist. St. Jerome in meditation; copied from *Albert Durer*. The Marriage of St. Catherine; *after D. Calvart*. The Sacrifice of Abraham; *after M. de Vos*. Christ taken down from the Cross; *after Otho Venius*. The Last Judgment; finely copied from the print of that subject, by *Martin Rota, after M. Angelo Buonarotti*. Christ taken down from the Cross; *after Bern. Passeri*.

HW or HEW WIERIX, Jerome, was the younger brother of the preceding born at Amsterdam in 1552. He is supposed to have learned the art of Engraving from John W., whose style he followed so closely that it would be difficult to distinguish their works, were it not that they are differently marked. His prints are more numerous than those of his brother, and chiefly consist of devout and allegorical subjects saints, and fathers of the church, many of which are from his own designs. He sometimes signed his prints Hieronimus Wierix, but usually with one of the above monograms, or simply with his initials, HI. W. or HI. W. F., or J. Hieronimus W. Fe. The following are among his best prints:

PORTRAITS.

The Emperor Charlemagne. Henry of Bourbon, King of Navarre. Queen Elizabeth. Sigismund III., King of Poland. Alessandro Farnese, Duke of Parma. Sir Francis Drake.

SUBJECTS FROM HIS OWN DESIGNS.

St. Cecilia. The Temptation of St. Anthony. St. Bruno, the founder of the Carthusians. St. Charles Borromeus The Virgin and Infant Christ, with St. Francis and St. Anthony. The Virgin and Infant, with a Glory of Angels. The Crucifixion. The Death of Lucretia.

SUBJECTS AFTER VARIOUS MASTERS.

Christ dead, supported on the knees of the Virgin; *after J. Mabuse*. Christ calling to him the little Children; *after C. van de Broeck*. The Death of the Virgin; *after Otho Venius*. Christ at Table, in the house of Simon the Pharisee; *do*. Christ crowned with Thorns; *after G. Mostaert*. The Four Doctors of the Church; *after M. Lucas Romanus*. The Scourging of Christ; *do*. One of his best prints. The Baptism of Christ by St. John; *after H. Hondius;* fine. The Vision of Daniel; *after van Haecht*. Jupiter and Danae; *do*. Christ expiring on the Cross; *after P. Aquila*, considered his best piece for purity of engraving. The Resurrection of Christ; *after L. Romanus;* a large and capital print.

WIERIX, Anthony, was the brother of the two preceding artists, and the youngest of the family, born at Amsterdam in 1554. His small plates are executed in the neat, finished style of his brothers, but his larger prints exhibit more freedom and facility. He engraved similar subjects, and frequently wrought in conjunction with them. The works of the Wierixes are exceedingly numerous; M. de Marolles had in his collection upwards of 1200 pieces by them. Anthony generally signed his prints with his name in full. The following are among his best prints:

PORTRAITS.

Pope Clement VII.; *Ant. Wierix*. Philip Emanuel of Lorraine, Duke de Mercœur. Isabella of Austria, Daughter of Philip II. of Spain. Margaret, Queen of Philip III. of Spain. Cardinal Bellarmin. Albert of Austria, Archbishop of Toledo, Governor of the Low Countries.

SUBJECTS FROM HIS OWN DESIGNS.

St. Theresa. St. Sebastian. St. Dominick receiving the Rosary from the Virgin. The Marriage of St. Catherine. The Entombing of Christ. St. Jerome praying, accompanied by two Angels; dated 1584; fine.

SUBJECTS AFTER VARIOUS MASTERS.

The Adoration of the Magi; *after M. de Vos*. The History of the Prophet Jonas; in four plates; *do*. The Holy Family reposing in Egypt; *after Cam Procaccini*. The Death of St. Francis; *do*. A set of sixty-nine plates, representing the Life and Passion of Christ, with the Death and Assumption of the Virgin; in which he was assisted by his two brothers.

WIGMANA, Gerard, a Dutch painter, born at Workum in Friesland, in 1673. It is not known by whom he was instructed, but after learning the rudiments of the art in his own country, he went to Italy, where he is said to have studied the works of Titian, Raffaelle, and Giulio Romano. On his return to his own country, he painted a great many cabinet pictures of subjects taken from sacred, Grecian, Roman, and fabulous histories, which are as remarkable for patient and laborious finishing and brilliant coloring, as for the vulgarity of the characters and the incorrectness of the design. His studies in Italy, instead of improving his taste and elevating his style, appear to have only served to render his affectation of the sublime more clumsy and preposterous. His pictures are sometimes tolerably well composed, his coloring is remarkably transparent and brilliant, and his pencil neat and delicate; but his figures are badly grouped, the expression of his heads very indifferent, his drawing incorrect, and he was an outrageous violator of costume. Yet, with all these imperfections, his vanity was unbounded; he styled himself the Raffaelle of Friesland, and asked such enormous prices for his pictures that he could not sell them. He demanded 300 pounds for his picture of the Death of Alexander, which in consequence was not sold till after his death. Not meeting with much success in his own country, he went to England, where he resided some time without receiving much encouragement. He returned to his own country, disappointed, and died at Amsterdam in 1741.

WILBORN, Nicholas. See Welbronner.

WILDE, Francis de, a Dutch engraver, who flourished at Amsterdam about 1705. He etched some small plates of views and historical subjects, with great neatness and spirit, apparently from his own designs, among which are the Angel appearing to Abraham, Venus rising from the Sea, and a View of the city of Chalons. He signed his plates *Fr. de Wilde, fec.*, with the date.

WILDE, Maria de. This lady was probably a relative of the preceding artist. She engraved a set of fifty plates of antique gems, which were published at Amsterdam in 1703.

WILDENS, John, an eminent Flemish painter, born at Antwerp in 1584. It is not known by whom he was instructed, but it is generally supposed that he was more indebted to his own genius, and a diligent study of nature, than to the precepts of a master. He was constantly in the fields and forests, carefully designing after nature every object which pleased his fancy, or appeared picturesque or remarkable. His skies, trees, grounds, and water, are all true imitations of what he had observed in his walks through the country. He had already acquired a distinguished reputation as a landscape painter, when his talents recommended him to Rubens, who employed him to assist in his numerous commissions, by painting the landscapes in the backgrounds of his pictures, which he did so much to the satisfaction of that great master, that he highly commended him for his skill, not only in imitating nature, but in adapting the freedom of his touch and the harmony of his coloring to the rest of the design, so that the whole appeared to be the work of one master. He had a good genius, an excellent choice of scenery, a pleasing and natural tone of coloring, and a free and spirited pencil. He also designed the human figure correctly. There are several grand landscapes by Wildens in the public edifices at Antwerp, several of which are embellished with figures by some of the ablest of his cotemporaries; two of the most capital are in the chapel of St. Joseph, representing the Holy Family and the Repose in Egypt, with figures by John Bronckhorst. Vandyck painted his portrait among the eminent artists of his country.

Brulliot and Zani say that Wildens was an engraver, as well as a landscape painter, and Brulliot attributes to him the following views of chateaux in Holland; Teylingen, Egmont op de Hoeff, T'Clooster tot Rynsburch, T'huys te Cleef by Haerlem, Werdenburch and Rossum. They are signed *J. W. fecit Robbertus de baudous excudit Amstelodami*, 1616. The same letters, *J. W.*, with *inv.*, are found on prints engraved after his designs by Peter Nolpe, consisting of six allegorical subjects relating to the House of Orange, and its connection with Great Britain by marriage. The name *Joan. Wild.*, and *J. Wild. inv.*, are found on two prints of a series of twelve subjects, representing the Months of the Year, engraved by Andrew Stock and J. Matham. Wildens died in 1644.

WILHELM, von Coeln, called Meister Wilhelm, a painter of Cologne, of whom little is known with certainty. He is thus noticed in the annals of the Dominican monks of Frankfort. "In that time (1380), there was at Cologne a most excellent painter, to whom there was not the like in his art; his name was Wilhelm, and he made pictures of men which almost appeared to be alive." The German writers have made profound researches concerning him, without eliciting anything beyond conjecture. There are several pictures in the Cathedral and churches of Cologne, painted, as is supposed, in the latter part of the 14th and first part of the 15th centuries, which are attributed to Wilhelm, and to Meister Stephan, his pupil; but they are of very doubtful authenticity, and possess little interest out of Germany.

WILKIE, Sir David, a British historical painter, and a very eminent delineator of scenes from common life, was born at the Manse of the parish of Cults, on the banks of Eden-water, in Fifeshire, Scotland, the 18th of November, 1785. He was the third son of David Wilkie, minister of Cults, and Isabella Lister, his third wife. During early childhood he manifested a strong love for art, and was afterwards heard to say that he could draw before he could read, and paint before he could spell. When seven years of age he was sent to the grammar school of Pitlessie, near his father's house, but he there learned little or nothing. From Pitlessie he was removed in his twelfth year to the grammar school of Kettle, but he there paid little attention to anything but drawing, and it became evident to his father that David would be nothing but a painter, greatly to his regret, for he did not see how a livelihood could be obtained by such a course. Accordingly, in 1799, at the age of fourteen, he was sent to the Trustees' Academy of Edinburg for the Encouragement of Manufactures, with a letter of introduction from the Earl of Leven to the Secretary, Mr. Thompson. The latter examined some of the young artist's drawings, and not being satisfied refused to admit him, but he afterwards did so at the particular request of the Earl of Leven. At this time John Graham was master of the Academy, and John Burnet, Alexander Fraser, and Sir William Allan, were among Wilkie's fellow pupils. The latter says of him, "The progress Wilkie made at this time, was marvelous. Everything he attempted showed a knowledge beyond his years; and he soon took up that position in art which he maintained to the last." In that description of drawings which requires academic taste and knowledge, he made little attainment compared with many others; his grand forte then, as ever after, was the delineation of character in scenes of humble life ; he frequented trystes, fairs, and market-places, in order to observe the diversified specimens of humanity; and his works were distinguished for admirable truth and simplicity. He invariably painted slowly, and required models on all occasions. In 1803, he won the premium of ten guineas, awarded to the painting of Callisto in the Bath of Diana, and in the same year made the sketch of his celebrated picture of the Village Politicians. In 1804, in his 19th year, he left the Academy and returned home, where he painted for Kinnear of Kinloch, a picture of Pitlessie Fair, in which he inserted about 140 figures, many of them sketched while at church, as he had no other means of procuring them. For this picture he received only £25. At this time he painted many portraits in small and in miniature, and the picture called the Village Recruit.

About this time Wilkie went to London and entered the Royal Academy as a student. His first patron was Stodart, a piano-forte maker, who had married a lady named Wilkie. He sat for his portrait, and commissioned Wilkie to paint two pictures for him, introduced him to a valuable connexion, and procured him several sitters. The Earl of Mansfield, whose acquaintance he made through Stodart, commissioned him to paint a picture from his sketch of the Village Politicians, which was exhibited at the Academy in 1806, and excited universal admiration. This work indicated a branch of the art, quite new to the painters of that day, and various comments were made upon it by the Academicians. Northcote termed it the "pauper style," and Fuseli, when he met Wilkie after he had seen it, said "Young man, that is a dangerous work. That picture will either prove the most happy or the most unfortunate work of your life." It apparently proved the most fortunate ; and although Wilkie was only twenty-one when he painted it, as a painting he never surpassed it afterwards, although in subject he produced several happier pictures. From this time commissions were abundant, and instead of returning to Scotland, as he had always intended, he found it necessary to establish himself in London. He received commissions from Mr. Whitbread, Lord Mulgrave, and Sir George Beaumont, who until his death proved a most valuable and sincere friend to Wilkie. His next works were the Blind Fiddler, for Sir George Beaumont, Alfred in the Neat-herd's Cottage, for Mr. Davidson ; the Card Players, for the Duke of Gloucester ; and the Rent-day, for the Earl of Mulgrave, painted in 1807 and 1808. After these came the sketch of the Reading of the Will, the Wardrobe Ransacked, the Game-keeper, and the Ale-house door, afterwards called the Village Festival, painted for Mr. Angerstein for 800 guineas, and now in the National Gallery ; all in the three succeeding years. In 1809 he was elected an Associate of the Royal Academy, and a member in 1811.

Wilkie's incessant application to his profession obliged him about this time to suspend all exertion, being naturally of a weak constitution ; and he made a short visit to his native place in Scotland. In 1812, he opened an exhibition of his own pictures in London, which extended his reputation, but was not very profitable. In December of the same year he lost his father, and invited his mother and sister to come and live with him in London, where he engaged a commodious house in Kensington for their reception. In 1813, he exhibited his picture of Blindman's Buff, painted for the Prince Regent. In 1814, he visited Paris, in company with his friend Mr. Haydon, where he studied the great collection of the gems of European art then gathered in the Louvre, particularly the pictures of the Flemish school. Some idea of the character of his taste, may perhaps be gathered from the following remark in his journal. "I was especially struck with the pictures of Ostade and Terburg, the latter of whom has risen greatly in my estimation from what I have seen here. He possessed a most perfect style of coloring, and represents his objects with a manner of handling the most beautiful and least artificial of any I ever saw. I observed to-day, that a number of pictures which did not strike at first, begin to gain upon me exceedingly. The Ostades and the Rembrandts improve greatly ; the Tenierses and others in that style, rather lose. The picture of the Marriage at Cana, which struck me so much at first, now begins to look common, and does not bear to be dwelt upon like the other pictures painted with much care and thinking." After his return to London, he painted the Distraining for Rent, purchased by the proprietors of the British Institution for 600 guineas. In the summer of 1816, he visited Belgium, in company with Raimbach the engraver, and on his return continued to produce various works, a catalogue of which would be too long for insertion. In 1820, he finished the Reading of the Will, for the king of Bavaria, which is now in the gallery at Schleissheim, and in point of character and composition is one of Wilkie's masterpieces, though inferior to many of his works in execution. His Chelsea Pensioners, painted for the Duke of Wellington for 1200 guineas, is esteemed Wilkie's masterpiece. The character, composition, and execution are exquisite, the drawing good, and the coloring sober and true ; it is said to be the finest work of its class in England, and gives Wilkie rank among the celebrated artists of the Dutch school.

After this time, Wilkie changed his subjects, and his style of execution, but it is generally allowed that he did not add anything to his reputation. In his own peculiar style he was without a rival, but in historical painting he had many. One of the worst and earliest of these new productions was the Entrance of George IV. into Holyrood. At the death of Sir Henry Raeburn, in 1823, he was appointed limner to the king in Scotland. Two years after he started for the Continent, on account of ill-health, and passed eight months in Italy ; after which he made the tour of Germany, and at Vienna had the honor of dining *en famille* with Prince Metternich. Returning to Italy, a public dinner was given him at Rome, by the Scotch artists and amateurs, at which the Duke of Hamilton presided. During his second visit to Italy, his health began to revive, and he painted three pictures at Rome. Passing through the south of France, he entered Spain October, 1827, and painted his Defence of Saragossa, with the portrait of Gen. Palafox inserted, the defender of the place. He returned to England in the following year, and exhibited seven pictures painted while abroad, five of which were purchased by George IV. Some of these pictures were much admired by his friends, but less so by the public. The principal characteristics are effect of color, and of light and shade; which, with breadth and facility, he seems to have considered the proper objects of what is termed "high Art," and an advance on the truth, simplicity, and character of his earlier works; thus voluntarily enrolling himself among those who allowed themselves to be engrossed by technicalities, and, to use his own words, "seem to have painted more for the artist and connoisseur, than for the untutored apprehensions of ordinary men."

After the death of Lawrence in 1830, Wilkie was appointed in his place, painter in ordinary to his Majesty. Two years after, he exhibited his picture of John Knox preaching the Reformation in St. Andrew's, painted for Sir Robert Peel for 1200 guineas, which is a work of very high class, though a less glowing color and more careful style of execution are necessary to constitute it a work of first-rate excellence; it has been well engraved by Mr. Doo. In 1836, Wilkie received the honor of knighthood from King William IV. Various other works came from his pencil during the succeeding years, among them, Columbus submitting to the Spanish authorities the Chart of his Voyage for the Discovery of the New World, is a work of much fine character, and very richly colored. His greatest historical effort, however, is the picture of Sir David Baird discovering the body of the Sultan Tippoo Saib, after storming Seringapatam, painted for Lady Baird for 1500 guineas. In 1840, Wilkie started for the East, in company with his friend Mr. Woodburn, on account of some reason, which probably is not certainly known, although various rumors were circulated at the time. He went by Holland and the Rhine to the south of Germany, and thence to Constantinople, where he painted a portrait of the young Sultan, said to have been done at the suggestion of Queen Victoria. After visiting the Holy Land, he went to Alexandria, and painted the portrait of Mehemet Ali. Wilkie's health had never been vigorous, and he had felt unwell for three months before arriving at Alexandria. On the 21st of May, 1841, he embarked on board the Oriental for England; on the 26th he arrived off Malta, where he indulged imprudently in fruit and iced lemonade; and he finally expired off Gibraltar, on the 1st of June.

Sir David Wilkie was tall and of sandy complexion, with sharp eyes; was polite and mild in his manners, and a staunch lover of everything Scotch. His works are well known to the world through the excellent engravings of Raimbach, Burnet, Cousins, Doo, and C. Fox. At the sale of his effects, which realized several thousand pounds, there were many unfinished works, which sold at high prices. In August, 1841, a public meeting of his friends was held in London, at which Sir Robert Peel presided. The result of this meeting was, that a subscription was started for the purpose of erecting a suitable monument to his memory: £2,000 were collected, and it was agreed that a statue of Sir David Wilkie, by the sculptor Joseph, should be placed in the National Gallery. The statue is now in the inner hall of that institution.

WILKINS, William, a distinguished English architect, was born at Cambridge in 1778. He was the son of a builder, and received an academic education in the university of that place. In 1801, he obtained a traveling bachelorship, and visited Italy and Greece. On returning to England, he published his *Antiquities of Magna Grecia*, folio, 1807, which, containing little of particular interest to professional students, was rather coldly received by architects; but it was well calculated to recommend the author to scholars, and obtain the patronage of the University. Accordingly, in the same year of its publication, Wilkins was appointed architect of Downing College, and the buildings were begun forthwith. In this work, instead of adopting the Grecian style as far as it could be used, and adding for the occasion what the style would not admit of, he merely applied it just as he found it; and the result is quite unsatisfactory, both in the exterior architecture, and the interior accommodations.

Wilkins was afterwards appointed architect to the East India Company, at the resignation of Mr. Cockerell, and erected the East India College at Haileyburg, Herts, also in the pure Grecian style. He subsequently succeeded better in the additions and alterations which he executed for the three colleges of Trinity (1823), Corpus (1823), and King's (1828), at Cambridge. In these works he was obliged to use the Gothic style, and he had moreover seen the necessity of treating the Grecian with freedom, as is evident from the façade which he subsequently erected to University College, Gower-street, originally called the University of London, exhibiting a dome in combination with a Grecian portico, the latter being elevated upon a substructure the height of the basement floor, and forming a most picturesque arrangement of flights of steps. This is esteemed Wilkins' best performance, and has gained for him the most praise, both from critics and professional architects. His next work was the National Gallery, which has been criticised perhaps more than any of his edifices. He was made a member of the Royal Academy in 1834, and at the death of Sir John Soane in 1837, he was chosen to succeed him as Professor of Architecture. His talents would doubtless have conferred honor upon that institution, but he died in 1839, before the term (two years) allowed to a new professor to prepare lectures had expired. Besides the above mentioned edifices, he erected among others, the Nelson Pillar, in Dublin, 1808; and St. George's Hospital, Hyde Park Corner, which is pleasingly remarkable for the tetrastyle portico of square columns in its east front.

WILLAERTS, Adam, a Flemish painter, born at Antwerp in 1577. He distinguished himself as a painter of marines, coast scenes, and sea-ports, with a variety of shipping and boats. His pictures are generally embellished with groups of numerous small figures, correctly drawn, and touched with neatness and spirit. He also painted conflagrations, representing villages and ships on fire; his works of this description are well colored, and produce a striking effect. He obtained considerable reputation in his day, but his works are not so much esteemed as they were formerly; for, though his coloring is clear and transparent, his manner is somewhat dry and hard, and his figures are deficient in elegance. In 1600 he left Antwerp, and settled at Utrecht, where he died, according to the best authorities, in 1640. Balkema, differing from all other writers, says he was Regent of the Hospital of St. Job, in that city, from 1639 to 1660, but doubtless he has confounded him with the following artist.

WILLAERTS, Abraham, was the son of the preceding, born at Utrecht in 1613. After receiving instruction from his father, he studied some time with John Bylert, and afterwards went to Paris, where he became the pupil of Simon Vouet. On returning to his own country, he acquired considerable reputation as a painter of history and portraits. He was taken into the service of Prince Maurice of Nassau at Brussels, in whose employment he continued some years. He afterwards went to Africa, and made numerous sketches of the scenery of that country, as well as the manners and costumes of the inhabitants. He died at Utrecht in 1671.

WILLE, John George, an eminent German engraver, born at Koningsberg in 1717. After learning the rudiments of design in his native city, he went to Paris at the age of nineteen, where he applied himself to stroke engraving, which he afterwards carried to such a high state of perfection that few engravers have equalled him in the clearness and beauty of his execution. He particularly excelled in representing the brilliancy and softness of silk and satin draperies, and the delicacy of his burin was admirably adapted to express the polished finishing of the most celebrated Dutch painters. He engraved several charming plates from the pictures of Douw, Mieris, Metzu, Schalcken, Netscher, and other eminent painters, which give a very perfect idea of the style of the original paintings. He also executed some admirable portraits after the French masters. He acquired great distinction, and was elected a member of the academies of Paris, Rouen, Augsburg, Vienna, Berlin, and Dresden; was appointed engraver to the king of France, the Emperor of Germany, and the King of Denmark. Several sovereigns sent pupils to him to be instructed in the art; he also had many other scholars, some of whom followed his style with considerable success. Among the most distinguished may be named Schultze, Schmutzer, J. G. Müller, Bervic, Chevillet, the brothers Guttenberg, Halm, and Dennel. Charles le Blanc, in his valuable work entitled "Le Graveur en Taille Douce," gives a detailed account of one hundred and seventy-five engravings, with all their variations, by Wille. Very full lists may also be found in Nagler's Kunstler Lexicon, and Bartsch's Peintre Graveur. He died in 1807. The following are among his most esteemed prints:

PORTRAITS.

James Francis Edward Stuart, called the old Pretender. Charles James Edward Stuart, called the young Chevalier. Henry Benedick Stuart, Cardinal York. Prospero, Cardinal Colonna; *after Pompeo Battoni.* Frederick II., King of Prussia; *after Pesne.* Marshal Saxe; *after Rigaud.* Woldemar de Loevendael, Marshal of France; *after de la Tour.* Louis Philipeaux, Count de St. Florentin; *after Tocqué.* Abel Francis Poisson, Marquis de Marigny; *do.* C. E. Briseux; Architect. Margaret Elizabeth de Largilliere; *after N. de Largilliere.* Elizabeth de Gouy, wife of H. Rigaud; *after Rigaud.* Joseph Parrocel, Painter; *do.* John de Boullogne, Comptroller-general of Finance; *do.*

SUBJECTS AFTER VARIOUS MASTERS.

The Death of Cleopatra; *after Netscher.* The Death of Mark Antony; *after Pomp. Battoni.* Le Maréchal-des-Logis; *after P. A. Wille.* Les bons Amis; *after Ostade.* Le Menagere Hollandoise; *after G. Douw.* La Liseuse; *do.* L' Instruction Paternelle; *after Terburg.* La Gazettiere Hollandoise; *do.* La Tricoteuse; *after Mieris.* L' Observateur Distrait; *do.* La Cuisiniere Hollandoise; *after Metzu.* Le Concert de Famille; *after Schalken.* Les Musiciens Ambulans; *after Dietricy.* The first impressions of this plate are before the letter *c*, in the word electorale in the dedication. Les Offres Reciproques; *do.* La Petite Ecoliere; *after J. E. Schenau.* La Maitresse d'Ecole; *after P. A. Wille.* Les Soins Maternelles; *do.* Les Delices Maternelles; *do.*

WILLE, Peter Alexander, was the son of the preceding, born at Paris in 1748. His father intended him for his own profession, and instructed him in the rudiments of art, but the son manifesting a genius for painting, was permitted to study that branch. He accordingly frequented the Academy, and afterwards studied with Vien and Greuze. He distinguished himself as a painter of domestic and familiar subjects, conversations, &c., and was elected a member of the Academy. A good idea may be formed of his abilities, from the prints engraved after his pictures by his father. He also etched a few plates from his own designs, and after other masters.

WILLEBORTS. See Boschaert.

WILLEMANS, or WILLMAN, Michael, an eminent German painter, born at Lubec in 1630. Desirous of procuring better instruction than he could obtain in his native city, he went to Amsterdam, and first studied with Jacob Backer; but he afterwards became the disciple of Rembrandt, with whom he continued several years. On returning to Germany, he acquired distinction as an historical painter, and found abundant employment. He was much patronized by the Elector of Brandenburg, for whom he executed several considerable works, particularly a large picture of Vulcan forging the Arms of Mars, which is highly commended. He was also employed at several other courts of Germany, where his works are highly esteemed; and many of the churches and the palaces of the nobility in Germany, are adorned with his productions. He died in 1697.

WILLEMS, Mark, a Flemish painter, born at Mechlin about 1527. He studied with Michael Coxcis, and became a very eminent painter of history in his time. He painted with great facility; his pictures are well composed, and agreeably colored; his figures are correctly designed. When Philip, king of Spain, made his public entry into Mechlin, Willems, then but twenty-two years of age, was employed to paint the triumphal arch, which gained him great credit. There is a fine picture by him, representing the Decollation of St. John, in the cathedral at Mechlin. He died in 1561.

WILLIAMS, Robert, an English engraver born in Wales, who flourished at London about 1715. He distinguished himself as an engraver in mezzotinto, and executed a great number of portraits of distinguished personages, after Wissing, Vandyck, Kneller, and others, which are interesting as illustrations of English history. Some of them are finely executed, and are accounted excellent likenesses. Among others are the following:

Charles I.; *after Vandyck.* Edward, Lord Littleton, Lord Keeper; *do.* Charles II.; two plates; *after Lely* and *Kneller.* James II., when Duke of York; *after Cooper.* Mary Beatrix, his Queen; *after Wissing.* William III., when Prince of Orange; *do.* Mary, Princess of Orange; *do.* Henry Somerset, Duke of Beaufort; *do.* William Russell, Duke of Bedford; *do.* James Fitzroy, Duke of Monmouth. James Butler, Duke of Ormond; *do.* Charles Somerset, Marquis of Worcester; *do.* The Countess of Derby. Sir Charles Cotton; *after Riley.* Theophilus, Earl of Huntingdon; *after Kneller.* George, Prince of Denmark; *after Wissing.* Anne, Princess of Denmark; *do.* Lord Cutts, when Mr Cutts; *do.* George Fitzroy, Duke of Northumberland; *do.* Charles Lennox, Duke of Richmond; *do.* Sir George Rook; *after Dahl.* Sir John Houblon, Alderman of London; *after Closterman;* scarce. Sir Edmund King, M. D; *after Lely.* Barbara Villiers, Duchess of Cleveland; *after Kneller.* Ann Scott, Duchess of Monmouth; *after Wissing.* Catherine Sedley, Countess of Dorchester; inscribed *Mrs. Sidley; do.* Dorothy Cressy; *after Kneller;* scarce. Thomas Betterton, Actor; *do.* John Campbell, Duke of Argyle; *after Closterman.* Sir Richard Blackmore, M. D., and Poet; *do.;* fine and scarce. William, Earl of Portland; *after Simon de Bois.*

WILLIAMS, John, an English portrait painter, who flourished about 1775. He is supposed to have been a scholar of Richardson. He was an excellent artist, and his portraits are deservedly admired.

WILLIAMS, William, an English engraver, who was probably an amateur. His name is affixed to two slight etchings of views of the town of Halifax.

WILLIAMSON, F., an English engraver and printseller, who flourished at London about 1667. He engraved a few portraits, and some small plates illustrating the Concealment of Charles II., dated in that year.

WILLINGEN, Peter vander, a Dutch painter, born at Bergen-op-Zoom in 1607. He painted subjects of still-life—vases of gold and silver, books, and musical instruments, ingeniously composed, agreeably colored, and very highly finished, producing a very natural and pleasing effect. He died in 1665. There was another artist of this name, who flourished about the same time, and painted interiors of churches and other edifices. Nothing is known of him except by his pictures.

WILS, or WILTS, John, a Dutch landscape painter, who flourished at Haerlem about 1650. Little is known of him, except that Nicholas Berghem married his daughter, and is said to have frequently embellished his landscapes with cattle and figures. Such are now attributed entirely to the latter.

WILSON, Richard, R. A., an eminent English landscape painter, was born of a respectable family at Pinegas, in Montgomeryshire, in 1714. He was the third son of seven children; at the time of his birth, his father was a clergyman in Montgomeryshire, but he was shortly afterwards collated to the living of Mold, in Flintshire. Young Wilson early manifested a taste for drawing, and gave such promise that his relative, Sir George Wynne, took him to London, and placed him under an obscure portrait painter, named Thomas Wright, who lived in Covent Garden. With this master he made great progress, but nothing is known of his earlier studies; he must, however, have attained some rank as a portrait painter, for in the year 1748 he painted a large picture of the Prince of Wales and his brother the Duke of York, for their tutor Dr. Hayter, bishop of Norwich.

After practicing for some time with success in London as a portrait painter, Wilson went to Italy in 1749, to study the great works of the Italian masters. He had as yet tried little, if anything, in landscape painting, and seems not to have known his abilities in that branch; but while stopping at Venice, he paid a visit to Zuccarelli, the landscape painter, who happened to be from home, and Wilson, to pass the time until he came, made a sketch in oils of the view from the painter's window. Zuccarelli thought so highly of this sketch, that he recommended Wilson to relinquish portrait, and take to landscape painting. Another occurrence which happened to him in Rome induced him to follow this advice. Vernet, the celebrated French landscape painter, visited him in his studio at Rome, and was so much struck with a landscape by Wilson which he saw there, that he offered one of his best pictures in exchange for it; the proposal was readily accepted, and the picture delivered to Vernet, who placed it in his exhibition room, and often spoke highly of Wilson's talents. Years after, when established in Paris, Vernet would frequently tell his English patrons that they had no need of coming to him for pictures, while they possessed such a painter as Wilson.

From this time, Wilson devoted himself to landscape, and soon acquired so great a reputation that he had many scholars, even while in Rome; and Mengs painted his portrait, receiving a landscape in return from Wilson. He did not follow the example of many, in copying the works of celebrated masters; but he went immediately to the source of all art, and confined his studies to nature. After an absence of six years, Wilson returned to England in 1755. In 1760 he exhibited, in the great room at Spring Gardens, his celebrated picture of Niobe, which was purchased by William, Duke of Cumberland. This work established his reputation in England, as one of the first landscape painters of his time. In 1765, he exhibited in the same place a View of Rome from the Villa Madama, which was purchased by the then Marquis of Tavistock. He was one of the first members of the Royal Academy, founded in 1768; and at the death of Hayman in 1776, he was appointed librarian in his place. This appointment brings a very small emolument with it, yet small as it is, Wilson solicited the place; for although a few discriminating connoisseurs purchased some of his best pictures, he was neglected by the public, and was in a state of indigence compared with the majority of his fellow members of the Academy. Many of the Academicians had a personal dislike to him, among whom the president, Reynolds, was the foremost. The friends of the latter attribute this to Wilson's unprepossessing appearance, and uncouth manners, but these unfavorable circumstances do not account for the active and persevering animosity of the president. Wilson's uncouthness, however, was seemingly only external, according to the account of Northcote, who says that "his mind was as refined and intelligent as his person and manners were coarse and repulsive; and discernment and familiarity with him were necessary to discover the unpolished jewel beneath its ferruginous coat." Like many other talented artists, he received no adequate encouragement during his life-time; but the prophecy of Peter Pindar (Dr. Wolcott) has been abundantly verified, and the pictures for which Wilson received only a few pounds, have since been sold for as many hundreds. During the last two or three years of his life he lived in affluence, owing to some property which he inherited from a brother. He retired to the house of his relative, Mrs. C. Jones, called Colomondie, in Wales, where he died in 1782.

The style of Wilson is altogether original. Following nature as his guide, he adopted a varied and interesting manner, distinguished for its boldness and fidelity to nature, yet entirely classical. He avoided the acquisition of all adventitious beauties, and escaped the mannerism which generally arises from the too partial study of favorite masters. His views in Italy are selected with judgment and taste. In the words of a just criticism which appeared at London many years ago, in the "Sun" paper: "In many of these pictures Italy is realized, and at one glance we are enabled to enter into all the great and powerful feelings which are awakened by the recollection of what our earlier studies taught us respecting that land of heroes, that seat of stupendous empire which virtue raised and luxury withdrew, till it presented those melancholy scenes in the representation of which Wilson so preëminently excels. They are fine compositions, mingling the loveliest appearances of nature, where nature is most beautiful, with dreary and dark desolation, and every touching image which decaying grandeur in the noblest works of art could suggest to a classical imagination." It has also been observed, in a similar strain, that "in his pictures the waving line of mountains, which bound the distance in every point of view, the dreary and inhospitable plains, rendered solemnly interesting by the mouldering fragments of temples, tombs, and aqueducts, are all indicated in a masterly manner, exhibiting that local character which cannot but be considered as peculiarly grand and classical." In his representations of scenes from his native country, Wilson was frequently employed to paint particular views, which were less picturesque than he would have selected, and consequently partake of the formality of portraiture; but they are invariably treated with taste and ingenuity, and are distinguished for their fresh and dewy brightness of verdure.

In 1814, about seventy of Wilson's pictures were exhibited with some other works, at the British Institution. Among his principal works are, Niobe; Phaeton; a large View of Rome; Villa of Mæcenas at Tivoli; Hadrian's Villa; Temple of Bacchus, near Rome; View on the Tiber; Cicero at his Villa; Ceyx and Atalante; View from Wilton House; St. James's Park; Carnarvon Castle; and many others. Some of them he repeated several times with little variation, particularly the Villa of Mæcenas at Tivoli, which he repeated five times; and this circumstance has sometimes given rise to a suspicion of the originality of some of his works, which are really the productions of his pencil. Many of them have been engraved by Woollett, Byrne, Elliott, Hodges, Middiman, Earlom, and others; and many yet remain to be engraved.

WILSON, Benjamin, an English portrait painter, born at Leeds in Yorkshire. He went early to London, where Dr. Berdmore, Master of the Charter House, took him under his protection. He became a reputable painter of portraits, and was one of the first who endeavored to introduce into his pictures a better style of relief and of the chiaro-scuro. His heads are colored with more warmth and nature than those of the generality of his cotemporaries. He had considerable knowledge of natural philosophy, and was a member of the Royal Society. He executed a few etchings, among which are two or three in imitation of Rembrandt. He was appointed master-painter to the Board of Ordnance, and died in 1788.

WILSON, Andrew, a distinguished Scottish landscape painter in water colors, was born at Edinburgh in 1780. After acquiring some knowledge of painting under Nasmyth, he went to London at the age of seventeen, and entered the Royal Academy. When he had completed his studies there, he went to Rome about 1799, and studied the great works of art in that city, besides designing the finest views in the vicinity, and making close investigations into the ancient modes of painting at Pompeii and the Neapolitan Museum. After returning to London, he was induced to revisit Italy in 1803, for the purchase of works by the old masters; and while in Genoa he purchased fifty-four, among which was Rubens' picture of the Brazen Serpent, now in the National Gallery. He was also elected a member of the Ligurian Academy.

In 1806, Wilson returned to England, and exhibited several admired pictures at the Royal Academy. In 1808 he married, and subsequently accepted one of the Professorships in the Royal Military College at Sandhurst; he resigned his appointment after a time, and returning to Scotland, became master of the Trustees' Academy, a post which he held for some years, during which time he was the instructor and warm friend of a number of young men who have since done honor to Scottish Art. Guided by Wilson's knowledge and taste, the Board of Manufacturers extended their collection of casts, which is now one of the finest in the kingdom. As Manager of the Royal Institution, he was employed to purchase the collection of engravings now preserved in their galleries; and his opinion was consulted on all matters relating to the collection of works of art and the promotion of taste. During this period he painted many fine pictures, which found a ready sale. His morning and evening scenes were greatly admired for their truth and beauty; his pictures were distinguished for their classic forms and arrangement, correct and elegant drawing, and vigorous touch.

Aided by a small accession of fortune, Wilson determined to revisit Italy in 1826; and during the succeeding twenty years he lived alternately at Rome, Florence, and Genoa, painting many pictures, some of which were purchased for the royal and noble collections. He also purchased many fine works of art for the English private galleries and formed the collection in Edinburgh which was subsequently intended to occupy the National Gallery of Scotland, and is probably located there at the present time. In 1847, Wilson returned to England, and died at Edinburgh in the following year.

WILSON, W., an English mezzotinto engraver of little note, who executed a few portraits, among which is one of the Countess of Newburg; *after Dahl.*

WILSON, William, an English engraver, who executed with the graver, in a neat, clear style, several landscapes after Claude Lorraine, Poussin, and other masters.

WILT, Thomas vander, a Dutch painter and engraver, born, according to Brulliot, at Piershil in 1659. He studied under John Verkolie, and settled at Delft, where he painted portraits and familiar subjects. He also executed a few portraits in mezzotinto, marked with the above monogram. There is some discrepancy about him; Laborde quotes Brulliot, saying that his name was F. vander Wilt; Zani calls him Ferdinand; but the monogram would indicate Thomas. He was living in 1729.

WILTON, Joseph, R. A., an eminent English sculptor, was born at London, according to Allan Cunningham, in 1722. His father, though a common plasterer, acquired a fair fortune by manufacturing ornaments for ceilings and furniture, and as Wilton manifested a strong inclination for sculpture, he sent him over the channel to Brabant, and placed him under Laurent Delvaux. At the age of 22, Wilton proceeded to Paris, where he entered the school of Pigalle, learned the art of working marble, and drew the silver medal at the Academy. In 1747 he removed to Rome, where he distinguished himself so much to the satisfaction of the Academy of St. Luke, that in 1750, Pope Benedict XIV. presented him with the Jubilee Gold Medal. During a residence of eight years in Italy, Wilton was chiefly occupied in copying the antique statues. He returned to London in company with Cipriani the painter, Chambers the architect, and a skillful modeller named Capizzoldi.

About this time the Duke of Richmond formed a gallery in Spring Gardens for students in art, offering premiums to the most meritorious, and appointed Wilton and Cipriani directors. Before the termination of Wilton's engagement he was appointed State Coach Carver to the King, and he made the coronation coach for George III. According to Cunningham, the English sculptors before this time were employed by the architects, and Wilton was the first who had passed through a regular course of instruction and travel. His father having left him a considerable fortune, he was enabled to follow his own inclinations, and he succeeded at length in elevating British sculpture to its proper footing as an independent art. The first public work of importance from his chisel was the monument to Gen. Wolfe, in Westminster Abbey; after which he executed many other works, among which were the monuments to Admiral Holmes, the Earl and countess Montrath, and Stephen Hales. He also executed a large number of busts, particularly those of Swift, Wolfe, Chesterfield, Chatham, Cromwell, Bacon, and Newton. His design was tolerably good, he was intimately acquainted with anatomy, and notwithstanding the defects in his composition, which was frequently ill-conceived, too crowded, and too minute in accessories, his execution was excellent, and all his productions were admirably worked in the marble. Wilton acquired a large fortune, and lived in great style. He had a very beautiful daughter, who was married to Sir Robert Chambers. He was one of the founders of the Royal Academy, and when he retired from his profession, accepted the office of Keeper of that institution. He died in 1803. There is a bust of him in the Royal Academy, executed by Roubilliac, and presented by his daughter, Lady Chambers.

WINCKEL, Theresa Emilia Henrietta, a German paintress, was born at Dresden in 1784. She studied in the gallery of her native city, and attained great excellence in copying after the old masters. In 1806 she visited Paris in company with her mother, and remained there about two years and a half. Her talents were highly esteemed by David, who said that no artist could equal her in copying Correggio. Her mother having lost her fortune, the daughter employed her talents in music and painting for their com mon support. Several of her paintings have been used as altar-pieces. The time of her death is not recorded.

WINDHAM, Joseph, an English artist, antiquary, and writer on art, was born at Twickenham in 1739. After his educational course at Eton, and Christ's College, Cambridge, he visited the Continent, and traveled through France, Italy, Istria, and Switzerland, in 1769. While residing at Rome, he studied and measured the remains of ancient architecture there, particularly the baths; and his numerous plans and sections of them were engraved in Mr. Cameron's great work on the Roman Baths. To this he also furnished a considerable and valuable portion of the letter-press; he also drew up the greater part of the letter-press of the second volume of the Ionian Antiquities, published by the Society of Dilettanti; and Mr. Stuart received material assistance from him in the second volume of his Athens. For many years Windham was a member of the Royal and Antiquarian Societies; and in the latter was for many years one of the council. He died in 1810.

WINDTER, J. W., an engraver, who died at Nuremberg in 1765. There is much contradiction about his name, but he signed his prints *J. W. Windter del. et sculps.*, or J. W. W. He engraved a few portraits and other subjects.

WINGANDORP, F., a German engraver, who flourished about 1672. He engraved some frontispieces and other book plates, indifferently executed with the graver.

WINGHEN, Jodocus, or Josse van, a Dutch painter, born at Brussels in 1544. He went young to Italy, and studied four years at Rome. On returning to his native city, he was appointed painter to the prince of Parma. In 1584 he went to Frankfort, and painted history with considerable reputation till his death, which happened, according to Füessli and Brulliot, in 1603, and Zani, in 1613. His pictures are marked with one of the following monograms; he is sometimes called *th Old*, to distinguish him from his son Jeremiah called the *Young*.

WINGHEN, Jeremiah van, was the son of the preceding, born at Brussels in 1578. He showed an early genius for art, and after receiving instruction from his father, he went to Italy, where he painted history with great reputation, and his works obtained him great applause in every city that he visited. He afterwards returned to his own country, and settled at Frankfort, devoting himself chiefly to portraits, in which he was truly excellent. He obtained a striking likeness, his coloring was clear and natural, and his pictures were finished with diligence and care. He died in 1648.

WINSTANLEY, Henry, an English architect of considerable distinction. He was the projector, designer, and builder of the first Eddy-stone lighthouse, and perished with his edifice in the great storm of 1704.

WINSTANLEY, Hamlet, an English painter, was the son of the preceding. After studying under Sir Godfrey Kneller, he went to Italy, where he resided some years. On returning to England, he abandoned painting and devoted himself entirely to engraving. He etched a set of twenty plates from pictures in the collection of the Earl of Derby by Titian, Tintoretto, Paul Veronese, Bassano, Guido, Castiglione, Spagnoletto, Carlo Maratti, Rubens, Vandyck, Rembrandt, and other eminent masters. He also engraved a set of plates from the paintings of Sir James Thornhill in the cupola of St. Paul's cathedral. He died about 1760.

WINTER, Giles de, a Dutch painter, born at Leeuwarde in 1650. He studied under Renier Brakenburg, whose style he followed with considerable success. He painted similar subjects to those of his master, representing the amusements and recreations of the peasantry, Dutch boors regaling themselves, interiors of cabarets, &c.—His pictures are ingeniously composed, and his coloring is clear and brilliant, but his design is often very incorrect, as his imagination was so strong, that he never gave himself the trouble to study after nature, or make any preparatory designs, but composed and painted at once on his canvass, and wrought with the negligence and despatch of a mannerist. His pictures are little known out of his own country. He died at Amsterdam in 1720.

WINTER, or WINTNER, Joseph George, a German designer and engraver, who flourished about 1787. He engraved and published a large number of plates from his own designs, and after the works of Teniers, Berghem, Wouwerman, Melchior Roos, Peter de Laer, and other masters, fifty-three of which were in the Rigal collection. There were several other painters and engravers of little note, named *Winter*. Zani mentions a Gio. Guglielmo Winter, a painter of animals, and an engraver, who flourished in 1764.

WIRZ, John, a Swiss painter and engraver, born at Zurich in 1640. He studied under Conrad Meyer, and painted portraits with considerable success; but he is chiefly known out of his own country by his engravings. He designed and etched a set of forty-two plates for a book written by himself, entitled *Johannis Wirzii Romæ Animale Exemplium*, &c., 1677. They are etched in a neat, spirited style, resembling that of John William Baur. He also etched a few plates of portraits, and other subjects, after Holbein, Meyer, and others. He died in 1710.

WISCHER, Theodore. See Visscher.

WISSING, William, a Dutch painter, born at Amsterdam in 1656. He studied under William Doudyns, a painter of history at the Hague, but his genius leading him to portraiture, he adopted that branch of the art. On leaving his instructor, he went to Paris, and soon afterwards to England, where he was employed by Sir Peter Lely to assist him in his numerous works, and on the death of that master, he succeeded to much of his business. He imitated the style and coloring of Lely very successfully. He painted the portrait of the Duke of Monmouth several times, which ingratiated him with the King, and procured him the commission to paint all the members of the Royal Family, as well as the principal ladies and nobility of the court. Although he found a formidable rival in Sir Godfrey Kneller, he was still extensively employed, and at the death of Charles II., was appointed principal painter to his successor, James II., who sent him to the Hague to take the likeness of William and Mary, Prince and Princess of Orange. He died at Burleigh, the seat of the Earl of Exeter, in 1687.

WIT, or WITTE, Pieter de, called by the Italians, Pietro Candido, a Flemish painter, sculptor, and architect, born at Bruges in 1548. After studying in his native city, under some unknown master, he went young to Italy, and formed an intimacy with Giorgio Vasari, who employed him to assist in his works in the Vatican. He painted equally well both in oil and fresco, and was afterwards employed to execute several considerable works for the palace of the Grand Duke of Tuscany; also some cartoons for tapestry. He was invited to Munich by the Elector of Bavaria, who appointed him his painter, and he remained there during the rest of his life. He was the intimate friend of John Sadeler, who engraved some of his principal works, among which are the Annunciation, the Last Supper, the Holy Women at the Tomb of the Saviour, and Christ with the Disciples at Emmaus. De Wit painted, under the arcade of the long gallery of the Hof-garten at Munich, a series of frescos, representing the deeds of Otto of Wittelsbach, and the Departure of the Emperor Ludwig I. from Rome, in 1327. The paintings are now defaced, but the designs are preserved in the tapestries worked from them, and in the prints engraved by Amling from the tapestries. These are thirteen in number, marked with the name of *Pietro Candido*, as the painter. He was a monk, and most of his works are of a religious character.

De Wit probably acquired the knowledge of sculpture and architecture under Vasari. He practiced those arts at Munich, where the Elector, Maximilian I., employed him in the great palace, entrusting to him the embellishment of the interior, and probably the principal part of the whole work. Milizia praises the staircase as a master-piece of architecture. As a sculptor, he executed, among other works, the mausoleum of the Emperor Ludwig, in the church of Our Lady at Munich, decorated at the four angles with four statues of soldiers, larger than life, with lances and various insignia. Milizia says this work is worthy of being placed in St. Peter's. There is some confusion in the different accounts of this painter, and that part of his history connected with the Elector of Bavaria, is attributed in the *Biographie Universelle*, to one Lievin Wit, an historical and glass painter, whose birth is placed at Ghent, about 1510; but this is most probably erroneous, as the artist of this name who visited Munich, was employed by the Elector Maximilian I., who succeeded to the government in 1596. His death is placed by some in 1599, but this probably refers to some other artist; as the works he executed for Maximilian would seem to have occupied at least ten or fifteen years, if not longer. Others place it after 1620, which is the most reliable account.

WIT, or WITTE, CORNELIUS DE, was a younger brother of the preceding, but the accounts of him are strangely confused. He is said to have been very eminent as a landscape painter.

WIT, or WITTE, GASPAR DE, a Flemish painter, born at Antwerp in 1621. After studying in his native city he went to Italy, and gained considerable reputation for his landscapes of small size, designed in the Italian manner, and enriched with ancient ruins and edifices, also with small figures, correctly designed. His pictures were exquisitely finished, in the Flemish style. After several years he returned to the Low Countries, and painted numerous pictures, many of them from designs he had made in Italy, which were much admired. He died at Amsterdam in 1673.

WIT, or WITTE, PETER DE, sometimes called JUNIOR, or the YOUNGER, to distinguish him from the elder Peter de Wit, was the brother of Gaspar de Wit. He was born at Antwerp in 1620, and died in or about 1669. He was a good landscape painter, and acquired considerable reputation.

WIT, or WITTE, EMANUEL DE, an eminent Flemish painter, born at Alkmaer in 1607. He studied under Evert van Aelst at Delft, a painter of still-life, but did not adopt the style of his instructor. He applied himself to portraits, and occasionally to history, for some time; but not meeting with much encouragement, he studied perspective and architecture, and became one of the most eminent artists of his country in this branch. His best pictures represent the interiors of churches, temples, and magnificent edifices, which he embellished with numerous figures, correctly drawn, and touched with great neatness and spirit. He frequently gave a striking and picturesque appearance to his pieces, by representing the sun shining through the windows on part of the building, which is finely contrasted with that which is in shadow, and produces a natural and pleasing effect. The different ornaments of the buildings are designed with the greatest precision, and every object is touched with a bold and masterly pencil. Wit resided most of his life at Amsterdam, and his pictures usually represent the interiors of churches in that city, with every object correctly delineated, as the organs, monuments, pulpits, clergymen, and seats crowded with the audience. His style of composition is so peculiar, that his pictures once seen, can be instantly recognized. His best works are highly esteemed, and are to be found in the choice collections of his country. He died in 1692, aged 85 years.

The fair fame of this talented artist has probably been grossly libeled, for some unaccountable reason. He is said to have been dissipated in his habits, of a sour and morose disposition, and too much inclined to depreciate the works of his brother artists, which procured him universal hatred and contempt, and reduced him to poverty. It is also related that he was found drowned in a canal at Haerlem, with a rope about his neck, in 1692. It is not very likely that a debauchee would live to the age of 85 years; and his style was so different from any of his cotemporaries, that he could have little fear of competition from them, or they from him. The following anecdote, however, would indicate that he was of a passionate temper. He had received a commission from the son of Admiral de Ruyter to paint a View of the choir of the new church at Amsterdam, where the monument of the famous Dutch commander was erected.—Young de Ruyter dying before the work was finished, the family refused to pay the stipulated price, but offered a moiety. As the artist had exerted all his energies to produce a capital work, he was so exasperated, that he destroyed the picture.

WIT, JACOB DE, a Dutch painter, born at Amsterdam in 1695. He first studied with Albert van Spiers for three years, after which he went to Antwerp, to improve himself by studying the works of Rubens and Vandyck. While there, he studied some time with Jacob van Halen, a painter of little note; but he derived his principal improvement from a diligent study of the works of the great Flemish masters. In 1712 and 1713, he made designs from the famous paintings by Rubens, on the four ceilings in the church of the Jesuits in that city, in thirty-six compartments; and we are indebted to him for the preservation of those admirable compositions, as the originals were destroyed with the church by lightning, in 1718. The engravings by John Punt, were executed from the designs of de Wit. He was principally employed in painting ceilings, and decorating the mansions of the nobility with historical, emblematic, and allegorical subjects, which he composed with great ingenuity, designed correctly, and colored agreeably. He was particularly successful in designing children, and some of his pictures of Cherubs, or Cupids sporting, painted in chiaroscuro, are remarkably fine, and are held in the highest estimation. In 1736, he was employed by the magistrates of Amsterdam, to embellish the great Council Chamber with several subjects from the Old Testament, in which he discovers great inventive genius, and uncommon facility of execution. He also painted many works for the churches in Holland. He died in 1744.

WIT, or WITTE, DE. There were several other painters and engravers of this name, but they were of little note, and the accounts are so confused that little reliance can be placed upon them; such are Anthony, Francis, E. and B. de Wit.

WITDOECK, HANS or JOHN, an eminent Flemish engraver, born at Antwerp about 1600. His name is variously inscribed on his plates; generally *Witdoeck*, sometimes *Withouck*, and occasionally *Witdouck*. His talents recommended him to the notice of Rubens, and he engraved several plates from the pictures of that great painter under his immediate inspection. His plates, though less correct in drawing, and less admirable in the mechanical part of the execution than those of Vorsterman, Bolswert, and Pontius, are still estimable for their powerful effect, and they are in several instances the only prints existing of the capital pictures from which they were engraved. He also executed some plates from the works of

Cornelius Schut, and other masters. The following are his most esteemed prints:

SUBJECTS AFTER RUBENS.

Melchisedeck presenting Bread and Wine to Abraham. The Nativity. This plate has undergone several alterations, chiefly to add to the effect. The first impressions are without the address of Corn. Coeberchs; the second are with that address. The plate afterwards came into the possession of S. Bolswert, who retouched it, by which it was greatly improved. He also effaced the name of Coeberchs, and inserted his own. The Adoration of the Magi; engraved in 1683. There are also different impressions of this plate. The Elevation of the Cross, in three sheets. His most capital print. Christ with the two Disciples at Emmaus. There are some impressions of this plate printed in chiaro-scuro, under the direction of Rubens, which are very scarce. The Assumption of the Virgin. The impressions of this plate with the address of Corn. van Merlen, are retouched. The Holy Family, with St. John. The first impressions of this plate are before the address of Moermans. Another Holy Family, with St. Elizabeth and St. John. The best impressions have the address of R. J. de Bert. St. Cecilia. This plate was retouched and improved by Bolswert.

WITHOOS, MATTHEW, a Dutch painter, born at Amersfort in 1627. After studying six years under Jacob van Campen, a painter of history and an architect, he went to Italy in company with Otho Marcellis. Observing that the works of the latter were eagerly sought after from their novelty, he abandoned history, and applied himself to the same branch, in which he greatly excelled. He painted fruit, flowers, curious plants, insects, serpents, lizards, toads, and other reptiles to the life. He drew everything from nature with wonderful precision, truthfulness, and beauty of penciling, that procured him many admirers. During a residence of two years at Rome, he was much employed by the Cardinal de' Medici to paint a great variety of subjects of that description, for which he was liberally rewarded. He returned to Holland in 1650, and found abundant employment, at high prices, his pictures bringing him five or six hundred florins each. On the approach of the French army in 1672, he retired to North Holland, and settled at Hoorn, where he died in 1703. See *Otho Marcellis*.

WITHOOS, JOHN, was the son of the preceding, born at Amersfort in 1648. After receiving instruction from his father, he went to Italy, and diligently studied nature; he made an immense collection of highly finished water-colored drawings of the beautiful scenery, and views in the environs of Rome, which were greatly admired, and readily sold at high prices. He also painted landscapes in oil, from these drawings, with equal success. Though he met with very flattering encouragement at Rome, he was induced after several years to return to Holland, at the solicitation of his friends. His works were not less admired in his own country, and he was invited to the court of the Duke of Saxe-Lawenburg, in whose service he continued till his death, in 1695.

P. W. WITHOOS, PETER, was the second son of Matthew W., born at Amersfort in 1654. He studied with his father, and painted similar subjects in water-colors on vellum. His works are very highly and delicately finished, correctly designed, and colored after nature; they are highly esteemed in Holland by the curious collector, still commanding considerable prices and admitted into choice collections. He died at Amsterdam in 1693.

WITHOOS, FRANCIS, was the youngest son of Matthew W., by whom he was instructed. He painted the same subjects as his brother, in water-colors, on vellum, but with much less ability. He made a voyage to Batavia, in the island of Java, where he executed a great many drawings of the plants, insects, and reptiles peculiar to that climate and country, but on returning to Holland, his performances were thought inferior to his earlier productions. He died at Hoorn in 1705.

WITSEN, NICHOLAS, an engraver, probably a native of Holland, who flourished about 1659.—He engraved a few landscapes after the Dutch masters.

WITTIG, BARTHOLOMEW, a German painter, born at Oels in Silesia, about 1620. He excelled in painting festivals and concerts of music. In the gallery of the Louvre is a fine picture by him, representing a sumptuous banquet. He died in 1684.

WIVELL, ABRAHAM, an English portrait painter, born at London in 1786. He devoted but little attention to the art until 1820, when he sketched a portrait of Queen Caroline, at the balcony where she appeared to receive the congratulations of the public. The sketch was much admired, and, on being shown to the Queen, she expressed a desire to have it completed, and sat for it accordingly. Soon after, Wivell was engaged by Kelly to draw the portraits of the principal personages on the trial of the Queen, to be engraved for a work then publishing. He gained admittance to the court, and sketched several portraits of the judges and other honorable members, which were handed around, and pleased the parties so well, that most of them gave him a sitting or two after the trial, to enable him to finish their portraits. Among these were the Attorney General, Mr. Brougham; the Solicitor General, Mr. Denman; Mr. Copley, the son of John Singleton C., now Lord Lyndhurst, and others. He now advanced rapidly in public favor, and was commissioned to execute the portraits of many of the nobility, among whom were the Duke of York, the Duke of Clarence, Lord John Russell, Lord Suffield, Lord Holland, and others. He also painted portraits of about 200 members of the House of Commons, for a view of the interior of the House, published by Bowyer and Parkes. Most of his portraits have been engraved. He died in 1849.

WOERIOT, or WOEIRIOT, PIERRE, a French designer and engraver, born at Bar-le-duc in Lorraine in 1532. He chiefly resided at Lyons, and is said to have followed the business of a goldsmith as well as that of an engraver; but from his numerous prints it is probable that he devoted his attention chiefly to engraving. Robert Dumesnil gives a descriptive account of four hundred and one pieces by him. His prints are chiefly from his own designs, and are executed in a neat style, though the drawing is not very correct, and there is little effect, from the lights being scattered, and a want of depth in the shadows. Woeriot engraved both on copper and wood, and usually marked his copper plates with the above monogram, composed of the initials P. W. D. B. His wooden cuts, which are executed with great neatness and delicacy, are marked with a double cross, called the Cross of Lorraine. The Biographie Universelle mentions a print by him in the Royal French Cabinet, marked *P. Woeriotius Bozæus;* from which it is supposed that he was a native of the town of Bozé, or Bouzy.

WOLFAERTS, Arthur, a Flemish painter, was born at Antwerp in 1625. His instructor is not mentioned, but he gained considerable reputation among the artists of his time as a painter of history. His compositions are grand and simple, evincing a thorough knowledge of the principles of design and coloring, and his backgrounds are decorated with rich architecture; his sacred subjects are distinguished for their elevated character, and appropriate landscapes, and he was scrupulously attentive to costume. Wolfaerts also represented allegorical subjects, which evince that he was no stranger to literature, and he occasionally painted small compositions in the manner of Teniers, remarkable for their gayety and originality. He died at Antwerp in 1687.

WOLFGANG, George Andrew, a German designer, engraver, and goldsmith, born at Chemnitz in Saxony, in 1631. He engraved a few portraits, historical and other subjects, which are executed with the graver, in a dry, stiff, and formal style, and possess little merit. He also scraped some mezzotints. He died in 1716.

WOLFGANG, Andrew Matthew, was the son of the preceding, born at Augsburg in 1662, and died there in 1736. He was instructed by his father, and engraved some indifferent portraits of distinguished personages of Germany.

WOLFGANG, John George, was the youngest son of George Andrew W., born at Augsburg in 1664. He was instructed in the art by his father, whom he greatly surpassed. He had acquired considerable reputation, when he was invited to the court of Berlin in 1704, and appointed engraver to the king. He engraved a considerable number of portraits of distinguished personages, executed with the graver, in a much neater style than those of his father and brother; besides a set of plates for a work in folio, published at Frankfort in 1707, entitled *Notitia Universitatis Francofurtanæ.* He died in 1743.

WOLFGANG, Gustavus Andrew, was the son of Andrew Matthew W., born at Augsburg in 1692, and died in 1774. He studied with his uncle John George, and engraved some portraits in the neat style of his instructor.

W or W WOLGEMUT, or WOLGEMUTH, Michael, an old German painter and engraver, born at Nuremberg in 1434. He has been the subject of deep research and much disquisition, yet little has been elicited beyond conjecture. As a painter, many works executed in the dry, gothic style which characterized the German school previous to the time of Albert Durer, are attributed to him, most of which, if not all, are of very doubtful authenticity. Two pictures attributed to him, which connoisseurs generally consider authentic, are Christ brought before Pilate, now in the Louvre, and St. Jerome, in the Imperial Gallery at Vienna, painted in 1511, when the artist was a very old man; the latter is considered his masterpiece. There are five others at Munich, representing the Nativity, the Agony in the Garden, the Crucifixion, the Descent from the Cross, and the Resurrection, which are variously attributed to Wolgemut, to Hugo vander Goes, and to Justus of Ghent.

As an engraver, the accounts and opinions of Wolgemut are exceedingly contradictory. He flourished soon after the commencement of engraving in Germany, and is supposed to have been instructed by Jacob Walch. This supposition, however, is very improbable, as Walch was probably born many years after Wolgemut, and never engraved on wood. (See *Walch.*) Strutt says he engraved both on wood and copper, and attributes to him some cuts marked with a W. surmounted with a small o.; but Bartsch is decidedly of the opinion that he only engraved on wood, and that the copper plates marked with the letter W. belong rather to *Wenceslaus d' Olmutz.* Zani, on the other hand, expresses great surprise that Bartsch should deprive Wolgemut of the honor of engraving on copper, and stoutly affirms that he never engraved on wood. It is very generally considered that he designed and executed a part of the wooden cuts for the large folio work compiled by Hermann Schedel, usually known by the appellation of the Nuremberg Chronicle, published in 1493. Ottley attributes to him the invention of *cross-hatching*, but Jackson says that "Ottley is wrong in attributing this material improvement in the art to Michael Wolgemut," and goes on to say that Wolgemut "has too long been decked out with borrowed plumes"; also that "he considers it extremely questionable if either he or Albert Durer ever engraved a single block!"—This much appears certain, that he was a painter and a designer, and probably an engraver on wood; that Albert Durer studied with him for some time, and painted his portrait three years before his death, which happened in 1519, at the age of 85 years. His portrait is in the gallery at Munich. The reader who wishes to pursue this subject further, must be referred to Strutt's Dictionary of Engravers, Ottley's Notices of Engravers and their Works, Jackson's Treatise on Wood Engraving. Bartsch's Le Peintre Graveur, and Zani's Enciclopedia delle belle Arti. See also, *Jacob Walch, Wenceslaus of Olmutz, Martin Schoen,* and *Albert Durer.*

WOLKOW, F., a Russian architect of the last century, who studied in the Academy at St. Petersburg, and afterwards visited Paris for improvement. While in that city, he was employed by Duval in the construction of the *Theatre Française.* He subsequently returned to St. Petersburg, where he was employed in constructing numerous works, and in designing some plans for the Prince Potemkin. He died in 1803.

WOLTERS, Henrietta, a celebrated Dutch paintress, born at Amsterdam in 1692. She was the daughter of Theodore van Pee, a painter of little note, who perceiving in her a genius for painting, instructed her in the rudiments of the art, and then placed her under the tuition of James Christopher le Blond, a miniature painter. It was not long before she surpassed her preceptor in delicacy of touch and beauty of coloring. She afterwards greatly improved herself by studying the works of Vandyck, which she copied on a small scale with surprising accuracy, preserving not only the likeness, but the suavity of coloring and freedom of touch, which characterize the originals. Her extraordinary talents soon attracted public admiration, and she was employed to paint the portraits in miniature of many of the first families of Amsterdam. When Peter the Great visited that city, he sat to her for his portrait, and invited her to his court, with the most flattering offers of protection and favor; but she declined. The King of Prussia also invited her to Berlin, with no better success. She resided in her native city, highly respected, until her death, in 1741.

WOOD, John, an English architect, commonly spoken of as "Wood of Bath" who flourished during the second quarter of the eighteenth century, in the time of King George II. His taste and abilities were little if at all inferior to his cotemporaries, although he has obtained less notice than some of them, and little is now known concerning him, except some incidental facts in his "Description of Bath." That city is indebted to him for its architectural fame, and he may be considered as having there introduced a style of street architecture till then quite unknown in England, by combining a number of private houses into one general design; and although this mode of producing continuous façades was afterwards adopted by the Adams, was followed by Nash, and has since become very general, yet Wood still continues to be nearly the first in point of merit, as he is of date.

About the year 1726, Wood began his erections at Bath, which he carried on uninterruptedly for about twenty years, within which time he entirely changed the architectural character of the place, and conferred upon it even a degree of magnificence, at least as is displayed in such parts as the Parades, the Circus, the Royal Crescent, Queen Square, and some of the public edifices. These works have several faults, but a part of them were injured by alteration of the original designs, and Mitford says that notwithstanding the errors in parts of the Crescent at Bath, he "must reckon it among the finest modern buildings at this day (1809) existing in the world." Although Wood distinguished himself rather as the founder of a general system than as the author of any individual structures of importance, yet he produced some works of the latter class that alone would save his name from oblivion. Among them are the noble mansion at Prior Park; that of Buckland, for Sir John Throckmorton; and the Exchange at Bristol, first opened in September, 1743. The last is a very handsome structure, and the principal front presents a very tasteful specimen of the Palladian style. Wood wrote a philosophical treatise on his art, entitled The Origin of Building, or the Plagiarism of the Ancients, folio, 1741. He died in 1754.

WOOD, John, an English engraver, who flourished at London about 1745. He engraved some plates of landscapes after Claude Lorraine, Gaspar Poussin, Salvator Rosa, Wilson, and other masters, which possess considerable merit.

WOODCOCK, Robert, an English marine painter, born in 1691. He first practised the art merely for amusement, and held a place under the government, which he quitted, to devote himself entirely to art. He began to paint in oil in 1723, and in two years had copied above forty pictures by Vandervelde. The Duke of Chandos gave him thirty guineas for one of his pictures. He died in 1728. Woodcock possessed great natural abilities, and would have attained eminence, had he early received proper instruction.

WOOLLETT, William, a preëminent English engraver, was born at Maidstone, in Kent, in 1735. He studied under John Tinney, an obscure engraver in London; but he soon adopted an original style, from the resources of his own genius. He early acquired a great reputation as a landscape engraver, and was appointed engraver to George III. Woollett stands at the head of the artists in that branch; by a skillful union of the etching needle and burin, he produced the most admirable effect of depth and vigor in his foregrounds, and of tenderness and delicacy in his distances. In the latter part of his life, he practised historical engraving, and in this department he also produced some of the finest plates of which the English school of engraving can boast, particularly the Death of Gen. Wolfe, and the Battle of the Hogue, which are considered his best historical pieces. In figures, and especially in flesh, he was not so successful as in the varied departments of landscape. Woollett was the first who conceived and embodied in practice the great improvement of uniting in one plate the three methods of engraving—aquafortis, the burin, and the dry point—constituting a great advance in the art. Longhi remarks that he "exhibited so much artistic accuracy, so much vivacity and boldness of touch, so much force and harmony of chiaro-scuro, so much variety of tint, so much intelligence in aërial perspective, so much truth, in fact, and so much pictorial illusion, that he was, for all cotemporary engravers, and is for those of the present time, the marvel and the example."

The private character of Woollett is highly praised for its modesty and amiability. He never censured the works of others, or omitted pointing out their merit. The following anecdote, related by Benjamin West, evinces an extraordinary degree of patience and perseverance: Woollett, when he had finished his plate of the Battle of the Hogue, took a proof to West for his inspection: at first the president expressed himself perfectly satisfied with the plate, but upon a longer examination, he observed that in some parts alterations might be made, and in others additional color might be added, which would, in his opinion, improve the effect of the plate; and taking a port-crayon, with white and black chalk in it, showed in a few minutes the effect that he wished to be produced, remarking at the same time that it was of no great consequence, but it might improve the appearance of the plate. Woollett, however, immediately consented to make the alterations and additions pointed out. "But how long will it take you, Mr. Woollett?" said the president. "Oh, about three or four months," said the engraver. "And the patient creature," said Mr. West, in relating the circumstance, "actually went through the additional labor without a murmur." His admirable prints are rendered much more valuabl by the careful supervision which he exercised ove the printing, destroying all impressions that ex hibited any imperfection. His plates after th landscapes of Richard Wilson are among his mas terpieces, presenting the very mind and feeling o that classic painter; he also engraved after Claude Zuccarelli, the Smiths of Chichester, and others and he executed some plates after views draw from nature by himself. He died in 1785. The following list comprises Woollett's best works:

PORTRAITS.

George III., King of Great Britain; *after Ramsay.* Peter Paul Rubens; *after Vandyck.*

LANDSCAPES AND SUBJECTS AFTER VARIOUS MASTERS.

A View of the Hermitage of Warkworth; *after Hearne.* The Merry Villagers; *after Jones.* A Landscape, with Æneas and Dido; *after Jones and Mortimer.* A Landscape, with Buildings; *after John Smith.* Another Landscape; *after George Smith;* the first premium print. The Hay-makers; *do.* The Apple-gatherers; The Rural Cot; *do.* The Spanish Pointer; *after Stubbs.* A View of Snowdon; *after Wilson.* Celadon and Amelia; *do.* Ceyx and Alcyone; *do.* Cicero at his Villa; *do.* Solitude; *do.*: by *Woollett* and *Ellis.* Niobe; *do.* Phaeton; *do.* Meleager and Atalanta; *do.* The Jocund Peasants and Merry Cottagers; *after C. Dusart*; a pair. The Fishery; *after Wright.* The Boar-hunt; *after Pillement.* Diana and Acteon; *after Fil. Lauri.* A pair, Morning and Evening; *after Swanevelt.* A Landscape, with figures and a Waterfall; *after An. Caracci.* Macbeth and the Witches; *after Zuccarelli.* The Enchanted Castle; *after Claude,* by *Woollett* and *Vivares.* The Temple of Apollo; *do.* Roman Edifices in ruins; *do.* A Landscape, with the Meeting of Jacob and Laban; *do.* The Death of General Wolfe; *after West.* The Battle of La Hogue; *do.*

WOOTTON, John, a celebrated English painter of landscapes and animals, who flourished about 1720. He is said to have studied with John Wyck. He particularly excelled in painting horses and dogs, and distinguished himself in designing field and turf sports, in which he was much employed. His animals are correctly designed, and touched with uncommon spirit. Among his most esteemed works were seven pictures of fox-hunting, engraved by Canot. Wootton's talents were not confined to this branch; he painted portraits and landscapes with considerable success, in the latter sometimes imitating Claude Lorraine and Gaspar Poussin. He died in 1765.

WORLIDGE, Thomas, an English painter, and engraver, who flourished about 1760. He first practised miniature painting, and afterwards attempted portraits in oil, but not meeting with much encouragement, he devoted himself entirely to engraving. He adopted a style resembling that of Rembrandt, and finished his plates with the point of the graver, or the scratchings of the dry point. His prints are very numerous, consisting chiefly of heads and portraits, in the manner of Rembrandt, which possess considerable merit. He also engraved quite a number of antique gems, from which he struck some proofs on satin, and a complete set of these now command a high price. His drawings on vellum in India ink and black lead are highly esteemed. He died at Hammersmith in 1766, or 1768, aged about 65.

or WORMS, Anthony von, a German engraver, who flourished about 1530. He was a native of Worms, in the Palatinate of the Rhine, from which city he derived his name. Florent le Comte miscalls him Vuormace. He executed some wooden cuts, which, though in the old gothic style, possess considerable merit. Bartsch describes eleven prints by him, marked with the first monogram, except one, which is signed *Coloniae, per Anthonium de Vormacia Pictorem.*—Brulliot says he engraved both on wood and copper, and that some of his prints are marked with the second monogram.

WORSDALE, James, an English painter of little note, who studied with Sir Godfrey Kneller, and married his wife's niece. His works are now unknown. He died in 1767, at an advanced age.

WORST, John, a Dutch landscape painter, born in 1625, and died in 1680. After studying in his own country, he went to Italy, where he resided some time. After returning to Holland, he painted many pictures from his drawings made from Italian scenery, which gained him considerable employment.

WORTMAN, Christian Albert, a German engraver, who was a native of Pomerania, according to Huber, and flourished about 1730. He studied with Wolfgang, and at the age of twenty-five, was invited to the court of Hesse-Cassel, and appointed engraver to the Landgrave. In 1727, he went to St. Petersburg, where he engraved some portraits of the Imperial Family, and the principal personages of the court.

WOUTERS, Francis, an eminent Flemish painter, born at Liere, in Brabant, in 1614. After receiving some instruction in his native city, he went to Antwerp, and entered the school of Rubens. He devoted himself chiefly to landscape, and became one of the most eminent artists of his time in that branch. His pictures usually represent the most picturesque views in the Forest of Soignes, near Brussels, and woodland scenes with vistas, through which the eye was agreeably deluded to an immense distance. These subjects he embellished with figures taken from mythological or fabulous history, as Pan and Syrinx, Venus and Adonis, Venus attended by Cupids, Nymphs, Satyrs, &c., generally naked, correctly designed, delicately pencilled, and freely touched. His pencil is bold and free, his coloring clear and brilliant, and his style resembles that of his instructor. He sometimes painted history on a large scale, but in these subjects he was less successful, than in those of a smaller size. He was much patronized by the Emperor Ferdinand II., who appointed him his principal painter, and for whom he executed many of his choicest works. He accompanied the Imperial Ambassador to England, where he was well received by Charles I., and appointed principal painter to the Prince of Wales, afterwards Charles II. When the Royal Family fell into misfortune, he returned to Antwerp, where he passed the rest of his days, and was appointed director of the Academy. He was killed by the accidental discharge of a gun in 1659. There are some altar-pieces by Wouters in the churches in Flanders, the best of which are Christ giving the Keys to St. Peter, in the church of that saint at Louvain, and the Visitation of the Virgin, in the church of the Augustines at Antwerp. He also etched a few plates of landscapes, in a free and masterly style, among which is a set of four, dated 1649. His name is sometimes erroneously written *Wauter.*

WOUTERS, Gomar, a Flemish historical and landscape painter, of whom little is known, except by some pictures bearing his name. He went to Italy, and is said to have passed much of his artistic life in Rome. He flourished towards the end of the 17th century. There are some large prints representing views in and near Rome, executed in a spirited and masterly style, resembling that of Callot, inscribed *G. Wouters, Cavalier, del. et sculp.*, doubtless by this artist.

WOUTERS, James, called also *Vosmeer*, a Dutch painter, born at Delft in 1584. Little is known of him. He is said to have excelled in landscape; but he afterwards quitted that branch for fruit and flowers, in which he displayed great talents. He went to Italy, but returned to his native place, where he died in 1641.

WOUWERMAN, Philip, one of the most popular of the Dutch landscape painters, was born at Haerlem in 1620. He was the son of Paul Wouwerman, an obscure historical painter, from whom he received his first instruction in art; but his genius inclining to landscape, he studied under John Wynants, and made very rapid progress, manifesting great ability in figure painting, as well as in landscape, and frequently decorating the works of Wynants with his admirable figures and animals. On leaving his instructor, he applied himself to the study of nature with the greatest assiduity, and attained a very high degree of excellence, so that he may unquestionably be reckoned one of the most masterly painters that ever lived, unless mastery consists in something else than fully accomplishing the proposed end. It is reported that he never quitted Haerlem; but although he probably never went to Italy, the mountainous character of many of his landscapes constitutes almost a certain refutation of this assertion. The pictures of Wouwerman are held in the highest estimation; they usually represent hunting and hawking parties, horse-fairs, encampments, halts of travelers, and other subjects into which he could introduce horses, which he designed with a correctness and spirit that has never been equalled. It is commonly reported that he never painted a picture without introducing a white or grey horse; but this is most probably incorrect. Some of his landscapes are simply composed, and others are enriched with architecture, fountains, or edifices of a beautiful construction. His invention was so abundant that none of his pictures have either the same grounds or distances, varying perpetually, with inexpressible skill. His figures are admirably drawn, and grouped with uncommon taste and ingenuity. He had the perfect command of his pencil, so that he instantly and effectually expressed every idea conceived in his mind, and gave to his pictures astonishing force, by broad masses of light and shadow, contrasted with excellent judgment. The pencil of Wouwerman is firm, yet delicate; his distances recede with true perspective beauty, and his skies, atmosphere, trees, and plants, are all exact and lovely imitations of nature. Although his pictures exhibit the appearance of the most precious finishing, he must have painted with extraordinary facility, as between seven and eight hundred pictures are ascribed to him in Smith's catalogue, part 1., and Supplement. In his latter time, his pictures had too much of the grayish and blue tint; but in his best days he was not inferior, either in correctness, coloring, or force, to any of the artists of Italy.

Very little is known with certainty concerning the events in the life of this eminent painter. According to Nieuwenhuys, about fifty years after Wouwerman's death, Houbraken collected various anecdotes concerning him, derived, according to his own account, altogether from hearsay. Among other things, he states that Wouwerman destroyed all his drawings when near the close of his life, from the apprehension that his son, if left in possession of them, might be too indolent to study from nature; while others (Houbraken's verbal informants) have reported that, not being on friendly terms with his brother Peter, he destroyed them lest the latter should derive any advantage from them; while there were yet other reports, stating that the drawings in question were not his own, but the work of other masters. D'Argenville, assuming the truth of the statement that the drawings were Wouwerman's own, draws the inference that the painter's talents were not appreciated during his life-time, that he died in indigence, and destroyed the drawings in order to prevent his son from entering a profession in which he had made so signal a failure! This gratuitous supposition has been adopted by various writers, and generally believed, notwithstanding Houbraken also states that, though his pictures rose immensely in value after his death, he was nevertheless a fortunate painter; and in corroboration of this, he says that Wouwerman gave his daughter 20,000 florins (about $8,000), upon her marriage with the painter of flowers and fruit, Hendrick de Fromantjou. The distinction he gained while in the school of Wynants, and the fact that he was employed by that master to insert the figures and animals in his pieces, would almost refute the assertion of D'Argenville; but when we consider that he flourished in the best era of Dutch painting, and produced so many admirable works, we are astonished that such a report should have been credited. Wouwerman produced many grand battle-pieces, and sporting pieces, almost all carefully finished, particularly when of large dimensions, and full of incident; which would never be expected from a necessitous artist. His finished drawings are indeed very rare; but it is probable, from his great facility, that he never bestowed much care upon them, and generally made only slight preparatory sketches of his works. The proof that he did not meet the encouragement which his merits deserved, amounts to very little, if indeed to anything at all, and there is every probability that this painter, one of the best that the world has produced, lived and died in affluence.

Wouwerman died in 1668. Bartsch mentions two etchings by him, one of which represents a horse tied by the bridle to the stump of a tree. It is executed in a masterly style, and has been copied; the original is very rare, marked W. *fec.* 1643, the letters being reversed.

WOUWERMAN, Peter, was the brother of the preceding, born at Haerlem about 1625. He was instructed in the rudiments of the art by his father, and next studied under Roland Rogman, but afterwards with his brother, whose style he followed with so much success, that some of his best works have frequently been mistaken for the earlier productions of Philip. He painted similar subjects to those of his brother, representing huntings, fairs, farriers' shops, &c. His figures are not so correctly drawn as those of Philip, his pencil is less spirited and delicate, and his coloring less clear and transparent. His works, however, possess considerable merit, and are admitted into choice collections. He died in 1683.

WOUWERMAN, John, was the younger brother and scholar of Philip W., born at Haerlem in 1629. He painted landscapes, with figures and buildings, in a very pleasing style, with an agreeable tone of coloring, and a free and masterly pencil. His works are not numerous, as he died young in 1666.

WRAY, Robt. Batemen, an eminent English engraver on gems, was born at Broadchalk, in Wiltshire, in 1715, and was allied to several of the best families in that county. His uncle, Edward Byng, was a good pupil, and assistant of Kneller, who directed in his will that the portraits which his sitters had contracted for, should be finished by Byng. During the years occupied in his education, Wray learned of his uncle to draw the human figure with grace and precision; and acquired such a taste for the fine arts, that when it became necessary for him to choose a profession, he selected seal engraving—an art which at that time was scarcely advanced beyond the delineation of heraldic figures, and was therefore open to great improvement. He was placed under a seal engraver named Gosset, residing in Berwick-street, Soho, to learn the mechanical part of the business, where his rapid progress excited a degree of jealousy that led to a speedy dissolution of the connection. Although his first works were engraving the types of ancient heraldry, yet his choicer hours were devoted to the delineation of nature, and especially of the human figure. until he had succeeded in representing some of the most distinguished personages of English history, or remains of ancient sculpture, or the ideal designs of modern cotemporary artists. Before completing his twenty-fourth year, he had executed the front face and one of the profiles of Milton, and in another the second profile. Tassie, the inventor of a very perfect method of copying ancient engraved gems, was so much impressed with the merits of Wray's works of the same kind, that he sold copies of them together with those of his own collection. In this manner the reputation of Wray became more widely extended, and his original productions were sought after with avidity, even in Italy.

In 1759, after residing over thirty years in the metropolis, Wray removed to Salisbury, where he produced some of his best works, and those on which his reputation with posterity will chiefly depend. The difficulty of engraving figures on hard stones, in the manner of the ancient Greeks, is evinced by its rarity in modern times; and although it has been cultivated in Italy with great success, in England Wray scarcely had a rival. If some of the Italians have surpassed him in facility of execution, and in the number of their works, none have been his superiors in expressing the affections, and in female grace and beauty. That he never acquired more than a decent competence by his talents, is evident from the amount received for his best and most difficult work, the Head of the Dying Cleopatra, which was purchased by the Duke of Northumberland for £20. The following are the most remarkable of Wray's works, and they are here placed in the order in which they are supposed to rank by competent judges: Dying Cleopatra; Head of Medusa, a copy from the Strozzi Medusa; a Magdalen, Flora; the Madonna; three ideal Female Heads; Milton, fron face; two of Milton, profiles; Cicero; Pope; Shakspeare; Zingara; Antinous.

WREN, Sir Christopher. This eminent English architect, born at East Knoyle, Wilts, October 20th, 1632, was of good family, being the son of Dr. Christopher Wren, chaplain in ordinary to Charles I., and dean of Windsor; and nephew to Dr. Matthew Wren, successively bishop of Hereford, Norwich, and Ely. From the former he seems to have inherited a taste for scientific and literary studies, that of architecture included. Though in childhood of weak bodily constitution, Wren was of a most precocious mind, and early manifested a strong inclination for the paths of science and philosophy; at the age of thirteen he invented an astronomical instrument, a pneumatic engine, and another instrument of use in gnomonics. When fourteen years old he was entered as a gentleman commoner at Wadham College, Oxford; and during the period of his collegiate course he associated with Hooke (whom he assisted in his *Micrographia*,) and other scientific men, whose meetings laid the foundation of the Royal Society. In 1653, he was elected a fellow of All Souls' College; and by the age of twenty-four, he was known to the learned of Europe for his various theories, inventions and improvements, a list of which would be too long for insertion. In 1657, he was appointed to the professor's chair of astronomy at Gresham College, London, and three years after to that of the Savilian professor at Oxford, when he resigned the Gresham chair. On the establishment of the Royal Society, soon after the Restoration, Wren contributed not a little to the reputation of that body.

Thus far, Wren had attained to high eminence among his cotemporaries, but it was such that he might have remained known only to a few; whereas at present his celebrity as an architect has swallowed up all his other titles to distinction. At that time his architectural genius had hardly dawned, and it was probably chiefly owing to his general reputation for scientific skill that he was appointed by Charles II., in 1661, assistant to Sir John Denham, the surveyor-general, and was commissioned, in 1663, to survey and report upon St. Paul's Cathedral, with a view to its restoration, or rather the entire rebuilding of the fabric, so as to reconcile it with the Corinthian colonnade added by Jones. This scheme met with great opposition from the clergy and citizens; dissensions and protracted discussions followed, and nothing was decided upon for three or four years. In the meantime, however, Wren was employed upon the Sheldonian Theatre at Oxford, and the Library and Neville Court, at Trinity College, Cambridge; he also visited Paris in 1665, where the works of the Louvre were then in progress. On returning to London, he found matters no nearer adjustment in regard to the proposed Cathedral; but an event soon after happened, most calamitous in itself, which changed the face of affairs; the Great Fire not only decided that St. Paul's should be rebuilt as one consistent whole, entirely of Wren's own idea, but also opened an extensive field for his talents in various other metropolitan buildings. One immediate labor arising from the conflagration was to make a survey of the whole of the ruins, and a plan for laying out the devastated space in a regular and commodious manner, with wide streets and piazzas at intervals, which Wren laid before Parliament. Yet so far was this plan from being adopted, that the proprietors refused to yield any part of their ground, and the new streets arose in that dense and intricate maze of narrow lanes, which are even now but slowly disappearing before the modern improvements. Furthermore, instead of the line of spacious quays along the Thames, which Wren proposed, the river is entirely shut out from view by wharfs and warehouses, to such an extent as to render any adequate scheme for the improvement of its banks hardly practicable. London might have arisen from her ashes the finest city in the world, if Wren's plan had been followed.

Thus frustrated in his idea for planning an entire city, Wren was compelled to confine the exertion of his talents within narrower limits.—Among the earliest of his individual edifices were the Royal Exchange, Custom House (both since destroyed by fire and rebuilt), Temple Bar, the Monument, and several churches, including that of St. Stephen's, Walbrook; all of which were erected before St. Paul's was begun. Previous to that great event in his professional life, he received the honor of knighthood, in 1672; and in 1674, he married a daughter of Sir John Coghill, after whose decease he took for his second wife a daughter of Viscount Fitzwilliam, an Irish peer; and by both these ladies he had issue. During this time he had not been idle in regard to the proposed Cathedral, but had prepared various designs and models. That one, however, which he was solicitous to see adopted, was set aside for that now executed; the composition of his favorite plan was compact and simple, forming a single general octagonal mass, surmounted by a cupola, and extended on its west side by a portico, and a short nave or vestibule within; and there is also a great deal of play produced by the alternate curved sides of the main body of the edifice. The plan which was finally adopted, exhibits an almost opposite mode of treatment, both as to arrangement and proportions. While the first exhibits concentration and uniform spaciousness, the other is more extended as to length, but contracted in other respects, and the diagonal vistas that would have been obtained in the other case are altogether lost. The first stone of the present edifice was laid June 21, 1675; the choir was opened for divine service in December, 1697; and the whole was completed in thirty-five years, the last stone on the summit of the lantern being laid by the architect's son Christopher, in 1710. Taken altogether, the present St. Paul's is a truly glorious work, and its cupola is matchless in beauty; yet all noble as it is, the spirit of criticism, as usual, has not failed to detract from its merit, particularly for the coupling of the columns, and other departures from the general application of the orders. There are few churches, however, of the past or present day, that can vie with it in richness of design; and St. Peter's, with its single order and attic, appearing of much smaller dimensions than it really is, cannot be put in comparison with it. Some parts of the design are of exquisite beauty, particularly the two semicircular porticos of its transepts, worthy models for church façades.

As an architect, Sir Christopher Wren possessed an inexhaustible fertility of invention, combined with good natural taste, and profound knowledge of the principles of the art. His architecture is the perfection of that modern style, which, with forms and models essentially Gothic, adopts for the purpose of decoration, the orders and ornaments of classical antiquity. The west front of St. Paul's consists of a noble portico of two orders, the lower Corinthian, composed of twelve columns, and the upper Composite, consisting only of eight; all of which are coupled and fluted, and rest on a basement formed by a double flight of steps. The whole is surmounted by a spacious pediment, and along the other parts of the summit of this front are statues of St. Peter, St. James, and the Four Evangelists. On the north and south sides of the Cathedral, at each end of the principal transept, placed upon a flight of steps, is a large semicircular portico, formed by six Corinthian columns, each four feet in diameter, supporting half a dome. The east end, or choir, is terminated semicircularly, and is of beautiful proportions. The whole of the outer walls are decorated with two stories of coupled pilasters, Composite above, and Corinthian below. The intervals between the latter are occupied by large windows, which light the side aisles, and those between the Composite pilasters by ornamental niches; the entire summit is surrounded by a regular balustrade. The whole of this upper order is of no further use than to conceal the flying buttresses, which are constructed after the manner of a Gothic cathedral, for the purpose of counteracting the thrust of the vaulting of the roof. The most conspicuous feature of the building is the dome, which rises in great majesty at the junction of the cross. On a circular stylobate are placed thirty-two Corinthian columns, forming a circular peristyle, every fourth intercolumniation being closed with masonary, and ornamented with a niche. Above the entablature of this colonnade, but not resting upon it, rises an attic story, with pilasters and windows over the cornice, on which springs the exterior dome, covered with lead, and ribbed at regular intervals. Round the aperture, or summit, is another gallery; and from the centre rises the stone lantern, which is surrounded by Corinthian columns, and crowned by a majestic ball and cross. Few buildings can produce more grandeur of perspective than St. Paul's, particularly as entered from the western door. The nave and choirs have on each side three arches, the transept one, resting on piers, decorated towards the middle aisle with Corinthian pilasters. The nave is further lengthened by the morning and corresponding chapel at the end. The central area below the dome is octangular, formed by eight massive piers. The entire length of the edifice, including the porch, is 500 feet; breadth of the front, including the turrets, 110 feet; breadth of the three naves, 130 feet; outward diameter of the cupola, 145 feet; inward diameter of the same, 108 feet; outward diameter of the lantern, 18 feet; the diameter of the ball six feet; height from the ground without, to the top of the cross, 340 feet; that of the turrets 222 feet; the general depth of the foundations below the surface of the ground, is 22 feet, and in some places 35 feet.

The other churches erected by Wren are by no means equal to this, his grand performance; they are very numerous, but do not remind the beholder of the architect of St. Paul's. Even in his campanili, the far-famed steeples of St. Bride's and Bow church, there is little to admire except the general outline, for they are strange compounds of incongruous parts, oddly put together, and not particularly elegant in themselves. The church of St. Stephen's, Walbrook, has also been greatly overrated; for, allowing all the merit that is claimed for it in regard to the dome and columns, the effect that would else be produced by them is sadly marred by the poverty and tastelessness of the rest. Among the other edifices erected by Wren, were St. James's, Westminster; St. Clement's, Eastcheap; St. Martin's, Ludgate; Temple Bar, Christ Church, Newgate; Marlborough House, London; and Westminster Abbey, towers of west front; besides many more. One work which would probably have not a little augmented his fame, was a design for a magnificent mausoleum to the memory of Charles I.; yet, though parliament voted £70,000 for this purpose in 1678, the design was abandoned, and the money applied more conformably with the personal tastes of Charles II. Wren had been thwarted in his ideas for another monument, namely, the Column so-called, which he had conceived very differently and very characteristically, the shaft being adorned with gilt flames issuing from the loop-holes; but that design was set aside for the very commonplace affair which we see at present. He had resigned the office of Savilian professor in 1673; he accepted that of President of the Royal Society in 1680, and he also sat several times in Parliament; but his numerous and important professional engagements left him little leisure for other pursuits or duties. Enjoying the favor of successive princes, he was employed by Queen Mary to complete the buildings at Greenwich, to be appropriated as a Royal Naval Hospital; and Wren's additions to that noble pile are well worthy of the architect of St. Paul's, although less quoted as proofs of his genius than several of his inferior performances. In his additions to Hampton Court for William III., he was less successful; perhaps unfortunate in being controlled by the taste of the king. If not actually a blot upon his fame, like his work at Windsor Castle, Hampton Court adds nothing to it, whereas, he might perhaps have produced a piece of palatial architecture at Windsor, had his plan for erecting a distinct pile of building on the south side of the Upper Ward been adopted.—Still, palaces do not appear to have been Wren's forte, if an opinion may be formed from the specimens he has left us at Marlborough House, and some portions of St. James's.

After the death of Anne, the last of his royal patrons, Wren was dispossessed of his office of surveyor-general (which he had held forty-nine years), very little to the credit of George I., and to the disgrace of "one Benson," the man who, by succeeding him in that capacity, has preserved a name from oblivion, by perpetuating it for everlasting shame and contempt. To Wren himself, however, this discharge from office must have been rather a welcome release than otherwise; for, verging towards ninety, he could then have little further worldly ambition, even had he not already amply gratified it. The close of his life was not so much to be pitied as to be desired, for if he passed the last five years of his existence in retirement and comparative obscurity, he passed them in serenity of mind and placid content. The struggles of dissolution were spared him, for without any previous symptoms of approaching death he was found dead, reposing in his chair after dinner, February 25, 1723, in the 91st year of his age. He received the tardy honor of a splendid funeral in St. Paul's where his remains, were deposited in the crypt, with no other adornment to his tomb than the inscription on it, with the sublimely eloquent legend—"*Si Monumentum quæris, circumspice.*"

Christopher, the architect's son by his first marriage, composed the chief part of the "Parentalia, or Memoirs of the family of the Wrens;" it was completed by Stephen Wren, the grandson of Sir Christopher, and published in 1750. It forms a valuable and authentic record. In All Soul's Library, at Oxford, there is a collection of Wren's original drawings.

WRIGHT, Inigo, an English engraver in mezzotinto, who flourished about 1770. He executed a few plates of portraits and other subjects, among which are the Family of van Goyen, *after J. van Goyen;* and St. John preaching in the Wilderness, *after F. Lauri.*

WRIGHT, Joseph, an eminent English painter, born at Derby in 1734, and hence called Wright of Derby. He studied under Thomas Hudson in London, on leaving whom, he returned to his native place, and devoted himself chiefly to portraiture with great success. He also painted candlelights and conflagrations, which were much admired. In 1773 he went to Italy, where he diligently studied two years. During his residence there he had an opportunity of seeing a very memorable eruption of Mount Vesuvius, and he depicted the sublime spectacle with extraordinary effect. He returned to Derby in 1775, and devoted himself to history and landscape, chiefly the latter, in which he greatly excelled, and his best works of this description are ranked with the productions of Wilson. Among his historical pictures are the Dead Soldier, the Destruction of the Floating Batteries at Gibraltar, Edwin at the tomb of his Ancestor, Belshazzar's Feast, Hero and Leander, and the Storm Scene in the Winter's Tale, painted for the Shakspeare Gallery, a most spirited performance. His Eruption of Vesuvius and View of Ulswater, are powerful examples of skill in representing nature under totally different aspects. He was a very modest and retiring man, and never would leave his native place to settle in London, although frequently recommended and solicited to do so, that his talents might be brought more conspicuously before the public. His works, however, were appreciated even when he did not paint them by commission, for they were generally purchased as soon as finished. Many of his pictures were engraved by Middiman, James Heath, and other artists. He was elected an Associate of the Royal Academy in 1782, but having taken offence at Mr. Garvey's being chosen Academician before him, he resigned his Associate's diploma in disgust. He was a man of estimable character, much beloved by his fellow-citizens. He died in 1797, of a disease brought on, as is supposed, by excessive professional application.

WRIGHT, Richard, an English painter, born at Liverpool about 1735. He was originally a house painter, but devoting himself to marine subjects, acquired considerable distinction by the force of his talents, and an attentive study of nature. On two occasions, in 1764 and 1766, he gained the first premium of fifty guineas, for two marine subjects, from the Society for the Encouragement of Arts, &c.; the latter, called the Fishery, was engraved by Woollett, whose print was afterwards copied by a French engraver, and the name of Vernet substituted for that of Wright. He died in 1775. He had two daughters, whom he instructed in the art, and who painted fruit, landscapes, and still-life.

WRIGHT, Thomas, an English painter and engraver of the present century. He attained some reputation in engraving by his portraits in a work published by Mrs. Jameson, entitled "The Beauties of the Court of Charles II." He afterwards went to St. Petersburg, where he was patronized by the Imperial family, many of whom sat to him for their likenesses, which he painted in water-colors and in miniature. He was also employed by the eminent personages at that court, and engraved several of their portraits, after his own paintings. On returning to England he commenced a plate of Reynolds' Infant Hercules, but did not live to complete it. He died in 1850.

WULFHAGEN, Francis, a German painter, born at Bremen in 1620, and died there in 1678. He was a scholar of Rembrandt, whose style and subjects he is said to have imitated with considerable success.

WULFRAET, or WULFRAAT, Matthias, Mathys, or Matthew, a Dutch painter, born at Arnheim, in 1648. He was the son of an eminent physician, who intended him for that profession; but as he attended more to drawing than to his medical studies, his father yielded to his decided disposition for art, and placed him under the tuition of Abraham Diepraam, a painter of drolls and drunken frolics. The latter took great pains with him, but Wulfraet did not follow his style or subjects. On leaving Diepraam, he improved himself by a diligent study of nature, and painted history, portraits, and domestic subjects, which were held in great estimation throughout Germany and the Low Countries. He particularly excelled in painting portraits in small; also conversations and assemblies of persons above the common rank, composed with taste, and delicately finished. He chiefly resided at Amsterdam, and died there in 1727.

WURSCH, M., a Swiss painter, born at Stanz, in the canton of Underwalden, in 1718. He painted history with considerable reputation, and there are some of his works in the Abbey of Engelberg, which are much admired for fine expression and beautiful coloring. He was for many years professor of painting in the Academy of Besançon. Some time before his death he lost his eyesight, and retired to his native place, where he was killed by the French troops in 1798.

WUST, Charles Louis, a German engraver, who flourished about 1760. He executed some plates of historical subjects with the graver, in a neat, but labored style, and incorrectly drawn.

WYATT, R. J., an English sculptor, born in 1795. He studied under Charles Rossi, R. A., for seven years, during which time he gained two medals from the Royal Academy. When Canova visited England, Wyatt was introduced to him through the kindness of Lawrence, and by his advice and instruction, the young artist gained great improvement. In 1821, Wyatt visited Paris, and studied for some time under the celebrated Bozio after which he went to Rome and remained there the rest of his life, except in 1841, when he made a short visit to his native land. During Canova's life-time, the closest intimacy subsisted between him and Wyatt, as also between the latter and Gibson, who was at that time a pupil of Canova. Wyatt was singularly industrious, rising constantly at five in the morning, and sometimes continuing his work until midnight; consequently he produced a large number of works, which are distinguished for their exquisite purity of style. Among his best productions are, a group of Ino and the Infant Bacchus; a statue of Glycera; a statue of Musidora; two statues of Nymphs; and an admirable statue of Penelope, ordered by Her Majesty, in 1841. Wyatt died in 1850.

WYATT, James, a distinguished English architect, was born in 1746, at Burton Constable, in Staffordshire, where his father was both a farmer and a dealer in timber. Little is known concerning his early life, but he manifested sufficient talents in architecture at the age of fourteen to gain the patronage of Lord Bagot, who took him with him to Rome, on an embassy to the Pope. Wyatt spent three or four years in the metropolis of art, examining and measuring the principal monuments of ancient architecture, but, as it would seem, without imbibing any taste for its modern ones, since no traces of it are discoverable in his own works. On quitting Rome, he proceeded to Venice, where he studied for about two years more under Vicentini, an architect and painter, and then returned to England, after being absent altogether about six years. His first work in London was the Oxford-street Pantheon, finished and opened in 1772. This edifice was remarkably attractive, as being the resort of the gay world, and was esteemed a master-piece of architecture, although it is impossible to say how far it merited the encomiums it received, as it has since been destroyed by fire, and the original designs have never been published. The Pantheon, however, established the reputation of its architect, and commissions poured in upon Wyatt in great abundance, chiefly for private residences in the country, of which the majority hardly aspired to the character of mansions. These edifices exhibit more of clever mannerism and uniformly respectable mediocrity, than of style or artist-like treatment, as they are nearly all variations of the same design. He seems to have devoted his attention mostly to the useful department of the art, and England is greatly indebted to him and Adam for the superior accommodation and refinement of comfort which they introduced into domestic architecture. According to Lord Kames, this should be the chief consideration in country mansions; but, accustomed to this mode of proceeding, Wyatt could scarcely rise above it when necessary, as is evinced in his design for Downing College, Cambridge, which was not executed. Neither did Chiswick inspire him with a desire to execute anything really noble, for though the wings which he added to the house rendered it more commodious as a residence, they sadly marred its original grace as a finished specimen of Palladian architecture.

About the time of the death of James Essex (1784), the only architect of the period who had shown any knowledge of Gothic architecture in regard to its details, if not its principles, Wyatt began to turn his attention to that style. As there were then no drawings or publications upon this subject, he was obliged to study it from the original examples; and it is very greatly to his credit that, under such difficult circumstances, and engaged in many other avocations, he gained the insight into it which he did, attaining to correctness in his details and individual features. His first essay in that style was Lee Priory, near Canterbury, in 1783, which gained for him great celebrity. Extolled by Horace Walpole, it served to bring thenceforward into vogue for modern residences, a style of Gothic comparatively pure for the time. Although Wyatt did not attain to a correct perception of the spirit and true character of the Gothic style, he certainly effected very much for its practical revival, and he is allowed to have been preeminent as the restorer of ancient architecture in England, standing as he did, singly, without equal or rival. He was also extensively employed in making alterations and restorations in the older edifices of that style, particularly in the Oxford Colleges, and the Cathedrals of Salisbury and Litchfield. In the latter, however, he was not very successful, and his splendid edifice of Fonthill Abbey is criticised as manifesting more magnificence than propriety of character.

While employed upon the last mentioned edifice, Wyatt succeeded Sir W. Chambers, in 1796, as surveyor-general; which led to his being employed at Woolwich and the House of Lords, and by George III., in making alterations at Windsor Castle, and in erecting a Gothic palace at Kew, which has since been demolished. In 1802, on West's retiring from the office of President of the Royal Academy, Wyatt became his successor; but in the following year, West was re-elected. After this time, scarcely any materials are recorded of his life. He died in 1813, in consequence of being overturned in a carriage, while traveling from Bath to London. He left a widow and four sons, one of whom, Benjamin, was the architect of Drury Lane theatre.

WYATTVILLE, Sir Jeffry, an eminent English architect, nephew of the preceding, and son of Joseph Wyatt, was born at Burton-upon-Trent, in Staffordshire, in 1766. During boyhood, he was bent upon going to sea, and made two attempts to do so, but was pursued and brought back on both of these occasions. At the age of seventeen, he was to have gone out with Admiral Kempenfeldt, in the Royal George; but being prevented from joining that vessel in time, he escaped the disaster at Spithead. Thus thwarted, he betook himself to the Metropolis, in the hope of finding some opportunity of engaging in the naval service, but as the American war had terminated, no such opportunity offered. These disappointments finally threw him into that course which he followed with so much distinction; his uncle Samuel, a London architect and builder of some distinction (who erected Tatton Hall; Trinity House, London; Heaton House, Lancashire, &c.,) took him into his office for seven years. During this period he became fully acquainted with the routine and business of his profession; and at its termination, he served a sort of second apprenticeship with his uncle, James Wyatt, from whom he doubtless imbibed his preference for the Gothic and old English styles. While with his uncle James, he was brought into contact with several persons of high rank and influence, among whom was his future royal patron, the Prince of Wales.

It would appear that no opportunities were at that time extended to him from the Prince, for in 1799, he accepted the proposal made him by an eminent builder, John Armstrong, who had extensive government contracts, to join in partnership with him. This line of business, though highly respectable and eminently lucrative, proved for about twenty years a bar to his being admitted to the Royal Academy, although he was very extensively employed as an architect by many noblemen and gentlemen in various parts of the country, either in improving and making additions to their mansions, or erecting new ones. Nearly all his works are of this class, excepting the new front of Sidney Sussex College, erected in 1833.

Early in 1824, parliament granted £300,000 for the improvement of Windsor Castle. Four architects were called upon for designs, Soane, Nash, Smirke, and Jeffry Wyatt. The first declined the affair altogether; the designs of the second and third were rejected; and it was probably unexpected to himself, when Wyatt was summoned to Windsor Castle by King George IV., and commissioned to remodel that celebrated edifice. This great work occupied him nearly all the rest of his life. The first stone was laid by the King himself, Aug. 12th, 1824, on which occasion the architect received the royal authority for altering his name to Wyattville; and when the King took possession of the private apartments, about four years after, he received the further distinction of knighthood. Until renovated and remodelled by Sir Jeffry, the exterior of Windsor Castle had very little of either architectural character or dignity, or even of picturesqueness, except that arising from situation; whereas it is now marked by many bold features and well-defined masses, presenting a series of parts all varied, yet more or less interesting. Though open to criticism in respect to details, and the intermixture in several parts of the earliest and latest styles of Gothic, it is still a noble specimen of architecture, and deserves very high praise. A long and detailed critique upon this edifice may be found in the Penny Cyclopædia, article Windsor Castle. Sir Jeffry beheld his great work brought to completion by himself, and intended to publish the designs which he directed to be done by his executors. He died at Windsor in 1840, and was buried in St. George's chapel. The designs were published on a magnificent scale in two vols. large folio, in 1841. During the period of his work upon Windsor Castle, he made very extensive additions to the princely seat of Chatsworth; he was also employed at Longleat Castle, Wilts; Wollaton Hall, Notts; and completed Ashridge, Notts, the seat of the Earl of Bridgewater, commenced by James Wyatt.

WYCK, Thomas, a Dutch painter, born at Haerlem in 1616. After studying in his native city, he went to Italy, where he resided some years, and on returning to Holland, he distinguished himself as one of the ablest artists of the time. He painted sea-ports, with a variety of shipping, which frequently represent the ports in the Mediterranean, particularly those from Leghorn to Naples. They are usually embellished with a great number of small figures, decked in the costumes of different nations, correctly designed, and touched with great spirit, in a style resembling that of Peter de Laer.

He also painted Italian markets, fairs, and mountebanks; he represented the interior of chemists' laboratories, with their furnaces and utensils, in an admirable manner. His pictures are well composed, his coloring is warm and transparent, his pencil bold and free, and he had an excellent knowledge of the chiaro-scuro, which enabled him to give his objects a fine relief; his distances show a charming truth of perspective, and the eye is agreeably deluded to a great distance. Wyck visited England about the time of the Restoration, where he found considerable employment. There are a few etchings of landscapes and views by him, executed with neatness and spirit, but they are now very scarce. He died in 1686. His name is often written *Wycke.*

WYCK, John, was the son of the preceding, born at Haerlem about 1640. He was instructed by his father, and distinguished himself as a painter of battles, sieges, and huntings of deer and other animals, processions, and landscapes, in which he appears to have imitated the style of Philip Wouwerman, but on a larger scale. Though inferior to his model in the neatness and delicacy of his finishing, his animals and figures are correctly designed, and touched with great spirit and animation. His pictures are well composed, and his scenery very agreeably chosen. He sometimes painted pictures of a large size, as the Battle of the Boyne, and the Sieges of Naarden and Namur; but they are inferior to his smaller productions. He accompanied his father to England, where he found considerable employment, and passed the rest of his life. He also etched some spirited plates from his own designs, which are very scarce; Bartsch describes twenty-one, and says they are so extremely scarce, that few oollections contain a complete set of them. Weigel, in his supplement to Bartsch, has added four more, and pointed out the variations which occur in the others. Wyck made the designs for a book on hunting and hawking. He died at Mortlake in Surrey, in 1702.

WYKEHAM, William de. This eminent English Bishop, distinguished also for his knowledge of architecture, was born in the village of Wykeham, according to Lowth, in 1324. His parents were poor, but of creditable descent, and of reputable character. Although he studied in the school of Winchester, aided by Nicholas Uvedale, Lord of Wykeham, he did not obtain a scholastic education; but after leaving school he acted as secretary to his patron, and subsequently to the Bishop of Winchester; after which he was presented at court to king Edward III. His strength lay in his natural genius, in his knowledge of mankind and talents for business; and probably the only art or science he had much cultivated, was architecture. In the year 1356, he was successively appointed clerk of all the King's works in his manors of Henle and Yethampstead, and surveyor of the King's works in the castle and park of Windsor. Wykeham seems to have progressed rapidly in the royal favor, and at his instigation the king gave orders to demolish a great part of Windsor Castle, which he afterwards rebuilt. Queenborough castle, in the Isle of Sheppy, was also restored by him. He had probably taken orders at an early age, and being made an ecclesiastic, he was presented with a number of benefices. Many honors were successively heaped upon him, of which a long detail is given by Lowth; he became Secretary of State, Bishop of Winchester, and Lord High Chancellor of England. He held the two latter posts in the church and state at the same time, until 1371, when the Lords and Commons presented a petition to the king, complaining of the abuses which had resulted from this feature of state policy; whereupon Wykeham resigned the latter office. His first undertaking after obtaining possession of the see, was to thoroughly repair the twelve castles or palaces furnished and maintained for the bishops of Winchester; he also proceeded to erect a preparatory college at Winchester, and purchased the ground at Oxford for the New College.

Wykeham's prosperity had not failed to excite jealousy, and during the last year of Edward's reign the parliament took possession of the superannuated and dying king; a series of false charges were instituted against Wykeham in 1376, and he was deprived of his bishopric; but the clergy immediately took up his cause with such zeal that it was speedily restored. The benevolent bishop then went on with his architectural and educational projects. The college at Oxford, still called New College, was completed in 1386, and that of Winchester in 1393. The chapel and hall of the latter edifice are beautiful specimens of Gothic architecture. As soon as these were erected, he entered upon another great work, which still remains a monument of his taste and magnificence. He rebuilt the Cathedral at Winchester in the greater part of its extent, commencing it in 1395, and completing the work just before his death, which occurred in 1404. This magnificent and interesting edifice is 545 feet long; from the west entrance to the choir is 356 feet; the length of the choir is 135 feet; and the Lady Chapel at the east end is 54 feet, which makes the total length. As a distinct part, the nave is 250 feet long, 86 feet wide including the isles, and 78 feet high. The length of the transepts is 186 feet. The square of the tower is 48 feet by 50, and the height is 138 1-2 feet, which is only about 26 feet above the roof. The tower, with part of the nave and transepts, was built in 1079 by Bishop Walkelyn; but the grandeur of the west front is due to William de Wykeham. Viewed from the exterior, this is by far the most imposing part of the building; the deeply recessed entrance doorway, with the ornamental gallery above it; the large and beautiful window, the rich effect of the mouldings, the buttresses, the pinnacled towers, and the gable termination surmounted by the canopied statue of Wykeham, cannot be looked upon without great admiration. On entering the building, the view from the west end to the east is magnificent; the vast length of the vista formed by the nave and choir, with the splendid ceiling, the columns and arches on each hand and overhead, and the eastern window casting its dim, softened light from behind the choir, produce a combined result of solemnity and beauty equalled by few cathedrals in Europe.

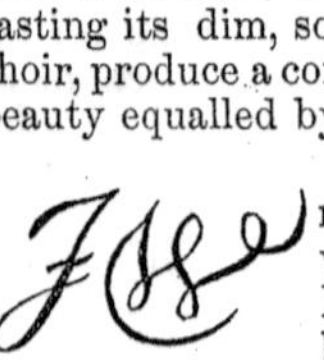

WYNANTS, John, an eminent Dutch landscape painter, was born at Haerlem in 1600. His instructor is not mentioned, but he owed his excellence mostly to his own abilities and perseverance. By an attentive study of nature, he formed an original style, and painted many admirable works, which gained him great reputation. They represent views in Holland, generally flat and confined, but distinguished for such simplicity and truthfulness to nature, that they are very highly esteemed, and are placed in the choicest collections. The following remarks on the works of Wynants are to be found in Smith's Catalogue, with a list of about two hundred of his pictures. "His early works generally represent the picturesque habitation of the peasant, or the ruins of some ancient mansion, an adjacent road, and the surrounding country.—These are always painted in a neat and careful manner, in a tone of color tending to brown or blackish hues. In his second period he becomes more excursive, breaks into an open country, and encounters a wide expanse of landscape, composed of hill and dale, woods and rivers, embellishing the lovely scene with a rich variety of objects, such as sandy banks, winding roads, withered trees, and wild plants. Occasionally his views are more confined, and the eye is entertained with a faithful picture composed of a clayey bank, a rugged road, an old tree, wild flowers, herbage, and a sedgy pool. Such, with few deviations, compose the views of the whole of his productions; but, notwithstanding the similarity of the scenes represented, there is great disparity in their quality, those of his middle time being clear and luminous in effect, and delightfully delicate in the execution. No artist furnished more luxuriantly the foregrounds of his pictures, or gave greater variety of form and tint to the soil in which the dock, the thistle, and the bramble, appear to be indigenous. In the lattea years of his life, his execution is frequently coarse, and his coloring brown and heavy ; defects by no means compensated by the great practical knowledge and masterly handling which such pictures always exhibit.

Very little is known concerning the personal history of Wynants. He established an academy, which produced some of the ablest painters of the Dutch school, among whom were Adrian Vandervelde, Philip Wouwerman, and other eminent masters. His landscapes are often embellished with figures and animals from their pencils. Bryan places his death in 1670 ; but Dillis, in his *Gemalde zu Schleissheim*, states that there is a picture by him in the gallery at Schleissheim, dated 1673 ; his name also is written in the book of the Company of Painters at Haerlem, for the year 1677. It is said that Wynants was addicted to indulgence in debauchery, which carried him off long before age would have enfeebled his talents ; but the facts above stated, show that he lived to the age of seventy-seven, and this piece of information may therefore be classed among the numerous apocryphal anecdotes of Dutch artists.

WYNGAERDE, Francis vander, a Flemish designer and engraver, who flourished at Antwerp about 1640, where he also carried on the business of a printseller. He executed some spirited etchings, principally after Rubens, which possess great merit, though the drawing is frequently incorrect.

WYNTRANCK, or WYNTRACK, a Dutch painter of whom little is known, except that he flourished in the time of Wynants, Ruysdael, and other eminent landscape painters, whose works he often enriched with wild ducks, and other aquatic birds, painted in an exquisite manner, and adding much to the beauty and value of their compositions. His own landscapes represent marshy grounds, with pools, backed by willows and alders, serving merely as the scene in which to display his skill in painting water-fowl. His birds are full of life and activity, correctly designed, and their plumage has all the softness, delicacy, and brilliancy of nature. Pictures entirely by Wyntranck are very rare, though he may be frequently recognized in the works of his cotemporaries.

WYON, William, R. A., an eminent English medalist, was born at Birmingham in 1795. In 1809, he was apprenticed to his father, an engraver of some celebrity in his native place, under whom he evinced much taste and feeling, heightened considerably by his studies of the designs of Flaxman. In 1813 he received the gold medal of the Society of Arts, for his die of the head of Ceres, purchased by the Society, and used to strike the gold medal for the agricultural prize ; and he also received another gold medal from the same institution, for his group of Victory in a Marine Car, drawn by Tritons. In 1815, Wyon visited London, for the purpose of assisting his uncle Thomas W. in engraving the public seals ; and in the following year, at the age of twenty, he was appointed second engraver at the Royal Mint, upon the judgment or recommendation of Sir Thomas Lawrence. In 1824, he entered upon the duties of chief engraver, though he did not receive his official appointment until four years after. During the remainder of his career, he executed many works, which numbered up to 1837, according to the memoir of Carlisle, about eighty coins, nearly one hundred medals and twenty public seals. His medals include the war medals of the Peninsula, Trafalgar, Jelallabad and Cabul ; the civic medals of the Royal Academy, the Royal Society, the Royal Institution, the Geological Society, the Geographical Society, the Bengal Asiatic Society, and indeed of almost every learned Society of Great Britain. Some of these bear on the obverse, heads from the antique, from modern and from living personages. The Harrow School Medal given by Sir Robert Peel, bears a head of Cicero ; the Royal Institution medal, the head of Lord Bacon ; the prize medal of the University of Glasgow, the head of Sir Isaac Newton ; the Art Union medal, the head of Sir Francis Chantrey. His medal of Sir Walter Scott bears a reverse after Stothard, and his coronation medal of William IV., a reverse of Queen Adelaide, after Chantrey.

The great merit of all Wyon's portrait medals is their truth, force, and delicate execution; and his designs for the rewards of honorary medals are always to the purpose, and conceived in a purely classic spirit. In 1831, he was elected an Associate of the Royal Academy, and in 1836, Academician—an honor never before conferred upon one in his particular department of art. Wyon's high reputation extended across the Channel ; he was invited to Lisbon, to execute a medallion portrait of Queen Donna Maria ; and other foreign governments also availed themselves of his services. Among his last works were the obverses of the exhibition medals, bearing the portraits of the Queen and Prince Albert. He died on the 29th of October, 1851.

WYTMAN, Matthew, a Dutch painter, born at Gorcum in 1650. He first studied under Henry Verschuring, and for some time painted landscapes in the style of that master ; but he afterwards became the scholar of John Bylaert, and applied himself to painting conversations and domestic subjects, in which he imitated the style of Gaspar Netscher with considerable success, though he differs from that master by introducing very elegant landscapes in his back-grounds, highly finished, with a very agreeable tone of coloring. He also painted fruit and flowers in a style of excellence. He died in the prime of life, in 1689.

# X

XAVERY, Jacob, a Dutch painter, born at the Hague in 1736. He was the son of Jacob Xavery, the sculptor, and was instructed in painting by Jacob de Wit. Little is known of him, and the accounts of his life are contradictory. He is said to have painted history, portraits, landscapes, seaports, fruit, and flowers; in his landscapes he imitated Berghem, and painted bas-reliefs in chiaroscuro, in the manner of his master. There was a Gerard Joseph Xavery, probably his brother, who flourished about the same time, and is said to have painted the same kind of subjects.

XAVIN, Paul and Hubert, two French engravers on wood, born at Paris, according to Papillon, and flourished about 1540. He does not specify any of their works.

XENOPHILES, a Greek sculptor of uncertain age, by whom Pausanias cites a statue of Esculapius at Argos, which was esteemed the most remarkable representation of that deity. The figure of the god in white marble, was accompanied by a statue of the goddess Hygeia, and two figures seated, which were said to represent Xenophiles and Strato, the authors of the work; although M. Quatremére de Quincy supposes, and with considerable probability, that these figures were intended as statues of Machaon and Podalyrius, the famous sons of Esculapius, or some other mythological personages, and that the former tradition arose from the artists having sculptured several of their own features on the heads of the statues, to immortalize their own names. This was perhaps suggested by the contrivance of Phidias, who when prevented from inscribing his name upon his great statue of Minerva, introduced his own portrait as an old man throwing a stone, upon the shield, in the battle between the Athenians and Amazons.

XENOPHON, an Athenian sculptor, who flourished about B. C. 300. According to Pausanias, he executed, in concert with Cephisodotus, the throne of Jupiter at Megalopolis, where the god was represented seated, on his right hand an impersonification of the city of Megalopolis, and a statue of Diana on the left. It was wrought in pentelic marble. Another more celebrated work was the statue of Fortune at Thebes, bearing in her arms the infant Pluto, of which he executed the head and arms of the goddess; the rest was the work of Callistonicus, the Theban. There was another sculptor named Xenophon, a native of the island of Paros.

XIMENES, or ZIMENES, Juan Fernandez. See Mudo.

XIMENES ANGEL, Jose, a Spanish painter, who studied under Antonio Rubio at Toledo, and succeeded Claudio Coello as painter to the Cathedral in that city, in 1695. He executed several works for the churches of Toledo, and a series of frescos representing incidents from the life of the Virgin, for the Hermitage of Fonseca.

XIMENES DE ILLESCAS, Bernabe, a Spanish amateur painter, born at Lucena in 1613. He was an officer in the Spanish army, and while serving several years in Italy, he studied the works of the great masters. On his return to Spain, he executed some works for various individuals. Count Raczynski mentions a picture by him, representing the battle of Santiago, in the collection of Count di Taroca at Lisbon. Leonard de Castro and Miguel Parrilla were his scholars. He died at Andujar in 1671.

XIMENES DONOSO, Juan, a Spanish painter and architect, born at Consuegra in 1628. He was the son of Antonio X., a painter of little note, and after receiving his instructions, he studied under Francisco Fernandez at Madrid. At the death of the latter he went to Rome, and studied there seven years, applying himself particularly to perspective and painting in fresco, and paying little attention to the antique or the works of the great masters. On returning to Spain he formed an intimacy with Claudio Coello, and executed some works in conjunction with him, for the Cathedral at Toledo; he also painted some works entirely by himself. Ximenes' chief merit lay in the excellence of his coloring. According to Bermudez, he was much employed as an architect, but he exhibited inferior taste in all his designs. He died in 1690.

XIMENES, Don Francisco, a Spanish painter, born at Saragossa in 1598. After studying in his native city, he went to Rome, and resided there several years. After returning to Spain, he executed many works for the churches, which, according to Bermudez, are more remarkable for excellence of coloring than correctness of design. He painted two large pictures for the Cathedral of Saragossa, and an Adoration of the Kings for the chapter of the Cathedral of Teruel, which is borrowed from the performance of Rubens in the palace at Madrid. The greater part of his works were executed in fresco or distemper, and have mostly perished. Ximenes, however, acquired considerable reputation in his time, and was much employed. He left his property to form a fund for the education of the orphan sons of painters, and for marriage portions to their daughters. He died at Saragossa in 1666.

XIMENO, Jose, a Spanish designer and engraver who flourished at Madrid in the latter part of the last century. He designed and engraved the plates to illustrate the magnificent edition of Solis' History of the Conquest of Mexico, published at Madrid in 1783, besides many vignettes and other plates for the booksellers. He was living in 1791.

XIMENO, Matias, a Spanish painter, of Old Castile, who flourished about the middle of the 17th centuty. He executed some works for the churches, among which are four lateral altar-pieces for the church of the Jeronymites of Siguenza, representing the Incarnation, the Nativity the Epiphany, and the Presentation.

# Y.

YANES, Hernando, a Spanish painter, born at Almedina. Little is known of him or his works, but he is said to have visited Italy, and studied under Raffaelle. On returning to Spain, he painted some altar-pieces for the churches at Cuenca, the principal of which are the Adoration of the Magi, and a Dead Christ in the Lap of the Virgin.—These pictures, according to Bermudez, resemble the works of Lionardo da Vinci more than those of Raffaelle; the same writer commends his works for the drawing, expression, coloring, and elaborate execution. He died about 1550.

YANUS, an engraver on wood, mentioned by Papillon. He does not specify any of his cuts, but commends them for their delicate execution.

YEATES, Nicholas, an English engraver, who flourished about 1680. He executed a few portraits in a very indifferent style.

YEPES, Thomas de, a Spanish painter, and a native of Valencia, who excelled in painting flowers, fruit, fish, and dead game. There are many of his works in the collections at Madrid, Seville, and Valencia, where they are highly esteemed. He died in 1674.

YOUNG, John. This English engraver wrought in mezzotinto, but is better known by his outlines of various celebrated galleries in England, which he published with descriptions. He held the office of Keeper of the British Institution, and was an active promoter of the Artist's Benevolent Fund. He died in 1825.

YPRES, Karel van, a Flemish historical painter, was born at Ypres in West Flanders in 1510. He acquired a knowledge of art in his own country, but after practising there for a number of years, he went to Italy for improvement, and studied particularly the works of Tintoretto. On returning to his own country, he gained considerable reputation for his subjects of history, in the style of his model, among which are the Resurrection, in the city of Tournay; and the Last Judgment, in a church between Bruges and Ypres. He executed many designs with the pen, for the painters on glass, which are highly praised by van Mander for their excellence of composition and correctness of design. Van Ypres is said to have been of a melancholy temper, and he put an end to his own life in 1564.

YUSO, Fray Matias Antonio Trala, a Spanish painter, born at Valencia in 1680. He became a monk of the order of St. Francis, and was principally employed in painting pictures of the Virgin, and Holy Families, for the church of his monastery, which, according to Bermudez, possess considerable merit. He died in 1753.

YVER, Peter, a Dutch engraver, who flourished at Amsterdam about 1747. He executed a few portraits and other subjects.

YVRART, Baudrin, a French painter, born at Boulogne in Picardy in 1610, and died in 1690. Little is known of him, but he is said to have been a good painter of history.

# Z.

ZAAGMOOLEN, Martin, a Dutch painter, who flourished at Amsterdam about 1670. He painted history with some reputation. Houbraken mentions a picture of the Last Judgment by him, with a great number of figures, incorrectly drawn and feebly colored. He was the instructor of John Luyken and Michael van Musscher.

ZAAL, J., a Flemish engraver, by whom there is a large etching of a Boar Hunt, *after Snyders*. It is executed in a bold masterly style, and the masses are broad and powerful; but the drawing is not very correct.

ZABAGLIA, Niccolo, an Italian architect and celebrated mechanician, was born at Rome in 1674, of obscure parentage. He was first employed as a common laborer on the works in the Vatican, but gained so much esteem by his talents, as to be finally appointed architect of St. Peter's. He invented some machines, and made various discoveries in mechanics, of such value that Caylues commends him as approaching the ancients in genius. It would also appear that he constructed a number of castles and bridges. In 1743, Giovanni Bottari published a work at Rome, in grand folio, containing fifty-four plates with explanations, of which thirty-six represented machines and instruments invented by Zabaglia. This work is highly esteemed by architects; it is entitled *Castelli e ponti di Niccolo Zabaglia, con alcune ingegnose pratiche e con la descrizione del trasporto del obelisco Vaticano e di altri del Dom. Fontana.* Zabaglia died in 1750

ZABELLI, or ZABAGLIO, Antonio, an Italian engraver, born at Florence about 1740. He engraved some portraits for the collection published by Allegrini, at Florence; also several subjects after Guido, Guercino, Caracci, and other masters.

ZABELLO, Giovanni Francesco, an Italian engraver, who was a native of Bergamo, according to Orlandi, and flourished about 1546. He engraved some plates after the Italian masters, marked with a die and the date.

ZACCAGNA, Turpino, a painter born at Cortona, of a noble family, who was a pupil of Luca Signorelli, according to Bottàri, and executed some works for the churches in his native city, and other places in the vicinity, with considerable reputation. He was living in 1537.

ZACCHETTI, Bernardino, a painter born at Reggio, who flourished about 1523. Tiraboschi and others conjecture from his style that he was a scholar of Raffaelle. Lanzi says, "his picture in the church of S. Prospero, designed and colored in the taste of Garofolo, and others which partake of the style of Raffaelle, may probably have given rise to this opinion. But Italy then abounded with the disciples of that great master, who no longer instructed by his voice, but by his paintings and engravings. The works said to have been produced by him at Rome, and the assistance he afforded to Michael Angelo in the Sistine Chapel are assertions of Azzari, which remain unquestioned by any ancient writer.

ZACCHIA, Paolo, called il Vecchio (the Elder), a painter of Lucca, who flourished about 1527. Lanzi supposes he was educated at Florence. He painted history with considerable reputation, and there are several altar-pieces and other works in the churches and public edifices at Lucca, which display much study and elegance in design, though his outline is somewhat harsh and cutting. His principal works are, the Marriage of the Virgin, the Assumption of the Virgin, in the church of S. Agostino, and the Ascension in S. Salvatore. Rosini has given an etching of the Marriage of the Virgin, which resembles the old Florentine school in simplicity of composition.

ZACCHIA, Lorenzo, called il Giovane (the Younger), was probably a relative of the preceding, and flourished at Lucca about 1550. Lanzi says he showed more softness of contour, and more strength of coloring, than the elder Z., but in every other respect, he was held in less estimation. He is sometimes called Lorenzo di Ferro Zacchia.

ZACCOLINI, Padre Matteo. This artist, according to the best authorities, was born at Cesena, in the Roman States, in 1590, and died at Rome in 1630. He was a reputable painter of history, but chiefly excelled in painting architecture and perspective, in which he is said to have instructed Domenichino and Niccolo Poussin. He became a monk of the order of the Theatines, and his principal works are in their church of S. Silvestro, on Monte Cavallo. Lanzi says he wrote some excellent treatises on perspective, the manuscripts of which are preserved in the Barberini Library.

ZACHTLEVEN. See Saftleven.

ZAECH, Bernard, a German engraver, of whom nothing is known except by a few prints, the chief of which are a Set of Ruins *after Jonas Umbach.* They are etched and finished with the graver in a very neat style. Brulliot mentions twelve pieces of designs for goldsmiths, consisting of vases and goblets, marked B. Z., 1581, which he conjectures to be from his hand, but erroneously, as Umbach, after whom he engraved, was born in 1624. There was a Daniel Zaech, a painter, goldsmith, and engraver of little note, who was living in 1613.

ZAGANELLI. See Cotignola.

MZ or [monogram] ZAGEL, Matthias, an old German artist, of whom little is known, and about whom there is a great deal of conjecture and discrepancy among writers. He is supposed to have been a painter, engraver, and goldsmith. There is a picture of the Crucifixion attributed to him in the Imperial Gallery at Vienna. He is variously called *Matthias* and *Martin Zagel, Zingler, Zasinger, Zatzinger. Zeyssinger,* and *Zinck.* Bartsch describes about twenty prints by him, usually marked with one of the above monograms, and dated from about 1500 to 1505. As an engraver, he may be ranked with Martin Schoen and Michael Wolgemut, and from the style of his engraving, he is supposed to have been a goldsmith. Zagel's plates are executed with the graver in a neat, but stiff, formal, and Gothic style, and his composition and drawing are very indifferent.

[monogram] ZAGEL, or ZAGHEL, Theodore, an engraver, who marked his plates with the above monogram. He is mentioned by Orlandi, who only specifies by him one print, representing an old woman.

ZAGNANI, Antonio Maria, a Bolognese painter, who excelled, according to Crespi, in painting fruit and flower pieces, which were so greatly admired, that " he received numerous commissions, even from princely foreigners." He was living in 1689.

ZAGO, Santo, a Venetian painter, who flourished, according to Ridolfi, about 1550, and was educated in the school of Titian. He followed the style of that master with considerable success, and executed some works for the churches at Venice, which are highly commended, particularly an altar-piece, representing Tobit and the Angel, in S. Caterina. Lanzi also commends him as an able painter in fresco.

ZAIS, Giuseppe, a Venetian painter, who studied under Francesco Zuccarelli, during that artist's residence at Venice, and followed his style. Lanzi says, " in point of invention, he was more copious and varied than his master, but inferior to him in the mellowness of his tints. He had acquired from Simonini, who resided also a long time at Venice, the art of painting battle-pieces, in which he showed equal skill, but unfortunately he fell into dissipated habits, and died a common mendicant in the hospital of Trevigi." Others say that he died at an *advanced age* in 1784, and Lanzi himself, in his index, says he *died old* in 1784.

ZAIST, Giovanni Battista, a painter born at Cremona in 1700, and died in 1757. He studied under Giuseppe Natali, an eminent architectural painter, whose style he followed. Lanzi commends him as an able artist. He wrote the Lives of the Painters, Sculptors, and Architects of Cremona, which was published after his death in 1774, by his pupil Antonio Maria Panni at Cremona, in two quarto volumes.

ZAMBONI, Matteo, a Bolognese painter, who was educated, according to Crespi, in the school of Carlo Cignani. He imitated the style of his instructor with considerable success in two altar-pieces in the church of S. Niccolo at Rimini, representing a history from the Life of St. Pietro Celestino, and another from that of St. Benedetto. He also painted some pictures for the collections, but he died in the flower of his life.

ZAMBONO, Michele, a celebrated Venetian worker in mosaic, who flourished about 1505. According to Zanetti, he decorated the chapel of the Mascoli with histories of the Life of the Virgin, designed in the best style of the Vivarini, and executed with such extraordinary care, that Vasari observed with surprise, "that it would not be possible to effect more with colors."

ZAMBRANO, Juan Luis, a Spanish painter, born at Cordova, according to Palomino, in 1599. He was a pupil of Pablo de Cespedes, whose style he followed with great success. His principal works are in the Cathedral at Cordova, and in the church of the convent of Los Martyros; in the latter he painted the Stoning of Stephen, and the Martyrdom of St. Acisclo, and St. Victoria. In the College of Santa Catalina are two fine pictures of the Guardian Angel and St. Christopher, which Palomino says are designed by him, in the grand style of Michael Angelo. He passed the latter part of his life at Seville, where he painted three large pictures for the church of St. Basil, representing the history of that saint, which are highly commended. Zambrano also painted easel pictures, which are highly esteemed; his design was correct, his figures animated, and his coloring warm and harmonious. He died in 1639. It is agreed by the Spanish writers, that he was instructed by Cespedes, who died in 1608; therefore the date of his birth must be erroneous.

ZAMORA, Diego, a Spanish painter, who flourished at Seville, according to Bermudez, in the latter part of the 16th century, and executed some works in the cathedral of that city. There are no further particulars recorded of him.

ZAMORA, Juan de, a Spanish painter, born at Seville, who flourished from about 1650 to 1671. He distinguished himself as a painter of landscapes, embellished with subjects taken from sacred and profane history, in which he imitated the highly finished style of the Flemish masters. Some of his best works are in the Episcopal palace at Seville. He also painted some sacred subjects; but he was less successful in his large figure pieces, in which his landscape backgrounds were the best part.

ZAMPEZZO, Giovanni Battista, a painter born at Cittadella, near Bassano, in 1620. He studied under Jacopo Apollonio, the grandson and imitator of Jacopo Bassano. Zampezzo possessed great talents, and adhered tenaciously to the precepts of his master. He copied and imitated the works of Bassano so closely that they now readily pass with the unlearned for the genuine productions of that master. Lanzi says, "he devoted himself to copying the works of Bassano. So well did he imitate his Santa Lucilla, baptized by Saint Valentine, in La Grazie at Bassano, that Scaligero pronounced it comparable to the original." There are some of his works in the churches at Bassano, which are esteemed little inferior to those of Apollonio. Though he lived to a great age, his works are scarce, being doubtless mostly attributed to Bassano, whose fame swallowed up all his imitations. He died at Bassano in 1700. See *Bassano* and *Apollonio*.

ZAMPIERI, Domenico. In the sketch of this great artist, given in this Dictionary, under the head of Domenichino, it was omitted to mention his architectural distinction, excepting his appointment by Gregory XV., as architect to the pontifical palace. Besides his superintendence of that edifice, he executed various other works, particularly two designs for the church of S. Ignazio at Rome. Instead of his being allowed to execute one of them, according to the principles of justice and propriety, the designs were combined by the Jesuit Grassi, who produced from them that which was executed. Upon this, Zampieri, indignant at such unworthy treatment, refused to design the façade, and according to Milizia, the building was transferred to Algardi. It is said that if his original design had been carried into effect, Rome would have boasted of a temple which would have astonished succeeding generations. In S. Maria in Trastevere, he designed the rich and ingenious entablature, also the chapel, called della Madonna di Strada Cupa. Domenichino designed the greater part of the elegant Villa Belvidere at Frascati and designed and erected the picturesque Villa Lodovisi at Rome, the gardens of which he laid out with a number of verdant walks, and divided the grove in exquisite taste. His family name was Zampieri, but he is almost universally called Domenichino, to which name the reader is referred for his character as a painter.

ZAN, Bernard, an engraver mentioned by Orlandi in his Abbecedario, who flourished about 1571. He marked his plates with the initials B. Z., with the date, but his works are not specified.

ZANARDI, Gentile, a Bolognese paintress, who flourished about the first part of the 18th century, and studied, according to Orlandi, with Cav. Marc' Antonio Franceschini. She possessed an extraordinary talent for copying the works of the principal Italian masters, with a softness of color and delicacy of outline, that surprised the best judges. She also painted historical subjects of her own composition.

ZANATA, Gioseffo, a Milanese painter, who studied, according to Orlandi, under Carlo Francesco Nuvolone, called the Guido of Lombardy, and followed his style with great success, being "extremely well versed in the art." There are some of his works in the churches at Milan, and other cities of Lombardy. He was living in 1718.

ZANCARLI, Poliphilos, an Italian designer and engraver, who flourished at Venice in the first part of the 17th century. Among other works he engraved a set of twelve plates of antique foliage for friezes. Many of his designs were engraved by Odoardo Fialetti, of which an account may be found among the prints of that artist, in Bartsch, P. G., tom. xvii. He is sometimes called Giancarli, Gian and Zan being synonymous in different dialects.

ZANCHI, Antonio, a painter born at Este, near Venice, in 1639. He was a scholar of Francesco Ruschi, and was more noted, according to Lanzi, for the number of his works than for their excellence. Lanzi says he belonged to the sect of naturalists called by the Italians Tenebrosi (dark colorists, or followers of Cortona and Caravaggio). "Such at least appears the cast of his genius; common in its forms, sombre in its colors; but nevertheless exciting surprise by a certain fullness and felicity of hand, by its picturesque spirit, by its effect of chiaro-scuro, and by a grand general result which imposes upon us by its power. If we examine more particularly into his manner, we shall not unfrequently discover an incorrectness of design, along with that kind of indecision, and indistinctness of outline, which is mostly the resource of weak, or at least very hasty artists. He chiefly attached himself to Tintoretto, some traces of whom may be found in his style. In the college of S. Rocco, where that great master rendered his name immortal, we behold one of the best specimens of Zanchi. The subject, admirably fitted to his manner, contributed greatly to his success. He has there given a bold exhibition of the great plague that afflicted Venice in 1630, a picture filled with a concourse of the sick, the dying, and the dead, bound to one universal grave." There are several of his works in the church of S. Girolamo, the best of which are the Good Samaritan and the Prodigal Son. He died in 1722.

ZANCHI, Filippo and Francesco, two painters of Bergamo, brothers, of whom, according to Tassi, there are notices from 1544 to 1567. They were reputable artists, and executed some works for the churches. Filippo assisted Girolamo Colleoni in some of his works.

ZANELLA, Francesco, a painter of Padua, who was living in 1717. It is not known under whom he studied, but Lanzi says that he "deserves to be recorded as an artist of spirit, though not very diligent, nor very learned in the art. He is esteemed almost the Giordano of this city, from the great number of his works, conducted in a short time; and he may be considered almost as the last of the school of Padua."

ZANETTI, Count Antonio Maria, a Venetian nobleman, who was celebrated not only as the possessor of a rich collection of rare works of art, but also as an engraver on wood and copper. He was born at Venice in 1680, and was taught drawing as an accomplishment; but his inclination for art soon became strongly manifested, and at the age of fourteen he designed and etched a set of twelve plates, representing studies of heads and figures. Assisted by his relative, Antonio Maria Zanetti, and others, he executed and published a great number of etchings and engravings on wood, in chiaro-scuro, from the drawings of Raffaelle, Parmiggiano, and other celebrated painters, many of which he had purchased at the sale of the Arundelian collection. They are divided into two sets, consisting in all of ninety-nine prints on copper and wood, with the portrait of the artist, engraved by Faldoni, from a painting by Rosalba, in the front of the work. Zanetti executed numerous other works, the principal of which are a set of twelve etchings of animals and figures, *after B. Castiglione;* a set of eighty prints of antique gems; and a collection of the statues in the palace of St. Mark, and other public places in Venice, which are highly commended. Lanzi says "he revived the art of taking prints from wooden blocks, with more than one color, which was invented by Ugo da Carpi, but afterwards lost." He usually marked his prints with a monogram composed of his initials, A. M. Z., as above. His death is generally placed at Venice, in 1757, but Lanzi says he was living at an advanced age, in 1765.

ZANETTI, Antonio Maria, called the Younger, was the nephew of the preceding, born at Venice in 1716. Being well versed in literature, he was appointed to the office of Librarian of St. Mark, and was not less distinguished than his uncle for his zealous attachment to the art. In 1760 he published a set of eighty plates, designed and etched by himself, from the works of the Venetian painters, entitled *Varie Pitture a fresco de principali Maestri Veneziani, &c.* Lanzi says he also displayed considerable skill as a painter. He is known as a learned and able writer on art by his *Pittura Veneziana*, a work highly commended by Lanzi, treating of Venetian painting and the public works of the principal Venetian masters, in five books, published at Venice in 1771, 8vo. He died in 1778.

ZANGRIUM, John Baptist, a Flemish engraver who resided at Louvain about 1602, in which year he published a book of dresses, entitled, *Album Amicorum habitibus Mulierum Omnium nationum Europæ.* By the side of each figure is an ornamental mantle, with a helmet, and a blank left for a coat of arms. They are neatly executed, but without much taste. In the beginning of the work, he introduced the portraits of the Duke of Brabant, Isabella Clara his duchess and Justus Lipsius.

ZANI, Giovanni Battista, an Italian designer and engraver, who flourished, according to Bartsch, in 1660; Zani says he *operated* in 1640. He formed the design of making a collection of etchings from the works of the most distinguished Bolognese painters, and for this purpose had completed the drawings from those in the cloisters of S. Michele in Bosco, when he died young, before the etchings were finished. Bartsch describes only one print by him, a Glory, *after L. Caracci.*

ZANIMBERTI, Filippo, a painter born at Brescia in 1585. He was educated in the school of Santo Peranda, with whom he continued ten years. He distinguished himself as an historical painter, and executed many works for the churches of Brescia and Venice, besides being much employed in decorating the palaces of the nobility. He had a fertile genius, and a lively imagination; he designed correctly and with facility; his heads have a fine expression, and his coloring is very natural. Lanzi says "he was never appreciated at Brescia; but at Venice, where he resided many years, and where he painted with real genius and skill for the churches, he is very highly esteemed. In Santa Maria Nuova, is to be seen his grand picture of the Manna, so much commended by Ridolfi, by Boschini, and by Zanetti; though he seems to have chiefly employed himself in ornamenting the palaces. He possessed a singular talent for drawing small figures, and composing histories and fables, which were eagerly sought after, insomuch that the poet of the Venetian paintings affirms that whoever possesses one of Zanimberti's pictures was sure of his money."

ZANNA, Giovanni, a painter who flourished at Rome, according to Baglioni, in the pontificate of Paul V. He painted history with reputation, and was an excellent figurist. He formed an intimacy with Tarquinio di Viterbo, and they both wrought in conjunction, Tarquinio painting the landscape and architectural pieces, and Zanna adorning them with figures.

ZANNICHELLI, Prospero, a painter born at Reggio in 1698, and died in 1772. According to Tiraboschi, he was an excellent painter of perspective, and was much employed in decorating theatres.

ZANOBRIO. See Carlevariis.

GANOTTI, Giovanni Pietro. This artist was born at Paris, of Italian parents, who sent him while young to Bologna. He was educated in the school of Lorenzo Pasinelli, and became a correct designer, a good colorist, exhibiting also an excellent knowledge of the chiaro-scuro. He painted several altar-pieces for the churches at Bologna, the principal of which are the Incredulity of St. Thomas, in the church of that Saint; the Resurrection in S. Pietro; and the Nativity, in La Puritâ. In the Palazzo Pubblico, is a large picture by him, representing the Ambassadors of Rome swearing fidelity to the Bolognese. He re sided a great part of his life at Cortona, where he distinguished himself by painting several pictures for the churches, particularly Christ appearing to Mary Magdalene, Christ bearing his Cross, and the Murder of the Innocents. Lanzi says he excelled in easel pictures of historical and mythological subjects, which are frequently to be met with in private houses, and are greatly admired. "They display much poetical imagination, this artist delighting in poetical compositions, very different from Lomazzo's and Boschini's, to an extreme old age."

Zanotti is also well known as a laborious and intelligent writer on art; of his numerous publications, the most considerable is his *Storia dell' Accademia Clementina di Bologna*, published in two volumes quarto in 1739. Lanzi says few have been more successful in wielding with equal excellence both pen and pencil. He died in 1765, at the great age of 91 years.

ZAPPI, Lavinia, a name by which Lavinia Fontana is sometimes called, from a family of Imola, into which she married. See *Fontana*.

ZARATO. See Luzzo.

ZARIÑENA, Francisco, a Spanish painter, born at Valencia about 1550. According to Palomino, he went to Italy while young, and had the advantage of studying in the school of Titian. On returning to Spain, he executed some works for the churches and convents of his native city, the principal of which are in the monastery of San Miguel de los Reyes. "In composition and coloring, they are worthy of the school in which he was educated." Bermudez says he was a scholar of the elder Ribalta, and commends his works, but says nothing of his studying under Titian. He died at Valencia in 1624.

ZARINENA, Cristobal and Juan, were the sons and disciples of the preceding, in whose style they painted history with considerable reputation. There are some of their works in the public edifices at Valencia.

ZARLATTI, Gioseffo, an Italian designer and engraver, was born at Modena about 1635, and died very young. We have by him a few etchings of historical and fancy subjects, from his own designs, executed in so spirited and pleasing a style, and evincing so lively a genius, that his premature death is deeply regretted.

ZATZINGER. See Zagel.

ZAUNER, Francis von, a distinguished German sculptor, was born at Feldpatan in German Tyrol, in 1746. He early evinced a decided taste for sculpture, and went to Vienna in 1766, where he studied and wrought with great assiduity under Prof. Schletterer, for a period of five years. His talents were noticed by Prince Kaunitz, who ordered him to execute within fifteen days a model for a spring, representing the three largest rivers of Austria. The work was approved, and was afterwards executed on a large scale. The Empress Maria Theresa took Zauner into favor; and, in 1776, he received assistance from the government to go to Rome, where he studied four years. In 1781 he was appointed Professor of Sculpture in the Academy at Vienna. He improved the manner of studying this art in the Austrian capital, and executed a number of works; among others, the colossal statue of the Emperor Joseph II., which Francis II. caused to be erected in honor of his uncle, in the Joseph Square, in 1807. It is one of the largest statues in Europe, and was cast by Zauner in a new method of his own invention, which succeeded perfectly. There are by this artist many busts, statues, and bas-reliefs; also the monument of the Emperor Leopold II., in white marble, in the church of St. Augustine. He died at Vienna, in 1822.

ZE, De. The name of this artist is affixed to a small print representing Christ dead in the Tomb, attended by an Angel. It is executed with the graver, in a style resembling that of John Sadeler, and is apparently from his own design.

ZEEMAN, Remy. See Nooms.

ZEEMAN, Enoch, a Dutch painter, who resided many years in London, and died there in 1744. He painted portraits in the labored style of Denner, and met with considerable employment. He had a son named Paul, who followed the same profession. Isaac Zeeman, the brother of Enoch, was also a portrait painter, and died in 1751, leaving a son, who pursued the same branch.

ZEGHERS. See Seghers.

ZEITBLOOM, Bartholomew, an ancient German painter of Ulm, to whom many pictures of the old German school are attributed. Dr. Kügler, in his Hand-Book of the German and Flemish Painters, mentions several pictures of sacred subjects by him, two of which are in the Pinacothek at Munich, and others are dispersed in various churches and collections. They are designed in the old, dry, gothic style, but the coloring is strong and rich. Nothing is known of his history, or the time when he flourished.

ZELOTTI, Battista, an eminent Italian painter, born at Verona, in 1532. He was brought up in the school of Antonio Badile, and was the fellow student and friend of Paul Veronese, with whom he coöperated in several important works in the public edifices at Venice. Vasari calls him Battista da Verona, and includes him among the disciples of Titian. Lanzi also thinks that he studied with Titian after he left Badile. "His Holy Family in the Carrara collection, frequently extolled by us before, is entirely in the style of Titian, and from such a studio it would appear we are to look for that warmth of tint in which for the most part he excels Veronese, as well as that power of design in which Zanetti is of opinion that he also surpassed him, although others think very differently. He often surpasses him, likewise, in grandeur, and in what appertains to painting in fresco, a circumstance that Paolo was fully aware of, and for that reason sought to obtain his assistance in works of that kind. He possessed great fertility of invention, and a rapid hand, while he was profound and judicious in his compositions. Indeed, he might have been esteemed another Paolo, had he been able to compete with him in the beauty of his heads, in variety and in grace. In truth, his productions were frequently given to Veronese; even those he painted for the grand hall of the Council of Ten, were engraved under the name of the latter by Valentine le Febre. He was doubtless one of the first artists of his time, though not estimated according to his merits, from his having worked chiefly in fresco, and at a distance from capital cities, in villages, in country seats, and in palaces. One of his grandest works is seen at Cataio, a villa belonging to the Marchese Tommaso Obizzi, where, about 1570, he represented in different rooms, the history of that very ancient family, distinguished no less in the council than in arms. The place is continually sought after by foreigners, attracted thither by its splendor, by the fame of these pictures, and the valuable museum of antiquities collected by the Marchese. In his oil paintings, Zelotti could not compete with Caliari, though he approached him near enough in his Conversion of St. Paul, and Christ with his Disciples in the Fishing bark, which he executed for the cathedral of Vicenza, to merit the honor of having them attributed to the pencil of Veronese. This city was his chief theatre of action, where, together with Veronese, and the help of one of his best pupils, he established a school, which partook of the taste of both these masters." Zelotti died in 1592.

ZELTER, Carl Friedrich, a German architect, was born at Berlin in 1758. He received a liberal education, and at the age of seventeen was articled to his father, who was also an architect. During the succeeding eight years he was occupied in professional pursuits, and in 1783 was admitted as a master-builder. During this time, however, he conceived a passion for music, and devoted himself to that art after completing his architectural course. He attained the position of Professor of Music to the University and the Royal Institute of Berlin; and it does not appear that he erected any edifices. Zelter died in 1832.

ZENALE, Bernardo, called also Bernardo da Trevilio, an Italian painter and architect, born at Trevilio in the Milanese. He was a pupil of Civerchio, and painted history and architecture, and excelled particularly in perspective. According to Lanzi, he was an eminent artist in his time, and the intimate friend of Lionardo da Vinci. Lomazzo relates that Vinci in his Last Supper had endued the countenances of both the saints James with so much beauty, that despairing of making that of the Saviour more imposing, he went to advise with Bernardo Zenale, who to console him, said, "Leave the head of Christ unfinished, as it is, for you will never be able to make it worthy of Christ, among these Apostles;" and this Lionardo is said to have done. (See, however, Vinci.) Vasari calls Zenale Bernardino da Trevio, and says he was an engineer at Milan, in the time of Bramante, "a very able designer, and esteemed an excellent master by Vinci, though his manner was somewhat harsh and dry in his pictures; and he then goes on to cite his picture of the Resurrection in the cloister of the Grazie, among other works, as exhibiting some beautiful foreshortenings.

As an architect, Zenale gained considerable distinction, and was entrusted with the restorations in the Cathedral at Milan. In 1520 he was invited to Bergamo by the magistrates of that city, to give his opinion concerning the proposed embellishments in the basilica of S. Maria Maggiore.

In his old age, in 1524, he published a work on perspective, containing many original and excellent observations. Few of his works now remain. He has been confounded by several Italian writers with Bernardo Butinone, a native of the same town, and his fellow-pupil. Tassi erroneously calls him *Bernardino da Trevigi*. Zani says he was born in 1426, and died in 1526; if so, he was ninety-eight years old when he published his work on perspective.

ZENCI, Domenico, an Italian engraver, who flourished about 1570. His style resembles that of Marco da Ravenna, and he is supposed to have been a disciple of that master, though his works are inferior, and incorrectly drawn. He engraved a set of portraits entitled *Illustrium Jureconsultorum Imagines*. It is said that his name was Zenoi, or Zenoni, and that he engraved some prints after Raffaelle, and other masters.

ZENOBRIO. See Carlevariis.

ZENODORUS, a celebrated Greek sculptor, who flourished in the first century of the Christian era, during the reigns of Claudius and Nero. Invited to the province of Auvergne in Gaul, he was commissioned by the prefect Vibius Avitus to execute a metallic colossal statue of Mercury. He was engaged ten years upon this work, and received for it the sum of 40,000,000 sesterces; but this amount probably covered also the cost of the materials. He also copied for Avitus the precious vases by Calamis the Greek sculptor, with such skill that they could scarcely be distinguished from the originals, which had been bequeathed by Germanicus to his instructor Cassius Silanus, and thence descended to Avitus, nephew of the latter. The works of Zenodorus gained him so much reputation, that he was employed by Nero to execute the colossal statue of that monarch, 110 or 120 feet high, erected in the vestibule of his Golden Palace. This immense height can hardly be credited, however; it is probably an error of some copyist. After the tyrant's death, the statue was overthown, and Vespasian subsequently ordered a head with seven rays to be substituted for that of Nero, and consecrated the statue to the Sun, in the fourth quarter of the city. There is a passage in Pliny's account of Zenodorus, which is translated thus: "This statue shows that the art of founding in bronze was lost: for Nero was ready to furnish all the necessary gold and silver; and Zenodorus yielded to no artist of antiquity in the art of chiseling and modeling." It would appear from this, that the statue was composed of some other material than bronze, and probably of brass; since not even the prodigality of Nero was able to revive the art of bronze casting.

ZENONI, Duce, an Italian engraver, who flourished in 1634. He engraved some plates of portraits, neatly executed with the graver, but in a stiff and formal style. He was probably also a goldsmith, as he signed his prints *Duce Zenoni Orefice*.

ZENTNER, J. L., a German engraver, who resided at Paris about 1780, and afterwards visited England, where he engraved some plates of landscapes, animals, and dead game. His plates are etched and finished with the graver, in a neat, clear style.

PZ *Sculp* ZETTER, Paul de. This artist was a native of Hanover, and flourished about 1630. He was chiefly employed in engraving portraits from his own designs, executed in a neat, but stiff and tasteless style. He engraved several plates for Boissard's Collection of Portraits. He sometimes marked his prints with the above monogram, and at others with his initials P. D. Z. *fec.*

ZEUXIS. This great artist, one of the most celebrated painters of antiquity, and the most eminent of his time, was born at one of the ancient cities named Heraclea, between B. C. 460 and B. C. 450. Pliny fixes the time when he flourished at B. C. 400; but he could scarcely have been born later than B. C. 450, as he was in the height of his reputation during the reign of Archelaus of Macedon, which was from B. C. 413 to B. C. 399; and Harduin and others are therefore probably incorrect in fixing upon Heraclea in Lucania, in Italy, as the birth-place of Zeuxis, since that city was not founded until after the destruction of Siris, B. C. 433; and the only reason that seems to be urged for their supposition, is a very insufficient one, namely, that Zeuxis was commissioned to paint a picture by the Crotoniats. When he had made himself rich by his profession, and must accordingly have been advanced in years, he gave away some of his works; and Archelaus was then living, for he presented a picture of the god Pan to that king. From the complaint of Apollodorus, who lived at Athens, Zeuxis must also have been early in that city; he was most likely a native of one of the Heracleas in Greece, and probably, from his connection with Archelaus, of Heraclea Lyncestis of Macedonia.

Zeuxis was instructed in art by Demophilus of Himera, or Neseas of Thasos; artists of whom nothing is known, except that one of them was his instructor. He soon far outstripped his master, as Apollodorus intimated, in verses expressive of his indignation that Zeuxis should have moulded to his own use all previous inventions, and stolen the graces of the best masters; thus paying a fine involuntary compliment to his great rival. Apollodorus having first practised chiaro-scuro, could not endure that his glory should be eclipsed by a younger artist, who availed himself of his own improvements to rise to a higher degree of excellence. The complaint of Apollodorus, that his rival had robbed him of his art, shows also that Zeuxis excelled in coloring, as effect of coloring and of light and shadow were the peculiar excellencies of Apollodorus. Lucian terms Zeuxis the greatest painter of his time, saying that he was immediately preceded by Apollodorus of Athens, whom he surpassed; and he was immediately followed by Parrhasius of Ephesus, who surpassed him. Parrhasius however, was defective in coloring and chiaro-scuro; and it is quite doubtful whether the latter part of this assertion is correct. Unlike Polygnotus, Zeuxis did not employ himself upon large compositions. He drew well, and in a grand style; and the beauty and grandeur of his forms were so predominant, that he was said by Aristotle to have failed in expressing mind, but Pliny says that in a picture of Penelope bewailing the loss of her husband, not only form, but character were vividly expressed; he censures him, however, for the too great size of the heads and joints in comparison with the other parts of the figures. Quintilian says that Zeuxis followed Homer, who loved powerful forms, even in women; he likewise notices his excellence in light and shade. He was also distinguished for a dramatic effect of composition, and he made a peculiar choice of subject; for he seldom or never, says Lucian, exerted his powers upon such hackneyed subjects as gods, heroes, and battles; but he always selected something new and unattempted, and when he had chosen a subject, he labored his utmost to render it a master-piece, painting very slowly, and with great care. Lucian instances, as an example, a picture of a family of Centaurs, of which he saw a copy at Athens, that excited his wonder at its extraordinary excellence. The original was lost at sea, on its way to Rome, whither it was sent by Sylla. He describes it as follows: "On a grass plot of the most glossy verdure lies the Centauress, with the whole equine part of her stretched on the ground, the hind feet extending backwards, while the upper female part is gently raised and reclining on one elbow. But the fore feet are not equally extended, as if she lay on her side; yet one seems to rest on the knee, having the hoof bent backwards, whereas the other is lifted up and pawing the ground, as horses are wont to do when they are going to spring up. Of her two young, one she holds in her arms to give it the breast, the other lies under her sucking like a foal. On an elevation behind her is seen a Centaur, who appears to be her mate, but is only visiable to the half of the horse; he looks down upon her with a complacent smile, holding up in one hand the whelp of a lion, as if jocosely to frighten his young ones with it. In the male Centaur all is fierce and terrific: his shaggy mane-like hair, his rough body, his broad and brawny shoulders, and the countenance, though smiling, yet wild and savage; in short, everything bears the character of these compound beings. The Centauress, on the other hand, as far as she is brutal, resembles the finest mare of the Thessalian breed which is yet untamed, and has never been mounted; by the other moiety, she is a woman of consummate beauty, excepting only in the ears, which have somewhat of the satyr shape. The blending, however, of the human and animal natures is so artificial, and the transition of one to the other so imperceptible, or rather they so gently lose themselves in one another, that it is impossible to say where the one ceases and the other begins. Nor in my mind was it less admirable that the young ones, notwithstanding their tender age, have somewhat wild and fierce in their aspect, and that mixture of infantine timidity and curiosity with which they look up at the whelp, while at the same time they continue eagerly sucking, and cling as close as they can to their mother."

Zeuxis was not only successful in securing wealth, and the applause of the multitude, but was honored with the friendship of Archelaus of Macedon, for whose palace he executed several pictures, and received for them the sum of 400 minæ—about $8000; which, though a small sum, compared with what was paid the painters of the Alexandrine period, and later, was probably at that time comparatively a large one. Cicero says that the inhabitants of Crotona prevailed on Zeuxis to visit their city, and to paint there a number of pictures for the Temple of Juno, for which he was to receive a large and stipulated sum. On his arrival he informed them that he intended only to paint the picture of Helen, with which they were satisfied, as he was regarded peculiarly excellent in the delineation of women. He accordingly desired to see the most beautiful maidens of the city, from whom he selected five, copied all that was most beautiful and perfect in the forms of each, and thus completed a work of exquisite beauty. It was a very famous work in after times, and artists apparently traveled to Crotona to see it. The painter Nicomachus, seeing this picture, could not restrain the expression of his surprise and admiration, when a bystander, not equally capable of appreciating its excellence, demanded what he saw in the picture to excite such sensations. "Ah," replied the painter, "take my eyes, and you will see a goddess"! This was his most celebrated work. It seems probable that he painted a picture of Helen, besides that for the people of Crotona, which in the time of Pliny was in the Portico of Philip at Rome. Probably a greater work by Zeuxis, though less celebrated than his Helen, was his picture which he presented to the Agrigentines, of the infant Hercules strangling the Serpents sent by Juno to destroy him, in the presence of his panic-struck mother Alcmena, and of Amphitryon. Other famous works by him were —Jupiter in the Assembly of the Gods; Menelaus mourning over the fate of Agamemnon; a Marsyas bound, in the Temple of Concord at Rome in Pliny's time; an Athlete inscribed with the line, "It is easier to find fault than to imitate"; and a Cupid crowned with roses, which was in the Temple of Venus at Athens. The time and place of Zeuxis' death are unknown. Festus relates, on the authority of Verrius Flaccus, that he died with laughter at the picture of an old woman whom he had painted; but this extraordinary circumstance is mentioned by no other writer, and is probably fictitious.

Zeuxis is represented as having been very proud of his reputation, and ostentatious of his wealth. He appeared at the Olympic Games attired in a mantle on which his name was embroidered in letters of gold, a piece of most absurd display in one whose name was deeply impressed on the hearts and imaginations of those by whom he was surrounded. He does not, however, seem to be chargeable with avarice, or, at least, this passion, if it existed, was subservient to his pride; for, when he had attained the height of his fame, he refused any longer to receive money for his pictures, because he regarded them above all pecuniary value. In the earlier part of his career, he was accustomed, however, to exhibit his productions for money, especially his celebrated painting of Helen, whence the figure was denominated, "Helen the Courtesan." The truth seems to have been, that the ruling passion of Zeuxis was the love of pomp, an ever-restless vanity, a constant desire and craving after every kind of distinction. So far as money assisted in procuring this, he stooped to obtain it, and refused it when he could most successfully assume dignity by refusing further recompense.

The story respecting the contest between Zeuxis and Parrhasius, has been frequently related. It is said that the former painted a cluster of grapes with such perfect skill that birds came and pecked them as they were exhibited on the table. Elated with so unequivocal a testimony of his excellence, he called to his rival to draw back the curtain which he supposed concealed his work, anticipating a certain triumph. Now, however, he found himself entrapped, for that which he took for a curtain, was only a painting of one by Parrhasius; upon which he ingenuously confessed himself defeated, since he had deceived only birds, but his antagonist had beguiled the senses of an experienced artist. An anecdote is also related of a similar kind, in which he overcame himself, or rather one part of his work was shown to have been executed at the expense of another. He painted a boy with a basket of grapes, to which the birds resorted; on which he acknowledged that the boy could not be well painted, since, had the similitude been equal in both cases, the birds would have been deterred from approaching. It was, perhaps, from the former of these accounts that Lucian drew his assertion that Zeuxis was inferior to Parrhasius, and if so, it certainly proves very little. Regard must be shown to the description of objects represented, and the artist who could represent a curtain to perfection, would not necessarily be the greatest painter of Greece. There are many testimonies, scattered through the writings of antiquity, to the transcendent genius of Zeuxis.

Cicero remarks that the works of Zeuxis, of Aglaophon, and Apelles, are in different styles, but they are all three perfect in their respective styles. Zeuxis also painted pictures in white, or mere chiaro-scuro, which the Greeks termed monochroms. It is remarkable that Pausanias does not mention the name of this artist, and we may infer from this that Zeuxis painted easel pictures only, or upon tabulæ, wooden panels, which, from their perishable nature and facility of removal, are very easily lost, particularly if the works of eminent artists, whose productions are best worth removal. Cicero states that Zeuxis used only four colors; but this is probably an error; or he may mean in his carnations, in which four are all that are necessary. In regard to the idea which has generally obtained in modern times, that the ancient painters really knew the use of only four colors, the anecdotes above related are almost sufficient to refute it entirely; because, although the stories themselves may be valueless, the fact that they were circulated in ancient times, shows that the ancients believed that exact imitation could be accomplished in colors, which result they could never have arrived at except by the evidence of their senses. For a further dissertation on this point, see the article APELLES.

There was another ancient artist named Zeuxis, a Greek statuary, who was a disciple of Silanion, and flourished from B. C. 316 to B. C. 296.

ZEVIO. See STEFANO DA VERONA and ALTICHERIO.

ZIARUKO, JOHN. This artist was a native of Poland, and is supposed to have been a painter. He executed a set of large etchings in a slight, spirited style, from his own designs, representing the Coronation Ceremonies of Louis XIII. of France.

ZIFRONDI, ANTONIO, a painter born at Clusone, in the Bergamese territory, according to Count Tassi, in 1657. After acquiring the rudiments of the art, he went to Bologna, and entered the school of Marc' Antonio Franceschini, under whose able instruction he became a reputable painter of history. There are many of his works in the churches and private collections of his native city, which show that he possessed a ready invention, and great facility of hand. Lanzi says he had a genius and an imagination for grand compositions, and a wonderful facility and rapidity of hand, that enabled him to dash off a picture in two hours; but hi works are seldom free from errors of over-haste and carelessness. His name is sometimes written *Cifrondi.* He died in 1730.

ZILOTTI, Domenico Bernardo, a painter born at Borso, near Bassano, about 1730. He painted landscapes, in which he imitated the style of Francesco Zuccarelli with great spirit and correctness. He also executed quite a number of spirited etchings from his own designs and after other masters, which possess considerable merit.

ZINANI, Francesco, a painter of Reggio, who flourished in 1755. According to Tiraboschi, he studied under Francesco Bibiena, and became one of the most skillful painters of perspective in Lombardy. He was much employed in decorating theatres.

ZINCKE, Christian Frederick, an excellent painter in enamel, born at Dresden in 1685. He went to England in 1706, and studied under Boit, whom he surpassed; and Cunningham states that he even rivaled Petitot, but Stanley says this is an error, that though he surpassed most artists of his time, and his works are still held in high estimation, he did not equal that master by many degrees. He found abundant employment, was much patronized by George II. and Queen Caroline, and was appointed cabinet painter to the Prince of Wales. The Princess Amelia, daughter of George II., had ten portraits of her illustrious family painted by him. His works are numerous and highly esteemed. He died in 1767.

ZING, or ZINGG, Adrian, a Swiss engraver, who flourished in the latter part of the 18th century. He first studied under John Rudolf Holzhalb, at Zurich, and then for two years with Louis Alberli at Berne, after which he went to Paris, and became the pupil of John George Wille. He executed several plates in that metropolis, which gained him considerable reputation, and after a residence there of seven years, he was invited to Dresden by the Elector of Saxony, who appointed him his engraver. He was also elected a member of the Academy of that city, He engraved quite a number of plates of landscapes, marines, sea-ports, views, and other subjects, after Vernet, vander Neer, Dietricy, and other masters, which were executed in a neat, clear style, resembling that of Wille. The times of his birth and death are not recorded.

ZING, ———. See Zagel.

ZINGARO, Lo. See Solario.

ZINMERMAN, Michael, a German painter and engraver on wood, who flourished at Vienna, according to Papillon, about 1550. Nothing is known of his works as a painter. He executed the cuts of a large geographical chart consisting of ten parts, which joined together. It represents the kingdom of Hungary, with the arms of the province, and is described as a very fine performance.

ZOAN, Andrea, a real or supposed engraver, who flourished about 1516. There is a great deal of dispute as to his name, country, and works, which we cannot enter into, further than to say that Bartsch, P. G. tom. xiii., describes thirty-three prints by him, most of which are marked with the initials Z. A., and quite a number more are described by other writers. Some of these are copied from Albert Durer. Zani says, "the initials Z. A., stand for Zoan Andrea, which is the same as Giovanni Andrea, Zoan being the Venetian pronunciation of Gian, or Giovanni," hence he argues that he was a Venetian. For further information the reader must be referred to Bartsch, Zani, and other voluminous writers.

ZOBEL, Benjamin, the inventor of Marmotinto, was born in 1762, at Memmingen, in Bavaria. He received his education at the government school of that city, and acquired the rudiments of drawing from a monk belonging to the convent of Ottobeuern. In 1781, he went to Amsterdam, where he resided two years, chiefly occupied in portrait painting. In 1783, he visited London, where he formed an acquaintance with Morland and Schweickhardt, the latter of whom was employed at Windsor Castle, by George III.'s "table decker." It was then customary to ornament the royal dinner table by having a silver plateau extending along the centre, on which were strewed various colored sands or marble dust, in fanciful designs of fruit, flowers, arabesque work, &c. For this an artist was required, possessing considerable talent and great freedom of hand. On the retirement of Schweickhardt, Zobel was appointed; and he continued to fill the office for a considerable period. As the sands were not cemented by any substance, this mode of ornamenting the table was a daily occupation; but Zobel conceived the idea of producing a finished and permanent picture, by the use of some substance to fix the sands. After various experiments, a composition, consisting chiefly of gum-arabic and spirits of wine, was found to answer the best. The subject of the picture having been designed either on pannel or milled board, a coating of the glutinous substance was spread over it; the different colored sands were then used in a similar manner as that employed in decking the royal table, namely, by strewing them from a piece of card held at various elevations, according to the strength or softness of the tint required. Thus was formed a picture, not subject to decay, and permanent in all its parts; and this the inventor called Marmotinto. Some of the best specimens of this peculiar art were formerly in the possession of the Duke of York, but were sold at his death, a number of years ago, at Oatlands. Several are still among the collections of paintings belonging to the Duke of Northumberland, and Sir Willoughby Gordon. Zobel also practised painting on gold and silver grounds in transparent colors, for various purposes, with eminent success. He died in 1831.

ZOBOLI, Jacopo, a painter born at Modena, who first studied under Francesco Stringa, and afterwards at Bologna. From thence he went to Rome, where he settled, and "acquired," says Lanzi, "the reputation of a good artist. This he obtained in a high degree by his labors in the church of S. Eustachio, where he is distinguished among the more modern productions by his St. Girolamo, displaying singular diligence, polish, and harmony of color, by no means general in those times." He died at Rome in 1761.

ZOCCHI, Giuseppe, a painter and engraver, born at Florence in 1711. Lanzi says he displayed such talents when a boy, that the noble family of the Gerini took him under its patronage, and after his elementary studies at Florence, sent him to Rome, to Bologna, and to other parts of Lombardy for his instruction. "Zocchi had a genius fertile in invention, pliant in imitation, and judicious in selection; hence at the conclusion of such a course of study he was able to compose large works with skill, and to color beautifully. He painted four tolerably large frescos in the Villa Serristori, beyond the gate of St. Nicholas; some apartments in the Rinuccini palace, and one in the Gerini gallery; and these are believed to be his best works of this sort. In small pieces he was still greater, as in his oil pictures of the festivals at Siena, on the arrival of the Emperor Francis I., a work true in perspective and graceful in the multitude of figures." Zocchi also made drawings of the most remarkable views in Florence, and of the villas in its environs, which he caused to be engraved and published in sets; the figures in these were etched by himself. He also etched some plates after Guido, P. da Cortona, Simone da Pesaro, Solimena, and others. He died in 1767.

ZOCCHI. See Zucchi.

ZOCCOLI, Carlo, a distinguished Italian architect and engineer, was born at Naples in 1718. Milizia does not mention his instructor, but at the age of seventeen he entered the corps of engineers. He attained great distinction, was appointed master of fortifications, and took precedence of many of the older officers; but in consequence of delicate health, he devoted his talents to civil architecture, and was appointed Superintendent of Buildings to the city of Naples. The principal works by Zoccoli, are, the Cathedral, Seminary, and Episcopal Palace of Calvi; the Convent of the Alcanterini, on the mountain of Pignatoro; the church and Baronial palace in Cutignano, near Nola; the Villa of the Prince of Supino at Portici; and that of the Marquis Palomba at Cesa. Zoccoli also constructed two windmills at Capua, and nine others at Scilla in Calabria. He died in 1771, leaving a son named Raffaelle Z., who completed the restorations on the Castle at Scilla, commenced by his father.

ZOFFANY, John, a German painter, born at Frankfort-on-the Maine, in 1735; although Fiorillo places his birth at Regensburg, in Bavaria. It is said that his father, an architect of Bohemian descent, sent him to Italy while young; and after returning to Germany, that he practised portrait and historical painting at Coblentz for several years. He went to England when about thirty years of age, where he acquired considerable distinction by painting the portraits of Garrick and several other eminent performers in costume, also those of the Earl of Barrymore, and several members of the Royal Family. At the formation of the Royal Academy, Zoffany was chosen one of the original forty members, in 1768; and he painted a picture of the Academicians of 1772, considered among his best works. He also painted conversation pieces with considerable success. On his expressing a wish to visit Italy, George III. gave him a letter to the Grand Duke of Tuscany, who received him well, and permitted him to study in the Florentine gallery, of which he painted a picture, now in the royal collection. In 1782, soon after his return to England, he went to the East Indies, and resided several years at Lucknow, where he painted the portraits of several native princes, and many European residents. Three of his best performances were painted in the East Indies, and have been engraved in mezzotinto by Earlom; they represent an Indian Tiger Hunt; a Cock-Fight, with many figures; and the Embassy of Hyderbeck to Lord Cornwallis at Calcutta, a rich display of Indian costumes, with about one hundred figures, and several elephants and horses. After acquiring a handsome fortune, Zoffany returned, in 1796, to England, where he passed the rest of his days, and died at Kew, in 1810.

ZOLA, or ZOLLA, Giuseppe, a landscape painter, born at Brescia in 1675. Lanzi says, "he devoted himself to no single master, but formed his style upon many. He was exceedingly rich in conception, and in expedients; his buildings are of a rustic kind, his ruins partake of the modern, and are picturesquely covered with creeping plants and ivy; the back grounds are of an azure hue, and he inserts a great variety of objects and figures, in which he was less happy than in his landscape. His earlier works are held in most esteem. When he obtained greater commissions, he executed them with a more mechanical hand, and with the exeception of his coloring, which he always studied, he bestowed little care on the rest. Those pictures are in general most complete in which he introduced the smallest figures, and such may be seen even out of private houses, as in the Monte della Pietà, and in the sacristy of S. Lionardo at Ferrara." In his best works, his figures are elegantly designed, carefully finished, and touched with spirit, though generally not equal to his scenery. He resided the greater part of his life at Ferrara, where he died in 1743.

ZOMPINI, Gaetano, a painter born at Venice in 1702. According to Lanzi he was a pupil of the Cav. Niccolo Bambini, and afterwards by studying the works of Sebastiano Ricci, he formed a mixed style not destitute of originality. "He received honorable commissions from the court of Spain, in which he displayed a rich fund of imagination; he also, in a measure, distinguished himself by his engravings." He died in 1778.

ZONCA, Victor, an Italian architect, and talented mechanician, was born in 1580. In youth, he applied himself to the study of mathematics and architecture, and attained sufficient excellence to be appointed architect to the city of Padua. He seems, however, to have attained his chief distinction by the invention of many ingenious machines, entitled *Nuovo teatro di machine ed edifizj per varie e sicure operazioni*, in folio, Padua, 1607, or 1621. There are said to have been other editions published in 1653 and 1656, but this is quite improbable, as the volume is very rare.

ZOOLEMAKER. See Solemacker.

ZOPPO, Marco, a painter born at Bologna in 1451. He first studied under Dalmasio Lippi, and afterwards at Padua, in the school of Francesco Squarcione, where Andrea Mantegna was his fellow pupil. Lanzi says, "he also studied in the Venetian school, where he painted for the Osservanti at Pesaro, a picture of the Virgin on a throne crowned, with St. John the Baptist, St. Francis, and other saints, and signed it *Marco Zoppo da Bologna Dip. in Vinexia*, 1471. This is his most celebrated production, from which, and a few other pieces in the same church, and at Bologna, we may gather some idea of his style. He formed an epoch in the Bolognese school, and rose to equal eminence with Pizzolo and Dario da Trevigi; and, like them, vied with the genius of Mantegna, which gave a further spur to his exertions. His composition is that common to the quattrocentisti (artists of the 14th century), particularly the Venetians, and which he probably introduced into Bologna, a style which continued till the time of Francia and his school, for the most part unvaried, except in the addition of a church to the steps of the throne, sometimes with a harp, and sometimes without. It is not free and graceful, like that of Mantegna, but rather coarse, particularly in the feet; yet less rectilinear in the folds, and bolder and more harmonious perhaps, in the selections of the colors. The fleshes are as much studied as in Signorelli, and in others of the same age, while the figures and accessories are conducted with the most finished care. He was moreover a fine decorator of façades." He died in 1517.

ZOPPO, Paolo, a painter of Brescia, who flourished in the first part of the 16th century. There are some of his pictures in the churches of his native city, which show that he had studied the works of the Bellini, and approached near the modern manner. Lanzi says he was present at the terrible sacking of the opulent city of Brescia, by the French army, under Gaston de Foix, in 1512, and that he painted the desolation of the city in miniature, upon a large crystal basin, a work of immense labor, intended to be presented to the Doge Gritti; but in transporting it to Venice, the crystal was unfortunately broken, and the unhappy artist, overwhelmed with despair, died about 1530, though Ridolfi says about 1515.

ZOPPO, Rocco, a Florentine painter, who flourished in the first half of the 16th century. He was a disciple of Pietro Perugino, in whose style, according to Lanzi, his Madonnas are frequently to be met with in private houses in Florence.

ZOPPO, Lo, de Gangi, a Sicilian painter, who flourished, according to Lanzi, in the 18th century. There are some of his works in the Cathedral at Castro Giovanni.

ZOPPO, Lo, di Genova. See Micone.

ZOPPO, Il, di Lugano. See Discepoli.

ZOPPO, Lo, da Vicenza. See Pieri.

ZORG. See Rokes.

ZOROTI, Domenico, an Italian engraver, who resided in Germany, according to Florent le Comte, and executed some portraits.

ZOUST. See Soest.

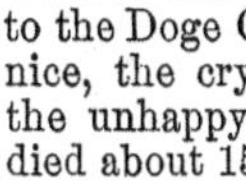

ZUBERLEIN, or ZIBERLEIN, Jacob, a German engraver on wood was born at Tubingen, and flourished at Frankfort about 1595. He executed a considerable number of wooden cuts, usually marked with a monogram of his initials, I. Z., to which he sometimes added a small tub. He is said to have been also a painter.

ZUBOZ, Alexis, an engraver in mezzotinto, who went to St. Petersburg, where he resided many years, and engraved a series of portraits of the Emperors of Russia; that of Peter the Great is dated 1729.

ZUCCARELLI, or ZUCCHERELLI, Francesco, an eminent landscape painter, born at Pitigliano, in Tuscany, according to Lanzi, in 1702. He studied first with Paolo Anesi, and afterwards successively with Gio. Maria Morandi and Pietro Nelli. For some time he applied himself to historical painting, but his natural genius leading him to landscape, he afterwards confined himself to that branch, in when he greatly excelled. His scenery is always pleasing, and usually embellished with ruins, cottages, and figures, elegantly designed, and touched with great neatness and spirit. His pictures were greatly admired and extolled, all over Europe. His principal field in Italy was in Venice, until the British Consul, Smith, induced him to visit England in 1752, where he met with very flattering encouragement, and was elected one of the original forty members of the Royal Academy. About 1773, he returned to Italy, and settled at Florence, where he invested a considerable sum of money, the produce of his talents, in the security of one of the monasteries, intending to pass the rest of his days in tranquil repose, but the monastery was soon afterwards suppressed by Joseph II. of Austria, and the unfortunate artist being reduced to indigence, was obliged to resume his pencil. He sometimes decorated the landscapes and architectural pieces of his cotemporaries with beautiful figures. He is said always to have marked his pictures with a pumpkin or squash, of large size, growing on a vine upon a shepherd's cot or fence, or stuck with a stick on a rustic's shoulder, as the rebus of his name, which in Italian signifies *little pumpkin*. We have a few spirited etchings by this artist from his own designs, and after other masters. He died at Florence in 1788.

ZUCCARO, Taddeo. This painter is sometimes miscalled Zucchero, and by Vasari, Zuccheri, or Zuccari; but Lanzi says that in his epitaph, and in the books of his brother Federigo, the name is Zuccaro. He was born at S. Angiolo in Vado, in the Duchy of Urbino, in 1529, and was the son of an obscure painter, named Ottaviano Zuccaro. At an early age he manifested a precocious genius, and after receiving instruction from his father, and from Pompeo da Fano, he went to Rome when only fourteen years old. Destitute of means, he was compelled to support himself by grinding colors for the shops; but he still devoted every available moment to the prosecution of art, and frequently, after passing the day in designing from the works of Raffaelle, he was compelled by poverty to sleep under the loggie of the Chigi palace. After perseverance under such difficulties, which would have daunted a less devoted lover of art, Taddeo was noticed by Daniello de Por, or da Parma, an artist then in repute, who favored him with his assistance and advice; and Lanzi says he "accomplished himself" under Giacomone da Faenza. His progress from this time seems to have been rapid; in 1547, at the age of eighteen, he was employed to decorate the façade of the Palazzo Mattei, with several emblematical subjects in chiaro-scuro.—Having accquired considerable reputation by this work, he was soon afterwards engaged by the Duke di Urbino to paint a series of frescos in a chapel of the Cathedral: Lanzi also mentions his picture of the Pentecost, in the church of S. Spirito at Urbino. During the pontificate of Julius III., he returned to Rome, and was employed by that pontiff, and by his successor, Paul IV., in the embellishment of the Vatican, and particularly of the apartments called Il Torrione. He painted in various parts of the Ecclesiastical States, and was entrusted by Cardinal Farnese with the entire decoration of his palace at Caprarola, where he represented the civil and military history of the Farnese family, in a variety of compartments, evincing great powers of invention, and a judicious style of composition. Lanzi says that the history of the Evangelists, in the church of the Consolazione at Rome, is among the best of his large fresco works in that city, but that none of his performances have added so much to his celebrity as those at Caprarola, and that strangers who visit that place generally return with a higher opinion of his abilities than they took with them. Lanzi also adds that a number of young artists, fully equal, and perhaps superior to Taddeo, were employed upon the same works at Caprarola, both in conjunction with him and after his death, whose works ought not to be confounded with his, though it is not always easy to distinguish them.

Most of Taddeo's performances are his grand works in fresco. He painted few pictures in oil, and is most pleasing in his small cabinet pictures, which are finished in the first style of excellence. Lanzi says that "from Giacomone da Faenza, and other good artists whom he assiduously studied, he acquired sufficient talent to distinguish himself. He adopted a style, which, though not very correct, was unconstrained and engaging, and very attractive to such as do not look for grandeur of design. He may be compared to that class of orators, who keep the attention of their hearers awake, not from the nature of their subject, but from the clearness of their language, and from their finding, or thinking they find, truth and nature in every word. His pictures may be cslled compositions of portraits; the heads are beautiful, the hands and feet negligently painted, nor yet labored, as in the Florentine manner; the dress and ornaments, and form of the beard, are agreeable to the times; the disposition is simple, and he often imitates the old painters in showing on the canvas only half figures in the foreground, as if they were on a lower plain. He often repeated the same countenance, and his own portrait. In his hands, feet, and the folds of his drapery, he is still less varied, and frequently errs in his proportions."

According to Vasari, Taddeo Zuccaro carried on a traffic in the art, similar to that of Pierino del Vaga before him, by contriving to abound in commissions, and securing to himself the services of other artists, in order to make them dependent on him, that they might not interfere with his own commissions and emoluments. He died at Rome in 1566, in his thirty-seventh year, worn out with continual exertion, and some disposition to excess. His monument is to be seen by the side of that of Raffaelle, in the Rotonda. In 1748, there were published a set of forty-five plates, engraved by John Joseph Prenner, from Taddeo's great work in the palace at Caprarola.

ZUCCARO, Cav. Federigo. This painter was the brother of Taddeo Z., and born at S. Angiolo in Vado, in 1543. He went to Rome at a very early age, and entered the school of his brother, where he had every advantage, and in a few years was so far advanced as to be able to assist Taddeo in his great works in fresco. In concert with Federigo Baroccio, he was employed by Pius IV. to paint in the Belvidere palace, the History of Moses and Pharaoh, and the Transfiguration, which gained him great reputation. He also assisted his brother in the works at the Vatican, and the Farnese palace at Caprarola; and he was invited to Florence by the grand duke Francesco I., to paint the great dome of the metropolitan church, S. Maria de' Fiori, commenced by Vasari, and left unfinished at his death. In this work Lanzi says there is little to admire, except vastness of conception; he designed more than three hundred figures, fifty feet in height, with outmentioning that of Lucifer, so gigantic that the rest appeared like children.

Federigo returned to Rome at the earnest solicitation of his brother; but the latter dying soon after, he was engaged to finish the various works upon which Taddeo had been engaged, in the Vatican, the church lá Trinita de' Monti, and various other places. He soon became the first artist in Rome, and every work on a large scale was assigned to him. Gregory XIII. engaged him to paint the vault of the Capella Paolina; but about this time, in order to revenge himself upon some of the principal officers of the Pope, who had treated him with indignity, he painted and exposed to public view an allegorical picture of Calumny,* introducing the portraits of all those individuals who had offended him, decorated with asses' ears. His enemies, upon this, made such complaints that he was compelled to quit the dominions of the Pope, and he traveled to France, where he was for some time employed by the Cardinal of Lorraine. Going on to Flanders he painted several cartoons for tapestry, and then crossed the Channel, arriving in England in 1574, where he met a favorable reception, and painted a number of fine portraits, among which, was that of Queen Elizabeth. Walpole also says that he painted the portrait of Mary, Queen of Scots, which was engraved by Vertue, and is now at Chiswick.

Federigo's stay in England was quite short, and on returning to Italy he was invited to Venice, to paint the Submission of the Emperor Frederick Barbarossa to Pope Alexander III. in the Palazzo Pubblico, which is praised by Zanetti as one of his best works, copious, beautiful, and well sustained. Lanzi says he was highly esteemed, and constantly employed in Venice; he was engaged, in concert with the most eminent Venetian masters of the day, to embellish the Grand Council Hall, where his performances were so much admired that he received the honor of knighthood.

The pontiff being by this time appeased, Federigo returned to complete his work in the Capella Paolina, which Lanzi commends as the best of all he executed in Rome, without the assistance of his brother. During the pontificate of Sixtus V., he was invited to Madrid by Philip II. He executed some frescos in the lower cloister of the Escurial, which, not giving satisfaction to his royal patron, were effaced, and their places supplied by Pellegrino Tibaldi. The king, however, compensated him liberally for his work, and sent him back to Italy with a pension. About this time, he was chosen by Gregory XIII. to put in execution the letters patent for the Academy of St. Luke, which Lanzi says was first organized in November, 1593, according to the account of Signor Barone Vernazza, although the Artists celebrated the year 1595 as the centenary of the Academy. By common consent Federigo was declared the first president of this

* This is not the large picture of the Calumny of Apelles, painted in distemper for the Orsini family, and engraved, which is now to be seen in the Palazzo Lante, and is one of the most finished productions of Federigo.

celebrated institution, of which he was one of the chief promoters.

Later in life, as it would appear, Federigo Zuccaro undertook a journey through the principal cities of Italy, everywhere leaving proofs of his abilities. Lanzi praises two of his pictures in a chapel at Loreto, representing scenes from the life of the Virgin, painted for the Duke of Urbino, for their simple and graceful style; he also mentions two large pictures in the library of the Cistercian monks at Milan, representing the Miracle della Neve, with a numerous assemblage of figures, in his usual lively manner, the coloring varied and well preserved. Federigo resembled his brother Taddeo in style; he possessed a ready and inventive genius, and his design is not incorrect: but his compositions are frequently incongruous and extravagant, and he was led into a greater degree of mannerism than Taddeo, by an affectation of grandeur, and a commanding facility, being more addicted to ornament, and more crowded in his composition. His works are frequently compositions of portraits, and his coloring, though vigorous, clear, and brilliant, possesses neither mellowness nor harmony.

After executing various works in Milan, Pavia, and other Italian cities, Federigo went to Turin, where he painted several pictures for the churches, and commenced the decoration of a gallery for the Duke of Savoy. Here he published his treatise entitled *La Idea de' Pittori, Scultori, e Architetti*, which Lanzi says he appears to have written with the intention of rivalling and excelling Vasari; but he chose an abstruse mode of writing, and concocted a mass of sterile and ill-directed speculations; for which reasons Lanzi says we derive more information from a single page of Vasari's plainly written work, than from the whole book of Zuccaro, which tends rather to raise disputes than to convey knowledge. In 1609, while returning to his native place, Federigo fell sick in Ancona, where he died, aged sixty-six years. He left his entire property to the Academy of St. Luke. This artist is said to have been versed in sculpture and architecture, but none of his works are mentioned. Baglioni admires his versatility of talent, but more his good fortune, in which he exceeded all his cotemporaries. He was distinguished for noble personal appearance, engaging manners, and great liberality; all of which qualities gained him the esteem and attachment of many individuals, and contributed in no small degree to his success.

ZUCCATI, Sebastiano, an old painter who was living at Trevigi in 1490. He painted in the gothic style of the time, and had the honor of being the first instructor of Titian.

ZUCCATI, Valerio and Francesco, two celebrated workers in mosaic, sons of the preceding, who were living at Venice in 1573. Lanzi, speaking of the perfection to which mosaic painting was carried before and during the time of Titian, says: "The same taste in mosaic work prevailed in the time of Titian, and to this he gave a renewed spirit, and even furnished several of these artists with designs. Marco Luciano Rizzio and Vincenzio Bianchini, are the first who, about 1517, succeeded in effecting a complete reform in the art. To the last is referred that celebrated Judgment of Solomon which adorns the portico or vestibule of San Marco. Both these, however, were surpassed by Francesco and Valerio Zuccati, or Trevigi, (or rather of the Valtelline), sons of the same Sebastiano who initiated Titian in the first rudiments of art. By them there likewise appear, in the portico of San Marco, among various prophets and doctors of the church, two histories that may be pronounced the best mosaic works produced during the age of painting. I have seen altar-pieces for churches, and pictures for private ornament, in the same taste. The Royal Gallery at Florence possesses a portrait from life of Cardinal Bembo, worked by Valerio; and a St. Girolamo by Francesco, is known to have been presented by the Republic to the court of Savoy. Subsequently to these, about 1585, Arminio, a son of Valerio, flourished, and was held in much repute. Nor did this family only possess the art of coloring glass and stone with admirable skill, but they understood the principles of design, more particularly Francesco, who had practised as a painter, before he entered upon mosaic works." Vasari erroneously calls these artists Zuccheri, and sometimes Zuccherini. See *Bianchini.*

ZUCCHI, Andrea, an Italian engraver, born at Venice about 1675. He engraved a part of the plates for a collection of prints from the most celebrated paintings at Venice, consisting of 57 plates, published by Lovisa. He also engraved a set of twelve plates of Venetian costumes. He died in 1740. The following are among his best works:

Tobit and the Angel; *after Titian.* St. John the Evangelist; *do.* St. John the Baptist; *after P. Veronese,* The Martyrdom of Paolo Erizzo; *after P. Longhi.* The Birth of the Virgin; *after Niccolo Bambini.* The Miracle of the Manna; *after G. Porta.* The Goddess Cybele in a Car, drawn by Lions; *after Tintoretto.* Aurora and Tithon; *do.* Æneas saving Anchises from the Burning of Troy; *after Seb. Ricci.*

ZUCCHI, Francesco, an Italian engraver, was the son and scholar of Andrea Z., born at Venice in 1698. He was invited to Dresden, where he engraved several plates from pictures in the Electoral Gallery, among which are the following. He died in 1764.

The Portrait of a Spaniard; *after Rubens;* in the Dresden Gallery. The Portrait of a Lady, resembling one of Rubens' wives; *after the same;* in the same collection. St. Helena worshipping the Cross; *after Gio. Bettini Cignaroli.* Two Allegorical Subjects; *after Antonio Balestra.*

ZUCCHI, Lorenzo, was the younger brother of the preceding, born at Venice, in 1704. He was instructed by his father, and in 1738 was appointed engraver to the Elector of Saxony, who employed him to execute several plates from pictures in the Electoral Gallery, for the collection known as the Dresden Gallery. The following are by him. He died about 1779.

The Seven Sacraments; *after Spagnoletto.* The Martyrdom of St. Peter and St. Paul; *after Nic. del Abati.* The Crowning of St. Catherine; *after Rubens.* A Sacrifice to Venus; *after Ger. Lairesse.* The Flaying of Marsyas, *after Langetti.* St. Michael combating the Dragon; *after Torelli.* The Tribute-Money; *after Titian.* David with the Head of Goliah; *after Luc. Giordano.*

ZUCCHI, Antonio, an Italian fresco painter, who accompanied Robert Adam, the architect, to England. He was employed to decorate some of the mansions of the nobility, among others a ceiling at Buckingham House. His subjects were usually mythological, with ruins and other embellishments, which he painted in a light and pleasing manner, though without much force. He died at Rome in 1795.

ZUCCHI, Jacopo, called also Della Zucca, a painter born at Florence about 1541. He was a pupil of Giorgio Vasari, whom he assisted in some of his works. Lanzi says: "his works exhibit none of the carelessness of Giorgio. He sometimes imitated him, but his style is better and more refined. He lived long at Rome, under the protection of the Cardinal de Medici, whose palace, and more especially the Palazzo Rucellai, he decorated with frescos, with incredible diligence. His picture of the Birth of the Baptist, in S. Giovanni Decollato, is esteemed the best picture in the church; and he appears more a follower of Andrea del Sarto than of any other master. He usually introduced portraits of distinguished characters and men of letters into his compositions, and showed a peculiar grace in the figures of children and young people." There are several altar-pieces, and other works by him in the churches at Rome, one of the best of which is the Descent of the Holy Ghost, in S. Spirito in Borgo. He died in the pontificate of Sixtus V. He had a brother named Francesco, who was a good artist in mosaic, according to Baglioni, and Lanzi says he likewise excelled in painting fruit and flowers.

ZUCCO, Francesco, a painter born at Bergamo. According to Tassi, he first studied in the school of the Campi at Cremona, and afterwards under Pietro Moroni, the disciple of Paul Veronese. Lanzi says, "From Moroni he acquired the art of giving a singular degree of spirit to his portraits, and from Veronese the mode of ornamenting them with most taste and fancy. Even in his larger compositions, he sometimes adhered so closely to Paolo, that several of his works were ascribed, even by his fellow-citizens, to that artist, a circumstance that occurred to his pictures of the Nativity and of an Epiphany in the church of S. Gottardo at Bergamo. He adopted, moreover, a variety of manners, apparently ambitious of displaying to the public his power of imitating Cavagna or Talpino, as he pleased." He died in 1627.

ZUGNI, Francesco, a painter born at Brescia, according to Ridolfi, in 1574, and died in 1636, aged 62; Zani says he was born in 1557, and died in 1621; and Lanzi places his death in 1621.—He studied under the younger Palma, and was his ablest disciple. Though inferior to him in beauty of forms and attitudes, he surpassed him in vigor and *impasto* of coloring, and in the spirit in which he conducted his works. He particularly excelled in fresco, and frequently embellished with his figures the architectural and perspective pieces of Tommaso Sandrini, with whom he was employed in the hall of the Podesta, in that of the Capitano, and in several villas. Zugni displayed great excellence in his oil paintings, one of the most esteemed of which is the Circumcision, in S. Maria delle Grazie, at Venice. He was also much employed by individuals.

ZUMMO, Gaetano Giulio, a celebrated Sicilian modeler in colored wax, was born of a noble family, at Syracuse, in 1656. His name is often incorrectly spelt Zumbo. He early devoted himself to the study of sculpture, and combining with it a careful investigation of the anatomy of the human body, he produced some good works, and various anatomical preparations in colored wax, prepared after a method of his own. He acquired considerable reputation in various Italian cities—in Bologna, Genoa, and especially at Florence, where the grand duke Cosmo III. took him into his service. Among other works which he executed for that prince, are two most repulsive but ingenious performances, one representing the effects of the Plague; the other called "Corruption" (La Corruzione), consisting of a group of five figures, in high relief, showing different stages of decomposition in the human body, after death. De Piles mentions two beautiful works by him at Genoa, representing the Nativity, and the Descent from the Cross. From Genoa, Zummo went to Paris, where he died in 1701.

ZUPELLI, Giovanni Battista, a painter of Cremona, who flourished about the close of the 15th century. He painted landscapes, usually embellished with figures representing subjects from sacred history. His style, though dry and gothic, exhibits much originality, and there is a graceful air in his figures, which distinguishes his works beyond the generality of his cotemporaries. In the church of the Eremitani, at Cremona, is a landscape with the Holy Family, by him, which is highly commended by Lanzi and others. Zani says he died in 1520, and others in 1536, aged 62. Lanzi says he flourished at the close of the 15th century.

ZURBARAN, Francisco, an eminent Spanish painter, was born, according to Palomino, at Fuente de Cantos, near Seville, in 1596. His father was a husbandman, and intended him for the same employment; but he manifested such a strong inclination for painting, that he was placed in the school of Juan de las Roelas, under whose direction he applied himself with such diligence and success, that he soon acquired the reputation of an eminent painter of history. He determined to copy nature in everything, and followed the style of Michael Angelo Caravaggio, at the same time discarding the extravagance and caprice of that master, whose bold effects and vigorous light and shadow he adopted with such great ability, that he was called the Spanish Caravaggio. In 1625, he was commissioned by the Marquis of Malazon to paint some pictures for the chapel of St. Peter, in the cathedral of Seville, representing scenes from the life of that Apostle, which he executed in a very able manner; and about the same time he painted his famous picture of St. Thomas Aquinas for the altar of the church of the college of that saint at Seville. This is esteemed his best performance in respect of correct imitation of nature, and vigor of chiaro-scuro; and it is said to equal the best productions of the Spanish school. He afterwards went to Guadaloupe, and painted eleven pictures from the life of St. Jerome, for the Hieronymite Friars in that city, besides various altarpieces, which were greatly admired. On returning to Seville, he executed three admirable works for the Carthusians of S. Maria de las Cuevas, evincing great skill and close observance of nature; also various other pictures in the churches and monasteries of that city, among which was a Crucifixion in the church of S. Pablo, remarkable for its boldness of relief, and dated in 1627.

Zurbaran's merit gained him an invitation to Madrid about 1630. He was appointed painter to the King, and employed in the palace of the Buon Retiro, where he painted a series of pictures representing the Labors of Hercules. It constitutes a high commendation of his abilities, that he was greatly favored by King Philip IV., (who is said to have frequently visited him while at work,) at the time when Velasquez was in his full career. Stirling places him in the first rank of the Spanish school, equal to Velasquez in coloring, though not in other respects; and that writer commends him as "the peculiar painter of monks, as Raffaelle is of Madonnas and Ribera of martyrdoms." His picture of the History of San Pedro Nolasco, painted for the cloister of La Merced Calzada at Seville, was greatly admired, particularly for the infinite art and delicacy displayed in the white draperies of the monks. It would appear also that he excelled in the more agreeable departments of the art, for his picture of the Infant Jesus sleeping, in the gallery at Madrid, is said to equal in beauty and grace, the same subject by Guido and Murillo. Zurbaran died in the service of King Philip IV., in 1662. There are many of his works in the Casa de Campo, and other royal palaces, in the churches and monasteries of Seville, Cordova, Guadaloupe, and Madrid, besides many in the private collections. The best are said to be in the Museum at Seville. They are quite uncommon out of Spain; but Marshal Soult brought away some, and others have been removed more recently. In the Spanish Museum at the Louvre there is a room devoted chiefly to his works, and it contains, according to the catalogue, eighty-one pictures from his pencil; but many of them are very indifferent, and doubtless by some other artist. In the Duke of Sutherland's collection, is a picture by Zurbaran of the Virgin and Infant, with St. John, which is greatly admired. It is dated 1653.

ZUSTRUS, or SUSTRIS, Lambert, a German painter, who flourished towards the close of the 16th century. After receiving at Munich the instructions of Christopher Schwartz, he went to Venice, and became the scholar of Titian. He imitated successfully the style of that great master in coloring, and also in design, though not without some mixture of the Gothic style of his country. There was an excellent work by Zustrus in the cabinet of the King of France, representing the Baptism of Christ by St. John; and another is also mentioned in the Louvre, of Venus and Cupid, with Mars in the background. See *Lambert Suterman*.

ZWOTT, or ZWOLL, J. Ancker de. This old German engraver flourished about 1500. His name is usually spelt *Zwoll*, in English works, but Bartsch calls him Zwott, and Zani expressly says that the other orthography is incorrect. His plates resemble the style of Israel von Mecheln, whence he is supposed to have been a pupil of that master, though very inferior to him, his compositions being crowded and confused, and his drawing of the figure meagre and incorrect. They are quite interesting from their age and rarity. Bartsch describes eighteen as follow. Zwott is called the *Master of the Shuttle*, from the circumstance of his prints being marked with a shuttle.

The Adoration of the Kings. The Last Supper. Christ at the Mount of Olives. Christ taken in the Garden. Christ crucified between two Thieves. The same subject differently treated. The Entombing of Christ. The Saviour standing, holding an open Book in one hand, and giving benediction with the other. The Virgin with the Infant holding a Cross. The Virgin with the Infant, who is turning the leaves of a Book. St. Augustine seated between Statues of SS. Jerome and Lawrence. St. Christopher on Horseback bearing the Saviour on his shoulders. St. George encountering the Dragon. St. Gregory celebrating Mass. St. Anne with the Virgin, Infant, and figures of Angels. A youth in conversation with an aged Pilgrim. A Skeleton in a vaulted Tomb. A design of Gothic Architecture, resembling the upper part of an Altar, with statues and coats of arms.

ZYL, Gerard Pietersz van, called also Gerard van Leyden, a Dutch painter, was born at Amsterdam in 1606. He acquired a knowledge of art in his native country, and seems to have attained there considerable excellence in portrait painting; after which he went to England, in 1635, and formed an intimacy with Vandyck, who employed him in his draperies and backgrounds. By this intercourse, Zyl greatly improved his own style, and after residing several years in London, he returned to Amsterdam, where he received plentiful encouragement. He painted many portraits, distinguished for their chaste and clear coloring, and the beauty of the hands, so that he acquired the appellation of the second Vandyck. There are also some conversations and familiar subjects attributed to him. He died in 1667.

ZYLVELT, Adam van, a Dutch engraver, born at Amsterdam about 1635. He imitated the style of John Visscher with some success, and engraved a set of plates representing sea-ports, &c., from the designs of John Lingelbach; also various portraits, several of which are from his own designs. Among them are the following:

Dirk Volkhertz Coornhaert, or Cuernhaert, Engraver. Stephen le Moine, Doctor in Theology at Leyden. Christopher Wittichius, Professor of the University of Leyden. Hermann Witsius, Professor of Theology at Franecker. John Hasius, Minister of the Church of Haerlem. Cornelius Bosch.

ZYNNDT, or ZUNDT, Mathias, an engraver of little note, who flourished about 1566, and executed a few plates, among which Bartsch mentions three: a View of the city of Grodno, in Lithuania, 1568; a portrait of John de Raleta, Grand Master of Malta, 1566; and a portrait of Louis III. de Bourbon-Conde, 1568.

# SUPPLEMENT.



ARUNDALE, Francis, an English architect, born in London, August 9, 1807; died at Brighton, September 9, 1853. Mr. Arundale's professional instructor was Mr. Pugin, the Gothic architect, with whom he traveled on the Continent. He afterwards spent many years in Egypt and the Holy Land in company with Messrs. Catherwood and Bonomi, engaged in the study of ancient architectural remains. He published "Travels in Asia Minor," 2 vols. 8vo., and a work on Egyptian Antiquities in conjunction with Mr. Bonomi in 1 vol. 4to. Mr. Arundale was one of the most highly cultured architects of the day, and was employed on several buildings of importance at the time of his premature decease.

BARRY, Sir Charles, R. A., an English architect, born at Westminster, May, 1795; died there, May 12, 1860. When young he evinced a decided taste for the pursuit of architecture, and was articled by his father to a firm of builders and surveyors in Lambeth. On his father's death in 1817, he inherited a small property, and left England for the Continent, with the view of carrying out a plan of study. He was absent nearly four years, and during that time made himself familiar with the ancient remains of Italy, Greece, Egypt, and Syria, and executed beautiful drawings of the most remarkable, which were much admired. His skill as a draftsman was conducive to his future advancement, all his designs being distinguished for finish and perfection of detail. When on his return to England he commenced a professional career, the new Church of St. Peter's, Brighton, was the first work of consequence intrusted to him. This proved very successful, and led to his frequent employment at Manchester, Birmingham, Liverpool, and other provincial cities. His first important work in the metropolis was the Traveller's Club-House, in Pall Mall, a charming design in the Italian palazzo style, then a novelty in London architecture. The Reform Club House in the same street, a more imposing mass of building, remarkable for the sumptuousness of its interior decoration, was designed by Mr. Barry, and also the College of Surgeons in Lincoln's Inn Fields, and the Treasury Buildings, Whitehall. In 1834 the conflagration of the House of Parliament led to the construction of the building now officially known as the New Palace, Westminster. The designs furnished to the competition, by Barry, in the Tudor Gothic of Henry VIIIth's time, were by far the most magnificent, and were unanimously adopted for execution. For the remainder of his life—twenty-four years—this national work occupied almost the entire attention of the architect, who died before the completion of the structure. He was elected associate of the Royal Academy in 1839, and Academician in 1842. Sir Charles Barry was knighted by Queen Victoria when in 1852 she made her first entry to the new palace by the Victoria Tower. He was remarkable for kindness of heart, liberality of feeling, and urbanity of manner. His funeral took place in Westminster Abbey. The New Houses of Parliament are unquestionably among the most important architectural works of modern times; decorations of every kind are lavishly employed, and the whole effect is one of unsurpassed richness and splendor, worthy of a great nation. The design has sometimes been criticized for tameness and want of the picturesque irregularity of outline so characteristic of Gothic building, but any faults it may have are amply compensated for by its beauties, and the impetus which the edifice has given to the sister arts of Painting, Sculpture, and Architecture.

BARTLETT, William Henry, an English artist and author, born in Kentish Town, Middlesex, March 26, 1809; died on board the steamer Egyptus, between Malta and Marseilles, September 13, 1854. Mr. Bartlett, when a youth, evinced great taste for drawing, and was placed by his parents, in 1823, with John Britton, the antiquarian, with whom his business was to travel about England making highly finished water-color drawings of the various ancient buildings, ruins, and remains of all kinds, illustrated in the richly embellished publications of that gentleman. In this employment Mr. Bartlett acquired a wonderful facility of execution, combined with rare truthfulness of detail, and accuracy in rendering the natural expression of the scenes represented. He afterwards travelled most extensively through nearly all the countries of Europe, Eastern Asia, and North Africa, including four voyages to America, engaged in the preparation of drawings for the embellishment of illustrated works on the scenery of various countries. Many of his tours were accompanied by Dr. Beattie, who generally contributed the letter-press. Mr. Bartlett's series extends to nineteen volumes in quarto, embracing over one thousand fine steel engravings, made entirely from his finished drawings. On the production of one of these works alone—Scotland—in 2 vols. 4to, forty thousand pounds were expended by the publishers. No works of art were ever so extensively circulated, and the effect on public taste has been in the highest degree beneficial. Mr.

Bartlett afterwards, still continuing his travels, brought out a series of books, both written and illustrated by himself, the most popular of which are "Walks about Jerusalem" (1844), "The Nile Boat" (1849), "The Pilgrim Fathers" (1853); and he was engaged in the collection of material for others, at the time of his death. Mr. Bartlett's works were principally executed in water colors, and rank high as specimens of that style; in number they probably exceed those of any other artist of the day.

BEHNES, William, an English sculptor, born in London, 1794, died there, January 7, 1864. His father was a Hanoverian, a pianoforte maker, who married an English wife and settled in London. He was at first intended to follow his father's trade, and became a remarkably skillful workman. His taste for the arts was however very decided, and determining on leaving home, he supported himself for some time as a portrait painter, with unusual success, and in after life frequently expressed his regret at having abandoned the brush for the chisel and mallet. His first works in sculpture were universally admired, and brought to the artist the most exalted patronage in the kingdom. He was distinguished by various members of the Royal family, and was equally favored by commissions from public bodies for statues, monuments, &c. His busts of Lord Lyndhurst, Clarkson, Mr. Grote, Mr. D'Israeli, and others, are of very high character. He was especially famous for his marble portraitures of children. He executed several colossal statues, the best of them being that of Dr. Babington, in St. Paul's Cathedral, and one of Sir Robert Peel, for the city of London. Early success had an unfortunate effect on Mr. Behnes; it led him into expenses from which he never recovered, and though constantly engaged in the production of works that commanded a high price, and possessing great rapidity of execution, he gradually grew more and more embarrassed, and at last died in Middlesex Hospital. In the number of his works he probably exceeds any other modern sculptor, and many of them will preserve his reputation as one of the first of the time for clearness of conception and vigor of execution.

BROCKEDON, William, an English landscape painter, born at Totnes in Devonshire, October 13, 1787, died in London, August 29, 1854. Mr. Brockedon showed in early life a decided taste for art, and first came to London as a student of the Royal Academy in 1809. He afterwards visited France and Italy for purposes of study, and exhibited at the Royal Academy and British Institution several historical paintings of Scripture subjects with great success. In 1824 he made an excursion to the Alps, for the purpose of investigating the route of Hannibal. This journey suggested his great work, "The Passes of the Alps," in 2 vols. 4to. He also published a splendid illustrated folio, "Italy," embellished with engravings from his paintings. The last year in which he exhibited his pictures at the Royal Academy was 1836. His paintings are distinguished by bold and correct drawing, particularly of mountain forms, and great truth of effect. Mr. Brockedon was, in addition to his abilities as an artist, celebrated for his scientific acquirements, and his name is connected with many popular inventive processes now in general use.

CAMPBELL, Thomas, an English sculptor, born at Edinburgh, May 1, 1790, died in London, February 12, 1858. His parents being in humble circumstances, he was apprenticed to a marble cutter, but displayed so much intelligence and taste in that employment, that a gentleman for whom he had put up a chimney-piece furnished him with means to study in London, at the Royal Academy schools. Here his improvement was rapid, and in 1818 he visited Italy. He resided at Rome some years, and executed there a statue of the Princess Pauline Borghese, sister of Napoleon I., for the Duke of Devonshire, which attracted much notice and secured him numerous commissions. The statue is now at Chatsworth. On Campbell's return to London he was much engaged in monumental sculpture, and was successful in obtaining the execution of many public works both in Scotland and England. His statue of Mrs. Siddons, of the heroic size, placed in Westminster Abbey, is one of his most admired works, from the elevated expression and character given to her features. He executed for her Majesty busts of Earl Grey and the Duke of Wellington, and was more employed by the nobility than any sculptor of the time. Among his public works are statues of the Duke of York (on the Castle Hill), and Lord Hopetown, at Edinburgh, and of Lord George Bentinck, in Cavendish Square. In St. Paul's Cathedral, London, are some of his finest productions.

CANINA, Luigi, an Italian architect and archæologist, born at Rome, 1790, died at Florence, October 17, 1856. He was educated as an architect, and early became remarkable for his devotion to the remains of ancient architectural art in his native country, to the illustration of which almost his whole life was devoted. His first important work was a general history of ancient architecture, comprising the Egyptian, Greek, and Roman, in three folio volumes of plates, and nine octavos of text. The ancient Basilican churches of Northern Italy next engaged his attention, and after them the edifices of classical Rome, and the Campagna, especially the Forum, and on them he has left behind him a series of volumes unsurpassed or perhaps unequalled, in their peculiar department, by the productions of any other single individual. Canina had traveled much in Europe, and studied on the sites themselves the monuments of Greece and Sicily. He was director of the Museum of the Capitol, with the title of *Commendatore*, and ranked as such among the Forty Nobles of Rome. In 1849 he received the royal gold medal of the Institute of British artists. His death occurred as he was on his return to Rome, from a prolonged stay in England. He was devoted to the study of art for its own sake, and during his life was the highest authority on classical subjects of the Italian school of archæologists. His days were passed among the monuments now inseparably connected with his name by the successful labors of a life of study.

CHALON, Alfred Edward, R. A., an English painter, born in Geneva, 1777, died at Hampstead, October 3, 1860. The family of Chalon was of Swiss extraction. He was the brother of John Chalon, also a Royal Academician, and early in life devoted himself to water-color painting. His portraits executed in that style are remarkable for grace and refinement, so that for many years he enjoyed almost a monopoly of the feminine fashionable world. They have been largely reproduced by engraving, particularly during the reign of favor of the illustrated gift books known as "Annuals." His pictures were first exhibited in 1810. In 1816 he was elected member the Royal Academy, and the products of his free and sparkling pencil were seen annually at its exhibitions for nearly half a century. He was by Queen Victoria appointed "portrait painter to her Majesty," and was the first artist to whom she sat after she ascended the throne. He lived on terms of great intimacy with Leslie, and was generally popular with his brother artists. He left behind him a large collection of his own works.

CHALON, John J., R. A., an English painter, died at an advanced age in London, November 14, 1854. Mr. Chalon was regularly educated to art, and as a painter was conspicuous for great range of subject. He was equally at home in figures, animals, landscapes, and marine views. In 1820 he published a series of sketches of Parisian manners, that was very popular. He was fond of the scenery of Switzerland, and one of his most admired works is a View of the Castle of Chillon. He was one of the founders, and for forty years a regular attendant at the meetings of a sketching society, which, during six months of the year, met alternately at the houses of its members. The designs he made on these occasions exceed one thousand in number, and are remarkable for fertility and readiness of conception, and for masterly compositions of form, and light and shadow. Mr. Chalon was at his death one of the oldest of the Royal Academicians. A collection of one hundred and twenty of his pictures was formed and exhibited at the Gallery of the Society of Arts. Shortly after his death a notice of his life was written by Leslie, and published in the "The Art Journal."

CLINT, George, A. R. A., an English engraver and painter, born in London, April 12, 1770; died May 10, 1854. Mr. Clint's youth was passed in great privations, and his career is a striking instance of the power of perseverance to overcome untoward obstacles. He was originally apprenticed to a fishmonger, but was treated so brutally by his master that he ran away and found employment in a lawyer's office. From thence he took to house painting. During this time he married. Many years passed and great family privations were endured before he could establish himself as a miniature painter. In this occupation he was partially successful, when an acquaintance with Mr. Edward Bell, a mezzotinto engraver, initiated him into the mysteries of that art, which he afterwards practised with eminent success. His first oil painting, a portrait of his wife, brought him the favorable notice of Sir William Beechey, Sir Thomas Lawrence, and other influential artists of the day. A favorable turn was given to his fortunes by his receiving a commission to engrave a fine and popular picture, The Kemble Family, by Harlowe, containing portraits of Mrs. Siddons, John and Charles Kemble, &c. So successful was the print that three separate plates were required to supply the demand. It ranks high among works of its class, no engraver being more happy in truly rendering the touch of the painter than Mr. Clint. This engraving introduced him to a large theatrical connection, and led to his adoption of the class of art which chiefly occupied the remainder of his professional life. His series of fine dramatic pictures, of cabinet size, representing scenes from acting dramas of the day, including character portraits of the most eminent performers, has no rivals in the English school of painting, except the works of Zoffany, in the last century, and to them Clint's paintings are every way superior in composition, richness of coloring, and mastery over expression. Among the actors thus delineated for posterity are Munden, Kean, Wm. Farren, Knight, Harley, Young, Fawcett, Matthews, Liston, Miss Tree, Clara Fisher, Miss Foote, Mme. Vestris, &c., &c. Mr. Clint was an associate of the Royal Academy for sixteen years, but resigned the rank on being improperly passed over in the election for Academicians. He was one of the founders of the Artists' Benevolent and Annuity Fund, and was always ready to befriend young artists in struggles similar to those he had successfully emerged from. One of his pictures, a scene from Shakspeare, is in the British National Gallery, forming part of the Vernon donation, and many others are in the collection of the Garrick Club.

COCKERELL, Charles Robert, R. A., an English architect, born in London, 1788; died there 1863. His father was an architect of eminence, in whose office his preliminary professional studies were made. In 1809 he became chief assistant to to Sir Robert Smirke, then engaged in rebuilding Covent Garden Theatre. He was desirous of studying in a wider field, and in 1810 embarked for the East (as the Continent was then closed for Englishmen), being intrusted by the Secretary of State with despatches for the ambassador at Constantinople. His residence abroad, principally in Greece, Asia Minor, and Italy, was remarkable for the success which attended his archæological researches and excavations—the Ægina marbles, now in the Glyptothek at Munich, and the Phigaleian marbles, in the British Museum, being both discovered by Mr. Cockerell and the party with whom he was associated. On his return to England in 1817, he established himself professionally in London, and met with a large share of employment. His predilection for the classical styles of architecture was very marked. Most of the buildings designed by him show his devotion to Roman and Italian models. The University Galleries at Oxford, the London and Westminster Bank, the Sun Fire Office, London, are among his best-known works. He was elected Royal Academician in 1836, and succeeded Mr. Wilkins as Professor of Architecture to the Royal Academy, where his course of lectures was annually delivered. He was one of the eight foreign members of the Institute of France. Shortly before his death he completed and published a splendid work in folio, that had been more than thirty years in preparation, "The Temple of Jupiter Panhellenius at Ægina," descriptive of his explorations in Greece and its Islands.

COLLINS, William, R. A., an English painter, born in London, September 18, 1787; died there February 7, 1847. His father was a picture dealer, and friend of Morland, the painter, whose life he afterwards wrote; and when his son began to show a fondness for art, his early attempts were benefited by Morland's advice and example. In

1807 he entered as a student at the Royal Academy, and the same year exhibited two small pictures. From that time, with the exception of two years, when he was in Italy, his paintings were seen at every Academy exhibition for the remaining nine-and-thirty years of his life. This fact will show the steadiness with which he worked, and the constancy of his efforts in the pursuit of the excellence that he finally attained to. His father's death, in 1812, threw the young painter on his own resources, and for a time he was glad to paint portraits, as the readiest means of securing an income, but he gradually worked out his peculiar style of landscape and rustic groups, and year by year became more celebrated as a truthful and picturesque delineator of English rural life and scenery. In 1814 he was elected Associate, and in the same year exhibited his first marine picture, a Coast Scene. This was received with so much favor that subjects of the same description henceforth occupied a large portion of his professional career. He became Academician in 1820. In 1836 Mr. Collins visited Italy, and devoted two years to the careful study of the works of the great masters as well as the striking features exhibited by the modern aspect of the land and the people. On his return he adventured in a higher branch of art, historical painting, and produced some scenes from the Gospel history, that did credit to his talents, though they wanted the unique charm that attended his representations of more familiar life and nature. He had the wisdom to continue the practice of the style in which he was unrivaled, and never enjoyed more popularity than during the last three or four years of his life. As an artist his technical merits are high. He had an excellent eye for form, chiaroscuro, and color. He never slighted the execution of a picture, but always painted with the utmost conscientiousness, and with a perpetual reference to the truth of nature. His sympathy with child-life in all its varieties of aspect marks the amiable and genial character of the man, and gives to his pictures of rustic urchins a completeness and air of enjoyment that is scarcely found in the works of any other painter since Murillo. His life was written by his son, William Wilkie Collins (in 1848), who is distinguished as a novelist; another son, Charles Allston Collins, is a painter of repute, and author of several books of travels, &c.

COX, David, an English water-color painter, born in Birmingham, 1783; died there June 7, 1859. His father was a smith, and for some time the son worked as a lad at the same business. However, not being robust enough for the employment, he turned his attention to drawing, and was employed in ornamenting some of the manufactured articles for which that town is famous. At this occupation he continued until the Birmingham Theatre, then under the management of the elder Macready, wanted a scene painter, and Cox received the appointment. With the company—a migratory one—he travelled to the principal towns in the midland counties, and having visited London, was employed in a similar capacity at Astley's Amphitheatre. His parents being opposed to his connexion with the stage, he relinquished it, and set to work making drawings, which he offered to dealers and purchasers wherever he could find them. He also taught drawing, and for three years was engaged at Hereford giving lessons to the pupils in a boarding school. Here began his acquaintance with the scenery of Wales, that exercised so marked an influence on his future career as an artist. Returning to London, he slowly emerged into notice as a most truthful delineator of English landscape, in all its varying incidents of storm and sunshine, mist, rain, and tempest. He exhibited some oil paintings, but his attention was almost wholly given to water colors, and he was one of the early members of the society established for its promotion. For more than thirty years, his constant place of resort was Bettwys y Coèd, a small hamlet in the wildest district of the Welsh Mountains, and as the sketching ground of David Cox, the whole neighborhood grew familiar to artists. Mr. Ruskin celebrates "the looseness, coolness, and moisture of his herbage, the rustling, crumpled freshness of his broad-leaved weeds, the play of pleasant light across his deep-heathered moor or flashing sand, the melting of fragments of white mist into the dropping blue above,—all this has not been fully rendered except by him." A steady and conscientious worker, Mr. Cox executed a large number of paintings, which are in great demand, and bring high prices. In 1814, he published a work on landscape painting, now very scarce. An exhibition of his collected works, loaned by their various possessors, was open in London at the time of his death; this took place after an illness of two or three days only, as the painter, though in his seventy-sixth year, practised his art to the last. His personal character was simple and unassuming, and marked by intense devotion to his art.

CRAWFORD, Thomas, an American sculptor, born in New York, March 22, 1814; died in London, October 10, 1857. His early taste for the Fine Arts was encouraged by his father, who placed him in the establishment of a carver in wood. His talents for sculpture here developed so rapidly that he attended the school of the National Academy of Design, and entered the studio of Frazee and Launitz, monumental sculptors, of New York. After spending two years there, by the advice of his friends, he determined to visit Italy, and arrived at Rome in the summer of 1835. He was furnished with an introduction to Thorwaldsen, and the kindness of the Danish sculptor made up for the slender supply of means with which he had undertaken this journey. He invited Crawford to work in his studio, an offer that was gladly accepted, and by unremitting application to study and intense earnestness in his profession, he gradually made himself a name among the artists of Rome, and was intrusted with commissions for portrait busts and copies in marble. In 1839, having previously executed a few original subjects, he designed his "Orpheus," a statue that first brought him into notice in America, and was warmly praised by Gibson and Thorwaldsen. A subscription was raised in Boston under the auspices of Mr. Charles Sumner, for its execution in marble. It is now in the Gallery of the Boston Athenæum. The reception of this fine and classical work in America excited unusual enthusiasm in the artist's favor, and commissions for mythological and historical subjects enabled him to devote more time to ideal compositions; while his studio at Rome became the resort of art amateurs from all countries. In 1844, he revisited America, and married Miss Louisa Ward, of New York. He shortly returned to Italy, and with the exception of two brief residences in the United States in 1849 and 1856, spent the remainder of his life abroad. His artistic position at Rome was a very distinguished one, and is illustrated by the production of many fine works that will perpetuate his name and talents. One of the most remarkable of these is the statue of Beethoven, executed for the Music Hall at Boston. It was cast in bronze at the Royal Foundry, Munich, and deposited in its destined place at the expense of Mr. C. C. Perkins of Boston. In 1849, the State of Virginia issued proposals for the erection of a monument to Washington at Richmond. The design sent in by Mr. Crawford was unanimously adopted. Its principal feature was a colossal equestrian statue of Washington, twenty-five feet in height, placed on a pedestal resting on a star-shaped elevation, with six rays or points, on which were to stand statues of Patrick Henry, Jefferson, Lee, and other distinguished Virginians. The central figure was cast at Munich under the artist's superintendence, and was placed on the Capitol Hill, Richmond, in 1858. The remaining statues were in progress at the time of the artist's death. Important works for the Capitol at Washington also engaged his attention, including a colossal statue of the "Genius of America," intended to be placed on the pinnacle of the central dome. His career, however, was interrupted by an obscure disease of the brain, which baffled the skill of the most accomplished medical men of Europe, and in a few months put an end to his life. Mr. Crawford executed more than sixty works, many of them colossal, in marble, and left a large collection of models, sketches, &c., which were presented to the City of New York by his widow. He ranks highest among American sculptors, and left no branch of his art unpractised, or without trophies of his success.

DANBY, Francis, A. R. A., an English painter, born in Dublin, November 16, 1793; died at Exmouth, Devonshire, February 10, 1861. Having shown an early taste for drawing, he determined, with the reluctant consent of his parents, to follow the fine arts as a profession, and commenced his studies at the Dublin Society of Arts. He began oil painting when about eighteen, and sent a picture to the Dublin exhibition, A Sunset. It was purchased by a clergyman for fifteen guineas. With this sum he and a fellow student started for London, with an introduction to West, the president of the Royal Academy. He received them kindly, affording them the means of seeing all that interested them connected with art. On their return home, when at Bristol, their funds proved to be sufficient only for the passage of one to Ireland. Danby decided to stay, and in a short time met with great success as a teacher of painting, and was in the receipt of a large income, by the ready sale of his pictures to local amateurs. His first picture at the Royal Academy Exhibition, Sunset after a Storm, appeared in 1824, and was purchased by Sir Thomas Lawrence, who gave the painter double the price he asked for it. He continued to exhibit for many years: his most celebrated picture, The Opening of the Sixth Seal, was bought by Mr. Beckford, from the exhibition of 1828. From 1830 to 1840 he resided abroad, in Paris and Switzerland, and for the last twenty years of his life in Devonshire. He was elected Associate of the Royal Academy in 1825. In many of his earlier paintings, Danby rivals John Martin in his mastery over terrible and supernatural effects, and the choice of his subjects is of the same Scriptural character. Latterly he subsided into a quieter style of poetical and classical landscape, in which his fine taste, brilliant coloring, and facility of execution were very conspicuous. He had a genius for mechanics, and patented several useful inventions.

DAVID, Jean Pierre (D'Angers), a French sculptor, born at Angers, March 12, 1793, died at Paris, January 6, 1856. The father of David was a sculptor in wood, but fared so badly that he was violently opposed to the indulgence of his son's artistic tastes. With much difficulty he made his way to Paris, at the age of eighteen, with nine francs in his pocket, and soon after entered the studio of his namesake, David the painter, but his natural bias for sculpture continuing, he sought the instruction of Roland the sculptor, and, after gaining several academical prizes, was sent, in 1811, to Italy, where he studied five years, and attracted the attention of Canova. On his return from Rome, he was unwilling to settle in the capital under the Bourbons, and made an unsuccessful attempt to establish himself in England. Returning to Paris, he set earnestly to work, leaving politics to take care of themselves, and commenced a career of artistic employment that placed him among the first sculptors of the day. Many public and monumental works were intrusted to him throughout France, and his bust and medallion portraits are more numerous than those of any modern artist. In 1825 the king conferred on him the cross of the Legion of Honor. He was a member of the Institute, and professor at the Académie des Beaux Arts. The famous statue of Gutenberg, the first printer, at Strasbourg, is a favorable specimen of the style of his groups and figures. He was remarkable for earnestness and enthusiasm in his art: these were the great features of his character, and bore him onward to success.

DECAMPS, Alexander Gabriel, a French painter, born in Paris, March, 1803, killed by a fall from a horse in the forest of Fontainebleau, August 23, 1860. He was educated in the studio of Abel de Pujol, and early in life traveled in the East, whence he returned with an immense number of picturesque sketches, that afforded him material for many of his best works. He commenced exhibiting at the Salon in 1827, and became from that time one of the most popular artists of the French school, particularly in the style known as "genre" painting. His oriental subjects are remarkable for depicting the peculiar Turk and Arab physiognomy and rich costume, with a facile and brilliant pencil. He also painted subjects from familiar life, scenes from Don Quixote, Gil Blas, &c., and capriccios, or grotesque pictures, in which monkeys take the place of men, as painters, amateurs, cooks, &c., with great power of physiognomical expression. His large historical pictures are fewer in number, but of a very high class for originality of conception, vigor of execution, and mastery of chiaro-scuro. One of the principal of these is The Defeat of the Cimbri, exhibited at the great "exposition" of 1855, at Paris, with sixty others from the same hand. Decamps worked with great facility, and was equally at home with every species of painting or drawing implement. He was nominated chevalier of the Legion of Honor in 1839. His death occurred while hunting in the forest of Fontainebleau, where he was residing for the sake of his health.

DELACROIX, Ferdinand Victor Eugene, a French painter, born at Charenton, in 1798, died at Paris, August 13, 1863. His father, a member of the Revolutionary National Convention, filled several important posts under the Republic and Consulate, and intended his son for official life, but his taste for the fine arts was too decided to approve of that career, and at the age of eighteen he entered the studio of P. Guerin as a pupil. There he worked steadily and perseveringly. His first picture, Dante and Virgil Crossing the Styx, was so opposed to the reigning classicality of taste in its choice of subject and treatment, that, by the advice of his master Guerin, he refrained from exhibiting it. The Romantic School, however, daily gained favor, and in 1824, Delacroix's painting, The Massacre of Scio, was received with acclamation, and honored with a medal from the jury of the exhibition. His reputation from this time progressively increased, and his historical pictures were accounted among the glories of the modern French school. In 1831 he paid a visit to the East, the influence of which is visible in his later paintings of Scriptural subjects. At the great Paris Exhibition of 1855, Delacroix exhibited no less than thirty-five of his principal works. His historical compositions are most masterly; his drawing is vigorous and true, and in daring boldness of conception and execution reminds one of Rubens. He was buried with much pomp in Père la Chaise.

DELAROCHE, Paul, a French historical painter, born in Paris, 1797; died there, November 3, 1856. He commenced the study of art as a landscape painter, but relinquished this department on entering the studio of Baron Gros, then the most distinguished historical painter of the day. Delaroche early took a dislike to the classicism then prevalent in the French school; and determined to create a style for himself more in harmony with the age. His first picture, Naphthali in the Desert, was exhibited in 1819, but attracted little attention. In 1824 he obtained the gold medal for a picture of The Examination of Joan of Arc in Prison, and continued to increase in popularity during the whole of his artistic career. Many of his most popular paintings were drawn from events recorded in English history, as The Children of Edward IV. in the Tower, The Death of Queen Elizabeth (in the Louvre), Cromwell contemplating the body of Charles I. (owned by the Earl of Ellesmere), Charles I. in the Guard Room, and Lord Strafford going to Execution (in the Duke of Sutherland's Gallery), and many others. Three years of his life were devoted to the adorning of the Amphitheatre of the Fine Art School (Ecole des Beaux Arts) at Paris. His work is known as the "Hemicycle," covering the semicircular space fronting the auditory. Here he has represented the great painters, sculptors, and architects from the earliest time down to the present. From the centre, where Apelles, Phidias, and Ictinus are enthroned as the representatives of the arts of ancient Greece, the great sculptors and architects are ranged in groups, the painters occupying the extremities. The painting never fails to excite admiration for its elevated style, sobriety and refinement of treatment, and simple and effective arrangement and execution. In 1855, on his first visit to Italy, Delaroche married the only daughter of Horace Vernet, the Director of the French Academy at Rome. He returned to Italy in 1844 for a short time, and painted some fine portraits. One of the most striking of his recent works is Napoleon musing at Fontainebleau, but of late years he had almost withdrawn from the practice of his profession. Delaroche stands at the head of the modern French historical school of painting. Dramatic in his conceptions, and simple and truthful in expressing them, his paintings strike the spectator with an air of reality and an utter absence of the conventional treatment in vogue at the time of his appearance in art. His drawing is correct, and his coloring equal to that of any of the French school. As a teacher Delaroche was very popular. He attracted around him a large number of pupils from other countries as well as France, and knew how to inspire them with his own enthusiasm for art. Delaroche was a member of the Institute (1832) and an officer of the Legion of Honor. His head and face had much resemblance to the Emperor Napoleon. In social circles his influence was very great, and it was always exerted in furtherance of the objects of his beloved art. Most of his historical pictures have been engraved, and are well known throughout Europe.

DYCE, William, R. A., a British painter, born at Aberdeen, 1806, died February 14, 1864. He was the son of a physician of local celebrity, and, being intended by his father for a learned profession, studied at the University of the town, and took the degree of M. D. His early passion for art proved, however, too strong for his father's intentions, and he left Aberdeen for the purpose of entering the school of the Royal Academy in the metropolis. The departure of a friend, who admired his talents, for Italy, gave him an opportunity of visiting that country in 1825, and he studied there, with a brief exception, till his return to Scotland in 1828. His first picture, the Education of Bacchus, was exhibited at the Royal Academy in 1829. While residing in Rome, he painted a Madonna and Child that gained the applause of Overbeck, and attracted much attention from foreign artists. The style of art that Mr. Dyce had adopted while abroad was so little understood and met with such limited sympathy at home, that he actually laid down his pencil for some time, and applied himself to scientific pursuits. A new field of occupation was opened to him, however, in portraiture, which he successfully practised in Edinburgh till the year 1837. He was shortly afterwards attracted to the subject of the best means of applying the arts of design to the improvement of manufactures, and made a mission of inquiry to the art schools of the Continent at the request of the President of the Board of Trade. His report was printed by Parliament, and led to the remodeling of the schools of design, Mr. Dyce becoming a Director and Secretary to the Council under the new organization. His official connection with these institutions lasted about five years, during which his profession was almost entirely neglected. At the end of the time he reapplied himself vigorously to art, going systematically "to school" at the Life Academy in company with his friend Etty. The results of his application were readily seen in his easel pictures, cartoons, and frescos. He was one of the six artists selected to embellish the House of Lords in the New Palace at Westminster. His fresco, The Baptism of King Ethelbert, was completed in 1846, and by its success led to the use of that material for the artistic decoration of that structure. He was afterwards engaged in frescos for Buckingham Palace and Osborne House by desire of Prince Albert, and at the time of his death was occupied in painting in the Queen's Robing Room at the Houses of Parliament a series of frescos on subjects afforded by the "Morte d'Arthur." His application to these laborious works in great measure prevented the completion of easel pictures, but Mr. Dyce occasionally exhibited paintings that grew in public estimation from their high qualities of drawing, purity of color, and intensity of spiritual expression, which gradually overcame the indifference that was at first created by the severe and archaic style that he most generally adopted. He was one of the most accomplished men of the day in all that related to the fine arts. In church music he was a proficient, and published several works that promoted the revival of ancient sacred music. He is one of the few English artists whose reputation is widely spread on the Continent of Europe.

EGG, Augustus Leopold, R. A., an English painter, born in London in 1816, died at Algiers, March 26, 1863. His determination to become a painter was fixed soon after leaving school, and he was regularly educated to art in a private studio and at the schools of the Royal Academy. His first pictures were sent to provincial exhibitions. In 1838, one of his paintings was admitted to the Academy Exhibition. Ten years after he was elected an Associate, and in 1861, Academician. His subjects were generally selected from English history, about the Stuart period, or from well-known sources, such as Gil Blas, Shakspeare, &c. They exhibited great discrimination in the delineation of character, pure and harmonious coloring, and a free and delicate touch. Among the most admired are Pepys' Introduction to Nell Gwynne, the Life and Death of Buckingham, the Night before Naseby, and Catharine and Petruchio. Mr. Egg's health was always delicate, and frequently compelled him to abstain from painting, so that the number of pictures he executed is not large. He twice visited the East, and derived much benefit from the change of climate; but on his return to England from his second oriental tour, he fell a victim to a sudden attack at Algiers. He was the friend and associate of Dickens in the amateur theatrical performances for the endowment of a benevolent institution, and was universally beloved for the active philanthropy that he displayed in behalf of less flourishing members of his profession.

ETTY, William, R. A., an English historical painter, born at York, March 10, 1787; died there November 13, 1849. His father was a miller and baker in the city of York, and young Etty assisted in his shop until his twelfth year, when he was apprenticed to a painter at Hull. Here, through opposition and discouragement of all kinds, his taste for drawing was developed by stealthy exercise. At the end of a most irksome seven-years term of uncongenial labor, he went to London on the invitation of an uncle. This relative was a man of intelligence and liberality. Etty was introduced to Fuseli, and entered as a student at the Royal Academy schools in 1807. Shortly after he became an indoor pupil of Sir Thomas Lawrence, then in the height of his reputation, his uncle paying the hundred guineas required as a premium. From Lawrence he had little direct instruction, but derived facility of execution from seeing his method of painting and copying his pictures. In 1811 his first picture was exhibited at the Royal Academy, Telemachus Rescuing Antiope; but it made no sensation, and though he every year sent paintings to the British Institution and Academy Exhibitions, it was not until 1820 that any picture attracted much notice, when the Coral Finders, Venus and her Nymphs arriving at Paphos, was greatly admired. This was the first of what afterwards proved a long series of representations of the undraped feminine form in subjects suggested by classical poetry or legend. It was followed next year by Cleopatra's Arrival in Cilicia, which led to many commissions from patrons in art. Having achieved success, Etty visited Italy and studied at Venice for seven months the coloring of the great masters of the Venetian school. On his return to England a succession of important works followed, confirming him in the good graces of the public. He was elected Associate of the Royal Academy in 1824, and Academician in 1828. Little occurred to break the tenor of his life, which was devoted to art. His days were spent in painting, and his evenings during the academic session in making studies in oil from the models in the life school of the Academy; this practice he continued until the last year of his professional career. In 1848 failing health induced him to retire to his native city, but he only survived the change about a year. Soon after his death a collection of his paintings was made and exhibited at the rooms of the Society of Arts in honor of his genius. It comprised 130 paintings, many of them of very large size. Three of his finest works, the Judith Series, The Combat, and Benaiah, were purchased by the Royal Scottish Academy. The National Gallery possesses but one of his pictures. They are mostly in private collections, and among the most highly valued modern works of art. Etty is undoubtedly one of the greatest names of the modern English school. Though not a classical scholar, his choice of subjects from Greek and Roman history or mythology was almost exclusive, on account of the opportunity they afforded him for the display of the undraped human form, which he properly regarded as the highest development of art. As a colorist and painter of flesh he is unrivaled by any modern artists. The apparent freedom of his subjects frequently led to imputations on his character and motives that were entirely unfounded, as the painter was one of the purest and most simple-minded of men. Though always in love, he never was married, a niece regulating his household. His Life was written by Mr. Gilchrist, 2 vols. 8vo, Lond. 1855.

FIELDING, Copley Vandyke, an English

painter, born in 1787, died at Worthing, February 3, 1855. Mr. Fielding belonged to a family of artists, and first exhibited a picture in 1810. He practised landscape painting in oil and water colors, until the growing popularity of his drawings led to his confining himself to the latter branch of art exclusively. He was for many years president of the Society of Painters in Water Colors, and his position was generally recognized as that of head and representative of that art in England. Copley Fielding's subjects were drawn from nature, and, as true and simple renderings of natural scenery, have never been surpassed. A favorite class of subjects with him was afforded by the broad chalk-downs of Kent and Sussex on the southern coast of England, where a rich expanse of verdure is relieved by glimpses of the near or remote ocean, and sunny slopes of woodland in the hollows of the hills. Stormy marine views, including shipwrecks, &c., were also treated by him in a masterly manner. For general breadth of effect, delicate aerial tones, and pure and exquisite color, he is unrivaled. His drawing is of inferior quality. His manipulative facility enabled him to execute a large number of works. They are in great demand, and command higher prices than those of any of his cotemporaries, except J. W. M. Turner. At the sale of Mr. Bicknell's Gallery in 1863, a drawing, Cranborough Hill, which cost 25 guineas, sold for 760 guineas.

FINDEN, William and Edward, English engravers. The former, born in London, 1787, died there September 20, 1852. The latter, born in 1792, died February 9, 1857. The brothers Finden were both educated for the profession they adopted under the charge of Mr. James Mitan, the eminent engraver. Many of their works were executed in common, and it is difficult to appropriate the separate share of each. William Finden was the better engraver of the two. His plate from Sir Thomas Lawrence's portrait of George IV. is one of his finest works. He received for it 2000 guineas, a sum unparalleled for a portrait. His engravings from Wilkie's Village Festival and Smirke's Illustrations to Don Quixote were much admired. At the time when the popularity of the Annuals had caused a demand for small engravings of high finish, the two brothers established a complete manufactory for the production of line engravings, from whence issued the landscape and portrait illustrations of Lord Byron's Works, landscape illustrations of the Bible and the Waverley Novels, Heroines of the Poets, Beauties of Thomas Moore, and various other works that met with extensive popularity, and did much to diffuse a knowledge of art among the middle classes of England. A larger and more expensive undertaking of a higher nature, Finden's Royal Gallery of British Art, proved unsuccessful as a speculation, and its failure clouded the latter days of both brothers by sweeping away the fruits of all their previous labor.

GORDON, Sir John Watson, R. A., a Scotch painter, born in Edinburgh in 1790, died there June 1st, 1864. He studied art in the Academy of Trustees for the Encouragement of Manufactures, where Wilkie and many eminent Scottish artists received early instruction. His first desire was to become a historical painter, but he subsequently relinquished that pursuit, devoting himself exclusively, or nearly so, to portraiture. In this branch he attained an excellence second to none of his time. The vigor and power of his pencil was displayed in the portraits of almost all of his countrymen of renown. Among the best known examples, are his fine pictures of Dr. Chalmers, Sir Walter Scott, De Quincey, George Combe, Professor Simpson, and many others. In 1827, Gordon first commenced to exhibit his works in London at the Royal Academy, and continued to do so until his death. In 1841 he was elected Associate, and in 1851, Royal Academician. In 1859, on the death of Sir William Allan, he was appointed President of the Royal Scottish Academy, and was knighted on the occasion by Queen Victoria. Gordon never studied in London, and scarcely ever left his native country. His talents as an artist were only equalled by his urbanity and kindly disposition. Under him the Scottish Academy greatly advanced in character and usefulness.

GREENOUGH, Horatio. An American sculptor, born in Boston, September 6th, 1808, died in its vicinity December 18th, 1852. He entered Harvard College at the age of sixteen, but had already modelled in clay and attempted sculpture. There he enjoyed the friendship and advice of Allston, and produced the design of the Bunker Hill Monument. In 1825 he started for Rome, and improved himself by practice and observation among the sculptors of that city. A brief visit to Boston in 1826 was put to professional service, and afforded him an opportunity of modelling busts of John Quincy Adams, Chief Justice Marshall, &c. The next year he returned to Europe and established himself permanently at Florence. His Chanting Cherubs, executed in marble there for James Fenimore Cooper, was the first original group from the chisel of an American sculptor. In 1831 he went to Paris to model the bust of Lafayette, and shortly after received a commission from Congress to execute his colossal statue of Washington. This was finished in 1843, and now stands in front of the national Capitol. Many statues, bas reliefs, &c., were sculptured by him for private parties. The Athenæum Gallery at Boston possesses one of his finest works, the Venus Victrix. In 1851 he returned to the United States to superintend the placing in its position at Washington of a symbolical group of the triumph of civilization, The Rescue, commissioned for the Capitol. Vexatious delays and hindrances brought on an attack of brain fever, which was fatal to Mr. Greenough, shortly after he had commenced a course of lectures on Art at Boston. A memorial of Horatio Greenough was published in 1853 by H. T. Tuckerman.

GWILT, Joseph, an English architect, born in Southwark, January 17th, 1784, died at Henley-on-Thames, September 14th, 1863. He was educated at St. Paul's School, and in 1801 was admitted a student at the Royal Academy. A few years after he visited Italy, and on his return commenced practice as an architect in London. He was much employed by the city and corporation of London, and executed many designs for halls, insurance offices, and other public buildings. To the public generally he was better known as an author, and produced many books that were accepted as standard authorities in his profession. The principal of these are, "Encyclopædia of Architecture, Historical, Theoretical, and Practical," 1842; "The Architecture of Vitruvius, translated," 1826; a new edition of Sir William Chambers' "Treatise on the Decorative Part of Civil Architecture," 2 volumes, 1828, and several others. He was a person of great general accomplishments in the fine arts. The Treatise on Music in the "Encyclopædia Metropolitana" is from his pen.

HARDING, James Duffield, an English painter, born at Deptford in 1797, died at Barnes, near London, December 4, 1863. He was the son of a teacher of drawing, by whom he was educated for the same profession. He received lessons from Prout, and at first adopted his style, but gradually worked out for himself a freer and bolder mode of execution, particularly as applied to trees, foliage, &c., then a novelty in the art. He gained the silver medal of the Society of Arts for a painting in water colors, at the age of eighteen. The infant art of lithography attracted at this time his attention for the facility which it afforded for perpetuating the very touches of a drawing and transferring the spirit of a sketch in chalk or pencil with a truth that no other mode of engraving afforded. For many years nearly his whole time was devoted to its practice, during which he produced numerous works that procured him great reputation at home and abroad. Among these were "Elementary Art," "Lesson on Trees," "Sketches at Home and Abroad," which are dedicated to Louis Philippe, who rewarded the artist with a magnificent set of Sevres china and a diamond ring. Mr. Harding continued at intervals the practice of water colors, and was a member of the society. About 1842 he commenced painting in oil, and was regarded as one of the first landscape painters of the day. He traveled much in Europe for many years, furnishing subjects for the "Landscape Annuals," then in the height of their popularity. He was indefatigable in the practice of his art, and by his example has exercised a very potent influence on modern English landscape painting.

HESS, Henry, a German painter, born at Dusseldorf in 1798, died there March 28, 1863. He studied in the Academy of Munich, and was pursuing his profession in Rome, when (being already favorably known by the purity and refinement of his designs) in 1826 he received an order from the King of Bavaria to undertake a series of paintings, partly in fresco, for the new church of All Saints, designed by Von Klenze, and one of the architectural ornaments of the capital. They are about fifty in number, and were executed either by himself or in conjunction with his pupils. The subjects are taken from the Old and New Testaments. They are the most important works of Hess. In them he has shown himself not unworthy of being classed with some of the old painters of sacred history. Several fine pictures of them are known by engravings in Count Raczynski's "Histoire de L'Art Moderne en Allemagne." His oil paintings are not numerous, and are held in much esteem. Hess is one of the greatest modern designers in the field of sacred art. In addition to the reverent and solemn treatment of Scripture subjects, common to the school of Overbeck and Cornelius, he displays a grace and pathos of his own that secure a marked individuality for his works. His life was characterized by the same purity and simplicity that distinguished him as an artist.

HOGAN, John, an Irish sculptor, born at Tallow, Co. Waterford, in 1801; died at Dublin, March 27, 1855. He was originally placed with an attorney at twelve years of age; but showing very little taste for that profession, at the expiration of his term he entered the office of an architect. While there he was brought more in contact with art, studied anatomy, and executed several carvings. A number of gentlemen who felt an interest in his progress raised a subscription which enabled him to visit Rome and open a studio there, from which came forth many of his best works, including his statue of O'Connell, in the Dublin Exchange, and the Drunken Faun. This was pronounced by Thorwaldsen *a miracle.* It resulted from a challenge given to Hogan by Gibson, to produce any attitude or expression in the human figure not previously appropriated by the great sculptors of antiquity. At the time of his death, he was engaged on a statue of Father Mathew, and on a bas-relief for the Wellington Monument, Phœnix Park, for which he was to receive £1000. Hogan was preëminently national in his feelings as a man and as an artist, and found ample patronage from his warm-hearted countrymen. A pension of £100 per annum was conferred on his widow by the Queen after his unexpected decease.

HUNT, William Henry, an English water-color painter, born in London, 1790; died there February 10, 1864. He was the son of a London tradesman, a tin-plate worker in Longacre, who, unwillingly yielding to the boy's love for art, placed him with John Varley, the landscape painter. Here Hunt studied zealously, painting both in oil and water colors. His easel pictures were exhibited at the Royal Academy in 1807 and subsequent years, but he gradually gave himself up exclusively to the use of water colors, and became an associate of the Water Color Society in 1824. From that time to his death little change occurred in the line of study he had marked out for himself. Two classes of subjects he equally excelled in—humorous rustic figures of children, such as are seen in English farm life; and representations of various natural objects, as a sprig of May blossom, a cluster of grapes, a hedge sparrow's nest and eggs, a bunch of primroses, &c. Critics are never weary of praising the bold handling, the breadth of general treatment, and the comic sentiment and expression of the first class, or the brilliant color, exquisite drawing, and the subtle delicacy of touch that is exhibited in his perfect fac-similes of nature's most cunning handiwork. In no other hands have the same effects ever been produced by so simple means. His works are accepted as canons of color in its brightest and most evanescent shades. Mr. Hunt was devoted to his art, and worked unintermittently during a long life, having the satisfaction of finding the great qualities of his pictures gradually more and more appreciated.

INMAN, Henry, an American painter, born in Utica, N. Y., October 20, 1801; died in New York, January 17, 1846. His taste for art was early developed. When, in 1812, his parents removed to New York, he was first able to procure regular instruction in drawing. In 1814, he was preparing to enter the Military Academy at West Point, when Jarvis, the portrait painter, offered to receive him as a pupil, and he was bound to him for seven years. He accompanied his teacher to New Orleans and other cities, and on the conclusion of his apprenticeship, he established himself as a portrait painter in New York, where he resided until his death, with the exception of a short sojourn at Philadelphia. In 1844 he visited Europe on account of his health, and painted portraits of several distinguished men. Among them are fine heads of Lord Macaulay, Dr. Chalmers, and Wordsworth the poet, executed for James Lenox, Esq., of New York, and now in his gallery. On his return to New York, he commenced a picture for the Rotunda of the Capitol at Washington, in accordance with a government commission. The subject selected by him was Daniel Boone's Cabin in the Wilds of Kentucky: he was engaged on this painting at the time of his death. Inman painted landscape and genre subjects with success, though his chief excellence lay in portraiture. Among his best-known and characteristic heads of American worthies are the fine and life-like portraits of Chief Justice Marshall, Bishop White, Nicholas Biddle, and many others. A collection of one hundred and twenty-seven of his paintings was brought together and exhibited in New York shortly after his death.

ISABEY, Jean Baptiste, a French miniature painter, born at Nancy, April 11, 1767; died at Paris, April 18, 1855. At an early age he entered the studio of David with the view of becoming a historical painter; but commencing with portraits in chalk, he met with so much success that he resolved to try whether, by carrying the principles of high art into miniature painting, he could not elevate that branch of art in popular estimation. Isabey had been intimate with Napoleon when an officer of artillery; when the Empire was founded he continued in favor, and constantly occupied, to the end of his life, the position of first miniature painter of the day. His portraits of the Napoleon family are very numerous, and his most famous works are connected with the Imperial Court, as the "Table des Marèchaux," representing Napoleon and the most illustrious of his generals, painted on a large slab of porcelain. In 1818, Isabey accepted an invitation to Russia, where he painted the Emperor Alexander and his family, &c. On his return he painted Louis XVIII. He formed a new school of miniature painting in France. Its works are remarkable for force and delicacy. His likenesses have much character and are generally esteemed faithful. They are the chief medium for perpetuating to posterity the appearance of the great men of the first Empire.

KLENZE, Leo von, a Bavarian architect, born at Hildesheim, Lower Saxony, in 1784; died at Munich, February 5, 1864. In the adoption of a profession Von Klenze had, like most other artists, to contend against the prejudices of his parents. They finally yielded, however, and placed him at the Berlin Academy, whence, as a reward for his unusual progress, he was sent on a professional tour to France, Italy, and Greece. This lasted for three years, and on his return he was appointed architect in chief to the King of Westphalia. When, in 1814, that monarch was compelled to abdicate, Von Klenze went to Munich, and there attracted the notice of Ludwig, King of Bavaria, who was then entertaining the idea of transforming his capital from a third-rate mediæval city to a modern Athens, that should eclipse any other on this side the Alps. Von Klenze eagerly seconded the King's intentions, and from his designs arose the famous buildings, the Glyptothek, the Pinacothek, the Maximilian Palace, &c., now of European celebrity. The Walhalla, near Ratisbon, dedicated to the memory of the illustrious men of Fatherland, was also one of his works, and at Athens he built a splendid palace for the Bavarian prince, King Otho. Von Klenze was perfectly learned in all that related to classical architecture, and his buildings show great skill in modifying its inexorable characteristics to the requirements of modern purposes. He stood unquestionably at the head of the classical architects of the day.

LANCE, George, an English painter, born at Little Dunmow, in Essex, in 1802, died at Sunnyside, near Liverpool, June 18, 1864. Evincing when a youth a great desire to become an artist, he unceremoniously introduced himself to Haydon, the painter, who, on looking over his sketches, observed such signs of promise that he took him into his studio and gave him gratuitously for a long period all the instruction and aid in his power. His peculiar talent for the representation of objects of "still life" appeared in his execution of a group of fruit and vegetables, which attracted the notice of and was purchased by Sir George Beaumont. This brought him in commissions from other gentlemen, and contrary to the practice of his teacher he abandoned high art for a more certain and lucrative branch of painting. Though a few figure-pieces of "genre" character attest his versatility, yet the demand for his still-life pictures left him little opportunity for any other class of subjects. Though the labor bestowed on them was very great, four hundred of his paintings remain to testify to his industry and application. They are found in the best galleries of modern art, and have a very high commercial as well as artistic value. In his peculiar style, Lance rivals the chef-d'œuvres of the Flemish masters, exhibiting equal brilliancy of color and minuteness and delicacy of touch, combined with a breadth of general effect.

LEECH, John, an English artist, born in London, August 29, 1817; died at Kensington, October 29, 1864. He was brought up at the school of the Charterhouse in London, and was there a cotemporary of Thackeray, with whom he always maintained a warm friendship. On leaving school, his parents articled him to a surgical practitioner, with the purpose of bringing him up to medicine. While walking the hospitals and going through the routine of a medical education, his talent for humorous sketching became well known to his fellow students, and many of his early drawings are preserved, showing much of the ability that afterwards distinguished his maturer efforts. His first published work was produced at the age of eighteen, and was entitled "Sketches, by A. Pen, Esq." About the same time some of his drawings fell in the way of the Rev. Mr. Barham, author of "The Ingoldsby

Legends." He introduced Leech to Mr. Bentley, and an engagement was entered into between them, that caused him to give up medicine for the fine arts. Besides the monthly illustrations to "Bentley's Miscellany," he produced many other works, as "The Comic Latin and English Grammar," "The Children of the Mobility," &c. The comic periodical "Punch" was started January 17, 1841. In the fourth number, for August 7, Leech's first drawing appeared. It was nearly a year after this before he became regularly engaged for this work, which afterwards was the medium for the chief labors of his life. The number and unrivaled merit of the drawings that he furnished to "Punch" are known through the civilized world. They amount to several thousand. Six volumes of selections from them have been published. In addition to this continuous and exhaustive labor, he frequently appeared as a book illustrator. Among the best-known works from his pencil are, A. Beckett's "Comic Histories of Rome and England," Mr. Surtees' Sporting Novels, "Handley Cross," "Soapy Sponge," &c., and a multitude of smaller books. Mr. Leech was always of delicate constitution, and retiring in his habits. Unremitting professional exertions began to tell heavily on his health three or four years since. In the summer of 1864 he made a tour to Belgium and Germany, that was attended with some improvement to him, but he shortly relapsed into a distressing state of nervous irritability, and died from a sudden attack of angina pectoris. Two years before his death Leech had exhibited a series of his drawings, enlarged and colored in oil; and it was understood that he intended in future to cultivate this branch of art. No artist ever left a record of cotemporary habits, manners, sports, costumes, &c., equal to that furnished by Leech's "Sketches of Life and Character." His death is mourned as a public loss by all whom he has delighted with his genial humor.

LESLIE, Charles Robert, R. A., an English artist, born in London in 1794, died there May 5, 1859. His father was an American of Scottish descent, settled at Philadelphia as a watchmaker, who went to London with his wife and three children on a business scheme in 1793. The next year his son, the future artist, was born. In September, 1799, the family returned to America; but, owing to an adventurous voyage, during which their vessel was attacked by a French privateer, and was obliged to put into Lisbon for repairs, they did not arrive at Philadelphia until eight months afterwards. The elder Leslie died in 1804, leaving his family insufficiently provided for. Charles, by the advice of friends, was apprenticed to Messrs. Bradford and Inskeep, publishers. After serving three years, a likeness he made of Cooke, the actor, then at the height of his popularity, attracted much notice, and Mr. Bradford determined to send him to England for instruction in art. He was kindly received by West, and settled himself in London as a student of art, at first, under the instruction of West and Washington Allston, and afterwards in the schools of the Royal Academy. The first large picture he attempted was Saul and the Witch of Endor. This was purchased by Sir John Fleming Leicester for one hundred guineas. He did not persevere very long in this class of subjects, and in 1818, Sir Roger de Coverley going to Church, accompanied by the Spectator, was exhibited at the Royal Academy, and showed that the painter had already discovered and marked out for himself the path to future success and celebrity. It was one of the most popular pictures of the year with the public, and Leslie never lost the hold that he had gained on their sympathy and attachment. Anne Page and Master Slender followed, and was succeeded by May Day in the reign of Queen Elizabeth. In 1824 commences, with Sancho Panza in the apartment of the Duchess, the series of paintings from Don Quixote, from which work the painter continued during the remainder of his life to draw congenial inspiration. Leslie's career, outwardly speaking, was for many years an uneventful one, the chief occurrences it affords for record being the completion of his pictures, and the almost unvarying success that greeted them. He was elected Associate in 1821, and Royal Academician in 1826. The course of few painters could be named marked by more intense devotion to his art, or more steady improvement in it. In 1833 Mr. Leslie accepted the post of drawing master to the U. S. Military Academy at West Point. Finding the situation less adapted to his pursuits than he expected, and suffering from the severity of a winter's climate on the Hudson, he returned to England in April 1834, and resumed the course of life that had been temporarily interrupted. In 1838 he painted, by royal commission, the Queen Receiving the Sacrament after the Coronation in Westminster Abbey. At the death of Mr. Howard in 1847, he was elected Professor of Painting at the Royal Academy; this office he held till compelled to resign it by ill health in 1851. In 1843 Mr. Leslie published his Memoir of John Constable, a tribute to the memory of a dear friend and brother in art; and in 1855, a "Hand-Book for Young Painters," partly composed of the materials used in his Academy lectures, and forming a manual of great professional value for the youthful student. Perhaps more than any artist of the time, Leslie lived in intimate association with the great and good men of his era; he was distinguished by the friendship rather than the patronage of men like the Earl of Egremont, Lord Holland, Sir George Beaumont, Dr. Howley, Archbishop of Canterbury, and others, to whom he was endeared by personal merit. His artistic career continued until the time of his fatal illness, a liver complaint, brought on or aggravated by the loss of a daughter, whose death preceded his own by two months only. As an illustrator and pictorial embodier of other men's conceptions, Leslie ranks among the first, if not the very first, of English painters. Cervantes, Shakspeare, Addison, Sterne, are the names with which his own is indissolubly connected, as recollections of Don Quixote, Sancho Panza, Anne Page, Uncle Toby, Sir Roger de Coverley, and other characters of whom he has supplied the current type to educated minds, are recalled. His pictures are now very valuable. A finished sketch of his picture Sancho and the Duchess, which cost the poet Rogers seventy guineas, realized at the sale of his collection eleven hundred and twenty guineas. The English National Gallery contains the largest collection of his works, through the bequests of Mr Vernon and Mr. Sheepshanks, the latter of whom was one of his most constant and attached patrons

www.ingramcontent.com/pod-product-compliance
Lightning Source LLC
LaVergne TN
LVHW021056110826
845150LV00001B/86

* 9 7 8 1 4 2 5 5 6 6 9 9 9 *